ISBN 978-0-282-98956-9
PIBN 10875902

1 MONTH OF
FREE
READING

at
www.ForgottenBooks.com

By purchasing this book you are
eligible for one month membership to
ForgottenBooks.com, giving you
unlimited access to our entire
collection of over 1,000,000 titles via
our web site and mobile apps.

To claim your free month visit:
www.forgottenbooks.com/free875902

THAT ROYLE GIRL
Says

"A girl can be annoyed by men or not—just as she pleases."

"I'm just a lot of goods which is trying to get together. You've got to give me a chance."

"I hate a man who thinks the country is going to the dogs because it's running out of ready-mades like himself."

"When a man comes from God knows where and has got his name in electric lights at twenty-four—I'm for him."

"Sure I like him. He had his pick of a flock of chickens—but he had to have me."

"You'll have Joan Daisy Royle against you in this trial, Mr. District Attorney. And that's something for which Harvard Law School gives you no preparation a-tall."

"That's what trouble's for—to make real men and women out of us."

"How can I, with a home like mine, dream lovely things about anybody or get an ambition for something big? Well—I'll show you!"

This is the
$50,000
Prize Picture announced in
Paramount's

Fannie Hurst's $50,000 Prize Story
and the big Paramount Picture to be
produced from it will be entitled

"The Moving Finger"

*Y*OU read in Paramount's announcements of the Liberty
Special. Well, here it is: "The Moving Finger," by
Fannie Hurst, author of "Humoresque."

James Cruze will produce the picture. Miss Hurst is
now in Hollywood conferring with Cruze and with his scenario writer, Walter Woods.

So tremendous are the theme and the possibilities of
"The Moving Finger" that its production was entrusted to
the man who made "The Covered Wagon" and who has just
completed an equally great epic, "The Pony Express."

"The Moving Finger" will run in Liberty Magazine as a
serial. Liberty will advertise it in newspapers throughout
the United States.

The Liberty Contest, to which over 100,000 stories
were submitted, received nation-wide advertising in the
magazine and in newspapers. The same kind of advertising will continue.

A $50,000 story; $1,000,000 worth of advertising; a James
Cruze production, by Fannie Hurst.

"THE MOVING FINGER" IS BIG!

SAENGER
HAVE BOOKED UNIVERSAL'S

The PHANTOM

·with **LON CHANEY** and

Directed by **RUPERT JULIAN** *with supplementary*

57
of the Finest Th

21 SUBSEQUENT RUNS IN NEW ORLEANS

Capitol	Prytania	Arcade
Carrollton	Ivy	Avenue
Escorial	Mecca	Fern
Fine Arts	Napoleon	Happy Hour
Folly	National	Rivoli
Hipp	Poplar	Queen
Isis	Variety	Cosmopolitan

(WATCH FOR THE BIG
(ASTOR THEATRE, BROA

The Wildest Weirdest Most Wonderful

Off!

Amusement Co.
and their affiliations
GREATEST PICTURE of 1925-26
of the OPERA

MARY PHILBIN
NORMAN KERRY

FROM THE INTERNATIONALLY FAMOUS STORY BY.
– GASTON LEROUX –

direction and supervision by EDWARD SEDGWICK

eatres in the South!

36 FIRST RUNS

New Orleans, La.	Helena, Ark.	Texarkana, Texas	Crowley, La.	New Iberia, La.
Alexandria, La.	Meridian, Miss.	Vicksburg, Miss.	Donaldsonville, La.	Plaquemine, La.
Biloxi, Miss.	Monroe, La.	Beaumont, Texas	Franklin, La.	Ruston, La.
Clarksdale, Miss.	Natchez, Miss.	Port Arthur, Texas	Jackson, Miss.	Thibodeaux, La.
Greenville, Miss.	Pensacola, Fla.	Orange, Texas	LaFayette, La.	Brookhaven, Miss.
Greenwood, Miss.	Pine Bluff, Ark.	Baton Rouge, La.	Lake Charles, La.	Tupelo, Miss.
Gulfport, Miss.	Shreveport, La.	Columbus, Miss.	McComb, Miss.	Crystal Springs, Miss.
Hattiesburg, Miss.				

NEW YORK PREMIERE
DWAY, N. Y., SEPT. 6, 1925)ˣ

hole City Rocks

with laughter at picturization of Edgar Franklin's joyous story at B. S. Moss's Colony Theatre, Broadway!

of praise from all critics and audiences!

"Denny an artist—one of the screen's best comedy bets".
N. Y. Evening World

"Good for a row of laughs. Fast, bright, gay comedy".
N. Y. Sun

"A broad farce—better than the average".
N. Y. American

"People at the Colony laughed loudly. Denny as amusing as ever".
N. Y. Herald-Tribune

"A racy, amusing comedy. Action. Much excitement".
N. Y. Daily Mirror

"We found ourselves laughing continuously. Maintains its pace very nicely. Denny possesses the knack of being funny".
N. Y. Evening Post

"Moves rapidly. Many funny situations. Audiences will like it. Amusing, interesting, and well-produced".
N. Y. Morning Telegraph

The Dorothy
HOME

with ALICE JOYCE
A KING BAGGOT PRODUCTION

Canfield's

MAKER

and CLIVE BROOK

Presented by CARL LAEMMLE

"THE HOME MAKER" IS A STUDY IN realism not often seen on the screen. It is a picture for those who like something beyond the usual movie hokum. Clive Brook does much to make Knapp's character stand out. Alice Joyce, it seems to me, cannot be improved upon. Billy Kent Schaeffer reaches a state of perfection not always found in a juvenile performance. Universal might have moralized the "papa loves mama" element and made it ridiculous, but thanks to the direction of King Baggot, there is no such catastrophe.

—*N. Y. American*

EXCELLENT PICTURE! A WISTFUL, human fragment from life!

—*N. Y. Daily Mirror*

CLIVE BROOK DOES HANDSOMELY. George Fawcett does his share of the good work.

—*N. Y. Times*

REGISTERS HIT! CAREFULLY DIRECT-ed! Efficiently acted! Baggot has created a real living family on the screen. Billy Kent Schaeffer gives every appearance of being the most talented child actor to appear on the screen since Jackie Coogan.

—*N. Y. Herald-Tribune*

four LEATR

CECIL B. DE MILLE *presents*

Leatrice Joy
in
HELL'S HIGHROAD

Edmund Burns
Julia Faye
Robert Edeson
directed by
RUPERT JULIAN

by Ernest Pascal
adapted by
Eve Unsell &
Lenore Coffee

CECIL B. DE MILLE *presents*

LEATRICE JOY
in
The Wedding Song

by ETHEL WATTS MUMFORD
adapted by CHARLES WHITTAKER *and* DOUGLAS DOTY
with
ROBERT AMES
directed by
ALAN HALE

Released by
PRODUCERS DISTRIBUTING
CORPORATION

F. C. MUNROE, President   RAYMOND PAWLEY, Vice-President and Treasurer   JOHN C. FLINN, Vice-President and General Manager

ICE JOY
Star Productions

BEAUTY, artistry, and an irresistible magnetism, are the attributes that have made Leatrice Joy a star of tremendous appeal to the public and her name a guarantee of big box office receipts to the exhibitor.

It was Cecil B. De Mille, with his unerring faculty for discovering unusual talent, who first realized the possibilities of this New Orleans beauty and made her a star.

That De Mille again demonstrated he is the "showman supreme," is proved by the distinct personal triumphs of Miss Joy in such successes as "*Manslaughter*," "*The Dressmaker From Paris*," and "*The Ten Commandments*."

Cecil B. De Mille is capitalizing on the tremendous popularity won by Leatrice Joy in those productions by starring her in four pictures which in story value, lavishness of production and costuming, satisfy the public demand for real entertainment.

Stories that reflect life in its colorful complexes—
Settings that mark the last word in artistic richness—
Casts of screen favorites with an established following—
A star whose name is a proved box-office magnet—
Make These Leatrice Joy Starring Productions Sure-Fire Box Office Attractions.

LINE UP WITH THESE GREAT ATTRACTIONS *NOW!*
THE *LINE-UP* AT YOUR BOX OFFICE *LATER* WILL JUSTIFY YOUR SHOWMANSHIP WISDOM!

CECIL B. DE MILLE
presents
Leatrice Joy in
"EVE'S LEAVES"
by Harry Chapman Ford
with Clive Brook and Rockliffe Fellowes
directed by
Paul Sloane

Personally
Supervised by
CECIL B.
DE MILLE

CECIL B. DE MILLE
presents
LEATRICE JOY in MADE FOR LOVE

adapted from the novel
"The Valiant Gentleman"
BY M. J. STUART
directed by
PAUL SLOANE

Your fans will revel in the thrilling situations in this new

Bob Custer western, "That Man Jack!"

Presented by
JESSE J. GOLDBURG

Produced by
INDEPENDENT PICTURES CORP.

Directed by
WILLIAM J. CRAFT

There is enough action in this picture to satisfy the most insatiable of thrill-seekers—the story is filled with punch, with plenty of romance, a touch of mystery and a very unusual climax! Bob Custer's horsemanship is something that your patrons are going to talk about!

If you've been playing the Bob Custer pictures you know that the popularity of this young star is growing in leaps and bounds. If you haven't you've been missing one of the biggest Western bets of the industry!

Get aboard this one! ! !

Distributed by

FILM BOOKING OFFICES OF AMERICA, INC.

723 Seventh Ave., New York, N. Y.—Exchanges Everywhere

Exclusive Foreign Distributors: R-C Export Corp., 723 Seventh Ave., New York.

AGENTS: London, Berlin and Paris.

Thematic Music Cue Sheets Available on All Our Features

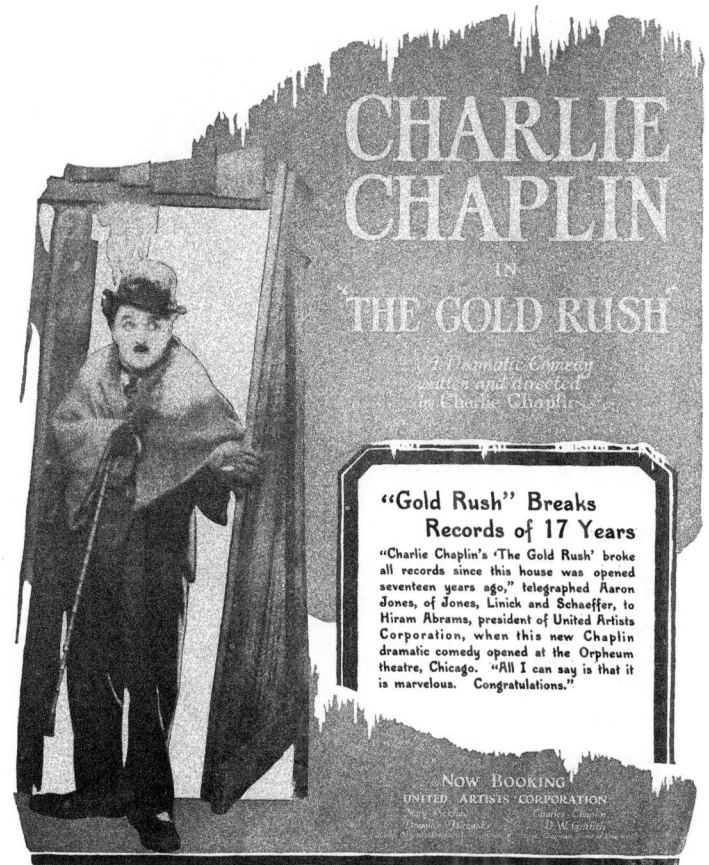

CHARLIE
CHAPLIN
IN
"THE GOLD RUSH"

A Dramatic Comedy
written and directed
by Charlie Chaplin

"Gold Rush" Breaks
Records of 17 Years

"Charlie Chaplin's 'The Gold Rush' broke
all records since this house was opened
seventeen years ago," telegraphed Aaron
Jones, of Jones, Linick and Schaeffer, to
Hiram Abrams, president of United Artists
Corporation, when this new Chaplin
dramatic comedy opened at the Orpheum
theatre, Chicago. "All I can say is that it
is marvelous. Congratulations."

NOW BOOKING
UNITED ARTISTS CORPORATION
Mary Pickford   Charles Chaplin
Douglas Fairbanks   D. W. Griffith

D.W.GRIFFITH

presents

SALLY OF THE SAWDUST

with
CAROL DEMPSTER
and **W.C.FIELDS**

Adapted by FORREST HALSEY *from a stage
story by* DOROTHY DONNELLY

"A Rogue Of a Movie"

"D.W.Griffith may have made better movies,but I
doubt it. At least, this one will be universally
liked. Gay and fun-streaked."—Daily News.
" 'Sally' is guaranteed to please both the young
and the adults."—Daily Mirror.
"You'll love Sally, and if you don't, then there
is something wrong with you."—Telegraph.
"There is sentiment to burn and, as a matter
of fact, all is as it should be in this film."—Post.
"Living, breathing characters that sway an
audience at will between rollicking mirth and
the greatest poignancy."—Evening World.

NOW BOOKING
UNITED ARTISTS CORPORATION

Mary Pickford   Charles Chaplin
Douglas Fairbanks   D.W.Griffith
Hiram Abrams, President   Joseph M.Schenck, Chairman, Board of Directors

JOHN GOLDEN

IN PRESENTING THE ATTRACTIONS LISTED IN THESE PAGES, WILLIAM FOX OFFERS TO EXHIBITORS *SEVEN* PICTURES THAT AS STAGE PLAYS HAVE *PROVED* THEIR POPULARITY.

THE TITLES ARE KNOWN THROUGHOUT THE WORLD; THEY ARE THE OUTSTANDING SUCCESSES OF A FOREMOST AMERICAN PRODUCER; THEY HAVE BEEN TRANSLATED INTO SCREEN PRODUCTIONS BY THE GREATEST DIRECTORS IN THE INDUSTRY, AND THE WORLD'S MOST POPULAR PLAYERS ARE IN THE CASTS. THEY COMPRISE

THE JOHN GOLDEN UNIT OF CLEAN AMERICAN PICTURES!

Fox Film Corporation.

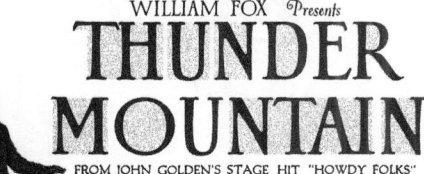

WILLIAM FOX
Presents

7th HEAVEN

JOHN GOLDEN'S MONUMENTAL SUCCESS

The screen version of Austin Strong's
stage play which ran three years in New
York—a guarantee of box-office value to
the exhibitor. For it will be assembled the
greatest cast ever seen in a motion picture.

SCENARIO BY FRANCES MARION   EMMETT FLYNN PRODUCTION

WILLIAM FOX OFFERS THE GREATEST GROUP OF
ESTABLISHED STAGE SUCCESSES EVER SCREENED

in

THE JOHN GOLDEN UNIT OF CLEAN AMERICAN PICTURES

Lightnin'	Thank You
The Wheel	Thunder Mountain
The First Year	Wages for Wives
7th Heaven	

JOHN GOLDEN
UNIT

Fox Film Corporation.

He's done it again!

Richard Talmadge

IN

"THE ISLE OF HOPE"

has made another thrilling action picture that will delight every fan in your community!

His skill, his recklessness, his athletic prowess, his speed, his breezy, buoyant personality have won him a host of friends, and when you announce this star your profits are as good as in the bank.

Other Talmadge pictures your fans will want to see are "Tearing Through", "The Fighting Demon", "The Mysterious Stranger."

A Richard Talmadge Production

Presented by A. Carlos

Continuity by
James Bell Smith

Directed by
Jack Nelson

Released by
FILM BOOKING OFFICES
723 Seventh Ave., New York, N. Y.
EXCHANGES EVERYWHERE

Send For Your Copy of Theatre Lighting Booklet

Get Details of Lamp Contracts

Special contracts have been prepared to meet the lamp requirements of every theatre.

These contracts allow substantial discounts on yearly supplies of lamps. They guarantee a convenient and reliable source of supply of highest quality lamps in any size or style desired.

A contract for Edison Mazda Lamps will solve your lighting problems and save you money.

Ask for full information.

MAIL THIS COUPON

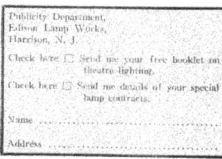

Publicity Department,
Edison Lamp Works,
Harrison, N. J.

Check here ☐ Send me your free booklet on theatre lighting.

Check here ☐ Send me details of your special lamp contracts.

Name ....

Address ....

E VERY Exhibitor should know how to use light most effectively in his theatre.

The proper uses of light for beauty, for comfort and for effective display are discussed in an interesting booklet prepared by our lighting specialists.

The booklet deals with such subjects as:

1. The use of direct and indirect lighting.
2. The proper intensity of light for each department of a theatre.
3. Decorative and ornamental lighting.
4. Coordination of light and music.
5. Orchestra lighting, etc.

Your copy of this theatre lighting booklet will be sent to you on request.

EDISON MAZDA LAMPS
A GENERAL ELECTRIC PRODUCT

SERVICE!

When Mr. Asher Levy recently opened the new Diversey Theatre in Chicago a Kinograms News Reel cameraman photographed the first audience to enter the doors

Before The Spectators Had Left Their Seats They Were Looking At Their Own Pictures On The Screen!

So Mr. Levy, who believes in giving credit where credit is due wrote us the following ---

> We have only the highest praise to offer for your services at the opening of our new Diversey Theatre, Chicago, when the motion pictures showing the first audience enter the theatre were projected on the screen one hour and five minutes after being taken. It was a remarkable feat in service and workmanship.
>
> (Signed) *Asher Levy*

This same service is yours for the asking

BOOK K I N O G R A M S

The News Reel Built Like a Newspaper

The wires are the news of

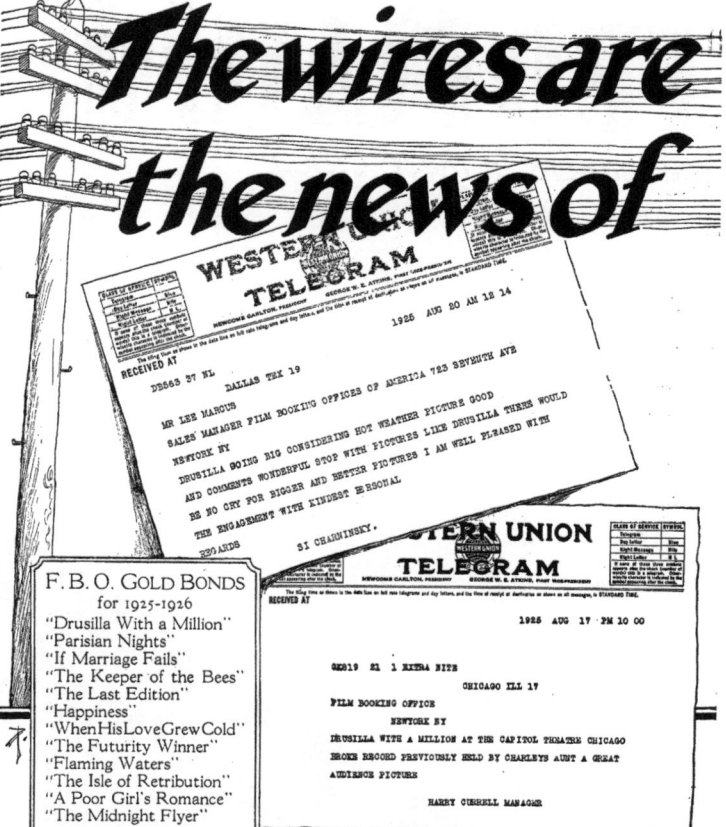

WESTERN UNION TELEGRAM

1925 AUG 20 AM 12 14

RECEIVED AT

DB563 37 NL   DALLAS TEX 19

MR LEE MARCUS FILM BOOKING OFFICES OF AMERICA 723 SEVENTH AVE

NEWYORK NY

DRUSILLA GOING BIG CONSIDERING HOT WEATHER PICTURE GOOD

AND COMMENTS WONDERFUL STOP WITH PICTURES LIKE DRUSILLA THERE WOULD

BE NO CRY FOR BIGGER AND BETTER PICTURES I AM WELL PLEASED WITH

THE ENGAGEMENT WITH KINDEST PERSONAL

REGARDS   SI CHARNINSKY.

WESTERN UNION TELEGRAM

1925 AUG 17 PM 10 00

RECEIVED AT

GK519 21 1 EXTRA NITE

CHICAGO ILL 17

FILM BOOKING OFFICE

NEWYORK NY

DRUSILLA WITH A MILLION AT THE CAPITOL THEATRE CHICAGO

BROKE RECORD PREVIOUSLY HELD BY CHARLEYS AUNT A GREAT

AUDIENCE PICTURE

HARRY CURRELL MANAGER

burning with
F.B.O.'s success

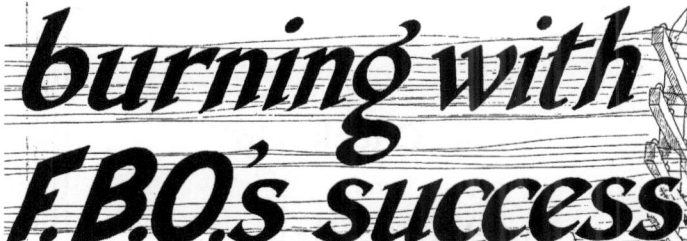

WESTERN UNION
TELEGRAM

GEORGE W. E. ATKINS, FIRST VICE-PRESIDENT
NEWCOMB CARLTON, PRESIDENT

CLASS OF SERVICE	SYMBOL
TELEGRAM	
DAY LETTER	BLUE
NIGHT MESSAGE	NITE
NIGHT LETTER	N L

1925 AUG 26 AM 3 00

SU 230 86 3 EXTRA NL

LOSANGELES CALIF 25

FILM BOOKING OFFICES

723 SEVENTH AVE NEWYORK NY

THE LOSANGELES NEWSPAPER CRITICISMS IN UNANIMOUSLY PRAISING
DRUSILLA WITH A MILLION ALSO EXPRESS THE OPINIONS OF PATRONS OF
THE FORUM THEATRE WHERE THIS EXCELLENT FEATURE PLAYED LAST
WEEK STOP NOT ONLY WAS THE BUSINESS MORE THAN SATISFACTORY BUT
THE AFTER EFFECTS OF THIS FEATURE WILL DO THE THEATRE
MUCH GOOD FOR SOME TIME TO COME

JOHN P GORING MANAGER FORUM THEATRE.

RECEIVED AT

SA71 41 NL

1925 AUG 19 PM 9 30

LOS ANGELES CALIF 19

FILM BOOKING OFFICES

723 SEVENTH AVE NEWYORK NY

WE ARE INDEED PLEASED TO STATE THAT OUR SELECTION OF YOUR PRODUCTION
PARISIAN NIGHTS FOR OUR TWENTY FIFTH ANNIVERSARY PICTURE HAS PROVEN
THAT OUR JUDGMENT OF THIS PICTURE WAS CORRECT WE HAVE PLAYED TO
CAPACITY EVERY DAY SINCE THE OPENING DAY REGARDS

PANTAGES LOSANGELES.

Distributed by
FILM BOOKING OFFICES
723 Seventh Avenue
New York, N. Y.
EXCHANGES EVERYWHERE

"The Check Up"

and

Box-Office Reports

as they now appear in the
NEWS provide the best and
quickest way of finding out
just what pictures are delivering the goods at the box-office.
Every week in Box-Office
Reports and once a month in
"The Check-Up," the real
"lowdown" is given on current releases in simple, concise form, based upon our own
direct-from-exhibitor reports.
They will aid you.

real box-office attractions
in a row –
all made, ready to see,
sold under a guarantee!

MONTY

in

"Keep Smiling"

with

ANNE CORNWALL, ROBERT EDESON
and a stellar cast

produced by Howard Estabrook
story by Herman Raymaker & Clyde Bruckman
directed by
Albert Austin & Gilbert W. Pratt

Four In a Row

Well, now that we are on the subject of box office successes—and we certainly are, right now—I can name you four independent ones in a row from any company. I know some more also but we are now dealing with the first four pictures for the new season from Associated Exhibitors.

To begin with, there is the picture "Headlines," a title I don't fancy much because it hasn't much lure but after all a lot of these lurid titles are falling flat on their noses and maybe, soon, the title won't be so important as the picture. "Headlines" is a story of a woman a sacrifice, not an old and ugly woman, but a woman young and sweet enough for any man's bother and happily played by Alice Joyce. Her sacrifice is for her crudely young daughter, a flapper with all the extreme selfishness of youth in the modern manner. Virginia Lee Corbin is the best flapper the screen has presented. She teaches a lesson as well as entertains and the picture, while broad, extreme and swift, can laugh at all excess because it actually shows the unlovely side of flapperism. It's better than a sermon because it's convincing.

One of my reviewers saw this picture and praised it with faint damns. Later he told me it was better than "Flaming Youth." He was so right in his private comment that I've given him another chance because this is one of the really great pictures of late years. It's well written, Peter Milne saw to that, it's topical, sane and with a fine and intriguing plot compelling, powerful and delicate and could run at the Capitol.

Mark for four weeks to everybody's profit.

I think Jack Woody is a conservative when he says he's just strong for that picture.

What it needs in every local community is exploitation, going to it in a showman's way, because it has everything that goes to make real compelling entertainment.

Well, so much for that, and now we come to the Monte Banks starring effort, called "Keep Smiling." I took the liberty of recommending some cuts which I was advised already had been made because I only saw the sample print. Not here really is a great big, fine exciting picture with danger and comedy walking along side by side like the Siamese twins and very nice too all the way. I don't know whether I regard Banks as really a comedian but certainly this is a picture of box office movies and attraction value. It's the sort of thing that can be exploited and make good on the exploitation and what more can those with money hunger ask?

Then there's "Under the Rouge," running to box and well deserved business at the Colony. Tom Moore is the star and its excellent support are Mary Alden, Eileen Percy, Chester Conklin and Carmelita Geraghty. Lewis H. Moomaw directed it from A. P. Younger's story and he has made one of the very best box office pictures of the year. It's a strong property sentimental play, gripping and absolutely satisfying as real entertainment. Mary Alden, the very magnificent on the screen, contributes tremendously to the power of the play. "Under the Rouge" is a real production.

Now we come to "Manhattan Madness" an Oscar Price offering with Jack Dempsey and Estelle Taylor. It is delightfully preposterous and has enough battle in it to satisfy all that could have been expected from the heavyweight champion of the world. The box office movie is of interest with this picture into money and there again we get into the thing that satisfies.

Four in a row! A fine start for the season. We congratulate the exhibitors who are using and who will use independent pictures.

ARTHUR JAMES

MOTION PICTURES TODAY

Physical Distributors
Pathé Exchange Inc.

Associated Exhibitors
JOHN S. WOODY *President*
FOREIGN REPRESENTATIVE INTER-GLOBE EXPORT CORP.

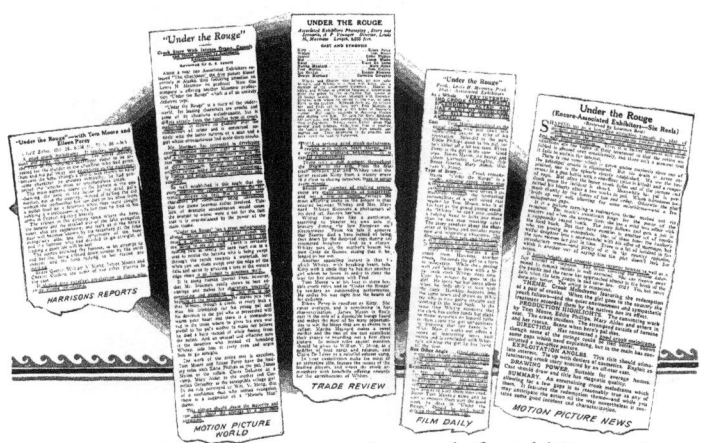

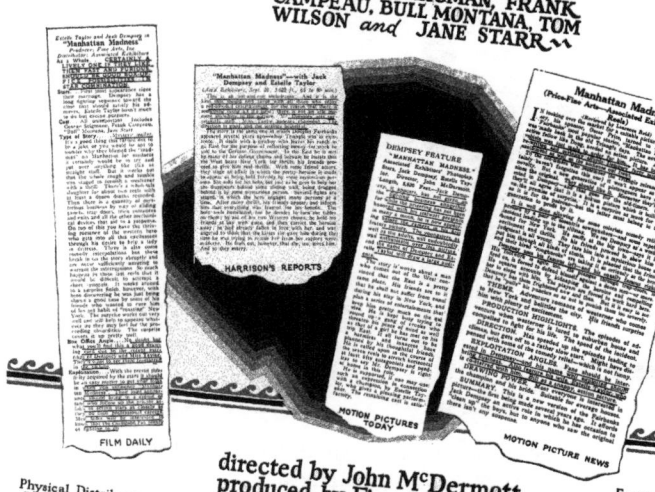

Short ubjects for howmen!

12 - The "Adventures of Mazie"

12 - "Fighting Hearts"

13 - Standard Comedies

13 - Blue Ribbon Comedies

26 - Bray Cartoons

Funniest Four in Filmdom

ALBERTA VAUGHN
LARRY KENT
AL COOKE & KIT GUARD

IN

The "ADVENTURES OF MAZIE"

NELL MARTIN wrote the stories, which are appearing in Top Notch Magazine, and RALPH CEDER directed. The same characters are in every episode, but each one is a separate story and each one contains a walloping climax that will literally drag your people back for the next one! You remember "The Telephone Girl", "The Go-Getters", "The Pacemakers"! The same artists appear in this series and they have a bigger laugh opportunity than they ever had before!

Follow the

12 more rapid-fire episodes to keep your box-office busy!

Sam Hellman

known to everybody in the country through his stories in the Saturday Evening Post and his writings for various newspaper syndicates wrote

"FIGHTING HEARTS"

Live-wire action stories that will start the red corpuscles dancing in the veins of every man, woman, boy and girl in the country. Sam Hellman's name will bring them in for the first episode; Sam Hellman's stories will keep them coming back for every one of the other episodes!

laugh line!

F.B.O SHORT SUBJECTS

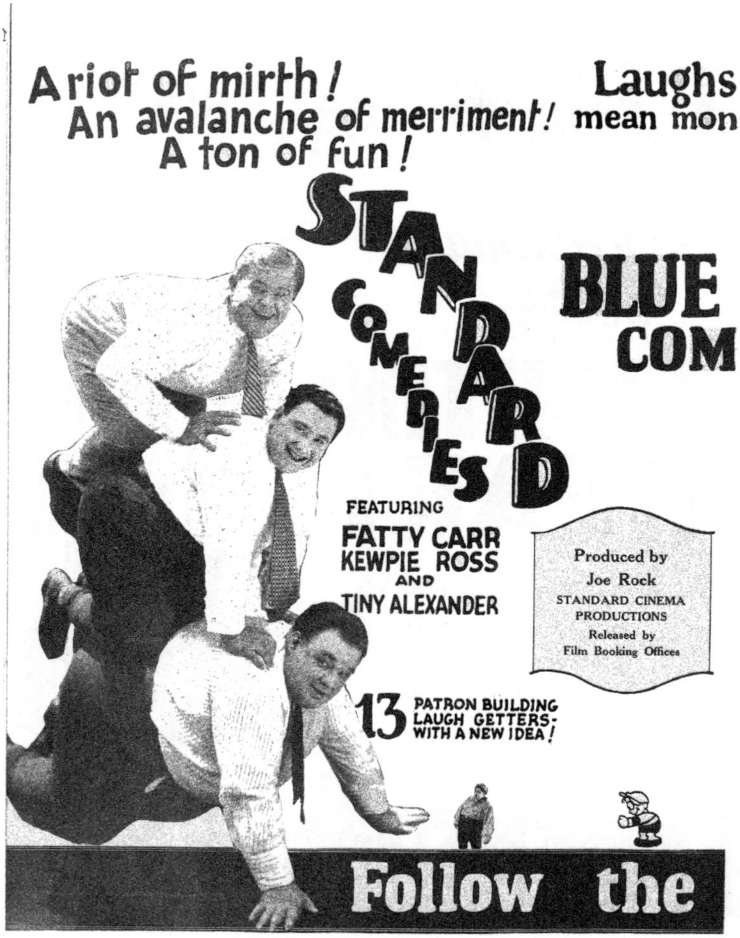

A riot of mirth!
An avalanche of merriment!
A ton of fun!
Laughs
mean mon
STANDARD
COMEDIES
BLUE
COM
FEATURING
FATTY CARR
KEWPIE ROSS
AND
TINY ALEXANDER
Produced by
Joe Rock
STANDARD CINEMA
PRODUCTIONS
Released by
Film Booking Offices
13 PATRON BUILDING
LAUGH GETTERS-
WITH A NEW IDEA!
Follow the

JOSEPH M SCHENCK
presents

Constance
in "Her Sister"

She captures New York!

Playing this week at the Capitol Theatre

New York Morning Telegraph: *"Capitol has a winner this week. Constance Talmadge is the main attraction at the Capitol theatre; and when we say attraction we mean attraction. Connie has never been more pert or charming than she is in this one."*

New York American: **"Do go to the Capitol if you want some light entertainment that will make you laugh and forget the serious side of life."**

New York Daily News: **"One Constance Talmadge is enough fun for any movie. *Two Constances are a riot."***

New York Tribune: *"We consider 'Her Sister from Paris' one of the most amusing pictures of 1925.* The direction is flawless, the acts are perfect and the entire cast acts as it never has before."

New York Times: **"A clever comedy with scintillating situations and deft directional touches. If you have felt like frowning all day and you need the pick-me-up of a bright and jolly entertainment the Capitol is a good place to go."**

"One of the most attractive pictures seen on Broadway in several weeks"

—New York Evening World

Motion Picture News

VOL. XXXII   ALBANY, N. Y., AND NEW YORK CITY, SEPTEMBER 5, 1925   NO. 10

Connecticut

WITH such facts as we have before us, before going to press, it is evident:

That producers, distributors and Connecticut exhibitors are agreed to take, if necessary, a very serious step, namely, the withdrawal of films from a State where legislation, confiscatory or equally unjust, has been imposed. This will be done in Connecticut when existing contracts between distributors and exhibitors have expired, several months hence;

That a revolving fund has been created by the M. P. T. O. of Connecticut and the New Haven and Boston Film Boards of Trade to take care of the payment of the tax in the meantime;

That exchanges are already closing in Connecticut; and there is talk of opening a distribution point at Port Chester, N. Y., just across the State line.

It is too early to make definite comment upon the Connecticut situation. We can only speak of its larger aspects.

This is the most flagrant instance of unfair legislation that has thus far confronted the industry. It combines censorship and a confiscatory tax. The leading newspapers of the State are of one voice in outspoken opposition to it. The Waterbury *American* characterizes the law as "simply one of those cases which are all too common in this free and unterrified land where a group of legislators saw what they thought was a chance to pluck a luscious plum from an overloaded tree and proceeded to do so."

Which quotation, in turn, lays bare the issue confronting this industry. There are forty-eight States in the Union and their legislators are not unlike those of Connecticut. If Connecticut can reap this tax harvest, so will other tax-anxious States. The Connecticut law, even after reading it a dozen times, is still vague to us, but assuming that it levies ten dollars a reel on every copy of a picture entering the State, a law of this kind adopted by all the States or a good measure of them would take away at one blow all the possible profits of the producing and distributing branches.

In passing we can't overlook a significant phrase in the Waterbury *American* editorial: "a luscious plum from an overloaded tree." What a pity it is that every legislator in the land, every politician, every statesman, let alone the public at large, still believes this to be a business swollen with easy profits and that no figures are ever issued to prove the contrary and true facts!

* * *

But there's the situation: confiscatory legislation, then, may well be national in scope and, if so, ruinous beyond any doubt.

What is the industry to do?

A boycott of films against a State is a radical step. But, also, decisive action is imperative—of some kind. What is there to do?

A most interesting fact to us is that the Connecticut papers—outspoken against the tax—are equally outspoken against a film boycott. "Silly," says one, "and causes offense." Don't punish the people of the State, say several, in effect; they pay the taxes anyway. Go after the legislators.

But how can you reach legislators except through the sentiment of the people they are supposed to represent? And how is that to be done so quickly and effectively as the urgency of the case demands? Bear in mind the fact that this is a national, not merely a State situation, so far as the interests—no, the life—of the industry is concerned.

We believe the sentiment of the industry, at this early day at least, favors a boycott. We can only hope that some other and better argument, plus an early and special session of the Connecticut legislature, will undo this arrant and ignorant injustice.

W. A. Johnston

MOTION PICTVRE NEWS

September 5   Vol. XXXII
1925   No. 10

Founded in September 1913

Publication Office: Lyon Block, Albany, N. Y.

Editorial and General Offices: Branch Offices\:
729 7th Ave., New York City   845 S. Wabash Ave., Chicago, Ill.
                        Room 616 Security Bldg., Hollywood, Calif.

A Letter From Glenn Harper

WILLIAM A. JOHNSTON, editor of MO-
TION PICTURE NEWS, is in receipt of a letter
from Glenn Harper, secretary of the California Division of the M. P. T. O. A., which is
reprinted below, without editorial comment, because
the letter is itself an editorial. It follows:

"DEAR MR. JOHNSTON:

"I wish to compliment you upon your editorial of
August 15. It is the most sensible manner of reporting our activity in Detroit that I have read, and
should receive the admiration of every Director of
the M. P. T. O. A.

"Too much recognition is always given by the
trade press to factional arguments, which results in
no good to all concerned, and too often clouds real
accomplishments of all our meetings.

"Your unusual departure is certainly to be com-
mended in the very highest terms.

"Yours very truly,
"GLENN HARPER".

What of the Future?

ALONG what lines will the future great developments in production come? This vital question is engaging the thought of the progressives
in the industry. Cecil B. De Mille has some interesting ideas on this subject.

"The purely mechanical side of motion pictures
has about reached its apex", he said the other day.
"We are near the limit of the great advance in the
technical lines of trick photography, strange lighting, unique sets and startling effects.

"We still have far to go, however, in the development of deft, new, subtle ways of transferring
thought of the screen; of inventing unusual methods
of driving home situation and ideas of especial
importance.

"In the next three or four years there will be
astounding advances made in the methods of screen
translation. Every day directors and writers are
discovering new points of 'technique' whereby a
thought or an emotion will be registered with more
surety and less effort.

"It was only a few years ago that if we wanted
to have a man do one bit of action in his home and
another at his office down-town we saw him go out
of the door, out of the house, enter his car, get off
at his office building, enter the elevator, etc. Now
we simply go from one scene to another with no
tedious, footage-wasting, intermediate steps. And,

because of this 'tightening up' tendency, our stories
will condense in action and increase in interest.

"The day of the purely butterscotch girl and pep-
permit boy love story is gone. The 'theme' photoplay that has something to say; something to add
for the general good of the world, in addition to its
entertainment values, will continue to advance and
increase in popularity and importance.

Short Subject Titles

WHAT are known as box office titles in relation
to feature pictures have been given weighty
consideration for years by all branches of the
industry, but at least one side of the trade, the exhibitor, seems to have forgotten that the growing importance of short subjects can be further extended by
taking advantage of the undoubted box office titles
which have been appended to many of the one and
two reelers up for current release.

An excellent example of this is to be found in the
Fox two-reeler "Failure," based on O. Henry's great
short story of the same title.

"O. Henry's Failure" in lights or bold face type
certainly would be a box office asset to even the
smallest theatre. The public's curiosity, if nothing
else, can be aroused if they see the name of America's
immortal writer and the title of the picture, a word
which is the common bugaboo of every normal man
or woman.

And there are many other short subject titles that
possess the same undoubted exploitation possibilities,
not only on the Fox program, which, by the way,
seems to be especially attractive in this connection,
but also in the productions by other distributors who
have attractive line-ups for the 1925-26 season.

September 6, 1925   MOTION PICTURE NEWS   Vol. XXXII, No. 10
Published twice weekly by MOTION PICTURE NEWS, INC., William A. Johnston,
President; E. Kendall Gillett, Vice-President; William A. Johnston, Editor; J. S.
Dickerson, Associate Editor; Oscar Cooper, Managing Editor; Fred J. Beecroft,
Advertising Manager; L. H. Mason, Chicago Representative; William McCormack,
Los Angeles Representative. Subscription price, $3 per year. Saturday Edition
$2. Mid Week $1, postpaid in United States, Mexico, Hawaii, Porto Rico, Philip-
pine Islands and some other countries; Canada, $5; foreign, $10.00. Copyright
1924, by MOTION PICTURE NEWS, INC., in the United States and Great Britain.
Title registered in the United States Patent Office and foreign countries. Western
Union Cable address is "Picknews," New York. Entered as second-class matter
January 31st, 1924, at the postoffice, Albany, N. Y., under the Act of March 3,
1879.

Mary Philbin and Hizzoner, Mayor John L. Davis of Oakland at the Greater Movie Season parade in that city, which was a great success.

PICTURES
AND
PEOPLE

THE NEW FEATURES

FIVE new pictures on Broadway this week, Constance Talmadge in "Her Sister From Paris" at the Capitol; Thomas Meighan in "The Man Who Found Himself," at the Rivoli, Ricardo Cortez and Greta Nissen in "In The Name Of Love," at the Rialto; Leatrice Joy, in "Hell's Highroad," at the Colony, and "Siegfried," the Ufa German production, at the Century.

Of these the Talmadge feature had the merriest appeal, with the inimitable Constance playing a dual role and proving herself, as ever, a mistress of the art of refined, sparkling comedy. Tom Meighan, as a self-sacrificing hero who takes another's guilt upon his shoulders and does time in Sing-Sing, hadn't a very original plot to back him up, but the Meighan personality always wins, and there was many a wet eye among the Rivoli audiences as Thomas suffered in silence behind bars, lost his sweetheart, got her back again and finally emerged into the sunshine of happiness.

Both Ricardo Cortez and Greta Nissen were excellent as the leads of "In The Name Of Love," a very entertaining attraction, with a French small-town atmosphere. Cortez is an extremely persuasive and, in a sense, pathetic lover, while Miss Nissen, the blonde beauty from Norseland, more than lived up to her reputation as a foreign star. "Hell's Highroad" proved to be a good audience film, replete with the luxurious settings for which every Cecil De Mille production is celebrated, and Leatrice Joy a fascinating figure as the girl in pursuit of wealth.

"Siegfried," with its beautiful photography, massive effects and wonderful orchestral score, for which latter Dr. Hugo Riesenfeld, who fitted the opera music to the film version, was given an enthusiastic reception at its first night showing, and certainly registers a triumph for the producers in this invasion of the hitherto shunned field of grand opera. Music-lovers in general will undoubtedly welcome the coming of "Siegfried," what the average fans will think of it, time only can tell.

Sam L. Warner, of Warner Bros., and his bride, formerly Lina Basquette of the Follies, on their arrival in Hollywood on their honeymoon.

A piquant pose of pert and pretty Alberta Vaughn, registering a come-hither look in "The Adventures of Mazie" (F. B. O.).

¶This is Eleanor Boardman as she appears in "The Exchange of Wives" (Metro-Goldwyn), but it's hard to see why anyone would want an exchange.

Spencer Bennet, who directed "Play Ball" for Pathe, and is now utilizing another type of sport in "The Green Archer" (Pathe).

Emanuel Cohen, editor of Pathe News and Pathe Review, was a recent visitor at the Hal Roach studios, where he was formally initiated as a member of "Our Gang."

George O'Brien, Fox film star, and the "O'Brien Smile," are great favorites with the kiddies. This is a new way of "picking 'em up on the beach."

Alexander Carr and George Sidney, who will again appear as Potash and Perlmutter in "Partners Again" (United Artists), in which they will be directed by Henry King.

DESANO MAKES GOOD

EVEN the hard-boiled critics who attended the projection showing of B. P. Schulberg's "The Girl Who Wouldn't Work", the other day, were loud in their outspoken praises of the hit scored by Director Marcel DeSano. It was the latter's initial effort in the directorial field, a fact which made the results achieved all the more surprising, for no veteran could have done better, and probably many an old-timer not nearly as well.

DeSano showed remarkable judgment in the careful building up of the story, the various situations interlocking smoothly and action moving at a fast clip. The work of the entire cast was excellent, with Lionel Barrymore and Marguerite De La Motte giving splendid performances in the leading roles. The sex problem entered into the story but was so delicately handled that no opportunity was given either censors or ultra-moralists to register objections. The picture fairly radiates sympathy, the human touch is ever in evidence and all in all can be listed as a credit to both director and players.

GLORIA AIDS GOVERNOR

GOVERNOR HOWARD M. GORE of West Virginia, went to Moundsville on business the other day, and incidentally became the unexpected guest of Gloria Swanson, who is making scenes for her new Paramount picture, "Stage Struck," at New Martinsville, W. Va. The Governor was returning to Charleston, capital of the State, and when he wired ahead to friends to get him a room at the Riverside Hotel, learned that the house was filled to the roof by the Swanson company and hosts of folks

whom the picture-making has drawn to New Martinsville. Miss Swanson then stepped into the breach by inviting the Governor to be her guest at the Noll residence, her temporary home, during a four-hour wait between trains. The invitation was accepted and the State's chief executive was the star's guest at dinner, and afterwards accompanied her to a local picture house to see "Manhandled."

And that isn't all! For while the Swanson company is at New Martinsville, an enterprising local printer is publishing a four page daily paper giving all up-to-date news of production activities. In view of which glories we ask—what has become of the old-fashioned party who was won't to spring the familiar crusted gag about an "industry that is still in its infancy"? Looks like the infant had learned to walk, anyhow.

SAY IT WITH SILK

CHARLES J. GIEGERICH writes that in the coming Cecil De Mille production—"The Wedding Song," starring Leatrice Joy, there will be seven dancers with only one veil, instead of the traditional one dancer with the famous seven veils. At first sight this looked like an economy note, designed to show that Mr. De Mille, in view of the high cost of silk, and repenting his lavish expenditures of the past; was beginning to "hedge," as the racing fans would put it. But not so! The real facts of the case are that Adrian, De Mille's Parisian designer, has developed an idea whereby seven dancers gracing a cafe scene will appear in one sweeping silk veil—"draped to make a sketchy and startling costume!" We quote verbatim from our correspondent, whose judgment in such matters is universally recognized as frightfully accurate.

HER MUSICAL SALARY

YOU will probably find it hard to believe that Wanda Hawley, the well-known star, once worked for a wage so small that if we were telling about it, we'd speak in a whisper. For Jake Rosenthal, of the Rose Theatre in Troy, N. Y. dug up an old payroll recently on which Wanda's name was set down as receiving the magnificent stipend of seven dollars per week, for services rendered as pianist at the Majestic Theatre in that city. How times have changed!

Incidentally, it's worth mentioning that Miss Hawley originally came from Troy, and what's more the Trojans haven't forgotten that fact. With result that whenever a picture featuring Wanda is shown her townsmen turn out and pack the theatre to capacity.

THE BELLS WILL RING

CONGRATULATIONS are in order to Lilyan Tashman, now playing in Metro-Goldwyn's "A Little Bit Of Broadway," on the announcement of her coming marriage to Edmund Loew, as soon as her part is completed. The congratulations, of course, go double. Miss Tashman recently came out boldly and made the important declaration on the set, stating that she expected the event to take place within a few days.

Some of the striking character types that will be seen in "Tumbleweeds," William S. Hart's first picture for United Artists. In the centre is Hart himself on the famous pinto pony; at the left is Barbara Bedford as Molly; and at the extreme right is Lucien Littlefield as Kentucky Rose.

GOLD THAT GLITTERS

CHARLIE CHAPLIN was recently presented by the Brunswick Company with a gold-plated phonograph record of two ballads "With You Dear In Bombay" and "Sing a Song," both composed by the comedian while he was producing "The Gold Rush," and which have just been placed on the market.

We furthermore learn that during the making of the records Charlie not only played the violin solo part, but conducted Abe Lyman's Cocoanut Grove Orchestra which did the recording. The old phrase—"Jack of all trades," might as well be revised to read—"Jack of all arts—so far as the renowned Charles and other celebrated screen stars are concerned. Not content with camera triumphs, they wander a far into other fields of endeavor, exploring the trails of fiction-land, poetry, music, painting, sculpture, etc. Maybe some day the intellectual stunts will become so commonplace that a wily publicist will stimulate fan curiosity by stating that his principal hasn't a single interest in life outside of a moving picture studio. To be "different" isn't such a bad way of making a bid for fame.

THE IRISH SHEIKS

EUGENE O'BRIEN, featured in Producers Distributing Corporations' "Simon The Jester," discoursed on the shiek question the other day. "Even though they used a different name," says O'Brien, "the most alluring lovers, fellows we now call shieks,

John C. Flinn, Marshall Neilan, P. A. Powers and Cecil B. De Mille at the De Mille studios after signing the contract under which Neilan becomes a contributor to the Producers Distributing Corp. program.

Miss Helene Sardeau, Belgian sculptress, sculping the trophy which will be awarded on September 10th at Atlantic City to the girl in the beauty pageant who screens best, who will also play the title role in "The American Venus" (Paramount).

originated in Ireland. Outside of the name, the devil a bit of change has there been in those conditions, for I'll book a bet any time that you care to take the average Irishman and, for persuasive lovemaking he'll come in first over the wire anywhere and everywhere."

Many years ago Charles Lever, the Irish author, expressed himself as follows:

> "Oh, I never cared much for hard work,
>   Sure it isn't the gift of the Bradies,
> But I'd make a most elegant Turk
>   For I'm fond of tobacco and ladies!"

Perhaps Mr. O'Brien is right, maybe he found his inspiration in the above lines, but, not caring to argue with him, we leave the fascinating subject to our readers' judgment.

KLAUSSEN CARRIES ON

ALTHOGH Vitagraph has passed away, some of the talent that distinguished that pioneer company is still to the fore. Among these is Dick Klaussen, the chap who for fourteen years handled titling, decorative effects and general artistic finishing-off touches of product for the concern. Dick is now in the business for himself and the many friends he has in the industry wish him all the luck in the world.

WOOING THE BLARNEY STONE

THE latest report from Ireland, transmitted to us by the industrious M. B. Blumenstock, conveys the startling tidings that Tom Meighan has kissed the Blarney Stone. To those not wise in Celtic lore this information may appear of scant consequence, some may even wonder why Mr. Meighan should waste caresses where no ardent return can be looked for. Wherefore, it seems fitting right here to insert the ancient Irish distich:

> "If the dear girls you'd always please
>   And win them" quoth Dan Carney,
> "There's but one way, Iv'e heard them say—
>   Go kiss the Stone of Blarney!"

From now on we can expect Tom Meighan to be a bigger matinee idol than ever. But isn't he taking a rather unfair advantage of his screen rivals who have never been helped by legendary magic? We may look for a swift exodus of male stars to the shores of the Emerald Isle in the near future when this news becomes public. In passing, it might be mentioned that to our certain knowledge Mr. Sidney Olcott, who has made many trips to Erin, never stepped on his native soil without paying tribute to the celebrated Stone. And yet—Sidney is a director, without any ambitions in the matinee idol direction. What could have been HIS object?

Universal chartered the S.S. Chauncey M. Depew the other day and all the employes of the home office, the Big "U" exchange and the laboratory, went up the Hudson river to Indian Point, where a good time was reported by one and all.

Marilyn Mills feeding a half dozen of her pets to be used in her next picture. She has just completed "Tricks" for the Davis Distributing Division.

Marion Davies, Cosmopolitan star, now working at the Metro-Goldwyn-Mayer studios, likes the Coast so well that she has purchased this handsome Beverly Hills home.

Richard Talmadge, star of "The Prince of Pep" F. B. O.), demonstrates the titular pep in a strenuous athletic performance caught in mid-air by the camera.

Another of George Kuwa's remarkable character interpretations is given in "Silver Treasure" (Wm. Fox), in which he has a colorful role.

DAN MASON'S BOOTS

THE only original "trooper boots" in captivity! That's the claim made by Dan Mason the Pa MacBirney of Fox's "Thunder Mountain, for he is willing to take oath that the boots he wears in the picture are the same he has utilized for more than twenty years.

It seems he first bought 'em to wear in the old musical comedy, "It Happened in Norland," in which he played the leading comedy role. They are now weatherbeaten, wrinkled and caked with Santa Cruz mountain mud, but he sticks to his ancient friends, stowing them away carefully whenever he is through using them, only to rout 'em out once more for "just another film."

We don't wish to cast a shadow upon Mr. Mason's veracity and accept his statement with child-like confidence. Only one thing—we wish he would give us his bootmaker's address.

A NEW EDITION

CHARLES E. McCARTHY, Paramount publicity director, is busily engaged answering phone calls these days, as stars, directors and executives ring him up incessantly to offer their good wishes on an extremely important event—the birth of a baby daughter! It is worthy of note that this is the third time Mr. McCarthy has starred in the father role, and THE MOTION PICTURE NEWS herewith joins his numerous friends in extending hearty congratulations.

Leatrice Joy, Cecil B. De Mille star, is a great believer in golf for keeping in form. She has started on "Her Wedding Song" (Producers Dist. Corp.).

Lou Tellegen, appearing in William Fox pictures, used to be the debonair hero, but look at him now, as the deep, dark and dastardly villain.

Howard Chandler Christy, the magazine illustrator, turns author and pounds out a few sequences for Jackie Coogan at the Metro-Goldwyn-Mayer studios, assisted by his wife, while Will H. Hays keeps a judicial eye on the proceedings.

Mada Gunn and Laty Florene, formerly of the Imperial theatre at Moscow, signed by B. P. Schulberg to act and direct for future releases.

Hays Now Announces Drastic Action in Connecticut

Exchanges Being Closed; Boycott Is Foreshadowed

Text of Official Statement by Will H. Hays on Connecticut Situation

FOLLOWING is the statement issued August 26 by Will H. Hays, President of the Motion Picture Producers and Distributors of America, Inc., on the Connecticut situation:

"The Connecticut Law which provides for a one-man political censorship of a method of expression and for a tax of a confiscatory nature is as unjust in its provisions and conception as it is impractical in its operation.

"The exhibitors, producers and distributors are united and unanimous in their conclusions as to the impossibilities of the situation.

"It is a most unfortunate condition, placing an entirely unnecessary and expensive burden on the amusement of the people and placing in the hands of one man the determination of what much of that amusement shall be. It is a serious economic problem. There is left for the motion picture theatre owners, producers and distributors scarcely any option. Producers and distributors will carry out their existing contracts; they will immediately remove their exchanges for the distribution of films from the State of Connecticut; and for the time being they will not make further Connecticut contracts."

DRASTIC steps were taken this week by the industry in the Connecticut tax situation. Official announcement was made Wednesday by Will H. Hays that producers and distributors will carry out existing contracts with theatres. No new contract will be made. And the distributors are closing their exchanges in New Haven and leaving the State.

The carrying out of this program will mean a virtual film boycott of Connecticut and the result will inevitably be the eventual closing down of the theatres, of which there are about 200.

Meanwhile, an appeal is being prepared to the United States Supreme Court, the Special Federal Court having decided last week that the Connecticut ten-dollar-a-reel tax was constitutional.

Existing contracts with theatres will expire in most cases, it is believed, about February, but theatres which have not booked films ahead will be without product.

This is an unprecedented situation. The statement by Mr. Hays, is printed in full above.

To meet the tangled situation brought about by the tax law, the Motion Picture Theatre Owners of Connecticut and the New Haven and Boston Film Boards of Trade have arranged a revolving fund of $60,000 to meet tax payments under the law.

This step followed a mass-meeting of exhibitors in New Haven and a meeting of the exhibitors committee with officials of the Hays organization in New York. The Board of Directors of the Hays organization met on Tuesday, and there was also a conference of the exchange managers comprising the two Film Boards of Trade with Charles C. Pettijohn.

The tax, which imposes a heavy burden on the industry, is the first State levy of the kind to be made, and it is felt that drastic action is necessary in order to make an object lesson of Connecticut.

A statement issued by Joseph W. Walsh, President of the Connecticut M. P. T. O., following the meeting with the Hays officials, declared that the revolving fund had been created to pay the tax on films now in Connecticut under contract for exhibition. "After existing contracts have been completed," said Mr. Walsh, "the exhibitors will leave to the distributors the problem of paying the tax."

The Franklin Film Company was the first exchange in New Haven to close. Instructions were issued from the main office in Boston to ship all prints out of the state

and cease operations. Similar instructions were being issued by other distributors when MOTION PICTURE NEWS went to press. It was said all the 16 exchanges in New Haven would probably be closed down by the end of the week.

Distributors will ship film to complete existing contracts from outside of Connecticut, and in this connection a central distributing agency at Port Chester, N. Y., just across the line is being discussed. Tax Commissioner Blodgett of Connecticut has ruled that express companies and mail service are not liable to taxation.

Present at the meeting of the Board of Directors of the Hays organization were: Mr. Hays, Major Edward Bowes, vice-president of Metro-Goldwyn; William Fox; E. H. Goldstein, treasurer of Universal; D. W. Griffith; E. W. Hammons, President of Educational; Arthur Kelly, United Artists; S. R. Kent, general manager of Famous Players-Lasky; Raymond Pawley, Producers Distributing Corporation; Saul Rogers, of Fox; Richard A. Rowland, general manager of First National; H. C. S. Thompson, managing director of F. B. O.; Nicholas M. Schenck, vice-president of Metro-Goldwyn; Harry M. Warner; and Adolph Zukor.

The exhibitor group, headed by President Walsh, included: Louis M. Sagal, C. M. Mansfield, N. J. Fournier, L. J. Hoffman and others.

Mr. Hays, after the conference with the exhibitors, declared that in many cases the tax on the picture would amount to six times the rental and that it was physically impossible for the theatres to continue business under such conditions.

(Continued on page 1134)

Request Annual Movie Season Drive

St. Louis Exhibitors Urge Campaign Be Made Yearly Event; Hays Announces Judges of Essay Contest

WILL H. HAYS, president of the M. P. P. D. A. this week received the first official request by an organized body of exhibitors for a Greater Movie Season Campaign next year. A wire to Mr. Hays from Joseph Mogler, president of the Exhibitors League of St. Louis, declared that the members of that organization at a special meeting to discuss the results of the Greater Movie Season Campaign, decided that the event should be made an annual affair.

The Hays organization reports that while this is the first official action by an exhibitor's organization, general managers of campaigns from "Los Angeles to Atlantic City, and from Atlanta to Seattle" have declared that their campaigns are giving the theatres the best August business they have had in years and report that exhibitors favor a Greater Movie Season drive every year.

Contest Judges Announced

Mr. Hays announced the names of those who will make up the board that will judge the essays submitted in the National Greater Movie Season Contest. These are Dr. S. Parkes Cadman, president of the Federal Council of Churches; George Barr McCutcheon, president of the Author's League of America; Richard Washburn Child, former United States Ambassador to Italy and Alice Duer Miller, noted author.

The contest has been conducted by leading newspapers throughout the United States to select the best essays on "What the Motion Picture Means to Me" or "What the Motion Picture Means to my Community." The three national prizes to be awarded by the judges are a trip for two around the world on the Red Star Liner Belgenland; a trip for two to Miami, and a trip for two to Los Angeles.

Warners Aid Greater Movie Season

WARNER BROTHERS made a material contribution to the Greater Movie Season campaign in New York last Tuesday, when they broadcasted a program of music and speech making from the steps of the United States Sub-Treasury, in Wall Street.

Major Andrew White was master of ceremonies, while among the speakers was a representative of each of the three leading religious faiths. These included Rev. Mr. Phillips assistant pastor of The Little Church Around the Corner, Protestant; Father Leonard, pastor of St. Malachi's Roman Catholic Church and Dr. Issac Landman, editor of The American Hebrew and Rabbi of Temple Israel. Mrs. Martin W. Littleton, wife of the former Congressman, was also a speaker.

The program was started at noon by the Vincent Lopez orchestra. They were followed by Vaughan De Leath, "the original radio girl," who sang, and Mae Breen and Peter De Rose, a versatile vaudeville team. The program was broadcast throughout the country.

N. J. Theatre Owners Combat Blue Laws

THE New Jersey Theatre Owners under the guidance of President Joseph M. Seider are enlisting the services of women's clubs to combat the blue law advocates. A number of women's clubs in Jersey last year endorsed the bill for local option on Sunday pictures.

The women will be welcomed to the Jersey theatre owners meetings so that they might be further informed regarding the problem of exhibitors. Last Thursday President Seider escorted a delegation of school teachers to the First National studios, where they were given first hand information on present methods of production. Milton Sills, Doris Kenyon and Lloyd Hughes cooperated with the Jersey president in enlightening the visitors.

Forty-two newspapers participated in the contest. In addition to the national prizes there will be many local awards of great value.

The Louisville, Washington, Tulsa and Minneapolis campaigns opened on August 15th. With the Motion Picture Theatre Owners of Western Pennsylvania, Inc., D. A. Harris, president, backing the campaign, Pittsburgh opened the season on August 24th.

Oklahoma City is advertising now the Season which will open there on September 7.

A feature of the Tulsa campaign was an eight page Greater Movie Season section issued by the Tulsa Tribune.

Taxis Carry Streamers

Charles W. Krebs, general manager of the Louisville Campaign, reports that 500 taxicabs in Louisville are carrying streamers reading, "Greater Movie Season. Let's Go." Mr. Krebs says that Louisville used practically every form of advertising suggested by the Greater Movie Season book, including the 30 foot banners over all the main streets.

The cooperation of the taxicabs in Louisville is equalled in Spokane by the cooperation of the street railway company, according to Ray A. Grombacher. All the street cars carried on their front fenders large banners reading "Greater Movie Season—Now. Go by Street Car."

The banner championship of the United States seems to be held by the Los Angeles Greater Movie Season campaign, of which Jack Retlaw is the general manager. The committee stretched sixty huge banners across the streets of Los Angeles and forty more in nearby towns.

One hundred thousand Greater Movie Season blotters were distributed in Los Angeles and adjoining towns by a dozen colored boys dressed as Arabian sheiks. Girls in chic French maid's costumes distributed 25,000 buttons. Not satisfied with the 100 banners, the committee stenciled every principal highway in and leading to Los Angeles. The street cars and interurban trains carried banners and a check up showed more than 100 theatres were elaborately decorated.

Laundries distributed 50,000 circulars in the packages. More than $4,000 was spent in newspaper advertising.

New Junior Orpheum House for Seattle

Erection within the next year of a $1,500,000 theatre in Seattle to house the Junior Orpheum vaudeville circuit, with its accompanying motion picture policy, was considered decidedly within the realm of possibility last week, following the visit of Marcus Heiman, president, and Joseph Finn, vice president of the Orpheum Vaudeville Circuit, to the Western city. It is understood that plans have already been prepared for the house, and that a site of an entire block in the northern business district of the city has been selected.

According to the present reports, the house would be operated as a combined vaudeville and motion picture theatre, running continuously from noon until midnight. Feature length pictures, short subjects, Junior Orpheum vaudeville and musical specialties would constitute the program.

Clark Robinson Joins Roxy in New Theatre Project

Clark Robinson, scenic artist and stage director, has resigned from the staff of the Capitol Theatre and will join the S. L. Rothafel organization in connection with the new Roxy Theatre which is to be built in New York City this fall. Robinson will accompany Mr. Rothafel to Europe when the latter sails on September 5th.

Decatur Theatre Managers Form Organization

The theatre managers of Decatur, Ill., have formed an organization to be known as the Decatur Theatre Managers' Association. Elmer Jerome, of the Empress, is president; E. Sigfried, of the Bijou, vice-president; Harry J. Wallace, of the Lincoln, secretary; and Paul Witte, of the Bijou, treasurer, of the new association.

Exhibitor Will Give Away $6,000,000

A VERY interesting news story about an exhibitor comes from Winnipeg, Manitoba, in the announcement that A. R. McNichol has decided to give away his fortune before he dies. Mr. McNichol is credited with having just $6,000,000 which he made in real estate and in moving picture theatres. He is 63 years of age and a bachelor so he has started to distribute his investments.

Not long ago he gave $250,000 to the hospital at Winnipeg and he has made other large donations, including gifts to relatives. He is the owner of a chain of Western Canadian theatres, including the Lyceum, Starland and College Theatres in Winnipeg.

Exibitors Logical Salvation of British Film Making

No. 6: Government Interference of Doubtful Value

By L. C. Moen

LEAVING behind the economic and financial considerations of last week, and getting down to brass tacks on the British film situation itself, we have this picture: An industrial nation where motion pictures are so well liked that, despite acute depression, business at the theatres thrives and American pictures easily gross $25,000 to $40,000 each, with specials rising much higher—yet a nation where production has waned to almost nothing and where domestic producers find difficulty in surviving.

Obviously, then, exhibitors are by far the healthiest branch of the British industry, and it is with them that any plan of production revival should start. After all, the future of better than three thousand exhibitors is of much greater moment than the prospects of a half dozen producers, and any scheme adopted, governmental or otherwise, should be primarily geared up to the needs and desires of the theatre owners themselves.

If the plan adopted gives British exhibitors good pictures on which they can make money, and which the public will like—well and good. But if it merely means that the goverment, by artificial and uneconomic means forces the production of a certain number of British pictures, willy-nilly, then the whole industry will suffer, exhibitors and all.

What is needed, in plain English, is not a method of forcing the production of British pictures, but of making possible the production of really good British pictures. Such pictures will stand on their own bottom anywhere, subsidy or no subsidy. Make no mistake about that. And a subsidized industry, unless it makes such pictures, will fall as soon as the prop is removed and the subsidy ceases.

Any plan of government paternalism that provides money and studio facilities and leaves out the factors of brains, creative imagination and temperament is fundamentally unsound, and will ultimately fail.

As outlined last week, the memorandum of the Federation of British Industries suggested four moves: A tax on the showing of foreign pictures to apply toward the subsidy of domestic production; a finance corporation to aid producers; a national studio; and the enforced showing by exhibitors of a definite number of British-made pictures.

Exhibitors Would Pay

The tax provision would mean, in effect, that exhibitors would furnish the money, through an indirect and involved channel, for the making of the pictures, and would presumably later pay rentals for those same pictures equivalent to those they pay on pictures which they have not financed. If it is rebated to them in amusement tax, the government will have furnished the money.

The more Brifish pictures are made, the greater the sum of money which will be needed—yet under the proposed system, the greater the number of British pictures played by exhibitors, the less revenue will be available for production in the form of duty.

Obviously, then, either the exhibitors or the government, or both, will furnish the money in the end—and how much more sane and practical it would be for either or both to put up the money directly, without wasteful and irritating taxes, duties, tariffs and what not! If exhibitors are to pay the piper, let them do so voluntarily, through a franchise plan or similar arrangement. If the government feels that motion pictures are sufficiently important as a propaganda and advertising medium, let it subsidise directly the making of such pictures as meet that need. But why, since it is a simple business problem, handle it in the most involved and circuitous manner possible? While it is true that the tax on the showing of alien pictures would tend to increase the number of British pictures played, the quota or contingent feature would assure an outlet for all the British films to be made for some time to come.

Studio Over-Stressed

The erection and equipment of a national studio is important, but is being stressed out of all importance to its moment in certain quarters. A studio, after all, is only a means to an end. The finest studios in the world can, and do, turn out some pretty bad stuff occasionally, and by the same token there are several memorable pictures on record that were made with utterly inadequate facilities. A gold-plated fountain pen does not make a gifted novelist.

In the last analysis, and assuming that subsidy will be but a temporary crutch, the British industry must accept one of two possibilities: 1. The making of pictures at a cost within the possible return from the British Empire market. 2. The making of pictures on a free and adequate scale, designed for the international market, with the government making up the deficit until such time as the income equals the outgo.

Swedish Plan

The first plan would be somewhat similar to that carried out with considerable success in Sweden. The Swedish industry, of its own volition, decided that it was desirable to keep natonal production alive. A certain number of productions were made at a cost within the possible revenue from the domestic market—and each picture was made just as entertaining and meritorious as could be done for that sum of money. Exhibitors voluntarily supported these pictures—and twenty-five of them took away the market for perhaps a hundred American pictures, since they played on the average four times as long in a given theatre. Thus Swedish production which was waning, was put back on its feet through a sane and healthy view-point. And this despite the fact that the best directors in Sweden had gone to America or to Germany.

If British exhibitors will pay rentals on such pictures equivalent to those they pay for American pictures, an average film might gross $25,000 in Great Britain. The remainder of the empire, including Canada and Australia, might perhaps return another $25,000. In the British market alone then, the sum of $50,000 might be grossed on each picture, provided that exhibitors were wholeheartedly back of the move to support British production.

Low Cost Necessary

It is true that not much of a picture can be made at a cost which will return a profit from a $50,000 gross, but it is absurd to say that it is impossible. Pictures of a certain type can be and are being made at such costs. One important American company has turned out outdoor program pictures at a figure as low as $8,000—and this is a national distributor. It can be done, but it means mixing large quantities of imagination, talent and showmanship with the money and materials.

The only other avenue is the making of pictures on a lavish and free-handed scale, planned for the world market and of such quality as that market demands. And that means a vigorous re-organization of British production from top to bottom. It means new blood, new talent, new ideas—and adequate financial backing. If such pictures are to be made, it means, first of all, studying the methods by which other countries have accomplished the same thing. It means, in other words, the absorption, tem-

(Continued on page 1138)

HENRY KING
Signed by Samuel Goldwyn

A NNOUNCEMENT has been made that Henry King, one of the most prominent of directors, has been signed by Samuel Goldwyn to produce a series of features, the first of which will be "Stella Dallas."

He will next direct "Partners Again," which will be the newest Potash and Perlmutter story to reach the screen. Both will be released through United Artists, and it is expected that "Stella Dallas" will be ready for distribution early in the fall.

Henry King's most widely known successes are "The White Sister" and "Tol'able David."

Iowa Exhibitor is Building New Theatre Chain

Clifford Niles, exhibitor of Anamosa, Iowa, is stepping into the magnates class. It is his desire to acquire a considerable string of theatres. He has just purchased the Cascade Theatre at Cascade, which was owned by R. J. Lane, the Princess Theatre at Monticello which was bought from V. Landis, and the Opera House at Wyoming which has not been operating as a theatre for some time.

Niles has options on eight or nine more theatres, but does not wish to give further information regarding these deals until the options are closed on September 1. Mr. Niles plans to operate twelve or thirteen theatres.

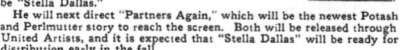

M. P. T. O. A. Showing Activity

Various Committees Are Functioning on Many Problems Being Presented

A WIDE variety of activities is being carefully handled by the different committees representing the Motion Picture Theatre Owners of America, according to a statement issued by President R. F. Woodhull.

A business manager is being sought by the Administrative Committee, which is composed of A. Julian Brylawski, Nathan Yamins, Harry Davis, M. E. Comerford and Jake Wells. A report from them on this matter will be made at a meeting to be held in New York City September 2nd.

The Contract Committee of which Mr. Joseph M. Seider is Chairman, has had several meetings and on Monday, August 24th, met with representatives of the Independent Motion Picture Association of America, with the purpose in view of fostering a simple equitable contract. A contract is being drawn up at this time for submission to a further meeting of the committees of both organizations.

The Legislative Committee has been busy laying out a program for various taxation relief to present to Congress when it convenes in December. These plans will require the cooperation of the theatre owners of the country and their intercession with their representatives at home.

Regarding the organization activities, President Woodhull said:

"We have been rendering practical business service through the Summer to exhibitors, including the securing of product for some of them, adjustments with accessory people, etc., and rendering aid in several Blue Law campaigns now under way in a number of states.

"A real evidence that theatre owners appreciate the necessity of the Motion Picture Theatre Owners of America continuing to function for their protection is the fact that with the direct membership in the National Organization we have members from every state in the Union, men who have paid their dues and are rendering us support and cooperation. This is most gratifying to our officers.

"With the functioning of the Business Manager, as has so long been recommended but which the lack of finances heretofore prevented, it is believed that theatre owners will feel the benefits and results of an even greater Motion Picture Theatre Owners of America, the Organization which has so consistently fought the cause of Independence

in their behalf, labored and secured taxation relief and been a bulwark against the encroachment of the forces bent on monopolization and control."

Radio Talking Picture is Broadcasted

Metro-Goldwyn-Mayer, in cooperation with the Los Angeles Examiner, West Coast Theatres and KFI radio station conducted a unique stunt in connection with the radioing of motion picture lines last week.

They broadcasted the speaking lines of a specially prepared film for the occasion with Norma Shearer and Lew Cody in the featured roles. The lines were read as the picture was shown on the screen in fourteen West Coast Theatres in and about Los Angeles. The lines were picked up and broadcasted by loud speakers to the audiences, giving the effect of radio talking pictures. It was necessary for each projection operator to grind by hand and with precision in order to properly maintain the synchronization of the picture and the lines.

New West Coast Theatres House for Los Angeles

West Coast Theatres is to build a handsome new theatre to cost $350,000 on the southwest corner of Wilshire Boulevard between La Brea and Syeamore Avenues in Los Angeles. Construction is to start immediately. The lease rental, it is said, will total over $1,000,000. The plans call for a class A fireproof structure with a 2000 seat theatre and many modern stores as part of the building.

Lichtbildbuehne is Launching New Trade Paper

Germany's leading film trade paper, "Lichtbildbuehne," will launch a new illustrated film trade paper starting October 1st and invites production stills, photos of leading players and all other interesting subjects from producing companies. These stills should be sent to Lichtbildbuehne, Friedrichstrasse 225, Berlin SW 48, Germany.

Edward Flanagan Funeral in St. Louis

Funeral services for Edward Flanagan, 41 years old, of Hollywood, Cal., motion picture actor and vaudeville performer were held in St. Louis, Mo., Monday morning, August 24. Services were conducted at St. Mark's Church and interment was in Calvary Cemetery.

Flanagan left St. Louis twenty-four years ago to go into vaudeville. Later he was one of the members of the "Hall Room Boys" motion picture comedies. He is survived by his wife and two children.

Skouras Has Organized New Operating Company

George P. Skouras, St. Louis, has organized the Columbus Amusement Company to operate his theatres. He recently took over the Congress Theatre owned by Hector M. E. Pasmezoglu and is also interested in the Aubert and Chippewa theatres, St. Louis.

Selznick Trustee Files $14,000,000 Suit

M ARK HYMAN, and Ralph B. Ittleton, lawyers; William J. Doolittle, formerly vice-president of the Utica Investment Company, and Walter Jerome Green, formerly of the Savage Fire Arms Company, have been made defendants in a suit for $14,000,000 damages brought by Arthur Y. Dalziel, as trustee in bankruptcy for the Selznick Distributing Corporation.

The suit charges a conspiracy to wreck the business of the company for the purpose of diverting assets and defeating the rights of the creditors. The action grows out of the reorganization in 1923 of various motion picture corporations owned or controlled by Lewis J. Selznick, the corporation being at the time embarrassed through lack of ready cash. The good will and net assets of the combined companies, it is alleged, had a value of $14,000,000.

The defendants, it is alleged, without any previous experience in the motion picture business, had themselves elected as officers and directors of a reorganized company and assumed absolute control of the new organization. It is charged that by reason of the acts of the defendants the assets of the corporation were dissipated, the confidence of motion picture producers in the company lost, the good will destroyed and the entire business wrecked.

Crandall Circuit Taken Over By Stanley Co.

Washington Deal One of Most Important of Year

OFFICIAL announcement has been made of the sale of the controlling interest in the Crandall Circuit to the Stanley Company of America. This deal has been foreshadowed for some weeks, but it was denied by the parties concerned until the papers were signed. Then Mr. Crandall himself made the announcement.

It is understood that between $4,000,000 and $5,000,000 was involved in the deal. Mr. Crandall retains 25% interest, and operations will be continued by the Crandall Corp., which has been formed.

The Crandall First National franchise is not affected by the transfer, according to reliable information. The Strand Theatre, Cumberland, Md., was not included in the sale, according to a letter to Motion Picture News from Robert Slote, general manager. Thirteen Crandall theatres in Washington, D. C., and houses in Maryland, West Virginia and Virginia were included.

The Stanley-Crandall deal is one of the largest circuit sales on record. In a year of big chain acquisitions, it takes rank with the operations of Balaban & Katz in the Middle West; the First National control of West Coast Theatres, Inc.; purchase by William Fox of 40% interest in that circuit; the extension of the Paramount holdings in several parts of the country; Universal's acquisition of the Hostettler chain in Iowa and Nebraska and the Sparks Enterprises in Florida; and others.

While the Crandall-Stanley deal was foremost in the news this week, other important deals were also noted. It became known that Paramount is completing work on a 4,400 seat house in Boston, to open in October, as part of a 12 story office building. This will give Famous Players-Lasky eleven houses in that city.

It was also reported, but not confirmed, that Paramount has taken over the Strand in Newport, R. I.

The Loew interests were also active. The Colonial Theatre, Reading, Pa., has been acquired from Carr and Schad. It has been the Paramount first-run house there, and it is reported the latter company is now seeking another outlet.

A contract has been signed by which the Loew interests secure control of the Empire Theatre, a famous West End house in London, which has been the home of many notable legitimate productions. It will become the principal Metro-Goldwyn first run theatre in the British capital.

Going back to Pennsylvania for a moment —announcement is soon to be made of plans for a new theatre to be built in Carbondale, Pa., by the Comerford Amusement Co. It will replace two small houses, the Victoria and the Majestic. The Comerford chain already controls the Irving, a modern house in Carbondale.

In Port Arthur, Texas, the Jefferson Amusement Co., of Beaumont, a subsidiary of the Saenger Amusement Co., New Orleans, has taken over all the picture houses.

The seven acquired are the Cameo, Liberty, Strand, People's, Pearce, Green Tree and Victor.

What is believed to be the foundation for another Texas chain is found in the announcement that C. C. Lindsey, operating houses at Lubbock, has formed a partnership with H. C. Houston of Sherman in the operation of the Gem and Travis theatres in the latter city. They plan another house in Memphis, Tex.

It has been announced that the Louis Marcus theatrical interests, Salt Lake City, have leased the Alhambra Theatrical Company of Ogden, Utah, for a period of ten years. The Alhambra Theatre has a seating capacity of 2,200. It is estimated that $20,000 will be spent in improving the theatre, during the next two weeks while the house is shut down. They propose to open September 5th, in connection with the Paramount Empress and Victory theatres in Salt Lake. This transaction has been confirmed by Louis Marcus, Division Manager for Famous Players-Lasky.

A deal that has been pending for some time was consummated the past week between Messrs. D. R. and C. B. Wilson, prominent manufacturers of Pontiac, and Col. W. S. Butterfield, president of the Bijou Theatrical Enterprise Company, Detroit, whereby the Messrs. Wilson plan the erection of a new theatre in Pontiac for Mr. Butterfield at a cost of $200,000.00.

The new theatre will be located on Saginaw Street, on a plot of ground sixty by

one hundred forty-five feet, across from the Oakland Theatre which was recently purchased by Mr. Butterfield and the occupancy of which he will secure in about a year and a half's time. Plans call for a fire proof building with a white cut stone and brick front to occupy the full extent of the property mentioned above. The theatre will be fully equipped with a stage, etc., so that it can be adapted for vaudeville and road attractions as well as pictures.

The seating capacity will be approximately thirteen hundred.

The Pryale Construction Company have been given the contract for the erection of the theatre while George Bachman of Flint will be the architect in charge.

Ground is to be broken this week and it is planned to have the theatre completed about February 1, 1926.

At the same time, Col. Butterfield announces that Articles of Association for the Bay City Theatre Company have been filed with the Secretary of State at Lansing, and all arrangements have been made with contractors for the building of a new theatre in Bay City.

John Eberson, the well known architect of Chicago, has completed plans for the erection of the new theatre which will be known as the Capitol Theatre in Bay City, Michigan. The estimated cost of this new theatre will be $350,000.00 and it will be the largest theatre and auditorium in Bay City, and when completed will be one of the most beautiful play houses in the State of Michigan.

The Capitol Theatre will have a seating capacity of 1,040 on the main floor and 620 in the balcony making a total capacity of 1,660. The theatre will have a front on Washington Avenue of 75 feet and will extend back to Adams Avenue, a depth of 220 feet. There will be two stores on either side of the lobby with a suite of four offices above each store. This theatre will be modern in every respect and furnished throughout with the latest equipment.

The theatre will have a large stage which will accommodate the larger road attractions as well as vaudeville and it is expected that it will be completed some time during the early part of the New Year.

The Bay City Theatre Company will build the theatre has the following officers:

President, W. S. Butterfield, Battle Creek; Vice-Presidents, William L. Clements, Bay City; E. C. Beatty, Detroit; Secretary and Treasurer, Arthur C. Harrison, Bay City; Directors: The officers and Herbert A. Rowles, Battle Creek; Edwin S. Clark, Bay City; C. L. Kendrick, Port Huron.

Mr. Butterfield announces that during the coming year he will build several other theatres in Michigan cities, and increase his holdings in many of the smaller towns. The Butterfield Circuit now comprises some forty-six theatres in Michigan.

Examiner Makes Report in Federal Trade Commission Case

E. C. ALVORD, examiner in the case of the Federal Trade Commission against Famous Players-Lasky and others, rendered his report to the Commission this week. His findings of facts in the case are against the respondents.

Copies of the examiner's report, which finds in effect that the so-called Famous Players group sought to secure control of the industry, will go to the respondents, and it is probable that oral arguments will be held before the whole Commission before that body hands down its decision.

The case is now in its third year. Testimony was taken in cities throughout the country. It appears likely that the decision of the Commission will not be rendered for two or three months.

The respondents in the case are: Famous Players-Lasky Corporation; Realart Pictures Corporation; the Stanley Company of America; the Stanley Booking Company; Black New England Theatres, Inc.; Saenger Amusement Company; Southern Enterprises, Inc.; Adolph Zukor; Jesse L. Lasky; Jules E. Mastbaum; Alfred S. Black; S. A. Lynch and E. V. Richards, Jr.

First National Holds Session

Sales Executives Are Enthusiastic at Three-Day Conference Held Last Week

WHAT was declared to-be the most successful and enthusiastic gathering of sales executives ever held by First National, was the three day convention held Tuesday, Wednesday and Thursday of last week at the Roosevelt Hotel in New York City. It was attended by every branch and district manager. They returned Thursday night and Friday morning to their respective territories keyed up to undertake what they say will be the biggest selling campaign the industry has ever seen.

E. A. Eschmann, director of distribution, who called the convention, imparted to his men his own enthusiasm for the product scheduled for the next fifty-two weeks and outlined to them the sales policies which he has worked out with the aid of his assistants and company executives for the new product.

On the first day of the session the managers were addressed by Mr. Eschmann, C. M. Steele, A. W. Smith, Jr., Stanley Hatch and C. W. Bunn of the distribution department on sales policies and problems, and by C. F. Chandler of the advertising department and Allan Glenn, supervisor of exploitation on advertising and exploitation possibilities of the new product. After dinner at the Hofbrau Haus the visitors were entertained at "Louis XIV" by Leon Errol, recently signed by First National to star in a series of pictures, the first of which will be "Clothes Make the Pirate."

Richard A. Rowland, general manager of production, and Samuel Spring, secretary and treasurer, were the principal speakers at the Thursday session, following a three-hour round table conference on selling problems and other important angles of operation.

A letter was read from President Robert Lieber regretting his inability to be present. Other speakers at the conferences were Earl Hudson, production manager at the Eastern studio; Mrs. Florence Strauss, scenario editor; R. W. Perkins, general counsel; W. C. Boothby, financial comptroller; Mark Kellogg, director of advertising and publicity; E. B. Johnson, manager of foreign distribution; Bruce Gallup, manager of advertising; Lynde Denig, manager of publicity.

Among those who attended the Convention were:

A. J. Herman, Albany; C. R. Beacham, Atlanta; T. B. Spry, Boston; F. J. A. McCarthy, Buffalo; F. P. Bryan, Charlotte; C. E. Bond, Chicago; R. H. Haines, Cincinnati; G. L. Sears, Cleveland; Leslie Wilkes, Dallas; J. H. Ashby, Denver, E. J. Tilton, Des Moines; F. E. North, Detroit; Floyd Brown, Indianapolis; T. O. Byerle, Kansas City; N. H. Brower, Los Angeles; Paul E. Krieger, Louisville; H. J. Fitzgerald, Milwaukee; L. E. Davis, Minneapolis; M. H. Keleher, New Haven; J. C. Vergesslieh, New Jersey; L. Connor, New Orleans; S. W. Hand, New York; E. D. Brewer, Oklahoma City; J. S. Abrose, Omaha; W. J. Heenan, Philadelphia; R. S. Wehrle, Pittsburgh; C. W. Koertner, Portland; Harry Weiss, St. Louis; William F. Gordon, Salt Lake City; Charles H. Muehlman, San Francisco; Fred G. Sliter, Seattle; Robert Smelzfer, Washington; E. H. Teel, Calgary; A. Gorman, Montreal; William J. Melody, St. John; B. D. Murphy, Toronto; W. H. Mitchell, Vancouver; J. C. James, Winnipeg; Fred Rodriguez, Mexico City; R. C. Seery, Chicago; H. A. Bandy, Cleveland; W. E. Callaway, New Orleans; Joseph S. Skirboll, Los Angeles, H. T. Nolan, Denver; C. J. Appel, Toronto.

McKean Made Officer in Military Society

Major S. H. MacKean, news editor of International Newsreel Corporation, was elected secretary of the Society of Military Intelligence Reserve Officers of the United States Army, an organization formed in New York last week. The purpose of the organization is to keep before the public at all times the defensive needs of the nation.

Hays Announces Drastic Connecticut Action

(*Continued from Page* 1129)

The Connecticut theatre owners committee were instructed by the mass meeting in New Haven "to fight to the last ditch to keep the theatres open." However, this appeared to be doubtful in view of the drastic action taken by the distributors. As an indication of what may be coming, all the Hartford theatres wth the exception of the Poli group, have given two weeks' notice to operators, stage hands and musicians, as required by union rules. This was done as a precautionary measure.

The statement issued by Mr. Walsh, on behalf of the exhibitors, follows:

"A committee appointed by the Motion Picture Theatre Owners of Connecticut at a mass meeting held in New Haven last Sunday night met with the committee of the New Haven Film Board of Trade and the Boston Film Board of Trade whose members distribute all the motion pictures shown in Connecticut. The uncertainty and the ambiguity of the Connecticut Tax law have aggravated the situation, which this very unpopular and unnecessary law created.

"Benedict M. Holden, general counsel for the producers and distributors, has advised his clients to remove their film exchanges from New Haven, and to ship all films into Connecticut by United States Parcels Post or the American Railway Express. Anticipating the confusion which will inevitably result when the New Haven exchanges are moved and deliveries are made through interstate commerce carriers, and to enable the exhibitors to keep open and show the pictures they have already contracted for the Motion Picture Theatre Owners of Connecticut, the New Haven Film Board of Trade and the Boston Film Board of Trade have arranged to borrow sufficient funds for the payment of the tax by theatre owners on the films now in Connecticut under contract for exhibition there. After existing contracts have been completed, the exhibitors will leave to the distributors the problem of paying the tax.

"This action was taken to relieve distributors who might be the first to receive films from interstate commerce carriers and be obliged to pay the entire tax before exhibiting them, as the tax on the film is several times the rental of it. Many theatres in Connecticut, not having pictures under contract for exhibition, will not come under the operation of this fund, and there are a great number of exhibitors who will be compelled to close their theatres and suffer a total loss on their entire investment."

Roxy Wins Popular Radio Entertainers Contest

RADIO WORLD, a fan publication in the radio field, has announced that S. L. Rothafel has won the Popular Entertainers Contest, which that magazine has been conducting for the past four months. The contest was open to announcers, singers, pianists and vocalists.

Roxy received over 3,000 votes more than his closest competitor, Ben Bernie. The Happiness Boys finished third. The prize, a gold medal, will be presented to the winner on the eve of Rothafel's departure for Europe.

Warner Brothers Take Over Theatres

Acquire Metropolitan in Baltimore and Circle in Cleveland for First Run Houses

WARNER BROTHERS now have first run houses in Baltimore and Cleveland, as a result of transactions concluded during the past week. They purchased the Metropolitan Theatre in Baltimore and took over the Circle in Cleveland. The houses go into immediate possession of Warners and they will inaugurate the same class of entertainment as planned for the New York Piccadilly.

The Metropolitan is situated in Baltimore's busiest section on Pennsylvania Avenue and was built about two and one-half years ago. It has a seating capacity of 1,800. Warners not only purchased the theatre, but the building in which it is located and the ground. Plans for improvements are already under way. It is intended to put in a new lobby and front. Bernard Depkin, the present manager will remain in charge.

Depkin is an efficient manager, up-to-date in every respect and every house that he has managed in his highly successful career since he started with Howard Bennett at the Little Piekwick Theatre (now extinct), in 1908, has been a success with the public.

When the Parkway Theatre was opened in 1912, Depkin was offered the management of it by Harry Webb, president of that company. At that time competition was extremely keen between the New and the Park-

Moberly Repeals Sunday Closing Bill

THE City Council of Moberly, Mo., on August 17th, by a vote of five to three decided to repeal the ordinance barring Sunday amusements, including motion pictures, despite the protests of ministers and others of the reform element.

The Ministers brought much influence to bear in connection with petitions circulated by them, but were able to secure only 3200 signers. Opposed to these Mayor Jefferies was presented with a petition bearing the signatures of 4200 persons who wanted Sunday shows. Whether the Mayor will sign the veto is problematical, but it seems certain the bill will pass over his veto.

The fight for Sunday picture shows was organized by William Cotter, owner-manager of the Fourth Street Theatre, who is given full credit for the victory.

way due to their being the largest film playhouses in Baltimore. Louis A. DeHoff, was manager then of the New Theatre and the battle for bookings continued for many years until the Parkway was bought out by The Whitehursts who then and still do own the New Theatre.

Depkin then managed a number of other houses and when the Metropolitan was ready to open, he was appointed manager of that playhouse by Dr. Frederick W. Schanze, president of the company. Dr. Schanze is also a pioneer in the industry in Baltimore. He built Schanze's theatre, just across the street from the Metropolitan on Pennsylvania Avenue and operated it for a number of years before selling it to Harry Reddisch, who now operates it.

The Circle in Cleveland is a 2,200 seat house situated at 101st Street and Euclid Avenue in a lively neighborhood. Built five years ago, it was recently remodeled and enlarged into an up-to-the-minute house with all the latest improvements for the comfort of its patrons. With the addition of Warner Entertainment, which means an eight unit, high-class program, with an augmented orchestra, the Circle will be ready to compete with any theatre in the city. Martin Printz, the former owner, will remain as resident manager.

George H. Dumond, general manager of all the Warner theatres, stated that it was the intention of the company to put the same class of entertainment in all the Warner first run houses.

The Metropolitan in Baltimore will be known as The Warner; the Circle in Cleveland will be Warner's Circle Theatre.

Student Theatre Men Start Classes

Paramount Training School Opened August 17 With Lectures on All Phases of House Management—42 in First Class

THE forty-two students registered in the first class of the Paramount Theatre Managers Training School, began their studies on August 17th, when the classes were opened with lectures at the Theatre Auditorium in New York.

The course, which covers a term of six months, will prepare men for positions as theatre managers. Instruction in all phases of theatre management, from the selection of a site for the theatre to the proper presentation and exploitation of pictures, will be included in the lectures and studies prescribed for the course.

The opening session was devoid of ceremony. There was an address welcoming the students by John F. Barry, director of the school. After reading some telegrams expressing the good wishes of those interested in the school, the work mapped out for the students was outlined by Mr. Barry and then lectures on certain of the subjects which will be a part of the course were given.

There were lectures on the History of the Motion Picture by Robert E. Welsh, editor of "The Moving Picture World," and by Joseph Seidleman, assistant manager of the foreign department of Famous-Players-Lasky who spoke on The History of the Motion Picture Abroad.

The trade papers were distributed and studied as night assignments with quizes on the following day.

Mr. Robert E. Welsh, editor of the "Mov-

ing Picture World," explained how this trade paper can be used effectively by managers.

Editors of the other trade papers will carry on this series during subsequent weeks so that members of the class will realize the part played by the trade papers in guiding their future work and how every section of these trade papers can be of service to the wide awake manager.

Norman Collyer, assistant secretary of Famous-Players-Lasky, lectured on "The Position of the Motion Picture in the Economic Structure of American Business."

Edmond Raeburn explained the United States Theatre Map and the economies which justify the theatre circuits.

Edwin Porter who directed the first motion picture, "The Great Train Robbery," explained how direction twenty-five years ago differed from the methods of today.

Lectures on the "Development of the Motion Picture Theatre Structure" were given by Lacey Johnson, by Robert E. Hall, who handled the technical phases of this development and by O. S. Geyer who spoke on theatre structures abroad.

The Organization Chart of the Famous-Players-Lasky Theatre Department was explained and the members of the class were introduced to the file systems used by the Theatre Departments.

The principles of choosing the theatre site and how these principles affect theatre management were explained by T. C. Young,

Louis Cohen and Lacey Johnson of the Theatre Realty Department of Famous-Players-Lasky.

The students visited two of the Class A theatres on Broadway and each department of these theatres was explained by experts in charge.

Five days of each week there are seven full hour periods with three full hour periods on Saturday. Each evening a definite assignment is given the members of the class on the material of the day.

Several Illinois Houses Added to B & K Circuit

The formation of the Great State Theatres, Inc., is announced, whereby Balaban & Katz secure an interest in theatres located in a number of cities outside of Chicago. All the houses involved are already affiliated with the Balaban & Katz Midwest circuit. They include the Strand, Fox and Rialto, Aurora; the Orpheum, Crystal, Prince and the new Rubens-Rialto in Joliet; the Crocker, Rialto and Grove in Elgin; the Orpheum and Majestic in Springfield; the Orpheum in Galesburg; the Majestic in Bloomington; the Midway in Rockford; and the De Kalb Theatre in De Kalb. The officers of the new corporation are: Sam Katz, president; J. J. Rubens, vice-president; Morris Rubens, J. J. Rubens, vice-president; Morris Rubens, secretary; and Barney Balaban, treasurer.

Fifty Theatres in New Buying Circuit With Cooney Brothers as Nucleus

A FTER several months of work, Joseph Hopp announces that a new buying circuit has been formed with the Cooney Brothers theatres as a nucleus, and that an operating company which will handle its business, the American Theatres Corporation, has been chartered under the laws of Illinois.

The new company will open offices on September 1st, on the fourteenth floor of the new Straus Building, according to Hopp, who will be general manager. He states that fifty theatres in Chicago and down state are interested in the corporation, through which they will buy film. A feature of the organization is that the corporation is owned and controlled by the interested theatre owners and will act as their agent in the purchase of the film, and on their recommendation.

Hopp further explained that the American Theatres Corporation will have no hand in the operation of the houses, except for an exchange of ideas and information at the meetings of the theatre men which will be held at frequent intervals. It is understood that a number of important Chicago houses have become affiliated with the new organization, but that the majority of the fifty theatres already signed up are down state. The names of the interested theatres will be made public in a few days.

Labor Trouble in Many Cities

Atlanta Operators Get New Contract—Conferences Continue in Denver and Baltimore

L ABOR difficulties face theatre operators in several cities in the United States. Conference between exhibitors and representatives of operators' and musicians' unions over proposed new working schedules and increased wage demands are being held in Atlanta, Denver and Baltimore.

The Atlanta theatre men have settled with the operators, a new 2-year contract providing for the continuance of the existing wage scale and working conditions for the period from September 1, 1925 to September 1, 1926, and an increase of $5 per man for the following year, having been signed last week. This contract disposes with the most serious aspect of the labor troubles which have existed in Atlanta for some time. So far no change has come about in the situation regarding the musicians. The orchestras are still out of all Atlanta houses. Conferences between the musicians and the theatre managers continue.

The attitude of the Atlanta exhibitors this year has been opposed to wage increases. The operators demanded a $60 a week scale in the contract to replace the one expiring the first of next month. The new agreement which will give an increase next year of $5 per week over the present scale of $50 per week represents a compromise move on the part of the theatre men and the operators both.

Union musicians, projection machine operators and stage hands of Denver and the local theatre managers who employ them are still very far from reaching an agreement on terms and conditions of the new contract which is to become effective September first. Several attempts have been made to settle their differences, but up to this time no progress whatever has been made. The union employees have steadfastly in-

sisted on a six day a week working schedule and 30% increase in pay. They have declared their intentions to strike in case these conditions are not granted. The theatre managers, on the other hand, have just as firmly refused to grant these conditions and it is reported they have made arrangements to fill all vacancies resulting from a general walk-out. The situation in Denver at this time is very bad.

Representatives of the Baltimore Operators' Union, Local 181, G. Kingston Howard, president; and those of the Motion Picture Theatre Owners of Maryland, Inc., Walter D. Pacy, president; were scheduled to meet and confer on the increase in wages and better working conditions asked by the Union, on Friday, August 21, but this failed to happen because of a misunderstanding.

The meeting was then scheduled to take place on Monday morning August 24.

The committee representing the Union will not confer with representatives of the Theatre Owners unless they have power of attorney for all moving picture theatre owners in the city it is reported.

Exhibitors of Ottawa, Ontario, have been having a serious labor problem through the demands of both the International Alliance of Theatrical Stage Employes and the Motion Picture Projection Machine Operators Union for substantial wage increases. The new scale demanded by the Operators is as high as 10 per cent over the agreement for 1924-25 while the Stage Employees are asking as much as 20 per cent more.

Quarterly Dividend for Loew's Inc.

T HE Board of Directors of Loew's, Inc., has declared a quarterly dividend of fifty cents per share on the capital stock of the company, payable September 30th, 1925, to stockholders of record at the close of business September 12th, 1925.

Stanley Company Has Signed Tetrazzini

Jules E. Mastbaum, president of the Stanley Company of America, who is now in Europe negotiating for the appearance of internationally prominent musical stars, has signed Madame Luisa Tetrazzini, noted operatic star for three one-week stands at the Stanley Theatres in Philadelphia, Atlantic City and Camden, at a salary said to be $27,000 for the three weeks.

Mastbaum will remain abroad until the latter part of September, but Frank Buhler, managing director of the Stanley Company, who accompanied him, is expected home shortly.

E MANUEL COHEN, Editor of Pathe News and Pathe Review, has returned to the home office in New York after a five weeks' tour of the country.

E DGAR B. HATRICK, vice-president of Cosmopolitan Productions, returned late last week from a four weeks' trip to the West Coast.

J. *CHARLES DAVIS, 2nd, left on the "Century" Monday for Chicago en route to the Coast. He will be joined by David R. Hochreich, president of Vital Exchanges, Inc.*

P ANDRO S. BERMAN, son of the late Harry M. Berman, general sales manager of F. B. O., has returned to Hollywood to resume work as assistant director at the F. B. O. studios.

L EE MARCUS, general sales manager of F. B. O., is on a tour of Southern exchanges. He will visit New Orleans, Dallas, Oklahoma City and Memphis.

T HOMAS A. CURRAN, *special representative of Rayart, sailed last week with Mrs. Curran for a six weeks' visit with his mother and friends in Australia.*

P AULA GOULD, general press representative for F. B. O., left Friday for a three weeks' trip to the Coast studios.

Business in Montreal Shows Increase

The moving picture business in Montreal, Quebec, during the past summer has been good and the theatre managers cannot deny it. Figures have just been issued by George Crump, chief inspector of amusement tax for the City of Montreal, for the month of July, which show that patronage has been far ahead of the corresponding month of last year, the difference being 374,879 more admissions at local theatres with a corresponding increase of $9,800.18 in the city's amusement tax revenue.

Local moving picture theatres are divided into two classes, those which give guarantee bonds by reason of which they are enabled to pay the amusement tax in lump sums according to their own box office records and the others at which the civic administration requires the actual use of amusement tax tickets in addition to the theatre's own ticket rolls.

In Montreal theatres holding the bonds, the number of patrons during July, 1925, was 1,079,623, with an amusement tax revenue of $33,406.62, as against an aggregate patronage of 890,054 admissions during July, 1924, giving a tax revenue of $30,142.15.

In theatres where tax tickets are issued, 450,341 persons were admitted as patrons during last July, bringing in a revenue of $8,333.54.

The total paid patronage at the Montreal theatres during July was therefore 1,529,964, as compared with 1,155,085 during the month of July, 1924, these being the official statistics of the local tax department as announced.

Marguerite Steppling in Cast of "Memory Lane"

John M. Stahl has cast Marguerite Steppling, sixteen year old daughter of John Steppling, screen character actor, for a role in "Memory Lane," which he is now filming for First National release. Miss Steppling is attending college and though she hopes to make a screen career will first complete her studies.

Another youthful actress, famous some years ago as a "baby star," in the cast of "Memory Lane" is Thelma Salter, who is returning to the screen after a long absence during which she attended school.

"Freshman" Premier Given in Jersey

"The Freshman," Harold Lloyd's newest comedy for Pathe, was given a world premier presentation in the Auditorium at Ocean Grove, New Jersey, last week. The picture was treated as a road show with prices ranging from 25 cents for children and 50 cents general admission to 75 cents, $1 and $1.50 for reserved seats. One performance a day was given starting at 8:15 P. M. The attraction drew summer residents and vacationists from a wide area.

Al Green Under Contract With First National

Alfred E. Green has signed a long term contract to direct for First National. He will begin work under the agreement as the director of "Spanish Sunlight," co-starring Barbara La Marr and Lewis Stone, which is to be filmed on the coast.

Production stills from "Without Mercy," a Producers Distributing Corporation release produced by George Melford

Nineteen Completed By Fox
Production Schedule Moving Rapidly With Several Others Well Under Way

NINETEEN leading attractions for the coming season have already been completed by the Fox Film Corporation, with several more in the course of production at the company's west coast studios. Five of the nineteen, "The Iron Horse," "As No Man Has Loved," "The Fool," "Lightnin'" and "The Lucky Horseshoe" have already had successful advance presentations on Broadway and elsewhere.

John Ford, with five completed productions to his credit heads the list of directors. Among these are, "The Iron Horse" and "Lightnin'." In addition he has completed "Kentucky Pride," a racing drama, with Henry B. Walthall, Gertrude Astor and J. Farrell MacDonald; "Thank You," a John Golden stage success, with Alec Francis, George O'Brien and Jacqueline Logan in the principal roles, and "The Fighting Heart," with George O'Brien and Billie Dove.

Victor Schertzinger has completed "The Wheel," with Harrison Ford, Claire Adams and Mahlon Hamilton, and "Thunder Mountain," taken from another Golden success, "Howdy Folks." Alec Francis, Madge Bellamy and Leslie Fenton are in the cast.

Frank Borzage's first contribution to the program is "Lazybones," with Charles "Buck" Jones in the starring role. Roland V. Lee, with "Havoc" and "As No Man Has Loved" to his credit is at Catalina Island preparing for "The Silver Treasure."

John Griffith Wray is cutting "The Winding Stair," which has Edmund Lowe, Alma Rubens and Mahlon Hamilton in the leading roles. Emmett Flynn is completing "East Lynne," with Alma Rubens, Edmund Lowe, Lou Tellegen, Frank Keenan, Belle Bennett, Marjorie Daw and Leslie Fenton in the cast.

Reginald Barker has completed his initial picture for Fox, "When the Door Opened," from the James Oliver Curwood story. Henry Otto is filming scenes for the sea fantasy, "The Ancient Mariner," based on the Coleridge poem, and Buck Jones has completed "A Man Four Square," based on William MacLeod Raine's novel. He had previously finished "The Timber Wolf" and "Durand of the Bad Lands."

Three Additions to "La Boheme" Cast

Three additions have been made to the Metro-Goldwyn-Mayer cast for "La Boheme," starring Lillian Gish, with John Gilbert in the leading male role. The newcomers are Tony D'Algy, Karl Dane and Leo White. Roy D'Arcy and Renee Adoree were previously announced for important roles. The production has just gone into rehearsal under the direction of King Vidor.

Malcolm McGregor Leading Man for Corinne Griffith

Malcolm McGregor will play the leading role opposite Corinne Griffith in "Caesar's Wife," the star's next vehicle for First National. The story is by W. Somerset Maugham and will be directed by Irving Cumings from a scenario by Albert Shelby LeVino.

Betty Bronson in "The Golden Princess," a Paramount picture.

Exhibitors Logical Hope of British Film Making

(Continued from page 1131)

porarily at least, of American production methods, right or wrong.

An excellent parallel is suggested by Mr. Cranfield, of Cranfield & Clarke, in the matter of Japanese shipping. For many years, while the Japanese navy and merchant marine were being built up, every important Japanese ship had a British captain and a Scotch chief engineer. The Japanese were not too proud to go to those who had accomplished results in that particular line, and to bring them in to teach their own men how to run ships as they should be run.

Even the American motion picture industry, remember, has never hesitated to do that same thing. Some of our earliest studios were built by Frenchmen who came here to erect them in the light of their wide experience at that time. The American industry has never hesitated to reach out across the sea for a foreign director or player who might bring some new contribution to the screen.

England, if she wants to produce in a big way, must do the same. Until she can develop new talent of her own, let her assemble a central production unit composed of the finest talent available anywhere in the world.

Let one strong central company be organized, as a beginning. Improve the equipment of the best existing studio. Bring from America a Chaplin or a De Mille or a Louis B. Mayer to direct and supervise the work of organization. Bring to Britain an American director of the very first rate. Bring one or two cameramen of the type who command $500 or $750 a week. Bring lighting experts and scenic artists from Germany. Bring a few selected players from other countries to fit the stories chosen.

Then take the best British stories and put this one central unit to work with a free hand. Throw overboard all antiquated ideas of technique, continuity, camera angles and settings. Finance the series on a franchise plan among British exhibitors, plus a suitable government guarantee against deficit.

And you will have pictures worthy the name. You will not give employment to the maximum number of British artists at the outset, but you will build for the future. Gradually, British artists and technicians will grow and develop, and their pictures will need neither contingent nor subsidy. But not otherwise.

Weil Heads Universal's Exploitation Dept.

UNIVERSAL has announced the appointment of Joe Weil as director of exploitation. Weil has been in charge of the Universal exploitation for the past five months and his appointment as director of the department, the Universal announcement states, is a reward for his accomplishments during that time.

For the past two years Weil has handled all of the Broadway showings for the company. A year ago he has detailed to put over "The Hunchback" in Paris, which he did in record breaking manner.

New Laboratory for New York

United Color Pictures to Offer New Process on Definite Commercial Scale

PURCHASE of a plot of ground in New York City last week by the United Color Pictures, Inc., for the erection of a three-story laboratory and factory building brought to light the fact that a new color process is soon to be offered to the industry on a definite commercial scale.

The new color process is the invention and development of Joseph Shaw, well known in the industry as a photographic expert, and until recent years, when he started to work on his color plans, associated with the Eastman Company for a period of twelve years. Mr. Shaw is authority for the statement that the new factory will be in operation by the middle of November and that orders for work are already being taken.

The process sponsored by the newly-organized United Color Pictures, Inc., was originally financed by George J. Gould, the nationally famous railroad man and capitalist. Since his death the interest of the estate has been taken over by the Barnes Finance Corporation, a strong Mid-West organization, which is now associated with Mr. Shaw in the United firm.

Representatives of the Barnes organization interviewed during the week were enthusiastic over the preliminary demand for the process in which they have become interested, and very optimistic regarding the probable market. More business has already been offered by concerns who have seen samples of the work than it will be possible to turn out at the start.

Virtues claimed for the new process include an exceptional range and softness of color; unusually close registering, and the fact that the process aids the blending with

the black and white. The inventor, previous to his association with Eastman, was prominent in photographic circles in England and Germany, and entered motion picture work with a background of firm scientific knowledge.

Concerning his new process, Mr. Shaw was reticent to speak preferring to allow the many samples of his work that have already been seen by picture experts to do the talking. "It is not for the inventor," he declares, "to proclaim the strong points of his own creation, for the parent is naturally enthusiastic. But practical picture producers who have viewed the United Color company's work are unanimous in telling me that at last it looks as though the picture industry is getting the color process for which it has been looking.

"Commercially practicable price and fineness of quality have been the demands. We will meet the market in price, thus putting natural color within reach of all, and as far as quality is concerned I feel confident that any picture men who view the new process on the screen will agree that we have finally got away from the jarring notes and limitations of color film work of the past."

James Mason in Cast of New Harold Lloyd Feature

James Mason will play a heavy role in the Harold Lloyd feature which is now in production for Paramount distribution. Mason will add to the group of underworld characters in the film, the group now including also Noah Young, Leo Willis and Constantine Romanoff, a heavyweight wrestler.

Kane Proposes Photoplay Chair

Offers $5,000 Annual Endowment for Picture Department in University

SUGGESTING a photoplay department for universities as the means of attracting to the picture industry college men trained in various phases of photoplay production, Robert T. Kane, head of the production company bearing his name, has offered an annual $5,000 endowment for that purpose.

In making this proposal Mr. Kane expressed the hope that other producers would share his views and lend their support toward establishing a photoplay chair in one of the larger universities of this country. Announcing his plan, Mr. Kane said:

"There is no other profession or business, in the world, wherein the financial reward is so great as in ours. I can name at the moment eight young men earning on an average of $1,000 a week in New York studios, and not one of them would be able to last a week if pitted against college trained, highly specialized and serious minded contemporaries. We must have creative thought and competent counsel. This is the only way of obtaining it.

"I have felt for years that we in the industry are paying genius prices to mediocrity. This must be curbed."

Kane restricted his annual gift toward a photoplay department to the following universities: Yale, Harvard, Princeton, University of California, University of Pennsylvania, University of Wisconsin, University of Chicago and Columbia.

Tearle Signs Contract to Star for Asher

Conway Tearle will be presented as the star in several productions to be made by E. M. Asher, of Corinne Griffith Productions, it was announced this week. A contract calling for Tearle's services as a star was signed on the coast by the actor and Mr. Asher.

The Tearle pictures will be an enterprise separate from the activities in which Asher participates with Corinne Griffith. Releasing arrangements will be announced soon, the producer said. The pictures are to be filmed at the United Studios in Hollywood. The first production will be "Good Luck," a London melodrama.

Rayart Companies Busy With Production

Three Rayart companies are busily engaged with production work on the west coast. Harry J. Brown Productions last week completed work on "The Patent Leather Pug," a five reel prize fight story starring Billy Sullivan, and will start next week on "The Windjammer," also featuring Sullivan. The same company also has in production "The Danger Quest," featuring Reed Howes, with a cast that includes Ethel Shannon, J. P. McGowan and Billy Franey.

Jack Perrin, another Rayart star, is working under the supervision of Harry Webb of Webb Productions, on a five reel western titled "Dangerous Fists."

Three Signed for "Sally, Irene and Mary"

Karl Dane, William Haines and Joan Crawford have been signed by director Edmund Goulding for three of the important roles in "Sally, Irene and Mary," a spectacular screen production for Metro-Goldwyn-Mayer.

The picture will be an adaptation from the Broadway stage success of three seasons ago by Edward Dowling. It was adapted for the screen by Louis Lighton and Hope Loring.

Dorothy Mackaill Signed by First National

Dorothy Mackaill has been placed under a five-year contract by First National. The agreement was signed by Miss Mackaill and John E. McCormick, western general manager of production for First National, recently. Her next appearance will be in "Joanna With a Million" to be produced by Edwin Carewe, producer of "Mighty Lak' A Rose," the photoplay in which Miss Mackaill achieved screen prominence.

Betty Bronson in Paramount's "A Kiss For Cinderella."

Highlights from the Frank Lloyd production "Winds of Chance," a First National release.

F. B. O. Presenting New Stars

Company Also Appointing New Directors in Building Up Its Production Forces

IN AN effort to present new talent on and back of the screen, F. B. O. has added to its personnel five stars and directors hitherto unknown in these capacities. Tom Tyler, new to stardom, is being guided by James Gruen, former Los Angeles newspaperman, and Robert De Lacey, who was for many years a star cutter. They are now filming "Let's Go, Gallagher," a western picture.

In the supporting role with Alberta Vaughn in "The Adventures of Mazie," is Larry Kent, a young juvenile with but little experience before the camera. James Wilkinson, formerly head cutter for F. B. O. is working with Director Ralph Ceder on the same series, and will probably be given his own unit in the near future.

In discussing the move for the presentation of new stars and directors, B. P. Fineman, general manager of F. B. O. studios, said:

"It is a sort of financial cowardice that has prevented the inculcation of new ideas and new blood to any appreciable extent heretofore. It is natural enough, in a way, but it is unfortunate. Producers have been afraid to 'gamble' with untried talent in almost any line, and have waited for talent to prove itself before accepting it as such. With no chance to prove itself, the situation has resolved into a vicious circle; men with ambition waiting to try and break in and show what they can do, while the producer says 'show me what you can do before I sign you.' I believe personally that the time for that sort of business conservatism is at an end. It is as archaic as Sanskrit. And I think, furthermore, that it is no gamble to utilize more or less unknown talent provided the men themselves are known and studied as individuals."

Six F. B. O. companies and ten independents are at work on the F. B. O. lot, keeping up the brisk production pace in Hollywood during the past several months.

Among the more important F. B. O. pictures now in the course of completion are "The Last Edition," Emory Johnson's newspaper melodrama; "Three Wise Crooks," Evelyn Brent's new vehicle; "Heads Up," the latest Lefty Flynn opus being produced and directed by Harry Garson; "Ridin' The Wind," the most recent Fred Thomson picture under the co-direction of Del Andrews and Al Werker; Dick Talmadge's "Dr. Jim," "Let's Go, Gallagher," and "The Adventures of Mazie," Alberta Vaughn's two reel starring series.

Douglas McLean is one of the outside companies which has just started work at this studio, beginning "Seven Keys To Baldpate." Other independents who are busy include the Hoffman company, the Sanford Productions, Howard Esterbrook Productions, Spitzer-Jones Pictures and Larry Semon.

Gotham Will Make Third Thunder Feature

A third Thunder feature for the Marvel Dog will be included in the program of twelve features by Gotham Productions for release through Gotham Productions. The new one titled, "The Phantom of the Forest" will take the place on the program previously announced for "The Forest of Destiny" and will be released early in the Spring as one of the final pictures of the current program.

Immediately upon his return from Germany, Thunder will start work on the second picture of the series titled, "The Sign of the Claw." The story was written especially for the dog by Lon A. Young. The third picture, "The Phantom of the Forest" is a melodrama of the lumber camps in Northern New York.

New William Fox Academy of Music Soon to Replace Famous Old Structure

THE old Academy of Music, New York's first home of the opera, opened on October 20th, 1853, will soon be no more. It is to be torn down to make way for a new skyscraper.

New York will not be without its Academy of Music, however, as directly across 14th street from the old site, William Fox, President of Fox Film Corporation who holds the lease on the building, is erecting a greater Academy of Music which will be opened March 1st, 1926, the date of the closing of the famous old playhouse.

The new Academy of Music has been planned by Mr. Fox as a "temple of Music" to the public. It is now under construction and was conceived as a center for true music lovers who abound in the 14th street district and below it. Motion pictures will also be shown.

The new structure will cost $1,500,000 and have a seating capacity of 4900, running through the block to 13th street. It will have an orchestra of 100 artists with a leader of international reputation. A refrigerating system will reduce the temperature of the auditorium 20 degrees lower than that in the street.

The lease of the Academy of Music was acquired by William Fox, through the New England Theatre Company, on February 12, 1910 and took possession on January 5, 1911. The last performance of the legitimate drama was given by E. H. Sothern and Julia Marlowe in "Hamlet" on June 6, 1910.

The New Academy of Music, which is nearing completion, will be one of the finest theatres of music and motion pictures in the city.

I. M. P. A. Membership Increases

Elliott Report Shows Enrollment Gains Forty-Five Per Cent in Two Months

THE membership of the Independent Motion Picture Association of America has increased 45 per cent in the past two months, according to the first formal report submitted to the Association by Frederick H. Elliott, general manager.

There were 71 members, 26 producers and distributors and 45 exchanges on June 15, the date on which Mr. Elliott assumed the duties of his office, and on August 15th there were 103 active members and two associate members enrolled. The active list now shows 25 producers-distributors and 78 exchanges.

"To the best of my knowledge," said Mr. Elliott in his report, this is the largest by far of any organization within the industry as regards corporate membership."

The Connecticut tax situation was the leading topic for discussion at the last meeting of the organization. Mr. Elliott submitted a proposal for special action by the Independents. His report was confirmed by Lester S. Tobias, of New Haven, regional director for the I. M. P. A. and the proposal received the unanimous indorsement of the meeting. A special legislative committee to consider the situation is to be appointed by I. E. Chadwick, president of the I. M. P. A.

New members elected at the meeting included the Krause Mfg. Co. to associate membership and the following to active membership: Freedom Film Co., Buffalo; Home State Film Co., Inc., Dallas; Independent Film Service, Inc., Dallas; Oklahoma Specialty Film Co., Oklahoma City; Standard Film Service, Inc., Oklahoma City; Lande Film Co., Pittsburgh; Renown Pictures, Indianapolis; Capitol Film Exchange, Indianapolis; Midwest Distributing Co., Milwaukee; Arkansas Specialty Film Co., Little Rock.

Leading Havana Theatre to Show Pictures

THE Teatro Nacional in Havana will be converted into a motion picture house with First National pictures as the basis of the program under an agreement signed by Fernando Poli, prominent Havana exhibitor, with First National. The Nacional will inaugurate its new policy on August 29th with "The Sea Hawk" as the attraction.

The Nacional, the foremost theatre in Cuba, has housed the annual presentation of opera in Cuba, and such famous operatic stars as Caruso, Tetrazini and Bonci have appeared there. The house has a seating capacity of 2,200 and was built in 1911.

A modern ventilating system and other improvements are being installed. The work will be conducted as a picture theatre under the direction of Mr. Poli, who is also the owner and operator of the Strand, Florencina, Palico Gris and Campoamor theatres in Havana.

Albany Zone Meeting to Adopt New By-Laws

There will be a meeting of the Albany and Buffalo Zones held in the latter city the fore part of September, according to an announcement made in the latter city this week by Louis Buettner, of Cohoes, chairman of the Albany Zone. The meeting, however, will be only of the two zone committees from each Zone and will be for the purpose of submitting and adopting by-laws and certain amendments that have been suggested by various exhibitors. Among these amendments will be one which would make it mandatory upon the exchange or the exhibitor bringing a case before the arbitration boards, to pay the sum of five dollars to meet expenses. It is contended that if such an amendment was adopted that it would do away with so many trivial cases being brought up before the Arbitration Board, requiring much valuable time on the part of exchange managers as well as exhibitors sitting on the Board. Whatever money accrued from such charges could be applied to meeting the running expenses of the two zones as well as the arbitration boards.

New Charters Granted in New York State

Motion picture companies incorporating in Albany and receiving charters which permit them to engage in the various branches of the industry in New York State during the past week, included the following, the names of the directors and the amount of capitalization, when specified, being given: Hubert's Museum, $10,000, D. Blum, J. H. Greenfeld, B. Selenks, New York city; United Stars Distributing Co., Inc., $5,000, Nat Nathensen, Samuel Goldfarb, W. Mason, New York City; Hudson Valley Theatres Corporation, with M. L. Elkin, M. Salit, Anne Eichel, New York city; Wellwood Amusement Co., Inc., Great Neck, $20,000, Fred Kilgour, Oyster Bay; George Duck, H. S. McKnight, Great Neck; H. E. R. Laboratories, Inc., David Bernstein, Morris L. Greenberg, Sylvia T. Stern, New York city; The Herkimer - Little Falls Corporation, with H. E. Hughes, New York; Louis Mehl, Charles B. Paine, Brooklyn; Little Neck Amusement Co., Inc., $5,000, Samuel Baker, Ozone Park; Daniel Kerner, Ozone Park; B. S. Michaelson, New York city; Magnus Film Sales Corporation, $5,000, Henry Arias, Edmund Souhami; Essie Bregstein, New York; A. and A. Amusement Corporation, $25,000, R. H. Clarke, F. C. Taylor, James T. Aspbury, New York city.

No Vacancies on New York Review Board

Despite the fact that there was a recent civil service examination in New York state for the position of reviewer on the New York State Motion Picture Commission, it is said that there is no possibility of any immediate appointments being made. While there were two vacancies existing some time ago, these were filled from the former eligible list. Many of those who took the examination a short time ago were under the impression that there was a chance for immediate appointment.

Preparing "Blue Law" Bill for New York State

Rev. John Ferguson, secretary of the Lord's Day Alliance, has served notice on the New York State Legislature that it may expect a "blue law" bill next January, very similar to the one that failed to pass last winter. It is said that the Lord's Day Alliance will support the bill and that preparations have already been made for its introduction. Among other things the bill will prohibit Sunday motion picture shows throughout New York state.

Blaisdell Organizes Producing Company

GEORGE BLAISDELL, former editor of the Exhibitors Trade Review and of Moving Picture World, this week announced the incorporation of Beacon Films Corporation, a California corporation, that will produce independent pictures in Hollywood. The company is headed by Robert Anthony Dillon, the author, as President and Mr. Blaisdell as Secretary and Treasurer.

The first production of the new company is in work and is "The Flame Fighter" a ten episode serial production starring Herbert Rawlinson. It will be released by Rayart Pictures.

Douglas Fairbanks' Niece in "Stella Dallas"

Flobelle Fairbanks, a niece of Doug, is making her screen debut with Samuel Goldwyn's "Stella Dallas," being directed by Henry King for United Artists release. She is playing the maid of honor at the wedding scene of Douglas Jr., as young Grovesnor, to Lois Moran as Laurel Dallas.

Conway Tearle Engaged by Tiffany

Conway Tearle has been engaged by Tiffany Productions for the principal role in "Morals for Men," suggested by "The Luck Serum," from the pen of Gouverneur Morris. A. P. Younger adapted the story for the screen. It will be the fourth of the Tiffany Big Twelve by famous authors.

S. F. Police Chief to Make Screen Debut

San Francisco's police chief, Dan O'Brien, will make his screen debut in "The Last Edition," Emory Johnson's newspaper story for early autumn release by F. B. O. He will have the role of the chief of police.

Barbara Starr Engaged for "Let's Go Gallagher"

Barbara Starr has been engaged for the feminine lead opposite Tom Tyler in "Let's Go Gallagher," his first western production for F. B. O., which is to be filmed in Hollywood.

Action stills from "The Meddler," a recent Universal feature.

Report New Independent Deals
Important Foreign and Domestic Sales Closed by States Rights Distributors

SALES of new independent productions for foreign and domestic territories show considerable buying activity on the part of exchange men and exporters. The foreign buyers figure prominently in the recent announcements of deals concluded by the states rights distributors, who also report the closing of more territory in this country on producers listed on the current year's program.

Sam Saxe this week announced the sale to Home State Film Co., Inc., of Dallas, Little Rock and Oklahoma City, of the twelve Gotham Productions for the Southwestern states of Texas, Oklahoma and Arkansas. The deal was concluded between Mr. Saxe and Jack K. Adams, of the Home State company, during his visit to New York this week. On his return Adams took with him prints of the first three releases, "The Overland Limited," "The Police Patrol" and "A Little Girl in a Big City."

Arrow Pictures Corporation, W. E. Shallenberger, president, reports the sale of "High Speed Lee" to the DeLuxe Film Company of Philadelphia, for their territory.

First Graphic Exchanges, Inc., of Albany and Buffalo have secured the rights to eight J. B. Warner pictures produced by Sunset Prod.

Jans Productions, Inc., announced that Charles LaLumiere, president of the Film DeLuxe, Ltd., had contracted for the Eastern Canadian Rights for the 1925-26 productions of that company. The announcement states that this sale practically closes the entire world distribution rights on the six features

which Jans will make this season.

Joe Rock Productions, making the series of 13 two-reel Standard comedies, and 13 Blue Ribbon comedies, to be distributed by F. B. O. in the United States and Canada, report that J. G. & R. B. Wainright of London, have bought the distribution rights to both series for the United Kingdom and Continental Europe.

The Wainright firm has also purchased for those territories the 26 single reel subjects being produced by J. R. Bray. These are in two series of 13 and are titled the "Unnatural History Cartoons," and the "Dinky Doodle Cartoons." These pictures, also, are being handled in the United States and Canada by F. B. O. The Bray product has also been sold to U. Ono for Japan.

Warner Bros. To Produce Stage Plays

Warner Brothers are mapping their plans to produce plays on the legitimate stage, according to Harry M. Warner. They are purchasing novels and plays for next season's schedule to be presented in Broadway playhouses. Casting will be under way shortly for two plays to be produced shortly before the holidays.

The first two stories being considered are "The Woman Tamer," by Stanley Shaw, and "The Florentine Dagger," a mystery story by Ben Hecht. "Bitter Apples," a recent novel by Harold McGrath, which has just been bought by the Warners, is another novel being considered for stage purposes.

Harold Lloyd in "The Freshman." Pathe Release.

Release stills from "Kentucky Pride," the John Ford production presented by Fox with J. Farrell Mac-Donald, Gertrude Astor and Henry B. Walthall in featured roles.

Warners Plan Sept. Releases

Four Features Are Scheduled for the Exhibitors During the Coming Month

THE first four releases of the 1925-26 schedule have been set for September by Warner Brothers. They include dramas, melodramas and comedies. The releases include "The Limited Mail," "The Wife Who Wasn't Wanted," "His Majesty Bunker Bean" and "Below the Line."

"The Limited Mail," starring Monte Blue, is set for release September 5th. It is an Elmer K. Vance story with Vera Reynolds, Willard Louis, John Roche, Eddie Gribbon, Tom Gallery and Otis Harlan in the prominent roles. George Hill directed.

Gertie De Wentworth James's "The Wife Who Wasn't Wanted" is to be released September 12th. Irene Rich is starred, with Huntly Gordon, John Harron, June Marlowe, Gayne Whitman, Elinor Faire and Don Alvarado in the supporting roles. James Flood directed.

"His Majesty Bunker Bean," a Harry Leon Wilson story, starring Matt Moore and Dorothy Devore, is the September 19th release. Louise Fazenda, Willard Louis, and John Patrick have the leading supporting roles. Harry Beaumont directed.

"Below the Line" is a Rin-Tin-Tin story by Charles A. Logue to be released September 26th. Among the players in the cast are John Harron, June Marlowe, Pat Hartigan and Charles "Heinie" Conklin. Herman Raymaker directed.

Katz Named Assistant F. B. O. Sales Chief

MAJOR H. C. S. Thomson, president and managing director of Film Booking Offices has announced the appointment of Sidney M. Katz as assistant sales manager. Katz has been associated with the company since its inception three and one-half years ago as assistant manager of the New York exchange and a district manager in the east.

Katz left this week for a swing around the exchanges of F. B. O. to further acquaint himself with the personnel of the company, though he is already widely known among eastern and mid-western exhibitors.

Two Added to Cast for "Masked Bride"

Chester Conklin and Fred Warren have been added to the cast supporting Mae Murray in her new starring vehicle, "The Masked Bride," for Metro-Goldwyn-Mayer. The production is now well under way under the direction of Christie Cabanne.

Francis X. Bushman has the leading male role in this production, while others in the supporting cast include Lew White, Roy D'Arcy, Basil Rathbone, Pauline Neff, Lawford Davidson and Andre Cheron.

Elinor Glyn Will Direct Own Picture

Metro-Goldwyn-Mayer have signed Elinor Glyn to direct her next picture, "The Only Thing," from an original story written by her. The story is now being adapted for the screen. Mme. Glyn has supervised her own productions in the past, but will be her first directorial effort.

Moomaw Will Produce at Tacoma Studios

Lewis H. Moomaw, who is under contract to make four pictures for Associated Exhibitors, will probably produce some of them at the H. C. Weaver productions studios in Tacoma, Washington. He visited the studios last week and was much pleased with them.

"Under the Rouge," Moomaw's second picture for Associated is now ready for release. It is his own story and features Tom Moore and Eileen Percy. Other important members of the cast are, Mary Alden, James Mason, Claire de Lorez, Chester Conklin, William V. Mong, Eddie Phillips, Carmelita Geraghty, Tom Gallery, Bruce Guerin, Aileen Manning, Peggy Prevost, William Dills and Stanley Blystone.

Ritter Technical Director for Monty Banks Unit

Frederick Ritter, technical director recently associated with the Douglas Fairbanks organization as technician for "Don Q," has been engaged by Howard Estabrook, president of the Monty Banks Pictures Corporation, as supervisor of the technical department working on "Keep Smiling," the new Banks feature-length comedy to be distributed by Associated Exhibitors.

Cullen Landis Opposite Dorothy Revier

Columbia Pictures has engaged Cullen Landis to play opposite Dorothy Revier in "Sealed Lips," a Waldorf feature. Antonio Gaudio who directed "The Price of Success" will handle the megaphone.

Highlight scenes from the Columbia production, "Stepin' Out."

New York Editorial Service for Doug and Mary

An editorial service bureau has been established in New York by Mary Pickford and Douglas Fairbanks with Arthur Zellner in charge. It will supply only special material on request to meet the needs and demands of specific publications and will give authoritative information of any sort regarding Miss Pickford and Fairbanks, as well as their photographs.

Zellner will have his headquarters at the home office of United Artists Corporation, 729 Seventh Avenue, New York City.

Kane Changes Title for the Initial Production

The title for Robert T. Kane's initial production for First National release will be changed from "Invisible Wounds" to "The New Commandment." It is being made at the Cosmopolitan studios. The picture is an adaptation by Sada Cowan and Howard Higgin from the story by Colonel Frederick Palmer and is being directed by Howard Higgin. In the cast are Blanche Sweet, Ben Lyon, Holbrook Blinn, Dorothy Cummings, Betty Jewel and Pedro De Cordova.

Griffith Completes His First Starring Vehicle

Raymond Griffith has completed his first starring vehicle for Paramount and the photoplay is now being edited. It is titled "He's a Prince" and is an adaptation by Keene Thompson from a story by Reginald Morris and Joseph Mitchell. Mary Brian plays the leading feminine role, while others featured in the cast are, Tyrone Power, Nigel de Brullière and Edward Norton. Edward Sutherland directed.

Arlen Coming for Pola Negri Production

Jesse L. Lasky, first Vice-President of Famous Players-Lasky has completed arrangements with Michael Arlen, famous English author, whereby the latter will arrive in Hollywood October 15th to personally aid in the screen adaptation of "Crossroads of the World," his original story for Pola Negri. This is Arlen's first original story for the screen.

Mix Making Progress on "Yankee Senor"

Good progress is being made on the new Tom Mix picture, "A Yankee Senor," at the Fox West Coast studios. It is an adaptation from the widely read novel, "Conquistador." Scenically this will be one of the most pretentious pictures ever made by Mix. It will show many shots in Yellowstone National Park and beautiful scenes in Chihuahua.

Van Dyke Again to Direct Buck Jones

Buck Jones will again be directed by W. S. Van Dyke in his next picture for Fox, "The Desert's Price." Montague Love is the only member of the supporting cast so far selected. It will be the first picture in which he has appeared for Fox.

Dramatic episodes from "With This Ring," a B. P. Schulberg production.

Educational Fixes Releases

Six Series of Two-Reelers Will Be Under Way by the End of September

BY THE end of September six different series of two-reel comedies on the Educational Pictures program for 1925-26 will be under way, with one or more subjects in each group released. In the three remaining groups, Hamilton Comedies, Lupino Lane comedies and Juvenile Comedies, the first subject will have appeared in pre-release showings, although set on the release schedules for October.

Late in August the Educational product made its first appearance with the release of a two-reel special, "Wild Beasts of Borneo," a single reel animated cartoon, "Felix the Cat Trifles with Time," and a two-reel Christy comedy, "Soup to Nuts," featuring Neal Burns.

The first week of September a Bobby Vernon Comedy "Watch Out" will be released. Jack Duffy and Frances Lee lend support to the star. "Pleasure Bound," a Mermaid Comedy with a cast headed by Lige Conley, is another two-reeler on this week's schedule. Included in the releases for the week is another "Felix the Cat" cartoon, "Felix Busts Into Business."

The week of September 13 is to have for its outstanding release "Off His Beat" starring Walter Hiers. A Cameo one-reel subject, "In Deep," with Cliff Bowes and Helen Foster, completes the schedule for this week.

Critics have pronounced "The Tourist" among the outstanding comedies. It is a two-reel Tuxedo Comedy being released the week of September 20. Johnny Arthur and Helen Foster have the leading parts. Two novelty releases, a "Felix the Cat" cartoon and Lyman H. Howe's Hodge-Podge "The Story Teller," are the single-reel offerings of the week.

The first Jimmie Adams Comedy, "Be Careful," makes its appearance the week of September 27. Long a favorite in Christie Comedies, this is Adams' first appearance in a production unit of his own. Another Mermaid Comedy is contributed this week by Al St. John in a picture called "Fair Warning." A one-reel Cameo Comedy "Who's Which" with Cliff Bowes and Phil Dunham, completes the comedy schedule.

In addition to the above, two releases of Kinograms, Educational's News Reel, will be issued each week.

Production highlights from "Fort Frayne," a Davis Distributing Division, Inc., release co-featuring Ben Wilson and Neva Gerber.

Cohn Developing New Directors

Head of Columbia Studios Says Present Need is for Fresh Directorial Talent

THAT directors with "new ideas, fresh viewpoints, and clever angles to movie material are the most vital need of the films today" is the belief of Harry Cohn, Columbia Pictures production manager. Mr. Cohn admits that there will be much good accomplished by the effort to bring new screen facts before the public, but maintains that even greater good may be accomplished toward bringing new interest into pictures by the encouragement and development of new director material.

Stating that the Columbia organization believed strongly in the idea, Mr. Cohn spoke of Antonio Gaudio, cameraman with D. W. Griffith twenty years ago, and for the past four years Norma Talmadge's chief cameraman, who was given his chance to direct a production when Mr. Cohn signed him to film "The Price of Success," a Waldorf feature. Gaudio's work was found so satisfactory by officials of the company that he was immediately reengaged and is now making "Sealed Lips" for the company.

Another directorial "find" of Cohn's is Frank Strayer, assistant director to Harry Beaumont for the past five years. Mr. Strayer's first work as a director was the filming of "Enemy of Men," a Columbia picture. He also has been reengaged on the strength of his initial work receiving a five-year contract to direct for Columbia. Mr. Cohn states that the Columbia company has in mind several other promising young men who will be given an opportunity to develop their talents as directors with that company in the near future.

Chaplin to Star Edna Purviance

CHARLEY CHAPLIN will supervise production of a number of pictures in which Edna Purviance will be starred following her return from Europe, for where she sailed last week on the steamship Majestic.

Miss Purviance was long leading woman for Chaplin in his earlier comedies and was the star of "A Woman of Paris," Chaplin's first serious dramatic production. The coming pictures are to be made at the Chaplin studio. The director has not been decided upon, but the pictures will be supervised by the comedian.

Casting Under Way for "First Year"

Casting is under way for "The First Year," a John Golden stage success, which Frank Borzage will direct for Fox. The picture will be made at the West Coast studios, where Borzage has just completed "Lazybones."

Harmon Weight Directing Evelyn Brent

Harmon Weight is directing Evelyn Brent for F. B. O. in "Three Wise Crooks," an original melodrama by John C. Brownell and Fred Kennedy of F. B. O. scenario staff. Following this story Weight will return to Associated to direct "Flaming Waters."

Carr to Play Perlmutter in "Partners Again"

Samuel Goldwyn has engaged Alexander Carr to play the role of Perlmutter in "Partners Again," the Montague Glass stage play which is to be filmed under the direction of Henry King. Carr created the role on the speaking stage and was seen on the screen in the Goldwyn production of "In Hollywood with Potash and Perlmutter." George Sidney will be the other member of the famous firm in "Partners Again." Production on the piece will be started by Mr. King immediately upon completion of "Stella Dallas," which he is now filming for Goldwyn.

Ricardo Cortez is Opposite Bebe Daniels

Ricardo Cortez has been assigned the leading role opposite Bebe Daniels in Paramount's "Martinique," which is being made on the west coast under the direction of William K. Howard.

The picture is an adaptation by Bernard McConville from the Laurence Eyre play. In the supporting cast are Wallace Beery, Arthur Edmund Carewe, Dale Fuller, Robert Perry, Eulalie Jensen, John Sainpolis and Emily Barrye.

Sterling to Make Another for Columbia

Columbia Pictures has signed Ford Sterling for another big production to follow "Steppin' Out," which he recently completed under the direction of Frank Strayer. The title of the new picture has not yet been announced, but it is said Harry Cohn, production manager, has a stage hit in mind for Sterling.

Scenes from Paramount's "In the Name of Love."

Associated Arts Title Contest Near End

With August 31st set as the closing date for the Associated Arts Corporation title contest, suggestions continue to pour in for a new title for "On the Stroke of Three." Every state in the union is represented in the hundreds of thousands of contributions.

There are to be 151 prizes in all, with the first prize $1,000 in cash. The second best title will be awarded $250, the third, $100 and the fourth $75. The next seven will receive $50, the next five $25 each, the next five $20 each, the next seventy $10 each and the next sixty, $5 each.

The motion picture trade paper editors, Goebel and Erb, producers of the picture and executives of Film Booking Offices, are the judges of the contest. Prominent in the cast of "On the Stroke of Three" are Madge Bellamy, Kenneth Harlan, Mary Carr, Eddie Phillips, Robert Dudley, John Miljan, Edward Davis and Dorothy Dahm. The picture is an F. B. O. release.

"Fifth Avenue" First for Belasco Productions

"Fifth Avenue," first Belasco production, will be the first 1925-1926 special produced on the program of Producers Distributing Corporation. It is described as an epic of Eastern America and will recount a vivid story of the famous street from which it takes its name.

The story is by Arthur Stringer and will be published serially in the Saturday Evening Post, with the picture due for release at about the time the last installment is printed.

Scenes from "The Book Boso," one of F. B. O.'s latest.

Buchowetzki Starts Work at Universal City

DIMITRI BUCHOWETZKI has started production at Universal City on "The Midnight Sun," an epic of Russia in the days of the Czar, which Universal announces will be made an even more elaborate scale than "The Hunchback" or "Phantom of the Opera."

An all-star cast will be assembled for the picture. Three principals have been selected to date. These are Laura La-Plante, Pat O'Malley and George Seigmann. Work is now under way on the construction of a replica of the Imperial Russian Ballet of Petrograd, where many of the important episodes of the play take place. The story, which was famous in Europe before the World War, is being repared for the screen by A. P. Younger.

Champion Pugilists With George Walsh

Twelve former champions or near champions of the pugilistic arena will appear in support of George Walsh in "The Prince of Broadway" for Chadwick Pictures Corporation. They are, Frankie Genaro, just relieved of the flyweight championship; James J. Jeffries, former heavyweight champion of the world; Billy Papke, former middleweight champion; Ad Wolgast, former lightweight champion; Leach Cross, Tommy Ryan, Joe Rivers, Captain Bob Roper, Gene Delmont, Babe Picato, Jerry Luvadis and Jerry McCarthy.

In addition to the fighters the cast includes Alyce Mills, who plays opposite the star, Alma Bennett, Frank Campeau, Freeman Wood and Dick Sutherland.

Fred Datig Made Casting Director for Paramount

Fred Datig will assume the duties of casting Director of Paramount's west coast studio to replace Tom White, who was given an indefinite leave of absence owing to ill health. Datig has held the position of casting Director at Universal City for the past twelve years and estimates that he has cast nearly a half million actors during that period.

Shirley Mason is Signed for "Lord Jim"

Paramount has signed Shirley Mason to play the only feminine role in Joseph Conrad's "Lord Jim," a story of the Far East and the Malay Islands. Other featured players in the cast, which Victor Fleming is directing are, Percy Marmont, Noah Beery and Raymond Hatton.

Ellis Plays Opposite Elaine Hammerstein

Harry Cohn, production manager for Columbia Pictures, has engaged Robert Ellis to play opposite Elaine Hammerstein, who is to be starred in "Ladies of Leisure." The production, directed by Tom Buckingham, is an adaptation from a story by Albert E. Lewin.

Noted Criminologist in "My Lady's Lips"

Chief of Police August Vollmer of Oakland, California, a noted criminologist appears in connection with the B. P. Schulberg Preferred Picture, "My Lady's Lips" to make an open declaration against third degree methods.

Chief Vollmer appears in a special insert preceding the third degree sequence of the police story, in which he declares that this police method must go to be replaced by a more scientific and more humane method of crime detection.

In giving his endorsement to the picture Chief Vollmer said: "It is interesting and as technically authentic in its picturization of the third degree as that sort of thing can be filled."

Lloyd Assembling Big Cast for "Splendid Road"

Frank Lloyd is busily engaged in the selection of a large cast for the production of a adaptation of "The Splendid Road" from the novel by Vingie E. Roe.

Anna Q. Nilsson has been chosen for the female lead and Robert Frazer will play opposite her. Among the others already selected for the support are Pauline Garon, Gladys Brockwell, Edward Earle, Russell Simpson, Edward Davis, DeWitt Jennings, George Bancroft, and Lillian Gray, who has been labelled a 1925 "discovery."

Richard Talmadge Picture Title Changed

Carlos Productions has changed the title of the new Richard Talmadge production now under way. Originally called "Dr. Jim," it will be released as "The Prince of Pep." The story, a stunt melodrama, is by James Bell Smith.

Six Leading Directors on Sennett Staff

Recent additions to the Mack Sennett directorial staff bring the number of leading comedy makers at that studio up to six. Among these are some of the screen's best known producers of photoplay comedy.

Alf Goulding, now directing Alice Day in her series for Sennett, gained wide recognition for his work in directing two feature length comedies for Metro-Goldwyn-Mayer. Another veteran of the comedy world now directing for Sennett is Eddie Cline. He has made feature-length comedies starring Buster Keaton, Viola Dana, Baby Peggy, Bert Lytell, Jackie Coogan and others. Del Lord, Harry Edwards, Lloyd Bacon and Gil Pratt, other members of the Sennett staff, are directors of distinction in the comedy field.

Second of Marilyn Mills Series Under Way

Casting is under way for the second picture of the Marilyn Mills series, which is being distributed by Davis Distributing Division and Vital Exchanges. Walter Emerson will play opposite Miss Mills and James McLaughlin will play the heavy. The picture is titled "Three Pals" and stars Miss Mills and her two horses, "Star" and "Beverly."

Leon Adams Signs Long Term Contract

Metro-Goldwyn-Mayer have signed Leon Adams to a long term directorial contract. He is the author of "The Masked Bride," Mae Murray's new starring vehicle and a former director in France.

Bruce Gordon Signed for "Three Wise Crooks"

Bruce Gordon will play the lead opposite Evelyn Brent in "Three Wise Crooks," her next F. B. O. vehicle now in production. Gordon appeared with Miss Brent in "Smooth as Satin" and "Midnight Molly."

"Thank You" Premiere at Cleveland

FIVE hundred ministers and members of women's clubs from Cuyahoga county, Ohio, were present at the first pre-release screening of "Thank You" at B. F. Keith's Palace Theatre, Cleveland, last Wednesday morning. This invitational screening preceded the world premiere of the picture which took place at the Palace Theatre the week of August 23d. Colonel Jason Joy, of the Public Relations Dept. of the Hays organization, came on from New York especially for this screening.

Colonel Joy explained to the audience the nature of the work being done by the Hays organization, and also told how "Thank You" came to be made through the co-operation of Will H. Hays, John Golden, William Fox and a group of twenty-eight ministers who sat in on the conferences preceding and during the making of this picture. Following its engagement at Keith's Palace theatre, Cleveland, "Thank You" will be withheld until October 24th, national release date.

Sax Announces Titles of New Gotham Productions

SAM SAX, head of Gotham Productions, distributed through Lumas Film Corporation, announces that five of the twelve features scheduled for the 1925-26 program have been completed.

Number six on the schedule will be "The Shadow on the Wall," an adaptation from the book of that title by J. Brenckenbridge Ellis. Eileen Percy and Creighton Hale will head the cast. "One of the Bravest" is the title of the seventh on the list. This will be a picturization of an original fire department story by James J. Tynan. Ralph Lewis has been chosen for the leading role. The eighth Gotham release will be "Hearts and Spangles," a circus story in the production of which it is planned to use an entire traveling show.

Charles Ray Will Return to Chadwick

Following the completion of his production for Metro-Goldwyn-Mayer, Charles Ray will shortly be back with Chadwick Pictures Corporation to continue his series for the coming year's program for that company.

"Some Pun'kins" and "Sweet Adeline" have already been finished for Chadwick and the former is now ready for release. The story was written by Charles E. Banks and Bert Woodruff, who also plays an important role in the picture. Duane Thompson plays opposite the star and the cast includes Hallan Cooley, George Fawcett, William Courtwright and Fanny Midgley. Jerome Storm directed.

Marion Ainslee Signs Long M-G-M Contract

Metro-Goldwyn-Mayer have placed Marion Ainslee under a long term contract to write titles for their forthcoming productions. For some time she has been a member of the company's staff of title writers. She has had wide experience in this line, her latest work being "The Merry Widow," starring Mae Murray and John Gilbert in this Erich von Stroheim production to be released in the early Fall.

Mildred Davis to Return in "Two Soldiers"

"The Two Soldiers," an adaptation from the Saturday Evening Post story, "The Spoils of War," by Hugh Wiley, is the vehicle which will bring Mildred Davis (Mrs. Harold Lloyd) back to the screen for Paramount. Hector Turnbull will supervise the production, which will be directed by Victor Fleming. Wiley is now preparing the screen treatment.

Clara Bow and Donald Keith in "Plastic Age"

Donald Keith and Clara Bow will again be featured in the leading roles of the B. P. Schulberg production, "The Plastic Age," now being picturized from the novel by Percy Marks. The same players were featured in "Parisian Love" and "Free to Love," others on the Schulberg program.

Columbia Engages Noted Color Specialist

Arnold Hansen, well known film color specialist has been engaged by Jack Cohn to do all of the color work for all of the Columbia pictures for the coming season. Hansen has perfected his new color system and is now applying it to Columbia product. It was shown in "Fighting the Flames," which played the Broadway Theatre in New York last week. Of the new series he has just completed "The Danger Signal" and "The Unwritten Law."

Norvin Haas Named Red Seal Branch Manager

Norvin Haas, with the Pathe office for the past four years on the coast, has been appointed Branch Manager of Red Seal in Los Angeles. The appointment was announced by Edwin Miles Fadman. Haas's headquarters will be at 915 South Olive Street.

"Fightin' the Wind" is the title of Fred Thomson's latest feature for F. B. O. These scenes are taken from the picture.

Exhibitors Service Bureau

With a background depicting New York City by night, and miniature automobiles, toy street cars and such, Manager Eddie Zorn of the Stratford theatre, Poughkeepsie, N. Y., put over an effective display recently for "Night Life of New York" (Paramount) during the showing of the picture.

Advisory Board and Contributing Editors, Exhibitors' Service Bureau

George J. Schade, Schade theatre, Sandusky.

Edward L. Hyman, Mark Strand theatre, Brooklyn.

Leo A. Landau, Lyceum theatre, Minneapolis.

C. C. Perry, Managing Director, Garrick theatre, Minneapolis.

E. R. Rogers, Southern District Supervisor, Famous Players-Lasky, Chattanooga, Tenn.

Stanley Chambers, Palace theatre, Wichita, Kan.

Willard C. Patterson, Metropolitan theatre, Atlanta.

E. V. Richards, Jr., Gen. Mgr., Saenger Amusement Co., New Orleans.

F. L. Newman, Managing Director, Famous Players-Lasky theatres, Los Angeles.

Arthur G. Stolte, Des Moines theatre, Des Moines, Iowa.

W. C. Quimby, Managing Director, Strand Palace and Jefferson theatres, Fort Wayne, Ind.

J. A. Partington, Imperial theatre, San Francisco.

George E. Carpenter, Paramount-Empress theatre, Salt Lake.

Sidney Grauman, Grauman's theatres, Los Angeles.

THE CHECK-UP

Weekly Edition of Exhibitors' Box Office Reports

Productions listed are new pictures on which reports were not available previously.

For ratings on current and older releases see MOTION PICTURE NEWS—first issue of each month.

KEY—The first column following the name of the feature represents the number of managers that have reported the picture as "Poor." The second column gives the number who considered it "Fair;" the third the number who considered it "Good," and the fourth column, those who considered it "Big." The fifth column is a percentage giving the average rating on that feature, obtained by the following method: A report of "Poor" is rated at 20%; one of "Fair," 40%; "Good," 70% and "Big," 100%. The percentage rating of all of these reports on one picture are then added together, and divided by the number of reports, giving the average percentage—a figure which represents the consensus of opinion on that picture. In this way exceptional cases, reports which might be misleading taken alone, and such individual differences of opinion are averaged up and eliminated.

TITLE	Poor	Fair	Good	Big	Value	Length
FAMOUS PLAYERS						
Lost—A Wife	—	4	6	—	58	6,420 ft.
Manicure Girl, The	—	4	8	—	60	5,959 ft.
Marry Me	2	3	3	—	51	5,539 ft.
FIRST NATIONAL						
Just a Woman	—	4	6	—	58	6,652 ft.
Making of O'Malley, The	—	1	10	2	72	7,571 ft.
Quo Vadis	1	2	9	9	78	8,945 ft.
VITAGRAPH						
Wildfire	—	—	12	—	70	6 reels

George E. Brown, Imperial theatre, Charlotte, N. C.

Louis K. Sidney, Division Manager, Loew's theatre, Pittsburgh, Pa.

Geo. Rotsky, Managing Director, Palace theatre, Montreal, Can.

Eddie Zorn, Managing Director, Broadway-Strand theatre, Detroit.

Fred S. Myer, Managing Director, Palace theatre, Hamilton, Ohio.

Joseph Plunkett, Managing Director, Mark Strand theatre, New York.

Ray Grombacher, Managing Director, Liberty theatre, Spokane, Wash.

Ross A. McVoy, Manager, Temple theatre, Geneva, N. Y.

W. S. McLaren, Managing Director, Capitol theatre, Jackson, Mich.

Harold B. Franklin, Director of Theatres, Famous Players-Lasky.

William J. Sullivan, Manager, Rialto theatre, Butte, Mont.

M. A. Albright, Manager, T. D. & L. theatre, Glendale, Calif.

Claire Meachime, Grand theatre, Westfield, N. Y.

Ace Berry, Managing Director, Circle theatre, Indianapolis.

See Complete "Check-Up" Sept. 12th

"Lost World" Campaign at Ocean City, N. J.

"The Lost World" played a week's engagement recently at the Moorlyn theatre, Ocean City, N. J. As is customary, the local management was assisted during the preliminary period by the personal co-operation of the Exploitation Department under the supervision of Allan S. Glenn, who prepared an elaborate campaign to stimulate interest in the advent of "The Lost World."

Ocean City is one of the largest seashore resorts in New Jersey comparable in size to Atlantic City and Asbury Park. Its population in the winter is only about 6,000 which is augmented to 100,000 in the summer. Lowell H. Stormont of the exploitation department, capitalized these facts in the operation of the campaign.

In addition to an especially heavy campaign in the newspapers and the rental of all the available billboard space, generous ads in the house programs and other such media, Stormont, with the aid of George Kline, resident manager, arranged many newspaper tie-ups of unusual quality and quantity.

Permission was obtained from the New York Times to reprint an article from its magazine section written by the scientist, Henry Fairchild Osborn, and illustrated by the caricaturist, Cesare. This article on the prehistoric animals and reptiles whose discovery in a lost world form the basis of Sir Arthur Conan Doyle's film, was used by the principal paper of Ocean City a week in advance.

In co-operation with the Sentinel-Ledger, Ocean City's principal newspaper, ten pairs of tickets were attached to balloons and sent into the air by the Mayor of the City. The ceremony was performed on the boardwalk and duly heralded in advance on the first page of the newspaper. Needless to say, a huge crowd was present to join in the chase for the coveted "Annie Oakleys." In addition to carrying the story in advance and afterwards, this paper also printed handbills and distributed them at its own expense announcing the stunt.

Jewelry provided an excellent window tie-up on "Pretty Ladies" (Metro-Goldwyn) when that picture was shown at Loew's Warfield theatre, San Francisco, recently.

The following day ten thousand toy balloons bearing the imprint of the theatre and the title of "The Lost World" were released from a captive balloon flying from the top of the theatre. Every kid in the sovereign State of New Jersey was present when the biggest balloon party in history was staged, judging from the movies made of the crowd which, incidentally, were unable to avoid reading the imprint on the captive balloon above the theatre giving the date and the title.

Five thousand stickers were attached to the front page of all the New York and Philadelphia newspapers announcing the opening date, by arrangement with the local newsdealers.

"Black Cyclone" Float is Seattle Prize Winner

Stealing circus parades has long been one of showman's popular outdoor sports, but L. A. Samuelson, manager of Pathe's Seattle Exchange and Robert Bender, manager of the Columbia theatre in Seattle not only crashed the American Legion's big parade in that city which more than two hundred thousand people viewed but won second prize; received additional newspaper publicity for their float which featured "Black Cyclone," and also received a letter of appreciation from the American Legion committee thanking them for their cooperation and help in making the parade a success and complimenting them upon the excellence of their float.

In advance of opening date, the exchange manager and the theatre manager got together and designed their beautiful floral float, procuring the only big wooden horse in the town which luckily happened to be black and was an excellent double for Rex. This they had mounted on the float with appropriate copy—"Hal Roach Presents Rex, the Wild Horse in Black Cyclone." Four Columbia ushers were also on the float. Although the float was a ballyhoo, it was so artistically done that the picture not only received a great boost from showing to the thousands who watched the parade but also every newspaper in town carried a story telling about the Columbia theatre winning second prize with a "Black Cyclone" float.

"Declasse" Advertised on 75-Foot Billboard

A feature of the billing given to "Declasse" by Loew's Vendome theatre, Nashville, was a seventy-five foot billboard in the heart of the business district, at the corner of Eighth avenue and Commerce street. All sizes of the paper except the 24's were used and the display was a brilliant one.

Night shot of the excellent specially painted lobby display prepared by P. H. Touney at the Majestic theatre, Fort Dodge, Iowa, for the engagement of "Tracked in the Snow Country" (Warner Bros.).

Warm Welcome for Trackless Train in Decatur

The Metro-Goldwyn-Mayer Trackless Train continues its journey across the continent to a series of welcomes of which that at Decatur, Ill., is typical. The Metro-Goldwyn-Mayer Trackless Train arrived there early in the morning. It was met at the city limits by a motorcycle detail of police and escorted through the principal streets and then to the Lincoln Square theatre. A crowd gathered and enthused over the train during the time that it was parked. Mr. Wallace, manager of the theatre, was taken aboard and was driven through the city to the city hall where the Mayor and other city officials went aboard for a trip around the city.

For fully two hours the train was driven about the city with whistle blowing and bell ringing, attracting thousands of people. Front page newspaper stories were repeated here as in other cities along the route of the train.

"I'll Show You the Town" on Realtors' Cards

By placing a special card reading "Come in, I'll show you the town," in every real estate window in Tampa, Manager John B. Carroll gained the maximum publicity for "I'll Show You the Town" at the Victory theatre. Due to the cards' attractive appearance, Manager Carroll experienced no trouble in placing them, realtors being most anxious to secure the cards for window display.

In connection with stills and photos in the lobby, Manager Carroll used a mounted three sheet cutout showing Reginald Denny and two girls, with the city skyline as a background. Appropriately mounted, the display made quite a flash.

Unique mounting for cut-out figures on "The Night Club" (Paramount) at the Howard, Atlanta, by Manager H. P. Kingsmore.

"Cheaper to Marry" Given Six Window Displays

Six window displays secured by Morris Abrams, Metro-Goldwyn exploiteer, recently exploited a showing of "Cheaper to Marry" at the Lyric theatre in Minneapolis. Three of these windows were contributed by cigar stores and featured stills in which Chesterfield cigarettes were used, and two others were donated by jewelry stores. The Gomossi Store for Ladies exhibited stills of Paulette Duval in lingerie in the center of an elaborate display of women's underclothing.

"Iron Horse" Drive Aimed at Railroad Employes

An outstanding feature of the recent "Iron Horse" engagement at Keith's Palace theatre, Cleveland, was the special exploitation campaign arranged by Manager John R. Royal and the Fox exploitation agent aimed at railroad men and their families.

Lists were secured of the vast army of railroad employees operating about Cleveland, and these employes solicited through the medium of a postal card bearing the following copy:

Railroad Men! "The Iron Horse," a tremendous drama of the building of the first transcontinental railroad, will make you prouder than ever to say "I am a Railroad Man." It is a picture for you and yours! Starting Sunday, July 5th, for one week only, B. F. Keith's Palace, world's most magnificent playhouse.

Another medium employed was a special one-sheet poster about railroad yards, near passenger and freight stations, and in fact at every point where there was a chance of a railroad man seeing it.

Ballyhoo Before Theatre for "Danger Signal"

An excellent exploitation stunt was put over by Manager MacDonald of B. S. Moss's Broadway Theatre then he showed "The Danger Signal."

On both sides of the marquee, MacDonald had huge arrows containing the cast, pointing to a large poster hung over the lobby entrance. The stunt that drew the crowds however, was a ballyhoo specialty in the form of a fat man dressed as a station agent. He delivered lectures on railroad life and incidents that amused the crowd, and his answers to hecklers often called forth roars of laughter.

Snappy music store window display of phonograph records and sheet music tying up effectively with "Sally" (First National) at the Arcade theatre, Jacksonville, of which Guy Kenimer is manager

With First Run Theatres

NEW YORK CITY

Rivoli Theatre—
Film Numbers—The Man Who Found Himself (Paramount), Rivoli Pictorial (Selected), Richard Wagner (S. R.).
Musical Program—"Richard Wagner" (picture with orchestra accompaniment), "Southern Rhapsody" (musical), Riesenfeld's Classical Jazz, "An Evening on a Plantation" (singing and dancing specialty).

Capitol Theatre—
Film Numbers—Her Sister From Paris (First National), Wings of the Fleet (U. S. Navy special), Capitol Magazine (Selected), The Lace Surf (S. R.).
Musical Program — "Raymond" (overture), "Liebstraum" (vocal and cellist), "Gallop" (ballet corps), Capitol Musicale (singing and dancing — "Drinking Song" and "Sampre Libera" from "La Traviata"), Organ.

Colony Theatre—
Film Numbers — Hell's Highroad (Producers Dist. Corp.), Cuba Steps Out (Fox), Colony Pictorial (Selected).
Musical Program—Selections from "Scandals" (overture), Marion Morgan (vocal), Ruth Granville (saxaphone virtuoso), Ray and Rose Lyte (dancers), Organ solo.

Cameo Theatre—
Film Numbers—Where Was I! (Universal), Beware (Educational), Cameo Pictorial (Pathe), Aesop's Fable (Pathe).
Musical Program—Selections from "Sally" (Overture), "Give Me All of You" (soprano solo), Organ solo.

Rialto Theatre—
Film Numbers—In the Name of Love (Paramount), With Pencil, Brush and Chisel (Fox), Rialto Magazine (Selected), Watch Out (Educational).
Musical Program—Ben Bernie and His Merrymakers in "Minstrel Week," Organ solo.

Strand Theatre—
Film Numbers—The Gold Rush

Two-column newspaper ad on "Just a Woman" (First Nat'l) at the Isis theatre, Houston, Texas.

Hand-drawn throughout, this three-column newspaper ad was used to announce the engagement of "The Woman Hater" (Warner Bros.) at the Liberty theatre, Kansas City.

(United Artists), Strand Topical Review (Selected).
Musical Program—Overture (orchestra), "The Monte Carlo Dance Hall" (prolog to feature). Organ solo.

Piccadilly Theatre—
Film Numbers—Winds of Chance (First National).
Musical Program—"Love Song Selections" (Overture), "Invictus" (baritone solo).

Embassy Theatre—
Film Numbers—The Merry Widow (Metro-Goldwyn-Mayer).
Musical Program—"Oriental Bacchanale" (prolog to feature).

Criterion Theatre—
Film Numbers—"The Wanderer (Paramount), continued.

LOS ANGELES

Criterion Theatre—
Film Numbers—The Scarlet West (First National), Unit Number Three (Universal), Fox News.
Musical Program—Melody Monarchs (Specialty).

Forum Theatre—
Film Numbers—Hell's High Road (Prod. Dist. Corp.), From Soup to Nuts (Educational), International News, Kinograms.
Musical Program—"Rose of My Heart" (vocal solo).

Hillstreet Theatre—
Film Numbers—The Texas Trail (Prod. Dist. Corp.), The Pace Makers (F. B. O.), Aesop's Fables (Pathe), International News.
Musical Program—Vaudeville.

Loew State Theatre—
Film Numbers—A Slave of Fashion (Metro-Goldwyn-Mayer), Felix The Cat Cartoon (S. R.), Loew's State Pictorial News (Selected).
Musical Program—Orchestral selections.

Metropolitan Theatre—
Film Numbers—The Lucky Devil (Paramount), Watch Out (Educational), Aesop's Fables (Pathe), Pathe News.
Musical Program—"Venetian Carnival" (Overture).

Pantages Theatre—
Film Numbers—The Silent Pal (Warner Bros.), Pathe News.
Musical Program—Vaudeville.

Rialto Theatre—
Film Numbers—Not So Long Ago (Paramount), Dirty Hands (Educational), Aesop's Fables (Pathe), Pathe News.
Musical Program—Orchestra.

CHICAGO

Chicago Theatre—
Film Numbers—The Making of O'Malley (First National), Scenic Wonders, International News (Universal), Comedy (Selected).
Musical Program — "Rienzi," (Overture), "Bercuese," from "Jocelyn," (Specialty), "The Evolution of 'Baby' Songs," (Organ Solo), "Under Spanish Skies," (Specialty).

Tivoli Theatre—
Film Numbers—The Lost World (First National), International News (Universal), Comedy (Selected).
Musical Program—"A Popular Fantasy," (Overture), "Voices of Spring." (Presentation), "Pomp and Circumstance," (Organ Solo), "The Pearl of Damascus," (Specialty).

Uptown Theatre—
Film Numbers — Wild, Wild, Susan (Paramount), Scenic, International News (Universal), Baby Blues (Educational).
Musical Program—"1812," (Overture), "Classical Jazz," (Specialty), "On The Desert Sands," (Presentation), "It's Up To You," (Organ Solo), "Roses," (Presentation).

Roosevelt Theatre—
Film Numbers—Don Q, Son of Zorro, (United Artists), Aesop Fable (Pathe).

Capitol Theatre—
Film Numbers—Not So Long Ago (Paramount), News and Views (Universal), Scenic, Kapitol Komedy Kreation.

Musical Program — "Selections From Katinka," (Overture), "Capitol Sport Revue," (Specialty), "Kinky Kids Parade," (Specialty), Leo Terry at the organ (Popular Selections).

Stratford Theatre—
Film Numbers—The Teaser (Universal), News Weekly (Fox), Scenic, The Pace Makers (F. B. O.).
Musical Program—The Four Girions in "The Cycling College Girl" (Specialty), Shelton & Toledo (Eccentric Dancing Specialty), "A Romance in 5 episodes," (Organ Solo), Miss Esther Nelson (Soloist).

Orpheum Theatre—
Film Numbers—The Gold Rush (United Artists).

Orchestra Hall—
Film Numbers—Broken Blossoms (United Artists).

McVickers Theatre—
Film Numbers—The Man Who Found Himself (Paramount), News Weekly (Pathe), Comedy (Pathe).
Musical Program—Paul Ash in "Jazz Rodeo," (Overture and Presentations, combined).

SALT LAKE CITY

American Theatre —
Film Numbers — The Desert Flower (First National), Hooked (Educational), Cartoon (F. B. O.), International News, Newspaper Fun (F. B. O.).

Kinema Theatre—
Film Numbers—East of Broadway (Associated Exhibitors), Accidents Can Happen (Pathe), Pathe News, International News.

Pantages Theatre—
Film Numbers—Slaves of Fashion (Metro-Goldwyn-Mayer).

Paramount-Empress Theatre—
Film Numbers—Don Q. Son of Zorro (United Artists), Pathe News.

Victory Theatre—
Film Numbers—Not So Long Ago (Paramount), What Price Goofy (Pathe), Pathe News.

Loew's Aldine theatre, Pittsburgh, used this newspaper ad on "New Toys" (First Nat'l).

ROCHESTER

Eastman Theatre—
Film Numbers—Paths to Paradise (Paramount), Eastman Theatre Current Events (Selected), On the Go (Fox).
Musical Program—"Fra Diavolo" (overture), "The Crapshooters," "Gringo Tango" and "Powwow —an Indian Reminiscence" Selections from "Suite of Five American Dances" (organ recital), "Indian Love Call" (soprano solo).

INDIANAPOLIS

Circle Theatre—
Film Numbers—The Knockout (First National), International News (Universal), Scenic Reel (Fox).
Musical Program—Ted Weems orchestra, and Miss Desa Byrd, organist.
Apollo Theatre—
Film Numbers—Never the Twain Shall Meet (Metro-Goldwyn), Comedy (Pathe), News Reel (Fox).
Musical Program—Orchestra and organist.
Colonial Theatre—
Film Numbers—A Woman's Faith (Universal), Comedy (Universal), International News (Universal), Aesop Fable (Pathe).
Musical Program—American Harmonists and Frank Owens, soloist.

ST. LOUIS

Loew's State Theatre—
Film Numbers—The Unholy Three (Metro-Goldwyn-Mayer), News, Views, Tours.
Musical Program — Orchestral overture. On stage: "Love Makes the World Go Round" (song and revue), Bragonette & Branz (Junior prima donnas of Grand opera), Lozier & Worth (novelty act).
Grand Central, Lyric Skydome and Capitol Theatres—
Film Numbers—Lightnin' (Fox), News and Views.
Musical Program — Orchestral selections. At Grand Central— The Kiddies Follies (song and dance numbers), "The Battle of Songs" (organ).

Art ad on "Winds of Chance" (First Nat'l) at Symphony Hall, Boston.

The Pantheon theatre's opening ad in Chicago Sunday papers for "Zander the Great" (Metro-Goldwyn) when that picture opened there recently.

Missouri Theatre—
Film Numbers—The Ten Commandments (Paramount), Missouri Magazine.
Musical Program—Special orchestral and organ music score.
William Goldman's Kings and Rivoli—
Film Numbers—The Lucky Horse Shoe (Fox), News and Views, Mary, Queen of Tots (Pathe), Married.
Musical Program — Orchestral overture and popular numbers.

OKLAHOMA CITY

Empress Theatre—
Film Numbers—The Half Way Girl (First National), Pathe News, Kinograms.
Musical Program—Organ recital.
Criterion Theatre—
Film Numbers—Wild Horse Mesa (Paramount), Below Zero Educational), The Troble With Wives (Paramount), Kinograms.
Musical Program—Organ recitals.
Capitol Theatre—
Film Numbers—My Ladies Lips (Schulberg S. R.), Kinograms.

DES MOINES

Capitol Theatre—
Film Numbers— Wild Horse Mesa (Famous Players), Fox News, Stereoscopic (Pathe), Watch Out (Educational).
Musical Program—Ten English Rockets (dancers), Russell Murphy (baritone).
Des Moines Theatre—
Film Numbers—Don Q, Son of Zorro (United Artists), News Weekly.
Musical Program—Organ and orchestra in special orchestration.
Strand Theatre—
Film Numbers—The Lucky Devil (Paramount), Kinograms, Hodge Podge Travel Treasures (Educational), Don Coo Coo (F. B. O.)
Rialto Theatre—
Film Numbers—One Way Street (First National).

CLEVELAND

Stillman Theatre—
Film Numbers—Romola (Metro-Goldwyn-Mayer).
Allen Theatre—
Film Numbers—Pretty Ladies (Metro-Goldwyn-Mayer), Plain Clothes (Pathe), Pictorial Proverbs (Educational), Topics of the Day (Pathe), Pathe News.
Musical Program — "Hungarian Impressions" (overture), "Meditation" (dance divertisement), Jazz Band in India.
State Theatre—
Film Numbers—The Half Way Girl (First National), Too Much Mother-in-law (Universal), Valentino and his Beauties (S. R.), International News (Universal).
Musical Program—Organ improvisations (overture), Vaudeville.
B. F. Keith's Palace—
Film Numbers — Thank You (Fox), Pathe comedy, Pathe News.
Musical Program—"No, No, Nanette (overture), Vaudeville.
Reade's Hippodrome—
Film Numbers — The Rainbow Trail (Fox), Pathe comedy, International News.
Musical Program—"William Tell" (overture), Vaudeville.
Park Theatre—
Film Numbers—Not So Long Ago (Paramount), Dirty Hands (Educational), Felix Finds Out (S. R.), Topics of the Day (Pathe), Kinograms, (Educational).
Musical Program—Old Timer's Selections (overture), "Ukelele Lady," "Sometime" and "Moonlight and Roses" (Jazz Unit), "Minuet Waltz" by Chopin (dance divertisement), "Let Me Call You Sweetheart" (love theme).
Keith's East 105th St.—
Film Numbers — The Rainbow Trail (Fox), Aesop's Fables (Pathe), Pathe comedy, Pathe News.
Musical Program — Hits from Friml (overture), Vaudeville.

ST. PAUL

Astor Theatre—
Film Numbers—The Talker (First National), The Tourist (Pathe), Madam Sans Gin (F. B. O.) News of the World.
Musical Program—Overture Astor Concert Orchestra, H. C. Christensen conducting, Organ Novelty, Kathryn Greenman.
Capitol Theatre—
Film Numbers—The Marriage Whirl (First National), Educating Buster (Educational), Capitol News Digest.
Musical Program—Overture Indian Fantasy, Capitol Theatre Concert Orchestra, Oscar Baum, directing; Anne Gray, harpist; Bernice Fetch and Roy Schmitt, Pierrot and Pierette.
Garrick Theatre—
Film Numbers—Little Annie Rooney (United Artists), Felix Cat Comedy, World News Pictures.
Musical Program—E. M. Stolurow and his Garrick Serenaders.
Princess Theatre—
Film Numbers—Lost—A Wife (Paramount), Don't Play Hookey, Kinograms (First half), Wildfire (Vitagraph), Nobody Works but Father (comedy), Kinograms (second half).
Musical Program—Organ concert.
Strand Theatre—
Film Numbers—The Lucky Horseshoe (Fox), Good News (Fox), Kinograms.
Musical Program—Organ program.

MINNEAPOLIS

New Astor Theatre—
Film Numbers—The Lucky Horseshoe (Fox).
Musical Program—Organ concert.
Garrick Theatre—
Film Numbers—The Unholy Three (Metro-Goldwyn), No Father to Guide Him (Comedy), Garrick News Weekly.
Musical Program—Avo Bombarger, tenor, from Roxy's radio gang, Bushels of Harmony (Norvy Mulliban and Jack Malerich).
New Lyric Theatre—
Film Numbers—Eve's Lover (Warner), Pleasure Bound (comedy), Pathe News.
Musical Program—David Rubinoff, Russian violinist, with Maurice Cook.
Strand Theatre—
Film Numbers—The Street of Forgotten Men (Paramount), comedy (Pathe), Pathe News.
Musical Program—Strand Concert Orchestra, Blaine Allen, conducting.
State Theatre—
Film Numbers—California Straight Ahead (Universal), The Masquerade (Red Seal), State News Digest.
Musical Program—Overture, Carmen Capers. State Concert Orchestra, William Warxvelle Nelson, conducting; organ novelty, Eddie Dunstedter; Sissle and Blake, stars of "Shuffle Along."

CINCINNATI

Capitol Theatre—
Film Numbers— Shore Leave (First National), King Cotton (Educational), Capitol News (Selected).
Musical Program—Orchestra.

Walnut Theatre—
Film Numbers—The Half Way Girl (First National), News Weekly, Topics of the Day (Pathe), Aesop's Fables (Pathe).
Musical Program—Orchestra.

Strand Theatre—
Film Numbers—A Broadway Butterfly (Warner Bros.), Never Weaken (Asso. Exhib. — reissue), Pathe News.

Lyric Theatre—
Film Numbers—The Re-Creation of Brian Kent (S. R.), Hello Goodbye (Comedy), Kinograms.
Musical Program—Orchestra.

Family Theatre—
Film Numbers—Riders of the Purple Sage (Fox), Felix Laughs Last (S. R.), Fox News.

Keith Theatre—
Film Numbers — The Cyclone Rider (Fox), News Weekly, Aesop's Fables (Pathe), Topics of the Day (Pathe).

PHILADELPHIA

Stanley Theatre—
Film Numbers—A Slave of Fashion (Metro - Goldwyn - Mayer), Mary, Queen of Tots (Comedy), Stanley Magazine.
Musical Program— "Poet and Peasant" (overture), "Echoes of Switzerland" (Yodeling Specialty), Gigli and Severn (Dance number).

Fox Theatre—
Film Numbers—Siege (Universal), Fox Theatre Screen Magazine, I Remember (Scenic).

Musical Program—"The Red Mill" (Overture), Macy and Scott (Singers), Layton and King (Dancers).

Stanton Theatre—
Film Numbers—The Ten Commandments (Paramount).

Karlton Theatre—
Film Numbers—Just a Woman (First National).

Palace Theatre—
Film Numbers—The Lady Who Lied (First National).

Victoria Theatre—
Film Numbers—The Making of O'Malley (First National).

Capitol Theatre—
Film Numbers—The Teaser (Universal).

To See it is to Love it!

A picture that justifies every superlative! And achievement in comedy, sentiment, drama, power and beauty!

A Serial Classic!

DRUSILLA
with a
MILLION

ELIZABETH GRIMES
PRISCILLA BONNER
PRISCILLA MORAN

JACK DEMPSEY
Mary's Time

LEASE OF INTEREST
STILL A LOT IN THE FLESH

AMERICA *NOW*

The America theatre's ad in Denver on "Drusilla with a Million" (F.B.O.)

DETROIT

Capitol Theatre—
Film Numbers—Her Sister From Paris (First National), Travelogue (S. R.), Aesop Fable (Pathe), Newsreel (Detroit News Pictorial and Pathe).
Musical Program — Orchestral overture, specialty presentation (piano and tenor), organ recessional.

Madison Theatre—
Film Numbers—A Slave of Fashion (Metro-Goldwyn), Sportreel (Pathe), Aesop Fable (Pathe), Newsreel (Detroit News Pictorial and Pathe).
Musical Program — Orchestral overture, specialty number (trio), organ recessional.

Adams Theatre—
Film Numbers—The Gold Rush (United Artists), Newsreel (Kinograms).
Musical Program — Orchestral overture, organ recessional.

Fox Washington—
Film Numbers—Poisoned Paradise (S. R.), On the Go (S. R.), Felix the Cat (S. R.), Newsreel (Fox).
Musical Program — Orchestral overture, vocal selections (tenor), organ recessional.

Broadway Strand—
Film Numbers—Tracked in the Snow Country (Warner Bros.), travelogue (Pathe), Newsreel (International).
Musical Program—Organ solos and recessional.

OMAHA

Strand Theatre—
Film Numbers—Don Q, Son of Zorro (United Artists), Newspaper Fun (F. B. O.), Fox News.

Rialto Theatre—
Film Numbers—The Knockout (First National), From Soup to Nuts (Educational), Kinograms.
Musical Program—"Hungarian Fantasy" (Overture), "Mamie" (Organ solo), "The Great Conquest" (Exit March). On the stage—Huston Ray, pianist.

Sun Theatre—
Film Numbers—Slave of Fashion (Metro-Goldwyn), The Marriage Circus (Pathe), Pathe Review.

World Theatre—
Film Numbers—Dangerous Innocence (Universal).
Musical Program—"Our Singing School" (Organ), Vaudeville.

Empress Theatre—
Film Numbers—A Woman's Faith (Universal).
Musical Program—"A Society Scandal," (Musical comedy).

Moon Theatre—
Film Numbers—The Wild Bull's

TODAY   *& ALL WEEK*

Playing with Love
♡ THEY PAID ♡
—AND PAID!
VIRGINIA VALLI — NORMAN KERRY
IN
"*The* PRICE *of*
PLEASURE"
Also FOX NEWS *and*
"PERMIT ME"
A CAMEO LAUGH NUGGET

Family

WEEK
AUG. 23   TOM MIX *in* "RIDERS *of the* PURPLE SAGE"

Pleasing single-column ad on "The Price of Pleasure" (Universal) at the Family theatre, Cincinnati.

Lair (F. B. O.), Looking for Sally (Pathe), Sunken Silver, Chapter No. 4 (Pathe).
Musical Program—Vaudeville.

KANSAS CITY

Newman Theatre—
Film Numbers— No So Long Ago (Paramount), Newman News and Views (Pathe and Kinograms), Newman Current Event (Local Photography).
Musical Program—Special Selections In Conjunction With "40 Clever Kiddies" In Prologue, Recessional (Organ solos).

Liberty Theatre—
Film Numbers—Drusilla With a Million (F. B. O.), Tame Men and Wild Women (F. B. O. Comedy), Aesop's Fables (Pathe), International News Pictorial, The Fighting Ranger (Universal).
Musical Program—Atmospheric Selections (overture), Recessional (Organ Solos).

Royal Theatre—
Film Numbers—The Ten Commandments (Paramount), continued, Royal Screen Magazine (Pathe and Kinograms), Royal Current Events (Local Photography).
Musical Program—Royal Syncopators on Stage (Overture), Recessional (Organ Solos).

Mainstreet Theatre—
Film Numbers—The Half Way Girl (First National), Educational Short Subjects and Pathe News.
Musical Program—Popular Selections (Overture), Recessional (Organ Solos).

Pantages Theatre—
Film Numbers— The Wizard Of Oz (Asso. Exhib.), Fox News and Fox Short Subjects.

BROOKLYN

Mark Strand Theatre—
Film Numbers—Kiss Me Again (Warner Bros.), George Frederick Handel (S. R.), Mark Strand Topical Review (selected).
Musical Program—"Kiss Me Again" (soprano solo), Harold Stern and his Brighton Beach Band—"March of the Toys", "Overture 1812," "Soldier's Dream" (cornet solo), "Evolution of the Toys," "Stars and Stripes Forever," "Toccata" (organ recessional).

MILWAUKEE

Garden Theatre—
Film Numbers — How Baxter Butted In (Warner Bros.), Comedy (Pathe), Fox News, Sport Light (Pathe).
Musical Program—"Knee Deep in Daisies (Organ Specialty).

Merrill Theatre—
Film Numbers—The Lost World (First National), International News, Felix Cartoon (S. R.).
Musical Program—Organ Overture.

Strand Theatre—
Film Numbers—My Son (First National), Hot and Heavy (Educational), Hodge Podge (Educational), Kinograms.
Musical Program—Cecelia (Overture).

Wisconsin Theatre—
Film Numbers — Are Parents People? (Paramount), Waiting (Educational), International News.
Musical Program—"Il Guarany" (Overture), "Collegiate" (On the Twin Organs), "In An Orange Grove in Italy" (Stage Presentation).

SAN FRANCISCO

California Theatre—
Film Numbers—Dangerous Innocence (Universal), Soup To Nuts (Educational), Pathe Review, International News (Universal).
Musical Program— "Hungarian Rhapsody No. 2" (Overture), "I Hear You Calling Me" (violin solo), "Waltz Pomone" and "Music As You Like It" (specialties).

Loew's Warfield Theatre—
Film Numbers—Her Sister From Paris (First National), International News and Kinograms, Saugerfest (Pictures with music).
Musical Program—"Hollywood's Own Review" (Fanchon and Marco Idea), "Pale Moon"

GRAND OPENING GREATER MOVIE SEASON AT KEARSE
KEARSE
ALL SEATS 25¢
MONDAY, TUESDAY, WEDNESDAY-COME EARLY

WINGS of YOUTH
(and how they were clipped~)
by Harold P. Montayne

with
MADGE BELLAMY
ETHEL CLAYTON
CHARLES FARRELL
FREEMAN WOOD
ROBERT CAIN
KATHERINE PERRY

Fully Laughs and the Fools Dance To Her Tune

AFTERNOONS 15¢ — ALL SEATS IN "POPPY" DAYS

Three-column opening ad on "Wings of Youth" (Fox) at the Kearse Theatre, Charleston.

(vocal), "Close Eyes" (violin solo).

Granada Theatre—
Film Numbers — Limited Mail (Warner Brothers), Iron Mule (Educational), Pathe News.
Musical Program—Monte Blue in person, "Review of Reviews" (automatic stage novelty with singing and dancing).

Cameo Theatre—
Film Numbers—Texas Trail (Producers Dist. Corp.), Crying For Love (Universal), International News.
Musical Program—"Indian Maid" (overture), "Parisian Knights" (specialty).

St. Francis Theatre—
Film Numbers—The Iron Horse (Fox), Felix Doubles For Darwin (S. R.), Kinograms, Sense and Nonsense (Educational).
Musical Program — "Kings of Rhythm" (special act).

Union Square Theatre—
Film Numbers—My Lady's Lips (S. R.), Stick Around (S. R.), Fox News.
Musical Program—Variety Revue including singing and dancing with Charleston contest.

Imperial Theatre—
Film Numbers—Don Q, Son of Zorro (United Artists), continued.

BEBE DANIELS
Wild Wild Susan
ROD LA ROCQUE

SUSAN was a slave to thrills with a kick. And when Susan went out into the world to go there, she GOT them—and then some!

Stepping out death and dash can keep "Wild Wild Susan" from stealing you hard.

Lloyd
HAMILTON
"Waiting"

Geo. Lee
Hamilton
Comedy

STRAND

Attractive use of stock material in the Strand theatre ad in the Birmingham on "Wild, Wild Susan" (Paramount).

SEATTLE

Blue Mouse Theatre—
Film Numbers—The Limited Mail (Warner Brothers), Isn't Life Terrible (Pathe), Over the Plate (Pathe), International News.
Musical Program — Selections from "Madame Modiste" (overture), "Tiger Rag" (orchestra specialty).

Coliseum Theatre—
Film Numbers—The Talker (First National), Cartoon (S. R.), Pathe Review, Kinograms

---

Musical Program — "Morning, Noon and Night" (overture), "Ida" (saxophone specialty).

Columbia Theatre—
Film Numbers—Drusilla With a Million (F. B. O.), Aesop's Fable (Pathe), International News.
Musical Program—"Medley of Italian Melodies" (overture). Selection from "Maytime" and "Crying for the Moon" (vocal solos).

Heilig Theatre—
Film Numbers—Never the Twain Shall Meet (Metro-Goldwyn-Mayer), Topics of the Day (Pathe), Pathe Review.
Musical Program — "Footloose" (orchestra specialty), "Trumpeter" (vocal solo).

Liberty Theatre—
Film Numbers—The Iron Horse

Newman
Hurrah! IT'S GREATER MOVIE SEASON
and, here's our first Greater Movie!

Clear the Road!

RICHARD DIX
and ESTHER RALSTON in
"THE LUCKY DEVIL"
(A Paramount Picture)

NEWMAN MIDSUMMER REVUE
a Teeple Parade of Scenes Entertainment With 11 Scenes
OTIS MITCHELL and THE MARYLAND SISTERS
THE IMPS ORCHESTRA
OUR GANG COMEDY

Action was the keynote of this newspaper ad on "The Lucky Devil" (Paramount) at the Newman theatre, Kansas City.

(Fox), continued.

Pantages Theatre—
Film Numbers—The Thorobred (S. R.), Aesop's Fable (Pathe), Pathe News.
Musical Program—Vaudeville.

Strand Theatre—
Film Numbers—The Fool (Fox), Felix Cops the Prize (S. R.), Fox News.
Musical Program—"William Tell" (overture), "By the Light of the Stars" (orchestra).

Winter Garden Theatre—
Film Numbers—The Midnight Express (S. R.), Home Scouts (comedy), Fox News.
Musical Program—"La Paloma" (overture).

BALTIMORE

Century Theatre—
Film Numbers—A Slave of Fash-

ion (Metro-Goldwyn), The Sky Jumper (Fox Van), Seas to the Sierras (Trio travel series), News Weekly (Fox), Local Lafs (Joke Film Tie-up with Baltimore News).
Musical Program—Selections from operetta "Count of Luxembourg" (Overture by Orchestra), "Sunrise" (Vocal and instrumental selection in special setting).

Garden Theatre—
Film Numbers—Taming the West (Universal), High Jinks (Fox), The Fortune Teller (S. R.), International News.
Musical Program—Vaudeville.

Keith's Hippodrome—
Film Numbers—The Mark of Zorro (United Artists), Won By Law (Universal), Aesop's Fable (Pathe), News Weekly (Pathe).
Musical Program—Vaudeville.

Metropolitan Theatre—
Film Numbers—Rugged Water (Paramount), Tender Feet (Educational), Boston (Pathecolor), News Weekly (Pathe).
Musical Program—Orchestra.

New Theatre—
Film Numbers—Gerald Cranston's Lady (Fox), Beware (Educational), A Day In Venice (Special film, part in colors from Pathe Reviews, Urban Chats and Pathe and Fox News, with special musical setting), News Weekly (Pathe).
Musical Program—"Concert Fantasia" (Overture by orchestra).

Exhibitors Box-Office Reports

Names of the theatre owners are omitted by agreement in accordance with the wishes of the average exhibitor and in the belief that reports published over the signature of the exhibitor reporting, is a dangerous practice.

Only reports received on specially prepared blanks furnished by us will be accepted for use in this department. Exhibitors who value this reporting service are urged to ask for these blanks.

Title of Picture	Population of Town	Location	Class of Patronage	Weather	Box Office Value	Check-up Percentage from other Reports
ASSOC. EXHIBITORS						
Back to Life	324410	Mo.	General	Warm	Good	70
Going Up	3600	Mich.	Mixed	Warm	Good	78
FAMOUS PLAYERS						
Air Mail, The	3600	Mich.	Mixed	Warm	Good	65
Are Parents People	29902	Kansas	General	Warm	Good	70
Beggar on Horseback	125000	N. Y.	1st Run	Hot	Fair	78
)	772897	Mo.	1st Run	Hot	Fair	—
Call of the Canyon	29902	Kansas	General	Warm	Good	78
In the Name of Love	120000	Fla.	1st Run	Warm	Good	70
	28535	Kansas	General	Cool	Good	—
Little French Girl	29902	Mo.	General	Warm	Good	73
Lucky Devil, The	120000	Fla.	General	Rain	Good	65
	72013	N. Y.	1st Run	Hot	Good	—
Night Life in New York	733826	Md.	1st Run	Warm	Fair	67
	158976	Texas	1st Run	Hot	Fair	—
	125000	N. Y.	General	Warm	Good	—
Rugged Waters	798841	Ohio	1st Run	Hot	Fair	60
Sideshow of Life, The	3395	Kansas	General	Cool	Good	59
Son of His Father, The	506676	Cal.	1st Run	Warm	Good	70
Ten Commandments, The	324410	Mo.	General	Warm	Big	89
	772897	Mo.	General	Hot	Big	—
Travelin' On	29902	Kansas	General	Warm	Fair	65
Trouble with Wives	506676	Cal.	1st Run	Warm	Good	70
Wild Horse Mesa	798841	Ohio	1st Run	Hot	Fair	70
	72013	N. Y.	1st Run	Cool	Good	—
Zaza	29902	Kansas	General	Warm	Fair	73
F. B. O.						
Drusilla with a Million	314194	Ind.	1st Run	Warm	Big	72
	315312	Wash.	1st Run	Warm	Good	—
	72013	N. Y.	General	Hot	Fair	—
In the Name of the Law	126468	Iowa	General	Warm	Good	73
Parisian Nights	120000	Fla.	1st Run	Warm	Good	70
Ridin' Comet, The	28535	Kansas	General	Cool	Good	63
FOX						
Arizona Romeo	75917	Pa.	General	Warm	Good	69
Dancers, The	733826	Md.	General	Warm	Fair	56
East Lynne	798841	Ohio	1st Run	Hot	Big	85
End of the Trail, The	3395	Kansas	General	Cool	Good	88
Hearts and Spurs	88723	N. Y.	1st Run	Hot	Good	55
Hunted Woman, The	8535	Kansas	General	Cool	Big	55
In Love with Love	733826	Md.	1st Run	Warm	Fair	58
Iron Horse, The (3d Week)	315312	Wash.	General	Warm	Good	88
Man Who Came Back	29902	Kansas	General	Warm	Fair	71
Rainbow Trail, The	28535	Kansas	General	Cool	Good	66
Roughneck, The	733826	Md.	General	Warm	Good	63
Stardust Trail, The	75917	Pa.	General	Warm	Fair	52
Teeth	3395	Kansas	General	Cool	Good	66
Troubles of a Bride	798841	Ohio	General	Hot	Fair	58
FIRST NATIONAL						
Born Rich	733826	Md.	General	Warm	Good	55
	3600	Mich.	Mixed	Warm	Fair	—
Enticement	3600	Mich.	Mixed	Warm	Fair	60
Frivolous Sal	158976	Texas	General	Hot	Poor	72
Girl in the Limousine	3600	Mich.	Mixed	Warm	Poor	63
Half Way Girl, The	125000	N. Y.	1st Run	Hot	Big	85
	120000	Fla.	1st Run	Storm	Good	—
	314194	Ind.	1st Run	Warm	Good	—
Her Sister from Paris	72013	N. Y.	1st Run	Cool	Good	71
	993678	Mich.	1st Run	Warm	Big	—
His Supreme Moment	29902	Kansas	General	Warm	Fair	64
Idle Tongues	3600	Mich.	Mixed	Warm	Good	63
Lost World, The	798841	Ohio	1st Run	Hot	Big	82
	126468	Iowa	1st Run	Warm	Good	70
Lady Who Lied, The	324410	Mo.	General	Warm	Good	60
	733826	Md.	1st Run	Warm	Good	—
New Toys	75917	Penna.	General	Warm	Poor	63
Quo Vadis	7320	Okla.	General	Warm	Good	79
Sandra	3600	Mich.	Mixed	Warm	Fair	53
Talker, The	315312	Wash.	General	Warm	Good	68
Thief of Paradise, A	88723	N. Y.	1st Run	Hot	Good	78
White Monkey, The	88723	N. Y.	1st Run	Hot	Fair	70
METRO-GOLDWYN-MAYER						
Great Divide, The	3885	Kansas	Mixed	Warm	Good	70
Never the Twain Shall Meet	315312	Wash.	1st Run	Warm	Good	70
	506676	Cal.	1st Run	Warm	Fair	—
Pretty Ladies	158976	Texas	1st Run	Hot	Fair	48
Romola	772897	Mo.	1st Run	Hot	Big	82
	120000	Fla.	1st Run	Warm	Fair	—
Sun Up	314194	Ind.	1st Run	Warm	Good	70
Slave of Fashion	993678	Mich.	1st Run	Warm	Good	84
Unholy Three, The	798841	Ohio	1st Run	Hot	Big	79
	401247	Ohio	1st Run	Warm	Fair	—
White Desert, The	324410	Mo.	General	Warm	Good	67
PATHE						
Black Cyclone, The	401247	Ohio	General	Hot	Fair	83
	75000	N. Y.	General	Hot	Good	—
PRODUCERS DIST. CORP.						
Beyond the Border	3600	Mich.	Mixed	Warm	Fair	66
Crimson Runner, The	75917	Penna.	General	Warm	Good	72
Friendly Enemies	75917	Penna.	General	Warm	Poor	70
Off the Highway	125000	N. Y.	1st Run	Warm	Fair	40
STATE RIGHTS						
Battling Buddy	38850	Kansas	Mixed	Warm	Good	62
Chin Chin Chinaman	506676	Cal.	General	Warm	Good	70
Crackerjack, The	75917	Penna.	General	Warm	Big	74
Danger Signal, The	126468	Iowa	1st Run	Warm	Good	70
Early Bird, The	401247	Ohio	General	Clear	Good	70
Hitting Hard	3885	Kansas	Mixed	Warm	Good	70
Midnight Express, The	315312	Wash.	General	Warm	Good	75
Poisoned Paradise	993678	Mich.	General	Warm	Good	62
Restless Wives	798841	Ohio	General	Hot	Fair	58
	3885	Kansas	Mixed	Warm	Good	—
Riding Mad	3885	Kansas	General	Warm	Good	70
Thoroughbred, The	315312	Wash.	General	Warm	Good	70
Two Fisted Justice	29902	Kansas	General	Warm	Fair	70
Speed Spook, The	3600	Mich.	General	Warm	Good	79
Walloping Wallace	3885	Kansas	Mixed	Warm	Good	70
Wasted Lives	506676	Cal.	General	Warm	Fair	70
Youth for Sale	3600	Mich.	Mixed	Warm	Fair	27
UNITED ARTISTS						
Don Q, Son of Zorro	126468	Iowa	1st Run	Warm	Big	92
Gold Rush, The	993678	Mich.	1st Run	Warm	Big	'93
Waking up the Town	733826	Md.	General	Warm	Fair	43
UNIVERSAL						
Dangerous Innocence	401247	Ohio	General	Warm	Poor	66
Gaiety Girl, The	3395	Kansas	General	Cool	Big	64
Hurricane Kid	3885	Kansas	Mixed	Warm	Good	66
K-The Unknown	8535	Kansas	General	Cool	Good	77
Price of Pleasure, The	401247	Ohio	General	Warm	Poor	71
Rose of Paris	29902	Kansas	General	Warm	Fair	60
Siege	772897	Mo.	1st Run	Hot	Fair	70
	120000	Fla.	1st Run	Storm	Fair	—
Tornado, The	29902	Kansas	General	Cool	Good	74
VITAGRAPH						
Baree-Son of Kazan	120000	N. Y.	1st Run	Hot	Good	73
School for Wives	158976	Texas	1st Run	Hot	Good	58
WARNER BROS.						
How Baxter Butted In	324410	Mo.	General	Warm	Good	60
Limited Mail, The	315312	Wash.	1st Run	Warm	Good	70
This Woman	401247	Ohio	General	Warm	Good	60
Tracked in Snow Country	993678	Mich.	1st Run	Warm	Fair	64
	3600	Mich.	Mixed	Warm	Good	—

Short Subjects and Serials

Dramatic Actors Signed by Hal Roach

Hal Roach has signed a number of well known dramatic actors to appear in his comedy casts for Pathe release. George Siegman and William J. Kelly will be seen in "The Caretaker's Daughter," a Charley Chase comedy directed by Leo McCarey.

Walter Long is one of the fun-makers in "There Goes the Bride," a Roach two-reeler, directed by James W. Horne. Gertrude Astor has a leading part in another two-reel star comedy.

Josephine Crowell, character lead in "The Birth of a Nation" and other big productions is in the cast of "No Father to Guide Him," an early September release . with Charlie Chase. Mickey Bennett will make his debut with the Hal Roach players in this same Pathe comedy.

Marshall Will Supervise All Fox Two-Reelers

George E. Marshall has been promoted to director-in-chief or all Fox two reel comedies. For the past several months he has been serving in that capacity for the Van Bibber, Helen and Warren and O. Henry comedies. Under the new arrangement Marshall supervises comedies made by Directors Ben Stoloff and Lew Seiler. He is directly responsible for the selection of all directors and players and seeing that scrips and stories are properly handled.

New Canine Performer in Hiers Comedy

Brownie II, son of the original Brownie, well known as a dog performer on the screen, is to make his film debut in a new comedy starring Walter Hiers, which is being made at Christies for distribution through Educational Film Exchanges.

Brownie II, was raised and trained by Charles Gee, who also trained his father. Gee claims the new Brownie will be even a better performer than his illustrious daddy.

"The Bad Man" is First of New Dinky Doodle Series

"The Bad Man" is the title of the first release in the new Dinky Doodle cartoon series for F. B. O. It is a burlesque of the western photoplays with the cartoon characters performing breath-taking stunts and feats of heroism of the order popularized by leading screen stars of the western melodramas. The picture will be released in October.

Charles Lamont to Direct Juvenile Comedy

Charles La Mont, recently signed to direct one-reel Cameo Comedies, will also direct the first of the Juvenile comedies for the season to be released by Educational Film Exchanges.

Release stills from "Mary, Queen of Tots," a new "Our Gang" comedy produced by Hal Roach for Pathe.

Pathe's Schedule for Sept. 6

Charlie Chase Comedy, "Stereoscopik" and Serial Episode on Program of Short Subjects

A WIDE range of short subjects will be offered by Pathe on the program for the week of September 6. The comedy will be supplied by a Hal Roach two-reeler starring Charlie Chase. Other releases of the week include a Grantland Rice "Sportlight," a "Stereoscopik" reel entitled "The Runaway Taxi," a chapter of "Play Ball," current Pathe serial, "Topics of the Day," "Aesop's Film Fables," a Pathe Review, and two issues of Pathe News.

"No Father to Guide Him" is the title of the Chase comedy. It shows the comedian as the father whose estranged wife will not allow him to see their son. The ingenious devices invented by the father to visit with his boy make up the comedy moments of the play. Katherine Grant appears as the wife and Josephine Crowell is .the mother-in-law.

"Barrier Busters," the latest Grantland

Rice "Sportlight," gives ample evidence that the so-called "weaker sex" is forging ahead in the world of sports. "A Runaway Taxi" permits spectators to experience the thrills of a wild ride through city streets and over country roads.

"Double Peril" is the title of the eighth chapter of the Pathe serial "Play Ball," written by Manager McGraw of the N. Y. Giants and adapted for the screen by Frank Leon Smith.

Pathe Review No. 36 offers the following subjects: "Understndying Ulm," the great German cathedral shown in miniature; "The Lost City," scenes of an ancient Moorish metropolis in Pathe color. "Barnyard Follies" is the title of Paul Terry's latest of the "Aesop's Film Fables" series. Completing the September 6th Pathe schedule are "Topics of the Day," and two issues of Pathe News.

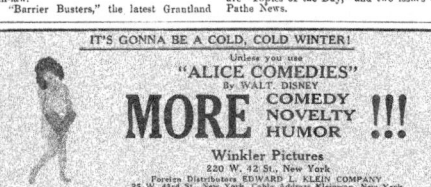

Harry Langdon in scenes from "Lucky Stars," a two- reel Mack Sennett production released by Pathe.

"We have only the highest praise to offer for your services at the opening of our new Diversey Theatre, Chicago, when the motion pictures showing the first audience enter the theatre were projected on the screen one hour and five minutes after being taken. It was a remarkable feat in service and workmanship."

Great credit, it is declared, is also due to the Rothacker Laboratory staff, who aided the Kinograms men. Special developing, printing and drying crews were placed at the disposal of the cameramen and orders given to push the film through in record time.

World Cartoonist Signed by Educational

Education-Mermaid Comedies has signed Charles Gordon Saxton, formerly a cartoonist on the New York World, to a contract as gag man. He is now at the new Educational studios in Los Angeles. Saxton was attached to the World for two years and his cartoons attracted wide attention.

F. B. O. Short Subjects Active

Four Comedy Units Busy With Production at West and East Coast Studios

SHORT subjects for the 1925-26 program are at the peak of their activity at the F.B.O. studio simultaneously with the arrival at the coast studios last week of vice-president J. I. Schnitzer and east coast scenario editor John Brownell. The four comedy units at the F.B.O. studio are functioning at full speed, while Walter Lantz of the Bray Studios in New York is turning out two series of animated cartoons for the distributing company.

Director Ralph Ceder has started work with Alberta Vaughn, Larry Kent, Kit Guard and Al Cook on the third episode of "The Adventures of Mazie". This episode is titled, "Or What Have You." There are twelve episodes in the series, which ran as short stories in Top Notch Magazine. Nell Martin is author of the stories and they are being continuitized by Doris Anderson.

Work on "Fighting Hearts," another series, is also under way. These stories are

being written especially for the company by Sam Hellman, well known humorist. Larry Kent will play the male lead in these new comedies.

Joe Rock units are producing two series of twenty-six comedies for F.B.O. The first two of the Standard Fat Men series, called "Tailoring" and "Three Wise Goofs" are already completed. They feature Fat Karr, Tiny Alexander and Kewpie Ross, three of the fattest men of the screen.

The first of the Blue Ribbon comedies, "Lame Brains," another Joe Rock contribution, featuring Alice Ardell, a young Parisian girl, has also been completed.

Walter Lantz of the Bray studios has finished two of the twenty-six cartoons he is scheduled to produce. The first of these a Dinky Doodle cartoon is called "The Bad Man," and the second is an Unnatural History cartoon called "How the Elephant Got His Trunk."

Helen Foster Given Lead With Lupino Lane

Helen Foster will play the leading feminine role opposite Lupino Lane in that star's next comedy for Educational. Miss Foster was formerly with Educational-Tuxedo comedies as leading lady with Johnny Arthur.

Kinograms Feat Stirs Chicago

News Reel Shows Pictures of Crowds Entering Diversey at Opening Performance of New House

VIEWS of the crowds entering the new Diversey Theatre, in Chicago, were shown on the screen at the opening performance of that house in a special film made in record time by Kinograms, Educational's news reel. Spectators were astonished to see flashed on the screen pictures of themselves entering the theatre just an hour and five minutes previously, the reel having been photographed, developed, printed and titled in time for screening before the first performance had been completed.

The remarkable feat, which is believed to set a record for fast developing and printing, was accomplished by Kinograms as part of its free service to Mr. Asher Levy,

manager of the Diversey Theatre, which is a unit of the Orpheum Circuit.

Though several surprise events were prepared for the opening of the theatre, the Kinograms stunt created the greatest comment and applause. The special reel showed exterior views of the theatre with the crowds collecting on the sidewalks and filing into the lobby. As few of the patrons noticed the news cameraman taking the scenes, the pictures came as a great surprise to the bulk of the spectators, who, midway through the performance, witnessed the pictures of the formal opening.

The following day Mr. Dave Lubin, of the Chicago Educational Exchange, received the following letter from Mr. Levy:

Scenes from the Wanda Wiley starring vehicle "Gridiron Gertie" a Century comedy released through Universal.

"Play Ball" Exploited in "Movie Season" Parade

Though presented on the same bill with a feature picture, the Pathe serial "Play Ball" was given the lion's share of the publicity and exploitation by Loew's Regent Theatre, Harrisburg, Pa., during the week of August 17th. Sydney J. Gates, manager of the house, used special newspaper advertising and in addition exploited the McGraw episode film by means of a float in the Regent's Greater Movie Season parade.

The float, mounted on a motor truck, featured a huge baseball made of canvas and inscribed with suitable advertising lines. Also there was a newspaper tieup with the Harrisburg Telegraph, in which "Play Ball" was featured.

Tolhurst Making Series for Pathe

Under the title of "The Magic Eye," Louis H. Tolhurst, noted scientist is making a series of cinema-microscopic studies of the most minute of living creatures for release through Pathe. The first of these will be a feature of Pathe Review No. 39 released in September.

"Seeing Things," is the title of the first Tolhurst release. In this subject various objects handled in everyday life are placed under the magic lens and shown in all-revealing detail. "Sun Power," demonstrating the sun as a fountain of all energy, is the title of the second release. "Walking on Water," the third subject, shows in close-ups how skating bugs and other tiny insects skim over the surface of the water.

Bryan Foy Will Direct Fox Comedy

Bryan Foy, son of Eddie Foy, and Fox comedy director is busy preparing a story which he will direct as a two-reeler. He has just been assisting Victor Schertzinger with the comedy situations in "Thunder Mountain."

F. B. O. Filming Second of "Mazie" Series

Alberta Vaughn is making the second episode in the "Mazie" series of two reel comedies at the F. B. O. studios in Hollywood. The picture is being made under the direction of Ralph Ceder.

"Every Comedy a Feature" is White Slogan

"EVERY comedy a feature production," is to be the slogan of Jack White Productions this year. The product is to be released through Educational. White declares there has been too much discrimination in the use of the word "feature" in its application to the longest picture on the exhibitor's program regardless of its quality or entertainment value.

"More footage does not make a feature," says White. "This theory was exploded two years ago at the time when directors were making short subjects in ten and twelve reels. A feature is the outstanding item of the program whether it is in one, two or ten reels and our pictures are all going to be features."

Production highlights of the William Fox presentation of the O. Henry story, "Shoes," with Marion Harlan as the O. Henry Girl.

Try Short Subject Programs

Cleveland Circuit Experimenting With "All Komedy Carnival"—Big Drive Announces Event

SCOVILLE ESSICK and Reiff are the first local circuit managers to give the all-short-subject-program a try out in Cleveland. They have arranged to offer a program of this sort at their Sunbeam theatre Wednesday, September 9th. If it works out as well as it is expected to do, then the policy will be introduced generally throughout the circuit.

The first program of short subjects to be offered will consist of ten reels of entertainment, and will be made up of the following: "Shooting Injuns," 2-reel Gang Comedy; "Black Hand Blues," 2-reel Spat Family Comedy; "Honey Moon Hardships," 2-reel Sennett comedy; "Daddy Goes a-Grunting," 2-reel Tryon comedy; and "All Night Long," a 2-reel Langdon comedy.

In order to introduce this program, Messrs. Scoville Essick and Reiff have draped their entire marquee with a banner announcing "All Komedy Carnival." They have been running slides several weeks in advance. Banners, with the names of the comedies, the names and pictures of the stars, have been prominently hung in the theatre lobby and five sets of photos on each comedy have been conspicuously placed outside the theatre on display frames. They are going after the comedy business in a big way, and big results are expected.

The use of the all short subjects program is gaining in popularity among the exhibitors in the Cleveland territory, where several houses have been using these bills as regular attractions for some time and others recently have reported favorable results from experiments with the idea.

Among the theatres in the territory which give the short subjects an equal break with the features in the advertising and exploitation is the Princess at Toledo. The house is managed by LeBolt and Brady who for a long while have followed the practice of dividing their newspaper advertising space equally between the feature and the short films of their programs. Also, their lobby displays include photographs of the comedy stars and the comedy pictures. Their outside frame displays carry comedy as well as feature advertising.

As a result of this policy, their business is fairly staple. Their patrons have been educated to size up a program as a whole instead of concentrating their entire attention on the feature attraction. The Princess theatre has played Educational comedies every week for four years without a single interruption.

La Mont Named to Direct Lupino Lane

Jack White, director-general in charge of production at the Educational studios, has assigned Charles La Mont to direct the second Educational-Lupino Lane comedy to be made for Educational. La Mont is one of the youngest directors in the industry.

Resume of Current News Weeklies

INTERNATIONAL NEWS NO. 70: Near Fez, Morocco—French armies turn tide in Morocco; Plymouth, Vt.—Vacationing with Mr. and Mrs. Coolidge; Hongkong, China—English soldiers round up Chinese coolies; Asconet, Mass.—Chief Stoupface lures summer tourists; Newport, R. I.—Scores of excursionists killed or injured in ship explosion; N. Y. City (N. Y. City only)—Delmonico's, famed restaurant, serves last banquet; San Diego, Cal. (Los Angeles only)—Congressional medal of honor awarded to two of world flyers; Kafus, Rhodesia, Africa—Prince of Wales rides in African race; Lake Geneva, Wis.—Hold tri-state yacht regatta; Indianapolis, Ind. (Indianapolis only)—Spectacular civic parade shows city's prosperity; Cape Gris-Nez, France—Merciless channel conquers Gertrude Ederle, American girl swimmer; Lakehurst, N. Y.—Navy daredevils leap from giant Shenandoah.

INTERNATIONAL NEWS NO. 71: Ain Defali, Morocco—French hurl reinforcements into Moroccoan war zone; Plymouth, Vt.—President and Mrs. Coolidge visit their own $32 a month cottage; Lake Ronkonkoma, L. I.—Shoot-the-chute furnishes thrills for jaded visitors to summer resort; Chicago, Ill.—Dr. Max Mason is named president of the University of Chicago; Washington, D. C. (Wash. only)—Swimmers compete for President's cup; N. Y. City (Pitts. only)—Record crowd sees Pirates take lead over Giants in pennant race; St. Louis, Mo. (St. Louis only)—Cops learn how to rescue drowning people; Tokio, Japan—Japanese youths and maidens in tribute to love God; Munich, Germany—Hindenberg acclaimed by vast crowds as national idol; Forest Hills, L. I.—Helen Wills retains Tennis Na-

"Soup To Nuts," with Neal Burns, featured, is the first of the new Educational-Christie Comedies. These scenes are taken from the picture.

tional Championship by defeating Kathleen McKane, British star; Kenley Airdrome, Eng.—British army flyers ready for defense of the air.

PATHE NEWS NO. 69: Daredevil teeters on roping 21 stories above Broadway; Cape Gris Nez, France—All nations represented by swimmers bent upon overcoming treacherous tides of Channel swim from France to England; Los Angeles, Cal.—Lucinda, 10 year old girl from Africa, shows promise as future operatic star; Dallas, Texas—Harry Cooper, Texas professional, sets golf record with score of 60 for eighteen holes; Berlin, Germany—Celebrate sixth anniversary of German Constitution; In the Limelight—McMillan Arctic expedition gives us polar sea flight; Washington, D. C.—Nation's city chiefs assemble; Newport, R. I.—Two score dead, 100 injured in excursion ship blast; Philadelphia, Pa. (Phila. only)—Honeymooners start for Hollywood and fame; Santa Rita, Cal.—Cowboys run afoul of tough ones in frenk rodeo; Brown Ripple, Ind. (Indianapolis only) Beach beauties charm in annual revue; Fort Sill, Okla.—Oklahoma City opth'—National Guard of 45th Division in review; Houston, Texas (Dallas only)—Unveil monument in honor of Gen. Sam Houston; Nevada, Missouri (Kansas city only)—Missouri National Guard Engineers hold annual maneuvers.

PATHE NEWS NO. 70: New York City—Record crowd sees Pittsburgh win lead of league in game with Giants; Borculo, Holland—4 dead, 150 injured as cyclone ravages town; N. Y. City—Belgian debt envoys sail for home; Northampton, Mass.—First Lady of the land visits her mother; Paris, France—French aviators complete 5,000 mile tour of continent in three days; London, England—Freemasons attend world's largest banquet; San Diego, Cal.—Test giant seaplane built for trans-Pacific flight; N. Y. City—Cameramen astray in Zoo finds new kind of taxicab; a giant turtle; Berlin, Germany—Hindenburg receives tremendous ovation during national celebration; Forest Hills, N. Y.—Helen Wills retains National tennis title; Charleston, W. Va. (Cincinnati only)—West Virginia troops answer in annual review; Rome, Ga.—Honor memory of Known Soldier.

KINOGRAMS NO. 5111: Gris Nez, France—Channel baffles 3 girl swimmers as Miss Ederle's name is added to that of Lillian Harrison, of Argentine, and Miss. Sion, of France; Newport, R. I.—Excursionists scalded to death when boiler blows up on steamer Mackinac; Washington, D. C.—Gen. Andrews summons state prohibition directors in biggest dry drive; Osaka, Japan—Jap flappers say "No" to bobbed hair and show latest styles in long tresses; New York—$150,000,000 is record sum spent since first of year to remake New York city; Berlin—500,000 Germans hold big celebration on anniversary of constitution; Lönghtyhed, Sweden—Swedish girls in equal drill show physical perfection in nation's womanhood; Middleboro, Mass.—Fire laddies stage exciting contests; Santa Cruz, Cal.—Army tries air and land defense while airplanes show what they can do.

KINOGRAMS NO. 5112: New York—130,000 in 3 days see Pirates beat Giants to hold league lead; Gloucester, Mass.—Girl scouts and relatives strew ocean with flowers to honor memory of fisher dead; Buenos Ayres—Millions of lights illuminate Argentine capital on Independence Day; Vishr, Isle of Gottland—Sweden's rulers attend 700th anniversary of St. Mary's cathedral; Marlow, Eng.—Crews drop from high bridge into boats in novel canoe race; San Francisco—Kiddie dancer graduates from Pine Arts Academy show their skill; Hamson, N. J.—Society girls ride jumpers in Monmouth Horse Show; Cape May, N. J.—Amateur anglers crowd boats as pan fish prove plentiful; Forest Hills, N. Y.—Helen Wills triumphs over Miss McKane gaining a, only outright, and then helps to also will doubles; Meriden, Conn.—Kaplan and Herman train for battle (New Haven only); Philadelphia—Choose Annette Jackson to represent city at Atlantic City beauty pageant (Philadelphia

only); Camp Sparta, Wis.—Reilly's Bucks riddle targets at artillery practice (Chicago only); Chicago—Mayor opens new giant market (Chicago only); Chicago—Dick Howell wins the marathon swim (Chicago only).

FOX NEWS VOL. 6 NO. 94: How a Big Ocean Liner Comes into New York; A pictorial record of the activities taking place when a ship docks; Washington, D. C.—Planning a new drive to make country bone-dry, prohibition enforcement chiefs meet in the capitol; Star Lakes, N. J.—Boys from New York's crowded East Side are carefree guests at the Salvation Army camp; Fort Sill, Okla.—National guardsmen of Forty-fifth Division end intensive training period with spectacular parade; Tredezer, Wales—James J. Davis, United States Labor Secretary visits birthplace which he left when a boy of 8; Indianapolis, Ind.—Four hundred girls vie for pulchritude prizes and five are selected as most beautiful in the city; Dublin, Ireland—The social and political leaders of Irish Free State attend race meet at Leopardstown Track; Brooklyn, N. Y.—Pete, a trustful sparrow, strikes up a friendship with Sassafras, the cat—and gets away with it; Stepping into space from a Navy Dirigible—Parachute jumpers leap from Shenandoah, over Lakehurst, N. J., at sunset.

News Reels Are Showing Big Gains Abroad

THE news reel is coming into its own abroad, according to a letter just received by E. W. Hammons, president of Educational Films, from Forrest Izard, managing editor of Kinograms News Reel.

Izard, who has been in England, France, and Italy for several weeks writes in part as follows:

"I was very much gratified to find that at last the news reel seems to be coming into its own in European countries. On my last trip here five years ago I found that the exhibitor looked upon the news reel as somewhat of a necessary nuisance. Two hundred feet was then the average length, and the pictures were either cut so short as to be flashes, or the photography poor.

"Now, however, I find a great improvement. In some of the English houses I discovered combination reels such as are made up in our Broadway and other big houses throughout America. Also in France there was marked improvement shown, and in my talks to several exhibitors I found that they are finally beginning to realize the intense interest attached to this product of our industry."

Hamilton Will Appear in "Straight" Makeup

Lloyd Hamilton will be seen in a "straight" makeup for the first time in twelve years in a new Education-Hamilton comedy now in production on the west coast. The comedian will play two characters. He will be seen in his regulation makeup in one, and as he would appear off the screen in the other. The production is being made under the direction of William Goodrich.

New Stage Erected for the Educational

An additional stage is being erected at the Educational studio in Los Angeles where the Lupino Lane, Hamilton, Mermaid, Tuxedo, Juvenile and Cameo Comedies are being made for release through Educational. The new stage occupies the second floor of the building.

CLASSIFIED AD SECTION

RATES: 10 cents a word for each insertion, in advance
except Employment Wanted, on which rate is 5 cents.

CLASSIFIED SERVICE

A classified ad in MOTION PICTURE NEWS offers the
full resources and circulation of the NEWS to the advertiser at a ridiculously low figure.

Whether you want to reach executives, branch managers,
salesmen, or theatre managers, you can accomplish this
quickly and economically through the NEWS Classified
Columns.

THE PEER OF ALL PROJECTION SURFACES
Mr. Exhibitor — The Radio Silver
Screens are the latest improve-
ment in stereopticon projecting
and for elimination of eye strain.
Sold under a positive guarantee.
Price 50c a square foot. For
particulars and samples apply to
JOHN MUNRO CRAWFORD,
48 Smith St., Newburgh, N. Y.

Wanted

EXPERT OPERATOR
and Electrician with 9 years'
experience in big houses;
married; wants to locate at
once. Address, Operator,
Box 282, Mason City, Iowa.

NOTICE. — Picture and
vaudeville theatre manager
of 10 years' experience in all
branches of show business
wishes to make change; will
go anywhere; references?
plenty. Box 370, Motion Picture News, New York City.

MOTION PICTURE
OPERATOR.—Experienced;
young man; wishing position
anywhere; nonunion. Nabeeh
Said, 349 West 51st St., New
York.

SITUATION WANTED.—
Projectionist wants position;
handle any equipment; go
anywhere, anytime; furnish
references if desired; single;
non-union. Robert W. Hous-
worth, Strand Theatre, Carrollton, Ga.

**Suburban Motion
Picture Theatre
For Sale**

Seating 400. Will show
good returns on a small
investment. Inquire

Tahen and Brenner
M and M Bldg.
Springfield, Ohio

THEATRE IN TOWN OF
4,000 or better, anywhere in
North Central states, Northern Indiana preferred. Can
either give satisfactory security on lease or buy outright.
Would consider buying interest in bona-fide proposition
where owner wishes to retire.
All replies absolutely confidential. Address Box 360,
Motion Picture News, New
York City.

MOTION PICTURE
OPERATOR.—Experienced;
young man; wishing position
anywhere. Write Dion Mol-
ler, 411a Prospect Ave.,
Brooklyn, N. Y.

For Sale

FOR SALE AT A SAC-
RIFICE.— Photoplayer; in
use less than 2 years. Orpheum Theatre, Orwigsburg,
Pa.

FOR SALE. — Modern
movie; priced for quick sale
account of illness; wonderful bargain; county seat of
10,000. Box 240, Motion
Picture News, New York
City.

CLOTH BANNERS—
$1.40 3 x 10 feet, 3 colors,
any copy up to 15 words.
One day service. Sent anywhere. Also Bargain Paper
Banners. Associated Advertisers, 111 W. 18th St., Kansas City, Mo.

FOR SALE.—Pathe Cam-
era; good as new; with new
Bell Howell tripod; com-
plete, $450; also new 200-
foot Universal Camera with
8 magazines, $250, or both
outfits for $600. H. Berger,
197 Hamilton St., Dorchester, Mass.

*Eight specimen newspaper ads on "The Lady Who Lied"
(First National) reproduced here, illustrate the varied
ways in which different theatres about the country have
announced the picture. The houses whose ads appear
here are: Princess theatre, Hartford, Conn.; Mainstreet
theatre, Kansas City; Leland theatre, Albany; Capitol
theatre, Detroit; Capitol theatre, Des Moines; Metropolitan theatre, Atlanta; Rivoli theatre, Baltimore, and
the Strand theatre, Providence, R. I.*

Opinions on Current Short Subjects

"No Father to Guide Him"
(Pathe—Two Reels)

(Reviewed by Thomas C. Kennedy)

A COMEDY with a sob-story plot about a father who is separated from his wife and child because of too-much-mother-in-law, serves as the current vehicle for Charlie Chase. The director and the author and the star aimed high enough, that is evident in several neatly done scenes, but the pace missed fire and so the two reels become more successful as serious sentimental fare than as comedy.

"No Father To Guide Him" lacks laughs. On the other hand it cannot be classed as dull, because there is some sentimental appeal to the situations and the characters are sympathetic. Moreover, the acting is good and the production up to the rather high standard of the Hal Roach Studios.

Sincerity and a certain amount of intelligence in the treatment of the play save the picture from failure. The action is slow and there is not sufficient incident to carry the story through two reels, but here and there the plot comes to the rescue and the flagging interest picks up.

Chase enacts his role with the easy, somewhat restrained grace which is winning him popularity as a screen farceur. The main support is rendered by Mickey Bennett, a boy actor possessing a box of tricks and a screen deportment somewhat beyond his years. Josephine Crowell, Duke Kahanamoku, famous aquatic star who gives a stirring exhibition of swimming, Kathrine Grant, and Leo Willis make up the balance of the cast.

"No Father To Guide Him" is not funny nor is its action stirring, though it may prove moderately entertaining to the bulk of the screen fans.

The Cast
The Milkman..................Charlie Chase
His Son.....................Mickey Bennett
His Wife....................Katherine Grant
Mother-In-Law............Josephine Crowell
A Hal Roach production. Directed by Leo McCarey.

The Story—A poor but honest milkman is driven from his wife and child by his tyrannical mother-in-law. To defeat his purpose the mother-in-law engages a detective to guard the boy. But Charlie spirits his son away and go to the beach for a swim, where the father is so buffeted by the waves that he loses his bathing suit. While trying to find a bathing suit for his father the boy is taken by the detective, but the father finally gets a barrel to cover his nakedness and takes up with the party. He has the mother-in-law arrested and there follows a family reunion.

Summary—Lacks comedy, incident and humor, but may succeed as passable entertainment on strength of likeable characters and an appealing play in which a sentimental plot is presented in the farce mood and brightened by moments of slapstick action.

"Ko-Ko Nuts"
(Red Seal—One Reel)

MAX FLEISCHER'S "Out-of-the-Inkwell" cartoon characters retain their interest remarkably well, or rather the devices by which the artist combines cartoons with actual photography continue to amaze and astonish the spectator because of the mechanical ingenuity involved in the process. At any rate the clown and the dog which assume their forms from the fluid in the inkwell have the quality to hold the interest of the spectator. Their adventure in this reel is concerned with the happenings in a lunatic asylum—a place we would not call

the most felicitous setting for comedy. However, there are some humorous moments and there are many extraordinary animated effects to sustain the interest and give the reel a rating as first-class cartoon comedy.—T. C. KENNEDY.

"Perils of the Wild"
(Adventure Serial-Universal—First Three Episodes)

(Reviewed by Edw. G. Johnston)

PIRATES, powder and sinking ships—not forgetting the rum and the gold. They are all in the picture and the younger element should fairly eat this one up. Also, a goodly portion of the grown-ups will probably enjoy it if they haven't too sharp an eye for detail. Right here, this reviewer can't help mentioning a most remarkable vividly striped shirt that is worn by the hero, Joe Bonomo. This shirt goes thru weeks of sailing, several terrific fights, is shipwrecked and emerges later on in perfect condition, with the starch still in the collar. It would not have been so noticeable but for its blazer pattern.

The first three episodes reviewed and those to follow, deal with the adventures of the Swiss Family Robinson, that old, impossible, but ever interesting story. After a free for all fight in a "Pub" in Liverpool, in the process of getting a crew together, the Family set sail with a cargo of flint-locks and gun powder and unknowingly, with a pirate crew. There is also another passenger, Emily Montrose, who develops as the heroine. As the ship nears the pirate's base, the ship is seized by the crew. A heavy sea and storm follow and the pirates thinking the ship doomed abandon it and row their boat to a tropical island, their headquarters. The Swiss Family, later on, land on the other side of the island, thinking it uninhabited except for the well mannered lions, leopards, monkeys, alligators, etc.

The cast is good and Joe Bonomo, well known as a "strong man" is given plenty of opportunities to demonstrate his remarkable strength. Margaret Quimby, as Emily Montrose, is very attractive and carries her part well. Jack Mower, as the wayward son and pirate chief also does good work. The crew are about as hard boiled looking lot of pirates that any one could want.

The Cast
Joe Bonomo, Margaret Quimby, Jack Mower, Alfred Allen, Eva Gordon, Francis Irwin, Howard Enstedt, Jack Murphy, William Dyer, Albert Prisco, Fannie Warren, John Wallace, James Welsh and Phil Ford.
An Adventure-Universal-Serial. Directed by Francis Ford.

The Story—The Swiss Family Robinson with Emily Montrose as passenger, sail for Australia with a cargo of gunpowder. Capt. William Robinson in command, Sir Charles Leicester, wayward son, sea rover and pirate chief is also aboard. He and Frederick Robinson are rivals for Emily's hand. During a storm a fire starts near the powder. Sir Charles and the crew take over the command of the ship. In the hold, Frederick is striving to keep the kegs from the flames. The ship founders, and the pirates abandon ship. After a calm the Robinsons make their way to a distant island. The island is the pirate's base and inhabited by followers of Sir Charles. The Swiss Family set up a tent and prepare to adjust themselves to their new home. The adventures that follow are many.

Summary—A fast-moving serial with a good cast, fairly well directed and excellently photographed. It should be good entertainment for audiences that like to follow aerials.

"Soup to Nuts"
Educational-Christie—Two Reels

(Reviewed by Thomas C. Kennedy)

AFTER a bad start this Christie comedy featuring Neal Burns works up to a hilarious finish and should be good for laughs and plenty of them in any man's theatre. Burns, Gale Henry and William Irving are fine comedy troupers and with the proper material can be depended upon to register fine performances. Here they have the material, essentially funny situations which William Watson, the director, has built up splendidly.

Especially amusing is the situation which shows Irving, ailing and closed in a room in a burning building, thinking the while that the digestive disturbance from which he suffers must be terribly bad because he has such a fever.

The plot is of a stock variety in the farce catalogue. A wife makes her husband masquerade as the butler while she allows her former sweetheart to act the role of husband in order to beguile her critical sister, a weekend visitor. Up to the time Burns, a bungling butler, cuts up the soap and puts it into the soup for toasted cubes of bread, there is not much to rave over in the play. But from that on things get sprightly and diverting. The fire scenes, with the excitement growing out of them, are corking and have been pointed up with a quantity of clever gags. "Soup to Nuts" is a clean, amusing picture—one that can be exploited and banked upon to satisfy.

The Cast
Henry.......................Neal Burns
Sally.......................Gale Henry
Belle......................Vera Steadman
The Cook...................Natalie Joyce
The Rival..................William Irving

The Story—Henry is expecting the new cook and when Sally, his wife's sister, appears, he immediately shows her the kitchen and orders her to serve food. When Henry's wife learns this she fears to present him as her husband, commands him to masquerade as the butler and calls in a friend to pose as her husband. The "butler" puts soap into the soup with the result that the sister-in-law and the other man become ill. When fire breaks out in the house the sister-in-law is trapped in her room and Bill thinks the terrible heat he feels is the result of fever from his illness. The fire brings on a climax in which the fire department performs and a series of hilarious gags are introduced.

Summary—A clean, highly diverting farce. It begins slowly but works up to a speedy and funny finish. Capital performances are given by Neal Burns, Vera Steadman, Gale Henry and William Irving. It is a picture which should register a hit everywhere.

"Marvels of Motion"
(Red Seal—One Reel)

THIS is issue "D" in the series of novelty reels produced by the Fleischer-Novagraph-Process. The slow motion camera is effectively used in depicting the feats of hurdling horses, a champion broad jumper, and other experiments in motion. The stop-motion is also used to show how the broad jumper accomplishes his long-distance leaps and to analyze the splash caused by dropping a lump of sugar into a glass of milk—a very interesting item, this latter. By means of reverse action the accidents occurring when a horse stumbles on a hurdle and throws its rider are corrected, the rider swinging back into the saddle and the mound going backwards over the hurdle. It is a novel and highly interesting reel.—T. C. KENNEDY.

"The Klynick"
(Davis Dist. Div.—Two Reels)
(Reviewed by Harold Flavin)

DUE to the numerous "gags" and the fast tempo at which the director has kept the action, this number of the "Hey Fellas" two-reelers manages to register a few laughs though the basic idea behind this series lacks originality. It's a pretty good bet for the kiddies but the grown-ups will probably prove laugh-proof through most of the scenes.

The scenes, in the beginning, deal with the efforts of one of the "crowd" to escape taking his medicine at the hospital in which he is incarcerated owing to a pronounced fondness for green apples which, however, fail to reciprocate his affection. His friends visit him and a pillow fight results. He escapes from the hospital and goes into consultation with the "crowd" being the opening of a "hospital" at which they experiment with dummies until a human prospect shows up. He is put through all the tortures of the Middle Ages by the "staff" in an effort to find some disease in his system and when he protests they prescribe mud baths from which he escapes after much trouble.

The most laughable bits of business are introduced in the last sequences in which the victim, fleeing from his persecutors, runs into a combination laundry shop and fireworks manufacturing plant and, being hot and dry, drinks a glass of nitro-glycerine and thereafter succeeds in putting fire to everything he breathes on.

Story by King Benedict and Clarence Hennecke.
Directed by Mark Goldaine.

The Story.—Mickey, convalescing in a hospital from a tummyache brought on by an overfondness for green apples is visited by his pals who, after much roughhousing, enable him to escape. They get together and start a hospital of their own which they operate with indifferent success until a live victim turns up. They "go to work" on him until he escapes and gets into a fireworks manufacturing plant where he drinks a glass of nitro-glycerine, immediately after which he is seized with a fit of sneezing which proves a combustible commodity as everything in sight goes up in a blaze. He goes back to the "hospital" and the "staff," using a stomach pump, succeeds in drawing off the explosive but it drops and scatters the gang.

Summary.—A not very amusing comedy as a whole but there are a number of ingenious "gags" introduced which make a good bid for laughter. It should prove a good bet for the children. But it is doubtful whether the older folks will get much out of it.

"Barrier Busters"
(Pathe—One Reel)

WOMAN'S invasion of the field of the strenuous sports such as hurdling, soccer, high-jumping, weight-throwing, etc., is the topic of this Grantland Rice Sportlight reel. It shows many actionful scenes, the major portion of which were made at a girl's school, and most of which, if memory serves, were presented in a previous issue of this series. But here is the unquestionable evidence of actual pictures to prove that the girls are acquiring physique and athletic skill which will put them into competition some day with the boys on the cinder-path and in the field.—T. C. KENNEDY.

"Pleasure Bent"
Universal—One Reel

CHARLES PUFFY registers an amusing performance as the central figure in this comedy about a woman who engages a detective to obtain evidence to be used in a divorce action. The wife explains that her husband is stepping out with fat ladies, so Puffy, the janitor of the building, is pressed into service to masquerade as a woman. He flirts with the husband and after some exciting adventures he and the detective learn that the woman has changed her mind about divorce. Not only that but the wife vents her ire on the "woman,"

with the result that Puffy takes another "drubbing." It is a good comedy, lively and supplied with some sure-fire laughs.—T. C. KENNEDY

"Stranded"
Universal-Century—Two Reels
(Reviewed by Thomas C. Kennedy)

EDNA MARIAN is the star of this Century offering, a frank piece of slap-stick in which she appears as the driver of the motor bus for a small-town hotel, as well as serving in the capacity of cook and waitress. The action is concerned with the doin's at the hotel when a stranded theatrical troupe signs up for accommodations.

The actors and chorines enjoy their experience, though they have no intention of paying the bill, a responsibility which they ultimately try to avoid but for which they are stripped of their luggage by the proprietor and the blond bus driver.

Miss Marion is given opportunity to display some of the dance steps she does so well and has the assistance of some gags which, though rather mechanical, are moderately successful in creating amusement. The picture should go well in the average house. There is action and there are some moments of the broad slapstick sort which seem always "in place" in the two reelers.

The Cast
The Girl ....Edna Marion
The Story.—Rival bus drivers vie with each other over getting a theatrical troup, stranded at the depot, into their conveyance. The girl wins and takes the troup to the hotel where she works as cook, floor clerk and char-woman as well. The rehearsals of the chorus in an upstairs room attracts a crowd, for it is a dress, or mayhap an undress rehearsal. At any rate things go swimmingly until the troupe seeks to depart without paying the bill, whereat there is a lively chase in which the actors are stripped of their valuable luggage in satisfaction of the hotel's claim.

Summary.—A slapstick comedy with some moderately amusing gags and a pleasant performance by Edna Marion as a slavey at a small-town hotel.

"Barnyard Follies"
(Pathe—One Reel)

THIS reel in the "Aesop's Film Fables" series produced by Paul Terry back-tracks over some former successful ground in cartoon comedy. The incongruous and the absurd is exploited for some rather amusing action concerning the show put on by the animals. A hippo does a toe dance and a very tat pig does a high dive from a spring board, but the greater part of the reel is devoted to showing the cute tricks employed by the gate-crashers, a familiar field but one which retains much good comedy material for the creator of animated cartoons.—T. C. KENNEDY.

"Props and the Spirits"
Educational—One Reel

THE further adventures of Earl Hurd's cartoon characters are followed in this "Pen and Ink Vaudeville" reel. There are two good gags, but both of them are overdrawn. However there is action here and the stunt in which the stage "prop" used a "stop and go" sign to silence the actors when they got too excited and start them off again on their conversation when he had assimilated what had been said so far. It it a fair to middlin' cartoon comedy.—T. C. KENNEDY.

"The Party"
Universal—One Reel

THIS is a comedy o fmix-up with Arthur Lake featured as the youth whose list of customers for the vanity cases he is selling is used as the invitation list for the party his parents are giving him. As the youth has sold most of his product in the slums the party

is patronized by a hard-boiled gang, which tears loose when the "eats" are served and starts a mild riot later. All this horrifies the parents and will amuse the screen patrons who like their comedy handed out in generous doses of obviousness. The climax, a fight with furniture being wrecked and features flattened, saves the reel from dullness.—T. C. KENNEDY.

"Dynamite's Daughter"
Universal—Two Reels
(Reviewed by Thomas C. Kennedy)

UNIVERSAL has found a way to give new life and vivacity to the hard ridin' scenes in western dramas. It is a simple formula—the studio solons merely draft Josie Sedgwick for the job and there you have it. Miss Sedgwick for screen purposes at least and we suspect for all practical purposes as well, can ride a hoss with the best of 'em, man or woman. She is a real queen of the saddle. Also she can put the vigor and power requisite to its success into the action typical of the short western melodrama.

Here is a two-reel western that should appeal to all the followers of this type of screen play. It has dash, the dash of fleet bronchs running at top speed across the plains, over the twisting trails of the mountains and taking in an easy leap the ditches which cut across the narrow paths forming the inevitable "short cut" without which no western plot is complete.

Miss Sedgwick is seen as "Lightning" Smith, Dynamite Smith's daughter. She is the spiritual, moral and physical leader of the little mining camp, where she conducts a saloon. There is a "Bill Hart" purpose and determination about "Lightning." This proves to be a vow that she will get the man who betrayed her sister before she will even think of her own happiness. A little boy, the son of the mine foreman, is her friend, and for his sake she refuses to kill the foreman when he proves to be the man who betrayed her sister. But the villain gets his deserts—he tumbles over the cliff.

The Cast
"Lightning" ....Josie Sedgwick
The Story.—A western melodrama concerned with a girl who runs a saloon, which she has inherited from her father. She has sworn to "get" the man who betrayed her sister. When the mine workers threaten to kill the foreman because he has withheld their pay, "Lightning" persuades them to be calm, but she is the first to set out after the crooked foreman when he tries to escape, after promising her he would pay off the boys. In his mad dash for freedom, the foreman is killed. He proves to be the man who deserted her sister and so "Lightning's" mission is filled and she is free to marry Bud, her handsome suitor.

Summary.—A western melodrama which has all the action and dash of the best of its kind, though the leading role and the assignment of the hard riding and heroism has been entrusted to a woman—Josie Sedgwick. She does her part splendidly. It should appeal strongly to the confirmed admirers of short western dramas.

Pre-release Reviews of Features

Peggy of the Secret Service
(Davis Distributing Division—4950 Feet)
(Reviewed by Harold Flavin)

FEATURED by some excellent settings, good performances by the principals and fast action, this production should prove popular with the fans of the smaller communities. Though having a somewhat slender story the numerous fight scenes, the desert "shots," the acting of Peggy O'Day and the rest of the cast will more than suffice to hold the interest of the spectator from beginning to end. This, the first of a series of detective yarns starring Miss O'Day, reveals her in the role of a female detective; she is assigned the task of recovering some jewels from an Eastern potentate and the way she goes about accomplishing her work proves an hour's entertainment.

THEME. Detective melodrama in which female detective is assigned task of recovering stolen jewels.

PRODUCTION HIGHLIGHTS. The desert scenes. The acting of the cast especially the star. The scenes in the home of Abdullah. The numerous fight scenes both aboard the ship and in the villian's home. The high grade settings.

EXPLOITATION ANGLES. Play up star. Hold matinee admitting free all girls named Peggy. Have masked girl travel about town in auto bearing banner reading "I Am Peggy of the Secret Service."

SUMMARY. A detective story that should get over well with most fans. Has slight story but incident and action help hold the interest. It is well mounted and directed.

THE CAST

Peggy	Peggy O'Day
Frank Jordan	W. H. Ryno
Spike Hennessy	Clarence Sherwood
Buck Brice	Dan Peterson
Mahmoud el Akem	Richard Neill
Hal Tracey	Eddie Phillips
Abdullah	V. L. Barnes
Abdullah's favorite wife	Ethel Childers

Produced by S. Cole. Story by Finis Fox. Directed by J. P. McGowan. Photographed by Bob Cline.

SYNOPSIS. Peggy, female detective, is assigned task of recovering stolen jewels from Abdullah, Algerian potentate. With the help of two assistants and her fiance she traps him and his cohorts but he eludes her and goes to his nephew's home. She follows him and after a series of exciting adventures succeeds in getting the jewels.

Peggy of the Secret Service
(Davis Dist. Div.)
PRESS NOTICE

BRINGING to the screen a thrilling drama based on the life of a Secret Service operator 'Peggy of the Secret Service' will be on the screen of the ———— theatre on ————. It is the first of a series starring winsome Peggy O'Day who will be remembered for some excellent characterizations in productions that proved popular. It is a colorful story combining good acting and some wonderful photography.

A brilliant cast of well known players support Miss O'Day in this stirring drama including Richard Neill, W. H. Ryno, V. L. Barnes and Ethel Childers. The outstanding thrill of the picture occurs in the climax when a terrific fight is staged between the forces of law and order and the thieves.

CATCH LINES

She postponed marriage for a life of service. Though beset by danger, may even death, at every step, she fought her way through.

Peggy O'Day

The Fighting Cub
(Truart—6000 Feet)
(Reviewed by George T. Pardy)

A MELODRAMA alive with human interest and deft sympathetic touches, clean wholesome and remarkably well adapted for exhibitors catering to the family trade. It will make an especial hit with the boys, who will be delighted with the work of Wesley Barry, the juvenile hero, who starts off as a copy kid on a newspaper, cherishes ambitions to rise in the profession, becomes a cub reporter and finally a star man on the sheet. Director Paul Hurst has done a remarkably good job here, putting over the thrills with a practiced hand and never passing an opportunity to make his young hero look like the real goods.

THEME. Melodrama of boy who wants to become a reporter and achieves his desire after passing through a medley of adventures.

PRODUCTION HIGHLIGHTS. The mother interest. Scene where Barry obtains admission to the presence of the big boss and gets interview with him.

DRAWING POWER. Should do capital business wherever family trade is chiefly sought for, has unfailing lure for juvenile patrons.

SUMMARY. Melodrama with kid hero and excellent mingling of humor and pathos, has several big punch situations and works up to satisfactory climax. Will make great impression on boys.

THE CAST

Tommy O'Toole	Wesley Barry
Jack Turner	Pat O'Malley
Maggie O'Toole	Mary Carr
J. William Toler	George Fawcett
Jane Toler	Mildred Harris
Margie Toler	Ann May
Spike Gory	Stuart Holmes
Detective Chief	Wilfred Lucas

Author, Adele Buffington. Directed by Paul Hurst.

SYNOPSIS. Tommy O'Toole, copy boy on the News, hears the editor assign police reporter to investigate a big jewelry robbery. Tommy asks for a chance at reporting and is told in jest he can have a job if he gets an interview with Toler, big political boss. He is thrown out of the Toler mansion by the butler, but scrapes acquaintance with Toler's youngest daughter and through her gets to see the father. The result is that he gets a job as reporter. Later he discovers the den of the Owls, the gang which stole the jewels. After a variety of thrilling adventures during which he is wounded by a bullet, he rounds up the thieves, proves the police reporter to be a crook, gets back the loot and is appointed star man on the paper.

The Fighting Cub (Truart)
PRESS NOTICE

"THE FIGHTING CUB" a stirring melodramatic story of the rise of a young copy boy on a big newspaper to the position of star reporter, comes to the ———— theatre on ————. Wesley Barry fills the role of the young hero and, according to the critics has never appeared to better advantage than in this thrilling, yet sympathetic tale of the lad who loves his mother and makes good.

Among the prominent players in support are such popular screen figures as Pat O'Malley, Mary Carr, George Fawcett, Mildred Harris, Walter Long, Ann May, Stuart Holmes, Wilfred Lucas, Otto Lederer and George Kuwa.

CATCH LINES

Romance and thrills in a corking melodrama of newspaper life.
A copy boy who had ambitions to advance in his profession and became star reporter after he ran down a gang of jewel thieves.
His love for his mother helped this lad to overcome all obstacles and makes himself famous.

Wesley Barry

The Man Who Found Himself
(Paramount—7168 Feet)
(Reviewed by George T. Pardy)

WHEN plenty of sympathy is worked up for a hero who also happens to be a great screen favorite there's not much risk in wagering that the film under consideration is sure to draw well at the box office. So Tom Meighan's latest vehicle may safely be listed as a money-getter, although the story, even with the prestige of Booth Tarkington's name as author, doesn't stand out as a particularly strong concoction. But it moves tolerably fast, wins unlimited pity for the self-sacrificing hero who goes to jail to shield a weak, erring brother, and as the martyr is righted in the end and gets the girl he loves, the average fan, as well as Mr. Meighan's countless admirers, will accept it as satisfactory entertainment.

THEME. Heart interest drama in which loyal hero goes to jail to cover up guilt of weak brother, temporarily loses his sweetheart, but regains her, and decides not to carryout intended scheme of revenge.

PRODUCTION HIGHLIGHTS. The fine photography. Realistic scenes in Sing Sing prison. Episode where hero, Tom Macauley escapes from jail and faces the man who tricked him on the night of latter's marriage to girl Tom loves. The revenge that misses fire and happy finish.

EXPLOITATION ANGLES. Feature Tom Meighan and Virginia Valli. Mention Booth Tarkington as author. Tell patrons Sing Sing scenes are genuine.

DRAWING POWER. A good attraction for any kind of house, large or small.

SUMMARY. A picture of the kind the public like to see Meighan starred in. Plot not of very original type, but spreads the sympathy salve heavily on hero and heroine and hits the heart target fairly.

THE CAST
Tom Macauley	Thomas Meighan
Nora Brooks	Virginia Valli
Lon Morris	Frank Morgan
Edwin Macauley, Jr.	Charles Stevenson
Evelyn Corning	Julia Hoyt
Mrs. Macauley, Jr.	Lynn Fontanne

Author, Booth Tarkington. Scenario by Tom J. Geraghty. Director, Alfred E. Green.

SYNOPSIS. Tom Macauley and his younger brother Edwin are directors in their father's bank. Edwin speculates with bank's money, loses, and Lon Morris a supposed friend of the brothers, plots successfully to have Tom sent to jail for his brother's crime. Morris marries Nora, but is confronted on his wedding night and beaten by Tom, who, having escaped, gives himself up again and is later released. Morris, now in control of the bank, is the object of Tom's revenge, but he gives it up when he learns Nora has been true to him and tricked by Morris. Latter, short in his accounts, is shot and killed by watchman when about to loot bank. Tom and Nora are wed.

The Girl Who Wouldn't Work
(B. P. Schulberg—5979 Feet)
(Reviewed by George T. Pardy)

WHILE the sex problem enters into this picture, director Marcel DeSano has handled it with such extreme delicacy and good judgment that it can safely be listed as a first-class production with strong general audience appeal. It represents Mr. DeSano's initial bid for fame in the directorial field and the hit he scores on this occasion speaks well for his future prospects. The action flows smoothly, briskly and there isn't an inch of padding in evidence, with the all-important human interest angle always predominant and a big thrill punch put over by the murder episode and hero's assumption of guilt from generous motives.

THEME. The romance of a girl department store clerk who wanted to be an actress, and wealthy young clubman; murder episode and melodramatic climax.

PRODUCTION HIGHLIGHTS. Clever acting of principals and support. First meeting of Mary Hale and Gordon Kent. Scene where she leaves home, joins Kent and is ousted from latter's apartments by angry rival.

EXPLOITATION ANGLES. Boost as a romance in which young working girl and wealthy admirer figure, stress love interest, the murder, hero's self-sacrifice and sunshine ending.

DRAWING POWER. Suited to needs of big and little houses, or any type of audience. Properly exploited, ought to do fine business.

SUMMARY. Picture has wide appeal, as it embraces romance, thrills and sympathetic lure. Presents sex problem, but so well handled as not to give offense. Skillfully directed and cleverly acted. Strong cast.

THE CAST
Gordon Kent	Lionel Barrymore
Mary Hale	Marguerite de la Motte
William Hale	Henry B. Walthall
Greta Verlaine	Lilyan Tashman
William Norworth	Forrest Stanley
District Attorney	Winter Hall
The Rounder	Thomas Ricketts

Author, Gertie D. Wentworth James. Adapted by Lois Hutchinson. Directed by Marcel DeSano.

SYNOPSIS. Mary Hale, department store clerk, wearying of her hard work and dull fiance, indulges in flirtation with wealthy clubman, Gordon Kent. Loses her job, is taken about by Kent and falls in love with him. Keeping late hours, she quarrels with her father and leaves home, Kent gives her shelter in his apartment, while he stays at club. Greta Verlaine, actress and former flame of Kent's, expels Mary. Latter's father, believing the worst, comes to apartment, shoots and kills Greta in mistake for supposedly erring daughter. To protect Mary's reputation, Kent gives himself up as the guilty man. Hale confesses, is tried but freed after three jury disagreements. Kent has gone broke, having spent fortune in Hale's defense, but wins Mary and settles down to work for his wife.

The Man Who Found Himself.
(Paramount)
PRESS NOTICE

Thomas Meighan

The Girl Who Wouldn't Work
(B. P. Schulberg)
PRESS NOTICE

Marcel De Sano

The Isle of Hope
(F. B. O.—5800 Feet)
(Reviewed by George T. Pardy)

ANOTHER of Richard Talmadge's whirlwind stunt films, stuffed to the limit with melodrama and comedy, as well as the breath-taking acrobatics in which this agile star always indulges. And in the later reels a fascinating mystery angle in which concealed pirate gold and life on a lonely island, with hero and heroine in the midst of perils, figure.

During the first half of the feature Mr. Talmadge is kept busy fighting aboard ship, climbing aloft with the activity of a monkey and swinging about the spars in his usual dare-devil style. The remainder shows less stunt stuff, but lots of melodramatic pep, with a satisfactory finish.

THEME. Fast stunt film with marine backgrounds, melodrama, comedy and mystery involved in search for concealed pirate treasure.

PRODUCTION HIGHLIGHTS. Good direction. Richard Talmadge's amazing stunt work. Fights aboard ship, the fire, wreck and landing on desert island. Scenes in old ruined castle. Comedy when Chink and negro cook are scared by skeletons. Heroine's capture by mutinous sailors, hero's scrap with mate. Discovery of gold.

EXPLOITATION ANGLES. Play up Talmadge's wild stunts, his adventures on board ship, the wreck and melodramatic happenings on the island. Stress the big fight, storm effects and finding of the treasure.

DRAWING POWER. Wherever Talmadge is a favorite or fast melodrama and stunt work are in demand, this film is sure to please.

SUMMARY. A good Talmadge stunt picture, with rather more plot to it than usual. Possesses melodramatic swing, love interest and provides timely comedy.

THE CAST
Robert Mackay	Richard Talmadge
Dorothy Duffy	Helen Ferguson
Captain Duffy	James Marcus
First Mate	Bert Strong
Second Mate	Howard Bell
Chinese Cook	Eddie Gordon
Colored Cook	George Reed

Author, James Bell Smith. Directed by Jack Nelson. Photographed by William Marshall and Jack Stevens.

SYNOPSIS. Bob Mackay, wealthy yachtsman, stows away aboard the Vulture for adventure's sake. Ship is commanded by Captain Duffy, sailing in search of gold hidden by ancient pirate. His stepdaughter, Dorothy, accompanies him. Bob and Dorothy fall in love. The crew mutiny and Duffy is killed. Ship takes fire and is wrecked. Bob and Dorothy land on island and find shelter in old ruined castle. Sailors who have escaped kidnap Dorothy. Bob pursues, whips giant mate in fight and carries her off. During storm lightning hits castle and exposes hidden treasure. Bob's friends from yacht club arrive and rescue him and his girl.

The Isle of Hope (F. B. O.)

PRESS NOTICE

RICHARD TALMADGE, famous stunt star, in "The Isle of Hope," will be the leading attraction on the bill of the —————— theatre on —————.

Besides showing Talmadge in the dare-devil feats for which he is justly renowned, this picture presents one of the most absorbing stories of wild adventure that has even been screened. There are fascinating marine backgrounds, a mutiny, a ship in flames, a wreck and landing on a deserted island and search for pirate gold.

No lover of exciting melodrama and romance can afford to miss this film, with its colorful atmosphere and endless succession of thrills. Helen Ferguson plays the pretty heroine.

CATCH LINES
Aerial acrobatics—mutiny aboard ship—terrific fighting—a vessel in flames—a wreck—pirate gold—Dick Talmadge in his most wonderful rôle. Watch for the big thrill in "The Isle Of Hope," when a lightning bolt splits the ruined castle and exposes the hidden treasure.

Richard Talmadge

Wreckage
(Banner—Six Reels)
(Reviewed by Paul Yawitz)

THERE is little in "Wreckage" to recommend it to first-run theatres, but sufficient melodramatic handling of a common place plot brings it to the level of good program entertainment. Throughout the picture is evidence of a director's strain to salvage-film values from a story that has been told a thousand and one times. Scott Dunlap does well in this respect and with the assistance of May Allison and Holmes Herbert will afford not-too-particular audiences a pleasant hour and a half.

THEME. Melodrama in which stormy seas, African jungles, and American vampires take a hand in the direction of a love affair.

PRODUCTION HIGHLIGHTS. A well executed ocean storm and ship-wreck. An under-sea fight. Fight in the country home.

EXPLOITATION ANGLES. The one certain element of this production to please audiences is the ship-wreck. Play this up and they will not be disappointed. The melodrama should be emphasized and also the fact that the story is an adaptation of a well known novel, "Salvage."

DRAWING POWER. Holmes Herbert and May Allison are deserving of much credit for the successful aspect of the picture and their previous performances bring them to the light of deserved advertising.

SUMMARY. The exhibitor whose audiences are not too fastidious in their tastes for continuity and well-developed plot will do well to book "Wreckage."

CAST
Rene	May Allison
Stuart Ames	Holmes Herbert
Maurice Dysart	John Miljan
Margot	Rosemary Theby
Grant Demarest	James Morrison

Author, Izola Forester. Directed by Scott Dunlap.

SYNOPSIS. Because of his knowledge of her selfishness, Dr. Stuart Ames attempts to put an end to her attentions to his best friend, Grant Demarest. Later that day Demarest is murdered and Ames is found in the apartment. The physician is acquitted by the coroner and embarks for the tropics. On board he meets Rene Jordon who is being followed by Maurice Dysart. In her father's cabin during a storm she sees Dysart in the act of robbing her father. The storm wrecks the ship and Dysart and Rene's father are apparently drowned. She is saved by Stuart and for three days are adrift together in a small boat. On her return to America she is a guest at the home of Margot and there meets a Count Bressing who in reality is Dysart in disguise. He continues his unwelcome attentions to the girl until Stuart returns from Africa, unable to stay away from the girl. A fight in Dysart's mountain cabin results in his being hurled over a cliff, but not before he had accidentally killed Margot in his battle with Ames. Margot confesses before her death that Demarest killed himself and thus clears all suspicion from Stuart. Rene and Stuart "are united and the wreckage of their lives salvaged."

Wreckage (Banner)

PRESS NOTICE

"WRECKAGE," a screen adaptation of Izola Forester's novel, "Salvage" comes to the ———— Theatre next ————. It is a stirring melodrama of life and love that carries the audience on board a ship during one of the most realistic ship-wrecks ever staged.

The great scene presents the Pacific in anger, with a vessel going down,, This shot is one of the finest ever caught by a camera. In order to make it, Ben Verschleiser, the producer, and Scott Dunlap, the director, took the entire cast into the Pacific on a small yacht fitted out to represent a liner. They sailed in the teeth of an ugly gale.

May Allison has the lead and is suported by Holmes Herbert, John Miljan, Rosemary Theby.

CATCH LINES
Love triumphs over intrigue and disaster in "Wreckage," the best sea story of the year.
A mighty drama of sea and society interwoven with an absorbing love story.

May Allison

Hell's Highroad

(Producers Distributing Corp.—6084 Feet)
(Reviewed by George T. Pardy)

THE luxurious atmosphere and magnificent settings always characteristic of Cecil De Mille productions are well to the fore in this picture, which was evidently made with a royal disregard for expense. The plot has nothing very new about it, but skilled direction and competent acting by principals and supporting cast carry it through to a triumphant finish. Also, the sub titles are excellent, some extremely witty, others terse and forcible—all helping the action along amazingly. Leatrice Joy is a winsomely alluring heroine, Edmund Burns a capable hero and Robert Edeson scores a hit as Sanford Gillespie, the millionaire who seems to be able to control Wall Street stocks by a mere wave of his hand.

THEME. Heart interest drama, showing how poor girl with lover in humble circumstances makes use of wealthy admirer to make the young chap wealthy, ruin him later when she thinks he is false; but begins life all over again with him.

PRODUCTION HIGHLIGHTS. Judy's visit to New York to claim supposed fortune, which turns out a disappointment. Scene where she quarrels with Ronald, her lover and that in which she meets and fascinates millionaire.

EXPLOITATION ANGLES. Boost this as another Cecil De Mille production of wonderful beauty as regards settings and gown display. Mention the director. Play up the love interest and feature Leatrice Joy and Robert Edeson.

DRAWING POWER. Has general audience appeal, is suitable for all classes of theatres.

SUMMARY. A good audience picture, has considerable heart appeal, is cleverly acted and sumptuously mounted in the usual ornate Cecil De Mille style and well directed.

THE CAST

Judy Nichols..Leatrice Joy
Ronald McKane...Edmund Burns
Sanford Gillespie...Robert Edeson
Anne Broderick..Julia Faye
Dorothy Harmon...Helene Sullivan

Author, Ernest Pascal. Directed by Rupert Julian.

SYNOPSIS. Ronald McKane comes to New York. Back in Chicago his sweetheart Judy Nichols dreams of wealth to come. She also journeys to New York to claim a supposed fortune, which turns out to be only a slim income. Refusing to face poverty with Ronald, she fascinates millionaire Gillespie and induces him to help the young fellow. Ronald makes money on the Stock Exchange and becomes entangled with wealthy Ann Broderick. In revenge Judy has Gillespie break Ronald. Latter seeks out Gillespie, finds Judy with him and is restrained by the millionaire from killing her. But Judy realizes her love for Ronald and they begin life anew.

A Fool and His Money

(Columbia Pictures—5800 Feet)
(Reviewed by George T. Pardy)

THIS flaring melodrama ought to "go over the top" in great shape, so far as the fans who wanted undiluted romance and snappy action for their money are concerned, while the members of the high-brow brigade will probably view it with amused tolerance. It's one of those yarns with an Old World fictitious country setting, in which a young American hero performs sundry deeds of valor and wins a fortune and charming bride. But it is uncommonly well directed and hasn't a dull moment in it, a good hot weather attraction which is sure to swell box office receipts in certain localities.

Madge Bellamy is an attractive figure as the Countess heroine, William Haines fights, writes and makes love as only a film hero could do, Stuart Holmes has one of those villain parts which suits him so well and Alma Bennett and Eugenie Besserer give excellent performances.

THEME. Romantic melodrama, with fictitious country setting, in which gallant young American aids and finally wins bride of noble birth.

PRODUCTION HIGHLIGHTS. The fast action and colorful atmosphere. Hero's adventures in old castle. Scene where heroine escapes in aeroplane, while lover covers her getaway by holding narrow bridge at sword point against pursuers. The comedy moments.

EXPLOITATION ANGLES. You can bill this as a cracking melodrama, full of fighting thrills, love interest and lively comedy. Play up the heroine's flight in a plane and the big scene where her lover is at sword's play on the bridge with the pursuing gang. Feature Madge Bellamy.

DRAWING POWER. An attraction which should make good in every respect at neighborhood and smaller houses.

SUMMARY. A lively melodrama whirling along at top-speed throughout. Has unlimited love interest and effective comedy relief. Will please the average fan.

THE CAST

Countess Von Pless ....Madge Bellamy
John Smart ....William Haines
Count Von Pless ....Stuart Holmes
Annette Ritazi..Alma Bennett
Mother ....Eugenie Besserer
Mrs. Schmick ....Carrie Clark Ward

Author, George Barr McCutcheon. Directed by Erle C. Kenton.

SYNOPSIS. John Smart, struggling American author, falls heir to a fortune and goes to country of Laupheim, where he has bought an old castle. He finds the beautiful Countess Von Pless in hiding there from her brutal husband and plans to help her out of the country, but is betrayed by a woman who had previously tried to vamp him. But the Countess escapes via aeroplane, while Smart, sword in hand fights off the Count and his men. He is wounded and the castle is confiscated by the authorities. Smart goes home broke, but his faithful servant whom he left behind, arrives with a great treasure he found in the castle and he weds the Countess.

Leatrice Joy

Madge Bellamy

In the Name of Love

(Paramount—5862 Feet)
(Reviewed by George T. Pardy)

EXCELLENT atmosphere, ornate settings, love intrigue, thrills and bright comedy combine to make this film a reliable investment for the exhibitor. It has a little of everything in the lineup and there can be scant doubt as to its box office pulling power. Incidentally there's something for the ladies to rave over in the up-to-date Paris fashion creation as exemplified by the gowns adorning the persons of Greta Nissen, Lillian Leighton and Edythe Chapman. Dramatic honors go to Miss Nissen, who gives a really wonderful performance in the role of the impetuous Marie Dufrayne, Ricardo Cortez is the handsome chap who wins her after much double and triple-crossing generally. Cortez is pleasing and the support capital.

THEME. Romantic drama with comedy and thrill interpolations. French atmosphere, heroine has several suitors, but finally weds one who loved her in boyhood.

PRODUCTION HIGHLIGHTS. Gorgeous mounting. Clever work of Greta Nissen, Ricardo Cortez and Wallace Beery. Attractive gown display. Fight between Beery and Cortez.

EXPLOITATION ANGLES. Street ballyhoo with pair dressed as bride and groom carrying banners bearing picture title. Feature Miss Nissen and Cortez. Window tie-ups on all kinds of articles that a man can buy for wife.

DRAWING POWER. Picture has universal appeal, should do good business anywhere.

SUMMARY. Film has snappy action, abounds in romantic lure, crisp comedy and thrills. French atmosphere well developed. Acting, photography, settings, direction all of first-chop quality.

THE CAST

Raoul Melnotte..................................Ricardo Cortez
Marie Dufrayne....................................Greta Nissen
M. Glavis:.......................................Wallace Beery
Marquis de Beaumont...........................Raymond Hatton
Mother Dufrayne...............................Lillian Leighton
Mother Melnotte...............................Edythe Chapman
Dumas Dufrayne..................................Richard Arlen
    Adapted from Edward Bulwer-Lytton's novel, "The Lady of Lyons" by Sada Cowan.
    Director, Howard Higgins. Photographed by C. Edgar Schoenbaum.

SYNOPSIS. Raoul Melnotte returns to France from U. S., to woo his boyhood sweetheart, Marie Dufrayne, but finds that she has become wealthy and has social aspirations. He starts a garage in the village, conceals his identity, and makes love to Marie so successfully that she turns down two other suitors, a poor nobleman and a rich brewer. The two ousted suitors join Raoul in a plot whereby he pretends to be the Prince of Como, intending to betray him at the last moment. But he outwits them and weds Marie. The real Prince arrives, the deception is exposed and Marie flies into a temper. She relents when she finds Raoul to be her childhood sweetheart, saves him from being killed by her brother and mutual happiness follows.

Greta Nissen

In the Name of Love (Paramount)

Tricks

(Davis Distributing Division, Inc.—5000 Feet)
(Reviewed by George T. Pardy)

THIS picture provides fair entertainment and is chiefly remarkable for the fact that for once, a heroine, of the much ill-used "wide open spaces" doesn't get herself up as a cowgirl, but is content to gallop around in ordinary feminine riding attire. It looks reasonable enough, too, for she is the daughter of a wealthy ranch-owner in lower California, equipped with a high grade education, and there are probably many young damsels of her type who don't care about living up to film tradition.

Two exceedingly handsome and intelligent horses figure prominently in the action, you might call them co-stars with Marilyn Mills, and those who like Westerners a bit different from the average output should find the feature amusing.

THEME. Part comedy, with girls' boarding school and society settings, part Western melodrama. Too vivacious heroine is expelled, goes to her father's ranch and has love affair with foreman.

PRODUCTION HIGHLIGHTS. Trix's rescue of a youngster from runaway horse. Comedy scenes in girls' boarding school. Her meeting with Jack Norton at the ranch.

EXPLOITATION ANGLES. Play up the feats of the two horses, Beverly and Star. Dwell on comedy relief. Tell patrons this Western has a different slant from the usual. Feature Marilyn Mills.

DRAWING POWER. Not strong enough to meet entertainment demands of big first-run theatres, but should get by in neighborhood and smaller houses.

SUMMARY. A mixture of melodrama and comedy. This variation from ordinary style of Western plot should please fans, who will also find exploits of two trained horses entertaining.

THE CAST

Angelica (Trix)...................................Marilyn Mills
The New Foreman............................J. Frank Glendon
Aunt Angelica....................................Gladys Moore
William Varden.................................Myles McCarthy
Buck Barlow....................................William Lowery
Ranch Housekeeper.............................Dorthy Vernon
Red..Harry Valeur
    Story and Scenario by Mary C. Bruning. Directed by Bruce Mitchell.

SYNOPSIS. Angelica, daughter of ranch-owner Varden, leaves her aunt's lawn party in disgust because it is too tame. Back in boarding school she gives a midnight supper which causes her expulsion. She visits her father's ranch, has her beautiful mare, Beverly, sent to her, and with a companion horse, Star, proceeds to enjoy herself by falling in love with the new foreman, Jack Norton. She overhears outlaws planning to steal cattle, is taken prisoner and sends Star for aid. Norton responds, rescues and wins her.

Tricks (Davis Distributing Div.)

Marilyn Mills

Regional News from Correspondents

Philadelphia

A L. FISHER, Jr., formerly salesman for Metro-Goldwyn, is now associated with American Feature Film Exchange, 1335 Vine Street.

J. S. Woody, president of Associated Exhibitors, was a recent visitor at the local office of the company.

C. C. Hite, special two-reel comedy salesman for Pathe, has returned from a motor trip to Ohio, where he visited his parents.

J. Howard Wiley, who has played in a number of important theatres in Philadelphia, is the new organist for the Hippodrome Theatre, York, Pa.

The Alcazar Theatre has been leased by Wolf & Berger, who operate the Ideal Theatre, the New Empress, the Manheim and the 56th St. theatres.

Denny Berkery, manager of the 69th St. Theatre, has returned

from a week's vacation in Bermuda.

R. C. Meigs, special salesman for Pathe, has been transferred from the local office to the Albany office, where he will act as special two-reel comedy salesman.

Tom Lark, cashier in the local Pathe office, has returned from a vacation in New York City.

While a fire was raging in a building in the rear of the Victoria Theatre, H. D. Cherry, manager, by his presence of mind quieted the patrons of the theatre and prevented a serious panic.

The Germantown Theatre has

reopened after having been closed for improvements. It has been thoroughly renovated and improved and presents a most attractive appearance.

J. S. Hebrew, manager of the local office of Warner Bros., has returned from a business trip to Boston.

O. Guilfoile, formerly with Vitagraph, has been appointed assistant cashier for Warner Brothers.

C. G. Powell, local manager of Associated Exhibitors, has returned from a vacation spent with his family in Atlantic City.

Mayer Milgram has purchased

a site and building in North Philadelphia which will be remodeled into a 500-seat theatre.

Sam E. Morris, general sales manager for Warner Bros., was a recent visitor in Philadelphia.

Miss Rhea V. Halpern, secretary to Mr. Ben Amsterdam and auditor of the Masterpiece Film Attractions, is spending a two weeks' vacation in Atlantic City.

The Wayne Theatre, Wayne Ave., Phila., has been sold by Harry Rosins to Elliott Goldman, acting for an undisclosed purchaser, for a price reported to be $57,000. Possession will be taken in September.

Erno Rapee, formerly conductor of the Fox Theatre Grand Orchestra, sailed for Berlin on the "Columbus" on August 10th, where he will organize an orchestra for a new theatre which the UFA expects to open in the fall.

Des Moines

E J. Deholt, owner of the Waterloo Theatre and the Strand Theatre of Waterloo, Iowa, is spending between $15,000 and $20,000 on each theatre in remodelling and redecorating. The Strand Theatre will be equipped with a stage. No vaudeville numbers are being planned for the Strand but Mr. Deholt is arranging for special presentations with his picture programs. The Waterloo Theatre will be completely redecorated, new light fixtures, etc.

L. R. Brager, formerly doing publicity from the New York office for First National, has been chosen to have charge of publicity for all the A. H. Blank theatres, now numbering more than thirty in Iowa. Mr. Brager was in Des Moines earlier this year for the exploitation of The Sea Hawk. Offices are being fitted up on the fourth floor of the Commonwealth Building which is owned by Mr. Blank for Mr. Brager. Dorothy Day, who has been handling publicity for the Des Moines theatres owned by Blank as well as those over the state, will also have her office on this floor. The A. H. Blank Enterprises occupy the entire third floor.

Lyle Utsler of the booking department at Famous Players is a proud papa. The baby is a bouncing nine pound girl and her name is Virginia Maude.

Hippie and Peak of the Past Time Theatre at Makoqueta are remodelling their theatre. D. L. DeNue has also remodeled his theatre, the Majestic Theatre. Mr. DeNue is exhibitor at De Witt.

The Garden Theatre at Iowa City of which Nate Chapman is owner as well as of the Inglert

Theatre there is being redecorated. The theatre will be equipped with new seats throughout. Mr. Chapman has bought two new machines with low intensity arcs.

John Waler and E. R. Coons who are joint owners of several theatres are opening up the Lyric Theatre at Seymour. They were operating the Majestic Theatre at Seymour but the lease on the Majestic Theatre building ran out and so they decided to build a theatre of their own. The owner of the Majestic Theatre will continue to run it.

Mr. Waller and Mr. Coons have the Idle Hour theatre and the Mills theatre at Tama, Iowa, which they recently purchased and also a house at Osceola.

Merle Anderson, advertising clerk for Famous Players, took a bad spill on his motor cycle. He was pretty well shaken up and one knee was badly hurt. He is about on crutches now.

Elmer Tilton, manager of the First National office, is in New York for the convention of branch managers there. He will be gone until the first of September.

Louise Wallensack lives at Batchtate, North Dakota, and is now spending her vacation days with her parents.

The picnic of DesMoines Film Exchange staffs, attended by about a hundred, was a grand success. Famous Players and First National made up a ball team and challenged a team made up of members of all other film exchanges. The challengers were defeated in decided manner. The score was 23 to 3. The game was not without its casualties. Gene Malone of First National was rather badly hurt when a fast

ball hit him in the side. And Mr. Clement, booker for Famous Players, was hit in the neck with a bat. The batter's intentions of hitting the ball instead of Clem went aglee. Everybody played some now and some then. Universal carried off the honors, it is believed, for champion sp忘ggers, their representatives winning in several races. Ruby Morgan and C. S. Baker of Universal were two of the winners. And others won the money as champion eaters. There were lots of chicken, etc. Altogether this gettogether was such a success that it is probable that it will be repeated.

The midwest district manager for Pathe, F. C. Aiken, visited the DesMoines office, coming to DesMoines from Chicago. R. S. Ballentyne, manager of the local exchange, accompanied Mr. Aiken to Omaha.

M. J. Weisfeldt, district manager for F. B. O., after a visit to the DesMoines exchange, made the Minneapolis office.

Miss Margaret McGreavy, secretary to Manager Banfard of Metro-Goldwyn, is on her vacation. She will visit Chicago. And, as some of the girls from this exchange have surprised them all with wedding bells, Miss McGreavy has already started the denials that she will be married on this trip.

A. C. Shuneman has bought a new screen for his theatre at Webster City, Iowa. The American Theatre at Cherokee, of which Dale Goldie is manager, has been equipped with a new electric fan. Wes Booth of Belle Plain also purchased new equipment. Wes bought two new condensing systems.

The Exhibitors Supply Company reports that a large number of theatres are purchasing new equipment. C. R. Coons of Seymour bought a new projection machine. He was purchasing for the new theatre, the Lyric. Mr. Ihers, owner of the theatre at Minlow, bought a new machine. Mr. Dehoet of Monroe purchased similar new equipment for his theatre. The Consolidated School of Dysart, Iowa, bought a machine. Supt. Ferrell of the Dysart schools has charge of the pictures and equipment bought for the school. Mr. Hundling, managing the Rialto Theatre at Newton for A. H. Blank, purchased his entire new lighting equipment from the Exhibitors Supply Company. He purchased new lighting fixtures as well as some special lighting effects. Mr. Deholt of Waterloo purchased the entire stage equipment for the Strand Theatre from the DesMoines Company and also for the Waterloo Theatre which he is planning to redecorate, adding new light fixtures, etc., at a cost of nearly $20,000. The Capitol Theatre at Davenport, which Milton Overman is managing for A. H. Blank Enterprises, has been equipped with two new Simplex machines with Peerless arcs.

The vacation schedule shows that Miss Gretchen Kelleher, billing clerk for Pathe, is visiting in Cedar Rapids, while Miss Novello Phillips, booker's stenographer, is in Omaha.

W. E. Banford, manager for Metro-Goldwyn, is planning the routing for The Trackless Train in the key towns.

Famous Players had fire drill last week. All escaped from the building without injury.

Salt Lake City

CLYDE H. MESSINGER, who has charge of the local Educational Pictures exchange leaves the beginning of this week to cover Southern Utah. He expects to be gone about two weeks. Walter Hiers, comedian, now playing in Educational Pictures, was through here last week, accompanied by his wife. They were en route to Yellowstone Park on a vacation trip. Clyde H. Messinger drove them to different points of interest during their brief sojourn in this city.

Miss Piper, booker for Educational here, has returned from her vacation.

L. L. Savage, Western Division Inspector Booker for Pathe, is leaving here this week for Denver. This will complete his trip in the Western Division. He expects to go direct to New York from Denver.

W. G. Seib, manager of the local Pathe exchange, is expecting Frank Harris, newly appointed Western Division Manager, to be in Salt Lake within the next two weeks.

R. D. Boomer, salesman for Pathe, is leaving this week for a three weeks' trip through Southern Utah.

Harold Pickering, exploitation manager for Famous Players-Lasky exchange here, is getting out the advertising for the eighth annual Paramount week which will be celebrated September 6th to 12th.

George L. Cloward, manager for Metro-Goldwyn in this city, has just returned from a trip

through Idaho in the interest of the new Metro-Goldwyn product.

W. F. Gordon, manager of the local Associated First National branch, is leaving for New York this week. Gordon expects to drive to Denver and complete the trip by train.

Vete Stewart who covers Southern Idaho and Nevada for Associated First National has left for this territory.

C. Hawks, salesman for Associated First National, has left for Idaho.

L. A. Davis, manager of F.B.O. local exchange, is leaving for a short trip into Idaho.

W. K. Bloom, Montana salesman for F. B. O., is now making a trip through Southern Utah.

Joe Soloman, F. B. O. salesman, is covering the Idaho territory.

E. M. Gibson, assistant manager for F. B. O. here, will return from his vacation next week.

Fred J. McConnel, short subject sales manager for Universal, is expected here from the home office the latter part of the week.

Samuel Henley, manager of the local Universal branch, returned last week from a trip through Southern Utah.

George Mayne, owner of Preferred Pictures and Super-Features exchange here, left for Idaho this week with his new pictures. He expects this trip to cover a period of about ten days.

Art A. Schuyer, who has charge of the local Fox exchange, is leaving this week to cover the Idaho branch.

Carl Stearn, manager of United

Jerry Abrams, Mid West District Manager for Renown Pictures, Inc.

Artists Exchange in this city, has just returned from a trip through Idaho with a large number of contracts.

James R. Keitz, manager of the local Greater Features exchange, leaves the first part of next week for Carbon County, Utah.

C. L. Pearce, who covers the Eastern Idaho and Western Wyoming territory out of the Greater Features exchange here, has just returned from an extended and very successful trip through this territory.

Miss Scott, booker for Greater

Features in this city, has returned from her vacation.

C. C. McDermond, salesman out of the local Producers Distributing Corporation exchange, is covering his territory in Southern Utah.

Harry Lustig, Western District Manager of Warner Brothers, will be in this week to hold a sales conference with R. S. Stackhouse, manager for Warner Brothers exchange here, and with all of the field representatives in this territory.

There are two new additions to the sales staff of Warner Brothers. They are Lawrence W. Hyde, who will cover the Utah and Nevada territory, and Harry Gibson who has been assigned to the Idaho and Wyoming branch.

Manager Stackhouse has just returned from a trip through the Montana territory.

Exhibitors visiting the local exchanges this week are: S. B. Stock, operating the Lyceum Theatre of Ogden, Utah; M. Clawson, owner of the Clawson Theatre, Morgan, Utah; A. L. Stallings, owner of the Kinema Theatre in Richfield, Utah; L. F. Brown and Cyrus Ward, operating the Isis Theatre at Preston, Idaho; Theodore M. Chessler, owner of the Princess Theatre, Bingham, Utah.

The motion picture operators of this city are staging a Movie Ball to be given this week at Pleasure Park, the outdoor moving picture theatre and dance hall.

Kansas City

THE Optimist Club of Kansas City met with exhibitors in a meeting and luncheon at the Kansas City Club Friday and Greater Movie Season was formally approved by the club.

Miss Emma Viets, chairman of the Kansas State Censor Board, was honored this week when word was received in Kansas City that she had been elected Most Worshipful Grand Matron of the Grand Chapter of the Eastern Star at Toronto, Canada.

Earl T. Cook, new manager of the Pantages theatre, Kansas City, concluded that a little publicity to start his reign would not be amiss, so he staged a free performance for newsboys of the Kansas City Star. He obtained the desired publicity—plenty of it—it is needless to say.

An average of thirty-eight essays a day is being received by Miss Katherine Prosser, motion picture editor of the Kansas City Star, in conjunction with the essay contest on Greater Movie Season, sponsored locally by a committee of exhibitors and exchange officials.

While Jack Quinlan, manager of the Mainstreet theatre, Kansas City, is spending a vacation in the

East, Fred Crowe of the American theatre, Chicago, is in charge. Mr. Quinlan is expected back soon.

Among the out-of-town exhibitors in the Kansas City market last week were: Charles Marshall, Palace, Golden City, Mo.; Charles Sears, Sears Circuit, Nevada, Mo.; C. M. Pattee, Pattee theatre, Lawrence, Kan.; William Cuff, Strand, Chillicothe, Mo.; Ben Levy, Hippodrome, Joplin, Mo.

There was not one whit of difficulty in "digging up" exchange news last week on Kansas City's movie row. M. A. Tanner, former Selznick branch manager, has accepted a position as booker at the Fox exchange, succeeding Edward Solig, who departed for Jacksonville, Fla.

Frank Baxter, former Universal salesman, has joined the Warner-Vitagraph force in Omaha.

J. R. Grainger, general sales executive for Fox, was in Kansas City on a business visit, being enroute to the Pacific Coast.

Lou Nathanson, former representative in Oklahoma and Kansas for P. D. C., has joined the United Artists force and will cover Oklahoma.

Miss Ruth Gershon, busy Fox

stenographer, is convalescing from an operation for appendicitis.

C. C. Knipe, formerly in charge of the accessories department for the Kansas City exchange, has been promoted to Universal Central West accessories manager, while Fred Herschorn, former Universal salesman, has been promoted to short subjects manager of that company.

George Priest has been employed as an extra salesman for the Fox exchange, while William Kaster of New York City has joined the Universal sales force.

It was hard punishment to take, but M. C. Brodsky, Universal salesman who was confined to his bed for a week with an infected foot, has returned to work, while it is understood Earl Reynolds, fellow salesman of the same office, has become so "fast" that he is considering trading in both of his motor cars for an airplane.

Strange and mystic is the power which E. C. Rhoden, manager of Midwest Film Distributers, Inc., Kansas City, has over the natives of Beloit and Concordia, Kan. Virtually no rain had fallen in the vicinity of those two towns all summer. The outlook was any-

thing but cheerful. Then along came Mr. Rhoden for a week of business and it rained each day he was there, much to his inconvenience. But city officials of the two towns, it is understood, are contemplating appointing Mr. Rhoden as the "Rain Maker."

William Gabel, Jr., of Beloit, Kan., and Harry Wareham of Manhattan, Kan., will leave soon to attend the Paramount Managers School in New York City, later to become managers of Paramount Manager School in New York City, later to become managers of Paramount theatres.

The Mayfield theatre, Seventy-first street and Prospect avenue, while it is understood that the natives of Beloit and Concordia, Kan. the Bonaventure theatre, a suburban house of Kansas City.

Untiring and efficient work as advertising manager of the Cuff Enterprises at Chillicothe, Mo., won the position as manager of the Strand theatre, owned by William Cuff, for John Creamer. Edward Smith, former manager of the theatre, is to become manager of the Strand hotel, owned by Mr. Cuff, and which adjoins the theatre.

New England

THE Immaculate Conception parish of Everett, Mass. will start at once on the erection of a moving picture theatre on Chelsea street, in which educationals, news reels, historic and scientific films will be shown. The building will be 42 x 100 feet, of wood and concrete construction and will cost about $30,000.

George and Oliver Ramsdell, proprietors of the Malden Orpheum, Malden, Mass. are back at their desks again with a fine coat of tan secured on the Maine coast. Work on their new theatre on Pleasant street is progressing rapidly and the building is expected to be ready by late fall.

Winchester, Mass., Boston's only suburb of more than 5,000 population without a motion picture theatre, may have the question again put up to the voters this fall of having such a theatre. Two Winchester men are looking the ground over and are planning to again seek a permit. On three occasions applicants in the past half dozen years have been refused licenses by vote of the town. Winchester's residents must attend shows in neighboring communities although it has a population of more than 15,000 people. Local capital is ready to build the playhouse and lease it if the permit is granted.

Apollo Theatres, Incorporated, is a newly incorporated company which plans presentation of motion pictures in Boston this winter at a new theatre which the company plans to build on a site yet to be selected, probably in the Back Bay district. John Henes of 1641 North Shore Road, Revere, Mass., is president and treasurer of the new company.

Charles A. Newhall, 73 Tremont street, Boston, will build a theatre in Harvard square, Cambridge, at a cost of $150,000 for which Architects Mowll & Rand, 21 School street, Boston, have prepared plans. Contracts will soon be let and construction work started so that the films may be shown for the first time about midwinter.

Astor Productions, Inc., has received its charter from Secretary of State Cook. It is understood that the new company has an option on a Boston theatre which it plans to remodel and open with motion pictures. Henry G. Segal of Brookline, Mass.; David L. Schoolman of Allston, Mass., and Louis R. Covner of Brookline are the officers of the company.

Parson's Theatre Enterprises, Inc., has been incorporated with $25,000 capital to conduct a motion picture theatre. Incorporators are Myron C. Parsons, president; A. Lillian Parsons, Rockport, Mass., treasurer, and Lillian H. Parsons, clerk.

Hyman Kronich has had plans prepared for the erection of a moving picture theatre at 63-67 Walnut street, Springfield. Work is to begin at once and the playhouse will be opened early in the winter.

Atlanta

MRS. JACQUES FUTRELLE, popular and well-known Atlanta writer, as well as the mother of the talented Virginia Futrelle, singer of distinction, has been appointed this week publicity director for the Howard theatre, taking up her duties in this connection at once.

N. W. Remond, who two years ago retired from the picture business, is this week back in the field again with the announcement of his purchase of the Scenic theatre at Lake Wales, Florida. He at one time owned several theaters in Jacksonville, and was also district supervisor for this territory under S. A. Lynch's regime a few years ago. His many friends here and elsewhere will be delighted to learn of his return to the fold, and to wish him unqualified success in his Florida house.

W. B. Fulton, Universal's salesman in the southwest Georgia and South Carolina territory, has been transferred to the Alabama territory this week to fill the place left vacant by Roy S. Campbell, who last week removed to St. Augustine, Florida to take charge of Universal's two theatres there. Mr. Campbell succeeds Ralph DeBruler in St. Augustine, who has gone to Houston, Texas. Mr. Fulton's territory will be taken over by S. C. Ware.

Mr. Herbert Furniss Kincey, otherwise known as "Mike," who has been associated with R. B. Wilby for many years, and with him is owner of the Academy and Walton theatres in Selma, Ala., announces his engagement this week to Miss Sara Elizabeth Bayne.

The marriage will be solemnized on September 1st in the First Presbyterian Church, Selma, Ala., at 4 o'clock in the afternoon. Mr. Kincey will be remembered by many in his connection for several years with Southern Enterprises, when he represented the booking department, together with Montgomery Hill and Ed. Brown. He has been in the motion picture business for nearly ten years, and the announcement of his coming marriage carries with it the felicitations of his large circle of friends.

Central Penn

BURGLARS entered and ransacked the box office of the Grand motion picture theatre, Centralia, near Mount Carmel, Pa., early in the morning of Sunday, August 16, and failing to find money, demolished a stout wooden cabinet, destroyed several rolls of tickets and committed other acts of vandalism.

Gaining entrance to the main auditorium by prying loose the lock on one of the exit doors, the burglars forced their way into the box office by cutting a large hole in the door, reaching a hand through the opening and turning the lock. It was evidently due to their disappointment at failing to find cash that they ruthlessly destroyed such articles as they could find. A description of men seen lurking near the theatre was given to the police.

The Family theatre, Hazleton, no longer will depend exclusively on the local electric power company to supply it with current for electric lighting. Because storms have in the past caused a temporary failure of the lights, under the present arrangement, it has been decided by the theatre management to install its own lighting

system to be used in emergencies, so that the theatre will be assured of never going dark during performances.

Charles K. Campbell, manager of the Victoria picture theatre, Harrisburg, went on a two weeks' vacation trip through Pennsylvania by motor in the latter part of August. In his absence the management of the Victoria was temporarily in the hands of Samuel A. Keubler, manager of the Colonial. Both theatres are Wilmer & Vincent houses.

Mr. and Mrs. Elmer H. Ley, the latter director of the Wilmer & Vincent Community Service Bureau in Harrisburg, left on August 19 for a vacation motor trip through the Pocono mountains to Delaware Water Gap, and other parts of Pennsylvania. Later they went to New York City to visit their daughter, Miss Naomi Ackley, known to the stage as Miss Sonya Leyton, who has appeared in several important roles with Schubert musical shows.

The opening date for the new Strand theatre, just built in York by the Nathan Appell theatre interests, was postponed from August 17, the date originally set, until

Thursday, August 27. Many newspapermen and motion picture exhibitors, film men, and other persons in most of the important cities of the state were invited to attend the dedicatory exercises.

As the feature of the annual picnic of the Carr & Schad, Inc., theatres, of Reading, held at Sinking Springs park on August 2, the baseball game between the Carr & Schad nine and the team representing the M. P. T. O. of Eastern Pennsylvania, South Jersey and Delaware, was highly exciting. The latter, who previously had won the Philadelphia motion picture league championship, were victors by a score of 4 to 3. Exhibitors and exchange men from all parts of Pennsylvania were guests at the picnic.

Dr. H. J. Schad, of Reading, president of the Motion Picture Theatre Owners of Eastern Pennsylvania, Southern Jersey and Delaware, and head of Carr & Schad Inc., which controls a chain of theatres in Reading and Lebabon, was host to a score or more of Reading's prettiest girls who competed in the recent contest to select "Miss Reading" to

take part in the Atlantic City pageant. The party was held at Dr. Schad's county home near Reading.

Miss Margaret Rudy, 18, of 2631 North Sixth Street, Harrisburg, an usher at the Majestic Theater, in that city suffered a severe injury about the head on August 20, when she slipped and fell in South Fourth street, below Market. She was admitted to the Polyclinic Hospital for treatment.

The Star motion picture theatre, Tower City, Schuylkill county, which had been closed for practically a year, has been reopened with nightly picture attractions for a period of at least two weeks.

William O. Heckman, manager of the Hippodrome, York, has engaged J. Howard Wiley, of Philadelphia, to become the organist for the theatre, and Mr. Wiley already has taken his place at the Wurlitzer instrument which the theatre uses. He succeeds John DePalma, who has become organist at the new Strand theatre, just opened in York by the Nathan Appell interests.

Milwaukee

H. J. FITZGERALD, manager of the Milwaukee branch of First National, has gone to New York to attend the convention of

First National branch managers at the Roosevelt Hotel. E. P. Vallendorf, office manager of the Milwaukee branch is enjoying a week's vacation in Minnesota, where he is visiting with relatives and friends.

Elmer Zieman, assistant manager of Saxe's Wisconsin Theatre, is sending picture post cards from Yellowstone National Park, where he is spending his two weeks' vacation.

The usual sunshine atmosphere of the Milwaukee office of F. B. O. has been missing for the past

few days. Miss Evelyn Benson, billing clerk and one of the most likeable young women in any local exchange, was killed in an auto accident on a county highway last week, and her escort, Robert Turner, F. B. O.'s poster clerk, was seriously injured. The two were occupants of a car which was crashed into at a curve in the road by a reckless driver. Miss Benson had been in the employ of the F. B. O. office for the past two weeks, and during that time had won the respect and admiration of everyone on the staff through her excellent qualities and her pleasant personality. The entire local F. B. O. force, from manager down to office boy attended the funeral services early Monday morning.

The inauguration of a better picture at higher prices policy at the Merrill Theatre seems to have been a wise move, for the house has been packed ever since the prices were raised from 25 to 50 cents, on August 15.

Milwaukee exhibitors are beginning to breath easier now that the summer season is drawing to an end without any serious box office casualties. While business has been nothing to brag about, taken as a whole, most houses had satisfactory returns each week, in spite of the fact that a large part of the population sought its amusement every evening at the lakes which are annoyingly handy.

Sidney Lawrence, who for the past twelve months has very successfully guided the destinies of Saxe's Modjeska Theatre, has resigned his position as manager of that house to take charge at Champaign, Ill., for the Orpheum Circuit. Sid not only established himself as an excellent house manager with a decided proclivity for nifty stage presentations, but also won himself a place in the heart of practically every other exhibitor in Milwaukee. Under his capable management the big south side picture house was prosperous throughout its entire first year, Sid having assumed charge soon after the grand opening last August.

Canada

D. C. Brown, formerly manager of the Algoma Theatre at Sault Ste. Marie, Ontario has been given a splendid promotion by the Famous Players Canadian Corp., in his appointment to the management of the Regent Theatre, Toronto, the big-time moving picture house of the Ontario Capital. Mr. Brown, who has had theatrical experience in South Africa, Australia and the United Kingdom, has been succeeded at the Algoma by J. D. Fletcher.

Another important change in the Famous Players circle in Canada has been the appointment of H. E. Wilton, until recently the manager of the Strand Theatre, Hamil-

ton, to the management of the Savoy Theatre, Hamilton, Ontario. Mr. Wilton's successor at the Hamilton Strand has not yet been announced.

B. E. Lang has returned to Montreal, Quebec, where he has been reappointed manager of His Majesty's Theatre, a large local house. Mr. Lang spent recent months in Asbury Park, N. J., but he had been the manager of His Majesty's at Montreal before going to the Jersey centre. The theatre has been modernized in recent weeks through the construction of new facilities and the replacement of old.

Exhibitors and exchange representatives of Winnipeg, Manitoba, mingled happily when they held their annual screen picnic at Selkirk Park on Sunday, August 14. The big sports programme was under the direction of Sam Swartz who secured no less than 80 prizes for the picnic competitions.

A successful competitor at the Ontario Rifle Ranges at Long Branch, Toronto, and at the Connaught Rifle Ranges, Ottawa, was Bert Palmer, usher of the Strand Theatre, Calgary, Alberta, who, between performances, has attained a high degree of marks-

manship. Mr. Palmer spent his annual vacation at the big Canadian rifle meets which were conducted under the auspices of the Dominion of Canada Rifle Association. He secured his share of the awards.

The Franklin Theatre, Ottawa, is losing its name, J. M. Franklin having decided to relinquish his lease of the house on August 31 in order to devote his whole attention to B. F. Keith's Theatre, Ottawa, of which he is the general manager. The "Franklin" signs are coming off the smaller house and it will probably be opened by other parties in the fall.

Cincinnati

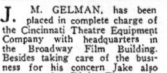

J. M. GELMAN, has been placed in complete charge of the Cincinnati Theatre Equipment Company with headquarters in the Broadway Film Building. Besides taking care of the business for his concern Jake also manages the Dixie Theatre in the West End. This theatre caters to the colored trade.

Bill Clark, in charge of the press for the Libson Houses returned from a vacation to the mountains of West Va.

Among the visitors to the local Paramount conference last week were, Bill Clark, manager of the Louisville exchange and Fritz Wagner, manager of the Indianapolis branch.

Pete Smyth of the Sylvia Theatre, Bellevue, Ky., is sporting a brand new Chandler sedan these days.

Godfry Kotzen, manager of the Lyric Theatre, Covington, Ky., predicts that he is in for one of the most successful seasons of his career as theatre manager. He is perfectly satisfied with his line up of pictures and all that he needs now is patrons. During his spare time Mr. Kotzen sells Hudson cars.

The Famous Players organization is now established in the new offices of the company on the second floor of the Broadway Film building. The offices look spick and span and the smell of fresh paint is rampant throughout.

Louis Damm, of the Damm Theatre, Osgood, Indiana, spent several days in the various exchanges lining up his pictures for the coming season.

Frank J. Ferguson of the Avondale Theatre, Columbus, O., spent several days with the various exchange managers last week.

David M. Gould, connected with the complete service department of Universal's New York office, has been spending some time at the local exchange and in the local territory boosting the short subjects of the firm. Just how soon he will get back home he does not know but he hopes that it will be soon.

Lou Snitzer, well known local exhibitor is the proud father of a baby boy. This is the third offspring in the Snitzer family and both baby and mother are doing fine.

H. R. Dixon, of the Ideal Theatre, Dry Ridge, Ky., and the Unique, Walton, Ky., was a visitor at Film Row last week.

John B. Elliott of the Strand Theatre, Lexington, Ky., is about to open a new hotel in his city which he will name the Paramount. He expects all the film boys to make their home with him while in Lexington.

Chas. Trieble and his son of the Pastime Theatre, Maysville, Ky., motored to Cincinnati last week and booked several pictures for future showing.

W. H. Wright and Wm. Gore of the Palace Theatre, Peech Creek, W. Va., and Gore Theatre, Cherry Tree, W. Va., spent several days in the film building booking pictures for the coming season.

Ralph Kinsler, who has been taking care of the F. B. O. offices during the illness of its manager Ed. Booth, who was in Indianapolis, has had his ring finger on his left hand broken, by a film can.

Henry Eger, former manager of the James Theatre, Columbus, O., will shortly be connected with one of the local film exchanges.

Sam Marks, Dayton salesman for F. B. O. is doubling these days. He is now doing special sales duty in the Kentucky territory.

Andy G. Hettesheimer, manager of the Orpheum Theatre of this city, is fastly recuperating from his recent severe illness and all his friends wish him a speedy recovery.

Fred Myers and Harry Silvers, of the Palace Theatre, Hamilton, O., came all the way to Cincinnati for their dinner the other evening. Evidently the food in this city is better than in their own. The writer stopped at their table for a few moments but could find no other evidence for their visit but food on the table.

Ned Beetx of the Liberty Theatre, Dayton, Ky., has purchased

the Princess theatre of the same city from A. C. Clayton.

L. J. Bugy with Dwyer Brothers Film Equipment Co. is spending his much needed vacation at Asbury Park.

Jim Hamilton, former salesman for Standard, is now on his way to Florida to enter the real estate field.

Johnny Hibner, of the Queen City Theatre, Cheviot, O., is another film man going to Florida soon to enrich himself in real estate.

Morris Frankel, of the Frankel Theatres, is spending his vacation in St. Louis, Mo. and Minneapolis, Minn.

Cliff Boyd, general decorative expert of the Libson theatres and manager of the Lyric theatre, returned from his vacation last week.

J. H. Stomphe, of the Orpheum Theatre, Lexington, Ky., spent several days in the city during which time he purchased several new reflector lamps.

Bill Gervis, local film man returned from a trip to New York, where he visited several theatres looking over their equipment.

M. O. Mullins will open a new theatre soon at 22nd and Eight ave., Huntington, W. Va. Name will be announced later.

Tom Morrow, who was connected for a number of years with the Kearse Theatre, Huntington, W. Va., has opened the Bennet Theatre at Logan, W. Va.

Denver

ED. SCHULTE, owner and manager of the Rialto Theatre, Casper, Wyoming, arrived in Denver last week enroute to Glenwood Springs, Colorado, for a month's vacation. He was accompanied by his son.

W. F. Gordon, First National branch manager of Salt Lake City, was in the city enroute to New York for the purpose of attending the annual convention for all First National branch managers. Mr. Gordon was a former salesman for the Denver branch of First National. He will be accompanied to New York by Joseph H. Ashby, Denver manager.

The new Alpine Theatre located at 33rd Avenue and Williams Street will be completed and ready for opening October first according to announcement made yesterday by Ed Nesbit, the builder and manager. The new suburban house is located on the East side and will contain approximately 625 seats. It will be a part of a new building 75 x 115 feet and will be two stories in height. The remainder of the building will be used for apartments. Mr. Nesbit, the owner, at present owns and operates the Mystic Theatre, a Denver suburban house.

Harry Lustig, district manager for Warner Brothers, has gone to Salt Lake City after spending

several days with the local branch of his company.

Gus Kohn of the Coronado Theatre, East Las Vegas, New Mexico, and his brother, Max Kohn, manager of the Rialto Theatre, Trinidad, Colorado, were among the exhibitors visiting exchanges during the past week.

Another prominent and well known exhibitor of the Denver territory who was in Denver was none other than Jim Zimmerman of the Lyric Theatre, Bridgeport, Nebraska. Jim seldom comes to Denver but when he does he manages to see all of his many friends among the exchanges. On this trip he was accompanied by his daughter.

Jasper J. Morgan, the popular president of the Denver Theatre Supply Company, is at present living on the Poudre River, about 25 miles from Ft. Collins, enjoying a two weeks' vacation, fishing, swimming and dodging rattle snakes. His camp is located at the foot of Rattle Snake Mountain, one of the most picturesque locations in the state of Colorado.

Eugene Gerbase, local Universal manager, and C. M. Van Horn, Pathe branch manager, have returned from sales trips into the New Mexico territory.

Harry Long, manager of the America Theatre, Universal first

run house on Curtis Street, is in Detroit, Michigan, taking a much needed vacation. Besides being in active management of a 1600 seat theatre, Harry was general director of the Greater Movie Season Campaign. He is expected to return to Denver about September first. During his absence the management is being conducted by Arthur Janisch, local Universal publicity manager.

Other exhibitors visiting Denver during the past week were

Max Kravetz, America Theatre, Ft. Collins, Colorado; Ray Allison, assistant manager, America Theatre, Colorado Springs; and J. E. Guild, owner and operator of the Peerless Theatre, Holyoke, Colorado.

Hugh W. Braly, manager of Famous Players-Lasky Exchange, is making an extensive sales trip by motor in the state of Wyoming. He is expected to return the latter part of the month.

Baltimore

THE New Preston is now the name of the old Flaming Arrow Theatre, 1108 East Preston street, which is now being operated under the management of Arthur B. Price, a pioneer in the moving picture business in Baltimore and who now also operates the Aurora Theatre, 7 East North avenue.

Mr. Price has christened the New Preston, "the perfect little playhouse," and says that about $10,000 have been spent on improvements and renovations. It is practically a new theatre because new seats, screen, projection machines, floor coverings, draperies, lighting fixtures, heating and ventilating plants have been installed.

The fight by William Cook, funeral director, to rebuild the fire damaged Lyceum Theatre, 1209-1213 North Charles street for use of funeral parlors, still goes on. After his application for rebuild-

ing had been disapproved by Building Inspector Charles H. Osborne, Mr. Cook immediately filed an appeal with the Zoning Board. The residents in the neighborhood will continue to protest against the building of such an establishment.

The lobby and foyer of the New theatre, 210 West Lexington street, managed by John T. Moore, have been redecorated with dull grey and gold and present a fine appearance. This playhouse is operated by the Combined Whitehurst Interests.

Dr. Milton M. Whitehurst, who is treasurer of the Garden Theatre Company, has been appointed treasurer of the New Theatre Company to succeed the late G. Edgar Smith. Both playhouses are operated by the Combined Whitehurst Interests.

T. M. Cushing, moving picture and dramatic critic of the Balti-

more Sun, is laid up at his home due to some torn ligaments in his right ankle. He has the ankle heavily bandaged and will have to stay at home for about two weeks.

Elmer Free, Automobile Editor of the Baltimore American, has been appointed publicity manager of Keith's Hippodrome to succeed Lee McLaughlin, who has just resigned that position to become associated with the James L. Kernan Company. Mr. Free held that position with the Hippodrome for a number of years some time ago. He will continue his work with the American.

Lee R. McLaughlin, formerly publicity manager of Keith's Hippodrome, has been appointed treasurer of the Academy Theatre, to be operated by the James L. Kernan Company as a legitimate playhouse. Frederick C. Schanberger, Jr., has been appointed manager of that playhouse.

Ford's theatre, which will show a series of legitimate attractions during the season, will reopen to the public on Labor Day under the management of Harry A. Henkel.

The Blue Bell Theatre, 1713 Hartford avenue, has been purchased from the Blue Bell Theatre Company, Arthur B. Price, president; Jack Whittle, secretary-treasurer; by Harry C. Mann, and will be conducted as a moving picture playhouse.

Music by a six-piece stringed orchestra under the direction of Emanuel Schwartz, will be a regular feature of the evening performances at the Victoria theatre, 415 East Baltimore street, beginning with Monday August 24. H. A. Blum, manager of that playhouse, says he will have them play a different overture for each new picture shown during the week, and will keep them on if patrons like the music.

Buffalo

THE original deal whereby the Kreiger Brothers of Batavia were to have taken over the three Border Amusement Company Buffalo houses is off. Now David Kreiger alone has taken over the Ellen Terry, one of the links in the chain, and will at once redecorate both interior and exterior and erect a big new electric sign.

Stanley Kozanowski, who operated the Rivoli theatre on Broadway, Buffalo, has leased the Circle theatre on Connecticut street and will reopen this community picture theatre the week of August 30. The Circle was operated the past season by Eugene A. Pfeil.

Charlie Bowe, manager of the Frontier, one of Buffalo's most popular community theatres, has gone to Hot Springs, on a health pilgrimage.

Chester A. Saunders has resigned from the sales staff of Warner Brothers exchange in the Queen City of the Lakes.

The Dellinger theatre has been closed for repairs in Batavia, N. Y. Harry D. Crosby and Edward Houghton have been showing pictures at the Dellinger Saturdays and Sundays for the past two years or more. The other day former Mayor William F. Haitz, owner of the house, received orders from the industrial board of the state department of labor to make certain changes to comply with the new theatre code adopted by the state.

The Columbia theatre has reopened in Erie, Pa. The house was visited by a destructive fire last spring. The house has been beautifully decorated inside, magenta, purple and brown being the predominant shades in the walls, drapes, curtains and floor coverings.

Walter Hays, vice president of the Mark-Strand interests, and former president of the M. P. T.

O. of N. Y., has returned to his home in Buffalo, following a 1700-mile motor tour with Mrs. Hays through the east.

Arthur L. Skinner, manager of the Victoria theatre, is spending a two-weeks' vacation at his summer home near Point Abino on the Canadian shore. During his absence, the house is in charge of Allen Hays, son of Walter Hays.

George E. Williams, Paramount exploiteer in the Buffalo territory, is busy preparing page ads for the annual Paramount Week splash.

J. H. Michael, chairman of Buffalo Zone, M. P. T. O. of N. Y., is arising at 6 A. M. these days and joining the Film Row pill chasers in Delaware Park. It is reported that J. H. is sporting a very nifty golf costume. Nothing like getting pepped up for the fall season.

Basil Brady, manager of the Buffalo Pathe exchange, has re-

turned from his vacation. Basil motored to New York and Brooklyn, his old stamping ground.

George T. Cruzen is putting over the new Palace in Lockport to the tune of record breaking business. And with the coming of fall and the addition of Keith vaudeville it is expected the receipts will register even larger figures.

Frank J. A. McCarthy, Buffalo First National manager, is attending the convention at the home office in New York City. Ray Powers, booker, and assistant manager, is vacationing.

Lillian Walker, former star of the screen, was in Buffalo this week, appearing as the headliner at the Loew's State. While in town Lillian made a trip out to Lancaster to visit her old friends, Mr. and Mrs. Bobby Albert of the Albert theatre.

Texas

THEO D. POLEMONAKOS and associates who started work a short time ago on a new 1200 seat popular price theatre, to be erected at 914 Preston Avenue, announced that the new theatre would be named the Cameo. Present plans point to an early opening in October. Aside from the fact that it will be a popular price theatre no other information regarding the new Cameo's policy has been made public.

Abe Silverberg, manager of the Crown and New Folly theatres, has announced that a contract had been let to remodel the interior of the Folly and the Crown, also that the machines from the Crown protection room would be sent to the

Folly and that two new type machines would be installed at the Crown. The present machines in the Crown are less than a year old. Both theatres have enjoyed a very successful run this summer and the management plans to condition them for a record fall season.

Abe Silverberg, local theatre owner, has returned from a week's vacation in Mineral Well and other north Texas points. Mr. Silverberg made the trip in his car with his brother-in-law.

Jeff Barnette, the Houston Chronicle theatre representative, has returned to his line of duty after a fifteen day vacation spent in central Texas on a ranch. Mr.

and Mrs. Barnette made the trip in an automobile.

Frank Starz, advertising and publicity manager for the entire Interstate circuit, plans to visit Houston next week, according to Eddie Breamer, local Interstate manager. Mr. Starz, before his promotion was writing advertising and publicity for the Interstate theatre in Houston. His headquarters are in Dallas, Texas.

Manson Floyd, house manager of the Queen theatre, has returned from a month's motor trip, including Chicago and New York and other eastern points.

Gerry Iselt of the Isis theatre, has returned from a month's vaca-

tion with the stars and producer in Hollywood. Mr. Iselt spent several days in the studios and witnessed the making of several big productions.

Greater Movie Ball went over with a bang according to Sam Abrams section of the Greater Movie Association (for Houston). A Houston lad in the garb of Jack Holt won first prize and the judges say that he was an exact double for the famous star.

Al Lever, manager of the Isis and Liberty theatres, has been host to his father, brother and sister-in-law for several weeks. They hail from Boston where Al first broke into the theatre game.

Cleveland

MRS. V. E. SAGER has sold her Southern Theatre, Akron to Miss Ethel Cooper, according to word received by the Film Board of Trade.

Meyer Fine and Abe Kramer, who recently announced the erection of a fine 2000-seat motion picture theatre at Broadview and West 25th St. now announce that they are going to build still another house this fall. It will be located on Kinsman Road at East 146th St. will have 1500 seats, and will play a combination vaudeville and picture policy. Nicola Petti of Cleveland is the architect. Work will be started not later than October 13th. Fine and Kramer are both prominent local exhibitors and are heavily interested in the Ohio Amusement Company which operates a chain of a dozen prominent local neighborhood picture houses.

Frank Porzinski of the New Victory theatre, Cleveland, has just returned from the gold rush in Florida and reports that pickings are still good down there. Paul Gusdanovic, who owns several local picture theatres and is now building some more, has gone to Florida in the interest of some property that he bought while on a previous trip there.

Manager Hoffman of theatres in Canton, Amsterdam and Alliance, is on his annual pilgrimage to the Ozark Mountains where he has a young brood of copper mines which are coming along very nicely, thank you.

Christie Deibel of the Liberty theatre, Youngstown, was in town last week swinging a mean golf stick at the Country Club. Deibel, captain of the Youngstown team won a tournament against a local team.

Forrest Templin, who has been managing the Duchess theatre in Warren has resigned to accept a position of the new Capitol Theatre in Steubenville. This is the new half million dollar house which is being erected by the Tri-State Amusement Company. It is scheduled to open on Labor Day.

Tom Birmingham of the Hazelton Dome theatre, Youngstown, is building a new picture house in the same town. He is literally building it. He dug the foundation himself. He is laying the brick himself. He's past the first story now, doing it when not on duty at the other theatre. He expects to get in under roof this fall, and during the winter, he will complete the inside work.

Leonard Hodgkin is a living proof of the fallacy of the old statement that you can't do two things at the same time. Hodgkin manages the Home theatre in Youngstown and at the same time attends law school in Washington, D. C. He's specializing in amusement law. Every two weeks he hops a train for Youngstown, sees that everything is being carried out according to his instructions and goes back to college. The beginning of the season he buys enough picture product to last until the Christmas holidays when he buys again to tide his house over until the next vacation period. Hodgkin began operating the Home theatre when he was fourteen years old, at a time when his father was taken ill. He's been doing it ever since, along with going to school.

Harry Rosenthal, manager of the Ohio Theatre, Ravenna, has just installed a new low intensity light system at a cost of $3000.

J. H. Ruben of the Strand theatre, Newton Falls, spent the week shopping. Among his purchases were a $6500 new organ and $3000 worth of new equipment.

The Film Bldg. register was much used last week, as many out-of-town exhibitors paid their personal respects to the exchanges. Among them were Earl C. Lair, Louisville theatre, Louisville; J. Perruzzi, Butler theatre, Niles; George Mock, Mock's theatre, Girard; Carl Fish, Alhambra and Arlington theatres, Akron; C. Wowra, Pastime, Barberton; John Arch, Palace, Tiltonsville; Phil Messina, Liberty, East Palestine; Ward Johnson, formerly of Ashtabula, now of the Liberty theatre, Geneva; H. L. Moranz, Grand, Lisbon; Charles Shearer, Lyric, Massilon; and all the exhibitors of Lorain, meaning George Zegiob, George Shenker and Joseph Solomon. Nat Charnas, movie magnate of Toledo was also an exhibitor guest last week, as were the Schagrin twins, Max and Joe, of Youngstown.

Reade's Hippodrome, Cleveland, will continue to play split weeks all through the coming season. This policy was inaugurated in the spring. It has been so successful that Manager Bill Raynor will keep it up.

C. H. Parker, assistant manager of the local Pathe office, has left for a two weeks' vacation in Washington—the old home town, y'know.

C. W. Allers, manager of the central poster department for Pathe, with headquarters in Cleveland, is off for a two weeks' vacation somewhere where there isn't such a thing as a one-sheet anywhere in sight.

George Wilson, who has had charge of the local sales of the Pathe two-reel comedies for the past two years has resigned. Mr. Wilson has accepted an offer to go into the real estate business in Florida.

H. E. Smith, for the past consecutive six years, a Pathe salesman out of the Cleveland branch, has permanently severed his connections with the picture business. Mr. Smith has gone into the radio business for himself. You can locate him in Lima.

Frank DeNoll, formerly with the Theatre Supply Company of this city, has been appointed short subject Pathe salesman, to succeed H. E. Smith, who has resigned.

George C. Chapman is the latest addition to the local film family. Mr. Chapman came out of the West.—Chicago, Salt Lake and Kansas City, to be exact—to take up sales work for the local branch of Associated Exhibitors.

Robert Cotton, P. D. C. division manager for District 4, made a tour of the exchanges under his wing last week. This included Detroit, Indianapolis and Cincinnati.

Garrett Graham is in town. Graham belongs to the Universal publicity department, and is here in advance of "Doc" Holah and the "See America First" Universal truck which is due to arrive in Cleveland in two weeks.

Morris Shlank of Anchor Film Corporation was in town last week. He's on his way to the west coast.

Herman Garfield spent part of last week in the city, renewing old acquaintances.

Anthony Xydeis, of Sunset Productions, of California, has been a guest, during the past week, of the local independent exchanges.

Mollie Goldstein, formerly with the Progress Pictures Company, has changed her address to the Warner Brothers Exchange. Mollie is now secretary to Warner Bros. exchange manager Harry P. Decker.

Southeast

E. F. DARDINE, Manager of the Universal Film Exchanges, office in Charlotte, N. C., had the misfortune to fall and break his left arm. This, however, did not stop Mr. Dardine's activities in covering his territory for the Company. He immediately drafted his wife as chauffeur and continued to cover his territory until his doctor called a halt.

S. S. Stevenson, of Henderson, N. C., who controls a chain of theatres through Eastern North Carolina, was a Charlotte visitor the past week. Mr. Stevenson stated that his new houses in Goldsboro and Burlington were rapidly nearing completion.

Charles Picquet, of Pinehurst, N. C., owner of the Carolina Theatre, was in Charlotte the past week. Mr. Picquet is Vice President of the M.P.T.O. of North Carolina.

R. D. Craver has just returned from a trip to Florida. Mr. Craver is very much enthused over the prospects in Florida and we understand he is considering transferring his activities to Florida.

Walter Price, Manager of the Fox Exchange, in Charlotte, has just moved his family into a new home in Charlotte. His family has been residing in Philadelphia.

The Exhibitors Supply Company has moved into their new quarters on Fourth Street, and we understand F. A. Abbott, who owns this business has restocked and put in a complete line of the latest Motiograph De Luxe machines.

A. B. Cheatham, Manager of the Ottoway Theatre, Charlotte, N. C., has just returned from a week-end visit to Greenwood and Abbeville, S. C.

W. L. Parker, advertising manager of Warner Brothers, who has been vitising his sister Mrs. J. U. McCormick in Charlotte, N. C., was carried to the hospital the past week to be operated on. We understand this is not a very serious operation but would confine Mr. Parker to the hospital for several days. Mr. McCormick is well-known to the exhibitors and distributors through this territory as manager of the Carolina Theatre Supply Company.

Aronson & Brown have sold their Almo Theatre property in Raleigh, N. C., to be used as store property. The Almo theatre was destroyed by fire on or about July 14th. The fire was discovered shortly after midnight, the flames spreading rapidly, and for a time it looked as though the whole block would be destroyed. According to the Raleigh papers the fire was believed to have originated in the operating room of the picture theatre. This theatre was a complete loss.

The Garing Theatre, of Greenville, S. C., a Southern Enterprise theatre was destroyed by fire the past week.

Lee Marcus, General Sales Manager, of F.B.O., was a Charlotte visitor last week.

Raleigh T. Goode, salesman of F.B.O. is being congratulted on the birth of a son.

New York and New Jersey

REPRESENTATIVES of the various big motion picture organizations in New York City at a well attended meeting last week took first steps toward formation of a baseball league, which, as now planned, will be all set and ready for a city schedule when the spring training season opens.

Those attending the meeting, and the prime movers in the proposed league, were, David Cassidy, Famous Players-Lasky; Harvey DuBois, United Artists Corporation; Fred Bullock, Jr., William Fox; Martin Hogan, First National; Philip Abrahams, Warner Brothers; George Ronan, Pathe; P. H. Cohen, Metro-Goldwyn-Mayer; and Ben Hyatt, Universal.

Fred Bullock, Jr., was chosen as temporary chairman, and Harvey DuBois, as temporary secretary. The general scope of the league organization was discussed at length, and it was decided that a permanent organization be formed at a meeting to be held early in October.

The representative of each company pledged that he would be personally responsible for seeing that a fully equipped baseball nine would be placed in the field next spring. At the next meeting the question of club rooms, training quarters, and the like will be settled.

The friends of George Bauman, manager of the Pioneer theatre, City, will regret to hear of the tragic death of Mrs. Bauman, resulting from an accident on a roller coaster at Coney Island. The accident occurred as the car was rounding a curve when Mrs. Bauman lost her balance and was swung out toward the supports by the speed of the car. Mr. Bauman did all in his power to help her regain the seat and had it not been for his efforts she would have fallen to the base of the structure. Mrs. Bauman suffered fracture of the skull and a broken spine and passed away the same day in the Coney Island Hospital where she was taken immediately after the accident.

Several more local theatre openings are reported. The old Rosehill theatre which has been closed

for sometime has had its name changed to the Hollywood and will reopen on Saturday, August 29th, under the management of S. Rich. The Hollywood is located at 2nd Ave. and 27th Street. The Royal theatre on 13th Ave., Brooklyn, and operated by S. Michaels, will reopen in September after having a complete renovation. Keith's Bushwick opened last Monday and Moe Kerman's Bluebird theatre, out in Brownsville, had a most successful first night last Friday.

In these columns of last week the News stated in error that Sam Zahler was operating several theatres under the firm name of the Rapthal Amusement Co. Mr. Zahler is no longer associated with these theatres, the officers of the Rapthal Amusement Co. being M. Bernstein, H. Turin and I. Kafko.

The Marcus's, whom readers will recall as having been recently married and both husband and wife bearing the same name before being married, have remodeled the Woodbridge theatre, a 600 seat house at Woodbridge, N. J., and had their opening last Thursday. Mrs. Marcus was formerly Secretary at the Jans Picture Corporation.

Ben Guttman, who has recently returned from a vacation, has, with his partner, Israel Sablove, bought the building at 2646 Atlantic Ave., Brooklyn. This includes the Atlantic theatre at that address which they will completely renovate and continue to operate.

Alec Okin of Cranford, N. J., and who is also the successful operator of the Cranford theatre in that city, was in town Tuesday shopping for film. Alec and the auburn moustache have received considerable publicity of late, so much so that it is reported that Mr. Okin has consulted his lawyer and will in all probability take some drastic action in the direction of one Ed Carroll whose sign hangs up in the New Jersey division of the Associated Exhibitors Exchange. M r. Okin has stated that the charge will be defamation of moustache.

John Dacy, assistant manager to Bill Raynor of the Pathe New

York Exchange, has returned from a very pleasant seventeen day vacation that he spent on the seventy-six-acre estate of his brother-in-law, down at Brookhaven, L. I. Mr. Dacy's brother-in-law is Charles Nelson, one of the executives of the Pictorial Review Co.

Recent callers among the exchanges include Rudy Gerard who operates a fine suburban theatre in Summerville, N. J., Fred Cross of the Rialto at Ridgefield Park, A. Hoffman, of the Park and Palace at Morristown, and John Metzger of the Rialto at Caldwell.

Aaron Saks, of the Associated Exhibitors sales staff is back from his vacation spent in the Adirondacks. While away he suffered extreme illness from contaminated water but is feeling well again at the present time.

Louis Goldberg of the M. & S. circuit was a busy man around the exchanges this week. Here and there and everywhere. He is opening the Mt. Morris theatre on Sept. 4th, and from all reports, M. & S. expect this house to be a most successful one.

The Madison, at Madison, N. J., will open about the 15th of September, and the Strand at Summit will follow along with its opening on October 15th. Both of these houses belong to Fred Faulkner.

Jos. Stern has broken ground for a new 1800 seat theatre in Cranford, N. J., and is also reported as looking about for a theatre site in Red Bank.

Milton Kronacker of the Pathe sales force had a very successful week. He disposed of one watch and three motometers. Next week he plans to have on hand a nice assortment of pocket knives.

Jack Hatton of the Small and Strassberg circuit has left for Florida via the Clyde Line. It will be a combination business and pleasure trip. They say that the Miami real estate bug has been buzzing around Jack.

Chas. Rosensweig, manager of the New York F. B. O. exchange, was seen along the South Jersey coast on a week end visit.

Moe Streimer of United Artists is smiling plenty of smiles these days. Well, why not!

A boxing club and theatre building is being planned for next season's opening at Asbury Park.

Manager Jacobs of the City and Grand at Newark and the Rialto at Westfield, N. J., is spending his vacation at Lyndhurst, N. J.

The Democratic candidate for Mayor of New York, "Jimmie" Walker, is certainly getting a great play from the local film trade. Yesterday they were putting up "Vote for Walker" banners on all the film delivery trucks.

Morris Ginsberg, who has leased the Berkshire theatre in Brooklyn, will open that house on Labor Day. The Berkshire has recently had entire new equipment installed and has a seating capacity of 1000.

Dave Solomon, of Howell's Cine Equipment Co., has returned from Detroit where he has been spending his vacation and is going out after a September prize that Joe Hornstein has offered to the man who brings in the most business during that month. Recent installations made by Howell's include Miss Gloria Gould's New Embassy which has its opening scheduled for August 22nd, the Kinema, Rosenaweig and Katz's latest theatre and the twelfth in their circuit, the Cumberland in Brooklyn, owned by the Brandt Brothers and the Inwood. Sol Brill's new theatre in the Dyckman Heights section of New York City. According to reports. Mr. Brill is spending a great deal of money on this theatre and to the extent that it will compare with the Broadway houses.

Rachmiel and Rinsler separated last Wednesday—but only for two weeks. Hyman Rachmiel is vacationing in the mountains.

Morris Sussman, general manager for Sydney Cohen has left on a two weeks' vacation through the New England States and Canada. Reports have it that Morris cleaned up enough at the Rockaway boom to take him around the world several times.

Joe Hornstein left last Friday on a ten days' trip to Memphis, Tenn., where he will attend the Motion Picture Supply Dealers' meeting.

Seattle

$10,000 in redecorating, recarpeting and renovating will be spent by John Hamrick, owner of the Blue Mouse Theatre of this city, on his house within the coming few weeks, according to reports made public last week. Work will be done without interrupting performances at any time, it is planned, and special apparatus and appurtenances are being obtained to make possible this plan. The Blue Mouse will be five years old in

December, and the present renovating is the first complete overhauling that the house has had in that time.

N. E. Huff, owner and manager of the Dream Theatre in Coeur D'Alene, Idaho, was a recent visitor in this city last week, for the first time in many months. Mr. Huff, accompanied by Mrs. Huff, drove to Seattle and return on a combined business and pleasure trip.

L. K. Brin, theatre magnate of

the Pacific Northwest, who has been leasing numerous houses in the Pacific Northwest in the interests of Warner Brothers, was scheduled to leave this week on a short trip to a number of smaller cities in Western Washington. His first stop was to be at Port Angeles, where negotiations are under way for the leasing of one of that town's newest houses.

A. J. Sullivan, former booker at the Producers' Distributing Corporation exchange here, last

week resigned that position and has returned to the Metro-Goldwyn office, under the management of Seth D. Perkins. Mr. Sullivan was formerly connected with the Goldwyn exchange, when it was managed by Mr. Perkins prior to the amalgamation with Metro. Following the combine, both Mr. Perkins and Mr. Sullivan joined the P. D. C. office, and now both are again associated with their first organization.

(*Continued on page 1176*)

St. Louis

AN overflow audience estimated at approximately 4000 persons in an orderly manner hurriedly left Loew's State Theatre, Eighth and Washington avenue, Sunday night, August 16 when a back-stage fire caused by a short-circuited electric wire did $250 damage to three curtains. And then it was that the efficiency of the well trained Loew's State organization came into play. Harry Greenman, managing director of the theatre, had schooled his forces to handle just such emergencies.

The evening's performances could have been carried through there was so little excitement, but Mr. Greenman decided to honor the seat checks at any performance during the balance of the week.

L. W. De Young, owner of Memorial Hall, Waterloo, Ills., has been ordered to the Artillery Officers Training School at Fortress Monroe, Virginia, for a seven weeks' course in the anti-aircraft school. De Young is a second lieutenant in the Officers Reserve Corps.

Claude McKean departed for Memphis, Tenn., August 21 to take over his new duties as manager of the new Fox exchange in that city. Prior to his departure he was presented with a beautiful brass engraved desk set from his friends among the exhibitors of St. Louis and vicinity while the Fox office force remembered him with a handsome diamond Masonic pin. He takes with him the well

wishes of all St. Louis filmdom.

A. C. Wilson, head auditor for Fox, was in town for several days.

G. E. McKean, manager of the local Fox office returned from a very successful trip to Quincy and Hannibal August 21.

The Famous Theatre on Franklin avenue, St. Louis, has reopened. Many other neighborhood houses will re-open during the next two weeks.

John Satterfield contemplates building a $10,000 motion picture theatre at Dardanelle, Ark. The theatre will be on Quay street and have a main floor and balcony. It will be of brick construction.

L. E. Talley is making all towns of 2500 and more inhabitants for Associated Exhibitors.

The Producers Distributing Corporation has leased the old Pathe offices on the ground floor of the Plaza Theatre building. Extensive alterations and improvements are contemplated for the offices. They will move some time in September. District Manager C. D. Hill has already opened a temporary office in the new quarters.

Mr. and Mrs. C. W. Lilly who recently resigned as manager of the Star, Orpheum, Opera House and Broadway theatres in Hannibal, Mo., are in St. Louis temporarily. It is reported they are considering the purchase of a theatre here if they can obtain a desirable house at a reasonable figure.

Paul De Outo has resigned from the sales staff of the local F. B. O.

office and has been succeeded by B. J. "Buns" Derby, formerly with Warner Brothers-Vitagraph. Derby will travel Southern Illinois.

C. L. Hickman resigned as manager of the F. B. O. office at Memphis, Tenn., and has accepted a position with the local Warner Brothers-Vitagraph office. He will make Arkansas, Kentucky and Tennessee.

Jim Duthie attached to the Pathe office at Memphis, Tenn., was in St. Louis for a few days.

M. F. Baker of Baker & Dodge, Keokuk, Ia., has returned from his vacation trip to Michigan.

The thousands who attended the Benton, Ill. Fair last week wondered why the musicians persisted in playing gallop music. Bill Keigley, popular exhibitor of Benton, was in charge of arrangements. He was roundly complimented on the success of the fair.

K. C. Whetstone, manager of the Regent Theatre, Keokuk, Ia., owned by Baker & Dodge, spent several days in St. Louis. He was accompanied by his wife and daughter.

Barney Lueken of the Macklind Theatre, St. Louis, was under the weather for about a week.

Arthur Schierstein, booker for the local F. B. O., has also been ill.

W. R. Richards of the Witt Theatre, Witt, Ill., has purchased a new Chrysler automobile and motored to La Salle, Ill., during the past week.

Harry Tanner will open his new house at Nokomis, Ill., about September 25. It will seat 500 persons and represents an investment of about $25,000.

Roy Dickson, manager for Associate Exhibitors, will spend his vacation fishing for Black Bass on the Black River near Noble, Ark. He has chartered an express car to bring back the fish he has promised his numerous friends.

Charley Werner, manager of the local Metro-Goldwyn-Mayer office, is in Rochester, Minn., undergoing a course of treatment at Mayo Brothers. Sam Burger, assistant manager, is in charge during his absence.

Ray Curran, formerly with Vitagraph, is now office manager for Metro-Goldwyn-Mayer.

Jim Lambert of the local Metro-Goldwyn-Mayer staff has gone to Kansas City, Mo., to become office manager of the M.-G.-M. office there.

Jack Flynn, district manager for Metro-Goldwyn-Mayer, has returned from a two weeks' vacation in Michigan.

Out-of-town exhibitors seen along the Row during the week were: Tom Reed, Duquoin; S. E. Pertle, Jerseyville, Ill.; K. C. Whetstone, Regent Theatre, Keokuk, Ia.; Jim Reilly, Alton, Ill.; Robert Stempfle, St. Charles, Mo.; Bill Karstetter, Columbia, Mo.; Walter Thimmig, Duquoin, Ill., and L. W. De Yong, Waterloo, Ill.

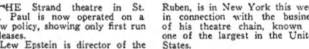

Minnesota

THE Strand theatre in St. Paul is now operated on a new policy, showing only first run releases.

Lew Epstein is director of the new eight-piece novelty orchestra just engaged at the Astor in St. Paul.

The St. Paul Princess is running split weeks of first run films under Finklestein & Ruben management.

Ben Ferris, publicity manager of F. & R. in St. Paul, mourns the loss of his mother who died Friday.

Hal Daigler, back from his Seattle vacation, is working up a style show for his patrons at the St. Paul Capitol. It will be the first of its kind in St. Paul in several years.

The Capitol has spent a lot of money on a great double panel of electric lighted transparent letters which not only advertises its attractions but illuminates the entire district in which the theatre is situated thus stirring the populace to patronize its ice-cool recesses.

Sarah Blumenthal, right hand bower in the Finklestein & Ruben auditing department is back in Minneapolis after an extended trip to the Pacific coast.

M. L. Finklestein, senior member of the firm of Finklestein &

Ruben, is in New York this week in connection with the business of his theatre chain, known as one of the largest in the United States.

Harvey Buchanan, manager of the Peoples' theatre, Superior, visited the main office of F. & R. last week.

The Advance Film Exchange, handling independent pictures, has moved its office from the third floor to the fifth floor of the Film Exchange building, Minneapolis, and is branching out. N. Lande is in charge.

Eph Rosen returned late in the week from another visit to the iron range of Minnesota and the Twin Ports on Lake Superior (Duluth and Superior). He is manager of Film Booking Offices in Minneapolis.

N. C. Rice, one of the F. B. O. exhibitors in Algona, Ia., visited the company's office in Minneapolis.

W. A. Steffes and associates are building a new theatre on West Broadway and Newton avenue N., Minneapolis. It will be one of the largest neighborhood theatres in the Twin Cities.

Fred Larkin, formerly of the Zelda theatre, Duluth, has been made manager of Finklestein & Ruben's St. Cloud theatre, the Sherman.

The Garrick theatre opened Saturday week with its new Metro Goldwyn policy. Everybody in the place has been known for a considerable period as an F. & R. employe.

Les Davis, manager of First National's Minneapolis office, is in New York city this week getting primed on how to handle his new job here.

Crop conditions continue as promising as possible in the Northwest section and theatre men here as well as film agencies are looking for satisfactory business.

I. H. Carr of the First National office staff made good use of his vacation last week. He wound up by sending in candy and cigars with the announcement of a strapping boy.

I. H. Ruben, M. L. Finklestein and Eddie Ruben of Finklestein & Ruben, spent several days in Indianapolis at the franchise holders conference of the First National company. The Messrs. Ruben are back in Minneapolis again now but Mr. Finklestein will return later.

Thomas A. Burke, manager of Warner Brothers northwest office in Minneapolis, took a flying trip to Northfield, Minn., the other day.

Lee Darling of the Lyceum theatre at Kenmare, N. D., was a recent visitor. Another visitor was E. A. Anderson of Aberdeen, S. D., who operates several theatres.

The Tower theatre in St. Paul was dark last week undergoing extensive and very rapid alterations to open with its new dance halls last Saturday. The two ballrooms just opened are capable of handling 2,000 persons at the same time. A new musical director has been selected to handle the dance orchestra and the symphonic orchestra to be used in the theatre.

Chicago

THE Fall tournament of the Midwest Golf Association, will held at the Bob-O-Link Golf Club, Highland Park, on September 16th. There will be the same number of events and the usual liberal prize list, so that even a larger number of film men than enjoyed the first two tournaments, is expected to participate. Bob-O-Link is one of the most exclusive and one of the very few "men only" clubs in the United States and the course is unsurpassed. Chairman R. C. Seery of the committee, urges those who desire to play to get their entries in early as only a limited number can be accommodated.

Archie Spencer, well known film salesman, is now connected with Warner Brothers and has been assigned to the south side territory.

Fred C. Dierking, who is interested in theatres located in Chicago and one in Fox River Grove, announces that he will build a 900 seat theatre, office and apartment building in Crystal Lake, Illinois, and that Architect Behrens already has plans under way for the new house.

Edward Grossman is representing Architect R. Levine and others, who have associated themselves to build and finance theatres, and for the present is making his headquarters in New York City, where he expects to open offices.

The death of Mrs. M. A. Osborn of Monmouth, who for many years conducted the Family Theatre of that city, is generally

Charles Rosenzweig, branch manager of the New York F. B. O. exchange.

regretted in film circles. Although suffering from ill health for many years, much of her time being spent in a wheel chair, Mrs. Osborn had a cheery smile and greeting for every one, which will be missed not only by patrons of her theatre, but by visiting exchange men.

F. O. Nielson, veteran film salesman, is now selling for Pathe and has been assigned to south side territory.

J. A. Seinson has resigned as manager of Warner Brothers Chicago exchange. While Mr. Steinson has not made any announce-

ment as to his future plans, it is rumored that he will become interested in the real estate business in Florida. Mr. Steinson, regarded in Chicago film circles as one of the most able and respected men connected with the industry, was for some years manager of Vitagraph's Chicago exchange and upon the merger of this company with Warner Brothers, was retained by the latter as exchange manager. According to Divisional Manager Eddie Silverman, of Warner Brothers, announcement of Mr. Steinson's successor cannot be expected for a week or ten days.

Brunhild Brothers are redecorating and improving their Temple, which has been operating but Theatre at 5241 N. Clark Street, three days a week, and expect to get back on their full time basis the early part of September.

Simon Simansky has returned from a trip to Elkart Lake, Wisconsin, where he had been vacationing for the past few days in the company of his wife and daughter.

Dave Dubin, for the past four and one-half years connected with Educational's Chicago exchange, as salesman and later sales manager, has been appointed exchange manager as successor to I. Maynard Schwartz, resigned. Mr. Schwartz became manager of the exchange when it opened five years ago, and his resignation came as a surprise to film row. Dave Dubin, one of the most

popular film men in the Chicago territory, has been Mr. Schwartz's right hand man during his long connection with the exchange, and his promotion is well deserved. Mr. Dubin has been connected with the film business for more than fourteen years, having started as an operator at the Little Boulevard Theatre on Taylor Street, after which he went with Abe Warner, and then with Mutual. Mr. Dubin's next step was to Bell & Howell's production department, where he took the first picture with a Bell & Howell camera, the location being Williams Bay. To round out his 100% experience as a film man, he conducted the Thome and Clarendon Theatres and was three years with Joe Friedman of Celebrated Players as a salesman, going from there to Educational.

G. G. Gregory, F. B. O. country salesman, last week was taken ill with appendicitis and was removed to the Wesley Hospital, where he underwent an operation. It is reported that Mr. Gregory is doing nicely.

Divisional Manager F. C. Aiken of Pathe, is spending most of his time on the road these days and at present is visiting Omaha and Des Moines exchanges of his company.

The Prairie Theatre, Ludwig Siegel's Prairie Avenue house, is again running seven days a week, the work of redecorating and refurnishing having been completed.

San Francisco

DAVE FRAZER special West Coast representative for P. D. C., spent ten days at the San Francisco office, after which he left for Los Angeles.

Sept. 1st marks the removal of the San Francisco offices of Producers to the corner of Golden Gate and Leavenworth, where the Selznick exchange formerly was located. The entire floor plan has been changed, and we are promished a splendid addition to the Golden Gate Row.

G. H. Schultheis, who has been handling the organ at the T. & D. Jr. Theatre at Paso Robles, is being transferred in the New Pacific Grove house, which the Monterey Theatres are planning on opening the 15th.

George Mann has moved his offices from 191 Golden Gate Ave. to 208 Turk St.

Hollis Osborne, Pathe salesman has married Miss Ruth Faught, and all his friends extend their congratulations.

J. A. Eustace, Aaron Goldberg's righthand bower, has returned from his vacation with his daughter at Feather River.

L. J. Darmour, vice president of the Standard Cinema Corporation, stopped in San Francisco long enough to make some friends. Mr. Darmour has been in Los Angeles for five weeks working

on the production of next year's product.

Joe Carrara, who formerly operated the Rex Theatre on 16th street, has taken over the Crown Theatre on Union, near Fillmore. He is thoroughly renovating the place and putting in many needed improvements.

Henry Bredhoff of the Hawaii Film Supply Company of Honolulu is in San Francisco on business. Mr. Bredhoff operates a film exchange supply house and theatre in Honolulu.

J. McInerny from Fairfield, Gus Johnson of Newman, Chas. Fraler of Tracey and M. Keller of Monterey were recent visitors.

Miss Browning of Supreme was in Dallas, Texas, her home town, where she spent her three weeks' vacation. Miss Roemer of L. A. substituted in her place.

Dutch Reimer has been vacationing at Mono Lake.

Harry Arthur, formerly of West Coast, stopped in San Francisco, en route to Seattle.

M. Montgomery of the Los Angeles office of Supreme spent several days in San Francisco and announced that Supreme is moving to the headquarters of Producers' Distributing Corporation as soon as P. D. C. vacate and move to their new home on Golden Gate Ave.

Preliminary work on the new theatre building planned by the T. & D. Jr. Enterprises at Tulare is well under way, and the estimated cost of the building is $165,000.

Howard W. Stubbins has purchased an interest in the Co-Operative Film Exchange in Los Angeles, and also becomes active manager effective at once. Mr. Stubbins many friends are pleased to hear of his affiliation, and are extending their earnest congratulations and good wishes.

Pathe has found it necessary to build two new vaults due to the increase in product. W. W. Kofeldt, local manager, is also making changes in the office, partitioning it off, so that his stenographer will be in practically the same office, while George Knowles, his assistant will have an office adjoining.

Tommy Thompson has become salesman for the Louis T. Dow Co. an advertising specialty company.

SEATTLE

(Continued from page 1174)
Ed Dolan, owner and manager of the D. and R. Theatre in Aber-

deen, spent a few days on Film Row last week, reporting that Greater Movie Season had begun in his territory and was apparently meeting with success as most of the houses in the Grays' Harbor country.

H. A. Black, manager of the Warner Brothers exchange, announced last week that William Rankin, former salesman for L. O. Lukan's Universal exchange, had joined the Warner Brothers organization, and would represent them in a sales capacity in the state of Washington generally.

Announcement was made at the First National exchange last week to the effect that J. W. Parry, former booker and office manager at Metro-Goldwyn had assumed that same position with First National. Harold Boehme, who has held that office for the last season, will again go on the road for Manager Fred G. Sliter's exchange according to present plans.

Charles W. Harden, manager of the United Artists office, has just returned to his office from a short sales trip around the local territory.

Albany

A NOTHER change came to Film Row during the past week, resulting in Jacob Klein, of Boston, succeeding Samuel Burns, as manager of the Warner Brothers exchange. Mr. Burns has not made any connections up to the present time but may go to New York to become associated with one of the companies there. The change came out of a clear sky and the first intimation that Mr. Burns received was when Mr. Klein arrived in town and announced that he would henceforth handle the exchange.

Morris Silverman, who runs the Happy Hour and Pearl theatres in Schenectady, is planning to erect a 900-seat theatre next spring that will take the place of the time-honored Pearl, which will be closed. The two houses, although small, have been a good business venture for Mr. Silverman during the years that have passed, enabling him to acquire a comfortable fortune.

George Dwore, who is running the Cameo, in Schenectady, a seventeen cent house, never books a western picture, claiming that his audiences demand society dramas. That Cameo is never run on Sundays, although the theatres in the rest of the city operate that day and generally make enough to meet any setbacks that may occur during the week. Mr. Dwore explains things by saying that residents in the section where he is located are solidly against a house operating in their midst on Sunday, although admitting that they frequently journey downtown for their Sunday night entertainment at other houses.

Cohen and Kornblite, of Binghamton, with seven theatres in that city and Endicott, are planning to remodel the Stone, in Binghamton, next spring. The State theatre in Schenectady is being redecorated at the present time, the furniture also being re-upholstered. The Albany theatre in Schenectady, may be closed for two or three weeks in September for renovation during which time its program of entertainment will be transferred to the Barcli which is scheduled to reopen the latter part of August or the forepart of September. The projection machines in the Barcli are now being overhauled. When the house is reopened it will change its program each day.

William Shirley, a former well known exhibitor in Schenectady, returned last week from Florida, where it is understood he made arrangements for the erection of apartment houses in Miami. Mr. Shirley expects to return to Florida almost immediately and may make his home permanently there. Myer Freedman, who is associated with Mr. Shirley in Schenectady, and who is now in the real estate business, is also planning to go to Miami in the near future, probably making the trip by automobile.

Burglars recently entered the Strand theatre in Schenectady, but secured nothing for their pains.

Ruth Stonehouse, now playing in "Wives of the Prophet", which is being produced by J. A. Fitzgerald Productions, Inc.

Examination revealed that they had jimmied the door leading into the private office and likewise had broken into a case containing several rolls of tickets. They carried off nothing. Constance Pedone, cashier at the Strand, is at a hospital in Schenectady, recovering from a recent operation for appendicitis.

Samuel Goldstein, of the Utica Theatre Corporation with houses in that city as well as a chain in Massachusetts, was in Albany the other day. Mr. Goldstein has a large farm in Massachusetts that is one of the show places of the region and on which he is a breeder of blooded stock.

Charles Walder's wife is in Miami, having preceded her husband there by a few weeks and whose real estate earnings are said to have largely influenced Mr. Walder's tendering his resignation recently as manager of the Fox exchange in Albany. Mrs. Walder is said to have cleaned up not less than $5,000 during her first week in Florida.

James Shultis opened Studio Hall in Woodstock on August 18.

William Morris, the well known theatrical manager, cabled fifty dollars recently to Dave Seymour, of the Pontiac in Saranac Lake, as a contribution to a benefit Mr. Seymour was giving for a local charity.

Among visitors in town during the week were Charles Charles, formerly of Albany, now manager of the Paramount exchange in Wilkesbarre, Pa.; John Rock, general manager for Vitagraph, and H. L. Berinstein, of Elmira, who is associated with his brothers in handling the several theatres in the Berinstein circuit. The Van Curler in Schenectady, a Berinstein house, reopened Monday night with A. J. Rachell as manager. Julius Berinstein announced during the week that managers for the Colonial and the Hudson theatres in Albany would be named from his own organization.

Oscar Perrin, who recently resigned as manager of the Buckley houses in Albany, was named last week as manager of the Capitol theatre, an Albany house, that will split weeks between burlesque and road shows. He succeeds Edward Lyons who has returned to New York. Herman Vineberg, manager of the Mark Strand in Albany, was named during the week as manager of the Albany and Regent theatres, acquired from the Sucknos. Mr. Vineberg will be succeeded by Tony Veiller, who has been handling the Lincoln in Troy, and who in turn will be succeeded by Ben Stern, assistant manager of the Troy theatre. Miss Carolyn Goodman, secretary of the Albany Zone, returned last week from a vacation spent at Lake Mohican.

Walter Hays, of Buffalo, former president of the New York State M. P. T. O., was in town on Tuesday on his way back from the White Mountains.

Alec Herman, manager of the First National exchange here, is in New York City, attending a convention of First National managers.

Myer Schine, one of the heads of the Schine circuit, is to forsake the ranks of bachelorhood on August 30, when he will claim Miss Feldman of Johnstown as his bride.

The deal whereby Famous Players was to acquire the Farley holdings in Schenectady, is said to be still hanging fire, although with the possibility of consummation in the near future. As a result of this the Farley houses are now booking pictures only from week to week.

Bob Wagner, former manager of the well known Gateway theatre in Little Falls, made his appearance on Film Row last week in a new role. Mr. Wagner is now the representative for Renown and knowing the exhibitors as he does, he has been given audiences by many with whom film salesmen generally have hard sledding.

Charles Miller reopened the Bright Spot, in Rensselaer, on August 22.

Irving Goldsmith, of Saratoga Springs, a former deputy Attorney-General, and part owner of one of the leading motion picture theatres in that city, came out last week with the announcement that he will run for the State Assembly on the Democratic ticket this fall.

J. B. Hart, of Bennington, Vt., owner of two theatres in that city, was along Film Row during the week. Mr. Hart went to Florida last winter and is said to have taken a small capital with him, which he turned over several times in real estate deals.

Mrs. Elizabeth Meeker announces that the Casino in Waterford will reopen the first week in September.

At the Olympic in Watertown last week, there was a personal presentation of the young woman who will represent that city at the Atlantic City Beauty Pageant in September. The presentation was made by A. B. Parker, manager of one of the newspapers in that city, the whole effecting an exceptionally good tie-up for the theatre.

The Graylin theatre, in Gouverneur, a Papayanakos house, switched from pictures last week while the county fair was in progress and presented a stock company with a change in program each night.

Claude Wade, of North Creek, owner of a theatre there as well as a hotel, is said to employ one of the best systems of bookkeeping of any theatre owner in the Adirondack region. Business has been exceptionally good with Mr. Wade this summer both at his hotel and the theatre.

William Smalley, of Cooperstown, has as his guest these days his mother and sister from Connecticut.

C. L. Gardner, of the Pine Hills theatre in Albany, encourages pipe smoking among his men patrons, providing a balcony where the men may go and enjoy a smoke as they watch the picture. As a result Mr. Gardner draws a heavy trade from among the men of the neighborhood, who generally bring their wives to view the picture on the lower floor.

Charles Dery, manager of the Empire theatre in Port Henry, and who recently adopted a three months old child, is now said to be considering adopting another as a companion to the first.

According to reports, Nate Robbins, who recently sold his chain of houses to Famous Players, but who was retained as manager, is to receive a handsome salary.

Albert Victor Howson, new head of Literary department of Warner Bros.

POWER'S
INCANDESCENT EQUIPMENT
MADE IN THE POWER'S PLANT
A GENUINE POWER'S PRODUCT

POWER'S INCANDESCENT EQUIPMENT

ADVANTAGES

1. Adaptability

An arc lamp gives a whiter, steadier, more effective light on direct current than on alternating current. Since the current supply to the theatre is usually alternating it is necessary to use an expensive motor-generator set to convert it to direct current.

The MAZDA lamp operates equally well on alternating and direct current and with equal illumination.

2. Steadiness

The MAZDA lamp provides a constant source of light. The intensity of illumination on the screen does not change. The MAZDA lamp does not vary in intensity and operates always in a fixed position. It assures continuous uniformity of screen illumination. This combination greatly reduces the possibility of eye strain.

3. Simplicity

The projectionist has no adjustments to make during operation. After the initial setting, no change is necessary during the life of the lamp. This permits more attention to the other details of presenting the picture in a successful manner.

4. Cleanliness

The MAZDA lamp is a hermetically sealed light source and because of its greater cleanliness inspires a cleaner general condition in the projection room.

5. Economy

The 900-watt MAZDA lamp compares favorably with a 40-amp. direct current arc. The advantage from an illuminating standpoint is in favor of the MAZDA lamp. Assuming an alternating current source of supply, the arc requires 60 volts at 50 amperes, and with converter losses, consumes 4 kw. per hour. The MAZDA lamp (including all losses) requires approximately 1 kw. per hour. The power bill is, therefore, cut to about one-fourth.

6. Utility

The new Incandescent Equipment can be used successfully in theatres having a main floor seating capacity up to 1,000 or having up to 16-ft. picture, or having a throw of approximately 100 feet. It gives better results than an alternating current arc and is the equal of the direct current arc up to 40 amps.

Power's Incandescent Equipment represents eight years' development and test in laboratories and theatres. It is therefore now possible to offer a reliable projection device, using a MAZDA lamp as the source of light, not only for theatres but also for schools, lodge rooms, community centers, and industrial establishments.

 IMPROVEMENTS and REFINEMENTS

Moulded Composition Knobs and Handles Thruout, and a New and Superior Vertical Adjustment on the Lamphouse. The Slideover Tracks are now Cold Rolled Steel, accurately finished and securely fastened to the top of the base casting.

Crystallized Lacquer Finish replaces plain Japan finish—all steel parts are Dull or Polished Nickel-plated. New Mirror and Power's Aspheric Condenser Mount are much superior to those heretofore supplied.

NICHOLAS POWER COMPANY
Ninety Gold St. New York, N. Y.

ENT

CONSTRUCTION & EQUIPMENT DEPARTMENT

Handles
Vertical

Beverly Theatre One of West Coast's Finest

California House Follows East-Indian Design; Elaborately Decorated and Appointed

AGAIN the West Coast adds to its ever increasing number of the country's finest theatres—and it can safely be added the world's finest. The West Coast Theatres, Inc., is responsible for one of California's most outstanding picture palaces built this year, which is as might be expected when it is recalled that this Company announced a several million dollar appropriation for theatre expansion during 1925.

It is of interest to note upon inspection of the photographs of the new Beverly Theatre, Beverly Hills, California, that once more California turns to architectural design patterned after the Far East; in this particular case East Indian design. The survey of the more recent theatres built in California would probably show an absolute lack of architectural treatment other than Spanish, Egyptian, Indian and the like. It still remains for some exhibitor to introduce an actual innovation among more important California theatres by designing some house along lines followed generally in the Eastern part of the country. However, under the influence of California atmosphere it remains a question whether the architecture of

Eastern theatres would prove a popular adjunct to California show places.

The following is a brief description of the Beverly Theatre:

Rising majestically at the intersection of two of Southern California's most traveled boulevards, and right in the center of the Movie Colony, the new Beverly theatre, owned and operated by the Hollywood Theatres, Inc., associated with the West Coast Theatres, Inc., recently opened in gala display. A large number attended the opening, and among those present were many of Filmdom's most notable stars and screen celebrities. Director Fred Niblo was Master of Ceremonies, and was introduced by Executive Director J. L. Swope, of the Hollywood Theatres, Inc. Mr. Niblo called upon all the stars who were present to appear before the spotlight. The important officials of the West Coast Theatres, Inc., including Messrs. M. Gore, President; A. L. Gore, Vice-President; Sol Lesser, Secretary and Adolph Ramish, Treasurer, were also introduced.

The big theatre, as noted in the photograph, is of strict East-Indian design, with the same motif followed out in the auditorium. Architecturally speaking, it is without question one of the most magnificent show palaces in the entire country, and in decorative scheme is wonderful.

Part of the equipment consists of a huge Wurlitzer Orchestral pipe organ. An eight-piece orchestra will be part of the house staff.

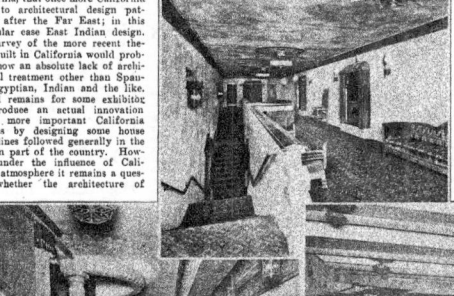

Three views of the new Beverly theatre recently opened by the West Coast Theatres, Inc., and Hollywood Theatres, Inc., at Hollywood, California. Note that the theatre is of strict East Indian design which is also followed out in the auditorium. E. S. Kuykendall is the resident manager under the supervision of J. Leslie Swope, Executive Director of Hollywood Theatres, Inc.

Chicago's new million dollar theatre, the Diversey, operated by Balaban and Katz and Jones Linick and Schaefer.

Importance of Lobby Wall Cases as Good Will Builders

By WM. F. LIBMAN, Pres. Libman-Spanjer Corp.

IN previous articles the writer has covered the subjects of the human leaning toward attractiveness, the psychology of pictures and mirrors, the value of lobby display, and the need for just the right kind of ticket booth. This, in following out the course of lobby subjects in the order in which they are laid out in the theatre, brings us up to the lobby wall case.

If ever there was an article built which served its purpose fully one hundred per cent, that article is the theatre wall-case. Practical, artistic, useful and ornamental, the wall-case has proven a boon wherever installed.

It is in the designing, and building of the up-to-date wall case that the contribution of the lobby frame maker to the art of theatre building makes itself most noticeable.

Where but a few years ago a simple frame of commercial stock moulding was considered "good enough," today we find lobbies that are visited and admired for their beauty alone, so great is the combined appeal which lies in the gilded carving, glittering mirrors, rich velvet, and sparkling French plate that go into the making of the modern wall case. Whether it is to cover up an awkward area of wall space, or to hide an ugly section of lobby architecture, the wall frame ease lends itself with admirable grace and practical purpose.

As a container or holder of photographs, lithographs, posters or announcements, the wall frame is indispensable. Add to this utilitarian value the inclusion of attractive mirrors and artistic bracket chandeliers, the place which the wall case has made for itself in the lobby of today is an important one indeed.

There are so many designs and adaptations as well as uses for wall cases that a chapter on each could well be written. The most popular series of this lobby requisite is the combination mirror and poster frame which is designed in types ranging all the way from the simple glass front with plain moulding to the heavy magnificently decorated and artistically lighted polychrome and gilded carving of the Empire, Cathedral, Tudor, and other periodic units.

The purpose of the wall case is two-fold. First of all it affords a practical medium for display, and secondly it arrests the attention of the prospective as well as the actual patron. Its mirrors particularly prove their lure to the gentler sex. In these days of indiscriminate use of make up, there are few ladies who do not linger if but a moment in front of a friendly garment as they enter or leave the theatre. To prove this, it is only necessary to stand in a theatre lobby at the close of a performance.

With the popularity and necessity of the mirror established, what better place then could be devised for the showing of photographs, posters and announcements than alongside these popular mirror spots?

The successful designer and maker of the best wall frames has standardized on the frames which are provided to contain or hold these photos and posters. Where formerly the pictorial or announcement matter was tacked up within the wall case with thumb tacks, (which method was un-

tidy, destructive and unattractive) today the wall cases are equipped with individual frames in units, each of them slotted so that the photo may be slipped into them and transforms the wall case at once into a group of uniformly framed pictures. That these cases do much to bring business to the theatre has been demonstrated time and again.

The writer is reminded of a theatre which was recently opened in a certain section of New York City. In this case a location long occupied by a large market was selected. The entrance of the old market adapted itself perfectly for lobby purposes. *But the walls were lined from floor to ceiling with glazed white tile* that admirably served its purpose as a sanitary feature of a market, but certainly had no place in the decorative scheme of a theatre.

To tear out this tiling and substitute marble, panelling or other architectural medium involved the spending of much money and considerable time. A group of combination wall cases were designed, and erected, while the tiling space in between these cases was covered with a polychrome coating to harmonize with the frames. Today this lobby could not be improved upon for attractiveness if ten thousand dollars had been spent on its complete renovation or rebuilding. In this case a sum little over $1,000 did the work.

The proper lighting of these wall cases too is an important item which is just beginning to get its due attention which the writer will cover in another article.

New $90,000 Theatre to Be Built in Hawthorne, Cal.

A new $90,000 theatre building will be built in Hawthorne, Calif., according to plans which have recently been completed. The theatre will be erected on the corner of Ballona avenue and Hawthorne Blvd., and have a seating capacity of 1,100. Mr. D. B. Vanderlip will be associated with the Venice Investment Co. and the West Coast Theatres, Inc., in building the new theatre building.

High Class Theatre to Be Built in Bergen, N. J.

West Bergen, N. J. is to have another high class theatre which will seat 1,500 persons. The theatre building will be erected at West Side and Communipaw avenues. The plans for this theatre have been drawn by George Flagg.

Work to Start on $500,000 San Francisco Theatre

A. SAMUELS has announced that work will begin in two weeks on a $500,000 theatre, market and stores project on the east side of Divisadero street, between Hayes and Grove, San Francisco, a property sold to Milton H. Lees and Samuel H. Levin for $200,000. Buildings on the southeast corner of Divisadero and Hayes, with a frontage of 75 ft. on Hayes and a depth of 82 feet, will be torn down to make room for the "Divisadero Public Market," part of the Lees-Levin project. New ornamental street lighting will surround the enterprise.

America's Finest Theaters are Equipped with

Peerless

REFLECTOR ARC LAMPS

Here are some Peerless installations in America's most successful theaters:

—and many others

The Peerless Reflector Arc Lamp provides the intense screen brilliancy in hundreds of the biggest and finest theaters in this country. Peerless Lamps are installed in these theaters because they give twice the light ordinary arc lamps give and spread it evenly over the entire surface of the screen. Peerless light, is an asset to your program—not a liability as the average arc. Not only do you get greatly increased light, but the Peerless Lamp, being a low amperage arc, saves 50% to 70% of your current cost and at least 70% of your carbon cost.

You can test the Peerless without cost on your own screen—send the coupon.

The J. E. McAuley Mfg. Co.

554 W. Adams St., Chicago

Omaha's new motion picture theatre which is to be erected by A. H. Blank Theatre Co., of Nebraska.   It has been announced that the house will cost over $1,000,000.

R. P. Elliot Named General Manager of Welte Organ Business

THE Welte-Mignon Corporation of New York has elected R. P. Elliot vice-president of the Corporation and general manager of their organ business. Elliot's previous connection was with the W. W. Kimball Company of Chicago, where he was manager of the organ division. Announcement has already been made that corporate control of the Hall Organ Company of West Haven, Connecticut, now rests with the Estey-Welte Corporation. No change in the officers of the Hall Company is contemplated, but it is obvious that the Welte connection is a matter of importance.

The Welte-Mignon Corporation, owns basic patents; and the Welte Library of recorded organ music is known throughout the music world. The new Welte organ factory adjoins the piano factory of the Estey Piano Company in New York. Both of these corporations are also owned by the Estey-Welte Corporation, and Mr. Gittins is the president of all of them.

Though comparatively a young man, Mr. Elliot's history covers the entire period of development of the modern organ. He started in with Granville Wood & Son, who, in the next year, became the foundation of the Farrand & Votey Organ Company, which shortly took over the Roosevelt patents and personnel, from which organization the Aeolian organ grew. He interested the first financial investments which established the Austin Organ Company, of which he was secretary and vice-president for years, selling his interest and also resigning the presidency of the Kinetic Engineering Company, which he had founded meanwhile, to take up an engineering career, eventually becoming a member of the American Institute of Mining Engineers.

The call of his old profession was too strong; however, and he returned to this country from England in 1909, to re-enter and remain in the organ business.

Robert P. Elliot recently named General Manager of the Welte Organ business.

Washington, D. C., Residents Form Theatre Company

Residents of the northeast residential section of Washington, D. C., have formed the West Woodridge Theatre Company, Inc., which will build a theatre, store and office building in the neighborhood of Sixteenth street and Rhode Island Avenue. Stock in the amount of $100,000 is to be sold at $10 per share, and construction of the house will begin about September 15. The theatre will have a capacity of 830. The building will be of fireproof construction, 55 feet wide, 166 feet long, and will contain two stores on the first floor and four offices or a hall on the second floor. W. S. Plager is the architect. A cash prize is offered to the child who submits the most acceptable name for the house.

The prospectus put out by the company estimates the receipts from the proposed theatre at $100 per night or $600 per week, against which there will be running expenses of $387 per week and fixed expenses for interest, taxes, insurance, etc., of $4,500 a year, leaving an annual net profit of $9,576.

Motion Picture House to Be Erected at Mt. Vernon

Plans are being drawn for a beautiful new theatre to be erected at the corner of First and Kineaid streets, Mt. Vernon, Washington. The structure will be of brick and tile. It has been intimated that the theatre department of the building has been leased to a Port Angeles theatre man.

Redding, Cal., to Have New Theatre Building

Chester Cole and E. Brouchard architects are drawing plans for new theatre to be erected in the Red Front Building in Market street near Butte, Redding, California. The theatre to be installed by J. H. Wood, manager of the Redding theatre.

One Thing More

In your modern motion picture house every detail of projection, decoration, ventilation, temperature, seating, has been carefully worked out to make the theatre attractive and comfortable.

But there's one thing more you can do— and it's a real factor from the box office point of view: make sure the picture is printed on Eastman Positive Film, the film that safeguards for the screen the quality of the negative so your public may enjoy it.

Eastman film is identified in the margin by the black-lettered words "Eastman" and "Kodak"

EASTMAN KODAK COMPANY

ROCHESTER, N. Y.

Projection
Optics, Electricity, Practical Ideas & advice

Inquiries and Comments

Lens Trouble

ARTHUR ALLEN, who confesses to being an "Operator" at the Lyric Theatre, Traverse City, Michigan, writes in asking for information about the causes for poor screen definition, without at the same time giving much information which would enable us to diagnose his trouble. Apparently, Friend Allen suspects us of supernatural powers whereby we can by merely knowing the nature of his trouble, instantly point out its cause and name a remedy.

His letter reads like this:

Dear Sir:

I am having considerable trouble getting a sharp picture on my screen so I am writing you with the hope that you can help me out. Would you please give me information as to what causes my picture to be slightly out of focus in the center and clear on the outer edges? Also, how can I remedy this?

I keep my objective lens very clean and no matter what I do I can not focus a sharp picture over the screen.

Would appreciate your help very much.

Very truly yours,
ART. ALLEN.

Number of Causes

Well, Friend Allen, we would say that there are a number of things which might cause the trouble you describe and it will have to be a matter of guesswork on our part to answer your questions.

In the first place, a heavy projection angle (projector off center with respect to perpendicular center-line of screen) would prevent you from getting a sharp focus over the entire picture area. This for the simple reason that any lens can only focus sharply in one given plane at a time. Thus, if the centerline of the projector beam is at an angle with the perpendicular center-line of the screen, it will be impossible to focus all parts of the picture simultaneously on the screen. This assumes, of course, that the screen is standing upright, and is not tilted, which is normally the case.

Under this condition if the center of the picture is sharply focussed, the edges will be out of focus and if the top is in focus the center and lower edge will be blurred, etc.

The focussing of any given picture area is thus secured at a sacrifice of definition in the remaining picture areas.

Of course, while this is strictly true for any angle, however slight, on small angles (up to about 12 degrees) the lack of definition in some parts of the picture is not readily noticeable but about 12 degrees it becomes increasingly bad.

Wrong Assembly

That is one cause of poor picture definition. Whether or not it applies to your case we do not know for there is not much to go on in your letter.

You mention being particular about keeping your lenses clean, so there is a strong possibility that there is just where your trouble lies. It frequently happens that when dissembling a projection lens for cleaning purposes the lens elements are wrongly replaced with respect to each in the lens barrel. There are a number of ways for wrongly assembling these lens elements and no doubt herein lies the source of your trouble.

The objective lens commonly employed for projection purposes is of the Petzval type. It consists of two principal lens combinations, one for correcting spherical aberration, the other for correcting chromatic aberration. The spacing between these two combinations, by the way, influences the equivalent focal length of the objective lens since, ordinarily the farther apart they are, the greater will be the E. F.

The rear lens combination (the one nearest the aperture) consists of one crown glass and one flint glass lens, nested together but with an air space between the lens elements and since it is possible to remove both of these elements from their holder, it may be that in replacing the elements their position with respect to each other may have been reversed. Or it is possible that the entire combination (two lenses) may have been turned about in the lens barrel which would again destroy the correction.

The front combination (nearest the screen) is a cemented doublet, the curvature of both adjacent lens surfaces being the same so as to secure a close nesting after which the two surfaces are brought into optical contact by means of Canada balsam which acts to cement the individual elements.

The only possibility for incorrect assembly here lies in reversing the position of the entire combination since, to all intents and purposes there is but one lens.

It is highly important in replacing the various lens elements, after their removal from the barrel and holders for cleaning purposes, to make certain that each and every element is returned to its exact former position as otherwise the effect on the screen picture will be disastrous. The reversal of but a single element will destroy the correction of the combinations and will result in the effects you describe, i. e.: poor screen definition.

The general rule to follow when re-assembling the elements of a projection lens is this: *All those lens surfaces having the greatest concavity should face toward the screen.*

So, Friend Allen, if in your zeal to have clean lens surfaces, you dissembled the elements, thinking to return them to their proper position you had better go over the job again and make certain that every element meets the rule quoted above. It is fairly safe to say that your trouble lies here.

An Old Argument

This subject brings to mind another question which was a bone of contention in the Society of Motion Picture Engineers and furnished much food for argument.

One side held that it was possible to have poor picture definition even though the objective lens was not at fault due to some peculiar quality in the light from the lamp. The other side held that screen definition is purely a function of the objective lens assuming, of course, a sharply defined object to start with.

The first side in supporting their claims spoke vaguely of "parallox" and some such similar animals arguing that if a "point source" of light could be obtained, no objective lens at all would be required since then a true image of the film picture, sharply defined, would be shown on the screen similar to that formed by a pinhole in a piece of cardboard.

Theory vs. Practice

Such reasoning is well enough as far as it goes but the hitch lies in the fact that a "point source" is purely hypothetical and is merely a creature of the brain devised in the early days of optical study in an effort to satisfactorily explain the action of lenses and mirrors.

The study of optics has since outgrown this purely theoretical consideration of light sources to such an extent that it is entirely useless as an aid in explaining optical phenomena.

Light sources should be looked upon as being extended areas endowed with *surface brightness*, which in truth they are, and when so considered it is possible to explain *all* optical phenomena satisfactorily. Such explanations can be backed up with tests to prove their correctness.

In closing this discussion we would like to give as our opinion that the matter of screen picture definition is purely a function of the objective lens and that nothing beyond the aperture in the way of light sources or condenser lenses can in any way affect the quality of picture definition.

The only action such elements can possibly have on the quality of picture on the screen is that of *even* screen illumination and intensity of illumination.

If your picture definition is not all it should be, then the first thing to investigate is the *objective lens*, not the light source.

Consolidated Theatre Co. to Build in San Francisco

The Consolidated Theatres Company have applied for a building permit for the theatre which they will erect on Polk and Green Sts., San Francisco. The estimated cost is $115,000. J. R. Miller and T. L. Pfleuger are the architects, and S. Malloch, the contractor.

N. A. M. L.

Dear Sir:—
I see by the MOTION PICTURE NEWS that you have got the bronze button ready. Since I joined I have found some very bad films but have tried to put them in the best of condition. I have two Powers 6A-S—just got a new one the other day.
Inclosed find 25 cents in stamps for a button. Also send me some more labels for I ran short.
Very truly yours, John A. George, No. 1207.

Dear Sirs:—
I hereby make application as a member of the National Anti-Misframe League. Am assistant to D. Eighmie at the Liberty Theatre, Poughkeepsie, N. Y.
Kenneth E. Tyrrell.

Dear Sirs:—
Am sending 25 cents in stamps also other membership requirements.
Very truly yours, A. S. Spillman, Piggott, Ark.

Dear Sirs:—
I am enclosing 25 cents in stamps for membership in the N, A. M. L. also the following information.
Name of theatre—Opera House, Uhrichsville, Ohio.
Name of Manager—L. E. Jones, Uhrichsville, Ohio.
Yours truly,
Clarence James,

Gentlemen:—
Please find enclosed 25 cents in coin and information asked for in return for membership to the N. A. H. L.
My name is Willie H. Lester. I am working for the Dixie Theatre at Sparkman, Ark., owned and managed by Mr. E. Roberts.
I have almost ten years experience as a projectionist.
Hoping I receive my membership by return mail I remain,
Yours truly,
Willie H. Lester.

Gentlemen:—
I received your letter concerning my application as a member of the National Anti-Misframe League. My name and address are above.
I work at the Lyric Theatre, 419 E. 6th St., Austin, Texas, and my manager's name is Ben May.
Enclosed find 25 cents in stamps.
Yours truly,
Raymond Dickson.

Plans Completed for Theatre in Sterling, Ill.

Plans for a new $40,000 vaudeville and motion picture theatre have been completed to be erected by William Tifft and William Schrader in Sterling, Illinois. The architects who have drawn the plans are Bradlev & Bradley, Brown Building, Sterling, Ill. There will be office suites over the front half of the building. The theatre will have a seating capacity of 800 persons.

New Pompeii Theatre, S. F., Leased by Markowitz

The Pompeii Theatre, adjoining the Granada, and the newest amusement palace on Market street, San Francisco, opened its doors to the public recently. The Pompeii, recently secured with the Egyptian, across the street, from Max and Louis Graf, on a tentative lease by Dan and N. L. Markowitz, will be devoted to the showing of second-run pictures.

Ground is Broken for New California Theatre

Ground has been broken for a new $70,000 theatre building in Mill Valley, Cal., for the Orpheus Theatre Co., operated by Max Blumenfeld and Rake. The theatre will contain approximately 900 seats

Hollywood to Have Another Large Theatre

Erection of a new theatre building to cost approximately $2,000,000 will be at the corner of Eleventh and Hill streets, Hollywood, Calif., according to plans which have recently been drawn. The playhouse will seat about 1,200. The Los Angles Theatre Co., will have a long term lease on the theatre.

Elizabeth, N. J., to Have $175,000 Theatre

Plans have been completed for the erection of a theatre building in Elizabeth, N. J., to cost approximately $175,000, to be erected at Jefferson avenue and East Jersey street by the Fabian Enterprise Co. The seating capacity of the theatre is to be 2,500 people.

Uptown Theatre, Chicago, Opened by Balaban and Katz.

BALABAN & KATZ new motion picture palace, the Uptown, opened to the Chicago public recently, and in size, beauty of design and elaborateness of decoration and equipment, is unsurpassed in Chicago.

It is located at Lawrence Avenue and Broadway, across the street from the Riviera which, for the past six years, has been Balaban & Katz's northside show house and during that period has become too small to accommodate the crowds which throng it nightly.

The great central uptown district, of which the theatre named for it becomes the amusement center, was so interested in the opening of the new house, that an elaborate pageant under the auspices of the Central Uptown Business Men's Association, was held in celebration of the event and lasted throughout the week.

Probably no theatre has been opened under more favorable auspices or with a greate amount of publicity, and on the day of its initial performance crowds blocked streets and filled the acre of seats throughout the day and evening.

The Uptown Theatre covers a city block of land and is Spanish Renaissance in design, after the plans of the architects, C. W. and George L. Rapp, the previous Balaban & Katz houses, the Tivoli, Riviera and Chicago, also designed by the same architects, having been French in architecture.

The structure is L shape with a grand lobby fronting sixty feet on Broadway and running back one hundred and twenty feet to the main auditorium. From Magnolia Avenue, there is also an entrance lobby.

The main auditorium is two hundred and thirteen feet in length and one hundred and seventy feet in width, with a ninety-two foot ceiling and some seventeen thousand electric light bulbs are used in the theatre, controlled by a multi-colored system dimmer board back stage.

The orchestra pit will hold sixty musicians and is on an immense elevator platform permitting the entire body of musicians to be raised or lowered as the program requires.

There are thirty-six feet of working space on the stage behind the picture screen, giving room for the staging of the largest productions.

One of the largest Wurlitzer organs yet built has been installed with a console which can be elevated as desired.

With the opening of the Uptown Theatre, Balaban & Katz are inaugurating a new system of alternating orchestra leaders and organists in their different houses and each week patrons will hear different talent. Nathaniel Finston, Leopold Spitalny and Adolph Dumont will be the leaders to circle from theatre to theatre and the organists with them will be Jesse Crawford, Milton Charles and Albert Hay Malotte.

The premier program was typical of the entertainment offered in the B. & K. houses

Comedy art card displayed by Manager E. A. Rogers of the Tivoli theatre, Chattanooga, in connection with "Introduce Me" (Associate Exhibits).

and included Tschaikowsky's "Capriccio Italienne," as the overture, with Nathaniel Finston wielding the baton; some fine syncopation specialties by the Oriole Orchestra of the Edgewater Beach Hotel; "Spain," a scenic; Weekly News Views; Jesse Crawford at the Wurlitzer Grand Organ, the musical production, "Under Spanish Skies," to harmonize with the Spanish motive which has been carried out in the architecture, and the feature picture "The Lady Who Lied."

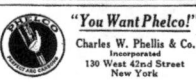

New Theatres Being Erected on West Coast

Theatre construction on the Coast continues brisk, work having been started on a $500,000 theatre in San Francisco, plans for a two thousand seat house in the same city have been completed and a site secured and in Fresno the White theatre is to be redecorated at an approximate cost of $30,000.

A. W. Thrasher of Wasco built and opened the New Wasco Theatre recently. It is a modern fireproof structure with a seating capacity of over 600, comfortably equipped throughout, and an especially pleasing feature is the indirect lighting system which permits the effects so necessary to picture presentation at the present time. A large orchestra pit contains the organ while the high ceiling and acoustics of the new building give full opportunity to the tone of the instrument.

Work was begun Aug. 22nd on a $500,000 theatre, market and store project on the east side of Divisadero street between Hayes and Grove, by Milton H. Lees and Samuel H. Levin following their purchase of the site. The site of the project which has a frontage of 162 feet 6 inches on Divisadero and a depth of 137 feet 6 inches was acquired for a consideration said to have been $200,000 in a deal conducted by Louis T. Samuels.

Max Blumenfeld has purchased an entire block of land and has completed plans for his Daylight block, with large public market and 2,000 seat theatre to be erected immediately on Taraval, near 29th Ave., in the center of the new business activity in the Parkside district. Reid Bros. are the architects. Planning for projection equipment and stage is being done by W. G. Preddy, who will outfit this theatre.

W. B. Armstrong and Robert E. Power of the Armstrong Power Studios, stopped at Fresno while en route to the Northwest and closed a contract for the redecoration of the old White Theatre, which the West Coast Theatres plan reopening Sept. 6th with Orpheum Vaudeville. It is planned to spend in the neighborhood of $30,000 for the redecoration, reconstruction and modernization of this theatre.

The Grove Theatre at Pacific Grove, a new 1,000 seat house, opened August 15th, under the management of A. Keller, who has so capably handled the Monterey Theatre Company's houses. Seating throughout was handled by the C. F. Weber Co., stage equipment by the Western Scenic Studios of Oakland, a growing and enterprising concern whose work is creating considerable comment; booth equipment by Tex Coombs; a Wurlitzer organ, while the interior decorating, Spanish in design, was handled by the Faggioni Studios.

A Correction

In the issue of August 22, an item was published under the heading "Reflector Arc Manufacturers," which gave the impression that the Morelite product was made by Howell's Cine Equipment Co. This is, of course, incorrect. The Morelite Reflecting Arc Lamp is manufactured by the Morelite Company, Inc., 600 West 57th street, New York. Howell's Cine Equipment ceased to be exclusive distributors in the Metropolitan district for Morelite about three months ago, S. Nickelsburg, President of Morelite, states.

Plans Complete for New Evanston, Ill., Theatre

Architect J. E. L. Pridmore has completed plans for the handsome new motion picture theatre which will be erected in Evanston, Ill., by the New Evanston Theatre Company which operates the New Evanston and Hoyburn theatres of that city and according to officials of the theatre company ground will be broken for the new house within thirty days. The architecture is to be of French Chateau type both as to exterior and interior, the theatre auditorium will represent the court yard of a chateau, with out door effects including sky with moving clouds and beautiful landscape vistas to be glimpsed through the openings in the court yard walls. It is the aim of the builders to make the structure artistic throughout, in keeping with Evanston's famous cultural atmosphere, and to embody the latest advanced ideas in theatre construction with the best in decorations, furnishings and equipment.

Plans Completed for 2,000 Seat Phila. Theatre

Plans are completed for a new 2,000 seat theatre to be erected on the hotel property at Ridge and Levering Avenues, Roxborough, Phila. It is stated that work on the new theatre, which it is estimated will cost approximately $250,000, will start this fall.

Newspaper Opinions on New Pictures

"The Gold Rush"—United Artists, Strand Theatre, N. Y. C.

Evening Journal: "The 'Gold Rush' is a great comedy, and by showing this play, the Strand, I should say, will be having a gold rush, too. It would be impossible to enumerate all the highlights of the film, but the best gag of them all is the bit called 'The Oceana Roll,' which is absolutely a riot. Chaplin is a delight, and it is to be regretted that his pictures come so few and far between."

Evening World: "With a little trimming 'The Gold Rush' would be one of the greatest comedies ever screened. As it is it contains some of the best work that Charlie Chaplin has ever done—and that means, of course, the best work of any screen comedian. 'The Gold Rush' is a positive scream—the kind that makes you pain from laughing. And, as is the case with all other Chaplin film, it also brings you very near to tears just when you are getting all set for another loud guffaw. If all audiences receive it as did the audience of experts at the Saturday night special showing 'The Gold Rush' is in for months and months of unprecedented success."

"Winds of Chance"—First National, Colony, New York City

World: "It is directed with great vim and vigor against a magnificent background of snow and pines and most energetically acted by Viola Dana, Ben Lyon and Anna Q. Nilsson."

Daily News: "The scenery is a treat—gorgeous mountains, vistas of snow-pelted peaks with long trains of adventurers staggering under their packs. The photography is fine, and here and there the picture is shot with humor and not a few thrills. The atmosphere of the gold craze days seemed especially good."

Mirror: "'Winds of Chance' blows icy melodrama and Klondike atmosphere into the Piccadilly this week." She says: "Much of the photography is beautiful. Anna Q. Nilsson intrigues as the beautiful Countess Courteau, who runs a hotel, manages a disreputable husband, and mothers childish men and women. Victor McLaglen, last seen as Hercules in 'The Unholy Three,' gives a spontaneous performance as the French trapper."

Times: "The best sequences in this effort are those dealing with the rapids. The torrents are good and the speed with which a barge is borne down the racing river is effective."

Morning Telegraph: "There is action enough crammed into 'Winds of Chance' to supply plots for a half dozen dramas. There are any number of angles of popular appeal, from the well known story by Rex Beach to the popular cast. A Frank Lloyd production can always be counted upon to offer good characterization and this one is no exception. The director's hand-picked cast is composed of some of the most gifted actors in celluloid, and they have every opportunity to prove their ability."

Evening World: "A gripping, virile Rex Beach story of the mad rush to the Yukon gold fields, and it is admirably enacted by one of the greatest casts ever assembled. It is packed from beginning to end with breathtaking thrills, some of its leading players in several of its sequences. It has the vast sweep of the Alaskan wilds, and Lloyd has imparted to it a gripping tempo."

Telegram: "An orthodox thriller truly depicting the historical period highly colored by fictionists of early Alaskan boom days. If Rex Beach has given you pleasure with his tales, then you should certainly see 'Winds of Chance.'"

"Don Q"—United Artists, Imperial, San Francisco

Chronicle: "'Don Q' has all the elements that make the pulses throb and the blood run faster—love, danger, suspense—magnificently done. 'Don Q' is good Fairbanks; the best for a long time. It is bound to please his immense following and to bring back those who may have felt he was getting too 'high-brow.'"

Call: "The very quintessence of romance—moonlight and roses, swords and sabers, treachery and intrigue, with love triumphant in the end — gorgeousness, novelty and action.

"Her Sister from Paris"—1st National, Capitol, New York

Times: "A clever comedy filled with scintillating situations and deft directional touches. Constance Talmadge adds much to the success of this vehicle with her captivating eyes, her charm and vivacity. Sidney Franklin has handled the scenes in an engaging manner, getting a great deal out of simple happenings through his imagination. It is a relief to view such a comedy."

Herald Tribune: "'Her Sister From Paris' presents Constance Talmadge in two different guises and those who can never get enough of Miss Talmadge will rejoice. We sat in an ecstasy of expectation from beginning to end. We consider 'Her Sister From Paris' one of the most amusing pictures of 1925. The direction is flawless, the acts are perfect and the entire cast acts as it never has acted before."

American: "If Hans Kraely had chosen guv Paree for his locale in 'Her Sister From Paris' instead of Vienna, we might have characterized Constance Talmadge's latest comedy as a smart French farce. There is that same sophistication and subtility of humor that makes French comedy so sprightly and amusing. The story is simple enough, but so well played by Constance and Ronald Colman and so deftly directed by Sidney Franklin, that we laugh with the rest of the delighted audience and say to ourselves 'Good girl, Connie.'"

Evening World: "Let it be reported right in the first sentence that 'Her Sister From Paris,' at the Capitol, is one of the most attractive pictures seen on Broadway in several weeks. True, it is as hoydenish as is its star. Constance Talmadge, and in places it gives signs of becoming a trifle daring. But there is a full-sized chuckle in every other scene, and the picture is altogether charming."

Evening Post: "Constance Talmadge in a dual role is enough to guarantee the happiness of most audiences. She is still her old amusing self with a dazzling array of Paris gowns as added attractions."

Journal: "'Her Sister From Paris' at the Capitol Theatre, is one of these delightfully frothy films. Hans Kraely wrote the story and he has a charming way of presenting situations with a scintillating effect. Colman is very good as the young husband, and George K. Arthur gets a chance to show what he can do. Connie, in her dual role, is cute and pert."

Telegraph: "Connie has never been more pert and more charming than she is in 'Her Sister From Paris.' It's as good as 'Her Night of Romance,' and you know what that means. What's better than Connie in a comedy? Answer: Two Connies. She plays a double role here and the thing is expertly contrived. It gives Constance Talmadge a chance to wear just twice as many gorgeous and darling gowns as usual."

Daily News: "One Constance Talmadge is enough fun for any movie. Two Constances are a riot. In 'Her Sister From Paris' Constance deals out the youth and gayety that are hers in a dual role. Constance, lest you forget it, is the suave and sure comedienne of the screen. The delightful farce written by Hans Kraely is the type that we usually tag 'French'—slight, teetering on the edge of the naughty, and generous with dots and asterisks that you fill in with your imagination."

"Mary, Queen of Tots"—Pathe, Stanley, Philadelphia

Daily News: "'Mary, Queen of Tots,' an 'Our Gang' comedy, was very funny and kept the audience in laughter."

Inquirer: "There was a corking good 'Our Gang' comedy called 'Mary, Queen of Tots,' which had many comedy surprises."

Record: "Another feature is the juvenile comedy entitled 'Mary, Queen of Tots,' a clever bit of romanticism, for which the imaginative mind of a child who falls asleep and starts to dream forms a rich field. It winds up as a realistic comedy. The startling vivification of inert dolls and puppets is a most remarkable piece of work turned out from the Hal Roach Studios."

Evening Bulletin: "The Stanley has a novel comedy, 'Mary, Queen of Tots,' by 'Our Gang,' in which 'The Rascals,' by trick photoplay, are reduced to Lilliputian proportions."

Evening Public Ledger: "'Mary, Queen of Tots' is a good specimen of Hal Roach's 'Our Gang' comedy, fresh as the 6-year-old young lady who stars in it."

"The Freshman"—Pathe, Auditorium, Ocean Grove, N. J.

Daily Press: "All roads from far and near seemed to have their journey's end last night at the Ocean Grove Auditorium where the world premiere was given 'The Freshman,' the latest triumph of Harold Lloyd, the justly popular screen comedian. They came from all parts of Monmouth County and as far away as Trenton and New Brunswick with a goodly delegation of New Yorkers in the world of motion pictures."

"When words fail just call it a 'wow' and have it all over with in one explosion. That describes 'The Freshman.' It is a truly refreshing comedy full of laughter and thrills. 'The Freshman' is literally crammed with gags—good ones—and Lloyd executes each so well that something whispers that many must have originated in his own head. In the first shot there is a chuckle. This develops into a laugh and the laugh into hilarity. It is by far the finest thing that Lloyd has ever done and it is difficult to imagine his ever doing anything better."

"Druilla With A Million"—F. B. O. Garden, Milwaukee

Sentinel: "What makes 'Druilla With A Million' stand above the average picture where the plot follows a sentimental groove is that the director by means of a cast of talented players has managed to impart a really beautiful lesson in the principles of unselfishness and devotion to the common good without using the too obvious varieties of hokum."

News: "It is a picture that will appeal to most every movie fan. Rich in laughs, tears and gripping moments, it is in every way decidedly worth seeing."

"Druzilla With A Million"—F. B. O., Rialto, Washington, D. C.

Post: "The story vividly portrays the naive and ingenuous methods adapted by the delightful little old lady who, being forced to work for her keep in a charity home, is suddenly left a million dollars."

Times: "It tells a powerful and enduring story, rich in character study. Mary Carr as the worn-out old servant, who suddenly inherits a million dollars and turns her beautiful home into a nursery for unfortunate children, gives a performance that dwarfs all her previous efforts."

FEATURE RELEASE CHART

Productions are Listed Alphabetically and by Months in which Released in order that the Exhibitor may have a short-cut toward such information as he may need. Short subject and comedy releases, as well as information on pictures that are coming, will be found on succeeding pages. (S. R. indicates State Right release.)

Refer to THE MOTION PICTURE NEWS BOOKING GUIDE for Productions Listed Prior to March

MARCH

Feature	Star	Distributed by	Length	Reviewed
Adventurous Sex, The	Clara Bow	Assoc. Exhib	5039 feet	Mar. 21
Air Mail, The	Special Cast	Paramount	6976 feet	Mar. 28
Beauty and the Bad Man	Special Cast	Prod. Dist. Corp	5794 feet	May 9
Beyond the Border	Harry Carey	Prod. Dist. Corp	4469 feet	April 25
Billy, The Kid	Franklyn Farnum	Inde. Pict. Corp. (S. R.)	4800 feet	
Blood and Steel	Desmond Holmes	Inde. Pict. (S. R.)	5300 feet	
Border Justice	Bill Cody	Inde. Pict. Corp. (S. R.)	5432 feet	Nov. 8
Coast Patrol, The	Kenneth McDonald	Barsky (S. R.)	5000 feet	
Confessions of a Queen	Terry-Stone	Metro-Goldwyn	5820 feet	April 4
Crimson Runner, The	Priscilla Dean	Prod. Dist. Corp	4775 feet	June 6
Daddy's Gone A'Hunting	Joyce-Marmont	Metro-Goldwyn	5851 feet	Mar. 7
Denial, The	Special Cast	Metro-Goldwyn	4791 feet	Mar. 21
Double Action Daniels	Buffalo Bill, Jr	Weiss Bros. (S. R.)	4650 feet	
Dressmaker from Paris, The	Rod La Rocque	Paramount	7080 feet	Mar. 28
Fighting Romeo, A	Al Ferguson	Davis Dist. Div. (S.R.)	5000 feet	Aug. 15
Fighting the Flames	Haines-Devore	C. B. C. (S. R.)	5800 feet	
Forbidden Cargo	Evelyn Brent	F. B. O	4850 feet	April 11
Goose Hangs High, The	Constance Bennett	Paramount	6186 feet	Feb. 14
Great Divide, The	Terry-Tearle	Metro-Goldwyn	7811 feet	Feb. 21
Head Winds	House Peters	Universal	5600 feet	Mar. 28
Hunted Woman, The	Seena Owen	Fox	4954 feet	April 4
I Want My Man	Sills-Kenyon	First National	6175 feet	April 18
Jimmie's Millions	Richard Talmadge	F. B. O	5167 feet	Feb. 28
Just Traveling	Bob Burns	Sierra Pict. (S. R.)	4400 feet	
Last Laugh, The	Emil Jannings	Universal	6519 feet	Dec. 20
Let'er Buck	Hoot Gibson	Universal	5547 feet	Jan. 3
Mad Whirl, The	May McAvoy	Universal	6184 feet	Dec. 6
Marriage in Transit	Edmund Lowe	Fox Film	4800 feet	April 11
Men and Women	Special Cast	Paramount	6223 feet	Mar. 28
Monster, The	L. Chaney-J. Arthur	Metro-Goldwyn	6435 feet	Feb. 28
My Wife and I	Special Cast	Warner Bros	6700 feet	June 6
New Lives for Old	Betty Compson	Paramount	6796 feet	Mar. 7
New Toys	Richard Barthelmess	First National	7250 feet	Feb. 21
One Year to Live	Special Cast	First National	6064 feet	Feb. 28
Percy	Charles Ray	Assoc. Exhib	5384 feet	Feb 28
Playing With Souls	Special Cast	First National	5831 feet	Mar. 14
Price of Pleasure, The	Valli-Kerry	Universal	6618 feet	June 13
Recompense	M. Prevost-M. Blue	Warner Bros	7480 feet	May 2
Renegade Holmes, M.D	Ben Wilson	Arrow (S. R.)	4947 feet	
Riders of the Purple Sage	Tom Mix	Fox	5578 feet	Mar. 28
Romance and Rustlers	Yakima Canutt	Arrow (S. R.)	4994 feet	Nov. 15
Sackcloth and Scarlet	Alice Terry	Paramount	6732 feet	Mar. 7
Sally	Colleen Moore	First National	8636 feet	Mar. 28
Scar Hanan	Yakima Canutt	F. B. O	4684 feet	April 4
Scarlet Honeymoon, The	Shirley Mason	Fox	5080 feet	Mar. 21
Seven Chances	Buster Keaton	Metro-Goldwyn	5113 feet	Mar. 28
Sign of the Cactus, The	Jack Hoxie	Universal	4938 feet	Jan. 10
Sky Raider, The	Capt. Charles Nungesser	Assoc. Exhib	6638 feet	April 4
Speed	Betty Blythe	Banner Prod. (S. R.)	6000 feet	May 30
Too Many Kisses	Richard Dix	Paramount	5759 feet	Mar. 14
Waking Up the Town	Jack Pickford	United Artists	4802 feet	April 11
Where Romance Rides	Dick Hatton	Arrow	4301 feet	
Zander the Great	Marion Davies	Metro-Goldwyn	5851 feet	May 16

APRIL

Feature	Star	Distributed by	Length	Reviewed
Adventure	P. Starke-T. Moore	Paramount	6713 feet	April 25
After Business Hours	Hammerstein-Tellegen	C. B. C. (S. R.)	5800 feet	
Bandit Tamer, The	Franklyn Farnum	Inde. Pict. (S. R.)	5000 feet	
Border Vengeance	Jack Perrin	Madoc Sales (S. R.)	4500 feet	
Charmer, The	Pola Negri	Paramount	6076 feet	April 18
Code of the West	O. Moore-C. Bennett	Paramount	6777 feet	April 25
Courageous Fool, The	Reed Howes	Rayart (S. R.)		
Crowded Hour, The	Bebe Daniels	Paramount	6558 feet	May 9
Dangerous Innocence	LaPlante-E. O'Brien	Universal	6759 feet	Mar. 21
Declasse	Corinne Griffith	First National	7869 feet	April 4
Eyes of the Desert	Al Richmond	Sierra Prod. (S. R.)	4500 feet	
Fifth Avenue Models	Philbin-Kerry	Universal	6581 feet	Jan. 24
Fighting Parson, The	Al Ferguson	Davis Dist. Div. (S.R.)	5000 feet	
Fighting Sheriff, The	Bill Cody	Inde. Pict. (S. R.)	4500 feet	May 30
Friendly Enemies	Weber and Fields	Prod. Dist. Corp	6288 feet	May 9
Galloping Vengeance	Bob Custer	F. B. O	5095 feet	April 11
Getting 'Em Right	George Larkin	Rayart (S. R.)	4669 feet	
Gold and the Girl	Buck Jones	Fox	4521 feet	April 4
Go Straight	Gladys Hulette	B. P. Schulberg (S.R.)	6107 feet	May 23
Heart of a Siren, The	Barbara La Marr	First National	6700 feet	Mar. 21
How Baxter Butted In	M. Moore-D. Devore	Warner Bros	6650 feet	July 11
Justice Raffles	Henry Edwards	Cranfield & Clarke (S. R.)	6000 feet	
Kiss in the Dark, A	Special Cast	Paramount	5767 feet	April 18
Kiss Me Again	M. Prevost-M. Blue	Warner Bros	7200 feet	June 6
Love's Bargain	M. Daw-C. Brook	F. B. O	5641 feet	April 25
Madame Sans Gene	Gloria Swanson	Paramount	9994 feet	May 2
Man and Maid	Special Cast	Metro-Goldwyn	5307 feet	April 18
My Son	Nazimova-J. Pickford	First National	6500 feet	April 25
Night Club, The	R. Griffith-V. Reynolds	Paramount	5732 feet	May 16
One Way Street	Special Cast	First National	5596 feet	April 11
Proud Flesh	Special Cast	Metro-Goldwyn	5770 feet	April 25
Rearing Adventure, The	Jack Hoxie	Universal	4657 feet	Feb. 14
Ridin' Comet, The	Yakima Canutt	F. B. O	4354 feet	May 16
Rough Going	Franklyn Farnum	Indep. Pict. Corp. (S. R.)	4800 feet	
Shackled Lightning	Frank Merrill	Hercules Prod. (S. R.)		
She Wolves	Alma Rubens	Fox	5783 feet	May 9
Spaniard, The	Cortez-Goudal	Paramount	6676 feet	April 18
Sporting Venus	Special Cast	Metro-Goldwyn	5938 feet	May 23
Stop Flirting	Special Cast	Prod. Dist. Corp	5161 feet	June 6
Straight Through	Wm. Desmond	Universal	4867 feet	
Tale of a Thousand and One Nights	Special Cast	Davis Dist. Div. (S. R.)	6500 feet	Feb. 14
Tearing Through	Richard Talmadge	F. B. O.	4714 feet	May 23
That Devil Quemado	Fred Thomson	F. B. O.	4768 feet	April 4
Two-Fisted Sheriff, A	Yakima Canutt	Arrow (S. R.)	4149 feet	Dec. 6
Way of a Girl, The	Boardman-M. Moore	Metro-Goldwyn	5025 feet	April 18
Western Engagement, A	Dick Hatton	Arrow		
Wings of Youth	Madge Bellamy	Fox	5340 feet	May 16
Winning a Woman	Perrin-Hill	Rayart (S. R.)	4865 feet	

MAY

Feature	Star	Distributed by	Length	Reviewed
Alias Mary Flynn	Evelyn Brent	F. B. O.	5559 feet	May 30
Any Woman	Alice Terry	Paramount	5963 feet	June 13
Awful Truth, The	Agnes Ayres	Prod. Dist. Corp	5917 feet	July 11
Bandit's Baby, The	Fred Thomson	F. B. O.	5291 feet	June 20
Baree Son of Kazan	Wolf (dog)	Vitagraph	7 reels	May 2
Barriers of the Law	Holmes-Desmond	Indep. Pict. (S. R.)	5400 feet	
Burning Trail, The	William Desmond	Universal	4783 feet	April 18
Chickie	Mackaill-Bosworth	First National	7767 feet	May 9
Crackerjack, The	Johnny Hines	C. C. Burr (S. R.)	6500 feet	May 23
Every Man's Wife	Special Cast	Fox	4365 feet	July 4
Eve's Lover	Irene Rich	Warner Bros	6540 feet	Aug. 8
Eve's Secret	Betty Compson	Paramount	6305 feet	May 9
Fear Fighter, The	Billy Sullivan	Rayart (S. R.)		
Fighting Demon, The	Richard Talmadge	F B O	5470 feet	June 20
Fugitive, The	Ben Wilson	Arrow	4892 feet	
Golden Trails		Sanford Prod. (S. R.)	5 reels	
His Supreme Moment	B Sweet-R Colman	First National	6600 feet	April 25
Lilies of the Streets	J. Walker-V. L. Corbin	F. B. O.	7160 feet	April 25
Little French Girl, The	Alice Joyce	Paramount	5628 feet	June 13
Lunatic at Large, A	Henry Edwards	Cranfield & Clarke (S. R.)	6000 feet	
Makers of Men	Kenneth McDonald	Barsky Prod. (S. R.)	5000 feet	
Necessary Evil, The	Dana-Lyon	First National	6307 feet	May 23
Old Home Week	Thomas Meighan	Paramount	6888 feet	June 6
Phantom Rider, The	Al Richmond	Sierra Prod. (S. R.)	4750 feet	
Private Affairs	Special Cast	Prod. Dist. Corp	6132 feet	Aug. 15
Quick Change	George Larkin	Rayart (S. R.)		
Raffles, The Amateur Cracksman	House Peters	Universal	5557 feet	May 30
Rainbow Trail, The	Tom Mix	Fox	5251 feet	April 25
Red Love	Lowell-Russell	Lowell Film Prod. (S. R.)	6500 feet	May 23
Saddle Hawk, The	Hoot Gibson	Universal	5468 feet	Mar 7
Silent Sanderson	Harry Carey	Prod. Dist. Corp	4841 feet	June 20
Scandal Proof	Shirley Mason	Fox	4400 feat	June 6
School for Wives	Tearle-Holmquist	Vitagraph	6750 feet	April 11
Shock Punch, The	Richard Dix	Paramount	6151 feet	May 23
Snob Buster, The	Reed Howes	Rayart (S. R.)		
Soul Fire	Barthelmess-B Love	First National	8262 feet	May 16
Speed Wild	Maurice B "Lefty" Flynn	F. B. O	4700 feet	June 20
Talker, The	A Nilsson-L Stone	First National	7861 feet	May 23
Texas Bearcat, The	Bob Custer	F. B. O	4770 feet	
Tides of Passion	Mae Marsh	Vitagraph	6279 feet	May 9
Up the Ladder	Virginia Valli	Universal	6023 feet	Jan 31
Welcome Home	Special Cast	Paramount	5909 feet	May 30
White Fang	Strongheart (dog)	F. B. O	6579 feet	June 20
White Thunder	Yakima Canutt	F. B. O.	4550 feet	
Wildfire	Special Cast	Vitagraph	6 reels	June 20
Wolves of the Road	Yakima Canutt	Arrow	4375 feet	
Woman's Faith	Reubens-Marmont	Universal	6023 feet	Aug 15
Woman Hater, The	Helene Chadwick	Warner Brothers	7000 feet	Aug. 22

JUNE

Feature	Star	Distributed by	Length	Reviewed
Are Parents People?	Bronson-Vidor	Paramount	6586 feet	June 6
Dangerous Odds	Bill Cody	Inde. Pict. (S. R.)	4800 feet	
Desert Flower, The	Colleen Moore	First National	6837 feet	June 13
Double Fisted	Jack Perrin	Rayart (S. R.)		
Down the Border	Al Richmond	Sierra Prod. (S. R.)	4750 feet	
Faint Perfume	Seena Owen	B. P. Schulberg (S.R.)	6228 feet	July 11
Grounds for Divorce	Florence Vidor	Paramount	5712 feet	July 4
Hearts and Spurs	Buck Jones	Fox	4600 feet	June 20
Human Tornado, The	Yakima Canutt	F. B. O.	4472 feet	
I'll Show You the Town	Reginald Denny	Universal	7400 feet	June 6
Introduce Me	Douglas MacLean	Assoc. Exhib	5980 feet	Mar. 21
Just a Woman	Windsor-Tearle	First National	6500 feet	June 6
Light of Western Stars	Special Cast	Paramount	6652 feet	July 4
Lost—a Wife	Special Cast	Paramount	6420 feet	June 27
Making of O'Malley, The	Milton Sills	First National	7571 feet	July 4
Man from Lone Mountain, The	Ben Wilson	Arrow	4530 feet	
Man in Blue	Herbert Rawlinson	Universal	5706 feet	Feb. 21
Marry Me	Special Cast	Paramount	5586 feet	
Meddler, The	William Desmond	Universal	4890 feet	May 23
Mike		Metro-Goldwyn		
Mist in the Valley	Alma Taylor	Cranfield & Clarke (S. R.)	5500 feet	
My Lady's Lips	Clara Bow	B. P. Schulberg (S.R.)	6609 feet	Aug 15
Off the Highway	Wm. V. Mong	Prod. Dist.	7641 feet	
Paths to Paradise	Bronson-R. Griffith	Paramount	6741 feet	June 27
Pioneers of the West		Sanford Prod. (S. R.)	5 reels	
Ridin' Easy	Dick Hatton	Arrow	4483 feet	
Ridin' Thunder	Jack Hoxie	Universal	4354 feet	May 23
Rough Stuff	George Larkin	Rayart (S. R.)		
Shattered Lives	Special Cast	Gotham (S. R.)	6 reels	July 4

Feature	Star	Distributed by	Length	Reviewed
Smooth as Satin	Evelyn Brent	F. B. O	6003 feet	July 4
Texas Trail, The	Harry Carey	Prod. Dist. Corp	4720 feet	July 18
Tracked in the Snow Country	Rin-Tin-Tin (dog)	Warner Brothers	6900 feet	Aug. 1
White Monkey, The	La Marr-T. Holding	First National	6121 feet	July 4
Wild Bull's Lair, The	Fred Thompson	F. B. O.	5280 feet	Aug. 15
Youth's Gamble	Reed Howes	Rayart (S. R.)		

JULY

Feature	Star	Distributed by	Length	Reviewed
Bloodhound, The	Bob Custer	F. B. O	4789 feet	
Cold Nerve	Bill Cody	Inde. Pict. (S. R.)	5000 feet	
Danger Signal, The	Jane Novak	Columbia Pict. (S.R.)	5502 feet	Aug. 15
Don Daredevil	Jack Hoxie	Universal	4810 feet	
Don't	S. O'Neill-B. Roach	Metro-Goldwyn		
Drug Store Cowboy, The	Franklyn Farnum	Ind. Pict. Corp. (S.R.)	5100 feet	Feb. 7
Duped	Holmes-Desmond	Ind. Pict. (S. R.)	5400 feet	
Fighting Youth		Columbia Pict. (S.R.)		
Lady Who Lied, The	L. Stone-V. Valli	First National	7111 feet	July 18
Lady Robinhood	Evelyn Brent	F. B. O	5582 feet	Aug 22
Manicure Girl, The	Bebe Daniels	Paramount	5959 feet	June 27
Marriage Whirl, The	C. Griffith-H. Ford	First National	7672 feet	July 25
Mysterious Stranger, The	Richard Talmadge	F. B. O	5270 feet	
Pipes of Pan	Alma Taylor	Cranfield & Clarke (S. R.)	6200 feet	
Ranger of the Big Pines, The	Kenneth Harlan	Vitagraph	5800 feet	Aug. 8
Scarlet West, The	Frazer-Bow	First National	8391 feet	July 25
Secret of Black Canyon, The	Dick Hatton	Arrow		
Strange Rider, The	Yakima Canutt	Arrow		
Taming the West	Hoot Gibson	Universal	5427 feet	Feb. 28
Trailed	Al Richmond	Sierra Prod. (S. R.)	4750 feet	
White Desert, The	Special Cast	Metro-Goldwyn	6345 feet	July 18

AUGUST

Feature	Star	Distributed by	Length	Reviewed
American Pluck	George Walsh	Chadwick	5000 feet	July 11
Beggar on Horseback, A	Ralston-Nissen	Paramount	6800 feet	June 20
Business of Love, The	E. Horton-M. Bellamy	Astor Dist. Corp		
Children of the Whirlwind	Lionel Barrymore	Arrow		
Don Q	Douglas Fairbanks	United Artists	10264 feet	June 27
Drusilla With a Million	Special Cast	F. B. O	7391 feet	May 30
Fine Clothes	L. Stone-A. Rubens	First National	6971 feet	Aug. 15
Girl Who Wouldn't Work, The	Lionel Barrymore	B. P. Schulberg (S.R.)		
Gold Rush, The	Charles Chaplin	United Artists	10 reels	Aug. 8
Halfway Girl, The	Doris Kenyon	First National	7570 feet	Aug. 8
Headlines	Alice Joyce	Assoc. Exhib.	6 reels	July 25
Her Sister From Paris	C. Talmadge	First National	7255 feet	Aug. 15
In the Name of Love	Cortez-Nissen	Paramount	5904 feet	
Isle of Hope, The	Richard Talmadge	Film Book. Offices		
Kivalina of the Ice Lands	Native Cast	Pathe	6 reels	July 11
Knockout, The	Milton Sills	First National		
Limited Mail, The	Monte Blue	Warner Brothers	6250 feet	
Love Hour, The	Ruth Clifford	Vitagraph	5900 feet	
Lover's Oath, The	Ramon Novarro	Astor Dist Corp		
Lucky Devil, The	Richerd Dix	Paramount	5935 feet	July 18
Lucky Horseshoes	Tom Mix	Fox	5000 feet	Aug. 29
Manhattan Madness	Dempsey-Taylor	Assoc. Exhib	5500 feet	July 25
My Pal	Dick Hatton	Arrow		
Night Life of New York	Special Cast	Paramount	6998 feet	July 4
Overland Limited, The		Gotham Prod. (S. R.)	6389 feet	Aug. 8
Parisian Love	Bow-Tellegen	B. P. Schulberg (S.R.)	6324 feet	Aug. 22
Penalty of Jazz, The		Columbia Pict. (S.R.)		
Quo Vadis	Emil Jannings	First National	8945 feet	Feb. 28
Range Justice	Dick Hatton	Arrow		
Romola	Gish Sisters	Metro-Goldwyn	About 12 reels	Dec. 13
Rugged Water	Special Cast	Paramount		
Shining Adventure, The	Percy Marmont	Astor Dist. Corp		
Slave of Fashion, A	Special Cast	Metro-Goldwyn	5906 feet	Aug. 1
Speed Demon, The		Columbia Pict. (S.R.)		
Street of Forgotten Men	Special Cast	Paramount	6366 feet	Aug. 1
Ten Commandments	Special Cast	Paramount	9980 feet	Jan. 5-24
Unholy Three	Lon Chaney	Metro-Goldwyn	6848 feet	Aug. 15
That Man Jack	Bob Custer	F. B. O	5032 feet	Aug. 22
Unwritten Law, The		Columbia Pict. (S.R.)		
Wife Who Wasn't Wanted, The	Irene Rich	Warner Brothers	6400 feet	
Wizard of Oz	Larry Semon	Chadwick	6300 feet	Apr. 25
Wrongdoers, The	Lionel Barrymore	Astor Dist. Corp		

SEPTEMBER

Feature	Star	Distributed by	Length	Reviewed
Amazing Quest, The	Henry Edwards	Cranfield & Clarke	5500 feet	
As No Man Has Loved	Edward Hearn	Fox	10000 feet	Feb. 28
Below The Line	Rin-Tin-Tin (dog)	Warner Brothers	6100 feet	
Black Cyclone	Rex (horse)	Pathe		May 30
Bobbed Hair	Prevost-Harlan	Warner Brothers	6700 feet	
California Straight Ahead	Reginald Denny	Universal		
Classified	Corinne Griffith	First National		
Coast of Folly	Gloria Swanson	Paramount		
Crack of Dawn	Reed Howes	Rayart (S. R.)		
Cyclone Cavalier	Reed Howes	Rayart (S. R.)		
Dark Angel, The	R. Colman-V. Dana	First National		
Freshman, The	Harold Lloyd	Pathe		July 25
Graustark	Norma Talmadge	First National		
Havoc	Special Cast	Fox	9200 feet	
High and Handsome	"Lefty" Flynn	F. B. O.	5669 feet	
If Marriage Fails	J. Logan-C. Brook	F. B. O	6006 feet	May 23
Keep Smiling	Monty Banks	Assoc. Exhib.		Aug. 1
Let's Go Gallagher	Tom Tyler	Film Book Offices		
Little Annie Rooney	Mary Pickford	United Artists		
Lost World, The	Special Cast	First National	9700 feet	Feb. 21
Man Who Found Himself	Thomas Meighan	Paramount		
Marrying Money		Truart (S. R.)	5800 feet	
Midshipman, The	Ramon Novarro	Metro-Goldwyn		
Never the Twain Shall Meet	Stewart-Lytell	Metro-Goldwyn	8143 feet	Aug. 8
New Champion, The		Columbia Pict. (S.R.)		
Not So Long Ago	Betty Bronson	Paramount	6943 feet	Aug. 8
Other Woman's Story		B. P. Schulberg		
Parisian Nights	E. Hammerstein - L. Tellegen	F. B. O	6278 feet	June 20
Pretty Ladies	Zazu Pitts	Metro-Goldwyn	5828 feet	July 25
Prince of Broadway, The	George Walsh	Chadwick		
Ridin' the Wind	Fred Thomson	Film Book. Offices		
Sealed Lips		Columbia Pict. (S.R.)		
Shore Leave	Barthelmess-Mackaill	First National	6856 feet	Aug. 29
Siege	Virginia Valli	Universal	6424 feet	June 20
Some Pun'kins	Chas. Ray	Chadwick		
Son of His Father	Special Cast	Paramount	7009 feet	
Souls for Sables		Tiffany (S. R.)	6500 feet	
S. O. S. Perils of the Sea		Columbia Pict. (S.R.)		
Spook Ranch	Hoot Gibson	Universal	5147 feet	May 2
Sun Up		Metro-Goldwyn		
Teaser, The	Laura La Plante	Universal	6967 feet	May 30
Three in Exile		Truart (S. R.)	5600 feet	
Three Weeks in Paris	M. Moore-D. Devore	Warner Brothers	5900 feet	
Three Wise Crooks	Evelyn Brent	Film Book. Offices		
Throwback, The	Special Cast	Universal		
Timber Wolf, The	Buck Jones	Fox	4809 feet	
Trouble With Wives, The	Vidor-T. Moore	Paramount	6374 feet	Aug. 15
Unchastened Woman, The	Theda Bara	Chadwick		
Wall Street Whiz, The	Richard Talmadge	Film Book. Offices		
What Fools Men	Stone-Mason	First National		
Wheel, The	Special Cast	Fox	7264 feet	
White Outlaw, The	Jack Hoxie	Universal	4830 feet	June 27
Wild Horse Mesa	Special Cast	Paramount	7221 feet	Aug. 22
Wild, Wild Susan	Bebe Daniels	Paramount		
With This Ring	Mills-Tellegen	B. P. Schulberg		

OCTOBER

Feature	Star	Distributed by	Length	Reviewed
Bells, The	Lionel Barrymore	Chadwick		
Dollar Down	Ruth Roland	Truart (S. R.)	5800 feet	Aug. 29
Everlasting Whisper, The	Tom Mix	Fox		
Fate of a Flirt, The		Columbia (S. R.)		
Flower of Night	Pola Negri	Paramount		
Golden Princess, The	Bronson-Hamilton	Paramount	8584 feet	
Great Sensation, The		Columbia (S. R.)		
His Buddy's Wife	Glenn Hunter	Assoc. Exhib	5600 feet	July 25
Iron Horse, The		Fox Film Corp	11335 feet	Sept. 13
John Forrest	Henry Edwards	Cranfield&Clark(S.R.)	5000 feet	
Lew Tyler's Wives		B. P. Schulberg (S. R.)		
Lovers in Quarantine	Daniels-Ford	Paramount		
Morals for Men		Tiffany (S. R.)	6500 feet	
New Brooms	Hamilton-Love	Paramount		
Pals		Truart (S. R.)	5800 feet	
Perfect Clown, The	Larry Semon	Chadwick		
Pony Express, The	Betty Compson	Paramount		
Sally of the Sawdust	Fields-Dempster	United Artists	9500 feet	Aug. 13
Sporting Chance, The		Tiffany (S. R.)	6500 feet	July 4
Thank U	Special Cast	Fox		
Tumbleweeds	Wm. S. Hart	United Artists		
Under the Rouge	Tom Moore	Assoc. Exhib	6500 feet	July 25
Winds of Chance	A. Nilsson-B. Lyon	First National	10 reels	Aug. 29

NOVEMBER

Feature	Star	Distributed by	Length	Reviewed
Ancient Highway, The	Holt-Vidor	Paramount		
Best People, The	Special Cast	Paramount		
Blue Blood	George Walsh	Chadwick		
Camille of the Barbary Coast	Busch-O. Moore	Assoc. Exhib	5600 feet	Aug. 1
Cobra	Valentino-Naldi	Paramount		
Fifty-Fifty	L.Barrymore-H.Hampton	Assoc. Exhib	5564 feet	June 20
Fight to a Finish, A		Columbia (S. R.)		
Fighting Heart, The	Geo. O'Brien	Fox	6978 feet	
King on Main St., The	Adolphe Menjou	Paramount		
Lightning		Tiffany (S. R.)	6500 feet	
Price of Success, The	Alice Lake	Columbia (S. R.)		
Silent Witness, The		Truart (S. R.)	5800 feet	
Stage Struck	Gloria Swanson	Paramount		
Transcontinental Limited	Special Cast	Chadwick (S. R.)		
Vanishing American	Dix-Wilson	Paramount		
Winner, The	Charley Ray	Chadwick (S. R.)		

Comedy Releases

Feature	Star	Distributed by	Length	Reviewed
Across the Hall	Edna Marian	Universal	2 reels	
Adventures of Adenoid	Aesop's Fables	Pathe	1 reel	April 25
After a Reputation	Edna Marian	Universal	2 reels	
Air Tight	Bobby Vernon	Educational	2 reels	June 13
Alice's Egg Plant	"Cartoon"	M. J. Winkler(S. R.)	1 reel	
Alice Stagestruck	Margie Gay	M. J. Winkler (S.R.)	1 reel	July 18
All Aboard		Fox	2 reels	
Almost a Husband	Buddy Messinger	Universal	2 reels	
Amateur Detective	Earle Foxe	Fox	2 reels	
Andy in Hollywood	Joe Murphy	Universal	2 reels	
Andy Takes a Flyer	"The Gumps"	Universal	2 reels	
Apache, The	Earle Foxe	Fox Film	2 reels	
Apollo's Pretty Sister		Fox	2 reels	
Are Husbands Human?	James Finlayson	Pathe	1 reel	April 11
Artists' Blues	G. Joy-J. Moore	Rayart (S. R.)	2 reels	
Ask Grandma	"Our Gang"	Pathe	2 reels	May 30
At the Seashore	Monkey	Fox	2 reels	
At the Zoo	Aesops Fables	Pathe	1 reel	
Baby Blues	Mickey Bennett	Educational	2 reels	
Bachelors	Special Cast	Universal		
Bad Bill Brodie	Charles Chase	Pathe	2 reels	
Bad Boy	Charles Chase	Pathe	2 reels	April 11
Balboa Discovers Hollywood	"Red Head"	Sering D. Wilson(S.R.)	1 reel	
Bark is the Woods	Harry Langdon	Pathe	2 reels	
Bashful Jim	Ralph Graves	Pathe	2 reels	Mar. 21
Be Careful	Jimmie Adams	Educational Film	2 reels	Aug. 22
Below Zero	Lige Conley	Educational	2 reels	July 4
Beware	Lige Conley	Educational Film	2 reels	Aug. 1
Big Chief Ko-Ko (Out of the Inkwell)	"Cartoon"	Red Seal Pict. (S. R.)	1 reel	
Big Game Hunter, The	Earle Foxe	Fox	2 reels	
Bigger and Better Pictures	"Aesop's Fables"	Pathe	1 reel	
Big Red Riding Hood	Charley Chase	Pathe	1 reel	May 9
Black Gold Bricks	Roach-Edwards	Universal	1 reel	April 18
Black Hand Blues	"Spat Family"	Pathe	2 reels	April 18
Bobby Bumbs & Co	Cartoon	Educational	1 reel	July 4
Boys Will Be Joys	"Our Gang"	Pathe	2 reels	July 25
Brainless Horsemen		Fox	2 reels	
Brass Button	Billy West	Arrow	2 reels	
Breaking the Ice	Ralph Graves	Pathe	2 reels	April 11
Bride Tamer, The	Milburn Moranti	Sierra Pict. (S. R.)	2 reels	
Bubbles	"Aesop's Fables"	Pathe	1 reel	Aug. 15
Bugville Field Day	"Aesop's Fables"	Pathe	1 reel	July 25

Feature	Star	Distributed by	Length	Reviewed
Business Engagement, A		Fox	2 reels	
Butterfly Man, The		Fox	2 reels	
California Here We Come	"The Gumps"	Universal	2 reels	
Cat's Shimmy, The	"Kid Noah"	Sering D. Wilson (S.R.)	1 reel	
Chasing the Chasers	Jas. Finlayson	Pathe	1 reel	July 4
City Bound	Charles Puffy	Universal	1 reel	
Clean-Up Week	"Aesop's Fables"	Pathe	1 reel	Mar. 7
Clear the Way	Buddy Messinger	Universal	2 reels	
Cleopatra and Her Easy Mark	"Cartoon"	Sering D. Wilson (S.R.)	1 reel	
Cloudhopper, The	Larry Semon	Educational	2 reels	June 6
Columbus Discovers a New Whirl		Sering Wilson (S. R.)	1 reel	
Cotton King	Lloyd Hamilton	Educational	2 reels	
Crime Crushers	Lige Conley	Educational	2 reels	
Crying for Love	Eddie Gordon	Universal	2 reels	Aug. 15
Cupid's Boots	Ralph Graves	Pathe	2 reels	July 25
Cure, The (Out of the Inkwell)	"Cartoon"	Red Seal Pict. (S. R.)	1 reel	
Curses	Al. St. John	Educational	2 reels	May 23
Daddy Goes A Grunting		Pathe	2 reels	July 18
Darkest Africa	"Aesop's Fables"	Pathe	1 reels	
Day's Outing, A	"The Gumps"	Universal	2 reels	
Depp Stuff	Aesop's Fables	Pathe	1 reel	April 25
Dinky Doodle and Cinderella	"Dinky Doodle"	F. B. O	1 reel	
Dinky Doodle and Robinson Crusoe	"Dinky Doodle"	F. B. O	1 reel	
Discord in "A" Flat	Arthur Lake	Universal	1 reel	July 25
Dog Days	"Our Gang"	Pathe	2 reels	Mar. 14
Dog 'On It	Bobby Dunn	Arrow	2 reels	
Dome Doctor, The	Larry Semon	Educational	2 reels	
Don't Pinch	Bobby Vernon	Educational	2 reels	April 25
Don't Worry	Wanda Wiley	Universal	2 reels	Mar. 21
Dragon Alley	Jackie McHugh	Educational	2 reels	May 16
Dr. Pyckle and Mr. Pride	Stan Laurel	Film Booking Offices	2 reels	
Dry Up	Singleton Burkett	Universal	2 reels	July 25
Dumb and Daffy	Al. St. John	Fox	2 reels	
Dynamite Doggie	Al. St. John	Educational	2 reels	Mar. 21
Echoes From the Alps	Aesop's Fables	Pathe	1 reel	May 23
End of the World, The	Aesop's Fables	Pathe	1 reel	
Etiquette	Jimmy Aubrey	Film Book. Offices	2 reels	
Excuse My Glove	"Spat Family"	Pathe	2 reels	Mar 21
Expensive Ebony	"Ebenezer Ebony"	Sering Wilson (S. R.)	1 reel	
Failure		Fox	2 reels	
Fares Please	Al. St. John	Educational	2 reels	May 16
Fast Worker, A	Aesop's Fables	Pathe	1 reel	
Felix Full O'Fight	"Cartoon"	M. J. Winkler (S. R.)	1 reel	
Felix Gets His Fill	"Cartoon"	M. J. Winkler (S. R.)	1 reel	
Felix Grabs His Grub	"Cartoon"	M. J. Winkler (S. R.)	1 reel	
First Love	"Our Gang"	Pathe	2 reels	
Fishermen's Luck	"Aesop's Fables"	Pathe	1 reel	
For Hire	Edward Gordon	Universal		
For Love of a Gal	"Aesop's Fables"	Pathe	1 reel	July 25
Found World, The	"The Gumps"	Universal	2 reels	
Fun's Fun	Bowes-Vance	Educational	1 reel	June 6
Getting Trimmed	Wanda Wiley	Universal	2 reels	April 18
Giddap	Special Cast	Pathe	2 reels	Mar. 21
Going Great	Eddie Nelson	Educational	2 reels	June 13
Goldfish's Pajamas	"Kid Noah"	Sering D. Wilson (S.R.)	1 reel	
Good Morning Nurse	Ralph Graves	Pathe	2 reels	May 30
Good Scouts	"Reg'lar Kids"	M. J. Winkler (S. R.)	2 reels	
Great Guns	Bobby Vernon	Educational	2 reels	Feb. 21
Gridiron Gertie	Wanda Wiley	Universal	2 reels	
Guilty Conscience, A	Eddie Gordon	Universal		
Gypping the Gypsies	"Ebonezer Ebony"	Sering Wilson (S. R.)	1 reel	
Half a Hero	Lloyd Hamilton	Educational	2 reels	Mar. 7
Half a Man	Stan Laurel	Pathe	2 reels	
Hard Boiled	Charley Chase	Pathe	2 reels	Mar. 21
Hard Working Loafer, The	Arthur Stone	Pathe		
Haunted Honeymoon	Tryon-Mehaffey	Pathe	2 reels	Feb. 28
Heart Trouble	Arthur Lake	Universal	1 reel	July 4
Hello, Goodby	Lige Conley	Educational	2 reels	May 30
Hello, Hollywood	Lige Conley	Educational	2 reels	Mar. 28
Helping Hand	Jimmy Aubrey	F. B. O	2 reels	
Help Yourself		Fox	2 reels	
Here's Your Hat	Arthur Lake	Universal	1 reel	May 9
Her Lucky Leap	Wanda Wiley	Universal	2 reels	
He Who Gets Crowned	Jimmy Aubrey	F. B. O	2 reels	
He Who Got Smacked	Ralph Graves	Pathe	2 reels	May 9
Hey! Taxi!	Bobby Dunn	Arrow	2 reels	
High Hopes	Bowes-Vance	Educational	1 reel	Feb. 14
High Jinx, A		Fox	2 reels	
His Marriage Wow	Harry Langdon	Pathe	2 reels	Mar. 7
Hold My Baby	Glenn Tryon	Pathe	2 reels	April 25
Home Scouts	Jimmie Aubrey	F. B. O.	2 reels	
Honeymoon Heaven		Sering Wilson (S. R.)	1 reel	
Horace Greeley, Jr	Harry Langdon	Pathe	2 reels	June 6
Horrible Hollywood		Lee-Bradford (S. R.)		
Hot and Heavy	Eddie Nelson	Educational	2 reels	July 18
Hot Dog	Animal	C B C (S. R.)	2 reels	
Hot Times in Iceland	Aesop's Fables	Pathe	1 reel	
House of Flickers, The		Fox	2 reels	
House that Dinky Built	(Cartoon)	F. B. O	1 reel	
Housing Shortage, The	"Aesop's Fables"	Pathe	1 reel	
Hysterical History (Series)		Universal	1 reel	
Ice Boy, An	"Ebonezer Ebony"	Sering D. Wilson (S.R.)	1 reel	
Ice Cold	Arthur Lake	Universal	1 reel	June 13
In Dutch	Aesop's Fables	Pathe	1 reel	
Innocent Husbands	Charley Chase	Pathe	2 reels	Aug. 1
Inside Out	Bowes-Vance	Educational	1 reel	Mar. 28
Into the Grease	James Finlayson	Pathe	1 reel	June 27
Iron Mule	Al St. John	Educational	2 reels	April 18
Iron Nag, The	Billy Bevan	Pathe	2 reels	Aug. 15
Is Marriage the Bunk?	Charles Chase	Pathe	1 reel	April 4
Isn't Life Terrible?	Charles Chase	Pathe	2 reels	July 4
Itching for Revenge	Eddie Gordon	Universal	2 reels	Mar 7
It's All Wrong	Karr-Engle	Universal		
James Boys' Sister		Sering Wilson (S. R.)	1 reel	
Jungle Bike Riders	Aesop's Fables	Pathe	1 reel	Mar. 14
Just in Time	Wanda Wiley	Universal	2 reels	July 11
Kicked About	Eddie Gordon	Universal	2 reels	Mar. 14
Kidding Captain Kidd	"Cartoon"	Sering Wilson (S. R.)	1 reel	
King Cotton	Lloyd Hamilton	Educational	2 reels	May 9
King Dumb	Jimmy Aubrey	F. B. O	2 reels	
Knocked About	Eddie Gordon	Universal	2 reels	June 13
Ko-Ko Trains Animals (out of the Inkwell)	"Cartoon"	Red Seal Pict. (S.R.)	1 reel	
Lead Pipe Cinch, A	Al Alt	Universal		
Lion Love		Fox	2 reels	Feb. 28
Lion's Whiskers		Pathe	2 reels	April 18
Little Red Riding Hood	"Dinky Doodle"	F. B. O	1 reel	
Locked Out	Arthur Lake	Universal	1 reel	May 30
Looking for Sally	Charles Chase	Pathe	2 reels	May 9
Look Out	Bowes-Vance	Educational Film	1 reel	Aug. 1
Lost Cord, The	Bert Roach	Universal	1 reel	Feb. 21
Love and Lions		Fox	2 reels	
Love Bug, The	"Our Gang"	Pathe	2 reels	April 4
Love Goofy	Jimmy Adams	Educational	2 reels	Mar. 7
Love Sick	Constance Darling	Universal	2 reels	May 23
Love's Tragedy		Sering Wilson (S. R.)	1 reel	
Lucky Accident, The	Charles Puffy	Universal	1 reel	July 18
Lucky Leap, A	Wanda Wiley	Universal	2 reels	
Lucky Stars	Harry Langdon	Pathe	2 reels	Aug. 15
Madame Sans Jane	Glenn Tryon	Pathe	2 reels	
Marriage Circus, The	Ben Turpin	Pathe	2 reels	April 11
Married Neighbors	Engle-Darling	Universal	2 reels	July 4
Mary, Queen of Tots	"Our Gang"	Pathe	2 reels	Aug. 22
Meet the Ambassador	Jimmy Aubrey	F. B. O	2 reels	
Mellow Quartette	Pen & Ink Vaudeville	Educational	1 reel	April 4
Merrymakers	Bowes-Vance	Educational	1 reel	Mar. 28
Met by Accident	Wanda Wiley	Universal	2 reels	
Milky Way, The	Charles Puffy	Universal	1 reel	July 25
Miss Fixit	Wanda Wiley	Universal	2 reels	
Monkey Business	"Pen & Ink Vaude"	Educational	1 reel	May 9
Moonlight Nights	Gloria Joy	Rayart (S. R.)	2 reels	
Nearly Rich	Charles Puffy	Universal	1 reel	
Neptune's Stepdaughter		Fox	2 reels	
Nero's Jazz Band		Sering Wilson (S. R.)	1 reel	
Never Fear	Bowes-Vance	Educational	1 reel	
Never on Time		Lee-Bradford	2 reels	
Never Weaken	Lloyd reissue	Assoc. Exhib	2237 feet	
Nice Pickle, A	Edwards-Roach	Universal	1 reel	
Nicely Rewarded	Chas. Puffy	Universal	1 reel	June 27
Night Hawks		Educational Film	2 reels	
Nobody Wins	Arthur Lake	Universal	1 reel	
No Place to Go	Arthur Lake	Universal	1 reel	
Now or Never (reissue)	Harold Lloyd	Assoc. Exhib	3 reels	
Office Help	"Aesop's Fables"	Pathe	1 reel	June 27
Official Officers	"Our Gang"	Pathe	2 reels	June 27
Oh, Bridget	Walter Hiers	Educational	2 reels	
Oh, What a Flirt	Jimmy Aubrey	Film Book. Offices	2 reels	
Oh, What a Gump	"The Gumps"	Universal	2 reels	
Old Family Toothbrush	"Kid Noah"	Sering Wilson (S. R.)	1 reel	
On Duty	Wanda Wiley	Universal	2 reels	
One Glorious Fourth	"Reg'lar Kids"	M. J. Winkler (S. R.)	2 reels	
On the Go		Fox	2 reels	
Orphan, The	Al Joy	Ricardo Films, Inc. (S.R.)		
Over the Bottom	Stan Laurel	F. B. O	2 reels	
Over the Plate	Aesops Fable	Pathe	1 reel	Aug. 22
Over Here	Harry Langdon	Pathe	2 reels	
Paging A Wife	Al Alt	Universal	2 reels	Aug. 1
Papa's Darling		Fox	2 reels	
Papa's Pet	Roach-Edwards	Universal	1 reel	April 11
Parisian Knight, A	Earle Foxe	Fox	2 reels	
Peacemakers, The		Fox	2 reels	
Pegg's Love Affair		Screen Art Dist		
Peggy the Vamp	Rosalie Morlin	Davis Distr	2 reels	Oct. 11
Permanent Waves	"Aesop's Fables"	Pathe	1 reel	
Permit Me	Bowes-Vance	Educational	1 reel	July 11
Pie-Eyed	Stan Laurel	F. B. O	2 reels	
Pie Man, The	"Aesop's Fables"	Pathe	1 reel	Mar. 21
Plain Clothes	Harry Langdon	Pathe	2 reels	Mar. 28
Plain and Fancy Girls	Charles Chase	Pathe	1 reel	Mar. 14
Plain Luck	Edna Marian	Universal	2 reels	
Pleasure Bound	Lige Conley	Educational	2 reels	Aug. 22
Plenty of Nerve	Edna Marian	Universal	2 reels	July 4
Polo Kid, The	Eddie Gordon	Universal	2 reels	July 18
Poor Sap, The		Fox	2 reels	
Powdered Chickens	Edna Marian	Universal	2 reels	Mar. 28
Props' Dash for Cash	Earl Hurd (Cartoon)	Educational	1 reel	
Putting on Airs	Edna Marian	Universal	2 reels	April 11
Puzzled by Crosswords	Eddie Gordon	Universal	2 reels	Mar. 7
Queen of Aces	Wanda Wiley	Universal	2 reels	May 16
Raid, The	Gloria Joy	Rayart Pictures	2 reels	
Raisin' Cain	Constance Darling	Universal	2 reels	April 4
Rapid Transit	Al. St. John	Educational	2 reels	
Rarin' Romeo	Walter Hiers	Educational	2 reels	Mar. 28
Raspberry Romance	Ben Turpin	Pathe	2 reels	Feb. 28
Red Pepper	Al. St. John	Educational	2 reels	Arpil 4
Regular Girl, A	Wanda Wiley	Universal	2 reels	
Riders of the Kitchen Range	Mohar-Engle	Pathe	1 reel	June 6
Remember When	Harry Langdon	Pathe	2 reels	April 25
Rip Without a Wink	"Redhead"	Sering Wilson (S. R.)	1 reel	
Ripe Melodrama, A		Sering Wilson (S. R.)	1 reel	
Rivals	Billy West	Arrow	2 reels	
Robinson Crusoe Returns on Friday	"Redhead"	Sering Wilson (S. R.)	1 reel	
Rock Bottom	Bowes-Vance	Educational	1 reel	May 9
Robbing the Rube		Lee-Bradford Corp	2 reels	
Rolling Stones	Charles Puffy	Universal	1 reel	May 30
Rough Party	Al Alt	Universal	2 reels	
Royal Four-Flush	"Spat Family"	Pathe	2 reels	June 13
Runaway Balloon, The	"Aesop's Fables"	Pathe	1 reel	June 27
Runt, The	"Aesop's Fables"	Pathe	1 reel	June 6
Sailor Papa, A	Glenn Tryon	Pathe	2 reels	April 4
Saturday		Davis Dist. Div	2 reels	
Say It With Flour		Fox	2 reels	
Sheiks of Bagdad		Pathe	1 reel	May 9
Sherlock Sleuth	Arthur Stone	Pathe	2 reels	July 11
Ship Shape	Vance-Bowes	Educational	1 reel	April 18
Shootin' Injuns	"Our Gang"	Pathe	2 reels	May 9
Short Pants	Arthur Lake	Universal	1 reel	Aug. 1
Should a Husband Tell?		Red Seal Pict. (S.R.)	1 reel	
Should Husbands Be Watched?	Charles Chase	Pathe	1 reel	Mar. 14
Sir Walt and Lizzie		Sering Wilson (S. R.)	1 reel	
Sit Tight	Jimmie Adams	Educational	2 reels	May 30
Skinners in Silk		Pathe	2 reels	May 16
Sky Jumper, The	Earle Foxe	Fox	2 reels	
Skyscraper, The	Harry Langdon	Principal Pict. (S. R.)	2 reels	
Sleeping Sickness	Edwards-Roach	Universal	1 reel	May 30
Slick Articles	Engle-Karr	Universal	2 reels	May 30
Smoked Out	Lake-Hasbrouck	Universal	1 reel	April 13
Sneezing Beezers	Billy Bevan	Pathe	2 reels	July 18
Snow-Hawk	Stan Laurel	F. B. O	2 reels	
Soap	"Aesop's Fables"	Pathe	1 reel	
S. O. S	"Aesop's Fables"	Pathe	1 reel	
Spanish Romeo, A (Van Bibber)		Fox	1 reel	
Speak Easy	Charley Puffy	Universal	1 reel	Aug. 22
Speak Freely	Edna Marian	Universal	2 reels	
Stick Around	Bobby Dunn	Arrow	2 reels	
Stop, Look and Whistle		Fox	2 reels	
Storm, The (Out of the Inkwell)	"Cartoon"	Red Seal Pict. (S.R.)	1 reel	
Stranded	Edna Marian	Universal	2 reels	
Super-Hooper-Dyne Lizzies		Pathe	2 reels	June 13
Sure Mike!	Martha Sleeper	Pathe	1 reel	May 23
Sweet Marie		Fox	2 reels	Aug. 29
Tame Men and Wild Women		Pathe	2 reels	Aug. 15

Feature	Star	Distributed by	Length	Reviewed
Teaser Island	"Redhead"	Sering Wilson (S. R.)	1 reel	
Tee for Two	Alice Day	Pathe	2 reels	Aug. 1
Tell It To a Policeman	Glenn Tryon	Pathe	2 reels	May 23
Tender Feet	Walter Hiers	Educational	2 reels	May 23
Tenting Out	Roache-Edwards	Universal	1 reel	Mar. 23
This Week-End		Lee-Bradford (S. R.)		
Thundering Landlords	Glenn Tryon	Pathe	2 reels	June 27
Too Young to Marry	Buddy Messinger	Universal	2 reels	
Tough Night, A	Jimmy Callahan	Aywon Film	2 reels	
Tourist, The	Harry Langdon	Educational Film	2 reels	Aug. 15
Tourists De Luxe	Hayes-Karr	Universal	2 reels	May 16
Transients in Arcadia		Fox	2 reels	
Transatlantic Flight, A	"Aesop's Fables"	Pathe	1 reel	
Twins	Stan Laurel	F. B. O	2 reels	
Two Cats and a Bird	"Cartoon"	Educational	1 reel	Mar. 14
Two Poor Fish	Earl Hurd cartoon	Educational	1 reel	May 30
Uncle Tom's Girl	Edna Marian	Universal	2 reels	
Unwelcome	Charles Puffy	Universal	1 reel	June 27
Waiting	Lloyd Hamilton	Educational	2 reels	July 11
Wake Up	Bowes-Vance	Educational	1 reel	June 13
Water Wagons	Special Cast	Pathe	2 reels	Feb. 21
Welcome Dangar	Bowes-Vance	Educational	1 reel	Feb. 23
West is West	Billy West	Arrow	2 reels	
What Price Goofy	Charley Chase	Pathe	2 reels	June 6
When Dumbells Ring		Fox	2 reels	
When Men Were Men	"Aesop's Fables"	Pathe	1 reel	July 25
White Wing's Bride	Harry Langdon	Pathe	2 reels	July 11
Whose Baby Are You?	Glenn Tryon	Pathe	2 reels	
Why Hesitate?	Neal Burns	Educational	2 reels	April 11
Why Sitting Bull Stood Up		Sering Wilson (S. R.)	1 reel	
Wide Awake	Lige Conley	Educational	2 reels	
Wild Papa	"Spat Family"	Pathe	2 reels	May 16
Wild Waves	Bowes-Vance	Educational	1 reel	May 23
Wine, Woman and Song	"Aesop's Fables"	Pathe	1 reel	
Wooly West, The	Buddy Messinger	Universal	2 reels	
Wrestler, The	Earle Foxe	Fox	2 reels	Aug. 29
Yarn About Yarn, A	Aesop Fable	Pathe	1 reel	Aug. 1
Yes, Yes, Nannette	Jas. Finlayson	Pathe	1 reel	Aug. 1

Short Subjects

Feature	Distributed by	Length	Reviewed
Action (Sportlight)	Pathe	1 reel	
All Under One Flag (Sportlight)	Pathe	1 reel	
Animal Celebrities (Sportlight)	Pathe	1 reel	June 27
Animated Hair Cartoon (Series)	Red Seal (S. R.)	1 reel	
Balto's Race to Nome (Special)	Educational	2 reels	May 23
Barbara Snitches (Pacemaker Series)	F. B. O.	2 reels	
Battle of Wits (Josie Sedgwick)	Universal	2 reels	July 18
Bashful Whirlwind, The (Edmund Cobb)	Universal	2 reels	
Beauty and the Bandit (Geo. Larkin)	Universal	2 reels	July 4
Beauty Spots (Sportlight)	Pathe	1 reel	April 18
Best Man, The (Josie Sedgwick)	Universal	2 reels	Aug. 15
Broken Trails	Denver Dixon (S.R.)	2 reels	
Cabaret of Old Japan	M. J. Winkler (S.R.)	1 reel	
Color World	Sering Wilson (S. R.)	1 reel	
Captured Alive (Helen Gibson)	Universal	2 reels	July 25
Close Call, The (Edmund Cobb)	Universal	2 reels	
Coccon to Kimona	M. J. Winkler (S.R.)	1 reel	
Come-Back, The (Benny Leonard)	Henry Ginsberg-S.R.	2 reels	
Concerning Cheese (Varieties)	Fox	1 reel	
Covered Flagon, The (Pacemaker Series)	F. B. O	2 reels	
Cowpuncher's Comeback, The (Art Acord)	Universal	2 reels	
Cross Word Puzzle Film (Comedy-Novelty)	Schwartz Enterprises (S. R.)	1 reel	
Cuba Steps Out (Variety)	Fox	1 reel	
Day With the Gypsies	Red Seal Pict. (S. R.)	1 reel	
Divertisement (Color Shots)	Sering Wilson (S. R.)	1 reel	
Don Coo Coo (Pacemakers)	Film Book. Offices	2 reels	
Do You Remember (Gems of Screen)	Red Seal (S. R.)	1 reel	
Dude Ranch Days (Sportlight)	Pathe	1 reel	May 30
Earth's Other Half (Hodge-Podge)	Educational	1 reel	June 6
East Side, West Side	DeForrest (S. R.)		
Fast Male, The (Pacemakers)	Film Book. Offices	2 reels	
Fighting Cowboy (Series)	Universal		
Fighting Ranger (Serial)	Universal	15 episodes	Feb. 7
Fighting Schoolmarm (Josie Sedgwick)	Universal	2 reels	Aug. 1
Film Facts	Red Seal (S. R.)	1 reel	
Fire Trader, The (Serial)	Universal	15 episodes	
Floral Feast, A	Sering Wilson (S.R.)	1 reel	
Frederick Chopin (Music Masters)	Jas. A. Fitzpatrick (S. R.)	1 reel	
From Mars to Munich (Varieties)	Fox	1 reel	April 4
Frontier Love (Billy Mack)	Denver Dixon	2 reels	
Fugitive Futurist	Cranfield & Clarke (S. R.)		
George F. Handel (Music Masters)	Jas. A. Fitzpatrick (S. R.)	1 reel	
Gems of the Screen	Red Seal (S. R.)	1 reel	
Ghost City, The (Serial)	Universal	15 episodes	
Golden Panther, The (Serial)	Pathe		
Great Circus Mystery, The (Serial)	Universal	15 episodes	
Great Decide, The (Pacemakers)	Film Book. Offices	2 reels	
He Who Gets Rapped (Pacemakers)	Film Book. Offices	2 reels	
Hittin' the Trail (Fred Hank)	Sierra Pict. (S. R.)	2 reels	
Idaho (Serial)	Pathe	10 episodes	Feb. 24
If a Picture Tells a Story	Cranfield & Clarke (S. R.)		
In a China Shop (Variety)	Fox	1 reel	
In the Spider's Grip (Novelty)	Educational	1 reel	April 11
Jazz Fight, The (Benny Leonard)	Henry Ginsberg (S. R.)	2 reels	
Judge's Cross Word Puzzle (Novelty)	Educational	1 reel	Jan. 31
Klondike Today (Varieties)	Fox	1 reel	
Knockout Man, The (Mustang)	Universal	2 reels	July 11
Land of the Navajo (Educational)	Fox	1 reel	
[illegible]earning How (Sportlight)	Pathe	1 reel	July 18
[illegible]pard's [illegible]	Universal	Serial	
[illegible] Paint	Cranfield & Clarke (S. R.)		
Line Runners, The (Arnold Gregg)	Universal	2 reels	
Little People of the Garden (Secrets of Life)	Educational	1 reel	
Little People of the Sea (Secrets of Life)	Educational	1 reel	Feb. 28
Lizzie's Last Lap	Cranfield & Clarke (S. R.)		
Loaded Dice (Edmund Cobb)	Universal	2 reels	April 4

Feature	Distributed by	Length	Reviewed
Luna-cy (Stereoscopik)	Pathe	1 reel	
Mad Miner, A (Western)	Hunt Miller (S. R.)	2 reels	
Magic Hour, The	Red Seal Pict. (S. R.)	1 reel	
Man Who Rode Alone, The	Miller & Steen (S.R.)	2 reels	
Marvels of Motion	Red Seal (S. R.)	1 reel	
Marvellous Manhattan	M. J. Winkler (S. R.)	1 reel	
Merry Kiddo, The (Pacemakers)	Film Book. Offices	2 reels	
Merton of the Goofies ... "Pacemaker"	F. B. O.	2 reels	
Mexican Melody (Hodge-Podge)	Educational	1 Reel	
Mexican Oil Fields	M. J. Winkler (S. R.)	1 reel	
Movie Morsels (Hodge Podge)	Educational	1 reel	April 4
My Own Carolina (Variety)	Fox	1 reel	Aug. 29
Mystery Box, The (Serial)	Davis Dist. Corp.	10 episodes	
Neptune's Nieces (Sportlight)	Pathe	1 reel	
New Sheriff, A (Western)	Hunt Miller (S. R.)	2 reels	
Olympic Mermaids (Sportlight)	Pathe	1 reel	
One Glorious Scrap (Edmund Cobb)	Universal	2 reels	
Only a Country Lass (Novelty)	Educational	1 reel	May 29
Ouch (Stereoscopik)	Pathe	1 reel	
Our Six-legged Friends (Secrets of Life)	Educational	1 reel	
Outlaw, The (Jack Perrin)	Universal	2 reels	
Paris Creations (Novelty)	Educational	1 reel	Feb. 7
Paris Creations in Color (Novelty)	Educational	1 reel	Feb. 28
People You Know (Screen Almanac)	Film Booking Offices.	1 reel	
Perfect View, The (Varieties)	Fox	1 reel	
Pictorial Proverbs (Hodge Podge)	Educational	1 reel	Aug. 15
Plastigrams (Novelty)	Educational		
Play Ball (Serial)	Pathe	10 episodes	June 27
Power God, The (Serial)	Davis Dist. Div. (S.R.)	15 episodes	
Pronto Kid, The (Edmund Cobb)	Universal	2 reels	June 27
Queen of the Round-Up (J. Sedgwick)	Universal	2 reels	June 13
Race, The (Van Bibber)	Fox	2 reels	
Record Breaker, The	Pathe	Serial	
Rim of the Desert (Jack Perrin)	Universal	2 reels	
River Nile, The (Variety)	Fox	1 reel	
Roaring Waters (Geo. Larkin)	Universal	2 reels	
Rock Bound Brittany (Educational)	Fox	1 reel	
Ropin' Venus, The (Mustang Series)	Universal	2 reels	July 11
R. Valentino and Eighty-eight Prize-winning American Beauties	Chesterfield (M. P. Corp.) (S. R.)	3 reels	
Secrets of Life (Educational)	Principal Pict. (S. R.)	reel	Feb. 21
Seven Ages of Sport (Sportlight)	Pathe	1 reel	Aug. 22
Shadow of Suspicion (Eileen Sedgwick)	Universal	2 reels	
Show Down, The (Art Acord)	Universal	2 reels	
Sky Tribe, The (Variety)	Fox	1 reel	
Smoke of a Forty-Five, The (Western)	Hunt Miller (S. R.)	2 reels	
Soft Muscles (Benny Leonard)	Ginsberg (S. R.)	2 reels	
Song Cartunes (Novelty)	Red Seal Pict. (S. R.)	1 reel	
Sons of Swat (Sportlight)	Pathe	1 reel	Aug. 15
Sporting Judgment (Sportlight)	Pathe	1 reel	Ma 9
Steam Heated Islands (Varieties)	Fox	1 reel	
Stereoscopic (Novelty)	Pathe	1 reel (Series)	May 16
Storm King (Edmund Cobb)	Universal	2 reels	
Straight Shootin' (Harry Carey)	Universal	2 reels	
Strangler Lewis vs. Wayne Munn	Educational	2 reels	July 4
Stratford on Avon (Gems of Screen)	Red Seal Pict. (S. R.)	1 reel	
Sunken Silver (Serial)	Pathe	10 episodes	April 18
Surprise Fight, The (Benny Leonard)	Henry Ginsberg (S. R.)	2 reels	
Thundering Waters (Novelty)	Sering D. Wilson (S. R.)	1 reel	April 25
Tiger Kill, The (Pathe Review)	Pathe		
Toiling for Rest (Variety)	Fox	1 reel	
Traps and Troubles (Sportlight)	Pathe	1 reel	Mar. 21
Travel Treasures (Hodge Podge)	Educational	1 reel	July 25
Turf Mystery (Serial)	Chesterfield Pict. Corp. (S. R.)	15 episodes	
Valley of Rogues (Western)	Universal	2 reels	April 18
Van Bibber and the Navy (Earle Foxe)	Fox	2 reels	
Village School, The (Hodge Podge)	Educational Film	1 reel	May 9
Voice of the Nightingale, The (Novelty)	Educational	1 reel	Mar. 28
Waiting For You (Music Film)	Hegerman Music Novelties (S. R.)		
Welcome Granger (Pacemakers)	Film Book. Offices	2 reels	
West Wind, The (Variety)	Fox	1 reel	
What Price Gloria (Pacemakers)	Film Book. Offices	2 reels	
Wheels of the Pioneers (Billy Mack)	Denver Dixon	2 reels	
Where the Waters Divide (Varieties)	Fox	1 reel	
White Paper (Varieties)	Fox	1 reel	
Wild West Wallop, The (Edmund Cobb)	Universal	2 reels	May 16
With Pencil, Brush and Chisel	Fox	1 reel	
Wonder Book, The (Series)	Sering D. Wilson	500 feet	April 25
Young Sheriff, The (Tom. Forman)	Miller & Steen (S. R.)	2 reels	
Zowie (Stereoscopik)	Pathe	1 reel	

Coming Attractions

Feature	Star	Distributed by	Length	Reviewed
Ace of Spades, The	Desmond-McAllister	Universal		
Age of Indiscretion		Truart (S. R.)	5800 feet	
American Venus, The	Special Cast	Paramount		
An Enemy of Men		Columbia Pict. (S. R.)		
An Old Man's Darling	Laura La Plante	Universal		
Another Woman's Life	Mary Philbin	Universal		
Aristocrat, The	Special Cast	B. P. Schulberg (S. R.)		
Ashes	Corinne Griffith	First National		
Atlantis		First National		
Back Wash	Mary Pickford	United Artists		
Bad Lands, The	Harry Carey	Prod. Dist. Corp.		
Barriers of Fire	Monte Blue	Warner Bros.		
Beautiful Cheat, The	Laura La Plante	Universal		
Beautiful City	R. Barthelmess	First National		
Before Midnight	Wm. Russell	Ginsberg (S. R.)	5895 feet	Aug. 8
Beloved Pawn, The	Reed Howes	Rayart (S. R.)		
Ben Hur	Special Cast	Metro-Goldwyn		
Beyond the Law	Jack Hoxie	Universal		
Big Parade, The	John Gilbert	Metro-Goldwyn		
Blackmail	Special Cast	Universal		
Blind Virtue	Special Cast	Atlas Educ. Co. (S. R.)		
Boden's Boy	Special Cast	Hepworth Dist. (S. R.)	5300 feet	
Border Intrigue	Franklyn Farnum	Inde. Pict. (S. R.)	5 reels	June 6
Border Women	Special Cast	Phil Goldstone (S.R.)	5000 feet	
Broken Hearts of Hollywood	Harlan-Miller	Warner Brothers		

Feature	Star	Distributed by	Length	Reviewed
Brown of Harvard		Metro-Goldwyn		
Captain Fearless	Reginald Denny	Universal		
Cave Man, The	Harlan-Miller	Warner Brothers		
Charity Ball, The		Metro-Goldwyn		
Circle, The		Metro-Goldwyn		
Claim No. 1	Special Cast	Universal		
Clean-Up, The	Richard Talmadge	F. B. O.		
Clinging Fingers	Special Cast	Universal		
Clod Hopper, The	Glenn Hunter	Assoc. Exhibitors		
Clothes Make the Pirate	Errol-D. Gish	First National		
College Widow, The	Syd Chaplin	Warner Brothers		
Coming of Amos	Rod La Rocque	Prod. Dist. Corp.		
Compromise	Irene Rich	Warner Bros.		
Conquered	Gloria Swanson	Paramount		
Count of Luxembourg, The	Larry Semon	Chadwick		
Crashing Through	Jack Perrin	Ambassador Pict. (S. R.)	5000 feet	
Cyclone Bob	Bob Reeves	Anchor Film Dist.		
Cyrano de Bergerac	Special Cast	Atlas Dist. (S. R.)	10 reels	July 18
Dance Madness	Pringle-Cody	Metro-Goldwyn		
Dangerous Currents		First National		
Dark Horse, The	Harry Carey	Prod. Dist. Corp.		
Deerslayer, The		Weiss Bros. (S. R.)	4780 feet	
Demon, The	Jack Hoxie	Universal		
Demon Rider, The	Ken Maynard	Davis Dist.	5000 feet	Aug. 22
Detour		Prod. Dist. Corp.		
Does Marriage Pay		Inde. Pict. Corp. (S. R.)		
Dollar Mark	Mildred Harris-Fraser	F. B. O.		
Down Upon the Swanee River	Special Cast	Lee Bradford (S. R.)		
Dumb Head		Tiffany (S. R.)	6500 feet	
East of the Setting Sun	Constance Talmadge	First National		
Enchanted Hill, The	Special Cast	Paramount		
Ermine and Rhinestone		H. F. Jans (S. R.)		
Exchange of Wives, An	Special Cast	Metro-Goldwyn		
Exquisite Sinner, The	Special Cast	Metro-Goldwin		
Extra Man, The		Universal		
Face to Face	Viola Dana	Metro-Goldwyn		
Face on the Air, The	Evelyn Brent	F. B. O.		
Fair Play	Special Cast	Wm. Steiner (S. R.)		
Fall of Jerusalem		Weiss Bros. (S. R.)	6800 feet	
Fast Pace, The	Special Cast	Arrow		
Fighter's Paradise, The	Rex Baker	Phil Goldstone	5000 feet	
Fighting Courage	Ken Maynard	Davis Dist. Div. (S.R.)	5 reels	July 11
Fighting Edge, The	Harlan-Miller	Warner Brothers		
Fighting Smile, The	Bill Cody	Inde. Pict. Corp. (S.R.)	4630 feet	
First Year, The	Special Cast	Fox		
Flaming Waters		F. B. O.		
Fool, The	Special Cast	Fox		April 25
Forest of Destiny, The		Gotham Prod. (S. R.)		
Forever After	Corinne Griffith	First National		
Fort Frayne	Ben Wilson	Davis Dist.	5000 feet	Aug. 29
Free to Love	C. Bow-R. McKee	B. P. Schulberg (S. R.)		
Friends	Special Cast	Vitagraph		
Frivolity		B. P. Schulberg (S.R.)		
Galloping Dude, The	Franklyn Farnum	Inde. Pict. Corp. (S.R.)	4700 feet	
Garden of Allah		United Artists		
Going the Limit	Richard Holt	Gerson Pict. (S. R.)		
Golden Cocoon		Warner Bros.		
Goose Woman, The	Special Cast	Universal	7500 feet	Aug. 22
Go West	Buster Keaton	Metro-Goldwyn		
Grass			10 reels	Mar. 7
Gulliver's Travels	Special Cast	Universal		
Handsome Brute, The	Columbia Pict. (S. R.)			
Happy Warrior, The		Vitagraph	6 reels	July 18
Hearts and Fists		Assoc. Exhib.		
Hearts and Spangles		Gotham Prod. (S. R.)		
Hell Bent for Heaven		Warner Bros.		
Hell's Highroad	Leatrice Joy	Prod. Dist. Corp.		
Heir's Apparent	Special Cast	First National		
Her Father's Daughter		F. B. O.		
Hero of the Big Snows, A	Rin Tin Tin (dog)	Warner Brothers		
His Jazz Bride	Special Cast	Warner		
His Majesty Bunker Bean	M. Moore-Devore	Warner		
His Master's Voice	Thunder (dog)	Gotham Prod. (S. R.		
His Woman	Special Cast	Whitman Bennett	7 reels	
Hogan's Alley	Harlan-Miller	Warner		
Home Maker, The	Alice Joyce	Universal	7755 feet	Aug. 8
Honeymoon Express, The	M. Moore-D. Devore	Warner Brothers		
Horses and Women		B. P. Schulberg		
Hurricane		Truart (S. R.)	5800 feet	
Inevitable Millionaires, The	M. Moore-Devore	Warner Bros.		
Invisible Wounds	Sweet-Lyon	First National		
Irene	Colleen Moore	First National		
Justice of the Far North		C. B. C. (S. R.)	5500 feet	
Kings of the Turf		Fox		
Kiss for Cinderella, A	Betty Bronson	Paramount		
Knockout Kid, The	Jack Perrin	Rayart Pict. Corp. (S. R.)		
La Boheme	Lillian Gish	Metro-Goldwyn		
Lady Windermere's Fan	Special Cast	Warner Brothers		
Lariat, The	William Desmond	Universal		
Last Edition, The	Ralph Lewis	Film Book. Offices		
Lawful Cheater, The	Bow-McKee	B. P. Schulberg	4946 feet	
Lazybones		Fox Film		
Lena Rivers	Special Cast	Arrow	6 reels	
Life of a Woman		Truart (S. R.)	6500 feet	
Lightnin'	Jay Hunt	Fox	7979 feet	Aug. 1
Lightning Jack	Jack Perrin	Ambassador Pict. (S.R.)	5000 feet	
Lightning Lover, The	Reginald Denny	Universal		
Lightning Passes, The	Al Ferguson	Fleming Prod. (S.R.)		
Lights of New York	Marion Davies	Metro-Goldwyn		
Limited Mail, The	Monte Blue	Warner Bros.		
Little Bit of Broadway	Ray-Starke	Metro-Goldwyn		
Little Girl in a Big City, A		Gotham Prod. (S. R.)		
Little Irish Girl, The	Special Cast	Warner Bros.		
Live Wire, The	Johnny Hines	First National		
Lodge in the Wilderness		Tiffany (S. R.)	6500 feet	
Lord Jim	Percy Marmont	Paramount		
Love Cargo, The	House Peters	Universal		
Love Gamble, The	Special Cast	Banner Prod. (S. R.)	5 reels	July 11
Lover's Island	Hampton-Kirkwood	Assoc. Exhib		
Love Toy, The	Lowell Sherman	Warner Bros		
Loyalties	Special Cast	Fox		
Lucky Lady, The	Lionel Barrymore	Paramount		
Lure of Broadway, The		Columbia Pict. (S. R.)		
Lying Wives	Special Cast	Ivan Abramson (S. R.)	7 reels	May 2
Man and the Moment		Metro-Goldwyn		
Man From Red Gulch	Harry Carey	Prod. Dist. Corp.		
Man of Iron, A	L. Barrymore	Chadwick	6 reels	July 4
Man on the Box, The	Sydney Chaplin	Warner Bros		
Man She Bought, The	Constance Talmadge	First National		
Man Without a Conscience	Louis-Rich	Warner Bros	6850 feet	May 2
Mare Nostrum	Special Cast	Metro-Goldwyn		
Married Hypocrites	Fredericks-La Plante	Universal		
Martinique	Bebe Daniels	Paramount		
Masked Bride, The	Mae Murray	Metro-Goldwyn		

Feature	Star	Distributed by	Length	Reviewed
Men of Steel	Milton Sills	First National		
Memory Lane	Boardman-Nagel	First National		
Merry Widow	Mae Murray	Metro-Goldwyn		
Message to Garcia, A		Metro-Goldwyn		
Miracle of Life, The	Busch-Marmont	Assoc. Exhib		
Miracle of the Wolves, The			10346 feet	Mar. 7
Midnight Flames		Columbia Pict. (S. R.)		
Miss Vanity	Mary Philbin	Universal		
Million Dollar Doll		Assoc. Exhib		
Moonlight Kisses	Mary Philbin	Universal		
Morganson's Finish		Tiffany (S. R.)	6500 feet	
Moving Finger, The	Special Cast	Paramount		
Mystic, The	Special Cast	Metro-Goldwyn		
Napoleon the Great		Universal		
Night Call, The	Rin-Tin-Tin (dog)	Warner Brothers		
Oats for the Woman	Special Cast	Universal		
Old Clothes	Jackie Coogan	Metro-Goldwyn		
Once to Every Man	O'Brien-Dove	Fox Film Corp		
Only Thing, The	Special Cast	Metro-Goldwyn		
Open Trail, The	Jack Hoxie	Universal	4800 feet	May 16
Outlaw Tamer, The	Clayton-F. Farnum	Inde. Pict. (S. R.)		
Pace That Thrills, The	Ben Lyon	First National		
Painted Woman, The	Kirkwood-Lee	Prod. Dist. Corp		
Paris	Pauline Starke	Metro-Goldwyn		
Paris After Dark	Norma Talmadge	First National		
Partners Again		United Artists		
Passionate Quest, The	Marie Prevost	Warner Bros		
Passionate Youth	Special Cast	Truart (S. R.)	6 reels	July 11
Part Time Wife, The		Gotham Prod. (S. R.)		
Peacock Feathers	Virginia Valli	Universal	6747 feet	Aug. 29
Peak of Fate, The		F. B. Rogers	8 reels	June 27
People vs. Nancy Preston	Bowers-De La Motte	Prod. Dist. Corp.		
Phantom of the Opera	Lon Chaney	Universal		
Pinch Hitter, The	Glenn Hunter	Asso. Exhibitors		
Pleasure Buyers, The	Irene Rich	Warner Brothers		
Police Patrol, The	James Kirkwood	Gotham Prod. (S. R.)		
Polly of the Ballet	Bebe Daniels	Paramount		
Pony Express, The	Special Cast	Universal		
Prairie Pirate, The	Harry Carey	Prod. Dist. Corp.		
Prince, The	Philbin-Kerry	Universal		
Purchased Youth	Anna Q. Nilsson	F. B. O.		
Quality Street		Metro-Goldwyn		
Quicker 'n Lightning	Buffalo Bill, Jr.	Weiss Bros. (S. R.)	5 reels	June 13
Racing Blood		Gotham Prod. (S. R.)		
Reckless Courage	Buddy Roosevelt	Weiss Bros. (S. R.)	4851 feet	May 2
Reckless Sex, The	Special Cast	Truart (S. R.)	6 reels	Feb. 14
Red Clay	William Desmond	Universal		
Red Dice	Rod La Rocque	Prod. Dist. Corp.		
Red Hot Tires	Monte Blue	Warner Bros.		
Resurrection		Principal Pict. (S. R.)		
Return of a Soldier	Special Cast	Metro-Goldwyn		
Rime of the Ancient Mariner, The		Fox Film		
Road to Yesterday, The	Special Cast	Prod. Dist. Corp.		
Road That Led Home, The		Vitagraph		
Romance of an Actress		Chadwick		
Ropin' Venus, The	Josie Sedgwick	Universal		
Rose of the World	Special Cast	Warner Bros		
Salvage		Truart (S. R.)	5800 feet	
Sap, The	M. Moore D. Devore	Warner Bros		
Satan in Sables	Lowell Sherman	Warner Bros		
Satan's Son	Special Cast	Inde. Pict. (S. R.)		
Savage, The	Ben Lyon	First National		
Scarlet Saint, The	Lyon-Astor	First National		
Scraps	Mary Pickford	United Artists		
Sea Beast, The	John Barrymore	Warner Bros.		
Sea Woman, The	Sweet-McLaglen	First National		
Seven Days	Lillian Rich	Prod. Dist. Corp.		
Seven Sinners	Marie Prevost	Warner Bros.		
Seventh Heaven	Special Cast	Fox		
Shadow of the Wall		Gotham Prod. (S. R.)		
Shadow of the Mosque	Odette Taylor	Cranfield & Clarke (S. R.)	6200 feet	
Shenandoah		B. P. Schulberg (S. R.)		
Ship of Souls	B. Lytell-L. Rich	Assoc. Exhib	6800 feet	
Shootin' Square	Jack Perrin	Ambassador Pict. (S.R.)	5000 feet	
Siegfried		Ufa		
Sign of the Claw		Gotham Prod. (S. R.)		
Silken Shackles	Irene Rich	Warner Bros.		
Silver Treasure, The	Special Cast	Fox		
Simon the Jester	Rich-O'Brien	Prod. Dist. Corp.		
Skyline of Spruce, The	Special Cast	Universal		
Social Highwayman, The	Harlan-Miller	Warner Brothers		
Some Pun'kins	Chas. Ray	Chadwick		
Souls Adrift	Rosemary Davies	Assoc. Exhib		
Souls That Pass in the Night	Special Cast	Universal		
Spanish Sunlight	LaMarr-Stone	First National		
Span of Life	Betty Blythe	Banner Prod. (S. R.)		
Speed Limit, The		Gotham Prod. (S. R.)		
Splendid Road, The	Anna Q. Nillsen	First National		
Steele of the Royal Mounted		Vitagraph	6 reels	June 27
Stella Dallas		United Artists		
Stella Maris	Mary Philbin	Universal		
Still Alarm, The	Chadwick-Russell	Universal		
Strange Bedfellows		Metro-Goldwyn		
Storm Breakers, The	House Peters	Universal		
Sunshine of Paradise Alley	Special Cast	Chadwick Pict.		
Super Speed	Reed Howes	Rayart (S. R.)		
Sweet Adeline	Charles Ray	Chadwick		
Tale of a Vanishing People		Tiffany (S. R.)	6500 feet	
Tearing Loose	Wally Wales	Weiss Bros. (S. R.)	4900 feet	June 13
Temptress		Metro-Goldwyn		
Ten to Midnight		Prod. Dist. Corp.		
Tenderfoot, The	Jack Hoxie	Universal		
That Man from Arizona	D. Revier-W. Fairbanks	B. F. O.		
That Royle Girl	Kirkwood-Dempster	Paramount		
This Woman	Special Cast	Fox		
Three Bad Men	Special Cast	Fox		
Three Faces East		Prod. Dist. Corp.		
Tower of Lies	Chaney-Shearer	Metro-Goldwyn		
Trailing Shadows	Edmond Lowe	Fox Film		
Travelin' Fast	Jack Perrin	Ambassador Pict. (S. R.)	5000 feet	
Travis Coup, The		Tiffany (S. R.)	6500 [illegible]	
Twin Sister, The	Constance Talmadge	First National		
Two Blocks Away	Special Cast	Universal		
Unchastened Woman, The	Theda Bara	Chadwick (S. R.)		
Unguarded Hour, The	Sills-Kenyon	First National		
Unknown Lover, The	Elsie Ferguson	Vitagraph		
Up and At 'Em	Jack Perrin	Ambassador Pict. (S. R.)	5000 feet	
Valiant Gentleman, The		Prod. Dist. Corp.		
Vengeance of Durand, The	Irene Rich	Warner Brothers		
Viennese Medley	Special Cast	First National		

WILLIAMS PRESS, INC.
ALBANY — NEW YORK

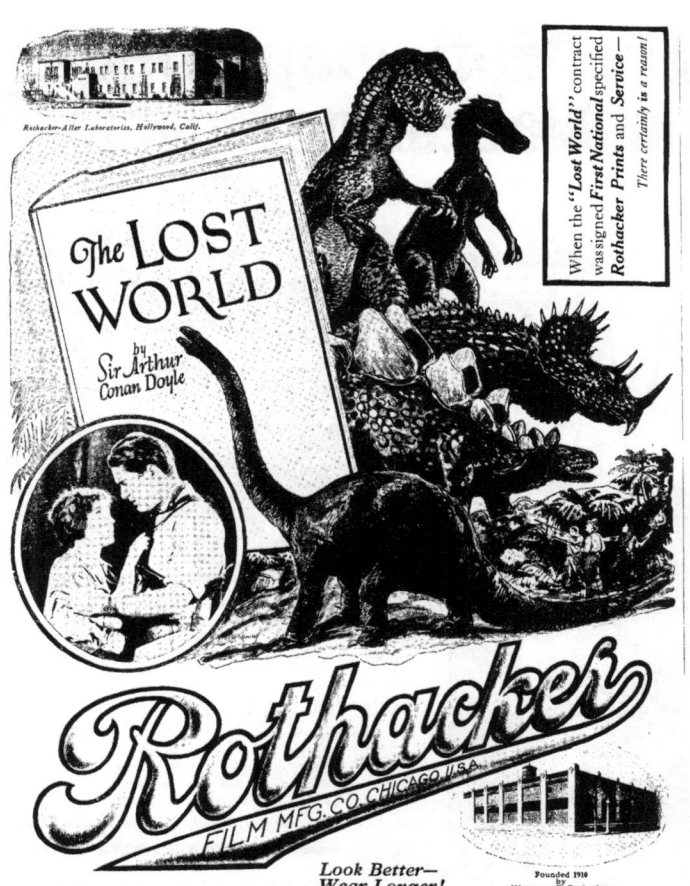

Rothacker-Aller Laboratories, Hollywood, Calif.

The LOST WORLD

by Sir Arthur Conan Doyle

Rothacker
FILM MFG. CO. CHICAGO U.S.A.

Look Better—
Wear Longer!

Founded 1910
by
Watterson R. Rothacker

September 12, 1925

Motion Picture
News

Reg. U. S. Patent Office

Entered as Second Class Matter

XXXII   No. 11

Published Every Week {
  Subscription, $2.00 Year
  Los Angeles, $3.00 Year
  Foreign Canada $3.00 Year
}

PRICE, 20 CENTS

Athens   —   Los Angeles   —   New York   —   Chicago

"The best picture Tom has had in a long, long time!" — N.Y. DAILY NEWS

Meighan in a great story of love and regeneration written especially for him by Booth Tarkington. Backed by the greatest all-star cast you've seen in months. Will top any Meighan week you've ever had—and that's going some! Get it and boost it. It's worth it.

ADOLPH ZUKOR and JESSE L. LASKY present

THOMAS Meighan
in
"THE MAN WHO FOUND HIMSELF"

with VIRGINIA VALLI

Adapted from the original screen story by BOOTH TARKINGTON
Scenario by TOM J. GERAGHTY   Directed by ALFRED E. GREEN

A Paramount Picture

On the right is a teaser ad idea used very successfully in New York. Get a still of Meighan and cut it off to show just a portion of face. Ask your public "Can you find 'The Man Who Found Himself'?" Start with very small portion of face and show more and more each day.

on't
yo
Goose Woman .

Says The New York Morning Telegraph

"An unusually good picture."
Evening World—New York

"An unusually interesting production. A drama well worth seeing."
New York Times

"The whole film is interesting. Ranks among the leaders."
Evening Telegram—New York

"The Goose Woman" does far better than the average.
Morning World—New York

"The Goose Woman" is well worth a visit.
The Sun—New York

"AT last a flaw-less production! Great crowd waited in the lobby"

Write Tom MacDonald, Florence Theatre, West Coast-Langley Circuit, Pasadena, Calif.

"Seizes attention from the first. Continuously interesting."
N. Y. Evening Post

"A fine film play finely played. Suspense well sustained."
St. Louis Post

"The uncanny charm in the story is retained in the screen."
St. Louis Star

"A darned fine picture should mean a lot at the box office."
Danny in Film Daily

"Among the best of the year. Business picked up tremendously at the Colony."
N. Y. Telegraph

"The Goose Woman" a splendid picture. Wonderful entertainment.
James R. Quirk—Ed. Photoplay Magazine.

Not in a long time has there been so good a picture. Should prove highly satisfactory to theatre goers.
Harrison's Reports.

Most remarkable picture I've seen in a long time.
Harry Carr—Los Angeles Times.

Audience picture with interest from start to fade-out.
Glendale Theatre—Los Angeles, Cal.

REX BEACH'S "GOOSE WOMAN"

with a great cast featuring Jack PICKFORD Louise DRESSER and Constance BENNETT
UNIVERSAL JEWEL
Presented by Carl Laemmle

A CLARENCE BROWN PRODUCTION

UNIVERSAL MILES AND MILES AHEAD OF ALL

STAR ONE SHEETS: *Available at regular cost at all Universal Exchanges.*

JUST BECAUSE YOU HAVE been given the chance of a lifetime to make money on a group of pictures sold to you at an unusually low rental in Universal's Complete Service Contract—don't stop after signing!

GET OUT AND ADVERTISE, exploit and boost these crackerjack box office pictures just as you would if you had bought them on an individual basis at the regular rental.

HERE IS YOUR GOLDEN opportunity to make EXTRA PROFITS! Don't miss the big chance. Step out!

UNIVERSAL IS STANDING BY ready to help you. It is offering you a special press sheet, posters, slides, ads and lobby cards *in addition* to the regular press sheets and accessories on the individual pictures.

FREE: *Slide announcing closing of Complete Service Contract.*

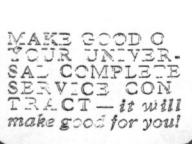

MAKE GOOD ON YOUR UNIVERSAL COMPLETE SERVICE CONTRACT — *it will make good for you!*

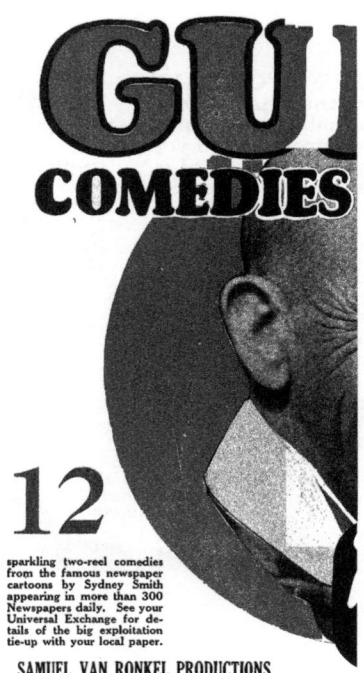

GU[
COMEDIES

12

sparkling two-reel comedies
from the famous newspaper
cartoons by Sydney Smith
appearing in more than 300
Newspapers daily. See your
Universal Exchange for details of the big exploitation
tie-up with your local paper.

SAMUEL VAN RONKEL PRODUCTIONS

ROWN
COMEDIES

12

hilarious comedy gems, two
reels each, made from the
world-famous newspaper
cartoons by R. F. Outcault.
Featuring the famous
comedy characters, Buster
Brown, Mary Jane and Tige,
enjoyed and loved by
readers of all ages for years
and years.

SAL

Produced by CENTURY COMEDIES

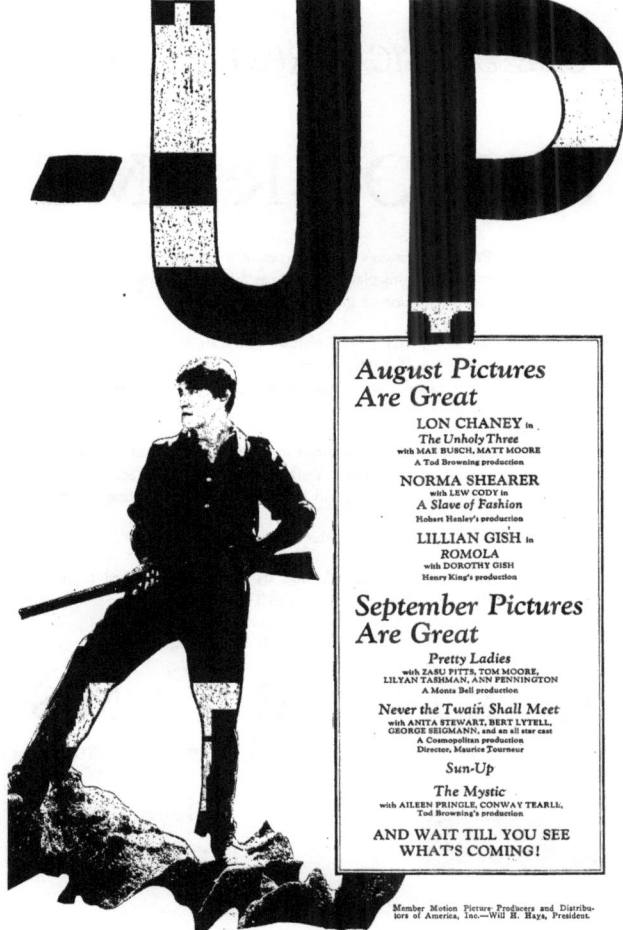

THE MAGIC CARPET of TODAY

--- IS ---

KINOGRAMS

Prince Houssain's magic carpet of oriental fable that flew with its owner from place to place at his slightest wish, never ran out of gasoline or got a puncture

It was a pretty good invention of the story teller of those times, and he could hardly be expected to foresee another kind of a magic carpet that brings the world to you and saves you the trouble and expense of travelling

KINOGRAMS the news reel in its latest issue whisked its audiences from New York to Japan, to Sweden, to Buenos Ayres, to California, and back again in the twinkling of an eye

KINOGRAMS is faster than lightning

Its scope is world-wide and its cameramen will be found in the out-of-the-way places as well as the big centres

See the news of the world with KINOGRAMS

BOOK # K I N O G R A M S
The News Reel Built Like a Newspaper

EDUCATIONAL
FILM EXCHANGES, Inc.

Member, Motion Picture Producers and Distributors
of America, Inc.   Will H. Hays," President

The William Fox
following theatres in
CIRCUITS

William Fox

United Booking Offices

Marcus Loew

B. L. M. Operating Co.

Leo Brecher

Walter Reade

Rachmille & Rinzler

Heights Theatres Inc.

A. H. Schwartz

Sol Brill

Sydney Cohen

Al Suchman

Schwartz & Muller

Allwon

Midtown

Wolff & Springer

Goldreyer & Gould

J. Fitzgibbons

Chas. O'Reilly

H. Botjer

Dave Snaper

Jenill & Pekilner

Wm. & Harry Brandt

Katz & Rosensweig

C. Frankenthal

M. Chrystmus

Joseph Stern

Louis Rosenthal

Haring & Blumenthal

Morris Kutinsky

Pete Woodhull

Walter Hoffman

Louis Nelson

Rosen & Salkin

Rosenblatt-Allen

Jack Ungerfeld

Charles Moses

Fred Baker

Hy Gainsborough

C. Newbury

RIDING HIGH
from the HARDBOILED

REVIEWS
FOX NEWS
MIGHTIEST OF ALL

REVIEWS
EARLE FOXE in
VAN BIBBER COMEDIES

"SHOES"
O. Henry Comedy

O. Henry, beloved of thousands, has finally reached the screen . . . one of the best short comedies ever screened. . . . Exploit this as an O. Henry story and do not hesitate to promise your patrons several thousand feet of merriment.—*Exhibitors Trade Review.*

You'll have to look a long time before you'll find a more amusing comedy. . . . Any exhibitor should be glad to get it. . . .—*Sunday Telegraph.*

"Shoes" is amusing and entertaining and there's the customary touch of O. Henry romance that makes it all the more pleasing. . . . Good clean comedy entertainment.—*Film Daily.*

It is all thoroughly amusing and holds the interest. There are lots of laughs.—*Moving Picture World.*

A delightful comedy worthy of feature honors in the theatre billing. . . . Excellently acted and produced . . . should score a big hit and a box office success.—*Motion Picture News.*

"A BUSINESS ENGAGEMENT"
Married Life of Helen and Warren Comedy

Has enough plot for a feature. More than many. . . . It has been produced on a lavish scale. . . . This series should be very popular.—*Exhibitors Trade Review.*

A step forward in its field. . . . Altogether a first-class offering which will be at home among the very best audiences.—*Morning Telegraph.*

Clean, wholesome comedy entertainment, nicely produced and with a good cast . . . brings its laughs along readily and has some quite new twists.—*Film Daily.*

There are a number of excellent touches and genuine laugh-provoking situations and the comedy is thoroughly worth while.—*Moving Picture World.*

"THE WRESTLER"
Earle Foxe in a Van Bibber Comedy

Exceptionally good comedy . . . does not rely upon slapstick humor . . . but gets smiles through logically developed humorous situations. . . .—*Exhibitors Trade Review.*

It is elaborately mounted and well cast. In fact it looks as if the Fox Company had determined to do right by Van Bibber.—*Morning Telegraph.*

The production is on a big scale and they've spent considerable in making these comedies. . . . Good comedy business . . . suitable for any program.—*Film Daily.*

A striking feature of the new Van Bibber series is the big scale on which they have been produced. . . . Great cleverness and ingenuity have been displayed.—*Moving Picture World.*

A highly amusing picturization of one of Van Bibber's adventures in Russia with several hilarious wrestling matches . . . sound entertainment value and high quality.—*Motion Picture News.*

"SWEET MARIE"
An Imperial Comedy

There is every indication that no expense or pains were spared to make this a good comedy. And it is good.—*Morning Telegraph.*

FOX $2,000,000 SHORT SUBJECT PROGRAM
Fox Film Corporation

WITH PRAISE
TRADE REVIEWERS

REVIEWS O. HENRY COMEDIES

REVIEWS THE MARRIED LIFE OF HELEN AND WARREN

REVIEWS Fox VARIETIES THE WORLD WE LIVE IN

REVIEWS Imperial COMEDIES

Is sure-fire comedy business that will get laughs anywhere and its gags draw howls more often than laughs.—*Film Daily.*

Thoroughly amusing and fast moving . . . good burlesque war stuff. . . . There is a real story. . . .—*Moving Picture World.*

Finely acted and produced . . . of the type which appeals to all classes of screen fans.—*Motion Picture News.*

"MY OWN CAROLINA"
Fox Variety

It is a beautiful scenic and cannot help but cause the city dwellers to long for Carolina or some place equally alluring.—*Exhibitors Trade Review.*

You are given some mighty beautiful views. The photography is essentially good and they've secured some very fine shots.—*Film Daily.*

There are a number of beautiful shots of forest, mountain and stream. . . . This has been varied by interesting scenes showing the hunting of quail with bird dogs. . . . A thoroughly entertaining subject.—*Moving Picture World.*

Here is the "travel" picture at its best. . . . The type of picture that will gain admiration for the screen and increase the prestige of the cinema. . . . It is entertaining, beautiful and instructive.—*Motion Picture News.*

FOX SHORT SUBJECTS—LITTLE GIANTS of the SCREEN
Fox Film Corporation.

Member Motion Picture Producers and Distributors of America, Inc.—Will H. Hays, President.

THE SEPTEMBER ISSUE

O F

The Booking Guide

listing releases from March
to September is now being
compiled. ℂ Producers and
distributors are requested to
cooperate in the publica-
tion of this valuable handbook by sending in usual data
pertaining to all pictures
released over this period.

in GRAUSTARK

Presented by . . . . JOSEPH M. SCHENCK
with EUGENE O'BRIEN
A MODERN ROMANCE
by GEORGE BARR McCUTCHEON
Screen version by FRANCIS MARION
A DIMITRI BUCHOWETZKI
PRODUCTION

Photography by . . . . . ANTONIO GAUDIO
Art Direction by CEDRIC GIBBONS and RICHARD DAY
Wardrobe by . . . . ETHEL T. CHAFFIN
Assistant Director . . . . . . WILLIAM COWAN

The most stupendous
box–office success
NORMA TALMADGE
has ever made.

A First National Picture

"GRAUSTARK" represents the very last word in showmanship valuations

1st—*Because* of its star, NORMA TALMADGE, who is second to none as a great attraction at any box office.

2nd—*Because* of the story. "Graustark," by George Barr McCutcheon, is one of the most popular selling novels ever written.

3rd—*Because* of the manner in which this exciting, romantic story has been modernized in every respect and given a treatment that has made it even more appealing than the book.

4th—*Because* of the magnitude of its cast. Directed by Dimitri Buchowetzki, we find the names of Eugene O'Brien, Marc McDermott, Albert Gran, Lillian Lawrence, Wanda Hawley, Winter Hall and Frank Currier as those lending support to Miss Talmadge.

5th—*Because* it will have back of it an extensive advertising campaign which will include use of the Saturday Evening Post.

6th—*Because* from the angle of audience appeal it will be immensely popular with every member of the family. It has action—adventure—romance—clothes—everything to make it a great box office magnet.

A First National Picture

They All See
Big Box-Office

"Will prove a big box-office magnet in any kind of house in any community."--M. P. News.

"A picture that appeals to the fans and brings box-office receipts."--M. P. Today.

"Will help you draw a crowd second only to the circus itself."--Trade Review.

"Filled with sure-fire stuff that will thoroughly entertain the majority. Should be big box-office draw."--World.

D.W.GRIFFITH
presents

SALLY OF THE SAWDUST

with

CAROL DEMPSTER
and W.C. FIELDS

Adapted by FORREST HALSEY *from a stage story by* DOROTHY DONNELLY

NOW BOOKING
UNITED ARTISTS CORPORATION

Mary Pickford	Charles Chaplin
Douglas Fairbanks	D. W. Griffith

Hiram Abrams, President   Joseph M. Schenck, Chairman, Board of Directors

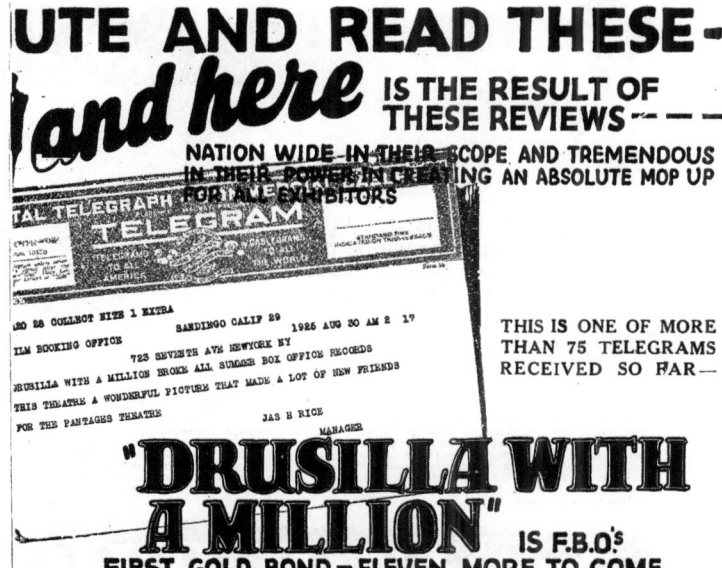

B.P. Schulberg

MARCEL

A new screen

WHAT DANNY SAYS
ABOUT HIS FIRST PRODUCTION

THE *Film* DAILY

EDITORIAL

HERE'S a picture out called, "The Girl Who Wouldn't Work." Get it. And run it. And make yourself not only money. But all that a good picture helps. In building patronage. B. P. ("Ben") Schulberg is the producer Franchise rights all around the country will allow you to get it wherever you are. And you should have it Because it has all the earmarks of a mighty fine box office attraction.

This happens to be what is called an "independent" production. This "independent" phrase has been over-worked to the limit. Frankly, we don't know just what an "independent" is, or is supposed to be But anyway the Schulberg picture is a real box office bet; a real picture, and the best of it is that it comes from practically a brand new director—Marcel de Sano. He made two for Universal several years ago. But they could not touch his latest. It is full of touches, full of delightful surprises, and with a tempo that makes you think it came from the Lubitsch school of expression. There are bits all the way that make you laugh, smile, or feel good. And then, after about five reels, the tempo changes, comedy is replaced with tragedy—a father presumably kills his own daughter And from there to the finish it moves with real dramatic force. This looks like a box office bet for any type of house. There is a fine cast. Incidentally, Marguerite de la Motte never appeared to such advantage as in this De Sano makes her troupe

The GIRL WHO

Presented by
B.P. Schulberg

with

LIONEL BARRYMORE
HENRY B. WALTHALL
LILYAN TASHMAN
WINTER

PREFERRED PICTURES

discover's

DE SANO

genius

WOULDN'T WORK

MARGUERITE De La MOTTE
FORREST STANLEY
THOMAS RICKETTS
HALL

Directed by
Marcel De Sano

B.P. SCHULBERG
PRODUCTIONS INC.

Playing to Tremendous Busine

The First of Forty

"The Lim
with Monte

In a Sensational George Hill Production

Adaptation and Scenario •

SAN FRANCISCO

Nationally Released

"Winds of Chance will blow money into the box-office"

FRANK LLOYD
presents

WINDS of CHANCE

by Rex Beach

with Anna Q. Nilsson, Ben Lyon,
Viola Dana, Victor McLaglen
and a great supporting cast including
Dorothy Sebastian, Robert Barrwth
Story by Rex Beach
Directed by Frank Lloyd
A First National Picture

SRO

FRANK
LLOYD
presents
"WINDS
of
CHANCE"

*and that is what
it sure is doing!*

another great

Jirst National special

Motion Picture News

VOL. XXXII   ALBANY, N. Y., AND NEW YORK CITY, SEPTEMBER 12, 1925   NO. 11

The Connecticut Situation

THERE are two big angles to the Connecticut Tax Matter.

One is the Connecticut situation itself. That is big enough, and its proper solution is going to take the level-headed and united action of the whole industry. For it deeply and gravely concerns the whole industry.

The other angle is the rest of the States of the Union—what they may do. Bear in mind one fact in this connection. There's a gasoline tax today in all of the forty-eight States but five and the District of Columbia. And Connecticut was the first State to impose a gasoline tax.

*   *   *

It is a gross libel upon our State legislative system, but it is a fact, that so mean a factor as a disgruntled employee may originate a bill threatening the existence of an industry. Legislative history is filled with these attempts at personal reprisals, and some have been astonishingly successful. For, once a bill is introduced and given any headway at all—no matter how vicious it may be, how openly and violently uneconomic and unnecessary—it may easily become a political football that in the melee of a closing session, is shot over the goal and into the statute books for no reason at all save gross political expediency.

We speak frankly to the trade because the true lesson of the unfortunate situation in Connecticut is eternal vigilance everywhere against a repetition of so outrageous an act. We are speaking particularly to the exhibitors, to their State organizations, for these State taxes are exhibitors' taxes—always. They affect us all; they are the concern of all, but they are borne by the exhibitor. They have to be.

*   *   *

In the Connecticut case everything is seemingly being done that can be done. We are told that the Association of Producers and Distributors is working in harmony with the State organization and the independent exchanges. Will H. Hays speaks highly of this cooperation. His Association's plan of action, summed up, is: serious procedure along economic and legal lines to correct a most unfortunate situation.

*   *   *

A rehearing has been asked for in Connecticut. In addition, an appeal has been made to the United States Supreme Court, and the case goes on the October Calendar as one of a preferred list.

A fund has been provided to help the State exhibitors meet the present and past taxes (due since the law went into effect). The exhibitors among themselves have arranged a sliding scale of tax payments to take care of over seventy small theatres which cannot meet the tax at all.

All existing contracts between distributor and exhibitor will be carried out, thus insuring a supply of pictures for the State for about six months.

But no further contracts for the exhibition of films within the State are to be made, so far as is now known.

And all exchanges, for good legal reasons, have been removed from the State.

This sums up the situation at this writing.

We are earnestly in hopes that united action and the utmost harmony will continue to prevail within the industry as its fight in Connecticut goes on. That is the only way we will win. The people of Connecticut do not want the law. The State does not need the tax. The newspapers are opposed to it. It is obviously uneconomic and uncalled for. Every right is on our side. And, united—we can win.

W. A. Johnston

MOTION PICTVRE NEWS

September 12
1925

Vol. XXXII
No. 11

Founded in September 1913

Publication Office: Lyon Block, Albany, N. Y.

Editorial and General Offices:
729 7th Ave., New York City

Branch Offices:
845 S. Wabash Ave., Chicago, Ill.
Room 616 Security Bldg., Hollywood, Calif.

"The Forgotten Man and Woman"

ONE of the most forceful editorials that has yet appeared on the Connecticut situation was printed the other day in the New Haven *Journal-Courier*. It goes to the very heart of the matter, and presents an unanswerable argument against the tax. The salient points of the editorial are these:

"Separating Lieutenant Governor J. Edwin Brainard, acting Governor in the absence of Mr. Trumbull from the State, from the subject which caused his comment, namely, the new tax on imported moving picture films, his views upon the subject of taxation in general cannot fail to interest students of economics and sociology. He is reported in the news columns of the local press as saying, apropos of a suggested compromise between the State and the producers, that 'there is nothing to compromise. The ultimate consumer is the only one who pays anything. You and I and the others who paid 20 cents to go to a show will now pay a quarter. That is the gist of the matter. If there is an overwhelming revulsion of public feeling, then there may be another step taken.'

"This brings up for consideration with a whoop Professor Sumner's 'Forgotten Man'. We have taken the liberty in our text to add 'The Forgotten Woman', and might add 'The Forgotten Child', for in the imposition of taxes all three are concerned. It was Professor Sumner's thesis, that too often the government in arranging its tax schedules forgets the forgotten man who in the last analysis pays the bill, which is to say, that it is not so much the welfare of the general run of taxpayers who are kept in mind in perfecting schedules as the more exclusive welfare of the petitioning party for legislative favors. Lieutenant Governor Brainard is sound in his contention, that the ultimate consumer, who is the forgotten man, is the chap who steps to the captain's office by an indirect process and settles, but 'that is not the gist of the matter'. There are other very important considerations to be treated in imposing taxes which Mr. Brainard overlooks. It would be a very simple matter—a mere legislative routine—if the undertaking began and ended with action by the halls of legislation and the cheerful paying of the bills by the ultimate consumer.

"In order to justify a tax, the State or the Federal Government must establish its need for the revenue produced, give assurance that the government itself is economically administered, and that the distribution of the burden shall be as nearly equal as it is possible to make it in human wisdom. In case of war, the need is always so great, and usually greater than was anticipated, that it covers every conceivable source of revenue and no specific explanations are given for utilizing all. The main complaint, which is made today against the federal taxes, is that to a fixed degree they have their justification in war needs only. In the case of this moving picture film tax, which Connecticut has imposed on producers and theatre patrons alike, not one excuse can be found for it under any one of the three heads mentioned above as essential to the determination of its justice. The State does not need the revenue which the tax is intended to create. There is no assurance that in the economical administration of the State government any additional revenue from any source is needed.

"It is impossible to speak of the even distribution of the burden involved, for there is no reason why the burden should be created. This reduces consideration of the tax to the level of at least a theoretical act in confiscation. Confiscation is not confined to taking property without due process of law. It is confiscation to take by State authority property, which with labor is the source of wealth, that is not definitely needed to sustain it.

"The addition of five pennies to the cost of an admission ticket to a moving picture house is just as much of a sin against good government, since it is not needed by the State, as if the additional cost was to be five dollars. The most contented community is that in which the tax rate is the lowest consistent with efficient government. In fact, that is the condition of the best government. Should the State of Connecticut undertake in a like spirit of resolution, which moves President Coolidge in his crusade for greater federal economy, a thorough survey of its balance sheet, and find that it could do the things required of it at half the cost, and set about doing it, an increase in the tax rate of any occupation would bring down upon its head severe condemnation. This would proceed from the indignation of the forgotten man who had suddenly found the courage of his convictions and discovered the hardness of his political muscles.

"Leaving entirely out of consideration the attitude of the moving pictures business, and the activities of its legal advisers and all the speculation as to the legality or illegality of the tax on films, it is an imposition, because it cannot be justified on economic grounds or sound business principles. To denounce the attitude of those directly concerned as a bluff, which may be translated to mean blackmail, is to disregard the false principle upon which the tax is grounded. The loftiest aim of the State should be to treat all of its people with a scrupulous sense of justice and solicitude. In this instance, it has been unjust and indifferent, and in protesting its action the moving picture industry is merely exercising the right which belongs to every citizen, individually or in group organization. The forgotten man had a real grievance as well. Government power has been abused."

September 12, 1925   MOTION PICTURE NEWS   Vol. XXXII, No. 11

Published twice weekly by Motion Picture News, Inc., William A. Johnston, President; E. Kendall Gillett, Vice-President; William A. Johnston, Editor; J. S. Dickerson, Associate Editor; Oscar Cooper, Managing Editor; Fred L. Beecroft, Advertising Manager; L. H. Mason, Chicago Representative; William McCormack, Los Angeles Representative. Subscription price, $3 per year. Saturday Edition $2. Mid Week $1, postpaid in United States, Mexico, Hawaii, Porto Rico, Philippine Islands and some other countries; Canada, $5; foreign, $10.00. Copyright 1924, by Motion Picture News, Inc., in the United States and Great Britain. Title registered in the United States Patent Office and foreign countries. Western Union Cable address is "Picknews," New York. Entered as second-class matter January 31st, 1924, at the postoffice, Albany, N. Y., under the Act of March 3, 1879.

PICTURES AND PEOPLE

Margaret Morris, Paramount featured player, is an expert swimmer, and in giving swimming lessons by radio dresses the part. She was in "The Best People" (Paramount).

E. M. Asher, of Corinne Griffith Productions, signs Conway Tearle to star on his own, the first picture to be "Good Luck," symbolized by the pose here.

SOME NEW FEATURES

AMONG the new feature arrivals on Broadway this week, Metro-Goldwyn's "The Merry Widow," at the Embassy; "The Mystic," at the Capitol; and Paramount's Gloria Swanson picture at the Rivoli, "The Coast Of Folly," register as the most important.

"The Merry Widow," lived up to its advance notices as an elaborate film of great box office possibilities and figures as a sterling example of director Von Stroheim's skill in shaping strong screen drama out of a comparatively slight plot. Mae Murray is pleasing as the heroine and John Gilbert's masterly performance as the gallant prince stands out in such bold relief that it wouldn't be surprising if this picture boomed his stock as a leading man as effectually as did "The Four Horsemen" in Valentino's case.

In general story interest the Swanson film does not rank with that noted star's best productions. Compared with "Manhandled" for instance, it fails in conveying the subtle, intimate human touch which distinguished that picture. This is partially accounted for by the fact that "Manhandled" dealt with a less artificial strata of society. But another reason is that in her latest vehicle Miss Swanson wanted to show what she could do in the line of extensive characterizations and a lot of footage was consequently sacrifice to her ambition. Her dual role called for portrayals of a modern flapper and elderly lady. Both are effective, but whether the Swanson fan cohorts will like their favorite in aged guise remains to be seen. . Colleen Moore, in "So Big," graduated from youth to middle-age, giving one of the finest dramatic performances of her career, yet her following didn't quite approve. They preferred the Colleen they knew and loved—vivacious, pretty, piquant. And assuredly the women folk at least, who gloat over Gloria's gorgeous gowns and slender grace, would sooner see her

Anita Garvin, one of the shapely beauties to be seen in support of Jimmie Adams in the comedies which he is making for Educational release. Lucky Jimmie!

The very newest camera portrait of Aileen Pringle, Metro-Goldwyn-Mayer featured player, who is shortly to begin work in "The Only Thing" (Metro-Goldwyn).

Director Emory Johnson wanted to knock off a bit early one afternoon and let everyone in "The Last Edition" (F. B. O.) go to the ball game—whereupon he was promptly mobbed by the irate staff. If you don't believe it, it isn't so.

Fred Cavens, former world's champion fencer, has taught fencing to the girls in Cecil B. De Mille's stock company—and now look what they're doing to him! Left to right, the embryo stars are Rita Carito, Jocelyn Lee, Josephine Norman, Sally Rand and Mabel Coleman.

First National Sales Convention lined up for the photographer; front row, left to right: I. C. Vergesslich, New Jersey; Charles M. Steele, Stanley Hand, New York; W. K. Callaway, Southern District Mgr.; R. S. Wehrle, Pittsburgh; F. G. Sliter, Seattle; Harry Weiss, St. Louis; C. W. Koerner, Portland; C. J. Appel, publicity, Toronto; C. F. Chan F. P. Bryan, Charlotte; Harry T. Nolan, Mountain District Mgr.; C. R. Beecham, Atlanta; W. H. Mitchell, Vancouver; Floyd Brown, Indianapolis; H. J. Fitzgerald, Milwaukee; E. A. Eßhmann, Manager of Distribution; C. W. Bunn, C. E. Bond, Chicago; W. J. Heenan, Philadelphia, Ad Dept., Home Office; second row: L. Conner, New Orleans; phia; E. H. Teel, Calgary; G. L. Sears, Cleveland; third row: R. E. Pritchard, studio; W. C. Boothby, William Fait, N. H. Brower, Los Angeles; A. W. Smith, Jr., J. S. Abrose, Omaha; T. O. Byerle, Kansas City; W. T. Melady, St. John; A. Gorman, Montreal; E. J. Tilton, Des Moines; J. C. James, Winnipeg; R. H. Haines, Cincinnati; F. E. North, Detroit; F. E. Krieger, Louisville; Leslie Wilkes, Dallas; back row: Robert Hage, Thomas B. Spry, Boston; Allan S. Glenn, Home Office; E. D. Brewer, Oklahoma City; R. C. Seery, Mid-West District Manager; C. H. Muehlman, San Francisco; I. H. Ashby, Denver; W. F. Gordon, Salt Lake City; L. E. Davis, Minneapolis; M. H. Keleher, New Haven; A. J. Herman, Albany; F. J. A. McCarthy, Buffalo; B. D. Murphy, Toronto; S. W. Hatch and Robert Smeltzer, Washington.

enshrined in lasting loveliness than obscured by the shadow of "the sere and yellow leaf."

The success of "The Unholy Three" apparently spurred director Tod Browning to fresh efforts in the underworld field, and he gives us "The Mystic," an entertaining melodrama in which an expose of fake spiritualism figures prominently. Browning has a positive genius for weird suggestion and the art of imparting darkling mystery to a situation, which bears full fruit in deft shaping of the seances held by the crooks to fool their victims.

"Seven Days," the Producers Distributing Corporation's Comedy, at the Colony, just missed being first-chop entertainment because it wasn't kept down to a reasonable length. It consists entirely of farce and slapstick, effective within a certain limit, beyond which they become distinctly monotonous. "The Limited Mail," Warner Brothers, was the attraction chosen for the newly baptized Piccadilly—now the Warner—and proved to be rattling melo of railroad life, with excitement plus, and a train wreck of gorgeous proportions and vivid realism.

Eugene Zukor recently purchased a snappy yacht, the Spendthrift II, and took Mel Shauer and two other friends on a two week cruise. Zukor may be seen with the hatchet, while Shauer has the glass. Judging from the action, the Spendthrift is about to be boarded by buccaneers with grappling irons and cutlasses.

"The Love Hour," Vitagraph, at the Rialto, looks like a throw-back to infantile movie days, offering an antiquated, unconvincing plot, with a shopgirl heroine, young millionaire and bleakly sinister villain cavorting around in the style originally copyrighted by sponsors of stage melodrama of the ten, twenty and thirty cent admission type. Willard Louis and Louise Fazenda contribute lively slapstick comedy that helps to keep the audience in good humor, but with this exception, the film fails utterly to "click".

WARNER THEATRE OPENS

LAST Saturday night the erstwhile Piccadilly theatre opened formally as The Warner, with a band on the outside discoursing familiar melodies, police reserves working heroically to keep the crowds from entirely blocking thoroughfares on Broadway and a crowd within that jammed the house to the S. R. O. mark. Stars, directors, leaders in every department of the industry sent telegrams of felicitation and good wishes. It was a gala night.

Not the least important of the innovations introduced by the new owners is the engagement of Herman Heller as musical director. Mr. Heller comes directly from the Sid Grauman theatres on the Pacific coast, where he has been a popular favorite with all music lovers for a period of many years, having swayed the baton over orchestras at the California in San Francisco, and later at the Metropolitan in Los Angeles. In 1904 he was the featured soloist at the celebrated Steel Pier in Atlantic City. The influence of his guiding hand was clearly to be noted in the greatly improved work of the enlarged orchestra, which from now on takes rank with the best of the symphony organizations.

A LONDON SOUVENIR

FROM Mr. and Mrs. Israel Davis come an elaborate souvenir program of a special showing held at the Shepherd's Bush Pavilion theatre, London, England, in aid of Earl Haig's British Legion Fund, at which the Duke and Duchess of York were in attendance. The subjects shown included the official "Tour of the Prince of Wales;" "Felix the Cat," "Britain's Birthright," being the record of the Empire Tour of the Special Service Squadron" and pictures of the Duke and Duchess, the distinguished guests as they appeared arriving at the Pavilion, presented on the screen one hour and thirty minutes after actual filming.

The Shepherd's Bush Pavilion was built by Mr. Israel, proprietor of the Marble Arch Pavilion and many other London Kinemas. Seating 3,000 people, it is the largest structure of its kind in Europe.

A FAMILY AFFAIR

THE heads of every department of First National, and their wives for gathered at dinner in the Ritz last week. You might call it a family affair, everything was so delightfully informal; business topics completely eliminated, having been thoroughly gone into for two days previous, and the executives looking forward to an early departure for their homes.

Tom Spry of Boston was toastmaster, among those who answered to his clarion call being Sam Spring, Earl Hudson, Al Rockett, Ben Lyon, Lloyd Hughes, Blanche Sweet, Dorothy Sebastian, Nathan Gordon, and others. Dick Rowland told a story, Johnny Hines danced, and the tide of merriment reached high-water mark with the appearance of the inimitable Leon Errol. But, according to Lynde Denig, the great event of the evening was when Tom Spry, stepped to the center of the floor, carrying a traveling bag and suitcase, which Tom informed those assembled were intended as a slight remembrance from the boys to Eddie Eschmann and wife, the donors hoping that Mrs. Eschmann would utilize the suitcase in journeying about the country with her husband.

Eddie Eschmann made a short speech of acknowledgment, thanking his associates for their gift and stating that anything he had accomplished he considered as due to their co-operation, square-dealing and loyalty to right principles. As to the token of comradeship extended to Mrs. Eschmann, he called it the most beau-

Dorothy Mackaill becomes a member of the First National family upon signing a five year contract with John McCormick. Her first under the new agreement will be "Joanna With a Million" (First Nat'l).

"I'm safe on home," says Walter Miller to Allene Ray in "Play Ball" (Pathe). "Just you wait," replies Allene, "we may have a retake."

tiful manifestation of friendship he had ever encountered in a business organization. It was one of those simple, straightforward addresses that has the ring of sincerity and reaches the hearts of an audience. Effective and appealing, because those who listened knew the speaker meant every word he said.

A real family party, this, which will be an inspiration to those present for a long time to come.

VETERAN FRANCONI

LEON FRANCONI, manager of the Film Editing Department at the Home Office of Pathe Exchange, Inc., recently celebrated his seventeenth anniversary with the pioneer film firm. He was the first editor of the Pathe Weekly, now released twice a week as Pathe News.

Mr. Franconi joined Pathe Freres August 16, 1908, when Pathe first invaded this country. Then, all Pathe pictures were made in France and Franconi, viewed the sample prints, cut, edited, titled, and then went forth and sold them to the small houses with which New York abounded. In 1914 he became head executive at the laboratory and studio in Jersey City. In 1915 he served as Charles Pathe's Special Representative, in 1916, was made assistant manager of the production and film editing departments, and in 1917 appointed to the post he now holds. A busy career, with no let-up Mr. Franconi stands elected to the real Veteran Brigade of filmdom.

SETS ARE ENORMOUS

IN the final sequences of "The Road To Yesterday" Cecil B. De Mille is using the largest sets he has made since his production of "The Ten Commandments". The biggest spectacle is a castle 100 feet high, where hundreds of extras assemble to portray a peasant celebration at a gala wedding ceremony.

So far, so good! But when we are further informed that two whole oxen and several suckling pigs were roasted to supply the dining arrangements and huge hogshead offered a continual flow of liquid refreshments, it's time to call a halt. Such statements turn us green with envy, create ravenous hunger, inflamed thirst, and provoke maledictions on the head of the publicist who taunts us thus. Too much realism is oppressive.

IT'S A GIRL!

HENRY CLAY BATE, Universal publicity expert, is wearing "the smile that won't come off," these days. The reason? Enough! For he is now a family man in the strict sense of the word, father of a little lady scaling nine pounds, who made her appearance quite recently. Both mother and child are progressing favorably. The wedding of Geneve Cole to Henry Bate took place last summer. Prior to her marriage, Mrs. Bate was well known as a short story writer, some of her work appearing in leading magazines. MOTION PICTURE NEWS extends due congratulations.

Exhibitors and their families at the Temple theatre, Mount Pleasant,

L. B. Jones, vice-president of the Eastman Kodak Company, presents Will H. Hays with the first of the new model Cine-Kodaks to be produced by that company.

Mike Newman, driving the "Seven Days" (Prod. Dist. Corp.) pre-view car on its cross-continent run, gets his first glimpse of New York from the Jersey meadows on the seventh day. It arrived in New York City on Wednesday.

Ann Pennington, who recently appeared in a special role in "Pretty Ladies" (Metro-Goldwyn), quite appropriately, demonstrated one of the steps that made her famous.

JOYOUS JOHNNY HINES

JOHNNY HINES made a personal appearance at the Hotel Plaza, New York, August 28, at the close of the successful premiere of C. C. Burr's "The Live Wire," this being his initial starring production under First National's banner. He was given a great "hand" by the big crowd, whose enthusiasm over the star was every whit as unbounded as that with which they greeted the picture. After the performance Johnny and C. C. Burr were hosts at a unique party among the guests being Helen Hudson, prima donna of George White's Scandals, and Helen Morgan, the McCarthy Sisters, Sally Starr, Evelyn Martin, Alice Weaver, Jean Williams, Chris Crane, Marjorie Shaw, Bert Kember, Jean Francis of the same show, John Irving Fisher and Miss Chalfonte. The premiere was attended by so many screen celebrities that lack of space prevents personal mention of the lineup, but you can take our word for it that it was a glorious gathering.

EVELYN BRENT HERE

Evelyn Brent, F. B. O. star, is staying at the Commodore Hotel, New York, intending to spent three weeks, solely "on pleasure bent." Miss Brent certainly needs a vacation as she has just completed a series of eight crook melodramas and on her return will start another series of eight for the same company. After attending school and playing in pictures a number of years in Gotham she went to England in 1918, where she appeared on the stage and before the camera for five years. In 1922 she returned to this country and was featured in Metro and Fox pictures. This is her first trip to New York in three years.

There's nothing high hat about Vilma Banky, Valentino's leading woman in "The Lone Eagle" (United Artists). She's merely posing in Rudy's Cossack hat from the film.

The latest thing in beach robes, the gaily pointed shawl, makes its appearance the other day about the shapely person of Shirley Mason, First National.

Hunt Stromberg in his office, making final plans for "The Last Frontier," the Ince production which he will carry to completion for Producers Dist. Corp.

The DeWitt Clinton train of 1831 which was paraded around New York to exploit "the Limited Mail" (Warner Bros.) at the Warner's theatre.

Sally O'Neill, pert and impertinent heroine of "Don't" (Metro-Goldwyn).

Connecticut Situation Still Involved: Plan Payments

Walsh Denies Rumors of Exhibitor Dissatisfaction

RUMORS of a split between the distributors and the Connecticut Motion Picture Theatre Owners over the payment of the tax and the affixing of stamps, credited in newspaper stories to Joseph W. Walsh, president of the Connecticut Theatre Owners, were emphatically denied by Walsh in a telegram to MOTION PICTURE NEWS on Wednesday in which he declared that there was "absolutely no truth in these rumors."

Although last minute reports from New Haven and Hartford were of a scattering and desultory nature, the telegram from Walsh shows that the Connecticut situation stands as follows, up to the time of going to press:

Walsh, Charles C. Pettijohn and Tax Commissioner William H. Blodgett are working out a practical plan for the payment of the tax along lines as convenient and equitable to the industry and to the State of Connecticut as possible. This will include a method for the affixing of the stamps, probably in New York and Boston, the computing of the tax on pictures now showing, and the making of the initial payment. A scale of payments is being worked out under which exhibitors will contribute to the revolving fund.

Application has been made for a rehearing on the constitutionality of the measure before a special term of the Federal court in Connecticut, on the grounds that its constitutionality was previously passed upon as a police power measure, whereas it is in reality a tax or revenue measure.

The case has also been filed with the U. S. Supreme Court, and as it now affects interstate commerce, it will be a preferred case in the matter of priority.

Practically all exchanges have moved out of the state and film shipments are being made from New York and Boston into the state. All contracts are being carried out, although new contracts are not being made for the present.

Tax Commissioner Blodgett has shown every disposition to work with the distributors and exhibitors in order to fix an equitable and effective way of collecting the tax. The proffer of a check earlier in the week was refused by the state, on the ground that no disposition of this money was provided for, but it was expected that a solution of this would be found during the week and that payments would commence.

Meanwhile, conferences are being held rally with Commissioner Blodgett, with distributors and with Connecticut exhibitors, in an effort to work out a plan under which theatres may continue operation despite the tax measure.

The revolving fund created for this purpose will be used in making the initial tax payments and in keeping them up for the present. A scale of payments is being worked out under which exhibitors will help to keep up this fund, one of the favored plans calling for this allotment:

A. 32 theatres at $31 a week, totalling $992 each week.

B. 42 theatres at $21 a week, totalling $882.

C. 48 theatres at $16 a week, totalling $768.

D. 73 theatres to pay nothing.

Under this plan, netting a revenue of $2,642 a week, the larger theatres would carry the smaller ones, many of which would be crippled or heavily handicapped, it is believed, by the imposition of even a small tax. These payments will not suffice to keep the revolving fund up to its present figure, but they are believed to be as heavy as exhibitors can be expected to bear at present.

As soon as the authorities can check up the list of films to be exhibited in Connecticut this week and next, it is expected that the first payment will be computed and collected. Until that time, the actual operation of the tax is held in abeyance.

The matter of affixing the stamps on the prints is also creating serious difficulty at present. Some means can be done in New York and Boston, since the individual exhibitor, who may be located at a great distance from Hartford, can do this only with the greatest difficulty.

As announced, all contracts are being carried out, so far as possible, but no new ones are being entered into for the present. It was rumored that some of the smaller independents were taking advantage of the situation by going out and making contracts for product. These will have to pay their own tax, according to the Hays office, since the revolving fund cannot be used to aid those whom it is felt are operating unfairly in the situation.

The Hartford-Connecticut Trust Co. of Hartford has been designated as the agency for the payment of taxes on all films exhibited in the state.

To date, few theatres have closed, and contracts now in force will provide product for the majority of houses for nearly six months. These contracts will all be carried out, it is emphasized, although the film will be shipped from Boston and New York. This places on the exhibitor a higher transportation cost, but every effort will be made to make shipments on time and get them to the Connecticut houses without delay.

The estimated revenue form the measure, which is admittedly problematical, has been placed at about $75,000 a year. This fact is the basis for the application for a hearing in Connecticut on the constitutionality of the measure. It is contended that the magnitude of the revenue to be derived makes the law a tax or revenue measure and not a police power measure or censorship act. The previous hearing in the Federal court tested the constitutionality of the law as a police power measure, which was upheld. Such a measure, however, must provide for a revenue which covers merely the cost of enforcement. If there is a substantial surplus over the above this, to go into the state treasury, the measure is automatically a revenue one.

The Connecticut hearing will be held as soon as possible, and if this fails, the matter will be carried to the U. S. Supreme court. where the case has already been filed. With the removal of the exchanges from New Haven, all shipments immediately come under the Inter-State Commerce regulations, and any case bearing on the restriction of this automatically takes priority over others in the Supreme court. There are, however, a great many such cases already on the calendar and there may be some little delay before it can be heard.

There is now only one small exchange in operation in New Haven, and 517 persons were thrown out of employment by the enforced closing down. These employes held a mass meeting, at which the mayor of New Haven spoke, and protested the tax law which brought about the situation.

Will H. Hays stated that his office would take "all possible serious procedure along economic and legal lines to correct a most unfortunate situation."

The independent exchange owners of New Haven, members of the Independent Motion Picture Association of America, have co-operated with the steps already taken, it being felt that the situation demanded unanimous action. Frederick H. Elliott, general manager of the association, issued the following statement:

"The Independent Motion Picture Association of America, representing producers,

(Continued on page 1242)

Attorney General's Forces Sift Film Monopoly Charge

New York Times Says Investigation Is Under Way

THE New York *Times* in its issue of September 3rd. carried an interesting news story concerning an investigation that has been instigated by the Department of Justice as to whether there are monopolistic combinations in the industry that violate the provisions of the anti-trust laws.

The trade in general has been aware that such an investigation has been under way but until the present no details have been available.

The *Times* prints the following relative to the action together with some of the details of the Federal Trade Commissions proceedings in the action brought against Famous Players-Lasky Corporation and other respondents all of which has been reported at length in MOTION PICTURE NEWS as the numberless hearings were held in various parts of the country.

The *Times* also says that an official of the Department of Justice stated that in complaints brought to the notice of the Attorney General it was specifically charged that certain moving picture producers and distributers had refused reels to theatres in many cases and that pictures were supplied in innumerable instances under conditions that were regarded as objectionable by exhibitors.

Department of Justice agents also were instructed to make a report on the operations of certain film boards of trade affiliated with the organization headed by Will Hays according to the official.

In prosecuting their inquiries the department agents have visited practically every moving picture centre in the country. They have also examined many individual exhibitors who have brought complaints. Department officials decline to indicate what conclusions have been drawn from reports already received.

The Times story bore a Washington date line and apparently was an exclusive article secured direct from the Department of Justice from authentic sources.

The important portions of the article follow:

A special investigation of the moving picture industry of the United States, conducted by agents of the Department of Justice, to determine whether any monopolistic combination or combinations dominate the trade in violation of the Federal anti-trust laws, is nearing completion and the results soon will be presented for consideration by Attorney General Sargent.

Particular attention has been paid to the activities of the Motion Picture Producers and Distributors of America, of which Will H. Hays, former Chairman of the Republican National Committee, is the head, and the film boards of trade affiliated with the Hays organization.

The investigation, now drawing to a close, was instituted three months ago by order of Attorney General Sargent and is based upon complaints of individual and group theatre owners that they have been damaged by discriminations in the matter of picture distribution, that combinations are in existence that tend to restrain trade in the industry and that these combinations are in violation of the provisions of the anti-trust laws prohibiting unfair practices and agreements as to price fixing.

Every distributing and producing picture group in the country, including so-called independents as well as those associated with the Hays organization and the Hays organization itself, have been and are being subjected to close scrutiny by agents of the Department of Justice, who will soon finish their work in the field and submit their final reports to the Attorney General and his assistants.

Two Investigations Run Parallel

The Department of Justice investigation in the moving picture field, it was said, runs parallel to the like inquiry into the industry made by the Federal Trade Commission, which was based upon an original complaint filed with that body Aug. 30, 1921, and an amended complaint submitted Feb. 14, 923. E. C. Alvord, the chief examiner of the Federal Trade Commission, has made a report in which he sustains charges of the commission against the Famous Players-Lasky Corporation and other picture producing and theatre owning firms named in the original and amended complaints.

It is the understanding that the data collected by the Trade Commission bearing on

the operations of a half dozen or more moving picture corporations shortly will be transmitted to the Attorney General for comparison with the reports on the same subject made by agents of the Department of Justice.

Whether a suit or suits will be filed in the Federal courts to dissolve an alleged combination or combinations in the moving picture field, on the ground that they are violating the anti-trust laws, will be determined at an early date.

Paragraph 5 of the original complaint filed with the Federal Trade Commission summarizes briefly the charges made against the Famous Players-Lasky Corporation and a number of like concerns. It reads:

"The respondents, Adolph Zukor, Jesse L. Lasky and Famous Players-Lasky Corporation have conspired and federated together and with respondents, Jules Mastbaum, Alfred S. Black, Stephen A. Lynch and Ernest V. Richards, Jr., and Realart Pictures Corporation, the Stanley Company of America, Stanley Booking Corporation, Black New England Theatres, Inc., Southern Enterprises, Inc., and Saenger Amusement Company to unduly hinder competition in the production, distribution and exhibition of motion picture films in interstate commerce and to control, dominate, monopolize, or attempt to monopolize the motion picture industry." It was further alleged :

Says Paramount Controls 6,000 Theatres

"As a further result thereof, Famous Players-Lasky Corporation is the largest theatre owner in the world, and in one week theatre owner in the world, and in one week —in the year 1920—more than 6,000 American theatres, or approximately one-third of all the motion picture theatres in the United States, showed nothing but Paramount Pictures, and about 67 cents of every dollar that was paid to enter motion picture theatres was paid to enter those theatres which displayed Paramount pictures."

Substantially, like charges as to other moving picture corporations were made in complaints filed with the Attorney General, with the result that he decided to probe the industry as a whole.

In their reply to the amended complaint of the Federal Trade Commission the Famous Players-Lasky Corporation denied each and every allegation contained in Paragraph 5. They deny the jurisdiction of the Trade Commission, and aver that the act creating the commission is "indefinite, uncertain and in violation of the Constitution of the United States." They declare further that the matters complained of do not constitute interstate commerce. They defend affiliations with certain corporations as a means of competing with other groups of producers. They assert that their acquisition of theatres was solely for investment that such acquisitions have not been lessened, but has been increased and that a monopoly has not been created, but has been prevented."

Germany Key to Important and Growing Film Market

No. 7: Production Prospers and Theatres Thrive

By L. C. Moen

ALTHOUGH Great Britain is today our most lucrative market for American pictures, Germany is pressing close behind and there is every indication that it may even surpass England in this respect. Although the operation of the Kontingent undoubtedly hampers matters somewhat, it also has its benefits. The revenue from Germany, per picture, is increasing and within a year or two should reach a very attractive figure.

While many things in Germany's financial and economic situation still require adjustment, for the most part things are moving toward normal prosperity probably faster in Germany than in any other large European nation.

As has been stated, England has more or less reached its maximum for the present; France has been somewhat poor but shows indications of becoming a good market within the next few years; Germany stands in a point between. A fairly good market, it is growing better and may be expected to reach a point of high development sooner than other countries on the Continent.

The Kontingent may be confidently expected to remain as long as German companies desire to have it, and its removal would be unlikely unless the effort came from them. At the same time, I am not so sure but that a system by which only selected product enters the market is better for everyone concerned than one which permits the indiscriminate dumping of all American films, good or bad, suitable or not.

According to recent statistics, compiled by the Lichtbild-Buehne, there are 3,669 theatres in Germany with a total of 1,315,246 seats. These afford in themselves a fairly lucrative market, and together with other markets available to the German producer offer him a fair chance to make money on productions of a modest type. Germany, of course, leads all other countries, exclusive of America, in scope and volume of production.

New theatre construction is fairly active in Germany—rather more so than elsewhere—and it is interesting to note that the number of theatres with more than 1,000 seats has increased from 58 to 67, since 1921, with several to open very soon. A steady increase is shown all along the line and the theatre field is all that could be expected, in view of conditions the last few years.

As Germany's export business grows, in general manufacturing lines, the prosperity of its people will grow with it. The people in Germany today are spending their money, and whether this is healthy or not, from an economic standpoint, it is profitable for any amusement enterprise.

Many German theatres are antiquated and inadequate—no one will dispute that—but new construction is proceeding as rapidly as can be expected. I am not so certain that the strictly American type of picture theatre would be either wanted or appreciated in Europe.

Our type of front, in particular, seems to be superfluous in Europe. Possibly a taste could be developed for it, but at the present time I do not believe that any elaborate front in the American style would have the slighest effect on business at the box-office. Europeans are accustomed to the severely plain façade and expect nothing more.

Comfort and attractiveness inside are, however, important, American types of ventilating and cooling systems would probably meet with favor. Electric displays before the theatre, such as I saw, were very bad. German poster art is excellent, but the Germans do not seem to have mastered electrical display. Some of the theatre fronts have as many lights as ours, but the placing of them is such as to give a rather cheap and tawdry effect, although the same materials might be rearranged to provide a brilliant and valuable display.

Projection is usually good; in fact, I found projection of surprising excellence throughout Europe. A leading German optical firm put out a projection machine of considerable size but great excellence, which gives clear, steady projection. In several European projection booths I saw devices and attachments of the greatest ingenuity which would undoubtedly be of value here.

The Ufa company has a projection room which deserves a whole article by itself, if space permitted, since it is probably the most remarkable to be found anywhere. Designed for experimental purposes, it has every type of apparatus, every attachment, every feature that could be imagined.

It is in practical features, therefore, that there is the greatest room for improvement. If a leading American theatre architect could go to Germany for some little time, make a thorough study of conditions there, and draw up certain standards and model plans, much good might be accomplished. At present, efforts are being made to copy leading American theatres, but there is some question about the success of this in the absence of experts thoroughly familiar with the building of American cinema palaces.

An effort is being made in Berlin at present to build up a theatre district around the Kurfurstendamm, a leading thoroughfare, where several of the new houses are going up. At the same time, Berlin has a certain similarity to a city such as Chicago, where large and magnificent neighborhood houses are the rule. There is a splendid opportunity in Berlin for the same thing, as the city consists of several "cities within a city," and there are a number of prosperous residential suburbs offering a good field. As an example of this, Ben Blumenthal's Scala theatre, located in a neighborhood district, has been used on a few occasions for showings of pictures, and no difficulty has been found in filling it, although it is the second largest in Berlin.

Your German does not just "drop in at a picture" because he happens to be walking along a certain street. His existence is too well ordered for that. He plans to see a certain picture, has his dinner at a certain hour—and wants to know that he will be able to see the picture. For that reason, the reserved seat policy is in favor, and a lobby display has little selling value. The neighborhood house profits by this, since it is convenient for persons in that particular district to reach.

In a general way, the German public likes good pictures, regardless of what country they were produced in. As far as I could learn, the fact that a picture is German-made neither helps nor hurts it. The questions is: "Is it a good film?" If so, it can be American, Italian, British or any other nationality.

Soon after the war, Western films were tremendously popular, since they came as a distinct novelty, but that popularity has waned. Now they like our big productions, pictures with some novel angle, society or problem plays, such comedians as Chaplin, Lloyd and Keaton—but especially novelty. The picture which has something strikingly unusual about it has an excellent chance on this market. Such pictures as "Nanook" and "King of the Wild Horses" are eagerly welcomed by the German public.

It must be remembered, too, that educational pictures enjoy a popularity in Germany which they have never held here. A special production of this sort, "Ways to Strength and Beauty," was running while I was in Berlin, and despite mid-summer conditions it was doing remarkable business, although the picture has no story or plot in any sense.

Under the Kontingent system, an equivalent footage of German-made film must be distributed for each foreign production, but this system does not guarantee exhibition and American films are heavily in the majority in the theatres. At the same time,

(Continued on page 1243)

Proposes Permanent Campaign Body

Buhler in Letter to Hays Suggests National Organization to Exploit Industry; Cites Movie Season Accomplishments

FORMATION of a permanent national organization of the active men in the Greater Movie Season Campaign to function the year round as an agency to exploit and promote the interests of the picture industry as a whole is proposed in a letter written to Will H. Hays by Frank W. Buhler, managing director of the Stanley Company of America.

In his letter suggesting such a movement Mr. Buhler says:

I am of the opinion that a permanent organization of the active men in the Greater Movie Season Campaign might be perfected —not only for Greater Movie Season each year, but for the general exploitation of the Motion Picture Industry as a whole, bringing it constantly before the public.

The will to do has been the thing that has made the picture industry and I am sure that the motion picture distributors would welcome and would help an organization that would be perfected for the purpose of selling pictures to the public.

Acting immediately upon Mr. Buhler's plan the Greater Movie Season Headquarters is communicating with the general managers of the Campaigns to learn their thoughts regarding the suggestion. If the active workers in the various campaigns favor such a move, the Hays organization will assist in every possible manner, serving the exhibitors with material and acting as a clearing house.

Dorothy Gish May Appear in Stage Play

DOROTHY GISH may make her debut on the speaking stage with her husband, James Rennie, in a contemplated stage version of the film production, "Clothes Make the Pirate," if plans of Sam Rork, producer of the picture, do not miscarry. Miss Gish, is considering the offer made by Rork, who is endeavoring to interest Flo Ziegfeld in associating with him in the venture.

Another name that would add lustre to Rork's plans, if arrangements could be made, is that of Leon Errol, star of "Louis the 14th," the current Ziegfeld New York musical comedy hit. Errol is now dividing his time between appearances in the stage play and the filming of "Clothes Make the Pirate," in which he is starring with Miss Gish. The picture is being produced for release through First National.

Whether or not a definite organization is perfected, the Hays Organization plans to furnish to all exhibitors who can use such material, a service of publicity and advertising matter that can be used as a follow up on this year's Greater Movie Season Campaign, and for leading into next year's. Announcement from the headquarters of the Greater Movie Season Campaign states

that there is no question now as to whether there will be a Greater Movie Season next year. Many exhibitors have declared that the drive should be made an annual affair. Among theatre men in smaller towns who have written to headquarters asking for another campaign next year is Billy Connors of Marion, Ind., who reported his business was "about forty percent better than last year. We certainly do want another next year." John C. Ingram, for the Midwest Amusement and Realty Co., of Scottsbluff, Neb., writes, "We're for Greater Movie Season strong. Please put our name down at the top of the list for 1926."

Charles W. Krebs, general manager of the Louisville campaign, writes, "I am informed that the box office receipts in a number of theatre increased from 20 to 50 percent over the same week last year in spite of the fact that the weather here Sunday to Wednesday was the hottest we have had in Louisville this summer. I have no doubt that Louisville will celebrate Greater Movie Season every year."

Earle D. Wilson of New Bedford, Mass., writes, "Unquestionably this campaign should be made an annual affair. Its business and showmanship possibilities are too evident to need even discussion."

Harry Crandall of Washington, D. C., believes that plans should be made for carrying on the campaign for at least five years.

Labor Strikes On in Four Cities

Musicians Quit Theatres in Des Moines and Cleveland: All Union Workers Out in Niagara Falls—Settlement in Baltimore

THEATRE men and representatives of the Musicians' Unions in Cleveland and DesMoines failed to reach an agreement over contracts calling for pay-increases and picture houses in those cities commenced to operate without music on September first as a result. A strike also hit three theatres in Niagara Falls, where the musicians, stage hands and operators walked out at the Strand, Bellevue and Cataract theatres. No agreement has been reached between the theatre managers and musicians in Atlanta and theatres there continue to show pictures without orchestral accompaniment. The difficulties arising over a new contract for operators in Baltimore have been ironed out after rather prolonged discussion of the terms of the new contract submitted theatre men by the operators' union there.

The union men in Niagara Falls quit the Strand, Bellevue and Cataract theatres on August 29 and their places were taken at once by 43 members of the National Theatrical Federated Union, all of whom were taken to Niagara Falls from New York City. The stage hands there demanded an additional man on every stage crew as well as a 12 per cent increase. Operators demanded thirty-three and one-third per cent increase in wages, while the musicians wanted an increase of 10 per cent. The Lumberg and Amendola theatres in Niagara

Falls both gave in to the demands of the unions.

After seven hours of battling on Saturday night, August 29, the stage hands of Buffalo theatres reached an agreement with the Buffalo Theatre Managers' association, whereby the men are to receive a five per cent increase in wages effective September 1 and covering a period of two years.

Des Moines' picture houses have been without musical accompaniment since September 1. A. H. Bland, head of the organization which operates the Des Moines, Capitol, Garden, Palace, Strand and Majestic theatres, today made public a statement in which he definitely announces that the theatres will not pay the increase in salaries demanded by the musicians' union.

"The contracts with the musicians and stage employees will expire August 31," Blank's statement says.

"Representatives of these bodies have approached us with a demand for a substantial increase in the wage scale and when we found it impossible to accede to these demands they notified us that with the ending of the existing contracts we will have no musical accompaniment in our motion picture houses."

So far as known the Casino theatre and Riverview park are the only theatres which

have reached an agreement with the unions.

The musicians playing in the first-run motion picture theatres of Cleveland have asked for a forty per cent increase for the coming season, starting September 1st. The other musicians have asked for a proportionate increase. Asked how this affects the leading first-run houses operated by Loew's Ohio Theatres, Inc., it was stated by an official of the company that the demand means an added expenditure of $100,000 a year for music at the Stillman, Allen and Park theatres.

"The public will not stand any boost in admission prices, and the theatres cannot stand $100,000 a year increase in operating expenses. So Cleveland fans can look forward to having their pictures served to them without music until an equitable settlement is made with the musicians," he added.

No change has been developed this week in the situation existing between the theatre managers of Atlanta and the Federation of Musicians. The orchestras in all first-run motion picture houses are still out, and notwithstanding the belief that a settlement of the existing controversy is impending, so far nothing definite has come about.

Most of the theatres continue to use special attractions in the way of dance revues and jazz orchestras, and report that business has not made any drop or appreciable change that may be attributed to the lack of orchestras.

Seider, For M. P. T. O. A., Offers New Form Of Contract

Important Changes on Arbitration Proposed

A NEW form of exhibition contract, whose adoption will be urged by the M. P. T. O. A., was made public this week by Joseph M. Seider, chairman of the organization's Contract and Arbitration Committee.

Mr. Seider made it clear that the contract was being submitted to the whole industry. "We offer it with the firm conviction that it contains a solution to our contract and arbitration difficulties; that it is equitable and that it affords every protection to both sides," said Mr. Seider.

"We do not demand that it be accepted without change," he continued. "We solicit and will welcome constructive criticisms and suggestions."

The chief provisions of the proposed contract were outlined in detail by the M. P. T. O. A. official as follows:

"We have given the subject much study, have investigated the application of the present contracts and arbitration system in many states and have gone far afield to obtain assistance so that this proposed contract should through its terms, brevity and simplicity serve to minimize disputes and thereby lessen, if not entirely eliminate, litigation through both law and arbitration.

"The proposed contract is in two sections. The contract proper and a set of rules or supplemental contract. We feel that the contract proper should cover those provisions which need be agreed upon at the signing of the contract, such as price, names of pictures, protection, run, etc. The terms that would assume importance only in the event of a controversy are covered in the Rules. There is provision made for the Rules being binding and a part of the main contract. Thus the theatre owner has only a short document to check up when signing for pictures and he will easily detect the addition or omission of clauses. This together with the fact that the proposed contract contains a warrantee that the contract is the approved Standard Exhibition Contract will assure a uniform contract.

"Mr. Nathan Burkan's suggestion for a solution of the designation of play dates problem is in our opinion the most feasible offered. We have incorporated in our proposed contract Mr. Burkan's clause relating thereto with the addition of a provision for specific dates for second or subsequent runs and a provision for relief in the event a theatre owner is forced into an overbought condition because the pictures he had contracted for had not been available to him.

"All pictures contracted for must be made available and played within a year. No run comes into another year. A playdate becomes a pay-date.

"The Arbitration clause in the proposed contract is in accordance with the law. It is fair to both sides and it is ample. It only exempts a dispute arising out of the violation or attempted violation of protection. In such a dispute provision is made for injunctive relief.

"The theatre owner who does not want to enter into a contract providing for compulsory arbitration is given the option of protecting the distributor through depositing with the distributor a sum equal to ten per cent (10%) of the amount of the contract as security for the faithful performance of the contract.

"The theatre owner who agrees to arbitration with such an option will not, if a dispute arises, refuse to submit same to an arbitration board. He will in every instance if it is against him carry out the decision or award of the Arbitration Board.

"This together with the provisions made for open hearings, for the availability of the records to the disputants and the press, for the right to the disputants to challenge the appointed arbitrators and replace them with their personal choice, for the refunding to the exhibitor who successfully defends an arbitration claim, his railroad fare and expenses, for the giving to the Arbitration Board jurisdiction over matters arising out of ethics and fair dealings and for a Contract Commission and Appeals Board, will win over many opponents of Arbitration.

"The theatre owner is entitled to and must have relief from the present contract and arbitration procedure. If distributors have honest objections we in all sincerity beg them to state them. If they have none they should not withhold a square deal from us any longer."

Rules Provided for in Proposed Contract

Following are the Rules provided for in the approved Standard Exhibition Contract and made a part thereof:

Identified this .... day of ...., 19......

1. The Board of Arbitration shall consist of four persons, two Distributors who do not own or operate theatres and two Exhibitors who are not directly or indirectly affiliated with a producer or distributor. The two Distributors' representatives shall be selected by the ....

.... to serve for one month. The two Exhibitors' representatives shall be selected by the Motion Picture Theatre Owners of America to serve for one month. No member of the Board of Arbitration shall sit in any case or controversy in which he has an interest direct or indirect.

In case of a tie vote the Board of Arbitration shall appoint a fifth arbitrator, and if they are unable to agree, then the Chairman of the Board of Arbitration shall request the presidents of the respective organizations of which both litigants are members to make the appointment and in the event they are unable to agree then the Chairman shall request the Mayor of the City in which the dispute is arbitrated to make the appointment.

The Exhibitor shall have the right to challenge the Exhibitors' representatives on the Arbitration Board appointed as herein provided and shall have the right to name the two exhibitors who shall serve on the Arbitration Board in his particular case or controversy.

Likewise, the Distributor shall have the right to challenge the Distributors' representatives on the Arbitration Board appointed as herein provided and shall have the right to name the two distributors who will serve on the Arbitration Board in his particular case or controversy.

2. The Board of Arbitration shall have general power, after a thorough and impartial hearing of every dispute or controversy (1) To determine such dispute or controversy, (2) to make findings thereon, (3) to direct what shall be done by either party or both parties with respect to the matter in dispute, (4) to elect its chairman, (5) to, in any decision or award, include a revision therein requiring the payment by one party to the other of compensatory damage and/or indemnity, (6) to also provide in any decision or award that the railroad fares and hotel bills incurred by the Exhibitor shall be paid to the Exhibitor by the Distributor, in the event the Board of Arbitration shall find in favor of the Exhibitor against the Distributor in the pending controversy or small dismiss the grievance brought by the Distributor against the Exhibitor, (7) to have jurisdiction over all matters in dispute arising under an application for a contract, (8) to have jurisdiction in all matters of fair dealing and ethics arising out of a contract, even though not specifically provided for therein.

3. There shall be formed an Arbitration Commission consisting of three Exhibitors and three Distributors. The exhibitor members shall be appointed by the Motion Picture Theatre Owners of America and the Distributor members shall be appointed by ....

.... This Commission to constitute and shall have the power of supervision of all Arbitration Boards, to review such decisions of Arbitration Boards as may in its discretion merit review and shall have the power to avoid or amend or modify the award thus reviewed and to make such changes in the Approved Standard Exhibition Contract and these rules as may from time to time become necessary.

4. The hearings before the Arbitration Boards shall be open. The records of the disputants shall be available and open to the Press, Exhibitor, Distributor and their organizations and counsel. Copies of complaints, awards, minutes and calendars shall be available to the Distributor and Exhibitor and their organizations.

5. If in the Distributor and the Exhibitor agree:

(a) None of the photoplays specified in the contract shall be reissues from old negative except it is so expressly noted therein.

(b) The photoplays specified in the contract shall not contain any paid advertising.

(c) Contracts may be assigned by either party providing the assignment is in writing and accepted in writing by the assignee and approved in writing by the Distributor or the Exhibitor as the case may be, in which event the assignor shall be released from his/or its liability hereunder.

(d) The exhibition date of each photoplay which has not otherwise been specified on the contract shall be fixed as follows:

(D-1) For all purposes herein the release date of such photoplay shall be construed to be the date when such photoplay shall have been exhibited for the first time in a first run theatre in the key city or exchange centre in the district in which the theatre specified in the contract is located.

Prompt notice of such exhibition date and the date of the expiration of the protection period of said first run theatre shall be given to the Exhibitor.

From and after the date of the expiration of such protection period, such photoplay shall forthwith become available to the Exhibitor for exhibition under his contract.

(D-2) If the Exhibitor is entitled to a first run of a photoplay the Exhibitor shall fix an exhibition date, such date to be within a period not exceeding three weeks following the expiration of the protection period aforementioned. The notice of the exhibitor fixing the exhibition as aforementioned shall be given to the Distributor at least two weeks prior to such exhibition date.

If the Exhibitor shall fail to fix such exhibition in the manner above provided, the Distributor shall promptly after the expiration of three weeks following the protection period, fix such exhibition date, such date to be within two weeks following such three week period and in such case the date so fixed by the Distributor shall, for all purposes hereunder, be deemed the exhibition date of the photoplay.

(D-3) In case the Exhibitor shall have a run subsequent to a first run, and the number of days subsequent to the run immediately prior to the Exhibitor named in the contract, after which the Exhibitor

"The Approved Standard Exhibition Contract"

Proposed for the Industry's Consideration by Joseph M. Seider, Chairman of the M. P. T. O. A. Contract and Arbitration Committee.

THE Distributor warrants that this contact conform in every respect and detail with the APPROVED STANDARD EXHIBITION CONTRACT, on file with ...., and identified by the signature of its President, on the .... day of September, 1925.

AGREEMENT, made in triplicate, this ...... day of ...., 19......, between ...., a corporation (hereinafter called the "Distributor") and .... operating the .... theatre, at .... City of .... and State of .... (hereinafter called the "Exhibitor") as follows:

1. The Distributor hereby grants to the Exhibitor, and the latter accepts, a license under the respective copyrights to the several photoplays hereinafter in the schedule below designated and described, subject to the terms and conditions herein specified, to exhibit, during and within the year commencing on the ...... day of .... , 19...... and ending the ...... day of .... , 19...... and the Distributor agrees to furnish to the exhibitor during and within the said period, each of such photoplays in the theatre herein specified only, for the number of successive days herein specified, and to deliver to a common carrier or to an agent of the exhibitor, a positive print of each of such photoplays, in time for exhibition at the theatre and on the dates herein specified or determined as herein provided.

2. The Exhibitor agrees:
   (a) To pay for such license as to each of such photoplays, the sums herein specified, at least three (3) days in advance of the date of shipment of each of such photoplays by the Distributor.
   (b) To pay the cost of the delivery of each of such photoplays to the theatre from the local exchange of the Distributor and their return to the said local exchange.
   (c) To return each of such photoplays in the same condition in which they were received, reasonable wear and tear excepted.
   (d) To be liable in an amount not exceeding four (4) cents per lineal foot for each foot of the positive prints of such photoplays, that is damaged, lost or stolen while in his possession.

3. The Distributor agrees not to permit or authorize or license the exhibition of any of such photoplays in violation of the run and protection granted to the Exhibitor as follows:
Protection .... days against .... Theatres run .... to follow .... days after .... Theatre.

4. Each of such photoplays shall be available to the Exhibitor, unless a definite exhibition date is specified herein, in the manner provided in the Rules hereinafter provided for.

5. SCHEDULE.

Release No.	Title of Production	Cast	No. of reels	Play dates	No. of days	Price

6. Excepting always and only the right of the Exhibitor to take such proceedings as he may deem advisable to enjoin any breach or threatened

breach or violation by the Distributor of any of the provisions relating to run or protection provided for herein, the Distributor hereby consenting to the granting of an injunction restraining such breach or threatened breach, it being agreed that in case of any such breach the damages to be sustained by the Exhibitor is irreparable and incapable of definite ascertainment and computation, the parties hereto agree that before either of them shall resort to any Court to determine, enforce or protect the legal rights of either hereto, he shall submit to a board of arbitration consisting of an equal number of Distributors and Exhibitors, which board of arbitration shall be formed and shall function as provided in a set of Rules on file with .... and identified by the signature of the President of said Association, which rules are made a part hereof the same as if they had been fully set forth herein, all disputes, claims and controversies arising hereunder, including those based upon a repudiation or rescission, or attempted repudiation or attempted rescission of this contract, for determination.

The parties herein further agree to abide by and forthwith comply with any decision or award of such Board of Arbitration in any such arbitration proceedings, and agree and consent that any such decision or award shall be enforceable in or by any court of competent jurisdiction pursuant to the Laws of the State of New York, now or hereafter in force and the parties consent to the introduction of such findings in evidence in any judicial proceedings.

7. The foregoing clause Six relating to arbitration shall become null and void and the parties hereto shall retain all their rights and powers at law and in equity in the event the Exhibitor deposits with the Distributor a sum equal to ten (10%) percent of the total sum payable by the Exhibitor to the Distributor under the terms of this contract, and in the event the Exhibitor so elects to deposit said sum of money with the Distributor, the Distributor agrees to pay to the Exhibitor interest on said sum or any balance remaining due from time to time at the rate of two (2%) percent per annum. Such moneys shall constitute trust moneys, and shall not be commingled with its other moneys unless and until and at the time when the sum shall be applied on account of the last sums payable hereunder. It is hereby expressly provided and understood however, that Clause Five of this Rules referred to and provided for in the said Clause Six shall at all times and in any event be in force and effect and a art of this contract.

8. This contract shall be deemed an application for a contract only and shall not become binding upon either party .... unless accepted in writing by an officer of the Distributor and notice in writing of acceptance sent to the Exhibitor within .... days from the date hereof. The Exhibitor may withdraw this application at any time prior to its acceptance by the Distributor as provided for herein.

9. No terms or representations have been made by either party to the other except as herein set forth.

(Insert here any special arrangements)

In witness whereof, the arties hereto have hereunto set their signatures and seals this day first above written.

....

....

Approved, for the Distributor
.... day of ...., 19...

---

is entitled to such photoplay is not specified, then the Exhibitor's exhibition date shall be fixed in like manner as herein above provided for the exhibition with respect to a first run, except that all periods shall run from the date of the expiration of the protection period of the exhibitor having a run immediately prior to that of the exhibitor named in the contract.

(D-4.) In the event any photoplays shall not be exhibited in a first run theatre in the key city or exchange center in the territory embracing the theatre named in the contract within a reasonable time after its production, and within such period no definite booking therefor shall have been fixed by any such first run theatre, then the Distributor obligates itself to fix a general release date which shall be within a

reasonable time after the completion of the production of the photoplay and such release date so fixed shall be deemed the release date for all purposes under this paragraph. Said photoplay shall thereupon forthwith after such date become available for exhibition under contracts, with the same force and effect as if such release date were the date of expiration of the protection period herein above in the preceding subdivision referred to.

(D-5) In case the contract shall embrace a series of featured photoplays featuring a particular star or director, the Exhibitor shall not be required to exhibit more than one photoplay of such series every five weeks.

(D-6) So far as the same may be feasible, the Distributor agrees to distribute the photoplays embraced under the contract at equal intervals apart, to the end that the Exhibitor shall be enabled to exhibit such photoplays within a year at approximately equal intervals.

(D-7) In the event of the failure of the Distributor to make available to the Exhibitor the photoplays embraced under the contract as provided herein, the Exhibitor may at his option cancel the contract embracing such photoplays not made available by giving written notice of cancellation to the Distributor.

(D-8) If any of the photoplays specified in the contract shall be released by the Distributor after the year specified in the contract, the Distributor shall be obliged to deliver such photoplays to the Exhibitor as though released within the year specified and the Exhibitor may at his option accept such photoplays at such later period and pay for and exhibit same pursuant to the terms of the contract.

In case the Exhibitor shall be delayed in or prevented from performance of the contract or any part thereof by the elements, accidents, strikes, fires, Court orders or Acts of God, such delay in or prevention of performance shall be excused and all damages arising therefrom are hereby expressly waived by the Distributor.

In case the Distributor shall be delayed or prevented from making deliveries of a photoplay or

photoplays as provided in the contract by reason of accidents, elements, strikes, fires, Censor Pulings or an Act of God, such delay in or prevent of delivery shall be excused and all damages arising therefrom are hereby expressly waived by the Exhibitor.

The Distributor or the Exhibitor as the case may be shall give prompt notice in writing to the other of the happening of any of the above mentioned contingencies, and the reasons therefor.

Identified by the resident of .... this .... day of .... 19...

West Coast Gets San Diego Houses

AS a result of the acquisition of the Balboa and Cabrillo theatres in San Diego, the West Coast Theatres circuit now extends from San Diego to Sacramento in California. A. M. Bowles, general manager of the West Coast concern, said the San Diego houses will be operated along the same lines as all others of the company. H. L. Hartman, recently manager for West Coast in San Bernardino, has been placed in charge of the company's interests in San Diego, with H. E. Holcomb as assistant, and Robert Collier in charge of Publicity.

Pantages Will Build Coast Chain

ALEXANDER PANTAGES, head of national vaudeville enterprises, announced last week in his home in Seattle that he would soon begin construction and operation of a chain of motion picture theatres on the Pacific Coast.

The first move in the plan will be the construction of large houses in Seattle and Tacoma, the estimated cost of which will be in excess of $1,000,000 each. Following the establishment of a chain of considerable proportions, Pantages declared it was his intention to enter the field of production. He will produce the pictures for his own and other independent theatres.

Washington Theatres Only in Deal

Crandall and Stanley Company Merger Also Includes First National Franchise

WASHINGTON theatres only, are involved in the merger of the Crandall Theatres and the Stanley Company of America, and the First National franchise and Crandall's Exhibitors Film Exchange are included in the deal, according to the latest announcement regarding the transaction.

Details of this big financial transaction, whereby the eleven Crandall Theatres in Washington are merged with the Stanley Company of America, were made public by Harry M. Crandall, founder of the circuit of fifteen motion picture houses of the first class in Washington and vicinity that have always been known by his name.

The monetary consideration involved in the deal was in the neighborhood of $8,000,-000 and the local theatres which become a part of the immense holdings of the Stanley Company, with headquarters in Philadelphia, Pa., are Crandall's Metropolitan, Tivoli, Ambassador, Central, Savoy, Avenue Grand, Apollo, York, Home, Lincoln and the new Colony under construction at the corner of Georgia Ave., and Farragut St., N. W. In addition to these popular picture houses control of the regional First National franchise for the Washington territory and the Exhibitors Film Exchange, owned by Mr. Crandall, passes to the Stanley Company. This integral unit in the vast Stanley combine will be known as The Stanley-Crandall Company.

While the Stanley Company of America acquires a majority of the stock in the new company through the merger, Harry M. Crandall is not eliminated from the local

amusement field. The deal resulting in the formation of the Stanley-Crandall Company was predicated upon an imperative stipulation that Harry Crandall sign a long-term contract to continue as the guiding genius in full control of the chain of playhouses which he established and has brought to such a high point of popularity and profit. It is also declared that the Crandall executive staff, as well as the operating personnels of the individual theatres will continue to function, without change, as in the past.

Harry M. Crandall retains a substantial stock interest in the Stanley-Crandall Company and by this new move becomes an important executive in the operation of an immense theatrical enterprise of which the total capitalization may conservatively be said to be $30,000,000.

The financial considerations involved were not paramount in the mind of Mr. Crandall in consummating this amalgamation. Under the expert advice of the leading legal and financial minds of this and other cities, he was convinced that at a time when mergers are the order of the day throughout the United States, with a probable final outcome of centralized control of the motion picture industry in its every ramification, he would best be serving the interests and safeguarding the hopes of the Washington public whose staunch support has been the basis of his success in the amusement field by affiliating his interests with one of the most powerful exhibiting concerns on the continent.

The operation of the various lines of service not directly allied with the box-office will be continued precisely as in the past.

The Public Service and Educational Department, which has never been looked upon as a source of revenue but merely as a valuable liason department between the Crandall Theatres and that segment of the public not directly concerned with the picture industry or any form of theatricals, will be continued under the personal direction of Harriet Hawley Locher, and the Crandall Saturday Nighters, the popular radio broadcasting unit that takes the air through station WRC every Saturday night from 10:30 P. M., to midnight, will not be stilled by the new arrangement.

The officers and directors of the Stanley-Crandall Company will be as follows for the period of one year:

Jules E. Mastbaum, president and director; Harry M. Crandall, vice-president, treasurer and director; Fritz D. Hoffmann, comptroller and director; George A. Crouch, assistant treasurer and director; Morris Wolf, secretary; Irving D. Rossheim, assistant secretary and director; Abe Sabolsky and John J. McQuirk, directors.

The local executive staff, as in the past, will consist of Joseph P. Morgan, general manager; John J. Payette, assistant general manager; Nelson B. Bell, director of advertising, publicity and broadcasting; Fritz D. Hoffmann, comptroller; Paul B. Davis, auditor; George A. Crouch, treasurer; George C. Larkin, assistant auditor; Nat B. Browne, private secretary, and Daniel Breeskin, musical director-in-charge. Nat Glasser will continue as head of the Crandall technical and mechanical department.

Famous Pennsylvania Deal Confirmed

Company Will Acquire a Number of Important Theatres From the Wilmer and Vincent Chain

POSITIVE confirmation was obtained in Harrisburg, Pa., on August 28, from Sydney Wilmer, president, and Joseph Egan, general manager of the Wilmer & Vincent Company, of New York, that, despite recent reports to the contrary, a big deal is about to be consummated whereby the Famous Players-Lasky Company will acquire a number of important theatres from the Wilmer & Vincent chain in Pennsylvania.

This confirmation came after the flood of conflicting rumors that had been in circulation all summer,—but without heretofore any official authority,—to the effect that Famous Players-Lasky were to purchase sixteen Wilmer & Vincent theatres in various Pennsylvania cities, including Harrisburg, Reading, Allentown, Altoona, Easton and elsewhere. Until Mr. Wilmer and Mr. Egan went to Harrisburg on August 28 the impression had become general that the reported negotiations had been abandoned, but the positive statement is now made in their behalf, through C. Floyd Hopkins, the Wilmer & Vincent Harrisburg representative, that a deal is now certain to be effected whereby Famous Players will get "at least some of the Wilmer & Vincent circuit."

Mr. Wilmer and Mr. Egan declined to be specific as to which theatres are to be included in the transaction, but gave assurance of a detailed announcement in Harrisburg at a very early date. The statement prepared by Mr. Hopkins and given to the press of Harrisburg for publication, said: "There has been some cause for the numerous rumors that have been floating thick and fast for the past several months concerning the possible transfer of one or more of the Wilmer & Vincent theatres in Harrisburg to the Famous Players-Lasky company, and transfers of other theatres in the state. Until this time no information as to the probable base for such rumors has been given by officers of either organization, although it has been known that the Famous Players-Lasky people have been endeavoring to locate here."

Prior to their coming to Harrisburg Mr. Wilmer and Mr. Egan, with Mr. Hopkins, attended the formal opening of the New Strand theatre, by the Nathan Appell interests, in York, Pa., on the night of August 27, where they were guests of Mr. Appell. They were in Harrisburg only a few hours and then went to Reading, where there are a number of Wilmer & Vincent theatres.

The purpose of Famous Players-Lasky in acquiring Central Pennsylvania theatres is understood to be to establish freer channels for the showing of Paramount pictures. Announcement already has been made in advertisements in Harrisburg that Paramount pictures are to be shown hereafter at the Victoria Theatre, one of the Wilmer & Vincent houses, and the unofficial impression in that city is strong that the Victoria and also the Colonial are two Harrisburg houses that Famous Players will include in the pending purchase.

It is pretty certain the Wilmer & Vincent company will retain the Majestic and the Orpheum in Harrisburg, the former a vaudeville house, which, however, will become a legitimate theatre this Fall, when the Orpheum, heretofore a legitimate theater, is rebuilt, at an expenditure of $750,000, for a vaudeville house that will seat 2,600.

Full details of the pending deal, as affecting Wilmer & Vincent theatres in various cities of the state, are expected to be forthcoming almost immediately.

WalkerDemonstrationPlanned

Luncheon and Rally at Hotel Astor.
September 9—Big Crowd is Expected

A LUNCHEON and demonstration in honor of Senator James J. Walker, Tammany candidate for mayor of New York City at the primaries to be held September 15, will be staged at the Hotel Astor on Wednesday, September 9.

A big attendance of representatives of the industry is expected and arrangements are being made by the Motion Picture Division of the Walker Campaign, with headquarters at 1600 Broadway, to take care of a record crowd.

It is planned to make the demonstration a monster rally in behalf of the Senator, who will of course be present and will speak. The names of the other speakers will be announced later. They will include prominent personages both in and outside the industry, and several surprises will be sprung. Everybody in the industry will be invited.

The Motion Picture Division, which has been actively at work since the campaign started, announced this week that its plans were now perfected for the final stretch of the battle, and made public the complete list of committees and officials in the drive.

Former State Senator Walter R. Herrick, a prominent attorney and personal friend of the Senator, is General Chairman. Samuel I. Berman, long a leader in exhibitor organization affairs, is the executive secretary and A. H. Schwartz is treasurer.

The Executive Committee is composed of the following: Charles L. O'Reilly, President of the Theatre Owners Chamber of Commerce, Chairman; Sydney S. Cohen, former President of the Motion Picture Theatre Owners of America and now Chairman of the board of that organization, Associate Chairman; J. Arthur Hirsch, prominent exhibitor, Secretary. The other members are: Harry L. Reichenbach and Mr. Schwartz.

Finance Committee — A. H. Schwartz, Chairman; Oscar A. Price, President of Tri-Stone, representing producers; Felix Feist, general manager of distribution, Metro-Goldwyn, representing distributors; Harry L. Reichenbach, representing publicity and advertising men; William A. Johnston, editor of Motion Picture News, representing the press; S. Eckman, representing exchanges; and Joe Hornstein, representing accessory dealers.

Publicity Committee—J. Arthur Hirsch, Chairman; Clarence Cohen, Marty Schwartz, Fred Wilson, I. Weinberg and H. Mackler.

Exhibitors Committee—Sol Raives, Manhattan; John Manheimer, Brooklyn; Rudolph Sanders, Brooklyn; Joseph Jaime, Bronx; B. Noble, Bronx; Sol Brill, Queens; Hy Gainsboro, Queens; Charles Moses and L. Rosenblatt, Richmond.

Salesmen's Committee — L. Weinberg, Bronx; S. Title, Manhattan; S. Trauner, and B. Schultz, Brooklyn.

An important feature of the campaign is the supplying of trailers and slides to theatres in New York and this work is being handled from headquarters.

Connecticut Situation Still Involved

(*Continued from page 1235*)

distributors and exchanges to the number of 105, has no war with the people of the State of Connecticut. It believes that the film tax law imposes a hardship which, if duplicated in the other states, would cripple the motion picture business, and which in the State of Connecticut imposes too great a penalty on an already too heavily taxed industry.

"It believes this law to be unfair, and, from information received from wide spread sources in Connecticut, that it is not a law popular with the people, who naturally must eventually bear its burden. It believes that this law should be repealed, but it also believes that the people of Connecticut, as part and parcel of a free commonwealth, have the right to settle their own propositions without outside interference.

"This Association is against depriving the people of the State of Connecticut of its amusement in the motion picture theatres by any boycott or other reprisal.

"It believes that the entire matter can be left with safety to the judgment and sense of fairness of the people of the State of Connecticut and that the local motion picture theatre owners are capable of presenting their case to the people fairly and openly, without the annoying aid and blundering interference on the part of paid attorney representating certain well meaning but misguided persons in the motion picture business.

"The motion picture theatre men of Connecticut have their business existence at stake and they foresee the sweeping away of their investments by the operation of this tax, because to them it is a problem as

Pathe Earnings for Year Equal to $9 a Share on Outstanding Stock

P ATHE EXCHANGE, Inc., earnings for 1924 were equal to $9 per share on 155,000 shares of stock outstanding, according to the Wall Street Journal. In an interview with a representative of the Journal, Bernhard Benson, vice-president, discussing Pathe's financial condition for the first six months of this year, is quoted as follows:

"Profits for the first six months of this fiscal year should be fully as large as in the corresponding period last year. Fall is usually the best season for the moving picture business, but current bookings are very satisfactory.

"The Pathex camera and projector recently placed on the market are meeting with pronounced demand and inquiries are coming in from all parts of the United States. Substantial orders have been received from leading department and sporting good stores.

"Business of du Pont-Pathe Film Manufacturing Corp. is showing improvement and ratio of profits to sales is satisfactory. We look for a very good year for Pathe from every standpoint."

Legislative Committee is Named by I. M. P. A.

B EFORE leaving for the Coast Saturday, President I. E. Chadwick, of the Independent Motion Picture Association of America, appointed a special Legislative Committee necessary. Selection of the committee to act for the Association wherever was authorized at a meeting of the Executive Committee of the Association last Friday, and one of its first duties will be to consider the Connecticut tax situation if it develops that a special session of the General Assembly is to be called by Governor Trumbull.

The committee is made up as follows:—

Oscar A. Price, Tri-Stone Pictures, Inc., chairman; W. E. Shallenberger, Arrow Film Corp.; Joseph Brandt, Columbia Pictures Corp.; M. H. Hoffman, Tiffany Pictures, Inc.; B. P. Schulberg, B. P. Schulberg, Inc.; W. Ray Johnston, Rayart Pictures Corp.; Sam Zierler, Commonwealth Film Corp.

Chairman Price said that he contemplated no immediate activity for the committee unless it develops that it may be of assistance in Connecticut.

to how it is possible for the public to absorb the burden.

"For the present at least nothing can be done toward having this burden shared by the public, the motion picture theatres of Connecticut have had to expend thousands of dollars in the middle of one of the worst seasons in their history, and there is no way that they now see that they can get it back.

"As far as the independent motion picture exchanges are concerned some have closed their New Haven offices, not from a desire to boycott anybody, but because their slim resources are in danger of being wiped out by the tax.

"This association is not in favor of any carpet-bagging activities, and does not desire in any way to enter into the situation except to give such aid as is necessary to keep the theatres open and the business running.

"If this can be made plain to the public, possibly the people would have a better understanding of the actual situation. It is the purpose of the Independent Motion Picture Association of America to co-operate insofar as possible with the Motion Picture Theatre Owners of Connecticut and the owners and managers of the independent exchanges serving theatres in htat state."

In and Out of Town

N AT G. ROTHSTEIN, of F. B. O., has returned to his desk after a four weeks' vacation in the Maine Woods.

P RESIDENT Joe Brandt, of Columbia, is back after a motor and golfing vacation in New York State, New England and Canada.

H ENRY GINSBERG left this week for a short business trip to Chicago.

K. HIRATA, of the Star Film Corp., Tokyo, Japan, is in New York making purchases of pictures for his territory.

F C. MUNROE and John C. Flinn of Producers Distributing Corp., are back after a trip to Hollywood.

Minnesota Court Upholds Theatre Bond Law

Discontinuance of free shows in Minnesota is forecast following the action of the district court at Mantorville in upholding the conviction and fine of William Jamieson, Claremont, Minn.

Jamieson was arrested on complaint of R. V. Morse, exhibitor and constable at Claremont, in a test case of the new Minnesota law providing that license from the state fire marshal and indemnity bond to cover possible damages must be taken out.

He waived a jury trial and was fined $15 to expedite appeal. The case may be taken to the state supreme court by the Community Amusement Association of Minneapolis which sponsored the project and which it is believed will be virtually eliminated from the state if the decision stands.

Montreal Poster Censor Change Effected

An important technical change is being made in the poster censor's bureau at Montreal, Quebec, which is under the direction of Martin Singher, a former local newspaperman. The bureau was opened a year ago as a division of the Montreal Police Department as it was considered as a disciplinary feature of the civic administration.

The bureau has now been transferred to the city treasurer's department because of the recognized and admitted fact that it has become more of a revenue producing office than anything else, local exchanges and exhibitors paying the bill. More than a $1,000 per month is being collected through the poster taxation locally.

Mason Building House in Goldsboro, N. C.

Rudolph Mason, who is now operating the Acme theatre in Goldsboro, N. C., is building a new theatre there, to be called the Maxon. It is understood the house will cost approximately $750,000, and will be ready for its opening October 1st. The theatre when completed will seat 1,000 people, and will be modern and attractive in every way.

Roxy Sails for Europe This Week

S. L. ROTHAFEL leaves for Europe September 5th in the interest of the new Roxy Theatre Corporation. He will return some time in October. His trip will take him to England, France and Germany. Accompanying Roxy will be Arthur H. Sawyer, one of the leading spirits of the new organization; Mrs. Arthur H. Sawyer, Dorothy Sawyer, Clark Robinson, Rothafel's art director and Yascha Bunchuk, cellist.

One of the purposes of the trip will be to make an exhaustive study of the folk lore and folk songs of various European countries, his intention being to present this folk music in conjunction with the contemplated entertainment program at the new Roxy Theatre.

During Rothafel's absence, Herbert Lubin and William E. Atkinson, his associates in the theatre building project, will push to completion the plans involving the contemplated Roxy chain of houses.

A. M. P. A. Nominations Announced

THE A. M. P. A. has placed in nomination the ticket that will be voted upon at the annual election to be held Thursday, September 10th. The ticket is headed by Glendon Allvine for the office of president, with Walter Eberhardt scheduled for the vice-presidency. For the Board of Directors Jerome Beatty is named to succeed Glendon Allvine, Charles P. Cohen to succeed Walter Eberhardt, and A. L. Selig to succeed Gordon White.

Many New Film Companies Get New York Charters

Motion picture companies incorporating in New York state during the past week included the following: Welcome Pictures, capitalized at $20,000, with A. W. Goldstein, H. A. Krein, Rachel Marmer, of New York city; Easy Terms Corporation, capitalization not specified, M. L. Elkin, M. Salit, Anne Eichel, New York city; Walker-Hamilton Distributing Company, Inc., $20,000, Henry Modery, Brooklyn; John H. Gould, Port Washington; Seward G. Spoor, Great Neck; Careda Theatres Corporation, $10,000, M. B. Jones, Jr.; R. Beattie, Ruth Rosenblatt, New York city; Sawyer and Lubin, Inc., capitalization not stated, H. G. Kosch, E. Bregstein, A. Thompson, New York city; Lariat Productions, Inc., capitalization not stated, H. B. Goldsmith, Haverstraw; J. F. Gerlach, Bayside; C. Hallmeyer, New York city; Rosie O'Grady Corporation, capitalization not specified, Thomas Bent, Pat Rooney, Marion Bent, New York city; Play C Company, Inc., $30,000, Charles Lorete, R. J. Joseph, New York; B. M. Mark, Brooklyn; Weak Sisters Production, Inc., $200,000, J. H. Harris, Charles Hertzman, H. N. Helde, New York city; Edeo Producing Unit, Inc., $200,000, I. M. Michelman, R. Liebhoff, A. J. Johnston, New York city; Hal Hodes Short Film Exchanges, Inc., $5,000, I. Steinberg, Brooklyn; Hal Hodes, P. Poger, New York city; College Point Amusement Co., capitalization not specified, Arthur Hoffman, Morris Fox, Rene Epstein, Brooklyn.

Wyoming Exhibitors Will Form Organization

A report is out that Wyoming exhibitors will soon organize, this being the report of a meeting which is scheduled to be held at Casper within the next ten days. All prominent Wyoming exhibitors have been invited to attend. Carl Ray of the Carl Ray Amusement Company Theatres of Cheyenne, Wyoming, is reported to be the moving power behind the idea. At present the only exhibitors organization in the Denver territory is the M. P. T. O. of Colorado.

Shelbyville, Ill., to Vote on Sunday Showings

Shelbyville, Ill., is scheduled to vote September 3 on an ordinance to permit the showing of motion pictures and the holding of other amusements on Sundays. The vote is expected to be close.

Germany Key to Growing Market

(*Continued from page 1237*)

the German producers are doing well and those who are content to make pictures at a reasonable cost are making money on them. A more critical condition will exist in regard to pictures now being made for the world market, at great expense, and the cost of which cannot be returned in Germany alone. If an outside market can be found for these, well and good. If not, the production branch of the industry may find itself in serious straits.

As mentioned in a previous article, Germany is the key to the Central European market, which includes also Austria, Hungary, the Balkans, Russia, perhaps Sweden and Holland. Austria and Hungary are small markets and are showing more and more American films. The Balkans are not a great factor. Russia is questionable. The time has not yet arrived when any great amount of money can be grossed there. There are many theatres in Russia, apparently, and doing good business, but the monopoly which exists makes it necessary to take the price offered for whatever pictures are desired, subject to acceptance by the censor board. All in all, it is not now especially profitable. Sweden, as mentioned last week, is strongly organized and taking care of much of her own wants, so that she is less open as a market than before. Holland is not grossing a great deal of money at present. Germany, however, is a rich and growing field, and her production methods are so interesting as to deserve separate consideration.

Yeggs Work as Policemen Prosecute

While 200 St. Louis policemen crowded the city courts to prosecute men and women for petty offenses such as playing pinnochle and lotto for doilies and the like, two youthful bandits held up three employees of the Grand Opera House, 514 Market Street at 10:40 a. m. Monday August 24, and escaped with the Saturday and Sunday receipts totaling $5,500. It was the third hold-up of the morning.

James P. Brennan, manager, Schuyler French treasurer, and Miss Agnes Rempe, stenographer, were the employees of the theatre stuck-up by the bandits.

Warners Acquire State in Pittsburgh

WARNER BROS. added this week to their rapidly extending list of first run theatres by taking over for a long term the State Theatre, Pittsburgh, Pa., from the Rowland & Clark interests. This is a downtown house, one of the best known in Pennsylvania.

The State is the latest acquisition of Warner Bros. who are taking over leading theatres in key centers throughout the country to assure first runs for their productions. It is acquired just following the formal opening of Warners Theatre, formerly the Piccadilly, New York, and almost simultaneously with the opening as a Warner house of the Circle, in Cleveland.

Announcement of the acquisition of several others also has been made recently.

Scenes from "The Knockout," a First National offering with Milton Sills in the starred role.

Schulberg Schedule Arranged
Will Deliver Fourteen by Middle of April, With Six Others to Follow

B. P. SCHULBERG, producer of Preferred Pictures, and J. G. Bachmann, general manager of distribution have mapped a production and release schedule providing for the delivery of fourteen pictures by the middle of April, the balance of six to follow by early Summer.

The first two pictures, "Parisian Love" and "The Girl Who Wouldn't Work" are already available for first runs. "With This Ring" is the third release and it is set for September 5th. Fred C. Windermere directed, while the cast includes Alyce Mills, Lou Tellegen, Forrest Stanley, Donald Keith and Dick Sutherland.

"Free to Love," directed by Frank O'Connor and featuring Clara Bow, will be delivered September 25th. "The Other Woman's Story," a Gasnier production, is due on October 16th. Robert Frazer, Alice Calhoun, Helen Lee Worthing, Mahlon Hamilton, Riza Royce and David Torrence are the principals.

Following this production on November 16th comes "The Plastic Age," one of the highlights of the Schulberg schedule. Clara Bow and Donald Keith head the cast. The picture story is an adaptation of the Percy Marks novel.

The second Marcel De Sano production on the schedule will be released November 27th. It is titled "Lew Tyler's Wives." The first De Sano production was "The Girl Who Wouldn't Work."

"The Lawful Cheater" is due for release on December 18th, with Clara Bow as the featured player. The production was directed by Frank O'Connor. The first

Schulberg release of the new year will be "Horses and Women," adapted from the L. B. Yates Saturday Evening Post novel, "The Biography of a Race Horse."

"Eden's Fruit," directed by Gasnier will be the release for January 28th, to be followed by "The Romance of a Million Dollars" on February 18th. This will directly precede the screen version of Bronson Howard's play "Shenandoah," to be released on March 11th.

"Dancing Days," another Gasnier production will be shown on April 2nd, while the Larry Evans story, "The Aristocrat" will follow on April 25th.

T. Roy Barnes Signed for Columbia Feature

T. Roy Barnes has been engaged to appear with Elaine Hammerstein in the Columbia Pictures production of "Ladies of Leisure," which Tom Buckingham is to direct, it has been announced by Harry Cohn, production head of the company. The picture will be offered on one of the Columbia specials.

Director Horne Completes One. Starts Another

James W. Horne has completed the direction of the Pathe comedy for which he took a company of thirty to Yosemite Valley recently, and has already started a new Hal Roach comedy in which Lucien Littlefield, Katherine Grant and Tyler Brooke have the principal roles.

"The Gold Rush" Screened for President Coolidge

Charlie Chaplin's "The Gold Rush" was screened for President Coolidge and a party of friends at White Court, Swampscott, the "Summer White House." A print of the picture was sent to White Court by Hiram Abrams, of United Artists at the request of the President.

Matt Moore in Male Lead With Marie Prevost

Warner Brothers have selected Matt Moore to play the leading male role opposite Marie Prevost in "The Jazz Bride," which Herman Raymaker is directing. Supporting Miss Prevost and Moore are, John Patrick, Mabel Julienne Scott, George Irving, Don Alvarado, Margaret Seddon and Helen Dunbar.

Beery and Hatton Chosen for "Two Solidiers"

Wallace Beery and Raymond Hatton will appear with Mildred Davis in "The Two Soldiers," the Paramount production which will bring Miss Davis back to the screen after an absence of some time. Camera work on the picture will start when Victor Fleming, who is to direct, completes "Lord Jim," which he is now filming.

Tom Ricketts to Appear in Dorothy Revier Feature

Tom Ricketts has been added to the cast which will support Dorothy Revier in her next Waldorf production, which Columbia Pictures will release. The leading male role is to be played by Cullen Landis and Antonio Gaudio will direct.

Conway Tearle and Aileen Pringle in "The Mystic", a Metro-Goldwyn-Mayer production.

M-G-M Get "The Mysterious Island" Rights

Metro-Goldwyn-Mayer have secured picture rights to "The Mysterious Island," by Jules Verne and it will go into production at an early date under the direction of Jack Conway.

From the Metro-Goldwyn-Mayer publicity offices comes the word that this will be the greatest underwater motion picture ever made. The underwater scenes will be filmed under the direction of J. E. Williamson, owner of the undersea equipment and laboratory at Nassau, Bahamas. Wyndham Gittens, M-G-M scenarist, is now adapting the story for the screen.

Ralph Lewis to Star in Gotham Feature

Ralph Lewis will play the starred role in "One of the Bravest," the Gotham Production now being filmed for distribution through Lumas Film Corporation, according to an announcement by Sam Sax, head of the organization. Lewis will have the role of a fireman, the central figure in this melodrama, which is to be staged under the personal supervision of prominent fire department officials.

Douglas Gilmore Joins Cast for "Only Thing"

The addition of Douglas Gilmore to the cast of "The Only Thing" is announced by Metro-Goldwyn-Mayer. He only recently joined that stock company. The story was written by Elinor Glyn and she will also direct it. Aileen Pringle and Conway Tearle have the leading roles in this production. The balance of the cast is now being selected.

Director Edward's Son Makes Screen Debut

J. Gordon Edwards, Jr., twenty years old son of the film director, will make his debut as a screen actor in a role in "The Plastic Age," a B. P. Schulberg Preferred Picture now in production under the direction of Wesley Ruggles.

$100,000 Improvements at F. B. O. Studios

IMPROVEMENTS amounting to approximately $100,000 have been completed at the F. B. O. studios on the coast, which are now housing five F. B. O. companies at work and ten other independent companies on a rental basis. The improvements embrace extension of construction in all departments of production.

Three new projection rooms have been built and stages 1 and 2 have been combined into one mammoth stage. Twenty new offices have been erected for occupancy of outside concerns. Additional dressing rooms and store rooms have also been provided.

Among the F. B. O. units at work are Fred Thomson in "Ridin' The Wind," Evelyn Brent in "Three Wise Crooks," Ralph Lewis in Emory Johnson's "The Last Edition," Dick Talmadge in "The Prince of Pep," Maurice Flynn in "Heads Up," Tom Tyler in "Let's Go Gallagher" and Alberta Vaughn in "The Marie Series."

Highlights from the Betty Bronson starring vehicle "Not So Long Ago." Paramount).

P. D. C. Opens British Offices

Eight Branches Established Throughout United Kingdom With London Headquarters

PRODUCERS Distributing Corporation has established eight branches throughout the United Kingdom and "supervising" offices in London and Berlin, it was announced this week. The organization which will handle the company's own product in Great Britain was established by William M. Vogel, general manager of the Producers International Corporation, the foreign division of P. D. C., who returned to the States last week after a three months trip in Europe.

The new British distributing agency has been incorporated as the Producing Distributing Company, Ltd., with headquarters in London at No. 12 Great Newport Street, and eight subsidiary exchanges throughout the provinces. Mr. A. George Smith who headed the British Goldwyn Limited prior to its merger with Metro, has been engaged as managing director of Producers Distributing Company, Ltd., and will be in complete charge of the release of the D. C. product in England, Scotland, Ireland and Wales.

Film Booking Offices of England handled the 1924-1925 releases of Producers Distributing Corp. during the past year.

While in Berlin Mr. Vogel arranged for the distribution of the P. D. C. releases throughout Germany with National Film, A. G., of which company Herman Rosenfeld is Managing Director.

The interests of Producers International Corp. are being supervised for France, Belgium, Switzerland, Spain, Portugal and Italy by Mr. F. de Saenduris with offices at No. 2 Rue de Lancry, Paris, France. And during the next thirty days an office will be

opened for the supervision of the P. D. C. distribution through Central and Northern European countries and the outright sale to other European markets reached directly from Berlin.

Charles Ray will be starred by Chadwick Pictures Corporation in "Some Punkins," from which these stills are taken.

Columbia Denies Sale Rumors
Cohn Says Company Will Stay Independent in Answer to the Rumors of Affiliation

AN emphatic denial that Columbia Pictures had been sold to a large producing and distributing company was issued this week by Jack Cohn, who with Joe Brandt and Mr. Cohn's brother Harry, are the owners of the Columbia company. Rumors to the effect that the company would be absorbed by one of the larger organizations gained currency recently and in his statement denying these reports as absolutely groundless Mr. Cohn declared that "Columbia would stay independent and is not on the market despite all the stories which have been published of late."

He stated that a number of offers have been made for the company within the past few weeks. In his statement Mr. Cohn said in part:

"As proof of the fact that we do not intend to sell out, we are formulating plans for a bigger production season the coming year and we have completed plans for the acquisition of one of the largest studio units on the coast.

"We have already acquired several plays, books and stories of wide circulation. And on top of this, because of the support of the exhibitors this year we have backed up our promises by our cash in order to help the exhibitors make more money.

"We have the support of the best exchange men in the country, men who know all the 'ins and outs' of picture distribution, to handle our product. They want us to continue making pictures for them. Such keen exchangemen as North, Charnas, Amsterdam, Ellman, Hyman, Sheffield, Oldknow, McConville and Montague Rosenthal & Steinberg, Mayne, Granman, Friedman, and H. & W. distribute Columbia Pictures everywhere successfully.

"We are in the business of making pictures as independents and as long as we have the support of the exhibitors we will continue as independents and we will not consider any offer to sell out no matter how flattering it may be."

Paul Whitcomb Made Studio Manager of Glendale Plant

Paul Whitcomb of Haverhill, Mass., has been appointed studio manager of the Whitman Bennett Studio at Glendale, according to an announcement this week. Mr. Whitcomb, who has been making a study of picture production, will assume his duties immediately. New electrical equipment is being installed at the plant and production on four pictures is expected to start soon.

Schuessler Appointed "U" Casting Director

Universal announces the appointment of Fred Schuessler as casting director at Universal City to succeed Fred Datig, who resigned last week. Schuessler has been in the employ of Universal for the past three years as assistant to Datig and is regarded one of the most capable casting directors in Hollywood.

"Madam Lucy" Now Titled "Madam Behave"

The Al Christie feature starring Julian Eltinge, famous female impersonator, will be released by Producers Distributing Corporation under the title of "Madam Behave" instead of "Madam Lucy," the original title.

Saxton Now Associated With Chadwick Pictures

Charles Saxton, formerly cartoonist with the New York World, is now associated with the Chadwick Pictures Corporation as title writer and gagman. Saxton first entered pictures with Chadwick in the capacity of gagman for productions in which Leon Lee was interested. Later he collaborated with Lee in titling Larry Semon's "The Wizard of Oz." He recently resigned as director of the art department of the Vanderbilt Newspaper Syndicate to return to the Chadwick company and he is now writing the titles for "The Perfect Clown," Semon's new feature comedy.

Leatrice Joy to Star in "Made for Love"

"Made for Love" is the title of the next feature in which Leatrice Joy will be starred by Cecil B. De Mille. The production, which will be released by Producers Distributing Corporation, will be put into work immediately upon completion of the star's current feature "The Wedding Song." Paul Sloane will direct "Made for Love," which was written by Garrett Ford.

Van Loan Writes Original Story for Fox

Fox will start production shortly on "Streets of Six," an original story just completed by H. H. Van Loan. Among the previous stories Van Loan has written for Fox production were "The Speed Maniac," "Three Gold Coins," "Red Terror" and "Winning With Wits."

Scenes from the Victor Seastrom production, "The Tower of Lies," for Metro-Goldwyn-Mayer.

Moberly Mayor Vetos Sunday Openings

The fight of Moberly, Mo., a town of 25,000 inhabitants, to obtain Sunday motion picture shows, apparently has just begun. J. M. Jefferies, mayor, Monday vetoed a measure passed by the city council providing for Sunday shows. The bill had passed the council by a vote of 5 to 3. The mayor in his veto said that if the ordinance went into effect it would produce a "long vexatious struggle and agitation through the prosecuting attorney, grand jury and others to enforce the law."

One more vote for the measure will be necessary to pass the ordinance over the mayor's veto. Ministers waged a warm fight against the proposed ordinance, obtaining a list of more than 2,000 names to a petition, but exhibitors, on the other hand, obtained a petition with more than 4,000 signed names, so the theatre owners are hopeful that the measure again will be passed by the city council.

Helen Lee Worthing Cast for Schulberg Feature

Helen Lee Worthing, former "Follies" girl who is now devoting herself exclusively to picture work, has been engaged for a principal role in "The Other Woman's Story," a Schulberg production being directed by Gasnier. Alice Calhoun is playing the wife with Robert Frazer as the husband in this feature.

"Eden's Fruit" to Be Next Gasnier Production

B. P. Schulberg has announced that "Eden's Fruit" will be produced by Gasnier as his next work for the Schulberg company. The story was written and adapted by John Goodrich. Gasnier is now filming "The Other Woman's Story" and upon its completion will start the Goodrich story.

Warners Announce New Sales Appointments

SAM E. MORRIS, general manager of distribution for Warner Bros., this week announced new appointments in the sales organization of that company.

Jacob M. Klein has become manager of the Albany office. His work previously has been largely in the Boston territory. Lloyd Willis, a veteran in film sales work, is now special representative out of the New York office, and Edwin Silverman in addition to his duties as district representative has taken over the management of the Chicago Exchange.

Appointments of managers for several of the Warner Bros. theatres in the South were announced by George H. Dumond, general manager of the company's theatres. B. H. Stough is now assistant manager of the Broadway in Charlotte, N. C. Ed. C. Pearce is manager of the Broadway in Columbia, S. C.; Ed. W. Williamson is the new manager of the Lexington Theatre, Lexington, S. C.; and M. Merriweather becomes manager of the New Concord at Concord, N. C.

JOSEPH SCHILDKRAUT
Signs Exclusive Contract With De Mille

JOSEPH SCHILDKRAUT, stage and screen star, has signed a long term contract to appear exclusively in Cecil B. De Mille productions after completion of his starring contract with the producers of "The Firebrand," the stage success.

The actor recently completed work in "The Road to Yesterday," De Mille's personally-directed production for Producers Distributing corporation release. He interrupted his work in "The Firebrand" to play the picture role and the engagement of the play was suspended to permit members of the cast a vacation and allow the star to fill his contract with De Mille.

Universal Purchasing Stories

Production Plans Are Practically Completed for Season of 1926-27

THOUGH the 1925-26 season is only just getting under way, Universal has already practically completed the story lineup for the 1926-27 season. With the exception of a half dozen stories and plays now being negotiated for, the schedule is all but provided for.

This announcement was made following the return from the coast of Mrs. Winifred Eaton Reeve, Universal's scenario editor. She was in conference for two weeks at Hollywood with Raymond L. Schrock, general manager of Universal City, and the coast production and scenario departments. It is likely there will be four more Jewel productions next year than this, in addition to three super-Jewels of the type of "The Phantom of the Opera."

Two of the Denny pictures have already been purchased. They are "Rolling Home" by John Hunter Booth and "Signs" by Dorothy Grundy. Of about ten stories which are under consideration, Universal will purchase three more in the next two or three weeks to complete the Denny schedule.

So far two stories have been chosen for Louise Dresser. They are "Perch of the Devil," a dramatic novel by Gertrude Atherton, and "The Vehement Flame" by Margaret Deland.

For Norman Kerry Universal plans a big racing story, a big naval story, and the Frederick Isham story, "This Way Out," which was announced for Reginald Denny but was crowded off of this year's Denny schedule. The racing story is entitled "Racing Blood" and was adapted by Winifred Eaton Reeve from the "Blister Jones" stories by John Tainter Foote. For the naval story Universal has purchased "The Big Gun" by Richard Barry, published first in the Argosy All Story Magazine.

For Mary Philbin Universal plans a production of the anonymous novel, "Another Woman's Life." "Folle Farine" by Ouida is already being put into film form, and two original stories are being written for Miss Philbin also.

For Laura La Plante are "Brides Will Be Brides," a newspaper serial by Lucille Van Slyke which ran in between four and five hundred daily newspapers this year.

"Click of the Triangle T" by Oscar J. Friend, which recently appeared in novel form, is the first of the Hoot Gibson stories to be purchased. Another Hoot Gibson story is "Cow Jerry" a novel by George W. Ogden.

Among the all-star pictures which have been purchased are "The Quest of Joan," by James Oliver Curwood; "The Old Soak" by Don Marquis, previously announced; "Crimes of the Arm Chair Club" by Arthur Somers Roche; "Spangles," a big circus story by Nellie Revell; "The Whole Town's Talking," a play by John Emerson and Anita Loos; "The Cow Girl" by Arthur Stringer; "Cap Fallon, Fire Fighter" by John Moroso.

Kane Changes Title of His First National Feature

Robert Kane has changed the title of his production for First National, based on Frederick Palmer's novel "Invisible Wounds" to "The New Commandment." The work is being filmed under the direction of Howard Higgin with Blanche Sweet, Ben Lyon, Holbrook Blinn, Claire Eames, Dorothy Cummings, Pedro de Cordoba, Effie Shannon, Lucius Henderson, George Cooper and Diana Kane in the principal parts.

Highlights from "The Girl Who Wouldn't Work," the B. P. Schulberg production.

Five From Fox Due This Month

Widely Varied Attractions Are Offered to Exhibitors During Month of September

FIVE widely varied attractions are on the Fox release schedule for the month of September. They are titled "Kentucky Pride," "As No Man has Loved," "The Wheel," "The Timber Wolf" and "Havoc."

"Kentucky Pride" is first on the list, scheduled for September 6th. It is the autobiography of a racing fillie. John Ford produced the picture in which such horses are seen as Man O'War, Negofol, Morvich, Fair Play and The Finn. In the cast are Henry B. Walthall, J. Farrell Mac Donald and Gertrude Astor.

"As No Man Has Loved" is based on Edward Everett Hale's story, "The Man Without a Country." It has already had a successful three months' run on Broadway. Edward Hearn enacts the title role, with Pauline Starke and Lucy Beaumont chief in the supporting cast. September 13th has been set as the release date.

The second attraction of the John Golden unit of clean American pictures, "The Wheel" by Winchell Smith, will be presented on September 20. Victor Schertzinger directed. Margaret Livingston, Harrison Ford, Claire Adams and Mahlon Hamilton head the cast.

On the same date as "The Wheel," Buck Jones will appear in his first starring vehicle of the season, "The Timber Wolf," based on Jackson Gregory's novel. Elinor Fair is the heroine and Dave Dyas, the villain.

The greatest picture of the five is "Havoc," based on the international stage success of the same name by Henry Wall. The action of the picture takes the hero and the villain, George O'Brien and Walter McGrail, to the front in France. Madge Bellamy is the heroine, and Margaret Livingston is the heartless woman who laid waste

men's hearts. Leslie Fenton, Bertram Grassby, Eulalie Jensen, David Butler and Harvey Clark have important roles. This is the second Rowland V. Lee production of the season.

Ochs on First Trip for Warner Brothers

Lee Ochs, until recently managing director of the Piccadilly, now the Warner Theatre in New York, has started on his first trip as field representative for Warner Brothers. It will take him through the Pittsburgh territory. Ochs is visiting first run exhibitors with a view to closing deals and remedying conditions existing in various territories.

"Free Lips" Next Vehicle for Norma Shearer

"Free Lips," by Carey Wilson, will be Norma Shearer's next starring vehicle for Metro-Goldwyn-Mayer. Hobart Henley will direct and Lew Cody is to have the leading male role. The story was adapted for the screen by Hope Loring and Louis Leighton.

Henry King Completes Work on "Stella Dallas"

Henry King has completed production work on "Stella Dallas," which he is producing for Samuel Goldwyn and scheduled for distribution by United Artists. The picture has been in production four months. A Broadway presentation of the picture will be given in October.

Louis N. Jaffe Enters Independent Field

Louis N. Jaffe, prominent New York lawyer and realtor, has entered the picture field as an independent producer, under the name of the Jaffe Art Film Corporation, of which he is president.

The new organization will produce a number of pictures during the coming season. The first work, now nearing completion at the Tec Art Studios, will star Lila Lee with Maurice Schwatz, noted Jewish dramatic actor, in the main supporting role. The story is based on a stage play of immigrant life.

Paramount's "Lord Jim" Cast Completed

Victor Fleming has completed the cast for Joseph Conrad's "Lord Jim" which he is directing for Paramount. The featured players are Percy Marmont, Noah Beery, Raymond Hatton, Joseph Dowling, George Magrill, Duke Kahanamoku and Madeline Hurlock. Others in the cast are Jules Cowles, J. Gunnis Davis and Nick de Ruiz.

Vignola to Direct "Fifth Avenue" for Belasco

Robert G. Vignola has been engaged to direct the production of "Fifth Avenue," which Belasco Productions, Inc., will make for distribution by Producers Distributing Corporation. The story is an adaptation of a work of the same title by Arthur Stringer and will be published in the near future by Saturday Evening Post.

Action stills from F. B. O's "Three Wise Crooks."

Two More of Warner Bros. Forty Finished

"The Clash of the Wolves" and "Compromise," two more of the Warner Brothers forty for the season have been completed at the Hollywood studios of the company and are now in the cutting room in preparation for distribution.

Rin-Tin-Tin is the star of "The Clash of the Wolves," and is supported by a cast that includes June Marlowe, Charles Farrell, Charles (Heinie) Conklin, Will Walling and Pat Hartigan. The story and scenario are by Charles Logue. Noel Smith directed.

Irene Rich is starred in "Compromise," which is an adaptation from the story by Jay Gelzer. In the supporting cast are Clive Brook, Louise Fazenda, Pauline Garon, Helen Dunbar, Winter Hall, Raymond McKee, Frank Butler, Muriel Frances Dana, Lynn Cowan and Edward Martindel. Alan Crosland directed.

Associated Arts Starts on "Flaming Waters"

Associated Arts Corporation was scheduled to start production this week on "Flaming Waters" for F. B. O. release. It is a melodrama of the oil fields from an original story by E. Lloyd Sheldon and was prepared for the screen by Fred Kennedy Myton, scenario editor at the F. B. O. studios. The production will be supervised by Ludwig Erb and direction will be by Harmon Weight.

Announce New Title for "The Sea Woman"

First National announces that the title of Edwin Carew's new production will be changed from "Dangerous Currents" to "Barriers Aflame." The story is based on Willard Robinson's play, "The Sea Woman." Blanche Sweet, Robert Frazer, Charles Murray, Russell Simpson, Fred Warren, Dorothy Sebastian and Edward Earle play the leading roles.

Murphy Named Universal Production Manager

Martin Murphy will succeed William Koenig as production manager at Universal City, according to an announcement by Raymond L. Schrock, general manager. Koenig resigned recently. Murphy has been in the employ of Universal for more than ten years, starting as an assistant director with the old I. M. P. company at the Fort Lee Studios.

Hobart Henley Has Signed Long Contract

HOBART HENLEY has signed a new long term contract with Metro-Goldwyn-Mayer to direct a series of pictures, the first of which will be "Free Lips," an original story by Carey Wilson. Hope Loring and Louis D. Leighton have been assigned to prepare the scenario.

The new contract is said to be largely the result of the good work done by Henley in the direction of "The Slave of Fashion," Norma Shearer's initial starring vehicle, and "Exchange of Wives," which has just been completed.

Film Booking Offices Will Produce "Life of Theodore Roosevelt"

F. B. O. is to produce "The Life of Theodore Roosevelt" as the most lavish production on the company's program since its inception.

J. I. Schnitzer, vice-president of F. B. O. in charge of production, now at the coast studios of the company, and B. P. Fineman, production manager are perfecting details so that actual production on the film may be started immediately.

The production will vividly depict the high lights in the romantic and interesting career of this great soldier and statesman. A graduate of Harvard, Roosevelt served in the New York state assembly from 1882 to 1884. Later he became Police Commissioner of New York. He then became a member of the National Civil Service Commission and from 1897 to 1898 he acted as Assistant Secretary of the Navy. He resigned that post to organize with Surgeon Leonard Wood, the 1st U. S. Cavalry, known throughout the world as Roosevelt's Rough Riders, which served in Cuba in the Spanish American War, and of which he became Colonel.

In 1898 he was elected Governor of New York and in 1900 was elected Vice-President. When President McKinley was assassinated in 1901, Roosevelt became President and in 1904 was elected by a vast majority to serve another term. Following his occupancy of the Presidential chair, Roosevelt spent the remaining years of his life largely in the hunting of wild game in Africa and South America.

The player who will impersonate Roosevelt and the director have not yet been announced. The picture will be included as a Gold Bond special on the 1926-27 program of F. B. O.

New Plan for F. B. O. Managers

Branch Heads to Be Placed on Percentage Basis Throughout the United States

BRANCH managers in all F. B. O. exchanges throughout the United States are to be placed on a percentage basis for remuneration of services in lieu of salary, according to announcement by Major H. C. S. Thomson, president and managing director of the company. The new arrangement is not a bonus plan in the commonly accepted sense of the word, but is a percentage that will be earned by managers on the business that is done by each exchange.

The executive heads of F. B. O. have long been considering a plan whereby the managers of the exchanges might share in the profits of the business, and finally evolved the percentage basis as being the simplest and most practicable.

In commenting on the percentage arrangement Major Thomson said:

"F. B. O. is moving forward at a fast pace. The organization has been built up in the past three years until today we have one of the finest selling organizations in the business. This plan of remuneration, we expect, will not only encourage the managers to the maximum sales effort, but will stabilize the organization and permanently settle the problem of remuneration. It means, on the basis of the present business, a raise for every manager in the organization."

F. B. O. is the second company in the industry to adopt the percentage plan of remuneration for branch managers.

Coogans Enter Theatre Field

Purchase One-Third Interest in the Langley Circuit in Southern California

JACKIE COOGAN PRODUCTIONS has entered the theatre field, according to word received from the west coast. The announcement is made that Arthur L. Bernstein, production manager of Jackie Coogan Productions has purchased from C. L. Langley, president of the West Coast Langley Theatres, the latter's interest in the Langley circuit, which constitutes one-third of a chain of twenty-one theatres.

This deal is reported to have come as a complete surprise to theatrical interests on the west coast. It is said that not even the closest associates of either the Coogans or Langley knew anything of the deal until the announcement was made in the morning papers. The consideration is said to have been around half a million dollars. The theatres included in the deal are located in Southern California towns.

There was no secret to the fact that the Coogan's were to enter the theatre field. Jack Coogan Sr. had announced that Jackie's money would be used to build a 3,000 seat house in Los Angeles and that that would be the first of a prospective chain. The nucleus of that chain undoubtedly will be the purchase just concluded. The 3,000 seat theatre will be built on Western Avenue between Fifth and Sixth Streets.

Scenes from the Paramount production "A Son of His Father."

Independent to Produce Only

Goldburg Announces Withdrawal From States Rights; Will Release Through National Co.

INDEPENDENT PICTURES CORPORATION will withdraw from distribution through state rights exchanges after completion of the current series of Bill Cody features and henceforth produce exclusively for release by national distributors, Jesse J. Goldburg, president of the company, announced this week.

Other than maintaining an office representation in New York, Mr. Goldburg's entire Eastern organization will move to the West Coast where production activities will be centered.

Mr. Goldburg, who returned from Hollywood last week, made the following statement:

"I have been an independent Producer and State Right Distributor for about thirteen years, but my activities were centered largely on the distribution end of my business. For the past two years my production activities were confined to California which necessitated my presence there in the personal supervision of my productions. The result was, that I had to abandon personal supervision of either distribution or production.

"I have been approached repeatedly by not alone National distributors operating their own exchanges, but also by National State Right Distributors to make pictures for them, and it is that end of the business that I will hereafter concentrate on.

"I find that one must specialize in this industry, and a Producer must be a Producer, and a Distributor must be a Distributor only, when the results are dependent largely on the efforts of the individual."

Mr. Jack Lustberg, in charge of the New York office of the Independent Pictures Corp., will be placed in charge of the studios and act as studio manager of that company on the West Coast.

Independent Completes "The Power of the Weak"

"The Power of the Weak" has been completed by Independent Pictures Corporation as its first special production. Alice Calhoun has the featured role and is supported by Spottiswood Aitken, Carl Miller, Arnold Gregg and Marguerite Clayton.

The story was written by James Ormont and produced under the personal supervision of Jesse J. Goldburg. There are to be six of these Alice Calhoun productions, the distribution plans for which have not yet been determined.

Betty Francisco is in Cast Supporting MacLean

Betty Francisco has been added to the cast which will support Douglas MacLean in "Seven Keys to Baldpate," the star's first production for Paramount. Others previously engaged for the picture, which is now being made under the direction of Fred Newmeyer, are Edith Roberts, who has the role of leading lady; Wade Boteler, William Orlamonde, Mayme Kelso, Edwin Sturgis, Ned Sparks, Anders Randolf and Craufurd Kent.

Swedish Star Signs Long M-G-M Contract

Lars Hansen, one of the most popular motion picture stars of Sweden and continental Europe, has been signed to a long term contract by Metro-Goldwyn-Mayer. He was scheduled to sail from Stockholm on September 4th.

Hansen, a discovery of Mayer's, has been connected with the Svenska Film Industrie of Stockholm, the same concern from which came Victor Seastrom and Benjamin Christianson, directors now serving under the M-G-M banner.

Leon Abrams Will Direct for M-G-M

Leon Abrams, author of "The Masked Bride," Mae Murray's next for Metro-Goldwyn-Mayer, has been signed as a director by that company. He was formerly a director for the late Sarah Bernhardt in France, and has been assigned to the direction of "Nocturne," the screen version of Frank Swinnerton's novel and play for M-G-M. It was erroneously announced last week that Leon Adams had been signed to direct for Metro-Goldwyn-Mayer.

"Checkered Flag" Script is Completed

The script for "The Checkered Flag" has been completed by Charles and Fanny Hatton and it will be made as the fourth of the Banner Productions for release through Henry Ginsberg. It is an adaptation from the novel of the same name by John Mersereau. Ben Verschleiser will be in charge of production.

"Tricks" is a Davis Distributing Division release. These scenes are from the production.

Rod La Rocque in "The Coming of Amos," a Cecile B. De Mille production released by Producers Distributing Corporation.

DeMille Buys Out Stromberg

"The Last Frontier" Among Properties Taken Over in P. D. C. Production Rearrangement

THE Cinema Corporation of America, the holding company back of Cecil B. De Mille's independent activities, has purchased the Hunt Stromberg Producers Distributing Corporation interests, it was announced this week. The company also has purchased the controlling interest in the Hollywood Studios from Charles and Al. Christie.

The transaction which has brought about a realignment of the Producers Distributing Corporation production program, means that De Mille's activities will be increased about fifty per cent over the twelve features originally announced as his production schedule for the year.

In the transaction with Hunt Stromberg,

the Cinema Corporation of America secured all of the Harry Carey pictures and Hunt Stromberg productions released and scheduled for release through Producers Distributing Corporation, including the producing rights of "The Last Frontier."

This spectacular western, for the filming of which elaborate preparations have already been made, will now be produced by Cecil B. De Mille, either under his personal direction or supervision. De Mille's producing activities will be still further increased by his assuming supervision of the filming of the several other stories, originally scheduled for production by Stromberg, and now, under the terms of the deal, the property of the Cinema Corporation of America.

Will Furnish Perfect Prints

Warners to Recondition Film After the First Run Showings in Own Laboratories

A PLAN for reconstructing prints after showings at the first run houses in order to insure the smaller theatres of perfect film has been worked out by Warner Bros., whose bookers have been instructed to send prints to the laboratories for inspection and servicing at certain intervals during a picture's currency.

Prints from all exchanges east of the Rockies will be shipped to the Laboratory in Brooklyn and western prints will go to the Hollywood plant of the company.

In announcing this service innovation Warners state that the plan will enable the company to furnish only perfect prints to

exhibitors large and small. While efforts have been made to give the smaller exhibitor as good a print as the bigger showman, of a necessity in receiving the prints after they had been used over the country the smaller house owner got the worst of the wear and tear on the film.

Under the new plan prints will be put into brand new condition after they have been in use by the bigger houses. Following the first run period of the prints' service they will go to the laboratories where all scratches, torn sprocket holes, etc., will be eliminated and repaired and the print put in as good condition as when it first left the laboratory.

"Kiki" to Be Next for Norma

"Kiki" will be Norma Talmadge's next production to follow "Graustark" on the First National program, according to an announcement just received.

Joseph M. Schenck has engaged Clarence Brown to direct this Andre Picard play. Hans Kraly will make the screen adaptation.

Bert Lytell Engaged for Warner Feature

Warners announce the engagement of Bert Lytell to play the role of Lord Windermere in support of Irene Rich in the Warner Brothers production of the Oscar Wilde classic, "Lady Windermere's Fan." May McAvoy will appear as Lady Windermere and Carry Daumery has been engaged for the role of the Duchess.

New Auditor Appointed by Arrow

W. E. Shallenberger, president of Arrow Pictures Corporation has appointed Louis L. Baudry auditor of the company to succeed Hugh Davis, resigned. Baudry has had wide experience as an accountant and auditor. He installed the audit system now in force at the Hotel Pennsylvania, New York, and also instituted an audit system used by the Congress Hotel in Chicago.

Anthony Paul Kelly Writing for Hines

C. C. Burr has engaged Anthony Paul Kelly to write the scenario of Hines' second First National vehicle, "Rainbow Riley," adapted from Thompson Buchanan's original stage play, "The Cub," in which Douglas Fairbanks appeared on the legitimate stage.

Alice Calhoun in scenes from "The Part Time Wife," a Gotham production.

Four More Selected for "Martinique" Cast

Edith Yorke, Brandon Hurst, Evelyn Sherman and Billy Franey have been added to the cast of "Martinique," Bebe Daniels next starring vehicle for Paramount. In addition to Miss Daniels the featured players already announced include Ricardo Cortez, Wallace Beery, Arthur Edmund Carew, Dale Fuller, Robert Perry, Eulalie Jensen and Emily Barrye. William K. Howard is directing.

Royal Pictures Completes "Big Pal" Cast

Royal Pictures has completed the cast for "Big Pal," second of the features to be distributed by Henry Ginsberg. William Russell is the featured star, while the main supporting roles are in the hands of Julianne Johnston, Mickey Bennett and Mary Carr. The production is scheduled for release in September.

Lionel Barrymore Signed for "The Splendid Road"

Lionel Barrymore has been engaged to play one of the three leading roles in "The Splendid Road," Frank Lloyd's next production for First National. Anna Q. Nilsson and Robert Frazer have the other two featured parts in this adaptation of Vingie E. Roe's novel.

Herrick in Chicago for New Picture

F. H. Herrick, who already has completed four of "The Fragment of Life" series, being distributed by the Davis Distributing Division, Inc., arrived in Chicago, to make the fifth of the series, which will be called "Memory Lane." Included in the cast according to Mr. Herrick are Eleanor King, Reginald Simpson, Harry Stone and William Calhoun. William J. Miller is the camera man.

Action stills from "Wall Street Whiz," an F.B.O. feature starring Richard Talmadge.

Forming 2 New Feature Units

First National Studios in East Ready to Start Errol Vehicle and "Mismates"

LEON ERROL'S new screen vehicle and a screen adaptation of "Mismates," a stage play by Myron C. Fagan, are scheduled to go into production at the First National studios in the east within the next few weeks.

The Errol picture will be "The Lunatic at Large," written by J. Storer Clouston. The book had an immensely successful career in England when it was first published and the continued popularity results in the two sequels "The Lunatic at Large Again," and "The Lunatic Still at Large," by the same author.

The cast for "Mismates" has not yet been selected. The script is being written by Earl Snell and C. L. Yearsley. It is a powerful melodrama, the story of a manicure girl who marries the son of a wealthy family who object to her.

Work on the filming of "The Unguarded Hour" and "The Scarlet Saint" now in production, is going on rapidly and the pictures are expected to reach the cutting room within a few weeks.

Other pictures in line for production in the near future by the eastern units include "Men of Steel," a super-special to be made with Milton Sills in the stellar role, "Mademoiselle Modiste," "Pals First," "The Savage," "Bed and Board" and "Atlantis," the big sequel to "The Lost World."

Opposed To Uniform Contract

Wisconsin M. P. T. O. Convention Appoints Committee to Discuss Revisions With Board

THE uniform contract and arbitration occupied the centre of the stage at the convention of the Wisconsin M. P.T.O. held in Milwaukee last week. The real basis of the complaints lodged by exhibitors against the present system was the contract, for while vigorous opposition to the existing method of handling disputes was generally expressed, the complaints cited cases resulting directly from the contract.

Definite action to bring revisions of the arbitration system was taken when the convention appointed a committee of three exhibitor members of the arbitration board to confer with the Film Board of Trade. The particular nature of the changes sought were not made known, the conference being relied upon to affect revisions which will make the system acceptable to the exhibitors.

Though a clash over the election of a new president of the organization was anticipated in some quarters no conflict on this score developed at the convention, and Fred Seegert, of the Regent, Milwaukee, was re-elected for a third term without opposition. Other officers elected include F. J. McWilliams, Madison, vice-president; Max Krofta, Milwaukee, recording secretary, and Ernest Langemack, Milwaukee, treasurer.

The Wisconsin exhibitors pledged their full support to Independence Week, to be held in October, a move which assumes added significance in view of the fact that the Greater Movie Season movement received no organized support there.

Editors to Collaborate on "U" Serial

Universal has inaugurated a contest that should be interesting to newspaper men. Members of the National Editorial Association will be asked to write a ten-episode chapter play for Universal production and $5,000 will be paid for the best story.

From the synopsis submitted the ten best will be chosen and the one then adjudged the best will be produced, while the writers of the other nine will collaborate by outlining in detail the action of one each of the chapters of the serial. Each of the ten winners will receive $500 for his synopsis.

Six months will be given to prepare the stories and the picture will be produced next year during the time the Editorial Association is convening in Los Angeles. It is more than likely more than one story will be suitable for production, in which event Universal will make offers for the successful ones.

Martha Franklin in Cast of "Masked Bride"

Martha Franklin, known thirty-five years ago to every theatre-goer in America, has been added to the cast of "The Masked Bride," Mae Murray's new starring vehicle for Metro-Goldwyn-Mayer. Francis X. Bushman plays opposite Miss Murray in this picture.

Miss Franklin played second lead in the original "Belle of New York" Company, the musical comedy that made Edna May the idol of Broadway. It later played for years in England with Miss Franklin in the cast. "The Masked Bride" is being directed by Christy Cabanne. Roy D'Arcy, Basil Rathbone and Karl Dane are in the supporting cast.

Rex Ingram Has Completed "Mare Nostrum"

"Mare Nostrum" has practically been completed in Nice for Metro-Goldwyn-Mayer by Rex Ingram. Alice Terry has completed her role and is due back in New York about September 8th. Tony Moreno, who played the leading male role, is scheduled to sail for America about the middle of September. Ingram will probably remain in France until he completes his next picture for Metro-Goldwyn-Mayer.

First Half of Gotham Program Completed

SAM SAX, head of Gotham Productions, this week announced that company has completed the first half of the schedule of features to be made for the 1925-26 season, sixty days ahead of schedule. The productions so far completed and delivered to exchanges with all exploitation material and ready for release are "The Overland Limited," "The Police Patrol," "A Little Girl in A Big City," "His Master's Voice," "The Part Time Wife," and "The Shadow on the Wall."

Camera work has been started on "One of the Bravest," the seventh Gotham for the season. This will be followed by "Hearts and Spangles," "The Phantom of the Forest," "Racing Blood," "The Speed Limit," "The Sign of the Claw," and the comedy special "McFadden's Row of Flats."

W. C. Boothby Appointed Comptroller of First National

FIRST NATIONAL PICTURES, INC., has appointed W. C. Boothby, formerly of the First National Bank of Boston, to the responsible executive position of Financial comptroller made vacant by the resignation of C. S. Pinkerton. Mr. Boothby has already assumed the duties of his new position.

He was born in Somerville, Mass., and after finishing the grammar and high schools of that city began his banking career in 1902. Four years later he joined the staff of the First National Bank of Boston, which is now one of the foremost financial institutions of America. He worked rapidly up through the various departments to the position of executive head of the loan and discount departments from which he was promoted to the First National Corporation, a subsidiary corporation owned entirely by the bank and one of the largest organizations of its kind in the country, as assistant treasurer. Three months later he was made treasurer and executive officer which position he held up to the time of joining the staff of First National Pictures, Inc.

Independents Report New Sales

Gotham Closes With Independent Films for Canada Rights—Chadwick Sells Cuba Franchise

IMPORTANT foreign territorial sales were announced this week by Chadwick and Gotham. The latter concern's program of twelve productions will be handled in Canada by Independent Films Limited. This deal was consummated by Sam Sax, of Gotham and Lumas Film Corporation, distributors of the Gotham pictures, and Jules Levine and L. Rosenfeld, representing the Canada company. The sale gives the Independent concern a total of 18 Gotham productions, as the latter's series of six features for last season were purchased by Levine and Rosenfeld.

In addition to the extensive territory already closed for the entire 1925-1926 product in Domestic and Foriegn territories, Chadwick Pictures Corporation this week completed arrangements with Carrera and Medina, one of the most prominent exchanges in Cuba, for the distribution of fourteen of its pictures in that territory.

Besides operating their important exchange, Carrera and Medina are also owners of a string of theatres in Cuba, and are planning an intensive exploitation campaign to put over these productions.

One of the most important domestic sales of the week past was negotiated by W. E. Shallenberger of Arrow Pictures and Richard Fox, of the Freedom Film Corporation of Buffalo. Under this deal the Freedom company acquired the franchise for the twenty-four Arrow features for 1925-26 for the Upper New York territory. Shallenberger also announced the sale of "Lost in the Big City," "North of Nome," "The Lost Chord," and "Lena Rivers," Arrow features, to W. D. Ward of Detroit for the district known as the Lower Michigan Peninsular.

Louis Weiss, Managing Director of Weiss Brothers' Artelass Pictures Corporation, announced that he has sold his new series of Six Single Reel Special Features entitled "Guess Who" to Mr. Bru, representing the Unity Film Company Ltd. of London, England.

The deal covers the distribution of the series in the United Kingdom and Continental Europe.

Nine Features Ready for Weiss

With the arrival in New York this week of "Action Galore" Weiss Brothers Artclass Pictures have nine pictures belonging to the 1925-26 program ready for release.

These nine are as follows: In the series of Fire-Reel Tough Riding Romances featuring Buddy Roosevelt, "Reckless Courage," in the Buffalo Bill Jr. Series "Quicker 'N Lightnin," "The Desert Demon" and "The Saddle Cyclone;" in the Wally Wales Series "Tear-in' Loose" and "The Hurricane Horseman;" and the first of the eight Westerns featuring Leo Maloney with Bullet, the Wonder Dog and Senator, the Human Horse "Win, Lose or Draw."

The fourth Buddy Roosevelt feature is ready to start and the third Wally Wales feature will be completed this week.

Leo Maloney is making active preparations to start the second of his series this week while nine stories have been completed on the following two.

With the two production schedules going along as they are Louis Weiss expects that his whole year's product will be in his office by the end of November.

Chadwick Has Acquired Full Ownership of Studio

I. E. Chadwick, head of Chadwick Pictures Corporation, has purchased from Jesse J. Goldberg the latter's interest in the Independent Studio at Sunset Boulevard and Gower Street, Los Angeles, it was announced this week. Under the purchase the Chadwick organization gains full ownership of the studio property, a half interest in which was bought from Goldburg a short time ago.

Chadwick will leave for Los Angeles soon to organize a complete studio staff to handle the future productions made by his company, which will do its producing at the Independent plant.

House Peters is featured in "Raffles," a new Universal Production. These stills are taken from the picture.

Meyer to Build New Theatre in Miami, Fla.

The Wolfson Meyer Theatre Enterprises corporation of Miami have announced plans to construct a new theatre on North Miami avenue there, to be named the Capitol, which will be a first-run theatre and modern in every respect. The company also own and operate the Lyric theatre, a colored house, in Miami.

Mr. Meyer has been in the motion picture industry for a great many years, and was formerly connected with Fox Film corporation in a sales capacity.

Arrested for Sunday Show in Test Case

O. W. McCutchin, owner of the motion picture house at Sikeston, Mo., has been arrested on a charge of operating his house on Sunday.

McCutchin announced in advance that he would give the Sunday show on August 23 so that he could be arrested and test the state law against employing labor on Sundays.

West Virginia Theatre is Destroyed by Fire

The Strand Theatre building Parkersburg, W. Va., was practically demolished by fire recently at 422 Market street. The estimated loss was about $50,000.

Gala Premiere For "Phantom"

Universal Makes Elaborate Plans for Presentation in New York Sunday Next

UNIVERSAL has completed elaborate plans for the gala premiere which "The Phantom of the Opera," spectacular screen production of Gaston Leroux's famous mystery romance, will be given at the Astor Theatre, New York, on Sunday, September 6th.

The Sunday night presentation will be surrounded by all the color and brilliance which a wide exploitation campaign and special invitations can accomplish for a first night. Celebrities of the stage and screen as well as prominent New Yorkers have accepted invitations to attend the affair, which will also be open to the public, Universal reporting a lively demand for tickets at the box office.

The Universal company has attempted to duplicate the lavishness of the production in the presentation that has been arranged for "The Phantom of the Opera." One of the main features of the presentation will be the musical accompaniment. A score based mainly on the opera "Faust" has been written for the picture and will be rendered by an orchestra under the direction of Eugene Conte, composer of the musical setting.

Another highlight in Universal's presentation plans will be the staging by Thurston, the famous magician, of the appearance of a "phantom" during the prologue. Universal offered a large cash prize to the person who would cause the appearance of a "spirit" during the premiere showing. Thurston took up the challenge.

A further interesting phase of Universal's presentation plan is a ballet which has been staged by Albertina Rasch, internationally noted ballerina.

$200,000 Theatre to Be Built in Santa Ana, Cal.

Santa Ana, California is to have a $200,000 theatre building in accordance with plans that are being drawn by Eugene Durfee, architect, with offices in Anaheim and Los Angeles, to be erected on the northeast corner of Fourth and Bush streets, to cost approximately $200,000. The site is 100 by 165 feet, and the seating capacity of the new theatre will be 2,000. In addition to the theatre there will be a number of shops, store room and studio.

Tennessee Theatre Suffers Fire Damage

The Bonita Theatre, Copper Hill, Tenn., was badly damaged by fire recently when several other buildings were caught also in a blaze that resulted in a loss of about $500,000.

Krafft Writing Titles for "The Pace That Thrills"

John W. Krafft, comedy title writer, is writing the titles for "The Pace That Thrills," the First National production co-featuring Ben Lyon and Mary Astor. The picture will be ready for release soon.

Wanda Wiley in "Just in Time," a new Century comedy released by Universal.

Seeking American Beauties for Universal Feature

Universal is conducting a nationwide search for the most beautiful girls in America to appear in "See America First," a forthcoming production. The search is being made by a director and cameramen who are touring the country in the automobile trailer built for Reginald Denny's "California Straight Ahead." Camera tests will be made of the winners of beauty contests to be held in various cities.

Edgar Norton Joins "Lady From Hell" Cast

The Associated Exhibitors cast for "The Lady From Hell" has been augmented by the addition of Edgar Norton, character actor, who has been assigned an important role. The picture is being directed by Stuart Paton and has Blanche Sweet and Roy Stewart in the featured roles. It will probably be released in the second group of Associated Exhibitors attractions for the new season.

Extended Run of "Phantom" at Roosevelt, Chicago

Universal's "The Phantom of the Opera" will have its Chicago premiere sometime in November at the Roosevelt Theatre, where it will play an indefinite engagement. The engagement was arranged by Ned Marin, Universal sales director and Balaban & Katz, operators of the theatre, during Marin's recent tour of the middle west.

Finish Casting for "The Scarlet Saint"

The principal roles for "The Scarlet Saint," which First National is producing in New York, have been filled, the most recent addition to the cast being Jack Raymond, who will have the role of a comedy valet. Other principals in the cast are Mary Astor, Lloyd Hughes, Frank Morgan and Jed Prouty. George Archainbaud is directing.

Valentino's "The Eagle" is Nearing Completion

Camera work on "The Eagle," Rudolph Valentino's first production for United Artists, will be completed in about two weeks, according to an announcement from the United Studios in Hollywood, where the feature is being filmed under Clarence Brown's direction.

"Lieber Month" Launched by First National

E. A. ESCHMANN, head of First National's sales department, announced that a "Lieber Month" sales contest would be launched by the company beginning September 14th next and extending to November 7th inclusive, at the three-day national sales convention held at the Hotel Roosevelt in New York last week.

Prizes aggregating more than $7,000 will be awarded to First National branches winning first, second and third place in the contest. In case of ties the full amount of the prizes tied for will be awarded to each tying contestant.

Patsy Ruth Miller and Monte Blue in "Red Hot Tires," a Warner Brothers production.

First National Convention Ends
Most Harmonious and Successful in the Organization's History, Declares Eschmann

THE recent national sales convention of First National, held last week, and attended by every branch and district manager was the most successful in the history of the organization, E. A. Eschmann, general manager of distribution declared this week.

In commenting on the convention, after it was over and the branch and district managers had returned to their territories, Mr. Eschmann said: "The convention was the most harmonious yet held by First National and was a developer of ideas, of unified spirit and of enthusiasm. We know from past performance what our sales force can do with good pictures, and we are giving them still greater box-office productions for the new season. First National has hit a stride that can't be beat; the momentum already attained will carry its sales to steadily increasing volume."

In his address to the convention at the Wednesday session, Richard A. Rowland, general manager of production, emphasized the spirit that animates the production end of First National.

He said in part:

"We in production know that you have to have pictures to sell that the market wants. We realize that you have to have good pictures and I assure you that we are doing everything in our power to give you good pictures.

"This year we have more than held our own and I am very hopeful for the future. I have recently returned from Hollywood and I can assure you that you have good product coming from the West Coast.

"You must not forget that a picture is not better than its cast value. The public wants names that are familiar to them—standard names.

"The big specials and the star productions are the box-office magnets. Next come the all-star productions. They are always a gamble, but they serve to develop the stars that the industry needs. This is a personality business and the public wants personalities. That is why we are constantly endeavoring to create stars. Star pictures are easier to sell and they bring in more revenue.

"The lack of good stories is another problem that we are constantly facing. In the course of the year it is impossible for all the companies combined to get more than twenty outstanding stories. We have to take the best we can get and give them the treatment necessary to turn them into photoplay entertainment."

Walter Long Engaged by Cecil De Mille

Cecil B. DeMille has engaged Walter Long for a leading role in "The Road to Yesterday." This will be De Mille's first personally directed production for release through Producers Distributing Corporation.

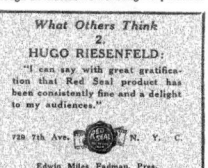

Exhibitors Service Bureau

Manager C. F. Creslin of the Rialto theatre, Augusta, Ga., used a shadow-box, a banner, a special strip and other accessory material to make up this attraction-compelling lobby display on "The Last of the Duanes" (Fox).

Advisory Board and Contributing Editors, Exhibitors' Service Bureau

George J. Schade, Schade theatre, Sandusky.

Edward L. Hyman, Mark Strand theatre, Brooklyn.

Leo A. Landau, Lyceum theatre, Minneapolis.

C. C. Perry, Managing Director, Garrick theatre, Minneapolis.

E. R. Rogers, Southern District Supervisor, Famous Players-Lasky, Chattanooga, Tenn.

Stanley Chambers, Palace theatre, Wichita, Kan.

Willard C. Patterson, Metropolitan theatre, Atlanta.

E. V. Richards, Jr., Gen. Mgr., Saenger Amusement Co., New Orleans.

F. L. Newman, Managing Director, Famous Players-Lasky theatres, Los Angeles.

Arthur G. Stolte, Des Moines theatre, Des Moines, Iowa.

W. C. Quimby, Managing Director, Strand Palace and Jefferson theatres, Fort Wayne, Ind.

J. A. Partington, Imperial theatre, San Francisco.

George E. Carpenter, Paramount-Empress theatre, Salt Lake.

Sidney Grauman, Grauman's theatres, Los Angeles.

Appealing float on "Drusilla With a Million" (F. B. O.) which carried off the prize in the Greater Movie Season parade in Minneapolis, where the picture was showing at Pantages theatre.

George E. Brown, Imperial theatre, Charlotte, N. C.

Louis K. Sidney, Division Manager, Lowe's theatres, Pittsburgh, Pa.

Geo. Rotsky, Managing Director, Palace theatre, Montreal, Can.

Eddie Zorn, Managing Director, Broadway-Strand theatre, Detroit.

Fred S. Myer, Managing Director, Palace theatre, Hamilton, Ohio.

Joseph Plunkett, Managing Director, Mark Strand theatre, New York.

Ray Grombacher, Managing Director, Liberty theatre, Spokane, Wash.

Ross A. McVoy, Manager, Temple theatre, Geneva, N. Y.

W. S. McLaren, Managing Director, Capitol theatre, Jackson, Mich.

Harold B. Franklin, Director of Theatres, Famous Players-Lasky.

William J. Sullivan, Manager, Rialto theatre, Butte, Mont.

H. A. Albright, Manager, T. D. & L. theatre, Glendale, Calif.

Claire Meachime, Grand theatre, Westfield, N. Y.

Ace Berry, Managing Director, Circle theatre, Indianapolis.

Complete "Check-Up" in this Issue

Two-Faced Winking Moon is "Forty Winks" Display

"Forty Winks" showing at the Superba, Raleigh, N. C., was uniquely exploited by Manager J. L. Williamson, who hung a winking two-faced moon from his attraction sign where it could be seen both up and down street for a considerable distance.

The double-faced moon was made of two pieces of beaverboard, each face painted gold and black to represent a smiling "man in the moon." Each face that two large eyes cut out and covered with yellow crepe paper with eyeballs and eyebrows painted on. One eye was equipped with a 40 watt lamp, remaining stationary, while other was equipped with a 60 watt lamp attached to a flasher which kept the eye winking at close intervals. The two-faced laughing moon with its winking eyes attracted a world of attention.

Local Girls Featured in Campaign on "Sally"

"Sally" at the Palace, Fort Worth, was aided by Manager Barry Burke's splendid campaign which embraced every available method of exploitation.

One of the highlights of the campaign was the publicity given the two Fort Worth girls appearing in a scene from the photoplay. This, Manager Burke accomplished by getting pictures of the two young ladies from their parents, which together with special write-ups were printed in the local newspapers. Both girls have won beauty prizes in their home town and are well-known there. Their pictures exhibited in the lobby of the theatre created a lot of attention.

Manager Burke entertained the Tarrant County Orphans at a special matinee, after which they were treated to ice cream and cake. The Kiwanis club provided automobiles which transported the children to and from the theatre. As the playhouse is lo-

C. D. MacGregor, the projectionist and exploiteer of the Princess theatre at Chatham, Ont., designed and carried out this snappy front for "Gold Heels" (Fox) recently.

cated in the heart of the business section, the arrival and departure of the orphans drew crowds. Pictures taken of the juveniles at the theatre were printed in the newspapers accompanied by special stories. The stunt added greatly to the good-will already enjoyed by the Palace, the management receiving many expressions of gratitude for the thoughtfulness.

Tie-ups were effected with all music stores on the song "Sally" and the theatre's orchestra and organist rendered special selections from the "Sally Hits."

The lobby had a beautiful cutout of the star, surrounded with stills and pictures from the photoplay.

Drawing Contest Given for "Black Cyclone"

In connection with his showing of "Black Cyclone" at the Rex, Spartanburg, Manager J. H. Stelling conducted a drawing contest, offering passes for the best drawing of Rex, the Wild Horse. The stunt, advertised both on the theatre screen and in the local newspapers, met with hearty response. The drawings received were put on display in the lobby during the showing of the picture, creating a lot of discussion.

Valuable word-of-mouth advertising was gained through the special morning matinee held for the boys and girls of Spartanburg on the opening day of the picture, the admission price of which was a horse shoe. Over 600 kiddies attended the matinee, and the horse shoes they brought were piled in the center of the theatre lobby, with a card announcing that to the one guessing the nearest the correct number, would be given passes to the Rex. In this way added interest was created for the photoplay.

Mirror Display Piece for "Proud Flesh" Showing

An ingenious lobby display piece was devised by Manager D. Roscoe Faunce for "Proud Flesh" at the Strand theatre, Birmingham.

The background consisted of beaverboard cut and painted to represent a beveled mirror on the surface of which was painted the figure of a woman getting a back view of herself in a small hand mirror in her left hand. Her reflection was visualised by artist's impression, giving a very realistic effect.

Several stills from the photoplay were artistically arranged on the mirror.

An important tie-up was arranged with the book department of a leading department store in which they displayed a large hand painted book, the cover of which carried advertising copy on the attraction with a line announcing that the book was on sale.

Good use was made of mounted poster paper in making up the lobby display on "Inez from Hollywood" (First Nat'l) at the Royal theatre, Laredo, Texas, recently.

"Goose Hangs High" Plays Take-a-Chance Week

"Take A Chance Week" was well put over at Peterson & Woods' Palace theatre, Jamestown, N. Y. "The Goose Hangs High" was the feature and "every unit on the program from overture to final curtain was shrouded in mystery." The entire campaign was very well handled with the assistance of George E. Williams, Paramount exploiteer.

Cuts from the press-sheet were used in the newspaper advertising with absolutely no hint about the production they represented. The cuts were used with the copy "you have taken a chance at fairs, carnivals, and bazaars, but never in your life have you bought a ticket to a theatre not knowing what you were going to see."

In the half-tone cuts used in the movie columns of the papers, the faces of the people in the cast were partially routed out so that it would be impossible to identify the players and thus get a clue to the picture.

The main catchline for all advertising was: "A Big Surprise Show—Will You Take A Chance?"

Trackless Train Succeeds Strongly in Chicago

America's first Trackless Train, now crossing the continent from New York to Los Angeles, has proved such a sensation in Chicago that Metro-Goldwyn-Mayer, the producing organization sponsoring its historic cross-country rtip, has acceded to demands made by exhibitors in the Windy City and extended the train's visit from three days to five.

Fully 150,000 people turned out to view the parade staged by the Illinois Automobile club, which was headed by the Trackless Train. The mayor and other city officials inspected the special at hte height of the ceremonies, while guests aboard it during the parade included the president of the

Lobby and marquee of the New Aster theatre, Minneapolis, as decorated for the engagement of "Lightnin'" (Fox) and Greater Movie season.

club, the vice-president and Ralph Ketter-ing, in charge of the Greater Movie Season campaign for the Hays organization. The Trackless Train bore banners exploiting Greater Movie Season, and was awarded first honorable mention by officials of the parade, no prizes being awarded.

Enormous crowds were attracted about the train when it parked before the Chicago theatre, while equally enthusiastic interest was aroused at every stop made in the Windy City. Other theatres visited by the special were the Balaban and Katz Riviera, Ascher's Chateau, the State and Lake, the Roosevelt, McVicker's, the Bugg, Standard, Plaza Ideal, Rosewood, Commodore, Rivoli, Vision, Hoyne, Biltmore, Rose, Sittners, LaSalle, Crown and numerous others.

Free Ticket Daily Boosts "Heart of a Siren"

A two-column head news reader, a two-column reader cut, and a quarter-page advertisement announced the coming of "The Heart of a Siren" at the Capitol theatre, Victoria, B. C., week commencing June 29th.

The free Loge Seat coupon is still appearing in all Capitol theatre advertisements and Manager Denham is absolutely positive that this form of advertising is bringing direct returns. The newspaper gives the space occupied by the coupon gratis and the Capitol furnishes three loge seats. The Colonist changes the name daily, the names being taken from their new subscription list. Manager Denham did not have to argue with the Colonist to try this stunt. They immediately fell in line and are of the opinion that they obtain new subscribers through this novel form of advertising.

As an added attraction Thomas McLean, baritone, of the International Opera Company, rendered a number of popular songs through the week.

Dailies Cooperate for "The Great Divide" Stunt

Arrangements were made with both local dailies in Newark, O., when "The Great Divide" played there recently at the Auditorium to award free tickets to names selected at random from their subscription lists and printed among the want ads. This stunt achieved front page space on both papers.

The leading music dealer contributed a window display, and special cut-outs decorated the lobby. The town was heavily billed for two weeks in advance, 100 one-sheets being used, 39 three-sheets, 15 six-sheets, 5 twenty-four sheets, 100 window cards and 5,000 heralds. There was also a special lobby display.

Snappy artwork and prominent lettering featured this lobby display on "The Unholy Three" (Metro-Goldwyn) at Keith's Majestic theatre, Louisville, Ky. Combined with the electric marquee signs, it made a splendid flash from any side.

"Making of O'Malley" is Advertised in Program

To build up the advertising in his program issued weekly as Gordon's Olympia Screen Review, Manager Harry ("Ted") Browning of Gordon's Olympia Theatre, New Haven, is offering a pair of free tickets to every person who makes a purchase at three of the firms advertising in the Screen Review. There is no restriction as to the amount of the purchase. All that is necessary to get a pair of free seats is to present receipt of purchase from three advertisers in the program together with the clipped ads.

In the current issue of the Screen Review, Browning is making the offer outlined above. He also advertises his coming attraction, "The Making of O'Malley," by running a cut of the star, as a policeman, on the front cover, with a few words of text, in black and orange. On an inner page appears his opinion of the picture in the form of an advance review. He continues to advertise his pictures in the local baseball score-cards.

Race Track Built in Lobby for "Gold Heels" Run

For his showing of "Gold Heels," Manager Oscar White of the Liberty theatre, Greenwood, converted his lobby into a veritable race track by the use of compoboard cutout and painted black and white to represent a fence, behind which was placed a huge cutout of a horse shoe with the head of a horse painted in the center.

Three bales of hay were used, one on each end and in front of fence. On top of hay pile in front of fence was placed a borrowed saddle, bridle and blanket. Vines decorated the fence, giving an added touch of color to the display, the effectiveness of which was only equalled by the attention it attracted.

Book-store window display on "The Keeper of the Bees" (F. B. O.) at Robinson's Book Store, Akron, Ohio.

Neat Miniature Display in Lobby for "Chickie"

For "Chickie," playing the Modjeska theatre, Augusta, Manager F. J. Miller built a miniature display in a shadow-box extending across lobby front.

The display depicted a couple canoeing on a lake with the sky and woodland greens for a background. A Japanese parasol held by the lady in the canoe gave a distinctive touch to the scene. Illuminated by colored lights which greatly enhanced its beauty, the exhibit brought forth many favorable comments from patrons.

Distribution of Newsettes Aids "The Monster"

The distribution of 10,000 attractively made-up Newsettes containing cuts and special stories were a feature of the campaign recently waged in connection with the showing of "The Monster" at Loew's Temple in Birmingham, Ala., by C. D. Haug, Metro-Goldwyn exploiteer, and E. A. Vinson, director of publicity for the theatre. Two thousand of these Newsettes were distributed through the Independent Laundry.

Sidewalk stencils reading "The Monster is Coming" were imprinted on all corners in the heart of the city and on sidewalks leading to the theatre. Thirty-one Yellow Cabs carried 30-inch signs over their spare tires, while street cars carried 100 dash cards on front and rear. Fifty window cards in gold frames were displayed to advantage in prominent locations, and 150 one-sheets were posted throughout the community.

Dallas House Ties Up With Newspaper Contest

Publicity Director R. B. Jones, at the Melba theatre, Dallas, recently tied-in with "The Times Herald Standard Brand Food Coloring Contest."

Every Friday, for three consecutive weeks, the newspaper printed a full page of ads, each featuring different products of the food company.

Prizes of 40 Melba tickets were awarded to the kiddies turning in the most effectively colored ads. All answers had to be sent direct to the newspaper's office, where pictures were passed upon by selected judges.

The contest proved valuable, not alone for the inspiration it afforded the children, but for the enviable publicity it brought theatre, merchant and newspaper.

Fantastic lobby display in brilliant colors, carrying out the style of the picture, by Manager Jean Wildenstein of the Princess theatre, San Antonio, on "Beggar on Horseback" (Paramount).

Striking Hat Shadow-Box on "Paths to Paradise"

The most striking feature of Manager D. Roscoe Faunce's campaign on "Paths to Paradise" in Birmingham, was the shadow-box used in the lobby of the Strand. This was in the form of a high silk hat made from compoboard and painted black. An opening was cut in the front of hat and faced with two layers of screenwire, in back of which was placed a scene painted to represent a room with Raymond Griffith and Betty Compson trying to open a safe. A powerful spotlight attached to an oscillating fan traveled all around the room and in its sweep revealed the figures at the safe. The moving light is especially noteworthy, its action arresting the attention of everybody. The cast and title were printed in white, directly underneath the opening.

The regular newspaper and billing campaign was augmented by the use of 2,000 special stickers carrying a huge black arrow with copy as follows: "Paths to Paradise"—Strand theatre—Now Playing.

Five Displays in St. Paul to Aid "Proud Flesh"

When "Proud Flesh" played recently at the Tower theatre in St. Paul, Minn., Morris Abrams, Metro-Goldwyn exploiteer, secured five striking window displays which attracted much attention to the run. Two were contributed by the leading cigar stores and featured stills showing Harrison Ford displaying a cigarette holder, and two more were donated to the caused by haberdashery stores, which exhibited stills of Pat O'Malley. A still showing Eleanor Boardman wearing a shawl was displayed by a dealer in women's apparel.

Special cut-outs decorated the lobby, and extra space was taken in the local dailies. The town was well posted in addition.

Mounted wood cut-out on the marquee of the Laughlin theatre, Long Beach, Calif., for "The White Outlaw" (Universal). E. D. Tracey is manager

Rag Patch Contest Boosts "Rag Man" Showing

A Jackie Coogan Rag Patch contest recently stimulated interest in a showing of "The Rag Man" at the Majestic theatre in Findlay, O. C. C. Deardourff planted this contest in the Findlay Republican-Courier and offered cash prizes amounting to $7, with 25 free tickets as consolation awards.

The town was lavishly posted in addition, and there was a vigorous press campaign which achieved the placing of special stories and cuts, as well as increased display space. Heralds were distributed and a trailer was brought into play at the Majestic.

Memphis Manicurists See "Manicure Girl"

When "The Manicure Girl" played the Strand theatre, Manager Walter League invited the manicurists of Memphis to attend a private showing of the picture.

A card with clever copy and attractive lay-out was issued to each girl, inviting her and an escort to attend the preview. The screening was well attended by the manicurists, their companions, and the press. Result was enviable word-of-mouth advertising and newspaper publicity.

In addition, every beauty parlor in the city had a framed 11 x 14 photo on their manicure tables.

The News Scimitar also furnished a lady reporter to cover the beauty parlors, interviews resulting in a feature story.

One of the strongest selling forces of the campaign was the exhibition of photos of Memphis manicurists held in the theatre lobby. This was the work of a local photographer who did same gratis in exchange for the advertising accorded his display.

Girl in Riding Habit Is "Sporting Venus" Aid

A young woman dressed in a snappy riding habit and mounted on a beautiful black horse recently exploited a showing of "The Sporting Venus" at Loew's State theatre in Boston, and proved a sensational feature of the campaign waged by Jerry Fraenkel, Metro-Goldwyn exploiteer.

This young woman rode through the principal streets daily for five days and attracted attention to the run which was announced in large letters on the saddle blanket. The best saddlery and sporting goods store in the city was tied up for a large window display, in which a 6-sheet cut-out was displayed.

A real circus in miniature provided the prologue to "Sally of the Sawdust" (United Artists) staged by Edward L. Hyman, managing director of the Brooklyn Mark Strand theatre, Brooklyn, the other week. The Mark Strand artists took part in it.

Treasure Hunt Put Over on "Paths to Paradise"

Manager Ed. Roberts got his inspiration for a "Treasure Hunt" on "Paths to Paradise" at the Majestic, from two sources. From an old "treasurer" map belonging to the Austin Statesman, and from an Aztec map found in the basement of the theatre several months ago when it was being remodeled.

Manager Roberts obtained possession of the Statesman's "treasure" map after reading an account of its discovery in a story printed by the paper a week prior to picture's opening.

A translation of the Aztec map, along with a picture, was published in the Statesman with the announcement that the Majestic theatre would conduct a "Treasure Hunt" on the evening before showing of "Paths to Paradise." Only requirements were that participants be at the Majestic at 7 p. m. with a car, a flashlight and plenty of perseverance. Upon starting out they were given numbered cards containing directions written in code, the solution leading to the next post, where another clew was given, and so on until entire route was covered.

The "hunt" started at the Capitol grounds, then to the dam on Colorado River, then to golf links a Lion's Club, then on to confectionery shop, famous for its "gem" sherbets, where "hunters" were given a "gem" cone free of charge. At drug store station, participants received samples of powder, tooth paste and shaving cream. The "hunt" ended with "the pot of gold" at the end of the trail.

A first prize of $10.00 was awarded to the Statesman to the first person completing the "Treasure Hunt," second prize, a month's pass to the Majestic, third prize, a year's subscription to the Statesman, fourth prize a three weeks' pass to the Majestic, fifth prize a two weeks' pass and sixth prize a one week's pass. Ten additional prizes of 2 passes each to see "Paths to Paradise" were given to the next ten winners.

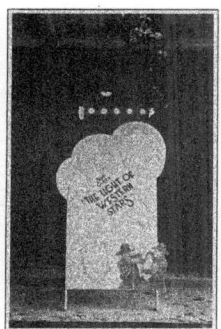

Illuminated lobby display piece on "Light of Western Stars" (Paramount), with lights behind yellow crepe paper star, done by Manager C. B. Stif of the Imperial theatre, Columbia, S. C.

Showing for Orphans Aids "Making of O'Malley"

Taking his cue from the fact that Milton Sills, in "The Making of O'Malley," plays the part of a big-hearted New York policeman who is a special friend of the children, the manager of the Savoy theatre, Wilmington, Del., captured much publicity through a special morning performance for the children of St. Peter's Female Orphanage, at Riverview.

The showing was five days in advance of the opening date and netted a good amount of newspaper space in addition to the word-of-mouth advertising it received.

Special Halifax Showing of "The Lost World"

Before its showing at the Casino theatre, Halifax, N. S., "The Lost World" came in for much excellent publicity through a private screening at the Casino, arranged for with W. J. Melody, branch manager in St. John for First National.

Newspaper men and many well-known resident were invited to the showing; among them the Archbishop and the Dean of Novia Scotia. Letters of commendation of an unusual sort were received from Mrs. Anne F. Worral, wife of the Most Rev. Clare L. Worrell, D.D., Archbishop of Nova Scotia, the very Rev. J. P. D. Lloyd, D.C.L., Dean of Nova Scotia; and Thomas Hilliard, president and managing director of the Dominion Life Insurance Company. Their opinion of the production not only carried weight in Halifax but throughout Nova Scotia and the Dominion.

Train of 1931 Advertises "The Limited Mail"

The showing of "The Limited Mail" at the Warners theatre (formerly the Piccadilly) in New York City was given the aid of a strong exploitation campaign put across by Warner Bros., which included one especially striking piece of advertising.

Through arrangement with the New York Central, the old De Witt Clinton train, the first operated by that railroad, was borrowed and mounted on motor trucks, one to each piece of historic rolling stock. This was paraded through the streets daily, exciting the greatest interest. A special guard was provided for the valuable property. On the first day of its use, the train was taken down to City Hall, where the Mayor made a talk.

As the showing came concurrently with Railroad Men's Week, the display and parade was especially appropriate.

The handsome facade of the Roosevelt theatre, Chicago, was decorated in true circus fashion for "Sally of the Sawdust" (United Artists), a regular "big top" being erected over the marque, as shown here.

Strong Campaign Made on "Don Q" Premiere

An effective advance publicity and advertising campaign was that which Mark Larkin, publicity director for the Douglas Fairbanks company, handled in connection with the New York World premiere of "Don Q, Son of Zorro," showing at the Globe theatre.

Perhaps the most important feature of the campaign was the policy under which it was conducted. Harry D. Buckley, special business representative for Douglas Fairbanks, who came to New York from Hollywood to handle the premiere showing, issued but one order. "No hokum," he said. "Run your campaign on a strict line of square dealing."

As a result absolute frankness featured the campaign. No attempt was made to hoodwink the newspapers with so-called exploitation stunts. No editor was tricked. The copy was written, for its genuine news or feature value, and placed solely on that basis. The same held true of the art. Every effort was made to oblige the newspapers, and when requests were made for special stories, they were supplied with despatch.

The advertising campaign consisted of outdoor display on billboards and in windows, and of paid-for newspaper space.

Eight days ahead of the opening of the picture, a one-half motion picture showing, consisting of 100 24-sheet stands, was posted. A "motion picture showing" in New York means billboards situated at the most advantageous spots in the city, none of them being in the theatrical district.

On Wednesday of the week preceding the opening, advertising began in the newspapers with 35 lines—two and one-half inches—in the five leading morning newspapers. No afternoon papers were used until the day of the opening, when the principal evenings were given an even break with fifty along with the morning papers.

A Tampa jeweler was induced to give this window display to "Paths to Paradise" (Paramount) at the Victory theatre, which John B. Carroll manages.

Most extensive window tie-ups were arranged, and included "Don Q" photographs in 500 windows; also department store window displays of productive costumes worn by Douglas Fairbanks and Mary Astor, his leading lady. Through the advertising managers of the stores, displays of these picturesque movie clothes were obtained for Fifth Avenue and other principal shopping centers. One man devoted two weeks to the placing in advantageous store locations of 500 beautifully made, and highly artistic photographs, each hand-lettered with the billing, of the picture, the theatre and opening play date.

Russian Dancers Support "Madonna of Streets"

When Manager Jack Rowley of the Royal theatre, at Laredo, Texas, began the exploitation work for "Madonna of the Streets," he did not depend upon the stars alone to put over the picture. Two popular Russian ballerines, Mlle. Gali de Mamay and Mons. Thaddeus Loboyko, the former a ballet dancer who had been a member of Pavlowa's ballet, and the latter formerly Pavlowa's dancing master, happened to be in Laredo on their way to Mexico City to fill an engagement.

When Manager Rowley learned that the Russian dancers would be detained in Laredo several days, he stated: "I am going to put on a prologue with these renowned Russian ballet dancers that will give the movie patrons a 'Russian' program and one of the best ever put on anywhere in Texas." He advertised extensively in the newspapers that in addition to the showing of "Madonna of the Streets," with Nazimova, the Russian motion picture star, and Milton Sills, two of the greatest Russian ballerines in this country would put on classical Russian interpretations of famous dances. Manager Rowley not only used this announcement in the newspapers in readers and advertisements, through handbills and heralds, but he had printed about a thousand announcements on fine linen paper and sent them through the mail to the citizens of Laredo.

On the opening date the front of the Royal Theatre was a mass of painted bulletins announcing the presence of the Russian dancers, while setting in the lobby, just inside the large double entrance, was a large cut-out of Nazimova and Milton Sills from a one-sheet and in this cut-out was arranged a smaller cut-out through which filtered a spotlight on the faces of the two stars, this effect being provided day and night.

Clever idea in billing the star's name used in the lobby of the Modjeska theatre, Augusta, Ga., by Manager F. J. Miller for "Paths to Paradise" (Paramount).

With First Run Theatres

NEW YORK CITY

Rivoli Theatre—
Film Numbers—The Coast of Folly (Paramount), A Seaside Frolic (Comedy), Rivoli Pictorial (Selected).
Musical Program—"Pique Dame" (Overture), Reisenfeld's Classical Jazz (Specialty), "Pal of My Cradle Days" (Organ solo).

Capitol Theatre—
Film Numbers — The Mystic (Metro-Goldwyn-Mayer), F i s h for Two (Scenic), Capitol Magazine (Selected).
Musical Program—"Marche Slav" (Overture), "The Wren" (Vocal solo), Modern Tango (Dance number), Ballet music from "Naila" (Piano solo), "Dreaming of Tomorrow" (Vocal solo and quartet), "Neptune's Daughters (Soloist and Ballet Corps), Organ solo.

Mark Strand Theatre—
Film Numbers—The Gold Rush (United Artists), continued.

Colony Theatre—
Film Numbers — Seven Days (Prod. Dist. Corp.), Colony Pictorial, Colony World Tour (Scenic).
Musical Program—"Morning, Noon and Night" (Overture), Colony Dance Creations "School Days to Jazz" (Special Jazz orchestra).

Cameo Theatre—
Film Numbers—Sally of the Sawdust (United Artists), Cameo Pictorial (Pathe News), Aesop's Fables (Pathe).
Musical Program—Orchestral overture, "One Little Dream of Love" (Soprano solo), Organ solo.

Warner's Theatre—
Film Numbers—The Limited Mail (Warner Bros.), Warner's News Weekly (Selected), Felix Dopes It Out (S. R.).
Musical Program—"Melodies You Know" (Orchestra), "Sweethearts" (Special vocal numbers by Trio), "Valse Bluette" (Soloist), Sam Herman (Xylophone solo).

Rialto Theatre—
Film Numbers—The Love Hour (Warner Bros.), Rialto Magazine (Selected), Felix Trifles With Time (S. R.).
Musical Program—Ben Bernie and the Rialto 'Gang' (Special number "In the Swiss Alps").

Embassy Theatre—
Film Numbers—The Merry Widow (Metro-Goldwyn-Mayer).
Musical Program—"Oriental Baccchanale" (prolog to feature).

Criterion Theatre—
Film Numbers—The Wanderer (Paramount), continued.

LOS ANGELES

Criterion Theatre—
Film Numbers—Wild Justice (Fox), Accidents Will Happen (Universal), Fox News.
Musical Program—Melody Monarchs (Specialty).

Forum Theatre—
Film Numbers—Seven Days (Prod. Dist. Corp), Ko Ko Nuts (S. R.), In the Spider's Grip (Educational), International

News, Kinograms.

Hill Street Theatre—
Film Numbers—The Kiss Barrier (Fox), The Pace Makers (F. B. O.), Aesop's Fables (Pathe), International News.

Loew's State Theatre—
Film Numbers—Shore Leave (First National), Marvels of Motion (Pathe), Loew's State Pictorial News (Selected).
Musical Program—Orchestra.

Metropolitan Theatre—
Film Numbers—The Street of Forgotten Men (Paramount), Aesop's Fables (Pathe), Pathe News.
Musical Program—"Light Cavalry" (Overture).

Million Dollar Theatre—
Film Numbers—The Freshman (Pathe), Aesop's Fables (Pathe).
Musical Program—"On the Campus" (Overture).

Pantage's Theatre—
Film Numbers—Faint Perfume, S. R., Pathe News.
Musical Program—Vaudeville.

CHICAGO

Capitol Theatre—
Film Numbers — Lightnin' (Fox), Capitol Theatre World Events (Pathe), Comedy Cartoon (Selected).
Musical Program—"A Medley of Popular Airs" (Overture), Miss Mamie Stillerman, playing "Staccato Etude" (Piano Solo), "The Three Harmony Aces" (Specialty), James J. Corbett and Capitol Abbott Ballet (Specialty), "Two Boys From Arkansas" (Musical Saw Specialty), "There Ain't No Flies On Auntie" (Organ), "Loves of the Evening Tide" (Presentation).

Stratford Theatre—
Film Numbers—The Danger Signal (S. R.), Stratford Pictorial (Fox), Scenic, Sneezing Beezers (Pathe).
Musical Program—Henderson & Weber (Specialty), "Are You Sorry?" (Organ Solo), "De Gray-Lester & Company" (Presentation).

Orchestra Hall—
Film Numbers—Seven Days (Producers Distr. Corp.).

Monroe Theatre—
Film Numbers—Lightnin' (Fox), International News.

Roosevelt Theatre—
Film Numbers—Don Q. Son of Zorro (United Artists).

Orpheum Theatre—
Film Numbers—The Gold Rush (United Artists).

McVicker's Theatre—
Film Numbers—Wild Horse Mesa (Paramount), News Weekly (Pathe), Remember When (Pathe).
Musical Program—"Jazz Grab Bag" (Stage Specialties and Presentations).

Chicago Theatre—
Film Numbers—The Unholy Three (Metro-Goldwyn), International News (Universal), Only a Country Lass (Scenic).
Musical Program—"Herbertiana" (Overture), "Meditation from Thais" (Organ Solo), "That Midnight Waltz," (Specialty).

Tivoli Theatre—
Film Numbers—The Marriage Whirl (First National), News Weekly (Universal), Comedy (Selected).
Musical Program—"Rienzi" (Overture), "Under Spanish Skies" (Presentation), "Classical Jazz" (Specialty), "Memories of Chopin" (Specialty), "The Evolution of Baby Songs" (Organ Solo).

Uptown Theatre—
Film Numbers—The Marriage Whirl (First National), News and Views (Pathe), Scenic Wonders, Felix Cat Cartoon.
Musical Program—"A Popular Fantasy" (Overture), "Voices of Spring" (Solo), "Pomp and Circumstance" (Organ Solo), "The Pearl of Damascus" (Presentation).

MILWAUKEE

Alhambra Theatre—
Film Numbers—The Gold Rush (United Artists), International News.
Musical Program—"Musical Madness and Titina (Overture),

"Tons of Ice" (Stage Presentation).

Garden Theatre—
Film Numbers—The Woman Hater (Warner Bros.), No Father to Guide Him (Pathe), Fox News.
Musical Program—"Dreams" (Organ Specialty).

Merrill Theatre—
Film Numbers—The Lost World (First National), International Weekly, Felix Cartoon (S. R.).
Musical Program—"The Lost World" (Myrtle Spangenberg and Spencer Rueter), Orchestra and Organ Overture.

Strand Theatre—
Film Numbers—In the Name of Love (Paramount), The Pacemakers (F. B. O.), Kinograms, Bray Magazine (F. B. O.).
Musical Program—"Red Hot" (Orchestra Presentation).

Wisconsin Theatre—
Film Numbers—Night Life of New York (Paramount).
Musical Program—Mardi Gras Week and Carnival of Syncopation (Stage Presentation).

BROOKLYN

Mark Strand Theatre—
Film Numbers—The Fool (Fox), Mark Strand Topical Review (selected).
Musical Program—"Southern Memories"—"My Old Kentucky Home" (Orchestra), "Heaven, Heaven" a negro spiritual, (quartette number), "Carolina in the Morning" (ballet), "Dry Yo' Eyes" (female quartette), "Dixie" and "Old Folks at Home" (Ensemble), "Russian Rag" (Xylophone solo), prologue to feature—"Omnipotence" and "Hallelujah Chorus" from the "Messiah" as the recessional.

DES MOINES

Capitol Theatre—
Film Numbers—Fox News, Watch Out (Educational), The Sporting Chance (Premier).
Musical Program—"Bunch of Harmony" (musical act).

Des Moines Theatre—
Film Numbers—Night Life of New York, Red Pepper (Educational), Barrier Busters (Pathe), International News.
Musical Program—Coster and Rich (Apache dancers).

Strand Theatre—
Film Numbers—Wild, Wild, Susan (Paramount), Oh, Bridget (Educational), Kinograms.
Musical Program—"A Sweet Hawaiian Moonlight" and popular numbers, musical instruments act.

Rialto Theatre—
Film Numbers—The Ten Commandments (Paramount).

BUFFALO

Shea's Hippodrome—
Film Numbers—The Unholy Three (Metro-Goldwyn-Mayer), Fox comedy, Current Events (Pathe and International News).
Musical Program—"Midsummer

Hand-drawn newspaper ad in three columns used recently by the Capitol theatre in Cincinnati on "Recompense". (Warner Bros.)

Night's Dream" (orchestra),
Florence Mills and Will Voc-
ery's orchestra.
Loew's State—
Film Numbers—The Lucky
Horse Shoe (Fox), King Cot-
ton (Educational), Current
Events (Pathe News).
Musical Program—Indian Jazz
Revue. Five acts of vaude-
ville.
Lafayette Square Theatre—
Film Numbers—Proud Flesh
(Metro-Goldwyn-Mayer), Pathe
comedy, Current Events (Fox
News).
Musical Program—Selection from
"The Student Prince" (orches-
tra), Henry B. Murtaugh play-
ing his orginal compositions on
the organ. Five acts of vaude-
ville.
New Olympic Theatre—
Film Numbers—My Lady's Lips
(B. P. Schulberg-S.R.), The
Man Without a Heart (S. R.),
Thundering Landlords (Com-
edy), Current Events (Interna-
tional News).
Musical Program—Overture to
"Mlle. Modiste" (organ).
Shea's North Park Theatre—
Film Numbers—The Dressmaker
from Paris (Paramount), Sher-
lock Sleuth (Pathe), Current
Events (Pathe and Inter-
national News).
Musical Program—Bits of Popu-
lar Hits (orchestra).

HOUSTON

Queen Theatre—
Film Numbers—Don Q, Son of
Zorro (United Artists), Pathe
comedy and Pathe News
(Pathe).
Musical Program—Queen Orches-
tra, featuring "La Ciabel"
organ numbers.
Iris Theatre—
Film Numbers—The Half Way
Girl (First National), Comedy
(Pathe), International News
(Universal).
Musical Program—Iris Concert
Orchestra, featuring "Merry
Wives of Windsor" (overture).
Organ numbers.
Majestic Theatre—
Film Numbers—Smooth as Satin
(F. B. O.), Aesop's Fables
(Pathe), Pathe News.
Musical Program—Majestic Or-
chestra, featuring popular pro-
gram. Organ numbers. Vaude-
ville.
Rialto Theatre—
Film Numbers — The Teaser
(Universal), comedy (Educa-
tional), Fox News.
Musical Program—Organ num-
bers.
Liberty Theatre—
Film Numbers—Rugged Waters
(Paramount), comedy (Educa-
tional), Pathe Review.
Musical Program—Organ num-
bers.
Capitol Theatre—
Film Numbers—The Lady Who
Lied (1st National), comedy
(Educational), Kinograms
(Educational).
Musical Program—Concert Or-
chestra, organ numbers.

MINNEAPOLIS

Astor Theatre—
Film Numbers — Havoc (Fox),
Wild Waves (S. R.), Fox News.
Musical Program—Organ over-
ture.

GORDON'S OLYMPIA - WASH. ST.

FIRST BOSTON SHOWING, BEGINNING TODAY (SUNDAY)

The MAKING OF A NATION

"*The* SCARLET WEST"

WITH A CAST OF 4000 including
2000 INDIANS and HUNDREDS
OF AMERICAN SOLDIERS *The*
The MOST SPECTACULAR PICTURE OF
OLD FRONTIER DAYS EVER FILMED

Also BIG VAUDEVILLE SHOW

*A two-column opening ad on "The Scarlet West" (First National) at
Gordon's Olympia theatre, Boston, recently.*

New Lyric Theatre—
Film Numbers — The Lucky Devil
(Paramount), Pathe News.
Musical Program — David Rubin-
off, Russian violinist, assisted
by Reginald Willis, Maurice
Cook, organist.
Garrick Theatre—
Film Numbers—A Slave of Fash-
ion (Metro-Goldwyn).
Musical Program — Avo Bombar-
ger, tenor, Santucci, accordion.
State Theatre—
Film Numbers — The Coast of
Folly (Paramount), Watch Out
(Educational), State News Di-
gest.
Musical Program — State Concert
Orchestra (overture), "Rhap-
sody Hongroise," Organ Novelty
"Sometime," E. J. Dunstedter.
"A Prince in Heidelberg, 18
voices.
Strand Theatre—
Film Numbers — The Lost World
(First National), Felix Doubles
for Darwin (Educational),
Strand News.
Musical Program—Strand Concert
Orchestra specialty "When
Shadows Fall."

ST. PAUL

Astor Theatre—
Film Numbers—I Want My Man
(First National), Three Bases
East (F. B. O.), News Events.
Musical Program — Neal Burns
and Vera Steadman (personal
appearance), Organ novelty,
George Getsey (baritone), Astor
Syncopating Gophers.
Capitol Theatre—
Film Numbers — California
Straight Ahead (Universal),
The Masquerade (Red Seal),
Capital News Digest.
Musical Program—Sissle & Blake,
Capitol Symphony orchestra
playing "Evolution of Dixie"
(Organ), Leonard Leigh.
Garrick Theatre—
Film Numbers — The Lost World
(First National), Napoleon Not
So Great (Comedy), World
Events in Pictures.
Musical Program—White Brothers
and Stendal, trio.
Princess Theatre—
Film Numbers—My Son (First
National), first half, Born Rich
(First National), second half,

Kinograms and Comedy.
Musical Program — Organ over-
ture.
Strand Theatre—
Film Numbers — Havoc (Fox),
Cartoon Comedy, Kinograms.
Musical Program — Organ over-
ture.

SAN FRANCISCO

California Theatre—
Film Numbers—Beggar on
Horseback (Paramount),
Pathe Review, No. 27, Barn-
yard Olympics (Pathe), Inter-
national News.
Musical Program—"Moments Mu-
sical" (Specialty), "Song of
Songs" (Vocal).
Loew's Warfield Theatre—
Film Numbers—Sun Up (Metro-
Goldwyn-Mayer), Waiting
(Educational). Kinograms and
International News.
Musical Program—"Oriental Fan-
tasy" (Fanchon and Marco idea
with Orientals and special
beauty chorus).
Granada Theatre—
Film Numbers—California
Straight Ahead (Universal)
Felix Finds 'Em Fickle (S. R.),
Pathe News.
Musical Program—"The Bridge,
The Bay Revue" (Special sing-
ing and dancing idea built
around Bridge idea).
Imperial Theatre—
Film Numbers—Don Q, Son of
Zorro (United Artists), contin-
ued).
Cameo Theatre—
Film Numbers—Head Winds
(Universal), Horace Greely, Jr.
(Pathe), International News.
Musical Program—Musical Maids
in Song.
Union Square Theatre—
Film Numbers—Slander (S. R.)
House of Flickers (Fox), Fox
News.
Musical Program—Variety revue
with singing, dancing and
jokes.
St. Francis Theatre—
Film Numbers—The Iron Horse
(Fox), continued.

ATLANTA

Howard Theatre—
Film Numbers—A Slave of Fash-

ion (Metro-Goldwyn).
Loew's Grand—
Film Numbers — Eve's Lover
(Warner).
Metropolitan Theatre—
Film Numbers—The Half-Way
Girl (First National).
Rialto Theatre—
Film Numbers—Beggar on Horse-
back (Paramount).

INDIANAPOLIS

Circle Theatre—
Film Numbers—Graustark (First
National), Comedy (Education-
al), Circle Presentation, "Old
Fashioned Movie Show, Twenty
Years Ago" (Short Film Syndi-
cate), Travel Film (Fox), Ani-
mated News Reel (Universal).
Musical Program—"March Slave"
(Circle concert orchestra), Hus-
ton Ray (pianist).
Colonial Theatre—
Film Numbers—Lightnin' (Fox),
Comedy (Universal), Interna-
tional News Reel (Universal),
Aesop's Fables (Pathe).
Musical Program—American Har-
monists and Frank Owens and
Bob Jones, soloists.
Apollo Theatre—
Film Numbers—The Mystic
(Metro-Goldwyn), Comedy
(Pathe), News Reel (Fox).
Musical Program—Emil Seidel
orchestra and Earl Gordon, or-
ganist.

CLEVELAND

Stillman Theatre—
Film Numbers—Romola (Metro-
Goldwyn-Mayer), continued.
Musical Program — "The Student
Prince" (overture), "Ave
Maria" (vocal, with elaborate
church setting, and light ef-
fects).
Allen Theatre—
Film Numbers—Her Sister from
Paris (First National). Dont
Pinch (Educational), Country
Life a la Mode (taken from
Pathe Review), Topics of the
Day (Pathe), Pathe News.
Musical Program—Magic Melodies
from Franz Lehar's operettas
(overture), Jazz Band in Spain,
playing "The Fire Bird" and
"St. Louis Blues."
State Theatre—
Film Numbers — Sun Up (Metro-
Goldwyn), Cupid's Victory
(Universal), The Iron Mule
(Educational), Pathe Review,
Literary Digest (S. R.), Inter-
national News (Universal).
Musical Program — Organ Over-
ture, Vaudeville.
Park Theatre—
Film Numbers—Poisoned Paradise
(S. R.), Call a Cop (Education-
al), Pathe Review, Topics of the
Day (Pathe), Kinograms (Edu-
cational).
Musical Program—"Capriccio
Italienne" (overture). Jazz
("Will You Remember
Me," "Sonya," "Alone at Last"
(baritone solo).
Keith's Palace Theatre—
Film Numbers — The Iron Horse
(Fox), repeat engagement,
Pathe comedy, Pathe News.
Musical Program—Medley of Old
American Melodies (overture),
Vaudeville.
Reade's Hippodrome—
Film Numbers—Hell's High Road
(Producers Distributing Corp.),
Pathe comedy, International
News (Universal).
Musical Program — "Rose Marie"

Snappy single-column ad on "The Manicure Girl" (Paramount) at the Karlton theatre, Philadelphia.

(overture), Vaudeville.

Keith's East 105th St.—
Film Numbers—Hell's High Road (Prod. Distr. Corp), Pathe comedy, Pathe News, Aesop's Fables (Pathe).
Musical Program—"Blossom Time" (overture), Vaudeville.

KANSAS CITY

Newman Theatre—
Film Numbers—Wild Horse Mesa (Paramount), Newman News and Views (Pathe and Kinograms), Newman Current Events (Local Photography).
Musical Program — Atmospheric Selections (Overture), Thirty Singing Cowboys (Vocal Novelty), Excerpts From "The Student Prince" (Novelty), Recessional (Organ Solos).

Liberty Theatre—
Film Numbers—The Teaser (Universal), Aesop's Fables (Pathe), International News Pictorial, The Fighting Ranger (Universal Serial).
Musical Program — Atmospheric Selections (Overture), Recessional (Organ Solos).

Royal Theatre—
Film Numbers—The Ten Commandments (Paramount), continued, Royal Screen Magazine (Pathe and Kinograms), Royal Current Events (Local Photography).
Musical Program—Royal Syncopators On Stage (Overture), Recessional (Organ Solo).

Mainstreet Theatre—
Film Numbers—The Knockout (First National), Educational Short Subjects and Pathe News.
Musical Program—Popular Selections (Overture), Recessional (Organ Solos).

Pantages Theatre—
Film Numbers — The Sporting Chance (Tiffany–S. R.), Fox News and Fox Short Subjects.
Musical Program—"Mamie" (Overture), Recessional (Organ Solo).

OMAHA

Rialto Theatre—
Film Numbers — Shore Leave (First National), Pleasure Bound (Educational), Kinograms.
Musical Program — "Hungarian

Rhapsody No. 2" (Overture), "Jack Tar" (Exit March), "The Mystery of Night" (Organ), "The Heart of Her" and "Characteristic Piece" (Theme for feature picture). On the stage—Gordon Green and His Imp Orchestra, assisted by Eddie Mathews.

Strand Theatre—
Film Numbers—Don Q, Son of Zorro (United Artists), continued, Fox News.

Sun Theatre—
Film Numbers— Pretty Ladies (Metro-Goldwyn), Boobs in the Woods (Pathe), Trip Through the Metro-Goldwyn Studios.

World Theatre—
Film Numbers — The White Desert (Metro-Goldwyn).
Musical Program—"Knee Deep in Daisies" and "Abie's Irish Rose," (Organ selections).

Moon Theatre—
Film Numbers—Taming the West (Universal).
Musical Program—Vaudeville.

Empress Theatre—
Film Numbers—Up the Ladder (Universal).
Musical Program—"For Love of a Girl" (Musical comedy).

ST. LOUIS

Grand Central, Lyric Skydome, West End Lyric and Capitol Theatres—
Film Numbers—The Iron Horse (Fox).
Musical Program—Orchestral overture and popular number. Organ accompaniment.

Missouri Theatre—
Film Numbers—Wild Horse Mesa (Paramount), Missouri Magazine.
Musical Program—"A Day at the Circus" (Missouri Symphony orchestra), "Just a Little Jazz." On stage—Circus Week (Many circus acts in one ring).

Loew's State Theatre—
Film Numbers—Sun Up (Metro-Goldwyn-Mayer), News, Views and Tours.
Musical Program—Don Albert's orchestra. Organ accompaniment. On stage: Dorma Lee (soloist), Musical comedy revue "The Revue D'Art."

William Goldman Kings and Rivoli Theatres—
Film Numbers—Lorraine of the Lions (Universal), Aesop Fable (Pathe), News and Views.
Musical Program—Orchestral overture and popular number. At Kings only on stage: Circus Week (Numerous Pony, dogs and monkeys and clowns). At Rivoli only film comedy "Going Good."

BALTIMORE

Century Theatre—
Film Numbers—Beggar On Horseback (Paramount), Soup to Nuts (Educational), News Weekly (Fox), Local Lafs (Joke film tie-up with Baltimore News.

Garden Theatre—
Film Numbers—The Mine With

---

the Iron Door (Principal Pictures), Galloping Bungalows (Pathe), International News (Universal).
Musical Program—Five acts of vaudeville. Organ Recessional.

Keith's Hippodrome—
Film Numbers—Barriers Burned Away (Associated Exhibitors), Crying For Love (Universal), Aesop's Fable (Pathe), News Weekly (Pathe).
Musical Program—Five acts of vaudeville. Organ recessional.

Metropolitan Theatre—
Film Numbers—The Street of Forgotten Men (Paramount), Bashful Jim (Pathe), Aesop's Fable (Pathe), Topical Review (Pathe).
Musical Program—Orchestra. Organ recessional.

New Theatre—
Film Numbers — The Crimson Runner (Producers' Distributing Corporation), Love and Lions (Fox), News Weekly (Pathe), Three Bears (F. B. O.).
Musical Program — "Morning, Noon and Night In Vienna" (Overture by Orchestra), Xylophone Selection (by Charles Soistman). Organ Recessional.

Parkway Theatre—
Film Numbers—Steele of the Royal Mounted (Warner Bros.), Buster Be Good (Universal), Fortune Teller (S. R.), Parkway Pictorial News (Educational), Kinograms.
Musical Program—"Pique Dame" (Overture by Concert Ensemble), Organ Recessional.

Rivoli Theatre—
Film Numbers—The Half Way Girl (First National), Rivoli News (Pathe).
Musical Program—"Fantasie Orientale" (Overture by Orchestra), Novelty Attraction (Musical Saw Music), Specialty Attraction (Harmonistic Humor by Macy & Scott), "Oberon" and "Indian Summer" (Organ Selections), "Magic Love" (Musical Theme for feature picture).

DETROIT

Madison Theatre—
Film Numbers—Romola (Metro-Goldwyn), News Weekly (Pathe), and Detroit News local pictorial; Aesop's Fable (S. R.).
Musical Program—Organ recessional.

Adams Theatre—
Film Numbers—"The Gold Rush" (United Artists), continued, Kinograms, News Weekly.
Musical Program—Orchestra Accompaniment and organ recessional.

Capitol Theatre—
Film Numbers—The Knockout (First National), News Weekly (Pathe and Detroit News), short subjects.
Musical Program—Stanley Perry (tenor), and Rosalyn Quintette (vocal), in stage presentation; orchestra and organ accompaniment.

Broadway-Strand Theatre—
Film Numbers—Drusilla With a Million (F. B. O.), International Newsreel Weekly; Organ solos, orchestra and organ accompaniment.

Fox Washington Theatre—
Film Numbers—Lover's Oath (S. R.), Felix, the Cat, Comedy (S. R.), Fox News Weekly.
Musical Program—Orchestra and organ accompaniment.

CINCINNATI

Capitol Theatre—
Film Numbers — The Knockout (First National), Dynamite Doggie (Comedy), Capitol News (Selected).
Musical Program—Orchestra.

Walnut Theatre—
Film Numbers—Not So Long Ago (Paramount), News Weekly, Topics of the Day (Pathe), Aesop's Fables (Pathe).
Musical Program—Orchestra.

Strand Theatre—
Film Numbers—Never the Twain Shall Meet (Metro-Goldwyn-Mayer), Pathe News, Topics of the Day (Pathe).

Lyric Theatre—
Film Numbers—The Ten Commandments (Paramount), Kinograms.

Family Theatre—
Film Numbers—Raffles (Universal), No Father to Guide Him (Comedy), Fox News.

Keith Theatre—
Film Numbers — How Baxter Butted In (Warner Bros.), News Weekly, Aesop's Fables, Topics of the Day (Pathe).

ROCHESTER

Eastman Theatre—
Film Numbers — The Unholy Three (Metro-Goldwyn-Mayer), Eastman Theatre Current Events, The Sky Jumper (Fox).
Musical Program — Overture to "Ruy Blas" Opus 95 (Overture), Echoes from the Metropolitan Opera (Organ), "Gypsy Airs" (Violin solo), "Nashville Nightingale" "I'll Build a Stairway to Paradise" (Jazz melodies).

SALT LAKE CITY

American Theatre—
Film Numbers — California Straight Ahead (Universal), A Ravin' Romeo (Educational), Newspaper Fun (F. B. O.).

Kinema Theatre—
Film Numbers — Bavee Son of Kazan (Warner Bros.), Cupid's Victory (Universal), Pathe Review, International News.

Pantages Theatre—
Film Numbers—The Unholy Three (Metro-Goldwyn-Mayer).

Paramount-Empress Theatre—
Film Numbers—Sally of the Sawdust (United Artists), Pathe News.

Victory Theatre—
Film Numbers—Beggar on Horseback (Paramount), Change the Needle (Pathe).

: : : : "THE CHECK-UP" : : : :

"The Check-Up" is a presentation in the briefest and most convenient form of reports received from exhibitors in every part of the country on current features, which makes it possible for the exhibitor to see what the picture has done for other theatre managers.

The first column following the name of the feature represents the number of managers that have reported the picture as "Poor." The second column gives the number who considered it "Fair"; the third, the number who considered it "Good"; and the fourth column, those who considered it "Big."

The fifth column is a percentage figure giving the average rating on that feature, obtained by the following method: A report of "Poor" is rated at 20%; one of "Fair," 40%; "Good," 70%; and "Big," 100%. The percentage ratings of all these reports on one picture are then added together, and divided by the number of reports, giving the average percentage — a figure which represents the consensus of opinion on that picture. In this way exceptional cases, reports which might be misleading taken alone, and such individual differences of opinion are averaged up and eliminated.

No picture is included in the list which has not received at least ten reports.

Title of Picture	Number Exhibitors Reporting "Poor"	Number Exhibitors Reporting "Fair"	Number Exhibitors Reporting "Good"	Number Exhibitors Reporting "Big"	Average Percentage Value	Length
ASSOCIATED EXHIB.						
Introduce Me	—		6	5	84	5,980 ft.
FAMOUS PLAYERS						
Adventure	—	9	15	4	65	6,603 ft.
Air Mail, The	2	1	12	4	69	6,976 ft.
Alaskan, The	4	13	42	16	69	6,736 ft.
Are Parents People	—		12	—	70	6,586 ft.
Argentine Love	—	15	19	4	61	6,470 ft.
Border Legion, The	—	6	39	11	73	7,048 ft.
Charmer, The	1	3	10	3	61	6,076 ft.
City That Never Sleeps, The	—	6	21	3	67	6,079 ft.
Code of the West, The	—	7	11	1	61	6,777 ft.
Coming Through	1	5	19	7	70	6,522 ft.
Contraband	—	8	10	2	61	6,773 ft.
Crowded Hour, The	1	2	10	3	67	6,558 ft.
Dangerous Money	3	12	33	2	61	6,846 ft.
Devil's Cargo, The	2	5	18	5	67	7,980 ft.
Dressmaker From Paris, The	—	3	13	9	73	6,186 ft.
East of Suez	6	5	20	2	58	6,821 ft.
Eve's Secret	—	2	10	—	65	6,338 ft.
Fast Set, The	8	9	24	—	54	6,754 ft.
Feet of Clay	5	7	32	31	76	9,746 ft.
Female, The	3		25	3	63	6 reels
Forbidden Paradise	8	8	33	4	60	7,543 ft.
Forty Winks	—	3	13	6	74	6,203 ft.
Garden of Weeds, The	4	14	3	58		6,230 ft.
Golden Bed, The	3	7	18	14	71	8,584 ft.
Goose Hangs High, The	—		8	4	72	6,186 ft.
Her Love Story	5	19	30	4	59	7 reels
Kiss in the Dark, A	—	4	13	1	65	5,776 ft.
Light of the Western Stars	—	6	14	2	65	6,869 ft.
Little French Girl, The	—	4	14	1	71	5,608 ft.
Locked Doors	2	11	14	—	56	6,221 ft.
Lost — A Wife	—	4	7	—	59	6,420 ft.
Madame Sans Gene	—	6	7	3	53	9,994 ft.
Manhattan	5	1	24	3	64	6,415 ft.
Manicure Girl, The	—	5	9	—	59	5,959 ft.
Man Must Live, A	3	3	19	3	65	7 reels
Man Who Fights Alone, The	13	11	23	6	55	6,337 ft.
Marry Me	2	3	6	—	53	5,529 ft.
Men and Women	2	3	7	1	59	6,323 ft.
Merton of the Movies	2	13	31	13	68	8 reels
Miss Bluebeard	2	2	20	7	72	7 reels
New Lives for Old	—	3	12	5	73	6,706 ft.
Night Club, The	1	1	14	4	73	5,732 ft.
Night Life of New York	—	4	7	1	63	6,998 ft.
North of 36	—	5	27	50	85	7,908 ft.
Old Home Week	—	1	15	3	75	6,888 ft.
Open All Night	24	7	15	—	39	5,671 t.f
Paths to Paradise	—	2	14	1	58	6,741 ft.
Peter Pan	2	8	34	25	76	6,593 ft.
Sackcloth and Scarlet	2	7	8	1	58	7,737 ft.
Sainted Devil, A	10	14	20	10	59	9 reels
Salome of the Tenements	—	2	6	2	51	7,017 ft.
Shock Punch, The	—	6	16	1	63	6,151 ft.
Side Show of Life, The	8	16	34	7	62	7,908 ft.
Sinners in Heaven	4	11	36	8	65	6,000 ft.
Spaniard, The	—	3	13	3	70	6,676 ft.
Story Without a Name, The	4	8	22	7	66	5,912 ft.
Swan, The	4	8	7	2	52	5,889 ft.

Title of Picture	Number Exhibitors Reporting "Poor"	Number Exhibitors Reporting "Fair"	Number Exhibitors Reporting "Good"	Number Exhibitors Reporting "Big"	Average Percentage Value	Length
Ten Commandments, The	—	1	11	25	89	12,000 ft.
Thundering Herd, The	1	5	14	19	79	7,187 ft.
To-Morrow's Love	1	3	12	2	66	5,903 ft.
Tongues of Flame	1	10	23	6	66	6,763 ft.
Too Many Kisses	1	1	10	1	67	6,373 ft.
Top of the World, The	—	6	12	2	64	7,167 ft.
Wages of Virtue	6	12	20	7	60	7 reels
Worldly Goods	4	11	18	3	58	6,055 ft.
FILM BOOKING						
Air Hawk, The	2	2	12	1	62	4,860 ft.
Bandit's Baby, The	—	2	15	6	75	5,291 ft.
Breed of the Border	2	3	15	—	61	4,930 ft.
Broken Laws	1	1	21	12	78	6,413 ft.
Cheap Kisses	—	7	9	2	62	6,538 ft.
Laughing at Danger	1	3	13	1	64	5,442 ft.
Life's Greatest Game	1	1	8	4	73	7,019 ft.
Millionaire Cowboy, The	3	5	11	2	60	4,841 ft.
No Gun Man	2	5	11	—	51	4,532 ft.
O. U. West	—	3	6	1	64	5,000 ft.
Range Terror	1	2	10	—	56	4,753 ft.
Stepping Lively	—	4	10	—	61	5,188 ft.
That Devil Quemado	—	5	22	14	77	5,641 ft.
Thundering Hoofs	—	2	15	15	79	5,003 ft.
Trigger Fingers	2	3	15	—	62	4,775 ft.
Vanity's Price	—	5	7	1	61	6 reels
White Fang	—	3	11	2	68	5,800 ft.
Youth and Adventure	4	5	3	65		5,525 ft.
FIRST NATIONAL						
Abraham Lincoln	3	—	21	54	89	9,759 ft.
As Man Desires	—	5	13	7	75	7,790 ft.
Born Rich	1	7	7	—	53	7,389 ft.
Chickie	—	5	13	5	70	7,767 ft.
Christine of the Hungry Heart	1	6	10	—	59	7,800 ft.
Classmates	1	1	21	22	83	6,800 ft.
Declassee	—	4	12	5	71	7,869 ft.
Desert Flower, The	—	2	11	3	70	6 reels
Enticement	1	4	13	1	63	6,497 ft.
Frivolous Sal	1	1	15	2	69	7,307 ft.
Heart of a Siren, The	—	9	6	—	56	6,780 ft.
Her Husband's Secret	1	8	3	—	46	6,300 ft.
Her Night of Romance	—	2	20	5	73	7,211 ft.
His Supreme Moment	1	7	9	3	62	6,600 ft.
Husbands and Lovers	—	1	15	9	80	7,823 ft.
Idle Tongues	2	2	9	1	61	5,447 ft.
If I Marry Again	—	3	11	4	72	7,400 ft.
In Every Women's Life	1	7	25	3	64	6,300 ft.
Inez From Hollywood	—	4	8	4	70	6,919 ft.
In Hollywood with Potash and Perlmutter	1	4	19	17	78	6,685 ft.
I Want My Man	—	5	19	1	66	6,173 ft.
Just a Woman	—	4	6	—	58	6,653 ft.
Lady, The	—	3	9	7	76	7 reels
Learning to Love	—	3	12	4	72	6,181 ft.
Love's Wilderness	—	3	16	1	67	6,900 ft.
Madonna of the Streets	4	3	25	15	72	7,507 ft.
Making of O'Malley, The	—	1	10	3	72	7,571 ft.
My Son	—	2	9	1	68	6,500 ft.
New Toys	—	3	16	2	62	7,250 ft.
One Way Street	—	4	10	—	61	5,506 ft.
One Year to Live	1	2	7	—	59	6,064 ft.

Title of Picture	Number Exhibitors Reporting "Poor"	Number Exhibitors Reporting "Fair"	Number Exhibitors Reporting "Good"	Number Exhibitors Reporting "Big"	Average Percentage Value	Length
Only Woman, The	—	—	19	5	76	6,770 ft.
Playing with Souls	1	2	4	2	62	5,831 ft.
Quo Vadis	1	3	11	10	78	8,945 ft.
Sally	—	1	13	21	87	8 reels
Sandra	6	10	13	2	53	6,800 ft.
Sea Hawk, The	3	3	25	36	80	12 reels
Silent Watcher, The	2	3	12	7	71	7,575 ft.
So Big	2	2	22	6	71	9 reels
Soul Fire	1	2	7	4	71	8,362 ft.
Sundown	3	12	15	1	55	8,640 ft.
Talker, The	—	2	12	1	68	7,861 ft.
Tarnish	2	6	10	6	66	6,685 ft.
Thief in Paradise, A	—	1	16	7	78	8 reels
FOX						
Arizona Romeo	1	1	11	2	69	4,694 ft.
Cyclone Rider, The	2	6	14	5	65	7 reels
Dancers, The	3	2	6	1	55	6,583 ft.
Dante's Inferno	1		16	8	72	5,484 ft.
Daughters of the Night	2	6	7	—	51	5,740 ft.
Deadwood Coach, The	—	5	9	13	79	6,346 ft.
Dick Turpin	—	3	13	6	78	6,716 ft.
Flames of Desire	5	4	2	—	36	5,439 ft.
Gerald Cranston's Lady	1	3	9	1	62	6,674 ft.
Gold Heels	2		16	—	63	6,020 ft.
Hunted Woman, The	6	3	11	2	56	6 reels
Last Man on Earth, The	3	1	7	4	66	6,637 ft.
Oh, You Tony	—	3	27	6	73	6,302 ft.
Painted Lady, The	—	3	18	—	66	6,938 ft.
Rainbow Trail, The	—	3	7	2	70	5,251 ft.
Riders of the Purple Sage	—	1	5	6	83	5,000 ft.
Roughneck, The	2	4	12	2	62	7,500 ft.
Teeth	—	3	22	—	66	6,190 ft.
Trail Rider, The	—	1	11	—	68	4,752 ft.
Warrens of Virginia	2	5	16	4	65	6,535 ft.
Winner Takes All	—	1	8	3	75	5,949 ft.
METRO-GOLDWYN						
Along Came Ruth	—	4	14	5	71	5,161 ft.
Bandolero, The	2	3	9	6	70	8,000 ft.
Beauty Prize, The	—	3	15	—	64	5,750 ft.
Cheaper to Marry	1	3	13	2	66	6,500 ft.
Chu Chin Chow	1	4	5	1	59	6,048 ft.
Circe, the Enchantress	1	4	20	3	61	6,882 ft.
Confession of a Queen	—	3	8	—	62	5,851 ft.
Daddy's Gone A Hunting	—	3	6	1	64	5,851 ft.
Denial, The	1	3	10	1	63	4,791 ft.
Dixie Handicap, The	—	1	21	7	76	7 reels
Excuse Me	1	—	9	9	82	5,747 ft.
Great Divide, The	—	3	23	3	70	7,811 ft.
Greed	3	3	7	1	55	10,067 ft.
He Who Gets Slapped	—	4	21	16	79	6,600 ft.
His Hour	2	—	29	—	71	6,300 ft.
Janice Meredith	—	4	15	10	80	12 reels
Lady of the Night	—	1	21	1	63	5,410 ft.
Married Flirts	2	5	18	3	63	6,765 ft.
Monster, The	—	7	12	4	66	6,435 ft.
Navigator, The	1	2	21	13	78	5,600 ft.
One Night in Rome	1	1	15	1	65	5,883 ft.
Prairie Wife, The	2	8	1	1	44	6,487 ft.
Proud Flesh	—	5	5	1	50	5,770 ft.
Rag Man	—		14	9	82	5,068 ft.
Red Lily, The	7	10	13	—	48	6,975 ft.
Seven Chances	1		15	13	82	5,113 ft.
Silent Accuser, The	2	1	20	9	74	5,885 ft.
Sinners in Silk	3	6	32	3	65	5,750 ft.
Snob, The	3		15	1	68	6,513 ft.
So This is Marriage	—	6	14	2	66	6,300 ft.
Sporting Venus	—	7	7	—	55	5,938 ft.
Way of a Girl, The	—	5	5	2	56	5,025 ft.
White Desert, The	2	1	9	—	67	6,345 ft.
Wife of the Centaur	2	1	19	4	69	6,700 ft.
Wine of Youth	1	4	15	5	69	6,600 ft.
Yolanda	1	4	15	—	70	10,125 ft.
Zander the Great	1	3	7	5	71	5,851 ft.
PATHE						
Battling Orioles	1	4	9	3	65	5,332 ft.
Dynamite Smith	8	10	9	1	45	6,400 ft.
Hot Water	—	3	22	33	86	4,899 ft.
White Sheep	—	4	5	1	61	6,091 ft.
PRODUCERS DIST. CORP.						
Another Man's Wife	—	5	10	—	60	5,015 ft.
Barbara Frietchie	1	5	16	20	80	7,149 ft.
Beyond the Border	—	5	14	—	62	4,469 ft.

Title of Picture	Number Exhibitors Reporting "Poor"	Number Exhibitors Reporting "Fair"	Number Exhibitors Reporting "Good"	Number Exhibitors Reporting "Big"	Average Percentage Value	Length
Cafe in Cairo, A	1	3	8	2	64	5,656 ft.
Chalk Marks	1	3	8	—	58	6,711 ft.
Charley's Aunt	—	2	9	38	92	6 reels
Chorus Lady, The	1	1	9	3	68	6,020 ft.
Flaming Forties, The	1	4	10	1	64	5,770 ft.
House of Youth, The	—	6	10	1	61	6,669 ft.
Ramshackle House	2	4	16	6	69	6,257 ft.
Reckless Romance	1	1	8	3	71	5,530 ft.
Roaring Rails	1		34	23	81	5,753 ft.
Silent Sanderson	1	3	6	—	56	4,841 ft.
Soft Shoes	1	3	13	—	61	5,527 ft.
Welcome Stranger	—	2	18	5	74	6,018 ft.
STATE RIGHTS						
Black Lightning	—	1	9	—	67	5,382 ft.
Breath of Scandal, The	—		11	2	75	5,700 ft.
Crackerjack, The	—		7	3	79	6,500 ft.
Early Bird, The	—	1	16	1	70	6,500 ft.
Fire Patrol, The	1	6	8	2	60	6,600 ft.
Helen's Babies	—	2	6	3	73	6,200 ft.
Lone Wagon, The	1	6	6	2	50	5,009 ft.
Midnight Express, The	—	4	2	1	56	5,067 ft.
Mine with the Iron Door, The	2		20	14	80	8,113 ft.
Recreation of Brian Kent, The	2	6	4	4	60	6,898 ft.
UNITED ARTIST 忍 帝						
America	—	3	23	56	90	11,442 ft.
Isn't Life Wonderful	—	3	6	1	51	8,600 ft.
Thief of Bagdad, The	4	2	19	33	87	10,000 ft.
UNIVERSAL						
Big Timber	1	4	14	1	63	5 reels
Butterfly	—	5	2	2	68	7 reels
Dangerous Innocence	1	1	8	—	62	6,739 ft.
Daring Chances	—		10	—	70	4,561 ft.
Family Secret, The	—	2	10	1	68	5,767 ft.
Fast Worker, The	—	3	18	5	74	7 reels
Fifth Avenue Models	—	4	8	1	63	6,581 ft.
Gaiety Girl, The	—	5	3	9	67	7,419 ft.
Head Wins	1	—	6	1	74	5,309 ft.
Hit and Run	—	4	22	8	71	6 reels
Hurricane Kid, The	—	3	18	1	67	5,396 ft.
I'll Show You the Town	—	3	23	5	79	5,898 ft.
K The Unknown	1	2	30	11	76	6,362 ft.
Last Laugh, The	3	3	3	2	54	6,519 ft.
Let 'Er Buck	—	1	11	4	75	5,547 ft.
Love and Glory	4	4	11	2	58	7 reels
Mad Whirl, The	1	3	5	1	50	6,184 ft.
Oh, Doctor	1	3	13	7	73	6,587 ft.
Price of Pleasure, The	2	1	12	1	58	6,018 ft.
Raffles	—	3	10	2	54	5,557 ft.
Ridin' Kid from Powder River, The	1	5	10	8	74	5,727 ft.
Rose of Paris	5	6	10	1	54	6,362 ft.
Saddle Hawk, The	1	1	7	1	65	5,468 ft.
Sawdust Trail, The	—	2	22	7	75	6 reels
Smouldering Fires	1	1	14	3	73	7,356 ft.
Tornado, The	—	3	24	9	74	6,375 ft.
Turmoil, The	1	4	20	4	68	7 reels
Up the Ladder	—	1	8	1	70	6,023 ft.
Woman's Faith, A	2	4	5	—	50	5,557 ft.
VITAGRAPH						
Baree, Son of Kazan	—	2	14	5	74	6,800 ft.
Beloved Brute, The	—	2	12	2	70	6,719 ft.
Captain Blood	2	3	20	25	81	10,608 ft.
Clean Heart, The	6	7	8	4	52	7,500 ft.
Fearbound	2	5	4	—	47	5,877 ft.
Greater Than Marriage	1	3	10	2	59	6,821 ft.
Pampered Youth	—	2	14	—	64	6,640 ft.
Redeeming Sin, The	5	5	6	—	45	6,227 ft.
School for Wives	—	5	8	—	58	6,750 ft.
Two Shall Be Born	1	3	8	1	59	5,443 ft.
Wildfire	—		13	—	70	6 reels
WARNER BROS.						
Age of Innocence, The	1	5	5	2	59	5 reels
Cornered	—	3	30	8	74	6,000 ft.
Dark Swan, The	1	3	11	1	63	6,700 ft.
Find Your Man	—	4	23	11	76	6,800 ft.
Lighthouse by the Sea, The	1	1	11	7	77	6,000 ft.
Lover of Camille, The	5	6	9	1	59	6,700 ft.
My Wife and I	3	4	5	1	54	6,700 ft.
Narrow Street, The	—	4	14	3	69	6,075 ft.
On Thin Ice	2	5	7	—	57	6,075 ft.
Recompense	1	5	7	—	53	7,480 ft.
This Woman	—	7	17	5	68	6,842 ft.

YOUR IDEA

IN THE MAIL

FROM Toledo, Ohio, comes an invitation to the dress rehearsal of the opening performance of the Temple theatre, extended by the Collins Theatre, Inc., which is to open the house with "The Iron Horse" on Friday evening, September 4th. By the time this appears, the opening will be over. A special music score is announced for the occasion, interpreted by the Temple Cinema Orchestra under the direction of Abram Ruvinsky. It is a source of real regret that it is not possible for us to attend more of these premieres of new theatres in person.

Another opening, though not a new house, is that of the renovated and redecorated Mount Morris theatre, in uptown New York City, under the managing directorship of MIKE EDELSTEIN. This event was also set for this Friday evening, on which occasion Johnny Hines and other stars were booked to appear, the feature being "The Crackerjack." A ten-piece orchestra under the direction of Mauritz Swanson will be a feature of the new policy.

FRANK W. PURKETT, enterprising pilot of the Kinema theatre, Fresno, Calif., sends in a comprehensive group of material and photographs on his Greater Movie Season campaign, built around "The Ten Commandments." Next week we hope to be able to reproduce some of it in the way it deserves.

BEN FERRIS, advertising director for the St. Paul theatres of Finkelstein & Ruben, mails us a remarkable full page ad on Greater Movie Season put over by that firm, which we hope to use. He recently sent us a remarkable story, with photos, on the personal appearance of Anna May Wong at the Capitol, when the F. & R. department "got away with murder" in the matter of space-grabbing, but to date we haven't had the opportunity to use it.

* * * * *

MORE TAKA-CHANCE STUNTS

SINCE the Take-a-Chance week idea was first described in these pages, some little time ago, the idea has traveled across the country and back. Paramount used it over its circuit for "The Goose Hangs High." But two of the best stunts of this nature have just come in from Greeley, Colo., and Vancouver, B. C.

In Greeley, the Sterling theatre carefully concealed the nature of the bill in all its Take-a-Chance week advertising, and in addition a strong mercantile line-up was obtained.

A string of leading local stores came in on the proposition, and page advertising was run. Question marks appeared frequently in the merchants' advertising. It was stated that every evening during the week advertising of an interesting and surprising variety would be presented at the Sterling theatre. The stores described no merchandise and quoted no prices whatever in their newspaper insertions.

The Sterling theatre said in part "and we're paging all of Greeley's gamblers to take a chance on the Sterling this week. Every number a secret! Every unit a surprise! And the whole show is a hit!

"Sh-h-h, just between frineds, here's the whole program:
"The overture. It's lilting, and fulla pep! You'll probably whistle the melody on the way home.
"The joker. This, number will be orally announced from the stage. Merchants named here are responsible.
"Novelty. The greatest surprise you've had since you saw your first movie. You can't see it with your own eyes!
Feature production. All we can tell you is that James Cruze directed it—nuf said! Let's go!"

The proposal is to make Taka-Chance week a semi-annual event in Greeley.

Ralph Ruffner, manager of the Capitol theatre, Vancouver, B. C., probably went further with the "Take-A-Chance Week" idea than any other theatre man and the stunt worked out very satisfactorily for all concerned. Manager Ruffner declares that when he decided to stage a "Sight-Unseen Week," he recognized the importance of delivering the goods in every respect so that there would be no comeback and he left no stone unturned to pack the show with unusual effects. The result was that there were fully a dozen real surprises in the mere presentation of the programme.

At the start of each show a request was made by trailer that every person in the audience treat as confidential anything and everything which was revealed. Each number on the bill was preceded with a trailer or slide detailing the subsequent item as "Surprise No. 2 or 3, etc."

The performance opened with a bugle call, followed by the playing of "O Canada" in place of the National Anthem, the latter having been used as the opener for over four years. Incidentally, the National Anthem was played at the end of the show instead. The orchestra overture was played without the announcement regarding the name of the selection and the audience was asked to "Guess the tune." After the news weekly and film magazine, the following announcement was screened.

"You've all been good sports and taken a chance, now the orchestra will take a chance. They will play that popular overture 'Light Cavalry' without a conductor; in other words, every man for himself."

After this the house lights were turned up and the orchestra director walked off sheepishly. Manager Ruffner reported that this got a laugh at every performance. An unknown young lady next rendered a solo, with piano accompaniment only, the soloist concealing her identity with a domino mask. The film comedy was introduced by a trailer reading "Surprise No. 6. Look who's here and in——." This revealed "A Raspberry Romance." A musical feature was presented without a title, a man and woman singing "Let it Rain." During the chorus, storm effects were used and, at the finish, the spotlight was switched suddenly to a remote section of the auditorium showing a traffic cop in oilskins with a traffic semaphore, the officer repeating the chorus. A moment later, a shapely girl in one-piece bathing suit appeared in the rain on the stage and sang the chorus, after which a chorus of 20 girls in one-piece thimble suits appeared when the stage lights were turned on full. As an encore, 10 little girls, 3 to 5 years, in bathing suits like their big sisters, paraded across the stage and tried to sing the chorus too. For this specialty, the whole orchestra also appeared in slickers and sou-westers.

"Surprise No. 8" was introduced by the following screen announcement: "This will thrill you to tears and tickle you pink—Watch——". This was the feature, "When the Goose Hangs High."

Here and there throughout the show were other little surprises and stunts but the above description, touching the high spots of the presentation, gives an indication of the manner in which Manager Ruffner worked out the mystery angle of the week's engagement.

Recording thermometer used in front of the Rivoli theatre, New York City, to prove to the skeptics just what the temperature is inside since the new air refrigerating system has been installed.

AND OURS

NOVEL REVIEWS

Columbus, OHIO, newspapers have recently put into action a novel means of advertising the current films at the theatres in the city by having several members of their staffs review the films on the opening night, and the following day the reports are printed in the papers over the initials of the reporters.

This system has given an added impetus to the public to attend the shows, since absolutely impartial reports are made and the shows are being given good boosts for the most part in a way that brings the theatre and the film into almost personal touch with the public.

The Columbus Citizen also plays another good stunt for the benefit of the motion picture houses in running a column under a catchy head entitled "Let's Go To The Movies." In this column, short and clever reviews are given and the attractions are thus placed before a busy public in such a way as to draw attention and attendance.

The Columbus Dispatch runs a longer column with several signed articles covering all of the current attractions, giving each a good write-up and thereby aiding the picture houses in more ways than one.

CONSTRUCTIVE PROPAGANDA

Not every theatre has a house organ, but most theatres have one way or another of getting constructive messages to the public on such things as censorship, the theatre as a community institution, house policies, Sunday opening, and the like, from time to time. A good piece of copy was run recently under the heading "Destructive Criticism is Valueless" in the Majestic Revue, a newspaper size house organ issued by the Majestic theatre, Grand Junction, Colo. This paper incidentally, is a splendid example of what can be done in the smaller cities with a house organ. The editorial in question, which might be easily adapted for use elsewhere, was as follows:

Getting up in club meeting and denouncing bad pictures will not accomplish a thing. Letters about the bad pictures, article about bad pictures, are all equally valueless—just as all destructive criticism inevitably must be valueless. The sure way, the quick way, the way that cannot fail, is to patronize those pictures which already exist and unquestionably are good. By patronize is meant go to see them, pay your money at the box office, make them financially successful.

Here is what will happen: The theatre owner of your community will find that he has had a prosperous day or a prosperous week. He will say to the producers, "I must have more pictures like that last one. I made money with it, and it pleased my patrons. That's the kind of pictures I want." The producer, whose business is to rent his pictures to the theatre owner, is bound to heed such a request. He says to his scenario chiefs, to his directors, "we must have more pictures like that one that we just turned out. It pleases the theatre owner because it pleases his folks, and shows good profit. There is a popular demand for that kind of a picture. Lets go ahead and do it.

When you see a good picture let us know on your way out of the theatre. If you will do that, then we know the kind of pictures you want. That is what we are striving and aiming to give you. We started out this Editorial about you getting up in club meetings and denouncing bad pictures. We know there are lots of bad pictures, but we are not present at that club meeting, and if instead of talking about the bad pictures to the theatre owner, you are giving us your criticisms on your way out of the theatre then you are hitting the nail on the head, and your criticism will bring results and be of value instead of being valueless. We are all hopped up on our ability to pick pictures, the kind we think you want and we are continually striving to pick only the best the market affords. In all fairness to our efforts you should at least tell us when leaving the theatre whether you like the picture or not, by doing so you are helping yourself to good entertainment. In last week's issue of The Revue our Editorial gave you a list of the pictures for the month of August. Last week we presented you with three of what we thought were big wonderful pictures and we believe we gave you the kind of entertainment you most desire, because the week proved one of the biggest we have enjoyed in a long time.

For this, the second week of August, and which we claim to be the one month of the best pictures we have ever booked into the Majestic we offer three more corking good pictures. Friday and Saturday, "The Code of the Wilderness," a western picture on which we have failed to find one single bad comment from the press critic or theatre manager that have already shown the picture. Sunday, Monday and Tuesday, we show "The Scarlet West," the picture that was made at Dolores, Colorado. This is one we feel sure that you will like better than any previous western pictures you have ever seen—not beca use it wa s ma de in Colorado, but because the picture actually is better.

The feature for next Wednesday and Thursday is "Inez From Hollywood." It will prove very interesting because it is Hollywood and the Movie Folks brought right to your door—we advise you to see every one of these productions—and when you leave the theatre tell us whether or not you enjoyed the picture.

BOB GETS UNDER WAY

Bob LA PINER, the new exploitation man for the Finkelstein & Ruben circuit, has started off with a variety of strong stunts that augur well for his future efforts. Just now he is working on a campaign which will be one of the strongest ever used in the Twin City territory, it is hoped.

It is to handle "The Iron Horse" and will tie up with every railroad in the Northwest with the display of gigantic modern locomotives as well as old timers, together with an automobile caravan which will accompany the picture.

The caravan will carry music, special lobby displays and a 15-foot captive balloon with 28 foot streamer. Essay contests will be organized for grade school children with a special sketching contest for those who would rather draw than write.

Several models of their new engines are being furnished by the Great Northern and Northern Pacific and negotiations are under way with the Hill estate to obtain use of the original oil painting of the picture "Jim Hill's Dream" showing the two types of engines, one used in the early days and the monster Mogul of today.

For exploitation of "The Wheel" F. & R. procured a roulette wheel from Tiajuana and displayed it in a downtown window with appropriate placard.

Harold Pontefract (left), Fox publicity and ad director in England, and the newspaper sellers who placards tied up so uniquely with the London trade shows of "Lightnin'" and "Havoc". (Fox).

CLASSIFIED AD SECTION

RATES: 10 cents a word for each insertion, in advance
except Employment Wanted, on which rate is 5 cents.

CLASSIFIED SERVICE

A classified ad in MOTION PICTURE NEWS offers the
full resources and circulation of the NEWS to the advertiser at a ridiculously low figure.

Whether you want to reach executives, branch managers,
salesmen, or theatre managers, you can accomplish this
quickly and economically through the NEWS Classified
Columns.

THE PEER OF ALL PROJECT ON SURFACES
Mr. Exhibitor — The Radio Silver
Screens are the latest improve-
ment in stereopticon projecting
and for elimination of eye strain.
Sold under a positive guarantee.
Price 50c a square foot. For
particulars, and samples apply to
JOHN MUNRO CRAWFORD,
45 Smith St., Newburgh, N. Y.

Wanted

EXPERT OPERATOR
and Electrician with 9 years'
experience in big houses;
married; wants to locate at
once. Address, Operator,
Box 282, Mason City, Iowa.

NOTICE.— Picture and
vaudeville theatre manager
of 10 years' experience in all
branches of show business
wishes to make change; will
go anywhere; references!
plenty. Box 370, Motion Picture News, New York City.

MOTION PICTURE
OPERATOR.—Experienced;
young man; wishing position
anywhere; nonunion. Nabeeh
Said, 349 West 51st St., New
York.

SITUATION WANTED.—
Projectionist wants position;
handle any equipment; go
anywhere, anytime; furnish
references if desired; single;
non-union. Robert W. Hous-
worth, Strand Theatre, Carrollton, Ga.

Suburban Motion
Picture Theatre
For Sale

Seating 400. Will show
good returns on a small
investment. Inquire

Tahen and Brenner
M and M Bldg.
Springfield, Ohio

THEATRE IN TOWN OF
4,000 or better, anywhere in
North Central states, Northern Indiana preferred. Can
either give satisfactory security on lease or buy outright.
Would consider buying interest in bona-fide proposition
where owner wishes to retire.
All replies absolutely confidential. Address Box 360,
Motion Picture News, New
York City.

MOTION PICTURE
OPERATOR.—Experienced;
young man; wishing position
anywhere. Write Dion Mol-
ler, 411a Prospect Ave.,
Brooklyn, N. Y.

For Sale

FOR SALE AT A SAC-
RIFICE.— Photoplayer; in
use less than 2 years. Orpheum Theatre, Orwigsburg,
Pa.

FOR SALE.— Modern
movie; priced for quick sale
account of illness; wonderful bargain; county seat of
10,000. Box 240, Motion
Picture News, New York
City.

CLOTH BANNERS—
$1.40 3 x 10 feet, 3 colors,
any copy up to 15 words.
One day service. Sent anywhere. Also Bargain Paper
Banners. Associated Advertisers, 111 W. 18th St., Kansas City, Mo.

Suddenly at liberty on account of union error.

Walter C. Simon

Noted composer, organist,
concert pianist and musical
director.
Original effects, presentations, and novelty over-
tures for motion pictures;
played Strand Theatre,
Boardwalk.
Address "The Haliburton."

309 Atlantic Ave.,
Atlantic City, N. J.

*Three two-column ads, two three-column and one four-
column display on "The Unholy Three" (Metro-Goldwyn) in six different cities throughout the United States.
A wide range of styles in picture advertising is represented in the ads of these theatres, which include the
Walnut theatre, Cincinnati; the Capitol theatre, Detroit;
B. F. Keith's Majestic theatre, Louisville; Loew's State
theatre, Los Angeles; Sun theatre, Omaha, and the Allen
theatre, Cleveland. They are special art ads.*

Opinions on Current Short Subjects

Scenes from "The Tourist," first of the 1925-26 series of Educational-Tuxedo Comedies featuring Johnny Arthur.

Fox Starts Third Story of O. Henry Series

Production was started this week at the Fox West Coast studios on "Failure," third of the two-reel comedies adapted from the O. Henry short stories. Daniel Keefe, who made the first two, is again directing. Kathryn McGuire has the feminine lead and the principal male character is played by Harvey Clark. The other principals include Maine Geary, William Bakewell, William Norton Bailey, Vivian Oakland and Roy Atwell.

Fox Starts Production on Imperial Comedy

A new Imperial Comedy has just been put into production at the Fox West Coast Studios under the working title of "All At Sea." Lew Seiler is directing this new short subject with Sid Smith and Judy King in the leading roles. The other principals are Stanley Blystone, James Farley and Nora Cecil.

"Crying for Love" Current Century Release

"Crying for Love" is the Century comedy for release this week through all Universal exchanges. Eddie Gordon is the featured player. The comedy was written and directed by Noel Smith. Blanche Payson plays opposite Gordon.

Century's Ambitious Schedule
Improved Product and Novelty Innovations Promised in Fifty-Two for New Season

CENTURY FILM CORPORATION has an ambitious schedule of Century Comedies for the 1925-26 season with a declared improvement in production and a number of novelty innovations. There are fifty-two of these comedies on the list, one for each week in the year.

A grouping of the season's output into star series is among the innovations. The pictures made by each star, such as Wanda Wiley, Edna Marian and others will be considered as separate brands. Another innovation was the acquisition of the screen rights for a novelty series of two-reel comedies. This is the Buster Brown Comedy Series, being made from the newspaper cartoons of R. F. Outcault.

The Century schedule shows a contemplated release of 52 comedies, one a week during the period from August 5th, 1925, to July 28th, 1926. In addition, there will be a Century special production, "Little Red Riding Hood." This is a novelty two-reeler made with Peter the Great and Baby Peggy. It is scheduled for release November 21st.

The 52 Centuries consist of a series of twelve Buster Brown Century Comedies, a series of twelve Wanda Wiley-Century Comedies, a series of twelve Edna Marian-Century Comedies, six comedies featuring Eddie Gordon, six featuring Al Alt and four featuring Charles King.

The Buster Browns are being made by Charles Lamont, one of Century's veteran comedy directors. Little Arthur Trimble has the role of Buster, Doreen Turner plays Mary Jane and Pete, the comedy dog, plays Tige Buster's famous canine companion. The two Buster Brown comedies already completed are "Educating Buster" and "Buster Be Good."

Sennett Adding Beauties to Roster

Mack Sennett is continuously adding beautiful girls to the Sennett roster. He now has eight under contract, five of whom have been signed in the past two months. Alice Day, Madeline Hurlock and Natalie Kingston have been appearing in Pathe-Sennett comedies for over a year.

The new girls recently signed to contracts are: Eugenia Gilbert, former bathing girl; Ruth Hiatt, leading ingenue with Harry Langdon; Thelma Parr, playing leads with Ralph Graves; Ruth Taylor, with Billy Bevan in Del Lord comedies and Marion McDonald, a newcomer from Boston, who has just been given a contract.

"Transients in Arcadia" is Finished by Fox

"Transients in Arcadia," second of the series of O. Henry stories, has been completed at the Fox West Coast Studios. The leading roles were played by Mary Akin and Hugh Allan. Daniel Keefe directed under the supervision of George T. Marshall. The scenario was by Beatrice Van.

"No Father To Guide Him" is a two-reel comedy from the Hal Roach studios with Charlie Chase featured. The above scenes are taken from this Pathe release.

Resume of Current News Weeklies

KINOGRAMS NO. 5113: Cape Gris-Nez, France—First pictures of Gertrude Ederle's brave but vain attempt to swim the English Channel; New York—Death list grows as Chinese Tongs renew feuds; Culver Lake, N. J.—Sunday services are held on the only floating church in the world; San Francisco—Japanese warship brings home body of Ambassador Bancroft and thousands pay tribute to late envoy; Hopewell, N. Y.—Girl pioneers demonstrate lessons in outdoor life; Swampscott, Mass.—President Coolidge presents cup to Navy flier who spent nearly 600 hours in air during the year; San Francisco—Navy airmen get ready for non-stop flight to Honolulu, 2418 miles away; Chicago—Dancers show their steps on top of building 523 feet high; New Rochelle, N. Y., Seattle, Wash., and Lake Geneva, Wis.—Water acrobats furnish thrills with daring stunts on skis and aquaplanes.

KINOGRAMS NO. 5114: Tamaqua, Pa.—158,000 miners in anthracite region strike for more pay, completely tying up hard coal industry; New York—Babe Ruth, defiant, after $5,000 fine and suspension imposed by Manager Huggins for training rule violations, returns home to appeal his case to Yankee club owner; Aurora, Ill.—Thousands are thrilled as big engines crash together in staged collision; New York—Three sailors cross ocean from Norway on 43-foot yawl, smaller than craft of Columbus; Ayer, Mass.—President Coolidge reviews training camp regiment and presents trophies after war games; New York—Six year old boy swims Hudson river, distance of mile and a quarter in 37 minutes; New Haven—Film men quit Connecticut in protest over state tax on industry; Port Clinton, Pa.—Dynamite blasts shift course of Schuylkill River; Berkeley, Cal.—California collegians engage in annual freshman-sophomore battle; Port Washington, N. Y.—Baby Bootlegger wins Gold Cup in stirring motorboat contest, averaging 48 miles per hour for 90 miles.

INTERNATIONAL NEWS NO. 72: San Diego, Cal.—Naval aviators learn catapult flying; Monster naval seaplanes leave for historic non-stop flight to Hawaii; Cuinn Deveus, Mass.—Corporal John Coolidge, son of Pres.

Coolidge, drills squad at Citizens' Military Training Camp; Ft. Ethan Allen, Vt.—Mounted cops risk necks in rough country riding; Frisco, Cal. (Frisco only)—Japanese cruiser brings home body of Ambassador Edgar A. Bancroft; Frisco, Cal.—Funny fashions o. a century shown at Diamond Jubilee; London, Eng.—British flying cadets learn to "stunt on ground;" St. Louis, Mo.—"Mike the Chimp" shows how he keeps himself fit; East Elhurst, L. I.—Another Mike (no relation) is pronounced a genuine hair restorer by Rudoly; Althena, his owner; Gris Nez, France—Pictures of Gertrude Ederle's brave effort to swim across English Channel.

INTERNATIONAL NEWS NO. 73: Aurora, Ill.—Trains in head-on crash as thriller for fair crowds; Montevideo, Uruguay—Prince o' Wales on World tour visits South America; Ballater, Scotland—King George on vacation in Scotland; Los Angeles, Cal.—Fidel L. Barba, 18-year-old schoolboy wins flyweight championship; Philadelphia, Pa.—Proclamation calling strike of anthracite coal miners is signed by Lewis; New York City—Speedograph studies of Babe Ruth, fined and suspended by Yankee manager; Atlantic City, N. Y.—Distinction is keynote of milady's fall furs; Rabat, Morocco—American flyers in Morocco pay visit to Sultan; Baltimore, Md. (Baltimore only)—Cops lose to postmen in big athletic meet; Portsmouth, N. Y. (Boston only)—New records mark national meet of women swimmers; Manhasset Bay, L. I.—Thrills aplenty in famous gold cup race for speedy motor boats.

PATHE NEWS NO. 71: Australians welcome American sailors; N. Y. City—Watermelon season at Zoo means lots of monkey business; Ft. Tilden, N. Y.—Test anti-aircraft guns in night "attack" on Fort; Cape Gris-Nez, France—Gertrude Ederle, first U. S. woman to try English Channel swim, fails after swimming 23½ miles in record time; St. Louis, Mo.—Youthful "Hercules" has "daily dozen" all his own; Uxbridge, Eng.—Britain's Royal Air Force in spectacular drills; San Diego, Cal.—Navy Seaplanes ready for non-stop flight to Hawaii; Philadelphia, Pa. (Phila. only)—Annette Jackson to represent Philadelphia in

national beauty contest; Gloucester, Mass. (Boston only)—Dedicate memorial to fishermen lost at sea; Rome, Ga. (Memphis only)—Honor memory of Known Soldier.

Release stills from "Butter Fingers," a Mack Sennett comedy released by Pathe.

FOX NEWS VOL. 6 NO. 96: Trivolof Islands—Senator Bill inspects government guarded seal rookeries in Alaska; The Passing of Famous New York Mansions—The encroaching tide of business dooms many Fifth Ave. show places; Cattolica, Italy—One of Europe's favorite summer resorts seldom visited by Americans; Ayer, Mass.—John Coolidge, soldier son of the President, is advanced to rank of corporal; Chicago, Ill.—Ballet picks cornice of world's highest building to rehearse new dances; Paris, France—Many a Frenchman gets a ducking in the Seine during tournament of the medival game of "joust;" Uploading Iron Ore on the Great Lakes—An engineering marvel are the giant scoops that take cargo from ships; Pictures of Gertrude Ederle's attempt to swim English Channel.

PATHE NEWS NO. 72: Wilkes-Barre, Pa.—158,000 anthracite miners go on strike; N. Y. City—6-year-old boy swims Hudson River; Rome, Italy—Mussolini inspects Italian cavalrymen; Chicago, Ill.—Babe Ruth suspended and fined $5,000 by Huggins for alleged misconduct; Dublin, Ireland—Honor memory of Free State Heroes; Washington, D. C.—Mexican-U. S. Labor Chiefs confer on immigration problems; Port Washington, N. Y.—Baby Bootlegger wins Gold Challenge cup for speedboats; Plymouth, Mass.—Coolidge on sight-seeing tour as vacation nears end; N. Y. City—Dancing masters approve new Charleston; Montevideo, Uruguay—South America gives Prince of Wales tremendous ovation; Salida, Colo. (Denver only)—Two killed, fifty injured in train crash; Clarksburg, W. Va. (Pittsburgh only)—Famous Blue Ridge division holds reunion; Lynn, Mass. (Boston only)—Coolidge attends flagpole dedication; Wilkes-Barre, Pa. (Phila. only)—Youths blow instruments for all they are worth in band contest.

Scenes from "Plenty of Nerve," a Century comedy starring Edna Marian, released through Universal.

Red Seal Will Release Nine in September

Nine subjects of the ninety-five featurettes on the Red Seal schedule for the season, will be released during the month of September. The first two are companion pictures titled "The Silvery Art" and "Flirting With Death." They reveal the possibilities of adventure lurking in a pair of skiis.

"Swanee River" is the first of a series of Ko-Ko Song Car Tunes. It was pre-released at the Capitol, New York. The first of the "Marvels of Motion" is also on the list. "Ko-Ko Nuts," of the Out of the Inkwell series, "Up the River Conway," a scenic, two "Animated Hair Cartoons" and another issue of "Film Facts" are also among the September releases.

Beth Brown Appointed Red Seal Editor

Max Fleischer and E. M. Fadman have appointed Beth Brown editor-in-chief of the Out-of-the-Inkwell Studio and Red Seal Productions. Miss Brown will assist Mr. Fleischer in writing scenarios and editing and titling the entire Inkwell product for Red Seal release.

Martha Sleeper to Appear With "Our Gang"

Martha Sleeper, who for the past year or two has been featured in grown-up roles in Hal Roach comedies, is to appear in the "Our Gang" comedy, "Better Movies." Miss Sleeper, who is but fifteen years old, will appear as one of the "gang." This two reeler is the "gang's" contribution to the national Greater Movie Season.

Scenes from a current Pathe comedy titled "The Iron Nag."

Pathe Announces New Schedule

Two Hal Roach Comedies on Program for September 13; Tryon and Finlayson Stars

GLENN TRYON and Jimmie Finlayson will be the comedy stars of the Pathe schedule for the week of September 13. The comedy contributions are both from Hal Roach studios and consist of a two-reeler titled "Madame Sans Jane," and "Unfriendly Enemies," a single reel offering with Finlayson appearing in the role of a volunteer cameraman with the A. E. F. in France.

The schedule also provides an episode of the "Play Ball" serial, in which Allene Ray and Walter Miller are featured. The chapter is titled "Into Segundo's Hands," and is the ninth release in this ten-episode play written by John J. McGraw of the N. Y. Giants.

Glenn Tryon appears as an ardent lover in "Madame Sans Jane," in which he has the support of Fay Wray as the object of his affections, Jimmie Finlayson in the role of an objecting father, and Lucien Littlefield in the principal roles. The picture was directed by James W. Horne. The story is concerned with the adventures of a very resolute young man who masquerades as a woman in order to get the job of traveling companion for his sweetheart on a trip to Europe, whither she is being sent by her father, who wants to get her away from the hero. At the last moment the father decides to make the trip himself, announcing that he will occupy one of the two staterooms he had engaged for the daughter and her companion.

Pathe Review No. 37 brings four interesting subjects to the screen: "The Swanee Shore," a sacred spot in the Southland; "Handle with Care," the story of glass manufacture; "Country Life a la Mode," the French idea of a good place to spend a vacation; and "Dog Days," a novelty produced by the new "process-camera," invented by Alvin V. Knechtel of the Pathe Review Camera Staff.

"The Ugly Duckling" is the animated cartoon release of the "Aesop's Film Fables" series. The release schedule for September 13th is completed with "Topics of the Day" and two issues of Pathe News.

Release stills from "Pleasure Bound," a new Mermaid Comedy for Educational.

Short Subjects and Serials

"Wild West"
(Pathe Serial)
(Reviewed by Thomas C. Kennedy)

THE first three episodes of this serial produced by C. W. Patton serve to demonstrate the fact that Pathe is about to release another elaborately staged episode play as a follow-up to "Play Ball," the current offering. Colorful and rather striking are the backgrounds for the action, concerning the affairs of a pretty bare-back rider with a circus, and a Carlisle graduate who manages a huge ranch in Oklahoma.

The scenarist chose two broadly appealing story elements for his play. There is in the west, the west of great open spaces with cattle-rustling as the basis of conflict between hero and villains, and the circus, the big top with its sawdust rings, its sympathetic clowns, plotting managers and charming bare-back rider. Both of these settings separately have served many photoplays that have made a great success at the box office. Their blending here is typical of a serial age wherein the producers put in two thrills where one was given before.

The play seems more a series proposition than the usual serial story. No "papers" are planted in the first chapter, as is usual. The initial episode of "Wild West" is concerned with the shuffling about of babies, as though they were cards in a deck and in view of the subsequent episodes it seems as though the scenarist has wasted much time setting his play. The action, however, holds immediate interest and is possibly justified on that count, even if it is now all necessary to the progress of the plot as developed later.

There are several well known players in the cast. Jack Mulhall is featured with Helen Ferguson. Then there are Eddie Phillips, Virginia Warwick, Milla Davenport, Fred Burns, Ed Burns, Dan Dix, George Burton, Inez Gomez and Larry Steers.

Most of the scenes were filmed at the Miller Brothers 101 Ranch in Oklahoma. The establishment has afforded the director ample material for "production" scenes and atmosphere as well as for the incidental situations which build up the story and characters.

It is a serial which the majority of the picture patrons should receive warmly. It may lack the story construction and plot substance of "Idaho" and "Play Ball," but there is certainly enough in the way of "action" and atmosphere to hold the attention and stir the emotions of the average serial devotee.

(The Cast)
Jimmy Whitehawk	Jack Mulhall
Polly Breen	Helen Ferguson
Bob Miller	Eddie Phillips
Elsie Withers	Virginia Warwick
Chalky Withers	Milla Davenport
Joe Miller	Fred Burns
Col. Hardcastle	Ed Burns
Pat Casey	Dan Dix
Dan Norton	George Burton
Wynta	Inez Gomez
Dr. Alonzo Powers	Larry Steers

Scenario by J. F. Natteford. Directed by Robert F. Hill

The Story.—Among the thousands who awaited the opening up of the Cherokee Strip in Oklahoma to homesteaders, were Dr. Powers, owner of a medicine show, Col. Hardcastle and his wife and the three Miller brothers, cowboy. Hardcastle is deserted by his wife, who takes their daughter with her. Twenty years after the land rush Hardcastle is the owner of a big ranch and is known as Tom Osborne. His property adjoins that of the Miller Brothers, one of whom has reared Powers' son as his own. The half-breed son of the showman is manager of the Hardcastle ranch and on a visit to see a traveling show he meets Polly Breen, the star performer of the troupe. The

boy adopted by the Millers is in league with cattle rustlers and has joined the circus "to see the world." When the show is sold at auction Bob Miller buys it with the money he has made from the cattle-stealing deals and brings the entire outfit to the 101 Ranch, an event which brings another meeting between Jimmy and Polly. At the conclusion of the third episode a maddened elephant is shown running head-on into the automobile in which Polly is riding with Bib and his foster-father

Summary.—A finely staged presentation of a Concentional serial play. The western local is enchanced by the introduction of a line of action dealing with a circus, the star performer of which is the heroine. The action is well-paced and the first three episodes close on rather stirring events, the outcome of which is illustrated at the beginning of the succeeding chapters.

"Spooky Spooks"
(Bischoff, Inc.—Two Reels)
(Reviewed by Thomas C. Kennedy)

THIS is all that its title implies. Mystery stories have been burlesqued to death in the film comedies and the proposition seems very cold at this time. Al Herman, the director, has crammed every gag on the list of "spook" stunts into the two reels and therefore keeps his action going at top speed.

There is a Sherlock Holmes character and several turbaned gentlemen, a heroine and an innocent messenger boy, the animated suit of armor, the trap doors, or trick panels, skeletons, etc., etc. If there is any fun left in these over-worked devices then "Spooky Spooks" may get laughs.

The detail of the production is fairly well handled and the settings and properties are as elaborate as the occasion demands. From the first the pace of the action is fast and it increases until a speedy climax, in which there is a sort of paper chase, with the valuable document passing from one person to another as the characters dash from one room to another.

The Story.—A messenger boy is halted by two mysterious men, who take the message he is bearing to a certain house and substitute another, commanding him under pain of death to deliver it. At the address he finds a beautiful girl. The note is a threat of death for herself and her father unless she delivers certain documents to the senders. The messenger boy goes to get Sherlock Bones, famous detective. Later the mysterious gentlemen get into the house and there is enacted a series of mystery, involving and baffling events, the outcome of which is that the messenger boy triumphs over the forces of evil and wins the girl.

Summary.—"Spook" slapstick of a very familiar variety. The gags are all standard and there is little sense or reason to the affair.

"The Merchant of Weenies"
(Bischoff, Inc.—Two Reels)
(Reviewed by Thomas C. Kennedy)

H. C. WITWER supplies the story presented in this two-reel production dealing with a certain "leather pusher" who takes to reading Shakespeare in order to improve his education. The story has novelty to recommend it. The fighter gives in slang his idea of how the "Merchant of Venice" could be brought up-to-date and be made vital and interesting to your modern.

There is a broad and farcical burlesque of the Shakespeare drama, with fighters and fight-managers making up the figures of the play. This is all very well, but the play does not last as long as the film, with the consequence that the last reel is padded out with fight scenes of the usual sort seen on the screen.

The story has an adequate production and fair acting. Its burlesque of "The Merchant"

may prove highly diverting to the lovers of obvious screen entertainment.

The Cast
Charles Delaney, Eddie Phillips, Charlotte Morgan	

The Story.—A not very successful fighter is in love with a girl who works in a book store and he yearns for education. He takes to reading Shakespeare and then gives a slang recital of the story as he would tell it. This becomes a visualized burlesque of "The Merchant of Venice" with a fighter and a manager serving as the central characters. The fighter, who has borrowed in advance from a promoter, is about to have the pounds he is overweight sliced from him, as per the contract, when the girl who waits on the book shop intervenes and renders Portia's decision. The last reel is devoted to some fight scenes which introduce comedy and some dramatic action.

Summary.—This "Classics in Slang" story presents a rather novel burlesque of "The Merchant of Venice" and on that count may score with the audiences of the smaller houses. There is not sufficient story to last through the two reels and the latter half is little more than pure action with nothing much in the way of plot to fold it together.

"Hollywouldn't"
(Bischoff, Inc.—Two Reels)
(Reviewed by Thomas C. Kennedy)

JOHNNY SINCLAIR, featured in this "Biff Comedy" is a mighty good tumbler and with the able assistance of Charlie King stages some acrobatic falls that make the action of this film as vigorous as the situations are broad.

The play goes behind the scenes at a picture studio, with a flash here and there of amusing burlesque of the masters of the megaphones. The director in this play is shown with an assortment of megaphones, one for closeups, one for long shots, etc.

The story is about a farmer boy who falls in love with a movie queen. He steals the family flivver and starts out for Hollywood. At the studio where the charmer works they need someone to do a spanish dance and the rural steps in which Johny is skilled seem to fill the need. So he gets a job. The heroine refuses to do the dance, asking for a double, a role in which another man is cast. He appears in make-up resembling the movie queen and Johnny is overjoyed to think he will dance with the famous actress. The dance starts as a dance and ends up as a wrestling match.

The picture provides some amusement in spots here and there but for the most part it is just knock-about action of the broadest slapstick type.

The Cast
Johnny Sinclair, Charlie King, Billy Jones, Dorothy Dorr, Sailor Sharkey	

The Story.—A farmer boy, infatuated with a movie queen whose pictures he has thrilled to, arrives in Hollywood to meet her. He is fortunate enough to get a job as extra at the studio where she makes her productions. The experience furnishes him thrills and excitement he had not banked upon and after a rough session with the villain he is glad to get back to his flivver and head her for home. . . . .

Summary.—A burlesque of the movie studios done in slapstick style. The picture has some amusing moments and plenty of action, which is supplied by the featured player, an expert tumbler.

"Wild Beasts of Borneo"
(Educational—Two Reels)
(Reviewed by Chester J. Smith)

MR. AND Mrs. Lou C. Hutt of San Francisco spent considerable time and quite evidently went through many hardships, for all of which they should be well repaid by returns from this good animal picture. It is nicely arranged, with some vivid and interesting shots

of wild animals of all kinds apparently taken as close up as those of the ordinary picture.

Not only is it interesting because it depicts these animals in their native haunts, but it is educational, because it shows their customs and various methods through which they are captured. The Hutt expedition was an eminently successful one and its results should be appreciated wherever pictures are shown. There have been other wild animal pictures, but none better arranged or showing the beasts under more intimate conditions.

The Hutts reveal that their lens brought an object ten times closer than it really was and then they take you down to the actual capturing and tieing of a leopard putting up the most desperate fight to avoid being tied.

A herd of the white elephants worshipped as Gods by the Siamese is first shown at a distance and then is revealed in a playful closeup which makes them appear but a few feet away. Later a pitfall was dug and camouflaged and the captured tusker is shown from the rim of the pit trying furiously to disentangle himself and make for his captors.

The capture of a crocodile, which animal is said to annihilate five percent of the local population, was shown in an interesting sequence. The native guides apparently tied the jaws of the beast within a few moments after capturing him with bait that consisted of a piece of meat on a block of wood.

A touch of humor is loaned to the picture by the artful manner of capture of several monkeys. A cocoanut trap is used with a cord that ties the wrist, but does not hurt. The evolutions of the monkeys when the traps were sprung were quite amusing. The capture of a giant python, most powerful of all reptiles was extremely interesting and should be most thrilling to any movie audience. All in all the picture is quite worth while.

"Madame Sans Jane"
(Pathe—Two Reels)
(Reviewed by Thomas C. Kennedy)

GLENN TRYON, featured in this Hal Roach comedy, essays a female impersonation as part of his contribution to the entertainment. The motive behind the masquerade is a desire to be with his sweetheart, whom the irascible father is sending to Europe in order to get her away from our hero. Not to be bested said hero gets himself up in finery and a wig and obtains the job of acting as companion to the girl.

The customary farce complications appear when the father announces at the last moment that he also is going to Europe and will use one of the two state rooms he has engaged for his daughter and her professional companion.

There are moments when "Madame Sans Jane" is amusing, some where it is dull and a few where the comedy is broader than it is clever or original. However, we think a fair majority of the screen fans will find the picture a satisfactory offering and will derive therefrom the fun and entertainment they seek in short comedies.

Fay Wray in the role of the girl has the leading feminine part—next of course to Tryon's masquerade as a lady of looks and importance. Jimmie Finlayson does his best with the part of the father and Lucien Littlefield does a good bit in the role of an inquisitive and knowing steward. The best single performance, we think, is that of Mr. Walker or whoever wrote the titles, which are funny and easily the most amusing thing about "Madame Sans Jane."

THE CAST

The Boy	Glenn Tryon
The Girl	Fay Wray
The Father	Jimmie Finlayson
The Steward	Lucien Littlefield

Directed by James W. Horne.

The Story—The hero, much in love with a girl whose father is sending her to Europe in order to get her out of his way, impersonates a woman and answers the advertisement of the father for a traveling companion for his daughter. He gets the job and it proves bigger than he at first thought when the father decides to go to Europe also, the father being much smitten with the companion. Aboard ship several complications arise when the boy arranges to have the captain marry him to his adored one, but finally the cat gets out of the bag and the father yields to the importunities of the hero for his daughter's hand.

Summary—Obvious but rather effective comedy situations are presented in first rate fashion, with the result that the picture should prove satisfactory in the majority of cases.

"Off His Beat"
(Educational—Two Reels)
(Reviewed by Chester J. Smith)

THIS is one of the Walter Hiers series of comedies and it is unfortunate a better vehicle could not have been provided for a comedian of his ability. It is just a hodge podge of slapstick and forced comedy situations that were hardly new or amusing.

Hiers has the role of a cop and his pal is a detective. A neglected baby is left on their doorstep and for two reels they go through some embarassing situations because of the youngster. Walter is accused of deception by his girl, when with his pal they try to secrete the youngster as the girl pays them a visit.

Later on the action takes the pair into the policeman's annual parade and having nothing else to do with the kid they take it with them. Both are members of the band and their difficulties are increased as both play horns.

Following the parade comes the drill with Walter as drillmaster, handicapped by the necessity of carrying the babe. The fact that a strange cat crawls up his trouser leg is also supposed to add to the general merriment. Back to his post as traffic cop Walter takes the youngster in its baby carriage. A speeding autoist hooks on to the carriage and the usual wild chase starts, with the youngster finally rescued by Hiers as it is about to be run down on a railroad crossing.

The Cast

The Cop	Walter Hiers
The big cop	Bill Blaisdell
The bandmaster	Jack Duffy
His daughter	Evelyn Francisco

Story by Earl Rodney. Direct by Archie Mayo. Photography by Gus Peterson and Frank Sullivan.

The Story—Hiers and his pal discover a neglected baby on their doorstep and take it in. Walter is accused of deception by his girl when he tries to hide the youngster. They participate in the policeman's parade and are compelled to take the baby with them. On his post as traffic cop Hiers lays the baby in its carriage beside him and a speeding autoist hooks the carriage in passing. A wild chase starts and the baby carriage becomes disentangled on a railroad crossing. Walter on the cowcatcher grabs the baby from the speeding train.

Summary. A story whose comedy situations are somewhat forced and whose action is almost devoid of new material. Hiers is worthy of a considerably better vehicle.

"Too Much Mother In Law"
(Universal-Century—Two Reels)
(Reviewed by Chester J. Smith)

THAT ever new theme of the newlyweds and the visiting mother-in-law supplies the comedy for this two reeler in which Beth Darlington is featured. The difference between this one and some of the others is that this is fairly good. At least it abounds with some fairly fast action and some comedy situations that should develop laughs.

All is happy as usual with the newlyweds until they reach the train with their motorcycle and its side-carriage to pick up mother. The latter as usual attempts to dominate the situation and unfortunately takes a dislike to the new son-in-law and his ways. But for all of that mother gets decidedly the worst of things. Riding atop her bundles the motorcycle gets stalled beside a truck on which is a pet dog that becomes enamored of mother-in-law to the point where he insists upon lavishing kisses upon her.

Upon arrival at the house a parrot adds to the gaiety of the occasion when he takes a dislike to the visitor and applies to her all of the names in his vocabulary. When she insists upon having tea, booze is poured into it, which adds considerable jazz to the party as the young friends of the newlyweds arrive. Finally in desperation, hubby lifts mother-in-law into his motorcycle and gives her a ride which makes her call quits. He slows down only when she agrees to leave town and he makes her exit sure by dumping her off at the railroad station.

The Cast

The Young Wife	Beth Darlington

The Story—Mother-in-law calls upon the newlyweds and proceeds as usual to make life miserable for them. She attempts to dominate the situation in the home and succeeds until liquor is poured into the tea. Then the young hubby with renewed nerve assumes command, hustles mother-in-law into his motorcycle and rides her dizzy. She agrees to leave town and he makes sure of it by dumping her right on to the train.

Summary—A good lively comedy with some clever situations that should be good for many laughs. It is well directed and well acted by a competent cast.

"Tricked"
(Universal-Mustang—Two Reels)
(Reviewed by Chester J. Smith)

EDMUND COBB is featured in this western which has more of the comedy element and less of thrills than most of the kind. The story is a simple one of cowboy life and cowboy fun, but it provides some good riding and enough action to make it fairly interesting.

Ten boys of the Diamond Bar Ranch figure largely in the action with Cobb and the new schoolteacher. The latter is fair to look upon and soon gets the entire bunch of cowboys enrolled in her class. Cobb is the last to succumb, which apparently makes his fall the most decisive.

When he discovers the others at the schoolhouse he works a successful ruse in the form of a fire to clear the road for himself. When they realize they have been tricked they decide upon revenge. They disguise one of their number as the new teacher and Cobb proceeds to make love to "her," to the amusement of all hands. Again they frame the abduction of the teacher, whom Cobb rescues, much to the amusement of the boys. In the end, however, the cowboys aid him in his suit and he wins the hand of the fair lady.

The Cast

The Ranch Foreman	Edmund Cobb

The Story—The new school teacher in a small town wins the admiration of the boys of the Diamond Bar Ranch, all of whom decide that higher education is a much desired thing. They enroll singly in the class, with Cobb the last to succumb. The latter frames a fire in order to more successfully ply his suit. In turn the cowboys frame a number of tricks to embarrass their leader, who eventually, with their aid wins the hand of the teacher.

SYNOPSIS—A fairly good western a trifle lacking in action, but containing some good comedy. It is well acted and well directed and should be an attraction wherever the western is liked.

Pathe Review No. 37
(One Reel)

THE Swanee River much sung but little seen in picture theatres has its innings on the screen as the leading article in this number of Pathe Review. Scenes along the beautiful and famed stream whose calm surface mirrows the moss draped trees which line its banks are offered in a short "travelogue" of sufficient visual appeal to justify its presentation in any theatre. "Handle With Care" is the title of some pictures made in a glass manufactory, where delicate articles are "knocked out" by huge machines. "Dog Days" gives some more "trick pictures" made with the Process Camera and "Country Life à la Mode," the color subject, completes the issue.—T. C. KENNEDY.

Newspaper Opinions on New Pictures

"Don Q"—United Artists, Roosevelt, Chicago

Tribune: "'Don Q' is magnificently staged, counts its thrills by the dozen, furnishes plenty to laugh at and has been an enormous box-office success wherever it has played. Some boy, Zorro! Some boy, Don Q! This follow-up to 'The Mark of Zorro' is full of stuff—the stuff that dreams of adventurous youth are made of. Douglas Fairbanks has never been in better form."

News: "'Don Q' is a tricky picture, full of the tricks of story-telling and of romance, and of death and danger. As an entertainment it is of 100 per cent quality. It beings with the aim of entertaining and when it ends it has accomplished its purpose of entertaining. As a piece of story-telling on the screen it is a rarely good picture. It is decidedly on the list of recommended and indorsed pictures."

Post: "A fine picture is 'Don Q' and as good an entertainment as you can ask for. It is a true melodrama de luxe. It is movie-esque, gorgeously so. It is the sort of gay, thrilling spectacular film drama which makes one realize how good a photoplay can be when it stays in its own field. Fairbanks is more than ever the acrobat and so graceful that his movements are a joy to watch."

Journal: "Douglas Fairbanks has struck twelve again in 'Don Q' which began an engagement at the Roosevelt amid applause and laughter. It is an ideal movie. The story is satisfactory in every detail and so are the direction, the photography and the supporting cast. The action is swift and long sustained, but so cleverly alternated between gayety and thrill that it never tires the eye or the nerves."

American: "Put down 'Don Q' as one of the things to see. It is of the fine stock of which that earlier stirring adventure melodrama, 'The Mark of Zorro,' was composed. There is never a let-up in the succession of thrills, moments of humor and other qualities that go to make up an hour of solid entertainment."

"Sun-Up"—M. G. M., Capitol N. Y.

Telegraph: "'Sun-Up' is a poignantly absorbing story of the hill people in South Carolina. While this play achieved success on the stage, it was rather difficult to conceive it as a picture. But Edmund Goulding has done a wonderful job and he should be very proud of himself. The ignorant mountain people are presented in such simple fashion that they become not merely shadows but living, breathing people, in whose fate the spectator takes keen interest."

Evening World: "Having conquered several other branches of the motion picture industry, Edmund Goulding has now tried his hand at direction. The result, a picture called 'Sun-Up', is a living, breathing proof that this interloper has leaped right into the

front rank of directors. For 'Sun-Up' rates extremely high. It tells a deeply moving story, as any one who saw the Vollmer stage version will attest, and it is admirably enacted."

Sun: "The motion picture version of 'Sun-Up' serves excellently as starring vehicle for Conrad Nagel and is excellently directed and acted and convincing photographed. There are, moreover, many scenes productive of authentic emotion—the films have seldom more sincerely and graphically portrayed an incident than is here portrayed the slow deciphering by Emmy Todd for the Widow Cagle of that fateful telegram telling of the death of Rufe."

Telegram: "'Sun-Up' is predestined for popularity. It passes the supreme test where movie votaries are concerned. It brings the handkerchiefs out and that hint of moisture in the manly eye. And that's that. Conrad Nagel gives a convincing impersonation of the boy who goes out to fight 'some enemy of the government called Huns.' But the histrionic palm undoubtedly goes to Lucille LaVerne, who duplicates in the movie role the shade popular on Broadway last year. The stern woman of the hills, who can neither read nor write, whose creed in life is to go out 'an' git' the family foes, stood out as a vivid thing of flesh and blood in her sensitive interpretation."

Mirror: "Director Goulding has turned out a powerful picture. With a heavy revenge story of ignorant backswoodsmen to deal with, Goulding has injected flashes of humor and developed his character with rare deftness. Pauline Starke gives a beautiful performance as Emmy Todd."

Tribune: "The cast is perfect. Lucille LaVerne plays the Widow Cagle quite as well as she played it in the original. Pauline Starke is fascinating as the girl and Conrad Nagel does better work than he ever has done in his life. Many of the scenes are poignant and thrilling."

"Hell's Highroad"—Prod. Dist. Corp., Forum, Los Angeles

Illustrated News: "You will of course see it. If anyone deserves to be a star of the first magnitude it is Leatrice Joy. Her gowns are beautiful, the sets spectacular, and the acting all that can be desired."

Herald: "The scenes are spectacular and gorgeous. There are beautifully gowned women, magnificently furnished mansions and all the scenes are typically 'De Millean.' Leatrice Joy lives up to the high standard of acting she has set for herself."

Herald-Tribune: "The cast is excellent. Leatrice Joy seems to have acquired a new archness and is a fascinating figure. There are big, big ballrooms, beautiful boudoirs, gorgeous gowns, gaudy girls, insurgent innocents, wealthy widows, recherche rich men, palpitating poor men, a warring wife, a happy husband and a daring denouement."

Journal: "Cecil De Mille's pictures are there when it comes to entertainment. Take 'Hell's Highroad,' the film at the Colony for instance."

American: "Pleasing entertainment with original touches that show the unmistakable hand of Cecil B. De Mille. It is well worth a visit to The Colony and is a credit to both Cecil De Mille and Producers Distributing Corporation."

"Don Q"—United Artists, Colonial, Boston

Telegram: "Douglas Fairbanks never was better than in 'Don Q'. With amazing agility and speed he races through a series of adventures and never once does he lose his pleasing powers. From the opening of the film until the end he sets a pace of thrills which never falters."

Traveler: "'Don Q' is a swift action melodrama, full of glamor and bravado and heroic deeds calculated to make the blood tingle and the breath come faster. The screen's most athletic star is as full of surprising stunts and feats, as resourceful and tireless as can be imagined. And there is as gallant a series of superhuman feats as ever an audience rose and cheered. It is a gorgeous production."

Post: "From the first crack of the whip 'Don Q' is a joyous, swaggering, thrilling romance. Mr. Fairbanks leaps through a series of breath-taking adventures without losing his high-powered smile."

Globe: "There is a dash and verve and thrill to 'Don Q' that keeps the spectators at fever heat. It is so good a picture that one doesn't even hear the music."

Herald: "Douglas Fairbanks has added another to his amazing list. The action in 'Don Q' is graphic and continuous. Never does it slacken for a moment."

American: "A hero of zestful deeds, in a role that hits the high mark of adventurous romance is Douglas Fairbanks in 'Don Q.' Once more Fairbanks proves that melodrama, infused with imagination and humor and dominated by his all-conquering vivacity can be fine film entertainment. There are many fine adventures and a grand finale of fighting."

Transcript: "'Don Q' is one continuous, often hilarious romp —sheer essence of Fairbanks, undiluted, self-confessed."

"The Gold Rush"—United Artists, Orpheum, Chicago

Herald: "Charlie Chaplin is still the world's greatest—an artist, a comedian, an entertainer .finer than any one else alive today. And his 'The Gold Rush' proves again that fact. A fine picture, I think, a picture taking Chaplin closer to the serious ambition that evolved 'A Woman of Paris' but not a step away from hilarious buffoonery. 'The Gold Rush' is a marvelous entertainment. It is far more elaborate than previous Chaplin productions and behind its laughs are tears."

Carmel Myers, now playing in Benjamin Christianson's initial production for Metro-Goldwyn-Mayer, as yet untitled.

Tribune: "Ten reels of Charlie Chaplin as you like him. Ten reels sounds like a heap, and it would be if 'The Gold Rush' weren't 'The Gold Rush.' The Lone Prospector gives you lots of original and fascinating comedy. And always there is the note of sadness. He's so lonesome and so game and so darned unlucky. 'The Gold Rush' really is a dandy, and you'd just better see Charlie's latest if you know what's good to see and what's good for you."

American: "He's the same old Charlie. Years may have grayed his hair and swelled his pocketbook, but in his screen characterizations he is still the same vagabond you've laughed at and many cried over since Keystone Comedy days. All in all, he is just as funny as ever he was. Go and see him, listen to the laughter of yourself and those around him, and see if you don't think so."

News: "Charlie Chaplin of the derby, cane, baggy trousers, funny mustache and wabbly walk, who has made the whole world laugh more than any other comedian, has built into 'The Gold Rush' a structure of fun and laughter. He has built what many say is the funniest and most hilarious comedy of his career. Pathos and suffering are converted into comedy and laughter—there is a laugh in every one of the 8,000 or so feet."

Journal: "There are many new things in Charlie Chaplin's new film. It has a plot. It has dramatic tensity. It has laughs of an order even Chaplin himself has never aroused before. Not content with making the whole world laugh, he now asks it to drop a trickling tear, a film that marks a new epoch in the account of Chicago movies."

Post: "It is hard to imagine anybody being disappointed in the treasure of comedy this newest Charlie Chaplin film, 'The Gold Rush' contains. It's pure gold from the first flicker to the end. The Gold Rush is gay and pathetic, fantastic and human."

Pre-release Reviews of Features

The Mystic
(Metro-Goldwyn—6147 Feet)
(Reviewed by George T. Pardy)

DIRECTOR Tod Browning, whose previous production of "The Unholy Three" created such a sensation, scores again with an extremely clever crook melodrama. This time, the members of a gang of fake spiritualists unite in fleecing the unwary and the revelations of their fraudulent tricks, as well as a pleasing romance, considerable suspense and not a few thrilling situations, combine to make this a very entertaining picture. Conway Tearle gives a uniformly excellent performance as the "master mind" of the band, Aileen Pringle offers a genuinely fine and artistic characterization of Zara, the gypsy medium, while Mitchell Lewis and Robert Ober distinguish themselves in their respective roles of Zazarack and Anton. The seance episodes are admirably handled, as are the scenes in which the detectives try to dope out the puzzling methods employed by the swindlers.

THEME. Crook melodrama, with fake spiritualists doing their stuff, numerous thrills and romantic interest.

PRODUCTION HIGHLIGHTS. The carnival settings in Hungary. Scene where phony clairvoyant is convinced she actually sees a ghost. The seances. Realistic atmosphere. Reform of hero.

EXPLOITATION ANGLES. Street ballyhoo with gypsy wagon and occupants. Lobby display including crystal ball on pedestal and fortune teller. Where possible, prologue with Hungarian dances, etc. Feature Conway Tearle and Aileen Pringle.

DRAWING POWER. Good attraction for any house.

SUMMARY. Crook melo, exposing methods utilized by fake spiritualists. Has heart interest, thrills and glints of comedy. An entertaining film with universal appeal.

THE CAST
Zara..Aileen Pringle
Jimmy Burton.......................................Conway Tearle
Zazarack...Mitchell Lewis
Anton..Robert Ober
Carlo...Stanton Heck
Bradshaw..David Torrence
Doris Merrick.......................................Gladys Hulette
Author and Director, Tod Browning. Photographed by Ira Morgan.

SYNOPSIS. Jimmy Burton, American crook, with Zara, fake gypsy medium, and her Hungarian associates, starts a criminal campaign, using phony spiritualistic methods. Bradshaw, Wall Street man and guardian of orphan Doris Merrick, is a victim. Doris is shown her father's ghost and learns that Bradshaw has speculated with her money. The remainder of her fortune is given the girl and annexed by the gang. In love with Zara, Jimmy reforms. He escapes with the loot during a police raid and returns it to Doris. Zara and the others are deported. Jimmy weds her abroad.

Aileen Pringle

Fighting the Flames
(Columbia Pictures—5800 Feet)
(Reviewed by George T. Pardy)

WHEREVER high-pressure melodrama is popular this picture should go over big. It's exactly what the average fan wants, stirring action, sustained love interest and comedy stuff interpolated just where it's needed. The title tells the story, for the hero is a formerly "bad boy," who joins the fire brigade, pulls off several thrilling rescues, wins a pretty girl and redeems himself generally in the eyes of his stern dad, who had chucked him out as a hard case. William Haines plays the lead, with Dorothy Devore as the heroine, and both acquit themselves satisfactorily, in fact the acting, not only of the principals, but the entire cast, is of a far higher average than one expects in films of this type.

The plot isn't strikingly original, but Director Reeves Eason has handled it with such skill that new angles are developed and everyone of the big punch situations gets home effectively.

THEME. Melodrama, with comedy relief, fireman hero, love interest and many thrills.

PRODUCTION HIGHLIGHTS. The realistic atmosphere and fast action. Fire and rescue scenes. Climax where hero fights crook as well as flames and saves boy and heroine.

EXPLOITATION. Play up as sensational melodrama of fire brigade. You can probably get local companies interested. Feature William Haines and Dorothy Devore.

DRAWING POWER. First-class attraction for neighborhood and smaller houses.

SUMMARY. Picture follows title closely. Is fast-moving sensational melo, with fireman hero, good love interest, and bunch of bully thrills.

THE CAST
Horatio Manly......................................William Haines
Alice Doran...Dorothy Devore
Mickey...Frankie Darrow
Judge Manly...David Torrence
Big Jim...Sheldon Lewis
Charlie Ryan.......................................William Welsh
Pawnbroker..Charles Murray
Scenario by Douglas Doty. Directed by Reeves Eason. Cameraman, Dewey Wrigley.

SYNOPSIS. Horato, (Racy) Manly, is cast off by his father on account of dissipated ways. He becomes pals with street Arab, Mickey, whose crook father is in jail. Racy joins the fire brigade, incidentally falling in love with Alice Doran, who lives in the same rooming-house. Fire breaks out in the jail and Mickey's dad, who has vowed vengeance on his kid, escapes. He finds Mickey in Alice's room and the girl fights him off. The house catches fire. Racy reaches Alice in time to rescue her and Mickey from the flames. He is reconciled to his father.

William Haines

The Limited Mail
(Warner Brothers—7144 Feet)
(Reviewed by George T. Pardy)

A GOOD box office attraction! They've taken Elmer Vance's old stage success and turned it into a film that vibrates with fast action sensational melodramatic thrills, seasoned yarn timely comedy relief and sentimental sauce. It's a railroad yarn and a snappy one, has a general audience appeal and tremendously realistic atmosphere. No spectator is likely to forget in a hurry the big punch scene where the Limited Mail and a fast freight smash into a head-on collision, and there are many other situations of similar tension which will startle the most hard-boiled fan and set the youngsters wild with enthusiasm. Monte Blue is the hero engineer, looks and acts like a real knight of the rail, and gives an admirable performance, ably assisted by Vera Reynolds, as the girl in the case, Willard Louis, as a fat, lovable hobo, with Master Jack Huff an uncommonly cute kiddie in the role of Bobby Fowler.

THEME. Western railroad melodrama with spectacular train-wreck scene, strong romantic interest, numerous thrills, comedy relief and happy climax.

PRODUCTION HIGHLIGHTS. Mountain landslide blocking tracks, train flagged and saved by three hobos. Collision between Limited and freight. Tunnel disaster, when Bob stops express from thundering into obstacles. Rescue of child from drowning by escaped convict.

EXPLOITATION ANGLES. Bill as sensational Western railroad melodrama, play up the big collision scene, flagging of train by tramps, Bob's mad rush to save Limited from tunnel wreck. Stress love interest, comedy touches. Feature Monte Blue, Vera Reynolds and Willard Louis.

DRAWING POWER. Should please the masses and do good business in any house.

SUMMARY. Offers a ripping tale of Western railroad life, with strong sentimental interest and well-balanced comedy. Well mounted and directed, a sure-fire melodramatic attraction.

THE CAST

Bob Wilson	Monte Blue
Caroline Dale	Vera Reynolds
"Dixie" Potts	Willard Louis
Jim Fowler	Tom Gallery
Bobby Fowler	Master Jack Huff
Spike Nelson	Edward Gribbon
Mrs. O'Leary	Lydia Yeamang Titus

Adapted from Elmer Vance's stage play by Darryl Kanuck. Director, George Hill, Cameraman, Charles van Enger.

SYNOPSIS. Jilted by Jane Gordon, Bob Wilson turns tramp, saves mail train from landslide disaster. Befrinded by mail clerk Fowler, he finally becomes engineer of Limited Mail. Bob loves Caroline Dale, their romance is temporarily checked when Jane reappears. The Limited collides with a freight. Bob escapes uninjured, as does Bobby, Fowlers little boy. Latter is saved from drowning by escaping convict, Tunnel caves in. Bob flages train and averts accident. He and Caroline find happiness together.

The Limited Mail (Warner Bros.)
PRESS NOTICE

A PICTURE sizzling with excitement and melodramatic power is "The Limited Mail," booked at the ———— theatre on ————. It's a railroad story of intense realism, packed with thrills, including one of the most spectacular wrecks ever filmed, when the Limited and fast freight crash in a head-on collision. The hero is an ex-hobo, who makes good, wins promotion to engineer and the love of a charming girl.

There's bright comedy too, and strong sentimental interest, with Monte Blue, as the heroic engineer and Vera Reynolds as heroine. A brilliant supporting cast is in evidence, including such favorite players as Willard Louis, Tom Gallery, Master Jack Huff, Edward Gribbon and Lydia Yeamans Titus.

CATCH LINES
A thrilling melodrama of the Colorado mountains, with realistic railroad settings, wherein a hobo regains his manhood and wins happiness.

Monte Blue.

Vic Dyson Pays
(Arrow—5000 Feet)
(Reviewed by George T. Pardy)

AN average Westerner, but with a plot which offers considerably more sentimental values than are usually found in these yarns of rough-and-ready ranch life, and sufficient speed to please those who like the red-blood, stressed-action stuff. Character drawing is generally at a discount in Westerners, therefore it is all the more surprising to find Ben Wilson, in the hero role of Vic Dyson, making the gent in question a very appealing sort of chap. True Vic scraps with the proper ferocity and effectiveness of a ranch film hero, but he also scores quite a bit in the sequences showing the effect pity for the injured heroine has upon him, while at the same time concealing his love for her, and there's a real bit of pathos in the climax, when he starts to ride away for good. But the girl follows him, so the picture finishes on a happy chord after all.

Director Jacques has done very well with a story of somewhat slight construction.

THEME. Western melodrama, with cattle man hero fighting against attempt to take his ranch for a railroad right-of-way.

PRODUCTION HIGHLIGHTS. Scene where hero has tussle with members of opposing faction, during which Neva falls over cliff. Episode where it develops that spinal injury causes loss of her eyesight. Her recovery and the happy climax.

EXPLOITATION ANGLES. Bill as Westerner with riding and fighting thrills, but stressing love story of more than common interst. Feature Ben Wilson and Neva Gerber.

DRAWING POWER. O. K. for neighborhood and smaller houses.

SUMMARY. Westerner a bit different from the usual kind in regard to plot, which has a good deal of sentimental lure in, all other respects an average melo.

THE CAST

"Mad" Vic Dyson	Ben Wilson
Neva	Neva Gerber
Skip	Archie Ricks
Albert Stacey	Mel McCormick

Author Not Credited. Directed by Jacques Jacard.

SYNOPSIS. Vic Dyson, cattleman, known as "Mad" Vic, because of his impetuous temper, vows vengeance when he learns that there is a plot on the part of certain business men to obtain possession of his ranch for use as a railroad right-of-way. He engages in a fight with certain members of the opposing faction, during which, Neva, a stenographer employed by the real estate contingent, is pushed over a cliff. She sustains spinal injuries which result in the loss of her eyesight. Vic, remorseful, takes care of the injured girl and falls in love with her. He is not aware that she returns his affection. On her recovery, Vic deeds his ranch over to her, is about to ride away, but she follows, and he realizes that she loves him.

Vic Dyson Pays (Arrow)
PRESS NOTICE

THERE is a tender love romance running through the exciting melodramatic trend of "Vic Dyson Pays," the Western picture which will be the principal attraction at the ———— theatre on ————. The story has for its theme a cattle man who combats the attempt of real estate men to secure his ranch for a railroad right-of-way. During a fight with his enemies, a girl stenographer is pushed over a cliff and seriously injured.

The hero blames himself for the mishap, takes care of the girl and deeds his ranch to her, when she recovers. He loves her, but starts to go away, is stopped by her and realizes that his affection is returned. Ben Wilson plays the leading role, with Neva Gerber as the heroine. Archie Ricks and Mel McCormick are members of the supporting cast.

CATCH LINES
A hero who was a terror to his foes, but tender hearted as a woman to the weak.

Ben Wilson.

Border Vengeance
(Aywon Film—4800 Feet)
(Reviewed by George T. Pardy)

THE best that can be said in this film's favor is that it will get by O. K. as an attraction for houses where a daily change is the policy, or as half of a double feature bill. It is a Westerner, introducing Jack Perrin as one of the fast-riding, hard scrapping star brigade, but not until near the finish does he get much of a chance to show what he can do in the strenuously active line. The trouble with the picture is that it lacks snappy action in most of the reels, a fatal handicap for a Westerner to carry. The fans may excuse incoherence of plot or similarity of events, but you must give them speed and plenty of thrills in the open-air adventure stuff, or they will turn thumbs down on the production.

However, there is this in Perrin's favor, he has a rather engaging smile, a free-and-easy way of getting around, is a muscular, agile chap and does his stuff with lots of pep and ginger in the few situations where he has an opportunity to pull stunt work. The last reel buzzes along at a merry clip and breezes into a slashing climax, making up in a measure for the tame sequences of the early stages of the film.

THEME. Western melodrama, with action taking place along and over Mexican border.

PRODUCTION HIGHLIGHTS. Western atmosphere and characteristic type. The big mine explosion. Jack Perrin's riding stunts. The smashing fight between Perrin and the villain at the close.

EXPLOITATION. Bill this as a straight Western melo, but don't promise too much as regards either story or action. Feature Jack Perrin, Josephine Hill.

DRAWING POWER. Suitable for daily change houses or as half of double feature bill.

SUMMARY. An ordinary Western. Misses fire in early stages because of lack of punch and decisive action. Speeds up in final reel and attains a good climax.

THE CAST

Wes Channing	Jack Perrin
Mary Sims	Josephine Hill
Mark Newman	Jack Richardson
Buck Littleton	Bud Osborne
Widow Jackson	Mina Redman
Bumps Jackson	Vandall Darr
Rufe Sims	Hugh Saxon
Flash Denby	Leonard Clapman

Author, Forret Sheldon. Director, Harry Webb. Photographed by William Thornley.

SYNOPSIS. Wes Channing's well-meaning but dissipated partner, Buck Littleton, loses his interest in their ranch to gambler Denby. Near the ranch is Rufe Sim's mining claim, an old chap whose life Wes saves when dynamite explodes prematurely in his mine. Wes opposes the sheriff's men who come to seize the ranch for Denby, but has finally to ride across the border. Denby tries to trick Rufe's granddaughter, Mary into surrendering the mine to him. Just as she signs the deed, Wes arrives. He and Denby engage in a savage encounter, which ends with Wes victor.

Jack Perrin.

Border Vengeance (Aywon Films)
PRESS NOTICE

In "Border Vengeance," a Western melodrama, a new star makes his appearance, Jack Perrin, who will be seen in this picture at the —————— theatre on ——————. The feature is what the title suggests, a story of adventure in the open, the action taking place on the Mexican border and offering a story rich in romantic interest as well as exciting situations.

A gambler who tries to cheat a young girl and her granddad out of a valuable mine is one of the central figures in the story, and meets his deserts at the hero's hands in a slashing fight at the finish. Josephine Hill is the heroine and Jack Richardson, Bud Osborne and other favorite players are in the cast.

CATCH LINES

Jack Perrin's riding and fighting stunts in this film, make them all "sit up and take notice."

The Wanderer
(Paramount—8173 Feet)
(Reviewed by Oscar Cooper)

COLORFUL, daring, spectacular, "The Wanderer" is produced on a big scale. It is acted by a first-rate cast, and presents an elaboration of the Biblical story of The Prodigal Son. It has big sets and scenes. There can be no question that it is a powerful dramatic document, but it does not have the breadth and sweep of "The Ten Commandments" with which it will inevitably be compared.

The dramatic action pivots on sex appeal of a very strong variety. Greta Nissen, in the role of the Temptress, displays her physical charms, as do many of the other feminine players. Her role is that of a wanton, who lures Jether, the shepherd boy from his home to the city.

THEME. A film version of the story of The Prodigal Son, who is ensnared by a temptress, spends his substance in riotous living and returns home, broken.

PRODUCTION HIGHLIGHTS. The acting by Miss Nissen, as a super-vamp; William Collier, Jr., as the black sheep—a remarkably fine, restrained performance; and Ernest Torrence, as a villain. The rich staging and scenes of pagan revelry. The destruction of the city. The feast of the Fatted Calf on the Prodigal's return. The big sets.

EXPLOITATION ANGLES. Should be built chiefly around the Prodigal Son story. Play up the cast and the big scenes as outlined above.

DRAWING POWER. O.K. for the best houses.

SUMMARY. Not one of the great pictures, but "strong medicine" dramatically and possessing many elements of popular appeal. Would have been still more impressive if less had been made of the physical and more of the spiritual.

THE CAST

Tola	Ernest Torrence
Jether	William Collier, Jr.
Tisha	Greta Nissen
Jesse	Tyrone Power
Huldah	Kathlyn Williams
Paris	Wallace Beery
Naomi	Kathryn Hill
Gaal	George Rigas

From the stage play, "The Lost Son," by Maurice V. Samuels. Scenario by J. T. O'Donohue. Directed by Raoul A. Walsh.

SYNOPSIS. Jether, the shepherd boy, is lured from his home by Tisha, a priestess. Her major domo, Tola, a villain, induces him to ask for his share of gold, and he goes with them to the city, where Tisha becomes his mistress. He lavishes jewels and fine clothes upon her, spends his substance in riotous living. The prophet warns him that destruction is coming. When all his money is gone, Tisha casts him out. While a big banquet is going on, the city is destroyed, but Jether escapes, and finds employment tending swine. Finally, he makes his way home and is welcomed at the Feast of the Fatted Calf.

Greta Nissen

PRESS NOTICE

THE famous Biblical story of The Prodigal Son, with a wonderful cast and elaborate scenes, is told in "The Wanderer," which comes to the —————— theatre on ——————. Raoul Walsh, who directed "The Thief of Bagdad," had charge of the making of the picture and was provided with a splendid cast, including Ernest Torrence, Greta Nissen, William Collier, Jr., Tyrone Power, Wallace Beery, Kathlyn Williams and others.

Miss Nissen appears as Tisha, the Temptress, in the most important role of her career thus far. Young Collier is great in the role of the Prodigal Son. Torrence gives a fine performance in a villainous role. Destruction of the wicked city while a big banquet and revel is in progress is the big scene.

CATCH LINES

The Wanderer (Paramount). He wasted his substance in riotous living, but his father killed the fatted calf for him.

The Love Hour
(Vitagraph—7036 Feet)
(Reviewed by George T. Pardy)

CONSIDERED even as an ordinary program attraction this picture fails to make the grade. It may get by in the "daily change" houses, but hasn't a Chinaman's chance of success elsewhere. The plot, with its virtuous shopgirl, suffering hubby and designing, black-hearted villain, brings memories of the worst examples of movies a generation ago. It would have been bad enough if confined to five reels, but dragged out to its present length it is inexcusably tiresome. The only bright spots in the film are the merry slapstick interludes for which Louise Fazenda and Willard Louis are responsible, a great comedy team whose work saves the feature from being altogether a blank failure. A slow start is registered, nearly a reel being consumed showing antics at a seashore resort before the story proper gets under way.

THEME. Melodrama with comedy relief, dealing with love of shopgirl for millionaire and pursuit of her by soulless villain.

PRODUCTION HIGHLIGHTS. The slapstick comedy. Scenes where Louise Fazenda and Willard Louis settle down in married life. Episode where heroine defends herself from villain's advances with gun and thunderstorm effects. The climax.

DRAWING POWER. May do for daily change houses, if bolstered up by lively short subjects.

SUMMARY. Romantic melo with hackneyed plot depicting adventures of shopgirl who weds millionaire, latter falling ill and going broke, while villain torments wife. A poor attraction, held up to some degree by interpolations of slapstick comedy.

THE CAST
Rex Westmore....................................Huntly Gordon
Jenny Tibbs....................................Louise Fazenda
Gus Yerger....................................Willard Louis
Betty Brown....................................Ruth Clifford
Ward Ralston....................................John Roche
Kid Lewis....................................Charles Farrell
Attorney....................................Gayne Whitman

Author, Bess Meredyth. Directed by Herman Raymaker. Photographed by E. B. Du Par.

SYNOPSIS. A chance meeting at an amusement park results in Betty Brown, shopgirl, wedding young Rex Westmore, millionaire, while her chum Jenny marries plumber Yerger. Rex loses all his money in stocks and falls ill. Ralston, a broker, sends him abroad to recuperate and makes advances to Betty. At a crucial moment she pulls a gun on him, just as a thunderstorm breaks. He falls and Betty runs away. Later, she learns that a lightning bolt killed Ralston. Rex regains health and fortune and they live happily.

PRESS NOTICE
The Love Hour (Vitagraph)

THE romance of a shopgirl and young millionaire is set forth in "The Love Hour," a melodrama of absorbing heart interest which is scheduled as the leading attraction at the —————— theatre on ——————. Betty Brown falls in love with and weds a man she meets at an amusement park, who turns out to be a wealthy society chap. He loses his fortune and falls ill and is sent abroad to recuperate by a broker, who makes advances to the young wife.

Betty pulls a gun on her tormentor, who falls just as a thunderstorm breaks. She runs away, but it transpires that he was killed by lightning. Rex regains his health and fortune. Bright comedy flashes enliven the action.

CATCH LINES
The romance of beauty and money, with a pretty shopgirl realizing her day-dreams when she meets and weds a young millionaire.

Huntly Gordon

The Merry Widow
(Metro-Goldwyn-Mayer—10,027 Feet)
(Reviewed by Oscar Cooper)

EVERY so often a picture comes along about which there can be no box-office doubt. "The Merry Widow" belongs in that class. It has great direction by Erich von Stroheim; Mae Murray really acting instead of posing her way attractively across the footage; John Gilbert scoring heavily as the hero; remarkable new villain, Roy D'Arcy, of whom more will be heard later; fine production values; and a story out of which first-class audience stuff has been made.

The picture can be shown at great length, as in the case of the opening of the Embassy Theatre, New York; or it can be, and we think should be trimmed, to fit the requirements of the majority of houses. In either case, it is a box-office certainty.

THEME. Mythical kingdom story, with the hero, a prince, eventually marrying the heroine, an American chorus girl.

PRODUCTION HIGHLIGHTS. Superb understanding of production values by the director. Heart interest and the splendor of court and Parisian life in admirable contrast. The uniformly high average of acting by the principals.

EXPLOITATION ANGLES. Capitalize the famous waltz and operetta. Tell them about Mae Murray, John Gilbert and D'Arcy, the villain, and the direction.

DRAWING POWER. O. K. for the best houses and all other classes of houses.

SUMMARY. A finely directed picture with sure-fire appeal because of the way in which it has been handled. Unusual combination of atmosphere, acting and direction.

THE CAST
Sally....................................Mae Murray
Danilo....................................John Gilbert
Crown Prince....................................Roy D'Arcy
Queen Milena....................................Josephine Crowell
King Nitika....................................George Fawcett
Baron Sadoja....................................Tully Marshall

There is also a large number of other players. By Franz Lehar, Victor Leon and Leo Stein. Directed by Erich von Stroheim. Adapted by von Stroheim and Benjamin Glazer. Cameraman, Ollie Marsh.

SYNOPSIS. Prince Danilo and the Crown Prince meet Sally O'Hara, a Follies dancer, and both seek to win her favor. Danilo wins, but the Crown Prince finds them in what seems to be a compromising position, whereupon Danilo announces he and Sally will wed. Danilo's parents force him to break off the engagement and Sally, broken-hearted, marries the Baron who dies on the wedding night. Sally thus becomes a rich widow and goes to Paris. The Crown Prince, seeking her money goes there, and Sally, thinking Danilo no longer loves her, tells him she is engaged to the Crown Prince. The two men quarrel, and a duel is arranged. Danilo is seriously wounded and is taken back to Monteblanco, followed by Sally. The Crown Prince is killed by an anarchist, the King and Queen having died, and thus Danilo and Sally become the rulers of the country.

PRESS NOTICE

THE wonderful screen version of the famous operetta, "The Merry Widow," comes to the —————— theatre on ——————. It has a great cast with Mae Murray, in the best role of her career; John Gilbert, as the dashing hero, a remarkable villain— Roy D'Arcy—and the picture was directed by Erich von Stroheim. There is a big group of supporting players.

The splendor of court life and glimpses of Parisian night life are shown. And the story is a fine romance, full of action, sword-play and all the other things you love in a mythical kingdom picture. Some of the finest color scenes ever shown on the screen are provided.

CATCH LINES
The Merry Widow (M-G-M)
An American chorus girl marries a Prince, but not until he is dangerously wounded in a duel.
See the famous "Merry Widow" waltz danced by Mae Murray and John Gilbert.

John Gilbert

The Live Wire

(C. C. Burr-First National—6850 Feet)
(Reviewed by Harold Flavin)

SCORE another hit for Johnny Hines. This comedian seems to have an uncanny faculty for making productions which have wide popularity as much their termination as the inevitable clinch at the finish of the last reel. And the titles! If your patrons don't get a laugh out of every one of them it will be due only to a lack of humor in their make-up.

As in Hines' previous pictures the story is incidental to the "gags" but then, who looks for plot in a production that combines all the thrills of a circus performance, an exhibition of the "Charleston," which incidentally, should go big at the present time, and the many other mirth-provoking stunts performed by this versatile funster.

As regards the romantic element—credit must be given the discerning eye of C. C. Burr for having picked so fair a vision of female loveliness as Mildred Ryan.

THEME. Comedy melodrama of adventures of circus performer, out of work, whose athletic ability and sense of humor win him wealth and a girl.

PRODUCTION HIGHLIGHTS. The circus scenes. The cafe sequence. The fight scene in the gymnasium. The many bits of business put over by Hines and Edmund Breese. John Krafft's titles.

EXPLOITATION ANGLES. The star's name ought to prove a good drawing card. Put on prologue featuring circus atmosphere. There are any number of tie-ups possible with electrical companies.

DRAWING POWER. An attraction that should go over with a bang in first runs and all other types of houses.

SUMMARY. A fast action comedy melodrama with a laugh in every scene. The "Gags" which occupy most of the footage, are novel and entertaining.

THE CAST

The Great Maranelli	Johnny Hines
"Sawdust" Sam	Edmund Breese
Henry Langdon	J. Barney Sherry
Dorothy Langdon	Mildred Ryan
George Trent	Bradley Barker
Pansy Darwin	Flora Finch

Adapted from Richard Washburn Child's "The Game of Light." Directed by Charles Hines. Photographed by Charles E. Gilson, John Geisel and Paul Strand. Titles by John Krafft.

SYNOPSIS. The Great Maranelli, forced to quit circus life, takes to the road accompanied by his chum "Sawdust" Sam, in search of adventure. In his travels he meets Dorothy Langdon, daughter of the president of the Power Company. Langdon gives Maranelli a position and Dorothy enlists the aid of Sam in putting over an amusement park of which her father has made her part owner the rest of the stock being in the possession of George Trent, Dorothy's suitor, who has failed in an attempt to get whole ownership. Though beset by difficulties put in their way by Trent the trio finally win out, Maranelli also succeeding Trent as Dorothy's fiance.

The Coast of Folly

(Paramount—6840 Feet)
(Reviewed by George T. Pardy)

THIS society drama has been produced with all the lavish disregard of expense for which Miss Swanson's pictures are usually noted, the star wearing gracefully a variety of magnificent gowns calculated to awaken the envy of all feminine patrons, and the interiors a veritable blaze of gorgeous settings. Its entertainment values are not quite up to the standard of "glorious Gloria's" best vehicles, chiefly because the actual story is subordinated to the leading lady's characterizations. She appears in a dual, or one might say a triple role, for we are first given a momentary flash of her attired in the early Victorian bustle and sweeping train, then as a modern flapper and later as an old French Countess. The Swanson fans won't care so much for their favorite in her elderly makeup, but they will wax enthusiastic over her girlish portrayal.

THEME. Society drama, with Palm Beach and New York atmosphere, in which mother comes to rescue of daughter involved in scandal.

PRODUCTION HIGHLIGHTS. The elaborate settings. Miss Swanson's clever characterizations. The fashion display. The masked ball. Scene where heroine's mother saves daughter's reputation.

EXPLOITATION. Feature Gloria Swanson's work, tell women patrons about her new gowns. Play up movie ball, luxurious atmosphere and settings. Boost love interest.

DRAWING POWER. Miss Swanson's popularity should bring good business at any house.

SUMMARY. Less action and more characterization footage than is customary in Swanson films, with consequent weakening of entertainment values. Lavishly produced society drama with Palm Beach settings and scandal theme. Star's fame the chief attraction.

THE CAST

Nadine Gathway	
Joyce Gathway	} Gloria Swanson
Larry Fay	Anthony Jowitt
Count de Tauro	Alec Francis
Constance Fay	Dorothy Cumming
Cholly Knickerbocker	Jed Prouty
Bather	Lawrence Gray

Author, Coningsby Dawson. Director, Allan Dwan. Photographed by George Webber.

SYNOPSIS. Nadine Gathway deserts her millionaire husband and disappears for twenty years. Her daughter Joyce becomes involved in a love affair at Palm Beach with Larry Fay, who is unhappily married. His wife Constance plans to blast Joyce's reputation. Nadine, now the wife of Count de Tauro in Paris, comes to Joyce's aid. She wheedles Constance into a compromising situation and saves Joyce. Nadine takes all the blame, but her husband believes in her. Larry and Joyce look forward to a peaceful future together.

Johnny Hines

Gloria Swanson

Seven Days
(Producers Distributing Corp.—6974 Feet)
(Reviewed by George T. Pardy)

IF they hadn't strung this picture out to an entirely unnecessary length it would probably have classed as first-rate entertainment. It takes mighty good comedy material to register successfully over the six reel limit, and when a film consists mostly of farce and slapstick stuff as this does, stretching its slender plot to the limit is a mistake. The story hinges on the efforts of the members of a house party to escape from a quarantine cordon established because of a supposed outbreak of smallpox, which proves at the last to be of the harmless chicken variety, and there is plenty of humming action with all sorts of funny complications which get the laughs for a while, but grow a trifle monotonous toward the close.

Lillian Rich and Creighton Hale do very nicely in the leading roles and are capably supported. The sub titles are uncommonly well written, terse, witty, and help out the action a whole lot.

THEME. House party quarantined on account of supposed smallpox outbreak which proves phony. Farce comedy.

PRODUCTION HIGHLIGHTS. Acting of Creighton Hale and Lillian Rich. The fast action. Scene where burglar is concealed in chimney. Chase up and down dumbwaiter, and other slapstick events.

EXPLOITATION ANGLES. Bill as adaptation of stage farce which had long Broadway run. Play up policeman and burglar episode and efforts of members of house party to beat the quarantine rule. Feature Creighton Hale and Lillian Rich.

DRAWING POWER. A fair program attraction for neighborhood and smaller houses.

SUMMARY. Farce comedy with some distinctly funny spots, fast action and plenty of slapstick. Spoiled by excess footage but holds up pretty well under that handicap and should pass muster as average attraction.

THE CAST
Kit Eclair	Lillian Rich
Jim Wilson	Creighton Hale
Bella Wilson	Lilyan Tashman
Anne Brown	Mabel Julienne Scott
Dal Brown	William Austin
Tom Harbinson	Hal Cooley
Aunt Selina	Rosa Gore

Adopted from stage farce by Mary Roberts Rinehart. Directed by Scott Sidney.

SYNOPSIS. Jim Wilson gives house party. Valet falls sick, police establish quarantine on suspicion of smallpox. Guests include Jim's discarded wife and Kit Eclair, who poses as his present spouse to help him get inheritance. A policeman and burglar are also involved. Wild and weird complications ensue until all are worn out. Valet's malady turns out to be only chickenpox. Jim wins his former wife back. Kit accepts a faithful suitor.

Seven Days (Prod. Dis. Corp.)

PRESS NOTICE

ADAPTED from a former big Broadway stage success, "Seven Days," billed as the leading attraction at the ———the-atre on ———, is a hilarious farce comedy that has won unstinted praise from the newspaper critics. It deals with a supposed outbreak of smallpox among the members of a house party and the wild complications which ensue when the panic-stricken guests, as well as a burglar and policeman who are caught within the established quarantine, try to escape.

There's a double love affair in progress, and romance vies with humor in holding the spectator's attention. In the finale, when all are about worn out, it transpires that the valet who caused the trouble only has chickenpox. The cast is headed by Creighton Hale and Lillian Rich.

CATCH LINES
Both as a stage play and musical comedy "Seven Days" scored tremendous hits. In film form it beats the originals hollow as a mirth-producer. See it, be convinced.

Lillian Rich

California Straight Ahead
(Universal-Jewel—7238 Feet)
(Reviewed by George T. Pardy)

ANOTHER Reginald Denny feature which is bound to have a tremendously wide audience appeal, offering as it does sure-fire thrills, uproariously funny comedy, and traveling at express speed. It's one of those pictures which winds up with an auto race crammed with furious action and hair-breadth escapes from death, but besides that big punch scene, there are countless other warranted to create gales of laughter and chase the blues away from all spectators. Nothing more amusing in the farcical line has been screened than the episode where a storm hits a circus, the animals escape and proceed to turn a number of tourists camping in the neighborhood, out of their sleeping places, and the adventures of the hero and his negro valet on the motor trip to the coast are a constant source of merriment.

It is a vehicle especially well suited to the talents of the versatile Denny, who works with his customary dash and gaiety, Gertrude Olmsted figuring as an extremely captivating heroine.

THEME. Lively comedy-drama, with farcical situations, and love affairs, ending in thrilling auto race.

PRODUCTION HIGHLIGHTS. Denny's adventures in big motor van along the National Highway. Scene where storms breaks, circus animals get loose and chase tourists. The fast action, the farcical comedy punches. Big thrill in auto race at finish.

EXPLOITATION ANGLES. Tell patrons this is one of Reginald Denny's best laugh-producers and nerve-thrillers. Praise the comedy the limit. Feature star and play up the dangers of big auto race.

DRAWING POWER. Good for any type of theatre.

SUMMARY. A comedy drama guaranteed to please everybody. Is replete with exciting situations and sure-fire farce comedy. Has love interest and great auto race at finish.

THE CAST
Tom Hayden	Reginald Denny
Betty Browne	Gertrude Olmsted
Sambo	Tom Wilson
Creighton Deane	Charles Gerrard
Mrs. Browne	Lucille Ward
Jeffrey Browne	John Steppling
Mr. Hayden	Fred Esmelton

Authors, Harry Pollard and Byron Morgan. Directed by Harry Pollard. Photographed by Gilbert Warrenton.

SYNOPSIS. A stag party stops Tom Hayden from attending his wedding, and his family disown him. He and Sambo, negro valet, start for coast on huge, double-decked auto, making expenses by selling chicken dinners and piping music to tourists. In the desert Tom encounters the girl he should have married, Betty Browne, and her indignant parents. During storm, animals break loose from nearby circus. Tom rescues the Brownes, but elopes with Betty, is pinched at Los Angeles, released, drives car for Browne in big auto race, wins, and gets Betty.

California Straight Ahead
(Universal)

PRESS NOTICE

REGINALD DENNY in his latest laughing success— "California Straight Ahead," will be seen on the screen of the ———— theatre on ———.

This comedy-drama is hailed by the critics as one of the most entertaining of its kind, a picture in which thrills and farcical situations mingle freely, concluding with an auto race, a whizz for strenuous action and hair-breadth escapes from sudden death.

Denny figures as a wild young chap who misses a wedding date, nearly loses the girl, but pushes on to the coast with his negro valet in a double-deck auto; has all kinds of funny adventures enroute, but wins a big race and the lady at the finish.

CATCH LINES
He missed his wedding date, was in universal disgrace, but made good in the end, winning a big auto race, and his girl back, into the bargain.

Harry Pollard

Souls for Sables
(Tiffany Productions—7600 Feet)
(Reviewed by J. S. Dickerson)

HERE we have one of the most dependable themes of the screen—logically developed, the final result being a first class production, in which good settings, nice clothes and excellent acting by an all-star cast headed by Claire Windsor and Eugene O'Brien, contribute about equally in making a production that will past muster in any class of theatre.

Minor faults can be found with the picture but we doubt if these will in any way effect its box office or audience values, unless in the fact that there is much excess footage in the early reels, some of which will probably register as silly with the average fan.

As a whole the picture telling the story of a luxury loving wife who almost wrecks her life by her indiscretions before being taught a lesson, builds to climax of logical melodrama without overstepping the bounds of reason and should prove a money maker for both exhibitor and its producers.

THEME—Dramatic story of a young wife who longs for luxuries and almost wrecks her life in an attempt to achieve them by questionable methods.

PRODUCTION HIGHLIGHTS. The good settings. Acting of the whole cast. The melodramatic climax where the disillusioned husband shoots his wife and then commits suicide. The dependable story and its logical development.

EXPLOITATION ANGLES—The all star cast. Presents an excellent opportunity for a fashion show tie-up. The theme with its possibilities for attention provoking catch lines.

DRAWING POWER—Has a wide variety of appeal. Good enough for the first runs and still not an impossibility for the neighborhood and small town houses.

SUMMARY—Just a good picture built along safe and sane lines that carries a variety of appeal but which could be improved by some intelligent trimming in the early reels, thereby speeding up the action and bringing the meat of the story to earlier attention. Contains some minor faults but these will probably not harm the picture's box office value.

THE CAST
Alice Garlan	Claire Windsor
Fred Garlan	Eugene O'Brien
Helen Ralston	Claire Adams
Mrs. Kendall	Edith Yorke
Mr. Nelson	George Fawcett
Esther Hamilton	Eileen Percy
Harrison Morrill	Anders Randolf
Jim Hamilton	Robert Ober

Suggested by the novel by David Graham Phillips, Harlan and Co. Directed by James C. McKay under the supervision of A. P. Younger.

Souls for Sables (Tiffany)
PRESS NOTICE

DAVID Graham Phillips famous novel, Harlan and Co. has been adapted to the screen under the title of "Souls for Sables" and will be the feature attraction at the ——— theatre for a ——— days run beginning ———

"Souls for Sables" is a strongly dramatic story of a young wife who almost wrecked her life before realizing that a woman's natural love for luxury can be carried to an extreme.

As the butterfly wife Claire Windsor is an ideal choice and the male lead is in the hands of Eugene O'Brien, always a great favorite with motion picture fans. In addition to Miss Windsor and Mr. O'Brien, there are other well known and popular players in the cast.

Miss Windsor wears 26 different varieties of new and modish gowns that will be the envy of every feminine patron of the movies.

CATCH LINES
She almost lost her soul because of her love for sables. Love of luxury is a woman's natural inheritance but should she risk her soul for sables?

Claire Windsor

Siegfried
(Ufa Films—9000 Feet)
(Reviewed by George T. Pardy)

THIS German film, an adaptation from the Wagnerian "Nibelungen Ring," offering a combination narrative of "Siegfried," "Gotterdaemmerung" and "Lohengrin," ranks as decidedly high achievement from the strictly artistic standpoint. The Teutonic facility for embroidering a fantastic tale with wild, weird, trimmings has never been better demonstrated, and the photography is exquisite. Presented at the Century Theatre, New York, with a large symphony orchestra which did full justice to the score supplied by Dr. Hugo Riesenfeld, it was greeted with generous enthusiasm by an audience of opera-goers and music-lovers for whom it possessed undeniable appeal. Considered as a commercial asset, excepting in the big theatres of large cities where it can be given adequate presentation, the film's outlook is not particularly rosy, as the average theatre simply couldn't handle it, and the average fan wouldn't find it entertaining.

THEME. A version of the Nordic sagas, adapted from combination of Wagner's "Siegfried," "Gotterdaemmerung" and "Lohengrin" operas.

PRODUCTION HIGHLIGHTS. The beautiful photography, impressive settings, fantastic atmosphere, Siegfried slaying dragon, adventures in the Land of the Dwarfs, magical encounters, death of Siegfried, suicide of Brunhilde.

EXPLOITATION ANGLES. Can only be boosted as great attraction where big orchestra of large theatres is qualified to render Wagnerian score effectively

DRAWING POWER. O. K. for large theatres only.

SUMMARY. A beautifully mounted and photographed film adapted from Wagner operas of "Siegfried" Gotterdaemmerung" and "Lohengrin." Appeal limited to music-lovers and opera patrons.

THE CAST
Brunhilde	Hanna Ralph
Siegfried	Paul Ritcher
Queen Ute	Gertrude Arnold
Runes Leader	Margarete Schoen
Kriemhild	Frida Richard
King Gunther	Theodor Loos
Mime, the Smith	Iris Robert

Adapted from the Nibelungen Lied. Scenario by Thea von Harbon. Directed by Fritz Lang. Photographed by Gunther Rittem and Carl Hoffman.

SYNOPSIS. Siegfried, son of King Siegmund, forges a great sword and journeys to win the princess of Bergundy, Kriemhild. En-route he slays a monstrous dragon, bathes in its magical blood and becomes invulnerable to mortal blade, excepting a spot on his shoulder where a leaf falls. During his adventurous career, he captures the treasure of the King of the Dwarfs and overpowers twelve other kings. Finally he conquers Brunhilde, strongest woman on earth and wins Kriemhild, but is slain by a spear-thrust in the unprotected place on his shoulder. Brunhilde commits suicide.

Siegfried (Ufa Films)
PRESS NOTICE

PATRONS of opera and music-lovers are promised an unusual treat when "Siegfried," the great German production, will be shown on the screen of the ——— theatre on ——— The story is based on a combination of the three Wagnerian operas, "Siegfried," "Gotterdaemmerung," and "Lohengrin." It is an impressive fantastic tale of magic, in which the hero slays a monstrous dragon, and has numerous weird adventures.

A large symphony orchestra will play Wagner's immortal music, for which a special score has been compiled. The beautiful photography and massive, splendid settings are an artistic triumph.

CATCH LINES
A marvelous adaptation of three great Wagnerian operas, moulded into a tale of weird fantasy and magical adventure. If you are a music-lover, see "Siegfried" and hear the strains of the symphony orchestra accompanying it.

Fitz Lang

Regional News from Correspondents

Chicago

L EE MITCHELL is now manager of the New Julian Theatre at 918 Belmont Avenue. During the summer the house has been redecorated and handsome new furnishings installed, so that it presents a brand new appearance. To mark the improvement Jimmy Coston has added "new" to the name of the house which was formerly called the Julian.

Cecil Maberry of Producers Distributing Corporation spent the week in New York City, where he attended the national conference of divisional managers. He is expected to be back in Chicago on September 7th.

Del Goodman, who is traveling around the world in the interest of Fox Film Corporation, postcards en route from Port Said to Arden, Arabia, that although the weather is very hot, he is having a good time. Mr. Goodman is well known in Chicago film circles, through his former connections with local exchanges. Manager C. C. Wallace of United Artists has appointed Fred R. Martin, former branch manager of Vitagraph in Mil-

waukee, as supervisor of sales for the Indiana territory. Mr. Martin will work out of Chicago. Cooney Brothers of Chicago and Bert Williams of Detroit, have entered into an agreement whereby the Capitol stage creations, produced by Francis A. Mangan, will go into the New Grand Riviera Theatre, Mr. William's Detroit house. It is said this is the first time that presentations will travel intact from city to city.

George Miller of the Park Theatre, one of the Simansky & Miller chain, has returned from an enjoyable vacation. Mr. Miller, accompanied by his wife, motored to his old home town, Buffalo, and also visited other points of interest in the east.

A recent visit to the big Diversey Parkway plant of the Rothacker Film Manufacturing Company, revealed the fact that an epidemic has been prevalent

there recently, but W. R. Rothacker is not taking any steps to suppress it; in fact he is for it. Pearl McClarey and Wade Parmalee had just returned from their vacation during which they were married; Charles Dixon shipping clerk was wed during the week, and George J. Kilgore of the industrial department surprised his fellow workers with the announcement that he had been married for several months.

Billie Troug, district manager for Universal, with headquarters in Kansas City, and Charle Sears, well known theatre man of that city, were Chicago visitors last week and made their headquarters at Universal's Chicago exchange.

Louis Laemmle has returned from a ten weeks' vacation abroad, having been one of the party that accompanied Carl Laemmle on his trip to Germany. Mr. Laemmle reports having had an enjoyable visit to the Black

Forest and leading German cities, and that the trip has greatly benefitted his health.

George Hopkinson, who has taken up golf in earnest since retiring from the management of the Hamlin Theatre, 3826 W. Madison Street, which he recently sold to H. Lutz, at present is enjoying a leisurely motor trip through the east, having left about two weeks ago.

More than one hundred exhibitors and exchange men gathered at the testimonial dinner tendered Dave Dubin, in honor of his appointment to the managership of Educational Pictures Chicago exchange. Al Sobler was in the chair as toastmaster and the occasion was most enjoyable. During the course of the evening Mr. Dubin was presented with a handsome desk set.

Eddie Grossman has returned from a trip to New York. Mr. Grossman recently became associated with Architect Levine, in building and financing motion picture theatres and reports that prospects in New York territory are excellent for considerable new building.

Milwaukee

E. C. ACCOLA, manager of the Bonham Theatre at Prairie du Sac, Wis., strolled into the various film exchanges here during the past week, and spread optimistic sentiments among the boys.

J. G. Frackman, Milwaukee manager for Progress Pictures Co., has taken a jaunt down to Chicago, where he is conferring with Frank Zambreno, president of the distributing organization, regarding the exploitation of Progress products in the Wisconsin territory during the coming months.

Goetz Brothers, operators of a chain of picture houses in Kenosha, Janesville, Beloit, Menasha and other Wisconsin cities, have added the Lincoln Theatre at Kenosha as their third house in that thriving city. The house has a capacity of approximately 600, and compares favorably with the Vogue and Butterfly Theatres, the other two Goetz houses in Kenosha.

Louis Holz, the active little manager of the Lorraine Theatre, Milwaukee, whose novel ideas and promotion stunts have made the house a paying proposition for its owner, Mrs. W. Smith, has negotiated the sale of the theatre to Rex and Randolph of New York, who will henceforth operate it. In recognition of his excellent work in the past, Louis will be retained as manager for the new owners, who will remodel the house into a 1,000 seat theatre. They will probably take over another local house in the near future.

Charlie Koehler, booker at the Milwaukee offices of Progress Pictures Co., has returned to his duties after a ten day seige at Deaconess Hospital, where he underwent treatment for gall stones. While he was a mighty sick boy for several weeks, he is now flashing his usual cheery smile on all visitors to the office and is rapidly catching up on the work which accumulated during his period of incapacity.

Sam Thirion, operator of the Bijou Theatre at Green Bay, Wis., spent a few days of the past week in Milwaukee arranging for tab shows to be booked into his house during the coming season. Business at the Bijou has been bounteous all summer and prospects for the winter are excellent, but Sam is a wise showman and believes his patrons would relish a little variety in their entertainment. Second run pictures will be run in connection with the one act tabs.

"Dad" Wolcott browsed about the Milwaukee film exchanges during the past week, lining things up for his Majestic Theater at Racine, Wis., where he says, business is going to be brisk this fall.

Establishing a precedent in local first run theatres, "The Lost World" was held over for a second week at Saxe's Merrill Theater. It is probable, according to Harry Jones, manager of the Merrill, that several of the other big pictures booked for the near future will be given two week runs, now that the experiment would seem to have bee nsuccessful. The Merrill, which has been

something of a step-child in the Saxe organization since its purchase last Spring, is now being frankly favored by the booking department, and in being given the choice of excellent pictures made available by Saxe's buying power.

All downtown Milwaukee picture houses are sporting dressed up fronts and lobby displays in honor of State Fair Week, which opened at the grounds just outside the city on Monday. Thousands of up-state visitors to the fair are dropping into the downtown picture houses for a real treat.

The Davidson Theatre, legitimate, which has been dark for several weeks, has re-opened for its annual season, thus entering into indirect competition with the picture houses once again.

E. Hoefer, manager of the Rex Theater at Sheboygan, has returned to his fair city to boost business again after a visit to the Milwaukee exchanges last week. Hoefer believes in availing himself of exploitation aids of distributors and has been very successful in that rtspect.

Interest in Milwaukee film circles during the past week was centered on the successful opening of the Alhambra Theatre under Universal management. During the two weeks the house was dark, the entire place was renovated and redecorated with most pleasing results, the key to the attractive interior being the elaborate front, featuring a large sign. The opening was staged in conjunction with *The Wisconsin News,* and took the form of a benefit party for that newspaper's Christmas Basket fund. The ad-

mission for the evening was boosted from 50 cents to one dollar, at which price a packed house was drawn. Howard Waugh, formerly manager of Paramount houses at Atlanta and Memphis, is in charge as resident manager for Universal theaters division. Heinz Roemheld, formerly concert master at Saxe's Wisconsin Theater, has returned to the city to become director of presentations at the Alhambra as well as conductor of the 25 piece concert orchestra. Other house executives are Ann McMurdy, publicity director; Robert Talbot, assistant manager, and Billy T. Hendricks, floor manager.

Lorraine Eason, the Hollywood girl in the Paramount Picture School. There were plenty of entrants in Hollywood, but Lorraine won out. Reason? See photo above.

New England

WILLIAM J. PRESTON, manager of the Fellsway Theatre in Medford, has resigned to take charge of the Victory Theatre in Holyoke, Mass. where pictures and vaudeville are given. He has been manager of the Medford house for eight months. The Fellsway Theatre was taken over when Mr. Preston became its manager by the Green & Ellenberg chain.

William J. Burke, who was formerly with Gordon's Olympia Circuit and more recently with the E. M. Loew circuit at Boston, Fitchburg and at the Capitol Theatre, Lynn, has resigned to become manager of the Majestic Theatre in Medford. He is succeeded as manager of the Lynn Capitol Theatre by Carl Hutchinson.

John P. Freeman, manager of the Strand, Malden, accompanied by Edward A. Aston, treasurer of the theatre, have been enjoying a motor trip through the Catskills and Adirondacks and Northern New York State.

Michael F. O'Brien of the Green Ellenberg chain has returned from a motor trip through New York, Pennsylvania and Washington to the Boston offices of the company.

Elizabeth Marbury, producer and designer, has purchased an estate of 68 acres at Mt. Vernon, near Belgrade Lakes, Maine where she is having plans drawn for a summer home.

A new motion picture house, to be known as the Cobb Theatre, is being erected at the junction of Cobb and Castle streets, Boston. A number of old wooden buildings on the site are now being torn down and construction work will start as soon as the site is cleared. A. J. Carpenter Jr. of Jamaica Plain district, Boston, has the plans and contracts in hand for the playhouse, which will be 81 by 195 feet and will have one balcony.

Winfield H. Bradley has bought the Standard Film Service at 23 Piedmont street, Boston.

W. Willson of the Wollaston Palace Theatre of Quincy, Mass., expects to start foundation work

next week for a new theatre at Hancock and Beale streets, Quincy which will be added to his present holdings. The theatre will be 60 feet wide and 200 feet deep. Tuck & Co. of Roxbury, Mass. have drawn the plans.

D. A. Pietroroia of Bristol, Conn. has organized four theatre companies and is getting information about film bookings. The theatres are the Bristol Theatre with capital of $50,000, Colonial Theatre with capital of $20,000, Circle Theatre with capital of $50,000, Princess Theatre with capital of $50,000 and Palace Theatre with capital of $50,000. The Circle Theatre will be located in Manchester, Conn., while the other four will be in Bristol.

The town of Winchester, Mass., has received an offer for the former Chapin school house for use as a motion picture theatre after extensive remodelling, provided the town will grant a license for a motion picture which it has heretofore refused to grant. The names of the persons making the offer are withheld. Winchester is the only large town in the state

without a moving picture theatre. Talk of remodelling the Auditorium theatre at Malden, Mass., into a moving picture house has been set at rest with the sale of the theatre and lease to James Hayden of the Brockton (Mass.) City theatre, who will continue the established policy of stock in the Auditorium, opening Sept. 14.

Following the incorporation of the Rhode Island Auditorium, Inc., with capital of $375,000 at Providence, R. I., by Edward P. Jastram, Walter A. Edwards and Ogden R. Lindsley, well known in theatrical enterprises, comes the announcement that the proposed Auditorium will be a big indoor amusement park and artificial ice skating rink. It is to seat 8600 people and will occupy an entire city block between North Main, Second and Third streets and Highland avenue and will be so constructed that it can be used for motion pictures during part of the year. It is expected to rush the building completion so it may be occupied about the middle of February.

Detroit

HARLAN STARR of the local Educational office is in Upper Michigan calling on exhibitors and outlining the coming year's product.

Charles G. Branham, former manager of the Majestic theatre here when that theater showed pictures, is now manager of the Howard theater in Atlanta, Ga., friends here learned this week. Until recently he was director of theaters for Famous Players theaters of Canada.

John H. Kunsky, Detroit theatre magnate, was among the prominent men on the committee which arranged the celebration honoring Ty Cobb's twentieth anniversary with

the Detroit Tigers, Saturday night, Aug. 29.

Ruhl Williams of the local Paramount forces married last week. His sister, Mrs. Harry W. Ross, and her husband, division manager in Chicago for Famous Players, came here to attend the ceremony.

Fred North, of First National, was in New York last week attending the sales convention of First National supervisors and branch managers.

Roy Tillson has been appointed general manager of the Fuller theater, Kalamazoo, following the departure of Lew Barnes for Florida. Barnes is motoring down. He will engage in real estate in the south.

Another new neighborhood the-

atre in Detroit is about to open. It is the Picadilly. Henry S. Koppin, owner of several other houses, is the owner.

The Fox Film Co. is in its new office at 66 Sibley street now, just back of the Colonial theatre. All new equipment has been installed.

The old Liberty theatre has closed. All its equipment is for sale. The Liberty was one of the first houses downtown. When the theatre section moved uptown, business fell.

The Capitol's new $60,000 Wurlitzer organ is being installed, replacing a smaller organ previously used. Two other organs of the same size have been purchased by

John H. Kunsky of the Kunsky theatre, and the other for the new Kunsky-Balaban and Katz theatre, The Michigan, both under construction.

The Laemmle-Universal Motorized studio unit is in Detroit taking pictures of interesting places in the city. The unit already has been in Niles, St. Joseph, Benton Harbor, Kalamazoo, Grand Rapids, Jackson and Ann Arbor.

E. O. Bahti, who operates the Star theatre at South Range, Mich., recently left via boat for Buffalo, N. Y. Mr. Bahti is accompanied by his wife and son and they will motor back home.

Des Moines

THE theatre at Nora Springs which has been changing hands rapidly of late has again gone into new management. Mr. Nonnunmaken who ran the Nora Springs house, which he called the Palace, sold to Mr. Kennedy.

"The Metro Goldwyn Trackless Train" is travelling through Iowa. This Pullman visited Des Moines last week.

Bill Ronning, booker of the F. B. O. exchange, has been trans-

ferred to the Sioux Falls office. He has been at the DesMoines office for a little over two months. D. McCullough who has been engaged to take his place came from Minneapolis where he was booker for the Universal office.

W. W. Watts, owner of the Casino Theatre at Sac City, Iowa has leased this theatre and also the Lyric Theatre including the dance hall to Mr. Wherry. The theatres have been leased for a year. Mr. Watts who has been

exhibiting in Sac City for some time has not yet bought another house.

Employees of the Pathe office are alternating on half day holidays to attend the State Fair now in DesMoines.

Elmer Tilton, manager of the First National office, returned September 1, from New York where he attended the national convention of First National exchange managers.

C. H. Nollen of Palmer, Eller Metzger of Greston, Wayne Dut-

ton of the Plaza at Manchester, William Johnson of the Rialto at Fort Dodge, C. H. Cookingham of the Opera House at Ayreshire were visitors in Film Row. E. P. Smith of Chariton dropped in at the Premier office and signed for a lot of pictures.

Ruby Dyer, stenographer of the First National office, visited Chicago on her vacation.

Thelma Washburn whose daughter is now getting along in months is back at the Pathe office making the typewriter click.

Seattle

JOHN G. VON HERBERG, general manager of the Jensen-Von Herberg circuit, left his office in this city last week for New York, Chicago and other Eastern centers, on a business trip that was expected to take a total of seven weeks duration. Mr. Von Herberg planned to visit the First National and Famous Players offices in New York City, and also was scheduled to visit a number of the large motion picture houses throughout the country on an informal tour of inspection.

Announcement was received here this week to the effect that Glenn Goff, former concert organist at the Pantages Theatre in this city, had just been selected as head organist at the California Theatre in San Francisco.

Lou Rosenberg, representative of Al Rosenberg's De Luxe Feature Film Exchange in the Oregon territory, arrived in Seattle last week with Mrs. Rosenberg on a brief business trip.

B. A. Kelsey, owner and manager of the Ruby Theatre in Chelan was included among the out-of-town exhibitors who visited Film Row during the last seven days. Mr. Kelsey bought and booked a number of fall products, for his house during his stay in this city.

Fred G. Sliter, manager of the First National exchange, left the local office last week for New York City, where he was to attend the meeting of branch managers being held there the latter part of August. The destinies of the local exchange were being controlled by J. W. Parry, booker, and A. C. Raleigh, advertising and exploitation manager during Mr. Sliter's absence. He was expected back in the city early in September.

A distinctly novel type of preview was staged in this city last week by Manager Al Finkelstein of the Strand Theatre. Instead of the ordinary press showing at night, Mr. Finkelstein extended invitations to representatives of the newspapers to attend Seattle's first "luncheon preview." This was held in the private projection room of the Greater Theatres Company.

Word was received by the film exchanges this week to the effect that the Fairfax Picture Club at Fairfax, Wash., was to reopen the latter part of August under the management of R. D. Moore. The Club is a cooperative institution owned and operated for and by the employees and owners of the industries of that territory.

Vic Gauntlett, rapid fire advertising and publicity manager of

John Hamrick's circuit of Blue Mouse Theatres, this week packed his little suitcase and departed for Tacoma Blue Mouse, where he was to occupy the manager's official chair for the coming week. Mr. Gauntlett's removal to Tacoma was only temporary, being effective only while Ned Edris, manager of the Tacoma house, was on his annual vacation.

Announcement was made last week by W. H. Drummond, manager of the Producers' Distributing Corporation exchange, of the appointment of Matt Apperton to a sales representative capacity with the P. D. C. organization. Mr. Apperton was formerly associated with Manager L. O. Lukan's Universal Exchange in this territory, and is expected to cover the same districts for the Producers' office.

Tom Olsen, well-known in this city for his various and sundry motion picture connections within the last two years, left last week for New York City to enter the Famous Players-Lasky School for the making of motion picture theatre managers.

Reports received in this city last week indicated that the Brewster Theatre at Brewster, Wash., had been taken over by C. D. Gillespie,

who will continue the operation of the house under its present policy. The former owner and manager of the theatre was Harry Dunning, whose departure from that venture was rather in the nature of a surprise.

Morris Siegel, sales representative in the Eastern Washington territory for Manager George P. Endert's local Famous Players-Lasky exchange, returned to Seattle last week, and present plans are that he will remain in this territory for the next number of weeks, at least. W. E. Nelson, who has been handling the books for Manager Endert, was expected to leave for the Spokane headquarters this week, to succeed Mr. Siegel for the first part of the coming season. Mr. Siegel is declared to be one of the foremost salesmen connected with the Famous Players organization in any city on the Pacific Coast.

A. H. Huot, manager of the Film Booking Offices exchange in this city has been absent from his office for the last week on a sales trip around the territory. He was expected back the latter part of August, according to E. A. Lamb, who has been in charge since his departure.

Central Penn

PRESENCE of prominent theatre owners, officials of theatre chains, exchange men and men conspicuous in public life of Pennsylvania, gave statewide importance to the formal opening on the night of August 27, of the beautiful $500,000 New Strand motion picture theatre, just erected in York, Pa., as the newest link in the big chain of theatres operated by the Nathen Appell interests in

A. H. McLaughlin, Branch Manager, Chicago Exchange for Renown Pictures, Inc.

that city, Reading and Lancaster. A feature of the construction of the house is that all the 1,800 seats are located on a single floor. The artistic murals and other decorations are original work of Willie Pogany, the New York artist, and the building was designed by E. C. Horn & Sons.

The theatre was dedicated with exercises including addresses by former Lieutenant Governor Edward E. Beidleman, of Harrisburg; Mayor E. S. Hugentugler, of York; Samuel K. McCall, city solicitor, of York; Martin J. O'Toole, of New York and Scranton, president of the Motion Picture Theatre Owners of America, and by the artist, Mr. Pogany.

A box party, as the guests of the management, included Nathan Appell, head of the Appell theatre enterprises; his son, Louis J. Appell, general manager; Sydney Wilmer, of New York, president, and Joseph Egan, of New York, general manager of the Wilmer & Vincent chain of theatres; C. Floyd Hopkins.

One of the most attractive features of the daily programs of the New Strand theatre, in "Shenandoah, which passed into the new management of the Burman Amusement Company, as lessee, on August 17, is the fine new orchestra, recruited from among the ranks of some of the best musical organizations of the country.

Writing from Paris to the Har-

risburg Chamber of Commerce, to assure the Chamber that he will be home from his European trip in time to join the members of that body in their annual "cruise," which starts September 8. Peter Magaro, pioneer motion picture exhibitor of the Pennsylvania capitol city, announced he would sail from France the latter part of August.

Pictures and vaudeville on the last three days of each week, have been resumed at the Mishler theatre, Altoona, which reopened under this policy on Thursday, August 27. This is a Wilmer & Vincent house.

The Easton Free Press contained the following announcement, of interest to motion picture exhibitors, in its issue of August 26: "All reviews of productions appearing on stage and screen in local playhouses will hereafter be written for the Free Press by members of the staff assigned to the work. Free Press readers and theatre managers alike will undoubtedly appreciate this innovation."

The week of August 24 was designated as "Elks' Convention Week," at the Colonial picture theatre, Bethlehem, in honor of the big state convention of the Elks in that city.

The management of the Lehigh Orpheum theatre, in Bethlehem, announces that the new Marr & Colton organ recently installed

there has been given a final test and, having proved entirely satisfactory, has been finally accepted. Hereafter the Orpheum theatre, in York, which was reopened on August 24 following extensive improvements which included new scenery, draperies and curtains, will cease to be a motion picture house.

PHILADELPHIA

THE outing of the Philadelphia Film Board of Trade was held on August 23rd at Pine Rock Country Club, Ambler, Pa. Field sports, dancing, base ball and contests of various kinds were among the features and all present report having spent a most enjoyable day.

Sam Blatt, who was manager of the Owl theatre, 23rd & South sts., Philadelphia, for a number of years is no longer connected with the motion picture industry but is now affiliated with H. Elmer & Co., real estate.

W. J. Heenan, Philadelphia manager of First National, attended the annual conference of First National district and branch managers from all parts of the country, held at the Roosevelt, New York, on August 25th, 26th, and 27th.

As a result of protests by local exhibitors the American Society of Composers, Authors and Publishers has discontinued cancellation of existing contracts, pending a conference.

Kansas City

ROY CHURCHILL, branch manager of the Kansas City F. B. O. exchange is busy receiving congratulations on the birth of a son, born August 20th. He has been named Roy Edmund Churchill, Jr., and reports from Kansas City indicate that the mother and child are doing nicely.

As a result of last minute change in plans, Kansas City's Greater Movie Season ball has been transferred from a segregated down town street to Convention Hall, which will seat 15,000 persons. Inability to obtain the proper lighting effects in a short length of time necessitated the change. A first prize of a gold engraved pass to all Kansas City theatres for one year will be awarded to the person best imitating a movie star. Second prize will be a set of personally autographed photographs of movie stars, while there will be several other awards. A 30-piece orchestra, supplied gratis by the Kansas City musicians' union will furnish the music for the event, the date of which was changed from Friday to Saturday, August 29. There will be no admission charge for contestants or spectators.

Never has a theatre in St. Joseph, Mo., had a more auspicious opening than the new Rivoli last week. The house, owned by the Sun Amusement and Realty Company and managed by Ben Greenberg, was constructed at a cost of about $75,000 and is the most modern theatre in that city. The admission price will be adults 25 cents, children 10 cents.

Just as the Orpheum theatre, Kansas City opened up for what is expected to be a big winter season, the fates decreed that Lawrence Lehman, manager, should be confined to his bed on account of illness. But he has assured friends that he will be on the job in three days, which is taken as being a rather short order.

So many droll faces has Samuel Carver, manager of the Liberty theatre, seen in the last week that he is on the verge of "D. T. S," according to his own admission. The Century Comedy company arranged with Mr. Carver to search Kansas City for comedy types to enter the slapstick field—and they were not hard to find.

Not only has Adolph Eisner, manager of the Circle theatre, Kansas City, been able to increase patronage each week for the last six weeks, but also has found time to make harried trips to St. Louis, Wichita and St. Joseph.

The thermometer and Kansas City's movie row ran a close race for the "count" last week. The fact that the First National branch has four salesmen—Curran, Lowery, Craddock and Cass —among the first six in the rankings of 133 First National exchanges is causing no little "puffing up" at the local exchange.

The Short Film Syndicate will have an exchange in Kansas City within the next sixty days, it was announced.

Harry Hollander, former Universal branch manager, has left for Buffalo, where he is to manage the Warner Bros. exchange.

W. C. Haynes, former Goldwyn and Selznick representative in Kansas City, has returned to join the local Universal sales force.

Ben Blotcky, Paramount manager, has returned from a vacation in Iowa.

O. H. Lambert, former assistant branch manager of Metro-Goldwyn, St. Louis, has been transferred to a similar position with the same company in Kansas City.

C. D. Hill, P. D. C. district manager, was busily engaged at the Kansas City branch last week as was R. L. McLean, district representative for P. D. C.

C. A. Schwann, former Vitagraph representative in St. Louis, has joined the Kansas City P. D. C. sales force.

M. A. Levy, Fox branch manager, is touring the Kansas territory for new business this week.

The Hall theatre, Columbia, Mo., is undergoing an extensive alteration program. Ornamental glass, reshaping and repainting of the ceiling, a new orchestra pit and a "re-vamped" front are the principal changes to be made.

The Isis theatre, one of Kansas City's largest suburban houses, managed by Jack Roth, celebrated its seventh anniversary last week.

Among the out-of-town exhibitors in the Kansas City market last week were: John Creamer, New Strand, Chillicothe, Mo.; H. Hedges and C. DeWolfe, Apex, Jamesport, Mo.; B. Wagner, Beldorf, Independence, Kas.; J. H. Thomas, Novelty, Winfield, Kas.; Sam Blair, Majestic, Belleville, Kas.; William Gabriel and H. Austin, Garden City, Kas.; Edward Frazier, Strand, Pittsburgh, Kas.; Charles Sears, Sears Circuit, Nevada, Mo.

J. H. Kelly, former manager of the Isis, Arkansas City, Kas., and the Rainbow, Kansas City has decided to try the "other side," having joined the Metro-Goldwyn sales force.

Two Motiograph Deluxe machines have been installed in D. Filizola's Empress theatre, Fort Scott, Kas. Peerless low intensity reflector arc equipment has been installed in the Royal theatre, Kansas City, owned by Paramount and managed by Bruce Fowler. Two Simplex projectors have been purchased by Charles L. Fisk of the Opera House, Butler, Mo., while Simplex equipment has been purchased by Jay Means, manager of the Murray and Prospect theatres and vice-president of the M. P. T. O. Kansas-Missouri.

Minneapolis

FINKELSTEIN & RUBIN have asked several occupants of offices and stores in the Loeb Arcade where their headquarters are located to take other space in the building. It is said that the F. & R. offices will take over every office on the fourth floor of the structure.

R. G. McCulloch, formerly of the Universal organization in Minneapolis has gone to Des Moines to become assistant to Fred Young, manager for Film Booking Offices there. He had been with Universal about five years.

Eph Rosen of F. B. O., Minneapolis, took a flying trip to Eau Claire during the week.

The Palace theatre, Minneapolis, opened September 5 with musical comedy and motion pictures with the McCall Bride company in charge.

Lee Darling, owner of ten theatres in North Dakota, with headquarters at Kenmare, spent a few days last week picking a part of his program.

Ray Stewart, of the Fox sales staff in the Northwest territory, is reported to be very ill. He was former Minneapolis manager of F. B. O.

Ned Marin, sales director for Universal, spent three days last week in the Minneapolis office looking over the field and conferring with Phil Dumas, branch manager.

Mark Ross, Twin City salesman for Universal, is back on the job after a two weeks' vacation, which he spent touring the Northern part of Minnesota and southern Manitoba.

Universal has a new exploitation manager in this district. He is William Prass, formerly of the publicity and house staff of the Metropolitan theatre, Minneapolis.

Because of its numerous small cities and towns, many of which are at a considerable distance from Minneapolis, Minnesota has been chosen by Universal for its second demonstration of the new "theatre party" plan of showing its product.

Dave Bader, personal representative of Carl Laemmle, is in Minneapolis arranging for the first of the Minnesota parties which will be held at Alexandria, Minn., Sept. 10.

The Tower theatre in St. Paul reopened Saturday night, Aug. 29, after being closed for a week for redecoration and renovation. In connection with the renewed theatre there was opened at the same time in adjoining space two beautiful dancing floors capable of handling 2,000 dancers.

Hugh Andress, and his staff in charge of the theatre worked under full pressure all week to get the place in shape for the grand occasion.

A new Twin City musical director is in charge of the two orchestras which work the theatre and the dance hall simultaneously. He is called "Maurice" and is well known in Detroit and Eastern cities, having made several orchestra records.

Resignation of "Billy" Koenig as production manager for Universal to take a similar position with Warner Brothers gives Minneapolis friends of his quite a kick for "Billy" was long known and liked here as manager of the Gayety, a burlesque theatre.

J. B. Munjar of the Robert-Mortno organ company, has announced that a sub-branch will be opened in Minneapolis.

Orrin F. Woody, brother of the head of Associated Exhibitors, made a special sales trip to Minneapolis last week.

Kenneth Cave is the new manager of McCarthy Theatre enterprises' Grand theatre at Enderlin, N. D.

Edward Furni, former Orpheum manager at Duluth, is the new manager of the Palace-Orpheum. Clarence S. Williams, former manager there, has gone to the Orpheum circuit's North Shore theatre in Chicago, the Riviera.

After being delayed by shortage of steel, work continues on the new F. & R. theatre in Sioux Falls, S. D., with Jan. 1 the probable opening date.

Looks like there was about to be a big ruckus in the Twin Cities over the musicians' contracts. Twenty dollars a week is said to be the raise demanded by the boys with the educated fingers.

Ramon Novarro, whose first starring vehicle, "The Midshipman" will be released by Metro-Goldwyn-Mayer early this fall.

Canada

PETE EGAN is back at his old desk at the Strand theatre, Calgary, Alberta. It was only a few weeks ago that he was transferred by Famous Players Canadian Corp. to Winnipeg, Manitoba, where the company operates the Capitol and Metropolitan theatres, but a reconsideration of the shift resulted in Mr. Egan returning to his old love, the Calgary Strand where he has made a name for himself as a capable manager.

Three prominent exhibitors of Western Canada figured in a bad automobile accident three miles out from Portage la Prairie, Manitoba. One of them, Henry Morton, owner of a chain of five theatres in Winnipeg, was seriously injured and is still feeling the effects of the smash although he has been able to return to his home. Two others in the car, J. Weiner of Winnipeg, owner of the

Regent and Colonial theatres there, and W. Narvey, manager of a theatre at Portage la Prairie, were not badly hurt but had miraculous escapes.

When the Savoy theatre, Hamilton, Ontario, re-opened August 17 after being closed for several months, H. E. Wilton, manager of the Strand theatre at Hamilton, was placed in charge of the house by Famous Players Canadian Corp. Announcement is now made that B. J. McKilliem has been appointed manager of the Hamilton Strand in succession to Mr. Wilton there. Mr. Wilton will now devote his entire attention to the Savoy.

Mr. McKilliem was Photoplay and Dramatic Editor of the Hamilton Herald until a few months ago when he became manager of the new Tivoli theatre, Hamilton.

Jack Welch of Toronto, former assistant manager of the Toronto branch of Regal Films, Limited, has gone to Vancouver, B. C., where he has become manager of the office of Canadian Educational Films, Limited.

Marjorie Stevens, popularly known for several years as the director of the ladies orchestra of the Palace theatre, Toronto, was recently married but she is continuing as conductor of the orchestra. The Palace staff, headed by Manager Charlie Querrie, gave Miss Stevens a kitchen shower and there were many personal gifts as well.

Five of the leading theatres of Winnipeg, Manitoba, were represented in the program which was presented at the Winnipeg Sports Carnival in a summer park on August 22 in aid of the Winnipeg

Amateur Lacrosse Association. Representatives of the Metropolitan, Dominion, Winnipeg, Playhouse and Orpheum theatres provided musical and other numbers as a community stunt.

The Papineau theatre, Montreal, has a crack baseball team, made up of members of the staff of the theatre. This team frequently breaks into print with the report of a snappy victory on the baseball diamond. Recently at Park Lafontaine, the Papineau team twice defeated the Joubert nine by 5 to 3 and 3 to 0.

The offices of the Calgary branch of First National Pictures have been moved from 405 Eighth Ave., West, to 300 Traders Building. Branch Manager E. H. Teel moved his force into the new quarters last week.

Buffalo

VINCENT R. McFAUL, managing director of Shea's Hippodrome, Buffalo, this week is celebrating the eleventh anniversary of the big picture palace.

George Roberts, district manager for Fox, is touring about western New York and the other evening stopped off in Niagara Falls to visit with A. C. Hayman, of the Strand and Cataract theatres.

J. Berkowitz, manager of the Buffalo First Graphic office, is all set for "First Graphic Month," to celebrate the third anniversary of the company in Buffalo.

Johnny Bykowski, former booker at the Buffalo Fox office, is now holding down the same job with Freedom Pictures corporation of which Richard G. Fox is manager. Lee Langdon has re-

signed from the Freedom sales staff to join Warner Brothers in Albany. Mr. Fox has just returned from New York where he booked several new features. Miss Ann Cahalan, formerly with Reynown, is now bookkeeper at Freedom.

The Cataract theatre, Niagara Falls, N. Y., operated by Charley Hayman, re-opened for the season Sunday, August 30.

Herman Lorence of the Bellevue, Niagara Falls, has signed up for all the First National and Metro-Goldwyn product for the coming season, first run in the Cataract City.

Workmen are installing signs on both the north and south sides of the marquee of the New Family theatre supplanting the signs that were installed when

the theatre was reconstructed. The new signs are much larger and of the latest design. Two rows of colored border lights inclose three lines where electrically lighted letters advertising the pictures may be placed.

Frank Cruikshank of Boston has been appointed manager of the Teck theatre, Buffalo, succeeding Edgar Healey. The Teck opens for the fall season on Labor Day. Eddie McBride, former Fox salesman, will again be in the box office.

J. C. Hilman, manager of the Peoples Theatre, Binghamton, N. Y., is the grandfather of a bouncing baby girl. That's the reason Phil Gentile of First Graphic had his pockets filled with cigars when he got in from the Southern Tier.

Plans have been made and bids called for on a new motion picture theatre which the Schine Theatrical corporation will erect in Fairport, N. Y. and which will be named the Capitol. The house will occupy the site of the Bucher property in West avenue, which was purchased some time ago by the Schine interests. Charles E. Clark will be the manager. Mr. Clark has been associated with the Schine company for several years.

The Jefferson theatre in Auburn has been re-decorated and refurnished and has opened for the fall season.

An old time song fest was staged in the Rialto theatre, Erie, Pa., the other night when Manager Partos arranged for slides of a number of Dixie and popular melodies.

St. Louis

CHARLES J. CELLA and Frank R. Tate, who less than three years ago purchased the corner of Sixth and St. Charles streets on which stands the Columbia Theatre and the adjoining Strand theatre, both of which they operated, for $458,000 have leased the property for a long term at a rental based on a valuation of $2,750,000.

The St. Louis police have arrested one man in connection with the robbery of Grand Opera House on the morning of August 24 and are looking for two well known police characters who are suspected of being the two men who went into the theatre office and stuck-up the treasurer, manager and stenographer escaping with the

Saturday and Sunday receipts.

According to the police the man under arrest has been positively identified as the driver of the automobile used by the stick-up men to make their getaway. The automobile license on the robber car had been issued to the arrested man but for a different make of automobile.

It is claimed that the theatre robbery plot was hatched in the City Jail to provide funds for the defense for a sextette of youths held in connection with the murder of a policeman and citizen on July 3 last. The pair were murdered when they frustrated a payroll hold-up at the H. S. Collins Printing Company, 1531 Washington avenue.

Charles Werner, manager of the

local Metro-Goldwyn-Mayer office, who recently underwent an operation at Mayo Brothers Sanitorium, Rochester, Minn., is said to be doing excellently. This will be pleasing news to his many friends throughout the St. Louis territory and the movie world at large.

Houses reported closed included Odin, Ill.; Delta, Mo., and Bethel, Mo.

The Southern Illinois coal mines are reviving and hundreds of additional miners are going to work every week in the territory below Springfield to the Ohio River. The threatened anthracite coal strike has proved a boon to the Southern Illinois coal fields. The increased activity will be welcomed by the owners of the motion picture houses throughout that territory,

as the miners, idle for months, have been without cash needed to patronize the shows.

C. R. Johnson is remodeling the Gem Theatre, Grafton, Ill., which he took over recently.

Tom McKean, manager for the local F. B. O. office spent several days out in the territory. He reports that conditions are much improved in the district around Carbondale and that general territory.

Many of the St. Louis neighborhood houses that have been closed for the Summer months will be reopened during September. It is anticipated that the lay-off has whet up the motion picture appetite of their patrons and that business will be good during the early Fall and Winter months.

Salt Lake City

GEORGE E. CARPENTER, managing director of the Louis Marcus Enterprises, announces that their new Articles of Incorporation have been filed for $150,000. The incorporators are Louis Marcus, George E. Carpenter, James Ingelbretsen and Carl A. Porter. Emmett F. Zorg from Louisville, Kentucky, will arrive here this week to manage the new Paramount Theatre in Ogden.

The Paramount Empress Theatre under the management of Geo. E. Carpenter, will inaugurate a new change of policy next week, showing big features only. They will have acts similar to those which play the big theatres on the Pacific Coast. This change will be accompanied by a raise in prices.

Fred and Carsten Dahnkin, owners of the American Theatre, have just arrived here from California according to manager Weir Cassady.

Clyde H. Messenger who has charge of the Educational exchange here is still in Southern Utah.

A. G. Pickett, Famous Players-Lasky local manager, is spending this week in the Idaho territory.

George L. Cloward, Metro-Goldwyn manager here, leaves this week to place the Metro-Goldwyn productions before the exhibitors of Montana.

W. B. Seib, manager for Pathe in this city, and Ed. C. Mix, manager out of the Associated exhibitors exchange, are both in Idaho for about ten days.

Bennett Brandon, Special Serial Representative from New York,

is en route to Butte, Montana, from here. Brandon just completed a swing through the entire Intermountain Territory.

Harry Lustig, Western District Manager of Warner Brothers is in Provo on a short trip with R. S. Stackhouse, manager of this exchange.

George E. Jensen, who covers the Montana territory out of the Warner Brothers exchange here, has returned to that section. Harry Gibson and L. W. Hyde, also out of this exchange, are now covering their respective territories in Idaho and Southern Utah.

E. M. Gibson, Assistant Manager for F. B. O. in this city has just returned from his vacation.

Joe Soloman, salesman out of F. B. O. office, has returned from a trip into Idaho. After remaining here for a few days he will be on his way to Wyoming.

Fred J. McConnell, Universal Short Subject Manager, has left here for Seattle. McConnell is making a trip from the New York offices taking in all of the offices in the Western Division. Salesman Joe McElhinney was in from Southern Utah, as was Milton Cohn from the Idaho territory to attend a sales meeting with Special Representative McConnell. They have now left to resume their respective territories. Manager Henley is leaving for the northern territory this week.

H. Bradley Fish, became manager for the local Fox office August 29th. Manager Fish was formerly Western Division Manager for Vitagraph for a number

of years, and is well known in this territory. He is spending the first week in preformance of his new duties in Salt Lake, and expects to make an extended trip through the entire territory within the next ten days.

J. L. Tidwell, who covers the Southern Utah territory out of the local Fox exchange, has left for an extended trip through this section where he expects to close the key cities.

A new man, in the person of W. H. Hughart, has been added to the Fox sales force. Hughart was formerly with Associated First National covering the Montana territory, and is now working this territory for Fox. A. Singelow, formerly the Montana salesman, has been transferred to the Idaho territory, succeeding C. L. Walker who is now taking charge of the booking in this exchange.

Carl Stearn, in charge of the United Artists exchange here, has left for Montana to cover the key cities there.

David T. McElhenney has been added to the United Artists sales force, and is now in Montana covering this territory out of the local office.

Dave Frazer, Producers Distributing Corporation Special Representative for Western Division, has just arrived here from Los Angeles, and is leaving for Denver within a few days.

C. F. Parr will return the latter part of this week from a months' trip through the Montana branch.

Allan Burke, manager of the local DeLuxe Feature exchange,

reports his recent trip into Idaho to have met with exceptional success.

James R. Keitz, local manager for Greater Features, is now making a trip through the coal camps of Carbon County, Utah. T. C. Pierce has been added to the Greater Features sales force.

The Victory Theatre, under the management of Carl A. Porter, reports the usual good business. The ushers here have been fitted up in nice style with new uniforms, according to Ray M. Hendry, assistant manager.

Among exhibitors visiting film row this week are: Burt Martin, operating theatres in Sunnyside, Winter Quarters, Castle Gate, and Clear Creek, Utah; I. Swenson of the Angelus Theatre, Spanish Fork, Utah; Fred Swenstrum, owner of The Angeles Theatre, Spanish Fork, Utah; S. M. Dugins, owner of the Casino Theatre, Goshen, Utah; J. E. Tietjien, operating the Jewel Theatre, Ogden, Utah; Harmon Peery, operating the Egyptain Theatre, Ogden, Utah; Paul De Mourdant, operating the Orpheum and Mission theatres, Blackfoot, Idaho; Thomas Berta, owner of the Rialto Theatre, Rocksprings, Wyoming; Ott Schmidt, operating the Colonial Theatre, Idaho Falls, Idaho; Whicker of Whicker and Bunker, exhibitors in Delta, Utah; A. L. Stallings, owner of the Kinema Theatre, Richfield, Utah, and J. A. Whitehead, who is opening a new house in Eureka, Utah, the first part of September, is here booking up for the opening weeks.

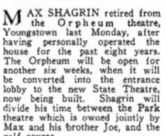 

Cleveland

MAX SHAGRIN retired from the Orpheum theatre, Youngstown last Monday, after having personally operated the house for the past eight years. The Orpheum will be open for another six weeks, when it will be converted into the entrance lobby to the new State Theatre, now being built. Shagrin will divide his time between the Park theatre which is owned jointly by Max and his brother Joe, and the golf course.

Henry S. Vogt has sold his Odessa Theatre in Malvern, Ohio, to Park C. Beatty. Peatty operates another picture house in Carrollton, O.

William Silverberg is putting his Ball Park theatre, Cleveland, right on the amusement map. He is doubling his seating capacity from 200 to 400 seats, installing a new $10,000 organ, and dressing up the whole place with new paint, and new fixings.

Mrs. Rose Stasny has purchased a lot of new projection equipment

for her Rex theatre, Cleveland, including new projection machines.

Caldwell Brown, prominent exhibitor in these parts, and manager of the Colonial theatre, Zanesville, is ill. He was recently removed to a local hospital.

A. H. Abrams, proprietor-manager of the Mozart and Odeon theatres, Canton, has just returned from a ten weeks' vacation fishing and hunting trip up in Michigan and made his first personal visit of the season to the exchanges last Friday. Mr. Abrams has a summer home up on the lakes, where he gets plenty of leisure to think up new stunts to exploit pictures.

The Film Bldg. register showed the following out-of-town exhibitor guests for the past week: Louis Mantho, the American theatre, Alliance; G. Gillia, National, Akron; A. J. Paul, Royal, Galion; M. Moran, Lincoln, Youngstown; Charles Mack, Strand, Sebring; H. J. Walters, Opera House, Burton; C. V. Rakestraw, Opera

House and State, Salem; M. E. Ames, Pastime, Jefferson; Dave Robbins and Frank Savage, Dome, Youngstown; Peter Rettig, Mystic, Galion; and "Mayor" Kelly, Lincoln theatre, Massilon.

Roger Ferri formerly of the staff of MOTION PICTURE NEWS is in town. He came to stay for a while, having been appointed residence publicity manager for the local Fox exchange covering the northern Ohio territory. Joe Shea, who has been here has returned to New York. Roy Crandall, who was out here in the interests of the pre-release engagement has also returned to New York.

Ward Scott, manager of the Cleveland Fox exchange, went out in the territory to call on the exhibitors last week instead of waiting for the exhibitors to come and call on him.

Robert Cotton, division manager for District 4 of Producers Distributing Corporation, held a local sales conference in the

Cleveland office last week. Frank Stuart, manager of the Detroit P.D.C. exchange came over for the talk. Cotton is now in New York attending a general conference of all P.D.C. division managers.

Dr. W. E. Shallenberg, president of Arrow Pictures, spent last Friday in Cleveland, as the guest of J. S. Jossey, head of the Progress Pictures Company, distributors of Arrow product in Ohio.

Frank Zambrino, president of Progress Pictures Company of Chicago, Milwaukee and Indianapolis, accompanied Dr. Shallenberg on his trip to Cleveland. Lou Rogers, representative for Arrow Film, was in town last week for a few days.

Charles Schwerin, we understand, has resigned as Metro-Goldwyn exchange manager in Pittsburgh to join the gold rush to Florida.

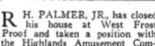

Florida

R H. PALMER, JR., has closed his house at West Frost Proof and taken a position with the Highlands Amusement Company of Sebring.

Jno. B. Carroll, City Manager of the Consolidated Amusements, Tampa, has returned from a three weeks vacation. Mr. Carroll, spent a week in New York lining up attractions for the four houses, and arranged to play the Keith Vaudeville for the first three days of each week, in the Victory, with the opening date announced for Sept. 14th. The other two weeks were spent in the mountains of North Carolina.

E. D. Tarbell, away back in 1911 and '12 was the manager of the two principal theatres of Tampa, and who passed us up and went up North to work for the Vitagraph Company, has finally given up the frozen north and is back with us again. Ed is looking fine, and says that he heard so much of Florida, and the boom, that he could not stay away longer. He is thinking of going into the real estate business.

Coral Gables, the new city on the East Coast, is going to have a theatre. Work has been started and it is planned to have the house ready by the first of the new year.

Work has started on a new theatre in Seminole Heights, a residential section of Tampa. The theatre will be called the Orpheum and will have a seating capacity of 1,000.

H. A. Kelly, a producer of motion pictures, and has been in films in Winter Haven, was taken ill while directing a scene and died shortly after. Mr. Kelly was only 53 years of age, but an old-timer in the film business, he having been connected with the industry for nearly twenty years. Another director is being selected to finish the picture Mr. Kelly was at work on.

George Connally, manager of the Grand and Howell theatres, Palatka, was married to Essie L. Woodruff, a native of Georgia, on Sunday, Aug. 23d. George is a great favorite in Tampa, he having been manager of the Grand here for some time. The Tampa bunch all sent congrats to George.

Hawkins & Hudson, who operate a string of theatres in cities through the central part of Florida, are opening another at Bushnell. The new house will be named the Sunland, and will open this week.

D. A. Stewart, owner of the open air theatre, the Hyde Park, on the west side of Tampa, has opened another one in the Latin section of Tampa, known as Ybor City. The new airdome is located at the corner of 7th Avenue and 19th Street, right opposite the Italian Club Theatre.

J. E. Ramos has taken over the Royal in West Tampa and will operate it in connection with his Franklin street house, the Prince.

Geo. B. Peck, manager of the Strand, Tampa, has been laid up with a game leg. It could not keep him away from his work however, for George propped the sore leg up on a stool and doped out his usual stunts.

Albany

Miss Florence Allen, winner the Princess title in Greater Movie Season Beauty contest on way to Universal City for tryout in Universal pictures.

MONDAY, September 14, will be the big red letter day along Film Row in this city, on account of the outing that has been arranged by the Albany Film Board of Trade, and to which all exhibitors and in fact everyone connected with the industry is invited. Transportation will be furnished for those without cars. The outing is scheduled for Saratoga Lake and tickets may be obtained from film salesmen, exchange managers, or from either the Albany Film Board of Trade or the Albany Zone. Charles Stombaugh, former manager of the Pathe exchange here, now in New York, is expected up for the occasion.

The employees in the Pathe exchange held a most enjoyable screen party and dance one night during the past week.

Among the exhibitors from out of town along Film Row during the past week, were Mr. and Mrs. A. T. Mallory, who run the Star in Corinth; Phil Markell, of Adams, Mass., with a chain of several theatres in that state, and George Nicholson, who runs Bennett Hall in Stottville.

Miss Mildred Coons, who has been doing the booking for some time past at Warner Brothers' exchange in this city, has transferred her affections to the Pro-Dis-Co office, where she will assist E. E. Lowe. Lee Langdon, who booked in several exchanges in years past, has taken over the job of booking for Warner Brothers. Jacob Klein, the new manager of the exchange here, arrived in town on Monday, and lost no time in getting out and becoming acquainted with the territory.

The lease which L. L. Conners holds on the Star theatre in Salem expires on October 1, when Mr. Conners announces that he will not operate the house from that time, but will turn over the house to the owner, John M. Gillies.

Vacations are about over for the exhibitors and the employees of the various exchanges in this city. Miss Lillian Nachman and Miss Helen Kestenbaum, of the Metro-Goldwyn force, are back at their desks, with a healthy coat of tan. T. J. McCarthy, owner of the Fair Haven theatre in Vermont, is back from a vacation spent in Ithaca. Harry Lazarus, of Kingston, has been enjoying a few days at Schroon Lake.

Lew Fischer, of Fort Edward, busy these days in getting the Bradley theatre in shape for opening in September, had a couple of guests at dinner the other night in Ted O'Shea, manager of the local Metro-Goldwyn exchange, and Alec Weissman, salesman.

J. H. McIntyre, who looks after the Famous Players exchange in Albany, and does it exceptionally well, is now on a ten day trip through northern New York.

Oscar Perrin made his first appearance during the past week as manager of the Capitol theatre in Albany. This theatre will run burlesque for the last three days of the week during the fall and winter season. This means that Harmanus Bleecker Hall will continue with pictures during the months to come, instead of splitting its week with burlesque.

The Rialto, in Little Falls, as it is now known, and which was formerly the Gateway theatre, is now being handled by a woman in the person of Mrs. Francis McGraw, who secured her experience in the running the Gem theatre. When the house was reopend a short time ago, Mrs. McGraw gave a short address of welcome and dedicated the theatre to the entertainment of not only Little Falls but the entire Mohawk Valley. Maurice Chase, of Buffalo, and others were on hand for the opening.

The Standard Silk mill at Chadwicks, will run motion pictures this fall and winter for its employees. The theatre in Averill Park, which is also a community house run by the Faith Knitting company, will also operate as a means of entertaining employees of the concern.

Bob Yates, who has been summering at Lake George and looking after his mother-in-law's theatre at the same time, was in town the other day on his way back from New York city.

Young, Whitney and Pierce are making fine progress these days in constructing the quarter million dollar motion picture theatre in Ilion and which will be known as the Capitol, and which will be run along lines similar to that of the New York city house bearing the same name. The theatre will have a seating capacity of about 1,600 persons and present plans call for its completion about October 15.

Earl Flack, of Potsdam is now planning to secure another theatre somewhere in northern New York and to that end is spending much of his time these days in driving over the territory.

Feldman and son, who recently bought the Lincoln theatre in Schenectady, are now planning to install a new organ. The son will probably play as he formerly served as organist at several theatres in both Albany and Troy.

Mrs. Robert Fonda, who runs the Grand theatre in Scotia, and who books the pictures for the house, is now being accompanied on her trips to Albany, by her baby that is just starting to walk.

Charles Dortic, of Pittsburg, who is connected with the Universal Film company as an advertising efficiency man, arrived in Albany during the past week, and will remain here for several days.

It was so cold in northern New York during the latter part of the week that in some places the mercury dropped to 28 degrees, making several exhibitors plan to start their furnaces.

Harry Hellman, who runs the Royal theatre in Albany, and who recently bought a summer home at Crooked Lake, near Troy, is planning to have the film boys out from Albany for some week-end in the near future.

Exhibitors in Saratoga Springs, are warning their cashiers to be on the lookout for counterfeit money as it is said there is considerable in circulation in that resort.

Bert Griffin, who runs the Lyceum in Red Hook, not only looks after his theatre, but also runs a dance hall and soft drink place, a confectionery store, and also superintends a chocolate factory. His theatre is now operating three nights a week.

It is planned to close the Albany theatre in Albany for two or three weeks in order that it may be redecorated and otherwise improved by the new owners.

The American theatre in Troy, which reopened last week, will run a serial on each Wednesday, Thursday and Friday, according to a placard in the lobby. Girl ushers in gray and white are being used in the theatre. Walter Hays, of Buffalo, and Moe Mark of New York, accompanied by Frank Dolan, of Albany, visited the American the other day and were much pleased in the transformation that had been made in the house. The operator is Louis Rinn.

Atlanta

NAT L. ROYSTER of Charlotte, N. C., general manager in charge of Warner Bros. theatres in this territory returned last Friday from a week's visit to the home office in New York.

Mr. Royster also announced important changes and an addition to the management of his Broadway theatre in Charlotte. S. H. B. Stough, former manager of the Rialto theatre, Birmingham, Ala., has been appointed by him assistant manager of the Broadway in Charlotte.

Thomas A. Little, who was last week appointed manager of the local Producers Distributing corporation office to succeed Mrs. Anna H. Sessions, entered into his new duties Monday morning of this week. He has been in Atlanta and in the office since last Friday week, however, familiarizing himself with local conditions and becoming settled in his new home.

Mr. Little comes to Atlanta from Charlotte, where he was manager of the Metro-Goldwyn exchange for nearly five years.

Harold E. Moore, an Atlanta man and son of Jno. L. Moore, optician of this city, announces his plans this week to construct a theatre in Haines City, Fla., where he has been living for the past few years.

Mr. Moore anticipates it will be ready to open on the 1st of January.

A. H. McCarthy, who owned the Mildred theatre, Barnesville, Ga., has this week sold the house to G. H. Goddard, and will take up his future residence in Florida, together with his family. Mr. Goddard will take over the theatre September 1st, it is stated.

J. F. Harris, manager of the Arcade and Airdome theatres in Fort Myers, Fla., spent this week in Atlanta visiting his mother. He was accompanied by his wife, Mrs. Harris, and they drove up to Atlanta in their car.

Dixie Graham, formerly booker at Producer's local exchange, is now traveling Georgia out of Atlanta for the company. Mr. Drum has taken his place as booker in the office here.

L. C. Lowe, who formerly traveled North and South Caro-

lina for Producers Distributing corporation, has been transferred to the Alabama and Tennessee territory.

C. Alexander, who has been with the Pathe office in Charlotte for the past ten years, has resigned this week to go with the Metro-Goldwyn exchange of that city.

R. H. Masterman, formerly advertising sales manager for Famous Players, is now traveling North Carolina for Metro-Goldwyn out of the Charlotte office. Mr. Masterman is an Atlanta man, and graduated at Georgia Tech.

Oscar Oldknow, president of Liberty Film Distributing corporation, accompanied by Rufus Davis, salesman for the company, left last Sunday night for Memphis and Asheville. From there Mr. Davis will proceed to Eaton, Ga., and Mr. Oldknow will return directly to Atlanta.

Miss Thelma McGinnis has joined the forces of the Educational Film Exchange this week in the capacity of contract clerk.

Ernest Neiman, district representative for Producers Distribut-

ing corporation and who has been in Atlanta this week doing special work, left Friday night going on to the Washington exchange.

Charles E. Kessnich, district manager for Metro-Goldwyn corporation, returned to the city Monday, having spent several weeks in the New Orleans territory.

Miss Hannah Blumensfeld of the Educational Film Exchange office, has been in Savannah and Baxley, Ga., this week on her vacation.

Frank L. Alig, auditor of Liberty Film Distributing corporation here, left town last week accompanied by Mrs. Alig for a two weeks' vacation. They go to visit Mrs. Alig's relatives in Illinois.

R. B. Wilby, well-known exhibitor, has permanently moved to Atlanta this week with his family, and has taken offices in the Glenn building.

C. R. Beacham, local branch manager of the First National exchange, and W. E. Calloway, district manager coming up from New Orleans, left for New York last Sunday to attend First National's big convention there.

Denver

SIDNEY D. WEISBAUM, local branch manager of Film Booking Offices of America, Arbitration Board member, and one of the most active and energetic members of the Denver Film Board of Trade, has been promoted. He received notification a few days ago to assume duties as branch manager of the San Francisco office of Film Booking Offices of America. Probably at no other time did the Film Board

Bob Lee Piner, new exploitation director for Kinkelstein and Rubin, Minneapolis.

of Trade and Arbitration Board so keenly feel the loss of a member. Mr. Weisbaum has held various offices in the Film Board of Trade and Arbitration Board membership, and at the present time is one of the outstanding members because of his activities in the Board. Besides being a member of various committees of the Denver Film Board, Mr. Weisbaum was elected last January a member of the joint Board of Arbitration. As a member of this Board, he more than once proved his ability as an arbitrator by his quickness in seeing the issue involved, in noting the merit of the argument presented by either side and suggesting an award which was usually fair and equitable to all parties concerned. Denver's loss is San Francisco's gain.

Harry Long, manager of the American Theatre, General Manager of Greater Movie Season Campaign of Denver, has returned after several weeks' visit with relatives and friends in Detroit, Michigan.

Thomas Love, owner and manager of the Hanna Circuit of theatres in Hanna, Wyoming, was a visitor in the city yesterday. He drove to Denver in a new Franklin car which was turned over to a garage for repairs immediately after his arrival. Tom says a cow disputed his right of way.

L. L. Savage, well known inspector booker of Pathe Exchange, Inc., of the Western ter-

ritory is at present working in the local branch of his organization relieving Jack Scott who is away spending a two week's vacation far up on the Poudre River. En route to Denver, Mr. Savage was aboard the train which was wrecked on the D. & R. G. Railroad near Granite, Colorado. He was one of the passengers who sustained no injuries. Immediately after the wreck, Mr. Savage took a number of pictures which were published by the Denver Post the day following the wreck. These pictures were the best if not the only pictures taken of this accident in which two were killed and many were seriously injured.

Hugh W. Braly, local branch manager of Famous Players-

Lasky, has returned to his desk after a two weeks' sales trip into the Wyoming territory.

The following theatres have reopened for business after having been closed most of the summer: Radium Theatre, Nucla, Colorado; G. Chrisman, manager; J. P. McKenna, Salt Creek, Wyoming; W. W. Davis, Fairplay Theatre, Fairplay, Colorado; Angus Linton, Meeteetse Theatre, Meeteetse, Wyoming; R. H. Cunningham, Howard Theatre, Howard, Colorado; and the Tomboy Club, Telluride, Colorado. This last theatre is owned and operated by C. F. Carpenter and is located high in the mountains at an altitude of 12,000 feet. It is probably the highest theatre in the world.

New York and New Jersey

JACOB FOX, executive of the Fox Amusement Company and successfully operating theatres in Riverside, Beverly and Burlington, New Jersey, has reopened the Bordentonian theatre and renamed it the Fox. The Bordentonian was at one time under the management of the Mercantini Brothers who are local merchants of Bordentown. Their other enterprises taking up too much of their time, the Mercantini's leased the theatre to the United Theatres of America, a Newark corporation that after a short period, gave up the project. Since then the house has been dark up until the time that Mr. Fox added it to his circuit. The whole theatre has been completely renovated and reconstructed, the lobby being entirely changed, new lighting fixtures installed, new scenic equipment, and many other changes made to make the house more comfortable. Feature pictures will be shown with changes on Mondays, Wednesdays, Fridays, and Saturdays.

Harold Blumenthal, formerly connected with the Capitol theatre at Passaic, N. J., is at present doing all the purchasing for the New Rivoli, Patterson, N. J.

Keith's Jersey City theatre, always a first run picture and vaudeville house, has for the first time in it's career, gone on a second run basis.

Dr. Harris, who at one time operated the Capitol theatre, Passaic, N. J., which was bought by the Fabians, is reported as negotiating for a theatre in Jersey City.

Friends of Bob Horn, Pathe Brooklyn salesman, will regret to hear of the severe illness of Mrs. Horn who is suffering from an attack of lockjaw.

Ned Malouf, formerly connected with the New York Fox exchange, is now covering the Bronx for Pathe.

Sobelson and Tanhauser have recently received a second deposit on the sale of their Strand theatre in Jersey City. The purchasers are contemplating tearing down the old structure and rebuilding a 2000 seat house on the same site.

Here is more evidence of the popularity of the Democratic Nominee for Mayor of the City of New York, "Jimmie" Walker, among the local film trade. The film salesmen have recently formed an association to further his cause. Milton Kronacher, city salesman for Pathe has lately become a member of the committee.

The City theatre, Union City, N. J., will open September the 7th under the new management of J. J. Goely. And by the way, Union Hill and West Hoboken are now known as Union City.

It is reported that Bound Brook, N. J. is being given the eagle eye in connection with a new theatre site and that Jos. Stern is

the owner of the eye. Mr. Stern operates at least ten theatres at the present time and it is further reported that his company plan to build about fourteen new houses in the Northern part of New Jersey.

Several more local theatre openings are reported this week. Loew's Alhambra in New York City opened on Tuesday and will change its policy. In the past the Alhambra has been devoted to vaudeville and stock and it will now run feature pictures. The Woodrow, at Wilson Ave, and Decatur St., Brooklyn, and operated by Abraham Manglin, started a full time schedule on August 31st. The Woodrow has been running on a three a week. The Crown theatre, Ditmas Ave., Brooklyn, will also go on full time September 3d. The Kinema, Rosenweig and Katz' new house at Pitkin Ave. and Berryman St. Brooklyn, will have its opening September the 4th.

And here is a piece of news—Filmland at Church and Nostrand Ave., Brooklyn, has at last been completed and will have its opening this month. Fred Dollinger, formerly connected with the Claremont and Our Civic theatres in Richmond Hill, will be the manager of this house. Filmland has been under construction for about two years or more.

L. Gold, formerly with the Newkirk theatre, Newkirk Ave., Brooklyn, is the new owner of the

Park at 451 East 169th St., Mr. Gold is doing considerable remodeling at nights, after shows.

Suchman Bros. opened their Hughes theatre, 189th St., Bronx, on Saturday, August 29th and the Tip Top, on Wilson Ave., Brooklyn, operated by the M. Heisler Amusement Co., will open this week Friday.

Miss Fannie Leighston, of the Select theatre, Pitkin Ave., Brooklyn, has gone to the mountains for a vacation.

Al Friedlander of the Garden theatre on New Utrecht Ave., Brooklyn, is back on the job again after spending a pleasant vacation up in Greene County.

Harry Bernstein, manager of Red Seal's New York Exchange, announced this week three additions to his sales force and a new territorial division, made necessary, according to his statement, by expansion of business.

As a consequence of this move, Chester Vanderbilt is covering Long Island; Harry Fogarty has charge of the New York division; S. Rubenstein is covering Brooklyn territory, and John Duffy is handling New Jersey.

Syd Falk, formerly manager of the Brandt Bros. Carleton theatre on Flatbush Ave., Brooklyn, is now the manager of the Cumberland, one of the Brandt circuit. The New Carleton is expected to be ready during the early part of December.

Cincinnati

MR. and Mrs. L. O. Davis, leading exhibitors of Hazard, Ky., are to be congratulated over the arrival of a new theatre manager in the family. Mr. Davis is already laying plans for a new theatre.

J. N. Gelman, returned from a trip to Lexington, Ky., where he claims to have made a rather profitable deal with J. B. Elliott, leading exhibitor of the blue grass city.

Katheryn Flavin formerly of the Famous Players organization in this city is now connected with the organ department of the Wurlitzer Chicago offices.

The Overlook Theatre will open early in November. This theatre is situated on one of Cincinnati's most beautiful hills and will be one of the most modern of houses of the suburban district.

Till Heichel, the ever smiling young lady who greets all visitors at the Cincinnati Theatre Equipment Co., returned from a two weeks' vacation in the Kentucky woods.

J. C. Fishman, general sales manager for Standard spent several days in the city going over the new product with local manager Nate Lefkowitz.

Abe Hyman, of the Hyman in-

terests of W. Va., was a welcome visitor to Film Row last week.

Howard Frankel, Columbus exhibitor, was seen in Coshocton, O., for a few days recently and it looks very much as if the latter metropolis of central Ohio is to have a new theatre.

Forrest Hathaway, former salesman for Vitagraph is now traveling for Metro Goldwyn.

Al Kaufman, for the past two years and a half manager for Metro Goldwyn has resigned from this firm. His immediate connections are not known at present but it has been intimated that he will be stationed in Detroit.

J. S. Davis of the Westland theatre, Portsmouth, O., was a visitor at film row last week.

John Kaiser, Jr., of the Royal theatre, Chilicothe, O., spent several days around film row.

J. F. McConnell of the Tripoli theatre, Mt. Washington, O., made his weekly pilgrimage to the Broadway Film building last week.

Gus Heichelman of the Glenway Price Hill was another suburban exhibitor to visit the boys at the film building.

The Opera House at Logan, O., was destroyed by fire last week. C. E. Oberly was the manager.

The Southern Ohio Golf Tournament held between the Ex-

change men and Exhibitors was pulled off Friday, August 28th at the Avon Fields, Cincinnati. A dinner at the Swiss Gardens followed the tournament. The winners of the affair were: 1st, Geo. Brown, manager of the Colonial theatre, Bluefield, W. Va., winning the silver trophy donated by Mike Silverglade, former local exhibitor, 2nd prize a traveling bag went to Lou Muchmore, manager of Associated Producers; 3rd prize, a traveling toilet set, went to C. E. Peppiatt, Famous Players manager; 4th prize, a dozen golf balls, went to Floyd Lewis, district manager for Asso. Seal, district sales manager for Educational. Lou Muchmore, Asso. Producers, manager, C. Johnston, manager for Educational, Dave Laughlin, salesman for Educational. Rudolph Skirbol, manager for Skirbol Gold

Seal, Clyde Congrove, salesman for Standard, C. E. Peppiatt, manager for Paramount, Mose Wilchins, manager for several of the Frankel theatres, Many Nagle, assistant city salesman for Paramount, Mose Strauss, manager for Progress and H. Nesbitt, salesman for F. B. O.

Alice Calhoun, loaned by Warner Bros. to Jesse J. Goldburg for one special Independent Pictures Corp. production.

CONSTRUCTION & EQUIPMENT DEPARTMENT

Selecting a Theatre Organ and Organist

Instrument Must Be of Special Design; Artist of Proper Training

By W. Meryle Hammond, Organist

THE exhibitor, who is planning on installing an organ in his theatre would do well to talk with some good theatre organist and be advised as to makes, tonal quality, ease of manipulation, etc. But for the benefit of the exhibitor who finds this impossible, I will say that there are a great number of firms who manufacture organs, but only a few who specialize in theatre organs. It would hardly be a wise act to install an organ designed expressly for church work in a theatre, for a great number of essential things would be lacking, such as drums, tambourine, wood block, wind siren, fire gong, bells, xylophones, etc., and also many sets of pipes which were designed especially for use in the church. All of these would in turn be just as far out of place in a church as they are essential to the theatre.

When installing the organ, great care should be taken to be positive that the organ boxes—the rooms where the organ proper is placed—are absolutely moisture proof. Nine-tenths of organ troubles can be traced to moisture either in the boxes or the console. Many use heavy building paper and wall board, but it is far better to be on the safe side and have the boxes plastered.

Immediately after the organ is installed, a wise manager would put an automatic heating unit in each box, thereby assuring himself that the organ would not drop out of tune on the first cold night that comes along.

The console should be placed in a position where the organist will have a good view of the screen at all times, and above all, where he can hear. Some consoles have been placed in such a position that the organist cannot really tell how loud he is playing and has to depend upon his knowledge of the stops to determine whether he is about to tear the house to pieces or whether he is playing too softly. If the boxes are three or four feet in front of him and eight, ten or more feet above him, you could not expect him to hear the true tones of the instrument, for the sound would first have to travel to the back of the house and return to him, thereby losing much of its volume. The console should be placed at least twenty feet away from the boxes, if they are on either side of the theatre parallel with it and facing the front. However, if they are in the ceiling, throwing the sound downward and outward, it would not be necessary to place them so far. Ten feet would be ample.

W. Meryle Hammond.

But no matter how fine an instrument you may buy, you might just as well have a tin pan, if you do not have an *organist* to play it.

The Organist

There are plenty of people who call themselves *organists*, but there are not so many who really *are*.

There is the person who calls himself an organist because he can play the piano nicely. He takes a few lessons on the "king of instruments," learns the fundamentals of pedaling and organ playing in general, and hangs out his shingle labeled "Organist." When he plays a picture, he uses all the popular music available, fakes a few chords for accompaniment, puts in a few pedal notes now and then, and blunders around melody with about three changes in registration in the process of an evening. He does not know that such a thing as synchronization exists. He may have the nucleus, but that's all.

There is the person who was quite a sensation as a church and concert organist and whom attractive salaries have lured into the interpretive field. He plays won-

derfully, it is a pleasure to hear him. But he does not understand when atmosphere stops and action begins. If he is playing "A Dream" and the villain captures the beautiful young heroine and makes way with her, he will calmly finish his "dream," apparently quite unconscious of the fact that the scene is quite dramatic. He cannot understand what all those traps were ever put on an organ for, and he abhors popular and jazz music, either because he can't play it or on general principles. He does not realize that popular dance music has its place in the theatre, as well as classical.

Then there is one who eats confections while on the job.

You want none of these! You want an honest to goodness organist—one who can deliver the goods and does it!

He plays really beautifully. You want to choke the villain when he captures the heroine, and just as they are about to drive the car off a steep cliff, you grab your seat and almost scream. And when the car finally runs off the cliff, after a thrilling chase, and the hero has captured his Lady Fair, you hear a deep rumble as the car starts falling and a dull thud as it strikes. You hear the fat man in the comedy laugh so gayly that you cannot suppress your emotions, and when he sees a bevy of pretty young girls walking down the avenue, you hear him say, "Oh Baby."

Your organist never eats in the pit, there is never anyone there gossiping with him. He doesn't watch the clock and he isn't afraid to practice. He's not the least bit afraid to start working ahead of time or quit after time and you can find him at the theatre almost all hours of the day. He does not play an organ in a theatre just to earn his bread, but because he loves it.

You sit down to see a new programme. You shed a few tears over some tragic scene and then you're laughing at grandfather's peaceful snoring, at the rooster crowing, and the mule braying. You get up and go to your office and say, "That's the best programme we've had in a long time, it ought to draw the crowd." But you were unconscious of the music. Why? Because the organist was good. He was tempered with feeling and knew how to portray it. He knew synchronization and knew many of the tricks of his profession. *That* is the kind of an organist you want. He is always a live wire and it is ones like him, who are making our profession and who mean something to it. The others will not last, they will drop by the wayside, for their days are numbered.

View of the grand stairway in the new West Coast theatre, San Bernardino, Calif., erected by West Coast Theatres, Inc.

West Coast Theatres, Inc. Open West Coast Theatre at San Bernardino, Cal.

WITH a decorative motif that is artistically beautiful in all its detail, a large stage with equipment unexcelled in any theatre of its size in the country and many other features including the little niceties for the comfort of its patrons the West Coast theatre at San Bernardino, California, opened recently by West Coast Theatres, Inc. stands as a model of twentieth century ingenuity.

This theatre is part of the Platt building in San Bernardino and the opening of the theatre and the building occurred simultaneously. A large gathering attended the opening the visitors including all the prominent officials of West Coast Theatres, Inc. and most of the representative citizens of San Bernardino. The speakers program was under the direction of the San Bernardino Chamber of Commerce. Mayor Holcomb was the principal speaker and A. M. Bowles, General Manager of the theatre company responded.

The appointments of the house are elaborate in every respect, with costly drapes, furnishings, lighting effects and decorative features. A large and elegantly furnished mezzanine floor provides ample lounging space for those who desire to rest prior to entering the auditorium.

Its policy calls for a three per week change, with high calibre pictures, elaborate stage presentations, produced by Fanchon and Marco, production experts of the West Coast Theatres, Inc., and two days of the week devoted to high class vaudeville bills.

San Bernardino is a city of 35,000, and the acquisition of this show-house at once places this city among the prominent theatrical

communities of Southern California. The theatre is under the direction of Gore Bros., Ramish, and Sol Lesser, and the building and completion of the theatre, was under the personal supervision of M. Gore, president. Mr. H. L. Hartman is in personal resident charge under the supervision of General Manager Bowles.

Capitol Machine Co. Market Miniature Projector

THE Capitol Machine Company was host to the motion picture trade press at a luncheon given at the Princeton Club, Friday, August 21.

Arthur Dunn, president of the corporation and prominent in local business enterprises, presided at the table and gave an interesting talk on the history of the organization and called attention to the tremendous field that is open to a machine of this kind.

Improvements in the machine made by the company and a tie-up with the National Trailer service were announced at the luncheon. The negative is to be developed at the Claremont Laboratories with whom the Capitol Machine Company is affiliated.

Walter E. Greene, President of the Claremont Laboratories, and well known in the film trade is Vice-president of the company. Julius Frankenberg, also well known, is another Vice-president.

Other officers and directors are: G. F. Zimmer, Milton H. Hall of the Mt. Vernon Trust Co.; Albert Banzhaf, connected with the United Artists Corp.; J. Walter Barnett, of the Lake Torpedo Boat Co.; Geo. C. Beach, of the Southwestern Utilities Co.; R. Henry Depew, Carlos Gardiner, of the Guarantee Trust Co.; A. Monson, of the Universal Stamping Co.; James Montgomery Irving and Frank K. Nebeker.

Zimm Theatre to Have Monsoon Cooling System

The Zimm theatre, at Winfield, Kansas, is continually under improvement, to make it more comfortable for its patrons. The latest addition is to be a great fan system which will change the air in the theatre every minute.

The system consists of two five foot fans working together. They are propelled by a five horse motor.

Lobby of the new West Coast theatre, San Bernardino, Calif., which is owned by West Coast Theatres, Inc.

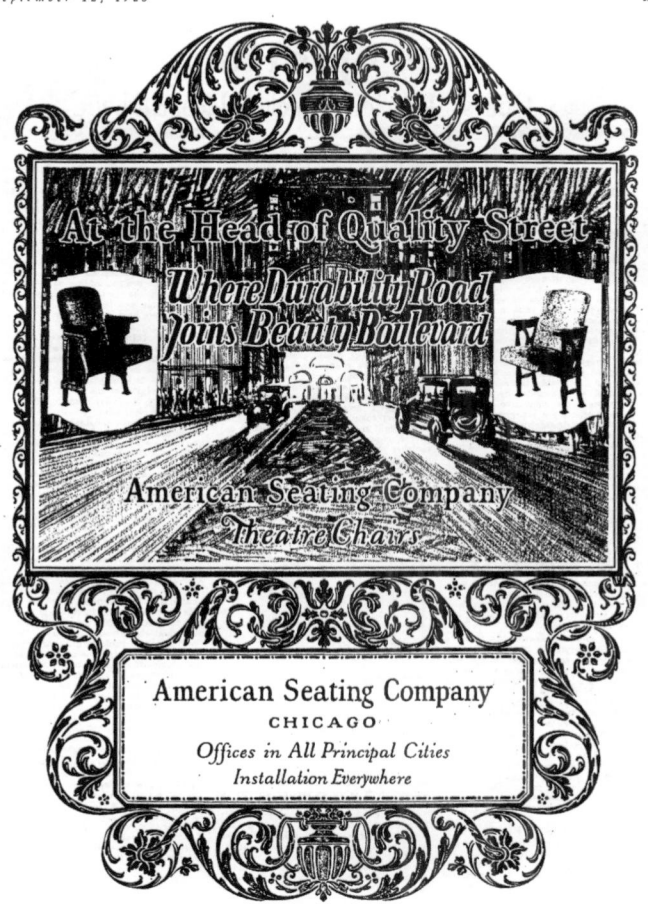

Inquiries and Comments

Color Vision and Screen Borders

SOURCE of much controversy among parties in the motion picture projection field has been the determination and selection of a suitable border for the illuminated picture on the screen. Common practice now consists of surrounding the lighted picture area with a jet black border unrelieved by any light or color so as to secure maximum contrast between the illuminated picture and the field outside of it.

This of course serves the purpose when comparing the picture area as a whole with the background but when the detail of the picture itself, as represented by the black and white tones are considered a serious loss of tonal effects are experienced not to mention other detrimental effects of which eyestrain is only one.

This entire subject of screen brightness and background contrast together with some interesting information on color vision in general is rather carefully explained in a paper by Dr. K. C. D. Hickman, presented before the Royal Photographic Society of England and which was published in the July issue of the Photographic Journal (English).

The entire paper is so interesting that it is being reprinted here in the hopes that some further light may be shed on the subject of screen surroundings on which the Martin Illuminated Border, incidentally, bears a direct relation.

Dr. Hickman gives as the first consideration "the structure of the eye and the elementary facts of vision."

Vision in General

Practically everyone is familiar with diagrams showing a cross section of the eye. The eye may be considered as a spherical camera having a lens of variable aperture at one pole (end) and the *retina*, or human equivalent of the photographic plate, at the other. Whereas the lens is small in relation to the sphere, the retina covers a large region and collects light from a wide spherical angle. On inspection it appears to be divided into *three* concentric zones. A large outside surrounding region, a smaller inside area called the *yellow spot*, and a very small central zone called the *fovea*. The units of structure of the retina surface are of two kinds, and have been called the *rods* and the *cones*.

Two Kinds of Vision

If these physical structures have any significance at all, we can conclude at once that visual perception occurs in *three regions* and is of *two kinds*. It is a matter of common experience that the outside peripheral region sees with poor definition and color sensitiveness, but is very alive to contrast and change of position. A change in brightness of movement to the side makes one turn the head immediately, even though the disturbing factor has not been recognized in shape or color. The next region, the yellow spot, is the zone of good color sensitiveness and general definition; it is the part used to recognize groups of letters in reading the perspective of small objects. In concentrating on any given letter, however, the rest of the word fades into insignificance, and the third region, the fovea, comes into play with its most critical resolving power of all.

That visual perception is of two kinds and can be demonstrated equally well by reference to other happenings of common experience. The classic examples cited in text books, are sunrise and sunset. (This was described once before in full by the Editor in discussing the general characteristic of vision.) In the blaze of daylight objects suggest their full brilliance of light, shade and color. As the illumination dies, though light and shade and form remain unaltered, objects become grayer and color vanishes. Let daylight be extinct and a full moon reign over the scene. The moon, perhaps, is silvery yellow, the sky purple black, with clouds of various pale hues drifting by. But the landscape, once so full of color, is now a study in monochrome (a single color).

Figure 1.

The detail is sharp and full of contrast, except when looked at directly. Who has not passed from a dark hall into a brilliant moonlit night and exclaimed that it is light enough to read, and on trying, found that even large newspaper print fails to reveal its legend? Therefore, though there is an impression of detail on peering directly the structure vanishes in a blur.

Pursuing our moonlight adventure further, we enter a small hut having its only window facing *North*. Standing well within and viewing the window, we see an apparently bright picture framed in blackness. Glancing away, the floors and walls nearby appear the deepest visible grey, fading to impenetrable darkness in the corners; yet we know there is light of some sort even in the farthest crevices—in daytime their contents would be visible, and they are receiving the same proportion of light from the window by night. It is merely that we are unable to perceive light when it is below a certain intensity (usually called the threshold of vision—Ed.) We see that there are two well marked *threshold* phenomena: firstly, the threshold of vision when faint light becomes just visible; secondly, the threshold when color makes its appearance. These are both phenomena of the dark—adapted eye—that is, the eye in which the sensitivity of the retina and the diameter of the iris opening have been increased by resting in a dim light.

Action of the Eye

We have mentioned that in twilight vision, although detail appears abundant, it does not increase on close inspection. This is because the dark adaptation only occurs for the outer region of the retina; the central fovea, which is *always* used for detail inspection, is *night blind*.

To return again to considerations of relative brightness, suppose we trace the reaction of the eye to light from the *least visible* to the greatest physically attainable brightness. Disregarding color, this could be done by viewing a metal-filament lamp in a dark room and increasing the current from zero to its maximum. The experiment was performed quantitatively by Abney by controlling the luminosity of two adjacent photometric fields. It will be simpler for us to consider the metal-filament lamp. When it is made to glow with its least visible brightness it is found that its candle-power has to be increased by a comparatively *large* amount before the eye notices any change. At feeble intensities the eye reacts sluggishly to alteration in brightness. When the brightness of the filament is increased to the order of 1 to 10 foot-candles the eye can detect an alteration with extreme delicacy. Now let the filament be made to glow strongly; the eye has again become insensitive to change; quite large alterations in brightness produce little difference in appearance, except, perhaps in the amount of dazzle. A practical example is the ceiling lamp of a railway carriage reflected from the windows at nighttime. Except that the dazzle is less, the filament appears as bright in the image as in the lamp itself. Yet calculation shows that one may be 20 times as bright as the other.

The Light Curve of the Eye

These facts can be expressed scientifically by plotting *apparent increase* in brightness against *actual increase* for a small object. We obtain what is called the *gamma curve* of the eye which expresses the relation and reaction to stimulus. This is shown in Fig. 1 for white, green, red and blue light. It is interesting to note that green light affects the eye exactly the same as white light but that red and blue lights behave differently. At the foot of the curve it will be seen that

(*Continued on page 1292*)

One Thing More

In your modern motion picture house every detail of projection, decoration, ventilation, temperature, seating, has been carefully worked out to make the theatre attractive and comfortable.

But there's one thing more you can do— and it's a real factor from the box office point of view: make sure the picture is printed on Eastman Positive Film, the film that safeguards for the screen the quality of the negative so your public may enjoy it.

Eastman film is identified in the margin by the black-lettered words "Eastman" and "Kodak"

EASTMAN KODAK COMPANY
ROCHESTER, N. Y.

Corner Cases as an Attention Compelling Force in Lobby Logic
By WM. F. LIBMAN, Pres., Libman-Spanjer Corp.

IN the last article, the writer went into the subject of wall cases and mirrors as adjuncts for the perfected lobby. There is still another type of case which is very popular and which is closely allied to the wall case, and that is the corner case. This type of case is used extensively in the very front of the lobby, and is usually attached to pilasters, columns, and pillars in such a manner as to attract the reading public travelling in two directions.

As an attention compelling force, there is hardly a finer medium to invoke the interest of the passer by than the corner case, properly located.

Built in 24, 36, and 48 inch widths, these cases are ideal enclosures in which to display photos, or posters. When placed in advantageous points bordering on the sidewalk or surrounding the pillars of the lobby front, they challenge interest indeed, in fact it has been proven that very few can resist the impulse to stop and peruse the contents of these attractive cases, so curious is the human race, and so alluring is the call of the small, neatly framed and appropriately titled photograph. Which reminds the writer of a little incident which took place some time ago, and which established in the writer's mind the value of the small dignified announcement as compared to the glaring, shrieking ballyho of the nickelodeon type of theatre which is rapidly disappearing.

A certain exhibitor who was operating in a community of the better kind, and who was a confirmed addict of the 6 sheet method of theatre front display, doubted the writer's assertion that in a certain type of house, and in a given neighborhood, an eleven by fourteen inch photograph is more effective in provoking genuine interest than is the case with a large poster. So heated did our debate become, that nothing less than an actual demonstration would swerve either of us from our respective grounds. So two opposite corners of the theatre front were chosen. On one of these corners a large poster depicting the usual pictorial matter was placed, while on the opposite corner, in a neat frame, was inserted a "still" taken from an actual scene in the feature with an appropriate explanatory title below it.

We both (the exhibitor and the writer) stood, watches in hand, anxious to test out our respective beliefs. To the exhibitor's surprise, fully ninety per cent of the people who showed any interest in the theatre front at all stopped in front of the small framed photograph, either to study the scene it depicted, or to read the title it contained, while none stopped at all to study the poster, contenting themselves with a glance as they passed it by.

Any advertising man will agree that the best mediums of advertising are judged by their circulation, and reader interest as they call it. In the case of the photo vs. the poster, the photo not only caused people to stop, but it caused them to read, which is the culmination of the advertiser's ambitions.

This case of course would not hold true everywhere, for certainly the exhibitor who hopes to attract the attention of the moving public that passes his front on street cars, taxis, autos, etc., must do so with a larger medium than a photo.

The writer once chided the manager of a theatre that was operating in a congested section of one of our larger cities. "Why do you spoil the front of your theatre with those awful crudely painted banners?" I asked him. "Why not some neat, dignified photo frames with titles explaining each photographed scene?"

He looked at me rather sadly I thought and said, "I'd do all that you say Bill, for I believe in it, but there's only one reason why I don't do it—*my patrons can't read!*"

So after all there are some cases where the poster banner must wave, but not many.

Then there is the new type of hand painted poster, that is beginning to enjoy its period of prosperity. In the larger theatres of the big key cities, these posters are really works of art, done by commercial artists of recognized ability. These high grade cards or posters are relatively expensive.

Many small exhibitors seeing the part that these attractive cards play in the big house lobby, resolve to follow suit. But where the big exhibitor can pay an artist $5 to $50 the little exhibitor pays his artist 50 cents, and surely the results are not comparable. Therefore it is far better to depend upon a good wall case or corner case, filled with several carefully chosen pictures, than to burlesque the feature by advertising it with a poorly or cheaply executed poster that will repell instead of attract.

The exhibitor should be careful of the arrangement of his lobby frames and of the pictures, photos or announcements that go into them. No matter how beautiful the lobby frames or cases may be that beauty is immediately negatived if the porter, or janitor, or some other simple soul is given carte blanche in the matter of filling the frames and case to overflowing with photos and pictures. Too many photos, like too much type in an advertisement, confuses and discourages the patron or reader.

Grand Riviera Theatre Opened by C. W. Munz Enterprises

DETROIT theatre goers this week had their first glimpse of the new Grand Riviera theatre at Grand River and Joy Road, the million dollar amusement house which was erected by the C. W. Munz theatrical enterprises.

The Grand Riviera is something that is different. The decorative scheme has been so perfectly carried out that the audience seems to be sitting in a beautiful outdoor park, with charming gardens on either side and the blue sky overhead.

Seating 3,000 persons, the auditorium has been modeled on the lines of an Italian garden nestling under the blue Mediterranean sky. Above the audience is the moonlight shining across the blue vaulted dome which has been so decorated that its extent seems limitless. On the right side is an Italian palace garden with a small temple building while above the whole are twinkling stars and moving clouds creating a complete illusion.

In front of the auditorium rises the proscenium which was conceived as a triumphal arch with supporting columns roofed with Roman tile mansard and a stone balustrade. The entire structure of this arch is richly ornamented in polychrome, lending a holiday atmosphere to the scene. Even above the proscenium is the sky and the impression of nature which coupled with the refrigerating and ventilating facilities of the theatre will create an atmosphere of the spacious outdoors.

The most effective examples of classical architecture to be seen in Europe have been

Plans Filed for New Buffalo Theatre

PLANS for the new motion picture theatre to be built at 1588-1598 Genesee street, including seven stores and offices, have been filed with the bureau of buildings in Buffalo. The new house will be built by Barney Vohwinkel, 2886 Main street, who has operated the Oriole theatre near the site for many years. When completed, the house will be leased by the Shea Amusement company. According to Mr. Vohwinkel the theatre and stores will cost $350,000. The seating capacity will be 1710. The frontage on Genesee street will be 168 feet. The house will have a depth of 32 feet.

faithfully copied in the design of the theatre. The unique lobby which represents a rotunda some 50 feet wide and 80 feet high has an interesting dome executed in rough texture plaster decorated in true Italian polychrome fashion and has a faience tile floor. Many of the motifs in this lobby are taken from the Villa Cambiasco and the doorheads are from those of St. Peter's in Rome.

The main foyer is richly carpeted and has a heavy Italian texture plaster wall, ornamented pilasters and a vaulted ceiling, giving the general effect of a stuccoed, cloistered arcade. Interesting detail of both these rooms are the handwrought iron gates, the wall lanterns and distance mirrors.

Architect's prospective rendering of the new Ambassador theatre, St. Louis, which is being erected by Skouras Bros. Enterprises.

The policy is to be the same as in the other Munz houses, which show moving pictures and vaudeville. Hugo Kalsow, well known orchestra leader has charge of the music.

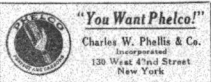
Walter C. Simon Discusses Music and Pictures

WALTER C. SIMON, organist and music writer, whose works have been published by many of the leading publishers of this country, and who claims to have written the first original score for a motion picture for the Kalem Company in 1911, in commenting on the relation of music to pictures says:

"A photoplay is enhanced 50 per cent by a good musical score. It is only a matter of time now when all pictures will have their individual score rather than having the theatre's musical director make up his program from published numbers which are suggested by a cue sheet supplied by the producer of the film."

Color Vision and Screen Borders

(*Continued from page 1288*)

the eye remains sensitive to blue light when red has long become invisible (at low intensities). At high intensities the reverse is true.

This unequal response to different colors has an important bearing on the *apparent* change of *hue* of a neutral object when the intensity of illumination is varied. Take any object which ordinarily appears white, therefore reflecting all colors at certain intensities. In diminishing illumination the red light reflected by the white object will become invisible rapidly, the green normally, and the blue less than normally; the white object will appear bluish as it dulls. Conversely it will appear *yellow* as the intensity continually raised. It has, therefore become natural to associate yellowness with brightness and blueness with night. In fact, the present Lord Rayleigh has shown that the objective color of the night sky is *yellow*, that the light coming from it is composed of radiations (wave lengths) which, if as bright as daylight would appear yellow and contain very little blue. As yellow is invisible to the dark-adapted eye, the actual subjective color of the night sky is blue.

Color, then, is largely an illusion, and the illusion produced under one lighting condition is not necessarily the same as under another. It is an experimental fact that the hue, but not the saturation, of any color can be imitated by the addition of three primary colors, red, green and blue. This has most naturally led people to suppose that there are three primary color-receiving mechanisms in the eye, spoken of as the three color sensations. It is another fact that any shade whatsoever can be imitated by the further addition of white, or the virtual addition of black.

(*Continued next week*)

Katherine C. Melcher Receives A. A. G. O. Degree

Miss Katherine C. Melcher who studied the organ under Wilhelm Middleschulte and Harrison Wild of Chicago has been elected an associate member of the American Guild of Organists. Miss Melcher, who was the first organist in Michigan also studied under Dr. Edward E. Manville, President of the Detroit Institute of Musical Art, for her A. A. G. O. degree.

Thos. C. Regan to Erect New Motion Picture Studio

Thomas C. Regan has purchased five acres of ground in Van Nuyes, a town close to Hollywood, and has started the erection of a motion picture studio. According to announcement, the plant will be fully equipped and will cost in the neighborhood of $150,000.

Besides all modern equipment for the studio proper, there will be constructed on the back lot several large streets of various kinds. These will include a New England street, a Spanish, a Northwest Cabin street and typical Western town. Other types of outdoor sets will be erected later, according to the needs of the producers using the studio.

Mr. Regan will use the studio for his own production work but space will be available for other producers.

New House to Succeed Pergola, Allentown

Work will be started in the late summer or early fall on a new theatre to succeed the present Pergola theatre, in Allentown. James K. Bowen, owner of the theatre, desires to make way for a new hotel which he is promoting on the present site, and he desires also to have a more modern theatre. The new picture house will be erected on a plot which he has just purchased at the rear of the present Pergola, and which will front at Nos. 28 to 34 North Ninth street. The frontage is 104 feet and the lot is 230 feet deep.

FEATURE RELEASE CHART

Productions are Listed Alphabetically and by Months in which Released in order that the Exhibitor may have a short-cut toward such information as he may need. Short subject and comedy releases, as well as information on pictures that are coming, will be found on succeeding pages. (S. R. indicates State Right release.)

Refer to THE MOTION PICTURE NEWS BOOKING GUIDE for Productions Listed Prior to March

MARCH

Feature	Star	Distributed by	Length	Reviewed
Adventurous Sex, The	Clara Bow	Assoc. Exhib	5039 feet	Mar. 21
Air Mail, The	Special Cast	Paramount	6976 feet	Mar. 28
Beauty and the Bad Man	Special Cast	Prod. Dist. Corp	5794 feet	May 9
Beyond the Border	Harry Carey	Prod. Dist. Corp	4469 feet	April 25
Billy, The Kid	Franklyn Farnum	Inde. Pict. Corp. (S. R.)	4800 feet	
Blood and Steel	Desmond Holmes	Inde. Pict. (S. R.)	5300 feet	
Border Justice	Bill Cody	Inde. Pict. Corp. (S. R.)	5432 feet	Nov. 8
Coast Patrol, The	Kenneth McDonald	Barsky (S. R.)	5000 feet	
Confessions of a Queen	Terry-Stone	Metro-Goldwyn	5820 feet	April 4
Crimson Runner, The	Priscilla Dean	Prod. Dist. Corp	4775 feet	June 6
Daddy's Gone A'Hunting	Joyce-Marmont	Metro-Goldwyn	5851 feet	Mar. 7
Denial, The	Special Cast	Metro-Goldwyn	4791 feet	Mar. 21
Double Action Daniels	Buffalo Bill, Jr	Weiss Bros. (S. R.)	4650 feet	
Dressmaker from Paris, The	Rod La Rocque	Paramount	7080 feet	Mar. 28
Fighting Romeo, A	Al Ferguson	Davis Dist. Div.(S.R.)	5000 feet	Aug. 15
Fighting the Flames	Haines-Devore	C. B. C. (S. R.)	5800 feet	
Forbidden Cargo	Evelyn Brent	F. B. O	4850 feet	April 11
Goose Hangs High, The	Constance Bennett	Paramount	6186 feet	Feb. 14
Great Divide, The	Terry-Tearle	Metro-Goldwyn	7811 feet	Feb. 21
Head Winds	House Peters	Universal	5600 feet	Mar. 28
Hunted Woman, The	Seena Owen	Fox	4954 feet	April 4
I Want My Man	Sills-Kenyon	First National	6175 feet	April 18
Jimmie's Millions	Richard Talmadge	F. B. O	5167 feet	Feb. 28
Just Traveling	Bob Burns	Sierra Pict. (S. R.)	4400 feet	
Last Laugh, The	Emil Jannings	Universal	6519 feet	Dec. 20
Let'er Buck	Hoot Gibson	Universal	5547 feet	Jan. 3
Mad Whirl, The	May McAvoy	Universal	6184 feet	Dec. 6
Marriage in Transit	Edmund Lowe	Fox Film	4800 feet	April 11
Men and Women	Special Cast	Paramount	6223 feet	Mar. 28
Monster, The	L. Chaney-J. Arthur	Metro-Goldwyn	6435 feet	Feb. 28
My Wife and I	Special Cast	Warner Bros	6700 feet	June 6
New Lives for Old	Betty Compson	Paramount	6796 feet	Mar. 7
New Toys	Richard Barthelmess	First National	7250 feet	Feb. 21
One Year to Live	Special Cast	First National	6064 feet	Feb. 28
Percy	Charles Ray	Assoc. Exhib	5384 feet	Feb 28
Playing With Souls	Special Cast	First National	5831 feet	Mar. 14
Price of Pleasure, The	Valli-Kerry	Universal	6618 feet	June 13
Recompense	M. Prevost-M. Blue	Warner Bros	7480 feet	May 2
Renegade Holmes, M.D	Ben Wilson	Arrow (S. R.)	4947 feet	
Riders of the Purple Sage	Tom Mix	Fox	5578 feet	Mar. 28
Romance and Rustlers	Yakima Canutt	Arrow (S. R.)	4994 feet	Nov. 15
Sackcloth and Scarlet	Alice Terry	Paramount	6732 feet	Mar. 7
Sally	Colleen Moore	First National	8636 feet	Mar. 28
Scar Hanan	Yakima Canutt	F. B. O	4684 feet	April 4
Scarlet Honeymoon, The	Shirley Mason	Fox	5080 feet	Mar. 21
Seven Chances	Buster Keaton	Metro-Goldwyn	5113 feet	Mar. 28
Sign of the Cactus, The	Jack Hoxie	Universal	4938 feet	Jan. 10
Sky Raider, The	Capt. Charles Nungesser	Assoc. Exhib	6638 feet	April 4
Speed	Betty Blythe	Banner Prod. (S. R.)	6000 feet	May 30
Too Many Kisses	Richard Dix	Paramount	5759 feet	Mar. 14
Waking Up the Town	Jack Pickford	United Artists	4802 feet	April 11
Where Romance Rides	Dick Hatton	Arrow	4201 feet	
Zander the Great	Marion Davies	Metro-Goldwyn	5851 feet	May 16

APRIL

Feature	Star	Distributed by	Length	Reviewed
Adventure	P. Starke-T. Moore	Paramount	6713 feet	April 25
After Business Hours	Hammerstein-Tellegen	C B. C. (S. R.)	5800 feet	
Bandit Tamer, The	Franklyn Farnum	Inde. Pict. (S. R.)	5000 feet	
Border Vengeance	Jack Perrin	Madoc Sales (S. R.)	4500 feet	
Charmer, The	Pola Negri	Paramount	6076 feet	April 18
Code of the West	O. Moore-C. Bennett	Paramount	6777 feet	April 25
Courageous Fool, The	Reed Howes	Rayart (S. R.)		
Crowded Hour, The	Bebe Daniels	Paramount	6558 feet	May 9
Dangerous Innocence	LaPlante-E. O'Brien	Universal	6759 feet	Mar. 21
Declasse	Corinne Griffith	First National	7869 feet	April 4
Eyes of the Desert	Al Richmond	Sierra Prod. (S. R.)	4500 feet	
Fifth Avenue Models	Philbin-Kerry	Universal	6581 feet	Jan. 24
Fighting Parson, The	Al Ferguson	Davis Dist. Div.(S.R.)	5000 feet	
Fighting Sheriff, The	Bill Cody	Inde. Pict. (S. R.)	4500 feet	May 30
Friendly Enemies	Weber and Fields	Prod. Dist. Corp	6288 feet	May 9
Galloping Vengeance	Bob Custer	F. B. O	5095 feet	April 11
Getting 'Em Right	George Larkin	Rayart (S. R.)	4669 feet	
Gold and the Girl	Buck Jones	Fox	4521 feet	April 4
Go Straight	Gladys Hulette	B. P. Schulberg(S.R.)	6107 feet	May 23
Heart of a Siren, The	Barbara La Marr	First National	6700 feet	Mar. 21
How Baxter Butted In	M. Moore-D. Devore	Warner Bros	6650 feet	July 11
Justice Raffles	Henry Edwards	Cranfield & Clarke (S. R.)	6000 feet	
Kiss in the Dark, A	Special Cast	Paramount	5767 feet	April 18
Kiss Me Again	M. Prevost-M. Blue	Warner Bros	7200 feet	June 6
Love's Bargain	M. Daw-C. Brook	F. B. O	5641 feet	April 25
Madame Sans Gene	Gloria Swanson	Paramount	9994 feet	May 2
Man and Maid	Special Cast	Metro-Goldwyn	5307 feet	April 18
My Son	Nazimova-J. Pickford	First National	6500 feet	April 25
Night Club, The	R. Griffith-V. Reynolds	Paramount	5732 feet	May 16
One Way Street	Special Cast	First National	5596 feet	April 11
Proud Flesh	Special Cast	Metro-Goldwyn	5770 feet	April 25
Rearing Adventure, The	Jack Hoxie	Universal	4657 feet	Feb. 14
Ridin' Comet, The	Yakima Canutt	F. B. O	4354 feet	May 16
Rough Going	Franklyn Farnum	Indep. Pict. Corp. (S. R.)	4800 feet	
Shackled Lightning	Frank Merrill	Hercules Prod. (S. R.)		
She Wolves	Alma Rubens	Fox	5783 feet	May 9
Spaniard, The	Cortez-Goudal	Paramount	6676 feet	April 18
Sporting Venus	Special Cast	Metro-Goldwyn	5938 feet	May 23
Stop Flirting	Special Cast	Prod. Dist. Corp	5161 feet	June 6
Straight Through	Wm. Desmond	Universal	4867 feet	
Tale of a Thousand and One Nights	Special Cast	Davis Dist. Div. (S. R.)	6500 feet	Feb. 14
Tearing Through	Richard Talmadge	F. B. O.	4714 feet	May 23
That Devil Quemado	Fred Thomson	F. B. O.	4768 feet	April 4
Two-Fisted Sheriff, A	Yakima Canutt	Arrow (S. R.)	4149 feet	Dec. 6
Way of a Girl, The	Boardman-M. Moore	Metro-Goldwyn	5025 feet	April 18
Western Engagement, A	Dick Hatton	Arrow		
Wings of Youth	Madge Bellamy	Fox	5340 feet	May 16
Winning a Woman	Perrin-Hill	Rayart (S. R.)	4865 feet	

MAY

Feature	Star	Distributed by	Length	Reviewed
Alias Mary Flynn	Evelyn Brent	F. B. O.	5559 feet	May 30
Any Woman	Alice Terry	Paramount	5963 feet	June 13
Awful Truth, The	Agnes Ayres	Prod. Dist. Corp	5917 feet	July 11
Bandit's Baby, The	Fred Thomson	F. B. O.	5291 feet	June 20
Baree Son of Kazan	Wolf (dog)	Vitagraph	7 reels	May 2
Barriers of the Law	Holmes-Desmond	Indep. Pict. (S. R.)	5400 feet	
Burning Trail, The	William Desmond	Universal	4783 feet	April 18
Chickie	Mackaill-Bosworth	First National	7767 feet	May 9
Crackerjack, The	Johnny Hines	C. C. Burr (S. R.)	6500 feet	May 23
Every Man's Wife	Special Cast	Fox	4365 feet	July 4
Eve's Lover	Irene Rich	Warner Bros	6540 feet	Aug. 8
Eve's Secret	Betty Compson	Paramount	6305 feet	May 9
Fear Fighter, The	Billy Sullivan	Rayart (S. R.)		
Fighting Demon, The	Richard Talmadge	F B O	5470 feet	June 20
Fugitive, The	Ben Wilson	Arrow	4892 feet	
Golden Trails		Sanford Prod. (S. R.)	5 reels	
His Supreme Moment	B Sweet-R Colman	First National	6600 feet	April 25
Lilies of the Streets	J. Walker-V. L. Corbin	F. B. O.	7160 feet	April 25
Little French Girl, The	Alice Joyce	Paramount	5628 feet	June 13
Lunatic at Large, A	Henry Edwards	Cranfield & Clarke (S. R.)	6000 feet	
Makers of Men	Kenneth McDonald	Barsky Prod. (S. R.)	5000 feet	
Necessary Evil, The	Dana-Lyon	First National	6307 feet	May 23
Old Home Week	Thomas Meighan	Paramount	6888 feet	June 6
Phantom Rider, The	Al Richmond	Sierra Prod. (S. R.)	4750 feet	
Private Affairs	Special Cast	Prod. Dist. Corp	6132 feet	Aug. 15
Quick Change	George Larkin	Rayart (S. R.)		
Raffles, The Amateur Cracksman	House Peters	Universal	5557 feet	May 30
Rainbow Trail, The	Tom Mix	Fox	5251 feet	April 25
Red Love	Lowell-Russell	Lowell Film Prod. (S. R.)	6500 feet	May 23
Saddle Hawk, The	Hoot Gibson	Universal	5468 feet	Mar 7
Silent Sanderson	Harry Carey	Prod. Dist. Corp	4841 feet	June 20
Scandal Proof	Shirley Mason	Fox	4400 feet	June 6
School for Wives	Tearle-Holmquist	Vitagraph	6750 feet	April 11
Shock Punch, The	Richard Dix	Paramount	6151 feet	May 23
Snob Buster, The	Reed Howes	Rayart (S. R.)		
Soul Fire	Barthelmess-B Love	First National	8262 feet	May 16
Speed Wild	Maurice B "Lefty" Flynn	F. B. O	4700 feet	June 20
Talker, The	A Nilsson-L Stone	First National	7861 feet	May 23
Texas Bearcat, The	Bob Custer	F. B. O	4770 feet	
Tides of Passion	Mae Marsh	Vitagraph	6279 feet	May 9
Up the Ladder	Virginia Valli	Universal	6023 feet	Jan 31
Welcome Home	Special Cast	Paramount	5909 feet	May 30
White Fang	Strongheart (dog)	F. B. O	6579 feet	June 20
White Thunder	Yakima Canutt	F. B. O.	4550 feet	
Wildfire	Special Cast	Vitagraph	6 reels	June 20
Wolves of the Road	Yakima Canutt	Arrow	4375 feet	
Woman's Faith	Reubens-Marmont	Universal	6023 feet	Aug 15
Woman Hater, The	Helene Chadwick	Warner Brothers	7000 feet	Aug. 22

JUNE

Feature	Star	Distributed by	Length	Reviewed
Are Parents People?	Bronson-Vidor	Paramount	6586 feet	June 6
Dangerous Odds	Bill Cody	Inde. Pict. (S. R.)	4800 feet	
Desert Flower, The	Colleen Moore	First National	6837 feet	June 13
Double Fisted	Jack Perrin	Rayart (S. R.)		
Down the Border	Al Richmond	Sierra Prod. (S. R.)	4750 feet	
Faint Perfume	Seena Owen	B. P. Schulberg(S.R.)	6228 feet	July 11
Grounds for Divorce	Florence Vidor	Paramount	5712 feet	July 4
Happy Warrier, The		Vitagraph	6075 feet	July 18
Hearts and Spurs	Buck Jones	Fox	4600 feet	June 20
Human Tornado, The	Yakima Canutt	F. B. O.	4472 feet	
I'll Show You the Town	Reginald Denny	Universal	7400 feet	June 6
Introduce Me	Douglas MacLean	Assoc. Exhib	5980 feet	Mar. 21
Just a Woman	Windsor-Tearle	First National	6500 feet	June 6
Light of Western Stars	Special Cast	Paramount	6652 feet	July 4
Lost—a Wife	Special Cast	Paramount	6420 feet	June 27
Making of O'Malley, The	Milton Sills	First National	7571 feet	July 4
Man from Lone Mountain, The	Ben Wilson	Arrow	4530 feet	
Man in Blue	Herbert Rawlinson	Universal	5706 feet	Feb. 21
Marry Me	Special Cast	Paramount	5586 feet	
Meddler, The	William Desmond	Universal	4890 feet	May 23
Mike		Metro-Goldwyn		
Mist in the Valley	Alma Taylor	Cranfield & Clarke (S. R.)	5500 feet	
My Lady's Lips	Clara Bow	B. P. Schulberg (S.R.)	6609 feet	Aug 15
Off the Highway	Wm. V. Mong	Prod. Dist.	7641 feet	
Paths to Paradise	Compson-R. Griffith	Paramount	6741 feet	June 27
Pioneers of the West		Sanford Prod. (S. R.)	5 reels	
Ridin' Easy	Dick Hatton	Arrow	4483 feet	
Ridin' Thunder	Jack Hoxie	Universal	4354 feet	May 23
Rough Stuff	George Larkin	Rayart (S. R.)		
Shattered Lives	Special Cast	Gotham (S. R.)	6 reels	July 4

Feature	Star	Distributed by	Length	Reviewed
Smooth as Satin	Evelyn Brent	F. B. O	6003 feet	July 4
Texas Trail, The	Harry Carey	Prod. Dist. Corp	4720 feet	July 18
Tracked in the Snow Country	Rin-Tin-Tin (dog)	Warner Brothers	6900 feet	Aug. 1
White Monkey, The	La Marr-T. Holding	First National	6121 feet	July 4
Wild Bull's Lair, The	Fred Thompson	F. B. O.	5280 feet	Aug. 15
Youth's Gamble	Reed Howes	Rayart (S. R.)	5264 feet	

JULY

Feature	Star	Distributed by	Length	Reviewed
Bloodhound, The	Bob Custer	F. B. O.	4789 feet	
Cold Nerve	Bill Cody	Inde. Pict. (S. R.)	5000 feet	
Danger Signal, The	Jane Novak	Columbia Pict. (S.R.)	5502 feet	Aug. 15
Don Daredevil	Jack Hoxie	Universal	4810 feet	
Drug Store Cowboy, The	Franklyn Farnum	Ind. Pict. Corp. (S.R.)	5100 feet	Feb. 7
Duped	Holmes-Desmond	Ind. Pict. (S. R.)	5400 feet	
Fighting Youth		Columbia Pict. (S.R.)		
Lady Who Lied, The	L. Stone-V. Valli	First National	7111 feet	July 18
Lady Robinhood	Evelyn Brent	F. B. O	5582 feet	Aug 22
Manicure Girl, The	Bebe Daniels	Paramount	5959 feet	June 27
Marriage Whirl, The	C. Griffith-H. Ford	First National	7672 feet	July 25
Mysterious Stranger, The	Richard Talmadge	F. B. O	5270 feet	
Night Life of New York	Special Cast	Paramount	6998 feet	July 4
Pipes of Pan	Alma Taylor	Cranfield & Clarke (S. R.)	6300 feet	
Ranger of the Big Pines, The	Kenneth Harlan	Vitagraph	5800 feet	Aug. 8
Scarlet West, The	Frazer-Bow	First National	8391 feet	July 25
Secret of Black Canyon, The	Dick Hatton	Arrow		
Strange Rider, The	Yakima Canutt	Arrow		
Taming the West	Hoot Gibson	Universal	5427 feet	Feb. 28
Trailed	Al Richmond	Sierra Prod. (S. R.)	4750 feet	
White Desert, The	Special Cast	Metro-Goldwyn	6345 feet	July 18

AUGUST

Feature	Star	Distributed by	Length	Reviewed
American Pluck	George Walsh	Chadwick	5000 feet	July 11
Beggar on Horseback, A	Ralston-Nissen	Paramount	6800 feet	June 20
Business of Love, The	E. Horton-M. Bellamy	Astor Dist. Corp		
Children of the Whirlwind	Lionel Barrymore	Arrow		
Don Q	Douglas Fairbanks	United Artists	10264 feet	June 27
Drusilla With a Million	Special Cast	F. B. O	7391 feet	May 30
Fine Clothes	L. Stone-A. Rubens	First National	6971 feet	Aug. 15
Girl Who Wouldn't Work, The	Lionel Barrymore	B. P. Schulberg (S.R.)	5979 feet	Sept. 5
Gold Rush, The	Charles Chaplin	United Artists	8500 feet	Aug. 8
Halfway Girl, The	Doris Kenyon	First National	7570 feet	Aug. 8
Headlines	Alice Joyce	Assoc. Exhib	5600 feet	July 25
Her Sister From Paris	C. Talmadge	First National	7255 feet	Aug. 15
In the Name of Love	Cortez-Nissen	Paramount	5904 feet	Sept. 5
Isle of Hope, The	Richard Talmadge	Film Book. Offices	5800 feet	Sept. 5
Kivalina of the Ice Lands	Native Cast	Pathe	6 reels	July 11
Knockout, The	Milton Sills	First National		
Limited Mail, The	Monte Blue	Warner Brothers	6250 feet	
Love Hour, The	Ruth Clifford	Vitagraph	5900 feet	
Lover's Oath, The	Ramon Novarro	Astor Dist Corp		
Lucky Devil, The	Richard Dix	Paramount	5935 feet	July 18
Lucky Horseshoes	Tom Mix	Fox	5000 feet	Aug. 29
My Pal	Dick Hatton	Arrow		
Overland Limited, The		Gotham Prod. (S. R.)	6389 feet	Aug. 8
Parisian Love	Bow-Tellegen	B. P. Schulberg (S.R.)	6324 feet	Aug. 22
Penalty of Jazz, The		Columbia Pict. (S.R.)		
Quo Vadis	Emil Jannings	First National	8945 feet	Feb. 28
Range Justice	Dick Hatton	Arrow		
Romola	Gish Sisters	Metro-Goldwyn	10875 feet	Dec. 13
Rugged Water	Special Cast	Paramount	6015 feet	Aug. 1
Shining Adventure, The	Percy Marmont	Astor Dist. Corp		
Slave of Fashion, A	Special Cast	Metro-Goldwyn	5906 feet	Aug. 1
Speed Demon, The		Columbia Pict. (S.R.)		
Street of Forgotten Men	Special Cast	Paramount	6366 feet	Aug. 1
Ten Commandments	Special Cast	Paramount	9980 feet	Jan. 5-24
Unholy Three	Lon Chaney	Metro-Goldwyn	6848 feet	Aug. 15
That Man Jack	Bob Custer	F. B. O	5032 feet	Aug. 22
Unwritten Law, The		Columbia Pict. (S.R.)		
Wife Who Wasn't Wanted, The	Irene Rich	Warner Brothers	6400 feet	
Wizard of Oz	Larry Semon	Chadwick	6300 feet	Apr. 25
Wrongdoers, The	Lionel Barrymore	Astor Dist. Corp		

SEPTEMBER

Feature	Star	Distributed by	Length	Reviewed
Amazing Quest, The	Henry Edwards	Cranfield & Clarke	5500 feet	
As No Man Has Loved	Edward Hearn	Fox	10000 feet	Feb. 28
Below The Line	Rin-Tin-Tin (dog)	Warner Brothers	6100 feet	
Black Cyclone	Rex (horse)	Pathe		May 30
Bobbed Hair	Prevost-Harlan	Warner Brothers	6700 feet	
California Straight Ahead	Reginald Denny	Universal		
Classified	Corinne Griffith	First National		
Coast of Folly	Gloria Swanson	Paramount		
Crack of Dawn	Reed Howes	Rayart (S. R.)		
Cyclone Cavalier	Reed Howes	Rayart (S. R.)		
Dark Angel, The	R. Colman-V. Dana	First National		
Freshman, The	Harold Lloyd	Pathe		July 25
Graustark	Norma Talmadge	First National		
Havoc	Special Cast	Fox	9200 feet	Aug. 29
High and Handsome	"Lefty" Flynn	F. B. O.	5669 feet	
If Marriage Fails	J. Logan-C. Brook	F. B. O	6006 feet	May 23
Keep Smiling	Monty Banks	Assoc. Exhib	5400 feet	Aug. 1
Let's Go Gallagher	Tom Tyler	Film Book. Offices		
Little Annie Rooney	Mary Pickford	United Artists		
Lost World, The	Special Cast	First National	9700 feet	Feb. 21
Manhattan Madness	Dempsey-Taylor	Assoc. Exhib	5500 feet	July 25
Man Who Found Himself	Thomas Meighan	Paramount	7168 feet	Sept. 5
Marrying Money		Truart (S. R.)	5800 feet	
Mystic, The	Special Cast	Metro-Goldwyn		
Never the Twain Shall Meet	Stewart-Lytell	Metro-Goldwyn	8143 feet	Aug. 8
New Champion, The		Columbia Pict. (S.R.)		
Not So Long Ago	Betty Bronson	Paramount	6943 feet	Aug. 8
Other Woman's Story		B. P. Schulberg		
Parisian Nights	E. Hammerstein - L. Tellegen	F. B. O	6278 feet	June 20
Pretty Ladies	Zazu Pitts	Metro-Goldwyn	5828 feet	July 25
Prince of Broadway, The	George Walsh	Chadwick		
Ridin' the Wind	Fred Thomson	Film Book. Offices		
Sealed Lips		Columbia Pict. (S.R.)		
Shore Leave	Barthelmess-Mackaill	First National	6856 feet	Aug. 29
Siege	Virginia Valli	Universal	6424 feet	June 20
Some Pun'kins	Chas. Ray	Chadwick		

Feature	Star	Distributed by	Length	Reviewed
Son of His Father	Special Cast	Paramount	7009 feet	
Souls for Sables		Tiffany (S. R.)	6500 feet	
S. O. S. Perils of the Sea		Columbia Pict. (S.R.)		
Spook Ranch	Hoot Gibson	Universal	5147 feet	May 2
Sun Up	Special Cast	Metro-Goldwyn		Aug. 29
Teaser, The	Laura La Plante	Universal	6967 feet	May 30
Three in Exile		Truart (S. R.)	5800 feet	
Three Weeks in Paris	M. Moore-D. Devore	Warner Brothers	5900 feet	
Three Wise Crooks	Evelyn Brent	Film Book. Offices		
Throwback, The	Special Cast	Universal		
Timber Wolf, The	Buck Jones	Fox	4809 feet	
Trouble With Wives, The	Vidor-T. Moore	Paramount	6489 feet	Aug. 15
Unchastened Woman, The	Theda Bara	Chadwick		
Wall Street Whiz, The	Richard Talmadge	Film Book. Offices		
What Fools Men	Stone-Mason	First National		
Wheel, The	Special Cast	Fox	7264 feet	Aug. 29
White Outlaw, The	Jack Hoxie	Universal	4830 feet	June 27
Wild Horse Mesa	Special Cast	Paramount	7221 feet	Aug. 22
Wild, Wild Susan	Bebe Daniels	Paramount		
With This Ring	Mills-Tellegen	B. P. Schulberg		

OCTOBER

Feature	Star	Distributed by	Length	Reviewed
Bells, The	Lionel Barrymore	Chadwick		
Circus Cyclone, The	Art Acord	Universal	4609 feet	Aug. 22
Dollar Down	Ruth Roland	Truart (S. R.)	5800 feet	Aug. 29
Everlasting Whisper, The	Tom Mix	Fox		
Exchange of Wives, An	Special Cast	Metro-Goldwyn		
Fate of a Flirt, The		Columbia (S. R.)		
Golden Princess, The	Bronson-Hamilton	Paramount	8584 feet	
Great Sensation, The		Columbia (S. R.)		
He's a Prince	Raymond Griffith	Paramount		
His Buddy's Wife	Glenn Hunter	Assoc. Exhib	5600 feet	July 25
Iron Horse, The		Fox Film Corp	11335 feet	Sept. 13
John Forrest	Henry Edwards	Cranfeild&Clark(S.R.)	5000 feet	
Lew Tyler's Wives		B. P. Schulberg (S. R.)		
Lovers in Quarantine	Daniels-Ford	Paramount		
Midshipman, The	Ramon Novarro	Metro-Goldwyn		
Morals for Men		Tiffany (S. R.)	6500 feet	
New Brooms	Hamilton-Love	Paramount		
Perfect Clown, The	Larry Semon	Chadwick		
Pony Express, The	Betty Compson	Paramount		
Sally of the Sawdust	Fields-Dempster	United Artists	9500 feet	Aug. 15
Sporting Chance, The		Tiffany (S. R.)	6500 feet	July 4
Thank U	Special Cast	Fox		
Tower of Lies	Chaney-Shearer	Metro-Goldwyn		
Tumbleweeds	Wm. S. Hart	United Artists		
Under the Rouge	Tom Moore	Assoc. Exhib	6500 feet	July 25
Winds of Chance	A. Nilsson-B. Lyon	First National	9753 feet	Aug. 29

NOVEMBER

Feature	Star	Distributed by	Length	Reviewed
Ancient Highway, The	Holt-Vidor	Paramount		
Best People, The	Special Cast	Paramount		
Blue Blood	George Walsh	Chadwick		
Camille of the Barbary Coast	Busch-O. Moore	Assoc. Exhib	5600 feet	Aug. 1
Cobra	Valentino-Naldi	Paramount		
Don't	S. O'Neill-B. Roach	Metro-Goldwyn		
Fifty-Fifty	L.Barrymore-H.Hampton	Assoc. Exhib	5564 feet	June 20
Fight to a Finish, A		Columbia (S. R.)		
Fighting Heart, The	Geo. O'Brien	Fox	6978 feet	
Flower of Night	Pola Negri	Paramount		
King on Main St., The	Adolphe Menjou	Paramount		
Lightning		Tiffany (S. R.)	6500 feet	
Little Bit of Broadway	Ray-Starke	Metro-Goldwyn		
Merry Widow	Mae Murray	Metro-Goldwyn		
Price of Success, The	Alice Lake	Columbia (S. R.)		
Silent Witness, The		Truart (S. R.)	5800 feet	
Stage Struck	Gloria Swanson	Paramount		
Time the Comedian		Metro-Goldwyn		
Transcontinental Limited	Special Cast	Chadwick (S. R.)		
Vanishing American	Dix-Wilson	Paramount		
Winner, The	Charley Ray	Chadwick (S. R.)		

Comedy Releases

Feature	Star	Distributed by	Length	Reviewed
Across the Hall	Edna Marian	Universal	2 reels	
Adventures of Adenoid	Aesop's Fables	Pathe	1 reel	April 25
After a Reputation	Edna Marian	Universal	2 reels	
Air Tight	Bobby Vernon	Educational	2 reels	June 13
Alice's Egg Plant	"Cartoon"	M. J. Winkler (S. R.)	1 reel	
Alice Stagestruck	Margie Gay	M. J. Winkler (S.R.)	1 reel	July 18
All Aboard		Fox	2 reels	
Almost a Husband	Buddy Messinger	Universal	2 reels	
Amateur Detective	Earle Foxe	Fox	2 reels	
Andy in Hollywood	Joe Murphy	Universal	2 reels	
Andy Takes a Flyer	"The Gumps"	Universal	2 reels	
Apache, The	Earle Foxe	Fox Film	2 reels	
Apollo's Pretty Sister		Fox	2 reels	
Are Husbands Human?	James Finlayson	Pathe	1 reel	April 11
Artists' Blues	G. Joy-J. Moore	Rayart (S. R.)	2 reels	
Ask Grandma	"Our Gang"	Pathe	2 reels	May 30
At the Seashore	Monkey	Fox	2 reels	
At the Zoo	Aesops Fables	Pathe	1 reel	
Baby Blues	Mickey Bennett	Educational	2 reels	
Bachelors	Special Cast	Universal		
Bad Bill Brodie	Charles Chase	Pathe	2 reels	
Bad Boy	Charles Chase	Pathe	2 reels	April 11
Balboa Discovers Hollywood	"Red Head"	Sering D. Wilson (S.R.)	1 reel	
Bark is the Woods	Harry Langdon	Pathe	2 reels	
Bashful Jim	Ralph Graves	Pathe	2 reels	Mar. 21
Be Careful	Jimmie Adams	Educational Film	2 reels	Aug. 22
Below Zero	Lige Conley	Educational	2 reels	July 4
Beware	Lige Conley	Educational Film	2 reels	Aug. 1
Big Chief Ko-Ko (Out of the Inkwell)	"Cartoon"	Red Seal Pict. (S. R.)	1 reel	
Big Game Hunter, The	Earle Foxe	Fox	2 reels	
Bigger and Better Pictures	"Aesop's Fables"	Pathe	1 reel	
Big Red Riding Hood	Charley Chase	Pathe	1 reel	May 9

Feature	Star	Distributed by	Length	Reviewed
Black Gold Bricks	Roach-Edwards	Universal	1 reel	April 18
Black Hand Blues	"Spat Family"	Pathe	2 reels	April 18
Bobby Bumbs & Co.	Cartoon	Educational	1 reel	July 4
Boys Will Be Joys	"Our Gang"	Pathe	2 reels	July 25
Brainless Horsemen		Fox	2 reels	
Brass Button	Billy West	Arrow	2 reels	
Breaking the Ice	Ralph Graves	Pathe	2 reels	April 11
Bride Tamer, The	Milburn Moranti	Sierra Pict. (S. R.)	2 reels	
Bubbles	"Aesop's Fables"	Pathe	1 reel	Aug. 15
Bugville Field Day	"Aesop's Fables"	Pathe	1 reel	July 25
Business Engagement, A		Fox	2 reels	
Butterfly Man, The		Fox	2 reels	
California Here We Come	"The Gumps"	Universal	2 reels	
Cat's Shimmy, The	"Kid Noah"	Sering D. Wilson (S.R.)	1 reel	
Chasing the Chasers	Jas. Finlayson	Pathe	1 reel	July 4
City Bound	Charles Puffy	Universal	1 reel	
Clean-Up Week	"Aesop's Fables"	Pathe	1 reel	Mar. 7
Clear the Way	Buddy Messinger	Universal	2 reels	
Cleopatra and Her Easy Mark	"Cartoon"	Sering D. Wilson (S.R.)	1 reel	
Cloudhopper, The	Larry Semon	Educational	2 reels	June 6
Columbus Discovers a New Whirl		Sering Wilson (S. R.)	1 reel	
Cotton King	Lloyd Hamilton	Educational	2 reels	
Crime Crushers	Lige Conley	Educational	2 reels	
Crying for Love	Eddie Gordon	Universal	2 reels	Aug. 15
Cupid's Boots	Ralph Graves	Pathe	2 reels	July 25
Cure, The (Out of the Inkwell)	"Cartoon"	Red Seal Pict. (S. R.)	1 reel	
Curses	Al. St. John	Educational	2 reels	May 23
Daddy Goes A Grunting		Pathe	2 reels	July 18
Darkest Africa	"Aesop's Fables"	Pathe	1 reels	
Day's Outing, A	"The Gumps"	Universal	2 reels	
Depp Stuff	Aesop's Fables	Pathe	1 reel	April 25
Dinky Doodle and Cinderella	"Dinky Doodle"	F. B. O	1 reel	
Dinky Doodle and Robinson Crusoe	"Dinky Doodle"	F. B. O	1 reel	
Discord In "A" Flat	Arthur Lake	Universal	1 reel	July 25
Dog Days	"Our Gang"	Pathe	2 reels	Mar. 14
Dog 'On It	Bobby Dunn	Arrow	2 reels	
Dome Doctor, The	Larry Semon	Educational	2 reels	
Don't Pinch	Bobby Vernon	Educational	2 reels	April 25
Don't Worry	Wanda Wiley	Universal	2 reels	Mar. 21
Dragon Alley	Jackie McHugh	Educational	2 reels	May 16
Dr. Pyckle and Mr. Pride	Stan Laurel	Film Booking Offices	2 reels	
Dry Up	Singleton Burkett	Universal	2 reels	July 25
Dumb and Daffy	Al. St. John	Fox	2 reels	
Dynamite Doggie	Al. St. John	Educational	2 reels	Mar. 21
Echoes From the Alps	Aesop's Fables	Pathe	1 reel	May 23
End of the World, The	Aesop's Fables	Pathe	1 reel	
Etiquette	Jimmy Aubrey	Film Book. Offices	2 reels	
Excuse My Glove	"Spat Family"	Pathe	2 reels	Mar 21
Expensive Ebony	"Ebenezer Ebony"	Sering Wilson (S. R.)	1 reel	
Failure		Fox	2 reels	
Fares Please	Al. St. John	Educational	2 reels	May 16
Fast Worker, A	Aesop's Fables	Pathe	1 reel	
Felix Full O'Fight	"Cartoon"	M. J. Winkler (S. R.)	1 reel	
Felix Gets His Fill	"Cartoon"	M. J. Winkler (S. R.)	1 reel	
Felix Grabs His Grub	"Cartoon"	M. J. Winkler (S. R.)	1 reel	
First Love	"Our Gang"	Pathe	2 reels	
Fisherman's Luck	"Aesop's Fables"	Pathe	1 reel	
For Hire	Edward Gordon	Universal		
For Love of a Gal	"Aesop's Fables"	Pathe	1 reel	July 25
Found World, The	"The Gumps"	Universal	2 reels	
Fun's Fun	Bowes-Vance	Educational	1 reel	June 6
Getting Trimmed	Wanda Wiley	Universal	2 reels	April 18
Giddap	Special Cast	Pathe	2 reels	Mar. 21
Going Great	Eddie Nelson	Educational	2 reels	June 13
Goldfish's Pajamas	"Kid Noah"	Sering D. Wilson (S.R.)	1 reel	
Good Morning Nurse	Ralph Graves	Pathe	2 reels	May 30
Good Scouts	"Reg'lar Kids"	M. J. Winkler (S. R.)	2 reels	
Great Guns	Bobby Vernon	Educational	2 reels	Feb. 21
Gridiron Gertie	Wanda Wiley	Universal	2 reels	
Guilty Conscience, A	Eddie Gordon	Universal		
Gypping the Gypsies	"Ebonezer Ebony"	Sering Wilson (S. R.)	1 reel	
Half a Hero	Lloyd Hamilton	Educational	2 reels	Mar. 7
Half a Man	Stan Laurel	Pathe	2 reels	
Hard Boiled	Charley Chase	Pathe	2 reels	Mar. 21
Hard Working Loafer, The	Arthur Stone	Pathe		
Haunted Honeymoon	Tryon-Mehaffey	Pathe	2 reels	Feb. 28
Heart Trouble	Arthur Lake	Universal	1 reel	July 4
Hello, Goodby	Lige Conley	Educational	2 reels	May 30
Hello, Hollywood	Lige Conley	Educational	2 reels	Mar. 28
Helping Hand	Jimmy Aubrey	F. B. O	2 reels	
Help Yourself		Fox	2 reels	
Here's Your Hat	Arthur Lake	Universal	1 reel	May 9
Her Lucky Leap	Wanda Wiley	Universal	2 reels	
He Who Gets Crowned	Jimmy Aubrey	F. B. O	2 reels	
He Who Got Smacked	Ralph Graves	Pathe	2 reels	May 9
Hey! Taxi!	Bobby Dunn	Arrow	2 reels	
High Hopes	Bowes-Vance	Educational	1 reel	Feb. 14
High Jinx, A		Fox	2 reels	
His Marriage Wow	Harry Langdon	Pathe	2 reels	Mar. 7
Hold My Baby	Glenn Tryon	Pathe	2 reels	April 25
Home Scouts	Jimmie Aubrey	F. B. O.	2 reels	
Honeymoon Heaven		Sering Wilson (S. R.)	1 reel	
Horace Greeley, Jr	Harry Langdon	Pathe	2 reels	June 6
Horrible Hollywood		Lee-Bradford (S. R.)		
Hot and Heavy	Eddie Nelson	Educational	2 reels	July 18
Hot Dog	Animal	C B C (S. R.)	2 reels	
Hot Times in Iceland	Aesop's Fables	Pathe	1 reel	
House of Flickers, The		Fox	2 reels	
House that Dinky Built	(Cartoon)	F. B. O	1 reel	
Housing Shortage, The	"Aesop's Fables"	Pathe	1 reel	
Hysterical History (Series)		Universal	1 reel	
Ice Boy, An	"Ebonezer Ebony"	Sering D. Wilson (S.R.)	1 reel	
Ice Cold	Arthur Lake	Universal	1 reel	June 13
In Dutch	Aesop's Fables	Pathe	1 reel	
Innocent Husbands	Charley Chase	Pathe	2 reels	Aug. 1
Inside Out	Bowes-Vance	Educational	1 reel	Mar. 28
Into the Grease	James Finlayson	Pathe	1 reel	June 27
Iron Mule	Al St. John	Educational	2 reels	April 18
Iron Nag, The	Billy Bevan	Pathe	2 reels	Aug. 15
Is Marriage the Bunk?	Charles Chase	Pathe	1 reel	April 4
Isn't Life Terrible?	Charles Chase	Pathe	2 reels	July 4
Itching for Revenge	Eddie Gordon	Universal	2 reels	Mar. 7
It's All Wrong	Karr-Engle	Universal		
James Boys' Sister		Sering Wilson (S. R.)	1 reel	
Jungle Bike Riders	Aesop's Fables	Pathe	1 reel	Mar. 14
Just in Time	Wanda Wiley	Universal	2 reels	July 11
Kicked About	Eddie Gordon	Universal	2 reels	Mar. 14
Kidding Captain Kidd	"Cartoon"	Sering Wilson (S. R.)	1 reel	
King Cotton	Lloyd Hamilton	Educational	2 reels	May 9
King Dumb	Jimmy Aubrey	F. B. O	2 reels	
Knocked About	Eddie Gordon	Universal	2 reels	June 13
Ko-Ko Trains Animals (out of the Inkwell)	"Cartoon"	Red Seal Pict. (S.R.)	1 reel	
Lead Pipe Cinch, A	Al Alt	Universal		
Lion Love		Fox	2 reels	Feb. 28
Lion's Whiskers		Pathe	2 reels	April 18
Little Red Riding Hood	"Dinky Doodle"	F. B. O	1 reel	
Locked Out	Arthur Lake	Universal	1 reel	May 30
Looking for Sally	Charles Chase	Pathe	2 reels	May 9
Look Out	Bowes-Vance	Educational Film	1 reel	Aug. 1
Lost Cord, The	Bert Roach	Universal	1 reel	Feb. 21
Love and Lions		Fox	2 reels	
Love Bug, The	"Our Gang"	Pathe	2 reels	April 4
Love Goofy	Jimmy Adams	Educational	2 reels	Mar. 7
Love Sick	Constance Darling	Universal	2 reels	May 23
Love's Tragedy		Sering Wilson (S. R.)	1 reel	
Lucky Accident, The	Charles Puffy	Universal	1 reel	July 18
Lucky Leap, A	Wanda Wiley	Universal	2 reels	
Lucky Stars	Harry Langdon	Pathe	2 reels	Aug. 15
Madame Sans Jane	Glenn Tryon	Pathe	2 reels	
Marriage Circus, The	Ben Turpin	Pathe	2 reels	April 11
Married Neighbors	Engle-Darling	Universal	2 reels	July 4
Mary, Queen of Tots	"Our Gang"	Pathe	2 reels	Aug. 22
Meet the Ambassador	Jimmy Aubrey	F. B. O	2 reels	
Mellow Quartette	Pen & Ink Vaudeville	Educational	1 reel	April 4
Merrymakers	Bowes-Vance	Educational	1 reel	Mar. 28
Met by Accident	Wanda Wiley	Universal	2 reels	
Milky Way, The	Charles Puffy	Universal	1 reel	July 25
Miss Fixit	Wanda Wiley	Universal	2 reels	
Monkey Business	"Pen & Ink Vaude"	Educational	1 reel	May 9
Moonlight Nights	Gloria Joy	Rayart (S. R.)	2 reels	
Nearly Rich	Charles Puffy	Universal	1 reel	
Neptune's Stepdaughter		Fox	2 reels	
Nero's Jazz Band		Sering Wilson (S. R.)	1 reel	
Never Fear	Bowes-Vance	Educational	1 reel	
Never on Time		Lee-Bradford	2 reels	
Never Weaken	Lloyd reissue	Assoc. Exhib	2237 feet	
Nice Pickle, A	Edwards-Roach	Universal	1 reel	
Nicely Rewarded	Chas. Puffy	Universal	1 reel	June 27
Night Hawks		Educational Film	2 reels	
Nobody Wins	Arthur Lake	Universal	1 reel	
No Place to Go	Arthur Lake	Universal	1 reel	
Now or Never (reissue)	Harold Lloyd	Assoc. Exhib	3 reels	
Office Help	"Aesop's Fables"	Pathe	1 reel	June 27
Official Officers	"Our Gang"	Pathe	2 reels	June 27
Oh, Bridget	Walter Hiers	Educational	2 reels	
Oh, What a Flirt	Jimmy Aubrey	Film Book. Offices	2 reels	
Oh, What a Gump	"The Gumps"	Universal	2 reels	
Old Family Toothbrush	"Kid Noah"	Sering Wilson (S. R.)	1 reel	
On Duty	Wanda Wiley	Universal	2 reels	
One Glorious Fourth	"Reg'lar Kids"	M. J. Winkler (S. R.)	2 reels	
On the Go		Fox	2 reels	
Orphan, The	Al Joy	Ricardo Films, Inc. (S.R.)		
Over the Bottom	Stan Laurel	F. B. O	2 reels	
Over the Plate	Aesops Fable	Pathe	1 reel	Aug. 22
Over Here	Harry Langdon	Pathe	2 reels	
Paging A Wife	Al Alt	Universal	2 reels	Aug. 1
Papa's Darling		Fox	2 reels	
Papa's Pet	Roach-Edwards	Universal	1 reel	April 11
Parisian Knight, A	Earle Foxe	Fox	2 reels	
Peacemakers, The		Fox	2 reels	
Pegg's Love Affair		Screen Art Dist		
Peggy the Vamp	Rosalie Morlin	Davis Distr	2 reels	Oct. 11
Permanent Waves	"Aesop's Fables"	Pathe	1 reel	
Permit Me	Bowes-Vance	Educational	1 reel	July 11
Pie-Eyed	Stan Laurel	F. B. O	2 reels	
Pie Man, The	"Aesop's Fables"	Pathe	1 reel	Mar. 21
Plain Clothes	Harry Langdon	Pathe	2 reels	Mar. 28
Plain and Fancy Girls	Charles Chase	Pathe	1 reel	Mar. 14
Plain Luck	Edna Marian	Universal	2 reels	
Pleasure Bound	Lige Conley	Educational	2 reels	Aug. 22
Plenty of Nerve	Edna Marian	Universal	2 reels	July 4
Polo Kid, The	Eddie Gordon	Universal	2 reels	July 18
Poor Sap, The		Fox	2 reels	
Powdered Chickens	Edna Marian	Universal	2 reels	Mar. 28
Props' Dash for Cash	Earl Hurd (Cartoon)	Educational	1 reel	
Putting on Airs	Edna Marian	Universal	2 reels	April 11
Puzzled by Crosswords	Eddie Gordon	Universal	2 reels	Mar. 7
Queen of Aces	Wanda Wiley	Universal	2 reels	May 16
Raid, The	Gloria Joy	Rayart Pictures	2 reels	
Raisin' Cain	Constance Darling	Universal	2 reels	April 4
Rapid Transit	Al. St. John	Educational	2 reels	
Rarin' Romeo	Walter Hiers	Educational	2 reels	Mar. 28
Raspberry Romance	Ben Turpin	Pathe	2 reels	Feb. 28
Red Pepper	Al. St. John	Educational	2 reels	Arpil 4
Regular Girl, A	Wanda Wiley	Universal	2 reels	
Riders of the Kitchen Range	Mohar-Engle	Pathe	1 reel	June 6
Remember When	Harry Langdon	Pathe	2 reels	April 25
Rip Without a Wink	"Redhead"	Sering Wilson (S. R.)	1 reel	
Ripe Melodrama, A		Sering Wilson (S. R.)	1 reel	
Rivals	Billy West	Arrow	2 reels	
Robinson Crusoe Returns on Friday	"Redhead"	Sering Wilson (S. R.)	1 reel	
Rock Bottom	Bowes-Vance	Educational	1 reel	May 9
Robbing the Rube		Lee-Bradford Corp.	2 reels	
Rolling Stones	Charles Puffy	Universal	1 reel	May 30
Rough Party	Al Alt	Universal	2 reels	
Royal Four-Flush	"Spat Family"	Pathe	2 reels	June 13
Runaway Balloon, The	"Aesop's Fables"	Pathe	1 reel	June 27
Runt, The	"Aesop's Fables"	Pathe	1 reel	June 6
Sailor Papa, A	Glenn Tryon	Pathe	2 reels	April 4
Saturday		Davis Dist. Div	2 reels	
Say It With Flour		Fox	2 reels	
Sheiks of Bagdad		Pathe	1 reel	May 9
Sherlock Sleuth	Arthur Stone	Pathe	2 reels	July 11
Ship Shape	Vance-Bowes	Educational	1 reel	April 18
Shootin' Injuns	"Our Gang"	Pathe	2 reels	May 9
Short Pants	Arthur Lake	Universal	1 reel	Aug. 1
Should a Husband Tell?		Red Seal Pict. (S.R.)	1 reel	
Should Husbands Be Watched?	Charles Chase	Pathe	1 reel	Mar. 14
Sir Walt and Lizzie		Sering Wilson (S. R.)	1 reel	
Sit Tight	Jimmie Adams	Educational	2 reels	May 30
Skinners in Silk		Pathe	2 reels	May 16
Sky Jumper, The	Earle Foxe	Fox	2 reels	
Skyscraper, The	Harry Langdon	Principal Pict. (S. R.)	2 reels	
Sleeping Sickness	Edwards-Roach	Universal	1 reel	May 30
Slick Articles	Engle-Karr	Universal	2 reels	May 30
Smoked Out	Lake-Hasbrouck	Universal	1 reel	April 11
Sneezing Beezers	Billy Bevan	Pathe	2 reels	July 18
Snow-Hawk	Stan Laurel	F. B. O	2 reels	
Soap	"Aesop's Fables"	Pathe	1 reel	
S. O. S.	"Aesop's Fables"	Pathe	1 reel	
Spanish Romeo, A (Van Bibber)		Fox	1 reel	
Speak Easy	Charley Puffy	Universal	1 reel	Aug. 22
Speak Freely	Edna Marian	Universal	2 reels	
Stick Around	Bobby Dunn	Arrow	2 reels	

Feature	Star	Distributed by	Length	Reviewed
Stop, Look and Whistle		Fox	2 reels	
Storm, The (Out of the Inkwell)	"Cartoon"	Red Seal Pict. (S.R.)	1 reel	
Stranded	Edna Marian	Universal	2 reels	
Super-Hooper-Dyne Lizzies		Pathe	2 reels	June 13
Sure Mike!	Martha Sleeper	Pathe	1 reel	May 23
Sweet Marie		Fox	2 reels	Aug. 29
Tame Men and Wild Women		Pathe	2 reels	Aug. 15
Teaser Island	"Redhead"	Sering Wilson (S. R.)	1 reel	
Tee for Two	Alice Day	Pathe	2 reels	Aug. 1
Tell It To a Policeman	Glenn Tryon	Pathe	2 reels	May 23
Tender Feet	Walter Hiers	Educational	2 reels	May 23
Tenting Out	Roache-Edwards	Universal	1 reel	Mar. 23
This Week-End		Lee-Bradford (S. R.)		
Thundering Landlords	Glenn Tryon	Pathe	2 reels	June 27
Too Young to Marry	Buddy Messinger	Universal	2 reels	
Tough Night, A	Jimmy Callahan	Aywon Film	2 reels	
Tourist, The	Harry Langdon	Educational Film	2 reels	Aug. 15
Tourists De Luxe	Hayes-Karr	Universal	2 reels	May 16
Transients in Arcadia		Fox	2 reels	
Transatlantic Flight, A	"Aesop's Fables"	Pathe	1 reel	
Twins	Stan Laurel	F. B. O	2 reels	
Two Cats and a Bird	"Cartoon"	Educational	1 reel	Mar. 14
Two Poor Fish	Earl Hurd cartoon	Educational	1 reel	May 30
Uncle Tom's Girl	Edna Marian	Universal	2 reels	
Unwelcome	Charles Puffy	Universal	1 reel	June 27
Waiting	Lloyd Hamilton	Educational	2 reels	July 11
Wake Up	Bowes-Vance	Educational	1 reel	June 13
Water Wagons	Special Cast	Pathe	2 reels	Feb. 21
Welcome Dangar	Bowes-Vance	Educational	1 reel	Feb. 23
West is West	Billy West	Arrow	2 reels	
What Price Goofy	Charley Chase	Pathe	2 reels	June 6
When Dumbells Ring		Fox	2 reels	
When Men Were Men	"Aesop's Fables"	Pathe	1 reel	July 25
White Wing's Bride	Harry Langdon	Pathe	2 reels	July 11
Whose Baby Are You?	Glenn Tryon	Pathe	2 reels	
Why Hesitate?	Neal Burns	Educational	2 reels	April 11
Why Sitting Bull Stood Up		Ser'ng Wilson (S. R.)	1 reel	
Wide Awake	Lige Conley	Educational	2 reels	
Wild Papa	"Spat Family"	Pathe	2 reels	May 16
Wild Waves	Bowes-Vance	Educational	1 reel	May 23
Wine, Woman and Song	"Aesop's Fables"	Pathe	1 reel	
Wooly West, The	Buddy Messinger	Universal	2 reels	
Wrestler, The	Earle Foxe	Fox	2 reels	Aug. 29
Yarn About Yarn, A	Aesop Fable	Pathe	1 reel	Aug. 1
Yes, Yes, Nannette	Jas. Finlayson	Pathe	1 reel	Aug. 1

Short Subjects

Feature	Distributed by	Length	Reviewed
Action (Sportlight)	Pathe	1 reel	
All Under One Flag (Sportlight)	Pathe	1 reel	
Animal Celebrities (Sportlight)	Pathe	1 reel	June 27
Animated Hair Cartoon (Series)	Red Seal (S. R.)	1 reel	
Balto's Race to Nome (Special)	Educational	2 reels	May 23
Barbara Snitches (Pacemaker Series)	F. B. O.	2 reels	
Battle of Wits (Josie Sedgwick)	Universal	2 reels	July 18
Bashful Whirlwind, The (Edmund Cobb)	Universal	2 reels	
Beauty and the Bandit (Geo. Larkin)	Universal	2 reels	July 4
Beauty Spots (Sportlight)	Pathe	1 reel	April 18
Best Man, The (Josie Sedgwick)	Universal	2 reels	Aug. 15
Broken Trails	Denver Dixon (S.R.)	2 reels	
Cabaret of Old Japan	M. J. Winkler (S.R.)	1 reel	
Color World	Sering Wilson (S. R.)	1 reel	
Captured Alive (Helen Gibson)	Universal	2 reels	July 25
Close Call, The (Edmund Cobb)	Universal	2 reels	
Coccon to Kimona	M. J. Winkler (S.R.)	1 reel	
Come-Back, The (Benny Leonard)	Henry Ginsberg-S.R.	2 reels	
Concerning Cheese (Varieties)	Fox	1 reel	
Covered Flagon, The (Pacemaker Series)	F. B. O	2 reels	
Cowpuncher's Comeback, The (Art Acord)	Universal	2 reels	
Cross Word Puzzle Film (Comedy-Novelty)	Schwartz Enterprises (S. R.)	1 reel	
Cuba Steps Out (Variety)	Fox	1 reel	
Day With the Gypsies	Red Seal Pict. (S. R.)	1 reel	
Divertisement (Color Shots)	Sering Wilson (S. R.)	1 reel	
Don Coo Coo (Pacemakers)	Film Book. Offices	2 reels	
Do You Remember (Gems of Screen)	Red Seal (S. R.)	1 reel	
Dude Ranch Days (Sportlight)	Pathe	1 reel	May 30
Earth's Other Half (Hodge-Podge)	Educational	1 reel	June 6
East Side, West Side	DeForrest (S. R.)		
Fast Male, The (Pacemakers)	Film Book. Offices	2 reels	
Fighting Cowboy (Series)	Universal		
Fighting Ranger (Serial)	Universal	15 episodes	Feb. 7
Fighting Schoolmarm (Josie Sedgwick)	Universal	2 reels	Aug. 1
Film Facts	Red Seal (S. R.)	1 reel	
Fire Trader, The (Serial)	Universal	15 episodes	
Floral Feast, A	Sering Wilson (S.R.)	1 reel	
Frederick Chopin (Music Masters)	Jas. A. Fitzpatrick (S. R.)	1 reel	
From Mars to Munich (Varieties)	Fox	1 reel	April 4
Frontier Love (Billy Mack)	Denver Dixon	2 reels	
Fugitive Futurist	Cranfield & Clarke (S. R.)		
George F. Handel (Music Masters)	Jas. A. Fitzpatrick (S. R.)	1 reel	
Gems of the Screen	Red Seal (S. R.)	1 reel	
Ghost City, The (Serial)	Universal	15 episodes	
Golden Panther, The (Serial)	Pathe		
Great Circus Mystery, The (Serial)	Universal	15 episodes	
Great Decide, The (Pacemakers)	Film Book. Offices	2 reels	
He Who Gets Rapped (Pacemakers)	Film Book. Offices	2 reels	
Hittin' the Trail (Fred Hank)	Sierra Pict. (S. R.)	2 reels	
Idaho (Serial)	Pathe	10 episodes	Feb.28
If a Picture Tells a Story	Cranfield & Clarke (S. R.)		
In a China Shop (Variety)	Fox	1 reel	
In the Spider's Grip (Novelty)	Educational	1 reel	April 11
Jazz Fight, The (Benny Leonard)	Henry Ginsberg (S. R.)	2 reels	
Judge's Cross Word Puzzle (Novelty)	Educational	1 reel	Jan. 31
Klondike Today (Varieties)	Fox	1 reel	
Knockout Man, The (Mustang)	Universal	2 reels	July 11
Land of the Navajo (Educational)	Fox	1 reel	
Learning How (Sportlight)	Pathe	1 reel	July 18
Leopard's Lair	Universal	Serial	
Let's Paint	Cranfield & Clarke (S. R.)		
Line Runners, The (Arnold Gregg)	Universal	2 reels	
Little People of the Garden (Secrets of Life)	Educational	1 reel	
Little People of the Sea (Secrets of Life)	Educational	1 reel	Feb. 28
Lizzie's Last Lap	Cranfield & Clarke (S. R.)		
Loaded Dice (Edmund Cobb)	Universal	2 reels	April 4
Luna-cy (Stereoscopik)	Pathe	1 reel	
Mad Miner, A (Western)	Hunt Miller (S. R.)	2 reels	
Magic Hour, The	Red Seal Pict. (S. R.)	1 reel	
Man Who Rode Alone, The	Miller & Steen (S.R.)	2 reels	
Marvels of Motion	Red Seal (S. R.)	1 reel	
Marvellous Manhattan	M. J. Winkler (S. R.)	1 reel	
Merry Kiddo, The (Pacemakers)	Film Book. Offices	2 reels	
Merton of the Goofies ... "Pacemaker"	F. B. O.	2 reels	
Mexican Melody (Hodge-Podge)	Educational	1 Reel	
Mexican Oil Fields	M. J. Winkler (S. R.)	1 reel	
Movie Morsels (Hodge Podge)	Educational	1 reel	April 4
My Own Carolina (Variety)	Fox	1 reel	Aug. 29
Mystery Box, The (Serial)	Davis Dist. Corp.	10 episodes	
Neptune's Nieces (Sportlight)	Pathe	1 reel	
New Sheriff, A (Western)	Hunt Miller (S. R.)	2 reels	
Olympic Mermaids (Sportlight)	Pathe	1 reel	
One Glorious Scrap (Edmund Cobb)	Universal	2 reels	
Only a Country Lass (Novelty)	Educational	1 reel	May 29
Ouch (Stereoscopik)	Pathe	1 reel	
Our Six-legged Friends (Secrets of Life)	Educational	1 reel	
Outlaw, The (Jack Perrin)	Universal	2 reels	
Paris Creations (Novelty)	Educational	1 reel	Feb. 7
Paris Creations in Color (Novelty)	Educational	1 reel	Feb. 28
People You Know (Screen Almanac)	Film Booking Offices.	1 reel	
Perfect View, The (Varieties)	Fox	1 reel	
Pictorial Proverbs (Hodge Podge)	Educational	1 reel	Aug. 15
Plastigrams (Novelty)	Educational		
Play Ball (Serial)	Pathe	10 episodes	June 27
Power God, The (Serial)	Davis Dist. Div.(S.R.)	15 episodes	
Pronto Kid, The (Edmund Cobb)	Universal	2 reels	June 27
Queen of the Round-Up (J. Sedgwick)	Universal	2 reels	June 13
Race, The (Van Bibber)	Fox	2 reels	
Record Breaker, The	Pathe	Serial	
Rim of the Desert (Jack Perrin)	Universal	2 reels	
River Nile, The (Variety)	Fox	1 reel	
Roaring Waters (Geo. Larkin)	Universal	2 reels	
Rock Bound Brittany (Educational)	Fox	1 reel	
Ropin' Venus, The (Mustang Series)	Universal	2 reels	July 11
R. Valentino and Eighty-eight Prize-winning American Beauties	Chesterfield (M. P. Corp.) (S. R.)	3 reels	
Secrets of Life (Educational)	Principal Pict. (S. R.)	reel	Feb. 21
Seven Ages of Sport (Sportlight)	Pathe	1 reel	Aug. 22
Shadow of Suspicion (Eileen Sedgwick)	Universal	2 reels	
Show Down, The (Art Acord)	Universal	2 reels	
Sky Tribe, The (Variety)	Fox	1 reel	
Smoke of a Forty-Five, The (Western)	Hunt Miller (S. R.)	2 reels	
Soft Muscles (Benny Leonard)	Ginsberg (S. R.)	2 reels	
Song Cartunes (Novelty)	Red Seal Pict. (S. R.)	1 reel	
Sons of Swat (Sportlight)	Pathe	1 reel	Aug. 15
Sporting Judgment (Sportlight)	Pathe	1 reel	May 9
Steam Heated Islands (Varieties)	Fox	1 reel	
Stereoscopic (Novelty)	Pathe	1 reel	May 16
Storm King (Edmund Cobb)	Universal	2 reels	
Straight Shootin' (Harry Carey)	Universal	2 reels	
Strangler Lewis vs. Wayne Munn	Educational	2 reels	July 4
Stratford on Avon (Gems of Screen)	Red Seal Pict. (S. R.)	1 reel	
Sunken Silver (Serial)	Pathe	10 episodes	April 18
Surprise Fight, The (Benny Leonard)	Henry Ginsberg (S. R.)	2 reels	
Thundering Waters (Novelty)	Sering D. Wilson (S. R.)	1 reel	April 25
Tiger Kill, The (Pathe Review)	Pathe		
Toiling for Rest (Variety)	Fox	1 reel	
Traps and Troubles (Sportlight)	Pathe	1 reel	Mar. 21
Travel Treasures (Hodge Podge)	Educational	1 reel	July 25
Turf Mystery (Serial)	Chesterfield Pict. Corp. (S. R.)	15 episodes	
Valley of Rogues (Western)	Universal	2 reels	April 18
Van-Bibber and the Navy (Earle Foxe)	Fox	2 reels	
Village School, The (Hodge Podge)	Educational Film	1 reel	May 9
Voice of the Nightingale, The (Novelty)	Educational	1 reel	Mar. 28
Waiting For You (Music Film)	Hegerman Music Novelties (S. R.)		
Welcome Granger (Pacemakers)	Film Book. Offices	2 reels	
West Wind, The (Variety)	Fox	1 reel	
What Price Gloria (Pacemakers)	Film Book. Offices	2 reels	
Wheels of the Pioneers (Billy Mack)	Denver Dixon	2 reels	
Where the Waters Divide (Varieties)	Fox	1 reel	
White Paper (Varieties)	Fox	1 reel	
Wild West Wallop, The (Edmund Cobb)	Universal	2 reels	May 16
With Pencil, Brush and Chisel	Fox	1 reel	
Wonder Book, The (Series)	Sering D. Wilson	500 feet	April 25
Young Sheriff, The (Tom. Forman)	Miller & Steen (S. R.)	2 reels	
Zowie (Stereoscopik)	Pathe	1 reel	

Coming Attractions

Feature	Star	Distributed by	Length	Reviewed
Ace of Spades, The	Desmond-McAllister	Universal		
Age of Indiscretion		Truart (S. R.)	5800 feet	
American Venus, The	Special Cast	Paramount		
An Enemy of Men		Columbia Pict. (S. R.)		
Aristocrat, The	Special Cast	B. P. Schulberg (S. R.)		
Ashes	Corinne Griffith	First National		
Atlantis		First National		
Back Wash	Mary Pickford	United Artists		
Bad Lands, The	Harry Carey	Prod. Dist. Corp		
Barriers of Fire	Monte Blue	Warner Bros.		
Beautiful Cheat, The	Laura La Plante	Universal		
Beautiful City	R. Barthelmess	First National		
Before Midnight	Wm. Russell	Ginsberg (S. R.)	5895 feet	Aug. 8
Beloved Pawn, The	Reed Howes	Rayart (S. R.)		
Ben Hur	Special Cast	Metro-Goldwyn		
Big Parade, The	John Gilbert	Metro-Goldwyn		
Border Intrigue	Franklyn Farnum	Inde. Pict. (S. R.)	5 reels	June 6
Border Women	Special Cast	Phil Goldstone (S.R.)	5000 feet	
Broken Hearts of Hollywood	Harlan-Miller	Warner Brothers		
Brown of Harvard		Metro-Goldwyn		
Cave Man, The	Harlan-Miller	Warner Brothers		
Charity Ball, The		Metro-Goldwyn		
Circle, The		Metro-Goldwyn		
Clean-Up, The	Richard Talmadge	F. B. O.		
Clod Hopper, The	Glenn Hunter	Assoc. Exhibitors		
Clothes Make the Pirate	Errol-D. Gish	First National		
College Widow, The	Syd Chaplin	Warner Brothers		

Feature	Star	Distributed by	Length	Reviewed
Coming of Amos	Rod La Rocque	Prod. Dist. Corp.		
Compromise	Irene Rich	Warner Bros.		
Conquered	Gloria Swanson	Paramount		
Count of Luxembourg, The	Larry Semon	Chadwick		
Crashing Through	Jack Perrin	Ambassador Pict. (S. R.)	5000 feet	
Cyclone Bob	Bob Reeves	Anchor Film Dist.		
Cyrano de Bergerac	Special Cast	Atlas Dist. (S. R.)	9500 feet	July 18
Dance Madness	Pringle-Cody	Metro-Goldwyn		
Dangerous Currents		First National		
Dark Horse, The	Harry Carey	Prod. Dist. Corp.		
Deerslayer, The		Weiss Bros. (S. R.)	4780 feet	
Demon, The	Jack Hoxie	Universal		
Demon Rider, The	Ken Maynard	Davis Dist	5000 feet	Aug. 22
Detour		Prod. Dist. Corp.		
Down Upon the Swanee River	Special Cast	Lee Bradford (S. R.)		
Dumb Head		Tiffany (S. R.)	6500 feet	
East of the Setting Sun	Constance Talmadge	First National		
Enchanted Hill, The	Special Cast	Paramount		
Ermine and Rhinestone		H. F. Jans (S. R.)		
Exquisite Sinner, The	Special Cast	Metro-Goldwin		
Extra Man, The		Universal		
Face to Face	Viola Dana	Metro-Goldwyn		
Face on the Air, The	Evelyn Brent	F. B. O.		
Fair Play	Special Cast	Wm. Steiner (S. R.)		
Fall of Jerusalem		Weiss Bros. (S. R.)	6800 feet	
Fast Pace, The	Special Cast	Arrow		
Fighter's Paradise, The	Rex Baker	Phil Goldstone	5000 feet	
Fighting Courage	Ken Maynard	Davis Dist. Div. (S.R.)	5 reels	July 11
Fighting Edge, The	Harlan-Miller	Warner Brothers		
Fighting Smile, The	Bill Cody	Inde.Pict. Corp.(S.R.)	4630 feet	
First Year, The	Special Cast	Fox		
Flaming Waters		F. B. O.		
Fool, The	Special Cast	Fox		April 25
Forest of Destiny, The		Gotham Prod. (S. R.)		
Forever After	Corinne Griffith	First National		
Fort Frayne	Ben Wilson	Davis Dist.	5000 feet	Aug. 29
Free to Love	C. Bow-R. McKee	B. P. Schulberg (S. R.)		
Friends	Special Cast	Vitagraph		
Frivolity		B. P. Schulberg (S.R.)		
Galloping Dude, The	Franklyn Farnum	Inde.Pict.Corp.(S.R.)	4700 feet	
Garden of Allah		United Artists		
Going the Limit	Richard Holt	Gerson Pict. (S. R.)		
Golden Cocoon		Warner Bros.		
Goose Woman, The	Special Cast	Universal	7500 feet	Aug. 22
Go West	Buster Keaton	Metro-Goldwyn		
Grass			10 reels	Mar. 7
Gulliver's Travels	Special Cast	Universal		
Handsome Brute, The	Columbia Pict. (S. R.)			
Hearts and Fists		Assoc. Exhib.		
Hearts and Spangles		Gotham Prod. (S. R.)		
Hell Bent for Heaven		Warner Bros.		
Hell's Highroad	Leatrice Joy	Prod. Dist. Corp	6084 feet	Sept. 5
Heir's Apparent	Special Cast	First National		
Her Father's Daughter		F. B. O.		
Hero of the Big Snows, A	Rin Tin Tin (dog)	Warner Brothers		
His Jazz Bride	Special Cast	Warner		
His Majesty Bunker Bean	M. Moore-Devore	Warner		
His Master's Voice	Thunder (dog)	Gotham Prod. (S. R.		
His Woman	Special Cast	Whitman Bennett	7 reels	
Hogan's Alley	Harlan-Miller	Warner		
Home Maker, The	Alice Joyce	Universal	7755 feet	Aug. 8
Honeymoon Express, The	M. Moore-D. Devore	Warner Brothers		
Horses and Women		B. P. Schulberg		
Hurricane		Truart (S. R.)	5800 feet	
Inevitable Millionaires, The	M. Moore-Devore	Warner Bros.		
Invisible Wounds	Sweet-Lyon	First National		
Irene	Colleen Moore	First National		
Justice of the Far North		C. B. C. (S. R)	5500 feet	
Kings of the Turf		Fox		
Kiss for Cinderella, A	Betty Bronson	Paramount		
Knockout Kid, The	Jack Perrin	Rayart Pict. Corp. (S. R.)		
La Boheme	Lillian Gish	Metro-Goldwyn		
Lady Windermere's Fan	Special Cast	Warner Brothers		
Lariat, The	William Desmond	Universal		
Last Edition, The	Ralph Lewis	Film Book. Offices		
Lawful Cheater, The	Bow-McKee	B. P. Schulberg	4946 feet	
Lazybones		Fox Film		
Lena Rivers	Special Cast	Arrow	6 reels	
Life of a Woman		Truart (S. R.)	6500 feet	
Lightnin'	Jay Hunt	Fox	7979 feet	Aug. 1
Lightning Jack	Jack Perrin	Ambassador Pict. (S.R.)	5000 feet	
Lightning Lover, The	Reginald Denny	Universal		
Lightning Passes, The	Al Ferguson	Fleming Prod. (S.R.)		
Lights of Old Broadway	Marion Davies	Metro-Goldwyn		
Limited Mail, The	Monte Blue	Warner Bros.		
Little Girl in a Big City, A		Gotham Prod. (S. R.)		
Little Irish Girl, The	Special Cast	Warner Bros.		
Live Wire, The	Johnny Hines	First National		
Lodge in the Wilderness		Tiffany (S. R.)	6500 feet	
Lord Jim	Percy Marmont	Paramount		
Love Cargo, The	House Peters	Universal		
Love Gamble, The	Special Cast	Banner Prod. (S. R.)	5766 feet	July 11
Lover's Island	Hampton-Kirkwood	Assoc. Exhib		
Love Toy, The	Lowell Sherman	Warner Bros		
Loyalties	Special Cast	Fox		
Lucky Lady, The	Lionel Barrymore	Paramount		
Lure of Broadway, The		Columbia Pict. (S. R.)		
Lying Wives	Special Cast	Ivan Abramson (S. R.)	7 reels	May 2
Man and the Moment		Metro-Goldwyn		
Man From Red Gulch	Harry Carey	Prod. Dist. Corp.		
Man of Iron, A	L. Barrymore	Chadwick	6 reels	July 4
Men on the Box, The	Sydney Chaplin	Warner Bros		
Man She Bought, The	Constance Talmadge	First National		
Man Without a Conscience	Louis-Rich	Warner Bros	6850 feet	May 2
Mare Nostrum	Special Cast	Metro-Goldwyn		
Married Hypocrites	Fredericks-La Plante	Universal		
Martinique	Bebe Daniels	Paramount		
Masked Bride, The	Mae Murray	Metro-Goldwyn		
Men of Steel	Milton Sills	First National		
Memory Lane	Boardman-Nagel	First National		
Message to Garcia, A		Metro-Goldwyn		
Miracle of Life, The	Busch-Marmont	Assoc. Exhib		
Miracle of the Wolves, The			10346 feet	Mar. 7
Midnight Flames		Columbia Pict. (S. R.)		
Miss Vanity	Mary Philbin	Universal		
Million Dollar Doll		Assoc. Exhib		
Moonlight Kisses	Mary Philbin	Universal		
Morganson's Finish		Tiffany (S. R.)	6500 feet	
Moving Finger, The	Special Cast	Paramount		
Napoleon the Great		Universal		
Night Call, The	Rin-Tin-Tin (dog)	Warner Brothers		
Oats for the Woman	Special Cast	Universal		
Old Clothes	Jackie Coogan	Metro-Goldwyn		
Once to Every Man	O'Brien-Dove	Fox Film Corp		
Only Thing, The	Special Cast	Metro-Goldwyn		
Open Trail, The	Jack Hoxie	Universal	4800 feet	May 16
Outlaw Tamer, The	Clayton-F. Farnum	Inde. Pict. (S. R.)		
Pace That Thrills, The	Ben Lyon	First National		
Painted Woman, The	Kirkwood-Lee	Prod. Dist. Corp		
Pals		Truart (S. R.)	5800 feet	
Paris	Pauline Starke	Metro-Goldwyn		
Paris After Dark	Norma Talmadge	First National		
Partners Again		United Artists		
Passionate Quest, The	Marie Prevost	Warner Bros		
Passionate Youth	Special Cast	Truart (S. R.)	6 reels	July 11
Part Time Wife, The		Gotham Prod. (S. R.)		
Peacock Feathers	Virginia Valli	Universal	6747 feet	Aug. 29
Peak of Fate, The		F. B. Rogers	8 reels	June 27
People vs. Nancy Preston	Bowers-De La Motte	Prod. Dist. Corp.		
Phantom of the Opera	Lon Chaney	Universal		
Pinch Hitter, The	Glenn Hunter	Asso. Exhibitors		
Pleasure Buyers, The	Irene Rich	Warner Brothers		
Police Patrol, The	James Kirkwood	Gotham Prod. (S. R.)		
Polly of the Ballet	Bebe Daniels	Paramount		
Pony Express, The	Special Cast	Universal		
Prairie Pirate, The	Harry Carey	Prod. Dist. Corp.		
Prince, The	Philbin-Kerry	Universal		
Purchased Youth	Anna Q. Nilsson	F. B. O.		
Quality Street		Metro-Goldwyn		
Quicker 'n Lightning	Buffalo Bill, Jr	Weiss Bros. (S. R.)	5 reels	June 13
Racing Blood		Gotham Prod. (S. R.)		
Reckless Courage	Buddy Roosevelt	Weiss Bros. (S. R.)	4851 feet	May 2
Reckless Sex, The	Special Cast	Truart (S. R.)	6 reels	Feb. 14
Red Clay	William Desmond	Universal		
Red Dice	Rod La Rocque	Prod. Dist. Corp.		
Red Hot Tires	Monte Blue	Warner Bros.		
Resurrection		Principal Pict. (S. R.)		
Return of a Soldier	Special Cast	Metro-Goldwyn		
Rime of the Ancient Mariner, The		Fox Film		
Road to Yesterday, The	Special Cast	Prod. Dist. Corp		
Road That Led Home, The		Vitagraph		
Romance of an Actress		Chadwick		
Ropin' Venus, The	Josie Sedgwick	Universal		
Rose of the World	Special Cast	Warner Bros		
Sally, Irene and Mary	Special Cast	Metro-Goldwyn		
Salvage		Truart (S. R.)	5800 feet	
Sap, The	M. Moore D. Devore	Warner Bros		
Satan in Sables	Lowell Sherman	Warner Bros		
Satan's Son	Special Cast	Inde. Pict. (S. R.)		
Savage, The	Ben Lyon	First National		
Scarlet Saint, The	Lyon-Astor	First National		
Scraps	Mary Pickford	United Artists		
Sea Beast, The	John Barrymore	Warner Bros.		
Sea Woman, The	Sweet-McLaglen	First National		
Seven Days	Lillian Rich	Prod. Dist. Corp.		
Seven Sinners	Marie Prevost	Warner Bros.		
Seventh Heaven	Special Cast	Fox		
Shadow of the Wall		Gotham Prod. (S. R.)		
Shadow of the Mosque	Odette Taylor	Cranfield & Clarke (S. R.)	6200 feet	
Shenandoah		B. P. Schulberg (S. R.)		
Ship of Souls	B. Lytell-L. Rich	Assoc. Exhib	6800 feet	
Shootin' Square	Jack Perrin	Ambassador Pict. (S.R.)	5000 feet	
Siegfried		Ufa		
Sign of the Claw		Gotham Prod. (S. R.)		
Silken Shackles	Irene Rich	Warner Bros.		
Silver Treasure, The	Special Cast	Fox		
Simon the Jester	Rich-O'Brien	Prod. Dist. Corp.		
Skyline of Spruce, The	Special Cast	Universal		
Social Highwayman, The	Harlan-Miller	Warner Brothers		
Some Pun'kins	Chas. Ray	Chadwick		
Souls Adrift	Rosemary Davies	Assoc. Exhib		
Souls That Pass in the Night	Special Cast	Universal		
Spanish Sunlight	LaMarr-Stone	First National		
Span of Life	Betty Blythe	Banner Prod. (S. R.)		
Speed Limit, The		Gotham Prod. (S. R.)		
Splendid Road, The	Anna Q. Nillsen	First National		
Steele of the Royal Mounted		Vitagraph	6 reels	June 27
Stella Dallas		United Artists		
Stella Maris	Mary Philbin	Universal		
Still Alarm, The	Chadwick-Russell	Universal		
Strange Bedfellows		Metro-Goldwyn		
Storm Breakers, The	House Peters	Universal		
Sunshine of Paradise Alley	Special Cast	Chadwick Pict.		
Super Speed	Reed Howes	Rayart (S. R.)		
Sweet Adeline	Charles Ray	Chadwick		
Tale of a Vanishing People		Tiffany (S. R.)	6500 feet	
Tearing Loose	Wally Wales	Weiss Bros. (S. R.)	4900 feet	June 13
Temptress		Metro-Goldwyn		
Ten to Midnight		Prod. Dist. Corp.		
Tenderfoot, The	Jack Hoxie	Universal		
That Man from Arizona	D.Revier-W.Fairbanks	F. B. O.		
That Royle Girl	Kirkwood-Dempster	Paramount		
This Woman	Special Cast	Fox		
Three Bad Men	Special Cast	Fox		
Three Faces East		Prod. Dist. Corp.		
Trailing Shadows	Edmond Lowe	Fox Film		
Travelin' Fast	Jack Perrin	Ambassador Pict. (S. R.)	5060 feet	
Travis Coup, The		Tiffany (S. R.)	6500 feet	
Twin Sister, The	Constance Talmadge	First National		
Two Blocks Away	Special Cast	Universal		
Unchastened Woman, The	Theda Bara	Chadwick		
Unguarded Hour, The	Sills-Kenyon	First National		
Unknown Lover, The	Elsie Ferguson	Vitagraph		
Up and At' Em	Jack Perrin	Ambassador Pict. (S. R.)	5000 feet	
Valiant Gentleman, The		Prod. Dist. Corp.		
Vengeance of Durand, The	Irene Rich	Warner Brothers		
Viennese Medley	Special Cast	First National		
Volga Boatman, The		Prod. Dist. Corp		
Wanderer, The	William Collier, Jr	Paramount	8173 feet	
Warrior Gap	Wilson-Gerber	Davis Dist	4900 feet	Aug. 22
Wedding Song, The	Leatrice Joy	Prod. Dist. Corp		
We Moderns	Colleen Moore	First National		
What Will People Say		Metro-Goldwyn		
Where the Worst Begins		Truart(S. R.)	5800 feet	
White Chief, The	Monte Blue	Warner Bros		
White Mice	Jacqueline Logan	Sering D. Wilson(S.R.)		
Why Girls Go Back Home		Warner Bros		
Wild Girl		Truart (S. R.)	5800 feet	
Wild Justice	Peter the Great	United Artists	6 reels	Aug. 1
Wild Ridin'	Buck Jones	Fox		
Winning of Barbara Worth		Principal Pict. (S. R.)		
Wise Guy, The	Lefty Flynn	Film Book. Offices		
Without Mercy	Vera Reynolds	Prod. Dist. Corp		
Womanhandled	Richard Dix	Paramount		
Women and Wives		Metro-Goldwyn		
World's Illusion, The		Metro-Goldwyn		
Worst Woman, The	Special Cast	B. P. Schulberg (S. R.)		
Wrong Coat, The		Tiffany Prod. (S. R.)	6500 feet	

The Pinnacle

of
printing intensities is
reached through the

DUPLEX AUTOMATIC LIGHT CHANGE

It has a range of 18 gradations of light and operates instantly and auto. matically *for* 60 consecutive scenes.

Other Sizes
21 and 40 Scenes.

DUPLEX MOTION PICTURE INDUSTRIES, INC.
Long Island City, New York

WILLIAMS PRESS, INC.
ALBANY — NEW YORK

Why Exhibitors Rely on Simplex

The Simplex Projector was designed by engineers who based their plans on the result of years of study and experience in Motion Picture Projection work.

These men fitted the most modern principles of machine design to the specific requirements of perfect projection and built with a view to maximum efficiency and minimum operating costs.

In the actual construction of each Simplex Machine every precaution is taken to insure that each part conforms in quality of material and fractional measurement with the specifications laid down by the designers of the machine.

The correctness of design and the detail thoroughness of construction is evidenced by the unanimous approval given Simplex Projectors by exhibitors in all parts of the world.

Says Tom Magruder of Kansas,

"I think Simplex Machines are in class by themselves. I have used other makes, but none of them comes up with the Simplex for a steady and true picture, and I think they are the most durable machines on the market today."

THERE is no single factor that contributes so much to the quality of a screen presentation as the projector itself. If the projector is correctly designed and conscientiously constructed it will show clear, steady and uninterrupted pictures.

The theatre that continually features good projection becomes known as a reliable source of good entertainment. Casual visitors become steady patrons. And steady patronage is the secret of success for the majority of Motion Picture houses.

Simplex Projectors have won their place of leadership because of their dependability and good performance. Not only in exclusive characteristics of design, but also through exceptional sturdiness of construction has the Simplex Projector proved its superiority.

Buy your projector from the standpoint of an investment. Consider performance, soundness of construction, cost of upkeep, repair facilities and the service back of the machine—your choice will inevitably be a Simplex.

For full description, prices, terms, etc., write to the Precision Machine Company, Inc., 317 East 34th Street, New York City

Rothacker-Aller Laboratories, Hollywood, Calif.

First National Pictures, Inc., Presents *"What Fools Men"*— Adapted from Henry Kitchell Webster's famous novel:— "Joseph Greer and His Daughter." With Lewis Stone, Shirley Mason, David Torrence, Barbara Bedford. June Mathis, editorial director. Scenario by Eve Unsell. The Photography by Norbert Brodin, A.S.C. Art direction by E. J. Shulter. Film edited by Bert Moore. All Directed by George Archainbaud. *A First National Picture.* **Rothacker Prints and Service.**

Lewis Stone
and
Shirley Mason
in
" What Fools Men."

CHICAGO-U.S.A.

N.Y. Telegraph
Aug. 30, 1925

The Talk
of The
Industry

Metro-
Goldwyn-
Mayer's

The Quality 52

Metro-Goldwyn Has The Pictures

Mr. Exhibitor

LAST Wednesday night the writer attended the premiere of Eric Von Stroheim's "The Merry Widow." It is with a sense of real satisfaction that I can truthfully say it is the best Metro-Goldwyn picture yet released, and the finest thing Von Stroheim has ever done.

Which brings me to the point of these few words. Metro-Goldwyn has an exceptionally fine product this season. If one is to judge from their pictures presented the last few weeks at the Capitol, exhibitors will do well to get in the swim, pick up the pencil and sign on the much-ly-publicised dotted line. "Pretty Ladies," a real picture; "The Unholy Three," another; "Sun Up," still another; all box-office attractions which have been built with an eye to truly please the public. To my mind, Metro-Goldwyn is far and away in the lead with presentations to date. There will be a merry little war between Paramount and First National to see whose product plays the big time, for their pictures are, as a general run, good entertainment, yet it seems that the real race between Famous and First should be to see which company can put out as consistent a group of winners as Metro-Goldwyn has to date.

The Editor

WURLIEZER
UNIT ORGANS

LUNA AMUSEMENT COMPANY

GENERAL OFFICE MARS THEATRE   LAFAYETTE INDIANA

April 7, 1921

Mr. A. Liebte
Manager Organ Dept.
The Rudolph Wurlitzer Company
Chicago, Illinois

Dear Mr. Liebte:

Just a few lines to tell you that the
Style 200 Wurlitzer Hope Jones Unit Pipe Organ is city,
proving it's worth at our box office.

A good pipe organ such as this one,
certainly goes a long way in putting over the "ever so
often very ordinary picture" that every theatre has
out of necessity present. It is so important that
produces handsome dividends, the better the organ the
safer the investment.

To me a pipe organ occupies a place
in the theatre that cannot be filled otherwise - no
other combination of musical instruments can bring it
the goal of its picture so effectively.

Very truly yours,

LUNA AMUSEMENT COMPANY

HHJ/CAM.

Address All Inquiries and Correspondence to

*Send for
the
beautiful
new
Theatre
Organ
Catalog.*

THE MARS THEATRE
LAFAYETTE INDIANA

Not the least of its accomplishments is that the
Wurlitzer Unit Organ has enabled the exhibitor in
the smaller cities to present musical programs of
real metropolitan distinction.

The RUDOLPH WURLITZER CO.

CINCINNATI   NEW YORK   CHICAGO   SAN FRANCISCO   LOS ANGELES
121 E. 4th St.   120 W. 42nd St.   329 S. Wabash Ave.   250 Stockton St.   814 S. Broadway

And Forty Other Branches in Thirty-Three Cities

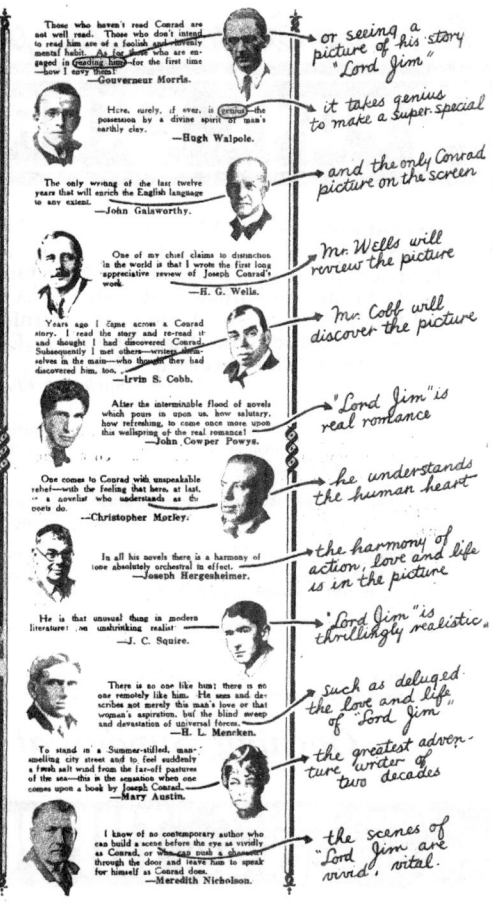

HIGHWAY"

from
Tom Gallon's *famous*
novel "*TATTERLY*"
with
a big cast headed by
William V. Mong
John Bowers
Marguerite De La Motte

A HUNT STROMBERG
ALL~STAR SPECIAL

RELEASED BY PRODUCERS DISTRIBUTING CORPORATION

F. C. MUNROE, President   RAYMOND PAWLEY, Vice-President and Treasurer   JOHN C. FLINN, Vice-President and General Manager

A Drama of Conflict and Romance in old Mexico

Scenario by
EVE UNSELL

EMMETT FLYNN
production

THANK YOU ∿ ∿ John Golden's play hit!
Fox Film Corporation.

WILLIAM FOX *Presents*

Tom Mix

and TONY, *the wonder horse, in*

The YANKEE SEÑOR

with

Margaret Livingston ~ Olive Borden
Alec B. Francis ~ Martha Mattox
Francis McDonald

From the novel "Conquistador" by
Katharine Fullerton Gerould

THANK YOU WITH GEORGE O'BRIEN · JACQUELINE LOGAN · ALEC FRANCIS **THANK YOU**
GEORGE FAWCETT · J.FARRELL M^cDONALD · CYRIL CHADWICK

Fox Film Corporation

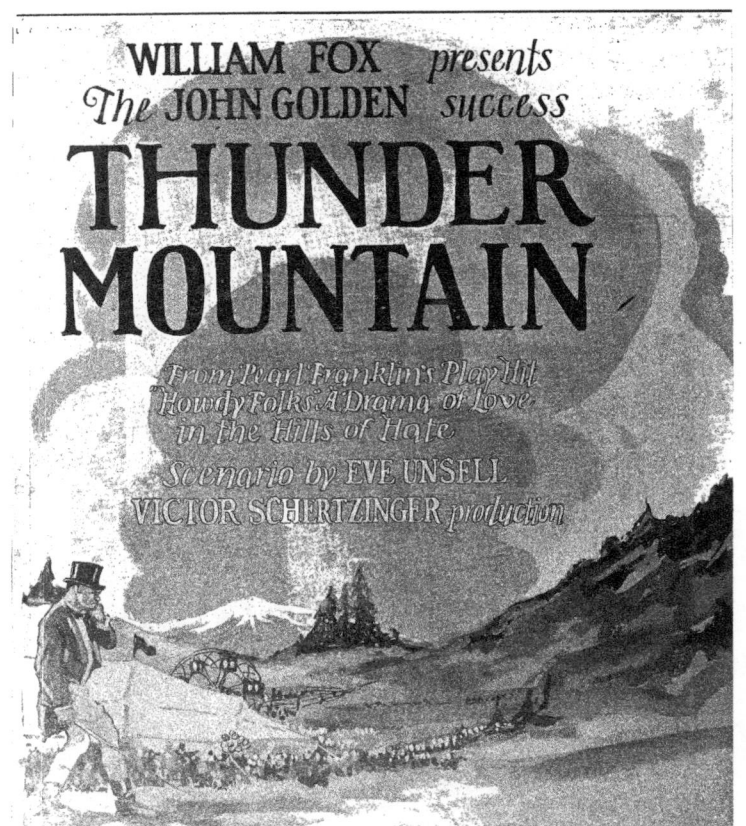

WILLIAM FOX presents
The JOHN GOLDEN success
THUNDER MOUNTAIN

From Pearl Franklin's Play Hit
"Howdy Folks." A Drama of Love
in the Hills of Hate

Scenario by EVE UNSELL
VICTOR SCHERTZINGER production

Fox Film Corporation.

with
MADGE BELLAMY - ZASU PITTS
LESLIE FENTON - ALEC FRANCIS
PAUL PANZER - OTIS HARLAN

Fox Film Corporation.

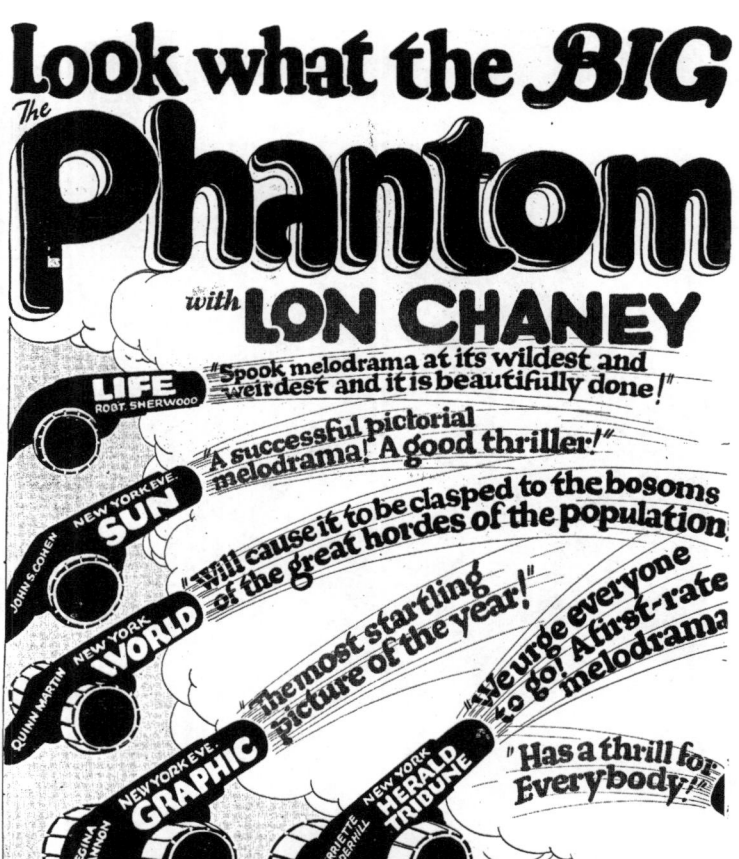

Look what the *BIG*

The **Phantom**

with **LON CHANEY**

"Spook melodrama at its wildest and weirdest and it is beautifully done!"
LIFE — ROBT. SHERWOOD

"A successful pictorial melodrama! A good thriller!"
NEW YORK EVE. **SUN** — JOHN S. COHEN

"Will cause it to be clasped to the bosoms of the great hordes of the population."
NEW YORK **WORLD** — QUINN MARTIN

"The most startling picture of the year!"
NEW YORK EVE. **GRAPHIC** — REGINA CANNON

"We urge everyone to go! A first-rate melodrama"
NEW YORK **HERALD TRIBUNE** — HARRIETTE UNDERWILL

"Has a thrill for Everybody!"

Now Playing to S. R. O. Busin

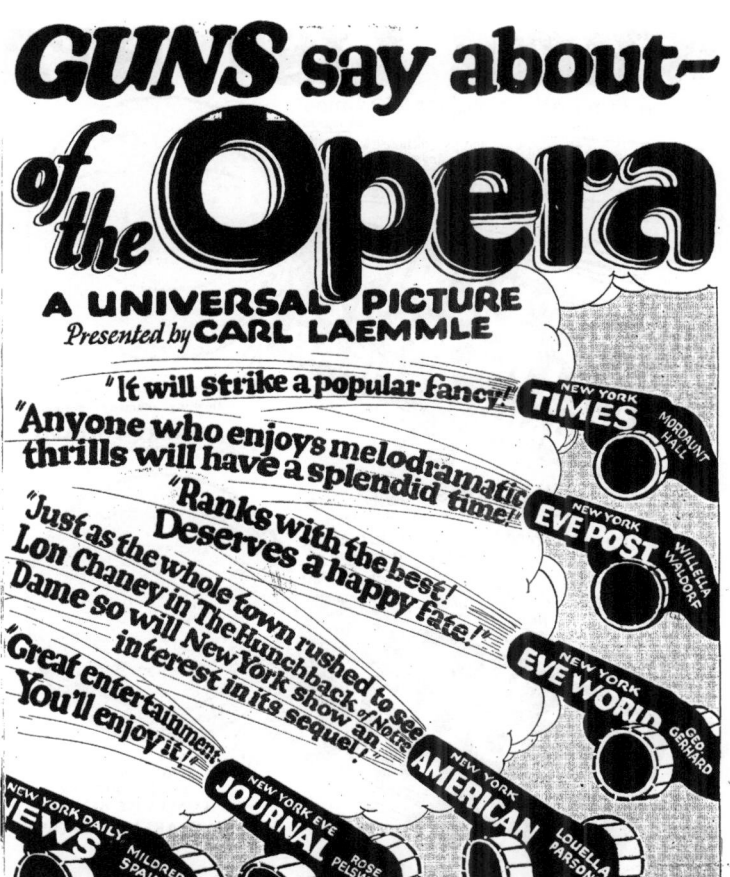

GUNS say about—
of *the* Opera
A UNIVERSAL PICTURE
Presented by CARL LAEMMLE

"It will strike a popular fancy!" — NEW YORK TIMES, MORDAUNT HALL

"Anyone who enjoys melodramatic thrills will have a splendid time!" — NEW YORK EVE POST, WILLELA WALDORF

"Ranks with the best! Deserves a happy fate!" — NEW YORK EVE WORLD, GEO. GERHARD

"Just as the whole town rushed to see Lon Chaney in The Hunchback of Notre Dame so will New York show an interest in its sequel!" — NEW YORK AMERICAN, LOUELLA PARSONS

"Great entertainment. You'll enjoy it!" — NEW YORK DAILY NEWS, MILDRED SPAIN

— NEW YORK EVE JOURNAL, ROSE PELSWICK

ess—**ASTOR Theatre** Broadway, N. Y. Twice Daily

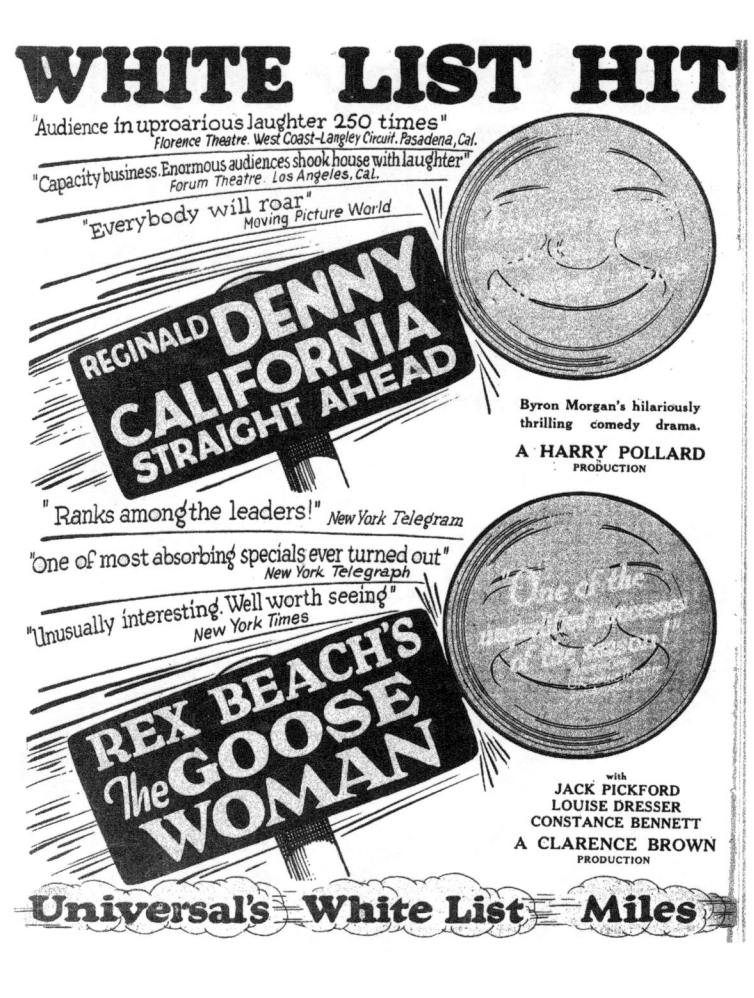

PERILS of the WILD

Adapted from the famous Adventure Story

Swiss Family Robinson

"A great box-office winner full of jungle stuff, wild animals and forest fires."
Exhibitors Trade Review

"Fast moving entertainment. They should fairly eat this one up."
Motion Picture News

"Young and old ought to revel in its thrills. Moves from the beginning".
Moving Picture World

Produced and Released by

UNIVERSAL

with an all-star cast including
BONOMO
MARGARET QUIMBY
JACK MOWER
Directed by Francis Ford

An ADVENTURE PICTURE

IT WILL TAKE YOU FOUR MINUTES TO READ THIS

BEGIN HERE

The majority of our first run accounts are sold.

We are "set" in practically every important spot in the United States.

And we haven't played second fiddle to anybody.

Our representation, so far, is as good as the best.

Before long it will be the best.

You know the reason.

It's because, we're not only big, but because we're constantly growing bigger.

Is this exaggeration?

You know it isn't.

We're delivering.

And why are we delivering?

The answer is this:

We know what it's all about.

We're showmen.

We know that an exhibitor has to make money on the attraction he plays—

That in order to do so, he has to show something in his ads., in his electric lights, and on the screen, that draws.

There's such a thing as the public.

We're out to boost ourselves, to increase the stock of our name, and all that, but—

We know that in last analysis, trademark or no trademark, good salesmanship or not, that the thing that a theatre needs is a good show.

We're aggressive, progressive, and we're overlooking no bets.

We cash in on angles.

And our biggest angle is to make you cash in.

That's that.

But to explain.

The Metro-Goldwyn-Mayer Studio in Culver City, California, is no place to have an afternoon tea.

It's a beehive of industry.

They're scheming things out all day long in that place. And our distributing organization is relaying the results, and adding a finishing touch of service.

For instance, we know the public likes stars.

We went and got 'em.

So that—

There isn't a week that you can't flash a big name in the lights.

Our first pictures of the season have Lon Chaney, Norma Shearer, Lillian Gish, Ramon Novarro, Marion Davies.

"The Unholy Three," (a bigger "Miracle Man").

"A Slave of Fashion" (Clothes).

"Romola" (The Gish Sisters).

"The Midshipman" (You read the front pages).

"Lights of Old Broadway" (Remember "Little Old New York").

"Pretty Ladies" (A Revue in Pictures).

"Never the Twain Shall Meet" (Breaking Records).

Look these over.

Each has a star, each is a good picture, each has an exploitation angle.

And that's our policy.

It's showmanship that brings over Erte, the great fashion creator, and gives his production the title "Paris."

It's a sense of the public that makes us do a picture called "The Mystic" which exposes fake spiritualists with their table-tapping.

It's a knowledge of what pleases the eye that makes us put technicolor sequences in our productions, and do the Sabatini story "Bardelys The Magnificent" entirely in color with John Gilbert as the star.

It's showmanship that inspires such stunts as America's first transcontinental trackless train.

And the opening of "The Merry Widow" on Broadway as a two dollar attraction with the society celebrity Gloria Gould as the managing directress of the theatre.

We have tricks up our sleeve constantly.

As the days wear on we're unfolding them one by one.

For you to cash in on.

So

It's good showmanship for you too, isn't it to hitch your wagon to

More stars than there are in Heaven—

The talk of the industry.

Metro-
Goldwyn-
Mayer's

SUCCESS
IS DUE
TO
SHOWMANSHIP

Don't Say "News Reel"

SAY KINOGRAMS

One of our exhibitor friends writes to us as follows:-

"The people of this town in calling up in reference to the shorter subjects refer to your single reel as 'The Kinograms,' which is proof that your subject is becoming more widely known as 'The Kinograms' than 'The News'."

This means that Kinograms has firmly established itself in the public mind as being synonymous with the word "News."

What Better Recommendation Can Kinograms Have Than This?

BOOK KINOGRAMS

The News Reel Built Like a Newspaper

EDUCATIONAL
FILM EXCHANGES, Inc.

Member, Motion Picture Producers and Distributors
of America, Inc.   Will H. Hays, President

E. W. Hammons

PRESENTS

"WILD BEASTS

of

BORNEO"

Produced by Mr. & Mrs. LOU C. HUTT

A TWO-REEL

Educational Pictures

SPECIAL

The most thrilling events of two years of adventure in the darkest jungles. The "high spots" of thousands of feet of close-ups of wild animals taken at constant peril to the lives of Hutt and his brave and charming wife.

A sensation when shown in five reels in San Francisco.

"The finest views of elephant herds, monkeys, cat animals and snakes ever secured."
—San Francisco Call and Post

NOW BOOKED TO THE CAPITOL THEATRE, NEW YORK

A big bet as the feature of an All Short Subjects program

"Time to Wake Up!"

You're sleeping on the job if you are not making extra profit out of your comedies. Exhibitors in all sections of the country are proving it can be done by DOING IT through better advertising and exploitation.

WALTER HIERS COMEDIES

provide a double appeal in your "ads" as well as on the screen—a star known to all, and pictures guaranteed in story, production and laugh values by Christie.

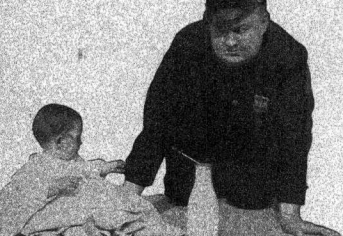

HIERS

cops the laughs in

"Off His Beat"

The first of a new series of six two-reel comedies. Have you booked them?

PRODUCED BY
Christie

Another whirlwind action picture!

The young star has packed more punch, more action, more speed into this one than you get in two or three ordinary pictures! He has a story that has all the elements of a Robert Louis Stevenson and a Robinson Crusoe rolled into one and it keeps him fighting, laughing, skylarking, leaping, punching, swarming all over the place.

It's Talmadge at his athletic best and your fans are going to go wild over him!

Another factor that will sell a lot of seats, particularly to your reading public, is the fact that Rupert Hughes, the eminent author, wrote all the titles for this picture.

Daring Richard Talmadge in "The Isle of Hope"

A Richard Talmadge Production

Presented by A. Carlos
Continuity by James Bell Smith
Directed by Jack Nelson

If you are a Talmadge exhibitor we don't have to tell you to hop aboard this one! If you are not—now is the time to get busy.

Distributed by

FILM BOOKING OFFICES OF AMERICA, INC.

723 Seventh Avenue, New York, N. Y.   *Exchanges Everywhere*

Exclusive Foreign Distributors, R-C Export Corp., 723 Seventh Avenue, New York. AGENTS: London, Berlin and Paris.
THEMATIC MUSIC CUE SHEETS AVAILABLE ON ALL FEATURES.

CHARLIE CHAPLIN

IN

"THE GOLD RUSH"

A Dramatic Comedy written and directed by Charlie Chaplin

JOHN H. KUNSKY
THEATRICAL ENTERPRISES

EXECUTIVE OFFICES

MADISON THEATRE BUILDING

BROADWAY AT GRAND CIRCUS PARK

DETROIT, MICHIGAN

JOHN H. KUNSKY
PRESIDENT AND TREASURER

GEO. W. TRENDLE
SECRETARY AND GENERAL MANAGER

FOR ALL LISTED COMPANIES

THE ADAMS THEATRE COMPANY
THE CAPITOL THEATRE COMPANY
THE MADISON THEATRE COMPANY
THE STATE THEATRE COMPANY
THE COLUMBIA THEATRE INC
THE ALHAMBRA THEATRE INC
THE DE LUXE OPERATING COMPANY
THE STRAND THEATRE INC
JOHN H KUNSKY THEATRICAL ENTERPRISES

THE MADISON REALTY COMPANY
THE CAPITOL BUILDING COMPANY

THE FIRST NATIONAL PICTURES INC.
THE BROADWAY-STRAND FILM EXCHANGE
THE MADISON FILM EXCHANGE

August 25, 1925.

Mr. Hiram Abrams,
United Artists Corp.,
729 Seventh Ave.,
New York, N.Y.

Dear Mr. Abrams:-

I wanted to take this occasion to con-
gratulate you upon having broken all records at the Adams
Theatre on the opening week with the Charlie Chaplin pro-
duction, "The Gold Rush". This picture played to 8,266
more people on the opening week than "The Hunchback of Notre
Dame", which has held the record for attendance at the Adams
Theatre ever since its opening , some seven years ago, and
I felt that you should know it.

With best wishes, I am,

Sincerely,

John H. Kunsky.

NOW BOOKING

UNITED ARTISTS CORPORATION

Mary Pickford   Charles Chaplin
Douglas Fairbanks   D. W. Griffith

Hiram Abrams, President.   *Joseph M. Schenck, Chairman, Board of Directors*

DOUGLAS FAIRBANKS

Hits the Bulls-eye

"Fairbanks has hit the bulls-eye again. A perfect example of showmanship, and it's for everybody from seven to seventy. Some picture." —Daily News.

"One of the most entertaining films that ever came from the studio." —Post.

"The best picture Fairbanks ever made, for sheer entertainment." —Journal.

Film patrons will gorge themselves on this picture." —Telegram.

"Certain to be a cleanup for the exhibitors everywhere." —Variety.

"DON Q
SON OF ZORRO"

NOW BOOKING
UNITED ARTISTS CORPORATION

Mary Pickford   Charles Chaplin
Douglas Fairbanks   D. W. Griffith
Hiram Abrams, President.   Joseph M. Schenck, Chairman, Board of Directors

S y d C

From the Novel and Celebrated Stage Play
by HAROLD MacGRATH
Cast Includes

DAVID BUTLER
ALICE CALHOUN
HELENE COSTELLO

Directed by Charles "Chuck" Reisner
Scenario by Charles Logue

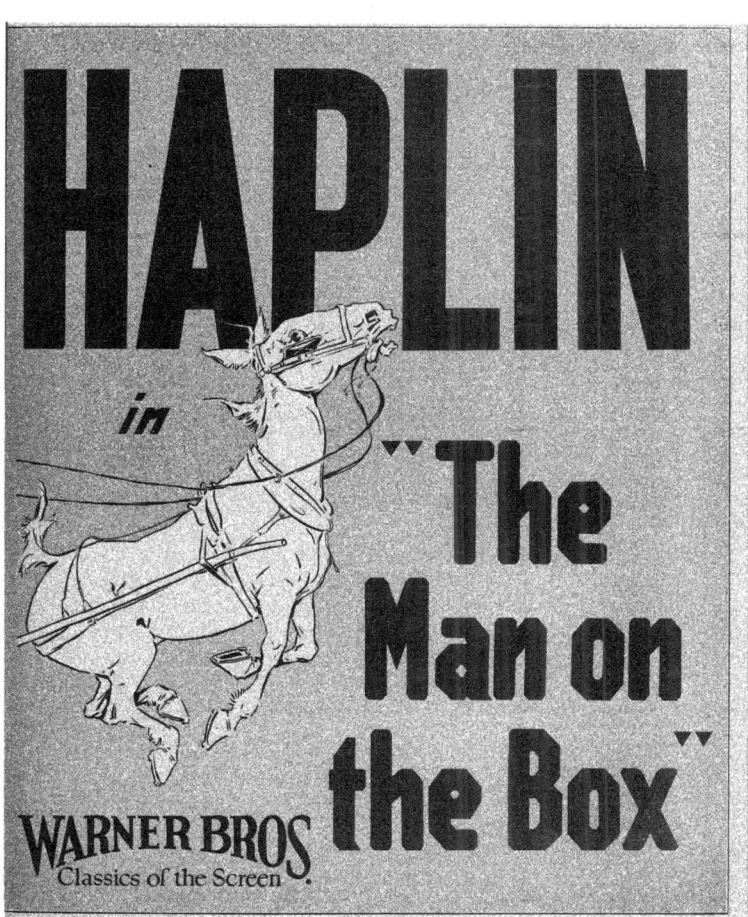

Now Get All the Facts
On Incandescent Lamp Projection

A handbook on incandescent lamp projection, the most complete ever published, has been prepared by our engineers to give exhibitors unbiased information on this important subject.

The incandescent lamp has many advantages over the arc but it is not recommended for use in every theatre. The types and sizes of theatres that can adopt this method of projection are described in the handbook; comparisons are made between the cost of operating the incandescent lamp and different types of arc lights; detailed descriptions of each part of the optical system is given; complete operating instructions are included and many other important subjects are covered.

Whether or not you are considering installing incandescent lamp projection you will find this book interesting and valuable.

Your copy is ready. Just mail the attached coupon and it will be sent to you promptly without charge or obligation.

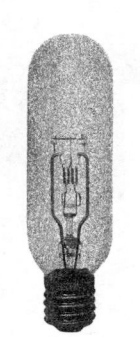

Supply Dealers Handling Edison MAZDA Lamps

MAIL THIS COUPON

Publicity Department,
Edison Lamp Works,
Harrison, N. J.

Check here ☐ Send me your free booklet on theatre lighting.

Check here ☐ Send me details of your special lamp contracts.

Name ....

Address ....

Southern Theatre Equipment, Atlanta, Ga.
Exhibitors Supply Co., Boston, Mass.
Robert Burroughton Co., Manchester, N. H.
United Theatre Equip. Co., Boston, Mass.
Robert Stereopt. Adv. Sup. Co., Manchester, N. H.
Capitol Mdse. Co., Chicago, Ill.
E. E. Fulton Co., Chicago, Ill.
Movie Supply Co., Chicago, Ill.
Amusement Supply Co., Chicago, Ill.
Denver Theatre Sup. Co., Denver, Colo.
Anderson Theatre Sup. Co., Okla. City, Okla.
Universal Film Exch., El Paso, Texas
David Parker, Dallas, Texas
Southern Film Service Co., Houston, Texas
Southern Theatre Equip., Dallas, Texas
Southern Theatre Equip., Okla. City, Okla.
R. D. Thrash, Dallas, Texas
Cole Theatre Sup. Co., Kansas City, Mo.
C. M. Stebbins Picture Supply Co., Kansas City, Mo.
Peskie Amusement Sup. Co., Los Angeles, Cal.
Northern Theatre Supply, Duluth, Minn.
Minto Co., Minneapolis, Minn.
Standard Theat. Equip., Minneapolis, Minn.
Hantol Motion Pic. Industries, Inc., New Orleans, La.
Southern States Film Co., New Orleans, La.
Chas. Beseler & Co., New York City
Capitol Motion Pic. Sup. Co., New York City
Herbert & Huesgen Co., New York City

Howells Cine Equip. Co., New York City
Independent Movie Supply Co., New York City
Sam Kaplan, New York City
Standard Slide Corp., New York City
United Cinema Co., New York City
Becker Theatre Supply Co., Buffalo, N. Y.
Empire Theatre Supply Co., Albany, N. Y.
Robertson-Cataract Elec. Co., Syracuse, N. Y.
Conn. Independent Movie Sup., New Haven, Conn.
H & S Film Supply Co., Pittsburgh, Pa.
Washington Thea. Supply Co., Washington, D. C.
National Elec. Sup. Co., Washington, D. C.
Phila. Theatre Equipment Co., Phila., Pa.
Louis M. Swab, Phila., Pa.
Theatre Sup. Co., Scranton, Pa.
S. F. Dusman, Baltimore, Md.
Carolina Theatre Sup. Co., Charlotte, N. C.
Service Film & Supply Co., Portland, Ore.
Theatre Equip. Co., Seattle, Wash.
E. H. Kemp, San Francisco, Cal.
Western Theatre Sup. Co., San Francisco, Cal.
Salt Lake Theatre Sup., Salt Lake City, Utah.
Erker Bros., St. Louis, Mo.
Amusement Supply Co., Detroit, Mich.
Theatre Equipment Co., Detroit, Mich.
E. E. Fulton Co., St. Louis, Mo.
B. E. Fulton Co., Indianapolis, Ind.

EDISON MAZDA LAMPS
A GENERAL ELECTRIC PRODUCT

Turn her vibrant
personality into
box-office dollars!

Evelyn Brent
IN
"LADY ROBINHOOD"

is a picture that will delight every type of fan!
She's making one big entertainment picture
after another. "Forbidden Cargo," "Alias
Mary Flynn," "Smooth as Satin" are a few of
the others! They're showmanship gold-mines!

Released by
FILM BOOKING OFFICES
723 Seventh Ave., New York, N. Y.
EXCHANGES EVERYWHERE

Exclusive Foreign Distributors
R-C Export Corporation
723 Seventh Avenue,
New York

Story by
Clifford Howard and
Burke Jenkins

Continuity by
Fred Myton

Directed by
Ralph Ince

$ 30,6

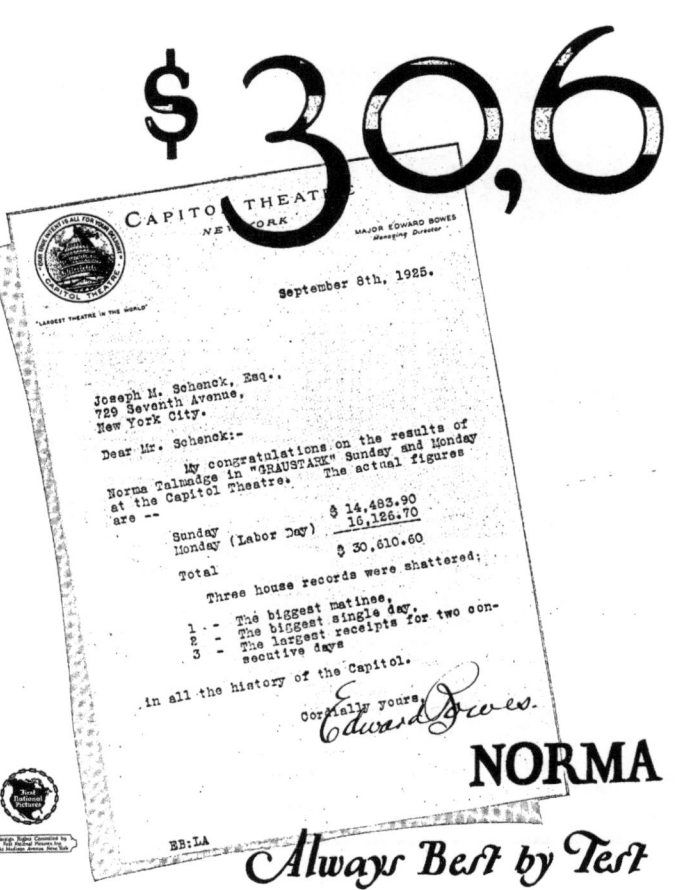

CAPITOL THEATRE
NEW YORK

MAJOR EDWARD BOWES
Managing Director

September 8th, 1925.

Joseph M. Schenck, Esq.,
729 Seventh Avenue,
New York City.

Dear Mr. Schenck:-

My congratulations on the results of
Norma Talmadge in "GRAUSTARK" Sunday and Monday
at the Capitol Theatre. The actual figures
are --

Sunday	$ 14,483.90
Monday (Labor Day)	16,126.70
Total	$ 30,610.60

Three house records were shattered:

1 - The biggest matinee,
2 - The biggest single day,
3 - The largest receipts for two con-
    secutive days

in all the history of the Capitol.

Cordially yours,
Edward Bowes.

EB:LA

NORMA

Always Best by Test

10.60
in *two* days!

~"biggest matinee"
~"biggest single day"
~"largest receipts for
two consecutive days
in the history of the
Capitol Theatre"~

And why not~why not~It's
TALMADGE'S biggest picture!

First National Pictures

Members of Motion Picture Producers and Distributors of America, Inc.~Will Hays President

wham!

MILTON SILLS
The Knockout
A First National Picture

Presented by
FIRST NATIONAL PICTURES

Here's a picture that
is sure going to make
new box office history
for this popular star.
Get it on your sched-
ule at once. Yes sir/

First National certainly
have the money makers.

Motion Picture News

VOL. XXXII   ALBANY, N. Y., AND NEW YORK CITY, SEPTEMBER 19, 1925   NO. 12

Let the Exhibitor Know It

I HAD a talk with an independent exhibitor the other day, which I will set down here just as it happened. First, let me say that he is a thoroughly experienced exhibitor, gets about a good deal, and is a close reader of the trade papers.

"I want to get your advice," said he, "your very best. And please be very frank. The matter involves all my money and considerable from investing friends; my credit, too.

"My houses (several in number and a new one is building) are now edged in between producer-owned chains. I can hold my own from a management standpoint. But what I want to know is this: can I get enough good pictures and at a live and let live price? A lot of other exhibitors similarly situated must be worrying about the same problem—available product. In fact, I know they are. I talk with them. Of course, the problem differs everywhere. Now, in my case, one of the theatre chains around me is owned by a so-called Independent Company. The pictures of another Independent Company are too high priced for me, much as I would like them. That narrows the field down to, say, two big national distributors and importantly, the State Rights group."

I assured him that to my best knowledge, he could be assured of satisfactory product, adequate in quantity and quality. That his problems were: (1) keen selection and (2) bang-up advertising. Especially the latter. As for product, we went over the pictures available, and he finally agreed with me, and heartily so, that there was plenty to be had and that he could hold his own with it against his competitors. It was evidently a relief to him to arrive at this decision.

"But why," he asked, "don't these independents play up their pictures more forcefully to the exhibitor? Here am I, an average exhibitor, we'll say, only vaguely informed as to their united strength. I don't know, and I'm doubtful. It would pay them, I should think, to go to it and leave no doubt anywhere but that they have got the goods."

The exhibitor is right. His contention has been our contention right along; not merely this season, but every season since the cry of independently owned theatres was raised at the Cleveland Convention. Plenty of pictures—good pictures, were available for every exhibitor that year, and have been every year since then. And there always will be an adequate supply. But the advertising of them has never been such as to convince the exhibitor that this true.

In making this assertion we will, of course, raise the suspicion that we are promoting trade paper advertising. Very well, and, to avoid any argument, we are. But the issue involved is much greater than that of trade papers—all of them combined. It concerns the welfare of several thousand exhibitors and of the entire body of independent producers and distributors.

Their problem is a straight out-and-out business one. Sentimental appeals, banner raising, orations and editorials, knocking the alleged trust, etc., will accomplish nothing. It's a plain case of having the goods and letting the customer know it.

In this issue of MOTION PICTURE NEWS we are presenting the announcement of the independent field. It is a goodly line-up. And we have little doubt but that a good many exhibitors will go over it carefully, estimate the pictures offered as to individual worth, and weigh it all as a factor in the new season's market.

W. A. Johnston

E. C. King, general manager of the Paramount Long Island studio, which are now celebrating their fifth anniversary by working "full speed ahead" on several Paramount pictures.

Several of the Albertina Rasch dancers rehearsing atop the new Steinway building for their prologue to "The Phantom of the Opera" (Universal) at the Astor, New York City.

PICTURES
AND
PEOPLE

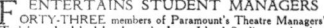

A 1ST NATIONAL LUNCHEON

AT noon last Tuesday First National gave a luncheon in the International Studio, 128th Street and Second Avenue, to representatives of the trade, daily press and fan magazines. Sam E. Rork was host, assisted by production manager Chester Beecroft. It was a merry and memorable gathering, with the underground wires working incessantly and providing real news, near news and shadowy run rumors of filmland doings for conversation purposes. And it may be said that the conversation ball never stopped rolling, excepting when the guests dutifully observed the silence rule while watching the filming of scenes for "Clothes Make the Pirate."

Leon Errol is the star of this picture, which will be completed in a couple of weeks, with Dorothy Gish and Nita Naldi as two of its leading lights. The consensus of opinion was that First National has a real box office winner here, and that the inimitable Errol's funny stunts will give the fans something to laugh over for a long time to come.

F ENTERTAINS STUDENT MANAGERS

FORTY-THREE members of Paramount's Theatre Managers' Training school had lunch at the Long Island Studio one day last week, and were introduced to a number of screen students who hope to be stars in their own right some time in the glittering future. Assistant manager Wingate escorted the guests around the studio, and showed them the various stages and sets where pictures were in the making.

Lectures were delivered by Jesse L. Lasky and Ralph Block, the entire day being utilized as part of the managerial training course. After six months of study the embryo managers will be stamped O.K. for all practical purposes and receive appointments to posts in all parts of the world.

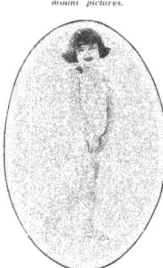

This is neither a Follies girl nor a Vanities or Scandals beauty—may we introduce Margie Gay, the dainty Alice of the "Alice Comedies" (M. J. Winkler).

The Gainsborough lady of the films—Alma Rubens, leading lady of "East Lynne" (Fox), whose cameo profile is the delight of artists.

Evelyn Brent, F. B. O. star, arrives in New York for a holiday and is met at the station by Frank Leonard, exploiteer, and Harry Osborne, of the ad department.

The first stages of the dream ball setting for "A Kiss for Cinderella" (Paramount), with Herbert Brenon (seated) in conference with J. J. Gain, assistant studio manager, and Julian Fleming, who designed the set.

Finis Fox chats over with Peggy O'Day the series of Secret Service pictures he is writing and supervising for her, to be released through Davis Distributing Division.

Marylin Mills snapped with Star and Beverly, the two clever horses who will support her in a series of starring vehicles for the Davis Distributing Division

Mr. and Mrs. Thomas Meighan and Lois Wilson (seated) returning on the Leviathan from Ireland after shooting "Irish Luck" (Paramount). (P. & A. Photo).

You've got to be in good trim to keep up with Harold Lloyd, and Jobyna Ralston, leading lady in his first for Paramount release, takes a work-out with Frank Merrill.

NOT SO DUSTY

KINOGRAMS news reel, released by Educational, was represented by a bunch of cameramen and helpers at the Gold Cup motorboat races, held at Port Washington, L. I. recently. Frank Dalrymple was one of the helpers.

Ray Haroun, with his flyer—"Fulford-by-the-Sea," found at the eleventh hour that he was shy a mechanician. As the rules insist on two men being in each boat, he was calling wildly for aid, when Frank butted in with the simple statement, that, although he didn't claim to rank as a mechanician, he had kept his flivver running for two years. It being any port in a storm, Haroun took him along. They got off to a bad start, but by degrees crept up to fourth place then third, then second—and crossed the finish line. Frank expressed regrets at having lost, but Haroun was satisfied.

It's O.K., "he said. You're the best mascot a driver ever had. With that rotten start I didn't expect to get better than sixh."

MIX PAYS THE BILL

TOM MIX has made good with Boy Scout contingents all over the country, or will, when they hear what he did for Avalon Ship I, several days ago. The government sent along a fine big whaling boat, which was eagerly unpacked by the boys. But gloom came in the shape of a freight bill which took all the wind out of the Seascouts' sails.

Just then Tom's cruiser made port and he stepped ashore, marked the disgusted faces turned toward him and asked what the trouble was. They told him, and a check to cover the intruding bill was promptly forthcoming. Mix says he was a Scout once and hasn't forgotten the "do a good turn daily" slogan.

WEDDING BELLS CHIME

ON September 1st, Miss Lilyan Tashman, Metro-film star, and Edmund Lowe, star of Fox Film Company, were united in marriage at San Francisco, having motored there from Hollywood. The ceremony was performed by Justice of the Peace A. T. Barnett. Sentiment may be said to have urged Mr. Lowe to select San Francisco as the place for tying the nuptial knot, as it was in that city he began his movie career and scored early successes. The bride is a former Follies girl, who made good on the screen, progressing swiftly until she reached her present altitude as head of her own company.

ONLY TWO WINNERS

MEMBERS of the National Committee For Better Films were chary of bestowing decorations on pictures registered in their weekly photoplay guide for week ending September 5. Only two were marked with the coveted "star," these being "Siefried," Ufa Films; and Pathe Review number I, the latter consisting of shots along the Swanee River; glass manufacturing; country life in France; and a dog days novelty. Both were classed under heading—For general audience and special "Family," audience including children of Grammar School age and up.

A violet phosphorescent diamond necklace (whatever that is!) is being worn by Mae Murray in "The Masked Bride" (Metro-Goldwyn), and is the only one in existence.

Jetta Goudal in a picturesque (and dangerous) looking pose from "The Road to Yesterday" (Producers Dist. Corp.) in which she is being featured under the direction of "C. B."

Yola d'Avril, whose Gallic personality has brightened many features, and who is now appearing in current Christie comedies for Educational release.

Lloyd Hughes, who is in the East working in "The Scarlet Saint" (First Nat'l), puts a little punch into the daily workout in the studio gymnasium.

John Barrymore, the star, Director Millard Webb, and members of the company engaged in filming "The Sea Beast" (Warner Bros.) from the classic whaling story, "Moby Dick."

STARS' HALL OF FAME

LIFE-SIZED portraits of screen stars by the world's greatest artists to hang in a Hollywood Hall of Fame and edify generations yet unborn! That's the idea sponsored by Sid Grauman, said Hall to be a bully show-place and one of the units in conjunction with his new $5,000,000 theatre, to be erected on Hollywood Square.

Norma Talmadge is the first star to have her portrait painted for this purpose, for whom Howard Christy Chandler was engaged. He will also turn out portraits of Constance Talmadge, Buster Keaton and Joseph M. Schenck, Grauman states that he will bring prominent artists from all parts of the earth, among those already selected being Frederic Beltran-Masses, Zulucaga, noted Spanish painter, Robert Henri, Weyman Adams, Charles Dana Gibson, Seymour Thomas and Joseph Kleitsch. "I fully believe" says Mr. Grauman, "that art lovers and motion picture enthusiasts will come to Hollywood just to see this wonderful art gallery of the brightest lights in filmdom, their personality transferred to canvas by master craftsmen of all time."

We were considering the framing-up of an Art Gallery of editorial personalities, not on canvas, but through the simpler medium of photos, $v per dozen, with crayon portraits thrown in for good measure. But the project is dead! Too much competition, besides we aren't at all sure the fans and art lovers would flock to see 'em. The field is clear for Mr. Grauman.

Colleen Moore, First National star, takes Richard A. Rowland, head of the organization, for a quiet little spin along Hollywood Boulevard. No casualties were reported among the traffic cops of that city.

THE MATERNAL ANGLE

MRS. Emilie Johnson, mother of Emory Johnson, producer and director of the "The Last Edition," is one of Hollywood's genuine screen parents. For Paula Gould, F. B. O.'s astute publicist, informs us that Mrs. Johnson is the author of every scenario used by her son and it is a treat to watch them co-operate on a production.

When they get an idea for a picture they consider it from all points, scribble a legion of notes, and then Mrs. Johnson starts her work. When the script is ready there comes the discussion between mother and son as to the possibilities of stars and supporting cast, the qualities of each "prospect" are freely gone over and finally a settlement made.

An unique pair, none other like them in the industry's production end. That their judgment is excellent is proved by the popularity attained by "The Third Alarm," "In the Name of the Law," and other pictures for which this remarkable mother-and-son combination is responsible.

BEAUTY IN DEMAND

SHE mustn't be over five feet three, nor under five feet. She must not weigh over one hundred and five pounds, nor scale under ninety-five. She must not have passed the twenty-year old mark. She must have studied dancing or have been an artist's model. She must be well formed and have tiny hands and feet.

Send any girl, or girls, you know who can qualify under the above specifications to Edmund Goulding, director of "Sally, Irene and Mary" for Metro-Goldwyn, now engaged in selecting a suitable ensemble of beauties for that production. The publicity expert says he needs 'em badly, not that there's any lack of lovely ladies among the "extra" brigade, but applicants must be constructed along certain lines in order to fill the bill. And there aren't as many of these as the innocent bystander might imagine.

Two old-time troupers of the original Biograph stock company meet —Henry B. Walthall and Lionel Barrymore, who talk over old times during the filming of "The Girl Who Wouldn't Work" (Preferred).

TOM MEIGHAN RETURNS

AFTER a month spent in Ireland working on "Irish Luck," his latest Paramount picture, Tom Meighan returned on the Leviathan Monday with Lois Wilson, Director Victor Heerman and twenty technical members of the company. The Lambs chartered a tug and sailed up the bay to welcome the star, who looked hale and hearty after his sojourn in the Emerald Isle.

They certainly made a big fuss over Thomas on the old sod. Ten thousand persons assembled to greet him when he reached Dublin and the thoroughfares of that ancient city were packed with interested spectators watching him work in the street scenes. Also, he hob-nobbed with the next thing to royalty or as the Celts would put it, "something a great dale better," in the person of President Cosgrave of the Irish Free State Altogether a memorable trip for the star and his associates, the events of which they aren't likely to forget in a hurry.

THE NEW FILMS

OF the five features on Broadway this week First National's "Graustark," at the Capitol; and Universal's "The Phantom of the Opera" at the Astor; stand well in the lead. In "Graustark" Norma Talmadge, as the lovely Princess Yetive, wooved and won in the face of death and dangers by a dashing young American hero, gives a really enchanting performance, while Eugene O'Brien as the aforesaid gallant, boosts the Stars and Stripes with George Cohanesuqe vigor, brushes aside enemies like flies as a film champion should do, and emerges from the imbroglio triumphant possessor of the blood-royal lady.

It is twenty years since George Barr McCutcheon wrote "Graustark" and started a host of imitators turning out fiction yarns of mythical countries with similar settings. A lengthy period for the most popular best-seller of its day to lie in seclusion so far as the screen is concerned! But the wait was worth while, considering the general excellence and commercial value of the film version. Director Dimitri Buchowetzki had fine melodramatic material to work on and made the best of his opportunities by surrounding the story with a wealth of colorful atmosphere, scenery and sets that for sheer appeal of beauty has few equals today.

"Wake up!" says Kit Guard to Al Cooke. "It's time we were at the F. B. O. studio cutting up for 'The Adventures of Mazie.'" "G'wan," says Cooke, "we ain't shootin' scenes by moonlight."

Chaps, bandana and the other cowboy trappings—and the familiar pancake hat—make up Buster Keaton's outfit in "Go West" (Metro-Goldwyn), the latest picture to include in its cast a large herd of cattle—this time for comedy effect.

"The Phantom of the Opera" is best described as the first super-mystery picture, even as "The Covered Wagon" ranked as the initial super-Western. Universal's widely advertised feature puts over the horror stuff in fine gruesome style, with Lon Chaney's grisly, inhuman make-up of grotesque ugliness sending chills down the spectator's spines, aided and abetted by the singularly fantastic trend of the narrative. The sets are gorgeous in the extreme, that of the celebrated Paris Opera House is a wonderfully faithful reproduction of the original edifice and the colored sequences of Faust, the ballet and masked ball are miracles of prismatic splendor. The acting is as good as might well be expected with such prominent players as Mary Philbin, Norman Kerry, Arthur Edmund Carewe, Snitz Edwards, Gibson Gowland, John Sainpolis, Virginia Pearson, and others helping that arch-creator of weird effects—Mr. Chaney, to promote goose-flesh among the onlookers. Certainly Universal has a genuine ghostly thriller here that should make even the hard-boiled fans sit up and shiver.

"The Golden Princess," at the Rivoli, is a good average Western melodrama and nothing more. Billed as an adaptation of a Bret Harte story, it doesn't contain a single line, scene or situation fathered by that author. But viewed merely as a straight screen Western it gets O.K. Betty Bronson, far-famed heroine of "Peter Pan," is starred, but her role is such an inconsequential thing that it doesn't throw much light on the question of her ability to handle a real grown-up part requiring dramatic intensity and emotional power. All that is asked of Betty in this production is to smile, look

pleasing and piquant, and with her youth, beauty and engaging personality that is an easily accomplished task.

The Colony presents "The Coming of Amos" a love romance with many melo punches which ought to do well enough at the box office. Rod La Rocque, as the hero, impersonates a young Australian shepe-rancher who lands on the Riviera equipped with uncouth garb and glorious disregard of social etiquette. But Rod brings a boomerang along, not exactly the sort of thing one would expect to figure as an aid to lovemaking, yet his expertness in hurling this singular weapon helps him mightily in winning the affections of a beautiful, mysterious Russian Princess. No—he doesn't bash her with the native war-tool, in cave-man fashion, even a sheep-rancher from the Antipodes would scarcely revert to such primitive methods. But the boomerang comes in very handy, just the same, as anyone who has seen the film will admit.

At the erstwhile Piccadilly, now Warner's Theatre, Irene Rich holds forth as the star of "The Wife Who Wasn't Wanted," a Warner Brothers Production. Miss Rich is cast in the, to her, exceedingly familiar role of a wife with an unappreciative hubby, and, as usual scores a dramatic triumph. It's a society drama and an interesting one, wherein the wife opposes her marital partner when he refuses to help a son held on a manslaughter charge, because the father is district attorney and handicapped by a sense of duty. The star's flawless acting is decidedly the highlight of the picture, but she receives adequate support, all of which, combined with James Flood's skilled direction, results in a good box office card.

Clyde Cook, fun-maker in Hal Roach comedies for Pathe, has a simple method of keeping comfortable in hot weather. A bottle of soda, a life-jacket and a derby hat is all that is required. Don't forget the derby.

WATCH Pathe this year for some very interesting announcements. Elmer Pearson has been quietly at work on production matters for some time, nearly a year, in fact. And now, at last, there's the scratching of pens on important contracts. Takes a long time to arrange these matters between New York and Hollywood; but the good ones are worth waiting for.

We venture to say that Pathe's shop window will be dressed more attractively this year than ever before in the history of this steady going, excellent organization. New kinds of comedies, new kinds of serials, and some electric light names to illuminate the whole window. Exhibitors will stop and look.

* * *

SPEAKING of comedies—they're difficult to make; that we all know. Always have been. I once handled the fiction desk of a popular magazine, and when a comedy story—a good one—appeared in the deluge of fiction which the U. S. mail gave us every week, the entire office stopped work to read it. The proportion of light to serious stories seemed as rare as one in ten thousand. As a matter of fact, we couldn't wait for comedy stories to come along; we had to go forth and capture them. So, at one time, a group of editors used to sit daily on O. Henry's doorstep—and shortened his life.

Yes, they're hard to make—that is, good comedies. But there would be more good ones, if the exhibitor would take a hand in the matter.

In other words, exhibitors will permit more and better comedies to be made if they will pay better prices for them.

The ruling price for comedies has lagged 'way behind in the swift advance in cost and price of dramatic features. You can make a fair feature today for say around $25,000 a reel; not often, at that. The ruling demand for big names all around—stars, casts, stories and plays, directors—shoves the cost away above $25,000 a reel, to double that amount, in fact. The cry everywhere is against, not for, the moderate cost program feature. Yet comedy producers would be happy if they could even have very much less per reel to spend than the ordinary feature costs.

Educational and Pathe, the distributing divisions of Fox, Universal, F. B. O., will increase their advances to the producer just as soon as the exhibitor will permit the increase. That's the long and short of the matter. The exhibitor can write the ticket—as he chooses; he knows the importance of comedies on his program.

* * *

THE very same situation applies to serials. They are damned only by the insistence that they must be cheaply made. Which unfolds a unique situation. In the popular magazine field today—so closely akin in every way to the picture field—serials are a prime factor. A magazine of large general circulation, going to the very people who go to movies, would give up anything in its editorial program rather

AN EDITOR

The Week in Review

than the serial. But—the best authors write them. They pay heavily for them. Harold Bell Wright received $50,000 for his latest magazine serial.

There's a very large and distinct field for the serial picture—much larger than the small communities where the need for the serial is not argued about. There's a very large field—if we make serials with the stories, cast and stars—in other words, with the moneys which go into dramatic features. Which, again, is up to the exhibitor, and the prices he will pay.

* * *

LEON ERROL is finishing "Clothes Make the Pirate," the Sam Rork special which bids fair to rank as one of the big attractions of the season. A notable cast includes Dorothy Gish, Nita Naldi, George Marion, Tully Marshall, James Rennie and others. Then Errol starts his two-year contract term as a First National star.

The wise ones are saying that Errol will take rank as one of the great comedians of the screen. Given the requisite production material, there seems little doubt but that he will score brilliantly. Here is what George Marion says: "Errol is the greatest Pierrot on the stage today. He is the superb clown—trained to his finger tips, laugh-provoking but whimsically appealing, capable of pathos, that great trick of the true comedian.

"It seems to me," Marion went on to say, "that the screen has caught up with Errol's art, that henceforth your audiences will continue to expect a breadth and finesse in your comedy offerings."

* * *

GEORGE MARION has other interesting things to say. He always has. When I want to know about things dramatic I go straight to this eminent actor, producer and scholar. "You write often," said he, "about the need for showmen in the entertainment world. True, of course, but how do you gage showmen? The term cannot be loosely applied. So many claim to be, even think they are, who are not. I believe a showman is simply a part of the audience, their representative back of the stage, or behind the screen. He is trained to think and feel as do the people in front. He knows what to give them, so much of this and so much of that, so they'll leave satisfactorily filled with their emotional meal."

Which we offer as the best definition of a showman. How many can claim this measure of training and innate ability?

* * *

BEGINNING with "The Unholy Three" and "Sally of the Sawdust," the Fall season has opened with the best pictures any season ever put forth. It's getting so that the exceptional attraction doesn't command exceptional attention. Consider

ON BROADWAY

By William A. Johnston

these: "The Gold Rush," "The Freshman," "Phantom of the Opera," "The Lost World," "The Wanderer," "The Merry Widow," "Havoc," "Don Q," and now comes "Graustark," making new records at the Capitol Theatre—over $30,000 in .two days. James Cruze's "Pony Express" is due at the Rivoli next week, following the two-weeks run of "The Coast of Folly," which, while the critics may disagree, will prove one of Gloria Swanson's best box-office bets. And Edwin Schallert writes from the coast of two forthcoming big ones: "The Big Parade" and "The Dark Angel."

Here's some more of the box-office kind. The list is impressive: "Kiss Me Again," "Her Sister from Paris," "The Lucky Horseshoe," "The Limited Mail," "Souls for Sables," "Fighting the Flames," "Seven Chances," "I'll Show You the Town," "Drusilla with a Million," "Friendly Enemies," "The Overland Limited," "The Girl Who Wouldn't Work," "The Crackerjack," "The Home Builder," "The Goose Woman," "The Danger Signal," "The Live Wire."

Quite a formidable list, here, and it doesn't cover all the good bets and the many more to come, including some big ones. In fact it's just rolling up the curtain. As I say, the average today is so good that the exceptional ones go by with scarcely a flurry. We used to get out special editions on them.

* * *

THERE are many good lessons on production to deduce from the above list: One that seems to stand out is that these pictures come from a good many sources. I count, hurriedly, seventeen different producing organizations and units. You certainly couldn't expect such a group of shows from one source; the actual truth is that you couldn't get them from five or ten. Seventeen is the count and seventeen sets of brains were required. And so it will always be. The better the pictures, the more producers we will need, for the simple reason that more producers supply more ideas, and ideas count mostly in the show world.

Scan these pictures over, and you will agree with me that it was—mostly—the idea back of each that made it succeed. Production ability, yes, of course; that counts heavily. We are agreed that it takes an organization today to make a picture. Stars, stories, cast, sets, photography—all important. But the idea looms biggest.

I can imagine, in the mind's eye, the very epitome of a smooth running, finely manned, fully equipped producing organization, splendidly efficient and with all the atmosphere of high endeavor. And I can imagine a finely finished product coming steadily from such an organization. But its very smoothness of operation would damn it for the show market because there would be sameness. And while sameness would be highly desired for most any factory product, it is just what the show business doesn't want. Shows want ideas, a lot of them, often crazy ones. And when there are not lots of ideas, fresh ones, inspiring ones, the show business gets into a rut.

Just so long as we have plenty of sources of production we will have plenty of box-office pictures and industrial property. May the contrary situation never exist.

* * *

ONE of the best campaign books ever to reach our desk is the one prepared on "The Freshman," by S. Barret McCormick. Looks like the summing of a rich and rare experience in picture exploitation. Barret McCormick's copy for the Circle Theatre of Indianapolis marks the first chapter of history in theatre exploitattion. We recall that exhibitors used to subscribe to Indianapolis newspapers—special delivery, too—to get his advertisements.

* * *

THE Eastman theatre, Rochester, is celebrating its third anniversary. During the three years of its existence the house has attracted worldwide attention through its plan of operation and the idealistic aims of its founder. Dedicated to the "enrichment of community life," it has established itself as a real community center of entertainment. Attendance at its various performances in the three years is said to have exceeded 6,000,000.

Illustrative of the magnitude of the details involved in the theatre's service are the facts that in the last year the orchestra played more than 1500 different musical numbers, and that about 3500 miles of motion picture film were run through the theatre's projection machines.

A survey of the best drawing pictures of the year at the Eastman demonstrates that in Rochester at least it is not the sex play nor the lurid drama that finds the readiest response from the public. Big dramatic and historical productions, comedies and clean romance have found the greatest measure of popular appreciation. The ten most popular pictures of the year, in order of their drawing power, were: "The Covered Wagon," "Hot Water," "The Rag Man," "The Sea Hawk," "Peter Pan," "Classmates," "Abraham Lincoln," "Sally," "He Who Gets Slapped," "A Thief in Paradise." Following closely were "The Navigator," "The Only Woman," "Secrets" and "Black Cyclone."

* * *

THE anniversary week attraction was Harold Lloyd in "The Freshman." The first public demonstration of dynamic color was also given in "Flowing Color Harmonies." The presentation was arranged through the co-operation of Lloyd A. Jones and Clifton Tuttle of the Eastman Research Laboratories. The demonstration presented with the accompaniment of Debussy's First Arabesque by the orchestra, illustrated some possibilities in the use of changing color and form.

MOTION PICTVRE NEWS

September 19
1925

Vol. XXXII
No. 12

Founded in September 1913

Publication Office: Lyon Block, Albany, N. Y.

Editorial and General Offices:
729 7th Ave., New York City

Branch Offices:
845 S. Wabash Ave., Chicago, Ill.
Room 616 Security Bldg., Hollywood, Calif.

What the Motion Picture Means

THE first prize in the National Greater Movie Season Contest was won by Mrs. Ruth Griffith Burnett, of Indianapolis. Here is her essay:

" 'Sing us a song!' was the demand of yore and the wandering minstrel complied. As he sang the song of valor there unrolled before the eyes of his listeners a picture to teach, to inspire and to entertain them.

" 'Tell us a story!' was the demand of our fathers from the oasis of the firelight. And as the story-teller, beloved and admired, told the story there unfolded, before the eyes of his hearers a picture to teach, to inspire and to entertain them.

" 'Show us a picture!' is our demand, and lo, we are given the magic of a real picture with the enchantment of the minstrel and the charm of the story-teller. .

"In the broadness of its scope and its capacity for the portrayal of things great and small, the motion picture shows me history, science, art and literature. From India, with its swarming highways, to barren Alaska, the world is mine, the generous gift of the camera.

"Because it depicts humanity the motion picture inspires. Its subtle sermons are abiding. It takes from my tongue the timid 'I can't,' and in its place puts a brave 'I'll try!' It lightens the corners of pride and indifference and makes me a little more sympathetic, more tolerant and more fit to take my place beside my fellow men.

"It entertains me. It draws me without my accustomed self and lets me laugh until the tears come, or sit upon the edge of my seat in suspense. It makes me glad to be alive.

"Education, inspiration and entertainment. These three the motion picture mean to me."

A Happy State of Affairs

THIS year, for the first time in nine years, no bills antagonistic to the industry were introduced in Georgia. The industry in that State has carried on a systematic campaign, familiarizing the lawmakers with actual conditions, giving them a comprehensive idea of the type of pictures now being presented, and acquainting them thoroughly with facts bearing on the financial end of the industry.

This has brought about a very happy state of affairs. Just before the Legislature adjourned, the other day, the following resolution was unanimously passed:

"Whereas, Throughout the 1925 session of the General Assembly of the State of Georgia in the City of Atlanta, members of both houses have been repeatedly the guests of the motion picture theatres, including the Grand and Forsyth theatres of said city, and

"Whereas, Members of the Legislature have found this form of entertainment not only clean and wholesome, instructive and educational, but it has generously contributed to the pleasure of our stay in the Capitol City.

"Therefore, Be It Resolved by the Senate, the House concurring, That the thanks of the General Assembly be hereby tendered to the managers of the various theatres for this courtesy so graciously extended."

The Box-Office Tells the Tale

THE other night, at a Broadway premiere, a slender little gray-haired man made his way from an orchestra seat to the stage to respond to the cheers of the crowd. It was Charlie Chaplin, and the crowd wanted to hear him speak. What he said was a graceful acknowledgment of the applause. He preferred to do his "talking" on the screen. And he had done it in such fashion that the box-office at the Strand Theatre has been resounding with the echo ever since.

This reminds us that, every once in a while, somebody bobs up with the prediction that "Charlie can't repeat". Well, "The Gold Rush" is his first appearance on the screen since 1922, and he has more than confounded the prophets of evil.

September 19, 1925   MOTION PICTURE NEWS   Vol. XXXII. No. 12
Published twice weekly by MOTION PICTURE NEWS, INC., William A. Johnston, President; E. Kendall Gillett, Vice-President; William A. Johnston, Editor; J. S. Dickerson, Associate Editor; Oscar Cooper, Managing Editor; Fred J. Beecroft, Advertising Manager; L. H. Mason, Chicago Representative; William McCormack, Los Angeles Representative. Subscription price, $3 per year. Saturday Edition $2, Mid Week $1, postpaid in United States, Mexico, Hawaii, Porto Rico, Philippine Islands and some other countries; Canada, $5; foreign, $10.00. Copyright 1924, by MOTION PICTURE NEWS, INC., in the United States and Great Britain. Title registered in the United States Patent Office and foreign countries. Western Union Cable address is "Picknews," New York. Entered as second-class matter January 21st, 1924, at the postoffice, Albany, N. Y., under the Act of March 3, 1879.

New Idea in Coming Pictures is to Create Striking Moments

"Big Parade" Cited As Example of Healthy Innovation

By Edwin Schallert, Los Angeles Times

(Editor's Note.—This is the seventh of a regular series of articles by the Editor of the Los Angeles Times Pre-View. Mr. Schallert writes exclusively for Motion Picture News *in the trade field)*

BIG moments *make* big pictures. Big moments of drama; big moments of acting. Big thrills; big climaxes; big scenes and ensembles, and sometimes even huge mobs and spectacles.

Recall a few instances:

The return of Henry Walthall to the Southern homestead, and the ride of the Clansmen in "The Birth of a Nation." Always unforgettable.

The poignant pain of sacrifice written on the faces of Rudolph Valentino and Alice Terry in "The Four Horsemen."

The beaten and oppressed Tol'able David's revolt and embittered battle for freedom.

The flaring brilliance of the mass effects in "Robin Hood," with its glory of setting.

More recently—a tragic seriousness flinging its shadow across a mood of laughter as in the New Year's Eve sequence in Charles Chaplin's "The Gold Rush."

Zorro to the rescue in "Don Q"—an idea of surpassing ingenuity and cleverness. The last two are perhaps not so generally known because so recently released, but they have the same vital spark.

If a picture has one such moment as I have mentioned, it will, as a rule, with other things even moderately in harmony, be talked about. The audience will remember it after they leave the theatre. They will tell their friends and acquaintances. Arguments may spring up over the effectiveness of the dramatic episode, the scene or the acting. There may be disagreements even—but all the better. It's the same as that rooting and shouting that goes on at a prize-fight or a football game.

This season I believe we will have a number of such pictures. Plots and situations (at least the reality of certain situations) are showing a sudden increase in health and vigor. Old formulae are being discarded. New and novel ideas for treatment, if not for the stories themselves, are being sought out. More daring, more initiative, more individuality is in evidence all along the line, at least in the bigger productions. It is a healthy state, disclosing an increased energy being thrown into productions as productions, rather than productions as vehicles merely for stars.

One picture I have seen lately that I know will start something: It will have both supporters and enemies, but it is not going to be allowed to languish. It is going to be both praised and damned vehemently, and it may even put some in a fighting mood, but above all it will attract attention. It is (significantly!) a *war* picture — "The Big Parade."

The story for this production, as is now doubtless pretty widely known, was written by Laurence Stallings, co-author of "What Price Glory." The feature was directed by King Vidor, and when they decided that they had something really big, Metro-Goldwyn-Mayer expanded their plans and spent a lot of extra money, procuring war scenes to give it a big epical character. When it is released it will be in the super-production class as to length—some twelve reels in all, with a break arranged for an intermission. And not too long at that!

I have hardly ever been conscious of such tensity in an audience, taken as a whole, at any time recently, than there was at the preliminary preview in Pasadena. The film was not at that time in its final shape, and some of the later episodes were a little weak, but it went over with a thundering bang.

More than once there was general applause.

The outstanding characteristic of this picture is that it does not take itself too seriously. Despite its length, it rarely touches the note of heaviness. For two-thirds of the film comedy and laughter are gloriously emphasized. It is life as it was lived behind the front during the World War that is depicted—an accurate, intimate and telling impression—a true inside story of the conflict abroad, that every ex-soldier will recognize as touching his own experiences at some point, and that every mother, father, wife, sweetheart, and even distant relative of an ex-soldier will appreciate because of still unforgettable associations.

Tragedy there is of course in "The Big Parade"—deep and pathetically—appealing sort of tragedy too, but not "Greed"-like and forbidding. All the bitterness of war comes to the surface in the scenes showing the death of one of a group of three soldiers—Three Musketeers you might call them—about whom the action of the picture centers. War hate is expressed in all its gaunt reality—a reality bordering on madness. Yet, the soldier who hated and would slaughter the Germans because they had killed his companion, gives a wounded one his last cigarette, when they find themselves together in a shell hole. There is a still older twist to this scene, when he takes the same cigarette out of the man's mouth after his death, and puts it absentmindedly into his own.

That particular scene is one that is going to be talked about. It represents in one brief glimpse all the horrors of war, and its humanness. It is a dreadful and terrible thing in a way, but one that the audience will watch with bated breath if perhaps with a shudder almost of distaste. Only the deftness of Jack Gilbert's acting as the American soldier, and Vidor's direction make it acceptable, as it doubtless will be to a large majority of people, for its terrific dramatic effect.

To many who see "The Big Parade" this will not be the only big moment. There is another equally as fine in a large way, which shows the first entrance of soldiers into battle. They have heard about war, thought about war, talked about war, laughed about war, and here they actually face its reality, seemingly when they had least anticipated it, when they are worn of body and soul

(Continued on page 1351)

Famous Players Net Profits $2,051,532.72 for Six Months Ending June 27

THE Famous Players-Lasky Corporation in its consolidated statement (which includes the earnings of subsidiary companies) reports net profits of $695,-724.61 for the three months and $2,051,532.71 for the six months to June 27, 1925 after deducting all charges and reserves for Federal income and other taxes.

After allowing for payment of dividends on the preferred stock, the above earnings amount to $2.16½ per share for the three months and $7.04 per share for the six months, on the 243,431 shares of common stock outstanding on June 27, 1925.

Hunt Stromberg Joins Executive Staff of Metro-Goldwyn-Mayer

Hunt Stromberg, Harry Rapf, Louis B. Mayer, Irving G. Thalberg

HUNT STROMBERG, one of the industry's foremost producers, has entered into an agreement with Metro-Goldwyn-Mayer whereby he will act in a supervisory capacity and will augment the work of Irving G. Thalberg and Harry Rapf, associate executives at the Culver City studios.

An enlarged production schedule is soon to be put into effect at the Metro-Goldwyn-Mayer studios and Stromberg will participate actively in its execution.

In addition to acting in a supervisory capacity he will assume the direction of several pictures.

In making the announcement Louis B. Mayer said: "Under the enlarged producing program about to be launched we will need the additional services of a producer who can achieve M-G-M quality in pictures. In Stromberg Messrs. Thalberg, Rapf and myself feel we have acquired such a man. He enjoys an eviable record and under his arrangement with us he will, I feel sure, achieve the greatest work of his career."

Hunt Stromberg was recently producing for P. D. C., and made several successes for them. A short time ago he disposed of all of his interests in such pictures and turned over four or more stories to them. Considerable speculation as to just why he had sold out his interests has been going the rounds, but the true cause, namely, the offer made to him by Louis B. Mayer on behalf of Metro-Goldwyn-Mayer, has just come to light with Mr. Mayer's announcement. Stromberg, felt that the opportunity to work wit M-G-M was one not to be lost, one that would provide him with the finest of facilities for the production of pictures along the lines that have brought him into the limelight.

Marion Fairfax Resigns Post

Quits as First National Editorial Director to Enter Production Field

MARION FAIRFAX has resigned as editorial director for First National to enter the production field as a personal venture. She has purchased screen rights to three novels which have had wide circulation during the past two years, and they will serve as her first vehicles for production.

The resignation of Miss Fairfax was to have become effective July 9th, but, at the urgent request of R. A. Rowland and Sam E. Rork, she cancelled a scheduled South American trip to remain in New York and supervise the Rork production, "Clothes Make the Pirate," which First National will release as a special, with Leon Errol and Dorothy Gish starring.

Miss Fairfax is one of the leading playwrights of the New York stage and an author scenarist, editorial and production supervisor of film plays. She has already achieved success as a picture producer, as the head, several years ago, of Marion Fairfax Productions.

Among the well known pictures with which Miss Fairfax has been identified in an editorial capacity are "Flaming Youth," "The Lost World," "So Big" and "The Talker," which is an adaptation of her own Broadway stage play. She has been editorial director of First National units since the entry of that organization into the producing field. Previously she served in a like capacity with Marshall Nilan and Famous Players-Lasky.

Miss Fairfax wrote the scenario of "Clothes Make the Pirate," adapting it from Holman Day's novel and preparing the continuity. She is now supervising the filming and the editing.

The scenario from which First National produced "The Lost World" was written by Miss Fairfax, who performed what was believed to be an almost impossible task in working out the adaptation of Conan Doyle's novel so that the effects of the prehistoric monsters could be put on the screen as part of drama of human characters.

New $350,000 Theatre for Wilshire, California

Plans have been completed for the erection of new theatre building and stores to be erected on Wilshire Boulevard between La Brea and Sycamore Avenues, Wilshire, California, to cost approximately $350,000. The theatre will be of old Spanish architecture and will be a fireproof construction with a seating capacity of 2,000. The owner of the new theatre will be the West Coast Company.

Five Companies Granted New York Charters

Motion picture companies entering the business in New York state during the past week, and receiving charters from the secretary of state, were: George Choos, Inc., capitalization not specified. George Choos, Edward J. Clarke, J. R. Elliott. New York city; Kirby-Marlowe, Inc., capitalization not stated, Mildred Singer, Morris Vogel, Saul Streit, New York city; Allegany Theatres Corporation, Batavia, capitalization not stated, J. R. Osborne, E. B. Westcott, Clara St. John, Batavia; Daly Avenue Theatre Corporation, capitalization not stated, Max Sheinart, Brooklyn; F. V. Goldstein, Benjamin Sherman, New York city.

First National Has Appointed Canadian Manager

E. A. Eschmann has appointed William A. Bach Canadian District Manager for First National to succeed Louis Bacine, who has resigned. Bach has long been a salesman of picture product in the Canadian market. Before joining First National he was manager of Famous Players in Toronto and prior to that was special representative of the Fox Film Corporation in Canada. He will make his headquarters in Toronto.

Shimon Resigns from Milwaukee Theatre

Louis C. Shimon, assistant manager of the Milwaukee theatre, 1080 Teutonia Ave., Milwaukee, Wis., has left that organization and will take a short vacation at Cedar Lake before announcing a new affiliation.

Mr. Shimon was popularly known at the Milwaukee as George Fischer's right-hand man. Besides being assistant manager, he was also advertising manager and head of the exploitation and copy department.

Canadian Conference on Copyrights

AN IMPORTANT conference on Musical Copyright and Performing Rights was held in the office of the Motion Picture Distributors & Exhibitors Association in Toronto on Thursday, September 3rd.

The Motion Picture interests were represented by Colonel John A. Cooper, President of the Association and Mr. Jack Arthur, Musical Director for Famous Players Canadian Corporation. The Canadian Society of Authors and Composers was represented by Professor Watson Kirkconnell of Winnipeg, Honorary Secretary. Musical Writers and Publishers were represented by G. V. Thompson.

The main topic under discussion was what attitude should be taken towards the Canadian Performing Right Society which has recently been formed in this country, at the instance of the Performing Right Society of London, England. While the conference was informal it is expected that the result will have a very considerable affect upon the Musical Copyright situation in Canada. Professor Kirkconnell will make a report on the subject to the National Executive of his Association.

Connecticut Film Tax Proves Burden on Industry

Exhibitors Decide Not to Increase Admission Prices

OUTSTANDING developments in the Connecticut tax situation this week:

Decision by the M. P. T. O. of Connecticut not to pass along the tax to patrons at least for the present.

Abandonment of Paramount Week in Connecticut in consequence of the tax situation.

Announcement that the State would receive $55,210 as the first tax payment, including all prints up to September 12, according to an agreement reached by Tax Commissioner Blodget and Charles C. Pettijohn, general counsel for the Hays organization.

A survey by the Connecticut exhibitor organization to determine the situation of its members with regard to product, in view of the announcement by distributors that no new contracts will be made after the present ones expire. This survey is being conducted under the supervision of President Joseph W. Walsh, of the Connecticut association.

Closing of a theatre because of the tax burden.

The New Haven meeting was attended by National President R. F. Woodhull, of the M. P. T. O. A., who assured the theatre owners that the entire resources of the National organization were behind them in the fight against the taxation and censorship measure.

Reports to *The Film Daily*, from its special correspondent in Connecticut, indicate that legislators who voted for the Durant bill now regret their action, in view of the difficulties imposed on the exhibitors. Statements to this effect were reported made to Mrs. W. A. Gill, proprietor of the Colonial and Walnut Beach theatres near Milford, Conn., by Representatives David A. Clarke and Hubert L. Pratt.

Senator Johnson and Representative E. Marshall Smith of East Haddam are quoted as having said that they were not aware the bill would place the burden on the theatre men and bring about the closing of the exchange. At the time the bill was brought up for passage the impression prevailed, it was stated, that the distributors would pay the tax.

Theatres in the Connecticut M. P. T. O. have been assessed according to their seating capacity and the money will be turned into the revolving fund created by the Hays organization. It will be paid to Tax Commissioner Blodgett through the Hartford-Connecticut Trust Company.

In order to take care of these payments the exhibitor organization has created a

central bureau, with quarters in the Kilfeather Building, which formerly housed most of the exchanges prior to their withdrawal from the State.

Numerous conferences have been held within the past ten days by Charles C. Pettijohn, general counsel for the Hays organization, and the Tax Commissioner, and these conferences have been entirely harmonious, as indicated by a statement issued by Mr. Blodgett. He praised Mr. Pettijohn for his efforts toward readjusting the difficulties brought about by the law, and declared Mr. Pettijohn was one of the few men who really understood the situation.

Eugene Treiber, President of the Motion Picture Operators' Union, has sent out questionnaires, through the members of the association, asking legislators if they voted for the measure and why and also if they are for repeal.

At the M. P. T. O. meeting in New Haven on Sunday steps were taken for a survey of product to find out how exhibitors stand on bookings. Announcement has been made by distributors that they will not make further contracts when the present agreements expire, so the association is gathering the information in view of the threatened film famine.

The meeting also discussed problems brought about by the removal of the exchanges. Nearly all the large theatres are using one delivery service, and the new arrangements are reported to cost the theatres about 15 per cent more than ordinary express service. Numerous difficulties have arisen in the delivery of film, but these, it is reported, are being ironed out to some extent.

Theatre Circuits Add More Houses

Famous and Warners Acquire New Holdings; Schwalbe to Build in Philadelphia—Fox Plans San Francisco Theatre

AMONG the important developments of the week in the theatre field is the formal announcement by Wilmer & Vincent, operators of a chain of theatres in Pennsylvania, that the Victoria at Harrisburg-Lasky. The announcement follows rumors current for some time that Famous was angling for the entire holdings of the Wilmer & Vincent company.

New theatre projects which came to light during the past week include the announcement that Fox would build a new house of more than 4,000 seating capacity in the Bronx and reports that Fox is negotiating for a theatre site in the downtown section of San Francisco, will build a 5,000 seat house on Figueroa St., Los Angeles and is preparing to erect a first-run theatre of about 3,500 seating capacity, in Chicago, the building to occupy a plot in the downtown section which Fox got some time ago.

It was reported in Philadelphia that Harry Schwalbe, formerly secretary of First National, and H. A. Winters, are having plans drawn for the construction of a large theatre, store and garage to be located at Fifty-second Street below Wyalusing Ave., that city. According to the report the building will occupy a plot 229 x 353 feet. The theatre will seat 2,000, will include thirteen stores in an arcade running through to Fifty-third Street. In the rear of the building there will be sixty-seven individual garages. The total cost of the structure according to estimates will be in excess of $600,000.

Warner Brothers this week announced the purchase of the Cameo Theatre, Bridgeport, Conn. The Warners have acquired full title to the property, including the real estate. The purchase was made from the Brandt

interests. The Cameo has a seating capacity of 1,600 and was built two years ago. It will be known hereafter as Warner's Cameo. Howard W. Foerste has been appointed manager.

In addition to the Victoria in Harrisburg, Famous Players this week acquired the Imperial Theatre at Pawtucket, R. I. Famous also holds a controlling interest in the Strand there. The Imperial was leased for an indefinite period. Walter G. Hartford and Thomas E. Marsden, who sold out their interests in the Imperial to Famous, opened the theatre in February, 1916 and have operated it since that time.

In taking over the Wilmer & Vincent house in Harrisburg, Famous obtained exclusive rights to the theatre. The transaction does not include the transfer of the real estate, C. Floyd Hopkins, Harrisburg representative of Wilmer & Vincent said.

PATHE SIGNS HARRY CAREY
Will Make Series of Westerns

BY THE terms of an agreement just entered into between Elmer Pearson of Pathe Exchange, Inc., and Charles R. Rogers, producer of Harry Carey films, Harry Carey will make a series of Western features for release through Pathe.

The same organization that has been making Carey pictures for Hunt Stromberg for the past two years will continue to produce the Carey pictures. Charles R. Rogers will devote his personal attention to the production activities, which will center at Universal City in California.

An adaptation of the story, "Buck Up," written by Basil Dickey and Harry Haven, will be Carey's first feature Western for Pathe. Harvey Gates prepared the continuity and Scott Dunlap will direct. Production will start at once. The initial release will probably be ready late in the Fall.

Carey has long been popular as a Western star. His three most recent successes were, "The Texas Trail," "Silent Anderson," and "Beyond the Border."

M. P. T. O. A. Committees Meet
Matters of Importance to Industry Are Submitted at Conferences

WEDNESDAY, September 2nd, was a day of great activity at the National headquarters of the Motion Picture Theatre Owners of America at 25 West 43rd Street, New York City. It was the occasion of several important committee meetings—Administrative—Legislative—Contract and Play Date.

The Administrative Committee, represented by A. Julian Brylawski, Washington, D. C., Chairman, Nathan Yamins, Fall River, Mass., and Harry Davis, Pittsburg, Pa., met and considered the report by President R. F. Woodhull on the various activities of the organization since the last meeting of the Board of Directors. Conferences were held with several prospective business managers, and these conferences are still continuing with the prospect of an early announcement being made of their final selection for this important post. Definite arrangements were also made for carrying on all the various work of the organization.

The Legislative Committee, particularly the Music Tax branch, submitted a report, and were authorized to continue their activities and to engage counsel to the end of securing an amendment to the Copyright law at the next session of Congress.

The Contract Committee represented by Joseph M. Seider, Newark, N. J., Chairman, together with Messrs. Yamins and Brylawski

met with Fred Elliott and Oscar Neufeld, representing Independent Motion Picture Association of America and a long and important conference was held. Seider presented a form of equitable contract and a form of Arbitration, which will be taken up by the other organization at an early date. Another meeting will be held as soon as is feasible.

The Play Date Committee, Messrs. Harry Davis, Chairman, Sydney S. Cohen, L. M. Sagal, Nathan Yamins and J. J. Harwood, met with A. Carlos, W. E. Shallenberger, Joseph Klein, A. Weiss and Fred Elliott of Independent Motion Picture Association of America.

President Woodhull was in attendance at all of the committee meetings. A resolution was adopted by all of the National Board of Directors present, pledging their support to the Theatre Owners of Connecticut in their present crisis, induced by the oppressive and confiscatory tax and censor law recently enacted, the repeal of which, or, relief from the restrictions of which, they are at present seeking.

New Auditor Appointed by Arrow

W. E. SHALLENBERGER, president of Arrow Pictures Corporation, has appointed Louis L. Beaudry auditor of the company to succeed Hugh Davis, resigned. Beaudry has had wide experience as an accountant and auditor. He installed the audit system now in force at the Hotel Pennsylvania, New York, and also instituted an audit system used by the Congress Hotel in Chicago.

$250,000 Theatre is to Be Erected in Oakland, Cal.

Plans for the erection of a $250,000 motion picture theatre on the east side of Broadway south of Fortieth Street, Oakland, California, are being completed. The theatre is to have a seating capacity of 2,500. The owner of the new structure is the Transbay Theatre Corporation.

New Theatre of Egyptian Design at Lynwood, Cal.

Lynwood, California is to have a new theatre building of Egyptian design to be erected on Long Beach Boulevard near the center of Lynwood. The seating capacity of the new house is to be 1,400. J. D. Marian has been appointed manager.

Henry King Signs Agreement With Sam Goldwyn

Samuel Goldwyn this week announced a contract with Henry King under which the latter will be associated with him in the production of a series of pictures covering a period of several years.

King will direct the film version of "Partners Again,' the next Potash '& Perlmutter story to reach the screen. Work on the Montague Glass play will start as soon as Mr. King completes "Stella Dallas," which he is now producing for Goldwyn.

Plans Announced for New $200,000 Monterey House

Plans are being prepared by Read Brothers, prominent San Francisco architects, for the erection of motion picture theatre building on Alvarado Street, Monterey, Cal. The approximate cost of the theatre will be $200,000 and it will have a seating capacity of from 1,000 to 1,500 persons. The owners of the new theatre will be the T. and D. Theatres Company.

Meyer Schine Joins Ranks of Benedicts

Miss Hildegard Feldman, of Gloversville, became the bride of J. Meyer Schine, one of the heads of the Schine circuit at a wedding performed Sunday in the Italian room of the hotel Utica. Mrs. Louis Schine was matron of honor, while the groom was attended by his brother, Louis.

De Mille Signs Hale to Long Contract

Cecil B. DeMille has signed Alan Hale to a long term directorial contract as the result of his work in the direction of Leatrice Joy in "The Wedding Song." The next story to be assigned Hale is "Braveheart," a Rod La Roque starring vehicle.

Cohen Declines Proffer of Testimonial Dinner

SYDNEY S. COHEN, Chairman of the Board of Directors of the M. P. T. O. A., has "finally and irrevocably" declined the proffer of a banquet or testimonial dinner which the Independent Motion Picture Association members proposed to tender him on October 18th. In a letter to I. E. Chadwick, president of the I. M. P. A., Mr. Cohen expresses his appreciation of the honor and compliment implied by the proffer of the association, but declines again to accept that honor, and suggests that the dinner which will open "Independence Week" be dedicated to the whole cause of "Independence."

Mr. Cohen concludes his letter with the following: "Trusting that you will see this in the same light and that your Committee will go forward to make this dinner so 'Independent' the biggest thing that has ever occurred in the industry, because it is a testimonial to the biggest cause which can exist—'Independence,' I must insist that this decision of mine be considered final and irrevocable."

Greater Movie Essay Winners Named

Indianapolis Woman Takes First Prize on Subject. "What the Motion Picture Means to Me"

A MOTHER of a three months old baby, living in a little house on the shady side of the road on Rural Route C, not far from Indianapolis, found time a few weeks ago to write an essay on "What the Motion Picture Means to Me." She sent it to the Indianapolis News, where it won first prize in the local Greater Movie Season Contest, sponsored by the Motion Picture Producers and Distributors of America, Inc., of which Will H. Hays is President.

The judges of the National Contest announced that it was the best of the thousands that were written in this nation-wide competition. And so, on November 25th, Mrs. Ruth Griffith Burnett, of Route C, Indianapolis, Ind., with her husband, Jesse Burnett—who always told her that she ought to try her hand at writing—will sail from New York City on the Red Star liner Belgenland on a tour of the world that will bring her back to New York City on April 6th, 1926. The cost of meals, stateroom and all sightseeing trips is paid.

Second prize in the contest—the choice of two trips to Los Angeles or two trips to Miami—goes to Mrs. Lawrence G. Wood of 1218 North Boston Place, Tulsa, Oklahoma, who submitted her entry through the Tulsa Tribune. Mrs. Wood has chosen to take the trip to Los Angeles.

The third prize was whichever trip was not selected by the second prize winner and the trip for two to Miami goes to a Civil War Veteran of Breckenridge, Colo. who—

in spite of his almost eighty years—is still an active man. His essay was entered by the Rocky Mountain News and Denver Times.

This winner of the third prize enlisted in the 108th Illinois Regiment when he was 17 years old. He served through the Civil War and was in the first and last attack on Vicksburg.

Many years ago Mr. Westerman moved to Colorado where he was engaged in mining and mine promotion for years. He has been elected State Representative from the counties of Summit and Grand and served in the Ninth, Tenth and a special session of the Colorado State General Assembly. Mr. Westerman has been deaf since the Battle of Vicksburg and his essay is a remarkable expression as to the part motion pictures have played in his life.

The winners of the trips to Los Angeles and to Miami will be the guests of the Chamber of Commerce in those two cities. Each prize winner and the person he or she selects as a companion, will have all traveling and hotel expenses paid for a two week visit.

The National judges were George Barr McCutcheon, president of the Author's League of America; Alice Duer Miller, noted author; Richard Washburn Child, famous writer and former Ambassador to Italy; and Dr. S. Parkes Cadman, president of the Federal Council of Churches. Dr. Cadman was called abroad and could

not return in time to take part in judging the contest and he appointed as his representative Dr. George Reid Andrews, Chairman of the Committee on Educational and Religious Drama, of the Federal Council of Churches.

Two hundred thousand essays were submitted to the forty-two prominent newspapers throughout the United States, that conducted the contest. The greatest number was received by the committee for the State of Michigan—which contest was conducted through the Detroit Times and other Michigan newspapers associated in the State Contest. The Michigan essays numbered 50,000.

Each newspaper, after selecting the local prize winners, sent its three best essays to New York for the National Judges. As fast as these essays were received in the office of the Motion Picture Producers and Distributors of America, Inc., they were copied and numbered and sent to the National judges who segregated the best ones as the essays were received. After nearly a week of deliberation each National judge had selected those that seemed to him to be the best.

They finally worked their way down to ten that all the judges agreed represented the best of those submitted. And finally, after a great deal of reading and re-reading of the essays, they named the winners, basing their final judgment on the originality of thought expressed and the sincerity of the author.

Demonstration for Senator Walker

Parade Through Film District is Followed by Enthusiastic Meeting at Hotel Astor

A SPECTACULAR demonstration in behalf of the candidacy of Senator James J. Walker for Mayor of New York City was staged by the Motion Picture Division of the campaign on Wednesday, September 9.

A luncheon, at which the Senator was the guest of honor and the chief speaker, was held at the Hotel Astor. This was preceded by a parade of a large number of automobiles, with Senator Walker leading, through the film district from Seventh avenue and Fifty-eighth to the hotel.

As the procession passed Forty-ninth street a big banner stretching across the street was unfurled. Film folk in 729 Seventh avenue and the other film buildings in the district turned out en masse and gave the candidate a great greeting. From the windows of the tall structures confetti and streamers rained down until the scene resembled the demonstration on Armistice Day.

Many representative men of the industry gathered at the luncheon. At the speakers' table, besides the guest of honor, were: Adolph Zukor, President of the Famous Players-Lasky Corporation; Felix F. Feist, distribution manager for Metro-Goldwyn; Ben F. Schreiber, manager of the Walker campaign; Nathan Burkan, prominent at-

torney and member of the Board of Directors of United Artists; Louis Mann, the actor; M. E. Comerford, head of the Comerford Circuit; Samuel I. Berman, secretary of the Motion Picture Division of the Walker campaign; Charles L. O'Reilly, President of the Theatre Owners Chamber of Commerce; A. H. Schwartz, prominent Brooklyn theatre owner; Former State Senator Walter Herrick, General Chairman of the Picture Division of the campaign, and Rudolph Sanders, well-known Brooklyn exhibitor.

Other prominent men present were William A. Johnston, Motion Picture News; Hiram Abrams, President of United Artists; John McGuirk and Abe Sablosky, of the Stanley Circuit, Philadelphia; and scores of exhibitors and exchangemen.

Senator Herrick introduced Mr. Burkan as the toastmaster. He at once sounded the keynote of the luncheon as a protest meeting against the blatherskite campaign that was being conducted in some quarters against the Senator.

Mr. Burkan evoked a demonstration when he paid warm tribute to Senator Walker as a friend and a citizen who stood for the best in public life. "Every man in the industry owes a debt to Senator Walker," said Mr. Burkan. When the Senator was introduced he was received with cheering that

lasted several minutes, after which he made a characteristic speech, punctuated with his accustomed wit and brilliant sallies.

Speaking in serious vein, Senator Walker ridiculed the charges of his enemies that he was linked with "the underworld," and referred to a resolution passed the night before in his behalf by the Grand Street Boys Club of which he is a vice-president.

He declared that he was proud of New York and grateful for what New York had done for him and scored those who were knocking the town in order to gain political advantage. "I know New York," he continued. "Just because I know it so well, when I become Mayor I may be more severe, if there is anything wrong with it, than some who does not know it."

One of the sallies that caught the crowd was this: "A lot of dust has been swept under the sofa in City Hall, and I am the designated vacuum-cleaner." This was typical of his speech, which made a great impression on the crowd.

Just before the Senator spoke, Harry Cooper sang the Walker campaign song composed by Irving Berlin, entitled "Walk in With Walker" and ending with the line "Everybody's out of step but Jim." The crowd voted it a hit and joined in the chorus with great enthusiasm.

Italy Refuses to Permit Control of Theatres by Americans

THE Italian interests behind the theatres of Italy are eager to welcome American film productions for display in their theatres, but they are loath to permit control of their theatres to pass into American hands.

This in substance is the observation of Peter Magaro, pioneer Harrisburg exhibitor, who returned about September 1 from a European trip during which, he said, he sought to negotiate the purchase or lease for big American financial interests of 138 of the leading Italian picture houses, the object being to provide a better output in that country for American film products.

Mr. Magaro, who last May sold his Regent Theatre in Harrisburg to the Marcus Loew interests, is a native of Italy and has kept in close touch with the theatre situation in that country.

"While in Italy this summer" he said, "I inquired, in behalf of American interests which desire to get control of the Italian theatres, on what terms they could be bought, and whether there was a popular demand among Italian theatre patrons for American film products. I negotiated with some of the leading men in control of 138 allied Italian theatres, and they said without hesitation that American films are the most popular in Italy,—in fact that the Italian people demand them in preference to any other makes.

It was made very evident to me, however, by these same Italian interests, that they are unwilling to dispose of control of their theatres to American capital, no matter how liberal the offer, so that I am convinced that further negotiations to that end would be unavailing."

Mr. Maggaro declined to say what American interests he represented abroad.

Chandler to Succeed Kellogg

First National Announces Appointment as Director of Advertising and Publicity

C. F. CHANDLER, one of the best known and most popular men associated with the publicizing of motion pictures, has been appointed Director of Advertising and Publicity of First National Pictures, Inc., to take effect September 15th. Mr. Chandler succeeds Mark Kellogg, who has resigned after occupying the post since January 1st, 1924. Mr. Kellogg has not yet announced his future plans.

Mr. Chandler is a newspaper and advertising man of long experience having been associated with First National Pictures since 1919, when he became a member of the Advertising Department under the direction of C. L. Yearsley. For the past two years he has been in charge of the Exhibitors Service Department. He has been notably successful in this capacity and is directly responsible for the high quality of First National's poster work during the past year.

Before his connection with First National,

he was for five years advertising manager and director of publicity for the Essanay Film Manufacturing Company in Chicago.

Mr. Chandler was born in Foo Chow, China, the son of Rev. Dr. David W. Chandler and Mary E. Stanley Chandler. He received preparatory school training at Mt. Union College at Alliance, Ohio, preceeding four years at the University of Michigan, where he was awarded a B.A. degree. Immediately after leaving college, he went into newspaper work becoming a reporter on the Cleveland Plain Dealer, later associate editor of the Cleveland Press, associate night editor of Philadelphia North American, on the re-write and copy desk of the New York Evening World, foreign editor New York World, head of the copy desk of the Chicago Examiner and managing editor of the Cleveland News, a post that he resigned in order to join the Essanay Company.

One Policy for Warner Houses

Plan is Mapped for Uniformity of Service in All Theatres of Chain

ONE policy will control all Warner Brothers theatres, according to an announcement from the home office of that organization. A plan is now being mapped for uniformity of service, which will embrace the same attention to detail in the entire string of Warner theatres as was bestowed upon patrons of the New York house during its opening week recently.

These new plans are in the capable hands of George H. Dumond, who was appointed general manager of all Warner theatres a few weeks ago. Under his managing directorship each house will have its managing director and a full complement of house attaches. Dumond had charge of arrangements for the opening night of Warners in New York and then proceeded to Cleveland

to direct the opening of the Cirele last week.

Under the plan as devised all attaches in each of the theatres will wear special uniforms, which will be identical for persons performing the same class of service in all Warner houses. Girl ushers are to be employed throughout and in every instance they are to be garbed as are those in the New York theatre. Their costume, a particularly chic creation suggestive of the French "Blue Devils," was designed by George W. Bonte, Warner Brothers' art director.

Dumond, new general manager of theatres, was home office representative of Warner Bros. for two years up to a year ago, when he went to Cleveland and became managing director of the State Theatre, in charge of production for all the Loew houses.

In and Out of Town

HARRY M. WARNER left late last week on one of his regular visits to the Warner studio in Hollywood. He will return within two or three weeks.

LESLIE WHELAN, exploitation manager of the Harold Lloyd Corp., left this week on an extended tour through the Middle West.

COL. W. F. CLARKE, of Cranfield & Clarke, has returned from a business trip to Canada.

COMPTROLLER David A. O'Malley, of Columbia Pictures, has gone to the Coast for a conference with Harry Cohn.

DWIGHT C. LEEPER, vice-president of Richmount Pictures and associated with Harry J. Brown in productions for Rayart, has returned from a European tour.

HARRY CARR, special photoplay writer for the Los Angeles Times, is in New York on a visit.

ALBERT WARNER was scheduled to sail for New York on the Berengaria this week. He has been in Europe for several weeks.

Ten Per Cent of Montreal Posters Rejected

MORE than ten per cent of all posters, window cards and placards of theatres were rejected in Montreal by the Montreal Poster Censor Bureau, according to the first annual report of the bureau, the director of which is David A. O'Malley, a former Montreal newspaper man. The statistics, which were issued September 6 by Jules Crepeaux, director of city departments, show that 109,249 display cards, posters and still photographs were submitted for approval from September 1, 1924, to the same date this year, or an average of about 350 pieces of printed matter per day. Of this number, 98,450 were accepted and 10,799 were rejected as unfit for public view.

Because of the revenue derived from the inspection of all posters, the Montreal bureau was recently transferred from the Police Department, under whose jurisdiction the branch was first established, to the City Treasurer's department.

Manning New Production Manager for F. B. O.

ROGER MANNING, who for the past two years has been in charge of all locations for all F. B. O. uits, has been appointed production manager of the F. B. O. studios to succeed Clarence White, according to announcement by B. P. Fineman, general manager of the studios. Manning has been affiliated with several of the foremost motion picture companies during the past few years.

White, whom Manning succeeds, has joined S. S. Hutchinson, pioneer motion picture producer, who has returned to activity on a large scale. White will serve as production manager for all of the Hutchinson units which will operate at the F. B. O. studio.

Labor Difficulties Being Adjusted

Controversies Between Exhibitors and Labor Unions Are Nearing a Settlement in Many Cities

LABOR troubles throughout the United States continue to occupy much of the attention of exhibitors, though in many cities they are being straightened out through arbitration or other methods, with both sides yielding on some points.

Efforts to adjust the wage differences between the musicians, stage hands and moving picture operators employed in the Strand, Cataract and Bellevue theatres, Niagara Falls, N. Y., and theatre managements have been unsuccessful. The theatre employes who at first asked for wage increases of $5 and $10 a week for musicians and 10 per cent increases for the stage hands and operators, announced they would agree to take a boost of $2.50 a week per man, but this offer also was rejected by the theatre managements, who refuse to grant any pay increases and it is now reported that the houses involved never again will sign up with the unions but will go "open shop" in the future.

The controversy between the musicians and trades craft union employees of Denver theatres will be settled by arbitration. After several weeks of unsuccessful negotiations between the two parties, the industrial commission of the state of Colorado was agreed upon as the arbitrator of the dispute over the new contract. Both sides have agreed to accept the decision of the industrial commission as final. The arguments before the commission will be presented on October 5th.

Differences that arose between the motion picture operators' union of Baltimore. Local No. 181, and the moving picture theatre owners of that city, have been amicably adjusted with the operators conceding a few points but in the main getting all the demands they made for increases in wages and better working conditions.

Negotiations were on all day Thursday of last week between the representatives of the Atlanta Federation of Musicians and the theatre managers of Atlanta, looking toward the settlement of the differences between the musicians and the theatres on Labor Day.

For a time it looked as though a compromise was going to be brought about, in which all the musicians would be able to return to the theatres, but at midnight no agreement had been reached, and the executive committee of the Federation of Musicians, through their representative, Cy Karston, declared that all negotiations were off.

The Cleveland Motion Picture Exhibitors Association and the Motion Picture Operators' Union have come to an agreement on the wage scale issue. Class A and Class B houses will pay a 10 per cent increase over the present scale. Class C will pay a 15 per cent increase. This scale covers a period of two years beginning September 1, 1925. This increase means an expenditure of between $60,000 and $70,000 to the Cleveland exhibitors.

Recall of the demand of the Musicians' Union, served on moving picture operators August 11th, for six months contracts covering musicians in orchestras, was approved at the meeting of the union at its headquarters on Sept. 1st in San Francisco.

Fox to Build First Run Theatre in Bronx

WILLIAM FOX, head of Fox Film Corporation and the Fox Circuit of theatres, has completed plans for the erection of a new theatre at East Tremont Ave., between Park and Washington Aves., the Bronx. The theatre will be directly across the street from the Crotona, which is also owned by Fox. The new house will have a seating capacity of more than four thousand five hundred, the announcement.

The theatre will be run along the same lines as the New Academy of Music, now being built, with presentations of operettas and operas in tabloid form in addition to big picture productions. The theatre will be equipped with a modern refrigerating system.

The entrance to the theatre lobby and business office will be on East Tremont Ave. There will also be an entrance to the theatre auditorium on the Park Ave. side. The frontage of the combined lots on East Tremont Ave. which are owned by the Treepark company is approximately ninety-seven feet.

Officials of the union refused to comment, other than to state, that a general feeling prevails that the controversy will be settled amicably.

The "silent drama" is not silent any more. The musicians' walkout in Omaha was settled September 4 after four silent nights in the Rialto and Sun theaters.

The wage dispute was settled September 4 after a long conference participated in by musicians headed by Rangval Olson, president, and Harry Goldberg representing the Sun and Harry Watts the Rialto and Strand.

The musicians had demanded $60 the year around, a considerable increase from their former $45 in summer and $50 in winter. The theatre managers countered with an offer of $52 a week, which was turned down.

The settlement now made provides for a three-year wage agreement which specifies $55 for the ensuing winter and $60 for the next two winters.

Labor troubles cropped up during the past week in both Schenectady and Albany, but with every indication that they will be smoothed out within the next few days, although they may result in Schenectady in a change of plans calling for the installation of orchestras in the State and Strand theatres in that city. Members of the orchestra are demanding $2 a week more, while organists in theatres without orchestras, are asking $90 a week instead of the $55 they are now receiving.

The strike of union musicians and stage hands at all DesMoines theatres following the refusal of the theatres to raise the wage scale did not take place. Monday, September 1, was the date set by the union for the theatre men to come to their terms but the union musicians did not leave any of the theatres; continuing to work with the expectation that arbitration would bring about settlement to the satisfaction of both sides. The union stage men are now working after having walked out for one day, despite the fact that agreement has not been reached.

New Idea in Coming Films is Striking Moments

(Continued from Page 1345)

through long hours of traveling and marching into battle.

We have been made acquainted with the armament of battle, and its terrifying destructive power. We know what the soldiers are going to face when they finally get into the arena of the conflict. We see them spread out into a loose formation preparatory to entering the wood, infested by Germans.

A French soldier has previously thrown up his hands in horror at the thought of their doing aught but turn back from that horrible death-dealing region. The commanding officer of the troops listens to his prophecies of terrors and dangers. He smiles while he listens, and after the Frenchman is through with his talking and gesticulating, he says—"Well, my boys have come a long ways to fight, and I'm afraid that they would be a trifle disappointed if they turned back now." The Frenchman rushes off throwing his arms in the air, wagging his head, at the idea of such insanity.

The troops advance. Slowly, watchfully, steadily, a step at the time through the wood. Ears and eyes are strained. You can see every muscle taut and tense.

Suddenly you catch a glimpse of a German sniper in a tree in the distance. He raises his rifle and fires. The first shot, and the first victim. One of the American soldiers answers immediately with a rifle ball, and the German falls. The troops continue to move on as if nothing had happened—Pershing's organized mob, which knew too little about war to be frightened, and too much about pioneer courage to be daunted—even as they remain undaunted when their ranks are riddled by the fire of machine guns and shells as step by step, in a veritable death march, they go on into No Man's Land.

I feel that "The Big Parade" is a picture that deserves the consideration that I have given it in this article, because it is one of the season's big pictures—perhaps in certain of its qualities the biggest. The bulk of the audiences will, I believe, be keenly susceptible to it. It is a far-reaching achievement, the most important in the war line without a doubt since "The Four Horsemen." The only weakness in the film when I saw it, was the love interest, and that is because its culmination is rather conventionally treated. I have no doubt that it will be improved somewhat before the first public showing. I am conscious of the fact that the picture is going to be a very radical one for the small-town audience, but even in this case I believe that it has sufficient patriotic interest to prove popular. While there may be some troubles with the censors over details, "The Big Parade" as a whole is going to encounter very little difficulty. One important item—

(Continued on Page 1352)

Governor Would Support School System by Amusement and Luxury Tax

COMPLETE support for the public school system of the state by revenue derived solely from a special state tax on amusements and luxuries is being considered by Governor Samuel A. Baker of Missouri.

The Governor plans to submit his measure as an amendment to the state constitution at the general elections in November, 1926, and is now gathering data.

He contemplates supporting all of the public grade and high schools of the state through the tax as well as the higher state educational institutions like Missouri University, the five State Teachers Colleges, Lincoln University, the Missouri School for the Deaf at Fulton and the Missouri School for Blind in St. Louis.

Originally the Governor considered a special 2 mill levy on real and personal property as a means of obtaining additional revenue for the state school system.

It is probable that he will recommend a 5 or 10 per cent state tax on all amusement admissions such as motion picture, vaudeville, dramatic and burlesque theatres, baseball, football and soccer games, etc., and also on cigarettes, cigars and other luxuries.

One-third of all state revenues collected is now used for the public schools. Under Baker's plan the present taxes would be abolished and all funds needed for the schools obtained by cutting into the receipts of amusement places and the sale of luxuries.

Paramount Studio Celebrates

Long Island Plant Five Years Old on Sept. 11; 80 Features Filmed There

THE Paramount Long Island Studio will be five years old on September 11 and will celebrate the anniversary in the midst of the greatest activity it has housed since its founding. For on the date of its fifth birthday the Paramount plant in Long Island will have six companies at work on productions.

Since it was established five years ago the studio has turned out eighty feature length photoplays, among them some of the most notable the Paramount company has offered. It is regarded as one of the best equipped, if not the best, in the world. At the time of its opening the plant was considered a costly experiment, but the work which has been accomplished there has conclusively proved that pictures can be just as successfully made in New York as California.

The big plant has been busy continuously with the exception of one span of ten months, two years ago, when a surplus of Paramount production caused a cessation of activity. In pointing to the success of the eastern producing project, Paramount officials accord a generous share of the credit for its success to Edwin C. King, its general manager.

The first picture made there was filmed by John Robertson, who started work on "Sentimental Tommy" in September, 1920.

Complete Photography on "Clodhopper"

Associated Exhibitors have completed photography on "The Clodhopper," the Oscar Price production starring Glenn Hunter. The production was made at the Universal Studios in Fort Lee, N. J., under the direction of Joseph Henaberry. The picture is now being cut and edited and will be ready for release in the near future.

Mildred Ryan has the leading feminine role opposite Hunter, while others in the cast include, Antrim Short, Margaret Irving, Citana Kamp, Beryl Halley, W. T. Hays, William Black, Marion Stephenson, Edward Poland, Isobel Vernon, George Graham and the dancing team of Bishop and Lynn.

De Sano Denies He Will Leave Schulberg

Marcel De Sano denies a persistent rumor that he will leave the directorial forces of B. P. Schulberg in the following statement:

"The report that I am leaving Mr. Schulberg is totally untrue. It is probably explained by the fact that following the completion of 'The Girl Who Wouldn't Work' I received four flattering offers from other organizations. The fact of the ease is that I will continue to make Preferred Pictures for some time to come."

Prominent English Actors in Meighan Cast

Cecil Humphrey and Robert English, prominent English film actors, play important roles in support of Thomas Meighan in "Irish Luck," portions of which were filmed in Ireland recently. The actors are returning with the star to the United States to finish their parts at the Long Island studio, where this new Paramount starring vehicle for Meighan will be completed.

M-G-M to Make Fire Prevention Film

BY AN arrangement just concluded between Louis B. Mayer and Chief Jay W. Stevens, fire marshall of the state of California and head of the Pacific Coast Fire Prevention Bureau, Metro-Goldwyn-Mayer will produce a feature film in the interest of fire prevention.

There will be a feature production of unusual entertainment value and not merely a preachment, though it will strongly advocate closer attention to fire prevention. Leading players of the Metro-Goldwyn-Mayer forces will appear in the picture and a large percentage of the net proceeds from the picture are to be given to the International Association of Fire Chiefs for their prevention work and a portion of the sum realized will be used by fire departments in various communities for sick, benefit and pension funds.

New Idea in Coming Films is Striking Moments

(Continued from Page 1351)

it is going to offer opportunities for a great musical score—one based to a large extent on those stirring songs which were associated with the period of the war. It arrives, too, at a propitious time, because the public, I feel, is just about ready for a production dealing both lightly and pathetically with soldier life during the conflict.

Beside Jack Gilbert, the leading player in the cast is Renee Adoree, but a chap by the name of Karl Dane, who does the part of the soldier who is killed, is going to make his everlasting reputation on the strength of his characterization. He is the real star.

Another war picture that merits high commendation in advance is "The Dark Angel." Ronald Colman has given his finest performance to date in this. His portrayal of the blind English soldier, who doesn't want to burden the girl whom he loves with his infirmity, is a splendid study in sacrifice as he interprets it, and Vilma Banky, as the heroine, is a newcomer of promising loveliness. She expresses a refinement in her character drawing which rather associates itself with that of Norma Shearer. Her acting is not quite so striking as her personality, but the general impression she evokes is very attractive. Colman's acting attains that height which may well be termed "big." He is going to be talked about, and more comparisons even than usual between his work and that of Jack Gilbert are bound to be made. Than which, there is just now probably no better stimulus for popular argument.

Douglas Fairbank's plans for his new buccaneering feature have been shaping up more rapidly lately, and ere this is printed he should be at work. Good news, perhaps, is the fact that he contemplates filming his production, "The Black Pirate," in seven reels instead of the customary ten or twelve. Doug feels that the story as it has been outlined can be told much more effectively in a shorter length, although it may stretch out during the filming.

The experiments with the color process, which were very exhaustive, have been brought to completion, and unless there is some last minute change, the entire picture is to be made that way. "Pirates suggest color to the imagination," declared Doug to me recently, "and I now feel that it would be impossible to film a story of them satisfactorily in black and white. We have never really had a pirate story as yet on the screen —with real pirates in all their picturesqueness. 'The Sea Hawk' was a great adventure story, great romance, but it was not a pirate story. I feel, therefore, that we have an absolutely clear field for what we are attempting."

There is no doubt that Doug has a great opportunity. Color is all but established for certain types of pictures, and if he proves the effectiveness of its use in this instance, a new vista will be opened up in the field of production. Whether, "The Black Pirate" will have the needful great moment or not is, of course, a question that can only be answered definitely when it is finally finished. Knowing Doug's invariably bright ingenuity, I imagine that it will have. It is an easy gamble, in any event, that his production is one that *will be talked about.*

Warners Start Production on "Fighting Edge"

Warner Brothers have started a new combination which co-features Kenneth Harlan and Patsy Ruth Miller. Their first picture, which has just gone into production is titled "The Fighting Edge." E. T. Lowe, Jr., and Jack Wagner adapted this William McLeod Raine novel to the screen. It is the first Warner production to be directed by Henry Lehman. Supporting Harlan and Miss Miller are Gayne Whitman, Charles Conklin, Pat Hartigan, Eugene Palette and Lew Harvey.

Company Coming to Make "Fifth Avenue"

Director Robert Vignola will shortly head a company east from Hollywood to make scenes in New York for "Fifth Avenue," an A. H. Sebastian production for Producers Distributing Corporation release. It is said that the biggest actual street scenes ever made in the metropolis will feature the production.

Color Sequence to Feature Gloria Swanson's Next

A color sequence will be among the features of Gloria Swanson's coming picture, "Stage Struck," which Alan Dwan is directing. Miss Swanson has the role of a poor little waitress who dreams she is a great actress. The color sequence is the dream.

Coleman Joins Lubitsch Cast for Warners

Warner Brothers have secured Ronald Coleman through arrangement with Samuel Goldwyn to play a prominent part in "Lady Windermere's Fan," the Ernst Lubitsch picturization of Oscar Wilde's celebrated drama.

M-G-M Purchase Rights to Hatton Story

Metro-Goldwyn-Mayer have purchased from Frederick and Fanny Hatton their first original story for the screen, "Single Beds." No director has as yet been selected, but the picture will go into production in the near future.

"Mare Nostrum" Now Practically Finished

ALICE TERRY has completed her role in "Mare Nostrum" which her husband, Rex Ingram, is producing for Metro-Goldwyn, and sailed on the Majestic arriving in New York September 8. Miss Terry is returning to the United States to visit her mother in California and to enjoy a short vacation after which she will go back to Europe to appear in Mr. Ingram's next picture.

Ingram suspended work at his studio in Nice to go to Paris to bid bon voyage to his wife but returned as soon as the Majestic sailed as he is in the midst of cutting his latest directorial effort.

"Mare Nostrum" has practically been completed. Tony Moreno, who played the leading male role, is planning to sail for America shortly after the middle of the month. Ingram himself will probably remain in France until after his next picture has been completed.

"Shore Leave" is Richard Barthelmess' latest starring vehicle for First National. These scenes are taken from the picture.

Ten from F. B. O. in October

Four Features and Six Short Subjects Due for the Exhibitors Next Month

F. B. O. has arranged a releasing schedule of ten pictures for the month of October. Four of these will be features and the other six short subjects.

"The Keeper of the Bees," a Gold Bond picture from a story by Gene Stratton-Porter heads the list of features. The cast is headed by Robert Frazer in the title role, with Gene Stratton, Clara Bow, Alyce Mills, Martha Mattox and Josef Swickard in support. It will be released October 18th.

The sixth Thomson production, tentatively titled "All Around the Frying Pan," based on the magazine story by Frank Richardson Pierce, will also be distributed on October 18th. Another for the same date will be the next of the Texas Ranger series starring Bob Custer, but as yet untitled. It is an Independent Pictures Corporation production.

"Heads Up," starring Maurice B. (Lefty) Flynn is scheduled for release October 25th. The story is by A. E. Barranger. It is being produced under the direction of Harry Garson.

The short subjects are headed by "Three Wise Goofs," the second Standard Fat Men Comedy, in which "Fatty" Karr, "Tiny" Alexander and "Kewpie" Ross, the three fattest men on the screen, are featured. "Three Wise Goofs" comes from the Joe Rock Studios, and will be distributed on October 4th.

The same day will see the distribution of a one reel novelty from the Bray Studios, as yet untitled, featuring Dinky Doodle.

"Or What Have You?" the third episode of "The Adventures of Mazie," starring Alberta Vaughn, will be released on October 11th. "The Adventures of Mazie" comes from the pen of Nell Martin and originally appeared in Top Notch Magazine. Larry Kent, Kit Guard and Al Cooke support Miss Vaughn, while Ralph Ceder is directing.

A Blue Ribbon comedy as yet untitled, starring Alice Ardell, Joe Rock's latest Paris importation, will be shown to exhibitors on October 18th, while the third Bray cartoon, also untitled, will be released on the same day.

"Mazie Won't Tell," the fourth episode of the Mazie series, will be distributed on October 25th.

Colleen Moore to Start "Irene" in October

With "We Moderns" nearing completion, Colleen Moore is already preparing to start work on "Irene," her next production for First National. Shooting will probably get under way under the supervision of John E. McCormick early in October.

John Francis Dillon will be retained as director of "Irene," the continuity for which is being prepared by Rex Taylor. Lloyd Hughes will again be Miss Moore's leading man. Others engaged for the new production include Charlie Murray, Kate Price and Dorothy Seastrom.

Radio Corp. of America Aids With Picture

First National had the assistance of the Radio Corporation of America in the filming of some of the scenes for "The Unguarded Hour." In this picture Milton Sills is an Italian Duke engaged in wireless experimentation. The Radio Corporation volunteered to fit out the laboratory and sent Joseph Wanbecker, technical expert, who planned the set.

Monte Blue in "The Limited Mail," in Warner Brothers production.

Pathe Fixes Weekly Releases

Final Chapter of Serial, "Play Ball,"
Heads Program for Week of Sept. 20

THE final chapter of the Patheserial, "Play Ball," heads the short-subject release program of Pathe for the week of September 20th. In addition there will be two Mack Sennett comedies, "Hurry Doctor" and "A Rainy Knight," a Hal Roach two-reeler, "Somewhere in Somewhere," and the usual weekly features.

"Hurry Doctor" is a two-reeler with Ralph Graves featured as an ambitious paper-hanger. Thelma Parr is the girl, Frank Whitson is Dr. Welland Strong, and Vernon Dent is a traffic cop of heroic proportions. Lloyd Bacon directed.

"A Rainy Knight" is another Mack Sennett two-reel comedy with an all-star cast, including Raymond McKee, Marvin Lobach, Eugenia Gilbert and Ruth Taylor. Lloyd Bacon also directed this subject.

"Somewhere in Somewhere" is a Hal Roach two-reel comedy, featuring Charlie Murray and Lucien Littlefield. James W. Horne directed under the supervision of F. Richard Jones, Supervising Director.

"A Home Plate Wedding," the tenth and final chapter of "Play Ball," brings this exciting Patheserial, written by Manager McGraw of the New York Giants, to a happy ending. Allene Ray as Doris Sutton agrees to become the bride of Walter Miller as Jack Rolling; while Mary Milnor as Mabelle Pratt joins hands with Wally Oettel as Rutger Farnsworth in "A Home Plate Wedding." Frank Leon Smith adapted this story for the screen and Spencer Bennett directed the ten-episode chapter play.

"Starting an Argument," a Grantland Rice "Sportlight," pictures various phases of the ever-present arguments wherever sportsmen meet.

Pathe Review No. 138 presents an interesting diversity of subjects: "The Hand-Made Jungle," papier-mache animals and what makes them go; "The Canyon of Champagnole," a village in the Franco-Swiss Mountains in Pathecolor scenes; and "Brides of the Orient," one of the "Here Comes the Bride" series picturing quaint marriage customs.

"Nuts and Squirrels" is the title of the Paul Terry cartoon of the "Aesop's Film Fables" series. The release schedule for September 20th is completed by "Topics of the Day" and two issues of Pathe News.

Schulberg to Start Two Productions

B. P. Schulberg plans to start production next week on "Lew Tyler's Wives" and "Eden's Fruit." Marcel De Sano will handle direction of the former and Gasnier the latter.

"Lew Tyler's Wives" is an adaptation of the Wallace Irwin novel. It is being adapted by Lois Hutchinson. "Eden's Fruit," by John Goodrich, is now ready for Gasnier, the script having been completed by the author some weeks ago.

Many Screen Favorites in "Wages for Wives" Cast

The cast which has been assembled by Frank Borzage for "Wages for Wives," the Fox screen version of John Golden's stage success, "Chicken Feed," includes Jacqueline Logan, Creighton Hale, Earle Fox, Zasu Pitts, Margaret Livingston, David Butler, Dan Mason, Claude Gillingwater, Margaret Seddon and Tom Ricketts Production on the play, which was written by Guy Bolton, has started at the studios in Los Angeles.

Archie Mayo is Signed for Special Directing

Metro-Goldwyn-Mayer has signed Archie L. Mayo for some special directorial work. For the past two years he has been directing two-reel subjects at the Christie studios and prior to that directed Lloyd Hamilton and Mermaid comedies. His work under the new contract will be in the nature of special directing of scenes calling for his particular line of ability.

Larry Semon Buys "Stop, Look and Listen"

Larry Semon has purchased screen rights to "Stop, Look and Listen," and will produce it as his first big comedy feature under Pathe release. The adaptation of this Charles Dillingham play has already been completed and preparations are now being made to shoot the initial scenes. Dorothy Dwan will play opposite the comedian, who will direct himself.

"Road to Yesterday" Now Being Edited

Photography has been completed by Cecil B. De Mille on "The Road to Yesterday" and he is now supervising the cutting of the picture, which will be released through Producers Distributing Corporation. Joseph Schildkraut, Jetta Goudal, Vera Reynolds, William Boyd, Casson Ferguson and Trixie Friganza have the featured roles.

P. D. C. Will Distribute "Rocky Moon"

Metropolitan Pictures has purchased screen rights to "Rocky Moon" and the picture will be made for release through Producers Distributing Corporation. The novel is by Barrett Willoughby. It will be filmed in part in the Hollywood studio and in Alaska, the natural locale called for in the story.

Columbia Retains "Thrill Hunter" Title

The title of "The Thrill Hunter," recently announced by Universal will be changed because of the fact that a picture of the same title is being released by Columbia Pictures Corporation with Dorothy Revier as the star. As soon as Universal learned that this condition existed they volunteered to change the title on their production.

"Freshman" Release Due September 20th

COINCIDENT with the opening of the college football season, Harold Lloyd's "The Freshman" will be released nationally through Pathe exchanges on September 20th. The production has been declared the most ambitious effort in the career of Lloyd. The story is of college life devised by Sam Taylor, John Grey, Ted Wilde and Tim Whelan, and was directed by Taylor and Fred Newmeyer.

Jobyna Ralston is again leading lady for Lloyd, while in the supporting cast are, Brooks Benedict, Pat Harmon, Hazel Keener, James Anderson and Joseph Harrington.

Neilan Starts Work on "The Great Love"

Marshall Neilan has started work on his next production for Metro-Goldwyn-Mayer. It is titled "The Great Love" and features Viola Dana opposite Bobby Agnew. In the supporting cast are Junior Coughlan, Malcolm Waite, Chester Conklin, and Frank Currier. The story is by Randall McKeever and was adapted to the screen by Neilan and Benjamin Glazer.

Abbett Renown Manager in Indianapolis

Renown Pictures, Inc., has appointed Ralph W. Abbett manager at Indianapolis. He will make his headquarters at 432 North Illinois Street. Abbett is well known in the central division. He entered the film business with Universal as salesman in Indianapolis in 1912 and was made manager of the office after two years of road work.

Five Episodes Completed on "Flame Fighter"

Photography has been completed on the first five episodes of Beacon Film Corporation's "The Flame Fighter," which Robert Dillon is producing. Herbert Rawlinson is starred in this serial play. A print of the first episode was received in the Rayart New York office this week.

Douglas Gilmore Signed to Long Contract

Douglas Gilmore has been signed to a long term contract by Metro-Goldwyn-Mayer and becomes a member of that stock company to play important roles in forthcoming releases this Fall. Gilmore only recently concluded playing the leading role in the stage success, "White Cargo."

Lloyd Hamilton Laid Up With Infected Foot

Lloyd Hamilton, Educational comedy star, is taking a rest from studio work in a Hollywood hospital where he is being treated for an infected foot. Physicians advised the comedian to give the infected member a rest after he had completed "The Movies," his first picture for the new season.

Marion Davies Signs Long Contract

MARION DAVIES has signed a new contract under which she will appear in Metro-Goldwyn-Mayer pictures for a number of years. The original contract called for the making of but one picture for this company, but following the completion of "Lights of Old Broadway," directed by Monta Bell, a new arrangement was entered into whereby Miss Davies will soon start work at the Culver City Studios on the first of a series of Cosmopolitan pictures for M-G-M.

"Lights of Old Broadway" is scheduled for release in October. It is based on the Laurence Eyre stage success, "Merry Wives of Gotham," and was adapted for the screen by Carey Wilson. Conrad Nagel plays opposite the star.

First National Finishes Four

Photography Completed on Features, While Five Others Enter Production

PHOTOGRAPHY was completed last week by First National on four feature releases, with the exception of a few clean-up shots, and work is scheduled to start on five new features by the end of next week.

The four pictures completed are Colleen Moore's starring vehicle, "We Moderns," "Memory Lane," "The Beautiful City" and "The New Commandment." The stories going into production are "Ceasar's Wife," "Joanna With a Million," "Rainbow Riley," "Just Suppose" and "Bluebeard's Seven Wives."

"We Moderns," with Colleen Moore, is ready to go into the cutting room. In the supporting cast are Jack Mulhall, Claude Gillingwater, Dorothy Seastrom, Louis Payne and Cleve Morison.

John M. Stahl finished photography on his own original story, "Memory Lane." Cutting was due to get under way this week. In the cast are Eleanor Boardman, Conrad Nagel, William Haines, Dot Farley, John Standing, Kate Price and Earl Metcalf.

"The Beautiful City" is an Inspiration picture with Richard Barthelmess as the star. Cutting and editing are now under way.

"The New Commandment" is Robert T. Kane's initial production for First National. It is an adaptation from the Frederick Palmer novel, "Invisible Wounds." Howard Higgin directed and in the cast are Blanche Sweet, Ben Lyon, Claire Eames, Holbrook Blinn, Dorothy Cummings, Effie Shannon, Pedro de Cordoba, George Cooper, Diana Kane and Lucius Henderson.

The first of the new stories to go into production on September 3rd was the Corinne Griffith picture, "Ceasar's Wife," with Irving Cummings directing. Edwin Carewe started work on "Joanna With a Million," with Dorothy Mackaill in the leading role. C. C. Burr got under way with Johnny Hines in "Railbow Riley," from Thompson Buchanan's play, "The Cub."

Two pictures are scheduled to start next week. They are the Inspiration picture with Richard Barthelmess, "Just Suppose," and the Robert T. Kane production, "Bluebeard's Seven Wives."

Lon Chaney's Next to Be "Mocking Bird"

Lon Chaney's next starring vehicle for Metro-Goldwyn-Mayer will be "The Mocking Bird," an original story by Tod Browning, who will direct the production. The story is said to be of the Limehouse district of London, with an underworld plot and a strong love theme.

William Wellman Engaged by Columbia

William Wellman has been signed by Columbia Pictures to direct a feature starring Dorothy Revier. Wellman has been engaged in picture production for the past ten years, starting as an assistant director. He directed features for Fox Film and other big producers.

M.G.M. Assigns Leading Roles

Leading Players Are Engaged to Play in Productions Soon to Get Under Way

A NUMBER of important roles have been assigned to leading players in Metro-Goldwyn-Mayer productions. Norman Kerry has been signed to play the leading role in Rex Beach's "The Barrier," which is to be directed by George Hill. The picture is scheduled to go into production this month.

Rosita Ramirez, Cuban beauty and granddaughter of General Colixto Garcia, makes her motion picture debut in Rex Ingram's production of "Mare Nostrum." Ingram met the Cuban beauty in Europe and made a screen test of her. It was so satisfactory he cast her for the role of Pepita. Alice Terry and Antonio Moreno have the leading roles in "Mare Nostrum."

Another selection made by Metro-Goldwyn-Mayer was that of Edmund Lowe for the leading male role in Elinor Glyn's production of "The Only Thing." This is an original story written by Madame Glyn directly for the screen. Lowe was borrowed from the Fox Film Company, to whom he is under contract.

Constance Bennett has been engaged to play the role of Sally in Edmund Goulding's production of "Sally, Irene and Mary." Miss Bennett, daughter of Richard Bennett, has been in the east making a series of pic-

tures, but will leave immediately for the west coast and will start work in the Goulding production within the next few days.

Actual shooting of La Boheme, starring Lillian Gish, has been started at the Metro-Goldwyn-Mayer studios under the direction of King Vidor. John Gilbert plays opposite the star, while other roles are in the hands of Renee Adoree, Roy D'Arcy, Karl Dane and Edward Everett Horton.

Associated Starts Work on "North Star"

Associated Exhibitors have started production at the F. B. O. studios in Hollywood on "North Star," starring Strongheart, the wonder dog, under the direction of Paul Powell. The story was adapted for the screen by Charles Horan from the novel by Rufus King.

The appearance of Strongheart on the Associated Exhibitors program followed an arrangement made by Howard Estabrook with Miss Jane Murfin, owner of the dog, whereby the canine star will be loaned to the producer for his new series of outdoor pictures, all of which will be released by Associated Exhibitors.

Alice Ardell and Chester Conklin in scenes from "Lame Brains," a two-reel comedy released by F. B. O.

Fox Production Units All Busy

Various Companies Ahead of Schedule Planned for the West Coast Studios

FOX production units are well ahead of their production schedules, but there is no slackening of the pace set at the West Coast studios. In fact the various companies are busier now than they have been at any time during the season.

With "Lazybones" completed, Frank Borzage has started shooting on his second Fox picture, "Wages for Wives," based on the John Golden stage success, "Chicken Feed." He has selected a cast including Jacqueline Logan, Creighton Hale, Zasu Pitts, Earle Foxe, David Butler, Claude Gillingwater, Margaret Seddon, Dan Mason and Tom Ricketts.

John Ford has left for Jackson's Hole, Wyoming, with a crew numbering more than a hundred to start filming "Three Bad Men."

Tom Mix has just finished "The Yankee Senor," scheduled as his second starring vehicle of the season and is engaged in casting for his next, as yet untitled.

"The Silver Treasure," Fox screen version of Joseph Conrad's "Nostromo," has just been finished under the direction of Rowland V. Lee and is now in the cutting room. George O'Brien is Nostromo.

Henry Otto has finished filming the fantasy sequences in "The Ancient Mariner," based on Samuel Taylor Coleridge's poem.

Buck Jones is well along on the season's schedule. He is now in the midst of filming "The Desert's Price," based on William MacLeod Raine's novel, under the direction of W. S. Van Dyke.

Casting has started on "The First Year," one of the John Golden stage successes, in which Matt Moore will play the leading male role.

George O'Brien has been selected as the dashing young cavalry hero of "The Golden Strain," first of the Peter B. Kyne stories.

'Phantom' Opens in New York

Premiere of Universal Spectacle Attracts Capacity Audience to Astor Theatre

UNIVERSAL'S new super-production "The Phantom of the Opera" had its New York premiere at the Astor Theatre, Sunday night, September 6. The performance which was attended by a capacity audience, took its place with the notable motion picture "first nights" staged on Broadway.

An elaborate lobby decoration, featuring a dungeon-like interior designed by the Eastman Studios, New York, carried out the atmosphere of the mystery story. Special interior decorations were installed in the Astor and the vivid colorings were further stressed by the red uniforms worn by the ushers. There was a ballet number, staged

by Albertina Rasch, and the orchestra, which rendered the special music score was under the direction of Eugene Conte, composer of the accompaniment. An added feature of the presentation was the "phantom" produced by Thurston, famous magician.

Among those who were present at the premiere were many representatives of foreign governments, including Sir Harry Armstrong, consul general of Great Britain, and Lady Armstrong; M. Mongendre, consul general of France; M. Brouget, consul of France; Senor Don Mariano Vidal, acting consul for Spain. Prominent motion picture officials and screen celebrities were also present.

"Wandering Footsteps" to Be Third Banner Release

Henry Ginsberg, distributor of Banner productions, announces that the third release in the series of Banner pictures will be "Wandering Footsteps" instead of "The Checkered Flag," originally announced for that position on the schedule. "Wandering Footsteps" will be released October 15. Featured in the cast are Estelle Taylor, Bryant Washburn, Alec B. Francis, Frankie Darro and Eugenie Besserer. The work was adapted from the Charles Sherman novel "A Wise Son," and was produced under the direction of Phil Rosen.

Promotions Announced in F. B. O. Ranks

A number of promotions are announced in the organization of the Film Booking Offices. S. D. Weisbaum, manager of the exchange in Denver, has been made exchange manager in San Francisco, and W. E. Matthews, former manager at Portland now heads the Denver exchange. H. F. Moore, salesman in San Francisco succeeds Matthews in Portland. All three of the appointees have been with the company for several years.

Valli and Hersholt to Be Co-Featured by Moomaw

Universal has loaned Virginia Valli and Jean Hersholt to Lewis F. Moomaw, who will co-feature these two Universal players in a production to be filmed in Portland, Ore., for release by another company. Miss Valli, who has been playing in pictures abroad will go to Portland upon her return to this country next week. Hersholt will accompany the producer to Portland, where production is scheduled to start soon.

Ethel Wales Cast for Role in "Penalty of Jazz"

Ethel Wales has been selected for a prominent part in "The Penalty of Jazz," a forthcoming Waldorf feature for Columbia Pictures with Dorothy Revier in the featured role.

World Premiere of "Pony Express" in Frisco

THE world premiere of "The Pony Express," James Cruze's latest production for Paramount, took place at the Imperial Theatre, San Francisco on the evening of September 5th. The event was attended by screen luminaries and notables in every walk of life.

The picture, an epic of California and offered as Cruze's sequel to "The Covered Wagon" was named by the Diamond Jubilee photoplay and will play a part in the celebration commemorating the seventy-fifth anniversary of California's admission into the Union. Senator Samuel Shortridge made the closing talk preceding the showing of the picture. The usual huge crowds attracted to premieres to get a glimpse of the stars and celebrities packed Market Street and held up traffic. The production was heartily acclaimed by the first night audience.

Exhibitors Service Bureau

The nightmare idea was carried out in cubist fashion in Manager Walter League's lobby for "Beggar on Horseback" (Paramount) at the Strand theatre, Memphis. Brilliant color in odd shapes and designs made the display one that couldn't be overlooked.

Advisory Board and Contributing Editors, Exhibitors' Service Bureau

George J. Schade, Schade theatre, Sandusky.

Edward L. Hyman, Mark Strand theatre, Brooklyn.

Leo A. Landau, Lyceum theatre, Minneapolis.

C. C. Perry, Managing Director, Garrick theatre, Minneapolis.

E. R. Rogers, Southern District Supervisor, Famous Players-Lasky, Chattanooga, Tenn.

Stanley Chambers, Palace theatre, Wichita, Kan.

Willard C. Patterson, Metropolitan theatre, Atlanta.

E. V. Richards, Jr., Gen. Mgr., Saenger Amusement Co., New Orleans.

F. L. Newman, Managing Director, Famous Players-Lasky theatres, Los Angeles.

Arthur G. Stolte, Des Moines theatre, Des Moines, Iowa.

W. C. Quimby, Managing Director, Strand Palace and Jefferson theatres, Fort Wayne, Ind.

J. A. Partington, Imperial theatre, San Francisco.

George E. Carpenter, Paramount-Empress theatre, Salt Lake.

Sidney Grauman, Grauman's theatres, Los Angeles.

: THE CHECK-UP :

Weekly Edition of Exhibitors' Box Office Reports

Productions listed are new pictures on which reports were not available previously.

For ratings on current and older releases see MOTION PICTURE NEWS—first issue of each month.

KEY—The first column following the name of the feature represents the number of managers that have reported the picture as "Poor." The second column gives the number who considered it "Fair;" the third the number who considered it "Good;" and the fourth column, those who considered it "Big."

The fifth column is a percentage giving the average rating on that feature, obtained by the following method: A report of "Poor" is rated at 20%; one of "Fair," 40%; "Good," 70%, and "Big," 100%. The percentage rating of all of these reports on one picture are then added together and divided by the number of reports, giving the average percentage—a figure which represents the consensus of opinion on that picture. In this way exceptional cases, reports which might be misleading taken alone, and such individual differences of opinion are averaged up and eliminated.

TITLE	Poor	Fair	Good	Big	Value	Length
FAMOUS PLAYERS						
Are Parents People?..........	—	1	14	—	68	5,585 ft.
Eve's Secret...............	—	4	11	—	62	6,338 ft.
Night Life of New York......	—	4	7	1	65	6,998 ft.
FIRST NATIONAL						
Just a Woman.............	—	4	6	—	58	6,652 ft.
Making of O'Malley, The....	1	10	2	72		7,571 ft.
METRO-GOLDWYN						
White Desert, The..........	—	1	10	—	67	6,345 ft.
WARNER BROS.						
Tracked in the Snow Country	—	3	5	2	67	5,900 ft.

George E. Brown, Imperial theatre, Charlotte, N. C.

Louis K. Sidney, Division Manager, Loew's theatres, Pittsburgh, Pa.

Geo. Rotsky, Managing Director, Palace theatre, Montreal, Can.

Eddie Zorn, Managing Director, Broadway-Strand theatre, Detroit.

Fred S. Myer, Managing Director, Palace theatre, Hamilton, Ohio.

Joseph Plunkett, Managing Director, Mark Strand theatre, New York.

Ray Grombacher, Managing Director, Liberty theatre, Spokane, Wash.

Ross A. McVoy, Manager, Temple theatre, Geneva, N. Y.

W. S. McLaren, Managing Director, Capitol theatre, Jackson, Mich.

Harold B. Franklin, Director of Theatres, Famous Players-Lasky.

William J. Sullivan, Manager, Rialto theatre, Butte, Mont.

H. A. Albright, Manager, T. D. & L. theatre, Glendale, Calif.

Claire Meachime, Grand theatre, Westfield, N. Y.

Ace Berry, Managing Director, Circle theatre, Indianapolis.

See Complete "Check-Up" Oct. 10th

Varied Campaign on "Her Sister From Paris"

Exploitation on "Her Sister From Paris," at the Empress theatre, Owensboro, Ky., included a 10-foot banner, cut-outs from 24-sheets, and a five-foot cut-out made of beaver board, as well as extra newspaper advertising, and an overhead billboard.

A telegram from the First National representative at Louisville was used verbatim several days before the three day showing, calling attention to the fact that Owensboro was getting the second Kentucky showing on "Her Sister From Paris."

A lighted billboard over the marquee carried posters announcing the coming attraction half a week ahead of the showing.

A Sunday lobby showing included the hat-box cut-out made and painted by a local artist, Herbert Williams, two cut-outs from 24-sheets, and frames. The ten-foot banner went up Saturday night when lobby display was fixed for Sunday showing. These banners are huge and can be seen coming and going for blocks.

The hat-box cut-out was the same on both sides and during the showing was placed on the curbing, with cut-outs turned one to the street and one to the pavement. Connie's bandbox was done in red and white stripes, with lettering in black.

Manager G. M. Pedley found this layout something new for his patrons.

Twin Contest in Raton on "Ten Commandments"

Although there is nothing in "The Ten Commandments" to inspire the idea of a Twin Contest, nevertheless Al. Bireh, Paramount exploiteer for the Denver territory, put on a twin contest at Raton, N. M., when the picture played at the Shuler, which had Raton and all the rest of the territory burned up with curiosity trying to find out

The transcontinental automobile exploiting "Seven Days" (Producers Dist. Corp.) before the Colony theatre, New York City. (Photo by Underwood & Underwood).

how many twins there were; who they were; how thin they were, and how fat they were. That's the way the contest was staged. Not only did every pair of twins that presented themselves at the box-office of the Shuler get a pair of tickets free, but there were cash prizes for the prettiest, the fattest, the thinnest, the oldest, and the youngest twins.

The Raton Daily Reporter tie-up with the theatre carrying several amusing human interest stories about the various types of twins applying for the cash prizes which were scaled from $5 for the youngest, to $20 for the prettiest pair of girl twins between 18 and 20 years of age.

"Greed" Passes to Those Opening Bank Account

For every new savings account opened at the Oil City, Pa., National Bank, during the week of the showing of "Greed" at the Venango theatre, two tickets were given away in accordance with terms arranged by Norman W. Pyle, Metro-Goldwyn exploiteer, who advertised the offer prominently in the local dailies and also in the windows of the bank. A teaser campaign ran in the press for a week preceding the premiere.

The lobby was decorated with cut-outs and stuffed money bags illuminated by green lights. Twenty-four-sheets were posted throughout the entire county and brought much business into town. Six-sheets, one-sheet, and window cards were prominently displayed throughout the downtown district.

A trailer was used in the theatre and 100 inches of extra advertising space was contracted for. Manager Marks collaborated actively with Exploiteer Pyle throughout this campaign.

"Light of Western Stars" Given Beauty Tie-up

By tying-up with the "Miss Oklahoma City" local beauty contest, during the showing of "The Light of Western Stars," Manager Pat McGee of the Criterion cut in on the front page publicity given the event.

This was accomplished by having a special cameraman take motion pictures of the choosing of "Miss Oklahoma City." The camera carried a sign advising that the film would be shown at the Criterion the next day. This stunt caused a lot of favorable comment.

In addition to showing the special film, Manager McGee had "Miss Oklahoma City" appear on the Criterion stage the last two days of "The Light of Western Stars."

Painted display with ingenious panel across the top for "The Desert Flower" (First National) by Manager F. J. Miller of the Modjeska theatre, Augusta, Ga.

Cosmetic Showing on "The Slave of Fashion"

Crowds gathered around the window of a Standard Drug store in Cleveland, O., recently, in which C. C. Deardourff, Metro-Goldwyn exploiteer, had placed an attractive young woman in negligee to demonstrate the correct use of cosmetics in connection with the appearance of "A Slave of Fashion" at the Stillman theatre. The young woman was attended at her toilet table by a smartly costumed colored maid.

Two other young women, equally attractive, each having a small dog painted on either leg just below the knee, strolled through the town's busiest section with announcements to the effect that this new style had been inspired by the new film, "A Slave of Fashion," at the Stillman. A special story with photographs broke into the press on this stunt. Other special stories were carried by the Plaindealer, the Press and the News.

One hundred and fifty special cards were carried on the street car fronts, and the town was lavishly posted. A teaser campaign initiated the active press campaign which was waged, and there was a special lobby display. A trailer was used at the theatre.

Palette Display Stand for "The Painted Lady"

For his showing of "The Painted Lady" at the Rialto, Augusta, Manager C. F. Creslin used a large cut-out of an artist's palette on an easel in the center of lobby.

On palette was painted the head of a man facing a pasted cut-out of Dorothy Mackaill. Daubs of various colors ornamented the palette, which also bore the wording: "The Painted Lady" with Geo. O'Brien and Dorothy Mackaill.

Kings Theatre Garden, St. Louis, took a 24-sheet cut-out of Tom Mix and built a hat over it for "The Lucky Horseshoe" (Fox).

Handkerchief Stunt Boosts "As No Man Has Loved"

An old but never-failing interest arouser was used by the Fox exploitation forces for the Cleveland run of "As No Man Has Loved." This consisted of neat linen handkerchiefs enclosed in white envelopes, with the envelopes carrying the line "For Ladies Only." In one corner of the handkerchief was imprinted:

"For a good cry go to B. F. Keith's Palace theatre, beginning Sunday July 19th. "As No Man Has Loved," greatest love story ever told.

hile the device has been used before, it is nevertheless a telling exploitation medium, inasmuch as the theatre had difficulty keeping stocked with the handkerchiefs, so great was the demand for them.

Diversified Campaign for "Beggar on Horseback"

"Beggar on Horseback," playing the Strand, Memphis, was the recipient of extensive and forceful campaigning at the hands of Manager Walter League, who played up the 'dream' angle in all his exploitation.

Campaign was launched two weeks in advance, with trailer on screen. Two thousand "Morning-Evenings" were distributed by newsboys two days prior to opening. They also made all outgoing trolleys at principal intersections during the five o'clock rush with "Extra Special Free Extra." A special banner was displayed in lobby two weeks in advance, and afterwards moved to lobby of leading hotel where it remained throughout run.

An exceptionally fine window tie-up was effected with the Houck Piano Company made up of various musical instruments and featuring sheet music with the word 'dream' in its title. A large card on the attraction, with a number of stills and photos from the picture were prominently displayed in the window.

Another window display with a local jeweler exhibited beautiful pieces of jewelry with a card announcing the photoplay at the Strand. A tie-up with the Betty Brown Candy Stores resulted in a window display carrying a large card advertising the attraction along with attractively mounted display cards of a fantastic nature.

With the co-operation of Station WMC, a radio dream contest was held, the station announcing that 20 pairs of Strand tickets, good for "The Beggar on Horseback," would be awarded to the persons submitting the best account of their funniest or strangest dream. The passes proved good bait, the contest going over with a 'bang.'

Manager Oscar White of the Liberty theatre, Greenwood, S. C., built this front on "Just a Woman" (First National) from odds and ends of beaver board at trifling cost. Natural vines were used on the front of the small "house" in the centre.

"Havoc" Showing Boosted by Automobile Parade

An outstanding feature of the exploitation campaign that accompanied the St. Louis showing of "Havoc" was an auto parade that toured the streets for several days preceding the showing.

The auto parade was made possible by a tie-up, arrangement with the Durant Motor Car company, who loaned fifteen new Star cars for the stunt. The cars bore large banners reading: "You Won't Play Havoc If You Buy A Star," "Buy A Star And You Won't Play Havoc With Your Bank Roll," etc. Other banners also carried the names of the cast, and play date. Two laundry wagons, one car advertising a shock-absorber and two Chevrolets also took part in the turnout. The laundry wagons carried signs reading: "The National Laundry Won't Play Havoc With Your Wash," with the car demonstrating the shock-absorber,and the Chevolets carrying similar Havoc signs.

The great length of this stunt touring all the principal thoroughfares attracted great attention, and undoubtedly contributed largely to the interest in "Havoc" at the Kings and Rivoli theatres.

Striking front display for "Le Monde Perdu" ("The Lost World"), First National's picture now in an extended run at Reginald Ford's Cameo theatre, Paris. The dinosaur was lighted from the inside.

Novelty Wedding Rings as "Marry Me" Advertising

Thomas Shrader, manager of the Olympic theatre, Pittsburgh, put over an effective campaign for "Marry Me" when it played there. The outstanding feature of the campaign was a small envelope on which was printed, "If he says Marry Me tell him here's the ring." Then followed the name of the theatre, play date, title, etc. In this envelope was a small wedding ring.

A few foot lines in the Sunday newspaper advertisement stated that every lady attending the matinees at the Olympic would receive a wedding ring free.

Punch Served in Lobby as "Old Home Week" Stunt

FOR the two days showing of "Old Home Week," patrons of the Sunset theatre, Ft. Lauderdale, were treated to "punch" which was served in the lobby by three girls.

In addition to the conventional campaign and a special lobby befitting "Old Home Week," Manager J. L. Denton had the theatre's orchestra play in front of the playhouse each night from 6:45 to 7:15, their performance drawing crowds.

Fire Chief Ties Up With "Smouldering Fires"

The Fire department of Wilmington, Del., entered wholeheartedly into the campaign which Al Feinman, Universal exploiter, arranged for "Smouldering Fires" at the Arcadia theatre. Members of the department personally distributed 2,500 cards to factories, department stores, cigar shops, lofts, etc., with the following copy on them:

"Notice! Be careful with smoking stubs, lighted matches, open flames, gasoline and oil tanks. Don't put ashes in wooden receptacles. Smouldering fires always result from carelessness. 'Let the citizens be the fire preventers and the firemen the fire fighters.' Bureau of Fire, William J. Lutz, Chief. See 'Smouldering Fires' at the Arcadia theatre."

Feinman also addressed letters to the secretaries of the four women's clubs in Wilmington asking them to notify their members at the next meeting of the presentation of "Smouldering Fires." He referred to it as "a woman's picture for the women of Wilmington."

A tie-up with the Wilmington Evening Journal brought about a contest for essays on "What is the happiest age for men and women to marry?" There were two cash prizes of $5 each and tickets for each contestant whose contribution was published.

Clever Auto Banner Copy for "The Mad Whirl"

A clever automobile banner for "The Mad Whirl" was designed by F. Raoul Cleaver, the exploitation man working out of Universal's Detroit exchange. It was used in Grand Rapids, Mich., for the "Mad Whirl" engagement at the Isis theatre.

The banner read: In The Mad Whirl of Traffic the lady driver needs the new snappy Essex Six. Drive *Your* Essex to see "The Mad Whirl" at the Isis theatre—Now.

Through this tie-up with the Hudson-Essex distributors, the Isis had Essex coaches carrying this banner on the street all day at no charge to the theatre whatsoever.

Display set up in Evansville, Ind., for the engagement of "The Sporting Venus" (Metro-Goldwyn) at the Strand theatre in that city.

Police Association Helps "Heart of a Siren" Run

George J. Schade, of the Schade theatre, Sandusky, O., had the membership of the Ohio Police Association — wives, children, friends and all—as guests one evening not long since. There was something like two hundred of them; more than four hundred taking in everybody. "The Heart of a Siren" was the attraction.

The chiefs were holding a convention at Cedar Point, a Lake Erie summer resort across Sandusky bay from Sandusky. Schade's theatre party was down on the official program. And by reason of its being on the program Schade and the Schade got a lot of newspaper notice that they wouldn't have gotten otherwise.

Everybody wanted to be at the Schade because it was known that the chiefs were to be there. Those who didn't want to be on hand for that particular reason had another, to wit:

Schade had offered a police dog pup to the person getting the most votes in a popularity contest arranged to further the interest of 'Tracked in the Snow Country," the attraction that gave way to "The Heart of a Siren." There was much interest in the competition.

The winner of the pup was to be announced at the conclusion of the presentation of "The Heart of a Siren" that had been arranged for the chiefs and their party.

The pup went to Chief C. Al Weingates of the Sandusky police department, who received something like 2,900 votes to about 2,800 for the party second in the race and 2,700 for the party third. .

Liar Contest Exploitation for "Lightnin'" Run

An exploitation feature of the Cleveland showing of "Lightnin'" was a Liars Contest that created no end of amusement, and incidentally directed a lot of extra attention to the picture.

As everybody knows, "Lightnin'" Bill Jones, from whom the picture takes its name, is one of those likeable old characters who, no matter how big a tale is told him, can always top it with a more impressive, if not entirely truthful tale.

Arthur Swanke's shadow-box for "The Lady" (First National) at his Rialto theatre, El Dorado, Ark., recently.

John R. Royal, the manager of Keith's Palace, that housed the showing, acting in concert with the Cleveland Plain Dealer, and the Fox exploitation forces, ran a series of announcements a week before "Lightnin'" opened, giving all details of the contest. Under a heading of "Here is One Time When Lying Will Be Rewarded," a bid was made for the cooperation of all those having elastic conceptions of the verities. Ananias, Baron Munchausen and all of history's great prevaricators proved that they have many exponents carrying on their work in Cleveland, if the deluge of "lies" which poured in on the contest judges is any criterion.

For the most gigantic falsehood turned in, $10 was awarded. For the second biggest "lie," $7.50. For the third best tale, $5, and twelve pairs of seats for the next twelve best. The judges who decided on the output of the Loyal Order of Myth Makers was John R. Royal, W. Ward Marsh and the Fox exploitation representative.

Home Products Displayed on "Old Home Week"

One of the many splendid features of Manager E. B. Roberts' elaborate campaign on "Old Home Week" at the Majestic, Austin, was the exhibit of Home Products staged in the lobby of the theatre during the picture's run.

Merchant displays ranged from machinery to real estate, the latter firm exhibiting a miniature plaster of Paris building model. Caldwell's Products gave away samples of potato chips, potato salad, popcorn, peanuts, etc. All the merchants who displayed in the theatre lobby had a full page truck in the Austin American on the opening day of the picture. This page carried a heading which tied-up Old Home Week directly with the picture coming to the Majestic.

The lobby was decorated in white and purple, the City's colors, and all lights were dyed to carry out this effect. Through the courtesy of the Mayor, the official City Flag was artistically draped in the lobby. A copy of the Mayor's proclamation, in which he designated week of June 28th as Old Home Week, appropriately mounted, occupied a conspicuous place in the theatre lobby.

At the Chamber of Commerce picnic, attended by 500 members and their families, Manager Roberts distributed a special attendance card, specially numbered. This card was a direct tie-up with "Old Home Week" coming to the Majestic.

Puzzles Introduced as Ad for "Dixie Handicap"

When "The Dixie Handicap" played recently at the Lyceum theatre in Thief River Falls, Minn., Morris Abrms, Metro-Goldwyn exploiteer, discovered that cross word puzzles had never been used in the town in connection with exploitation and induced both local papers to run contests with free tickets to the picture as prizes. This innovation proved immensely popular and exploited the picture effectively.

Two thousand heralds were distributed in addition and extra display space was taken in the press. Slides were also used to popularize the picture and the town was well posted.

Left, display of the Frisco lines on Grand Boulevard in St. Louis, virtually a state fair in condensed form, for "The Iron Horse" (Fox) at the Grand Central, Lyric, Capitol and Skydome theatres; right, the panorama on rollers and one of the model locomotives displayed by the Missouri Pacific.

Queen of Tresses Contest Given "Pretty Ladies"

A Queen of Tresses contest proved an exceedingly popular feature of the elaborate campaign waged by W. J. Murphy, Metro-Goldwyn exploiteer and the management of Loew's Warfield in San Francisco when "Pretty Ladies" opened there recently. The first prize for the most beautifully dressed head of hair was a week's vacation at Hotel Capitola, a vacation outfit contributed by the Emporium Sportswear Shop and a three weeks' engagement under Fanchon and Marco. The second prize was $50 in cash, and there were 15 additional prizes.

Eight elaborate window displays each featuring a number of artistically mounted stills were secured, while street cars carried cards exploiting the showing also. Five hundred strips reading "Pretty Ladies, Take a Ride With Me" were distributed among automobilists and proved popular, drivers pasting them up eagerly on their windshields and windows. A large number of brilliantly colored 24-sheets were posted, together with many other posters of varied sizes.

Rare Mechanical Display for "The Speed Spook"

The noteworthy feature of Manager Rodney Bush's lobby for "The Speed Spook," playing the Galax, Birmingham, was the mechanical nature of the display, which consisted of a huge racing car cut out of Upson board with a white spook standing behind it, pointing a warning finger. The wheels of the car were made separate from the centerpiece and mounted on fan blades which actuated the wheels to a speed attained by an ordinary electric fan. A stiff piece of leather placed on back of car, where one end of it hit the protruding fan blade on each revolution, produced a motor effect that even attracted the attention of motorists. The car was

Animated display piece in "The Speed Spook" (C. C. Burr) by Rodney Bush, manager of the Galax theatre, Birmingham, Ala. Electric fans made the wheels revolve and one fan slapping a leather flap made the engine noise.

painted a light chrome yellow with a blue streak running the length of the body. As an attention getter, the display couldn't be excelled.

Enviable word-of-mouth advertising and newspaper publicity was accorded the picture through the Post newsboys who were the guests of the management at an evening performance of "The Speed Spook." In addition to the advance stories given the invitation, the Post expressed its gratitude in a special article on closing day of photoplay.

Branford's Wow Contest on "Heart of a Siren"

D. J. Shepard, the live managing director of the Bradford theatre of Newark, N. J., was quick to see the merits of the Wow Contest exploitation stunt arranged for "The Heart of a Siren," and arranged with the Newark Star-Eagle to conduct the contest during the engagement of this production of his theatre.

The Star-Eagle gave "The Heart of a Siren Contest" space on its front page for the entire week prior to the opening of the feature an dincreased the space each day of the engagement as the contest gained momentum. The novel contest proved extremely popular with Star-Eagle readers and the hundreds of clever and humorous definitions submitted made the selection of winners a difficult task.

Twelve Star-Eagle trucks carried banners reading "Wow! Follow the Star-Eagle Branford Tehatre Contest" all during the contest. The newspaper campaign on contest and picture was backed up by atractive window displays in the windows of leading book merchants which were arranged through E. P. Dutton & Co. assisting in the contests.

The first prize of $25 given by the Branford theatre was won by Gladys B. Machter for her definition of a wow as "something unexpected, unrivalled, or extraordinary, that prompts a spontaneous outburst of enthusiastic approval." The set of Roget's Thesaurus (donated as second prize by E. P. Dutton & Co.) was won by C. T. Johnson who described a wow as "That which excited an extraordinary enthusiastic outburst of good feeling." The Star-Eagle published fifteen of the best definitions received each day and they were awarded pairs of seats for "The Heart of a Siren" at the Branford theatre. Many of the definitions sent in were written in a humorous vein exciting not a few laughs and many smiles with their slang wording.

Attractively arranged window display for "Lost—a Wife" (Paramount) when that photoplay showed at the Rialto theatre, Chattanooga, of which J. L. Cartwright is manager.

WE BEG TO REPORT

MEMBERS NOW ENROLLED

26 Producer-Distributors - 82 Exchanges

The INDEPENDENT MOTION PICTURE ASSOCIATION OF AMERICA is growing in Strength and Influence every day, BECAUSE—

Its membership includes the best of the Honest-to-Goodness Independents in the industry, unaffiliated with any theatre-owning organizations, and standing as the Protectors of Theatres against Monopoly.

Its members work in CO-OPERATION, not in COMPETITION with exhibitors. They are producing and purveying a greater number of High Class Pictures— *honestly made and honestly sold*—than any other group.

WHAT WE STAND FOR

To foster, standardize and stabilize on the highest possible plane the business relationship among Independent Producers, Distributors, Exchanges, Theatres and other branches of the industry.

To foster and encourage the Independent production of the Highest type of motion pictures for distribution through Reputable Independent Exchanges.

To establish uniform methods and practices in the business relationships between the Members of this Association and their contacts.

This Seal is a Symbol of
Protection

For Independent
Producers, Distributors,
Exchanges, Theatres

INDEPENDENT MOTION PICTURE ASSOCIATION OF AMERICA

1650 Broadway   Frederick H. Elliott
New York City   General Manager

MEMBER
INDEPENDENT
MOTION PICTURE ASSOCIATION OF AMERICA INC.

Chadwick Pictures Corporation
— presents —

THE FINEST ASSEMBLY of STARS
OFFERED IN THE INDEPENDENT MARKET.

— IN —

A SERIES of HIGHLY
IMPORTANT
PRODUCTIONS

CHARLES RAY

LIONEL BARRYMORE

THEDA BARA

LARRY SEMON

EACH PICTURE A BOX OFFICE ACHIEVEMENT

Charles Ray	George Walsh	Larry Semon	Lionel Barrymore	Theda Bara
	in	in		in
"Dyna Paradise"	"American Pluck" "Blue Blood"	"The Wizard of Oz"	Lionel Barrymore	"The Unchastened Woman"
—	and	and	in	
"Sweet Adeline"	"The Prince o. Broadway"	"The Perfect Clown"	"The Bells"	

AND A HUNT STROMBERG SPECIAL PRODUCTION – PAINT and POWDER

THE PICK OF
for
INDEPENDENCE

GENERAL CHARLES KING
Frontier Features
starring
Ben Wilson and Neva Gerber

Ready { "Warrior Gap," "Under Fire," "Fort Frayne," "Tonio, Son of the Sierras," "A Daughter of the Sioux."

Secret Service Stories
starring
PEGGY O'DAY
"The Thrill Girl"
Ready—"Peggy of the Secret Service"

Society-Athletic Features
starring
F. SCHUMANN-HEINK
Ready—"Hills Aflame"
"Youth's Highway"

Comedy Dramas
co-starring
FORREST TAYLOR
and
ANNE BERRYMAN

Two-Reel Herrick
Unique Featurettes
"FRAGMENTS OF LIFE"
"Tales Told Without Titles"
Four Now Ready

Super Feature
"RED LOVE"
starring
John Lowell and
Evangeline Russell

Ready

Super Special
RED

Being Produced by and With
MRS. WALLACE REID

Pictures from the Novels of
JAMES OLIVER CURWOOD
"My Neighbor's Wife"
Ready "The Gold Hunters"
1 Lawson Haris Production
"LAW or LOYALTY"—*Ready*

Episode Serial
BEN WILSON and NEVA GERBER
in
"THE MYSTERY BOX"
Now Ready

"BETTER PICTURES
DAVIS DISTRIBU'
T. Charles

218 West 42nd Street

for

PROFIT

Arabian Nights
Super Special

TALES OF A THOUSAND
AND ONE NIGHTS   **Ready**

Super Feature
"KING LOG"
(working title)
from a story by
Clarence Buddington Kelland
featuring
John Bowers, Marguerite de la Motte,
Dan Mason, Allan Hale.
NOW READY

Splendid

AL FERGUSON

Features

Ready—Seven Pictures

Super-Serial
Nationally Advertised and
Exploited
"THE POWER GOD"
starring
Ben Wilson and Neva Gerber
For Fall Release

EPISODES

De Luxe Series
starring
MARILYN MILLS
and her intelligent horses
"Star" and "Beverly"
Ready—"Tricks" *Next*—"Three Pals"

Productions Starring

" KEN " MAYNARD
(acclaimed as the new star of Westerns)
and "Tarzan" King of All Horses
Ready—"50,000 Reward," "Fighting
Courage," "The Demon
Rider," "The Haunted Range"

"HEY FELLAS"!
Kid Komedies

The Doin's and "Disasters"
of Young America

Six Ready—(Released Every Other Week)

"SHEIKS and SHEBAS"
Comedies of

Flapper Americans

Six Ready—(Released Every Other Week)

Single Reel Novelties

" CINEMA STARS "
Intimate glimpses of film favorites
—at home, at work and at play
ALL READY NOW

W. RAY JOHNSTON
presents

"THE PATENT LEATHER PUG"

A HARRY J. BROWN
PRODUCTION
Starring
BILLY
SULLIVAN
DIRECTED BY
ALBERT ROGELL

RAYART
PICTURES

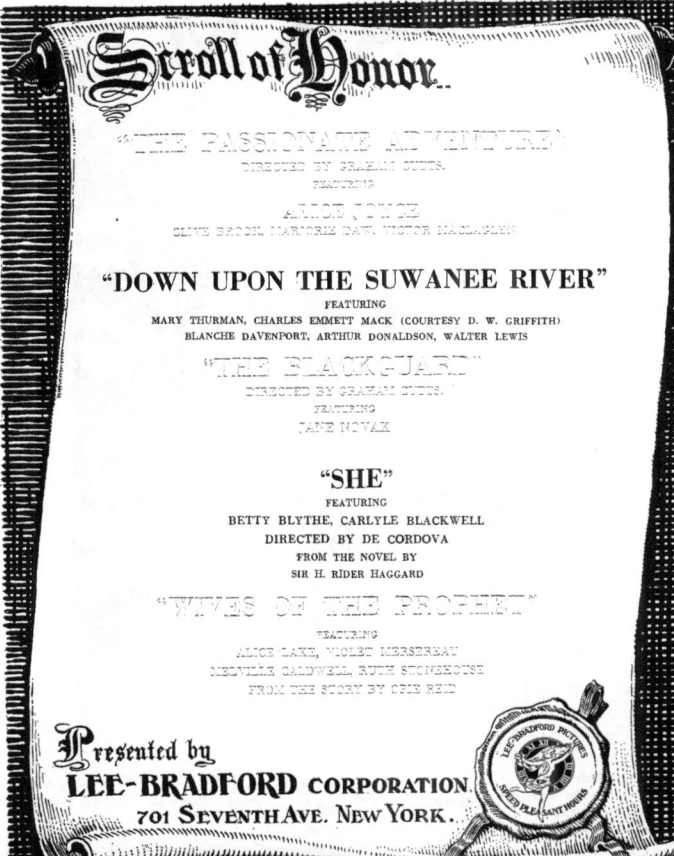

Scroll of Honor

"THE PASSIONATE ADVENTURE"
DIRECTED BY GRAHAM CUTTS
FEATURING
ALICE JOYCE
CLIVE BROOK, MARJORIE DAW, VICTOR McLAGLEN

"DOWN UPON THE SUWANEE RIVER"
FEATURING
MARY THURMAN, CHARLES EMMETT MACK (COURTESY D. W. GRIFFITH)
BLANCHE DAVENPORT, ARTHUR DONALDSON, WALTER LEWIS

"THE BLACKGUARD"
DIRECTED BY GRAHAM CUTTS
FEATURING
JANE NOVAK

"SHE"
FEATURING
BETTY BLYTHE, CARLYLE BLACKWELL
DIRECTED BY DE CORDOVA
FROM THE NOVEL BY
SIR H. RIDER HAGGARD

"WIVES OF THE PROPHET"
FEATURING
ALICE LAKE, VIOLET MERSEREAU
MELVILLE CALDWELL, RUTH STONEHOUSE
FROM THE STORY BY OPIE READ

Presented by
LEE-BRADFORD CORPORATION
701 SEVENTH AVE. NEW YORK.

LOUIS N. JAFFE

PRESENTS

LILA LEE

WITH Maurice Schwartz

IN

BROKEN HEARTS

A Struggle for the right to Love

NOW BOOKING JAFFE ART FILM CORP. Jaffe Building 317 BROADWAY NEW YORK CITY

A BOX OFFICE ATTRACTION FOR ANY KIND OF A HOUSE

The gripping story of life under the knout of the Czar and the shadows of the Statue of Liberty.

A JAFFE ART FILM

"WANDERING FIRES"

Produced & Directed by MAJOR MAURICE CAMPBELL

with

Constance Bennett, George Hackathorne & Wallace MacDonald

From the story by Warner Fabian, Author of "FLAMING YOUTH"

ES

∥TESSIE∥

Produced & Directed by DALLAS M. FITZGERALD

with

Jonald
TH"

May McAvoy, Bobby Agnew, Myrtle Stedman & Lee Moran

From the Saturday Evening Post Story by SEWELL FORD

SPEED - ACTION - THRILLS

HIGH SPEED WESTERN
COMEDY DRAMAS
FEATURING
(BiLL) PATTON

SPEED DRAMAS
FEATURING

 O

ONE REEL PRODUCTIONS WITH A
NATIONAL NEWSPAPER TIE-UP—GET IN
ON THIS AT ONCE—IT WILL CLEAN UP
NG H L YWOOD"
WITH A NEWSPAPER REPORTER

WRITE OR WIRE FOR TERRITORIES

Product Plentiful for Present Season

Independents Go Through With Big Programs

By Thomas C. Kennedy

MORE than 300 independent productions will be offered on the market this season, according to estimates based on actual accomplishments at studios in the east and on the west coast to date. To a precedented degree the independents are adhering to the production plans announced by them in the spring and features of every type, from the high-class modern society play down to the low cost westerns will be available to exhibitors from state rights operators this year.

The number of features from the independents this year exceeds by far that for any previous twelvemonth. Taking 300 as the total —and, in view of the large number of producers who are well along with their schedules, that is a conservative figure—the volume of state rights pictures this year is fifty per cent. greater than that of 1924-25, when there were about 200 features, and 100 per cent. greater than in 1923-24, a period during which there were less than 150 independently released features. In 1922-23 the state rights features totaled slightly more than 100.

The independent producers have made heavy investments this year and with a majority of the territories sold to exchanges the crucial period approaches as the booking season opens. Whether the producers will do as well proportionately on an increased volume, as they did last year, when many of the leading organizations in the field turned a neat profit on their investments, remains to be seen—the exhibitors with their play dates being the factors which will determine that.

The producers and distributors are in an optimistic mood. They have received a high order of encouragement in the success achieved in their producing activities to date. To begin with the better established firms are on a sounder financial basis than ever before, for money is available at reasonable rates. Their studio organizations have functioned competently and with a minimum of waste. And finally and most importantly, the pictures so far made have measured up to a very high standard. The initial productions of several of the companies have been shown and have received the highest praise from screen critics and trade observers.

While there is optimism, and just cause for it probably, there is also now a spirit of watchful waiting on the part of the producers. The exchanges are beginning to sell to the exhibitors and the results of those campaigns will tell the tale of whether or not the exhibitors want the state rights producers to survive on their present rather flourishing basis or not.

The year will be a veritable bonanza for the exhibitors seeking products from the independent channels. With a great volume of pictures from which to select there will be no difficulty, or should not, in obtaining high-class programs at fair prices. The majority of the producers have striven for quality pictures and with so many attempting to hit the mark it is reasonable to suppose that the supply of good attractions, up to the present day standards of feature pictures, will be plentiful.

Because of the number and quality of pic-

tures which will be offered on the state rights market this year the exhibitors will be in a stronger position than ever before to book for quality and profit. An imposing list of box office names have been attracted to the state rights productions and books and plays of some reputation are among the literary properties which have been selected for production. In fact the independents have taken a bold step forward and even now are planning to attempt even more ambitious programs next year. Whether these plans ever materialize will depend upon the circulation they can get for their pictures this season. It has been said that an increase of 25 per cent in the number of play dates over last year will suffice to see the independents through on their present schedules and afford them the encouragement necessary for them to make an even better showing as producers of box office attractions next year.

The following list gives the number of features which will be made this year by the prominent state rights producers:

Anchor	16
Arrow	32
Artclass	24
Astor	13
Aywon	18
C. C. Burr	1
Chadwick	17
Columbia	18
Davis	70
Ginsburg	12
Independent	18
Ivan	4
Jans	6
Rayart	36
Schulberg	18
Sunset	13
Tiffany	12
Truart	14

To this list must be added productions from other companies who have not announced definite programs but will nevertheless make several features. The list above shows a total of 342, so a shrinkage, which is likely, will still leave the number above 300.

A fact which has been commented upon this year is the absence of "orphan features". For the past few seasons these "orphans" have appeared with considerable regularity. Made by some organization formed to produce a single picture "with an idea" or with some particular exploitation angle, these orphans usually drift about the market seeking a release and with their backers hoping against hope to place them and thus get a start in the production field. The backers of such enterprises have been howled down by the bigger independent producers as fly-by-nights and to the operations of many them has been laid the blame for the difficulty which the independents formerly experienced in getting financial backing. The independents of today form a sort of "middle class" in the motion picture social scheme. They have gained a reputation among the bankers as being substantial enough to merit financial support and their operations are considered legitimate fields for investment.

So far the well organized state rights producers have measured up to standard in their studio accomplishments. The early crop of pictures, which number many now being discussed as box office attractions of great potential value, appears to justify the early claims of the producers.

The remarkable strides made by the majority of the independent producers during the past few months clearly demonstrates that their studio organizations are capable of turning out pictures of high quality on scheduled time. The fact that many have gone ahead of their production programs also illustrates that the independents may be taken at their word, for advance announcements of the schedules are now shown to have been conservative in the estimates on which the release programs of these companies were based. Several companies have already finished a major portion of the pictures they scheduled for the 1925-26 season. Columbia, for example, has completed camera work on 14 of the eighteen pictures to be offered this year, and the remaining four are now in production.

The finished works show that the state rights people are making their grand gesture this year and are determined to demonstrate that they can make better and bigger pictures if the exhibitors want them to. The answer as to whether they will operate on an even larger scale next year lies with the exhibitors, and now that exchangemen are beginning to offer the pictures for booking the question will be answered soon.

Lee-Bradford Offering Five Features

WITH four productions completed and the fifth now in work, the Lee-Bradford Corporation is in readiness to offer exhibitors the entire program for 1925-26 well in advance of release dates. Much of the territory on these features has been closed already and the early offerings on the company's list soon will be available for screening before exhibitors at the various exchanges handling the product.

The program will be initiated by "The Passionate Adventure," a Graham Cutts production made in England with Alice Joyce, Clive Brook, Marjorie Daw and Victor MacLaglen. This production is considered by exchange men to be in the class of first run class "A" attractions and is pointed out by its sponsors as the standard of feature which they will offer through state right exchanges this year.

The next picture on the list is "The Blackguard," another Graham Cutts production,

in which Jane Novak is featured. This will be followed by "Shea," an elaborate screen adaptation of the novel by Sir H. Rider Haggard. Betty Blythe and Carlyle Blackwell play the principal roles and the picture was directed by De Cordova.

"Wives of the Prophet," the fifth picture is now in production. The company, in which Alice Lake, Violet Mersereau, Melville Caldwell and Ruth Stonehouse will be features, now is working on location in West Virginia. The film will be based on the story of the same title by Opie Reid.

With the completion of "Wives of the Prophet" the Lee-Bradford schedule bill for the coming season will be ready for the market. In all these productions special exploitation material will be issued and substantial aid will be given exhibitors in launching publicity campaigns well before

the date of the opening engagements of the pictures at their theatres.

Arthur A. Lee, president Lee-Bradford Corporation.

Anchor Schedule Lists 24 Productions

NOTEWORTHY progress on the schedule of 16 features and 12 short comedies to be offered independents this season by Anchor Film Distributors, Inc., has been made at the studios of the company in Hollywood.

With a series of eight Helen Holmes features, eight starring Al Hoxie, and eight Bob Reeves features, with a series of 12 two-reel comedies featuring Bobby Ray, the Anchor company this year is essaying a most ambitious program and an enlarged organization has been formed to handle the schedule. The result is that production is well ahead of the producing program and exhibitors are now assured that the pictures will be delivered to exchanges well in advance of release.

The Helen Holmes series will be composed of railroad thrillers of the type in which this star established herself as a favorite with a host of screen patrons. The pictures are being directed by J. P. McGowan, who filmed the Helen Holmes successes of the

The program from Anchor Film Distributors for the coming season includes the following series of features and short comedies.

8 Railroad Thrillers Starring Helen Holmes.

8 Western Melodramas Starring Al Hoxie.

8 Western Stunt Dramas Starring Bob Reeves.

12 Two-Reel Comedies Starring Bobby Ray.

past. The titles of the pictures, in the order of their release, are: "Perils of the Rail," "Webs of Steel," "The Train Wreckers," "The Open Switch," "Mistaken Orders," "The Lost Express," "The Mainline Wreck," and "The Fast Freight."

Al Hoxie, a western star, will be presented in a group of colorful western melodramas specializing in speed, stunts and ro-

mance. These pictures also will be directed by J. P. McGowan. Particular attention will be given the backgrounds, every effort being made to lend pictorial flavor and the atmosphere of the great open spaces to these features. Al Hoxie's first of the series will be titled "Riding Romance." This will be followed by "Unseen Enemies," "The Texas Terror," "Red Blood," "Ace of Clubs," "A Lost Trail," "Hidden Gold," and "The Road Agent."

Larry Wheeler is the producer of the series in which Bob Reeves, another sprightly western star, is to be featured by Anchor. These action and stunt dramas of the far west are titled "Cyclone Bob," "Ambushed," "Riding Straight," "Fighting Luck," "The Iron Fist," "A Desperate Chance," "Riding for Life," and "A Narrow Escape."

Speed and situations will be stressed in the twelve two-reelers in which Bobby Ray, a popular comedy personality, is to be starred.

Rayart Ahead on Production Schedule

SIX producing units are pounding away on the coast on the Rayart Product for the 1925-6 according to W. Ray Johnston, President of Rayart.

"Our releases for the months of Septem-

W. Ray Johnston, president of Rayart.

ber, October and part of November are already in the house," states Mr. Johnston, who continued.

"Next week we will release our serial attraction 'The Flame Fighter,' a ten-chapter thriller starring Herbert Rawlinson. This was directed by Robert Dillon and produced by Beacon Films Corporation.

"Also in September we will release 'Starlight, the Untamed,' a Harry Webb production, 'The Crack O'Dawn,' starring Reed Howes, and 'The Fear Fighter,' starring Billy Sullivan. Also a two-reel comedy produced by Billy West and featuring Gloria Joy entitled 'Wood Simps.'

"For October we will release Reed Howes in 'The Cyclone Cavalier,' a Central American revolution story, Jack Perrin in 'Dangerous Fists,' a Whirlwind Western, and Billy Sullivan in 'The Goat Getter,' a Harry J. Brown attraction.

"Of especial interest in our October program will be the Gerson Production 'The Pride of the Force,' directed by Duke Worne. This is an unusual police story with

a cast that includes Tom Santschi, Gladys Hulette, Francis X. Bushman, Jr., Cranford Kent and Edith Chapman.

"For November we will again have an attractive lineup headed 'The Golden State Limited,' a railroad story, Reed Howes with Bull Montana, Dorothy Dwan, Sheldon Lewis and Jimmy Aubrey in 'The Bashful Buccaneer,' and Billy Sullivan in 'The Speed Champion.' Also a new comedy feature entitled 'The Thrill Chaser,' starring Billy West with Virginia Pearson, Kathleen Myers, John Miljan and Lionel Belmore. This will be the first of a series of four features length comedies starring Billy West.

"Other productions on our list for this fall include 'The Danger Quest,' a South African story in which Reed Howes will appear. 'The Beloved Pawn,' from the Harold Titus novel of that name. 'The Last Alarm,' a fire story; 'Somebody's Mother,' 'The Call of the Klondyke,' 'The Coast Guard Patrol,' 'The Patent Leather Pug,' 'Fighting Fate,' and 'The Windjammer.'"

Bischoff Schedule Half Completed

SAMUEL BISCHOFF'S guarantee to the independent market that he would produce and deliver thirty-six two reel comedies of merit and quality this season is being fulfilled with great expedition at the California Studios in Hollywood.

To date Bischoff has completed fifteen of his comedies, has three more in production and three more in preparation for filming the minute the last trio are photographed.

Bischoff has three sets of comedies. The first set is the H. C. Witwer "Classics in Slang." These in the main are travesties on the works of Shakespeare and other famous authors. Another is the Biff Thrill comedies series. In these comedies the object is to thrill and produce laughter at the same time. The other series are Gold Medal comedies,

> **Comedies completed by Samuel Bischoff include the following:** "Classics In Slang" Series: "Mac's Beth," "Battling Romeo," "Taming of the Shrewd," "The Merchant of Weenies," "Account of Monte Cristo."
> Biff Thrill Comedies: "The Live Agent," "Six Miles to Go," "Working for the Best," "Hollywouldn't," "The Starvation Hunters."
> Gold Medal Comedies: "Play Ball," "Assorted Nuts," "Spooky Spooks," "Roomers Afloat" "Vauda Villains."

stories of swiftly moving action from start to finish.

To insure the scenes in these productions going over with the utmost laughter and thrills Bischoff assembled what is considered

the greatest array of laugh producers gathered under one banner. Notable in the list are Al St. John, Eddie Gribbon, Mildred June, Chester Conklin, Charles Delaney, Eddie Phillips, Charlotte Morgan, Johnny Sinclair, Al Alt, Jack Richardson, Dot Farley, Jack Cooper, Cliff Bowes, Billy Franey and others.

The comedies that Bischoff has completed to date are five of the Witwer series, namely, "Mac's Beth," "Battling Romeo," "Taming of the Shrewd," "The Merchant of Weenies," and "Account of Monte Cristo."

The five Biff Thrillers are "The Live Agent," "Six Miles to Go," "Working for the Rest," "Hollywouldn't" and "The Starvation Hunters." Then there are five of the Gold Medal variety, namely, "Play Ball," "Assorted Nuts," "Spooky Spooks," "Roomers Afloat" and "Vauda Villians."

New Artclass Short Subjects Series

LOUIS WEISS, managing director of Weiss Brothers' Artclass Picture is offering a new series of six single reel special short subjects on the independent market this week. The series is titled "Guess Who," and comprises a series of guessing contests with well known screen stars as the object of the contest.

Each reel will contain pictures of twenty-five well-known stars, who will be seen portraying their individual characteristics. Their names will be left for the spectators to guess. Cards will be provided for the fans to write out their answers to the questions as to which stars were shown on the screen in the "Guess Who" reels.

The names of the twenty-five stars will be printed in alphabetical order and in large type on the card so that all the parti-

cipant in the "Guess Who" contest has to do is to identify the star and mark the star's number on the reel along side of the star's name.

Prizes can be given for the individual reel and then a grand contest made of the series. It is anticipated that if the individual reels be shown for a number of days that a great many people will come back again to have another try at the names of the stars that were missed.

The press sheet gives the exhibitor a great number of possible ways of attracting attention to the contest and once it is started will work itself up. A brilliantly designed one sheet is made up for each reel showing the names of the stars who will appear in the reel. That alone with the drawing power

of the stars will prove a big number with the public.

Two reels of the series are already in New York for showing. In them is a great array of stars. Among those in the first reel are Wallace Beery, Betty Blythe, Hobart Bosworth, Margaret De La Motte, Percy Marmont, Nazimova, Anna Q. Nilsson, Pat O'Malley, Charles Ray, Alma Rubens, Milton Sills, Alberta Vaughn, Claire Windsor.

Some of the prominent stars in the second reel are Monte Blue, Ruth Clifford, Corinne Griffith, Elaine Hammerstein, Norman Kerry, Cullen Landis, Laura LaPlante, Jacqueline Logan, Ben Lyon, Bert Lytell, Dorothy Mackaill, Antonio Moreno, Marie Prevost, Anita Stewart, Lewis Stone.

Chadwick Star Units Hard at Work

I. E. CHADWICK, who has just departed for the Coast to supervise the production of several super-special films, has purchased outright the Independent Studios in Hollywood for the use of the Chadwick Pictures Corporation and they will now be called The Chadwick Studios.

The Chadwick Pictures Corporation's 1925-26 schedule is a gala one. Nine productions have already been completed and two more have been started by the West Coast Studios.

Larry Semon has finished two comedies, "The Wizard of Oz" and "The Perfect Clown," an original story written especially for Mr. Semon and directed by Fred Newmeyer.

Theda Bara, original screen vampire who has been in retirement for five years, has just completed "The Unchastened Woman," adapted from the drama by Louis K. Anspacher, directed by James Young and including an all-star cast—Wyndham Standing, Eileen Percy, John Miljan, Dale Fuller, Milla Davenport, Eric Mayne, Mayme Kelso and Frederic Kovert.

Another return is that of Charles Ray to the rural roles. Ray has just completed "Some Pun'kins" and "Sweet Adeline," the story based on the famous song. Jerome Storm, directed both of these comedies. The

cast of "Some Pun'kins" includes Duane Thompson, Bert Woodruff, George Fawcett, William Courtright and Fanny Midgely. For "Sweet Adeline" the following stars have been cast: Gertrude Olmstead, Gertrude Short, J. P. Lockne, Frank Austin, Sybil Johnson and Jack Clifford.

Three pictures with George Walsh have just been completed and three more are to follow. The first release starring Walsh is "American Pluck," adopted from the novel "Blaze Derringer," by Ralph Spece. Wanda Hawley plays the feminine lead, and the supporting cast include Sidney De Grey, Frank Leigh, Tom Wilson, Leo White and Dan Mason. "Blue Blood" and "The Prince of Broadway" are the two other completed productions, the former a story dealing with the "class problem," the latter a fight film including an all-star prize-ring cast. "The Prince of Broadway" was directed by John Gorman.

Elaine Hammerstein in "Paint and Powder" and Lionel Barrymore in a "Man of Iron" are also listed among the completed pictures.

Work on "The Count of Luxenbourg," a picture version of the operetta of the same name, has just been commenced, and will be filmed by Arthur Gregory, famous European director. And Lionel Barrymore has been

cast for the lead in "The Bells," a filmization of the world-famous play.

I. E. Chadwick, president Chadwick Pictures Corporation.

Davis Dist. Program Lists Big Features

By J. CHARLES DAVIS, 2nd, President, Davis Distributing Division, Inc.

THERE are lots of good pictures on the independent market and the exhibitors are playing them. Also they are paying fair prices for fair product. I know from my contacts with producers making pictures for the Davis Distributing Division, Inc., there is much good material available for distribution.

By the deal with the Vital Exchanges our product will receive national distribution. This means that companies making pictures for us will get national distribution and that the exhibitor throughout the country will get Davis Distributing pictures on a set release date.

Of the product which we will handle there are three super-specials. "Tales of 1001 Nights," the Arabian Nights Fantasy, and "Red Love" starring John Lowell and Evangeline Russell are now ready; Mrs. Wallace Reid has cast and is producing the "Red Kimono".

We have a series of five James Oliver Curwood pictures of which "My Neighbor's Wife" and "The Gold Hunters" are completed. This will be followed by "Tentacles of the North," "The Courage of Captain Plum" and "The Wolf Hunters". The eight pictures from the books of Gen. Chas. King U. S. A. are well under way and five have been completed, "Under Fire," "Warrior Gap," "Fort Frayne," "A Daughter of the Sioux," and "Tonio, Son of the Sierras". In the Marilyn Mills series of eight, one

has been completed and is ready for release "Tricks". The second, "Three Pals," is in production. Among the titles of the other six to be made are "Long Odds," "Fleet Foot," "White Fury," "The Killer," Ken Maynard is making a series of eight westerns for us. The series will feature "Tarzan," Ken's pal and the Hollywood Beauty Sextette in every picture. "$50,000 Reward," "Fighting Courage," "The Demon Rider," and "The Haunted Range" have been completed. "The Grey Vulture" is in production and will be followed shortly by the "Lights of Mojave," "The Texan's Oath" and "Timber Wolves."

Peggy O'Day is making a Secret Service Series of eight pictures dealing with the adventures of a girl secret service operative. The first, "Peggy of the Secret Service" is ready and "Peggy in Chinatown" is being cast.

We will have two series of pictures starring Al Ferguson. The first six, "Shackles of Fear," "Trail of Vengeance," "Phantom Shadows," "Scarlet and Gold," "A Fighting Romeo" and "The Fighting Parson" are already completed. "Lawless Love," the first of the second series has been finished and the second is in production.

F. Schumann-Heink is making a series of pictures under the direction of J. J. Fleming in Beaverton, Oregon, and has completed two pictures—"Hills Aflame" and "Youth's Highway". The same producer will also have for us a series of eight comedy-dramas co-starring Forest Taylor and Anne Berryman.

We have the most complete line-up of independent short product on the market. For the coming season there will be fifty-two comedies, two serials, six "Fragments of Life" (2 reel novelties, "Tales Told Without Titles") and fifty-two "Cinema Star" reels.

J. Charles Davis, 2nd, President Davis Distributing Division, Inc.

I. M. P. A. Now Lists Hundred Members

ONE of the concrete facts of "Independence Year" is the growth of the Independent Motion Picture Association in America.

Started less than two years ago by a handful of earnest men who came to the conclusion that the state righter's salvation lay in organization, it has developed into an association of great force and now has 108 members—26 producer-distributors and 82 separate exchanges.

Since June 15th, when Frederick H. Elliott was called in as General Manager, it has grown 45 per cent.

The I. M. P. A. has dignified the state right market and raised it to a position where its

members command the respect of the industry. I. E. Chadwick, as president, has been at the helm since the organization's birth, with W. E. Shallenberger, Chairman of the Board of Directors. Others who have been factors in its advancement are Ben Amsterdam, first vice-president; Oscar A. Price, second vice-president; Joe Brandt, third vice-president; Nathan Hirsh, treasurer; Jack Bellman, recording secretary.

Committee heads include William Steiner, M. H. Hoffman, W. Ray Johnston, Louis Weiss, Abe Carlos, Herman Gluckman, Jack Cohn, B. P. Schulberg, J. G. Bachmann, Harry Thomas, S. S. Krellberg, Oscar Neufeld, Joe Klein, John Lowell Russell, Joseph

L. Friedman and H. W. Pearlman.

The business and responsibilities of the association became so diversified this year it was found necessary to call in a general manager to direct its affairs. Frederick H. Elliott, a potent force in the organization and upbuilding of the old National Association, was summoned from another field of activity to handle the job.

The I. M. P. A. offices at 1650 Broadway, New York, maintained as "Independence Hall," are the headquarters for the independents of the country. An information bureau, with telephone, mail, publicity and stenographic service included, is maintained for the benefit of the visitors.

Jaffe Company Completing First Feature

Hanna Jaffe, vice-president Jaffe Art Film Corporation.

THOUGH a comparative newcomer into the field of independent picture production and distribution the Jaffe Art Film Corporation, formed recently by Louis N. Jaffe, a New York lawyer and realtor, is completing the first of a series of features to be offered this season at the Tec Art Studios in New York.

The picture is titled "Broken Hearts" and with Lila Leet in the featured role is scheduled for release in October. The principal male role is being played by Maurice Schwartz, a noted Jewish dramatic actor. It is a drama dealing with immigrant life and is based on a stage play.

Hanna Jaffe, an active addition to the many women who have chosen the pictures as a career, is vice-president of the producing and general manager of the producing and distributing end of the Jaffe Art Film

Company. It was she who selected "Broken Hearts" as the first work for production by the organization. The story is said to be based on the true life story of two lovers. The action is played against a background of immigrant life and is said to afford many opportunities for the introduction of the realism and atmosphere which gives the picture supremacy over the stage.

It is probable that the other features which Jaffe will produce will be filmed in New York. The pictures will be distributed by the company which produces them. Territorial rights on "Broken Hearts," which will be ready for release in October, are now offered to state rights exchanges.

The organization has been perfected and both the sales and production branches of the enterprise are now going forward with an ambitious program.

Seven of 32 Arrow Features Completed

"NEVER before in the history of the motion picture industry has the exhibitor been offered the opportunity of booking as many good pictures as will be his experience this season," says W. E. Shallenberger, President of the Arrow Pictures Corporation, one of the most important of the Independent Producing and Distributing organizations.

"In outlining the policy of my company for the season of 1925-26, I determined that over and above all things, good pictures would be our aim. Preparations for this objective were not made over night. The twenty-four pictures which will represent the Golden Arrow Franchise of first run features for this season will be the result of the policy outlined above.

In the pre-view showing of "Children of the Whirlwind," a Whitman Bennett Production, the cast of which is headed by Lionel Barrymore, Johnny Walker and Marguerite De La Motte, "The Primrose Path," an Arthur Beck production, directed by Harry Hoyt, in which Clara Bow, Wallace McDonald, Stuart Holmes, Tom Santchi and Arline Pretty are employed in the principal roles;

W. E. Shallenberger, president Arrow Film Corp.

"Tessie," a Sewell Ford story, produced and directed by Dallas M. Fitzgerald, with May McAvoy, Bobby Agnes, Myrtle Stedman, Lee Moran and Gertrude Short; "The Substitute Wife," another Whitman Bennett production, directed by Wilfred Noy, starring Jane

Novak, with Niles Welsh, Louise Carter and others in the cast; "Scandal Street," with Madge Kennedy, Niles Welsh, Louise Carter, Edwin August and others; "The Unnamed Woman," directed by Harry Hoyt, for Arthur Beck, with a cast headed by Katherine McDonald, Wanda Hawley and Herbert Rawlinson; "Wandering Fires," directed by Major Maurice Campbell, with a cast embracing Constance Bennett, Wallace McDonald, Henrietta Crosman, Effie Shannon and George Hackathorn, without exception, every one who was privileged to see these pictures declared in no uncertain terms they would take rank with the very best pictures shown by any producing organization, irrespective of affiliations in the past two years.

"I am proud," continued Dr. Shallenberger, "of the work of all concerned in the production of these first seven of the twenty-four Bolden Arrow features. How can I feel otherwise, for it is a feat, almost unprecedented, to produce seven of what are considered by competent judges, "knock-out" features of the first magnitude in seven attempts. It means that the organization is hitting on every cylinder, with an efficiency of 100%."

18 on Hollywood Films Sales Program

HOLLYWOOD Film Sales Service are listed among important state rights distributors contributing to the 1925-26 program with a list of 14 features and four single reel comedies. The pictures are being made in Hollywood and many of the territories have been closed for the product well in advance of release date.

The features consist of six high speed western comedy dramas starring Wm. (Bill) Patton, eight speed dramas featuring Johno Wells, and four comedies in a series called "Seeing Hollywood With a Newspaper Reporter." The comedies will show many "be-

hind the screen" scenes of the great motion picture producing centre.

Wm. Patton is known to a large portion of the picture-going public. He has specialized in western characterizations of a very breezy and likeable type and his pictures generally have blended fast action and thrill stunts with humorous situations prominent throughout. Patton will be supported by casts assembled from groups of players well skilled in the western type of play and the great out of doors will figure importantly and pictorially in assisting the star

to accomplish his entertaining characterizations.

Pace and movement keyed to a high pitch will furnish the special flavor which is claimed for the eight dramas featuring Johno Wells, an actor whose dash will carry him far along the road toward widespread popularity with the screen fans.

Hollywood Film Sales Service will have the scheduled productions ready for release well in advance of the scheduled time, according to M. S. Rosenfield, eastern representative with offices in the Loews State Theatre Building in New York.

Columbia Supplying Popular Demand

WHEN President Joe Brandt of Columbia Pictures made the statement three years ago that the public wants melodramas—of a better sort of course than those which flourished on the legitimate stage about a quarter century ago, he made a prediction which since has been borne out by the repeated success of screen productions of this type.

"Today," Mr. Brandt explained, "I find after visiting all parts of the country, repeatedly, and conferring with the biggest, as well as some of the smallest of exhibitors, that they all shout for honest-to-goodness melodrama. Of course such pictures must have really worth while stories.

"They want action. And more action, all the time. Not without reason did those great producers of melodrama, Al Woods, Charles Blaney and Corse Payton attract the greatest audience numbers to their box offices by giving them powerful melodramas—crude and ridiculous though they seem to us when weighed by our modern standards of screen play craft, but powerful plays, nevertheless.

"From the very start we have borne this fact in mind and the success we achieved with 'More to be Pitied,' 'Only a Shopgirl,' 'Temptation,' 'Fighting the Flames,'

and 'The Midnight Express,' have proven that this form of entertainment is what the vast majority demands.

"Polite dramas, and dramas that treat over-much of sex, even when they are brilliantly done, and have excellent stories for plots, never achieve the mark which a fairly good melodrama reaches. And an overdose of sexy and polite society drama only paves the way for melodramas of 'The Bat' and 'The Gorilla' order.

"When we prepared our present season's production schedule we had this angle in mind and worked hard to put it over. 'The Danger Signal,' first of our Columbia series, as well as 'Enemy of Men,' first of our Waldorf series, our fast action Perfection Series, and those pictures which follow, are all carefully constructed along such lines.

"In our forthcoming productions for the future seasons, we expect to adhere to this technic. It is essential so long as the public retains its desire for powerful action drama. We have realized this need from the start, and the film fans who have filled the theatres to see Columbia pictures have attested to our judgment."

Joe Brandt, president Columbia Pictures Corporation.

CLASSIFIED AD SECTION

RATES: 10 cents a word for each insertion, in advance except Employment Wanted, on which rate is 5 cents.

CLASSIFIED SERVICE

A classified ad in MOTION PICTURE NEWS offers the full resources and circulation of the NEWS to the advertiser at a ridiculously low figure.

Whether you want to reach executives, branch managers, salesmen, or theatre managers, you can accomplish this quickly and economically through the NEWS Classified Columns.

THE PEER OF ALL PROJECTION SURFACES Mr. Exhibitor — The Radio Silver Screens are the latest improvement in stereoptican projecting and for elimination of eye strain. Sold under a positive guarantee. Price 50c a square foot. For particulars and samples apply to JOHN MUNRO CRAWFORD, 45 Smith St., Newburgh, N. Y.

Wanted

EXPERT OPERATOR and Electrician with 9 years' experience in big houses; married; wants to locate at once. Address, Operator, Box 282, Mason City, Iowa.

WANTED immediately in Buffalo, a man with considerable experience in laboratory and camera work. Applicants should state full details as to experience, giving names of former employers and present occupation if not now employed in laboratory work. Also state salary expected. Address "Experience" c/o Motion Picture News, New York City.

THEATRE IN TOWN OF 4,000 or better, anywhere in North Central states, Northern Indiana preferred. Can either give satisfactory security on lease or buy outright. Would consider buying interest in bona-fide proposition where owner wishes to retire. All replies absolutely confidential. Address Box 360,

Motion Picture News, New York City.

For Sale

FOR SALE.—Theatre Equipment of all descriptions; Immediate shipment of used chairs,' any quantity. Will also buy used chairs and equipment. Theatre Seating Company, 845 South State Street, Chicago, Illinois.

FOR SALE.—Hope Jones Wurlitzer type 135, excellent condition. Will trade for cheaper instrument with cash difference. A bargain if you are looking for a fine organ. H. E. Skinner, Box 882, Ogden, Utah.

FOR SALE AT A SACRIFICE.— Photoplayer; in use less than 2 years. Orpheum Theatre, Orwigsburg, Pa.

FOR SALE. — Modern movie; priced for quick sale account of illness; wonderful bargain; county seat of 10,000. Box 240, Motion Picture News, New York City.

CLOTH BANNERS— $1.40 3 x 10 feet, 3 colors, any copy up to 15 words. One day service. Sent anywhere. Also Bargain Paper Banners. Associated Advertisers, 111 W. 18th St., Kansas City, Mo.

Here are nine different ads showing how nine different theatres announced the showing of "Fine Clothes" (First National in recent weeks. The houses represented in the lay-out are: Olympia theatre, New Haven; Capitol theatre, Cincinnati; Loew's State theatre, Cleveland; Rialto theatre, Omaha; Palace theatre, San Antonio; Criterion, Los Angeles; Leland theatre, Albany; Capitol theatre, Detroit, and the Circle theatre, Indianapolis. These displays were two and three columns wide in the original.

GLENN TRYON

in

Madame Sans' Jane

(Madame Don't Give a Whoop)

He wanted the girl but her father didn't want him.

To lose him the old man set sail for Europe with his daughter. But on the same boat, disguised as a movie vamp, was the boy, prepared to do or die and stand the old man on his addled bean.

Tryon as the movie vamp is one of the choicest bits of humor your eyes have seen in many a long day. It will outshine all but the very biggest features.

You can only get all that's coming to you IF you advertise it.

F. Richard Jones, Supervising Director

Pathécomedy

TRADE MARK

When he saw—a Charming and Skittish Woman with the face he'd love to kiss.

What he saw—the face he'd love to punch.

...th First Run Theatres

NEW YORK CITY

Rivoli Theatre—
Film Numbers—The Golden Princess (Paramount), Life's Greatest Thrills (International Newsreel), Marvels of Motion (S. R.), Rivoli Pictorial (Selected).
Musical Program—"Wagneriana" (overture), Six Brown Brothers (jazz band), "Yes Sir, That's My Baby" (organ).

Capitol Theatre—
Film Numbers—Graustark (First National), The Dahlia (color), Montana Clouds (Scenic), My Bonnie (S. R.).
Musical Program—Overture: "Espana" (orchestra), "Li'l Black Rose" (vocal solo), "Ave Maria" (cornet solo), "Mignonette" (dance), "Leonore" (duet), "Nutcracker Suite" (ballet corps), Organ recessional.

Strand Theatre—
Film Numbers—The Gold Rush (United Artists), continued, Strand Topical Review (Selected).
Musical Program—Orchestral Overture, "The Monte Carlo Dance Hall" (Prologue to feature), Organ solo.

Colony Theatre—
Film Numbers—The Coming of Amos (Producers Dist Corp.), Colony Pictorial (Selected), Life's Greatest Thrills (International Newsreel).
Musical Program — "Pucciniana" (Overture), Memphis Five (jazz orchestra), "Butterfly Ballet" (ballet), Organ solo.

Warners Theatre—
Film Numbers—The Wife Who Wasn't Wanted (Warner Brothers), News Weekly (Selected), Hodge Podge (Educational).
Musical Program—"Melodies You Know" (orchestra and soloists), Russian Interpretative Dancer, "Traviata" (vocal solo), Imperial Balalaika Quintette, Organ solo.

Rialto Theatre—
Film Numbers—The Coast of Folly (Paramount), Rialto Magazine (Selected).

Two-column ad on "Drusilla with a Million" (F.B.O.) at the Garden theatre, Baltimore.

BROOKLYN

Brooklyn Mark Strand Theatre—
Film Numbers — "Winds of Chance" (First National), Mark Strand Topical Review (selected).
Musical Program—Selections from Bizet's "Carmen" (Orchestra), "Toreador" (baritone solo), "Oh How I Miss You Tonight" (soprano solo), "Reminiscences of Franz Schubert"—"Marche Militaire" (Orchestra), "Song of Love" (soprano and basso duet), "Moment Musicale (ballet), "Who is Sylvia"! (tenor solo), "Serenade" (contralto solo), and "Song of Love" (Ensemble), and Wagner's "Tanhauser March" (organ recessional).

THEATRE COOLED WITH WATER-WASHED AIR
GARDEN THEATRE

THE RIDING ACE OF ACES!
In the Fastest Fighting—Shooting Thriller Ever Made

Carl Laemmle presents

HOOT GIBSON IN TAMING THE WEST

A Corking Comedy "HIGH JINX"

A Riot of Fast Action!
In the Wildest Romance Hoot Has Ever Screened.
A Million Thrills!
A Million Gasps!
A Million Laughs!

The Garden theatre in Baltimore prepared this attractive opening ad recently to announce the showing at that house of "Taming the West" (Universal).

Musical Program — Ben Bernie and the Rialto Gang in "A Day at the Beach."

Cameo Theatre—
Film Numbers—Sally of the Sawdust (United Artists), Cameo Pictorial (Pathe), Aesop's Fable (Pathe).
Musical Program—Orchestral overture, "One Little Dream of Love" (soprano solo), Organ solo.

Astor Theatre—
Film Numbers—The Phantom of the Opera (Universal).
Musical Program—Ballet (Albertina Rasch conception), Phantom effects (by Thurston).

Embassy Theatre—
Film Numbers—The Merry Widow (Metro-Goldwyn-Mayer), continued.
Musical Program—"Oriental Bacchanale" (prologue to feature).

Criterion Theatre—
Film Numbers—The Wanderer (Paramount), continued.

LOS ANGELES

Criterion Theatre—
Film Numbers—The Iron Horse (Fox), Fox News.
Musical Program—Indian Airs (overture).

Forum Theatre—
Film Numbers—Off the Highway (Prod., Dist. Corp.), Sweet Marie (Fox), International News.
Musical Program—"Chinese Lullaby" (overture).

Hill Street Theatre—
Film Numbers — Go Straight (Schulberg), Pacemakers (F. B. O.), Aesop's Fables (Pathe), International News.
Musical Program—Vaudeville.

Loew's State Theatre—
Film Numbers—Never the Twain Shall Meet (Metro-Goldwyn), Loew's State Pictorial.
Musical Program — "Tamea" (overture), South Sea Ideas (Fanchon and Marco Revue).

Metropolitan Theatre—
Film Numbers—Wild Horse Mesa (Paramount).
Musical Program—Operetta selections prologue to feature.

Pantages Theatre—
Film Numbers — The Lucky Horseshoe (Fox), Pathe News.
Musical Program—Vaudeville.

Rialto Theatre—
Film Numbers—Sally of the Sawdust (United Artists), Pathe News.
Musical Program—Orchestra (prologue to feature).

Million Dollar Theatre—
Film Numbers—The Freshman (Pathe).
Musical Program — "On the Campus" (overture).

CHICAGO

Capitol Theatre—
Film Numbers—The Man Who Found Himself (Paramount), Capitol Theatre World Events (Universal), Capitol Review (Selected), Cartoon (S. R.).
Musical Program — "Raymont" (Overture), Delano Dell, comedian (Specialty), "Music That Charms" (Specialty), Romeo & Juliet (Presentation), "Alone at Last," (Organ Solo), "An Iceland Frolie" (Specialty).

Stratford Theatre—
Film Numbers — Trouble With Wives (Paramount), Stratford Pictorial (Fox), Nature's Book of Scenic Wonders, Cartoon (Selected).
Musical Program—'The' Diamond Horseshoe of Girls" (Presentation), "Some Time," (Organ solo), Eva Tanguay, comedian (Specialty).

Roosevelt Theatre—
Film Numbers—Don Q, Son of Zorro (United Artists).

Orpheum Theatre—
Film Numbers—The Gold Rush (United Artists).

Randolph Theatre—
Film Numbers — Spook Ranch (Universal), International News (Universal).

Monroe Theatre—
Film Numbers—As No Man Has Loved (Fox).

Orchestra Hall—
Film Numbers — His Majesty Bunker Bean (Warner Brothers).

McVickers Theatre—
Film Numbers—The Golden Princess (Paramount), News Weekly (Pathe), Review (Pathe).
Musical Program—Paul Ash in "Bowery Night Life," (Stage Specialties and Presentations).

INDIANAPOLIS

Circle Theatre—
Film Numbers — Shore Leave (First National), Travel Film (Educational) and Fox), International News (Universal).
Musical Program — "The Playmates" orchestra.

Colonial Theatre—
Film Numbers—Seven Days (Producers Dist. Corp.), Comedy (Universal), International News (Universal), Aesop Fable (Pathe).
Musical Program—American Harmonists and Frank Owens, Bob Jones and Floyd Thompson, soloists.

Apollo Theatre—
Film Numbers—Wild, Wild, Susan (Paramount), Comedy (Fox), News Weekly (Fox).
Musical Program—Organ selections.

RIVOLI

A BIG, WONDERFUL STORY OF HEARTS AND HEROES!

MILTON SILLS
DOROTHY MACKAILL
The MAKING *of* O'MALLEY

The Rivoli theatre, Baltimore, announced "The Making of O'Malley" (First Nat'l) with this three-column ad.

CLEVELAND

Stillman Theatre—
Film Numbers—The Ten Commandments (Paramount).
Musical Program—Compilation by Maurice Spitalny (overture), Musical prologue, consisting of a desert scene, with lone wanderer singing "Eli Eli" (tenor solo).

Allen Theatre—
Film Numbers—The Man Who Found Himself (Paramount), Going Great (Educational), Topics of the Day (Pathe), Pathe News.
Musical Program—"Jewels of the Madonna" by Wolf-Ferrari (overture), "Bell Song" from "Lakme" (soprano solo), Phil Spitalny's Jazz Boys "In Honolulu."

State Theatre—
Film Numbers — Trouble With Wives (Paramount), Cupid's Victory (Universal), Hot Sheiks (Pathe), Pathe Review, Literary Digest, International News (Universal).
Musical Program—Organ overture —Vaudeville.

Park Theatre—
Film Numbers—Wild, Wild Susan (Paramount), Mary, Queen of Tots (Pathe), Felix Brings Home the Bacon (S. R.), Topics of the Day (Pathe), Kinograms (Educational).
Musical Program—Second Hungarian Rhapsody by Liszt (overture), "Red Hot Henry Brown," "I Miss My Swiss," "Twilight, the Stars and You." (Jazz Unit).

Reade's Hippodrome Theatres—
Film Numbers—I'll Show You the Town (Universal), Comedy (Universal), Pathe News.
Musical Program—Popular Jazz Medley (overture), Vaudeville.

Keith's East 105th St. Theatre—
Film Numbers—I'll Show You the Town (Universal), Aesop's Fables (Pathe), Pathe News.
Musical Program—"No, No, Nanette" (overture), Vaudeville.

Circle Theatre—
Film Numbers—The Limited Mail (Warner Bros.), Daddy Goes A-Grunting (Pathe), The Window Washer and Barnyard Follies (Pathe).
Musical Program—"William Tell" (overture), "Legend of the Canyon" by Cadman (violin solo), Jazz program by Austin Wylie's Golden Pheasant Band, "The Charleston" (dance specialty).

DES MOINES

Capitol Theatre—
Film Numbers—The Man Who Found Himself (Paramount), Treasure Bound (Educational), Fox News.
Musical Program—"Lego Minia" (dancing specialty).

Des Moines Theatre—
Film Numbers—The Coast of Folly (Paramount), Pathe Review, International News, Butter Fingers (Pathe).

PRINCESS
ENTIRE WEEK STARTING TODAY

BEBE DANIELS
in Wild Wild Susan
with ROD LA ROCQUE
"Pleasure Bound"

Sunday, newspaper ad on "Wild, Wild, Susan" (Paramount) at the Princess theatre, Toledo.

Musical Program — Popular Jazz Selections (orchestra).

Strand Theatre—
Film Numbers—The Son of His Father (Paramount), Miss Me Again (F. B. O.), Kinograms.

Rialto Theatre—
Film Numbers—The Street of Forgotten Men (Paramount), Cold Turkey (Pathe).

ATLANTA

Howard Theatre—
Film Numbers—The Ten Commandments (Paramount).

Loew's Grand Theatre—
Film Numbers — California Straight Ahead (Universal).

Metropolitan Theatre—
Film Numbers—Graustark (First National).

Rialto Theatre—
Film Numbers—Wild, Wild, Susan (Paramount).

MILWAUKEE

Alhambra Theatre—
Film Numbers—The Gold Rush (United Artists), International News.
Musical Program — "Musical Madness" and Titina (Overture), "Tons of Ice" (Stage Presentation).

Garden Theatre—
Film Numbers — Seven Days (Prod. Dist. Corp.), Fox News, Topics of the Day (Pathe), Scenic (Fox), Felix Cartoon (S. R.).
Musical Program—"Knee Deep in Daisies" (Organ).

Merrill Theatre—
Film Numbers—The Ten Commandments (Paramount), Kinograms (Educational), Two Poor Fish (Educational).
Musical Program—Orchestra Overture.

Strand Theatre—
Film Numbers — Wild, Wild Susan (Paramount), Tender Feet (Educational), Kinograms.
Musical Program—Joie Lichters' Orchestra on the Stage.

Wisconsin Theatre—
Film Numbers—The Coast of Folly (Paramount), International News.
Musical Program—"Hits From Friml Operettas" (Orchestra), "Sextette From Lucia" (Organ), "The California Mocking Bird" (Margaret McKee), "Dancers Supreme" (Martinez and Marion Randall).

OMAHA

Strand Theatre—
Film Numbers—The Coast of Folly (Paramount), Newspaper Fun (F. B. O.), Fox News, The Tourist (Educational).
Musical Program—Gordon and His Imp Orchestra.

Rialto Theatre—
Film Numbers—Wild Horse Mesa (Paramount), Off His Beat (Educational), Kinograms.
Musical Program—On stage—Ten English Rockets.

World Theatre—
Film Numbers — The Price of Pleasure (Universal).

Oh Doctor
REGINALD DENNY
MARY ASTOR
OTIS HARLAN

Family

Two-column newspaper display on "Oh, Doctor" (Universal) at the Family, Cincinnati.

Musical Program—"A Musical Chop Suey" (Organ), Vaudeville.

Sun Theatre—
Film Numbers—Romola (Metro-Goldwyn), Pathe News.

Empress Theatre—
Film Numbers—Back to Life (Associated Exhibitors).
Musical Program — "Broadway Rose" (Musical Comedy).

Moon Theatre—
Film Numbers—The Bad Lands (Producers Dist. Corp.), Hold My Baby (Pathe).

SALT LAKE CITY

American Theatre—
Film Numbers—The Last of the Duanes (Fox), High Gear (Educational), Babes in the Woods (F. B. O.), International News.

Kinema Theatre—
Film Numbers — The Painted Lady (Fox), Crowning the Count (Universal), Pathe News, International News.

Pantages Theatre—
Film Numbers—The Wife Who Wasn't Wanted (Warner).

Paramount-Empress Theatre—
Film Numbers—The Coast of Folly (Paramount), Pathe News.

Victory Theatre—
Film Numbers — Wild Horse Mesa (Paramount), High Society (Pathe), Pathe News.

PHILADELPHIA

Stanley Theatre—
Film Numbers—Shore Leave, (First National), Koko Nuts (S. R.), Country Life A La Mode (Scenic), Stanley Magazine (Selected).
Musical Program—Overture "Mignon" (orchestra), "Heart That's Free," "Rose in the Bud" and "My Little One" (Junior Prima Donnas), "Moth and Flames" (musical), Dance Divertisement, "When You Smile" (organ).

Fox Theatre—
Film Numbers—Lucky Horseshoe (Fox), Life of Stephen Foster (S. R.), Shoes (Fox), Fox News.
Musical Program—Overture (orchestra), Pianologue, Favorite Operatic Arias by Gondolfi & Kurkjian.

Stanton Theatre—
Film Numbers—The Ten Commandments (Paramount).

Arcadia Theatre—
Film Numbers—The Lost World (First National).

Karlton Theatre—
Film Numbers — The Sporting Venus (Metro-Goldwyn-Mayer).

Palace Theatre—
Film Numbers—A Slave of Fashion (Metro-Goldwyn-Mayer).

Victoria Theatre—
Film Numbers—The Unholy Three (Metro-Goldwyn-Mayer).

Capitol Theatre—
Film Numbers—Just A Woman (First National).

STILLMAN
A CONAN DOYLE'S STUPENDOUS STORY
THE LOST WORLD
WALLACE BEERY
BESSIE LOVE
LLOYD HUGHES
LEWIS STONE

Bold action in newspaper ad on "The Lost World" (First Nat'l) at the Stillman, Cleveland.

ST. PAUL

Astor Theatre—
Film Numbers—The Lucky Devil (Paramount), The Merry Kiddo (F. B. O.), News Film (Selected).
Musical Program—Organ novelty Astor Syncopating Gophers—William Lae and Joe Huey, soloists.

Capitol Theatre—
Film Numbers—The Coast of Folly (Paramount), Watch Out (Educational), Capitol News (International).
Musical Program—Capitol Theatre Orchestra—"A Prince in Heidelberg," featuring Alice Lilligren, soprano, Charles Gash, tenor, Gold Medal Radio quartet and chorus of 12 men.

Garrick Theatre—
Film Numbers—The Lost World (First National), Napoleon Not So Great (S. R.), World Events in Pictures (Selected).
Musical Program—Riley Turner and his saxophone.

Princess Theatre—
Film Numbers—First Half—Marry Me (Paramount), Too Much Mother in Law (Universal), Second half — Rugged Water (Paramount), Kinograms.
Musical Program — Organ overture.

Strand Theatre—
Film Numbers—Kentucky Pride (Fox), The Bouncer (Pathe), Kinograms.
Musical Program — Organ overture.

Tower Theatre—
Film Numbers—A Slave of Fashion (Metro-Goldwyn), Tea for two (Pathe), Pathe News.
Musical Program — Tower Symphony orchestra.

KANSAS CITY

Newman Theatre—
Film Numbers—The Coast of Folly (Paramount), Newman News and Views (Pathe and Kinograms), Newman Current Events (Local Photography).
Musical Program—"Melodyland" (Overture), "Berceuse" (Vocal Prelude), "Old Pal" (Song Interpretation), Fifteen Syncopators in Conjunction with Prologue; Recessional (Organ Solo).

Liberty Theatre—
Film Numbers—The Iron Horse (Fox), Aesop's Fables (Pa-

Opening ad for "Black Cyclone" (Pathe) at the Capitol theatre in Cincinnati.

the), The Fighting Ranger (Universal Serial); International News.
Musical Program — "Give A Thought To Music" (Overture), Recessional (Organ Solo).

Royal Theatre—
Film Numbers—The Beggar On Horseback (Paramount), Royal Screen Magazine (Pathe and Kinograms), Royal Current Events (Local Photography).
Musical Program—Royal Syncopators On Stage (Overture), Recessional (Organ Solos).

Pantages Theatre—
Film Numbers—The Overland Limited (S. R.), Fox News and Fox Short Subjects.
Musical Program — Atmospheric Selections (Overture), Recessional (Organ Solos).

Mainstreet Theatre—
Film Numbers — Shore Leave (First National), Pathe News and Educational Short Subjects.
Musical Program—Popular Selections (Overture), Recessional

MINNEAPOLIS

Astor Theatre—
Film Numbers—The Wheel (Fox), A High Jinx (Fox), Fox News.
Musical Program — Organ overture.

Lyric Theatre—
Film Numbers—The Wild Horse Mesa (Paramount), Pathe News and comedy.
Musical Program—David Rubinoff, Russian violinist.

State Theatre—
Film Numbers—Takachance week
—No film numbers announced.
Musical program — Takachance week—Musical numbers not announced.

Art ad announcing the showing of "Smouldering Fires" (Universal) at the Strand, Cincinnati.

Strand Theatre—
Film Numbers—The Lost World (First National),—second week — Kat Comedy (Education), Strand News (selected).
Musical program—Orchestra.

Garrick Theatre—
Film Numbers—Romola (Metro-Goldwyn), Kat Comedy (Educational).
Musical Program—Oscar Moss and the Manning Sisters, musical comedy favorites.

BUFFALO

Shea's Hippodrome Theatre—
Film Numbers—(Eleventh Anniversary Week)—The Coast of Folly (Paramount), Your Own Backyard (Pathe), Current

Events (from Pathe and International News).
Musical Program—Selections by Paul Zinn's Chicagoans, Overture by Hippodrome orchestra.

Shea's North Park Theatre—
Film Numbers—The Marriage Whirl (First National), Sherlock Sleuth (Pathe), Current Events (from Pathe and International News).
Musical Program—"Musical Comedy Memories" (orchestra).

Loew's State Theatre—
Film Numbers—The Street of Forgotten men (Paramount), Tame Men and Wild Women (Pathe), Current Events (Pathe News).
Musical Program—"Festival overture" (orchestra), Five acts of vaudeville.

Lafayette Square Theatre—
Film Numbers—Souls for Sables (S. R.), Comedy (Pathe), Current Events (Fox News).
Musical Program—Selections from Victor Herbert's musical com-

edies (orchestra), Organ solos by Henry B. Murtagh, Five acts of vaudeville.

New Olympic Theatre—
Film Numbers—Speed (S. R.), The Truth About Women (S. R.), Comedy (Universal), Current Events (International News).
Musical Program—Medley of Popular Airs (organ).

Victoria Theatre—
Film Numbers—Sally (First National), Radio Mad (Pathe), Current Events (Pathe News).
Musical Program—Selection from "Sally" (Orchestra).

WASHINGTON

Metropolitan Theatre—
Film Numbers — Shore Leave (First National), Current Events (Pathe), Boys Will be Joys (Pathe), Pathe Review.
Musical Program—"Home Sweet Home the World Over" (Overture); "Hearts and Flowers" (Jazz Arrangement).

Rialto Theatre—
Film Numbers—The Iron Horse (Fox), Current Events (Universal).
Musical Program—American Fantasy (Overture), "Thine Alone" (Soprano-Tenor duet).

Columbia Theatre—
Film Numbers—Coast of Folly

PAULINE FREDERICK
MALCOLM MacGREGOR
LAURA LA PLANTE
WANDA HAWLEY
TULLY MARSHALL

Smouldering Fires

Strand

(Paramount), (continued), Current Events (Universal), Pleasure Bound (Educational).
Musical Program—"The Fortune Teller" (Overture).

Earle Theatre—
Film Numbers—The Lucky Devil (Paramount), Current Events (Educational).

Palace Theatre—
Film Numbers—Sun Up, (Metro-Goldwyn), Current Events (Pathe), Off His Beat (Educational), Topics of the Day (Pathe).
Musical Program — "Southern Rhapsody" (overture).

Strand Theatre—
Film Numbers—Capital Punishment (S. R.), Current Events (Fox).

DETROIT

Capitol Theatre—
Film Numbers — Shore Leave (First National), Sportreel (Pathe), Aesop's Fable (Pathe), Detroit and Pathe News.
Musical Program—Overture (orchestra), Solo (vocal), Organ recessional.

Madison Theatre—
Film Numbers—In the Name of Love (Paramount), Detroit News and Pathe News, Aesop's Fable (Pathe), Comedy (S. R.).

Broadway-Strand Theatre—
Film Numbers—The Teaser (Universal), International News.
Musical Program — "Charleston Steppers" (dancers with jazz band accompaniment), Organ recessional.

Adams Theatre—
Film Numbers—The Gold Rush (United Artists), Kinograms.
Musical Program—Orchestra accompaniment and organ recessional.

Fox Washington Theatre—
Film Numbers—The Lucky Horseshoe (Fox), Fox News Reel, Felix (S. R.).
Musical Program — Orchestra, Vocal solos and organ recessional.

HOUSTON

Queen Theatre—
Film Numbers—Coast of Folly (Paramount), Comedy (Educational), News (Pathe). Musical Program — Melodies of Popular Numbers—"That's My Baby," "Yearning," "Your Just a Flower From an Old Bouquet (Queen orchestra), Organ numbers.

Isis Theatre—
Film Numbers—Sun-Up (Metro-Goldwyn), Comedy (Pathe), News (International). Musical Program — Overture "Pique Dame" (Van Suppe), Isis Concert Orchestra, Organ numbers.

Rialto Theatre—
Film Numbers—Seige (Universal), Comedy (Educational), News (Fox). Musical Program—Organ.

Capitol Theatre—
Film Numbers—The Street of Forgotten Men (Paramount), Comedy (Educational), News (Kinograms). Musical Program—Orchestra, Organ numbers.

Majestic Theatre—
Film Numbers—The Lucky Horseshoe (Fox), Aesop's Fables (Pathe). Musical Program—Vaudeville.

Liberty Theatre—
Film Numbers—The White Man (Producers Dist. Corp.), Comedy (Pathe), Scenic (Pathe). Musical Program—Organ.

SAN FRANCISCO

California Theatre—
Film Numbers—Wild, Wild Susan (Paramount), Isn't Life Terrible (Pathe), Pathe Review, International News.

The Strand, Birmingham, made clever use of stock cuts and rule border in this ad on "The Street of Forgotten Men" (Paramount).

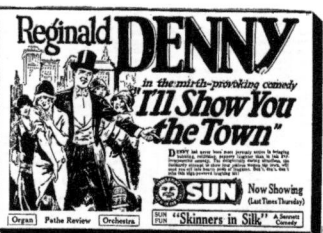

Bold newspaper ad designed by the Sun theatre, Omaha, and used by that house in advertising its run of "I'll Show You the Town" (Universal).

Musical Program — "Spanish Nights" (Max Donlin Diamond Jubilee Presentation with Spanish songs and dances).

Loew's Warfield Theatre—
Film Numbers — Shore Leave (First National), San Francisco of Long Ago (Special), International News and Kinograms Wings of the Fleet. Musical Program — "Midnight Waltz" (Fanchon & Marco Idea with singing and dancing), U. S. S. Savannah Naval Band (specialty).

Imperial Theatre—
Film Numbers—The Pony Express (Paramount), Off Stage Reel of James Cruze Company on Location (Special), Fox News. Musical Program — Selections from "The Chocolate Soldier."

Granada Theatre—
Film Numbers—The Man Who Found Himself (Paramount), Pathe Review. Musical Program — "Diamond Jubilee Review" (Singing and dancing—old Spanish California Songs).

Cameo Theatre—
Film Numbers—Parisian Nights (F. B. O.), The Burglar (Fox), International News. Musical Program — "Song of Songs" (Apache dancers), "Lapolana" (organ).

Union Square Theatre—
Film Numbers—Overland Limited (S. R.), Help Yourself (Fox), Fox News. Musical Program—Union Square Variety Revue (singing and dancing).

St. Francis Theatre—
Film Numbers—The Iron Horse (Fox), continued.

ST. LOUIS

Missouri Theatre—
Film Numbers—The Street of Forgotten Men (Paramount), Don't Tell Dad (Pathe), Missouri Magazine. Musical Program—Orchestral overture and popular number, Organ accompaniments. On stage—Second Edition of the St. Louis Fashion Pageant (fashion revue and bathing girl act).

Delmonte Theatre—
Film Numbers—In the Name of Love (Paramount), The Hunted

Woman (Fox), Delmonte News and Views (Selected). Musical Program—Orchestral and vocal selections.

Loew's State Theatre—
Film Numbers—The Mystic (Metro-Goldwyn-Mayer), News and Views (Selected). Musical Program—In Shadowland," Overture presentation, Don Albert's orchestra. On stage—"A Study in Marble" with Yureiva and Svoboda Lazier & Worth, Dorma Lee and State Ballet Corps.

William Goldman's Kings Garden and Rivoli Theatres—
Film Numbers—Hell's Highroad (Producers Dist. Corp.), No Father to Guide Him (Pathe), News and Views (Selected), Aesop Fable (Pathe).

Grand Central, Lyric Skydome and Capitol Theatres—
Film Numbers—Shore Leave (First National), News and Views (Selected). Musical Program—Orchestral overture and popular numbers, Ralph Errolle (Tenor).

BALTIMORE

Century Theatre—
Film Numbers — Proud Flesh (Metro-Goldwyn-Mayer), Sweet Marie (Fox), News Weekly (Fox). Musical Program—Popular Medley (Overture by Orchestra), Violin Quartette (The Romany Four), Organ Recessional.

Garden Theatre—
Film Numbers—The Trail Rider (Fox), Scandal Hunters (Universal), Felix Outwits Cupid (S. R.), International News (Universal). Musical Program—Five acts of vaudeville, Organ recessional.

Keith's Hippodrome Theatre—
Film Numbers—The White Sheep (Pathe), Stranded (Universal), News Weekly (Pathe), Aesop's Fable (Pathe). Musical Program—Five acts of vaudeville, Organ recessional.

Metropolitan Theatre—
Film Numbers—The Recreation of Brian Kent (Principal Pictures), Oh, Joy (Educational), Topical News (Pathe), Aesop's Fable (Pathe). Musical Program—Orchestra, Organ recessional.

New Theatre—
Film Numbers—Dangerous Innocence (Universal), A Speedy Marriage (Universal), News Weekly (Pathe). Musical Program—"Creme de la Creme" (Overture by Orchestra), "My Heart at thy Sweet Voice" (Vocal selections), Organ recessional.

Parkway Theatre—
Film Numbers—Daddy's Gone A-Hunting (Metro-Goldwyn-Mayer), In a China Shop (Fox), Look Out (Educational), Parkway Pictorial News (Educational Kinograms). Musical Program—Selections of Well-Known Songs (Overture by Parkway Concert Ensemble), Organ recessional.

Rivoli Theatre—
Film Numbers—Her Sister from Paris (First National), The Iron Nag (Pathe), Rivoli News (Pathe). Musical Program—"No, No, Nanette" Selections (Overture by Orchestra), Specialty Attraction (Morton Downey Irish Tenor in vocal selections), "The Enchantress" and "By the Light of the Stars" (Organ Selections).

CINCINNATI

Capital Theatre—
Film Numbers—Beggar on Horseback (Paramount), Wild Beasts of Borneo (S. R.), Capitol News (Selected).

Now Playing 2d Big Week

MARY PICKFORD in "Little Annie Rooney"

Don't miss Peter Chapman and Irving Pichery of "The Toonerville Follies" in an atmospheric prologue to feature picture.

NEXT—

"THE LOST WORLD"

Garrick

Snappy single-column ad on "Little Annie Rooney" (United Artists) at the Garrick theatre, St. Paul.

Short Subjects and Serials

Pathe Acquires Series of Holy Land Films

Pathe has acquired a series of twenty one-reel Holy Land films, which they describe as "ideal subjects for forthcoming Christmas season programs, as the first six subjects depict scenes of Christ's activity upon earth from the time of His birth to the resurrection. "A pilgrimage to Palestine" is the title of the series, which was produced by Holy Land Film Company of Cincinnati.

The first six subjects which will be available on October 4th are as follows: Bethlehem; Nazareth; Scenes of Christ's Early Ministry, showing the Sea of Galilee, Capernaum and adjacent territory; Scenes of Christ's Later Ministry, showing scenes around Jerusalem and Bethany; Gethsemane, showing the scenes of His Trial, the home of Caiphas, the high priest, etc., Via Dolorosa (The Sad Way), showing the road to the Cross, the Church of the Holy Sepulchre, Christ's Tomb and scenes of Jerusalem.

Comedian Billy Moon in Production Field

Billy Moon, comedian, has entered the production field and will produce a series of twelve Billy Moon Comedies, featuring himself. They will be released one each month. Lyle Salveaux will direct the series, and Eugene E. Voltaire will serve as general manager of the unit. Negotiations are now being completed for the distribution of these comedies and Voltaire will leave for New York shortly to complete these arrangements.

Bray Productions Start "Unnatural History"

Bray Productions are making interiors at the Ter-Art studios in New York for the first of the "Unnatural History" subjects which will be released by F. B. O. The initial picture is titled, "How the Elephant Got his Trunk." Walter Lantz is featured. This Bray subject, in addition to real actors employs a number of cartoon characters.

Helen Ferguson in New Pathe Serial

Helen Ferguson is to be featured opposite Jack Mulhall in the new Pathe serial, "Wild West," staged at the famous Miller Brothers 101 Ranch in Oklahoma. It is a C. W. Patton production in ten episodes directed by Robert F. Hill from the scenario by J. F. Netteford. This marks Miss Ferguson's debut as a Pathe serial player.

Jess Robbins Directing All Star Cameo Cast

Jess Robbins is directing an all star cast in Educational-Cameo Comedies. The cast includes Helen Marlowe, Phil Dunham, George Davis and Babe London.

Highlights from "Half A Man," a two-reel comedy starring Stan Laurel and released by F. B. O.

Many Fox Short Subjects Due

Splendid Progress Being Made Under the Supervision of George Marshall

WITH the Fox comedy units now all under the supervision of George E. Marshall, splendid progress is being made in production. Marshall is devoting all of his time to the supervision of Van Bibber, O. Henry, Helen and Warren and Imperial comedies.

At the present time five Imperial Comedies are finished and being rushed through the laboratories. Four others of the series are being rushed to completion. Two of the O. Henry comedies have been completed and the third is under way. The first three of the Helen and Warren series have been completed and are scheduled for early release. Five of the Van Bibbers are finished.

Earle Fox is the star of the Van Bibber series, with Florence Gilbert, Frank Beal and Lynn Cowan in support. "The Big Game Hunter," directed by Robert P. Kerr, was the first of the series released on August 16th. "The Sky Jumper" is due September 20th, "The Wrestler," November 1st and 'A Parisian Knight," December 13th. "The Feud" has been completed but no release date set.

Kathryn McGuire and Harvey Clark have the leading roles in the O. Henry stories. "Shoes," first of the series was released September 6th. "Transients in Arcadia" is due October 18th.

Kathryn Perry and Hallam Cooley have the leading roles in the Helen and Warren comedies which are being directed by Albert Ray. August 30th was the release date of

"A Business Engagement," first of this series. "All Aboard" is set for October 11th and "The Peacemakers" will be presented November 22nd.

The first of the Imperial Comedies, "On the Go," went to the exhibitors August 23rd. This was followed by "Sweet Marie" on September 6th. "Love and Lions" will be released September 20th and "A Cloudy Romance," October 4th. There are twenty Imperials in the series.

Resume of Current News Weeklies

KINOGRAMS NO. 5115. San Francisco.— Air fight fails as Navy plane is lost on ill-fated flight to Honolulu; London, Eng.— Last of the old horse buses still does a thriving business; New York—Six year old boy swims the Hudson river in fast time; Aurora, Ill.— Thousands see locomotives crash in staged collision; Fort Slocum, N. Y.—Football season begins with New York University squad in practice; Newton, Mass.—Boston College eleven also limbers up; Augusta, Me.—Seventy-five year old club in Maine has many members; Asbury Park, N. J.—Children are awarded prizes in annual baby show; Washington—30,000 see Senators tighten hold on another pennant by besting the Athletics (Washington Philadelphia and Pittsburgh only); Oakland, Cal.—Dons of Peralta in annual festival (San Francisco only); Chicago—88,000 watch police in annual games (Chicago only).

KINOGRAMS NO. 5116, Oakmont, Pa.— Bobby Jones retains amateur golf title by beating young Watts Gunn, his former pupil, 8 and 7; Washington, D. C.—Col. Mitchell accuses superiors in controversy over air tragedies and faces a court martial while Lieut. Richardson, a Shenandoah survivor tells Secretary of Navy Wilbur what happened in terrible disaster; Pemberton, N. J.—Farmers spray cranberry vines from the air to protect them for Thanksgiving trade; New York— Governor Smith and Mayor Hylan and Senator Walker, rival mayoralty candidates shun politics in addressing Labor Day crowd from same platform; Philadelphia—Girls take part in Slovak gymnasts drill; El Monte, Cal.— Charles Gay drills lions on his farm; Paris— French fliers get ready for hop across Atlantic to New York; Chicago—Charleston jazz exhibition in Loop district ties up traffic; Pittsburgh —Pirates and Senators await world's series clash (First pictures of the Pittsburgh regulars), Washington—Manager Bucky Harris has Senators ready for big post season clash (First pictures of entire 1925 Washington club).

INTERNATIONAL NEWS, No. 74: Asbury Park, N. J.—Aristocrats of babydom hold impressive parade; San Francisco, Cal.—Abandon hope for safety of navy's Hawaiian plane; Hazelton, Pa.—Coal miners on strike till their fields and repair homes; Spooner, Wis.—Summer is over and Thanksgiving approacheth so farmers start to fatten turkey flocks; Comfort, Texas—Armadillo hunt provides great sport; Centralia, Wash.—(Seattle only)—Pacers and trotters set Pacific coast records; Newton, Mass. (Boston only)—Boston college starts fall football practice; Ava, Ohio—Shenandoah breaks in half while on western flight,—scenes of wreckage of great navy craft and other famous dirigibles.

INTERNATIONAL NEWS NO. 75. Ava, Ohio—Naval inquiry board probes tragic end of Shenandoah; Wash., D. C.—Secretary of the Navy Wilbur congratulates Lt. W. L. Richardson, one of those who escaped with only minor injuries when giant airship crashed; Lakehurst, N. J.—Return of Shenandoah's survivors accompanied by touching scenes; Pittsburgh, Pa.—"Bobby" Jones holds national amateur golf title; Camp Le Ble, N. Y.,—Large families refute claim of race suicide; London, Eng.—Infant airplane arrives with millions of gold marks, German indemnity to Great Britain; N. Y. City—Fire chiefs witness successful test of non-explosive tank; Gromer, Eng.—Princess Ilena of Rumania plays part in picturesque pageant; Hamilton, Mass. (Boston only)—Crowds see Whippets race in speedy American derby; Milwaukee, Wis. (Milwaukee only)—Governor sees prize cattle at State Fair; Pawahuska, Okla. (Okla. City only)—World War Vets parade at legion convention; Grand Rapids, Mich.—Pathos and joy mingle as Grand Army veterans march; Yellowstone National Park—Indians round-up Uncle Sam's big buffalo herd.

PATHE NEWS No. 74. Grand Rapids. Mich.—Civil War soldiers in line once again; Pisa, Italy—Flies over historic Pisa; Detroit. Mich.—Lawyers from all parts of

Stills from "Three Wise Goofs," one of the series of Pat Man comedies produced by Standard for F. B. O.

U. S. attend 48th annual meeting; Salford, England—Animal hospital-on-wheels brings relief to pets of poor; Munich, Germany—Brave rushing waters of Isar in collapsible boats; Scranton, Pa.—Meet the Whaleus—America's family—Pathe awards prize to parents and 7 children; Pittsburgh, Pa.—"Bobby" Jones, retains amateur golf championship; Ava, Ohio— Navy investigates Shenandoah disaster.

Alberta Vaughn Resumes Comedy Series

Alberta Vaughn has returned from a brief vacation and has started work at the F. B. O. studios in Episode No. 3 of the "Adventures of Mazie," her new series of two-reel comedy features. It is titled, "Or What Have You." Larry Kent, new juvenile lead, Al Cook and Kit Guard are supporting Miss Vaughn.

Standard Selects Title for Comedy

"A Ton of Fun in a Beauty Parlor" is the title decided upon for the third of the Standard Comedies which Joe Rock is producing for F. B. O. release. The series features the trio of heavyweight comedians, "Fatty" Karr, "Tiny" Alexander and "Kewpie" Ross.

Rene Marvelle in Comedy Leads With Bowes

Rene Marvelle, a French-Canadian girl from Montreal, is playing leading roles with Cliff Bowes in Educational-Cameo Comedies under the direction of Hugh Fay. Previous to her entry into Cameo Comedies, Miss Marvelle played parts in feature pictures.

Scenes from "The Constant Simp," second episode in the "Adventures of Mazie" series of two-reel comedies offered by F. B. O. with Alberta Vaughn in the starred role.

First "Buster Brown" Released

First of Series Offered This Month;
Four Other Century Comedies in Sept.

UNIVERSAL has announced that "Educating Buster," first of the series of "Buster Brown" comedies produced by Century, will be released in September. The picture will initiate a group of 12 two-reelers based on the famous newspaper comics of R. F. Outcault.

"Educating Buster" has had pre-release showings in many important first-run theatres throughout the country and has received praise from reviewers of the trade press and daily papers. Arthur Trimble is starred in the name role, and "Tige," the faithful dog is played by Pete the Dog. Mary Jane is played by Doreen Turner, and others in principal roles are Charles King, Emily Gerdes, Hilliard Karr and several clever young screen players. It will be released on September 23.

"Stranded" is a two-reeler directed by William Watson, with Miss Marian supported by Hilliard Karr and the Century Follies Girls. In it she portrays the role of a country girl who is bus driver, baggage tosser, cook and waitress and general utility girl for a country hotel.

"Officer 13," Eddie Gordon's latest comedy, was directed by Edward I. Luddy and has a strong supporting cast including Frank Whitson and Betty Browne. This picture has been played in many houses and is hailed as Gordon's best film work to date.

"Too Much Mother-in-law" brings a new Century star to the screen in the person of Constance Darling. This picture was directed by Noel Smith. The cast includes Blanche Payson, as the mother-in-law, and Charles King, as the bride-groom.

"Cupid's Victory," the Wanda Wiley comedy for September release is a two-reeler directed by Charles Lamont, with Earl McCarthy and Tony Hayes as the chief supporting players. It shows Miss Wiley in the role of a dignified bespectacled clerk in a law office.

A trio of scenes from "The Fighting Cub," a Truart Production co-featuring Mary Carr and Wesley Barry.

Pathe Contests Aid Business

Storey and Comedy Competitions Develop
Keen Rivalry in Many of the Exchanges

BOSTON, New York, Detroit, Dallas, Los Angeles, Milwaukee, New Orleans, Salt Lake and Memphis proved the winners of the Storey Victory Campaign and the Special Two-reel Comedy contest conducted by Pathe Exchange, Inc. The contests have just been concluded and according to the Pathe office resulted in the greatest Summer business for a given period in the history of the organization.

As an incentive to better business, Pathe instituted a billings campaign, named in honor of Assistant General Manager, J. E. Storey, then General Sales Manager. This campaign started on April 19th and was continued for sixteen weeks. At the same time a special Two-Reel Comedy Contest was started and run coincidentally with the Victory Campaign. Every employee entered actively into the spirit of the drives and results have been better than were ever anticipated.

To add zest to the campaigns the various branch offices were arranged in groups and given the names of military divisions.

The Boston Branch under the management of Ross G. Cropper, won the Storey Victory Campaign, while in the same division New York, under the management of William T. Raynor, won the comedy contest.

In the artillery division the Storey Victory campaign was won by Detroit under the management of Oscar Hanson. The comedy contest was won in the same division by Dallas.

Los Angeles, under the managership of William Jenner, won the Cavalry division in the Storey campaign and in the same division Milwaukee won the comedy contest. New Orleans took both ends of the contest in the Engineer Division.

Manager W. G. Seib and his crew of Salt Lake took the Storey competition in the Aviation Division, while Memphis took the other angle of the contest.

amounts to half of the entire lobby display.

"This is by no means an experiment with me, for I have proved the value of exploiting the short subject through a long period of such exploitation, and have shown conclusively that good short subjects will attract people to the box-office when properly advertised."

In Milwaukee there has been a very noticeable increase in newspaper space devoted to comedy subjects.

"As a matter of fact," writes Max Stahl, manager of the Educational exchange in that city, "every two reel comedy which is used at our first run theatres in Milwaukee is advertised in the newspapers with the one or two column ads illustrated in our press sheets, for which we furnish exhibitors with free mats."

Give Shorts Bigger Ad Space

Educational Says Northwest Leads in Comedy
Exploitation; Ad Material in Demand

EDUCATIONAL reports that information received at the home offices from branches throughout the country show that exhibitors are increasing their ad space on short subjects and that the briefer comedies are exploited more extensively in the Northwest than in other sections of the country at present. An increased demand for theatre aid material issued by Educational in connection with its comedy and novelty reels is reported from all branch offices.

One of the theatres cited as notable among the houses which give short subjects adequate advertising support is the Fuller at Kalamazoo, Mich. This theatre, managed by Roy Tillson, has long made a practice of 100 per cent advertising for every item on the program.

For, as Mr. Fuller explains, "there are a whole lot of my patrons come to see the comedy as much as they do the feature and the vaudeville."

"I devote a good conspicuous box in my newspaper ad layout to my comedy, and make it especially forceful when I have stars like Lloyd Hamilton. Comedy stars such as Hamilton get 50 per cent of the electric sign display and I consider that any comedy that is worth showing in the theatre is worth giving a good display in front of the theatre. This display generally

Perez Will Direct Blue Ribbon Comedy

Marcel Perez, known to film fans as "Tweedy" has been signed by Joe Rock to direct the third of the Blue Ribbon Comedies in which Alice Ardell and a well known comedian will be starred. The subject will be released by F. B. O. in November.

Franey Joins Joe Rock Comedy Cast

Billy Franey has been added to the cast of Joe Rock's second Blue Ribbon Comedy in which Alice Ardell and Lee Moran are starred. The series is to be released through Film Booking Offices.

Exhibitors Box-Office Reports

Names of the theatre owners are omitted by agreement in accordance with the wishes of the average exhibitor and in the belief that reports published over the signature of the exhibitor reporting, is a dangerous practice.

Only reports received on specially prepared blanks furnished by us will be accepted for use in this department. Exhibitors who value this reporting service are urged to ask for these blanks.

Title of Picture.	Population of Town.	Location.	Class of Patronage.	Weather.	Box Office Value.	Check-up Percentage from other Reports.
F. B. O.						
Bandit's Baby, The.....	2996	Ark.	Farm	Warm	Big	75
Broken Laws..........	1748	Neb.	Small town	Hot	Big	79
Drusilla With a Million..	993678	Mich.	Mixed	Fair	Good	—
	120000	Fla.	Mixed	Fair	Fair	—
	158796	Texas	Mixed	Fair	Good	—
Life's Greatest Game...	1748	Neb.	Small town	Hot	Good	73
Lillies of the Street.....	113344	N.Y.	Mixed	Fair	Good	—
Range Terror, The......	2996	Ark.	Farm	Warm	Good	56
Speed Wild..........	2996	Ark.	Farm	Warm	Good	—
White Thunder.......	2996	Ark.	Farm	Warm	Fair	—
Youth and Adventure...	2996	Ark.	Farm	Warm	Good	65
PARAMOUNT						
Are Parents People?....	113344	N.Y.	Mixed	Fair	Big	68
Beggar on Horseback...	158976	Texas	Mixed	Fair	Poor	—
Big Brother..........	2996	Ark.	Farm	Warm	Fair	—
Changing Husbands....	2996	Ark.	Farm	Hot	Good	71
Coast of Folly, The.....	297000	Ohio	Mixed	Hot	Fair	—
Contraband..........	2793	Pa.	Mixed	Warm	Fair	62
Fighting Coward, The...	2996	Ark.	Farm	Hot	Poor	—
Forty Winks.........	2793	Pa.	Mixed	Warm	Good	74
Kiss in the Dark......	2793	Pa.	Mixed	Warm	Good	65
Light of Western Stars..	297000	Ohio	Mixed	Hot	Good	65
Lucky Devil, The......	297000	Ohio	Mixed	Warm	Good	—
	113344	N.Y.	Mixed	St'my	Good	—
	113344	N.Y.	Mixed	Fair	Good	—
Male and Female.....	772897	Mo.	Mixed	Hot	Fair	—
Manhandled.........	2996	Ark.	Farm	Warm	Good	77
Monsieur Beaucaire....	2996	Ark.	Farm	Hot	Fair	74
Night Life of New York..	113344	N.Y.	Mixed	Fair	Big	63
Not So Long Ago......	796841	Ohio	Mixed	Fair	Fair	—
Old Home Week.......	2793	Pa.	Mixed	Warm	Big	75
Rugged Water........	733826	Md.	Mixed	Hot	Fair	—
Salome of the Tenements	2793	Pa.	Mixed	Warm	Poor	58
Ten Commandments, The	772897	Mo.	Mixed	Hot	Big	89
	34324410	Mo.	Mixed	Hot	Big	—
Thundering Herd, The..	2793	Pa.	Mixed	Warm	Big	79
Unguarded Women.....	2996	Ark.	Farm	Hot	Fair	59
Wanderer of Wasteland.	2996	Ark.	Farm	Warm	Good	75
Welcome Home.......	297000	Ohio	Mixed	Hot	Good	—
Wild Horse Mesa......	772897	Mo.	Mixed	Fair	Fair	—
	113344	N.Y.	Mixed	Stormy	Good	—
	34324410	Mo.	Mixed	Fair	Good	—
Wild, Wild Susan......	120000	Fla.	Mixed	Fair	Big	—
FIRST NATIONAL						
Born Rich...........	2793	Pa.	Mixed	Warm	Fair	53
Flirting with Love......	2793	Pa.	Mixed	Warm	Big	74
Half Way Girl, The.....	113344	N.Y.	Mixed	Fair	Fair	—
	796841	Ohio	Mixed	Fair	Fair	—
	401247	Ohio	Mixed	Fair	Good	—
Her Sister from Paris....	113344	N.Y.	Mixed	Fair	Big	—
Husbands and Lovers...	2793	Pa.	Mixed	Warm	Good	80
Knockout, The........	113344	N.Y.	Mixed	Fair	Good	—
	314194	Ind.	Mixed	Fair	Big	—
	993678	Mich.	Mixed	Fair	Good	—
	324410	Mo.	Mixed	Fair	Good	—
Lady Who Lied, The....	113344	N.Y.	Mixed	Fair	Good	—
Marriage Whirl, The....	733826	Md.	Mixed	Hot	Big	—
	120000	Fla.	Mixed	Fair	Good	—
One Way Street.......	126468	Iowa	Mixed	St'my	Good	61
Quo Vadis..........	120000	Fla.	Mixed	Fair	Good	78
Shore Leave.........	401247	Ohio	Mixed	Warm	Fair	—
FOX						
Cyclone Rider, The.....	401247	Ohio	Mixed	Warm	Good	65
	1748	Neb.	Small town	Warm	Good	—
Deadwood Coach, The..	1748	Neb.	Small town	Warm	Big	79
	2793	Pa.	Mixed	Warm	Big	—
Gerald Cranston's Lady.	733826	Md.	Mixed	Hot	Good	62
Iron Horse, The........	772897	Mo.	Mixed	Hot	Good	—
Lightnin'............	772897	Mo.	Mixed	Hot	Fair	—
Lucky Horseman, The...	772897	Mo.	Mixed	Hot	Fair	—
Oh, You Tony.........	1748	Neb.	Small town	Warm	Good	73
Rainbow Trail........	796841	Ohio	Mixed	Warm	Good	70
Riders of the Purple Sage	401247	Ohio	Mixed	Warm	Big	83
Thank U............	796841	Ohio	Mixed	Fair	Good	—
Troubles of a Bride.....	1748	Neb.	Small town	Warm	Good	—
Wings of Youth.......	158796	Texas	Mixed	Fair	Poor	—
METRO-GOLDWYN-MAYER						
Along Came Ruth......	2996	Ark.	Farm	Hot	Good	71
Beauty Prize, The......	2996	Ark.	Farm	Hot	Good	64
Broken Barriers.......	2996	Ark.	Farm	Warm	Good	59
Circe, The Enchantress..	2793	Pa.	Mixed	Warm	Good	61
Dixie Handicap, The....	1748	Neb.	Small town	Warm	Good	76
Excuse Me..........	1748	Neb.	Small town	Warm	Big	82
Great Divide, The......	1748	Neb.	Small town	Warm	Fair	70
Married Flirts........	1748	Neb.	Small town	Hot	Good	63
Never the Twain Shall Meet..............	314194	Ind.	Mixed	Fair	Good	—
Prairie Wife..........	2996	Ark.	Farm	Hot	Fair	44
Pretty Ladies.........	796841	Ohio	Mixed	Fair	Good	—
Revelation...........	2996	Ark.	Farm	Hot	Fair	83
Romola.............	993678	Mich.	Mixed	Fair	Good	—
	796841	Ohio	Mixed	Fair	Good	—
Slave of Fashion.......	120000	Fla.	Mixed	Fair	Good	—
	158796	Texas	Mixed	Hot	Good	—
Snob, The...........	1748	Neb.	Small town	Warm	Fair	68
Sporting Venus, The....	158796	Texas	Mixed	St'my	Fair	55
	324410	Mo.	Mixed	Fair	Fair	—
Sun Up.............	772897	Mo.	Mixed	Hot	Fair	—
Unholy Three, The.....	158796	Texas	Mixed	Fair	Big	—
	772897	Mo.	Mixed	Warm	Good	—
PROD. DIST. CORP.						
Hell's Highroad.......	113344	N.Y.	Mixed	Fair	Big	—
B. P. SCHULBERG						
Boomerang, The.......	297000	Ohio	Mixed	Hot	Fair	—
UNITED ARTISTS						
Don Q, Son of Zorro....	126468	Iowa	Mixed	St'my	Big	—
Dorothy Vernon of Haddon Hall...........	1748	Neb.	Small town	Warm	Big	—
Gold Rush, The.......	993678	Mich.	Mixed	Fair	Big	—
Isn't Life Wonderful....	297000	Ohio	Mixed	Hot	Poor	—
Mark of Zoro, The.....	733826	Md.	Mixed	Hot	Big	—
UNIVERSAL						
Lorraine of the Lions....	772897	Mo.	Mixed	Fair	Fair	—
	120000	Fla.	Mixed	Fair	Good	—
Love and Glory........	1748	Neb.	Small town	Hot	Fair	58
Ridin' Pretty.........	2793	Pa.	Mixed	Warm	Good	—
Sign of the Cactus.....	2793	Pa.	Mixed	Warm	Good	—
Teaser, The..........	324410	Mo.	Mixed	Fair	Good	—
VITAGRAPH						
Empty Saddle, The.....	2996	Ark.	Farm	Hot	Fair	—
Man From Brodney's...	2996	Ark.	Farm	Hot	Fair	—
Midnight Alarm, The...	2996	Ark.	Farm	Hot	Fair	—
Mystery of Lost Ranch..	1748	Neb.	Small town	Warm	Fair	—
One Law for Women....	2996	Ark.	Farm	Hot	Poor	—
Santa Fe Pete........	2996	Ark.	Farm	Hot	Fair	—
WARNER BROS.						
Broadway Butterfly, A...	401247	Ohio	Mixed	Warm	Good	—
Printer's Devil, The....	2793	Pa.	Mixed	Warm	Poor	—
STATE RIGHTS						
Bandit Tamer, The.....	2996	Ark.	Farm	Warm	Poor	—
Fearless Lover, The.....	2996	Ark.	Farm	Warm	Poor	—
Re-Creation of Brian Kent, The..........	314194	Ind.	Mixed	Warm	Poor	60
Speed Spook, The.....	1748	Neb.	Small town	Warm	Good	78
Women First........	2996	Ark.	Farm	Warm	Good	—

Pre-release Reviews of Features

Speed Mad
(Columbia Picture Corp.—4442 Feet)
(Reviewed by George T. Pardy)

THIS one lives up to its title in point of lively action, featuring some great thrill stuff in the auto racing line, with an aeroplane stunt worked in toward the climax for good measure. Director Jay Marchant didn't allow William Fairbanks many restful moments while producing the feature, for that energetic star, seen in the role of a young chap whose great delight lay in breaking speed laws, is continually gyrating around like an unchained devil on wheels, making love impetuously, beating up his foes, escaping from kidnappers, finally leaping from a plane into his car and winning an auto race in a furious finish. Of course there's a love affair which winds up satisfactorily and the net result is a good program attraction which ought to please a majority of fans.

THEME. Auto-racing comedy drama, with love interest and numerous thrills.

PRODUCTION HIGHLIGHTS. Fairbank's speeding thrills. The brisk comedy situations and romance. Scene where Fairbanks jumps from plane to auto and wins race.

EXPLOITATION ANGLES. Play up Fairbank's daredevil stunts. Stress love affair, the comedy stuff. Feature the big auto race and hero's leap from plane to car.

DRAWING POWER. Should do good business wherever William Fairbanks is popular and fast comedy drama, with exciting punch stuff, gets the patrons.

SUMMARY. Lightning action comedy drama, with romantic appeal and sensational stunts in plenty. Features big auto race in finale, with aeroplane side-kick.

THE CAST
```
Bill Sanford.....................................William Fairbanks
Betty Hampton.........................................Edith Roberts
Alan Lawton..........................................Lloyd Whitlock
John Sanford................................Melbourne MacDowell
Freckles Smithers...............................Johnny Fox, Jr.
Grandma Smithers....................................Florence Lee
```
Author, Dorothy Howell. Director, Jay Marchant. Photographed by George Meehan.

SYNOPSIS. Bill Sanford, broke, leaves home with his dog, Buddy, and racing car. He meets and falls in love with Betty Hampton, whose folks have met with financial reverses, but she scrapes up an entrance fee for Bill to participate in a big auto race. He is kidnapped by a rival, but escapes with the aid of Buddy. A friendly aviator takes him to the track. Bill jumps from the plane to his car, throws out the chauffeur hired by his rival to run it, wins the event, money prize and Betty.

Edith Roberts in "Speed Mad," a Truart picture.

The Call of Courage
(Universal—4661 Feet)
(Reviewed by George T. Pardy)

THERE is more variety in the plot of this picture than distinguishes the average Westerner, and in point of quick action and thrills it stacks up even with the best of its kind. Those who like animal stuff will find additional interest in the film because of the bits of drama and comedy contributed by two four-footed actors, a horse and dog, both the faithful adherents of the cowboy hero, who are always on the job to help their master out of a tight corner. The scene where this intelligent pair, Raven and Rex, restore Art Acord after he has been knocked unconscious and help him to escape, scores a great hit, and one can imagine how juveniles, in particular, will enjoy it.

THEME. Western melodrama, cowboy hero falsely accused of murder, proves innocence, wins pretty girl.

PRODUCTION HIGHLIGHTS. Chase after stage coach. Scene where dog and horse release their bound master and help him escape. Rescue of Hazelton by hero from powder magazine. Acord's riding stunts, comedy relief, climax.

EXPLOITATION. Bill this as a fast Westerner offering plot somewhat out of ordinary. Stress love romance, Art Acord's horsemanship, powder magazine incident. Feature Art Acord and Olive Hasbrouck.

DRAWING POWER. Good box office attraction wherever Western melo is popular.

SUMMARY. A lively Westerner, story gets out of the stereotyped rut, presents interesting complications. Has some dog and horse stuff that will amuse old and young.

THE CAST
```
Steve Caldwell.........................................Art Acord
June Hazelton...................................Olive Hasbrouck
Sam Caldwell.............................................Duke Lee
Slim...................................................Frank Rice
Jeff Hazelton.......................................John T. Prince
Jimmy.............................................Turner Savage
The Cook.......................................Floyd Shackelford
```
Author, Harold Shumates. Director, Clifford Smith. Photographed by Edward Linden.

SYNOPSIS. Lazy Steve Caldwell, cowpuncher, is falsely accused of shooting Jeff Hazelton, his brother Sam being guilty of the crime. Steve, arrested, finds that the supposed dead man's daughter believes him innocent. His horse and dog free him. He hides in powder magazine of mine and is astonished to find old Hazelton there alive, victim of Sam's plot. The two men go after Sam who is drowned trying to escape. Steve wins June.

Art Acord, Universal star in "The Call of Courage."

Some Pun'kins

(Chadwick Picture Corp.—6500 Feet)
(Reviewed by George T. Pardy)

CHARLES RAY returns to the sort of role which made him famous, as the hero of this attraction. It is a rural comedy drama, with the star cast as Lem Blossom, chief of the local fire department in the village of Mosville, who falls in love with Mary Griggs, tries to corner the pumpkin market, has his courtship continually interrupted by fire alarms, most of them false and the work of a rival, finally saves the girl's life from the flames, wins her and makes a fortune. Mr. Ray is thoroughly at home in this kind of a characterization, and the fans who remember his similar portrayals in "String Beans" and "The Egg Crate Wallop," ought to welcome their favorite in such a setting.

There's just sufficient melodramatic urge to balance the comedy values nicely, lively action and a whale of a climax. Duane Thompson plays the heroine sweetly and the support is all that could be desired.

THEME. Comedy drama. Hero fire chief in rustic village, who tries to corner pumpkin market and has courtship constantly interrupted by alarms.

PRODUCTION HIGHLIGHTS. Charles Ray's work in lead. Pleasing rustic atmosphere and village types.

EXPLOITATION ANGLES. Tell patrons that Charles Ray again assumes the kind of role which brought him film fame. Praise his work as awkward country youth, stress the funny situations and crashing climax. Mention Duane Thompson.

DRAWING POWER. Wherever Ray is a favorite this ought to please. Should do particularly well in neighborhood houses.

SUMMARY. Comedy drama, village locale, hero fire chief, who falls in love with girl, is continually interrupted in courting her by fire bell, tries to corner pumpkin market, finally saves sweetheart from flames. Presents Charles Ray in country youth role, the kind that made him famous. Pleasing film.

THE CAST
Lem Blossom	Charles Ray
Mary Griggs	Duane Thompson
Joshua Griggs	Bert Woodruff
Ma Blossom	Fanny Midgley
Jake Blossom	George Fawcett
Tom Perkins	Hallam Cooley

Author, Charles E. Banks. Directed by Jerome Storm.

SYNOPSIS. Lem Blossom, fire chief of village of Mosville, falls in love with Mary Griggs. His rival, Tom Perkins, purchasing pumpkins for a cannery, frequently interrupts Lem's courtship by turning in false fire alarms. When Lem learns that pumpkin crop in the North has been destroyed by frost, he conceives idea of cornering the pumpkin market in the county. The Griggs home catches fire. Lem saves Mary and quenches fire with pump of his own invention. With old Grigg's aid he sells pumpkins at record prices, makes a fortune and wins Mary.

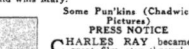
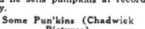

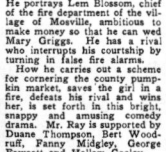

Charles Ray, star of "Some Pun'kins," a Chadwick feature.

The Knockout

(First National—7450 Feet)
(Reviewed by L. C. Moen)

MILTON SILLS continues to deliver in good shape in starring vehicles, and "The Knockout" is a worthy successor to "The Making of O'Malley." Here he portrays a gentleman pugilist who becomes involved in a lumber fight in the north woods. The course of the action includes two ring fights, a rough and tumble fight that starts in a cabin and continues to the river bank, a mighty log jam, the effort to dynamite it, and some remarkable shots of log-rollers in action.

It is a he-man picture, with vigorous action from start to finish, and the Sills fans should "eat it up." Sills makes a pretty convincing sort of fighter, even though the winning of a world's championship bout with one arm disabled savours a bit of the miraculous. The log jam and river scenes are the most remarkable we have seen.

THEME. Story of a gentleman pugilist who becomes involved in a lumber fight, is the unwitting tool of a crook and ultimately fights a championship battle to pay off the mortgage on the girl's timber land.

PRODUCTION HIGHLIGHTS. The log jam and river scenes. The dynamiting, in which Sills is trapped after lighting the fuse. The two ring fights. The rough-and tumble fight with Black Jack. Sills' good work in the stellar role.

EXPLOITATION ANGLES. Get the sporting editor of your paper to review it, round by round. Aim your advertising at the Sills fans. Tell them this is another picture with a punch from the star of "The Sea Hawk."

DRAWING POWER. Should prove popular in any sort of house.

SUMMARY. Well produced melodrama of the prize ring and the lumber camps in the north woods, with star well cast in a sympathetic and vigorous role.

THE CAST
Sandy Donlin	Milton Sills
Jean Farot	Lorna Duveen
Black Jack Ducane	John Philip Kolb
Mike Leary	Edward Lawrence
Steve McKenna	Harry Cording
Brown	Frank Evans
Farot (Jean's father)	Harlan Knight
Mac	Jed Prouty
Parker	Claude King

Adapted from "The Come-Back" by M. D. C. Crawford. Directed by Lambert Hillyer.

SYNOPSIS. Sandy Donlin, light heavyweight champion, tears a ligament in his arm and takes an enforced rest. His friend, Parker, a crooked lumber magnate, sends him to his north woods camp to tame a rival boss, who blocks his schemes. This rival camp is headed by heroine, with whom Donlin falls in love. His men dynamite the dam and tie up her timber, preventing payment of mortgage. Donlin, with last minute encouragement from girl, who hates fighting, wins championship bout and money to meet payment.

Milton Sills, star of First National's "The Knockout."

The Coming of Amos
(Producers Distributing Corp.—5677 Feet)
(Reviewed by George T. Pardy)

A GOOD box office attraction! It's romantic melodrama, staged against a Riviera background, with turreted castles galore, dark dungeons, a beautiful Russian princess in distress and Australian hero, peculiarly expert in throwing the boomerang, who comes to her aid when she needs him worst. All the elements here for a story sure to win the favor of picture patrons in general. It isn't the most probable yarn in the world, but carries its interest to the finish just the same, and being a Cecil B. De Mille film, is naturally rich in gorgeous settings. There's a sprinkling of comedy too, and if the hero chap gets the worst of it at first in a duel with the arch villian, he evens matters up nicely when he reverts to the native boomerang as a weapon. Noah Beery is the bad man of the narrative, plays the part with his usual sinister leer, and is lamented by none when trapped and drowned at the finish.

Rod La Rocque is the hero lad and gives a convincing performance, with Jetta Goudal the most graceful of heroines, and smooth support contributed by the rest of the company.

THEME. Romantic melodrama. Australian hero wooing and winning Russian princess on the Riveria, after many adventures.

PRODUCTION HIGHLIGHTS. The attractive sets. Hero's boomerang-throwing stunts. The Rose Carnival. Kidnapping of princess. Flooded dungeon scene. The rescue. Death of villain. Comedy relief.

EXPLOITATION ANGLES. Book-store tieups on author William J. Locke's novel. Boost the De Mille settings. Stress story's romantic intensity and melodramatic situations. Play up Rod La Rocque, Jetta Goudal, Noah Beery.

DRAWING POWER. Should do well in any house.

SUMMARY. Romantic melo, with attractive backgrounds and fine sets, action laid on Riveria. Moves fast, has general audience appeal, a likely boxoffice bet.

THE CAST

Amos Burden	Rod La Rocque
Princess Nadia Ramioff	Jetta Goudal
Ramon Garcia	Noah Beery
David Fontenay	Richard Carle
Bendyke Hamilton	Arthur Hoyt
Duchess of Parth	Trixie Friganza
Pedro Valdez	Clarence Burton

Adapted from Novel by William J. Locke. Director, Paul Sloane. Photographed by Arthur Miller.

SYNOPSIS. Wealthy sheep-rancher Amos Burden from Australia visits his uncle on the Riviera. He falls in love with Russian princess Nadia. Latter is followed and persecuted by Ramon Garcia, who wounds Amos in a duel. Garcia kidnaps Nadia and takes her to his inland castle. Amos arrives just as she collapses. He rescues her, and in a fight with Garcia throws him into a water-filled dungeon where he drowns. Nadia and Amos are united.

The Coming of Amos (Prod. Dis. Corp.)

PRESS NOTICE

THE management of the _____ theatre has secured Cecil De Mille's latest screen success, "The Coming of Amos," for presentation on _____. This is a romantic melodrama, staged in the gorgeous style for which this producer's films are noted, an appealing love story, numerous sensational thrills and bright comedy relief.

Rod La Rocque is the hero, with Jetta Goudal as the princess. The supporting cast is rich in talent, including Noah Beery, Richard Carle and other distinguished lights of the screen.

CATCH LINES

A rich, handsome, uncouth lad, after 31 years on an Australian sheep ranch, suddenly set down amid the gay throngs and wild pleasures of the Riviera and Monte Carlo.

Rod La Rocque in "The Coming of Amos," a Producers Distributing Corp. release.

The Police Patrol
(Gotham-Lumas—6000 Feet)
(Reviewed by George T. Pardy)

PICTURES with police and firemen heroes are having quite a run in the film markets just now, and this latest addition to the cycle of cop features holds its own with the best of them. It's the sort of entertainment that has a sure mass appeal because it mixes melodramatic punches with sentimental lure, while dealing with the everyday folks of everyday life, easy to understand and follow, without making any undue drain on the mental faculties. James Kirkwood looks good in uniform, a real handsome specimen of a patrolman, and plays the role in refreshingly natural fashion, with Edna Murphy doubling as heroine and the adventuress who is her living image; and proving herself a versatile performer, possessed of considerable physical attractions.

The support is good, director Burton King has kept the action moving swiftly throughout, and introduced several shots of police parades and annual field games which add to the picture's realism. Photography is excellent.

THEME. Melodrama with policeman hero and dressmaker heroine, latter having crook double who causes her lover lots of trouble.

PRODUCTION HIGHLIGHTS. Scene where cop, Jim Ryan, stops runaway horse and saves heroine's little brother. Police station stuff. Realistic slum shots. Race of pursuing patrol boat down river. The climax.

EXPLOITATION ANGLES. You should be able to get the local police force interested. Might put on special police night. Stress film's melodramatic strength and romance. Play up James Kirkwood and Edna Murphy.

DRAWING POWER. Good for the neighborhood and smaller houses.

SUMMARY. A rousing melo with policeman hero and poor girl heroine, has sure audience appeal, outside of highbrow element. Skillfully directed and acted.

THE CAST

Jim Ryan	James Kirkwood
Alice Bennett	Edna Murphy
Dorothy Stone	Edna Murphy
Lieutenant Burke	Edmund Breese
Maurice Ramon	Robert McKim

Adapted from stage play by A. Y. Pearson. Director, Burton King. Supervised by Lon Young. Cameraman, C. J. Davis and Jack Brown.

SYNOPSIS. Patrolman Jim Ryan falls in love with Alice Bennett, a dressmaker. During a tussle with fur thieves he fancies he recognizes a woman confederate as Alice. Later he realizes that Alice has a double in Dorothy Stone, a noted thief. Ordered to arrest Alice as Dorothy, Jim tells the captain he is mistaken, and is suspended. Jim realizes that to clear Alice's name he must run down her double. With Alice posing as Dorothy he gets in touch with the gang. Dorothy is killed in a fight, Alice kidnapped. Jim pursues in patrol boat, captures abductor and rescues Alice, whom he weds, after being reinstated.

The Police Patrol (Gotham-Lumas)

PRESS NOTICE

IF YOU want to see a rousing melodrama, with a gallant policeman for hero, thrills galore, a bit of the underworld, clean sentiment and pleasing romance, don't fail to be on hand when "The Police Patrol" occupies the place of honor on the _____ theatre's screen, on _____. This tells how the cop falls in love with a girl who turns out to have a double. And the double is a daring and skillful thief. Suspicion falls on the innocent girl, and her lover himself suffers suspension because he refuses to believe her guilty. A wonderfully interesting story with a happy climax. James Kirkwood is the star, with Edna Murphy as heroine. In support are Edmund Breese, Bradley Barker, Tammany Young, Blanche Craig and others.

CATCH LINES

The man who "travels beat" is often a humble hero who doesn't get the credit due him.

Edna Murphy in "The Police Patrol," Gotham-Lumas.

Graustark

(First National—5900 Feet)
(Reviewed by George T. Pardy)

THEY'VE made a great audience picture out of this hot-paced romantic story, written by George Barr McCutcheon some twenty years ago, and the first of a long series of best sellers, wherein a young American performs heroic exploits in a mythical foreign country and wins a royal bride. Norma Talmadge as the lovely princess Yetive is a truly fascinating figure giving an exquisite performance which will surely delight all her numerous admirers. Eugene O'Brien in a clean-cut, vigorous portrayal of the handsome young fellow from the U. S., shares dramatic honors with the star, and every member of the carefully selected cast contributes to the picture's well-deserved success. Full credit must be given Dimitri Buchowetzki for his masterly direction. He has handled the big melodramatic situations with just the right amount of reserve, stressing them almost to the breaking point, but never to excess.

THEME. Romantic story with strong melodramatic punches, depicting adventures of young American who mingles in politics of foreign State and wins princess.

PRODUCTION HIGHLIGHTS. First meeting of princess and hero out West. Hero's arrival in Graustark, The melodramatic situations. Well sustained suspense. Gorgeous settings. Climax where princess's marriage to rival is halted.

EXPLOITATION ANGLES. Arrange tieup with book stores on McCutcheon novel. Boost the tremendous heart-interest, the exciting action. Tell them this is one of Norma Talmadge's finest. Feature star and Eugene O'Brien.

DRAWING POWER. Any house, big or little, should pack 'em in with this one.

SUMMARY. A fine audience picture adapted from George Barr McCutcheon's well known novel "Graustark." Crammed with melodramatic punches, alive with heart interest. Well directed, beautifully photographed.

THE CAST

Princess Yetive	Norma Talmadge
Grenfall Lorry	Eugene O'Brien
Prince Gabriel	Marc McDermott
Dangloss	Roy D'Avey
Count Halfont	Albert Gran
Dagmar	Wanda Hawley
King	Frank Currier
Countess Halfont	Lillian Lawrence

Author, George Barr McCutcheon. Directed by Dimitri Buchowetzki.

SYNOPSIS. Grenfell Lorry goes to Graustark, where he finds Yetive, whom he met in the West, to be a princess of the blood royal. She loves him but is betrothed to Prince Gabriel. The latter has Lorry arrested and sentenced to death on a fake murder charge. He escapes with Yetive, but they are captured. Lorry is freed, Yetive prepares to wed Gabriel. Lorry forces a confession from a spy that the prince plotted against him. He comes in time to halt Yetive's marriage and all ends well.

Norma Talmadge, starred in "Graustark," First National.

The Golden Princess

(Paramount—6395 Feet)
(Reviewed by George T. Pardy)

A WESTERN melodrama, action taking place in the days of '49; this feature is neither better nor worse than scores of similar pictures whose plots dealt with the gold rush period, presenting rugged but honest miners, dastardly villains, innocent maidens and gallant heroes. The story is said to have been adapted from Bret Harte's "Tennessee's Partner," but except for the name of one of the principal characters, there is nothing whatever in the photoplay to even recall the Harte masterpiece of fiction. There's a good cast in evidence, headed by Betty Bronson, who is delightfully winsome and charming in the heroine role, and well supported by her associates. Miss Bronson's part doesn't really demand much acting ability, but such as it is, she plays it in sprightly fashion, and, due to the interest she excited in her never-to-be-forgotten impersonation of Peter Pan, registers as the best box office asset of "The Golden Princess."

Theme. Western melodrama of California gold rush period, romance, thrills and happy finish.

PRODUCTION HIGHLIGHTS. Realistic and colorful atmosphere and backgrounds. Comedy bits. Fast action. Melodramatic punches. Betty Bronson's personal appeal.

EXPLOITATION ANGLES. Don't use Bret Harte's name as author. People who like his works would come prepared to welcome a Harte story on the screen, and feel that they had been tricked. Bill as straight melo of '49 days, with lots of excitement, sentimental values, romance. Feature Betty Bronson.

DRAWING POWER. Miss Bronson's widely advertised fame as Peter Pan should bring the fans to see how she makes out in a different role. Picture suited for average house.

SUMMARY. Conventional Western melo of California-flush gold-mining period. Has plenty of stirring action, sentimental and romantic angles, comedy glints. Follows familiar plot trail. Star's name should draw at box office.

THE CAST

Betty Kent	Betty Bronson
Tennessee Hunter	Neil Hamilton
Tom Romaine	Rockcliffe Fellowes
Kate Kent	Phyllis Haver
Padre	Joseph Dowling
Gewilliker Hay	Edgar Kennedy
Bill Kent	George Irving

Directed by Clarence Badger. Photographed by McKinley Martin.

SYNOPSIS. In '49 Bill Kent's wife Kate elopes with Tom Romaine. Bill pursues, is shot, killed, and his boy friend Tennessee takes charge of Bill's deserted baby girl, putting her under care of padre. Fifteen years later Betty goes to gold mining camp, meets Tennessee, also Romaine and Kate, not suspecting her relationship to latter. Romaine plots to obtain Betty's property, is prevented by Tennessee. Romaine is killed after trapping Tennessee, Betty and Kate in mine. Cave-in causes Kate's death. Tennessee wins Betty.

Betty Bronson, starred by Paramount in "The Golden Princess."

The Phantom of the Opera
(Universal—8464 Feet)
(Reviewed by L. C. Moen)

IN this picture we have a complete novelty, in that it has been filmed on a spectacular scale from a mystery story, and is the first production of the "super" type in its field. We have had spectacular war specials, historical dramas, pioneer epics, and the like, but just as "The Covered Wagon" was the first "super" western, this is the first "super" mystery thriller. We imagine there will be more of them.

It is also unique in that almost all of the action takes place in, around, above and under the Paris Opera. This has been faithfully reproduced and photographed in color, in many of the scenes. Chaney's long awaited make-up is gruesome enough to satisfy the most exacting.

A splendid cast, both as to type and ability, interprets the Gaston Leroux story. Mary Philbin is a charming Christine, with Kerry as the ardent lover, and Carewe, Gowland, Edwards, Gravina and others are excellent in supplementary roles.

THEME. Melodramatic spectacle, in which insane criminal hides in underground passages of Paris Opera, from where he brings malignant influence to bear on life of heroine and events at the Opera.

PRODUCTION HIGHLIGHTS. Chaney's make-up. The settings of the Opera. The crash of the chandelier. The excellent cast. The pursuit of Erik. The ballet and opera scenes. The general production.

EXPLOITATION ANGLES. Exploit this along big lines with a dignified and forceful campaign. Feature Chaney, Philbin, etc. Tie up with the photoplay edition of the novel. Tell them about the vast settings in color.

DRAWING POWER. Suitable for any house and a good opening campaign should be all that's necessary.

SUMMARY. Represents a novel departure in the production of elaborate spectacles, with a strong, gripping story, enacted by a brilliant cast against backgrounds of unusual beauty.

Elliot ..: .. ------------
direction by Edward Sedgwick.

SYNOPSIS. Christine Daae, understudy of the Paris Opera, is aided in her career by a strange Phantom whom she has never seen. Through his efforts she sings a leading role with great success, but he demands that she give up her fiance. When she refuses, he kidnaps her and takes her into the underground passages of the Opera. Ultimately she is rescued by her lover and the Phantom, an escaped insane criminal, dies.

Kentucky Pride
(Fox—6597 Feet)
(Reviewed by George T. Pardy)

A RACING melodrama which radiates both human and horse interest, intensely sympathetic and starting from an odd and entertaining angle by having the equine heroine tell her own story. This animal really holds the centre of the stage, although several great race horses of national fame are introduced, including Man O'War, Fair Play, Ladkin, Morvich, The Finn, Negofol and others whose names live in turf history. Interwoven with this is a well developed narrative in which mere human figure, with thrills, pathos and comedy in rich profusion, but when all is said and done, the chief interest lies in the tale of "Virginia's Future," the horse that broke down at the commencement of a glorious racing career, became the drudge of a junk-dealer, but lived to see her colt Confederacy become the sensation of the turf world and finished as a contented old pensioner in the blue grass pastures.

Henry B. Walthall, in the owner role, and J. Farrell MacDonald, as Donovan, are excellent and receive well balanced support from others in the cast.

THEME. A melodrama of the turf in which a broken-down race-horse tells its life story.

PRODUCTION HIGHLIGHTS. The great racing scenes. The admirable photography, sympathetic interest, suspense, thrills and comedy touches.

EXPLOITATION ANGLES. Feature this as a turf story handled from an entirely new direction. Play up the horse romance, the racing sequences, the sympathetic interest, the comedy seasoning.

DRAWING POWER. Should get the money anywhere and please masses as well as high-brow element.

SUMMARY. A melodrama of the turf, with story narrated by horse, handled in unique fashion, strong in sympathetic lure, puts over numerous thrill punches, offers splendid racing shots. A good box office attraction.

THE CAST

Mr. Beaumont	Henry B. Walthall
Donovan	J. Farrell MacDonald
Mrs. Beaumont	Gertrude Astor
Carter	Malcolm Waite
Mrs. Donovan	Belle Stoddard
Danny Donovan	Winston Miller
Virginia Beaumont	Peaches Jackson

Author, Dorothy Yost. Directed by John Ford.

SYNOPSIS. Mr. Beaumont, Kentucky horseman, loses all when his mare, Virginia's Future, falls and is injured when about to win the Futurity. His wife deserts him. Trainer Donovan nurses the horse back to health. She is sold, gives birth to a colt named Confederacy and passes into the possession of a junk man by whom she is ill-treated. Confederacy, ridden by Donovan's son, enters a big race. Donovan and Beaumont bet heavily on Confederacy, who wins. They buy back Virginia's Future and give her a happy home.

Lon Chaney, featured in "The Phantom of the Opera," Universal.

John Ford who directed "Kentucy Pride" for Fox.

Thank You

(A John Ford Prod.-Fox—Seven Reels)
(Reviewed by Frank Elliott)

IN "Thank You" John Ford has transferred to the screen one of the most delightful and entertaining stories of the season, a clean tale with a golden rule message that should find its way into every city, town and hamlet of these United States. The picture is an adaptation of the play by Winchell Smith and Tom Cushing, which was presented for a long run on Broadway by John Golden. The action is packed with human interest, situations that strum on the heart strings, moments of quaint humor and some of the finest character portraits registered on the silver sheet in many moons.

THEME. A comedy drama of small town life showing how the hypocrites were made to see the error of their ways by a modern girl and how a hard working but underpaid pastor came into his own.

PRODUCTION HIGHLIGHTS. The acting of Alec B. Francis and other members of the cast. The scene in which the "ladies' aid" discuss the horrors of Paris. The sequence in which David is informed of a cut instead of an increase in salary. The hunt for the lost pastor.

EXPLOITATION ANGLES. Part of the proceeds of this picture will go to the pension fund for aged and infirm ministers, so go after the co-operation of your local clergy.

DRAWING POWER. The excellent cast, the fame of the authors and producers of the play and the appeal of the story should make this one a welcome attraction

SUMMARY. Appealing comedy drama of "back home" folks, containing much fine acting, many dramatic sequences, a wealth of sure fire humor and a mounting that is a credit to the director.

THE CAST

David Lee	Alec B. Francis
Diane	Jacqueline Logan
Kenneth Jamieson	George O'Brien
Cornelius Jamieson	George Fawcett
Andy	J. Farrell McDonald
Mr. Jones	Cyril Chadwick
Mrs. Jones	Edith Boswick
Milly Jones	Marion Harlan

Based on the play by Winchell Smith and Tom Cushing. Scenario by Frances Marion. Directed by John Ford. Photographed by George Schneiderman.

SYNOPSIS. David Lee, the "thank you" pastor of Dedham, has a salary which consists mostly of stingy donations from miserly vestrymen. David asks for an increase, but the vestrymen use the arrival of a niece from Paris and an unjust "scandal" story about her and the hero, as an excuse for a decrease. The blow is too much for the kindly old minister and he becomes seriously ill. The millionaire father of the hero, grateful to David for aiding in the regeneration of his son, "shows up" the hypocritical vestrymen. David recovers, gets his increase and all ends well.

George O'Brien, appearing in "Thank You" for Fox.

Thank You (Fox)
PRESS NOTICE

ANOTHER of the clean, splendid films being produced by William Fox in association with John Golden, based on the wholesome plays which the latter has sponsored on the stage, comes to the ——— theatre next ——— when "Thank You" will be the feature attraction.

Intermingled with a story of small town life and a charming love interest is a powerful theme, based on the hardships of the underpaid pastor. This character is portrayed with great feeling by Alec B. Francis, the sterling character actor, while George O'Brien and Jacqueline Logan are the young lovers. George Fawcett and J. Farrell McDonald are also prominent.

CATCH LINES

He was only the "Thank You" minister, but he finally won out.
Are ministers underpaid? See "Thank You."

A Son of His Father

(Victor Fleming Prod.-Paramount—6925 Feet)
(Reviewed by Frank Elliott)

VICTOR FLEMING has made a good western out of this Harold Bell Wright tale. While it is slow in getting started, the early reels being somewhat retarded with unnecessary hokum, the picture picks up later and comes to a close with a satisfactory climax. The plot is not one of startling originality. The villain threatens to foreclose on the mortgage, wanting the ranch as a passing point over the border for contraband. The hero wins out in foiling his attempt and in the end retains the old homestead. The story is unfolded against an ever changing background of rugged western landscapes.

THEME. A straight western in which the hero thwarts the plans of the villain to get his hands on a rich ranch, the only point not being watched for the latter's contraband smuggling activities.

PRODUCTION HIGHLIGHTS. The scene in which Morgan goes alone after his stolen horses and gets them back after some exciting stunts. The good fights. The stirring climax in which the hero turns the tables on the smugglers and with the aid of the border patrol rounds

EXPLOITATION ANGLES. Play up the Harold Bell Wright end. Put over book store window tie-ups. Put on a father and son night. Play up the names of the stars.

DRAWING POWER. A good attraction for houses whose patrons like westerns. This one will please because of its good cast and interesting story.

SUMMARY. There are millions who read Harold Bell Wright's works and Paramount has transplanted this novel into a fairly diverting screen drama, which, while possessing nothing new in features of this kind, is well acted and beautifully mounted and has a good quota of thrills.

THE CAST

Morgan	Warner Baxter
Nora	

has gone over to the Holdbrook camp, where he is made to believe smuggling is a "noble profession." Larry's sister, Nora, arrives from Ireland. Morgan does not tell her where her brother is. She learns soon and is induced by Holdbrook to visit him. Holdbrook seeks to keep her a prisoner and she knows of the smuggling. Morgan and his men, rescue her and save Larry from the border police.

Victor Fleming now producing "Lord Jim" for Paramount.

A Son of His Father (1st Nat'l)
PRESS NOTICE

THE leading attraction at the ——— theatre on ——— will be "A Son Of His Father" starring Bessie Love and Warner Baxter. This is a colorful and thrilling version of Harold Bell Wright's famous novel, directed by Victor Fleming, who was responsible for many of the big Zane Grey successes. The action takes place in the West, with a hero making a fight against smugglers running contraband across the border.

It is brimful of thrills and romantic interest, much hard riding, gunfights, and attains a rattling climax that will please the most enthusiastic admirers of Westerns. In support of the principals are Raymond Hatton, Walter McGrail, Carl Stockdale, Billy Eugene and other screen favorites.

CATCH LINES

A fast Western melodrama with a great cast, and fine story. Adapted from a novel by one of America's most popular author Harold Bell Wright

Fair Play
(William Steiner Prod.—5035 Feet)
(Reviewed by George T. Pardy)

STARTING off at a rather deliberate gait, this picture gradually develops speed and gets a hold on the audience which doesn't relax until it swings into a highly satisfactory climax. It stands out as an uncommonly "good buy" for the state rights field, offering an interesting plot with love angles and crook atmosphere ingeniously blended. Its drawing power is intensified by a strong cast, featuring Edith Thornton and Lou Tellegen, with several well-known players in support, each name possessing box office value. The film has general audience appeal, is well directed and O. K. for the family trade, despite its sensational developments.

Edith Thornton gives a colorful performance as heroine Norma Keith, Lou Tellegen has a role which doesn't win him much sympathy until toward the close, when he finally makes good with the girl who has sacrificed so much for him.

THEME. Heart interest drama with crook atmosphere, depicting devotion of heroine to her employer, who weds the wrong woman but afterwards turns to girl who clears him of murder charge.

PRODUCTION HIGHLIGHTS. Acting of Edith Thornton and Lou Tellegen. Scene where murder is committed. Suspense and melodramatic punches. Situation where hero finally realizes that he loves girl who has stuck by him through trouble.

EXPLOITATION ANGLES. Play up the woman's devotion and self-sacrifice angles. Stress the realistic crook atmosphere, sensational trend and love interest. Feature Edith Thornton and Lou Tellegen.

DRAWING POWER. An excellent attraction for neighborhood and smaller houses.

SUMMARY. Heart interest drama with strong crook angle and romantic lure and heroine who dares all to save man she loves from murder charge. Has universal appeal, well directed and acted.

THE CAST

Norma Keith	Edith Thornton
Bruce Elliot	Lou Tellegen
Dickie Thane	Gaston Glass
Rita Thane	Betty Francisco
Bull Mong	David Dunbar
Charlie Morse	Simon Greer

Author, Charles Hutchinson. Director, Frank Crane. Photographed by Ernest Miller.

SYNOPSIS. Norma Keith, in love with her employer, Bruce Elliot, a lawyer, has worked faithfully to help him succeed in his career. Bruce is fascinated by Rita Thane, an unworthy woman and weds her. Rita's lover, masquerading as her brother, kills her and takes her jewels. Suspicion falls on Bruce, who is arrested on a murder charge. Norma devotes herself to clearing him. After many adventures she identifies the real murderer. Bruce at last realizes that Norma is the only woman in the world for him.

Lou Tellegen in "Fair Play" a Wm. Steiner production.

Fair Play (William Steiner Prod)
PRESS NOTICE

A STRONG heart interest drama, with fascinating crook atmosphere, a sensational murder mystery and continuous thrills, is outlined in "Fair Play" the feature film scheduled for the screen of the ——— theatre on ———. Edith Thornton, in the heroine role, is wonderfully appealing as the girl who is willing to sacrifice herself for the man she loves, and Lou Tellegen gives a powerful performance as the hero.

The story deals with the infatuation of lawyer for an unworthy woman whom he weds, the love of his faithful girl-secretary for him, and her successful efforts to clear him of a murder charge when his wife is slain by her lover. Gaston Glass and Betty Francisco appear in important roles.

CATCH LINES

He wed the wrong woman, but the girl who really loved him was rewarded in the end.

The Thoroughbred
(Truart—5481 Feet)
(Reviewed by George T. Pardy)

AN acceptable program offering, skilfully directed by Oscar Apfel and presenting a cast of standard merit. It is snappy comedy drama, with a full quota of thrills, well-turned love angle, and there's an exciting horse race in which an entry backed by hero and heroine actually loses—this being a totally unprecedented event in filmland, especially when the leading man is supposed to have bet his last nickel on the result. But so it runs with the losers reaching happiness goal by another route than that of the turf. Maclyn Arbuckle, as the testy millionaire uncle, and Carter De Haven, in the role of a society hanger-on, broke but cheerful, are responsible for the laughs and get a lot of fun out of their respective roles. Theodore Von Eltz and Gladys Hulette are the lovers around whose varying fortunes the plot swirls. Both work with considerable vim and decided appeal and the support is adequate.

THEME. Comedy drama, with racing sequence, in which he has to make the high society grade in order to please wealthy uncle.

PRODUCTION HIGHLIGHTS. Arbuckle and De Haven's comedy work. Development of love affair. Scene in which Drummond is thrashed by Bob Bemis. The horse race, with unusual ending. Acting of Theodore Von Eltz and Gladys Hulette.

EXPLOITATION ANGLES. Feature as amusing comedy drama in which hero is compelled to break into social running because his rich uncle wants to boost the family name. Play up heroine's rescue by lover from assailant and big fight which ensues. Horse race worth mentioning, but not as main thing in picture. Advertise Von Eltz, Gladys Hulette, Maclyn Arbuckle and De Haven.

DRAWING POWER. Suitable for neighborhood and smaller houses.

SUMMARY. Fast comedy drama with well sustained love interest, thrill stuff, horse race and bright, gingery comedy. A good program attraction.

THE CAST

Peter Bemis	Maclyn Arbuckle
Robert Bemis	Theodore Von Eltz
Mitzi Callahan	Gladys Hulette
Dan Drummond	Hallam Cooley
Gwendolyn Vandemere	Virginia Brown Faire

Author, Leet Renick Brown. Director, Oscar Apfel.

SYNOPSIS. Wealthy uncle insists nephew Bob Bemis must break into society. He tries, but only succeeds in falling in love with chorus girl Mitzi Callahan. He buys old racehorse from Mitzi's improverished father, thrashes man who makes insulting advances to girl, is arrested on false charge of giving bad check and horse loses race. Uncle comes to Bob's rescue, villain is exposed. Bob and Mitzi are united.

Carter De Haven in "Thorobred"; Truart.

The Thoroughbred (Truart)
PRESS NOTICE

SENSATIONAL incident, an appealing love romance and bright comedy are combined in "The Thoroughbred," which is due to appear on the screen of the ——— theatre on ———. The plot hinges on the desire of a wealthy uncle to have his nephew break into high society, instead of which the young fellow falls in love with a pretty chorus girl and buys a racehorse, which loses in a thrilling race.

Maclyn Arbuckle and Carter De Haven furnish the laughs, with Theodore Von Eltz and Gladys Hulette doing great work as hero and heroine. A large supporting cast is in evidence, with Hallam Cooley, Virginia Brown Faire, Lillian Langdon, Thomas Jefferson and other favorites playing important roles

CATCH LINES

His uncle wanted him to break into society, but Bob Bemis preferred the quiet life and the girl he loved.

Regional News from Correspondents

Central Penn.

A CAMERAMAN of the Wilmer & Vincent organization accompanied the 400 members of the Harrisburg Chamber of Commerce on its annual "cruise" during the four days of which they visited nine cities, going as far west as Detroit. He shot pictures of the cruisers' activities everywhere and these are to be shown later in the various Wilmer & Vincent theatres in Harrisburg. This was the largest excursion of the kind from the viewpoint of the number participating ever made by the business and professional men of any city of the United States, and included visits to Lewiston, Altoona, Johnstown, Pittsburgh, Youngstown, Cleveland, Detroit, Buffalo and Williamsport.

C. Floyd Hopkins, manager of the Wilmer & Vincent theatres in Harrisburg, and a former president of the Chamber of Commerce, was chairman of the Program and Stunts committee of the cruise, which provided the entertainment for the excursionists. This included a big theatre party in Cleveland. The cruisers left Harrisburg on the morning of September 8 and returned the evening of the 11th, covering a total of 900 miles, part by rail and part by steamships on the Great Lakes.

Announcement has been made of the complete personnel of the executive staff of the half-million-dollar New Strand picture theatre that was formally opened by the Nathan Appell Amusement Enterprises, in York, on August 27. Louis J. Appell is general manager of this and the other Appell theatres in York; the manager of the New Strand is C. C.

Pippin; house manager, C. W. Hofman; organist, John De Palma; assistant organist, J. Howard Wiley; chief projectionist, W. E. Raffensberger; treasurer, Marie Rhoads; chief usher, Raymond Landis; chief doorman, Daniel Petrie, and special officer, E. J. Smith. Individual motion pictures of each of these employees was displayed on the New Strand screen as a feature of the program on the opening night.

Special Labor Day programs were provided in many of the Central Pennsylvania picture theatres, some of which put on four instead of three performances for the holiday. A feature of the Labor Day Program at the Alto theatre, Columbia, Lancaster county, was a display of local films of the thousands who attended the Lancaster City bathing revue at which the final selection was made of Miss Estella Wittell as "Miss Lancaster" for the 1925 Atlantic City bathing beauty pageant. The feature film for Labor Day at the Alto was "A Thief in Paradise," with Doris Kenyon, Aileen Pringle and Ronald Colman.

The new fire-proof steel and concrete theatre erected by Julius Freedman, in Forest City, with a seating capacity of 1,000, was formally opened on Labor Day.

James McFadden, at one time proprietor of the Lyric theatre, Kulpmont, died very suddenly at his home in Dalmatia. He was 40 years old.

The Strand theatre, Shamokin, operated by the Chamberlain Amusement Enterprises, Inc., was formally opened on Labor Day for the 1925-1926 season. It is devoted to pictures and vaudeville. Announcement was made that the Strand Concert Orchestra will be under the direction of Jack Dale.

The Columbia Opera House, Columbia, Lancaster county, had a special Labor Day program of pictures and vaudeville, at which special prices were made for the holiday. Admittance to the matinee was 10 cents for children and 25 for grown-ups, while the evening prices were, children 10 cents and adults 25 and 40 cents. The feature film was "Paths to Paradise," with Betty Compson and Raymond Griffith.

The Feeley theatre, Hazleton, put on four programs instead of the usual three, for Labor Day. The feature film was "The Mine With the Iron Door." There were two matinees and two night shows.

Improvements recently made under direction of Manager F. E. Barry, to the interior of the Jackson picture theatre, York, include a new system of colored lights, a new silk curtain and extensive redecorations and renovations.

Herman Fisher, of New York, special exploiteer for the Metro-Goldwyn-Mayer company, and Mr. Pyle, of the Philadelphia office, have arranged with the Harrisburg Evening News to print in serial form the story,

"The Unholy Three," on which the film play of that name is based.

There is speculation rife in Harrisburg as to whether Peter Magaro, pioneer picture exhibitor of that city, who last spring sold his Regent theatre to the Marcus Loew interests' will re-enter the picture business in Harrisburg. Upon his return recently from a summer spent in Europe, Mr. Magaro was asked whether he has any such intentions, to which he replied: "That is a matter which I cannot discuss at this time." He said, however, that for the present he will devote his entire time to the management of his Coliseum dance hall and amusement building and to his large Harrisburg real estate interests.

Several motion picture exhibitors are reported to be negotiating for control of the theatre in the new Moose Temple, in Reading, which is soon to be completed, at 1018 Penn street, but at this writing no lease has been made.

Wilmer & Vincent's Hippodrome theatre, Reading, has a new manager in the person of William Masard, of New York, who succeeds Frank S. Mickley who has been made manager of the Rajah, pictures and vaudeville, which has just been reopened for the Fall season.

Among the Pennsylvania theatres reopened on Labor Day for the Fall season, is the Poli theatre, Wilkes-Barre, which has been renovated during the summer and which has increased its seating capacity by the removal of the lower boxes, devoting the space to several rows of new seats. Fred Herman is manager.

Houston

CURTIS DUNHAM, publicity man for Paramount in the southwest was in town this week enroute to Galveston. Mr. Dunham won fame and promotion with his organization last spring when he dug up the original heroine of "North of 36" the Emerson Hough novel which Paramount filmed in Texas. South of San Antonio in the cattle country Dunham found the original Tessie Lockhart around whose ranch this famous story was laid. He plans to have a big publicity campaign on Paramount's forthcoming production "The Pony Express." From Galveston Mr. Dunham will go to San Antonio, stopping again in Houston enroute.

Word has reached Houston that Earl E. Crabb, for the past two years district manager for Southern Enterprises, Inc., of Texas has been promoted to the directorship of Paramount's biggest theatre in Boston which will be open in about seven weeks. Mr. Crabb was very popular with the theatre men and public in general and

many regret that he is leaving but wish him good luck in his new field. He will be succeeded by T. L. Freedle who has been director of the Palace theatre, Dallas for two years. Prior to his connection in Dallas he was a publicity man for Paramount in the West.

Sam Abrams and family of the Rialto theatre left Sunday morning for a motor trip through north Texas. They plan to be out of the city about ten days.

S. L. Lowery, manager for Progress Film Exchange was in town this week booking his new product with the Crown and Folly theatre.

Harve Holland Tent Theatre has opened an indefinite engagement on Harrisburg Blvd, just outside the city limits. This is the first tent theatre to open in Houston for more than three years, the last one played a 54 weeks' engagement.

E. L. Bickert, road man for Saenger Amusement Co. who has been in Houston for several days has returned to Dallas, where his

company control the Old Mill Theatre, a former Paramount Theatre.

The Majestic, the local Interstate Amusement Co., vaudeville theatre is featuring a picture attraction above their vaudeville number. This is the first time in the history of the Majestic that this policy has been followed. Tom Mix is the star that is being featured at the Majestic. They are doing extensive advertising both newspaper and outdoor.

Virgil E. Siner and his company who have been playing at the Prince theatre for the past ten weeks will close their engagement Sept. 12th. For the final week they are featuring Ollie Bebrow, a Houston black face comedian, who has played in vaudeville for several seasons also with "The Follies" for one season.

The new popular price theatre being erected at 914 Preston avenue has a new name, however it won't be open for several weeks yet. It was first called

the Cameo theatre and signs were posted to that effect but a few days later the signs were hauled down and it will make its bow to the world under the title of the RITZ Theatre. Work is progressing at a fast clip and the management is sure they will be able to open before many days of the fall season have passed.

Work on the new million dollar theatre has been held up, temporarily. This theatre is being built by Jesse H. Jones, local capitalist, and will be leased to the Famous-Players organization. It will rank with the best in the South when completed.

Sam Abrams, manager of the Rialto theatre, is giving the film boys a whiz in his brand new Hudson car. Sam plans to take a few weeks off in a short time and motor through Texas.

Hal. H. Norfleet, newly appointed exploitation manager for Fox Film Exchange, southern district, is in Houston for a short time.

Chicago

PRESIDENT Al Steffes of the Motion Picture Theatre Owners of the Northwest, was in Chicago last week in the interests of his organization.

General Manager F. M. Brockell of the Balaban & Katz Midwest Theatres, Inc., has appointed C. E. Bond, well known exchange manager, to an executive position with the Midwest organization. Mr. Bond resigned the managership of Associated First National's Chicago office to accept the new post. He had been manager of the First National office for the past five years and prior to that was associated with Paramount as sales manager for more than three years.

Lou Metzger, manager of the Complete Plan Service Department of Universal, is making his headquarters in Chicago for a few days and while here conferred with Manager Alexander and held several sales meetings in which all salesmen participated. Mr. Metzger is making a complete tour of Universal exchanges and will go as far west as the Pacific Coast before returning to New York City.

Bill Brimmer is now handling the north side territory for First National, formerly covered by Carl Leserman, who was promoted to city sales manager and Tom Gilliam has been appointed to the south side.

Ward P. Woolbridge of the Hays organization is in Chicago, promoting the Saturday Morning Movie Movement. Distribution of programs which have been specially prepared for children, will be made through Universal's Chicago exchange.

M. Siegel, former owner of the New Home Theatre, has returned to Chicago after a three month's vacation in the east, which included visits to the principal cities and a sojourn at a Catskill Mountains summer resort.

Manager Frank Scott of the Iris Theatre, has returned from a motor trip to the Dells of Wisconsin, which he enjoyed in the company of Mrs. Scott.

Starting on September 3rd the Rialto Theatre at Altamont, Illinois, will be opened on Thursday and Friday nights.

Frank Marshall, popular Wurlizer salesman, is back on the job selling organs after an illness of three weeks. Mr. Marshall was overcome with the grippe while on the road and had to be brought back to Chicago.

The committee in charge of the Midwest Film Golf Tournament has sent out notices to the effect that the fall tournament will be held on Friday, September 18th at Olympia Fields, it having been necessary to make this change in playing arrangements to accommodate the large crowd that has entered. Entries should be sent, at the earliest possible time, to F. M. Brockell, 162 N. State Street, Chicago.

Charles Pyle, who expects to open his beautiful new theatre at Danville, Illinois, at an early date, has taken over the Victory Theatre at Kokomo, Indiana, from Manager Heller. The new Danville house will be one of the handsomest theatres in the state and will accommodate 600 patrons.

The eight motion picture theatres located in Champaign and Urbana are operating despite the strike of operators, whose demand for a substantial wage increase was refused. The strike was called at 2:30 A. M. and before 1:00 P. M. that day, a sufficient number of operators to keep the machines going in all the houses, was on hand and performances went on as usual.

J. J. Schmuck is now connected with Associated Exhibitors as a salesman covering Illinois territory. Mr. Schmuck came from New York to take this position.

A group of independent producers have chartered Premier Films, Inc., under the laws of Illinois, with I. E. Chadwick as president and Henry Ginsberg as vice-president, and have completed arrangements with Joe Friedman of Celebrated Players Film Corporation, whereby the latter company will distribute in Illinois and Indiana the pictures produced or purchased by Premier Film Company. According to Mr. Friedman, the new connection assures Celebrated of fifty feature releases for the year.

Rubens Rialto Square, the big theatre now under course of construction in Joliet will be ready for opening about January 31st, according to Morris Rubens, who states it will be one of the finest houses in the middle west with a seating capacity for about three thousand. A feature of this house will be the lobby which Mr. Rubens states will be even larger than that of Balaban & Katz's recently opened Uptown Theatre.

Regge Doran of Pathe's Public Relations Department, is making her headquarters at this company's Chicago office for the present and while here will work to establish closer relations between the exhibitors and their patrons.

Joe Lyons is now selling film for Renown on Chicago's south 'side, after several years' connection with Fox Film Corporation.

Bill Cook who has been covering the south side for Associated First National, is going to Florida, where it is said he may remain. Another former Chicago film man who is now located in Florida, is J. A. Steinson, who recently severed his connection with Warner Brothers.

The Stratford Theatre is presenting Miss Eva Tanguay to its patrons this week, in addition to the "Diamond Horseshoe," a sensational stage presentation produced by Francis A. Mangan, as well as the usual program of pictures.

The Enterprise Theatre Company, Inc., celebrated anniversary week at their Empress Theatre, 6230 S. Halsted Street, starting on August 31st. As a feature of the occasion they dedicated their new Robert Morton Unit Organ with Harry Wagner solo organist at the console. Many floral offerings were received by Billy Fearson, manager, and quite an assemblage of film men helped make the affair a success.

C. R. Johnson has taken over the Gem Theatre at Grafton, Illinois, and will start remodeling the house some time in September.

Milwaukee

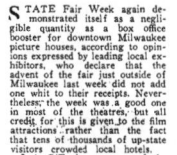

STATE Fair Week again demonstrated itself as a negligible quantity as a box office booster for downtown Milwaukee picture houses, according to opinions expressed by leading local exhibitors, who declare that the advent of the fair just outside of Milwaukee last week did not add one whit to their receipts. Nevertheless, the week was a good one in most of the theatres, but all credit for this is given to the film attractions rather than the fact that tens of thousands of up-state visitors crowded local hotels.

Jack O'Toole, manager of the Minneapolis branch of the Producers Distributing Corporation, stopped in Milwaukee for a short visit with friends among the film men and exhibitors, enroute to Chicago on a business trip.

Paramount Week was celebrated in Milwaukee by having a Paramount picture in each of the downtown Saxe houses, including the Wisconsin, Strand, Merrill and Miller theatres. The Saxe organization has contracted for the Paramount product this year and is distributing the pictures among its various first run houses as listed.

Elmer Zieman, assistant manager of the Wisconsin Theatre, has returned from a two week's vacation in Yellowstone National Park. Among the souvenirs brought back is one set of blisters on Elmer's foot, acquired through the unique expedient of inserting said pedal extremity into an ambitious geyser at the park. Elmer also tried his luck at broncho busting while in the west. It is expected that he will be able to sit down without a groan as early as next Thanksgiving.

Carl Ebert, formerly of Metro-Goldwyn, has joined the sales force of F. B. O. at Milwaukee, replacing Lee Anger, resigned. He will travel in the Wisconsin territory.

Frank Trottman, manager of the Gem Theatre, Milwaukee, has left for the Northland to indulge in his annual four weeks of fishing. In order to satisfy the expectations of only half his friends at Milwaukee, who all look for a shipment of fish within the next few days, he will have to catch every scaled inhabitant of the Great Lakes as well as the inland waters of the Wisconsin Land O'Lakes. He probably will, at that.

Sam Abrams, Milwaukee manager for F. B. O., has just returned from a very successful sales boosting trip through Northern Wisconsin, and plans within the next few days to go to the Upper Michigan peninsula, to work in cooperation with Dick Scheinbaum, who with headquarters at Crystal Falls, Mich., has been promoting F. B. O. interests in that territory.

The advent of two double week first runs on Grand Avenue during the same overlapping period is something new in Milwaukee. This week the Alhambra is holding its opening program, featuring "The Gold Rush," for a second week, while the Merrill is doing excellent business with the first week of the two week run of "The Ten Commandments."

Buffalo

E. O. WEINBERG, one of the best known theatre men in the state, is back in the business again, after dabbling in real estate for several months in Buffalo. Eddie is now manager of the Cataract theatre in Niagara Falls, N. Y. Eddie formerly managed the old Strand, Elmwood and other houses, including the Olympic in Buffalo, the State in Schenectady and the Strand in Syracuse. He also was manager for a time of the Buffalo branch of Renown Pictures corporation. The Cataract is owned by the Cataract Amusement company of Niagara Falls, of which Charley Hayman is the head.

L. Weidrich, former manager of theatres in Costa Rica and Panama has come to Buffalo to manage the Ellen Terry theatre, recently acquired by Mr. Kreiger from the Border Amusement company.

Percy E. Brown, 52 years old, 408 Washington street, Jamestown, N. Y., who was granted a permit September 1 to build a $100,000 theatre in Taylor street, in the Chautauqua lake city, died suddenly of heart disease at his home on the evening of the same day. Mr. Brown was returning from a stroll when he collapsed in front of his home. For the past eight years Mr. Brown has operated the Royal theatre in Jamestown.

Falling 90 feet down an elevator shaft at the new Shea's Buffalo theatre, Daniel Shea, 46 years old, 20 North Pearl street, suffered serious internal injuries and a possible fracture of the skull. He is in the Millard Fillmore hospital. Shea was working alone on a ladder at the top of an elevator shaft. The cause of his fall could not be learned. He landed on a pile of planks at the foot of the shaft. He was employed by the Elevator Company of America, which is installing elevators in the theatre.

Stewart Parmalee, former manager of the Capitol theatre in South Park section of Buffalo, is now selling flivvers for a Main street lizzie agency. Many of his distributor friends along Film Row have been in to look over the new models and several have filed orders with Stewart.

Howard Waugh, who for many years was connected with moving picture theatres in Jamestown, N. Y., has been appointed manager of the remodeled Alhambra theatre in Milwaukee, which has been acquired by Universal. Mr. Waugh had been managing houses for Paramount before accepting the Milwaukee post, his last positions having been in Memphis and Atlanta.

Paramount will build a new exchange building in Buffalo in North Pearl street which will be

the last word in structures of this type. It is expected the building will be ready for use soon after the first of the new year.

"Hub" Taylor, Pathe plugger in the Southern Tier, was seen the other day, all dolled up in the latest things in golf togs. Another good man has fallen for the famous Scotch game. Tom North, Pathe publicity representative, was in Buffalo the other day for a visit with local manager Basil Brady.

Al Beckerich, manager of Loew's State, pulled a good one when he arranged to have "Miss Pittsburgh" (Miss Mildred Walker) appear at his house for one day when she arrived in Buffalo on her way to the beauty tournament in Atlantic City. As a result Al got a lot of publicity gained in tieups with local auto and other merchants.

Richard C. Fox, president of Freedom Film corporation of Buffalo, announces the signing of a contract for the distribution of 24 Golden Arrow features for 1925-26 in upper New York state. "I am more than fortunate in securing the Golden Arrow franchise," said Mr. Fox, "and am thoroughly impressed with the fact that the independent producer is making a product on par with the best pictures turned out by the big combinations."

Ray S. Averill, manager of the

Olympic, Buffalo, is distributing house programs in which is printed a free ticket good one night of the week. Fair enough.

Lionel Edel, manager of the Ritz theatre, Niagara Falls, N. Y., took a half page ad in the local newspaper to announce the booking of the entire Fox product for 1925-26. "Lightning" the first of the bookings is being shown this week.

Harry Gribbon, Mack Sennett comedian, was in Buffalo this week, with a company, appearing on the vaudeville program at the Lafayette Square.

The week of September 20 promises to be a big one at the Palace theatre, Lockport, when Manager George T. Cruzen will offer a new Paramount feature, five acts of vaudeville and Sousa's Band, all at regular prices. Mr. Cruzen is plastering every highway leading into the Lock City with three sheets and continuing to wake up the natives with his live wire exploitation stunts. He has just put up large photos of all the Paramount stars in the barber shop next door to the theatre.

Jim Savage, manager of the Buffalo office of Chase Pictures corporation, announces that Eugene Sternman, formerly with film companies in Philadelphia, is now representing the firm in Albany.

San Francisco

MORTIMER THOMAS, pioneer in the San Francisco motion picture world, has sold his interest in the Golden State Theatre & Realty Corporation at a figure reputed to be $100,000. The transaction is said to have involved the sale of 10,000 shares of stock in the corporation, which was taken by associates in the company. The Golden State Theatre and Realty Corporation operates a circuit of theatres in Northern California. Thomas retains his individual holdings in various theatres in San Francisco and Oakland.

Harry Goldberg, of the Famous-Lasky organization, accompanied by his wife, arrived in San Francisco on the President Polk. He was rounding up a tour of the company's properties while vacationing. Goldberg has just been made head of the Southern Division of theatres, according to word received from New York.

Featured in Fanchon and Marco's novelty act, "Screenland Beauties of 1925" a the Loew's Warfield is Miss Nelly Kelly, a native daughter of San Francisco, who recently completed a successful tour of the Orpheum circuit, and has just signed a contract

whereby she will be featured by Larry Semon in his next big productions which will soon be under way at the F. B. O. Studio where Larry produces his features pictures.

A. M. Bowles, general manager of the West Coast Theatres, Inc., was in San Francisco for a conference with Marco, of the producing firm of Fanchon & Marco, on the stage attractions for the coming weeks at Loew's Warfield.

Ann Dempsey, who has been connected with the Imperial Theatre for almost seven years, and is one of the most popular young women connected with a motion

picture house, has taken a trip to New York.

Samuel H. Levin has plans under way for four theatres. One at Balboa Street and 38th Ave. is already under construction. The others are to be at Divisadero and Hayes streets, Polk street at Broadway and Fillmore and California streets.

Plans for a jubilee cruise of the motion picture industry in which motion pictures stars and directors will make a special trip to San Francisco during jubilee week, were announced. The cruise will be taken on board the steamer H. F. Alexander.

Denver

THE new State Theatre, formerly the Strand, is being rapidly remodeled, redecorated and generally overhauled in preparation for a grand and glorious opening September 18th. The new theatre promises to be the most beautiful one on Curtis Street, both exterior and interior. The people of Denver will be refunded with something entirely new in the way of artistic decorations. The theatre will be strictly first-run opening Friday night, September 18th with "Hell's Highroad".

Joe Roth, manager of Fox Theatres in Denver, and Mel

Wilson, manager of the branch of Fox Film Corporation, met James R. Grainger, the general sales manager of Fox Organization, in Cheyenne, Wyoming a few days ago. They accompanied Mr. Grainger to North Platte, Nebraska, holding a business conference with their manager while riding on the train. They returned to Denver from North Platte, Mr. Grainger going on to New Mexico.

An unusual number of exhibitors visited Denver during the past week. Some of those who visited film row were Fred Lee, owner and operator of the Victory

Theatre, Lamar, Colorado; R. C. Geeting, owner of the Lyric Theatre, Chappel, Nebraska; W. B. Cook and wife, who operate the Dawson Opera House, Dawson, New Mexico; William Ostenburg Jr., owner and manager of the Orpheum Theatre, Scottsbluff, and a small chain in Western Nebraska.

Charles Klein of the Black Hills Amusement Company has returned to Deadwood, So. Dakota, after visiting his many friends among the exchanges and also contracting and dating service for the coming year.

Joseph H. Ashby, manager of First National, and Harry Nolan, district supervisor of First Nation, have returned from New York, where they attended the general sales convention held recently. They were accompanied to Denver by W. F. Gordon, manager of the First National office of Salt Lake City.

H. E. Brooker, for many years past associated with the local branch of Fox Film Corporation as salesman, has resigned. His future plans have not been announced.

Salt Lake City

CLYDE H. MESSINGER who is in charge of the Educational exchange here, has returned this week from a trip to Southern Utah.

A. G. Pickett, manager of the local Metro-Goldwyn exchange, is leaving within a few days for the Montana territory. Manager Pickett has just returned from the Idaho branch, and he reports that Walter Mendenhall, first run exhibitor there, is confined to his bed through illness. All film men connected with Mendenhall are looking forward to his immediate recovery.

George Carpenter, managing director for the Louis Marcus enterprises, announces that the new Paramount Theatre in Ogden, Utah, will open on September 9th, with Richard Dix in "The Lucky Devil." This new house will run Paramount, Metro-Goldwyn and United Artists Pictures, with Pathe and Educational comedies, and Fox News.

Louis Marcus leaves here for Chicago tomorrow to attend a film meeting.

The Paramount Empress Theatre had a very unique entrance arrangement this week in connection with their showing of "Sally of the Sawdust." They carry one in imagination to the big circus tent, by the sawdust under foot, the tent awning overhead, the ticket wagon in place of the box office, and a real honest-to-goodness lemonade and peanut stand, arranged by Carpenter.

George L. Cloward, of Metro-Goldwyn-Mayer here, is making the key towns in Montana and expects to be gone about two weeks. All Metro-Goldwyn salesmen are still in their respective territories sending in large numbers of contracts.

W. B. Seib, manager of the local Pathe branch, has returned from a short trip through Idaho in the especial interest of "The Freshman."

Word from New York has just been received at the Pathe exchange that the Salt Lake office has won the contest for the Storey Victory Campaign. The winning of the first prize in this division will mean $1,300 for this office.

C. J. Hamal, Pathe salesman, has just left for a two weeks' trip in Idaho. R. D. Boomer is still in Southern Utah where he has been for the past three weeks. He is expected in the office within the next few days.

R. S. Stackhouse, in charge of the Warner Brothers exchange in this city, leaves in a few days for a short trip into Montana.

L. W. Hyde, who covers the Southern Utah and Nevada territory out of the local Warner Brothers office, is still in Southern Utah, doing a very consistent business. Harry Gibson is sending in the contracts from Idaho, and George E. Jensen from Montana.

It is reported at the Associated First National exchange here that manager W. F. Gordon will return from New York the latter part of this week.

Ed. C. Mix, manager for Associated Exhibitors in this city, has returned from the Idaho branch.

James R. Keitz, who has charge of the local Greater Features exchange, reports upon his return from the coal camps of Southern Utah, that business is good, as usual.

Samuel Henley, who manages the Universal exchange here, just returned from Idaho. Henley has closed with all of the Universal products at the Egyptian Theatre of Ogden, Utah, including "The Phantom of the Opera," which production he has also sold to the American Theatre here for a showing in October.

Milton Cohn and Joe McElhenney, selling out of the local Universal exchange, are still making their respective territories in Idaho and Southern Utah.

A trade showing of "The Keeper of the Bees," Mrs. Gene Stratton Porter's latest picture, has been arranged by L. A. Davis, manager for the F. B. O. branch here. This pre-view will be held the latter part fo this week for all of the Salt Lake exhibitors.

All of the F. B. O. salesmen will be in the city next week for a sales conference with manager Davis.

George Mayne, owner of the Preferred Pictures and Super-Feature Independent exchange here has returned from his trip through Idaho where he introduced his new pictures.

The new manager of the local Fox branch, H. Bradley Fish, has left for a trip through the Idaho territory.

Carl Stearn, manager of the United Artists exchange in this city, is still in Montana, where he has lined up the key cities for United Artists fall product. He is expected to return within a few days.

A new salesman has been added to the United Artists' sales force, in the person of J. C. Dowd, who has been assigned the Utah and Idaho territory, and according to reports his first trip has been very successful.

C. F. Parr, who has charge of the local Producers Distributing Corporation exchange, has just returned from an extended trip through Montana, which proved to be very successful, as he sold every key point in this territory.

L. W. Weir, Western Division Manager for the Producers Distributing Corporation, passed through here this week enroute to New York.

Dave Schayer, selling out of the local Producers Distributing Corporation exchange, is just completing an extensive tour through the Idaho territory, and is due in the office here the latter part of the week. C. C. McDermond, Southern Utah salesman is completing a successful trip in his territory, and is also returning the latter part of this week, to the local office, where a sales conference will be held with manager Parr.

Mitts Lillian Hansen has just returned to the Producers Distributing Corporation exchange from a vacation spent in the scenic section of Southern Utah.

Exhibitors visiting Exchange Place this week are: F. M. White, operating the Real Art Theatre, American Fork, Utah; Gordon Thornberg and wife, operating the Blue Bird Theatre at Garfield, Utah; Ben Wensler, owner of the Liberty Theatre, Tremonton, Utah; George Lindsey, owner of the Star Theatre, Eureka, Utah, and John H. Miller, operating the Ideal Theatre, Heber, Utah.

Cincinnati

W. H. KAISER, of the Kaiser Film Co., returned from a trip in the East where he negotiated for some new additions to his already large interests.

Harry Bugie of Dwyer Bros. Supply Co. returned from a trip in the field and announces that many exhibitors are re-equipping their theatres with modern appliances.

Miss Alice Morgan of the Strand Theatre interests of Huntington, W. Va., spent several days in the city visiting with the many exchange managers and looking over the product for the season.

Dol Holland of the Darmar Theatre, Portsmouth, O., was seen around film row last week. He has just recovered from an operation and looks much improved in health.

Don Baker of the Perkins Campbell Co., neighbors to the Broadway Film Bldg., is making several radio sets of high power to be used by the Cincinnati Theatre equipment. J. Gelman however, is of the opinion that the sets will never be finished for the simple reason that he paid for the parts in advance and he is very suspicious. Not that Don needs the money, for he has purchased the parts, but it has been too blame hot to work on a radio set up till now and pretty soon it will be too cold to work on anything.

M. D. Devere of the Palace Theatre, Sabina, O., spent several days in the city last week.

John Gregory of the Liberty and Colonial Theatres, Springfield, O., paid his monthly visit to film row.

Much news could be gathered at the F. B. O. offices from Ralph Kinsler, the genial office manager, were it not for the weekly sales meetings held and presided over by Ed. Booth the hustling manager of the local exchange. Anything to better your sales, Ed., say we.

Gus Schifos of the Strand Theatre, Middletown, O., is ill in a local hospital.

Clarence Bell and John Haggerty are checking for Paramount on "The Ten Commandments."

Chas. Regan, district manager for Famous Players, with offices in Cincinnati, returned the other day from Chicago where he attended a convention of district managers of his firm.

Dick Roche has resigned as salesman for Paramount. His immediate connections have not been announced as yet, but will be at an early date.

The Hollywood Theatre in Portsmouth, O., opened to the public last week under the management of Miss Julia Law. The opening was an auspicious occasion for Miss Law and the city on the river with the following theatre and exchange men in attendance: Nat Lefkowitz, manager for Standard; J. M. Johnston, manager for Educational; Nick Shafer, manager for Producers; the Myer Brothers, leading exhibitors of Chillicothe, O.; Gus Sun, well-known theatrical man from Springfield, O., Al Sugarman, short subjects manager for Universal and Chas. Lowenburg, Universal exploiter.

On Wednesday, September 9th, the Gem Theatre, Newark, Ohio, under the management of Shell & Gallagher, will open as a strict Universal house. The theatre has been entirely decorated and a new twenty thousand dollar organ has been installed. Attendance at the opening will be strictly by invitation.

An extra Universal trade showing will be held at the Grand Theatre, Ironton, O., on September 16th. L. G. Frecka is manager of the house. Chas. Lowenburg, Universal exploiter, is making all the arrangements.

L. B. Wilson, manager of the Liberty Theatre, Covington, Ky., has secured the Tom Mix pictures for release in his house. He is of the opinion that they will do big business for him.

Atlanta

CHARLES E. KESSNICH, district manager for Metro-Goldwyn, left last week for Dallas, where he will participate in the welcome arranged for the arrival of Metro-Goldwyn's "Trackless Train" in that city.

Dixie Graham, traveling Georgia for Prod. Dist. Corp., came in off the road for the week end and left town again Tuesday morning, having come in principally to meet Mr. Little, the new manager of this office.

Frank Sheppard, Georgia and South Carolina salesman for F. B. O., has been confined to his bed at the Robert Fulton hotel for the past ten days. He does not show signs of much improvement since the first days of his sickness, but it is hoped that he will soon be able to get on his feet again.

W. W. Anderson, manager of the local Pathe exchange, returned this week from his two weeks' vacation, looking "fit as a fiddle" and reporting that he feels much benefited by his rest.

Earle E. Griggs, exploiteer for Universal, was ill with a slight attack of influenza last week and confined to his bed for several days. He has fully recovered, however, and is busy attending to his many duties in the territory again.

H. L. Forman, F. B. O. auditor, was in town for a few days last week and left town Saturday for Cincinnati, where he will spend his two weeks' vacation.

L. C. Lowe, Alabama and Tennessee salesman for Prod. Dist. Corp., came in last Saturday for the week-end and left again Tuesday morning for his territory.

F. L. Davie, manager of the F. B. O. Atlanta exchange, returned to the city last Saturday after completing a very successful trip through their Tennessee territory.

Miss Izolla Dodd, popular switchboard operator at the Paramount exchange, has been promoted this week to the position of ledger clerk in the office. Miss Hannah Echols, formerly of the Inspection department, will take Miss Dodd's place the switchboard.

Jack Cook, Florida representative for Producers Distributing Corporation, came in town Saturday and left again Tuesday morning to take up his work again.

Harry G. Ballance, district manager for Famous Players, left Tuesday for New York, where he will accompany executives of the home office to the meeting of the district managers in Chicago.

C. D. Haug, Metro-Goldwyn-Mayer exploiteer, has been busy for the past week throughout the territory arranging with many newspapers for the serialization of "The Unholy Three," which is one of Metro-Goldwyn's big feature pictures.

S. A. Castellow, recently resigned accountant of the Paramount exchange here, has taken over the management of the Strand theatre in Winder, Ga., and has the best wishes of his former office associates for his success in this enterprise.

W. M. Minder, salesman for F. B. O., had recovered sufficiently from his operation for appendicitis that he was able to leave this week to take up again his work in his territory, which is Alabama and Tennessee.

A tribute was paid Louis Rosenbaum in particular, and the Muscle Shoals Theatres, Inc., an organization of which Tony Sudekum, of Nashville, head of the Crescent Amusement company also, is president; Harry Sudekum, secretary and treasurer, and Mr. Rosenbaum general manager, by the Florence Times in their big 1925 Muscle Shoals Opportunity Edition which came out last Sunday. The Muscle Shoals Theatres, Inc., owns the Princess Theatre, Florence, Alabama, and leases the Majestic, in Florence, the Strand at Tuscumbia, and the Palace in Sheffield, Alabama. The four theatres are under the management of Mr. Rosenbaum.

L. S. Drum, who has filled Dixie Graham's place as booker in the local Producers Distributing company office since July 20, has gotten away to a good start in his new position as salesman by winning this week first prize in the bookers' contest conducted by the home office. The prize is $50 in cash, and a large and beautiful pennant in red and gold, bearing the words "Champion Booker of the United States, Producers Distributing Corporation" and at the bottom "Energy-System-Perseverance."

When the Grand Riviera theatre, Detroit's newest and most beautiful motion picture and vaudeville playhouse opened last week, it listed among its outstanding features for the first week's program the presentation of George Lee Hamrick, celebrated organist, playing the $40,000 organ installed in the house.

Jan Rubini, nationally known violinist, made his bow this week

to Atlanta audiences at the Howard theatre, where he has become a permanent part of that theatre's musical entertainment.

Rufus Davis, one of the most popular men in Southern film circles, who has been the North Carolina representative for Liberty Film Distributing corporation up until the present time, is to assume on the 15th of September the management of an exchange in Charlotte, the newly created North and South Carolina office of Liberty Film Distributing corporation. Formal announcement of the addition of this exchange in their chain was made by Oscar Oldknow, president, of the company. It will be located at 223 West Fourth Street, where Metro-Goldwyn also have their quarters. The office will be opened on September 15th.

Phelp Sasseen will be star salesman for the new exchange and will represent the company on the road. Miss Bertha Schindelhauer, will be another member to transfer to the Charlotte office, where she will have the position of bookkeeper. It is planned at present that Mr. Davis will select the rest of his office force in Charlotte, no other transfers being reported at this time.

Reynolds Wilbanks and O. L. Freeman, members of the local Paramount exchange, left town Wednesday on a business trip through the southern part of Georgia. They will return to the city shortly.

Mrs. E. C. Dunn has assumed the duties of chief accountant in the Paramount exchange this week.

Charlotte

C. D. Turner, of the Carolina Theatres Incorporated, Asheville, N. C., announces they have taken over the Rivoli Theatre at Lincolnton, N. C., and the Rivoli Theatre at Hickory, N. C. These theatres were formerly managed by Claude Lee. Turner announces they have taken over the Grand Theatre at Newton, N. C., which is being remodeled and put in first class condition.

Claude Lee, who was formerly manager of the Rivoli Theatres at Hickory and Lincolnton, N. C., has disposed of his interests and accepted a position with Universal as manager of one of their theatres in Florida.

F. P. Bryan, manager of First National is attending a sales meeting of his Company in New York.

E. C. Pearce, who formerly owned the Amuzu Theater, of Winston-Salem, N. C. and sold same to A. F. Sames, of that city, is now manager of the Broadway Theatre, Columbia, S. C., for Warner Brothers.

The Carolina Theatre Supply Company has moved to their new

quarters in the new Film Building. J. U. McCormick, owner, stated that he had put in a complete line of equipment and theatre supplies and that he would now be in a position to place on the floor of his exhibition room models of the new Superior Machine of which he has sold a large number in this territory. McCormick states that he was unable to place a machine on the floor previously as the factory could not keep up with his sales as they were behind in their orders.

Nat L. Royster, General Manager in charge of Warner Brothers Theatres in this territory, returned last Friday from a week's visit to the Home Office in New York and reported that everything was moving a top speed in Warner Brothers production schedule. Royster also announces important changes in additions to the management of the Broadway Theatre, in Charlotte, N. C. S. H. B. Stough, formerly manager of the Rialto Theatre, Birmingham, Ala., has been appointed by him

to assistant managership of the Broadway. Plans have been completed for the installation of a fourteen piece orchestra in the Broadway on September 14th. This theatre will on September 14th begin presenting vaudeville sketches and musical numbers, which on and after that date will be a part of the weekly program.

Thomas A. Little, has been appointed manager of the Producers & Distributors Corporation in Atlanta, to succeed Anna H. Sessions. Little entered into his new duties the past week. Little, who was connected with Metro-Goldwyn Exchange in Charlotte for almost five years, was also associated with the Hodkinson Corporation before it became Producers & Distributors Corporation, for a period of about eighteen months. Executives of the Producers & Distributors feel they have secured in Mr. Little a man thoroughly versed in film exchange work.

R. H. Masterman, formerly advertising manager of Famous Players is now traveling North

Carolina for Metro-Goldwyn out of the Charlotte office.

Ernest Neiman, District representative, for Producers & Distributors, has left the past week for Atlanta and will make a trip covering all the exchanges in the Southeast.

N. Miras is building a new theatre in Greensboro, N. C., which will seat about 800. This house will be a colored theatre.

E. F. Dardine, Manager of the Universal Exchange, Charlotte, N. C. has just returned from a two weeks vacation.

The New Charlotte theatre will open it's doors to the public on Labor Day. This was formerly the old Ideal Theatre. This house has been torn out completely and rebuilt and redecorated. They will seat about 500 and we understand they will play large productions second run. This theatre will be managed by Harry Lucas, and it is also one of a chain of theatres owned by the Sunset Amusement Company controlled by Arthur Lucas.

Cleveland

NORMAN MORAY, late manager of the local First National Exchange, now a bona fide Florida real estate broker, was in town for just one day last week. "Nothing like it," says Moray. "After you get the first million, everything's clear sailing." Both Moray and Nat Baruch, also a former local exchange manager now located in Florida, have taken to commuting between Miami and Cleveland.

J. E. Beck, for the past nine years connected with the local Vitagraph exchange, first as assistant manager, and then as manager, is now with the Cleveland office of Producers Distributing Corporation. He's visiting the exhibitors in the Youngstown territory in person.

G. C. Johnson, who used to be the local Producers Distributing Corporation's sales force, is now with Fox Film in Cincinnati.

Robert Cotton, P. D. C., division manager for District No. 4 held a central sales meeting last Saturday at the Statler Hotel, where he passed on to the exchange managers of his territory, the sales policies of the company as expounded at the recent division managers' convention in New York. Among those present were: George W. Erdman, Cleveland exchange manager; Frank Stuart, Detroit manager; G. R. Ainsworth, Pittsburgh manager; N. G. Shafer, Cincinnati manager; Dudley Williston, Indianapolis manager; Chester Loewe, district representative; Carroll S. Trowbridge, Christy representative; and H. O. Duke, assistant secretary of the corporation.

Ike Lipston, southern Ohio motion picture magnate, has purchased all of W. N. Skirboll's Gold Seal productions for showing in his Cincinnati and Dayton houses.

George Moore, theatre owner of Bucyrus and Bellevue is very ill in a hospital at Bellevue. He had a sudden attack of appendicitis. Before he could be operated upon, the appendix burst. His many friends in Cleveland are anxiously awaiting word of his condition.

Max Marcus, proprietor of the

U. S. Theatre has sent out announcements to his many patrons, of the formal opening of his house on Labor Day for the season. True, the U. S. has never been closed. The "opening" means simply the beginning of the new season's pictures. He sent out 2,000 notices on Sunday, the day before the opening, and another 2,000 on Monday, the day of the opening. The U. S. is the only picture theatre in Cleveland that operates all the year through without a break and without any tears. All seasons are good. All weather is good. The 1,400 seats in the U. S. are always filled, regardless of the thermometer, be it too high or too low. And the reason for this is Price. Marcus charges five and ten cents admission. Never more. And his motto is "WHY PAY MORE?" He gives his patrons a daily change, each program consisting of a feature, a comedy, a news and a novelty. Also there is a symphony orchestra. The U. S. theatre is located in a district of toilers. They need entertainment. Max Marcus gives to them, good entertainment, at a price that makes it available for the whole family. So the ten cent pieces mount up until Marcus is rated one of the most successful exhibitors in the territory.

E. Mandlebaum has issued invitations to a pre-release showing of "The Iron Horse" at his Temple theatre, Toledo, for Friday night. The picture opens its Toledo engagement at the Temple the following Saturday. City officials, railroad officials and friends received invitations to the party. This is the first opening of the Temple since Mandelbaum remodelled the house.

The Film Bldg. register was much in use last week. The following out-of-town exhibitors were signed; Paul Muelle, manager of the Palace theatre, Ashtabula; Arthur Dunlevy, Strand, Akron; J. S. Beidler, Eastwood, Royal and East Auditorium, Toledo; Charles Menches, Liberty, Akron. And Charles Barbian of Akron was here. Barbian is interesting in the new Keith building in Akron, which will play a combination vaudeville and picture

policy, so it is understood.

The Standard Film Service Company of Cleveland has issued invitations to a midnight screening on Friday, September 11, of two of their pictures of the season, namely, "Souls for Sables," and "The Girl who wouldn't Work." Harry Charnas, president of the Standard Film Service Company, has purchased in excess of 200 pictures for release in Ohio, Michigan, West Virginia and western Pennsylvania, the largest number of pictures to be released by any independent exchange in the country. Charnas states that he has over a hundred pictures now in his exchange, all finished and ready for release. The private screening is the first of a series by which Charnas will introduce the type of product to be released through his exchanges.

One hundred theatres in this territory were playing Paramount pictures during Paramount week. Paramount pictures were being advertised everywhere — on bill boards, in store windows, with stunts, through the newspapers, and with co-operative merchants ads. All of which helped both the exhibitor and Paramount week.

The Capitol theatre, Steubenville, opened Monday September 7th, with the Warner feature, "The Wife Who Wasn't Wanted." The Capitol is a very beautiful new house erected by the Tri-State Amusement company of Steubenville. J. K. Papulias is president of the Tri-State Amusement Company. A. G. Constant is general manager. The new theatre is said to be the finest of its kind in the country, equipped to the last detail. The second floor is to be used as a dance hall.

The Ambassador is Cleveland's newest motion picture theatre. It opened on Saturday night for the first time. Messrs. Lustig, Stotter and Berkowitz, who also built and own the Ritz and other local houses, built the Ambassador, which is located on Superior Ave., and East 124th St. Oscar Stotter is manager.

The local Metro-Goldwyn exchange has come up in the world from the fifth floor to the eighth in the Film Exchange Bldg. They

can go no higher. More space and better service facilities caused the move.

Jack Flannigan, Pathe news service man out here, had some bad luck in his efforts to get pictures of the wrecked Shenandoah. As soon as news of the disaster reached Cleveland, Flannigan hopped on a plane headed straight for Ava, where the disaster occurred. He had gone only a short distance when his plane refused to travel further. He had to make the rest of the trip by train. And when he reached Ava, it was too dark to get any pictures. Nevertheless, Flannigan was the first one on the scene in the morning, took the pictures, and sent them to New York by plane, where they were printed and delivered again in Cleveland on Saturday, ready for the screen.

Samuel Bradley, who formerly had a film laboratory in Cleveland, has now organized the Bradley Players. He has offices in the Hippodrome Bldg. Bradley is training aspirants to the stage. He has already placed several of his pupils in prominent New York Productions.

Charles Miller of the F. B. O. exchange in Chicago spent a few days in Cleveland last week visiting his brother D. C. Miller, who is a son-in-law of Max Marcus of the U. S. theatre.

Garrett Graham, advance manager for "Doc" Holah and his "See America First" Universal train, has left the Cleveland territory and is now on his way west with stops at St. Louis, Kansas City and then on out to the coast. Holah is due in Cleveland about Wednesday. He has been held up on the roads by heavy rains.

Gabriel Hess, general attorney for the Film Boards of Trade was in Cleveland last week to try to effect peace between the exchange and exhibitor factions of the Board of Arbitration. The board has not been operating smoothly for some time. It is understood that Hess' visit bore no satisfactory results, and that C. C. Pettijohn will be here early in the week to see what he can do to iron out the existing difficulties.

Omaha

VERA MAY GOODSELL, Strand theatre organist, who has been ill in the hospital for several weeks, is well on the way to recovery.

By special request, "The Black Cyclone" is again being shown at the Muse theatre. It appeared first at the Sun theatre which like the Muse is operated by the World Realty company.

After a frantic search by their

mother and the police, two little lost girls, Jean and Violet Lipp, 8 and 10 years old, were found sound asleep in the Moon theatre at 2:30 a. m. The theatre had been closed several hours.

Manager Sutphen of the Brandeis theatre welcomed kiddies of Omaha to a four o'clock special movie show featuring Buster Brown and Tige September 4. Newsboys of the Omaha Bee

were guests of Manager Art Cunningham of the Strand theatre September 2, at a performance of "Don Q."

When temperatures soar in Omaha, Manager Harry Watts of the Rialto, delights in demonstrating his cooling plant. He has a big thermometer just outside the theatre door and another just inside and Harry can be seen making frequent trips between

the two. The other day when it registered 108 outdoors the inside mark was 72.

A special showing of "The Gold Rush" was given at the Strand theatre last week before members of the motion picture industry and newspaper critics. "The Iron Horse" will be shown at the Sun theatre Saturday, September 12, according to Harry Goldberg, manager of the World Realty theatres.

Albany

C. H. BUCKLEY, who first entered the ranks of exhibitors just three years ago, observed his third anniversary in the theatre business last week and announced that three years hence would find him the owner of more theatres than at present. He is now running the Leland and Clinton Square theatres in Albany and the Empire in Glens Falls. J. F. Gilmore is the new organist at the Leland, starting his duties on Labor day. Mr. Gilmore was at one time organist at the Avon in Utica, as well as the Empire in Syracuse.

Jacob Golden, of the Griswold, in Troy, established a new house record an amateur night last week, when he gave eight acts of vaudeville along with double features. The house was packed by seven o'clock. Mr. Golden is also using a Miss Brewer, of Albany, a soloist at the WGY broadcasting station, in illustrated songs.

The Pastime theatre in Granville, which was recently taken over by new parties, and after being renovated, was opened to the public last week. Despite the fact that Granville is but a small village, over 1,000 persons attended the opening presentation.

The fact that Governor Alfred E. Smith and C. H. Buckley, the latter operating the Empire theatre in Glens Falls, are firm friends is entirely responsible for the fact that Mr. Buckley has offered the use of the Empire on September 24, when Governor's day will be observed in Glens Falls.

Clarence Fish, of the American in Schenectady, has once more settled down to the ordinary run of an exhibitor's existence, the Saratoga track having closed. Mr. Fish is presenting some high class pictures at the American this fall.

Lew Fischer was unable to secure a delivery of the new seats for the Bradley theatre in Fort Edward in time to permit him to open the house as he had hoped on Labor Day. The house has been closed for the past month or so, during which time it has been improved in many ways. A complete new installation has been made in the electric light system throughout the entire theatre.

The Woodlawn, in Schenectady, a residential house, appears to be taking more than ordinary interest in the political scrap now on in that city. The entryway of the theatre was plastered last week with placards in the interest of John G. Myers, one of the candidates for the nomination for Mayor at the coming primaries.

The Palace in Oneonta, is now serving on Sunday as a church for the Methodists of that city, with a morning and an evening service. On the other six days of the week, the theatre is showing pictures. In explanation, it appears that a new Methodist church is being constructed and after looking over the city, members of the congregation decided to lease the theatre as a place of worship.

Bess Meredyth, Warner Bros.' staff scenario writer who wrote the script for John Barrymore's "The Sea Beast" and who will prepare the script for "Don Juan."

There is no use talking, William Smalley is a great advertiser. Entering Cooperstown a week ago, one's eye was naturally caught by the whole front of Mr. Smalley's theatre in that place, advertising the attraction of the day and in a way that could not be overlooked even by a blind man. Mr. Smalley is also using Ford cars in carrying his message of current attractions over the highways in that part of New York state.

The State theatre in Schenectady smells of paint these days as workmen are engaged in going over various sections of the house. The work continues throughout the afternoons. A painter will now be retained throughout the year, and will be employed on other of the Farley houses as soon as the State theatre job has been finished.

L. B. Tefft, of Berlin, N. Y., was a caller along Film Row during the week. Mr. Tefft has a 250 seat house in the small village, but is using big pictures whenever opportunity presents itself. He recently ran "The Hunchback of Notre Dame" two nights to the capacity of the theatre.

Miss Wilhelmina Wenzel, cashier at the Pathe exchange, and Miss Rea M. Carmody, sales control clerk at the same office, are once more back at their duties following a two week's vacation. George Doolittle is also once more back in the Pathe shipping room. Leon Medem, local manager for Pathe, and Charles Boyd manager for Associated Exhibitors, spent the weekend in New York city.

Amateur acts are simply overwhelming Morris Silverman at the Pearl theatre in Schenectady. No less than 13 acts applied to Mr. Silverman last week, and he used six. Exhibitors who are now running an amateur night each week are cooperating with each other and making it less hard to secure the right sort of acts to run along with their pictures.

Ben Apple, who for years was one of Troy's best known exhibitors, and who recently disposed of the King theatre, left last week for Florida, and may remain there throughout the winter. Charles Walder, who resigned as local manager for Fox, to go to Florida, must have journeyed over to Havana a week or so ago, as postals have been received here from him, bearing the Havana postmark.

Jake Rosenthal, of the Rose in Troy, allowed all children in that city to attend his matinees last week for five cents admission. He did this in appreciation of the business which has come to his theatre during the vacation when the boys and girls of that city, threw many dollars away on Mr. Rosenthal.

Everybody who is anybody along Film Row, as well as in the ranks of exhibitors in central New York, is planning to attend the outing of the Albany Film Board at Saratoga Lake, on Monday, September 14. Those who do not own cars will be provided with transportation by notifying any of the exchange managers. The exchanges will be closed the entire day in order that everyone may attend the blowout.

F. C. Adams, who has theatres in Copake and Dover Falls, was along the Row last week and gave an interesting account of conditions as they exist in Dover Plains, a place of 600 inhabitants. There are three motion picture theatres in the village, each running a couple of nights a week, although only one will probably operate throughout the winter. The village is without a newspaper and the exhibitors are forced to depend on bill boards and heralds to advertise their attractions.

Herman Vineberg, who has been handling the Mark Strand in Albany in a way beyond criticism and who was recently promoted to the management of two houses, took over the Albany and Regent theatres on Labor Day, and plans to bring these houses to as high a standard of entertainment, as the Mark Strand.

Handsome invitations were received in this city during the past week for the reopening of the Liberty theatre in Herkimer, which is now one of the Schine houses. The house was formerly handled by Charles Moyer, and ranks as one of the handsomest motion picture theatres in the entire Mohawk Valley.

Amos Leonard, of the Pathe sales force, covering northern New York, is enjoying a two weeks vacation at his camp near Boonville. He expects to have as his guest for a short time, Charles Stombaugh, of New York city, former manager of the Pathe office here. R. S. Coyle, inspectorbooker for Pathe, has been in Albany for the past week.

Maurice Chase, who was district manager for Universal some time ago, and who is now head of the Chase Pictures Corporation of Buffalo, paid a visit to Albany last week, and received a warm welcome along Film Row.

On account of the vast amount of work ahead of him, through the reopening of the American in Troy; the acquisition of two additional theatres in Albany and the construction of another house in the same city, Uly S. Hill, managing-director of the Strand group of theatres here, has decided that he can not spare the time to go to Buffalo for the coming conference between the Albany and Buffalo committees on new by-laws governing the two zones. No date has yet been fixed for the conference.

Employees of the Pathe exchange continue to hold frequent screenings which are also social affairs for the office, the last occurring Tuesday night when "The Coast of Folly" was screened, followed by a dance.

Fred Mausert is having some little delay in securing the seats for the theatre which he is building in Glens Falls these days by transforming the old Presbyterian church of that city into a first class motion picture house. Mr. Mausert has decided to name the house "The State." It will have a seating capacity of 1,200 and the paneled walls will be in a lavender and blue color design.

William Shirley, of Schenectady, has returned to his real estate interests in Florida, and will probably not return north for some little time to come. Meyer Freedman is still in Schenectady. When someone asked James Roach, manager of the Farley houses in Schenectady, last week, if he had yet taken his vacation, he simply replied by saying that during the past two months or so, since he became the active manager of the three theatres, he has had time to make but one trip to Albany's Film Row.

Ernest J. Wolfe, who breeds prize winning Great Danes, as well as running the Bijou theatre in Lowville, had the satisfaction of seeing one of his dogs appear on the screen last week in several scenes in "Miss Manhattan." The news that the dog, which is known to practically the entire village, was in the picture, brought much additional business to the house.

New Orleans

ACCORDING to official announcement received here, J. A. Bertram, manager of the Palace theatre, a first run photoplay house, New Orleans, La., will succeed Earl Steward, who has resigned to engage in real estate business in Miami.

Steward is regarded as one of the most efficient showmen in the country. It was his idea that the Orpheum introduced summer vaudeville combined with motion pictures. Bertram has been equally successful with the Palace, the Junior Orpheum here.

Vic Meyer, one of the most popular treasurers that ever served of the New Orleans public, has been named manager of the Palace to succeed Bertram.

Vincent Guerrano has been named treasurer at the Orpheum.

Minnesota

BEN FERRIS, formerly director of St. Paul publicity for Finkelstein & Ruben, has been promoted to circuit advertising director for all the F. & R. houses. He has moved his headquarters to Minneapolis where he will be in direct contact with the F & R. officers.

E. J. Kelly of the Pioneer Press, St. Paul, will succeed Ferris on the St. Paul publicity job, taking the position corresponding to that of Frank Woolen in Minneapolis..

The Minneapolis publicity office of F & R. has been moved into new and larger quarters as a part of the expansion of the office to take over the most of the fourth floor of the Loeb Arcade.

Minneapolis Universal has a new assistant manager. He is H. J. Quinn. He will assist Phil Dunas, relieving him of numerous onerous duties. The arrangement was authorized by F. W. Frankson of the New York office.

E. T. Gomersall, Minneapolis, manager of Fox Film, is back from another three-day trip to Chicago where he conferred with the Fox general sales manager.

Thomas Gavin, Fox exploitation man for this district, was in Dubuque, Ia., this week.

George W. Johnson, manager of the Metro theatre at Red Wing, Minn., has been scouting around in Minneapolis recently. He reports renewed interest in the pictures attributable to Greater Movie Season.

Thomas A. Burke, Warner Brothers' Minneapolis manager, has been in Fargo for several days.

Twin City picture men have been standing around with their mouths open watching Charles Lee Hyde of the Grand theatre at Pierre, S. D., do his stuff with the Pierre polo team. He conducted himself very creditably in the Twin City tournament much to the delight of his trade associates.

George Bromley who recently took over the State theater at Alexandria paid his first visit to the Twin Cities since the deal the other day. He is said to be planning to take over other theatres in the vicinity.

Carl Sather of Annandale is said to be about to open a new theater at Robbinsdale, Minneapolis most famous suburb. The house will be completed shortly.

Dick Dickinson has released the Opera House at Brimsmade, N. D., to the McCarthy circuit.

The Lyric theater at Little Falls has been reopened by A. J. Hand after a period of darkness.

John Piller of Valley City is plastering his new $75,000 theater there and expects to have the lights on October 1. It is one of the finest theatres in North Dakota, they say, having every modern equipment including ventilation system and a $15,000 pipe organ. It will seat 946 persons.

A second theater is contemplated in Little Falls, Minn. The promoters of the project have not yet revealed their identity but there is said to be no question but that H. R. Smoots who has had things his own way with the Lowell theater in this town of 5,500, will soon have competition.

Mrs. M. E. Brinkman of the Grand theater, Bemidji, did her film shopping in Minneapolis the other day.

Joe King of the State Theater at Zumbrota, Minn., visited Producers' Distributing company offices last week.

Ray Zerbel who has the Delf theaters at Marquette and Escanaba, Mich., spent a few days recently in Minneapolis.

Sam Hess and Rowe, owners of the Metropolitan and Lyric theaters at Watertown, S. D., have been visiting Minneapolis.

Al Anson, manager of the Lyceum theater at Duluth, got into Minneapolis the other day just when the heat was at its hottest and he soon hurried back to the place where they have one month poor sleighing.

Bill Bennett who has been a member of the Metro sales force for five years in Minneapolis has gone over to Producers' Distributing corporation to work for Jack O'Toole. He will continue to handle southern Minnesota.

Fred Hines of Cresco, Ia., visited at Crockett Brown's Lyric theater in Nashwauk recently.

W. J. Rogenbeck has taken over the opera house at Webster, S. D., formerly owned by Harry Nelson.

Mrs. Thomas Kirk of Ortonville, writes that her new theater is nearly done and she is looking for an operator.

Gus Winegreene of Bismarck's Capital theater has been visiting in the Twin Cities.

E. E. Anderson has taken over from H. B. Hazlet the Electric theater of Langdon, N. D. Hazlet bought the house from a receivership and now turns it over to the new man.

J. E. O'Toole Minneapolis manager of Producers' Distributing corporation has been spending a few days in Chicago conferring with Cecil Mayberry and some of the others of his company.

Eph Rosen, F. B. O. manager for Minneapolis, looked over the situation at Fargo in person last week. He is back on the job now.

W. A. Steffes announces that his new theater at Oliver avenue N. and West Broadway, Minneapolis, will be ready for business about October 15. Mr. Steffes was in Chicago two or three days last week.

Finkelstein & Ruben expressed some surprise the other day at the announcement of John E. Mason that the Northern Theater company's new house at Chippewa Falls would be leased to the Twin City organization. J. F. Cubberley, general manager of the F & R. theater chain said it was the first he had heard about the proposal.

Jack Hellman, exploitation man of Minneapolis Paramount office is in charge of Greater Movie Season at Sioux Falls which opened recently with a grand ball.

The Dakota theater, formerly the Hess, has been reopened at Yankton, S. D., with O. C. Johnson manager.

The Casino theater at Milaca, Minn., has been purchased by Dr. F. O. Krejci and Herbert J. Nelson. William H. Swadling is the manager.

The Garrick theater at Hawley, Minn., has been reopened by McCarthy Brothers.

The Welch family is busy in South Dakota theaterdom. Edward is managing the Shamrock at Letcher, while his father, W. H., is the new owner of the Opera House at Doland.

The Opera House at Bisbee, N. D., has been taken over from Charles Gerard by I. K. Lund.

Warren Snakenburg takes the Princess theater at Kiester, Minn.

The Legion theater at Dazey, N. D., will be managed for the American Legion post by Berg and Roth.

A new theater is being built at Onamia, Minn., by Lindquist & Son. It will be the Arrowhead and will seat 275 persons.

Arch Zacheri and William Allen have resigned from Metro-Goldwyn and Famous Players-Lasky staffs respectively.

Reno Wilk who has been managing the Lyric in Duluth for F. & R. has resigned to go to the Majestic at Cedar Rapids, Ia.

The Strand theater at Parker's Prarie, Minn., has been reopened by Henry Arvidson and Everett Nelson.

The Palace theater at Paisade, Minn., has been reopened under new management.

The Opera House at Egan, S. D., has been taken over by Montie Hodge and H. E. Randolph.

Indianapolis

WASHINGTON THEATRE, Richmond, Ind., has re-opened after having been completely remodeled. Exhibitors Supply Co. of Ind., Indianapolis, installed new Simplex Projectors equipped with Peerless Reflecting Arc Lamps at the Washington prior to their opening.

Rex Theatre, 30th and Northwestern Ave., Indianapolis, Ind., opened with a tremendous crowd. The entire equipment, opera chairs, Simplex Projectors, etc., were furnished by Exhibitors Supply Co. of Ind., Indianapolis.

Bob Gunn, President and General Manager of the Exhibitors Supply Co. of Ind., has returned from a month's vacation spent in Minnesota.

Work on the new theatre for Harry P. Vanderschmidt, at Greencastle, Ind., is progressing rapidly. Equipment for the new theatre was installed by the Exhibitors Supply Co. of Ind., Indianapolis.

The owners of the new Grand Theatre at Henderson, Ky., have purchased from the Exhibitors Supply Co. of Ind., Indianapolis, Peerless Reflecting Arc Lamps to use on their Simplex machines.

Harry Kiene, Manager of the Royal and Palms theatres, Indianapolis, has leased the Wild Opera House at Noblesville, Ind., and will remodel. Equipment, including Simplex Projectors equipped with Peerless Reflecting arc lamps has been purchased from the Exhibitors Supply Co. of Ind., Indianapolis.

New England

A REHEARSAL not on the program provided a few minutes of genuine thrills at the Gayety Theatre, Boston, the other night when an automobile left parked by Isaac G. Holmes on the incline of Boylston square, rolled down the incline, crashed through the stage doors and rolled out to the edge of the stage. Only the earliest arrivals among the patrons witnessed the scene, however, the screen was soon replaced and other damage repaired before the show started.

Arrangements have been made by the trustees of the Jewett Repertory Theatre Fund, Inc., in Boston with the Yale University Press Film Service to present the entire series of "Chronicles of America" photoplays to the school children of Greater Boston free, commencing early in November.

The performances will be given Saturday mornings.

Lou Radkin, manager of the Maplewood theatre, Malden, Mass., had the honor of purchasing the first of the new model Willys-Knight cars to reach New England.

Philadelphia

BEGINNING with the second Friday in September, meetings of the Philadelphia Film Board of Trade will be held every Friday. The new arbitration committee appointed by the F. B. T. to serve for four weeks is composed of Jerome Safron, Jay Emanuel and C. S. Goodman. A nominating committee consisting of Ben Amsterdam, of Masterpiece, W. J. Heenan, of First National, and C. S. Goodman, of Electric Theatre Supply Co., has been appointed to suggest names to be voted upon for president, vice-president, secretary and treasurer for the coming year.

Three new salesmen on the local Warner force are Harry Weiner, of Independent, A. Fisher formerly with Metro-Goldwyn, and Tom Mason, who formerly covered the Chicago territory for Warner.

It is announced that Jules E. Mastbaum, president of the Stanley Company of America, who is now in Europe, has secured two options on sites for a 5,000 seat

theatre in Paris, where it is planned to build a motion picture house to be operated along the most improved American lines. Mr. Mastbaum will visit Spain before returning to America the latter part of September, for the purpose of securing additional acts for the Stanley circuit.

San Stiefel, vice-president and treasurer of the De Luxe Film Exchange, is back at his desk after a month's vacation in Maine.

A charter has been granted to the Penn Production Company, Philadelphia, with $25,000 capital, $2,500 paid in, the purpose of the corporation being to buy and least motion picture films.

Several hundred persons attended the basket picnic held August 23rd at Silver Lake Park, N. J. by employees of the Stanley Theatres on East Market St., Phila., under the management of Joe Murphy. It was reported a great success.

The Grant Theatre, 40th & Girard Ave., which has been operating on a part-time schedule, will op-

erate on a fulltime basis after September 7th.

Philadelphia will not be represented at the Atlantic City Beauty Pageant. The "Daily News" announces the disqualification and withdrawal of Miss Annette Jackson, who was selected to be the 1925 "Miss Philadelphia" from Atlantic City Pageant. It was found that Miss Jackson had signed a contract in which she agreed to appear professionally after September 1st, which is in direct violation of the rules of the contest. Miss Jackson was first brought to public notice at the Movie Ball given by the M. P. T. O. of Eastern Penna. last summer on the Garden Pier. She is well known in the motion picture industry and is personally acquainted with many exhibitors and exchangemen.

Miss Anna Gillard, of the Penn Production Exchange was married September 1st to Mr. Albert Bergner.

The Howard Theatre, Front St. & Lehigh Ave., with a seating capacity of 700, will be opened

during the latter part of September.

S. Witman, manager of the local office of Universal, spent his vacation motoring through New York State.

Jack McFadden, assistant manager of the local F. B. O. office, spent a two weeks' vacation at Delaware Water Gap.

Fred F. Sully, associate editor of "The Exhibitor," who is touring Europe, will interview King Alphonso of Spain for "Liberty" magazine. Arrangements have been completed for the interview. Mr. Sully will return to Philadelphia on the "La France."

Morris Wax, proprietor of the Stratfors, Keystone, Bellevue and Royal theatres, who has been spending a two months' vacation in Europe, visiting France, Germany and Czecho-slovakia, returned to America on the Leviathan on September 1st.

The new Littleton theatre, which has been built on the site of the old Tuxedo at 40th & Lancaster Ave., will be opened to the public on September 14th.

Baltimore

THE McHenry Theatre, 1032 Light street, which was taken over several months ago by Walter D. Pacy, president of the Motion Picture Theatre Owners of Maryland, Inc. and proprietor of Pacy's Garden theatre, has had extensive renovations and improvements made on it costing about $10,000, according to Mr. Pacy. The operating room has been entirely remodeled and refitted, he says, at a cost of about $2,500 alone. Other improvements consisted of redecorating and repainting, and fixing the chairs and other furnishings. This playhouse has a seating capacity of 1,000 persons and is located in a residential section of South Baltimore.

A cat, a rat and a mouse, have furnished excitement recently in two large Baltimore theatres. The other night a pet white mouse seemingly came from nowhere and plopped into the lap of a woman

seated in the audience. She immediately became panicky and shrieked, throwing the house into an uproar and a police sergeant captured the disturber of the peace, placed it under arrest, took it to the Central station where it is now keeping the telephone clerk company and answers to the name of "Oswald." The house cat at another playhouse downtown did a star act "in one" when it calmly walked across the stage in the glare of the footlights with a rat in its mouth as the orchestra was playing the overture. The rat was still wriggling and while some women shrieked, some men gave cat calls and others applauded while the majority howled with laughter.

The Garden Theatre, a large downtown playhouse, was the only Baltimore Theatre to show the special section of the International News reel giving the

details of the Shenandoah Disaster, on Friday night, September 4 and Saturday, September 5. H. M. Messiter, of the Whitehurst Combined Theatrical Interests, saw the film in Washington, D. C. immediately phoned Dr. Whitehurst about it booked it, and it was shown that night. The assistant publicity man, well known as a Baltimore newspaper man, was called in in the absence of the regular advertising man on business, and back page ads were flashed for Saturday and a front page story was run in the American Saturday morning with a two column head.

A new theatre is being built at Richwood, W. Va., on the lot formerly occupied by the Star theatre destroyed by fire about three years ago. The Cherry River Amusement Company with which J. C. Holt and others are connected, is backing the project. The playhouse will be completed

by the first of next year it is thought.

From Asheville, N. C., comes word that a theatre building may be erected by Olive Tiford Dargan of that city, as a memorial in honor of her late husband.

The Flag Theatre, 1318 East Fort avenue, has been reopened under the management of J. J. Hartlove, well-known exhibitor and exploitation man of Baltimore. This is a residential playhouse of South Baltimore with a seating capacity of 500 persons. About $2,000 was spent on renovating that theatre.

Dr. J. H. Whitehurst, president of the Whitehurst Combined Theatrical Interests, operating the Century, New, Garden, and Parkway theatres, Baltimore, Md., has returned from a vacation of three weeks to Atlantic City, which he enjoyed very much.

St. Louis

THE American Theatre, Twelfth and Barton streets, St. Louis, Mo., has been purchased by Sam Lewis who also conducts the New Shenandoah Theatre, Broadway and Shenandoah 'avenue. The American was owned by Joseph Wagner, who operates the adjoining airdome. The theatre contains about 700 seats and is said to be a nice money-maker.

During the week Lewis also closed a deal for the purchase of the New Shenandoah theatre building. He has operated the house under lease for some time. It seats about 1400 persons. It is reported that the deal for the two

houses will aggregate $250,000. A large airdome was included.

The St. Louis Amusement Company controlled by Skouras Brothers and Harry Koplar owns some fourteen theatres and several large airdomes in St. Louis.

Maurie Stahl who recently took over the New Delmar Theatre, Delmar boulevard near Kingshighway, St. Louis, has changed the name of the house. He calls it the Embassy Theatre. It was formerly operated by Hector M. E. Pasmezoglu, but was leased by Stahl several weeks ago. About the same time Pasmezoglu leased his Criterion and Congress Theatres

and is dickering on deals involving his Plaza and Yale theatres. He plans to take a trip to Greece after he has disposed of his theatre and other holdings in St. Louis.

Ernest Scherler, 43 years old, of Cleveland, O., was overcome by heat Sunday, August 30, a few minutes after he had entered the Lyric Theatre, 114 North Sixth street, St. Louis.

Paul Haynes and Leslie Mace, salesmen for the local First National office were on the sick list the past week.

The Rialto Theatre, Altamont, Ill., opened September 3 and plans to operate on Thursday and Fri-

day evenings until further notice. G. P. Bates has purchased the Grand Theatre, Salem, Mo., from Lulu Donaldson.

The Barlow Theatre, Barlow, Ky., is closed while undergoing extensive alterations and repairs.

The Eureka, Eureka, Mo., and the Belle High School, Belle, Mo., are closed.

The Crescent Theatre, 118 West 2nd street, Little Rock, Ark., is being required. J. M. Ensor operates the house under lease.

Herbert J. Krause, manager for Paramount, on a trip to Cairo, Ill., closed a contract with I. W. Rodgers for his houses.

Canada

THE labor situation at Montreal, Quebec, had reached a tense situation early in September, following the refusal of Local 56 of the International Alliance of Theatrical Stage Employes to accept a five per cent increase in wages and no annual vacation with pay. The Montreal Theatre Managers Association, made up of members representing His Majesty's, Princess, Imperial, Loew's, Capitol, Palace, Gayety, St. Denis, Orpheum, and many other houses, negotiated with the stage hands and projection machine operators, the spokesman for the theatres being B. M. Garfield, manager of one of the local houses operated by United Amusements, Limited.

Announcement was made by Theatrical Enterprises, Limited, Montreal, that it had cancelled all but one road show for the whole of the coming season because of the demands of organized labor and it was announced that B. E. Lang had been appointed agent for the J. B. Sparrow Amusement Co., Limited, Montreal, the company owning His Majesty's Theatre building for the purpose of renting the house to any who would care to take it over. This practically meant that the Theatrical Enterprises, Limited, which operated the house last year, ceased to exist.

Robert Knevel, assistant manager of the Pantages Theatre, Toronto, has returned from an important trip to Elkhart, Indiana,

where he was quietly married without advance notices to any of his friends in Toronto.

N. L. Nathanson of Toronto, managing director of Famous Players Canadian Corp., operating 100 theatres across Canada, and also an executive officer of Regal Films, Limited, Trans-Canada Bookings, Limited, and other important affiliated companies, has returned home after a three months stay in England and on the Continent for business and pleasure. Mr. Nathanson conferred with leading moving picture producers and theatre men in London, Paris, Berlin and other cities.

The Regent Theatre, Toronto, started on its fourth week with Charlie Chaplin's "The Gold Rush" on Saturday, September 5, this being the first run of the feature for Canada. The Regent, which specializes in outstanding productions for extended engagements, is now under the management of D. C. Brown, formerly manager of the Orpheum Theatre at Fort William, Ontario.

Prior to taking over the management of the Savoy Theatre, Hamilton, Ontario, H. E. Wilton was honored by the staff of the Strand Theatre, Hamilton, of which he had been the manager for the past four years. George Murray, in behalf of the house staff, presented him with a handsome ebony brush set and a bouquet of roses to Mrs. Wilton.

After the ceremony, refreshments were served and dancing enjoyed. B. J. McKilliam is now the manager of the Strand.

Every night is a "special" at the Strand Theatre, Calgary, Alberta, according to the schedule which has been drawn up by Manager Pete Egan. Monday is merely "opening night" for the week's presentations but on Tuesday it is "Aluminum Night" when cooking utensils are distributed among the patrons under an arrangement with a local firm; on Wednesday there is a "Lady's Guest Matinee" when every lady patron can bring another lady free while every Wednesday evening a $15 lady's hat is given away thanks to a tie-up with a local millinery shop. Thursday night is "Pay Night" when every purchaser of a ticket gets a pay envelope in which is enclosed a coin anywhere from one cent to $2.50. Friday night is "Dad's Night" when every father can bring his whole family of kids for the price of one ticket. Saturday has "Community Singing Night" when the audiences are encouraged to participate in both new and old songs with slides and a special song leader.

Jimmie Crang, manager of the Oakwood Theatre, Toronto, one of the largest of suburban houses, gave his employes and their friends a very enjoyable outing to his father's farm, a few miles out from Toronto, on Sunday, August 30. About 100 persons were pres-

ent. A big feature was a baseball game in which the Oakwood Theatre team defeated a rival aggregation by 28 to 1. There were many picnic races and, in the evening, a dance was held with music furnished by the Oakwood Theatre orchestra under Ernie Knaggs.

T. J. McDougall, who was recently appointed manager of the Danforth Theatre, Toronto, a former Allen suburban house, has been compelled to take a vacation in search of health. Jack Laver, of the Bloor Theatre, Toronto, is pinch-hitting for Mr. McDougall until the latter's return.

Charles A. Dentelbeck, director of the technical department of Famous Players Canadian Corp., Toronto, has blossomed forth as a tournament golf player. Mr. Dentelbeck, who has been president of the Toronto Local of the Motion Picture Projection Machine Operators for years and an authority on film projection, is in the running for the club championship of the Century Golf Club at Cedarbrook, near Toronto.

At a recent stage in the second half of the championship series of the Moving Picture Baseball League at Toronto, Ontario, no less than three teams were tied for the first position in the league standing. The trio were Regal Films, Limited; Famous Lasky Film Service and Famous Players Canadian Corp., followed by First National Pictures, Limited.

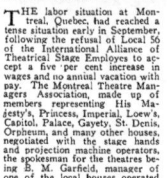

Des Moines

BESS DAY, manager of the Strand Theatre, Des Moines, broke into print and on the front page of the Des Moines Tribune-News with the kind of publicity that does the motion picture business good in more ways than one. Mr. Day was host at a special performance at ten o'clock on Saturday at which the box office receipts were all turned over to the widow of Ollie Thomas of the city police force who was shot dead by burglars caught in the act of entering one of the downtown business houses. The tickets were sold by the members of the police force and the complete sum, amounting close to four hundred dollars was presented to Mrs. Thomas. The house, which seats 1250, was sold out at a twenty-five cent admission price. The film, "A Son of His Father" was given for the performance by Famous Players without charge and all the employees of the Strand donated their services whether members of the union or not. As it is the rule that union members cannot work for nothing they took their pay but made donations of their wages. Zola Palmer and her Kirkwood Serenaders also gave their musical act for the special show. The Strand's special show put the Ollie Thomas trust fund which had reached $1,808.59 well over the two thousand mark.

A. H. Blank, motion picture magnate, and his wife paid a combined income tax of $13,660. Which isn't so bad. There were several other Des Moines men whose individual tax income receipts showed bigger amounts, so Mr. Blank was not listed as the largest payer.

Joe Jacobson, salesman for Pathe, was quite seriously hurt last week when his car took a complete somersault off the road near Independence, Iowa. Mr. Jacobson pulled to the side of the road to avoid hitting a car which was parked without lights and went off on the other side. The car which turned over several times, was completely demolished while Mr. Jacobson was badly bruised. He was at the hospital in Independence for a week and Mr. Ballentyne, manager of the Pathe office, went down to Independence to bring him back to Des Moines as soon as he could travel. Mr. Jacobson is still much the same and for wear but sustained no serious injuries.

F. B. O. entertained 150 exhibitors of Iowa at their Open House during Fair Week. Following out the plan which proved so successful last year Mr. Young sent invitations to all the exhibitors of the state to attend the

State Fair and the F. B. O. Open House at the expense of the Des Moines office. The railroad fare to Des Moines and back was paid by the exchange. A number of exhibitors who had never come to Des Moines to see their pictures took advantage of F. B. O.'s offer and were pleased to meet the men who are furnishing them with film service.

Mr. Jack Nixon who was transferred to Des Moines from the office at New Haven, Conn., is serving Pathe on the sales staff. He takes the place vacated by Mr. Hermann who is now managing the Orpheum Theatre at Clinton for A. H. Blank Enterprises.

C. O. Baker who came to Des Moines from Kansas City to act as booker for Universal has won a very nice promotion. He was transferred to the San Francisco exchange where he will be the assistant manager. Harry Harsha who has been with Universal before as salesman and in the office as assistant manager will fill the post.

Van Dyke and Young of Pella, Iowa, have sold their house there to Chris Nelson. The theatre has been closed for about a month while it was being redecorated. Another change of ownership

took place at Independence, Iowa. Ernie Young, owner of the Grand Theatre at Independence bought from Ralph Farrand. Mr. Young was in Des Moines buying pictures.

A string of theatres were bought by Miles and Coston of Chicago through Clifford R. Niles, exhibitor of Anamosa, Iowa. Mr. Niles sold his house, the Crystal Theatre, at Anamosa to the Chicago consolidation and the theatres at Cascade, Lowden, Mechanicsville, Bryersville, Wyoming and Monticello. The theatre at Monticello was bought from E. T. Landis.

The Exhibitors Supply Company sold the equipment for the booth of the new Waterloo Theatre at Waterloo to A. J. Debolt, manager and owner of the theatres, the Waterloo and the Rialto at Waterloo.

Fred Mendenhall, manager of the Sioux Falls office and his booker, John Fritcher, visited the Des Moines office of Famous Players. Ernie Frase, manager of the Minneapolis office was also again it has been a busy time for the booking staff and Mr. Clement, head booker, has been burning the midnight oil making the wheels go round.

Kansas City

ARTHUR McKAY, state movie house inspector, has returned to his home in Galena, Kans., after an overland motor trip inspecting theatres in this district.

Mr. and Mrs. J. D. Wineland, owner of a theatre at Picher, Ok., have returned from an extended motor trip through the East.

Gov. Paulen's son-in-law, Mr. Ellis, state fire inspector, was in Galena, Kans., recently inspecting the Electric Theatre at that place. He was accompanied by Mr. Johns, county fire inspector, of Cherokee Co. The manager of the Electric Theatre was complimented over the way they found the theatre.

W. W. Holliday returned to Carthage, Mo., Sunday, from Manhattan, Kans, where he has been managing a theatre. He will resume the managership of the Crane theatre, at Carthage.

The Palace Theatre, at Little Rock, Ark., has reopened with W. A. Hodges as manager. A. E. Hanger, has resigned.

The Lyric Theatre, at Perry, Ok., has been purchased by N. B. Hinds, from O. L. Sullivan.

The Princess Theatre, at Sayre, Ok., has been purchased by Mrs. J. H. Taylor.

The Lyric Theatre, at Bartlesville, Ok., has been purchased by the Berryman Bros.

Hugh Gardner, Orpheum Theatre, Neosho, Mo., Ben Levy, Hippodrome Theatre, at Joplin, Mo., and M. J. Aley, and wife of Eureka, Kans., were Kansas City visitors.

Wm. Parsons, manager of the Pershing Theatre, at Joplin, Mo., says that "Sunken Silver" and "Play Ball" series, sure gets the business for him.

Fred and Albert Jackson, will reopen the Jackson theatre, at Pawhuska, Ok., in the near future.

A. C. Stalcup, manager of the Hippodrome Theatre, Okmulgee, Ok., visited in Oklahoma City, this week.

Fred Cantz, manager of the Star Theatre, at Sand Springs, Ok., and Mr. Layman, of the Layman Film Co., were in Oklahoma City, last week. Mr. Layman, is producing two reel comedies, at Sand Springs, and Mr. Cantz, is interested in the company.

A new theatre to be called the "Rialto" will open in October, in Hobart, Ok., under the mangement of Miss Ruth Talbert.

John A. Collins has leased the new $65,000 Majestic Theatre, at Paragould, Ark. Collins has also purchased the house at Wynne, Ark., formerly owned by G. Carey.

The Liberty Theatre, at Fort Sill, Ok., a government-owned house is being repainted and repaired.

The Amusy Theatre, at Frederick, Okla., is building a fifty-foot extension to the building, and adding other improvements, among which a stage for road attractions will also be added.

One of the best run picture houses in the Southwest is being run by John and Pete Sinolpolo, where they are making the Orpheum Theatre, at Oklahoma City, one of the best vaudeville and first run picture house in the Southwest. Nightly they have capacity houses as they show first-class attractions and first-run pictures booked at all times.

Tom Boland, manager of the Empress Theatre, at Oklahoma City, is a go-getter and a winner in all of his undertakings and has never been beaten for anything that he went after. At Oklahoma City, he is being extensively talked of for nomination for mayor of the city at the next election and afterwards as governor of the state.

The Electric Theatre, at Joplin, Mo., is reopened for the fall showing after being closed for redecoration. The opening show was "Night Life of New York."

A new theatre building is being erected at Ponca City, Okla., by Dr. J. A. Douglas, Eugene Wetzel, George Brett, and C. T. Calkins.

The Palace Theatre, at Eufaula, Okla., was destroyed by fire last week, but the owners intend to rebuild in the near future.

Can a down town first run theatre in a city of more than 500,000 population operate successfully with only a pipe organ for music? That question seems to be definitely answered, as far as Kansas City is concerned. About a year ago Universal leased the Liberty theatre from Samuel and David Harding, Kansas City. Up to that time the theatre had maintained an orchestra and done a good business in opposition to the Newman theatre, Kansas City's largest first run house, which has an orchestra of 46. But the orchestra was abandoned at the Liberty. Business continued fair for a while, but there were some "tough weeks." Now the Liberty is to have an orchestra again. Samuel Carver is the manager.

Miss Emma Viets, chairman of the Kansas state censor board, returned last week from a three weeks' trip in which she conferred with motion picture censors of Ohio, Maryland, Virginia, Pennsylvania and New York.

The Studebaker car, carrying the first print of "Seven Days," Christie production, from the West Coast to New York, was worth a liberal news story in Kansas City newspapers Saturday. A. H. Holdson a Pacific Coast driver, and M. H. Newman, stunt performer, were in charge of the trip.

Miss Lois Bridge and Edgar Barnett of the Globe theatre personnel, Kansas City, were $3,850 poorer in jewelry and $7.50 in cash the other night, as a result of being held up by two bandits shortly after they left the theatre.

Joseph Schildkraut and Jack Pickford, screen stars, were visitors in Kansas City last week, the former being a target for humor by the Kansas City Star when he retired at his hotel at 9 o'clock.

The on-rush of fall business made Kansas City's movie row a hub of activity last week. A large gathering of exhibitors attended a pre-view showing of "The Winds of Chance," a print of which was received at the First National exchange, while the personnel of the Universal exchange was elated over the fact that virtually all of the smaller daily newspapers in the Kansas City territory are to carry in serial form "The Phantom of the Opera." C. A. Schultz, Warner-Vitagraph manager, was named as branch manager of the Kansas City P.D.C. office, while Truly B. Wildman, formerly with Enterprise Distributing Corp., has accepted a position as special representative and assistant district manager for P.D.C. in Kansas City. R. L. McLean, assistant to C. D. Hill, P.D.C. district manager, was in temporary charge of the P.D.C. exchange pending the change in management. Bob Withers, Enterprise branch manager, returned from the territory with this assertion: "The best week's business we ever have had." Russell Borg, the energetic assistant branch manager of Educational, left for a two weeks' vacation on the Great Lakes. A record sheet of the Warner-Vitagraph branch for one day last week showed eighty-nine shipments for the day, putting to flight the "bad business" wails. T. O. Byerle, First National branch manager, left behind a busy office to attend a meeting of sales chiefs in New York City. The Midwest Film Distributors, Inc., will move from 130 West Eighteenth Street to new quarters at 1710 Baltimore avenue.

Among the out-of-town exhibitors in the Kansas City market last week were: Hugh Gardner, Orpheum, Neosho, Mo.; and Mrs. M. J. Aley, Regent, Eureka, Kas.; I. W. Maple, Bethany, Kas.; C. L. McVey, Herrington, Kas.; H. McGuire, Darlington, Mo.; Roy Spurlock, St. Joseph, Mo.; L. Brenninger, Topeka, Kas.; William Gabriel and H. Austin, Garden City, Kas.; G. L. Rugg, Robinson, Kas.; C. M. Pattee, Pattee theatre, Lawrence, Kas.; G. L. Germain, Bonner Springs, Kas.; M. M. Myers, Topeka, Kas.; H. Terry, Grain Valley, Mo.

Glenn Dickinson, Lawrence, Kas., exhibitor who operates a circuit of theatres, has obtained Claire Woods, formerly of the shipping department of the Kansas City United Artists branch, to act as publicity manager.

Lawrence Lehman, manager of the Orpheum theatre, Kansas City, "dressed up" the house a bit last week with the installation of two new Motiograph projectors with G. E. high intensity arcs.

A special warning to exhibitors in the Kansas City territory has been issued by the First National exchange, as a result of an incident which occurred last week. Several small green bugs, which are common about any type of electric lights in the summer months, were found caught in a film which had been returned. When the insects were removed the emulsion came off on every part of the film where one had been, ruining the film.

"Well, well, it's finally come," signed C. E. Cook, business manager of the M. P. T. O. Kansas-Missouri, as he walked away from his desk Tuesday night for a two weeks' vacation.

For the last three months Cook has been working "double time" on the Greater Movie Season campaign and careworn lines have found their way on his face. He will visit his relatives in Maryville, Mo., a short time, then go to Colorado.

Samuel E. Morris, general manager of distribution, announced this week the appointment of Louis Reichert as manager of the Warner Bros. branch exchange in Kansas City. Reichert is a veteran salesman and executive. He was at one time assistant general manager of General Films, and later served as special Pacific coast representative of several companies and as branch manager of Select in Washington.

Ralph W. Abbett, manager of Renown's Indianapolis exchange.

Aileen Bernard, musical comedy favorite, who is soon to make her appearance on the screen.

CONSTRUCTION&EQUIPMENT DEPARTMENT

Proper Method for Ventilating Theatres

Special Consideration Necessary for Motion Picture Houses; Installations Prove Excellent Investments

By F. R. Still*

MOST of the owners of theatres and the engineers who design heating and ventilating plans for theatres have largely failed to consider the wide difference in the requirements of a standard theatre and moving picture theatre. There is hardly any more resemblance in their respective requirements than there is in the provisions to be made to ventilate a school house or a church, yet it has been the general practice to apply the same proportions and employ about the same standards of apparatus for both types of theatre buildings.

The Standard Theatre is occupied for perhaps three hours at a time usually after sundown during six days of the week, and is closed throughout the warm summer months. An adequate and dependable heating system is, of course, necessary to maintain a comfortable temperature in cold weather. The usual standards for ventilating auditoriums will apply to such theatres, and will prove to be entirely adequate under normal weather conditions.

In winter weather there is very little moisture in the outside air. As the temperature of the outside air is raised to the room temperature, the relative humidity is lowered; hence the air should be humidified in cold weather so as to maintain 40 to

*Vice President American Blower Co.—paper before the Society of Motion Picture Engineers.

45% relative humidity inside the building. In the late spring and early fall, the outside temperature and humidity sometimes becomes almost as high as during the summer. During these periods it may become uncomfortable inside, but these periods are so short that artificial cooling is hardly warranted.

The Moving Picture Theatre is an altogether different problem. It is occupied, more or less to full capacity, for twelve hours per day, every day in the week including Sundays, and every week throughout the year. The heating and ventilating plant must be designed to meet the requirements of the two extremes of outside weather conditions, viz., winter and summer, both of which extend over several months.

In the winter time, the place must be heated to a comfortable temperature. The air must be clean and pure, devoid of odors and humidified to a comfortable extent.

In the summer time, both the temperature and the relative humidity must be reduced to get satisfactory results. It is impossible to reduce the temperature of the air discharged into the building very much below the normal inside temperature without causing discomfort; hence it becomes necessary to provide for the circulation of a very much larger volume of air in the summer than during the winter to absorb the natural heat radiated from the walls, the roof, the

lights and the people. If this large volume is properly distributed and diffused over the whole area of the house, an excellent air motion can be maintained which has a most marked effect on the comfort of the audience in warm weather, because it feels as though the temperature is much lower than it really is, instead of feeling chilly and clammy as is so noticeable in those theatres wherein an attempt has been made to cool them with a small volume of air circulated air which has been lowered to a very low temperature so as to absorb the heat.

It is not infrequent that the volume of air required to maintain comfortable conditions in a Moving Picture Theatre in the summer time will be two or more times the volume of air that would be normally provided for a Standard Theatre of the same size, yet we see plans and specifications right along wherein this difference is entirely ignored, and no greater provision is made for a movie house than would be made for a Standard Theatre.

There are two reasons for this. One is that few designers understand exactly what sort of atmospheric condition should prevail to attain perfect comfort. The other is, that the majority of the architects and engineers did not appreciate fully the great difference there is in the requirements of a Standard Theatre and a Moving Picture

Where the Paramount school for theatre managers is being conducted; left, the model theatre, equipped with all projection and lighting apparatus; right, the library and reception room.

The Beverly theatre, opened recently by the West Coast Theatres, Inc. The auditorium of this house is of an unusual design following East Indian design.

Theatre. They knew that certain standards as applied to the older type of theatres gave reasonably satisfactory results, and it naturally followed in the course of their everyday operations that the same would apply to moving picture theatres.

It is only within the last two or three years that any reliable data has been available to work with which would indicate what the atmospheric conditions should be inside of a building to attain the same comfort that a person feels on a fine June day in the open country. Apparatus was available to maintain any temperature, any relative humidity and produce any air motion, but the right combination was not known. Not until the American Society of Heating and Ventilating Engineers established a Research Laboratory at the U. S. Bureau of Mines, Pittsburgh, and induced the U. S. Department of Public Health Service to take up the investigation of this subject, was any real progress made. This was started nearly seven years ago. The work is now nearing completion, but the whole scope of the problem required nearly five years of constant experimentation and investigation before any definite results were available.

Some years ago Dr. Leonard Hill of London, England, made an investigation of the wet and dry bulb temperatures all over the world. He took particular note of those atmospheric conditions which seemed to be most comfortable. As a result of his observations he found the prevailing wet bulb temperature was somewhere between 54° and 58° and that the dry bulb temperature

must vary, depending on the wind velocity and the occupation of the subject, to attain perfect comfort.

With this as a starting point the Research Laboratory at Pittsburgh persuaded Dr. Sayers of the Department of Public Health Service, Washington, D. C., to take charge of the experiments, to definitely determine the reactions of human beings to varying wet bulb temperatures, dry bulb temperatures, air velocities, when naked, lightly clothed and normally clothed; when at rest, at light work, and when vigorously exercising.

As the greatest demand for refined ventilation is in those buildings where the occupants are at rest, the work so far completed covers that condition quite fully. One or two examples will illustrate how the data obtained may be applied.

Supposing a person normally clothed is exposed to a dry bulb temperature of 71° and a relative humidity of 30%; the wet bulb will be 54°. Again supposing the dry bulb temperature is 69° and the relative humidity is 76%; the wet bulb temperature will be 55.75°. Either of these temperatures will afford about the same degree of comfort in still air.

In the first instance if, instead of still air, the air velocity should be 100 ft., the effect will be the same as though the apparent dry bulb temperature was only 69°; at 200 ft. velocity the apparent temperature will be 68°; at 300 ft. velocity the apparent temperature will be 66°.

In the second case, if the velocity should be 100 ft. the apparent temperature would be 68°; at 200 feet. velocity the apparent temperature would be 65°; at 300 ft. velocity the apparent temperature would be 63°.

If a person was stripped to the waist, under these air motions he would soon shiver as though it was 10° to 15° colder.

These citations are given merely to indicate the scope of the work being done and to impress upon you that real comfort can not be obtained by merely heating or cooling air. There is a relationship existing between the wet and the dry bulb temperatures which must be maintained in a still atmosphere. As soon as an air motion is set up, the relationship changes and it varies more or less as the air motion increases or decreases.

Another important factor that affects the comfort of many persons is odors. To what extent the effect they have on some people is physiological or psychological has not yet been definitely determined. A strong odor of musk in a warm, unventilated room has been known to cause some women to faint, yet others enjoy it. Some people can live and thrive in the midst of conditions that are to others most abhorrent and, perhaps, nauseating.

Odors can always be completely eliminated by passing the air through a properly proportioned air washer. Adding a heater to warm the spray water, the humidity of the air can be increased and by cooling the water the humidity can be lowered. With

(*Continued on page 1418*)

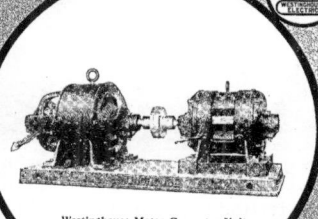

Exterior View of the new West Coast theatre, San Bernardino, Calif., opened recently by West Coast Theatres, Inc.

Proper Method for Ventilating Theatres

(Continued from page 1416)

suitable automatic controlling instruments any desired relative humidity can be obtained that is best suited for the air motion maintained regardless of outside atmospheric weather conditions, in addition to the complete elimination of the odors and the removal of the floating dust and dirt in the air as previously mentioned.

Many owners of theatres fail to realize the value in an air washer. The preservation of the decorations and furnishings will alone make it a good investment in many cities, even if its value as an essential adjunct to the ventilating plant is entirely discounted. But the time is fast approaching when there will be no argument about the necessity of properly humidifying and cooling the air. The theatres that are so equipped will soon become generally known and the public will demand the same comfortable atmospheric condition in all of them by refusing to patronize the houses which have failed to put in such equipment.

While the building and operation of theatres is a business proposition from the standpoint of the owner or manager, it is a place of recreation and pleasure for those who patronize them, and as the patrons begin to realize it is unnecessary to endure uncomfortable atmospheric conditions they are sure to seek out and favor those places where they are comfortable.

Architectural beauty, pleasing and colorful decorations, comfortable roomy seats and good acoustics have all come about because the public has shown it appreciates such things, but none of them would count for much if the place smelled badly, or the atmosphere was close and stuffy, or if it became too warm, or it was drafty and cold.

While there are now quite a number of theatres equipped with ventilating plants of ample capacity to maintain a reasonable, comfortable, thermometric temperature throughout most of the auditorium, we only know of two buildings in which the designer apparently fully recognized the opposite requirements during the cold and warm weather by arranging for a reversal of the air movement during the two periods. That is, the warm air enters the house through the floor, beneath the seats in the winter and finds an exit mostly through the ceiling. In the summer the cool air is admitted through the ceiling and is largely removed through the floor beneath the seats.

Cold air striking a person shortly after it escapes from the ducts always causes great discomfort and complaint. Hence it must be introduced at a considerable distance from the occupants. On the other hand, the warm air coming into immediate contact with the occupants in cold weather is very agreeable provided the velocity of the air is not excessive.

In both of the theatres referred to, this reversal of air currents is accomplished by shifting two or three dampers. Of course the fans are speeded up to get a larger volume in the summer than is required in the winter, and the velocity can be very much greater owing to the air entering at a distance so remote from the audience.

The question uppermost in your mind is likely "What does it cost to install an efficient ventilating plant such as has been herein described?"

That is a very difficult question to answer with any degree of definiteness, because there are so many variables in the construction and location of the buildings, the climatic conditions prevailing in different parts of this country, the size of the building, its exposure and the type of refrigerating plant used.

It may be stated that it requires approximately from 75 to 100 tons of refrigeration per thousand people, and a complete ventilating plant with refrigeration will cost anywhere from $200.00 to $800.00 per ton refrigeration.

In other words, a house seating 3000 people, with a ventilating plant designed to cool it to 70 degrees when it is 95 degrees outside, recirculating 80% of the air would require about 285 tons capacity. This is based on an initial dewpoint of 40 degrees. With the same dewpoint and outside temperature, if the inside temperature is 85 degrees instead of 70 degrees, it will require about 267 tons of refrigeration, or about 6½% less.

With the same outside temperature and a dewpoint of 50°, to maintain 70° inside will require about 284 tons, and to maintain 85° inside will require only 250 tons capacity. Thus there is only 15% difference in the extremes of refrigeration required in these examples, which are fairly representative of conditions encountered in the summer in this section of the country. It also indicates the possibility of obtaining very comfortable temperatures even when it is impossible to reach an anticipated low dewpoint.

Such a plant would cost from $50,000 to $85,000 complete. This includes blowers, motors, heating surface, humidifying equipment, pumps, ducts, automatic controlling instruments, etc., all installed on foundations and adjusted ready for use.

The next question is the testimony of those who have tried it. The lowest estimate we have obtained from any manager is an average increase of 26¼% in the attendance of patrons during the months of June to

(Continued on page 1421)

The Capitol Self-Operating motion picture projector which projects film continuously without rewinding. This machine is designed for the display of short film lengths of coming attractions in the lobby of theatres as well as many other commercial uses. This projector is manufactured by the Capitol Machine Co.

One Thing More

In your modern motion picture house every detail of projection, decoration, ventilation, temperature, seating, has been carefully worked out to make the theatre attractive and comfortable.

But there's one thing more you can do— and it's a real factor from the box office point of view: make sure the picture is printed on Eastman Positive Film, the film that safeguards for the screen the quality of the negative so your public may enjoy it.

Eastman film is identified in the
margin by the black-lettered
words "Eastman" and "Kodak"

EASTMAN KODAK COMPANY
ROCHESTER, N. Y.

Projection
Optics, Electricity, Practical Ideas & advice

Inquiries and Comments

Vision by Contrast and Color Illusion

OME time ago we published an article explaining the general characteristics of vision in which he statement was made that isism was of two principal kinds—that is, by means of color difference or by a difference in brightness.

In a more specific article on the theory of vision, Dr. Hickman of the Royal Photographic Society explains in detail just how this is accomplished and uses it as a prelude in support of his recommendations regarding the proper treatment of contrasts between the lighted motion picture screen and its background.

In continuation of last week's article, he takes up next the subject of *contrast* after having first explained the action of color vision. Contrast vision treats primarily of the colors "black" and "white", which, strictly speaking are not colors at all. While objectively black is merely the absence of light, physiologically and subjectively black is a definite sensation. If we stand in a perfectly dark room we are much more conscious of not being able to see than of actual blackness. The blackness is lit up with a starry mist, a graininess of texture. There is a definite living background of grey-black, against which one is able to picture true blackness. If, now, the dark-adapted eye is turned for a few seconds to a feebly illuminated card, after withdrawal there remains an after image of the card painted in a blackness more intense than the darkness itself. A piece of black velvet held in sunlight appears definitely black, even though it reflects sufficient light to suggest texture in its parts. Wandering along a bright seashore, the illumination being, perhaps, 5000 foot-candles (Dr. Hickman suggests 15,000 meter-candles or approximately 1,500 f. c. but intensities of from 2,000 to 10,000 foot-candles are common in summer in the open) when one comes across a cave, though the very air between you and the cave is reflecting light, the cave, subjectively, suggests a forbidding blackness. As a general fact, then, one can produce the sensation of black by contrast, either temporal or spatial. One can dilute a color, virtually, with black by looking first at a bright object, or by placing it against a bright background.

Flicker Effect

There is one other point we must consider, and that is *flicker*. The Talbot-Plateau law states that when the eye receives a certain number of quickly succeeding impressions the resulting stimulus is the mathematical addition of all the light and dark intervals. It is the quantitative law of the persistence of vision, and on it depends the whole of kinematography. There is a minimum slowness at which impressions can be received to blend without flicker—about 16 per second. It is not generally known that the number is variable and depends on *two factors—color* and *brightness*. (These two points were emphasized in the recent series of articles on flicker presented in this department.) The vanishing-flicker frequency for any color and any screen brightness can be expressed in the form of an equation by means of which it can be calculated for any color of light and any intensity. Increasing the screen illumination 10 *times* means that the picture frequency must be *doubled* to give the same continuity.

Color in Tinted Pictures

We are now in a position to examine the question of picture tinting and projection. Films are generally tinted yellow, blue or blue-green. We have seen that the effect of increasing the brightness of white light is to make it yellower. By yellowing a *dull light we endow it with warmth and apparent brightness*, deluding the eye that the illumination is increased; also we *steepen the contrast*. Blue and blue-green washes

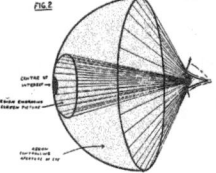

FIG. 2

Figure two.

are used to convey two illusions, *night* and *purity of texture*. Blue is the color associated with the sky, with distance, water, snow and ice. In tinting blue we not only induce the sensations associated with these, but also produce a physiological sense of quietness. In blue light appearance of flicker is reduced by two-thirds, and contrast is so diminished that inequalities due to scratches, dust, or grain pattern become less obvious, and we have an improvement in the quality of projection which suggest placidity and purity.

Where a deep blue is used to depict night the "Purkinje" effect is being utilized. Because neutral tones become bluer on diminishing, artificially bluing the light suggests a dimness to the eye. When first the blue-dyed night scene follows a yellow film the illusion is excellent, but presently the eye becomes adapted to the blue, to which it is more sensitive at these illuminations,

and all sense of dimness is lost, and there remains nothing but the residue of conventional color to convey the feeling of night. Although blue tinting is quite rightly used to suggest darkness, the illusion is only a temporary one—as indeed, to a lesser extent, is the brightness from the yellow-dyed film.

Wrong Contrast

The reason for this is that in the motion picture the simultaneous contrast is all wrong. Only a small portion of the retina is being used, the central detail revealing area. The outside surrounding region, anywhere but in a picture dark, whereas anywhere but in a picture house it would be subject to the same illumination as the yellow spot (See last week's article).

It is the field of view embraced by this outside region (See Fig. 2) which determines the sensitiveness of the eye and the diameter of the pupil. Viewing a bright picture in a darkened room the eye is being persuaded to open too widely and too receptively. This has the effect, firstly, of increasing contrast and apparent brightness, giving the picture a fictitious strength and brilliancy, and secondly, *it induces eye-strain*. A collateral effect is the *destruction of all sense of blackness*. It is impossible to appreciate as black the shadows in scenes which are projected in such a manner that their darkest parts are always more luminous (lighter than the surrounding mask or the picture house itself. It is analogous to viewing a solitary picture in a room "papered" with black velvet. The shadows of the finest etching would lose tone in such surroundings.

This has been the contention of the writer for a long time—that the black bordered screen practically destroys the tonal values in the screen picture and it also explains the illusion of "depth" and contrast obtained by the light bordered screen of which the Martin Illuminated Border is an extreme example.

Recommendations for obtaining the proper harmony between picture and border will be given in next week's article.

(*Continued next week*)

Helios Reflector Arcs on Market Over Two Years

IN THE issue of August 22 on page 972 of this publication a statement was made to the effect that the Helios Reflector Arc, manufactured by the Warren Products Company was not yet placed on the market. This was an error as the Helios Reflector Arc has been on the market now for over two years and numbers of these lamps are in use in all parts of this country.

Proper Method for Ventilating Theatres

(Continued from page 1418)

August inclusive. The maximum report we received was a statement that the house had always lost money during the hot weather; that they afterward advertised daily the outside and inside temperatures and people actually admitted that they came quite as much to get cooled off as they did to see the show. This may not speak very well for the show, but in indicates whether or not it pays to make such an investment.

In Minneapolis and St. Paul there is a basin of very cold water at depths varying from 400 ft. to 800 ft. This water is supposed to come through a stratification leading from Lake Superior.

The Astor Theatre in St. Paul is so located that it gets a severe exposure from the sun and hot winds blowing in from the prairies. The attendance at this house fell off to almost nothing in the summer. A cooling system was installed, using artesian water from the basin mentioned. The house not having been built to admit of a highly efficient plant being installed, maximum results could not be obtained, but the conditions are so improved that the manager claims there is hardly any noticeable difference in the attendance, summer or winter.

The State Theatre in Minneapolis is very well known to all theatre owners in the middle west as being about the first theatre wherein a real effort was made to install an up-to-date cooling plant. Cold water is obtained from the same basin above referred to at a depth of about 800 ft. The tempera-

Photograph of the design of the theatre which Rowland & Clark will build in the East Liberty section of Pittsburgh, Pa.

ture of the water is 49°. The satisfaction obtained from this installation was so marked that many owners, managers, architects and engineers have visited it from all parts of the country. It is our belief that this plant has had a greater influence on the attitude of theatre owners toward cooling plants than anything that had been done up to that time.

Cold water not being obtainable in most places it is necessary to cool it artificially by a refrigerating plant. This adds greatly to the cost. In fact, it becomes the most expensive unit of the entire system.

Many other instances could be cited than the two referred to, but both being pioneers in that line and still giving a good account of themselves, it seems hardly necessary to mention that about fourteen or more other

houses have been since equipped with cooling plants using refrigeration to cool the water.

We hope that out of this discussion you will have been convinced of the coming and certain necessity for cooling theatres that the problem must receive special treatment by somebody who is conversant with proper relative atmospheric conditions and how to obtain them so that the results will be entirely satisfactory; that the cost, though considerable, is not prohibitive, and in fact that it costs less than many other things that go into theatres from which less returns can be measured on the investment.

In closing, we want to suggest that good, substantial, efficient, dependable apparatus is the cheapest in the end.

The Grand Riviera Theatre, Detroit, which has a seating capacity of 3,000.

Propose Modification of the Hartford Building Code

Recommendation that the city's building code be made less stringent as regards motion picture theatre construction will be made to the Common Council of Hartford, Conn., by the City Building Commission. A 20 per cent reduction of all fees for new construction involving more than $1,000 will also be made by Supervisor Mason.

The Hartford code, which in many respects is even more exacting than that of New York City, provides among other requisites that picture theatres have a passage way to the street both from the front and the rear. In New York only one passage is required. The action of the Commission in recommending the changes is the result of appeals from several local men who plan to build a theatre on State St.

Ground Broken for 2000 Seat House at Cambridge, Mass.

Harvard Square, Cambridge, Mass., will soon have a modern motion picture house. Ground will be broken next week at 1434 Massachusetts avenue for the foundations of the University Theatre, which is to have a seating capacity of two thousand. Charles E. Hatfield, county treasurer of Middlesex county and former mayor of Newton, Mass. is president and treasurer of the University Theatre, Inc., which will own the house. The main auditorium will be located in the rear of the present College House and will have an entrance through the College House. Land in the rear has been purchased by the company while a long lease has been taken for the entrance site.

Marr & Colton Organ for California Theatre

The Marr & Colton Company of Warsaw, N. Y., was recently awarded the contract for the New Tempest Theatre at Los Angeles, California. This theatre is going to be opened late in the year.

The Marr & Colton organ will be one of the feature attractions, played by a prominent organist.

C. W. Hodgdon Reopening Princess Theatre, Wakefield

Charles W. Hodgdon is reopening the Princess theatre in Wakefield, Mass. after making extensive improvements in the house. On Saturdays and holidays three acts of B. F. Keith vaudeville will be added to the regular picture program. The house is reseated with air cushion seats, new stage and border lights have been installed, a new property house has been erected adjoining the rear of the stage and a spacious parking space for autos has been acquired and is being paved for patrons. I. M. Berg continues as house manager of the Princess and Wakefield theatres.

Plans Filed for New Buffalo Theatre

Plans for the new motion picture theatre to be built at 1588-1598 Genesee street, including seven stores and offices, have been filed with the bureau of buildings in Buffalo. The new house will be built by Barney Vohwinkel, 2886 Main street, who has operated the Oriole theatre near the site for many years. When completed the house will be leased by the Shea Amusement company. According to Mr. Vohwinkel the theatre and stores will cost $350,000. The seating capacity will be 1710. The frontage on Genesee street will be 168 feet. The house will have a depth of 132 feet.

New Theatre Planned for Malden, Mass.

Ramsdell Brothers of the Malden Orpheum Theatre of Malden, Mass., have commenced the construction of a second theatre to be known as the Middlesex Theatre, on Dartmouth and Pleasant streets, Malden. Associated with the Ramsdell Brothers in the new enterprise is Fred Green, who conducts the Mystic Theatre in Malden. It is the plan at present to use the new playhouse for vaudeville and moving picture purposes and to use the existing playhouses in Malden in which they are interested exclusively for motion pictures.

Plan Addition for New States Theatre, East Grand Forks

McDonald Bros., owners of the New States Theatre in East Grand Forks, Minn., are spending $15,000 on an addition to their present theatre building which will be used as a dance hall. When complete, it will be one of the largest dance halls in the Northwest and will be well patronized by the number of students attending college in Grand Forks, North Dakota, just across the river.

Plans Prepared for Theatre at Waterbury, Conn.

Waterbury, Conn., is to have a new theatre. Alfonso E. Sirica has had plans prepared by Architect Joseph DeLauretis for a brick and steel structure at 101 Sherry street, the main auditorium of which will be 45 by 108 feet with spacious lobby.

Newspaper Opinions on New Pictures

"Black Cyclone"—Pathe, Eastman, Rochester

Herald: "If anyone should come away from the Eastman Theatre this week and feel that he hasn't gotten his money's worth of entertainment there must be something wrong with his digestion. On the screen bill the feature is provided by Rex, the wild horse, in 'Black Cyclone,' a combination of equine and human romance. 'Black Cyclone' is something different in the way of screen entertainment. Its principal character is Rex, a black horse, who shows a degree of understanding which almost passes belief."

Democrat and Chronicle: "Supplanting human beings as stars, the sleek black horse, supported by his companions, Lady and The Killer, thrilled Eastman Theatre audience with the opening performances of this week's program, 'Black Cyclone.'"

"Merry Widow"—M-G-M., Embassy, New York

Mirror: "The most notable event of the current cinema year occurred last night at the new Embassy Theatre, when social and celluloid lights turned out en masse to view the premiere of Erich von Stroheim's 'The Merry Widow.' 'The Merry Widow' is a gem. This production unfolds with beautiful precision, artful subtlety and magnificent sets. Mae Murray and Jack Gilbert cover themselves with glory as hero and heroine of this rich romance."

Herald-Tribune: "Erich von Stroheim's pictures are peerless pictures. Perhaps another director could have made as interesting and alluring a version of 'The Merry Widow' as the one Miss Gould presented last night, but we doubt it. It seems to be the first musical play that has been transferred to the screen successfully. If one touched on all the fine points of 'The Merry Widow' one would write columns about it."

American: "What a picture! There are touches that are so original and so brilliant we feel an impatience that von Stroheim has wasted his time without giving us more of this type of entertainment. Miss Murray is enchanting. She is not only beautiful but she gives a fine, sincere performance that is not to be named in the same breath with her other film work. The whole thing is done with a deftness that commands our admiration."

World: "I don't think that I have ever seen more delightful photographic effects than last night in the Embassy. They have spared no time nor expense, it would seem, in constructing realistic settings into which to cast this grand old music play. No young man in the films today would have stood up so bravely and so snappily and so romantically as did John Gilbert to the part of the soldier Prince. And who could have been expected to dance into the camera as Miss Murray would dance!"

Telegraph: "The first night audience applauded to the echo. When the orchestra glided into the 'Merry Widow Waltz' the enthusiasm reached its height; and there was no doubt that 'The Merry Widow' as conceived by Metro-Goldwyn-Mayer, has found a home on Broadway as long as it cares to stay. Directed by Erich von Stroheim, starring Mae Murray and Jack Gilbert, it is a predestined success."

Times: "The picture is one of strong passion. The Widow is, of course, impersonated by Mae Murray, who demonstrates true acting ability in this effort. Both Mr. Gilbert and Roy D'Arcy as the two Princes, acquit themselves with distinction, especially Mr. D'Arcy, who is seen in the role of the Crown Prince. And we must mention the skillful performance rendered by Tully Marshall."

Sun: "A captivating picture fraught with the exquisite beauty of a new Mae Murray and having further the charm of John Gilbert's restrained and intelligent, yet full blooded and robust acting. It is a masterpiece of direction. It is a picture with an appeal to the mind; a thing done with sophistication, poise and intelligence. The picture is magnificently photographed."

Journal: "If I could reproduce here a bar from the waltz of 'The Merry Widow' it would describe better than words the lilting romance and the provocative charm of the photoplay which opened at the new Embassy Theatre last night. It's the kind of love story of which you imagine yourself the hero or heroine when you shut your eyes and dance to an alluring melody. Had I a hat on I'd take it off to Erich von Stroheim for the delightful picture he made of 'The Merry Widow.'"

Graphic: "The opening of the Embassy Theatre last night was both a social and a cinema triumph. The 'Merry Widow' is von Stroheim at his best. In point of artistry, directing, acting and photography nothing better has ever been seen on Broadway."

"Unholy Three," M-G-M., Allen, Cleveland

News: "When the present season draws to a close there will not be many pictures ranked ahead of 'The Unholy Three.' It seems to be one of those productions that contain every requisite of first class screen entertainment. First of all the story is unusualness itself. Second, the cast has been so carefully chosen that the players seem to live their parts. Third, it has been produced in a careful and true to life manner. Lastly, the principal part has been placed in the hands of Lon Chaney. Chaney has never done better work in his whole career than he does in 'The Unholy Three.'"

Plain Dealer: "We have with us this week a greater picture than 'The Miracle Man.' It is 'The Unholy Three,' with Lon Chaney and Mae Busch. More

stark in its realism and lacking the semi-religious flavor and the near heart-agonies of the other. Chaney's new one is better than the one which served to introduce him because it is more artistically created, because its players are better actors and because, finally, pictures have really advanced in their methods of making."

"Coast of Folly" — Paramount, Rivoli, N. Y.

Times: "One is impressed by the lofty aspirations of the popular actress. She virtually fills three roles. Miss Swanson is singularly well made up as the Countess. She looks old, but always Miss Swanson. These scenes are amazingly well pictured and quite a credit to Miss Swanson."

The Mirror: "Gloria Swanson is a revelation. Gloria portrays three different roles. As the Victorian gal, dolled in flowing skirts, pompadour hair and coy manners, she shows promise of being the Mommer she later becomes. As Mommer, she looks like she may be twenty years from now. She gives a splendid account of herself in this part. Her walk is a marvel, her pecky affectations very good, and her makeup a work of art. As the modern flapper she manages to act with youthful buoyancy."

Telegraph: "Bravo, Gloria Swanson!"

American: "No one, after seeing Gloria Swanson in the hard make-up of a froway, middle-aged woman fighting for youth in 'The Coast of Folly' can accuse her of being vain."

Daily News: "To say that the film is all Gloria and a yard wide is putting it mildly. Gloria Swanson has never had the chance to show her versatility as she does in this high-voltage drama of life as it is lived on the coast of folly (not Hollywood, but Florida). She is the pompadour girl of twenty years ago. She is a dashing debutante, the playgirl of the eastern world. She is the kittenish old woman with ratty hair and ruddied cheeks. And she gives an imitation of Mary Pickford!"

Journal: "The photoplay, which deals with an unjust society scandal, is entertaining, and has several amusing touches."

Telegram: "Although we have ever been a Gloria Swanson fan it was somewhat of a revelation to discover that Madame La Marquise is capable of acting the role of an elderly Countess—French, of course—as pleasingly as she does in her new film, an adaptation by James Creelman of Coningsby Dawson's successful novel.

Sun: "In her impersonation of the elderly countess—which saves the young Gloria from scandal—Miss Swanson gives perhaps the most interesting study that she has yet revealed to the camera. The 'Coast of Folly' is good box office entertainment."

Evening World: "This feature is all Swanson. In fact, this story is overshadowed by the star's

characterizations and in all three she is admirable."

"The Gold Rush"—United Artists, Victory, Denver

Post: "'The Gold Rush' is with us, and a box-office record which had stood at the Victory theatre for five years has departed. 'The Gold Rush' is Charlie Chaplin; typically Charlie Chaplin; more elaborate and possibly funnier than ever before. It can be said without fear of contradiction, this is his greatest effort."

"Drusilla With A Million"— F. B. O., Forum, L. A.

Times: "Heart interest has at last been rediscovered for the screen, and as a consequence, audiences may as well be forewarned to be sure and take extra pocket handkerchiefs with them when they go to see 'Drusilla With A Million.' It is the best feature of the tearful type, destined to make everybody happy, that has been shown on the screen, seemingly in ages, and I imagine that owing to this fact alone there will be an unusual pilgrimage to the Forum Theatre where it is on view this week."

Record: "The question 'Does a million dollars mean anything to you?' brings forth some of the most wholesome comedy and greatest heartthrobs of the season . . . Priscilla Bonner gives a supreme performance. This little lady is destined to travel far along the road of perfect screen portrayals. Her abundant ability shows in her every appearance on the screen. Mary Carr repeats her triumph in 'Over the Hill.' Personally, I believe that she surpasses her efforts in the latter film. She has an appealing manner that touches your heart strings."

Express: "When a picture takes such hold of the emotions of an audience that it bursts into applause at the turn of affairs which confound the forces arrayed against the distressed heroine, the critics may as well sheathe their arrows. Mary Carr is 'Drusilla' and so delightful is her portrayal, so tender, so humorous, so pathetic by turn that it is one of the histrionic gems of the year."

News: "One of the most dramatic situations that has ever been filmed is incorporated into the story of 'Drusilla With A Million' this week's Forum offering. Scenes are so intensely dramatic, in which the suspense is prolonged so effectively that one suspects the director of a flash of real genius."

"Soup to Nuts" — Educational, Forum, L. A.

Examiner: "The surrounding program at the Forum is brilliant, 'Soup to Nuts,' a Christie Comedy featuring Neal Burns, and its fledgins spontaneous laughter with its action, but its subtitles run apace."

Express: "A Christie Comedy on the Forum bill, 'Soup to Nuts,' featuring Neal Burns, is one of the funniest but made under this brand and kept the audience in a high state of merriment."

FEATURE RELEASE CHART

Productions are Listed Alphabetically and by Months in which Released in order that the Exhibitor may have a short-cut toward such information as he may need. Short subject and comedy releases, as well as information on pictures that are coming, will be found on succeeding pages. (S. R. indicates State Right release.)

Refer to THE MOTION PICTURE NEWS BOOKING GUIDE for Productions Listed Prior to March

MARCH

Feature	Star	Distributed by	Length	Reviewed
Adventurous Sex, The	Clara Bow	Assoc. Exhib	5039 feet	Mar. 21
Air Mail, The	Special Cast	Paramount	6976 feet	Mar. 28
Beauty and the Bad Man	Special Cast	Prod. Dist. Corp	5794 feet	May 9
Beyond the Border	Harry Carey	Prod. Dist. Corp	4469 feet	April 25
Billy, The Kid	Franklyn Farnum	Inde. Pict. Corp. (S. R.)	4800 feet	
Blood and Steel	Desmond Holmes	Inde. Pict. (S. R.)	5300 feet	
Border Justice	Bill Cody	Inde. Pict. Corp. (S. R.)	5432 feet	Nov. 8
Coast Patrol, The	Kenneth McDonald	Barsky (S. R.)	5000 feet	
Confessions of a Queen	Terry-Stone	Metro-Goldwyn	5820 feet	April 4
Crimson Runner, The	Priscilla Dean	Prod. Dist. Corp	4775 feet	June 6
Daddy's Gone A'Hunting	Joyce-Marmont	Metro-Goldwyn	5851 feet	Mar. 7
Denial, The	Special Cast	Metro-Goldwyn	4791 feet	Mar. 21
Double Action Daniels	Buffalo Bill, Jr	Weiss Bros. (S. R.)	4650 feet	
Dressmaker from Paris, The	Rod La Rocque	Paramount	7080 feet	Mar. 28
Fighting Romeo, A	Al Ferguson	Davis Dist. Div. (S.R.)	5000 feet	Aug. 15
Fighting the Flames	Haines-Devore	C. B. C. (S. R.)	5800 feet	
Forbidden Cargo	Evelyn Brent	F. B. O	4850 feet	April 11
Goose Hangs High, The	Constance Bennett	Paramount	6186 feet	Feb. 14
Great Divide, The	Terry-Tearle	Metro-Goldwyn	7811 feet	Feb. 21
Head Winds	House Peters	Universal	5600 feet	Mar. 28
Hunted Woman, The	Seena Owen	Fox	4954 feet	April 4
I Want My Man	Sills-Kenyon	First National	6175 feet	April 18
Jimmie's Millions	Richard Talmadge	F. B. O	5167 feet	Feb. 28
Just Traveling	Bob Burns	Sierra Pict. (S. R.)	4400 feet	
Last Laugh, The	Emil Jannings	Universal	6519 feet	Dec. 20
Let'er Buck	Hoot Gibson	Universal	5547 feet	Jan. 3
Mad Whirl, The	May McAvoy	Universal	6184 feet	Dec. 6
Marriage in Transit	Edmund Lowe	Fox Film	4800 feet	April 11
Men and Women	Special Cast	Paramount	6223 feet	Mar. 28
Monster, The	L. Chaney-J. Arthur	Metro-Goldwyn	6435 feet	Feb. 28
My Wife and I	Special Cast	Warner Bros	6700 feet	June 6
New Lives for Old	Betty Compson	Paramount	6796 feet	Mar. 7
New Toys	Richard Barthelmess	First National	7250 feet	Feb. 21
One Year to Live	Special Cast	First National	6064 feet	Feb. 28
Percy	Charles Ray	Assoc. Exhib	5384 feet	Feb 28
Playing With Souls	Special Cast	First National	5831 feet	Mar. 14
Price of Pleasure, The	Valli-Kerry	Universal	6618 feet	June 13
Recompense	M. Prevost-M. Blue	Warner Bros	7480 feet	May 2
Renegade Holmes, M.D	Ben Wilson	Arrow (S. R.)	4947 feet	
Riders of the Purple Sage	Tom Mix	Fox	5578 feet	Mar. 28
Romance and Rustlers	Yakima Canutt	Arrow (S. R.)	4994 feet	Nov. 15
Sackcloth and Scarlet	Alice Terry	Paramount	6732 feet	Mar. 7
Sally	Colleen Moore	First National	8636 feet	Mar. 28
Scar Hanan	Yakima Canutt	F. B. O	4684 feet	April 4
Scarlet Honeymoon, The	Shirley Mason	Fox	5080 feet	Mar. 21
Seven Chances	Buster Keaton	Metro-Goldwyn	5113 feet	Mar. 28
Sign of the Cactus, The	Jack Hoxie	Universal	4938 feet	Jan. 10
Sky Raider, The	Capt. Charles Nungesser	Assoc. Exhib	6638 feet	April 4
Speed	Betty Blythe	Banner Prod. (S. R.)	6000 feet	May 30
Too Many Kisses	Richard Dix	Paramount	5759 feet	Mar. 14
Waking Up the Town	Jack Pickford	United Artists	4802 feet	April 11
Where Romance Rides	Dick Hatton	Arrow	4301 feet	
Zander the Great	Marion Davies	Metro-Goldwyn	(851 feet	May 16

APRIL

Feature	Star	Distributed by	Length	Reviewed
Adventure	P. Starke-T. Moore	Paramount	6713 feet	April 25
After Business Hours	Hammerstein-Tellegen	C B. C. (S. R.)	5800 feet	
Bandit Tamer, The	Franklyn Farnum	Inde. Pict. (S. R.)	5000 feet	
Border Vengeance	Jack Perrin	Madoc Sales (S. R.)	4500 feet	
Charmer, The	Pola Negri	Paramount	6076 feet	April 18
Code of the West	O. Moore-C. Bennett	Paramount	6777 feet	April 25
Courageous Fool, The	Reed Howes	Rayart (S. R.)		
Crowded Hour, The	Bebe Daniels	Paramount	6568 feet	May 9
Dangerous Innocence	LaPlante-E. O'Brien	Universal	6759 feet	Mar. 21
Declasse	Corinne Griffith	First National	7869 feet	April 4
Eyes of the Desert	Al Richmond	Sierra Prod. (S. R.)	4500 feet	
Fifth Avenue Models	Philbin-Kerry	Universal	6581 feet	Jan. 24
Fighting Parson, The	Al Ferguson	Davis Dist. Div. (S.R.)	5000 feet	
Fighting Sheriff, The	Bill Cody	Inde. Pict. (S. R.)	4500 feet	May 30
Friendly Enemies	Weber and Fields	Prod. Dist. Corp	6288 feet	May 9
Galloping Vengeance	Bob Custer	F. B. O	5095 feet	April 11
Getting 'Em Right	George Larkin	Rayart (S. R.)	4669 feet	
Gold and the Girl	Buck Jones	Fox	4521 feet	April 4
Go Straight	Gladys Hulette	B. P. Schulberg (S.R.)	6107 feet	May 23
Heart of a Siren, The	Barbara La Marr	First National	6700 feet	Mar. 21
How Baxter Butted In	M. Moore-D. Devore	Warner Bros	6650 feet	July 11
Justice Raffles	Henry Edwards	Cranfield & Clarke (S. R.)	6000 feet	
Kiss in the Dark, A	Special Cast	Paramount	5767 feet	April 18
Kiss Me Again	M. Prevost-M. Blue	Warner Bros	7200 feet	June 6
Love's Bargain	M. Daw-C. Brook	F. B. O	5641 feet	April 25
Madame Sans Gene	Gloria Swanson	Paramount	9994 feet	May 2
Man and Maid	Special Cast	Metro-Goldwyn	5307 feet	April 18
My Son	Nazimova-J. Pickford	First National	6500 feet	April 25
Night Club, The	R. Griffith-V. Reynolds	Paramount	5732 feet	May 16
One Way Street	Special Cast	First National	5596 feet	April 11
Proud Flesh	Special Cast	Metro-Goldwyn	5770 feet	April 25
Roaring Adventure, The	Jack Hoxie	Universal	4457 feet	Feb. 14
Ridin' Comet, The	Yakima Canutt	F. B. O	4354 feet	May 16
Rough Going	Franklyn Farnum	Indep. Pict. Corp. (S. R.)	4800 feet	
Shackled Lightning	Frank Merrill	Hercules Prod. (S. R.)		
She Wolves	Alma Rubens	Fox	6723 feet	May 9
Spaniard, The	Cortez-Goudal	Paramount	6676 feet	April 18
Sporting Venus	Special Cast	Metro-Goldwyn	5938 feet	May 23
Stop Flirting	Special Cast	Prod. Dist. Corp	5161 feet	June 6
Straight Through	Wm. Desmond	Universal	4867 feet	
Tale of a Thousand and One Nights	Special Cast	Davis Dist. Div. (S. R.)	6500 feet	Feb. 14
Tearing Through	Richard Talmadge	F. B. O.	4714 feet	May 23
That Devil Quemado	Fred Thomson	F. B. O.	4768 feet	April 4
Two-Fisted Sheriff, A	Yakima Canutt	Arrow (S. R.)	4149 feet	Dec. 6
Way of a Girl, The	Boardman-M. Moore	Metro-Goldwyn	5025 feet	April 18
Western Engagement, A	Dick Hatton	Arrow		
Wings of Youth	Madge Bellamy	Fox	5340 feet	May 16
Winning a Woman	Perrin-Hill	Rayart (S. R.)	4865 feet	

MAY

Feature	Star	Distributed by	Length	Reviewed
Alias Mary Flynn	Evelyn Brent	F. B. O.	5559 feet	May 30
Any Woman	Alice Terry	Paramount	5963 feet	June 13
Awful Truth, The	Agnes Ayres	Prod. Dist. Corp	5917 feet	July 11
Bandit's Baby, The	Fred Thomson	F. B. O.	5291 feet	June 20
Baree Son of Kazan	Wolf (dog)	Vitagraph	7 reels	May 2
Barriers of the Law	Holmes-Desmond	Indep. Pict. (S. R.)	5400 feet	
Burning Trail, The	William Desmond	Universal	4783 feet	April 18
Chickie	Mackaill-Bosworth	First National	7767 feet	May 9
Crackerjack, The	Johnny Hines	C. C. Burr (S. R.)	6500 feet	May 23
Every Man's Wife	Special Cast	Fox	4365 feet	July 4
Eve's Lover	Irene Rich	Warner Bros	6540 feet	Aug. 8
Eve's Secret	Betty Compson	Paramount	5305 feet	May 9
Fear Fighter, The	Billy Sullivan	Rayart (S. R.)		
Fighting Demon, The	Richard Talmadge	F B O	5470 feet	June 20
Fugitive, The	Ben Wilson	Arrow	4892 feet	
Golden Trails		Sanford Prod. (S. R.)	5 reels	
His Supreme Moment	B Sweet-R Colman	First National	6600 feet	April 25
Lilies of the Streets	J. Walker-V. L. Corbin	F. B. O.	7160 feet	April 25
Little French Girl, The	Alice Joyce	Paramount	5628 feet	June 13
Lunatic at Large, A	Henry Edwards	Cranfield & Clarke (S. R.)	6000 feet	
Makers of Men	Kenneth McDonald	Barsky Prod. (S. R.)	5000 feet	
Necessary Evil, The	Dana-Lyon	First National	6307 feet	May 23
Old Home Week	Thomas Meighan	Paramount	6888 feet	June 6
Phantom Rider, The	Al Richmond	Sierra Prod. (S. R.)	4750 feet	
Private Affairs	Special Cast	Prod. Dist. Corp	6132 feet	Aug. 16
Quick Change	George Larkin	Rayart (S. R.)		
Raffles, The Amateur Cracksman	House Peters	Universal	5557 feet	May 30
Rainbow Trail, The	Tom Mix	Fox	5251 feet	April 25
Red Love	Lowell-Russell	Lowell Film Prod. (S. R.)	6500 feet	May 23
Saddle Hawk, The	Hoot Gibson	Universal	5468 feet	Mar 7
Silent Sanderson	Harry Carey	Prod. Dist. Corp	4841 feet	June 20
Scandal Proof	Shirley Mason	Fox	4400 feet	June 6
School for Wives	Tearle-Holmquist	Vitagraph	6750 feet	April 11
Shock Punch, The	Richard Dix	Paramount	6151 feet	May 23
Snob Buster, The	Reed Howes	Rayart (S. R.)		
Soul Fire	Barthelmess-B Love	First National	8262 feet	May 16
Speed Wild	Maurice B "Lefty" Flynn	F. B. O	4700 feet	June 20
Talker, The	A Nilsson-L Stone	First National	7861 feet	May 23
Texas Bearcat, The	Bob Custer	F. B. O	4770 feet	
Tides of Passion	Mae Marsh	Vitagraph	6279 feet	May 9
Up the Ladder	Virginia Valli	Universal	6023 feet	Jan 31
Welcome Home	Special Cast	Paramount	5909 feet	May 30
White Fang	Strongheart (dog)	F. B. O	6579 feet	June 20
White Thunder	Yakima Canutt	F. B. O.	4550 feet	
Wildfire	Special Cast	Vitagraph	6 reels	June 20
Wolves of the Road	Yakima Canutt	Arrow	4375 feet	
Woman's Faith	Reubens-Marmont	Universal	6023 feet	Aug 15
Woman Hater, The	Helene Chadwick	Warner Brothers	7000 feet	Aug. 22

JUNE

Feature	Star	Distributed by	Length	Reviewed
Are Parents People?	Bronson-Vidor	Paramount	6586 feet	June 6
Dangerous Odds	Bill Cody	Inde. Pict. (S. R.)	4800 feet	
Desert Flower, The	Colleen Moore	First National	6837 feet	June 13
Double Fisted	Jack Perrin	Rayart (S. R.)		
Down the Border	Al Richmond	Sierra Prod. (S. R.)	4750 feet	
Faint Perfume	Seena Owen	B. P. Schulberg (S.R.)	6228 feet	July 11
Grounds for Divorce	Florence Vidor	Paramount	5712 feet	July 4
Happy Warrior, The		Vitagraph	6075 feet	July 18
Hearts and Spurs	Buck Jones	Fox	4600 feet	June 20
Human Tornado, The	Yakima Canutt	F. B. O.	4472 feet	
I'll Show You the Town	Reginald Denny	Universal	7400 feet	June 6
Introduce Me	Douglas MacLean	Assoc. Exhib	5950 feet	Mar. 21
Just a Woman	Windsor-Tearle	First National	6500 feet	June 6
Light of Western Stars	Special Cast	Paramount	6652 feet	July 4
Lost—a Wife	Special Cast	Paramount	6420 feet	June 27
Making of O'Malley, The	Milton Sills	First National	7571 feet	July 4
Man from Lone Mountain, The	Ben Wilson	Arrow	4530 feet	
Man in Blue	Herbert Rawlinson	Universal	5706 feet	Feb. 21
Marry Me	Special Cast	Paramount	5586 feet	
Meddler, The	William Desmond	Universal	4890 feet	May 23
Mike		Metro-Goldwyn		
Mist in the Valley	Alma Taylor	Cranfield & Clarke (S. R.)	5500 feet	
My Lady's Lips	Clara Bow	B. P. Schulberg (S.R.)	6609 feet	Aug 15
Off the Highway	Wm. V. Mong	Prod. Dist.	7641 feet	
Paths to Paradise	Compson-R. Griffith	Paramount	6741 feet	June 27
Pioneers of the West		Sanford Prod. (S. R.)	5 reels	
Ridin' Easy	Dick Hatton	Arrow	4483 feet	
Ridin' Thunder	Jack Hoxie	Universal	4354 feet	May 23
Rough Stuff	George Larkin	Rayart (S. R.)		
Shattered Lives	Special Cast	Gotham (S. R.)	6 reels	July 4

Feature	Star	Distributed by	Length	Reviewed
Smooth as Satin	Evelyn Brent	F. B. O	6002 feet	July 4
Texas Trail, The	Harry Carey	Prod. Dist. Corp	4720 feet	July 18
Tracked in the Snow Country	Rin-Tin-Tin (dog)	Warner Brothers	6900 feet	Aug. 1
White Monkey, The	La Marr-T. Holding	First National	6121 feet	July 4
Wild Bull's Lair, The	Fred Thompson	F. B. O.	5280 feet	Aug. 15
Youth's Gamble	Reed Howes	Rayart (S. R.)	5264 feet	

JULY

Feature	Star	Distributed by	Length	Reviewed
Bloodhound, The	Bob Custer	F. B. O	4789 feet	
Cold Nerve	Bill Cody	Inde. Pict. (S. R.)	5000 feet	
Danger Signal, The	Jane Novak	Columbia Pict. (S.R.)	5502 feet	Aug. 15
Don Daredevil	Jack Hoxie	Universal	4810 feet	
Drug Store Cowboy, The	Franklyn Farnum	Ind. Pict. Corp. (S.R.)	5100 feet	Feb. 7
Duped	Holmes-Desmond	Ind. Pict. (S. R.)	5400 feet	
Fighting Youth		Columbia Pict. (S.R.)		
Lady Who Lied, The	L. Stone-V. Valli	First National	7111 feet	July 18
Lady Robinhood	Evelyn Brent	F. B. O	5582 feet	Aug 22
Manicure Girl, The	Bebe Daniels	Paramount	5959 feet	June 27
Marriage Whirl, The	C. Griffith-H. Ford	First National	7672 feet	July 25
Mysterious Stranger, The	Richard Talmadge	F. B. O	5270 feet	
Night Life of New York	Special Cast	Paramount	6998 feet	July 4
Pipes of Pan	Alma Taylor	Cranfield & Clarke (S. R.)	6200 feet	
Ranger of the Big Pines, The	Kenneth Harlan	Vitagraph	5800 feet	Aug. 8
Scarlet West, The	Frazer-Bow	First National	8391 feet	July 25
Secret of Black Canyon, The	Dick Hatton	Arrow		
Strange Rider, The	Yakima Canutt	Arrow		
Taming the West	Hoot Gibson	Universal	5427 feet	Feb. 28
Trailed	Al Richmond	Sierra Prod. (S. R.)	4750 feet	
White Desert, The	Special Cast	Metro-Goldwyn	6345 feet	July 11

AUGUST

Feature	Star	Distributed by	Length	Reviewed
American Pluck	George Walsh	Chadwick	5000 feet	July 11
Beggar on Horseback, A	Ralston-Nissen	Paramount	6800 feet	June 20
Business of Love, The	E. Horton-M. Bellamy	Astor Dist. Corp		
Children of the Whirlwind	Lionel Barrymore	Arrow		
Don Q	Douglas Fairbanks	United Artists	10264 feet	June 27
Drusilla With a Million	Special Cast	F. B. O	7391 feet	May 30
Evolution		Red Seal	4200 feet	Aug. 15
Fine Clothes	L. Stone-A. Rubens	First National	6971 feet	Aug. 15
Girl Who Wouldn't Work, The	Lionel Barrymore	B. P. Schulberg (S.R.)	5979 feet	Sept. 5
Gold Rush, The	Charles Chaplin	United Artists	8500 feet	Aug. 8
Halfway Girl, The	Doris Kenyon	First National	7570 feet	Aug. 8
Headlines	Alice Joyce	Assoc. Exhib	5600 feet	July 25
Her Sister From Paris	C. Talmadge	First National	7255 feet	Aug. 15
In the Name of Love	Cortez-Nissen	Paramount	5904 feet	Sept. 5
Isle of Hope, The	Richard Talmadge	Film Book. Offices	5800 feet	Sept. 5
Kivalina of the Ice Lands	Native Cast	Pathe	6 reels	July 11
Knockout, The	Milton Sills	First National		
Lightnin'	Jay Hunt	Fox	7979 feet	Aug. 1
Limited Mail, The	Monte Blue	Warner Brothers	6250 feet	
Love Hour, The	Ruth Clifford	Vitagraph	5900 feet	
Lover's Oath, The	Ramon Novarro	Astor Dist Corp		
Lucky Devil, The	Richard Dix	Paramount	5935 feet	July 18
Lucky Horseshoes	Tom Mix	Fox	5000 feet	Aug. 29
My Pal	Dick Hatton	Arrow		
Overland Limited, The		Gotham Prod. (S. R.)	6389 feet	Aug. 8
Parisian Love	Bow-Tellegen	B. P. Schulberg (S.R.)	6324 feet	Aug. 22
Penalty of Jazz, The		Columbia Pict. (S.R.)		
Quo Vadis	Emil Jannings	First National	8945 feet	Feb. 28
Range Justice	Dick Hatton	Arrow		
Romola	Gish Sisters	Metro-Goldwyn	10875 feet	Dec. 13
Rugged Water	Special Cast	Paramount	6015 feet	Aug. 1
Shining Adventure, The	Percy Marmont	Astor Dist. Corp		
Slave of Fashion, A	Special Cast	Metro-Goldwyn	5906 feet	Aug. 1
Speed Mad		Columbia Pict. (S.R.)		
Street of Forgotten Men	Special Cast	Paramount	6366 feet	Aug. 1
Ten Commandments	Special Cast	Paramount	9980 feet	Jan. 5-24
Unholy Three	Lon Chaney	Metro-Goldwyn	6848 feet	Aug. 15
That Man Jack	Bob Custer	F. B. O	5032 feet	Aug. 22
Unwritten Law, The		Columbia Pict. (S.R.)		
Wife Who Wasn't Wanted, The	Irene Rich	Warner Brothers	6400 feet	
Wizard of Oz	Larry Semon	Chadwick	6300 feet	Apr. 25
Wrongdoers, The	Lionel Barrymore	Astor Dist. Corp		

SEPTEMBER

Feature	Star	Distributed by	Length	Reviewed
Amazing Quest, The	Henry Edwards	Cranfield & Clarke	5500 feet	
As No Man Has Loved	Edward Hearn	Fox	10000 feet	Feb. 28
Below The Line	Rin-Tin-Tin (dog)	Warner Brothers	6100 feet	
Black Cyclone	Rex (horse)	Pathe		May 30
Bobbed Hair	Prevost-Harlan	Warner Brothers	6700 feet	
California Straight Ahead	Reginald Denny	Universal		
Classified	Corinne Griffith	First National		
Coast of Folly	Gloria Swanson	Paramount		
Crack of Dawn	Reed Howes	Rayart (S. R.)		
Cyclone Cavalier	Reed Howes	Rayart (S. R.)		
Dark Angel, The	R. Colman-V. Dana	First National		
Freshman, The	Harold Lloyd	Pathe		July 25
Graustark	Norma Talmadge	First National		
Havoc	Special Cast	Fox	9200 feet	Aug. 29
High and Handsome	"Lefty" Flynn	F. B. O.	5669 feet	
If Marriage Fails	J. Logan-C. Brook	F. B. O	6006 feet	May 23
Keep Smiling	Monty Banks	Assoc. Exhib	5400 feet	Aug. 1
Let's Go Gallagher	Tom Tyler	Film Book Offices		
Little Annie Rooney	Mary Pickford	United Artists		
Lost World, The	Special Cast	First National	9700 feet	Feb. 21
Manhattan Madness	Dempsey-Taylor	Assoc. Exhib	5500 feet	July 25
Man Who Found Himself	Thomas Meighan	Paramount	7168 feet	Sept. 5
Marrying Money		Truart (S. R.)	5800 feet	
Mystic, The	Special Cast	Metro-Goldwyn		
Never the Twain Shall Meet	Stewart-Lytell	Metro-Goldwyn	8143 feet	Aug. 8
New Champion, The		Columbia Pict. (S.R.)		
Not So Long Ago	Betty Bronson	Paramount	6943 feet	Aug. 8
Other Woman's Story		B. P. Schulberg		
Outlaw's Daughter, The	Josie Sedgwick	Universal	4375 feet	
Parisian Nights	E. Hammerstein - L. Tellegen	F. B. O	6278 feet	June 20
Pretty Ladies	Zaru Pitts	Metro-Goldwyn	5828 feet	July 25
Prince of Broadway, The	George Walsh	Chadwick		
Ridin' the Wind	Fred Thomson	Film Book. Offices		
Sealed Lips		Columbia Pict. (S.R.)		
Shore Leave	Barthelmess-Mackaill	First National	6856 feet	Aug. 29
Siege	Virginia Valli	Universal	6424 feet	June 20
Some Pun'kins	Chas. Ray	Chadwick		

Feature	Star	Distributed by	Length	Reviewed
Son of His Father	Special Cast	Paramount	7009 feet	
Souls for Sables		Tiffany (S. R.)	6500 feet	
S. O. S. Perils of the Sea		Columbia Pict. (S.R.)		
Spook Ranch	Hoot Gibson	Universal	5147 feet	May 2
Sun Up	Special Cast	Metro-Goldwyn		Aug. 29
Teaser, The	Laura La Plante	Universal	6967 feet	May 30
Three in Exile		Truart (S. R.)	5800 feet	
Three Weeks in Paris	M. Moore-D. Devore	Warner Brothers	5900 feet	
Three Wise Crooks	Evelyn Brent	Film Book. Offices		
Throwback, The	Special Cast	Universal		
Timber Wolf, The	Buck Jones	Fox	4809 feet	
Trouble With Wives, The	Vidor-T. Moore	Paramount	6489 feet	Aug. 15
Unchastened Woman, The	Theda Bara	Chadwick		
Wall Street Whiz, The	Richard Talmadge	Film Book. Offices		
What Fools Men	Stone-Mason	First National		
Wheel, The	Special Cast	Fox	7264 feet	Aug. 29
White Outlaw, The	Jack Hoxie	Universal	4830 feet	June 27
Wild Horse Mesa	Special Cast	Paramount	7221 feet	Aug. 22
Wild, Wild Susan	Bebe Daniels	Paramount		
With This Ring	Mills-Tellegen	B. P. Schulberg		

OCTOBER

Feature	Star	Distributed by	Length	Reviewed
Bells, The	Lionel Barrymore	Chadwick		
Circus Cyclone, The	Art Acord	Universal	4609 feet	Aug. 22
Dollar Down	Ruth Roland	Truart (S. R.)	5800 feet	Aug. 29
Everlasting Whisper, The	Tom Mix	Fox		
Exchange of Wives, An	Special Cast	Metro-Goldwyn		
Fate of a Flirt, The		Columbia (S. R.)		
Golden Princess, The	Bronson-Hamilton	Paramount	8584 feet	
Great Sensation, The		Columbia (S. R.)		
He's a Prince	Raymond Griffith	Paramount		
His Buddy's Wife	Glenn Hunter	Assoc. Exhib	5600 feet	July 25
Iron Horse, The		Fox Film Corp	11335 feet	Sept. 13
John Forrest	Henry Edwards	Cranfield&Clark(S.R.)	5000 feet	
Lew Tyler's Wives		B. P. Schulberg (S. R.)		
Lights of Old Broadway	Marion Davies	Metro-Goldwyn		
Lovers in Quarantine	Daniels-Ford	Paramount		
Midshipman, The	Ramon Novarro	Metro-Goldwyn		
Morals for Men		Tiffany (S. R.)	6500 feet	
New Brooms	Hamilton-Love	Paramount		
Perfect Clown, The	Larry Semon	Chadwick		
Pony Express, The	Betty Compson	Paramount		
Sally of the Sawdust	Fields-Dempster	United Artists	9500 feet	Aug. 15
Sporting Chance, The		Tiffany (S. R.)	6500 feet	July 4
Thank U	Special Cast	Fox		
Tower of Lies	Chaney-Shearer	Metro-Goldwyn		
Tumbleweeds	Wm. S. Hart	United Artists		
Under the Rouge	Tom Moore	Assoc. Exhib	6500 feet	July 25
Winds of Chance	A. Nilsson-B. Lyon	First National	9753 feet	Aug. 29

NOVEMBER

Feature	Star	Distributed by	Length	Reviewed
Ancient Highway, The	Holt-Vidor	Paramount		
Best People, The	Special Cast	Paramount		
Blue Blood	George Walsh	Chadwick		
Camille of the Barbary Coast	Busch-O. Moore	Assoc. Exhib	5600 feet	Aug. 1
Cobra	Valentino-Naldi	Paramount		
Don't	S. O'Neill-B. Roach	Metro-Goldwyn		
Fifty-Fifty	L.Barrymore-H.Hampton	Assoc. Exhib	5564 feet	June 20
Fight to a Finish, A		Columbia (S. R.)		
Fighting Heart, The	Geo. O'Brien	Fox	6978 feet	
Flower of Night	Pola Negri	Paramount		
Fool, The	Special Cast	Fox		April 25
King on Main St., The	Adolphe Menjou	Paramount		
Lazybones		Fox Film		
Lightning		Tiffany (S. R.)	6500 feet	
Little Bit of Broadway	Ray-Starke	Metro-Goldwyn		
Merry Widow	Mae Murray	Metro-Goldwyn		
Price of Success, The	Alice Lake	Columbia (S. R.)		
Silent Witness, The		Truart (S. R.)	5800 feet	
Stage Struck	Gloria Swanson	Paramount		
Time the Comedian		Metro-Goldwyn		
Transcontinental Limited	Special Cast	Chadwick (S. R.)		
Vanishing American	Dix-Wilson	Paramount		
Winner, The	Charley Ray	Chadwick (S. R.)		

Comedy Releases

Feature	Star	Distributed by	Length	Reviewed
Across the Hall	Edna Marian	Universal	2 reels	
Adventures of Adenoid	Aesop's Fables	Pathe	1 reel	April 25
After a Reputation	Edna Marian	Universal	2 reels	
Air Tight	Bobby Vernon	Educational	2 reels	June 13
Alice's Egg Plant	"Cartoon"	M. J. Winkler(S. R.)	1 reel	
Alice Stagestruck	Margie Gay	M. J. Winkler (S.R.)	1 reel	July 18
All Aboard		Fox	2 reels	
Almost a Husband	Buddy Messinger	Universal	2 reels	
Amateur Detective	Earle Foxe	Fox	2 reels	
Andy in Hollywood	Joe Murphy	Universal	2 reels	
Andy Takes a Flyer	"The Gumps"	Universal	2 reels	
Apache, The	Earle Foxe	Fox Film	2 reels	
Apollo's Pretty Sister		Fox	2 reels	
Are Husbands Human?	James Finlayson	Pathe	1 reel	April 11
Artists' Blues	G. Joy-J. Moore	Rayart (S. R.)	2 reels	
Ask Grandma	"Our Gang"	Pathe	2 reels	May 30
At the Seashore	Monkey	Fox	2 reels	
At the Zoo	Aesops Fables	Pathe	1 reel	
Baby Blues	Mickey Bennett	Educational	2 reels	
Bachelors	Special Cast	Universal		
Bad Bill Brodie	Charles Chase	Pathe	2 reels	
Bad Boy	Charles Chase	Pathe	2 reels	April 11
Balboa Discovers Hollywood	"Red Head"	Sering D. Wilson(S.R.)	1 reel	
Bark is the Woods	Harry Langdon	Pathe	2 reels	
Bashful Jim	Ralph Graves	Pathe	2 reels	Mar. 21
Be Careful	Jimmie Adams	Educational Film	2 reels	Aug. 22
Below Zero	Lige Conley	Educational	2 reels	July 4
Beware	Lige Conley	Educational Film	2 reels	Aug. 1
Big Chief Ko-Ko (Out of the Inkwell)	"Cartoon"	Red Seal Pict. (S. R.)	1 reel	
Big Game Hunter, The	Earle Foxe	Fox	2 reels	
Bigger and Better Pictures	"Aesop's Fables"	Pathe	1 reel	
Big Red Riding Hood	Charley Chase	Pathe	1 reel	May 9

Feature	Star	Distributed by	Length	Reviewed
Black Gold Bricks	Roach-Edwards	Universal	1 reel	April 18
Black Hand Blues	"Spat Family"	Pathe	2 reels	April 18
Bobby Bumbs & Co	Cartoon	Educational	1 reel	July 4
Boys Will Be Joys	"Our Gang"	Pathe	2 reels	July 25
Brainless Horsemen		Fox	2 reels	
Brass Button	Billy West	Arrow	2 reels	
Breaking the Ice	Ralph Graves	Pathe	2 reels	April 11
Bride Tamer, The	Milburn Moranti	Sierra Pict. (S. R.)	2 reels	
Bubbles	"Aesop's Fables"	Pathe	1 reel	Aug. 15
Bugville Field Day	"Aesop's Fables"	Pathe	1 reel	July 25
Business Engagement, A		Fox	2 reels	
Busts Into Business	Felix the Cat	Educational	1 reel	
Butterfly Man, The		Fox	2 reels	
By the Sea	Charles Puffy	Universal	1 reel	
California Here We Come	"The Gumps"	Universal	2 reels	
Cat's Shimmy, The	"Kid Noah"	Sering D. Wilson (S.R.)	1 reel	
Cat's Whiskers, The	Neely Edwards	Universal	1 reel	
Chasing the Chasers	Jas. Finlayson	Pathe	1 reel	July 4
City Bound	Charles Puffy	Universal	1 reel	
Clean-Up Week	"Aesop's Fables"	Pathe	1 reel	Mar. 7
Clear the Way	Buddy Messinger	Universal	2 reels	
Cleopatra and Her Easy Mark	"Cartoon"	Sering D. Wilson (S.R.)	1 reel	
Cloudhopper, The	Larry Semon	Educational	2 reels	June 6
Columbus Discovers a New Whirl		Sering Wilson (S. R.)	1 reel	
Cotton King	Lloyd Hamilton	Educational	2 reels	
Crime Crushers	Lige Conley	Educational	2 reels	
Crying for Love	Eddie Gordon	Universal	2 reels	Aug. 15
Cupid's Boots	Ralph Graves	Pathe	2 reels	July 25
Cupid's Victory	Wanda Wiley	Universal	2 reels	
Cure, The (Out of the Inkwell)	"Cartoon"	Red Seal Pict. (S. R.)	1 reel	
Curses	Al. St. John	Educational	2 reels	May 23
Daddy Goes A Grunting		Pathe	2 reels	July 18
Darkest Africa	"Aesop's Fables"	Pathe	1 reels	
Day's Outing, A	"The Gumps"	Universal	2 reels	
Depp Stuff	Aesop's Fables	Pathe	1 reel	April 25
Dinky Doodle and Cinderella	"Dinky Doodle"	F. B. O	1 reel	
Dinky Doodle and Robinson Crusoe	"Dinky Doodle"	F. B. O	1 reel	
Discord In "A" Flat	Arthur Lake	Universal	1 reel	July 25
Dog Days	"Our Gang"	Pathe	2 reels	Mar. 14
Dog 'On It	Bobby Dunn	Arrow	2 reels	
Dome Doctor, The	Larry Semon	Educational	2 reels	
Don't Pinch	Bobby Vernon	Educational	2 reels	April 25
Don't Worry	Wanda Wiley	Universal	2 reels	Mar. 21
Dragon Alley	Jackie McHugh	Educational	2 reels	May 16
Dr. Pyckle and Mr. Pride	Stan Laurel	Film Booking Offices	2 reels	
Dry Up	Singleton Burkett	Universal	2 reels	July 25
Dumb and Daffy	Al. St. John	Fox	2 reels	
Dynamite Doggie	Al. St. John	Educational	2 reels	Mar. 21
Echoes From the Alps	Aesop's Fables	Pathe	1 reel	May 23
Educating Buster	Trimble-Turner	Universal	2 reels	
End of the World, The	Aesop's Fables	Pathe	1 reel	
Etiquette	Jimmy Aubrey	Film Book. Offices	2 reels	
Excuse My Glove	"Spat Family"	Pathe	2 reels	Mar 21
Expensive Ebony	"Ebenezer Ebony"	Sering Wilson (S. R.)	1 reel	
Failure		Fox	2 reels	
Fair Warning		Educational	2 reels	
Fares Please	Al. St. John	Educational	2 reels	May 16
Fast Worker, A	Aesop's Fables	Pathe	1 reel	
Felix Full O'Fight	"Cartoon"	M. J. Winkler (S. R.)	1 reel	
Felix Gets His Fill	"Cartoon"	M. J. Winkler (S. R.)	1 reel	
Felix Grabs His Grub	"Cartoon"	M. J. Winkler (S. R.)	1 reel	
Fireflies		Davis Dist	2 reels	
First Love	"Our Gang"	Pathe	2 reels	
Fishermen's Luck	"Aesop's Fables"	Pathe	1 reel	
For Hire	Edward Gordon	Universal		
For Love of a Gal	"Aesop's Fables"	Pathe	1 reel	July 25
Found World, The	"The Gumps"	Universal	2 reels	
Fun's Fun	Bowes-Vance	Educational	1 reel	June 6
Getting Trimmed	Wanda Wiley	Universal	2 reels	April 18
Giddap	Special Cast	Pathe	2 reels	Mar. 21
Going Great	Eddie Nelson	Educational	2 reels	June 13
Goldfish's Pajamas	"Kid Noah"	Sering D. Wilson (S.R.)	1 reel	
Good Morning Nurse	Ralph Graves	Pathe	2 reels	May 30
Good Scouts	"Reg'lar Kids"	M. J. Winkler (S. R.)	2 reels	
Great Guns	Bobby Vernon	Educational	2 reels	Feb. 21
Green-Eyed Monster, The	Arthur Lake	Universal	1 reel	
Gridiron Gertie	Wanda Wiley	Universal	2 reels	
Guilty Conscience, A	Eddie Gordon	Universal		
Gypping the Gypsies	"Ebenezer Ebony"	Sering Wilson (S. R.)	1 reel	
Half a Hero	Lloyd Hamilton	Educational	2 reels	Mar. 7
Half a Man	Stan Laurel	Pathe	2 reels	
Hard Boiled	Charley Chase	Pathe	2 reels	Mar. 21
Hard Working Loafer, The	Arthur Stone	Pathe		
Haunted Honeymoon	Tryon-Mehaffey	Pathe	2 reels	Feb. 28
Heart Trouble	Arthur Lake	Universal	1 reel	July 4
Hello, Goodby	Lige Conley	Educational	2 reels	May 30
Hello, Hollywood	Lige Conley	Educational	2 reels	Mar. 28
Helping Hand	Jimmy Aubrey	F. B. O	2 reels	
Help Yourself		Fox	2 reels	
Here's Your Hat	Arthur Lake	Universal	1 reel	May 9
Her Lucky Leap	Wanda Wiley	Universal	2 reels	
He Who Gets Crowned	Jimmy Aubrey	F. B. O	2 reels	
He Who Got Smacked	Ralph Graves	Pathe	2 reels	May 9
Hey! Taxi!	Bobby Dunn	Arrow	2 reels	
High Hopes	Bowes-Vance	Educational	1 reel	Feb. 14
High Jinx, A		Fox	2 reels	
His Marriage Wow	Harry Langdon	Pathe	2 reels	Mar. 7
Hold My Baby	Glenn Tryon	Pathe	2 reels	April 25
Home Scouts	Jimmie Aubrey	F. B. O.	2 reels	
Honeymoon Heaven		Sering Wilson (S. R.)	1 reel	
Horace Greeley, Jr	Harry Langdon	Pathe	2 reels	June 6
Horrible Hollywood		Lee-Bradford (S. R.)		
Hot and Heavy	Eddie Nelson	Educational	2 reels	July 18
Hot Dog	Animal	C B C (S. R.)	2 reels	
Hot Times in Iceland	Aesop's Fables	Pathe	1 reel	
House of Flickers, The		Fox	2 reels	
House that Dinky Built	(Cartoon)	F. B. O	1 reel	
Housing Shortage, The	"Aesop's Fables"	Pathe	1 reel	
Hysterical History (Series)		Universal	1 reel	
Ice Boy, An	"Ebenezer Ebony"	Sering D. Wilson (S.R.)	1 reel	
Ice Cold	Arthur Lake	Universal	1 reel	June 13
In Deep		Educational	1 reel	
In Dutch	Aesop's Fables	Pathe	1 reel	
Innocent Husbands	Charley Chase	Pathe	2 reels	Aug. 1
Inside Out	Bowes-Vance	Educational	1 reel	Mar. 28
Into the Grease	James Finlayson	Pathe	1 reel	June 27
Iron Mule	Al St. John	Educational	2 reels	April 18
Iron Nag, The	Billy Bevan	Pathe	2 reels	Aug. 15
Is Marriage the Bunk?	Charles Chase	Pathe	1 reel	April 4
Isn't Life Terrible?	Charles Chase	Pathe	2 reels	July 4
Itching for Revenge	Eddie Gordon	Universal	2 reels	Mar. 7
It's All Wrong	Karr-Engle	Universal		
James Boys' Sister		Sering Wilson (S. R.)	1 reel	
Jungle Bike Riders	Aesop's Fables	Pathe	1 reel	Mar. 14
Just in Time	Wanda Wiley	Universal	2 reels	July 11
Kicked About	Eddie Gordon	Universal	2 reels	Mar. 14
Kidding Captain Kidd	"Cartoon"	Sering Wilson (S. R.)	1 reel	
King Cotton	Lloyd Hamilton	Educational	2 reels	May 9
King Dumb	Jimmy Aubrey	F. B. O	2 reels	
Klynick, The		Davis Dist	2 reels	
Knocked About	Eddie Gordon	Universal	2 reels	June 13
Ko-Ko Trains Animals (out of the Inkwell)	"Cartoon"	Red Seal Pict. (S.R.)	1 reel	
Lead Pipe Cinch, A	Al Alt	Universal		
Lion Love		Fox	2 reels	Feb. 28
Lion's Whiskers		Pathe	2 reels	April 18
Little Red Riding Hood	"Dinky Doodle"	F. B. O	1 reel	
Locked Out	Arthur Lake	Universal	1 reel	May 30
Looking for Sally	Charles Chase	Pathe	2 reels	May 9
Look Out	Bowes-Vance	Educational Film	1 reel	Aug. 1
Lost Cord, The	Bert Roach	Universal	1 reel	Feb. 21
Love and Lions		Fox	2 reels	
Love Bug, The	"Our Gang"	Pathe	2 reels	April 4
Love Goofy	Jimmy Adams	Educational	2 reels	Mar. 7
Love Sick	Constance Darling	Universal	2 reels	May 23
Love's Tragedy		Sering Wilson (S. R.)	1 reel	
Lucky Accident, The	Charles Puffy	Universal	1 reel	July 18
Lucky Leap, A	Wanda Wiley	Universal	2 reels	
Lucky Stars	Harry Langdon	Pathe	2 reels	Aug. 15
Madame Sans Jane	Glenn Tryon	Pathe	2 reels	
Marriage Circus, The	Ben Turpin	Pathe	2 reels	April 11
Married Neighbors	Engle-Darling	Universal	2 reels	July 4
Mary, Queen of Tots	"Our Gang"	Pathe	2 reels	Aug. 22
Meet the Ambassador	Jimmy Aubrey	F. B. O	2 reels	
Mellow Quartette	Pen & Ink Vaudeville	Educational	1 reel	April 4
Merrymakers	Bowes-Vance	Educational	1 reel	Mar. 28
Met by Accident	Wanda Wiley	Universal	2 reels	
Milky Way, The	Charles Puffy	Universal	1 reel	July 25
Miss Fixit	Wanda Wiley	Universal	2 reels	
Monkey Business	"Pen & Ink Vaude"	Educational	1 reel	May 9
Moonlight Nights	Gloria Joy	Rayart (S. R.)	2 reels	
Nearly Rich	Charles Puffy	Universal	1 reel	
Neptune's Stepdaughter		Fox	2 reels	
Nero's Jazz Band		Sering Wilson (S. R.)	1 reel	
Never Fear	Bowes-Vance	Educational	1 reel	
Never on Time		Lee-Bradford	2 reels	
Never Weaken	Lloyd reissue	Assoc. Exhib	2237 feet	
Nice Pickle, A	Edwards-Roach	Universal	1 reel	
Nicely Rewarded	Chas. Puffy	Universal	1 reel	June 27
Night Hawks		Educational Film	2 reels	
Nobody Wins	Arthur Lake	Universal	1 reel	
No Place to Go	Arthur Lake	Universal	1 reel	
Now or Never (reissue)	Harold Lloyd	Assoc. Exhib	3 reels	
Off His Beat	Walter Hiers	Educational	2 reels	
Office Help	"Aesop's Fables"	Pathe	1 reel	June 27
Official Officers	"Our Gang"	Pathe	2 reels	June 27
Oh, Bridget	Walter Hiers	Educational	2 reels	
Oh, What a Flirt	Jimmy Aubrey	Film Book. Offices	2 reels	
Oh, What a Gump	"The Gumps"	Universal	2 reels	
Old Family Toothbrush	"Kid Noah"	Sering Wilson (S. R.)	1 reel	
On Duty	Wanda Wiley	Universal	2 reels	
One Glorious Fourth	"Reg'lar Kids"	M. J. Winkler (S. R.)	2 reels	
One Wild Night	Neely Edwards	Universal	1 reel	
On the Go		Fox	2 reels	
Orphan, The	Al Joy	Ricardo Films, Inc. (S.R.)		
Over the Bottom	Stan Laurel	F. B. O	2 reels	
Over the Plate	Aesops Fable	Pathe	1 reel	Aug. 22
Over Here	Harry Langdon	Pathe	2 reels	
Paging A Wife	Al Alt	Universal	2 reels	Aug. 1
Papa's Darling		Fox	2 reels	
Papa's Pet	Roach-Edwards	Universal	1 reel	April 11
Parisian Knight, A	Earle Foxe	Fox	2 reels	
Peacemakers, The		Fox	2 reels	
Pegg's Love Affair		Screen Art Dist		
Peggy in a Pinch		Davis Dist	2 reels	
Peggy's Pests		Davis Dist	2 reels	
Peggy's Putters		Davis Dist	2 reels	
Peggy the Vamp	Rosalie Morlin	Davis Distr	2 reels	Oct. 11
Permanent Waves	"Aesop's Fables"	Pathe	1 reel	
Permit Me	Bowes-Vance	Educational	1 reel	July 11
Pie-Eyed	Stan Laurel	F. B. O	2 reels	
Pie Man, The	"Aesop's Fables"	Pathe	1 reel	Mar. 21
Plain Clothes	Harry Langdon	Pathe	2 reels	Mar. 28
Plain and Fancy Girls	Charles Chase	Pathe	1 reel	Mar. 14
Plain Luck	Edna Marian	Universal	2 reels	
Pleasure Bound	Lige Conley	Educational	2 reels	Aug. 21
Plenty of Nerve	Edna Marian	Universal	2 reels	July 2
Polo Kid, The	Eddie Gordon	Universal	2 reels	July 18
Poor Sap, The		Fox	2 reels	
Powdered Chickens	Edna Marian	Universal	2 reels	Mar. 28
Props' Dash for Cash	Earl Hurd (Cartoon)	Educational	1 reel	
Putting on Airs	Edna Marian	Universal	2 reels	April 11
Puzzled by Crosswords	Eddie Gordon	Universal	2 reels	Mar. 7
Queen of Aces	Wanda Wiley	Universal	2 reels	May 16
Raid, The	Gloria Joy	Rayart Pictures	2 reels	
Raisin' Cain	Constance Darling	Universal	2 reels	April 4
Rapid Transit	Al. St. John	Educational	2 reels	
Rarin' Romeo	Walter Hiers	Educational	2 reels	Mar. 28
Raspberry Romance	Ben Turpin	Pathe	2 reels	Feb. 28
Red Pepper	Al. St. John	Educational	2 reels	Arpil 4
Regular Girl, A	Wanda Wiley	Universal	2 reels	
Riders of the Kitchen Range	Mohar-Engle	Pathe	1 reel	June 6
Remember When	Harry Langdon	Pathe	2 reels	April 25
Rip Without a Wink	"Redhead"	Sering Wilson (S. R.)	1 reel	
Ripe Melodrama, A		Sering Wilson (S. R.)	1 reel	
Rivals	Billy West	Arrow	2 reels	
Robinson Crusoe Returns on Friday	"Redhead"	Sering Wilson (S. R.)	1 reel	
Rock Bottom	Bowes-Vance	Educational	1 reel	May 9
Robbing the Rube		Lee-Bradford Corp	2 reels	
Rolling Stones	Charles Puffy	Universal	1 reel	May 30
Rough Party	Al Alt	Universal	2 reels	
Royal Four-Flush	"Spat Family"	Pathe	2 reels	June 13
Runaway Balloon, The	"Aesop's Fables"	Pathe	1 reel	June 27
Runt, The	"Aesop's Fables"	Pathe	1 reel	June 6
Sailor Papa, A	Glenn Tryon	Pathe	2 reels	April 4
Saturday		Davis Dist. Div	2 reels	
Say It With Flour		Fox	2 reels	
Sheiks of Bagdad		Pathe	1 reel	May 9
Sherlock Sleuth	Arthur Stone	Pathe	2 reels	July 11
Ship Shape	Vance-Bowes	Educational	1 reel	April 18
Shootin' Injuns	"Our Gang"	Pathe	2 reels	May 9
Short Pants	Arthur Lake	Universal	1 reel	Aug. 1
Should a Husband Tell?		Red Seal Pict. (S.R.)	1 reel	

Feature	Star	Distributed by	Length	Reviewed
Should Husbands Be Watched?	Charles Chase	Pathe	1 reel	Mar. 14
Sir Walt and Lizzie		Sering Wilson (S. R.)	1 reel	
Sit Tight	Jimmie Adams	Educational	2 reels	May 30
Skinners in Silk		Pathe	2 reels	May 16
Sky Jumper, The	Earle Foxe	Fox	2 reels	
Skyscraper, The	Harry Langdon	Principal Pict. (S. R.)	2 reels	
Sleeping Sickness	Edwards-Roach	Universal	1 reel	May 30
Slick Articles	Engle-Karr	Universal	2 reels	May 30
Smoked Out	Lake-Hasbrouck	Universal	1 reel	April 13
Sneezing Beezers	Billy Bevan	Pathe	2 reels	July 18
Snow-Hawk	Stan Laurel	F. B. O.	2 reels	
Soap	"Aesop's Fables"	Pathe	1 reel	
S. O. S.	"Aesop's Fables"	Pathe	1 reel	
Spanish Romeo, A (Van Bibber)		Fox	1 reel	
Speak Easy	Charley Puffy	Universal	1 reel	Aug. 22
Speak Freely	Edna Marion	Universal	2 reels	
Stick Around	Bobby Dunn	Arrow	2 reels	
Stop, Look and Whistle		Fox	2 reels	
Storm, The (Out of the Inkwell)	"Cartoon"	Red Seal Pict. (S.R.)	1 reel	
Stranded	Edna Marian	Universal	2 reels	
Super-Hooper-Dyne Lizzies		Pathe	2 reels	June 13
Sure Mike!	Martha Sleeper	Pathe	1 reel	May 23
Sweet Marie		Fox	2 reels	Aug. 29
Tame Men and Wild Women		Pathe	2 reels	Aug. 15
Teaser Island	"Redhead"	Sering Wilson (S. R.)	1 reel	
Tee for Two	Alice Day	Pathe	2 reels	Aug. 1
Tell It To a Policeman	Glenn Tryon	Pathe	2 reels	May 23
Tender Feet	Walter Hiers	Educational	2 reels	May 23
Tenting Out	Roache-Edwards	Universal	1 reel	Mar. 23
This Week-End		Lee-Bradford (S. R.)		
Thundering Landlords	Glenn Tryon	Pathe	2 reels	June 27
Too Young to Marry	Buddy Messinger	Universal	2 reels	
Tough Night, A	Jimmy Callahan	Aywon Film	2 reels	
Tourist, The	Harry Langdon	Educational Film	2 reels	Aug. 15
Tourists De Luxe	Hayes-Karr	Universal	2 reels	May 16
Transients in Arcadia		Fox	2 reels	
Transatlantic Flight, A	"Aesop's Fables"	Pathe	1 reel	
Twins	Stan Laurel	F. B. O	2 reels	
Two Cats and a Bird	"Cartoon"	Educational	1 reel	Mar. 14
Two Poor Fish	Earl Hurd cartoon	Educational	1 reel	May 30
Uncle Tom's Gal	Edna Marian	Universal	2 reels	
Unwelcome	Charles Puffy	Universal	1 reel	June 27
Waiting	Lloyd Hamilton	Educational	2 reels	July 11
Wake Up	Bowes-Vance	Educational	1 reel	June 13
Watch Out	Bobby Vernon	Educational	2 reels	
Water Wagons	Special Cast	Pathe	2 reels	Feb. 21
Welcome Dangar	Bowes-Vance	Educational	1 reel	Feb. 23
West is West	Billy West	Arrow	2 reels	
Westward Ho	Charles Puffy	Universal	1 reel	
What Price Goofy	Charley Chase	Pathe	2 reels	June 6
When Dumbells Ring		Fox	2 reels	
When Men Were Men	"Aesop's Fables"	Pathe	1 reel	July 25
White Wing's Bride	Harry Langdon	Pathe	2 reels	July 11
Whose Baby Are You?	Glenn Tryon	Pathe	2 reels	
Who's Which	Bowes-Vance	Educational	1 reel	
Why Hesitate?	Neal Burns	Educational	2 reels	April 11
Why Sitting Bull Stood Up		Sering Wilson (S. R.)	1 reel	
Wide Awake	Lige Conley	Educational	2 reels	
Wild Papa	"Spat Family"	Pathe	2 reels	May 16
Wild Waves	Bowes-Vance	Educational	1 reel	May 23
Wine, Woman and Song	"Aesop's Fables"	Pathe	1 reel	
Wooly West, The	Buddy Messinger	Universal	2 reels	
Wrestler, The	Earle Foxe	Fox	2 reels	Aug. 29
Yarn About Yarn, A	Aesop Fable	Pathe	1 reel	Aug. 1
Yes, Yes, Nannette	Jas. Finlayson	Pathe	1 reel	Aug. 1

Short Subjects

Feature	Distributed by	Length	Reviewed
Action (Sportlight)	Pathe	1 reel	
All Under One Flag (Sportlight)	Pathe	1 reel	
Animal Celebrities (Sportlight)	Pathe	1 reel	June 27
Animated Hair Cartoon (Series)	Red Seal (S. R.)	1 reel	
Balto's Race to Nome (Special)	Educational	2 reels	May 23
Barbara Snitches (Pacemaker Series)	F. B. O.	2 reels	
Battle of Wits (Josie Sedgwick)	Universal	2 reels	July 18
Bashful Whirlwind, The (Edmund Cobb)	Universal	2 reels	
Beauty and the Bandit (Geo. Larkin)	Universal	2 reels	July 4
Beauty Spots (Sportlight)	Pathe	1 reel	April 18
Best Man, The (Josie Sedgwick)	Universal	2 reels	Aug. 15
Broken Trails	Denver Dixon (S.R.)	2 reels	
Cabaret of Old Japan	M. J. Winkler (S.R.)	1 reel	
Color World	Sering Wilson (S. R.)	1 reel	
Captured Alive (Helen Gibson)	Universal	2 reels	July 25
Cinema Stars (Novelty)	Davis Dist	1 reel	
Close Call, The (Edmund Cobb)	Universal	2 reels	
Cocoon to Kimono	M. J. Winkler (S.R.)	1 reel	
Come-Back, The (Benny Leonard)	Henry Ginsberg-S.R.	2 reels	
Concerning Cheese (Varieties)	Fox	1 reel	
Covered Flagon, The (Pacemaker Series)	F. B. O	2 reels	
Cowpuncher's Comeback, The (Art Acord)	Universal	2 reels	
Crooked (Elinor King)	Davis Dist	2 reels	
Cross Word Puzzle Film (Comedy-Novelty)	Schwartz Enterprises (S. R.)	1 reel	
Cuba Steps Out (Variety)	Fox	1 reel	
Day With the Gypsies	Red Seal Pict. (S. R.)	1 reel	
Divertisement (Color Shots)	Sering Wilson (S. R.)	1 reel	
Don Coo Coo (Pacemakers)	Film Book. Offices	2 reels	
Do You Remember (Gems of Screen)	Red Seal (S. R.)	1 reel	
Dude Ranch Days (Sportlight)	Pathe	1 reel	May 30
Earth's Other Half (Hodge-Podge)	Educational	1 reel	June 6
East Side, West Side	DeForrest (S. R.)		
Fast Male, The (Pacemakers)	Film Book. Offices	2 reels	
Fighting Cowboy (Series)	Universal		
Fighting Ranger (Serial)	Universal	15 episodes	Feb. 7
Fighting Schoolmarm (Josie Sedgwick)	Universal	2 reels	Aug. 1
Film Facts	Red Seal (S. R.)	1 reel	
Fire Trader, The (Serial)	Universal	15 episodes	
Floral Feast, A	Sering Wilson (S.R.)	1 reel	
Frederick Chopin (Music Masters)	Jas. A. Fitzpatrick (S. R.)	1 reel	
From Mars to Munich (Varieties)	Fox	1 reel	April 4
Frontier Love (Billy Mack)	Denver Dixon	2 reels	
Fugitive Futurist	Cranfield & Clarke (S. R.)		
George F. Handel (Music Masters)	Jas. A. Fitzpatrick (S. R.)	1 reel	
Gems of the Screen	Red Seal (S. R.)	1 reel	
Ghost City, The (Serial)	Universal	15 episodes	
Golden Panther, The (Serial)	Pathe		
Gold Trap, The ... Fred Humes	Universal	2 reels	
Great Circus Mystery, The (Serial)	Universal	15 episodes	
Great Decide, The (Pacemakers)	Film Book. Offices	2 reels	
He Who Gets Rapped (Pacemakers)	Film Book. Offices	2 reels	
Hittin' the Trail (Fred Hank)	Sierra Pict. (S. R.)	2 reels	
Idaho (Serial)	Pathe	10 episodes	Feb. 28
If a Picture Tells a Story	Cranfield & Clarke (S. R.)		
In a China Shop (Variety)	Fox	1 reel	
In the Spider's Grip (Novelty)	Educational	1 reel	April 11
Invention, The (Elinor King)	Davis Dist	2 reels	
It Might Happen to You (Evangeline Russell)	Davis Dist	2 reels	
Jazz Fight, The (Benny Leonard)	Henry Ginsberg (S. R.)	2 reels	
Judge's Cross Word Puzzle (Novelty)	Educational	1 reel	Jan. 31
Just Cowboys ... Corbett-Holmes	Universal	2 reels	
Klondike Today (Varieties)	Fox	1 reel	
Knockout Man, The (Mustang)	Universal	2 reels	July 11
Land of the Navajo (Educational)	Fox	1 reel	
Learning How (Sportlight)	Pathe	1 reel	July 18
Leopard's Lair	Universal	Serial	
Let's Paint	Cranfield & Clarke (S. R.)		
Line Runners, The (Arnold Gregg)	Universal	2 reels	
Little People of the Garden (Secrets of Life)	Educational	1 reel	
Little People of the Sea (Secrets of Life)	Educational	1 reel	Feb. 28
Lizzie's Last Lap	Cranfield & Clarke (S. R.)		
Loaded Dice (Edmund Cobb)	Universal	2 reels	April 4
Luna-cy (Stereoscopik)	Pathe	1 reel	
Mad Miner, A (Western)	Hunt Miller (S. R.)	2 reels	
Magic Hour, The	Red Seal Pict. (S. R.)	1 reel	
Man Who Rode Alone, The	Miller & Steen (S.R.)	2 reels	
Marvels of Motion	Red Seal (S. R.)	1 reel	
Marvellous Manhattan	M. J. Winkler (S. R.)	1 reel	
Merry Kiddo, The (Pacemakers)	Film Book. Offices	2 reels	
Merton of the Goofies ... "Pacemaker"	F. B. O.	2 reels	
Mexican Melody (Hodge-Podge)	Educational	1 Reel	
Mexican Oil Fields	M. J. Winkler (S. R.)	1 reel	
Movie Morsels (Hodge Podge)	Educational	1 reel	April 4
My Own Carolina (Variety)	Fox	1 reel	Aug. 29
Mystery Box, The (Serial)	Davis Dist. Corp.	10 episodes	
Neptune's Nieces (Sportlight)	Pathe	1 reel	
New Sheriff, A (Western)	Hunt Miller (S. R.)	2 reels	
Olympic Mermaids (Sportlight)	Pathe	1 reel	
One Glorious Scrap (Edmund Cobb)	Universal	2 reels	
Only a Country Lass (Novelty)	Educational	1 reel	May 29
Ouch (Stereoscopik)	Pathe	1 reel	
Our Six-legged Friends (Secrets of Life)	Educational	1 reel	
Outlaw, The (Jack Perrin)	Universal	2 reels	
Paris Creations (Novelty)	Educational	1 reel	Feb. 7
Paris Creations in Color (Novelty)	Educational	1 reel	Feb. 28
People You Know (Screen Almanac)	Film Booking Offices	1 reel	
Perfect View, The (Varieties)	Fox	1 reel	
Perils of the Wild (Serial)	Universal		
Pictorial Proverbs (Hodge Podge)	Educational	1 reel	Aug. 15
Plastigrams (Novelty)	Educational		
Play Ball (Serial)	Pathe	10 episodes	June 27
Power God, The (Serial)	Davis Dist. Div.(S.R.)	15 episodes	
Pronto Kid, The (Edmund Cobb)	Universal	2 reels	June 27
Queen of the Round-Up (J. Sedgwick)	Universal	2 reels	June 13
Race, The (Van Bibber)	Fox	2 reels	
Raid, The ... Edmund Cobb	Universal	2 reels	
Record Breaker, The	Pathe	Serial	
Rim of the Desert (Jack Perrin)	Universal	2 reels	
River Nile, The (Variety)	Fox	1 reel	
Roaring Waters (Geo. Larkin)	Universal	2 reels	
Rock Bound Brittany (Educational)	Fox	1 reel	
Ropin' Venus, The (Mustang Series)	Universal	2 reels	July 11
R. Valentino and Eighty-eight Prize-winning American Beauties	Chesterfield (M. P. Corp.) (S. R.)	3 reels	
Secrets of Life (Educational)	Principal Pict. (S. R.)	reel	Feb. 21
Seven Ages of Sport (Sportlight)	Pathe	1 reel	Aug. 22
Shadow of Suspicion (Eileen Sedgwick)	Universal	2 reels	
Show Down, The (Art Acord)	Universal	2 reels	
Sky Tribe, The (Variety)	Fox	1 reel	
Smoke of a Forty-Five, The (Western)	Hunt Miller (S. R.)	2 reels	
Soft Muscles (Benny Leonard)	Ginsberg (S. R.)	2 reels	
Song Cartunes (Novelty)	Red Seal Pict. (S. R.)	1 reel	
Sons of Swat (Sportlight)	Pathe	1 reel	Aug. 15
Sporting Judgment (Sportlight)	Pathe	1 reel	May 9
Steam Heated Islands (Varieties)	Fox	1 reel	
Stereoscopic (Novelty)	Pathe	1 reel	May 16
Storm King (Edmund Cobb)	Universal	2 reels	
Story Teller, The (Hodge-Podge)	Educational	1 reel	
Straight Shootin' (Harry Carey)	Universal	2 reels	
Strangler Lewis vs. Wayne Munn	Educational	2 reels	July 4
Stratford on Avon (Gems of Screen)	Red Seal Pict. (S. R.)	1 reel	
Sunken Silver (Serial)	Pathe	10 episodes	April 18
Surprise Fight, The (Benny Leonard)	Henry Ginsberg (S. R.)	2 reels	
Thundering Waters (Novelty)	Sering D. Wilson (S. R.)	1 reel	April 26
Tiger Kill, The (Pathe Review)	Pathe		
Toiling for Rest (Variety)	Fox	1 reel	
Traps and Troubles (Sportlight)	Pathe	1 reel	Mar. 21
Travel Treasures (Hodge Podge)	Educational	1 reel	July 25
Turf Mystery (Serial)	Chesterfield Pict. Corp. (S. R.)	15 episodes	
Valley of Rogues (Western)	Universal	2 reels	April 18
Van Bibber and the Navy (Earle Foxe)	Fox	2 reels	
Village School, The (Hodge Podge)	Educational Film	1 reel	May
Voice of the Nightingale, The (Novelty)	Educational	1 reel	Mar. 28
Waiting For You (Music Film)	Hegerman Music Novelties (S. R.)		
Welcome Granger (Pacemakers)	Film Book. Offices	2 reels	
West Wind, The (Variety)	Fox	1 reel	
What Price Gloria (Pacemakers)	Film Book. Offices	2 reels	
Wheels of the Pioneers (Billy Mack)	Denver Dixon	2 reels	
Where the Waters Divide (Varieties)	Fox	1 reel	
White Paper (Varieties)	Fox	1 reel	
Wild West Wallop, The (Edmund Cobb)	Universal	2 reels	May 16
With Pencil, Brush and Chisel	Fox	1 reel	
Wonder Book, The (Series)	Sering D. Wilson	500 feet	April 26
Young Sheriff, The (Tom. Forman)	Miller & Steen (S. R.)	2 reels	
Zowie (Stereoscopik)	Pathe	1 reel	

Ace of Spades, The	Desmond-McAllister	Universal		
Age of Indiscretion		Truart (S. R.)	5800 feet	
American Venus, The	Special Cast	Paramount		
An Enemy of Men		Columbia Pict. (S. R.)		
Aristocrat, The	Special Cast	B. P. Schulberg (S. R.)		
Ashes	Corinne Griffith	First National		
Atlantis		First National		
Back Wash	Mary Pickford	United Artists		
Bad Lands, The	Harry Carey	Prod. Dist. Corp.		
Barriers of Fire	Monte Blue	Warner Bros.		
Beautiful Cheat, The	Laura La Plante	Universal		
Beautiful City	R. Barthelmess	First National		
Before Midnight	Wm. Russell	Ginsberg (S. R.)	5895 feet	Aug. 8
Beloved Pawn, The	Reed Howes	Rayart (S. R.)		

Coming Attractions

Feature	Star	Distributed by	Length	Reviewed
Ben Hur	Special Cast	Metro-Goldwyn		
Big Parade, The	John Gilbert	Metro-Goldwyn		
Border Intrigue	Franklyn Farnum	Inde. Pict. (S. R.)	5 reels	June 4
Border Women	Special Cast	Phil Goldstone (S.R.)	5000 feet	
Broken Hearts of Hollywood	Harlan-Miller	Warner Brothers		
Brown of Harvard		Metro-Goldwyn		
Cave Man, The	Harlan-Miller	Warner Brothers		
Charity Ball, The		Metro-Goldwyn		
Circle, The		Metro-Goldwyn		
Clean-Up, The	Richard Talmadge	F. B. O.		
Clod Hopper, The	Glenn Hunter	Assoc. Exhibitors		
Clothes Make the Pirate	Errol-D. Gish	First National		
College Widow, The	Syd Chaplin	Warner Brothers		
Coming of Amos	Rod La Rocque	Prod. Dist. Corp.		
Compromise	Irene Rich	Warner Bros.		
Conquered	Gloria Swanson	Paramount		
Count of Luxembourg, The	Larry Semon	Chadwick		
Crashing Through	Jack Perrin	Ambassador Pict. (S. R.)	5000 feet	
Cyclone Bob	Bob Reeves	Anchor Film Dist.		
Cyrano de Bergerac	Special Cast	Atlas Dist. (S. R.)	9500 feet	July 18
Dance Madness	Pringle-Cody	Metro-Goldwyn		
Dangerous Currents		First National		
Dark Horse, The	Harry Carey	Prod. Dist. Corp.		
Deerslayer, The		Weiss Bros. (S. R.)	4780 feet	
Demon, The	Jack Hoxie	Universal		
Demon Rider, The	Ken Maynard	Davis Dist	5000 feet	Aug. 22
Detour		Prod. Dist. Corp.		
Down Upon the Swanee River	Special Cast	Lee Bradford (S. R.)		
Dumb Head		Tiffany (S. R.)	6500 feet	
East of the Setting Sun	Constance Talmadge	First National		
Enchanted Hill, The	Special Cast	Paramount		
Ermine and Rhinestone		H. F. Jans (S. R.)		
Exquisite Sinner, The	Special Cast	Metro-Goldwin		
Face on the Air, The	Evelyn Brent	F. B. O.		
Fair Play	Special Cast	Wm. Steiner (S. R.)		
Fall of Jerusalem		Weiss Bros. (S. R.)	6800 feet	
Fast Pace, The	Special Cast	Arrow		
Fighter's Paradise, The	Rex Baker	Phil Goldstone	5000 feet	
Fighting Courage	Ken Maynard	Davis Dist. Div. (S.R.)	5 reels	July 11
Fighting Edge, The	Harlan-Miller	Warner Brothers		
Fighting Smile, The	Bill Cody	Inde.Pict. Corp.(S.R.)	4630 feet	
First Year, The	Special Cast	Fox		
Flaming Waters		F. B. O.		
Forest of Destiny, The		Gotham Prod. (S. R.)		
Forever After	Corinne Griffith	First National		
Fort Frayne	Ben Wilson	Davis Dist.	5000 feet	Aug. 29
Free to Love	C. Bow-R. McKee	B. P. Schulberg (S. R.)		
Friends	Special Cast	Vitagraph		
Frivolity		B. P. Schulberg (S.R.)		
Galloping Dude, The	Franklyn Farnum	Inde.Pict.Corp.(S.R.)	4700 feet	
Garden of Allah		United Artists		
Going the Limit	Richard Holt	Gerson Pict. (S. R.)		
Golden Cocoon		Warner Bros.		
Goose Woman, The	Special Cast	Universal	7500 feet	Aug. 22
Go West	Buster Keaton	Metro-Goldwyn		
Grass			10 reels	Mar. 7
Handsome Brute, The	Columbia Pict. (S. R.)			
Hearts and Fists		Assoc. Exhib.		
Hearts and Spangles		Gotham Prod. (S. R.)		
Hell Bent for Heaven		Warner Bros.		
Hell's Highroad	Leatrice Joy	Prod. Dist. Corp	6084 feet	Sept. 5
Heir's Apparent	Special Cast	First National		
Her Father's Daughter		F. B. O.		
Hero of the Big Snows, A	Rin Tin Tin (dog)	Warner Brothers		
His Jazz Bride	Special Cast	Warner		
His Majesty Bunker Bean	M. Moore-Devore	Warner		
His Master's Voice	Thunder (dog)	Gotham Prod. (S. R.		
His Woman	Special Cast	Whitman Bennett	7 reels	
Hogan's Alley	Harlan-Miller	Warner		
Home Maker, The	Alice Joyce	Universal	7755 feet	Aug. 8
Honeymoon Express, The	M. Moore-D. Devore	Warner Brothers		
Horses and Women		B. P. Schulberg		
Hurricane		Truart (S. R.)	5800 feet	
Inevitable Millionaires, The	M. Moore-Devore	Warner Bros.		
Invisible Wounds	Sweet-Lyon	First National		
Irene	Colleen Moore	First National		
Justice of the Far North		C. B. C. (S. R)	5500 feet	
Kings of the Turf		Fox		
Kiss for Cinderella, A	Betty Bronson	Paramount		
Knockout Kid, The	Jack Perrin	Rayart Pict. Corp. (S. R.)		
La Boheme	Lillian Gish	Metro-Goldwyn		
Lady Windermere's Fan	Special Cast	Warner Brothers		
Lariat, The	William Desmond	Universal		
Last Edition, The	Ralph Lewis	Film Book. Offices		
Lawful Cheater, The	Bow-McKee	B. P. Schulberg	4946 feet	
Lena Rivers	Special Cast	Arrow	6 reels	
Life of a Woman		Truart (S. R.)	6500 feet	
Lightning Jack	Jack Perrin	Ambassador Pict. (S.R.)	5000 feet	
Lightning Passes, The	Al Ferguson	Fleming Prod. (S.R.)		
Limited Mail, The	Monte Blue	Warner Bros.		
Little Girl in a Big City, A		Gotham Prod. (S. R.)		
Little Irish Girl, The	Special Cast	Warner Bros.		
Live Wire, The	Johnny Hines	First National		
Lodge in the Wilderness		Tiffany (S. R.)	6500 feet	
Lord Jim	Percy Marmont	Paramount		
Love Cargo, The	House Peters	Universal		
Love Gamble, The	Special Cast	Banner Prod. (S. R.)	5766 feet	July 11
Lover's Island	Hampton-Kirkwood	Assoc. Exhib		
Love Toy, The	Lowell Sherman	Warner Bros		
Loyalties	Special Cast	Fox		
Lucky Lady, The	Lionel Barrymore	Paramount		
Lure of Broadway, The		Columbia Pict. (S. R.)		
Lying Wives	Special Cast	Ivan Abramson (S. R.)	7 reels	May 2
Man and the Moment		Metro-Goldwyn		
Man From Red Gulch	Harry Carey	Prod. Dist. Corp.		
Man of Iron, A	L. Barrymore	Chadwick	6 reels	July 4
Man on the Box, The	Sydney Chaplin	Warner Bros		
Man She Bought, The	Constance Talmadge	First National		
Man Without a Conscience	Louis-Rich	Warner Bros	6850 feet	May 2
Mare Nostrum	Special Cast	Metro-Goldwyn		
Married Hypocrites	Fredericks-La Plante	Universal		
Martinique	Bebe Daniels	Paramount		
Masked Bride, The	Mae Murray	Metro-Goldwyn		
Men of Steel	Milton Sills	First National		
Memory Lane	Boardman-Nagel	First National		
Message to Garcia, A		Metro-Goldwyn		
Miracle of Life, The	Busch-Marmont	Assoc. Exhib		
Miracle of the Wolves, The			10346 feet	Mar. 7
Midnight Flames		Columbia Pict. (S. R.)		
Miss Vanity	Mary Philbin	Universal		
Million Dollar Doll		Assoc. Exhib		
Morganson's Finish		Tiffany (S. R.)	6500 feet	
Moving Finger, The	Special Cast	Paramount		
Napoleon the Great		Universal		
Night Call, The	Rin-Tin-Tin (dog)	Warner Brothers		
Old Clothes	Jackie Coogan	Metro-Goldwyn		
Only Thing, The	Special Cast	Metro-Goldwyn		
Open Trail, The	Jack Hoxie	Universal	4800 feet	May 16
Pace That Thrills, The	Ben Lyon	First National		
Pals		Truart (S. R.)	5800 feet	
Paris	Pauline Starke	Metro-Goldwyn		
Paris After Dark	Norma Talmadge	First National		
Partners Again		United Artists		
Passionate Quest, The	Marie Prevost	Warner Bros		
Passionate Youth	Special Cast	Truart (S. R.)	6 reels	July 11
Part Time Wife, The		Gotham Prod. (S. R.)		
Peacock Feathers	Virginia Valli	Universal	6747 feet	Aug. 29
Peak of Fate, The		F. B. Rogers	8 reels	June 27
People vs. Nancy Preston	Bowers-De La Motte	Prod. Dist. Corp.		
Phantom of the Opera	Lon Chaney	Universal		
Pinch Hitter, The	Glenn Hunter	Asso. Exhibitors		
Pleasure Buyers, The	Irene Rich	Warner Brothers		
Police Patrol, The	James Kirkwood	Gotham Prod. (S. R.)		
Polly of the Ballet	Bebe Daniels	Paramount		
Pony Express, The	Special Cast	Universal		
Prairie Pirate, The	Harry Carey	Prod. Dist. Corp.		
Prince, The	Philbin-Kerry	Universal		
Quality Street		Metro-Goldwyn		
Quicker 'n Lightning	Buffalo Bill, Jr.	Weiss Bros. (S. R.)	5 reels	June 13
Racing Blood		Gotham Prod. (S. R.)		
Reckless Courage	Buddy Roosevelt	Weiss Bros. (S. R.)	4851 feet	May 2
Reckless Sex, The	Special Cast	Truart (S. R.)	6 reels	Feb. 14
Red Clay	William Desmond	Universal		
Red Dice	Rod La Rocque	Prod. Dist. Corp.		
Red Hot Tires	Monte Blue	Warner Bros.		
Return of a Soldier	Special Cast	Metro-Goldwyn		
Rime of the Ancient Mariner, The		Fox Film		
Road to Yesterday, The	Special Cast	Prod. Dist. Corp		
Road That Led Home, The		Vitagraph		
Romance of an Actress		Chadwick		
Ropin' Venus, The	Josie Sedgwick	Universal		
Rose of the World	Special Cast	Warner Bros		
Sally, Irene and Mary	Special Cast	Metro-Goldwyn		
Salvage		Truart (S. R.)	5800 feet	
Sap, The	M. Moore D. Devore	Warner Bros		
Satan in Sables	Lowell Sherman	Warner Bros		
Savage, The	Ben Lyon	First National		
Scarlet Saint, The	Lyon-Astor	First National		
Scraps	Mary Pickford	United Artists		
Sea Beast, The	John Barrymore	Warner Bros.		
Sea Woman, The	Sweet-McLaglen	First National		
Seven Days	Lillian Rich	Prod. Dist. Corp.		
Seven Sinners	Marie Prevost	Warner Bros.		
Seventh Heaven	Special Cast	Fox		
Shadow of the Wall		Gotham Prod. (S. R.)		
Shadow of the Mosque	Odette Taylor	Cranfield & Clarke (S. R.)	6200 feet	
Shenandoah		B. P. Schulberg (S. R.)		
Ship of Souls	B. Lytell-L. Rich	Assoc. Exhib	6800 feet	
Shootin' Square	Jack Perrin	Ambassador Pict. (S.R.)	5000 feet	
Siegfried		Ufa		
Sign of the Claw		Gotham Prod. (S. R.)		
Silken Shackles	Irene Rich	Warner Bros.		
Silver Treasure, The	Special Cast	Fox		
Simon the Jester	Rich-O'Brien	Prod. Dist. Corp.		
Social Highwayman, The	Harlan-Miller	Warner Brothers		
Some Pun'kins	Chas. Ray	Chadwick		
Spanish Sunlight	LaMarr-Stone	First National		
Span of Life	Betty Blythe	Banner Prod. (S. R.)		
Speed Limit, The		Gotham Prod. (S. R.)		
Splendid Road, The	Anna Q. Nillsen	First National		
Steele of the Royal Mounted		Vitagraph	6 reels	June 27
Stella Dallas		United Artists		
Stella Maris	Mary Philbin	Universal		
Still Alarm, The	Chadwick-Russell	Universal		
Strange Bedfellows		Metro-Goldwyn		
Storm Breakers, The	House Peters	Universal		
Sunshine of Paradise Alley	Special Cast	Chadwick Pict.		
Super Speed	Reed Howes	Rayart (S. R.)		
Sweet Adeline	Charles Ray	Chadwick		
Tale of a Vanishing People		Tiffany (S. R.)	6500 feet	
Tearing Loose	Wally Wales	Weiss Bros. (S. R.)	4900 feet	June 13
Temptress		Metro-Goldwyn		
Ten to Midnight		Prod. Dist. Corp.		
That Man from Arizona	D.Revier-W.Fairbanks	F. B. O.		
That Royle Girl	Kirkwood-Dempster	Paramount		
This Woman	Special Cast	Fox		
Three Bad Men	Special Cast	Fox		
Three Faces East		Prod. Dist. Corp.		
Trailing Shadows	Edmond Lowe	Fox Film		
Travelin' Fast	Jack Perrin	Ambassador Pict. (S. R.)	5000 feet	
Travis Coup, The		Tiffany (S. R.)	6500 feet	
Twin Sister, The	Constance Talmadge	First National		
Two Blocks Away	Special Cast	Universal		
Unchastened Woman, The	Theda Bara	Chadwick		
Unguarded Hour, The	Sills-Kenyon	First National		
Unknown Lover, The	Elsie Ferguson	Vitagraph		
Up and At' Em	Jack Perrin	Ambassador Pict. (S. R.)	5008 feet	
Vengeance of Durand, The	Irene Rich	Warner Brothers		
Viennese Medley	Special Cast	First National		
Volga Boatman, The		Prod. Dist. Corp		
Wanderer, The	William Collier, Jr.	Paramount	8173 feet	
Warrior Gap	Wilson-Gerber	Davis Dist	4900 feet	Aug 22
Wedding Song, The	Leatrice Joy	Prod. Dist. Corp		
We Moderns	Colleen Moore	First National		
What Will People Say		Metro-Goldwyn		
Where the Worst Begins		Truart(S. R.)	5800 feet	
White Chief, The	Monte Blue	Warner Bros		
White Mice	Jacqueline Logan	Sering D. Wilson(S.R.)		
Why Girls Go Back Home		Warner Bros		
Wild Girl		Truart (S. R.)	5800 feet	
Wild Justice	Peter the Great	United Artists	6 reels	Aug. 1
Wild Ridin'	Buck Jones	Fox		
Winning of Barbara Worth		Principal Pict. (S. R.)		
Wise Guy, The	Lefty Flynn	Film Book. Offices		
Without Mercy	Vera Reynolds	Prod. Dist. Corp		
Womanhandled	Richard Dix	Paramount		
Women and Wives		Metro-Goldwyn		
World's Illusion, The		Metro-Goldwyn		
Worst Woman, The	Special Cast	B. P. Schulberg (S. R.)		
Wrong Coat, The		Tiffany Prod. (S. R.)	6500 feet	

Williams Press, Inc.
Albany — New York

ph De Luxe
rake

LEWIS STONE

SIR ARTHUR CONAN DOYLE

WALLACE BEERY

BESSIE LOVE

LLOYD HUGHES

We point with pride to the significant fact that **Sir Arthur Conan Doyle's** stupendous story **"The Lost World"** is presented and protected on the screen by virtue of *Rothacker Prints* and *Service.*

Rothacker

FILM MFG. CO. CHICAGO, USA

Look Better — Wear Longer!

Founded 1910
by
Watterson R. Rothacker

September 26, 1925

Motion Picture
News

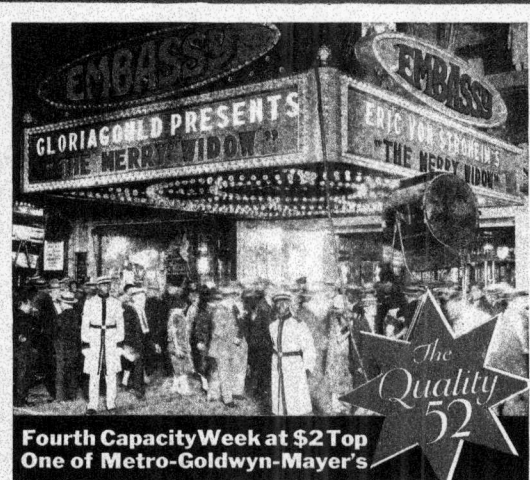

GLORIA GOULD PRESENTS
"THE MERRY WIDOW"

ERIC VON STROHEIM'S
"THE MERRY WIDOW"

Fourth Capacity Week at $2 Top
One of Metro-Goldwyn-Mayer's

The Quality 52

Member Motion Picture Producers and Distributors of America, Inc.—Will H. Hays, President.

Vol. XXXII   No. 13   PRICE, 20 CENTS

THE TOWER OF LIES

Norma Shearer   Lon Chaney

Perhaps you heard rumors about this production.

The studio said: "Something marvelous."

We have kept it as a surprise—and what a surprise it is!

Victor Seastrom has made a picture that's going to be the talk of this broad land within a few weeks.

Of course, after "He Who Gets Slapped" we knew that we could expect a money-maker from Seastrom.

But this exceeded our wildest hopes.

Seastrom has put Life on the screen as no one has ever done it before.

He took Selma Lagerlof's world-prize novel "The Emperor of Portugallia" and made a world-prize screen epic out of it.

He probes the depths of the heart, finding there the joy of living and loving, the despair of Fortune's fickleness.

What moments of tenderness and beauty—with the magnificent Norma Shearer!

What moments of towering passion—with Chaney, the genius!

A box-office triumph indeed—with dramatic story-telling that never lets up a moment!

You've seen Chaney, you've seen Shearer, you know Seastrom's magic hand.

Combined they have made one of the greatest motion picture achievements of our day!

from
Metro-Goldwyn-Mayer Is The

It Will Do the Same in <u>YOUR</u> Town!

——— San Francisco ———

All records for the city smashed by "The Pony Express" opening night at the Imperial Theatre.

S.R.O. at every subsequent performance despite extra shows at 9 A.M. and midnight.

Newspapers unanimously hail it as "greater than 'The Covered Wagon'"

AND YOU GET IT AS ONE OF THE REGULAR GREATER FORTY

Paramount Pictures

WITH SUCH BOX OFFICE GIANTS AS THESE COMING RIGHT AFTER:

"THE VANISHING AMERICAN"
Zane Grey's Epic of the American Indian

GLORIA SWANSON in "Stage Struck"

"THE AMERICAN VENUS"
with "Miss America" and Atlantic City Bathing Beauties

D. W. GRIFFITH'S "That Royle Girl"

RAYMOND GRIFFITH in "He's A Prince!"

DOUGLAS MacLEAN in "Seven Keys to Baldpate"

and more~more~more!

Now~as always~the REAL BIG ONES *are*

Paramount Pictures

ont Theatre,
  Chicago, Ill.
axeiner & Trottman, Gem Theatre,
  Milwaukee, Wisc.
Dreamland Theatre,
  Elyria, O.
  R. B. R. Amusement Co.,
    Laredo, Texas.
  Mecca Theatre,
    New Orleans, La.

Clip
and mail
Coupon
Today

ROBERT
MORTON
ORGAN CO.
Send me without
obligation full details
of your New Selling Plan

Name ....
Theatre ....
Seating Capacity.... ....
City and State . ...

men
go together!
FOX pictures

Lefkowitz Circuit in Cleveland	**S. Z. Poli Circuit** in Connecticut
Feiber & Shea Goodrich and Colonial Theatres Akron, Ohio	**Peery Brothers** Egyptian Theatre Ogden, Utah
Leitich & Pryor Circuit In North Carolina	**Ackerman & Harris** Franklin Theatre Oakland, Cal.
P. J. Schlossman Regent and Strand Theatres Muskegon, Mich.	**Frank Durkee Circuit** in Baltimore, Md.
G. L. Hooper Grand-Isis-Orpheum Theatres Topeka, Kan.	**Moe Mark** Worcester and Lynn, Massachusetts
Interstate Amusement Co. Majestic Theatre Little Rock, Ark.	**Leland Theatre, Inc.** Leland and Clinton Square Theatres Albany, N. Y.

for your profit's sake!

THUNDER MOUNTAIN
from JOHN GOLDEN'S *Play "Howdy Folks"*

with MADGE BELLAMY ~ ZASU PITTS
LESLIE FENTON ~ ALEC B. FRANCIS
PAUL PANZER ~ OTIS HARLAN

Fox Film Corporation

admittedly—

The best comedies that any exhibitor can buy!

The most popular stories of these world known authors:

O. HENRY
 RICHARD HARDING DAVIS
  MABEL HERBERT URNER

Produced on a lavish scale hitherto seen only in superproductions with strong box office casts—directed by the world's leading comedy directors.

Snappy titles—eye catching photography and—

no slapstick

Acclaimed by critics everywhere the ultimate in real humor

IT HAS BECOME THE MARK OF DISTINCTION

Presented by

Fox Film Corporation.

meaning—

IMPERIAL
COMEDIES

20 Releases for the Season

Now Available!

"On The Go"

"Sweet Marie"

"Love and Lions"

"A Cloudy Romance"

O. HENRY
COMEDIES
Gems of Fiction

Now Available!

''Shoes''
and
"Transients in
Arcadia"

Directed by Daniel Keefe
Supervised by George Marshall

**EARLE FOXE in
VAN BIBBER**
Polite Society Comedies
By Richard Harding Davis

Now Available!

"The Big Game Hunter"
"The Wrestler"
Directed by Robert P. Kerr
Supervised by George Marshall

"The Sky Jumper"
Directed by George Marshall

THE MARRIED LIFE
OF HELEN
AND WARREN
by Mabel Herbert Urner

Now Available!

"A Business Engagement"
and
"All Abroad"

Directed by Albert Ray
Supervised by George Marshall

TO PLAY THESE LITTLE GIANTS OF THE SCREEN
WILLIAM FOX

Fox Film Corporation,

Member Motion Picture Producers and Distributors of America, Inc.—Will H. Hays, President.

CHARLIE CHAPLIN

IN

"THE GOLD RUSH"

*A Dramatic Comedy
written and directed
by Charlie Chaplin*

**A World's Record on
Broadway; New House
Records Everywhere**

Setting a box-office mark for the whole
motion picture industry to shoot at

"The Gold Rush"

Has made swift history. A world's record
for receipts and attendance, and a run of four
weeks at the Mark Strand, in New York; a
world's record for income per seat per day
at the Orpheum, Chicago, and new box-office
records everywhere - in big city or small - East,
West, North or South - that's the story of
"The Gold Rush."

NOW BOOKING
UNITED ARTISTS CORPORATION
Mary Pickford   Charles Chaplin
Douglas Fairbanks   D. W. Griffith

Ever since the opening—every single performance—afternoon and evening—holidays and workdays—sees the S.R.O. dangling in the Astor Theatre lobby. "The Phantom of the Opera" is now in its second week and going stronger than ever. Typical of the kind of business you are sure to get.

THE PHANTOM OF THE OPERA

NOW PLAYING AT THE
ASTOR
THEATRE
Broadway, N. Y.
TWICE DAILY
Tickets
Four Weeks In Advance
$1.50 Top

Starring

LON CHANEY

MARY PHILBIN NORMAN KERRY

Directed by RUPERT JULIAN

Supplementary direction
by EDWARD SEDGWICK

Presented by CARL LAEMMLE

A UNIVERSAL PRODUCTION

An Unsolicited Tribute on Universal's Comp

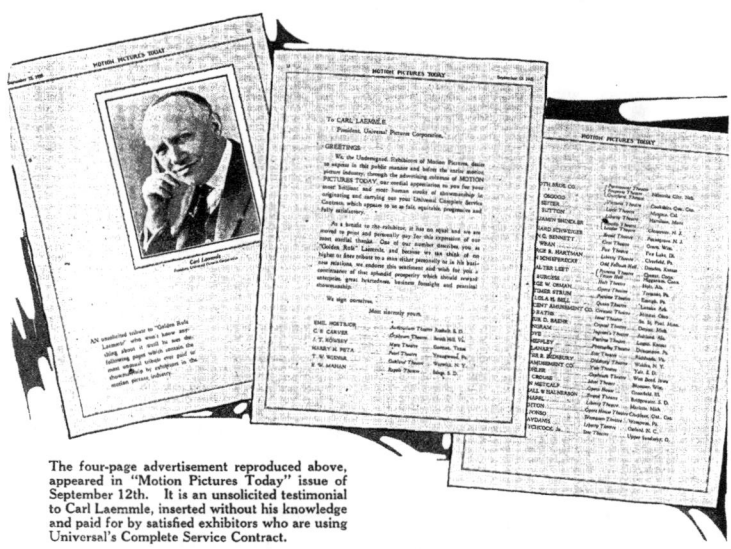

The four-page advertisement reproduced above, appeared in "Motion Pictures Today" issue of September 12th. It is an unsolicited testimonial to Carl Laemmle, inserted without his knowledge and paid for by satisfied exhibitors who are using Universal's Complete Service Contract.

Universal miles and miles ahead of all

to "Golden Rule Laemmle"
lete Service Contract

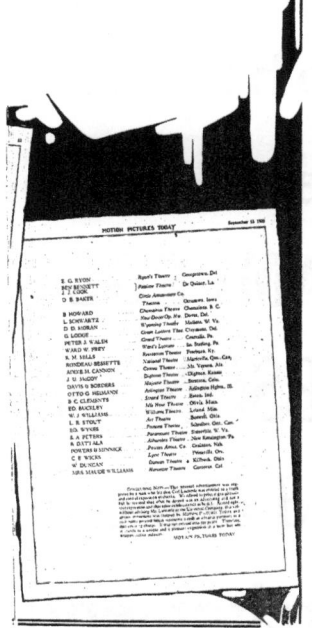

The exhibitors who have tendered this unique expression of appreciation to Carl Laemmle are a very small part of the many who have signed his Complete Service Contract and are reaping its benefits. To date there are 2525 of them with more coming every day. These exhibitors from every section of the country are loud in their praise and sincere in their thanks because Universal's Complete Service Contract will keep their theatres running in season and out. It will make money for them every week in the year.

Look at this from a purely business angle. Isn't it convincing evidence to the live-and-let-live policy inaugurated by Carl Laemmle with this contract? These exhibitors have tried and tested it and have found it to be just what Mr. Laemmle said it was—a Godsend to exhibitors.

That's the reason we reproduce this testimonial here. We want you to know from other exhibitors just what a wonderful business proposition it is. We want you to call in your Universal salesman and get your share of this prosperity.

oh what a wallop!

oh what a wallop!
oh! oh! oh! oh!
we've just seen "THE
CALGARY STAMPEDE"
with **HOOT GIBSON** and
we're knocked coo-coo
with joy and excitement!

The Whole Darned Universal Family

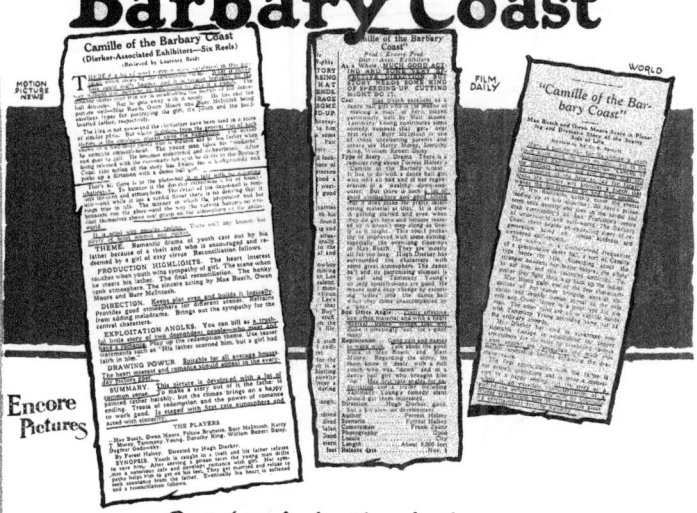

Glenn Hunter
and Edna Murphy
in His Buddy's Wife
with Douglas Gilmore, Flora Finch and Marcia Harris

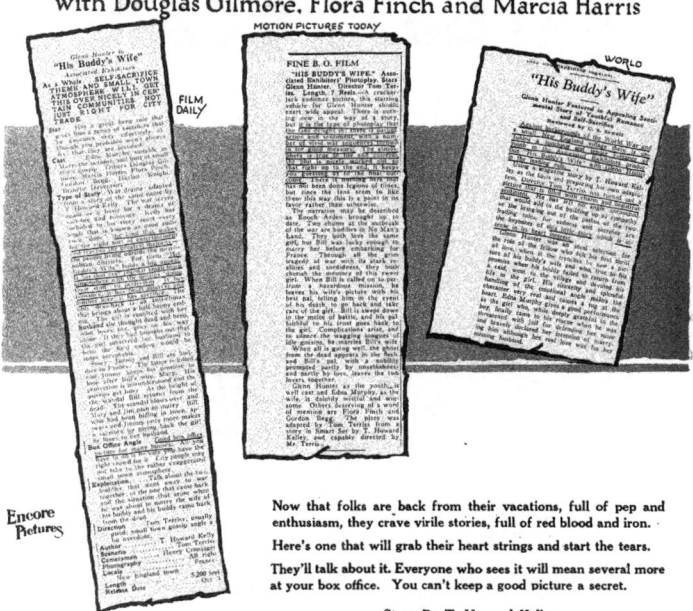

Now that folks are back from their vacations, full of pep and enthusiasm, they crave virile stories, full of red blood and iron.

Here's one that will grab their heart strings and start the tears.

They'll talk about it. Everyone who sees it will mean several more at your box office. You can't keep a good picture a secret.

Story By T. Howard Kelly

Produced and directed by Tom Terriss

Associated Exhibitors

PHYSICAL DISTRIBUTOR
PATHE EXCHANGE, INC   JOHN S. WOODY,   PRESIDENT   FOREIGN REPRESENTATIVE
INTER-GLOBE EXPORT CORPORATION

Lionel Barrymore
Hope Hampton
and Louise Glaum
in Fifty-Fifty

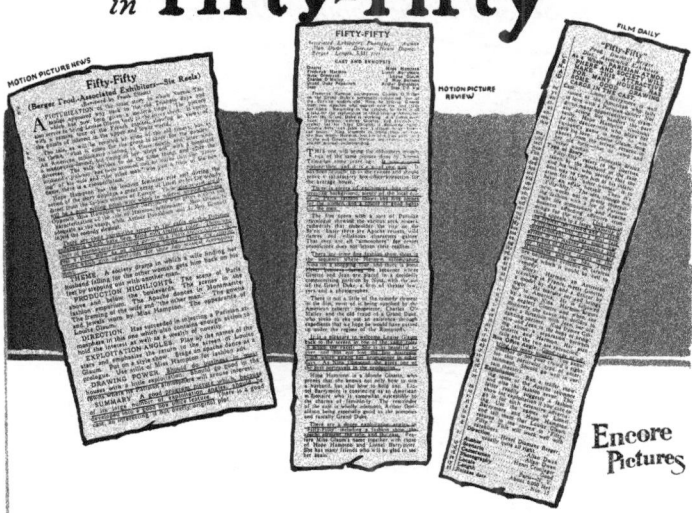

Encore
Pictures

·Crisp and spicy like a rare tropical fruit.

Settings and costumes that fairly dazzle.

French underworld, American high-life, all in one picture..

Looks class, IS class.

Has names that count on your theatre front.

A Henri Diamant Berger Production

Associated Exhibitors

PHYSICAL DISTRIBUTOR
PATHE' EXCHANGE, INC   JOHN S. WOODY,   PRESIDENT   FOREIGN REPRESENTATIVE
INTER-GLOBE EXPORT CORPORATION

Hal Roach *Presents*

Harold Lloyd
in "Never Weaken"

(The Second of the Popular Demand Series)

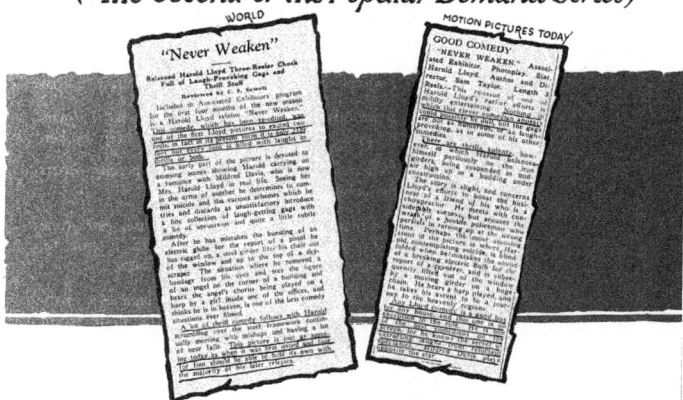

"Now or Never," the first of the Popular Demand Series, was a clean-up everywhere.

Knocked a score of house records galley west.

Salvaged lots of weeks that exhibitors had charged off in advance as bloomers.

All you have to do is to advertise this one—

For there's only one Harold Lloyd, and "Never Weaken" is a pip.

Associated Exhibitors

PHYSICAL DISTRIBUTOR
PATHÉ EXCHANGE, INC.

JOHN S. WOODY, PRESIDENT

FOREIGN REPRESENTATIVE
INTER-GLOBE EXPORT CORPORATION

KINOGRAMS
NEVER CHARGES FOR
"EXTRA   SERVICE"

A Kinograms contract has no strings to it

Any of its exhibitor friends will tell you that

It promises full service and during its six years
of progress its promise has never been broken

When an "extra special" news happening occurs
the exhibitors get the benefit

No matter how much extra expense, extra time
and extra trouble KINOGRAMS is put to,
nothing extra is asked of the exhibitor

Remember the Roma disaster, Japanese earthquake, Kentucky Derby, and the more recent
Shenandoah crash

Each a special with extra service to the exhibitor
without extra charge

BOOK KINOGRAMS
The News Reel Built Like a Newspaper

Writing Movie

Who?	Warner Bros.
How?	By building ad
On What?	The entire War
Where?	Everywhere. Big
How do they do it?	In many ways.

plishing more in
ever dreamed of.
papers. Not in a
Serial stories that
is ready for re
fit of a tremendous
picture aroused by
your local paper.

Never before

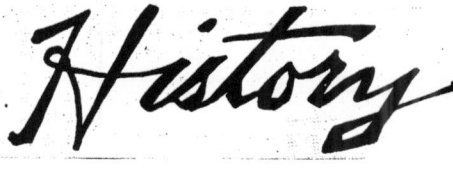

History

vance interest.

ner product for 1925-26.

cities and small cities.

SERIALIZATION, for one. Accom-
this big service than was
Stories placed in daily news-
few cities, but in hundreds.
appear when the picture
lease. You reap the bene-
advance interest in your
the fascinating fiction in

could you buy such

"The Wife
Who Wasn't
Wanted"
Now being
Serialized
in

**400
DAILY**
Newspapers

PLUS
SERVICE

12
GIANT
REASONS
WHY

Gene Stratton-Porter's

WILL BE A NATION WIDE MOP-UP
FOR THOUSANDS OF EXHIBITORS

Watch for these reasons—To be published every week from now on

REASON
—No. 1—

These newspaper ads you see reproduced here in miniature are now running in forty (40) leading Metropolitan dailies throughout the Nation telling millions of people about Mrs. Porter's latest and by far greatest story.

As America's best known, best loved fiction author, she has a reading public of more than 10,000,000 people—a force to reckon with. The publishers of the book—Doubleday Page & Co. thru these newspaper ads are selling thousands upon thousands of the books to new readers of Mrs. Porter as well as her huge following.

We've got 11 more giant reasons coming why "THE KEEPER OF THE BEES" will be an absolute miop for exhibitors.

Watch For
REASON
No. 2
NEXT WEEK

It means MONEY to you

FILM BOOKING OFFICES
723 Seventh Ave., New York
Exchanges Everywhere

Direction by
James Leo Meehan.

Shines at every box office

Live wire exhibitors are all rushing to book this live wire star in his greatest money maker.

Constance Talmadge

in. "HER SISTER

presented by
JOSEPH M. SCHENCK
with

RONALD COLMAN

Story by . . . . . HANS KRAELY

A SIDNEY FRANKLIN
PRODUCTION

Photography by . . . . . ARTHUR EDESON
Art Direction by . . . . WILLIAM C MENZIES
Wardrobe by . . . . ADRIAN
Assistant Director . . . . . . SCOTTY BEAL

A First National

From
PARIS"

The beautiful scene
of the Follies Bergere

Picture

Motion Picture News

VOL. XXXII   ALBANY, N. Y., AND NEW YORK CITY, SEPTEMBER 26, 1925   NO. 13

Special Attractions

IN reply to a recent editorial here, asking for the special picture and more of them, an editorial elsewhere takes up a counter plea for the average picture on behalf of the average picture theatre-goer.

We don't want to be unfair to another editorial. But we strongly contend for the general principle that it is dangerous to the box-office at large to advocate a supply of average pictures for it.

In the creative world, whether you write stories, or make books, paintings, or pictures, it is difficult to keep on hitting the high spots. They are reached out of the ruck of clever and sincere endeavor. But quantity production always tends to breed mediocre stuff. It makes hack writers and hack producers of pictures. Maybe an amazing lot of people will stand for it and pay for it. But they would pay better for better material. The average movie-goers are sharply critical these days. They don't want average pictures. Ask the exhibitor.

Before Chaplin's "Gold Rush" came along, every exhibitor I talked with urged that it be hurried to the theatres. Picture houses, they said, were starving for it. People keep going to the movies, but the things they hanker for don't come along as fast as they hope; and then the theatres everywhere suddenly report apathy. And it gets serious.

Last Spring William Fox announced that he was through with program pictures. He would make no more of them. The Fox Announcement of this season's product created a lot of attention. Why? Because it was tuned up to special attractions. Tom Mix pictures, by the way, are of course special attractions. A star of such appeal, aided and abetted always by the best stories he can get—that is always essential—is a special attraction. And, all in all, I do not define a special attraction, or a greater movie, or whatever you call it, as one of lavish production and high cost. F. B. O. turns out some specials each year at very moderate cost. Nor do I merely mean the outstanding picture sure to result from the large output of a finely equipped producing organization. I mean the picture that a good showman has taken time enough to originate and then has concentrated upon its production.

The fact of the matter is that every producing company ranks in the exhibitor mind today as to the specials they turn out.

The thing that works against good pictures is their wholesale production. It always has. It always will.

The exhibitors of this country and Great Britain object to block booking. Well, block booking—and the public objects primarily—is a necessary outcome of block production.

As one who has written for a living, I know well enough that you can't hit the peaks all the time. But you certainly can't if you set a pace of quantity production; and you can come mighty near it if you have the creative ability and do a few things and do them well. That is equally true of picture making.

There still exists a belief that a man who wants to make money—and he may be a commercial genius, too—can also make pictures the public wants. Well, he can't. And again you can't make them by imitation. A man may look at the models in a Fifth Avenue shop—study them, and then produce wonderful imitations for a lower price. That goes with gowns, but not at all with pictures. And money alone won't make them. Nor can we rely upon accident.

Well, what does make them? Concentration upon fewer pictures by men who can create for the show world. That's the one answer we know of.

And we repeat: the exhibitors of this country want this kind of attraction, and Europe wants them. And the business needs them. By the end of this year, it is said, 5,000,000 out of the 25,000,000 families of the country will own radio sets. That's one thing to consider; and another is that the legitimate stage business lost its hold when it went into the quantity production of road shows.

W. A. Johnston

MOTION PICTVRE
NEWS

September 26 1925

Vol. XXXII No. 13

Founded in September 1913

Publication Office: Lyon Block, Albany, N. Y.

Editorial and General Offices: 729 7th Ave., New York City

Branch Offices: 845 S. Wabash Ave., Chicago, Ill. Room 616 Security Bldg., Hollywood, Calif.

Senator Walker's Great Victory

SENATOR JAMES J. WALKER, outstanding friend of the industry, has won a smashing victory in the Democratic primaries for the nomination for Mayor of New York City. His plurality at the polls on September 15 was 100,000; a decisive tribute to an honest, faithful, brilliant public servant.

In the forefront of his battle was another staunch friend of the motion pictures—Governor Alfred E. Smith. So the victory has double significance for film folk everywhere.

The Motion Picture Division of the campaign played an important part; and it will continue its activities in the no less important campaign leading up to the election in November.

And all this is done without thought of partisanship. It is a simple acknowledgment of friendship toward the great friendship that Jimmy Walker has always borne the motion picture. It is an emphatic demonstration of appreciation by the exhibitors of Greater New York and the industry generally.

MOTION PICTURE NEWS, first among the trade papers to hail Jimmy Walker's candidacy several weeks ago, joins with his thousands of friends throughout the country, in rejoicing at his great success in the primaries. There will be still further cause for rejoicing when he becomes—as he surely will—the Chief Magistrate of the world's greatest city.

What Attracts the Public

THE CLEVELAND PLAIN DEALER has recently completed a survey among its readers on the subject: "What Attracts the Public to the Movies?" Incidentally, the compilation of the hundreds of letters received is being sent to all producers by the Stillman Theatre.

The table showing the preferences of those who took part in the questionnaire is as follows:

Number who go to see their favorite star, 252.

Number who go because reviewers recommend it, 193.

Number who go to see favorite book or story filmed, 177.

Number who go because attracted by advertising, 158.

Number who go because of director of picture, 157.

Number who go because of the title of the picture, 144.

Number who go because of nature or standard play, 138.

Number who go because of musical setting, 135.

Number who go to favorite theatre, 133.

Number who are attracted by newspaper publicity, 121.

Number who go because of word of mouth boosting, 117.

Number who are attracted by magazine publicity, 96.

Number who go because of author of story, 73.

Number who go because of posters and photo displays, 49.

Number who are attracted by general publicity, 38.

September 26, 1925   MOTION PICTURE NEWS   Vol. XXXII, No. 13
Published weekly by Motion Picture News, Inc., William A. Johnston, President; E. Kendall Gillett, Vice-President; William A. Johnston, Editor; J. S. Dickerson, Associate Editor; Oscar Cooper, Managing Editor; Fred J. Beecroft, Advertising Manager; L. H. Mason, Chicago Representative; William McCormack, Los Angeles Representative. Subscription price, $3 per year, post paid in United States. Mexico, Hawaii, Porto Rico, Philippine Islands and some other countries; Canada, $5; foreign, $10.00. Copyright 1924, by Motion Picture News, Inc., in the United States and Great Britain. Title registered in the United States Patent Office and foreign countries. Western Union cable address is "Picknews," New York. Entered as second-class matter January 31st, 1924, at the postoffice, Albany, N. Y., under the Act of March 3, 1879.

Little Mary Pickford paints her famous aunt as she appears in "Little Annie Rooney" (United Artists), where she returns to her original type of role.

PICTURES AND PEOPLE

LIL'S IN TOWN

THERE'LL be genuine atmosphere in "Fifth Avenue," for A. H. Sebastian and members of his producing unit have arrived in New York to film scenes on the world famous thoroughfare, and expect to finish "shooting" there within the next ten days.

In the Sebastian party are Marguerite de La Motte and Allan Forrest, principals, director Robert G. Vignola, Sally Long, Josephine Norman, Maurice Sebastian, producer's assistant, Phillip Carle, assistant director and cameraman J. C. Van Trees and Lillian R. Gale.

Miss Gale, formerly a member of MOTION PICTURE NEWS editorial staff, forsook the journalistic grind several years ago and sought the congenial atmosphere of Hollywood, where she has since distinguished herself in picture roles. It was no new experience for her, however, as prior to taking up newspaper work, she had yielded to the camera's compelling lure. And having been lured back again she expects to stay lured, for according to Lillian—it's the only life. Between attending to her professional duties and receiving calls from a multitude of friends who haven't seen her in a dog's age, for this is a long-delayed visit to the big town, she is having a strenuous time, and will probably find Hollywood real restful, when the company returns there to complete production, after the Gotham scenes have been filmed.

THE NEW FEATURES

PARAMOUNT'S long heralded production, "The Pony Express," occupies both the Rialto and Rivoli Theatres this week, playing to crowded houses and amply fulfilling the promises made in its behalf by advance advertising. James Cruze has every reason to feel proud over his latest directorial accomplishment. It's a fine spectacle depicting a particularly vivid phase of American history of equal value as an educational and entertaining factor.

Mr. Cruze's name is naturally enough inseparably associated with the making of "The Covered Wagon," a fact which led most

Harold Lloyd, now at work on his first for Paramount release, presents his director, Sam Taylor, with a megaphone as a souvenir of their fifth anniversary together.

Norman Alley, International Newscameraman in Chicago, who flew to the scene of the "Shenandoah" disaster, then flew on to New York with his negative. (Int'l Newsreel Photo.)

Evelyn Brent, F. B. O. star, now on a brief trip to New York, who was the guest of honor last week at a luncheon to the trade paper and daily fraternity.

Nazimova, who returned recently from Paris, more youthful and charming than ever, and has gone on to Hollywood, where she will resume picture work.

At the left, Brownie I, the former educated bull terrier of the Christie Comedy studio; and at the right, Brownie II, his successor, a remarkably intelligent dog who will appear in forthcoming releases through Educational.

Robert McGowan, director of Hal Roach's "Our Gang" comedies for Pathe, with his own "gang" consisting of Mrs. Bob and the two Miss McGowans.

of the picture critics to draw comparisons between that screen masterpiece and his latest contribution to the silent drama, giving a majority vote in favor of the former. Personally, we agree with this verdict, yet "The Pony-Express" stands out in bold relief from the general ruck of films as a feature of superlative merit.

It's no small task to smoothly weave melodramatic and sentimental lure into a historical tapestry, but this has been neatly done in the present instance, a very necessary box office slant, for the fans must have their romance at any cost. A curious angle in the picture is the disposal of the murderous Mr. Slade, who instead of being punished after the traditional style of screen villains, wins promotion, and no doubt the increased respect of his ruffianly following. While it is historically true that Slade achieved temporary success, it is a matter of record that he was later hanged by the outraged members of a community who finally wearied of his crime revels. Somehow, we fancy the average movie patron would have been better pleased had the picture, given at least a hint of his abrupt finish. This could have been accomplished

D. J. McGowan and D. McBeath of the First National Home Office, and A. Haggerty and G. Campbell of the Boston exchange, checking up the posters and accessories coming into Boston as the result of the New Haven shut-down.

without swerving an inch from the exact historical trail and satisfied the spectators who yearned to see a cold-blooded monster meet with his just deserts.

In First National's "Shore Leave" at the Mark Strand, Richard

This is not, as you might imagine, a trick double exposure shot; it's Marie Prevost, Warner Bros. star, with her sister, Peggy, a dancer of no little ability.

Dorothy Crooker, who represents the Christie studios in "Screen and Beauties of 1925," a vaudeville act, does the split, supported by Jimmie Adams and Bobby Vernon, both starring in comedies for Educational release.

Barthelmess scores a distinct hit in the hero role of one of Uncle Sam's jolly sailor lads. It is an admirable characterization of the careless, free-and-easy gob who is at home in any port. Dorothy Mackail sharing honors with the star by her pleasing performance as Connie Martin, the little dressmaker who fears she is drifting on the rocks of eternal spinsterhood, but steers clear and has Dick take her in tow after all. The picture is strong in human interest and heart appeal, varied by a flow of bright comedy calculated to keep any audience in good humor.

"Souls For Sables," a Tiffany production, holds forth at the Colony, and registers as acceptable entertainment. It is a dramatic story of a young wife who longs for luxuries and almost wrecks her domestic happiness in an attempt to obtain them by questionable methods. The action is handicapped by excess footage in the opening reel, but handsome settings, elaborate gowns and excellent acting by an adequate cast, headed by Claire Windsor and Eugene O'Brien, are big helps in boosting the picture

The Warner Theatre presents "His Majesty Bunker Bean," a Warner Brothers offering. They had material obtained from Harry Leon Wilson's novel and stage play which could have been wrought into a delightful comedy, but director Harry Beaumont elected to make it merely slapstick. The result is a film which misses altogether the subtle humor and delicate shades of pathos originally woven by the author into one of the most appealing of modern fiction tales. Matt Moore, far too mature for the leading role of youthful Bunker, conforms to his director's slapstick ideas, also investing the luckless hero with a feverishly effeminate personality which succeeds in thoroughly eliminating any sympathetic interest the spectators might have felt in the career of the young gent who imagined himself the reincarnation of an Egyptian king.

VERSATILE ALMA

WHEN Alma Rubens made her appearance in Fox's "The Winding Stair," and her lithe figure bent and swayed in the sinuous measure of a wild African dance, all Hollywood marveled over the grace and ease of her performance. What Hollywood didn't know was that prior to her entry into movie land she distinguished herself both as singer and dancer in a San Francisco musical comedy company, and this engagement led to her becoming leading lady for Douglas Fairbanks in "The Half Breed."

Later she played leading roles in English, French and German productions, and when traveling in the Orient perfected herself in the dances peculiar to the Far East, her training in this respect resulting in the surprise she gave the movie colony. Last season William Fox signed Miss Rubens to a contract, and she scored heavily as Lady Hermione in "Gerald Cranston's Lady," as well as in the feminine lead of "She Wolves." Her forthcoming characterization of Lady Isable in "East Lynne", and dancing interlude in "The Winding Stair" should win her fame as one of the most versatile of screen actresses.

CONCERNING FAY LAMPHIER

ON September 12, Fay Lamphier, winner of the 1925 Beauty Pageant at Atlantic City, received the coveted title of "Miss America" from the judges with which goes the designation of "the most beautiful girl in the United States." And that isn't all, for she is signed up to appear in Paramount pictures under a long term contract; her first starring role being in "The American Venus."

Jesse L. Lasky, first vice-president of the Famous Players-Lasky Corporation enthusiastically predicts that within a year Fay Lamphier will be as well known to the public as Betty Bronson and Esther Ralston, both of whom quite recently emerged from obscurity into filmland fame. Mr. Lasky was at Atlantic City just prior to the windup of the beauty tournament, saw Fay Lamphier, entered as Miss California, on the Boardwalk, and then and there voiced an emphatic agreement with Roy Hunt, head cameraman of the Frank Tuttle outfit, who pointed her out as "the prettiest girl of the whole batch!"

At that time no selection had been made or prizes awarded. Paramount's committee consisted of three men, Frank Tuttle, director of "The American Venus," Larry Hitt, art director, and Armand T. Nichols, director general of the pageant. Their task was to name from among sixty-four entries the girl who was to fill the title role in the picture, and win Miss Helene Sardeau's American Venus trophy. A separate committe of fifteen judges on the grandstand cast approving eyes on the beauty brigade and that afternoon dropped their ballots for the Miss America award. Debating in a hotel room three other judges finally agreed upon Miss Lamphier. That night on the Million Dollar pier thousands sat eagerly awaiting the result.

"It was a sight not easily forgoten," said Mr. Lasky, "and it pleased me beyond measure when Miss Olive Anne Alcorn, styled 'th world's most beautifully formed girl,' presented the American Venus trophy to the latter. There was real drama and suspense as the director of judges, Mr. Louis St. John, read out the names, and it was finally made clear that the same girl selected by our committee for the picture lead had won the grand award.

"This double selection of Fay Lamphier proves conclusively to me that the feminine fad of boyish bob and boyish figure is passing. For Miss Lamphier is a perfect example of girlish beauty such as men worshipped in the past. Her hair is long, golden and curly. She scales 138 pounds, a real American Venus, not so plump as the Venus de Milo, but with grace in every line. A year from now I am willing to confirm the prediction I now make—that Miss Lamphier will set a new beauty style and the vogue in attractive young women will be the wholesome, distinctively feminine type she represents.

On the screen she will appear as Miss Alabama, in competition with Miss Centreville, played by Esther Ralston. Olive Anne

Ken Maynard stopped work at Lake Arrowhead the other day long enough to take part in his marriage ceremony. The bride was Miss Leeper, a society girl of South Bend, Ind. Among those witnessing the ceremony were Stuart Holmes, Monty Banks, Paul Powell and Virginia Lee Corbin.

Alcorn portrays Miss Greentown and Louise Brooks of the Ziegfeld Follies, fills the Miss Bayport role. Local competitions will be held in each city where a Paramount Exchange is located, the winning girl in each case to be known as American Venus of Chicago, of Omaha, of Denver, and so on. Arrangements will be made for the holding of an American Venus Ball in all large cities, part of the proceeds to go to charity."

OPEN CLEVELAND HOUSE

ON Saturday evening, September 5, Warner Brothers opened another theatre, this time the Circle, at 102nd Street and Euclid Avenue, Cleveland, Ohio. The house was formerly operated under management of Martin Printz. Some months ago it closed for extensive alterations, including the installation of a new balcony, raising the seating capacity to 2,000, and the redecorating and refurnishing of the theatre from back to front. The opening was attended by huge crowds and proved an unqualified success. It was personally supervised by George H. Dumond, head of the Warner theatre division. Mr. Printz continues as executive manager, with the general policy dictated by Warner Brothers through Mr. Dumond, who will take flying trips to Cleveland frequently.

Paramount participated in the Atlantic City Beauty Pageant this year, and will make a picture, "The American Venus," around it. At the left is seen Jesse L. Lasky, vice-president, on the famous boardwalk, and at the right, Fay Lamphier, Miss San Francisco, who won the pageant and the title role in "The American Venus," snapped with Ernest Torrence, made up as Father Neptune.

TO MEET MISS BRENT

NAT ROTHESTEIN, F. B. O. director of publicity and advertising, arranged a luncheon at the Biltmore on September 10th, whereby members of the New York dailies, fan magazines and trade papers were enabled to make the acquaintance of Evelyn Brent, well enough known on the screen hereabouts, but not so familiar in person.

Major Thomson, F. B. O. president, and Mr. Herbert B. Yates occupied posts of honor on either side of the star. There were no speeches, or business discussions, such things being utterly forbidden, as announced officially beforehand, and the promise was sacredly kept. However, it did leak out that Miss Brent will return to the Coast next week to begin work on a new crook drama, "Light Fingers," and Nat Rothestein wouldn't deny that she had signed a new contract to make pictures for the organization during the current year.

Among those present were: Louella O. Parsons, of the N. Y. American; Irene Thirer, of the Daily News; Regina Cannon, of the Evening Graphic; Ethel Rosemon, of Moving Pictures Stories; Dorothy C. Jordon, of the N. Y. World; Mary Jane Warren, of Motion Pictures Today; Clio Lor, of Women's Wear; Rose Pelswick, of the Evening Journal; Helen Klumph, of the Morning Telegraph; Dorothy Herzog, of the Daily Mirror; Major Thomson, of F. B. O.; Herbert J. Yates, Mr. Litell of Zit's; J. A. Milligan and George Bradley, of the Morning Telegraph; Arthur James, of Motion Pictures Today; Jay M. Schreck; John Spargo, of the Exhibitors Herald; M. W. Liebler, of the Evening Post; Kelcey Allen, of Women's Wear; John A. Archer, Tom Waller, C. Schottenfels, of Moving Picture World; George Gerhard, of the Evening World; Pete Milne, of the Trade Review; Chester J. Smith, of the MOTION PICTURE NEWS; Larry Reid and W. Adolphe Roberts, of the Brewster Publications; Maurice ("Red") Kann, of Film Daily; Julius Cohen, of Staats-Zeitung; Lee Marcus, Colvin W. Brown, Edna Williams, Al Boasberg, D. A. Poucher.

Norma Shearer, who recently completed work in "The Tower of Lies" for Metro-Goldwyn-Mayer, snapped in a bit of snappy action on the tennis court.

PEREZ HERE; SIMMONS EN ROUTE

PAUL E. PEREZ, for the past year director of advertising, publicity and exploitation for European in London, returned to the United States last week and is engaged at the Home Office of Universal, where he was an assistant to Paul Gulick before his departure for foreign shores.

While in Great Britain, Paul distinguished himself for his exploitation and advertising campaigns, particularly that which he put over in England, Scotland and Wales for "The Hunchback". An arrangement which he made with the Woolworth stores resulted in the first nation-wide tie-up in Great Britain.

He made himself widely popular in the trade, and with Horace Judge was active in the formation of the British Motion Picture Advertisers association, known there as the "Bumpas". A luncheon was given him on his departure, at which he was presented with a silver-headed stick. The trade press also paid high tribute to his ability and personal qualities.

Also, Michael L. Simmons, for the past six months handling exploitation in association with Perez for European, sailed this week on the Mauretania and will arrive in New York any day, after serving for a time as acting director of exploitation. He has organized a service which will continue to function along American lines.

Simmons' association with European was a sequel to six months of travel through Italy, Austria, Germany and France, where he studied local conditions and showmanship. He writes that he plans an independent press and publicity service for exhibitors on his return.

Henry B. Walthall, the Little Colonel, who is now contributing one of his inimitable characterizations to "The Plastic Age," a Preferred Picture.

SAM GOLDWYN'S FIND

LOIS MORAN, the sixteen year old girl, who fills the role of Laurel in "Stella Dallas," the United Artists release sponsored by Samuel Goldwyn, was discovered and brought into screen prominence by the latter while visiting Paris last winter. On the stage she made a successful appearance in Marc Connelly's "The Wisdom Tooth," at Baltimore and Atlantic City, and will play the leading feminine role in that production on Broadway this Fall. Which doesn't mean that she will discard the movies, for after the play has finished its New York run, she will return to the Goldwyn fold.

Fannie Hurst, noted author, who won Liberty's $50,000 contest with "The Moving Finger," which she has helped adapt at the Paramount West Coast studio.

Paramount - Balaban and Katz Deal Reported Closed

F. P. - L. To Create Separate Theatre Corporation?

THE long-expected deal between Famous Players Lasky and Balaban & Katz was this week reported practically closed. At the same time, it became known that the Famous Players theatre activities would be entirely separated, according to present plans, from the parent company. This, it appears, will happen whether the B. & K. deal is consummated or not.

The chances that the deal will fall through are considered very slim. Official announcement will no doubt be made shortly. Meanwhile, no statement could be obtained from the principals.

The merger with B. & K.—if "merger" is the word—means that the vast theatre holdings of that concern will come into the Paramount fold, under a joint management plan. That is to say, the separate corporation will be formed, according to the present outlook, and Sam Katz

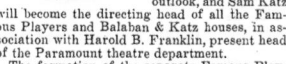

Adolph Zukor

will become the directing head of all the Famous Players and Balaban & Katz houses, in association with Harold B. Franklin, present head of the Paramount theatre department.

The formation of the separate Famous Players theatre corporation, in itself an unprecedented step by a film producer-distributor was rumored months ago; and it was believed then that its actual consummation hinged upon the signing of the papers with Balaban & Katz.

At the same time, it was strongly evident then that the creation of this corporation was inevitable sooner or later, in the natural course of circumstances.

The future theatre operations of Famous Players, then, would be conducted under a separate corporate identity, but the stock of the company would be owned outright by Paramount, if present indications are correct. This would mean, no doubt, that the theatre activities would be run from a different headquarters entirely separate from the Paramount executive offices.

Indications that the Famous Players B. & K. deal was nearing the signature mark were contained in the following dispatch from Chicago to The Wall Street Journal:

"Barney Balaban, vice-president of Balaban & Katz, says prospects for closing a transaction with Famous Players-Lasky are bright. Mr. Balaban was in New York last week and returned for consultation with other principals in the company. He is leaving for New York again."

Sam Katz was in New York this week and could not be reached for a statement. Neither was any comment available at Paramount.

The virtual merger of Balaban & Katz with the Famous Players theatres would give the latter upwards of six hundred

houses, by far the greater portion of which are strategic exhibition points, and would make it by all odds the giant corporation of the industry.

It will be recalled that, according to a statement made by Emil Shauer, head of the Paramount foreign department several months ago, and never denied, Famous Players owned or controlled at that time 358 theatres in America. The latest figures on the B. & K. holdings place their total at 100, but this does not include theatres under construction.

Since the statement by Mr. Shauer, Famous Players has acquired a number of theatres. It is of course well known that, included in the Balaban & Katz chain, are the important Kunsky and A. H. Blank circuits; and there is a further ramification in the fact that First National, in which Mr. Katz is a dominant figure, recently brought the West Coast Theatres, Inc., comprising over 100 houses, under its virtual control as a corporation.

In the opinion of close observers, these latest developments may be taken to mean that Famous Players is gradually bringing

about the creation of a theatre chain, which will not only be the biggest numerically, but will also have far-reaching effects on the distribution problem, an angle which is sometimes overlooked when theatre acquisitions are discussed.

In other words, the acquisition of a great number of theatres would reduce both the cost and the problem of distribution.

It is a safe observation that the B. & K. deal and the creation of the separate theatre concern, considered together, will write new history in the industry. What the ultimate result will be, no one can foretell.

Reports were widely current, but could not be confirmed, that Sam Katz, as associate chief of the new theatre corporation, would receive a salary of $100,000 annually, besides other financial considerations.

Sam Katz

Earl Crabb to Manage New Paramount Boston House

Earl L. Crabb, for nineteen months district manager for Southern Enterprises of Texas, left Dallas, his headquarters, September 7 for Boston where he will become managing director of the New Paramount house which will possibly be named The Plymouth. John J. Friedl, for nineteen months, managing director of the Palace Theatre in Dallas has been named by Harold Franklin to succeed Mr. Crabb as Texas district manager for Southern Enterprises. His successor as managing director of the Palace has not been named. Mr. Friedl is one of the youngest district managers with Famous Players being but 27 years old. He joined Paramount six years ago as an exploiteer on Claud Saunders' staff.

Pearl Keating is Signed as Scenario Chief

Metropolitan Pictures, Inc., has engaged Pearl Keating to head its eastern scenario department. She will make her headquarters in New York at the home office of Producers Distributing Corporation. In addition to her work for Metropolitan she will purchase material for the Christie Comedies, under personal arrangements made by Charles Christie.

Miss Keating was for several years head of Warner Brothers scenario department. She has had wide experience in both the theatrical and motion picture fields.

Beaudry Made Secretary of Arrow

Louis L. Beaudry was elected secretary of Arrow Pictures Corporation at a meeting of the board of directors held on Wednesday, September 9th, at which W. E. Shallenberger, president of the company, presided.

Seider Discusses New Form Contract

Clarifies Certain Points Raised by Ohio Exhibitor in Letter to Motion Picture News

JOSEPH M. SEIDER, chairman of the M. P. T. O. A. Contract and Arbitration Committee, in an exclusive statement to MOTION PICTURE NEWS this week clarified certain points in his proposed new contract. This was done in response to a letter written to the NEWS by G. M. Bertling, of the Favorite Theatre, Piqua, Ohio, which Mr. Seider was asked to comment upon. Mr. Bertling's letter follows:

"I was reading over your News of Sept. 12th and also was reading over Mr. Seider's new form of Contract. As an exhibitor I wish to say that Mr. Seider surely was making out the contract to suit the Distributor. I think now is about the time that the Exhibitor should be given a little thought on this contract matter. Where has the Exhibitor got a half a chance on his contract or the present contract? What does the Exhibitor have to do when he buys, pictures? When a salesman comes to him and tries to sell him pictures he has to buy the whole product or nothing. If there are a half dozen pictures that is O. K. for his house and there are half a dozen that is not, what does the Exhibitor get. He either buys them all or he don't get any. What has become of the contract that has the Cancelation clause in it? Why it was put on the shelf because it did not suit the Distributor.

"There isn't a contract in force now that gives the. Exhibitor a fair chance, and I don't think that there is anyone that can show me a contract that does. What are the Film Boards for? Just to suit a few of the Distributors. Arbitration boards, what do they do for the Exhibitor? Nothing. I think that the M. P. T. O. A. should think of the Exhibitor and give him a chance to have a little to say as to how he should buy his service and also stop this BLOCK BOOKING. How many exchanges can you do business with if you don't buy the whole product? There isn't any. I do business with about ten or twelve exchanges and there isn't any that you can get along with unless you buy all of their product.

"The M. P. T. O. A. may mean alright but the way I get their new form of contract is not suiting me and a lot of other exhibitors. I think that the time has come when the Exhibitor should have a little to say and we all know that we are paying enough for our service that we ought to be able to have a little to say pretty soon.

"I also noted where Mr. Seider has it fixed where the Exhibitor is to pay for the shipment both ways of film. Does that look like the Exhibitor is getting anything? I think that it is time for us to get busy and have a contract where we can buy as many pictures as we want to without buying the exchange out and also the exchange to pay one way on the shipment and also give us the Cancelation Clause. If we buy ten pictures and lose money on them we haven't got a chance. I may be wrong on the way I am taking Mr. Seider's new form of contract, but it don't look good to me. I may not just understand the contract, but if you can show me where the EXHIBITOR has a chance in it, why I am going to be the first Exhibitor to O. K. Mr. Seider's contract."

Mr. Seider's comment follows:

Missouri Exhibitors War on Sunday Ordinances

WITH the arrival of fall it appears that Missouri exhibitors are to be presented a new series of annual "problems" to work. O. W. McCutcheon, Sikeston, Mo., exhibitor who was arrested last week for operating his theatre on Sunday, is out on bond. Mr. McCutcheon has appealed the case and will test the validity of the law, as there is no state Sunday closing law.

Then there is the battle in Moberly, Mo., a town of 25,000, which comes to a decision in the next few days, the mayor having vetoed an ordinance permitting Sunday shows. William Gotter of the Fourth Street theatre, leader in the fight against a group of ministers, feels confident the exhibitors will win out. However, the big issue to be settled, as far as Sunday shows are concerned, is whether or not city ordinance can prohibit Sunday shows when the statutes of the state do not. The Sikeston case may throw a light upon this.

"Mr. G. M. Bertling, Manager, Favorite Theatre, Piqua, Ohio, is correct when he says that he may not just understand our proposed contract. Otherwise, there could not be any explanation for his assumption that it has been written solely from the viewpoint of the Distributor.

"It is an absolutely mutually fair contract. Practically all the old clauses that have been so objectionable to the theatre owners have been eliminated. Provisions have been added to clarify the rights of the parties under the contract and to eliminate most of the difficulties the theatre owner has encountered under the old contract and, yet, the new contract is shorter and in plain language.

"Many theatre owners are complaining against the 'block booking sales policy' used by many distributors. However, the new contract is not a medium through which this condition can be remedied. In the territories where the distributors meet sales resistance, they sell on an individual picture basis.

"The cancellation clause, referred to by Mr. Bertling, was an optional clause in the old contract and the clause, suggested for this contract, was as follows:

"'If this contract designates certain photoplays by title, it shall be non-cancellable as to such photoplays. If it embraces a series of photoplays, not designated by title, it may be cancelled, as to such series by either party after two photoplays of such series have been played and paid for, by notice in writing to the other party within ten days after playing the second of said photoplays, such cancellation to take effect after ———— additional photoplays shall have been played and paid for."

"The Independent Motion Picture Association's Contract Committee objected to this clause being a part of the contract and requested that it be made an optional clause and that its incorporation in the contract should be left to negotiations between the parties at the time the contract is signed.

"That this clause was not written on our proposed draft of the contract, is not the fault of the Distributors, but entirely my fault in having overlooked its incorporation in the contract.

"We have not fixed it where the Exhibitor is to pay for the shipment of film both ways. It is a condition in the old contract, the practice has been in effect for the past eight years and no objections to it have been made to us.

"In answer to Mr. Bertling's statement, 'If we buy ten pictures and lose money in them, we haven't got a chance,' we can only say that if the money is lost through no fault of the exhibitor and through the fault of the distributor or through the misrepresentations of the distributor, then the exhibitor has a chance, because there is a definite provision made in the proposed contract giving the right to the arbitration board to determine the matter and the power to award a refund or damages to the exhibitor.

"Mr. Bertling is opposed to the present arbitration system and Film Boards of Trade. We also are opposed to the present arbitration system and the Film Boards of Trade and their methods. In our contract we have offered a solution to this vexatious problem."

$10,000 Fire Destroys Colorado House

The Rialto Theatre, Delta, Colorado, was almost completely destroyed by fire Saturday night, September 5th. The extent of the damage will reach an approximate total of $10,000. The cause of the fire is unknown although it occurred immediately after the last show. About ten people were in the house at the time. All safely retired from the building.

Part of the estimated damage resulted from the destruction of a print of "The Ten Commandments" and several reels and short subjects which were in the booth at the time the fire started. The Rialto Theatre was a 500 seat house, the largest and best theatre in Delta. The theatre is one of a chain owned and operated by Western Enterprises. Rick Ricketson, one of the managers of the company, announced plans have been completed for a new 1,100 seat theatre to replace the Rialto, to be the finest on the Western Slope.

Ohio Exhibitor Succumbs to Appendicitis

George Moore, for the past twelve years an exhibitor of Bellevue and Bucyrus, Ohio, passed away suddenly last week, a victim of peritonitis following appendicitis. Moore was well and favorably known by exhibitors and exchangemen around the Cleveland territory. He was on the executive board of the Motion Picture Theatre Owners of Ohio. His wife and two children survive him. Funeral services were held at Bellevue last Saturday.

Typical German Efficiency Seen in Studio Organization

No. 8: Equipment and Methods of Highest Precision

By L. C. MOEN

PERHAPS nothing in Europe is more interesting to the American visitor than the German film studios. Most of the theatres must suffer by comparison with our best, distribution is a comparatively simple matter—but in the application of sensible system and efficiency to production routine, the Germans need take second rank to no one.

It is not so much in outward appearance that the difference is noticeable. To the casual eye, a studio is a studio, and save for the glass roofs still present abroad, the external face of things is not much different, and is steadily growing less so.

It is rather in the administration of affairs and the handling of details that a distinct national flavor appears. Organization is the keynote of German production, and there is little glorification of the individual. Entertainment value aside, technical excellence has probably reached its highest point in the Berlin ateliers. Throughout Europe, the Germans are looked to for the salvation of Art—with a capital A—in picture making, but I did not find that the Germans themselves favored this view especially. They feel, I believe, that this opinion is rather prejudicial to their commercial success. As a matter of fact, the period that produced "Dr. Caligari," "The Golem," and the like, is at an end, and "box-office values" are as great a concern today in Berlin as in Hollywood. Inevitably, however, their pictures will always be different. The national temperament, the type of men engaged in the work, the taste of the public which must be pleased, insure a certain originality and artistry not present in the production of any other country, save perhaps Sweden.

The studio at Neubabelsberg may be taken as typical. Babelsberg is a suburb of Berlin, and can be reached by train or automobile about as easily as Long Island from New York City. Formerly the property of the Decla-Bioscop, it passed into the hands of the Ufa when the companies merged. The Ufa studio at Templehof was retained, however, and there many of the interiors are shot. Templehof is another suburb, not far away.

The Babelsberg plant can be best compared to Universal City, since it is in actuality a film city, complete in every detail. Getting past the gate (fully as difficult as in an American studio), you come upon the "main street" of the Babelsberg studios. Long rows of buildings line both sides of this street. At the left is the pleasant studio canteen, where food and drink may be had by the studio force, from the highest to the lowest—but not all in the same dining room! The class system holds in picture making as elsewhere in Europe.

At the right is the administration building, with offices for the directors and their aides, together with cutting and projection rooms for each. Dressing rooms for the principals are also here. All the dressing rooms I saw, even those for the Komparserie (or extras), were clean and comfortable in the extreme.

Passing on down the street, you see in turn, the fire station, with several men on constant duty, a fully equipped hospital, a splendid power station which is being

enlarged, large storage sheds for props and material, the "mud room" where plaster work is done, the carpenter shops, machine shops, and the like.

In one of these sheds I had the pleasure of inspecting the dragon which plays so important a part in "Siegfried." Large it was, but much simpler than might have been expected. No machinery in it save a few automobile springs to lend motion to the head.

Miniature Methods

In one of the buildings I saw a group of miniatures which deserve a word of mention. Instead of the "glass shots" which we are now using frequently, the Germans are adhering to solidly built miniatures, constructed with amazing ingenuity by a man who, a few years ago, was a day laborer about the studio.

I saw, for instance, the Hotel Atlantic setting for "Der Letzte Mann" (here "The Last Laugh"). This exterior was built up to a height of one story. Here we would have painted the upper stories on glass, but the Germans built them solidly in miniature, and suspended this near the camera.

Another thing which is being done with the greatest of engineering skill is the use of miniature sets in the foreground, in combination with full size settings. I saw, for example, a miniature lake, perhaps ten feet across, with tiny natural surroundings and little boats. Far beyond this was a castle, built full size. The miniature setting, being so much nearer the camera,

comes up to the same scale as the enormous castle. Little "toy" automobiles and trains run directly before the camera appear in combination with living actors and full sized sets. The scientific and engineering skill of the Germans shows up to particular advantage in this sort of thing. Another development is what they call "perspectivie" construction, in which an intentional distortion of perspective is introduced, giving effect of enormous space and size within a limited area.

Some remarkable cameras have been developed for this special trick work, including one that will do double-exposure and even triple-exposure effects at one operation. In photographing a ghost or vision scene, for instance, it is not necessary to run the film through the camera twice, with elaborate timing methods. It can all be done at one time, the ghost being at one side of the camera and the scene in front. With this camera, through its ingenious arrangement of prisms and its utilization of both faces of the negative film at once, one might conceivably shoot a group of actors on a miniature set one-tenth their size, with a ghost appearing in their midst—all at one operation! The possibilities, needless to say, are endless.

German Set Building

Especially interesting, however, is the construction of exterior sets on the lot. Their plans, to begin with, are somewhat more detailed than ours usually are, for the reason that the script is built more carefully in advance. The architects are not forced to hurriedly lay out the sets at the last moment, but rather develop them concurrently with the progress of the continuity. These plans, in fact, form a part of the working script.

Because of the high cost of lumber in central Europe, oa system of fabricated assembly is used, not unlike the "Mecanno" toy building sets for children here. Strips of lumber are cut to standard lengths, with bolt holes bored at a uniform distance apart. The architects' drawing specify these lengths, and the strips are simply bolted together to form the desired framework.

An unusual feature is the fact that all of these buildings are constructed on "stilts," some distance off the ground. Earth is then filled in under the building, which can be sodded with grass, or landscape gardened in any fashion desired. If trees are needed, they are set in. This is naturally more flexible than if the set were built on flat ground.

Over the assembled framework is fastened a layer of barcuta—a material which comes in rolls, consisting of narrow, lath-like strips, wired together—which can be shaped to fit anything. This takes plaster splendidly, and once the barcuta is on, the plasterers go to work and finish the building. This is then painted, and it is worthy of mention

(Continued on Next Page)

The strike of musicians, stage hands and operators is still in force in Niagara Falls, N. Y., with indications pointing to a long drawn out affair and eventual open shop condition. In Syracuse the motion picture operators have asked for a wage boost, but it is reported that exhibitors are prepared to "grind their own," if necessary rather than grant the requests.

Carl A. Porter, president of the Managers Association in Salt Lake City, reports that the recent demands of the operators for an increase in wages, was flatly refused at the meeting of this organization last week.

Managers of the Pantages, Paramount Empress, Victory, Gem, Kinema, American, Star. Cozy and Ises theatres were represented at the meeting.

The controversy between the Musicians' Union and the Allied Amusement Industries in San Francisco is at an end. Members of the union met in special session and voted

ment is reached arrangements will be made to furnish some type of music to accompany the picture presentations.

Mr. Blank, in New York on business for First National, sent word to Des Moines that the next move must be on the part of the union.

Blank left Des Moines after an agreement with the officers of the musicians association that the wage scale controversy would be arbitrated after five days and that the musicians would continue to work until the arbitration decision was handed down.

Despite the fact that officials of the musicians' association had publicly announced they were in favor of arbitration, a majority of the members voted at a meeting Tuesday afternoon to reject Blank's arbitration proposal and failed to report for duty.

Many of the operators are not in favor of striking for higher wages but are satisfied with the present wage scale.

German players do not make themselves up, as here, but it is all done by this department. Even a star has nothing to say about his or her make-up; it must be what the cameraman and the producer decree.

Many other features might be described, but these will serve to give some idea of the technical marvels of Babelsberg. A zoo is being built up. Tracks and a tiny, narrow-gauge railway connect the various parts of the lot, drawn by a tractor. Everything that is needed is manufactured on the spot. Babelsberg is entirely self-contained; it depends on the outside world for nothing.

The absence of Cooper-Hewitts in great numbers is notireable. This is what results in the relatively hard, contrasty lighting of European pictures. At the same time an interesting new type of mercury lamp has been developed which can be held in the hand and placed wherever desired for the lighting of close-ups, and the like.

Despite the work and study which have gone into the development of methods and machines at Babelsberg, nothing is concealed from the visitor. The attitude taken is that when the executives visit American studios, they are shown everything, and reap many ideas which they can utilize—so that it is no more than fair that America should be given full opportunity to use any of the German technical developments which may be of value.

Allvine A.M.P.A. President

Advertising Organization Selects Officers for the Coming Year

GLENDON ALLVINE was elected president of the Associated Motion Picture Advertisers, Inc., at the annual election of officers of the organization, held Thursday, September 10, at the Hofbrau Haus on Broadway.

Walter F. Eberhardt was elected vice president, S. Charles Einfeld treasurer and A. S. Rittenburg, secretary. The following were elected to serve on the board of directors with the officers: Charles Barrell, E. O. Brooks, Gordon White, Charles P. Cohen and A. L. Selig.

For the auditing committee: Sam Palmer, Chairman, H. C. Bate and Hal Howe.

For Managing Editor the Bulletin: W. E. Mulligan.

For Business Manager the Bulletin: Ed. McNamee.

For trustees of Treasurer's Fund: Paul Gulick, three years; Victor Shapiro, two years; P. A. Parsons, one year.

For Councillor of the Chamber of Commerce: John C. Flinn.

E. O. Brooks was elected to serve on the finance committee with the president, secretary and Charles Burrell, the senior member of the Board of Directors.

A. M. Botsford, the retiring president,

who presided in his best and wittiest style, made a very snappy report of "fifty-two weeks of progress." He read a communication from his successor, Glendon Allvine, who during the past year served in the capacity of treasurer.

The treasurer's report covering a year's custody of the funds of the A. M. P. A. showed the resources on hand to be the greatest in the history of the organization.

Another important bit of business transacted was the passing of a motion which calls for a future A. M. P. A. affair along the lines of functions given in the past by the W. A. M. P. A. S. with a view to raising funds to establish a permanent home for the A. M. P. A. This motion, introduced by Mr. Kopstein, was carried unanimously.

Charles Barrell, retiring vice president, made a brief presentation speech which carried with it the gift of a handsome cowbell which he insisted on calling a bull bell to be delivered to the incoming president, who in turn must hand it down to his successor and so on ad infinitum. On motion of P. A. Parsons, the outgoing president was tendered a vote of thanks for his efficient administration and "for the best speech of the year."

United Artists Joins All Film Boards of Trade

MANAGERS of all United Artists branch offices which are not now members of Film Boards of Trade in their territories have been instructed by the home office of the corporation to immediately apply for membership in the Boards.

Heretofore United Artists held membership in Film Boards in Boston, Butte, Cincinnati, Cleveland, Dallas, Denver, Des Moines, Detroit, Kansas City, Minneapolis, New Haven, Omaha, Portland, Salt Lake City, Seattle, St. Louis and Washington.

The decision of officials of the corporation to become 100 per cent members of the Film Boards will bring affiliations of the company's Atlanta, Buffalo, Chicago, Los Angeles, New York, Philadelphia, Pittsburgh and San Francisco offices, with the Boards in those cities.

First National Signs Harry Langdon

Screen Comedian Affixes His Signature to Contract That Will Cover a Long Period of Years

HARRY LANGDON, famous screen comedian, for whose services the biggest companies in the film world have been bidding vigorously for months, has affixed his signature to a contract with First National Pictures, Inc.

While definite figures are not mentioned it is understood to be the biggest individual contract of the year, insuring an almost fabulous income for the star. First National, which launched Charlie Chaplin on his first great screen successes a number of years ago, plans, according to Richard A. Rowland, general manager to give Langdon opportunity to develop as the new Comedy King of the Movies.

With the signing of Langdon all rumors of contractional relationship with various film corporations which have been buzzing about the picture world are set at ease and from now on the comedian will sail under the First National banner.

John E. McCormick, general manager of production for First National on the West Coast, represented his organization in the transaction in Hollywood after a series of conferences between William H. Jenner, general business manager, and Jerry Geisler,

Harry Langdon, who has been signed to a starring contract by First National.

attorney, representing Harry Langdon, covering many months.

Sol Lesser, vice president of First National, signed on behalf of that organization, Attorney Geisler of Woolwine and Geisler, represented Langdon and Blaire Evans, of Cruickshank, Brooks and Evans, represented the film company's interests.

The contract covering a period of years for full efature length comedies which will be made under the personal supervision of Langdon. The first series consists of four pictures and it is estimated they will consume sixteen months in the making.

Langdon has been sought after by practically every producing and distributing organization in the industry. Rumors were to the effect he had signed with this or that company, but nothing definite was settled until Sept. 16 when the principals, together with attorneys and managers, met in Hollywood and once and for all closed the subject with the signing of the agreements.

According to Jenner, Langdon expects to start on his first production for First National about November 15th, his contract with Mack Sennett expiring early in November. His first picture will be ready for release by the First National organization on or about April 15th, 1926.

Court Sustains Film Board Demurrer

Cleveland Body and Several Exchanges Upheld in Answer to Conspiracy in Restraint of Trade Charge

FEDERAL Judge E. C. Westenhaver of the Northern District of Ohio of the Eastern Division last week sustained the demurrer filed by Squires, Sanders and Dempsey, representing the Film Board of Trade of Cleveland, Pathe Film Exchange, Ohio Educational Exchange, Gold Seal Productions and Progress Pictures Company in answer to the petition of John Romwebber of the State Theatre, Akron, charging the Film Board of Trade of Cleveland and the several exchanges named, with conspiracy in restraint of trade.

Romwebber filed his petition in the Federal Court of the Cleveland district. Squires, Sanders and Dempsey, representing the defendants, based their demurrer on the ground that Romwebber's petition failed to establish a claim of recognition by the Federal Court. Judge Westenhaver simply endorsed the demurrer.

The demurrer was based first on the ground of failure to establish a diversity of citizenship between the plaintiff and the defendant. Diversity of citizenship is one of the requirements of a Federal Court action. Because the plaintiff is a citizen of Akron, and because the Film Board of Trade of Cleveland and the exchanges named in the Romwebber petition are corporations duly organized and existing under and by virtue of the laws of the state of Ohio, the petition failed to come under the jurisdiction of Federal Court of the Northern District of Ohio, the ruling held.

The second point of the demurrer which was sustained by Judge Westenhaver stated that, by the allegations of the plaintiff's petition, it is not shown that a Federal question is involved. The demurrer contended that action cannot be brought under the combination of conspiracy provision of the Sherman Law for the reason that the allegations of the petition are not sufficient to establish conspiracy.

The attorneys for the defendants went on, in their demurrer, to say that if the allegations of the plaintiff are true, he may have cause of action in the proper forum, but, for the reasons stated, the petition does not state a cause of action on the ground of diversity of citizenship, and his allegations are so indefinite that they do not bring him under the condition which conferred jurisdiction upon the Federal Court.

The rule of the law which was invoked in this demurrer is found in a number of cases of the Supreme Court of the United States and other Federal Courts, which is stated in the case of The Western Union Telegraph Company, vs. Ann Arbor Railroad Company which says:

"When a suit does not really and substantially involve a dispute or controversy as to the effect or construction of the Constitution or Laws of the United States upon the determination of which the result depends, it is not a suit involving the Constitution and Laws, and it must appear on the records by a statement in legal and logical form, such as is required in good pleading, that the suit is one which does not really and substantially involve dispute or controversy as to the right which depends on the construction of the constitution or some law or treaty of the United States before jurisdiction can be maintained on this ground."

The suit of Romwebber against the Film Board of Trade of Cleveland and the exchanges named in the petition, was the first of a series of similar suits which were to follow as a protest against the method of operation of the Cleveland Board of Arbitration. Romwebber charged that, through conspiracy between the exchanges and the Film Board of Trade he was deprived of film service and that his business as an exhibitor was ruined.

Romwebber will file another petition immediately in which he will seek to meet the requirements for Federal recognition.

Errol to Start New Film Next Month

Leon Errol's second feature for First National will be started in production about October 1st at the studios in New York. The comedian is now working in the Sam Rork production "Clothes Make the Pirate," from Holman Day's novel of that title. His next work will be "The Lunatic at Large Again," an adaptation from the novel by J. Storer Clouston.

Vancouver Wins Summer Drive

First National Sales Contest Victors Announced; Atlanta in Second Place

THE Vancouver Branch is the winner of First National's "Summer Drive," a sales contest for play dates to mature between May 31st and August 29th. Atlanta was in second place at the close of the drive, which First National announces raised the national percentage of summer business for 1925 up to 115.50, taking 100 per cent for the volume of business for the summer months of 1924.

The Vancouver branch, W. H. Mitchell, manager, won first place with 160.88 per cent.; Atlanta, C. R. Beacham, manager, second with 153.01 per cent.; Philadelphia captured third place with 148.21 per cent. W. J. Heenan is manager of the Philadelphia branch.

The summer drive was instituted by E. A. Eschmann of First National last March when he appealed to his field force for a performance during the summer of 1925 that would eclipse the big record of sum-

mer business done during 1924.

The prizes awarded by First National's distribution department to the winners of the summer drive follows.

Vancouver—First Prize. Manager W. H. Mitchell, a trip to Hollywood with all expenses paid; Joseph Plottel, salesman; Albert Brooks, shipper, W. Etris, booker; Mary Macauley, biller; Miss M. E. Middleton, stenographer; J. S. Mulhall, cashier, and Mrs. L. L. Patterson, inspector, each one week's salary.

Atlanta—Second Prize. Manager C. R. Beacham, a platinum watch; salesman George C. Almon, Lewis W. Carter, P. A. Strachan and James M. Young their choice of cuff links or a cigarette case.

Philadelphia—Third Prize. Manager W. J. Heenan, a gold watch; Salesmen P. F. Duffy, A. F. Hickox, F. J. Leonard, F. A. Loftus, W. G. Mansell and W. H. Schwalbe their choice of cuff links or cigarette case.

Wyoming Exhibitors Organize

State Theatre Owners and Managers Association Formed at Casper Meeting

AT a meeting held last week in Casper, the Wyoming exhibitors formed a state oranization, which is to be known as the Wyoming Theatre Owners and Managers Association. It is probable that the new orgnization will affiliate with the M.P.T.O.A. later.

The meeting at which the organization was formed was attended by eighteen exhibitors of the State, who met in a two-day convention which culminated with the election of officers to serve for the coming year and various committees.

James Lynch, of Laramie, was elected president with John Bangs of Rawlins, vice-president and M. H. Todd, of Casper, secretary and treasurer. The executive board and trustees are composed of the following: Thomas Berta, Rock Springs, Fred Besold, Sheridan, Earl Nye, Cheyenne; E. J.

Schulte, Casper; Thomas Love, Parco, and John Bangs, Rawlins.

The Casper meeting was attended by the following:

Thomas Berta, Rialto theatre, Rock Springs; Mrs. W. R. Logan, Rex, Basin; J. S. Ward, Princess, Douglas; Mrs. M. M. Young, Bison, Buffalo; John Bangs, Strand, Rawlins; P. J. Johnson, Strand, Rawlins; Mrs. LeMote, Acme, Riverton; Geo. Stewart, Bishop-Cass Co., Casper; M. H. Todd, Rialto, Casper; E. J. Schulte, Rialto, Casper; Fred Besold, Lotus, Sheridan; Earl Nye, Princess and Atlas, Cheyenne; O. P. Fish, Grand, Lander; Florence Ward, Midwest, Midwest; Esther Ward, Edgerton, Edgerton; Chas. Reeder, Castle Creek, New Lavoye; James Lynch, Empress, Laramie; John Lynch, America, Laramie; Mr. Lee, Empress, Glenrock.

A. S. Kane To Produce Series

Pictures to Be Released by Universal; Deal Calls for Group of Six Features

ARTHUR S. KANE, well known in the industry as a production and distribution executive, will re-enter the production field as a contributor to the Universal release schedule, according to a report this week from the Coast, where Mr. Kane has been located for some months as a contact executive for the Universal company. Complete arrangements regarding Mr. Kane's production activities have not been worked out as yet, but a tentative deal has been concluded with Universal. It is probable that the pictures may be filmed at Universal City, though this has not been decided upon as yet. However, it is understood that Mr. Kane's production headquarters will be established on the Coast.

There will be about six pictures in the first group he will make for the Universal program.

Kane became associated with Universal several months ago to act as contact executive between the production and sales departments of the company. His most recent association before joining Universal was with Associated Exhibitors.

Zabin Transferred to Ad Department of Famous

James Barton Zabin, for the past two years assistant to Glendon Allvine at Famous Players, has been transferred to the theatre advertising department of that company. Zabin will assist Lem Stewart and Bill Johnson in the advertising work of the theatre division of Famous.

Find No Violation by the Scenic Artists' Union

No evidence of violation of the Federal laws by The Scenic Artists, an organization composed of designers and creators of scenes and settings for theatrical productions who are members of a union holding a charter under the Brotherhood of Painters, Decorators and Paper Hangers of America, has been developed by an investigation undertaken by agents of the Department of Justice, and the matter has been closed.

Representations were made to the department that the organization was violating the law in various ways, but investigation disclosed only the maintenance of a credit bureau by the union, such as was upheld recently by the Federal courts in the case of other organizations. No element of interstate commerce was found, and the department could not determine that the union's activities had any effect in restraining interstate commerce.

Lon Ramsdell Joins "U" Publicity Department

Lon Ramsdell, veteran publicity and exploitation man, has joined the Universal exploitation and publicity department. Ramsdell will exploit Universal pictures in the Pittsburgh territory, succeeding Jack Hays, who has resigned.

Ramsdell has had a wide experience in publicity and picture theatre management, serving as manager for Loews' Victoria in New York for a year; B. F. Keith's Hippodrome in Baltimore for two years, and the Ramsdell Opera House in Frederick, Md. He has been associated with D. W. Griffith, First National and Warner Bros. in publicity work.

Urges Special Session to Act on Connecticut Tax

Governor May Issue Call; Feeling Against Bill Grows

WITH a growing public sentiment hostile to the tax to back them in their attack on the Durant Bill, exhibitors of Connecticut are pinning their faith on a special session of the Legislature, which Governor Trumbull has been urged to call, to afford them early relief from the measure which places a state impost of $10 per reel on motion picture film for exhibition there.

As the theatre situation in Connecticut becomes more chaotic in consequence of the removal of exchanges from New Haven and a cessation of booking contracts for the future, the feeling within the state against the tax bill grows apace and the motion picture men see signs of encouragement for their move to have a special session of the lawmakers assemble to hear the industry's case against the Durant Bill.

The move for a special session gained impetus when the M. P. T. O. sent a formal petition to the Governor requesting him to take this action. At a meeting of the state exhibitors' body to discuss ways and means to meet the present situation it was decided in favor of a special session of the Legislature.

The State Federation of Labor in convention last week passed a resolution asking for an extra session of the assembly. The resolution was introduced by Eugene Treiber, secretary of the State Federation and president of the New Haven Operators' local, who in introducing the resolution predicted that all theatres in the state will be closed within six months unless something is done to relieve the situation. A general close down he said would throw 300 operators out of employment.

The operators are waiting upon members of the legislature from their districts to learn if they voted for the Durant measure and if they favor the plan of the exhibitors to obtain a special session. Treiber reported that these solicitations were developing the fact that the majority of the legislators who voted for the bill were under the impression at the time that the distributors would pay the tax, and all who have been interviewed so far expressed sympathy with the stand of the theatre men and were for a special session to take action on the tax.

President Joseph W. Walsh and other members of the M. P. T. O. have conferred with several Assemblymen, the majority of whom declared they will vote to kill the bill if they have the opportunity for action on it at another session.

The exhibitors will seek written requests of members of the Assembly for a special session, and the support of social, civic and political organizations, including the Kiwanis, Lions and Rotary Clubs, and Chambers of Commerce will be sought. Petitions will be circulated throughout the state by the exhibitors.

Criticism of the tax bill has been expressed in many quarters. Among those who have voiced their emphatic disapproval of the bill are the Rev. Oscar F. Maurer, pastor of the Center Congregational Church and a prominent figure in the civic life of New Haven, who is quoted as declaring that the state should avoid making a direct tax on the picture industry. With regard to the censorship phases of the bill, Rev. Maurer said that in his opinion the picture men had little to fear. "Motion Pictures have assumed a higher moral tone under the supervision of Will Hays," he said. The clergyman condemned the action of the distributors in removing their offices from the state, asserting that they would have won more sympathy had they paid the tax under protest and worked for the repeal of the law while continuing their exchanges in New Haven.

The removal of the exchanges has resulted in a delivery situation which is at least temporarily in a muddle. The situation has been somewhat relieved by the extension of service by the Rosen Film Delivery Service, which increased its trucks from three to seven and is working on a day and night schedule to get programs to the theatres on time for showing.

According to Lester Tobias of the Yale Film Exchange and regional director of the I. M. P. A., there is much speculation among exhibitors as to whether the distributors will re-establish exchanges in Connecticut after the situation is cleared up, many feeling, he says, that now that the distributors have moved out and found that they can deliver from outside sources at a lower over-head, it will be difficult to induce them to return.

Tobias declared that all differences between the independents and the national distributors over the Connecticut situation have been smoothed out and that now the greatest harmony exists between them in their concerted efforts to solve the situation. He said that the soliciting of new contracts for films in Connecticut had been definitely discontinued by all distributors both national and independent. He expressed the opinion that it would not be long before the whole problem in the state would be cleared up.

Theatre operation costs have mounted greatly as a result of the removal of the exchanges. The delays in film deliveries is causing the greatest difficulty to theatre managers and adds to the expense because several of the theatres are now holding extra reels on hand for use in the event that their programs do not arrive on time. J. F. Clancy, manager of Poli's theatre, estimates that the present situation if maintained for a year would increase the cost of operation of that house by at least $25,000. Other theatre men give figures proportionately high and affirm that present conditions cannot exist long without bringing ruin upon the entire picture theatre enterprise in Connecticut.

Albany and Buffalo Zones Adopt New By-Laws

At the meeting of the directors of the Albany and the Buffalo zones, held at the Hotel Onondaga in Syracuse last week, a set of by-laws was adopted under which each zone will be responsible for any expense incurred. William Dillon, of Ithaca, presided. Among those present were: Robert Wagner, of Little Falls; Ben Davis, of Gloversville; Louis Buettner, of Cohoes; Charles Hayman, of Niagara Falls; William Callahan, of Rochester, and Jules Michaels, of Buffalo. The by-laws provide, among other things, that zone directors shall meet at least quarterly. The Connecticut situation was discussed, but no definite action taken. It was decided to give all possible support to Senator James J. Walker, candidate for mayor of New York city, in view of the important work done by Mr. Walker in the pest in the interests of the exhibitor.

Find Body in Wreckage of Gillis Theatre

The Gillis theatre of Kansas City, destroyed by an explosion June 25, yielded another body this week, which makes the fifth. It was found at the side of the balcony railing at the bottom of the debris. It was that of a youth about 20 years old. Nothing could be found about the body which might lead to identification. The inquest into the tragedy will be re-opened soon, according to authorities. Four bodies were removed from the ruins soon after the explosion and fire, the search being stopped shortly afterwards as all missing persons were believed accounted for.

Zambreno Buys Interest in Jossey Exchanges

Frank Zambreno, president of Progress Pictures Corporation, with offices in Chicago, Milwaukee and Indianapolis, has purchased an interest in two exchanges operated in Cleveland and Cincinnati by J. S. Jossey. Zambreno owns the Golden Arrow Franchise for Illinois, Wisconsin and Indiana and may sign up the Arrow feature product for Ohio as well now that he has entered that territory.

Paramount Class Progressing

Students in Training School for Managers Undergoing Strenuous Course

STUDENTS in the Paramount Theatre Managers' Training School are being put through a rigid course of lectures and practical training in preparation for the positions they will be called upon to fill after the expiration of the six months term. The schedule of the second, third and fourth weeks of the term included activities that kept them busy throughout every day and many nights.

Rocky T. Newton, city manager of the Paramount Little Rock Theatres, explained the management of the small town theatre as differentiating from the New York first run house. The interrelation of production, distribution and exhibition was discussed with the students by the following Paramount executives: Norman Colyer, W. B. Cockell, Myke Lewis, Joseph Seidelman, Miss Maude Miller, B. G. J. Frawley, Edmond Raeburn and George M. Spidell.

Following a visit of the class to the Long Island studio, E. C. King and Earl Wingart explained the departmental organization of the studio. The class then visited each department and saw pictures in the making. The New York exchange was also visited and its workings were explained by Joseph Unger. Henry Salsbury pointed out the necessity of "audience reaction reports."

Trade paper editors explained how each department of these papers could be of serv-

ice to the theatre manager. Those who addressed the class on these points were William A. Johnston, editor of MOTION PICTURE NEWS, and J. S. Dickerson, associate editor of the same paper, and Martin J. Quigley, editor of *Exhibitors' Herald.*

Austin Keough lectured on "Legal Relationship Between Patrons and Theatre Managers." To apply the principles outlined in lectures by Theodore C. Young, Louis Cohen and Lacey Johnson on "The Theatre Site." The class was divided into five groups and sent to the following towns: Englewood, New Rochelle, Mount Vernon, Flushing and Yonkers.

Henry Anderson, manager of the Insurance Department, gave a series of lectures on "Theatre Insurance and Fire and Accident Prevention." He was assisted by C. E. Cherry, superintendent of the New York Claim Department of the Employers' Liability Assurance Corporation, Ltd. The class will spend an entire week at the Edison Lamp Works, where eleven lecturers, experts secured by the Edison Lamp Works, will cover every phase of theatre lighting. Special bulletins have been prepared for the class by the Edison Lamp Works, and their institute has been equipped to meet the needs of the school with complete demonstration facilities.

Mrs. Anna A. Sessions, named assistant to First National's European Director General.

Colleges Interested in Kane Endowment

Yale University and the University of California are much interested in the offer of Robert T. Kane of an annual $5,000 endowment fund for the establishment of a chair of photo-play in one of the nine leading universities of the country.

Queries have come to Kane from both Yale and California asking more information regarding the fund. George Parmly Day, treasurer of Yale wrote for further particulars so that he may submit the matter to the Yale Corporation's committee on Educational policy, and subsequently to the members of the corporation for their consideration.

From the University of California came the following telegraphic communication: "Am advised you are offering endowment fund to University of California for chair of cinema arts. Consider this much needed and wonderful step forward. Will you kindly telegraph me at my expense if this is authentic as I wish to communicate with you."

"U" Trade Show Plan Extended

Success of Laemmle's Theatre Parties in Iowa Initiates Country-Wide Application

THE Carl Laemmle Universal Theatre Parties, inaugurated a few weeks ago in Iowa for the purpose of letting small town exhibitors view Universal features in advance of release, are to be employed nationally, Universal announced this week.

The first showing under the plan was held at Des Moines, and this was followed last week by a Theatre Party in the Omaha territory for the benefit of theatre owners of Northwest Iowa. The showing took place at the Empress theatre at Cherokee. The Cherokee Chamber of Commerce co-operated with Max Drefke, manager of the Empress, and Universal executives. Nearly 100 guests attended the screening, at which "The Teaser," "California Straight Ahead," and "The Goose Woman" were presented.

The second party to be conducted by the Omaha exchange took place at the Strand theatre, Pierce, Neb., last Monday, and the next is scheduled for Lexington, Nebr., where a Laemmle party will be staged at the Majestic theatre Monday, September 21.

The first of the Universal theatre parties given for Minnesota exhibitors was held at the State theatre, Alexandria, Minn., Thursday and was attended by 110 persons, including 25 exhibitors and their families. Weather was excellent for the event and some of the exhibitors came as far as 250 miles to look over the company's product.

Manager Bromley made a little talk at 10 a. m. after which "The Teaser" and "Siege"

were shown. There was a luncheon at the Alexandria hotel at 12:30 where the visitors were welcomed by Paul Kinney, president of the Alexandria Commercial club.

Films of the crowd and some of the individuals were taken and then the exhibitors had a little surprise for Phil Dumas, Universal's Minneapolis manager. They presented him with a silver service. Thereafter the films "California Straight Ahead," "The City of Stars," a comedy, and "The Homemaker" were shown.

Ralph B. Williams, manager of Universal's Atlanta branch, entertained exhibitors at a trade showing at the Strand theatre, Tullahoma, Tenn., last Tuesday. The theatre was placed at the disposal of Mr. Williams by R. T. Hill, the owner.

Earle E. Griggs, Universal's publicity director, went to Tullahoma, Sunday and Monday for the purpose of arranging the details of the event. It is planned to make motion pictures of the exhibitors and their families who will be the guests of Universal at this unusual trade showing.

Yola D'Avril is Loaned to Universal Company

Yola D'Avril, new Educational-Christie beauty and former Parisian dancer, has been loaned to Universal where she is playing an important role in "The Midnight Sun" in support of Laura La Plante and Pat O'Malley.

Dorothy Seastrom Signs With First National

DOROTHY SEASTROM, blonde beauty who made her screen debut in comedies and later appeared in a feature under the direction of C. B. De Mille, has been signed to a long term contract by First National, for whom she has played in two recent productions, Corinne Griffith's "Classified" and "We Moderns," the newest Colleen Moore vehicle.

"We are looking forward to excellent results from Miss Seastrom," said John McCormick, production chief for First National's West Coast Studios. "She is possessed of camera technique and has received a firm foundation through work already accomplished in motion pictures. Our organization, realizing her ability and beauty, will endeavor to develop in her every charm and talent necessary for the screen."

"U" Entering Canada Theatre Field

Pantages. Finkelstein & Ruben and Fitzpatrick-McElroy Among Circuits Which Add to Holdings

THE activities of circuits and producer-controlled chains in expanding their operations and holdings figure prominently in reports emanating from various parts of the country concerning recent developments in the theatre field.

Announcement that Universal has purchased three theatres in Canada is taken as an earnest of that company's intention of invading the Canadian field on a large scale. The company has taken long-term leases on the Lyceum, Starland and College theatres in Winnipeg, where rumors have it that this is the first step in a move by Universal to enter Canada as a large operator in the picture theatre field. The three theatres which Universal has leased are owned by A. R. McNichol. Charles A. Meade, manager of the Lyceum, will be in charge of all three houses.

Fitzpatrick-McElroy have acquired a lease on a theatre to be built at Richmond, Indiana. This will make the second Indiana deal of this organization, which has large theatre holdings in Michigan, Illinois and Wisconsin, and which recently extended its operations into the Hoosier State by the acquisition of a house at Michigan City. As in the latter deal Harry Katz, brother of Sam Katz, of Balaban & Katz, is associated with Fitzpatrick-McElroy in the Richmond theatre lease. The new house is to be built by the Quaker City Realty Co.

These recent moves by Fitzpatrick-McElroy are considered to be the forerunner of a big chain of houses which the company

Admission Tax Totaled $30,907,809 Last Year

COLLECTIONS from the admission tax during the fiscal year ended June 30, last, totaled $30,-907,809, according to figures just issued by the Internal Revenue Bureau. This was a decrease of $46,804,714 from the collections of $77,712,253 reported in the fiscal year 1924, due to the exemption from tax of admissions of not over 50 cents, which became effective the beginning of the 1925 fiscal year.

New York City paid approximately one-fifth of the total admission taxes of the country, the figures show, the collections in the Third New York District totaling $6,113,904. The other districts reporting the heaviest collections of admission taxes were: First New York, $1,395,939; First Illinois, $3,018,-337; First California, $998,120; Sixth California, $1,429,907; Maryland, $901,-728; Massachusetts, $1,723,602; First Michigan, $1,064,133; Eighteenth Ohio, $920,890; and First Pennsylvania, $1,362,-333.

will establish in Indiana. At the present writing the organization controls 45 theatres. During the past year this company has expanded rapidly and its continued extension has led to much discussion of what the future will bring forth in connection with its development as a steadily growing circuit.

Finkelstein & Ruben gained full control of the theatre situation at Brainerd, Minn., through the acquisition of the Lyceum there in a deal with Clinton-Meyers, former operators of the house. F. & R. has also taken over the Lyceum and Rex at Virginia. This latter move narrows competition in Virginia, recently the scene of a bitter price war, down to two factions, the other house in the city being operated by Roy McMinn, who owns the Royal. A report from Huron, S. D., states that Finkelstein & Ruben are negotiating for a theatre in that city, the report claiming that a representative of the company is seeking interests to erect a 1,000 seat house for lease to F. & R.

Alexander Pantages is said to be making a survey of Milwaukee, Minneapolis, Omaha and Des Moines with a view to building first-run theatres in those cities. It is said that Pantages is planning to enter the production field and with that view in mind will establish a chain of picture theatres throughout the country. In Minneapolis it was reported that he would go there soon to seek a site for a theatre.

Marked changes in the theatre situation of New Britain, Conn., took place when a half interest in the Capitol, Palace and Scenic theatres was purchased by Israel J. and Bernard E. Hoffman of Ansonia. The owners of the theatres, Contaras Bros. and Perokas, in turn have taken a half interest in the new theatre which the Hoffman Bros. intend to build in New Britain at an estimated cost of $500,000.

Fox Assets Placed at $24,509,469

Consolidated Balance Sheet Shows $8,334,761 Cash on Hand; 400,000 Shares of Stock Admitted to Big Board

ASSETS of $24,509,469 are shown by the Fox Film's consolidated balance sheet as of March 21, 1925, which also shows profits of $535,352 for the twelve weeks ending on that date.

The company's net profits for 1924 totaled $2,099,044 as against $1,808,165 as reported in a statement of the company filed with the Board of Governors of the New York Stock Exchange, to which 400,000 shares have been admitted to trading. The Fox stock was previously traded in on the New York Curb Market.

The consolidated balance sheet of Fox shows the following:

Assets: Cash $8,334,761; marketable securities and mortgages $143,352; accounts receivable $637,402; inventories $6,541,439; cash in hands of trustees $11,833; land, buildings, machinery, equipment, etc., less reserves $7,594,646; charges against foreign branches $265,756; deferred charges $080,-280; total $24,509,469.

Liabilities: Notes payable $350,000; accounts payable $802,742; federal taxes $86,-664; advance payments for film service $215,067; remittances from foreign branches held in abeyance $605,182; funded debt guaranteed by Fox Film Corp., $3,207,900;

Maryland Body Pledges Loyalty to M. P. T. O. A.

THE Motion Picture Theatre Owners of America is just in receipt of an official communication from the Secretary of the Motion Picture Theatre Owners of Maryland, Inc., advising that at a meeting of their body the organization went on record endorsing their loyal support to the National Organization, and further stating that it stands ready and willing to be of every service it can to the Motion Picture Theatre Owners of America at any time.

other mortgages $509,677; capital stock and surplus (represented by 400,000 no par shares of Class A stock and 100,000 no par shares of Class B stock) $18,732,237; total $24,509,469.

Sales of Fox Film on the New York Stock Exchange on Monday reached a total of 3,200 over a price range of from 71 3/8 high to a low of 70. The stock closed that day at 71½.

The 400,000 shares of Fox capital stock were admitted to the New York Stock Exchange by the Board of Governors last week,

and brought the number of motion picture enterprises represented on the Big Board up to five, the others being Famous Players, Eastman Kodak, Metro-Goldwyn, and Loews Inc.

Ask George M. Cohan to Title MacLean Feature

George M. Cohan is being sought by Bogart Rogers, general manager of Douglas MacLean Productions, to write the titles for the film version of "Seven Keys to Baldpate," the Cohan play in which MacLean will make his debut as a Paramount star. At the time MacLean purchased the screen rights to the play Cohan is reported to have declared his willingness to contribute to the making of the photoplay comedy.

Father of B. F. Fineman Dies Suddenly

Dennis Fineman, father of B. F. Fineman, studio manager for F. B. O., died suddenly at his residence, 73 West 116th Street, New York City, on Tuesday morning, September 8th.

Independents Make New Sales

Sax Announces Gotham Program is Sold 100%; Freedom Film Buys Arrow Product

INDEPENDENT distributors are rapidly closing territories on the programs they will offer this season. The product of several concerns has been sold solid to exchanges throughout the country. Among the most recent to close all territories is the Lumas Film Corporation, distributors of the Gotham pictures.

Sam Sax, of Lumas, announced this week that the first series of six Gotham Productions have been sold one hundred per cent. All territories on these pictures were closed with the signing last week by F. & R. Film Co., Minneapolis, for the product in that territory. The world's rights outside of the United States and Canada were taken over by the Apollo Trading Corp. The first Gotham six have been sold to 25 exchanges in this country.

The pictures in the first Gotham series are "Women and Gold," "Unmarried Wives," "The Night Ship," "Shattered Lives," "The Silent Pal," and "Black Lightning," the latter two featuring "Thunder," the dog.

The F. & R. Film Co. also signed with Lumas for the second group of Gotham Productions, which includes eighteen features. The new series of twelve was recently sold in the New England territory to Independent Films, Inc., of Boston. This group of pictures also figured in another deal last week. This was the purchase by Stoll Films, Ltd., of the British rights through Inter-Ocean Films. The Stoll company was represented by Herbert Case Hoagland, managing director of the organization.

W. E. Shallenberger, president of Arrow, announced that Freedom Film Corporation has acquired the Golden Arrow franchise for twenty-four features, for the Upper New York territory. The deal was concluded between Dr. Shallenberger and Richard Fox, president of Freedom. Mr. Fox is planning an extensive exploitation campaign to publicize the twenty-four Arrow features in his territory. The product will be handled from the offices of Freedom Film in Buffalo.

Wardour Films, Ltd., of London have the sales rights for the entire Ginsberg product of Royal and Banner Productions throughout the United Kingdom. This deal was made at the opening of the season by Jeffrey Bernerd, European representative of the Ginsberg Corporation.

Nathan Hirsh reported as among his recent territorial sales on the Gordon Clifford series that the Texas, Oklahoma and Arkansas section had been acquired by Southern Enterprises, the Liber company had contracted for the Indiana territory, Fisher Films for Ohio and that Argentine American films had signed contracts for Argentine, Paraguay, and Uruguay.

Louis Weiss, managing director of Weiss Brothers Artclass Pictures Corporation announces that he has sold his series of six single reel specials entitled "Guess Who" to I. Maynard Schwartz' Short Film Exchange of Chicago to be distributed in the territory included in Northern Illinois and Indiana.

Warners at Production Peak

Indications Are That Forty Features Will Be Completed by First of Year

FROM present indications the forty features on the Warner schedule for the season will be completed by January 1st, in accordance with the promise of Jack Warner. Production at the coast studios is now at its peak. In addition to the pictures already finished and released or ready for release, twelve are now in the process of cutting, preparation or in actual work.

Lowell Sherman has completed "The Love Toy," his second picture for Warners, and left for New York to fulfill a stage engagement. The next to be completed will probably be John Barrymore's "The Sea Beast." Much of the action is being taken aboard a whaling vessel now cruising in the Pacific. It is expected the company will return in about three weeks. With the return of Barrymore he will start work in "Don Juan," his next Warner vehicle. The scenario is being prepared by Bess Meredyth and Maude Fulton.

Syd Chaplin is also preparing to put into production "Nightie Night, Nurse," by Robert E. Sherwood and Bertram Bloch. Chuck Reisner will direct.

"The Cave Man" is being adapted for the screen by Julien Josephson from the story by Gillett Burgess. This will probably be a vehicle for Matt Moore and it will be a wide deviation from anything he has done to date. Lewis Milestone will direct.

"Broken Hearts of Hollywood," a special that will have all the Warner players in its cast is to be the grand finale on the year's program. Roy del Ruth will direct and Bennie Zeidman will personally supervise the production.

King Baggott Signs a New Contract With Universal

King Baggott, associated with Universal for almost ten years, has signed a new long-term contract to direct pictures for that company, according to an announcement from Raymond L. Schrock, studio manager. Baggott left the company for a short time to direct William S. Hart in his current production for United Artists. He will return to Universal City when his present work is completed.

Barbara Bedford Opposite "Bill" Hart

Barbara Bedford has been chosen as leading woman for "Tumbleweeds," William S. Hart's first production for United Artists Corporation, which is now in work.

Universal to Produce "Gulliver's Travels"

UNIVERSAL is to make a big super-jewel production of "Gulliver's Travels" adapted from the world famous story written by the English satirist Jonathan Swift in 1726. The production has been under consideration for some time, but only this week Carl Laemmle cabled from Europe to start work on it.

"Gulliver's Travels" is composed of four different sections his visit to Lilliputia, his visit to Brobdingnag, where he is thrown in with the giants; his experiences in Laputa, an island city and fortress that floats in the air, and his trip to Huoynhhym, the realm of the intelligent horses. It is not yet known whether Universal will embrace all four sections in the coming production, which, it is said will be made on a larger scale than "The Hunchback of Notre Dame" and "The Phantom of the Opera."

Ginsberg Productions Lined Up for Season

The production schedule has been arranged for the product to be handled by the Henry Ginsberg Distributing Corporation during the season. In the Banner production series of six, two have already been released. They are "The Love Gamble" and "Wreckage." The third will be "Wandering Footsteps," featuring Estelle Taylor, Alec B. Francis and Bryant Washburn. It will be directed by Phil Rosen.

The fourth Banner will be "Checkered Flag," which will shortly go into production under the direction of John Adolfi. The fifth and sixth will be made under the titles of "Whispering Canyon" and "Brooding Eyes."

"Before Midnight" and "Big Pal" of the Royal Production series of six have been completed. They will be followed in order by "A Desperate Moment," "The Millionaire Policeman," "The Taxi Mystery" and "The Phantom Express."

Many Universal Features in Cutting Room

Several of the important forthcoming Universal features are now in the cutting rooms at the Universal City plant. Among the pictures now being edited and prepared for screening are "Stella Maris," which was produced by Charles Brabin with Mary Philbin starred; "His People," a feature directed by Edward Sloman; "The Still Alarm," a melodrama of the fire-fighters directed by Edward Laemmle; and "My Old Dutch," which Laurence Trimble directed.

Among the Universal directors who have completed pictures recently and are preparing to start new productions is Svend Gade. The company has about six features now in active production.

Adolfi to Direct Fourth for Banner

John Adolfi will direct "The Checkered Flag," fourth of the Banner productions for the season. The book of the same title by John Mersereau was adapted for the screen by Charles and Fanny Hatton. The story is of the automobile industry and the speedway racing game.

Many Nations Represented in Fox Cast

Nineteen nations are represented in the cast and technical staff making "The Silver Treasure" for Fox. The picture was adapted from Joseph Conrad's story, "Nostromo."

In the cast, George O'Brien is Irish; Lou Tellegen, French-Greek-Dutch; Helen D'Algy, Spanish; Evelyn Selbie, Italian; Otto Matiesen, Danish; David Makarenko, Russian; Stewart Rome and Hugh Crumplin, English, and George Kuwa, Japanese.

In the technical staff the representatives are from Australia, Canada, France, Norway, Russia, England, Wales, Scotland, Peru and Mexico, while among the extras there are Argentinians, Chileans and Brazilians.

Play by English Playwright Bought by M-G-M

The film rights to "Bellamy the Magnificent" by Roy Horniman, well known English actor, playwright and novelist, have been purchased by Metro-Goldwyn-Mayer. The work is scheduled for early production at the Culver City plant of the company. "Bellamy the Magnificent" made its first appearance as a novel in 1908 and was dramatized by the author later. It was a London stage success some seasons ago.

"Merry Widow" Villain is Signed by Mayer

Louis B. Mayer has exercised his option to retain the services of Roy D'Arcy, who scored so emphatically in "The Merry Widow." D'Arcy is now playing a villain role in "La Boheme," which King Vidor is directing with Lillian Gish in the name part.

Mulhall Opposite Dorothy MacKaill In "Joanna"

Jack Mulhall has been cast for the leading male role opposite Dorothy MacKaill in "Joanna With a Million," Edwin Carewe's forthcoming First National Production, which is to be started this week.

Tom Mix Starts Fourth on Fox Schedule

THOUGH Tom Mix has only just completed "The Yankee Senor," he had already plunged into production on "The Best Bad Man," his fourth starring vehicle of the season for Fox from a story by Max Brand. J. G. Blystone is directing the new picture. In the past he has directed Mix in such pictures as "Dick Turpin," "Teeth," and "Soft Boiled."

Clara Bow has the leading feminine role in the new picture, while others in support of the star are: Cyril Chadwick, Tom Kennedy, Paul Panzer, and Frank Beal.

The three of the seven Mix pictures already completed are "The Lucky Horseshoe," which has already had a successful engagement on Broadway; "The Yankee Senor," which will be presented October 11th, and "The Everlasting Whisper," which will be presented later in the season.

Lieber Month Promises Big Returns

FIRST NATIONAL branch managers expect to exceed the success scored during the Eschmann month drive of last autumn with the Lieber month drive in honor of Robert Lieber, president of the company, which was announced for this fall late in August. Telegrams and letters from the field staffs express determination to show the biggest sales results ever obtained in a similar drive.

First National executives declare they have never had such an enthusiastic response from the field as that made following the August announcement.

Cunningham Signs With Metropolitan

Jack Cunningham, scenarist of "The Covered Wagon," "Don Q" and other successes has been signed by Metropolitan Pictures as head of the film editorial department. The new appointee will supervise selection of stories, research on selected plays and stories, the preparation of scenarios and continuities, the cutting of film and the writing of sub-titles.

"Rocking Moon" with Lilyan Tashman in the lead is the first of the pictures Cunningham will devote his talents to. Like the others of the Metropolitan pictures, it will be released through Producers Distributing Corporation.

Pathe Will Make Feature Version of Serial

Pathe has decided to make a feature version in six reels of "Wild West," their latest serial, made on the Miller Brothers 101 Ranch in Oklahoma, with Jack Mulhall and Helen Ferguson heading the cast. "Wild West" is based upon actual happenings in the early history of Oklahoma and was adapted for the screen by J. F. Natteford.

Clara Bow Opposite Tom Mix With Fox

Clara Bow has been loaned by B. P. Schulberg to the Fox organization and she will appear opposite Tom Mix in the latter's forthcoming production. Miss Bow will start work at once in order to be free later in the Fall to undertake her next featured role with Preferred Pictures.

Marguerite De La Motte and Bowers Sign

Metropolitan Pictures, whose product is released through Producers Distributing Corporation, has signed Marguerite De La Motte and John Bowers to contracts which call for their exclusive services to Metropolitan for the coming year.

Edgar Kennedy Will Direct Universal Comedy Series

Edgar Kennedy, well known actor and director, has been signed by Universal to direct the next series of "Sweet Sixteen" comedies starring Arthur Lake and Eddie Clayton.

Two for First National Near Completion

Two pictures are nearing completion for First National and another has reached the cutting room. Photography has about been finished on "The Scarlet Saint," with the final scenes being shot on the Empire City and Belmont race tracks. Mary Astor and Lloyd Hughes have the featured roles, with George Archainbaud directing.

"The Unguarded Hour" company, of which Milton Sills is the star, returned during the week from Greenwich, Conn., where a number of sequences were shot.

"The Pace That Thrills," the automobile racing story written by Byron Morgan with Ben Lyon and Mary Astor in the featured roles, was shipped to Chicago last week for printing.

Three Added to "Morals for Men" Cast

Three have been added to the cast of "Morals for Men," fourth of the Tiffany "Big Twelve" for the season. They are Robert Ober, Mary Beth Milford and Otto Matieson. The picture was suggested by "Love Serum," by Gouverneur Morris and was adapted to the screen by A. P. Younger, who is supervising the production. Conway Tearle and Agnes Ayres are the featured leads.

Chaney to Be Starred in "The Mocking Bird"

Lon Chaney's next starring vehicle for Metro-Goldwyn-Mayer will be "The Mocking Bird," an original story by Tod Browning, who will direct the film. The locale of the play is the Limehouse district of London. Waldemar Young is writing the screen adaptation.

Wellman Named to Direct "Penalty of Jazz"

Columbia Pictures has assigned William Wellman to the direction of "The Penalty of Jazz," one of the forthcoming Waldorf features. Dorothy Revier is to head the cast, with Ethel Wales in a character role.

Roland West Buys Picture Rights to "The Bat"

SCREEN rights to "The Bat," the Mary Roberts Rhinehart-Avery Hopwood stage melodrama, were acquired this week by Roland West. The price paid for the picture privileges was $75,000. West will produce the story for release by United Artists.

"The Bat," which scored as one of the most sensational stage successes of recent times, was the object of spirited bidding by several big picture companies. Its success on the stage ushered in an era of "thrill plays" in the American theatre. The play is said to have netted its sponsors over $1,800,000.

Negotiations for the deal under which Roland West obtained the film rights were completed by Wagenhals and Kemper, theatrical agents, who represented the authors. It is planned to have the screen version ready for release by United Artists in January.

Committees Agree on Contract

M. P. T. O. A. and I. M. P. A. Groups
Reach Complete Accord on Form for Submittal

THE final meeting of the joint contract and arbitration committees of the Motion Picture Theatre Owners of America and the Independent Motion Picture Association was held at the headquarters of the Motion Picture Theatre Owners of America at 1 P. M. on Wednesday, September 16th.

The work of the committees was completed and a contract form was agreed upon. The final form is virtually the same as recently promulgated with the addition of a provision limiting the time, after the rendering of the award by the local arbitration board, in which the award can be reviewed by the national arbitration commission, and a provision for the right to both the distributor and the exhibitor to challenge the arbitrators appointed or selected by the other side. Each side is limited to three challenges.

The committees will submit the contract to their respective organizations with a recommendation for its acceptance. The Independent Motion Picture Association of America will hold a convention in the very near future, at which time its contract committee will render its report and recommendation.

Copies of the proposed contract have been sent to all of the members of the Independent Motion Picture Association of America, to the presidents of the various theatre owner state organizations, the officers of the Motion Picture Theatre Owners of America, to Will H. Hays, president of the Motion Picture Producers and Distributors of America and Mr. Nathan Burkan.

Melford to Leave for Alaska for "Rocking Moon"

Director George Melford was scheduled to leave Los Angeles this week with a company from Metropolitan Studios bound for Sitka, Alaska, to make most of the scenes for "Rocking Moon," which will be released through Producers Distributing Corporation.

"Rocking Moon" is an adaptation from the Barrett Willoughby novel. Lilyan Tashman will play the leading role and will be featured in the production with John Bowers. The supporting cast has not yet been announced.

Clever Child Actors in "Baby Be Good"

Malcolm Sebastian, eighteen months old, and Bonnie Barrett, four-year-old screen actress, will head a cast of clever youngsters in the Jack White comedy "Baby Be Good," which will be released this fall by Educational. Many of the young screen players were assembled by White from the hosts which went to the studio in response to his "want ad" in newspapers and an appeal for children to appear in a film which was broadcast by radio.

Ken Maynard Completes "Grey Vulture"

Ken Maynard has completed his fifth picture for release through Davis Distributing Division. It is a western titled, "The Gray Vulture." The horse, Tarzan, is featured with Maynard, while in the supporting cast are Hazel Deane, Boris Bullock, "Sailor" Sharky, Whiteborne and the Hollywooy Beauty Sextette.

Schulberg Releases Two This Month

J. G. BACHMANN, general manager of distribution for B. P. Schulberg productions announces two features for release during the month of September. "With This Ring" went to the exhibitors September 5th. It is based on a Saturday Evening Post novel by Fanny Heaslip Lea, and was directed by Fred C. Windermere. The principal players in the cast are Alyce Mills, Lou Tellegen, Forrest Stanley, Donald Keith, Joan Standing, Martha Mattox, Eulalie Jensen and Dick Sutherland.

"Free to Love" is scheduled for release September 25th. This is the screen version of Adele Buffington's story, directed by Frank O'Connor. Clara Bow and Donald Keith have the featured roles and are supported by Raymond McKee, Hallam Cooley, Winter Hall and Charles Mailes.

features were announced this week by First National. Edwin Carewe's screen version of "The Sea Woman," will be titled "Why Women Love," "Dangerous Currents" and "Barriers Aflame," having been discarded.

The Sawyer-Lubin production from Anthony Pryde's novel "Spanish Sunlight," will be released as "The Girl From Montmatre." Barbara La Marr and Lewis Stone will be co-featured in this production.

John Ford Starts "Over the Border" for Fox

John Ford, who directed "The Iron Horse" for Fox has started on another production of the same magnitude for the Fox company. He has departed Hollywood with a large company for Jackson's Hole, Wyoming, where camera work will be started on "Over the Border."

The story was prepared for the screen by John Stone and will have George O'Brien and Olive Borden in the leading roles. In the supporting cast are J. Farrell MacDonald, Thomas Santschi, Frank Campeau, Lou Tellegen, Jay Hunt, Otis Harlan, Zasu Pitts, Grace Gordon, George Harris and Walter Perry.

Mrs. Wallace Reid Starts "Red Kimono"

"The Red Kimono," Mrs. Wallace Reid's newest production is under way and will be distributed by Davis Distributing Division. Shooting started this week with the following in the cast, in addition to Mrs. Reid; Sheldon Lewis, Mary Carr, Virginia Pearson, Tyrone Power, George Seigman, Nellie Bly Baker, Priscilla Bonner, Max Ancher, Theodore Von Eltz and Emily Fitzroy. In order to speed up production three directors are shooting scenes in three different locations.

Tiffany Signs Tearle and Agnes Ayres

CONWAY TEARLE and Agnes Ayres have been signed by Tiffany Productions for the principal roles in "Morals for Men," suggested by "The Love Serum" by Gouverneur Morris, and adapted to the screen by A. P. Younger. This will be the fourth production on the schedule of twelve for Tiffany.

Two New Westerns Under Way at Universal

William Crinley is directing Fred Humes in "The Man Without a Scar," a two-reel western for Universal. In the supporting cast to the star are, Colin Chase, Jack Pratt, Dan Paterson, Anton Vaverka and Morgan Brown.

"The Pinnacle Rider," another two-reel western is also in course of production at Hollywood, with Jack Mower as the star, under the direction of Willie Wyler. Velma Connor has the feminine lead, while others in the cast are, Stanhope Wheatcroft, Nellie Parker Spaulding, Billy Engle and Al Hart.

"Miss America" Signed for Paramount Feature

Jesse L. Lasky has signed Miss Fay Lamphier, Oakland, Calif., beauty who was crowned "Miss America" at the Atlantic City Beauty Pageant last week, to appear in "The American Venus," a forthcoming Paramount feature. In addition to signing Miss Lamphier to play the name role in "The American Venus," Mr. Lasky awarded a free scholarship in the Paramount School of Acting to Adrienne Dore, of Los Angeles, who was runner-up in the Atlantic City contest.

Moore Loaned to Fox' for "First Year"

Matt Moore has been loaned by Warner Brothers to Fox, for whom he will play the leading role of the young husband in "The First Year," the screen version of Frank Craven's stage success of the same name. On the completion of the Fox production Moore is to return to Warners to make "The Sap," under the direction of Lewis Milestone.

Larry Semon Starts First for Pathe Release

Photography has been started by Larry Semon on his first female comedy for release through Pathe. It is an adaptation of the Broadway musical comedy success, "Stop, Look and Listen." In addition to starring in the production, Semon is also directing. Dorothy Dwan is appearing opposite the star, and is the only member of the cast so far selected.

Beers Appointed Warners' Casting Director

Fred C. Beers has been appointed casting director of Warner Brothers west coast studio. In the past he has served in the same capacity for Metro and Famous. He started in the picture business eight years ago as an extra for the Triangle Company at Inceville.

O'Brien is Made Red Seal Manager on Coast

Thomas O'Brien, formerly special representative of Red Seal Pictures Corporation, has been appointed resident manager of that company's west coast exchanges with headquarters in San Francisco. C. P. Thostenson has been added to the selling staff of the same company at Los Angeles.

Jaffe Company to Film Eight Features

THE recently organized Jaffe Art Film Corporation will produce eight features this year. The first of the group "Broken Hearts," with Lila Lee in the featured role has been completed at the Tech Art Studios in New York. Maurice Schwartz, eminent Jewish dramatic actor and the director of several important European films will direct the productions.

Included in the eight Jaffe productions will be a special scenario which Israel Zangwill, famous British playwright and author, has been asked to write. Zangwill is to be invited to come to America and supervise the production of the picture. Jaffe also intends to produce a film based on one of the Biblical stories, the production to be made in the Holy Land, Egypt, and America.

Hollywood Studios Renamed Metropolitan

The Cinema Corporation of America, recent purchasers of the controlling interest in the Hollywood Studios, have changed the name of the plant to the Metropolitan Studios. An ambitious program of production is being mapped by Charles and Al Christie and William Sistrom.

Among the first productions to go into work under the new regime will be "The Million Dollar Handicap," an adaptation of the W. A. Frazer novel, "Thoroughbreds," and "Rocking Moon," which George Melford will direct from an adaptation of the Barrett Willoughby novel.

Warners Purchase Two for Next Season

Warner Brothers have purchased two additional stories for the 1926-27 schedule. They are "The Footloose Widow," by Beatrice Burton, and "White Flannels," from the pen of Lucien Cary.

"The Footloose Widow" is now running serially in a number of newspapers and will later appear in novel form. "White Flannels" appeared in the Saturday Evening Post.

Ill Health Compels De Sano to Quit

Because of ill health, Marcel De Sano has been released from his directorial contract with B. P. Schulberg. He has expressed his intention of taking an extensive vacation at a mountain health resort before resuming work. De Sano was scheduled to make "Lew Tyler's Wives" as his next Schulberg picture, but another director will be substituted.

Arrow Acquires Rights to "Protecting Prue"

"Protecting Prue," a comedy by Edgar Franklin has been purchased by Arrow Pictures Corporation and will be one of the twenty-four attractions on the program for the coming season. It will be produced and directed by Dallas M. Fitzgerald as the second of the series of features he will make for Arrow.

Rupert Julian Again to Play ex-Kaiser

In addition to directing "Three Faces East" for Producers Distributing Corporation, Rupert Julian will again impersonate the German ex-Kaiser, as he did in "The Beast of Berlin," the successful production released during the world war. Since that picture he has devoted his time to directing but will again don make-up for this role.

Clive Brook is another who has been assigned to the cast by Cecil B. De Mille. He will be featured with Jetta Goudal and Robert Ames. The picture was adapted by C. Gardner Sullivan from the stage success by Anthony Paul Kelly.

Charley Murray Signs for "Steel Preferred"

Charles Murray has been signed by Metropolitan Pictures for a leading comedy role in "Steel Preferred," which is being directed by James Hogan. He will join the company on its return from the Pittsburg steel mills, where scenes are now being shot.

The cast, in addition to Murray is composed of Vera Reynolds, William Boyd, Hobart Bosworth, Walter Long, William V. Mong, Nigel Barrie and Helene Sullivan.

Valli and O'Brien Leads in Moomaw Production

Changes in the cast originally named for "How To Train a Wife," a Lewis H. Moomaw feature for Associated Exhibitors, were announced this week. In the picture, which is now in production on the Pacific Coast, will co-feature Virginia Valli and Eugene O'Brien, with Jean Hersholt, George Nichols, Boris Karloff, Bryant Washburn and Cissy Fitzgerald prominent in the support.

Metro-Goldwyn-Mayer Buys Packard Novel

Metro-Goldwyn-Mayer has purchased the screen rights to "The Four Stragglers," one of the recent novels of Frank L. Packard, author of "The Miracle Man." The story offers a mystery plot centering about four odd characters. The work was first published by the Munsey publications and later in book form.

Thomson to Star in Story by Buckley Oxford

Fred Thomson has purchased the screen rights to an original story, as yet untitled, by Buckley Oxford. The story will be put into production with Thomson in the star role upon the completion of "All Around The Frying Pan," which Thomson is now making for F. B. O. release.

Carlotta Monterey Will Join Menjou Cast

Carlotta Monterey, well known as an actress on the New York speaking stage, will play opposite Adolphe Menjou for Paramount in "The King of Main Street." It will be her second screen appearance, her first having been with Richard Barthelmess in "Soul Fire."

Exhibitors Service Bureau

Manager Pat Argust's atmospheric lobby display for "The Gold Rush" (United Artists) at the Rialto theatre, Colorado Springs. It got over the effect of coolness and the theme of the photoplay at the same time.

Advisory Board and Contributing Editors, Exhibitors' Service Bureau

George J. Schade, Schade theatre, Sandusky.

Edward L. Hyman, Mark Strand theatre, Brooklyn.

Leo A. Landau, Lyceum theatre, Minneapolis.

C. C. Perry, Managing Director, Garrick theatre, Minneapolis.

E. R. Rogers, Southern District Supervisor, Famous Players-Lasky, Chattanooga, Tenn.

Stanley Chambers, Palace theatre, Wichita, Kan.

Willard C. Patterson, Metropolitan theatre, Atlanta.

E. V. Richards, Jr., Gen. Mgr., Saenger Amusement Co., New Orleans.

F. L. Newman, Managing Director, Famous Players-Lasky theatres, Los Angeles.

Arthur G. Stolte, Des Moines theatre, Des Moines, Iowa.

W. C. Quimby, Managing Director, Strand Palace and Jefferson theatres, Fort Wayne, Ind.

J. A. Partington, Imperial theatre, San Francisco.

George E. Carpenter, Paramount-Empress theatre, Salt Lake.

Sidney Grauman, Grauman's theatres, Los Angeles.

: : THE CHECK-UP : :
Weekly Edition of Exhibitors' Box Office Reports

Productions listed are new pictures on which reports were not available previously.

For ratings on current and older releases see MOTION PICTURE NEWS—first issue of each month.

KEY—The first column following the name of the feature represents the number of managers that have reported the picture as "Poor." The second column gives the number who considered it "Fair"; the third the number who considered it "Good"; and the fourth column, those who considered it "Big." The fifth column is a percentage giving the average rating on that feature, obtained by the following method: A report of "Poor" is rated at 20%; one of "Fair," 40%; "Good," 70%; and "Big," 100%. The percentage rating of all of these reports on one picture are then added together, and divided by the number of reports, giving the average percentage—a figure which represents the consensus of opinion on that picture. In this way exceptional cases, reports which might be misleading taken alone, and such individual differences of opinion are averaged up and eliminated.

TITLE	Poor	Fair	Good	Big	Value	Length
FAMOUS PLAYERS						
Lucky Devil, The............	—	1	11	1	70	5,935 ft.
Night Life of New York.......	—	4	8	2	66	6,998 ft.
FILM BOOKING						
Druscilla with a Million.........	—	2	5	3	73	7,391 ft.
FIRST NATIONAL						
Just a Woman.............	—	4	6	—	58	6,652 ft.
METRO-GOLDWYN						
Unholy Three, The............	—	1	6	4	78	6,848 ft.
White Desert, The...........	—	1	10	—	67	6,345 ft.
WARNER BROS.						
Tracked in the Snow Country.	—	3	5	2	67	6,900 ft

George E. Brown, Imperial theatre, Charlotte, N. C.

Louis K. Sidney, Division Manager, Loew's theatres, Pittsburgh, Pa.

Geo. Rotsky, Managing Director, Palace theatre, Montreal, Can.

Eddie Zorn, Managing Director, Broadway-Strand theatre, Detroit.

Fred S. Myer, Managing Director, Palace theatre, Hamilton, Ohio.

Joseph Plunkett, Managing Director, Mark-Strand theatre, New York.

Ray Grombacher, Managing Director, Liberty theatre, Spokane, Wash.

Rose A. McVey, Manager, Temple theatre, Geneva, N. Y.

W. S. McLaren, Managing Director, Capitol theatre, Jackson, Mich.

Harold B. Franklin, Director of Theatres, Famous Players-Lasky.

William J. Sullivan, Manager, Rialto theatre, Butte, Mont.

H. A. Albright, Manager, T. D. & L. theatre, Glendale, Calif.

Claire Meachime, Grand theatre, Westfield, N. Y.

Ace Berry, Managing Director, Circle theatre, Indianapolis.

See Complete "Check-Up" Oct. 10th

The Sure Test of a Really Big Picture---
When the Attendance Grows and Grows and Grows!

EASTMAN THEATRE
DEDICATED TO MUSIC AND MOTION PICTURES
ROCHESTER · N · Y
Telephone Main 7140

August 27th 1925.

Reply to Mr. Clarke

Mr. Basil Brady,
Pathe Exchange,
505 Pearl Street,
Buffalo, N. Y.

Dear Mr. Brady:

You will by now have received the daily statements of box office receipts for the showing of Black Cyclone here last week and will understand why we are so glad that a showing of this unusual feature was arranged in this theatre.

Your claims in regard to Black Cyclone are more than justified. The attendance grew steadily during the week that we showed the picture and we are greatly interested that the general run of patrons came from the usual run of pictures.

It can particularly pleasing to us to find that the footage of Black Cyclone was such that we were able to present a well diversified program, two included the Harry Langdon comedy (The Sea Squawk), we noted and a novelty film. Our only wish is that we might have more frequent opportunities to present pictures of this kind.

With best personal regards, I am

Very truly yours,

EASTMAN THEATRE,
Manager.

HAL ROACH
presents

BLACK CYCLONE

with REX The Wild Horse

DIRECTED BY
FRED JACKMAN

WRITTEN BY
HAL E. ROACH

Pathépicture
TRADE MARK

Broadway 'Phantom' Campaign

Joe Weil Puts Over Smashing Line-Up of Stunts for Astor Theatre Showing

AN exploitation campaign of unusual importance has been used throughout Greater New York during the past few weeks, heralding the premiere of "The Phantom of the Opera" at the Astor theatre on Broadway, put across by the exploitation department of Universal under the direction of Joe Weil.

The opening gun in this campaign was the permission of the Textile Color Card association, which has a membership of 16,000 in the textile trade, to name the predominating Fall color, "Phantom Red." The association sent a letter to its entire membership telling of the new color and enclosing a sample of the shade.

Universal canvassed all millinery houses, cloak and suit manufacturers, resident buyers, etc., telling of the new color and offering an attractive window card to be used with a "Phantom Red" display.

Many exclusive Fifth Ave. establishments have tied-up with "The Phantom." Dutton's book shop has an attractive display, Brentano's, Sarnoff, the Astor Hat Shop, and many others have put in a "Phantom Red" window. Capezio's, a fashionable shoe shop on West 48th St., placed a few red shoes in their window for a tie-up and then, because of the instantaneous demand, gave the entire window over to a red display.

A window card showing Mary Philbin listening-in on her radio set afforded a tie-up with all the Radiola stores in the Greater New York territory, 1,000 in all. These dealers gave prominent window displays on the new picture.

A manufacturer of lipsticks was induced to put out a "Phantom Red" lipstick which all the big drug stores along Broadway will soon be featuring.

Even the restaurants along Broadway felt that they could not permit the "Phantom" opening to go by unnoticed. The chef of the El Dorado carved a giant cake out of vegetables, showing a full-length figure of "The Phantom," which was placed in the restaurant's window.

A special book cover was made up of heavy manilla paper with "The Phantom of the Opera" in large bold red letters. These were furnished drug stores selling popular priced fiction and circulating libraries to place on all outgoing books. Hundreds of persons were seen on the subway, trolley cars and ferries, ostensibly reading "The Phantom of the Opera."

Universal placed 200 copies of the photoplay edition of the book in hotel lobbies and public terminals where scores of people were seen reading it.

Twenty thousand "Phantom" post cards with trick printing which was not visible until held up to the light brought the message to beauty parlors, barber shops, hotels and a picked mailing list. It was figured that if the barbers and the beauty specialists could be interested in the new picture that Universal would have gained powerful advertising allies, through their well known conversational possibilities.

Double truck rotogravure sheets were distributed to the number of several thousand in the lobby of the Astor and by crews of boys who delivered them to stores in picked neighborhoods. Boys were also posted in railroad terminals with these sheets.

A special sniping campaign was used along all roads leading into the city backed up by space in the subways and railroad cars. Returning vacationists were made aware of the fact that "The Phantom" was ready for their inspection.

The Exploitation Department worked hand in hand with the Publicity Department on special stunts with the ballet girls who appear in the prologue at the Astor. Every New York newspaper made use of one or more pictures of these girls taken on the roof of the Steinway building and the Heckscher building.

Illuminated display piece for "Her Sister from Paris," (First National) at the Saenger theatre, Shreveport, La., built by George E. Findley. Lights threw the silhouette on a lightly clad dancer on the small screen.

The walls of the Astor lobby have been entirely covered with plaster "stone," carrying out the dungeon-like atmosphere of the picture. A faint half-light adds to the general spookiness of the effect, and a red silk clothed figure of the "phantom" lying in a niche over the entrance to the auditorium sends cold shivers up and down the spines of entering patrons. The ushers carry out the "spirit" of the picture by wearing red silk robes.

Auto Firm Gives Display to "The Tourist" Run

Something of a precedent for exploitation of two-reel comedies on Broadway has been established through a window display tie-up in one of the most prominent locations on the Great White Way boosting "The Tourist," showing at the Rialto theatre.

The display arranged by the Rialto theatre is in the big window of the Picard Motor Sales Company, Inc., authorized Ford Dealers, on Broadway, between 51st and 52nd streets, opposite the Piccadilly theatre.

A life sized painted cut-out of Johnny Arthur, star of "The Tourist," showing him seated before a dilapidated Ford, the engine of which serves the tourist as his complete kitchen equipment, is featured in the window dislay opposite a new Ford coupe. In the foreground of the window are displayed ten stills from "The Tourist," mounted and each carrying a caption tying up the comedy, the Ford car and the Picard company. A card, the size of a one-sheet, mounted on an easel, announces prominently that "The Tourist" is showing at the Rialto theatre.

Womanless Wedding Stunt on "Marriage Whirl"

As a prologue to "The Marriage Whirl," Manager Geo. Rea of the Grand Theatre, Columbus, staged a unique presentation, "A Womanless Wedding." The bridal party consisted of the bride and bridegroom, best man, minister, choir boy and two young girl and boy attendants. All the actors were collegians, even the bride and her girl attendants being impersonated by college boys.

The prologue was inexpensive, being produced at the cost of six theatre tickets and the cost of renting wigs for the "young ladies." Flowers were also purchased for the wedding.

Don Nichols, manager of the Savoy theatre, Durham, N. C., arranged this attractive front display on "The Prairie Wife" (Metro-Goldwyn). The center frame was worked on a flasher.

"Unholy Three" is Greater Movie Season Opener

"The Unholy Three" was the attraction which ushered in "Greater Movie Season" at the Imperial Charlotte. Manager Warren Irvin played it up as a special feature, stressing the fact that this film was also the opening attraction for the season at the Capitol theatre, New York.

A valuable publicity stunt was the throwing away of a thousand tickets from an airplane at Lakeview Park, among which were several passes, good for any of the three Paramount houses in Charlotte during the first week of the "Greater Movie Season." The railway company operating the street cars to and from the Park, carried signs on all their cars advertising the airplane stunt.

Splendid co-operation was received from the merchants of the city, fifteen of whom permitted the theatre to paint "Greater Movie Season is here—Let's go—" on their windows.

A week in advance all theatre employees wore ribbons reading: "It starts August 17." This teaser aroused curiosity, many asking for details. Balloons were used in lobby and some given to children. Banners and pennants decorated marquee, announcing "Greater Movie Season."

Dinosaurus Ballyhoo Given "Lost World" Showing

Rowland and Clark's theatres staged a rather unique street ballyhoo for "The Lost World" in Pittsburgh. Several days before the advance advertising of the picture at the Liberty theatre, a huge dinosaur, measuring 14 feet long, and towering 12 feet 6 inches in the air, mounted on a two-ton truck was put on the streets. A bellows arrangement, fed with red confetti belched forth apparent fire from his ferocious mouth. The animal was designed and built at the Rowland and Clark studios at Pittsburgh.

The effect on the people was not only startling, but as it was in advance of the campaign on "The Lost World," it led to much discussion.

A living model, attended by her maid, attracted attention to "A Slave of Fashion" (Metro-Goldwyn) at the Stillman theatre, Cleveland, in this window.

A vacant store building in Jamestown, N. Y., which Paterson & Woods, managers of the Jamestown Palace, decorated with stills and so on as a "museum" to advertise "The Iron Horse" (Fox).

Portland "Iron Horse" Drive

Oregon City is Scene of Heavy Campaign for Majestic Theatre Showing of Picture

AN unusually comprehensive and far reaching campaign was put over very recently in Portland, Ore., by Charles E. Couche, director of publicity, and Frank Lacey, house manager, at the Majestic theatre in that city for the engagement of "The Iron Horse." They started the ball rolling three weeks in advance of the opening with an elaborate newspaper announcement and plenty of pertinent press notices.

A score of De Luxe painted boards 12 by 60 feet were arranged on the four main vacation highways. The boards were not merely painted, but had old style engine heads built of wood and beaver board projecting about two feet from surface of sign. The boards were brilliantly illuminated with flood lights at night, and constituted a valuable flash for the campaign. Forty ordinary 24-sheet boards were also utilized for "Iron Horse" stands.

The "Oregonian" — Portland's leading newspaper was tied up with the drive, and in a manner that secured over 200 inches of free space, including two front page stories. The Oregonian consented to act as host to local pioneers, who came to Portland by railroad prior to 1885. The newspaper also acted as host to orphan children at special matinees. The local lodge of Elks co-operated by providing transportation for the children at these performances.

The Union Pacific Railways responded liberally to an invitation for reciprocal advertising courtesies, and displayed special 8x10 "Iron Horse" ad cards throughout their shops, offices, etc. The railroads also allowed an advertising slip on the picture to be attached to every month-end pay check issued to their employees, approximating 10,000.

The Union Pacific helped put over the biggest advertising parade over staged in Portland. They furnished their 40 piece shop band to lead the procession, which consisted of section crew, floats, equipment, Indians and Portland's first railway engine. The old engine being transported on a tractor-drawn truck. The parade was ten blocks long and secured 260 inches of free publicity for the picture.

The parade was the climax of the advance campaign—being staged on Saturday morning immediately preceding the opening. After it was over, the band gave a concert in front of the theatre, where the engine was parked by special permit for the run of the engagement.

Motion pictures of the parade were made during its progress. These pictures were run at the three other big downtown houses. The orchestra at one theatre, and the orchestra of the biggest and most popular hotel cafe, put on "Iron Horse" musical novelties.

The local County Fair opening the week before the picture's opening, a booth was engaged, in which an "Iron Horse" trailer was shown to 60,000 people for five days preceding the opening engagement.

A number of display windows in the downtown section were also brought into play. One window using a trailer, and two displaying miniature model engines.

Oilcloth signs were used on the spare tires of taxicabs, and Portland street cars carried "Iron Horse" dash board cards as well. A distinctive feature of the drive was the broadcasting from local wireless station of an orchestra rendering "Iron Horse" musical novelty. This number comprised in its rendition, whistles, bells and imitations of railroad effects.

Exhibitors Box-Office Reports

Names of the theatre owners are omitted by agreement in accordance with the wishes of the average exhibitor and in the belief that reports published over the signature of the exhibitor reporting, is a dangerous practice.

Only reports received on specially prepared blanks furnished by us will be accepted for use in this department. Exhibitors who value this reporting service are urged to ask for these blanks

Title of Picture	Population of Town	Location	Class of Patronage	Weather	Box Office Value	Check-up Percentage from other Reports
ASSOC. EXHIB.						
Barriers Burned Away...	733826	Md.	Mixed	Warm	Big	—
PARAMOUNT						
Air Mail, The.........	2000	Ohio	Farm	Warm	Fair	69
Alaskan, The.........	15000	Mich.	Farm	Fair	Good	69
Beggar on Horseback, The	200616	Ga.	Mixed	Warm	Fair	—
	324410	Mo.	Mixed	St'my	Good	—
	733826	Md.	Mixed	Warm	Fair	—
Border Legion, The....	2000	Ohio	Farm	Warm	Good	73
Coast of Folly, The.....	324410	Mo.	Mixed	St'my	Good	—
Dressmaker from Paris, The.........	2000	Ohio	Farm	Warm	Fair	73
Eve's Secret.........	140000	Mass.	Mixed	Warm	Fair	65
Goose Hangs High, The.	2000	Ohio	Farm	Warm	Fair	72
Grounds for Divorce....	140000	Mass.	Mixed	Warm	Fair	—
In the Name of Love...	772897	Mo.	Mixed	Warm	Fair	—
	993678	Mich.	Mixed	Fair	Good	—
Little French Girl, The..	140000	Mass.	Mixed	Warm	Fair	72
Lucky Devil, The......	60000	Mont.	Mixed	Warm	Big	—
Manicure Girl, The....	140000	Mass.	Mixed	Hot	Fair	59
Man Who Found Himself	796841	Ohio	Mixed	Hot	Fair	—
Night Club, The.......	2000	Ohio	Farm	Warm	Fair	72
Night Life of New York.	126468	Iowa	Mixed	Hot	Good	63
Not So Long Ago.......	324410	Mo.	Mixed	Fair	Good	—
	401247	Ohio	Mixed	Warm	Fair	—
	120000	Fla.	Mixed	Fair	Big	—
Paths to Paradise.......	140000	Mass.	Mixed	Hot	Good	58
Rugged Water.......	258288	Ore.	Mixed	Fair	Poor	—
Sainted Devil, A.......	15000	Mich.	Farm	Fair	Fair	59
Son of His Father, A.....	120000	Fla.	Mixed	Fair	Good	—
Street of Forgotten Men.	158976	Texas	Mixed	Hot	Poor	—
	993678	Mich.	Mixed	Warm	Good	—
	772897	Mo.	Mixed	Warm	Fair	—
	120000	Fla.	Mixed	Warm	Good	—
	733826	Md.	Mixed	Warm	Good	—
Ten Commandments, The.................	401247	Ohio	Mixed	Warm	Good	89
	120000	Fla.	Mixed	Fair	Big	—
	796841	Ohio	Mixed	St'my	Fair	—
	324410	Mo.	Mixed	Fair	Good	—
	126468	Iowa	Mixed	Hot	Good	—
Tongues of Flame.......	2000	Ohio	Farm	Warm	Good	66
Too Many Kisses.......	2000	Ohio	Farm	Warm	Fair	—
Trouble with Wives, The	796841	Ohio	Mixed	Hot	Fair	—
Wild, Wild Susan.......	796841	Ohio	Mixed	Hot	Good	—
	126468	Iowa	Mixed	Hot	Good	—
Wild Horse Mesa......	772897	Mo.	Mixed	Warm	Good	—
FIRST NATIONAL						
Chickie.............	258288	Ore.	Mixed	Fair	Poor	70
Desert Flower, The.....	158976	Texas	Mixed	Hot	Poor	70
Graustark...........	314194	Ind.	Mixed	Warm	Big	—
Half-Way Girl, The....	200616	Ga.	Mixed	Warm	Fair	—
	324410	Mo.	Mixed	Fair	Good	—
	733826	Md.	Mixed	Warm	Big	—
Heart of a Siren, The...	158976	Texas	Mixed	Hot	Poor	52
Her Sister from Paris...	796841	Ohio	Mixed	Hot	Big	—
If I Marry Again......	140000	Mass.	Mixed	Warm	Fair	72
I Want My Man......	60000	Mont.	Mixed	Warm	Good	66
Knockout The........	401247	Ohio	Mixed	Warm	Fair	—
Lost World, The.......	69272	Maine	Mixed	Hot	Good	—
	450000	Minn.	Mixed	Hot	Big	—
Madonna of the Streets.	15000	Mich.	Farm	Warm	Fair	72
Sally.............	60000	Mont.	Mixed	Warm	Good	87
Self-Made Failure, A....	15000	Mich.	Farm	Fair	Poor	—
Shore Leave.........	772897	Mo.	Mixed	Warm	Good	—
	258288	Ore.	Mixed	Fair	Fair	—
	324410	Mo.	Mixed	St'my	Fair	—
	993678	Mich.	Mixed	Fair	Good	—
	158976	Texas	Mixed	Hot	Good	—

Title of Picture	Population of Town	Location	Class of Patronage	Weather	Box Office Value	Check-up Percentage from other Reports
F. B. O.						
Drusilla With a Million..	324410	Mo.	Mixed	Fair	Good	—
Speed Wild...........	200616	Ga.	Mixed	Warm	Good	—
White Fang..........	140000	Mass.	Mixed	Warm	Big	68
	200616	Ga.	Mixed	Warm	Good	—
Wild Bull's Lair, The....	2000	Ohio	Farm	Warm	Good	—
FOX						
Dick Turpin..........	140000	Mass.	Mixed	Hot	Good	78
Every Man's Wife......	140000	Mass.	Mixed	Warm	Good	—
Iron Horse, The.......	324410	Mo.	Mixed	St'my	Big	—
	258288	Ore.	Mixed	Fair	Good	—
	314194	Ind.	Mixed	Warm	Big	—
Lucky Horseshoe, The..	993678	Mich.	Mixed	Fair	Good	—
	158976	Texas	Mixed	Hot	Poor	—
METRO-GOLDWYN-MAYER						
Daddy's Gone A Hunting	140000	Mass.	Mixed	Hot	Good	64
Mystic, The..........	314194	Ind.	Mixed	Warm	Big	—
	772897	Mo.	Mixed	Warm	Good	—
Never the Twain Shall Meet...............	120000	Fla.	Mixed	Fair	Good	—
	401247	Ohio	Mixed	Warm	Fair	—
Romola..............	796841	Ohio	Mixed	Hot	Good	—
Slave of Fashion, A.....	200616	Ga.	Mixed	Warm	Fair	—
Sporting Venus, The	140000	Mass.	Mixed	Hot	Fair	55
Sun-Up.............	796841	Ohio	Mixed	Hot	Good	—
PATHE						
Girl Shy............	15000	Mich.	Farm	Fair	Big	—
PROD. DIST. CORP.						
Crimson Runner, The..	733826	Md.	Mixed	Warm	Good	—
Hell's Highroad.......	796841	Ohio	Mixed	Hot	Fair	—
	772897	Mo.	Mixed	Warm	Good	—
Seven Days..........	60000	Mont.	Mixed	Warm	Good	—
STATE RIGHTS						
Overland Limited, The..	324410	Mo.	Mixed	St'my	Fair	—
Mine With the Iron Door	733826	Md.	Mixed	Warm	Big	80
Poisoned Paradise.....	796841	Ohio	Mixed	Hot	Fair	—
Wizard of Oz, The.....	324410	Mo.	Mixed	Fair	Good	—
UNITED ARTISTS						
Gold Rush, The.......	993678	Mich.	Mixed	Fair	Big	—
	993678	Mich.	Mixed	Warm	Big	—
Isn't Life Wonderful...	2000	Ohio	Farm	Warm	Poor	51
Loving Lies.........	2000	Ohio	Farm	Warm	Fair	—
One Exciting Night	2000	Ohio	Farm	Warm	Good	—
Salvation Hunters, The..	2000	Ohio	Farm	Warm	Poor	—
Waking Up the Town...	2000	Ohio	Farm	Warm	Fair	—
Woman of Paris, A.....	2000	Ohio	Farm	Warm	Poor	—
UNIVERSAL						
California Straight Ahead	993678	Mich.	Mixed	Warm	Good	—
Head Winds........	140000	Mass.	Mixed	Warm	Fair	74
I'LL Show You the Town	796841	Ohio	Mixed	Hot	Fair	79
Last Laugh, The......	200616	Ga.	Mixed	Warm	Good	54
Raffles.............	401247	Ohio	Mixed	Warm	Fair	64
Siege..............	258288	Ore.	Mixed	Fair	Poor	—
Teaser, The..........	993678	Mich.	Mixed	Fair	Good	—
The White Outlaw.....	60000	Mont.	Mixed	Warm	Fair	—
WARNERS BROS.						
Eve's Lover.........	200616	Ga.	Mixed	Warm	Good	—
George Washington, Jr..	15000	Mich.	Farm	Fair	Poor	—
How Baxter Butted In...	401247	Ohio	Mixed	Warm	Fair	—
Limited Mail, The.....	796841	Ohio	Mixed	Hot	Good	—
Lover of Camille, The...	15000	Mich.	Farm	Fair	Poor	59
Steele of the Royal Mounted............	733826	Md.	Mixed	Warm	Good	—

Thank you, Mr. Comerford –

Richard Talmadge

THE COMERFORD AMUSEMENT COMPANY
207 WYOMING AVENUE
STATE THEATRE BLDG
SCRANTON, PA.

September 11, 1925.

Mr. R. Talmadge
F.B.O. Studios
780 Gower Street
Los Angeles, Calif.

Dear Talmadge:

I congratulate you on the clean pictures you have been making. Your releases thru F.B.O. have been fine examples of clean and entertaining pictures.

Your "Tearing Thru" - "The Fighting Demon" - "The Isle of Hope" - and your latest "The Wall Street Whiz" are real entertainment.

Keep up your good work.

Yours for continued success.

THE COMERFORD AMUSEMENT COMPANY

MEC:K   For *M. E. Comerford*

RICHARD TALMADGE PRODUCTIONS
are today acknowledged by thousands of exhibitors to be the best drawing box office
action pictures on the market.

Presented by ABE CARLOS - - - Distributed by

FILM BOOKING OFFICES
723 Seventh Ave., New York
Exchanges Everywhere

Exhibitors Box-Office Reports

Names of the theatre owners are omitted by agreement in accordance with the wishes of the average exhibitor and in the belief that reports published over the signature of the exhibitor reporting, is a dangerous practice.

Only reports received on specially prepared blanks furnished by us will be accepted for use in this department. Exhibitors who value this reporting service are urged to ask for these blanks

Column headers (diagonal): Title of Picture · Population of Town · Location · Class of Patronage · Weather · Box Office Value · Check-up Percentage from other Reports

Title of Picture	Population	Location	Class	Weather	Box Office	Check-up
ASSOC. EXHIB.						
Barriers Burned Away...	733826	Md.	Mixed	Warm	Big	—
PARAMOUNT						
Air Mail, The.........	2000	Ohio	Farm	Warm	Fair	69
Alaskan, The.........	15000	Mich.	Farm	Fair	Good	69
Beggar on Horseback, The	200616	Ga.	Mixed	Warm	Fair	—
	324410	Mo.	Mixed	St'my	Good	—
	733826	Md.	Mixed	Warm	Fair	—
Border Legion, The.....	2000	Ohio	Farm	Warm	Good	73
Coast of Folly, The.....	324410	Mo.	Mixed	St'my	Good	—
Dressmaker from Paris, The.................	2000	Ohio	Farm	Warm	Fair	73
Eve's Secret........	140000	Mass.	Mixed	Warm	Fair	65
Goose Hangs High, The.	2000	Ohio	Farm	Warm	Fair	72
Grounds for Divorce....	140000	Mass.	Mixed	Warm	Fair	—
In the Name of Love...	772897	Mo.	Mixed	Warm	Fair	—
	993678	Mich.	Mixed	Fair	Good	—
Little French Girl, The..	140000	Mass.	Mixed	Warm	Fair	72
Lucky Devil, The......	60000	Mont.	Mixed	Warm	Big	—
Manicure Girl, The....	140000	Mass.	Mixed	Hot	Fair	59
Man Who Found Himself	796841	Ohio	Mixed	Hot	Fair	—
Night Club, The......	2000	Ohio	Farm	Warm	Fair	72
Night Life of New York.	126468	Iowa	Mixed	Hot	Good	63
Not So Long Ago......	324410	Mo.	Mixed	Fair	Good	—
	401247	Ohio	Mixed	Warm	Fair	—
	120000	Fla.	Mixed	Fair	Big	—
Paths to Paradise.......	140000	Mass.	Mixed	Hot	Good	58
Rugged Water.........	258288	Ore.	Mixed	Fair	Poor	—
Sainted Devil, A.......	15000	Mich.	Farm	Fair	Fair	59
Son of His Father, A....	120000	Fla.	Mixed	Fair	Good	—
Street of Forgotten Men.	158976	Texas	Mixed	Hot	Poor	—
	993678	Mich.	Mixed	Warm	Good	—
	772897	Mo.	Mixed	Warm	Fair	—
	120000	Fla.	Mixed	Fair	Good	—
	733826	Md.	Mixed	Warm	Good	—
Ten Commandments, The................	401247	Ohio	Mixed	Warm	Good	89
	120000	Fla.	Mixed	Fair	Big	—
	796841	Ohio	Mixed	St'my	Fair	—
	324410	Mo.	Mixed	Fair	Good	—
	126468	Iowa	Mixed	Hot	Good	—
Tongues of Flame......	2000	Ohio	Farm	Warm	Good	66
Too Many Kisses......	2000	Ohio	Farm	Warm	Fair	67
Trouble with Wives, The	796841	Ohio	Mixed	Hot	Fair	—
Wild, Wild Susan......	796841	Ohio	Mixed	Hot	Fair	—
	126468	Iowa	Mixed	Hot	Good	—
Wild Horse Mesa......	772897	Mo.	Mixed	Warm	Good	—
FIRST NATIONAL						
Chickie..............	258288	Ore.	Mixed	Fair	Poor	70
Desert Flower, The.....	158976	Texas	Mixed	Hot	Poor	70
Graustark...........	314194	Ind.	Mixed	Warm	Big	—
Half-Way Girl, The....	200616	Ga.	Mixed	Warm	Fair	—
	324410	Mo.	Mixed	Fair	Good	—
	733826	Md.	Mixed	Warm	Big	—
Heart of a Siren, The...	158976	Texas	Mixed	Hot	Poor	52
Her Sister from Paris...	796841	Ohio	Mixed	Hot	Big	—
If I Marry Again......	140000	Mass.	Mixed	Warm	Fair	72
I Want My Man......	60000	Mont.	Mixed	Warm	Good	66
Knockout The........	401247	Ohio	Mixed	Warm	Fair	—
Lost World, The......	69272	Maine	Mixed	Hot	Good	—
	450000	Minn.	Mixed	Hot	Big	—
Madonna of the Streets.	15000	Mich.	Farm	Fair	Fair	72
Sally...............	60000	Mont.	Mixed	Warm	Good	87
Self-Made Failure, A....	15000	Mich.	Farm	Fair	Poor	—
Shore Leave..........	772897	Mo.	Mixed	Warm	Fair	—
	258288	Ore.	Mixed	Warm	Fair	—
	324410	Mo.	Mixed	St'my	Fair	—
	993678	Mich.	Mixed	Fair	Good	—
	158976	Texas	Mixed	Hot	Good	—

Title of Picture	Population	Location	Class	Weather	Box Office	Check-up
F. B. O.						
Drusilla With a Million..	324410	Mo.	Mixed	Fair	Good	—
Speed Wild..........	200616	Ga.	Mixed	Warm	Good	—
White Fang..........	140000	Mass.	Mixed	Warm	Big	68
	200616	Ga.	Mixed	Warm	Good	—
Wild Bull's Lair, The...	2000	Ohio	Farm	Warm	Good	—
FOX						
Dick Turpin.........	140000	Mass.	Mixed	Hot	Good	78
Every Man's Wife.....	140000	Mass.	Mixed	Warm	Good	—
Iron Horse, The......	324410	Mo.	Mixed	St'my	Big	—
	258288	Ore.	Mixed	Fair	Good	—
Lightnin'............	314194	Ind.	Mixed	Warm	Big	—
	993678	Mich.	Mixed	Warm	Good	—
Lucky Horseshoe, The..	993678	Mich.	Mixed	Fair	Good	—
	158976	Texas	Mixed	Hot	Poor	—
METRO-GOLDWYN-MAYER						
Daddy's Gone A Hunting	140000	Mass.	Mixed	Hot	Good	64
Mystic, The.........	314194	Ind.	Mixed	Warm	Big	—
	772897	Mo.	Mixed	Warm	Good	—
Never the Twain Shall Meet..............	120000	Fla.	Mixed	Fair	Good	—
	401247	Ohio	Mixed	Fair	Fair	—
Romola..............	796841	Ohio	Mixed	Hot	Good	—
Slave of Fashion, A....	200616	Ga.	Mixed	Warm	Fair	—
Sporting Venus, The ...	140000	Mass.	Mixed	Hot	Fair	55
Sun-Up.............	796841	Ohio	Mixed	Hot	Good	—
PATHE						
Girl Shy............	15000	Mich.	Farm.	Fair	Big	—
PROD. DIST. CORP.						
Crimson Runner, The..	733826	Md.	Mixed	Warm	Good	—
Hell's Highroad......	796841	Ohio	Mixed	Hot	Fair	—
	772897	Mo.	Mixed	Warm	Good	—
Seven Days..........	60000	Mont.	Mixed	Warm	Good	—
STATE RIGHTS						
Overland Limited, The..	324410	Mo.	Mixed	St'my	Fair	—
Mine With the Iron Door	733826	Md.	Mixed	Warm	Big	80
Poisoned Paradise.....	796841	Ohio	Mixed	Hot	Fair	—
Wizard of Oz, The.....	324410	Mo.	Mixed	Fair	Good	—
UNITED ARTISTS						
Gold Rush, The......	993678	Mich.	Mixed	Fair	Big	—
	993678	Mich.	Mixed	Warm	Big	—
Isn't Life Wonderful....	2000	Ohio	Farm	Warm	Poor	51
Loving Lies..........	2000	Ohio	Farm	Warm	Fair	—
One Exciting Night	2000	Ohio	Farm	Warm	Poor	—
Salvation Hunters, The..	2000	Ohio	Farm	Warm	Poor	—
Waking Up the Town....	2000	Ohio	Farm	Warm	Fair	—
Woman of Paris, A.....	2000	Ohio	Farm	Warm	Poor	—
UNIVERSAL						
California Straight Ahead	993678	Mich.	Mixed	Warm	Good	—
Head Winds..........	140000	Mass.	Mixed	Warm	Fair	74
I'LL Show You the Town	796841	Ohio	Mixed	Hot	Fair	79
Last Laugh, The......	200616	Ga.	Mixed	Warm	Good	54
Raffles.............	401247	Ohio	Mixed	Warm	Fair	64
Siege..............	258288	Ore.	Mixed	Fair	Poor	—
Teaser, The.........	993678	Mich.	Mixed	Fair	Good	—
The White Outlaw.....	60000	Mont.	Mixed	Warm	Fair	—
WARNERS BROS.						
Eve's Lover.........	200616	Ga.	Mixed	Warm	Good	—
George Washington, Jr...	15000	Mich.	Farm	Fair	Poor	—
How Baxter Butted In...	401247	Ohio	Mixed	Warm	Good	—
Limited Mail, The.....	796841	Ohio	Mixed	Hot	Good	—
Lover of Camille, The..	15000	Mich.	Farm	Fair	Poor	59
Steele of the Royal Mounted..........	733826	Md.	Mixed	Warm	Good	—

Thank you, Mr. Comerford –

Richard Talmadge

RICHARD TALMADGE PRODUCTIONS
are today acknowledged by thousands of exhibitors to be the best drawing box office
action pictures on the market.

Presented by ABE CARLOS · · · Distributed by

FILM BOOKING OFFICES
723 Seventh Ave., New York
Exchanges Everywhere

Special Bus Tour Exploits "Don Q" at Lockport

In his exploitation of "Don Q" at the Palace, Lockport, Manager Geo. T. Cruzen introduced a novel and forceful agent in the form of a Special Bus Tour which covered twenty towns and villages in surrounding territory.

The bus, one of the Parlor Type Coaches, with a seating capacity of 54 people, was chartered for a day and manned with a 22 piece band, a ballyhoo man, poster-man, six bill-passers and an extra helper. Bus was put on a running schedule of 30 miles per hour, with time of arrival, departure and stop-over in each town timed.

At the instant of arrival in a town the most prominent position was monopolized. The bill-passers in charge of poster man flooded the community in all directions with heralds, while the poster-man sniped available out-door locations. Another one of the boys located window cards.

After the first selection by the band, the entire population was out en masse, whereupon the ballyhoo man proceeded to narrate the luxuries, appointments, etc., of the Palace theatre, stressing the point that it was built to serve, not only Lockport, but Niagara county as well. He finished his talk with an elaborate account of the merits of "Don Q," as well as those of future films to be shown at the Palace.

"Havoc" Heralds Dropped From Airplane Aloft

Among the many stunts employed to attract attention to the Cleveland engagement of "Havoc" was the distribution of heralds and passes from an aeroplane that soared over the entire city of Cleveland, on the day the picture opened. The heralds were 25,000 small cards bearing the following copy:

This Fell From An Aeroplane. If It Was a Bomb Havoc would be created in Cleveland during a war. See this greatest photoplay ever made—Now showing at B. F. Keith Palace theatre.

Three hundred of the cards had, imprinted across their face "This Ticket Good For One Admission." The backs of all the cards also bore a brief selling argument on the picture.

An extra large campaign on "Havoc" was waged in newspapers; the copy playing up principally the fact that this engagement constituted a world premiere.

The billboards were used for a veritable circus campaign of billing, a full showing being effected for one week preceding the opening.

Display of live bees in the lobby of Keith's Palace theatre, Cleveland, for the showing of "Lightnin'" (Fox), in which a bee story figures prominently.

"Night Life of New York" in Animated Display

The effective lobby display Manager Oscar White used on "Night Life of New York" when it played the Liberty, Greenwood, is well worth describing.

Cut-outs of buildings were placed against a sky background, one of the smaller ones being painted to represent a theatre with a tiny electric sign carrying the picture title. The effect was obtained by punching holes in the sign and backing it with a small electric bulb. A cement drive was put down in front of the buildings with three lamp-posts at each of sidewalk. A motor car was parked in a small park at right which was covered with sand and green dust sown to represent grass, with compobourd trees and shrubs enhancing its realism. A small car read "Keep Off The Grass." Another small racing car was placed on street with a card reading: "Coming Monday—Lucky Devil." The action appeal of the display was increased by a train of electric cars, which kept circling around the block of buildings.

"Sally" Trailer Projected in Liberty Lobby

Manager Oscar White during his showing of "Sally" at the Liberty theatre, Greenwood, pulled a lobby stunt which was a "knockout" from a publicity standpoint.

In the center of the lobby was placed a miniature stage, complete in every detail, with a screen and black curtains which were dropped when screen was not in use. A small toy motion picture machine was borrowed and placed outside on sidewalk, about six feet from screen. Permission was obtained from the city to cut off the lights around the theatre, so that when trailer on "Sally" and two or three others on coming attractions were flashed on small screen, they were clearly projected. Result was that sidewalk in front of theatre was jammed with people watching the exhibit.

A drug store window display of "Phantom Red" lipsticks, tying up with the engagement of "The Phantom of the Opera" (Universal) at the Astor theatre, New York City.

Trackless Train Receives Welcome in Twin Cities

The Trackless Train of the Metro-Goldwyn organization made stops at the Twin Cities last week and stirred the hearts of young and old alike. It was on hand for the opening of the Garrick under Metro policy Saturday and pulled out Saturday night for Des Moines and Omaha.

In Minneapolis it made a union depot of the Daily Star office. Friday afternoon a group of old men and women from Ebenezer home took a ride and one woman was nearly in tears because she missed it while another who made the trip was so pleased she refused to get off the train.

"Beggar on Horseback" is Given Dream Contest

The most noteworthy unit of Manager W. J. Melvin's campaign on "The Beggar on Horseback," was the Wierd Dream Contest conducted in the Daily News by the Plaza theatre, St. Petersburg.

Five dollars in gold and 25 pairs of Plaza theatre tickets were offered to the persons submitting the wierdest dreams. Stories were limited to 100 words and had to be sent to the photoplay editor of the News.

The winning dreams were published in a latter edition of the paper, along with the names of the winners.

Special Fight Film Given Sporting Page Ads

When the Educational Special on the Lewis-Munn Wrestling bout ran at the Washington theatre in Chester, Tenn., it was made the occasion of a very forceful appeal to the sporting element in the town through special adds in the sporting section of the Chester Times.

A two-column ad was placed in the Times calling the attention of the sport enthusiasts to this two-reel subject alone. The Washington theatre was satisfied that this special advertising appeal on a two-reel subject was productive of much interest.

Lobby display of miniature cut-outs on "I'll Show You the Town" (Universal) arranged by Manager Fred Walters of the Temple theatre, Toledo, recently.

Large Tarpon Displayed as "Rugged Water" Tie-up

In planning his campaign for "Rugged Water" playing the Imperial theatre, Jacksonville, fortune smiled on Manager Morrison, for in addition to having a great display of outdoor fisherman's paraphernalia in the window of a leading hardware and sporting goods store, a large tarpon, caught by the manager of the sporting goods department, was hung in front of store with a large sign reading:

Caught in the Rugged Water at Mayport. See "Rugged Water" Paramount Picture—Imperial—Now.

The sign, which was read by hundreds of persons daily who stopped to look at the catch, proved an extremely valuable advertising medium for the attraction.

A card calling attention to the works of Jos. C. Lincoln, author of "Rugged Water," was placed on display in the Public Library.

Poster Stamps Popularize Tom Mix in Germany

That the Germans are rapidly being converted to film exploitation is amply attested by the receipt in this country of a number of stamps bearing the likeness and name of Tom Mix. The stamps, which are twice as large as ordinary postage stamps, are being distributed by movie theatres and throughout the German offices as well.

The stamps are the regulation perforated edge, gummed back article, printed in a deep purple. They bear an excellent engraved likeness of Mix in the center, with the words "Tom Mix, Fox Star," surrounding the picture.

Giant on Shetland Boosts "Beggar on Horseback"

As advance publicity for "The Beggar on Horseback," during the five days preceding its opening at the Sterling theatre, Greeley, Manager C. T. Perrin had a man, six feet tall, ride a little Shetland pony across the stage each night, carrying a banner reading, "Beggar on Horseback"—Next Week—It's a Scream." The tall man in a bathrobe and high silk hat made quite a contrast to the very small pony and as a result their appearance evoked lots of laughter from patrons. Produced at very little cost, the stunt played up strongly the humorous angle of the photoplay.

Dressing Room in Lobby for "Pretty Ladies"

The Imperial lobby, Asheville, during the recent run of "Pretty Ladies," looked like a dressing room at the Follies depicted in the photoplay. The effect was produced by placing a long table with several chairs in center of lobby, with cut-out of a woman back of each chair. Various toilet requisites adorned the dressing table, while a large colored drop with matching drapes added much to the effectiveness of the display.

In addition to the above, Manager Ernest Morrison used the usual newspaper and billing campaign.

Painted red hearts with poster cut-outs were the basis of this attractive lobby on "In the Name of Love" (Paramount) at the Rex theatre Sumter, S. C., of which John Hanson is manager.

With First Run Theatres

NEW YORK CITY

Rivoli Theatre—
Film Numbers—The Pony Express
Musical Program — Overture:
"Tunes of 1860" (orchestra),
Organ recital.

Capitol Theatre—
Film Numbers—Graustark (First
National), My Bonnie (Red
Seal), The Dahlia (color), Capitol Magazine (Selected), Montana Clouds (S. R.).
Musical Program—Overture:
"Fifth Symphony" (orchestra),
"Eli, Eli" (vocal solo), "Ave
Maria" (trumpet), "Mignonette" (dance number), "Love
Me and I'll Live Forever"
(solo), "Nutcracker Suite"
(ballet), Organ recessional.

Strand Theatre—
Film Numbers — Shore Leave
(First National), Ko-Ko On the
Run (Red Seal), Strand Topical
Review (Selected).
Musical Program — Overture:
"Capriccio Italian" (orchestra),
"Bird Song" (vocal solo), Mandolin solos, "Bombay" (baritone
solo), "Sailor's Hornpipe"
(specialty with male ensemble),
Organ solo.

Colony Theatre—
Film Numbers—Souls For Sables
(S. R.), Colony News Pictorial
(Selected).
Musical Program—"The Land of
Jazz" (orchestra), "Save Your
Sorrow" (tenor solo), Olga

Sunday newspaper ad, three columns wide, for the engagement of "Drusilla
With a Million" (F. B. O.) at the Liberty theatre in Kansas City.

Mishka and the Harp Orchestra
(specialty), Organ solo.

Warners Theatre—
Film Numbers—His Majesty Bunker Bean (Warner Brothers),
News Weekly (Selected), Expose of American Coal Mining
Industry (Special).
Musical Program — "Beautiful
Galathea" and "Brown Eyes,
Why Are You Blue?" orchestra) "Susan" and "All Because
of You" (vocal), "La Paloma"
and "El Choclo" (Argentine
dancers), Organ recessional.

Rialto Theatre—
Film Numbers—The Pony Express
(Paramount).
Musical Program—Ben Bernie and
the Rialto Gang in "Black and
White," Organ solo.

Cameo Theatre—
Film Numbers—The Ten Commandments (Paramount), Pathe
News.
Musical Program — "Caucasian
Sketches" (overture), "The
Wandering Jew" (solo).

Astor Theatre—
Film Numbers—The Phantom of
the Opera (Universal), continued.
Musical Program—Ballet (Albertina Rasch conception), Phantom effects (by Thurston).

Embassy Theatre—
Film Numbers—The Merry Widow
(Metro - Goldwyn - Mayer), continued.
Musical Program—"Oriental Bacchanale" (prologue to feature).

Criterion Theatre—
Film Numbers—The Wanderer
(Paramount), continued.

BROOKLYN

Mark Strand Theatre—
Film Numbers—The Gold Rush
(United Artists), Mark Strand
Topical Review (Selected).
Musical Program — Prologue to
The Gold Rush, a short prelude
by the Mark Strand Orchestra,
and the organ recessional.

PHILADELPHIA

Stanley Theatre—
Film Numbers—Beggar on Horseshoe (Paramount), Betty and
Her Beasts (Comedy), Stanley
Magazine (Selected).
Musical Program—"Tannhauser"
(Overture), "A Spanish Festival" (solo), Eddie Clark.

Fox Theatre—
Film Numbers—As No Man Has
Loved (Fox), Fox Theatre
Screen Magazine (Selected).
Musical Program—"Sixth Hungarian Rhapsody" (Overture),
Weber Male Quartette, Pianologue.

Stanton Theatre—
Film Numbers—Coast of Folly
(Paramount).

Arcadia Theatre—
Film Numbers—The Lost World
(First National).

Karlton Theatre—
Film Numbers — Wild, Wild
Susan (Paramount).

Palace Theatre—
Film Numbers—Street of Forgotten Men (Paramount).

Victoria Theatre—
Film Numbers—Wild Horse Mesa
(Paramount).

Capitol Theatre—
Film Numbers—In the Name of
Love (Paramount).

ST. PAUL

Astor Theatre—
Film Numbers—The Son of His
Father (Paramount), What
Price Gloria (F. B. O.), Off His
Beat (Educational), News (Selected).
Musical Program—Organ Novelty,
Leland McEwen; Lew Epstein's
Syncopating Gang; Alice Lilligren and Charles Bennett.

Capitol Theatre—
Film Numbers—Takeachance week.
Musical Program — Organ overture; Capitol Theatre Concert
orchestra.

LOS ANGELES

Forum Theatre—
Film Numbers—The Goose Woman
(Universal), Hodge Podge (Educational), International News,
Kinograms.
Musical Program—Orchestral
Selections.

Hillstreet Theatre—
Film Numbers—The Happy Warrior (Vitagraph), Pacemakers
(F. B. O.), Aesop's Fables
(Pathe), International News.
Musical Program—Vaudeville.

Loew's State Theatre—
Film Numbers—Her Sister From
Paris (First National), Loew's

Garrick Theatre—
Film Numbers—The Half Way
Girl (First National), Comedy
and News reels (Selected).
Musical Program—Stolurow and
his Garrick Serenaders in a
Musical Novelette; Harry
Katzman and Everett Fritzberg, violin and piano.

Strand Theatre—
Film Numbers — East Lynne
(Fox), Head On (Fox), Kinograms.
Musical Program—Organ overture.

Tower Theatre—
Film Numbers — Romola (Metro-
Goldwyn Pathe News.
Musical Program—"Maurice" and
the Tower Concert orchestra
playing "Echoes from the
Metropolitan Opera."

State Pictorial News and Events (Selected).

Musical Program—Selections from the "Toy Box," Fanchon & Marco Revue.

Metropolitan Theatre—
Film Numbers—Wild, Wild Susan (Paramount), Mary, Queen of Tots (Pathe), Aesop's Fables, Pathe News.

Musical Program — "Rigoletto" (Overture).

Pantages Theatre—
Film Numbers—The Reckless Sex (S. R.), Pathe News.

Criterion Theatre—
Film Numbers—The Iron Horse (Fox), continued.

Musical Program—"Indian Airs" (overture).

Million Dollar Theatre—
Film Numbers — The Freshman (Pathe), continued.

Musical Program — "On the Campus" (overture).

Rialto Theatre—
Film Numbers—Sally of the Sawdust (United Artists), continued.

Musical · Program—O r c h e s t r a (prologue to feature).

CHARLIE CHAPLIN

Says:
"Hello everybody in St. Louis, I want you to see me at Loew's State in my latest comedy 'The Gold Rush,' starting Saturday."

Unique single-column advance ad on "The Gold Rush" (United Artists) at Loew's State theatre, St. Louis.

OMAHA

Strand Theatre—
Film Numbers—The Man Who Found Himself (Universal), Lion Love (Fox), Fox News, Newspaper Fun (F. B. O.).

Musical Program—"Chin Chin," (Overture), Fall Style Revue.

Rialto Theatre—
Film Numbers—Her Sister From Paris (First National), Amateur Detective (Fox), Kinograms.

Musical Program—"Maritana," (Overture), "Night Owl" (Exit March), "Blue Danube Waltz," and "Is the Girl You Married Still the Girl You Love?" (Themes for feature picture), "I Miss My Swiss," (Organ). Special stage feature—Billy Sharpe and His Revue.

World Theatre—
Film Numbers—Kentucky Pride (Fox), Paging the Wife (Universal), Pathe News.

M u s i c a l Program—"Deestrick Skule No. 13." (Organ.)

Empress Theatre—
Film Numbers—The Kiss Barrier (Fox), Play Ball (Pathe).

Musical Program—"The Girl in the Gingham Gown," (Musical comedy).

Sun Theatre—
Film Numbers—Lightnin' (Fox), The Super Hooper Dyne Lizzy (Pathe), Pathe Review.

Moon Theatre—
Film Numbers—The Lucky Horses h o e (Fox), Sunken Silver (Pathe), Isn't Life Terrible? (Pathe).

BOSTON

Fenway Theatre—
Film Numbers—Wild Horse Mesa (Paramount), The Wrongdoers (S. R.), Hot and Heavy (Educational), Fenway News (Selected).

Musical Program—Lloyd G. Del Castillo at the Wurlitzer, "Cecelia."

Gordon's Scollay Square Olympia Theatre—
Film Numbers—Half Way Girl (First National), Play Ball (Pathe), Hot and Heavy (Educational), m o r n i n g special, Cities That Never Sleep (Paramount).

Musical Program—Overture, orchestra. Seven acts vaudeville.

Loew's State Theatre—
Film Numbers—The Ten Commandments (Paramount) Cold Turkey (Pathe), Aesop's Fables (Pathe), Loew's State Pictorial News (Selected).

Musical Program—"C minor prelude" (overture), "By the Waters of Minnetonka," "Eli Eli," (solo).

Modern and Beacon Theatres—
Film Numbers—Hell's Highroad (Producers Dist. Corp.), Wild Horse Mesa (Paramount), Comedy (Pathe).

WASHINGTON

Metropolitan Theatre—
Film Numbers — Fine Clothes (First National), Fair Warning (Educational), The Canyon of Champagnole (Pathe), Current Events (Pathe).

Musical Program—"Echoes from the Metropolitan Opera House"

APOLLO
Greater Movie Season—Let's Go!

SUN·UP

Edward Goulding's production of Lulu Vollmer's Great Stage Success—A thrill at the Criterion, N. Y. where drama lives in the cabins of the lowbrow—in spite of lords, knaves, murderers, feuds and undernourished devotions.

Century Comedy—"Educating Buster"

Musical Program, Played Weekly
Emil Seidel and His Orchestra
EARL GORDON, at the Organ

Pictorial ad on "Sun Up" (Metro-Goldwyn) at the Apollo theatre, Indianapolis.

(Overture includes selections from "Rienzi," "Meistersinger," "Carman," "La Boheme," "Samson and Dalila").

Strand Theatre—
Film Numbers—Daddy's Gone a Hunting (Metro-Goldwyn), Current Events (Fox).

Palace Theatre—
Film Numbers—The Man Who Found Himself (Paramount), Current Events (Pathe), From Soup to Nuts (comedy).

Musical Program—"Bridal Rose" (Overture).

Earle Theatre—
Film Numbers—Parisian Nights (F. B. O.), Current Events (Educational).

Columbia Theatre—
Film Numbers—Ten Commandments (Paramount).

Rialto Theatre—
Film Numbers—Iron Horse (Fox), continued.

SALT LAKE CITY

American Theatre—
Film Numbers—Graustark (First National), Sit Tight (Educational), International News.

Kinema Theatre—
Film Numbers—Twenty Dollars A Week (Associated Exhibitors), High Jinks (Fox), Pathe Review.

Pantages Theatre—
Film Numbers—The Married Flirt (F. B. O.)

Paramount Empress Theatre—
Film Numbers—The Gold Rush (United Artists), Pathe News.

Victory Theatre—
Film Numbers—The Trouble With Wives (Paramount), The Iron Nag (Fox), Pathe News.

INDIANAPOLIS

Circle Theatre—
Film Numbers—The Lost World (First National), Cartoon Comedy (Educational), News Weekly (Universal).

Musical Program — Prologue to The Lost World by the Circle orchestra. Harlowe Dean, soloist.

Apollo Theatre—
Film Numbers—Wild Horse Mesa (Paramount), Comedy (Pathe), Fox News.

Musical Program—Emil Seidel orchestra and Earl Gordon, organist.

Colonial Theatre—
Film Numbers—The Goose Woman (Universal), Comedy (Universal), News Weekly (International), Aesop's Fable (Pathe).

Musical Program—American Harmonists and Frank Owens, Bob Jones and Floyd Thompson, soloists.

ROCHESTER

Eastman Theatre—
Film Numbers—Beggar on Horseback (Paramount), The Tourist (Educational), Eastman Theatre Current Events, Glimpses of the Orient (Scenic).

Musical Program—"The Sorcerer's Apprentice" (Overture), Nee Wong, Chinese Minstrel.

DES MOINES

Capitol Theatre—
Film Numbers—The Knockout (Famous Players), Fox News, From Soup to Nuts (Educational).

Musical Program—Violin special numbers by Erny Holmgrin.

DesMoines Theatre—
Film Numbers—Shore Leave (First National), International News, The Amateur Detective (First National).

Musical Program—"A Trip to the Hawaiian Islands," Imperial Hawaiian Singers.

Strand Theatre—
Film Numbers—T h e Mystic (Metro-Goldwyn), Kinograms, The Official Officer (Pathe), The Mystic (Metro-Goldwyn).

Musical Program—Johnny Ambrose Band.

Rialto Theatre—
Film Numbers—Havoc (Fox).

WE HAD TO PUT OUT THE
S. R. O. SIGN YESTERDAY!

DRAMA!
WILL ABSORBING, TENSE, AWE-INSPIRING DRAMA THAT WILL BE A STANDARD OF COMPARISON FOR MOTION PICTURES FOR YEARS TO COME

WILLIAM FOX presents
THE SCREEN VERSION OF THE INTERNATIONAL STAGE SUCCESS

HAVOC
A MIGHTY DRAMA OF WAR-DAZED WOMEN
with
GEORGE O'BRIEN · MADGE BELLAMY · LESLIE FENTON
MARGARET LIVINGSTON · WALTER McGRAIL · ERVILLE ALDERSON

Better Come Down Early Today to See This Story of Two Life-long Pals Who Loved a Woman Without a Soul.

MATS. 25c   EVES. 30c
Children Anytime 10c

NEXT—"KENTUCKY PRIDE"

STRAND
HOME OF 1ST RUN FOX PICTURES

The Strand theatre ad in St. Paul for the opening of "Havoc" (Fox) at that house.

ST. LOUIS

Loew's State Theatre—
Film Numbers—The Gold Rush (United Artists).
Musical Program—Special music score orchestra and organ. Prologue.

Delmonte Theatre—
Film Numbers—The Ten Commandments (Paramount).
Musical Program—Orchestral selections. Song prologue.

Missouri Theatre—
Film Numbers—The Lucky Devil (Paramount), The White Wing's Bride (Pathe), Missouri Magazine (Selected).
Musical Program—"The Life of Frederick Chapin" Joseph Littau orchestra. Milton Slosser at organ and Steve Cady (vocalist). On stage: Louis Panico and Jazz Orchestra.

Grand Central, Lyric Skydome and Capitol Theatre—
Film Numbers—Her Sister from Paris (First National), Kinogram News and Views.
Musical Program—At Grand Central only Gene Rodemich and Gang in "Struttin' the Charleston." Orchestral and organ number of Capitol. Silverman-Conley orchestra at Skydome.

William Goldman's Kings and Rivoli Theatres—
Film Numbers—California Straight Ahead (Universal), Selected News and Views, Aesop's Fables (Pathe).
Musical Program—Orchestral overtures and popular numbers.

HOUSTON

Queen Theatre—
Film Numbers—A Slave of Fashion (Metro-Goldwyn), Mack Sennett comedy, News (Pathe).
Musical Program — "Miserere" (Overture), Organ numbers.

Isis Theatre—
Film Numbers—The Scarlet West (First National), Comedy (Educational), News (International).
Musical Program—"Indian Love Song" (Overture). Organ numbers.

Players and action were featured in this "The Lost World" (First Nat'l) ad of the Lyric Skydome, Grand Central and Capitol, St. oviLa.

THIS WEEK **PRINCESS**
All Aboard For The Land of Thrills
CLAIRE WINDSOR
PAT O'MALLEY
ROBERT FRAZER
REGINALD BARKER'S
The **WHITE DESERT**
A Metro-Goldwyn

Stock out well used in the Princess theatre ad in Hartford on "The White Desert" (Metro-Goldwyn).

BALTIMORE

Century Theatre—
Film Numbers—Not So Long Ago (Paramount), A Business Engagement (Fox), News Weekly (Fox).
Musical Program — Vocal selections by Van and Schenck. Organ recessional. Orchestra.

Garden Theatre—
Film Numbers—The Rainbow Trail (Fox), Nursery Troubles (Universal), Seven Ages (Educational), International News (Universal).
Musical Program—Five acts of vaudeville. Organ recessional.

Keith's Hippodrome Theatre—
Film Numbers—The Foolish Virgin (S. R.), Officer No. 13 (Universal), News Weekly (Pathe), Aesop's Fable (Pathe).
Musical Program—Five acts of vaudeville. Organ recessional.

Metropolitan Theatre—
Film Numbers—Wild, Wild Susan (Paramount), Tame Men and Wild Women (Pathe), Aesop's Fable (Pathe), Topical Review (Pathe).

Capitol Theatre—
Film Numbers—Wild, Wild Susan (Paramount), Comedy (Educational), News (Kinograms).
Musical Program — Orchestra playing popular selections for overture and feature. Organ numbers.

Rialto Theatre—
Film Numbers—American Pluck (S. R.), Comedy (Educational), News (Fox).
Musical Program—Organ numbers for feature, piano for comedy and news.

Majestic Theatre—
Film Numbers—As No Man Has Loved (Fox), Aesop's Fables (Pathe).
Musical Program—Jazz selections. Organ numbers, Vaudeville.

Liberty Theatre—
Film Numbers—The Wife That Wasn't Wanted (Warner), Comedy (Educational), Review (Pathe).
Musical Program—Organ selections.

Musical Program—Orchestra. Organ recessional.

New Theatre—
Film Numbers—The Lucky Devil (Paramount), Pleasure Bound (Educational), Thundering Waters (S. R.), News Weekly (Pathe).
Musical Program—"Orpheus in the Underworld" (Overture by Orchestra), Vocal and instrumental selections "Lopa's Chinese Oriental Band). Organ recessional.

Parkway Theatre—
Film Numbers—Stop Flirting (Prod. Dist. Corp.), Baltro's Race to Nome (Paramount), Parkway Pictorial News (Educational), Paris Creations (Educational).
Musical Program — Selections from "Carmen" (Overture by Parkway Concert Ensemble). Organ recessional.

Rivoli Theatre—
Film Numbers—Shore Leave (First National), The White Wing's Bride (Pathe), Rivoli News (Pathe).
Musical Program—"American Fantasie" (Overture by Orchestra), Specialty Attraction (Royal Accordian Orchestra), "Anchor's Aweigh" and "If You Hadn't Gone Away" (Organ Selections).

BUFFALO

Shea's Hippodrome Theatre—
Film Numbers—The Freshman (Pathe), The Guest of Honor (Fox), Current Events (from Pathe and International News).
Musical Program—"Morning, Noon and Night in Vienna" (orchestra), Selections by Frederick Patton, Chicago Opera company tenor.

Loew's State Theatre—
Film Numbers—The Rag Man (Metro-Goldwyn), Love Goofy (Educational), Current Events (Pathe News).
Musical Program—Selections by Harry Ellsworth and His Orchestra. Five acts of vaudeville.

Lafayette Square Theatre—
Film Numbers—Enticement (First National), Current Events (Fox News).
Musical Program—Selection from "Lady Be Good" (orchestra), Five acts of vaudeville.

Shea's North Park Theatre—
Film Numbers—The Unholy Three (Metro-Goldwyn), Comedy (Fox), Current Events (from Pathe and International News).
Musical Program—Overture to "Stradella" (orchestra).

New Olympic Theatre—
Film Numbers—Spook Ranch (Universal), Three Keys (S. R.), Stranded (Universal), Current Events (International News).
Musical Program—Selections from "The Student Prince in Heidelberg," (organ).

Victoria Theatre—
Film Numbers—The Little French Girl (Paramount), My Wife and I (Warner Brothers). Current Events (Pathe News).
Musical Program—"Southern Rhapsody" Hosmer (Orchestra).

Criterion Theatre—
Film Numbers—A Son of His Father (Paramount), Tame Men and Wild Women (Pathe), Thirty Years Ago Pictures (S. R.), Kinograms.

Empress Theatre—
Film Numbers—Drusilla With a Million (F. B. O.), Pathe News.

Capitol Theatre—
Film Numbers—The Man Who Found Himself (Paramount), Cold Turkey (Pathe), Kinograms, The Golden Princess (Paramount).

Liberty Theatre—
Film Numbers—Riders of the Purple Sage (Fox), International News.

Majestic Theatre—
Film Numbers—Her Love Story (Paramount), Two Wagons Both Covered (Pathe).

KANSAS CITY

Newman Theatre—
Film Numbers—A Son of His Father (Paramount), Watch Out (Educational), Newman News and Views (Pathe, Kinograms and International News), Newman Screen Magazine (Local Photography).
Musical Program—"Peaceful Valley" (Overture in conjunction with Song Specialty), Margaret McKee (Whistling Novelty), Recessional (Organ Solos), Pavley Oukrainsky Chicago Opera Ballet (Specialty).

Liberty Theatre—
Film Numbers—The Iron Horse (Fox Second Week), Aesop's Fables (Pathe), International News, The Fighting Ranger (Universal).
Musical Program—"Give a Thought to Music" (Overture), Recessional (Organ Solos).

Royal Theatre—
Film Numbers—Proud Flesh (Metro-Goldwyn), Hot Shieks (Pathe), Royal Screen Magazine (Pathe, Kinograms and International News), Royal Current Events (Local Photography).
Musical Program—Royal Syncopators on Stage (Overture), Recessional (Organ Solos).

Mainstreet Theatre—
Film Numbers—Fine Clothes (First National), Educational Short Subjects and Pathe News.
Musical Program—Popular Selections (Overture), Recessional (Organ Solos).

Pantages Theatre—
Film Numbers—The Silent Pal (S. R.), Fox News and Fox Short Subjects.
Musical Program — Atmospheric Selections (Overture), Recessional (Organ Solos).

DETROIT

Capitol Theatre—
Film Numbers—Wild Horse Mesa (Paramount), Aesop's Fable (Pathe).
Musical Program—Singing by Harry Jolson, black face comedian, and colored men.

Madison Theatre—
Film Numbers—Street of Forgotten Men (Paramount), Capt. Wanderwell's pictures of Chinese Revolution and Soviet Russia, Aesop's Fable (Pathe), Pathe News, Comedy (Educational).
Musical Program — Orchestra accompaniment and organ recessional. Capt. Wanderwell appearing in person.

Adams Theatre—
Film Numbers—The Gold Rush (United Artists), continued, Kinograms.

Musical Program—Orchestra accompaniment and organ recessional.

Fox Washington Theatre—
Film Numbers—Lightnin' (Fox), Felix Comic (S. R.), Fox News.

Broadway Strand Theatre—
Film Numbers — California Straight Ahead (Universal), International News.

CINCINNATI

Capitol Theatre—
Film Numbers—Lightnin' (Fox), Felix Comedy (S. R.), Capitol News.
Musical Program—Orchestra selections.

Walnut Theatre—
Film Numbers—Her Sister From Paris (First National), Why Kids Leave Home (Comedy), Topics of the Day, Aesop's Fable.
Musical Program—Orchestra selections.

Strand Theatre—
Film Numbers—The Woman Hater (Warner), Official Officers (Pathe), Pathe News.

Lyric Theatre—
Film Numbers—The Ten Commandments (Paramount), third week, Kinograms.
Musical Program—Orchestra selections.

Gifts Theatre—
Film Numbers—The Boomerang (S. R.), Too Much Law (Universal), Kinograms.

Family Theatre—
Film Numbers — The Rainbow Trail (Fox), The Bouncer (comedy), Fox News.

CLEVELAND

Stillman Theatre—
Film Numbers—Graustark (First National), The Big Game Hunter (Fox), International News (Universal).
Musical Program—Overture to "Rienzi" by Wagner (overture), Seranade from "The Student Prince" (vocal duet—musical prologue).

Allen Theatre—
Film Numbers — Shore Leave (First National), Baby Blues (Educational), Topics of the Day (Pathe), Pathe News.

Special art ad for "Don Q, Son of Zorro" (United Artists) at the A. H. Blank Strand, Omaha.

Musical Program—"If I Were King" by Adams (overture), "Stranssiauna" (Johann Strauss airs arranged by Philip Spitalny with soprano), "In Deep Water" (Phil's Jazz Boys in a musical prologue).

State Theatre—
Film Numbers—A Son of His Father (Paramount), Uncle Tom's Girl (Universal), Shoes (S. R.), Pathe Review—Literary Digest (S. R.)
Musical Program — Organ overture, Vaudeville.

Park Theatre—
Film Numbers — The Mystic (Metro-Goldwyn), Savage Love (Educational), Pathe Review, Topics of the Day (Pathe), Kinograms (Educational).
Musical Program—"Danza della Orre" by Ponchielli (overture), Violin specialty numbers by Henri Kubheki: "To a Wild Rose," "Hungarian Russian Semphonic Medley," "Kingdom Within Your Eyes," and a Medley of Popular Airs on the Hawiian Harp with orchestral accompaniment.

Reade's Hippodrome—
Film Numbers—The Goose Woman (Universal), Century Comedy (Universal), Pathe News.
Musical Program—"Rose Marie" (overture), Vaudeville.

Keith's East 105th St.—
Film Number—The Goose Woman (Universal), Madame Sans Jane (Pathe), Aesop's Fables (Pathe), Patin News.
Musical Program — Friml Hits (Overture), Vaudeville.

Warner's Circle—
Film Numbers—The Wife Who Wasn't Wanted (Warner Bros.), Aesop's Fables (Pathe), Innocent Husbands (Pathe), Pathe News.
Musical Program — "Mme. Modiste" by Victor Herbert (Symphonic overture), Austin Wylie Jazz band playing "My Gal Sal," "I'm Tired ofEverything But You," "River Boat Shuffle," and "Rock a Bye My Baby Blue" with vocal accompaniment, Sam Herman (xylophone virtuoso-specialty number).

ATLANTA

Howard Theatre—
Film Numbers—The Ten Commandments (Paramount) International News.
Musical Program — Prologue staged by Jan Rubini; Virginia Futrelle soprano singing "Vissi D'Arte" from "Tosca," Song of "Ramsees" by Solon Drunkenmiller, Ballet dance of the Temple by Howard Ballet.

Metropolitan Theatre—
Film Numbers—Graustark (First National), Fox News, Official Officers (Pathe).

Loew's Grand Theatre—
Film Numbers—California Straight Ahead (Universal), Timely Topics and Aesop's Fables (Pathe), Comedy (Educational), Spotlight (Pathe).
Musical Program—Five acts of vaudeville.

Rialto Theatre—
Film Numbers—Wild, Wild Susan (Paramount), Pathe News, Comedy (Educational).

Alamo No. 3 Theatre—
Film Numbers—The Sporting Chance (S. R.), Pal O'Mine (S. R.), Comedy (Pathe).

Two-column art ad on "Siege" (Universal) recently run in Washington, D. C., by the Rialto theatre.

Musical Program—Orchestra rendering popular selections.

Tudor Theatre—
Film Numbers—The Red Rider (Universal), Comedy (Pathe).

MINNEAPOLIS

Aster Theatre—
Film Numbers—East Lynne (Fox), News and Comedies (Selected).
Musical Program—Organ overture.

Garrick Theatre—
Film Numbers—Never the Twain Shall Meet (Metro-Goldwyn), Off His Beat (Educational).
Musical Program—George Barton, Jr. saxophone, Garrick Concert orchestra.

Lyric Theatre—
Film Numbers—Marry Me (Paramount), Comedy (Selected), Pathe News.
Musical Program—Dave Rubinoff, Russian violinist.

State Theatre—
Film Numbers—Shore Leave (First National), Fair Warning (Comedy), Animated Hair Cartoon (S. R.), State News Digest (Selected).
Musical Program—State Concert Orchestra under William Warvelle Nelson; Lionel Bilton, English cellist; E. J. Dunstedter, organist; Zimmermann and Grandville in a Yodling Romance.

Strand Theatre—
Film Numbers—The Lost World (First National), third week, Felix Doubles for Darwin (S. R.) Strand News (Selected).
Musical Program—Strand Concert Orchestra "When Shadows Fall."

SEATTLE

Blue Mouse Theatre—
Film Numbers—The Wife Who Wasn't Wanted (Warner), The Big Game Hunter (Fox), The Ugly Duckling (Comedy), International News.
Musical Program—Selections from "Firefly": (Overture), "Twenty-five Years from Now," (Jazz Specialty).

Coliseum Theatre—
Film Numbers—As No Man Has Loved (Fox), Alice Cartoon (S. R.), Kinograms, Pathe News.
Musical Program—Selections from "Spring Maid." (Overture).

Columbia Theatre—
Film Numbers — California Straight Ahead (Universal), continued.

Helig Theatre—
Film Numbers—The Lucky Horseshoe (Fox), Topics of the Day, Pathe Review, Aesop Fable, Pathe News.
Musical Program—Medley of Jazz Favorites (Overture).

Liberty Theatre—
Film Numbers—Havoc (Fox), Felix Dopes It Out (S. R.), Pathe Review, International and Liberty News.
Musical Program—Vocal and musical prelude featuring "Tipperary," "Katy" and other war songs.

Strand Theatre—
Film Numbers—The Lost World (First National), continued.

SAN FRANCISCO

California Theatre—
Film Numbers—The Coast of Folly (Paramount), Alice Solves the Puzzle (S. R.), Pathe Review, International News.
Musical Program—"Tannhauser" (Overture), "Rondo" (Violin), "Vienna Beauties," (Dolin Orchestra Novelty).

Loews Warfield Theatre—
Film Numbers—The Tower of Lies (Metro-Goldwyn). Tender Feet (Educational). Marvels of Motion (Red Seal). International News, Kinograms.
Musical Program—Selections from "Merry Widow" (Overture), "Song of India" (Solo), "Orchid Ideas" (Fanchon & Marco Idea Singing & Dancing).

Granada Theatre—
Film Numbers—The Teaser (Universal), Remember When (Pathe). Fox News.
Musical Program—"Evolution of the Charleston" (Automatic stage creation with dancing and singing.

Imperial Theatre—
Film Numbers—The Pony Express (Paramount), continued, Off Stage Reel of James Cruze Company on Location (Special).
Musical Program—Selections from "The Chocolate Soldier."

Union Square Theatre—
Film Numbers—Daughters Who Pay (S. R.), When Dumb Bells Ring (Fox), Fox News.
Musical Program—Singing and dancing by Union Square Revue.

St. Francis Theatre—
Film Numbers—The Iron Horse (Fox), continued.

CLASSIFIED AD SECTION

RATES: 10 cents a word for each insertion, in advance
except Employment Wanted, on which rate is 5 cents.

CLASSIFIED SERVICE

A classified ad in MOTION PICTURE NEWS offers the
full resources and circulation of the NEWS to the advertiser at a ridiculously low figure.

Whether you want to reach executives, branch managers,
salesmen, or theatre managers, you can accomplish this
quickly and economically through the NEWS Classified
Columns.

The Peer of All Projection Surfaces

The Radio Silver Screens (Guaranteed). Price 50 cents per square
foot. For Particulars and sample
apply to Manufacturer
JOHN MUNRO CRAWFORD
45 Smith St., Newburgh, N. Y.

Wanted

WANTED—To lease the-
atre, equipped with stage, in
city not less than eight thousand. Would consider house
somewhat run down. Address
Box 330, Motion Picture
News, New York City.

EXPERT OPERATOR
and Electrician with 9 years'
experience in big houses;
married; wants to locate at
once. Address, Operator,
Box 282, Mason City, Iowa.

WANTED immediately in
Buffalo, a man with considerable experience in laboratory
and camera work. Appli-
cants should state full details
as to experience, giving
names of former employers
and present occupation if not
now employed in laboratory
work. Also state salary expected. Address "Experi-
ence" c/o Motion Picture
News, New York City.

THEATRE IN TOWN OF
4,000 or better, anywhere in
North Central states, Northern Indiana preferred. Can
either give satisfactory security on lease or buy outright.
Would consider buying interest in bona-fide proposition
where owner wishes to retire.
All replies absolutely confidential. Address Box 360,
Motion Picture News, New
York City.

For Sale

MOVIE THEATRE for
sale, 950 seats. Corner loca-

tion, west side. $20,000 cash
required. David Krieger, 367
Grant street, Buffalo, N. Y.

FOR SALE.—Theatre
Equipment of all descrip-
tions; Immediate shipment of
used chairs, any quantity.
Will also buy used chairs and
equipment. Theatre Seating
Company, 845 South State
Street, Chicago, Illinois.

FOR SALE.—Hope Jones
Wurlitzer type 135, excellent
condition. Will trade for
cheaper instrument with cash
difference. A bargain if you
are looking for a fine organ.
H. E. Skinner, Box 882, Ogden, Utah.

FOR SALE AT A SAC-
RIFICE.— Photoplayer; in
use less than 2 years. Orpheum Theatre, Orwigsburg,
Pa.

FOR SALE. — Modern
movie; priced for quick sale
account of illness; wonderful bargain; county seat of
10,000. Box 240, Motion
Picture News, New York
City.

CLOTH BANNERS—
$1.40 3 x 10 feet, 3 colors,
any copy up to 15 words.
One day service. Sent anywhere. Also Bargain Paper
Banners. Associated Advertisers, 111 W. 18th St., Kansas City, Mo.

Suddenly at liberty on account of union error.

Walter C. Simon

Noted composer, organist,
concert pianist and musical
director.
Original effects, presentations, and novelty over-
tures for motion pictures;
played Strand Theatre,
Boardwalk.
Address "The Haliburton."

309 Atlantic Ave.,
Atlantic City, N. J.

*Nine selected ads from nine different cities, which were
used to announce showings of "Shore Leave" (First
National). The houses whose ads are reproduced are:
B. F. Keith's Colonial theatre, Dayton, Ohio; Capitol
theatre, Cincinnati; the Grand Central, Lyric, Skydome
and Capitol theatres, St. Louis; Mainstreet theatre,
Kansas City; Circle theatre, Indianapolis; Leland
theatre, Albany; Stanley theatre, Philadelphia; Capitol,
Detroit, and the Rialto, Omaha.*

Short Subjects and Serials

Fox Scenario Department is Busy With Stories

The Fox scenario department is busy turning out stories for four units, the Helen and Warren stories, the O. Henry stories, the Imperial comedies and the Van Bibbers, which are soon to be released.

The script for "The Peacemakers," the next of the Helena and Warren series, has been prepared, as has "The Hypothesis of Failure," next of the O. Henry series. The latter will be directed by Daniel Keefe, with Roy Atwell, Vivien Oakland, William Bailey, Kathryn McGuire and Harvey Clarke in the cast.

Another Imperial comedy story is being completed and will be put into production this week, with Sid Smith and Judy King in the leading roles.

New Screen "Find" Signed by Universal

Janet Gaynor, an eighteen year old Los Angeles girl, and a new screen "discovery" has been added to the Universal stock company, where she will play ingenue roles in Westerns. Her first role is the feminine lead in a two-reeler featuring Gilbert Holmes and Ben Corbett. She was a visitor at the Universal lot when she was discovered by Isadore Bernstein, western supervisor. Successful screen tests were made and she was immediately signed as a member of the company.

William Crinley to Direct Desmond Serial

Universal announces that William Crinley has been assigned to direct "The Radio Detective," an Arthur B. Reeve story to be produced in serial form with William Desmond in the name role. Crinley was given his first opportunity to direct by Universal about four months ago, when he took charge of a unit making 2-reel westerns. Previously he was an assistant director with the company.

Fox Short Subject Drive Shows Results

THE increased efforts of the Fox publicity department in connection with that company's short subjects are showing results in the growing tendency of newspaper editors to give space to news items about the briefer pictures and the general use by exhibitors of added exploitation material furnished with these releases, according to a report from Fox Film following a check-up of the short subject department.

According to this check-up reproductions of stories about Fox short subjects have increased 100 per cent in recent months and reports from the branch offices state that exhibitors are employing the theatre aid material to a much greater degree than heretofore. The O. Henry, Van Bibber and "Helen and Warren" comedies have been widely exploited by Fox.

Production stills from "The Invention," featuring Elinore King, released by Davis Distributing Division.

New Pathe Serial September 27

First Chapter of "Wild West" Heads List of Short Subjects Announced for Week

THE first chapter of "Wild West," Pathe's new 10 episode serial produced by C. W. Patton, will head that company's schedule of short subjects for the week of September 27th. "The Land Rush" is the title of the first episode of the play in which Jack Mulhall and Helen Ferguson are co-featured and which was produced at the Miller Brothers "101 Ranch" in Oklahoma.

Also on the program for the week of the 27th are two double reel comedies, a single reel comedy, an issue of Pathe Review, "Aesop's Film Fables," "Topics of the Day" and the regular issues of Pathe News.

"The Land Rush" is concerned with the opening of the Oklahoma territory in 1893. The action in this chapter of "Wild West" introduces the important characters of the play to be presented in two reel installments. Those who appear in support of Mulhall and Miss Ferguson are Eddie Phillips, Virginia Warwick, Inez Gomez, Ed and Fred Burns, and Gus Seville. The scenario for "Wild West" was written by J. F. Natteford and the picture was directed by Robert F. Hill.

"Your Own Back Yard," a Hal Roach comedy starring the "Our Gang" comedians, is one of the two-reel pictures on the program. Farina appears in the principal role in this fun-film directed by Bob McGowan. Farina is declared "out" by the gang be-

cause his goat ate up two radio sets and a bicycle and the dusky dot gets his revenge in a beautiful dream in which he becomes wealthy and spends his riches lavishly before the very eyes of the rest of the Gang.

"Love and Kisses" is a two-reel comedy featuring Alice Day, produced by Mack Sennett and directed by Eddie Cline. Raymond McKee plays the boy opposite Miss Day, and Sunshine Hart is a matchmaker. Jack Cooper is her son and her choice for Alice. Preparations for the wedding progress right up to the eventful day, which becomes brimful of excitement for the groom-who-would-be and the groom-to-be. Barbara Tennant plays the role of the matchmaker's daughter, and Vernon Dent appears as the family butler.

"The Big Kick" is a Hal Roach one-reeler directed by Fred L. Guiol. Billy Engle appears as "Dinky" Dubbs, Earl Mohan is "Cuckoo" Kelly, work dodger de luxe. The plot concerns Dubbs' efforts to make a knockout champion out of Kelly.

Pathe Review No. 39 offers: "Fireside Factories," how the peasants of Picardy manufacture cloth in their own homes; San Antonio, Texas, one of the series of American Cities in Pathecolor; and "Seeing Things," chapter one of "The Magic Eye" series photographed by Louis Tolhurst. "Hungry Hounds" is the cartoon comic of "Aesop's Film Fables."

Resume of Current News Weeklies

FOX NEWS CONTINUITY VOL. 6, NO. 90: Sydney, N. S. W.—Australia's welcome to U. S. Fleet; New York City—Gov. Smith, Mayor Hylan and Senator Walker talk from same platform at Labor Day celebration; St. Louis, Mo.—How St. Louis open air opera trained its own ballet to appear in "Aïda;" Tifton, Ga.—Harvesting $15,000,000 tobacco crop; Oregon Caves, Ore.—Students of Agricultural college choose a weird place to hold a dance; French aviators plan Paris-New York hop—Will try trans-Atlantic flight; New York City—Introducing "Corn Willy," a fastidious fox terrier with a funny fondness for cooked corn-on-the-cob; Venice, Italy—Every tourist returning from Venice tells about the pigeons of St. Mark's—and here they are; How the business girl spends her vacation; Yellowstone Park—Visitors travel by stage to see Old West revived in a roundup.

KINOGRAMS NO. 5117: Arlington, Va.—Nation honors Shenandoah's dead at impressive funeral expression in National Cemetery; San Francisco—Missing Hawaiian fliers are found after being given up for lost in P.N.-9-1, while cripples sister girl returns to port; Berlin—German troops invent a moving boat to foil police; Jacksonville, Fla.—Major Edward James Monroe, who according to his records is a son of President Monroe, is hale and hearty at age of 110 years; Los Angeles—Ostriches are ready if fashion turn to feathers; Ulm, Germany—Turnverein athletes parade in garb of the time of Frederick; Sydney—U. S. fleet officers are feted at garden party at which Governor of New South Wales is host; Jerusalem—Kinograms camera man takes a ride on a real "ship of the desert;" Washington, D. C.—Unofficial over, President and Mrs. Coolidge return to Washington.

KINOGRAMS NO. 5118: Atlantic City—Miss California is picked as nation's fairest in annual beauty pageant on boardwalk; Philadelphia—U. S. tennis team beats French stars and retains the Davis international trophy; Sacramento, Cal.—Prize cattle of coast stage a $1,000,000 parade; Washington—President Coolidge receives an airplane all his own; Los Angeles—Vice President Dawes is received by motion picture stars on his visitation to studioland; San Francisco—Million cheer as California celebrates its seventy-fifth anniversary of admission to statehood; New York—Million children begin study on vacation cash and school shoes; Belmont Park, N. Y.—Pompey wins the $80,000 Futurity, turf's richest classic, in $35,000 cheer favorite; Chicago—Lincoln Park has interesting naturalized citizens (Chicago only); New York—State Legislators in brilliant array (Albany and Buffalo only); Boston—Crowds cheer heroes of Massachusetts (Boston only).

INTERNATIONAL NEWS NO. 76: Atlantic City, N. J.—Nation's fairest daughters compete for beauty crown; Osaka, Japan—Jap youngsters battle for wrestling title; St. Louis, Mo. (St. Louis only)—Bike speed demons race for national title; Baltimore, Md. (Baltimore only)—East's best oarsmen race in big regatta; Swampscott, Mass.—President and Mrs. Coolidge leave summer home for the capital; North Manchester, Ind.—Presidential timber, the aerial elephant—alias Rita and Dima; Arlington Cemetery, Wash.—Heroic officers who perished in Shenandoah disaster buried in Nation's cemetery; Rochester, N. Y. (Buffalo only)—Horse show opens with exhibition of jumping; El Monte, Cal.—Beauties dance on Eton's den; Chanute Field, Rantoul, Ill.—Pupils in Uncle Sam's thrift school pass their first fall "exam;" Germantown, Pa.—France defeated by U. S. tennis stars for Davis Cup.

INTERNATIONAL NEWS NO. 77: Buenos Aires, Argentine—Vast crowds gather for glimpse of the Prince of Wales; Atlantic City, N. J.—"Miss California" crowned beauty queen of 1925; New York City—Jumbo, style dictator of the Zoo, announces season's crop for straw hats; Sacramento, Cal.—A million dollars in live stock on parade at big fair; Newark, N. J.—Fred Spencer wins 7-mile bicycle championship; Baltimore, Md. (Baltimore only)—Hundreds of ministers attend National News Baptist Convention, N. Y. City (New York territory only)—Civil war veterans cheer American Legion boys on parade; Ponca City, Okla.—Speed demons broken in great terrapin derby; Boston, Mass. (Boston only)—State Legion veterans hold stirring parade; Wenatchee, Wash.—Cloudburst spreads ruin over vast area; Helsingfors, Finland—King Gustave and Queen Victoria of Sweden visit their neighbors in Finland; Near Ellensburg, Wash.—Vice President Dawes views scenic beauties of the Cascades; Chicago, Ill.—Jade Bay deserts cheer path for the boxing ring; Belmont Park, L. I.—$80,000 Belmont futurity won by Pompey; Roosevelt Field, L. I.—Newaired daredevil rides on wing of an airy express.

PATHE NEWS NO. 75: Auckland, New Zealand—U. S. Fleet visits New Zealand; Pikes Peak, Colo.—Drivers speed up Pikes Peak in record time; In The South Atlantic—Find crossing the equator is event long to be remembered; Arlington, Va.—Final tribute to Shenandoah's heroic dead; Casablanca, Morocco—French poilu big drive against Riffs; Philadelphia, Pa.—U. S. wins Davis Cup final matches from French challengers; Kiel, Hawaiian Islands—Hawaii fliers found after drifting in Pacific for 10 days; Atlantic City, N. J.—Nation's beauties vie for honor of "Miss America;" Altoona, Pa. (Pittsburgh only)—Drives without stop to win 250-mile auto speed race; Bucktown, Texas (Dallas only)—Flappers invade action fields; Ft. Des Moines, Ia. (Des Moines only)—Boy soldiers march in annual review; Kansas City, Mo. (K. C. only)—Boys start two-year hike in interest of Detroit; Boston, Mass. (Boston only)—Maine organizes Three-Quarter Century Club; St. Louis, Mo. (St. Louis only)—Playground children take part in colorful pageant; Detroit, Mich. (Detroit only)—Playground children take part in city's 11th annual pageant; Ft. Snelling, Minn. (Minneapolis only)—Ft. Snelling polo-ists capture grand championship match.

PATHE NEWS NO. 76: Philadelphia, Pa.—United States wins Davis Cup; Ch. Elton, Wash.—Daring pilots file own train on scenic trip; Lakehurst, N. J.—Boys' bunnies buy new flag for dirigible Los Angeles; Mare Island, Cal.—Pacific-flight planes damaged torpedo while being towed to navy yard; Detroit, Mich. (Detroit only)—Cobb celebrates 20th anniversary as big league player; Langley Field, Va. (Wash. only)—Test new amphibian planes; Belmont Park, N. Y.—Pompey captures rich Futurity; Atlantic City, N. J.—"Miss California" wins title of "Miss America;" Augusta, Sicily—King of Italy reviews battle fleet; Philadelphia, Pa.—Interesting pets tumpey opens; Ardmore, Okla.—Girl daredevil makes dive from speeding plane; Buenos Aires, Argentina—Argentina hails Prince of Wales; Detroit, Mich. (Detroit only)—Steelhead sets new record in Sweepstakes; Hendersonville, N. C. (Charlotte only)—Break ground for new hotel; Muncie, Ind. (Indianapolis only)—Dedicate new mid-west flying field; N. Y. City (New York territory only)—15,000 veterans march in American Legion parade; Boston, Mass. (Boston only)—4,000 veterans parade in American Legion parade.

Century Releases "Crying for Love"

Universal exchanges this week released a new two-reel Century Comedy titled "Crying For Love." Eddie Gordon is starred and Blanch Payson plays the leading feminine role.

The story, written and directed by Noel Smith, centers about the courtship and marriage of a small, meek man and a woman who is tall and commanding.

Lloyd Hamilton breaks into the movies in his new Educational comedy titled "The Movies," release stills from which are shown above.

"Inkwell" Reel to Be Hand Colored by Brock Process

Another Max Fleischer "Out-of-the-Inkwell" reel is to be produced in colors by the Brock Process, Red Seal, releasing these subjects, announces. The color process was used for "Ko-Ko Celebrates the Fourth," recently issued, and the reception accorded the picture has decided sponsors of the pictures to employ the same color in connection with "Ko-Ko's Thanksgiving," a forthcoming "Inkwell" film.

Short Subjects Publicized In National Magazines

Single reel pictures released by Educational are the subjects of two feature articles in the current issues of American Magazine and Vanity Fair. The article in American Magazine is by John Monk Saunders and deals with Louis H. Tolhurst and his "Secrets of Life" series.

In Vanity Fair Mr. Aldous Huxley, well known critic, devotes a long article to a discussion of "Felix the Cat," which he describes as his favorite dramatic hero.

Kathryn McGuire Has Lead in Fox Comedy

Kathryn McGuire has been assigned the leading role in "Failure," another of the William Fox O. Henry two-reeler series, which is being directed by Daniel Keefe under the personal supervision of George E. Marshall.

Fox offers "Transients in Arcadia," from the O. Henry story.

Production highlights from "The Land Rush," first chapter of Pathe's new serial "Wild West," produced at the Miller Brothers "101 Ranch," with Jack and Helen Ferguson in the leading roles.

Showmen Value News Reels

Day, of Kinograms, Reports "Topicals" Are Big Factor of Most Theatre Programs

DECLARING that he found that the majority of successful exhibitors unhesitatingly pronounce the news reel as important a factor as the feature itself in building patronage, Harvey Day, general sales manager for Kinograms who recently returned from a tour of the Educational Exchanges, which release the Kinograms reels, has made an extensive report to E. W. Hammons, president of Educational, in which he states that the topical reels are firmly established as indispensable units of every motion picture program.

In discussing the results of his trip Mr. Day said:

"The position of the news reel on every exhibitor's program is firmly established, and it will continue to remain so as long as there are motion pictures. This has come about in two ways, first, through the wonderful strides made in the last few years by the news reels themselves in quality of production, speed in getting the news on the screen and higher entertainment value, and

second, because the public has created a demand for news reels by increasing interest, which has been brought to the attention of the exhibitor.

"In Milwaukee I talked with Tom Saxe, of the Saxe Amusement Co., and in Philadelphia with Frank Buhler, Managing Director of The Stanley Co., both of whom have devised valuable systems whereby they are in constant touch with their customers. I personally looked over hundreds of letters received in which the writers criticised, suggested or in some manner commented on the shows they had seen in the various theatres under the supervision of these gentlemen. In every one there was a mention of the news reel, showing that this portion of the program remained in their minds as vividly as the feature. Both Mr. Saxe and Mr. Buhler told me that their selection of news reels was given exactly as much care as that of their features, which is as high a compliment to the progress of this branch of the industry as one could expect."

Pathe Busy With Production

Directors Busy With New Comedies After Vacation Period at Roach Studios

WITH the vacation period at an end, production activities on Pathe comedies are booming at the Hal Roach studios. Executives, directors, stars and players are prepared to plunge into a busy season. F. Richard Jones, director general at the Roach lot is leading the rush, following a three weeks' vacation.

Among those who have just gotten under way are Leo McCarey, who has started production on a Charley Chase two-reel comedy, in which Katherine Grant has the leading feminine role. Robert McGowan is lining up his forces preparatory to launching another "Our Gang" comedy. He is scheduled to start production during the week.

Director Fred L. Guiol and Glenn Tryon are busy with a new story in which Tryon will be starred. Clyde Cook, Lucien Little-

field, Tyler Brooke and Jimmie Finlayson will start productions in the immediate future.

Fred Wood Jackman, who for the past five months has been busy with "Rex," the equine wonder in the production of "The Devil Horse," is getting down toward the final shots of that picture. Jackman is making the picture in Eastern Montana with Roy Clements as associate director and Yakima Canutt, Gladys McConnell and Robert Kortman handling the human roles.

Two additions have been made recently to the scenario staff at the Roach studios. They are C. R. Wallace, associated with Universal during the past two years in a scenario and co-directorial capacity, and Frank Terry, who has been identified with a number of the leading producers.

Opinions on Current Short Subjects

" Life's Greatest Thrills "
(Universal—International—Two Reels)

(Reviewed by L. C. Moen)

MORE thrills than there are in a feature, might well be taken as the slogan for this amazing novelty release, for it would be no overstatement of the facts. Few features within the memory of this reviewer have carried the genuine "wallop" that these two reels pack. And why not? For within the narrow space of two spools of film has been crowded the dramatic highlights of years of work by International Newsreel. Its outstanding achievements are all here. The only wonder is that no one has thought before of making a compilation of this sort.

The opening scenes show how a newsreel is put together—how the cameramen, editors, laboratory men and others put together these newspapers of the screen. Following this brief introduction we are led into such thrilling moments as the air flight over the Grand Canyon, the arrival in America of the ZR-3, the Los Angeles breaking through a smoke-curtin, a racing driver tossed to his death when his car crashes, the revolution in Berlin, the parachute drop, the close-ups of Mt. Vesuvius in action, Woodrow Wilson reviewing the American troops on French soil, the first pictures made of the pope, the earthquake in Japan, a cruiser among the ice floes, an accident-filled steeplechase, a ship pounding to pieces on the rocks, a storm at sea—but why enumerate more?

These scenes have a punch that no staged scenes could ever have, for each and every one bears the stamp of truth and reality—we know that it actually happened and get a corresponding "kick" out of it. This is, in every way, an outstanding novelty release.

" Somewhere in Somewhere "
(Pathe—Two Reels)

(Reviewed by Thomas C. Kennedy)

CHARLIE MURRAY and Lucien Littlefield, than whom there are no more seasoned screen comedians, are co-featured in this Hal Roach two-reeler directed by James W. Horne. It is a "war play" with its action centering about the farcial happenings to a pair of buddies in the trenches in France. They are sent on heroic missions and fumble and falter into ultimate success.

The incident which has been introduced here is familiar and over-familiar to the screen fans. After seeing this picture there is the feeling that perhaps the comedy producers would do well to leave the war out of their operations until such time as there is some bit of inspiration to employ it as a background for an idea which has fundamental humor. Surely there is no longer any fun left in the device which places a weakling soldier in the situation of going out almost single handed to meet the enemy —particularly when there is so much realism in the background.

The picture may succeed moderately well in the majority of theatres, but it cannot class as something uproarous or stimulating. Laughs that develop will result from individual items of action, such as when a shell, propelled by a wire, follows a fleeing

soldier and eventually reaches its target in the seat of his pants, but nothing in the way of characterization or story continuity is there to carry a humorous mood. It all may be very funny, this jumble of tumbles, consternation over the pungent smell of a piece of Limberger cheese, and running away from shells, but this reviewer found it all distractingly dull and stupid.

The Cast

Patrick O'Brien .... Charlie Murray
Livingston Toots .... Lucien Littlefield
Captain .... Noah Young

Directed by James W. Horne

The Story—An Irishman and a Boston chap are buddies in a forward trench on the battlefields of France. Toots is unskilled in the ways of a warrior and thinks the gas alert is a call to dinner. Later when a piece of Limber cheese is brought into the trench he rings the alarm for the men to don their gas masks. The captain sends the two boys "over the top" to establish a line of communication with the trench. Toots proves a great handicap to the more skillful O'Brien, but after several narrow escapes, including victories in races with shells, they succeed and are hailed as heroes.

Summary—A very conventional slapstick affair with the battlefield as its setting. The material is worn and the incident familiar, though a pair of good comedy actors make every effort to produce laughs. The action moves along with some pace and the production is good.

" I Remember "
(Short Films Syndicate, Inc.—Two Reels)

(Reviewed by L. C. Moen)

VENTURINI has produced n this picture a visualization of Thomas Hood's immortal poem which is a charming pastoral study. It is, in effect, a recollection of boyhood days, with the subtitles in the form of verses from the poem, together with others that Hood overlooked.

The outstanding merit of "I Remember" is in the lovely rural backgrounds, many of which are exquisitely photographed. Through these scenes wanders a carefree boy, splendidly acted by an unnamed youth, whose trials and triumphs make up the thread of the story. He is accompanied in some of these by his little crippled brother, who lends a note of wistful pathos to the whole. In others, it is the childhood sweetheart who figures prominently. The ol' swimmin' hole, Sunday School, the swing in the highest tree, climbing for birds' nests, and such incidents make up the principal action.

"I Remember," then, is rather a novelty subject—partly a scenic with a novel twist, and partly a miniature drama. It should prove a pleasing contrast to a rough-and-tumble comedy feature of hair-raising melodrama, by virtue of its quiet charm.

"Flirting with Death"
(Red Seal—Two Reels)

THIS short subject, a secuel to "The Silvery Art," shows what can be accomplished on skis if you've followed out the instruction outlined in the above named subject.

Three daring climbers commence the task of climbing Mount Rosa, the highest point of the Swiss Alps. It's a hard climb, necessitating bridging chasms and banks of ice and snow. And then the descent, during which the men are tied to each other at first, for safety's sake, but break away at the finish and then it's a case of every man for himself. Pictorially the film leaves nothing to be desired.

This should prove an attraction in any house.
—HAROLD FLAVIN.

"Fair Warning"
(Educational-Mermaid—Two Reels)

(Reviewed by Chester J. Smith)

AL ST JOHN has been a lot funnier in many of his comedies than he is in this one. He displays all his gymnastic ability, but his gags are hardly up to the usual standard he has set in the past. The story too, is a trifle weak and too slow in the telling. It is merely a vehicle to permit of his tumbling about and indulging in a lot of slapstick.

Al is the bank messenger entrusted by his boss with the delivery of valuable bonds much sought by a pair of ex-convicts. Those bonds and the theft of a costly pearl necklace, which also passes into the possession of Al furnish much of the comedy in the picture. The pearls become unstrung in a chicken coop and are consumed as hen fodder so Al delivers the pearls to their rightful owner via the fowls. The bonds also eventually find their proper destination after the crooks have switched a black bag containing a bomb for the original package. There's a lot of suspense lurking in those black bags and also some good comedy, but the comedian has done so much better in the past that too much is probably expected of him.

The Cast

The Bank Messenger .... Al St John
A Crook .... Otto Fries
Another Crook .... Bert Young
The Banker's Daughter .... Virginia Vance
A Jack White production written and directed by Stephen Roberts.

The Story—Al the bank messenger is entrusted with the delivery of a bag of bonds to the home of the banker. The bonds are sought by a pair of crooks. All three arrive at the height of a lawn party and the crooks steal a valuable necklace from one of the guests. They slip it into Al's pocket and then substitute a black bag containing a bomb for the original package of bonds. Al eventually delivers both the necklace and the bonds after a series of episodes in which the crooks are bested.

Summary—A slapstick comedy that offers St John an opportunity to display his acrobatic ability, but hardly up to the standard set by the comedian in the past. There are a number of good comedy situations however and they should provide some laughs in the neighborhood houses.

"Silvery Art"
(Red Seal—Two Reels)

THIS two-reeler should prove interesting both from the knowledge of skiing one draws from it as well the ocular appeal resulting from the beautiful scenes among the Swiss Alps, where the action takes place.

The spectator is initiated into the art of skiing from starting operation—attaching the skis to the feet— and thence the proper method of walking, skating, climbing and descending cliffs. The reel winds up with some fancy stunts.

"Silvery Art" will probably go better in the larger houses.—HAROLD FLAVIN.

" The Ugly Duckling "
(Pathe—One Reel)

A HUMAN interest tale about the ugly duckling's sublime gesture of gratitude toward the young chicks which beg their mother to receive him into the brood, is revealed in this animated cartoon in the "Aesop's Film Fables" series produced by Paul Terry. It makes a fairly amusing and interesting reel.—T. C. KENNEDY.

Regional News from Correspondents

THE transfer of the control of the Acme Amusement Company into the hands of three prominent Maine amusement operators has been completed. The corporation is capitalized at $10,000 and owns theatres at Kennebunk and Vinalhaven.

Leon P. Gorham of this city and Wilfred Duffy and Howard Duffy, managers of the Old Orchard Pier, are the three new owners. Mr. Gorham is manager of the Maine Theatre Supply Company and operates motion pic-

Portland

ture theatres in Yarmouth, Gorham and South Portland.

The house at Kennebunk will be closed a week for alterations.

Arthur F. Kendall, leader of the Strand Theatre orchestra has completed an orchestral arrangement entitled "The Evolution of Famous pieces between the dates 1894 and

Jazz" which made a big hit at the Strand this week.

Permission has been sought to include this overture in the United States Marine Band program with credit given Mr. Kendall for the arrangement. The overture is composed of the most popular 1925 and opens with "The Bowery"

and "The Sidewalks of New York." "Seminola" closes the selection.

Mary Bourbeau, assistant contract clerk for Universal, who broke her arm horse back riding, has just returned to work.

W. E. Branson, former booker for Pathe, is now on the road covering southern Nebraska. L. D. Chapman, formerly connected with the Educational Film Company here, has been made booker for Pathe.

Philadelphia

OFFICERS of the Stanley Company of America have been instrumental in forming the Stanley Musical Club of Philadelphia, the plan of which will be one of the most pretentious ever undertaken by motion picture interests in this city. The object of this club is primarily the cultivation of a fraternal spirit among the better class of musicians and it is planned to provide the public with high-class concerts on Sundays and such other times as the concerts will be available to those who otherwise would not be able to attend them. The officers of the Club are: Jules E. Mastbaum, honorary president; Leopold Stokowski, vice-president; Frank W. Buhler, general manager of the Stanley Company, second vice-president; Irving D. Rossheim, controller of the Stanley Company, treasurer. Leopold Stokowski, conductor of the Philadelphia Orchestra, has promised that his organization will give several concerts as part of the program of the Club.

Oscar Neufeld, president of the De Luxe Film Exchange was re-elected president of the Film Board of Trade for the fourth successive year at the September meeting of the Board. Mr. Neufeld has given unstintedly of his time and effort to bring about the present efficiency of the organization and has been largely instrumental in eliminating many of the evils that prevailed in the motion picture industry in Philadelphia prior to the functioning of the Board. Percy A. Bloch, manager of the Philadelphia exchange of Famous Players Lasky, was re-elected vice-president; Ben Amsterdam of Masterpiece Film exchange, was elected treasurer; and Jack Greenberg, secretary. The board of directors will be named by the chair at the October meeting.

Mel Sokolow, of the Paramount sales force, has returned to his duties after an illness which confined him to his home for several weeks.

R. Rosenbaum and James Clark, special representatives of the ad sales department of Paramount, were recent visitors on Vine Street and called a meeting of the sales force of the Philadelphia office to familiarize them with the forthcoming product.

It is understood that the Stanley Company is negotiating for the four theatres owned by the Whitehurst interests in Baltimore and in the event of being unable to acquire the Whitehurst holdings, has secured options on two desirable sites in Baltimore on which it is intended to build.

Ben Amsterdam, representing the independent exchanges in Philadelphia, has returned from New York, where he attended the meeting of independent distributors and has announced plans for the general observation of Independence Week, which will be held in October.

Jules Levy, one of the assistant general sales managers of Universal, was a recent visitor in Phil-

adelphia. Mr. Levy at one time made his headquarters in the Philadelphia exchange as district manager.

South Philadelphia exhibitors are co-operating with the Business Men's Association of Philadelphia in order to put across a Special Movie Week during the latter part of September. It is the first time in Philadelphia that a business organization has tied up with the motion picture men to promote a sectional boosting campaign. The theatres will reciprocate the advertising which will be given them by the merchants and it is believed that the plan will work out for the general benefit of South Philadelphia interests.

Leonard Deery, shipper at the local office of F. B. O. was married recently to Miss Elsie Pettit, of Rosemont, Pa.

The Sherwood Theatre, 54th & Baltimore Ave., which has been closed while undergoing extensive improvements, reopened September 12th.

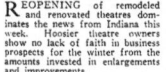

Indianapolis

REOPENING of remodeled and renovated theatres dominates the news from Indiana this week. Hoosier theatre owners show no lack of faith in business prospects for the winter from the amounts invested in enlargements and improvements.

The Circle symphony orchestra at Indianapolis is back in the pit with Bakaleinikoff directing, after being supplanted during the summer with name acts and jazz bands. The return of the orchestra was one of the features of the ninth anniversary week celebration of the Circle.

Forrest McMurtry has leased the Ladoga opera house to C. W. Rhon and Son. The new management is redecorating and will run pictures two nights a week.

With redecorated interior and exterior, a new $10,000 cooling system and many new stage ef-

fects the Grand, vaudeville and feature pictures, at Evansville, has been reopened. Allen C. Carter remains house manager. He has appointed Ray Koenig treasurer, succeeding Morris Blacker, who resigned at the close of last season. Miss Fredia Thiele is cashier.

Manager Frank Ford of the renovated Lyric at Fort Wayne is offering a $100 prize to patrons for a new name for the theatre on the score that improved facilities and pictures warrant the change.

Mr. and Mrs. Frank Walters, proprietors of the Orpheum at Hartford City, have opened their new picture house, the Jefferson.

The Sourwine at Brazil, Ind., has been reopened after a three months' closing. R. W. McCray is manager.

A new electric system, redecorating, new stage, new orchestra pit, increase of seating capacity

to 650, two new pianos and a number of minor changes are improvements in the Grand, reopened after two weeks of work at Newcastle, Ind.

The Hamilton and Orpheum theatres, Indianapolis neighborhood houses, which have booked films together, switching the same reels nightly have changed policy and are running different pictures.

George W. Anstead and Axel Pearson have reopened the Auditorium at Connersville, Ind., after installing new doors from the lobby, refinishing walls in polychrome and gold, installing all new scenery, new screen, new silk screen drop, and making other extensive improvements.

James E. Huckleberry of Indianapolis has leased the Princess at Williamsport, Ind.

George W. Anstead and Axel terests in the Princess and Castle

at Rushville, Ind., to his partner, Fred S. Casady.

Business friends sent numerous huge boquets to the management of the Grand at Gary, Ind., when the house was reopened after many improvements.

Harry Vonderschmidt of Bloomington has decided to name his new theatre at Greencastle, the "Voncastle." Completion is expected about Nov. 1.

A. M. Robertson, manager of the Palace at Rensselaer, Ind., has leased the New Ellis for a long term.

Fire destroyed the Anderson photoplay theatre at Syracuse, Ind., with $8,000 loss.

Clyde Noble, formerly connected with the Noble at Princeton, Ind., has bought the "Arcade" at Brookhaven, Miss., and is moving his family there to take charge of his property.

Kansas City

THREE youthful bandits held up the Miller theatre, one of the largest downtown houses in Wichita, Kas. Saturday night and escaped with $2,800. The robbery was the most daring one attempted in Wichita in several years.

"And they think it incongruous if a woman who has been in pictures for ten or twelve years plays anything else but 'mother' parts in a white wig and a ficha."

That was the outburst of Clara Kimball Young in Kansas City this week. Miss Young, who celebrated her thirty-fifth birthday Monday, said there no longer remained any doubt about her statement that she was "through" with the screen.

The arrangement of the Orpheum theatre, Kansas City, for staging "Charleston" contests each night this week not only proved a popular move, but was good for liberal newspaper support, including cuts and stories on the winners.

The honor in Kansas City of being first to the newspapers with the news that the destruction of the Shenandoah would be in a Pathe reel "now on the road" was won by Lawrence Lehman of the Orpheum theatre, or, rather, Fred Spear, his publicity man.

Every one was "brushing up" in anticipation of a big fall business along Kansas City's movie row last week. There was activity aplenty.

Louis Reichert, former P. D. C. branch manager, accepted a position as Warner-Vitagraph branch manager.

The Universal trade showing was held at Chillicothe, Mo., Tuesday, attended by a large number of small town exhibitors.

About 150 exhibitors and friends of the operators attended a special screening of "Manhattan Madness," which marked the graduating exercises of a class of the Kansas City School of Motion Picture Projection, operated in conjunction with the M. P. T. O. Kansas-Missouri for non-union operators.

Sidney M. Katz, formerly with F. B. O., has been appointed assistant sales manager of that branch in Kansas City.

Roy Churchill, F. B. O. branch manager, contends that business is better right now than it has been in three or four years.

Fred Hershorn, Universal short subjects manager at Kansas City, became a benedict and left for Buffalo with the bride, Miss Mildred Wilson, to join the Warner-Vitagraph force.

Lloyd Willis, special Warner-Vitagraph representative, spent a busy week in Kansas City, as did C. S. Baker, who was on his way to San Francisco, where he will become Universal assistant branch manager.

An exhibitor of Garden City, Kas., called C. A. Schultz on the telephone—a distance of 400 miles —to congratulate him upon being appointed P. D. C. branch manager.

J. L. Grantham has been made assistant booker at the Warner-Vitagraph branch.

Earl Cunningham, Paramount exploiteer, is putting in a busy week on the road this week.

Rebecca Joffe, home office manager of the sales promotion department for Universal, was a Kansas City visitor.

W. E. Truog, Universal district manager, made a hurried trip to New York, while J. A. Epperson, Pathe branch manager, returned from a gratifying trip through the Kansas and Missouri territory.

Harold Cass, First National salesman, who covers his territory in a motor car, took his vacation last week and went on a tour with his car.

"Yep, my show's 'blown up'," said the voice of H. E. Schildhter, Madison, Kas., exhibitor to C. W. Allen, assistant branch manager of Warner-Vitagraph branch at Kansas City, "unless an airplane can be obtained."

There was no airplane, no fast train—merely a "used" model of Ford touring car belonging to Allen, who made the trip of 162 miles over bumpy roads in a little more than four hours.

Among the out-of-town exhibitors in the Kansas City market last week were: F. G. Weary, Farris theatre, Richmond, Mo.; Roy Burford, Arkansas City, Kas.; C. M. Pattee, Pattee theatre, Lawrence, Kas.; Ben Levy, Hippodrome, Joplin, Mo.; S. E. Wilhoit, Jefferson, Springfield, Mo.

Last week marked much projection room improvement in theatres in the Kansas City territory. Peerless reflector arc equipment was installed in the Newman theatre, Kansas City, while G. E. High Intensity lamps were installed at the Orpheum, Kansas City. A new Simplex projector and Raven Haftone screen equipment was installed at the Grand theatre, Winfield, Kas. Two Simplex projectors were installed in the Plaza theatre, Leoti, Kas., while two Simplex projectors also were installed in the Pantages theatre, Kansas City.

Not in a long time has any exploitation stunt received the wide publicity and space given Metro-Goldwyn's trackless train in Kansas City this week. Aside from a "run-in" with a "hard boiled" traffic patrolman, who refused to let a safety zone be blocked, the 3-day visit in Kansas City was a pleasant and successful one.

St. Louis

WHILE hundreds of persons were enjoying the show at the Lindell Airdome, Grand boulevard and Natural Bridge avenue, St. Louis, one night recently a sneakthief gained entrance to the cashier's cage and escaped unnoticed with the evening's receipts $305.65.

Mrs. Lili Torline, 4938 Leahy avenue, cashier had bundled the money into a newspaper which she placed on a chair. She then departed from the cage for a few minutes. When she returned ten minutes later the money had disappeared.

Negotiations have been opened looking to the purchase of Stolberg Lake at Belleville, Ill., by a St. Louis syndicate. It is planned to convert the resort into a first class amusement park.

Harry Greenman, manager for Loew's State Theatre, Eighth and Washington avenue, was host to the orphans of St. Louis at a special performance of Charlie Chaplin's "The Gold Rush" the morning of Saturday, September 12. Arrangements were perfected for caring for upwards of 4000 orphans, the capacity of the big first run palace. Every orphanage in the city sent its quota to the show.

Steve Kaiman, owner of the O'Fallon Park and Baden theatres has had plans prepared for a new theatre to be erected at 8200 North Broadway. Theodore Steinmeyer, International Life Building, is the architect and contractors will be asked to submit bids this week. The house will be two-stories, 60 by 130 feet and cost upwards of $50,000. It will have 800 seats.

Mr. and Mrs. S. W. Lilly, formerly of Flandreau, Mo., have purchased the Irma Theatre, Bartmer avenue, from Dave Nelson and associated. The price paid has not been revealed.

Tom McKean, manager of the local F.B.O. office, accompanied by his wife departed Saturday, September 12, on a two weeks' vacation tour of the East. He will call at the home office before returning to St. Louis.

A local syndicate headed by Louis Dremer has purchased the Elite and Cozy theatres at Metropolis, Ill., from J. A. Weece. The houses have a total of 1150 seats.

W. W. Watts of Springfield, Ill., is vacationing in Cuba.

S. E. Pertle of Jerseyville, Ill., motored to Champaign and Danville during the past week.

The Pekin theatre, a negro house, opened for business in Springfield, Ill., during the past week. Amos Duncan is the proprietor.

Claude McKean, manager of the Memphis, Tenn., Fox exchange spent last Tuesday and Wednesday in St. Louis.

Eva Bolson, assistant booker for Fox is vacationing in Kentucky.

C. D. Williams has purchased the theatre at Thebes, Ill. Moses Lesar formerly operated the house.

C. D. Hill, district manager for Producers' Distributing Corporation, presided at a sales conference for his various branch office managers in the local exchange Saturday, September 12.

In attendance were the following managers: Eddie Lipson, Des Moines, Ia.; Frank De Lorenzo, Omaha, Nebr.; Clarence A. Schultz, Kansas City, Mo., and Art La Plant, St. Louis, Mo. Russell McLean, special representative for Hill was also in attendance.

Producers Distributing Corporation has opened its beautiful new exchange on the ground floor of the Plaza Hotel Building. It is among the finest in the city and gives ample room for handling the increase in business this company has experienced in recent months.

It is reported that some other exchanges will move into new quarters during the next few months.

Metro-Goldwyn-Mayer is said to have under consideration the taking over of the old United Artists and Selznick office at 3332 Olive street. If that move is made it is believed United Artists will go into the present Metro headquarters at 5330 Olive street.

E. Borg, assistant manager of the Educational office at Kansas City, Mo., motored through on the way back from a vacation trip to Chicago, Detroit and points north.

St. Louis friends of Mike Doyle former proprietor of the Orpheum Theatre, Cape Girardeau, Mo., were grieved to learn of the death of his mother in that city Monday, September 7.

Visitors of the week included: John Rees, Wellsville, Mo.; H. C. Tuttle, Desloge, Mo., and Jim Reilly, Alton, Ill.

Central Penn

FOUR hundred members of the Harrisburg Chamber of Commerce who returned on Friday, September 11, from their four-day annual cruise were invited with their wives to be the guests of the Wilmer & Vincent Theatre Company in Harrisburg, in the Victoria theatre.

The cruisers accepted the invitation and the occasion served as a sort of a reunion of those who took the trip. During the cruise a Wilmer & Vincent camera man took motion pictures of all the important incidents. These and other film pictures of the cruise were taken under direction of C. Floyd Hopkins, Harrisburg, manager of the Wilmer & Vincent theatres, to be displayed in the Harrisburg theatres. Another feature of the cruise was a visit to witness a performance in the Keith Palace theatre, in Cleveland.

Peter Magaro, veteran motion picture exhibitor, of Harrisburg, gained the distinction of being the member of the Harrisburg Chamber of Commerce Cruise who traveled the longest distance in order to go along on the trip. Mr. Magaro was in Paris at the time he decided to make the tour with the Chamber, it having been his original intention not to return to America until late in the Fall. He altered this plan, however, and arranged to cut short his Conti-

nental tour to reach Harrisburg in time for the cruise.

Advertisements in the Easton newspapers state that the Fox Film Company has again selected the Strand Theatre in that city for the presentation of their "1925-1926 master productions."

On September 14, when Loew's, Inc., took over control of the Colonial Theatre, Reading, which they purchased from Carr & Schad, Inc., the Carr & Schad office force moved from the Colonial to the Arcadia theatre building. Carr & Schad control a number of theatres in Reading and Lebanon. Dr. H. J. Schad, president of the company, stated while it is the ultimate plan to build a new theatre with seating capacity of 3,200 on the site of the Arcadia and adjacent properties that have been acquired, the construction work cannot be started for several years because of leases held by tenants occupying some of the buildings that are to be razed.

A special added attraction to the program of motion pictures at Nixon's Academy, Hagerstown, Md., during the week of September 7, was a series of local films showing Hagerstown industries, stores, merchants and other business and professional men and scenes about some of the public schools. A number of free tickets for these shows were dropped from an airplane which flew over the city.

Marian Nixon, Universal leading woman

New projection machines and a large amount of other new equipment have been installed in the Opera House, Mauch Chunk, by the Comerford Amusement Company, of Scranton, which controls the theatre.

The Chicago Stock Company, which was holding forth at the Park Theatre, Altoona, during the summer, terminated its engagement there.

Each day in its newspaper advertisements the Rialto theatre, Allentown, prints a local telephone number and announces "if this is your telephone number come to

the box office and receive two free tickets."

As an added attraction at the Cambria picture theatre, Johnstown, during the week of September 14, Edna Wallace Hopper, the actress, appeared in person four times daily in an act written and staged for her by Raymond Hitchcock.

Carr & Schad, Inc., have just completed extensive alterations in the Strand theatre, Reading, to equip it for the presentation of combined vaudeville and picture shows. The stage has been made larger, a number of dressing rooms installed and the orchestra pit extended. New electrical devices have been provided.

The Savoy theatre, Bethlehem, which was formerly the Lorenz, and which was recently acquired by Lou Berman, of Philadelphia, is now being managed by Mrs. Bertha Emmett, formerly manager of the Colonial, a Wilmer & Vincent house in Harrisburg, and the leading picture theatres in Allentown.

C. Wilbur Hoffman, camera man, has been employed by the management of the New Strand theatre, recently opened in York by the Nathan Appell interests, to film local things of interest in and around York. The regular showing of local events on the Strand screen is a new feature of the theatre's programs.

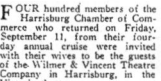

Denver

HICKMAN PRICE, representative of the fire prevention department of the Motion Picture Producers and Distributors of America, was a visitor in Denver

Eugene O'Brien, featured player in First National's "Graustark."

last Tuesday. He spent a short time with the President and Secretary of the Film Board of Trade, after which a few fire drills were held. Mr. Price arrived in connection with his department. He left Denver Tuesday noon for Dallas, Texas.

Harry Nolan, district supervisor for First National Pictures, Inc., left early in the week for Salt Lake City, Utah, for a few days visit with the local branch of his organization in that city.

Dave Bader, personal representative of Carl Laemmle, President of Universal Film Corporation, has been a visitor in the city for the past few days spending most of his time in the local branch of Universal at Broadway and Stout. Bader arrived in Denver from Kansas City, Missouri, and will leave shortly for Oklahoma City. It is reported that he is arranging to put into force a system whereby all small exhibitors will be afforded an opportunity to review Universal products in the projection room.

Bill Mathews has arrived in Denver to take charge of the local

office of Film Booking Offices. He will succeed Sid Weisbaum who was recently transferred to the San Francisco office. Bill has a host of friends in this territory who are glad to see him back. He was formerly salesman working out of the Denver office.

Charles Gilmour, manager of Warner Brothers, made a short business trip to Cheyenne, Wyo. Hugh Braly, manager of Famous Players-Lasky, motored to Chadron, Nebraska, for a visit to James Pace who owns and operates the theatres in that city.

H. I. Mason, former assistant manager of Warner Brothers, has been engaged by the local branch of Fox to assume the duties of booker. Since the taking over of Vitagraph Mr. Mason has been engaged in other lines outside of the industry. His many friends are glad to see him back and wish him the best of success in his new connection.

All Denver theatres enjoyed capacity houses Saturday, Sunday and Monday of last week for the reason that several railroads gave exceptionally low excursion rates into Denver. It is estimated that approximately 15,000 visitors were

in the city during that time. Every theatre on Curtis Street was crowded. Another low excursion rate will be given in the near future.

S. H. Horner, owner and manager of the Emblem Theatre, popular suburban house of Denver, has been appointed by Mr. Huffman, President of the M. P. T. O. of Colorado, as a permanent exhibitor member of the Board of Arbitration succeeding Jacob Enpler who recently resigned from the Board. Mr. Eppler has severed his connection with the Ogden theatre and will leave for California in the near future. Mr. Horner is an experienced theatre owner and safe to say this selection is made with a great satisfaction among his fellow exhibitors.

Les Weir, district manager for Producers Distributing Corporation, was a visitor in Denver for a few days having just arrived from New York City. While in Denver he closed contracts with the new State theatre of Curtis Street for practically the entire output of Producers. Mr. Weir will leave shortly for Los Angeles.

Albany

IF Arthur Whyte, of New York, and of the Peerless Booking agency, pays a visit to this section, let him bring his golf clubs for some of the exchange managers along Film Row are planning to take his measure on the links.

Mr. and Mrs. Meyer Schine are back in Gloversville, from a honeymoon spent during the last week or ten days, as the couple swung over New York State, with a day or so at Lake Placid, another in Richfield Springs, and two or three in New York City. During the time, Mr. Schine simply refused to talk business, but now that he is back home it's a different story.

The Rialto, in Glens Falls, which was badly damaged by fire some months ago, is expected to be in shape for reopening not later than November 1. Last Saturday witnessed the opening of Fred Mausert's new house in Glens Falls. The theatre was constructed out of an old church which Mr. Mausert purchased late in the spring.

E. J. Smith, district manager for Vitagraph, was in town during the past week, and after a conference with J. N. Klein, local manager, the two departed for Utica, where they saw Nate Robbins and some of the other exhibitors.

Joe Miller, who handles Renown product out of Buffalo, working as far east as Albany, was in town during the past week. Mr. Miller announced that Robert Wagner, of Little Falls, a former exhibitor, who became a salesman for Renown in this territory a few weeks ago, had tendered his resignation and returned to Little Falls. It is the general expectation that Mr. Wagner will later associate himself with some theatre in the capacity of manager.

Mr. and Mrs. C. H. Boyd, of this city, together with Mr. and Mrs. Charles Stombaugh, of New York, have been guests during the week of Mr. and Mrs. Amos Leonard, of Syracuse, at their camp near Boonville. Mr. Boyd is local manager for Associated Exhibitors.

Charles R. Rogers, who is giving his personal attention to the making of a new series of Westerns starring Harry Carey for Pathe Release.

The fascination of Florida real estate is still manifest among the exhibitors of New York state. William Dillon, of Ithaca, president of the New York state M. P. T. O., has just returned from Florida, while Mrs. W. C. Carpenter, an exhibitor in Lake George, is planning to spend the winter in the south.

Ted O'Shea, local manager for Metro-Goldwyn, held a sales meeting during the past week, with Lester Wolf, Louis Mendley, and Alex Weisman, present. Mr. O'Shea's sister, Margaret, of Buffalo, has been spending a couple of weeks here as the guest of her brother.

The theatres in Syracuse are once more back on standard time, much to the satisfaction of the managers and owners. The city has been operating on new time up until September 11.

Joe Weidman, who with his brother, Charles, owns the Central theatre in Albany, is becoming more and more convinced that something must be done next year to save the motion picture theatres from the inroads and losses caused by daylight saving. While the summer has been but fair at the Central theatre, the fact remains, said Mr. Weidman, that the evening shows, despite advertising and every other effort, were confined to but one show a night, as it was impossible to get the people out on account of daylight saving.

Joe Saperstein, manager of Harmanus Bleecker Hall in Albany, encounters no trouble in securing entries in his Charleston dance contest, staged each Monday night, with the finals on November 2. But when it comes to getting amateur talent for each Thursday night, Mr. Saperstein employs scouts, and as a result is able to present some highly commendable acts. Through admitting children, unaccompanied by parents, free, at all matinees except on Saturday, Mr. Saperstein has been able to maintain good business throughout the summer.

Richard Bloomingdale, who has been with Julius Berinstein, at the Palace in Troy, has been promoted by Mr. Berinstein to the management of the Hudson theatre in Albany. At the Palace, Thomas Norris has been made manager, which allows Mr. Berinstein more time to give to the various theatres in this section that are being run by the Berinstein brothers. The Palace and Hudson theatres started off last week with double features, which will prevail each Tuesday, Thursday and Saturday from now on.

The Regent theatre in Albany is still closed, but will reopen the latter part of this month, by which time it is expected that the work of redecorating and otherwise improving the house, will have been completed. While this work is in progress, Herman Vineberg will devote his entire attention to the Albany theatre.

Mr. and Mrs. Alec Herman, were in Sharon Spa, a week ago, visiting Mrs. Herman's mother

Dwight C. Leeper, vice-president Richmount Pictures who recently returned from Europe.

who is spending a few weeks there.

Charles L. Reed has taken over the theatre in Windsor, according to letters received on Film Row. Visitors along the Row last week included Julius Byck, of Tannersville, as well as G. H. Garvey, who has theatres in Clinton and Oriskany Falls. It was Mr. Garvey's first trip to Albany in quite some time, and with the numerous changes that have taken place along the Row, it was necessary for him to introduce himself in some places.

Louis Schine was in New York city during the week. Vic Warren, of Massena, who is busy these days in putting up a business block as well as in looking after his theatre, was also in New York during the week.

Harry Hellman, owner of the Royal theatre in Albany, is planning to make certain improvements to his summer camp on Crooked Lake, in order that he can spend weekends during the fall, when there is good partridge shooting nearby and when the surrounding mountains will be a blaze of color. The camp is known as Camp Neil, being named after Mr. Hellman's son. Incidentally, the Royal is observing its sixth anniversary this week, and both Mr. and Mrs. Hellman are the recipients of many congratulations. The theatre is one of the best run of any in this part of the state.

Sol Manheimer, manager of the Robbins theatres in Watertown, used to be a film salesman, so it it not to be wondered at that when some of the exchange managers and salesmen from here, hit the northern city, that he sees to it that they have a good time. There is always a plate of cheese and crackers and maybe something to wash it down. Mr. Manheimer is using fourteen models this week in connection with the showing of "The Dressmaker from Paris," at the Olympic. At the Neighboring Avon, vaudeville and pictures will be shown from now on. Mr. Manheimer reports business as having been good throughout the entire summer.

Keeping his admission prices on Labor Day the same as on any other day, Julius Berinstein, of the Colonial in Albany, pulled a good stroke on Labor Day, and packed his theatre even during the afternoon, so that the gallery was even filled. The price of admission was ten cents. It must be that many of those who attended expected to pay holiday prices, for nine out of ten sat down more than a dime for their admission and appeared surprised when they were told that no increase prevailed.

Alec Papayanakos, of Canton, his brother James, of Gouverneur, and still another brother, Harry of Potsdam, are now setting the pace in that part of northern New York in pictures shown and in business done. This is not to be wondered at, however, when one stops and reminisces a bit for years ago, when movies were in their infancy, it was the Papayanakos brothers that provided entertainment for Watertown and in return started the groundwork for the fortune which later came their way.

When Claude Fredericks, owner of the Capitol theatre in Pittsfield, Mass., ran "The Covered Wagon" a year ago last Labor Day, he established a house record that lasted for exactly one year. On the recent Labor Day, Mr. Fredericks, playing "The Coast of Folly," made a new house record and one which he says he is now out to smash a year hence.

Bob Landry, of Ogdensburg, used "The Ten Commandments" as his feature for four days last week while the city was filled with persons attending the county fair. In conjunction with another party, Mr. Landry also has a theatre in Malone, and here he played "The Ten Commandments" for three days.

Otto Eigen is still devoting himself to his novelty store in Sharon Springs, and will probably not return to the motion picture theatre. Mr. Smalley is running Mr. Eigen's house, but whether he will keep it open throughout the winter is not known.

Perhaps Alec Weisman and Ted O'Shea, of the Metro-Goldwyn exchange didn't get a thrill last week as they were driving back to Albany through the Adirondack region. All of a sudden, out of the brush near North Creek, jumped a couple of deer and further along appeared two red fox. Mr. O'Shea and Mr. Weisman stopped with C. H. Wade, who runs a theatre and a hotel in North Creek. Mr. O'Shea is still talking of a wonderful bookkeeping system installed by Mr. Wade, at an expense of $1,200.

Bob Yates, of Lake George, was in town Tuesday on his way to New York. Louis Buettner, of Cohoes, was in Syracuse last week, attending a meeting of the Albany and Buffalo zones. George Dwore, of Schenectady, secretary of the Albany zone, was unable to be present.

Buffalo

A PITIFUL condition arose the other day when the champion pinochle shark of New York state was taken into camp by an amateur. The champion, one Walter Hays of Buffalo, vice president of the Mark-Strand interests, has been having things his own way on the trains between New York and Buffalo for lo, these 20 years, until he met up with Charley Hayman of Niagara Falls, who, it seems, also plays a wicked game when he gets warmed up. But the worst part of this contest was that the champeen advised his best friend, Eugene Falk, secretary-treasurer of the Mark-Strand organization, to lay his wad on the well known Hays' pinochle ability with the result that the Falk bank roll faded away. J. H. Michael, sparring partner, for Charley, bet on the Cataract City kid's tricks to win and as a result made enough to pay his expenses at the Syracuse meeting of the boards of directors of the Buffalo and Albany zones. Moral—Every champeen gets a knockout some day.

E. S. Sharaf has resigned as Syracuse representative of the Buffalo Paramount office. George E. Williams, exploiteer, is in charge of a handsomely decorated Paramount booth at the state fair in Syracuse.

Joe Schuchert, Sr., has been bitten by the Florida real estate boom bug and has gone to that state to take a wallop at some land deals. Joe owns the Colonial and Columbia theatres in Buffalo.

Henry Lally, Dunkirk fillum magnate, has also "cleaned-up," a barrel of coin of realm in Florida lots.

Ben Wallerstein, manager of the Broadway theatre, Buffalo, was host at a party given in honor of Harry T. Dixon, F.B.O. manager in the Hotel Statler, Saturday evening, September 12. It was surprise party for Harry, who was marched right into the banquet room by Basil Brady, Pathe branch manager. There was a goodly representation of exchange men and exhibitors. Harry gave a pathetic speech which moved everyone present to tears. Because of this condition there was no response.

Buffalo exhibitors will be interested to know that their old friend, Bill "Victrola," Mack, former Pathe manager who left town a few years ago to take over the Philadelphia office of the same company, is now short subject sales manager at the home office. Congratulations, Bill. Theatre men in this neck of the woods used to hear all the new stories from Bill, who used to get the boys shaking with laughter and then he would guide their hands in a signature on a fat contract.

Al Beckerich, manager of Loew's State, Buffalo, landed on the front page of the Evening News with a photo of himself and an army of newsboys, through a tie-up with the News on a free screening for the boys of Jackie Coogan in "The Rag Man."

Bob Demming, left, organist, George T. Cruzen, right, manager new Palace theatre, Lockport, N. Y.

Frank Noel of Akron, O., has been appointed director of publicity at Keith's theatre in Syracuse, succeeding Nelson Mirick of the Salt City. Ruby Belle Mason, former Buffalonian, has been engaged to preside at the console of the new organ. The house is now operating under its new combination policy at 50 cents top, instead of $1.

Manager J. Berkowitz is tickled pink with the success so far of First Graphic Month which was launched September 1 to celebrate the company's third anniversary.

Fay's theatre in Rochester has

tied up with the Rochester Herald in a Local Lafs Contest. Each week the offerings of the ten best are filmed on the Fay screen.

Obeying a court order, the Buffalo city council has granted a permit to build a motion picture theatre at 822 Tonawanda street. It is reported that this house will be leased by the Shea Amusement company.

Frank Moynihan has joined the sales staff of Freedom Film corporation of Buffalo. Richard C. Fox, manager, has signed up the new Arrow product 100 per cent. with the Michaels Theatres Enterprises, operating the Plaza, New Ariel, Avon and Cameo theatres in the Queen City of the Lakes.

Nothing like being an all around theatre man. The other night when the operator fainted in the book at the Cataract theatre, Niagara Falls, Manager Eddie Weinberg sprang at the projection machine and stood by until the end of the show.

Jess Kaufman, who has been representing Chase Pictures corporation of Buffalo in the Syracuse territory, has resigned. He has not as yet announced his plans for the future.

Vassiliadis Bros., have taken over the "Linden Theatre" Jefferson Ave., near High St., and are planning big improvements all around. They will continue operating the theatre while improvements are being made.

They also operate the Strand Theatre on Clinton St.

San Francisco

G. C. PARSONS has returned to Film Row in the capacity of exchange manager after a year's association with the National Theatre Syndicate. Prior to this time Parsons was for a good many years manager of the Goldwyn office, but at the time the consolidation of Metro and Goldwyn took place, he affiliated himself with the National Syndicate and Frank Voigt took over the office. Mr. Voigt's health, however, has been very poor for some time and it became imperative for him to resign.

John Spickett, owner of the Palace Theatre, Juneau, Alaska, paid Film Row a visit recently.

Charles Muehlman, manager of the First National Exchange, returned from New York after attending a convention of managers.

Finding the Turk street quarters too small for their increasing business, the Producers Distributing Corporation found it necessary to obtain larger quarters. The old Selznick office at the corner of Golden Gate and Leavenworth had possibilities and appreciating this, Manager M. E. Corey personally worked out a floor plan whereby this corner has now been remodeled into an ideal film exchange.

A serious fire damaged the Orpheum Theatre at Red Bluff put-

ting this house temporarily out of business. Plans by Opera House Ass'n are under way for the immediate repair of same.

Negotiations for a new theatre building in the Hestor District on the Alameda in San Jose, have been completed by the H. R. Roth Realty Co., on the Victor W. Benson property. Ennos Lion and E. Rosenthal, former theatre owners of San Francisco, are to lease the building, which will contain a thousand seats and which will be used for motion pictures only. It is expected that the building will be ready for occupancy within six months.

Max Blumenfeld announces the opening of a San Francisco general headquarters office located at 298 Turk street. This circuit has grown very rapidly within a short year and a half. It now constitutes eight theatres. Joe Blumenfeld, son of the managing director of the circuit, will be in charge of the San Francisco office.

Mortimer M. Thomas, who has been connected with the Golden State Theatre and Realty Corporation and in fact one of the organizers, disposed of his stock in the corporation to a group of his present associates about Aug. 26th. The transaction is understood to have involved upwards

of $100,000. Thomas retains his individual theatre holdings, the deal in question embracing only the interest in the G. S. T. & R. Corporation.

G. N. Aaronson of the Western Poster Co., in Seattle, spent a couple of weeks in San Francisco at the local office.

Independent Exchange that has for some time operated at 284 Turk street, have taken over the more extensive offices heretofore occupied by the Producers Distributing Corporation at 294 Turk street.

The Red Seal Corporation of New York represented by General Sales Manager Thomas O'Brien, is opening offices on the Pacific Coast. Their San Francisco headquarters are with the All Star Exchange and Abe Markowitz has been appointed manager. Breaking a hard and fast rule which he has always followed since he first became a star, Fred Thomson, F. B. O. western luminary, made his first public appearance in San Francisco, as a feature of the Greater Movie Week parade.

R. M. Ford, for 'a large number of years associated theatrically in San Francisco and more recently at the Broadway Theatre in Oakland, has just purchased the interest of Mortimer Thomas in

this theatre, which now makes him the heaviest stockholder in that house.

Joseph Bauer, formerly of the Wigwaum Theatre, has just returned from Alaska with his family, where they spent the summer.

L. Borg states construction is well under way on the Parkway Theatre, Park Blvd. and East 19th street, Oakland, a new 1,000-seat house, being built by the West Berkeley Theatres, and Golden State Theatres Corporation.

The Robert Morton Organ Co. have opened offices on Golden Gate avenue. The old office of Nat Magner and the adjoining store are being made into one large office.

Mr. Hull of the Ely theatre at Ely, Nevada, and B. B. Byard, Eureka, Cal., both paid visits to this city in quest of pictures.

Miss Edna Escher, Pathe, Los Engeles cashier, stopped off between boats, both coming and going to Vancouver, where she went on her vacation visiting friends in Seattle and Portland.

Rex Midgley of the American Theatre in Oakland left for New York in company with some of the First National delegates, where he will be gone for approximately a month.

Atlanta

F A. LEATHERMAN an-
nounces this week the ap-
pointment of Florey W. Russell
as salesman in the North and
South Carolina territory. Mr.
Russell is a native of North Carolina, one of the best known service men in the south, and an
authority on musical instruments.
He will have offices in the United
Film Building, Charlotte, N. C.
and will endeavor to make the
North and South Carolina exhibitors more widely acquainted
with the merits of the Reproduco
Pipe Organ.

L. J. Davies, who for the past
five years has been general representative for F. A. Leatherman
and the Reproduco Pipe Organ
line, has been given charge of the
Birmingham territory for the company. Mr. Davies will move immediately to Birmingham with his
family, and plans to open a branch
office there, where he will welcome
his many friends and endeavor to
take care of their musical necessities.

M. C. Coyne, otherwise known
as "Mike," formerly Atlanta manager of United Artists office, later
road manager in the south for
"The Ten Commandments," and

more recently exploitation man of
the southern territory for Greater
Movie Season, has been appointed
by United Artists Corporation as
their exploiter in the Los
Angeles and San Francisco exchanges. Mr. Coyne will have
charge of the exploiting of all
United Artists' product. "Mike"
has demonstrated his intention of
becoming a good Californian by
recently buying a farm near Los
Angeles, and has become
thoroughly settled there.

John L. Crove, former manager
of the Lyric Theatre, Atlanta, who
has been affiliated with Famous
Players Lasky corporation for the
past several years as managing
director of various theatres
throughout the country, has completed arrangements with the
Beaux-Art Amusement Company
of Dallas, Texas, whereby he will
organize and direct for the season
a dramatic stock company to play
in the Circle theatre, Dallas.

In spite of the fact that the extreme heat under which Atlanta
has been suffering all summer
continued and even seemed to grow
more intense on Labor Day, and
added to the continued absence of

orchestras in the ¿its of all local
picture houses, theatres unanimously reported one of the biggest
Labor Day businesses they have
known in a period of several
years' time.

Information from Miami is to
the effect that David and Myron
Selznick, former executives of the
Selznick Pictures Corporation,
now bankrupt, are in Miami at the
present time promoting a motion
picture studio to be located there.

Lee L. Castleberry ¿of the Bell
Theatre, Gadsden, Alabama, who
is one of the most popular exhibitors in these woods, was in the
city this week on business.

Louis C. Ingram, Georgia representative for Metro-Goldwyn, was
in town the first of this week and
left on Wednesday for Newman.
He will probably return to the
city for the week-end.

J. F. Worsley, formerly with
Grosset and Dunlap company, and
who is well-known to local film
folk, was visiting in Atlanta this
week. Mr. Worsley recently resigned managership of a Florida
theatre.

George Jones of the local
Metro-Goldwyn exchange, is
authority for the statement that

cigars are not the proper smoke
for aspiring young bookers. His
many friends in the industry will
be pleased to know that George
has recovered from his trying experience, which experience he says
justifies him in the expression of
his opinion on the subject.

Fanny Lee Zimmerman, secretary to Arthur Lucas of the Educational Exchange, left town
Saturday for a two-weeks vacation. Miss Zimmerman is
traveling through the Carolinas in
her car, and expects to return to
Atlanta within ten days or so.

C. D. Haug, Metro-Goldwyn
exploiteer, has been in the city
several days this week, following
his activities in various Georgia
points in connection with one of
their big features.

F. S. Shepard, who represented
F. B. O. in the Georgia and Tenn-
esee territory, has resigned from
his position on account of ill
health. Mr. Shepard leaves this
week for the East.

F. L. Davie, manager of the
local F. B. O. exchange, plans to
take a two weeks' vacation beginning next week. Mr. Davie has
not decided yet where he will
spend his much needed rest.

Cleveland

HARRIS WOLFBERG is in
town, working out of the
Cleveland Metro-Goldwyn office.
Wolfberg is a home office representative. He expects to be in this
territory for several weeks. This
is not the first time Wolfberg has
been out here. Some six or seven
years ago he was manager of the
Foursquare exchange in Cleveland.
He was also associated with the
local Famous-Players-Lasky exchange at one time. So there's a
wholesale greeting going on, with
Wolfberg as the central figure.

Fred C. Quimby, short subject
sales manager for Fox Film Corporation, paid the local Fox office

a visit one day last week. Quimby
was on his way east.

C. C. Pettijohn is due here on
Tuesday to preside at a special
meeting of the Arbitration Board.

D. W. Griffith is scheduled to
be in Cleveland on Sunday, September 20, for the opening of
"Sally of the Sawdust" at the
Allen theatre. Carroll Dempster
will accompany him. As the plans
now stand, Griffith and his party
will spend Sunday here, and will
leave the following Monday for
Chicago, to start work on a new
play.

J. S. Jossey, president of Progress Pictures Company has purchased the Arrow franchise for

the 24 Golden Arrow productions
for the whole state of Ohio. Jossey plans to put on a big advertising campaign for this series, starting next with an invitational
showing of "Tessie."

John F. Royal, manager of
Keith's Palace theatre, Cleveland,
who showed a combination vaudeville and picture policy during the
summer, has returned to the
straight vaudeville policy—almost.
Hal Roach comedies have been
maintained as a steady weekly attraction at the Palace. The comedy will take the place of an act,
and has been the opening position
on the bill.

L. B. Cool, manager of Feiber

and Shea's Colonial theatre, Akron, opened the house last week
under a combination picture and
vaudeville policy. This the first
time the Colonial has ever offered mixed entertainment. Last
season it played straight vaudeville. The season previous it offered stock. Manager Cool thinks
that today's public likes plenty of
variety. That's why he adopted
pictures and vaudeville for this
season.

Frankel and Malott are the new
owners of the Windsor theatre,
Canton. They bought the house
last week from Wagonner and
Hoffman. Howard Frankel will
manage the house.

Cincinnati

LOUIS, Phil and Harry Chekeras, prominent exhibitors of
Springfield and Middletown, O.,
paid a sort of a family visit to
the various film exchanges last
week.

The Shifas has sold his Columbia Theatre, Middletown, O., to
Pete Chekeras who now manages
the Majestic in the same city.

Chas. Lowenburg, Universal exploiteer returned from Newark.
Ohio, last week loaded with a
machine full of squash and
pumpkins. It is not known
whether Charlie is going into the

wholesale vegetable business or
the pie baking business.

Julius Leopold of the Mecca and
Midget theatres. Dayton, Ohio,
spent several days in the city
last week.

Ed. King of the Oxford Theatre, Oxford, O., visited film row
the other day with a view of
booking several pictures suitable
for a college town.

Lawrence Barnes of the Champion Theatre. Columbus, O., was
another visitor at the Broadway
film building.

H. G. Passe and his girl friend

visited in the city with the various exchange managers this week.
Passe manages the Forum Theatre at Hillsborough, O.

C. E. Henderson of the Kentucky Theatre, Olive Hill, Ky.,
spent several days with the bookers.

Fred Tines of the Columbia.
Portsmouth, O., was seen at the
film offices last week.

C. A. Smith, manager of the
Sherman Theatre, Chillicothe, O.,
spent several days in the city
booking pictures for early showing.

Robert Baer and family of the
Palace Theatre, Beckly, W. Va.,
were in the city last week.

V. E. Giffofl and wife, of the
Virginia Theatre, Wellston, O.,
spent several days in the city
booking pictures and purchasing
new equipment for his theatre
which he is redecorating.

E. Davidson, of the American
Theatre. Welsh, W. Va., spent
several days in the city buying
new equipment for his theatre
from J. Gelman of the Cincinnati
Theatre Equipment Co.

Salt Lake City

GEORGE L. CLOWARD, manager of the Metro-Goldwyn exchange here, has left for a short trip into the Wyoming territory.

Clyde H. Messinger, in charge of the local Educational exchange, is in the Idaho branch at present.

A fine tieup has been obtained with a prominent down town store in connection with the eighth annual Paramount week, which is being celebrated here from Sept. 5th to 12th. A window display has been arranged showing different models which have been used in making Paramount pictures, among which is Peter Pan's doll house.

Harold Pickering, exploitation manager for Famous Players-Lasky, has been busy distributing an abundance of advertising matter for Paramount week.

The formal opening of the new Paramount house at Ogden, Utah, was very successful according to George E. Carpenter, managing director for the Louis Marcus Enterprises here. Many people were turned away, scores of telegrams were received from different stars, and many beautiful floral offerings were sent as is the usual custom upon opening a new and large theatre.

Manager Fish announces that the Fox exchange here, has just returned from a very successful trip through the Idaho territory. Fish has a sign attached to his car proclaiming loudly that William Fox presents "The Iron Horse." "The Iron Horse" is being presented this week at the Salt Lake Theatre here. An elaborate prologue is being shown in connection with this picture. The publicity and exploitation work has been taken care of by Weir Cassady, manager of the American Theatre of this city.

A tieup which is attracting much notice is displayed in the window of a local music store, showing many historic articles of furniture and musical instruments which were brought to this section of the country before the entering of The Iron Horse.

Max Roth, Fox home office representative, who was here to install H. Bradley Fish as manager of the local office, has left for Buffalo, New York. Roth planned to meet Jimmie Grainger, sales manager for Fox at Ogden. Grainger is also returning to New York from the coast.

Manager Fish announces that upon his return trip from Idaho he closed the Egyptian Theatre at Ogden, Utah, with the 1925-26 Fox product. J. L. Tidwell, selling out of the Fox exchange here, has returned from the Southern Utah territory. Miss Pearl Cardwell, assistant cashier for Fox, has changed her name to Mrs. R. S. Brown.

Joe McElhenney and Milton Cohn out of the Universal office here, have come in and left again for their territories in Southern Utah and Idaho.

L. J. Schlaifer, Western Division Manager for Universal, is expected to be in this city this week.

E. S. Winward, booker, and C. W. Peck, assistant manager at the Universal office here, report that their week end trip spent in chicken (grouse) hunting was highly successful.

"The Keeper of the Bees" was sold to the American Theatre here by manager L. A. Davis of the F. B. O. exchange, after the trade showing last week. This will be the world premier showing of this picture, which will open September 19th. An exploitation man is being sent here direct from the studios to work with Weir Cassady, general exploitation manager at the American Theatre, to handle the exploiting of this picture.

W. K. Bloom, salesman for F. B. O., was in this city for two days and has now left for the Duschene County in Southern Utah.

Manager Davis is leaving for Montana this week to make the key towns with his Fox product.

Miss Madee Mitchell, F. B. O. cashier, is spending her vacation at the studios in Los Angeles.

W. F. Gordon, in charge of the Associated First National exchange here, has just returned to his managerial chair from New York.

R. S. Stackhouse local manager for Warner Brothers is now making the Montana territory. L. W. Hyde, selling out of this office, has returned from Southern Utah and left within a few days for Northern Utah and Nevada. Harry Gibson is on his way to the Yellowstone Branch in Idaho, and G. E. Jensen is doing his work in Montana.

The Kinema Theatre here has adopted a new policy within the last week, and will have a change of program three times a week in place of once, as was their previous custom.

Local Pathe exchange manager W. G. Seib, has taken the fatal step and is spending his honeymoon and vacation some place in Colorado.

According to Charles Epperson, booker for Pathe here, they are expecting a visit from the new District Manager, Frank Harris, who is enroute to the District Managers' Convention in New York.

C. J. Hamal, selling for Pathe, has left for Idaho for about five or six weeks, and R. D. Boomer is headed for Southern Utah as usual.

Ed. Mix, Associated Exhibitors local manager, is leaving the later part of the week for a short trip into Idaho to make the key towns with his next year's guaranteed product sales.

Manager C. F. Parr of the Producers Distributing Corporation exchange here, is expecting L. W. Weir, Western Division Manager, to be in this city soon enroute back to the coast from New York.

C. C. McDermond, salesman for Producers Distributing Corporation, has returned from a trip into Southern Utah with contracts by the score. Dave Schier, Idaho salesman, is still in the midst of an extensive campaign there.

A display featuring Warner Brothers stars, pictures and directors, and telling of the outstanding pictures of the new season, has been given a conspicuous place this week in the lobby of the Victory Theatre here.

Carl Stearn, who has charge of the United Artists exchange in this city, has just closed a seven day engagement for "The Gold Rush" at the Egyptian Theatre of Ogden, Utah. This picture also opens in Salt Lake at the Paramount Empress Theatre. Stearn closed every key center in Montana during his recent trip, and has closed practically all of the key cities in this whole territory.

T. C. Pierce, who covers the Idaho territory out of the local Greater Features branch, was here for a brief stay and has left for his territory again.

Among exhibitors seen on "Film Row" this week are: J. Whitehead, who has a new house which he calls Recreation Hall, at Eureka, Utah; John Ruger of the American Theatre at Park City, and who has just completed plans for a new house to be built there; Isaac Swenson, owner of The Angelus Theatre, Spanish Fork, Utah; J. W. Hedges operating the Meridian Theatre, Meridian, Idaho; Gordon Thornberg, owner of the Blue Bird Theatre, Garfield, Utah; J. J. Gillett of the Strand Theatre, Tooele, Utah, and Don Carrothers of the C. & A. Amusement Company of Pocatello, Idaho.

Canada

WHEN Lambert Hillyer, First National director, made "The Knockout" in Northern Quebec, a number of lumberjacks, log rollers and river men were engaged to appear in the picture. Noted among these jacks were the Letang Brothers of Gatineau Point, Quebec, and since the time last spring when they shot the rapids on logs they have been busy filling engagements throughout the Ottawa Valley. Not long ago they put on the stunt of log rolling at the Brighton Beach regatta, Ottawa, and their last appearance of the season was on Sunday, September 13, at Luna Park, Aylmer, Quebec, where they staged their log riding specialty.

Starting September 12, a reduced scale of prices went into effect at the Regent Theatre, Ottawa, the manager of which is Leonard Bishop, but even under the new schedule the admissions are no lower than those charged by houses playing both vaudeville and pictures. The Regent shows pictures exclusively. The prices now range from 65 cents for loges and 50 cents for the orchestra floor down to 25 cents for children.

Rodolph Pelisek, for years the conductor of the Regent Theatre orchestra at Ottawa, Ontario, resigned to his post of duty at the theatre on September 12 after an absence of two months in which he was seriously ill in a hospital at Montreal, Quebec. During his illness, the orchestra was directed by Rodolph's brother, Joseph Pelisek.

A startling development occurred at Chambly, Quebec, a few nights ago in Columbus Hall when the discovery was made that the moving picture projection machine had been stolen from the booth. The theatre was well filled with patrons and the show was about to get under way when it was found that the machine was not in its place. No trace of it has been found either. It was valued at $1,250.

Independent Films, Limited, Toronto, has been making excellent headway during recent months on its avowed independent basis. The company has offices in Toronto, Montreal and other cities. The company has signed for the Canadian distribution of the 12 Gotham Productions in the 1925-26 schedule to follow the six Gotham features previously booked. L. Rosenfeld, formerly with the Allens at Toronto, and J. Levine are identified with the Independent Films, Limited.

Exhibitors of Calgary and Edmonton, Alberta, interviewed Hon. Alex. Ross and Attorney-General Brownlee of the Alberta Provincial Government at Edmonton a few days ago to enter objections regarding the stringency of the examination regulations for projection machine operators. A request was made for a board of three or more examiners in place of the one inspector at present who issues licenses. Arrangements have been made for a board of appeal to reconsider several cases of license applicants.

Omaha

THE old Majestic theatre in South Omaha has been remodeled and decorated and is now called the Tivoli. A new pipe organ has been installed and new seats, new stage and other theatre equipment provided. August Herman, who has been assistant manager at Rialto theatre of the Blank Syndicate, is looking after the management of the new house for the present time.

Earl A. Bell, recently appointed branch manager here for Warner Brothers, is on the job. According to the contracts coming into the office, Mr. Bell is 'on the job' in every way.

Charlie Chaplin's impersonator, who goes under the name of Charlie Aplin, is in town. It is reported that he may appear in the prologue during the showing of "The Gold Rush," coming to the Strand, Sept. 19.

F. B. McCracken, sales manager of the United Artists, is out of town for a few days covering the territory. T. Y. Henry, from the New York home office, is spending a few weeks here. After leaving here he will make Kansas City and St. Louis.

Bill Strickland, assistant manager and booker for Universal, just returned from a vacation in Sioux Falls, reporting low golf scores and high fishing scores.

W. C. Wallace, who formerly covered northern Nebraska for Warner Brothers, has gone to Florida to enter the real estate game.

Maud Carville, cashier at the Pathe exchange, just returned from spending two weeks' vacation at Denver and Colorado Springs.

Mrs. Art Johnson, wife of the First National booker in Des Moines, spent a few days here last week.

Ned Marin, of New York, sales director of Universal, spent a day here this week.

C. J. Riggs, sales manager for southern Nebraska for Metro-Goldwyn, is driving around in a new Nash brougham. Mr. Riggs reflects good business.

Art Stokes, general manager for A. H. Blank in Des Moines, was here early this week.

F. M. De Lorenzo, manager of the Omaha office of the Producers' Distributing Corporation plans to leave Friday for St. Louis to attend a managers' meeting at the district manager's office.

T. B. McConnel, formerly with Paramount in Milwaukee, has been made salesman for the Producers' Distributing Corporation and will cover the Iowa territory. The Producers office has undergone a

complete redecoration and presents a cheerful aspect.

L. J. Goodall and J. A. Goodall have been added to the staff of United Artists. These brothers will look after U. A. interests during bigger engagements in large towns.

Frank Bacon's "Lightnin'" which will be shown at the Sun theatre beginning Friday September 11, will have more than ordinary interest to Omahans. It will be remembered that Frank Bacon, who wrote the play and also played the leading role on the stage, played in stock here.

J. L. Kelley has been added to the staff of Metro-Goldwyn and will cover an Iowa territory. He reports business so far very good.

V. B. Trent, cashier for Metro-Goldwyn, injured his hand severely while handling a box in the rear of the office. He is recovering satisfactorily.

W. E. Trout, assistant sales director of the Omaha division of Universal, is in New York on business.

J. E. Flynn, district manager for Metro-Goldwyn, spent Monday

and Tuesday of this week here. He held a sales conference at the local exchange.

O. H. Dutton, manager of the Exhibitor's Supply Company, early last week drove to Menomonie, Wis., to bring back his family, which had been spending the summer there. Upon his arrival he found them quarantined with diphtheria. After assuring himself that the family was recovering nicely, he drove back to Minneapolis. From there he made a flying trip back to Omaha, leaving Minneapolis at 7 a. m. and driving the 400 odd miles to Omaha by 11 p. m.

A big theatre party was given at the Empress theatre at Cherokee, Iowa, Tuesday, September 8, by Universal for exhibitors. H. F. Lefholtz and salesmen of the Omaha office attended. A score of features and many comedies were shown during the all-day party.

J. D. Blossom is a new salesman for Warner Brothers. He is new to the film field, but his pleasing personality and proven salesmanship are sure to win him success.

Hulda Bowen, stenographer for the Universal exchange, has just returned from a vacation spent at Denver.

Baltimore

E. A. LAKE, manager of Keith's Hippodrome, was taken suddenly ill several days ago and had to be rushed to the Maryland General Hospital.

Broughton Tall, correspondent for Variety in Baltimore, will pinch-hit for Gustav Klemm, in writing reviews for the Baltimore Evening Sun, while the latter is on his vacation during the weeks beginning September 21 and 28.

J. M. Shellman, motion picture editor of the Baltimore Sun does not understand what has happened to the publicity department of many of the film companies he has been receiving so little mail re-

cently. There was a time, he says, when at least two barrels full came in every week, but it has dwindled to about half a barrel now. He enjoys attention from press agents.

Mrs. E. K. Cross has succeeded Miss Frances Kresslein as bookkeeper at the New Theatre. Miss Kresslein has been on a vacation and has not received her new appointment up to the present time.

H. J. Brooks, came to town during the week beginning Monday, September 21, and exhibited the film entitled "Are You Fit to Marry?" at Lubin's Theatre, 404 East Baltimore street, for men only while here.

M. Henderson, assistant to Frank H. Durkee, who controls the Palace Theatre, Gay and Hoffman streets, and several other Baltimore Theatres is now away on a two weeks' vacation.

A Charleston dance contest is being conducted by the Capitol Theatre, one of those controlled by the Associated Theatres Company, which will continue for five weeks. One is held every Wednesday night and by previous try-outs three couples are selected. At the end of the five weeks those three couples having the highest number of successes to their credit dance for the prizes in the finals.

J. Louis Rome, general manager of the Associated Theatres Company enjoyed a short trip to Virginia Beach and Ocean View, Va., recently.

H. Elliott Stuckel, who handled the publicity for the road company that presented "The Hunchback of Notre Dame," in Baltimore for its first run, was married to Miss Gertrude Rutland, of Boston, recently in Baltimore. Miss Rutland is a feature dancer in musical comedies. The couple will reside in New York. Mr. Stuckel is now handling the publicity work at Carlin's Park here.

Butte

THROUGH a contract signed recently between Merle Davis, lessee of the Ansonia Amusement company theatres, that include the Broadway, Ansonia and Empress theatres of Butte, and C. F. Parr of Salt Lake, district manager for the Producers Distributing corporation, the entire output of the company has been arranged to be shown at the Broadway. The Producers films will begin with the season opening the first of September.

The hot summer days are passing into history and once more the

theatres are crowded to capacity. The Rialto theatre made a big hit all summer by using tons of ice over which the big electric fans of the Rialto, played to keep the theatre cool and many sought the popular theatre just to cool off as well as to enjoy some of the fine programs that Manager W. J. Sullivan always has on his programs.

This is Paramount Week, a celebration of their eighth annual and the various theatres all over the state are tied up in a universal exhibit of the Paramount pictures

in which Butte and Anaconda join. The 8th, 9th and 10th will be devoted to the celebration. Paramount salesmen have been working hard to see that the company not only receive the felicitations of all their friends but that these congratulations can be gilt edged with a large cash value.

During the summer Miss Harriet McConnell, motion picture star for the Hal Roach Motion Picture company, visited Butte in company with her mother. During the brief visit in the city City Passenger Agent Cooke of the

Union Pacific escorted the distinguished guests on a tour of Butte. Miss McConnell expressed herself greatly interested. She has been working on a picture at Lodge Grass, Montana.

During August, as a special treat and a compliment to the crippled children of Butte and vicinity Manager W. J. Sullivan of the Rialto theatre gave an invitation to attend the afternoon performance. In addition many of the contestants who have appeared at the Monday evening song contests, were on hand to give a special program for the guests.

Des Moines

SEVERAL thousand dollars damage resulted from a fire which injured the interior of the Family Theatre at Davenport last Sunday. The theatre is one of the Blank circuit. The fire which started in the projection booth destroyed the booth and did damage to the seats, walls and screen. The operator was also badly hurt. The house will be redecorated, the seats gone over, the screen refinished and new booth supplies provided. The whole job of refurnishing the Family Theatre has been given by Mr. Blank to the Exhibitors Supply Company of Des Moines. Two new Simplex machines with Peerless arcs have been purchased.

Changes have been taking place in the personnel of the Des Moines film exchanges. At Famous Players Bill Curry and Merrill Anderson have been added to the booking staff from the ad sales department. Gene Stephenson has been promoted to the ad sales department from the shipping room and Lyle Utsler who was in the booking office is now in the shipping department. Raymond Fisher, who was in the shipping department, has been added to the ad sales section under Jack Curry.

Harry Herman, who traveled the southern part of Iowa for Metro-Goldwyn, is now managing the Orpheum Theatre at Clinton for A. H. Blank Enterprises. His place at Metro-Goldwyn has been taken by J. A. Nixon who comes to Des Moines from New Haven, Conn.

Grace Gannon resigned her position as stenographer for F. B. O. She seems to have retired to private life and whether wedding bells has anything to do with her giving up her work, none seems to know. Miss Anna Vigel is the new stenographer for F. B. O. Bill Ronning who was the booker for F. B. O. was transferred to the Sioux Falls office of F. B. O. He had only been with the Des Moines office about a month. R. C. McCulloch, who takes his place comes from Minneapolis where he was with Universal.

Joe Jacobson, salesman for Pathe, is back on the road again after his bad spill near Independence, Iowa, when his car was rather completely smashed up and he was too. He was in Independence in the hospital for a week. While his car is being patched together again, Mr. Jacobson is traveling the territory with several of the other salesmen.

Harry M. Wilkinson, manager of the Rialto Theatre at Sioux City for A. H. Blank, has resigned his managership without statement as to what his future plans will be. None has been secured to take Mr. Wilkinson's place at the Rialto. Homer Gill, manager of the Princess, has taken charge temporarily.

Florida is calling Ben Harding, manager of the Liberty Theatre at Council Bluffs. He has gone to Florida but he says that it is a visit and that he does not plan to locate there.

The Royal Theatre at Sioux City has just been equipped with some new fixtures. Morrie Smith, who is manager of the Royal, has installed a new Day Lite screen.

The Alamo Theatre at Pella has been bought by Chris Nelson. He bought the house from Van Dyke and Young who have just spent a considerable amount in the redecoration of the Alamo.

Grace Allen, inspector of the Pathe office, is now in Los Angeles, Calif., where she plans to locate. Miss Bab Pence has taken her place with Pathe.

The K. P. theatre at Hastings, Iowa, has been bought by O. L. Davis.

S. S. Swara, Premier booker, is a family man again. His wife and three daughters, Adele, Corinne and Eleanor, have spent the summer at Highland Nature Camp at South Sebago, Maine. Corinne won the tennis championship gold medal. Last year she was voted the best all around athlete of the camp. And next week Corinne and Adele leave for Grinnell College.

F. C. Anderson, cashier of Pathe, is away on a two weeks' vacation. He spent a week in Sioux City and then he is coming back to spend the other week at the Des Moines golf links and at the baseball park.

Fred W. Young, manager of the F. B. O. office, says that over a hundred exhibitors attended the F. B. O. Open House during State Fair week and that a great many exhibitors have been in the last week.

A. H. Blank made a flying trip to New York on First National business but, following telephone conversation with Des Moines he took the opportunity while in New York to converse with officials of the musicians union. Union musicians and stage hands walked out of Blank's houses, the Capitol, Des Moines, Strand, Rialto, Palace, Garden and Majestic on September 10.

Omar J. Kenyon, manager of the Majestic theatre for the last five years, and R. B. Armstrong, of New Bern, N. C., a theatrical producer, have leased the Majestic and opened the new season September 13.

The Majestic is owned and has been operated by the A. H. Blank interests. The house was closed last Saturday night, however.

It is the plan of the new firm to install "The Majestic Players" in the local theatre to present musical comedy programs. Principals will be changed every two weeks and the entire company will change places with other companies occasionally in order to give the public an opportunity to see new faces.

There will be four shows each day and entirely new programs each Sunday and Thursday.

Detroit

B. F. KEITH'S Temple theatre here exploited Pathe's "Our Gang" two-reel comedies in the newspapers, bill boards and in screen announcements. The first picture proved pleasant and held the audience in rapt attention. Incidentally other Pathe subjects are used at this house: Pathe News, Aesop's Fables, and Topics of the Day.

Lew and Ben Cohen signed one of the biggest contracts of the week when they contracted for 100 per cent Warner Bros. product in their houses here, the Colonial, Rex, Victory and Coliseum.

W. S. Butterfield predicts the biggest season so far on the occasion of the fall opening of his 35 theatres in Michigan. He credits the general prosperity of the country for the public's increasing desire for entertainment.

Keith vaudeville is now being played at the Orpheum, Bay City, in addition to pictures. Before only pictures were presented.

New Butterfield theatres are under construction in Pontiac, Owosso and Bay City.

The Motion Picture Theatre Owners of Michigan will hold their convention in Grand Rapids, October 7 and 8.

First run pictures and musical tabloid comedies are to be shown at the Capitol, Lansing, and the Regent, Jackson, this winter.

Burglars stole $100 from the Park theatre one night last week.

A leather pocketbook was presented E. R. Reed, bookkeeper of the Metro-Goldwyn exchange here, on the occasion of his 78th birthday. He was at work as usual.

Lester Sturb, Manager of Metro-Goldwyn here, reports that he gets several requests every week for "The Four Horsemen of the Apocalypse," which brought fame to Valentino. The picture is off the market for another year at least.

Film men and exhibitors attended the premiere of Harry S. Koppin's New Picadilly theatre last week.

Golden Brothers are building their second theatre in Brightmoor. They recently opened the Franklin theatre in another part of town.

The Cinderella and DeLuxe theatres are back on fall schedule, pictures and vaudeville.

Louis D. Hick, formerly of Cleveland, is now covering the eastern half of Michigan for Standard.

Jack Young won praise from Lloyd Willis, special home office representative for Warner Bros., for his conduct of the Detroit office, when Willis visited here this week.

Charles H. Miles, owner of the Miles theatre and other theatre properties in Detroit and Cleveland, has offered his Ferry Field theatre, residential district picture and vaudeville house, for sale.

Howard E. Sweet, former manager of the Colonial theatre, Lansing, now is managing the Strand, Grand Rapids.

George Davidson and S. K. Decker are busy rolling up new business for A. B. C.

The East End theatre, on East Jefferson avenue, is being torn down to make way for a new theatre seating 1,000. Glenn Watkins will operate the new theatre.

Detroit's newest theatre, the Roosevelt, out Gratiot avenue, will open this week. It is one of the chain operated by the James H. Robertson Enterprises. It is reputed one of the finest residential theatres in the middle west. It will seat 2,000 and present pictures and vaudeville. The latest equipment has been installed to make it ultra-modern.

Preparing for the opening of the new Michigan and State theatres, the former to seat 5,000 and the latter almost 4,000, the John H. Kunsky organization has made several promotions in its personnel. George W. Trendle remains general manager and attorney with increased responsibilities. Thomas D. Moule, supervising manager of the Capitol, Madison and Adams, has been promoted to be general supervising manager of the Capitol, Madison, Adams and State. Malcolm C. MacInnes, of the Adams, will go to the State as manager; Bertram W. Winstanley, assistant manager of the Capitol, becomes manager of that house; Russell C. Chapman, house manager of the Madison, becomes full manager of that house; and Rex W. Minkley takes over the managership of the Adams. Howard O. Pierce will remain in charge of advertising and publicity and stage direction and presentations. Herbert Straub, director of the Madison theatre orchestra, will direct the orchestra at the new State.

New England

INDEPENDENT Films, Inc., has closed up its offices at 128 Meadow street, New Haven, and brought its entire force to the Boston offices except Louis Astor, who was manager of the Connecticut offices. He remains to look after the Independent interests in Connecticut.

Manager Harold Eskine of the Franklin-Film Booking office remains in Connecticut to look after his firm's interests but the offices at 134 Meadow street have been closed and the staff transferred to Boston.

A Montague, treasurer of the Independent Films, Inc., is back at his desk at 10 Piedmont street, Boston, with a splendid coat of tan and a new sparkle in his eye. He spent several weeks in Northern Maine with rod and line and with a better assortment of fish stories than ever before.

Mrs. M. S. Ayer, owner of the Exeter Street Theatre, Boston, returned from Paris on Tuesday and stopped for a few minutes to greet friends along the row on her way from the pier to her home.

Warner Brothers have purchased the Cameo theatre at New Haven from David Brand and have already assumed management of the house.

Louis Gordon, nephew of Nathan H. Gordon of the Olympia circuit has resigned from the Paramount Theatres and has become interested in theatres in Bristol, Manchester and Torrington, Conn. He was formerly with the booking department of the Olympia Theatres.

Al Somerby, manager of the Bowdoin Square Theatre, and Howard Athenaeum in Boston is the recipient of all kinds of congratulations upon the advent of a daughter at his home. Al was recently feted by a group of friends upon the completion of a quarter century as manager of the two Boston houses so that present felicitations mark the second great event in his life in a single year.

But Al is dividing honors with

James McManus of Marlboro, general manager of the Elm Amusement circuit, who is likewise receiving good luck tokens from his friends, due to the arrival of a son and heir in his home. Between Al and James, the Row is being plentifully supplied with fragrant Havanas.

Gus Shaffer of the Famous Players-Lasky company, who leaves soon to take up his duties as special representative of Paramount in Germany, was tendered a little surprise party by a host of business friends and associates during the week and presented with a huge stein to take along with him to his new fields. The stein stands about eighteen inches high and Gus promised to fill it to overflowing when he reaches the other side of the pond, just to let the boys back home know what they are missing.

James Greeley of Portland, Me., formerly manager of the Opera House in Bangor, has joined the United Artists as special representative.

Phillip Markell has taken over the Magnet Theatre at 301 Washington street, Dorchester, which was formerly operated by the Buckley interests.

Arthur Lockwood has bought the property and taken over the Circle Theatre at South Manchester, Conn. This house was formerly owned by John Sullivan.

Power's Theatre at Caribou, Me., was visited by fire on Labor Day resulting in the closing of the theatre until extensive repairs are made, probably a matter of several weeks. The fire started in the balcony from undetermined origin and badly damaged the balcony and rear of the main auditorium before being put out. As a result of the blaze the town will be without motion pictures until repairs are made.

William Farnum, temporarily back on the legitimate stage, will appear in the title role in "The Buccaneer," a play based on the life of the pirate Morgan, at the Tremont theatre, Boston, commencing Sept. 14.

Charlotte

N. MERRIWETHER, Manager of the New Concord Theatre, Concord, N. C., a Warner Brothers house, was in Charlotte the past week and made a trip around Film Row visiting his many friends.

Mr. Maydanis, who operates the Liberty Theatre, at Oxford, N. C., a colored theatre, was a Charlotte visitor the past week buying product for Fall and Winter use and setting in dates.

Frank Bryan and R. D. Craver spent Labor Day at the lake at Rockingham, N. C., fishing, and now the managers in Film Row are hearing innumerable fish stories from these two nimrods.

A. B. Huff, General Manager of the Broadway, American, Orpheum and Rose Theatres at High Point, N. C., was a Charlotte

visitor the past week. Huff states that he expects to have one of the best seasons in the history of High Point.

J. M. Davis, owner of the Capitol and Iris theatres of Salisbury, N. C., who has been ill for some time, is able to be out again, so we understand.

Rufus Davis, Manager of the Liberty Film Exchange, has now become a resident of Charlotte. His wife has joined him here and they have set up house-keeping in Dilworth. We understand that the Metro-Goldwyn office will handle the physical distribution of the Liberty Film Exchange and they will open for business on September 15th.

George Glegg, district auditor, of Universal Film Exchanges, Inc., is in Charlotte to audit the

records of the Universal Exchange at this point.

W. S. Scales, of the Rex and LaFayette Theatres, of Winston-Salem, N. C. was a Charlotte visitor the past week to arrange dates on the new product for the coming year.

The Metro-Goldwyn office has a visitor in Mr. Berry, the auditor of their company.

The Broadhurst Theatre, of High Point, N. C., a beautiful $100,000 structure opened its doors on Monday, September 7th. This is one of the most modern theatres in this section. It is beautifully decorated and has every modern device obtainable. The theatre is owned by the Liberty Amusement Company, and Geo. W. Crater is manager.

The Charlotte Theatre, at 23 W.

Trade Street, opened its doors at 10 o'clock September 7th. This picture house is modernly equipped throughout, has a seating capacity of 500 and all seats are of the air cushion variety. With the opening of this house a new plan of picture production will be produced in Charlotte. Big pictures previously shown here will be brought back for return engagements at this house. The charges for admission will be popular prices, 10 and 20 cents. Harry K. Lucas, the manager, states the plan has proven very satisfactory in many other large cities. The theatre will be one of the theatres operated by the Sunset Amusement Company, of Atlanta. The slogan of chairs, ventilation and projection is enforced.

Houston

ABE SILVERBERG, manager of the Folly theatre says: "back to pre-war prices" and has cut the admission of the Folly to 10 cents for adults. This is the only theatre in Houston with a 10 cent admission price. Mr. Silverberg says "a theatre can be run on a 10 cent admission base and no better proof is wanted than the fact that I reduced the admission price of the Crown theatre" (Mr. Silverberg is also manager of the Crown) "from 30 cents to 15 cents several months ago and since that time my business has been wonderful and I am sure that I can operate the Folly at a bigger profit with the lower admission price." The admission price of

the Folly was 15 cents for adults before the reduction. The same picture policy will be used as heretofore.

Famous-Players will film another picture in Houston. The first picture "North of 36" was filmed in Houston last fall and another Paramount company is on its way to Houston to film "Woman Handled." It will be filmed on the Bassett Blakley ranch the scenes of the first picture and part of the thousands of head of cattle used in that picture will also be used in this production. The company plans to remain in Houston for about four weeks.

A. L. DeBuer who was connected with the Howard theatre, Atlanta, Ga., for several years has moved his family to Houston where he has accepted a position with the Interstate Amusement Company who control two theatres here.

Gene Finley former publicity manager of the Palace and Old Mill theatres is in Houston on a business trip. Mr. Finley is at the head of his own company who have several pictures which are being shown throughout Texas and Oklahoma.

Work on the Jesse H. Jones new

million dollar theatre has been resumed and the basement is ready for the cement. This theatre is being built for Famous Players and will be one of the finest in the south when completed. As yet it is unnamed.

Sam Abrams and family have returned from a week's vacation spent in Dallas and other north Texas towns. He made the trip in automobile.

Mrs. Edna W. Sauners has returned from a motor trip through the middle west. She has reopened her office and is getting affairs lined up for the coming opera season.

Minneapolis

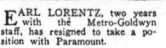

EARL LORENTZ, two years with the Metro-Goldwyn staff, has resigned to take a position with Paramount.

Sam Sandon of the Sandon theatre, Blue Earth, looked over the fair during the week.

Smith and Trimble of the State theatre, Devil's Lake, are putting in an orchestra for this winter's expected rush of prosperity business.

Archie Miller of the Grand theatre, Devil's Lake, isn't worrying much about the coming season. He got 20 bushels of wheat to the acre from a little farm of only 1,000 acres that is only a side issue with him. With wheat selling well above $1.50 a bushel it looks as though Archie would not have to hock the base drum to get his overcoat out of pawn.

The new F. & R. theatre at Fargo is said to be coming on at a great rate and will soon be in shape for opening.

Milton Pay of the Colonial theatre, Sioux Falls, is expecting to put in an orchestra this winter after several years without one in the lean period.

Benny Berger of the Metropolitan theatre, Grand Forks, is shedding fewer tears than usual this year, according to Morris Abrams and it looks like he must be almost making a little money. They say luck has to be too good to be true before Benny turns off the cascade.

Former District Judge Robert S. Kolliner of Hennepin county was called in as a seventh arbitrator in the case of W. M. Miller of the Western Theatres incorporated and the F. & R. Film company the other day. The three representatives from the Exhibitors' Association and three from the Film Board of Trade were unable to come to an agreement on the matter of a contract Miller declared was void.

The disagreement arose over the matter of a film ordered by Miller from F. & R. which was delivered to him by Vitagraph, now in the hands of Warner Brothers. Miller declared that his contract had been assigned to Vitagraph without his consent and insisted he was relieved from further obligation. The F. & R. company asserted that it had merely hired the Vitagraph company to handle its delivery of the film and that it still held the contract.

Judge Kolliner decided that the contract had not been assigned and that Miller must make good on it.

The question of whether a theatre owner has as much right to a dance hall license as a non-theatre owner is considerably agitated in Minneapolis just now. W. A. Steffes sought to acquire such a license for the operation of a dance hall in connection with his new theatre on Broadway which will soon near completion.

Other theatre owners in North Minneapolis insisted that it he got a license they must have one too and then opposition to the granting of dance hall licenses to theatres

popped up in spite of the fact that Minneapolis already has one large combination of this kind and a new one has recently gone in at the Tower in St. Paul.

The matter was threshed out before a city council committee and later before the council itself on a minority report but at last information there was virtually no hope that Steffes or the others would get the license.

Les Davis of First National is back from a little trip to Litchfield and vicinity.

Mrs. A. B. Muller of the Rex theatre at Maple Lake brightened the Pathe office here recently.

Bob La Piner had a good idea go wrong on him the other day. In his exploitation work for F. & R. he sought to put over one on the "Iron Horse" by suggesting that the theatre manager promote an "Iron Horse" sundae in St. Paul drug horse.

"I can't do it," the man came back. "I'm only running it Monday, Tuesday and Wednesday."

Bill Biesel, new exploiteer of United Artists here, is getting his feet under him in the Twin Cities and will soon make a little visit to surrounding territory.

Finkelstein & Ruben have taken over the Lyceum theatre at Brainerd which for several years has been run by Clinton and Meyers, and the Lyceum and Rex theatres at Virginia. The Garrick there is already owned by F. & R. This ends the price war at Virginia.

Thief River Falls, Minn., is not going to let its motion picture man fall a prey to "large financial interests." The city council has passed a resolution to limit the number of motion picture houses in the city to two, the Lyceum and Majestic, owned by H. A. Brummond.

Jack Rothschild, veteran film man in Minneapolis, has begun business as a theatre broker under the name Rothschild Theatres company. It will buy, sell or lease theatres and now has the Old Mill, Minneapolis, and the Orpheum at Forest Lake.

The new theatre at Little Falls is to be opened by William Anderson, A. J. Hand and Herbert Griff. The building is being remodeled now and will soon be ready.

E. E. Gomersall of the Fox organization is back from his conference with Jimmy Grainger in Chicago.

Vincent Soweija has sold his equipment at Swanville, Minn., and gone to work for the New Lyric theatre at Little Falls, which leaves Swanville without a picture house.

The Majestic theatre at Lake Benton, Minn., has been purchased by L. W. Liddle of Carthage, S. D., from Carlsten Gehlsen.

Otto Parlitz is running his Crystal theatre at Glencoa, Minn., six days a week, keeping it dark on Thursdays.

The Shen theatre at Lakeville

was reopened recently by Robert Shen.

The old Olympia theatre operated by O. S. Adams at Sioux Falls has been taken over by Rehfield & Knapp and named the Royal.

J. F. Cubberly of Finklestein & Ruben's outlying theatres, took a trip into Dakota during the week.

Ben Ferris in his new job as director of all F. & R. advertising has been giving special attention to "Drusilla With a Million" at the Capitol theatre, St. Paul.

M. L. Finkelstein, senior partner of the Finkelstein & Ruben organization, has gone to Europe. He sailed on Sept. 16 for Cherbourg and will take a three weeks' vacation on the continent with several New York leaders of First National. Although the trip is to be an outing without any definite business in view it is safe to say that the Minneapolis theatre man will look over some of the foreign product with a view to possible use in this locality.

Frank Buckley of the Princess and Capitol theatres at Superior has been visiting around in Minneapolis.

Pat Dowling of Los Angeles studios of Christie Comedies paid a call on Jack O'Toole of Producers Distributing Corporation in Minneapolis during the week.

Fred Knispel, division representative of Producers Distributing corporation also paid a visit in the Minneapolis office of that company in his new capacity. He was formerly one of the Minneapolis staff until Cecil Mayberry came along and grabbed him for an assistant.

M. Radwin of the Regent Theatre in Eveleth, Minn., took in the Fair in the Twin Cities last week.

Mr. and Mrs. Everett Dilley of the Grand Opera House at Northfield drove up again last week. They are getting to be regular visitors in the Twin Cities.

The safe in the Minneapolis office of Warner Brothers was tapped for $40 the other night and now there is a great deal of rushing to get all work done in the daytime and leave the office to the exclusive use of the world of yeggdom at night.

Thomas A. Burke, manager of Warner's was off on a trip through Fargo, Fergus Falls and nearby places when the excitement was going on.

C. J. Howard, associate sales manager of Pathe's office here has resigned effective September 12. They say he is going to California.

F. L. McMillan, of the Princess theatre in Winnebago, said it was the best Fair Week he had ever seen in the Twin Cities.

Morris Abrams, Metro-Goldwyn exploiteer, is just back from a visit to Devil's Lake, Fargo, Grand Forks and Aberdeen. He reports that both North and South Dakota are going wild over the prosperity brought them by the fing crops of last year and this.

H. L. Walker of the Rialto, Lyric and Orpheum theatres in Aberdeen is putting in a new $12,000 pipe organ in his Rialto theatre.

Carl Michaels, old Twin City exchange man, has gone to Southern Minnesota and Wisconsin territory for Metro-Goldwyn which has also put Max Berenson on its staff. Max will handle North Dakota.

Lou Metzger, manager of the company's complete service contract department, visited Manager Dunas at the Minneapolis office during the week.

Film Booking Offices took occasion during Fair week in Minneapolis to hold open house for all exhibitors who happened to be in town for the big Minnesota State Fair and Livestock Exposition. Eph Rosen and his staff had their hands full most of the week.

Among those who paid their respects were Mr. and Mrs. Ole Viste of the Murray theatre, Slayton, Minn.; Harvey Thorpe of the People's theatre, Crosby, Minn.; Harry Nelson of the Princess theatre, St. James, Minn.; Manager Joffe of the Lyric at Kenyon; Mrs. Peterson of the Happy Hour at Excelsior, Minn.; George Clow of Ogilvie, Minn.; Manager Ankrum of the Gem at Balaton, Benson of the Community theatre at Minnesota; Ed Kienholtz of the Eagle theatre at Buffalo, Minn.; Ed Buckley of the Idle Hour, Olivia.

Pre-release Reviews of Features

The Timber Wolf
(Fox—4809 Feet)
(Reviewed by George T. Pardy)

BUCK JONES makes a ten-strike in this film. It's a Western far above the average, there's the usual melodramatic punches, hard fighting and fast riding, but the story is much stronger in point of direct human interest and clever characterizations than one is accustomed to find in this type of picture. Buck is simply great as the reserved, yet strenuous man of action, who knows what he wants, and gets it, the "it" in this case being a girl, hard to woo and manifesting extreme dislike for Mr. Jones to the extent of bashing his face and checking him with a bullet. Buck cuts the Gordian knot by abducting her, and the cave-man method wins out. The star is also all to the good when he goes on the war-path and demonstrates his right to the nickname of "Timber Wolf" by tearing into and eliminating his foemen.

THEME. Melodrama. Western logging camp atmosphere, with silent hero, who defeats enemies through sheer fighting ability, and wins girl by cave-man methods.

PRODUCTION HIGHLIGHTS. The good photography and fast action. Buck's battles with the villain and latter's confederates. His kidnapping of heroine.

EXPLOITATION ANGLES. You can safely boost this as an uncommonly good Western, a winner for Buck Jones, showing him in one of the best roles of his career.

DRAWING POWER. A sure-fire attraction wherever first-class Westerns are in favor.

SUMMARY. A Western of superior brand. Has plenty of melodramatic power and stages customary thrill stuff, but plot values are of particularly high grade for this sort of picture. A fine Buck Jones vehicle, with star in unusual role of woman-tamer.

THE CAST
```
Bruce Standing...................................Buck Jones
Reenee Brooke...................................Elinor Fair
Babe Deverill...................................David Dyas
Joe Terry......................................Sam Allen
Sheriff.........................................William Walling
The Boy.........................................Jack Craig
Billy Winch.....................................Robert Mack
```
Author, Jackson Gregory. Directed by W. S. Van Dyke.

SYNOPSIS. Old prospector Terry is backed by Bruce Standing in attempt to find gold mine. Babe Deverill and latter's pal, the sheriff, throw Terry in jail and ill-treat him in order to make him reveal location of the rich claim. He is released by Bruce, who thrashes Deverill, thereby earning hatred of the latter's fiancee, Renee Brooke. Renee wounds Bruce, who kidnaps her in return. She nurses him and finally realizes that she loves him. Bruce finally discomfits the thieves and weds Renee.

The Timber Wolf (Fox)
PRESS NOTICE

LOVERS of thrilling Western melodrama and the many admirers of Buck Jones, can look forward to a decided treat when that star's latest picture, "The Timber Wolf" is featured as the principal attraction at the ———— Theatre on ————.

Besides the usual hard fighting and fast riding episodes for which all Mr. Jones' vehicles are noted, this one offers an unusual love story in which the hero kidnaps a girl who thinks she hates him, and teaches her to love him in the end.

It's a great film with a splendid cast, with Elinor Fair as the fascinating heroine and Dave Dyas, Sam Allen, William Walling and Robert Mack supporting the principals.

CATCH LINES
They called him the "Timber Wolf" and he lived up to the nickname when the time came for demonstrating how he could fight.
From intense hatred this girl's mind turned to love.

Buck Jones in "The Timber Wolf," Fox production.

The Great Sensation
(Columbia Pictures—4470 Feet)
(Reviewed by George T. Pardy)

REGISTERS as a good average program attraction, with William Fairbanks executing several of the lively thrill stunts for which he is famous, and more comedy stuff to balance the heroics than is usual in this star's vehicles. The melodramatic sequences are built upon the scheming of a couple of crooks to pull off a jewel robbery, and these are well handled, rounding into a rattling climax, the hero having a strenuous mixup with the underworld villain and his confederate, from which he naturally emerges victorious. Bill, disguised as a chauffeur in the employ of the girl he loves, who is aware of his identity and invents all sorts of disagreeable jobs for him to tackle, gets a lot of fun out of these situations.

Pauline Garon plays the mischievous heroine prettily.

THEME. Melodrama, with comedy relief and hero who poses as chauffeur for girl he loves, defeats crooks and regains proceeds of jewel robbery.

PRODUCTION HIGHLIGHTS. Wreck of heroine's auto. The comedy bits. Fast action. Fairbanks' high dive from cliff to rescue girl. His rough house scrap with crooks in finale.

EXPLOITATION ANGLES. Bill this as a rapid melodrama, with comedy episodes that get the laughs. Stress the thrills, Fairbanks' stunts, particularly dive from cliff, jewel robbery scene and hero's fight with crooks.

DRAWING POWER. Should please patrons in neighborhood and small houses.

SUMMARY. O. K. as program attraction. Fast-moving melo, with lively comedy here and there. Suspense well developed, with Fairbanks doing customary thrill stunts, battling with crooks, and winning girl.

THE CAST
```
Jack Curtis.....................................William Fairbanks
Peggy Howell....................................Pauline Garon
Captain Winslow.................................Lloyd Whitlock
Harry Ruby......................................William Franey
Mrs. Franklin Curtis............................Winifred Landis
Mrs. Howell.....................................Adelaide Hallock
Maid............................................Pauline Pacquette
```
Author, Douglas Z. Doty. Director, Jay Marchant. Photographed by George Meehan.

SYNOPSIS. Wealthy Jack Curtis, disguised as chauffeur, works for Peggy Howell, a flapper in search of thrills. Peggy discovers his identity but keeps up the deception. She becomes involved with a society crook introduced as Captain Winslow. Jack saves her from drowning. Winslow and a confederate steal Mrs. Howell's jewels. Jack pursues, regains gems after a battle and wins Peggy.

The Great Sensation
(Columbia Pics)
PRESS NOTICE

A PICTURE which more than lives up to its suggestive title, "The Great Sensation" is listed as the big screen attraction at the ———— Theatre on ————. It's a rousing melodrama, with fast action all the way, balanced by crisp comedy and pleasing love interest. William Fairbanks is seen as a wealthy chap who, disguised as a chauffeur, works for the flapper he falls in love with, eventually winning her, after saving her from drowning and the wiles of a crook who steals her mother's jewels.

Pretty, vivacious Pauline Garon is the heroine.

CATCH LINES
You know what William Fairbanks is capable of in the line of executing marvelous stunt work. Watch for his high dive in this picture as well as other extraordinary feats.
He had everything he wanted in this world, except a certain girl's love.

Pauline Garon in "The Great Sensation," a Columbia Pictures Release.

The Haunted Range

(Davis Distributing Div.—4900 Feet)

'(Reviewed by George T. Pardy)

A GHOST mystery angle introduced into this picture renders its plot a bit different from that of the usual Western, even if the spook turns out after all to be just the villain in disguise and not a visitant from spirit-land. Outside of which there are the customary scrapping thrills, spectacular riding stunts, and so on, which one looks for in open air adventure tales. The action rattles along at top speed, with never a hitch, the racing event, won by the hero after his ill-wishers have tried all sorts of dodges to bump him into eternity, including the dynamiting of the road-course, is unique and startling, and, taken as a whole, the feature ought to prove an excellent program attraction.

Ken Maynard and his clever horse Tarzan are a well matched pair, the star rides well, puts lots of ginger into his work, and the equine actor earns plenty of applause. Alma Rayford is an exceedingly attractive heroine and Harry Moody a strenuous performer in the heavy role.

THEME. Western melodrama, villain playing ghost to hide cattle-thieving operations.

PRODUCTION HIGHLIGHTS. Rapid, well sustained action. Exploits of horse Tarzan. Maynard's riding stunts, his fights with Slade. Racing scene. Roundup of rustlers.

EXPLOITATION ANGLES. Feature Ken Maynard, Tarzan and Alma Rayford. Title has advertising value, boost the ghost angle as something new in Westerns. You can safely praise the picture as a galloping melo, alive with thrills and offering an appealing romance.

DRAWING POWER. Good stuff for any house where lively Westerns are in demand.

SUMMARY. A rousing Western, with a ghost mystery issue which lends variety to plot. Puts over numerous melodramatic punches, offers many fast riding and fighting situations. Has romantic values. Stunts of Ken Maynard and his horse enjoyable. A good program attraction.

THE CAST

Terry Baldwin	Ken Maynard
Judith Kellerd	Alma Rayford
Alex Forester	Harry Moody
Charlie Titus	Fred Burns
Executor	Al Hallett
Ralph Kellerd	Bob Williamson
Terry's Horse	Tarzan

Author, Frank H. Clark. Director, Paul Hurst. Photographed by Frank Cotner.

SYNOPSIS. Terry Baldwin's uncle leaves him a cattle ranch on condition that he clears the dead man's name of a murder accusation and eliminates a ghost that haunts the property. Failing this, the ranch goes to Alex Forester, half-brother of deceased. Judith Kellerd and her brother Ralph live on the ranch. After many adventures Terry proves Buck Slade, leader of cattle-thieves to be the supposed spirit, rounds him up and his gang and weds Judith.

Ken Maynard, star of "The Haunted Range," Davis Distributing Division.

The Haunted Range (Davis Dis. Div.)

PRESS NOTICE

"THE Haunted Range," a Western picture with a ghost angle, of exceptional melodramatic power, is billed as the big screen attraction at the .... Theatre on ....

The film is brimful of exciting action and suspense, with a well developed love romance furnishing sentimental interest, is beautifully photographed and speeds into a splendid climax. Ken Maynard is the star, and, with the assistance of his wonderhorse Tarzan, does some great work in the perilous riding line.

CATCH LINES

A ghost has no business on a cattle ranch! That was hero Terry Baldwin's idea, and he refused to be scared away by an angry spirit. But it took considerable battling on his part before he solved the mystery of the Haunted Range.

Mystery, melodrama ,and romance. They're all present in this picture, with a thrill in every foot, lightning action and a climax that will please everyone.

Sporting Life

(Universal-Jewel—6709 Feet)

(Reviewed by George T. Pardy)

S EVERAL years ago Director Maurice Tourneur turned out a film version of this reliable old Drury Lane stage melodrama, which proved a good box office attraction. His second essay with the same material results in a picture superior in every way to its predecessor. The new "Sporting Life" is a genuine "corker" of its type. Lovely ladies, noble race horses, prize fighters, a dashing hero and villain of the deepest dye, are all present in a feature vibrating with fast action, loaded with suspense and projecting thrills by the score. Bert Lytell is immense as the athletic young Lord Woodstock, who takes on and knocks out the ring champion, when the chap he backs against the pug is doped; Marian Nixon makes a palpable hit as heroine Nora Cavanaugh, and the support is perfect.

THEME. Melodrama of London Sporting and society circles.

PRODUCTION HIGHLIGHTS. The fine photography and rattling action. Scene where fighter is doped, and killing of woman responsible for his misfortune. The ring contest. Scene where hero, his fighter and girl are trapped in Limehouse den. Winning of the Derby.

EXPLOITATION ANGLES. Tell patrons this is adaptation of famous melo which was great London Drury Lane success and scored two years run in this country with Robert Hilliard as star. Go the limit on boosting fight and race scenes, the appealing romance, the tremendous thrills. Feature Bert Lytell and Marian Nixon.

DRAWING POWER. Should get the money in any house.

SUMMARY. A realistic and thrilling picture version of celebrated old Drury Lane melo, and fine box office attraction. Stages stirring ring contest and view of Epsom Downs, with hero's horse winning Derby.

THE CAST

Lord Woodstock	Bert Lytell
Norah Cavanaugh	Marian Nixon
Olive Carteret	Paulette Duval
Wainwright	Cyril Chadwick
Joe Lee	Charles Delaney
Dan Crippen	George Seigmann
Cavanaugh	Oliver Eckhard

Authors, Cecil Raleigh and Seymour Hicks. Director, Maurice Tourneur. Photographed by Arthur Todd.

SYNOPSIS. Young Lord Woodstock loses money backing theatrical revue, but enters his horse Lady Love for Derby, and bets on Joe Lee to whip middleweight champion. Gambler Wainwright has Lee doped by woman aid. Woodstock takes Lee's place and knocks out champion. Nora Cavanaugh, the girl Woodstock loves, is lured to Limehouse den. He rescues her and reaches racecourse in time to foil plot by Wainwright to prevent Lady Love from running. Lady Love wins. Woodstock and Nora face happy future together.

Maurice Tourneur, director of "Sporting Life," Universal.

Sporting Life (Universal-Jewel)

PRESS NOTICE

A MAGNIFICENT film version of the great London Drury Lane stage success, "Sporting Life," which had a two years run before the footlights in this country, comes to the screen of the .... Theatre on .... It is an elaborate melodrama of London sporting and society circles, vibrating with thrills, offering a sympathetic love story, a furious prizefight, and great scene visualizing the running of the Derby at Epsom Downs.

Bert Lytell plays the role of hero Lord Woodstock, supported by Marian Nixon, Paulette Duval, Cyril Chadwick and other well-known screen favorites.

CATCH LINES

When the man he backed to win the fistic championship was doped, young Lord Woodstock took his fighter's place and won by a knockout. He rescued his girl from a Limehouse den and saw his racehorse run to victory in the Derby.

His Majesty Bunker Bean

(Warner Brothers—7291 Feet)

(Reviewed by George T. Pardy)

THE novel by Harry Leon Wilson from which this film was adapted is rich in the finer shades of subtle humor, its hero an amusingly credulous and, at times, rather pathetic figure. Translated to the screen in its present form it registers as mere slapstick comedy, and pretty crude slapstick at that, not a single trace of the story's lovable human appeal being retained. As a program attraction in localities where continuous horseplay delights patrons, it may do well enough at the box office, but critical audiences will find it simply tiresome.

Matt Moore is badly cast in the lead. He is years too old for the role, which calls for a callow youth. As portrayed by Moore, this Bunker Bean is just an effeminate near-imbecile. Director Harry Beaumont seems to have sacrificed all sense of true comedy proportions to clowning tactics which are in evidence all through the picture. These get the laughs here and there, but the general impression the feature makes is that of strained, over-done burlesque.

THEME. Farce comedy steered along slapstick lines, dealing with love adventures of male stenographer who thinks he is the reincarnation of an Egyptian king.

PRODUCTION HIGHLIGHTS. Scene in which mummy reaches hero's apartment. Bunker's "sideplays" when taking dictation from employer. Romance development. Slapstick stuff, culminating in climax with Bean and rival fighting in pond.

EXPLOITATION ANGLES. Bill this as a comic feature with wildly absurd situations. Tell patrons about Bunker's ambition to imitate royal ancestor and his love affair with boss's daughter.

DRAWING POWER. Not suitable for first-class houses. May pass where fans are satisfied with knockabout clowning and not particular as to story or acting values.

SUMMARY. Starts as straight comedy, but whirls abruptly into slapstick, pushed to excess and maintained up to climax. Rough-house work amusing in spots, doesn't hold interest. No appeal for sophisticated movie fans.

THE CAST

Bunker Bean	Matt Moore
Marie Breede	Dorothy Devore
Bud Matthews	David Butler
Jim Breede	George Nichols
Mrs. Breede	Helen Dunbar
Grandma Breede	Gertrude Clair
Bert Hollins	Gayne Whitman

Adapted from Novel and Stage Play by Harry Leon Wilson. Director, Harry Beaumont.

SYNOPSIS. Bunker Bean, millionaire Jim Breede's stenographer, inherits money, is persuaded by phoney clairvoyants that he is a reincarnation of an Egyptian king, and buys from them a mummy supposed to be his royal self. Full of conquering confidence, he wins the love of Breede's daughter, Marie. The mummy turns out to be a fake. Bunker becomes timid again, but finally rallies and weds Marie.

Matt Moore in "His Majesty Bunker Bean"—Warner Bros.

Was It Bigamy

(William Steiner Prod.—5000 Feet)

(Reviewed by George T. Pardy)

AN inferior production and poor investment for the exhibitor, excepting as half of a double bill, or in houses where a daily change policy prevails. Its plot is rather absurd, decidedly unconvincing and the director hasn't improved matters any, padding it out with entirely superfluous detail. The heroine finds herself in a fix because she has married two men, although in each case it is made clear that she is "a wife in name only." She dreads being prosecuted for bigamy, which, under the circumstances, isn't surprising, even if she acted under generous motives, wedding hubby number one to reform him, and the second in order to save her beloved guardian from going to jail. The trouble with the yarn is that you can't imagine any female outside of a half-wit, getting snared in such a foolish fashion.

The acting of Edith Thornton and Earle Williams in the leading roles is the film's best box office asset. But even Miss Thornton, with all her charm and sincerity, can't do much with an impossible part. Williams, as Steele, isn't quite so badly handicapped, and gives a capable performance.

THEME. Domestic drama, wherein girl, to save guardian from jail, weds second husband while first is still alive.

PRODUCTION HIGHLIGHTS. Acting of principals. Scene where Ruth Sedley finds first husband a drunken degenerate, living with native woman, and his death by an avenging bullet.

EXPLOITATION ANGLES. Your best plan is to play up Edith Thornton and Earle Williams as much as possible, as both are well-known players. The title may draw, feature it, but don't promise too much as regards story.

DRAWING POWER. Only suitable for daily change house, or as half of double bill.

SUMMARY. Domestic drama, weak, unconvincing plot, with heroine in trouble because she weds two men and fears prosecution. Edith Thornton and Earle Williams, the leads, save the picture from being a complete flop, but it won't do for discriminating audiences.

THE CAST

Ruth Sedley	Edith Thornton
Carlton Steele	Earle Williams
Judge Gaynor	Thomas Ricketts
Harvey Gaynor	Charles Cruz
Attorney	Wilfred Lucas

Author, Forrest Sheldon. Directed by Charles Hutchison.

SYNOPSIS. Harvey, son of Judge Gaynor, induces Ruth Sedley, his father's ward, to marry him under promise of reformation from his idle life. He goes to South America. Judge discovers son has stolen bonds belonging to client Carlton Steele. Ruth overhears Judge threatened with prison by Steele, unless she weds latter. She consents second marriage with Steele. Later, she goes to Harvey, Steele following. Finds Harvey a drunkard, living with native woman. Harvey is killed by native. Steele and Ruth admit their mutual love.

Charles Hutchinson, who directed "Was It Bigamy!" for William Steiner Productions.

The Prairie Pirate
(Producers Distributing Corp.—4603 Feet)
(Reviewed by George T. Pardy)

A BORDER tale melodrama which sizzles with speedy action and puts the thrill punches over in decisive style! Wherever good Westerners are in demand this picture will surely please and hold its own at the box office. As is the case with most features of the kind, the probabilities are considerably stretched, but this fact does not detract from the film's market value as entertainment for an extremely large class of movie-goers, the members of which are content, so long as they get enough excitement for their money.

Harry Carey, as the young ranchman who turns outlaw to avenge his sister's murder, plays the role with unfailing dash and energy, and Trilby Clark, a bewitching little brunette, registers as a very fascinating Spanish heroine. Director Edmund Mortimer has had especially good luck with his color effects, all the backgrounds are exceedingly picturesque and the shots of the Mexican fiestas oddly alluring, with their display of quaint costumes and graceful charm.

THEME. Border melodrama in which young ranchman turns bandit to avenge sister's death, accomplishes purpose and wins beautiful senorita for wife.

PRODUCTION HIGHLIGHTS. Melodramatic sweep and speed of action. The picturesque surroundings. Colorful atmosphere. Harry Carey's virile acting, horsemanship and athletic activities. Big scene where he overcomes enemy he sought.

EXPLOITATION ANGLES. Bill this as a rip-roaring border melodrama, crammed with suspense, exciting sequences, and offering a pleasing love romance. Feature Carey, and tell the fans this is one of his very best.

DRAWING POWER. A banner attraction for any house where Westerners are popular.

SUMMARY. Colorful Westerner, charged with fast action and thrills, has romantic appeal, a strenuous border melodrama, with Harry Carey in a part that will please all his admirers.

THE CAST
Brian Delaney..Harry Carey
Ruth Delaney..Jean Dumas
Howard Steele..Lloyd Whitlock
Teresa Esteban...Trilby Clark
Jose...Tote Ducrow
Don Esteban..Robert Edeson
Aguilar..Fred Kohler
Adapted from "The Yellow Seal," by W. C. Tuttle. Director, Edmund Mortimer. Photographed by Georges Benoit.

SYNOPSIS. His sister's murder causes Ranchman Brian Delaney to become a bandit seeking revenge. He raids Steele's gambling house and aids Don Esteban and latter's daughter Teresa, who are in gambler's power. Later, he stops wedding between Steele and the girl, is wounded, but carries her off. When Steele comes to his hiding place, he overcomes him, disguises him in his clothes and the gambler is killed by posse in pursuit of Brian. It transpires that Steele was the murderer. Brian and Teresa are united.

The Pony Express
(Paramount—9929 Feet)
(Reviewed by George T. Pardy)

DIRECTOR JAMES CRUZE has added another brilliant success to his screen triumphs, "The Pony Express." It would be futile to indulge in comparisons between the new feature and its predecessors of historical significance, the worth-while facts being that this picture excels in its own particular period, offers splendid entertainment, and having lived up to its advance notices, should, with the great advertising campaign made by Famous-Lasky in its behalf, register a sure-fire box office hit.

The exploits of the pony-riders and undercurrent of events leading up toward the outbreak of the Civil War are fused into a stirring melodrama which is curiously convincing in its colorful realism, because the on-looker knows it stands upon a firm historical foundation, and a love affair between the hero and Betty Compson supplies the necessary sentimental lure. The work of the entire cast is superb, with performances by Ernest Torrence, George Bancroft, Wallace Beery, Ricardo Cortez and Miss Compson standing out in bold relief.

THEME. Melodrama, with American historical background, staged during days of pony express riders.

PRODUCTION HIGHLIGHTS. The feature's spectacular appeal, magnificent scenic shots and melodramatic thrills; good direction and work of cast.

EXPLOITATION ANGLES. Feature this as another triumph for the man who directed "The Covered Wagon." Stress the picture's historical accuracy and educational values, melodramatic thrills and scenic beauty. Every member of the cast is worth advertising.

DRAWING POWER. Should get the money in any theatre, large or small.

SUMMARY. A great historical feature with melodrama and romance craftily interwoven. Crammed with thrills, ablaze with colorful scenery. Has sure spectacular appeal for all classes of movie patrons.

THE CAST
Molly Jones..Betty Compson
Jack Weston...Ricardo Cortez
Ascension Jones...Ernest Torrence
Rhode Island Red...Wallace Beery
Jack Slade..George Bancroft
Charlie Bent..Frank Lackteen
Billy Cody...John Fox, Jr.
William Russell...William Turner
Senator Glen..Al Hart
Sam Clemens..Charles Gerson
Author, Henry James Forman. Director, James Cruze. Photographed by Karl Brown.

SYNOPSIS. In 1860 Jack Weston, pony express rider, is rival of Jack Slade, gunman and superintendent Overland Express Company, for the hand of Molly Jones, belle of Julesberg, Colorado. Slade plans to send fake dispatch announcing Lincoln's defeat in Presidential election. Jack foils him by riding West with the true news. California declares for the Union. Jack and Molly wed, as war between North and South is declared.

Harry Carey, star of "The Prairie Pirate," Producers Distributing Corporation.

The Prairie Pirate (Producers Dis. Corp.)
PRESS NOTICE

HARRY CAREY appears as the dashing hero of "The Prairie Pirate," a stirring Western melodrama slated for the screen of the .... Theatre on .... This is a border tale, remarkable for its colorful settings, breath-taking thrill scenes, and virile work of the star, whose horsemanship stunts and fighting ability have never been so successfully demonstrated. There's an appealing love romance involved, with beautiful Trilby Clark as a Spanish senorita heroine.

The hero turns outlaw to avenge a sister's murder, fulfills his oath and wins the Spanish girl.

CATCH LINES
He turned bandit to avenge his sister's murder, and became the scourge of the border, helping the poor, robbing the rich and defying his pursuers.

Harry Carey as "The Yellow Seal," the border bandit who trailed to death the man who slew his sister and won the love of a lovely senorita.

James Cruze, production of Paramount's The Pony Express.

The Pony Express (Paramount)
PRESS NOTICE

"THE PONY EXPRESS," a huge and colorful epic of American history, crammed with melodramatic thrills aglow with spectacular shots of wonderful scenic beauty, and offering an alluring love romance, will be the main attraction at the .... Theatre on ....

James Cruze, the man who produced "The Covered Wagon" directed this amazing film, which no patron of the silent drama can afford to miss.

Ricardo Cortez and Betty Compson play the hero and heroine.

CATCH LINES
A picture that will awaken patriotic pride in the breast of every true American who sees it.

A wonderful spectacle of scenic beauty, a crashing melodrama, a beautiful love story, a great educational factor.

Children and adults alike will thrill to the sensational punches and intense human interest of this vivid American historical epic.

The Dark Angel
(First National—7311 Feet)
(Reviewed by George T. Pardy)

TRAGIC suggestion and intense pathos are the mainsprings of this Samuel Goldwyn production, which nevertheless ends on a cheerful note, is brimful of sentimental lure, never carried to excess, and always convincing. It is well directed and beautifully photographed, the views of the hunt, the quiet beauty of the English landscapes, symbolic touches showing Death's shadowy angel hovering overhead, are all perfect examples of camera technique, and a couple of battle shots, with trench backgrounds and artillery in action register as the very acme of war realism. Also, the picture introduces in the personality of Vilma Banky, who plays the feminine lead, an actress of genuine talent who must be reckoned with in considering the future's lineup of budding screen stars.

Physically attractive, she is natural and wistfully appealing in the emotional phases of a difficult role. Ronald Colman has never appeared to such good advantage as in the part of hero Captain Trent, and the support is faultless.

THEME. Heart drama in which soldier hero goes blind and is willing to sacrifice future happiness by dissuading sweetheart from marrying him, but girl remains faithful.

PRODUCTION HIGHLIGHTS. Charming scenic views, realistic battle shots. Sustained heart interest. Scene in which hero conceals his blindness and greets fiancee coldly. Fine acting of Ronald Colman, Vilma Banky and support.

EXPLOITATION ANGLES. Make it plain that this is not a straight war play, although some battle stuff is shown. Stress the sympathetic side, the lover's attempted self-sacrifice, the exquisite scenery and good acting.

DRAWING POWER. Should satisfy all classes of patrons in big and little houses.

SUMMARY. A gripping drama of love and devotion, with war angle on which plot revolves. Is beautifully photographed, well acted and directed. Possesses universal appeal.

THE CAST

Captain Trent	Ronald Colman
Kitty Vane	Vilma Banky
Captain Shannon	Wyndham Standing
Lord Beaumont	Frank Elliott
Sir Hubert Vane	Charles Lane
Miss Pindle	Helen Jerome Eddy
Roma	Florence Turner

Adapted from H. B. Trevelyan's Stage Play. Directed by George Fitzmaurice.

SYNOPSIS. Ordered suddenly back to the front, Captain Trent and his fiancee, Kitty Vane, spend their parting night together at an inn. Trent is blinded, taken prisoner, and reported dead. Time passes, and Kitty finally consents to wed Gerald Shannon, a friend of Trent's. Gerald finds Trent alive and writing for a living. He is loyal and tells Kitty. She goes to Trent, who conceals his blindness and pretends he no longer cares for her. But Kitty discovers the ruse and they are united.

Vilma Banky, star of "The Dark Angel." First National.

The Cyclone Cavalier
(Rayart—4928 Feet)
(Reviewed by George T. Pardy)

AN amusing comedy, with occasional melodramatic splurges verging close on the mock-heroic margin, this picture classes as a sufficiently entertaining program attraction. It has the familiar background of a Central American revolution and equally familiar U. S. hero, whose activities in dodging and overcoming foes and making love to a pretty Spanish girl are constantly in evidence. Not much to the plot, but plenty of slapstick fun and startling acrobatic stunts performed by Reed Howes, the good-looking, agile star. Director Albert Rogell keeps the action pot boiling over all the time, there certainly isn't a dull moment in the film, and the chances are strong that it will score a hit with a majority of the fans.

Carmelita Geraghty gives a vivaciously pleasing performance as the girl in the case, Jack Mower is a sinister figure as he stalks about in cloak and sombrero, as the villainous El Diablo, and the support is effective.

THEME. Comedy-melodrama, with young American foiling Central American revolutionists and winning President's daughter.

PRODUCTION HIGHLIGHTS. The ceaseless swing of action. Attractive scenic shots. Reed Howes' acrobatic stunts. Amusing slapstick comedy. Scene where Howe displays swordmanship and holds palace stairs against attacking party. Romantic interest.

EXPLOITATION ANGLES. Feature Reed Howes as the handsome lover and play up his gymnastic stunts. Bill as amusing comedy with melodramatic thrills and love affair. Mention colorful backgrounds and Carmelita Geraghty's good work.

DRAWING POWER. O. K. for neighborhood and smaller houses.

SUMMARY. Offers Central American background, with U. S. hero upsetting revolutionary plans, winning President's gratitude and pretty daughter. Lively comedy with melo thrills interpolated, burlesque suggestion and fast action throughout. Pleasing program production.

THE CAST

Ted Clayton	Reed Howes
Rosita Gonzales	Carmelita Geraghty
Hugh Clayton	Wilfred Lucas
President Gonzales	Eric Mayne
El Diablo	Jack Mower
Micky	Johnny Sinclair
Van Blatten	Ervin Renard

Author, Krag Johnson. Directed by Albert Rogell.

SYNOPSIS. Ted Clayton goes to Central America on father's business. He gets in bad with the President, but falls in love with latter's daughter. His pal Micky, Ted overhears the plans of one El Diablo to overthrow Government. After many adventures, he convinces President of his friendship, defends the palace against revolutionaries until loyal troops arrive, wins the father's gratitude and girl's love.

Reed Howes starred by Rayart in "The Cyclone Cavalier."

Going the Limit

(Gerson Pictures—5000 Feet)

(Reviewed by George T. Pardy)

A BRISK mystery melodrama, chiefly remarkable for its lively action and agile stunt work of the star, Richard Holt. The plot isn't much out of the ordinary, but by speeding it up to the 'steenth degree and never allowing Mr. Holt a chance to sit down and recuperate, Director Duke Worne has turned out an amusing film which should prove acceptable entertainment for the fans who like the leading man's stuff and welcome exciting jolts. The heiress heroine is abducted early in the game and when Richard gets after the crooks who trapped her, there is always something doing in the fervid thrill line. The finale comes after a wild chase up and down hill that is full of fresh and thoroughly unexpected angles and a decided novelty of its kind.

As in his previous films, Dick Holt is at his best when dodging around in the stunt situations, but his performance on the whole is creditable, and Ruth Dwyer figures as a very appealing and good-to-look-atheroine, with other members of the cast rendering adequate support.

THEME. Crook melodrama, with hero performing neck-breaking stunts and rescuing girl from underworld gang.

PRODUCTION HIGHLIGHTS. The athletic stunts pulled by Richard Holt. Scene where heroine is kidnapped by crooks. The fast action and bewilderingly rapid chase of gangsters which winds up story.

EXPLOITATION ANGLES. Feature the stunt work of star and mystery plot. Play up the big climax, with the hunt after the crooks through San Francisco streets.

DRAWING POWER. Good for any house where Holt is popular and the patrons want fast melodrama, with vivid stunt trimmings.

SUMMARY. Mystery melodrama, puts over decisive punches and thrills, with Dick Holt performing all kinds of amazing stunts. A good card, if your patrons are strong for exciting screen fare.

THE CAST

Ted Van Brunt	Richard Holt
Helen Hayward	Ruth Dwyer
Lung Duck	Garry O'Dell
Meg.	Miriam Fouche
Eddie	Robert Cosgriff
Dr. Rosaro	Hal Stephens
Lorenzo Hayward	Rupert Drum

Author, Grover Jones. Director, Duke Worne. Photographed by Alfred Gosden.

SYNOPSIS. While touring Japan, Ted Van Brunt meets and falls in love with Helen Hayward, American girl. He returns to the U. S. Later Helen arrives home. She finds her father in the power of Dr. Rosaro, who has interested the old man in occult teachings. Helen is carried off by one of Rosaro's henchmen. Ted follows, and after a wild pursuit, rescues Helen, who promises to wed him.

Richard Holt, in "Going The Limit."— Gerson Pictures.

The Storm Breaker

(Universal-Jewel—6064 Feet)

(Reviewed by George T. Pardy)

A WHIRLWIND of human emotions and salt sea gales off the rock-bound coast of Nova Scotia, this picture, with its impressively natural settings and fine direction gives House Peters an opportunity to again demonstrate his ability as a de-lineator of strong character roles of which he takes full advantage. As the physically powerful and blatantly confident fisher king of a small isle, Mr. Peters scores heavily, and ends up as a very pa-thetic figure when realization comes that he like other ordinary men, is but the sport of destiny after all. Yet, the finish cannot be listed as unhappy, for it is plainly suggested that the temporarily dis-appointed man, will later find solace in the affections of Judith Nyte, his mother's orphan ward. The feature as a whole is enter-taining and is a likely box office asset.

THEME. Drama with marine atmosphere, depicting fisher-captain's mistaken love for wrong woman, and his sacrifice for brother's sake.

PRODUCTION HIGHLIGHTS. The forceful, appeal-ing work of House Peters in leading role. Picturesque sea views. Romantic complications. Big storm scene when lifeboat is launched and John Strong rescues drowning brother.

EXPLOITATION ANGLES. Play up the magnificent maritime shots, the conflict between hero's affection for brother and love for the girl he desires. Boost House Peters' splendid work and the rescue-dash of lifeboat through raging gale.

DRAWING POWER. Should do good business in any house.

SUMMARY. A drama rich in conflict of emotions, with fine character sketch of rugged, overbearing self-confident fisher-captain by the star. Has strong romantic values and puts over tremendous thrill in big storm and lifeboat rescue scene. Will please any audience.

THE CAST

John Strong	House Peters
Lysette DeJon	Ruth Clifford
Judith Nyte	Nina Romano
Neil Strong	Ray Hallor
Tom North	Jere Austin
Parson	Lionel Belmore
Elspeth Strong	Gertrude Claire
Malcolm	Mark Fenton

Author, Charles Guernon. Director, Edward Sloman. Photo-graphed by Jack Rose.

SYNOPSIS. John Strong, powerful fisher-captain, lives on small isle off Nova Scotia coast with mother, her ward Judith and his younger brother Neil. John falls in love with dainty Lysette DeJon and brings her home. Later it transpires that Neil and Lysette are mutally attracted. The shock of the discovery almost destroys John's confidence in himself. But he rallies and when Neil is lost in a gale, puts out in the life boat and saves him. John leaves home, but it is understood that he will come back for Judith.

House Peters, star of Universal's "The Storm Breaker."

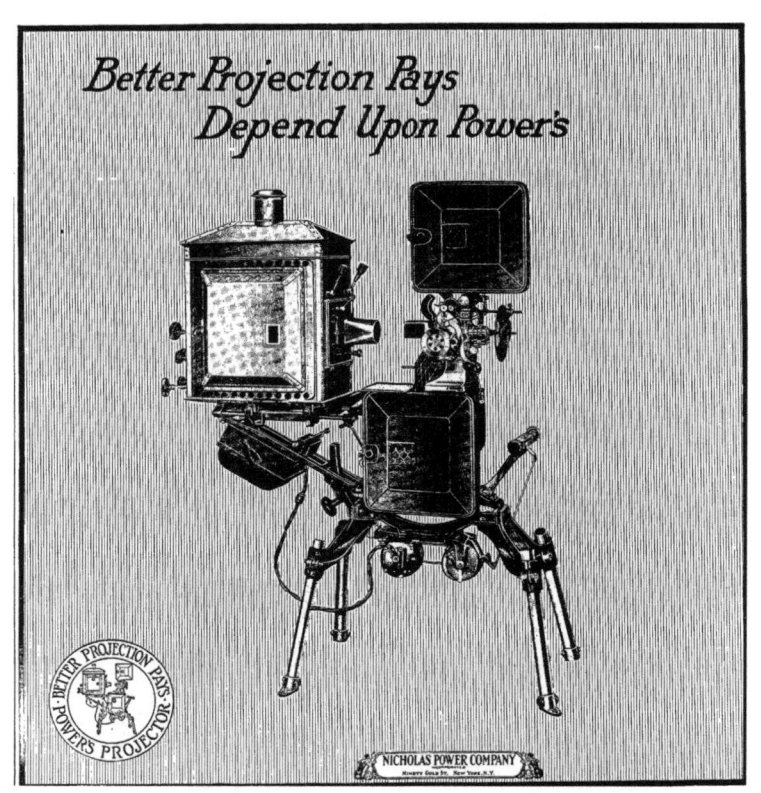

CONSTRUCTION & EQUIPMENT DEPARTMENT

New 600 Seat Theatre Opens on Broadway

Embassy, Managed by Society Leader, Creates Interest Through Unusual Features

A NEW and altogether delightful development in motion picture theatres has come to the fore with the opening of the new Embassy Theatre, Broadway, New York City. This theatre is a small and intimate playhouse dedicated exclusively to the showing of motion pictures without auxiliary features, other than an accompanying orchestra, and as such is proving an unqualified success. Gloria Gould, well known society girl, has been placed in charge of the theatre by Metro-Goldwyn, who controls it.

The Embassy seats but 600 people, and the entire audience views the screen from one floor, there being no balconies, no mezzanines and no boxes. The auditorium is richly and profusely decorated in French baroque, applied in decorative plaster and gilt carvings enhanced by silk damask hangings of deep carmine. Arcade-like side aisles gives access to both auditorium and stage, and wide and graceful side aisles between elaborately ornamented piers outline the wall decorations. These decorations consist of paintings reproducing Gobelin and are chiefly architectural in subject matter. Two of them flank the proscenium and conceal the organ enclosures, and have been painted by Arthur Crisp.

The color scheme, of gold and carmine, has been tastefully executed and is reflected in the richly ornamented ceiling, which is a large indirectly lighted dome surrounded by illuminated art glass panels. The aisles are wide, and the seats, which are covered with tapestry and have carmine lacquered arms and black lacquer and gold standards and

Construction Starts on New Roxy Theatre

CONSTRUCTION is to start immediately upon the New York Theatre to be built for Samuel (Roxy) Rothafel, according to Walter W. Ahlschlager of Chicago, who is completing plans for the big New York structure. According to the architect the theatre will be the largest, and he believes, the finest in the world. It will have 6,210 seats, consisting of 3,200 on the main floor 910 seats on the loge and 2,100 seats in the balcony.

There will be three high speed passenger elevators to the balcony and separate and private stairways leading from the foyer to the loge. Entrance from Seventh Avenue will be by means of an outer foyer 100 feet wide, 120 feet long and 20 feet high, which will lead to a grand salon 60 feet wide and 100 feet deep and 60 feet long. The project, it is estimated will cost $6,000,000.

The president and managing director will be Samuel (Roxy) Rothafel, until recently managing director of the Capitol Theatre, situated 150 feet away from the entrance to the new house.

backs, are roomy and comfortable. A proper balance of direct and indirect lighting has contributed effective illumination, added to the decorative ensemble and established a most pleasing atmosphere. The lighting fixtures, which were especially designed for

this theatre, are of bronze and cut glass.

The lobby and vestibule have been done in marble, the stone panels being set off with bronze display frames, mirrors and decorative plaster work. A richly carved circassian walnut and marble advertising kiosk takes the usual place of the ticket booth, the ticket office having been placed in the lobby. The men's smoking rooms and ladies' retiring rooms are accessible from the lobby and have canvas covered walls portraying decorative subjects in, respectively, the style of the Francis I and Chinese Chippendale periods. The marque is distinctive, varying radically in design from the usual canopy. Public telephones are available in the rest rooms off the lobby, and elaborate heating and ventilating systems have been installed, insuring clean, comfortable atmosphere at all times.

Perhaps the most notable feature of the presentation is the excision of all auxiliary program features with the exception of the accompanying orchestra, which in this case delivers the famous Franz Lehar score with brilliant effect. All seats are reserved, and it is planned to continue to play attractions on the long run policy at a two dollar top. The theatre, having entrances on both Broadway and 46th Street, is well located in the very busiest center of New York's theatrical district.

Exhibitors throughout the industry are watching closely the progress of the Embassy. It is prophesied that the theatre will be largely copied in size and in details of management throughout the country.

Two views of the interior of the Embassy Theatre, Broadway, New York City, which has a seating capacity of only 600, and which incorporates many unusual features in its design. The house is complete in all its appointments and presents an exceedingly attractive appearance.

Interior of the Embassy Theatre on Broadway, New York City, of which Gloria Gould, society leader, is managing director. This house is owned by the Metro-Goldwyn Corporation and was opened recently to a brilliant first night.

Theatre Construction News From Central Section

Theodore Gray, South Eleventh Street, Springfield, Ill., has let a building contract to O'Shea Brothers, 1214 East Jefferson Street, for a one-story, 65 by 115 ft. theatre building on North Grande, between 8th and 9th Streets. It is reported that the house will cost $250,000.

Hagerman & Harshman have the contract for the construction of a new theatre at Sul-

livan, Ill. The building will be two story, 40 by 70 feet and cost about $30,000. The names of the owners are being withheld for the time being.

J. M. Ensor who operates the Crescent Theatre in Little Rock, Ark., plans to build a new house at 2618 East Sixth Street and has taken bids from contractors. The house will be one story, 60 by 140 feet and cost about $25,000. Wittenberg, Delony & Watts, 408 Southern Trust Building, Little Rock, are the architects.

ROME THEATRE, PLEASANTVILLE N.Y.   OSCAR VATET
                                                  ARCHITECT

$250,000 Theatre is to Be Erected at Lankershim, Cal.

Plans have been announced for a $250,000 theatre to be erected at Lankershim Boulevard and Weddington Avenue on plot 100 x 210 ft. on Lankershim, California. The theatre will be of latest design and will have a seating capacity of 1500 persons. This site has been leased by the Hollywood Theatres, Inc., from The Weddington Investment Company for a period of ninety-nine years.

New Theatre on Walnut St., Springfield, Mass.

John W. Foster is drawing plans for the erection of a theatre building on Walnut Street near Union Street, Springfield, Mass. The building will have three stores on the street front. The approximate cost is to be $65,000. The owner of the new structure is Hyman Kroniek, of Springfield, Mass.

New House to Be Erected in Sullivan, Illinois

Sullivan, Illinois, is to have a new movie theatre to be erected on the east side of the Square. The theatre building will cost in the neighborhood of $30,000. The owner of the new structure will be J. H. Ireland of 608 South Haworth Avenue, Decatur.

Projection
Optics, Electricity, Practical Ideas & advice

Inquiries and Comments

Proper Screen Borders

HE field immediately surrounding a motion picture screen exercises considerable influence on the appearance of the projected picture as explained in the preceding article and for this reason

Figure three.

should receive rather careful consideration if best results are desired.

The psychology of most exhibitors is rather difficult to understand. Some will go to considerable expense in the way of installing first class projection room equipment and accessories but will attempt to struggle along with an antiquated screen which bears the accumulations of three years' dust. When the quality of projection is not up to snuff they are at a loss to account for it and will usually blame everything in sight but the thing that is actually causing the trouble.

Others will concentrate their efforts at improvement on the screen to the neglect of everything else and will ordinarily arrive at the same conclusions reached by the first class; i.e., that any money spent for projection equipment is just so much good money tossed out the window.

There is a third group, quite small to be sure, but growing, who conscientiously provide what they honestly believe to be all the necessary equipment for good screen results but fall down on the final step—that of providing the proper projection environment.

This is due not so much to unwillingness to meet the necessary requirements but rather to a lack of knowledge as to just what is required in the way of screen surroundings to secure the desired effect.

Recommendations

The requirements for perfect projection may be summarized as follows:

(1) The illumination of the picture must be sufficiently brilliant to eliminate the Purkinje effect for normal untinted films.

(2) It will be an advantage if the brilliance is increased till the eye is at its maximum sensitiveness for contrast and change of tone, i.e., at the steepest part of its gamma curve (see Fig. 1, preceding articles).

(3) Dazzle should be eliminated by bringing the general lighting of the theatre *right up to the margins of the picture.*

(4) This should be in such a way that the general light does not reach the screen itself. When un-illuminated by the projector the screen should appear darker than the walls or background.

(5) The contrast illumination of the background should be of such an order that the highest lights of the picture have at least *ten times* its intrinsic brilliancy and the shadows less than *one-third.* An actual black will be obtained in the shadows of normal pictures and the true illusion of night in the dark-blue scenes will be preserved. The border will provide a standard light for scaling tone values and determine the iris aperture of the eye. (The scheme of theatre lighting developed and recommended by the research laboratory of the Eastman Kodak Co., seems to bear this out.)

The question now remains, how are these points to be achieved in practice? The problem is divided naturally into two parts —the improvement of existing theatres and the design of new ones.

How to Do It

In Fig. 3 is shown a sketch of the interior of a typical small theatre, looking toward the screen, with the faults of illumination emphasized. The screen is set in a ground actually or virtually black—that is to say, maintained at an illumination much less than the darkest part of the picture. The walls being darker in body color than the screen, and the side lamps exposed in every direction, the screen receives more scattered light than any part of the house. The rows of lamps down the sides do not provide peripheral illumination of the right kind to influence the iris aperture. During projection the center of interest wanders from point to point on the screen and is followed by movements of the eye to bring the center on to the yellow spot and favea (for sharp vision). The outer part of the yellow spot is therefore sometimes focussed on the black surrounding border and sometimes on the bright picture. The images of the side lamps wander similarly on the peripheral region. *This induces alternate contrast of the worst kind and leads to eyestrain and faulty appreciation (of the picture.)*

The first thing to be done is to shield the lamps with large diffusers towards the audience and with opaque masks, towards the screen. Then any dark curtains or background should be removed from the

latter and a uniformly distempered border substituted. This could be illuminated in various ways, of which two will be indicated. If the screen could be brought forward a little, lamps could be placed behind and supplied with current through resistances to provide exactly appropriate lighting. Or a suitable stereoptican lantern might be housed in the projection room ("Projector box" was the author's phrasing) and, with a transparent slide having a central opaque rectangle (of exact aperture proportions), throw an annular (hollow) beam of light on the border and background.

Improvements

Apart from the improved tone values such an arrangement would give, it would remove the effect, so noticeable at present, of the picture being suspended without human aid in space. It would give the much truer illusion of gazing through a window on a scene taking place outside. (This explains the effects obtained in the United States by Mr. Martin with his illuminated border which, incidentally, the inventor himself seemed unable to satisfactorily explain.

The effect might be developed by giving the background some form associated with walls and windows—*not colonnades or elaborate framing* which, guessed at in the semi-darkness, would only distract the eye, but a *symmetrical paneling or graining.* The presence of a regular pattern, as illustrated in Fig. 4, would emphasize the structural purity of the picture and minimize its granularity.

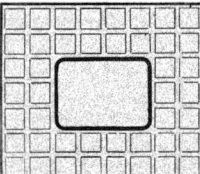

Figure four.

It will be recalled that the editor of this department has consistently recommended a scheme of picture border similar in general effects to that described by Dr. Hickman—that is, placing a jet black narrow border (about 4 to 6 inches wide depending on picture size) around the picture area and then using a large surrounding border of gray material (such as velvet) to prevent eyestrain and bring forth the tonal values of the picture at the same time giving the illusion of perspective.

(*To be concluded next week*)

MODERN THEATRE SEATING

Beauty and Value

THERE are two very sound reasons for the amazing growth of popularity which Steel Furniture Company seating is now enjoying.

First, is outstanding beauty of design. In fine color harmonies, skillfully balanced proportions, and luxurious upholsteries, Steel Theatre Chairs are masterpieces of their kind.

Second, is the equally important fact that this better seating is offered at prices which indicate truly remarkable value.

If you are contemplating seating for a new theatre or new seating for an old one, you owe it to yourself to investigate the Steel line. The complete catalog and the services of experienced seating engineers are yours for the asking.

STEEL FURNITURE CO.
GRAND RAPIDS, MICHIGAN

Architect's drawings of the new Roxy (Samuel Rothapfel) theatre which is to be built between 50th and 51st Streets on Seventh Avenue, New York City. According to the architect, the theatre will be the largest in the world, with a seating capacity of 6,210. There will be three high speed elevators to the balcony, and separate and private stairways leading from the foyer to loges.

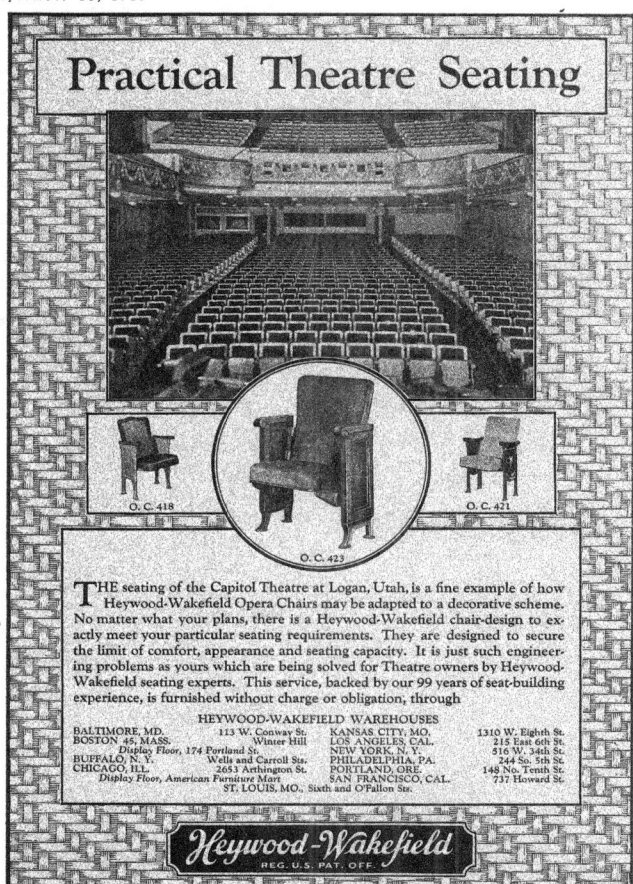

assured that its appeal is negatived 50 per cent or over. It is difficult for the public to become interested in any thing that is hard to decipher or that is not clearly defined.

To bring out the value of proper lobby illumination we can again best illustrate by reverting to the store window simile. Just imagine the strides that have been taken in the lighting of store windows. From the period when merchants with the advancement of superior police protection began dispensing with the heavy shutters and blinds that were used to cover their entire windows at night, up to the present day of brilliantly lighted store fronts that are visible for blocks, the matter of utilizing window space for night displays of merchandise, has demanded the attention of experts, an attention that has reached not only into the offices of the greatest advertising geniuses the Columbus Circle district, at a time nearest dusk. The crowds, buildings, streets, differ but little from the other cities.

But all of a sudden, one by one the theatre, window front, and roof sign and flashers are turned on, and what a transformation. That which a few minutes ago was a scene that could be duplicated in almost any large city, is now the only and incomparable Broadway. It was light that caused this transformation. That and nothing more. And so it is with the lighting of the lobby. There isn't a theatre lobby anywhere that shouldn't look infinitely better at night than it does in the daytime. Gilded frames with their high spots of burnished gold, mirrors with their candelabras or bracket lamps, and crystals, are all of them designed and calculated to individually send out their appeal with the aid of proper illumination.

This element in lobby attractiveness is but mounted, and if the subject is a well executed one, is about the most attractive means of lobby advertising. First of all, being a bright spot in itself, it catches the eye at once. Then the rear lighting, if arranged properly, gives added color, tints, and values to the painting or poster, which enhanced by a pretty frame, forms an almost irresistible combination.

Through the proper lighting of mirrors we have another wonderful and valuable night attraction for the lobby. As has been pointed out in previous articles, the lobby mirror is a feminine requisite as well as an ornamental medium, but when properly illuminated, through means of strategically located lamps and candles, several mirrors can transform a modest entrance into a spacious, commodious, magnificent lobby, all through the means of reflection and illusion, superinduced by mirror lighting.

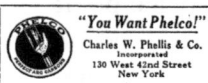

Lyric Theatre in Virginia, Minn., Being Renovated

The old Lyric theatre in Virginia, Minn., is being renovated and repaired for formal opening sometime in October. This house belongs to the Clinton-Meyers Company of Duluth, who also operate the Rex Theatre in Virginia. The name of Lyric will be changed to Lyceum and will be under the management of H. O. Whelpley, who will take care of both theatres.

Pulaski Heights, Ark. to Have New House

Pulaski Heights, Arkansas, is to have a new motion picture theatre, to be erected near Prospect Avenue and Beach Street in the rear of the Nicholson drug store. The new theatre will be 40 x 140 ft. with a seating capacity of 750 persons. It will be a fireproof construction, and the approximate cost of the new theatre will be $25,000. The owner of this new theatre is T. W. Sharp.

Plans Being Drawn for Playhouse for Springfield, Ill.

E. P. Rupert of Chicago is drawing plans for the erection of a playhouse to be erected in Springfield, Illinois, at Fifth and Jefferson Streets, to cost approximately $1,250,000. The theatre is expected to seat 3,000 persons. The new theatre is expected to be one of the most beautiful over which Balaban & Katz, the new theatre merger has assumed charge.

Palace, Toledo, Remodeled, Opens in September

The Palace Theatre, Toledo, Ohio, is now being remodeled and will open this month. New seating, projection machines, screen and many other new equipments are being installed by The Theatre Supply Co., Cleveland, Ohio.

Shea Announces Decorating Plans for New House

Michael Shea, head of the Shea amusement enterprises, announces that more than $300,000 will be spent for decorations and furnishings in the new Shea Buffalo theatre, the exterior work of which is practically completed.

Plans for $100,000 Theatre at Crystal Lake Announced

Plans have been announced for the erection of a theatre building to be erected on Brink Street on plot 82½ x 132 ft. in Crystal Lake, Ill. The new theatre is to have a seating capacity of 1000. It will be of Spanish style and will cost approximately $100,000. The owner of the new theatre is Fred C. Dierking of Chicago.

Theatre and Office Building for New Haven

Contracts have been let by the College Street Corporation of New Haven, Conn. for a theatre and office building on College street near Chapel street, to cost approximately $1,000,000. The J. D. Harrison Construction Co. of New York City are doing the work and A. W. Johnson, 70 East 45th street, New York, is architect.

Blanchard Brothers Doubling Size of Southbridge House

Blanchard Brothers of 291 Main street, Southbridge, Mass., will erect an addition to their theatre at Elm and Main streets which will practically double the present seating capacity. The addition will be 92 feet wide and 100 feet in length. Remodeling of the structure will start at once.

Newspaper Opinions on New Pictures

"Seven Days"—Prod. Dist. Corp., Colony, N. Y.

American: "It is a rattling good comedy. The titles are almost as full of laughs as the action. Some one with a fine sense of comedy wrote them."

Telegraph: "Liberally sprinkled with the good old Al Christie gags, provides a lot of laughs. Eddie Gribbon, as the burglar, takes first honors for fun making with Tom Wilson, as the cop, a close second."

Journal: "You'll enjoy 'Seven Days' at the Colony Theatre. It's packed with every conceivable comedy gag. The fun is fast and furious."

World: "At the Colony there is much to laugh at, as the picture stands, and Mr. Hale, always a free and easy light comedian, is worth anybody's trip there to see him no matter how far in the suburbs you may live. He and the person who thought up snappy sayings with which to hang together the episodes have made the film worthy of Broadway showing."

Herald-Tribune: " 'Seven Days' is the feature at the Colony this week and, having been the rounds, it looks to us like the most amazing picture on Broadway. Al Christie has gathered together a most effective cast for this comedy. Lillian Rich is one of the handsomest and most subtly amusing young stars on the screen."

Mirror: "This is an uproariously funny farce. Director Scott Sidney has packed the picture with hilarious situations, comically interpreted by the players who seem to have entered into the spirit of the yarn with infectious vengeance. Lillian Rich does surprisingly good work as the heroine. Eddie Gribbon is a yell as the burglar while Mabel Julienne Scott, as the spiritualistic novice, is simply corking. Even the subtitles, of which there are comparatively few, contribute to the fun."

Daily News: "'Seven Days' is the happiest choice for the movie-going on Broadway this week. The audience laughed and chuckled and chuckled and laughed. Spanking good entertainment. If you don't laugh you're just pretending."

"Seven Days"—Prod. Dist. Corp., Forum, L. A.

Herald: "Laughing incessantly until their sides ached, the first night audiences accorded a riotous welcome to 'Seven Days' at the Forum. Lillian Rich takes full advantage of opportunity displaying her skill as comedienne and laugh follows laugh from the time she is first flashed on the screen until the end of the picture. Recent comedies have been notoriously lacking in plot, but here is a picture which not only has a main plot that is bound to be humorous, but also subplots galore."

Examiner: "'Seven Days' at the Forum keeps audiences shrieking with laughter. Laughs?

Thousands of them! 'Seven Days' is the last word in merriment. The audiences roared, chuckled and shrieked all day yesterday at the Forum."

Times: "'Seven Days' proves a hilarious joy fest."

"The Mystic"—M.-G.-M., Capitol, N. Y.

American: "I should say 'The Mystic' is rattling good entertainment. Who doesn't like to see the tricks of a successful medium revealed in a way that makes one chuckle at one's stupidity? The gypsy costume and free and easy manners suit Aileen Pringle, who makes Zara, the gypsy medium, a person of distinction and interest. The psychic powers of Zara are laid bare in a screen drama that is unusual enough to insure the Capitol Theatre a very profitable week."

Times: "Tod Browning has another original and stirring production at the Capitol this week. Conway Tearle and Aileen Pringle are excellent in their particular roles."

Sun: "Mr. Browning reveals himself once more as possessed of an unusual aptitude for casting a weird, tense atmosphere around a given melodramatic plot. The shadowy composition of scenes is excellent. I should say that 'The Mystic' is worth seeing."

Telegram: "If the true test of any form of entertainment is its capacity for holding interest, then 'The Mystic' is good entertainment, for you never weary of it during the hour it is on. So artfully has Browning worked that the Capitol audience yesterday was tense and amused during the seances in the film."

Mirror: " 'The Mystic' is an enthralling crook drama with a refreshing new touch. Aileen Pringle puts fire and zip into her role, and Mitchell Lewis is simply priceless. The story gallops in the wake of Jimmie Burton, clever crook, who utilizes the mediumistic guiles of a Hungarian gypsy and her two assistants, polishing these off into entertaining rogues."

Evening World: "'The Mystic' is bound to prove very popular, if only for its revelations of fraudulent tricks employed at spiritist seances and for the inguious manner in which these revelations are screened. Aileen Pringle does one of the best characterizations of her career as Zara, the gypsy medium."

Graphic: " 'The Mystic' is an engaging film, the story is by Tod Browning, whose production 'The Unholy Three' stamped him as a master director. In 'The Mystic' Browning has done an equally splendid piece of directing. It is a very good story and extremely well told. There are no cumbersome side issues, no long waits, nor over-sustained situations. The story moves forward rapidly, concisely and logically from the opening scenes to the finish."

"Pony Express"—Paramount Imperial, S. F.

Chronicle: "The Pony Express' has swing, sweep, thrill. There is romance, suspense, strength, beauty, in its tale of the brave men who rode the pony express. The picture thrilled an elite and critical crowd and aroused it to applause throughout the length of the film. The Pony Express' is a worthy successor to 'The Covered Wagon.'"

Herald: "It is a lesson in visualized history. Wallace Berry's masterly performance will linger in memory. Several of his scenes are as fine acting as the motion picture camera has recorded."

Examiner: "There has perhaps never been such a moving picture audience as that which crowded the Imperial theatre last night for the premiere of 'The Pony Express.' Gowns and jewels created a replica of the Diamond Horseshoe. A roll call might have been made from the Blue Book and Social Register. Last night's affair at the Imperial will live in the annals of the city's theatrical history as one of brilliance and impressiveness. 'The Pony Express' is more exciting than 'The Covered Wagon.'"

Call: "While Betty Compson, Ricardo Cortez and Ernest Torrence were convincing and picturesque, the picture was stolen by Wallace Berry in the role of Rhode Island Red, a happy-go-lucky tramp, the greatest work of his versatile career. 'The Pony Express' is a truly effective picture—a truly constructive picture —one that must not be missed."

Bulletin: "Brilliant in every particular, spectacular in its introduction and finished throughout, the opening of 'The Pony Express' last night at the Imperial was in every sense of the word a real motion picture premiere. It would have been difficult to have selected a more fitting subject for the Diamond Jubilee week commemorating California's seventy-fifth birthday of her admission to the Union."

News: "Possibly 'The Pony Express' is not as great a picture panoramically as 'The Covered Wagon,' yet it is a greater picture in plot, more thrilling, a great picture historically, with true epic sweep against which is set a moving, thrilling humorous and emotional story. If memory serves right, this is the first time a director who has made an enormous success such as 'The Covered Wagon' has ever repeated with as big a picture. James Cruze is to be congratulated. He has done it again."

"Iron Horse"—Fox, St. Francis, San Francisco.

Call-Post: "Whatever else you do, don't miss 'The Iron Horse.' We ask it for your own sakes. A truly glorious motion picture dramatically, photographically, romantically, historically — came to the St. Francis Theatre last Saturday; and, if salvos of applause at its conclusion are any

criterion, it should still be here when the Christmas holidays roll around."

Examiner: "'The Iron Horse' is a salutary and highly educational picture. A schoolboy who witnesses it may be given a month's vacation, for he has acquired more history than he can usually cram into his head in two months of dull reading. Lest this frighten anybody who hankers for entertainment and hates to be beaned by a textbook in the process, let us qualify the verdict by saying it is as full of action and humor as 'The Covered Wagon.'"

Bulletin: "History and fiction are combined in 'The Iron Horse,' the truly remarkable picture this week at the St. Francis. When it is all said and done, however, it is the historical portion of the picture which furnishes the thrills and the fact that the director, John Ford, followed the true story of the great railroad building epoch of the West makes the film far more interesting than if the scenario had been purely fiction."

Chronicle: "John Ford has created something memorable in 'The Iron Horse,' which is being shown at the St. Francis Theatre; a great picture, one in which the glow of beauty and the glamor of romance cover a tale of vast labor with glory."

"Limited Mail"—Warners, State-Lake, Chicago

American: "Monte Blue, of course, can act. He is whole-souled and natural. Bless him, he makes the whole show whole-souled."

Post: "If you crave action on the screen 'The Limited Mail' was made expressly for you. Don't fail to see it. From the pictorial standpoint, too, it ranks high. Also, the picture has a heart interest story, with Monte Blue, Vera Reynolds, Tom Gallery and little Jackie Huff as the principals. The humor is supplied by Willard Louis. The train episodes, most of them taken in the Royal Gorge of Colorado, are gorgeous. 'The Limited Mail' will amply satisfy those who want to be thrilled."

"The Love Gamble"—Henry Ginsberg, Garden, Milwaukee.

Sentinel: "It is a pleasure once in a while to turn from a picture of the wide open spaces to the more limited confines of a shabby studio on Beacon Hill, the Bohemian Quarter of Boston. A man may be a man, or a woman may be a heroine, riding a hobby instead of a broncho. It also seems to indicate that one may shoot at a high ideal to greater purpose than at a fellow man in chaps and sombrero. Mr. Frazer and Miss Rich do exceptionally fine work and have the support of a clever cast in which James Marcus, Pauline Garon and Arthur Rankin lend admirable support. Robert Frazer has just the right blase manner."

FEATURE RELEASE CHART

Productions are Listed Alphabetically and by Months in which Released in order that the Exhibitor may have a short-cut toward such information as he may need. Short subject and comedy releases, as well as information on pictures that are coming, will be found on succeeding pages. (S. R. indicates State Right release.)

Refer to THE MOTION PICTURE NEWS BOOKING GUIDE for Productions Listed Prior to March

MARCH

Feature	Star	Distributed by	Length	Reviewed
Adventurous Sex, The	Clara Bow	Assoc. Exhib	5039 feet	Mar. 21
Air Mail, The	Special Cast	Paramount	6976 feet	Mar. 28
Beauty and the Bad Man	Special Cast	Prod. Dist. Corp	5794 feet	May 9
Beyond the Border	Harry Carey	Prod. Dist. Corp	4469 feet	April 25
Billy, The Kid	Franklyn Farnum	Inde. Pict. Corp. (S. R.)	4800 feet	
Blood and Steel	Desmond Holmes	Inde. Pict. (S. R.)	5300 feet	
Border Justice	Bill Cody	Inde. Pict. Corp. (S. R.)	5432 feet	Nov. 8
Coast Patrol, The	Kenneth McDonald	Barsky (S. R.)	5000 feet	
Confessions of a Queen	Terry-Stone	Metro-Goldwyn	5820 feet	April 4
Crimson Runner, The	Priscilla Dean	Prod. Dist. Corp	4775 feet	June 6
Daddy's Gone A'Hunting	Joyce-Marmont	Metro-Goldwyn	5851 feet	Mar. 7
Denial, The	Special Cast	Metro-Goldwyn	4791 feet	Mar. 21
Double Action Daniels	Buffalo Bill, Jr	Weiss Bros. (S. R.)	4650 feet	
Dressmaker from Paris, The	Rod La Rocque	Paramount	7080 feet	Mar. 28
Fighting Romeo, A	Al Ferguson	Davis Dist. Div. (S.R.)	5000 feet	Aug. 16
Fighting the Flames	Haines-Devore	C. B. C. (S. R.)	5800 feet	
Forbidden Cargo	Evelyn Brent	F. B. O	4850 feet	April 11
Goose Hangs High, The	Constance Bennett	Paramount	6186 feet	Feb. 14
Great Divide, The	Terry-Tearle	Metro-Goldwyn	7811 feet	Feb. 21
Head Winds	House Peters	Universal	5600 feet	Mar. 28
Hunted Woman, The	Seena Owen	Fox	4954 feet	April 4
I Want My Man	Sills-Kenyon	First National	6175 feet	April 18
Jimmie's Millions	Richard Talmadge	F. B. O	5167 feet	Feb. 28
Just Traveling	Bob Burns	Sierra Pict. (S. R.)	4400 feet	
Last Laugh, The	Emil Jannings	Universal	6519 feet	Dec. 20
Let'er Buck	Hoot Gibson	Universal	5547 feet	Jan. 3
Mad Whirl, The	May McAvoy	Universal	6184 feet	Dec. 6
Marriage in Transit	Edmund Lowe	Fox Film	4800 feet	April 11
Men and Women	Special Cast	Paramount	6223 feet	Mar. 28
Monster, The	L. Chaney-J. Arthur	Metro-Goldwyn	6435 feet	Feb. 28
My Wife and I	Special Cast	Warner Bros	6700 feet	June 6
New Lives for Old	Betty Compson	Paramount	6796 feet	Mar. 7
New Toys	Richard Barthelmess	First National	7250 feet	Feb. 21
One Year to Live	Special Cast	First National	6064 feet	Feb. 28
Percy	Charles Ray	Assoc. Exhib	5384 feet	Feb 28
Playing With Souls	Special Cast	First National	5831 feet	Mar. 14
Price of Pleasure, The	Valli-Kerry	Universal	6618 feet	June 13
Recompense	M. Prevost-M. Blue	Warner Bros	7480 feet	May 2
Renegade Holmes, M.D.	Ben Wilson	Arrow (S. R.)	4947 feet	
Riders of the Purple Sage	Tom Mix	Fox	5578 feet	Mar. 28
Romance and Rustlers	Yakima Canutt	Arrow (S. R.)	4994 feet	Nov. 15
Sackcloth and Scarlet	Alice Terry	Paramount	6732 feet	Mar. 7
Sally	Colleen Moore	First National	8636 feet	Mar. 28
Scar Hanan	Yakima Canutt	F. B. O	4684 feet	April 4
Scarlet Honeymoon, The	Shirley Mason	Fox	5080 feet	Mar. 21
Seven Chances	Buster Keaton	Metro-Goldwyn	5113 feet	Mar. 28
Sign of the Cactus, The	Jack Hoxie	Universal	4989 feet	Jan. 10
Sky Raider, The	Capt. Charles Nungesser	Assoc. Exhib.	6638 feet	April 4
Speed	Betty Blythe	Banner Prod. (S. R.)	6000 feet	May 30
Too Many Kisses	Richard Dix	Paramount	5759 feet	Mar. 14
Waking Up the Town	Jack Pickford	United Artists	4802 feet	April 11
Where Romance Rides	Dick Hatton	Arrow	4801 feet	
Zander the Great	Marion Davies	Metro-Goldwyn	5851 feet	May 16

APRIL

Feature	Star	Distributed by	Length	Reviewed
Adventure	P. Starke-T. Moore	Paramount	6718 feet	April 25
After Business Hours	Hammerstein-Tellegen	C B. C. (S. R.)	5800 feet	
Bandit Tamer, The	Franklyn Farnum	Inde. Pict. (S. R.)	5080 feet	
Border Vengeance	Jack Perrin	Madoc Sales (S. R.)	4500 feet	
Charmer, The	Pola Negri	Paramount	6076 feet	April 18
Code of the West	O. Moore-C. Bennett	Paramount	6777 feet	April 25
Courageous Fool, The	Reed Howes	Rayart (S. R.)		
Crowded Hour, The	Bebe Daniels	Paramount	6558 feet	May 9
Dangerous Innocence	LaPlante-E. O'Brien	Universal	6759 feet	Mar. 21
Declasse	Corinne Griffith	First National	7869 feet	April 4
Eyes of the Desert	Al Richmond	Sierra Prod. (S. R.)	4500 feet	
Fifth Avenue Models	Philbin-Kerry	Universal	6581 feet	Jan. 24
Fighting Parson, The	Al Ferguson	Davis Dist. Div. (S.R.)	5000 feet	
Fighting Sheriff, The	Bill Cody	Inde. Pict. (S. R.)	4500 feet	May 30
Friendly Enemies	Weber and Fields	Prod. Dist. Corp	6288 feet	May 9
Galloping Vengeance	Bob Custer	F. B. O	5095 feet	April 11
Getting 'Em Right	George Larkin	Rayart (S. R.)	4669 feet	
Gold and the Girl	Buck Jones	Fox	4521 feet	April 4
Go Straight	Gladys Hulette	B. P. Schulberg (S.R.)	6107 feet	May 23
Heart of a Siren, The	Barbara La Marr	First National	6700 feet	Mar. 21
How Baxter Butted In	M. Moore-D. Devore	Warner Bros	6659 feet	July 11
Justice Raffles	Henry Edwards	Cranfield & Clarke (S. R.)	6000 feet	
Kiss in the Dark, A	Special Cast	Paramount	5767 feet	April 18
Kiss Me Again	M. Prevost-M. Blue	Warner Bros	7200 feet	June 6
Love's Bargain	M. Daw-C. Brook	F. B. O	5641 feet	April 25
Madame Sans Gene	Gloria Swanson	Paramount	9994 feet	May 2
Man and Maid	Special Cast	Metro-Goldwyn	5307 feet	April 18
My Son	Nazimova-J. Pickford	First National	6500 feet	April 25
Night Club, The	R. Griffith-V. Reynolds	Paramount	5732 feet	May 16
One Way Street	Special Cast	First National	5596 feet	April 11
Proud Flesh	Special Cast	Metro-Goldwyn	5770 feet	April 25
Roaring Adventure, The	Jack Hoxie	Universal	4657 feet	Feb. 14
Ridin' Comet, The	Yakima Canutt	F. B. O	4354 feet	May 16
Rough Going	Franklyn Farnum	Indep. Pict. Corp. (S. R.)	4500 feet	
Shackled Lightning	Frank Merrill	Hercules Prod. (S. R.)		
She Wolves	Alma Rubens	Fox	57.3 feet	May 9
Spaniard, The	Cortez-Goudal	Paramount	6676 feet	April 18
Sporting Venus	Special Cast	Metro-Goldwyn	5938 feet	May 23
Stop Flirting	Special Cast	Prod. Dist. Corp	5161 feet	June 6
Straight Through	Wm. Desmond	Universal	4867 feet	
Tale of a Thousand and One Nights	Special Cast	Davis Dist. Div. (S. R.)	6500 feet	Feb. 14
Tearing Through	Richard Talmadge	F. B. O.	4714 feet	May 23
That Devil Quemado	Fred Thomson	F. B. O.	4768 feet	April 4
Two-Fisted Sheriff, A	Yakima Canutt	Arrow (S. R.)	4149 feet	Dec. 6
Way of a Girl, The	Boardman-M. Moore	Metro-Goldwyn	5025 feet	April 18
Western Engagement, A	Dick Hatton	Arrow		
Wings of Youth	Madge Bellamy	Fox	5340 feet	May 16
Winning a Woman	Perrin-Hill	Rayart (S. R.)	4865 feet	

MAY

Feature	Star	Distributed by	Length	Reviewed
Alias Mary Flynn	Evelyn Brent	F. B. O.	5559 feet	May 30
Any Woman	Alice Terry	Paramount	5963 feet	June 13
Awful Truth, The	Agnes Ayres	Prod. Dist. Corp	5917 feet	July 11
Bandit's Baby, The	Fred Thomson	F. B. O.	5291 feet	June 20
Bares Son of Kazan	Wolf (dog)	Vitagraph	7 reels	May 2
Barriers of the Law	Holmes-Desmond	Indep. Pict. (S. R.)	5400 feet	
Burning Trail, The	William Desmond	Universal	4783 feet	April 18
Chickie	Mackaill-Bosworth	First National	7767 feet	May 9
Crackerjack, The	Johnny Hines	C. C. Burr (S. R.)	6500 feet	May 23
Every Man's Wife	Special Cast	Fox	4365 feet	July 4
Eve's Lover	Irene Rich	Warner Bros	6540 feet	Aug. 8
Eve's Secret	Betty Compson	Paramount	6305 feet	May 9
Fear Fighter, The	Billy Sullivan	Rayart (S. R.)		
Fighting Demon, The	Richard Talmadge	F B O	5470 feet	June 20
Fugitive, The	Ben Wilson	Arrow	4892 feet	
Golden Trails		Sanford Prod. (S. R.)	5 reels	
His Supreme Moment	B Sweet-R Colman	First National	6600 feet	April 25
Lilies of the Streets	J. Walker-V. L. Corbin	F. B. O.	7160 feet	April 25
Little French Girl, The	Alice Joyce	Paramount	5628 feet	June 13
Lunatic at Large, A	Henry Edwards	Cranfield & Clarke (S. R.)	6000 feet	
Makers of Men	Kenneth McDonald	Barsky Prod. (S. R.)	5000 feet	
Necessary Evil, The	Dana-Lyon	First National	6307 feet	May 23
Old Home Week	Thomas Meighan	Paramount	6888 feet	June 6
Phantom Rider, The	Al Richmond	Sierra Prod. (S. R.)	4750 feet	
Private Affairs	Special Cast	Prod. Dist. Corp	6132 feet	Aug. 15
Quick Change	George Larkin	Rayart (S. R.)		
Raffles, The Amateur Cracksman	House Peters	Universal	5557 feet	May 30
Rainbow Trail, The	Tom Mix	Fox	5251 feet	April 25
Red Love	Lowell-Russell	Lowell Film Prod. (S. R.)	6500 feet	May 23
Saddle Hawk, The	Hoot Gibson	Universal	5468 feet	Mar 7
Silent Sanderson	Harry Carey	Prod. Dist. Corp.	4841 feet	June 20
Scandal Proof	Shirley Mason	Fox	4400 feet	June 6
School for Wives	Tearle-Holmquist	Vitagraph	6750 feet	April 11
Shock Punch, The	Richard Dix	Paramount	6151 feet	May 23
Snob Buster, The	Reed Howes	Rayart (S. R.)		
Soul Fire	Barthelmess-B Love	First National	8262 feet	May 16
Speed Wild	Maurice B "Lefty" Flynn	F. B. O	4700 feet	June 20
Talker, The	A Nilsson-L Stone	First National	7861 feet	May 23
Texas Bearcat, The	Bob Custer	F. B. O	4770 feet	
Tides of Passion	Mae Marsh	Vitagraph	6278 feet	May 9
Up the Ladder	Virginia Valli	Universal	6023 feet	Jan 31
Welcome Home	Special Cast	Paramount	5909 feet	May 30
White Fang	Strongheart (dog)	F. B. O	6679 feet	June 20
White Thunder	Yakima Canutt	F. B. O.	4550 feet	
Wildfire	Special Cast	Vitagraph	6 reels	June 26
Wolves of the Road	Yakima Canutt	Arrow	4375 feet	
Woman's Faith	Reubens-Marmont	Universal	6023 feet	Aug 15
Woman Hater, The	Helene Chadwick	Warner Brothers	7000 feet	Aug. 22

JUNE

Feature	Star	Distributed by	Length	Reviewed
Are Parents People?	Bronson-Vidor	Paramount	6586 feet	June 6
Dangerous Odds	Bill Cody	Inde. Pict. (S. R.)	4800 feet	
Desert Flower, The	Colleen Moore	First National	6837 feet	June 13
Double Fisted	Jack Perrin	Rayart (S. R.)		
Down the Border	Al Richmond	Sierra Prod. (S. R.)	4750 feet	
Faint Perfume	Seena Owen	B. P. Schulberg (S.R.)	6228 feet	July 11
Grounds for Divorce	Florence Vidor	Paramount	5712 feet	July 4
Happy Warrior, The		Vitagraph	6075 feet	July 18
Hearts and Spurs	Buck Jones	Fox	4600 feet	June 20
Human Tornado, The	Yakima Canutt	F. B. O.	4472 feet	
I'll Show You the Town	Reginald Denny	Universal	7400 feet	June 6
Introduce Me	Douglas MacLean	Assoc. Exhib.	5980 feet	Mar. 21
Just a Woman	Windsor-Tearle	First National	6500 feet	June 6
Light of Western Stars	Special Cast	Paramount	6652 feet	July 4
Lost—a Wife	Special Cast	Paramount	6420 feet	June 27
Making of O'Malley, The	Milton Sills	First National	7571 feet	July 4
Man from Lone Mountain, The	Ben Wilson	Arrow	4530 feet	
Man in Blue	Herbert Rawlinson	Universal	5706 feet	Feb. 21
Marry Me	Special Cast	Paramount	5586 feet	
Meddler, The	William Desmond	Universal	4890 feet	May 23
Mike		Metro-Goldwyn		
Mist in the Valley	Alma Taylor	Cranfield & Clarke (S. R.)	5500 feet	
My Lady's Lips	Clara Bow	B. P. Schulberg (S.R.)	6609 feet	Aug 15
Off the Highway	Wm. V. Mong	Prod. Dist.	7641 feet	
Paths to Paradise	Compson-R. Griffith	Paramount	6741 feet	June 27
Pioneers of the West		Sanford Prod. (S. R.)	5 reels	
Ridin' Easy	Dick Hatton	Arrow	4483 feet	
Ridin' Thunder	Jack Hoxie	Universal	4354 feet	May 23

Feature	Star	Distributed by	Length	Reviewed
Rough Stuff	George Larkin	Rayart (S. R.)		
Shattered Lives	Special Cast	Gotham (S. R.)	6 reels	July 4
Smooth as Satin	Evelyn Brent	F. B. O	6003 feet	July 4
Texas Trail, The	Harry Carey	Prod. Dist. Corp	4720 feet	July 18
Tracked in the Snow Country	Rin-Tin-Tin (dog)	Warner Brothers	6900 feet	Aug. 1
White Monkey, The	La Marr-T. Holding	First National	6121 feet	July 4
Wild Bull's Lair, The	Fred Thompson	F. B. O.	5280 feet	Aug. 15
Youth's Gamble	Reed Howes	Rayart (S. R.)	5264 feet	

JULY

Feature	Star	Distributed by	Length	Reviewed
Bloodhound, The	Bob Custer	F. B. O	4789 feet	
Cold Nerve	Bill Cody	Inde. Pict. (S. R.)	5000 feet	
Danger Signal, The	Jane Novak	Columbia Pict. (S.R.)	5502 feet	Aug. 15
Don Daredevil	Jack Hoxie	Universal	4810 feet	
Drug Store Cowboy, The	Franklyn Farnum	Ind. Pict. Corp. (S.R.)	5100 feet	Feb. 7
Duped	Holmes-Desmond	Ind. Pict. (S. R.)	5400 feet	
Fighting Youth		Columbia Pict. (S.R.)		
Lady Who Lied, The	L. Stone-V. Valli	First National	7111 feet	July 18
Lady Robinhood	Evelyn Brent	F. B. O	5582 feet	Aug 22
Manicure Girl, The	Bebe Daniels	Paramount	5959 feet	June 27
Marriage Whirl, The	C. Griffith-H. Ford	First National	7672 feet	July 25
Mysterious Stranger, The	Richard Talmadge	F. B. O	5270 feet	
Night Life of New York	Special Cast	Paramount	6998 feet	July 4
Pipes of Pan	Alma Taylor	Cranfield & Clarke (S. R.)	6200 feet	
Ranger of the Big Pines, The	Kenneth Harlan	Vitagraph	5800 feet	Aug. 8
Scarlet West, The	Frazer-Bow	First National	8391 feet	July 25
Secret of Black Canyon, The	Dick Hatton	Arrow		
Strange Rider, The	Yakima Canutt	Arrow		
Taming the West	Hoot Gibson	Universal	5427 feet	Feb. 28
Trailed	Al Richmond	Sierra Prod. (S. R.)	4750 feet	
White Desert, The	Special Cast	Metro-Goldwyn	6345 feet	July 18

AUGUST

Feature	Star	Distributed by	Length	Reviewed
American Pluck	George Walsh	Chadwick	5000 feet	July 11
Beggar on Horseback, A	Ralston-Nissen	Paramount	6800 feet	June 20
Business of Love, The	E. Horton-M. Bellamy	Astor Dist. Corp		
Children of the Whirlwind	Lionel Barrymore	Arrow		
Don Q	Douglas Fairbanks	United Artists	10264 feet	June 27
Drusilla With a Million	Special Cast	F. B. O	7391 feet	May 30
Evolution		Red Seal	4200 feet	Aug. 15
Fine Clothes	L. Stone-A. Rubens	First National	6971 feet	Aug. 15
Girl Who Wouldn't Work, The	Lionel Barrymore	B. P. Schulberg (S.R.)	5979 feet	Sept. 5
Gold Rush, The	Charles Chaplin	United Artists	8500 feet	Aug. 8
Halfway Girl, The	Doris Kenyon	First National	7570 feet	Aug. 8
Headlines	Alice Joyce	Assoc. Exhib	5600 feet	July 25
Her Sister From Paris	C. Talmadge	First National	7255 feet	Aug. 15
In the Name of Love	Cortez-Nissen	Paramount	5904 feet	Sept. 5
Isle of Hope, The	Richard Talmadge	Film Book. Offices	5800 feet	Sept. 5
Kivalina of the Ice Lands	Native Cast	Pathe	6 reels	July 11
Knockout, The	Milton Sills	First National	7450 feet	Sept. 19
Lightnin'	Jay Hunt	Fox	7979 feet	Aug. 1
Limited Mail, The	Monte Blue	Warner Brothers	6250 feet	
Love Hour, The	Ruth Clifford	Vitagraph	5900 feet	
Lover's Oath, The	Ramon Novarro	Astor Dist Corp		
Lucky Devil, The	Richard Dix	Paramount	5935 feet	July 18
Lucky Horseshoes	Tom Mix	Fox	5000 feet	Aug. 29
My Pal	Dick Hatton	Arrow		
Overland Limited, The		Gotham Prod. (S. R.)	6289 feet	Aug. 8
Parisian Love	Bow-Tellegen	B. P. Schulberg (S.R.)	6324 feet	Aug. 22
Penalty of Jazz, The	Dorothy Revier	Columbia Pict. (S.R.)		
Quo Vadis	Emil Jannings	First National	8945 feet	Feb. 28
Range Justice	Dick Hatton	Arrow		
Romola	Gish Sisters	Metro-Goldwyn	10875 feet	Dec. 13
Rugged Water	Special Cast	Paramount	6015 feet	Aug. 1
Shining Adventure, The	Percy Marmont	Astor Dist. Corp		
Slave of Fashion, A	Special Cast	Metro-Goldwyn	5906 feet	Aug. 1
Speed Mad		Columbia Pict. (S.R.)	4442 feet	Sept. 19
Street of Forgotten Men	Special Cast	Paramount	6366 feet	Aug. 1
Ten Commandments	Special Cast	Paramount	9980 feet	Jan. 5-24
That Man Jack	Bob Custer	F. B. O	5032 feet	Aug. 22
Unholy Three	Lon Chaney	Metro-Goldwyn	6848 feet	Aug. 15
Unwritten Law, The		Columbia Pict. (S.R.)		
Wife Who Wasn't Wanted, The	Irene Rich	Warner Brothers	6400 feet	
Wizard of Oz	Larry Semon	Chadwick	6300 feet	Apr. 25
Wrongdoers, The	Lionel Barrymore	Astor Dist. Corp		

SEPTEMBER

Feature	Star	Distributed by	Length	Reviewed
Amazing Quest, The	Henry Edwards	Cranfield & Clarke	5500 feet	
As No Man Has Loved	Edward Hearn	Fox	10000 feet	Feb. 28
Below The Line	Rin-Tin-Tin (dog)	Warner Brothers	6100 feet	
Black Cyclone	Rex (horse)	Pathe		May 30
Bobbed Hair	Prevost-Harlan	Warner Brothers	6700 feet	
California Straight Ahead	Reginald Denny	Universal		
Call of Courage, The	Art Acord	Universal	4661 feet	Sept. 19
Classified	Corinne Griffith	First National		
Coast of Folly	Gloria Swanson	Paramount		
Crack of Dawn	Reed Howes	Rayart (S. R.)		
Cyclone Cavalier	Reed Howes	Rayart (S. R.)		
Dark Angel, The	R. Colman-V. Dana	First National		
Freshman, The	Harold Lloyd	Pathe		July 25
Graustark	Norma Talmadge	First National	5900 feet	Sept. 19
Havoc	Special Cast	Fox	9200 feet	Aug. 29
High and Handsome	"Lefty" Flynn	F. B. O.	5669 feet	
If Marriage Fails	J. Logan-C. Brook	F. B. O	6006 feet	May 23
Keep Smiling	Monty Banks	Assoc. Exhib	5400 feet	Aug. 1
Let's Go Gallagher	Tom Tyler	Film Book Offices		
Little Annie Rooney	Mary Pickford	United Artists		
Lost World, The	Special Cast	First National	9700 feet	Feb. 21
Manhattan Madness	Dempsey-Taylor	Assoc. Exhib	5500 feet	July 25
Man Who Found Himself	Thomas Meighan	Paramount	7168 feet	Sept. 5
Marrying Money		Truart (S. R.)	5800 feet	
Mystic, The	Special Cast	Metro-Goldwyn		
Never the Twain Shall Meet	Stewart-Lytell	Metro-Goldwyn	8143 feet	Aug. 8
New Champion, The		Columbia Pict. (S.R.)		
Not So Long Ago	Betty Bronson	Paramount	6943 feet	Aug. 8
Other Woman's Story		B. P. Schulberg		
Outlaw's Daughter, The	Josie Sedgwick	Universal	4375 feet	
Parisian Nights	E. Hammerstein - L. Tellegen	F. B. O	6278 feet	June 20

Feature	Star	Distributed by	Length	Reviewed
Pretty Ladies	Zazu Pitts	Metro-Goldwyn	5828 feet	July 25
Prince of Broadway, The	George Walsh	Chadwick		
Ridin' the Wind	Fred Thomson	Film Book. Offices		
Sealed Lips		Columbia Pict. (S.R.)		
Shore Leave	Barthelmess-Mackaill	First National	6856 feet	Aug. 29
Siege	Virginia Valli	Universal	6424 feet	June 20
Some Pun'kins	Chas. Ray	Chadwick	6530 feet	Sept. 19
Son of His Father	Special Cast	Paramount	7009 feet	
Souls for Sables		Tiffany (S. R.)	6500 feet	
S. O. S. Perils of the Sea		Columbia Pict. (S.R.)		
Spook Ranch	Hoot Gibson	Universal	5147 feet	May 2
Sun Up	Special Cast	Metro-Goldwyn		Aug. 29
Teaser, The	Laura La Plante	Universal	6967 feet	May 30
Three in Exile		Truart (S. R.)	5800 feet	
Three Weeks in Paris	M. Moore-D. Devore	Warner Brothers	5900 feet	
Three Wise Crooks	Evelyn Brent	Film Book. Offices		
Throwback, The	Special Cast	Universal		
Timber Wolf, The	Buck Jones	Fox	4809 feet	
Trouble With Wives, The	Vidor-T. Moore	Paramount	6483 feet	Aug. 15
Unchastened Woman, The	Theda Bara	Chadwick		
Wall Street Whiz, The	Richard Talmadge	Film Book. Offices		
What Fools Men	Stone-Mason	First National		
Wheel, The	Special Cast	Fox	7264 feet	Aug. 29
White Outlaw, The	Jack Hoxie	Universal	4830 feet	June 27
Wild Horse Mesa	Special Cast	Paramount	7221 feet	Aug. 22
Wild, Wild Susan	Bebe Daniels	Paramount		
With This Ring	Mills-Tellegen	B. P. Schulberg		

OCTOBER

Feature	Star	Distributed by	Length	Reviewed
Bells, The	Lionel Barrymore	Chadwick		
Circus Cyclone, The	Art Acord	Universal	4609 feet	Aug. 22
Dollar Down	Ruth Roland	Truart (S. R.)	5800 feet	Aug. 29
Everlasting Whisper, The	Tom Mix	Fox		
Exchange of Wives, An	Special Cast	Metro-Goldwyn		
Fate of a Flirt, The		Columbia (S. R.)		
Golden Princess, The	Bronson-Hamilton	Paramount	6395 feet	Sept. 19
Great Sensation, The		Columbia (S. R.)		
Heads Up	Fred Thomson	F. B. O		
He's a Prince	Raymond Griffith	Paramount		
His Buddy's Wife	Glenn Hunter	Assoc. Exhib	5600 feet	July 25
Iron Horse, The		Fox Film Corp	11335 feet	Sept. 13
John Forrest	Henry Edwards	Cranfield&Clark(S.R.)	5000 feet	
Keeper of the Bees, The	Robert Frazer	F. B. O		
Lew Tyler's Wives		B. P. Schulberg (S. R.)		
Lights of Old Broadway	Marion Davies	Metro-Goldwyn		
Lovers in Quarantine	Daniels-Ford	Paramount		
Midshipman, The	Ramon Novarro	Metro-Goldwyn		
Morals for Men		Tiffany (S. R.)	6500 feet	
New Brooms	Hamilton-Love	Paramount		
Peacock Feathers	Virginia Valli	Universal	6747 feet	Aug. 29
Perfect Clown, The	Larry Semon	Chadwick		
Pony Express, The	Betty Compson	Paramount		
Sally of the Sawdust	Fields-Dempster	United Artists	9500 feet	Aug. 15
Sporting Chance, The		Tiffany (S. R.)	6500 feet	July 4
Thank U	Special Cast	Fox	7 reels	Sept. 19
Tower of Lies	Chaney-Shearer	Metro-Goldwyn		
Tumbleweeds	Wm. S. Hart	United Artists		
Under the Rouge	Tom Moore	Assoc. Exhib	6500 feet	July 25
Winds of Chance	A. Nilsson-B. Lyon	First National	9753 feet	Aug. 29

NOVEMBER

Feature	Star	Distributed by	Length	Reviewed
Ancient Highway, The	Holt-Vidor	Paramount		
Best People, The	Special Cast	Paramount		
Blue Blood	George Walsh	Chadwick		
Camille of the Barbary Coast	Busch-O. Moore	Assoc. Exhib	5600 feet	Aug. 1
Cobra	Valentino-Naldi	Paramount		
Don't	S. O'Neill-B. Roach	Metro-Goldwyn		
Fifty-Fifty	L. Barrymore-H. Hampton	Assoc. Exhib	5564 feet	June 20
Fight to a Finish, A		Columbia (S. R.)		
Fighting Heart, The	Geo. O'Brien	Fox	6978 feet	
Flower of Night	Pola Negri	Paramount		
Fool, The	Special Cast	Fox		April 25
King on Main St., The	Adolphe Menjou	Paramount		
Lazybones		Fox Film		
Lightning		Tiffany (S. R.)	6500 feet	
Little Bit of Broadway	Ray-Starke	Metro-Goldwyn		
Merry Widow	Mae Murray	Metro-Goldwyn		
Price of Success, The	Alice Lake	Columbia (S. R.)		
Silent Witness, The		Truart (S. R.)	5800 feet	
Stage Struck	Gloria Swanson	Paramount		
Time the Comedian		Metro-Goldwyn		
Transcontinental Limited	Special Cast	Chadwick (S. R.)		
Vanishing American	Dix-Wilson	Paramount		
Winner, The	Charley Ray	Chadwick (S. R.)		

Comedy Releases

Feature	Star	Distributed by	Length	Reviewed
Across the Hall	Edna Marian	Universal	2 reels	
Adventures of Adenoid	Aesop's Fables	Pathe	1 reel	April 25
After a Reputation	Edna Marian	Universal	2 reels	
Air Tight	Bobby Vernon	Educational	2 reels	June 13
Alice's Egg Plant	"Cartoon"	M. J. Winkler(S. R.)	1 reel	
Alice Stagestruck	Margie Gay	M. J. Winkler (S.R.)	1 reel	July 18
All Aboard	Perry-Cooley	Fox	2 reels	
Almost a Husband	Buddy Messinger	Universal	2 reels	
Amateur Detective	Earle Foxe	Fox	2 reels	
Andy in Hollywood	Joe Murphy	Universal	2 reels	
Andy Takes a Flyer	"The Gumps"	Universal	2 reels	
Apache, The	Earle Foxe	Fox Film	2 reels	
Apollo's Pretty Sister		Fox	2 reels	
Are Husbands Human?	James Finlayson	Pathe	1 reel	April 11
Artists' Blues	G. Joy-J. Moore	Rayart (S. R.)	2 reels	
Ask Grandma	"Our Gang"	Pathe	2 reels	May 30
At the Seashore	Monkey	Fox	2 reels	
At the Zoo	Aesops Fables	Pathe	1 reel	
Baby Blues	Mickey Bennett	Educational	2 reels	
Bachelors	Special Cast	Universal		

Feature	Star	Distributed by	Length	Reviewed
Bad Bill Brodie	Charles Chase	Pathe	2 reels	
Bad Boy	Charles Chase	Pathe	2 reels	April 11
Balboa Discovers Hollywood	"Red Head"	Sering D. Wilson (S.R.)	1 reel	
Bark is the Woods	Harry Langdon	Pathe	2 reels	
Bashful Jim	Ralph Graves	Pathe	2 reels	Mar. 21
Be Careful	Jimmie Adams	Educational Film	2 reels	Aug. 22
Below Zero	Lige Conley	Educational	2 reels	July 4
Beware	Lige Conley	Educational Film	2 reels	Aug. 1
Big Chief Ko-Ko (Out of the Inkwell)	"Cartoon"	Red Seal Pict. (S. R.)	1 reel	
Big Game Hunter, The	Earle Foxe	Fox	2 reels	
Bigger and Better Pictures	"Aesop's Fables"	Pathe	1 reel	
Big Red Riding Hood	Charley Chase	Pathe	1 reel	May 9
Black Gold Bricks	Roach-Edwards	Universal	1 reel	April 18
Black Hand Blues	"Spat Family"	Pathe	2 reels	April 18
Bobby Bumbs & Co.	Cartoon	Educational	1 reel	July 4
Boys Will Be Joys	"Our Gang"	Pathe	2 reels	July 25
Brainless Horsemen		Fox	2 reels	
Brass Button	Billy West	Arrow	2 reels	
Breaking the Ice	Ralph Graves	Pathe	2 reels	April 11
Bride Tamer, The	Milburn Moranti	Sierra Pict. (S. R.)	2 reels	
Bubbles	"Aesop's Fables"	Pathe	1 reel	Aug. 15
Bugville Field Day	"Aesop's Fables"	Pathe	1 reel	July 25
Business Engagement, A	Perry-Cooley	Fox	2 reels	
Busts Into Business	Felix the Cat	Educational	1 reel	
Butterfly Man, The		Fox	2 reels	
By the Sea	Charles Puffy	Universal	1 reel	
California Here We Come	"The Gumps"	Universal	2 reels	
Cat's Shimmy, The	"Kid Noah"	Sering D. Wilson (S.R.)	1 reel	
Cat's Whiskers, The	Neely Edwards	Universal	1 reel	
Chasing the Chasers	Jas. Finlayson	Pathe	1 reel	July 4
City Bound	Charles Puffy	Universal	1 reel	
Clean-Up Week	"Aesop's Fables"	Pathe	1 reel	Mar. 7
Clear the Way	Buddy Messinger	Universal	2 reels	
Cleopatra and Her Easy Mark	"Cartoon"	Sering D. Wilson (S.R.)	1 reel	
Cloudhopper, The	Larry Semon	Educational	2 reels	June 6
Cloudy Romance, A		Fox		
Columbus Discovers a New Whirl		Sering Wilson (S. R.)	1 reel	
Cotton King	Lloyd Hamilton	Educational	2 reels	
Crime Crushers	Lige Conley	Educational	2 reels	
Crying for Love	Eddie Gordon	Universal	2 reels	Aug. 15
Cupid's Boots	Ralph Graves	Pathe	2 reels	July 25
Cupid's Victory	Wanda Wiley	Universal	2 reels	
Cure, The (Out of the Inkwell)	"Cartoon"	Red Seal Pict. (S. R.)	1 reel	
Curses	Al. St. John	Educational	2 reels	May 23
Daddy Goes A Grunting		Pathe	2 reels	July 18
Darkest Africa	"Aesop's Fables"	Pathe	1 reels	
Day's Outing, A	"The Gumps"	Universal	2 reels	
Depp Stuff	Aesop's Fables	Pathe	1 reel	April 25
Dinky Doodle and Cinderella	"Dinky Doodle"	F. B. O	1 reel	
Dinky Doodle and Robinson Crusoe	"Dinky Doodle"	F. B. O	1 reel	
Discord In "A" Flat	Arthur Lake	Universal	1 reel	July 25
Dog Days	"Our Gang"	Pathe	2 reels	Mar. 14
Dog 'On It	Bobby Dunn	Arrow	2 reels	
Dome Doctor, The	Larry Semon	Educational	2 reels	
Don't Pinch	Bobby Vernon	Educational	2 reels	April 25
Don't Worry	Wanda Wiley	Universal	2 reels	Mar. 21
Dragon Alley	Jackie McHugh	Educational	2 reels	May 16
Dr. Pyckle and Mr. Pride	Stan Laurel	Film Booking Offices	2 reels	
Dry Up	Singleton Burkett	Universal	2 reels	July 25
Dumb and Daffy	Al. St. John	Fox	2 reels	
Dynamite Doggie	Al. St. John	Educational	2 reels	Mar. 21
Echoes From the Alps	Aesop's Fables	Pathe	1 reel	May 23
Educating Buster	Trimble-Turner	Universal	2 reels	
End of the World, The	Aesop's Fables	Pathe	1 reel	
Etiquette	Jimmy Aubrey	Film Book. Offices	2 reels	
Excuse My Glove	"Spat Family"	Pathe	2 reels	Mar 21
Expensive Ebony	"Ebenezer Ebony"	Sering Wilson (S. R.)	1 reel	
Failure		Fox	2 reels	
Fair Warning		Educational	2 reels	
Fares Please	Al. St. John	Educational	2 reels	May 16
Fast Worker, A	Aesop's Fables	Pathe	1 reel	
Felix Full O'Fight	"Cartoon"	M. J. Winkler (S. R.)	1 reel	
Felix Gets His Fill	"Cartoon"	M. J. Winkler (S. R.)	1 reel	
Felix Grabs His Grub	"Cartoon"	M. J. Winkler (S. R.)	1 reel	
Fireflies		Davis Dist	2 reels	
First Love	"Our Gang"	Pathe	2 reels	
Fisherman's Luck	"Aesop's Fables"	Pathe	1 reel	
For Hire	Edward Gordon	Universal		
For Love of a Gal	"Aesop's Fables"	Pathe	1 reel	July 25
Found World, The	"The Gumps"	Universal	2 reels	
Fun's Fun	Bowes-Vance	Educational	1 reel	June 6
Getting Trimmed	Wanda Wiley	Universal	2 reels	April 18
Giddap	Special Cast	Pathe	2 reels	Mar. 21
Going Great	Eddie Nelson	Educational	2 reels	June 13
Goldfish's Pajamas	"Kid Noah"	Sering D. Wilson (S.R.)	1 reel	
Good Morning Nurse	Ralph Graves	Pathe	2 reels	May [illegible]
Good Scouts	"Reg'lar Kids"	M. J. Winkler (S. R.)	2 reels	
Great Guns	Bobby Vernon	Educational	2 reels	Feb. 21
Green-Eyed Monster, The	Arthur Lake	Universal	1 reel	
Gridiron Gertie	Wanda Wiley	Universal	2 reels	
Guilty Conscience, A	Eddie Gordon	Universal		
Gypping the Gypsies	"Ebenezer Ebony"	Sering Wilson (S. R.)	1 reel	
Half a Hero	Lloyd Hamilton	Educational	2 reels	Mar. 7
Half a Man	Stan Laurel	Pathe	2 reels	
Hard Boiled	Charley Chase	Pathe	3 reels	Mar. 21
Hard Working Loafer, The	Arthur Stone	Pathe		
Haunted Honeymoon	Tryon-Mehaffey	Pathe	2 reels	Feb. 28
Heart Trouble	Arthur Lake	Universal	1 reel	July 4
Hello, Goodby	Lige Conley	Educational	2 reels	May 30
Hello, Hollywood	Lige Conley	Educational	2 reels	Mar. 28
Helping Hand	Jimmy Aubrey	F. B. O	2 reels	
Help Yourself		Fox	2 reels	
Here's Your Hat	Arthur Lake	Universal	1 reel	May 9
Her Lucky Leap	Wanda Wiley	Universal	2 reels	
He Who Gets Crowned	Jimmy Aubrey	F. B. O	2 reels	
He Who Got Smacked	Ralph Graves	Pathe	2 reels	May 9
Hey! Taxi!	Bobby Dunn	Arrow	2 reels	
High Hopes	Bowes-Vance	Educational	1 reel	Feb. 14
High Jinx, A		Fox	2 reels	
His Marriage Wow	Harry Langdon	Pathe	2 reels	Mar. 7
Hold My Baby	Glenn Tryon	Pathe	2 reels	April 25
Home Scouts	Jimmie Aubrey	F. B. O.	2 reels	
Honeymoon Heaven		Sering Wilson (S. R.)	1 reel	
Horace Greeley, Jr	Harry Langdon	Pathe	2 reels	June 6
Horrible Hollywood		Lee-Bradford (S. R.)		
Hot and Heavy	Eddie Nelson	Educational	2 reels	July 18
Hot Dog	Animal	C B C (S. R.)	2 reels	
Hot Times in Iceland	Aesop's Fables	Pathe	1 reel	
House of Flickers, The		Fox	2 reels	
House that Dinky Built	(Cartoon)	F. B. O	1 reel	
Housing Shortage, The	"Aesop's Fables"	Pathe	1 reel	
Hurry Doctor	Ralph Graves	Pathe		
Hysterical History (Series)		Universal	1 reel	
Ice Boy, An	"Ebenezer Ebony"	Sering D. Wilson (S.R.)	1 reel	
Ice Cold	Arthur Lake	Universal	1 reel	June 13
In Deep		Educational	1 reel	
In Dutch	Aesop's Fables	Pathe	1 reel	
Innocent Husbands	Charley Chase	Pathe	2 reels	Aug. 1
Inside Out	Bowes-Vance	Educational	1 reel	Mar. 28
Into the Grease	James Finlayson	Pathe	1 reel	June 27
Iron Mule	Al St. John	Educational	2 reels	April 18
Iron Nag, The	Billy Bevan	Pathe	2 reels	Aug. 15
Is Marriage the Bunk?	Charles Chase	Pathe	1 reel	April 4
Isn't Life Terrible?	Charles Chase	Pathe	2 reels	July 4
Itching for Revenge	Eddie Gordon	Universal	2 reels	Mar. 7
It's All Wrong	Karr-Engle	Universal		
James Boys' Sister		Sering Wilson (S. R.)	1 reel	
Jungle Bike Riders	Aesop's Fables	Pathe	1 reel	Mar. 14
Just in Time	Wanda Wiley	Universal	2 reels	July 11
Kicked About	Eddie Gordon	Universal	2 reels	Mar. 14
Kidding Captain Kidd	"Cartoon"	Sering Wilson (S. R.)	1 reel	
King Cotton	Lloyd Hamilton	Educational	2 reels	May 9
King Dumb	Jimmy Aubrey	F. B. O	2 reels	
Klynick, The		Davis Dist	2 reels	
Knocked About	Eddie Gordon	Universal	2 reels	June 13
Ko-Ko Trains Animals (out of the Inkwell)	"Cartoon"	Red Seal Pict. (S.R.)	1 reel	
Lead Pipe Cinch, A	Al Alt	Universal		
Lion Love		Fox	2 reels	Feb. 28
Lion's Whiskers		Pathe	2 reels	April 18
Little Red Riding Hood	"Dinky Doodle"	F. B. O	1 reel	
Locked Out	Arthur Lake	Universal	1 reel	May 30
Looking for Sally	Charles Chase	Pathe	2 reels	May 9
Look Out	Bowes-Vance	Educational Film	1 reel	Aug. 1
Lost Cord, The	Bert Roach	Universal	1 reel	Feb. 21
Love and Lions		Fox	2 reels	
Love Bug, The	"Our Gang"	Pathe	2 reels	April 4
Love Goofy	Jimmy Adams	Educational	2 reels	Mar. 7
Love Sick	Constance Darling	Universal	2 reels	May 23
Love's Tragedy		Sering Wilson (S. R.)	1 reel	
Lucky Accident, The	Charles Puffy	Universal	1 reel	July 18
Lucky Leap, A	Wanda Wiley	Universal	2 reels	
Lucky Stars	Harry Langdon	Pathe	2 reels	Aug. 15
Madame Sans Jane	Glenn Tryon	Pathe	2 reels	
Marriage Circus, The	Ben Turpin	Pathe	2 reels	April 11
Married Neighbors	Engle-Darling	Universal	2 reels	July 4
Mary, Queen of Tots	"Our Gang"	Pathe	2 reels	Aug. 22
Meet the Ambassador	Jimmy Aubrey	F. B. O	2 reels	
Mellow Quartette	Pen & Ink Vaudeville	Educational	1 reel	April 4
Merrymakers	Bowes-Vance	Educational	1 reel	Mar. 28
Met by Accident	Wanda Wiley	Universal	2 reels	
Milky Way, The	Charles Puffy	Universal	1 reel	July 25
Miss Fixit	Wanda Wiley	Universal	2 reels	
Monkey Business	"Pen & Ink Vaude"	Educational	1 reel	May 9
Moonlight Nights	Gloria Joy	Rayart (S. R.)	2 reels	
Nearly Rich	Charles Puffy	Universal	1 reel	
Neptune's Stepdaughter		Fox	2 reels	
Nero's Jazz Band		Sering Wilson (S. R.)	1 reel	
Never Fear	Bowes-Vance	Educational	1 reel	
Never on Time		Lee-Bradford	2 reels	
Never Weaken	Lloyd reissue	Assoc. Exhib	2237 feet	
Nice Pickle, A	Edwards-Roach	Universal	1 reel	
Nicely Rewarded	Chas. Puffy	Universal	1 reel	June 27
Night Hawks		Educational Film	2 reels	
Nobody Wins	Arthur Lake	Universal	1 reel	
No Place to Go	Arthur Lake	Universal	1 reel	
Now or Never (reissue)	Harold Lloyd	Assoc. Exhib	3 reels	
Nuts and Squirrels	"Aesop's Fables"	Pathe	1 reel	
Off His Beat	Walter Hiers	Educational	2 reels	
Office Help	"Aesop's Fables"	Pathe	1 reel	June 27
Officer 13	Eddie Gordon	Universal		
Official Officers	"Our Gang"	Pathe	2 reels	June 27
Oh, Bridget	Walter Hiers	Educational	2 reels	
Oh, What a Flirt	Jimmy Aubrey	Film Book. Offices	2 reels	
Oh, What a Gump	"The Gumps"	Universal	2 reels	
Old Family Toothbrush	"Kid Noah"	Sering Wilson (S. R.)	1 reel	
On Duty	Wanda Wiley	Universal	2 reels	
On the Go		Fox		
One Glorious Fourth	"Reg'lar Kids"	M. J. Winkler (S. R.)	2 reels	
One Wild Night	Neely Edwards	Universal	1 reel	
Orphan, The	Al Joy	Ricardo Films, Inc. (S.R.)		
Over the Bottom	Stan Laurel	F. B. O	2 reels	
Over the Plate	Aesops Fable	Pathe	1 reel	Aug. 22
Over Here	Harry Langdon	Pathe	2 reels	
Paging A Wife	Al Alt	Universal	2 reels	Aug. 1
Papa's Darling		Fox	2 reels	
Papa's Pet	Roach-Edwards	Universal	1 reel	April 11
Parisian Knight, A	Earle Foxe	Fox	2 reels	
Peacemakers, The	Perry-Cooley	Fox	2 reels	
Pegg's Love Affair		Screen Art Dist		
Peggy in a Pinch		Davis Dist	2 reels	
Peggy's Pests		Davis Dist	2 reels	
Peggy's Putters		Davis Dist	2 reels	
Peggy the Vamp	Rosalie Morlin	Davis Distr	2 reels	Oct. 11
Permanent Waves	"Aesop's Fables"	Pathe	1 reel	
Permit Me	Bowes-Vance	Educational	1 reel	July 11
Pie-Eyed	Stan Laurel	F. B. O	2 reels	
Pie Man, The	"Aesop's Fables"	Pathe	1 reel	Mar. 21
Plain Clothes	Harry Langdon	Pathe	2 reels	Mar. 28
Plain and Fancy Girls	Charles Chase	Pathe	1 reel	Mar. 14
Plain Luck	Edna Marian	Universal	2 reels	
Pleasure Bound	Lige Conley	Educational	2 reels	Aug. 24
Plenty of Nerve	Edna Marian	Universal	2 reels	July 2
Polo Kid, The	Eddie Gordon	Universal	2 reels	July 18
Poor Sap, The		Fox	2 reels	
Powdered Chickens	Edna Marian	Universal	2 reels	Mar. 28
Props' Dash for Cash	Earl Hurd (Cartoon)	Educational	1 reel	
Putting on Airs	Edna Marian	Universal	2 reels	April 11
Puzzled by Crosswords	Eddie Gordon	Universal	2 reels	Mar. 7
Queen of Aces	Wanda Wiley	Universal	2 reels	May 18
Raid, The	Gloria Joy	Rayart Pictures	2 reels	
Rainy Knight, A	Special Cast	Pathe		
Raisin' Cain	Constance Darling	Universal	2 reels	April 4
Rapid Transit	Al. St. John	Educational	2 reels	
Rarin' Romeo	Walter Hiers	Educational	2 reels	Mar. 28
Raspberry Romance	Ben Turpin	Pathe	2 reels	Feb. 28
Red Pepper	Al. St. John	Educational	2 reels	Arpil 4
Regular Girl, A	Wanda Wiley	Universal	2 reels	
Riders of the Kitchen Range	Mohar-Engle	Pathe	1 reel	June 6
Remember When	Harry Langdon	Pathe	2 reels	April 25
Rip Without a Wink	"Redhead"	Sering Wilson (S. R.)	1 reel	
Ripe Melodrama, A		Sering Wilson (S. R.)	1 reel	
Rivals	Billy West	Arrow	2 reels	

Feature	Star	Distributed by	Length	Reviewed
Robinson Crusoe Returns on Friday	"Redhead"	Sering Wilson (S. R.)	1 reel	
Rock Bottom	Bowes-Vance	Educational	1 reel	May 9
Robbing the Rube		Lee-Bradford Corp.	2 reels	
Rolling Stones	Charles Puffy	Universal	1 reel	May 30
Rough Party	Al Alt	Universal	2 reels	
Royal Four-Flush	"Spat Family"	Pathe	2 reels	June 13
Runaway Balloon, The	"Aesop's Fables"	Pathe	1 reel	June 27
Runt, The	"Aesop's Fables"	Pathe	1 reel	June 6
Sailor Papa, A	Glenn Tryon	Pathe	2 reels	April 4
Saturday		Davis Dist. Div.	2 reels	
Say It With Flour		Fox	2 reels	
Sheiks of Bagdad		Pathe	1 reel	May 9
Sherlock Sleuth	Arthur Stone	Pathe	2 reels	July 11
Ship Shape	Vance-Bowes	Educational	1 reel	April 18
Shootin' Injuns	"Our Gang"	Pathe	2 reels	May 9
Short Pants	Arthur Lake	Universal	1 reel	Aug. 1
Should a Husband Tell?		Red Seal Pict. (S.R.)	1 reel	
Should Husbands Be Watched?	Charles Chase	Pathe	1 reel	Mar. 14
Sir Walt and Lizzie		Sering Wilson (S. R.)	1 reel	
Sit Tight	Jimmie Adams	Educational	2 reels	May 30
Skinners in Silk		Pathe	2 reels	May 16
Sky Jumper, The	Earle Foxe	Fox	2 reels	
Skyscraper, The	Harry Langdon	Principal Pict. (S. R.)	2 reels	
Sleeping Sickness	Edwards-Roach	Universal	1 reel	May 30
Slick Articles	Engle-Karr	Universal	2 reels	May 30
Smoked Out	Lake-Hasbrouck	Universal	1 reel	April 13
Sneezing Beezers	Billy Bevan	Pathe	2 reels	July 18
Snow-Hawk	Stan Laurel	F. B. O.	2 reels	
Soap	"Aesop's Fables"	Pathe	1 reel	
Somewhere in Somewhere	Murray Littlefield	Pathe		
S. O. S.	"Aesop's Fables"	Pathe	1 reel	
Spanish Romeo, A (Van Bibber)		Fox	1 reel	
Speak Easy	Charley Puffy	Universal	1 reel	Aug. 22
Speak Freely	Edna Marion	Universal	2 reels	
Stick Around	Bobby Dunn	Arrow	2 reels	
Stop, Look and Whistle		Fox	2 reels	
Storm, The (Out of the Inkwell)	"Cartoon"	Red Seal Pict. (S.R.)	1 reel	
Stranded	Edna Marian	Universal	2 reels	
Super-Hooper-Dyne Lizzies		Pathe	2 reels	June 13
Sure Mike!	Martha Sleeper	Pathe	1 reel	May 23
Sweet Marie		Fox	2 reels	Aug. 29
Tame Men and Wild Women		Pathe	2 reels	Aug. 15
Teaser Island	"Redhead"	Sering Wilson (S. R.)	1 reel	
Tee for Two	Alice Day	Pathe	2 reels	Aug. 1
Tell It To a Policeman	Glenn Tryon	Pathe	2 reels	May 23
Tender Feet	Walter Hiers	Educational	2 reels	May 23
Tenting Out	Roache-Edwards	Universal	1 reel	Mar. 23
This Week-End		Lee-Bradford (S. R.)		
Three Wise Goofs	Special Cast	F. B. O		
Thundering Landlords	Glenn Tryon	Pathe	2 reels	June 27
Ton of Fun in a Beauty Parlor, A		F. B. O		
Too Much Mother-in-Law	Constance Darling	Universal		
Too Young to Marry	Buddy Messinger	Universal	2 reels	
Tough Night, A	Jimmy Callahan	Aywon Film	2 reels	
Tourist, The	Harry Langdon	Educational Film	2 reels	Aug. 15
Tourists De Luxe	Hayes-Karr	Universal	2 reels	May 16
Transients in Arcadia		Fox	2 reels	
Transatlantic Flight, A	"Aesop's Fables"	Pathe	1 reel	
Twins	Stan Laurel	F. B. O	2 reels	
Two Cats and a Bird	"Cartoon"	Educational	1 reel	Mar. 14
Two Poor Fish	Earl Hurd cartoon	Educational	1 reel	May 30
Uncle Tom's Gal	Edna Marian	Universal	2 reels	
Unwelcome	Charles Puffy	Universal	1 reel	June 27
Waiting	Lloyd Hamilton	Educational	2 reels	July 11
Wake Up	Bowes-Vance	Educational	1 reel	June 13
Watch Out	Bobby Vernon	Educational	2 reels	
Water Wagons	Special Cast	Pathe	2 reels	Feb. 21
Welcome Dangar	Bowes-Vance	Educational	1 reel	Feb. 28
West is West	Billy West	Arrow	2 reels	
Westward Ho	Charles Puffy	Universal	1 reel	
What Price Goofy	Charley Chase	Pathe	2 reels	June 6
When Dumbells Ring		Fox	2 reels	
When Men Were Men	"Aesop's Fables"	Pathe	1 reel	July 25
White Wing's Bride	Harry Langdon	Pathe	2 reels	July 11
Whose Baby Are You?	Glenn Tryon	Pathe	2 reels	
Who's Which	Bowes-Vance	Educational	1 reel	
Why Hesitate?	Neal Burns	Educational	2 reels	April 11
Why Sitting Bull Stood Up		Sering Wilson (S. R.)	1 reel	
Wide Awake	Lige Conley	Educational	2 reels	
Wild Papa	"Spat Family"	Pathe	2 reels	May 16
Wild Waves	Bowes-Vance	Educational	1 reel	May 23
Wine, Woman and Song	"Aesop's Fables"	Pathe	1 reel	
Wooly West, The	Buddy Messinger	Universal	2 reels	
Wrestler, The	Earle Foxe	Fox	2 reels	Aug. 29
Yarn About Yarn, A	Aesop Fable	Pathe	1 reel	Aug. 1
Yes, Yes, Nannette	Jas. Finlayson	Pathe	1 reel	Aug. 1

Short Subjects

Feature	Distributed by	Length	Reviewed
Action (Sportlight)	Pathe	1 reel	
All Under One Flag (Sportlight)	Pathe	1 reel	
Animal Celebrities (Sportlight)	Pathe	1 reel	June 27
Animated Hair Cartoon (Series)	Red Seal (S. R.)	1 reel	
Balto's Race to Nome (Special)	Educational	2 reels	May 23
Barbara Snitches (Pacemaker Series)	F. B. O.	2 reels	
Battle of Wits (Josie Sedgwick)	Universal	2 reels	July 18
Bashful Whirlwind, The (Edmund Cobb)	Universal	2 reels	
Beauty and the Bandit (Geo. Larkin)	Universal	2 reels	July 4
Beauty Spots (Sportlight)	Pathe	1 reel	April 18
Best Man, The (Josie Sedgwick)	Universal	2 reels	Aug. 15
Broken Trails	Denver Dixon (S.R.)	2 reels	
Cabaret of Old Japan	M. J. Winkler (S.R.)	1 reel	
Color World	Sering Wilson (S. R.)	1 reel	
Captured Alive (Helen Gibson)	Universal	2 reels	July 25
Cinema Stars (Novelty)	Davis Dist	1 reel	
Close Call, The (Edmund Cobb)	Universal	2 reels	
Cocoon to Kimono	M. J. Winkler (S.R.)	1 reel	
Come-Back, The (Benny Leonard)	Henry Ginsberg-S.R.	2 reels	
Concerning Cheese (Varieties)	Fox	1 reel	
Covered Flagon, The (Pacemaker Series)	F. B. O	2 reels	
Cowpuncher's Comeback, The (Art Acord)	Universal	2 reels	
Crooked (Elinor King)	Davis Dist	2 reels	
Cross Word Puzzle Film (Comedy-Novelty)	Schwartz Enterprises (S. R.)	1 reel	
Cuba Steps Out (Variety)	Fox	1 reel	
Day With the Gypsies	Red Seal Pict. (S. R.)	1 reel	
Divertisement (Color Shots)	Sering Wilson (S. R.)	1 reel	
Don Coo Coo (Pacemakers)	Film Book. Offices	2 reels	
Do You Remember (Gems of Screen)	Red Seal (S. R.)	1 reel	
Dude Ranch Days (Sportlight)	Pathe	1 reel	May 30
Earth's Other Half (Hodge-Podge)	Educational	1 reel	June 6
East Side, West Side	DeForrest (S. R.)		
Fast Male, The (Pacemakers)	Film Book. Offices	2 reels	
Fighting Cowboy (Series)	Universal		
Fighting Ranger (Serial)	Universal	15 episodes	Feb. 7
Fighting Schoolmarm (Josie Sedgwick)	Universal	2 reels	Aug. 1
Film Facts	Red Seal (S. R.)	1 reel	
Fire Trader, The (Serial)	Universal	15 episodes	
Floral Feast, A	Sering Wilson (S.R.)	1 reel	
Frederick Chopin (Music Masters)	Jas. A. Fitzpatrick (S. R.)	1 reel	
From Mars to Munich (Varieties)	Fox	1 reel	April 4
Frontier Love (Billy Mack)	Denver Dixon	2 reels	
Fugitive Futurist	Cranfield & Clarke (S. R.)		
George F. Handel (Music Masters)	Jas. A. Fitzpatrick (S. R.)	1 reel	
Gems of the Screen	Red Seal (S. R.)	1 reel	
Ghost City, The (Serial)	Universal	15 episodes	
Golden Panther, The (Serial)	Pathe		
Gold Trap, The ... Fred Humes	Universal	2 reels	
Great Circus Mystery, The (Serial)	Universal	15 episodes	
Great Decide, The (Pacemakers)	Film Book. Offices	2 reels	
He Who Gets Rapped (Pacemakers)	Film Book. Offices	2 reels	
Hittin' the Trail (Fred Hank)	Sierra Pict. (S. R.)	2 reels	
How the Elephant Got His Trunk (Bray)	F. B. O		
Idaho (Serial)	Pathe	10 episodes	Feb. 28
If a Picture Tells a Story	Cranfield & Clarke (S. R.)		
In a China Shop (Variety)	Fox	1 reel	
In the Spider's Grip (Novelty)	Educational	1 reel	April 11
Invention, The (Elinor King)	Davis Dist	2 reels	
It Might Happen to You (Evangeline Russell)	Davis Dist	2 reels	
Jazz Fight, The (Benny Leonard)	Henry Ginsberg (S. R.)	2 reels	
Judge's Cross Word Puzzle (Novelty)	Educational	1 reel	Jan. 31
Just Cowboys ... Corbett-Holmes	Universal	2 reels	
Klondike Today (Varieties)	Fox	1 reel	
Knockout Man, The (Mustang)	Universal	2 reels	July 11
Land of the Navajo (Educational)	Fox	1 reel	
Learning How (Sportlight)	Pathe	1 reel	July 18
Leopard's Lair	Universal	Serial	
Let's Paint	Cranfield & Clarke (S. R.)		
Line Runners, The (Arnold Gregg)	Universal	2 reels	
Little People of the Garden (Secrets of Life)	Educational	1 reel	
Little People of the Sea (Secrets of Life)	Educational	1 reel	Feb. 28
Lizzie's Last Lap	Cranfield & Clarke (S. R.)		
Loaded Dice (Edmund Cobb)	Universal	2 reels	April 4
Luna-cy (Stereoscopik)	Pathe	1 reel	
Mad Miner, A (Western)	Hunt Miller (S. R.)	2 reels	
Magic Hour, The	Red Seal Pict. (S. R.)	1 reel	
Man Who Rode Alone, The	Miller & Steen (S.R.)	2 reels	
Marvels of Motion	Red Seal (S. R.)	1 reel	
Marvellous Manhattan	M. J. Winkler (S. R.)	1 reel	
Merry Kiddo, The (Pacemakers)	Film Book. Offices	2 reels	
Merton of the Goofies ... "Pacemaker"	F. B. O.	2 reels	
Mexican Melody (Hodge-Podge)	Educational	1 Reel	
Mexican Oil Fields	M. J. Winkler (S. R.)	1 reel	
Movie Morsels (Hodge Podge)	Educational	1 reel	April 4
My Own Carolina (Variety)	Fox	1 reel	Aug. 29
Mystery Box, The (Serial)	Davis Dist. Corp.	10 episodes	
Neptune's Nieces (Sportlight)	Pathe	1 reel	
New Sheriff, A (Western)	Hunt Miller (S. R.)	2 reels	
Olympic Mermaids (Sportlight)	Pathe	1 reel	
One Glorious Scrap (Edmund Cobb)	Universal	2 reels	
Only a Country Lass (Novelty)	Educational	1 reel	May 29
Ouch (Stereoscopik)	Pathe	1 reel	
Our Six-legged Friends (Secrets of Life)	Educational	1 reel	
Outlaw, The (Jack Perrin)	Universal	2 reels	
Paris Creations (Novelty)	Educational	1 reel	Feb. 7
Paris Creations in Color (Novelty)	Educational	1 reel	Feb. 28
People You Know (Screen Almanac)	Film Booking Offices	1 reel	
Perfect View, The (Varieties)	Fox	1 reel	
Perils of the Wild (Serial)	Universal		
Pictorial Proverbs (Hodge Podge)	Educational	1 reel	Aug. 15
Plastigrams (Novelty)	Educational		
Play Ball (Serial)	Pathe	10 episodes	June 27
Power God, The (Serial)	Davis Dist. Div. (S.R.)	15 episodes	
Pronto Kid, The (Edmund Cobb)	Universal	2 reels	June 27
Queen of the Round-Up (J. Sedgwick)	Universal	2 reels	June 13
Race, The (Van Bibber)	Fox	2 reels	
Raid, The ... Edmund Cobb	Universal	2 reels	
Record Breaker, The	Pathe	Serial	
Rim of the Desert (Jack Perrin)	Universal	2 reels	
River Nile, The (Variety)	Fox	1 reel	
Roaring Waters (Geo. Larkin)	Universal	2 reels	
Rock Bound Brittany (Educational)	Fox	1 reel	
Ropin' Venus, The (Mustang Series)	Universal	2 reels	July 11
R. Valentino and Eighty-eight Prize-winning American Beauties	Chesterfield (M. P. Corp.) (S. R.)	3 reels	
Secrets of Life (Educational)	Principal Pict. (S. R.)	reel	Feb. 21
Seven Ages of Sport (Sportlight)	Pathe	1 reel	Aug. 22
Shadow of Suspicion (Eileen Sedgwick)	Universal	2 reels	
Shoes (O. Henry)	Fox	2 reels	
Show Down, The (Art Acord)	Universal	2 reels	
Sky Tribe, The (Variety)	Fox	1 reel	
Smoke of a Forty-Five, The (Western)	Hunt Miller (S. R.)	2 reels	
Soft Muscles (Benny Leonard)	Ginsberg (S. R.)	2 reels	
Song Cartunes (Novelty)	Red Seal Pict. (S. R.)	1 reel	
Sons of Swat (Sportlight)	Pathe	1 reel	Aug. 15
Sporting Judgment (Sportlight)	Pathe	1 reel	May 9
Starting an Argument (Sportlight)	Pathe	1 reel	
Steam Heated Islands (Varieties)	Fox	1 reel	
Stereoscopic (Novelty)	Pathe	1 reel	May 16
Storm King (Edmund Cobb)	Universal	2 reels	
Story Teller, The (Hodge-Podge)	Educational	1 reel	
Straight Shootin' (Harry Carey)	Universal	2 reels	
Strangler Lewis vs. Wayne Munn	Educational	2 reels	July 4
Stratford on Avon (Gems of Screen)	Red Seal Pict. (S. R.)	1 reel	
Sunken Silver (Serial)	Pathe	10 episodes	April 18
Surprise Fight, The (Benny Leonard)	Henry Ginsberg (S. R.)	2 reels	
Thundering Waters (Novelty)	Sering D. Wilson (S. R.)	1 reel	April 25

Feature	Star	Distributed by	Length	Reviewed
Tiger Kill, The (Pathe Review)		Pathe		
Toiling for Rest (Variety)		Fox	1 reel	
Traps and Troubles (Sportlight)		Pathe	1 reel	Mar. 21
Travel Treasures (Hodge Podge)		Educational	1 reel	July 25
Turf Mystery (Serial)		Chesterfield Pict. Corp. (S. R.)	15 episodes	
Valley of Rogues (Western)		Universal	2 reels	April 18
Van Bibber and the Navy (Earle Foxe)		Fox	2 reels	
Village School, The (Hodge Podge)		Educational Film	1 reel	May
Voice of the Nightingale, The (Novelty)		Educational	1 reel	Mar. 28
Waiting For You (Music Film)		Hegerman Music Novelties (S. R.)		
Welcome Granger (Pacemakers)		Film Book. Offices	2 reels	
West Wind, The (Variety)		Fox	1 reel	
What Price Gloria (Pacemakers)		Film Book. Offices	2 reels	
Wheels of the Pioneers (Billy Mack)		Denver Dixon	2 reels	
Where the Waters Divide (Varieties)		Fox	1 reel	
White Paper (Varieties)		Fox	1 reel	
Wild West Wallop, The (Edmund Cobb)		Universal	2 reels	May 16
Wild West		Pathe	Serial	
With Pencil, Brush and Chisel		Fox	1 reel	
Wonder Book, The (Series)		Sering D. Wilson	500 feet	April 26
Young Sheriff, The (Tom. Forman)		Miller & Steen (S. R.)	2 reels	
Zowie (Stereoscopik)		Pathe	1 reel	

Coming Attractions

Feature	Star	Distributed by	Length	Reviewed
Ace of Spades, The	Desmond-McAllister	Universal		
Age of Indiscretion		Truart (S. R.)	5800 feet	
American Venus, The	Special Cast	Paramount		
An Enemy of Men		Columbia Pict. (S. R.)		
Aristocrat, The	Special Cast	B. P. Schulberg (S. R.)		
Ashes	Corinne Griffith	First National		
Atlantis		First National		
Back Wash	Mary Pickford	United Artists		
Bad Lands, The	Harry Carey	Prod. Dist. Corp.		
Barriers of Fire	Monte Blue	Warner Bros.		
Beautiful Cheat, The	Laura La Plante	Universal		
Beautiful City	R. Barthelmess	First National		
Before Midnight	Wm. Russell	Ginsberg (S. R.)	5885 feet	Aug. 8
Beloved Pawn, The	Reed Howes	Rayart (S. R.)		
Ben Hur	Special Cast	Metro-Goldwyn		
Big Parade, The	John Gilbert	Metro-Goldwyn		
Border Intrigue	Franklyn Farnum	Inde. Pict. (S. R.)	5 reels	June 6
Border Women	Special Cast	Phil Goldstone (S.R.)	5000 feet	
Broken Hearts of Hollywood	Harlan-Miller	Warner Brothers		
Brown of Harvard		Metro-Goldwyn		
Caesar's Wife	Corinne Griffith	First National		
Cave Man, The	Harlan-Miller	Warner Brothers		
Charity Ball, The		Metro-Goldwyn		
Circle, The		Metro-Goldwyn		
Clean-Up, The	Richard Talmadge	F. B. O.		
Clod Hopper, The	Glenn Hunter	Assoc. Exhibitors		
Clothes Make the Pirate	Errol-D. Gish	First National		
College Widow, The	Syd Chaplin	Warner Brothers		
Coming of Amos	Rod La Rocque	Prod. Dist. Corp	5677 feet	Sept. 19
Compromise	Irene Rich	Warner Bros.		
Conquered	Gloria Swanson	Paramount		
Count of Luxembourg, The	Larry Semon	Chadwick		
Crashing Through	Jack Perrin	Ambassador Pict. (S. R.)	5000 feet	
Cyclone Bob	Bob Reeves	Anchor Film Dist.		
Cyrano de Bergerac	Special Cast	Atlas Dist. (S. R.)	9500 feet	July 18
Dance Madness	Pringle-Cody	Metro-Goldwyn		
Dangerous Currents		First National		
Dark Horse, The	Harry Carey	Prod. Dist. Corp.		
Deerslayer, The		Weiss Bros. (S. R.)	4780 feet	
Demon, The	Jack Hoxie	Universal		
Demon Rider, The	Ken Maynard	Davis Dist	5000 feet	Aug. 22
Detour		Prod. Dist. Corp.		
Down Upon the Swanee River	Special Cast	Lee Bradford (S. R.)		
Dumb Head		Tiffany (S. R.)	6500 feet	
East of the Setting Sun	Constance Talmadge	First National		
Eden's Fruit		B. P. Schulberg (S.R.)		
Enchanted Hill, The	Special Cast	Paramount		
Ermine and Rhinestone		H. F. Jans (S. R.)		
Exquisite Sinner, The	Special Cast	Metro-Goldwin		
Face on the Air, The	Evelyn Brent	F. B. O.		
Fair Play	Special Cast	Wm. Steiner (S. R.)	5035 feet	Sept. 19
Fall of Jerusalem		Weiss Bros. (S. R.)	6800 feet	
Fast Pace, The	Special Cast	Arrow		
Fifth Avenue		Prod. Dist. Corp		
Fighter's Paradise, The	Rex Baker	Phil Goldstone	5000 feet	
Fighting Courage	Ken Maynard	Davis Dist. Div. (S.R.)	5 reels	July 11
Fighting Edge, The	Harlan-Miller	Warner Brothers		
Fighting Smile, The	Bill Cody	Inde.Pict. Corp.(S.R.)	4630 feet	
First Year, The	Special Cast	Fox		
Flaming Waters		F. B. O.		
Forest of Destiny, The		Gotham Prod. (S. R.)		
Forever After	Corinne Griffith	First National		
Fort Frayne	Ben Wilson	Davis Dist.	5000 feet	Aug. 29
Free to Love	C. Bow-R. McKee	B. P. Schulberg (S. R.)		
Friends	Special Cast	Vitagraph		
Frivolity		B. P. Schulberg (S.R.)		
Galloping Dude, The	Franklyn Farnum	Inde.Pict.Corp.(S.R.)	4700 feet	
Garden of Allah		United Artists		
Going the Limit	Richard Holt	Gerson Pict. (S. R.)		
Golden Cocoon		Warner Bros.		
Goose Woman, The	Special Cast	Universal	7500 feet	Aug. 22
Go West	Buster Keaton	Metro-Goldwyn		
Grass			10 reels	Mar. 7
Great Love, The	Dana-Agnew	First National		
Handsome Brute, The	Columbia Pict. (S. R.)			
Hearts and Fists		Assoc. Exhib.		
Hearts and Spangles		Gotham Prod. (S. R.)		
Hell Bent for Heaven		Warner Bros.		
Hell's Highroad	Leatrice Joy	Prod. Dist. Corp	6084 feet	Sept. 5
Heir's Apparent	Special Cast	First National		
Her Father's Daughter		F. B. O.		
Hero of the Big Snows, A	Rin Tin Tin (dog)	Warner Brothers		
His Jazz Bride	Special Cast	Warner		
His Majesty Bunker Bean	M. Moore-Devore	Warner		
His Master's Voice	Thunder (dog)	Gotham Prod. (S. R.		
His Woman	Special Cast	Whitman Bennett	7 reels	
Hogan's Alley	Harlan-Miller	Warner		
Home Maker, The	Alice Joyce	Universal	7755 feet	Aug. 8
Honeymoon Express, The	M. Moore-D. Devore	Warner Brothers		
Horses and Women		B. P. Schulberg		
Hurricane		Truart (S. R.)	5800 feet	
Inevitable Millionaires, The	M. Moore-Devore	Warner Bros.		
Invisible Wounds	Sweet-Lyon	First National		
Irene	Colleen Moore	First National		
Justice of the Far North		C. B. C. (S. R.)	6500 feet	
Kentucky Pride	Special Cast	Fox	6597 feet	Sept. 19
Kings of the Turf		Fox		
Kiss for Cinderella, A	Betty Bronson	Paramount		
Knockout Kid, The	Jack Perrin	Rayart Pict. Corp. (S. R.)		
La Boheme	Lillian Gish	Metro-Goldwyn		
Lady Windermere's Fan	Special Cast	Warner Brothers		
Lariat, The	William Desmond	Universal		
Last Edition, The	Ralph Lewis	Film Book. Offices		
Lawful Cheater, The	Bow-McKee	B. P. Schulberg	4946 feet	
Lena Rivers	Special Cast	Arrow	6 reels	
Life of a Woman		Truart (S. R.)	6500 feet	
Lightning Jack	Jack Perrin	Ambassador Pict. (S.R.)	5000 feet	
Lightning Passes, The	Al Ferguson	Fleming Prod. (S.R.)		
Limited Mail, The	Monte Blue	Warner Bros.		
Little Girl in a Big City, A		Gotham Prod. (S. R.)		
Little Irish Girl, The	Special Cast	Warner Bros.		
Live Wire, The	Johnny Hines	First National		
Lodge in the Wilderness		Tiffany (S. R.)	6500 feet	
Lord Jim	Percy Marmont	Paramount		
Love Cargo, The	House Peters	Universal		
Love Gamble, The	Special Cast	Banner Prod. (S. R.)	5766 feet	July 11
Lover's Island	Hampton-Kirkwood	Assoc. Exhib.		
Love Toy, The	Lowell Sherman	Warner Bros		
Loyalties	Special Cast	Fox		
Lucky Lady, The	Lionel Barrymore	Paramount		
Lure of Broadway, The		Columbia Pict. (S. R.)		
Lying Wives	Special Cast	Ivan Abramson (S. R.)	7 reels	May 2
Man and the Moment		Metro-Goldwyn		
Man From Red Gulch	Harry Carey	Prod. Dist. Corp.		
Man of Iron, A	L. Barrymore	Chadwick	6 reels	July 4
Man on the Box, The	Sydney Chaplin	Warner Bros		
Man She Bought, The	Constance Talmadge	First National		
Man Without a Conscience	Louis-Rich	Warner Bros	6850 feet	May 2
Mare Nostrum	Special Cast	Metro-Goldwyn		
Married Hypocrites	Fredericks-La Plante	Universal		
Martinique	Bebe Daniels	Paramount		
Masked Bride, The	Mae Murray	Metro-Goldwyn		
Men of Steel	Milton Sills	First National		
Memory Lane	Boardman-Nagel	First National		
Message to Garcia, A		Metro-Goldwyn		
Miracle of Life, The	Busch-Marmont	Assoc. Exhib		
Miracle of the Wolves, The			10346 feet	Mar. 7
Midnight Flames		Columbia Pict. (S. R.)		
Miss Vanity	Mary Philbin	Universal		
Million Dollar Doll		Assoc. Exhib		
Mocking Bird, The	Lon Chaney	M-G-M		
Morganson's Finish		Tiffany (S. R.)	6500 feet	
Moving Finger, The	Special Cast	Paramount		
Napoleon the Great		Universal		
Night Call, The	Rin-Tin-Tin (dog)	Warner Brothers		
North Star, The	Strongheart (dog)	Assoc. Exhib		
Old Clothes	Jackie Coogan	Metro-Goldwyn		
Only Thing, The	Special Cast	Metro-Goldwyn		
Open Trail, The	Jack Hoxie	Universal	4800 feet	May 16
Pace That Thrills, The	Ben Lyon	First National		
Pals		Truart (S. R.)	5800 feet	
Paris	Pauline Starke	Metro-Goldwyn		
Paris After Dark	Norma Talmadge	First National		
Partners Again		United Artists		
Passionate Quest, The	Marie Prevost	Warner Bros		
Passionate Youth	Special Cast	Truart (S. R.)	6 reels	July 11
Part Time Wife, The		Gotham Prod. (S. R.)		
Peak of Fate, The		F. B. Rogers	5 reels	June 27
People vs. Nancy Preston	Bowers-De La Motte	Prod. Dist. Corp.		
Phantom of the Opera	Lon Chaney	Universal	8464 feet	Sept. 19
Pinch Hitter, The	Glenn Hunter	Asso. Exhibitors		
Pleasure Buyers, The	Irene Rich	Warner Brothers		
Police Patrol, The	James Kirkwood	Gotham Prod. (S.R.)	6000 feet	Sept. 19
Polly of the Ballet	Bebe Daniels	Paramount		
Pony Express, The	Special Cast	Universal		
Prairie Pirate, The	Harry Carey	Prod. Dist. Corp.		
Prince, The	Philbin-Kerry	Universal		
Quality Street		Metro-Goldwyn		
Quicker 'n Lightning	Buffalo Bill, Jr.	Weiss Bros. (S. R.)	5 reels	June 13
Racing Blood		Gotham Prod. (S. R.)		
Reckless Courage	Buddy Roosevelt	Weiss Bros. (S. R.)	4851 feet	May 2
Reckless Sex, The	Special Cast	Truart (S. R.)	6 reels	Feb. 14
Red Clay	William Desmond	Universal		
Red Dice	Rod La Rocque	Prod. Dist. Corp.		
Red Hot Tires	Monte Blue	Warner Bros.		
Return of a Soldier	Special Cast	Metro-Goldwyn		
Rime of the Ancient Mariner, The		Fox Film		
Road to Yesterday, The	Special Cast	Prod. Dist. Corp		
Road That Led Home, The		Vitagraph		
Romance of an Actress		Chadwick		
Ropin' Venus, The	Josie Sedgwick	Universal		
Rose of the World	Special Cast	Warner Bros		
Sally, Irene and Mary	Special Cast	Metro-Goldwyn		
Salvage		Truart (S. R.)	5800 feet	
Sap, The	M. Moore D. Devore	Warner Bros		
Satan in Sables	Lowell Sherman	Warner Bros		
Savage, The	Ben Lyon	First National		
Scarlet Saint, The	Lyon-Astor	First National		
Scraps	Mary Pickford	United Artists		
Sea Beast, The	John Barrymore	Warner Bros.		
Sea Woman, The	Sweet-McLaglen	First National		
Seven Days	Lillian Rich	Prod. Dist. Corp.		
Seven Sinners	Marie Prevost	Warner Bros.		
Seventh Heaven	Special Cast	Fox		
Shadow of the Wall		Gotham Prod. (S. R.)		
Shadow of the Mosque	Odette Taylor	Cranfield & Clarke (S. R.)	6200 feet	
Shenandoah		B. P. Schulberg (S. R.)		
Ship of Souls	B. Lytell-L. Rich	Assoc. Exhib	6800 feet	
Shootin' Square	Jack Perrin	Ambassador Pict. (S.R.)	5000 feet	
Siegfried		Ufa		
Sign of the Claw		Gotham Prod. (S. R.)		
Silken Shackles	Irene Rich	Warner Bros.		
Silver Treasure, The	Special Cast	Fox		
Simon the Jester	Rich-O'Brien	Prod. Dist. Corp.		
Social Highwayman, The	Harlan-Miller	Warner Brothers		
Son of His Father, A	Special Cast	Paramount	6925 feet	Sept. 19
Spanish Sunlight	LaMarr-Stone	First National		
Span of Life	Betty Blythe	Banner Prod. (S. R.)		
Speed Limit, The		Gotham Prod. (S. R.)		
Splendid Road, The	Anna Q. Nillson	First National		
Steele of the Royal Mounted		Vitagraph	6 reels	June 27
Stella Dallas		United Artists		

Feature	Star	Distributed by	Length	Reviewed
Stella Maris	Mary Philbin	Universal		
Still Alarm, The	Chadwick-Russell	Universal		
Strange Bedfellows		Metro-Goldwyn		
Storm Breakers,The	House Peters	Universal		
Sunshine of Paradise Alley	Special Cast	Chadwick Pict.		
Super Speed	Reed Howes	Rayart (S. R.)		
Sweet Adeline	Charles Ray	Chadwick		
Tale of a Vanishing People		Lefty Flynn		
Tearing Loose	Wally Wales	Weiss Bros. (S. R.)	4900 feet	June 13
Tempress		Paramount		
Ten to Midnight		Prod. Dist. Corp.		
That Man from Arizona	D.Revier-W.Fairbanks	F. B. O.		
That Royle Girl	Kirkwood-Dempster	Paramount		
This Woman	Special Cast	Fox		
Thoroughbred, The	Special Cast	Truart	5481 feet	Sept. 19
Three Bad Men	Special Cast	Fox		
Three Faces East		Prod. Dist. Corp.		
Trailing Shadows	Edmund Lowe	Fox Film		
Travelin' Fast	Jack Perrin	Ambassador Pict. (S. R.)	6060 feet	
Travis Coup, The		Tiffany (S. R.)	6500 feet	
Twin Sister, The	Constance Talmadge	First National		
Two Blocks Away	Special Cast	Universal		
Unchastened Woman, The	Theda Bara	Chadwick		
Unguarded Hour, The	Sills-Kenyon	First National		
Unknown Lover, The	Elsie Ferguson	Vitagraph		
Up and At' Em	Jack Perrin	Ambassador Pict. (S. R.)	5809 feet	
Vengeance of Durand, The	Irene Rich	Warner Brothers		
Viennese Medley	Special Cast	First National		
Volga Boatman, The		Prod. Dist. Corp.		
Wages for Wives	Special Cast	Fox		
Wanderer, The	William Collier, Jr.	Paramount	8173 feet	
Wandering Footsteps	H. Ginsberg (S. R.)			
Warrior Gap	Wilson-Gerber	Davis Dist.	4906 feet	Aug. 22
Wedding Song, The	Leatrice Joy	Prod. Dist. Corp.		
We Moderns		First National		
Where Will People Say		Metro-Goldwyn		
Where the Worst Begins		Truart (S. R.)	5800 feet	

Feature	Star	Distributed by	Length	Reviewed
White Chief, The	Monte Blue	Warner Bros.		
White Mice	Jacqueline Logan	Sering D. Wilson (S.R.)		
Why Girls Go Back Home		Warner Bros.		
Wild Girl		Truart (S. R.)	5800 feet	Aug. 1
Wild Justice	Peter the Great	United Artists	6 reels	Aug. 1
Wild Ridin'	Buck Jones	Fox		
Winning of Barbara Worth		Principal Pict. (S. R.)		
Wise Guy, The		Film Book. Offices		
Without Mercy	Vera Reynolds	Prod. Dist. Corp.		
Womanhandled	Richard Dix	Paramount		
Women and Wives		Metro-Goldwyn		
World's Illusion, The		Metro-Goldwyn		
Worst Woman, The	Special Cast	B. P. Schulberg (S. R.)		
Wrong Coat, The		Tiffany Prod. (S. R.)	5500 feet	
Voley Boatman, The		Prod. Dist. Corp.		
We Moderns	Colleen Moore	First National		
Wanderer, The	William Collier, Jr.	Paramount	8173 feet	
Warrior Gap	Wilson-Gerber	Davis Dist.	4906 feet	Aug. 22
Wedding Song, The	Leatrice Joy	Prod. Dist. Corp.		
What Will People Say		Metro-Goldwyn		
Where the Worst Begins		Truart (S. R.)	5800 feet	
White Chief, The	Monte Blue	Warner Brothers		
White Mice	Jacqueline Logan	Sering D. Wilson (S.R.)		
Why Girls Go Back Home		Warner Bros.		
Wild Girl		Truart (S. R.)	5800 feet	
Wild Justice	Peter the Great	United Artists	6 reels	Aug. 1
Wild Ridin'	Buck Jones	Fox		
Winning of Barbara Worth		Principal Pict. (S. R.)		
Wise Guy, The		F. B. O.		
With Kit Carson Over the Great Divide	Special Cast	Sunset Prod. (S. R.)		
Without Mercy	Vera Reynolds	Prod. Dist. Corp.		
Womanhandled	Richard Dix	Paramount		
Women		Banner Prod. (S. R.)		
World's Illusion, The		Metro-Goldwyn		
Worst Woman, The	Special Cast	Metro-Goldwyn		
Wrong Coat, The	Special Cast	Tiffany (S. R.)	6500 feet	
Yarn, The	Special Cast	Warner Brothers		
You Can't Live on Love	Reginald Denny	Universal		

Newspaper Opinions on New Features

"Drusilla With A Million" — F. B. O., Opera House, Easton, Pa.

Press: "'Drusilla With A Million' at the Opera House this week should play to crowded houses. It is a masterpiece of motion picture art and the biggest thing since 'Over The Hill' which it equals in pathos and heart interest. Mary Carr, who played the mother in 'Over The Hill' plays Drusilla with the delicious mother appeal that she knows how to invoke. It is remarkable how Miss Carr can portray age so realistically. Equally as noteworthy in the play is Priscilla Bonner's portrayal of Sally May, the orphanage waif. The story makes a picture that everyone will want to see."

"Drusilla With A Million" — F. B. O., Colonial, Indianapolis

Times: "One of the nation's best photoplays—that's 'Drusilla With A Million.' When the history of the American movie industry is written I am sure that 'Drusilla' will be included in the list of the very best pictures ever made. Because of its simplicity, its charm, the human acting of Mary Carr, Priscilla Bonner, Kenneth Harlan and the greatest lot of babies ever assembled in a movie studio, 'Drusilla With A Million' will be a picture to be remembered."

"Sally of the Sawdust"—United Artists, Rialto, L. A.

News: "'Sally of the Sawdust' is a great picture. The picture brings deep-seated guffaws with its comedy, and counts ten with its dramatic moments."

Times: "One glorious circus picture—'Sally of the Sawdust.' The Lord only knows when it will end its run here. It makes them laugh, it makes them cry, it makes them thrill."

Examiner: "The new Griffith film is deliciously funny."

Express: "As to entertainment in abundance, there cannot be a doubt."

"The Unholy Three" — M.-G.-M., State, New Bedford

Mercury: "It is a picture which, as shown at the State yesterday was the most engrossingly fascinating offering this far in a season that has started out brilliantly. Mr. Chaney's portrayal was another triumph in virile character-ization for that gifted actor. His portrayal was no less effective than that of the clown in 'He Who Gets Slapped.' Harry Earle's impersonation of Tweedledee was masterly, the midget's clever assumption of a baby role and his callous willingness to engage in any crime being delineated with a skill that contributed largely to the spooky tenseness of the dramatic situations."

Standard: "The photoplay 'The Unholy Three' being shown this week at the State Theatre is a crook melodrama of great power and refreshing originality. You may say that its excellence is due to the fine discrimination of its director, Tod Browning; to brilliant character acting by Lon Chaney and six more; or to the strange and unusual story of criminals, true to life; but the truth is, this picture is like Kipling's 'ship that found itself' during its first voyage,—it is one imaginative whole, commanding an imaginative response from its audience. We thought 'The Unholy Three' splendid entertainment."

Times: "A mystery picture that is off the beaten path and as thrilling as any melodrama has arrived. It's 'The Unholy Three,' the Metro-Goldwyn-Mayer picture which played to packed houses Sunday at its premiere showing at the State. Director Tod Browning has contributed his greatest work to the screen in this singular tale of the villainous careers of three undisciplined freaks thrown together in a dime museum."

"The Freshman"—Pathe, Million Dollar, L. A.

Times: " 'The Freshman' is one of Lloyd's top-notch triumphs. It is great, taken all in all, vastly amusing; refreshing and pepful to a high degree, with a touch of romance that makes the enjoyment of the audience seem ever to have extra zest. It is all mechanically perfect, with spontaneity, too, and proves Harold and his entire staff capable of amazing invention."

Express: "It was a field day for Momus. The god of ridicule must have scored his highest record in throwing humans into laughter spasms when Harold Lloyd's comedy 'The Freshman,' received at the Million Dollar Theatre its first showing. If it has ever been exceeded, it is not within the ken of anyone present. It sets a new mark for his powers for effective drama, for realism and for threading his attack on the risibles with sympathetic appeal. In the course of the story there are innumerable episodes that rouse the audience not merely to amusement but to 'belly laugh-ter' spontaneous and uncontrolled."

Record: "If there has ever been a doubt in your mind whether Harold Lloyd is our foremost screen comedian, then 'The Freshman' will certainly remove all doubts. Lloyd has given us many enjoyable hours through his past efforts at comedy, but it can be truthfully stated that this has them all beaten. Never have I ever witnessed such a storm of approval for any film as that yesterday afternoon during the first performance."

Herald: "You'll laugh. You'll feel a little catch at the throat. You'll go away saying that it is one of the most wholesome screen comedies you have ever seen. That is, if you are just an ordinary American with a good old-fashioned Yankee sense of humor.

That's the prediction of this reviewer after seeing Harold Lloyd's newest mirth-provoker, 'The Freshman' at the Million Dollar Theatre yesterday. The picture has everything, dramatically speaking."

News: "Howdy, Mister Lloyd! Heretofore I have always called you Harold. With utmost respect, it is true, but never with that particular brand to which your work in 'The Freshman' entitles you. 'The Freshman,' the mister substitution. Hence, the mister substitution. Your comedies have been bigger and better from the beginning. But 'The Freshman' leaves me speechless."

Examiner: "Fun gushes forth with the unfailing prodigality of a geyser in Harold Lloyd's new comedy, 'The Freshman.' This popular comedian finds an inexhaustible source of lively humor on the college campus. He has his audiences at the Million Dollar Theatre rocking in their seats at the vicissitudes of the young collegian he impersonates. Further than that, he has them cheering him to victory in the football scenes. 'Some achievement in the annals of the silent drama! Not since 'Grandma's Boy' has Lloyd had the opportunity to temper his clowning with pathos."

"His Buddy's Wife" — Associated Ex., Loew's, New York, N. Y.

Graphic: " 'His Buddy's Wife,' starring Glenn Hunter, is being featured at the Loew Theatres, and we want to say that the patrons of the outlying movie houses have a great treat in store for them. The picture is a Tom Terriss production and is as fine a bit of artistry as we've seen anywhere anytime. Glenn Hunter scores a hit as the hero, doing some of the best work we've ever seen him do—but then, Mr. Hunter never fails to register the ability he displays in this film. Edna Murphy is sweet, pretty, and altogether charming."

NDER the personal management of Gloria Gould, the Embassy Theatre draws its patronage from the elite of New York City.

Quality is the key note of this exclusive theatre. In selecting the furnishings Miss Gould chose for class, distinction — superiority.

The matter of selecting projection equipment was placed in the hands of experts. For, as the management expressed it, what could be more essential in this theatre than perfect picture presentation?

* * * * * *

Naturally Simplex projectors were unanimously chosen.

You have a critical audience to please, and they too will appreciate good projection. Why not follow the example of the best theatres? Install Simplex projectors and assure your audience perfect pictures. Simplex projectors cost no more and they pay bigger profits in the long run. Get full particulars as to prices, terms, etc., from your nearest supply dealer.

Simplex Projectors are Sold and Serviced
by the following Theatre Supply Dealers:

Rothacker-Aller Laboratories, Hollywood, Calif.

C. C. Burr presents Johnny Hines
In *"The Live Wire'* —adapted from
Richard Washburn Child's story,
"The Game of Light." Directed by
Charles Hines. Titles by John Krafft.
Photography by Charles E. Gilson and
Johnny Geisel. *A lively entertainment.*
A First National Picture.
Rothacker Prints and Service.

Johnny Hines
" The Live Wire "

Look Better —
Wear Longer!

Founded 1910
by
Watterson R. Rothacker

MARION DAVIES

in

MONTA BELL'S *Production*

Lights of Old Broadway

with CONRAD NAGEL

Directed by Monta Bell

Adapted by Carey Wilson from the play
"Merry Wives of Gotham" by LAURENCE EYRE

A Cosmopolitan Production

Metro-
Goldwyn
Mayer's

The
Quality
52

FALL PIPPINS!

RAYMOND **GRIFFITH** IN "He's A Prince!"

DOUGLAS **MacLEAN** IN "7 Keys to Baldpate"

JAMES CRUZE'S "THE PONY EXPRESS"

BEBE **DANIELS** IN "Lovers in Quarantine" with HARRISON FORD

WILLIAM de MILLE'S "NEW BROOMS"

BETTY **BRONSON** IN "The Golden Princess"

*A Pippin a week
Keeps receipts at the peak!*

And these
Pippin Paramount Pictures
All Come in One Month—October!

"MISS AMERICA" has been

THE EXPLOITA

Reason No.2

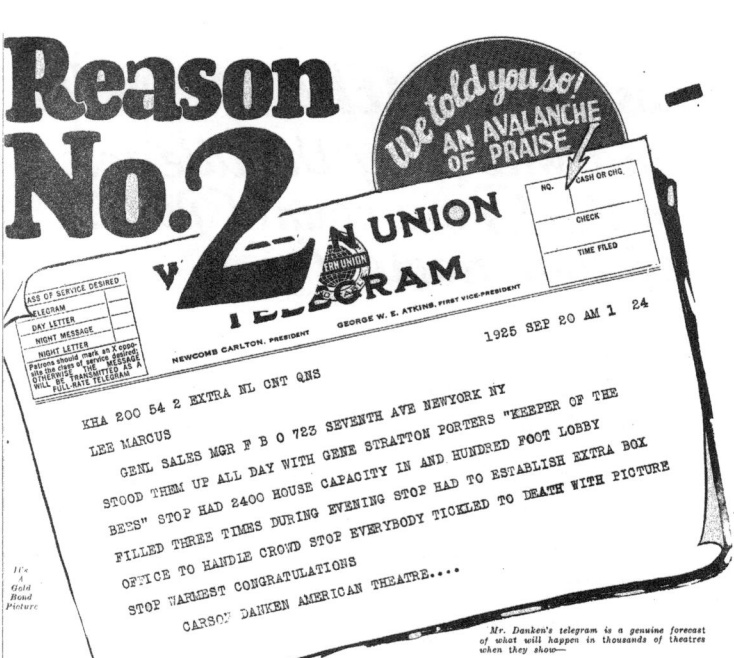

We told you so! AN AVALANCHE OF PRAISE

WESTERN UNION TELEGRAM

GEORGE W. E. ATKINS, FIRST VICE-PRESIDENT

NEWCOMB CARLTON, PRESIDENT

1925 SEP 20 AM 1 24

KHA 200 54 2 EXTRA NL CNT QNS

LEE MARCUS
GENL SALES MGR F B O 723 SEVENTH AVE NEWYORK NY
STOOD THEM UP ALL DAY WITH GENE STRATTON PORTERS "KEEPER OF THE
BEES" STOP HAD 2400 HOUSE CAPACITY IN AND HUNDRED FOOT LOBBY
FILLED THREE TIMES DURING EVENING STOP HAD TO ESTABLISH EXTRA BOX
OFFICE TO HANDLE CROWD STOP EVERYBODY TICKLED TO DEATH WITH PICTURE
STOP WARMEST CONGRATULATIONS
CARSON DANKEN AMERICAN THEATRE....

Mr. Danken's telegram is a genuine forecast of what will happen in thousands of theatres when they show—

Gene Stratton-Porter's greatest story,
"The KEEPER OF THE BEES"

Backed by a tremendous Advertising-Publicity and Exploitation Campaign in conjunction with Doubleday Page & Co. and backed by four solid months of display advertising in McCall's Magazine.

FILM BOOKING OFFICES OF AMERICA, Inc.
723 Seventh Avenue, New York · *Exchanges Everywhere*

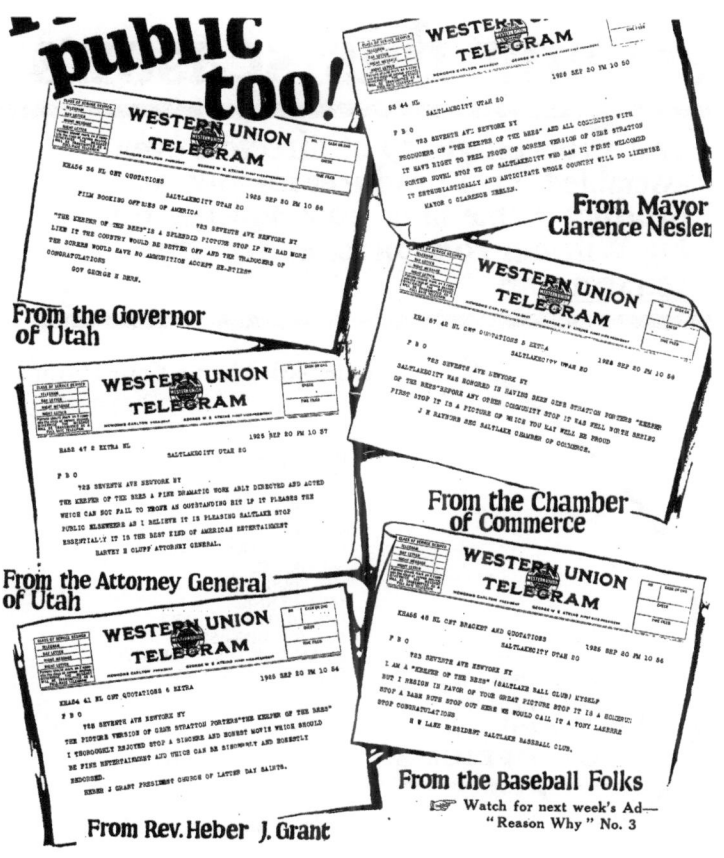

staging this season's

'The strongest group of directors ever assembled by a producer for any year's product ~~~ the men **now** **making** the big William Fox pictures for **this season** ~~~

Their Skill Means Your Profit

from

THE IRON HORSE
*LIGHTNIN'
THE LUCKY HORSESHOE
AS NO MAN HAS LOVED
KENTUCKY PRIDE
*THANK YOU
HAVOC
*THUNDER MOUNTAIN
LAZYBONES
*THE FIRST YEAR
EAST LYNNE
THE FIGHTING HEART
THE WINDING STAIR
WHEN THE DOOR OPENED
THE JOHNSTOWN FLOOD
THE SILVER TREASURE
THE FOOL
*THE WHEEL
*WAGES FOR WIVES
THE ANCIENT MARINER
THE BEST BAD MAN

*John Golden Unit of
Clean American Pictures

their work has stood the test ~ the acid test of the **BOX OFFICE**

Fox Film Corporation.

sensational FOX successes!

JOHN FORD—mention his name and you think of "The Iron Horse," one of the greatest pictures of all time. He has also produced "Lightnin'" and "Thank You"—John Golden plays—"Kentucky Pride" and "The Fighting Heart."

REGINALD BARKER, master director of outdoor pictures, has produced a screen triumph for Fox, based on James Oliver Curwood's "When the Door Opened." Now he's preparing to film "The Johnstown Flood," a dynamic American epic.

JOHN GRIFFITH WRAY has made A. E. W. Mason's novel, "The Winding Stair," into a photoplay that breathes the romance of Morocco and the dash of the French Foreign Legion. It strengthens Wray's well earned reputation for producing artistic box office successes.

J. G. BLYSTONE has added to the pleasure of millions of Tom Mix fans with "The Lucky Horseshoe," which followed the Blystone-Mix production, "Dick Turpin." Now they are filming a popular Max Brand novel, "The Best Bad Man."

VICTOR SCHERTZINGER has made "Thunder Mountain," based on "Howdy Folks," a real drama of love in the hills of hate. "The Wheel" has all the punch of the stage play. Both are Golden successes, with proved audience appeal.

FRANK BORZAGE has done some of the best work of his distinguished career in filming "Lazybones," Owen Davis' gripping stage drama. Borzage will also direct "Wages for Wives" and "The First Year," John Golden plays. All three have proved their box office pull.

ROWLAND V. LEE has made "Havoc" into a powerful film. In "As No Man Has Loved" he has caught the adventure and romance of Hale's story, "The Man Without a Country." He packed all the thrills of Conrad's "Nostromo" into "The Silver Treasure," a colorful South American romance.

HARRY MILLARDE has made the screen version of Channing Pollock's play, "The Fool," with the same intelligent sympathy that he put into world-renowned "Over the Hill," one of the greatest money-makers the screen has known.

EMMETT FLYNN'S name recalls "The Connecticut Yankee." Now he's made another masterpiece, "East Lynne." It's better than the original melodrama, which has always drawn patronage for three generations. The picture will pack them in.

HENRY OTTO is celebrated for his skill in bringing fantasy to the screen. In "The Ancient Mariner" he gives his imagination free play, and it promises to beat his former greatest achievements.

Fox Film Corporation.

WILLIAM FOX
Presents

The
WINDING
STAIR

THE FIRST YEAR
with Matt Moore
Frank Borzage *Production*
John Golden's Great Comedy Hit of Married Life

Fox Film Corporation.

From the novel by A.E.W. MASON

The Heroic Coward's Battle for Love

with

EDMUND LOWE ~ ALMA RUBENS
WARNER OLAND ~ MAHLON HAMILTON
EMILY FITZROY ~ CHESTER CONKLIN

Scenario by JULIAN La MOTHE
JOHN GRIFFITH WRAY Production

How Can We Im
Metro-Gold

1. LOBBY CARDS: Do you use them? Can you suggest improvements in their make-up?	**2.** POSTERS: What paper do you buy for a normal showing? Do you use block as well as pictorial 24-sheets?
3. ADVERTISING: What space do you use for an average showing? Indicate whether the following list of advertising material is sufficient for your average newspaper requirements: Three 1-col. ads. Two 2-col. ads. Two 3-col. ads. One 4-col. ad. One 6-col. ad. Five character line drawings. Assortment of 1-2-3 and 4-col. advertising slugs. Can you suggest any additions to this choice of advertising material?	**4.** LINE CUTS and HALF-TONES: Which type of advertisement do you prefer? Many exhibitors declare that half-tone reproduction is unsatisfactory. Are advertisements in line safest for your general needs?
5. MATS and CUTS: Which do you use in advertising? Do you find your present cut service satisfactory in the exchanges or does it appear that there is not a sufficient supply of cuts available?	**6.** SLIDES: Do you use them? Have you any suggestions to make regarding improvement in their selling value? Do you believe that slides should carry brief copy in addition to announcing the production?
7. HERALDS: Do you use them? What suggestions can you offer for making them more effective?	**8.** ROTOGRAVURE SUPPLEMENTS: Have you ever planted a Roto Supplement with your Sunday newspaper? Do you believe that their selling value is worth their expense? Do you advocate them on Special Productions only?

METRO-GOLDWYN-MAYER is making the outstanding box-office hits today. Pictures like "The Unholy Three," "Pretty Ladies," "A Slave of Fashion," "Sun up," "Never the Twain Shall Meet" deserve the most effective promotion that it is possible to offer to exhibitors.

prove Our Service?
wyn-Mayer

Believing that the only intelligent cooperation is the one arrived at by getting the
opinion of the exhibitor who is in direct contact with the public, offers these questions:

9. SERIALIZATION OF PICTURE STORIES: Do you find that serials running in local newspapers help build interest in attractions? Is your local newspaper interested?	**10. RHYMED REVIEWS:** Do you think a Rhymed Review on each picture would be a welcome addition to your press and advertising service? Would you use a Rhymed Review on a panel in your lobby?
11. PRODUCTION CUTS: Do you get production cuts of the right kind for your press work? Can you make any suggestions that might be of help to you in bettering this service?	**12. PRESS MATERIAL:** Are you getting publicity and feature stories of the kind your editor requires? Have you any ideas for improving this service?
13. ACCESSORIES: Which is your most valuable accessory? Have you found a need for any additional advertising aid which is not furnished by your exchange?	**14. STILLS:** Do you find the production stills furnished are satisfactory for your needs? For newspaper reproduction? For use in lobby frames? Do you favor including straight portraits of all prominent players in the cast?
15. PICTURE REVIEWS SERVICE: We have recently instituted the new Picture Reviews Service, the first time this has been done. What do you think of it?	**16. CAMPAIGN BOOKS:** What could we have added to the campaign book on for example "The Unholy Three" (you can get a copy from your exchange) that you would need?

WHEN you fill out this questionnaire you are helping
us to help you. Fill in these answers and mail
to: Service Editor, Metro-Goldwyn-Mayer, 1540 Broadway,
New York City. Your opinion will be appreciated and
every effort made to follow your helpful suggestion.

Carl Laemmle
presents

Sporting Life

with

BERT LYTELL
PAULETTE DUVAL
and **MARIAN NIXON**

*from the famous Drury Lane melo-
drama by Seymour Hicks and
Cecil Raleigh - A Maurice Tourneur
Production - Universal Jewel.*

Monday

I've got my horse in training
for the Derby race. He must
win! I've got 50,000 pounds
up on him. And every nobleman, all England, will be
there. I met Nora for the first time
today. Between a horse and
a woman I've got
TROUBLES!

Saturday

DIARY

What a race! The Derby was the
greatest ever run. Talking
about excitement! And — Nora
won! loves me!
Glorious
World!

UNIVERSAL — WHITE LIST — MILES AND MILES — AHEAD — OF — ALL

"GO OVER BIG IN ANY THEATRE! JAM FULL OF ACTION AND EXCITEMENT!

— Motion Pictures Tod

Tuesday DIARY

What a battle! I found Nora and her kidnappers in a dark cellar where she was being held for ransom. How I lit into those scoundrels! They'll need an ambulance to carry them away. I grabbed Nora and jumped into my racer and what a chase they gave me!

Wednesday DIARY

Just because I've fallen in love with Nora, they've kidnapped her, to keep my attention from the Derby race. I'd rather lose all my money than this new happiness in loving Nora. I've got to find her! If they injure so much as her little finger I'll have their heads!

Thursday DIARY

Olive should be more sensible. I'm in love with Nora and that's that. I'm thru with Olive. What a howl she raised backstage tonight. Being wealthy and eligible has its drawbacks when a woman decides a man can't stop loving her. She's going to stir a lot of trouble.

Friday DIARY

Trouble never stops comin'! My fighter backed down and I had to take his place in the ring, to cover my big bet. And I'm there when it comes to a fight! What I did to that fellow is a shame. He looks like a moth-eaten turnip now. And I've got 10,000 pounds in my pocket.

Just Another Showmanship Picture on Universal's Great White List!

A

becom

C

To the Editor of Greater Amusements:

Seeing so much about Universal's complete service plan, or contract, I may say that I have booked this service and believe it is the only sane thing that the small town exhibitor can do. I had to discontinue my mid-week shows until Universal's salesman came along with the complete service proposition, and I took him up with the idea that there was another hitch somewhere that would cost me as much in the long run as the old system of contracts.

However, I am pleased to say that I find that I can run my mid-week shows, change shows on Sunday, and besides realize a small profit on Wednesday. I double my patronage Saturday and Sunday and the program for the week sets me back just a trifle less than when I ran three nights per week, with two programs. Universal comedies fill a long felt want, and their features never fail to please. I am strong for the complete service plan, and if other producers would open their eyes and hearts to the needs of the small town showman as Universal has, there would be less weeping, wailing and gnashing of teeth.—

A. W. Martin, Legion Theatre, Blunt, S. D.

Already
bigger

WARNING!

It has come to our notice that certain scenes from INTERNA-TIONAL NEWSREEL, and particularly some of those which appear in INTERNATIONAL NEWSREEL'S two-reel production, "LIFE'S GREATEST THRILLS," which is creating such a tremendous sensation throughout the country, are being offered for sale to various producing companies.

Attention is hereby called to the fact that every issue of INTERNATIONAL NEWSREEL is copyrighted, and that every scene appearing in each issue is fully protected under these copyrights. This protection covers also all scenes in the two-reel production, "LIFE'S GREATEST THRILLS." All persons are warned against showing these pictures, either publicly or privately, unless authorized by INTERNATIONAL NEWSREEL, which is released exclusively by Universal Film Exchanges, Inc. Any violation of this warning will be prosecuted to the fullest extent of the law.

Attention is also called to the fact that the title, "LIFE'S GREATEST THRILLS," is registered in the patent office at Washington, and is the exclusive property of INTERNATIONAL NEWSREEL, which forbids its use by any person or corporation.

INTERNATIONAL NEWSREEL

Released Through Universal

"Be Careful"

Not to miss one of the best box-office bets of the season among Short Subjects by letting the other fellow beat you to the new series of six two-reel

JIMMIE ADAMS COMEDIES

PRESENTS

Jimmie Adams

in his first starring comedy

"This is a comedy fairly bulging with humorous situations"—M. P. NEWS

"BE CAREFUL"

Produced by
CHRISTIE

Popular demand raised Adams to the head of his own comedy company after a long series of unbroken laugh successes on the *Educational Pictures* program. Popular demand will make the Jimmie Adams Comedies producers of Extra Profit for You if you get back of them with proper advertising and exploitation.

EDUCATIONAL
FILM EXCHANGES, Inc.
E.W. Hammons
President

Member, Motion Picture Producers
and Distributors of America, Inc.,
Will H. Hays, President

Educational Pictures
"THE SPICE OF THE PROGRAM"

"KINOGRAMS

GOES ON EVERY SHOW
OUR PUBLIC DEMANDS IT"

So wrote Earl Hall Payne, Managing Director of the Kentucky Theatre, Kentucky, to the editor of Film Daily, *and the editor thought so much of the letter that he printed a whole page of it with a picture of Mr. Payne's theatre in the issue of Sept. 26 last*

Mr. Payne also wrote in part:-

"We have proved that our news can be made to bring in money, and not used just as a reel of film to open the show with in order to kill 12 minutes. With long shows when it means that something must come out, *it is never the news reel."*

That Is How Mr. Payne Puts Over His News Reel Which Happens To Be

KINOGRAMS
The News Reel Built Like a Newspaper

TEN YEARS'

FOR TEN YEARS THE STAMP OF
HAS BEEN THE STANDARD OF QUALITY

Absolute Supremacy in the

Your Guarantee

The Life-saver

Success Founded

The Standard

Al Christie

CHRISTIE FILM COMPANY, Inc.
Member, Motion Picture Producers and Distributors
of America, Inc.   Will H. Hays, President

LEADERSHIP

**CHRISTIE ON TWO-REEL COMEDIES
IN BEST THEATRES EVERYWHERE**

SEASON OF

1925-6

Field of "Short Features"

of a Full Quota of Laughs

of Many a Bill ———

on Audience Appreciation

Comedy all over the World

10 CHRISTIE COMEDIES
6 BOBBY VERNON COMEDIES
6 WALTER HIERS COMEDIES
6 JIMMIE ADAMS COMEDIES

Released through
EDUCATIONAL FILM EXCHANGES, Inc.

An audience

THE SATURDAY EVENING POST

THE SATURDAY EVENING POST

FIFTH AVENUE By ARTHUR STRINGER

A.H. SEBASTIAN
PRESENTS

'FIFTH AVENUE'

WITH
MARGUERITE
DE LA MOTTE
ALLAN
FORREST
LOTTIE PICKFORD
LOUISE DRESSER
SALLY LONG
WILLARD LOUIS

adapted by ANTHONY COLDEWEY from the
SATURDAY EVENING POST STORY
by ARTHUR STRINGER
Directed by
ROBERT G. VIGNOLA

of TEN
MILLION

A N audience limited only by the number of people who can read, is waiting to see "FIFTH AVENUE" on the screen!

The number of readers of The Saturday Evening Post is conservatively estimated at 10,000,000.

Here is your patronage *guaranteed in advance!*

Arthur Stringer is a writer whose stories are eagerly looked for by readers of the popular publications. They are vivid, realistic, colorful and human. He knows the highways and the byways of metropolitan life. He knows Fifth Avenue — its splendor and its sophistry — its sophistication and its shams — and he has put his first-hand knowledge into a story that is thrilling millions of readers today.

Filmed on the actual scenes, the local color and sense of reality of New York's most famous thoroughfare are visualized as they have never been before on the screen.

A GREAT STORY!   A WONDERFUL CAST!
A SUMPTUOUS PRODUCTION!

An Audience Waiting to
Storm Your Box Office!

RELEASED BY
PRODUCERS DISTRIBUTING CORPORATION

F. C. MUNROE, President   RAYMOND PAWLEY, Vice-President and Treasurer   JOHN C. FLINN, Vice-President and General Manager
Member of: Motion Picture Producers and Distributors of America, Inc.—Will H. Hays, President

hitting the high spots!

Melodrama
"The Limited Mail"
with
Monte Blue

Society Drama
"The Wife Who
Wasn't Wanted"
with
Irene Rich

There's Varied

The Warner

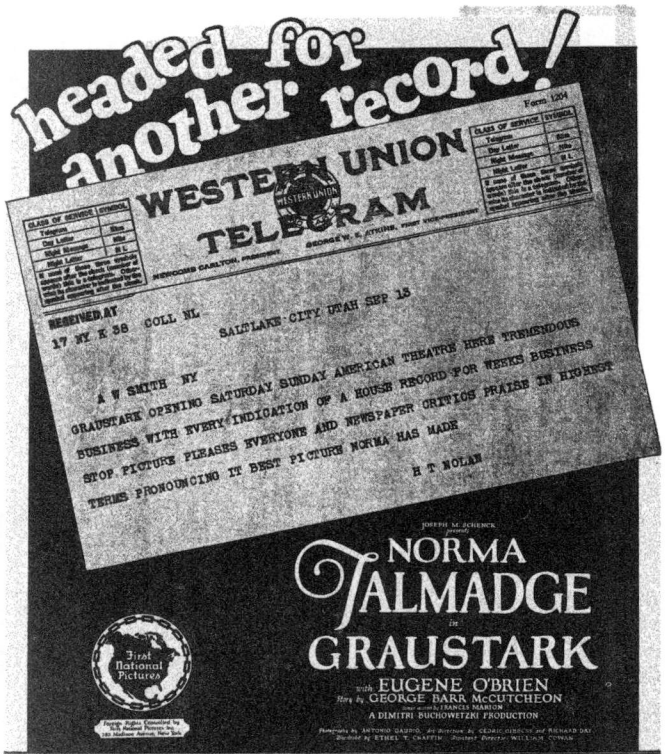

headed for another record!

WESTERN UNION TELEGRAM

Form 1204

SALT LAKE CITY UTAH SEP 13

A W SMITH NY

GRAUSTARK OPENING SATURDAY SUNDAY AMERICAN THEATRE HERE TREMENDOUS
BUSINESS WITH EVERY INDICATION OF A HOUSE RECORD FOR WEEKS BUSINESS
STOP PICTURE PLEASES EVERYONE AND NEWSPAPER CRITICS PRAISE IN HIGHEST
TERMS PRONOUNCING IT BEST PICTURE NORMA HAS MADE

H T NOLAN

JOSEPH M SCHENCK presents

NORMA TALMADGE in GRAUSTARK

with EUGENE O'BRIEN

Story by GEORGE BARR McCUTCHEON

Scenario by FRANCES MARION

A DIMITRI BUCHOWETZKI PRODUCTION

First
National
Pictures

First National have the big money making pictures

Motion Picture News

VOL. XXXII   ALBANY, N. Y., AND NEW YORK CITY. OCTOBER 3, 1925   NO. 14

"Getting Away With Murder"

THE motion picture business is taken severely to task in a bulletin recently issued by a newspaper trade publication. It seems that during the Greater Movie Season week the press agents in one of the key cities not only "grabbed" a lot of valuable newspaper space, but so loudly acclaimed the fact that the noise echoed through the business offices of most every prominent newspaper in the country; and then back to New York City, whence a special notice was issued warning all newspapers against marauders from the ranks of the movies and a further repetition of such "grabs."

Obviously, if you "get away with murder" it doesn't pay to shout it from the housetops. The successful second story operator is a very mum individual. So, at least, our press agents can sign the pledge to stop bragging. We assume, of course, that the publicity interests of the pictures and the theatres of the land are greater than the interests of the press agents themselves. The man who gets away with newspaper murder also murders himself, his firm and his industry.

Everybody knows or should know that the clever and successful press agent is the man who convinces the newspapers that he is working for them, not against them. He has their continuing confidence; certainly he doesn't let them think he is rifling their safes. Their respect for him is his one great asset.

But the larger question is this: does free space really pay? And this: hasn't the industry grown too high in stature to rely upon publicity donations?

On the one hand it may be said that we are dealing in a commodity of vast public interest. People want photoplay news, and so the newspapers want to give it to them. And so the newspapers want to receive it. There's a large and important field of work here for the press representatives of the theatres, producers and distributors. This isn't space grabbing; it is space feeding.

＊ ＊ ＊

But at its best it doesn't merchandise pictures; this can only be done by straight advertising. That's true of pictures and any other commodity; it is so true that it is beyond any argument. And it is proved year in and out by the profitable expenditure of hundreds of millions of dollars.

This industry has acquired its merchandising stature. Today, with any picture the advertising money to be spent upon it ranks—or should rank—right along with the important costs of production, prints and distribution. Any individual or firm unable or unwilling to enter into adequate advertising is handicapped as severely as by inadequate facilities for production, distribution and sales.

＊

The fallacy long prevailed in the amusement business that only free space counted, that the advertisement itself was a perfunctory matter, and necessary only to get a reader. Which is one good and solid reason why the legitimate stage business is just where it is today.

I don't know of any business today where the advertising man and the publicity man—men of ideas, writing ability, sales and newspaper experience—are more important than in this. But, by the same token, I don't believe that any theatre or producer or distributor can get by, today, by grabbing space for which someone else pays.

[signature]

Judy King, clever comedienne in Fox Imperial comedies, displays her ability to perform the Charleston, now all the rage on the West Coast.

PICTURES
AND
PEOPLE

A GENUINE FALL

LEON ERROL, famous stage comedian, cast in the leading role with Dorothy Gish for First National's—"Clothes Make the Pirate," is noted for his ability to take funny falls, which apparently would dislocate the limbs of any ordinary man. But Mr. Errol's ankles, or at least one of them, so often designedly twisted by the agile owner, got an unexpected twist while filming scenes for the comedy, and he flopped in dead earnest, tearing a ligament. The only consolation the comedian found in the incident was that he was able to save himself from a twenty-foot plunge down on a pile of rocks. In his current stage hit, Louie the 14th, Errol earns the designation because a millionaire picks him as a guest to avert the bad omen of having only thirteen persons at a banquet. His good luck persisted on before the footlights, but certain of his superstitious friends are now advising him to carry a rabbit's foot while performing for the camera.

FILM REPRESENTATIVE IN RADIO

TO ANNE DALE, young screen actress who will be remembered for her portrayal of the crippled girl in the Fox film version of "The Fool," went the honor of representing the picture industry on the elaborate radio program which marked the launching of the Forty-Second Street Centennial from station WRNY at the Hotel Roosevelt. Radio scouts report that it was in the clearest of diction and with the choicest of words that Miss Dale expressed the film industry's wish for the continued success of Forty-second Street. That her address over the air made an impression at so auspicious an occasion is the more remarkable for the fact that Miss Dale was sandwiched between two such experienced orators as George Gordon Battle and Louis Wiley, business manager of the New York Times.

An interesting character study of a sterling actor, Frank Currier, as he appears in "Light of Old Broadway" (Metro-Goldwyn-Mayer), soon to be released.

Max J. Weisfeldt, popular field sales veteran, who has rapidly risen to be Northwest Division Manager for Film Booking Offices, with headquarters in Minneapolis.

A strikingly unusual scene from "The Rime of the Ancient Mariner" (Fox), the first to be released, showing the Mariner (Paul Panzer) watching Death and Life-in-Death (Gladys Blackwell).

Harry Langdon, completely surrounded by Sol Lesser and John McCormick, signs the contract which will make him a First National star, to appear in feature comedies for that company.

A lovely figure among the newcomers on the Christie lot is Jean Lorraine, leading lady in comedies for current release on the Educational program.

Pauline Stark and Lilyan Tashman make a fascinating pair of choristers in "A Little Bit of Broadway" (Metro-Goldwyn), a story of chorus girl life.

Marion Ivy Harris, a beautiful Atlanta girl who is among the youthful students of the Paramount School at the Long Island studio.

Eleanor Boardman, with William Haines, her leading man, and John M. Stahl, her director, between scenes of "Memory Lane" (First Nat'l).

A CRUZE ANNIVERSARY

LANDMARKS are plentiful in the career of James Cruze as a screen director, but they grow in number—as witness the fact that "The Pony Express," in itself a notable accomplishment even for a record so brilliant as his, marks the director's golden film anniversary. The work is Cruz's fiftieth directorial effort, though the record dates back only nine years, at which time he first took up the megaphone for Famous Players-Lasky as the director of "Too Many Millions," in which Wallace Reid was featured. Statistics are sometimes interesting, and here's an instance where they are. For the facts show that Cruze is a workman as well as an artist. An average of more than five pictures a year over a period of nine years is testimony to the man's energy as convincing as the individual works have testified to his artistry.

Since starting his career as a director, Cruze has essayed a wide range of photoplay types. With equal skill and understanding of their inherent values he has brought to the screen comedies, dramas, melodramas, satires, in a variety of settings—and the record mind you, includes "The Covered Wagon," "The Pony Express" and "Hollywood." Owing to a striking quality individual to the material, these latter three stand as his most sensational successes, though from the standpoint of direction just as fine a quality of treatment was present in his productions of "The Fighting Coward," "Ruggles of Red Gap," "Merton of the Movies" and other works. Cruze has already started his fifty-first picture, the screen version of "The Mannequin,"Fannie Hurst's prize story, in which he is directing a cast headed by Warner Baxter, Dolores Costello and Zasu Pitts.

LIKES THE STUDIOS

VICE-PRESIDENT CHARLES G. DAWES is fast earning the reputation of a confirmed studio fan. He recently paid a visit to Metro-Goldwyn-Mayer studios, where he was greeted by Louis B. Mayer and welcoming committee of directors, stars and feature players, and after lunching, made a tour of the "Ben Hur" circus set, where stills and motion pictures of the inspection party were made. Also, having watched James Cruze film "The Pony Express" six weeks ago at Cheyenne, Wyoming, the General wasn't content until he appeared behind the scenes at Paramount's Los Angeles studio the other day, where technical work on the picture was completed. Mrs. Dawes, their daughter, Mrs. M. B. Ericson of Chicago, secretary E. Ross Bartley and several friends composed the party, which was taken in charge by General Manager Charles Eyton, who explained the mysteries of interior sets.

A GOLDEN GET-TOGETHER

THERE was a real "old timers" celebration enacted when Dan Mason and Charlie Evans met at the Fox studio. Mason, who has done many memorable screen characterizations, is playing Mr. Bailey in "Wages for Wives," the title under which John Golden's "Chicken Feed" is being produced on the screen by Fox. It is the role created on the stage by Evans. When the latter turned up at the studio he and Dan renewed old acquaintances and a statistical turn of the conversation revealed the fact that the two had played together in the old-time variey shows just fifty years ago. Thereupon was the idea of marking the anniversary with suitable celebration, and a celebration there was.

A LONE STAR ISSUE

AMONG the pictures selected for the week ending September 12 by the National Committee For Better Films, but one, Paramount's "The Pony Express" appeared in the bulletin bearing the "star," which brands a film as particularly good. James Cruze's big historical production is listed under the heading of—For the General Audience, and Special Family "Audience including children of Grammar School age and up."

MISS GOULD AT HOLLYWOOD

PAULA GOULD, press and fan magazine representative, whose regular habitat is the F. B. O. Home Office, is sojourning at the organization's West Coast studios, getting acquainted with executives, stars and directors, and absorbing local color. During her stay on the Coast Miss Gould will write a series of articles for a nationally known magazine.

First National executives off for Europe on the S. S. Deutschland; left to right: M. L. Finkelstein, Twin Cities theatre magnate, Richard A. Rowland, general manager of First National, and Robert Lieber, president.

A super-vamp de luxe, 1925 model, is Myrna Loy, who is here shown in the costume which she will wear in "The Love Toy" (Warner Bros.), now in production.

Allene Ray, Pathe serial star, is an ardent aquatic fan, and is here seen about to dive off, while Walter Miller, her leading man, and other players are the "gallery."

AN EDITOR

The Week in Review

THE Famous Players-Balaban & Katz deal which has been shaping for some time has at length been officially announced. It has created, naturally, a good deal of discussion and a large variety of opinions. If it will serve at all to clear the air, we give here our own general opinion on the situation.

The legal phase of the matter we can dismiss by saying:—that's that. We are not competent to discuss the whys and wherefores. There are the past, the present and the future to consider, in this respect.

But, important as the legal phase may be, we are inclined to regard the banking angle as at least, a more definite influence.

This business, as we have pointed out before, is now in its capitalistic era. The stocks of some dozen film enterprises are now quoted on the stock exchanges. Large banking resources are back of some and the shares of stock are being widely distributed.

Now, in the merchandising of stocks, tangible assets like brick and mortar are highly desirable sales arguments. So it -is only natural—and you could say economic—for theatres to enter heavily in the situation. After all, the other side of the business—the making and selling of pictures—is a very intangible thing. Men are not fixed assets—nor are stars.

Fox, Universal, Warners are right out after theatres—and if the banking resources match up, they may figure just as heavily as any one else. Of course, theatre management is going to count as well as money. When theatre chains first started I asked the head of one how far they would go. His reply was "as far as managers go." And that holds good today.

All this, of course, is beside the argument that producer-owned theatres are needed to get pictures adequately before the public. But that argument won't altogether hold water. As an instance: United Artists doesn't own a single theatre. Yet, from all accounts, this concern isn't having much difficulty in getting its goods to market. In fact, in a year when producer-ownership is at its height United Artists is, apparently, in its strongest position.

We are not going to argue with the man who says: "All right, but such and such a city is closed up." True, it is closed for some pictures—for the present. It will be hard sledding here and there and maybe generally in the key cities for a period—until the pinch is over. It will be mighty hard sledding for poor pictures everywhere, not merely right now but for all the future.

Nor can we well argue with the man who claims that Famous is out after enough theatres to pay for its production. That's stiff competition for the other fellow; but, if it is enterprise—and without a legal mind we can only view it that way—what about it?

The one phase of this entire business that still rises supreme in our minds is—pictures.

Suppose a farmer spent all his time and interest in improving his barns and let his crops and cattle go their own way. He would be in a pretty fix, wouldn't he?

It would seem right now that there's a lot of over-attention to theatres and other matters and too little to pictures. Yet right along pictures are making the big dividing lines among our business forces, and in all probability and in the final analysis they will determine commercial supremacy, and the general welfare of this industry at large in the show world. At least, that is our best guess.

* * *

LAST Spring in Hollywood I saw a number of pre-release showings of pictures.

Mostly they were too disappointing to write about, and all in the same way. The picture would start and build admirably. The story unwound logically, clearly, illuminatingly. The audience was tense, expectant, pleased. And then, about half way along, something happened. The story paused and looked about anxiously. It drifted into several eddies. It started this way and then tried another tack and finally plunged for the shore.

I assumed that in some cases a good deal of re-vamping would be done, after the tryout; but found later that it wasn't. Probably it was impossible to do much. I also laid the trouble to the story; that it was not meant for pictures. Pictures need simple and compact themes; at least they do at this stage of picture production.

But after viewing some pictures this Fall, and finding the same messing up of construction, one is forced to believe that it is due to some general studio practice.

What is the trouble?

It looks like a plain case of too many cooks.

Once I worked under an editor who used to approach his manuscript with sleeves rolled up and the grim jaw of a blacksmith. His attitude seemed to say: "Now, boys, let's all take a whack at this damn thing and beat it into shape." So we all rolled our sleeves up and went at it.

The result was always awful. Authors who cared only about their checks were uncomplaining. But the writer who took any pride in his name accepted his pay but refused to have his name appear—and justly so.

This remodeling process was not merely unnecessary and highly expensive, but disastrous. In every instance the creative threads were snapped and never nicely tied up. The patches showed glaringly; and the finished job was a plain mess.

Like the messy picture that is all too common.

* * *

WE hear a good deal these days about supervision of production. Most studios seem to be hunting supervisors just as producers ten years ago were seeking directors. At that time we had mighty few directors—good ones. Perhaps today we

ON BROADWAY

By William A. Johnston

have mighty few good supervisors and the rest are the ones who are messing up pictures.

I notice that where a director is good—and today we have a goodly list—their work isn't supervised. Probably they won't stand it—like the magazine writers who refused to lend their names to emasculated stories.

Supervision—of any kind of creative work—is, or should be, a delicately skilful and masterful job. Otherwise it makes chaos. It requires master skill and experience.

And, anyway, why isn't the supervision exercised while the picture is on paper? That's where the picture should be made; at least, there's where its construction should be settled once and for all. The extra bits of business—brain waves they are called by the English—can be added in the making. But in the making you can't throw the picture off the track without a wreck—and a sad one.

* * *

PROBABLY too much blacksmithing is done to the story, too, by the supervisors or some other overseers; like the editor with his magazine articles.

Here's a new and true story, in that connection, straight from Hollywood: a friend of mine was waiting outside of a studio executive office, when suddenly a terrific commotion started inside. It kept right up, and he kept his eye anxiously on the door, expecting to see someone come crashing through the panels. A young lady came out with an armful of papers. "What is it?" he whispered, "a fight?" "Why, no," said she. "It's a story conference."

* * *

I LEARNED a lot at the Paramount managers' school last week—a lot about trade papers.

First let me say that this school is a real honest-to-goodness one, where some forty picked men are putting in a lot of hours and hard work every day for a period of six months. If this school as conducted doesn't turn out good managers I don't know what will.

Mr. Dickerson and I undertook to explain the various departments of MOTION PICTURE NEWS, and for two and a half hours answered questions—sharp and pertinent ones.

My reactions were these:

That it would be fine and helpful all around if the high executives of this business knew as much about trade papers as these embryo managers of theatres.

That said executives, had they been present, would have learned how essential a trade paper is to modern theatre management—what a force it is in stimulating and stabilizing the retail sales of pictures.

That these managers were little interested in trade news, in particular the stilted and dreary utterances of and the doings of prominent trade personages;

that they spotted at once and resented any inspired publicity; that they were, however, vitally concerned with all those departments having to do with the booking and presentation and merits and exhibition of pictures. In fact, they were still asking questions and making suggestions long after our allotted time was up; and it was apparent that, to satisfy them, we should about double the size of the paper.

We repeat: how gratifying it would be if New York understood just how the theatre managers use a trade paper, so that New York in turn could help us make it still more useful to the theatres.

* * *

A YOUNG lady came in to our office the other day and, after talking a good hour with her— she asked for but ten minutes—we decided that public relations would be a telling force in this business, and that she will be very successful in this field of work. Her name is Regge Doran. She ran the public relations department of West Coast Theatres, and now she is with Pathé. She has just returned from Chicago, where censorship will be a big issue next Spring when the Illinois legislature meets. She's a college graduate, but has gotten well over it; she is highly intuitive and intelligent—and she speaks box-office language. Any exhibitor in the country will be mighty glad to talk with her and, I surmise, after that talk, will come pretty near to entering heartily into her scheme of work.

I have before me a well-written treatise on the public relations of a theatre. But what it all amounts to—from an exhibitor's standpoint, at least—is this: getting to know your public and thereby to work with your public so that out of the harmony there will grow a substantially better box-office. Of course, there's a lot to be said about public relations: how the motion picture carries a great public responsibility, how it moulds the home life and thought, how it—public relations—will be the one way to solve censorship, Sunday closing and other pressing problems. But Miss Doran talks about the box-office, and that's why she is going to succeed. She will give us later some exact figures as to how her work increases the Saturday business and even makes it carry over into Sunday and Monday.

Of course, the great point of contact is the children —the proper and successful amusement of the children. But it doesn't end with the children— from a box-office standpoint. Not by any means. If the children **are** handled rightly, you have them advertising the picture and the theatre in each of their homes. It is the one sure way to bring the parents out.

Mostly children are regarded as puppets and treated so. We treat them much as the reformers treat us adults. On the contrary, as Miss Doran points out, children are the real, dyed-in-the-wool fans of the country. You can't fool them. You've got to give them the real goods, not sugar coated pills.

(Continued on next page)

MOTION PICTVRE
NEWS

October 3
1925

Vol. XXXII
No. 14

Founded in September 1913

Publication Office: Lyon Block, Albany, N. Y.

Editorial and General Offices:
729 7th Ave., New York City

Branch Offices:
845 S. Wabash Ave., Chicago, Ill.
Room 616 Security Bldg., Hollywood, Calif.

An Editor on Broadway

(Continued from Preceding Page)

And there are plenty of pictures high in entertainment value and suitable for children and family patronage.

We suggest that exhibitors give Regge Doran as much time as Sam Katz gladly tendered her, namely a three-hour interview. We don't know of a more important service to the exhibitor.

* * *

Again—the British Situation

A DEFINITE move toward reviving British production seems to have been made. Thomas Ormiston, President of the Cinematograph Exhibitors' Association, met representative producers at a meeting in London the other day, and the upshot was the appointment of a committee to meet the Government Board of Trade.

Mr. Ormiston's activities are directed toward establishing a national studio aided by Government subsidy. He does not, however, look upon the studio proposition as a complete solution of the situation. On the contrary, he declares it is "only part of the general scheme which we are preparing for the Government, but it does, I honestly think, go some way towards remaking British pictures.

"My idea is that such a studio can be erected for the sum of 200,000 pounds (about $1,000,000), and it should be located within forty or fifty miles of London outside the foggy area.

"I do not," continued Mr. Ormiston, interviewed by *The Film Renter and Moving Picture News*, "intend to ask the Government for a great deal of money. Whilst I am convinced that the Government are very anxious to see more British films as they are, undoubtedly, uneasy at the thought of the entire Americanization of our screens, at the same time it is my belief that the money for the studio can be got from the trade itself with some slight monetary assistance from the Government, some 10,000 or 20,000 pounds.

"We have got to realize," continued Mr. Ormiston, "that the exhibitor has to play his part in this problem and we are not shirking our responsibility. In collaboration with my colleagues I have seen producers and convinced them that a quota system is useless. As a matter of fact the quota or kontingent system is not, I am convinced, the way to tackle this problem. The reciprocity idea is excellent and one that we shall prosecute in the near future, but it is no use asking America to take a number of our pic-

tures unless they have merit. They cannot possess that merit unless they are made in proper studios, that is why I think the National Studio will be a big advantage. Personally, I believe that American producing houses are wise and sensible enough to see that it will be to their advantage to take a number of British pictures to be released in their programs in return for the enormous number of pictures they show here. If they do not, then we shall, as exhibitors, have to bring pressure to bear, but I do not think this is likely to be necessary."

What is evidently another step in "the general scheme" is the announcement of a drastic campaign by the C. E. A. against block-booking. The General Council of the exhibitor association passed this resolution: "On and after January 1, 1927, no film to be booked unless it has first passed the Censor, then to be trade-shown, and the playing date is not to be more than six months from the date of the signing of the contract."

Mr. Ormiston and his associates are ready, they state, to ask for Government legislation against block-booking, if that step becomes necessary.

The campaign against block-booking is part of the plan to aid British production. "If British pictures are to have a chance," said Mr. Ormiston, "it is no good choking up our screens eighteen months and two years ahead, which does not give the British producers a chance to live."

All of which is highly interesting to the industry here, particularly as it is the exhibitor who has taken the lead in attempting to solve the British dilemma.

October 3, 1925   MOTION PICTURE NEWS   Vol. XXXII, No. 14

Published weekly by Motion Picture News, Inc., William A. Johnston, President; E. Kendall Gillett, Vice-President; William A. Johnston, Editor; J. S. Dickerson, Associate Editor; Oscar Cooper, Managing Editor; Fred J. Beecroft, Advertising Manager; L. H. Mason, Chicago Representative; William McCafmack, Los Angeles Representative. Subscription price, $3 per year, post paid in United States, Mexico, Hawaii, Puerto Rico, Philippine Islands and some other countries; Canada, $5; foreign, $10.00. Copyright 1924, by Motion Picture News, Inc., in the United States and Great Britain. Title registered in the United States Patent Office and foreign countries. Western Union cable address is "Picknews," New York. Entered as second-class matter January 31st, 1924, at the postoffice, Albany, N. Y., under the Act of March 3, 1879.

Resume of European Situation As It Affects Industry

No. 9: Probable Trend in Foreign Field Forecast

By L. C. Moen

IN the eight articles which have preceded this, an effort has been made to depict some of the highlights, at least, in the European-American film situation as it affects this complex industry. Many volumes could be devoted to the subject, if one were to enter into all its ramifications, and in the limited space of these articles it has been possible only to sketch lightly a few of the outstanding developments.

The response that has been accorded them, however, shows convincingly the keen interest that is felt on both sides of the water in the matter of international film relations. Foreign trade journals have been generous in their comment, and distribution executives in America as well, indicating that the problem is of equal concern on both sides of the Atlantic.

As matters stand today, it is likely that the gross foreign business done by American companies is about 30% of the domestic total. Few figures have ever been given out, but it can be stated that in the case of one leading company it is 42%, of another, 35%, and in several instances, 28 to 30%. Some of the smaller companies, who sell outright, do not do as well as this, but the large distributing organizations, which handle the bulk of the business, do very well, so that our estimated percentage is probably not far wrong.

It can easily be seen that every American exhibitor thus has a direct personal interest in the foreign situation. With this considerable revenue removed, conditions would become quite different in the American film industry. Yet, despite that fact, few companies have come to accord their foreign organizations the attention and importance they deserve—the attention they receive, for example, from such corporations as the U. S. Rubber Company, Standard Oil or International Harvester.

This is not the fault of the foreign personnel. In some instances, these men abroad are struggling valiantly against the handicap of limited facilities, lack of co-operation and even jealous inappreciation of the importance of their work. In other cases, men of high ability in the American field prove unfitted to the altogether new conditions which they meet abroad. Still others, happily in the minority, have created antagonism toward American pictures through their misunderstanding of the manner in which business must be conducted there.

Accidental Beginnings

The foreign branch of the American industry was, in the beginning, virtually an accident—and it has not yet quite come into its rightful position. There is no more reason for considering foreign revenue as "velvet" than for rating American bookings in the same manner. At least two companies—perhaps three— have been kept going during recent trying periods by their foreign business. One of them has admitted it publicly.

The foreign distribution machinery deserves all the consideration that can be given it. No country in Europe today, except perhaps England, is yielding the revenue which it might yield and which it can reasonably be expected to yield within a few years.

But—that increase is dependent upon keeping the channels of commerce free and open. Duties, tariffs, contingents, red tape —all of these things can, and will, throttle our foreign business if permitted to multiply indefinitely. Germany has a Kontingent. England is threatening something similar. Italy will put more rigid restrictions into force the first of the year. Australia has put a duty into effect which diminishes the profit from that field. Hungary is taxing imported pictures to help keep domestic production alive.

Whether such handicaps continue to increase or abate depends in a large measure on the attitude and tactics of the American industry. Men of the right sort, working hand in glove with the U. S. Department of Commerce and the American consuls, together with various local organizations throughout Europe, could create a lasting and cordial alliance based upon sincerity and mutual understanding of each other's problems.

Graham's Position

As an excellent and outstanding example, it seems only fair to mention John Graham, the Famous Players head in England. Graham, through his tact and intelligent understanding has made himself literally idolized by British exhibitors. While retaining his own individuality, he has fitted himself into their scheme of things in a frictionless manner. They regard him as one of them, if I judge rightly, and the prestige and advantage that have accrued to Famous Players are boundless. Not that Graham is the only one—but he is so excellent an example

that I do not believe others will feel slighted if he is cited as a model.

Business in Europe, it must be remembered, is not conducted as it is in America. You can talk as you will of the fact that "people are pretty much the same the world over," but you cannot alter the fact that American sales methods in Europe, like the Heiry Ape, "don't belong." To the European, the principal characteristic trait of the American is his materialistic absorption in business—"chasing the dollar." Not that Europeans are in business for their health exclusively. Nevertheless, they do not permit it to monopolize all their waking hours.

Many of the European buyers and executives are men of old and distinguished families, with a rigid code as to what is done and what is not done. The "sign on the dotted line" school of salesmanship has little effect on them. The sort of representative who can successfully do business with them is the man who can fraternize with them at their clubs—the sort of man whom they will invite into their own homes gladly. Such men can do business with them—but not outside of business hours, remember!—on a far different basis from the man who does not fit into their scheme of things. Whatever our prejudices may be in regard to European traditions and customs, we cannot alter them by ignoring their existence, and the road to success lies through shaping our policy to them.

Fitting In

Men sent out by the U. S. Rubber company, Standard Oil, and other big corporations, are expected to become a part of the community where they take up their residence. They are expected to study and master local conditions and customs, and to shape their business practices to them. They are expected to aid the home office in developing new products, new ways of packing and shipping, and the like, which will increase business and improve foreign commercial relations.

There are men in the European field who are perfectly capable of doing this sort of thing, but they receive scanty encouragement in most instances. Until foreign business is given the recognition and support which it deserves it cannot come into its own.

Tribute should be paid at this point to Fox and Universal. The industry owes these two companies a great deal for their pioneer work in the operation of exchanges in all parts of the world. They virtually blazed the trail which others today are following, and they have benefitted accordingly in the prestige which their trademarks carry in all quarters of the globe today.

Now, with first run theatres coming into the limelight, Famous, First National and Metro-Goldwyn are thoroughly aware of the need for show window theatres in London, Paris and Berlin, at least. How far they will go remains to be seen. If they can get adequate first run representation in suitable

(Continued on next page)

Resume of European Situation
By L. C. Moen

(continued from preceding page)

houses, probably they will be satisfied—but if they cannot, it is not unlikely that some new theatre construction will be chalked up.

Europe does need better theatres. No one will gainsay that, but as we have pointed out before, their construction and operation must be planned with European tastes in mind. Merely transplanting American methods, system and ideas will not turn the trick. Alien enterprises are no more popular in Europe than in America, and the native touch must be given to any venture if it is to be established on a solid basis. The company which is affiliated with a leading local organization on a proper basis will be stronger in the long run than the purely alien corporation.

Production abroad will help, undoubtedly, but only if it is handled properly. Some such experiments in the past have worked more harm than good. The sporadic making of one or two or three pictures will be interpreted merely as a sop to European interests, and discounted accordingly.

Opportunity Desired

The Europeans do not so much desire that we produce pictures in Europe, as that we give an opportunity to their own producing forces. Their principal grievance might be summed up thus: "You have made your profit in our market, we have purchased your pictures freely—and you have closed your own market to us, making it difficult, if not impossible, for us to continue.

Right or wrong, that is the opinion now held, and no amount of argument will move them from that position.

Consequently, the most lasting move toward good will and a free, open market which any American company could make would be to create a free, open market to produce for the market in these United States. The screen admittedly needs novelty—new backgrounds, new faces, new stories, new ideas—and there are persons and places in Europe that can supply all of these.

Difficult it may be, but it is certainly not impossible, to work out reciprocal plans by which these forces could profit by our own better knowledge of this market and be directed along lines that would enable them to make pictures suitable for distribution here.

Perhaps I shall draw the charge of being a propagandist when I assert that the *successful* distribution here of a certain amount of European product is vital to continued profitable existence and development of our foreign trade—but I believe that any one who surveys the situation dispassionately and with an open mind will reach the same conclusion.

If this is not done, it seems to me that we shall face a continually increasing hostility—an attitude that will mean the constant menace of legislation and tariffs both unpleasant and unprofitable.

The Paramount experiment of some years ago, in producing in London and Berlin, was undoubtedly unfortunate; not alone was it a failure in itself but it gave the impression that the whole idea was unsound. As a matter of fact—and I believe that those closest to the venture will bear me out—

the move was ahead of its time. Conditions were not yet right—are only just beginning to be so now.

But if production is to be carried out abroad, alone or in association with European companies, then it must be done rightly. The best directors, the best stars, the best studios, the best artists, should be employed. Too often, in the past, these things have been taken for granted on someone or another's say-so. If there is to be co-operation, let it be between the best elements on both continents, so that it may have a fair chance of success.

Bruce Johnson, at First National, has made a significant gesture in the encouragement of British production. He has guaranteed the distribution, in all countries under his jurisdiction, of "The Only Way," and now, with the inclusion of Dorothy Gish in the cast of "Nell Gwynn," an effort will be made, apparently, to meet the requirements of the American maket as well. Richard A. Rowland, accompanied by Robert Lieber and M. L. Finklestein, have gone abroad, and it may be that there will be further developments in this direction.

The first company, it would seem, that makes a strong, firm move in this direction will occupy a place in the European field now unknown. Perhaps it will not be done in the manner we have suggested. Perhaps something altogether different will develop. But this much we can state without fear of contradiction:

Our trade depends upon two things, quality of product aside: 1. The buyers' attitude, including both the exhibitor and the ultimate consumer, the public; and 2. The governmental attitude, as reflected in tax and restrictive legislation.

Buyer in Control

As regards the first, the buyer, after all, is in control of any commercial situation. You can create a demand, but you cannot force a man to buy your product, and a friendly attitude here is essential.

As regards the governmental attitude, it is likely to be, in the main, a reflection of the other. If the European industry generally is hostile to the American product, it will always be able to put through a certain number of measures to handicap it.

If, on the other hand, we so conduct our affairs that Europe is convinced of our good will and "live and let live" spirit, the attitude toward us will be one of friendliness and reciprocity—and the channels of trade will remain free and clear, with the greatest ultimate profit to all concerned. This, I am certain, is no Utopian babble—but the expression of a truth which will hold in any industry that carries its trade to foreign shores.

In bringing this series to a close, I take this opportunity of again expressing my appreciation to the men, here and abroad, who have made it possible for me to collect this fragmentary data, and who have given unselfishly of their time and knowledge to assist me. And if any of the readers of MOTION PICTURE NEWS have derived from this series a tithe of the pleasure which I have received in its preparation, I have, to quote the hoary and inevitable bromide, "been well repaid." So, with the hope that

Abe Warner Back After European Survey

ALBERT WARNER of Warner Brothers returned to New York last week following a three months' survey of the theatre situation in a number of European countries. He visited Russia, Poland, Italy, Germany, England and the Balkan states.

Warners have admitted they intended to open theatres in Europe where it was necessary for them to have first class representation, but Albert Warner refused to comment on his trip until he has met in conference the other executives of the Warner organization.

American films may continue to blaze the trail of American commerce around the globe, and that the free interchange of the best product of all nations may bring about better international understanding of each other's problems and hopes and ideals, we write

THE END.

United Artists Announce German Branch Chiefs

A. C. Berman, in charge of United Artists Corporation interests in Germany, which recently purchased the Ifa-Film-Verleih-G. m. b. H., sends word to the New York office of the appointment of branch sales managers as follows:

Berlin, 8 Friedrichstrasse, Alfred Peters; Dusseldorf, 46 Graf Adolfstrasse, Rudolf Saklikowsty; Frankfort am Main, 52-60 Taunesstrasse, Benno Lachmann; Hamburg, 6 Esplanade, Louis Segall and Leipzig, 1 Karlstrasse, Arthur Peters.

New Sunday Ordinance Test Draws Interest

Minnesota theatre owners are watching with a good deal of interest the fight in Cumberland, Wis., on the Sunday closing ordinance. Mrs. W. W. Zimmerman, owner of the Zim Zim theatre there, has been paying a $10 fine every Monday morning for running every Sunday. She has now carried the case to the higher district court to test the ordinance.

Famous Declares Regular Quarterly Dividend

The Board of Directors of Famous Players-Lasky Corporation have declared the regular quarterly dividend of $2.00 per share on the preferred stock, payable November 2nd, 1925, to stockholders of record at the close of business on October 15, 1925. The books will not close.

Ex-Mayor of Quincy, Mass., Building 1500 Seat House

Ex-Mayor William J. Bradford of Quincy, Mass., has started construction of his new theatre at Maple and Chestnut streets which will have a seating capacity of about 1,500. The structure is expected to be completed late in the fall.

Coast Concerns Deny Coercion Charge

West Coast Theatres and Other Respondents File Answers to Complaint Brought by Federal Trade Commission

GENERAL denial in their answers has been made by respondents to the complaint of the Federal Trade Commission charging restraint of trade and various other offenses against West Coast Theatres, Inc., West Coast Theatres of Northern California, Venice Investment Company, Hollywood Theatres, Inc., All Star Feature Distributors, Inc., Educational Film Exchange, Principal Pictures Corp., H. M. Turner, Fred Dahnken, C. L. Langley, and F. W. Livingstone, partners doing business under the name of Turner, Dahnken & Langley, Herbert L. Rothchild Entertainment, Inc., and A. L. Gore, Michael Gore, Sol Lesser, Adolph Ramish and Dave Bershon.

The Commission has made public the answers of Principal Pictures Corp. and Sol Lesser, and of Herbert L. Rothchild Entertainment, Inc. Principal Pictures Corporation and Sol Lesser deny that 60 per cent or more of its stock, as charged by the Commission, or that any percent or part of its stock is owned or held by West Coast Theatres, Inc. In his joint answer with the concern, Lesser denies he is engaged in the leasing of films or the operation of theatres. All deny the charges of the Commission in so far as they further relate to combination in restraint of trade.

Among the charges brought by the Commission are that the respondents combined and cooperated themselves for the purpose of:

(1) "Hindering, restraining and preventing producers and distributors of motion picture films in other States from leasing their said films to said competitors of respondents or any of them and from shipping said films into the State of California and delivering them to said competitors, and (2) restraining and preventing competition among the respondents and between respondents and other exhibitors in the State of California in negotiating for and leasing motion picture films to be shipped from other States and delivered to said exhibitors respectively in the State of California as aforesaid. In pursuance of and to carry out said mutual purposes respondents and each of them are alleged to have done and still do the following acts and things:

(a) "Seek by threats of withholding patronage and by actually withholding patronage, to coerce and compel, and do coerce and compel said motion picture producers and distributors to discontinue dealing with competitors at respondents' theaters in all towns where respondents or any of them have competition.

(b) "Seek by similar threats and action, to coerce and compel, and do coerce and compel said producers and distributors to cease from dealing with particular competitors of the respondents, or to withhold certain pictures from said competitors for the purpose and with the effect of preventing said competitors from obtaining an adequate and necessary supply of suitable films for the operation of their respective theatres.

Warner Brothers Launch Accessory Contest

WARNER BROTHERS have inaugurated an advertising accessory contest with all of the thirty-six branch exchanges in the United States and Canada taking part. To the exchange selling the largest quantity of accessories in proportion to its allotment will go a silver loving cup. In addition there will be $500 in cash prizes to be divided among bookers and poster clerks. First prize will be $250, second, $100, and third will be made up of three awards of $50 each.

The contest started the week of September 20th and will be concluded the week ending December 12th. The winners will be announced Christmas Eve and the prizes wired the winners in time to contribute to their Christmas celebration. The bookers and poster clerks in the winning exchanges are to share equally in the prize money.

(c) "Seek by similar threats and action to coerce and compel, and do coerce and compel said producers and distributors to withhold from, and refrain from leasing to competing theatres for repeat runs, films that have been previously run in respondents' theatres, until after the expiration of such a long time after such previous run that said films have become practically valueless for exhibition purposes.

(d) "Seek by threats of withholding patronage and by actually withholding patronage to coerce and compel and do coerce and compel said producers and distributors to lease their films to respondents at prices arbitrarily fixed by respondents, without regard to the cost of production and distribution of said pictures, and at prices substantially less than the usual and normal exhibition values of said films in the respective towns and cities in which respondents exhibit them, and at prices substantially less than competitors of respondents would have been willing to pay for them in the same towns were they not prevented by said acts of the respondents from having an opportunity to lease said films.

(e) "Lease films which they cannot use and do not expect to use, in order to prevent their exhibitors from securing same for their theatres.

(f) "Use other cooperative and individual means to carry out and make effective their aforesaid purposes and undertakings.

"The effect and result of the above alleged acts and things done by respondents have been and now are to unduly hinder and restrain interstate commerce between the said producers and distributors on the one hand and the said exhibitors on the other hand in the distribution, leasing, transportation into the State of California and delivery to exhibitors of motion picture films; to close to both said producers and distributors and said exhibitors certain of the outlets or channels through which they would otherwise be enabled to obtain trade and pursue their respective business; and to deprive them of the advantages which they would enjoy under

the natural and normal conditions of competition which would exist among respondents and between respondents and the other exhibitors in the absence of the matters and things herein set out.

Missouri Defies the Sunday Closing Ordinance

The policy of opening on Sundays in defiance of city ordinances and smiling upon being arrested appears to be on a decided increase in Missouri. This week two exhibitors were arrested—C. R. Wilson, his wife and the operator of the Liberty theatre, Liberty, Mo., and J. W. Cotter, Moberly, Mo., exhibitor.

An old fashioned "town row," such as were common in Civil War days, is brewing in Liberty, a college town of about 6,000, among groups of the populace on the streets. For a week or more there has been a bitter fight between the "pros" and "cons" on Sunday motion picture shows. So Sunday the pastors of the Presbyterian, Baptist and Christian churches denounced Sunday shows, while Wilson was playing to a good sized house. When the case comes before the police court on September 23 he said. There is no state Sunday amusement law in Missouri.

After being arrested in the Moberly case, Mr. Cotter was released on bond and his theatre continued operation Sunday. The Moberly city council recently passed an amendment to an old city ordinance and paved the way for Sunday shows, but it was vetoed by the mayor. Moberly exhibitors still are hopeful that the council again will pass the measure over the mayor's veto.

Pasadena Raymond Robbed of $1,800

The Raymond Theatre of Pasadena was robbed during the week of over eighteen hundred dollars. The house is running two changes of Orpheum vaudeville and feature pictures weekly, a policy which was adopted two weeks ago. It is one of the West Coast-Langley chain, management of which was acquired only three weeks ago by Arthur L. Bernstein, formerly production manager for Jackie Coogan, from C. L. Langley. This is the fourth time in the past four years the Raymond has been robbed.

Three Corporations Given New York Charters

Motion picture companies incorporating in New York state during the past week included the following: Open House, Inc., capitalized at $10,000, with R. J. Joseph, C. F. Collins, Jr., Jacob Rosenfeld, New York city; Goodwill Distributing Corporation, $10,000, Toby Hodes, Henry Senenshine, Jack Ferst, New York city; John G. Jermon, Inc., $50,000, I. L. Baldwin, P. E. Jacobs, J. G. Germon, New York city.

New Problems in Exibition

Eric Thacher Clarke.

"**P**ARADOXICAL as it may seem, the screen offerings have ceased to be the major concern of managers of large motion picture theatres, for other forces have been set in motion to assure high-grade film fare, and audiences no longer enraptured over the 'miracle' of the silver sheet, demand something more than the feature, the news weekly and the comedy before they are willing to call it an evening."

Thus speaks Eric Thacher Clarke, managing director of the Eastman theatre, Rochester, N. Y., in discussing the new order of things in the exhibiting end of the motion picture business.

"Our connection with the University of Rochester has not proved the practical handicap that was foreseen by some prophets. It has proved a great advantage; people told us that we should find ourselves in difficulties because we would be forced to be showing 'highbrow' pictures and because we should be prevented from showing 'box office' pictures, which I take to be a polite term for sex pictures.

"Now it is a fact that the list of our biggest successes fails to show where in any single instance the slightest question of morality could be involved.

Audiences demand something more than program of pictures, declares manager of Eastman Theatre

"I do not believe in prologues. What is the rationale in presenting an act based on a picture which the audience has not seen? Preludes—yes, sometimes. Take a picture like 'The White Sister' and it is easy to arrange an atmospheric prelude; the audience has preliminary knowledge to appeal to and a well devised prelude can induce a sympathetic mood.

"A carefully prepared score will enhance the feature amazingly. We go about our score preparation very carefully to suit the music to each change of mood. Usually 50 or more pieces of music are on each orchestra desk at our performances. I do not believe in music that is too well known for an accompaniment to a feature film; a popular tune or a famous song easily diverts attention from film to music, which is not the motive of picture accompaniment.

"But we have no quarrel with music and its aid to our program problem. It is the suitable act that is hard to find. This much I think I know; the successful motion picture program is not made by transplanting bodily into it vaudeville, grand opera or ballet divertisements.

"Operatic music can be used with discretion in our programs in various ways, but you cannot get an audience into the right frame of mind for grand opera in connection with pictures; the time is too limited and to the audience bent on a picture program, an act of grand opera comes as a bolt from the blue not relished, even if it is respected. And the ballet divertisement, bodily transplanted, is not successful with audiences.

"But there is possible a form of dramatic action to music and of dance pantomime that will meet our program needs, I am confident.

Michigan M. P. T. O. Will Meet October 5-6

WILL H. HAYS has assured the committee in charge of, the sixth annual convention of the Motion Picture Theatre Owners of Michigan that he will make every effort to be present. The meeting, the first to be held in the Western part of the state, will occur at Grand Rapids on October 5 and 6.

John M. Lovett of the Michigan Manufacturers Association is also expected to be present.

The third annual Michigan Golf Tournament for exhibitors and exchangemen will be held on October 5th in connection with the convention. H. M. Richey, general manager of the Michigan M. P. T. O., is offering a silver loving cup as the winner's trophy.

New Iowa Theatre Co. Takes Over Seven Houses

The Eastern Iowa Theatre Company, recently formed in that state, has acquired control of seven theatres. These are the Cozy at Dyersville, the Grand and Crystal at Anamosa, Cascade at Cascade, Pastime at Mechanicsville, and Princess at Monticello.

Mrs. Stella Fackenthall was the former owner of the Dyersville house and the Anamosa houses were bought from Clifford Niles, who will serve as one of the officials of the company. The Princess at Monticello was bought from E. T. Landis. In most cases the owners of the theatres were retained as managers for the new company.

Motion Picture Exposition in Germany This Month

The first motion picture exposition to be held in Germany will open at the large exhibition hall at Kaiserdamm, Berlin, on September 25th and continue to October 4th. The event is being arranged by the Berliner Messe-Amt. The entire available floor space for exhibits has been engaged and all phases of the art of motion and still photography will be demonstrated by organizations represented by display booths.

Paramount B. & K. Deal is Announced

Plan to Create Separate Theatre Corporation Also Officially Made Known

OFFICIAL announcement has been made of the closing of the Famous Players-Balaban & Katz deal along the lines forecast in last week's issue of MOTION PICTURE NEWS. The statement issued by Paramount said:

"Famous Players-Lasky Corporation decided to separate their theatre interests from their production and distribution departments. A new corporation will be formed under separate management, but will be wholly owned by the Famous Players Lasky Corporation. The theatres will thus be operated as a separate unit and will rent and exhibit both Paramount and other pictures strictly according to their merit and suitability.

"After protracted negotiations Famous Players-Lasky Corporation have been able to effect a mutually satisfactory agreement with Balaban & Katz Corporation of Chicago, whereby Famous Players-Lasky Corporation secures the advantages of the Balaban & Katz management for the new theatre corporation, working in association with those officers who have already built up the Famous Players theatre department to its present efficient standard.

"The enviable record and reputation of Messrs. Balaban & Katz as eminently successful and progressive theatre operators is generally recognized among those familiar with the film industry."

Balaban & Katz are losing no time in taking over the associate management of the Paramount theatres throughout the country, the first move in this direction becoming known in Chicago this week, when Balaban & Katz's Director of Publicity, William Hollander, Service Manager Harry Marks, and a number of Balaban & Katz's mechanical staff, left for Boston, to make preparations for the opening of the Metropolitan Theatre in that city, which is scheduled for October 15th.

The second big theatre project announced since the combination of the Balaban & Katz and the Lubliner & Trinz interests, is for a 2,500 seat theatre to be erected on Cicero Avenue, north of Belmont. Rapp & Rapp, noted theatre architects, have completed plans for the house which will front 175 feet and have a depth of 180 feet. The first theatre announced by the combined firms was the house to be erected at Washington Boulevard and West End Avenue.

Pettijohn Presides at Cleveland Session

C. C. PETTIJOHN, counsel for the Film Boards of Trade, and W. E. Wilkinson, his assistant, were in town last week and presided over a special meeting composed of the members of the Cleveland Film Board of Trade, members of the Joint Arbitration Board, officers and board members of the Cleveland Motion Picture Exhibitors Association, and officers and board members of the M. P. T. O. of Ohio.

At this meeting it was definitely concluded that the secretary of the Film Board of Trade could not act as secretary of the Joint Arbitration Board. This has been a bone of contention in Cleveland for some months.

Dillon and O'Reilley to Confer at Syracuse

The indications are that the conference between William Dillon, president of the New York State M. P. T. O., and Charles L. O'Reilly, of New York city, president of the Theatre Owners Chamber of Commerce, and others, relative to according exhibitors in the New York city zone representation in the state association, and ironing out certain differences that have existed for several months, will be held in Syracuse some time this month. Letters between Mr. Dillon and Mr. O'Reilly, have apparently crossed, with the result that they have been considerably delayed. Mr. O'Reilly has also been away on his vacation while Mr. Dillon has been in Florida.

Cleveland Gives Screen to Safety Council

The motion picture theatres of Cleveland, through the Cleveland Motion Picture Exhibitors Association, have donated their screen to the National Safety Council. One hundred theatres have agreed to run a 100-foot trailer which calls attention to everyday carelessness. The National Safety Council will hold its annual convention in this city the end of September.

Built Theatre with Own Hands

Small Iowa town boasts home made theatre that wins patronage through its hominess

T. W. THOMPSON, owner of the Rex Theatre of Albia, Iowa, is a man of countless trades and much ingenuity. Proof is his cozy, if not pretentious, Rex in the little town of Albia—on the direct route to Burlington and Chicago traveling from Des Moines.

Thompson built the little house with his own hands. His son Kenneth assisted him, but doing them right is the senior Thompson's. For the Rex had been many other things in the distant days, including B. V. (Before Volstead!) It had been a busy small-town saloon—it had been a livery stable in which the best horses of the surrounding country had been housed—it had been a bicycle hospital—it had been a garage before Fords were plentiful. Now it is the Rex Theatre, named after a son who fell for his country in the late war.

Here in a town of three theatres, the Rex stands forth like a beacon light. It breathes homeliness and home! It winks its home-made electric sign as dusk falls, through the summer and winter months. It is a home-made theatre, with a home-made electric sign, with a home-made projection booth—but with the same kindred spirit of wholesomeness we all know in "things" that are home-made.

Here, assisted by Mrs. Thompson who acts as treasurer and ticket-seller of the Rex, T. W. Thompson wields his wand. He purchases good film, he furnishes consistent music—and above all he extends *friendliness* to his patrons.

The entrance of the Rex is plain. There are several nicely arranged frames for 11 x 14 lobby photos, a place for a window card here and there—and several frames for

T. W. Thompson.

posters, cut neatly to get the most out of them. As you enter the theatre there is a very pretty little table lamp, taken directly out of Mrs. Thompson's home.

Of the 786 seats the Rex has—seven hundred are given over to men, women and children. There is a lower and there is an upper floor. The lower floor seats seven hundred—and the upper floor eighty-six. These eighty-six are reserved for couples—and couples only!

Talking about ingenuity—it runs in the family. Kenneth the son is the one who built the home-made electric sign. He had a sign cut out of wood, under his and his father's direction, painted it to suit himself and had it hoisted in place with the assistance of a gray mule and a pulley and rope. Then he set to work putting together a device that would regulate the systematic winking of the electric bulbs.

Thompson gives much attention to courtesy and cleanliness and sincerity in welcoming and greeting his patrons. His patrons leave with a smile, and when one speaks of the Rex they may not eulogize its appearance, inside and out—but dollars to corn-husks they *do* eulogize the friendly Thompsons.

Pathe Buys Chaplin Re-Issue Rights

Comedian Paid $500,000 for "A Dog's Life," "Shoulder Arms," "A Day's Pleasure" and "Sunnyside"

UNDER a contract involving $500,000 concluded this week between Elmer R. Pearson, vice-president and general manager of Pathe Exchange, Inc., and Charles Chaplin, Pathe has acquired the re-issue rights to four of the famous comedian's screen successes—"A Dog's Life," "Shoulder Arms," "A Day's Pleasure," and "Sunnyside," are the pictures which Pathe will bring back into circulation as a result of the arrangement with Chaplin.

The payment of half a million dollars for the re-issue rights to these four pictures is equivalent to the purchase price paid by First National for the original issue of these comedies together with four others under its famous million dollar contract with Chaplin in 1917. It is the first instance in which the same price has been paid for re-issue rights on a group of comedies as was paid for their initial issue.

"It is not at all necessary to indulge in a long dissertation upon Charlie Chaplin and his magic drawing power at the box-office," said Mr. Pearson in discussing the contract. "Past and present results amply attest volumes as to the merits 'of these exceptional comedy subjects.

"Chaplin's professional and business career is probably the most remarkable of any man alive today. His pictures have undoubtedly played to over five hundred thousand bookings, and I don't believe anybody ever heard of any booking that was not a success. His pictures have undoubtedly played to eight to ten billion admissions and I don't suppose anybody ever heard a customer kick about the entertainment. Several exchange systems have distributed his pictures and they have all

made money and friends beyond their fondest expectations.

"It is a well known fact that no matter what the competition offers it cannot make a noticeable dent in the attendance of a theatre that is playing a Chaplin picture—no matter how often the same Chaplin picture had previously played that locality.

"Just this week we closed a contract with Charles Chaplin for the reissue rights to the first four pictures made by Chaplin for First National at the same price First National paid for them upon original issue.

"We have given the matter much study and truly do not know where we or anybody else could secure anywhere near an equal amount of potential box-office value for an equal amount of money."

Continued on page 1583

Advertising Plan Is Endorsed

Hays Organization Approves Protective Measures of Advertising Clubs

DIRECTORS of the Hays organization formally set the seal of approval of the film industry on the public protection plan operated by the National Better Business Bureau of the Associated Advertising Clubs of the World and the forty-four affiliated local Bureaus, which they have reviewed for more than a year. The Directors of this group, the Motion Picture Producers & Distributors of America, include Will H. Hays, Chairman, and D. W. Griffith, Adolph Zukor, William Fox, Charles Christie, Marcus Loew, Richard A. Rowland, R. H. Cochrane, Harry M. Warner, Jos. M. Schenck, Hal E. Roach, E. W. Hammons, Frederick C. Munroe.

The text of the resolution follows:

"*Whereas:* The Associated Advertising Clubs of the World, through their National Better Business Bureau and affiliated Bureaus in forty-four cities, and through more than three hundred Advertising Clubs in fourteen countries, is aiding the Motion Picture Producers & Distributors of America in their efforts to protect the public and the legitimate advertiser in the motion picture industry, and

"*Whereas:* The Motion Picture Producers & Distributors stands firmly for wholesome, truthful and constructive advertising and has been co-operating to this end with the Associated Advertising Clubs of the World.

"*Now, Therefore, Be It Resolved:* That the Board of Directors of the Motion Picture Producers & Distributors of America heartily reciprocate, and they hereby do reciprocate the expressions of endorsement heretofore given by the Executive Committee of the Associated Advertising Clubs of the World to the effort being made by the Motion Picture Producers & Distributors of America and the Associated Advertising Clubs of the World for the betterment of motion picture advertising."

M.-G.-M. Arbitration Winners

Board Favors Exchange in Controversy With Star Company of Seattle

A DECISION of interest to exhibitors throughout the entire country was handed down last week, in a case brought against the Metro-Goldwyn exchange by C. A. Swanson of the Star Amusement Company in Everett, Wash. The case centered around the claim of the Star Company that "Romola" should be supplied them on their Metro-Goldwyn contract, which called for "two King-Gish productions." The decision was in favor of the Metro-Goldwyn company.

In the hearing, the Star claimed that "Romola" should be supplied them because it was directed by Henry King, and Dorothy Gish appeared therein. It was brought out at the meeting that Metro-Goldwyn, while not specifying in their contract accordingly, had extensively advertised that they would have two King-Gish pictures during the 1924-1925 season, and it was these that were included in the Star's contract. The pictures were never made, and Metro-Goldwyn notified all holders of such contracts, in July, that these could not be supplied.

Metro-Goldwyn claimed that they knew in advance the box office value of "Romola," and would not have sold the Star Company any Lillian Gish pictures at the price the King-Gish attractions were scheduled on the contract. Their further release was signified by their request in July to the exhibitors to cancel the King-Gish pictures as originally scheduled. The decision of the Board of Arbitration was in favor of the Metro-Goldwyn company, who by their victory are generally accepted to have warded off many similar complaints from other exhibitors of the Pacific Northwest.

Court Decides Against Amador

Injunction in Suit Brought by Chaplin Sustained in Defendant's Appeal Action

THE decision in favor of Charlie Chaplin in his suit against Charles Amador and Western Features Productions to prohibit either from producing and distributing pictures which Chaplin alleged were in imitation of those in which he was the featured actor, has been sustained by the Superior Court in a judgment rendered on the appeal from the lower court by Amador and Western Features.

In its judgment the Superior Court enjoined the defendants from "producing or exhibiting pictures in which the public might be mislead into thinking the featured actor" was Chaplin. The judgment also restrained the defendants from releasing a picture entitled "The Race Track" which had been produced at the time Chaplin filed his original suit three years ago.

Counsel for the defendants had asked for a new trial following the lower court restrictions, and a modification of the ruling that would permit of the releasing of "The Race Track" film. In the final order the court held that this film was made, in his belief, as an imitation of Chaplin's pictures; that this imitation inhered in "The Race Track" to an extent that would make it impossible of elimination—as promised by the defendants—and for this reason refused to modify the original judgment so as to permit the defendants to release the picture.

HOWARD DIETZ, director of publicity and advertising for Metro-Goldwyn-Mayer, is on a short vacation.

DOROTHY GISH sailed on the Olympic late last week for England to appear in "Nell Gwynn" for Herbert Wilcox Productions.

DAVID R. HOCHREICH, president and general manager of Vital Exchanges, and his assistant, Milton Kempner, are on a tour of exchanges throughout the East and South. Canada and the Middle West are being covered by Max Goosman, assistant general manager. Hochreich and Kempner will meet J. Charles Davis, 2nd, President of Davis Distributing Division on the Coast.

SIR WILLIAM JURY, of Jury-Metro-Goldwyn, and Major William Evans, of Provincial Cinematograph Theatres, of England, arrived on the Leviathan for conferences with Marcus Loew.

HARRY RATHNER, President of Astor Distributing Corp., has returned to New York from a tour of the country and is completing plans for the production of "Child Wives." The picture will probably be made in Hollywood.

WALTER W. IRWIN, of the Railway Express Film Transport Co., returned on the Leviathan this week from a vacation in Europe.

MARSHALL NEILAN and Leeds L. Baxter, his business manager, are in town to finish scenes for "Ups and Downs."

GEORGE K. SPOOR left for Chicago this week to start work on a third dimension picture at the old Essanay studio.

CURTIS MELNITZ, press representative for Charlie Chaplin, is leaving for the Coast.

Winners of "Power God" Contest Named

Mary Crane of Chicago and John Battaglia of New York were the winners of the national contest conducted by the Montgomery Circulation Service and the Cloverleaf Magazines of St. Paul of roles in the Ben Wilson serial, "The Power God." The contest was conducted in sixty magazines and six hundred newspapers, the two winners to receive feature roles in the serial.

The four runners-up were Albert Stogel of Brooklyn, James Zarris of Indianapolis, Marguerite Bakas of Pueblo and William Sabo of Dundee, Michigan. They will be given tryouts by Ben Wilson and if found suitable will have parts in the serial.

Production on "The Power God" is to start shortly. The stars of this serial are Ben Wilson and Neva Gerber, who have a long list of serials and other pictures to their credit.

Playhouse is Planned for Tacoma, Washington

B. Marcus Priteca is drawing plans for erection of a theatre building to be erected in Tacoma, Washington, which may cost $1,000,000. The new theatre will be modern in every respect.

Universal Acquires New Theatres

Purchase Sears Houses in Western Missouri and Others in Same Territory; Many Transactions Reported

UNIVERSAL figures prominently in the acquisition of new theatres by big companies during the week, with their activities centering largely around the Missouri and Kansas territory. A deal was concluded with Charles T. Sears for his theatres in Western Missouri, including the Lyric at Boonville, Star at Nevada, De Graw at Brookfield and Auditorium at Marshall. The deal does not include the purchase of the property, which Sears still retains. Sears also has been retained as manager of Universal theatres in the Kansas City territory.

The Royal and Crystal theatres of Atchison, Kansas, were purchased by "U" from Lee Gunnison, and the Best of Parsons, Kansas, was bought from Fees Brothers. Walter Fenny, formerly Pantages manager in Kansas City, has been placed in charge of the Parsons house, while Lee Jones has been made manager of the Atchison theatres. The Apollo of Kansas City was also added to the Universal string, being leased.

A persistent rumor has been current that Universal would purchase the theatres operated by Capitol Enterprises, one of the largest chains in the middle west. This, however, has been emphatically denied by officials of Capitol Enterprises, who insist there are no grounds for the rumor.

The Stanley Company of America is making persistent efforts to purchase the Century, Garden, Parkway and New theatres in Baltimore. John J. McGuirk and Abe Sablosky of the Stanley Company have made several trips to Baltimore to negotiate for the houses with the estate of C. E. Whitehurst and the other owners.

While details have not been completed for the acquisition by the Stanley Company of the Crandall houses in Washington it is said that the new company will be capitalized at $4,000,000 based on preferred stock issue, in addition to which there will be 1,000 shares of common stock at no par value.

It is planned under the reorganization, to convert the stock of the various companies into the preferred stock of the new company, which will be known as the Stanley-Crandall Company of Washington. The details of the transfer are now being arranged and the exact amount of cash that

Sills Signs New First National Contract

MILTON SILLS, First National star, has signed a new contract with that company, it was announced this week. The contract is for a period of three years and will go into effect at the expiration of his present agreement.

Sills was elevated to stardom by First National some time ago. He had played featured parts in several outstanding productions for a long period. His last starring vehicle was "The Knockout," and he is now making "Men of Steel." Among the several important screen plays in which he played leading roles are "The Sea Hawk," "Flowing Gold," "Flaming Youth," "The Isle of Lost Ships," "The Spoilers," "Skin Deep" and "Adam's Rib."

Screen Advertisers Meet at Dayton Next Month

THE Fall Meeting of the Screen Advertisers Association will be held at Dayton, Ohio, on October 29th and 30th. The association members will be the guests of the National Cash Register Company and will hold their sessions at that concern's big plant in Dayton.

The Screen Advertisers Association, of which Douglas D. Rothacker of the Rothacker Film Mfg. Company is president; M. J. Caplan of the Metropolitan Motion Picture Company and Elmer G. Kuhn of the Atlas Educational Film Company, vice-presidents; and George J. Zehrung, of the National Council of the Y. M. C. A., secretary and treasurer, is a department of the Associated Advertising Clubs of the World.

will change hands, and the final purchase price will be determined within the next few days.

The announcement has been made that the Chamberlain Amusement Company of Shamokin and the M. E. Comerford Amusement Company of Scranton have consolidated with New York interests in promoting a large hotel and theatre at Pottsville. The theatre will seat 2,500 and will take about eight months to complete. It will give Pottsville one of the largest houses in the eastern part of Pennsylvania.

Loew's, Inc., has purchased the Aldine theatre, Wilmington, which for many years has been operated by the Topkis-Ginns interests. Four other motion picture houses in Wilmington which were operated by the same company, were recently acquired by the Stanley Company and therefore Loew's and the Stanley Company are running opposition value.

Another link was forged in the chain of Butterfield theatres last week when the Dawn theatre at Hillsdale was sold by Nick Pappas to the Bijou Theatrical Enterprise Company of Detroit, better known as the Butterfield organization. This addition means that the Butterfield circuit now has a total of thirty-seven theatres in operation in Michigan and several new houses under construction. Actual transfer of the Dawn theatre property to its new owners will take place at midnight, October 3rd.

M. H. Jacobs, treasurer of the Central Enterprises, operating a chain of motion picture theatres in New Orleans, recently announced that the firm will begin work immediately on a new house to be located on Washington avenue near South Broad street. The name for the new theatre has not yet been chosen. The contract was let through Emile Weil, architect, to Charles Gilbert, contractor, and is for a building to cost $150,000.

What is said to be the largest theatrical lease ever consummated was announced recently in San Francisco, by the A. J. Rich Company for the property on Market, Hayes, Polk and Larkin streets by the Capital Company, a subsidiary of the

Bank of Italy, to the Fox Film Corporation for a period of 25 years at an aggregate rental of $6,000,000. A 5,000-seat theatre is to be erected on the property with a Market street entrance, a depth of 200 feet through to Hayes street and a 150-foot frontage on that thoroughfare. According to A. J. Rich, Jr., the construction of the new theatre will begin as soon as A. P. Giannini of the Bank of Italy concludes final arrangements with the heads of the Fox Film Corporation in the East.

Pathe Buys Chaplin Group of Comedy Re-Issues

(*Continued from Page 1581*)

The Pathe contract just closed marks another notable chapter in the career of the famous comedian. Back in the days of the General Film the name of Chaplin began to mean the smashing of box-office records. Chaplin's last picture released through General Film, titled "Police," proved a veritable sensation.

The Mutual Film Company, seeking for a sure-fire attraction with which to bolster up their program, signed a contract with Chaplin the financial terms of which were so unprecedented as to astound the entire industry. Yet the connection resulted in amazing profits both for the company and its exhibitor customers.

At the time that First National was formed its leaders realized that to strengthen their position they were under the necessity of contracting a star whose box-office value could not be questioned by even the severest of their critics. Chaplin was their choice, and again a contract was signed for the star's services that made the trade literally gasp with amazement. One million dollars for a group of eight pictures was the arrangement agreed to. "A Dog's Life" was the first release of the series, and it smashed records from one end of the country to the other. "Shoulder Arms," followed, playing to greater receipts than any contemporary release. "A Day's Pleasure" and "Sunnyside" were subsequently produced and established new box-office records.

New Film Corporations Are Chartered in New York

Motion picture companies incorporating in New York state during the past week, included the following, the names of the directors being given, as well as the amount of capitalization, when such was specified in the papers as filed with the secretary of state: Cohen Weidberg Theatre Corporation, $20,000, Abraham and Beckie Cohen, Isidore Cohen, New York city; VanWyck Amusement Corporation, $420,000, Julius Gulkie, Ridgewood; Isaac Katz, Mitchell Kay, Brooklyn; Self-Protection Pictures, Inc., $10,000, M. R. Loewenthal, A. C. Gratz, Grace Ahearn, New York city; Rogowsky Amusement Company, Port Chester, $10,000, Sarah, Jacob and Samuel Rogowsky, Port Chester.

Labor Troubles Being Righted

Conferences in Many Cities Bring Settlement With Musicians and Operators

LABOR troubles between operators, musicians and exhibitors are rapidly being adjusted with every indication that in most cities they will be a thing of the past for another year, in the near future.

A faint possibility of an operators' strike is the latest development in the wage controversy between Milwaukee theater managers and their operator and stage hands. While a strike was laughed at by both sides until a few days ago, a somewhat different aspect was brought into the thing when musicians publicly stated that if the operators and stage hands wanted to strike the musicians would join in sympathy.

After a number of conferences between representatives of the Exhibitors Association of Chicago and the Musicians Union, a new working agreement has been entered into. Under its terms the musicians in theatres seating six hundred and over will receive an increase of ten per cent. The original demands of the union included a twenty-five per cent increase in wages, increase in the number of musicians in certain theatres from four to seven, and a clause whereby musicians proving satisfactory on a two weeks' tryout could not be dismissed for a year, and fifty-two weeks' work a year. The exhibitors' representative refused to consider these demands and final compromise was arrived at which left matters as they were before with the exception of the ten per cent increase.

Negotiations to settle their differences and reach an amicable agreement occupied the attention of the Atlanta Federation of Musicians and Famous Players-Lasky Corporation representatives in a series of conferences held last week, and culminated Sunday night in the signing of a contract between the musicians and Famous Players' theaters here.

According to the terms of the settlement reached, practically every demand made by the Federation of Musicians was conceded by Famous Players. The terms of the contract provide a scale of $50 per week minimum, the number of men to be not less than fifteen at all times; $10 extra for doubling, and that all men used on the stage for numbers are to receive $1 per performance additional.

Thalberg to Supervise Program

Louis B. Mayer in East Announces Fall Production Schedule for M-G-M Studios

THE Fall production schedule for the Metro-Goldwyn-Mayer studios, on which several special features are listed, to be made under the supervision of Irving G. Thalberg, was announced by Louis B. Mayer on his arrival in the east for conferences with Marcus Loew, Nicholas M. Schenck, Major Edward Bowes and other officials of Metro-Goldwyn-Mayer, this week. In addition to discussing production matters Mr. Mayer will also discuss arrangements for the presentations of "Ben Hur" and "The Big Parade."

Mr. Mayer said that the schedule which Thalberg has mapped out is the most pretentious ever launched at the Culver City plant. One of the first pictures to go into production will be the next Marion Davies Cosmopolitan vehicle, "Beverley of Graustark," the George Barr McCutcheon story. Syd Franklin has been loaned to M-G-M to direct the production. Another unit soon to start work is the Lon Chaney company

which will make "The Mocking Bird," an original story written and to be directed by Tod Browning.

Upon completion of "La Boheme," in which Lillian Gish will be starred, King Vidor will direct a picturization of "Bardleys the Magnificent," by Rafael Sabatini. This picture will be done in color with John Gilbert in the starred role. Another picture soon to be produced by Thalberg will be "The Temptress," by Blasco Ibanez. This will be a Cosmopolitan production.

Among the recent pictures which have been produced under Thalberg's supervision are "The Unholy Three," Lon Chaney's recent success; "The Midshipman," Ramon Novarro's initial starring vehicle for M-G-M; "Lights of Old Broadway," the Cosmopolitan production starring Marion Davies, and "The Tower of Lies," directed by Victor Seastrom and co-starring Norma Shearer and Lon Chaney.

St. Louis Company Expanding

Skouras and Koplar Concern Planning to Acquire Many St. Louis Theatres

THE St. Louis Amusement Company, controlled by Skouras Brothers and Harry Koplar, on Tuesday, September 22, took over the Cinderella Theatre, 2731 Cherokee street, owned by Freund Brothers under a long term lease calling for a substantial yearly payment to the former owners.

Co-incident with the leasing of the Cinderella it was learned that the St. Louis Amusement Company plans to purchase or lease ten other prominent neighborhood theatres in St. Louis and also has perfected plans for the construction, purchase and lease of other theatres in the St. Louis territory. The deal for the ten St. Louis houses will be concluded within the next few weeks.

In furtherance of the expansion plans of the company the officers of the St. Louis Amusement Company have perfected arrangements for the floating of the $600,000 first mortgage 6 per cent real estate gold bond issue due serially from October 1, 1927 to 1935.

The St. Louis Amusement Company now operates and owns in fee simple ten moving picture houses and airdomes and in addition has attractive leases on eleven other amusement places. It has also leases on three other theatres and an airdome which are closed at present.

The properties owned in fee simple by the company recently was appraised at $1,232,500. This does not take into consideration any value accruing from the leaseholds. An audit of the company's books showed annual earnings before Federal Income Taxes of $125,451.43 after allowing $124,618.81 for depreciation.

The audit made by Ernst and Ernst, certified public accountants, covered the two-year period ended on December 31, 1924.

For the six months' period to June 30, 1925, the company had earnings before estimated Federal income taxes of $87,601.69 or the rate of $165,203 a year.

The officers of the St. Louis Amusement Company are: Spyros P. Skouras, president; Harry Koplar, first vice-president; Charles P. Skouras, second vice-president; W. A. Stickney, secretary, and Sol E. Koplar, treasurer. Recently Sam Hamburg, Jr., disposed of his stock in the company and was succeeded as treasurer by Sol E. Koplar.

In addition to their stock in the St. Louis Amusement Company, the Skouras Brothers control the Skouras Brothers Enterprises which owns the Grand Central, West end and Lyric, Lyric Skydome and Capitol theatres and is building a $4,500,000 theatre and office building at Seventh and Locust street.

Universal Buys Scenario by New York School Girl

"Signs," an original scenario written by Dorothy Grundy, eighteen-year old New York school girl, has been purchased by Universal and will be produced as a starring vehicle for Reginald Denny. The production will be started this week under the direction of William A. Seiter. "Signs" according to the announcement, "contains a highly original and diverting idea which has to do with the automobile business."

Irving G. Thalberg, production supervisor at the Metro-Goldwyn-Mayer studios.

Famous Players At New Peak

Wall Street Journal Reports Business 28% Ahead of 1924 for Eight Month Period—Earns $7.04 Per Share in Half Year

ACCORDING to an article in the Wall Street Journal Famous Players-Lasky Corporation's business for the first eight months of 1925 was 28% ahead of that for last year, when a new high record for profits was established. The corporation is now doing the biggest business in its history, the Journal article states with earnings for the first six months of the year at $2,051,532, equal to $7.04 a share on 243,-431 shares. Earnings for the similar period in 1924 were $1,350,801, or $4.32 a share. The earnings for the full year of 1924 were $5,422,349, equal to $20.08 a share, a new high peak for the company, which the article states, will be considerably exceeded this year from present indications.

The foreign business of Famous shows a remarkable increase, foreign receipts being reported as 30% above those for the first eight months' period of 1924. The increase in foreign business is pointed out as especially notable in view of the fact that this is one of the most profitable branches of the corporation's operations.

"The financial position of the company at the end of the first half year," the Journal continues, "was stronger than at any other similar period on record. This is without giving effect to sale of new common stock, which will add over $10,000,000 to the company's resources. Cash on hand June 30 was $3,748,000 compared with $3,197,000 at

end of June, 1924, while bills payable were only $2,000,000 compared with $4,450,000. Inasmuch as the middle of the year is the height of the production season, when obligations for new films are at their peak, this position is particularly good and shows the success of the company's efforts to handle their production without the aid of the banks. In former years, notes payable at this season ran as high as $6,000,000.

"Proceeds from sale of stock will go in large part into theatrical properties which will more than provide for dividends on the additional common.

"Famous Players in spite of its position as the most important producer of moving pictures in the world has always been conservatively capitalized. Expansion in the last five years has been largely out of earnings although from time to time small amounts of common have been issued in exchange for new properties. This is the first important increase in common stock since 1919.

"Title has been taken recently to the Gordon chain of 38 theatres in New England and new theatres are being acquired in St. Petersburg, Fla., London, Eng., and Paris, France. It is probable that the acquisition of other properties is planned. Income from these new properties will be large and the additional capital should produce a corresponding increase in earnings.

"The large office and theatre building being erected on the Putnam site in New York will be handled as an ordinary real estate transaction without serious drain on the company's resources or need for financing.

"In a recent statement to stockholders Adolph Zukor, president, pointed out that in the last six years over $18,000,000 has been spent by the company in fixed assets, amortization of mortgages and retirement of preferred stock.

"Earnings and financial position in recent years as of December 31 have been as follows:

	1924	1923	1922	1921
Earnings	$5,422,349	$4,545,734	$4,110,987	$4,694,499
Per share	$20.08	$14.96	$14.72	$19.01
Cash	3,768,839	3,560,602	2,250,622	3,390,693
Bank loans....	None	2,385,000	2,567,416	3,065,222
Owned assets..	21,224,584	20,406,596	18,672,606	20,662,911
Cur. liabilities.	3,491,654	1,606,066	8,227,069	8,339,589
Work. capital..	13,732,677	13,065,612	10,446,457	15,823,392

"As Famous Players has been improving its financial position from year to year the investment qualities of its common and preferred are becoming more and more evident. In the past the only flaw in the position of Famous has been its large bank loans but now these have been cleared up. Famous has the extraordinary record of having earned a total of $90.16 a share on its common in the last five years, an annual average of $18.03 a share. In this time, only $40 a share has been paid out in dividends."

Connecticut Committee Maps Plans

Intensive Campaign Being Arranged to Seek Relief for Exhibitors From Drastic Durant Film Tax Law

THE committee of five named by the Motion Picture Theatre Owners of Connecticut have mapped an intensive campaign plan looking to the interest of the exhibitors in relief from the film tax law. This committee appointed at first temporarily to map a solution of the producers and distributors' difficulties has now been made a permanent one and will be ready to announce its program within the next few days. The foregoing information was given by Joseph W. Walsh, president of the Connecticut M. P. T. O.

Further discussing the present status of the matter, Walsh said:

"We feel that the sensible way out of our difficulties is to try to convince the officials of the state that the law has been miscarried and placed the burden where it was never intended. The M. P. T. O. has at all times since the trouble started tried to maintain an even balance and find the solution of the problem in a sane, constructive way.

"I want to express my appreciation to the members of our state organization for the manner in which they have conducted themselves and for the splendid united front they are presenting in the face of the most troublesome times that the industry has ever seen in Connecticut."

Various members of the Connecticut Legislature have come forward with statements that the Durant law was passed under a misapprehension. Among these is Mrs.

Mary M. Hooker, representative from Hartford, who said:

"I am in favor of revising the Durant film tax law at the next regular session of the Legislature. I feel that when the measure passed it was misunderstood. I voted for the bill under the impression that it would affect New York, not Hartford and Connecticut in general. As I believe the workings of the act were mis-interpreted I am wondering whether or not it can legally stand as a law."

Answers to a questionnaire sent legislators by the M. P. T. O., querying them on their attitude toward the law, are already coming in. Senator Samuel C. Doty from the first district expressed himself as being sold on the Durant tax because the law would "make the wealthy motion picture companies stand the bills." He feels that for the measure because the distributors "could well afford to pay taxes to the state of Connecticut."

William H. Mead, secretary of the Hartford Chamber of Commerce, attributes the passage of the bill to the reputed prosperity of the picture industry. He feels the producers and distributors lost out because of the widespread reports concerning the high salaries paid stars and executives of the busines and that pictures therefor were probably considered a lucrative source of revenue to the state.

Exhibitors are having more than their share of troubles because of the withdrawal from the state of exchanges. Edward J. McMahon, one of the owners of the Empire in Hartford, has said there will be a raise in prices at the Empire in case the tax law is not killed. The house, which changes daily during the warm weather, is having difficulty especially in securing its short subjects as the bookings. Inability to get paper on time is another hardship. Occasionally film booked fails to put in an appearance on time and some unannounced picture must be used. When the exchanges were located at New Haven these matters were easily righted, but now it is necessary to get relief from New York and Boston.

Find Second Skeleton in Gillis Theatre Debris

The skeleton of still another body, making the second within two weeks and a total of six, found in the abandoned ruins of the Gillis theatre, destroyed by an explosion June 25, has caused an active investigation to be launched by city authorities to determine if any more bodies remain undiscovered. The body found this week was about six feet from the one found last week, near the balcony ruins, and as yet has not been identified.

Sponsoring New Florida Studio

H. P. Carver Heads "Studio Park" Development; Was in New York Conferring With Picture Men

H. P. CARVER, former general manager of Cosmopolitan Productions, has become associated with the organization which will erect a large motion picture studio near St. Petersburg, it was announced this week. The new film development in Florida is known as "Studio Park," located in Pinnellas County, about two miles from St. Petersburg.

James Sayles, formerly advertising and publicity director for the Hearst motion picture enterprises, is another well known figure who is now identified with the studio undertaking on the Florida West Coast.

On a recent visit to New York for conferences with motion picture men, Mr. Carver said he received assurances from many producers that they would welcome the facilities which a well equipped studio in Florida would offer . He stated the Studio Park development had progressed far beyond the stage of projected enterprises, asserting that the tract of six hundred acres which will be developed as an ultra residential community have been cleared and that work soon would be started on the erection of a modern motion pic-

ture studio. Owing to its location, he said, Studio Park will afford adequate transportation facilities essential for a producing center and that the plant that has been planned will provide the necessary modern equipment for the efficient production of motion pictures.

Paramount Starts "Song and Dance Man"

Paramount has started production on a screen adaptation of George M. Cohan's stage play "The Song and Dance Man" with Herbert Brenon directing. The cast is made up of Tom Moore, in the title role; Harrison Ford, Bessie Love, George Nash, Norman Trevor, William B. Mack, and Josephine Drake.

Marian Warren Engaged to Act for Universal

Marian Warren, stage actress who has played in stock, vaudeville and on the musical comedy stage, has signed a contract to appear in Universal pictures. Miss Warren will make her screen debut in one of Universal's forthcoming features.

Novel Bought by Fox Goes Into Fifth Printing

The Century Company, publishers, announces that "The Chicken Wagon Family," a novel by Barry Benefield to be adapted to the screen by the Fox company, has gone into its fifth printing. The photoplay based on the book will be offered by Fox in January.

Gilda Gray Returns From Europe, to Start Film

Gilda Gray returned this week from France on the S. S. Paris and will soon start her first starring photoplay "Aloma of the South Seas" at the Paramount Long Island studios.

William De Mille Writes Photoplay Story

William de Mille has written an original story, tentatively titled "Magpie," which he will produce as his next for Paramount instead of "Polly of the Ballet," previously scheduled as his next work.

Sally Rand Joins Rod La Rocque Cast

Sally Rand, former vaudeville dancer, has won a featured role in support of Rod La Rocque in "Braveheart," which Alan Hale is directing for Cecil B. De Mille.

Cadman to Write Score for "The Vanishing American"

Charles Wakefield Cadman, one of America's leading composers and the writer of several famous songs based on the native music of the American Indian, has been engaged by Jesse L. Lasky to write the score to accompany "The Vanishing American," Paramount's screen version of the Zane Grey novel of that title.

In the work Mr. Cadman will include a song theme, "Little Wild Rose," dedicated to Lois Wilson, who, as the heroine of the screen story, is known by that name to the Indian hero portrayed by Richard Dix.

Metropolitan Increases Studio Staff

A number of additions have been made to the staff of Metropolitan Pictures, by William Sistrom, general manager. Edward Dillon has been signed to direct the first Priscilla starring vehicle and Randall C. Faye has been engaged to adapt the story and prepare the continuity. Don Hays has been signed to cut "Simon the Jester," the recent Frances Marion production which George Melford directed, while Jim Morley has joined the staff to cut "Steel Preferred."

Hart's "Tumbleweeds" Cast is Completed

The cast has been completed and production is well under way on "Tumbleweeds," William S. Hart's first production for United Artists release. Supporting the star are Barbara Bedford, Lucien Littlefield, J. Gordon Russell, Richard R. Neill, Jack Murphy, Lillian Leighton, Gertrude Claire, George Marion, Capt. E. T. E. Duncan, James Gordon, Fred Gamble, Turner Savage and Monte Collins. King Baggot is directing.

"Sally, Irene and Mary" in Production

"Sally, Irene and Mary" has gone into production at the Metro-Goldwyn-Mayer studios under the direction of Edmund Goulding, with John Crawford, Constance Bennett, William Haines and Karl Dale in the cast.

Dual Role for Chaney in "The Mocking Bird"

Lon Chaney will essay a dual role in "The Mocking Bird," his next starring vehicle for Metro-Goldwyn-Mayer. The story is an original by Tod Browning, who will direct the production, and deals with the Limehouse district in London.

Lois Moran Signed for "Just Suppose"

Inspiration Pictures has signed Lois Moran as leading woman for Richard Barthelmes in "Just Suppose," the star's next picture for First National release.

Judy King and Tom Wilson in Cast With Mix

Judy King and Tom Wilson have been added to the cast which will be seen in support of Tom Mix as the star of "The Best Bad Man," his next production for Fox. The picture is being made under the direction of J. G. Blystone. Others in the cast are Clara Bow, Paul Panzer, Cyril Chadwick, Buster Gardner, Tom Kennedy, and Frank Beal.

Cast Completed for "Rocking Moon"

Metropolitan Pictures has completed the cast for "Rocking Moon" with the addition of Rockliffe Fellowes, Laska Winters, Luke Cosgrave and Eugene Pallette, who will support John Bowers and Lilyan Tashman in the featured roles. George Melford will direct and the picture will be a Producers Distributing Corporation release.

New Wanda Wiley Comedy is Released

"Cupid's Victory," second of the Wanda Wiley Century comedies of the season, is released this week through Universal exchanges. The picture was directed by Charles Lamont, and in the cast with Miss Wiley are Earl McCarthy, Tony Hayes and a bevy of Century beauties from the Century Follies Girls.

Fanny Hurst Story Ready for Production

Walter Woods and Frances Agnew have completed the script of "The Mannequin," Fanny Hurst's $50,000 prize story, and work is now being rushed on the construction of the sets at the Paramount studio in Hollywood. Actual production is scheduled to start within a week.

Six First National Films Now Being Edited

Six of the features recently completed by directors for First National are now being edited and titled. They are "We Moderns," from the Israel Zangwill play and starring Colleen Moore; "Classified," a Corinne Griffith starring vehicle; "Why Women Love," an Edwin Carewe production based on "The Sea Woman"; "The Beautiful City," starring Richard Barthelmes; "Memory Lane," directed by John M. Stahl, and "The New Commandment," Robert Kane's production based on the Frederick Palmer novel "Invisible Wounds."

Von Stroheim is Preparing Continuity

Erich von Stroheim is at present at Catalina Island preparing the continuity for Joseph M. Schenck's next Constance Talmadge picture for First National release. In addition to preparing the story, Von Stroheim will direct and have a leading part in the picture. It is to be a screen version of George Barr McCutcheon's new Graustark story, "East of the Setting Sun," and photography is scheduled to get under way early in October.

Cast for "The Bat" Will Be Kept Secret

Casting is under way for the film version of "The Bat," screen rights to which were purchased by United Artists last week. It is the intention of the releasing company not to reveal the names of the cast until the picture is released, if possible. One of the features of the proposed film will be that none of the audience will be able to tell from an announced cast just whom is "The Bat."

"Plastic Age" Release Due This Month

B. P. Schulberg Productions has altered the release schedule somewhat so that "The Plastic Age," one of its most pretentious productions, may be released nationally on September 29th, instead of November 6th, as originally announced. Wesley Ruggles directed the production with a cast headed by Clara Bow, Donald Keith, Mary Alden, Henry B. Walthall and Gilbert Roland.

James W. Clark Joins M-G-M Exploitation Staff

James W. Clark, for the past two years art and publicity director of the Majestic Theatre at Tulsa, Oklahoma, has been appointed to take charge of all exploitation work for the Metro-Goldwyn exchanges in Oklahoma City and Dallas. Clark's territory will cover the large cities of Oklahoma, Texas and Arkansas.

Fantasy for "The Ancient Mariner" Completed

Henry Otto has completed the phantasy sequence which will be presented in the Fox screen version of "The Ancient Mariner." The allegorical scenes were filmed by Otto at Catalina Island. Paul Panzer is playing the title role in the production.

Will Add More Eastern Units

Rowland Says First National Will Continue Extensive Production at New York Studios

THE original intention of First National to produce extensively in the east, announced when several units were transferred from the West Coast to New York under the supervision of Earl Hudson, will be carried through, Richard A. Rowland, general manager of the company, said on the eve of his departure last week for Europe.

Mr. Rowland also announced that A. L. Rockett has succeeded Herman Bruenner, recently resigned, as general business manager of the Eastern studios. The appointment he said was requested by Earl Hudson when Bruenner gave notice three months ago of his intention to resign. At that time Rockett was on the Coast acting as West Coast representative during the absence of John McCormick in Europe.

The present slacking for four of five weeks at the First National plant in New York, Mr. Rowland said, is necessary to allow the scenario department to prepare stories ahead so that the production units may have time for preparation between the finishing of the scripts and the commencement of camera work. "During the coming year," he declared, "production both in the east and in the west is to be gradually expanded. Our eastern scenario department is being materially strengthened. Among the acquisi-

tions to this department recently are Olga Printzlau, John Fish Goodrich, Charles Whittaker, Jane Murfin and Harvey Thew."

This week will see the completion of production of "The Scarlet Saint," a picture being directed by George Archainbaud at the Eastern studio with Mary Astor and Lloyd Hughes in the co-featured roles. "The Unguarded Hour," a Milton Sills starring vehicle, with Doris Kenyon featured, was completed last week. According to Rowland's plan the next cycle of three pictures to be made at that studio are to go into production between October 1 and October 15. These are to be "Men of Steel," with Milton Sills starred; "The Lunatic at Large," a comedy, starring Leon Errol and "Mismates," a screen version of the Myron C. Fagan play, probably with Doris Kenyon in the leading role.

The second cycle will be begun, stated Rowland, immediately following the completion of those three, and will include "The Savage," with Lloyd Hughes, "The Boss of Little Arcady," an adaptation of Henry Leon Wilson's story, a screen version of the famous musical comedy "Mademoiselle Modiste." The following series will include a special "Atlantis," an original fantasy by Earl Hudson.

Report New Territorial Sales

Sax Announces Additional Contracts for Gotham Product; Levine on Exchange Tour

AMONG the independent distributors announcing new sales this week is the statement from Sam Sax, head of Lumas Film Corporation, distributors of the Gotham Productions, that he has closed contracts with H. Lieber Co. of Indianapolis and Progress Features of Salt Lake City and Denver.

These deals cover the distribution rights for the Gotham program of twelve features. Both companies distributed the Gotham product for last season. The Lieber Co., represented by John Sertas, took over the Gotham pictures for the state of Indiana, while George Mayne, representing Progress Features, signed the program for the states of Colorado, Utah, Wyoming, New Mexico, and Southern Idaho.

Nat Levine, recently returned from a general sales tour in the middle west and south, closed contracts for the distribution of Sam Bischoff's comedy output, to the following independent exchanges: Tom Brannon, of Eltabran, for Atlanta; Bill Underwood, of Specialty Films, for Dallas; Bobby North, of Bond, for Upper New York State; Ben Amsterdam, Masterpiece, Philadelphia and Washington; Harry Lande, Lande, Pittsburgh; Benny Judell, Judell Film Co., Chicago; Elmer Rhoden, Midwest Film Exchange, Kansas City; H. O. Mugridge, Celebrated, Minneapolis; Gene Emmick, Peerless, San Francisco; G. L. Sheffield, Greater Features, Seattle and Denver; Jimmy Minter, A.B.C., Detroit; Harry Asher, American

Features, New England; Harry Thomas, Merit, Greater New York and Northern New Jersey; Bobby North, for all of the foreign market.

In Mr. Levine's portfolio included with the Bischoff contracts were blanks for the sale of his series of six westerns starring Big Boy Williams and Wolfheart, the dog wonder. The following signatures were affixed, after this tour which lasted six weeks: Nathan Hirsch, for New York, First Graphic, for Upper N. Y. State; Tony Luccbesse, for Philadelphia; Abe Steinberg, Pittsburgh; Mayer Fisher, Greater New York; Charles Trampe, Milwaukee; H. O. Mugridge, Minneapolis; Joe Stern, Omaha; Frank Warren, Kansas City; Sam Werner, St. Louis; Jack Adams, Dallas; Tom Brannon, Atlanta and New Orleans; Sam Flax, Washington; W. H. Bradley, New England; J. H. Hoffberg, for the foreign market.

Mr. Levine sold every territory in the United States, with the exception of two. The two remaining territories are expected to be closed in a few days, he states.

$6,000,000 Company Incorporated in Delaware

The Far West Theatre Corporation, with a capital of $6,000,000, has been incorporated in Delaware. Oscar M. Bate, Winthrop H. Kellogg, and S. M. Wolfe, of New York, are the incorporators.

Conrad Nagel and Pauline Starke in "Sun Up," Metro-Goldwyn-Mayer's screen adaptation of the successful stage play.

Fox Adds 7 Specials To List

Announcement of New Productions Increases Original Schedule Arranged for 1925-1926

FOX Film this week announced the titles of seven productions which will be added to the list of Supreme Attractions originally listed on the schedule for 1925-26. This makes an increase of nine specials over the program as announced at the beginning of the current season, the others being "The Ancient Mariner," and "Streets of Sin."

The seven new Supreme Attractions are "Dangers of a Great City," "The Road to Glory," "Daybreak," "Separate Rooms," "Manhood," "The Golden Butterfly" and "Palace of Pleasure."

Fox also announced that two more stories have been decided upon for the list of Tom Mix features the company will release this season. These are "My Own Pal" and "Tony Runs Wild." To date Mix has completed "The Lucky Horseshoe," "The Everlasting Whisper," and one as yet untitled. He is now making "The Best Bad Man."

Title changes which have been made by Fox are the substitution of "The Golden Strain" for "Throughbred," a Peter B. Kyne story to be directed by Victor Schertzinger with George O'Brien in the leading role; and "Married Cheats" for "Part Time Wives," the title originally announced for the screen version of Bessie Beatty's magazine story "Part Time Marriage." This production will be directed by Emmett Flynn.

Paramount Coast Studio Busy

No Let-Down in Production Activities: New Production Schedule is Started

THOUGH no less than eight features were completed at the West Coast studios of Famous Players-Lasky in the past ten days, there will be no let-down in the heavy production activities at the company's plant in Hollywood, where several new photoplays will be started within the next ten days, under the new schedule announced by Hector Turnbull, supervising editor at the West Coast studios.

James Cruze will commence work this week on "The Mannequin." This is the Fannie Hurst story that won the authoress a $50,000 prize offered by Liberty Magazine. "The Tattooed Countess," will furnish Pola Negri her next starring vehicle under the direction of Malcolm St. Clair.

Raymond Griffith is soon to commence work on another starring comedy "Stage Door Johnny," under the direction of Clarence Badger.

With Bebe Daniels starring and Neil Hamilton playing the male lead, William de Mille's next production for Paramount will be "Polly of the Ballet."

After an absence of nearly three years, the Klieg lights will shine soon on Mildred Davis (Mrs. Harold Lloyd) under the direction of Victor Fleming. "The Two Soldiers" will be the picture, and prominent in the cast will be Wallace Beery and Raymond Hatton.

"Hassan" is the title of the next Raoul Walsh production for Paramount, and Irvin Willat will start work next on "The Enchanted Hill."

Paramount Places Alice Joyce Under Contract

PARAMOUNT has engaged Alice Joyce under long-term contract, it was announced last week by Jesse L. Lasky, first vice-president of Famous Players-Lasky. The contract was signed in Hollywood by Miss Joyce and Charles Eyton, manager of Paramount's West Coast studio.

Miss Joyce will make her first appearance under the new agreement in the leading role of "Mannequin," James Cruze's next picture, which is an adaptation of Fannie Hurst's prize winning story in the Liberty magazine contest.

Technicolor Used in Tom Mix Latest

Technicolor will feature many of the scenes in "The Yankee Senor," Tom Mix's latest production for Fox. It is a colorful story of Old Mexico adapted from "The Conquistador," the novel by Katharine Fullerton Gerould and was directed by Emmet Flynn.

The cast supporting Mix in "The Yankee Senor" includes Margaret Livingston, Kathryn Hill, Martha Mattox, Francis Mac Donald, Alec Francis and others. "Tony" also figures prominently.

Schulberg Adds Two to Gasnier Cast

B. P. Schulberg has added Charles Clarey and Joseph Girard to the cast of "The Other Woman's Story," the new Gasnier production to be released in the Fall as a Preferred picture. Alice Calhoun and Robert Frazer are playing the leading roles, while others in important parts are Helen Lee Worthing, Mahlon Hamilton, Riza Royce, David Torrence, Gertrude Short and Joan Standing.

Fox Starts "East Side, West Side"

Fox has started production on "East Side, West Side," an Imperial comedy in which George Harris and Barbara Leddy have the leading roles. The action is laid on New York's east side. In the supporting cast are George Williams, Tom McGuire and "Red" Thompson. Benjamin Staloff directed.

Mack Swain Cast for Role in Valentino Vehical

Mack Swain has been added to the cast which will support Rudolph Valentino in "The Eagle," his first vehicle for United Artists. Swain will appear in a prominent role. "The Eagle" is nearing completion at the United Studios under the direction of Clarence Brown.

Lefty Flynn's Next Will Be "Between Men"

Lefty Flynn's next picture for F. B. O. will be "Between Men." It will be produced and directed by Harry Garson. The story is by Rob Wagner.

Revier Vehicle Named 'When Husbands Flirt'

Columbia Pictures announces that "When Husbands Flirt" is the title selected for the Dorothy Revier starring vehicle based on the story "Penalty of Jazz," written by Dorothy Arzner and Paul Gangelin.

The cast assembled to support Miss Revier in the picture includes Forrest Stanley, Tom Ricketts, Ethel Wales, Maude Wayne, Frank Wood and Edwin Connelly. William Wellman will direct.

Gaylord Lloyd to Return to Screen Acting

Gaylord Lloyd, brother of Harold Lloyd, will return to the screen as a character actor. He will be succeeded as casting director for the Harold Lloyd company, a position he has held since quitting the screen two years ago, by Nora Ely, for several years associated with Hal Roach as casting director. Gaylord will be seen prominently in support of Harold Lloyd in his first picture for Paramount.

Semon Names Cast of "Stop, Look and Listen"

Larry Semon has completed casting for "Stop, Look and Listen," his first feature comedy for Pathe release. The principals who will appear in support of the star in this screen adaptation of the stage play of the same title are Dorothy Dwan, "Babe" Hardy, William Gillespie, Curtis McHenry, Frederick Kovert, B. F. Blinn, Joseph Swickard and Bull Montana.

Alyce Mills Loaned for Truart Picture

Alyce Mills has been loaned by B. P. Schulberg to Truart, for whom she will play the leading feminine role opposite Conway Tearle in "Morals for Men." Miss Mills has been with Schulberg for the past six months.

Gloria Swanson's Latest is Completed

Director Allan Dwan has completed "Stage Struck," Gloria Swanson's starring vehicle for Paramount. It is scheduled for release November 16th. The first and final sequences are in color to suggest the periods of happiness in the life of the heroine.

Molnar to Write 3 Plays for M-G-M

FERENC MOLNAR, Hungarian playwright and author of successes on the American stage as "Lilion," "The Swan," "Fashions for Men" and "The Guardsman," has signed a contract to write three original plays for screen production by Metro-Goldwyn-Mayer, according to an announcement by Louis B. Mayer.

The plays will be this author's first contributions directly to the photoplay, though several of his dramatic works have been adapted to the screen.

Lon Chaney and Norma Shearer in the Victor Seastrom production for Metro-Goldwyn-Mayer, "The Tower of Lies."

New F. B. O. Pictures Started

Second Half of Gigantic Program is Inaugurated at the Coast Studios

F. B. O. has inaugurated the second half of its production activities in connection with the gigantic program announced for the season. Production is already under way on some pictures, while the continuity writers are busy completing work on others.

"The Midnight Flyer," a railroad melodrama, got under way last week when the first scenes were shot. Tom Forman is directing the cast which includes Cullen Landis, Dorothy Devore, Charles Mailes, Claire McDowell, Frankie Darrow, Barbara Tennant, Elmo Billings and Buddy Post. The story is by Arthur Guy Empey and was adapted by J. Grubb Alexander.

A second of the Gold Bond pictures will be launched this month when "Flaming Waters," a melodrama of the oil industry goes into production. It is an original story by E. Lloyd Sheldon and will be produced by Associated Arts Corporation.

The continuity is being completed for "When His Love Grew Cold," first of the Laura Jean Libbey specials. Filming will start within two weeks.

Fred Thomson is on location with Silver King and a big company shooting exteriors for "All Around the Frying Pan." Scenes shot at the Alturas Roundup will be a feature of this production, which is being directed by Dave Kirkland.

Maurice Flynn is at work on "Between Men," which Harry Garson is producing and directing. Dick Talmadge is preparing his ninth comedy for F. B. O., while a suitable vehicle is being arranged for Tom Tyler. Bob Custer is completing "The Man of Nerve."

Alberta Vaughn is at work on the fourth episode of "Adventures of Mazie," the two-reel series being directed by Ralph Ceder.

Jackie Coogan Completes "Old Clothes"

Jackie Coogan has completed "Old Clothes," his first production under his new contract with Metro-Goldwyn-Mayer and will start work on his second comedy simultaneously with the release of "Old Clothes" the last week in November. In the cast with Jackie in his latest picture are, Max Davidson, Joan Crawford, James Mason, Alan Forrest, Lillian Elliott and Stanton Mack.

"U" Signs Harry Pollard to Long Contract

Universal has signed Harry Pollard to a directorial contract that will cover a period of several years. He is now directing "Two Blocks Away" with a cast headed by Charlie Murray, Vera Gordon and George Sidney.

Ernest Gillen Leading Man for Elaine Hammerstein

Ernest Gillen has been engaged by Columbia Pictures to play the leading role opposite Elaine Hammerstein in "Ladies of Leisure," a forthcoming Columbia Special. Gillen has appeared with several leading screen stars.

Names Two Supervisors of Paramount Production

Julian Johnson, title writer, and Townsend Martin, scenarist, associated for some time with Paramount's Long Island studio, have been appointed supervisors of production at that plant, Jesse L. Lasky announced this week.

The various units at work on Long Island are assigned as follows: Gloria Swanson and D. W. Griffith pictures are in charge of Le Baron. Sheldon is responsible for the Adolphe Menjou-Monta-Bell unit, Allan Dwan, Bebe Daniels and Gilda Gray. Julian Johnson has Herbert Brenon and Betty Bronson under his wing, and Townsend Martin will supervise Richard Dix and Frank Tuttle productions. Tom Geraghty is both supervisor of production and adapter of all Thomas Meighan stories.

"Tumbleweeds" Soon Will Be Completed

Photography will be completed in about two weeks on "Tumbleweeds," William S. Hart's first production for United Artists release. The big scene of the production was shot last week at La Aguerro Rancho in California, where was reenacted a homestead land rush depicting actual happenings at the opening by the Government of the Cherokee land strip to homestead.

Some three hundred wagons, about a thousand horses and mules, scores of dogs, goats, etc., and eight hundred men, women and children, took part in the rush. Nineteen cameras cranked on the scene.

Columbia Signs Harry Kerr to Contract

HARRY KERR, late executive of Metro-Goldwyn-Mayer, has been signed as production manager in charge of the various producing units of Columbia Pictures, as the first step toward the enlargement of the production staff of Columbia. For the past few days he has been devoting himself to all of the new Columbia productions, the signing of several new directors and the shifting of the personnel of the business staff of the organization.

"Three Faces East" Cast is Completed

With the signing of Edythe Chapman, Cecil B. De Mille completed his cast for "Three Faces East," which Rupert Julian will direct for release through Producers Distributing Corporation. In the featured roles, in addition to Miss Chapman, are Jetta Goudal, Robert Ames, Clive Brook, and Henry Walthall.

George Hassel Added to "La Boheme" Cast

George Hassel has been chosen to interpret the role of "Schunard" in the Metro-Goldwyn-Mayer screen production of "La Boheme," in which Lillian Gish will be starred. The picture is being filmed under the direction of King Vidor.

"Rex" Unit Returns to Hal Roach Studios

Fred Jackman, director, and his company making a new feature starring "Rex" the horse, has returned to the Hal Roach studios in Culver City following a location tour in Montana of four months. Jackman and his unit returned with the picture, which is titled "The Devil Horse," two-thirds completed.

The players appearing with "Rex" in "The Devil Horse" include Yakima Canutt, Gladys McConnell and Robert Kortman.

Lloyd French, business manager; Floyd Jackman, head cameraman; Carl Himm, film editor; "Jack-the-Swede" Lindale, Rex's trainer, and twenty other people were in the company.

"Lady Windermere's Fan" Cast Completed

Ernst Lubitsch has completed the cast for "Lady Windermere's Fan," which he will produce for Warner Brothers. The last member signed was Ronald Colman, who comes to Warners by arrangement with Samuel Goldwyn for the role of Lord Darlington.

The cast, in addition to Colman, includes Irene Rich, May McAvoy, Edward Martindel, Bert Lytell, Helen Dunbar and Carrie Daumbry.

The cast has also been completed for "His Jazz Bride," and includes Marie Prevost, Matt Moore, John Patrick, Mabel Julienne Scott, George Irving, Don Alvarado, Margaret Seddon, Helen Dunbar and Gayne Whitman. Herman Raymaker is directing.

Production highlights from the William Fox presentation, "Thunder Mountain," an adaptation from the John Golden stage success, "Howdy Folks."

Next Hines Continuity is Being Prepared

George Amy, Bradley Barker and Charles Hines, comprising the C. C. Burr scenario staff, are at Delaware Water Cap with Burr and Johnny Hines where they are putting the finishing touches to the continuity for "Rainbow Riley," Hines' second starring vehicle for First National release.

"Rainbow Riley" is an adaptation of "The Cub," which served as the last legitimate stage production for Douglas Fairbanks. It has its locale in the Kentucky mountains.

Extensive Improvements at F. B. O. Studios

Extensive improvements, which are said to have involved an outlay of $250,000 have been completed at the F. B. O. studios in Hollywood. The construction work includes new projection rooms, offices, dressing rooms, and the joining of stages 1 and 2 into one mammoth stage. Eight independent companies are carrying on production activities at the F. B. O. studios. The business end of the studios is being carried on by Fred Smith.

Dillon Again Will Direct Colleen Moore

Colleen Moore will again be directed by John Francis Dillon in "Irene," the new starring vehicle for First National. Dillon has just completed the direction of Miss Moore in "We Moderns." He also handled the megaphone for her in "Flaming Youth" and "The Perfect Flapper." The director is now engaged on the script for "Irene," while Miss Moore is taking a short vacation in the mountains.

"Lure of the Wild" Will Star Jane Novak

"Lure of the Wild" with Jane Novak in the leading role will be the sixth Columbia production, it was announced by Joe Brandt, president of the company, last week. The announcement states that "Lure of the Wild" will be one of Columbia's biggest and most important releases of the 1925-26 season.

B. Grimm Heads Warner Theatre Publicity Dept.

BEN H. GRIMM has resigned as advertising manager of Moving Picture World to join the Warner Bros. Theatres Inc., as head of the publicity and advertising department of all Warner houses. Mr. Grimm's headquarters will be at the Warners theatre in New York.

Mr. Grimm has been associated with the picture industry for several years and has a wide circle of friends in the business. He quit newspaper work in New York to join the publicity department of Metro. Later he went to England for Universal and managed a theatre in London for that company. He will organize the publicity and advertising departments for each of the fourteen theatres now being operated by Warner Bros.

P. A. Powers Heads Board of Directors of Reorganized Associated Exhibitors

FURTHER Details of the reorganization of Associated Exhibitors were made known this week. Oscar A. Price is the new president of the organization, which will be completely divorced from Pathe, it is announced, except for the physical handling of film.

At the instigation of the banking interests involved in the purchase of the company, P. A. Powers has been appointed Chairman of the Board of Directors with the other members of the board consisting of Elmer Pearson, Vice-President and General Manager of Pathe; Oscar Price; W. B. Levy, R. M. Hamilton, Henry Kelly and Harold Donnegan. W. B. Levy was made treasurer of the corporation, while R. M. Hamilton was elected secretary.

John S. Woody was made general manager and placed in charge of the company's affairs. Jay A. Cove remains general sales manager.

Plans are now on foot to enlarge every department in the organization and to install new departments to handle the work formerly done by Pathe. The home office quarters will be increased to allow for the installation of art, advertising, publicity and exploitation departments.

The releasing program for the coming season will number thirty features. Several specials will be added. Selling plans remain as they were originally started by General Manager Woody.

Warners Start Two Features

"Lady Windermere's Fan" and "Nightie Night Nurse" Under Way on Coast

WORK was started during the past week on two of Warner Brothers important productions. They are "Lady Windermere's Fan" and a new Syd Chaplin picture, "Nightie Night Nurse."

"Lady Windermere's Fan" is to be an Ernst Lubitsch production adapted from the Oscar Wilde classic, which enjoyed a tremendous stage success for many years. The principal roles are taken by Irene Rich, Ronald Colman (by arrangement with Samuel Goldwyn), May McAvoy, Edward Martindel, Bert Lytell, Helen Dunbar and Carrie Daumery. The scenario was prepared by Julien Josephson.

Charles Reisner, who seems to be achieving as much success as a director as he did as an actor, is handling the megaphone on "Nightie Night Nurse," the new Syd Chaplin vehicle.

Plans are being completed for two other productions to get under way in the near future at Warners' west coast studios. Julien Josephson is writing the scenario and Louis Milestone has been selected to direct Gillette Burgess', "The Cave Man," Matt Moore's next Warner picture.

"The Night Cry" will be the next starring vehicle for Rin-Tin-Tin, the Warner wonder dog. Both story and scenario are by Phil Klein and Edward Meagher. The director has not yet been assigned.

John Barrymore will complete his work in "The Sea Beast" within the next three weeks and will immediately start "Don Juan," which is being prepared by Bess Meredyth and Maude Fulton. "The Sea Beast" is being directed by Millard Webb.

"U" Will Start Six New Features

Production Work at Its Height With Five Others Already Under Way

UNIVERSAL is at the height of one of the busiest production seasons of its career, with six pictures ready to start production this week and five others being filmed.

Charles Brabin has just finished "Stella Maria," and is ready to start an ordinal story not yet titled ,written by Raymond L. Schock ,with Mary Philbin as the star. "Wives for Rent" is ready for production immediately. It was done by Svend Gade in collaboratio nwith Charles Whittaker and is based on a Swedish novel.

Reginald Denny is due to start work this week on "Skinner's Dress Suit," which William A. Seiter will direct. Denny has just finished "What Happened to Jones," also directed by Seiter.

Henry McRae is selecting a cast to support William Desmond in "Strings of Steel," a chapter play chronicling the building of the railroads, and Jack Daugherty will be featured in "The Radio Detective," another chapter play adapted from the Arthur B. Reeve mystery novel.

Among the Universal features already in production are "The Midnight Sun," a super-Jewel directed by Dimitri Buchowetzki; "Two Blocks Away," directed by Harry Pollard; an untitled historical production directed by Edward Sedgwick with Hoot Gibson in the starring role, and "The Scrapping Kid," with Clifford Smith directing and Art Acord a the star.

In addition to the features the regular schedule of comedies starring Neely Edwards, Charles Puffy and the "Sweet Sixteen" troupe, headed by Arthur Lake, will be made.

Hoffman Casting "Phantom of Forest"

Renaud Hoffman, supervising director for Gotham Productions, has started casting for "The Phantom of the Forest," with Thunder, the marvel dog as the star. This will be the eighth of the season's twelve pictures for Gotham. Eddie Phillips has the leading male role and Betty Francisco the feminine lead. Others so far selected are Barbara Tennant and James Mason.

The story is an original by Frank Foster Davis, owner and trainer of Thunder and will be directed by Henry McCarty. The picture will be shot at the Government redwood reservation at Santa Cruz, California.

Warner Players Loaned to Other Companies

Two of Warner Brothers most popular players have been loaned to other producing companies for important roles in productions now in the making. Dolores Costello, who has just completed the feminine lead opposite John Barrymore in "The Sea Beast," goes to Famous for an important feminine part in "The Mannequin," Fannie Hurst's prize story, which James Cruze is to direct.

Willard Louis has been loaned to Metro-Goldwyn-Mayer for an important role in the Hobart Henley offering, "Free Lips," which is now under way.

Editor Will Cooperate in "False Pride"

H. A. Keller, editor of True Detective Mysteries, a Macfadden publication, will cooperate with director Hugh Dierker in the murder sequences of "False Pride," second of the series of pictures to be made by the Macfadden True Story Film Company. Whenever crook atmosphere has a part in a Macfadden production it is the plan to have Keller cooperate with the director.

Sidney to Direct "Million Dollar Handicap"

Scott Sidney has been selected by Metropolitan Pictures to direct "The Million Dollar Handicap," which is scheduled to go into production the end of the month. It is an adaptation of W. A. Fraser's "Thoroughbreds." Scott Sidney and F. McGrew Willis are preparing the continuity. The picture will be released through Producers Distributing Corporation.

Pathe District Managers Meet in New York

A CONVENTION of the District Managers of Pathe will be held at the Hotel Roosevelt in New York from Wednesday, September 23 to Sunday the 27th. The convention will discuss new methods for exploiting the company's pictures.

Harry Scott, General Sales Manager, is chairman of the convention, which will hear addresses by all of the home office executives and department managers. It is also planned to have several of the producers contributing to the Pathe program address the district managers.

Wilson to Make Series for Davis

DAVIS DISTRIBUTING DIVISION has signed Al Wilson, well known as a stunt aviator, for a series of six aviation stunt pictures to be released on the 1925-26 schedule through Vital Exchanges.

The first picture, titled, "Flying Thru" has already been completed. The second, which has not yet been given a title is in production at the Al Wilson studios in Hollywood.

True Story Names Cast for "Broken Homes"

The principals selected for the cast of "Broken Homes," Bernarr Macfadden's third production for distribution by Astor are Alice Lake and Gaston Glass, it was announced this week. Other important roles are to be filled by Betty Jewell, Barney Sherry and Rita Allen.

The picture, to be made by True Story Film Company, will be directed by Hugh Dierker from a scenario by Lewis Allen Browne. The story of "Broken Homes" will be published in two installments in the Macfadden True Story Magazine.

Valentino's "The Eagle" is Ready for Editing

Director Clarence Brown has completed photography on "The Eagle," Rudolph Valentino's first production for United Artists release. Editing is under way and the picture will be rushed to the theatres for early release. George Marion, Jr. has been engaged to title "The Eagle." Valentino plans to take a trip to Europe as soon as the finishing touches have been put on the picture. He will visit England, France and Italy, returning to the United States as soon as a suitable story is found.

Production is Resumed at Whitman Bennett Studio

Following a period of idleness during which new equipment was installed the Whitman Bennett Glendale Studio has resumed activities as a production center with three units making features for the Golden Arrow program about to begin camera work. Major Maurice Campbell started work on a feature as yet untitled, while Mr. Bennett is due to begin soon the production of a feature he will direct and Jane Novak is ready to start the second of a series that she will make for Arrow.

Wellman Replaces De Sano With Schulberg

William A. Wellman has been signed by B. P. Schulberg to take the place left vacant on the directorial staff by the resignation of Marcel De Sano, whom ill health compelled to retire temporarily from the picture field. Wellman's first Preferred picture will be the screen version of Wallace Irwin's novel, "Lew Tyler's Wives." The direction of this picture was originally assigned to De Sano. Camera work will start as soon as the cast is selected.

Training Camp Feature Made by M-G-M for Government

Metro-Goldwyn-Mayer will turn over to the Government a six reel feature film of incidents in connection with the recent Military Training Camp at Del Monte, California to stimulate interest in the National Defense Program. Thirty-three reels of air, land and sea maneuvers were recorded by the camera.

Colonel William J. O'Loughlin, training officer in charge of the recent Del Monte camp, and Major Horace G. Foster of the Presidio, San Francisco, have arrived at Culver City to supervise the editing and titling of the film. Upon completion of the picture it will be turned over to Major General Davis, Adjutant General of the American Army to be shown throughout the country to stimulate interest in defense and especially in annual training camps.

Texas Welcomes Richard Dix on Location Trip

Richard Dix and the unit producing "Womanhandled," his next starring vehicle for Paramount, received a hearty welcome upon his arrival at Houston, Tex., last Monday. Dix made his first appearance as a leading man with a stock company in Dallas several years ago, and his return to the state was greeted by a "welcome home" celebration in which 2,000 admirers of the star participated.

The incoming party included Director Gregory La Cava, Esther Ralston, who will play the leading feminine role, Margaret Morris, a new screen find, Edmund Breese, the veteran character actor, and others.

"Agony Column" Next for Monte Blue

Monte Blue's next starring vehicle for Warner Brothers will be "The Agony Column," an adaptation from the Earl Derr Bigger's Saturday Evening Post story. E. T. Lowe, Jr. is writing the scenario and Erle Kenton will direct.

Two Added to Cast for "Free Lips"

Director Hobart Henley has added Gwen Lee and Antonio D'Algy to the cast of "Free Lips," the Metro-Goldwyn-Mayer production in which Norma Shearer is starred. It is a Carey Wilson story and Lew Cody has the leading male role.

Einfeld Promoted by First National

S. CHARLES EINFELD has been appointed by First National to the position of director of the exhibitors' service division, made vacant by the recent promotion of C. F. Chandler as director of advertising publicity for First National.

Einfeld has been in the company's service division ever since 1919 and at the time of his present appointment was assistant to Chandler. He also holds an executive position with the Leo Brecher chain of theatres in New York City.

Exhibitors Service Bureau

Klondike lobby display arranged at the Victory theatre in Denver for "The Gold Rush" (United Artists), with silhouetted trees and a cut-out of Charlie, against a sky backdrop.

Advisory Board and Contributing Editors, Exhibitors' Service Bureau

George J. Schade, Schade theatre, Sandusky.

Edward L. Hyman, Mark Strand theatre, Brooklyn.

Leo A. Landau, Lyceum theatre, Minneapolis.

C. C. Perry, Managing Director, Garrick theatre, Minneapolis.

E. R. Rogers, Southern District Supervisor, Famous Players-Lasky, Chattanooga, Tenn.

Stanley Chambers, Palace theatre, Wichita, Kan.

Willard C. Patterson, Metropolitan theatre, Atlanta.

E. V. Richards, Jr., Gen. Mgr. Saenger Amusement Co., New Orleans.

F. L. Newman, Managing Director, Famous Players-Lasky theatres, Los Angeles.

Arthur G. Stolte, Des Moines theatre, Des Moines, Iowa.

W. C. Quimby, Managing Director, Strand Palace and Jefferson theatres, Fort Wayne, Ind.

J. A. Partington, Imperial theatre, San Francisco.

George E. Carpenter, Paramount-Empress theatre, Salt Lake.

Sidney Grauman, Grauman's theatre, Los Angeles.

George E. Brown, Imperial theatre, Charlotte, N. C.

Louis R. Sidney, Division Manager, Loew's theatres, Pittsburgh, Pa.

Geo. Rotsky, Managing Director, Palace theatre, Montreal, Can.

Eddie Zorn, Managing Director, Broadway-Strand theatre, Detroit.

Fred S. Myer, Managing Director, Palace theatre, Hamilton, Ohio.

Joseph Plunkett, Managing Director, Mark-Strand theatre, New York.

Ray Grombacher, Managing Director, Liberty theatre, Spokane, Wash.

Ross A. McVoy, Manager, Temple theatre, Geneva, N. Y.

W. S. McLaren, Managing Director, Capitol theatre, Jackson, Mich.

Harold B. Franklin, Director of Theatres, Famous Players-Lasky.

William J. Sullivan, Manager, Rialto theatre, Butte, Mont.

H. A. Albright, Manager, T. D. & L. theatre, Glendale, Calif.

Claire Meachime, Grand theatre, Westfield, N. Y.

Ace Berry, Managing Director, Circle theatre, Indianapolis.

THE CHECK-UP

Weekly Edition of Exhibitors' Box Office Reports

Productions listed are new pictures on which reports were not available previously.

For ratings on current and older releases see MOTION PICTURE NEWS—first issue of each month.

KEY—The first column following the name of the feature represents the number of managers that have reported the picture as "Poor." The second column gives the number who considered it "Fair"; the third the number who considered it "Good"; and the fourth column, those who considered it "Big".

The fifth column is a percentage giving the average rating on that feature, obtained by the following method: A report of "Poor" is rated at 20%; one of "Fair," 40%; "Good," 70%; and "Big," 100%. The percentage rating of all of these reports on one picture are then added together, and divided by the number of reports, giving the average percentage—a figure which represents the consensus of opinion on that picture. In this way exceptional cases, reports which might be misleading taken alone, and such individual differences of opinion are averaged up and eliminated.

TITLE	Poor	Fair	Good	Big	Value	Length
FAMOUS PLAYERS						
Beggar on Horseback	1	4	5	1	57	7,168 ft.
FIRST NATIONAL						
Half Way Girl, The	—	2	6	2	70	7,570 ft.
Lost World, The	—	—	6	5	84	9,700 ft.
METRO-GOLDWYN						
Romola	—	2	5	4	75	10,875 ft.
Slave of Fashion, A	—	2	7	1	62	5,906 ft.
PATHE						
Black Cyclone	—	1	6	3	76	5,508 ft.
WARNER BROS.						
Eve's Lover	1	2	8	1	63	6,540 ft.

See Complete "Check-Up" Oct. 10th

"Old Home Week" Tied Up With Issue of Life

Wm. N. Robson, Paramount's Exploitation representative, sends in a story of an exploitation campaign put on by Carl Maple, manager of Barney's theatre at Point Marion for "Old Home Week" that shows how timely events work to the benefit of the live showman who is willing to think as well as work.

The week he played "Old Home Week" was the week "Life" came out with an "Old Home Week" number. Everything in it was made to order for the exploitation of "Old Home Week."

Maple bought up all the copies on the news stands not only in Point Marion but in surrounding towns. To make sure he missed none he sent several of his assistants over the same trail. The publicity this aroused itself was substantial as all the drug stores, news stands, etc., told all who inquired for "Life" of the "crazy fools" from Barney's theatre buying them all up.

With a rubber stamp Maple said on every page of these copies of "Life" "See Thomas Meighan in 'Old Home Week' at Barney's theatre." Then he put them in each barber shop, waiting room, soda fountain, restaurant and every place in town where people congregate, with a result that was all that he could desire.

Dignified Campaign Given "Winds of Chance" Run

"Winds of Chance" opened a fortnight's engagement at Warner's theatre in New York City recently. The exploitation campaign was concentrated on the week prior to the opening and was characterized by dignity and restraint.

The opening gun of the campaign was a co-operative tie-up with Frank Munsey's Evening Telegram-Mail which started publication of the serialization of "Winds of Chance" simultaneously with the opening date. Realizing the value of the serial and the following of Rex Beach as circulation boosters, The Telegram-Mail instituted a vigorous advertising campaign in its columns, giving due credit to First National and Frank Lloyd.

The publication will continue in daily instalments for forty consecutive days.

Illuminated marquee display and costumed usherettes at the Strand theatre, Seattle, for the engagement of "The Fool" (Fox).

A tie-up was next arranged with Hearst's Daily Mirror in connection with their distribution of "Uncle Sam's Lucky Two Dollar Bill." This stunt, frankly fathered by the Hearst paper as a circulation booster was the talk of the town from its inception. The Mirror daily distributed two dollar bills, and then announced prizes of $50.00 each for those bearing the numbers published in its columns. The theatre was one of the chief distributing points of the "lucky deuces," due mention being made daily of the theatre and "Winds of Chance."

Arrangements were next consummated with Gimbel Brothers broadcasting station WGBS and Colonel William Green's famous station WMAF at South Dartmouth, Mass., for the broadcasting of a personal appearance of Ben Lyon, one of the featured principals of the cast of "Winds of Chance."

This radio hook-up had a double-barrelled value as the South Dartmouth station acted as a preliminary campaign for the Boston engagement which opened at Symphony Hall the following week.

"I'll Show You the Town" Given Photo Contest

The amateur photographers of Toledo, Ohio, were out to win the $50 camera and carrying case which the Gross Photo Supply Company offered as a prize for an "I'll Show You the Town" contest at the instigation of A. J. Sharick, exploitation man from Universal's Cleveland exchange, when the picture was about to play the Temple theatre. The contest was for the best set of photographs by an amateur photographer showing the main points of interest of Toledo.

The Chamber of Commerce became so interested in Sharick's contest that the secretary appointed a special committee to decide which set of views was the best. All three newspapers gave publicity to the stunt.

The kodak store mailed out 1,000 cards telling about the contest and incidentally something about the picture. They also gave a big window display with the prize camera the center attraction.

In a corner of the Temple's lobby, Sharick and Manager Fred Walters arranged a very clever display. A triangular lobby stage draped with curtains was set with a miniature 24-sheet board at one side and cut-out figures of Denny and three girls walking along in front. Cut-out trees, miniature yellow taxis, and a toy aeroplane in the sky completed the novel set.

Mail Trucks Placarded for "The Air Mail" Showing

Every mail truck in Fresno, Cal., and every U. S. Mail letter box in town was placarded for the showing of "The Air Mail" at the Kinema theatre. The mail trucks carried banners covering the two sides of the machines reading, "The Air Mail—Neither snow nor rain, nor wind, nor night can stay the pilot in his flight." On the letter boxes were regular window cards for the production.

On the canopy in front of the theatre Manager Purkett had a small airplane displayed which was visible for several blocks on either side of the theatre.

Two of the features in the ten block parade arranged by the Union Pacific Railway and the Majestic theatre, Portland, Ore., to exploit the engagement of "The Iron Horse" (Fox). One view shows some of the 60 real Umatilla Indians in full war paint, while the other depicts a U. P. section crew laying track on a truck.

Elaborate Style Revue is "Slave of Fashion" Aid

An elaborate fashion revue held under the auspices of Peggy Hamilton, fashion expert of the Los Angeles Times, was the outstanding feature of the campaign recently waged on "A Slave of Fashion," by Bert Lennon, Metro-Goldwyn exploiteer, in Los Angeles where this picture played at Loew's State. Twelve models and two pages assisted Miss Hamilton, more than $57,000 worth of gowns and furs loaned by local merchants being displayed. Director Henley acted as master of ceremonies. Press notices were contributed by the Los Angeles Times.

Several thousand copies of a letter written by Norma Shearer to the Sehuck Dry Cleaning company commending their service were mailed out by the company and a copy enclosed with every package delivered. Twenty-six Owl Drug stores featured "A Slave of Fashion" sundaes and distributed cards exploiting them to their patrons. Soda clerks wore badges recommending these sundaes, which proved popular. One of the leading jewelry firms, Feagan and Company, devoted three windows to displays of solid gold frames in which pictures of Miss Shearer were mounted.

"Fast Express" Tickets as Retail Tie-up Medium

Joseph W. Springer who owns the Strand theatre in Elizabethtown, Ind., has found an excellent means of starting a new chapter play off. He tried it on "The Fast Express."

In a co-operative arrangement with the merchants of his town he sells them tickets for the first episode of the serial which they in turn give away to their customers. Since he charges only one cent a ticket for these, the merchants feel free to give them away with all purchases of ten cents or more. While the charge is small, it enables Mr. Springer to pay out on his show; the stunt gives the customers practically a free show and at the same time generates much good will for the merchants.

Special display piece in the lobby of the Royal theatre, Laredo, Texas, announcing the showing of "A Thief in Paradise" (First National) at that house.

Clever window display for "Beggar on Horseback" (Paramount) by Manager Walter League of the Strand theatre, Memphis, in a music store. Each song featured centered about a "dream" idea, tying up with the dream sequence of the film.

Smashing "Shore Leave" Stunt

Loew's Warfield in San Francisco Makes Navy Tie-up During Diamond Jubilee Week

LAST year, when Loew's Warfield theatre, San Francisco key house of West Coast Theatres., Inc., played "Classmates," they secured the co-operation of the U. S. Army in putting across a splendid and spirited stage presentation which was calculated to stir patriotism and an added admiration for Uncle Sam's army. The idea went across beautifully.

This year a combination of events and circumstances again lent themselves to the West Coast people and a new high mark in interest and enthusiasm was created.

"Shore Leave" was booked into Loew's Warfield from September 5th to the 11th —day and date with the Diamond Jubilee, the biggest celebration San Francisco, a city which prides itself upon civic celebrations, had ever staged. Hundreds of thousands of visitors swarmed into the city and parades, fetes, and carnivals were hourly occurrences.

The U. S. S. "Savannah," mother ship to the division of submarines in the Pacific, had been ordered to dock at San Francisco to participate in the celebration and as the big battle cruiser, leading the flotilla of submarines, swung into the harbor of the Golden Gate and dropped anchor off California City to coal for its stay, Frank Whitbeck, publicity director of West Coast Theatres, Inc., climbed aboard a power boat and sped down the bay to greet Captain John R. Thompkins, the commander, and invite him to participate with the theatre in bringing home a rousing "Navy Week" at Loew's Warfield—to thoroughly sell the idea of the navy to the thousands of visitors from inland points who were to be in the city for the celebration.

Captain Thompkins, seeing the possibility of navy propaganda by appearance of the 30 piece band from the Savannah upon the stage of Loew's Warfield before approximately 100,000 people, agreed to the press agent's proposition and sent his organization to Loew's Warfield for the first three days of the seven day engagement.

Fanchon and Marco conceived a splendid presentation with the band on stage and with the addition of the "Wings of the Fleet," the two reel educational film of navy aviation sponsored by the Naval Board of the United States, Loew's Warfield theatre was able to put across a smashing week.

Co-operation such as this builds for a better and finer understanding between the theatre management and the federal and city governments and even though many cities are not situated as well as San Francisco in matters of this sort an effort can be made to bring the theatre into closer contact when pictures such as "Shore Leave" or "The Midshipman" are available.

"I'll Show You the Town" Aided by Ballyhoo

At the Liberty of Puyallup, Wash., with the aid of Frederic Babcock, Universal exploiteer out of the Seattle exchange, Manager Mike Barovic stepped on "I'll Show You the Town."

A man on horseback was secured to gallop through the streets and countryside round about Puyallup. Signs hanging from his saddle proclaimed that he was hurrying to see "I'll Show You the Town" at the Liberty theatre.

Manager Latts of the Royal theatre, Ashland, Wisc., was the creator of this attractive parade stunt for "Classmates" (First Nat'l). The can non, soldiers and cadets on the truck were the talk of the town.

Collegiate "Freshman" Stunts

Feature Comedy at Colony, New York, Given Lively Prologue and Displays

THE run of "The Freshman" at the B. S. Moss Colony theatre on Broadway, New York City, opened recently after an intensive campaign. The Moss management has surrounded the feature with an elaborate prologue entitled "Campus Capers," produced under the personal supervision of George Choos and featuring Jack Broderick and Betty Felsen, Hill's Blue Devils orchestra, Senmon Krevoff, five members of the "University of Southern California Trojans"—Clark, Eaton, Scott, Shutts and Magee—who appear in the Lloyd picture in the scenes staged at the University, and the famous Colony ensemble. This merry musical melange was staged by Harry Shaw. Lighting effects are by J. De Rosa, scenic art is by Nat Eastman, costumes were provided by Textile Mills, Hilton Company and Tams. Jack Glogan arranged the music.

In keeping with the type of the picture the opening overture is "Jolly Fellows" by Suppe, rendered by the Colony Melody Masters, with Dr. Edward Kilenyi and E. Chas. Egget as associate directors. John Priest is at the Colony Grand Organ console.

The lobby was decked with extensive displays of paintings of Lloyd in character as "The Freshman" and punch scenes from the picture. As a ballyhoo, a sightseeing bus was employed. Three large cutouts were perched on the roof and colorful streamers hung along the sides. With a full crew of "college boys," garbed as Lloyd appears in the campus scenes of the picture, cheering through megaphones and waving Harold Lloyd flags, the bus was driven practically all over the city.

A special painted sign of twenty-four sheet size was placed high on the front of the Colony some time previous to the opening of the picture, and an extensive poster campaign was worked out with good displays in the most advantageous locations throughout the city and vicinity. Extensive advertising was carried in the daily newspapers.

Pioneer Oregonians Free to See "Iron Horse"

The Morning Oregonian, published at Portland, Oregon, recently acted as host at a theatre party to all pioneer Oregonians who came to that state by rail between the years of 1869 and 1885. The guest party was arranged with Jensen & Von Herberg and J. J. Parker, proprietors of the Majestic theatre, as part of the exploitation of the feature "The Iron Horse."

A booth was erected in the Oregonian offices, where those eligible to be guests were invited to register. The registrations were afterward checked up, and tickets for the opening sent to those who qualified. The Oregonian played the matter up prominently in front page stories, and also announced that guests would not even be required to walk to the theatre, but would be driven in cars which would line up in parade formation and make a short tour of the downtown streets before the performance.

The Oregonian made much of the event, due to the fact that at that time, the Central Pacific and the Union Pacific forged the connecting link across the continent in 1869, that veteran news sheet was already in its 19th year.

The pioneers who attended the guest performance were not only carried to the theatre in cars, but returned to their homes by the same means.

Exhibitors Box-Office Reports

Names of the theatre owners are omitted by agreement in accordance with the wishes of the average exhibitor and in the belief that reports published over the signature of the exhibitor reporting, is a dangerous practice.

Only reports received on specially prepared blanks furnished by us will be accepted for use in this department. Exhibitors who value this reporting service are urged to ask for these blanks.

Title of Picture	Population of Town	Location	Class of Patronage	Weather	Box Office Value	Check-up Percentage from other Reports
ASSOC. EXHIBITORS						
Camille of Barbary Coast	350000	Wash.	General	Clear	Good	70
FAMOUS PLAYERS						
Beggar on Horseback...	401247	Ohio	1st run	Hot	Fair	57
Coast of Folly, The....	113344	N. Y.	1st run	Clear	Big	70
	506675	N. Y.	1st run	Clear	Good	—
	126468	Iowa	1st run	Bad	Good	—
	550000	Cal.	1st run	Clear	Good	—
In the Name of Love....	401247	Ohio	General	Hot	Poor	63
Lucky Devil, The......	772987	Mo.	1st run	Hot	Good	72
	733826	Md.	1st run	Hot	Good	—
Man Who Found Himself, The...............	85000	Pa.	1st run	Hot	Good	50
	550000	Cal.	1st run	Clear	Good	50
	72012	N. J.	1st run	Clear	Good	50
	500000	N. J.	1st run	Clear	Good	50
	126468	Iowa	1st run	Bad	Good	50
	258288	Ore.	General	Clear	Fair	50
Not So Long Ago....	350000	Wash.	General	Clear	Poor	64
	733826	Md.	1st run	Hot	Good	—
Pony Express, The.....	550000	Cal.	1st run	Clear	Big	89
Shock Punch, The......	506675	N. Y.	1st run	Clear	Fair	63
Son of His Father.....	324410	Mo.	1st run	Bad	Fair	70
	72012	N. Y.	1st run	Clear	Good	—
	126468	Iowa	1st run	Bad	Good	—
	796841	Ohio	1st run	Clear	Good	—
Street of Forgotten Men	126468	Iowa	1st run	Bad	Good	61
	401247	Ohio	1st run	Hot	Fair	61
	506675	N. Y.	1st run	Clear	Good	—
Ten Commandments,The	401247	Ohio	General	Clear	Poor	89
	401247	Ohio	1st run	Hot	Good	—
	772897	Mo.	1st run	Hot	Good	—
	500000	N. J.	1st run	Clear	Fair	—
	200616	Ga.	1st run	Clear	Big	—
Trouble With Wives, The	72012	N. Y.	1st run	Hot	Good	60
	85000	Pa.	1st run	Hot	Fair	—
Wild Horse Mesa......	314194	Ind.	1st run	Clear	Good	70
Wild, Wild Susan......	550000	Cal.	1st run	Clear	Good	63
	200616	Ga.	General	Clear	Big	—
	258288	Ore.	1st run	Clear	Good	—
	401247	Ohio	1st run	Hot	Poor	—
	993678	Mich.	1st run	Clear	Good	—
	733826	Md.	1st run	Hot	Good	—
	314194	Ind.	1st run	Bad	Big	—
	350000	Wash.	1st run	Clear	Good	—
F. B. O.						
Bloodhound, The.......	200616	Ga.	General	Clear	Good	70
If Marriage Fails......	72012	N. Y.	General	Clear	Fair	55
Parisian Nights........	550000	Cal.	1st run	Clear	Good	70
FIRST NATIONAL						
Enticement............	506675	N. Y.	General	Clear	Good	63
Fine Clothes..........	324410	Mo.	General	Bad	Good	58
Graustark.............	796841	Ohio	1st run	Clear	Good	85
	200616	Ga.	1st run	Clear	Big	—
Half Way Girl, The.....	993678	Mich.	1st run	Clear	Good	70
	430000	Mich.	1st run	Clear	Poor	—
Her Sister From Paris..	772897	Mo.	1st run	Hot	Good	79
	733826	Md.	1st run	Hot	Big	—
	401247	Ohio	1st run	Clear	Fair	—
I Want My Man.......	85000	Pa.	General	Warm	Big	66
Knockout, The........	126468	Iowa	1st run	Bad	Poor	65
Lost World, The.......	350000	Wash.	1st run	Clear	Big	84
	314194	Ind.	1st run	Clear	Big	—
	258288	Pa.	1st run	Clear	Good	—
My Son..............	85000	Pa.	General	Hot	Fair	70
Shore Leave..........	126468	Iowa	1st run	Bad	Good	24
	314194	Ind.	1st run	Bad	Big	—
	550000	Cal.	1st run	Clear	Big	—
	796841	Ohio	1st run	Clear	Good	—
	113344	N. Y.	1st run	Clear	Big	—
	733826	Md.	1st run	Hot	Big	—
FOX						
Iron Horse, The........	550000	Cal.	General	Clear	Big	77
	324410	Mo.	1st run	Bad	Big	—
(6th week)	258288	Ore.	1st run	Clear	Good	—
Kentucky Pride........	796841	Ohio	General	Clear	Fair	50
	500000	N. J.	General	Clear	Fair	—
	993678	Mich.	General	Clear	Good	—
Lightnin'............	401247	Ohio	1st run	Clear	Fair	53
Rainbow Trail, The.....	733826	Md.	General	Hot	Good	70
	401247	Ohio	Mixed	Clear	Good	—
Trail Rider, The.......	733826	Md.	General	Hot	Fair	68
METRO-GOLDWYN-MAYER						
Daddy's Gone a-Hunting	733826	Md.	General	Hot	Fair	65
Mystic, The...........	126468	Iowa	1st run	Bad	Poor	63
	796841	Ohio	1st run	Clear	Fair	—
	500000	N. J.	1st run	Clear	Fair	—
Pretty Ladies..........	350000	Wash.	1st run	Clear	Fair	50
Proud Flesh...........	733827	Md.	General	Hot	Fair	59
	324410	Mo.	General	Bad	Good	—
Rag Man, The........	506675	N. Y.	General	Clear	Good	82
Romola..............	258288	Ore.	General	Clear	Good	75
Unholy Three, The.....	506675	N. Y.	General	Clear	Big	78
PATHE						
Freshman, The (2d week)	506675	N. Y.	General	Clear	Big	92
White Sheep..........	733826	Md.	General	Hot	Good	58
PRODUCERS DIST. CORP.						
Hell's Highroad........	72012	N. Y.	General	Clear	Fair	70
Roaring Rails.........	72012	N. Y.	Mixed	Hot	Big	81
Seven Days...........	314194	Ind.	General	Bad	Good	90
Stop Flirting..........	733826	Md.	General	Hot	Good	54
Without Mercy........	113344	N. Y.	General	Hot	Poor	59
STATE RIGHTS						
Boomerang, The.......	401247	Ohio	General	Clear	Fair	58
Daughters Who Pay....	550000	Cal.	General	Clear	Fair	50
Foolish Virgin, The....	733826	Md.	General	Hot	Fair	63
Pal O' Mine..........	200616	Ga.	General	Clear	Fair	60
Recreation of Brian Kent	733826	Md.	General	Clear	Good	88
Silent Pal, The........	324410	Mo.	General	Bad	Fair	70
Souls for Sables.......	506675	N. Y.	1st run	Clear	Good	70
Sporting Chance, The...	200616	Ga.	Mixed	Clear	Good	70
Trip to Hawaian Islands.	126468	Iowa	General	Bad	Good	60
UNITED ARTISTS						
Gold Rush,The (6thweek)	993678	Mich.	1st run	Clear	Big	93
	500000	N. J.	1st run	Clear	Big	—
	772897	Mo.	1st run	Hot	Big	—
UNIVERSAL						
California Straight Ahead	772897	Mo.	1st run	Hot	Fair	70
	200616	Ga.	General	Clear	Big	—
	350000	Wash.	1st run	Clear	Good	—
Dangerous Innocence...	733826	Md.	Mixed	Hot	Good	63
Goose Woman, The.....	500000	N. J.	1st run	Clear	Good	85
	314194	Ind.	1st run	Clear	Big	—
Red Rider, The.......	200616	Ga.	General	Clear	Fair	63
Siege...............	993678	Mich.	General	Clear	Good	48
Spook Ranch, The.....	506675	N. Y.	General	Clear	Good	—
Teaser, The..........	550000	Cal.	1st run	Clear	Good	64
VITAGRAPH						
Baree, Son of Kazan....	85000	Pa.	General	Clear	Good	73
	120000	N. Y.	General	Clear	Good	—
Wildfire.............	550000	Cal.	1st run	Clear	Good	—
WARNER BROS.						
Wife Who Wasn't Wanted	796841	Ohio	1st run	Clear	Fair	68
The Woman Hater......	401247	Ohio	1st run	Clear	Poor	48

With First Run Theatres

NEW YORK CITY

Mark Strand Theatre—
Film Numbers—Don Q, Son of Zorro (United Artists), Mark Strand Topical Review, (Selected).
Musical Program—"La Pintura Blanca" (Dance Duet), "Moonlight Dreams" (Tenor Solo), Organ Solo.

Colony Theatre—
Film Numbers—The Freshman (Pathe), Colony Pictorial News (Selected).
Musical Program—Campus Capers (Special prologue to feature).

Capitol Theatre—
Film Numbers—The Circle (Metro-Goldwyn), Capitol Magazine (Selected), Wild Beasts of Borneo (Educational).
Musical Program—"Second Hungarian Rhapsody" (Overture), Persian Sword Dance (Dance solo), "Scherzo" from "La Source" (Dance solo), "Waltz Song" from "Romeo and Juliet" (Vocal solo), "Kol Nidre" (Vocal duet assisted by Capitol Singers).

Warner's Theatre—
Film Numbers—Below the Line (Warner Bros.), Warner's News Weekly (Selected), Alice's Tin Pony (S. R.).
Musical Program — "Southern Rhapsody" and "Rythmical Ragtime" (Orchestra), Vocal Selections (Female soloist), "Midnight Waltz" (Dance solo), "Light Cavalry" "Popular Medley" "Chopin Waltz" (Special Orchestra).

Rialto Theatre—
Film Numbers—The Pony Express (Paramount).
Musical Program—"Beauty Review" (Ben Bernie and his orchestra), "Readin' for Home" "By the Waters of the Minnetonka" (Orchestra).

Rivoli Theatre—
Film Numbers—The Iron Horse (Fox).
Musical Program — "Mignon" (Overture), Clasical Jazz (Reisenfeld's Specialty).

Cameo Theatre—
Film Numbers—Souls for Sables (S. R.), Pathe News, Aesop's Fables (Pathe), Pleasure Bound (Educational).
Musical Program—Popular Melodies (Orchestral overture), "Listening" (Soprano solo), Organ solo.

LOS ANGELES

Criterion Theatre—
Film Numbers—Never the Twain Shall Meet (Metro-Goldwyn-Mayer), In Deep (Fox), Fox News.
Musical Program—"My Sweetie Turned Me Down" (Overture).

Forum Theatre—
Film Numbers—The Wife Who Wasn't Wanted (Warner Bros.), The Live Agents (Educational), International News, Kinograms.
Musical Program—Orchestra.

Hillstreet Theatre—
Film Numbers—Steele of the Royal Mounted (Warner Bros.), The Pace Makers (F. B. O.), International News, Aesop's Fables (Pathe).
Musical Program—Vaudeville.

Loew's State Theatre—
Film Numbers—The Tower of Lies (Metro-Goldwyn-Mayer), Beware (Educational), Loew's State Pictorial News (Selected).
Musical Program — "Futuristic Ideas" (Fanchon and Marco Ideas).

Metropolitan Theatre—
Film Numbers—The Trouble With Wives (Paramount), Aesop's Fables (Pathe), Pathe News.
Musical Program—"Forge of the Forest" (Overture).

Pantages Theatre—
Film Numbers—Every Man's Wife (Fox), Pathe News.
Musical Program—Vaudeville.

Million Dollar Theatre—
Film Numbers—The Freshman (Pathe), continued.
Musical Program — "On the Campus" (Overture).

Rialto Theatre—
Film Numbers—Sally of the Sawdust (United Artists), continued.
Musical Program — Orchestra (prologue to feature).

BROOKLYN

Mark Strand Theatre—
Film Numbers—The Gold Rush, continued (United Artists), Mark Strand Topical Review (selected).
Musical Program—Short prelude to the feature by the Mark Strand orchestra; atmospheric prologue and organ recessional.

CHICAGO

Chicago Theatre—
Film Numbers—Never the Twain Shall Meet (Metro-Goldwyn-Mayer), Felix Cartoon (S. R.), International News.
Musical Program — "Faust," (Overture), "Khartum," the Pianist," (Specialty), "How's

Your Voice?" (Organ Solo), "A Twilight Romance," (Presentation).

Tivoli Theatre—
Film Numbers — Pretty Ladies (Metro-Goldwyn-Mayer).
Musical Program — Syncopation Week including "Ray Miller and His Brunswick Orchestra with Eddie Chester;" "White & Manning;" "Adler, Weil & Herman;" "Edythe Blossom;" "Joe Whitehead;" "Jimmy Dunn;" and "The Kinky Kid Parade," (Organ Solo), "Charleston Echoes," (Tivoli Theatre Orchestra.)

Uptown Theatre—
Film Numbers — The Coast of Folly (Paramount), Cartoon (Selected), Fun From the Press (Prod. Dist. Corp.), Pathe News.
Musical Program—"Dance of the Hours" (overture), "Treumerei" (Specialty), "Salut a Peuth" (Organ solo), "On The Levee" (Presentation).

Capitol Theatre—
Film Numbers—The Wheel (Fox), Aesop's Fable (Pathe), International News.
Musical Program — "Hungarian Rhapsody" and "Classical Jazz Peer Gynt's Pep," (overture), "The Moonlight Ballet," (Specialty), "Ladies of the Evening," (Presentation), "Moonlight and Roses," (Organ solo), "South Sea Revue," (Specialty).

Stratford Theatre—
Film Numbers—Parisian Nights (F. B. O.), Krazy Kat Cartoon (S. R.), International News.
Musical Program—"Popular Melodies" (Overture), "Laces and Graces" (Specialty), "In The Land of Dreams" (Specialty), "Melvisto Phanto Revue" (Presentation).

Roosevelt Theatre—
Film Numbers — The Freshman (Pathe).

Monroe Theatre—
Film Numbers—The Wheel (Fox).

Orchestra Hall—
Film Numbers—The Miracle Man (Paramount).

Orpheum Theatre—
Film Numbers—The Gold Rush (United Artists).

Randolph Theatre—
Film Numbers—Enemy of Men (Universal), International News (Universal).

SEATTLE

Blue Mouse Theatre—
Film Numbers—His Majesty Bunker Bean (Warner Bros.), Dragon Alley (Pathe), International News.
Musical Program — "Poet and Peasant" (Overture), "Down on the Farm" (Orchestra specialty).

Coliseum Theatre—
Film Numbers—Wild Horse Mesa (Paramount), The Bouncer (Comedy), Kinograms and Pathe News.
Musical Program—Selections from "Kid Boots" (Overture), Knickerbocker Trio in popular songs.

Columbia Theatre—
Film Numbers—The Goose Woman (Universal), Waiting (Educational), International News.
Musical Program—Selections from favorite light operas (Overture), "At Close of Day" (Orchestra).

Heilig Theatre—
Film Numbers — The Mystic (Metro-Goldwyn-Mayer), Topics of the Day (Pathe), Aesop's Fables (Pathe), Pathe Review and News.
Musical Program—Medley of popular musical numbers (Overture).

Liberty Theatre—
Film Numbers—Don Q, Son of Zorro (United Artists), Pathe Review and International News.
Musical Program—"Serenade of Love" (Vocal and instrumental overture), Spanish Dance (prelude).

Pantages Theatre—
Film Numbers—Do It Now (F. B. O.), Aesop's Fables (Pathe), Pathe News.
Musical Program — Vaudeville — Baby Peggy in person.

Strand Theatre—
Film Numbers—Lightnin' (Fox), Felix Doubles for Darwin (S. R.), Screen Snapshots (S. R.), Fox News.
Musical Program—Selections from "The Fortune Teller" (Overture), "Crying for the Moon" (Orchestral and vocal specialty).

Two-column art ad by the Walnut theatre, Cincinnati, for "The Half Way Girl" (First Nat'l).

INDIANAPOLIS

Circle Theatre—
Film Numbers—Romola (Metro-Goldwyn-Mayer), Circle News Reel Weekly (Universal), Cartoon (Educational).
Musical Program—"Classmates" harmony quartette.

Colonial Theatre—
Film Numbers—Parisian Nights (F. B. O.), Life's Greatest Thrills (Universal), Comedy (Universal), Aesop Fable (Pathe).
Musical Program—American Harmonists, Frank Owens, Bob Jones, Floyd Thompson, soloists; Miss Blanche Wilson, pianiste.

Apollo Theatre—
Film Numbers—The Freshman (Pathe), Bray Picturegraph F. B. O.)
Musical Numbers—Emil Keidel orchestra, Earl Gordon, organist and Bill Chandler, soloist.

CLEVELAND

Stillman Theatre—
Film Numbers—Graustark (First National), continued, The Big Game Hunter (Fox), Starting an Argument.
Musical Program — "Rienzi" (overture), "Sometime" (novelty song film with violin solo), with orchestral accompaniment), "Deep in My Heart" (prologue, vocal).

Allen Theatre—
Film Numbers—Sally of the Sawdust (United Artists), Topics of the Day (Pathe), Pathe News. Personal appearance of D. W. Griffith and Carroll Dempster.
Musical Program—"Il Guarnay" (overture), "Allah's Holiday" and "I'll See You Tuesday Night" (encores), "A Hicktown Rehearsal" (Jass Band).

State Theatre—
Film Numbers—He's a Prince (Paramount), Piping Hot (Universal), Love and Lions (Fox), Pathe Review, Fun from the Press (Prod. Dist. Corp.)
Musical Program—Organ overture, Vaudeville.

Park Theatre—
Film Numbers—The Circle (Metro-Goldwyn-Mayer), A Business

Engagement (Fox), Felix Goes Hungry (S. R.), Pathe Review, Topics of the Day (Pathe), Kinograms (Educational).
Musical Program — "Carmen" (overture), "Alone at Last," "Cecelia," "Normandy" (Jazz Unit).

Reade's Hippodrome—
Film Numbers—The Goose Woman (Universal), Pathe Comedy, Pathe News.
Musical Program—"Tales of Hoffman" (overture), Vaudeville.

Keith's East 105th St.—
Film numbers—The Goose Woman (Universal), Somewhere in Somewhere (Pathe), Pathe News, Aesop's Fables (Pathe).
Musical Program—Excerpts from "The Student Prince" (overture), Vaudeville.

The Metropolitan theatre's ad in Baltimore for "Rugged Water" (Paramount).

ROCHESTER

Eastman Theatre—
Film Numbers—The Ten Commandments (Paramount), Eastman Theatre Current Events (Selected), Pencil, Brush and Chisel (Fox).
Musical Program—"Military Polonaise" (Overture), "The Golden Calf" (Prologue).

CINCINNATI

Capitol Theatre—
Film Numbers—Wild Horse Mesa (Paramount), Fares Please (Comedy), Capitol News (Selected).
Musical Program—Orchestra.

Walnut Theatre—
Film Numbers—The Freshman (Pathe), Pathe News, Aesop's Fables (Pathe), Topics of the Day (Pathe).
Musical Program—Orchestra.

Strand Theatre—
Film Numbers—A Son of His Father (Paramount), Don't Tell

Dad (Comedy), Pathe News.

Lyric Theatre—
Film Numbers—The Lost World (First National), Kinograms.
Musical Program—Orchestra.

Gifts Theatre—
Film Numbers—The Breath of Scandal (Prod. Dist. Corp.), Educating Buster (Universal), Kinograms.

Family Theatre—
Film Numbers—I'll Show You The Town (Universal), Battles by Banjoes (S. R.), Fox News.

ST. LOUIS

Grand Central, West End Lyric and Capitol Theatres—
Film Numbers—Sally of the Sawdust (United Artists), Kinogram News and Views (Educational).
Musical Program—At Grand Central Conley-Silverman Band in "Russian Capers", supported by singers and dancers. At West End Lyric, Gene Rodemich and His Gang in "Struttin' the Charleston." At Capitol, orchestral and organ selections.

Missouri Theatre—
Film Numbers—The Coast of Folly (Paramount), Tee for Two (Pathe), Missouri Magazine.
Musical Program—Joseph Littau and Missouri Symphony Orchestra in "Aieda" Milton Slosser at organ with Steve Cady and Harry Kessell (vocalists) in "Medley." On stage.

The Madison theatre's ad in Detroit newspapers on "Proud Flesh" (Metro-Goldwyn).

Louis Panico and his Steamer J. S. Jazz Band, Jack Hanley (comedian), in "Making the World Safe for Hokum."

William Goldman's Kings and Rivoli Theatres—
Film Numbers—The Coming of Amos (Producers Distributing Corporation), William Goldman's Magazine (Selected), Comedy.
Musical Program—Orchestral and vocal selections.

Lowe's State Theatre—
Film Numbers—The Gold Rush (United Artists), News and Views.
Musical Program—"The Spell of the Yukon" (colorful prologue), Orchestral overture and popular numbers. Organ accompaniments. On stage—Lou Girlie-Senia & Company (Eccentric dancers).

Delmonte Theatre—
Film Numbers—Tomorrow's Love

(Paramount), Back Home and Broke (Paramount), Delmonte News and Views.
Musical Program—Orchestral and vocal numbers.

BUFFALO

Shea's Hippodrome—
Film Numbers — The Freshman (Pathe, continued; The Guest of Honor (Fox), Current Events, Pathe and International News.
Musical Program—Medley of College Airs (orchestra).

Loew's State Theatre—
Film Numbers—Sun Up (Metro-Goldwyn-Mayer), The Love Bug (Pathe), Current Events, Pathe News.
Musical Program—Selections from "When You Smile" (orchestra), Five Acts of Vaudeville.

Lafayette Square Theatre—
Film Numbers—The Price She Paid (S. R.), Pathe comedy, Current Events (from Kinograms).
Musical Program—Hits from "The Student Prince" (orchestra), organ solo, Five Acts of Vaudeville.

Shea's North Park Theatre—
Film Numbers—The Coast of Folly (Paramount), Your Own Back Yard (Pathe), Current Events (Pathe and International News).
Musical Program—"Caprice Viennoise" (orchestra).

New Olympic Theatre—
Film Numbers—How Baxter Butted In (Warner Bros.), The Snob Buster (S. R.), Current Events (International News).
Musical Program—Medley of Popular Airs (organ).

DES MOINES

DesMoines Theatre—
Film Numbers—What Fools Men (First National), International News, Curtess (Educational).
Musical Program — " Ach der Lieber Augustine" (Dutch Schmidt and His Little German Band).

Capitol Theatre—
Film Numbers—The Freshman (Pathe), Fox News; Wild Beasts of Borneo (Educational).
Musical Program—Dance numbers (Morton and Mayo).

Strand Theatre—
Film Numbers—Lightnin (Fox), Shoes (Fox), Kinograms.

Opening ad for "The Gold Rush" (United Artists) at the Adams theatre in Detroit recently.

SALT LAKE CITY

American Theatre—
Film Numbers—The Keeper of the Bees (F. B. O.), The Big Game Hunter (Fox), Newspaper Fun (F. B. O.), International News.

Kinema Theatre—
Film Numbers—Every Man's Wife (Fox), Piping Hot (Universal), Pathe Review, International News.

Pantages Theatre—
Film Numbers—Hearts of Oak (Fox).

Paramount-Empress Theatre—
Films Numbers—The Gold Rush (United Artists), Pathe News.

Victory Theatre—
Film Numbers—A Son of His Father (Paramount), Plain Clothes (Pathe), Pathe News.

BALTIMORE

Century Theatre—
Film Numbers—Lightnin' (William Fox), Mary Queen of Tots (Pathe), News Weekly. Musical Program—Dancing Specialty (Albert and Adelaide Gloria), Orchestra, Organ recessional.

Garden Theatre—
Film Numbers—Spook Ranch (Universal), Taxi War (Universal), Felix Rests In Peace (S. R.), International News (Universal), Scenic (Educational).
Musical Program—Five acts of vaudeville, Orchestra, Organ, recessional.

Keith's Hippodrome—
Film Numbers—Fighting the Flames (S. R.), News Weekly (Pathe), Aesop's Fable (Pathe), Too Much Mother In Law (Universal).
Musical Program—Five acts of vaudeville, Orchestra, Organ recessional.

Metropolitan Theatre—
Film Numbers—The Limited Mail (Warners Brothers), Around the World in Twelve Minutes (Compiled by Bernard Delepin, Jr., and shown with special music), The Ugly Duckling (Pathe), Metropolitan Topical Review (Pathe), The Tourist (Educational).
Musical Program—"Maratina" (Overture by Orchestra), organ recessional.

New Theatre—
Film Numbers—I'll Show You the Town (Universal), A

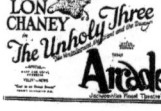

Three-column announcement of 'The Unholy Three' (Metro-Goldwyn) at the Arcade, Jacksonville.

Cloudy Romance (Fox), News Weekly (Pathe).
Musical Program—"Smile All the While," "Whose Woozie Mazie Are You," and "Shadowland" (Vocal selections), "Zampa" (Overture by Orchestra).

Parkway Theatre—
Film Numbers—Wildfire (Vitagraph), With Pen, Brush and Chisel (Fox), Educating Buster (Universal), Parkway Pictorial News (Educational Kinograms).
Musical Program—"Home Sweet Home, the World Over" (Overture by Parkway Concert Ensemble). Organ recessional.

Rivoli Theatre—
Film Numbers — Fine Clothes (First National), Butter Fingers (Pathe), Rivoli News (Pathe).
Musical Program—"Pizzica tio Polka" (Overture by Orchestra), Special Attraction (Janet Hall and Hilda Barr), Special Attraction (Aeolian Trio, vocal and instrumental selections). "Mlle. Modiste" and "When I Think of You" (Organ Selections).

NEWARK

Mosque Theatre—
Film Numbers—Ten Commandments (Paramount), Pictorial (Selected).
Musical Program—Overture, "Processional March" from "Queen of Sheba," "Eli, Eli" (tenor solo), Ella Daganova, (dancer), ballet, and prologue with combined artists.

Striking newspaper ad on "Black Cyclone" (Pathe) at the Keith State theatre, Dayton.

Capitol Theatre—
Film Numbers — Gold Rush (United Artists), International News (Universal).

Branford Theatre—
Film Numbers—Night Life of New York (Paramount), News (Pathe), Comedy (Educational).
Musical Program—Overture (Selected), "The Only Girl," Marion and Martinez Randall (dancers), Philine Falco (soprano), "Gianina Mia" and "Kol Nidre" (vocal).

Fox Terminal—
Film Numbers—As No Man Has Loved (Fox), News (Fox), Comedy (Fox).
Musical Program—Four specially arranged jazz numbers termed "Greater Syncopation."

MINNEAPOLIS

Aster Theatre—
Film Numbers—As No Man Has Loved (Fox), A Scientific Husband (Fox), Fox News.
Musical Program—Organ overture.

Garrick Theatre—
Film Numbers—Pretty Ladies (Metro-Goldwyn-Mayer), In Your Own Back Yard (Fox), Howe's Hodge Podge (Educational), Garrick News Weekly.
Musical Program—The English Rockets with Edward Allen and Ten Tiller Girls.

Lyric Theatre—
Film Numbers—Wild, Wild Susan (Paramount), Comedy, Pathe News.
Musical Program—Dave Rubinoff (Russian violinist), organ numbers

State Theatre—
Film Numbers—The Goose Woman (Universal), Felix Busts into Business (Educational), State Theatre Digest (International).
Musical Program—State Concert Orchestra with William Mervelle Nelson conducting, playing "Pomp and Circumstance," Dayton Style Revue.

Strand Theatre—
Film Numbers—The Half Way Girl (First National), The Big Game Hunter (Pathe), Strand News.
Musical Program—State Concert Orchestra, playing "Save Your Sorrows," White Brothers and Stendal in late songs.

BOSTON

Fenway Theatre—
Film Numbers—A Son of His Father (Paramount), Without Mercy (Prod. Dist. Corp.) Fenway News (Special).
Musical Program—Lloyd G. Del Castillo at the organ; overture and recessional.

Gordon's Washington Street Olympia Theatre—
Film Numbers—Her Sister from Paris (First National), Rainy Night (Pathe), News (Pathe).
Musical Program—Southern Plantation Songs. Five acts vaudeville.

Loew's State Theatre—
Film Numbers—Sally of the Sawdust (United Artists), Aesop's Fables (Pathe), Topics of the

The Bijou, New Haven, used this ad on "Rugged Water" (Paramount) recently.

Day (Pathe), Sportlight (Pathe), Weekly News (Pathe).
Musical Program—The Masked Countess in "Love Call" and other selections. Dock Isenberg's orchestra.

Beacon Theatre—
Film Numbers—A Beggar on Horseback (Paramount), Off the Highway (Producers Dist. Corp.), Comedy (Educational), International News (Universal).
Musical Program—Organ overture.

Modern Theatre—
Film Numbers—Beggar on Horseback (Paramount), Off the Highway (Prod. Dist. Corp.), Comedy (Educational), International News.

ATLANTA

Howard Theatre—
Film Numbers—The Coast of Folly (Paramount), Easy Pickings (Educational), International News Reel.
Musical Program—"Patriotic" (Charles Joseph Possa and New Special Organ), "June Brought The Roses," (stage presentation with ballet and vocal duet), "The Chinest Plate" (prologue, with Chinese dancers, Mandarin and Maid), "Morning, Noon and Night" (orchestra), "Rosary" violin solo by Jan Rubini.

Loew's Grand Theatre—
Film Numbers—The Unholy Three (Metro-Goldwyn-Mayer), Pathe News, Sportlight (Pathe), Aesops Fables (Pathe), "Safe and Sane" (Educational), Topics of the Day (Pathe).
Musical Program—Five acts of vaudeville.

Metropolitan Theatre—
Film Numbers—Shore Leave (First National), Fox News, Giddap (Pathe).

Alamo No. 2 Theatre—
Film Numbers—The Midnight Express (S. R.), O..cer 16, (Universal).
Musical Program—Alamo's Jazz Orchestra.

Tudor Theatre—
Film Numbers—The Crimson Runner (Producers Dist. Corp.), Mary Queen of Tots (Pathe).

KANSAS CITY

Newman Theatre—
Film Numbers—The Unholy Three (Metro-Goldwyn-Mayer), Newman News and Views (Pathe), Kinograms and International News, Newman Current Events (Local Photography).
Musical Program—Excerpts from "L'Pagliucci" (Overture), Agnes Neudorff (Prima Donna), Arthur Corey & Co. (Novelty Orchestral Number on Stage). Recessional (Organ Solos).

Liberty Theatre—
Film Numbers—California Straight Ahead (Universal), Aesop's Fables (Pathe), International News Pictorial, The Fighting Ranger (Universal).
Musical Program—Selections by Special Augmented Orchestra (Overture), Recessional (Organ Solos).

Royal Theatre—
Film Numbers—The Freshman (Pathe), Royal Screen Magazine (Pathe), Kinograms and International News, Royal Current Events (Local Photography).
Musical Program—Royal Syncopators On Stage (Overture), Recessional (Organ Solos).

Pantages Theatre—
Film Numbers—The Police Patrol (S. R.), Fox News and Fox Short Subjects.
Musical Program — Atmospheric Selections (Overture), Recessional (Organ Solos).

Main Street Theatre—
Film Numbers—The Scarlet West (First National), Pathe News and Educational Short Subjects.
Musical Program—Popular Selections (Overture), Recessional (Organ Solos).

OMAHA

Rialto Theatre—
Film Numbers—A Son of His Father (Paramount), Remember When (Pathe), Kinograms.
Musical Program — Themes for feature picture, "The Breath of an Irish Smile," and "Misteriono alla Valse," "Loyal Comrades" (Exit March). On the stage: Fall Style Revue and Billy Sharpe's revue with Mlle. Marionne and M. J. Cook.

Strand Theatre—
Film Numbers—The Gold Rush (United Artists), continued, Fox News.

Hand-drawn newspaper ad on "In the Name of Love" (Paramount) at the Strand theatre, Des Moines.

Musical Program—"The Alaskan" (Overture).

World Theatre—
Film Numbers—Siege (Universal), Wild Papa (Pathe), Pathe News.
Musical Program — "Someone," (illustrated organ number), Vaudeville.

Sun Theatre—
Film Numbers — California Straight Ahead (Universal), Dog Days (Pathe), Pathe Review.

Empress Theatre—
Film Numbers—Beauty and the Bad Man (Prod. Dist. Corp.), Play Ball No. 9 (Pathe).
Musical Program—"Seaside Sirens" (Musical Comedy).

Moon Theatre—
Film Numbers — The Crimson Runner (Prod. Dist. Corp.), Sunken Silver No. 8 (Pathe), Sherlock Sleuth (Pathe).
Musical Program—Vaudeville.

HOUSTON

Queen Theatre—
Film Numbers—The Freshman (Pathe), Comedy (Pathe), News (Pathe).
Musical Program—College Capers (overture), Queen Orchestra, Organ Numbers.

Capitol Theatre—
Film Numbers—The Trouble with Wives (Paramount), Comedy (Pathe), News (International-Universal).
Musical Program—Capitol Orchestra playing popular selections. Organ numbers.

Rialto Theatre—
Film Numbers—Hell's Highroad (Producers Dist. Corp.), Educational, Comedy, News (Fox).
Musical Program—Organ numbers and piano.

Majestic Theatre—
Film Numbers — The Wheel (Fox), Aesop's Fables (Pathe).
Musical Program—Jazz Overture and selections (Orchestra), Organ numbers, Vaudeville.

Liberty Theatre—
Film Numbers—His Majesty Bunker Bean (Warner Bros.), Comedy (Fox), Review (Pathe).

Isis Theatre—
Film Numbers—Romola (Metro-Goldwyn-Mayer), Educational Comedy, Kinograms (Educational).
Musical Program — "The Love Song" (Overture), Organ numbers.

SAN FRANCISCO

San Francisco Theatre—
Film Numbers—The Golden Princess (Paramount), Big Game Hunter (Fox), Pathe Review, International News.
Musical Program—"Il Trovatore" (Overture), "Salut D'Amour" (Violin solo), "Oh Katherina" (Novelty).

Loew's Warfield Theatre—
Film Numbers—The Winds of Chance (First National), Life's Greatest Thrills (Universal).
Musical Program—Charleston versus Waltz (Fanchon and Marco idea with singing and dancing).

Granada Theatre—
Film Numbers—In The Name of Love (Paramount), Pleasure Bound (Educational), Pathe News.
Musical Program—Second edition "Evolution of the Charleston"

(Special act with singing and dancing).

Imperial Theatre—
Film Numbers—The Pony Express (Paramount), continued.

Cameo Theatre—
Film Numbers — Black Cyclone (Pathe), Grief in Bagdad (Universal), International News.
Musical Program—"Indian Maid" (Baritone solo).

Union Square Theatre—
Film Numbers—Black Lightning (S. R.), Blue Blood (Fox), Fox News.
Musical Program—Five acts of vaudeville.

St. Francis Theatre—
Film Numbers—The Fool (Fox).
Musical Program—Miracle scene from feature enacted on stage.

DETROIT

Broadway-Strand Theatre—
Film Numbers—Siege (Universal), Newsreel (International), organ accompaniment.

Adams Theatre—
Film Numbers — Gold Rush (United Artists), Newsreel (Kinograms), orchestra accompaniment and organ recessional.

Capitol Theatre—
Film Numbers—The Half Way Girl (First National), Newsreel (Pathe and Detroit News), Keystone Serenaders, (orchestra in stage presentation), Dexter Sisters (singers and banjoists in stage presentation), orchestra accompaniment and organ recessional.

Madison Theatre—
Film Numbers—Wild, Wild Susan (Paramount), Newsreel (Pathe and Detroit News pictorial), Captain Wanderwell's film journey around the world; orchestra accompaniment and organ recessional.

Fox-Washington Theatre—
Film Numbers—Kentucky Pride (Fox), Newsreel (Fox), Felix the Cat (S. R.), Stereoscopiks (Pathe).
Musical Program—Organ accompaniment.

MILWAUKEE

Alhambra Theatre—
Film Numbers—The Iron Horse (Fox), International News.
Musical Program—"Will He Tell Or Won't He?" (Overture), "The Iron Horse" (Atmospheric Prologue).

Garden Theatre—
Film Numbers—The Lost Battalion (S. R.), Topics of the Day, Fox News, Comedy.
Musical Program—Organ Specialty.

Merrill Theatre—
Film Numbers—The Freshman (Pathe), Wild Beasts of Borneo (Educational), Kinograms.
Musical Program—Orchestra Overture.

Strand Theatre—
Film Numbers—The Shock Punch (Paramount), Hodge Podge (Educational), Hot Stleks (Comedy), Cross Word Puzzle (Educational), Kinograms.
Musical Program—"Charlestown" (Overture).

Wisconsin Theatre—
Film Numbers—Fine Clothes (First National), International News, Felix Comedy.
Musical Program—"Ballet Egyptian" (Overture), "Moments Musical" (The Dore Sisters), "Oh, How I Miss You Tonight" (Organ Overture), "The American Siamese Twins" (Violet and Daisy Hilton).

ST. PAUL

Astor Theatre—
Film Numbers—Wild Wild Susan (Paramount), Hodge Podge (Educational), Felix Gets the Can (Educational), Don Coo Coo (F. B. O.).
Musical Program—Organ Novelty, Lew Epstein and His Gang in "Rubetown."

Capitol Theatre—
Films Numbers — Shore Leave (First National), Fair Warning (Educational), Capitol Digest (Selected).
Musical Program—Capitol Symphony orchestra playing "Il Guarany;" Lionel Hilton (cellist), Zimmerman and Grandville in "A Yodling Romance," organ recessional.

Garrick Theatre—
Film Numbers—The Iron Horse (Fox), Oat Comedy (Educational), News Reel.
Musical Program—Garrick Serenaders in "A Merry Melange of Jazz;" Prolog, "The Three Musketeers."

Princess Theatre—
Film Numbers—The Overland Limited (S. R.), On the Go (Fox), Kinograms.
Musical Program—Mrs. Robert E. Gehan, organ specialty.

Strand Theatre—
Film Numbers—As No Man Has Loved (Fox), He Who Gets Socked (F. B. O.) Kinograms.
Musical Program—Organ overture.

Tower Theatre—
Film Numbers—Never the Twain Shall Meet (Metro-Goldwyn-Mayer), Lucky Stars (Pathe), Pathe News.
Musical Program—"Maurice" and his Tower Symphony, Organ overture.

Short Subjects and Serials

Sennett Studios Still Busy Making Pathe Comedies

Though the Sennett comedy units worked without let-down during the summer months that company is about to enter upon a very busy production schedule for the fall season.

Among the directors now starting new comedies for the Pathe program are Eddie Cline, who is filming a yachting comedy starring Alice Day; Lloyd Bacon, who is directing Ralph Graves in a two-reeler in which Thelma Parr and Marvin Lobach have the principal supporting roles; Gil Pratt is in charge of a unit making a comedy featuring Billy Bevan, Andy Clyde and Natalie Kingston; and Harry Langdon has started a comedy in which he will be seen as a henpecked husband. Harry Edwards is directing Langdon.

Red Seal and Fleischer Sign New Contract

Red Seal Pictures and Max Fleischer, cartoonist, have signed a new three year contract whereby Red Seal will distribute the entire film output of the Fleischer Studios, including the "Out-of-the-Inkwell" cartoons, "Ko-Ko Song Car-Tunes," "Marvels of Motion" and "Film Facts" series.

Scenes from "All Aboard," a two-reel comedy based on "The Married Life of Helen & Warren" stories by Mabel Herbert Urner. Produced by Fox with Hallam Cooley and Kathryn Perry in the name roles.

"Your Own Back Yard" is the title of the latest "Our Gang" comedy, produced by Hal Roach for Pathe. The above scenes are taken from the picture.

Izard Returns From Europe
Managing Editor of Kinograms Back After Extensive Tour in Interest of News Reel

FORREST IZARD, managing editor of Kinograms, the news reel released by Educational has returned from an extended trip abroad. Mr. Izard completed arrangements for the extension of Kinograms' foreign service and staff of camera men abroad. Among the arrangements which he completed is a contract with one of the leading "Gazette" producers of the British Isles whereby their product and staff of camera men, numbering twenty operators, are available for Kinograms. This includes service from England, Ireland, Scotland, Wales and nearby islands.

For Continental Europe Mr. Izard first established a main office or clearing house in Paris which serves as a main shipping point for all news reel negative from Europe (except England), Turkey, Asia Minor, Africa, Arabia and India. Points in the Orient such as China and Japan will continue to ship across the Pacific. The Paris office consists of a manager, Mr. Louis Dansee, and a staff of cameramen who cover Belgium, Austria and Switzerland as well as France.

Another most important affiliation was made in Germany with one of that country's leading news reel producers whereby Kinograms is assured of full and prompt service of all news events, and special news features from Germany, Holland and Russia. Another contact was made in Stockholm giving Kinograms full service in Sweden, Norway, Finland and Denmark.

Mr. Izard then journeyed to Rome, where a staff was organized to cover fully Italy and Greece. Special staff representatives were also secured in Spain, Portugal and Malta.

Other foreign points are being built up as rapidly as possible. Contacts already in existence include Japan, China, South and Central America, Mexico and Australia. A complete Canadian staff has always been a complement of the Kinograms' domestic staff.

Joe Rock Producing Four F. B. O. Comedies

Joe Rock, comedy producer who is making Blue Ribbon and Standard Comedies for F. B. O. release, now has four productions in work. "A Ton of Fun," the third Standard comedy, and "Salute," second Blue Ribbon comedy with Alice Ardell in the featured role, are in the cutting room; while at Universal City Rock's trio of heavyweight comedians, "Tiny" Alexander, "Kewpie" Ross and "Fatty" Karr, are working on another comedy under the direction of Jimmy Davis.

Rock will return to the screen in the leading comedy role opposite Alice Ardell in her next Blue Ribbon picture. Standard is also ready to begin camera work on the second of the "Unnatural History" comedies, which are being produced at the Bray Studios.

Resume of Current News Weeklies

KINOGRAMS NO. 5110: Oyster Bay, N. Y.—Scandinavian yachts in close races with United States craft: Washington, D. C.—Special air board is named by President to probe aircraft situations; Notre Dame, Ind.—Knute Rockne prepares another eleven to seek championship laurels; New York—Gertrude Ederle returns declaring she will make another attempt to swim channel; George Arliss, actor, and Irish officials also arrive on Mauretania: Sheridan, Wyo.—Oliver H. Wallop, Wyoming rancher, who is now the Earl of Portsmouth, poses exclusively for Kinograms on his Western ranch; Dublin—Ireland turns out to greet Tom Meighan, who is greeted by President Cosgrave and John McCormack; San Francisco—Western girl stages boxing bout between cats; New York—Uncle Sam tests gas masks for horses in a Kinograms exclusive.

KINOGRAMS NO. 5120: Forest Hills, L. I.—Tilden is again crowned tennis king when he beats "little Bill" Johnston in grueling match of national finals; Manchester, N. H.—"Super-Brownies" perform thrilling high diving feats; Urbana, Ill.—Red Grange and his brother get in action as Illinois begins 1925 football campaign with hard practice; Washington, D. C.—Army heads differ on aviation inquiry opens in nation's capital; Braemar, Scotland—Clans gather for annual games; Los Angeles—Circus folk cheer crippled youngsters; Madison, Wis.—Young Bob La Follette is victor in primaries for Republican nomination to succeed his father in United States Senate; Topsfield, Mass.—Horses make daring dives into shallow pool; Philadelphia—Knights Templar in annual field day; Philadelphia only); Chicago—Chicago University and Northwestern pigskin chasers begin fall practice (Chicago only); Ellensburg, Wash.—Annual rodeo thrills ranchers (Seattle only); Madison, Wis.—University of Wisconsin football candidates begin strenuous training (Milwaukee only).

FOX NEWS VOL. 6. NO. 102: Rome, Italy—Boy Scouts from all parts of world, call at Vatican: Interesting Figures in the News of the Day—James J. Walker wins Democratic nomination for Mayor of New York: Pearl Islands—A paradise for anglers in this island group near Panama; Cambridge, Mass.—Harvard football squad opens fall training; Tuscaloosa, Ala.—University of Alabama football team start training for season; Brooklyn, N. Y.—Natholia Crane, poetess at 12, is elected member of the British Society of Authors; Venice, Italy—Splendor of the Middle Ages is revived in gondola regatta; El Paso, Tex.—The mountain lioness presents two cubs to the city's zoo; New South Wales—Twin rocks are haven of millions of sea-birds; President Calls Parley to Decide Air Policy.

INTERNATIONAL NEWS NO. 78: Venice, Italy—Gay gondoliers revel in biggest regatta; Paris, France—Sculptured beauties put Paris models out of job; Rochester, N. Y.—High-jumping horses try gamely for new records; Rome, Italy—Boy Scouts from many lands on visit to Pope came in shadow of St. Peter's; Wilmington, Cal.—Inventor displays new one-man submarine in which he hopes to sail around world; Eastport, Me. (Boston only)—After long career on the ocean seas barge Canada is consigned to flames; Jerusalem, Palestine—Sacred wailing wall thronged on eve of Holy Days; Ellensburg, Wash.—Stampeding steeds defy cowboys in wild race; An International Newsreel Special—Gridiron warriors of many colleges begin training.

INTERNATIONAL NEWS NO. 79: Rotorua, New Zealand—Maori was "jazz" greets men of U. S. battle fleet; Benares, India—Thousands of India Natives take their yearly bath; Los Angeles, Cal.—Movie stunt daredevil puts a new peril in marriage; Vancouver, B. C.—International peace memorial to late President Harding unveiled in Canada; N. Y. City—The Bolsters, Mr. and Mrs. and eight little Bolsters, comprise one of Manhattan's prize families; Chicago, Ill.—Sets new streaking record with hit of 621 feet iced off from skyscraper roof; Forest Hills, N. Y.—Tilden retains national tennis championship title; Washington, D. C.—Air board inquiry opens; Washington, D. C. (Washington only)—Mrs. Jessie Dell takes oath as member of Civil Service Commission; Frisco, Cal. (Frisco only)—Trolley car runs wild, crashes into house; Jacksonville, Fla.—Disastrous explosion wrecks big tanker; Indianapolis, Ind. (Indianapolis only)—Scenes of havoc as explosion wrecks garage; Madrid, Spain—Queer "Hicopter" plane tried out; Topsfield, Mass.—Horses in daredevil dives thrill crowds at fair.

PATHE NEWS NO. 77: Ulster, Ireland—Motorcycle daredevils furnish thrills in Ulster Grand Prix; Washington, D. C.—Special board to probe aviation services; Rab Mendoll, Morocco—French continue drive against Abd-el-Krim; Pacific Beach, Cal.—Here's where they place Atlantic City's beauty pageant in the shade—Dusky mermaids open most exclusive beach, exclusively dusky; Venice, Italy—City of gondolas holds regatta; Milford, Pa.—Discuss coal strike problems; Chicago, Ill.—World's bag-puncher champion is jazz artist; N. Y. City—U. S. takes drastic measures to end Tong warfare; Detroit, Mich.—Octogenarian constructs model yacht; Columbus, Ga.—Kiddies stage auto race of their own; Buenos Aires, Argentina—Prince of Wales reviews Argentine troops; Newark, N. J.—Fighting fire furnishes thrills; Ponca City, Okla. (Okla. City only)—Daring cowboys perform at rodeo; Boston, Mass. (Boston only)—City liquor squad destroys seized stills; Olathe, Kansas (K. C. only)—Highway completed at impressive ceremony; Wheeling, W. Va. (Pittsburgh only)—Pedigreed stock exhibited at annual State Fair; El Dorado, Ark. (Memphis only)—State legionnaires attend annual convention; Bayfield, Wis. (Minneapolis only)—Chippewa Indians present historic pageant; New York City (Newark & N. Y. only)—Primaries decide Mayoralty candidates.

PATHE NEWS NO. 78: Mecklenburg, Germany—Hindenburg inspects National Defense Guard; Washington, D. C.—Air Board inquiry opens; Forest Hills, N. Y.—Tilden again wins national tennis championship; Manchester, N. H.—Youths show skill in spectacular high dives; Braemar, Scotland—Britain's king attends rally of highland clans; Westbury, N. Y.—Spirited contest marks first play for polo open championship; Lihue, Kauai Island, T. H.—Royal Hawaiian fliers speed; Boston, Mass. (Boston only)—Dedicate Boston's new Fire Alarm building; Washington, D. C. (Washington only)—President Coolidge appoints Miss Jessie Dell to Civil Service Commission.

Completing New Stage at Educational Studio

The new stage being erected at the Educational studio in Los Angeles is nearing completion and will soon be ready for use by the comedy units under the charge of Jack White. The stage measures eighty by one hundred and twenty feet and is said to mark a new departure in studio construction.

Brook Loaned by Warners to De Mille

Clive Brook has been loaned by Warner Brothers to Cecil B. De Mille for the role of Valdar in "Three Faces East," an adaptation of the successful stage play. Rupert Julian is directing the picture from the scenario by C. Gardner Sullivan. Jetta Goudal and Robert Ames have important roles.

International Cast in New Clyde Cook Comedy

The comedians who support Clyde Cook in "Moonlight and Noses," his first Hal Roach two-reeler for Pathe, hail from so many different parts of the globe that the picture is said to have an "international cast."

Cook, himself, is from Australia, while Stan Laurel, who directed the picture, came from England with the original Charley Chaplin vaudeville company. Tyler Brook, juvenile hero in the film, was born of French parents. Fay Wray, the leading lady, was born in Canada, Jimmy Finlayson, seen in a character role, was born in Scotland, and Noah Young, the heavy, is a product of the West of these United States.

Taurog Completes New Lige Conley Two-Reeler

Norman Taurog, directing Lige Conley in Mermaid Comedies, has finished his third two reeler of the year. The latest work is a fast action comedy revolving around a game of auto polo. Eight auto polo cars are used in the contest, which was staged last week at Griffith Park, Los Angeles.

Hugh Fay Signed to Direct Educational Comedies

Hugh Fay has signed a contract to direct a series of Educational Cameo Comedies in which Cliff Bowes and Helen Marlowe are the leading players. Fay, a well known comedy specialist, has started work at the Educational studios in Hollywood under his new agreement.

Helen Foster Leading Lady for Lupino Lane

Helen Foster has been selected to play the role of leading lady opposite Lupino Lane in a comedy he is making for release by Educational Film Exchanges. Miss Foster scored an individual hit in "The Tourist," in which she appeared at lead opposite Johnny Arthur.

Walter Hiers Injures Hand Acting Comedy Scene

Walter Hiers suffered a serious injury to his hand while on location making one of his new Educational-Walter Hiers Comedies. He is confined to his home, stopping work on the picture temporarily. A large iron pipe nearly severed one of Hiers' fingers, which has been saved by skilful surgery.

"All At Sea" Title of New Fox Imperial Comedy

Work has been completed on a new Fox Imperial Comedy in which Sid Smith and Judy King have the leading roles. The picture will be released under the title "All At Sea."

Charles LaMont is Directing Lane Comedy

Charles La Mont has started camera work on the second Educational comedy starring Lupino Lane, stage comedian. The supporting cast is headed by Helen Forster.

New Universal Serial to Be Started Soon

Camera work on "The Radio Detective," a mystery story by Arthur B. Reeve to be made in serial form by Universal, will soon be started at Universal City. Jack Daugherty will be featured in the picture and Margaret Quimby will have the leading role opposite the star. Principal supporting roles are to be played by Jack Mower, John T. Prince, Vern James and Howard Enstedt. William Crinley will direct the production.

"Failure" by O. Henry is Completed by Fox

The Fox comedy unit making "Failure," an adaptation of the story of that title by O. Henry, has completed camera work on the picture, a two-reel offering. The leading roles are played by Harvey Clark and Kathryn McGuire. Daniel Keefe directed the production.

Helen Forster is Lead for Lupino Lane

Helen Forster will make her next appearance in an Educational comedy starring Lupino Lane. Miss Forster scored a personal triumph recently in the leading feminine role in "The Tourist," which starred Johnny Arthur.

Billy Dooley in scenes from "The Misfit Sailor." his first comedy, produced by Christie and released on the Educational Program.

A trio of scenes from "Dry Up," a two-reel Century Comedy released by Universal.

Clyde Cook's Pathe Debut Soon

Schedule for Week of October 4 Brings First of New Hal Roach Comedy Series

CLYDE COOK, English comedian who has starred in vaudeville and pictures in this country, will make his debut as a Pathe star on that company's program of releases for the week of October 4th, when the first of a series of two-reel comedies produced by Hal Roach, will be offered. Other important short subjects listed on the program for that week are the second chapter of "Wild West," current Pathe serial, a Grantland Rice "Sportlight" reel, "Aesop's Film Fables," Pathe Review No. 40, and the regular issues of Pathe News.

"Moonlight and Noses" is the title of the vehicle which presents Clyde Cook. It presents the comedian in the role of a burglar who is captured and who is offered freedom if he will obtain a corpse for a professor who wants to prove one of his pet scientific theories. The picture was directed by Stan Laurel, former star comedian who is now devoting his talents to the filming of comedies for Hal Roach. Those who appear in support of Cook are Noah Young, Fay Wray, Jimmie Finlayson and Tyler Brooke.

"On the Show" is the title of the second chapter of "Wild West" produced on the 101 Ranch in Oklahoma with the Miller Brothers' Wild West Show supporting the stars, Jack Mulhall and Helen Ferguson. This episode presents the various child characters introduced in the opening chapter as grown-ups, and the circus lot and big top provide most of the background for the two-reels.

"Outings For All" is the Grantland Rice "Sportlight" release. Pathe Review No. 40 features a prominent Broadway star, Ann Pennington, in one of the three subjects comprising the reel. Miss Pennington appears in a dancing novelty made by Alvin V. Knechtel's "Process camera" which presents the former Follies star "Charlestoning" in multiple action. Other subjects in this issue of the Pathe Review are: "A Gem of the Jura," Pathecolor scenes of Salina-les-Bains, and "The Rock of Ages," revealing scenes of mining in the world's greatest quarries at Barre, Vermont.

"The Lion and the Monkey" is the new release of the "Aesop's Film Fables" series.

Del Andrews Will Direct "Andy Gump" Series

Samuel Van Ronkel, producer of "Andy Gump" comedies for Universal release, has signed Del Andrews to direct the forthcoming series. The first of the new productions now being made is titled "Min Walks in Her Sleep."

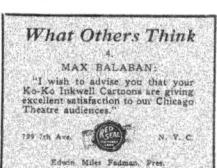

Opinions on Current Short Subjects

"The Movies"
(Educational-Hamilton—Two Reels)
(Reviewed by Chester J. Smith)

LLOYD HAMILTON has a comedy here that is very good in spots, but is rather spotty. There are some good gags in it that are bound to bring laughs, but for the most part it is the usual Hamilton material. It is a bit unusual for this comedian to be seen in a straight makeup, as he is in parts of the picture. Some double exposure shots show him in his street attire and as a double for himself in the movies.

The story is somewhat above the average for this type comedy and permits Hamilton to run full scope of his comedy talents. He leaves home, a small towner, admonished by his mother to keep his neck clean and to keep away from the movies. And then he wanders into Hollywood and is drafted into the service as a picture actor when Hamilton of the comedies injures his foot and it is necessary to get some one to finish the picture for him.

There is some good comedy when he gets on to the set for the first time and meets up with the leading lady in a love scene that is interrupted by the arrival of his big brother in the cast. Big brother proves to be a giant with whom Hamilton has had a run-in early in the picture and who is seeking revenge. There is a wild and humorous chase when big brother discovers his late adversary.

The Cast
A Country Boy	Lloyd Hamilton
An Actress	Marcella Daly
The Villain	Arthur Thalasso
The Director	Frank Jonnasson
A Traffic Officer	Glen Cavender

A Hamilton comedy written and directed by William Goodrich.

The Story.—Hamilton a country boy leaves home for the big city and immediately gets into difficulties with a Giant, whom he outwits and turns over to a policeman. Lloyd then wanders into a motion picture studio just at a time when the star of the picture is disabled. He is impressed into the service to double for the star and in the midst of a love scene is interrupted by the giant, who is a member of the cast. Lloyd makes his getaway after an exciting chase and is welcomed back to the family home.

Summary.—This is a good two-reel comedy with a story well above the average and one that shows Hamilton off to the best advantage. It should go well in any house where the short subject is appreciated.

"Uncle Tom's Gal"
(Universal-Century—Two Reels)
(Reviewed by L. C. Moen)

EDNA MARIAN is the star of this breezy little release, which seems to us about the best we have seen her in. "Uncle Tom's Cabin" in burlesque form makes its appearance once more, this time as a movie being made by an itinerant film company, with Edna as the simple country miss who takes the place of the leading lady when that person fails to put in an appearance.

Many of the gags are rather fresh and lively, and the whole should be good for a generous quota of laughs. The part involves just the sort of foolery that Miss Marian does to best advantage, and the mechanical props provide her with several ludicrous moments.

There is more continuity than usually obtained in two-reel releases of this sort, and it builds up to a suitable climax.

The Story.—Dolly, a farmer maiden longs to become a screen star. A visiting film company wants to shoot "Uncle Tom's Cabin" on the farm and she gives permission. When the leading lady fails to arrive, Dolly is cast and Little Eva, Topsy and Eliza. Various laughable sequences occur in the filming of the venerable classic along somewhat unique lines. At the end of the day, Dolly draws all of the undeveloped film from the camera magazines, hoping to see her "pitcher," thus ruining the most original version of the "Tom" show ever screened.

Summary.—Fairly original and thoroughly amusing slapstick comedy, with plenty of action and an abundance of laughable gags.

"Love and Kisses"
(Pathe—Two Reels)
(Reviewed by Thomas C. Kennedy)

ALICE DAY seems to be specializing in "Peg O' My Heart" roles in the two-reel comedies presented by Mack Sennett. For she is again the poor girl who is really rich and who is first received very cooly into the home of some social climbers and then made a great fuss over when they learn that her father has struck oil in Oklahoma.

The plot is about the efforts of the family to land a rich youth for their daughter and Alice for their somewhat worthless son. In places the play is too plotty, but once Eddie Cline, the director, dispensed with that and cleared the way for some of his gags, "Love and Kisses" started to come to life, and as it now stands, the work rates as an amusing and diverting film, capable of injecting merriment into any program.

Miss Day seems more facile in action comedy than she is in the situation play. She performs with telling effect when there is a gag to put across, but when characterization is called for, she appears to be quite unimpressed with its importance and appears impatient to reach the "laugh" which is the proper goal and destination of these pictures she is making for Pathe. In this offering she has the able support of Raymond McKee, Sunshine Hart, Jack Cooper, Barbara Tennant and Vernon Dent.

There are several diverting incidents toward the end, which offers a laughable satire of the conventional "movie" wedding in which the heroine is being married to the villain while the hero contrives to arrive on time to prevent the disastrous pronouncement of the officiating clergyman or justice. The action picks up here and the incident is broadly amusing.

The Cast
Matchmaker	Sunshine Hart
Her Daughter	Barbara Tennant
Her Son	Jack Cooper
The Girl	Alice Day
The Boy	Raymond McKee
Butler	Vernon Dent

The Story.—The hero is being sought as a husband for a girl who has been seeking husbands for years. He nearly "falls" when he meets Alice, who has just come from the west and who at first is taken as the new servant. Alice is differently regarded when it is learned that her father has made millions in oil in Oklahoma and the matchmaking mother tries to force a marriage between Alice and her son. It nearly succeeds, but the hero frames a situation and stops the wedding ceremony, which has been subject to several delays, as when the justice drops his glasses and cannot read the contract, a situation which becomes worse when the groom's mother proffers her lorgnette which so distorts the print and dizzies the justice that he falls backward through the window and into the courtyard where the action comes to a fast finish.

Summary.—A "situation comedy" which moves slowly at times but picks up well toward the climax and at that point succeeds in producing several hilarious bits. It should score as a satisfactory comedy offering in the majority of houses.

"Your Own Back Yard"
(Pathe—Two Reels)
(Reviewed by Thomas C. Kennedy)

THIS new "Our Gang" comedy from the Hal Roach studios amounts to a starring vehicle for Farina—and of all the screen comedians none can carry more blithely the burdens of stellar honors in a film. The climax of the play gives the picture a rating as first-rate comedy, one that will register strongly with any audience.

Assisting Farina are Mickey Daniels, Jackie Condon, Joe Cobb, Mary Cornman, Johnny Gray, and H. M. Walker, whose titles are one of the best things about "Your Own Back Yard."

Bob McGowan, the director of the "Our Gang" pictures, has contrived a series of gags of certain appeal to supply his stars with acting material. There are a couple of "Joe Millers" brought in to help things along. There is the one about the bet of a cent that a boy can eat an ice cream cone right before its owner without the latter seeing him, with the bet lost and the forfeit cheerfully paid.

But "Your Own Back Yard" is better than these items—much better when the time arrives for Farina to come into sudden wealth—he falls asleep in a "blind man's chair" with the tin cup in his hand. With the proceeds he buys a dandy outfit of clothes and an express wagon full of toys and struts on by the pals who threw him down because his pet goat ate a radio aerial of a bicycle. Some good "chase action" is introduced when the cops are called out to shoot three dogs declared mad by a woman who sees them after the Gang have tried out some tooth paste which has been donated by a sample dispenser. "Your Own Back Yard" is a corking good comedy.

The Cast
Farina, Mickey Daniels, Mary Kornman, Jackie Condon, Joe Cobb, Johnny Gray.

A Hal Roach comedy directed by Robert McGowan.

Story.—Farina is "in bed" with the gang because his goat ate a radio set and a bicycle. Also he is ordered to remain in his own back yard by his mother. But he slips out when he finds a nickel and buys an ice cream cone. Further adventures lead him to sit in a chair belonging to a blind beggar. He holds the tin cup and goes to sleep and upon awakening finds the cup filled with coins. Farina thereupon buys some new clothes and a lot of toys. He starts for his own back yard in grandeur, scorning the pleas of the Gang for a chance to play with him now that he is rich.

Summary.—A corking good "Our Gang" comedy with Farina in the star role. It is a finely presented and cleverly acted piece treating with the triumph of a little "down and outer" who becomes wealthy and sort after by those who scorned him when he was "poor."

"My Bonnie"
(Red Seal—One Reel)

THIS "KO-KO Song Car-tune" produced by Max Fleischer presents "My Bonnie Lies Over the Ocean" in a novel and interesting manner. The device to indicate the beat of the tune and the several bits of amusing cartoon effects should make it a popular reel and successful as an inducement to audience singing. They will all join in the song when this is flashed on the screen if there is any song in them. The words of the song are shown and the time is indicated by having a little ball or disk bounce from one word to another in beat. It is a very ingenious device for directing choral singing and the reel should be hailed as an entertaining novelty in any theatre.—T. C. KENNEDY.

"A Misfit Sailor"
(Educational-Christie—Two Reels)
(Reviewed by Chester J. Smith)

HERE is a comedy with a lot of humorous situations and a story that should provoke many a laugh in the progress of the two reels. Billy Dooley and Vera Steadman are the featured players and Dooley proves himself a comedian of no mean ability. He is really funny without overdoing it. Miss Steadman also gets everything possible out of a part that does not call for too much. Eddie Baker of the supporting cast is particularly good in the role of the hard boiled sailor, who steals the parrot from the cage given Dooley to deliver to the Senator's beautiful daughter and substitutes a brick in the cage in place of the parrot.

This incident provides the comedy for the picture and it waxes fast and furious when Dooley arrives at the house, following the arrival of Baker, in the midst of the party. Dooley presents the wrapped up brick in the cage after Baker has presented the real parrot. Baker meantime explains an accompanying note by apprising those present that Dooley has irrational fits and can only be subdued with cold water. As may be imagined, water buckets and a hose figure prominently with the guests at the house all but having to tread water to make their escape.

The Cast

A Gob...Billy Dooley
Gunner George...................................Eddie Baker
Patricia...Vera Steadman

A Christie Comedy by Frank Roland Conklin; directed by William Watson; photography by Paul Garnett and Frank Sullivan.

The Story.—Dooley is entrusted with the delivery of parrot to the Senator's daughter. Baker sees a photo of the girl and decides to deliver the parrot himself. He steals the bird from the cage and substitutes a brick. Arriving at the house he presents it to the girl at the height of a party. Dooley arrives later and presents the cage containing only the brick. Baker tells the hostess of Dooley's occasional fits of insanity and that the only cure for them is to hurl cold water on him. This is done on frequent occasions, but Dooley emerges triumphant and with the complete admiration of the Senator's daughter.

Summary.—A fast moving comedy full of humorous situations and well acted and well directed with a story well above the average. It should go well in almost any type house.

"Moonlight and Noses"
(Pathe—Two Reels)
(Reviewed by Thomas C. Kennedy)

CLYDE COOK'S debut as a Hal Roach star is auspicious and there is good fun in the occasion for the screen patrons. There are laughs, and plenty of them, in "Moonlight and Noses." Equally notable is the fact that the laughs are of a sort which promises well for the future works of this comedian under his present regime, which places Stan Laurel in the position of his director.

Laurel and Cook are of the same school of acting, and from this picture we assume that the actor understands the director and conversely the director has a deep understanding and appreciation of the kind of work the actor can do best.

The director must receive a large share of the applause due the sponsors of this comedy, which we think capable of scoring as a thoroughly entertaining number for any theatre. Laurel has done something notable in devising a new type of "spook" comedy. These are new "ghosts" for the comedy and the plot is built of amusing stuff, even though it does employ a rather grisely premise in the incident dealing with the attempted robbing of a grave in order to receive a reward from a doctor bent upon proving a theory concerning water on the brain. A title assures us that the doctor "could not tell water on the brain from rain on the roof."

The comedian's acrobatics and comic expressions find a wide scope for their activities in the series of gags invented for "Moonlight and Noses." The scene where he believes he is carrying a corpse in a sack on his back when in reality it is a very live suitor for the hand of the doctor's daughter, and also his experiences on the dissecting table, where he dons a suit of armor to protect him from the keen edge of the operator's instruments, are hilarious pieces and they are accompanied by a number of equally amusing items.

Cook is ably supported by Noah Young, Fay Wray, Jimmie Finlayson and Tyler Brooke. "Moonlight and Noses" offers the exhibitor an opportunity to book a two-reel comedy he can bank upon to amuse and win the applause of his patrons.

The Cast

Burglars................................{ Clyde Cook
　　　　　　　　　　　　　　　　{ Noah Young
The Doctor...............................Jimmie Finlayson
The Girl....................................Fay Wray
Her Sweetheart............................Tyler Brooke

A Hal Roach comedy directed by Stan Laurel.

Story.—An eccentric doctor captures two burglars who enter his house. He promises them freedom and a reward of $1,000 if they will go to the cemetary and obtain for him the body of a man whom the doctor contends died of water on the brain. They agree. A suitor for the hand of the doctor's daughter, who has been forbidden to enter the house, passes himself off as a corpse and is carried to the doctor. The suitor escapes and in order to obtain the reward Cook is forced to act as the "body." An attempt to carve him up leads to the greatest activity on the part of the doctor.

Summary.—Though it employs scenes in a cemetery and an attempt to steal a corpse, this comedy avoids all traces of the offensiveness that might easily arise in depicting such situations. It is a "spook" comedy with an entirely new twist and novel gags. The acting, directing and production are first-rate and the picture superior in conception and execution to the average two-reel comedy.

"Westward Ho"
(Universal-Blue Bird—One Reel)

CHARLES PUFFY, the rotund comedian is the hero of this one-reeler in which he is seen to good advantage. It is the wildest kind of slapstick but should be good for a few laughs.

Puffy, on a world walking tour makes an impressive entrance into the town when he is thrown from the rear of a speeding car and bumps into Gopher Gus, the bad man, knocking the latter out. He becomes a hero and is idolized by the fair and much sought Mildred, only to encounter a second bad man, who gives him chase. Puffy mounts a broncho and a wild ride follows. It terminates when he is thrown over a fence and in his fall knocks out both of the bad men, who flee from him in terror. The girl again hails him as her hero and they proceed on their way to the minister.—CHESTER J. SMITH.

"A Runaway Taxi"
(Pathe—One Reel)

THRILLS are the goal of these "Stereoscopik" films produced by Ives-Leventhal, and here are some new thrills for the screen patrons. "The Runaway Taxi" is the name of a strip of stereoscopic film which presents a series of sensational effects. The spectator is given a ride in a runaway taxi and experiences all the chilling sensations which might come from a mad dash through traffic in the city and around the curves of a country road winding through a mountain. To furnish a stirring finish there is a repetition of the scenes taken in a roller coaster, the subject of one of the former pictures in this series. It should succeed for the novelty has not yet worn off these realistic screen adventures.—T. C. KENNEDY.

"The Invention"
(Herrick-Davis Dist. Div.—Two Reels)
(Reviewed by Harold Flavin)

PROVING once more that a story may be told clearly and logically without the aid of subtitles the sponsors of this production, one of the "Fragments of Life" series, have turned out a picture that takes its place with the best of the "short features." It is a distinct departure from the usual run of two-reelers in that the entire plot is unfolded without a single written line of explanation but, owing to a compact script and the fact that the cast embraces only four characters, the spectator need have no fear of experiencing a "what's it all about" feeling after the final fade-out.

The theme is one of those "Comedy of Errors" affairs in which the hero, a hard-working inventor in a small town, is hounded by the "wide-awake" constable due to a mistaken idea of the marshall's that the aforementioned inventor is the perpetrator of a bank robbery; the reason for his suspicion being the fact that he observed the embryo Edison examining fire-arms just before the hold-up.

The cast all turn in creditable performances, the work of Elinor King and Reginald Simpson, who are featured, being worthy of special mention. Miss King has a likeable screen personality in addition to which she can act though in this instance she seemed hampered by the director who evidently has a flair for violent gestures as regards expressing emotion.

The Cast

William Calhoun, Harry Stone, Elinor King and Reginald Simpson.

The Story.—Simpson, a young inventor and sportsman, has nearly completed a new process of colored photography but lacks the necessary funds to complete it. Meeting his sweetheart, Elinor, he shows her a shotgun in the window of a hardware store, and is observed by the sheriff. The local bank is held up and the sheriff conceives the idea that the inventor is the bandit and gives chase. Simpson is warned by Elinor and they start for his laboratory with the sheriff in hot pursuit. On arriving they find a tramp has broken in and wrecked the plant but has accidently completed the inventors process. They arrest him and discover he is the bank robber so all ends well.

Summary.—A distinct novelty owing to the absences of subtitles. It is a well told story and the cast is uniformly good.

"Ko-Ko on the Run"
(Red Seal—One Reel)

A RACE between the well-known "Ko-Ko" and a fat boy furnishes the plot for this Out-of-the-Inkwell cartoon reel made by Max Fleischer. The fantastical is exploited in several novel situations. In once instance "Ko-Ko" is supplied a donkey to aid him in covering the course, the animal being drawn on the run as it were with the back and head speeding along even before the cartoonist completes the lines which form the legs. The cartoons are blended with photographed images and there is a surprising bit when "Ko-Ko" is shown dancing on the eyelid of his creator, Mr. Fleischer. This seems a marvelous trick and will no doubt stir considerable wonderment in the theatre.—T. C. KENNEDY.

"The Story Teller"
(Educational—One Reel)

THIS Lyman H. Howe tale is as well presented as those of the series that have gone before. It is related by a fisherman to his boy as the pair are fishing from a bridge. The elder fisherman relates experiences he has had fishing in different parts of the world. This provides the opportunity for displaying a number of beautiful pictorials, as well as several educational and interesting details of exploits in many different countries.—CHESTER J. SMITH.

CLASSIFIED AD SECTION

RATES: 10 cents a word for each insertion, in advance except Employment Wanted, on which rate is 5 cents.

CLASSIFIED SERVICE

A classified ad in MOTION PICTURE NEWS offers the full resources and circulation of the NEWS to the advertiser at a ridiculously low figure.

Whether you want to reach executives, branch managers, salesmen, or theatre managers, you can accomplish this quickly and economically through the NEWS Classified Columns.

The Peer of All Projection Surfaces

The Radio Silver Screens (Guaranteed). Price 50 cents per square foot. For Particulars and sample apply to Manufacturer
JOHN MUNRO CRAWFORD
48 Smith St., Newburgh, N. Y.

Wanted

WANTED—Producer who is well known and has contracts for series of pictures wishes motion picture partner with fifty thousand dollars. Box 848, Motion Picture News, New York City.

SITUATION WANTED—At liberty, one non-union operator with ten years' experience. Will go anywhere at any time. Can give good reference if necessary. Write care Grand Theatre, Prattville, Ala.

WANTED—To lease theatre, equipped with stage, in city not less than eight thousand. Would consider house somewhat run down. Address Box 330, Motion Picture News, New York City.

EXPERT OPERATOR and Electrician with 9 years' experience in big houses; married; wants to locate at once. Address, Operator, Box 282, Mason City, Iowa.

WANTED immediately in Buffalo, a man with considerable experience in laboratory and camera work. Applicants should state full details as to experience, giving names of former employers and present occupation if not now employed in laboratory work. Also state salary expected. Address "Experience" c/o Motion Picture News, New York City.

THEATRE IN TOWN OF 4,000 or better, anywhere in North Central states, Northern Indiana preferred. Can either give satisfactory security on lease or buy outright. Would consider buying interest in bona-fide proposition where owner wishes to retire. All replies absolutely confidential. Address Box 360, Motion Picture News, New York City.

For Sale

SALE — DeVry portable projector, Type E, accessories. Used at home. Perfect screen results. $170. Lumley, 1054 Ackerman Ave., Syracuse, N. Y.

MOVIE THEATRE for sale, 950 seats. Corner location, west side. $20,000 cash required. David Krieger, 367 Grant street, Buffalo, N. Y.

FOR SALE.—Theatre Equipment of all descriptions; Immediate shipment of used chairs, any quantity. Will also buy used chairs and equipment. Theatre Seating Company, 845 South State Street, Chicago, Illinois.

FOR SALE.—Hope Jones Wurlitzer type 135, excellent condition. Will trade for cheaper instrument with cash difference. A bargain if you are looking for a fine organ. H. E. Skinner, Box 882, Ogden, Utah.

FOR SALE AT A SACRIFICE.—Photoplayer; in use less than 2 years. Orpheum Theatre, Orwigsburg, Pa.

FOR SALE. — Modern movie; priced for quick sale account of illness; wonderful bargain; county seat of 10,000. Box 240, Motion Picture News, New York City.

The most widely diversified group of advertisements we have presented here in some time is shown above. Nine newspaper ads from various sections of the country are reproduced, all on "A Slave of Fashion" (Metro-Goldwyn), as follows: Loew's State theatre, Indianapolis; Madison theatre, Detroit; Century theatre, Baltimore; Stanley theatre, Philadelphia; Loew's Aldine theatre, Pittsburgh; Garrick theatre, Minneapolis, and the Palace theatre in Dallas.

Pre-release Reviews of Features

The Bad Lands
(Producers Distributing Corp.—5833 Feet)
(Reviewed by George T. Pardy)

THIS picture goes back to the old frontier days, presenting Harry Carey as an Indian fighter in one of the best Westerns yet filmed as a vehicle for this popular star. It's a colorful production in the true sense of the phrase, with cunning redskins, fair women, U. S. cavalrymen and a scout hero played up to the limit in the rousing events which go to the making of a genuine thrill melodrama. The Indian fighting scenes are intensely realistic and it would be a peculiarly cold-blooded critic who couldn't get excited when the attack of Fort Sumner and the burning of Porterville is flashed upon the screen.

From a strictly spectacular standpoint this feature registers big, but it must also be conceded that the director has managed to instill an unusual amount of straight human interest into the story.

THE CAST
Patrick Angus O'Toole	Harry Carey
Colonel Owen	Wilfred Lucas
Captain Blake	Lee Shumway
Hal Owen	Gaston Glass
Charlie Squirrel	Joe Ricksen
Mary Owen	Trilby Clark

Author, Kate Corbaley. Director, Dell Henderson. Photographed by Sol Polito and George Benoit.

SYNOPSIS. Sergeant O'Toole finds Indians attacking wagon train, joins fight and at conclusion he and boy named Freckles are only survivors. At Fort Sumner O'Toole discovers Captain Blake forcing unwelcome attentions of Mary B. Owen—and beats him up. Through Blake's plotting O'Toole is suspected of robbing the mails and imprisoned. Indians attack the fort and O'Toole heads the defense, which is maintained successfully until cavalry arrive and scatter savages. O'Toole's name is cleared and he wins Mary.

THEME. Western melodrama with scout hero, staged in Indian fighting days on the frontier.

PRODUCTION HIGHLIGHTS. Indian attack on wagon train. Burning of Porterville. Assault on Fort Sumner and scout's perilous journey through enemy lines to obtain cavalry assistance.

EXPLOITATION ANGLES. Feature Harry Carey and Trilby Clark. Make it plain that this is an unusual Westerner, blazing with color and thrills, and giving an accurate outline of strenuous life in the old frontier days.

DRAWING POWER. Should get the money in neighborhood and smaller houses.

SUMMARY. An unusually high-class Western, action taking place in frontier days. Indian fighting scenes particularly realistic and colorful. Impressive melodramatic effects, appealing romance. A good box office attraction.

Trilby Clark in the Producers Distributing Corp. release, "The Bad Lands."

The Bad Lands (Producers Dis. Corp.)
PRESS NOTICE
A STIRRING tale of old frontier days, when Indians were on the warpath and U. S. cavalrymen fought as the savages, is outlined in "The Bad Lands" scheduled as the principal attraction on the screen of the ...... Theatre on ...... Harry Carey appears as the lead in one of the best roles of his brilliant career, to which he does full justice, with beautiful Trilby Clark winning all hearts

The story deals with the adventures of a dashing sergeant of the U. S. regulars, renowned for his clever scouting work, who is double-crossed by a villain, but clears himself

CATCH LINES
A Red-blooded tale of Frontier Days, a gripping story of men fighting a painted menace, a love theme of tenderness and beauty.

Harry Carey has one of his most thrilling roles as the man who overcomes obstacles of disgrace and lack of rank to save Fort Sumner for civilization.

With This Ring
(B. P. Schulberg Prod.—5333 Feet)
(Reviewed by Harold Flavin)

THIS one registers as a good picture for cosmopolitan audiences with some excellent South Sea Island sequences and capable acting by the cast, especially Alyce Mills, Donald Keith and Lou Tellegen.

Though possessing good entertainment value for certain classes it misses being placed in the "above the ordinary" class due to the director's insistence on dragging sex into every possible sequence with the result that it will not prove a good buy for houses catering to family trade.

With better treatment this story could have been made into a production that would stand out from the ordinary run of pictures as the story has fine possibilities.

THEME. Melodrama in which boy and girl, shipwrecked on an Isle in the Pacific become man and wife before God, with many ensuing complications after their rescue.

PRODUCTION HIGHLIGHTS. The marriage before God. The fight between Keith and Dick Sutherland on the island. The sequences in which the wife is harrassed by the elder Van Buren.

EXPLOITATION ANGLES. Play up the names of the featured players-Alyce Mills, Donald Keith and Lou Tellegen. Put on South Sea Island dance as prologue.

DRAWING POWER. Should draw well in second run and houses catering to the younger element. Not so good for family consumption.

SUMMARY. A fair offering that will probably entertain the younger folks but which, due to director's flair for exploiting sex, won't get by with either the intellegentsia or family trade.

THE CAST
Cecilie Vaughn	Alyce Mills
John Wendell	Forrest Stanley
Rufus Van Buren	Lou Tellegen
Donald Van Buren	Donald Keith
The Portuguese	Dick Sutherland
Luella Van Buren	Martha Mattox

From the novel by Fanny Heaslip Lea. Directed by Fred C. Windermere.

SYNOPSIS. Donald Van Buren and Cecilie Vaughn, wrecked on an island become man and wife before God. Attacked by a mad Portuguese Donald is stunned and Cecilie, believing him dead leaves the island with a rescuing party. She goes to Donald's brother who refuses his help but offers to 'keep' her which she refuses. Donald's lawyer offers his hand which she accepts, as a measure of protection, on the lawyer's promise not to demand his nuptial rights. Donald is rescued and returning home finds Cecilie and the lawyer who returns her to him.

Alyce Mills, appearing in "With This Ring," Schulberg Preferred.

With This Ring (B. P. Schulberg)
PRESS NOTICE
A PICTURE of outstanding merit "With This Ring" will be the big screen attraction the ...... Theatre on ...... It is a heart-stirring tale of struggles of a woman, forced by circumstances to wed before God, to carry on and care for a child after the supposed death of her husband.

Alyce Mills, an actress of rare charm and personality portrays the role of the wife with an emotional fibre that is the acme of acting. The part of the husband is played by Donald Keith who gives an excellent performance.

CATCH LINES
Though believing her husband dead she nevertheless strove to rear a child without resorting to a sordid arrangement with the husband's brother.

You will experience nervous tremors up and down your spine during the fight scene between the husband and the mad Portuguese.

Makers of Men
(Bud Barsky Prod.—5500 Feet)
(Reviewed by George T. Pardy)

HARDLY strong enough to stand a week-run test, this picture will do nicely for the daily change houses, or can be utilized as half of double bill. It isn't badly acted and most people will feel a certain amount of sympathy for hero Jimmy Jones, whose nervous weakness made a coward of him in civilian life, until he went to war and developed a tough spine, with the aid of a sergeant buddy and familiarity with danger and death. The picture's worst fault is its tangled continuity, due to the frequent use of cut-backs, and having the tale related by one of a group of rusties, instead of making a straight yarn of it.

Kenneth MacDonald furnishes a good character sketch of Jimmy Jones, but chief dramatic honors go to Clara Horton, as the heroine, and J. P. MacGowan, whose portrayal of the canny sergeant, the chap responsible for the hardening of Jimmy's physical and mental fibre, stands out as a bully bit of acting. The photography is O. K., but as much cannot be said for Forrest Sheldon's direction, which fails signally in bringing out the story's best points.

THEME. Heart drama with hero whose weak character becomes developed and strengthened by war experience, returns home a new man and wins the girl he loves.

PRODUCTION HIGHLIGHTS. Jimmy Jones' first meeting with Sergeant Banks, his experiences abroad, his return home. Scene where he man-handles rival. The romance and happy ending.

EXPLOITATION ANGLES. Kenneth MacDonald, J. P. McGowan and Clara Horton are all well known and worth featuring. You might be able to interest your local American Legion Posts in this tale of a returned soldier. Play up the romantic interest, comedy touches and acting of principals.

SUMMARY. Drama with heart interest, few melodramatic punches, chief character, chap who gets courage through war experiences. Has some comedy value. Plot rather poorly developed, continuity bad. Picture will get by as attraction for daily change houses, or half of double bill.

THE CAST
Jimmy Jones..............................Kenneth MacDonald
Lillian Gilman...Clara Horton
Sergeant Daniel Banks............................J. P. MacGowan
Hiram Renfrew...William Burton
Steppling..William Lowery
Shiftless Poole..Ethan Laidlow
Author, William E. Wing. Director, Forrest Sheldon.

SYNOPSIS. Jimmy Jones is the victim of a nervous trouble which causes him to start and tremble at any unexpected noise. Although he cannot help this weakness, try as he may, the townsfolk made no excuse for him and he is generally looked upon as a coward. To make matters worse, the girl he admires, Lillian Gilman, shares in the popular opinion. War breaks out, Jimmy goes to France. Under the tutelage of Sergeant Banks he forgets his nervousness, returns home a new man, whips his rival and wins Lillian.

J. P. McGowan, who appears in "Makers of Men", a Bud Barsky production.

Makers of Men (Bud Barsky Prod.)
PRESS NOTICE

"MAKERS OF MEN" is the attraction scheduled for the screen of the ———— Theatre on ————. This is a story with a great deal of heart interest, the hero a young fellow who suffers from a nervous complaint which makes all the townsfolk, as well as the girl he admires, look upon him as a coward. But war breaks out and Jimmy goes to the front. There, under the tutelage of Sergeant Banks, who doesn't know what fear is, Jimmy developes into a new-man.

. Kenneth MacDonald plays the hero, with pretty Clara Horton as the girl. Others in cast are, J. P. MacGowan, William Burton and Ethan Lowery.

CATCH LINES
It isn't always safe to mistake a timid man for a coward. Jimmy Jones was nervous, but he proved there was fighting stuff in him at the finish!

The Fighting Heart
(Fox—6978 Feet)
(Reviewed by George T. Pardy)

LOOK like a reliable program attraction! Director John Ford has managed to put over a double audience appeal, those who like the strenuous, scrapping stuff will find it here in abundance, while on the other hand the story registers well from the human interest standpoint. Its hero not only proves himself a capable man with his fists, but wins a moral decision, for he combats successfully against the curse of heredity, his forefathers having been notorious for their heavy drinking habits. But he comes out victor on the hootch issue, and as a rough-and-tumble scrapper registers in the top-notch class. As a ring artist he doesn't do so well and we are offered the very unusual sight of a screen hero taking the count before a gloved opponent. But this untoward event is balanced nicely later when the defeated boxer whips his conqueror in a go-as-you-please gutter battle. George O'Brien is excellent in the hero role, Victor MacLaglen, a perfect example of a champion pug, Billie Dove charming as Doris, and the support is adequate.

THEME. Melodrama with hero who overcomes drink heredity handicap, is whipped in glove contest, but beats conqueror in street fight, achieves success and wins girl he loves.

PRODUCTION HIGHLIGHTS. Contrasts of small town and Broadway atmosphere. The swift action. The ring and street fights. Romantic lure. The climax.

EXPLOITATION ANGLES. Feature George O'Brien, Billie Dove and Victor MacLaglen. Stress story's romantic interest and play up the fighting scenes to the limit.

DRAWING POWER. O. K. for the neighborhood and small houses.

SUMMARY. A likely program attraction. Registers a number of good melodramatic punches, fighting stuff is capital and there's a lot of sympathetic interest aroused in hero's behalf. Plot rather out of the ordinary, acting first-class.

THE CAST
Denny Bolton................................... George O'Brien
Doris Anderson....................................Billie Dove
Jerry ....J. Farrell MacDonald
Soapy Williams...............................Victor MacLaglen
Helen Van Allen......................................Diana Miller
Grandfather ....Bert Woodruff
Town Fool...Francis Ford
Author, Larry Evans. Director, John Ford.

SYNOPSIS. Denny Bolton's family has produced a large crop of men drunkards. Knowing that the townsfolk look down upon him, and that even his sweetheart, Doris Anderson, distrusts him, Denny heads for New York. Having licked soapy Williams, pugilistic champion, in a street fight, Denny tackles him in the ring. But he loses, due to lack of training. Later he trades wallops again with Williams outside the ring and thrashes him soundly, going back triumphantly to Doris.

George O'Brien, who is starred in the Fox production "The Fighting Heart."

The Fighting Heart (Fox)
PRESS NOTICE

AS its title indicates, there is lots of fierce battling in the story of "The Fighting Heart," billed as the main attraction on the screen of the ———— Theatre on ————. Fans who rejoice in sharp fistic encounters within and outside the ring, will find plenty to satisfy them in this picture. But there is also a strong human interest angle and tender romance.

The Hero leaves his small-town home because of the bad reputation all the men-folks of his family have earned through hard drinking. Even the girl he loves distrusts him. In the big city he becomes a professional fighter, loses to the champion, but evens matters up by whipping him in a straight fist fight. Things finally break well for him and he finds happiness with the girl.

CATCH LINES
This man fought successfully against the handicap of a bad reputation earned by his ancestors. He won a moral fight, lost one in the ring, but proved himself an efficient scrapper by thrashing his conqueror.

A Daughter of the Sioux
(Davis Dist. Div.—Five Reels)
(Reviewed by Harold Flavin)

A FAST action production of the "western" type is this starring Ben Wilson and Neva Gerber in which Wilson also did the directing turning in a good bit of work in both roles. This is the type of picture that goes over with the youngsters as well as the old folks.

It is really a "two in one" proposition as the explanation of the heroine's true identity consumes a lot of footage in the telling but it is all very interesting and that part of the explanation dealing with the fording of the river by the prairie schooners is one of the best bits of photography and direction yet seen by this reviewer.

The supporting cast, consisting of Robert Walker, Fay Adams, William Lowery and Rhody Hathaway, contribute excellent performances in their respective roles. It is a good bet for the second run and neighborhood houses and you may tell your patrons that it's fit for the entire family to view.

THEME. Western historical drama dealing with the efforts of the early settlers to prevent being annihilated by Indians. There's a romance thrown in for good measure.

PRODUCTION HIGHLIGHTS. The superb horsemanship of Neva Gerber. Ben Wilson's capable acting and direction. The fight at the top of the cliff between Wilson and Walker. The fording of the river by the prairie schooners. The Indian attack on the settlers.

EXPLOITATION ANGLES. Play up the names of Ben Wilson and Neva Gerber as they are well known among the fans. Have man dressed in Indian costume walk up and down in front of the house.

DRAWING POWER. Should do good business in second run and neighborhood houses. Good bet for the entire family.

SUMMARY. A fast action story with good performances by the entire cast. The direction is good. Mountings and photography are first rate.

THE CAST

John Field	Ben Wilson
Nanette "Daughter of the Sioux"	Neva Gerber
Eagle Wing	Robert Walker
Trooper Kennedy	Fay Adams
Big Bill Hay	William Lowery
Major John Webb	Rhody Hathaway

Author, Brig. General Charles King, U. S. A. Adapted by George W. Pyper. Directed by Ben Wilson, assisted by Archie Ricks. Photographed by William Fildew.

SYNOPSIS. John Field, Government surveyor, suspects that Nanette, known at Fort Frayne as the "Daughter of the Sioux," is giving information about the fort to the Indians. Eagle Wing, a renegade Indian, incites the Indians to attack the settlers. Field follows him and a fight ensues in which Field emerges the victor. Nanette, recognized by an old scout as a white woman, confesses to Eagle Wing being her foster brother—also stating he is the son of 'Big Bill' Hay. Field, learning Nanette is white declares his love for her which she reciprocates.

Let's Go Gallagher
(F. B. O.—5182 Feet)
(Reviewed by George T. Pardy)

T OM TYLER, new F. B. O. cowboy star, makes his debut in this picture, and looks as though he is destined to forge to the front rank of screen heroes engaged in furnishing amusement for the countless admirers of Western features. Physically, Mr. Tyler is certainly "the goods;" over six feet, built like a Hercules and as nimble as a cat. They've given him a regulation Western plot, with lots of riding and fighting to do, and he acquits himself well at all times. The film is chock-full of exciting situations, the thrills are numerous and a side-line of timely comedy balances the melodramatic sweep of the story nicely.

Wherever the fans like Western pictures this one should get the money, as it amply fulfils the demand for open-air romances and fast furious action. The photography throughout is of excellent quality, including a wealth of fine exteriors, with some remarkably attractive long shots. Barbara Starr plays the heroine role of Dorothy Manning with vivacity and charm, Alfred Huston gets the laughs by a clever portrayal of the hero's rheumatic pal, Bendy Mulligan, and the support as a whole is capital.

THEME. Western melodrama. Cowboy hero becomes foreman of girl's ranch, defeats schemes of cattle-rustlers and wins her for wife.

PRODUCTION HIGHLIGHTS. Tom Tyler's riding and fighting stunt work. The fast action. Hero's rescue of little boy and dog from being killed by train. Scene in which he saves Dorothy from death in runaway.

EXPLOITATION ANGLES. Boost personality of new star, mention that he was selected out of one thousand other candidates by F. B. O. for Western pictures. You can praise the feature as melodrama of the kind that makes the spectators wild with enthusiasm over its forceful appeal.

DRAWING POWER. Good for any house where Western melodrama holds the patrons.

SUMMARY. Western melodrama introducing new star in person of Tom Tyler, who works fast and looks like a real attraction for the box office. Plot has nothing very new to offer but moves briskly, is alive with thrills and should go over O. K. **THE CAST**

Tom Gallagher	Tom Tyler
Dorothy Manning	Barbara Starr
Black Carter	Olin Francis
Thug Peters	Sam Peterson
Bendy Mulligan	Alfred Huston
Little Joey	Frankie Darrow

Author, Percy Heath. Directed by Robert De Lacey and James Gruen.

SYNOPSIS: Tom Gallagher, cowboy, looks for job at Dorothy Manning's ranch, is made foreman and incurs enmity of Perkins and latter's cattle-rustling bang. Perkins obtains a mortgage on the ranch and has Dorthy kidnapped. Tom comes to her aid and gets to ranch with the money necessary to pay mortgage and keep Perkins from taking possession. The discovery of oil on the property ends Dorothy's financial troubles and she weds Tom.

A Daughter of the Sioux
(Davis Dist. Div.)
PRESS NOTICE

A DRAMATIC story of frontier life in this country will be unfolded on the screen of the ———— Theatre on ————

It is replete with tense situations and moments fraught with suspense. Ben Wilson, as the Government surveyor gives a performance that will be long remembered. Neva Gerber, as the heroine, gives a wonderful exhibition of horsemanship in addition to a marvelous characterization of an Indian squaw.

There are many thrilling fight scenes incorporated in this tale of the hardships endured by the early settlers.

Robert Walker, Fay Adams, William Lowery and Rhody Hathaway complete the cast.

CATCH LINES

Racial prejudices had no terrors for Field—he loved Nanette though he thought she was of Indian blood. Although positive of her guilt he, nevertheless, tried to shield her.

Neva Gerber in "Daughter of the Sioux," released by Davis Distributing Division.

Lets Go Gallagher (F. B. O.)
PRESS NOTICE

T OM TYLER, a new star, appears in the leading role of "Let's Go Gallagher," an exciting Western melodrama which comes to the screen of the ———— Theatre on ————

Critics all over the country hail Mr. Tyler as one of the finds of the season. He is a big fellow, as active and powerful as he is good-looking, and shows to great advantage in this film. He is seen as a youthful cowboy who becomes foreman of a ranch run by a girl, defeats the schemes of cattle-rustlers and others who try to obtain her property, and weds her.

There's action and thrills in every foot of this feature. Barbara Starr is the heroine, with Olin Francis, Sam Peterson and Alfred Huston in support.

CATCH LINES

The build of Hercules, the horsemanship of a cowboy champion and dynamic personality—these are the characteristics of the new star—Tom Tyler.

Tom Tyler, new F. B. O. Western star, who appears in "Let's Go Gallagher."

Regional News from Correspondents

Detroit

TWO new theatres are to be built on Michigan avenue by Arthur D. Baehr, William Burnstein and Jacob Cohn. They own the Crystal theatre. One of their new theatres will seat 2,000; the other, 1,000.

Dave Chatkin, assistant to the president of Educational, visited local exhibitors this week.

E. P. Strong, theatre and dance hall owner, has entered a new line. In addition to his other interests he now owns a gasoline company.

Alex and Jake Schreiber are back from Florida, where they made some money in real estate.

Producers is sending Henry Zapp and Carl Chalit out into the state.

The Family theatre, Flint, has closed.

Charles W. Perry is now working in the Chicago district for Fox. He formerly worked here. Fred Wuerth of Ann Arbor and Ypsilanti have gone to Florida on a real estate jaunt.

Miss Julia Kramer has quit the Theatre Supply Company and gone into real estate. She was with the theatre concern eight years.

Roy Fricken has gone to Miami, and Harold Hefferan is now doing publicity for the Miles interests.

The Detroit Board of Commerce has elected Oscar W. Smith of the John H. Kensky Enterprises to the Board of Directors. George W. Trendle of Kensky's has retired as vice president of the Board.

The Detroit Pathe office won first prize in the central division in the campaign for new business.

The new Roosevelt theatre opened last week. James N. Robertson is owner. George W. Sampson is general manager.

St. Louis

HENRY CHOTEAU, owner of the Odeon theatre and office building and International Life building, St. Louis, Mo., has purchased the Liberty Theatre building, Delmar boulevard, west of Grand boulevard. The deal included a residence on an adjoining 50-foot lot and is said to have approximated $300,000.

Choteau plans to expend about $200,000 in redecorating and remodeling the theatre.

The house is under lease to Oscar Dane who puts on stock burlesque shows. Choteau stated that Dane's lease would continue.

George P. Skouras has organized the Sarah & Olive Amusement Company to operate the Congress Theatre which he recently leased from Hector M. Passemoglu. The capital of the new company is listed at $10,000.

Carrol Gridley, cashier of the First National Bank at Libertyville, Ill., has had plans prepared for a $50,000 theatre, store and apartment building for Libertyville. Bids will be taken from contractor shortly.

Otto Zehnder, custodian of the Aubert theatre, Aubert and Easton avenues, St. Louis, believes that he frustrated plans of safe blowers to rob the theatre a few nights ago.

Shortly after Zehnder had closed the house for the night a well dressed woman, apparently much excited, called at his home and stated that her son had fallen asleep in the theatre and was locked in. She asked that the custodian return to lease the boy. As Zehnder neared the theatre two men started to follow him. He increased his pace, met a patrolman and the two men disappeared. There was no boy in the theatre.

The Aerial Theatre, Annapolis, Ill., has closed.

The Star Theatre, Paris, Mo., has closed for three weeks.

The employees of the First National exchange had a luncheonette dance Saturday, September 12. As the country editors say a very enjoyable evening was had by all.

C. D. Hill, district manager for Producers Distributing Corporation, accompanied by Russell McLean, his personal representative, attended the district sales managers convention in Chicago.

Jack Weil of Jack Weil Productions is back from a tour of the Northern Missouri key towns.

The new Opera House at Shelbina, Mo., opened on Monday, September 14. Dale Smith is the owner-manager. The house seats 700.

A. C. Wilson traveling auditor for Fox is back in town following a trip to New York to attend the wedding of his daughter.

William Hamilton has sold the Gem Theatre, Marissa, Il., to Singer & Degen.

Tom McKean and wife spent several days in Boston according to a wire received at the local F. B. O. office of which Tom is manager. They are vacationing Down East.

Jack Walsh of F. B. O. returned from a trip to Chicago during the week.

G. E. McKean, manager for the local Fox exchange visited Duquoin, Cairo, Carbondale and other Southern Illinois towns.

The Ivanhoe Theatre on Southwest avenue at Watson Road is almost ready for the grand opening. It will seat 600 persons. It is reported that Mrs. Frank Tabler has been offered the management of the new house.

Dick Rosenbaum and Jimmy Clarke, Paramount famous road crew were visitors. They departed Friday, September 18, for Kansas City.

Visitors seen along Picture Row were: Walter Thimmig, Duquoin, Ill.; Ed. Fellis, Hillsboro; L. E. Fondaw, Fairyland Theatre, Kensett, Ark.; W. E. Malin, Lura Theatre, Augusta, Ark.; Tom Reed, Duquoin; Jim Reilly, Alton; J. Keuse, New Athens, Ill.; A. L. Crichlow, Alton, Ill. and Charley Barber, Tilden, Ill.

The general contract has been let on the new Senate theatre to be erected at 7 and 9 North Broadway. The house has been leased to Charles Goldman and Julius Leventhal. It will be of re-inforced concrete construction with glazed whitebrick exterior and terra cotta trim. The house will adjoin the Astor Theatre, 5 North Broadway, now operated by Goldman and Leventhal.

Canada

BEN LOBAN, one of the most distinguished of Winnipeg's violinists, has been appointed director of the new orchestra which was installed at the Lyceum Theatre, Winnipeg, Manitoba, a week ago, by Manager Charles A. Meade.

An important business tour of Western Canada has been made by H. L. Nathanson, brother of N. L. Nathanson of Toronto, managing director of Famous Players Canadian Corp., and G. W. Brady of New York, representing the Producers Distributing Corp. H. L. Nathanson represents Regal Films, Ltd., Toronto, distributors in Canada of Metro-Goldwyn, Pathe, Warner, British and other features.

The Toronto Moving Picture Baseball League is enjoying a hotly contested race for championship honors. At the middle of September, no less than three teams were tied for premier position in the league standing, these being the teams of Regal Films, Limited, Famous Lasky Film Service and Famous Players Canadian Corp. Trailing these teams is the Associated First National club.

The Garrick Theatre, Winnipeg, Manitoba, is now under the control of D. E. L. Fisher, who has had charge of the theatre for some months past. Some four years ago the Garrick was erected with Winnipeg capital by Walter Wilson, now manager of the Capitol Theatre at Edmonton, Alberta. The Garrick struck a financial snag early in 1924 but the creditors arranged to have the theatre continue in operation with D. E. L. Fisher as managing director. Mr. Fisher eventually secured a number of creditors' claims and, in association with other creditors, organized a new company which has proved a distinct success. The Garrick is notably independent, Mr. Fisher being the president of the Manitoba Moving Picture Exhibitors Association, the oldest continuous exhibitor organization in the Dominion.

Griffin's Theatre at St. Catharines, Ontario, has re-opened after being dark for two months, under the management of George J. Forlan with a mixed policy of pictures and vaudeville. Mr. Forlan has been able to secure some very effective advertising for the theatre through the distribution of special window cards among local merchants. These cards announce to American tourists that they can take back with them to the United States Canadian goods to the value of $100, duty free. At the bottom of the card there is a reference to the theatre. The merchants of St. Catharines, which is only a short distance from the Niagara border, have been eager to make use of the theatre cards as designated.

W. G. Rupay, manager of Griffin's Theatre at Woodstock, Ontario, arranged a corn roast and outing for the staff of the Griffin's Theatre on a farm near Woodstock a few nights ago, about 75 people enjoying the event. The farm was gaily decorated with Japanese lanterns and a huge bonfire was used for the roast. There was music'n everything.

Florida

THE past week marked the opening of the Fall Season. All of the theatres used extra space in the papers and built up special lobbies. The most elaborate of these special displays was the lobby arranged by Manager George B. Peck, of the Strand, Tampa. The entire lobby was covered with wall boards, attractively gotten up with hand painted floral designs and the words "Opening of the Fall Season" spelled out with electric lights.

The Victory, Tampa, opened the fall season with Keith Vaudeville the first three days of the week. Manager Jno. B. Carroll was called away by sickness in his family, and George Peck, of the Strand officiated for him. Peck was right there with his bright smile and glad hand to greet the regulars and make them feel they were appreciated.

John S. Jackson, who operates the Jalms in New Port Richey, has opened a house in Odessa. This is a saw mill city and there are over two thousand workmen on the pay roll, so it looks like he picked out a live one.

The Greystone Casino in Kissimmee is being re-modeled and it is stated that the seating capacity will be nearly doubled by the new arrangements.

Cecil A. Ross has sold his string of three houses in Apopka, Mount Dora and Tavares to Jas. O. Dean. Mr. Dean is planning to make a number of changes in the houses to make them more attractive to the winter visitors.

Somewhere in Tampa, some one is having a fine time smoking up several thousand cigarettes and cigars that were stolen from the stand in the lobby of the Central theatre. The hasp and padlock was pried from the door and the place ransacked. Beside the smokes a small amount of change that was left in the cash register was taken.

The Rivoli gave away the Ford touring car last Tuesday night and Manager N. V. Darley says he never had any idea the Rivoli would hold so many people. Seemed like everybody in Ybor City was there. The stunt proved so successful that Mr. Darley is thinking of giving away another.

The Italian Club Theatre, Ybor City, is putting on musical acts with their picture programs. The people seem to like the stunts and good business is the rule.

A. Juran, manager of the Casino in West Tampa and Ybor City, has had both houses repainted and decorated. New lobby display frames have been ordered also.

Fred L. Freeman, who operated the Grand in Lake City for several years, has sold his house there and bought the Alimar at Live Oak from C. C. Price. After a needed rest Mr. Price is going to return to South Florida and get back in the game.

Philadelphia

W. A. V. MACK, local manager of Pathe, who was recently tendered a farewell dinner at the Rittenhouse Hotel, has been succeeded by Miles Gibbons from the New York office of Pathe. Mr. Mack has been promoted to Short Subject Manager of Pathe, in charge of the thirty-four offices in the United States. Mr. Gibbons assumed his new duties on September 14th.

Fred G. Nixon-Nirdlinger, who has been associated with the Stanley Company for many years and has a controlling interest in a large number of motion picture theatres as well as three of the leading legitimate theatres in Philadelphia, will return to his office in the Stanley Company building at 1916 Race Street the latter part of October. Mr. Nirdlinger, who has been in Paris for about two years, will sail on the "Majestic" from Cherbourg on October 14th.

Leon Behal, well known to theatre men in this territory, has opened the Ben Franklin Film Exchange, at 1318 Vine Street. The new exchange will distribute short subjects only.

It is understood that work will start immediately on the erection of a new theatre to be built for William Freihofer at 4700 Frankford Ave., this city. Messrs. Hodgens & Hill are the architects and the contract has been awarded to the George Kessler Contracting Co., which recently completed the Colney Theatre, 5th St. and Olney Ave.

Superseding the plans of Famous-Players-Lasky for the acquisition of Wilmer & Vincent theatres in Pennsylvania, a contract has been closed between the two companies whereby the latter will play all Paramount releases in the Victoria Theatre at Harrisburg and the Capitol and Hippodrome Theatres in Reading.

Abe L. Einstein, publicity director of the Stanley Company, has returned to his duties in this city after having given more than a fortnight of his time to the Atlantic City Beauty Pageant. Mr. Einstein found this year's Pageant one of the most turbulent enterprises with which he was ever associated. He was in charge of publicity and some of the general arrangements for the Pageant.

Abe Resnick, who has been manager of the Grand Theatre and also of the Jackson Theatre, has been appointed manager of the Grant Theatre, 40th & Girard Ave.

Leo Hannan, assistant booker for First National's local office, is spending his vacation on a motor trip through Canada.

Dembow Brothers recently purchased the Coulter Street Theatre, Germantown, for an amount said to be $45,000.

Seattle

ANNOUNCEMENT was made public last week of the appointment of C. M. Hill as manager of the Metro-Goldwyn branch office in this city, succeeding Seth D. Perkins, who has been made a sub-District Manager with jurisdiction over the Metro-Goldwyn offices in Seattle, Denver and Salt Lake City. Mr. Hill was associated with the Paramount forces in Portland for seven years, and has more recently been connected with the Vitagraph exchange in Los Angeles. He assumed his new duties in this territory early in September.

Mr. and Mrs. E. J. Potter, owners and operators of the Clinton Theatre in Portland, last week announced the opening of their new Moreland Theatre in that city. The house is situated at Milwaukee and Bybee Streets, in one of the larger residential districts. It will be operated as part of the Multnomah Theatres Circuit of that city.

Moving of the film and office equipment of the Educational Pictures Exchange to new quarters at the corner of Third and Virginia was completed last week, and Manager J. A. Gage is now proudly entrenched in his attractive new space, formerly occupied by the L. K. Brin enterprises. The new Educational office is elaborately decorated in a light green and mahogany color scheme, and is one of the show places of Film Row.

Charles W. Harden, manager of the United Artists exchange, recently announced the appointment of H. M. Glanfield as sales representative in the local territory. Mr. Glanfield was formerly associated with various concerns in this city, and more recently has been connected with the First National exchange in Portland.

R. C. Hudson, assistant manager of the new Producers' Distributing Corporation exchange in Portland, and R. A. Tracey, cashier of the same office, spent several days in this city recently in conference with W. H. Drummond, manager of the local P. D. C. office. Several conferences relative to fall plans were held, despite the disruption caused by the preparations for moving the local office to new quarters at 308 Virginia Street, the location formerly occupied by the Educational exchange.

After a closed summer season, the American Theatre in Spokane has again resumed operation under a combined motion picture and musical program policy.

Louis Goldsmith, one of Seattle's leading suburban exhibitors, last week announced that he had sold his Society Theatre of this city to W. F. Ackles, former owner and manager of a downtown second run theatre several years ago. Mr. Goldsmith, who has owned and operated the Society for many years, has as yet announced no plans for the future, but at present is enjoying the use of a brand new motor car around the streets of this city.

Edwin B. Rivers, former advertising and publicity manager for C. W. McKee's Heilig Theatre, and more recently manager of one of the West Coast Theatres in Southern California, returned to this territory last week to assume the office of general manager of the John Danz Circuit of theatres. He will soon occupy offices in the Capitol Theatre, from which location he will direct the activities of Mr. Danz's rapidly growing string of houses.

The Angier Theatre, Seattle's suburban photoplay house catering to the colored trade, last week was purchased by F. S. Barkus, formerly connected with the West Coast circuit in California, according to announcement made by Roy Cooper, former owner. The house will continue under the same second run policy, with four changes weekly.

Arthur Bishell was announced last week by L. K. Brin as manager of the Connell Theatre in Aberdeen, now operated by Mr. Brin in the interests of the Warner Brothers. Mr. Bishell was formerly general manager of the Will Starkey Amusement Company of Spokane, operating houses in that city and in Montana towns.

Al Rosenberg, owner and manager of the De Luxe Feature Film Exchange, last week announced the appointment of A. A. Bruce as sales representative for DeLuxe in the Eastern Washington territory. Mr. Bruce has been associated on Film Row for several seasons, and has just recovered from a severe illness that has kept him off the road for several weeks.

Frank Graham and A. H. St. John recently announced that they had just purchased the interests of Messrs. Cormier, Fitzgerald and Robertson of the Twin Cities Theatres Company, and hereafter will own and operate the entire string of seven houses in the Chehalis and Centralia territories. The agreement was to become effective early in September, it was announced.

J. J. Lowenstein, president of the newly incorporated Elbe Theatres, Inc., owning and operating theatres in Aberdeen, Astoria and Ellensburg, recently opened general offices in the American Bank Building of this city. L. K. Brin, representing the Warner Brothers organization, is in complete charge of booking attractions for these houses.

Fred McConnell, short subject sales manager for the Universal Film Company, from New York City, left this territory last week after several days spent here with Manager L. O. Lukan and his staff. Following his visit here, Mr. McConnell was scheduled to stop off at the Portland exchange, en route to Universal City for a brief visit.

Jack Sullivan, manager of the Fox Film Exchange, last week announced the appointment of H. Lawrence as publicity and exploitation manager of the local office. Mr. Lawrence was formerly associated with Loew's State Theatre in Los Angeles, and also has been connected with First National and Metro-Goldwyn in Los Angeles in exploitation capacities. His duties in this territory will include assisting exhibitors of the smaller cities to properly advertise and exploit their Fox pictures.

Central Penn

THE twentieth anniversary of the entrance of the Wilmer & Vincent interests into the theatrical life of Reading was celebrated in the company's four theatres in that city during the week of September 14.

Two of the company's Reading theatres, according to claims of the management, have the largest seating capacity of any theatres in that city. In addition to these theatres, Wilmer & Vincent, with Nathan Appell, of York, operate the Orpheum in Reading, having controlled a lease on this house since twenty years ago.

In connection with the Reading anniversary celebration Wilmer & Vincent pointed out that the firm now operates about 40 theatres, having acquired, since its first entry to Reading, theatres in Allentown, Harrisburg, Easton, Altoona, Norfolk, Richmond and Savannah. Sidney Wilmer and Walter Vincent, the original members of the firm, which was formed in Utica, N. Y., in 1901, are still at its head.

The managers of the four Wilmer & Vincent theatres in Reading are: Frank S. Micklay, Rajah; Joel L. Levy, Capitol; William Masard, Hippodrome, and James Kelly, Orpheum. C. Floyd Hopkins, director of the Wilmer & Vincent theatres in Harrisburg, is also in general charge of the company's interests in the district embracing Reading.

The Victoria theatre, Mahanoy City, has re-engaged the Slowitsky orchestra for the Fall and Winter season.

Since his acquisition of the Strand theatre, Shenandoah, Lou Berman, of Philadelphia, has installed as manager, Nash Weil, who formerly managed the Rialto, in Washington, D. C.

Confusion was averted through the cool-headed action of the attaches of the Majestic theatre, Pottsville, in quietly informing the patrons when a slight fire occurred in the theatre recently. The house was emptied quickly and without the trace of panic. The flames were caused by a film igniting, and they were quickly conquered by a fire company.

The Victoria theatre, Mount Carmel, has a new organist in the person of George Gross, formerly with the Wilmer & Vincent circuit in the Rajah theatre, Reading, and elsewhere.

The Victory theatre, DuPont, has been added to the chain operated by Louis Marinos.

The management of the new $500,000 Strand picture theatre, opened by the Nathan Appell interests in York, on August 27, has begun the publication of a weekly four-page news folder, relating to the news of the theatre and coming attractions.

Announcement is made that new pipe organs are to be installed in the Refowich theatre, Freeland, and in the Elks theatre, Mahanoy City. Eugene McAtee is manager of the latter house.

Baltimore capitalists who were said to have been considering the erection of a new picture theatre at Frackville, in the Pennsylvania coal mining regions, are now reported to have abandoned the project.

Mrs. Florence Ackley Ley, director of the Community Service Bureau maintained in Harrisburg by the Wilmer & Vincent theatres of that city, is recovering from a recent severe illness to the extent that she is now able to be out-of-doors again.

Sydney J. Gates, manager of Loew's Regent theatre, Harrisburg, has announced the appointment of Girard Newkirk as assistant manager of this picture theatre.

A number of boys who made a practice of sneaking their way into the Strand theatre, Easton, without paying, were recently arrested and fined $2.50 each. The management took this step in order to break up the practice, and apparently has succeeded.

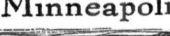

Minneapolis

SEVERAL changes in the management of Finkelstein & Ruben theatres in the Twin Cities have just been announced.

Al Kvool, former house manager of the State Theatre, Minneapolis, has been transferred temporarily to the Rialto theatre there. He is said to be slated to handle the new F. & R. theatre in Fargo which is rapidly nearing completion.

George Kruger, formerly manager of the Rialto, has been transferred to the St. Clair theatre, St. Paul.

Gus Carlson of the Grand theatre, Minneapolis, has gone to take charge of the Zelda theatre in Duluth.

Mal Herz, former assistant manager of the Capitol theatre in St. Paul becomes assistant manager of the Garrick at Duluth.

Ed Cornell, house superintendent of the State, has been promoted to house manager of the big F. & R. Minneapolis house.

W. J. Roggenbeck who has just opened the Liberty theatre at Webster, S. D. was a recent visitor at the Fox office in Minneapolis.

George Johnson, manager of the T. B. Sheldon Memorial Auditorium at Red Wing, came to Minneapolis the other day to arrange for his winter program in that theatre which is one of the few municipal motion picture theatres in the world.

E. S. Noreen, of the Rex theatre at Hutchinson, Minn., was in the Twin Cities the other day.

The Sandon brothers operating the Sandon in Jackson and the Sandon in Blue Earth have been visiting in Minneapolis.

Minneapolis distributors were called upon by J. Diener for the new program of his Capitol theatre at Dubuque, Ia. The theatre has just been reopened by Mr. Diener after being renamed. It was formerly the Family.

Finkelstein & Ruben are said to have taken over the Palace theatre at Mandan, N. D., from Joe Maitland.

Fox recently closed a sales conference in Minneapolis. E. T. Gomersall and Don Nairn, the manager and his assistant, were cast in the role of orators and among those who told them what was going on in the territory were F. G. Hallowell of Jamestown, W. W. Adams of Sioux Falls and Ray Stewart of LaCrosse in addition to those who make their headquarters in Minneapolis, Frank I. Mantzke and Jack Raper.

Jack O'Toole, manager of Producers' Distributing Corporation for Minneapolis, took a run down to LaCrosse recently.

Harry Olin of the Orpheum Theatre at Grand Forks dropped in at Producers' office last week.

Cecil Mayberry, district supervisor of Producers', was in Minneapolis for a couple of days again last week.

Max Weisner of the Badger theatre, Milwaukee, was a weekend visitor in Minneapolis, combining business with more business.

Floyd Lewis of Chicago, supervisor for Associated Exhibitors is here picking out a new assistant manager to take the place of Charley Howard.

Harry Bailey, manager of the Pathe exchange here, has just returned from a trip on the Northern border of Minnesota, attending to business in that locality which was formerly considered hopeless wilderness but which is now taking on a development that centers around International Falls and the Rainy Lake.

Fred H. Knispel stopped in Minneapolis for a few days on his way back to Chicago after a trip through the Northwest for Producers' Distributing corporation. He is assisting Cecil Mayberry as division man. They are in Chicago now taking part in the sales meeting of district men from all over the United States.

J. R. Banty of the Majestic theatre, Rhinelander, has been stopping in Minneapolis. He says that Wisconsin is getting its share of the film business this year with general conditions encouraging.

John Pillar of Valley City spent nearly a week here arranging for the program of his new theatre there. Pillar has done something that probably has never been done in the United States before. He has persuaded the whole town of Valley City to take a holiday on the occasion of the opening of his house.

Lloyd Willis, special representative from the New York office has been a guest this week at Warner Brothers office in Minneapolis.

T. A. Burke, Warner manager, has just returned from a swing around the key center towns in the district.

Morris Abrams, exploiteer at Metro-Goldwyn office, has been looking around at Alexandria.

Earl Lorentz has completed his first week on the Paramount staff. He invaded Wisconsin through the port of Hudson and is said to have made good progress.

The Minneapolis Paramount office is bursting buttons off its chest this week. Out of 40 district offices in the United States it stood second in the annual contest. Manager A. V. Leak was congratulated by his company.

Not only that but Leak's staff boasts the champion of all the Paramount salesmen and another salesman who stands third in the United States. The champion is Fred B. Benno whose work in the North Dakota territory won the honor of placing first among 173 in the United States. F. W. Thayer, another North Dakota man, was in third place on the list.

The Garrick theatre of Hawley, Minn., has broken away from the McCarthy circuit and is operating independently once more.

Sid Heath of Wells is burnishing up the Pastime theatre at Mapleton which he recently took over and expects to make it one of the finest theatres in the district so far as service and appointments go.

Clinton & Meyer have given over the Two Harbors theatre to independent management.

Bill Biesel of United Artists is getting well underway his exploitation program for the territory.

Jack Hellman came back with a prize from his Greatest Movie Season ball in Sioux Falls, S. D., not long ago. He was master of ceremonies for the event which raised $700 for the town band. One of the stunts arranged by himself with H. J. Chapman, Ted Mendenhall and Harry Weinberg assisting was a star impersonation contest. To make it a success they all entered and the vote of the fans gave Jack the prize for his impersonation of Larry Semon. Hellman is exploiteer for Paramount.

Minneapolis may have a new first run picture house. Alexander Pantages, head of the Pantages circuit with its chain of vaudeville theatres, is said to be about to include this city with Milwaukee, Omaha, Des Moines and others in a string of first run movie houses that will eventually be extended throughout the country. The first theatre of this string is to be built in Seattle.

Lee Marcus, sales manager of Film Booking Office is on a tour of inspection of the company's offices in Des Moines, Omaha, Sioux Falls, Minneapolis and Milwaukee. He was in Minneapolis Thursday. Max Weisfeldt, district manager, accompanied him throughout most of the tour.

Universal held more of its famous theater parties for managers and owners last week and this. Fairmont entertained on the 13th, Owatonna on the 18th and Devils Lake on the 22d.

Howard Whelpley, former manager of the Rex and Lric theaters, Virginia, is now in charge of the Doric at Duluth. H. E. Billings, late of the Garrick, has been given charge of the Virginia houses recently taken over by F. & R.

Walter Hiller who has managed the Brainerd Lyceum for Clinton & Meyer has been given charge of the Park there as well under F. & R. ownership. George Irwin is now in charge of the Palace theater, Minneapolis.

Remodeling of the Tower City, N. D., theater is being completed and John Pierson will soon offer films there.

Louisburg, Minn., will have a picture theatre. Carl G. Hagan is making plans.

H. N. Turner now has two houses. In addition to the Family theater at Pine City, he is again in charge of the Family at North Branch, recently operated by Philip Fagerstrom.

Ole Midthbruget has installed a second projection machine at Union hall, Hanska, Minn.

Frank Burke, new publicity man for the Hennepine-Orpheum, Minneapolis, is putting on an orchestra contest in cooperation with the Daily Star. Bookings are to be offered the musical organizations most popular with the fans.

Salt Lake City

CLYDE H. MESSINGER has returned from the Idaho branch to his managerial chair at the Educational exchange here.

Harold Pickering, Exploitation Manager for the local Famous Players-Lasky office, is now in the Southern Utah territory, and is expected back within a few days.

George L. Cloward, manager for Metro-Goldwyn in this city, has returned from a short trip into Wyoming.

W. G. Seib, in charge of the local Pathe exchange, is still in Colorado on his vacation and honeymoon. He is expected to return to the office next week.

Frank Harris, Pathe Western Division Manager, has been here this week, and has just left for Denver, Colorado, where he intends to meet local manager Seib for a conference on the forthcoming year's productions.

R. D. Boomer, selling out of the local Pathe exchange, has left for a trip into Southern Utah. Salesman Charlie Hamal is in the midst of a six weeks' trip in Idaho.

Ed. C. Mix, in charge of the local Associated Exhibitors exchange, has just returned from a trip through central Utah. Mix is leaving right away for a short trip through the Yellowstone Branch in Idaho.

R. S. Stackhouse, Manager of the Warner Brothers exchange here, is still in the Montana territory and is expected to return soon.

George E. Jensen, who covers the Montana territory for Warner Brothers, is still on an extended trip in that part of the country. L. W. Hyde has been in the Nevada and Northern Utah territory for the past two weeks, and will return to the local office soon.

W. F. Gordon, local Associated First National exchange manager, is leaving this week for the Montana branch.

Walter Lindlar is here from New York, conducting an exploitation campaign for Associated First National.

H. T. Nolan, formerly Associated First National District Manager, is here from Denver and is leaving this week for Montana points with manager Gordon. Nolan has resigned his position as District Manager, his resignation becoming effective October 1st. He intends to devote all of his time now to his theatre interests.

Vete Stewart has left for an extended trip into the State of Montana.

Samuel Henley, who manages the Universal exchange here, left this week to cover the Idaho territory. Henley held a sales meeting before leaving the office, to which Milton Cohn and Joe McElhenney were called in from their respective territories.

L. J. Schaifer, Universal District Manager, was here during the sales conference, and has left for the Universal office at Butte, Montana. He is enroute to the coast.

Mrs. Ione Barrett, who has charge of the poster department for Universal here, is spending her vacation in Wyoming and Colorado.

H. Bradley Fish, local manager for Fox, has left this week for a two weeks' trip into Montana.

A new salesman has been added to the Fox salesforce in the person of Dave McElhenney who was formerly with United Artists. McElhenney has been assigned to the Idaho branch in place of A. Singelow, who has resigned. J. A. Tidwell has left to cover Northern Utah.

R. A. Walsh, director of "The Wanderer" for Paramount.

W. H. Hughart is still making them sign in Montana.

Carl A. Stearn, manager of the local United Artists exchange, has left for a short trip into Southern Utah.

J. C. Dowd is covering the Nevada territory out of the United Artists exchange this week.

L. W. Weir, Division Manager for Producers Distributing Corporation, is here from Denver conferring with local manager C. F. Parr. Weir is said to be on his way to the coast.

Dave Schayer is expected back at the local Producers Distributing Corporation exchange after a two months' trek into Idaho.

James R. Keitz, manager for Greater Features in this city, has left to cover the Idaho territory.

Weed Dickenson, West Coast Exploitation Manager for the Film Booking Offices, arrived in this city last week.

W. K. Bloom, selling out of the local F. B. O. exchange, is in town from a trip through the Southern Utah territory. Joseph K. Soloman is still in Idaho.

George Mayne, owner of the Preferred Picture exchange in this city, has taken over the DeLuxe Feature exchange here, and will handle these pictures in connection with his own product. Mayne is leaving for the Idaho branch immediately. He expects to put a new man out into the Southern Utah territory soon.

The DeLuxe Feature exchange has been closed, and the owner, E. J. Drucker has returned to Denver.

E. E. Tucker, in charge of the open air motion picture and dancing resort here, reports that they have just closed a very successful season and will reopen next spring.

Among out of town visitors seen on the local Film Mart this week are: Frank Hoor, manager for the Gem Theatre at Bingham, Utah; Joe Krakis, owner of the Isis Theatre, Bingham, Utah; Jack Ryan of the Ryan circuit at Brigham City, Garland, and Tremonton, Utah; Steve Diehl, owner of the Star Theatre, Springville, Utah; C. A. Linsley, owner of the Opera House, Soldiers Summit, Utah; Frank White, operating the Real Art Theatre, American Fork, Utah; R. M. Chesler of the Princess Theatre, Bingham, Utah:

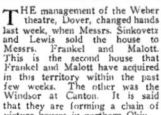

Cleveland

THE management of the Weber theatre, Dover, changed hands last week, when Messrs. Sinkovetz and Lewis sold the house to Messrs. Frankel and Malott. This is the second house that Frankel and Malott have acquired in this territory within the past few weeks. The other was the Windsor at Canton. It is said that they are forming a chain of picture houses in northern Ohio.

F. L. Olds has sold his Opera House in Middlefield and his Opera House in West Farmington to Garland Shetler. Shetler is associated with Old in the management of a Middlefield newspaper.

Frank Zambrini has acquired an active interest in the Progress Pictures Company, in association with J. S. Jossey. Zambrini now has an interest in five offices, namely Chicago, Indianapolis, Milwaukee, Cincinnati and Cleveland. Jossey will continue to remain in Cleveland as head of the Cleveland office.

H. A. Bandy, formerly First National division manager for the central states, and now representing First National in England, has been heard from. Bandy was in Ireland at the time he wrote to his Cleveland associates and says it's very fine over there.

James R. Grainger, Fox general sales manager, paid local exchange manager Ward Scott a short visit one day last week on his way to New York.

Jack Tierney, Pathe film and poster room inspector, was here to give the local Pathe exchange the once-over but failed to find anything that needed correction.

San Francisco

POLICE were stationed in the State Theatre in Oakland Sept. 4th to prevent a possible panic when a fire broke out on the roof of the structure. The audience, did not learn of the fire however, and the performance went on without interruption. The fire, starting in the ventilator system in the basement of the building, damaged the roof and one wall to the extent of approximately $1500. The blaze is supposed to have been caused by a faulty electric motor.

Homer Curran, owner of the Curran Theatre, returned recently from his summer abroad.

Leo Laughlin, popular house manager of Loew's Warfield theatre recently returned from his vacation in Catalina Island. All were pleased to see him back again.

The first week in September some robbers entered the Alexandria, one of the Pacific Coast's largest residential motion picture palaces, and after gagging the janitor early in the morning, attempted to open the safe, but to their embarrassment they could not do so and were forced to leave the theatre.

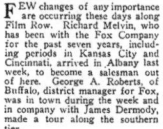

Albany

FEW changes of any importance are occurring these days along Film Row. Richard Melvin, who has been with the Fox Company for the past seven years, including periods in Kansas City and Cincinnati, arrived in Albany last week, to become a salesman out of here. George A. Roberts, out of Buffalo, district manager for Fox, was in town during the week and in company with James Dermody, made a tour along the southern tier.

Many exhibitors and others will be interested in knowing that N. I. Filkins, one of the veterans in the business, is now residing in Syracuse, and running a printing establishment that specializes in theatrical and motion picture work.

William Tweedy, who runs the Star theatre in Mechanicville, has been confined to his home for the past three weeks with a most severe attack of hay fever. Mr. Tweedy's theatre has about 500 seats, and while it has no particularly advantageous location, it has always been a good drawing house. The severe storm which swept over this section last Saturday night, however, gave Mr. Tweedy and his assistants more than a half hour of worry. Transmission lines went out of service on two occasions, leaving the house in darkness for fifteen minutes and then again for thirty-five minutes.

Charles Sesonske, of the Grand theatre in Johnstown, was among the exhibitors who attended the Film Board of Trade's outing. While Mr. Sesonske and Frank Empsall have been leasing the Grand, they have now bought the house and Mr. Sesonske will continue at its head.

Mr. and Mrs. Morris Silverman, of Schenectady, took a day off last week and attended the outing.

Mr. and Mrs. Louis Buettner have a novel way of spending their odd hours. They reside in Cohoes, where Mr. Buettner has his theatre. Late each afternoon they may be seen driving along some country road, with Mrs. Buettner scanning the fields with glasses on the lookout for woodchucks. The other Sunday, Mr. Buettner shot not less than thirty-five. The Buettners have been away on an automobile trip, circling through New England for ten days with not a day of rain.

Claude Wade, of North Creek, was probably the most interested exhibitor in all New York state in the outcome of the recent fight in New York, when Slattery of Buffalo dropped under the blows of his opponent in the eleventh round. Slattery did his training a few miles from North Creek and a warm friendship developed between Wade and Slattery.

B. J. Straus, of the Palace in Saratoga, announces that he has dropped admission prices to 25 cents, and that the program is changed four times during the week. During the month of August, the Saratoga houses boost their prices and at the same time show some of the biggest pictures that can be secured. But from September on, the months bring only the ordinary run of business, with the exhibitors looking forward to another summer.

Last week was a banner one for Mr. and Mrs. Harry Hellman, of the Royal theatre in Albany, for not only was their daughter home for a few days, but their gifted son-in-law, Jack Little, broadcast his latest songs, including "Normandy" from WGY in Schenectady and WHAZ in Troy. Mr. and Mrs. Hellman rigged up the radio in the theatre and gave their patrons the selections as they came through the air.

Ben Davis, who is now living at the Hotel Ten Eyck in Albany, and who was connected for some years with the Schines in Gloversville, is now in hopes of being able to purchase a motion picture theatre for himself.

William Dillon, of Ithaca, president of the New York State M. P. T. O., has invested $150,000 in Florida real estate in the vicinity of West Palm Beach, according to word that has reached Film Row.

Ben Apple, who recently disposed of the King theatre in Troy, has started in selling real estate in Florida, according to postcards that are now reaching here. The last one came from Palm Beach. On it, Mr. Apple said that he had met Charles Walder, former manager of the Fox exchange in Albany, on the second day after his arrival.

George Trembly is making a good record these days in his new position as manager of the reopened American theatre in Troy. It must be admitted that Mr. Trembly is on the job for he appears each morning about nine o'clock and remains until 11:30 at night.

Illustrated songs on Monday and Tuesday nights are being used by Jacob Rosenthal, of the Rose theatre in Troy, as a means of bolstering up business. Mr. Rosenthal recently played the part of host to 200 or more boys and girls who had been declared winners in the inter-park contests in baseball, track, swimming, basketball and other events.

There was a great baseball game on Sunday between employees of the Troy theatre and a team made up from those who work at the Mark Strand in Albany. The game was a part of an outing held on the Williams farm. Ben Stern did the twirling for the Troy crowd, with Joe Wall behind the bat. At the end of the game, no one seemed to know exactly what the score was.

The Griswold, in Troy, managed by Jake Golden, a former newspaper man, has been drawing big crowds each Monday night with Charleston dance contests along with the pictures.

Mr. and Mrs. Harry McNamara of Valatie, were along Film Row during the week, with Mrs. McNamara doing the booking. Business was reported as being good.

Children's Saturday morning movies will be held this fall and winter at the Strand in Schenectady and the Avon in Utica, through arrangements just completed last week. Jason Joy, of the Hays organization, was in town two or three weeks ago arranging matters.

Allan Hawley, former husband of Wanda Hawley, the actress, and a resident of Troy, died Saturday at the summer home of his mother near here, after a long illness. He was thirty years of age. He was identified with the motion picture interests in Hollywood for ten years or so, but several months ago his health failed and he returned to the home of his mother.

Harry Berinstein, of Elmira, was in town last week attending the unveiling of a monument erected to the memory of his father and mother. Mr. Berinstein remained over for two or three days as the guest of his brother, Julius, who has houses in Troy, Albany and Schenectady.

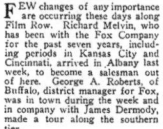

Atlanta

THE newly completed Charlotte Theatre opened on Labor Day in Charlotte, N. C., to excellent business and many congratulations from the many friends of the management.

The theatre is operated by the Sunset Amusement Company, and will be under the management of Harry K. Lucas, well-known in southern film circles. It is a motion picture house entirely, and has a seating capacity of about 750.

Due to the long drouth under which practically the entire South has suffered for the last four months, which has caused farmers and many industries to experience serious losses, the Georgia Railway and Power Company of Atlanta recently asked all theatres to cooperate with them in an effort to so conserve on light that a further cut in power consumption will not become necessary.

Fred Martin, Liberty salesman who was taken ill several months ago in Chattanooga and has only recently been moved to an Atlanta hospital, is still in quite a serious condition after having survived several operations.

W. M. Minder, F. B. O. representative in Alabama and Tennessee, returned to the city this week from Birmingham.

Henry Hury of Birmingham. Ala., reopened the Frolic Theater (colored house) there last week after having closed for a short time to redecorate the house.

Bill Specht, Tennessee representative for Liberty Film Distributing Corporation, was in the city last week leaving Tuesday to resume his work in his territory. "Shag" Jordan, popular Georgia salesman for Universal, came in town for the week-end, leaving again Tuesday morning.

Carl Bausch, recently connected with the Columbus theatres, is now with F. B. O. He will work out of the local office as salesman, although his territory has not yet been assigned. Mr. Bausch will take up his new duties next week.

J. R. McTheran, secretary-treasurer and manager of the Theater Supply and Equipment Company, returned this week from Florida, where he attended the opening of the new Capitol Airdome Theater in St. Petersburg last week. The house is reported to have cost $35,000, and John Gillooley is manager of the new theatre.

C. B. Ellis, branch manager of the Jacksonville F. B. O. office, was in the city last week for a few days on business. He returned to Jacksonville the latter part of the week.

Frank Rogers, Liberty's Florida representative, was in town for a few days during the week, returning to his territory with plans for an intensive sales campaign for the Fall.

O. K. Bourgeois, local manager for Associated Exhibitors, has returned to Atlanta after having spent a week in Florida on business.

H. B. Vinson, resident manager of Universal's four theatres in Orlando, Fla., the largest of which is the Beacham Theatre, was in Atlanta for several days last week transacting business and visiting part of the week.

Ira P. Stone, branch manager of Vitagraph-Warner Exchange, left Monday night for Birmingham and Bessemer, Ala. He is expected to return to the city the end of the week.

New York and New Jersey

PRESIDENT JOSEPH M. SEIDER'S occasional few hours absence from his office during the last week or so is explained by the fact that he is placing his two boys, Daniel and Henry, aged eleven and eight years, respectively in the Kohut School for Boys at Harrison, N. J. Daniel, who has been sick of fate, has entirely recovered and both boys will leave for school this week Wednesday, accompanied by their father. Any one who has had the experience of sending children off to school will appreciate Joe's efforts in getting together the two outfits. Mr. Seider will place his Brooklyn home on the market and in the future will take up his residence at the Hotel Robert Treat in Newark.

Charles Hildinger and William Keegan of the Hildinger Circuit of New Jersey are back in their Trenton homes after spending the summer in Belmar, N. J.

Leon Rosenblatt has reopened his Lyceum theatre at Bayonne, N. J. This house has been closed during the summer months.

The next meeting of the M. P. T. O. of New Jersey will be held at Asbury Park on September the 24th where the attending members will be the guests of Messrs. Hildinger, Keegan and Newberry.

E. Thorton Kelly, who operates the Grantley theatre at Palisades, N. J., and who has recently been elected an assistant director of the M. P. T. O. of N. J., has returned from a trip through the west. Mr. Kelly will attend the meeting this week at Asbury Park.

Joseph Seider has received a post card from A. A. Adams, who is vacationing in Greece, accompanied by Mrs. Adams. Joe says that the post mark of the town "Greek" to him. Mr. Adams is the proprietor of the Newark Theatre, Newark, N. J.

J. B. Fox who operates a string of theatres over in Jersey has recently recovered from a bad attack of hay fever.

Several more September openings are reported for local theatres. Keeney's Bedford and Bay Ridge houses are open again and will continue their usual policy of vaudeville and feature pictures. The Plaza theatre located at South Jamaica and under the management of Baker and Craft opened about ten days ago. The Plaza is a brand new 600 seat house.

Somer's Highway theatre, Brooklyn, has had its name changed to just 'Highway' and the house had its reopening on the 14th of September.

Joe Finger has put his American theatre, Fort Hamilton Ave., Brooklyn, on full time. The American has been running three days a week.

There are also several closings in order about town. The Victoria on St. John's Place, Brooklyn has definitely closed its doors on the expiration of the lease. A banking company is the owner of this property and they will convert the building to another use. The Auditorium at Ocean Grove, N. J. has closed its doors after a prosperous summer season and will not open again until next year. It is reported that the management will then adopt a policy of showing a pre-release of super-specials.

George H. Engelage has closed the Bijou theatre at Rockaway Point until next season and has already started on his usual winter pilgrimage to Florida.

Albert Delia, formerly connected with the Electra theatre on Third Ave., in the Bay Ridge section of Brooklyn, had bought the Park theatre at 941 East 180th street, New York City and will close it for a short time in order to effect improvements and to renovate the entire house.

The residents of Gerritsen Beach will have motion picture entertainment for four days a week at the Gerritsen Club. This is a Community project.

The New Classique theatre at Marcy Ave. and Fulton St., Brooklyn and owned by John Cappadona had a little scare the other day when a fire started in the projection room. A complete show was burned up.

William "Bill" Hermann, Manager of Universal's "Big U" has forsaken North Asbury for his winter quarters in New York. Bill will undoubtedly be missed by the remaining travelers on the Jersey Central, with whom he had been commuting—or will he be missed? They say that Bill's bridge game is pretty good.

Charles Stombaugh, manager of the Pathe Newark branch has been vacationing with Mrs. Stombaugh and friends up in the Adirondacks.

Moe Saunders, booker for the New York Fox Exchange, is the proud father of a brand new baby boy. Moe, with the rest of the Fox Sales staff held a big party at the old Fox exchange on 45th street and during the evening Moe was presented with a handsome cover for the kids go-cart.

Harry Buxbaum, popular manager of the local Fox Exchange and Charlie Schwartz, prominent Brooklyn exhibitor, are becoming keen competitors for honors at golf, which by the way has come to be recognized as the standard form of relaxation for the harried captains of our industry. Mr. Schwartz was recently in receipt of a letter signed "Bronco," presumably from Mr. Buxbaum's young son and to the effect that his father had stated that Mr. Schwartz's game wasn't any good. However, the report is that Mr. Schwartz has the edge.

The sales staff at the Fox exchange are still preparing their appetites for that "Million Dollar" dinner which has expanded to a "Two Million" affair. Maybe they will make it a three million one before they get through.

E. Solkin who operates the Eagle theatre at 103d Street and 3rd Ave., New York City has bought the building next door to the Eagle and will increase the seating capacity from 600 to 2000. The theatre will also be completely renovated and extensive improvements made throughout.

Walter Reade, of the Walter Read Enterprises of New York and New Jersey has returned from his summer residence at Deal, N. J.

Two more local theatres are opening this week. The Arcadia at 59th St. and 3d Ave., will start on Wednesday, the 24th and the Inwood located in the Dyckman Heights section will have its opening on Friday, the 26th.

Denver

FRANN HARRIS, new Western District manager for Pathe, spent Wednesday and Thursday of last week in Denver visiting Mr. C. M. Van Horn, manager of the local branch of Pathe Exchange, Inc. Mr. Harris left Thursday evening for New York City to attend a conference which will be held here September 24th for all district managers of Pathe.

The State Theatre, Denver's most gorgeous motion picture theatre was officially opened Friday night, September 18th, with the brilliance pomp and ceremony which usually accompanies an occasion of this kind. The management of the theatre carried out all statements in regard to giving Denver a grand and glorious opening of one of the most beautiful and high-class theatres in the West. The remodeling of the theatre was under the personal direction of Harold Horne who has been directing a hundred workmen for the past two weeks. The result has been the change of an ordinary second-run ten cent theatre into an extremely elaborate and high-class amusement house. Some of the new features which greeted the first-night audience was the large tapestries on the walls and an ascending organ console. The opening night was strictly an invitation affair, some of the leading citizens and officials of Denver and the State of Colorado being among those present.

W. G. Seib, manager of Pathe Exchange, Inc., of Salt Lake City, and his bride, formerly Mrs. Doris Tinge, motored to Denver last week for a honeymoon vacation. They were married at Salt Lake September 2d. Mrs. Seib was formerly secretary of her husband in his office at Salt Lake. Mr. Seib, or better known as Bill in and about these parts, was formerly employed in the old Denver office of Pathe on Walton Street during the days of Ward Scott. The bridal party was accompanied to Denver by Mrs. Larry Barrett, a sister of the bride.

Messrs. Brown and Waterson spent last week in Denver purchasing equipment for a new 350 seat house in Rapid City, South Dakota. The change of the new theatre will take place about November 1st, and from all indications it will be high-class and up-to-date in every sense of the word. Mr. Brown is an old theatre owner and manager in South Dakota, having just recently operated the Colonial Theatre at Aberdeen, South Dakota.

Ben Fish, special representative for Pathe, is back in Denver for a few days after spending two weeks in New Mexico and Southern Colorado territory.

Albert Haehnel, decorator from Salt Lake City, plunged thirty feet from a scaffold in the Avalon Theatre at Grand Junction, Colorado, landing on the seats. He died a few moments after the fall. The Avalon Theatre is the largest theatre in Grand Junction, containing some 1,500 seats. It is managed by Walter Walker.

Arthur L. Janisch, who for the past year has been associated with the local branch of Universal, as publicity manager, has resigned. He has accepted a position as publicity manager for First National office in Portland, Oregon. Mr. Charles Lounsbury, formerly on the editorial staff of the Denver Post, has succeeded Mr. Janisch as publicity manager of the local Universal office.

F. M. Drexel, owner and manager of the Crawford Theatre, Crawford, Colorado, was a visitor in film row last week. Mr. Drexel says this is his first visit in Denver for over a year. He states that the honey business and the picture business is in first class condition. Mr. Drexel is known as a honey man in Crawford as well as a movie man.

C. Leslie Barnard, former dramatic editor of the Denver Post, is now associated with the management of the new State Theatre in Denver, in charge of the publicity department. Mr. Barnard has been with the Denver Post a comparatively short period, having succeeded Frederick Babcock a few months ago. Mr. Barnard, because of his thorough and interesting criticisms which appeared on the dramatic page of the Denver Post was soon recognized as one of the leading critics in the West.

All theatre managers of the Black Hills Amusement Company held a business meeting in Sheridan, Wyoming, Friday, September 18th.

Charles R. Gilmour, manager of Warner Brothers, made a hurry trip to Pueblo, Colorado Springs and Albuquerque, New Mexico, last week with very good results.

Kansas City

THE northeast corner of Eighteenth and Wyandotte streets, "big corner" of Kansas City's movie row, was bought last week for $45,000 by Dr. Nathan Zoglin from Milton Tootle of St. Joseph, Mo. The building will be remodeled into a modern two-story affair, the present tennants, the Midwest Film Distributors, Inc., having already arranged for space in the new building.

The Metro-Goldwyn trackless train, which passed through Kansas City the other day, was in a ditch near Emporia, Kas., having ran off the concrete road, according to reports reaching Kansas City. No one was injured, however.

The management of the Alamo theatre, Kansas City suburban house, by turning the theatre over to the American Legion Tuesday night, the proceeds going to disabled veterans, received liberal publicity in Kansas City newspapers.

Last Tuesday was an eventful day in Chillicothe, Mo. It marked the first of a series of trade showings in smaller towns by Universal. More than 150 exhibitors attended and newspapers "splattered" their front pages with the event. Among those in attendance were: George H. Clarkson, Eversonville, Mo.; C. A. Sunk,

Ravenwood, Mo.; F. C. Bingham, Galt, Mo.; Mrs. Minnie Newton, Missouri City, Mo.; T. R. Sullivan, Miami, Mo.; J. W. Baird, Pattonsborg, Mo.; Mrs. Fay Barr, Hale, Mo.; Mr. and Mrs. Robert Brisco, Hale, Mo.; Mr. and Mrs. G. W. Summers, Unionville, Mo.; Mr. and Mrs. R. R. Gladdish, Higginsville, Mo.; J. B. Carter and J. B. Moore, Carter, Mo.; Mr. and Mrs. W. F. Casper, Laredo, Mo.; Mrs. W. P. Wood, Laredo, Mo; E. W. McClelland, Gilmon, Mo.; F. W. Silverman, Princeton, Mo.; Sam Minnich, Macgiline, Mo.; K. H. Waldin, Hardin, Mo.; Dr. C. D. Weakley, Hardin, Mo.; H. T. Chelton, Norborne, Mo.; Marvin Beery, Hardin, Mo.; Mr. and Mrs. C. Logan, Cainsville, Mo.; H. H. Ingan, Ludlow, Mo.; Mr. and Mrs. W. I. Pope, Mendan, Mo.; E. A. Dickerson, Bogard, Mo.; Hugo Martin, Meadeville, Mo.; Mr. and Mrs. L. W. Winfield, Chillicothe, Mo.; I. J. Aye, Wheeling, Mo.; Mrs. Nancy Dowell, Gilham City, Mo.; Edwin L. Dwyer, Kansas City, Mo.

There was no mistake about increased business with cool weather along Kansas City's movie row last week. W. F. Senning, Educational branch manager, returned from a trip to Leavenworth, Kas. He then announced that the Kan-

sas City office would undergo a complete remodeling.

H. F. Butler joined the Kansas City - Vitagraph-Warner sales force, while J. J. Gilmore, Fox exploiteer from the home office, had a busy week in the territory.

Russell Borg, Educational booker, returned from a vacation just in time to find work at its thickest.

Sherman S. Krelberg, general manager of Chadwick Pictures Corporation, was a Kansas City business visitor.

J. J. McCarthy, former First National salesman, again has joined the sales force of that company in Kansas City. C. A. Schultz and C. W. Allen, manager and assistant manager, respectively, of the P. D. C. branch, made a hurried business trip to Omaha.

Harry Taylor, Universal branch manager, blocked sidewalk traffic last week displaying his new Elgin watch which he won in the Universal managers sales contest.

Fred Young, F. B. O., Des Moines, Iowa, manager, was a Kansas City visitor. Lou Nathanson joined the Universal sales force as special representative, while Bert Edwards, formerly with First National, now is with Associated Exhibitors.

Among the out-of-town exhibitors in the Kansas City market last week were: D. L. Zimmerman, Leland theatre, Troy, Kas.; C. M. Pattee, Pattee theatre, Lawrence, Kas.; Ben Levy, Hippidrome, Joplin, Mo.; Edward Frazier, Strand, Pittsburg, Kas.; Walter Wallace, Orpheum, Leavenworth, Kas.

The Gayety theatre of Richmond, Mo., which has been closed, has been re-opened by E. J. Lime and Guy Cooper of Kansas City, while C. A. "Bones" Smith, former secretary of the M. P. T. O., Kansas-Missouri, has been named as manager of the Electric theatre, first run house of Kansas City, Kas. He formerly was manager of the Tenth Street theatre, Kansas City, Kas.

Not until after he had been honeymooning in Kansas City for two weeks was it discovered that J. B. Tackett of the Tackett and Southtown theatres, Coffeyville, Kas. had taken a bride unto himself. Then it "was" a honeymoon.

The Royal theatre, down town first run house of Kansas City, owned by Paramount, has changed its opening policy from Sunday to Saturday. The Pantages and Liberty theatres, other first run houses, already have adopted that policy.

Baltimore

ED HEIBER has resigned as Baltimore representative for Universal Film Corporation and has become associated with Warner Brothers, Inc., to cover the Virginia territory.

So popular has the Charleston contest proved at the Capitol Theatre, operated by the Associated Theatre Company of which J. Louis Rome is general manager, that a similar series of contests has begun at the Apollo, also controlled by the company. At each playhouse the series cover a period of five weeks with three of the most popular couples in the finals. They are held on Monday nights at the Capitol and on Wednesday nights at the Apollo.

Starting with the week beginning Monday, September 21, the Capitol Theatre, controlled by the Associated Theatres Company, began to distribute window cards again. About 200 were given out during that week.

The Garden Roof, located over the Garden Theatre and operated by Thomas J. Tobin for the Whitehurst Combined Theatrical Interests, reopened to the public on Saturday night, September 12. While it was closed during the summer, extensive redecorating was done and a special dias like a sea shell was made for the orchestra to sit in.

About 350 patrons had to leave the New Preston Theatre, 1108 East Preston street, one night recently when C. Robert Moore, the operator discovered a small blaze

in a reel of film in the projection room.

The audience was warned by Gustav Beck, housemanager of the theatre and while they were leaving in an orderly manner Miss Bessie Westguard, the pianist, kept on with her music.

An alarm was turned in and the fire was soon extinguished with very little damage resulting. This house is controlled by Arthur B. Price.

Baltimore's oldest film exchange will be vacated by an order from Charles H. Osborne, head of the Bureau of Buildings, which was issued after a complaint had been made by Walter K. Hough, president of the Fire Board.

This exchange is located on the second floor of the building at 412 East Baltimore street, in the downtown section. It is the Federated and operated by Peter Oletzky, who also operates the Comedy Theatre on the first floor of the same building and the Waverly Theatre, 3211 Greenmount avenue.

According to Mr. Hough, in his report to the Board of Zoning Appeals, one of the "most serious fire menaces of the city" was constituted by the exchange.

The offices of Harry Van Hoven advertising manager of the Whitehurst Combined Theatrical Interests, on the third floor of the Century Theatre Building, have been completed almost and the carpenters will soon have finished their work. Mr. Van Hoven now

has a reception room where his secretary does her work and receives callers and then there is another office where Mr. Van Hoven can conduct his own work and receive visitors quietly.

Improvements to cost about $10,000 are to be made on the Brodie Theatre, 1118 Light street, owned by the Riviera Amusement Company. The renovations will include an entire new front with interior improvements. The alterations are being made from plans by A. Lowther Forrest, architect. The work is being done by the Mervis Construction Company. This theatre has a seating capacity of 700 and was built in 1910. It is located in a South Baltimore

neighborhood section.

A steel and concrete moving picture theatre measuring 138 by 135 feet is being constructed by J. A. Hincher at Richwood, W. Va., with a seating capacity of 615 persons. Plans were drawn by Levi J. Dean, architect. Huntington, W. Va.

Several locations are being considered now in Huntington, W. Va., on which to build a playhouse by the United Theatre Enterprises of which A. B. Hymen, is president, it is said. The plans call for a theatre with a seating capacity of 3,000 persons, it is understood and it is claimed that Keith vaudeville will constitute the main part of the program.

Des Moines

WILLIAM YOUNGCLUAS has bought the Amuzu Theatre at Scranton. He is also owner of the Majestic Theatre at Jefferson and will operate both theatres. G. J. Connors has bought the Alamo at New London. Mr. Johnson of Yankttown, S. D. has bought the Grand Theatre at Estherville. He bought the house from F. H. Graff.

The theatre at Red Oak, Iowa, is on the market. Mr. H. Simons, owner of the Red Oak theatres, is planning to move to Florida and wants to sell out.

Jack Nixon who came to Iowa following the boycott of Connecticut by the film men was formerly associated with Metro-Goldwyn at New Haven, Conn. He is now covering southern Iowa in the territory formerly covered by Harry Herman, serving Metro-Goldwyn. He ran into a goodly chunk of Iowa mud last week, which was a bad shock after the paving about New Haven. He spent eleven and a half hours making about forty miles and finally broke a wheel two and a half miles out of Libertyville. After his car was hauled back to town he made the rest of the week's run on the train. He plans to go back after the car this week. But he has nothing pretty to say about Iowa mud.

B. A. Mitchell, of Lynnville, may not open his theatre this fall,

he states the business last year was not satisfactory. His house, the Isis, has been closed all summer while he was on the road, booking a merry-go-round at the state fairs, etc.

Park Agnew, booker for Metro-Goldwyn, has bought a theatre. He has purchased the theatre at Carlyle, Iowa, and will name it the Metro. Metro-Goldwyn pictures will be featured. On Wednesdays and Saturdays, Mr. Agnew will have charge of the picture shows of the theatre and will also continue his duties as booker.

W. H. Gilbert, who was owner of the Princess Theatre at Stewart, Iowa, died on September 9 very suddenly after an attack of heart trouble. Mr. Gilbert was located at Stewart for the past year. Mrs. Gilbert will operate the theatre for the present.

B. A. Voltsey, owner of the Unique Theatre at Bussey, has added another theatre to his string. He is opening up a house at Tracy but has not yet given the new theatre a name.

Mr. Boeke, banker of Hubbard, Iowa and also owner of the Opera House there has sold the theatre. Mr. E. O'Hara, owner of the Orpheum at Fairfield, has also sold. Mr. Pederson who had the Princess Theatre at West Union has sold his house to Pace and Bauma of Pocohontas. Mrs.

Coinder has sold the Victory Theatre at Fairfield. Mr. Hoffman is the new owner.

Joe Cowan, formerly salesman for Universal, is now one of the star salesmen of the Premier office. He is covering northeastern Iowa.

C. R. Coons, who has built a new theatre at Seymour, opened the house last week. The theatre is very good looking, cost between six and seven thousand and will seat 275. The theatre has been named the Lyric.

Joe Jacobson, salesman for Pathe, is now pretty well recovered from his bad spill two weeks ago.

R. S. Ballentyne, manager for Pathe, and E. L. Meyers, associate manager, made a trip to Chicago for the sales conference.

Callers in Movie Row were Mr. and Mrs. Byron Watson of Knoxville and R. C. Metzger of the Strand at Creston.

The Strand Theatre at Des Moines, of which Jess Day is manager for the A. H. Blank Enterprises, has put in a staff of seven boy ushers. Girls have always been ushers for the Strand before this. Hubert Schrodt is head usher for the Strand. The new uniforms have blue trousers with a gold stripe, maroon vests and a royal blue jacket.

The girl ushers at the Capitol have also come out in new uni-

forms, much like those of the boy ushers at the Des Moines Theatre. They have red skirts and jackets, a black vest and red caps.

MOTION PICTURE NEWS wishes to make the following correction in regard to Jack Nixon's transfer and the following is taken from Mr. Nixon's letter: "In your issue of September 19th, you have under the Des Moines Iowa page, information regarding Jack Nixon's transfer as follows: 'Mr. Jack Nixon who was transferred to Des Moines from the office at New Haven, Conn. is serving Pathe on the sales staff. He takes the place vacated by Mr. Herrmann who is now managing the Orpheum Theatre at Clinton for A. H. Blank Enterprises.'

"This error is I'm not with Pathe, but with Metro-Goldwyn-Mayer Distributing Corporation. Since there is a little difference selling comedies and Metro-Goldwyn Quality '52' I will appreciate you making the necessary change in your next issue, because when I walk into an exhibitor, he will try to buy comedies instead of Metro-Goldwyn pictures."

"Mr. Hermann is not managing the theatre for A. H. Blank Enterprises but is managing the Orpheum Theatre in Clinton, Iowa, for Frank Amusement Co."

Cincinnati

LAW'S Hollywood theatre, Portsmouth, O., the latest addition to the city's theatres, formally opened its doors to the public on September 6th. The policy is pictures and vaudeville.

Manny Naegel, assistant city salesman for Famous Players, made his first trip into the surrounding territory last week.

Ned Depinet, sales manager for Universal, paid a visit to the local exchange, taking up matters of sales importance with Fred Strief, branch manager.

Danny McNutt, manager for Libsons' State theatre in Dayton, O., is making good at his job and is very happy in his surroundings. The writer paid him a visit last week and found Danny hustling every moment of the day. This is an old trait with Danny for we worked together at the Capitol, Cincinnati, in the Asher regime.

The Universal theatre party at the Grand theatre, Ironton, O., on September 16, turned out to be a huge success. Many prominent exhibitors from Ohio, Kentucky and West Virginia attended, among them: George Laws and wife of the Hollywood, Portsmouth, O.; Chas. Triebel and daughter of the Pastime theatre, Maysville, Ky.; Wm. Maddox and wife O. H., Ripley, O., and

Ed. Burns of the O. H., Bainbridge, O. L. J. Frecka, manager of the Grand, entertained his guests in royal style and everyone was much pleased with the party.

J. M. McCoy of the Lamox theatre, Wilmington, O., spent several days around the various exchanges.

J. F. Robertson of the Dreamland theatre, Blanchester, O., was seen around film row last week booking pictures for the near future.

Ben. C. Almond, of the Garden theatre, Westerville, O. Princess theatre, Plain City, O., and Kingdome theatre, Grove City, O., paid a hurried visit to Cincinnati last week booking pictures and purchasing supplies for his chain of houses.

C. M. DeWeese, owner and manager of the Majestic theatre, Sidney, O., was a visitor to film row last week.

W. E. Parks, manager of the Grand theatre, Lancaster, Ky., spent a few days in the city with the various film managers.

A. W. Jordan of the Jenkins theatre, Jenkins, Ky., was another exhibitor at film row last week.

Frances Brown, Myrtle Freeman and Marie Dorsel of the local Paramount exchange office force, will leave the company this

week. The first two to get married and the last named to open a Modiste Shoppe. Wonder which is entering the right business.

I. Lisbon announces that the Strand theatre, Cincinnati, will enter upon a new policy on Sunday, September 27. An orchestra is to be installed in the theatre under the direction of Theo. Hahn, Jr., general musical director for the Libson houses, with Harry Wiltsey conductor of the Lyric theatre orchestra wielding the baton. An advance in prices will also be effected.

Chester Leowe, assistant district manager for Producers Distributing Corporation, was in the city last week making arrangements for a school for film salesmen. He will come back soon to start the school on its merry way.

L. O. Davis of the Virginia Amusement Co., Hazard, Ky., was in the city last week and it is said that he was splendidly entertained by Ralph Kinsler of F. B. O. and Levitt Bugie of Dwyer Brothers.

Andy Hettesheimer, genial manager of the Orpheum theatre, made his first appearance at the exchanges in six months. He has been very ill during this time but his health is much improved and

his complete recovery is being looked forward to with a great deal of pleasure by all film men and the members of the Stage and Screen Scribes of which Andy is an active member.

Chas. Gross of the Columbia theatre, Dayton, O., drove down the other day and booked several pictures while here.

Colvin Brown, one of the heads of the distribution department of F. B. O., spent several days with Ed. Booth, local manager.

A. M. Potts, owner of the Eastland theatre, Maysville, Ky., is building a new theatre in his city.

J. Barbour Russell of the Washington theatre, Maysville, Ky., was in the city last week booking several large features for his house.

Ralph Kinsler of F. B. O., has collected the insurance on his broken finger which he sustained while cranking Bugie's Ford. The bandages are all off and Ralph is now looking for another Ford to crank.

Homer Guy of the Apollo theatre, Dayton, was in the city last week purchasing new equipment.

Bill Kunzman, representative for the National Carbon Co., and motion picture engineer, was in the city last week visiting his old friends in the film industry.

Milwaukee

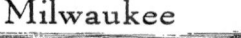

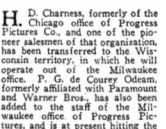

H. D. Charness, formerly of the Chicago office of Progress Pictures Co., and one of the pioneer salesmen of that organization, has been transferred to the Wisconsin territory, in which he will operate out of the Milwaukee office. P. G. de Courey Odeam, formerly affiliated with Paramount and Warner Bros., has also been added to the staff of the Milwaukee office of Progress Pictures, and is at present hitting the high spots in the state.

Art Deasuarmeaux, manager of the Strand Theatre at Madison, has been dubbed "The Speed Boy" by the Milwaukee exchange men who have visited him in recent weeks. Art has a mania for screening pictures at top speed, and several of the boys who individually dropped in on him recently, have come back with tales of seeing reel after reel raced through on his special projection machine. Art does everything that way,—fast but thoroughly,—and the excellent box record of his house gives testimony of the effectiveness of his methods.

Eddie Weisfeldt, production manager of Saxe's Wisconsin Theatre, is sporting a brand new Wills St. Clair coupe. Eddie is one of the hardest working men affiliated with Milwaukee picture houses, and everyone wishes him much pleasant recreation in his "wonder car."

Pat Dowling, press agent for the Christy Film Co., spent the past week and at the Milwaukee Educational exchange, getting the stage all set for properly exploiting his company's product.

Henry Goldman, manager of the Colonial Theatre at Green Bay, has announced that his remodelled house will be opened as soon as the new chairs have been received and installed. Original plans called for having the theatre in operation again by now, but delays in obtaining the seats have postponed the re-opening dates. Film men who have seen the interior of the house since the contractors finished their part of the job, declare that it is one of the finest theatres in that section.

Leon Goetz of Goetz Bros., operators of a chain of picture houses in various Wisconsin cities, visited with Milwaukee distributors during the past week. He reports business as being good at this time in all the Goetz houses.

Frank Fisher of the Fisher Theatre Co., of Madison and Fond du Lac, was another prominent operator, who honored the Badger metropolis with his presence during the past week. He was accompanied by Sam Miller, who buys the films for the Fisher theatres. Both men reported optimism.

J. G. Frackman, manager of the Milwaukee office of Progress Pictures Co., has just returned from Chicago.

Ernst Hoefer, operating the Gem and Rex Theatres at Sheboygan, took time out for a Milwaukee stop-over en route to New York to bring his family back from a vacation in the family motor.

Ed Prinzer of the Fond du Lac

Theatres Co., also stopped here while on his way back to his headquarters after a visit to Chicago. Like the other visiting exhibitors of the week, Ed has great hopes for the coming season.

Heinz Roemheld's Clown Week took its place this week as the first big stage presentation at the Alhambra Theatre since its acquisition by Universal. Heinz first became a drawing card in Milwaukee while concert master at the Wisconsin Theatre. After a summer in the East he has been brought back as director of presentations at the Alhambra. His first big offering is being well received.

Max Stahl, manager of the Milwaukee office of Educational, has just returned from a two weeks' trip through the northern Wisconsin territory, where he found business good practically without exception.

Fred Martin, formerly covering Northern Wisconsin for Fox, has resigned to join the Chicago force of United Artists. His friends in the territory regret his leaving the state.

The feminine element among Wisconsin exhibitors was represented in Milwaukee's film row this week by Mrs. Kelly, manager of the Badger Theatre at Reedsburg who paid a business visit to the city.

Gerald T. Gallagher, formerly manager of Universal's Cameo Theatre at Pittsburgh, Pa., has been definitely assigned as exploitation expert for the Milwaukee branch of the Fox Film Corporation. The Milwaukee branch has been established for only a few weeks, prior to which the local office was a sub-station of the Chicago branch. The advent of a permanent exploitation expert at the Milwaukee office is heralded by Manager John Lorentz as one of the many features that will be offered here for the convenience and profit of Wisconsin exhibitors.

Owen McKivett, operator of the Bijou Theatre at Racine, Wis., paid one of his rather frequent visits to the Milwaukee exchanges last week. McKivett is a frequent but ever welcome figure on the local "Rialto."

Ed Harris, who runs the Princess and Columbia Theatres at Peoria, Ill. stopped off to visit his old friend J. G. Frackman, manager of the Milwaukee office of Progress Pictures Co., on his return trip to Peoria from a vacation spent in Northern Wisconsin with his son. They were

Lee Marcus, general sales manager for F. B. O., spent Friday of last week at the Milwaukee office conferring with local officials. He was accompanied by M. J. Weisfeldt, district manager, who remained in the city and on Saturday conducted a sales conference attended by the following members of the local F. B. O. staff: Sam Abrams, manager; Art Roberts, assistant manager; Dick Scheinbaum, Carl Ebert and Art Schmitz. An elaborate program for further boosting F. B. O. interests in the Milwaukee and Wisconsin territory.

Letters have been received by several local film men during the past week from Walter Hickey, formerly traveling the Wisconsin territory for Warner Bros. Walt is now selling real estate in Florida and judging by the letters, is knocking 'em dead. Figures used in the telling about his recent biggest deals looked like telephone numbers.

Gerald T. Gallagher, exploitation expert for the Milwaukee branch of the Fox Film Corporation, is receiving a warm welcome from exhibitors throughout Wisconsin during his initial trip through the state.

Lou Holz, formerly manager of the Lorraine Theatre, Milwaukee, has tendered his resignation and plans to indulge in a several weeks' trip through the Northland. Although he has made no definite plans for the future, he is bound to get back into the picture business, which has engrossed his attention for many years past and in which he established a reputation as one of the most resourceful managers of neighborhood theatres in this section. His specialty for the past ten years has been the rejuvenation of business in houses which no one else could operate successfully.

Rapid progress is being made in the remodeling of the Idle Hour Theatre in Milwaukee, and Max Krofta, manager, has announced that it is soon to be reopened to the public. An entirely new front is being constructed and extensive changes are being made on the interior.

New pep was instilled into the Milwaukee office of Progress Pictures Co., by the announcement that Frank Zambreno, president of the organization, had taken over the Progress Pictures exchanges of Cleveland and Cincinnati, formerly operated independently of the organization by the same name in Chicago, Milwaukee and Indianapolis. The merger makes Progress Pictures one of the largest state rights organizations in the country.

John Herzinger, prominent exhibitor of Neenah and Menasha, Wis., has set out for the hunting regions in the northern part of the state. He is an inveterate sportsman and will no doubt strike terror into the wild life of Northern Wisconsin.

Charlie Lundgren, manager of the Milwaukee branch of the Producers Distributing Corporation, has returned from Chicago, where he attended the district meeting of P. D. C. managers held at the Congress Hotel. He is highly enthusiastic about the plans for the coming season.

Eddie Prinzer of the Fond du Lac Theatres Co., of Fond du Lac, Wis., was among the prominent exhibitors who made the rounds of the Milwaukee exchanges during the past week.

Dan Roche, exploitation agent for the Producers Distributing Corporation, working out of the Chicago offices, is at present making a trip through the state of Wisconsin.

Frank Cook, operator of the Bijou Theatre at Appleton, Wis.,

spent several days in Milwaukee setting dates for his fall films. Frank is one of Wisconsin's pioneer exhibitors.

The Allis Theatre at West Allis, Wis., a suburb of Milwaukee, is soon to be reopened after being extensively remodeled, according to Eugene Felon, manager. The house will be one of the most attractive in West Allis when the contractors take their last scaffoldings and paint cans from the premises.

Ed Gavin, formerly with Universal has joined the sales force of the Walter Baier Film Exchange of Milwaukee, and is soon to make his first rounds of the state in his new capacity.

Al Segals, shipping clerk at the Milwaukee branch of P. D. C., has been most generous with cigars lately. Al is the proud papa of a brand new baby boy.

J. S. Wolff, district auditor for P. D. C., has left Milwaukee after making contacts with the books of the branch. He has gone on to Chicago, where he will remain for some time.

The new Barton Organ that is being installed in Saxe's Strand Theatre at Milwaukee will be dedicated during the first week in October, according to Stan Brown, manager. During the interval between the removal of the old organ and the completion of the new one, a three piece string orchestra is supplementing Joje Lichter's Record Makers in furnishing music during the showing of films.

Charlie Oasis, manager of the Grand Theatre at Racine, Wis., dashed into the Milwaukee film exchanges on business during the past week. A little pleasure was, of course, mingled with the business.

Henry Goldman, manager of the Colonial and Grand Theatres at Green Bay, Wis., also looked up his Milwaukee friends last week. He states that the Colonial will soon be re-opened, after undergoing complete remodeling.

Omaha

THE annual convention of the Motion Picture Theatre Owners of Nebraska and Western Iowa division will be held at the Hotel Loyal, September 22 and 23. There will be an election of officers and general business will be discussed.

W. W. Booth, of the Empress and Strand theatres, Belle Plaine, Iowa, paid a visit to film row this week.

S. B. Rahn, special representative for the Harold Lloyd productions, was a visitor in town this week.

"Bill" Troug, popular district manager for the Universal with headquarters at Kansas City, is in town this week.

A. B. Seymour, who covers the North Platte territory for Universal, is whizzing around in a new Hudson coach.

C. W. Schaefer, owner of the Opera house at Petersburg, Nebr., who died recently, is mourned by many friends in the theatrical circles.

Mick Larson, owner of the Majestic theatre at Oakland, Nebr., has been improving his theatre, putting in a new booth and adding an extra machine. He has redecorated throughout.

Jimmie Rogers, Omaha branch manager for the Enterprise Distributing Corporation, is slowly recovering from an operation he underwent last week.

M. E. Schrieber, Wisner, Nebr., exhibitor, was a visitor on film row between times of watching the ponies at the Ak-Sar-Ben races.

Esther Powers, stenographer for O. H. Dutton, manager of the Exhibitors' Supply Company, will report back for work Monday after a vacation.

C. D. Hill St. Louis district manager of the Producers' Distributing Corporation, is in town placing new product throughout the larger cities of the territory.

Manager F. M. De Lorenzo, of the Producers' office here, spent Friday at Lincoln with Mr. Hill.

C. J. Sonin, of the New York office of Metro-Goldwyn, arrived here September 19.

S. N. Fogman, booker at the Producers' Distributing Corporation, won the national prize of $30 for obtaining the most bookings for a four-week period.

E. J. Lipson, manager of the Des Moines office of the Producers' Distributing Corporation, was here for a couple of days this week.

Catherine Nodean, inspector for the Metro-Goldwyn exchange, is spending the week at Kansas City.

Manager M. L. Stearn of the Independent Films exchange, has taken to his home this week after a period of serious illness at the Wise Memorial hospital. He is not expected to be able to be back at the office for a month.

Miles Radler, owner and exhibitor of West Point, Nebr., took a week off from his theatrical duties to play in a band at the county fair at Albion, Nebr.

F. A. Van Husan, manager of the Western Theatre Supply Company has been out of town on several small trips the last couple of weeks. He expects to leave for the east in a few days on buying tour.

Madeline Sudmeier, secretary to F. A. Van Husan of the Western Theatre Supply company, has returned to her duties after a two weeks' illness.

Cupid has "booked" Mildred Gratsfield, biller at the Metro-Goldwyn exchange. She is to be married in October to an Omaha man, Richard Mockler. Marie Kralizek will take Miss Gratsfield's place. She was formerly on the staff of Metro.

It is rumored that Alexander Pantages is contemplating building a house in Omaha.

Bruce Merrill of the Lyric theatre at Edgar, Nebr., while convalescing from a recent illness, paid a visit here.

The son of A. C. Cloidt, who operates the Parmalee theatre at Plattsmouth, Nebr., is here in a hospital for an operation.

Many exhibitors were in town this week. Among them were Anthon Jonata from the World theatre, Howell, Nebr.; L. W.

Splichler, owner of the Empress theatre at Bancroft, Nebr.; W. A. Bowker, Opera House, Omaha, Iowa; A. F. Jenkins, Community theatre, David City, Nebr.; H. F. Kennedy, Lyric theatre, Broken Bow, Nebr.

Mrs. W. Cohn, mother of J. J. Cohn, a production manager for Metro-Goldwyn films, and her daughter Mrs. A. C. Terens, passed through here Tuesday evening, September 15, on the Los Angeles limited, enroute to New York, their home. They have been spending a two months' vacation with Mr. Cohn in Hollywood.

A new theatre is being contemplated for Benson, a suburb of Omaha, by the Metcalfe company, which is platting the former Country club.

Eighty exhibitors from Nebraska and South Dakota gathered at Pierce, Nebr., for the second party to be given by Universal, and Joe Douglas, manager at the Strand theatre at Pierce.

The president and secretary of the Commercial Club, Frank Pilger and Arnold Stienbraun, assisted Mr. Douglas in putting over the party. The town band turned out and headed a procession up the main street to the Pohlman hotel, where the banquet was held.

A new 1200-seat theatre which will cost $250,000 according to reports, is going to be built at Grand Island by Universal.

Buffalo

J BERKOWITZ, manager of the Buffalo office of First Graphic Exchanges, has returned from a trip to New York city.

"Jimmy" Grainger, general sales manager of the Fox Film corporation was in Buffalo last week end. During his visit he held a sales conference at the Buffalo exchange during which he pumped three or four ton of TNT enthusiasm into the boys all of whom promised Jimmy to break all former records at the local exchange. The fellahs at Fox, by the way, have fallen for bowling and one night this week the Fox team assembled at the Central alleys for practice. In the gang were Emmy Dickman, Carl Fahrenholtz, Clarence Ross, O. T. Schroeppel, Norman Sheehan, brother of General Manager W. R. Sheehan, Tom Stapleton and Moe Grassgreen. Otto Schroeppel bowled the high mark and Carl Fahrenholtz got the booby prize, the last hair from Emmy Dickman's head. Now the Fox bowlers are ready to challenge any other exchange in town.

It is reported that Vassiladis Brothers who operate the Clinton-Strand have taken over the Linden theatre on Jefferson street, Buffalo. Rumor also has it that they have leased the Central Park. Both are community houses.

John M. Sitterly, after a try at the auto sales game, is back on Film Row again as a member of

the United Artists' sales force. John is one of the veteran film men in this neck of the woods.

Charles W. Anthony has resigned from the Buffalo staff of Warner Brothers. Mr. Anthony was manager of the local Vitagraph exchange for several years. He expects to announce future plans on his return from New York city where he has gone for a few days.

The Cataract Theatre corporation of Niagara Falls, N. Y., operating the Strand and Cataract theatres, has declared the semi-annual dividend of eight percent.

The members of the boards of directors of the Buffalo and Albany zones of the M. P. T. O. of N. Y. will meet with the officers of the Producers and Distributors of America in New York city, October 5 to discuss arbitration matters.

The Amendola theatre, another of the houses in Niagara Falls which is paying the increased scale asked by the various unions, as well as the Ritz theatre, are co-operating with the unions through the issuance by the members of the unions of a Special Courtesy Ticket with which if presented at either theatre before October 1 the holder can obtain an additional seat with one paid admission. This ticket is inserted in the ad placed by the unions.

Ben Wallerstein, manager of the Broadway theatre, Buffalo, has

a new one. He is putting on "Moonlight Shows." Or perhaps they are nolight shows. Last week at the height of the picture presentation and on several evenings, all the lights in the house went out. Everyone swore, including Ben. But it seems there was no kick from the shieks and shebas. Seeking light on the subject, Ben went before the electric officials who promised to push more water over Niagara Falls to get more power to get more light for the house that Ben built.

J. W. Straub and F. N. McCullough are reported to be interested in a new theatre to be built in Oil City, Pa. Plans call for the utilization of the vacant McGuigan lot on Elm street and the Straub and Cunningham property.

Colonel Howard F. Brink, manager of the Buffalo Educational exchange, never was an admiral but he knows how to navigate that I'll old bus of his through water puddles up to the roof. The colonel encountered many of these young floods down state last week when he visited Syracuse and Rochester.

Fred M. Zimmerman, manager of the Producers Distributing corporation office in Buffalo returned to town last week and from a down state tour nursing a beautiful cold caused when Fred got caught in some of those cloud bursts.

Well, Charlie Bowe, manager of the Frontier has gone and done it. Yep, stepped right up to the parson and said "I do!" comes back from his honeymoon looking as spry as ever and all set for a busy season at the popular Buffalo westside neighborhood theatre.

Again this season the Rochester Parents and Teachers' association will cooperate with the Eastman theatre in presenting the special-Saturday morning movies for children. Although each program has been carefully selected and reviewed by the representatives of national welfare organizations, it will be subjected to an additional local scrutiny before going on the screen. Each week a committee from the Parents and Teachers association, headed by Mrs. Charles Thomas, president, who will review the program selected for the coming Saturday morning and will make such suggestions and recommendations as seem proper. The first of the Saturday morning performances was given Saturday, September 19 and there was a great outpouring of youngsters on hand. These Saturday morning shows are not a commercial enterprise, but were arranged for the sole purpose of providing specially selected programs for juvenile tastes. They will be continued every Saturday this fall and winter. All admissions are 10 cents.

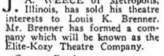 # Chicago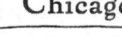

J. A. WEECE of Metropolis, Illinois, has sold his theatre interests to Louis K. Brenner. Mr. Brenner has formed a company which will be known as the Elite-Kozy Theatre Company.

Cooney Brothers expect to remove their offices to 1404-10 Straus building this week where the headquarters of the American Theatres Corporation will also be located. The latter corporation is the booking circuit recently organized with Joe Hopp as general manager, and of which Cooney Brothers are reported to be members.

After remaining in his Chicago headquarters for two weeks, Divisional Manager Aiken of Pathe is again out on the road and when last heard from was visiting Detroit.

City Clerk Huff of Galesburg, Illinois, who operates the Empress theatre of that city, is going on a three months' vacation to California where he will be accompanied by his wife. Mr. Huff is said to be Galesburg's most popular citizen and the recent election, in which he was elected city clerk by a twenty to one majority, bears out the assertion.

Manager Jimmy Gillick of Pathe Exchange, expects to move into his company's handsome new building at 1021 S. Wabash avenue on November 1st. Mr. Gillick states that the building is scheduled to be completed by October 15th, but in order to avoid any possible slip up the moving date has been set two weeks later.

Renown Exchanges is now operating four offices, having established a branch in Indianapolis, Indiana, with Ralph Abbott in charge.

H. A. O'Brien, Metro-Goldwyn salesman, has had additional territory assigned to him and will, hereafter, cover Central as well as Northern Illinois.

Frank Evans is rushing work on his handsome new Hinsdale theatre with the expectation of having it ready to open the last week in September.

William Pearl of the Pearl theatre, whose fine new theatre in Highland Park is rapidly nearing completion, plans to open its doors to the public by the end of the month.

Special Representative Floyd Lewis of Associated Exhibitors, who makes his headquarters in St. Louis, was in Chicago for a conference with Manager Harris this week and then went on to Minneapolis.

S. J. Gregory of the S. J. Gregory Company, was in New York this week seeing his mother and father off on a trip to Greece. Mr. Gregory expects to be back at his desk the first of next week.

Pat Dowling, short subject representative for Christy, and Carroll Trowbridge, feature representative, met in Chicago Monday, Mr. Trowbridge coming from New York and Mr. Dowling from the coast. While here Mr. Trowbridge conferred with Manager Lorch of Producers Distributing Corporation, which handle the feature productions, and Mr. Dowling took up sales plans with Manager Dave Dubin of Educational, distributors of the short subjects.

A. E. Alger of Urbana, has taken over the Rialto theatre at Bloomington, Illinois, and has appointed Tom Larson, manager of his latest acquisition. Other houses operated by Mr. Alger include the Majestic at Paxton, the Central at Fairbury, Colonial at Urbane, Park at La Salle, and the Peru at Peru, Illinois.

Thomas Fox of the Star theatre, Bradford, Illinois, reports business good and that indications for a profitable winter are excellent. Mr. Fox recently was in Chicago and booked a number of pictures.

Frank Thomshack, secretary of the American Legion Post at Leda, Illinois, has been giving the people of his town free movies all summer, through the courtesy of the Business Men's Association, and this fall expects to move from an airdome into the Legion Hall and continue the shows.

The Echo theatre at Des Plaines is being remodelled, redecorated and enlarged to one thousand seats. A feature of the remodelled house will be a new organ which is being installed at the present time.

Walter Taylor, former owner of the Rialto at Bloomington, is now booking for the Lyceum Theatre at Chenoa.

The Majestic Theatre at Belvidere, Illinois, reopened on Labor Day and is now operating on a seven day schedule.

M. D. Martin of Mineral Point, Wisconsin, advises us that he and E. S. Perkins have sold the Alamo Theatre at New London, Iowa, to J. O'Connor of Chesterton, Indiana.

I. Maynard Schwartz, who has been visiting New York since his resignation as manager of Educational's Chicago exchange, on his return stated that it is his intention to open the short subject exchange on Wabash Avenue as soon as he can secure a desirable location.

Mr. Schwartz in point of service, if not in age, is one of the old timers on film row and enjoys one of the widest acquaintances of any film man in Chicago. Five years ago he opened the Educational exchange in this city and continued as manager until his recent resignation, all that time being in close touch with the distribution of short subjects.

Jack Corbett of Universal's New York office, has been visiting the local exchange for the last few days.

Sam Katz of Balaban & Katz, returned from New York the first of the week, after negotiations had been concluded for the operation of the Paramount Theatres by Balaban & Katz. Mr. Katz, however, only remained in Chicago for a couple of days, going back to New York on Wednesday.

Clyde Elliott of the Evanston and Hoyburn Theatres of Evanston, has recently opened the Riley, formerly the New Lyric, at Fort Wayne, Indiana.

M. Whitmoyer is now selling for Security Pictures. Mr. Whitmoyer was formerly connected with Renown.

Clyde Quimby will reopen his Allen Theatre in Fort Wayne as a second run house. This follows

the reopening of the Strand, which will be operated under a big picture policy. The Strand, during the summer, had been completely redecorated and refurnished, and presents a very handsome appearance. The other Fort Wayne houses operated by Mr. Quimby include the Jefferson, Palace and Colonial.

Samuel Abrahams, popular owner of the Gold Theatre, returned from a three month's trip to the Holy Land last week, and reports having had a very enjoyable vacation. The object of Mr. Abrahams' long journey was to visit his father, who lives near Jerusalem, whom he had not seen for several years.

Renown sales staff surprised manager Jerry Abrams with the announcement that they are putting on a "Jerry Abrams Week" on the west and north side starting November 8th and on the south side starting November 5th. The boys completed all their plans including preparation of necessary paper, announcements, etc., before passing the word to Mr. Abrams.

The Midwest Film Golf Tournament, which was scheduled for September 18th, has again been postponed and will be played on October 2nd at Olympic Fields. The change in the date was made necessary by the holiday which came on September 18th, and which was overlooked by those in charge of the tournament at the time the date was originally announced.

Jimmy Scofield, who is well known in this territory, where he formerly worked as a salesman, has returned from a state on the west coast and has taken a position with United Artists covering northern Indiana territory.

John Flinn of Producers Distributing Corporation, was a Chicago visitor this week.

V. T. Lynch, Charles L. Casanave and Jack Miller, were among Chicago exhibitors visiting New York last week.

Lyman Ballard, Wisconsin representative for United Artists, was in the city Saturday for a conference with Divisional Manager Cress Smith.

 # Houston

A BE SILVERBERG, manager of the Crown and Folly theatres, has announced an extensive re-modeling program for the Crown theatre. When completed it will be one of the most modern western theatres in this city. He plans to re-decorate the entire interior and rebuild the back of the theatre adding several rows of seats. The lobby will be entirely new and will be finished off with bright colors, new special built lobby frames are being made to replace the old type frames now in use. Two

new type B Powers machines were installed in the Crown less than a month ago.

Ed Bloomingthal, south Texas representative for F. B. O. was in town for several days last week. Mr. Bloomingthal has just returned from the Rio Grande Valley and reports that the recent rains have improved business throughout his territory. Wm. Horwitz, Jr., owner and manager of the New Texan and Iris theatres, has just completed the job of hanging over 100 heads, mounted, and old fashioned guns

in the lobby and alongside the stair cases of his Texan theatre. Mr. Horwitz says that he knows no better way to carry on the name than this method of interior advertising. The Texan was thrown open May 1, 1925 and has enjoyed a sensational run since that time. It is the only popular price theatre in Houston with an orchestra.

Bill Branch former publicity man throughout Texas writes from California that he will book several road productions through

Houston and other Texas towns this season.

Mrs. Milton S. Gross, of Beaumont and Port Arthur, has arrived in Houston to open an office for the winter season. It will be located in the Auditorium Building.

Frank Star, publicity manager for the Interstate Amusement company, is due in town this week on a business trip.

Curtis H. Dunham stopped off in Houston enroute from Galveston to San Antonio.

Newspaper Opinions on New Pictures

"Unholy Three"—M-G-M., Garrick, Minneapolis

Tribune: "A better crook drama than 'The Unholy Three' has not been filmed. This picture should please a greater percentage of its audiences than any photoplay shown locally for weeks. One must hark back to 'The Green Goddess,' 'Wild Oranges' and 'He Who Gets Slapped' to find a film comparable to 'The Unholy Three' in its thoroughly sustained interest, its restless suspense and its refreshing uniqueness of plot and characterization."

Star: "Those who saw Mr. Chaney in 'The Miracle Man,' 'The Penalty,' 'He Who Gets Slapped' and 'The Hunchback of Notre Dame' will want to see him again in 'The Unholy Three,' which is one of the cleverest characterizations of his screen career. The film has a series of absorbing love scenes which mingle with the high-tensioned crook episodes and with the numerous thrilling incidents that are part of the plot."

"Unholy Three"—M-G-M., Tower, St. Paul

Pioneer Press: "Here is a picture which may legitimately claim distinction, because it depends for effectiveness on none of the stereotyped devices with which experience has made us familiar. It is unique in the structure of scenario, daring in its characterization and for the most part unchangingly consistent in the development of its extraordinary story. The picture has the merit of setting appropriately the unusual talents of Lon Chaney. 'The Unholy Three' should not be missed by those who are interested in moving picture developments."

Daily News: "'The Unholy Three' is unquestionably one of the best melodramas ever put on film. For one thing, it has a novel, enthralling story — an ironic really suspensive tale of crime. Unlike most of the movie melodramas, 'The Unholy Three'

Del Lord, comedy director who has signed a new contract with Mack Sennett to direct pictures for the Pathe program.

contains little or no unbelievable, rough-and-tumble action. It is simply and thoughtfully directed by Tod Browning and superbly played by Lon Chaney, a giant and a first-rate little actor as the third and tiny member of 'The Unholy Three.' It is a first-rate picture, vastly superior to the run of films."

"Never The Twain Shall Meet"—M-G-M., Warfield, San Francisco

Examiner: "Here is that South Seas' glamour in sizeable chunks on the screen at the Warfield. For two days the crowd have been piling into see it. The background is smitingly volcanic. Not before in any photoplay has the life of the South Seas, in its gorgeous aspect, been so well transcribed to the films."

Call: "Beautiful Anita Stewart is the central figure of this most absorbing picturization of the famous novel by Peter B. Kyne. Never, it can safely be said, has Miss Stewart appeared to better advantage. The same can be said for Justine Johnstone, Bert Lytell, Huntly Gordon and George Seigmann. The outstanding feature of the production, however, is not so much the fine acting or the dramatic story, but the glorious photography—most of which was done on the islands of Tahiti and Moorea. There are a thousand and one South Sea 'shots' which provoke gasps of awesome ecstasy on the part of each audience."

News: "'Never the Twain Shall Meet' reaches the zenith of atmospheric treatment carried in a solid body of downright entertainment that is a positive delight. Maurice Tourneur directed the players through the intriguing action of the Kyne story. He took them to the South Seas where he found many beautiful scenic backgrounds. He made real actors out of the natives, a novelty in itself and which adds materially to the realism of the pictured events."

Herald: "In 'Never the Twain Shall Meet' the Warfield is presenting a screen drama no San Franciscian should miss. The scenes are laid in San Francisco and the South Sea Islands, and the photography is something to shout about. The unfolding of the age-old story of the impossibility of the east meeting the west is achieved in a novel and most interesting manner. The cast is as fine as any seen on a local screen in a year."

"Drusilla With A Million"—F. B. O, Rialto, Washington

Herald: "Personally I rather had the sneaking notion that 'Greater Movie Season Week' was going to be just so much pretzel dust. Then Lee Somers told me willing to publicly kiss Will Hays' fingertips in the lobby of the Rialto Theatre any day at

John Ford, who directed "Kentucky Pride," for Fox.

high noon by way of contrition. For 'Drusilla' is a knockout—a wow, in other words."

News: "There is a climax that actually brought the customers to their feet."

Star: "A throbbing love story woven into the plot brings the main characters together in an intensely dramatic climax with one of the most effective bits of staging ever witnessed. Mary Carr gives a perfect characterization from her first carework smile, with which she walks straight into the hearts of her audience, to her last radiant beam, which capitulates the judge and routs the opposing lawyer in the thrilling court scene."

"The Freshman"—Pathe, Eastman, Rochester

Herald: "It is difficult to establish the relative place of this new picture among the star's achievements, for each one of his pictures seems to be the best he has done. Judged by the number of laughs this picture certainly measures up to any of the star's previous successes. Anyone who understands anything about football and most of those in yesterday's audience seemed to have at least an inkling of the game, can realize the ludicrous possibilities of the football arena."

Democrat and Chronicle: "The reviewer enjoyed 'The Freshman' even better than 'Safety Last.' In both productions there are provided materials, commonly called in producing circles 'Gags' that are about of equal merit. To the youth of the land, who are the most devoted patrons of the bespectacled comedian, the college background of the new production will, very likely, make a great appeal. Then, to replace the hair-raising stunts that thrilled millions in 'Safety Last,' Lloyd's directors have introduced into the plot of 'The Freshman' the more dependable dramatic element of pathos. Lloyd comedy, always cleanly and inoffensive to every class of patron, with this commendable quality of heart appeal

added, is just about 100 per cent entertainment for the average class of movie patrons."

"Off the Highway"—Prod. Dist. Corp., Forum, L. A.

Daily News: "'Off The Highway,' is a photoplay abounding in atmosphere and color and possessing a strangely haunting theme. This picture is a notable achievement for many reasons: the first being the work of William V. Mong. This veteran plays a dual role and the double exposures that result are the most remarkable I have ever seen."

Times: "'Off The Highway' is interesting and unusual. William V. Mong plays the dual role and he gives a fine performance—finished and convincing. Charles Gerrard is unforgettable as the sleek hypocrite. His scene with Mong, where he piously explains his aims in life, is one of the cleverest pieces of acting seen on local screens for a long while."

Examiner: "'Off The Highway,' showing this week at the Forum is well named. It is quite out of the beaten path . . . the points of the story have been skillfully brought out. William V. Mong plays the dual role splendidly."

Herald: "A gripping story totally different from any heretofore seen on the screen. Forman has taken this novel of the super life of Caleb Fry and made an entertaining study of human nature. The realism of some of the sequences remind one forcibly of some of Poe's immortal hairraisers."

Record: "While the character acting of William V. Mong dominates the picture, the photographic work, which allows Mong to shake hands with himself, pass in front of himself and change clothes with himself is uncanny."

(Continued on page 1635)

Edith Roberts, who appears in "Speed Mad," a Columbia picture.

CONSTRUCTION & EQUIPMENT DEPARTMENT

Fabian Opens Large Theatre in New Jersey

Mosque, Part of Salaam Temple, Has 3,500 Seats and Elaborate Appointments

THE theatre that lays claim to being the largest and finest in New Jersey, the Mosque, was opened in Newark recently. Stupendous in size and marvelously constructed, the Mosque measures favorably in comparison with the largest theatres of the country. The large auditorium contains 3,500 seats, a capacity that is said to be only surpassed by a few theatres in this country.

The Mosque is expected to boom big business on the southern portion of Broad street where it rises majestically near the busy intersection of Clinton avenue. The residential mansions of this part of the city have given way before the encroaching development of the automobile industry and the theatre is expected to send realty values up 100 per cent. The entire section was decorated by the business men welcoming the coming of the playhouse.

Architecturally, the Mosque is one of the distinctive achievements of the city. The entire building was designed by George W. Backoff, Frank Grad and Henry Baechlin, architects. The outside follows the Greek manner and the auditorium is modern Greek in treatment.

The building, which is 116 feet wide on Broad street and 476 feet deep, is known as Salaam Temple, A. A. O. N. M. S. It contains besides the huge theatre, a ballroom, a grill, a banquet hall, lodge rooms, stores, and concessions. The theatre was leased from the shriners by Jacob Fabian for a long period of years. This theatre is the twentieth he now controls in New Jersey.

The grand foyer of this fine temple of entertainment is 131 feet long by 52 feet wide. On the extreme left is the ladies retiring room, in the center the hostess' quarters and the checkroom, and on the right, the gentlemen's room. Three dormitories lead from the foyer to the auditorium. From the end of the foyer to the curtain line is 175 feet. The balcony is reached by two spacious stairways in the foyer.

Flanking each side of the auditorium are two colonades with five openings. These apertures can be utilized as loges if necessary. A huge chandelier hangs from the center of the dome which is sixty-five feet in diameter. The chandelier weighs two tons.

The proscenium is 67 feet wide and 34 feet high. The depth of the stage, from the curtain line to the rear wall, is 45 feet thus giving ample room for prologues and stage

presentations. From this wall to the street, there are an additional 30 feet which are used as scene dock. There are nineteen dressing rooms, a property room, showers and toilets, and a musician room and library also back of the stage.

More than 1,000 seats are lodged in the lone balcony. The sight line of this section to the front of the stage is 50 feet. The balcony, which has two promenades, is reached by three elevators which stop at the upper and lower levels. The exits are through fire towers on each side of the building.

The expansiveness of the theatre is seen in the arrangement of seats. Comfort was the first consideration. There is no jamming of seats and a stout person can be as comfortable as a long shanked one.

The orchestra pit is roomy enough to accommodate 100 musicians. In its entirety, the theatre has 2½ more space area than is required by the fire laws. The illumination is by indirect lighting.

Crowds flocked to the Mosque on the opening day. Long queues stood before the ticket booths throughout the showing and police help was necessary to hold the people.

The theatre is controlled and directed by Mr. Fabian. H. M. S. Kendrick is the manager; A. Gordon Reid, director of production, and J. E. Firnkoess, director of publicity. Mr. Fabian's policy will be first run pictures with appropriate scenic and stage presentations.

The organ is a four manual, and the projection is of the latest models. A 40 piece orchestra is part of the house staff.

The new Mosque Theatre which was recently opened in Newark, New Jersey. This house lays claim to being the largest and finest in that state, having a seating capacity of 3,500 and magnificently appointed throughout. The theatre is on a long term lease by Jacob Fabian.

Interior of the Mosque Theatre, Newark, New Jersey, which was recently opened by Jacob Fabian. This theatre is a part of the Salaam Temple and is claimed to be one of the finest amusement palaces in the world.

How to Maintain Attractive Appearing Lobby Display Frames

By W. F. LIBMAN of Libman Spanjer Corp.

THE value of an attractive lobby, the psychology of lighting, as well as the effect of beauty upon the eye and mind, have all been touched upon in preceding articles.

The descriptive detail, and the individual merits of the various types of frames have also received attention. It would seem then that it would be quite in order to go into the construction and material used in these frames and cases that form so important a basis for all lobby background and design.

As the writer pointed out in the first article, the question of atmospheric conditions and elements play a most important part in the life and upkeep of all exterior work on theatre fronts and lobbies.

It is necessary wherever wood is used, particularly for exterior purposes, to cover the wood surface with some medium of protection. This protection may take the form of paint, varnish, shellac or similar bodies, depending entirely upon its decorative purpose or location.

Wood of every kind is porous, some more so than others, depending upon its species, firmness and growth. When once these pores or tiny openings, that correspond to the pores of the human skin, are exposed to rain, sand, dirt and sunshine they become infected so to speak, either one or the other form of disintegration or rot then takes place. Dry rot usually occurs, where moisture without air prevails, while damp rot occurs where animal or vegetable life accompanies the moisture.

These facts are touched upon merely to show the need for proper wood covering, and should in no wise be regarded as negativing the value of wood for construction or design.

The most expensive material that can be used for construction or ornamentation is bronze. Here we have a practically indestructible medium, as is evidenced by the fact that instruments and utensils fashioned from this metal are constantly being dug up on the sites of ancient and buried cities, the metal in all cases being untouched by its long interment. But while in the writer's opinion, nothing is better than bronze for the purpose of building accessory, yet its price is almost prohibitive for theatre use; a fact which can be easily checked up by pricing just an insignificant looking little bronze ornament in a convenient art shop.

Next in the metallic line we find brass and copper, both of them high in value when used in solid cast or moulded form, or high in upkeep if constructed in sheet form when almost daily polishing or burnishing is required to keep up appearances of attractiveness.

Then comes iron, which unless constantly painted, which also spells upkeep, or maintenance, is particularly susceptible to atmospheric conditions. Unless carefully and frequently covered with a suitable paint, iron either peels or flakes in unprotected spots, causing a shabby and rundown appearance, or else corrosion takes place and causes a rapid destruction of joints, ornamentation and surface.

So after all, of the various materials of which decorative and artistic frames and wall cases can be best built, wood, of the proper sort, and when properly selected, is the most desirable and inexpensive in the long run, as well as the most easily worked.

It is well understood that any thing which is built by man, whether texture, clothing, machinery, or building, must be kept up, or maintained in some way. Neglect shows, either quickly or gradually, depending upon the use of the article or its original construction. A pair of shoes, a suit of clothes, an automobile or frame house, when constantly used, and never cleaned, painted, polished or adjusted, soon shows the results of neglect and usage.

And so it is with lobby equipment. The writer makes the following assertion without fear of contradiction, based upon years of observation and experience: A good well built wooden frame if varnished every six months, and refinished approximately every two years, will last from ten to fifteen years. This length of service over which the original investment costs may be spread, brings the price of a beautiful lobby down to a very low figure indeed.

Many of the largest theatres, include in their regular routine the repainting of their lobby equipment every six months regularly, with the result that the lobbies are at all times the same sparkling, shiny, attractive mediums of attention that they were in the beginning.

The writer can think offhand of hundreds of theatres that are today running with the original frames that they opened with years and years ago, merely through intelligent upkeep.

Mass. Theatre Reopens After Fire Caused by Film

The Day Street Olympia Theatre in Somerville, Mass., has reopened after repairs following a recent fire. The theatre was closed just a week and a day. The fire started in the booth and did about $3,000 damage. Repairs were rushed to the balcony and rear of the auditorium and rear walls and the house is now reopened. A. D. Rubenstein is manager.

Exterior of the Mosque Theatre, Newark, N. J., which is housed in the building which is known as the Salaam Temple. This Theatre has created a great amount of comment on its splendor and unique design.

Projection
Optics, Electricity, Practical Ideas & advice

Inquiries and Comments

Interior Illumination as Related to Projection

IN THIS concluding section of Dr. Hickman's paper on Motion Picture Theatres the point of interior illumination is stressed and suggestions are advanced to assist one in securing the proper balance and harmony be-

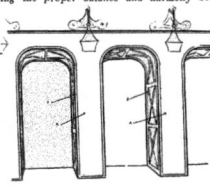

Figure Five.

tween the general illumination of the theatre and the projected picture.

Whether or not his suggestions are applicable without change to American theatres is open to question but the principles on which he bases his contentions certainly seem to have considerable foundation in fact.

General Lighting System

Where it is not a question of adapting an existing theatre, improved lighting might be provided in a number of ways. The pendent side lamps might be replaced by a series of hollow arches, depicted in Fig. 5. Inside each upright pillar would be a lamp of small wattage. The faces (A) of the arches would be opaque, but the interior panelled with translucent material on the sides away from the screen (B). Each lamp

would give a diffused area of light about 10 feet square of a low order of brightness. Viewed in enfilade by the audience, they would suggest a dimly lit wall; viewed from the screen they would be practically invisible.

If it were required to fill the arches with boxes the system would have to be modified so that the bright pillars did not trouble the occupants. They would be made triangular, opaque on one side, transparent on the other, with the apex angle so contrived that no light reached the box and little the screen. Both systems are indicated in plan Fig. 6, where the plain arches are shown on one side and the box system on the other. The projection and back lamp lighting of the screen surround is also shown.

The more ambitious theatres, of which in London the Stoll and Tivoli will serve as examples, present greater difficulties. The circular galleries and boxes, the staging arrangements and orchestra convert the cubical shell, from a lighting point of view, into a broken surfaced sphere. Such buildings are generally tall, and the contrast lighting might be carried out as in Fig. 7.

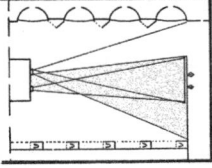

Figure Six.

A large area (A) round the screen (B) might derive its light from a lantern (C) and would in turn light the house. Subsidiary lighting by lamps in deep consical shades suspended from the roof would augment that received by the middle and back seats. This simple arrangement would not limit in the slightest any gorgeous display from other lights during the intervals from projection.

With regard to the color of the contrast lighting, this might be varied to suit the subject, but round the screen, at least, it should not depart much from a neutral hue. By common consent the side lamps in most kine theatres are red or orange. Whatever the origin of the convention, it is founded on scientific truth, for contrast in the red is greater than in other colors. This means that a red light which is bright near its source and sufficient for the needs of the theatre attendants becomes invisible most rapidly as the distance from the lamp in-

creases. The shadows on the screen suffer less with red than other colors.

The possibilities with contrast lighting are so great that in the same way that the better theatres arrange their musical programme with care so that appropriate music greets each change of scene, so also can one imagine a contrast lighting programme being arranged to throw into correct relief each successive film. The blue night or dungeon scene could be emphasized by increasing the contrast lighting to a warm orange. The brilliance of blue water and distance might go further and arrange the matter automatically by allowing notches or contacts on the film to control appropriate lights.

Much more might be said for a system of rational lighting. The foregoing remarks are intended merely to be suggestive. If they appear dogmatic in places it is because time and space have not permitted the very full argument merited by so controversial a subject.

Plan to Erect $500,000 Theatre in Chicago

Plans have been completed for the erection of a $500,000 theatre to be erected at the southwest corner of Chicago and Monticello Avenues on a plot 133 x 299 by A. F. Sass and V. T. Lynch. The building will consist of a theatre which will have a seating capacity of 2000 persons, four stores and eight apartments.

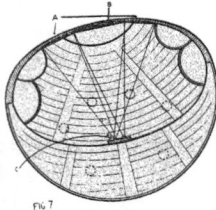

Figure Seven.

New Theatre for Northwest Side, Chicago, Planned

Plans are being prepared for the erection of a motion picture theatre, apartments, stores and garages to be erected on Cicero Avenue just north of Belmont, Chicago. The theatre will seat 3000 persons. This theatre will be owned by one of Chicago's big movie chains.

The lower left section of the foyer of the new Mosque Theatre, Newark, N. J.

Simplex Dealer Reports Good Business for August

That business is good in the theatre equipment and supply phase of this business is well illustrated by the number of Simplex projectors that were sold by one dealer, Howell Cine Equipment Co., New York, during the month of August. The total machines sold were thirty-one to theatres listed as follows: Band Box Theatre (2), Bronx, N. Y.; Orpheum Theatre (2), Newark, N. J.; Kinema Theatre (2), Brooklyn, N. Y.; Pathe Theatre, New York, N. Y.; Rialto Theatre (2), Glens Falls, N. Y.; Proctor's Theatre (2), Yonkers, N. Y.; Public School, New York, N. Y.; Plaza Theatre (2), Jamaica, N. Y.; Colonial Theatre (2), Albany, N. Y.; Cumberland Theatre (2), Brooklyn, N. Y.; Cameo Theatre (2), Yonkers, N. Y.; New Theatre (2), Rockaway, N. Y.; Oxford Theatre (2), Plainfield, N. J.; Salaam Temple Baldwin, N. Y.; Royal Theatre (2), Roosevelt, N. Y.

Cooling System Installed in Angela Theatre, Cleveland

Mrs. G. Robinson has redecorated her Angela theatre, Cleveland and has also installed a cooling and ventilating system of modern design. The house now presents a much improved appearance due to Mrs. Robinson's efforts.

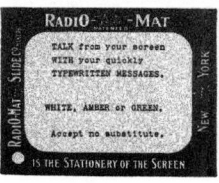

Automatic Ticket Register Corp. Wins Suit

An important decision has just been rendered in the U. S. District Court with reference to a suit for infringement of certain claims on ticket selling machine patents.

This suit was brought by the National Electric Ticket Register Co., against Automatic Ticket Register Corp. of New York.

District Judge Augustus N. Hand, in his decision states that Automatic Ticket Register Corp. does not in any manner infringe on the patent in question, and dismisses the bill of complaint with costs against the National Electric Ticket Register Co.

The contention of the manufacturers of the Gold Seal Ticket Register has been upheld by Judge Hand.

Bush Brothers Are to Build $100,000 Theatre in S. D.

G. A. Bush and Kent G. Bush, formerly operating the Superba Theatre and other motion picture houses in San Diego, Cal., and vicinity, and still controlling several, announce that they will soon start the construction of a new house to be known as the Bush Egyptian Theatre at Park boulevard and University avenue, in that city, to cost approximately $100,000.00, and to have a seating capacity of 1000. Work will be commenced as soon as the architect's detailed plans are completed. It is said that the new house will be the finest neighborhood theatre in southern California, and will be second only to the Pantages and Balboa theatres in the down town section of the city.

Woodlawn, Pa., to Have New $30,000 House

Plans are being drawn by F. M. Stetson. Archt., 425 Franklin Ave. for the erection of a theatre building to be erected on Franklin Avenue on site 25 x 100 at an approximate cost of $30,000. The structure is to be of brick and steel construction. The owner is Anthony P. Jin, c/o Strand Theatre, Franklin Avenue.

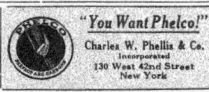
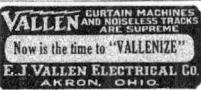
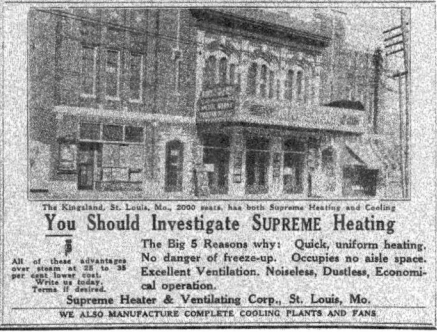

FEATURE RELEASE CHART

Productions are Listed Alphabetically and by Months in which Released in order that the Exhibitor may have a short-cut toward such information as he may need. Short subject and comedy releases, as well as information on pictures that are coming, will be found on succeeding pages. (S. R. indicates State Right release.)

Refer to THE MOTION PICTURE NEWS BOOKING GUIDE for Productions Listed Prior to March

MARCH

Feature	Star	Distributed by	Length	Reviewed
Adventurous Sex, The	Clara Bow	Assoc. Exhib.	5039 feet	Mar. 21
Air Mail, The	Special Cast	Paramount	6976 feet	Mar. 28
Beauty and the Bad Man	Special Cast	Prod. Dist. Corp.	5794 feet	May 9
Beyond the Border	Harry Carey	Prod. Dist. Corp.	4469 feet	April 25
Billy, The Kid	Franklyn Farnum	Inde. Pict. Corp.		
		(S. R.)	4800 feet	
Blood and Steel	Desmond Holmes	Inde. Pict. (S. R.)	5300 feet	
Border Justice	Bill Cody	Inde. Pict. Corp.		
		(S. R.)	5437 feet	Nov. 8
Coast Patrol, The	Kenneth McDonald	Barsky (S. R.)	5000 feet	
Confessions of a Queen	Tarly-Stone	Metro-Goldwyn	5570 feet	April 4
Crimson Runner, The	Priscilla Dean	Prod. Dist. Corp.	4776 feet	June 6
Daddy's Gone A'Hunting	Joyce-Marmont	Metro-Goldwyn	5851 feet	Mar. 7
Denial, The	Special Cast	Metro-Goldwyn	4791 feet	Mar. 21
Double Action Daniels	Buffalo Bill, Jr	Weiss Bros. (S. R.)	4660 feet	
Dressmaker from Paris,				
The	Rod La Rocque	Paramount	7080 feet	Mar. 28
Fighting Romeo, A	Al Ferguson	Davis Dist. Div.(S.R.)	5000 feet	Aug. 15
Fighting the Flames	Haines-Devore	C. B. C. (S. R.)	5600 feet	
Forbidden Cargo	Evelyn Brent	F. B. O.	4830 feet	April 11
Goose Hangs High, The	Constance Bennett	Paramount	6100 feet	Feb. 14
Great Divide, The	Terry-Teech	Metro-Goldwyn	7811 feet	Feb. 21
Head Winds	House Peters	Universal	5600 feet	Mar. 28
Hunted Woman, The	Seena Owen	Fox	4954 feet	April 4
I Want My Man	Sills-Kenyon	First National	6175 feet	April 18
Jimmie's Millions	Richard Talmadge	F. B. O.	5167 feet	Feb. 28
Just Traveling	Bob Burns	Sierra Pict. (S. R.)	4400 feet	
Last Laugh, The	Emil Jannings	Universal	6119 feet	Dec. 20
Let'er Buck	Hoot Gibson	Universal	5175 feet	Jan. 3
Mad Whirl, The	May McAvoy	Universal	5184 feet	Dec. 6
Marriage in Transit	Edmund Lowe	Fox Film	4800 feet	April 11
Men and Women	Special Cast	Paramount	6233 feet	Mar. 28
Monster, The	L. Chaney-J. Arthur	Metro-Goldwyn	5432 feet	Feb. 28
My Wife and I	Special Cast	Warner Bros	6790 feet	June 6
New Lives for Old	Betty Compson	Paramount	6796 feet	Mar. 7
New Toys	Richard Barthelmess	First National	7250 feet	Feb. 21
One Year to Live	Special Cast	First National	6310 feet	Feb. 28
Pefcy	Charles Ray	Assoc. Exhib.	5584 feet	Feb. 28
Playing With Souls	Special Cast	First National	5831 feet	Mar. 4
Price of Pleasure, The	Valli-Kerry	Universal	6616 feet	June 13
Recompense	M. Prevost-M. Blue	Warner Bros	7480 feet	May 2
Renegade Holmes, M.D.	Ben Wilson	Arrow (S. R.)	4947 feet	
Riders of the Purple Sage	Tom Mix	Fox	5578 feet	Mar. 28
Romance and Rustlers	Yakima Canutt	Arrow (S. R.)	4869 feet	Nov. 15
Sackcloth and Scarlet	Alice Terry	Paramount	5732 feet	Mar. 7
Sally	Colleen Moore	First National	8426 feet	Mar. 28
Scar Hanan	Yakima Canutt	F. B. O.	4684 feet	April 4
Scarlet Honeymoon, The	Shirley Mason	Fox	4660 feet	Mar. 21
Seven Chances	Buster Keaton	Metro-Goldwyn	6110 feet	Mar. 28
Sign of the Cactus, The	Jack Hoxie	Universal	4929 feet	Jan. 10
Sky Raider, The	Capt. Charles Nun-			
	gesser	Assoc. Exhib.	4638 feet	April 4
Speed	Betty Blythe	Banner Prod. (S. R.)	6000 feet	Mar. 28
Too Many Kisses	Richard Dix	Paramount	5726 feet	Mar. 14
Waking Up the Town	Jack Pickford	United Artists	4927 feet	April 11
Where Romance Rides	Dick Hatton	Arrow	4901 feet	
Zander the Great	Marion Davies	Metro-Goldwyn	5951 feet	May 16

APRIL

Feature	Star	Distributed by	Length	Reviewed
Adventure	P. Starke-T. Moore	Paramount	6713 feet	April 25
After Business Hours	Hammerstein-Tellegen	C. B. C. (S. R.)	5000 feet	
Bandit Tamer, The	Franklyn Farnum	Inde. Pict. (S. R.)	5000 feet	
Border Vengeance	Jack Perrin	Madoc Sales (S. R.)	4500 feet	
Charmel, The	Pola Negri	Paramount	6076 feet	April 18
Code of the West	O. Moore-C. Bennett	Paramount	6777 feet	April 25
Courageous Fool, The	Reed Howes	Rayart (S. R.)		
Crowded Hour, The	Bebe Daniels	Paramount	6585 feet	May 9
Dangerous Innocence	LaPlante-E. O'Brien.	Universal	6759 feet	Mar. 28
Declasse	Corinne Griffith	First National	7869 feet	April 4
Eyes of the Desert	Al Richmond	Sierra Prod. (S. R.)	4500 feet	
Fifth Avenue Models	Philbin-Kerry	Universal	6581 feet	Jan. 24
Fighting Parson, The	Al Ferguson	Davis Dist. Div.(S.R.)	5000 feet	
Fighting Sheriff, The	Bill Cody	Inde. Pict. (S. R.)	5000 feet	May 30
Friendly Enemies	Weber and Fields	Prod. Dist. Corp.	6888 feet	May 9
Galloping Vengeance	Bob Custer	F. B. O.	5095 feet	April 11
Getting 'Em Right	George Larkin	Rayart (S. R.)	4500 feet	
Gold and the Girl	Buck Jones	Fox	4521 feet	April 4
Go Straight	Gladys Hulette	B. P. Schulberg(S.R.)	5986 feet	June 20
Heart of a Siren, The	Barbara La Marr	First National	6700 feet	Mar. 21
How Baxter Butted In	M. Moore-D. Devore	Warner Bros	6450 feet	July 11
Justice Raffles	Henry Edwards	Cranfield & Clarke		
		(S. R.)	6000 feet	
Kiss in the Dark, A	Special Cast	Paramount	5767 feet	April 18
Kiss Me Again	M. Prevost-M. Blue	Warner Bros	7700 feet	June 6
Love's Bargain	M. Daw-C. Brook	F. B. O.	5641 feet	April 25
Madame Sans Gene	Gloria Swanson	Paramount	9994 feet	May 2
Man and Maid	Special Cast	Metro-Goldwyn	5607 feet	April 18
My Son	Nazimova-J. Pickford	First National	6980 feet	April 25
Night Club, The	R. Griffith-V.Reynolds	Paramount	5732 feet	May 16
One Way Street	Special Cast	First National	5703 feet	April 11
Proud Flesh	Special Cast	Metro-Goldwyn	5770 feet	April 25
Raging Adventure, The	Jack Hoxie	Universal	4657 feet	Feb. 14
Ridin' Comet, The	Yakima Canutt	F. B. O.	4850 feet	May 16
Rough Going	Franklyn FaPnum	Inde. Pict. Corp.		
		(S. R.)	4354 feet	May 16
Shackled Lightning	Frank Merrill	Hercules Prod. (S. R.)		
She Wolves	Alma Rubens	Fox	4785 feet	May 9
Spaniard, The	Cortez-Goudal	Paramount	6676 feet	April 18
Sporting Venus	Special Cast	Metro-Goldwyn	5939 feet	May 23

MAY

Feature	Star	Distributed by	Length	Reviewed
Slop Flirting	Special Cast	Prod. Dist. Corp.	5161 feet	June 6
Straight Through	Wm. Desmond	Universal	4967 feet	
Tale of a Thousand and				
One Nights	Special Cast	Davis Dist. Div.		
Tearing Through	Richard Talmadge	F. B. O.	4500 feet	Feb. 14
That Devil Quemado	Fred Thomson	F. B. O.	4714 feet	May 23
Two-Fisted Sheriff, A	Yakima Canutt	Arrow (S. R.)	4764 feet	April 4
Way of a Girl, The	Boardman-M. Moore	Metro-Goldwyn	4749 feet	Dec. 6
Western Engagement, A	Dick Hatton	Arrow	5025 feet	April 18
Wings of Youth	Madge Bellamy	Fox	5340 feet	May 16
Winning a Woman	Perrin-Hill	Rayart (S. R.)	4665 feet	

Feature	Star	Distributed by	Length	Reviewed
Alias Mary Flynn	Evelyn Brent	F. B. O.	5559 feet	May 30
Any Woman	Alice Terry	Paramount	5963 feet	June 13
Awful Truth, The	Agnes Ayres	Prod. Dist. Corp.	5917 feet	July 11
Bandit's Baby, The	Fred Thomson	F. B. O.	5291 feet	June 20
Barriers of the Law	Holmes-Desmond	Indep. Pict. (S. R.)	5400 feet	May 2
Before Trail, The	William Desmond	Universal	4763 feet	April 18
Chickie	Mackaill-Bosworth	First National	7567 feet	May 9
Crackerjack, The	Johnny Hines	C. C. Burr (S. R.)	6500 feet	May 23
Evely Man's Wife	Special Cast	Fox	4365 feet	July 4
Eve's Lover	Irene Rich	Warner Bros	6549 feet	Aug. 8
Eve's Secret	Betty Compson	Paramount	6305 feet	May 9
Fear Fighter, The	Billy Sullivan	Rayart (S. R.)		
Fighting Demon, The	Richard Talmadge	F. B. O.	4470 feet	June 20
Fugitive, The	Ben Wilson	Arrow	4892 feet	
Golden Train		Sanford Prod. (S. R.)	5 reels	
His Supreme Moment	B Sweet-R Colman	First National	6800 feet	April 25
Lilies of the Streets	J. Walker-V. L. Corbin	F. B. O.	7160 feet	April 25
Little French Girl, The	Alice Joyce	Paramount	5628 feet	June 13
Lunatic at Large, A	Henry Edwards	Cranfield & Clarke		
		(S. R.)	6000 feet	
Makers of Men	Kenneth McDonald	Barsky Prod. (S. R.)	5600 feet	
Necessary Evil, The	Dana-Lyon	First National	5907 feet	May 23
Old Home Week	Thomas Meighan	Paramount	6588 feet	June 6
Phantom Rider, The	Al Richmond	Sierra Pict. (S. R.)	4750 feet	
Private Affairs	Special Cast	Prod. Dist. Corp.	6132 feet	Aug. 15
Quick Change	George Larkin	Rayart (S. R.)		
Raffles, The Amateur				
Cracksman	House Peters	Universal	5557 feet	May 30
Rainbow Trail, The	Tom Mix	Fox	5211 feet	April 25
Red Love	Lowell-Russell	Lowell Film Prod.		
Saddle Hawk, The	Hoot Gibson	Universal	5465 feet	May 9
Silent Sanderson	Harry Carey	Prod. Dist. Corp.	4841 feet	June 20
Sealed Proof	Shirley Mason	Fox	4400 feet	June 6
School for Wives	Yearle-Hornquist	Vitagraph	6750 feet	April 11
Shock Punch, The	Richard Dix	Paramount	6151 feet	May 23
Snob Buster, The	Reed Howes	Rayart (S. R.)		
Soul Fire	Barthelmess-B. Love	First National	8282 feet	May 16
Speed Wild	Maurice B "Lefty"			
	Flynn	F. B. O.	4780 feet	June 30
Talker, The	Special Cast	First National	7061 feet	May 23
Texas Bearcat, The	Bob Custer	F. B. O.	4770 feet	
Tides of Passion	Mae March	Vitagraph	6379 feet	May 9
Up the Ladder	Virginia Valli	Universal	6623 feet	Jan. 31
Welcome Home	Special Cast	Paramount	5909 feet	May 30
White Fang	Strongheart (dog)	F. B. O.	5770 feet	June 20
White Thunder	Yakima Canutt	F. B. O.	4550 feet	
Wildfire	Special Cast	Vitagraph	6 reels	June 20
Wolves of the Road	Yakima Canutt	Arrow	5000 feet	
Woman's Faith	Reubens-Marmont	Universal	6022 feet	Aug. 15
Woman Hater, The	Helene Chadwick	Warner Brothers	6000 feet	May 23

JUNE

Feature	Star	Distributed by	Length	Reviewed
Are Parents People?	Bronson-Vidor	Paramount	6586 feet	June 6
Dangerous Odds	Bill Cody	Inde. Pict. (S. R.)	4600 feet	
Desert Flower, The	Colleen Moore	First National	6837 feet	June 13
Double Fisted	Jack Perrin	Rayart (S. R.)		
Down the Border	Al Richmond	Sierra Prod. (S. R.)	4500 feet	
Faint Perfume	Seena Owen	B. P. Schulberg(S.R.)	6226 feet	July 11
Grounds for Divorce	Florence Vidor	Paramount	5712 feet	July 4
Happy Warrior, The	Special Cast	Vitagraph	6073 feet	July 18
Hearts and Spurs	Buck Jones	Fox	4600 feet	June 20
Human Tornado, The	Yakima Canutt	F. B. O.	4472 feet	
I'll Show You the Town	Reginald Denny	Universal	7400 feet	June 6
Introduce Me	Douglas MacLean	Assoc. Exhib.	5980 feet	Mar. 21
Just a Woman	Windsor-Tearle	First National	6700 feet	June 6
Light of Western Stars	Special Cast	Paramount	6853 feet	July 4
Lost—a Wife	Special Cast	Paramount	6420 feet	June 27
Making of O'Malley, The	Milton Sills	First National	7371 feet	July 4
Man from Lone Mount-				
ain, The	Ben Wilson	Arrow	4530 feet	
Man in Blue	Herbert Rawlinson	Universal	5706 feet	Feb. 21
Marry Me	Special Cast	Paramount	5546 feet	
Meddler, The	William Desmond	Universal	4680 feet	May 23
Miss Morgan's		Metro-Goldwyn		
Mind in the Valley	Alma Taylor			
My Lady's Lips	Clara Bow	B. P. Schulberg(S.R.)	6609 feet	Aug. 15
Off the Highway	Wm. V. Mong	Prod. Dist.	6600 feet	June 27
Paths to Paradise	Compson-R. Griffith	Paramount	5741 feet	June 27
Pioneers of the West	Special Cast	Sanford Prod. (S. R.)	5 reels	
Ridin' Easy	Dick Hatton	Arrow	4463 feet	
Ridin' Thunder	Jack Hoxie	Universal	4354 feet	May 23

Feature	Star	Distributed by	Length	Reviewed
Rough Stuff	George Larkin	Rayart (S. R.)		
Shattered Lives	Special Cast	Gotham (S. R.)	6 reels	July 4
Smooth as Satin	Evelyn Brent	F. B. O	6003 feet	July 4
Texas Trail, The	Harry Carey	Prod. Dist. Corp	4720 feet	July 18
Tracked in the Snow Country	Rin-Tin-Tin (dog)	Warner Brothers	6900 feet	Aug. 1
White Monkey, The	La Marr-T. Holding	First National	6121 feet	July 4
Wild Bull's Lair, The	Fred Thompson	F. B. O.	5280 feet	Aug. 15
Youth's Gamble	Reed Howes	Rayart (S. R.)	5264 feet	

JULY

Feature	Star	Distributed by	Length	Reviewed
Bloodhound, The	Bob Custer	F. B. O.	4789 feet	
Cold Nerve	Bill Cody	Inde. Pict. (S. R.)	5000 feet	
Danger Signal, The	Jane Novak	Columbia Pict. (S.R.)	5502 feet	Aug. 15
Don Daredevil	Jack Hoxie	Universal	4810 feet	
Drug Store Cowboy, The	Franklyn Farnum	Ind. Pict. Corp. (S.R.)	5100 feet	Feb. 7
Duped	Holmes-Desmond	Ind. Pict. (S. R.)	5400 feet	
Fighting Youth		Columbia Pict. (S.R.)		
Lady Who Lied, The	L. Stone-V. Valli	First National	7111 feet	July 18
Lady Robinhood	Evelyn Brent	F. B. O	5582 feet	Aug 22
Manicure Girl, The	Bebe Daniels	Paramount	5959 feet	June 27
Marriage Whirl, The	C. Griffith-H. Ford	First National	7672 feet	July 25
Mysterious Stranger, The	Richard Talmadge	F. B. O	5270 feet	
Night Life of New York	Special Cast	Paramount	6998 feet	July 4
Pipes of Pan	Alma Taylor	Cranfield & Clarke (S. R.)	6200 feet	
Ranger of the Big Pines, The	Kenneth Harlan	Vitagraph	5800 feet	Aug. 8
Scarlet West, The	Frazer-Bow	First National	8391 feet	July 25
Secret of Black Canyon, The	Dick Hatton	Arrow		
Strange Rider, The	Yakima Canutt	Arrow		
Taming the West	Hoot Gibson	Universal	5427 feet	Feb. 28
Trailed	Al Richmond	Sierra Prod. (S. R.)	4750 feet	
White Desert, The	Special Cast	Metro-Goldwyn	6345 feet	July 18

AUGUST

Feature	Star	Distributed by	Length	Reviewed
American Pluck	George Walsh	Chadwick	5000 feet	July 11
Beggar on Horseback, A	Ralston-Nissen	Paramount	6800 feet	June 20
Business of Love, The	E. Horton-M. Bellamy	Astor Dist. Corp		
Children of the Whirlwind	Lionel Barrymore	Arrow		
Don Q	Douglas Fairbanks	United Artists	10264 feet	June 27
Drusilla With a Million	Special Cast	F. B. O	7391 feet	May 30
Evolution		Red Seal	4200 feet	Aug. 15
Fine Clothes	L. Stone-A. Rubens	First National	6971 feet	Aug. 15
Girl Who Wouldn't Work, The	Lionel Barrymore	B. P. Schulberg (S.R.)	5979 feet	Sept. 5
Gold Rush, The	Charles Chaplin	United Artists	8500 feet	Aug. 8
Halfway Girl, The	Doris Kenyon	First National	7570 feet	Aug. 8
Headlines	Alice Joyce	Assoc. Exhib	5600 feet	July 25
Her Sister From Paris	C. Talmadge	First National	7255 feet	Aug. 15
In the Name of Love	Cortez-Nissen	Paramount	5904 feet	Sept. 5
Isle of Hope, The	Richard Talmadge	Film Book. Offices	5800 feet	Sept. 5
Kivalina of the Ice Lands	Native Cast	Pathe	6 reels	July 11
Knockout, The	Milton Sills	First National	7450 feet	Sept. 19
Lightnin'	Jay Hunt	Fox	7979 feet	Aug. 1
Limited Mail, The	Monte Blue	Warner Brothers	6250 feet	
Love Hour, The	Ruth Clifford	Vitagraph	5900 feet	
Lover's Oath, The	Ramon Novarro	Astor Dist Corp		
Lucky Devil, The	Richard Dix	Paramount	5935 feet	July 18
Lucky Horseshoes	Tom Mix	Fox	5000 feet	Aug. 29
My Pal	Dick Hatton	Arrow		
Overland Limited, The		Gotham Prod. (S. R.)	6389 feet	Aug. 8
Parisian Love	Bow-Tellegen	B. P. Schulberg (S.R.)	6324 feet	Aug. 22
Quo Vadis	Emil Jannings	First National	8945 feet	Feb. 28
Range Justice	Dick Hatton	Arrow		
Romola	Gish Sisters	Metro-Goldwyn	10875 feet	Dec. 13
Rugged Water	Special Cast	Paramount	6015 feet	Aug. 1
Shining Adventure, The	Percy Marmont	Astor Dist. Corp		
Slave of Fashion, A	Special Cast	Metro-Goldwyn	5906 feet	Aug. 1
Speed Mad		Columbia Pict. (S.R.)	4442 feet	Sept. 19
Street of Forgotten Men	Special Cast	Paramount	6366 feet	Aug. 1
Ten Commandments	Special Cast	Paramount	9980 feet	Jan. 5-24
That Man Jack	Bob Custer	F. B. O	5032 feet	Aug. 22
Unholy Three	Lon Chaney	Metro-Goldwyn	6848 feet	Aug. 15
Unwritten Law, The		Columbia Pict. (S.R.)		
Wife Who Wasn't Wanted, The	Irene Rich	Warner Brothers	6400 feet	
Wizard of Oz	Larry Semon	Chadwick	6300 feet	Apr. 25
Wrongdoers, The	Lionel Barrymore	Astor Dist. Corp		

SEPTEMBER

Feature	Star	Distributed by	Length	Reviewed
Amazing Quest, The	Henry Edwards	Cranfield & Clarke	5500 feet	
As No Man Has Loved	Edward Hearn	Fox	10000 feet	Feb. 28
Below The Line	Rin-Tin-Tin (dog)	Warner Brothers	6100 feet	
Black Cyclone	Rex (horse)	Pathe		May 30
Bobbed Hair	Prevost-Harlan	Warner Brothers	6700 feet	
California Straight Ahead	Reginald Denny	Universal		
Call of Courage, The	Art Acord	Universal	4661 feet	Sept. 19
Classified	Corinne Griffith	First National		
Coast of Folly	Gloria Swanson	Paramount		
Crack of Dawn	Reed Howes	Rayart (S. R.)		
Cyclone Cavalier	Reed Howes	Rayart (S. R.)	4928 feet	Sept. 26
Dark Angel, The	R. Colman-V. Banky	First National	7311 feet	Sept. 29
Free to Love	C. Bow-R. McKee	B. P. Schulberg (S. R.)		
Freshman, The	Harold Lloyd	Pathe		July 25
Graustark	Norma Talmadge	First National	5900 feet	Sept. 19
Havoc	Special Cast	Fox	9200 feet	Aug. 29
High and Handsome	"Lefty" Flynn	F. B. O.	5669 feet	
If Marriage Fails	J. Logan-C. Brook	F. B. O	6006 feet	May 23
Keep Smiling	Monty Banks	Assoc. Exhib	5400 feet	Aug. 1
Let's Go Gallagher	Tom Tyler	Film Book Offices		
Little Annie Rooney	Mary Pickford	United Artists		
Lost World, The	Special Cast	First National	9700 feet	Feb. 21
Manhattan Madness	Dempsey-Taylor	Assoc. Exhib	5500 feet	July 25
Man Who Found Himself	Thomas Meighan	Paramount	7168 feet	Sept. 5
Marrying Money		Truart (S. R.)	5800 feet	
Mystic, The	Special Cast	Metro-Goldwyn		
Never the Twain Shall Meet	Stewart-Lytell	Metro-Goldwyn	8143 feet	Aug. 8
New Champion, The		Columbia Pict. (S.R.)		
Not So Long Ago	Betty Bronson	Paramount	6943 feet	Aug. 8
Other Woman's Story		B. P. Schulberg		
Outlaw's Daughter, The	Josie Sedgwick	Universal	4375 feet	
Parisian Nights	E. Hammerstein - L. Tellegen	F. B. O	6278 feet	June 20

Feature	Star	Distributed by	Length	Reviewed
Pretty Ladies	Zazu Pitts	Metro-Goldwyn	5828 feet	July 25
Prince of Broadway, The	George Walsh	Chadwick		
Ridin' the Wind	Fred Thomson	Film Book. Offices		
Sealed Lips		Columbia Pict. (S.R.)		
Shore Leave	Barthelmess-Mackaill	First National	6856 feet	Aug. 29
Siege	Virginia Valli	Universal	6424 feet	June 20
Some Pun'kins	Chas. Ray	Chadwick	6500 feet	Sept. 19
Son of His Father	Special Cast	Paramount	7009 feet	
Souls for Sables		Tiffany (S. R.)	6500 feet	
S. O. S. Perils of the Sea		Columbia Pict. (S.R.)		
Spook Ranch	Hoot Gibson	Universal	5147 feet	May 2
Sun Up	Special Cast	Metro-Goldwyn		Aug. 29
Teaser, The	Laura La Plante	Universal	6967 feet	May 30
Three in Exile		Truart (S. R.)	5800 feet	
Three Weeks in Paris	M. Moore-D. Devore	Warner Brothers	5900 feet	
Three Wise Crooks	Evelyn Brent	Film Book. Offices		
Throwback, The	Special Cast	Universal		
Timber Wolf, The	Buck Jones	Fox	4809 feet	Sept. 26
Trouble With Wives, The	Vidor-T. Moore	Paramount	6489 feet	Aug. 15
Unchastened Woman, The	Theda Bara	Chadwick		
Wall Street Whiz, The	Richard Talmadge	Film Book. Offices		
What Fools Men	Stone-Mason	First National		
Wheel, The	Special Cast	Fox	7264 feet	Aug. 29
White Outlaw, The	Jack Hoxie	Universal	4830 feet	June 27
Wild Horse Mesa	Special Cast	Paramount	7221 feet	Aug. 22
Wild, Wild Susan	Bebe Daniels	Paramount		
With This Ring	Mills-Tellegen	B. P. Schulberg		

OCTOBER

Feature	Star	Distributed by	Length	Reviewed
Bells, The	Lionel Barrymore	Chadwick		
Bustin' Through	Jack Hoxie	Universal	4506 feet	
Circus Cyclone, The	Art Acord	Universal	4609 feet	Aug. 22
Dollar Down	Ruth Roland	Truart (S. R.)	5800 feet	Aug. 29
Everlasting Whisper, The	Tom Mix	Fox		
Exchange of Wives, An	Special Cast	Metro-Goldwyn		
Fate of a Flirt, The		Columbia (S. R.)		
Golden Princess, The	Bronson-Hamilton	Paramount	6395 feet	Sept. 19
Great Sensation, The	W. Fairbanks-P. Garon	Columbia (S. R.)	4470 feet	Sept. 26
Heads Up	Fred Thomson	F. B. O		
He's a Prince	Raymond Griffith	Paramount		
His Buddy's Wife	Glenn Hunter	Assoc. Exhib	5600 feet	July 25
Iron Horse, The		Fox Film Corp	11335 feet	Sept. 13
John Forrest	Henry Edwards	Cranfield&Clark(S.R.)	5000 feet	
Keeper of the Bees, The	Robert Frazer	F. B. O		
Lew Tyler's Wives		B. P. Schulberg (S. R.)		
Lights of Old Broadway	Marion Davies	Metro-Goldwyn		
Lovers in Quarantine	Daniels-Ford	Paramount		
Midshipman, The	Ramon Novarro	Metro-Goldwyn		
Morals for Men	Tearle-Ayers	Tiffany (S. R.)	6500 feet	
New Brooms	Hamilton-Love	Paramount		
Peacock Feathers	Logan-Landis	Universal	6747 feet	Aug. 20
Perfect Clown, The	Larry Semon	Chadwick		
Pony Express, The	Betty Compson	Paramount		
Sally of the Sawdust	Fields-Dempster	United Artists	9500 feet	Aug. 15
Sporting Chance, The		Tiffany (S. R.)	6500 feet	July 4
Storm Breaker, The	House Peters	Universal	6064 feet	Sept. 26
Thank U	Special Cast	Fox	7 reels	Sept. 19
Tower of Lies	Chaney-Shearer	Metro-Goldwyn		
Tumbleweeds	Wm. S. Hart	United Artists		
Under the Rouge	Tom Moore	Assoc. Exhib	6500 feet	July 25
Winds of Chance	A. Nilsson-B. Lyon	First National	9753 feet	Aug. 29

NOVEMBER

Feature	Star	Distributed by	Length	Reviewed
Ancient Highway, The	Holt-Vidor	Paramount		
Best People, The	Special Cast	Paramount		
Blue Blood	George Walsh	Chadwick		
Camille of the Barbary Coast	Busch-O. Moore	Assoc. Exhib	5600 feet	Aug. 1
Cobra	Valentino-Naldi	Paramount		
Don't	S. O'Neill-B. Roach	Metro-Goldwyn		
Fifty-Fifty	L. Barrymore-H. Hampton	Assoc. Exhib	5564 feet	June 20
Fight to a Finish, A		Columbia (S. R.)		
Fighting Heart, The	Geo. O'Brien	Fox	6978 feet	
Flower of Night	Pola Negri	Paramount		
Fool, The	Special Cast	Fox		April 25
King on Main St., The	Adolphe Menjou	Paramount		
Lazybones		Fox Film		
Lightning		Tiffany (S. R.)	6500 feet	
Little Bit of Broadway	Ray-Starke	Metro-Goldwyn		
Merry Widow	Mae Murray	Metro-Goldwyn		
Price of Success, The	Alice Lake	Columbia (S. R.)		
Silent Witness, The		Truart (S. R.)	5800 feet	
Stage Struck	Gloria Swanson	Paramount		
Time the Comedian		Metro-Goldwyn		
Transcontinental Limited	Special Cast	Chadwick (S. R.)		
Vanishing American	Dix-Wilson	Paramount		
Winner, The	Charley Ray	Chadwick (S. R.)		

Comedy Releases

Feature	Star	Distributed by	Length	Reviewed
Absent Minded	Neely Edwards	Universal	1 reel	
Across the Hall	Edna Marian	Universal	2 reels	
Adventures of Adenoid	Aesop's Fables	Pathe	1 reel	April 25
After a Reputation	Edna Marian	Universal	2 reels	
Air Tight	Bobby Vernon	Educational	2 reels	June 13
Alice's Egg Plant	"Cartoon"	M. J. Winkler (S. R.)	1 reel	
Alice Stagestruck	Margie Gay	M. J. Winkler (S.R.)	1 reel	July 18
All Aboard	Perry-Cooley	Fox	2 reels	
Almost a Husband	Buddy Messinger	Universal	2 reels	
Amateur Detective	Earle Foxe	Fox	2 reels	
Andy in Hollywood	Joe Murphy	Universal	2 reels	
Andy Takes a Flyer	"The Gumps"	Universal	2 reels	
Apache, The	Earle Foxe	Fox Film	2 reels	
Apollo's Pretty Sister		Fox	2 reels	
Are Husbands Human?	James Finlayson	Pathe	1 reel	April 11
Artists' Blues	G. Joy-J. Moore	Rayart (S. R.)	2 reels	
Ask Grandma	"Our Gang"	Pathe	2 reels	May 30
At the Seashore	Monkey	Fox	2 reels	

Feature	Star	Distributed by	Length	Reviewed
Raid, The	Gloria Joy	Rayart Pict. (S. R.)	2 reels	
Rainy Knight, A	Special Cast	Pathe		
Raisin' Cain	Constance Darling	Universal	2 reels	April 4
Rapid Transit	Al. St. John	Educational	2 reels	
Ratin' Romeo	Walter Hiers	Educational	2 reels	Mar. 28
Raspberry Romance	Ben Turpin	Pathe	2 reels	Feb. 28
Red Pepper	Al. St. John	Educational	2 reels	Arpil 4
Regular Girl, A	Wanda Wiley	Universal	2 reels	
Riders of the Kitchen Range	Mohar-Engle	Pathe	1 reel	June 6
Remember When	Harry Langdon	Pathe	2 reels	April 25
Rip Without a Wink	" Redhead "	Sering Wilson (S. R.)	1 reel	
Ripe Melodrama, A		Sering Wilson (S. R.)	1 reel	
Rivals	Billy West	Arrow	2 reels	
Robinson Crusoe Returns on Friday	" Redhead "	Sering Wilson (S. R.)	1 reel	
Rock Bottom	Bowes-Vance	Educational	1 reel	May 9
Robbing the Rube		Lee-Bradford Corp.	2 reels	
Rolling Stones	Charles Puffy	Universal	1 reel	May 30
Rough Party	Al Alt	Universal	2 reels	
Royal Four-Flush	" Spat Family "	Pathe	2 reels	June 13
Runaway Balloon, The	"Aesop's Fables "	Pathe	1 reel	June 27
Runt, The	"Aesop's Fables "	Pathe	1 reel	June 6
Sailor Papa, A	Glenn Tryon	Pathe	2 reels	April 4
Saturday	" Hey Fellas "	Davis Dist. Div.	2 reels	
Say It With Flour		Fox	2 reels	
Scrambled Eggs		Educational		
Sheiks of Bagdad		Pathe	1 reel	May 9
Sherlock Sleuth	Arthur Stone	Pathe	2 reels	July 11
Ship Shape	Vance-Bowes	Educational	1 reel	April 18
Shootin' Injuns	" Our Gang "	Pathe	2 reels	May 9
Short Pants	Arthur Lake	Universal	1 reel	Aug. 1
Should a Husband Tell?		Red Seal Pict.	1 reel	
Should Husbands Be Watched?	Charles Chase	Pathe	1 reel	Mar. 14
Sir Walt and Lizzie		Sering Wilson (S. R.)	1 reel	
Sit Tight	Jimmie Adams	Educational	2 reels	May 30
Skinners in Silk		Pathe	2 reels	May 16
Sky Jumper, The	Earle Foxe	Fox	2 reels	
Skyscraper, The	Harry Langdon	Principal Pict. (S. R.)	2 reels	
Sleeping Sickness	Edwards-Roach	Universal	1 reel	May 30
Slick Articles	Engle-Karr	Universal	2 reels	May 30
Smoked Out	Lake-Hasbrouck	Universal	1 reel	April 13
Sneezing Beezers	Billy Bevan	Pathe	2 reels	July 18
Snow-Hawk	Stan Laurel	F. B. O.	2 reels	
Soap	"Aesop's Fables"	Pathe	1 reel	
Somewhere in Somewhere	Murray-Littlefield	Pathe	2 reels	Sept. 26
S. O. S.	"Aesop's Fables"	Pathe	1 reel	
Spanish Romeo, A (Van Bibber)		Fox	1 reel	
Speak Easy	Charley Puffy	Universal	1 reel	Aug. 22
Speak Freely	Edna Marion	Universal	2 reels	
Spot Light		Educational	2 reels	
Stick Around	Bobby Dunn	Arrow	2 reels	
Stop, Look and Whistle		Fox	2 reels	
Storm, The (Out of the Inkwell)	" Cartoon "	Red Seal Pict.	1 reel	
Stranded	Edna Marian	Universal	2 reels	
Super-Hooper-Dyne Lizzies		Pathe	2 reels	June 13
Sure Mike!	Martha Sleeper	Pathe	1 reel	May 23
Sweet Marie		Fox	2 reels	Aug. 29
Tame Men and Wild Women		Pathe	2 reels	Aug. 15
Teaser Island	" Redhead "	Sering Wilson (S. R.)	1 reel	
Tee for Two	Alice Day	Pathe	2 reels	Aug. 1
Tell It To a Policeman	Glenn Tryon	Pathe	2 reels	May 23
Tender Feet	Walter Hiers	Educational	2 reels	May 23
Tenting Out	Roache-Edwards	Universal	1 reel	Mar. 23
This Week-End		Lee-Bradford (S. R.)		
Three Wise Goofs	Special Cast	F. B. O		
Thundering Landlords	Glenn Tryon	Pathe	2 reels	June 27
Ton of Fun in a Beauty Parlor, A		F. B. O		
Too Much Mother-in-Law	Constance Darling	Universal		
Too Young to Marry	Buddy Messinger	Universal	2 reels	
Tough Night, A	Jimmy Callahan	Aywon Film	2 reels	
Tourist, The	Harry Langdon	Educational Film	2 reels	Aug. 15
Tourists De Luxe	Hayes-Karr	Universal	2 reels	May 16
Transients in Arcadia		Fox	2 reels	
Transatlantic Flight, A	"Aesop's Fables "	Pathe	1 reel	
Twins	Stan Laurel	F. B. O	2 reels	
Two Cats and a Bird	" Cartoon "	Educational	1 reel	Mar. 14
Two Poor Fish	Earl Hurd cartoon	Educational	1 reel	May 30
Ugly Duckling, The	"Aesop's Fables "	Pathe	1 reel	Sept. 26
Uncle Tom's Gal	Edna Marian	Universal	2 reels	
Unwelcome	Charles Puffy	Universal	1 reel	June 27
Waiting	Lloyd Hamilton	Educational	2 reels	July 11
Wake Up	Bowes-Vance	Educational	1 reel	June 13
Watch Out	Bobby Vernon	Educational	2 reels	
Water Wagons	Special Cast	Pathe	2 reels	Feb. 21
Welcome Dangar	Bowes-Vance	Educational	1 reel	Feb. 23
West is West	Billy West	Arrow	2 reels	
Westward Ho	Charles Puffy	Universal	1 reel	
What Price Goofy	Charley Chase	Pathe	2 reels	June 6
When Dumbells Ring		Fox	2 reels	
When Men Were Men	"Aesop's Fables "	Pathe	1 reel	July 25
White Wing's Bride	Harry Langdon	Pathe	2 reels	July 11
Whose Baby Are You?	Glenn Tryon	Pathe	2 reels	
Who's Which	Bowes-Vance	Educational	1 reel	
Why Hesitate?	Neal Burns	Educational	2 reels	April 11
Why Sitting Bull Stood Up		Sering Wilson (S. R.)	1 reel	
Wide Awake	Lige Conley	Educational	2 reels	
Wild Papa	" Spat Family "	Pathe	2 reels	May 16
Wild Waves	Bowes-Vance	Educational	1 reel	May 23
Wine, Woman and Song	"Aesop's Fables "	Pathe	1 reel	
Winning Pair, A	Wanda Wiley	Universal	2 reels	
Wooly West, The	Buddy Messinger	Universal	2 reels	
Wrestler, The	Earle Foxe	Fox	2 reels	Aug. 29
Yarn About Yarn, A	Aesop Fable	Pathe	1 reel	Aug. 1
Yes, Yes, Nannette	Jas. Finlayson	Pathe	1 reel	Aug. 1
Your Own Back Yard	" Our Gang "	Pathe		

Short Subjects

Feature	Distributed by	Length	Reviewed
Action (Sportlight)	Pathe	1 reel	
All Under One Flag (Sportlight)	Pathe	1 reel	
Animal Celebrities (Sportlight)	Pathe	1 reel	June 27
Animated Hair Cartoon (Series)	Red Seal	1 reel	
Balto's Race to Nome (Special)	Educational	2 reels	May 23
Barbara Snitches (Pacemaker Series)	F. B. O.	2 reels	
Battle of Wits (Josie Sedgwick)	Universal	2 reels	July 18
Bashful Whirlwind, The (Edmund Cobb)	Universal	2 reels	
Beauty and the Bandit (Geo. Larkin)	Universal	2 reels	July 4
Beauty Spots (Sportlight)	Pathe	1 reel	April 18
Best Man, The (Josie Sedgwick)	Universal	2 reels	Aug. 15
Broken Trails	Denver Dixon (S.R.)	2 reels	
Boundary Line, The (Fred Humes)	Universal	2 reels	
Cabaret of Old Japan	M. J. Winkler (S.R.)	1 reel	
Color World	Sering Wilson (S. R.)	1 reel	
Captured Alive (Helen Gibson)	Universal	2 reels	July 25
Cinema Stars (Novelty)	Davis Dist	1 reel	
Close Call, The (Edmund Cobb)	Universal	2 reels	
Cocoon to Kimono	M. J. Winkler (S.R.)	1 reel	
Come-Back, The (Benny Leonard)	Henry Ginsberg-S.R.	2 reels	
Concerning Cheese (Varieties)	Fox	1 reel	
Covered Flagon, The (Pacemaker Series)	F. B. O	2 reels	
Cowpuncher's Comeback, The (Art Acord)	Universal	2 reels	
Crooked (Elinor King)	Davis Dist	2 reels	
Cross Word Puzzle Film (Comedy-Novelty)	Schwartz Enterprises (S. R.)	1 reel	
Cuba Steps Out (Variety)	Fox	1 reel	
Day With the Gypsies	Red Seal Pict.	1 reel	
Divertisement (Color Shots)	Sering Wilson (S. R.)	1 reel	
Don Coo Coo (Pacemakers)	Film Book. Offices	2 reels	
Do You Remember (Gems of Screen)	Red Seal	1 reel	
Dude Ranch Days (Sportlight)	Pathe	1 reel	May 30
Earth's Other Half (Hodge-Podge)	Educational	1 reel	June 6
East Side, West Side	DeForrest (S. R.)		
Fast Male, The (Pacemakers)	Film Book. Offices	2 reels	
Fighting Cowboy (Series)	Universal		
Fighting Ranger (Serial)	Universal	15 episodes	Feb. 7
Fighting Schoolmarm (Josie Sedgwick)	Universal	2 reels	Aug. 1
Film Facts	Red Seal	1 reel	
Fire Trader, The (Serial)	Universal	15 episodes	
Flirting With Death	Red Seal Pict.	2 reels	Sept. 26
Floral Feast, A	Sering Wilson (S.R.)	1 reel	
Frederick Chopin (Music Masters)	Jas. A. Fitzpatrick (S. R.)	1 reel	
From Mars to Munich (Varieties)	Fox	1 reel	April 4
Frontier Love (Billy Mack)	Denver Dixon	2 reels	
Fugitive Futurist	Cranfield & Clarke (S. R.)		
George F. Handel (Music Masters)	Jas. A. Fitzpatrick (S. R.)	1 reel	
Gems of the Screen	Red Seal	1 reel	
Ghost City, The (Serial)	Universal	15 episodes	
Golden Panther, The (Serial)	Pathe		
Gold Trap, The Fred Humes	Universal	2 reels	
Great Circus Mystery, The (Serial)	Universal	15 episodes	
Great Decide, The (Pacemakers)	Film Book. Offices	2 reels	
He Who Gets Rapped (Pacemakers)	Film Book. Offices	2 reels	
Hittin' the Trail (Fred Hank)	Sierra Pict. (S. R.)	2 reels	
How the Elephant Got His Trunk (Bray)	F. B. O		
Idaho (Serial)	Pathe	10 episodes	Feb. 28
If a Picture Tells a Story	Cranfield & Clarke (S. R.)		
In a China Shop (Variety)	Fox	1 reel	
In the Spider's Grip (Novelty)	Educational	1 reel	April 11
Invention, The (Elinor King)	Davis Dist	2 reels	
I Remember	Short Films Synd.	2 reels	Sept. 26
It Might Happen to You (Evangeline Russell)	Davis Dist	2 reels	
Jazz Fight, The (Benny Leonard)	Henry Ginsberg (S. R.)	2 reels	
Judge's Cross Word Puzzle (Novelty)	Educational	1 reel	Jan. 31
Just Cowboys Corbett-Holmes	Universal	2 reels	
Klondike Today (Varieties)	Fox	1 reel	
Knicknacks of Knowledge (Hodge Podge)	Educational	1 reel	
Knockout Man, The (Mustang)	Universal	2 reels	July 11
Land of the Navajo (Educational)	Fox	1 reel	
Learning How (Sportlight)	Pathe	1 reel	July 18
Leopard's Lair	Universal	Serial	
Let's Paint	Cranfield & Clarke (S. R.)		
Life's Greatest Thrills	Universal	2 reels	Sept. 26
Line Runners, The (Arnold Gregg)	Universal	2 reels	
Little People of the Garden (Secrets of Life)	Educational	1 reel	
Little People of the Sea (Secrets of Life)	Educational	1 reel	Feb. 28
Lizzie's Last Lap	Cranfield & Clarke (S. R.)		
Loaded Dice (Edmund Cobb)	Universal	2 reels	April 4
Luna-cy (Stereoscopik)	Pathe	1 reel	
Mad Miner, A (Western)	Hunt Miller (S. R.)	2 reels	
Magic Hour, The	Red Seal Pict.	1 reel	
Man Who Rode Alone, The	Miller & Steen (S.R.)	2 reels	
Man Without a Scar	Universal	2 reels	
Marvels of Motion	Red Seal	1 reel	
Marvellous Manhattan	M. J. Winkler (S. R.)	1 reel	
Merry Kiddo, The (Pacemakers)	Film Book. Offices	2 reels	
Merton of the Goofies .... " Pacemaker "	F. B. O.	2 reels	
Mexican Melody (Hodge-Podge)	Educational	1 Reel	
Mexican Oil Fields	M. J. Winkler (S. R.)	1 reel	
Movie Morsels (Hodge Podge)	Educational	1 reel	April 4
My Own Carolina (Variety)	Fox	1 reel	Aug. 29
Mystery Box, The (Serial)	Davis Dist. Corp.	10 episodes	
Neptune's Nieces (Sportlight)	Pathe	1 reel	
New Sheriff, A (Western)	Hunt Miller (S. R.)	2 reels	
Olympic Mermaids (Sportlight)	Pathe	1 reel	
One Glorious Scrap (Edmund Cobb)	Universal	2 reels	
Only a Country Lass (Novelty)	Educational	1 reel	May 29
Ouch (Stereoscopik)	Pathe	1 reel	
Our Six-legged Friends (Secrets of Life)	Educational	1 reel	
Outlaw, The (Jack Perrin)	Universal	2 reels	
Paris Creations (Novelty)	Educational	1 reel	Feb. 7
Paris Creations in Color (Novelty)	Educational	1 reel	Feb. 28
People You Know (Screen Almanac)	Film Booking Offices.	1 reel	
Perfect View, The (Varieties)	Fox	1 reel	
Perils of the Wild (Serial)	Universal		
Pictorial Proverbs (Hodge Podge)	Educational	1 reel	Aug. 15
Plastigrams (Novelty)	Educational		
Play Ball (Serial)	Pathe	10 episodes	June 27
Power God, The (Serial)	Davis Dist. Div.	15 episodes	
Pronto Kid, The (Edmund Cobb)	Universal	2 reels	June 27
Queen of the Round-Up (J. Sedgwick)	Universal	2 reels	June 13
Race, The (Van Bibber)	Fox	2 reels	
Radio Detective, The	Universal	Serial	
Raid, The Edmund Cobb	Universal	2 reels	
Record Breaker, The	Pathe	Serial	
Rim of the Desert (Jack Perrin)	Universal	2 reels	
River Nile, The (Variety)	Fox	1 reel	
Roaring Waters (Geo. Larkin)	Universal	2 reels	
Rock Bound Brittany (Educational)	Fox	1 reel	
Ropin' Venus, The (Mustang Series)	Universal	2 reels	July 11
R. Valentino and Eighty-eight Prize-winning American Beauties	Chesterfield (M. P. Corp.) (S. R.)	3 reels	
Secrets of Life (Educational)	Principal Pict. (S. R.)	reel	Feb. 21
Seven Ages of Sport (Sportlight)	Pathe	1 reel	Aug. 22

Feature	Star	Distributed by	Length	Reviewed
Shadow of Suspicion (Eileen Sedgwick)		Universal	2 reels	
Shoes (O. Henry)		Fox	2 reels	
Shootin' Wild (Corbett-Holmes)		Universal	2 reels	
Show Down, The (Art Acord)		Universal	2 reels	
Silvery Art		Red Seal Pict.	2 reels	Sept. 26
Sky Tribe, The (Variety)		Fox	1 reel	
Smoke of a Forty-Five, The (Western)		Hunt Miller (S. R.)	2 reels	
Soft Muscles (Benny Leonard)		Ginsberg (S. R.)	2 reels	
Song Cartunes (Novelty)		Red Seal Pict.	1 reel	
Sons of Swat (Sportlight)		Pathe	1 reel	Aug. 15
Sporting Judgment (Sportlight)		Pathe	1 reel	May 9
Starting an Argument (Sportlight)		Pathe	1 reel	
Steam Heated Islands (Varieties)		Fox	1 reel	
Stereoscopic (Novelty)		Pathe	1 reel	May 16
Storm King (Edmund Cobb)		Universal	2 reels	
Story Teller, The (Hodge-Podge)		Educational	1 reel	
Straight Shootin' (Harry Carey)		Universal	2 reels	
Strangler Lewis vs. Wayne Munn		Educational	2 reels	July 4
Stratford on Avon (Gems of Screen)		Red Seal Pict.	1 reel	
Sunken Silver (Serial)		Pathe	10 episodes	April 18
Surprise Fight, The (Benny Leonard)		Henry Ginsberg (S. R.)	2 reels	
Thundering Waters (Novelty)		Sering D. Wilson (S. R.)	1 reel	April 25
Tiger Kill, The (Pathe Review)		Pathe		
Toiling for Rest (Variety)		Fox	1 reel	
Traps and Troubles (Sportlight)		Pathe	1 reel	Mar. 21
Travel Treasures (Hodge Podge)		Educational	1 reel	July 25
Turf Mystery (Serial)		Chesterfield Pict. Corp. (S. R.)	15 episodes	
Valley of Rogues (Western)		Universal	2 reels	April 18
Van Bibber and the Navy (Earle Foxe)		Fox	2 reels	
Village School, The (Hodge Podge)		Educational Film	1 reel	May
Voice of the Nightingale, The (Novelty)		Educational	1 reel	Mar. 28
Waiting For You (Music Film)		Hegerman Music Novelties (S. R.)		
Welcome Granger (Pacemakers)		Film Book. Offices	2 reels	
West Wind, The, (Variety)		Fox	1 reel	
What Price Gloria (Pacemakers)		Film Book. Offices	2 reels	
Wheels of the Pioneers (Billy Mack)		Denver Dixon (S. R.)	2 reels	
Where the Waters Divide (Varieties)		Fox	1 reel	
White Paper (Varieties)		Fox	1 reel	
Wild West Wallop, The (Edmund Cobb)		Universal	2 reels	May 16
Wild West		Pathe	Serial	
With Pencil, Brush and Chisel		Fox	1 reel	
Wonder Book, The (Series)		Sering D. Wilson	500 feet	April 26
Young Sheriff, The (Tom. Forman)		Miller & Steen (S. R.)	2 reels	
Zowie (Stereoscopik)		Pathe	1 reel	

Coming Attractions

Feature	Star	Distributed by	Length	Reviewed
Ace of Spades, The	Desmond-McAllister	Universal		
Age of Indiscretion		Truart (S. R.)	5800 feet	
American Venus, The	Special Cast	Paramount		
An Enemy of Men		Columbia Pict. (S. R.)		
Aristocrat, The	Special Cast	B. P. Schulberg (S. R.)		
Ashes	Corinne Griffith	First National		
Atlantis		First National		
Back Wash	Mary Pickford	United Artists		
Bad Lands, The	Harry Carey	Prod. Dist. Corp		
Barriers of Fire	Monte Blue	Warner Bros.		
Beautiful Cheat, The	Laura La Plante	Universal		
Beautiful City	R. Barthelmess	First National		
Before Midnight	Wm. Russell	Ginsberg (S. R.)	5895 feet	Aug. 8
Beloved Pawn, The	Reed Howes	Rayart (S. R.)		
Ben Hur	Special Cast	Metro-Goldwyn		
Best Bad Man, The	Tom Mix	Fox		
Big Parade, The	John Gilbert	Metro-Goldwyn		
Border Intrigue	Franklyn Farnum	Inde. Pict. (S. R.)	5 reels	June 6
Border Women	Special Cast	Phil Goldstone (S.R.)	5000 feet	
Broken Hearts of Hollywood	Harlan-Miller	Warner Brothers		
Brooding Eyes		Ginsberg Dis. Corp. (S. R.)		
Brown of Harvard		Metro-Goldwyn		
Caesar's Wife	Corinne Griffith	First National		
Cave Man, The	Harlan-Miller	Warner Brothers		
Charity Ball, The		Metro-Goldwyn		
Checkered Flag, The		Ginsberg Dist. Corp. (S. R.)		
Circle, The		Metro-Goldwyn		
Clean-Up, The	Richard Talmadge	F. B. O.		
Clod Hopper, The	Glenn Hunter	Assoc. Exhibitors		
Clothes Make the Pirate	Errol-D. Gish	First National		
College Widow, The	Syd Chaplin	Warner Brothers		
Coming of Amos	Rod La Rocque	Prod. Dist. Corp	5677 feet	Sept. 19
Compromise	Irene Rich	Warner Bros.		
Conquered	Gloria Swanson	Paramount		
Count of Luxembourg, The	Larry Semon	Chadwick		
Crashing Through	Jack Perrin	Ambassador Pict. (S. R.)	5000 feet	
Cyclone Bob	Bob Reeves	Anchor Film Dist.		
Cyrano de Bergerac	Special Cast	Atlas Dist. (S. R.)	9500 feet	July 18
Dance Madness	Pringle-Cody	Metro-Goldwyn		
Dangerous Currents		First National		
Dark Horse, The	Harry Carey	Prod. Dist. Corp.		
Deerslayer, The		Weiss Bros. (S. R.)	4780 feet	
Demon, The	Jack Hoxie	Universal		
Demon Rider, The	Ken Maynard	Davis Dist	5000 feet	Aug. 22
Detour		Prod. Dist. Corp.		
Devil Horse, The	Rex (horse)	Pathe		
Down Upon the Suwanee River	Special Cast	Lee Bradford (S. R.)		
Dumb Head		Tiffany (S. R.)	6500 feet	
East of the Setting Sun	Constance Talmadge	First National		
Eden's Fruit		B. P. Schulberg (S.R.)		
Enchanted Hill, The	Special Cast	Paramount		
Ermine and Rhinestone		H. F. Jans (S. R.)		
Exquisite Sinner, The	Special Cast	Metro-Goldwin		
Face on the Air, The	Evelyn Brent	F. B. O.		
Fair Play	Special Cast	Wm. Steiner (S. R.)	5035 feet	Sept. 19
Fall of Jerusalem		Weiss Bros. (S. R.)	6800 feet	
Fast Pace, The	Special Cast	Arrow		
Fifth Avenue		Prod. Dist. Corp		
Fighter's Paradise, The	Rex Baker	Phil Goldstone	5000 feet	
Fighting Courage	Ken Maynard	Davis Dist. Div. (S.R.)	5 reels	July 11
Fighting Edge, The	Harlan-Miller	Warner Brothers		
Fighting Smile, The	Bill Cody	Inde. Pict. Corp. (S.R.)	4630 feet	
First Year, The	Special Cast	Fox		
Flaming Waters		F. B. O.		
Forest of Destiny, The		Gotham Prod. (S. R.)		
Forever After	Corinne Griffith	First National		
Fort Frayne	Ben Wilson	Davis Dist.	5000 feet	Aug. 29
Friends	Special Cast	Vitagraph		
Frivolity		B. P. Schulberg (S.R.)		
Galloping Dude, The	Franklyn Farnum	Inde. Pict. Corp. (S.R.)	4700 feet	
Garden of Allah		United Artists		
Going the Limit	Richard Holt	Gerson Pict. (S. R.)	5000 feet	Sept. 26
Golden Cocoon		Warner Bros.		
Goose Woman, The	Special Cast	Universal	7500 feet	Aug. 22
Go West	Buster Keaton	Metro-Goldwyn		
Grass			10 reels	Mar. 7
Great Love, The	Dana-Agnew	First National		
Grey Vulture, The	Ken Maynard	Davis Dist. Div.		
Gulliver's Travels		Universal		
Handsome Brute, The	Columbia Pict. (S. R.)			
Haunted Range, The	Ken Maynard	Davis Dist. Div.		
Hearts and Fists		Assoc. Exhib.		
Hearts and Spangles		Gotham Prod. (S. R.)		
Hell Bent for Heaven		Warner Bros.		
Hell's Highroad	Leatrice Joy	Prod. Dist. Corp	6084 feet	Sept. 5
Heir's Apparent	Special Cast	First National		
Her Father's Daughter		F. B. O.		
Hero of the Big Snows, A	Rin Tin Tin (dog)	Warner Brothers		
His Jazz Bride	Special Cast	Warner		
His Majesty Bunker Bean	Moore-Devore	Warner	7291 feet	Sept. 26
His Master's Voice	Thunder (dog)	Gotham Prod. (S. R.		
His Woman	Special Cast	Whitman Bennett	7 reels	
Hogan's Alley	Harlan-Miller	Warner		
Home Maker, The	Alice Joyce	Universal	7755 feet	Aug. 8
Honeymoon Express, The	M. Moore-D. Devore	Warner Brothers		
Horses and Women		B. P. Schulberg		
How to Train a Wife	Valli-O'Brien	Assoc. Exhib.		
Hurricane		Truart (S. R.)	5800 feet	
Inevitable Millionaires, The	M. Moore-Devore	Warner Bros.		
Invisible Wounds	Sweet-Lyon	First National		
Irene	Colleen Moore	First National		
Justice of the Far North		C. B. C. (S. R.)	5500 feet	
Kentucky Pride	Special Cast	Fox	6597 feet	Sept. 19
Kings of the Turf		Fox		
Kiss for Cinderella, A	Betty Bronson	Paramount		
Knockout Kid, The	Jack Perrin	Rayart Pict. Corp. (S. R.)		
La Boheme	Lillian Gish	Metro-Goldwyn		
Lady Windermere's Fan	Special Cast	Warner Brothers		
Lariat, The	William Desmond	Universal		
Last Edition, The	Ralph Lewis	Film Book. Offices		
Lawful Cheater, The	Bow-McKee	B. P. Schulberg	4946 feet	
Lena Rivers	Special Cast	Arrow	6 reels	
Life of a Woman		Truart (S. R.)	6500 feet	
Lightning Jack	Jack Perrin	Ambassador Pict. (S.R.)	5000 feet	
Lightning Passes, The	Al Ferguson	Fleming Prod. (S.R.)		
Limited Mail, The	Monte Blue	Warner Bros.		
Little Girl in a Big City, A		Gotham Prod. (S. R.)		
Little Irish Girl, The	Special Cast	Warner Bros.		
Live Wire, The	Johnny Hines	First National		
Lodge in the Wilderness		Tiffany (S. R.)	6500 feet	
Lord Jim	Percy Marmont	Paramount		
Love Cargo, The	House Peters	Universal		
Love Gamble, The	Special Cast	Banner Prod. (S. R.)	5766 feet	July 11
Lover's Island	Hampton-Kirkwood	Assoc. Exhib		
Love Gamble, The		Ginsberg Dist. Corp. (S. R.)		
Love Toy, The	Lowell Sherman	Warner Bros		
Loyalties	Special Cast	Fox		
Lucky Lady, The	Lionel Barrymore	Paramount		
Lure of Broadway, The		Columbia Pict. (S. R.)		
Lying Wives	Special Cast	Ivan Abramson (S. R.)	7 reels	May 2
Man and the Moment		Metro-Goldwyn		
Man From Red Gulch	Harry Carey	Prod. Dist. Corp.		
Man of Iron, A	L. Barrymore	Chadwick	6 reels	July 4
Man on the Box, The	Sydney Chaplin	Warner Bros		
Man She Bought, The	Constance Talmadge	First National		
Man Without a Conscience	Louis-Rich	Warner Bros	6850 feet	May 2
Mare Nostrum	Special Cast	Metro-Goldwyn		
Married Hypocrites	Fredericks-La Plante	Universal		
Martinique	Bebe Daniels	Paramount		
Masked Bride, The	Mae Murray	Metro-Goldwyn		
Memory Lane	Boardman-Nagel	First National		
Men of Steel	Milton Sills	First National		
Message to Garcia, A		Metro-Goldwyn		
Million Dollar Handicap, The		Prod. Dist. Corp.		
Miracle of Life, The	Busch-Marmont	Assoc. Exhib		
Miracle of the Wolves, The			10346 feet	Mar. 7
Midnight Flames		Columbia Pict. (S. R.)		
Miss Vanity	Mary Philbin	Universal		
Million Dollar Doll		Assoc. Exhib		
Mocking Bird, The	Lon Chaney	M-G-M		
Morganson's Finish		Tiffany (S. R.)	6500 feet	
Moving Finger, The	Special Cast	Paramount		
Napoleon the Great		Universal		
Night Call, The	Rin-Tin-Tin (dog)	Warner Brothers		
North Star, The	Strongheart (dog)	Assoc. Exhib		
Old Clothes	Jackie Coogan	Metro-Goldwyn		
Only Thing, The	Special Cast	Metro-Goldwyn		
Open Trail, The	Jack Hoxie	Universal	4800 feet	May 16
Pace That Thrills, The	Ben Lyon	First National		
Pals		Truart (S. R.)	5800 feet	
Paris	Pauline Starke	Metro-Goldwyn		
Paris After Dark	Norma Talmadge	First National		
Partners Again		United Artists		
Passionate Quest, The	Marie Prevost	Warner Bros		
Passionate Youth	Special Cast	Truart (S. R.)	6 reels	July 11
Part Time Wife, The		Gotham Prod. (S. R.)		
Peak of Fate, The		F. B. Rogers	8 reels	June 27
Penalty of Jazz, The	Dorothy Revier	Columbia Pict. (S.R.)		
People vs. Nancy Preston	Bowers-De La Motte	Prod. Dist. Corp.		
Phantom of the Opera	Lon Chaney	Universal	8464 feet	Sept. 19
Pinch Hitter, The	Glenn Hunter	Asso. Exhibitors		
Pleasure Buyers, The	Irene Rich	Warner Brothers		
Police Patrol, The	James Kirkwood	Gotham Prod. (S.R.)	6000 feet	Sept. 19
Polly of the Ballet	Bebe Daniels	Paramount		
Pony Express, The	Special Cast	Universal	9929 feet	Sept. 26
Prairie Pirate, The	Harry Carey	Prod. Dist. Corp.	4603 feet	Sept. 26
Prince, The	Philbin-Kerry	Universal		
Quality Street		Metro-Goldwyn		
Quicker 'n Lightning	Buffalo Bill, Jr.	Weiss Bros. (S. R.)	5 reels	June 13
Racing Blood		Gotham Prod. (S. R.)		
Reckless Courage	Buddy Roosevelt	Weiss Bros. (S. R.)	4851 feet	May 2
Reckless Sex, The	Special Cast	Truart (S. R.)	6 reels	Feb. 14
Red Clay	William Desmond	Universal		
Red Dice	Rod La Rocque	Prod. Dist. Corp.		
Red Kimono, The	Mrs. Wallace Reid	Davis Dist. Div.		
Red Hot Tires	Monte Blue	Warner Bros.		

Feature	Star	Distributed by	Length	Reviewed
Return of a Soldier	Special Cast	Metro-Goldwyn		
Rime of the Ancient Mariner, The		Fox Film		
Road to Yesterday, The	Special Cast	Prod. Dist. Corp		
Road That Led Home, The		Vitagraph		
Rocking Moon		Prod. Dist. Corp		
Romance of an Actress		Chadwick		
Ropin' Venus, The	Josie Sedgwick	Universal		
Rose of the World	Special Cast	Warner Bros		
Sally, Irene and Mary	Special Cast	Metro-Goldwyn		
Salvage		Banner (S. R.)	5880 feet	
Sap, The	M. Moore-D. Devore	Warner Bros		
Satan in Sables	Lowell Sherman	Warner Bros		
Savage, The	Ben Lyon	First National		
Scarlet Saint, The	Lyon-Astor	First National		
Scraps	Mary Pickford	United Artists		
Sea Beast, The	John Barrymore	Warner Bros		
Sea Woman, The	Sweet-McLaglen	First National		
Seven Days	Lilian Rich	Prod. Dist. Corp		
Seven Sinners	Marie Prevost	Warner Bros		
Seventh Heaven	Special Cast	Fox		
Shadow of the Wall		Gotham Prod. (S. R.)		
Shadow of the Mosque	Odette Taylor	Cranfield & Clarke (S. R.)	6200 feet	
Shenandoah		R. P. Schulberg (S. R.)		
Ship of Souls	K. Lytell-L. Rich	Assoc. Exhib	5800 feet	
Shootin' Square	Jack Perrin	Ambassador Pict. (S.R.)	5000 feet	
Siegfried		Ufa		
Sign of the Claw		Gotham Prod. (S. R.)		
Silken Shackles	Irene Rich	Warner Bros		
Silver Treasure, The	Special Cast	Fox		
Simon the Jester	Rich-O'Brien	Prod. Dist. Corp		
Social Highwayman, The	Marian-Miller	Banner Prod		
Son of His Father, A	Special Cast	Paramount	6915 feet	Sept. 19
Spanish Sunlight	LaMarr-Stone	First National		
Sons of Life	Kelly Blythe	Banner Prod (S. R.)		
Speed Limit, The		Gotham Prod. (S. R.)		
Splendid Road, The	Anna Q. Nilsson	First National		
Sporting Life	Special Cast	Universal	6799 feet	Sept. 26
Steel Preferred	Special Cast	Prod. Dist. Corp		
Steele of the Royal Mounted		Vitagraph	6 reels	June 27
Stella Dallas		United Artists		
Stella Maris	Mary Philbin	Universal		
Still Alarm, The	Chadwick-Russell	Universal		
Strange Bedfellows		Metro-Goldwyn		
Sunshine of Paradise Alley	Special Cast	Chadwick Pict		
Super Speed	Reed Howes	Rayart (S. R.)		
Sweet Adeline	Charles Ray	Chadwick		
Tale of a Vanishing People		Tiffany (S. R.)		
Tearing Loose	Wally Wales	Weiss Bros. (S. R.)	4900 feet	June 13
Temptress		Metro-Goldwyn		
Ten to Midnight		Prod. Dist. Corp		

Feature	Star	Distributed by	Length	Reviewed
That Man from Arizona	D. Revier-W.Fairbanks	F. B. O		
That Royle Girl	Kirkwood-Dempster	Paramount		
This Woman	Special Cast	Fox		
Thoroughbred, The	Special Cast	Truart	5481 feet	Sept. 19
Three Bad Men	Special Cast	Fox		
Three Faces East	Special Cast	Prod. Dist. Corp		
Trailing Shadows	Edmund Lowe	Fox Film		
Travelin' Fast	Jack Perrin	Ambassador Pict. (S. R.)	5800 feet	
Travis Coup, The		Tiffany (S. R.)	5500 feet	
Twin Sister, The	Constance Talmadge	First National		
Two Blocks Away	Special Cast	Universal		
Unchastened Woman, The	Theda Bara	Chadwick		
Unguarded Hour, The	Stile-Kenyon	First National		
Unknown Lover, The	Elsie Ferguson	Vitagraph		
Up and At 'Em	Jack Perrin	Ambassador Pict. (S. R.)	5000 feet	
Vengeance of Durand, The	Irene Rich	Warner Brothers		
Viennese Medley	Special Cast	First National		
Voigs Boatman, The	Special Cast	Prod. Dist. Corp		
Wages for Wives	Special Cast	Fox		
Wanderer, The	William Collier, Jr.	Paramount	8173 feet	
Wandering Footsteps	Special Cast	Ginsberg Dist. Corp		
Warrior Gap	Wilson-Gerber	Davis Dist	4900 feet	Aug. 22
Was It Bigamy	Edith Thorton	Wm. Steiner (S. R.)	5000 feet	Sept. 26
Wedding Song, The	Leatrice Joy	Prod. Dist. Corp		
Wie Modern	Colleen Moore	First National		
What Will People Say		Metro-Goldwyn		
Where the World Begins		Truart (S. R.)	5800 feet	
Whispering Canyon		Ginsberg Dist. Corp		
White Chief, The	Monte Blue	Warner Brothers		
White Mice	Jacqueline Logan	Sering D. Wilson (S. R.)		
Why Girls Go Back Home		Warner Brothers		
Wild Girl		Truart (S. R.)	5850 feet	
Wild Justice	Peter the Great	United Artists	6 reels	Aug. 1
Wild Ridin'	Buck Jones	Fox		
Wild West	Mulhall-Ferguson	Pathe		
Winning of Barbara Worth		Prod. Dist. Corp		
Wise Guy, The	Lefty Flynn	F. B. O		
Without Mercy	Vera Reynolds	Prod. Dist. Corp		
With Kit Carson Over the Great Divide		Special Cast	Sunset Prod. (S. R.)	
Without Mercy	Vera Reynolds	Prod. Dist. Corp		
Womanhandled	Richard Dix	Paramount		
Women		Banner Prod. (S. R.)		
Women and Wives		Metro-Goldwyn		
World's Illusion, The		Metro-Goldwyn		
Wotd Woman, The	Special Cast	Ginsberg Dist. Corp		
Wreckage		Banner (S. R.)		
Wrong Coat, The		Tiffany (S. R.)	5200 feet	
Yankee Senor, The	Tom Mix	Fox		
Yoke, The	Special Cast	Warner Brothers		
You Can't Live on Love	Reginald Denny	Universal		

Newspaper Opinions on New Features

(Continued from page 1024)

"Graustark" — First National, Capitol, N. Y.

Times: "Miss Talmadge gives an extraordinarily fine performance, always restrained and always effective. She is delightfully sincere in the love scenes. This is a production which is thoroughly enjoyable. It has been handled by an expert."

Herald Tribune: " 'Graustark' is a delightful picture. Dimitri Buchowetski directed 'Graustark' and it is the best picture he ever made. Everyone in the cast was remarkably good. Norma Talmadge and Eugene O'Brien were fine as the lovers. If you want an hour of romance go and see 'Graustark.' "

World: "An uncommonly fine picture. Romance and excitement invests this latest screen version. For this, most of the credit goes to the gleaming and shadowy scenes of Dimitri Buchowetski and the presence of Norma Talmadge, Eugene O'Brien and Marc Mac-Dermott in its cast. McCutcheon himself probably never dreamed of a more pensive and appealing heroine than the picture made by Miss Talmadge. He evolved the perfect movie plot, for in this screen version 'Graustark' has fulfilled its destiny."

American: "The regular Sunday crowd at the Capitol lost itself in admiration of the gorgeous sets, the absorbing story and in Norma Talmadge as the lovely Yetive. We admire the sheer beauty of scenes and settings and admit that 'Graustark' will always prove a love story of absorbing interest. Miss Talmadge is exquisite as the princess. Her admirers will be delighted. 'Graustark' is an audience picture."

Telegraph: "The two greatest screen lovers acquit themselves creditably. Norma's personal popularity will never diminish. The drama moves along with swiftness and smoothness. Sets are sumptuous, there is plenty of comedy relief and the story will please the fans. Better see Norma at the Capitol this week."

News: " 'Graustark' is an interesting, beautiful picture, dominated by that charming lady, Norma Talmadge. Norma is her gracious self as Yetive. The story is skillfully set forth. The scenes are prints from a fairy tale. The sets are glittering, magnificent. Think you'll adore seeing Norma once more as is."

Journal: "There is nothing quite like a romance. Norma is lovely. She always is. And the royal costumes make her even more so. The settings are very beautiful, and there's a good cast. It's a colorful picture."

Mirror: "If you're in the mood for romance look no further than the Capitol. It is confectionery entertainment."

Telegram: "Dear old 'Graustark' has been given a Steinach treatment to the greater glory of the flickering films. Beside—The Merry Widow, 'The Prisoner of Zenda,' 'Graustark' makes a brave showing. Norma Talmadge is the leading luminary, with the attractiveness that is Miss Talmadge's own."

"Coming of Amos"—Prod. Dist. Corp., Colony, N. Y.

Graphic: "'The Coming of Amos' is easily the best bet among the Broadway film offerings. Take it from us, this is a picture that everybody will like."

Mirror: "'The Coming of Amos' has the earmarks of being a box office wow. It is raving melodrama, wild carnivals and hectic action."

Herald-Tribune: "'The Coming of Amos,' we are sure, will mean the bounding of the fans to the box office of the Colony."

Times: "Mr. La Rocque is capital as Amos. This is an unusually jolly picture, with capable acting by all the cast. It is beautifully photographed."

Daily News: "Direction—careful. Sets—splendiferous. Acting —fine. Effect—just swell."

Evening World: "It is full of carnivals, gorgeous settings and Continental sophistication. The net result is a picture which will afford entertainment for most movie fans."

Journal: "The story continues with a set of the cleverest subtitles flashed on the screen in months. It's nonsensically, melodramatically, delightfully amusing."

"Pony Express" — Paramount, Rivoli, Rialto, N. Y.

Daily News: "Cruze has fashioned one of those 'you must see' pictures from the rich story of the building of the West."

Mirror: "James Cruze, who gave us 'The Covered Wagon' has scored another sensational winner in this stirring dramatization of the American West of 1860. He has enhanced it with a 14-karat gold cast. Wallace Beery is superb as Rhode Island Red, a humorous disreputable soul—the diamond in the rough sort."

American: "Taken as a whole 'The Pony Express' is an excellent picture. If you like a drama with action and historical interest, one that is exceptionally well done, visit either the Rivoli or Rialto, or both, and you will find your kind of entertainment."

Times: "This pictorial document which causes one's heart to throb with delight, is another chapter in American history."

Telegraph: "In 'The Pony Express' at the Rivoli and Rialto this week, the Paramount company has another great winner. It is a genuinely thrilling tale peopled with glorious characters, replete with humor and doubly appealing because it is the history of our forebears."

6th Week of record attendance at $2 top

"METRO-GOLDWYN-MAYER'S "THE MERRY WIDOW" IS THE HIT OF N. Y. AT GLORIA GOULD'S EMBASSY THEATRE

The Quality 52

CLEAN UP!

The big stage comedy hit Brodway roared at for over a year is now on the screen!

A GREATER FORTY *Paramount Picture*

"NEW BROOMS"

D E MILLE has his biggest comedy hit since "Grumpy" in this breezy laugh picture of the son who took over his father's business so the father could take over the son's girls. And it comes to you in the same month (October) as James Cruze's "The Pony Express," DOUGLAS MacLEAN in "7 Keys to Baldpate," BEBE DANIELS in "Lovers in Quarantine," RAYMOND GRIFFITH in "He's a Prince" and BETTY BRONSON in "The Golden Princess"!

A  William de Mille
PRODUCTION

WITH
 BESSIE LOVE
NEIL HAMILTON
PHYLLIS HAVER

FROM THE PLAY BY
FRANK CRAVEN
SCREEN PLAY BY
CLARA BERANGER

This man showed TOM MEIGHAN'S new picture to 1000 convicts, He writes (unsolicited):

PARTING OF THE WAYS HOME
216 EAST STOCKTON AVENUE
PHONE. FAIRFAX 0280

N. S., PITTSBURGH, PA.

Sept. 21, 1925

My dear Mr. Robson,

We desire at this moment to thank you for permitting the use of Tom Meighan's newest picture "The Man Who Found Himself" which was put on at the Western Penitentiary before a Standing Room Only crowd this morning.

How true to life Tom Meighan played his prison part can only be vouched for by the 1000 men who witnessed his wonderful work. They cheered as no actor on the speaking stage is cheered today.

1000 men behind the gray walls that witnessed today "The Man Who Found Himself" earnestly urge that the inmates of all institutions might have the same privilege, because it will make them better men for the future.

We trust that Pittsburgh will give this picture the earnest interest that was granted it this morning. If they will, "The Man Who Found Himself" will mean much to the lives of others.

Very sincerely,

Rollo McBride

Rollo McBride is the official Public Defender in Pittsburgh. He takes men when they leave prison walls and provides them with a home, a job and a new viewpoint. He is nationally known. His supporters are the best element in the community.

"THE MAN WHO FOUND HIMSELF"

WILL DO MORE THAN YOUR POCKETBOOK GOOD – IT WILL DO YOUR FELLOW MEN GOOD. *HERE'S THE PROOF!*

a GREATER FORTY *Paramount Picture*

WITH
VIRGINIA VALLI
ADAPTED FROM THE
ORIGINAL SCREEN STORY
BY
BOOTH TARKINGTON
SCENARIO · · · · BY
TOM J. GERAGHTY
DIRECTED BY
ALFRED E. GREEN
PRESENTED BY
ADOLPH ZUKOR
JESSE L. LASKY

LIGE CONLEY

Educational Pictures

"THE SPICE OF THE PROGRAM"

AL ST. JOHN

Two Great Daredevil Comedy Stars in One Series

No stunt is too daring, no speed too great, for Lige Conley or Al
St. John, if it will add thrills to the rapid succession of laughs in

MERMAID COMEDIES

JACK WHITE PRODUCTIONS

have been for years the leaders among the broad, fast action
comedies. "Faster and funnier" is always the object. Every
picture in the new series of 18 will be a real feature.

E.W. Hammons Presents

"PLEASURE BOUND"

with **Lige Conley**

Directed by Norman Taurog

"FAIR WARNING"

with **Al St. John**

Supervised by JACK WHITE

For foreign rights address
FAR EAST FILM CORPORATION
729 Seventh Avenue, New York, N. Y.

EDUCATIONAL
FILM EXCHANGES, Inc.
E.W. Hammons
President

Member, Motion Picture Producers
and Distributors of America, Inc.,
Will H. Hays, *President*

KINOGRAMS
CAMERA EXPERTS
COVER THE WORLD

KINOGRAMS is building up a service for exhibitors that comes as close to perfection as is humanly possible

In all parts of the world it has camera representatives, wide-awake, live-wire, hand-picked craftsmen who are constantly *on the job*

That is why Kinograms is *consistently good*

From the product of this enormous staff its editors enjoy the choice of a wide variety of subjects, *a steel-clad guarantee to exhibitors of first class entertainment at all times*

$\overline{BOOK}$ KINOGRAMS
The News Reel Built Like a Newspaper

adapted by Frederic
and Fanny Hatton
from the play by
Cosmo Hamilton

HOBART
HENLEY'S *production*
Excha

with
EW CODY ELEANOR BOARDMAN
Renee Adoree   Creighton Hale

Wives

in

Reason #3

straight wire from

CARSON DAHNKEN

American Theatre, Salt Lake City

JUST CLOSED WEEKS RUN ON KEEPER
OF THE BEES TO BIGGEST ATTENDANCE
WE HAVE HAD IN YEARS.....

PLAYED TO TWENTY TWO THOUSAND
FIVE HUNDRED SIXTEEN PEOPLE......

I RECOMMEND THIS PICTURE TO EVERY
EXHIBITOR IN THE WORLD AS A BOX-
OFFICE ATTRACTION AND REAL AUDIENCE
PICTURE......

WESTERN UNION TELEGRAM

SALT LAKE CITY UTAH SEPT. 26th 1925

LEE MARCUS   FILM BOOKING OFFICES OF AME. 723 Seventh Ave. N. Y. C.

JUST CLOSED WEEKS RUN ON KEEPER OF BEES TO THE BIGGEST ATTENDANCE
WE HAVE HAD IN YEARS STOP PLAYED TO TWENTY TWO THOUSAND FIVE
HUNDRED SIXTEEN PEOPLE RECEIPTS FIVE THOUSAND SIX HUNDRED FIFTY
FOUR FORTY FIVE STOP I RECOMMEND THIS PICTURE TO EVERY EXHIBITOR
IN THE WORLD AS A BOX OFFICE ATTRACTION AND REAL AUDIENCE PICTURE
LETS HAVE SOME MORE LIKE THIS ONE KINDEST REGARDS.

CARSON DAHNKEN

MGR AMERICAN THEATRE

Predestined to Sweep The Country in A Wave of Popularity

Gene Stratton-Porter's *The* KEEPER OF THE "BEES"

Distributed by
FILM BOOKING OFFICES of AMERICA, Inc.
723 Seventh Ave., New York, N. Y.
EXCHANGES EVERYWHERE

A torrent of thrills from the Western Pine Forests

FOX $2,000,000 SHORT SUBJECT PROGRAM

Fox Film Corporation.

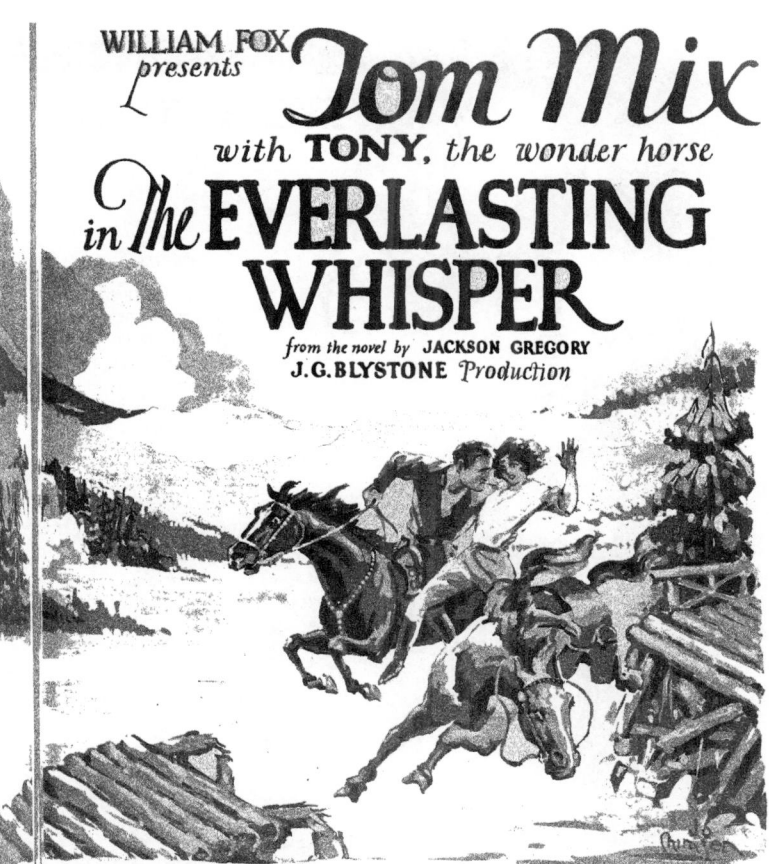

EVERY TIME

The Cast

George O'Brien
Jacqueline Logan
Alec B. Francis
J. Farrell MacDonald
George Fawcett
Cyril Chadwick
Frankie Bailey
Francis Powers
Marion Harlan
Mark Fenton

THE FIRST YEAR

with Matt Moore
Frank Borzage *Production*

John Golden's Great Comedy Hit of Married Life

Fox Film Corporation.

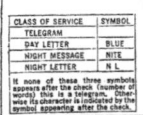

John W. Considine Jr. *presents*

PETER
THE
GREAT
in
WILD
JUSTICE

by C. Gardner Sullivan

A
Chester M. Franklin
PRODUCTION

NOW BOOKING
UNITED ARTISTS CORPORATION

Mary Pickford   Charles Chaplin
Douglas Fairbanks   D. W. Griffith
Joseph M. Schenck   *Hiram Abrams*
Chairman Board of Directors   *President*

This Dog Film in
Blue Ribbon Class

"Straight melodrama that should go well with juvenile patrons and offers entertainment classy enough for elders." —News.

"Peter easily qualifies for the blue ribbon class. This dog is good. All dog lovers will want to see this one." —Film Daily.

"This is one of the most thrilling of the dog pictures, and should prove above the average with most audiences. There is lots of action and plenty of melodrama, with exceptional punch" —Motion Picture World.

"Peter the Great is just about the best of the screen's dog performers, and this film is well worth seeing." —Daily News

Action
Melodrama
Thrills

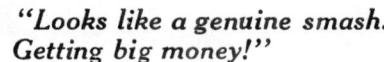
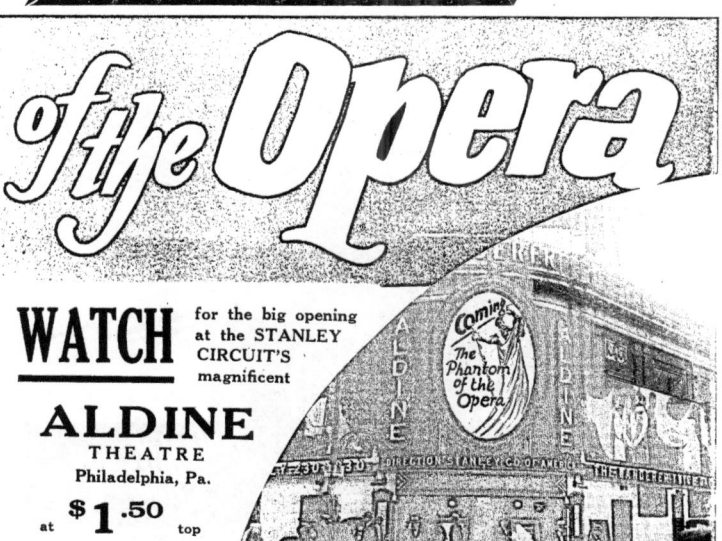

Get in on the
World's Complex

"MODERN MADNESS"

The New
Sensational
Screen Drama of
Humanity's Maddening
Clamour for a Thrill

Produced by A.M. FOOTE PRODUCTIONS
Under the Able Direction of

JOHN P. McCARTHY

WILL MAKE BOX OFFICE HISTORY

Be a Maker of History and get
this one on your schedule

BEFORE
IT'S TOO LATE

World Distribution
Controlled by
HOLLYWOOD FILM SALES
SERVICE
of
Hollywood, Calif.

Eastern Representative: M. S. Rosenfield, 1001 Loew's State Bldg., New York

SYD CHAPLIN

MERRIER, HAPPIER, FUNNIER THAN EVER

IN

"THE MAN ON THE BOX"

with

DAVID BUTLER - ALICE CALHOUN - HELENE COSTELLO

by Harold McGrath

Directed by Charles "Chuck" Reisner

The Check-up

The most complete and comprehensive form of exhibitors box office reports yet originated giving at a glance the consensus of opinion on any picture released within the year.

This department is a feature of Motion Picture News and appears in the first issue of each month.

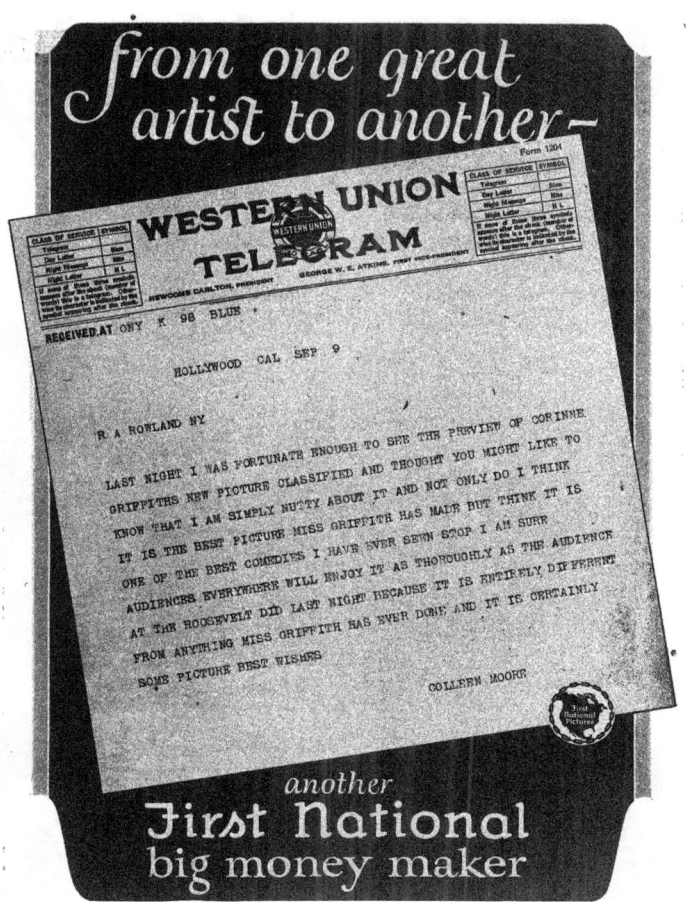

Motion Picture News

VOL. XXXII   ALBANY, N. Y., AND NEW YORK CITY, OCTOBER 10, 1925   NO. 15

Reciprocity

WE HAVE just concluded a series of articles designed to present clearly the European film situation—from the European angle as well as from the American.

It seems to simmer down to this: Great Britain, France and Germany want to stimulate production. They want to market their goods here. That is highly essential. But it is just as essential to American producers that they continue to market their pictures abroad.

This whole situation—and it is of the utmost importance to the progress of the motion picture—calls, therefore, for reciprocal relations. That is the only way out.

But the problem is: what kind of reciprocal relations between Europe and America will be best for each, and best for the motion picture?

It seems to us that it will be fatal to all these interests to approach a solution from the hard and fast angle—the material angle, you might say—of a Kontingent or a tariff.

This might apply to material goods, though even there you can't jam goods into a market when they haven't been thoughtfully adapted to the market, nor the market well tilled to receive them.

The writer recalls, from a year's residence in London, that American goods had a stiff time getting sales there. Some never got by the dealers at all; and some were only accepted by the public after a spirited and costly advertising and selling campaign.

But pictures, because they are more intangible merchandise—more subtle in appeal to the public—are still further beyond the grasp of reciprocal tariff rules.

Great Britain makes the mistake of believing this to be largely a nation of Nordic peoples. It is far from that. It is a vast mixture, a melting pot of many races; and over here we have to make pictures to fit this polyglot taste. German pictures for the Teutons, British pictures for the Anglo-Saxons, French pictures for the Latins, are one thing: American pictures for Americans are another.

I have always believed that American-made pictures go well the world over because America is a world of peoples in itself and because, for years, our entire entertainment business, stage, screen and what not, has been trained and tuned up to the exactions of pleasing many varying types of the public.

The reciprocal relations—it would seem—will have to be reciprocal film relations. By that I mean a joining of American and European resources in the making of pictures suitable for the world market. And that, happily, is under way. Metro-Goldwyn, First National, Famous, Fox, Universal, Warners—all are entering into such alliances. And it is to be hoped that this good work will progress and succeed so well that the dangerous alternative of arbitrary regulations will be, quickly enough, found unnecessary.

This making of pictures of international appeal is not merely a matter of studios and studio facilities, nor of technique, nor even of directors and casts. It is primarily a matter of ideas. Stories, if you will, but the broader term is better. Ideas. Ideas that will appeal to and be understood by various peoples of varying training, environment and heredity. And that, of course, is not a simple matter.

[signature]

MOTION PICTVRE NEWS

October 10
1925

Vol. XXXII
No. 15

Founded in September 1913

Publication Office: Lyon Block, Albany, N. Y.

Editorial and General Offices:
729 7th Ave., New York City

Branch Offices:
845 S. Wabash Ave., Chicago, Ill.
Room 616 Security Bldg., Hollywood,
Calif.

A Constructive Suggestion

THE Motion Picture Theatre Owners of Brooklyn have taken the initiative in suggesting to the Independent producers and distributors that the latter supply exhibitors with free trailers on their productions.

An excellent idea—which ought to to be followed out.

The Brooklyn suggestion has been endorsed by national headquarters of the M. P. T. O. A. and has been transmitted to the Independent Association by President R. F. Woodhull in the following letter:

"We are presenting for the consideration of the members of your Association, a resolution adopted by the Motion Picture Theatre Owners of Brooklyn urging the Independent Producers and Distributors to furnish theatre owners with free trailers on their productions, as in their opinion such a course will result in increased business both for the distributors and the theatre owners.

"They point out the exploitation possibilities of such trailers and the great publicity value.

"We are very pleased to transmit this resolution to you at the request of these theatre owners, and would urge your giving the same your serious consideration at the earliest opportunity. We join in the belief of the Brooklyn theatre owners that such a practice will prove of great benefit and advantage to the producers, distributors and theatre owners."

Messrs. Zerner and Phillips of the Brooklyn organization point out that the trailer is of genuine service in selling pictures to the public, and their argument is right. We must agree with them that the independents would do far better to supply trailers than to spend large amounts on press-books which cannot affect directly the attendance of the public at the theatres.

"Give us tools to work with," sums up the exhibitors' attitude. "And give them to us consistently and on a definite plan."

They further suggest that a scheme of careful routing be worked out for the trailer service—just as careful as that used if feature prints are to arrive on time and in good condition at the theatres.

We have pointed out several times that the proper advertising of independent productions is an imperative need. The trailer service is a constructive suggestion along this line.

...u.com " big boy" Sebastian, in picture since he was three weeks old, has reached the mature age of 18 months, in recognition of which he has been awarded the role of chief comic in "Baby Be Good," an Educational Juvenile comedy.

More Radio Concerts

ANNOUNCEMENT has been made of thirty radio concerts to be given during the coming Winter by the leading opera stars, the programs to be broadcast by WEAF through a hook-up of a large number of stations.

This is an expansion of the radio concert plan put into effect last Winter. What its effect will be on theatre attendance remains to be seen. Until the facts are gathered—and they cannot be until the programs are actually under way—predictions are unwarranted.

October 10, 1925   MOTION PICTURE NEWS   Vol. XXXII, No. 15

Published weekly by Motion Picture News, Inc., William A. Johnston, President; E. Kendall Gillett, Vice-President; William A. Johnston, Editor; J. S. Dickerson, Associate Editor; Oscar Cooper, Managing Editor; Fred J. Beecroft, Advertising Manager; L. H. Mason, Chicago Representative; William McCormack, Los Angeles Representative. Subscription price, $3 per year, post paid in United States, Mexico, Hawaii, Porto Rico, Philippine Islands and some other countries; Canada, $5; foreign, $10.00. Copyright 1924, by Motion Picture News, Inc., in the United States and Great Britain. Title registered in the United States Patent Office and foreign countries. Western Union cable address is "Picknews," New York. Entered as second-class matter January 31st, 1924, at the postoffice, Albany, N. Y., under the Act of March 3, 1879.

Zukor Discusses B. & K. Deal In Exclusive Interview

Makes Statement on F.P.-L. Theatre Policy

Adolph Zukor, President of the Famous Players-Lasky Corporation.

By William A. Johnston

(*Copyright,1925,by Motion Picture News, Inc.*)

THERE have been a thousand and one surmises about the Famous Players-Balaban & Katz theatre deal—what it was and what it portended. We ourselves did some surmising. So we decided it would be a good idea to go direct to Adolph Zukor and let him tell about it; that this might clear the air.

"Certainly I'll tell about it," said Mr. Zukor. "There's nothing at all to conceal, and just a few simple facts to state.

"Famous Players-Lasky owns theatres. We are in the theatre business because there's money in it. That's our privilege, I take it.

Discusses Balaban & Katz Deal

"We own a good many theatres. The investment is large. We've got to have the best management obtainable. Mr. Lasky attends to production, Mr. Kent to distribution; I don't know anything about theatre operation. It has grown to be a highly specialized business. We have our own theatre department, a very good one. But we wanted the best. Balaban and Katz have specialized in theatres all during the twenty years I have specialized in pictures. They have developed a man-power organization of the finest: they have vision, initiative. Their wonderful success speaks altogether for itself. What more natural than that we should seek their management for our theatres? I put the proposition to them some time ago. They held back at first. 'Well, think it over,' I said. And now the terms of management have been agreed upon and the matter closed. They get a commission as managers, a share in the profits.

Will Book Best Product

"These theatres must make money. We expect they will. Balaban and Katz expect they will. That's their business. Therefore the theatres will be run strictly on their own bottoms. Do you think Balaban and Katz or any other management would be agreeable to having them run any other way? The theatres will book the best product available. They will have to. And they will pay the right rentals. They will have to—to succeed. And we intend they will succeed."

"Will you buy more theatres?" I asked.

"I don't know," said Mr. Zukor. "Any more than any other theatre concern knows at the moment. Theatre conditions are changing all the time. We may buy; we may sell. I simply repeat I am in the theatre business to make money, like any theatre firm. And I propose to. I will act accordingly. What that action will be I don't now know. I will announce it when I do know."

"Has your ownership of theatres anything to do with your production and distribution problems?"

"No. I see it only as a theatre enterprise. It is purely an economic matter all its own.

"Exhibiting End is the Best," Says Zukor

In Interview with William A. Johnston

(Continued from Preceding Page)

"Exhibiting End is the Best"

"The exhibiting end of this business is the best end—by far. It is about time someone said so and said it fearlessly. It is the stable, substantial, profitable side. Production is pure and simple speculation; stars are grief and worry. I know. Making pictures is a heart-breaking game.

"I put five hundred thousand dollars—or six or seven hundred thousand—into a picture. At its best, it's speculative. For the same money I could build a beautiful theatre and safely make money on product on which the other fellow risked his money and health. I repeat—the stable, sure end of the business is the exhibiting end. The profits have been vast and swiftly had. They are increasingly alluring. The people who have my sympathy, my utter sympathy, are the producers—every one of them. Nobody ever weeps over them; but most everybody takes a whack at them. If anyone thinks production is profitable, let them try it. Let them at least get a fair notion of what it means to build and run a producing unit, to create entertainment ideas, to buy at high competitive prices all the values demanded by the box-office success everyone clamors for. It is high time the producer had some sympathetic and intelligent understanding and recognition of the fact that he, with his courage, nerve-wracking enterprise and heavy risk, has advanced the industry and its theatre profits as far as they are today.

A Plain, Candid Statement

"I have now given you," said Mr. Zukor, "a plain, candid statement about my own business affairs. It's my business and my affair. Yet I give it willingly, to correct, as you say, a lot of gossip. But why must this gossip be? The greatest trouble with this business is that everyone is minding the other fellow's affairs. And knowing very little, he imagines very much. Let him devote himself to his own business and thereby not only improve his own fortunes but those of the whole industry. We have plenty of big problems facing us. There's the European situation, for instance. We have brought these muddles on by our own sheer thoughtlessness. If each man would spend in serious thought and analysis the time he uses in gossiping about his neighbor's affairs we would all be better off. We would stop butting our heads blindly against stone walls."

Scenes of the navy seaplane, PN-9 No. 1, in a recent issue of Pathe News. In one view is shown the damaged wing where the men, adrift in the Pacific, tore off wing fabric to make buckets to catch rain water for drinking; in the other is shown the U. S. S. Pelican bringing the lost seaplane into Pearl Harbor, Honolulu, after the rescue. (Pathe News photos).

Metro-Goldwyn-Mayer's latest acquisition is Lars Hanson, a Swedish film star, who is here shown as he arrived on the boat in New York.

Texas contributes another dazzling figure to the screen in the person of Dorothy Seastrom, signed to a five-year contract by First National, and seen in "We Moderns."

Fay Lamphier, crowned Miss America at Atlantic City, and who is playing the title role in "The American Venus" at the Paramount Long Island studios.

PICTURES
AND
PEOPLE

GOLDEN ASTERISKS

TWO of the coveted asterisks from the National Board of Review, denoting "a particularly good picture," were awarded this week, according to the bulletin just received. Both, it so happens, are based on stage plays. One is the Paramount picture, "New Brooms," and the other is the Warner Brothers slapstick farce, "The Man on the Box."

Three of the little stars were handed out last week, but could not be listed for lack of space. One was a feature, while the other two were what managers usually bill as "added attractions," that is, special novelty short subjects. The feature subject was "The Calgary Stampede," Universal's rodeo romance, while the two short subjects were "Thirty Years Ago" and "I Remember," both of the Short Films Syndicate.

SAM RORK'S MASTERPIECE

SPLENDID things are being heard along Film Row of Sam Rork's newest and biggest production, "Clothes Make the Pirate." These whispers assert that this picture is by far Rork's "magnum opus," which is considerable of an assertion, in view of the success of "Ponjola," "The Talker," and some of his others.

The story is a unique one, telling, as it does, of pirate adventure in the early days of Massachusetts. The central character, played by Leon Errol, is a meek, hen-pecked tailor, who dreams himself the hero of pirate adventures in strong contrast to his timidity—and who suddenly falls in with real pirates. They carry him out to sea, thinking him their chief, which leads to myriad complications, laughs and thrills.

TO RESTORE MISSION

SEVERAL of the Metro-Goldwyn-Mayer stars and featured players were among those booked to appear this Saturday at a mammoth benefit performance at the Olympic auditorium in Los Angeles to raise funds for the restoration of the Santa Barbara Mission. This was badly damaged in the recent earthquake, and the plan for its restoration has aroused widespread sympathy and interest.

MYSTERY PLUS

NOT even the members of the cast will know the identity of the villain in "The Green Archer," according to the plan of Production Manager Frank Leon Smith. The title character is a mysterious masked figure, who shoots death-dealing green arrows, and each member of the cast, in turn, is suspected by the others of being the evasive archer. It is Smith's belief that if the players themselves do not know the answer to the riddle, the mystery atmosphere will be greatly intensified in this Pathe Serial.

CRITICS OF YESTERYEAR

AN unusual idea has already been worked out for the premiere of "The Road to Yesterday," Cecil B. De Mille's personally directed production. Producers Distributing corporation has made preliminary arrangements to have at this showing as many as possible of the old time New York dramatic critics who covered the opening of the play at the Herald Square theatre in 1906. At that time they were warm in their praise of the play, and it is felt that it will be interesting to learn of their reaction to the picturized version.

Col. and Mrs. Fred Levy of Louisville, Ky., snapped aboard the Paris as the First National Franchise Holder returned from a five weeks' tour abroad.

Stella Doyle, an English girl, is an important member of the Christie stock company, appearing in Christie comedies for Educational release.

Eastern film circles are brightened just now by the presence of Esther Ralston, who is working in "A Kiss for Cinderella" (Paramount) at Long Island studios.

Dinner tendered Pathe producers and the Home Office executives at the Hotel Roosevelt, New York, on Friday evening, September 25th. In the picture may be seen most of the executives, as well as the men producing for Pathe release.

THAT PATHE ROOSTER

PATHE'S rooster trade-mark which appears on all this firm's films, has been translated from a silent to an animated fowl. Strange as it may seem, the bird to properly fill the role was mighty hard to find. They wanted a real, live rooster who would flop his wings and crow incessantly while the camera was cranking, but despite numerous excursions into the environs of Culver City, the Roach camera crew realized that not every rooster will oblige. It wasn't until the services of Billy Knight and his roosters, a well-known international vaudeville act, were secured that the difficulty was solved.

For Billy brought forth his loudest crowing artist, and in an hour's time enough negative was shot of a crowing rooster to keep the Pathe trade-mark going strong for the next twenty years or so. But the Hal Roach boys are convinced that there is a whole lot of difference between the barnyard variety and a rooster that will exert his lungs for the benefit of the camera.

OLCOTT 'TWEEN PICTURES

IN AN age which likes to inquire into the methods of the celebrated while at work and their occupations while at play, it seems fitting enough to ask the question "what do directors do when they are not directing?" If there is a generic answer to the question we know nothing about it. But taking individual cases now and then the want can be supplied. Thus Sidney Olcott is now between pictures—having completed "The Best People" at the Famous Players-Lasky studio in Hollywood—and it can be reliably stated

The signing of the contract by which United Artists acquires an interest in the IFA distributing corporation in Germany; left to right: Rudolf Buerstein Meinert, Dr. Raphael Strauss, Hermann Saklikower, A. C. Berman, Gustav Schwab, William S. Harrison.

that now he is not directing Olcott is vacationing at Big Bear Lake, where may be found much rugged natural beauty, air that tingles and stimulates, and where there are no studios, though the pictures have been there many times in the form of production units on location. Upon his return to the studios announcement will be made of his next production. His last work "The Best People" is from the play of the same title by David Grey and Avery Hopwood, and those who will be seen in the principal roles are Warner Baxter, Kathlyn Williams, Esther Ralston, Margaret Livingston, Margaret Morris, Joseph Striker and Edward Davis.

UTILIZE HOME TALENT

EXTRAS including branch and district managers and home office executives of First National's distribution department will appear in the racing sequence of "The Scarlet Saint." They were visiting at the studio when director George Archainbaud invited the whole crowd to take part as "railbirds" at the race. They were duly rehearsed in expressing frantic enthusiasm and cheered until they were hoarse. The results were highly satisfactory and Archainbaud asserted that he never had a bunch of extras who were so thoroughly infatuated with their jobs and ready to give good service.

AN AMERICAN DEAUVILLE

WILLIAM FOX is heading a new real estate development corporation which, while it has no connection with his motion picture or theatrical enterprises, is of more than passing interests. The company, Deauville Estates, Inc., has taken title to the Floyd-Jones estate at Massapequa, Nassau county, L. I., which has a remarkable history, having been in the same family for nearly 300 years.

In carrying out the ideas that have been conceived for the purpose of creating a real estate development that will be unique and at the same time of a high order, Deauville Estates, Inc., proposes to construct a series of tide water canals of sufficient depth to adequately provide for the clearance of large sized motor driven craft at low tide.

In the plotting of the acreage, provisions have been made for 35,000 feet of water frontage, the owner of every lot having a natural or a man-made water-way at his door. Dredging of these canals will begin at Great South Bay and will be carried back into the property in accordance with the plans.

FIFTH AVENUE—AND BACK

MEMBERS of the "Fifth Avenue" unit, who came East recently to film exteriors along the world's most famous thoroughfare, returned to the Coast in two parties, one of which remained behind for a few days to clean up a number of special scenes. Director Robert C. Vignola departed last Friday, together with Jim Van Trees, cameraman, Allan Forrest, Marguerite de la Motte and Lillian R. Gale, formerly of the MOTION PICTURE NEWS staff. A. H. Sebastian, the producer, his son, Maurice Sebastian, Phil Carle, assistant director, Sally Long, former Follies beauty, Josephine Norman, of the De Mille stock company, and Anthony Caldewey, veteran scenarist.

A recent experience on the part of Miss Long well illustrates the uncertain vicissitudes of this ever changing industry. Leaving the New York stage, she determined to seek the wider opportunities of the silver screen, and trekked to Hollywood, having previously played in a D. W. Griffith production, thereby adding to the list of Griffith "discoveries." On the Coast, her striking beauty procured her parts in several features. Then, with climactic suddenness, she was assigned the much coveted role of leading lady to Valentino in "The Hooded Falcon"—but with equal suddenness the "Falcon" was shelved and another war-like bird, "The Eagle," substituted. This called for a blonde leading lady, which Miss Long is not, so her appearance with the Great Lover has been indefinitely postponed. Meanwhile, since she could not afford to remain off the screen for so long, she has gone ahead with other roles. Quite by coincidence, Caldewey, who did the "Falcon" script, has also done the "Fifth Avenue" continuity. It almost seems as if the motion picture industry should extend a testimonial of some sort to Ziegfeld for discovering so many of the girls who later desert him for the celluloid drama.

MASTBAUM'S ART TREASURES

PHILADELPHIA art circles brightened to the cabled news that Jules E. Mastbaum, head of the Stanley Company and prominent Philadelphian, had acquired ninety-eight bronzes by the famous August Rodin while in Paris on a recent European trip which ended with his arrival in New York last week. These art treasures make Mr. Mastbaum the largest individual owner of Rodin bronzes in the world, he having acquired several of this sculptor's masterpieces last year. The entire collection, Mr. Mastbaum has notified the officials of the Sesquicentennial art exhibition to be held in Philadelphia next year and of which he is a director, will be exhibited publicly for the first time at that event, which its sponsors are ambitious to make the most representative of any collections of works ever held in this country.

Up until the time of Mr. Mastbaum's recent acquisitions, the Thomas Fortune Ryan collection, now in the Metropolitan Museum of Art, held first place as the largest individual collection of Rodin's works. The Mastbaum art treasures are destined ultimately to become the property of Philadelphia, long noted for its works of art. Paris reluctantly parted with the Rodin works, as is evinced by the fact that Mr. Mastbaum has been negotiating with the Minister des Beaux Arts for a long time. When he purchased several bronzes last year Parisians voiced their surprise and shock when it became known that the directors of the Rodin Musee had sold the works to a collector who would take them to America. The proffer to exhibit the collection at the Sesquicentennial exhibition is warmly appreciated in Philadelphia. Mayor Kendrick acknowledging the offer with words of thanks to Mr. Mastbaum and enthusiastic praise of this public spirited move.

CHAPLIN ENTERTAINS

CHARLIE CHAPLIN presided at a luncheon last week at the Ritz-Carlton hotel, New York, among his guests being the picture reviewers and several editors and special writers. He was good naturedly "kidded" on his proclivity for attending luncheons by proxy. In a short talk to the writers, the comedian freely discussed plans for his next picture, "The Dandy," and said that, since the public seem to prefer him as a laugh-provoker, he would forget all serious motifs in his forthcoming vehicle.

EVELYN BRENT ENDS TOUR

WITH a radio engagement in Providence, coupled with a personal appearance at Fay's theatre, Evelyn Brent concluded her country wide tour last week and is en route to the West Coast. During her trip across the country she appeared before the microphone at several leading broadcasting stations, with excellent results in the way of fan mail and publicity.

SYD'S NEWEST HAS PREMIERE

AT 11:30 p.m. last Friday, at Warner's theatre, New York City, "The Man on the Box" was given its world premiere before one of the most distinguished audiences ever assembled for such an occasion. The audience was liberally dotted with celebrities of the screen, stage, literary and diplomatic circles in greater numbers than is usual for such an affair. The Warners should be very happy over the reception given this feature comedy at its initial performance.

PAUL PROGRESSES

PAUL A. YAWITZ, who made a reputation for himself as director of foreign publicity for Fox, and later with MOTION PICTURE NEWS, was this week appointed director of publicity for all the Ned Wayburn enterprises in New York and throughout the United States. The prominent Cheese Clubman will be in complete charge of the direction of all future publicity policy for all the companies under Wayburn's management, including the producing firm, which has three musical comedies scheduled for early winter production, the large group of vaudeville acts, and the Wayburn school of stage dancing. With his wide acquaintance in editorial circles, and his undisputed ability, Paul should do much to add to the lustre of the already illustrious Mr. Wayburn, who glorified the American girl for many years for Monsieur Ziegfeld, and is now on his own.

A remarkable demonstration of the power of make-up to work a complete transformation: at the left, Jack Duffy, the Christie comedian, as the young man that he is in real life; and at the right, Jack Duffy as he appears under the Kliegls and Cooper-Hewitts.

THE MACDONALD STAR LOOMS

HISTORY tells of an instance where Destiny made a star for a corporal, the Little Corporal who later was an Emperor, and now there is news that stardom is in the making for Corporal Casey, humorous and loveable discharged Union soldier and gang boss who figures so prominently in "The Iron Horse." For though J. Farrell MacDonald has done many striking roles since, it is as Corporal Casey that he is known best. That characterization will be associated with him even after MacDonald, who a year ago was practically unheard of, has attained to the stardom which William Fox is planning for the actor. Even now a suitable vehicle to serve as his first starring picture is being sought by the Fox scenario heads and it is indicated that it will not be long before J. Farrell MacDonald will be written in large type at the top of a poster with below it the word "in" and below that the title of a Fox feature production. Since making his screen debut in "The Iron Horse" MacDonald has essayed important roles in "Lightnin'," "Kentucky Pride," "The Fighting Heart," "The Lucky Horseshoe" and "Thank You." He was a "trouper" who became tired of roaming and settled down to make a career in the pictures. MacDonald is a Yale man and started his career after leaving college as a newspaper man, later taking up acting on the legitimate stage.

The technical staff doesn't usually get much of a publicity "break," so here is Corinne Griffith surrounded by the able corps which made "Classified" for First National.

Myer Lesser, director-general of advertising, publicity and exploitation, and Sam E. Morris, general manager of distribution of Warner Bros., talk over plans.

Milton Sills signs his new First National contract under which he will continue as a star; left to right: E. A. Eichmann, general manager of distribution, Samuel Spring, secretary-treasurer; Mr. Sills, Roy Rockett, of production department, B. W. Perkins, general counsel.

One of the principal figures in the Laurence Stallings story, "The Big Parade" (Metro-Goldwyn-Mayer) is Renee Adoree, in the role of Melisande, a peasant.

A new version of the "infernal triangle" is furnished by Hallam Cooley, Kathryn Perry and Marion Harlan in "The Peacemakers" (Fox).

MORE INDIANA AUTHORS

IT has been asserted, with some little reason, that every person has an unproduced play stuck away in his trunk, or on the attic shelf. Every person, apparently, at some time during his or her life decides to write the Great American Drama.

Sometimes, however, they go a step further and actually get them produced. Such is the case with two men connected with the justly famous Circle theatre in Indianapolis. There seems to be something in the Indiana atmosphere that leads irresistably to the fields of play and novel writing. If you don't believe it, look over your Who's Who, and see how many of them come from the Hoosier state.

The two latest are Constantin Bakaleinikoff, director of the Circle Theatre Concert orchestra, and Carl Niesse, auditor at the same cinema temple. Together they have written a musical comedy entitled "On Time," which has been accepted by the George Milam Production company of Chicago and Los Angeles for staging. Early in October it is to receive its premiere on the Pacific coast. It is to be an elaborate production in seven scenes, with some two score persons in the cast.

Perhaps, if "On Time" goes the way of "Sally," "The Merry Widow" and other musical dramas that have found their way later to the screen, Bakaleinikoff may yet be conducting the Circle Theatre orchestra through an accompaniment to "On Time" on the Circle screen, while Niesse audits the staggering receipts. Anyway, we wish 'em the best o' luck!

MARY'S RAGGED BAND

NINE small children are appearing in Mary Pickford's new film, "Scraps," now in production, a quaint ragged army, clad entirely in cast-off adult clothing obtained from the Salvation Army and Los Angeles second-hand stores. They are an interesting and rather pathetic sight, as they toddle around the "baby farm," led by "Mama Molly," in whose care they are. Tom McNamara, the artist, celebrated for his comic children pictures, arranged the attiring of the youngsters. The kiddies enjoy themselves thoroughly, and, as might be expected, fairly idolize "our Mary" whose love for kiddies is wide enough to embrace them all.

Among the youngsters who have already "won their camera spurs," are Muriel McCormac and Billy Butts. Monty O'Grady, who plays the little bug-picker, is said to be a "find." Others are Billy Jones, Jack Levine, Mary McLane, Florence Rogan, Camilla Johnson, Sessel Anne Johnson, Sylvia Bernard and Mary Louise Miller, all cast in baby roles.

NO GREASE PAINT HERE

AN interesting fact in connection with "The Pony Express" is that Cruze has produced a picture in which, with one exception, no make-up is used and no false whiskers appear. The one exception is in the case of Johnny Fox as young Bill Cody. Make-up was used to cover Johnny's freckles, since Buffalo Bill had none, legend avers.

Dorothy Dwan, who comes under the Pathe banner as Semon's leading lady in "Stop, Look and Listen" adopts the famous rooster as a head-piece.

W. Collinson, general manager of the Palace Cinema, Walton-on-Thames, Surrey, England, visits Ben Lyon during the filming of "The New Commandment" (First Nat'l) in New York.

Bobby Vernon, starring in comedies on the Christie lot, for release by Educational, listens to words of wisdom from the lips of Felix, the feline funster.

Subsidiary of Firm Affiliated With P. D. C. Forms Circuit

60 to 100 Houses in North American Theatres

By Thomas C. Kennedy

NORTH American Theatres Corporation, a subsidiary of Motion Picture Capital Corporation, the financing organization back of Producers Distributing Corporation, has entered the theatre field as the latest large-scale circuit operator. Financing and booking arrangements have been acquired with more than sixty houses through affiliations with independent theatre groups in Northern and Southern California, Oregon, Washington, and Iowa. The exact number of theatres affiliated with the organization at present is not known, but is understood to range from sixty to one hundred.

The theatre company has the backing of Motion Picture Capital Corporation, which numbers among its large stockholders many influential financial groups which hitherto had had no connections with enterprises in the amusement field. These include leading Wall Street operators and officials of some of the largest industrial and commercial organizations in the country.

It is known that the Motion Picture Capital Corporation has served as the medium for bringing into the industry interests never before identified with amusement enterprises. Its stockholders include financiers of the highest standing, including men whose names rarely appear as the holders of shares in companies of this kind, so the report from reliable sources goes. Among these are said to be three men who are partners of the firm of J. P. Morgan and Company and whose stock in the Capital Corporation is held in the names of their brokers.

Frank R. Wilson, president of the Capital Corporation, is also president of North American Theatres Corporation, which is a closed syndicate with no stock being offered on the market. Harry C. Arthur, formerly associated with West Coast Theatres, Inc., is vice-president and general manager of the theatre company, the stockholders of which will hold a meeting this week to elect a board of directors.

Motion picture men who are represented on the directorate of Motion Picture Capital Corporation are Cecil B. De Mille and Charles Christie, whose productions are released by Producers Distributing Corporation.

Included in the circuits which have become affiliated with North American Theatre Corporation is the Far West Theatres, Inc., formed in Los Angeles by a consolidation of theatres controlled by Fred Miller and L. L. Bard, which brought six theatres into the combination and which has since acquired leases on several others. The combination now controls about 20 theatres in Southern California and has plans for the erection of several others there. This group also controls the State, formerly the Strand, theatre in Denver, Colo., recently taken over by North American.

According to Mr. Wilson, who with Harry Arthur is directing the operations of North American in acquiring theatres, the present status of the company's circuit represents only a beginning of the large undertakings which have been planned and are ready for execution.

Mr. Wilson told MOTION PICTURE NEWS that the company is in the field to make profits operating theatres. The move he says is in no way designed to create a "forced outlet" for product, but is aimed to develop the buying power necessary to the successful operation of picture houses.

The plan being followed is to form affiliations with independent theatre groups, which provides the financial backing and booking facilities of the parent company to its subsidiaries.

The company has eight or nine houses in Iowa. These are located at Waterloo, Sioux City, Clinton, Olewein, Dubuque and Cedar Rapids. Through leases and ownership of theatres, North American controls large groups of houses in Oregon and Northern California, where corporations subsidiary to the company have been formed with the holdings of local circuits as the nucleus of the operation in those states.

North American made its entrance into Washington last week, when plans were completed in Seattle for the beginning of construction within the next thirty days of a $1,500,000 theatre and office building on the half block at Fifth Avenue and Union Streets, in the heart of the business district. The theatre will be operated under a lease by the Washington Theatre Corporation, the North American organization in that state. The new theatre will occupy an area of 120 by 335 feet and have a seating capacity of 3,000, making it the largest theatre on the Pacific Coast outside of California.

North American plans to enter other states in the course of its operations during the immediate future. Those districts in which the company now has theatre interests include territory where companies without theatre connections find great difficulty in getting theatre representations for their product. In Iowa, for example, where the Blank circuit dominates the theatre situation, Producers Distributing is said to have found the booking situation a difficult one to solve.

Trade observers credit the entry of Motion Picture Capital Corporation, originally formed to finance the production of pictures, into the theatre field to the natural gravitation of capital toward the theatre branch of the industry, which many producers claim is a more profitable enterprise than that of producing. According to this view, the policy of organizations with their own theatres will be to continue production mainly as a reliable and self-controlled source of supply for those theatres.

The Board of Directors of Motion Picture Capital Corporation is comprised of the following:

Cecil B. De Mille, Charles H. Christie, H. A. Richards, New York; Theodore Schulze, New York; John E. Barber, Los Angeles; Steven Leonard, chairman of the board of directors of Arnold Constable Company; Theodore Watson, of Watson & White Co.; John T. Pratt, of the Standard Oil Company; Clarkson Potter, of Hayden Stone & Co., New York stock brokers; Jules E. Brulatour; John B. Miller, Los Angeles, president of the Southern California Edison Company; H. Lester Cuddihy, and Delos Blodgett.

Officers of the corporation are Frank R. Wilson, president; T. H. Brownell, associated with Jeremiah Millbank, vice-president; H. A. Richards, Treasurer; Oscar M. Bate, attorney and secretary.

Brooklyn Theatre is Robbed of $1400

Early on the morning of September 28th, burglars forced their way into the Filmland theatre, Church and Nostrand Avenues, Brooklyn, blew the safe and made their getaway with the week end receipts that amounted to $1400. After dragging the safe from the office to the stage, a distance of over one hundred feet, they cut down the curtain, gathered seat cushions and piled both over the safe, saturating them with water to muffle the explosion.

Filmland is owned by Filmland Players, Inc. and under the management of Fred Dollinger. The theatre held its premiere only about two weeks ago.

Picture Machine Exports Show Increase

Preliminary Department of Commerce figures show that 166 motion picture machines valued at $35,890 were exported from the United States during the month of August as against 99 valued at $23,699 in July and 64 valued at $16,484 in August 1924.

Robt. E. Welsh Joins Associated

Becomes Director of Advertising and Publicity for Company Under New Regime

ROBERT E. WELSH, until last week Editor of *Moving Picture World*, has been secured for an executive post in Associated Exhibitors, Inc. Since it became known two weeks ago that Mr. Welsh was about to relinquish the editorial reins there has been considerable speculation as to the connection he had planned. His acquisition by Associated Exhibitors rounds out a home office staff that gives strong promise of the big things planned for that organization.

It is only two weeks ago that announcement was made that Oscar Price had completed negotiations to assume control of Associated. Exhibitors which will hereafter be divorced from Pathe in every respect except physical distribution. Then last week he crashed into the headlines with the news that Associated's new Board of Directors would include such prominent picture figures as P. A. Powers and Elmer Pearson, while John S. Woody was named for the post of Gen-

eral Manager and Jay A. Gove retained as General Sales Manager.

The current headline means the bringing to Associated of one of the best known figures in the editorial end of motion pictures. He assumes the duties of Director of Advertising and Publicity, and is preparing to organize one of the most complete and efficient departments in the industry. In this respect the new Associated Exhibitors starts entirely from scratch, these departments having in the past been handled through the Pathe organization.

Through his service as managing editor of Motion Picture News for five years, and in recent years as editor-in-chief of *Moving Picture World*, Robert E. Welsh has been known to exhibitors throughout the country for ten years. Through young in years he is a veteran of the picture industry and probably numbers as many exhibitors as personal friends as any other figure in the business.

Pathe Convention is Sucessful

Home Office Executive Discus Problems With District Representatives

DISTRICT Managers and Pathe executives gathered at a convention in New York last week at which the problems of all hands were openly discussed and from which ways and means will be devised for the improvement of conditions in the field in connection with the most formidable releasing program this year ever attempted by the company.

Harry Scott, general sales manager of the company presided at the sessions and struck the key-note of the convention in his opening address by urging the field representatives present to lay their problems and recommendations before the assembly with the utmost frankness.

"We desire to base the decisions of this convention on first hand knowledge of actual conditions in the field," declared Mr. Scott. "What we are after are facts, not theories. If old methods and established procedure have outlived their time, we want to know it. We must proceed in accord with actual conditions as found in the field." The district managers heartily approved the recently established staff of field exploitation men who are at work under the supervision of S. Barret McCormick, exploitation manager. Plans were also discussed in detail for national advertising of a kind that exhibitors can tie up with their benefit to their box offices. Every phase of the huge production program was discussed in detail and plans perfected for the adequate presentation of the various units involved to the field.

Those who attended the regular convention sessions included: Harry Scott, General Sales Manager (Chairman); Pat Campbell, Feature Sales Manager; Stanley B. Waite, Sales Manager of Two-Reel Comedies Dept.; E. Oswald Brooks, Serial Sales Manager; W. A. V. Mack, Short-Feature Sales Dept.; Charles Henschel, Eastern District Manager; Fred C. Aiken, Mid-West

District Manager; R. S. Schrader, Central District Manager; Oscar Morgan, Southern District Manager; Frank Harris, Western District Manager; L. S. Diamond, Manager of Sales Statistical Dept.; S. Barret McCormick, Exploitation Manager; P. A. Parsons, Advertising Manager; E. F. Supple, Publicity Manager; Miss Regge Doran, Manager of Public Relations Dept.; Mrs. E. R. Dessez, Manager of Educational Dept.; George Gray, Editor of Pathe Sun; and W. C. Smith, Comptroller.

At the banquet in honor of the Pathe producers, held on Friday evening, September 25th, at the Hotel Roosevelt, there were present in addition to those already named, E. C. Lynch, Chairman of the Board of Directors; Paul Fuller, President of Pathe Exchange, Inc.; Elmer R. Pearson, Vice-President and General Manager of Pathe Exchange, Inc.; J. E. Storey, Assistant General Manager; Hal Roach and W. B. Frank for the Hal Roach Studios; William R. Fraser and John Ragland for the Harold Lloyd Corporation; Pete Carroll and John Waldron for the Mack Sennett Studios; A. Van Beuren and Charles MacDonald for "Aesop's Film Fables" and "Topics of the Day"; Emanuel Cohen for Pathe News and Pathe Review; and Irving Green for the Yale University Press.

Blank Reaches Settlement With Musicians

The Des Moines musicians' union and the A. H. Blank Enterprises have settled their differences and reached a compromise. The settlement is based on a two year contract with an increase of three dollars per week per man. The union had asked an increase of five dollars. The orchestras, which walked out of the Blank houses when the strike was declared are back at work in all houses controlled by the organization.

New Companies Launched in New York State

Motion picture companies filing papers of incorporation in the secretary of state's office and entering the business in New York state, during the past week, included the following: Lanscape Amusement Corporation, capitalized at $50,000, with Matthew N. and Fannie Chrystmos, Athenas P. Terris, of Yonkers; Calderone Valley Stream Corporation, Hempstead, $100,000, S. Calderone, C. W. Carman, Hempstead; G. L. Maggie, New York City.

B. R. Producing Company, Inc., capitalization not specified, H. Baron, M. Weiss, F. Risser, New York city; E. C. Fielder Co., Inc., $10,000, W. L. Worrall, E. C. Fielder, New York; M. J. Warner, Pine Orchard, Conn.; Ace Productions, Inc., $10,000, Jack McClellan, A. Sauk H. Goldman, New York city; Swingalong Movie Productions Inc., $50,000, E. E. Hart, B. C. Hart, William G. Bitzer, New York city.

Sears Amusement Corporation, capitalization not stated, Louis Mehl, Anna Radeloff, Adolph Schimel, New York city; Forest Avenue Studios, Inc., $25,000, A. S. D'Agostino, Elmhurst; Charles Ohmann, A. T. Mannon, New York city; K. W. F. Productions, Inc., $10,000, Clark Rose, M. W. Dixon, Dorothea Hein, New York city; Universal Artists Inc., capitalization not stated, Ruth Sherman, Muriel Borrman, P. D. Kaufman, New York city.

Albany Exhibitors Adjust Labor Troubles

Wage and working conditions have been adjusted between the exhibitors of Albany, N. Y., and the motion picture machine operators. Several conferences, however, were necessary before matters were finally ironed out. Each side compromised to some extent. While the operators desired a six hour day, it was decided that seven hours would constitute a day's work and that hereafter doing away with apprentices. Under this arrangement a union operator will do the relief work for two theatres.

Bowes Engages New Ballet Master for Capitol

Chester Hale, featured dancer who has arranged ballet numbers for several musical productions, has been engaged by Major Edward Bowes as Ballet Master of the Capitol theatre to succeed Mlle. Gamberelli, who hereafter will devote herself entirely to her work as prema ballerina.

Montreal Leads "Lieber Month" Contest

AT the end of the first week of First National's "Lieber Month" sales contest, Montreal, A Gorman, manager, held first position with a standing of 197.94. Indianapolis was second, with a narrow margin over the Portland branch, and New York was in fourth place. Salt Lake and Cleveland were next.

First National reports that a large percentage of the branches had exceeded their quota at the close of the first week of the drive.

Government Seeks Divorce of F.P.-L. Theatres

Also Asks Commission to Ban Block Booking

By Clarence L. Linz

Washington Correspondent, Motion Picture News

AN order requiring the Famous Players-Lasky Corporation, Adolph Zukor, Jesse L. Lasky, Jules E. Mastbaum, the Stanley Company of America, the Stanley Booking Corporation, the Saenger Amusement Company and Ernest V. Richards, Jr., to divest themselves of all interests which they have in theatrical property where motion picture film is exhibited, is asked of the Federal Trade Commission in a 280-page brief filed with that body by its attorneys in the Famous Players case.

Famous Players-Lasky has already announced that a separate theatre corporation is in process of formation.

Block-booking would also be banned under the order contemplated by the commission's counsel, both being characterized as unfair methods of competition.

The brief follows the history of the case from its inception in 1921 to the present time. Block booking and producer ownership of theatres are characterized as the most important phases of the case, and are considered exclusively, the other charges being left for oral argument.

The attorneys express the opinion that the evidence in the case would not warrant an action under the Clayton Act, and that it is only the virtue of the power granted the Federal Trade Commission that the continuance of these alleged unfair methods and practices can be stopped "and the door opened to a free and open market for the sale of motion pictures, where every producer will have an equal opportunity freed from the undue restraints now imposed as a result of these respondents' conspiracies to unduly restrain the sale of pictures, and the unfair methods in attempting to monopolize the industry."

Citing testimony submitted during the hearings to the effect that a good feature to be successful must have a first-class, first-run showing, and that a town with more than one theatrical seat for every twelve inhabitants was "overseated," it is declared to be "very obvious" that all of the producers cannot own theatres in the key cities, nor can all the distributors own such theatres, "so that if it is not an unfair method of competition for producers or distributors to own such theatres it means the practical elimination of all small producers of pictures and distributors from the business, and that the entire picture industry will shortly be controlled and monopolized by those companies which have the financial power to own and control the first-run motion picture theatres."

To require the various respondents to divest themselves of the theatre holdings, it is asserted, is a step of great magnitude. "Your counsel, in asking this commission to issue an order directing those respondents in this proceeding that are producers and/or distributors, engaged in the exhibition of motion pictures, to divest themselves of all interests, either direct or indirect, which they may have in theatrical properties which exhibit picture films, or divest themselves of the interests which they may have in producing and/or distributing companies, in the United States, realize the far-reaching results of such an order, and in that it contemplates the disposal of property of a probable value of more than one hundred million dollars. This commission, in considering the power that it has to make such an order under the Federal Trade Commission Act, is in the same position as the Supreme Court in the American Tobacco Company case, where Chief Justice White, in rendering the decision, stated:

" 'If the anti-trust Act is applicable to the entire situation here presented and is adequate to afford a complete relief for the evils which the United States insists that situation presents it can only be because that law will be given a more comprehensive application than has been affixed to it in any previous decision. This will be the case because the undisputed facts as we have stated them involve questions as to the operation of the Anti-trust Act not hitherto presented in any case.' "

The block booking situation is outlined in detail, the brief declaring it to be "not only an unfair method of competition against other producers and distributors, but an outrage on the exhibitors as well as the public who patronize the picture shows."

The record shows, it is asserted, that it was the policy of the Famous-Players Lasky Corporation to coerce and attempt to coerce and intimidate exhibitors who refused to buy all or substantially all of its pictures by various means and methods. This sales policy was usually pursued with exhibitors who refused to take the Paramount pictures because of the exorbitantly high rentals asked for them by the respondent. Threatening to open opposition theatres. "shock advertising" and "clocking" are declared to have been among the methods resorted to.

Discussing the results of block booking, the testimony of various witnesses is cited to show that block booking and theatre ownership by producer-distributor is fatal to the industry, "because it corners or closes the market, especially the first-class, first-run theatres in the big cities, and if it continues will eliminate the independent producers, who are producing the bigger and better pictures with their own money, and with a restricted market they will not be able to get their money out of their pictures. The producer-distributor-theatre owner dictates the policies and prices they pay for the pictures irrespective of the artistic merits.

"It is absolutely necessary for the picture industry to have an open market and an open field for the independent producers, or for all producers who want to make good pictures. If the exhibitor was not compelled to take the bad pictures with the good pictures, the bad pictures would soon be eliminated."

Considerable attention is paid by the attorneys to the contention of the respondents in the case that the Commission has no jurisdiction in the matter, it being pointed out that to sustain a proceeding under the Federal Trade Commission Act against a respondent engaged in interstate commerce the commission must have reason to believe that the alleged unfair methods of competition are of interest to the public. Testimony by Thomas A. Edison, H. H. Cotnick, Dr. John J. Tigert, United States Commissioner of Education; Colonel Alvin M. Owsley, former Commander of the American Legion; Douglas Fairbanks and others is cited to show the great educational value of motion pictures, and statistics are quoted to show the magnitude of the industry in the United States.

"These figures show the magnitude of the industry," it is declared, "and the testimony of the above witnesses—who are the best qualified in America to testify as to the potential power of the screen—have given us facts to show that never before has there been a case brought by the Government in which the general public has been more vitally concerned.

"It is astonishing to learn that within so short a time this new science for imparting knowledge has developed a greater potential power to influence the character, habits, dress, morals and general conduct of our youth than our public school system.

"As an advertising agency in business, it is equally effective. The screen being the first and only universal language in existence, and the effect of its use in foreign trade and in bringing about a better understanding among nations, cannot be overestimated.

"It follows necessarily that the public is

(*Continued on Next Page*)

First National and B. & K. Status Unchanged, Katz Declares

B ALABAN AND KATZ'S recent
theatre deal with Famous Players will in no way alter its longstanding affiliation with First National
Pictures. This fact was emphasized
in a telegram sent by Sam Katz to all
First National's original franchise
holders. Mr. Katz's wire reads:

Sam Katz

"Knowing your interest in the
negotiations between Balaban and
Katz and Famous Players, I want to
advise you that our board of directors
today ratified our deal with Famous
Players. The first and most important
thing is that the status of Balaban and
Katz remains unchanged. Balaban
and Katz remain the original franchise
holder of First National and intend to contribute in
the future as they have in the past to the continued development and success of First National. The success of First National is an integral part of your business and
ours and our efforts will be directed to maintain the important
position First National now holds in the industry."

(Signed) SAM KATZ.

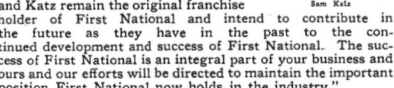

vitally interested in such a medium for enlightenment, which has such a tremendous
influence over every phase of American life
and over every phase of business, both foreign and domestic.

"Whether the motion picture will prove to
be a blessing or a curse to the world will
depend upon whether or not each of the
three branches of the industry, to-wit, the
production, distribution and exhibition of
motion-picture film, can be kept free from
the evil influences of monopolistic control.

"We do not contend that the Government
should own and operate this industry, but
the same rules that have been found necessary to prevent unfair methods in competition, and monopoly, in other great industries
must be rigidly applied to this new industry, at least to the extent sought in this case
that the independent theatre owner should
be left free to lease from any and all producers, and free to lease only such films as
he deems suitable for his locality and acceptable to his patrons, and the theatres
kept free from the control and domination
of producers and distributors."

The brief, in addition to the statement of
the case and a discussion of the commission's
jurisdiction, reviews the organization of
Paramount and Famous Players and the
acquisition of the former by the latter; the
acquisition of producing and distributing
companies and theatres by Zukor's new company prior to January, 1917; the effect of
these different mergers resulting in the
organization of the First National e *hibitors'*
circuit; Zukor's "attempt to destroy First
National exhibitors' circuit and to merge it
with his company;" affiliations of Famous
Players with independent producers; the
raising of $10,000,000 to buy first-run theatres in key cities; the organization of
Southern Enterprises and agreements with

Lynch; acquisition and control of theatres
in various States; block booking; Realart
Pictures Corporation as "a bogus independent;" the connections of the various respondents; the coercive methods employed in
foreing block booking, and the effect of
block booking upon the motion picture industry.

The Commission has set November 10 as
the date for the hearing. The attorneys for
the respondents have twenty days in which
to answer the complaint.

Motion Picture Exposition Under Way in Berlin

All of the different branches of the film
industry are represented at the Berlin Motion Picture and Photographic Exposition
now under way at Kaiserdamm, Berlin, W.,
Germany. It is the first exhibition of the
kind ever held in Germany and attracted
wide attention. The dates are from September 25th to October 4th. The exposition
was arranged by the Berliner-Messe-Amt in
co-operation with the leading film and photographic associations of Germany.

Des Moines Theatre Strike is Terminated

The Des Moines theatre strike is over.
Differences have been settled after three
weeks during which stink bombs were once
used. The union men returned to work
Thursday. Mort Singer and Asher Levy,
negotiating for the Orpheum circuit, said
both sides made concessions. The theatre had
been picketed until a week ago Monday.
The settlement includes a two-year agreement retroactive to Sept. 1.

Jersey M. P. T. O. Meeting Held At Asbury Park

Directors of the Motion Picture Theatre
Owners of New Jersey met at Asbury
Park Thursday, September 24th. Joseph M.
Seider, president of the organization presided at the gathering, which was attended
by Charles Hildinger, Peter Adams and
Louis Rosenthal, vice-presidents; Leon
Rosenblatt, secretary; William Keegan,
treasurer, and Directors Sidney E. Samuelson, Benjamin Schindler, I. M. Hirshblond,
Jacob Fox, J. J. Unger, Lee Newbury, E.
Thornton Kelly and Louis Gold.

Among the subjects discussed at the meeting were legislation, industrial reels and the
Play Date Bureau. Data collected during
the past year for the purpose of obtaining a
reduction in the Power Rate has been prepared for presentation to the Public Utility
Commission. A large increase in the payment of dues was reported by the treasurer.

San Francisco Coliseum Has Changed Hands

Sale and immediate leasing of the Coliseum property in the Richmond District of
San Francisco, the entire transaction involving $1,600,000, was announced Sept.
19th by Louis R. Lurie, realtor, who acquired the large holding from Samuel H.
Levin. Lurie purchased the property for
$225,000 from Levin and then leased the
holding back to Levin for 99 years.

The total rental was $1,470,150 net, the
lessee paying all insurance and taxes and
expenses of the property. The theatre seats
2,200 persons. Levin sublets the holding
for a total rental of $29,000 a month net
after deducting for taxes and insurance.

Glens Falls Rotarians Hosts to Hays

Will H. Hays, president of the Motion
Picture Producers and Distributors of America, was the guest of honor last week at a
Rotary Club luncheon in Glens Falls, N. Y.
Mr. Hays was spending a few days at Lake
George, as the guest of Lucius Greve, a
friend. Exhibitors of Glens Falls and vicinity, anxious to see Mr. Hays, flocked to the
luncheon and listened to his talk.

O'Toole Made Major in Reserve Army

I N RECOGNITION of the work
done for the army through Motion
Picture Theatre screens while he was
president of the Motion Picture
Theatre Owners of America and
chairman of the Public Service Department of that organization, M. J.
O'Toole has received an appointment as
Major in the Reserve Corps of the United
States Army. The appointment was
made at the direction of President
Coolidge.

Major O'Toole, associated with the
Comerford Amusement Company in different theatrical enterprises will serve as
required in the office of Secretary of War
at Washington and in General Summerall's Second Army Corps Area, with
headquarters at Governor's Island, New
York. During his association with the
motion picture business, Major O'Toole
evolved different processes whereby
screen publicity has been made to serve
the interests of Nation, State, City and
Town.

First National Alters Sales Plan

Franchise Holders Replace District Managers as Sales Representatives: System Worked Out At Indianapolis Meeting

SWEEPING alterations in the sales and distribution system of First National provides among other changes for the replacement of district managers by First National franchise holders. Under this new arrangement the company's field forces will operate under twenty-six district managers instead of seven as heretofore.

The new plan, which has already been put into effect, was evolved at the last meeting of the Franchise holders at Indianapolis. The plan was submitted by E. A. Eschmann and received the indorsement of the franchise holders, who agreed to take over the duties of managing the sales in their districts without compensation.

Mr. Eschmann pointed out that while they are exhibitors primarily, the franchise holders are also partners in First National and contended that as partners they are vitally interested in the sales of the company's pictures as they are in their own exhibitions of its product. The franchise holders volunteered full co-operation in the execution of the plan, agreeing to go out into the field if necessary and to lend their assistance if such were required, in smoothing out difficulties which may arise in dealings between seller and buyer.

Mr. Eschmann explained that the change in no way reflected upon the ability of the former district managers. In fact, under

E. A. Eschmann, who has inaugurated a new First National sales plan.

his new plan, they will remain with the company, but in the capacity of branch managers.

Canada will remain under the supervision of a general manager, who will act as district manager, as well.

In this manner, it is believed that considerably greater strength can be maintained throughout the field. For, while functioning ordinarily in the territory mapped out for them, provision is also made whereby any one or more of the branch managers, as required, can be switched at a moment's notice to any other territory that might show signs of weakening.

A still more direct contact between the field agencies and distribution headquarters is also incorporated into the new arrangement. It is Mr. Eschmann's intention that executives from the personnel of the distribution department will circulate constantly around the cycle of the exchanges so that there will be no loss of direct contact between them and the home office. He holds that this will be one of the vital aims of his organization.

By this change in policy Mr. Eschmann is calling to his distribution strength, the brains, acumen and force of the owners and partners of First National, and at the same time bringing about a closer and more direct coordination between the home office and the branches, as at least one of his associates in the home office will be making the round of the various branches, when he is not doing so himself.

Seider Makes Protest To Will Hays

Attacks Clause Which He Declares Has Been Added to Exhibition Contracts

A PROTEST has been sent to Will H. Hays by Joseph M. Seider, Chairman of the M. P. T. O. A. Contract and Arbitration Committee, with reference to a clause which Mr. Seider states has been added to the present exhibition contracts by members of the Hays organization.

The effect of this clause, Mr. Seider declares, is to require the exhibitor to accept a contract the terms of which are unknown to him. Mr. Seider's letter says:

"You, no doubt, are aware of the fact that the members of your organization, without advice to their customers, have added a clause to the exhibition contracts that they enter into with theatre owners as follows:—

"'This contract and each and every term and condition hereof, except the matter set forth in the Schedule, shall be deemed amended, modified, added to and/or abrogated by the terms and conditions of the proposed new uniform exhibition contract if and when finally adopted and approved by Motion Picture Producers and Distributors of America, Inc., insofar as the terms and conditions of such new uniform exhibition contract shall or may be inconsistent with or additional to the terms and conditions hereof, and the provisions, terms and conditions of such new uniform contract, when so adopted and approved, shall be deemed to be incorporated herewith, to form a part hereof and to be binding upon the parties hereto.'

Mr. Seider then declares that when a distributor adds a clause to a contract that con-

Hays Office is Drafting New Contract

AT the Hays office it was said no comment would be made on the letter from Mr. Seider. It is understood that the Hays organization is drawing up a new contract.

While no official statement of any kind is available it is understood from sources usually well informed that the view of the Hays office is that the new contract will be an improvement from the exhibitor's standpoint on the contract now in use.

tains in bold face type the words "Uniform Exhibition Contract," he is leading his customer to believe that the contract that he is signing is the so-called Uniform Contract without change from the form promulgated by the Hays organization. The letter continues:

"The clause is so drawn that it would give the impression upon a first reading that the proposed new uniform exhibition contract referred to is the form of contract proposed by us and it is only after a careful reading that it becomes apparent that it refers to a

contract that your organization is obviously preparing.

"We have no objection to your organization ignoring our proposed form and instead preparing one from your own viewpoint. On the contrary, we will welcome a contract drawn by you that is fair to both sides.

"We must, however, protest, on behalf of our membership, against this newly added clause.

"Through this clause an exhibitor agrees in advance to accept a contract, the terms of which are unknown to him. Your members require of the exhibitors to sign a check in blank for your organization to fill in the amount and the payee.

"We have tried very hard, but in vain, to find a reason for this section other than an effort by your organization to overcome sales resistance because of the demand of the theatre owners for a fair contract to forestall the acceptance of our proposed contract by the Independent Motion Picture Association of America and to provide against a possible decision adverse to the form of contract now in use by your members.

"In the event a decision is rendered, holding the present contract inequitable, we assume it is the intention of your members to substitute a new form for the present one and this clause makes it possible for you to do so. You purpose, thereby, to make valid the present contracts, which we claim are invalid because they lack mutuality."

New York Congressman Will Ask Probe of Copyright Law Exactions

CONGRESSMAN MacGREGOR, of New York, has announced that at the opening of Congress he will ask for an investigation of the American Society of Composers, Authors and Publishers, so it may be determined precisely how the organization is using the Copyright Law to exact tribute from the public.

"It is unthinkable," said Congressman MacGregor, "that the American Society of Composers, Authors and Publishers should be permitted to continue the practices it indulges in under cover of the Copyright Act. I propose immediately upon the opening of Congress to ask for the appointment of a committee to investigate its practices to the end that there be some curb put to the indefensible methods it has pursued in extracting money from the public.

"Congress never intended to put into anybody's hands such extraordinary power as seems to be exercised by this Society in the institution of a system of spies, the imposition of fines and penalties and the extraction of license fees. I understand that every movie house, every broadcasting station, every hotel, every place in the United States where music is played or songs sung for the pleasure of the people that can in any way be classed as for profit must pay tribute to this society.

"It is unthinkable that any person or group can be permitted to continue such a course. It is contrary to the American sense of fairness or decency."

Buffalo exhibitors are greatly pleased with the announcement by Representative MacGregor of Buffalo that he will seek congressional help to "throttle the music trust." J. H. Michael, chairman of Buffalo Zone, M. P. T. O. of N. Y., declares the fight to repeal this tax is just as important as the campaign to repeal the admission tax and urges every exhibitor in the state as well as the country to support Mr. MacGregor in his proposed battle.

A. M. P. A. Committees Named

Hold Second Meeting Under New Regime; Start Plans for the Naked Truth Dinner

APPOINTMENTS to the various committees of the A.M.P.A. were published at the second meeting under the new administration held at the Hofbrau house, September 24th. The meeting, presided over by Glenn Allvine, newly elected president, also settled questions relative to the policy of the new regime and named Saturday, February 7th, 1926, as the tentative date of the next Naked Truth Dinner.

The appointments to the committees follow:

Advisory Council—Jerome Beatty, Arthur Brilant, John Flinn, Paul Gulick, C. L. Yearsley, Lon Young and A. M. Botsford; Membership — P. A. Parsons, Chairman, Paul Gulick and Julian M. Soloman; Finance—G. Allvine, C. Einfeld, A. Rittenberg, W. Barrell, and E. O. Brooks; Publicity—W. E. Mulligan, Edward Klein, E. F. Finney and Dave Weschner; Entertainment — Harry Reichenbach, Russell Holman, Tom Wiley,

Bert Adler, Irving Green, Herman W. Fisher, Jack Kopstein, Nat Rothstein and the Board of Directors, the Advisory Council and the Past Presidents; Guests—V. M. Shapiro, W. F. Eberhardt and H. W. Fisher; Art — Vicent Trotta, Chairman, Harry Lewis, Karoly Gross, Hal Phyffe and C. L. Yearsley; Auditing—Sam Palmer, Chairman, H. C. Bate and Hal Howe; A.M.P.A. Bulletin—W. T. Mulligan, Mng. Editor, Edward McNamee, Bus. Mgr.; National Chancellor of U. S. Chamber of Commerce — John Flinn; and the newly appointed Space Buyers on Trade Paper and other Amusement mediums, Audit.

The last named committee, an active one sometime back in the history of the association has been revived to determine the number and classification of the various subscribers and value of each of the periodicals in question.

Saenger Theatres Bond Issue

Float $1,500,000 Issue at 6½% Secured by Mortgage on Real Estate

A $1,500,000 issue of first mortgage and collateral trust gold bonds, paying 6½% and due in 15 years, has been floated by Saenger Theatres, Inc., operating 44 theatres in Louisiana, Texas, Mississippi, Florida and Arkansas, through Hibernia Securities Co., Inc., of New Orleans and Hemphill Noyes & CoS., and Merrill, Lynch & Co., of New York.

The bond issue will be secured by a first mortgage on the real estate holdings of the Saenger company, appraised as of August 1st, 1925, at $2,313,003. The net assets of the company as shown by the consolidated balance sheet as of June 30, 1925, are $4,-526,425. Saenger Theatres owns one-third of the stock of the Canal Realty & Improve-

ment Co., Inc., and as co-guarantor with two other parties, has a contingent liability of a total amount of $500,000 first mortgage bonds issued by the Canal Realty & Improvement company.

In addition to the 44 theatres which the company operates, Saenger holds an interest in 23 others. Sixteen of the 44 houses are owned outright and the others operated on long term leases. Saenger Theatres was chartered in 1913, at which time it operated five theatres. Consolidated net earnings of the company and its subsidiaries after depreciation, available for bond interest and Federal taxes, for the five and a half years ended June 30, 1925, averaged over $411,570 per annum.

LESLIE F. WHELAN, exploitation manager for the Harold Lloyd Corporation, has returned from a trip through the Middle West in the interest of "The Freshman." He assisted in the exploitation of Lloyd's latest production at Chicago, Milwaukee, Buffalo, Des Moines, Kansas City, St. Louis, Cincinnati and Pittsburgh.

A. W. SMITH, Jr., assistant to E. A. Eschmann, is on a three weeks' trip to the company's branch offices in the Mid-West and Central districts.

HARRY COHN, vice-president of Columbia Pictures, is on a flying trip to New York from the Coast.

PAULA GOULD, general press representative for F. B. O. in the East, returned Sept. 28 from a four weeks' visit to the Hollywood studios of the company.

RICHARD TALMADGE, starring in comedy dramas for F. B. O. arrived from the Coast this week for a month's stay.

A LARGE number of film notables arrived from Los Angeles during the past week. They included: Joseph M. Schenck, Norma Talmadge, Harry M. Warner, B. P. Schulberg, Joe Engel, Harry Rapf, Joseph I. Schnitzer and Charles Whittaker.

WINFIELD R. SHEEHAN, general manager of Fox, arrived late last week on the Aquitania from Europe.

Bunn Wins Appointment by First National

E. A. Eschmann has placed C. W. Bunn in charge of the open market selling of First National pictures, exclusive of the specials. The appointment became effective September 28th. Bunn has been conducting the work for the past two months.

E. V. Richards Jr., of Saenger Theatres, Inc., which is floating $1,500,000 bond issue.

Pathe Stock on New York Exchange

156,208 Shares of Class A Common Stock Are Admitted to Market; Statement Shows Rapid Growth

STOCK of Pathe Exchange, Inc., has been admitted on the New York Stock Exchange. The Board of Governors of the exchange has admitted to trading 156,208 share of class A common stock. This company, one of the oldest and largest concerns engaged in the picture industry has shown consistent growth during the past eight years. Its gross revenue in 1916 was $4,277,003, and in 1924, $16,459,386.

According to the story in the Wall Street Journal, Pathe expects to do a gross business of $18,000,000 in the current year, from which net profits of $1,500,000 will be available for dividends. This figure after dividends on the $848,200 of 8% preferred stock outstanding, would be equivalent to nearly $9 a share on the outstanding 160,133 common shares, according to the Journal. In 1924 on a gross of $16,459,385 the net was $1,312,000, or $7.77 a share on the common.

For the first 28 weeks of the current year net of $705,058 was realized on sales of $3,-805,268, or $4.19 a share.

The consolidated balance sheet as of July 11th lists assets and liabilities as follows:

Assets: Cash $1,247,252; advances to producers $3,017,168; inventories $1,168,352, other current assets $883,619, real estate, equipment, etc., after depreciation, $757,172, investments at cost $150,000, residual value of films, written off, $1, deferred charges

Missouri Still Fights the Sunday Closing

ONE Missouri exhibitor has hoisted the proverbial white flag in the Sunday show battle among several smaller town exhibitors and citizens, while another, despite a fine and judgment against him, battles stubbornly on, determined to see the fight to a finish.

J. W. Cotter, Moberly, Mo., exhibitor, pleading not guilty to operating his theatre on Sunday in violation of a Sunday ordinance was fined $50 in a police court. He then gave notice of an appeal to the state circuit court and announced his theatre would be open on Sunday, as usual.

In Liberty, Mo., after those who sympathized with Sunday shows, had threatened to close up all drug stores and filling stations if Sunday shows were prohibited, Mr. and Mrs. C. R. Wilson, owners of the Liberty theatre and leaders in the fight, agreed, after a conference with sixteen business men, to let bygones be bygones and cease operating their theatre on Sunday without making the town a "blue law" mecca.

$226,885, goodwill and contracts $2,214,907; total, $9,665,356.

Liabilities: Accounts payable and federal taxes $655,533, advance payments on film rentals $197,378, reserve for amortization of contract $819,915, 8% gold bonds due 1931

$1,184,600, 8% preferred stock $848,200, common stock (represented by 150,133 no par shares of class A and 10,000 no par shares of class B) $2,073,254, reserve for sinking fund for retirement of preferred stock $86, surplus $3,886,390; total $9,665,-356.

The product of Pathe includes special features, serials, the Pathe News, one and two-reel comedies, the Pathe Review, animated cartoons, topics of the day and educational pictures. Through a subsidiary, Pathex, Inc., a new popular priced motion picture camera and projector has been recently placed on the market. This instrument is meeting with increasing demand and is beginning to contribute to profits. The price of the film used in the camera includes its development in Pathe's laboratories and its return on a camera ready to screen. While profits on the camera are substantial, the greater return lies in the sale of the film. The number of cartridges of film per camera sold to date has far exceeded preliminary estimates, and the company expects revenues from this subsidiary will materially swell profits.

The company also owns 49% of the common stock of the du Pont Pathe Film Manufacturing Corp. This company was recently organized to manufacture raw and non-inflammable film under the process of Pathe Cinema of France. Present production of film is sufficient to take care of all Pathe's requirements.

West Coast Now Controls 250 Houses

New Subsidiary Corporations Are Launched, Bringing in Additional Theatres; Many More to Be Added

AS THE result of the organization of a new subsidiary company, and other expansion proceedings, West Coast Theatres now embrace close to 250 theatres along the western coast. West Coast Theatres of Northern California, of which Mike Nafy and Nasser Brothers are the guiding spirits, have organized the Bear State Theatres Corporation, a $2,000,000 concern which will take over the T. and D. Junior Circuit. West Coast owns a half interest in the new unit and the other half is owned by Nafy and Nassers.

The Bear State company will not secure complete control of the T. and D. houses, but will hold a majority interest. The T. and D. holdings at present include about thirty houses, but will eventually expand to include about 75 houses, all in Northern California. Nafy individually controls seven houses and Nasser Brothers eight. This in time, will probably be included in the holdings of the new company. Five new houses are on the program to be built by T. and D.

West Coast Theatres is now operating 111 houses in the principal California key cities and has seventeen others in course of construction. West Coast Junior, operating in Southern California is rapidly e panding its activities and it is said will shortly annex some sixty additional houses in the smaller towns in the Southern part of the state. The

Junior Circuit is under the guidance of Mike Rosenberg and Harry Gore.

Theatres already purchased by the new Junior organization include the Royal, Seventeenth and Main streets, Los Angeles, to be remodeled at a cost of $40,000; the Crystal on Whittier Boulevard, the June on Whittier Boulevard, three houses in Redlands, one of which is the Opera House, which is to cater to legitimate plays, road shows and feature films. A site for a new $200,000 theatre was also purchased in Ontario, California. This house will have a seating capacity of 1,500, a Wurlitzer organ and all modern facilities. Work is to be started immediately.

According to the Junior Theatre Circuit policy a motion picture house will be established in every town in Southern California not covered already by the West Coast Theatres, Inc. Millions of dollars, it is said, will be spent on the new houses and the reconstruction of acquired houses within the next twelve months.

West Coast is also said to be planning an invasion of the Colorado Theatre field. A deal, said to be of considerable proportions, is now in process of consummation. According to A. L. Gore, who is in New York on business with First National, the T. and D Junior holdings involved in Bear

State Theatres Corporation deal include three houses in Alameda, two in Lodi, one in Merced, one in Paso Robles, one in Petaluma, one in Oakland, three in Reno, three in Sacramento, one in Selma, one in Susanville, one in Tulare and ten or twelve others in various towns in California.

East Side Theatre Wrecked by Safe-Blowers

In an effort to obtain the cash box containing $500, amateur yeggs caused an explosion which wrecked the Florence Theatre, largest motion picture house on lower East Side, New York, resulting in damage to the amount of $15,000. The bandits used an excessive charge of nitro-glycerine in their attempt to blow open the safe in which the cash box was locked. The bandits escaped without obtaining the cash box which was found intact near the wrecked safe.

The attempted burglary was the fifth raid to be made on the Florence Theatre this year. The explosion, which hurled pieces of the steel safe a distance of 100 feet, started a fire. Orchestra seats, the proscenium arch, organ and other musical instruments were ruined by the flames and by smoke and water.

Laemmle Is Due From Europe

Universal President Returning After Spending Entire Summer Abroad

CARL LAEMMLE, president of Universal, accompanied by his secretary, Harry H. Zehner, and his two children, Carl Jr. and Miss Rosabelle, is due back from Europe this week. He has been away all Summer and has visited all of the important film centers on the Continent in furtherance of Universal's interests.

During his stay abroad Laemmle conducted a Universal sales convention in Berlin. It was attended by the company's office managers from France, Czechoslovakia, Italy, Spain, Holland, and Sweden, and was the first convention of the kind ever held by Universal.

This convention was similar in scope to the sales conventions held in the United States. The visiting managers reported the current conditions in their territories and previewed coming Universal films.

Laemmle was the guest of honor at two important banquets in Europe. The first was held in the Hotel Pupp, Prague, Czechoslovakia, and was given in his honor by the exhibitors of Prague. The second was given in Berlin by the film writers and critics of that city. Both dinners were marked with enthusiasm and amity. In each case the Universal president was hailed for the excellence of Universal's product and assured that Universal pictures had won for themselves a warm spot in the hearts of the Continental film fans.

During his stay in Berlin, Laemmle was the guest of the Ufa organization on a tour through the big Ufa studio plant at Neubabelsberg, on the outskirts of the German metropolis.

Shortly before he returned to America, the Universal chief acquired the rights to an important invention recently developed in Germany. It is a method of trick photography said to be very simple and very effective. The discovery of this invention led directly to the recent decision by Laemmle to make "Gulliver's Travels" as a big super-picture.

Sixteen Columbias Completed

Harry Cohn Here, Lauds Independents for Their Service to Exhibitors

SIXTEEN of the eighteen Columbia Pictures for the season have been completed and the other two are now in work, according to Harry Cohn, who is in New York from Hollywood to confer with his associates, Jack Cohn and Harry Brandt.

The product is made up of six Columbias, six Perfections and six Waldorfs.

The Columbia pictures are, "The Danger Signal," "The Unwritten Law," "Steppin' Out," "S. O. S. Perils of the Sea," "Ladies of Leisure" and "The Lure of the Wild." The six Perfections are, "Fighting Youth," "Speed Mad," "The New Champion," "The Great Sensation," "A Fight to the Finish" and "The Handsome Brute." The Waldorfs are, "Enemy of Men," "The Prince of Success," "Sealed Lips," "When Husbands Flirt," "The Fate of a Flirt" and one unentitled.

Discussing the Columbia product and the independents in general Cohn said:

"Of course I am personally proud of the pictures I have made for Columbia this year. But I want to say more than a mere passing word of praise for men like Ben Schulberg, Ike Chadwick, Phil Goldstone, Renaud Hoffman, Hunt Stromberg, Whitman Bennett, Charles Burr, Abe Carlos and a host of other real independent producers who have kept their promise one hundred per cent to give to the exhibitors who have had the courage to stand by the independent producers a series of pictures that will stand the acid test of hard box office values.

"A few of this season's finished independent pictures which illustrate this contention and prove that this statement is accurate and that the independent boys are delivering the goods is borne out with 'The Danger Signal,' a Columbia; 'Souls for Sables,' Goldstone-Tiffany; 'The Girl Who Wouldn't Work,' Schulberg; 'Steppin' Out,' Columbia; 'Wizard of Oz,' Chadwick; 'Overland Limited,' Gotham; 'Romance of an Actress,' Stromberg; Richard Talmadge specials, and many others, too numerous to mention."

August Film Exports Show Increase

PRELIMINARY figures just issued by the Department of Commerce show that exports of motion picture films, sensitized but not exposed, from the United States to all countries reached, in August 1925, a total of 9,577,243 linear feet valued at $175,816. This is nearly 13,000,000 linear feet under the unprecedented total of 22,000,000 linear feet of raw film exported in July 1925, but it tops by slightly over 3,000,000 feet the amount of raw film exported in August 1924.

Exports of negatives for August 1925 amounted to 1,750,117 linear feet valued at $260,475 as against $671,765 linear feet valued at $106,559 in July and 1,188,238 feet valued at $244,339 in August 1924.

Exports of positives also showed a slight increase for August 1925 over the two previous periods, the figures reading, 20,368,923 linear feet valued at $572,782 for August 1925 as against 17,589,806 linear feet valued at $552,633 in July and 19,636,791 linear feet valued at $685,140 in August 1924.

Fisher Plans Studio in Florida Soon

Victor B. Fisher, well-known independent producer, was in New York this week. He is planning a studio development in Florida.

Famous-Daily News Tie-up to Seek Potential Star

FAMOUS PLAYERS-LASKY and the Daily News of New York have entered a tieup in which a search will be made for a girl to play a prominent role in a forthcoming Paramount production titled "New York." The girl selected to portray the Spirit of New York will be given a year's contract with Paramount at a salary of $5,200. Four other girls, one from each borough of the Greater City will be selected for the cast of "New York." They will be paid at current studio rates for the time employed.

The judges who will make the selection are to be appointed by Governor Alfred E. Smith.

Weaver Seattle Studios to Be Enlarged

Enlargement of the H. C. Weaver Productions, Inc., studio at Titlow Beach, Wash., according to announcements made in Seattle last week by Mr. Weaver upon his return from New York City. Growth of the company is a result of the contract signed recently by Mr. Weaver, whereby he will produce within the next year eighteen pictures, at an approximate cost of $1,300,000, which will be distributed by the Vital Pictures Corporation.

The improvements being made in the studios will cost in excess of $25,000, but will make it possible to work twenty-four hours a day on the production of the films. General James M. Ashton of the Weaver organization was expected in Seattle next week, after having signed a contract for the production of eight additional pictures for the Associated Exhibitors' release schedule.

Anthracite Withheld From Massachusetts Theatres

Eugene C. Hultmnn, chairman of the Emergency Fuel Board, has issued orders to Massachusetts theatre owners and managers that no anthracite coal will be sold for the present time to theatres or to other large buildings. Deliveries are also forbidden to all who have half or more of their year's fuel supply in their bins. Most of the theatres have their fuel supply already on hand, anticipating some such order. Distributing offices are also well fixed as to their supply.

Archer First National's Vancouver Manager

J. E. Archer has been named manager of First National's Vancouver branch, succeeding W. H. Mitchell, who was assigned by E. A. Eschmann to assist William A. Bach, manager of First National's Canadian business.

William Rau Seriously Ill With Pneumonia

William Rau, production manager of the Harry Pollard unit for Universal, is seriously ill with pneumonia at his home in Hollywood. He was soaked in the skin taking rain scenes in a production last Saturday and his illness followed.

Lumas Will Distribute "The "Northern Code"

"The Northern Code," a Jerry Mayer production, has been taken over for distribution by Lumas Film Corporation. It will be handled as an individual production and sold on a territorial basis independent of any of the Gotham productions released by Lumas.

The story is of the Canadian Northwest and the cast includes Eva Novak and Robert Ellis in the featured roles, Josef Swickard, Claire De Lorez, Francis McDonald and others. Leon De La Mothe directed.

Mary Pickford Cameraman Signs With Ufa

Charles Rosher, who has been with Mary Pickford for the past eight years as cameraman, has signed a contract with Ufa, the German film concern and will go abroad immediately upon the completion of Miss Pickford's "Scraps," now in production. In Germany Rosher will be associated with Murnau, director of "The Last Laugh." While with Miss Pickford, Rosher has photographed fifteen of the star's productions.

Metro-Goldwyn-Mayer Sign Expert Cameraman

Metro-Goldwyn-Mayer have signed Oliver Marsh, expert cameraman to a new contract which provides for his exclusive services to the Culver City organization. Among other successful pictures he photographed von Stroheim's "The Merry Widow" and Christy Cabanne's "The Masked Bride."

Norma Talmadge in scenes from the First National production, "Graustark."

Ten Productions Made In East

First National Units Complete One Feature a Month at New York Studios

SINCE their transfer to New York from Hollywood last October, the First National production units under the supervision of Earl Hudson, have made a record of turning out a feature a month, ten productions having been completed from November, when actual camera work was first started in the East, to the end of August.

The final scenes for "The Scarlet Saint" were completed last week and is now in the cutting room at First National's New York studios, where Arthur Tavares is assembling the work.

The first production made by First National under Hudson's supervision in the East was "One Way Street." This was started in the middle of November last. This was followed by "I Want My Man," with Milton Sills and Doris Kenyon in the featured roles. On the completion of these two "The Necessary Evil" and "Chickie" were filmed. "The Making of O'Malley," Milton Sills' first starring vehicle, and "The Half Way Girl" comprised the next pair. Then followed "The Pace That Thrills," "The Knockout," "The Unguarded Hour," and "The Scarlet Saint."

Five noted scenario writers have just been added to First National's eastern production units at New York. These writers who will do the scenarios for pictures going into production this Fall under the supervision of Earl Hudson are: Olga Printzlau, John Fish Goodrich, Charles Whittaker, Jane Murfin and Harvey Thew.

Highlight scenes from "The Best People," Paramount.

Editing "Road To Yesterday"

De Mille Also Prepares to Start New Feature; Three Other Units at Work

THE peak of production activity at the Cecil B. DeMille studios has been reached by the units making features for the Producers Distributing Corporation program at the Culver City plant, where three pictures are now in course of filming and Mr. DeMille is editing his personally directed production "The Road to Yesterday."

Upon completion of his editing and titling of this work, Mr. DeMille will immediately hold conferences with Jeanie Macpherson on the adaptation of "The Volga Boatman," his next personally directed feature based on a story especially written for him by Konrad Bercovici.

The units engaged in camera work on Producers Distributing features are headed by Rupert Julian, directing a screen adaptation of Anthony Paul Kelly's stage success "Three Faces East;" Alan Hale, who is making "Braveheart," the second Rod LaRocque starring vehicle, and Paul Sloane, filming "Made for Love," an original story by Garrett Fort in which Leatrice Joy will be starred.

The cast which will appear in "Three Faces East" includes Jetta Goudal, Robert Ames, Clive Brook and Henry Walthall. La Rocque's supporting company in "Braveheart" includes Lillian Rich, Robert Edeson, Tyrone Power, Jean Acker and Sally Rand.

Betty Jewel to Play Lead in "Broken Homes"

Betty Jewel has been cast for the second lead in "Broken Homes," the Bernarr McFadden True Story production being filmed at the Whitman Bennett Glendale studio under the direction of Hugh Dierker.

Jackie Coogan in his newest Metro-Goldwyn-Mayer production, "Old Clothes."

Outline Students' Schedules

Paramount Training School Takes Up Subjects of Lighting and Projection

STUDENTS of the Paramount Theatre Managers Training School continued their instruction in the details of house management during the fifth and sixth weeks of the six-months course for which they have entered.

The schedule for the fifth and sixth weeks included the following:

Mr. L. E. Schneider concluded his instruction on "The Operation of the Warehouse"—Mr. Leo Gafney of the American Seating Company outlined "The History of Theatre Seating"; Mr. Albert L. Baum of Jarvis & Baum, gave instructions on "Theatre Heating"; Mr. C. Buensod of the Carrier Engineering Corporation, explained "Theatre Ventilation"; Mr. Arthur J. McEntee of the Robert E. Hall Company explained "The Building Code as it Applies to Theatres." Further instruction in "Equipment" will be continued at the Edison Lighting Institute, Harrison, N. J. during the week's training in "Theatre Lighting"; also by Harry Ruben's instruction in "Projection Machines," by Mortimer Norden's instruction in "The Care of Electric Signs" and by instruction in "The Care of Carpets, lobby frames, drapes, motors, the cleaning of woodwork, doors and marble, etc.

Edward J. Myrick continued the training in "House Service." As this training is positional, the class will serve as ushers in the Broadway Theatres, each student serving during the evenings of two weeks under the direction of Mr. Cruse. The men will wear the theatre usher uniforms and go through the regular training given ushers.

The class visited 75 New York motion picture theatres to prepare the House Service Inspection Report. A. D. Scovel, Public Relation Expert of the New York Telephone Company, gave instruction on "The Employment of the Telephone Operator and in the Proper Handling of Typical Problems of the Theatre Operator."

John Grierson, psychological expert from England, who is concluding a two years' study of American motion picture audiences, gave the second series of his lectures The Attitude of Patrons Toward the Different Types of Stories and how this can be Applied in Building Campaigns.

Beauty Contest Winners in "Best People"

Sidney Olcott has signed twelve girls who have won beauty contests in various parts of the country for the tea dansant scene in "The Best People," his latest production for Paramount. Among them are Evelyn Atkinson, "Miss Seattle," in two Atlantic City Pageants; Barbara Cloatman, "Miss Hollywood"; Jane de Vaney, artist model and winner of several beauty contests, and Rosaline Borland, acclaimed the prettiest girl in Evansville, Ind. Featured in the cast are Esther Ralston, Margaret Morris and Margaret Livingston.

Cortez is to Play Opposite Gilda Gray

Paramount has selected Ricardo Cortez for the leading male role opposite Gilda Gray in "Aloma of the South Seas." This is Miss Gray's first starring vehicle in pictures, though she has been a featured dancer in some of Broadway's foremost musical comedies.

Gotham Release Schedule is Rearranged

Gotham Productions have rearranged their release schedule, though with one exception the productions will be the same as originally announced. "The Phantom of the Forest," with Thunder, the Marvel Dog, will be substituted for "The Forest of Destiny."

Under the new release schedule "One of the Bravest," a fire picture, starring Ralph Lewis, will be the November release in place of "The Shadow on the Wall," the mystery drama, which will be released in December. "The Phantom of the Forest" will go to the e hibitors in January, and "The Sign of the Claw" will be the twelfth and last release on the program.

Jans Engages Burton King to Direct Feature

Herman F. Jans, of Jans Productions, has signed Burton King to direct the screen version of "Ermine and Rhinestones," a magazine story by Louis Winter which will be the fourth offering on the Jans schedule for the current season. The picture will be filmed at the Whitman Bennett Studios at Glendale, Long Island.

"Abraham Lincoln" Third in London Contest

In a recent voting contest conducted by the London Daily Chronicle to determine the most popular films shown in England, First National's "Abraham Lincoln" won third place with 698,000 votes. The highest vote given a picture was 735,000.

"The Pace That Thrills" is a First National Picture, from which these scenes were taken.

I. M. Schwartz Opens Short Subject Exchange

I. Maynard Schwartz, for four years manager of Educational's Chicago exchange, has resigned from that organization to open his own exchange offices in Chicago and Indianapolis. The new distributing company will specialize in short subjects and is to be known as the Short Subject Exchange. Temporary offices have been opened at 806 South Wabash Avenue, Chicago.

The new company has signed for Rayart's "The Flame Fighter," a serial starring Herbert Rawlinson, the twelve Rayart Comedies, and the twelve two-reel Bobby Ray comedies offered by Anchor Film Distributors.

Grainger Makes Shifts in Fox Sales Staff

A number of changes have been made in the Fox staff of sales managers by James R. Grainger, general sales manager. George T. Landis takes over the Indianapolis exchange from Harry J. Bailey on September 28th. Bailey replaces W. C. Rowell as Buffalo manager October 5th and Rowell will take up the duties of salesman in the Buffalo territory.

Griffith is Assembling "That Royle Girl"

"That Royle Girl," D. W. Griffith's first picture for Paramount under his new contract, is being assembled and cut. The production features Carol Dempster, W. C. Fields, Harrison Ford and James Kirkwood.

Scenes from "The Wife Who Wasn't Wanted," a Warner Brothers production.

Lefty Flynn in highlight scenes from the F. B. O. production, "Heads Up."

F. B. O. Production Activity

Studio Personnel to Be Increased; Plans Made for Completion of Current Schedule

A SCHEDULE of great production activity has been mapped out for the F. B. O. studios in Hollywood during October and November. Production executives are concentrating on the completion of the 1925-26 program of 64 pictures and the plans which they have completed call for the addition of several directors and players to the present personnel of the organization.

At the close of September the F. B. O. plant completed one of the busiest months in its history. There are now six companies actively producing, with four more units about ready to start camera work.

Tom Forman, filming the "Midnight Flyer," a railroad melodrama by Arthur Guy Empey, is on location with a cast which includes Dorothy Devore, Cullen Landis, Buddy Post, Claire McDowell and Frankie Darro. And other F. B. O. units on location at present are the Fred Thomson company making "All Around the Frying Pan," a Frank Richardson Pierce story being directed by David Kirkland, and Maurice Flynn and his associates in the cast of "Between Men," a comedy melodrama being directed by Harry Garson.

Richard Talmadge is at work on an untitled story under the direction of Sam Nelson, and Tom Tyler, F. B. O.'s new western star, is being directed by Bob De Lacey and Jimmy Gruen. The fourth episode in the "Adventures of Mazie" series is being made by Alberta Vaughn and the comedians who will support her in these pictures.

Productions for which the preliminary plans are now being made are "A Poor Girl's Romance," to be adapted from the Laura Jean Libbey story of that title, "Flaming Waters," an original story by E. Lloyd Sheldon, the Emory Johnson production to follow "The Last Edition," and the next starring vehicle for Evelyn Brent, who will return to the studio soon from a month's vacation in New York.

John Lowell Russell Starts New Production

John Lowell Russell left on September 30th, for Knoxville, Chattanooga and points South where he will join the Miller Bros. 101 Ranch Outfit with whom a special production will be made.

The story is by Mrs. L. Case Russell and George Terwilliger will direct. John Lowell and Evangeline Russell are to be starred and the title and releasing arrangements will be later announced.

Cast Completed for Harry Carey Feature

Charles R. Rogers has assembled the cast for the first of a series of Western features he will produce with Harry Carey as the star for release through Pathe. Harriette Hammond has been chosen as leading lady, while in the supporting roles will be Bert Woodruff, Ruth King, Pat Harmon, Stanton Heck, Raymond Nye and Joseph Gerard. The first feature is an adaptation of "Buck Up," a story by Basil Dickey and Harry Haven. Scott Dunlap will direct.

A group of scenes from "The Everlasting Whisper," a Wm. Fox production in which Tom Mix is starred, accompanied as usual by Tony, the Wonder Horse.

Seven Units Working on Coast

Paramount Launches Busy Fall Schedule at Hollywood Plant; Eastern Units on Location

WITH seven production units now at work on important features for the Paramount program and plans completed for the launching of eight additional pictures in November, the Hollywood studios of Famous Players-Lasky are now well under way on the heavy Fall production schedule outlined for them by Jesse L. Lasky. There is little activity at present at the Long Island studios owing to the fact that three features were completed last week and the other units producing there are now on location.

The companies working at the Hollywood studios include the Pola Negri unit, now filming "The Tattooed Countess," adapted from the Carl Van Vechten novel and being directed by Malcolm St. Clair.

James Cruze is directing "Mannequin," the Fannie Hurst prize story of the Liberty Magazine contest; while Irvin Willat recently started the cameras on "The En-

chanted Hill," written by Peter B. Kyne.

New productions which it is expected will be started this week at the Hollywood plant are "Magpie," William de Mille's next feature, in which Bebe Daniels will have the starred role, and "Two Soldiers," adapted from the story by Hugh Wiley. This picture will bring Mildred Davis, Mrs. Harold Lloyd, back to the screen after an absence of two years. Victor Fleming will direct the work and Wallace Beery and Raymond Hatton are to head the cast supporting Miss Davis.

The productions completed within the past week at the Eastern plant are "The King on Main Street," with Adolphe Menjou, Greta Nissen, Bessie Love and Oscar Shaw and directed by Monta Bell; "Stage Struck," Gloria Swanson's new vehicle, and Herbert Brenon's "A Kiss for Cinderella," from the Barrie play and featuring Betty Bronson and Tom Moore.

Warner Plans For Next Season

Current Schedule Well Up; Preliminary Arrangements for 1926-27 Under Way

WARNER BROS. will make forty pictures for the 1926-27 season, the program to be headed by six superspecials of which two will be directed by Lubitsch, two will be vehicles for John Barrymore and two will star Syd Chaplin, it was stated by H. M. Warner, who returned to New York last week from a visit to the company's studios in Hollywood.

The current production schedule, Mr. Warner said, was so well advanced at this time that considerations looking toward the product to be offered next season were already under way. Twenty-five of the forty

Warner features for this year have been completed and according to present indications the studios will be ready to start on the 1926-27 product as early as January next.

Twelve of the fifteen remaining pictures to be made for the current program are well along in production now. Warner officials, he said, have found the results of advanced production so gratifying to both the production and distribution branches of the organization that every effort will be made to take advantage of the plan during the 1926-27 season.

Fifty Candidates for Role of Theodore Roosevelt

F. B. O. reports that more than fifty applications have been received from candidates for the role of Theodore Roosevelt in the production based on the noted statesman's career to be filmed by that company. Each of the applicants have been granted a personal interview at which their qualifications to portray the character on the screen have been minutely inspected. The choice, it is reported, has narrowed down to twelve. Work on the scenario for the picture will be started soon at the F. B. O. studios in Hollywood.

Kelley Color System in Novelty Pictures

A new series of pictures in which the Kelley Color system has been applied, is announced for release. It offers diversified subjects, consisting of novelty reels, such as "Escotypes" and "Babyland," and scenics such as "Feathered Braves," Indian pictures; "Sky High and Blue," showing the Canadian Rockies, the "Gardens of Victoria" and "Golden Apples."

Florence Auer in "King on Main Street"

Florence Auer has been assigned the role of Queen of Molvania in "The King on Main Street," which Monta Bell is producing at Paramount's Long Island studio. Miss Auer has just completed an engagement with D. W. Griffith in "That Royle Girl."

Scenes from "Borrowed Finery," a Tiffany Productions offering.

"Modern Madness" Print is Due in New York

"Modern Madness," a new A. M. Foote production has been completed under the direction of J. P. McCarthy, and F. J. Hawkins of the Hollywood Film Sales Service will leave for New York October 1st with a print of the picture. Dorothy Hope, an actress from England, makes her initial American appearance in "Modern Madness."

M. S. Rosenfield is the eastern representative of Hollywood Film Sales Service and will handle the sales of the Foote series. His offices are in the Loew State Theatre building in New York.

New Production Managers for Metropolitan

George Bertholon, production manager of Metropolitan Studios has appointed two assistant production managers to take care of pictures now in the making for release through Producers Distributing Corporation. E. J. Babille, recently with Cosmopolitan Productions, has been assigned to the "Rocking Moon" company, and Bob Ross has taken charge of the "Steel Preferred" company.

M-G-M Buy Screen Rights to "Monte Carlo"

Metro-Goldwyn-Mayer have purchased screen rights to "Monte Carlo," a new and original story by Carey Wilson, and will produce it on an elaborate scale this year. Wilson has contributed a number of recent stories to the screen, among them being, "Free Lips," Norma Shearer's new starring vehicle for Metro-Goldwyn-Mayer and "The Midshipman," starring Ramon Novarro.

Action stills from "Exchange of Wives," Metro-Goldwyn-Mayer's film version of the Cosmo Hamilton story

M-G-M to Double Production

Most Extensive Schedule in History of Organization Under Way on Coast

THE usual Fall production schedule of Metro-Goldwyn-Mayer will be more than doubled, according to Louis B. Mayer, who is now in the east conferring with other executives of the organization. Within the next four months at least twenty productions, many of them super specials, will be sent east either completed or near completion.

King Vidor has started his Fall productions with the direction of Lillian Gish in "La Boheme," in which John Gilbert will also appear. Elinor Glyn will direct one of her own stories for the first time when "The Only Thing" goes into production.

Tod Browning is ready for the production of his underworld story, "The Mocking Bird," which will star Lon Chaney. Waldemar Young, who wrote the continuity for "The Unholy Three" is preparing the script and the story will go into production in the near future.

George Hill has been assigned to direct Rex Beach's "The Barrier," adapted by Harvey Gates, and Leon Abrams will handle the megaphone on the English novel, "Nocturne," the work of Frank Swinnerton.

Benjamin Christianson, noted Swedish director, will start "The Light Eternal," some time this month. After a brilliant record on the continent, this will be Christianson's first picture in this country.

Hobart Henley is scheduled to start production this week on "Free Lips," an original story by Carey Wilson. Norma Shearer will be starred and Lew Cody featured in the supporting cast.

One of the most pretentious efforts on the Metro-Goldwyn-Mayer schedule will be the filming in technicolor of "Bardelys the Magnificent" from the story by Raphael Sabatini. This will be directed by King Vidor, it is announced by Mayer.

Paul Bern will direct "Paris" as his initial M-G-M picture. The story is an original by Carey Wilson, adapted by Jessie Burns. Edmund Goulding has completed his script for "Sally, Irene and Mary," adapted from the successful musical play and was scheduled to start direction this week.

Robert Z. Leonard is directing his first Fall picture, "A Little Bit of Broadway," co-starring Charles Ray and Pauline Starke. The story is by Richard Connell.

Marshall Neilan is completing "The Great Love," based on his own original story, and Christy Cabanne has been assigned to the direction of "Dance Madness." "The Mysterious Island" is to be directed by Jack Conway.

One of the super specials of the year to be made under the supervision of Hunt Stromberg will be a propaganda picture on the peril of fire, by arrangement with the International Order of Fire Chiefs.

Among other stories slated for Fall production are Vincente Blasco Ibanez' "The Temptress," an original by Donald Ogden Stewart, and a superspecial by William Slavens McNutt. There will also be three original stories by Ferenc Molnar.

Louise Dresser Added to Cast of "Fifth Avenue"

Louise Dresser, well known stage and screen actress, has been added to the cast of "Fifth Avenue," now being filmed under the direction of Robert G. Vignola for release on the Producers Distributing Corporation program. Miss Dresser will join the company on its return to Hollywood from New York, where exterior scenes were filmed.

Dramatic episodes from "Free To Love," a B. P. Schulberg Preferred Picture.

Mae Murray and John Gilbert in the Von Stroheim directed production, "The Merry Widow," for Metro-Goldwyn-Mayer.

Foreign and Domestic Sales

Rayart Selling New Serial; Columbia Reports Deal With Canadian Exchange

ANNOUNCEMENTS of new sales by independent distributors this week include the following:

Columbia Picture Corporation has closed a contract with the Film de Luxe of Montreal, whereby the entire Columbia output for 1925-26, comprising eighteen feature productions, will be distributed in Canada by the latter concern. The Film de Luxe is headed by Charles Lalumiere. Besides Columbia he is handling Banner and other independent pictures from this country. Lalumiere recently took out a charter for a new half-million dollar organization with offices in the Dominion.

Rayart announced the sale in several territories of "The Flame Fighter," a serial produced by Beacon Films Corporation with Herbert Rawlinson in the starred role. The following territories have been closed on this new episode play:

Greater New York and Northern New Jersey to Merit Film Corporation of New York; Upper New York to First Graphic Exchanges, of Buffalo, and Albany; The New England States to Independent Films, Inc., of Boston. Eastern Pennsylvania, Southern New Jersey and Delaware to Liberty Film Corporation of Philadelphia. Western Pennsylvania and West Virginia to S. & S. Film & Supply Co., of Pittsburg. Michigan to the American Booking Corporation of Detroit, Kentucky and Tennessee, to Big Feature Rights Corporation of Louisville. Northern Illinois and Indiana to Short Subject Exchange, of Chicago, Eastern Missouri and Southern Illinois to Columbia Pictures Corporation of St. Louis. North and South Carolina, Georgia, Florida and Alabama to Progress Pictures Corporation of Atlanta. Louisiana and Mississippi to Progress Pictures of New Orleans, and Tex-

as, Oklahoma and Arkansas to Progress Pictures of Dallas.

Richmount Pictures, Inc., have secured the entire foreign territory exclusive of the United States and Canada. Other Rayart sales include: The Billy Sullivan Series and the Superior melodramas for Texas, Oklahoma and Arkansas to Home State Film Corporation of Dallas. Billy Sullivan Series for New England (exclusive of Connecticut) to Standard Film Corporation of Boston. The Butterfly Comedies for Western Pennsylvania and Western Virginia to Lande Film Company of Pittsburg. The same comedies to American Booking Corporation of Detroit, who also purchased the Billy West feature series and the Rayart-Superior Melodrama series; Eltraban Film Company of Atlanta, purchased the four Billy West Features for the eight southeastern states, while Short Subject Exchange of Chicago secured the Butterfly Comedies for Northern Illinois and Indiana. The latter series were also sold for Iowa and Nebraska to Fontenelle Feature Film Co.

The serial "Secret Service Sanders" was sold to Ludwig Film Co. of Milwaukee for Wisconsin and to the same concern of Minneapolis for Minnesota, North and South Dakota.

Another Rayart sale during the week was the sale of Six Reed Howes features, four Billy West Features, Six Superior Melodramas and "For Another Woman" and "Easy Money" to Aywon Film Company of Montreal.

Harry Grelle of Pittsburg secured "For Another Woman" for the Pittsburg territory and Pena Film Service of Philadelphia, secured "Easy Money" for the Philadelphia zone.

Schulberg in New York for Story Material

B. P. SCHULBERG, producer of Preferred Pictures, arrived in New York the end of last week to confer with J. G. Bachmann, production manager, on the purchase of story material for the 1926-27 season. He will look over the current Broadway stage productions and best sellers from the lists of current fiction.

Schulberg brought with him the master print of the latest Preferred Picture, "The Other Woman's Story," an adaptation from the novel by Peggy Gaddis. Before leaving Hollywood he supervised the initial steps in the production of "Lew Tyler's Wives," by Wallace Irwin; John Goodrich's original screen drama, "Eden's Fruit," and J. J. Bell's "Dancing Days."

Cleve Moore Plays Brother Role With Colleen

Cleve Moore, young brother of Colleen Moore, will make his screen debut in "We Moderns," the Israel Zangwill play which will serve as Miss Moore's next starring vehicle for First National. Cleve will be seen as the brother to the star in her role as the heroine of "We Moderns."

Moore gained admission to the studios as an office boy, later becoming script holder, a position which he filled on three of his sister's productions, "So Big," "Sally" and "The Desert Flower."

Margette De La Motte and John Bowers in "The People vs. Nancy Preston," a Hunt Stromberg production for Producers Distributing Corporation's release.

"Sally, Irene and Mary" Cast Completed

Three players for the name role have now been selected by Metro-Goldwyn-Mayer for "Sally, Irene and Mary." Sally O'Neill is the latest choice and will play Mary. Constance Bennett had previously been announced for Sally and Joan Crawford for Irene. The picture is in production at the Culver City Studios under the direction of Edmund Goulding.

Other late additions to the cast, which is now about completed are, Ray Howard, Aggie Herrin, Kate Price, Henly Kohlker, Edna Mae Cooper, Gene Miller and Voya Georges. Those previously announced were, William Haines, Karl Dane, Belva McKay, Doris Cleveland and Douglas Gilmore.

George Bancroft Now Under Contract to Famous

Famous Players-Lasky has signed George Bancroft, interpreter of the villain role in "The Pony Express," to a long-term contract. Bancroft's performance as Jack Slade in the new Cruze production was highly applauded by the photoplay critics. He is a former stage actor and made his first screen appearance as the mountaineer in "Driven." His first work for Paramount was in a heavy role in "Code of the West."

Seery Chicago Manager for First National

First National has named R. C. Seery manager of the Chicago branch in place of C. E. Bond, who resigned. Seery has been manager of First National's Mid-West district for a number of years. The latter post will now be vacated in accordance with the company's policy of eliminating the offices of district managers in the distribution organization.

Mary Brian Joins Cast of "Enchanted Hill"

Irvin Willat has assigned Mary Brian to a featured role in "The Enchanted Hill," which he will produce for Paramount. Players previously announced for the picture include Jack Holt, Florence Vidor and Noah Beery. It is an adaptation of the Peter B. Kyne story.

New Foreign Exchanges for First National

WITH the arrival on the Continent of E. Bruce Johnson, foreign manager of First National, new exchanges will be opened in France, Germany, Belgium, Holland, Poland, Checko-Slovakia, Hungary and Italy. Up to a short time ago the Berlin and Paris office were selling agents, but have been transformed into distributing main offices.

The new subsidiary branches are located in Lille, Marseilles, Strassburg, Brussels, Amsterdam, Prague, Vienna, Warsaw, Turin and Rome. This makes a total of fifteen new exchanges for First National in foreign territory since January 15th. The others are in Havana, Cuba, and Kobe and Tokio, Japan.

Scenes from "Typhoon Love," a Norman Dawn production released for Sering D. Wilson.

Tourneur Signs to Direct Gilda Gray Feature

Maurice Tourneur has been engaged by Famous Players-Lasky to direct Gilda Gray in her first screen starring vehicle for Paramount, an adaptation of "Aloma of the South Seas." Production on the picture will start next week at the Long Island studios. Ricardo Cortez, Percy Marmont and William Powell will appear in the cast supporting Miss Gray.

Edward Dillon to Direct Priscilla Dean Feature

Edward Dillon has been engaged to direct Priscilla Dean in her first starring vehicle for Metropolitan Pictures. The story will be of the fast action type in which Miss Dean has won her popularity. Producers Distributing Corporation will release the production.

Warners Sign Crosland to Long Contract

Warner Brothers have signed Alan Crosland to a long term directorial contract. His first work will be the direction of "Don Juan," second of John Barrymore's specials for Warners, which will go into production in the near future.

Sally Long Signed for Cast of "Fifth Avenue"

Sally Long, Ziegfeld Follies beauty, has been engaged by A. H. Sebastian for a prominent role in "Fifth Avenue," a feature now being produced under the direction of Robert Vignola for release by Producers Distributing Corporation.

Ginsberg Units Completing Second Half of Program

Banner Productions and Royal Pictures, producing features for distribution by Henry Ginsberg Distributing Corporation, will start work on the second half of the schedules they have arranged for the current season. Plans for the filming of the latter portions of these schedules are being completed.

"The Checkered Flag," "Whispering Canyon" and "Brooding Eyes" are the three productions on the second half of the Banner program, while Royal will make "The Millionaire Policeman," "A Desperate Moment" and "The Phantom Express" as the final group of the six productions the company has listed for 1925-26.'

Sebastian Signs Clift to Direct Own Story

A. H. Sebastian has signed Dennison Clift to direct a big production titled "The City of Play," for release through Prodneers Distributing Corporation. Clift recently returned from England, where he directed a series of eleven productions for Ideal Films, Ltd. "The City of Play" is Clift's own story and will not be released until some time next year.

Kane Starts "Bluebeard's Seven Wives"

"Bluebeard's Seven Wives," Robert T. Kane's second production for First National is under way at the Cosmopolitan studios in New York under the direction of Alfred A. Santell. The cast so far selected includes Blanche Sweet, Ben Lyon, Dorothy Sebastian, Nita Naldi, Andrew Mack and Dick Bernard. The story calls for seven leading women.

Open Radio Station at De Mille Studios

The radio sending and receiving station recently erected at the Cecil B. De Mille studios in Culver City is ready to operate and has been designated as station K J U. Entertainment programs will not be broadcast from this new station, which is to used solely for business communication while De Mille is on yachting trips, it is announced.

Marmont Signs Exclusive Contract With Famous

PERCY MARMONT this week signed a long-term agreement to act exclusively in Paramount productions, it was announced by Jesse L. Lasky, of Famous Players-Lasky. The actor has appeared in several productions of the company since his entry into pictures several years ago.

Marmont is of English birth. He started his career on the stage in London at the age of 16. He appeared with Sir Herbert Tree, Cyril Maude and other noted English actors. In the United States he acted in plays in which Ethel Barrymore starred and for a time was under the management of Belasco. He has contributed many notable screen characterizations, his most famous, perhaps, being the heroic role in "If Winter Comes."

Cast Assembled for New Tiffany Production

The cast has been assembled for "Morals For Men," the fourth Tiffany Production based on "The Love Serum" by Gouverneur Morris. Those who will be seen in the principal roles are Conway Tearle and Agnes Ayres, the featured players; Alyce Mills, Otto Matieson, Robert Ober, John Miljan, Mary Beth Milford, Eve Southern and Margery O'Neill.

"U" Writers Adapting Two Film Stories

Edward L. Montagne, Universal scenario editor, and Harry Dittmar are busy with the adaptation of Richard Barry's "The Big Gun" for screen production. It will be directed by Edward Sedgwick as one of next season's features. Rex Taylor is also adapting "Rolling Home" as a starring production for Reginald Denny.

Columbus Student Heads Paramount Class

Charles Brokaw, Columbus, O., has been elected president of the first class of the Paramount Picture School, Inc., Miss Mona Palma, New York City, has been chosen vice-president. With the formal organization, the students voted unanimously to adopt the name "Paramount Junior Stars."

Engages Beauties for Cast of "Sally, Irene and Mary"

Edmund Goulding, directing the Metro-Goldwyn-Mayer screen version of "Sally, Irene and Mary," a former Broadway musical comedy success, has selected Belva McKay, winner of the red-haired beauty contest at Venice, Cal., and Doris Cleveland.

Victory Bateman Added to Neilan's Cast

Marshall Neilan has added Victory Bateman, well known stage actress, to the cast he is directing in "The Great Love," a Metro-Goldwyn-Mayer production in which Viola Dana and Bobby Agnew have the leading roles.

Stromberg to Supervise Six for M-G-M

IN HIS new post as assistant studio executive at the Metro-Goldwyn-Mayer studios, Hunt Stromberg will supervise six big productions for this season. Preliminary work on them has already been started.

The first of the six to go into production will be Rex Beach's "The Barrier," which George Hill is to direct from the adaptation by Harvey Gates. "Monte Carlo," a new and original story by Carey Wilson, is another Stromberg picture scheduled for early production. Robert Z. Leonard will direct.

The other four to be supervised by Stromberg are Rupert Hughes' "Money Talks," which Archie Mayo will direct; "The Mysterious Island," by Jules Verne; "Bellamy the Magnificent," the stage success by Roy L. Horniman, and Blasco Ibanez' "The Torrent."

Dramatic episodes from "The Price of Success," a Waldorf production, released by Columbia Pictures.

Chadwick Selects "Count of Luxembourg" Cast

Chadwick Pictures has selected the principal players for the super-special production, "The Count of Luxembourg" and work has been started on the picture. In the leading roles are, George Walsh, Helen Lee Worthing, James Morrison, Lola Todd and Joan Meredith. Arthur Gregor, prominent European director, is handling the megaphone.

Walthall and Barrymore Join "Barrier" Cast

Hunt Stromberg, assistant studio executive at the Metro-Goldwyn-Mayer studios, had added Henry Walthall and Lionel Barrymore to the cast of George Hill's production, "The Barrier," by Rex Beach. Norman Kerry is to play Meade Burrell. No leading woman has yet been announced. Production is to be under way within the next fortnight.

M-G-M Appoint Lancaster to Important Post

Metro-Goldwyn-Mayer have named John Lancaster for an important executive post with the company. He will supervise a number of departments, including the casting department, and will have charge of the permanent M-G-M stock players. For a number of years Lancaster has headed his own casting organization.

"Nightie Night Nurse" Cast Selected

Warner Brothers have made good progress with the selection of the cast to support Syd Chaplin in "Nightie Night Nurse," which has already gone into production. Patsy Ruth Miller will play opposite Chaplin, while others in important roles are, Gayne Whitman, Pat Hartigan, Edith Yorke, David Torrance and Raymond Wells. Charles (Chuck) Reisner is directing.

Camera Work Soon to Start on "Beverly of Graustark"

"Beverly of Graustark," a screen adaption of the George Barr McCutcheon work of that title, is to be started soon at the Metro-Goldwyn-Mayer studios in Culver City. The picture will be made by Cosmopolitan with Marion Davies in the starring role. Sydney Franklin will direct.

Featured Players Named for "Hassan"

Ernest Torrence, William Collier, Jr., and Greta Nissen will be the featured players in "Hassan," Raoul Walsh's production for Paramount from the Arabian Nights tale. Five gigantic sets are now under way for the production. The story was adapted for the screen by James T. O'Donohoe.

Tom Buckingham Again Fox Comedy Director

Tom Buckingham, who for a number of years directed Fox Comedies, has again been appointed to the directorial staff of a comedy unit, by George T. Marshall, Fox comedy supervisor. Buckingham is preparing a new Imperial comedy which will shortly go into production.

Two Universal Serials in Production

Universal has put two serial pictures into production. They are "Strings of Steel," starring William Desmond and Eileen Sedgwick, and "The Radio Detective," starring Jack Daugherty. Henry McRae will direct the former and William Crinley the latter.

M-G-M Planning Third Annual Ball

ELABORATE preparations are being made for the third annual Loew-Metro-Goldwyn-Mayer ball scheduled to be held at the Astor Hotel in New York City, Saturday evening, October 31st. Louis B. Mayer, vice-president in charge of production, is at present in the east arranging for the personal appearance of practically all of the M-G-M stars and featured players.

Major Edward Bowes and the entire house and technical staff of the Capitol Theatre are at work on a number of novelties to be presented, while Nils Granlund, master of ceremonies, is lining up the talent that will appear from all of the leading Broadway shows.

Dancing will be enjoyed to the music of several of the leading orchestras and an elaborate banquet will be served.

"The Brown Derby" Next Star Vehicle for Hines

C. C. BURR announces the purchase of the motion picture rights to "The Brown Derby," a comedy by Francis S. Merlin and Brian Marlow which is soon to be produced on the New York stage, as a screen vehicle for Johnny Hines on the First National Program.

The picture will be produced after "Rainbow Riley," which Hines is now making at Delaware Water Gap. "The Brown Derby" will complete the group of three productions which the Burr-Hines combination will contribute to the First National schedule this year.

MacIntyre Now Production Manager for Goldwyn

Samuel Goldwyn has engaged Robert D. MacIntyre, for the past four years casting director for Metro-Goldwyn-Mayer, as production manager. Mr. MacIntyre will assume his new duties immediately and will supervise George Fitzmaurice, Potash and Perlmutter and Henry King productions, the three Goldwyn production units.

Paramount Appoints New Title Editor

Paramount has appointed John Peale Bishop, former managing editor of Vanity Fair, as title editor of the company's eastern made productions. He succeeds Julian Johnson, who has been promoted to production supervisor.

Elaine Hammerstein in "Paint and Powder," a Chadwick picture.

Douglas MacLean in "Seven Keys to Baldpate," a Paramount production.

Five Fox Features in October

"Iron Horse" Heads List of Releases Due Exhibitors During Coming Month

FIVE feature pictures, four two-reelers, two one-reelers and the usual twice a week issue of the news reel comprise the month's releases for October of Fox Film Corporation. The features are "The Iron Horse," "Thunder Mountain," Tom Mix in "The Everlasting Whisper," George O'Brien in "The Fighting Heart" and "The Winding Stair."

October 4th is the release date set for "The Iron Horse," which has already had sensational runs in New York, Chicago, Los Angeles, Cleveland and other cities. It is a John Ford production, an epic of the building of the first transcontinental railroad.

Two feature attractions will be released October 11th. They are the Tom Mix starring vehicle, "The Everlasting Whisper," and "Thunder Mountain." The former is an adaptation of Jackson Gregory's story of the same name. J. G. Blystone directed. Tony, the Mix horse is of course featured with him, while in the supporting cast are Alice Calhoun, Robert Cain, George Berrell, Walter James, Virginia Madison and Karl Dane.

"Thunder Mountain" is an adaptation of John Golden's stage success, "Howdy Folks," by Pearl Franklin. It was directed by Victor Schertzinger. Madge Bellamy, Leslie Fenton and Alec B. Francis have the leading roles. In the supporting cast are Jay Hunt, Zasu Pitts, Paul Panzer, Otis Harlan, Arthur Houseman, Emily Fitzroy, Dan Mason, Natalie Warfield, Maine Geary and Russell Simpson.

George O'Brien's starring vehicle, "The Fighting Heart," is scheduled for release October 18th. It was directed by John Ford, and supporting the star are Billie Dove, J. Farrell Mac Donald, Victor Mac Laglen, James Marcus, Francis Powers, Harvey Clark, Colin Chase, Bert Woodruff, Edward Piel, Jack Herrick and Hazel Francis Ford, Lynn Cowan, Diana Miller, Howell.

"The Winding Stair" is set for release October 28th. It is John Griffith Wray's first directorial effort for Fox. Alma Rubens and Edmund Lowe are the featured players. Others in the cast are Warner Oland, Mahlon Hamilton, Emily Fitzroy, Chester Conklin and Frank Leigh.

"A Cloudy Romance" and "With Pen, Brush and Chisel" head the short subject releases on October 4th. The former is an Imperial comedy directed by Lew Seiler, with Harold Austin, Hazel Dawn, Harry Dunkinson and Jules Cowles in the leading roles.

"All Aboard," second of the "Married Life of Helen and Warren" series, is scheduled for release October 11th.

On October 18th Fox will release the one-reel variety, "Cuba Steps Out," the two-reel Imperial, "The Heart Breaker" and the second of the O. Henry series, "Transients in Arcadia."

Seven Featurettes Due From Red Seal

Seven featurettes are announced for October release by Red Seal. "Daisy Bell," taken from the old song, "On a Bicycle Built for Two," is the Ko-Ko Song Car-tune. The second of the "Marvels of Motion" is also on the list, while "Ko-Ko on the Run" is the month's "Out of the Inkwell" contribution. "Land's End," another release is of the Gems of the Screen series. Two more of the "Animated Hair Cartoons", and another issue of "Film Facts" titled "Dance of All Nations," complete the list.

: : : : "THE CHECK-UP" : : : :

"The Check-Up" is a presentation in the briefest and most convenient form of reports received from exhibitors in every part of the country on current features, which makes it possible for the exhibitor to see what the picture has done for other theatre managers.

The first column following the name of the feature represents the number of managers that have reported the picture as "Poor." The second column gives the number who considered it "Fair"; the third, the number who considered it "Good"; and the fourth column, those who considered it "Big."

The fifth column is a percentage figure giving the average rating on that feature, obtained by the following method: A report of "Poor" is rated at 20%; one of "Fair," 40%; "Good," 70%; and "Big," 100%. The percentage ratings of all of these reports on one picture are then added together, and divided by the number of reports, giving the average percentage—a figure which represents the consensus of opinion on that picture. In this way exceptional cases, reports which might be misleading taken alone, and such individual differences of opinion are averaged up and eliminated.

No picture is included in the list which has not received at least ten reports.

Title of Picture	Number Reporting "Poor"	Number Exhibitors "Fair"	Number Exhibitors "Good"	Number Exhibitors "Big"	Average Percentage Value	Length
ASSOCIATED EXHIB.						
Barriers Burned Away	1	2	6	2	65	6,474 ft.
Introduce Me	—		8	5	82	5,980 ft.
FAMOUS PLAYERS						
Adventure		9	17	4	64	6,602 ft.
Air Mail, The	2	2	16	5	70	6,976 ft.
Are Parents People?	—	2	15	1	68	6,586 ft.
Argentine Love		16	19	4	61	5,970 ft.
Begger on Horseback	1	6	5	1	55	7,168 ft.
Charmer, The	1	2	11	3	69	6,076 ft.
City That Never Sleeps, The	—	6	21	3	67	6,097 ft.
Code of the West, The		8	16	3	63	6,777 ft.
Coming Through	1	9	21	8	63	6,521 ft.
Contraband	1	11	10	2	57	7,173 ft.
Crowded Hour, The	3		12	2	66	6,558 ft.
Dangerous Money	3	15	13	2	60	6,846 ft.
Devil's Cargo, The	2	7	18	5	65	7,980 ft.
Dressmaker from Paris, The	1	7	17	9	73	6,186 ft.
East of Suez	6	5	20	2	58	6,821 ft.
Eve's Secret		5	13	—	62	6,338 ft.
Female, The	3	9	25	3	62	6 reels
Forbidden Paradise	8	8	33	4	60	7,543 ft.
Forty Winks		3	16	6	74	6,303 ft.
Garden of Weeds, The	4	8	14	3	58	6,230 ft.
Golden Bed, The	3	7	21	14	71	8,584 ft.
Goose Hangs High, The		4	12	4	70	6,186 ft.
Grounds for Divorce	5	5	3	—	39	6,420 ft.
Her Love Story	5	17	39	4	59	7 reels
In the Name of Love	1	3	8	—	58	5,904 ft.
Kiss in the Dark, A	1	4	15	1	63	5,707 ft.
Light of the Western Stars		6	16	4	64	6,850 ft.
Little French Girl, The	—	1	16	1	70	6,628 ft.
Locked Doors	3	11	14	—	53	6,221 ft.
Lost — A Wife	1	7	9	—	55	6,420 ft.
Lucky Devil, The		2	15	3	72	5,935 ft.
Madame Sans Gene	7	8	11	4	54	9,994 ft.
Manhattan	5	1	25	3	64	6,415 ft.
Manicure Girl, The	3	6	10	—	54	5,059 ft.
Man Must Live, A	3	4	19	2	63	7 reels
Marry Me	2	4	9	—	51	5,549 ft.
Men and Women	2	2	8	1	60	6,223 ft.
Merton of the Movies	2	13	34	13	68	8 reels
Miss Bluebeard	2	2	22	9	73	7 reels
New Lives for Old		5	12	5	70	6,796 ft.
Night Club, The	1	5	16	4	67	5,732 ft.
Night Life of New York		4	11	3	66	6,998 ft.
North of 36	1	5	38	51	84	7,908 ft.
Old Home Week		2	16	6	75	6,888 ft.
Open All Night	25	7	15	—	39	5,671 ft.
Paths to Paradise		2	16	1	68	6,741 ft.
Peter Pan	2	8	36	25	76	9,593 ft.
Sackcloth and Scarlet	3	7	9	6	63	6,732 ft.
Sainted Devil, A	10	17	20	10	58	9 reels
Salome of the Tenements	9	3	6	2	46	7,017 ft.
Shock Punch, The	—	7	17	1	63	6,151 ft.
Spaniard, The		4	14	3	69	5,676 ft.
Story Without a Name, The	4	8	23	7	64	5,912 ft.
Street of Forgotten Men, The	1	3	12	1	65	6,366 ft.
Swan, The	4	9	8	2	52	5,889 ft.
Ten Commandments, The	1	3	19	42	87	12,055 ft.
Thundering Herd, The	2	5	17	25	80	7,187 ft.
To-Morrow's Love	1	3	14	1	66	5,903 ft.
Tongues of Flame	2	11	25	6	64	6,763 ft.
Too Many Kisses	1	3	16	1	65	6,373 ft.
Top of the World, The	—	8	15	1	63	7,167 ft.
Wages of Virtue	6	13	22	7	60	7 reels
Welcome Home	1	1	8	—	60	5,909 ft.
Wild Horse Mesa		3	7	2	68	7,221 ft.
Wild, Wild Susan	2	4	6	3	61	5,774 ft.
Worldly Goods	4	11	18	4	59	6,055 ft.
FILM BOOKING						
Air Hawk, The	2	3	15	1	64	4,860 ft.
Bandit's Baby, The		3	23	16	80	5,291 ft.
Breed of the Border	2	4	16	—	60	4,030 ft.
Broken Laws	2	8	27	15	77	6,413 ft.
Cheap Kisses		8	9	13	65	6,538 ft.
Cloud Rider		4	5	2	65	5,070 ft.
Druscilla With a Million		2	9	3	73	7,301 ft.
Jimmies Millions		2	9	—	65	5,167 ft.
Just A Woman		4	6	—	58	6,052 ft.
Laughing at Danger		5	13	1	62	5,442 ft.
Midnight Molly	1	1	7	1	65	5,400 ft.
Millionaire Cowboy, The	3	6	12	2	58	4,841 ft.
No Gun Man	8	12	—	55		4,522 ft.
O. U. West	3	9	1	65		5,000 ft.
Range Terror	1	4	12	—	60	4,753 ft.
Ridin' Comet, The		3	7	—	61	4,354 ft.
Scar Hanan		2	10	—	65	4,684 ft.
That Devil Quemado		6	25	15	76	5,541 ft.
Thundering Hoofs		3	27	16	78	5,933 ft.
Trigger Fingers	2	2	17	—	62	4,775 ft.
White Fang	1	4	15	5	69	5,800 ft.
Wild Bull's Lair, The		5	7	5	79	5,280 ft.
Youth and Adventure		5	8	5	04	5,525 ft.
FIRST NATIONAL						
Abraham Lincoln	3	1	22	54	88	9,759 ft.
As Man Desires		4	19	8	74	7,790 ft.
Born Rich	1	9	9	—	53	7,389 ft.
Chickie		2	18	5	68	7,767 ft.
Christine of the Hungry Heart	3	6	10	1	55	7,500 ft.
Classmates	2	2	23	24	82	6,800 ft.
Declasse		4	14	3	71	7,869 ft.
Desert Flower, The	1	2	15	3	69	6 reels
Enticement	1	4	15	1	63	6,407 ft.
Frivolous Sall	1	2	19	2	68	7,307 ft.
Half Way Girl, The	1	2	7	2	66	7,570 ft.
Heart of a Siren, The	1	11	7	—	50	6,780 ft.
Her Husband's Secret	1	8	4	—	48	6,300 ft.
Her Night of Romance		1	25	5	71	7,311 ft.
Her Sister From Paris		3	4	76		7,255 ft.
His Supreme Moment	1	8	12	3	62	6,000 ft.
Husbands and Lovers	1	1	16	10	77	7,823 ft.
Idle Tongues	2	2	11	1	62	5,447 ft.
If I Marry Again		5	12	4	67	7,866 ft.
Inez From Hollywood		4	9	4	70	6,919 ft.
I Want My Man		5	23	3	67	6,173 ft.
Lady, The		2	9		76	7 reels
Learning to Love		9	15	5	73	6,181 ft.
Lost World, The			7	8	83	9,700 ft.
Love's Wilderness		4	17	1	66	6,800 ft.

Title of Picture	Poor	Fair	Good	Big	Avg % Value	Length
Madonna of the Streets	4	4	28	11	70	7,307 ft.
Making of O'Malley, The	—	1	11	3	74	7,371 ft.
Marriage Whirl, The	—	3	6	1	64	7,073 ft.
My Son	—	3	12	2	72	6,500 ft.
Necessary Evil, The	—		4	1	58	6,307 ft.
New Toys	2	6	19	1	61	7,250 ft.
One Way Street	—	4	13	—	63	5,596 ft.
One Year to Live	1	3	16	—	58	6,064 ft.
Only Woman, The	—	1	19	5	75	6,770 ft.
Playing with Souls	1	4	7	2	62	5,831 ft.
Quo Vadis	1	2	13	11	78	8,945 ft.
Sally	—	1	15	25	88	8 reels
Sandra	8	10	13	2	50	6,800 ft.
Sea Hawk, The	4	3	25	56	86	12 reels
Shore Leave	—		8	4	80	6,856 ft.
Silent Teacher, The	2	4	13	7	70	7,375 ft.
So Big	2	2	29	7	71	9 reels
Soul Fire	1	2	8	4	71	8,262 ft.
Sundown	4	13	17	1	54	8,640 ft.
Talker, The	—	3	14	1	67	7,861 ft.
Thief in Paradise, A	—	1	17	9	79	8 reels
FOX						
Arizona Romeo	1	2	15	2	68	4,694 ft.
Dancers, The	3	4	6	1	55	5,583 ft.
Daughters of the Night	3	6	9	1	50	5,740 ft.
Deadwood Coach, The	—	5	15	15	79	6,346 ft.
Dick Turpin	—	5	19	6	70	6,976 ft.
Flames of Desire	5	4	2	—	36	5,439 ft.
Gerald Cranston's Lady	3	3	11	1	59	6,974 ft.
Gold Heels		7	17	—	60	6,020 ft.
Hearts of Oak	6	3	13	2	56	6 reels
Hunted Woman, The	—	5	7	2	64	5,954 ft.
Iron Horse, The	—	5	8	50		11,335 ft.
Last Man on Earth, The	3	1	8	4	66	6,037 ft.
Man Who Played Square	—	3	8	3	78	6,500 ft.
Rainbow Trail, The	—	3	12	3	72	5,251 ft.
Riders of the Purple Sage	—	1	7	9	84	5,534 ft.
Roughneck, The	2	5	14	4	65	7,500 ft.
Star Dust Trail	—	5	4	—	52	4,800 ft.
Teeth	—	4	27	4	70	6,190 ft.
Trail Rider	—	2	15	—	66	4,752 ft.
Warrens of Virginia	3	6	16	4	63	6,538 ft.
Winner Takes All	—	2	10	3	72	5,949 ft.
METRO-GOLDWYN						
Along Came Ruth		5	17	5	70	5,161 ft.
Bandolero, The	3	3	10	6	70	8,000 ft.
Beauty Prize, The	—	5	19	—	64	5,750 ft.
Cheaper to Marry	1	4	16	3	65	6,500 ft.
Chu Chin Chow	2	4	5	1	54	6,048 ft.
Circe, the Enchantress	3	5	12	3	61	6,882 ft.
Confessions of a Queen	1	3	8	—	58	5,651 ft.
Daddy's Gone A Hunting	1	3	9	1	61	5,851 ft.
Denial, The	1	6	10	1	59	4,791 ft.
Dixie Handicap, The	—	2	26	7	74	6 reels
Excuse Me	1	—	12	11	82	5,747 ft.
Great Divide, The	—	6	23	4	68	7,821 ft.
Greed	5	3	10	1	54	10,067 ft.
He Who Gets Slapped	—	3	21	17	79	6,600 ft.
Janice Meredith	—	4	17	16	80	12 reels
Lady of the Night	1	7	12	2	61	5,419 ft.
Married Flirts		7	22	3	64	6,765 ft.
Monster, The	—	8	15	5	67	6,435 ft.
Navigator, The	1	4	24	13	75	5,600 ft.
Prairie Wife, The	3	12	2	1	43	6,487 ft.
Proud Flesh	—	6	6	1	56	5,770 ft.
Rag Man, The	—	—	16	9	81	5,967 ft.
Romola	—	2	5	4	75	10,875 ft.
Seven Chances	—	3	17	14	80	5,113 ft.
Silent Accuser, The	2	1	25	9	74	5,883 ft.
Slave of Fashion, A	—	3	7	1	67	5,906 ft.
Snob, The	—	4	20	1	60	6,513 ft.
So This is Marriage	1	8	16	3	63	6,300 ft.
Sporting Venus	—	2	11	—	52	5,938 ft.
Unholy Three, The	—	4	6	5	72	6,848 ft.
Way of a Girl, The	3	8	5	—	52	5,025 ft.
White Desert, The	—	2	7	1	67	6,345 ft.
Wife of a Centaur	2	3	20	4	68	6,700 ft.
Zander the Great	1	3	17	6	72	5,851 ft.
PATHE						
Battling Orioles	1	6	12	3	64	5,333 ft.
Black Cyclone	—	1	6	3	76	5,508 ft.
Dynamite Smith	8	13	8	3	46	6,400 ft.
Hot Water	—	3	23	38	86	4,899 ft.
White Sheep	—	6	6	1	58	5,091 ft.

Title of Picture	Poor	Fair	Good	Big	Avg % Value	Length
PRODUCERS DIST. CORP.						
Beyond the Border	—	5	14	—	62	4,469 ft.
Cafe in Cairo, A	1	3	9	2	65	5,656 ft.
Charley's Aunt	—	2	10	40	92	6 reels
Chorus Lady, The	1	1	11	2	69	6,020 ft.
Flaming Forties, The	2	6	17	1	60	5,770 ft.
Girl on the Stairs, The	1	3	7	1	61	6,314 ft.
House of Youth, The	—	6	11	1	62	6,669 ft.
Reckless Romance	1	2	11	3	69	5,530 ft.
Roaring Rails	1	2	36	23	79	5,753 ft.
Silent Sanderson	1	5	7	3	63	4,841 ft.
Soft Shoes	3	3	14	—	58	5,557 ft.
Trouping with Ellen	3	4	4	—	45	6,452 ft.
STATE RIGHTS						
Black Lightning	—	1	11	1	70	5,382 ft.
Crackerjack, The	—	—	8	3	78	6,500 ft.
Early Bird, The	1	1	18	2	71	6,500 ft.
Helen's Babies	—	2	6	3	73	6,200 ft.
Lone Wagon, The	1	6	6	2	59	5,009 ft.
Midnight Express, The	—	2	13	4	73	5,967 ft.
Mine With the Iron Door, The	—	2	23	16	81	8,115 ft.
Re-creation of Brian Kent, The	3	6	6	4	59	6,878 ft.
UNITED ARTISTS						
Isn't Life Wonderful?	7	4	6	1	51	8,600 ft.
Thief of Bagdad, The	—	2	20	34	87	10,000 ft.
UNIVERSAL						
Butterfly	—	6	17	2	65	7 reels
Dangerous Innocence	1	1	11	—	64	6,750 ft.
Daring Chances	—	—	12	—	70	4,561 ft.
Fast Worker, The	—	2	10	5	73	7 reels
Fifth Avenue Models	1	4	9	1	61	6,581 ft.
Flying Hoofs	—	1	10	1	70	4,474 ft.
Gaiety Girl, The	—	5	10	3	67	7,419 ft.
Head Winds	1	1	7	3	71	5,309 ft.
Hit and Run	—	4	25	9	74	6 reels
Hurricane Kid, The	—	2	19	3	70	5,296 ft.
I'll Show You the Town	—	2	14	5	74	7,396 ft.
K-the Unknown	1	2	20	12	77	6,362 ft.
Last Laugh, The	3	4	4	2	54	6,519 ft.
Let 'Er Buck	—	1	14	4	75	5,547 ft.
Love and Glory	4	7	11	2	55	7 reels
Mad Whirl, The	1	3	6	1	60	6,184 ft.
Oh, Doctor	1	3	15	7	73	6,587 ft.
Price of Pleasure, The	2	2	5	3	64	6,518 ft.
Raffles	1	7	7	3	58	5,557 ft.
Ridin' Kid from Powder River, The	2	3	19	8	73	5,727 ft.
Ridin' Pretty	1	2	7	—	48	5,613 ft.
Rose of Paris	5	7	10	2	53	6,326 ft.
Saddle Hawk, The	1	1	10	2	69	5,468 ft.
Sign of the Cactus	3	1	6	—	54	4,938 ft.
Smouldering Fires	—	2	18	4	69	7,356 ft.
Taming the West	—		12	2	74	5,427 ft.
Tornado, The	1	5	16	7	74	7,375 ft.
Up the Ladder	—	1	9	1	70	6,023 ft.
Woman's Faith, A	2	5	5	—	49	5,587 ft.
VITAGRAPH						
Baree, Son of Kazan	—	2	22	6	74	6,800 ft.
Beloved Brute, The	—	3	13	4	68	6,719 ft.
Clean Heart, The	6	9	10	4	56	7,500 ft.
Empty Saddle	—	4	7	—	60	5 reels
Fearbound	—	2	7	1	67	7,200 ft.
Greater Than Marriage	1	5	10	2	62	6,821 ft.
Pampered Youth	—	2	10	—	65	6,940 ft.
Redeeming Sin, The	5	—	8	—	47	6,227 ft.
School for Wives	—	7	8	—	56	6,750 ft.
Two Shall be Born	2	3	10	1	54	5,443 ft.
Wildfire	—	2	17	—	67	6 reels
WARNER BROS.						
Age of Innocence, The	2	4	11	1	57	5 reels
Dark Swan, The	2	4	11	2	59	6,700 ft.
Eve's Lover	1	3	8	1	62	6,540 ft.
Kiss Me Again	—	2	7	1	67	7,200 ft.
Lighthouse by the Sea, The	1	1	13	1	76	6,000 ft.
Lost Lady, A	3	3	3	2	57	7,111 ft.
My Wife and I	3	6	5	1	60	6,700 ft.
Narrow Street, The		5	17	8	73	6,700 ft.
On Thin Ice	2	2	5	1	57	6,675 ft.
Recompense	2	5	7	—	57	7,450 ft.
This Woman	—	7	16	5	68	6,842 ft.
Tracked in the Snow Country	—	4	6	3	68	6,900 ft.

WRITE YOUR OWN TICKET

The Box-Office Value of Pathe Two Reel
Comedies is up to You!

Under a new long term contract with the Hal Roach Studios, Pathe agrees, to advance to the producer *for production purposes* every dollar indicated- by an expectancy table that quite reliably forecasts at six month intervals what the eventual collections per picture are going to be.

If there has been another similar contract between producer and dis- tributor, I have yet to hear of it. If there is a fairer contract to producer, distributor and exhibitor, I don't know of it.

Increased receipts are at once reflected in pictures that cost more, are worth more, and will bring more at the box office.

The chief concern of every exhibitor is, and should be, not so much what a picture *costs* him but what it will *bring* him. If a moderate increase in film rentals will insure him an immoderate increase in profits, it is mighty good business to pay more to get more.

A producer must get an adequate return on his pictures in order to go on producing. Better pictures mean increased production cost. The busi- ness is not interested in more pictures. It only wants better ones.

The production cost of a feature picture that is just fair, is low at $25,000.00 per reel. Mr. Wm A. Johnston of the MOTION PICTURE NEWS in their issue of Sept. 19 says: "The cry everywhere is against, not for, the moderate cost program feature. Yet *comedy producers would be happy if they could have as much per reel to spend as the average feature costs.* . . . . Distributors of comedies will increase their advances to the producer just as soon as the exhibitor will permit the increase."

Putting the biggest part of your program cost, reel for reel, into the feat- ure, and giving to the comedy what's left, is neither fair to the comedy, nor is it good business for you. On a footage basis, entertainment value considered, *the comedy is as important to you as your feature.*

To make the most money you've got to get the best pictures that it is possible to make. The public is hungry for *quality* entertainment. You and you only can make it possible, by encouraging the producer to make his pictures better.

You, then, write your own ticket. Both the production cost of Pathe Two Reel Comedies and their value at your box office are up to you!

ELMER PEARSON
Vice President and General Manager
PATHE EXCHANGE, Inc.

Two Reels

Exhibitor

Advertising

Mack Sennett
Comedies

"She's a good gal. Why not
treat her right?"

A hungry man wouldn't be satisfied with humming bird's tongues on toast or a dill pickle.

He wants a real square meal, like good rare roast beef, potatoes and brown gravy.

The "subtle stuff" may go with a Browning Club, but your crowd likes to haw haw. They don't like to guess at the laughs.

When you give them a Mack Sennett you give them a good square meal of comedy, and they thank you for it.

Take a look at "Over There-Abouts" and "Dangerous Curves Behind." When you get through laughing, plan to advertise them. What's the profit in having a good thing if you don't tell them about it?

Wild

with
Jack Mulhall *and*
Helen Ferguson

You know how they greet westerns. You know how they
eat up circus pictures. Why not give your patrons both?

Here it is! A breath-taking, spine-tingling, Western with
an exciting circus atmosphere.

A large cast of popular, well-known players, supported
by the whole Miller Brothers' 101 Ranch outfit.

Produced by C. W. PATTON

The gigantic struggle for life in the Cherokee Strip in Oklahoma at a time when a gun was the best argument, and the man who first pulled the trigger won. Thrilling stunts of courageous cowboys, plunging herds of cattle rustlers, roping wild steers in the rodeos, etc.

Cast? Listen!

Jack Mulhall, himself. Helen Ferguson, of "Racing Luck" and "Never Say Die" fame. Eddie Phillips, co-star with Mary Pickford in "The Love Light" and leading man in a number of Cosmopolitan and First National Productions. Virginia Warwick, a former member of that well-known group—the Mack Sennett bathing beauties.

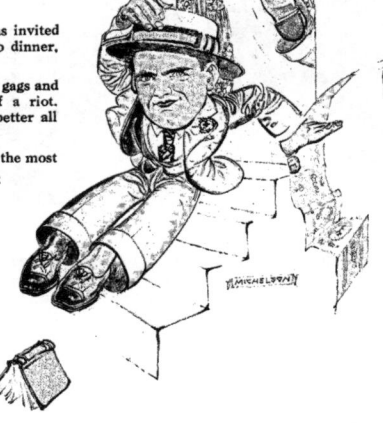

Exhibitors Service Bureau

The management of the Imperial theatre, San Francisco, tied up with the Wells Fargo bank in that city for this display on "The Pony Express" (Paramount), consisting of an old-time pony express station of the Wells Fargo company.

Advisory Board and Contributing Editors, Exhibitors' Service Bureau

George J. Schade, Schade theatre, Sandusky.

Edward L. Hyman, Mark Strand theatre, Brooklyn.

Leo A. Landau, Lyceum theatre, Minneapolis.

C. C. Perry, Managing Director, Garrick theatre, Minneapolis.

E. R. Rogers, Southern District Supervisor, Famous Players-Lasky, Chattanooga, Tenn.

Stanley Chambers, Palace theatre, Wichita, Kan.

Willard C. Patterson, Metropolitan theatre, Atlanta.

E. V. Richards, Jr., Gen. Mgr. Saenger Amusement Co., New Orleans.

F. L. Newman, Managing Director, Famous Players-Lasky theatres, Los Angeles.

Arthur G. Stolte, Des Moines theatre, Des Moines, Iowa.

W. C. Quimby, Managing Director, Strand Palace and Jefferson theatres, Fort Wayne, Ind.

J. A. Partington, Imperial theatre, San Francisco.

George E. Carpenter, Paramount-Empress theatre, Salt Lake.

Sidney Grauman, Grauman's theatres, Los Angeles.

THE CHECK-UP

Weekly Edition of Exhibitors' Box Office Reports

Productions listed are new pictures on which reports were not available previously.

For ratings on current and older releases see MOTION PICTURE NEWS—first issue of each month.

KEY—The first column following the name of the feature represents the number of managers that have reported the picture as "Poor." The second column gives the number who considered it "Fair"; the third the number who considered it "Good"; and the fourth column, those who considered it "Big." The fifth column is a percentage giving the average rating on that feature, obtained by the following method: A report of "Poor" is rated at 20%; one of "Fair," 40%; "Good," 70%; and "Big," 100%. The percentage rating of all of these reports on one picture are then added together, and divided by the number of reports, giving the average percentage—a figure which represents the consensus of opinion on that picture. In this way exceptional cases, reports which might be misleading taken alone, and such individual differences of opinion are averaged up and eliminated.

TITLE	Poor	Fair	Good	Big	Value	Length
FAMOUS PLAYERS						
Beggar on Horseback	1	4	5	1	57	7,168 ft.
FIRST NATIONAL						
Half Way Girl, The	—	2	6	2	70	7,570 ft.
Lost World, The	—	—	6	5	84	9,700 ft.
METRO-GOLDWYN						
Romola	—	2	5	4	75	10,875 ft.
Slave of Fashion, A	—	2	7	1	67	5,906 ft.
PATHE						
Black Cyclone	—	1	6	3	76	5,508 ft.
WARNER BROS						
Eve's Lover	1	2	8	1	63	6,340 ft.

George E. Brown, Imperial theatre, Charlotte, N. C.

Louis K. Sidney, Division Manager, Loew's theatres, Pittsburgh, Pa.

Geo. Rotsky, Managing Director, Palace theatre, Montreal, Can.

Eddie Zorn, Managing Director, Broadway-Strand theatre, Detroit.

Fred S. Myer, Managing Director, Palace theatre, Hamilton, Ohio.

Joseph Plunkett, Managing Director, Mark-Strand theatre, New York.

Ray Grombacher, Managing Director, Liberty theatre, Spokane, Wash.

Ross A. McVoy, Manager, Temple theatre, Geneva, N. Y.

W. S. McLaren, Managing Director, Capitol theatre, Jackson, Mich.

Harold B. Franklin, Director of Theatres, Famous Players-Lasky.

William J. Sullivan, Manager, Rialto theatre, Butte, Mont.

H. A. Albright, Manager, T. D. & L. theatre, Glendale, Calif.

Claire Meachime, Grand theatre, Westfield, N. Y.

Ace Berry, Managing Director, Circle theatre, Indianapolis.

See Complete "Check-Up" on Pages 1694-5

Window Displays Featured on "Wife of Centaur"

Elaborate window displays were a feature of the campaign on "Wife of the Centaur" recently waged by Charles Glickauf in connection with the showing of this production at the Strand theatre in Evansville, Ind. Five drug stores displayed copies of the novel on which the film is based, and the town's leading jeweler contributed an exhibit of Richelieu pearls, vanity boxes, fancy compacts and toilet articles. Tobacco shops featured a popular brand cigar with stills showing John Gilbert smoking one. Art cards were displyed in all these windows.

Three slides and a trailer were used, and there was a special lobby display. Special stories achieved space in the press and three slides and a trailer were brought into play.

Old Time Stars Made Basis of Effective Contest

The ability to recognize famous screen stars of yesterday was rewarded in Brooklyn, N. Y., by passes to the Meserole theatre. J. Hartman, exploiteer from the Big U Exchange, secured a photograph of former favorites taken at Universal City during the recent Anniversary celebration and used it as a basis of a contest which a neighborhood newspaper, The Greenpoint Home News, conducted for him. Under a two-column cut of the photograph, which showed such celebrities as Francis Ford, King Baggot, Max Asher, Cleo Madison, Carmen Phillips, Grace Cunard, Rosemary Theby, Ella Hall and Dorothy Phillips, was this copy:

"With the rapid progress of the 'movie' productions the stars that you knew 'yesterday' have retired to either private life or other fields, but few remain to carry on in the 'land of make believe.'

Manager George Schenck of Loew's Metropolitan theatre, Brooklyn, and Carl Levi, of Loew's, Inc., arranged this striking front for "Never the Twain Shall Meet," Cosmopolitan's production for Metro-Goldwyn-Mayer.

"In this group are a number of players who were popular players in the Universal productions within the past ten years. How many do you recognize? How many were your favorite players?

"It would take but an instant to recognize Dorothy Phillips, seated in the second row, third from the right. Perhaps it is easy to recall one of her greatest triumphs, 'Once to Every Woman.'"

The story went on to say that the Meserole theatre would give a pass to every reader of the paper who could send in a correct list of the pictured stars. In addition to the cut in the newspaper there was an enlarged reproduction of the group in the lobby of the theatre.

Lillian and Dorothy Pairs See "Romola" Gratis

When "Romola" played in Cleveland, O., at the Stillman theatre, M. A. Malaney, publicity director for the house, assisted by C. C. Deardourff, Metro-Goldwyn exploiteer, waged a campaign that attracted considerable attention to the showing.

The most notable feature of their campaign was the publishing of a telegram from Lillian and Dorothy Gish in the Cleveland Press reading "Will you kindly invite all sisters in Greater Cleveland whose names are Lillian and Dorothy to be our guests next week at the Stillman theatre during the presentation of our latest picture, 'Romola'? Please have them send their names and addresses to you and our representative in Cleveland will provide them with tickets. Our sincere thanks to you and best wishes to our many friends in our home state." Twenty-one letters were received on the day following the appearance of this letter in the Press, and several on each day succeeding, the stunt attracting enormous attention. In the event that any one of the sisters was sick a two-pound box of candy was forwarded. Each pair was checked up and all found authentic.

The Catholic Alumni association, Cleveland branch, co-operated in distributing 20,000 tickets good for a five per cent discount in the afternoon and 10 per cent in the evenings, and seventeen displays of photographs were made in branch libraries, through which 10,000 book marks exploiting the showing were distributed. Forty 24-sheets and twenty-one 8-sheets were posted, and copies of the novel were featured in a window display. Ads were bought extensively in all local papers including the Italian, and letters from the Will Hays office endorsing the picture were liberally distributed. Street cars carried cards throughout the showing.

Display of Warner Bros. stars in one of the many windows arranged by Frank W. Purkett of the Kinema theatre, Fresno, Calif., for Greater Movie Season in that city. Other windows featured the stars of other companies.

Toledo "Iron Horse" Drive a Model

Temple Theatre Engagement Supported by Exploitation Campaign of Smashing Magnitude and Force

ONE of the most complete and carefully planned exploitation campaigns on record is that staged recently in Toledo, Ohio, for the showing of "The Iron Horse" at the Temple theatre. The management of this house, in conjunction with the Fox exploitation forces, left no stone unturned to let Toledo know the calibre of the attraction.

The first step taken by the exploiters was to organize the local railroad officials and employees, which was done at a special invitational showing, in which the executives of the different roads entering Toledo, together with the heads of the various unions were asked to pledge their support. Toledo being the third largest railroad center in the world, the railroadmen's showing took on all the aspects of a convention or political demonstration.

A similar screening was held for the Toledo Chamber of Commerce, and the aid of this body was pledged to make the Temple engagement a success. Then an afternoon tea was held at the Fort Meigs hotel, to which were invited the heads of all the women's business and social organizations, together with all the local school teachers. The women were organized to act in concert with the railroad men and the Chamber of Commerce.

A replica of "The Iron Horse" built upon an auto chassis, toured the streets for one week preceding the opening, and throughout the engagement as well.

The Mayor of Toledo, cognizant of the tremendous local interest in the engagement, offered his services in helping put the picture over. At a special invitational showing, held on the evening before the engagement opened, the Mayor headed the list of celebrities present, and also rode in the cab of the engine ballyhoo on the streets.

Oliver Slocum, aged 94 years, and reputed to be the oldest railroad man in the world, was guest of honor at this showing. The old railroader was brought to the theatre in the cab of the engine ballyhoo, accompanied by a special military guard of honor from the state barracks at Columbus.

Animated marquee display by Manager Charles H. Amos of the Carolina theatre, Greenville, S. C., for "Don Q" (United Artists).

So enthusiastic was the crowd gathered before the theatre, on seeing the old timer that it was necessary to take him to one of the windows of the theatre overlooking the street, where an announcer with megaphone, introduced him, incidentally making a short talk on the picture.

The recruiting division of the army was tied up with the attraction, through a number of specially painted one-sheet boards placed about town in advantageous locations. A recruiting meeting was held before the post office on one evening before the opening, at which plenty of railroad flares were burned, and speeches made by civic officials, together with liberal mention of "The Iron Horse."

Special vaudeville gags bearing on humorous aspects of "The Iron Horse" were compiled. These gags were used the week before the engagement by Mack and Tempest, and Ryan and Walker in the routine of their acts at the local Keith house.

A railroadmen's parade was staged during the run, in which members of the Engineer's, Fireman's, Conductor's and Trainmen's organizations took part. The American Express Co. contributed a float to this turnout.

The local radio station was used for a sales talk on the attraction, and the Toledo newspapers played this and the many other stunts up heavily in their columns.

Forty-two window tie-ups were secured in the shopping district, through the co-operation of the Chamber of Commerce. The Chamber also displayed a large announcement in the windows of their offices. Each window bearing a single letter, and the whole spelling the title.

Taking advantage of the new "Lucky Buck" craze that is sweeping the country, the Toledo News-Bee ran a contest in which passes to the theatre were given to the winners of the money prizes.

The Lion and Milner's department stores wrapped up "Iron Horse" heralds with all bundles for a week before the opening.

The Boy Scouts organization was tied up with the showing, on the angle that the hero of the picture, as a child was the original Boy Scout. The boys paraded with the railroad men, as did also the Toledo G. A. R. posts, and the Sons of Italy, a fraternal organization.

In most exploitation campaigns, it is customary to have some kind of a newspaper contest. The Toledo exploiters had two. The News-Bee ran a Railroad Men's Popularly Contest, while the Blade ran an essay contest on "What The Iron Horse Has Done For The Civic Development of Toledo."

The members of the Board of Education, school principals and teachers were also invited to one of the special showings.

Tags made up after the fashion of Auto Violation Cards, and carrying "Iron Horse" copy, were tied to all cars parked in the downtown district.

Three of the attractive window displays in the campaign on "The Pony Express" (Paramount) at the Imperial theatre, San Francisco, featuring costumes and properties actually used in the filming of the picture.

YOUR IDEA

A SCRIP BOOK PLAN

AS AN introductory feature for the fifth season of Capitol Entertainment at the F. P.-L. houses in Canada, the company has launched a Scrip Book plan. Books of tickets have been placed on sale simultaneously in 57 of the corporation's theatres from Montreal to Vancouver, B. C., the ticket coupons being offered in five, 10 and 25 cent denominations for the convenience of patrons. The books of admission tickets, which are transferable and acceptable at any of the 57 theatres, were issued at prices that represented a considerable saving to purchasers. The $10 scrip books are sold at $8.50 and the $5 books are sold for $4.50. The scrip books have practically no restrictions, the coupons being detachable, interchangeable and transferable.

This feature was worked out and put through by Walter F. Davis, former manager of the Metropolitan theatre, Winnipeg, Manitoba, who was transferred to the head office staff of Famous Players at Toronto to take charge of the Scrip Book department for the 57 theatres. The principal cinema halls of the corporation were selected for the feature and it is a noteworthy fact that no less than 14 theatres in Toronto come under the plan.

Large advertising space was used simultaneously in the various cities in which the 57 theatres are located for the first "flash" on August 22 and other literature and screen announcements were employed for the purpose. The cities which come under the plan include Toronto, Montreal, Winnipeg, Vancouver, Calgary, Brandon, Brockville, Brantford, Cobourg, Chatham, Edmonton, Fort William, Guelph, Galt, Hamilton, Kitchener, Kingston, London, Moose Jaw, Nanaimo, Nelson, Ottawa, Oshawa, Owen Sound, Port Arthur, Paris, Peterboro, Port Hope, Regina, Saskatoon, Stratford, Victoria, Welland, Woodstock, Sault Ste. Marie and St. Catherines.

The 14 theatres listed for Toronto include the Hippodrome, Oakwood, Bloor, College, Palace, Alhambra, Beaver, Parkdale, Teck, Family, Beach, Capitol, St. Clair and York Theatres.

The Scrip Book feature is one of the most important innovations for chain theatres in the Dominion in recent years.

REISENFELD ON MUSIC

THE all-important matter of musical accompaniment for pictures is dealt with interestingly in a past issue of *The Close-Up*, published by Famous Players for its theatre employes, by Dr. Hugo Riesenfeld, who has charge of the Rivoli, Rialto and Criterion, New York City. Some of the highlights of the Riesenfeld article are:

In scoring a picture, I think it is unwise to use tunes that are too familiar. They distract attention from the screen. By this I do

Naval band from the U. S. S. "Savannah," mother ship to the Pacific division of submarines, which appeared in a Naval Week at Loew's Warfield theatre, San Francisco, in conjunction with "Shore Leave" (First National).

Race between an ancient automobile and a foot racer, patterned after the picture, used to exploit "Not So Long Ago" (Paramount) by Manager George T. Crusen of the Palace theatre, Lockport, N. Y.

not mean that well-known music should never be used. Often it gives exactly the right atmosphere. When we show boys playing on the poorer streets of New York City, nothing is more appropriate than to play "The Sidewalks of New York," which everybody knows. What I do mean is that one should avoid using a too well-known aria, such as "Celeste Aida," or a song like "Love's Old Sweet Song" for a love theme. But then again, in a Southern picture it might be very suitable to play "Swanee River" or "My Old Kentucky Home." A good thing to remember is that the audience should never be consciously listening to the music. The score should never become obtrusive.

The film should be divided into moods and then every effort be made to find music that represents each mood. Ideally, of course, all motion picture theatres should be equipped with an extensive music library, with the compositions so catalogued that reference is a simple matter.

With the exception of set arias, operatic music is admirably suited to film accompaniment. In opera one finds practically every emotion and situation expressed. If a certain film has oriental scenes there is "L'Africana" and "Aida" and "Coque D'Or" to draw upon.

Musical settings cannot be standardized. If Charlie Chaplin in one of his comedies slips and falls, he may well be accompanied with a roll of drums and crash of cymbals. But it would be fatal to use such an accompaniment for a scene where Valentino falls to a tragic death.

Scoring has become a science of split seconds. A melody that perfectly enhances one scene may prove ruinous if it is allowed to run over raggedly into a subsequent one. A scene of dancing and gaiety may perhaps be immediately followed by one of sadness and tears. In such a case the tune that is used for the former must not be allowed to run over even a fraction of a second into the other. The method that I have found to be most satisfactory in scoring a film is to divide it roughly into moods, and then select from the library such compositions as seem to be suitable. While the picture is being run off in the projection room, a pianist plays these compositions while the scorer marks off on the sheet the point that is reached when the scene stops. Afterwards the whole picture with the accompaniment is run off, timed absolutely, and the accompaniment carefully modulated so that the changes will not be too abrupt.

I finish with a plea to the conductor that however he arranges the score, when it comes to the actual performance, not to halt in the middle of a musical phrase because of a scene change. It gives an impression of jerkiness that makes the audience unconsciously fidgety. Of the two evils, having a musical phrase run over too far, or breaking it up, the former is far more desirable.

AND OURS

PRESS BOOKS

DOROTHY CLEVELAND, direc-
tor of advertising and publicity for Rayart
Pictures, has just brought out a press book
which is an excellent example of the useful-

ANOTHER HYMAN PRESENTATION

TYPICAL of the atmospheric prologue which he consistently
delivers, Edward L. Hyman, managing director of the Brooklyn Mark Strand theatre, Brooklyn, recently staged a most
effective presentation for "Sally of the Sawdust." Not so elaborate
as to detract from the picture, it blended pleasantly with the feature
and created just the right mood for it.

This prologue, which opened "in one" and gradually worked to
a full stage, was preceded by an art-title announcement introducing
the purpose of the prologue and the characters. A basso, made
up as W. C. Fields in the photoplay, came on in front of the purple
spangled draw-curtains of the production stage for some business
built around the character. In a moment the premiere danseuse, as
Sally, made her appearance. For the two a special number was
written, both music and lyrics, which embodied many of the sayings
of McGargle in the picture, among them "the old army game."

As the pair finished their number, the purple draw-curtains
opened, disclosing the outside of a huge circus tent. There was a
group of performers in various poses and costumes, listening to a
woman-whistler, made up as a boy, whistling "Invitation." Then
a hobo, who had been lounging around the tent, picked up a football
balloon and played two numbers on it, "When You and I Were
Young" and "My Best Girl." Then the clown of the group, following the example set by the hobo, picked up a saw and played
"Old Pal" on it. This was followed by the popular xylophonist
of the orchestra, who dressed as the ringmaster, played "Ruffen-
ready," while Sally danced and the rest of the performers swayed
to the rythm of the music.

Then the ensemble on the stage and in the orchestra took up the
final, "The Gallop" from "Faust," after which the performers were
seen packing their belongings in preparation to move. As the production stage was cleared, lights dimmed down on the circus tent,
which was rigged on a traveller, slowly opened for the final scene
which was that of the circus leaving town.

This final scene was the climax of this pretentious and elaborately
staged prologue. The scene depicted circus band wagons and animals, one behind the other, with lights on the sides, moving slowly
along and disappearing in the distance. The calliope was heard
playing as the circus left, gradually growing fainter and fainter as
the curtains closed on the prologue and the feature picture "Sally
of the Sawdust" was flashed upon the screen.

*Unusual enterprise in exploiting a news weekly subject was shown by
Manager Barry Burke of the Palace theatre, Fort Worth, in connection
with the Pathe News shots of the Shenandoah disaster. This working
model, with revolving propellors, drew great attention to the lobby.*

ness and value that can be crammed into these exhibitor aids when
they are intelligently prepared, with an eye to showmanship and
practical conditions. The press book in question is on "The
Cyclone Cavalier," and in its sixteen pages is embraced a valuable
collection of worth while ideas and material.

A number of unusually compelling newspaper ads, a cartoon
feature for the photoplay page, a mailing card and theatre program
cover, a special lobby panel, prepared reviews, snappy catch lines,
and the like, are included in the meaty pages, several of which are
inclosed in highly decorative art borders.

CANINE EXPLOITATION

HOW many dogs are there in your town? Unless they are
conspicuous by their absence, there is one sure-fire exploitation
angle for you to use on any of the dog-star pictures that come along,
and that is the dog contest for the youngster. Every kid is proud
of his "mut" and confident that it would beat the bluest-blooded
thoroughbred.

Announce a dog contest, with prizes for the dogs most nearly
resembling Rin-Tin-Tin or Strongheart, whoever the star may be,
and also for the biggest dog, the smallest, the handsomest, the
homeliest, and so on. Give a pass to each of the boys who enters a
dog. If it could be arranged, you would attract a lot of attention
by rigging up temporary kennels at one side of the lobby and leaving
the dogs there for an evening. But just the contest, alone, should
bring you a lot of publicity and talk. The prizes need not be large.
The appeal is rather to the children's pride in their pets, and their
anxiety to see them win.

$5,000 REWARD

HAVE you ever used the "Reward" and "Lost" bulletins as
heralds, by way of getting variety into your throwaways?
If printing isn't too expensive in your town, little cost attaches to the
stunt. The thing to do is to get one of the regular police "Reward"
heralds and copy its general style.

If there is a "Lost" or a "Missing" in the title of the picture, so
much the better. Use a cut of the villain and announce $5,000 re-
ward for his capture, dead or alive. Then use the line: For information, phone—followed by the theatre phone number. If they
phone in, give them a brief sales talk on the picture.

Manager Walter League of the Strand theatre in Memphis used
a similar idea on "Lost—a Wife," when he had printed bulletins
carrying a picture of Greta Nissen as a lost wife, with a suitable
reward offered for her return. He followed this up with classified
ads in the "Lost and Found" section of the paper. These stated
that she was expected in Memphis the following week.

*Unique shadow-box on "The Gold Rush" (United Artists) at the Tivoli
theatre, Chattanooga. This same idea might be worked out on a large
scale and made the basis of an effective prologue, using the drop cut-out
in the shape of a Chaplin shoe.*

Elaborate Ballyhoo Boosts "Never the Twain"

Loew's Metropolitan in Brooklyn, N. Y., played "Never the Twain Shall Meet!" recently following a vigorous campaign waged by Carl Levi, of Loew's, Inc., and Manager George Schenck.

A massive float which toured the busiest sections of Brooklyn four days before the opening and an exceedingly elaborate lobby display were the features of this campaign. The float carried a setting reproducing a South Sea Island, and two attractive young women costumed as natives, who played ukeleles and at intervals gave short exhibitions of native dances. Special scenic sets transformed the lobby into a South Sea island grove, with Yuba leaves five feet long hanging from the edges of the marquee. Large palm leaves were used in abundance and over 500 real cocoanuts in the husk helped decorate the lobby. A thatched hut was built over the box office and water boards and shields grotesquely painted stood at each corner. Four live monkeys, brilliantly colored macaws, tropical plants, palms and flowers, spears, tom-toms, cocoanuts and fibre mats completed the display.

Teaser cards were distributed in abundance through the city, and 10,000 Chinese puzzles, walking dolls and colored balloons, all bearing announcements of the showing, were donated to patrons of the theatre the week preceding the showing.

Handsomest Man Passes as "Lightnin'" Publicity

An interesting method of acquainting Indianapolis with the fact that "Lightnin'" was shortly to make its local screen debut has just been executed by Bingham and Cohen, managers of the Colonial, and the Fox exploitation department.

The stunt consisted in sending a letter signed by the theatre management, and enclosing two complimentary tickets to the secretaries of the local civic and fraternal bodies. The letter stated that the Colonial management had been requested by Miss

Old-fashioned carriage, with its passengers garbed in the period of the picture, used as an advance ballyhoo on "East Lynne" (Fox) at Keith's Palace, Cleveland.

Madge Bellamy to present the tickets to the two best looking men in the local lodge, society or fraternity, as the case might be.

The Indianapolis Rotary club, Real Estate board, Traffic club, Luncheon club, and in fact, every social body to which the passes were sent, held voting contests to determine which of their members were most qualified to wear the laurels as beauties. That the eliminations, tests and balloting created no end of amusement is putting it mildly. The picture—in the meantime—coming in for no small amount of word-by-mouth advertising.

On the evening appointed for the Adonises to attend the theatre, not only were Indianapolis's "handsomest" on hand, but their less decorative brothers as well, turned out and gave them a cheer as they entered the theatre. The cheer was responded to, by a set of such fiery blushes that the Marquee lights for the moment seemed to have lost their "kick."

Unique Display Arranged for "Iron Horse" Ad

A unique display was arranged in the lobby of the Grand Central theatre in connection with the premiere St. Louis showing of the "Iron Horse" at the Skouras houses opening on August 29.

The display was arranged by Jack Fuld, exploitation man for Fox, in conjunction with the St. Louis, San Francisco railway. It included a miniature working model of the finest engine on the Frisco system in 1904, incased in glass, while above was displayed a photograph of the new "1500" type of engines now in use on the Frisco lines.

The model was in the Frisco exhibit at the Louisiana Purchase World's exposition in St. Louis in 1904 and last week was shown at the Missouri State fair in Sedalia.

The lobby exhibit also included various farm products raised along the Frisco lines.

A similar exhibit has been arranged by the Missouri Pacific railroad and will be displayed at Eighth and Pine Streets in the down-town business section.

Stickers on Newspapers as "Unholy Three" Stunt

Three thousand stickers exploiting "The Unholy Three" were distributed among newsboys in Minneapolis when this production played at the Garrick theatre, and were attached to lower corners of every paper sold on the town's busiest corners. Exceedingly prominent exploitation was secured in this way at a nominal cost. Morris Abrams, Metro-Goldwyn exploiteer, and Eddie Gallinagh, publicity man for the Garrick, achieved this feat.

Twenty thousand cards tying up the impending arrival of Metro-Goldwyn-Mayer's Trackless Train with the showing were distributed, and the town was lavishly posted. Three thousand 1-sheet and thirty-five 24-sheets were used, and extra display space was taken in all the papers. A trailer was used and there was a special lobby display.

Circus wagon, with personal appearance of Joe Bonomo, before the Theatre De Luxe, Los Angeles, for "The Great Circus Mystery" (Universal). The star showed his strength by drawing the wagon along the street.

With First Run Theatres

NEW YORK CITY

Capitol Theatre—
Film Numbers—The Tower of Lies (Metro-Goldwyn-Mayer), Capitol Magazine (Selected), The Friendly Breast of Earth (Scenic).
Musical Program — "Queen of Sheba" (Overture), "The Lorale!" (Vocal solo), "Autumn Leaf" (Dance solo), Musical selections (Saxophone solo), "Home Sweet Home the World Over" (Soloist and ballet corps).

Colony Theatre—
Film Numbers — The Freshman (Pathe), continued.

Mark Strand Theatre—
Film Numbers—Don Q, Son of Zorro (United Artists) continued.

Rialto Theatre—
Film Numbers—A Son of His Father (Paramount), Rialto Magazine (Selected).
Musical Program—Ben Bernie and the Rialto Gang at the "Country Club."

Cameo Theatre—
Film Numbers—What Fools Men (First National), Cameo Pictorial (Selected), Aesop's Fables (Pathe), The Idle Class (Chaplin re-issue).
Musical Program — "Katinka" (Overture), "Alone at Last" (Soprano solo), Organ solo.

Warner's Theatre—
Film Numbers—The Man on the Box (Warner Bros.), Warner's News Weekly (Selected), The Smoke Eater (Educational).
Musical Program—"Milestones to Jazz" (overture), "Moonlight and Roses" (Dance number) "A Bit of Russia" (Dance and accordion solo), From Waikiki (Dance solo), Southern Impression (Dance and Banjo solo), On Broadway (Dance solo), "The Man on the Box" (Dance).

BROOKLYN

Mark Strand Theatre—
Film Numbers — Shore Leave (First National), Anniversary Greeting (S. R.), Mark Strand Topical Review (selected).
Musical Program—Prologue from "Pagliacci" (baritone solo), overture "Second Hungarian

Strikingly original ad on "Don Q" (United Artists) at the Colonial theatre, Boston.

Rhapsody" (with original piano cadenza), "Divertissements Populaire"—"If I Had a Girl Like You" (dance orchestra), "Pal of My Cradle Days" (contralto solo), "Heebee Geebees" (banjo solo), "Let Me Linger Longer in Your Arms" (soprano solo), "Twelfth Street Rag" (xylophone solo), "Carme Carme" (baritone solo), "Let It Rain, Let It Pour" (ensemble), atmospheric prologue to feature— "Three for Jack" (baritone solo).

LOS ANGELES

Criterion Theatre—
Film Numbers—Lightnin' (Fox), Wild Waves (Educational), Fox News.
Musical Program—"Neapolitan Nights" (Overture).

Forum Theatre—
Film Numbers—The Home Maker (Universal), Props (Universal), Cash (Fox), International News, Life's Greatest Thrills (Universal).
Musical Program—Orchestra and organ.

Hillstreet Theatre—
Film Numbers—A Man of Iron (S. R.), The Pace Makers (F. B. O.), Aesop's Fables (Pathe), International News.

Loew's State Theatre—
Film Numbers—The Dark Angel (First National), Life's Greatest Thrills (Universal).
Musical Program—Impressionistic revue of "Lady Be Good" (Specialty), "Neapolitan Nights" (Orchestra).

Metropolitan Theatre—
Film Numbers — The Coast of Folly (Paramount), The Iron Nag (Pathe), Pathe News.
Musical Program—40 "Il Trovatore" (Overture).

Pantages Theatre—
Film Numbers — The Bandit's Baby (F. B. O.), Pathe News.
Musical Program—Vaudeville.

Million Dollar Theatre—
Film Numbers — The Freshman (Pathe), continued.

Hand-drawn ads are the rule among the first run houses of Cincinnati, and this one on "Her Sister from Paris" (First National) is a typical specimen.

Musical Program — "On the Campus" (Overture).

Rialto Theatre—
Film Numbers—Sally of the Sawdust (United Artists), continued.
Musical Program—Orchestra (prologue to feature).

CHICAGO

Chicago Theatre—
Film Numbers—The Mystic (Metro-Goldwyn), Comedy (Selected), Scenic, International News.
Musical Program—"2nd Hungarian Rhapsody" (Overture), 'A Sea Fantasy" (Specialty), "A Polonaise Militarie" and "Chopin Up to Date," (Organ Solos); "An Evening at Home," (Presentation).

Tivoli Theatre—
Film Numbers—The Making of O'Malley (First National), Cartoon (S. R.), International News.
Musical Program — "Classical Jazz," "Faust," (Overture), "M. Kharam, pianist," (Specialty), "How's Your Voice?" (Organ Solo), "A Twilight Romance" (Presentation).

Uptown Theatre—
Film Numbers—Pretty Ladies (Metro-Goldwyn-Mayer).
Musical Program — Syncopation Week, including "Ray Miller and His Brunswick Orchestra with Eddie Chester," "White & Manning," "Adler, Weil & Herman," "Edythe Blossom," "Joe Whitehead," "Jimmy Dunn," and "The Kinky Kid Parade," (Organ Solo), "Charleston Echoes" (Tivoli Theatre Orchestra).

Capitol Theatre—
Film Numbers—California Straight Ahead (Universal), Comedy Cartoon, International News and Scenic.
Musical Program—"Tutti Frutti" (Overture), "Evening Star" (Specialty), "Arnold Johnson and His Jazz Band of Golf Enthusiasts" (Presentation) "The

Restaurant Problem" (Organ Solo), "California Straight Ahead" (Prologue).

Stratford Theatre—
Film Numbers—He's A Prince (Paramount), Stratford Magazine (Universal), Prisma, The Adventures of Maxie (F. B. O.)
Musical Program—"Light Cavalry" (Overture), "The Beautiful Lady" (Specialty), "Navigating On the Ocean of Joy" (Specialty), "A Trip to the Land of Memories" (Organ Solo), "The Love Boat" (Specialty).

Castle Theatre—
Film Numbers—Some Punkins (S. R.).

Roosevelt Theatre—
Film Numbers—The Freshman (Pathe).

Monroe Theatre—
Film Numbers— Kentucky Pride (Fox).

Orpheum Theatre—
Film Numbers—The Gold Rush (United Artists).

Randolph Theatre—
Film Numbers—California Straight Ahead (Universal), International News (Universal).

SAN FRANCISCO

California Theatre—
Film Numbers—He's a Prince (Paramount), Don't Tell Dad (Pathe), Pathe Review, International News.
Musical Program—"Merry Wives of Windsor" (Overture), "By The Waters of the Minnetonka" (Violin Solo), Orchestra novelty.

Loew's Warfield Theatre—
Film Numbers—The Midshipman (Metro-Goldwyn-Mayer), The Dark Angel (First National), International News and Kinograms.
Musical Program—"On the Firing Line" (Fanchon and Marco idea with singing and dancing).

Granada Theatre—
Film Numbers — The White Desert (Metro-Goldwyn-Mayer), Cold Turkey (Pathe), Pathe News.
Musical Program—"Charleston on the Bowery" (Special act with singing and dancing.

Imperial Theatre—
Film Numbers—The Pony Express (Paramount), continued.

Cameo Theatre—
Film Numbers—Kivalina of the Icelands (Pathe), Circus Cyclone (Universal), International News.
Musical Program—Selection of southern melodies (orchestra).

St. Francis Theatre—

Union Square Theatre—
Film Numbers—The Fearless Lover (S. R.).

Mr. Exhibitor: Ask at the Film Exchanges for the

It's little to ask for, but it's the only reliable aid you can give your musicians to help put the picture over

Two-column ad on "Her Sister from Paris" (First Nat'l) at the Grand Central, Lyric, Skydome and Capitol.

DES MOINES

Capitol Theatre—
Film Numbers—The Trouble With Wives (Paramount), Fox News.
Musical Program—"Cecilia" (special organ number).

Desmoines Theatre—
Film Numbers—Sun Up (Metro-Goldwyn), The Amateur Detective (Fox), Pathe Review, International News.

Strand Theatre—
Films Numbers—Souls for Sables (S. R.), Kinograms, Boys Will Be Boys (Pathe).

Rialto Theatre—
Film Number—The Lost World (First National). —

CINCINNATI

Capitol Theatre—
Film Numbers—The Coast of Folly (Paramount), Dragon Alley (Pathe), Capitol News.
Musical Program—Orchestra.

Walnut Theatre—
Film Numbers—The Freshman (Pathe), continued.

Strand Theatre—
Film Numbers—A Slave of Fashion (Metro-Goldwyn-Mayer), Tender Feet (Pathe), Pathe News.

Lyric Theatre—
Film Numbers—The Lost World (First National), Kinograms.
Musical Program—Orchestra.

Gifts Theatre—
Film Numbers — The Sporting Chance (Metro-Goldwyn-Mayer), Cupid's Victory (Universal), Kinograms.

Family Theatre—
Film Numbers—The Man Without a Conscience (Warner Bros.), All Balled Up (S. R.), Fox News.

CLEVELAND

Stillman Theatre—
Film Numbers—Coast of Folly (Paramount), Wide Awake (Educational), With Pencil and Brush (Fox), International News (Universal).
Musical Program—"Gypsy Love Song" (Overture), "Caprice Venoise" by Kriesler (prologue).

Allen Theatre—
Film Numbers—The Dark Angel (First National), The Iron Nag (Pathe), Pathe Review, Topics

THE FOUNDATION FOR EVERY GREAT MODERN DRAMA!
'EAST LYNNE'

Playwrights for years have been drawing inspiration from this great play because it has every element of truly wonderful entertainment—pathos—suspense—humor and heart interest. Since 1861 it has been regarded by millions, in every town and city, as the world's greatest love story. Now it has been screened, and on a more lavish and wonderful scale than was ever possible on the legitimate stage, and with five great favorites—Alma Rubens, Lou Tellegen, Edmund Lowe, Marjorie Daw, Frank Keenan—in the wonderful cast.
It is fitting that the world's most magnificent playhouse should be chosen for the world premiere of the film version of America's greatest drama.

PALACE

B. F. KEITH THEATRE
WITH GREAT KEITH-ALBEE VAUDEVILLE
AFTERNOONS all 30c EVENINGS 50c & 75c
Now Playing "The Wheel" and 6 Big Acts Keith-Albee Super Vaudeville

Dignified and forceful ad for the premiere of "East Lynne" (Fox) at the B. F. Keith Palace, Cleveland.

of the Day (Pathe), Pathe News.
Musical Program — "Finlandia" (overture), "Mignon" (soprano solo), "Brown Eyes Why are You Blue," "The Kiss I Can't Forget," "Tiger Rag" (Jazz Unit).

State Theatre—
Film Numbers—The Knockout (First National), A Winning Pair (Universal), On the Go (Fox), Fun from the Press (Prod. Dist. Corp.), Pathe Review.
Musical Program—Organ overture, vaudeville.

Park Theatre—
Film Numbers—What Fools Men (First National), Why Hesitate (Educational), Pathe Review, Topics of the Day (Pathe), Kinograms (Educational).
Musical Program—Largo and Finale from "The New World Symphony" (overture), Vocal duet from "Norma" (vocal), "My Sweetie Turned Me Down",

---

"Angry," "Save Your Sorrows" (Jazz).

Reade's Hippodrome—
Film Numbers—Seven Days (P. D. C.), Pathe Comedy, Pathe News.
Musical Program—Potpourri of Jazz (overture), Vaudeville.

Keith's East 105th St. Theatre—
Film Numbers—Seven Days (P. D. C.), Aesop's Fables (Pathe), Moonlight and Noses (Pathe), Pathe News.
Musical Program—Selections from "No No Nanette" (overture), Vaudeville.

Circle Theatre—
Film Numbers—Below the Line (Warner Bros.), No Father to Guide Her (Pathe), Pathe News, sportlight (Pathe), Aesop's Fables (Pathe).
Musical Program—"Songs of Uncle Sam" (overture), "Let Me Linger Longer in Your Arms," "Indian Love Call," "Someshine," "Everybody Stomps" (Jazz).

SEATTLE

Blue Mouse Theatre—
Film Numbers — East Lynne (Fox), Hungry Hounds (Comedy), International News.
Musical Program — "Orpheus" (Overture).

Coliseum Theatre—
Film Numbers—The Coast of Folly (Paramount), Alice Cartoon (Educational), Kinograms and Pathe News.

VICTORIA
9th & Market—8 A. M. to 11:15 P. M.
MILTON SILLS in The Making of O'Malley
TONIGHT—MIDNIGHT SHOW

Compact and effective single-column ad on "The Making of O'Malley" (First Nat'l) at the Victoria theatre, Philadelphia.

Musical Program — Descriptive Fantasy (Special Overture).

Columbia Theatre—
Film Numbers—Hell's Highroad (Prod. Dist. Corp.), Life's Greatest Thrills (Universal), The Green Eyed Monster (Comedy), International News.
Musical Program—"Sixth Hungarian Rhapsody" (Overture), "Sometime" (Novelty selection).

Heilg Theatre—
Film Numbers—Sun-Up (Metro-Goldwyn-Mayer), Pathe Reviews, Topics of the Day (Pathe), Pathe News.
Musical Program—Popular medley (Overture).

Liberty Theatre—
Film Numbers—Don Q, Son of

Zorro (United Artists), continued.

Pantages Theatre—
Film Numbers—Kentucky Pride (Fox), Hungry Hounds (Comedy), Pathe News.
Musical Program—Vaudeville.

Strand Theatre—
Film Numbers—The Lady Who Lied (First National), Felix Cartoon (Educational), Fox News.
Musical Program — Fifteen minutes in a Broadcasting Studio (Novelty overture).

KANSAS CITY

Newman Theatre—
Film Numbers—The Man Who Found Himself (Paramount), Newman Mirror of the World (Pathe), Kinograms and International News, Newman News and Views (Local Photography).
Musical Program—Atmospheric Selections (Overture), "Hawaii the Beautiful" (Novelty with Chorus of Ten), Recessional (Organ solos).

Liberty Theatre—
Film Numbers—Lightnin' (Fox), Officer No. 13 (Universal), Aesop's Fables (Pathe), International News Pictorial.
Musical Program—"The Fortune Teller" (Overture), Recessional (Organ solos).

Royal Theatre—
Film Numbers—The Freshman (Pathe), continued, Royal Screen Magazine (Pathe), Kinograms and International News, Royal Current Events (Local Photography).
Musical Program—Royal Syncopators in Collegiate Frolic on Stage (Overture), Recessional (Organ Solos).

Mainstreet Theatre—
Film Numbers—Don Q, Son of Zorro, (United Artists), Pathe News and Educational Short Subjects.
Musical Program—Popular Selections (Overture), Recessional Organ Solos).

Pantages Theatre—
Film Numbers—The Crackerjack (C. C. Burr-S. R.), Fox News and Fox Short Subjects.
Musical Program — Atmospheric Selections (Overture), Recessional (Organ Solos).

The A. H. Blank Strand theatre, Des Moines, ran this ad on "The Mystic" (Metro-Goldwyn) recently.

SALT LAKE CITY

American Theatre—
Film Numbers—The Lost World (First National), Newspaper Fun (F. B. O.), International News.

Kinema Theatre—
Film Numbers—Friendly Enemies (Prod. Dist. Corp.), Nursing Trouble (Universal), Pathe Review, International News.

Pantages Theatre—
Film Numbers—The Tower of Lies (Metro-Goldwyn-Mayer).

Paramount-Empress Theatre—
Film Numbers—The Pony Express (Paramount), Pathe News.

Victory Theatre—
Film Numbers—The Man Who Found Himself (Paramount), No Father to Guide Him (Pathe), Pathe News.

INDIANAPOLIS

Circle Theatre—
Film Numbers—The Live Wire (First National), News Reel Weekly (Universal), Comedy (Educational).
Musical Program — Van and Schenck, entertainers; overture by Circle concert orchestra.

Colonial Theatre—
Film Numbers — California Straight Ahead (Universal), Comedy (Universal), Aesop Fable (Pathe), International News Reel (Pathe).
Musical Program — American Harmonists and Miss Blanche Wilson pianologues.

Apollo Theatre—
Film Numbers—The Freshman (Pathe) News Reel Weekly (Fox), Bray picturegraph (F. B. O.).
Musical Program—Ralph E. Duncan, soloist, and Earl Gordon, organist.

PHILADELPHIA

Stanley Theatre—
Film Numbers—Little Annie Rooney (United Artists), Stanley Magazine, A Night in the Forest (Scenic).
Musical Program—"Eileen" (Stanley Symphony Orchestra), "Faust" (Organ), Vocal & Terpsichorean Novelty, Stanley Theatre Ballet.

Fox Theatre—
Film Numbers—The Iron Horse (Fox).

Effective double-colum ad on "Hell's Highroad" (Producers Dis. Corp.) at Orchestra Hall, Chicago.

Stanton Theatre—
Film Numbers—The Gold Rush (United Artists).

Karlton Theatre—
Film Numbers—The Desert Flower (First National).

Palace Theatre—
Film Numbers—Shore Leave (First National).

Victoria Theatre—
Film Numbers—Son of His Father (Paramount).

Capitol Theatre—
Film Numbers—The Scarlet West (First National).

ST. PAUL

Astor Theatre—
Film Numbers—Hell's Highroad (Producers), Miss 'Me Again (F. B. O.), News.
Musical Program—Smiling Lew Epstein and his Merry Gang in "Sunny Spain" assisted by Alice Lilligren and Bennet Charles.

Capitol Theatre—
Film Numbers—Drusilla With a Million (F. B. O.), News.
Musical Program—Capitol Symphony Orchestra; The Lyric Four; Muldoon & Franklin, dancers.

Garrick Theatre—
Film Numbers—The Iron Horse (Fox), Felix Cat Comedy (S. R.), News Weekly.
Musical Program—Garrick Serenaders.

Strand Theatre—
Film Numbers—Riders of the Purple Sage (Fox), Uncle Tom's Gal (Pathe), News.
Musical Program—Organ Overture.

Opening ad on "The Teaser" (Universal) at the Plaza theatre in San Diego.

Tower Theatre—
Film Numbers — Pretty Ladies (Metro-Goldwyn-Mayer), Unfriendly Enemies (Pathe), Pathe News.
Musical Program—Miss Los Angeles (runner up in the Atlantic City contest), in toe dance numbers.

MILWAUKEE

Alhambra Theatre—
Film Numbers — Siege (Universal), The Cat's Whiskers (Universal), International News, Journal-Alhambra Pet Show (Special reel).

Musical Program — "The House of David Band" (Specialty).

Garden Theatre—
Film Numbers—The Lucky Horseshoe (Fox), Fox Weekly, Topics of the Day (Pathe), The West Wind (Fox), A Business Engagement (Fox).
Musical Program—"Brown Eyes" (Organ).

Merrill Theatre—
Film Numbers—The Freshman (Pathe), Wild Beasts of Borneo (Educational). Kinograms.
Musical Program—Orchestra Overture.

Strand Theatre—
Film Numbers — The Mystic (Metro-Goldwyn), Below Zero (Educational), Twenty-five Years Ago (S. R.), Kinograms.
Musical Program—"Prisma" (Violin Duet), "Hoodwinks" (Overture).

Wisconsin Theatre—
Film Numbers—The Man Who Found Himself (Paramount), Comedy (Educational), Here, There, Everywhere, with the Wisconsin Theatre Cameraman (International News Reel).

Two-column newspaper ad on "Siege" (Universal) at the America theatre, Denver.

Broadway Strand Theatre—
Film Numbers—The Crackerjack (S. R.), Universal comedy, International news reel.
Musical Program—Stage presentation, fashion revue with jazz orchestra, dancer and soloist, organ accompaniment.

Fox Washington Theatre—
Film Numbers—As No Man Has Loved (Fox), Felix the Cat comedy (S. R.), Fox news reel, other short subjects.
Musical Program—Organ accompaniment.

Capitol Theatre—
Film Numbers—The Man Who Found Himself (Paramount), Aesop's Fable (Pathe), Detroit News and Pathe pictorial, scenic short subject, stage presentation.
Musical Program—Slavic orchestra, organ accompaniment.

MINNEAPOLIS

Aster Theatre—
Film Numbers—Kentucky Pride (Fox), Tons of Trouble (Pathe), Fox News.
Musical Program—Organ overture.

Garrick Theatre—
Film Numbers — The Mystic (Metro-Goldwyn-Mayer), Comedy, News.
Musical Program—Jack Malerich (organist), Augmented Orchestra, Fred Heiscke, director; Lai Mon Kim, Chinese John McCormack.

Lyric Theatre—
Film Numbers—Hell's Highroad (Producers), Lyric Comedy; Pathe Weekly.
Musical Program—Maurice Cook, organ specialty.

Single-column art ad on "The Rainbow Trail" (Fox) at the Family theatre in Cincinnati.

Musical Program—"The Ten English Rockets," Comedy Dance (Edward Allen), Two Boys and a Piano (Brundage and Kramer), Originator of the Charleston (Jean Collins), Zimmerman and Granville (International Record Artists), "Making the World Safe for Hokum" (Jack Hanley).

DETROIT

Adams Theatre—
Film Numbers—The Gold Rush (United Artists) continued.

Madison Theatre—
Film Numbers—Never the Twain Shall Meet (Metro-Goldwyn), Detroit News and Pathe pictorial, Aesop's Fable (Pathe).
Musical Program—Organ and orchestra accompaniment.

State Theatre—
Film Numbers—Her Sister From Paris (Paramount), News Digest.
Musical Program—State Concert Orchestra; Eddie Dunstedter, organist; The Vanity Dolls featuring Kay and Muriel Sisters.

Strand Theatre—
Film Numbers—The Iron Horse (Fox), Kat Comedy (Educational), Strand News.
Musical Program—Strand Concert Orchestra.

BOSTON

Beacon Theatre—
Film Numbers—Son of His Father (Paramount), Without Mercy (Producers Dist. Corp.), Comedy (Educational), International News (Universal).
Musical Program—Overture, organ.

Fenway Theatre—
Film Numbers—The Man Who Found Himself (Paramount), The Bad Lands (Prod. Distributing Corp.), Comedy (Educational), News (Pathe).
Musical Program—Lloyd G. Del Castillo at the Wurlitzer.

Gordon's Washington St. Olympia Theatre—
Film Numbers—Winds of Chance (First National), Comedy (Pathe), News (Pathe).
Musical Program—Overture, five vaudeville acts.

Loew's State Theatre—
Film Numbers—The Coast of Folly (Paramount), Comedy (Pathe), Screen Snapshots (S. R.), Topics of the Day (Pathe), Aesop's Fables (Pathe), Weekly (Pathe).
Musical Program—Doek Isenberg's Orchestra.

Modern Theatre—
Film Numbers—A Son of His Father (Paramount), Without Mercy (Prod. Dist. Corp.), Comedy (Educational), International News.
Musical Program—Overture (Orchestra), organ.

BUFFALO

Shea's Hippodrome—
Film Numbers—A Slave of Fashion (Metro-Goldwyn), Super Hooper Dyne Lizzies (Pathe), Current Events (Pathe and International News).
Musical Program—Paul Whiteman and His Orchestra of 28 men in half hour program.

Loew's State Theatre—
Film Numbers—A Son of His Father (Paramount), Waiting (Educational), Current Events (Pathe News).
Musical Program—Selections from "Susanne" (orchestra). Five vaudeville acts.

Lafayette Square Theatre—
Film Numbers—Hell's Highroad (Prod. Dist. Corp.) Pathe comedy, Current Events (Kinograms).
Musical Program—"Sally" (orchestra), Organ solo, Five acts of vaudeville.

New Olympic Theatre—
Film Numbers—Lorraine of the Lions (Universal), Off the Highway (Prod. Dist. Corp.), Universal comedy, Current Events (International News).
Musical Program—Musical comedy Memories (Organ overture).

Shea's North Park Theatre—
Film Numbers—The Freshman

ACTION! THRILLS! ACTION!

GARDEN
Whitehurst Theatre

A Hair-Raising Story of Taming the Wild West

HUNT STROMBERG
PRESENTS

HARRY CAREY
IN
"The Bad Lands"

A tale of Romance and Adventure, in the days when brave hearted and sturdy cavalrymen outwitted and outfought the Indians to push America's boundary ever Westward.

Added Comedy
Al Alt in
"Helpful Al"

Effective action in three-column space on "The Bad Lands" (Producers Dist. Corp.) run in connection with the eng gement of that picture at the Garden theatre, Baltimore.

(Pathe), Guest of Honor (Fox), Current Events (Pathe and International News).
Musical Program—Overture to "Norma" (orchestra).

Palace Theatre—
Film Numbers—Jimmy's Millions (F. B. O.), Chaplin comedy (re-issue), Current Events (International News).

HOUSTON

Queen Theatre—
Film Numbers—A Son of His Father (Paramount), Comedy (Pathe), News (Pathe).
Musical Program—"The Evolution of Dixie" (overture), Organ numbers.

Isis Theatre—
Film Numbers—The Limited Mail (Warner), comedy (Pathe), News (International).
Musical Numbers—"Love Call" (overture), Organ numbers.

Capitol Theatre—
Film Numbers—Wild Horse Mesa (Paramount), Comedy (Educational), News (Kinograms).
Musical Program—Popular selections, orchestra, organ numbers.

Rialto Theatre—
Film Numbers—The Coming of Amos (Producers Dist. Corp.), comedy (Educational), News (Fox).
Musical Program—Organ and piano numbers.

Majestic Theatre—
Film Numbers—Lady Robin Hood (F. B. O.), Aesop's Fables (Pathe).
Musical Program—"In the Garden of To-Morrow" (overture), Organ numbers, Vaudeville.

Liberty Theatre—
Film Numbers—The Night Ship (S. R.), Comedy (Fox), Review (Pathe).
Musical Program—Organ and piano selections.

BALTIMORE

Century Theatre—
Film Numbers—The Coast of Folly (Paramount), Fair Warning (Educational), News Weekly (Fox).
Musical Program—Eccentric Dances (Rita Owin), Dancing

(Johnny Hamp's Kentucky Serenaders), Organ recessional, Orchestra.

Garden Theatre—
Film Numbers—The Bad Lands (Producers Distributing Corporation), Barrier Busters (Pathe), Helpful Al (Universal), International News (Universal).
Musical Program—Five acts of vaudeville, Orchestra, Organ recessional.

Keith's Hippodrome—
Film Numbers—Who Cares (S. R.), Aesop's Fable (Pathe), News Weekly (Pathe), Cupid's Victory (Universal Century Comedy).
Musical Program—Five acts of vaudeville, Organ recessional, Orchestra.

Metropolitan Theatre—
Film Numbers—The Wife Who Wasn't Wanted (Warner Brothers), Nuts and Squirrels (Pathe), Topical Review (Pathe), Country Life a la Mode and The Swanee Shore (Pathe), No Father to Guide Him (Pathe).
Musical Program—Selections from "No-No Nanette" (Overture by Orchestra), Organ recessional, Orchestra.

New Theatre—
Film Numbers—The Rag Man (Metro-Goldwyn-Mayer), Going Good (Universal), News Weekly (Pathe).
Musical Program—Selections from "Babes in Toyland" (Overture by Orchestra), Mandolin selections (Bernado de Pace), Organ recessional, Orchestra.

Parkway Theatre—
Film Numbers—The Teaser (Universal), Parkway Pictorial News (Kinograms), The Amazing Mazie (F. B. O.).
Musical Program—"Raymond" (Overture by Parkway Concert Ensemble), Organ recessional, Orchestra, "Gypsy Love Song" (Violin Solo).

Rivoli Theatre—
Film Numbers—The Knockout (First National), In the Spider's Grip (Educational), Rivoli News (Pathe), Fashion Snap Shots (Made by Baltimore shop).

Musical Program — "Hungarian Rhapsodie No. 6" (Overture by Orchestra), "A Half Ton of Harmony" (Vocal and piano selections by Haynes, Lehman and Kaiser), "The Firefly" and "My Heart at Thy Sweet Voice" (Organ selections).

ST. LOUIS

Loew's State Theatre—
Film Numbers — Little Annie Rooney (United Artists), News.
Musical Program—Orchestral overture and popular number. Organ accompaniment. On stage "Garden of Dreams" "The Sacrifice" (Stage presentation.

Missouri Theatre—
Film Numbers—The Man Who Found Himself (Paramount), Missouri Magazine, Comedy.
Musical Program—Overture "The Life of Franz Liszt" (Missouri Symphony Orchestra), "I'm Knee Deep in Daisies" (organ). On stage—Harry Jolson and Southern Serenaders. "The World Is Such a Lonesome Place," (tenor solo).

Grand Central, West End Lyric and Capitol Theatres—
Film Numbers—The Knockout (First National), Kinogram News and Views (Educational).
Musical Program—At Grand Central: Gene Rodemich and His Gang in "The Schoolmaster." At West End Lyric: Conley-Silverman Band and Frank Libure in "Russian Capers."

Delmonte Theatre—
Film Numbers—Rugged Waters (Paramount), The Timber Wolf (Fox), Delmonte News and Views.
Musical Program—Orchestral selections. Vocal numbers.

William Goldman's Kings and Rivoli Theatres—
Film Numbers—Souls for Sables (S. R.), Somewhere in Somewhere (Pathe), Madame Sans Jane (Pathe).
Musical Program—Orchestral and vocal numbers.

ATLANTA

Howard Theatre—
Film Numbers—The Freshman (Pathe), Life's Greatest Thrills (International News).
Musical Program—"Three O'Clock in the Morning", (organ) prologue "Campus Life," Jazz hits "Collegiate" "Mighty Lak' a Rose" (vocal solo), "Just a Little Love," (violin solo) "Souvenir" and pianos playing "Kitten on the Keys," Howard ballet of sixteen in eccentric dances.

Metropolitan Theatre—
Film Numbers—Her Sister From Paris (First National). Curses (Educational), International News.
Musical Program—"Home Coming" (Overture), "If You Hadn't Gone Away" (Jazz), Special Numbers—Phil and the Carolina Trio (pianist and male trio singing popular numbers).

Rialto Theatre—
Film Numbers—Not So Long Ago (Paramount), Horseshoes (Warner), Pathe News.

Loew's Grand—
Film Numbers—Sun Up (Metro-Goldwyn), Sportlight, Aesop's Fables, Topics of the Day, (Pathe releases), Dandelion (Educational).
Musical Program—Five acts of vaudeville.

Short Subjects and Serials

Pathe Fixes Release for "A Dog's Life"

"**A** DOG'S LIFE" will be the first of the Charley Chaplin comedies brought back to the screen by Pathe under the terms of the contract recently signed by the comedian and the distributing concern. The release date has been set for November 22nd.

Edna Purviance is Chaplin's leading lady in this one, with Albert Austin prominent in the supporting cast. In addition to "A Dog's Life," Pathe secured the rights to three others of Chaplin's old comedies; "Shoulder Arms," "A Day's Pleasure" and "Sunnyside."

Pathe will provide exhibitors a complete line of campaign books and accessories on the Chaplin series.

F. B. O. to Film New Series by H. C. Witwer

F. B. O. announces the purchase of the screen rights for a new series of H. C. Witwer stories now running in Cosmopolitan Magazine under the title "Bilgrim's Progress." The stories will be made as a series of two-reel productions.

The stories are concerned with the adventures of a taxi driver and are done in the slang style of "Fighting Blood," "The Telephone Girl" and "The Pacemakers," all of which were screened by F. B. O.

Edna Marion is starred in "After A Reputation," a two-reel Century Comedy released by Universal. These scenes are from the picture.

"Be Careful" is the first of the 1925-26 series of Educational-Jimmie Adams comedies. These stills are taken from the picture.

Comedies Top Pathe Releases

Mack Sennett and Hal Roach Two-Reelers
Feature Program for Week of October 11

THE Pathe program of releases for the week of October 11th is headed by comedies from the Mack Sennett and Hal Roach studios. A single reel Roach comedy, the third chapter of "Wild West," the current serial, and the usual weekly features make up the balance of the program for the week.

The Sennett two-reeler is "Over There-Abouts," with a cast headed by Billy Bevan. The Roach two-reel subject is "The Caretaker's Daughter," with Charley Chase. Katherine Grant plays opposite Chase, while in the supporting cast are William J. Kelly, Jimmy Finlayson, Jimmie Parrott and Symona Boniface. Leo McCarey directed.

Madeline Hurlock plays opposite Billy Bevan in "Over There-Abouts," a comedy of war times. In other prominent roles are Ernest Woods, and Sunshine Hart. Arthur Rossen directed.

The Hal Roach one-reeler is "Solid Ivory," a comedy of the prize ring, with Earl Mohan and Billy Engle heading the cast. Ralph Cedar directed.

The third chapter of "Wild West" is titled "The Outlaw Elephant." Jack Mulhall and Helen Ferguson are the featured leads in this serial made on the 101 Ranch of Miller Brothers. Other players appearing in this chapter are, Eddie Phillips, George Burton, Virginia Warwick, Milla Davenport and Gus Seville. Robert F. Hill directed.

Pathe Review No. 41 presents three subjects: "The City of Half-and-Half," Ronda, Spain, shown in Pathecolor; "Lively But Refined," the manufacture of rubber bands

and rubber balls; and "There She Blows!", scenes of whaling in the Antarctic.

"The Hero Wins" is the latest animated cartoon of the "Aesop's Film Fables" series, and the schedule for October 11 is completed by "Topics of the Day" and two topical issues of Pathe News.

Felix Adler to Write Fox Comedy Titles

Fox Film Corporation has signed Felix Adler, former vaudeville headliner and short story author, as chief title writer for the comedy units at the West Coast studio. Adler served in a similar capacity for several years at the Mack Sennett studios. He will write titles for the "Helen and Warren," O. Henry and "Van Bibber" comedies, as well as all the Fox Imperials.

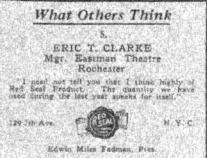

Fox Launches Comedy Program

Helen and Warren, O. Henry and Van Bibber Stories Are Ready for Production

GEORGE E. MARSHALL, supervising director-in-chief of Fox comedies has launched an extensive program of comedy productions for this season. Among the first to get under way will be Director Albert Ray who will start production on a new "Helen and Warren" picture titled, "Hold Everything," with Kathryn Perry and Hallam Cooley again playing Helen and Warren. In the supporting cast will be Sidney Bracey and Frank Rice. This will be the fourth of the series to be produced at the West Coast studios.

Director Ben Stoloff has just completed "East Side, West Side," first of a series of Irish-Jewish comedies with George Harris and Barbara Luddy in the leading roles.

Stoloff has already started preparing the script for the second of the series which will go into production shortly.

The scenario for the next O. Henry comedy is being prepared by Beatrice Van. It is titled, "Cupid A La Carte" and will be directed by Daniel Keefe. This will be the fourth of the series.

Robert Kerr has started production on "The Brain Storm," an Imperial comedy with Sid Smith and Katherine Bennett in the two principal roles. Director Lou Seiler is preparing the script for another of the Imperial comedies, as yet untitled, while a third Imperial is being prepared by Tom Buckingham, recently added to the Fox directorial staff.

Al St. John in the Educational Mermaid comedy, "Fair Warning."

Educational Announces Lineup

Lloyd Hamilton and Lupino Lane Stars of October Schedule; Will Offer Ten Comedies

EDUCATIONAL has announced a program of 10 comedies for the current month. The schedule will introduce the new series of Lloyd Hamilton two-reelers and the series in which Lupino Lane is starred. In addition to the pictures of these stars there will be three other two-reel comedies, with the customary twice-a-week releases of Kinograms, Educational's news reel.

"The Movies," the first of this season's Hamilton Comedies, will be released on Oc-

tober 4th. It shows the star as a country boy who leaves home to make his fortune in Hollywood. He endeavors to follow his mother's instructions to "keep away from the movies," yet in spite of all, he finds himself pressed into service as a "double" for the well known star, Lloyd Hamilton.

Lupino Lane will be seen in "Maid in Morocco," the first of Educational's 1925-26 series of six releases which will star him. It will be released October 11. Charles Lamont directed the first of the Lupino Lane Comedies.

Educational's October 4 releases will also introduce a new Christie comedian, Billy Dooley in "A Misfit Sailor." The role is similar to the part in which he built up a reputation in vaudeville circuits. A one-reel animated cartoon "Felix, the Cat On The Farm," completes the schedule for this week.

Coincidentally with the first Lane two-reel subjects on October 11 there will be released a one-reel Cameo Comedy "Dog Daze."

The first of the new season's two-reel Juvenile, "Baby Be Good," appears on October 18, introducing Bonnie Barrett and "Big Boy" (Malcolm Sebastian), "Felix the Cat On The Job" and "Knickknacks of Knowledge," a Lyman H. Howe's Hodge-Podge, both one-reel offerings complete this week's schedule.

A Mermaid Comedy, "Spot Light," the two-reel release for the final week of October, features Lige Conley in a satire on "back stage" life. Another Cameo one-reeler, "Scrambled Eggs," completes the comedy schedule for October 25.

Fox Will Continue Van Bibber Stories

George E. Marshall, Fox comedy supervisor plans resuming the screening of Richard Harding Davis Van Bibber stories early in December at the Fox West Coast studios. Earle Foxe and Florence Gilbert will continue in the leading roles. These two are now appearing in important roles in other Fox pictures. Foxe is playing in "Wages for Wives" and Miss Gilbert is appearing in her second leading role opposite Buck Jones in "The Desert Price."

Action stills from Universal's "The Great Circus Mystery."

Resume of Current News Weeklies

KINOGRAMS NO. 5121; Washington—French debt mission arrives in nation's capital to discuss payment of $4,211,000,000 debt; Schwerin, Germany—President von Hindenburg appears in full army uniform to review troops; Speonk, N. Y.—Largest duck farm in the world raises 120,000 birds for holiday trade; Gilboa, N. Y.—New reservoir to supply New York city with water will obliterate historic town; Paris—KINOGRAMS discovers a "lost" African village on the Seine; Chicago—Pick of professional golfers strive for title in championship tournament; Amherst, Mass.—Amherst sophomore class, of which John Coolidge, the President's son is a member, engage freshmen in college scrap on registration day; Pago Pago—Samoans entertain U. S. fleet officers.

KINOGRAMS NO. 5122; Off Block Island—Rescue ships and divers strive to save S-51 crew from ocean's bottom; Chicago—Walter Hagen beats Bill Mehlhorn in finals for professional golf championship; Washington—President Coolidge joins the Washington Baseball club, world's champions, to have his picture taken; San Francisco—Coast thousands turn out to greet Commander Rodgers and crew of P.N. 9 No. 1 upon their return from Hawaii; Paris—Four hundred thousand francs go up in elaborate demonstration of fireworks; Fairmount Park, Ill.—Crowds brave rain to witness return of racing to St. Louis district after lapse of twenty years; Philadelphia—Forty-three-year-old excursion steamer is consigned to the flames; New York—George Chapman wins motor paced bicycle title for sixth year in succession while crowd of 20,000 looks on; Atlantic City—Shore crowds see Shriners in march (Philadelphia only); Bloomington, Ill.—New training tricks for Indiana football candidates (San Francisco, Chicago and Indianapolis only).

PATHE NEWS NO. 79; Oyster Bay, N. Y.—U. S. captures 6 meter yacht series in international match; Arica, Chile—Pershing directs Tacna-Arica plebescite; Scott Field, Ill.—Prepare Army's new dirigible; Pendleton, Ore.—"Wild West" color abounds at big round-up; Auckland, New Zealand—American sailors in gala farewell parade; N. Y. City—Envoys arrive to settle French debt to U. S.; Honolulu,

Hawaii—Pay honors to Pacific flight heroes; St. Paul, Minn. (Minneapolis only)—Girl catches baseball dropped from 257-foot tower; Arvada, Colo. (Denver only)—Catholics march in first pilgrimage to Shrine of St. Anne; Dallas, Tex. (Dallas only)—Forth Worth wins sixth straight pennant in Texas League; Springfield, Mass. (Boston only)—Maine Building dedicated.

PATHE NEWS NO. 80; Olympia Fields, Ill.—Walter Hagen again wins national professional golf title; Chicago, Ill.—Mid-West Democrats hail Gov. Smith; Philadelphia, Pa.—Forty thousand football fans see Penn's eleven defeat Ursinus; Osaka, Japan—Japan's Venice celebrated summer boat festival; San Francisco, Cal.—Hawaii fliers back in U. S.; Riff War Zone—Spain joins France in united drive against Moors; Off Block Island, R. I.—U. S. submarine S-51 sunk in collision with steamer City of Rome.

FOX NEWS VOL 6, NO. 104; Caillaux comes to U. S. to settle French debt; Rome, Italy—The war veterans of ten allied nations are greeted by Premier Mussolini; Springfield, Mass.—Throngs attend Eastern States Exposition; Yalesville, Conn.—Farm animals form their own League of Nations; Dublin, N. H.—A camera interview with Charles MacVeagh, new Ambassador to Japan; Mullens, W. Va.—World's largest electric locomotive is tested for power; Chicago, Ill.—Autoists compete for the 1925 speed title of the U. S.; Montana—Vast sheep herds come down from the mountains; Broadway enters upon Fall theatre season; Pendleton, Ore.—Men master mustangs in thrilling contest of skill.

INTERNATIONAL NEWS NO. 80; Along the Whyngapoo River, China—Chinese junks race to supply Shanghai as boycott ends; Mecklenburg, Germany—von Hindenburg dons war uniform to review army; N. Y. City—French Finance Committee arrives to arrange payments to U. S.; Little Rock, Ark.—Sam S. Sloan, state treasurer, without use of hands signs hundreds of warrants; Miami Beach, Fla.—Jackie Ott, champion baby diver, tries a new stunt; Pago-Pago, Samoa—Samoan festival honors visit of battle fleet; Los Angeles, Cal. (Los Angeles only)—S. C. students begin

new term with hard work; Pendleton, Ore.—Girl riders rival cowboys in exhibition of horsemanship at round-up; Washington, D. C.—Fight for independent air force stirs nation.

INTERNATIONAL NEWS NO. 81; Homewood, Ill.—Walter Hagen retains professional golf title of U. S.; Roosevelt Field, L. I. (N. Y. City only)—Newsreel daredevil rides on wing of sky express; Hollywood, Cal.—Unique banquet for animal actors only; Notre Dame, Ind. (Indianapolis only)—Notre Dame opens football season with smashing victory; Underwood, Wash.—Salmon begin annual uphill battle to reach spawning grounds; Pewsey, England—Old-time town-crier has his day in unique tournament; Frisco, Cal.—Rescued Pacific flyers arrive home; Worely, Tenn. (New Orleans and Memphis only)—Disastrous collision between express trains; Near Kent, Wash. (Portland and Seattle only)—Interurban trains meet head-on in fog; Washington, D. C. (Washington only)—Pres. Coolidge congratulates Senators on winning second pennant; Southend, England—Strange football game on muddy river bed; Larchmont, N. Y.—Sea-sled expressers new speed commuters to work; Off Block Island, R. I.—U. S. submarine rammed and sunk with 34 men.

Pathe Makes Changes in Branch Managers

Pathe has effected a number of changes in branch manager personnel. H. L. Knappen has been appointed manager at New Orleans, succeeding P. A. Schmuck, who has been transferred to the Charlotte branch, while E. E. Heller, formerly Charlotte branch manager, has been appointed special district serial representative.

Seiler Starts Production on Fox Comedy

"All at Sea," the latest Fox Imperial comedy has gone into production on the west coast under the direction of Lew Seiler with Sid Smith and Judy King in the lead-in roles. Stanley Blystone, James Farley and Nora Cecil have the chief supporting roles.

Sees No Need to Change Name of Short Subjects

THE agitation to find a new name for Short Subjects is aimless and mere wasted effort, according to an official of the Short Subject Division of Fox Film Corporation, who points out that "the changing of the class name will not change the quality of the films themselves."

Declaring that the name Short Subjects has in no way interfered with the success of meritorious short pictures and has not proved a handicap to the "Van Bibber," "Helen and Warren," "O Henry," and other series offered by his company, the Fox official states that his organization is glad to foster "anything that will give the short subject its well earned place in the sun; that will bring in extra dollars at the box office through adequate advertising of the short screen offering." But he doubts strongly whether that end will be attained by lost motion in creating a new name for the short product, which, when found, will be little used.

It is better, he states, to devise ways to help exhibitors in getting results from this class of product than to waste time over a name that will not give them any added value.

Scenes from "Peggy's Heroes," a Davis Distributing Division release.

CLASSIFIED AD SECTION

RATES: 10 cents a word for each insertion, in advance
except Employment Wanted, on which rate is 5 cents.

CLASSIFIED SERVICE

A classified ad in MOTION PICTURE NEWS offers the
full resources and circulation of the NEWS to the advertiser at a ridiculously low figure.

Whether you want to reach executives, branch managers,
salesmen, or theatre managers, you can accomplish this
quickly and economically through the NEWS Classified
Columns.

**The Peer of All
Projection Surfaces**

The Radio Silver Screens (Guaranteed). Price 50 cents per square
foot. For Particulars and sample
apply to Manufacturer
JOHN MUNRO CRAWFORD
45 Smith St., Newburgh, N. Y.

Wanted

WANTED—Producer who
is well known and has contracts for series of pictures
wishes motion picture partner with fifty thousand dollars. Box 848, Motion Picture News, New York City.

SITUATION WANTED
—At liberty, one non-union
operator with ten years' experience. Will go anywhere
at any time. Can give good
reference if necessary. Write
care Grand Theatre, Prattville, Ala.

WANTED—To lease the
atre, equipped with stage, in
city not less than eight thousand. Would consider house
somewhat run down. Address
Box 330, Motion Picture
News, New York City.

EXPERT OPERATOR
and Electrician with 9 years'
experience in big houses;
married; wants to locate at
once. Address, Operator,
Box 282, Mason City, Iowa.

WANTED immediately in
Buffalo, a man with considerable experience in laboratory
and camera work. Applicants should state full details
as to experience, giving
names of former employers
and present occupation if not
now employed in laboratory
work. Also state salary expected. Address "Experience" c/o Motion Picture
News, New York City.

THEATRE IN TOWN OF
4,000 or better, anywhere in
North Central states, Northern Indiana preferred. Can
either give satisfactory security on lease or buy outright.
Would consider buying interest in bona-fide proposition
where owner wishes to retire.
All replies absolutely confidential. Address Box 360,
Motion Picture News, New
York City.

For Sale

FOR SALE — Pathe
Camera; good as new; with
new Bell & Howell tripod;
complete, $450; also new 200-foot Universal Camera with
7 magazines, $250, or both
outfits for $600. H. Berger,
197 Hamilton St., Dorchester,
Mass.

SALE — DeVry portable
projector, Type E, accessories. Used at home. Perfect
screen results. $170. Lumley,
1054 Ackerman Ave., Syracuse, N. Y.

FOR SALE.—Theatre
Equipment of all descriptions; Immediate shipment of
used chairs, any quantity.
Will also buy used chairs and
equipment. Theatre Seating
Company, 845 South State
Street, Chicago, Illinois.

FOR SALE.—Hope Jones
Wurlitzer type 135, excellent
condition. Will trade for
cheaper instrument with cash
difference. A bargain if you
are looking for a fine organ.
H. E. Skinner, Box 882, Ogden, Utah.

IS THERE ROOM in your organization
for a young man with initiative, energy,
and proven ability? Ten years experience
in the profession business devoted to
selling, exploitation, and publicity. Last
five years as editor of a well-known
motion picture house organ running N.
Y. N. Y. state and Pennsylvania.
Would like to associate myself with a
sound organization either in New York
or New England, where important specialization and hard work will be rewarded.
Box 340, Motion Picture News, New
York City.

*Ten selected ads on "The Freshman" (Pathe), showing
billing of this feature comedy. The various ads were
originated by these houses: Shea's theatre, Buffalo;
B. F. Keith's Mary Anderson, Louisville; Strand
theatre, Birmingham; the Howard, Atlanta; Walnut
theatre, Cincinnati; Balaban & Katz Roosevelt, Chicago, Community theatre, Miami; Royal theatre, Kansas
City; Eastman theatre, Rochester, N. Y.; and an advance ad from the Chicago Roosevelt.*

Opinions on Current Short Subjects

"The Raid"
(Universal-Mustang—Two Reels)
(Reviewed by Chester J. Smith)

THIS is a western of considerable action with Edmund Cobb in the featured role. The action is provided largely by a series of fist fights in which Cobb finds no more difficulty in conquering a half dozen tough cattle rustlers than he does in subduing one. He's a demon with his mitts, is Cobb, though his punches apparently do not carry the heft of a Mickey Walker or a Jack Dempsey. Nevertheless, when he hits them they go down and that is what wins for Cobb against such tremendous odds.

But for the athletic prowess of this hero, Jessica, daughter of the owner of the ranch and the owner of the ranch himself would be victims of these rustlers. They are both captured by them in the process of a raid and are held captive in an abandoned cabin until Cobb dashes to the rescue. He bowls the rustlers over one after another until the ranch hands, apprised of the raid by a cowardly suitor of the girl swoop down upon the place, make prisoners of the rustlers and rescue the victims.

(The Cast)

Jerry Smith, a Cowboy.....................Edmund Cobb

The Story.—Jessica, daughter of the owner of the Raymond ranch implores her father to employ Jerry Smith, cowboy, to put an end to rustling on the ranch. He acquiesces only after another raid, in which both Raymond and the daughter are abducted. Jerry gives chase and overtakes the party at an abandoned cabin. A fierce fight ensues, with Jerry getting the better of it as the other ranch hands come to the rescue. The raiders are captured and the girl admits her love for Jerry.

Summary.—A fast action Western, replete with lively fighting and some good riding. The story is of the ordinary run for these pictures and will doubtless be approved where the short western is liked.

"Just Cowboys"
(Universal-Mustang—Two Reels)
(Reviewed by Chester J. Smith)

THIS western which features Ben Corbett and Pewee Holmes is decidedly more of a comedy than the usual type of western. It is devoid of the thrills that mark these two reelers, and is somewhat of a relief, though the comedy situations could well be improved upon. The story too, is one that has often been seen in the past.

The two cowboys, fired by the ranch manager, seek a new job and encounter a moving picture outfit on location making a thriller. They think it serious action and go to the rescue when the child is abducted. They also take seriously the bank robbery until they are apprised that it is only a motion picture. And then they fall heavily for the beauteous leading lady.

With but one suit between them to do their courting, they cut the cards for that, but it is burned in the process of being gasoline-cleaned. They succeed in getting other clothes of ridiculous cut and then pursue their comedy antics in the courting of the movie queen. The action is considerably forced and strives too hard to corral laughs.

The Cast

A Cowboy.............................Ben Corbett
Another Cowboy.....................Pewee Holmes

A Mustang picture featuring Ben Corbett and Pewee Holmes.

The Story.—Two discharged cowboys seeking a new job encounter a motion picture company on location. They become alarmed when the child is abducted and give chase. They

also prevent the bank holdup, until they are apprised of the fact that it is a motion picture stunt. They are then urged to play the role of bank bandits, are slugged by real bandits, who proceed to hold up the bank in reality. Both cowboys fall in love with the leading lady and apparently are making good progress until the husband of the heroine puts in an appearance. They are paid off in motion picture money to the amusement of the entire company.

Summary.—A comedy western without the usual thrills. The story is somewhat old and hackneyed and the comedy situations not too humorous, but it may be appreciated in the neighborhood houses.

"Piping Hot"
(Universal-Century—Two Reels)
(Reviewed by Chester J. Smith)

THERE is very little in the way of slap-stick and hokum they have neglected to put in this picture. It is more a succession of alleged comedy incidents than an attempt at a story. Al Alt and the others in the cast apparently were rushed around until some one thought of something considered funny that they might turns their hands to and then the cameras started grinding.

The result is just another comedy based upon the recovery from a spree of Alt and his fat buddy. It all happens after an all night session with a bottle and with Alt going through his maneuvers in a semi-stupor and not realizing what he is doing. He jumps or falls from one incident to another without any of them having any bearing on the one immediately preceding it.

There are a few comedy situations that may bring an occasional laugh, and there is a touch of the aerial stuff that seems now to be the vogue in these short comedies. The latter angle is not well executed however and decidedly lacking in the thrill it should provide.

The Cast

A Plumber...............................Al Alt

The Story.—Al, with his buddy wakes to a semi-stupor following an all-night session with the bottle. He walks out of the window on a wire rope to a building across the way. As his buddy approaches with an undertaker Al apparently walks off the end of the building but is seen being lowered atop a safe. Alt next emerges from a barber shop, his face covered with shaving cream, and proceeds to shave himself, first walking down the street and then on the rear of a truck. Later Alt is a plumber and with his buddy all but destroys a house in an effort to repair a leaky pipe.

Summary.—This is a comedy of hokum and slapstick without the semblance of a story. It is a collection of incidents shot in a vain effort to gain laughs, only a few of which may be forthcoming.

"The Big Kick"
(Pathe—One Reel)

SOME good slam-bang slap-stick is provided by this single reeler from the Roach plant. The story is about a fight manager who has his troubles but triumphs over them when his badly beaten "champ" is saved by using a bean shooter to pepper his opponent and thus make an opening for his wide and wild swings. The bulk of the reel is devoted to a burlesque boxing bout. The bout is funnier than we thought one could be at this date. The picture was ably directed by Fred Gulol and makes a better than average single reel comedy offering. Billy Engle plays the manager and Earl Mohan and Noah Young do efficient work as the fighters.—T. C. KENNEDY.

"A Cloudy Romance"
(Fox-Imperial—Two Reels)
(Reviewed by Chester J. Smith)

THIS Fox comedy is a combination of humorous situations, slapstick and hokum and it makes for a pretty lively two-reeler that should be good for a lot of laughs. The story is smoothly told with the action brought about naturally, except for the aerial stunts which provide considerable comedy as well as an abundance of thrills. The story for a change, is an exceptionally good one with complications that are taken the fullest advantages of by the director and players.

There is rather a strain to get the players on the huge steel girders on which a lot of the action takes place, but even this is fairly cleverly done and the situation adds much to the picture.

The cast is an exceptionally good one, with Harold Austin, Connie Dawn, Harry Dunkinson and Jules Cowles in the principal roles. Austin as the young suitor gets all the comedy possible out of a humorous role, as does Connie Dawn as the prospective bride.

The Cast

A Match Mate......................Harold Austin
A June Bride......................Connie Dawn
Her August Father................Harry Dunkinson
A December Cloud...................Jules Cowles

An imperial comedy, directed by Lew Seiler.

The Story.—The young couple eloping is brought before the Judge, the girl's father, and the unwelcome suitor is sentenced to thirty days, to make way for the foppish sort of man whom the Judge selects for the daughter. The real sweetheart at the expiration of his term disguises himself as a negro maid and gets a position in the Judge's house. The butler falls in love with the distinguished hero and abducts "her." The hero returns in time to stop the girl in bridal clothes going into a hotel. He sits on the end of a girder and is hoisted to the window of the room in which the marriage ceremony is about to take place. The girder swings through the window and in turn lifts out the bride and minister. The marriage ceremony with the hero takes place on the girder in mid-air.

Synopsis.—A good, lively, well told story that is well acted and well directed. It contains a number of good comedy situations, as well as some hokum and slapstick that is entertaining. The serial thrills add to the effectiveness of the picture and it should be appreciated in almost any type of house.

Pathe Review No. 40
(One Reel)

ANN PENNINGTON'S dancing, revealed with novel photographic effects produced by the "Process Camera," lends spirit and spice to this issue of the Review. She is a splendid subject for the trick camera, which numbers among its stunts the ability to reproduce several images of the subject on the screen at the same time. The camera made five Ann Penningtons grow where one grew before, and beholding this magic we for the first time realized that this particular trait of Mr. Knechtel's machine must be listed among other virtues which were more readily apparent with its previous demonstrations. The Pennington pictures are entertaining and compelling and they are supplemented by a color feature showing some pretty scenes of Salin-LesBains, a French vacation resort, and some views of the granite quarries at Barre, Vermont.—T. C. KENNEDY.

" The Caretaker's Daughter "
(Pathe—Two Reels)
(Reviewed by Thomas C. Kennedy)

THIS new Charley Chase two-reeler from the Hal Roach studios specializes in mistaken identity, and, with two men and a woman, all with different purposes in view impersonating the caretaker, whose outstanding characteristics are a flowing moustache and a stiff leg, a skull cap and a linen duster, there is bound to be some audible response from audiences viewing "The Caretaker's Daughter" on the screens of their favorite picture theatres.

We would not say that the offering measures up to the exceptionally high standard of Chase's best work in the brief comedies. It is not so fresh as to idea nor as subtle in execution as some of his works in the past. However, there is humor in the picture and all of it reaches toward, even though it does not entirely grasp, the spontaniety and brightness which distinguishes the pictures of this unit directed by Leo McCarey.

In the cast supporting Chase are several excellent actors. Among them is George Seigman, who has scored many personal hits in big features. Here Seigman essays the role of the jealous husband, whose wife is carrying on a flirtation with a banker, the employer of our hero. The latter agrees to drive the lady to his employer's lodge in the country. He is followed by his own not too trusting wife, the banker and the other woman's husband. All are brought together at the lodge and the hero as well as the rather adventurous lady seek to escape by wearing a make-up similar to that of the faithful caretaker. The latter is much on the job and more complications arise when a prohibition agent assumes a get-up like that of the other three. This situation is worked for all it is worth at this rather late date in its career, and the result is a comedy that will score many laughs even though it does not create a sensation.

The Cast

The Clerk...........................Charley Chase
His Wife...........................Katherine Grant
The Banker.........................William J. Kelly
The Vamp...........................Symona Boniface
Her Husband........................George Seigman
Caretaker..........................Jimmie Parrott
Sleuth.............................Jimmy Finlayson

A Hal Roach comedy. Directed by Leo McCarey.

The Story.—Charley agrees to help out his employer by driving a lady, whose husband has just gotten out of jail, to a favorite rendezvous. On the way he is seen by his wife, who follows in a taxi. Also following are the adventurous lady's jealous husband and the banker. The banker invites the husband and Charley's wife to stay for luncheon, a situation which makes it difficult for Charley and the vamp to escape. They try impersonating the caretaker by wearing a make-up similar to his, but the appearance of "the caretaker" here, there and everywhere almost simultaneously results in a general investigation and an exciting chase, with the jealous husband and Charley's wife leading the pursuit.

Summary.—A rather lively comedy specializing in mistaken identity. It offers nothing very original but there is substance to the plot and the situations while the acting and direction of the piece are of the highest order.

" The Gold Trap "
(Universal-Mustang—Two Reels)
(Reviewed by Chester J. Smith)

LOVE, intrigue, action and thrills, none of them new elements in a two-reel western, mark this Mustang picture, whose story is perhaps a little better than the average. It is the old, old tale of the salted mine and the young mining engineer who saves the girl's father from investing the last of his remaining fortune in the crooked scheme.

However, the story is well told with the situations not so incredulous as in the majority of pictures of this type. There is some good lively scrapping in the picture, some daring horseback riding and the action

is continuously sustained without the story diverting from its main object. There is enough suspense to add to the effectiveness of the story which is exceptionally well directed. Fred Humes is the featured player and he gets everything possible out of a sympathetic role.

The Cast

A Mining Engineer...................Fred Humes

The Story.—Major Fairfax and his daughter, southern aristocrats attempt to retrieve a dwindled fortune in the gold hills. They are persuaded by an unscrupous promoter to invest in a worthless mine that has been salted. Jack Craig, a young mining engineer has just discovered a rich vein before saving the newcomers from death in a stage coach and falling in love with the daughter. Jack is told of the prospective investment and goes to the salted mine with the girl. They are seized by Craven's men and made prisoners. Jack escapes, rescues the girl and they proceed to the headquarters of the swindling outfit in time to prevent Major Fairfax turning over his fortune. He is then permitted to invest his money in the new Jack Craig mine presided over by his daughter and the young mining engineer.

Summary.—This western tells a better story than the usual run. It is well acted and well directed, with sufficient thrills, love and intrigue to make it interesting from start to finish. It should be well received wherever the western is appreciated.

" Peggy's Heroes "
(Davis Dist. Div.—Two Reels)
(Reviewed by Harold Flavin)

THIS is a mildly amusing two-reeler consisting of a miscellaneous assortment of "gags" with lots of hard work by the cast in an effort to coin laughs in which endeavor it partly succeeds. The production is another of the "Sheiks and Shebas" series the general theme of which seems to be a race for the hand of Peggy indulged in by various types of youngsters, stout, thin, juvenile Harold Lloyds and cake-eaters.

This particular number of the series revolves around the efforts made by Cudgy and Specks, two of Peggy's boy friends, to curry favor with her by taking her gouty dad to the beach for a day but their clumsiness only increases the old gentleman's irritableness and at the same time provides a few chuckles for the spectators. The latter portion of the chase concerns itself with a conglomeration of mishaps which occur at a party when a number of burglars break in and a general chase ensues which results in a complete route of the thieves due purely to dumb luck on the part of the "heroes."

This subject should find favor with the patrons of the smaller houses.

A McKnight-Womack production. Story by King Benedict. Titles by Pinto Colvig.

The Story.—Cudgy and Specks visit Peggy and, in an attempt to gain her favor, volunteer to take her father, who is troubled with gout, to the beach for a day's outing. They succeed in balling things up to such an extent that the party returns from the beach. That evening during the peaceful progress of a party a gang of thieves gain entrance to the house and succeed in demoralizing both the people and the furniture until aided by Peggy's heroes.

Summary.—A fairly entertaining two-reeler with a number of funny gags which should cause laughs in houses where physical mishaps to the players get a mirthful response from the audience. The titles are fair and it has been given a good production. The action moves at a fast pace.

" In Deep "
(Educational-Cameo—One Reel)

THIS is the story of the henpecked husband, whose wife goes to the country and who determines to let no grass grow under his feet while she is away. As a consequence he brings a lot of trouble upon himself and

his boy friend. They are arrested for speeding and as an excuse offer a sick wife and child.

The cop is suspicious and makes them display the wife and child. A young lady friend is inducted to serve as the wife and a monkey as the child. At about the time the cop is satisfied everything is all right the irate wife unexpectedly returns and the complications arise. The cop overhears the retelling of the ruse and the whole gang are rustled off to the station house. Cliff Bowes, George Davis, Blanche Payson and Helen Foster make up the cast in this comedy which is well above the average.—CHESTER J. SMITH.

" By the Sea "
(Universal-Bulls Eye—One Reel)

THE rotund comedian Charles Puffy is featured in this one-reeler, which provides him the best vehicle he has had in the series to date. Puffy, posing as a sheik is in reality a hod carrier. He has a successful flirtation with Betty Burton until the latter's real lover takes a hand. To escape the latter's vengeance, the girl plunges from a pier at the seashore and Puffy dives to the rescue. The inexperienced life savers attempt their rescue by a crane that has a happy faculty of going amiss just as the pair reach the level of the pier. They are finally rescued by a passing racing launch. There is a lot of good comedy in this one, which should win many admirers for Puffy.—CHESTER J. SMITH.

Pathe Review No. 41
(One Reel)

A TRIO of interesting subjects are presented in Pathe Review No. 41, which includes a color sequence devoted to picturesque spots in Ronda, Spain; a sketch of the manufacturing processes which go into the making of rubber balls, and scenes illustrating the ever-fascinating adventure of whaling. The latter contribution covers pretty completely the enterprises and experience of a ship which sets out to sea in search of the monsters of the deep. Pictures of icebergs as well as scenes showing a whale being harpooned by the modern method of a gun and its landing by the crew prove highly entertaining. It is a very good number of Pathe Review.—T. C. KENNEDY.

" The Lion and the Monkey "
(Pathe—One Reel)

PAUL TERRY, maker of the "Aesop's Film Fables," was in rare form when he produced this contribution to the series of cartoon comedies. It relates the stirring and touching tale of an appreciative monkey who comes to the rescue of the farmer who befriended him when the farmer is attacked by a lion. The grotesque movements of the characters and the cartoonist's brilliant flair in achieving ludicrous situations are here displayed for the delight of the spectator. It is an uproarious reel and its unreeling should be accompanied by gales of laughter everywhere.—T. C. KENNEDY.

" Who's Which "
(Educational-Cameo—One Reel)

PHIL DUNHAM, Helen Marlowe and James Hertz are featured in this one reeler directed by Jules White. There is some fairly good comedy in it of the slapstick variety, though the material is no newer than the story. A masquerade party provides the theme. Eleanor is the hostess and her sweetie phones her he is coming as a burglar. On the way he is apprehended by a policeman and a real burglar puts in an appearance at the party. He is welcomed as the sweetie, and the real boy interloper until he proves his identity, after which the usual comedy chase begins. The picture is a little better than the run of this type.—CHESTER J. SMITH.

Pre-release Reviews of Features

The Calgary Stampede
(Universal—5924 Feet)
(Reviewed by Harold Flavin)

FOR thrills, natural scenic beauty and, to a certain extent, the suspensive element, there haven't been many of the outdoor type of pictures made that can surpass this vehicle. Hoot Gibson is starred in this production which, in the opinion of this reviewer, is the best he has made to date.

Though having a conventional theme, the riding of the star, the authentic scenes taken at the Rodeo staged at Calgary, which are even better than that put on at Pendleton, and the good work of the entire cast more than compensate for any familiarity in story outline that might be noticed.

THEME. Melodrama of the Northwest. Rodeo champion, accused of murder of fiancee's father, is forced into hiding. Reveals himself at Rodeo when employer's ranch is at stake. Wins rodeo event, is cleared of murder charge and wins girl.

PRODUCTION HIGHLIGHTS. The murder of the fiancee's father and Gibson's subsequent ride in search of the murderer. The many thrilling scenes at the Rodeo.

EXPLOITATION ANGLES. Play up the horsemanship of the star. Advertise the fact that the Rodeo scenes are authentic. Stress the romantic element.

DRAWING POWER. Good picture for all types of houses but especially those catering to audiences with a bent for outdoor stories.

SUMMARY. An excellent production that combines beautiful outdoor scenes, superb horsemanship, good direction and character delineation.

THE CAST
Dan Malloy	Hoot Gibson
Marie LeFarge	Virginia Brown Faire
Jean LaFarge	Clark Comstock
Neenah	Ynez Seabury
Fred Burgess	Jim Corey
Callahan	Philo McCullough

Story by E. Richard Schayer and Don Lee. Directed by Herbert Blache. Photographed by Harry Neuman.

SYNOPSIS. Dan Malloy, champion Roman rider of the United States, roaming through Canada, meets and falls in love with Marie LaFarge but her father refuses to allow their marriage. Fred Burgess, poacher, just released from prison, kills Marie's father and is observed in the act by Neenah, Marie's maid, who shields him. Malloy, accused of the murder, flees and gets employment on the Bar-O ranch. Mounted police get on his trail but fail to identify him until day of Rodeo event, when Malloy, to save employer's ranch, rides in and wins Roman race. He is arrested by M. P. but saved by confession of Neenah whom Burgess has betrayed.

The Tower of Lies
(Metro-Goldwyn-Mayer—6849 Feet)
(Reviewed by L. C. Moen)

IN "The Tower of Lies" Victor Seastrom approaches more nearly to the artistic masterpieces which he produced abroad than in anything he has made here. Not that it is finer than "He Who Gets Slapped," but that it approaches his Swedish pictures more nearly in theme and mood. This is partly due, no doubt, to the fact that it is based upon Selma Lagerlof's Swedish novel "The Emperor of Portugallia," and concerns itself with Swedish peasants.

Many of the scenes of rural life have the artistic charm and force of a painting by Millet. Like "The Man with the Hoe," it presents the man who toils with his hands, living from day to day, feeling neither sorrow nor joy. To this man there comes an infant daughter, and with it a sudden interest in life. Her girlhood increases his pride in her, and finally, when she falls, his reason leaves him and he returns to their childhood game, the Emperor and Empress of Portugallia.

THEME. Intimate drama of a farmer who awakens to the beauty of life through his daughter, and who loses his reason when she goes astray. His death brings the girl back to herself, and she finds happiness with her childhood sweetheart.

PRODUCTION HIGHLIGHTS. The remarkable atmosphere and background which Seastrom has created. The vivid characterization contributed by Chaney.

EXPLOITATION ANGLES. Play up Chaney and Shearer, if you have any Scandinavian element in your community, appeal to them. Advertise along high class lines.

DRAWING POWER. High class production, appealing to intelligent audiences.

SUMMARY. A sincere and forceful story of rural life, produced and acted with feeling and skill.

THE CAST
Glory	Norma Shearer
Jan	Lon Chaney
Lars	Ian Keith
Katrina	Claire McDowell
August	William Haines
Eric	David Torrence

Adapted by Agnes Christine Johnston from the novel, "The Emperor of Portugallia" by Selma Lagerlof. Directed by Victor Seastrom. Photographed by Percy Hilburn.

SYNOPSIS. Jan, a farmer, finds an interest in life in his daughter, Glory. She goes away to earn money to meet mortgage on farm, and is seduced. When she does not return, Jan loses his reason. She returns, but villagers try to drive her away, leading to Jan's death. Girl finds happiness with childhood sweetheart.

Hoot Gibson, star of "The Calgary Stampede," a Universal picture.

Norma Shearer, who appears in "The Tower of Lies" a Metro-Goldwyn-Mayer production.

The Wrongdoers
(Astor Distributing Corp.—Six Reels)
(Reviewed by Frank Elliott)

THIS is just a fair program picture with the work of Lionel Barrymore the saving factor. Otherwise the offering recalls films of other days, being somewhat crude in direction and unconvincing in incident and characterization. The players seem to move as being guided about the scenes on strings like mannequins.

Mr. Barrymore assumes the role of a philanthropic druggist who like Robin Hood of old, heads a gang to rob from the rich to help the poor. The gang meets in a secret room, which is discovered one day by an adopted son who unable to see his dad's attitude toward life, rushes to a costume ball to foil a planned jewel robbery. He gets the jewels from dad, but is caught with them himself and arrested. Both hero and villain pass out at the end.

THEME. A melodrama of New York's lower strata life in which the career of a modern Robin Hood ends in disaster but brings happiness to others.

PRODUCTION HIGHLIGHTS. The jewel dance and robbery. The climax in which villain and hero take each other's lives. The artist's studio scenes.

EXPLOITATION ANGLES. Play up the name of Lionel Barrymore. Stage a jewel dance as a prologue patterned after the one in the picture. Tell the folks this is a Bernarr MacFadden True Story picture.

DRAWING POWER. Suitable for the smaller houses downtown, some community theatres and towns. Also O. K. for double feature programs.

SUMMARY. Just another program picture, weak in direction and story and saved only by the work and fame of Lionel Barrymore.

THE CAST
Daniel Abbott	Lionel Barrymore
Helen Warren	Anne Cornwall
Jimmy Abbott	Henry Hull
Sylvester Doane	Henry Sedley
Honora	Blanche Craig
Society woman	Flora Finch
Butler	William Calhoun
Solemn Man	Harry Lee
Crook	Tammany Young
Little Jimmy	Tom Brown

A Bernarr MacFadden "True Story" production. Directed by Hugh Dierker. Scenario by Lewis Allen Brown. Photographed by John Holbrook and Fred Chasten.

SYNOPSIS. Daniel Abbott, druggist and philanthropist, visits court with his adopted son, Jimmy Nolan. There he finds a "Mrs. Warren," charged with attempted suicide. He takes mother and baby home. Abbott is also head of a gang that steals from the rich to aid poor. They plan to rob Sylvester Doane, tenement owner, who has also been attracted to Helen Warren, now grown to beautiful girlhood. Jimmy, also now a youth, learns of his father's dual role and rushes to the Doane home to stop the robbery. He takes the gems and is himself jailed. Eventually Abbott kills Doane, but is shot himself. Jimmy and Helen are married and the identity of Mrs. Warren solved.

Lionel Barrymore, who plays the lead in "The Wrongdoers," an Astor release.

The Man on the Box
(Warner Bros.—7481 Feet)
(Reviewed by L. C. Moen)

IT seems to be the fashion these days to turn famous light farces of other days into slapstick comedies, and the result, in this case, is productive of much merriment. The ingredients are nine-tenths Syd Chaplin and one-tenth Harold McGrath, for the resemblance to the story is rather slight. The characters still bear the same names, and the hero still enters the heroine's employ as her groom, but not much else of the original plot remains.

Many of the sequences are riotously funny, some of the best being those in which Chaplin impersonates a maid. The humor is laid on with broad, sure strokes, and Chaplin's remarkable pantomimic ability is brilliantly displayed. Plenty of entertainment here for the comedy fans.

THEME. Comedy of mistaken identity in which hero, a wealthy young man, masquerades as the groom, and later the maid, of the girl he has fallen in love with, ultimately foiling the villainous spies and winning the girl.

PRODUCTION HIGHLIGHTS. Chaplin's pantomime. His impersonation of the maid. Chuck Reisner's direction and his own acting. The scenes in which Chaplin is left on the street in his pajamas.

EXPLOITATION ANGLES. Bill this as the successor to "Charley's Aunt," and tell them that Chaplin does a female impersonation which is just as funny. Play up the cast. Good chance for a street ballyhoo of a man impersonating girl and handing out heralds or cards on the picture.

DRAWING POWER. Should do well in view of past record of star, popularity of story and present taste for comedy.

SUMMARY. A comedy which is extremely funny in spots, and drags in others, but which on the whole should register well with comedy fans. Some of the gags are distinctly original and general production is satisfactory.

THE CAST
Bob Warburton	Syd Chaplin
His brother-in-law	David Butler
Betty Annesly	Alice Calhoun
Mrs. Lampton	Kathleen Calhoun
Inventor Lampton	Theodore Lorch
Bob's sister	Helene Costello
Col. Annesly	E. J. Ratcliffe
Badkoff	Charles F. Reisner
Count Karaloff	Charles Gerard
Warburton, Sr.	Henry Barrows

Adapted from the novel by Harold McGrath. Directed by Charles F. Reisner. Photographed by Nick Barrows.

SYNOPSIS. Bob Warburton is backing the invention of Lampton, which the government seeks. Lampton misunderstands Bob's attentions to his wife. Bob flees, and becomes groom of Betty, with whom he has fallen in love. Here he foils foreign spies, seeking to steal plans from Betty's father, and ultimately wins girl.

Sydney Chaplin, starred in the Warner Bros. feature comedy, "The Man on the Box."

East Lynne

(Emmett Flynn Production-Fox—Nine Reels)
(Reviewed by Frank Elliott)

ONCE again this famous old melodrama comes to the shadow stage. This time it is Emmett Flynn who has transferred the half-century old love story to the screen. He has achieved a creditable production from an acting viewpoint, but has taken entirely too much footage to tell the story and has given the picture a mounting that smacks too much of artificiality.

However, there are many fine dramatic moments and a climax that will move most audiences to tears. The scene in which Lady Isabel dies in her husband's arms after she has nursed her child back from death's door to health is sure to strum on the heart strings. The biggest selling point is the cast. It is an all-star one in the true sense of the word.

THEME. A melodrama dealing with the eternal triangle in English life of yesteryear.

PRODUCTION HIGHLIGHTS. The murder of Mr. Hallijohn by Levison. The scene in which Lady Isabel leaves for France with Levison. The train wreck. The scene in which Levison returns to woo Afy Hallijohn.

EXPLOITATION ANGLES. Go after the women folks by playing up the love story. Plaster the town with the title. Boost the names of the all-star cast.

DRAWING POWER. The strong cast, the fame of the director and the popularity of the story should make this a drawing card in most houses, although especially suited for the towns.

SUMMARY. A well acted version of the noted stage meller laid against an artificial background, which is much too long, but which has a goodly quota of dramatic incident, a fine climax and some comedy. Will appeal to women everywhere.

THE CAST

Lady Isabel	Alma Rubens
Archibald Carlyle	Edmund Lowe
Sir Francis Levison	Lou Tellegen
Chief Justice Hare	Frank Keenan
Barbara Hare	Marjorie Daw
Richard Hare	Leslie Fenton
Afy Hallijohn	Belle Bennett
Mr. Hallijohn	Paul Panzer
Mrs. Hare	Lydia Knott

Based on the play by Mrs. Henry Wood. Directed by Emmett Flynn. Scenario by Lenore J. Coffee.

SYNOPSIS. Left alone by the death of Lord Mount Severn, Lady Isabel is wooed and wed by Archibald Carlyle, new owner of East Lynne. Seeking the aid of Carlyle in behalf of her brother, charged with murder, Barbara Hare arranges a rendezvous with Carlyle. Levison, a ne'er-do-well, persuades Isabel the meeting is one of many. Isabel, believing there is an affair on, leaves her husband and children, and goes to France with Levison. Injured in a wreck, Isabel recovers, assumes another name, returns to East Lynne and nurses her child back to health. Later she dies in her husband's arms. Carlyle weds Barbara. Levison is convicted of the murder of which Barbara's brother had been charged.

Alma Rubens, who has an important role in the Wm. Fox picture, "East Lynne."

Thunder Mountain

(Fox—Eight Reels)
(Reviewed by Chester J. Smith)

"THUNDER MOUNTAIN" has perhaps gained in effectiveness in its transition from John Golden's "Howdy Folks" of the legitimate stage. Some of its bigger dramatic moments lend themselves more readily and with more telling effect on the screen than on the speaking stage.

The story is undoubtedly a strong one and one that holds the interest throughout despite the fact that the continuity is rather jumpy in spots. It is well produced and well acted by a cast headed by Madge Bellamy, Alec Francis, Leslie Fenton and Zasu Pitts.

THEME. A melodrama of the Kentucky Hills, in which the hero, influenced by the visiting preacher, attempts through education to put an end to lawlessness, only to himself be accused of murder and threatened with hanging, which is avoided with the aid of the heroine.

PRODUCTION HIGHLIGHTS. The blowing up of the mountain side as a warning from above that an unjustifiable crime is to be committed in the hanging of the hero.

EXPLOITATION ANGLES. Playing up the feud angle always makes for interest at the box office. You can offer them a thrill in the blowing up of the mountain side.

DRAWING POWER. The story is of a type that should appeal strongly to houses of all classes. With its diversified angles there should be something to interest all.

SUMMARY. This is a grim story of the Kentucky Hills, with thrills, suspense and love. It has been given a good production and should interest picture goers of all classes.

THE CAST

Azalea	Madge Bellamy
Sam Martin	Leslie Fenton
Preacher	Alec B. Francis
Morgan	Paul Panzer
Joe Givens	Arthur Houseman
Mandy Coulter	Zasu Pitts
Ma MacBirney	Emily Fitzroy
Pa MacBirney	Dan Mason
Jeff Coulter	Otis Harlan
Mrs. Coulter	Natalie Warfield

SYNOPSIS. Sam Martin, befriended by the preacher, leaves for three years to acquire an education. He returns to the mountains determined to build a school and instruct his townsfolk in the rudiments of learning. He goes to Simon Pace the miserly money lender for funds, but is turned down. Azalea, a former circus queen deserts the show in the mountain town, falls in love with Sam and attempts to get the necessary funds for him from the miser. The latter is slain following a visit of the pair, and suspicion is turned upon Sam. Azalea rushes to the preacher for aid as the townsfolk proceed to the mountain side for the purpose of executing the hero. The preacher plants dynamite in the mountain side and eventually dynamites it as a sign of God's wrath against the action about to be taken. The real murderer of the money lender, in his fear, acknowledges his guilt. Sam builds his school and marries Azalea.

Madge Bellamy, who appears in "Thunder Mountain," a Wm. Fox production.

The Plastic Age
(Schulberg—6488 Feet)
(Reviewed by Thomas C. Kennedy)

THIS is a "Jazz" story with a collegiate background, the central character being a country youth who goes away to college to make good in studies and athletics and then nearly comes a cropper through associations with the riotous and reckless youngsters he finds there. The work is based on a novel of the same title by Percy Marks and has been filmed with a view to the sprightliness of photoplay scenes depicting petting parties, dances at which there is plenty of stimulating punch, etc., and so forth. The interest which screen patrons have evinced in previous plays of this type no doubt will work in favor of "The Plastic Age," and as there is a general triumph of virtue over its opposite as depicted here, there is reason to suppose that this offering will succeed at the box office.

THEME. Modern drama of youth, in which a young man takes up dissipation at college but learns in time that scholarly and athletic attainments are more worth while.

PRODUCTION HIGHLIGHTS. The scenes on the football field where hero makes good. The scene in which flapper tells hero she and he must reform.

EXPLOITATION ANGLES. A tieup with book dealers offers the best exploitation bet. Stress football sequence as of great timely interest and the fact that story concerns the adventures of a youth at college.

DRAWING POWER. Designed for general audiences and capable of gaining the interest of a big majority of the screen patrons.

SUMMARY. A drama of youth, zestful material in that regard and cut to a pattern which has succeeded on the screen of late. It is somewhat conventional dramatic fare.

THE CAST
Cynthia Day	Clara Bow
Hugh Carver	Donald Keith
Mrs. Carver	Mary Alden
Henry Carver	Henry B. Walthall
Carl Peters	Gilbert Roland
Norrie Parks	J. Gordon Edwards, Jr.
Merton Billings	Felix Valle
Coach Henry	David Butler

Author, Percy Marks. Scenario by Eve Unsell and Frederica Sagor. Directed by Wesley Ruggles.

SYNOPSIS. Hugh Carver, a promising athlete, takes up with a fast set at college. One of his companions is Cynthia Day, a young and rather too carefree girl. Carver, out of condition, loses a race at the big meet, an event which brings the wrath of his father and sobers the youth. With Cynthia's assistance, Hugh settles down to work and as a result makes good in his studies and on the football gridiron as well. His reward is the love which Cynthia offers and his own and her triumph over the frivolity which threatened their happiness.

Donald Keith featured in "The Plastic Age," released by B. P. Schulberg.

The Plastic Age (Schulberg)
PRESS NOTICE

THE screen version of "The Plastic Age," Percy Marks' tremendously popular novel of college life, will be presented at the .... on .... Clara Bow, the screen's most popular interpreter of "flapper roles" appears as Cynthia Day, a young beauty whose carefree attitude toward life a l m o s t wrecks the career of Hugh Carver at college and threatens her own happiness.

Donald Keith appears as Hugh Carver and other screen celebrities appearing in principal roles are Henry B. Walthall, Mary Alden, David Butler, Gilbert Roland, J. Gordon Edwards, Jr., and Felix Valle.

CATCH LINES
Hugh Carver went to college to make good as a scholar and an athlete—he did ultimately, but not until he defeated himself by joining in the dissipations of a jazzy young set whose occupations were petting parties and dances where there was gaiety and well-filled punch bowls.

What Fools Men
(George Archainbaud-First Nat'l—Eight Reels)
(Reviewed by Frank Elliott)

THE usual excellent characterization contributed by Lewis Stone is the feature of this picture which is entirely too long for the material at hand and which in spots is weighted down with exaggerated situations and one sequence showing life in a ne'er-do-well society set which tends to cheapen the otherwise dignified atmosphere. The title seeks to set forth that many men are fools because they are unable to distinguish the sham from the real in other men and to understand workings of the mind of a modern flapper.

Mr. Stone dominates the action throughout and he is given some good support. There are some tense scenes between Stone and Miss Mason as the former seeks to curb the latter's unruly ways. The picture is artistically mounted.

THEME. A drama of frenzied finance and society sham in which an inventor is ruined by crooked bankers and fails in his efforts to "mother" a wild daughter.

PRODUCTION HIGHLIGHTS. The scene in which Greer reprimands Williamson's wife for her unwelcome advances during the storm. The return of Greer to find his daughter arriving home with her chauffeur.

EXPLOITATION ANGLES. The title. The stars. Bookstore tie-up on the Webster novel. Put man on street dressed in jester's costume with appropriate advertising. Photos of Miss Mason as theme of fashion window.

DRAWING POWER. Popularity of Lewis Stone and the strong supporting cast should make this a welcome attraction in any house. With a little exploitation should do business.

SUMMARY. A fairly entertaining picture which is saved by the excellence of the acting, the artistic mounting and the dramatic incident. Too long, however, and would be improved by careful cutting.

THE CAST
Joseph Greer	Lewis Stone
Beatrice	Shirley Mason
Jennie McArthur	Barbara Bedford
Lancing Ware	John Patrick
John Williamson	David Torrence

Adapted from Henry Kitchell Webster's novel, "Joseph Greer and His Daughter." Directed by George Archainbaud. Editorial Director, June Mathis. Photographed by Norbert Brodin.

SYNOPSIS. Joseph Greer agrees to have a group of financiers market linen made by his new process, knowing that the methods of the group are questionable. He hopes his new connection will aid his daughter climb the social ladder. Vi Williamson, wife of head of group financing him, makes advances to Greer. He reprimands her. Wife twists facts of incident, so that husband brings about Greer's ruin. His daughter elopes with his chauffeur and he is injured in an auto accident. He takes to drink. He learns true character of chauffeur, daughter returns and so does his secretary, Jennie. He starts to fight the game anew.

Lewis Stone, prominent in the cast of First National's "What Fools Men."

What Fools Men (1st Nat'l)
PRESS NOTICE

LEWIS STONE, one of the most popular stars now appearing on the silver sheet, comes to the .... theatre on .... in "What Fools Men," adapted from Henry Kitchell Webster's novel, "Joseph Greer and His Daughter." The plot has to do with an inventor who, hoping to aid his daughter climb the ladder to association with the "400," sells his new linen making process to a gang of crooked financiers. The gang brings about his ruin and his daughter elopes with a chauffeur, so that he retires to a poor section of the city and takes to drink. The Chauffeur proves true blue, however, and offers the inventor laboratory space in his home and inspires him to start the fight again.

CATCH LINES
A photoplay for men who think they know their women—and for women who learn their men. The latest tips for ladies on what to do in love.

Regional News from Correspondents

AN important reorganization of managers in Winnipeg, Manitoba, has been effected by H. M. Thomas, Winnipeg, Western Division manager of Famous Players Canadian Corp., Toronto. L. Charles Straw has been appointed manager of the Metropolitan Theatre in succession to H. A. Bishop and the latter has been made assistant to Mr. Thomas in the general supervision of theatres. E. A. Retallick of Winnipeg has been appointed house manager of the Capitol Theatre, Winnipeg, over which Mr. Thomas has general personal direction.

Mr. Straw is a former Winnipeg exhibitor but has had charge of the Strand Theatre at Brandon, Manitoba, where he scored signal triumphs in popularizing that

Canada

house. Mr. Bishop's promotion is of wide interest as he is well-known in theatrical circles of Winnipeg, Calgary and other Western centers and also of Los Angeles where his family resides.

Mr. Retallick has been the dramatic editor of the Winnipeg Tribune for the past five years and has handled the publicity for the Capitol Theatre for a considerable period.

The Bijou Theatre has become one of the recognized first run theatres of Winnipeg, Manitoba, this development having taken place along with other important local happenings. Announcement is made by Manager Levy that the Bijou will be the "outlet" in the Manitoba Capital for all releases of the Film Booking Offices and will specialize in independent bookings.

Recently Universal Films acquired the leases of three important Winnipeg theatres, the Lyceum, Starland and College

Theatres, appointing Charles A. Meade general manager of the group, a specialty to be made of Universal attractions. Famous Players have two large theatres in Winnipeg, the Capitol and the Metropolitan.

Famous Players Canadian Corp. has no immediate use for the large central site which it acquired several years ago in Ottawa, Ontario, at a cost of several hundred thousand dollars, judging by a notice which has been erected on the location offering the property on a rental basis for a parking station, gasoline service station or other purposes. Famous Players has a fine moving picture house in Ottawa, the Regent, which is managed by Leonard Bishop.

Albany

ANOTHER shift took place along Film Row during the past week, when Bert Gibbons, one time manager for Vitagraph here, and later transferred to Canada, only to return to Albany, to become associated with Universal, succeeded Bob Wagner, of Little Falls, who has been looking after Dependable's interests in this section since the theatre which he managed in Little Falls, was taken over by the Schines. Henry Randall, former manager for Dependable in this section, but who is now residing in Miami, where it is said he has massed a considerable fortune, was in town during the week, on his way to Montreal, with his bride of a few days. Mr. Randall was married in New York City a week ago. He received a warm welcome in Albany, although admitting that there were many strange faces along The Row.

Mike Freedman, who was associated with Mr. Shirley in Schenectady, is reported about to reopen the Rialto in that city, and to operate it along with the Woodlawn.

William Smalley, of Cooperstown, who already operates a dozen or more motion picture theatres in this part of the state, has just bought the site for another which he will erect in Stamford next spring. Mr. Smalley is already running a theatre in Stamford, but it is located on the second story of a business block and not very well adapted for theatrical purposes. Mr. Smalley has been running a Fashion Show along with pictures in St. Johnsville, Walton and Fort Plain, drawing immense crowds in each place. "Al" Bothner, who has been associated with Mr. Smalley for the past year or so, has returned to Mohawk and will get busy booking amateurs over the Smalley circuit for the fall and winter months.

Rae Candee, of Utica, well known in Albany, and associated with Nate Robbins, is looking forward anxiously for the opening of the hunting season. It's a safe bet that Mr. Candee will bring

back a deer this fall as he never failed in this respect.

Alex Weismann, who is associated with the Metro-Goldwyn office here, is bemoaning the theft of his car last week. It bears license 6L 8-784.

William Benton, of Saratoga Springs is rushing matters in Mechanicville these days, where he is building a new theatre which was originally scheduled to open on October 12. Various matters, however, have delayed things so that the opening is now set for October 19. All the exchange managers and exhibitors in this part of the state are to be invited by Mr. Benton and will be on hand.

Although Lew Fischer opened his remodeled theatre at Fort Edward last week, in what he terms an informal opening, rather than wait for additional seats to replace those broken in shipment, the real opening to occur in the near future.

Frank Pelon, a well known exhibitor of Indian Lake, managed to save his new Studebaker car last week, when it caught fire as he was driving between North Creek and Indian Lake. It so happened that Mr. Pelon was traveling a rather sandy road which enabled him to scoop up a few handsful of sand and put out the blaze.

William Tweedy, of Mechanicville, was along Film Row during the week, having recovered from an unusually severe attack of hay fever.

Charles Walder, former manager of the Fox exchange in Albany, but who resigned to engage in the real estate business in Miami, arrived back in town from Florida last week, but plans to return south in about four weeks.

Ben Apple, an exhibitor in Troy, who went to Florida a month or so ago, also returned home last week and like Mr. Walder, expects to wing his way southward in the near future.

The Arbitration Board, which has been meeting but once a month during the summer, is now back on its schedule of two meetings a month.

Clarence Gardner has discontinued his Wednesday matinees at the Pine Hills theatre in Albany, now that school has reopened. Mr. Gardner has a balcony in his theatre which enables male patrons to enjoy their cigars along with the pictures.

Leon Medem, manager for Pathe in Albany, is back home from a vacation, spent in Edgemere, L. I. The vacation, however, cost Mr. Medem his wrist watch which was lost while he was in bathing. He has replaced it with a brand new one.

R. J. Meigs and Jack Coudert, connected with the New York office of Pathe, were in town during the week.

Mr. and Mrs. John Moran, of Coxsackie, who run the Opera House there, were also along Film Row during the week.

The week also brought to town Walter Hays, of Buffalo, former president of the New York State M. P. T. O., and one of the owners of the Strand group of houses in this city and Troy. Mr. Hays reported business as being good throughout the territory. The Regent in Albany, which was recently leased by Mr. Hays and his associates, reopened on Thursday under the management of Herman Vineberg. The theatre presents a very attractive appearance. W. W. Farley, of Albany, owner of houses in Schenectady and Yonkers, was in Binghamton during the week on a business trip.

Louis Scott, an exhibitor in Cazenovia, who also is manager of a canning works in that village, has just about completed his labors with the canning factory and will now devote most of his time to furnishing the villagers with the best pictures obtainable.

Between the Holy Rollers, holding an outdoor meeting on Tuesday nights, and the Socialists on Friday nights, each directly across from the Lincoln theatre in Troy, Benjamin Stern, manager of the house, is well nigh frantic.

Zeb, handyman at the Troy theatre, is declared to have carried off eating honors at a clam steam held by employees of the Troy, and Mark Strand theatres, a week ago. Walter Roberts, manager of the Troy theatre, declares that Zeb consumed four chickens and fifty clams and then asked for more. Incidentally, the Troy theatre trimmed the Mark Strand at a baseball game by a score of 25 to 8.

Louis Saperstein, was named as manager of the Palace theatre in Troy, last week. His brother, Joe Sapterstein, manages Harmanus Bleecker Hall in Albany.

Patrons of motion picture theatres in Troy, appear to be superstitious when it comes to two dollar bills, invariably tendering such when they have one in their possession, for their tickets. The other night, Mrs. Walter Roberts, cashier at the Troy theatre, took in eighty-six in an hour.

Barcli theatre, in Schenectady, one of the Farley group of houses, and which has been closed for several months, has reopened, giving Mr. Farley control of the down town situation. Orchestras have been installed at the State and Strand theatres in Schenectady, also owned and operated by Mr. Farley.

Harold Filkins, a local F.B.O. salesman, is passing around the cigars these days as he announces that it was a nine pound boy.

Ben Young, is busy these days in Ilion, rushing matters in the construction of a new theatre that will be in readiness to open about December 1.

Another exhibitor in that section of the state, W. H. Linton, is also starting to rebuild in Utica.

The many friends of George Goldberg, a salesman in the local Producers Distributing Company office, will be pleased to know that the operation which he underwent last week at an Albany hospital, was successful, and that he will up and around within a couple of weeks.

Southeast

OSCAR OLDKNOW, President, and Hank Hearne, General Manager, of the Liberty Film Exchanges, have been visiting in Charlotte the past week to supervise the opening of their exchange on September 14th. Rufus Davis will manage the branch and the Metro-Goldwyn office will handle the physical distribution.

Warner's Broadway, of Charlotte, N. C., opened with vaudeville on the 21st of September, 5 acts and feature pictures. While this theatre is not advertising the vaudeville at Keith they are buying through Jules Delmare, and have published a facsimile letter from the Keith Office in New York as to their bill.

The New Municipal theatre at Durham, N. C., which seats 1800 and is fully equipped for road shows and pictures, has been completed and on September 21st they are opening the bids which they

have asked for and will lease the theatre through this system.

The Garden Theatre, Hendersonville, N. C., which has been running stock all summer has closed.

A. L. Cook, of the Muzu Theatre, Maiden, N. C., was in Charlotte the past week setting in service for the Fall and Winter.

Otto Haas, owner of the Ottoway Theatre, Charlotte, who has been abroad for several months, sailed for home from Cherbourg, on the steamer Aquitania on the 18th of September.

The Moving Picture Fraternity of Charlotte were very much elated when they received the information that James Walker had won the democratic nomination of New York City with such a decisive victory. "Jim" as he was known to the Moving Picture Fraternity of Charlotte, was very well liked here and several years

ago was a Charlotte visitor to attend a moving picture exposition. He made several addresses during his visit and made innumerable friends who are all well pleased that he won the nomination.

The Star Theatre, York, S. C., was destroyed by fire Friday night. J. G. Wray, Manager and Owner, stated that the fire originated in the adjoining building. It was a total loss without any insurance but Mr. Wray was fortunate in saving the moving picture film.

T. B. Smith, Gem Theatre, Clinton, N. C., was a Charlotte visitor the past week. We understand Mr. Smith is one of the bidders for the New Municipal Theatre at Durham.

James Estridge and wife, of Gastonia, are spending a couple of weeks vacation at the Hodgwell, Hendersonville, N. C. Mr. Estridge is Manager and Owner of

the Gastonia Theatre, Gastonia, N. C.

Jake Wells who owns the Rex and Queen Theatres, Hendersonville, N. C., has transferred Ben Caplon from his Richmond circuit to Hendersonville to manage these theatres. Mr. Caplon is an old timer and there is no question as to his succeeding with these houses.

W. L. Sherrill, of the Strand Theatre, Canton, N. C., was a Charlotte visitor the past week and states that business is gradually getting better and he is looking forward to a good season.

C. L. "Hank" Henry, former salesman of F. B. O., has resigned from this company to take charge of the Marvin-Wise Estate Theatre circuit of six houses, and left for Birmingham to assume his new duties. Hank is well liked by the Film Fraternity and they indeed regretted to see him leave this section.

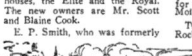

Des Moines

L. H. KOHLER, exhibitor of Pella, Iowa, has sold his house, the West End Theatre, to T. E. VanDyke. Another theatre to change hands last week is the Princess Theatre at Eagle Grove which is now under the management of Leland Hanson. The Feldhans Theatre at Galva was sold by the Feldhans Brothers to the Loeb Motor Company. Mr. Eichor is now owner of the theatre at Minlow and L. E. Carnes has bought the Sun Theatre at Sioux City from Homer Gill. J. W. Kelley, representing the American Legion at Elkorn, sold the Princess Theatre there to C. Jones, Mrs. W. H. Hoffman at Le Mars, Iowa has sold her two houses, the Elite and the Royal. The new owners are Mr. Scott and Blaine Cook.

E. P. Smith, who was formerly

in partnership with W. H. Dewey at the Strand and Lincoln at Sheraton, recently bought the Newtonia. Mr. Dewey has charge of the Lincoln and the Strand. He has secured his nephew, Boyd Haskins, who has been associated with Fred F. Harvey Company of Kansas City, to manage the two theatres for him. Mr. Haskins used to be in the picture game some years ago and this is his first return to the theatre business.

The Des Moines office of Universal, announces Manny Gottlieb, manager, won fourth place in the national contest for the Laemmle Trophy Cup.

C. L. Knipe, accessory sales representative of the western division for Universal, is visiting Des Moines.

The Gem Theatre at Little Rock, Iowa, which had been

closed for some time; was reopened last week.

Theatre men of western Iowa met with exhibitors of Nebraska on September 22 and 23 at the Hotel Lloyd for the discussion of some matters important to theatre owners. Election of officers for the new year was held.

De Moines is one of the places which has been discussed as a possible location of a motion picture house to be built by Alexander Pantages of the Pantages vaudeville circuit.

The Casino Theatre, owned by Abe Frankel who also has charge of Riverview Amusement Park, has added several acts of vaudeville to the motion picture bill. The Casino is one of the oldest theatres in Des Moines and has always played motion pictures before. During the recent controversy between the union musi-

cians and stage hands and the theatre men, the Casino was asked to increase the number of their orchestra from two to three. This request was complied with.

Bean and Prusha of the Paramount Theatre at Winterset and Ted Bryant of the Gem Theatre at Oelwein were in Des Moines on business. Mr. Bryant says that business in Oelwein is fine.

Leo Moore of the Majestic Theatre, at Centreville made a trip to Kansas City.

The Des Moines Film Board of Trade has had little to do for the past few months. The cases which have come up for arbitration have been settled without the board passing upon them. Mrs. Mary Benjamin, secretary and treasurer of the Film Board, reports an amiable time being had by all.

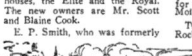

Baltimore

THE fall season of the Apollo Theatre, 1500 Harford avenue, managed by John G. Volz, began on Monday, September 28, with the opening of the balcony in which all the seats have been renovated and the starting of the new schedule of opening daily at 2 P. M., with the performances continuous until 11 P. M. The ushers also have been dressed in new uniforms.

This is a residential house with a seating capacity of 1200 persons. The distribution of about 200 window cards has been started and Mr. Volz is trying now to get several 24-sheet stands in the neighborhood.

The exterior of the Aurora Theatre, 7 East North avenue, operated by Cook Brothers and managed by Arthur B. Price, has been given a new coat of grey paint;

a new electric sign and interchangeable electric board has been installed by the Flexiume Sales Company of Maryland. George C. Easter, who formerly operated a film exchange here and was associated with the Jans Pictures Company, installed the electric signs.

George W. Jacobs, manager of the Goldfield Theatre, 913 Warner street, is a proud and happy papa for he was presented with a ten pound baby girl by his wife recently. Both mother and daughter are getting along fine at the Hebrew Hospital.

H. M. Messiter, manager of the Parkway Theatre, spent several days during the week beginning Monday September 21 in New York.

Levinia and Olinda, the two little daughters of William M. Whitehurst, assistant to Dr. J. H.

Whitehurst, president of the Whitehurst Combined Theatrical Interests, underwent throat operations on Tuesday, September 22.

A number of the pupils of the dancing school of Professor Cockey, give exhibition dances at the Poplar Theatre, 611 Poplar Grove street, every Tuesday evening. George F. Burgan, manager, says it appeals to the patrons. The Poplar is a residential house.

T. M. Cushing (T. M. C.) reviewer of the Morning Sun of Baltimore, is also busy with his activities for the Play-Arts Guild, here. A cozy little theatre with a seating capacity of 150 persons is being made ready at Twentysecond and Morton streets and the season for little plays will begin in November.

The electric fixtures of The

Tent, a cabaret over the Academy of Music here, which recently opened to the public, were installed by J. F. Dusman, consulting engineer, who is well known to the moving picture theatre owners and managers of Baltimore for his work on the electrical equipment of various film playhouses.

The Century Roof, over the Century Theatre, will reopen to the public Saturday night, October 3.

The Kentucky Theatre, Lexington, Ky., managed by Earl Payne was damaged by fire which also badly damaged the building next to it, it is reported.

The Star Theatre, York, S. C. was caught in the fire which recently damaged a residence and warehouse badly in that city. The playhouse is owned by J. Q. Wray.

New England

SAM BERG, familiarly known to his associates as Barry, has been promoted from the sales force of the Boston office of the Fox Film Corporation to chief booker, succeeding Walter Gillis.

Harry Campbell, Fox district manager at Boston, has been burning up the rails between Boston and New York during the week having made three round trips. He says he knows every curve in the rails of the New Haven over the whole distance and could call out the stops without looking out the window.

Harry E. Noble, formerly manager of the New Haven offices of Educational Films, Inc., has rejoined the New York sales force since the closing of the Connecticut offices and is renewing acquaintances through the Empire state. He was with the New York forces before taking charge at New Haven.

Eddie Golden of the Boston office of Film Exchange is keeping active in Connecticut despite the situation facing the distributors there, but just how he does it is puzzling his Boston friends.

President Joseph E. McConville and Treasurer A. Montague of the Independent Films, Inc., Boston, are back from a business trip to the Metropolis.

Joseph Donahue, who besides his activity in Florida real estate and fishing in the rapids of Canada finds time to own and operate the Park and Rialto theatres at Woonsocket, was a recent visitor to Boston.

G. A. Hickey, divisional supervisor of Metro Goldwyn at Boston, is on a two weeks' trip in the South.

It is understood that the plans of the Sigfrid Amusement Co. for a new theatre in Derby, Conn., are progressing satisfactorily and that the business men of the town are anxious to have a modern theatre erected there. The fund is well along towards the $50,000 mark, it is said, and the proposed theatre is expected to be built in the near future. Sigfrid Malm, head of the company, was in Derby for a few days last week and consulted with engineers and contractors regarding the proposed playhouse. It is also understood that negotiations for the lease of the theatre are progressing satisfactorily.

I. J. Hoffman of the Capitol theatre, Ansonia, Conn., and Bernard Hoffman of New Haven, Conn., have purchased a site on Main street, New Britain, for a new theatre. The property purchased is the former property of the S. M. Davidson Co., and the price paid is said to have been $209,000. The Hoffmans plan the erection of a modern playhouse with a seating capacity of approximately 2,500 on this site, to cost in the vicinity of $500,000. They now own and operate, besides the Capitol theatre, theatres in Hartford, Waterbury and the Sterling theatre in Derby, Conn.

Announcement is also made that the Hoffmans have bought a half interest in the Capitol, Palace and Scenic theatres in New Britain and that Contaras Brothers & Perokas, owners of these three playhouses, have purchased a half interest in the new theatre which the Hoffman Brothers are to build in New Britain. It is said that the transactions involve in the vicinity of $1,250,000.

Goldstein Brothers Amusement Co., of Springfield, Mass., have leased the main hall of the West Boylston Manufacturing Co. at Easthampton and are making extensive alterations remodelling it into a theatre for motion pictures. It will be known as the Strand theatre and Fred P. Belmont, manager of the Northampton, Mass., theatres of the Goldstein company, will direct the programs while Jack Mahar of Easthampton is to be resident manager. The playhouse is expected to open some time during the present month.

James F. Ray, assistant manager of the Merrimack Square theatre in Lowell, Mass., has been appointed manager of the Salem theatre at Salem, Mass., according to announcement made by Manager David F. Perkins of the Lowell theatre. The promotion is made by William P. Gray, general manager of the Famous Players-Lasky Corporation in New England. Before going to Lowell, Mr. Ray managed the Lawrence, Mass., Opera House and the Fitchburg, Mass., Majestic theatre. He had been assistant manager at Lowell for several months.

The S. & S. Corporation has been organized at Middletown, Conn., with capital of $50,000 to conduct theatrical enterprises. The corporation is headed by Alessandro Saraceno of Middletown.

Benjamin I. Coone of Worcester, Mass., has awarded contract for the erection of a motion picture theatre to the Central Building Company of Worcester. The new playhouse will be built in the rear of the Bancroft Trust Company building on Franklin street with spacious lobby on Franklin street and will cost approximately $350,000. No intimation is made as to the probable lessee of the theatre when completed. It is understood that construction work is to start immediately.

Mrs. M. N. Wolf, wife of the general manager of Metro in Boston, and their son, Norton Jerome Wolf, have returned from a visit to Mrs. Wolf's relatives in Denver, Colo.

Albert J. Locatelli, owner of a chain of theatres bearing his name in suburban Boston and of the new theatre being erected in Arlington, Mass., was bereaved this week by the death of his son, Mrs. John E. Locatelli of Somerville, Mass. Besides her son, Mrs. Locatelli is survived by a husband, well known Boston

contractor, and a daughter, Mrs. Felix Forte.

Earl L. Crabb, who is to be manager of the new Metropolitan Theatre, has arrived in Boston and established his headquarters at the Copley Plaza Hotel until he has a few spare minutes to hunt up a more permanent residence. Mr. Crabb was for a year and a half district manager of Southern Enterprises with headquarters in Dallas.

Manager Laurence F. Stuart of the Fenway Theatre, Boston, has gone to the New York offices of the Paramount company and George E. Guise, formerly of Detroit, is now acting manager of the Fenway.

Philip Feldman of Everett, Mass. is having plans prepared by Architect Samuel E. Moffie of Boston for a motion picture theatre.

Work is progressing rapidly on the new Grand Theatre at Southbridge street and Burns court, Worcester, for S. Z. Poli of New Haven. Walls are up for the first floor.

Andrew Pegu of St. Johnsbury, Vt. is to erect a motion picture theatre in that city at a cost of approximately $150,000. Plans for the structure are being prepared by Haynes & Mason of Fitchburg, Mass. and will probably be completed within a week so that contracts may be let and work started before severe weather.

James McMann and Ben G. Desmarais are the new owners of the Star Theatre Co. at 1480 Pleasant street, Fall River, Mass.

E. S. Sharaf, who recently resigned as Syracuse representative of Paramount, was a visitor in Boston's film row recently.

A fur revue is to be staged at Loew's State theatre, Boston early in October, to be presented just before the feature film.

Edwin G. Hiscock, well known in Massachusetts and until a few years ago a resident of Malden, Mass., who entered the motion picture field in Boston's Film Row, has just been appointed exploitation director for the United Artists Corporation with headquarters in Kansas City. Hiscock is but 26 years old and is said to be the youngest exploitation director in the country. He is a World War veteran. He was dramatic editor of the Los Angeles Record for a while after returning from war and resigned to become publicity director for several theatres in Los Angeles including the Famous Players-Lasky Theatres.

The Broadway Theatre in Springfield, Mass. has engaged a 15-piece orchestra for its musical program. The theatre also will give feature films instead of short reels and vaudeville.

Nathan H. Gordon, one of the most prominent men in the theatrical field in New England and until his recent retirement, head of the Gordon chain of theatres, left Boston for New York Tuesday to board a steamship for Europe.

Mr. Gordon is accompanied by his family and will spend at least a year in travel in Continental Europe. More than 200 friends were on hand to bid them godspeed and many beautiful bouquets were forwarded to their ship.

Mr. Gordon recently underwent a serious operation and takes this much needed rest for his health. His children will accompany him part of the trip but will remain in Switzerland after visiting the principal Continental cities while Mr. and Mrs. Gordon continue their trip.

The Famous Players-Lasky Corporation acquired Mr. Gordon's theatres recently when he retired from their active management.

The Acme Amusement Company of Portland, Me., which operates motion picture theatres in Kennebunk and Vinalhaven in that state, has been purchased by Leon P. Gorman of Portland and Wilfred Duffy and Howard Duffy, both of Old Orchard, Me. The Duffy brothers manage the Pier at Old Orchard while Mr. Gorman, who is manager of the Maine Theatre Supply Co. at Portland, conducts theatres at Gorham, South Portland and Yarmouth, Me.

Houston

R. C. LEAVES, representative of the newly formed Liberty Film Exchange, was in town last week visiting Wm. Horwitz Jr. of the New Texan and Iris theatres.

John Smith, former publicity man for the Interstate circuit at Houston, Texas, and later connected with the home office at Dallas, Texas, dropped into town for a short visit early last week. Mr. Smith is now connected with Wm. Lytle of the San Antonio Amusement Co., San Antonio, Texas.

L. M. DeBruler, local representative of the Interstate circuit announced that stock would open in the Palace theatre about October 11th if a director and a company could be gotten together by that time. The Palace will try to bring to Houston Mickie Finn, a producer who directed at the Palace last season.

The walls of the new Ritz theatre are rapidly going skyward and the management hopes to open for the fall season in a short time. This 1500 seat western theatre is located on a side street about half block off Main St., where most of the theatres are located.

Peter Crown, former owner of the Folly theatre is in Miama, Fla. where he will spend the winter.

Abe Silverberg left Dallas last week on a business trip.

Atlanta

MRS. ANNA AIKEN PATTERSON, publisher of the Weekly Film Review, who has been on an extended motor tour through Europe since June 1st covering England, France, Germany, Holland, Switzerland, Belgium and Italy, returns to America on the S. S. Ryndam October 10th.

F. E. Williamson, well-known Winter Haven, Fla., exhibitor, spent most of this week in Atlanta on business and visiting Oscar Oldknow. Mr. Williamson left for Florida Thursday night, and reported he had had a most enjoyable stay in Atlanta.

L. C. Lowe, representing Producers Distributing Corporation in the Alabama territory, was in Atlanta for a few days this week.

Tom Little, branch manager of Producers' Atlanta exchange, left Thursday night for Charlotte. He will return Monday morning.

Barrett C. Keisling, director of Publicity for Producers Distributing Corporation at the Cecil B. De Mille studio on the coast, arrived in Atlanta this week to attend the hearing on the Famous Players' suit involving the author-

ship of De Mille's "The Ten Commandments."

William J. Clark, formerly with the Goldwyn Pictures Corporation in Atlanta, is now manager of the Paramount exchange in Louisville, Ky. Mr. Clark was a popular member of the local film fraternity during his stay here, and the news his present connection in Louisville with Famous Players will be of interest to many.

George F. Lenehan, district manager for Producers Distributing Corporation in this territory, is due in Atlanta Monday morning, after having met Tom Little in Charlotte on Sunday for a conference in the Charlotte exchange.

A. B. Cheatham, manager of the Ottoway Theatre, Charlotte, N. C. was in Atlanta this week on business. He left during the weekend for his home.

Otto Haas, owner of the Ottoway Theatre, Charlotte, is scheduled to arrive in New York sometime next week on the S. S. Mauretania, after having completed an extensive tour abroad.

Charles E. Kessnigh, branch manager of the Atlanta Metro-

Goldwyn exchange, returned to the city Thursday after having completed a successful trip throughout the territory.

M. W. Smith, manager of the Potomac branch of the United States Army, Motion Picture Service, was in Atlanta this week on one of his regular trips to the city, purchasing pictures for the soldiers in the camp at Fort Worth.

N. V. Darley, who will be remembered as the manager of the Alpha Theatre, Atlanta, for a number of years, is now manager of the Strand Theatre, Ybor City, Fla., and made a trip to Atlanta this week, visiting many of his old friends.

James Jackson, popular manager of the Tudor Theatre, Atlanta, returned this week after having spent his two-weeks' vacation at his old home in Danville, Va.

E. E. Geyer, Paramount exploiter, left for Columbus, Ga., Tuesday night. He returned to Atlanta Friday night, after a successful trip.

W. E. Wilkinson, who is assistant to Charlie Pettijohn, general

counsel of the Film Boards of Trade, stopped over in Atlanta Monday to visit with friends. He is on his way East after having enjoyed a visit to his old home, Montgomery, Ala., last week.

Invitations were sent out this week bearing the signatures of A. J. Amm, district manager for Southern Enterprises, and H. Somerville, resident city manager for the company in Daytona Beach, Fla., to the opening Monday night, September 28th, of the new Florida Theatre there.

It is understood that the Florida Theatre will be an exceptionally fine house, modern throughout in every respect. It is a Paramount house, and H. Somerville will have its management in charge.

C. L. Price, who bought the Alamo Theatre, Gainesville, Ga., from Bob Addington of Cornelia the latter part of August, has just completed the sale of the Alamo, originally owned by Mrs. Cinciolla, to Frank Plaginos, who also operates the State theatre, Gainesville. The sale is to become effective October first.

Philadelphia

MEMBERS of the Philadelphia office of Paramount are now sporting the prizes awarded to them for taking third place in the drive for summer business which has been in progress in Paramount exchanges throughout the country since early summer. Manager Heenan received a beautiful platinum watch, while Bill Schwalbe, Phil Duffy, Frank Loftus, Bill Mansell and Frank Leonard, members of the sales force, received their choice of platinum cuff links or gold cigarette cases.

Gordon Lenhart, former manager of the Rialto theatre, Wilmington, has succeeded Dave Rosen, shipper at the Fox Exchange for the past nine years. Mr. Rosen recently resigned to become foreman of the shipping room of Warner Brothers' Exchange.

Recent hearings before the Arbitration Board include those of

the Chautauqua Auditorium, Mt. Gretna, defendant against action brought by the Producers Distributing Corporation, and the Cayuga Theatre, Phila., for complaints filed by the Film Booking offices. In the first instance the Board ruled that the defendant must pay P.D.C. $90.00 for failure to lift three pictures under the terms of the contract and in the second instance the Cayuga Theatre was ordered to accept an unplayed picture of a contract for thirteen before October 31st for $20.00, a price much less than the amount originally agreed upon.

Sidney Montor, who has been manager of the Princess Theatre on Market Street for the Stanley Company, has been transferred to the Southwark Theatre and Sigmund Schwartz for some time manager of the Savoy has succeeded Mr. Montor at the Princess.

Manager Edgar Ross, of the Fox Exchange, has taken a lease on the second floor of the building at 1228 Vine St., which will be converted about November 1st into a production room and poster department.

Frank Hardey, is now managing the Arcadia Theatre, Wilmington, recently acquired by the Stanley Company from Topkis-Ginns. Frank Cook is now managing the Orient theatre for the Stanley Company and Marcus Benn, succeeding Mr. Hardey.

Ray Nugent is now covering the New Jersey territory for the De Luxe Exchange. Mr. Nugent was at one time booker for Metro-Goldwyn and later bookkeeper for George Bennethum, a position now being filled by Jacob E. Ernst.

Robert E. Long, who was formerly connected with motion pic-

ture theatres in Washington, is now managing the Aldine Theatre for the Stanley Company, succeeding William Scott, who has been transferred to the new Stanley Theatre at Atlantic City.

Miss Alice McMahon has succeeded Miss Julia Barry as secretary to Percy A. Bloch, manager of the Philadelphia Paramount exchange. Miss Barry, who has been associated with Vine Street exchanges for a number of years, will be married on October 24th to Dr. T. S. Collins.

A. C. Benson, until recently a salesman in the Philadelphia office of Paramount, a position which he left to become sales manager in the Washington exchange, has been transferred to Toronto, Canada, to assume the management of the Famous Players Exchange there.

Milwaukee

WILLIAM MORGAN, general sales manager for the Producers Distributing Corporation, and Cecil E. Mayberry, district manager, spent Thursday of last week at Milwaukee, where they conferred with Charles Lundgren, branch manager, Fred Knispel, assistant to the district manager, also dropped in during the week, while E. S. Wagner, representing the accessory department at New York, is spending some time at the Milwaukee exchange.

Buddy Stewart, manager of the Fenway Theatre, Boston, Mass., and Phil Tyrrell of the Phil Tyr-

rell Attractions, came up from Chicago last week to pay a visit to their old bosom friend, Howard Waugh, manager of Universal's Alhambra Theatre at Milwaukee. Their stay in the city was brief but filled with enjoyment.

Harry Jones, manager of Saxe's Merrill Theatre since it was taken over by the Saxe organization six months ago, has resigned his position. He is succeeded by S. P. Kennedy, former house manager for the Finkelstein & Ruben interests in Minneapolis. Jones has not yet announced his plans for the future, but it is expected that he

will soon again step into the limelight as manager of a high class house.

Dale Larisch, who for some time past has been first assistant to Stanley Brown, manager of Saxe's Strand Theatre, has resigned his post to complete his college course, and is now enrolled at Rippon College. Dale plans to be an architect and hopes in the not too remote future to be a designer of theatres beautiful.

Formal opening of the remodeled Colonial Theatre has been scheduled for Saturday, October 3, according to advises received from

Henry Goldman, manager, by his friends on Milwaukee's film row. The house now boasts of 900 seats, an excellent pipe organ, and newly redecorated interior.

Leo Behring, who has developed his Pastime Theatre from a liability at the time of its acquisition, to one of the best paying neighborhood houses in the city, has just completed an ambitious remodeling program. The house now boasts of a well illuminated front, featured by a large sign, a new lobby arrangement, and a redecorated interior.

Salt Lake City

CLYDE H. MESSINGER has left his managerial chair at the Educational exchange here, and is on his way to the Idaho branch.

J. F. Burke, Educational travelling auditor, was here from Seattle, and found the local office in good shape. Burke has left for Denver, Colorado.

Harold Pickering, Famous Players-Lasky local exploitation Manager, has returned from his trip through Southern Utah.

George I. Cloward, manager for Metro-Goldwyn in this city, has been in Wyoming and has gone direct from there to cover the Montana territory.

The Victory Theatre, under the management of Carl A. Porter, has installed a radio by which they are broadcasting their musical programs. These concerts may be heard over K. S. L.

Ed. C. Mix, manager of the local Associated Exhibitors exchange, is expected back within a few days from a short trip to Ogden, Utah.

W. G. Seib, Pathe exchange manager here, has returned from Denver, Colorado, where he met and had a conference with Frank Harris, where Associated Manager for Pathe. Harris is now enroute to New York to attend a managers convention there.

R. D. Boomer, who covers the Southern Utah territory out of the local Pathe office, has been unable to get out on the road during the last few days on account of a very bad cold which has confined him to his bed.

C. J. Hamal, Pathe salesman, is still in Idaho. Miss Max Hansen, inspector at this exchange, has been married recently and is now Mrs. Turner.

Warner Brothers national drive this week is the cause of much enthusiasm at the local exchange according to manager R. S. Stackhouse, who says there will be no sleeping nor eating going on until they put it over in this section. George E. Jensen is hitting the ball in Montana; L. W. Hyde just returned from Nevada and Northern Utah and is returning immediately for Idaho. Stackhouse has returned from Montana and is leaving for the key towns of Utah. Harry Gibson, formerly connected with Warner Brothers here has returned to Denver.

W. F. Gordon, local Associated First National exchange manager, is expected in this week from his trip to Montana. Vete Stewart, salesman out of this office, is also in the Montana territory. Claude Hawkes has just returned from the Idaho branch.

W. K. Bloom, F. B. O. salesman has just left for a four weeks' trip into Montana. Joseph K.

Soloman has left for the Northern Utah territory. Miss Gladys Illingworth is now doing the cashier work in this office while Miss Mitchel is on her vacation. Another marriage on Film Row of late is that of Miss Gladys Grow, F. B. O. inspector, who has changed her name to Mrs. Stoddart.

H. Bradley Fish, manager of the local Fox exchange, has returned from a trip through the Montana territory. Dave T. McElhenney has just come in from his first trip into Idaho which was very encouraging. J. A. Tidwell left this office for Southern Utah immediately after coming in from Northern Utah.

The former secretary and legal counsel here for the Film Board of Trade, Judge Loofbourow, has resigned this office because of it taking up too much of his time.

L. W. Weir, Western District Manager for Producers Distributing Corporation, left here last week for Portland, Oregon, where they are opening a new office.

C. C. McDermond, selling out of the local Producers Distributing Corporation exchange, is leaving right away for an extended trip into Southern Utah.

James R. Keitz, who has charge of the Greater Features exchange here, is expected in from Idaho the later part of this week. Clifton Pierce, salesman for Greater Fea-

tures, came in from the Idaho branch and left immediately for Southern L'tah.

Carl A. Porter, manager of the Victory Theatre in this city, announces that the movie golfers are getting ready for their fall tournament. This promises to be a very interesting event, and keen rivalry is expected between the contestants. The Paramount Empress and the Victory theatres have put up a cup, and the players of all of the theatres are getting prizes. A meeting will be held within a few days and the players will be paired off according to their handicaps.

M. Stringham who formerly owned the houses at Price and Raines, Utah, has purchased the Colonial Theatre at Ogden, Utah, from H. S. Skinner.

George Brewerton has purchased the Iris Theatre at Murray, Utah, and the Rialto and Princess theatres at Magna, Utah, from Frank Burgener.

Other exhibitors visiting the exchanges this week are: A. L. Stallings, owner of the Kinema Theatre, Richfield, Utah; Chas. Simmons of the Orpheum Theatre, Oakley, Idaho; H. W. Howdeshell, operating the Baugh Theatre, Shoshone, Idaho and Ed Ryan, owner of the Liberty Theatre, Brigham City, Utah.

Seattle

R. R. NAVE, former booker for L. K. Brin's Kwality Pictures Exchange, and more recently associated with Manager H. A. Black's Warner Brothers office, last week took over the booking details at Manager W. H. Drummond's Producers' Distributing Corporation exchange. Mr. Nave is succeeded at Warner Brothers by G. G. Maxey, former salesman in the Eastern Washington territory, who is well known by exhibitors of the Northwest through his former connections with Selznick and First National.

Guy D. Haselton, owner and manager of the Rialto Theatre in Missoula, Montana, was a visitor in this city last week, buying and booking pictures for his house for the coming season.

Two Universal notables, both former residents of this city, were the guests of Manager L. O. Lukan at the local "U" office last week. These were Jack Schlaifer, former local manager and now western district manager for Universal, and Lou Metzger, former Film Booking Offices manager here, and now a special representative for Carl Laemmle.

Charles Code, well-known as a film representative of this city and more recently associated with Manager W. K. Beckwith's Warner Brothers Exchange in Portland, last week joined Manager Jack Sullivan's local Fox office. He will cover the Eastern part of

the state for Fox in a sales executive capacity, with headquarters in Spokane.

Reports received on Film Row from Cheney, Wash., last week indicated that Frank Carlon's Rose Theatre in that town had been purchased by Miss L. Neilson, who was scheduled to take over the management of the house within a few weeks time.

George P. Endert, manager of the Famous-Players-Lasky exchange in this city, left last week for San Francisco, where a coast managers' convention was called by District Manager Herman Wobber. On the way south Mr. Endert stopped off long enough in Portland to pick up Neal East who manages the Paramount interests in the Oregon territory.

Erection of a 600 seat theatre in Wenatchee, Wash., directly across the street from the Jensen-Von Herberg Liberty Theatre, was announced this week. It will be built and managed by M. Lillis, who expects to have it ready for a grand opening on January 1, 1926.

W. J. Murphy, publicity director for the Metro-Goldwyn-Mayer interests on the Pacific Coast, spent a few days in this territory last week around Manager C. M. Hill last week.

Something new in the art of theatre construction and design was promised last week by G. W. Swope, a former exhibitor of Cal-

ifornia, who has begun construction in Longview, Wash., of the Pekin Theatre, which will be entirely Chinese in architecture. The house will seat approximately 600, will cost in excess of $25,000, and is expected to be ready for occupancy within three months.

Roy Cooper, exhibitor of this city, and former manager of the Anzier Theatre here, last week announced his marriage to Miss Adelaide Salinger, also of this city, the latter part of September.

W. H. Burke, a special representative of the Educational Pic-

tures Corporation from New York City, spent several days here last week with Manager J. A. Gage in the new Educational quarters. Wallie Rucker, Educational salesman, also was "among those present" for the week.

W. V. Ginn, formerly an exhibitor of Trinidad, Colorado, last week announced that he had taken a lease on the Rialto Theatre of Brownsville, Oregon, and would take over the management of the house immediately. The Rialto is owned by R. W. Kessel of Harrisburg and Junction City.

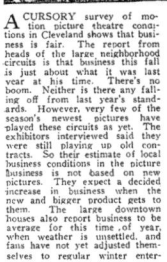

Cleveland

A CURSORY survey of motion picture theatre conditions in Cleveland shows that business is fair. The report from heads of the large neighborhood circuits is that business this fall is just about what it was last year at his time. There's no boom. Neither is there any falling off from last year's standards. However, very few of the season's newest pictures have played these circuits as yet. The exhibitors interviewed said they were still playing up old contracts. So their estimate of local business conditions in the picture business is not based on new pictures. They expect a decided increase in business when the new and bigger product gets to them. The large downtown houses also report business to be average for this time of year, when weather is unsettled, and fans have not yet adjusted themselves to regular winter entertainment.

Howard Christman has resigned as secretary of the Cleveland Film Board of Trade. Christman's resignation will become effective just as soon as his successor has been appointed. Howard Christman has been the one and only secretary of the Film Board of Trade of Cleveland. He was appointed to the position when the Film Board of Trade was organized in 1922 and has continued in that post ever since. Under his secretaryship, many important things have been successfully accomplished by the Board. The two big constructive things that they have accomplished is to stabilize contracts and to establish confidence between the distributing and exhibiting branch of the industry. The zoning system, whereby the city is divided into zones, with each theatre classified

so as to regulate booking precedence, has also been put into operation under Christman. He resigned in order to accept a bigger job in the east.

Dr. B. I. Brody is the successful bidder for the lease of the new motion picture theatre now in course of construction at the Cedar Lee intersection on Cleveland Heights, a residence suburb of Cleveland. The house has been leased from the Cedar-Lee Realty Company, composed of Charles D. Simmons and Malcolm B. Vilas of the Law firm, Simmons, Dewitt and Vilas. The lease is for seventeen years at an aggregate rental of nearly $300,000. The theatre, which will be finished in about two months, will have 1200 seats, and is located in the rear of a business building. Entrance will be on Lee Road. Dr. Brody also owns and operates the Detroit, Kinsman, Homestead and New Broadway theatres. The new Broadway and Kinsman were built early in 1925. The Detroit is two years old. All of them are night class first-run neighborhood houses. All of them play a straight picture policy with the exception of the Kinsman which plays a combination vaudeville and picture policy. It is expected that the new Cedarlee Theatre will play straight pictures.

The Cameo theatre, Euclid Ave. near East Sixth St. will be ready to open about November 1st. This is a Loew house and the ninth Loew. house in the city. As the Star Theatre, it was for many years the home of burlesque. Recently the property was acquired by the Laronge Company, and has been entirely rebuilt for a picture house. The policy to be inaugurated has not been established other than that it will be devoted to pictures only. But whether it

will play first run pictures, for second runs, or both, has not been determined.

The Park Theatre at Barberton has changed hands, the change to become effective on October 5th. Messrs. Makinson and Gaethke have purchased it from John Buck- hor. The new owners have closed the house for several weeks, during which time they will put it through a complete course of renovation, including remodeling and re-decorating.

Fred Schram has resigned as city representative for Producers Distributin- Corporation. Schram has been with the company ever since it opened its Cleveland exchange. He will announce his future plans shortly.

R. C. Struve, owner and manager of the Orpheum theatre, Canton, has returned from a summer abroad. Struve wrote his Cleveland friends to get the band out some day this week, when he plans to visit the exchanges in person.

J. B. Cohen has been advanced from a sales position to that of manager of the Producers Distributing Company's exchange in Pittsburgh. He succeeds G. R. Ainsworth, who has resigned.

Chester Loewe, district representative for P. D. C. and Robert Cotton, division manager, attended a meeting in Chicago, last week, of all district representatives.

Pat Dowling, in charge of publicity for Metropolitan Studios was in the city early in the week. Dowling called on the local newspapers, and paved the way for further publicity on his product.

A. W. Smith, in charge of First National specials, was a guest of the local First National family for a day or two in the beginning

of the week, and left on Thursday for Detroit.

Margaret Moir, who has served First National, and First National customers faithfully for a number of years, has resigned to take a new position as wife of Arthur Ayers. It was a Film Bldg. romance, as Ayers was employed in the building when he met Miss Moir. The wedding took place Thursday, September 24th at the Pilgrim Congregational Church. The entire First National office force was in attendance, both at the ceremony and the dinner which followed. They presented the bride and groom with a set of flat silver.

The Film Bldg. register was much in use during the past week. The list of out-of-town exhibitor guests included: Bat B. Charnas, Lyric theatre, Toledo; Garland Shetler, the new owner of the Opera House in Middlefield and the Opera House in West Farmington; Mrs. S. E. Chuba, Empire theatre, Amherst; A. Stalder, Spicer Theatre, Akron; N. D. Schworm, Grand, Massilon; Mike Shea, of Feiber and Shea theatres; Max Young, McKinley theatre, Canton; C. O. Frederick, Moose theatre, Norwalk; A. Moranz, Grand, Lisbon; J. Rubin, Strand, Newton Falls; Leo Burkhart, Hippodrome, Crestline; W. J. Powell, Lonet, Wellington; Ben Yudelvitz, Princess, Medina; Mike Ratoff, Pastime, Akron; J. Stein, Utopia, Painesville; John Damm, Strand, Wadsworth; J. A. Martin, Pastime, Berea, and A. Fish, Alhambra, Canton.

Lou Geiger, manager of F. B. O.'s Cleveland office, is spending a few weeks' vacation in Hollywood at the F. B. O. Studios. Much of his time is being spent in conferences with production managers at work on F. B. O.'s next season product.

Denver

PUEBLO, COLORADO, will soon have another beautiful theatre. On the corner of Broadway and Abriendo Street is being erected a large building most of which will be occupied by what will be known as the Broadway Theatre. The capacity of the new house will be about 1,000 seats. No expense is being spared to make the new motion picture house one of the finest in the state as far as beauty and modern equipment are concerned. The owners of the lease and operators of the theatre are Messrs. Lucy and Wilkinson. The theatre will be finished and open on or about December 15th.

The entire Pathe sales force working out of the local Denver exchange were called into Denver this week. While here, several conferences were held with their manager, Mr. C. M. Van Horn.

Aaron Epstein, auditor for the Fox Theatres in Denver, was

taken seriously ill a few days ago while working at his desk. He was immediately removed to a local hospital where he is now reported to be steadily improving. Mr. Epstein has been auditor for the Fox theatres for over a year with offices in the Isis Theatre, during which time he has become one of the most popular and well known theatre men among the Curtis Street first run houses. His present location is J C R S Sanatorium, Sanatorium, Colorado. His many friends wish him a speedy recovery.

Mrs. B. A. Tyo was in Denver visiting her many friends among the exchanges a few days ago. Mrs. Tyo is one of the few lady exhibitors in the Denver territory, being the owner and manager of the Tyo Theatre in Wray, Colorado.

Senator and Mrs. Frank Kelly, who own and operate the Empress Theatre, Salida, Colorado, also

made the rounds at film row this week. Their trip to Denver was primarily for the purpose of purchasing service and equipment for their theatre's use during the coming winter months.

J. B. Melton of the Colonial Amusement Company is now in Florida on a business trip. Mr. Melton is also visiting his son who is a real estate operator in Ft. Lauderdale, Florida. He expects to return to Denver October 10th.

The active management of the new State Theatre which opened last week in Denver has been taken over by H. D. McBride. Mr. McBride is a well known theatre manager of the Pacific Coast having until recently managed the theatre at Santa Barbara, California. He was located in that city at the time of the recent disastrous earthquake.

R. V. Mallory has disposed of all his interests in the Rialto

Theatre at Brighton, Colorado, to W. A. Seaman. Mr. Seaman is a veteran exhibitor in and near Brighton having operated in that vicinity for the past nine years. Mr. Mallory as yet has not announced his future plans but states that his fellow exhibitors will probably soon see him in the territory as a salesman for one of the leading exchanges.

Exhibitors visiting Denver during the past week were Otto Bachechi of the Pastime Theatre, Albuquerque, New Mexico; J. E. "Tommy" Tompkins, American Theatre, Colorado Springs; Paul Krier, Star Theatre, Walesburg, Colorado; and A. H. Stewart, present manager of the Iris and American Theatres, Casper, Wyoming.

Harry Nolan, district supervisor for First National, will leave for New York City on a business trip about October 1st.

St. Louis

THE addition of the Cinderella Theatre to the St. Louis Amusement Company's chain has caused the transfer of many managers for that company.

J. F. Brinkmeyer moves into the Cinderella from the Grand Florissant. Ralph Walsh takes over the Grand-Florissant while Joe Greene moves up from the Lafayette and Russell airdrome to the Maffitt to replace Walsh. Harry O'Brien goes from the Gravois to the Lafayette and Russell J. Smith is managing the Gravois now.

Lou Hess of Universal entertained three home office executives the past week. They were Dave Bader and Julius Singer, special representatives of Carl Laemmle and Ned Depinet, Southern Division Sales Director.

Sol Rose, Central Missouri Salesman for Universal who spent his vacation in New York is back on the job. Louis E. (Nickey) Goldhammer, city salesman, returned from Minneapolis.

Bruce Lewton, popular film hauler is the proud daddy of a baby boy.

George McBride has gone up again. Recently he was made chief booker for the local Uni-

versal office following a considerable period as short products booked. He is now a valued member of Lou Hess' sales staff. Elmer Sedin who was Universal's booker until about a year ago returned to his old job. Bill Collins continues as short products booker.

David E. Russell, manager of the Columbia and Strand theatres, has been reappointed manager for the Municipal Opera for the season 1926 which opens next May. The opera runs twelve weeks at the Municipal theatre in Forest Park. Russell has always managed it.

T. W. Sharp of Little Rock took bids September 28 on his new theatre in Pulaski Heights. The house will be one story, 40 by 150 feet and cost about $50,000.

Manager J. Greenberg of the New Bond Theatre, 3600 Bond avenue, East St. Louis, Ill., gave a benefit show for St. Regis Church on Sunday evening, September 27.

C. D. Hill, district manager for Producers Distributing Corporation departed for Kansas City and Omaha September 26. Russell McLean, personal representative for Hill has gone to Des Moines.

Charley Werner, manager for the local Metro-Goldwyn-Mayer office has returned from Mayo Brothers Sanitarium at Rochester, Minn. He was accompanied by his brother Sam, who operated the United Films Exchange. Charley's numerous friends will be pleased to learn that he is greatly improved and will be his old self again within a few weeks. His recent operation was entirely successful.

Tom McKean, manager for F. B. O. and Mrs. McKean returned from the Eastern tour on Monday, September 28. They had a dandy time amid the Effete East. Tom denies that he bought the Woolworth Tower or Grant's Tomb.

The Opera House at Jonesburg, Mo., was destroyed by fire recently. The entire business section of the town was wiped out.

L. C. Crow has sold the Star Theatre, Paris, Mo., to K. K. Stephens. The new owner changed the name to Liberty Theatre.

J. W. Etherton has sold the Opera House, Edinburg, Ill., to P. A. McCarth. Etherton will manage an automobile salesroom for his brother at Carbondale, Ill.

H. W. Haines is now sole owner of the Star, Rockport, Ill. The Majestic Theatre, Mammoth Springs, Ark., is scheduled to close on October 1.

May Stewart, prize winning beauty who formerly ornamented Universal's local office, has resigned to complete her course of study at Cleveland High School. Representing the Kingland Theatre Miss Stewart was chosen as St. Louis' Film Queen and later she landed top honors in the city's Midwinter Bathing Beauty contest.

Among the other millionaires who vacationed at Wildwood Country Club, Steeleville, Mo., was Bernard (Tim) Temforius, cashier for Universal here. He returned to town with a handsome coat of tan and a flattened bankroll.

Sam R. Alexander has purchased the house at Pawnee, Ill., formerly operated by Tony Serva.

The theatre at West Salem, Ill., will be converted into a poultry house.

A new theatre will be erected at Bowen, Ill.

Visitors were Tom Reed, Duquoin; S. M. Francis, Charleston, and O. W. McCutcheon of Sikeston, Mo.

Kansas City

MRS. MARY WILLIAMS of Sedalia, Mo., mother-in-law of Fred Spear of the Orpheum theatre, Kansas City, died unexpectedly while visiting Mr. and Mrs. Spear in Kansas City Monday.

Theatre construction in Kansas City appears to have shifted from the southern section of the city to the older district of the city in the northeast section. One new theatre has been completed, another is under course of remodeling and enlarging, a third is under construction, while a fourth is planning to increase its seating capacity. The Vista theatre has opened under the management of L. J. Lenhart, who also operates the Roanoke theatre, while the Belmont theatre, which is under construction, is nearing completion. At Independence avenue and Harrison street Frank Garnier is constructing a new theatre which he has contemplated for years, while A. P. Vaughan, owner of the Maple theatre, announces that the house will be remodeled to seat 1,000 and a 10-cent policy adopted.

The Twelfth Street theatre, which originally was built as a down town first run house of Kan-

sas City, has changed its policy to burlesque, having entered into a 30-week agreement with the Gus Sun and Ackerman and Harris vaudeville chain.

Several openings and changes of management of theatres in the Kansas City territory have occured in the last week. The New Regent theatre, Winfield, Kas., owned by O. K. Mason, has re-opened after having been remodeled. I. S. Campbell will manage the house. The Elliott and Electric theatres of Independence, Mo., have been added to the string of Glenn Dickinson, he now controlling all three theatres in that town. Three theatres, the Gem at Cassville, Mo., the Star at Exeter, Mo., and the Cozy at Seligman, Mo., have been purchased by Mrs. H. L. Karr of Monett, Mo., who also owns the Gem at Monett and the Strand at Pierce City, Mo. H. L. Karr will manage the entire string and will buy for all the theatres.

The Burford theatre, Arkansas City, Kas., operated by William Burford, was robbed Sunday night of $1,000 when the safe of the theatre was blown by nitroglycerine.

Work on the new $150,000 Gil-

lioz theatre at Springfield, Mo., will start soon, all contracts having been let. The house, which will seat 1,700 persons in the parquet and balcony, also will contain a full sized stage. It will be a first run house and, according to reports from Springfield, will be leased by United Studios, Inc., of Chicago.

Light top-coats were necessary along Kansas City's movie row this week, but there was no "cooling off" of business by any means. C. A. Schultz, P. D. C. branch manager, returned from a managers' meeting in St. Louis and started his men out in the territory to "get 'em." M. A. Levy, Fox branch manager, conducted a peppy sales meeting all of his own. F. J. Warren and Jack Langan, general manager and manager, respectively, of the Standard Film Exchange, returned from the territory to report that cooler weather had stimulated box offices. George Priest, Fox salesman, has resigned. "Alexander Bill" obtained excellent results on his first week in the territory for the Standard Film Exchange. Sam Black, formerly with Warner Bros., has accepted a position as shipping clerk with

P. D. C. E. H. Goldstein, treasurer for Universal, and A. E. Fair, general manager of Universal's Hostetter circuit, were in Kansas City last week on their way to the West Coast. Few rivals on movie row has Harry Silverman for being an "in-and-outer." Scarcely had the Independent Film Corp., representative arrived home last week than he was on his way back to the territory. The P.D.C. branch is undergoing many new improvements and alterations, much to the satisfaction of C. E. Schultz, branch manager.

Among the out-of-town exhibitors in the Kansas City market last week were: R. E. Christian, Casino, Excelsior Springs, Mo.; F. A. Robinson, LeRoy, Kas.; Louis Griefe, Windsor, Mo.; Bryan Hawkins, Drexel, Mo.; S. E. Wilhoit, Jefferson theatre, Springfield, Mo.

"Yes, after spending a rather strenuous vacation playing golf, fishing and swimming, I'm glad to get back to work," said C. E. Cook, business manager of the M. P. T. O. Kansas-Missouri, who returned from Northern Missouri and Colorado this week.

New York and New Jersey

INVITATIONS are out this week for at least two new theatre openings. Sol Brill's Inwood at Dyckman Street and Post Ave. New York City, will have its Premiere on Thursday evening, October 1st. The Inwood is under the management of the Haven Amusement Corporation with Sol Brill as President.

Small and Strassburg will open their new Terminal theatre at Fourth Ave. and Dean Street, Brooklyn, on Wednesday evening, September 30th. Further details of both these opening nights will be given in next week's MOTION PICTURE NEWS.

Peter Adams, of Newark and Paterson theatrical circles, has been presented by Mrs. Adams, with a baby girl. Mrs. Adams is in the Paterson hospital and the report is that she is getting along finely.

Joseph M. Seider, President of the M. P. T. O. of N. J., and Director Hirschblond attended the Shriners Convention at Atlantic City and while there did not lose the opportunity of talking over Sunday legislation with the Reverend Samuel Steinmetz of Trenton, N. J.

President Seider is scheduled for Tom's River on Saturday of this week and will go on to Camden, Sunday. Both stops will be made in the interest of Jersey organization matters.

On the completion of Joseph Stern's new theatre in Red Bank, N. J., it is reported that a booking arrangement will be formed between Mr. Stern and Walter Reade of the Walter Reade Enterprises. Mr. Stern's theatre is now under construction and when it is finished, both circuits will be represented in Red Bank.

Fred Mertens, of the Fulton theatre, Jersey City, whose policy has been first and second runs will change his theatre over to a strictly first run house. Mr. Mertens has been experimenting with first runs of late and with such success that it is the reason for the change.

Mr. and Mrs. Max Pear appeared at the Astor theatre recently with a brand new chauffeur driven Marmon Sedan which was delivered to him during the past few weeks. Max had a brace of box seats and after looking over their location, decided that the orchestra was a better bet. Dave Brill of the Big U exchange had to help him out. Mr. Pear operates a circuit of six theatres in New York City. Messrs. Jutkwitz and Smollen of Red Bank and Perth Amboy, N. J., were also observed in the Astor theatre lobby on the same night.

Arthur Rapf, brother of Harry Rapf of Metro-Goldwyn-Mayer, has gone up to the mountains for a two weeks' vacation. Mr. Rapf's interests included the Highway, Benson, Montauk and Park theatres in Brooklyn.

John J. Heagney has recently joined the sales staff of the local Associated Exhibitors exchange and will cover Northern New Jersey. Mr. Heagney's former connections were with the Fox and Warner-Standard exchanges in Michigan and he has also worked under the Hodkinson banner in New Jersey.

Goldreyer's Manor theatre, reported to be a beautiful new 1800

William De Mille, who has written the story for his next Paramount production "Magpie."

seat house that is strictly up to the minute in every respect, recently held its opening. The Manor is located at Avenue K and Coney Island Ave., Brooklyn.

It is reported that A. Sobelson, of the Sobelson and Tannhauser Enterprises over in Jersey, has lately become interested in a big real estate deal in Bergen County. No theatre sites are said to be involved.

Phil Meyer, the New York manager of the Associated Exhibitors exchange has bought himself a new Hupmobile Sedan.

Louis Gold and E. Thornton Kelly, both recently elected Associate-Directors of the M. P. T. O. of N. J., attended for their first time the last meeting held at Asbury where the members were the guests of Messrs. Hildinger, Keegan and Newberry.

Several more local theatres have changed over to a full time schedule. They include J. Wolff's Miller theatre on Saratoga Avenue, Brooklyn, Small-Strassberg's Washington, Myrtle Ave., Brooklyn and also the S. & A. theatre, the latter of late only being operated for two nights a week.

Lee Simon, assistant Pathe shipper, is back at work again after a two weeks' vacation in the mountains.

The Ritz theatre at 1901 Fulton Street, Brooklyn, which has been closed for several months, was reopened on Saturday, September 25th, by H. Lightstone.

The Forest Park theatre in Brooklyn, owned by Rossasy, has been sold to a former Connecticut exhibitor by name of Crystal.

Abe Puder and Harry Lowe, as heads of a syndicate, took over the property at 172-174 Clinton avenue, formerly the home of James R. Nugent, Democratic boss of Essex County, and will erect a combined theater, store and office building. The transaction was made through Murray Applebaum, Inc., realtors, with Attorney Seymour Solomon representing the syndicate.

Along with the property, a tract of land at 170 Clinton avenue and having a depth of 219 feet was also bought. The combined properties are valued at $100,000.

Central Penn

SPECIAL exercises on Labor Day marked the formal opening of the new 1000 capacity Freedman Theatre, erected by Julius Freedman, in Forest City. Among the prominent theatre men in attendance was M. E. Comerford, of Scranton, head of the Comerford Amusement Company, which operates a big chain of theatres in the hard coal mining regions of Pennsylvania. He had just recently returned from Europe. The new theatre is a modern one in every respect, being of steel and concrete construction.

A ten-year lease on the Moose picture theatre, Mahanoy City, has been granted to Charles Haussman. He will make extensive alterations and renovations and operate it under the name of the Hippodrome. It was formerly known as the Family. Mr. Haussman is manager of the Hippodrome in Pottsville. He has appointed Frank Hill, formerly of the Hippodrome in Reading, to act as manager of the theatre in Mahanoy City.

The new Arcadia theatre, in Shenandoah, which is to replace the old theatre of the same name, is nearing completion, and will soon be ready for formal opening,

according to Oppenheimer & Sweet, the owners. They purchased the old property from Porter Seiwell.

The management of the Hippodrome theatre, York, has announced an engagement of the expert motion picture organist, Walter C. Simon.

The Poli theatre, Scranton, was reopened for the Fall season on September 14, and the Poli in Wilkes-Barre, on September 21. Both are affiliated with the Comerford Amusement Company chain of theatres. Both theatres have undergone improvements.

Reports from the hard coal mining regions of Pennsylvania are that the miners' strike, which started September 1, did not, during the first three weeks of the month, have the adverse effect on the motion picture theatre business that had been anticipated. It is now predicted by the more optimistic theatre men that the falling off in theatre patronage may not become very serious in the anthracite sections unless the strike becomes prolonged. They point out that while the strikers' incomes are reduced, the fact that the men have more time on

their hands since they have become idle, gives them more leisure in which to attend picture shows and other forms of amusement.

An increase in wages of about four dollars a week has been granted by the Comerford Amusement Company, of Scranton, to the stage hands employed in the Capital, Academy, Gaiety and Poli theatres in that city, effective September 1.

The Victoria theatre, of Mahanoy City, has a new chief electrician in the person of Raymond Clarke, formerly of Barnesville. This is one of the Chamberlain Amusement Company theatres.

A new theatre with a seating capacity of 350 is about to be opened in Swayersville, by Michael Manchutas.

Arthur Lichtenthaler, prominent theatre man in Pittsburgh, proprietor of the Family theatre there, and owner of a motion picture and dance pavilion at the Mt. Gretna summer resort, on the evening of Saturday, September 19, formerly opened his new $100,000 Community Auditorium, at Cumberland street, near Fifth, in Lebanon. It provides accommodations not only for dances, lectures and public as-

semblies of a general character, but also is designed for conventions, expositions and all kinds of meetings where large space is required. It has floor space two times as great as that of the Lebanon Armory which heretofore had been the city's largest assembly hall. The opening exercises were featured by a large public dance.

The State theatre, Altoona, recently acquired by the Wilmer & Vincent interests, has been formally reopened under their management, after having undergone extensive interior improvements. Announcement is made that Professor J. F. Keith has been engaged as organist for the theatre which is one of the finest and largest in Western Pennsylvania, outside of Pittsburgh.

New scenery, curtains and lighting effects have just been added to the equipment of the Academy of Music, in Lebanon. The curtains are of asbestos, decorated in plain, straight-line trimmings. An emergency lighting system has been installed so that in event of the city light failing the theatre can be lighted by means of storage batteries.

Minneapolis

MINNEAPOLIS city ordinance requirements having to do with fire protection have been so altered as to make it necessary for most of the film companies here to change the arrangement of their plants, cutting exits and increasing the thickness of the walls. One company which, at the time its plant was built, went far beyond the requirements of the time in the matter of construction has been put to a good deal of inconvenience in spite of this and some alterations have been ordered with most of the others.

S. F. Heath of the State theatre at Wells, Minn., was a visitor in the Fox office at Minneapolis last week.

R. H. Byram of the New Dream theatre at Redwood Falls, paid a visit to the Twin Cities recently.

George W. Ryan has taken over the Palace theatre at Hector, Minn., from E. P. Nelson.

Waldorf and Johnson have taken over the management of the Grand theatre at Estherville, Ia., Minneapolis film men report.

Ray D. Stewart of the Fox sales force, who makes his headquarters at LaCrosse, is not half so sick as he was supposed to be. In fact, he denies having been sick at all in spite of the story that went the rounds that he was in bad shape. He was formerly with F. B. O. here.

W. J. Morgan, sales manager. and Cecil E. Mayberry, district manager, of Producers' Distributing Corporation, spent a few days with Jack O'Toole, local manager. last week.

Lloyd Willis, formerly with the Will Hays organization, has come out from the home office of Warner Brothers as special representative. It is understood that he will become division manager.

Warner Brothers force of five salesmen, supervised by T. A. Burke, manager, and M. E. Montgomery, assistant manager, has been making high marks in the drive now being conducted throughout the United States. Last week this organization went well over its quotas.

H. B. Smoots of the Lowell theatre at Little Falls has gone back home after a visit to Minneapolis.

J. Dudley of the Dudley theatre at Bradley, S. D., has been paying calls at the exchanges here.

John Millar of Valley City, N. D., is getting to be a familiar figure on the film row here. The opening of his new Rex theatre sent him back to the Twin Cities again last week.

Stanley B. Waite, two-reel comedy salesmanager for Pathe, dropped into Minneapolis office and stayed a few days last week.

J. O. Sholseth let the Princess theatre at Sioux Falls run itself for a day or two last week and came to the cities.

E. P. Nelson of Hector was looking around in Minneapolis last week after selling out the Palace in Hector.

L. R. Campion, Capitol theatre, Chatfield, Minn., has been in the city looking over product for his fall program.

M. A. Manning came in a few days ago from the Opera House at Baldwin, Wis., and continued the story that Wisconsin is doing well in the film line.

E. S. Noreen of the Rex at Hutchinson told the Pathe force the other day that it looked like a good year in "Hutch."

Morris Abrams, the genial and high-minded exploiteer of Metro-Goldwyn is in Watertown, S. D., thinking up one for that fast growing town.

Charles Sonin, purchasing agent of Metro Goldwyn, has come on from New York to look over the needs of the local office.

Everett Dilley is keeping the road hot between Northfield, his field of operations and the Twin City exchange. No sooner is the news published of a former visit than he is back on a new one. The results are showing in his program, however. His theatre is the Grand.

From the Garden theatre at South - Hibbing comes Louis Deutsch on a visit to film row. He pronounces the Iron Range prosperous.

M. Kleinholtz of Buffalo, Minn., was in the Metro offices last week.

Schultz and Zetter are now handling the Dreamland theatre at Tappan, N. D.

Isabelle Getter who formerly operated a small theatre at Staples,

Minn., is taking over the Caughren opera house at Sauk Center.

Alexandria is still facing a big battle on the Sunday show proposition and is getting the unanimous backing of the exchanges in Minneapolis.

Virginia Woodward, Owatonna's Metropolitan theatre high light is back from a long vacation and the theatre is running right again.

Mrs. Mayme Comer, secretary to A. V. Leak, the Paramount manager in the Northwest, is resigning and is said to be going down east. She has been with the Paramount for a long time.

Dick Rosebaum, district manager, and Jimmy Clark, special representative, of Paramount are in the Twin Cities, trying to find out how the Northwest organization came to make such a record in the last drive.

J. E. O'Toole, Producers Distributing corporation manager, is back from a series of jaunts including La Crosse, Wisconsin, Duluth and Superior and the Iron Range cities.

The McMinn brothers, Roy and Os, are attending to the theatre business in Virginia and Superior. Roy is back at the Capitol in Superior and Os has taken the Royal at Virginia, which his brother formerly handled.

Billy Biesel, Minneapolis exploiteer for United Artists, has been invading the British Empire. He has spent the last two or three weeks in Winnipeg.

Jack Wiesian from the New York office has gone back home after filling in for Biesel here in his absence.

Phil Dunas, manager of Universal here, and William Prass, his exploitation man, are back on the job again this week after completing the series of Universal parties to theatre owners and managers at which the company's product was shown. Their last appearance as troupers was at Devils Lake.

Eddie Ruben is back from New York. He brought back several nice arrangements for service to the Finkelstein & Ruben string for which he does all the booking.

M. L. Finkelstein notified the folks in his F. & R. office here that he found the ship all right in

New York and is now on the way to France. He is with the party which includes Mr. and Mrs. Robert Lieber, the First National president and his wife.

B. J. Benfeld who handles theatres at Morris and Graveville, Minn., stopped in at First National's office recently.

The arbitration committee of the Film Board exchange is said to have broken all records for cases handled last week.

F. M. Honey has purchased the Moon theatre, Tecumseh, Neb., which he sold out a year ago. He has been operating the Isis at Cedar Rapids, Ia.

Newly redecorated the Pastime theatre at Maquoketa, Ia., is now doing business again.

The Palace theatre at Nora Springs, Ia., has been bought by R. D. Williams.

The Cozy theatre at Dyersville, Ia., has been taken over by Clifford Niles of Anamosca.

The Lyric theatre, Columbus Junction, Ia., recently purchased by Ludy Boston is now managed by Harry Dilley.

The Pastime theatre, Brandon, Ia., has been reopened.

The Palace theatre at Federal Dam, Minn., has been taken over by F. J. Mack.

The house in the City hall, Lake Norden, S. D., recently operated by Robert Redburn, is now in the hands of Henry Horton.

The Sawyer theatre at Doland, S. D., is now in the hands of W. H. Welch, whose son is operating the Letcher house.

The New Palace theatre now being built at Rapid City, S. D., will open Nov. 1 under direction of Zack Watterson and A. L. Brown, formerly of the Dreamland there. This brings the first competition since the Elks theatre was taken over by the Black Hills Amusement company.

Conrad Mahowald, son of J. J. Mahowald of the Alabama theatre, Garrison, N. D., is known as the heaviest 16-year-old high school student in the state. He tips the scales at around 250 and is much sought after by football scouts. Fat men's seats are being installed in part of Nate Chapman's Garden theatre, Iowa City, Ia. A whole row of 22 inch seats is being used in addition to the usual 17-inch places.

Cincinnati

JIM DUNBAR, general publicity agent for the Hyman Interests in Huntington, W. Va., is ill in the hospital with typhoid fever.

J. E. McCauley of the Peerless Reflector Lamp Co. visited last week with Jake Gelman of the Cincinnati Theatre Equipment Co.

The Midland Mining Co. of Triby, Ky., has purchased a complete new equipment for its show house in Trilby, Ky.

Fred Meyer and Harry Silvers

of the Palace Theatre, Hamilton, Ohio, paid their weekly visit to Film Row the other day.

The Universal Trade Showing at the Manding Theatre, Middleboro, Ky., was a huge success. Otto Brown, the manager of the house, and Chas. Lowenburg, Universal exploiteer, were in charge.

Miss Katherine Roush of the Dreamland Theatre, Waverly, Ohio, visited the various film buildings last week.

W. H. Shull of the Gem The-

atre, Newark, Ohio, made a flying trip to film row last week.

Del Holand, manager of the Delmar Theatre, Portsmouth, O., was another visitor to the Roadway film building last week.

Tony Cassinelli of the Bulan Theatre, Bulan, Ky., paid his regular monthly visit to the city and exchanges last week.

A welcome visitor to film row the other day was Charles Gross, owner and manager of the Columbia Theatre, Dayton, Ohio.

George Kirby, for the last five years booker for Metro-Goldwyn is now serving in the same capacity with the local F. B. O. exchange.

S. H. Nesbeitt, W. Va. salesman for F.B.O. is having his tonsils removed during his vacation period this week.

Ed. Booth manager for F.B.O. and C. Kendall Columbus salesman for the same firm made a flying trip through the surrounding towns.

Buffalo

THE strike of musicians, stage hands and operators is still in force in the Strand, Cataract and Bellevue theatres, Niagara Falls, N. Y., and promises to continue indefinitely. High officers of the stage hands union were in the Cataract City last week end but were unable to get together with the theatre interests so they returned to New York. A. C. Hayman, president of the Cataract Amusement company, operating the Strand and Cataract, has left for the wilds in northern Ontario for a two weeks' hunting and fishing trip, and Herman Lorence, manager of the Bellevue has started on a motor tour to the Adirondacks and New York city. The Strand is celebrating its third anniversary this week.

Members of the Rochester Parent-Teachers' association heard Mrs. A. S. Mattice outline the work for the Eastman theatre educational program committee the other day. The association is co-operating in arranging the programs for the Saturday morning children shows at the big house.

Four thousand, two hundred and twenty-seven different articles have been picked up during the past ten months in the Eastman, Rochester, auditorium. A great majority of these articles were returned to their owners. A review of the collection displays a variety that would do justice to a five and ten cent store. They range all the way from prayer books to soldering irons and lipsticks. Handkerchiefs head the list with a total of 1,890, the majority of which are women's. The women also left behind some 106 vanity cases, along with 55 pairs of rubbers, 80 umbrellas and 102 combs. House Manager John J. O'Neill must be a busy man.

George Biehler, the genial Hamburg, N. Y. film magnate, expects

to have his new theatre ready soon after the first of the year for the entertainment of the villagers.

Charlie Bowe, manager of the Frontier, a Buffalo community house, has received a letter from Mayor Frank X. Schwab congratulating him on his recent marriage. Other local celebrities are doing the same thing.

It is reported that Buffalo theatre interests have leased the old Browning-King site on Main street, opposite Shea's Hippodrome, on which they will build a house and lease to someone.

William L. Sherry, one of the organizers of the Famous Players-Lasky a decade ago and who has the first F. P. L. franchise in western New York, has resigned as manager of the Buffalo United Artists' exchange and is going to Florida to seek wealth and the fountain of eternal youth.

Pat Dowling, funnybone doctor and delegate for Al Christie, was in Buffalo last week end, visiting leading exhibitors and conferring with Colonel Howard F. Brink, local Educational exchange manager.

Mayor William J. MacFarlane won out in the primaries in Canandaigua, N. Y., the other day, over his opponent by a bare plurality of 28 votes. Mayor Bill is also interest in the exhibitor end of the business. He was one of the officers of the old Associated Theatres, Inc., which was headed by Harold P. Dygert.

There have been some changes at the Buffalo Fox exchange. Bill Rowell is now a sales representative instead of branch manager. Charlie Johnston has resigned and has accepted a position with the Freedom Film corporation as a salesman. O. R. Rieffel, former manager of the Albany office and recently Rochester representative, has also re-

signed from the Buffalo sales force.

C. H. Smith, manager of the Shattuck Opera House in Hornell, N. Y., has taken over the Peerless theatre in the same Southern Tier town, The Peerless was formerly operated by Mrs. Grace Flint.

Al Root, former Olean exhibitor, is coming back in the business when he takes over the management of the new Thurston road theatre which will open about November 1 in Rochester, N. Y.

Allan S. Moritz has resigned as manager of the Buffalo office of Dependable Pictures Corporation in the Beyer building. He is now devoting his time to the operation of the Ritz theatre in Niagara Falls, N. Y.

The Strand theatre, operated by Bill Dillon in Ithaca, N. Y., is now offering vaudeville the last half of the week. Pictures are being shown the first half. Bill has booked all the big features for the Cornell town house.

The Cataract theatre in Niagara Falls, N. Y., has inaugurated a policy of double feature bills, changing the program Sunday and Thursdays. Eddie Weinberg is managing this house for the Cataract Amusement company, which is headed by A. C. Hayman, the bird who recently took Walter Hays into camp in a pinochle game.

Batiste Madalena, head of the Eastman theatre poster department, was awarded a gold medal as the first prize in the figure and portrait class of the Art Exhibit held at the Rochester exposition. Mr. Madalena's canvas which is a huge decorative panel in oil ten feet long and five feet high, is titled "Prosperity."

It is reported that Ben Fitzer of Syracuse has closed for the lease of the new theatre being built in Kenmore, N. Y., and

which will be ready for the public early in the new year. It is understood the Shea Amusement company was negotiated with for the lease of the house but considered the rental asked too high.

Negotiations are said to be under way by Al Sherry and Ben Levine for the lease of the Main-Central market building, at 640 Main street, which they plan to remodel into a 1700 seat vaudeville and picture house.

Through a mutual agreement between the management of the Strand-Cataract theatre the disorderly conduct charge preferred in Niagara Falls police court last week against William Sarginson, Jr., secretary of the local Musician's union, has been withdrawn and the case disposed of. This course was taken when officers of the union handed the complainant a written guarantee that there would be no further molestation of theatre employes on the part of union members.

The Universal motor bus which has been making a cross country trip, blew into Buffalo the other day and after giving Mayor Schwab a ride and visiting some of the theatres in town, parked for several hours in front of the Olympic on Lafayette Square where it attracted a large crowd.

Charles W. Anthony, a former manager of the local Vitagraph, and later the Warner Brothers exchange, has been appointed branch manager for Associated Exhibitors in Buffalo. Harry E. Lotz, who has held this position, has been promoted to a district managership in the same organization.

Fred Schweppe will open the remodeled Amusu theatre in Elmira soon under the name of the Capitol. A $30,000 organ has been installed in the house which will offer pictures. The capacity is now 1,000.

San Francisco

A FREE-FOR-ALL distance race began through the streets of Oakland when a suspect declared to be Jose Herrera, 20, of 1244 Helen St., thrust his hand into the ticket office of the State theatre, seized a roll of currency and took to his heels on Sept. 16th. The first competition was provided by E. A. Smith, manager of the theatre, who was standing in the lobby when the cashier cried out. As the chase swept from 14th and Broadway across another street intersection Traffic Officer A. L. Seydn deserted his post and set the pace for the mob. The crowd closed in quick and the chase was over. A roll of bills amounting to $50 was found in Jose's pocket.

W. J. Clark, well known theatre man, formerly Eureka and who some months ago acquired the Vacaville theatre from J. A. Harvey, Jr., has completed plans

to practically build a new theatre on the site of the present house now under his management. The new theatre, when completed, will have just double the seating capacity of the present house, A. W. Cornelius, the San Francisco architect, has made the plans. Work will start shortly.

Harry Fontana, formerly local manager of the Unique Theatre in San Francisco, for the Wobber Bros., has just completed rehabilitation of the Glade Theatre at Lindsay opening on Sept. 16th. Motion pictures exclusively will be the policy.

H. L. Beach of Beach and Krahn Amusement Co. controlling the Chimes Strand and Lorin theatres in Oakland and Berkeley, accompanied by Mrs. Beach returned from a vacation trip to the southern end of the state. Beach is mixing duty, pleasure and a little observation business with his trip.

Thos. H. Tucker, former exchange employee and more recently for two years past with Grauman's Egyptian Theatre in Hollywood, is now at the Temple Theatre in San Francisco.

Frank Newman, who directs the affairs of the State-Orpheum at Stockton was a visitor along Golden Gate row recently.

San Cargano of the Golden Gate Theatre in Oakland is commencing work on his new 1500-seat theatre on San Pablo Avenue.

Robert E. Power Studios and the Armstrong-Power Studios have under preparation plans to give the T. & D. Theatre in Oakland a complete rejuvenating from dome to cellar.

Another of the chain of M. Blumenfeld theatres opened Sept. 15th at Berkeley under the customary auspicious program attending the inaugural of the Blumenfeld theatre openings. Officialdom of the college city was on

hand as well as the film industry to wish Max success in his latest amusement enterprise to open.

Visitors from out of town were Mr. and Mrs. Leslie Hables of King City, Sam Gordon of Napa, Mr. McDannell of Santa Rosa and Charles Fraler of Tracy.

Rex Midgely, manager of the American, Oakland's big picture theatre, returned recently from a trip to New York City, where he attended the First National clan gathering.

Charlie Kaufman of the Gem Theatre at Colusa, made his regular monthly sojourn to film row recently.

Hickman Price, a prominent official of the M. P. P. and D. of New City was a visitor in San Francisco at the office of Milton A. Nathan, local attorney, also interviewing a number of the local exchange managers.

CONSTRUCTION & EQUIPMENT DEPARTMENT

Theatre Analysis Reveals Interesting Data

Reports of Four Weeks Show Investment of $21,000,000; Sixty Projects Average $360,000

ANALYZING the reports on new theatre projects which have been received by MOTION PICTURE NEWS, the remarkable showing of sixty new motion picture theatres is recorded within the last four weeks. The reported investment called for by these new projects totals approximately $21,500,000, a figure which would tend to indicate that the estimate of over $200,000,000 for theatre construction and equipment during 1925 would be exceeded, especially when it is realized that this total of over $21,000,000, is solely for the purpose of construction of new houses and does not take into consideration the very material expenditure constantly required for the re-equipment of the thousands of theatres already in operation.

Further analyzing of these reports shows that Illinois leads with a $5,340,000 building program, though the number of projects calling for this figure is only eight. New York with thirteen projects will require $4,440,000 being very closely pressed for second place by California with a building program of $4,400,000 to be invested in eleven new theatres. New Jersey follows next in line with a schedule of $1,575,000 for six houses. Three other states call for $1,000,000 or more new theatre construction. They are: Virginia, $1,250,000, 1 project; Washington, $1,175,000, 4 projects; Wisconsin, $1,000,000, 1 project. Ten additional states report building programs varying from $700,000 down to $50,000. They are: Connecticut, $700,000; Massachusetts, $515,000; Arizona, $400,000; North Dakota, $150,000; Ohio, $125,000; Georgia, $110,-000; Kansas, $100,000; Pennsylvania, $70,-000; Minnesota, $50,000; Tennessee, $50,000.

These new theatre project reports call for a total seating capacity of approximately 84,000, which brings the average per theatre very nearly 1400. This unusually high average only forcibly illustrates the general tendency of the times towards large pretentious houses located in relatively large centers of population. However, it is well to note here that there are included in this building program quite a number of theatres calling for a seating capacity from 350 up to 800 seats.

Individual reports from which the above analysis was compiled follow:

ARIZONA

Phoenix—Plans have been announced for erection of theatre bldg., to cost approx. $400,000 to be erected at southwest corner of Second Avenue and Adams Street on site 100 x 137½ ft. Seat Cap. 2,000. Bldg. will be theatre-office. Owners—The Rickard Nace Amusement Co., Arizona.

CALIFORNIA

Hawthorne—Plans have been completed for erection of theatre bldg. on corner of Ballona Ave. & Hawthorne Blvd. Seat. Cap. 1100; Approx. Cost $90,000.

Hollywood—Plans are being drawn for erection of theatre bldg. to be erected at corner of Eleventh & Hill Sts. Seat. Cap. 1200; Approx. Cost $2,000,000—Los Angeles Theatre Co. will have long lease on theatre.

Pasadena—J. H. Woodworth & Son, Archts. are drawing plans for erection of two story colonial type theatre, store and office bldgs. to be erected at Chester Ave. & Colorado Sts., Seat. Cap. 1200—Approx. Cost $194,000—Owners, Liberty Players Inc.

Redding—Chester Cole & E. Brouchard, Archts., are drawing plans for new theatre bldg. to be erected in the Red Front Bldg. at Market St. nr. Butte. The theatre is to be installed by J. H. Wood, Mgr. of Redding Theatre.

Santa Ana—Eugene Durfee, Archt., of Anaheim and Los Angeles is drawing plans for theatre bldg. to be erected on the northeast corner of Fourth and Bush Sts. Approx. Cost $200,000; Site 100' x 165'; Seat. Cap. 2000.

Los Angeles—G. Albert Lansburgh is completing plans for the erection of a $1,250,000 theatre bldg. to be erected at Hollywood Blvd. and Wilcox St. by Warner Brothers. Seating cap. to be 3,600.

Los Angeles—Plans are being completed for the erection of theatre bldg. at Vermont Ave. and 87th St. to cost approx. $250,000; owners, West Coast Theatres.

San Francisco—Plans are being drawn for the erection of theatre bldg. on Haight St. nr. Fillmore. Approx. cost $160,000. Owner, W. S. King. Seat cap. 1,500.

Lankershim—Plans have been announced for a $250,000 theatre bldg. to be erected at Lankershim Blvd. and Weddington Ave. on site 100 x 210 ft. Seat. Cap. 1,500. Site leased by Hollywood Theatres Inc. from Weddington Investment Co. for period of 99 years.

Monterey—Plans are being drawn by Read Bros., San Francisco, Archts., for erection of theatre bldg. to be erected on Alvarado St. Approx. Cost $200,000. Seat. Cap. 1,500. Owners—The T. & D. Theatres Co.

Oroville—Plans are being drawn by Arthur H. Lamb, Sacramento, Archt., for the erection of theatre bldg. at Meyers and Robinson Sts. Seat. Cap. 1,400; Approx. Cost $200,000.

CONNECTICUT

Winsted—L. J. Thompson of New Britain is drawing plans for the erection of theatre bldg. on Main St. Owner, John E. Panara.

New Britain—Plans are being drawn for the erection of theatre bldg. office bldg. and stores on West Main St. Site 109' x 200' Approx. Cost $700,000.

GEORGIA

Atlanta—Plans are being drawn for erection of theatre bldg. at 57 Gordon St. The bldg. will also have stores and will cost approx. $60,000. Bldg. will be erected on site 50 x 200. Owner—Adolph Samuels.

Atlanta—Plans have been completed for the erection of theatre bldg. at 201 Lee St. Approx. Cost $50,000. Seat. Cap. 1000. Owners—Southern Development Corp.

ILLINOIS

Crystal Lake—Plans are being drawn for erection of theatre bldg. to be erected on Brink Street on site 82½ x 132 ft. in Crystal Lake, Ill. The theatre will have seating capacity of 1,000. Approx. Cost $100,000. Owner—Fred C. Dierking, Chicago.

Springfield—Plans are being drawn for theatre bldg. to be erected at 5th and Jefferson Streets. Approx. Cost $1,250,000. Seat. Cap. 3,000. Owner—Balaban & Katz.

Sullivan—Plans are being drawn for erection of theatre bldg. on the East side of Square. Approx. Cost $30,000. Owner— J. H. Ireland, 608 South Haworth Avenue, Decatur.

Chicago—Rapp & Rapp are drawing plans for theatre bldg. to be erected at Washington Blvd., Crawford & West End Avenues. Site 165 x 125. Approx. Cost $4,000,000. Owners —Balaban & Katz.

Sterling—Plans are being drawn for theatre bldg. to be erected in Sterling. Archts. drawing plans are Bradley & Bradley, Brown Bldg., Sterling, Ill. Seat. Cap. 800; Approx. Cost $40,000. Owners William Tifft & William Schrader, Sterling.

Chicago—Levy & Klein, 111 W. Washington St. are drawing plans for the erection of theatre bldg. 1 story brick on Irving Park Blvd. nr. Central Park. Approx. cost $225,000. Owners, Knipp & Shapiro; ¾ Architect.

Springfield—Plans are being drawn for the erection of theatre bldg. at North Grand Ave. E. bet. 8th and 9th Sts. Seat cap. 600. Approx. cost $25,000. Owners, Theodore Gray and Charles Coutrakon.

Paris—Plans are being completed for the erection of theatre bldg. to be erected on North Central Ave. and to occupy all available space between the Paris Auto Co. and the Central Hotel. Seating cap. 850.

KANSAS

Topeka—Thos. W. Williamson, archt. is drawing plans for erection of theatre bldg. to be erected on Seventh St., Topeka, Kansas. New theatre will have seating cap. of 1,500.

MASSACHUSETTS

Malden—Plans have been completed for the erection of theatre bldg. to be erected in Malden Square at a cost of $450,000. Seating cap. 3,000. Owners, Messrs. Green and Ellen-

(Continued on page 1732)

Where the Goetz optical and film products are manufactured. Bird's eye view of the large plant at Berlin, Germany.

Final O. K. Placed on Plans for New Grauman Theatre at Hollywood

THE first definite authentic announcement concerning the much heralded new Grauman theatre in Hollywood was given out yesterday by Sid Grauman, following his placing the final okay on the plans for the $5,000,000 edifice as designed, executed and engineered by Mendel Meyer of Meyer and Holler, working under ideas created by the California showman, who has raised the prologue from a vaudeville skit to an extravaganza, and developed film playhouses from the nickelodeon to the bizarre picture palace palatial.

The new temple to Thespis will be located on the North Side of Hollywood boulevard, between Orange Drive and Orchid Avenue, with a frontage of 140 feet on the boulevard and a depth of 250 feet. The seating capacity will be 2,000.

The motif of the theatrical palace is to be that of the classical Chinese dynasties, and inspiration has been drawn from those magnificent Celestial temples which bear the same relation to the architecture of the Orient as do the Greek Acropolis and the Roman Forum to the architecture of the Occident.

The approach to the Thespian palace will be through a great tropical garden, elliptical in form, and surrounded by a wall 45 feet high.

No expense will be spared in creating such surroundings that when the visitor enters the court he will be conscious of entering another world.

The auditorium will be absolutely unique in its plan, patrons passing through great colonnades or corridors on either side, formed by towering lacquered columns seven feet in diameter.

In developing the scheme for painted decoration, the marvelous colorings and designs developed to such a high degree in early days by the Chinese people have furnished the inspiration for the architect.

One of the largest and finest pipe organs in the country will be installed, with the music introduced into the auditorium through an elaborate grill in the ceiling. Provision will be made for a very large orchestra.

The proscenium arch at the asbestos curtain will be 65 feet wide. The stage from this line will be 40 feet in depth and 140 feet wide, designed to permit the staging on an elaborate scale of the most gigantic of stage productions.

The structure will be Class "A" construction throughout on a frame of steel. A highly developed system of ventilation will be incorporated, which will permit of the introduction of fresh air, cooled to the proper temperature in summer, in such a manner that the patrons will be unconscious of the mechanical circulation.

Ground will be broken for the theatre about November 1, and it is estimated that more than a year will be required to complete the structure.

Reports that Grauman is financially interested in other theatres to be constructed are vigorously denied, his only enterprises of this character being Grauman's Egyptian theatre and the new Grauman Chinese Theatre.

Effinger to Build 2,500 Seat House in Philadelphia

Plans are now being prepared for the erection of a 2,500-seat theatre at 67th avenue and Broad street, Philadelphia, for Herbert Effinger, who now operates the Strand, Leader, 69th Theatre and the Nixon at Glenside, all of which are booked through the Stanley Company. The lot is 125 x 200 feet and the specifications call for a structure, including stores, which will cost approximately half a million dollars. It will probably be ready for operation late next spring.

Atlanta, Georgia, to Have Another New Theatre

A new motion picture theatre is to be erected in the heart of the West End business district at 57 Gordon Street. There will be erected a motion picture theatre with stores and the cost of the new structure will be approximately $60,000. The site on which the new building will be erected is 50 x 200. The owner of the new theatre is Adolph Samuels.

Theatre Analysis Reveals Interesting Data

(*Continued from page 1731*)

berg of the Mystic Theatre, Malden and Ramsdell Bros. of the Orpheum Theatre, Malden.

MASSACHUSETTS
Springfield—John W. Foster is drawing plans for erection of theatre bldg. on Walnut St. nr. Union St. Bldg. will have three stores on street front. Approx. Cost $65,000. Owner—Hyman Kronick of Springfield, Mass.

MINNESOTA
Robbinsdale—Plans are being drawn for theatre bldg. to be erected on site at corner of West Broadway Avenue and the New Rockford Road. Approx. cost $50,000; Seat. Cap. 350. W. E. Westby is the Archt. and Wm. Mueller is the owner of the new building which will contain four stores.

NEBRASKA
Omaha—Plans are being drawn for the erection of a theatre bldg. on the Southwest corner of 20th and Farnam Sts. Seating cap. 3,200. Owner, A. H. Blank; site, 207' on Farnam St. x 132' on 20th St. Site leased from Creighton University.

NEW JERSEY
Long Branch—Plans are being drawn by Maximilian Zipkes, Archt. of 25 West 43rd St., N. Y. for erection of theatre bldg. at corner of North Broadway and Second Ave. Approx. Cost $350,000. Seat. Cap. 1,500. Plot 155 ft. x 145 ft. Owner—Lucinor Holding Corp. of N. Y.

Elizabeth—Plans have been completed for the erection of theatre bldg. to be erected at Jefferson Ave. & East Jersey St. Approx. Cost $175,000; Seat. Cap. 2500. Owner—Fabian Enterprise Co.

West Bergen—George Flagg is drawing plans for the erection of theatre bldg. at West Side and Communipaw Aves. Seat. Cap. 1500; Owners—The Wolcott Holding Co., Julius Krumgold, Pres. of 48 Van Reipen Ave.

Red Bank—W. E. Lehman of Newark is drawing plans for the erection of theatre bldg. to be erected at Maple Ave. & Monmouth St. by Joseph Stern of Theatrical Enterprises of Newark. The bldg. will contain stores and offices. Approx. cost $350,000.

Englewood—Plans are being drawn for the erection of a theatre bldg. at Palisade Ave and Van Brunt St., site 100 x 115 ft. Approx. cost $350,000. Seat cap. 2,000.

Jersey City—Plans are being completed for the erection of theatre bldg. on the west side of Ocean Ave. bet. Danforth and Cator Aves. in the Greenville section. Approx. cost $350,000. Seating cap. 1,800.

NEW YORK
Brooklyn—Plans are being prepared by Douglas Hall, Archt. for erection of theatre and roof garden to be erected on the southeast corner of Kings Highway and East Eighteenth St. Approx. Cost $1,000,000. Seat. Cap. 1,800. Owner—Charles A. Goldreyer and Maurice L. Fleishman.

East Bronx—Plans are being drawn for erection of theatre bldg. office suites, and store space to be erected on East Tremont Ave. between Park and Washington Avenues. Seat. Cap. 4,500. Owner—Fox Film Corporation.

New York City—From plans drawn by Charles N. Whinston and Bro. Archts. theatre bldg. will be erected in the rear at 2-3 South St. Approx. Cost $100,000. Owner—Whitehall Amusement Co.

West Bronx—Louis H. Kaplan, Archt. plans to erect theatre bldg. at the southeast corner of University and Tremont Avenues, West Bronx. Seat. Cap. 2,000. Owners—Louis H. Kaplan and Silverman, Willett & Ballatin.

(*Continued on page 1734*)

Interesting Program for Society of Motion Picture Engineers' Fall Convention

THE SOCIETY OF MOTION PICTURE ENGINEERS will hold their Fall Convention beginning Monday, October 5th and concluding Thursday the 8th at the Lakewood Farm Inn, Roscoe, N. Y. An exceptionally interesting program of papers and entertainment has been announced that promises to equal or surpass any previous convention. Another attraction that this meeting holds forth to the Society members and guests is the delightful auto trip to the meeting place for all those within a radius of 250 miles of Roscoe.

The program for the meeting is as follows:

October 5th—Registration, President's Address, Unfinished Business, New Business, Report of Arrangements Committee, Report of Advertising Committee; Papers: "Handling of Motion Picture Film in the Field Under Climatic Conditions" —R. J. Flaherty; "Washing of Motion Picture Film"—Kenneth Hickman; "Effect of Scratches on Motion Picture Film"—S. E. Sheppard and S. S. Sweet, Evening of Entertainment.

October 6th—Papers: "Importance of Village Theatre"—F. H. Richardson; "Color Photography Patents"—William V. D. Kelley; "A New Camera for News Screen Cinematographers"—J. H. McNabb; "A New Incandescent Spotlight"— L. C. Porter; Report of Progress Committee—"The Questionable Educational Value of the Motion Pictures"—A. W. Abrams; "Movies for Teaching; The Proof of their Usefulness"—Rowland Rogers; "An Exhibitors Problem in 1925"—E. T. Clark; "Transmission of Pictures Over Telephone Lines"—Dr. H. E. Ives; Evening of Entertainment.

October 7th—Papers: "A Prefocusing Base and Socket for Projection Lamps" —R. S. Burnap; "The High Intensity Arc"—Dr. Frank Benford; "Reflector Arc Projection; some Limitations and Possibilities in Theory and Practice"—S. Stark; "Standards and Nomenclature Committee Report; Recreation as scheduled for the afternoon; Banquet—Informal.

October 8th—Papers: "Importance of Proper Splicing"—E. J. Dennison; "Rack Marks and Air Bells Produced in the Development of Motion Picture Film by Rack System"—J. I. Crabtree; "The Pathe Camera and Projector"—W. R. Daniel.

Building Contracts Continue to Be Let for New England Theatres

CONTRACTS have been let and ground broken for the new theatre in Harvard square, Cambridge, Mass., which will probably be known as the University Theatre. It is being erected by Charles A. Newhall of Brookline, Mass., for the University Theatres, Inc., of which Charles E. Hatfield of Newton, Mass., is a leading factor. The company operates the Community Theatre and other playhouses.

The new theatre will be completed sometime in March, according to present plans. It will have a seating capacity of about 2,000 and will have a main entrance from Massachusetts avenue.

J. M. & C. J. Buckley of Boston have the contract and will push the theatre to completion at the earliest possible date. Programs of feature films with comedy and short subjects and news reels will be given and it is probable orchestral music will be provided.

Contracts for the new S & S Corporation theatre at 250 Main street, Middletown, Conn., have been let to Tracy Brothers Co. of Waterbury, Conn. The playhouse will be completed late in the spring and will cost approximately $150,000. The auditorium will be 60 by 150 feet with lobby 22 by 125 feet. It will be of brick and concrete construction with balcony.

Alterations costing about $25,000 are to be made on the former St. James Theatre, 239 Huntington avenue, Boston, by the new owners, the Keith-Albee company.

A new theatre is to be erected by the Singer Real Estate Trust of 84 Chauncey street, Boston, at 119 Dudley street in the Roxbury district. No announcement is

forthcoming at this time as to the lessees. The theatre will be 81 by 195 feet with auditorium and main balcony and will cost approximately $225,000. It will be completed late in the spring. M. Shapiro & Son of Boston have the general contract and plans were drawn by F. A. Norcross of Boston.

The Wakefield Theatre, Wakefield, Mass. which was gutted by fire a few weeks ago, has been entirely remodelled, enlarged and redecorated and this week the house reopened for the season. The theatre was practically reconstructed from basement to roof.

Broadway Theatre Corporation of Providence, R. I. is constructing foundations for its new theatre on Broadway, which will be 60 by 200 feet and will have a seating capacity of from 850 to 900.

The Globe Theatre on Chapel street, New Haven, Conn. is to undergo extensive remodelling, contracts for which have been let. A new front, new lobby, new toilets, new ceilings, and redecorating of the theatre will be done before reopening for the winter season.

Alexander Saraceno is to build a new theatre in Middletown, Conn. which, it is understood, will be linked up with the circuit operated by Israel Gordon of New Haven. The theatre will be located near the present Grand Theatre, owned by the D. & G. Corporation which also owns the Middlesex Theatre, the only other theatre in the city. It is understood the new theatre will cost in the vicinity of $100,000. Construction will commence within the next 30 days.

Theatre Analysis Reveals Interesting Data

(Continued from page 1732)

Coxsackie—Plans are being drawn for theatre bldg. and stores (2) to be erected at Mansion St. & Spencer Blvd. Seat. Cap. 600; Owner—Geo. E. Cornwell of Coxsackie.

Jackson Heights—Herbert J. Krapp, Archt. has completed plans for theatre bldg. to be erected at the southwest corner of Northern Blvd. and Eighty-Third St., Site 100 x 150; Approx. Cost $1,000,000—Owned by Max J. Kramer & Son, to be operated by Grob & Knobel, owners and operators of the Jackson Theatre.

Syracuse—Plans are being drawn for the erection of theatre bldg. at Westcott St. & Harvard Pl., Seat. Cap. 2000; Salt Springs Finance Corp. represented by Philip and Wm. Smith of the Denison Bldg. is said to be backing the enterprise.

Williamsville—Plans are being drawn for theatre bldg. to be erected on the site where the Glen Theatre originally was. Seating Cap. 300; Owners—Cardina Bros.

Albany—T. W. Lamb, Architect, is drawing plans for the erection of a theatre bldg. to be erected at South Pearl and Howard Sts. Approx. cost $1,000,000. Owner, Moe Mark.

Inwood—Eric O. Holdigren, Architect, 371 Fulton St., Brooklyn, N. Y., is drawing plans for the erection of theatre bldg. on Bayview Ave. on plot 121 x 49 ft. Owner, Facopoulos Bros., Cedarhurst Ave., Cedarhurst, N. Y. Approx. cost $50,000.

Washington Heights—Plans are being drawn by Eugene de Rosa for the erection of a theatre bldg. at 560 W. 181st St. on plot 150 x 100. Owner, Heights Theatre, Inc.

New York City—Eugene de Rosa is drawing plans for the erection of theatre bldg. to be erected at 176th St. and Jerome Ave. Seating cap. 2,200. Owner, Jerome Avenue Exhibition Company, Inc.

Westbury—Plans are being drawn for the erection of theatre bldg. to be erected on Post Ave. There will be 15 stores and apartments above them. Seating cap. 1,000. Owner, Hill-Calderone Corporation.

OHIO

Bowling Green—Plans are being drawn for the erection of theatre bldg. on site 44 x 200 ft. Seat cap. 800; approx. cost $125,000. Owners, Young Bros. of Bowling Green Amusement Company.

PENNSYLVANIA

Greenville—J. A. Altschuler, Pierson Bldg., New Castle, Pa., is drawing plans for the erection of theatre bldg. to be erected on Mercer St. Site 17 x 70; approx. cost $40,000. Owner, The Mercer Square Theatre, W. J. Silverberg, Mercer St., Greenville.

Woodlawn—Plans are being drawn by F. M. Stetson, Archt., 425 Franklin Ave., for erection of theatre bldg. on Franklin Ave., site 25x100, at approximate cost of $30,000. Owner—Anthony P. Jin, c/o Strand Theatre, Franklin Ave.

TENNESSEE

Memphis—Anker F. Hanson, Archt. with offices in the Shrine Bldg. is drawing plans for the erection of theatre bldg. in Linden Circle. Approx. Cost $50,000.

Memphis—George Maplan, Archt. is drawing plans for the erection of a theatre bldg. at Union Avenue and Avalon St.

VIRGINIA

Roanoke—Plans are being drawn for erection of theatre bldg. and office bldg. to be erected on northwest corner of Jefferson St. and Kirk Ave. Approx. cost $1,250,000; plot 75 x 170 ft. Owner—Sun Investment Corp.

(Continued on page 1738)

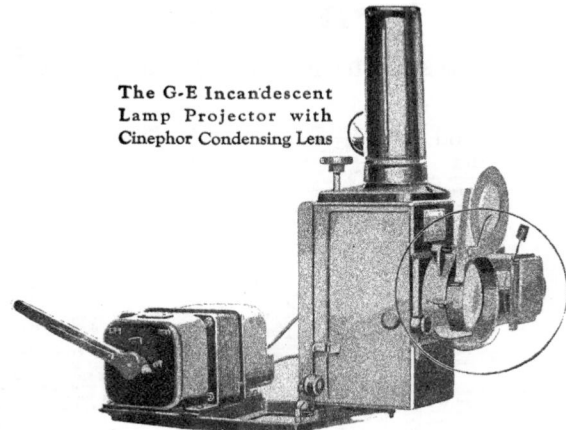

The G-E Incandescent
Lamp Projector with
Cinephor Condensing Lens

More Light from the Same Current

The Cinephor Condensing Lens, consisting of two specially designed parabolic condensers, makes the advantages of incandescent projection available to an increased number of theatres. This new lens is for use with the 30-volt, 30-ampere Mazda lamp, and can be adapted to all existing installations of the G-E incandescent lamp projector. Properly adjusted, it increases the amount of light on the screen nearly 50 percent over that obtained on the same sized picture with a standard prismatic condenser. In addition, the screen illumination is more even, the presentation of the picture improved.

For more than thirty years the General Electric Company has built electrical apparatus for service to every industry. In motion picture theatres all over the country, incandescent lamp projectors bearing the G-E monogram are providing the best, most even screen illumination.

General Electric specialists will be pleased to consult with any theatre owner or projectionist on the requirements of his theatre. Address the G-E office in any large city.

GENERAL ELECTRIC

GENERAL ELECTRIC COMPANY, SCHENECTADY, N. Y., SALES OFFICES IN ALL LARGE · CITIES

Projection
Optics, Electricity, Practical Ideas & advice

Inquiries and Comments

A Remarkable Change

FOR a considerable length of time a writer for a certain motion picture trade journal has been carefully nursing the idea that the laws governing the emission of light from primary sources —"open" sources he calls them—differed in some mysterious manner from those governing the projection of light by means of lenses and reflectors. We have looked high and low for a suitable definition of an "open" source—but all in vain, so we have come to the conclusion, much to our regret, that as far as "open" or "nude" sources, to speak with brutal frankness, are concerned, there simply "ain't no such animal."

Positive

Be that as it may, this writer was so positive in his convictions that the same laws did not apply in these two cases that he went so far as to accuse persons who thought otherwise of having seriously blundered. In this respect we call upon you to witness his rashness for yourself.

Sometime ago he wrote as follows: "Light intensity decreases inversely as the square of the distance from the source. It (the law) is mentioned here to caution you that *this law applies to light from an open light source only*, because many have committed the blunder of applying it to the light beam between the projection lens and the screen. The law does *not* apply to light after it has been acted upon by a *lens*."

Didn't Think So

The "information" contained in that paragraph did not strike us as being exactly correct; it didn't read right. With this thought in mind we undertook to explain in these columns how the "Inverse Square Law" *did* apply to projector beams and that the mere addition of lenses or reflectors did not, under average conditions, change its operation. This article appeared a little more than a year ago (MOTION PICTURE NEWS, July 26, 1924).

Immediately thereafter our friend defended his stand.

Third Party Agrees

He sent the article in question to a friend who is reputed to be well versed in optics. No doubt, much to the surprise of our literary contemporary, his friend agreed with our statements and proceeded to explain the whys and wherefores of his beliefs. In attempting this explanation he got considerably balled up and thus only served to increase our conviction that he, too, did not know what he was talking about.

In this connection let us quote from an article containing the discussions of our literary and optical friends which appeared a little less than a year ago.

Mr. Optics.—"Regarding the attached page (our article—Ed.) the following is a statement covering the situation: The fact that it is possible, with a given size crater, to project a given size picture at 50, 75, 100 or 125 feet projection distance, with practically the same screen illumination density in all cases, *merely by changing the* E. F. of the projection lens is sufficient proof that the inverse square law does *not* apply to the light action of the motion picture projector optical train as measured from light source to screen, although it does apply to that part of the light beam as measured from the condenser image (commonly referred to as the "aerial image") to the screen, when using an arc light source, and from the lens to screen when using a Mazda."

Just imagine securing a constant footcandle intensity on any throw between 50 ft. and 125 ft. "merely by changing the E. F. of the projection lens!" In other words if a certain system gave 8 footcandles on a 50 ft. throw and it was desired to secure the same intensity on a 300 ft. throw the only thing required would be "merely to change the E. F. of the projection lens" to a certain value and then—8 foot-candles would jump out of space and stare you in the face.

No Such Thing

The only effect that a change in projection lens E. F. will have, in any given optic system and where the throw is constant, is that the *total volume* of light on the screen will change in practically direct proportion to the *area* of the illuminated picture. *The intensity will remain constant.* The screen intensity will vary inversely *as the square of the throw regardless of projection lens* E. F.

The only things that effect *intensity* on the screen are *free diameter* of projection lens, source brightness, and aperture area. This assumes, of course that the system is properly adjusted to secure limiting illumination. As for the statement in the last part of the above quotation that the inverse square law is measured from the objective lens in one case and from the aerial image in another, why, that too is wrong. *It is measured from the objective lens in each case.*

Change in Attitude

In view of all the foregoing it is interesting to note a recent statement of our writing friend in which he confesses to a change of heart. He writes as follows:

"In conversation with —— he made the assertion that I was in error in saying that the inverse square law applies only to an open (Blast that word—Ed) light source— that the intensity of illumination decreased inversely as the square of the distance.

"—— holds that this law applies to anybeam of light, including the light from a projection lens. This I both concede and dispute. I concede that it applies to the beam from a projection lens, but dispute that it applies in just the same way. The light in a beam from a projection lens will decrease inversely as the square of the distance, provided that this does not always apply close to the lens; also I hold that it is stretching things to apply the inverse square law to the directed beam in the same way it is applied to the open (what again?—Ed) source.

"I am well aware of the fact that I could be cornered in this and put in a position where I would not exactly know how to prove my view correct, but all the same I do hold that, while granting the law to apply in both cases, still there is a difference. I think, however, the statement in the third paragraph of page 125 of —— is altogether too strong. I was in error when I made it."

A Trickey Law

Well, well! Will wonders never cease? After a solid year of heavy abuse the poor, old, inverse square law has come into its own. So it does apply to projector beams after all. And all the harsh things that were said about it, too.

The inverse square law is a fickle lady so she doesn't deserve much sympathy. She seems to be a very aristocratic person because she chooses her application in a critical manner. For instance, when our optical friend said the inverse square law applied to *any* beam of light he was wrong. Very much so. And yet in the strictest sense of the word he was right, too. When considering a spotlight flooding a stage, the inverse square law does *not* apply to the *beam* from the spot but only to individual points on the stage such as a person's head.

Nor does it apply to light beam between the collector and converging lenses of a plano-convex condenser, condenser set, although it does apply to the beam from the two lenses in combination.

Fundamental Law

The inverse square law is the *fundamental law of light*. In the *strictest sense* of the word, it applies to *all light radiation* no matter what the conditions of use are. It makes no difference whether lenses, mirrors, or other objects are placed in its path, the law always remains operative. The only possible effect such objects can have upon light is to change either its *direction* or *velocity* or both.

HOWEVER, the inverse square law in projection, is commonly understood to apply to *beams* (such as from mirrors or lenses) and in view of this it must be used with extreme caution.

The exact application of this law must be understood since the same factors in the law cannot be used for each condition, new factors are involved for each change.

Theatre Analysis Reveals Interesting Data

(Continued from page 1734)

WASHINGTON

Seattle—Wilson & Jones, Archts., Arcade
Bldg., have completed plans for erection of
theatre building at Green Lake, on plot 45 x 120,
on 72nd St. near Fifth Ave., northeast. Seat
cap. 700. Owner—Green Lake Theatre Company.

Tacoma—B. Marcus Priteca is drawing
plans for erection of theatre bldg. in Tacoma.
Approx. cost $1,000,000.

Mt. Vernon—Plans are being drawn for
erection of theatre bldg. at the corner of First
and Kincaid Streets. Theatre department of
the new bldg. has been leased by a Port Angeles man.

Seattle—B. Marcus Priteca and Fred J.
Peters are drawing plans for the erection of
theatre bldg. to be erected in the North Broadway district. Approx. cost $500,000. Owner,
Jensen and Von Herberg.

WISCONSIN

Milwaukee—Archts. Kick & Bauer, 811
State Street, are drawing plans for erection of
theatre bldg. on Farwell Ave. between Ivanhoe
and Kenilworth, to cost approximately $1,000,-
000. Owner—Mal Investment Co., Hy Weiss,
Manager, located at 425 E. Water Street, Milwaukee. Seat. Cap. 2,200.

Locatelli is Building Third House in Somerville, Mass.

Albert J. Locatelli, general manager of the
Ball Square and Central Theatres in Somerville, Mass., is building a third theatre on
Massachusetts avenue, corner of Lake street,
Arlington, Mass. which will be opened later
this season, probably around Nov. 1. The
construction work is being done by his father, John E. Locatelli of the J. E. Locatelli
Company. The new playhouse will be larger
than either of the two Somerville houses,
with a seating capacity of about 1,700. It is
located between Arlington square and North
Cambridge and will draw its patronage
largely from those sections of Arlington,
Cambridge, Somerville and Medford within
close proximity to the theatre.

Contracts to Be Let for New Arkansas House

T. W. Sharp, 114 Main street, Little
Rock, Ark., will let contracts shortly on the
new theatre he plans to erect at Beech and
Prospect avenue, Pulaski Heights. The
house will be one story, 40 by 140 ft. and
cost approximately $25,000 exclusive of
equipment. It will contain a balcony and
full size stage.

$50,000 Theatre to Be Built in Paris, Illinois

Paris, Ill., is to have a $50,000 theatre to
be erected between the Central Hotel and the
Paris Auto Company garage on site 47 x 147
ft. The theatre will have a seating capacity
of 800 persons. It will be up-to-date in
every respect.

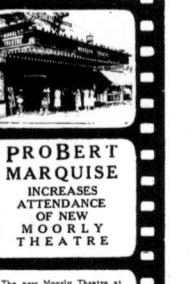

How Lobby Material and Equipment are Manufactured

By Wm. F. Libman, Libman-Spanjer Corp.

FROM the earliest days of the average normal youth, the desire to "see the wheels go round" is an inherent impulse in all of us; while the wish to see men working at some calling other than our own is always present.

And the urge to "look behind the scenes" is an even stronger one. So it seems to the writer that a brief trip through the factory of an up to date lobby equipment plant would not only be interesting, but fully in keeping with the subjects so far discussed in the present series of articles. As in every form of good construction, whether it be in the building or mechanical line, the material used, and the sort of labor engaged in its manipulation, determines to a great extent, the length of service, and the value to the user of the finished product.

As detailed in the last article, the very best medium that is most easily manufactured, that is most adaptable, readily worked, and at the same time most economical, is carefully chosen wood. It is but natural therefore, that woodworkers, carvers, and cabinet makers should predominate. Machinery for aiding the craftsmen mentioned is required, and forms a most important group of necessities in the frame building business.

Besides the artisans mentioned, the requirements also call for the inclusion of painters, decorators, glaziers, marble workers and electricians.

As we enter the factory, we pass through the shipping room where a completed order is ready waiting for shipment. The care necessary and the means employed in packing these easily-broken-in-transit frames will be touched upon in the natural sequence which will be followed—the building of a frame.

Lining the walls of this room, swathed in canvas, old velvets and sailcloths, are the finished frames, looking for all the world like the treasured objects that were brought, one by one, out of King Tut's tomb. And by the way, the art of carving, gilding and decorative surfacing aside from the modern machinery now employed, differs but little in process or application from that followed in the days of the Pharoahs where this art was followed by skilled masters.

First of all let us go into the stock room where long, ceiling high racks are filled with lumber, including everything used in frame building, from the thin, slender little beaded moulding, to the 16-inch wide board stock. Speaking of the latter, it might be well to mention that this stock in the rough costs the builders 24c a square foot, or 2c an inch, so it can be seen that careless cutting, or wasteful methods would quickly run into big sums.

All of the wood is kiln dried, and carefully selected, for the presence of warpage, or cracks in a finished frame will also spell losses for the manufacturer. The absence of knots, gnarls, and sap marks, is also an important item in selection.

Let us follow the progress of a wall case and watch it grow from the rough stock in the racks, to the shipping room. This frame

will have, let us say, a decorative, hand carved top with the name of the theatre, and includes French plate, mitre cut mirror, with a crystal chandelier or bracket lamp mounted against the mirror. First we see the frame itself being put into shape, the corners cut on the mitring machine, which produces a smooth, almost invisible joint where the corner edges come together. Behind each corner, an iron corner brace is attached, while the glued corners are held together in a viselike grip of a special screw press which exerts terrific pressure and insures a tight seam. The edges in which the glass is to set have already been cut out on the "rabbiting" machine, which forms a smooth even surface of any desired width or depth that is needed. The ornamental columns are now attached to the sides of the door openings on the top of which, caps or capitals are mounted in either Roman, Greek or Egyptian design.

Meanwhile in another section of the factory, the decorative top, or capping for the entire frame is being carved, and here indeed can be seen one of the most interesting phases of frame building, where the most skilled artisans are at work carving beautiful designs from single pieces of wood stock. The baseboard that is to be used for the top is roughly outlined with the band saw, and a piece of sugar pine, selected for its softness and freedom of fibres and knots, is tacked onto the baseboard. The design is transferred from the pattern to the sugar pine, and then the carver commences his work.

Through the use of native skill the proper tools, the plain pieces of wood very quickly becomes a beautiful example of hand carving, bringing out in bold relief, the central design of sea shell ornament, flanked with floral and leafy designs on either side. It is this real hand carving which gives so much distinction to the professionally built lobby frames, which is absent altogether when the hand of the local carpenter has fashioned his examples of framework.

While this is in progress, at another machine which operates as a large jig saw, a workman is busy cutting out of sugar pine, the lettering that is to be attached to the cap piece. These letters, resembling those seen on children's alphabet blocks and books, are also first traced and then cut out one by one, with the jig saw, which is of course power driven.

After being smoothed and finished up the letters are attached to the cap piece which is now ready to be fastened to the main frame, this being done with glue, dowels, and iron braces. The partially constructed frame is now ready for its trip to the paint shop, after which it will go to the decorator for the plush, then to the glazing department for the mirror, and the electrical shop for the chandelier, and lighting fixtures.

The interesting process followed out in the paint shop, will be described in another article. The writer might add, that in the covering of the wood in the right manner, a big element in the life and service of the frame is accounted for.

Newspaper Opinions on New Pictures

"Tower of Lies"—M-G-M., Warfield, S. F.

Call: "Another magnificent characterization by the marvelous Lon Chaney, quite as fine as anything he has done before; an almost equally startling portrayal of a Swedish peasant mother by Claire McDowell; Norma Shearer exceeding even her arresting work in 'He Who Gets Slapped' and 'Lady of the Night'; marvelous photography, deft direction and a heart-burning narrative — these are highlights of 'The Tower of Lies,' which will undoubtedly go down in cinematographic history as one of the finest five photoplays of 1925."

Chronicle: "'The Tower of Lies' has all the elements of a great success. Lon Chaney, Norma Shearer, Claire McDowell, William Haines and Ian Keith have principal characters to play, and Chaney and Miss Shearer set the pace for the others to follow. It's a good fast race to the goal, with Chaney giving one of the finest performances in his brilliant career."

Bulletin: "Maintaining in every particular the dramatic standard set in his other successes, Lon Chaney, the past master of screen make-up, has created a new, an impressive character, in Victor Seastrom's new picture, 'The Tower of Lies.' This picture can be taken as a shining example of the progress made in photoplay achievement. It is unquestionably the finest dramatic screen play thus far brought forward this season."

Examiner: "Unusually fine photography, subtle direction and a setting of Arcadian loveliness make all this a pretty and moving tale. There is pathos, as when Goldy comes back and her mad father, all bedecked with tinsel and medals, hails her as his empress. And retribution, as when the wicked cousin is drowned from the steamboat upon which the girl is sent out by her evil neighbors. The ending is happy, and Seastrom, a genuine artist among directors, proves that he can direct down to the popular taste."

News: "The principal claim for recognition offered by 'The Tower of Lies' is that it is the vehicle for carrying another wonderfully fine character portrayal by Lon Chaney in the role of Jan, the crazed 'emperor,' plus some very excellent direction by Seastrom."

"Black Cyclone"— Pathe, Sun, Omaha

World-Herald: "One of the most interesting films of the year is at the Sun Theatre this week. It is Hal Roach's production 'Black Cyclone,' which stars Rex, the handsome black stallion, as the hero. If you don't enjoy the love story of Rex and his Lady, then we miss our guess. It is only after seeing such a production that you can appreciate the art of direction."

Bee: "No audience ever pulled harder for a human hero to win than did the Sun audience for 'Rex' Sunday evening. Two fights are high points in that unique photoplay, 'Black Cyclone.' There are other big moments, though. 'Rex' kills a mountain lion; he drives away a pack of wolves which attacked 'Lady'; and finally he offers his flect legs to the man who saved him from the quicksands. It is a thrill to watch him run, with one of the two human characters in the picture on his back. The picture almost exudes the scent of the sage brush and the open spaces. It has the appeal of the primitive—the genuineness."

"Your Own Backyard"—Pathe, Keith's, Rochester

Democrat and Herald: "Not the least important offering on Keith's bill is the supplementary screen offering, an 'Our Gang' number, entitled 'Your Own Backyard.' Those who recall the plaintive melody of the name, popular a score or more years ago, remember how it tells the story of a mammy's consoling of her pickaninny because of his being neglected by white neighbors. Farina appears for the first time as a boy and gives evidence in this brief screen tale, which is a blending of comedy and melodrama, of unusually promising acting ability."

"The Freshman"—Pathe, Colony, New York

American: "Beg, borrow or steal, but get the price somewhere for a ticket to the Colony Theatre this week to see Harold Lloyd in 'The Freshman.' Put off the bridge game, the shopping expedition or whatever you have scheduled but by no means miss getting the best laugh of the year. Seeing 'The Freshman' is as good as a doctor's prescription for it makes you forget everything but the laugh you will surely get out of Harold's adventures at Tate College."

Times: "If laughter really is a panacea for some ills, one might hazard that a host of healthy persons were sent away from the Colony yesterday after regaling themselves in wild and rollicking explosions of mirth over Harold Lloyd's comic antics in his latest hilarious effusion, 'The Freshman.' Judging from what happened in the packed theatre in the afternoon, when old folks down to youngsters volleyed their hearty approval of the bespectacled comedian, the only possible hindrance to the physical well being of the throngs was an attack of aching sides."

Mirror: "Harold Lloyd charged the Colony yesterday and kicked a goal with his latest college football comedy, 'The Freshman.' Harold makes a nifty freshman. 'The Freshman' is a screamingly funny comedy. Jobyna Ralston makes a darling heroine. 'The Freshman' is clean entertainment. Yes, Harold Lloyd triumphs again in his latest comedy. This is one picture we go on record as advising everybody to see."

Daily News: "'Your money refunded if you don't laugh.' The Colony would have been perfectly safe in handing out laugh insurance to its audience yesterday—and for all days to come. It's a Harold Lloyd comedy, and to this reviewer's way of thinking his gayest."

Telegraph: "You'll forget that it is a symbol of bad manners to laugh out loud when you view 'The Freshman' at the Colony Theatre. In fact, you'll be lucky to be able to control your laughter at all. Just as soon as you are about over one good roar, something happens on the screen, and you start all over again. Which is my subtle manner of informing you that Harold Lloyd's latest picture is just about the funniest film he has ever made."

Herald-Tribune: "It's quite funny enough to suit the most exacting, and, thank heaven, most of its humor is derived from situations and not from throwing things and kicking people about. The picture is well cast, well directed, well played and well titled. 'The Freshman' has a fresh theme and is a refreshing picture."

Evening World: "'The Freshman' is Harold Lloyd at a new high level. Any one who has enjoyed other Lloyd pictures will enjoy the offering at the Colony, and 'The Freshman' shows development that should win many new friends for this popular comedian. 'The Freshman' has been cast, staged and photographed in a thoroughly adequate manner."

Graphic: "'The Freshman' is a succession of laughter-producing gags, each funnier than the other. Harold's mashed personality is particularly suited to this character, and while he is the college fall guy he is no sap. 'The Freshman' is much more than a fine comedy. It depicts a phase in the life of every individual whether he has been to college or not. You can't afford to miss it."

Post: "Harold Lloyd's newest comedy, 'The Freshman,' which opened at the Colony yesterday, is a very funny movie, and like all really funny movies, it contains, likewise, a distinct element of pathos. Everybody is sure to enjoy 'The Freshman.'"

Sun: "Laughter, loud, hearty laughter, filled the Colony yesterday when Harold Lloyd's new comedy, 'The Freshman'—a strikingly humorous slapstick affair which turned academic ways to burlesque account—made its first appearance hereabouts. 'The Freshman' is funny. Very funny. It is in the finely imagined, humorous details that it is superlative. 'The Freshman' must be seen at all costs."

Journal: "Three cheers and a five-letter word meaning a spotted animal, for Harold Lloyd's best picture to date—'The Freshman,' at the Colony. It's without a doubt one of the funniest, most spontaneous comedies that ever flickered to a happy fade-out. Jobyna Ralston, the little girl at the cigar counter, realizes that they're all making fun of him, and the result is humor and pathos and satire and understanding. It is very deftly directed by Sam Taylor and Fred Newmeyer, and the various gags and situations are joyously effective."

Telegram: "The fun is irresistible. There is a punch value that produces laughs in such rapid succession that even the most captious spectators will count his wait on the sidewalk line-up well worth while. Lloyd is at his best in his characterization of the well-meaning boob."

"Girl Who Wouldn't Work"— Schulberg, Broadway, N. Y.

American: "If you like your drama dished up with a new angle you will find this a film after your own heart. Here is a picture made with as much attention to direction, production and action as if it had been widely heralded as the greatest super-special of the year."

World: "An engrossing and continuously interesting play. Stark, bold melodrama, swift traveling and nicely charged with suspense, is 'The Girl Who Wouldn't Work.' Barrymore is far too good to miss."

Daily News: "A movie that is both sane and satisfying. There is but one suggestion. This is the one time a picture could be bettered by making it longer. You will like it. It is alive."

Journal: "A delightfully adroit piece of work. It was directed by an unknown, Marcel De Sano, and having seen his first effort, all we can say is long may Marcel wave!"

Post: "Turned into something different by intelligent and individual handling. One of the most interesting offerings of the season. De Sano prefers suggestion of mood and action to printed analyses of every detail."

Mirror: "Splendid entertainment. A youthful director shows that while there may be nothing new in the world there are new ways of doing old things."

"Below the Line" — Warner's, Warners' N. Y.

Herald Tribune: "A tale well fitted to the talents of Rin-Tin-Tin, filmland's wonder dog. A nice picture."

Sun: "There is something intriguing about Rin-Tin-Tin. He seems eloquent. I have never tired of seeing him in photoplays. His admirers may go to 'Below The Line' with the assurance that they will be satisfied."

Post: "There is a splendid fight between the police dog and a pack of bloodhounds, which is thrilling, indeed, and many of the scenes are unusually well photographed."

The World: "There is no surpassing the work of this young actor, the brightest of the dog stars. We can recommend 'Below the Line' heartily as a thrilling

(Continued on page 1747)

FEATURE RELEASE CHART

Productions are Listed Alphabetically and by Months in which Released in order that the Exhibitor may have a short-cut toward such information as he may need. Short subject and comedy releases, as well as information on pictures that are coming, will be found on succeeding pages. (S. R. indicates State Right release.)

Refer to THE MOTION PICTURE NEWS BOOKING GUIDE for Productions Listed Prior to March

MARCH

Feature	Star	Distributed by	Length	Reviewed
Adventurous Sex, The	Clara Bow	Assoc. Exhib	5039 feet	Mar. 21
Air Mail, The	Special Cast	Paramount	5976 feet	Mar. 28
Beauty and the Bad Man	Special Cast	Prod. Dist. Corp	5794 feet	May 9
Beyond the Border	Harry Carey	Prod. Dist. Corp	4469 feet	April 25
Billy, The Kid	Franklyn Farnum	Inde. Pict. Corp.		
	(S. R.)		4800 feet	
Blood and Steel	Desmond Holmes	Inde. Pict. (S. R.)	5300 feet	
Border Justice	Bill Cody	Inde. Pict. Corp.		
	(S. R.)		5432 feet	Nov. 8
Coast Patrol, The	Kenneth McDonald	Barsky (S. R.)	5000 feet	
Confessions of a Queen	Terry-Stone	Metro-Goldwyn	5830 feet	April 4
Crimson Runner, The	Priscilla Dean	Prod. Dist. Corp	4775 feet	June 6
Daddy's Gone A'Hunting	Joyce-Marmont	Metro-Goldwyn	5851 feet	Mar. 7
Denial, The	Special Cast	Metro-Goldwyn	4791 feet	Mar. 21
Double Action Daniels	Buffalo Bill, Jr	Weiss Bros. (S. R.)	4650 feet	
Dressmaker from Paris, The	Rod La Rocque	Paramount	7050 feet	Mar. 28
Fighting Romeo, A	Al Ferguson	Davis Dist. Div. (S.R.)	5000 feet	Aug. 15
Fighting the Flames	Haines-Devore	C. B. C. (S. R.)	5600 feet	
Forbidden Cargo	Evelyn Brent	F. B. O	4953 feet	April 11
Goose Hangs High, The	Constance Bennett	Paramount	6146 feet	Feb. 14
Great Divide, The	Terry-Tearle	Metro-Goldwyn	7611 feet	Feb. 28
Head Winds	House Peters	Universal	5600 feet	Mar. 28
Hogdled Woman, The	Seena Owen	Fox	4954 feet	April 4
I Want My Man	Sills-Kenyon	First National	6175 feet	April 19
Jimmie's Millions	Richard Talmadge	F. B. O	5167 feet	Feb. 28
Just Traveling	Bob Burns	Sierra Pict. (S. R.)	4400 feet	
Lady of the Night	Norma Shearer	Metro-Goldwyn		
Last Laugh, The	Emil Jannings	Universal	6118 feet	Jan. 3
Let 'er Buck	Hoot Gibson	Universal	5547 feet	Jan. 3
Mad Whirl, The	May McAvoy	Universal	6194 feet	Mar. 16
Marriage in Transit	Edmund Lowe	Fox	4500 feet	April 11
Men and Women	Special Cast	Paramount	5800 feet	Mar. 9
Monster, The	L. Chaney-J. Arthur	Metro-Goldwyn	6425 feet	Feb. 28
My Wife and I	Special Cast	Warner Bros	7000 feet	June 4
New Lives for Old	Betty Compson	Paramount	6796 feet	Mar. 21
New Toys	Richard Barthelmess	First National	7280 feet	Feb. 21
One Year to Live	Special Cast	First National	6064 feet	Feb. 28
Percy	Charles Ray	Assoc. Exhib	5384 feet	Feb. 28
Playing With Souls	Special Cast	First National	5651 feet	Mar. 21
Price of Pleasure, The	Valli-Kerry	Universal	6414 feet	June 13
Recompense	M. Prevost-M. Blue	Warner Bros	7490 feet	May 2
Renegade Holmes, M.D	Ben Wilson	Arrow (S. R.)	4947 feet	
Riders of the Purple Sage	Tom Mix	Fox	5578 feet	Mar. 28
Romance and Rustlers	Yakima Canutt	Arrow (S. R.)	4984 feet	Nov. 15
Sackcloth and Scarlet	Alice Terry	Paramount	6732 feet	Mar. 7
Sally	Colleen Moore	First National	8636 feet	Mar. 28
Scar Hanan	Yakima Canutt	F. B. O	4575 feet	Apr. 11
Scarlet Honeymoon, The	Shirley Mason	Fox	5000 feet	Mar. 21
Seven Chances	Buster Keaton	Metro-Goldwyn	4551 feet	Mar. 28
Sign of the Cactus, The	Jack Hoxie	Universal	4939 feet	Jan. 10
Sky Raider, The	Capt. Chetley Nungesser	Assoc. Exhib	6638 feet	April 4
Speed	Betty Blythe	Banner Prod. (S. R.)	6000 feet	May 30
Too Many Kisses	Richard Dix	Paramount	5758 feet	Mar. 14
Waking Up the Town	Jack Pickford	United Artists	4802 feet	April 11
Where Romance Rides	Dick Hatton	Arrow	4301 feet	
Zander the Great	Marion Davies	Metro-Goldwyn	5851 feet	May 16

APRIL

Feature	Star	Distributed by	Length	Reviewed
Adventure	P. Starke-T. Moore	Paramount	6712 feet	April 25
After Business Hours	Hammerstein-Tellegen	C. B. C. (S. R.)	5900 feet	
Bandit Tamer, The	Franklyn Farnum	Inde. Pict. (S. R.)	5000 feet	
Border Vengeance	Jack Perrin	Madoc Sales (S. R.)	4900 feet	
Charmer, The	Pola Negri	Paramount	6076 feet	April 18
Code of the West	O. Moore-C. Bennett	Paramount	6777 feet	April 25
Courageous Fool, The	Reed Howes	Rayart (S. R.)		
Crowded Hour, The	Bebe Daniels	Paramount	6432 feet	May 9
Dangerous Innocence	LaRocque-E. O'Brien	Universal	6759 feet	May 21
Declasse	Corinne Griffith	First National	7669 feet	April 4
Eyes of the Desert	Al Richmond	Sierra Pict. (S. R.)	4500 feet	
Fifth Avenue Models	Philbin-Kerry	Universal	6481 feet	Jan. 24
Fighting Parson, The	Al Ferguson	Davis Dist. Div. (S.R.)	5000 feet	
Fighting Sheriff, The	Bill Cody	Inde. Pict. (S. R.)	4900 feet	May 30
Friendly Enemies	Weber and Fields	Prod. Dist. Corp	6288 feet	May 9
Galloping Vengeance	Bob Custer	F. B. O	5095 feet	April 11
Gelling 'Em Right	George Larkin	Rayart (S. R.)	4465 feet	
Gold and the Girl	Buck Jones	Fox	4522 feet	April 11
Go Straight	Gladys Hulette	B. P. Schulberg (S.R.)	6307 feet	May 23
Heart of a Siren, The	Barbara La Marr	First National	6700 feet	Mar. 21
How Baxter Butted In	M. Moore-D. Devore	Warner Bros	6650 feet	July 11
Justice Raffles	Henry Edwards	Cranfield & Clarke		
	(S. R.)		4600 feet	
Kiss in the Dark, A	Special Cast	Paramount	5767 feet	April 18
Kiss Me Again	M. Prevost-M. Blue	Warner Bros	7200 feet	June 6
Love's Bargain	M. Daw-C. Hitrick	F. B. O	5641 feet	April 25
Madame Sans Gene	Gloria Swanson	Paramount	9994 feet	May 9
Man and Maid	Special Cast	Metro-Goldwyn	5307 feet	April 18
My Son	Nazimova-J. Pickford	First National	6500 feet	April 4
Night Club, The	R. Griffith-V. Reynolds	Paramount	5732 feet	May 16
One Way Street	Special Cast	First National	5100 feet	April 18
Proud Flesh	Special Cast	Metro-Goldwyn	5770 feet	April 25
Raging Adventure, The	Jack Hoxie	Universal	4527 feet	Feb. 14
Ridin' Comet, The	Yakima Canutt	F. B. O	4354 feet	May 16
Rough Going	Franklyn Farnum	Indep. Pict. Corp.		
			4800 feet	
Shackled Lightning	Franz Merrill	Hercules Prod.	4800 feet	
She Wolves	Alma Rubens	Fox	4772 feet	May 9
Spangled, The	Corliss-Goudal	Paramount	5675 feet	April 18
Sporting Venus	Special Cast	Metro-Goldwyn	5926 feet	May 23

Feature	Star	Distributed by	Length	Reviewed
Stop Flirting	Special Cast	Prod. Dist. Corp	5161 feet	June 6
Straight Through	Wm. Desmond	Universal	4967 feet	
Tale of a Thousand and One Nights	Special Cast	Davis Dist. Div		
	(S. R.)		6500 feet	Feb. 14
Teasing Through	Richard Talmadge	F. B. O	4714 feet	May 23
Thal Devil Quemado	Fred Thomson	F. B. O	4766 feet	April 4
Two-Fisted Sheriff, A	Yakima Canutt	Arrow (S. R.)	4149 feet	Dec. 6
Way of a Girl, The	Boardman-M. Moore	Metro-Goldwyn	5022 feet	April 11
Western Engagement, A	Dick Hatton	Arrow		
Wings of Youth	Madge Bellamy	Fox	5340 feet	May 16
Winning a Woman	Pettit-Hill	Rayart (S. R.)	4665 feet	

MAY

Feature	Star	Distributed by	Length	Reviewed
Alias Mary Flynn	Evelyn Brent	F. B. O	5559 feet	May 30
Any Woman	Alice Terry	Paramount	5962 feet	June 13
Awful Truth, The	Agnes Ayres	Prod. Dist. Corp	5817 feet	July 11
Bandit's Baby, The	Fred Thomson	F. B. O	5291 feet	June 30
Baree Son of Kazan	Wolf (dog)	Vitagraph	7 reels	May 2
Barriers of the Law	Sigmon-Desmond	Indep. Pict. (S. R.)	5000 feet	
Burning Trail, The	William Desmond	Universal	4783 feet	April 18
Chickie	Mackaill-Bosworth	First National	7767 feet	May 9
Chickie-Saint, The	Johnny Hines	C. C. Burr (S. R.)	5000 feet	May 23
Every Man's Wife	Special Cast	Fox	4365 feet	July 4
Eve's Lover	Irene Rich	Warner Bros	6540 feet	Aug. 8
Eve's Secret	Betty Compson	Paramount	6305 feet	May 9
Fear Fighter, The	Billy Sullivan	Rayart (S. R.)		
Fighting Demon, The	Richard Talmadge	F. B. O	5470 feet	June 20
Fugitive, The	Ben Wilson	Arrow	4992 feet	
Golden Train		Sanford Prod. (S. R.)	5 reels	
His Supreme Moment	B. Sweet-R. Colman	First National	6600 feet	April 25
Lilies of the Streets	J. Walker-V. L. Corbin	B. O.	7168 feet	April 26
Little French Girl, The	Alice Joyce	Paramount	5628 feet	June 13
Lunatic at Large, A	Henry Edwards	Cranfield & Clarke		
			(S. R.)	
Maker's of Men	Kenneth McDonald	Barsky Prod. (S. R.)	5000 feet	
Necessary Evil, The	Jane-Kenyon	First National	6307 feet	May 23
Old Home Week	Thomas Meighan	Paramount	6588 feet	June 6
Phantom Rider, The	Al Richmond	Sierra Pict. (S. R.)	4500 feet	
Private Affairs	Special Cast	Prod. Dist. Corp	6132 feet	Aug. 15
Quick Change	George Larkin	Rayart (S. R.)		
Raffles, The Amateur Cracksman	House Peters	Universal	5557 feet	June 20
Rainbow Trail, The	Tom Mix	Fox	5251 feet	April 25
Red Love	Lowell-Russell	Lowell Films Prod.		
			(S. R.)	
Saddle Hawk, The	Hoot Gibson	Universal	5456 feet	Mar. 7
Silent Sanderson	Harry Carey	Prod. Dist. Corp	4841 feet	June 20
Scandal Proof	Shirley Mason	Fox	4400 feet	June 6
School for Wives	Pearle-Holmquist	Vitagraph	6750 feet	April 11
Shock Punch, The	Richard Dix	Paramount	6161 feet	May 23
Snob Buster, The	Reed Howes	Rayart (S. R.)		
Soul Fire	Barthelmess-B Love	First National	8362 feet	May 16
Speed Wild	Maurice B " Lefty " Flynn			
	A. Nilsson-L. Stone	First National	4700 feet	June 20
Talker, The	Bob Custer	F. B. O	4770 feet	
Texas Bearcat, The	Max Marsh	Vitagraph	6279 feet	May 9
Tides of Passion	Virginia Valli	Vitagraph	6025 feet	Jan. 31
Up the Ladder	Special Cast	Paramount	3900 feet	May 30
Welcome Home	Stronghart (dog)		6579 feet	June 30
White Fang	Yakima Canutt	B. O	4530 feet	
White Thunder	Special Cast	Vitagraph	6 feels	June 20
Wildfire	Reuben-Marmont	Universal	6023 feet	Aug. 15
Wolves of the Road	Helene Chadwick	Warner Brothers	7000 feet	Aug. 22
Woman's Faith				
Woman Hater, The				

JUNE

Feature	Star	Distributed by	Length	Reviewed
Are Parents People?	Bronson-Vidor	Paramount	6586 feet	June 6
Dangerous Odds	Bill Cody	Inde. Pict. (S. R.)	4900 feet	
Desert Figwert, The	Colleen Moore	First National	6837 feet	June 13
Double Fisted	Jack Perrin	Rayart (S. R.)		
Drop the Border	Al Richmond	Sierra Pict. (S. R.)	4750 feet	
Faint Perfume	Seena Owen	B. P. Schulberg (S.R.)	6236 feet	July 11
Grounds for Divorce	Florence Vidor	Paramount	5712 feet	July 4
Happy Warrior, The		Vitagraph	6675 feet	July 18
Headis and Spurs	Burk Jones	Fox	4600 feet	June 20
Human Tornado, The	Yakima Canutt	F. B. O	4487 feet	
I'll Show You the Town	Reginald Denny	Universal	7400 feet	June 6
Introduce Me	Douglas MacLean	Assoc. Exhib	5900 feet	Mar. 21
Just a Woman	Windust-Tearle	First National	6600 feet	June 6
Light of Western Stars	Special Cast	Paramount	6633 feet	July 4
Lost—a Wife	Special Cast	Paramount	5430 feet	June 27
Making of O'Malley, The	Milton Sills	First National	7371 feet	July 4
Man from Lone Mountain, The	Ben Wilson	Arrow	4530 feet	
Man in Blue	Herbert Rawlinson	Universal	5706 feet	Feb. 21
Maffy Mc	Special Cast	Paramount	5586 feet	
Maddief, The	William Desmond	Universal	4690 feet	May 23
Mike		Metro-Goldwyn		
Mist in the Valley	Alma Taylor	Cranfield & Clarke		
			(S. R.)	
My Lady's Lips	Clara Bow	B. P. Schulberg (S.R.)	6609 feet	Aug 15
Off the Highway	Wm. V. Mong	Prod. Dist.	7641 feet	
Paths to Paradise	Compson-R. Griffith	Paramount	6741 feet	June 27
Pioneers of the West		Sanford Prod. (S. R.)	5 feels	
Ridin' Easy	Dick Hatton	Arrow	4483 feet	
Ridin' Thunder	Jack Hoxie	Universal	4354 feet	May 23

Feature	Star	Distributed by	Length	Reviewed
Rough Stuff	George Larkin	Rayart (S. R.)		
Shattered Lives	Special Cast	Gotham (S. R.)	6 reels	July 4
Smooth as Satin	Evelyn Brent	F. B. O	6900 feet	July 4
Texas Trail, The	Harry Carey	Prod. Dist. Corp	4730 feet	July 18
Trapped in the Snow Country	Rin-Tin-Tin (dog)	Warner Brothers	6900 feet	Aug. 1
White Monkey, The	Ia Marr-T. Holding	First National	6123 feet	July 4
Wild Bull's Lair, The	Fred Thomson	F. B. O	5280 feet	Aug. 15
Youth's Gamble	Reed Howes	Rayart (S. R.)	5264 feet	

JULY

Feature	Star	Distributed by	Length	Reviewed

AUGUST

Feature	Star	Distributed by	Length	Reviewed

SEPTEMBER

Feature	Star	Distributed by	Length	Reviewed

Feature	Star	Distributed by	Length	Reviewed

OCTOBER

Feature	Star	Distributed by	Length	Reviewed

NOVEMBER

Feature	Star	Distributed by	Length	Reviewed

DECEMBER

Feature	Star	Distributed by	Length	Reviewed
Lodge in the Wilderness, The		Tiffany (S. R.)	6500 feet	
Prince of Broadway	George Walsh	Chadwick		
Sweet Adeline	Charles Ray	Chadwick		

Comedy Releases

Feature	Star	Distributed by	Length	Reviewed
Absent Minded	Neely Edwards	Universal	1 reel	
Across the Hall	Edna Marian	Universal	2 reels	
Adventures of Adenoid	Aesop's Fables	Pathe	1 reel	April 25
Afry a Reputation	Edna Marian	Universal	2 reels	
Air Tight	Bobby Vernon	Educational	2 reels	June 13
Alice's Egg Plant	"Cartoon"	M. J. Winkler (S. R.)	1 reel	
Alice Staged Struck	Margie Gay	M. J. Winkler (S. R.)	1 reel	July 18

Feature	Star	Distributed by	Length	Reviewed
All Aboard	Perry-Cooley	Fox	2 reels	
All at Sea	Smith-King	Fox		
Almost a Husband	Buddy Messinger	Universal	2 reels	
Amateur Detective	Earle Foxe	Fox	2 reels	
Andy in Hollywood	Joe Murphy	Universal	2 reels	
Andy Takes a Flyer	" The Gumps "	Universal	2 reels	
Apache, The	Earle Foxe	Fox Film	2 reels	
Apollo's Pretty Sister		Fox	2 reels	
Are Husbands Human?	James Finlayson	Pathe	1 reel	April 11
Artists' Blues	G. Joy-J. Moore	Rayart (S. R.)	2 reels	
Ask Grandma	" Our Gang "	Pathe	2 reels	May 30
At the Seashore	Monkey	Fox	2 reels	
At the Zoo	Aesops Fables	Pathe	1 reel	
Baby Be Good		Educational	2 reels	
Baby Blues	Mickey Bennett	Educational	2 reels	
Bachelors	Special Cast	Universal		
Back to Nature	Charles Puffy	Universal	1 reel	
Bad Bill Brodie	Charles Chase	Pathe	2 reels	
Bad Boy	Charles Chase	Pathe	2 reels	April 11
Balboa Discovers Hollywood	" Red Head "	Sering D. Wilson (S.R.)	1 reel	
Bark is the Woods	Harry Langdon	Pathe	2 reels	
Bashful Jim	Ralph Graves	Pathe	2 reels	Mar. 21
Be Careful	Jimmie Adams	Educational Film	2 reels	Aug. 22
Below Zero	Lige Conley	Educational	2 reels	July 4
Beware	Lige Conley	Educational Film	2 reels	Aug. 1
Big Chief Ko-Ko (Out of the Inkwell)	" Cartoon "	Red Seal Pict.	1 reel	
Big Game Hunter, The	Earle Foxe	Fox	2 reels	
Bigger and Better Pictures	" Aesop's Fables "	Pathe	1 reel	
Big Kick, The	Engle-Mohan	Pathe	1 reel	
Big Red Riding Hood	Charley Chase	Pathe	1 reel	May 9
Black Gold Bricks	Roach-Edwards	Universal	1 reel	April 18
Black Hand Blues	" Spat Family "	Pathe	2 reels	April 18
Bobby Bumbs & Co	Cartoon	Educational	1 reel	July 4
Boys Will Be Joys	" Our Gang "	Pathe	2 reels	July 25
Brainless Horsemen		Fox	2 reels	
Brass Button	Billy West	Arrow	2 reels	
Breaking the Ice	Ralph Graves	Pathe	2 reels	April 11
Bride Tamer, The	Milburn Moranti	Sierra Pict. (S. R.)	2 reels	
Bubbles	" Aesop's Fables "	Pathe	1 reel	Aug. 15
Bugville Field Day	" Aesop's Fables "	Pathe	1 reel	July 25
Business Engagement, A	Perry-Cooley	Fox	2 reels	
Buster Be Good	Trimble-Turner	Universal	2 reels	
Butterfly Man, The		Fox	2 reels	
By the Sea	Charles Puffy	Universal	1 reel	
California Here We Come	" The Gumps "	Universal	2 reels	
Cat's Shimmy, The	" Kid Noah "	Sering D. Wilson (S.R.)	1 reel	
Cat's Whiskers, The	Neely Edwards	Universal	1 reel	
Chasing the Chasers	Jas. Finlayson	Pathe	1 reel	July 4
City Bound	Charles Puffy	Universal	1 reel	
Clean-Up Week	" Aesop's Fables"	Pathe	1 reel	Mar. 7
Clear the Way	Buddy Messinger	Universal	2 reels	
Cleopatra and Her Easy Mark	" Cartoon "	Sering D. Wilson (S.R.)	1 reel	
Cloudhopper, The	Larry Semon	Educational	2 reels	June 6
Cloudy Romance, A		Fox		
Columbus Discovers a New Whirl		Sering Wilson (S. R.)	1 reel	
Cotton King	Lloyd Hamilton	Educational	2 reels	
Crime Crushers	Lige Conley	Educational	2 reels	
Crying for Love	Eddie Gordon	Universal	2 reels	Aug. 15
Cupid's Boots	Ralph Graves	Pathe	2 reels	July 25
Cupid's Victory	Wanda Wiley	Universal	2 reels	
Cure, The (Out of the Inkwell)	" Cartoon "	Red Seal Pict.	1 reel	
Curses	Al. St. John	Educational	2 reels	May 23
Daddy Goes A Grunting		Pathe	2 reels	July 18
Darkest Africa	" Aesop's Fables "	Pathe	1 reels	
Day's Outing, A	" The Gumps "	Universal	2 reels	
Depp Stuff	Aesop's Fables	Pathe	1 reel	April 25
Dinky Doodle and Cinderella	" Dinky Doodle "	F. B. O	1 reel	
Dinky Doodle and Robinson Crusoe	" Dinky Doodle "	F. B. O	1 reel	
Discord In " A " Flat	Arthur Lake	Universal	1 reel	July 25
Dog Days	" Our Gang "	Pathe	2 reels	Mar. 14
Dog Daze		Educational		
Dog 'On It	Bobby Dunn	Arrow	2 reels	
Dome Doctor, The	Larry Semon	Educational	2 reels	
Don't Pinch	Bobby Vernon	Educational	2 reels	April 25
Don't Worry	Wanda Wiley	Universal	2 reels	Mar. 21
Dragon Alley	Jackie McHugh	Educational	2 reels	May 16
Dr. Pyckle and Mr. Pride	Stan Laurel	Film Booking Offices	2 reels	
Dry Up	Singleton Burkett	Universal	2 reels	July 25
Dumb and Daffy	Al. St. John	Fox	2 reels	
Dynamite Doggie	Al. St. John	Educational	2 reels	Mar. 21
East Side, West Side	Harris-Leddy	Fox		
Echoes From the Alps	Aesop's Fables	Pathe	1 reel	May 23
Educating Buster	Trimble-Turner	Universal	2 reels	
End of the World, The	Aesop's Fables	Pathe	1 reel	
Etiquette	Jimmy Aubrey	Film Book. Offices	2 reels	
Excuse My Glove	" Spat Family "	Pathe	2 reels	Mar 21
Expensive Ebony	"Ebenezer Ebony"	Sering Wilson (S. R.)	1 reel	
Failure	Kathryn McGuire	Fox	2 reels	
Fair Warning	Al St. John	Educational	2 reels	Sept. 26
Fares Please	Al. St. John	Educational	2 reels	May 16
Fast Worker, A	Aesop's Fables	Pathe	1 reel	
Felix, the Cat on the Farm	Cartoon	Educational	1 reel	
Felix Full O'Fight	" Cartoon "	M. J. Winkler (S. R.)	1 reel	
Felix Gets His Fill	" Cartoon "	M. J. Winkler (S. R.)	1 reel	
Felix Grabs His Grub	" Cartoon "	M. J. Winkler (S. R.)	1 reel	
Felix the Cat on the Job	Cartoon	Educational	1 reel	
Fire Flies	" Hey, Fellas "	Davis Dist.	2 reels	
First Love	" Our Gang "	Pathe	2 reels	
Fishermen's Luck	"Aesop's Fables "	Pathe	1 reel	
For Hire	Edward Gordon	Universal		
For Love of a Gal	" Aesop's Fables "	Pathe	1 reel	July 25
Found World, The	" The Gumps "	Universal	2 reels	
Fun's Fun	Bowes-Vance	Educational	1 reel	June 6
Getting Trimmed	Wanda Wiley	Universal	2 reels	April 18
Giddap	Special Cast	Pathe	2 reels	Mar. 21
Going Great	Eddie Nelson	Educational	2 reels	June 13
Goldfish's Pajamas	" Kid Noah "	Sering D. Wilson (S.R.)	1 reel	
Good Morning Nurse	Ralph Graves	Pathe	2 reels	May 30
Good Scouts	" Reg'lar Kids "	M. J. Winkler (S. R.)	2 reels	
Great Guns	Bobby Vernon	Educational	2 reels	Feb. 21
Green-Eyed Monster, The	Arthur Lake	Universal	1 reel	
Gridiron Gertie	Wanda Wiley	Universal	2 reels	
Guilty Conscience, A	Eddie Gordon	Universal		
Gypping the Gypsies	" Ebonezer Ebony "	Sering Wilson (S. R.)	1 reel	
Half Fare	Arthur Lake	Universal	1 reel	
Half a Hero	Lloyd Hamilton	Educational	2 reels	Mar. 7
Half a Man	Stan Laurel	Pathe	2 reels	
Hard Boiled	Charley Chase	Pathe	2 reels	Mar. 21
Hard Working Loafer, The	Arthur Stone	Pathe		
Haunted Honeymoon	Tryon-Mehaffey	Pathe	2 reels	Feb. 28
Heart Trouble	Arthur Lake	Universal	1 reel	July 4
Hello, Goodby	Lige Conley	Educational	2 reels	May 30
Hello, Hollywood	Lige Conley	Educational	2 reels	Mar. 28
Helping Hand	Jimmy Aubrey	F. B. O	2 reels	
Help Yourself		Fox	2 reels	
Here's Your Hat	Arthur Lake	Universal	1 reel	May 9
Her Lucky Leap	Wanda Wiley	Universal	2 reels	
He Who Gets Crowned	Jimmy Aubrey	F. B. O	2 reels	
He Who Got Smacked	Ralph Graves	Pathe	2 reels	May 9
Hey! Taxi!	Bobby Dunn	Arrow	2 reels	
High Hopes	Bowes-Vance	Educational	1 reel	Feb. 14
High Jinx, A		Fox	2 reels	
His Marriage Wow	Harry Langdon	Pathe	2 reels	Mar. 7
Hold My Baby	Glenn Tryon	Pathe	2 reels	April 25
Home Scouts	Jimmie Aubrey	F. B. O	2 reels	
Honeymoon Heaven		Sering Wilson (S. R.)	1 reel	
Horace Greeley, Jr	Harry Langdon	Pathe	2 reels	June 6
Horrible Hollywood		Lee-Bradford (S. R.)		
Hot and Heavy	Eddie Nelson	Educational	2 reels	July 18
Hot Dog	Animal	C B C (S. R.)	2 reels	
Hot Times in Iceland	Aesop's Fables	Pathe	1 reel	
House of Flickers, The		Fox	2 reels	
House that Dinky Built	(Cartoon)	F. B. O	1 reel	
Housing Shortage, The	" Aesop's Fables "	Pathe	1 reel	
Hurry Doctor	Ralph Graves	Pathe		
Hysterical History (Series)		Universal	1 reel	
Ice Boy, An	" Ebonezer Ebony "	Sering D. Wilson (S.R.)	1 reel	
Ice Cold	Arthur Lake	Universal	1 reel	June 13
In Deep		Educational	1 reel	
In Dutch	Aesop's Fables	Pathe	1 reel	
Innocent Husbands	Charley Chase	Pathe	2 reels	Aug. 1
Inside Out	Bowes-Vance	Educational	1 reel	Mar. 28
Into the Grease	James Finlayson	Pathe	1 reel	June 27
Iron Mule	Al St. John	Educational	2 reels	April 18
Iron Nag, The	Billy Bevan	Pathe	2 reels	Aug. 15
Is Marriage the Bunk?	Charles Chase	Pathe	1 reel	April 4
Isn't Life Terrible?	Charles Chase	Pathe	2 reels	July 4
Itching for Revenge	Eddie Gordon	Universal	2 reels	Mar. 7
It's All Wrong	Karr-Engle	Universal		
James Boys' Sister		Sering Wilson (S. R.)	1 reel	
Jungle Bike Riders	Aesop's Fables	Pathe	1 reel	Mar. 14
Just in Time	Wanda Wiley	Universal	2 reels	July 11
Kicked About	Eddie Gordon	Universal	2 reels	Mar. 14
Kidding Captain Kidd	" Cartoon "	Sering Wilson (S. R.)	1 reel	
King Cotton	Lloyd Hamilton	Educational	2 reels	May 9
King Dumb	Jimmy Aubrey	F. B. O	2 reels	
Klynick, The	" Hey, Fellas "	Davis Dist.	2 reels	
Knocked About	Eddie Gordon	Universal	2 reels	June 13
Ko-Ko Celebrates the Fourth (Out of the Inkwell)	" Cartoon "	Red Seal Pict.		
Ko-Ko Trains Animals (out of the Inkwell)	" Cartoon "	Red Seal Pict.	1 reel	
Lead Pipe Cinch, A	Al Alt	Universal		
Lion Love		Fox	2 reels	Feb. 28
Lion and the Monkey	" Aesop's Fables "	Pathe		
Lion's Whiskers		Pathe	2 reels	April 18
Little Red Riding Hood	" Dinky Doodle "	F. B. O	1 reel	
Locked Out	Arthur Lake	Universal	1 reel	May 30
Looking for Sally	Charles Chase	Pathe	2 reels	May 9
Look Out	Bowes-Vance	Educational Film	1 reel	Aug. 1
Lost Cord, The	Bert Roach	Universal	1 reel	Feb. 21
Love and Kisses	Alice Day	Pathe	2 reels	
Love and Lions		Fox	2 reels	
Love Bug, The	" Our Gang "	Pathe	2 reels	April 4
Love Goofy	Jimmy Adams	Educational	2 reels	Mar. 7
Love and Kisses	Alice Day	Pathe	2 reels	Oct. 3
Love Sick	Constance Darling	Universal	2 reels	May 23
Love's Tragedy		Sering Wilson (S. R.)	1 reel	
Lucky Accident, The	Charles Puffy	Universal	1 reel	July 18
Lucky Leap, A	Wanda Wiley	Universal	2 reels	
Lucky Stars	Harry Langdon	Pathe	2 reels	Aug. 15
Madame Sans Jane	Glenn Tryon	Pathe	2 reels	
Marriage Circus, The	Ben Turpin	Pathe	2 reels	April 11
Married Neighbors	Engle-Darling	Universal	2 reels	July 4
Mary, Queen of Tots	" Our Gang "	Pathe	2 reels	Aug. 22
Meet the Ambassador	Jimmy Aubrey	F. B. O	2 reels	
Mellow Quartette	Pen & Ink Vaudeville	Educational	1 reel	April 4
Merrymakers	Bowes-Vance	Educational	1 reel	Mar. 28
Met by Accident	Wanda Wiley	Universal	2 reels	
Milky Way, The	Charles Puffy	Universal	1 reel	July 25
Min Walks in Her Sleep	" Gumps "	Universal		
Misfit Sailor, A	Dovley-Steadman	Educational	2 reels	Oct. 3
Miss Fixit	Wanda Wiley	Universal	2 reels	
Monkey Business	" Pen & Ink Vaude "	Educational	1 reel	May 9
Moonlight Nights	Gloria Joy	Rayart (S. R.)	2 reels	
Moonlight and Noses	Clyde Cook	Pathe	2 reels	Oct. 3
Movies, The	Lloyd Hamilton	Educational	2 reels	Oct. 3
Nearly Rich	Charles Puffy	Universal	1 reel	
Neptune's Stepdaughter		Fox	2 reels	
Nero's Jazz Band		Sering Wilson (S. R.)	1 reel	
Never Fear	Bowes-Vance	Educational	1 reel	
Never on Time		Lee-Bradford (S. R.)	2 reels	
Never Weaken	Lloyd reissue	Assoc. Exhib	2237 feet	
Nice Pickle, A	Edwards-Roach	Universal	1 reel	
Nicely Rewarded	Chas. Puffy	Universal	1 reel	June 27
Night Hawks		Educational Film	2 reels	
Nobody Wins	Arthur Lake	Universal	1 reel	
No Place to Go	Arthur Lake	Universal	1 reel	
Now or Never (reissue)	Harold Lloyd	Assoc. Exhib	3 reels	
Nursery Troubles	Edna Marian	Universal		
Nuts and Squirrels	" Aesop's Fables "	Pathe	1 reel	
Off His Beat	Walter Hiers	Educational	2 reels	
Office Help	" Aesop's Fables "	Pathe	1 reel	June 27
Officer 13	Eddie Gordon	Universal		
Official Officers	" Our Gang "	Pathe	2 reels	June 27
Oh, Bridget	Walter Hiers	Educational	2 reels	
Oh, What a Flirt	Jimmy Aubrey	Film Book. Offices	2 reels	
Oh, What a Gump	" The Gumps "	Universal	2 reels	
Old Family Toothbrush	" Kid Noah "	Sering Wilson (S. R.)	1 reel	
On Duty	Wanda Wiley	Universal	2 reels	
On the Go		Fox		
One Glorious Fourth	" Reg'lar Kids "	M. J. Winkler (S. R.)	2 reels	
One Wild Night	Neely Edwards	Universal	1 reel	
Orphan, The	Al Joy	Ricardo Films, Inc. (S.R.)		
Over the Bottom	Stan Laurel	F. B. O	2 reels	
Over the Plate	Aesops Fable	Pathe	1 reel	Aug. 22
Over Here	Harry Langdon	Pathe	2 reels	
Paging A Wife	Al Alt	Universal	2 reels	Aug. 1
Papa's Darling		Fox	2 reels	
Papa's Pet	Roach-Edwards	Universal	1 reel	April 11
Parisian Knight, A	Earle Foxe	Fox	2 reels	
Peacemakers, The	Perry-Cooley	Fox	2 reels	
Peggy in a Pinch	" Sheiks and Shebas "	Davis Dist.	2 reels	
Peggy's Pests	" Sheiks and Shebas "	Davis Dist.	2 reels	
Peggy's Putters	" Sheiks and Shebas "	Davis Dist.	2 reels	

Feature	Star	Distributed by	Length	Reviewed
Peggy the Vamp	" Sheiks and Shebas "	Davis Dist.	2 reels	Oct. 11
Permanent Waves	" Aesop's Fables "	Pathe	1 reel	
Permit Me	Bowes-Vance	Educational	1 reel	July 11
Pie-Eyed	Stan Laurel	F. B. O.	2 reels	
Pie Man, The	"Aesop's Fables"	Pathe	1 reel	Mar. 21
Plain Clothes	Harry Langdon	Pathe	2 reels	Mar. 28
Plain and Fancy Girls	Charles Chase	Pathe	1 reel	Mar. 14
Plain Luck	Edna Marian	Universal	2 reels	
Pleasure Bound	Lige Conley	Educational	2 reels	Aug. 24
Plenty of Nerve	Edna Marian	Universal	2 reels	July 2
Polo Kid, The	Eddie Gordon	Universal	2 reels	July 18
Poor Sap, The		Fox	2 reels	
Powdered Chickens	Edna Marian	Universal	2 reels	Mar. 28
Props' Dash for Cash	Earl Hurd (Cartoon)	Educational	1 reel	
Putting on Airs	Edna Marian	Universal	2 reels	April 11
Puzzled by Crosswords	Eddie Gordon	Universal	2 reels	Mar. 7
Queen of Aces	Wanda Wiley	Universal	2 reels	May 16
Raid, The	Gloria Joy	Rayart Pict. (S. R.)	2 reels	
Rainy Knight, A	Special Cast	Pathe		
Raisin' Cain	Constance Darling	Universal	2 reels	April 4
Rapid Transit	Al. St. John	Educational	2 reels	
Rarin' Romeo	Walter Hiers	Educational	2 reels	Mar. 28
Raspberry Romance	Ben Turpin	Pathe	2 reels	Feb. 28
Red Pepper	Al. St. John	Educational	2 reels	Arpil 4
Regular Girl, A	Wanda Wiley	Universal	2 reels	
Riders of the Kitchen Range	Mohar-Engle	Pathe	1 reel	June 6
Remember When	Harry Langdon	Pathe	2 reels	April 25
Rip Without a Wink	" Redhead "	Sering Wilson (S. R.)	1 reel	
Ripe Melodrama, A		Sering Wilson (S. R.)	1 reel	
Rivals	Billy West	Arrow	2 reels	
Robinson Crusoe Returns on Friday	" Redhead "	Sering Wilson (S. R.)	1 reel	
Rock Bottom	Bowes-Vance	Educational	1 reel	May 9
Robbing the Rube		Lee-Bradford Corp.	2 reels	
Rolling Stones	Charles Puffy	Universal	1 reel	May 30
Rough Party	Al Alt	Universal	2 reels	
Royal Four-Flush	" Spat Family "	Pathe	2 reels	June 13
Runaway Balloon, The	"Aesop's Fables"	Pathe	1 reel	June 27
Runt, The	"Aesop's Fables"	Pathe	1 reel	June 6
Sailor Papa, A	Glenn Tryon	Pathe	2 reels	April 4
Salute	Alice Ardell	F. B. O.		
Saturday	" Hey Fellas "	Davis Dist. Div.	2 reels	
Say It With Flour		Fox	2 reels	
Scrambled Eggs		Educational		
Sheiks of Bagdad		Pathe	1 reel	May 9
Sherlock Sleuth	Arthur Stone	Pathe	2 reels	July 11
Ship Shape	Vance-Bowes	Educational	1 reel	April 18
Shootin' Injuns	" Our Gang "	Pathe	2 reels	May 9
Short Pants	Arthur Lake	Universal	1 reel	Aug. 1
Should a Husband Tell?		Red Seal Pict.	1 reel	
Should Husbands Be Watched?	Charles Chase	Pathe	1 reel	Mar. 14
Sir Walt and Lizzie		Sering Wilson (S. R.)	1 reel	
Sit Tight	Jimmie Adams	Educational	2 reels	May 30
Skinners in Silk		Pathe	2 reels	May 16
Sky Jumper, The	Earle Foxe	Fox	2 reels	
Skyscraper, The	Harry Langdon	Principal Pict. (S. R.)	2 reels	
Sleeping Sickness	Edwards-Roach	Universal	1 reel	May 30
Slick Articles	Engle-Karr	Universal	2 reels	May 30
Smoked Out	Lake-Hasbrouck	Universal	1 reel	April 13
Sneezing Beezers	Billy Bevan	Pathe	2 reels	July 18
Snow-Hawk	Stan Laurel	F. B. O.	2 reels	
Soap	"Aesop's Fables"	Pathe	1 reel	
Somewhere in Somewhere	Murray-Littlefield	Pathe	2 reels	Sept. 26
S. O. S.	"Aesop's Fables"	Pathe	1 reel	
Spanish Romeo, A (Van Bibber)		Fox	1 reel	
Speak Easy	Charley Puffy	Universal	1 reel	Aug. 22
Speak Freely	Edna Marion	Universal	2 reels	
Spot Light		Educational	2 reels	
Stick Around	Bobby Dunn	Arrow	2 reels	
Stop, Look and Whistle		Fox	2 reels	
Storm, The (Out of the Inkwell)	" Cartoon "	Red Seal Pict.	1 reel	
Stranded	Edna Marian	Universal	2 reels	
Super-Hooper-Dyne Lizzies		Pathe	2 reels	June 13
Sure Mike!	Martha Sleeper	Pathe	1 reel	May 23
Sweet Marie		Fox	2 reels	Aug. 29
Tame Men and Wild Women		Pathe	2 reels	Aug. 15
Teaser Island	" Redhead "	Sering Wilson (S. R.)	1 reel	
Tee for Two	Alice Day	Pathe	2 reels	Aug. 1
Tell It To a Policeman	Glenn Tryon	Pathe	2 reels	May 23
Tender Feet	Walter Hiers	Educational	2 reels	May 23
Tenting Out	Roache-Edwards	Universal	1 reel	Mar. 23
This Week-End		Lee-Bradford (S. R.)		
Three Wise Goofs	Special Cast	F. B. O		
Thundering Landlords	Glenn Tryon	Pathe	2 reels	June 27
Ton of Fun in a Beauty Parlor, A		F. B. O		
Too Much Mother-in-Law	Constance Darling	Universal		
Too Young to Marry	Buddy Messinger	Universal	2 reels	
Tough Night, A	Jimmy Callahan	Aywon Film	2 reels	
Tourist, The	Harry Langdon	Educational Film	2 reels	Aug. 15
Tourists De Luxe	Hayes-Karr	Universal	2 reels	May 16
Transients in Arcadia		Fox	2 reels	
Transatlantic Flight, A	"Aesop's Fables"	Pathe	1 reel	
Twins	Stan Laurel	F. B. O	2 reels	
Two Cats and a Bird	" Cartoon "	Educational	1 reel	Mar. 14
Two Poor Fish	Earl Hurd cartoon	Educational	1 reel	May 30
Ugly Duckling, The	"Aesop's Fables"	Pathe	1 reel	Sept. 26
Uncle Tom's Gal	Edna Marian	Universal	2 reels	
Unwelcome	Charles Puffy	Universal	1 reel	June 27
Waiting	Lloyd Hamilton	Educational	2 reels	July 11
Wake Up	Bowes-Vance	Educational	1 reel	June 13
Watch Out	Bobby Vernon	Educational	2 reels	
Water Wagons	Special Cast	Pathe	2 reels	Feb. 21
Welcome Danger	Bowes-Vance	Educational	1 reel	Feb. 23
West is West	Billy West	Arrow	2 reels	
Westward Ho	Charles Puffy	Universal	1 reel	Oct. 3
What Price Goofy	Charley Chase	Pathe	2 reels	June 6
When Dumbells Ring		Fox	2 reels	
When Men Were Men	"Aesop's Fables"	Pathe	1 reel	July 25
White Wing's Bride	Harry Langdon	Pathe	2 reels	July 11
Whose Baby Are You?	Glenn Tryon	Pathe	2 reels	
Who's Which	Bowes-Vance	Educational	1 reel	
Why Hesitate?	Neal Burns	Educational	2 reels	April 11
Why Sitting Bull Stood Up		Sering Wilson (S. R.)	1 reel	
Wide Awake	Lige Conley	Educational	2 reels	
Wild Papa	" Spat Family "	Pathe	2 reels	May 16
Wild Waves	Bowes-Vance	Educational	1 reel	May 23
Wine, Woman and Song	"Aesop's Fables"	Pathe	1 reel	
Winning Pair, A	Wanda Wiley	Universal	2 reels	
Wooly West, The	Buddy Messinger	Universal	2 reels	
Wrestler, The	Earle Foxe	Fox	2 reels	Aug. 29
Yarn About Yarn, A	Aesop Fable	Pathe	1 reel	Aug. 1
Yes, Yes, Nannette	Jas. Finlayson	Pathe	1 reel	Aug. 1
Your Own Back Yard	" Our Gang "	Pathe	2 reels	Oct. 3

Short Subjects

Feature	Distributed by	Length	Reviewed
Action (Sportlight)	Pathe	1 reel	
All Under One Flag (Sportlight)	Pathe	1 reel	
Animal Celebrities (Sportlight)	Pathe	1 reel	June 27
Animated Hair Cartoon (Series)	Red Seal	1 reel	
Balto's Race to Nome (Special)	Educational	2 reels	May 23
Barbara Snitches (Pacemaker Series)	F. B. O.	2 reels	
Battle of Wits (Josie Sedgwick)	Universal	2 reels	July 18
Bashful Whirlwind, The (Edmund Cobb)	Universal	2 reels	
Beauty and the Bandit (Geo. Larkin)	Universal	2 reels	July 4
Beauty Spots (Sportlight)	Pathe	1 reel	April 18
Best Man, The (Josie Sedgwick)	Universal	2 reels	Aug. 15
Broken Trails	Denver Dixon (S.R.)	2 reels	
Boundary Line, The (Fred Humes)	Universal	2 reels	
Cabaret of Old Japan	M. J. Winkler (S.R.)	1 reel	
Color World	Sering Wilson (S. R.)	1 reel	
Captured Alive (Helen Gibson)	Universal	2 reels	July 25
Cinema Stars (Novelty)	Davis Dist	1 reel	
Close Call, The (Edmund Cobb)	Universal	2 reels	
Cocoon to Kimono	M. J. Winkler (S.R.)	1 reel	
Come-Back, The (Benny Leonard)	Henry Ginsberg-S.R.	2 reels	
Concerning Cheese (Varieties)	Fox	1 reel	
Covered Flagon, The (Pacemaker Series)	F. B. O	2 reels	
Cowpuncher's Comeback, The (Art Acord)	Universal	2 reels	
Crooked (Elinor King)	Davis Dist	2 reels	
Cross Word Puzzle Film (Comedy-Novelty)	Schwartz Enterprises (S. R.)	1 reel	
Cuba Steps Out (Variety)	Fox	1 reel	
Day With the Gypsies	Red Seal Pict.	1 reel	
Divertisement (Color Shots)	Sering Wilson (S. R.)	1 reel	
Don Coo Coo (Pacemakers)	Film Book. Offices	2 reels	
Do You Remember (Gems of Screen)	Red Seal	1 reel	
Dude Ranch Days (Sportlight)	Pathe	1 reel	May 30
Earth's Other Half (Hodge-Podge)	Educational	1 reel	June 6
East Side, West Side	DeForrest (S. R.)		
Fast Male, The (Pacemakers)	Film Book. Offices	2 reels	
Fighting Cowboy (Series)	Universal		
Fighting Ranger (Serial)	Universal	15 episodes	Feb. 7
Fighting Schoolmarm (Josie Sedgwick)	Universal	2 reels	Aug. 1
Film Facts	Red Seal	1 reel	
Fire Trader, The (Serial)	Universal	15 episodes	
Flirting With Death	Red Seal Pict.	2 reels	Sept. 26
Floral Feast, A	Sering Wilson (S.R.)	1 reel	
Frederick Chopin (Music Masters)	Jas. A. Fitzpatrick (S. R.)	1 reel	
From Mars to Munich (Varieties)	Fox	1 reel	April 4
Frontier Love (Billy Mack)	Denver Dixon	2 reels	
Fugitive Futurist	Cranfield & Clarke (S. R.)		
George F. Handel (Music Masters)	Jas. A. Fitzpatrick (S. R.)	1 reel	
Gems of the Screen	Red Seal	1 reel	
Ghost City, The (Serial)	Universal	15 episodes	
Golden Panther, The (Serial)	Pathe		
Gold Trap, The ... Fred Humes	Universal	2 reels	
Great Circus Mystery, The (Serial)	Universal	15 episodes	
Great Decide, The (Pacemakers)	Film Book. Offices	2 reels	
He Who Gets Rapped (Pacemakers)	Film Book. Offices	2 reels	
Hittin' the Trail (Fred Hank)	Sierra Pict. (S. R.)	2 reels	
How the Elephant Got His Trunk (Bray)	F. B. O		
Idaho (Serial)	Pathe	10 episodes	Feb. 28
If a Picture Tells a Story	Cranfield & Clarke (S. R.)		
In a China Shop (Variety)	Fox	1 reel	
In the Spider's Grip (Novelty)	Educational	1 reel	April 11
Invention, The (Elinor Ki g)	Davis Dist	2 reels	Oct. 3
I Remember	Short Films Synd.	2 reels	Sept. 26
It Might Happen to You (Evangeline Russell)	Davis Dist	2 reels	
Jazz Fight, The (Benny Leonard)	Henry Ginsberg (S. R.)	2 reels	
Judge's Cross Word Puzzle (Novelty)	Educational	1 reel	Jan. 31
Just Cowboys ... Corbett-Holmes	Universal	2 reels	
Klondike Today (Varieties)	Fox	1 reel	
Knicknacks of Knowledge (Hodge Podge)	Educational	1 reel	
Knockout Man, The (Mustang)	Universal	2 reels	July 11
Ko-Ko on the Run ... (Ko-Ko Series)	Red Seal	1 reel	Oct. 3
Land of the Navajo (Educational)	Fox	1 reel	
Learning How (Sportlight)	Pathe	1 reel	July 18
Leopard's Lair	Universal	Serial	
Let's Paint	Cranfield & Clarke (S. R.)		
Life's Greatest Thrills	Universal	2 reels	Sept. 26
Line Runners, The (Arnold Gregg)	Universal	2 reels	
Little People of the Garden (Secrets of Life)	Educational	1 reel	
Little People of the Sea (Secrets of Life)	Educational	1 reel	Feb. 28
Lizzie's Last Lap	Cranfield & Clarke (S. R.)		
Loaded Dice (Edmund Cobb)	Universal	2 reels	April 4
Luna-cy (Stereoscopik)	Pathe	1 reel	
Mad Miner, A (Western)	Hunt Miller (S. R.)	2 reels	
Magic Hour, The	Red Seal Pict.	1 reel	
Man Who Rode Alone, The	Miller & Steen (S.R.)	2 reels	
Man Without a Scar	Universal	2 reels	
Marvels of Motion	Red Seal	1 reel	
Marvellous Manhattan	M. J. Winkler (S. R.)	1 reel	
Merry Kiddo, The (Pacemakers)	Film Book. Offices	2 reels	
Merton of the Goofies ... " Pacemaker "	F. B. O.	2 reels	
Mexican Melody (Hodge-Podge)	Educational	1 Reel	
Mexican Oil Fields	M. J. Winkler (S. R.)	1 reel	
Movie Morsels (Hodge Podge)	Educational	1 reel	April 4
My Bonnie ... (Ko-Ko Series)	Red Sea	1 reel	Oct. 3
My Own Carolina (Variety)	Fox	1 reel	Aug. 29
Mystery Box, The (Serial)	Davis Dist. Corp.	10 episodes	
Neptune's Nieces (Sportlight)	Pathe	1 reel	
New Sheriff, A (Western)	Hunt Miller (S. R.)	2 reels	
Olympic Mermaids (Sportlight)	Pathe	1 reel	
One Glorious Scrap (Edmund Cobb)	Universal	2 reels	
Only a Country Lass (Novelty)	Educational	1 reel	May 30
Ouch (Stereoscopik)	Pathe	1 reel	
Our Six-legged Friends (Secrets of Life)	Educational	1 reel	
Outings for All ... (Sportlight)	Pathe	1 reel	
Outlaw, The (Jack Perrin)	Universal	2 reels	
Paris Creations (Novelty)	Educational	1 reel	Feb. 7
Paris Creations in Color (Novelty)	Educational	1 reel	Feb. 28
People You Know (Screen Almanac)	Film Booking Offices.	1 reel	
Perfect View, The (Varieties)	Fox	1 reel	
Perils of the Wild (Serial)	Universal		
Pictorial Proverbs (Hodge Podge)	Educational	1 reel	Aug. 15
Plastigrams (Novelty)	Educational		

Feature	Star	Distributed by	Length	Reviewed
Play Ball (Serial)		Pathe	10 episodes	June 27
Power God, The (Serial)		Davis Dist. Div.	15 episodes	
Pronto Kid, The (Edmund Cobb)		Universal	2 reels	June 27
Queen of the Round-Up (J. Sedgwick)		Universal	2 reels	June 13
Race, The (Van Bibber)		Fox	2 reels	
Radio Detective, The		Universal	Serial	
Raid, The	Edmund Cobb	Universal	2 reels	
Record Breaker, The		Pathe	Serial	
Rim of the Desert (Jack Perrin)		Universal	2 reels	
River Nile, The (Variety)		Fox	1 reel	
Roaring Waters (Geo. Larkin)		Universal	2 reels	
Rock Bound Brittany (Educational)		Fox	1 reel	
Ropin' Venus, The (Mustang Series)		Universal	2 reels	July 11
R. Valentino and Eighty-eight Prize-winning American Beauties		Chesterfield (M. P. Corp.) (S. R.)	3 reels	
Runaway Taxi, A (Stereoscopic)		Pathe	1 reel	Oct. 3
Rustlen of Boulder Canyon (Edmund Cobb)		Universal	2 reels	
Secrets of Life (Educational)		Principal Pict. (S. R.)	reel	Feb. 21
Seven Ages of Sport (Sportlight)		Pathe	1 reel	Aug. 22
Shadow of Suspicion (Eileen Sedgwick)		Universal	2 reels	
Shoes (O. Henry)		Fox	2 reels	
Shootin' Wild (Corbett-Holmes)		Universal	2 reels	
Show Down, The (Art Acord)		Universal	2 reels	
Silvery Art		Red Seal Pict.	2 reels	Sept. 26
Sky Tribe, The (Variety)		Fox	1 reel	
Smoke of a Forty-Five, The (Western)		Hunt Miller (S. R).	2 reels	
Soft Muscles (Benny Leonard)		Ginsberg (S. R.)	2 reels	
Song Cartunes (Novelty)		Red Seal Pict.	1 reel	
Sons of Swat (Sportlight)		Pathe	1 reel	Aug. 15
Sporting Judgment (Sportlight)		Pathe	1 reel	May 9
Starting an Argument (Sportlight)		Pathe	1 reel	
Steam Heated Islands (Varieties)		Fox	1 reel	
Stereoscopic (Novelty)		Pathe	1 reel	May 16
Storm King (Edmund Cobb)		Universal	2 reels	
Story Teller, The (Hodge-Podge)		Educational	1 reel	Oct. 3
Straight Shootin' (Harry Carey)		Universal	2 reels	
Strangler Lewis vs. Wayne Munn		Educational	2 reels	July 4
Stratford on Avon (Gems of Screen)		Red Seal Pict	1 reel	
Sunken Silver (Serial)		Pathe	10 episodes	April 18
Surprise Fight, The (Benny Leonard)		Henry Ginsberg (S. R.)	2 reels	
Thundering Waters (Novelty)		Sering D. Wilson (S. R.)	1 reel	April 25
Tiger Kill, The (Pathe Review)		Pathe		
Toiling for Rest (Variety)		Fox	1 reel	
Traps and Troubles (Sportlight)		Pathe	1 reel	Mar. 21
Travel Treasures (Hodge Podge)		Educational	1 reel	July 25
Turf Mystery (Serial)		Chesterfield Pict. Corp. (S. R.)	15 episodes	
Valley of Rogues (Western)		Universal	2 reels	April 18
Van Bibber and the Navy (Earle Foxe)		Fox	2 reels	
Village School, The (Hodge Podge)		Educational Film	1 reel	May
Voice of the Nightingale, The (Novelty)		Educational	1 reel	Mar. 28
Waiting For You (Music Film)		Hegerman Music Novelties (S. R.)		
Welcome Granger (Pacemakers)		Film Book. Offices	2 reels	
West Wi d, The (Variety)		Fox	1 reel	
What Price Gloria (Pacemakers)		Film Book. Offices	2 reels	
Wheels of the Pioneers (Billy Mack)		Denver Dixon (S. R.)	2 reels	
Where the Waters Divide (Varieties)		Fox	1 reel	
White Paper (Varieties)		Fox	1 reel	
Wild West Wallop, The (Edmund Cobb)		Universal	2 reels	May 16
Wild West		Pathe	Serial	
With Pencil, Brush and Chisel		Fox	1 reel	
Wonder Book, The (Series)		Sering D. Wilson	500 feet	April 25
Young Sheriff, The (Tom. Forman)		Miller & Steen (S. R.)	2 reels	
Zowie (Stereoscopik)		Pathe	1 reel	

Coming Attractions

Feature	Star	Distributed by	Length	Reviewed
Ace of Spades, The	Desmond-McAllister	Universal		
Age of Indiscretion		Truart (S. R.)	5800 feet	
Agony Column	Monte Blue	Warner Bros		
All Around the Frying Pan	Fred Thompson	F. B. O		
Alma of the South Seas	Gilda Gray	Paramount		
American Venus, The	Special Cast	Paramount		
An Enemy of Men		Columbia Pict. (S. R.)		
Ancient Mariner, The	Special Cast	Fox		
Aristocrat, The	Special Cast	B. P. Schulberg (S. R.)		
Ashes	Corinne Griffith	First National		
Atlantis		First National		
Back Wash	Mary Pickford	United Artists		
Bad Lands, The	Harry Carey	Prod. Dist. Corp	5833 feet	Oct. 3
Barriers of Fire	Monte Blue	Warner Bros.		
Bat, The	Special Cast	United Artists		
Beautiful Cheat, The	Laura La Plante	Universal		
Beautiful City	R. Barthelmess	First National		
Before Midnight	Wm. Russell	Ginsberg (S. R.)	5895 feet	Aug. 8
Bells, The	Lionel Barrymore	Chadwick		
Beloved Pawn, The	Reed Howes	Rayart (S. R.)		
Ben Hur	Special Cast	Metro-Goldwyn		
Best Bad Man, The	Tom Mix	Fox		
Between Men	"Lefty" Flynn	F. B. O		
Big Parade, The	John Gilbert	Metro-Goldwyn		
Border Intrigue	Franklyn Farnum	Inde. Pict. (S. R.)	5 reels	June 6
Border Women	Special Cast	Phil Goldstone (S.R.)	5000 feet	
Boss of Little Arcady, The		First National		
Braveheart	Rod LaRocque	Prod. Dist. Corp		
Broken Hearts of Hollywood	Harlan-Miller	Warner Brothers		
Broken Himes	Lake-Glass	Astor Dist		
Brooding Eyes		Ginsberg Dis. Corp. (S. R.)		
Brown of Harvard		Metro-Goldwyn		
Caesar's Wife	Corinne Griffith	First National		
Cave Man, The	Harlan-Miller	Warner Brothers		
Charity Ball, The		Metro-Goldwyn		
Checkered Flag, The		Ginsberg Dist. Corp. (S. R.)		
Circle, The		Metro-Goldwyn		
Clean-Up, The	Richard Talmadge	F. B. O.		
Clod Hopper, The	Glenn Hunter	Assoc. Exhibitors		
Clothes Make the Pirate	Errol-D. Gish	First National		
College Widow, The	Syd Chaplin	Warner Brothers		
Coming of Amos	Rod La Rocque	Prod. Dist. Corp	5677 feet	Sept. 19
Compromise	Irene Rich	Warner Bros.		
Conquered	Gloria Swanson	Paramount		
Count of Luxembourg, The	Larry Semon	Chadwick		
Crashing Through	Jack Perrin	Ambassador Pict. (S. R.)	5000 feet	
Cyclone Bob	Bob Reeves	Anchor Film Dist.		
Cyrano de Bergerac	Special Cast	Atlas Dist. (S. R.)	9500 feet	July 18
Dance Madness	Pringle-Cody	Metro-Goldwyn		
Dangerous Currents		First National		
Dangers of a Great City		Fox		
Dark Horse, The	Harry Carey	Prod. Dist. Corp.		
Daybreak		Fox		
Deerslayer, The		Weiss Bros. (S. R.)	4780 feet	
Daughter of the Sioux, A	Wilson-Gerber	Davis Dist. (S. R.)	5 reels	Oct. 3
Demon, The	Jack Hoxie	Universal		
Demon Rider, The	Ken Maynard	Davis Dist	5000 feet	Aug. 22
Detour		Prod. Dist. Corp.		
Devil Horse, The	Rex (horse)	Pathe		
Down Upon the Suwanee River	Special Cast	Lee Bradford (S. R.)		
Dumb Head		Tiffany (S. R.)	6500 feet	
East of the Setting Sun	Constance Talmadge	First National		
Eagle, The	Rudolph Valentino	United Artists		
Eden's Fruit		B. P. Schulberg (S.R.)		
Enchanted Hill, The	Special Cast	Paramount		
Ermine and Rhinestone		H. F. Jans (S. R.)		
Exquisite Sinner, The	Special Cast	Metro-Goldwin		
Face on the Air, The	Evelyn Brent	F. B. O.		
Fair Play	Special Cast	Wm. Steiner (S. R.)	5035 feet	Sept. 19
Fall of Jerusalem		Weiss Bros. (S. R.)	6800 feet	
False Pride		Astor Dist.		
Fast Pace, The	Special Cast	Arrow		
Fifth Avenue		Prod. Dist. Corp		
Fighter's Paradise, The	Rex Baker	Phil Goldstone	5000 feet	
Fighting Courage	Ken Maynard	Davis Dist. Div. (S.R.)	5 reels	July 11
Fighting Edge, The	Harlan-Miller	Warner Brothers		
Fighting Smile, The	Bill Cody	Inde. Pict. Corp. (S.R.)	4630 feet	
First Year, The	Special Cast	Fox		
Flaming Waters		F. B. O.		
Flying Three	Al Wilson	Davis Dist. Corp.		
Forest of Destiny, The		Gotham Prod. (S. R.)		
Forever After	Corinne Griffith	First National		
Fort Frayne	Ben Wilson	Davis Dist.	5000 feet	Aug. 29
Free Lips	Norma Shearer	M-G-M		
Friends	Special Cast	Vitagraph		
Frivolity		B. P. Schulberg (S.R.)		
Galloping Dude, The	Franklyn Farnum	Inde. Pict. Corp. (S.R.)	4700 feet	
Garden of Allah		United Artists		
Going the Limit	Richard Holt	Gerson Pict. (S. R.)	5000 feet	Sept. 26
Golden Butterfly, The		Fox		
Golden Cocoon		Warner Bros.		
Goose Woman, The	Special Cast	Universal	7500 feet	Aug. 22
Go West	Buster Keaton	Metro-Goldwyn		
Grass			10 reels	Mar. 7
Great Love, The	Dana-Agnew	First National		
Grey Vulture, The	Ken Maynard	Davis Dist. Div.		
Gulliver's Travels		Universal		
Handsome Brute, The	Columbia Pict. (S. R.)			
Hassan		Paramount		
Haunted Range, The	Ken Maynard	Davis Dist. Div.		
Hearts and Fists		Assoc. Exhib.		
Hearts and Spangles		Gotham Prod. (S. R.)		
Hell Bent for Heaven		Warner Bros.		
Hell's Highroad	Leatrice Joy	Prod. Dist. Corp	6084 feet	Sept. 5
Heir's Apparent	Special Cast	First National		
Her Father's Daughter		F. B. O.		
Hero of the Big Snows, A	Rin Tin Tin (dog)	Warner Brothers		
His Jazz Bride	Special Cast	Warner		
His Majesty Bunker Bean	M. Moore-Devore	Warner	7291 feet	Sept. 26
His Master's Voice	Thunder (dog)	Gotham Prod. (S. R.		
His Woman	Special Cast	Whitman Bennett	7 reels	
Hogan's Alley	Harlan-Miller	Warner		
Home Maker, The	Alice Joyce	Universal	7755 feet	Aug. 8
Honeymoon Express, The	M. Moore-D. Devore	Warner Brothers		
Horses and Women		B. P. Schulberg		
How to Train a Wife	Valli-O'Brien	Assoc. Exhib.		
Hurricane		Truart (S. R.)	5800 feet	
Husband Hunters		Tiffany	6500 feet	
Inevitable Millionaires, The	M. Moore-Devore	Warner Bros.		
Invisible Wounds	Sweet-Lyon	First National		
Irene	Colleen Moore	First National		
Justice of the Far North		C. B. C. (S. R)	5500 feet	
Just Suppose	Richard Barthelmess	First National		
Kentucky Pride	Special Cast	Fox	6597 feet	Sept. 19
Kings of the Turf		Fox		
Kiss for Cinderella, A	Betty Bronson	Paramount		
Knockout Kid, The	Jack Perrin	Rayart Pict. Corp. (S. R.)		
La Boheme	Lillian Gish	Metro-Goldwyn		
Ladies of Leisure	Elaine Hammerstein	Columbia (S. R.)		
Lady Windermere's Fan	Special Cast	Warner Brothers		
Lariat, The	William Desmond	Universal		
Last Edition, The	Ralph Lewis	Film Book. Offices		
Lawful Cheater, The	Bow-McKee	B. P. Schulberg	4946 feet	
Lena Rivers	Special Cast	Arrow	6 reels	
Life of a Woman		Truart (S. R.)	6500 feet	
Lightning Jack	Jack Perrin	Ambassador Pict. (S.R.)	5000 feet	
Lightning Passes, The	Al Ferguson	Fleming Prod. (S.R.)		
Limited Mail, The	Monte Blue	Warner Bros.		
Little Girl in a Big City, A		Gotham Prod. (S. R.)		
Little Irish Girl, The	Special Cast	Warner Bros.		
Live Wire, The	Johnny Hines	First National		
Lodge in the Wilderness		Tiffany (S. R.)	6500 feet	
Lord Jim	Percy Marmont	Paramount		
Love Cargo, The	House Peters	Universal		
Love Gamble, The	Special Cast	Banner Prod. (S. R.)	5766 feet	July 11
Lover's Island	Hampton-Kirkwood	Assoc. Exhib		
Love Gamble, The		Ginsberg Dist. Corp. (S. R.)		
Love Toy, The	Lowell Sherman	Warner Bros		
Loyalties	Special Cast	Fox		
Lucky Lady, The	Lionel Barrymore	Paramount		
Lunatic at Large, The	Leon Errol	First National		
Lure of Broadway, The		Columbia Pict. (S. R.)		
Lure of the Wild	Jane Novak	Columbia (S. R.)		
Lying Wives	Special Cast	Ivan Abramson (S. R.)	7 reels	May 2
Manhood		Fox		
Man and the Moment		Metro-Goldwyn		
Mannequin, The		Paramount		
Man From Red Gulch	Harry Carey	Prod. Dist. Corp.		
Man of Iron, A	L. Barrymore	Chadwick	6 reels	July 4
Man on the Box, The	Sydney Chaplin	Warner Bros		
Man She Bought, The	Constance Talmadge	First National		
Man Without a Conscience	Louis-Rich	Warner Bros	6850 feet	May 2
Mare Nostrum	Special Cast	Metro-Goldwyn		
Married Cheats		Fox		
Married Hypocrites	Fredericks-La Plante	Universal		
Martinique	Bebe Daniels	Paramount		

Feature	Star	Distributed by	Length	Reviewed
Masked Bride, The	Mae Murray	Metro-Goldwyn		
Memory Lane	Boardman-Nagel	First National		
Men of Steel	Milton Sills	First National		
Message to Garcia, A		Metro-Goldwyn		
Midnight Flyer, The	Landis-Devore	F. B. O.		
Million Dollar Handicap, The		Prod. Dist. Corp.		
Miracle of Life, The	Busch-Marmont	Assoc. Exhib.		
Miracle of the Wolves, The			10346 feet	Mar. 7
Midnight Flames		Columbia Pict. (S. R.)		
Miss Vanity	Mary Philbin	Universal		
Million Dollar Doll		Assoc. Exhib.		
Mismates		First National		
Mocking Bird, The	Lon Chaney	M-G-M		
Morganson's Finish		Tiffany (S. R.)	6500 feet	
Napoleon the Great		Universal		
My Own Pal	Tom Mix	Fox		
Night Cry, The	Rin-Tin-Tin (dog)	Warner Brothers		
Nightie, Night Nurse	Syd Chaplin	Warner Brothers		
North Star, The	Strongheart (dog)	Assoc. Exhib.		
Old Clothes	Jackie Coogan	Metro-Goldwyn		
Only Thing, The	Special Cast	Metro-Goldwyn		
Open Trail, The	Jack Hoxie	Universal	4800 feet	May 16
Pace That Thrills, The	Ben Lyon	First National		
Palace of Pleasure		Fox		
Pals		Truart (S. R.)	5800 feet	
Paris		Metro-Goldwyn		
Paris After Dark	Norma Talmadge	First National		
Partners Again		United Artists		
Passionate Quest, The	Marie Prevost	Warner Bros.		
Passionate Youth	Special Cast	Truart (S. R.)	6 reels	July 11
Part Time Wife, The		Gotham Prod. (S. R.)		
Peak of Fate, The		F. B. Rogers	6 reels	June 27
People vs. Nancy Preston	Bowers-De La Motte	Prod. Dist. Corp.		
Phantom of the Forest	Thunder (dog)	Gotham Prod.		
Phantom of the Opera	Lon Chaney	Universal	8464 feet	Sept. 19
Pinch Hitter, The	Glenn Hunter	Assoc. Exhibitors		
Pleasure Buyers, The	Irene Rich	Warner Brothers		
Police Patrol, The	James Kirkwood	Gotham Prod. (S.R.)	6000 feet	Sept. 19
Polly of the Ballet	Bebe Daniels	Paramount		
Pony Express, The	Special Cast	Paramount	9929 feet	Sept. 26
Prairie Pirate, The	Harry Carey	Prod. Dist. Corp.	4603 feet	Sept. 26
Prince, The	Philbin-Kerry	Universal		
Quality Street		Metro-Goldwyn		
Quicker 'n Lightning	Buffalo Bill, Jr.	Weiss Bros. (S. R.)	4 reels	June 13
Racing Blood		Gotham Prod. (S. R.)		
Rainbow Riley	Johnny Hines	First National		
Reckless Courage	Buddy Roosevelt	Weiss Bros. (S. R.)	4851 feet	May 3
Reckless Sex, The	Special Cast	Truart (S. R.)	6 reels	Feb. 14
Red Clay	William Desmond	Universal		
Red Dice	Rod La Rocque	Prod. Dist. Corp.		
Red Kimono, The	Mrs. Wallace Reid	Davis Dist. Div.		
Red Hot Tires	Monte Blue	Warner Bros.		
Return of a Soldier	Special Cast	Metro-Goldwyn		
Rime of the Ancient Mariner, The		Fox Film		
Road to Glory, The	Special Cast	Prod. Dist. Corp.		
Road That Led Home, The		Vitagraph		
Rocking Moon	Bowers-Tashman	Prod. Dist. Corp.		
Romance of an Actress		Chadwick		
Ropin' Venus, The	Josie Sedgwick	Universal		
Rose of the World	Special Cast	Warner Bros.		
Sally, Irene and Mary	Special Cast	Metro-Goldwyn		
Salvage	M. Moore-D. Devore	Warner Bros.		
Satan in Sables	Lowell Sherman	Warner Bros.		
Savage, The	Ben Lyon	First National		
Scarlet Saint, The	Lyon-Astor	First National		
Screen	Mary Pickford	United Artists		
Sea Beast, The	John Barrymore	Warner Bros.		
Sea Woman, The	Sweet-McLaglen	First National		
Separate Rooms		Fox		
Seven Days	Lillian Rich	Prod. Dist. Corp.		
Seven Sinners	Marie Prevost	Warner Bros.		
Seventh Heaven	Special Cast	Fox		
Shadow of the Wall		Gotham Prod. (S. R.)		
Shadow of the Mosque	Odette Taylor	Cranfield & Clarke (S. R.)	6300 feet	
Shenandoah		B. P. Schulberg (S. R.)		
Ship of Souls	B. Lytell-L. Rich	Assoc. Exhib.	6500 feet	
Shootin' Square	Jack Perrin	Ambassador Pict. (S.R.)	5000 feet	
Siegfried		Ufa		
Sign of the Claw		Gotham Prod. (S. R.)		
Silken Shackles	Irene Rich	Warner Bros.		
Silver Treasure, The	Special Cast	Fox		
Simon the Jester	Rich-O'Brien	Prod. Dist. Corp.		
Skinners Dress Suit	Reginald Denny	Universal		

Feature	Star	Distributed by	Length	Reviewed
Social Highwayman, The	Haylan-Miller	Warner Brothers		
Song and Dance Man, The	Tom Moore	Paramount		
Son of His Father, A	Special Cast	Paramount	6915 feet	Sept. 19
Spanish Sunlight	LaMarr-Stone	First National		
Span of Life	Betty Blythe	Banner Prod. (S. R.)		
Speed Limit, The		Gotham Prod. (S. R.)		
Splendid Road, The	Anna Q. Nilsson	First National		
Sporting Life	Special Cast	Universal	6709 feet	Sept. 26
Stage Door Johnny	Raymond Griffith	Paramount		
Steel Preferred	Special Cast	Prod. Dist. Corp.		
Steele of the Royal Mounted		Vitagraph	6 reels	June 27
Stella Dallas		United Artists		
Stella Maris	Mary Philbin	Universal		
Still Alarm, The	Chadwick-Russell	Universal		
Stop, Look and Listen	Larry Semon	Pathe		
Strange Bedfellows		Metro-Goldwyn		
Streets of Sin		Fox		
Sunshine of Paradise Alley	Special Cast	Chadwick Pict.		
Super Speed	Reed Howes	Rayart (S. R.)		
Sweet Adeline	Charles Ray	Chadwick		
Tale of a Vanishing People		Tiffany (S. R.)	6500 feet	
Tattooed Countess, The	Pola Negri	Paramount		
Tearing Loose	Wally Wales	Weiss Bros. (S. R.)	4900 feet	June 13
Temptress		Metro-Goldwyn		
Ten to Midnight		Prod. Dist. Corp.		
That Man from Arizona	D. Revier-W. Fairbanks	B. O.		
That Royle Girl		Kirkwood-Dempster	Paramount		
This Woman	Special Cast	Metro-Goldwyn		
Thoroughbred	George O'Brien	Fox		
Thoroughbred, The	Special Cast	First National		
Three Bad Men	Special Cast	Fox		
Three Faces East	Special Cast	Prod. Dist. Corp.		
Tony Runs Wild	Tom Mix	Fox		
Trading Shadows	Edmond Lowe	Fox Film		
Travelin' Fast	Jack Perrin	Ambassador Pict. (S. R.)	5000 feet	
Travis Coup, The		Tiffany (S. R.)	6500 feet	
Twin Sister, The	Constance Talmadge	First National		
Two Blocks Away	Special Cast	Universal		
Two Soldiers, The	Mildred Davis	Paramount		
Unchastened Woman, The	Theda Bara	Chadwick		
Unguarded Hour, The	Sills-Kenyon	First National		
Unknown Lover, The	Elsie Ferguson	Vitagraph		
Up and At 'Em	Jack Perrin	Ambassador Pict. (S. R.)	5000 feet	
Vengeance of Durand, The	Irene Rich	Warner Brothers		
Viennese Medley	Special Cast	First National		
Volga Boatman, The		Prod. Dist. Corp.		
Wages for Wives	Special Cast	Fox		
Wanderer, The	William Collier, Jr.	Paramount	8172 feet	
Wandering Footsteps	Special Cast	Ginsberg Dist. Corp.		
Warrior Gap	Wilson-Gerber	Davis Dist.	4900 feet	Aug. 22
Was It Bigamy	Edith Thornton	Wm. Steiner (S. R.)	5000 feet	Sept. 26
Wedding Song, The	Leatrice Joy	Prod. Dist. Corp.		
We Moderns	Colleen Moore	First National		
What Happened to Jones	Reginald Denny	Universal		
What Will People Say		Metro-Goldwyn		
When His Love Grew Cold		F. B. O.		
When Husbands Flirt	Dorothy Revier	Columbia		
Where the Worst Begins		Truart (S. R.)	5500 feet	
Whispering Canyon		Ginsberg Dist. Corp.		
White Chief, The	Monte Blue	Warner Brothers		
White Mice	Jacqueline Logan	Bering D. Wilson (S. R.)		
Why Girls Go Back Home		Warner Brothers		
Wild Girl	Peter the Great	Truart (S. R.)	5500 feet	
Wild Justice		United Artists	6 reels	Aug. 1
Wild Ridin'	Josie Sedgwick	Fox		
Wild West	Mulhall-Ferguson	Pathe		
Winning of Barbara Worth		Principal Pict. (S. R.)		
Wise Guy, The	Lefty Flynn	F. B. O.		
Without Mercy	Vera Reynolds	Prod. Dist. Corp.		
With Kit Carson Over the Great Divide	Special Cast	Sunset Prod. (S. R.)		
Without Mercy	Vera Reynolds	Prod. Dist. Corp.		
Wives for Rent		Paramount		
Womanhandled	Richard Dix	Paramount		
Woman, A		Banner Prod. (S. R.)		
Women and Wives		Metro-Goldwyn		
World's Illusion, The		Metro-Goldwyn		
Worst Woman, The	Special Cast	Tiffany (S. R.)		
Wreckage		Ginsberg Dist. Corp.		
Wrong Coat, The		Tiffany (S. R.)	5500 feet	
Yankee Senor, The	Tom Mix	Fox		
Yoke, The	Special Cast	Warner Brothers		
You Can't Live on Love	Reginald Denny	Universal		

Newspaper Opinions on New Features

(Continued from page 1741)
melodrama on the merits of the best work of our favorite movie actor."

Evening World: "The dog is interesting and convincing."

Daily Mirror: "A cracker jack melodrama, packed with thrills. Herman Raymaker has turned out a picture that is a credit to him, while Cameraman John Mescall contributes greatly by splendid photographic effects. The actors are all good but it is Rin-Tin-Tin that makes 'Below The Line' a wow of a melodrama."

American: "A corking melodrama with a dog hero full of pep and zip. I only wish a few

of our leading men would steal his 'stuff' and forget the exalted position they occupy. Even if you are a high-brow and scorn the Nick Carters of the 'fillums,' you will adore Rin-Tin-Tin and wish you had him in your family."

Daily News: "For you who admire Rin-Tin-Tin, that noble canine; for you who enjoy a good, brisk melodrama; in fact, for you, and you and you. 'Below The Line' is heartily recommended. The director has a clever way of whipping up your interest."

Morning Telegraph: "The best dog picture that has been made in months. Rin-Tin-Tin, in himself, is enough to put over a film among fans who have dogs, and

here he has been given a good story, with great suspense, excellently directed by Herman Raymaker. Rin-Tin-Tin is marvelous; he can always express pathos as well or better than any human actor on the screen."

Graphic: "The dynamic personality of this fourfooted is truly amazing, and the audience watches his adventures with amused interest. If you think you've seen this cleverest of animal actors do everything possible for a canine to accomplish, you will have a few surprises in 'Below The Line.'"

"The Circle"—M-G-M, Capitol, N. Y.

Brooklyn Eagle: "In the hands

of a director less capable than Frank Borzage, W. Somerset Maughan's play might have turned out to be just another dull, unconvincing triangle picture. As it stands, however, it has sufficient originality to hold the interest. The group of players who appear in his tale are billed as an all-star cast, and, for once, that term does not prove a misnomer. Few recent films have had so many performers of equal merit."

Post: "An excellent cast has been assembled for the picture. The various roles are unusually well handled by people who look the parts. Our best advice is—go and see the picture."

DuplexFilm Cement

HOLDS

~and when the climax of the feature is reached—it won't be necessary to hold your breath and pray that your splice won't break.

for EVERY stock

No. 7 cements inflammable film to non-inflammable, or instantly patches either.

It works fast—dries immediately and the bottle may be used for weeks until all the cement is gone. It does NOT deteriorate with ordinary handling.

Yes No 7 HOLDS!

USE THIS COUPON

8 oz. Bottle $1 Plus Postage.

DUPLEX MOTION PICTURE INDUSTRIES, Inc.
Long Island City, New York.

DUPLEX
Long Island City

DATE_____

Here's a Quarter—let's try it!

1 oz. Bottle 25¢

Name_____

Address_____

City_____

For Better Projection

Incandescent lamp projection has many substantial advantages that are worthy of serious consideration by every exhibitor. There is no question about its economy. The incandescent lamp consumes only about one half the current required for the average arc light.

It assures steady pictures. The light source being fixed and constant, screen flicker, shadows, spots, etc. are entirely eliminated by this method of projection. The light is pleasing and easy on the eyes of the audience.

The incandescent lamp improves operating conditions. It gives off no fumes, carbon dust or excessive heat. The projection booth is cleaner and healthier.

MOST THEATRES CAN USE IT.

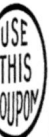

Incandescent lamp projection is adaptable to any theatre with seating capacity less than 1,000 throw not exceeding 120 feet and picture width not more than 16 ft. That includes about 80% of the theatres in the country.

But for maximum efficiency, incandescent lamp projection requires careful adjustment of the optical system. Because the Simplex incandescent unit is easily adjusted, its popularity is increasing every day. Many exhibitors who despaired of obtaining the advantages of this newer method of projection, found that the Simplex unit overcame every obstacle in the way.

Full information on the merits of incandescent lamp projection and detailed description of the Simplex Incandescent Unit is given in an interesting booklet that will be sent to you on request. It will pay you to have this information.

Mail the attached coupon. It may be a step towards a saving of hundreds of dollars.

MADE AND GUARANTEED BY
THE PRECISION MACHINE CO. INC.
317 East 34th St— New York

Rothacker-Aller Laboratories, Hollywood, Calif.

First National Pictures, Inc.,
Presents *"The Pace That Thrills"*
Adapted from an original story
By Byron Morgan—with Ben Lyon,
Mary Astor and Tully Marshall.
Scenario by Raymond Harris. The
Photography by T. D. McCord.
Milton Menasco, art director.
Film edited by Mr. Arthur Tavares.
Marion Fairfax, editorial direction.
All directed by Webster Campbell.
Supervised by Mr. Earl Hudson.
A First National Picture.
Rothacker Prints and Service.

Mary Astor
in
"The Pace That Thrills"

FILM MFG. CO. CHICAGO, U.S.A.

**Look Better—
Wear Longer!**

Founded 1910
by
Watterson R. Rothacker

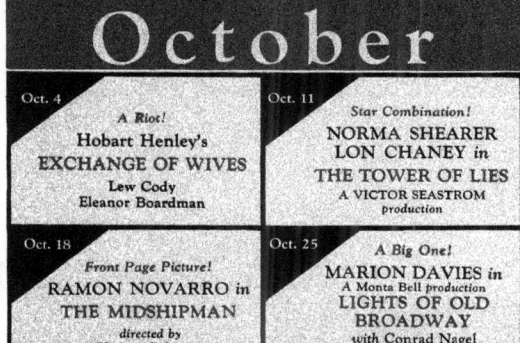

What a Quartet of Pictures for

October

Oct. 4

A Riot!
Hobart Henley's
EXCHANGE OF WIVES
Lew Cody
Eleanor Boardman

Oct. 11

Star Combination!
NORMA SHEARER
LON CHANEY *in*
THE TOWER OF LIES
A VICTOR SEASTROM
production

Oct. 18

Front Page Picture!
RAMON NOVARRO *in*
THE MIDSHIPMAN
directed by
Christy Cabanne

Oct. 25

A Big One!
MARION DAVIES *in*
A Monta Bell *production*
LIGHTS OF OLD
BROADWAY
with Conrad Nagel
A Cosmopolitan Production

PRODUCED BY THE SHOWMEN OF
METRO-GOLDWYN-MAYER

Member of Motion Picture Producers and Distributors of America, Inc.—Will H. Hays, President

WURLITZER
UNIT ORGANS

... the permanent attraction with a REAL Box Office POWER

EXHIBITORS from coast to coast are realizing every day the real box office value of the Wurlitzer Unit Organ. The steadily increasing number of Wurlitzer Unit Organ installations, in both newly constructed and long established houses, is conclusive evidence of this fact. And it is not always the largest of America's finest motion picture palaces that select the Wurlitzer, but the smaller houses as well, for there is Wurlitzer Music for every type of motion picture theatre, whether large or small. The convenient Wurlitzer plan of purchase is a boon to the small exhibitor and bears investigation. Write today and learn how easy it is to acquire this powerful and permanent box office attraction.

MIGHTY WURLITZER

THE accompanying illustrations show the interior and exterior views of the new Albee Theatre, Brooklyn. It is considered to be the finest house in Greater New York. After careful research and extensive investigation of numerous makes of organs, the mighty Wurlitzer has been selected. Thus again a Wurlitzer will furnish the musical accompaniment for the highest type of motion picture productions in another of America's finest motion picture palaces.

TWO UNUSUAL CATALOGS

A copy of the new Wurlitzer Unit Organ catalog is ready to be mailed to you. Write for it today—it's a genuine printing masterpiece. No obligation.

The Wurlitzer Grand Piano is used and highly endorsed by leading exhibitors in the orchestra pits and for feature sets. Write today for catalog.

The RUDOLPH WURLITZER CO.

CINCINNATI   NEW YORK   CHICAGO   SAN FRANCISCO   DENVER   LOS ANGELES
121 East 4th St.   120 W. 42nd St.   329 S. Wabash   250 Stockton St.   2106 Broadway   814 S. Broadway

And Forty Other Branches in Thirty-Three Cities

And It's Doing the Same All Over!

"They laughed and howled for more"

So raves the "Service Talks" editor in *Exhibitors' Herald* after seeing "Lovers in Quarantine" at McVickers Theatre, Chicago. He goes on: "Bebe Daniels, wild enough in 'Wild, Wild Susan', is wilder and funnier in 'Lovers in Quarantine'. The humor breaks in at the beginning of the picture and never subsides until it is done".

YOU CAN USE A GOOD SNAPPY LOVE-COMEDY RIGHT NOW!

"LOVERS IN QUARANTINE"

Starring

Bebe Daniels

Bebe as a bride on a tropical island!

WITH
HARRISON FORD
A
FRANK TUTTLE
PRODUCTION

FROM THE PLAY "QUARANTINE"
BY F. TENNYSON JESSE
SCREEN PLAY BY TOWNSEND
MARTIN AND LUTHER REED
PRESENTED BY
ADOLPH ZUKOR AND JESSE L. LASKY

A Greater 40 Paramount Picture

Money Magic for

Press and Public unite in praise !

Exhibitors are enthusiastic ~

because

The **WILLIAM FOX** $2,000,000 program of short subjects are **LITTLE GIANTS OF THE SCREEN**

The MARRIED LIFE *of* HELEN *and* WARREN

EARLE FOXE *in new series of* VAN BIBBER *society comedies*

O. HENRY *Series*

Fox Film Corporation.

your Box Office !

NEW FOX COMEDIES OF SURPASSING QUALITY

EARLE FOXE in
VAN BIBBER Comedies
Based on stories by
RICHARD HARDING DAVIS
With Florence Gilbert

Coming:
THE WRESTLER

Directed by Robert P. Kerr
Supervised by GEORGE MARSHALL

Now Playing:
The Big Game Hunter
The Sky Jumper

O. HENRY
COMEDIES

Book Now:
TRANSIENTS IN ARCADIA
with
Mary Akin as the O. Henry Girl
Directed by Daniel Keefe
Supervised by GEORGE MARSHALL

Now Playing:
Shoes

The MARRIED LIFE
of HELEN and WARREN
Based on the stories by
MABEL HERBERT URNER
with
Hallam Cooley   Kathryn Perry
as the Husband   as the Bride

Ready:
ALL ABROAD
Directed by Albert Ray
Supervised by GEORGE MARSHALL

Now Playing:
A Business Engagement

IMPERIAL
COMEDIES

New Releases:
THE HEART BREAKER
STRONG FOR LOVE

Now Playing:
On The Go
Sweet Marie
Love And Lions
A Cloudy Romance

Imperial Comedies   Fox News   Fox Varieties

Fox Film Corporation.

EXHIBITORS ~
you know how well
your patrons like

★ LEADING FAN MAGAZINES REPORT MORE
QUERIES ON GEORGE O'BRIEN THAN
ON ANY OTHER YOUNG STAR.

Fox Film Corporation.

It's two reels in length, but in its great comedy
star, excellent story, gorgeous settings, lavish costuming, and abundant laughs, it's a superfeature.

E.W. Hammons

Presents

LUPINO
LANE

in

"MAID IN
MOROCCO"

First of the six two-reel

Lupino Lane
Comedies

Better SEE this picture at your Educational Exchange RIGHT NOW. You're
going to regret it before the season is
over if you fail to get this remarkable
new star. By that time he is going to
be acknowledged one of the greatest
comedy stars the screen has produced.

Educational Pictures

"THE SPICE OF THE PROGRAM"

For foreign rights address
Far East Film Corporation
729 Seventh Avenue
New York, N.Y.

Member,
Motion Picture Producers and
Distributors of America, Inc.
Will H. Hays, *President*

EDUCATIONAL
FILM EXCHANGES, Inc.

E.W. Hammons
President

"BIG BOY"

This new baby star will captivate the hearts of any audience. He is just about the cutest kid that ever donned his daddy's derby and big shoes and "played big boy." If you want to hear the "Ohs" and "Ahs" of love and admiration from your audiences, as well as the laughs, show them "Big Boy" with the host of other clever youngsters in the new

Juvenile
•COMEDIES•

E.W. Hammons Presents

"BABY BE GOOD"

Directed by CHARLES LAMONT
First of a new series of six

Here's a great new selling feature for your advertising. Play up "Big Boy" and Juvenile Comedies for Extra Profit.

SOME PUMPKINS!!

When our General Sales Manager returned last week from a trip around the country he said:-

"Funny thing Tom Saxe in Milwaukee, and Frank Buhler in Philadelphia, told me. They both said that they have to pay as much attention to the selection of their news reels as to their features. Then they showed me the week's mail.

"Forty per cent of the letters related to the news reel. *I tell you we're getting to be some pumpkins.*"

Right, Mr. Sales Manager

We're not only getting to be some pumpkins, but we are some pumpkins already

Needless to say Messrs Saxe and Buhler, two of America's foremost exhibitors, *book* KINOGRAMS

PUT A PUMPKIN IN YOUR THANKSGIVING BASKET

WITH

KINOGRAMS
The News Reel Built Like a Newspaper

Apply These Savings to Your Credit

Every dollar you save on operating expenses is a dollar added to the earnings of your theatre. Incandescent lamp projection reduces your operating costs from 25% to 75%. It means an extra earning of hundreds of dollars annually.

The table above shows the saving affected by the incandescent lamp over various types of arc lights. For instance if you are operating a 50 amperage arc by rheostat control 10 hours a day, current rate 8c a K. W. hour, you can save $1,280.00 a year by replacing your arc with a 900 watt Edison MAZDA Incandescent lamp. If your arc control is by motor generator, compensator or rectifier your saving would be $623 per year. If you operate 5 hours a day your saving would be half as much in each case.

Apply these savings to the earnings of your theatre. Consider also the advantages to be gained through better projection and better operating conditions. Is it not a matter of good business to install incandescent lamp projection now?

The whole story of incandescent lamp projection is told in an interesting booklet prepared for theatre owners. A copy of this booklet will be sent to you free on request. Just mail the attached coupon.

EDISON MAZDA LAMPS
A GENERAL ELECTRIC PRODUCT

First Choice—
Cecil B. DeMille

"The policy of this theatre has always been to show only carefully selected pictures — Pictures that could offend no one — yet can delight and entertain the most particular people. Realizing the place the Rialto occupies in the hearts of the theatre-goers of this section, the management has recently made arrangements to be the —

Cecil B. DeMille House

in the future in Enid, showing all of this great director and producer's pictures.

It is with a great deal of pride that we make the above announcement because we believe the Rialto patrons are entitled to the best.

In addition to the

Cecil B. DeMille Productions

we will continue to show all of the FIRST NATIONAL PICTURES. The Pictures that have already made the Rialto famous among lovers of good shows."

RELEASED BY

PRODUCERS DISTRIB

RIALTO

Enid's Pioneer Theatre

A show house of Character and Quality—In a fast growing city, the greater movie season. The Rialto will maintain its leadership, its reputation—The house where the best show is to be seen

THE ROYAL THEATRE

run in connection with the Rialto, conducted on the same high plan of wholesome entertainment. The Royal shows all of the Out-Door plays including all the pictures made featuring

Tom Mix
Hoot Gibson
Buck Jones
Fred Thompson
Harry Carey

The Royal will continue to be the family theatre. Every Wednesday night the entire family can see the show for

40c

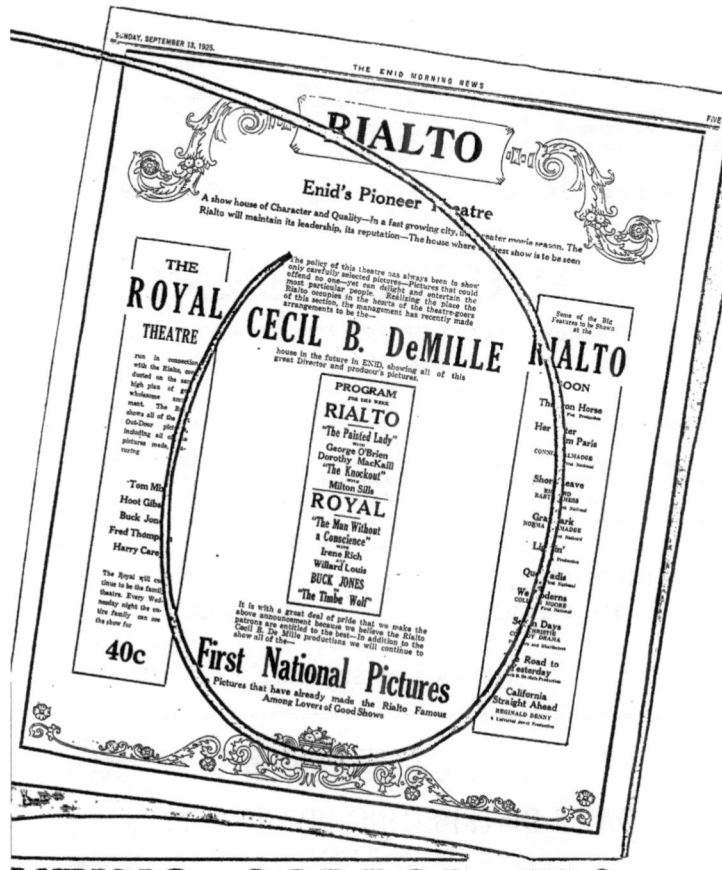

The policy of this theatre has always been to show only carefully selected pictures—Pictures that could offend no one—yet can delight and entertain the most particular people. Realizing its place the Rialto occupies in the hearts of the theatre-goers of this section, the management has recently made arrangements to be the—

CECIL B. DeMILLE

house in the future in ENID, showing all of this great Director and producer's pictures.

PROGRAM
FOR THE WEEK

RIALTO

"The Painted Lady"
George O'Brien
Dorothy MacKaill
"The Knockout"
Milton Sills

ROYAL

"The Man Without a Conscience"
Irene Rich
Willard Louis
BUCK JONES
"The Timber Wolf"

It is with a great deal of pride that we make the above announcement because we believe the Rialto patrons are entitled to the best—In addition to the show all of the—

First National Pictures

Pictures that have already made the Rialto Famous Among Lovers of Good Shows

Some of the Big Features to be Shown at the RIALTO SOON

The Iron Horse
Fox Production

Her Sister From Paris
CONSTANCE TALMADGE
First National

Shore Leave
RICHARD BARTHELMESS
First National

Graustark
NORMA TALMADGE
First National

Lightnin'
Fox Production

Quo Vadis

We Moderns
COLLEEN MOORE
First National

Seven Days
A COMEDY DRAMA
Pathe and Warner Bros.

Road to Yesterday
Cecil B. DeMille Production

California Straight Ahead
REGINALD DENNY
A Universal Jewel Production

UTING CORPORATIO

THE PHA OF THE *Beats*

"The PHANTOM" Beats
"The HUNCHBACK" in
PITTSFIELD, MASS.

"The Phantom" played to tremendous business at the Union Square Theatre, topping every established "Hunchback" figure for that city. As a result The Goldstein Circuit has booked "The Phantom" for all their houses in New England.

"The PHANTOM" Beats
"The HUNCHBACK" in
SAN FRANCISCO, CALIF.

"'The Phantom' opened better than 'Hunchback.' Consider it twice as good a picture from standpoint of good theatre entertainment."

Homer Curran, Mgr.,
Curran Theatre,
San Francisco, Calif.

"The PHANTOM" Beats
"The HUNCHBACK" in
KINGFISHER, OKLA.

"'The Phantom' is most wonderful production shown in my theatre for many years. Far greater than 'The Hunchback.' A great success."

Homer C. Jones, Mgr.,
Temple Theatre,
Kingfisher, Okla.

A UNIVERSAL PRODUCTION *starring* **LON CHANEY** MARY NORMAN

TOM
OPERA
he HUNCHBACK
OF NOTRE DAME

HOW I WON MISS PR

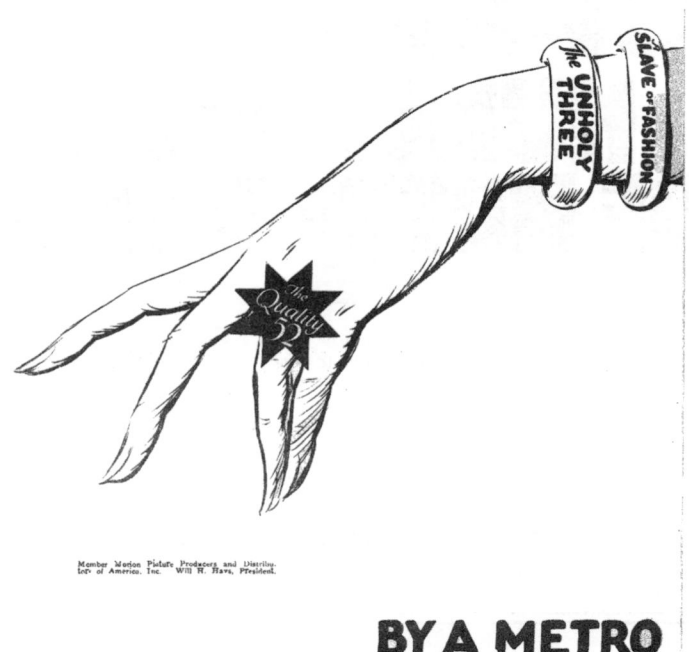

BY A METRO

OSPERITY

THE UNHOLY THREE
Starring Lon Chaney, with Mae Busch, Matt Moore. Tod Browning's production of the story by Tod Robbins.

A SLAVE OF FASHION
Starring Norma Shearer, with Lew Cody. Hobart Henley's production of the story by Samuel Shipman.

PRETTY LADIES
With Zasu Pitts, Tom Moore, Lillian Tashman, Ann Pennington. Monta Bell's production of the story by Adela Rogers St. Johns.

NEVER THE TWAIN SHALL MEET
With Anita Stewart, Bert Lytell and All Star Cast. By Peter B. Kyne. Maurice Tourneur, director. A Cosmopolitan Production.

SUN UP
With Pauline Starke, Conrad Nagel, Lucille La Verne. Edmund Goulding's production of Lula Vollmer's play.

THE MYSTIC
With Aileen Pringle, Conway Tearle. Tod Browning's production of his own story.

EXCHANGE OF WIVES
With Lew Cody, Eleanor Boardman, Renee Adoree, Creighton Hale. Hobart Henley's production of Cosmo Hamilton's play.

THE TOWER OF LIES
Starring Norma Shearer, Lon Chaney. Victor Seastrom's production of Selma Lagerlof's novel. With William Haines.

·GOLDWYN-MAYER EXHIBITOR

Out in October

The Next Issue of
Motion Picture News

Booking
Guide

!

Companies
Which Have Not
Yet Submitted Full
Data on All Productions
Should Do So Immediately

Some Speed!!

2nd LAFFIN'
CRASHIN'
CASH-IN
WEEK

at Warners Theatre – New York City

Syd **CHAPLIN**

"The Man on the Box"

Directed by
Chas. [Chuck] Reisner

WARNER BROS
Classics of the Screen

From the novel and
stage play by
Harold Mac Grath

RECORD: "Brimful of sentimental lure and is always convincing. Powerful drama of love and devotion."

EVENING HERALD: "One of the few great war pictures."

EVENING EXPRESS: "An intensely gripping story."

EXAMINER: "A drama of high romance and intensive emotion. A notable film which has attracted huge audiences ever since its opening."

TIMES: "'The Dark Angel' really proves to be a winning dark horse on the race course of romantic film drama.

"COLMAN and BANKY"
Great in 'Dark Angel' "

RECORD: "Vilma Banky, an actress of genuine talent. Must consider her in the future's line-up of stars. Ronald Colman gives a supreme performance."

EVENING EXPRESS: "Ronald Colman's acting the finest of his screen career. Vilma Banky acts with grace, delicacy and intensity.

"The DARK ANGEL"

The George Fitzmaurice PRODUCTION

Presented by **SAMUEL GOLDWYN**

From the stage play by H. B. Trevelyan   Scenario by FRANCES MARION

with

Ronald Colman and Vilma Banky

First National Pictures

Best by Test

The First National big 4 for October

CORINNE GRIFFITH
in "Classified"

This is Miss Griffith's greatest achievement. The story is by Edna Ferber, directed by Al Santell, with editorial direction by June Mathis, and has Jack Mulhall and Charles Murray in support of star. Presented by Corinne Griffith Productions, Inc.

RICHARD BARTHELMESS
with DOROTHY GISH
in "The BEAUTIFUL CITY"

Another money making picture for Dick. It was written for the screen by Edmund Goulding and was directed by Kenneth Webb. Presented by Inspiration Pictures, Inc. Just the type of picture the fans love to see him in.

"The PACE THAT THRILLS"
with Ben Lyon and Mary Astor

Here's a fast one. Adapted from an original story by Byron Morgan, directed by Webster Campbell, and produced under the supervision of Earl Hudson. Editorial director, Marion Fairfax.

"WHY WOMEN LOVE"
with Blanche Sweet

One of the most powerful dramas ever screened. From the famous play, "The Sea Woman," by Willard Robertson. Produced and directed by Edwin Carewe. Robert Frazer, Charles Murray, Dorothy Sebastian and Russel Simpson in cast. Scenario by Lois Leeson.

First National have the pictures

Motion Picture News

VOL. XXXII   ALBANY, N. Y., AND NEW YORK CITY, OCTOBER 17, 1925   NO. 16

Percentage

WE FEEL like adding our own observations to the much discussed subject of producer-owned theatres; and what is in our mind is best introduced by the following facts:

Said a prominent executive the other day: "Our company (a large producing-distributing concern) just took over a theatre in the State of ————. This theatre had rarely paid over $75.00 for our features—$150.00 occasionally for a longer run. Now we receive over $500.00. Why shouldn't—and why wouldn't—a manufacturer run his own retail outlets when he can sell his wares to the public for five times what the dealer will pay?"

Said another executive—and he is compiling a most interesting and significant set of figures: "By playing on a percentage basis instead of flat rentals our receipts thus far on (a well known star) have been increased 65%. I have a comparative box-office record from a list of towns of 400 to 17,000 population. It shows receipts of about $22,000 in flat rentals on another and just as good picture, as against $39,000 receipts on percentage playing."

* * *

Fully six years ago MOTION PICTURE NEWS came out flat-footedly for percentage playing—in the interests equally of producer, distributor and exhibitor. We didn't advocate any one scheme, especially any then in use. We said it was not an easy matter to work out; that unfairness from both sides would prevail at first, but that gradually a scientific, practical and equitable system would be evolved; that advertising done by the theatre would have to enter the equation; that traveling auditors would be necessary, etc.

We asserted that only through the picture's actual box-office receipts could producer, distributor and exhibitor—on some just sharing basis—be assured, each, of an equitable return.

For this stand we were pretty generally assailed. Not by all exhibitors; some even then saw the wisdom as well as the fairness of the scheme. But a resolution against percentage playing was then a stock procedure in practically every exhibitor convention.

We believed in percentage playing then; we believe in it as sincerely today. And today we are prepared to go further. We believe that, had percentage playing been entered into several years ago, producer-owned theatres today would be a minor factor in the layout of this industry—confined, at least, to the key cities; and possibly not a factor at all. Anyway, producing organizations would not have been tempted or forced into the buying or building of theatres, because they could make five dollars grow where, before, they reaped but one.

* * *

Everybody is talking pretty plainly, these days. And rightly so. There's no use in smoothing over facts that are glaring enough.

The truth of the matter is that a lot of theatres, in a position to force rentals down, have been making unreasonable profits.

There have been two inevitable results of this greed: one is to induce well-financed producing organizations to buy or build theatres; the other is to force a lot of other exhibitors to pay too heavy rentals. Someone has got to pay the freight. Production cost is high. If one exhibitor pays one-half of what he could well afford to pay, some other exhibitor has got to pay twice as much as he should pay.

Note the tax return figures from producing and exhibiting firms, as published in this issue. It is pretty evident that some are making a lot and some are losing a lot. There's little balance. And if you'll dig into the facts it will be found that theatres, not pictures, are the determining factor between big profits and heavy losses.

Percentage playing, where neither partner can gyp the other—and producer and exhibitor are partners, of course—would have leveled profits and losses, stabilized the whole business, and kept each business man in his own business field.

W. A. Johnston

MOTION PICTURE NEWS

October 17
1925

Vol. XXXII
No. 16

Founded in September 1913

Publication Office: Lyon Block, Albany, N. Y.

Branch Offices:
843 S. Wabash Ave., Chicago, Ill.
Room 616 Security Bldg., Hollywood.
Calif.

Editorial and General Offices:
729 7th Ave., New York City

Speaking Editorially

OUR observer on the film firing-line at Hollywood reports a distinct trend away from the program picture and a steady swing to specials—in fact as well as in name. This follows our own analysis of the situation some weeks ago—when we pointed out that the "average" picture no longer has a real place in the progressive march of the motion picture.

❋ ❋ ❋

THIS week we are happy to present the views of Joseph M. Schenck on the subject of producer-owned theatres. The interview with Adolph Zukor, printed last week, seems to have aroused unusual interest throughout the trade.

These are divergent views; both are highly significant, and are, we believe, real contributions to the discussion of the industry's major problems.

❋ ❋ ❋

FROM Washington comes the news that Representative John Q. Tilson, the majority leader of the House of Representatives, is squarely on record for the repeal of the admission tax on motion pictures. This is a development of unusual significance, and should give great encouragement to exhibitors—as well as to all the other divisions of the industry. The tax up to and including 50c admissions has, of course, already been lifted. Mr. Tilson now urges complete freedom of the screen from this out-of-date impost. His reasons, which are highly gratifying, are set forth in full elsewhere in this issue.

❋ ❋ ❋

THINGS are humming at Associated Exhibitors. With the inauguration of the new regime, headed by Oscar Price and P. A. Powers, the company's activity has been greatly increased. Mr. Price has given us an interview on what he hopes to accomplish. It is an elaborate plan; and the company, strongly financed and officered by film men of genuine skill, bids fair, as Mr. Price says, to make a very definite and standing place for itself in the industry.

❋ ❋ ❋

THAT was a very interesting communication sent by Mr. Hays to the convention of the Michigan M. P. T. O., in which he offers to take up for immediate adjustment any real grievances exhibitors may communicate to him against members of the M. P. P. D. A. A step forward—and a very necessary work. Incidentally, the Michigan organization now includes practically all the exhibitors of the State in its membership—some 475, we believe. It's a real organization.

Vice-President Charles G. Dawes (in the light suit) visits the Metro-Goldwyn-Mayer studios during his stay on the West Coast, and is piloted about the Culver City plant by Harry Rapf and Louis B. Mayer, at the left and right of Mr. Dawes, respectively.

AN authentic report comes to us that J. D. Williams is very active in England. As is well known, he went to the other side some time ago but the nature of his plans, up to the present moment, has not been disclosed. We learn now—from a source fully informed of the situation—that J. D. is in process of building another "First National" along the lines he followed as the author of First National here. Further news may be expected shortly. Meanwhile, this report in itself will be of great interest to the American industry.

October 17, 1925   MOTION PICTURE NEWS   Vol. XXXII, No. 16
Published weekly by Motion Picture News, Inc., William A. Johnston, President; E. Kendall Gillett, Vice-President; William A. Johnston, Editor; J. S. Dickerson, Associate Editor; Oscar Cooper, Managing Editor; Fred J. Beecroft, Advertising Manager; L. H. Mason, Chicago Representative; William McCormack, Los Angeles Representative. Subscription price $3 per year; post paid in United States, Mexico, Hawaii, Porto Rico, Philippine Islands and some other countries; Canada, $5; foreign, $10.00. Copyright 1925, by Motion Picture News, Inc., in the United States and Great Britain. Title registered in the United States Patent Office and foreign countries. Western Union cable address is "Picknews," New York. Entered as second-class matter January 21st, 1924, at the postoffice, Albany, N. Y., under the Act of March 3, 1879.

Schenck Defines Attitude on Producer-Owned Theatres

U. A. Prefers to Concentrate on Pictures

By William A. Johnston

(Copyright, 1925, by Motion Picture News, Inc.)

"UNITED ARTISTS have never owned theatres, do not now own theatres and expect never to own theatres," said Joseph M. Schenck, in an interview I asked for on the subject of producer-owned theatres.

"That is our policy, that's all. I do not criticize any other company for owning theatres. That is their business—not mine, nor anyone else's, it seems to me.

"I may, however, disagree with them on business grounds; and so I do.

"The buying of theatres, it seems to me, is a necessary result of indiscriminate production. If you make a great many pictures you cannot possibly make them all good. Some of them will be fine attractions and these find their way readily to market. The weak ones—and they are inevitable in bulk production—need theatres to bring back their negative cost. Mind you, I am not criticizing. It is just one business policy against another, that's all. And we mustn't forget to give a lot of credit to those big producing organizations that have given the theatres so many fine and profitable pictures.

: "Over-production is a seriously bad factor today. It raises production cost to an alarming point. There's just so much raw material to go around—stories, talent, etc. And naturally, intense production raises the competitive bids.

"I don't believe that block selling is an outgrowth of this bulk production. I think the exhibitor is largely to blame for that. He buys in block; he evidently prefers to.

"He rarely sees the pictures before he buys them. He figures that such and such a service made money for him last year. So he buys in advance, in bulk, sight unseen. If he would reform his buying methods you would see reform in production and distribution.

"But to get back to theatres. We don't own them because we feel we do not need the ownership. That's one reason. Secondly, we don't want the responsibility of ownership. A theatre, you know, is also an attraction, like a picture. You've got to make good theatres just as you should make good pictures. The public pays for the brick and mortar. Now, the making of

Joseph M. Schenck, Chairman of the Board of Directors, United Artists Corporation.

good theatres demands concentration. We, for our part, prefer to concentrate on pictures.

"Then there's a third reason. And an important one. It is this, that the theatre map is changing with incredible swiftness today. The theatre you want to own today you may not want tomorrow. Theatres get out of date very fast. Look at Chicago. Compare the theatres there today—the new Uptown, for instance—with the theatres of a few years ago. These changes are happening, will happen, in every big city and in many smaller ones. I look to see a great movement in the building of large and beautiful neighborhood houses. In fact, the future holds forth so much—and I feel I can see it so clearly—that I wouldn't tackle theatres on a large scale. I'd rather make pictures suitable for these present and future houses—whatever they may be.

"But, as I say, that is simply my own business program. I agree with Mr. Zukor, and I think it's fine, wholesome advice to give—that each one of us stick to his own job, do the best he can, and stop worrying about and throwing rocks at the other fellow.

"We are making pictures for the world to see. We hope to continue to. That's a man-sized job, a great responsibility for all of us."

Teddy Criswell, the attractive winner of Universal's "See America First" Beauty Contest in Milwaukee, conducted by the travelling studio unit now on tour.

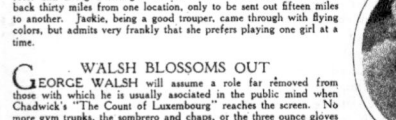

PICTURES
AND
PEOPLE

JACKIE'S CHANGING ROLES

JUST about the busiest person on the Fox lot last week was Jacqueline Logan, playing the leading feminine role in "Wages for Wives." Just before this she had been engaged in making "When the Door Opened," a James Oliver Curwood story, and when this was completely assembled and the work print screened it was found that several scenes would have to be added to complete it.

So for several days Miss Logan's services were in equal demand by Frank Borzage, director of "Wages for Wives," and Reginald Barker, in connection with the other picture. As it finally worked out, she played on one set in the morning and the other in the afternoon during one hectic week, portraying two entirely different roles and living a strange "double life." In one case, she came back thirty miles from one location, only to be sent out fifteen miles to another. Jackie, being a good trouper, came through with flying colors, but admits very frankly that she prefers playing one girl at a time.

WALSH BLOSSOMS OUT

GEORGE WALSH will assume a role far removed from those with which he is usually associated in the public mind when Chadwick's "The Count of Luxembourg" reaches the screen. No more gym trunks, the sombrero and chaps, or the three ounce gloves —for in the title role of the Franz Lehar operetta, in its celluloid transcription, he discards them all for the frock coat, the boiled shirt, the wing collar and the top hat. Nor is that all, for with them he has acquired a new decoration—a firm, dignified mustache —thus upsetting the screen tradition of long standing that only villians wear whiskers. The Sheik has run his vogue—perhaps it will be the Count that will replace him in the hearts of feminine fans.

The first heroine with a dirty face on record will be Doris Kenyon in "The Unguarded Hour." (First National). Director Lambert Hillyer is about to dish the dirt.

Peggy Hopkins Joyce (Countess Morner) who makes her debut as a star in "The Skyrocket," which Associated Exhibitors will release as a special.

Charlotte Bird, a clever and attractive miss engaged for "The Best People," which Sidney Olcott is now producing for Paramount on the West Coast.

Alice Ardell goes through a few rounds of shadow boxing prior to her strenuous work in Blue Ribbon comedies for F. B. O., in which she is leading woman.

A remarkable shot of wild elephants in their native habitat, as photographed by Mr. and Mrs. Lou C. Hutt and shown in their "Wild Beasts of Borneo," an Educational Pictures Special.

Yola d'Avril, a striking Gallic type, who lends color to the Christie comedies for Educational, caught by the photographer in an Apache pose. (Photo by Hurwitz).

Director Joseph Henebery shows Glenn Hunter how to "choke the bat" in a scene for "The Pinch Hitter" (Associated Exhibitors), recently produced.

TOM'S PROUDEST PRESENT

MANY strange gifts come to an actor in the course of his career, and Tom Mix, no exception to the rule, has accumulated as strange an array of trophies as any of them. Most of them mean little or nothing, but Tom acquired one on location for "The Best Bad Man" that he treasures with a great deal of pride.

The company was on location making outdoor sequences for this picture in the Columbia district (not to be confused with the District of Columbia) and Mix noticed a grizzled old miner watching him intently. When lunch time came, and the company knocked off, the old man approached and asked if he was Tom Mix. Tom allowed that he was. Then the prospector paid him the compliment of telling him that while he didn't go to pictures much, he had always fancied the Mix yarns, and had never seen Tom in a bad picture (something a good many folks would agree with). Then he ended up by fumbling about in his faded blue shirt and producing a shiny nugget. Presenting this to Mix, he explained that it was the first he had ever wrested from Mother Earth and that he wanted the Western star to have it. He had carried it for more than fifty years, but the work of Mix had made such an impression on him that he was happy to part with his treasure so that he might know that the nugget was in good hands.

Fay Lanphier, "Miss America," is declared to be a real find as a result of her work in "The American Venus" (Paramount), now in production at the Long Island studio.

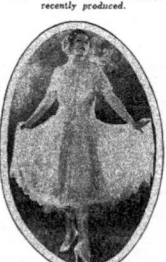

Lilyan Tashman, one of the most beautiful of the Follies graduates in pictures, whose current rôle is in "A Little Bit of Broadway" (Metro-Goldwyn-Mayer).

PATHE'S MERRY WASSAIL

AN interesting time is looked forward to by the press scribes this week on Friday, when Pathe will entertain in the "vast baronial hall of Bellamy Castle" erected at the Pathe studios in Astoria, Long Island for "The Green Archer." The party is to be held in honor of Allene Ray, the serial star, who appears in the picture.

A special feature of the day will be the coronation of Miss Ray as "queen of serials" with suitable ceremony and jollity. Just who will do the "crowning" is undetermined, since that will be decided at the party by the drawing of lots. The lucky person will then be photographed bestowing the coronet on the charming star, thereby going down to fame in a blaze of reflected glory. We shall doubtless have much more to say about the party and the coronation next week.

HIGH SPEED SHOOTING

AN unusual record for working under difficult conditions was made recently by James P. Hogan and his "Steel Preferred" company in Pittsburgh. Nearly two hundred scenes were filmed under considerable handicaps in exactly ten working days, right in and around the steel mills. And all of this was done without delaying or interfering in any way with the work of the mills.

These scenes against a background of Bessemer converters and furnaces, with flaming loads of liquid metal passing back and forth on the ladle trains, should provide some thrilling and beautiful shots.

Gilda Gray, Paramount's newest star, who leaves this week for Porto Rica in location for "Aloma of the Seas," her first production. (Photo by Abbe, Paris.)

Madge Bellamy, whose beauty and personality have steadily grown with each picture, has been an attractive feature of several recent Fox releases.

King Vidor directs Lillian Gish in a close-up for "La Bohème" (Metro-Goldwyn-Mayer), while Irving Thalberg, assistant executive, looks on to see how things are progressing.

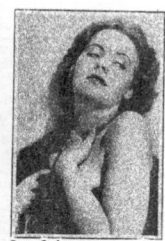

Greta Garbo, most recent of the imported beauties, who will be seen in Metro-Goldwyn-Mayer pictures. Sweden holds the honor of being her birthplace.

A "DARK ANGEL" TAKES FLIGHT

ATTENDED by a brilliant array of celebrities, "The Dark Angel" was given its professional premiere on the Coast this week at Loew's State theatre, Los Angeles, and was warmly received. In addition to those connected with the filming of the picture, notables on hand included: Edwin Carewe, Florence Turner, M. C. Levee, Sid Grauman and mother with party, John Gilbert, Matt Moore, Harry Wilson, Finis Fox, Robert D. McIntyre, Mrs. Wallace Reid, Florence Lawrence and many others.

Clayton P. Sheehan (at the left), Fox home office representative, clasps hands with Stanley S. Clark, Australian managing director, at laying of corner-stone for the new Fox building in Sydney, Australia. More than 250 prominent persons were on hand.

FIFTH AVENUE BEAUTIES

ONE of the high spots in the scenes obtained in New York by Robert Vignola and his company, filming exteriors in New York for the A. H. Sebastian production "Fifth Avenue," before their departure last week, was a group of shots of a corps of models said to rival the beauty brigade of Florenz Ziegfeld.

These models, employed as mannequins by one of New York's most fashionable shops where the clientele is of the most wealthy and aristocratic class, are selected with the utmost care, both as regards beauty and grace, and are paid proportionate salaries.

Naturally, such a shop does not seek publicity in the usual sense, and it was only through bringing considerable personal influence to bear that permission was obtained to photograph the showroom with its aggregation of exceptionally beautiful girls.

Meanwhile, Director Vignola, with his company of players, including Allan Forrest, Marguerite de la Motte and Sally Long, has arrived on the coast, where the cast will be augmented by the addition of Louise Dresser. He will at once plunge into the filming of the interiors to match up with the rich assortiment of exterior scenes taken on Fifth avenue, from Washington Square on the south to the new Ghetto on the north.

MEIGHAN'S TRAVEL RECORD

THOMAS MEIGHAN has certainly made himself eligible during the past 18 months, for membership in the ranks of confirmed travellers. All told, during the period named, he has knocked off 20,000 miles of touring on location for various pictures. No more does he get the trunk and make-up box unpacked than it becomes necessary to trek away in a new direction, and if he ever decides to expand his activities he might well open the Thomas Meghan Travel Bureau, for he could surely give all inquirers first hand information.

Four of the most lengthy trips have been as follows: To Alberta, Canada, for "The Alaskan," 6,000 miles; to Birmingham, Ala., for "Coming Through," 2,500 miles; to Ocala, Fla., for "Old Home Week," 2,500 miles; and now, to Dublin, Killarney, Cork and other Irish locations for "Irish Luck," 9,000 miles. Together with other and shorter location trips in New York state, the total for the 18 months is in the neighborhood of 21,000 miles.

A feature of Carl Laemmle's trip to Europe this summer was his visit to the Ufa studios, near Berlin, where the Universal chief looked over the latest German improvements; left to right: Carl Laemmle, Jr., Mr. Laemmle, Director Staub, Erich Pommer, General Director of Ufa, H. H. Zehner, secretary to Laemmle, Oscar Einstein and Director Ostermeyer.

UNIVERSAL'S NEW BEAUTIES

WEEK by week, Universal's "See America First" tractor and trailer studio unit has been going about the country from city to city, doing remarkable work. In each city a special film has been made, depicting the leading spots of interest, industries, and the like. C. E. Holah is in charge of the unit, and has gotten a remarkable publicity "break" for the stunt in every city. Now the outfit has arrived in New York, where the procedure is being repeated.

An important feature of the campaign in each city has been a contest to select a local beauty, the winner being awarded a six months' contract at Universal City. Such a contest is now being waged in New York in conjunction with the *Daily Mirror*, one of the tabloid newspapers. Already, it is said there are some thirty thousand entrants.

An interesting feature of these contests is the fact that the winners are actually being put to work at Universal City and given practical training from the outset. If they have any real ability, they will have every chance to show it.

Vanna Carroll, San Francisco, was cast first in "Sporting Life," and later in two-reel westerns, "The Winking Idol" and a special western feature. Dorothy Gulliver, Salt Lake City, has already played in "The Still Alarm," "The Winking Idol," "Two Blocks

Walter Lang directing a scene for "The Red Kimono" (Davis Distributing Division) in which Mrs. Wallace Reid, Virginia Pearson and Priscilla Bonnet appear. The picture is now in production on the West Coast.

Al Wilson, stunt flyer, signs with Davis Distributing Division for six pictures. Left to right, J. K. Adams, Wilson and J. Charles Davis, 2d.

Away" and "Strings of Steel." Blanche Fisher, Omaha, has worked in a comedy with Charles Puffy, in "Strings of Steel" and a western feature. Florence Allen, Chicago, is playing in "The Radio Detective." Emmaline (Teddy) Criswell, Milwaukee, has just arrived at Universal City, and is cast in a new western feature. Grace Parent, has appeared in "Two Blocks Away." Irene Franklin, Toledo, and Mabelle Perry, Cleveland, are undergoing preliminary training, and will be cast shortly.

A girl will be selected in New York City within a fortnight. She will first appear in a special film showing the high spots of the city, as have the other winners, after which she will journey to Universal City to take up serious training. This special film will be used for showing around New York.

THE LONE STAR

ONLY one of the significant little asterisks found its way to the list of pictures reviewed this week by the National Board, but if past performance is any criterion this one should be well deserved. The picture in question is Robert J. Flaherty's "Mona," a Samoan idyll, acclaimed a worthy successor to "Nanook of the North." Flaherty spent some two years in getting the precise shots at South Sea life that he wanted, and the few favored individuals that have seen the picture since his return have been tremendously enthusiastic about its beauty and interest.

Carlo Fescia, accordionest, celebrates his seventh anniversary on the Harry Carey set during the filming of "The Man From Red Gulch" (Producers Dist. Corp.). Carey carves the seventh notch, watched by Harriett Hammond, his leading lady.

ESKIMO EXPRESS SERVICE

THE exhibitor who has trouble with deliveries of film should ponder the case of the one lone Eskimo exhibitor, served out of Calgary. William Kelly, Paramount branch manager in that city, writes that this man's prints must each be shipped 300 miles by dog train over the frozen wastes. It is a remarkable testimonial to the popularity of the motion picture the world over that it should be in demand 300 miles from a railroad, where such influences penetrate only with the greatest of difficulty.

It's wonderful how stars and their producers get along together. Here are Leon Errol and Sam Rork having it out with cutlass and derringer between scenes of "Clothes Make the Pirate" (First National).

HUDSON DEFENDS TEMPERAMENT

THAT much maligned quality, Temperament, often condemned and the cause of many sleepless nights for producers, has at last found a warm defender in Earl Hudson, head of First National's Eastern production units at New York—who not only defends it but demands it in his players, and gives good reasons why.

"I wouldn't give ten cents for an actor or actress in the motion picture business who has no temperament," declares Hudson. "Temperament and imagination go hand in hand. What good is an actor without imagination? He may do everything the director tells him, but without imagination he will lack that something which the successful actor has. It is hard to describe, but it shows on the screen.

"Don't make the mistake so many people do and think that temperament means just a plain 'temper.' There is a vast difference. I have no use for alleged temperament which is a cloak for temper. Temperament is a special type of mental constitution and development or mixture of characteristics. In other words it is summary of intellectual and emotional tendencies. I figure, and believe I am right, that where there is no temperament there is little if any intellect; and of course, there can be no emotionalism. An actor surely needs emotionalism or he will not get very far.

"An actor with temperament reaches the heights that his untemperamental brother always strives vainly for.

A. M. P. A. AFFAIRS BOOM

UNDER the new administration headed by Glendon Allvine the weekly luncheons of the A. M. P. A. are doing an S. R. O. business, with seats in the hands of speculators, and no prospect of the attraction going into the cut-rates. Each week's program seems better than the one before it, with even more brilliant plans for the future.

Last week's meeting had on its bill the following headliners, a truly all-star aggregation: Phil Baker, comedian of "Artists and Models;" H. A. Snow, explorer and picture producer; Eileen Stanley, phonograph recording artist; James A. O'Gorman, candidate for alderman; and Jackie Taylor and his Rue de la Paix orchestra.

The guest of honor scheduled for this week is Richard Talmadge, the screen star, and several other surprises are promised.

JOHN BARRYMORE IN SPECIAL
Warners To Make "Tavern Knight"

AFTER several weeks of negotiations, Warner Bros. announce they will make a third picture with John Barrymore while that actor is on the coast. The signature of Barrymore was obtained this week out on the Pacific Ocean where he is making "The Sea Beast," and the Warners immediately purchased "The Tavern Knight" by Rafael Sabatini, author of "The Sea Hawk" and "Captain Blood" as the story in which Barrymore will be put out in a big special production.

This does not mean that the Warners are to abandon their plans to present the star in Lord Byron's "Don Juan." On the contrary work on this love story will be started with the completion of "The Sea Beast," which is nearing an end, and will practically be finished so far as Barrymore is concerned when the whaling episodes now being shot are completed.

"The Tavern Knight" is a period picture of the Seventeenth Century in England when Charles II attempted to regain the throne from the parliamentary rule of Oliver Cromwell. Barrymore will play the title role, that of Sir Crispin Ballaird.

This means that Barrymore is not likely to appear on the speaking stage this season, but it does not mean that he is deserting the footlights permanently.

"Two Thirty Three" Club Celebrates

The Two Thirty Three Club of Hollywood, composed of a restricted membership of 1,233 theatrical masons celebrated its first anniversary last week with a fourteen act vaudeville show made up of talent exclusively from the club roster. It was announced that the club would start work within a few months on a twelve story building, which will be used for headquarters.

Edwards Davis, character actor and former president of the N. V. A. of North America and the Green Room Club in New York is president of the club. Milton Sills, Frank Lloyd and Don Meaney are vice-presidents, Raymond McKee and Adam Hull Shirk, secretaries with Fred Douglas, recording clerk and Samuel Kress, treasurer. The board of directors comprises George Sargent, secretary of the Motion Picture Directors Association, chairman; John Ince, Lew Gill, Joseph Goldsmith, Jr., Raymond Hatton, Edward V. Rowland, Darwin S. Karr, George Davies, Parry Vekroff, Joseph Mary, Joseph Kilgour, Philip Hunt and J. L. Johnston. The membership committee comprises Wilfred North, chairman; Mitchell Lewis, Herbert Prior, William H. Turner and David Thompson.

Centralize Paramount Booking
Sam Dembow is Organizing New System; Five Districts Under Theatre Department

THE organization of a centralized booking system to be put into effect by the Paramount Theatre Department is being supervised by Sam Dembow, Jr. Under the plan there will be five district offices which will be in charge of physical operation and a master book will be maintained by the theatre department in New York.

William Saal, recently transferred to the home office from the Missouri theatre, St. Louis, will be in charge of the bookings under Dembow's supervision.

The district offices are now being established in New York, Charlotte, Atlanta, Jacksonville and Dallas. District No. 1 will have its headquarters at the home offices in New York and will be supervised by Saal. Bookings for New York State, Kansas City, St. Louis, Bay City, Denver, Lincoln, Los Angeles, San Francisco and other widely separated points not included in other districts, will be handled from this office.

District No. 2 will have headquarters in Charlotte, where bookings will be handled for Paramount theatres in North and South Carolina. District No. 3 will be established in Atlanta with A. C. Cowles in charge. Georgia, Alabama and Tennessee are in this district. Florida houses will be booked by J. N. Thomas, in charge of District No. 4, with headquarters in Jacksonville. District No. 5 will be located in Dallas and will be under the direction of Miss Bray.

The appointment of Earl L. Crabb as managing director of the Metropolitan, Boston, and the promotion of John J. Friedl to succeed him as district manager in Dallas, have entailed the following promotions in the Paramount theatre organization in Dallas:

Bary Burke succeeds Fredl as manager of the Palace, Dallas; Harry Gold succeeds Burke as manager of the Palace, Fort Worth;

Luther Strong succeeds Gould as manager of the Hippodrome, Fort Worth, and Tom Owens, formerly at the Melba, Dallas, goes to the Crystal, Dallas, as manager, succeeding Strong.

Eastman Holdup Averted by Treasurer

A daring attempt by a lone bandit to hold up Frank L. Smith, treasurer of the Eastman theatre, Rochester, in his office on the second floor of the big Kodak Town house last week was frustrated when Smith whipped out a revolver, covered the youthful robber and then chased him down a corridor to the main lobby and into the arms of House Manager John J. O'Neil.

While hundreds of patrons in the theatre watched the final performance, all unaware of the drama being enacted in the lobby, the youthful bandit, fighting for liberty was turned over to the police who had been notified of the attempted holdup and rushed to the scene. Taken to headquarters the youth gave his name as John Henderson, 24 years old, living at a Russell street boarding house.

Led Successful Fight for Open Sundays in Logan

R. E. Brown of the Pastime theatre, Logan, Ia., is given credit for the open Sunday victory there. Though new in the picture business he went to merchants and showed them how the closed Sunday was driving away business and hurting the town. Then he led them in a campaign for petition signatures. The victory was won only after several fines had been paid.

Bandits Take Receipts of St. Louis Maffitt

Two armed bandits held up the Maffitt theatre, 2812 North Vandeventer avenue, St. Louis, Mo., shortly before midnight Sunday, October 4th, escaping with Saturday and Sunday receipts, totaling $530.70.

The Maffitt is one of the string of theatres owned by the St. Louis Amusement Company.

Joseph Greene, manager; Miss Grace Hilliker, cashier, and Walter Bunte, usher, were about to depart from the showhouse when the two bandits entered. While one guarded Bunte and Miss Hilliker in the lobby the other robber forced Greene to enter the office and open the safe.

Mayer Attends Convention of Fire Chiefs

Louis B. Mayer, vice-president in charge of production for Metro-Goldwyn-Mayer, will attend the convention of International Fire Chiefs being held this week at Louisville, Kentucky. Mr. Mayer will consult with the officials of the organization and the fire chiefs regarding the picture which M-G-M will make in behalf of fire prevention.

August Film Exports Over Million Mark

MOVING picture exports again exceeded the million-dollar mark in August, figures just compiled by the Department of Commerce show. The shipments of positive film totaled 20,368,923 feet, valued at $572,782; negatives, 1,760,117 feet, valued at $250,475; and raw stock, 9,577,243 feet, valued at $170,816.

Approximately a third of the total exports went to the United Kingdom, whose imports included 6,705,925 feet of raw stock, valued at $94,446; 1,322,979 feet of negatives, valued at $190,515, and 1,540,129 feet of positives, valued at $49,038. Exports to Canada totaled $68,000, and to France $69,000.

House Republican Leader For Admission Tax Repeal

Tilson Advocates Complete Removal of Levy

Washington, D. C., Oct. 7
Special to Motion Picture News
By Clarence W. Linz

"THE tax on theatre admissions should go," declared Representative John Q. Tilson, of Connecticut, Republican Leader of the House, in an interview with the Washington correspondent of MOTION PICTURE NEWS. "This is a tax on a very important means of education and relaxation and should not be continued in effect after the enactment of the forthcoming revenue revision bill."

Mr. Tilson insisted that it should be clearly understood that he voiced his own sentiments only, and that he did not undertake to speak for anyone else. However, there is known to be a great deal of sentiment in favor of this proposal and the repeal of these taxes is likely to become an accomplished fact.

Representatives of the theatrical and moving picture industries will be given an opportunity to present their plea for removal of the admission tax either on October 24 or 26 when the House ways and means committee takes up the question of eliminating the so-called "nuisance taxes."

The committee has assigned ten days to hearings on the question of tax revision.

The Washington Bureau of MOTION PICTURE NEWS has received several inquiries of late as to what is likely to happen to the move to materially reduce the income taxes. There has been some talk of a maximum surtax rate of 15 per cent, but it is not believed that this can be procured, although it is quite likely that a 20 per cent rate will be finally agreed to.

To reduce the surtax maximum to 15 per cent would bring about a great dip in the income tax receipts to the Government, it is pointed out by leaders in Congress, and might be dangerous. On the other hand, if a 20 per cent rate proves satisfactory there will be plenty of opportunity later to make a further reduction. This latter proposal would represent a cut in the tax burden now placed upon the American people of about $100,000,000, and a like amount will be absorbed in the reduction of the present normal taxes from 2, 4 and 6 per cent, to 1, 3 and 5 per cent, respectively.

The Treasury Department is said to be opposed to any reduction in the corporate income tax rate at this time, although there is some sentiment in Washington for some relief to those corporations whose income is not in excess of $50,000 a year. The capital stock tax also will be retained.

Floor Leader Tilson expressed the belief that the permanent peace time maximum surtax rate should not exceed 15 per cent, adding that with such a rate in force the increase in the total amount of incomes returned for taxation will alone soon make good the initial loss of revenue, to say nothing of the tremendous indirect effect.

Analysis of Tax Returns

Nearly half of the corporations engaged in amusement enterprises in 1923 failed to show any net income, according to an analysis of the income tax returns for that year just issued by the Internal Revenue Bureau.

The report shows 5,446 corporations engaged in such enterprises, 2,191 of which had no net income, but reported losses aggregating $19,951,135. The 3,255 corporations showing net income reported a total of $56,659,551, on which profits and income taxes to the total of $6,233,548 were paid. These corporations deducted $3,169,461 from their net income for that year on account of losses suffered in prior years.

The detailed analysis shows 281 corporations engaged in the production of moving pictures in 1923, of which 176 reported no income, having losses aggregating $4,803,665. The 105 corporations showing net income reported $10,058,562, on which, after deducting $843,883 as losses in prior years, taxes aggregating $1,141,519 were paid.

Kansas and Missouri Fear Baker Tax Plan

FEARING the disastrous result of the film tax in Connecticut may be duplicated in Missouri and subsequently in Kansas, the M. P. T. O. Kansas-Missouri is launching a thorough investigation of the plan of Governor Baker to submit an amendment to the Missouri constitution calling for a 5 to 10 per cent levy on all amusement and luxuries.

"Missouri exhibitors are not to be caught asleep in this proposed action," said C. E. Cook, business manager of the M. P. T. O. K.-M. "We always have co-operated in constructive legislation and we are capable of fighting what we believe is unjust legislation just as hard as we have aided the government in various ways."

Four hundred and fifty-two corporations had theatres or theatrical enterprises, 169 reporting no net income and a loss of $1,919,126, and 283 reporting net income of $11,239,831, deducting $485,532 as losses in prior years, and paying taxes of $1,307,749.

Of 1,712 corporations engaged in moving pictures, 517 reported no net income, having deficits aggregating $3,492,285, and 1,195 reported net income aggregating $16,208,944, deducting $887,998 as losses in prior years and paying taxes of $1,725,640.

Tacoma Settles Its Troubles With Musicians

Reports were received this week from Tacoma to the effect that the differences between the management of the Pantages Theatre and the musicians' union had been settled, and the house would return to a combined vaudeville and motion picture program policy next week.

Demands made by the musicians recently were declared to be so exorbitant that vaudeville programs were discontinued, and motion pictures, with only organ accompaniments held sway. The basis of settlement of the differences was not stated, but it was generally understood to favor the theatre management.

Sunday Shows Issue Stirs Urbana, Ill.

The question of legality and morality of Sunday picture shows has divided Urbana, Ill., into two camps and the issue is being hotly contested between them. Students of Illinois University cheer the managements of the town's two theatres for defying the Sunday closing ordinance while the Puritan element clamors for a tight lid on the town. G. T. Freeman and E. E. Alger, the managers, declare they will fight the ordinance to the highest court. Merchants of the town have taken sides with the theatre owners and have signed a petition asking for the repeal of the Sunday Closing Ordinance.

Mrs. Moffett Secretary of Cleveland Film Board

Mrs. Georgia Moffett has been appointed secretary of the Film Board of Trade of Cleveland by C. C. Pettijohn. Mrs. Moffett has previously been engaged in field work for the national film board organization. She succeeds Howard Christman, who has resigned to become affiliated with the Hays organization in New York.

Maurice Sapier, manager of the Cleveland Exchange for United Artists, has been chosen president of the Cleveland Film Board of Trade. Ward Scott, Fox exchange manager, is vice president.

TRADE PAPER AUDIT

Rothstein Heads A. M. P. A. Committee

ANNOUNCEMENT has been made by President Glendon Allvine of the appointment by the Associated Motion Picture Advertisers of the following Space Buyers Audit Committee of Trade Papers and Other Amusement Mediums:

Nat Rothstein, chairman; Vivian Moses, P. A. Parsons, A. M. Botsford, Bruce Gallup, A. L. Selig, Gordon White, J. M. Solomon, Russell Holman, John C. Flinn and Paul Gulick.

The questionnaire decided upon to be sent to the publishers follows:

What is your total circulation?

What is your total exhibitor paid circulation?

How many copies do you deliver to others than bonafide exhibitors?

(a) To advertising departments of film companies.

(b) To publicity men or managers.

(c) To film executives' offices.

(d) To moving picture directors.

(e) To stars and other people in or out of the trade.

*Give classification and state exact number of copies absorbed.

What is your news stand sale if any?

How many copies do you send to Foreign counties?

Give list of countries and number of copies sent to each.

How can you prove to the satisfaction of space buyers that your paid exhibitor subscribers are actually exhibitor subscribers who pay for your paper?

How many bulk circuit subscriptions have you?

Give name of circuit and list of theatres and towns.

Canada Fights Copyright Law

Organized Exhibitors and Performing Right Society Debate Music Royalties

THE decks are being cleared in Canada for an action over the question of copyright royalties for music played in the moving picture halls, with the organized exhibitors on one side and the Performing Right Society of London, England, on the other. The music copyright question has been a live issue in the Dominion since last winter when E. R. E. Chevrier, Federal member for Ottawa, introduced amendments to the Canadian Copyright Acts in the Canadian House of Commons, Ottawa, to provide for the payment of royalties on music played by theatre orchestras. The changes were strenuously opposed by the Canadian M. P. T. O. and the Motion Picture Distributors and Exhibitors of Canada with the result that the amendments died a natural death in the committee stage in the Parliamentary proceedings at Ottawa.

There has been a new development, however, which has just been indicated by a notice of incorporation by the Secretary of State at Ottawa of the establishment of the Canadian Performing Right Society, Limited, with headquarters at Toronto, under a Canadian Federal charter, the capital stock being 10,000 shares of no nominal or par value. The Canadian company is a branch of the Performing Right Society of London, England, which had previously organized a branch in South Africa and which had also invited the Society of Composers and Authors in the United States to enter into a working agreement for mutual interests. It has been intimated that the society controls the copyright privileges on many musical works which are commonly played in moving picture houses and on which fees will have to be paid, it is stated, when the society gets going.

A conference was held recently at Toronto, however, to combat the Performing Right Society and announcement was made after this conference that the result would have a very considerable effect upon the musical copyright situation in the Dominion. Those attending the Toronto conference include President John A. Cooper of the Motion Picture Distributors and Exhibitors of Canada; John Arthur, musical supervisor of the Famous Players Canadian Corp., Toronto; Prof. Watson Kirkconnel of Winnipeg, secretary of the Canadian Society of Authors and Composers; Mrs. G. V. Thompson of Toronto, representing the Musical Writers and Composers Association.

Whitehurst Theatres to Change Hands

IT was learned on excellent authority this week that the important Whitehurst chain of theatres in Baltimore will shortly change hands and will pass into the control of one of the big factors in the industry.

The deal will be settled probably within a week. The Whitehurst circuit includes the Garden, New, Parkway and Century.

While the name of the prospective new owner could not be learned, it is known that several of the large film concerns have been active in bidding for the circuit.

British Film Exports and Imports Show Increase

Exports of British motion picture films during the first six months of 1925 totaled 54,894,482 feet, as compared with 27,598,472 feet in the corresponding period of 1924, it is declared in a report just received at the Department of Commerce from the American consulate in London.

The greater part of these exports—40,096,413 feet—were unexposed film, while shipments of positives amounted to 14,545,347 feet and the small balance was negative film.

Imports during the six-month period showed a great increase over the preceding year as a result of the announcement that the McKenna duties on British imports of films would be reimposed on July 1, 1925. The total imports for the first six months of this year were 154,742,426 feet, against 48,898,631 feet in the same period of 1924, when imports were withheld pending the removal of the duties in August, 1924.

Of the imports this year 112,070,968 feet were unexposed film, 36,051,101 feet positive film and 6,620,357 feet negative film.

Yeggs Get Jefferson City House Receipts

Yeggmen on Sunday night, October 4, robbed the safe of the Jefferson theatre, Jefferson City, Mo., getting the Saturday and Sunday receipts totaling $1,000. It was the first safe blowing job in the history of the Missouri capital city.

The yeggs broke a rear window then carried the safe from the office to the lower floor of the theatre auditorium, where the combination was knocked off and the safe rifled. William H. Mueller owns the Jefferson.

Production Trend Is Toward Bigger Features

Indications on Coast of Let-Down in Program Films

Belle Bennett as she appears in "Stella Dallas." (Samuel Goldwyn-United Artists.) Douglas Fairbanks in Costume for "The Black Pirate," (United Artists.) John Gilbert, in "The Big Parade" (M-G-M). Lillian Gish as she will appear in "La Boheme." (M-G-M).

By Edwin Schallert, Los Angeles Times

(Editor's Note:—This is the eighth of a regular series of articles by the Editor of the Los Angeles Times Pre-View. Mr. Schallert writes exclusively for MOTION PICTURE NEWS in the trade field.)

THERE is still a strong concentration of interest in Hollywood in the bigger features, with some indications of a let-down of activity in the smaller films. It portends, I believe, some scepticism regarding the worth of the routine program film during the ensuing months. Overproduction gives signs of seriously affecting the status of this smaller product — a fact which has already been called to the attention of MOTION PICTURE NEWS readers.

More than ever it would appear, a picture must have some sound reason for its existence to become a good salable commodity. It does not market itself in an overcrowded market simply because it is a picture.

Those companies that have adhered rather relentlessly to the policy of getting out their releases on a schedule are proceeding more cautiously than heretofore, awaiting developments and observing what will be the eventual outcome for the big productions.

This slowing-down process is interesting since it has not brought on any burden of real dullness. The feeling is that the late fall and winter will see a consistent if not a sweeping activity. And even though the number of cameras at work may be reduced, those that are on the job will crank busily enough, because there are so many larger productions under way or right in the offing.

Notable, of course, in their elaborate character are the scenes now being completed of the "Ben Hur" Circus Maximus—a feature in themselves; Douglas Fairbanks's "The Black Pirate"; John Barrymore's starring feature, "Don Juan," just about to start, as well as "La Boheme," which is turning out much more spectacular than might be anticipated; and the various starring films of Corinne Griffith, Colleen Moore, Pola Negri, and others.

Altogether, it is hardly a condition over which one may raise complaint, for the prominence of the big production has all the earmarks of a new phase of health in the industry, which is the most desirable thing of all.

I must mention that the color photography in "The Black Pirate," of which I spoke in my last article, has now been demonstrated as most amazing. It is color that is never going to bother or distract an audience if one may judge from the scenes already taken. It is most sensational in not giving the effect of color, so much as in adding stereoscopic depth to the screen. One's feeling on seeing it is that the screen had been suddenly enlarged toward the back —if I make myself clear—and that one is looking across rather than at a panorama. If anything, the color tones in which the picture is being made are more restful to the eye than the so-called black and white.

In my last article I devoted more space to advance glimpses of a new picture than to actual studio developments, but there was striking reason in the case of "The Big Parade," and again I find, after viewing "Stella Dallas" at a preview in Pasadena, that a single completed work of the studios assumes an outstanding position among the recent developments here.

For all that each season brings a considerable quota of films based on the ever dependable theme of mother-love, only a few of the features that have used it as the basis for their attraction, really stand out in the memory.

Recollections turn most readily to "Over the Hill" and "Madame X," with "The Old Nest" sharing in their tremendous popularity.

The majority of the others are for the most part not so brilliantly remembered. Too much similarity has been the fault of many of them—too much slobber of sentiment and a consequent lack of sincerity has destroyed the effectiveness of the others.

Actually, the mother picture has gone somewhat out of fashion. There have been only a very few examples in the past season or two that are worth remarking—"My Son," "So Big" and more recently "The Goose Woman."

There is, I believe, at this time, therefore, a genuine and logical place for a great mother-love picture, one that possesses a searching pathos and heart interest, and it is for this reason that I am inclined to predict big things for "Stella Dallas."

This production, made by Samuel Goldwyn, with Henry King as director, and Frances Marion as scenarioist, is, to my mind, a singularly splendid treatment of a justly outstanding modern novel. It is a story absolutely free from sugar-sweetness. It has the quality of tear-evoking drama, a pathos and a penetrating heart interest that give promise of reaching every kind of public.

(Continued on next page)

MILTON SILLS AN AUTHOR

Writes "Men Of Steel," His New Vehicle

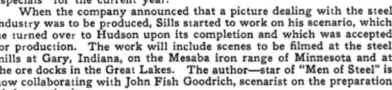

MILTON SILLS is the author of the drama of the steel industry to be produced by First National under the title "Men of Steel" with Sills as the star, it was announced this week by Earl Hudson, supervisor of First National's eastern production units. This picture will be one of the First National "specials" for the current year.

When the company announced that a picture dealing with the steel industry was to be produced, Sills started to work on his scenario, which he turned over to Hudson upon its completion and which was accepted for production. The work will include scenes to be filmed at the steel mills at Gary, Indiana, on the Mesaba iron range of Minnesota and at the ore docks in the Great Lakes. The author—star of "Men of Steel" is now collaborating with John Fish Goodrich, scenarist on the preparation of the continuity.

(Continued from preceding page)

The audience that left the theatre the evening of the preliminary showing recently in Pasadena, was an audience of glistening eyes and thoughtful demeanor, rather than one of casual laughing conversation. There were ample evidences that tears had been shed, particularly by the women who attended the preview. There were many who mentioned on leaving—"Why, I know a woman just like that woman in the picture." Despite the fact that "Stella Dallas" brought a deeply serious reaction, I venture that there was not a single one that would not have advised every friend and acquaintance to go and view it at the very first opportunity.

If, as a matter of fact, entertainment occasionally may mean something that will touch generously the heart, rather than merely amuse, then "Stella Dallas" has that quality in a way that will result in its being hailed far and wide as one of the year's sensations.

The story from which it was adapted has been widely read, and needs no detailed second telling. The book has been followed very faithfully right from the courtship between Stephen and Stella Dallas, to the very end where the mother, an outcast, beholds through a window and unrelenting iron fence bars the marriage of her daughter Laurel, from whom she has so willingly separated herself for the sake of the girl's future.

Some of the finest scenes in this production are those which build up to this separation.

Really, in this picture more pathos is secured through smiles than tears of the leading characters. The situation that would be termed good for a laugh in another feature, has been transformed into something heart-moving in this. The moment when, in the wash room of a railroad station, Stella Dallas weeps over the departure of her daughter until the mascara runs down from her eyes has every element to cause mirth, yet it is one of the most curiously pitiful that has ever been filmed.

Some audience members, strongly ruled by sentiment may, of course, not agree with the idea of the mother giving up her daughter to her divorced husband in the way that Stella Dallas does, and certainly the character of Stephen Dallas lacks something of bigness both in the book and in the picture, but there is not a single person who will not appreciate the terrible and tragic dilemma in which the mother found herself in the effort to do the best for the future of her child.

The performance by Belle Bennett in the title part is tremendous. It will be acclaimed as one of the great acting triumphs of the year.

Lois Moran as the child Laurel is a happy discovery—a girl who lives up fascinatingly to the term unsophisticated. She seems indeed to represent youthful refinement itself. A wise choice was made in putting the sympathetic Ronald Colman in the somewhat unsympathetic part of Stephen Dallas, and Alice Joyce's grace and dignity are very acceptable as Mrs. Morrison. Young Douglas Fairbanks is the fiancé of Laurel, while Jean Hersholt gives a broad but clever portrayal of Ed Munn, the uncouth riding master whom Stella marries when he is a wreck from drink, to force her daughter to leave her.

Receiver Asked for Ohio Amusement Company

Messrs. Schumann, Fine and Kramer have asked that a receiver be appointed for the Ohio Amusement Company, for the purpose of dissolving the company. The Ohio Amusement Company owns and operates one of the largest motion picture circuits of Cleveland. All of its theatres are first run neighborhood houses. They include the Dennison Square, Five Points, Jewel, Savoy, U-No, Yale, Capitol, Knickerbocker, Photoplay and Lakewood and Garden theatres. Beside Schumann, Fine and Kramer, founders of the firm, Leo Keller, Art Keller and John Kalafat are active members. The Ohio Amusement Company, however, has purchased the stock owned by John Kalafat, so his activity in the company automatically ceases when he has been paid out. Failure to agree on business policies is said to be the reason for the present action, calling for a receivership and dissolution of the firm.

Catholic Priest Operates Schroon Lake House

A Catholic priest in the person of Father Blais, of Schroon Lake, N. Y., is now included in the ranks of the exhibitors of New York state. He has taken over the Strand theatre in Schroon Lake, previously operated by Arthur Richardson, who has gone to Florida.

Father Blais tried out being an exhibitor during the summer, and was so successful that he has leased the theatre, a house of 350 seats, and will run it in the interests of the church over which he presides.

Ten Companies Chartered in New York State

Ten companies obtained charters from the secretary of state during the past week for the purpose of engaging in the motion picture business in New York state. This number is somewhat above the weekly average that has prevailed for the past month or so.

The companies incorporated during the week included the Rawig Amusement Corporation, capitalized at $10,000, with N. Ravitz, M. Gordon, of New York City; Samuel Witlin, Brooklyn; Deannsee Theatre Co., Inc., $11,000, Samuel and Anita Crystal, New York; Abraham Deitch, Middletown, Conn.; Playhouse at the Cross Streams, Inc., Hopewell Junction, $25,000; Marguerite Robertson, V. I. Boyer, Hopewell Junction; A. D. VanBuren, New York City.

Appearances Producing Corporation, $30,000, L. W. Sagar, Brooklyn; H. S. Wilkinson, Santa Rosa, Calif.; Fergus Wilkinson, Santa Rosa, Calif.; Prelude, Inc., $10,000, H. Ascher, R. Sattler, A. Medoff, New York City, the capitalization of the following not being specified; Bellcrene Amusement Corporation, H. Frieder, S. Price, F. J. Farrell, New York City; Albany Regent Theatre Corporation, Buffalo, Moe Mark, White Plains; E. B. Mark, New York; M. Sharaf, Boston, Mass.

Buffalo Strand Theatre Corporation, S. G. Falk, R. A. Williams, I. W. Smith, Buffalo; Highway Theatre Corporation, H. L. Jacobson, Alex Aaronson, Irene Feinburg, New York City; Fairchild Aerial Camera Corporation, S. M. Fairchild, F. N. Rondolf, Ernest Robinson, New York City.

Labor Troubles Settled in Montreal

The labor situation has been straightened out in Montreal, Quebec. The projection machine operators decided a short time ago to accept last year's wage scale of $40 and $45 per week but the stage hands held out for something different.

B. M. Garfield, secretary of the Montreal Theatre Managers Association and manager of the Rialto Theatre himself, has announced that a compromise has been effected with the stage employees in agreeing upon a five per cent increase in wages for 1925-26. The union had asked for a 10 per cent raise.

C. E. Williams Reelected by Nebraska M. P. T. O.

MOTION PICTURE THEATRE Owners of Nebraska and Western Iowa re-elected C. E. Williams to serve a third term as president of the organization at their annual convention held in Omaha last week. The convention drew the largest attendance of any ever held by the organization.

Others re-elected were H. F. Kennedy, vice president and George H. McCardle, treasure. Miss Esther Anderson was elected secretary. Members of the executive committee re-elected are the following: H. F. Kennedy, Baline Cook, Sam Epstein, H. A. Larson, W. H. Creal, A. Burrus, E. E. Gailey, J. E. Schoonover, R. B. Thomas, Wm. Hawley, W. H. Ostenburgh, R. W. Small, Lou Heal, Chas. Prokop, W. A. Bowker, F. A. Schlumberger, Max Drefke, B. B. Holdridge.

Hays Offers Aid to Exhibitors

Message to Michigan Convention States His Willingness to Help Adjust All Grievances and Complaints

IN his first direct message to the exhibitors of the country, Will H. Hays has expressed his willingness to aid any exhibitor or distributor who is a member of the Hays' organization. This statement was made in a speech by Jerome Beatty, delivered at the sixth annual convention of the Motion Picture Theatre Owners of Michigan, which opened Tuesday at the Pantlind hotel, Grand Rapids, with two hundred and fifty exhibitors present, representing nearly four hundred theatre owners. The memo from Mr. Hays, read by Mr. Beatty, included the following:

"You may further say for me to the exhibitors that this determination on our part to do everything possible for them and to co-operation, goes to the fullest extent the plan of co-operation, goes to the fullest extent of assuring them that if any exhibitor in Michigan or anywhere in the country has a real grievance against any of the producers or distributors who are members of this association and will call my attention to such grievance, that the good offices of the association will be immediately and sympathetically used to bring about such conferences and consideration........that a fair solution may be quickly sought."

The first high spot of the Tuesday session came in the report of Glen A. Cross, of Battle Creek, the retiring president, when in his farewell address he advised Michigan to cease pioneering for national exhibitor organization and not to spend any more of its time and money until new interests took a

H. M. Richey,   Glenn Cross,
Detroit.   Battle Creek.

guiding hand in the so-called national body. The cheers that greeted the statement was evidence that such a policy met with the hearty approval of the Michigan exhibitors.

In the report of General Manager Richey he pointed out that regardless of how big the circuits got in Michigan the time would never come when these circuits didn't need an organization and didn't need the little fellows, too, especially when it came to legislation. He warned exhibitors of Michigan to retain the interest in their organization pending the necessity of again putting the organization machinery in the field. He stated that the Connecticut situation was an example of the sort of thing they must be constantly on guard against.

The financial report as read by John E Niebes, treasurer, showed that there are now 475 theatres represented in the organization and that there had been added twelve thousand dollars to the surplus during the year, despite the fact that dues have been cut fifty per cent. The surplus of the organization now lacks only a few dollars of fifty thousand dollars, which is invested in bonds and which bring in dividends of nearly three thousand dollars a year. The report was enthusiastically accepted.

Tuesday afternoon John Lovett of the Michigan Manufacturers association addressed the convention, as did Martin J. Quigley of the Exhibitors Herald.

The convention was preceded by a golf tournament for the beautiful silver cup offered by Manager Richey, which resulted in a tie between Harold Frank of Jackson and C. J. Kendriek of Port Huron. This will be played off later. A board of directors' dinner was held Monday night, and on Tuesday the entertainment features included a luncheon for the ladies at the Highlands Golf club, given by the American Seating company, a theatre party in the afternoon and the banquet at six thirty.

The banquet was a colorful affair attended by three hundred and fifty, with addresses by James C. Ritter, the daddy of Michigan organization; Martin J. Quigley, John Lovett, Lieut. Governor Welch, Jerome Beatty of the Motion Picture Producers and Distributors of America, bringing a message *(Continued on page 1793)*

Laemmle To Produce In England

Universal Chief, Home From Abroad, Announces Extensions of Foreign Activities in Several Directions

CARL LAEMMLE, president of Universal, returned from Europe last week, accompanied by his children, Miss Rosabelle and Carl, Jr., and his secretary, Harry H. Zehner and Julius Bernheim, formerly director general of Universal City.

Mr. Laemmle's activities were widespread during the three months he was abroad. He made several appointments that will pave the way for greater Universal activities on the other side. He appointed Max Schach, well known German producer, distributor and theatre owner, to take charge of Universal activities in Germany. Schach will succeed Henry H. Heningson, who returned a few days ago and will have an executive position at Universal City.

Mr. Laemmle also opened a distributing organization in Poland in charge of Sam Burstein. Charles L. Brookheim, formerly Universal representative in Spain, succeeds I. Blofson as manager of the Paris office, and A. Torres succeeds Brookheim in Spain.

While in Germany President Laemmle became acquainted with a new double exposing process which prompted him to produce "Gulliver's Travels." With this invention he feels that the mechanical difficulties required in the production of the picture will be easily met.

Just prior to his sailing for New York,

Laemmle was the luncheon guest of the Cinematograph Exhibitors Association in London and he announced his acceptance of their invitation to produce pictures in England, using as far as possible the English backgrounds, English actors, experts and directors. Several American actors, whose names are well known, will also be sent to England to appear in the pictures.

In his speech to the C. E. A., Mr. Laemmle said in part: "I am going to produce pictures here for the sole and simple reason that I consider it good business. I may bring American stars over here, what of it? If I do, it will be solely because I consider it good business. I may bring American technical men for the same reason. But if I can find what I want right here, it would be poor business not to use them, wouldn't it? I am not going to employ any of the stuff you call eye wash. I am not pretending that I can make better pictures in England than English producers make. I am not coming here to teach you anything.

"I'm not here to reform anything, not even the climate. I am not here to perform miracles. I am not here to pretend to be anything I am not. I have too much respect for your hard common sense as well as your sense of humor to make any mistake about why American producers as a whole.

have been more successful than English producers as a whole. I know as well as you do that the war gave us a tremendous jump on you and I know as well as you do that we've got to fight and fight hard to keep you from giving us a licking.

"Your directors are just as brainy as ours. Your technical people are just as skilled. Your actors are just as able. Outside of the fact that the war crippled your production work fearfully while we went madly about our business, I think we've got you beaten in only one respect and that is our willingness to gamble on results. You always speak of Yankees as synonomous with money. You've got just as much money for picture producing as we have, if you'll go ahead and gamble with it as we do. Don't imagine we pick money off the trees. I've seen the occasion many a time, when I put the last dollar of cash and the best dollar of credit I could dig up into one season's pictures. I've been up against it just as hard and as often as you have. So I know exactly how you have been feeling for a long time.

"There's just one idea I want to pass along to you in closing. If I can make pictures in England which will sell all over the world, you can do it, too. No matter how I do it, if it helps to show you the way, then my efforts here will have been helpful."

Price Discusses Associated's Plans

Declares Company, Strongly Financed, Will Make Definite Plans for Itself in Industry

THERE is an atmosphere of mystery and suppressed excitement about the Associated Exhibitors' offices these days. Encounter Jack Woody and you get the impression of repressed enthusiasm. Then just as he is about to tell you an item of news, he catches himself, and says, "Well, I'd better wait awhile." Speak to J. A. Gove, Sales Manager, and you get the same impression; drop in on Bob Welsh's office and once more that feeling, "We've got big things to tell you, but we are biding our time."

So we determined to beard Oscar Price in his den and, by means of an interview for MOTION PICTURE NEWS, get an advance hint of Associated Exhibitors' plans. Those plans are big, there seemed no doubt of it; and after a leisurely talk with the calm, busine s-like, unaffected president of the organization we feel doubly certain of it.

"Of course our plans are big," said Mr. Price in response to our opening question. "If you will look over the names on the new Associated Exhibitors Board of Directors you will readily agree that they are not the sort of men to embark on so futile a mission as the running of 'just another picture company.' Associated isn't going to sit on the fence or just drift along with the current. Associated is going to have a definite personality, a definite mission, a definite place in this business, and I can tell you right here and now it is going to be a big place.

"There is a real and concrete need for the organization that the new Associated is going to be. The battle lines in this industry are growing tighter every day. The independent exhibitor's decision is coming closer to him every day. But speeches about independence aren't going to help him a bit. Mere shouting about independence isn't going to keep him on the right side of the ledger nor keep him in business. The natural desire on his part to line up with independents isn't going to be translated into action unless independents do their part by him.

"Pictures are the answer. Not merely good pictures, but pictures that rank in entertainment values with any that are offered to him from whatever source. Pictures that also offer the box office pull that he expects and needs. Then back those pictures up with service that is efficient and truly cooperative.

Request for Free Trailer Service Sent I. M. P. A.

AT the request of the Motion Picture Theatres Owners of Brooklyn. President R. F. Woodhull of the national organization, has forwarded to the Independent Motion Picture Association of America, a resolution urging members of the latter body to supply free trailer service with their productions. The resolution adopted by the Brooklyn theatre owners expresses the opinion that such a course would result in increased business both for the distributors and the exhibitors.

President Woodhull has referred the matter to the I. M. P. A. with the request that it be submitted to the members of the organization for their consideration.

Oscar A. Price, President of Associated Exhibitors.

"It's a simple calculation. You can't give the independent no choice but the choice of two evils. On the one hand he knows that support of the tendencies, with their growing strength and over-weening ambition is just hastening his doom. On the other hand he knows that the playing of mediocre or average pictures today will bring that doom just as certainly.

"Give him Grade A independent pictures, back them up with Grade A sincere service and his decision is automatically made.

"The independent with limited financial resources, or the independent with hampering distribution problems, will find difficulty in doing it. But the men who have taken over Associated know that they can do it. They have the capital, they have the machinery, they are sincere in their desire to go out and get the brains and the merchandise to go through with the job.

"They are not looking to today's profits, nor to this month's. They are looking towards the future. They are building solidly, brick upon brick, towards a goal that is clearly in sight and vividly in their minds.

"I could issue a thousand word policy statement to you and not tell exhibitors of the country any more than I can in a few words with the plain fact that practical, veteran picturemen have thrown their hats in the ring with Associated Exhibitors and they don't intend to give elbow room or take second place for anybody. It takes strong financial resources to feel that way—and it's going to take hard work to change the feeling into results' and both ways we'll meet the test.

"But that is enough in the way of forecast and ambitions for Associated Exhibitors. To tell the truth I would rather say nothing now and let the happenings of the next year do the ta'king. For that matter there are current happenings that carry a lesson or two of their own.

"Take one recent bit of Associated news for an example—the addition of Robert E. Welsh to the home office staff. For ten years Bob Welsh has been known to the exhibitors of the country as a square-shooting, straight-thinking editor. If he hasn't earned exhibitor confidence then no editor in this business ever will earn it. In addition, for over ten years he has been in intimate touch with the inside maneouvering and developments of the business—right on the ground in New York where the wheels are turning that decide next year's problems.

"When we set out to get Bob Welsh for the new Associated Exhibitors' executive staff you can be certain that we did so knowing of the many attempts that had previously been made to lure him from the editorial chair. And knowing that we would have to show him where we were heading and how we are going to go about getting there. A man who has been sitting on the inside for ten years is in a position for shrewd analysis and clear judgment.

"I consider the fact that we are able to 'show' Bob Welsh and add him to our forces almost the same as if he had been able to talk simultaneously to the thousands of e'hibitors who know him so well and lay our innermost plans before them. By the action of the editor whose film knowledge and independent spirit they have known for so many years they can readily gauge the pace that Associated Exhibitors intends to set."

Hays Offers to Adjust Exhibitors Complaints

(Continued from page 1793)
from Will H. Hays and Judge Alfred J. Murphy of Detroit.

Judge Murphy saw drastic changes taking place in the industry that demanded a closer, more compact exhibitor organization and he deplored that policies had prevented a truly national body.

Wednesday there was planned a luncheon for the ladies at the Pantlind hotel, a trip through the largest furniture exhibit in the world, and for the men a trip and luncheon at the American Seating Company plant. The Wednesday session opened at one o'clock and was featured by the report of E. E. Kirchner on arbitration in which he recommended an investigation of the arbitration law in the state and opposed the contract that Joseph M. Seider has proposed which would fix a board of appeals and leave the decision of disputed cases to this board. He stated that Mr. Seider, in making this offer, was not speaking for the exhibitors of Michigan.

Southern Office Reestablished by Loew

E. A. SCHILLER, general representative of Loew's Inc., this week announced that Howard McCoy, a member of the New York executive staff would re-establish a southern office to handle the expansion activities in the South and Southwest which the company will carry out in the near future.

Several Circuits Enlarge Holdings

West Coast Expanding in Northern California; Saxe Acquires Four More Theatres and Universal One

SEVERAL large theatre circuits increased their holdings as a result of deals concluded during the past week, which also brought forth official announcements of definite plans looking toward the expansion of other chain operators.

The Saxe circuit has acquired four more theatres in Milwaukee through a group of deals said to involve $4,000,000, the announcement being accompanied by the statement that this organization aims to have forty houses in its chain by another year.

The new deals include the outright purchase of the Mirth Theatre in the Bay View section of Milwaukee from George Busch, while Saxe obtained long-term leases on two large theatres being built by the Mal Investment Company. In addition to these Saxe interests will build on property at North and Lisbon Avenues. The additions of these new houses brings the total of theatres owned by Saxe up to thirty, ten of which are located in Milwaukee and the others in various parts of the state.

The Mirth has a seating capacity of 1,000 and was rebuilt two years ago. Saxe interests, it is reported, will buy the adjoining property so that the capacity of the theatre can be doubled. One of the two theatres leased from the Mal Investment Co. will be located at 27th and Wells Sts. It will be known as the Tower and will be completed in a few months. The other leased house will have a capacity of 2,300 and the Uptown, which Saxe will build, is to have a capacity of 2,000.

Herman Wobber, Pacific Coast Manager for Famous Players and Sol Lesser, Photographed in San Francisco on Lesser's arrival to initiate expansion of West Coast Theatres, Inc., in Northern California.

West Coast Theatres, Inc., has formed definite plans for further expansion in Northern California. Sol Lesser, vice president of the West Coast, was in San Francisco last week for conference with Jacob Samuel, senior counsel for his corporation, and Herman Wobber, Pacific Coast manager for Famous Players-Lasky.

Lesser's presence in San Francisco brought out a report that the West Coast company would buy four theatres from Louis R. Greenfield. Two of these houses are located in San Francisco, one in Santa Cruz and the fourth is in Honolulu.

At the present time West Coast is represented in San Francisco, Oakland, Berkeley, Richmond, San Jose, Stockton, Salinas, Watsinville, Sacramento and Fresno, these houses representing the northern division. Lesser definitely states that his company will go into Marysville and Chico with new theatres and that some fifteen houses now operated by others will be added to the present West Coast holdings which number over 100 theatres, all in the state of California.

From Chicago it was reported that Balaban & Katz have entered into a deal with Fitzpatrick & McElroy whereby the chain of houses owned by the latter would be operated by B & K under an arrangement similar to that which was recently entered into with Lubliner & Trinz. Sam Katz would make no comment on this report.

The Beldorf theatre, Independence, Kan., has been obtained by Universal, according to Charles T. Sears, general manager of Universal theatres in the Kansas City territory. The Royal and Crystal theatre, Atchinson, Kan., which were purchased by Universal, are to be managed by A. R. Zimmer, recently a First National salesman, it also was announced.

In Philadelphia the Independent Theatre Corporation of that city announced that three new theatres would be erected in that territory. The company, which now operates the Strand, Shenandoah, and the Savoy

(Continued on next page)

Connecticut Tax Relief Is Likely

Ninety Per Cent of Legislators Favor Special Assembly Session to Repeal Statute; 500,000 Signatures to Petition

THAT a special session of the Connecticut Assembly may be called for the purpose of repealing the Durant tax law, is not unlikely, according to Joseph W. Walsh, President of the State Motion Picture Theatre Owners. According to Walsh 90 per cent of the legislators are in favor of such a special session to consider the repeal of this drastic law. The M.P.T.O. recently sent out cards asking the legislators to express themselves regarding the matter. Up to the present time, according to Walsh, 80 members of the Assembly have expressed themselves as against the statute.

Governor Trumbull alone has the power to call such a special session, according to Connecticut law. He originally approved the Durant law after bearing the protests of film representatives, but it is understood at that time the Governor had the impression the law would hit only at the distributors. The law has admittedly miscarried, however, and in view of that fact it is thought the Governor may yield to the wishes of almost the entire Assembly.

According to one prominent exhibitor the film theatres cannot continue to operate under the crushing burden of the new tax. He said:

"If we are to receive the aid we need it must come immediately or it will be too late. Proponents of the law who argue concerning the $60,000 which a special legislative gathering would cost, should be informed that the film people have already paid considerably more than that amount under the Durant Law.

"The distributors and exhibitors have co-operated with the state tax department as much as possible in working out a plan for the collection of the assessments. Now it is up to the state to give the film interests equally fair treatment by at once nullifying the law which has frankly failed to achieve its purpose."

Charles Schneider, owner of the new Strand at New Haven has been unable to open his house for a week because of a lack of pictures available under the tax burden. He has an investment of $85,000 in his theatre and has appealed to the state M.P.T.O. to help him in his problem. President Walsh has promised to call a meeting of the special committee of five to see what can be done for Schneider.

At Stafford Springs in Connecticut, Joe Wood, owner of Town Hall Theatre is faced with a similar problem. He has suffered three dark nights in the past two weeks because of his inability to get delivery on pictures. Wood has talked with Alexander I. Mitchell and Benjamin P. Cooley, two representatives from the town concerning the law and both are said to have vowed they would help obtain a special session and will vote to repeal the statute.

Public opinion is being moulded by the M.P.T.O. and the operators' union toward the demand for a special session of the Assembly. Hundreds of residents of Connecticut are daily signing cards requesting a special session to reconsider the law. It is expected that well in excess of 500,000 of these signatures will be on hand in the near future. When the seat tax bill was fought five years ago 650,000 people e pressed their disapproval of the act in this manner and it is felt there is far more interest in the present tax situation.

The Strand Amusement Company has been active in Bridgeport in the securing of signatures. Houses of that company have secured over 5,000 signers to the petition asking the repeal of the tax measure. Jack Schwarts is running a slide explaining to his patrons the necessity and the reason for the substitution of pictures for others that have been advertised. Schwarts says his patrons have voluntarily signed cards and have in many instances expressed to him personally their disapproval of the law.

British Film Imports Increase

Reimposing of McKenna Duties in July Adds to the First Six Months' Imports

A RECENT report just released by the Department of Commerce from Alfred Nutting, clerk in the Consulate General, London, gives an interesting analysis of British foreign trade for the first six months of 1925 in comparison with similar periods in 1924 and 1923. The report follows:

Coincident with the announcement that the McKenna duties on British imports of films would be re-imposed on July 1, 1925, there was a great increase in the quantities received during the first half of the current year, far transcending the decrease recorded in 1924 (compared with 1923) when shipments were withheld pending the removal of such duties in August, 1924. Two years ago the amount imported aggregated 58,940,968 linear feet; last year the total was 48,808,-631 linear feet; while in the current period no less than 154,742,426 linear feet were imported. Against an average import value on total receipts in 1923 of 2d. per linear foot, the rate rose last year to just under 3d. and decreased in 1925 to 1½d.

Of the present year's imports 112,070,-908 linear feet (£315,070) comprised blank films, contrasted with 36,715,356 linear feet (£122,213) a year ago, and 44,997,838 linear feet (£128,107) in 1923. Positives rose to 30,051,101 linear feet (£186,100), against 8,961,679 linear feet (£74,638) in 1924, and 10,020,170 linear feet (£83,611) two years ago; while negatives increased to 6,620,357 linear feet (£427,833) contrasted with 3,-221,596 linear feet (£376,860) and 3,922,960 linear feet (£250,943) in 1924 and 1923 respectively. Countries of origin are not shown in the official returns of trade available.

British exports in the current period aggregated 54,894,482 linear feet, valued at £198,749, compared with 27,508,472 linear feet (£124,315) last year, and 21,063,515 linear feet (£77,147) in 1923; 40,096,413 linear feet (£104,410) comprised blank films, against 16,552,254 linear feet (£42,219) in 1924, and 222,180 linear feet (£1,012) in

1923; positives increased from 10,498,473 linear feet (£68,364) two years ago, and 10,825,906 linear feet (£71,380) in 1924, to 14,545,347 linear feet (£87,532) in the current six months, the comparatively small balances consisting of negative films.

Figures of total re-exports do not show any extensive movement, except, proportionately, in value, the aggregate of 6,875,880 feet re-exported in 1923, being valued at £146,410; of 8,268,949 linear feet a year ago, at £102,264; and in 1925 the total of 7,836,105 linear feet declining to £87,661.

Missouri Owners Advised to Pay Music Tax

Missouri exhibitors who use music controlled by the Society of Composers, Authors and Publishers have been advised by the M. P. T. O., Kansas-Missouri to make payment on a fair and consistent license until such time as Missouri can obtain the same 20 per cent rebate system as is in force in Kansas among e hibitor members, or, until the national copyright act is amended.

Kofeldt is Appointed Berlin Manager of P. D. C.

Walter W. Kofeldt has been appointed as Berlin Representative of Producers Distributing Corporation, it was announced this week by William M. Vogel, general manager of the P. D. C. International Corporation. Kofeldt has been associated with Pathe as manager of the San Francisco branch for several years.

Lauds Health Conditions of Chicago Theatres

Dr. Herman Bundesson of the Chicago Health Department is preparing to distribute a pamphlet telling the public of the splendid health conditions existing in Chicago motion picture houses, and recommending the theatres as a safe place to go on account of their adequate ventilation and cleanliness.

Troy Operators' Chief is Assembly Candidate

Harry Brooks, president of the Motion Picture Machine Operators' Union in Troy, N. Y., is a candidat for the New York State Assembly on the Republican ticket this fall and his opponent is Michael F. Breen, who is connected with the bill posters' organization in the Collar City.

Swedish Actor Arrives at M-G-M Studio

Lars Hanson, Swedish film actor and his wife are late arrivals on the coast, where Hanson is to appear in forthcoming productions of Metro-Goldwyn-Mayer. He was signed by Louis B. Mayer on the latter's last trip abroad.

Mastbaum Back, Declares Paris House Unlikely

J ULES E. MASTBAUM, President of the Stanley Company of America, is back at his home in Philadelphia following a vacation of several months in Europe. Upon his departure from America it was announced that an effort was being made to have him devote his personal attention to a big house in Paris.

No progress was made on the deal, according to Mastbaum, who declares the site near the Paris Opera House is still held, but that government interest is lacking. He declares too, he could not give his personal attention to the house because of the activities of the Stanley Company.

Regarding exhibition conditions abroad Mastbaum said:

"The motion picture situation abroad cannot be compared with that in this country. There isn't a picture house anywhere that compares with our Palace in Philadelphia. The entertainment is of the old type without large orchestras, special features, prologues and the like."

Several Circuits Enlarge Their Holdings

(*Continued from preceding page*)

in Bethlehem, is headed by L. L. Berman, owner of the Independent Film Exchange. The company has plans for a circuit of 15 first run theatres in the Philadelphia territory.

Independent has awarded the contract for the erection of a 1,600 seat house at 4th and Vine, South Bethlehem, while plans for another theatre to be located on Main St., Shenandoah, are now being drawn. The third theatre will be built in Easton, on Northampton St., and will seat 1,600.

Warners are reported to have purchased a theatre site in the business section of New London, Conn., for the erection of a theatre and office building to cost $700,000. Sam Morris of Warner Bros., refused to comment on the New London report, but denied rumors from New Haven that his company was interested in the new theatre now being built on College St., by Arthur S. Friend and a syndicate.

The Frank Amusement Company of Waterloo, Iowa, operating the Plaza and Rialto theatres, Waterloo; the Isis and Majestic Theatres in Cedar Rapids; the Orpheum Theatre, Clinton; and the Grand Theatre, Oelwein, Iowa, has taken over the Plaza Theatre, Sioux City, under a long term lease. The Plaza is a modern theatre with a seating capacity of 1,000.

Associated Calls Field Men for Conference

J. S. Woody, general manager of Associated Exhibitors, this week called the company's four field representatives to the Home Offices in New York for conferences regarding the new sales policy to be inaugurated by Oscar Price, the new president of Associated.

The four representatives are Harry E. Lotz, Melville E. Maxwell, Claude E. Ezell and Floyd Lewis. The plans for the coming season will be outlined to the representatives and the large advertising campaign to be launched soon is to be discussed.

Connecticut Exhibitor Buys Brooklyn House

An echo of the Connecticut theatre tax situation is heard in Brooklyn, N. Y. in the person of Manager Crystal who has recently purchased the Forest Park theatre from Rosassy. It is reported that Crystal gave up his Connecticut house on account of the added tax.

Fox Building Exchange Quarters in Australia

G OVERNMENT officials and prominent exhibitors of Australia attended the ceremonies marking the laying of the cornerstone for the new exchange quarters which Fox Film Corporation is erecting in Sydney. The ceremony was presided over by Clayton P. Sheehan, home office representative for Fox, and Stanley S. Crick, Australian managing director.

The building will provide the most modern exchange equipment. The Fox Company is the first of the overseas film concerns represented in Australia to build its own exchange quarters there.

Jaffe Company Completes "Broken Hearts"

Jaffe Art Film Corporation, recently organized to produce pictures for the independent market, announces the completion of "Broken Hearts," the company's initial production. The story is based on the stage play and deals with immigrant life.

The leading feminine role is played by Lila Lee, and Jacob Swartz, Jewish dramatic star and the director of several notable European films, will be seen in the leading male role. Mr. Swartz, also directed the picture.

Engage Leading Players for "Flaming Waters"

Malcolm McGregor, Mary Carr and Pauline Garon have been signed for the principal roles in "Flaming Waters," a melodrama of the oil industry to be produced by Associated Arts Corp., for F. B. O. distribution. Harmon Weight will direct the production. The story is an original written by E. Lloyd Sheldon.

"Knight of the Range" to Be Tyler's Next

Tom Tyler's next western starring vehicle for F. B. O. will be "The Knight of the Range," a melodrama to be directed by Bob DeLacey and James Gruen, directors of "Let's Go Gallagher," the star's first picture in the series for F. B. O.

George O'Brien in the William Fox presentation, "The Fighting Heart."

F.B.O. Picture Has Premieres
Salt Lake City American Enjoys First Showing of "Keeper of the Bees"

T HE World premiere of F.B.O.'s "The Keeper of the Bees" was held at the American Theatre, Salt Lake City on Saturday evening, September 19th and attracted an audience, which included among others, Governor George H. Dern of Utah; Hon. C. Clarence Neslen, Mayor of Salt Lake City; Harvey H. Cluff, Attorney General of Utah; Heber J. Grant, President of the Church of Latter Day Saints; J. H. Rayburn, Secretary of the Salt Lake City Chamber of Commerce; H. W. Lane, President of the Salt Lake baseball club, many officials of the Chamber of Commerce and social dignitaries.

The premiere was enthusiastically received and was followed by a brilliant run. Cut-

ting of the first print of the picture was completed barely in time to rush the negative by special airplane to the American Theatre. The print arrived only an hour before the rise of the curtain. J. Leo Meehan produced the picture for F.B.O., from the novel by Gene Stratton Porter. The picture is being released simultaneously with the publication of the book. The novel, however, was serialized in McCall's Magazine.

The New York premiere of "The Keeper of the Bees" took place in Town Hall last Monday evening and brought out an audience of society folks, stage and screen celebrities and members of the literary set.

Rod La Rocque in "The Coming of Amos," a Producers Distributing Corporation release.

Discuss New Franchise Play
Columbia Officials and Exchangemen Hold Meeting to Perfect System of Nationalization

E XCHANGE men handling the Columbia Pictures product and officials of that company held a meeting in New York to discuss a plan looking toward the nationalizing of exchanges distributing Columbia pictures. It was said that a system under which that end could be accomplished has been perfected and would be brought into operation within a very short time.

No detailed description of the plan was given out by Joe Brandt or Jack Cohn, president and treasurer of Columbia, but it was said the suggestion was made at the meeting that all exchanges handling the company's program restrict its activities to

the Columbia product for the coming season.

It is reported that all of the exchangemen who attended the meeting were in favor of the idea under which Columbia Pictures would receive simultaneous release throughout the United States.

A general meeting of all of the Columbia franchise holders will be held immediately upon the arrival of Harry Cohn in New York, which will be some time during the month of October. At that time, it is said, the working plan of the National system of Columbia distributors will be worked out in detail and put into execution.

Scenes from "Time, the Comedian," a Robert Z. Leonard production for Metro-Goldwyn-Mayer.

Fox Schedule Half Completed

Photography is Finished on Twenty-Two Features and Half of Short Subjects

FOX has completed practically half of its productions for the 1925-26 season. Twenty-two of the company's feature pictures have been finished so far as photography is concerned and half of the short subject program. Preparations are now being rushed to launch the remaining half of the program. Ten companies are shooting on the Fox lot on the west coast and five others are scheduled to start work in a few days.

Henry Otto is directing the final scenes in the allegorical sequence of "The Ancient Mariner." Tom Mix is busy on his fourth starring vehicle for the current season titled "The Best Bad Man," under the direction of J. G. Blystone. "Wages for Wives," the screen version of John Golden's stage success, "Chickenfeed," is progressing toward the final stages under the eye of Frank Borzage. Buck Jones, with R. William Neill wielding the megaphone, in on his fifth 1925-26 production, which has the title "Her Cowboy Prince."

The other films in work are two-reel comedies. Robert Kerr is back on the Fox lot and has another of the Van Bibber comedies under way. Albert Ray has the fourth of the Helen and Warren married life series, "Hold Everybody," at a point where it will be finished soon. Daniel Keefe is directing another of the O. Henry series and Bryan Foy, Lew Seiler and Benjamin Stoloff are at work on new Imperial Comedies.

The pictures that are scheduled to be put in work immediately are: "Daybreak," an adaptation of the stage play "The Outsider"; "The Golden Strain," Peter B. Kyne's first contribution to the Fox program from the Cosmopolitan magazine story "Thoroughbred"; "The Golden Butterfly," an original story by Evelyn Campbell; "My Little Pal," which is a Tom Mix starring vehicle from Gerald Beaumont's story, "The Gallant Guardsman," and "The First Year," the sixth of the John Golden Unit of Clean American productions.

Associated Signs "Sky Rocket"

Peggy Joyce Feature to Be a Special: S. S. Hutchinson to Produce for Program

ASSOCIATED Exhibitors announces that "The Sky Rocket," Peggy Hopkins Joyce's first screen vehicle which was produced under the direction of Marshall Neilan, would be released by that company. The picture will not be included in the program of thirty features announced for release by Associated, but will be handled as a special.

"The Sky Rocket" is an adaptation of the novel of the same title written by Adela Rogers St. Johns. Randall McKeever prepared the scenario and the cast assembled to support Miss Joyce includes Owen Moore, Earle Williams, Sammy Cohen, Gladys Brockwell, Gladys Hulette, Bernard Randall, Joan Standing and Lilyan Tashman.

Minimum of 12 Specials From F. B. O. Next Year

A MINIMUM of twelve specials will be offered on the F. B. O. production schedule for 1926-27, it was announced by J. I. Schnitzer, vice-president in charge of production, following conferences held at the company's studios in Hollywood regarding next year's program. Mr. Schnitzer arrived in New York from the Coast with John C. Brownell, home office scenario editor.

He said that F. B. O. will essay specials next season which will dwarf any previous efforts of the company in the production of elaborate photoplays. In addition to a list of specials the program he said would include several star series, among which the Evelyn Brent and Fred Thomson productions will be prominent.

Curran Joins Columbia as Publicity Director

Barry Curran has joined Columbia Pictures Corporation as director of advertising and publicity. He was recently associated with Chadwick Pictures in a similar capacity, resigning to fill his present position. Since leaving newspaper work for publicity film companies, Curran has served with Goldwyn and other companies. His newspaper experience includes the London Daily News, in England, the Dublin Independent, Ireland, The New York Tribune, the Providence Journal, the Pawtucket Times, and many others.

George Walsh in scenes from the Chadwick picture, "The Count of Luxembourg."

Warners Will Star Matt Moore in "The Sap"

Warner Bros. this week announced the purchase of photoplay rights to "The Sap," William A. Grew's comedy in which Raymond Hitchcock starred on the stage. The picture will be produced with Matt Moore in the leading role. Production will be started as soon as Moore finishes his part in "The First Year," for which he was loaned to William Fox by the Warners.

De Mille Selecting Cast for "Made for Love"

Cecil B. De Mille is giving his personal attention to the selection of the cast which will support Leatrice Joy in "Made For Love," her next picture for Producers Distributing Corporation which Paul Sloane will direct. Edmund Burns has the role opposite the star, and Ethel Wales and Bertram Grassby have prominent parts.

Agnes Christine Johnston Signs Contract

Metro-Goldwyn-Mayer have signed Agnes Christine Johnston, well known scenarist, to a long term contract. Miss Johnston wrote the scripts for such pictures as "Confessions of a Queen," "Exiles in Paris," "The Tower of Lies," "The Denial," "The Square Peg" and others.

P. D. C. Gets Prints of Five Features

MASTER prints of five big productions in the second batch of the 1925-26 pictures, were sent to the home office of Producers Distributing Corporation this week and shipments of duplicate prints were made to all the releasing company's branch offices directly from Los Angeles.

The five productions which will be available within the next few days are: "The People vs. Nancy Preston," with Marguerite De La Motte, John Bowers and William V. Mong in the leading roles; "Simon the Jester," with Lillian Rich, Eugene O'Brien and Henry B. Walthall; "The Man from Red Gulch," starring Harry Carey; "The Wedding Song," starring Leatrice Joy, and "Madame Behave," with Julian Eltinge and Ann Pennington.

Metropolitan Adds Benoit to Camera Staff

Georges Benoit has been added to the staff of camera men at the Metropolitan Pictures studio. Benoit has acted as chief camera operator with several big production units and is credited with the camera work on "Trilby," "Off The Highway," and other important features. Other cinematographers aligned with Metropolitan are Charles G. Clarke, Joseph La Shell, Devereaux Jennings and "Rube" Boyce.

Gala Opening for Warner's Cameo in Bridgeport

Mayor F. W. Behrens of Bridgeport, Conn., was the principal speaker at the ceremonies which marked the formal opening of Warner's Cameo theatre in that city last week. Irene Rich in "The Wife Who Wasn't Wanted" was the feature selected for the opening bill at the theatre under Warner's regime. The event attracted a capacity audience to the Cameo.

Arthur Beck Returns to California

Arthur Beck, who recently brought to New York prints of "The Unnamed Woman" and "The Primrose Path," both for distribution by Arrow, returned to California last week with several manuscripts from which he will select a story for his next production to be made under the direction of Harry O. Hoyt.

Campbell Starts Casting for New Feature

Major Maurice Campbell, who recently completed "Wandering Fires," an Arrow release, has started casting the story which he will make as his second contribution to the schedule of that company. The picture will be made at the Whitman Bennett Glendale Studios.

Highlights from Cecil B. De Mille's personally directed production for Producers Distributing Corporation, "The Road to Yesterday."

Niblo Films Chariot Race Scenes for "Ben Hur"

One thousand guests, among whom were many screen celebrities, witnessed the filming of the chariot race scenes for "Ben Hur." The scenes, directed by Fred Niblo, .ho is making the picture for Metro-Goldwyn-Mayer, were staged last week in a set reproducing the great Antioch Circus built near the Culver City studios of the Metro-Goldwyn-Mayer company. Niblo used 10,-000 extras in the scenes.

From special boxes outside the camera lines Douglas Fairbanks, Mary Pickford, Harold Lloyd, John Considine, Syd Grauman and many other prominent figures in the picture world viewed the event as guests of the director.

Gotham to Make "Butter and Egg Man"

Gotham Productions has started production activities in the east, as well as those being conducted by the company on the west coast. Work has been started at the Glendale, L. I. studios on "The Butter and Egg Man," adapted from the Peggy Gaddis story, in the Droll Stories Magazine.

"The Butter and Egg Man," will be released through Lumas Film Corporation in addition to the regular Gotham program of twelve productions, as a comedy special. It is scheduled to go to the exhibitors within the next six weeks.

Films Entertain President on Omaha Trip

Films were made part of the equipment of the Presidential train when President and Mrs. Coolidge left the Capital to attend the American Legion convention at Omaha.

While the train was in motion at night, the dining car was converted into a miniature theatre and pre-release films were shown. The Presidential party. The showings were arranged at the request of the President by Jack Connolly, Washington representative of the Hays organization.

Bennett Filming Kauffman Story at Glendale

Whitman Bennett has started the cameras on "Share and Share Alike," a magazine story by Reginald Wright Kauffman, at his studios in Glendale. The picture, which will be distributed by Arrow, will present Jane Novak in the starred role.

Astor Outlines Plans for Season

PRODUCTION and distribution plans of Astor Distributing Corporation were decided upon last week at a conference between Harry Rathner, president of the company, and Irving M. Lesser, vice president and general manager.

The first Astor "Aristocrat" will be "Child Wives," which will probably be produced in Hollywood. Following the completion of "Child Wives," Rathner will go to the northwest to arrange for the production of a railroad story. Another of the "Aristocrats" will be a sea story laid on the east coast.

In addition to the specials Astor is active with a number of super-state rights productions, including "A Lover's Oath," "Business of Love" and "The Shining Adventure." There will also be a separate series of eight "Macfadden Made Movies," the first two of which, "The Wrongdoers" and "False Pride" have been completed.

Washington Delegates See "Merry Widow"

Metro-Goldwyn-Mayer entertained delegates to the Interparliamentary Union Conference in Washington last week with a special showing of "The Merry Widow" at the Wardman Park Hotel. As a light opera the story was known to most of the delegates present, as it has played in practically all parts of the world.

Tom Ricketts Engaged for Waldorf Production

Tom Ricketts has been engaged for a prominent part in the cast of "The Fate of a Flirt," a Waldorf production for Columbia pictures. Dorothy Revier has the featured role and the picture is being directed by Frank Strayer.

Fitzgerald Engages Clara Bow for Leading Role

Dallas M. Fitzgerald has engaged Clara Bow for the leading feminine role in his next production for the Arrow schedule. The story, as yet untitled, is by Edgar Franklin, author of "White Collars," a current Broadway stage play.

Gerson Completes Series for Rayart

Gerson Pictures Corporation have completed shooting on six melodramas for release through Rayart Pictures Corporation. The last of the series, directed by Oscar Apfel is titled, "The Midnight Limited," starring Gaston Glass, Wanda Hawley and Richard Holt. It is due for November release.

The first of the Gerson series, produced by B. Berger, "The Pride of the Force," has just been booked by the Loew Circuit in New York for October release. The next picture the company will make will probably be "The Last Alarm," an Arthur Hoerl story.

Alice D. G. Miller Signs M-G-M Contract

Metro-Goldwyn-Mayer have signed Alice D. G. Miller to a long term contract to write continuities exclusively for that company. She is at present writing a screen version of "Monte Carlo," which will go into production under the direction of Robert Z. Leonard.

Miss Miller has been one of the feature writers with the M-G-M organization ever since the merger more than a year and a half ago. Listed among her successes are, "So This is Marriage," "Lady of the Night," "The Exquisite Sinner," "Pretty Ladies," and "Dance Madness."

Dorothy Revier Plays Lead in "The Fate of a Flirt"

Dorothy Revier has been cast for the leading feminine role in "The Fate of a Flirt," a Waldorf production for Columbia Pictures to be made on the West Coast under the direction of Frank Strayer. The story is by Janet Corthers and was scenarioized by Alfred Lewin. Forrest Stanley, Tom Ricketts, William Austin, Charles West and Clarissa Selwynne have been assigned prominent roles.

Buck Jones Starts Work on "Desert's Price"

Buck Jones, Fox star, has started work on "The Desert's Price" under the direction of W. S. Van Dyke. The story is an adaptation from the novel by William MacLeod Raine. In the supporting cast are, Florence Gilbert, Edna Marion, Ernest Ritterwooh, Arthur Houseman and Montague Love. The picture will be released January 31st.

Charles Ray in his latest picture for Chadwick Pictures Corporation, "Sweet Adeline."

"Lights of Old Broadway" to Have Los Angeles Premiere

"Lights of Old Broadway," Marion Davies' first starring vehicle for release through Metro-Goldwyn-Mayer, will have its world premiere at Loew State Theatre, Los Angeles, October 31st. The picture was recently completed at the Metro-Goldwyn-Mayer studio at Culver City. The photoplay was adapted by Carey Wilson from Laurence Eyre's Broadway stage success, "Merry Wives of Gotham." Monta Bell directed the production, which has Conrad Nagel in the leading male role.

Gotham Completes Three New Features

Three new Gotham features, "The Part Time Wife," "One of the Bravest" and "The Shadow on the Wall," were completed at the Hollywood studios of the company last week. Sample prints of the pictures have been shipped to the New York offices of Gotham.

"The Part Time Wife" will be released by Lumas Film Corporation, distributors of the Gotham Productions, on October 15. Alice Calhoun and Robert Ellis are featured.

Mrs. Reid Completing "The Red Kimono"

"The Red Kimono," Mrs. Wallace Reid's feature for release by Davis Distributing Division, is nearing completion at the studios in Los Angeles. Priscilla Bonner will be featured and has Mary Carr, Theodore Von Eltz, Sheldon Lewis, Tryone Power, Virginia Pearson, George Seigmann and other well known players. Walter Lang is directing.

Tom Ricketts Engaged for Waldorf Production

Tom Ricketts has been engaged for a prominent part in the cast of "The Fate of a Flirt," a Waldorf production for Columbia pictures. Dorothy Reviere has the featured role and the picture is being directed by Frank Strayer.

Steel Corporation to Aid With Picture

FIRST NATIONAL has concluded arrangements with the United States Steel Corporation whereby that organization will lend the producing company its complete cooperation in the filming of "Men of Steel," an original story of the steel industry written by Milton Sills, in which the author will also be the star.

C. L. Close, Manager of the Bureau of Safety, Sanitation and Welfare of the United States Steel Corporation is to represent his organization during the filming of the picture, which Earl Hudson will produce.

Scenes of the photoplay will be taken on the Mesaba Ridge in Minnesota, where the bulk of the company's iron ore is mined; at the docks in Duluth, where the ore starts its journey across the Great Lakes, and at the Gary, Indiana and Pittsburgh plants of the steel corporation. John Fish Goodrich has been assigned to write the scenario.

Corinne Griffith in scenes from "Classified," a First National release.

First National Sets Releases

Thirteen of Winner Group and Three Specials Due in Next Three Months

THIRTEEN productions will be released during the next three months by First National, in addition to the two specials, "The Lost World" and "Winds of Chance," and "The Sea Hawk," which was withdrawn from the market during June, July and August.

The thirteen pictures scheduled for release during October, November and December are a part of the Winner Group. In the order of their release they are: October 4th, "The Pace That Thrills," an original automobile racing story written for Ben Lyon and Byron Morgan; October 11th, Corinne Griffith's "Classified," from Edna Ferber's story.

October 18th, "Why Women Love," Edwin Carewe's production of Willard Robertson's play, "The Sea Woman."

October 25th, "The Beautiful City," Inspiration Pictures' new production starring Richard Barthelmess.

November 1st, "The New Commandment," Robert Kane's initial production for First National, adapted from Frederick Palmer's novel, "Invisible Wounds," directed by Howard Higgin.

November 8th, "We Moderns," the new Colleen Moore picture made from Israel Zangwill's play, directed by John Francis Dillon.

November 15th, "Clothes Make the Pirate," a Sam Rork production based upon Holman Day's novel of the same title, directed by Maurice Tourneur, starring Leon Errol, recently placed under contract for a long term by First National Pictures.

November 22nd, "The Unguarded Hour," starring Milton Sills, from Margaretta Tuttle's new novel. Lambert Hillyer directed.

November 29th, "The Scarlet Saint," directed by George Archainbaud from Gerald Beaumont's story, "The Lady Who Played Fidele." Mary Astor and Lloyd Hughes are the featured players.

December 6th, "The Splendid Road," the new Frank Lloyd production, adapted by J. G. Hawks from Vingie E. Roe's new novel. The cast includes Anna Q. Nilsson, Robert Frazer and Lionel Barrymore in the featured roles.

December 13th, "Caesar's Wife," starring Corinne Griffith, adapted from a story by Somerset Maugham and directed by Irving Cummings.

December 20th, "The Girl from Montmartre," Sawyer-Lubin's production based on Anthony Fryde's novel, "Spanish Sunlight." Alfred E. Green directed.

December 27th, "Kiki," the new Joseph M. Schenck production starring Norma Talmadge, adapted from David Belasco's stage production in which Lenore Ulric starred.

First National Scenario Staff in East Busy

Seven stories are being prepared for filming by the units under Earl Hudson's supervision by the scenario staff at First National's studio in New York.

The script for Milton Sills' next vehicle, "Men of Steel," is being written by John Fish Goodrich. Jane Murfin and Charles Whittaker are working together on the continuity of Mademoiselle Modiste." Olga Printzlau is writing the script for "Pals First." Harvey Thew is writing the script for "The Boss of Little Arcady," an adaptation of Harry Leon Wilson's magazine story of the same name. Eugene Clifford and Ray Harris are rapidly completing the continuity for "The Lunatic at Large," and Earl Snell is doing "Mismates," the screen version of Myron C. Fagan's stage play.

Independent Starts First of New Custer Series

Independent Pictures Corporation has started production on the first of the second series of eight Texas Ranger features starring Bob Custer. The story is titled, "No Man's Law," by Walter J. Coburn and was published in the Western Magazine. It is now being produced under the personal supervision of Jesse J. Goldburg. F. B. O. have exercised their option for the distribution of this second series.

Independent has also started production on the second series of Bill Cody stunt westerns for release through the state right market. The title of the first production is "A Man's Fight."

Wellman to Make "Dancing Days" First

William Wellman's first directorial assignment for B. P. Schulberg will be "Dancing Days," instead of "Lew Tyler's Wives," as originally announced. The change was necessitated because of the difficulty in securing a proper masculine lead for "Lew Tyler's Wives," which now will be the second of the Wellman productions.

Bern's First Production Will Be "Paris"

Paul Bern's first directorial effort for Metro-Goldwyn-Mayer will be "Paris," an original story by Carey Wilson, featuring Pauline Starke and Lew Cody. The production will also feature Erte fashion creations and a special pearl ballet designed by Erte.

Billings Plays Lincoln in "Hands Up"

Clarence Badger has assigned George A. Billings to the role of Abraham Lincoln in Raymond Griffith's new Paramount starring picture, "Hands Up." Billings, it will be recalled played the title role in the screen production, "Abraham Lincoln."

Two Join "Sally, Irene and Mary" Cast

Edmund Goulding had added Sam De Grasse and Lillian Elliott to the cast of "Sally, Irene and Mary," which he is producing for Metro-Goldwyn-Mayer.

Paramount Signs John Murray Anderson

FAMOUS PLAYERS-LASKY have engaged John Murray Anderson as director of production for the Metropolitan Theatre in Boston, a new Paramount house to be operated in conjunction with E. F. Albee. The first Anderson production will be presented at the opening of the Metropolitan, October 16th.

Anderson has organized his corps of assistants, with Herman Rosse as scenic director. The direction and training of the performers will be done in New York in order that Anderson may continue to supervise his interests in his theatre at Park Avenue and 58th street.

Anderson's production activities include the first "Greenwich Village Follies," "What's in a Name," last season's production of Irving Berlin's "Music Box Review" the production in London of "The League of Notions" and the new musical comedy, "Dearest Enemy" which recently opened on Broadway.

Anne Dale Added to "Keep It Up" Cast

F. Herrick-Herrick has signed Anne Dale for one of the main feminine roles in "Keep It Up," which will be released through Davis Distributing Division. Miss Dale played the crippled girl in the film version of "The Fool" and had a prominent part in "The Miracle," the spectacular production staged at the Century Theatre in New York.

Holmes Herbert Given Lead With Pola Negri

Holmes Herbert will be Pola Negri's leading man in her next Paramount starring vehicle to be made at the company's Long Island studio under the direction of Malcolm St. Clair. The production also calls for another male lead which has been assigned to Charles Emmet Mack.

Jack Conway Will Direct "The Reason Why"

Because of his success with the direction of Ellinor Glyn's "Four Flaming Days," Jack Conway will direct the same author's, "The Reason Why," in which Aileen Pringle will have the heroine role. Edmund Lowe will have the male lead. The picture will be produced for Metro-Goldwyn-Mayer.

Montagu Love is Added to "Hands Up" Cast

Clarence Badger has added Montagu Love to the cast of featured players in Raymond Griffith's new Paramount starring picture, "Hands Up." Marion Nixon, Virginia Lee Corbin, Mack Swain and George Billings are the other players so far selected.

British Players in Cast With Meighan

Cecil Humphreys and Louise Grafton, noted British players will be seen in the cast of Thomas Meighan's new Paramount production, "Irish Buck," exterior scenes of which were filmed in Ireland. The interiors are being made at the Paramount Long Island studio under the direction of Victor Heerman.

J. Barney Sherry Added to Johnny Hines' Cast

C. C. Burr has signed J. Barney Sherry as the first member of the supporting cast to Johnny Hines in "Rainbow Riley," Hines' second starring vehicle for First National, which went into production at Delaware Water Gap this week.

Burr also made the announcement that in addition to Charles Gilson and John Geisel, who have had the photographic assignment on all the Johnny Hines features, Al Wetzel had also been added to the camera force. Charles Hines is again directing, with Charles Berner as his assistant. Benny Berk continues as production manager, assisted by Joseph Bannon.

Officials of Navy Attend "Midshipman" Showing

Curtis D. Wilbur, Secretary of the Navy, headed a delegation of twenty-five officers of the Bureau of Navigation and the United States Naval Academy at Annapolis and their wives to Loew's Palace Theatre in Washington, October 5th, when "The Midshipman" was shown. The picture was made by Metro-Goldwyn-Mayer and is a photoplay of Naval Academy life, filmed at Annapolis, with Ramon Novarro in the leading role.

Myton to Write Special Stories for F. B. O.

Fred Myton, scenario writer for F. B. O., will continue with that organization to write special stories, it was announced this week by B. P. Fineman, general manager of the studio. Myton is now working on the script for "Flaming Waters," which is to be produced by Associated Arts and released by F. B. O.

Harry Morey in Cast With Gilda Gray

Harry Morey has been added to the cast which will support Gilda Gray in "Aloma of the South Seas," her Paramount starring vehicle now in production at the Long Island studios under the direction of Maurice Tourneur.

Tourneur Company Leaves for Porto Rico

Maurice Tourneur and a company of seventy-five Paramount players headed by Gilda Gray are scheduled to leave Thursday of this week for San Juan, Porto Rico, to make "Aloma of the South Seas."

Corinne Griffith's Next Will Be "Ashes"

Reginald Goode's "Ashes" will be Corinne Griffith's next picture for First National following "Caesar's Wife," which is now in production. Walter Pidgeon will be Miss Griffith's leading man

Neil Hamilton Opposite Bebe Daniels

William De Mille has selected Neil Hamilton to play opposite Bebe Daniels in the forthcoming Paramount production, tentatively titled, "Magpie."

J. G. Hawks Joins F. B. O. as Scenario Editor

J. G. Hawks, well known scenarist, has joined F. B. O. as scenario editor at the Hollywood studios of the company. Mr. Hawks entered scenario work in 1914 with the Thomas H. Ince organization, and since that time has written photoplays for several of the leading producers. He is the author of scenarios for many outstanding screen productions, including "Hearts Aflame," "Dangerous Age," "The Eternal Struggle," "The Sea Hawk," "The Silent Watcher," "Inez from Hollywood," "The Storm," and "Winds of Chance."

"Other Woman's Story" is Next Schulberg Release

"The Other Woman's Story," adapted from the novel by Peggy Gaddis, will be the next B. P. Schulberg release. It will be released October 15 and offers a cast including Alice Calhoun, Robert Frazer, Helen Lee Worthing, Mahlon Hamilton, David Torrence and Riza Royce. B. F. Stanley directed the picture.

Zasu Pitts is Assigned to "Mannequin" Cast

Zasu Pitts has been added to the Paramount Cast for "Mannequin," Fannie Hurst's $50,000 prize winning story which James Cruze is producing. Others in the cast are Alice Joyce, Warner Baxter, Dolores Costello and Walter Pidgeon.

Release stills from "Ranger of the Big Pines," a new Paramount feature.

Action stills from "Peggy of the Secret Service," a Davis Distributing Division release.

Mayer Concluding Conference

Will Return to Coast Soon to Launch Second Half of the M-G-M Schedule

LOUIS B. MAYER, vice-president in charge of Metro-Goldwyn-Mayer production, who arrived in the East recently to discuss production matters with Marcus Loew and other officials of the company, will soon return to California to launch the second half of the production schedule M-G-M will carry out this season.

In the production of the second half of the "Quality Fifty-Two," the executives associated with Mr. Mayer will be, as in the past, Irving Thalberg and Harry Rapf with the addition of Hunt Stromberg, recently signed. This announcement definitely refutes rumors concerning a change in the executive personnel of this organization.

"Under the producing schedule just prepared, provision has been made for vacations among the members of the executive staff," said Mr. Mayer. "Harry Rapf will shortly make a trip to Europe with his family where he will combine pleasure with M-G-M business. Upon his return Irving Thalberg will take a well earned rest and later, I myself will spend a month abroad. The addition of Hunt Stromberg and others with whom we are now in negotiation, will make it possible for members of the executive staff to take vacations which have thus far been denied them because of the rush of production."

Among the pictures to be produced during the coming months are: Elinor Glyn's "Four Flaming Days," "Free Lips," starring Norma Shearer; Tod Browning's "The Mocking Bird," starring Lon Chaney; "La Boheme," starring Lillian Gish and featuring John Gilbert; "Ben Hur," now nearing completion, and "Bardolys the Magnificent,"

a spectacular version of the Raphael Sabatini novel to be made entirely in technicolor and to star John Gilbert.

Chadwick Receives "Prince of Broadway" Print

The home office of Chadwick Pictures Corporation in New York has received the master print of "The Prince of Broadway," George Walsh's third starring vehicle, and it is now being titled by Leon Lee, with the assistance of five New York columnists and two sporting editors.

It is a prize fight picture with such luminaries of the ring appearing as James J. Jeffries, Ad Wolgast, Frankie Genaro, Capt. Bob Roper, Tommy Ryan, Gene Delmont and Leach Cross. The regular picture players in the cast in addition to Walsh are, Alyce Mills, in the feminine lead; Freeman Wood, Wade Turner, Frank Campeau and Alma Bennett.

Fox Completes Shooting on "Silver Treasure"

"The Silver Treasure" has been completed by Fox and the picture is now being cut. It is an adaptation of the novel, "Nostremo," by Joseph Conrad and was directed by Rowland V. Lee, with George O'Brien in the leading role. In the supporting cast are, Lou Tellegen, Joan Renee, Helena D'Algy, Hedda Hopper and Harvey Clark. The picture is scheduled for release December 6th.

Scenes from "The Dark Angel," Samuel Goldwyn's screen version of the stage play of that tile. A First National release.

Park French Art Director for Samuel Goldwyn

Samuel Goldwyn has signed Park M. French as art director for his third "Potash and Perlmutter" production, "Partners Again." French for a long time was associated with Joseph M. Schenck Productions. Henry King will direct "Partners Again" from the script prepared by Frances Marion in collaboration with Montague Glass. George Sidney will play "Potash" and Alexander Carr, "Perlmutter." The picture will be distributed by United Artists.

Metropolitan Fills Cast of "Steel Preferred"

Metropolitan this week completed the cast which will appear in "Steel Preferred," a feature to be distributed by Producers Distributing Corporation, with the signing of Pat Harmon, Herbert Pryor and Ivor McFadden for principal roles. William Boyd and Vera Reynolds have the leading parts, and others prominently cast are Hobart Bosworth, William V. Mong, Charles Murray, Nigel Barrie, Walter Long and Helene Sullivan. James Hogan is directing.

Final Title Selected for Mildred Davis Story

The vehicle which will bring Mildred Davis back to the screen for Paramount has been definitely titled "Behind the Front." The picture is an adaptation of Hugh Wiley's war story, "The Spoils of War," and was tentatively titled "Two Soldiers." Production is scheduled to start October 12th.

Midshipman In Capital

Secretary Wilbur and Naval Officers Attend Premiere at Loew's Palace

THE premiere of "The Midshipman," Ramon Novarro's initial starring vehicle for Metro-Goldwyn-Mayer, was held last Monday night at Loew's Palace theatre, Washington, D. C.

Secretary of the Navy Wilbur, Navy and Army officers and Government officials attended the presentation. Will Hays, who made the trip to the Capital from New York especially to be present at the showing, was another distinguished guest at the premiere.

The premiere of "The Midshipman" was celebrated as Navy Night at the Palace. The major portion of the exterior scenes in the production were filmed at the U. S. Naval Academy at Annapolis.

Among the distinguished people who attended were Secretary Wilbur, Will Hays, Rear Admiral W. R. Shoemaker, Admiral E. W. Eberle, Captain Gherardi, Mrs. Theo-

dore Douglas Robinson, Everett Saunders, President Coolidge's secretary; Rear Admiral Robinson, Brig. Gen. Williams, Brig. Gen. C. Richards, Major General J. A. Kejuenne, Rear Admiral C. F. Hughes, Rear Admiral J. O. Tawresey, Rear Admiral Charles Morris, Rear Admiral G. N. Burrage, Rear Admiral C. C. Block, Rear Admiral T. J. Senn, Captain W. W. Gallbraith, Captain W. D. Puleston, Captain J. R. Y. Blakely, Captain E. T. Pollock, Lt. Commander Hayes, Captain C. F. Brooks, Captain J. O. Richardson, Lieut Commander George M. Lowry, Lieut. Commander C. Cobb, Captain T. W. Lentz, Lieut. E. T. Spellman, Lieut. K. T. R. W. Grue'ich, Capt. George H. Rock, Capt. A. W. Dunbar, Capt. W. D. Leahy, Lieut. T John J. Fitzgerald, Capt. A. W. Johnson, and Robert M. May.

S. F. Sees Paramount Premiere

Public and Press Enthuse Over Initial Showing of "Vanishing American"

PARAMOUNT'S "The Vanishing American" had its world premiere at the St. Francis Theatre in San Francisco last week and was acclaimed a success by both public and critics. The opening performance was a brilliant affair which brought out the social set of San Francisco and a number of screen luminaries from Hollywood. Power wagons and arc lights in front of the theatre permitted newspaper photographers to photograph the celebrities entering the theatre.

Among those prominent in pictures who attended the opening performance, were,

Betty Bronson, Raymond Hatton, Zasu Pitts, Douglas Fairbanks, Jr., and George B. Seitz, director of the picture. Charles Wakefield Cadman, who wrote the musical score and theme song, "Little Wild Rose," journeyed to San Francisco especially to play the theme song at the opening performance.

"The Vanishing American" luncheon, given by Paramount on the day preceding the premiere was attended by Hollywood celebrities and all of San Francisco's dramatic critics and the city's leading newspaper men.

Scenes from the B. P. Schulberg Preferred Picture, "With This Ring."

Exhibitors Service Bureau

Rowland & Clark's Liberty theatre in Pittsburgh arranged a splendid lobby display recently on "The Iron Horse" (Fox), including authentic models of early locomotives, rare Indian bead work and bison heads, loaned by the Museum department of the Carnegie library.

Advisory Board and Contributing Editors, Exhibitors' Service Bureau

George J. Schade, Schade theatre, Sandusky.

Edward L. Hyman, Mark Strand theatre, Brooklyn.

Leo A. Landau, Lyceum theatre, Minneapolis.

C. C. Perry, Managing Director, Garrick theatre, Minneapolis.

E. R. Rogers, Southern District Supervisor, Famous Players-Lasky, Chattanooga, Tenn.

Stanley Chambers, Palace theatre, Wichita, Kan.

Willard C. Patterson, Metropolitan theatre, Atlanta.

E. V. Richards, Jr., Gen. Mgr., Saenger Amusement Co., New Orleans.

F. L. Newman, Managing Director, Famous Players-Lasky theatres, Los Angeles.

Arthur G. Stolte, Des Moines theatre, Des Moines, Iowa.

W. C. Quimby, Managing Director, Strand Palace and Jefferson theatres, Fort Wayne, Ind.

J. A. Partington, Imperial theatre, San Francisco.

George E. Carpenter, Paramount-Empress theatre, Salt Lake.

Sidney Grauman, Grauman's theatres, Los Angeles.

George E. Brown, Imperial theatre, Charlotte, N. C.

Louis K. Sidney, Division Manager, Loew's theatres, Pittsburgh, Pa.

Geo. Rotsky, Managing Director, Palace theatre, Montreal, Can.

Eddie Zorn, Managing Director, Broadway-Strand theatre, Detroit.

Fred S. Myer, Managing Director, Palace theatre, Hamilton, Ohio.

Joseph Plunkett, Managing Director, Mark-Strand theatre, New York.

Ray Grombacher, Managing Director, Liberty theatre, Spokane, Wash.

Ross A. McVoy, Manager, Temple theatre, Geneva, N. Y.

W. S. McLaren, Managing Director, Capitol theatre, Jackson, Mich.

Harold B. Franklin, Director of Theatres, Famous Players-Lasky.

William J. Sullivan, Manager, Rialto theatre, Butte, Mont.

H. A. Albright, Manager, T. D. & L. theatre, Glendale, Calif.

Claire Meachime, Grand theatre, Westfield, N. Y.

Ace Berry, Managing Director, Circle theatre, Indianapolis.

THE CHECK-UP

Weekly Edition of Exhibitors' Box Office Reports

Productions listed are new pictures on which reports were not available previously.

For ratings on current and older releases see MOTION PICTURE NEWS—first issue of each month.

KEY—The first column following the name of the feature represents the number of managers that have reported the picture as "Poor." The second column gives the number who considered it "Fair," the third the number who considered it "Good," and the fourth column, those who considered it "Big."

The fifth column is a percentage giving the average rating on the feature, obtained by the following method: A report of "Poor" is rated at 20%; one of "Fair," 40%; "Good," 70%; and "Big," 100%. The percentage rating of all of these reports on one picture are then added together, and divided by the number of reports, giving the average percentage—a figure which represents the consensus of opinion on that picture. In this way exceptional cases, reports which might be misleading taken alone, and such individual differences of opinion are averaged up and eliminated.

TITLE	Poor	Fair	Good	Big	Value	Length
FAMOUS PLAYERS.						
In the Name of Love	1	4	8	—	57	5,904 ft.
Street of Forgotten Men, The	1	2	13	1	65	6,386 ft.
Wild Horse Mesa	—	4	8	2	66	7,223 ft.
Wild, Wild Susan	2	4	6	3	51	5,774 ft.
FIRST NATIONAL.						
Her Sister from Paris	—	2	5	4	75	7,255 ft.
Shore Leave	—	—	8	4	80	6,856 ft.
UNITED ARTISTS.						
Gold Rush, The	—	1	1	8	91	8,500 ft.

See Complete "Check-Up" on Pages 1694-5

Ad-Line Contest in Daily Advertises "Chickie"

The Morning Press of Santa Barbara staged a "Chickie" Ad Line contest to help the showing of "Chickie" in the Granada theatre, Santa Barbara, as a direct tie-up with the newspaper serial, which had run previously in the paper, and the motion picture.

The contest was held one week in advance of the opening of the film, and more than 100 "ad lines" were received in the campaign. Readers of the story were advised of the coming of the picture through the contest and the resulting publicity.

The winning ad line was used in the Granada "splash" ad, while all prize winners were published in the news columns of the Press.

J. Frank Churchill, Managing Director of the Granada, and H. D. McBride, publicist for the California Theatre Co., operators of the Granada handled the campaign.

Scooter Sweepstakes Aids "California Ahead"

The great Seattle Star handicap, the Columbia Theatre derby, and the California Straight Ahead sweepstakes were big events this summer among the children of Seattle—and they gave the Columbia theatre front page publicity on "California Straight Ahead."

Robert Bender, manager of the Columbia, conceived the idea of a coaster wagon and kid automobile race, and sold it to the Seattle Star. The prizes were nine merchandise certificates, and in addition each kid who made the race received two tickets—one for himself and the other for his mechanic—for a special show of "California Straight Ahead" at the Columbia on the following Saturday morning.

When an escaped leopard recently monopolized the front pages of the Paris newspapers, Reginald Ford's Cameo theatre had this appropriate ballyhoo out for "The Lost World" (First Nat'l).

The races to find the speediest scooter wagon or home-built automobile in town were open to any boy under 14 years of age. All contestants were told to assemble at the race course—a downhill grade several blocks long patrolled by police to make it safe—with one of the entrance blanks properly filled out with the driver's name and that of his mechanic. When a boy turned in his blank, he was given his theatre tickets and racing number to hang on his back.

Here are the rules that were used:

First race: The Seattle Star Handicap: Pilots will ride on their cars; mechanics will be allowed to give them a 10-foot shove off. Three merchandise prizes.

Second: Columbia Theatre Derby: Same rules and similar prizes.

Third: California Straight Ahead Sweepstakes. The three winners of each of the first two races will be started over the course. Three merchandise certificate prizes of $15, $10 and $5.

Deaf Ballyhoo Stunt Used to Aid "Lightnin' "

Passengers on Seattle street cars were—for several days recently—amused greatly by the antics of two old soldiers, both deaf, who were continually getting on the wrong cars, and when not on cars were getting all tangled up in traffic. No matter how badly the two old fellows fared in their journeyings however, they managed to keep up a running fire of conversation in a loud tone about them being on their way to the Strand theatre to see their old comrade Jay Hunt in "Lightnin'."

Of course it was all an exploitation stunt for the Strand engagement of the picture, but it went over big. The stunt was pulled, after several days of careful rehearsing with the operatives—one 88, and the other 75. The two men were instructed to never accost each other, but to let people within earshot direct them. An exploitation man accompanied them everywhere on their travels, picking out the street cars they were to ride on, the crowded streets they were to get "lost" on, etc. The soldiers, of course, never accosted or paid any attention to their guide.

No G. A. R. insignia of any kind was worn by the men, and there was nothing about the stunt that could in any way reflect on the G. A. R. The uniform of that body not even being worn. The clothes worn by the men being makeshifts supplied by a local masquerade costumer.

The stunt was started each day, by the men boarding cars going in some direction away from the Strand Theatre. Then, feigning deafness, they would start to shout at each other, until passengers would volunteer directions, telling them they were on the wrong ear, etc. Then the "boys" would acquaint everybody present that they were on their way to see their old comrade, play the main part in that picture "Lightnin'" and how they expected to enjoy it.

A real, honest-to-goodness circus front, with sideshow banners and all, and a juvenile circus parade, featured the campaign of Manager Dick Durst of the Hollyway theatre, Los Angeles, on "The Great Circus Mystery" (Universal).

"Perils of Wild" Tied Up With Chicago Contest

Bruce Godshaw, Universal's new exploitation man in the Chicago territory, is turning out exploitation campaigns in rapid order. His latest tie-up, for "Perils of the Wild," is with The Hub (Henry C. Lytton & Sons) for essay contests in 35 theatres, the clothing store to furnish three boys' suits for prizes for each theatre. All the Lubliner and Trinz houses with the exception of the Pantheon, and the Monogram, 20th Century, Casino (Halstead St.) and the Casino (Madison St.) are already in on the stunt.

The prizes are to go to the writers of the best essays on the three following subjects:

Why do boys prefer to come to The Hub for their first long trouser suit?

Would you rather wear long trousers or knickers—why?

If the Hub organized a Boys' Club would you like to belong and what entertainment would you suggest?

In addition each boy who enters the contest will receive a free copy of a 48-page book containing batting averages, track records, Boy Scout data, All American football teams, radio dope, etc.

Miniature Skyscraper in "Shock Punch" Lobby

Manager E. B. Roberts of the Majestic theatre, Austin, in his recent exploitation of "The Shock Punch" used a miniature display in the lobby which effectively sold the picture.

The exhibit consisted of a small skyscraper, about 12 feet high, in course of construction. This was made from the toy construction apparatus, Erecto, and had a crane with a toy beam with toy men on it and an elevator such as is used for hauling up material. Both of the latter devices were kept moving up and down by means of a small concealed motor, their operation greatly enhancing the attention value of the display. A beaverboard background painted with the skyline of New York completed this interesting exhibit.

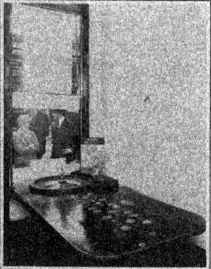

A real roulette wheel obtained and used as a special window display for "The Wheel" (Fox), showing at the New Aster theatre in Minneapolis, and attracted no little attention.

Eye-catching cut-out on "As Man Desires" (First Nat'l), mounted on rosin paper, and used in the lobby of the Rex theatre, Eugen, Ore.

Notable "Iron Horse" Parade
Majestic Theatre, Portland, Makes Tie-up With Union Pacific on Joint Advertising

INTENSIVE exploitation preceded the opening of "The Iron Horse" at the Majestic theatre, Portland, Ore., where a corking campaign was put over by Charles E. Couche and Frank Lacey, director of publicity and house manager, respectively.

The big Portland "push" started three weeks before the picture opened, with an elaborate newspaper announcement and plenty of press stories planted, on the signing of the contract.

A score of de luxe painted boards 12 by 60 feet were arranged on the four main vacation highways. The boards were not merely painted, but had old style engine heads built of wood and beaver board projecting about two feet from surface of sign. The boards were brilliantly illuminated with flood lights at night, and constituted a valuable flash for the campaign. Forty ordinary 24-sheet boards were also utilized for "The Iron Horse" stands.

The "Oregonian," Portland's leading newspaper, was tied up with the drive, and in a manner that secured over 200 inches of free space, including two front page stories. The Oregonian consented to act as host to local pioneers, who came to Portland by railroad prior to 1885. The newspaper also acted as host to orphan children at special matinees. The local lodge of Elks co-operated by providing transportation for the children at these performances.

The Union Pacific Railways responded liberally to an invitation for reciprocal advertising courtesies, and displayed special 8x10 "Iron Horse" ad cards throughout their shops, offices, etc. The railroads also allowed an advertising slip on the picture to be attached to every month-end pay check issued to their employees, approximating 10,000.

The Union Pacific helped put over the biggest advertising parade ever staged in Portland. They furnished their 40 piece shop band to lead the procession, which consisted of section crew, floats, equipment, Indians and Portland's first railway engine. The old engine being transported on a tractor-drawn truck. The parade was ten blocks long and secured 260 inches of free publicity for the picture.

The parade was the climax of the advance campaign—being staged on Saturday morning immediately preceding the opening. After it was over the band gave a concert in front of the theatre, where the engine was parked by special permit for the run of the engagement.

Motion pictures of the parade were made during its progress. These pictures, were run at the three other big downtown houses. The orchestra at one theatre, and the orchestra of the biggest and most popular hotel cafe, put on "Iron Horse" musical novelties.

The local County Fair opening the week before the picture's opening, a booth was engaged, in which an "Iron Horse" trailer was shown for five days preceding the opening engagement.

A number of display windows in the downtown section were also brought into play, one window using a trailer, and two displaying miniature model engines.

Oil cloth signs were used on the spare tires of taxicabs, and Portland street cars carried "Iron Horse" dash board cards as well. A distinctive feature of the drive was the broadcasting from local wireless station of an orchestra rendering "Iron Horse" musical novelty. This number comprised in its rendition, whistles, bells and imitations of railroad effects.

Lucky "Iron Horse" Stunt Put Across in Lima

Quick to take advantage of a newspaper circulation builder, now sweeping certain cities of the country like wildfire, the management of the Faurot Opera House, Lima, Ohio, and the Fox exploitation department, have the *The Lima News* of that city, running a Lucky Buck contest as an aid to the local "Iron Horse" showing.

In this contest, however, the Lucky Bucks are no longer designated as Lucky Bucks, but as "Iron Horses." *The Lima News* featuring the matter daily under a three column head in its most prominent front page position.

The *News* is further offering in all its contest announcements, a season pass for the Faurot, to holders of all lucky "Iron Horses." The offer stresses the fact that the cash prizes for bills carrying the lucky numbers are really of secondary value, as "The two season passes mean $600 in free shows for the whole year, the William Fox 'Iron Horse' being the first treat."

The contest is receiving in Lima, the same response that has marked its introduction at New York and other cities, with the exploitation on the picture receiving a valuable added impetus as a consequence.

Weird Lobby Display Made as "Monster" Flash

Attention was attracted to "The Monster" at the Egyptian, Greenville, recently by the uncanny lobby display Manager J. Wright Brown arranged for the attraction.

Mounted in a shadow-box was a large cutout figure, similar to the big black shadow on the six sheet, with the eyes cut out and faced with red crepe paper. The title also appeared in cutout lettering backed with similar colored paper. Equipped with a flasher socket which kept the eyes and title flashing on and off, the exhibit drew the eye unresistingly.

"Don Q, Son of Zorro" (United Artists) at the London Hippodrome, in London, was given this attractive window display in Piccadilly Circus by Swan & Edgar, Ltd.

"Lightnin'" Wins Tie-up With Bakery in Omaha

When "Lightnin'" played the Sun theatre, Omaha, Nebr., recently, N. N. Frudenfeld, director of publicity for the Sun theatre effected a tie-up with a local baking concern on Peter Pan Bread. The tie-up consisted of a large card, bearing a picture of Jay Hunt as "Lightnin'" and the statement. "Lightnin'" Bill Jones sez: "When I was a baker, I used to bake good bread just like 'Peter Pan,' the leading bread."

The card also carried the play date of the engagement, and a brief selling argument on the picture. The cards were distributed about town in cars, on billboards, and upon the wagons of the baking company.

"Slave Girl's Dream" Show With "Slave of Fashion"

Under the title of "The Slave Girl's Dream," a style show was presented at the Majestic, Austin, during the recent showing of "A Slave of Fashion," which was entirely "different" from any previous show of its kind.

Manager E. B. Roberts accomplished this with the cooperation of four local merchants, all of whom in addition to arranging window displays, ran a large cooperative display ad in the local newspaper, tying-up the style show with the picture at the Majestic.

Presentation opened with prison scene, done in futuristic style, with woman elaborately gowned wielding a whip over a ragged slave girl, who with wrists chained to floor, did a short dance in a spot. This unique opening was followed by full stage lighting, revealing several shop windows displaying gowns, millinery, jewelry, shoes and the like. In one window manikins posed as wax models, coming to life when orchestra started playing. Three girls at a time paraded before the audience showing off their finery, while others were seen inside shops trying on hats, shoes, and jewelry. While models changed gowns, popular singer entertained with group of songs, girls in pajamas closing show with jazz dance.

The models, university sorority girls, greatly enhanced the presentation's drawing power.

Horseshoe Matinee Strong "Lucky Horseshoe" Ad

One place where horseshoes brought good luck, was at Hagerstown, Md., where the Academy theatre played "The Lucky Horseshoe" recently. One of the stunts employed by the management and the Fox exploitation department, was a Horseshoe matinee to which any child who brought a horseshoe, was admitted free, provided they were accompanied by an adult. The adult, of course, paid admission.

So great was the amount of shoes collected that they were made into a huge pile in the lobby and appropriately placarded.

The America theatre, Colorado Springs, dressed its lobby attractively for the recent engagement of "Introduce Me" (Assoc. Exhibs.), as shown in the above photo. Poster paper was utilized both for mounted cut-outs and special lobby cards.

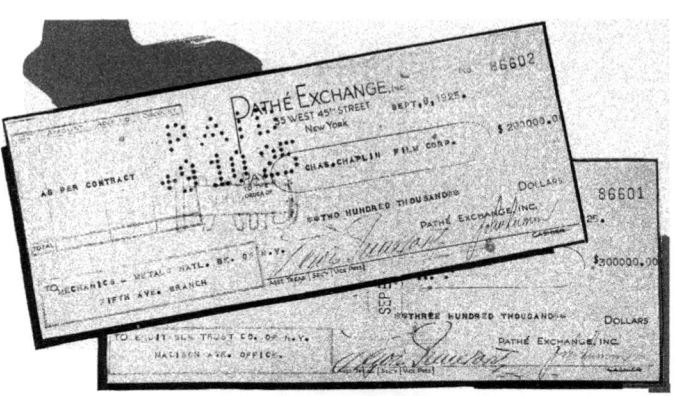

the screen the

made under his

ture

Four triumphant successes, "A Dog's Life," "Shoulder Arms," "A Day's Pleasure" and "Sunnyside," which include some of the greatest pictures this amazing screen personality has ever made!

Never before have pictures for re-presentation brought such a price. Only Chaplin productions could have done it.

These Chaplin pictures are always first runs. As box office attractions *today* they are in a class by themselves.

The first, "A Dog's Life," will be released Nov. 22.

When, a number of years ago, First National made a million dollar contract with Charlie Chaplin for eight two-reel pictures, the price was considered very high.

Since that time it has been amply demonstrated that the price, far from being excessive, made that contract one of the very best buys any distributor has ever made.

Every one of those pictures was good. Among them are some of the outstanding successes of the business.

Chaplin's screen career is absolutely unique. His pictures have undoubtedly played over 500,000 bookings, yet who ever heard of a booking that wasn't a success?

All of his pictures have made money for everyone. There is probably not one exhibitor in the many thousands all over the world but what has money he wouldn't have if he hadn't played Chaplin.

PATHE HAS JUST PAID HALF A MILLION DOLLARS FOR THE PRIVILEGE OF BRINGING BACK TO THE SCREEN THE FIRST FOUR CHARLIE CHAPLIN PICTURES MADE UNDER HIS FAMOUS MILLION DOLLAR CONTRACT WITH FIRST NATIONAL FOR EIGHT PICTURES

AND—

THE PRICE PAID IS THE SAME PRICE THAT WAS PAID FOR THEM ON ORIGINAL ISSUE.

"A Dog's Life" will be released on Nov. 22nd. "Shoulder Arms," "A Day's Pleasure" and "Sunnyside" will follow.

In all honesty I do not know where so much box-office value can be secured, dollar for dollar and foot for foot.

If there is any box-office certainty in any product, it is in these pictures. Like diamonds their value has grown with time. They are PROVEN product, the best that can be bought.

To be able to offer pictures so certain to make money for exhibitors is a privilege indeed.

We are confident that exhibitors will be as eager to welcome them as we were to get them.

ELMER PEARSON,
Vice-President and General Manager,
PATHE EXCHANGE, INC.

With First Run Theatres

NEW YORK CITY

Rialto Theatre—
Film Numbers—Thank You (Fox) Ko-Ko Nuts (Red Seal), Rialto Magazine (Selected).
Musical Program — "Toyland" (Overture by special orchestra).

Cameo Theatre—
Film Numbers — Shore Leave (First National), Pathe News, Aesop's Fables (Pathe), In the Spider's Grip (Educational), The Story Teller (Educational).
Musical Program—Chopiniana" (Overture), Organ solo.

Capitol Theatre—
Film Numbers — Exchange of Wives" (Metro-Goldwyn-Mayer), Tomorrow's Promise (Scenic), Capitol Magazine (Selected), Mixing in Mexico (S. R.).
Musical Program—"Les Preludes" (Overture), Special vocal solo, "At Dawning," "Erica Waltz," "Saxorella," "Saxophobia" (Saxophone solos), "Tres Delicat" (Dance number), Dance of the Elves (Soloist and ballet).

Mark Strand Theatre—
Film Numbers—The Lost World (First National), Mark Strand Topical Review (Selected).
Musical Program—Prelude (Orchestra), Prologue to "The Lost World" Organ solo.

Rivoli Theatre—
Film Numbers—A Regular Fellow (Paramount), Mozart-Haydn (S. R.), As You Like It (Pathe), Rivoli Pictorial (Selected).
Musical Program — "Serenade" (Overture), Riesenfeld's Classical Jazz (Specialty), Charleston Everywhere (Special dancing act), "The Mignight Waltz" (Organ solo).

Colony Theatre—
Film Numbers — The Freshman (Pathe), continued.

BROOKLYN

Mark Strand Theatre—
Film Numbers—Don Q, Son of Zorro (United Artists), Mark Strand Topical Review (selected).

Hand drawn newspaper ad on "The Goose Woman" (Universal) at the Rialto theatre in Washington, D. C.

Musical Program—Orchestral prelude by the Famed Mark Strand Orchestra; atmospheric prologue to "Don Q," introducing "La Paloma," (trio selection); "Pearl of Iberia" (ballet number); and "Iolita" (baritone solo).

LOS ANGELES

Criterion Theatre—
Film Numbers—The Talker (First National), Robinson Crusoe (Novelty), Fox News.
Musical Program—O r c h e s t r a selections.

Forum Theatre—
Film Numbers—The Coming of Amos (Prod. Dist. Corp.), Oh, Bridget (Educational), International News.
Musical Program—Organ selections.

Millstreet Theatre—
Film Numbers—Headlines (Asso. Exhib.), The Pace Makers (F. B. O.), Aesop's Fables (Pathe), International News.
Musical Program—Vaudeville.

Loew's State Theatre—
Film Numbers — The Midshipman (Metro-Goldwyn-Mayer), Felix the Cat (Educational), Loew's State Pictorial News and Events.
Musical Program—On The Road to Mandalay" (Overture), Middies in Mandalay (Fanchon and Marco Idea).

Metropolitan Theatre—
Film Numbers—The Man Who Found Himself (Paramount), Aesop's Fables (Pathe), Pathe News.
Musical Program—Orchestra.

Pantages Theatre—
Film Numbers—Kentucky Pride (Fox), Pathe News.
Musical Program—Vaudeville.

Million Dollar Theatre—
Film Numbers—The Freshman (Pathe), continued.
Musical Program — " On the Campus" (Overture).

Rialto Theatre—
Film Numbers—Sally of the Sawdust (United Artists), continued.
Musical Program—O r c h e s t r a (prologue to feature).

BOSTON

Beacon and Modern Theatres—
Film Numbers—Not So Long Ago (Paramount), Coming of Amos (Producers Distributing Corp.), Comedy (Educational), News (International).
Musical Program—Overture.

Fenway Theatre—
Film Numbers—Not So Long Ago (Paramount), The Coming of Amos (Producers Distributing Corp.), Comedy (Educational), News (Pathe).
Musical Program—Overture, Lloyd G. Del Castillo at the Wurlitzer.

Gordon's Washington Street Olympia Theatre—
Film Numbers—What Fools Men (First National), Dutch (Pathe), Comedy (Educational), Additional film at morning show. The Female (Paramount).

"His Majesty Bunker Bean" (Warner Bros.) was advertised in this manner at the Circle, Cleveland.

Musical Program—Overture. Five acts vaudeville.

New Boston Theatre—
F i l m N u m b e r s — California Straight Ahead (Universal), Comedy (Pathe), Topics of the Day (Pathe), News (Pathe).
Musical Program—Overture by 14-piece orchestra. Five acts vaudeville.

State Theatre—
Film Numbers—The Tower of Lies (Metro-Goldwyn-Mayer), Comedy (Pathe), News (Pathe), Topics of the Day (Pathe), Fables (Pathe).
Musical Program—Overture, orchestra and organ.
Special—Fur Fashion Revue.

PHILADELPHIA

Stanley Theatre—
Film Numbers—The Man Who Found Himself (Paramount), News Weekly, Better Movies (Pathe).
Musical Program—"Faust" (Overture), Paul Zim and his Band (Specialty), Piatov and Natalie (Dance), Organ selections.

Stanton Theatre—
Film Numbers—The Gold Rush (United Artists).

Karlton Theatre—
Film Numbers—Hell's Highroad (Prod. Dist. Corp.).

Arcadia Theatre—
Film Numbers—Winds of Chance (First National).

Palace Theatre—
Film Numbers — Pretty Ladies (Metro-Goldwyn-Mayer).

Victoria Theatre—
Film Numbers—The White Desert (Metro-Goldwyn-Mayer).

Capitol Theatre—
Film Numbers—The Goose Woman (Fox).

Fox Theatre—
Film Numbers—The Iron Horse (Fox), continued.

ROCHESTER

Eastman Theatre—
Film Numbers—Graustark (First National), Eastman Theatre Current Events (Selected), My Old Carolina (Scenic), Butter Fingers (Comedy).
Musical Program — "The Bat" (Overture), "Three Nell Gwyn

Dances" (Organ solos), "Save Your Sorrow" (Soprano solo), Forest Spell from "Siegfried" Hunting Chorus from "Der Freischutz" "The Night" (Horn Quartette specialty).

CLEVELAND

Stillman Theatre—
Film Numbers — The Gold Rush (United Artists), International News (Universal).
Musical Program—"Forgotten Roses" (Overture specialty).

Allen Theatre—
Film Numbers—Never Weaken (Pathe), Pathe Review, Topics of the Day (Pathe), Pathe News.
Musical Program—"Capriccio Espagnole" (Overture), "Days of Hearts and Flowers," "Worrying Blues," "Brown Eyes Why Are You Blue?" (Jazz).

State Theatre—
Film Numbers — The Live Wire (First National), Buster Be Good (Universal), Pathe Review, Fun from the Press (Prod. Dist. Corp.), Century of the Cycles.
Musical Program — Organ Overture, Vaudeville.

Park Theatre—
Film Numbers—The Golden Princess (Paramount), Hurry Doctor (Pathe), Felix Finishes First (S. R.), Topics of the Day (Pathe), Kinograms (Educational).
Musical Program—Classical Jazz Review.

Reade's Hippodrome—
Film Numbers — The Fighting Heart (Fox), Pathe Comedy, Pathe News.
Musical Program—Popular Classical Arias (Overture), Vaudeville.

Keith's East 105th St. Theatre—
Film Numbers — The Fighting Heart (Fox), Aesop's Fables (Pathe), The Caretaker's Daughter (Pathe), Pathe News.
Musical Program—March Militaire (Overture), Vaudeville.

Circle Theatre—
Film Numbers—The Man on the Box (Warner Bros.), Aesop's Fables (Pathe), Pathe Comedy, Pathe News.
Musical Program — Selections from "Sari" (Overture), "Gypsy Airs" (violin solo by Jean Nestoresco, director) Excerpts from "Faust," "Normandy," "Simple Simon," "Whoop 'Em Up" (special orchestra).

OHIO

Paramount Week

THOMAS MEIGHAN

in

"THE MAN WHO FOUND HIMSELF"

WITH VIRGINIA VALLI

THE Good Luck Star he is living, a reminding drama of the silent world behind prison walls and a star who's fight to "come back." Especially written for Tom by Booth Tarkington. Annual scenes of ding-ding prison.

Wonderful cast includes Frank and Ralph Morgan, Charles Barrendam, Julia Hoyt, Virnie Moore and Norman Trevor.

PATHE CURRENT EVENTS

CARTER DE HAVEN

in a comedy

"HOT SELLERS"

The Ohio theatre's ad in Indianapolis for "The Man Who Found Himself" (Paramount).

SALT LAKE CITY

American Theatre—
Film Numbers—The Fool (Fox), Cartoon (F. B. O.), International News.
Kinema Theatre—
Film Numbers—Steele of the Royal Mounted (Vitagraph), She Loved Him But (Universal), Pathe Review.
Pantages Theatre—
Film Numbers—Parisian Nights (F. B. O.).
Paramount-Empress Theatre—
Film Numbers — The Freshman (Pathe), The Movies (Educational), Pathe News.
Victory Theatre—
Film Numbers—The Midshipman (Metro-Goldwyn-Mayer), Pathe News.

DES MOINES

Capitol Theatre—
Film Numbers—Never the Twain Shall Meet (Metro-Goldwyn-Mayer), International News, Be Careful (Educational).
Musical Program — "Syncopated Fantasy" (dance numbers by the Desleys Sisters Review).
Des Moines Theatre—
Film Numbers—The Iron Horse

(Fox), International News.
Musical Program—Prolog presenting Indians in atmospheric sketch.
Strand Theatre—
Film Numbers—Zander the Great (Metro-Goldwyn-Mayer), International News.
Rialto Theatre—
Film Numbers—Rugged Waters (Famous Players).

ST. PAUL

Astor Theatre—
Film Numbers—The Trouble With Wives (Paramount), Be Careful (Comedy), News.
Musical Program—Leland Mc-

AT LAST!
CIRCLE
"The LOST WORLD"

*It is Truly the Marvel of the Screen
A Picture You Will Never Forget*

NO GUN PATHONS. Picture the trail your thrill be shot after features to wit that thing is stolen from

TRY THE MATINEES
NO ADVANCE IN PRICES

Unusually striking art as on "The Lost World" (First Nat'l) at the the Circle theatre, Indianapolis

Ewen (Organist), Smiling Lew Epstein and his Musical Gang in "Bowery Night Life."
Capitol Theatre—
Film Numbers — The Knockout (First National), Stage Fright (Comedy), Capitol Digest (Selected).
Musical Program — Capitol Symphony Orchestra playing "March of the Toys", Old Time Picture Show (Novelty), The Vanity Dolls in a song and dance.
Garrick Theatre—
Film Numbers—Winds of Chance (First National), Comedy (Selected), News Reel.
Musical Program—Garrick orchestra, Organ Novelty.
Princess Theatre—
Film Numbers—Wild Horse Mesa (Paramount), Love and Lions (Comedy), Kinograms.
Musical Program—Organ Specialty.
Strand Theatre—
Film Numbers—The Wheel (Fox),

Who's Which (Comedy), Kinograms.
Musical Program — Organ Overture.
Tower Theatre—
Film Numbers—The Mystic (Metro-Goldwyn-Mayer), Comedy (Pathe), Pathe News.
Musical Program—Symphony Orchestras, Organ Overture.

INDIANAPOLIS

Circle Theatre—
Film Numbers—Don Q (United Artists), News Reel Weekly (Universal).
Musical Program — Overture, "Carmen," by the Circle concert orchestra.
Apollo Theatre—
Film Numbers—The Freshman (Pathe), News Reel Weekly (Fox).
Musical Program — Emil Seidel orchestra, Ralph E. Duncan, soloist; Earl Gordon, organist.
Colonial Theatre—
Film Numbers—The Iron Horse (Fox), Aesop Fable (Pathe), News Reel Weekly (Universal).
Musical Program—American Harmonists.

CINCINNATI

Capitol Theatre—
Film Numbers—Graustark (First National), The Cloud Hopper (Educational), Capitol News (Selected).
Musical Program—Orchestra.

Stanley

MARY PICKFORD

Supreme in "OUR GANG" comedy

LITTLE ANNIE ROONEY

"The World's Sweetheart"

"THIS IS MY BEST PICTURE"
—MARY PICKFORD

ADDED FEATURE—SOMEWHAT DIFFERENT

"ANNIE ROONEY" PROLOGUE

ENACTED BY CAREFULLY-SELECTED CAST
WITH SPECIAL AND APPROPRIATE MUSIC

Presentation by Stanley Prolog unit staff

"Annie" Overture   Interpreted by
by Victor Herbert   Stanley Symphonical orchestra

The Stanley theatre's ad in Philadelphia for "Little Annie Rooney" (United Artists).

Walnut Theatre—
Film Numbers—The Freshman (Pathe), continued.
Strand Theatre—
Film Numbers — Pretty Ladies (Metro-Goldwyn-Mayer), Don't Pinch (Educational), Pathe News.
Musical Program—Orchestra.
Gifts Theatre—
Film Numbers—The Wizard of Oz (Chadwick), Uncle Tom's Gal (Universal), Kinorams.

Family Theatre—
Film Numbers—What Fools Men (First National), Felix Goes West (Educational), Fox News.

SAN FRANCISCO

Imperial Theatre—
Film Numbers — The Freshman (Pathe), Outings for All (Pathe), Fox News.
Musical Program — "Little Symphony" (Special college selections.)
California Theatre—
Film Numbers—Hell's Highroad (Prod. Dist. Corp.), The Smoke Eater (S. R.), Pathe Review and International News.
Musical Program—"Madame Butterfly" (Overture), "Hawaiian Serenade" (Violin Solo), "Serenade" (Violin solo and orchestra).
Loew's Warfield Theatre—
Film Numbers—The Dark Angel (First National), Don't Pinch (Educational), International News.
Musical Program—"Ideas Unique" (Fanchon and Marco idea with singing and dancing).
Granada Theatre—
Film Numbers—Seven Days (Prod. Dist. Corp.), The Story Teller (Educational), Pathe Weekly.
Musical Program — "Exclusive Drapery Style Review" (with singing and dancing).
Cameo Theatre—
Film Numbers — Spook Ranch (Universal), The Honeymoon Limited (Fox), International News.
Musical Program—"Kings of Harmony Trio" (Special songs), "Radio Songs" (Soloist).
Union Square Theatre—
Film Numbers — Back to Life (Asso. Exhib.), Battling Bunyan (Asso. Exhib.), Nobody Works but Father (Fox), Fox News.
Musical Program—Five vaudeville acts.
St. Francis Theatre—
Film Numbers—The Vanishing American (Paramount), Sportlight (Pathe), Felix the Cat (S. R.), Kinegrams.
Musical Program — "Seminole" (Overture).

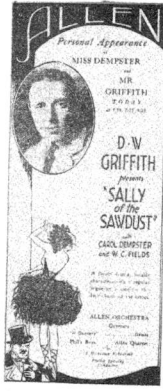

Two-column ad on "*Sally of the Sawdust*" (*United Artists*) at the Allen Theatre, Cleveland.

DETROIT

Madison Theatre—
Film Numbers—Never the Twain Shall Meet (M-G-M), Detroit News and Pathe News.
Musical Program — Orchestra accompaniment and organ recessional.

Adams Theatre—
Film Numbers—The Lost World (First National), Kinograms and Detroit News Weekly.

Capitol Theatre—
Film Numbers—The Trouble with Wives (Paramount), Detroit News and Pathe reel; stage presentation, Misses Schuilling and Thrasher and Messrs. Siebert and Warren in operatic bits; orchestra accompaniment.

Broadway Strand Theatre—
Film Numbers—Hell's Highroad (Prod. Dist. Corp.), International News reel; comedy.

Fox Washington Theatre—
Film Numbers—The Wheel (Fox), Fox News Weekly; Comedy.

NEWARK

Capitol Theatre—
Film Numbers—Don Q, Son of Zorro (United Artists), Pictorial (Pathe).

Mosque Theatre—
Film Numbers—Graustark (First National), Comedy (Educational), News (International).
Musical Program—"Il Guarany" (Overture), selection from "Prince of Pilsen" with thirty voices (tenor), "Swiss Military" (soloist and ballet), "Dance of Marionettes" (dance duet).

Branford Theatre—
Film Numbers—The Pony Express (Paramount), Pathe News.

Musical Program — Hemstreet singers and Ritz Male Quartette render in prologue, "Medley of Old Songs," "To a Wild Rose," "Joe Bowers," "Sylvia," "Serenade," "Maryland, My Maryland," "Battle Cry of Freedom," B. A. Rolfe, trumpeter, presented in conjunction with "1849" (Overture).

Rialto Theatre—
Film Numbers—Beggar on Horseback (Paramount), Just a Woman (First National), News (Kinograms).
Musical Program—Frank Dailey's Meadowbrook Orchestra in jazz numbers.

Three-column announcement of "*As No Man Has Loved*" (*Fox*) at the Coliseum theatre, Seattle.

HOUSTON

Queen Theatre—
Film Numbers—The Man Who Found Himself (Paramount), Comedy (Educational), News (Pathe).
Musical Program — "Poet and Pleasant" (overture), organ numbers.

Isis Theatre—
Film Numbers — The Knockout (First National), Comedy, (Pathe), News (Universal).
Musical Program—Melodies of New York (Overture), and organ numbers.

Rialto Theatre—
Film Numbers—The Unchastened Woman (Chadwick), Comedy (Educational), News (Fox).
Musical Program—Organ numbers and selections on the piano.

Majestic Theatre—
Film Numbers—Lightnin' (Fox), Aesop's Fables (Pathe), News (Pathe).
Musical Program—Echoes from "Ukulele Lady" (overture), and organ numbers. Vaudeville.

Liberty Theatre—
Film Numbers—If Marriage Fails (F. B. O.), Sunshine Comedy (Fox), Review (Pathe).
Musical Program — Organ and piano numbers.

Capitol Theatre—
Film Numbers — The Midshipman (Metro-Goldwyn), Our Gang Comedy (Pathe), Kinograms (Educational).
Musical Program—Popular selection by orchestra. Organ and piano numbers.

SEATTLE

Blue Mouse Theatre—
Film Numbers — Below the Line (Warner Bros.), Wild Waves (Comedy), Aesop's Fables (Pathe), International News.
Musical Program—"Wonderland" (Overture), "Oh How I Miss You Tonight" (Novelty selection).

Coliseum Theatre—
Film Numbers—The Wheel (Fox), Comedy, Kinograms and Pathe News.
Musical Program — "Raymond" (Overture), Boy saxophone soloist.

Columbia Theatre—
Film Numbers—Peacock Feathers (Universal), Little Red Riding Hood (Comedy), International News.
Musical Program—Selection from "The Chocolate Soldier" (Overture), "Song of India" (Orchestra specialty), Peacock Alley Dance and vocal prelude.

Opening ad on "*The Coming of Amos*" (*Producers Dist. Corp.*) at the Kings-Rivoli theatres, St. Louis.

Heilig Theatre—
Film Numbers—Tower of Lies (Metro-Goldwyn-Mayer), Pathe Review, Topics of the Day (Pathe), Aesop's Fables (Pathe), Pathe News.
Musical Program—Popular medley (Overture).

Liberty Theatre—
Film Numbers—Don Q, Son of Zorro (United Artists), continued.

Strand Theatre—
Film Numbers—The Man Who Found Himself (Paramount), Solid Ivory (Fox).

Musical Program — "Orpheus" (Overture), "Sad" (Orchestra).

Pantages Theatre—
Film Numbers—The Wrongdoers (Astor-S. R.).

ST. LOUIS

Missouri Theatre—
Film Numbers—The Trouble with Wives (Paramount), Moonlight and Noses (Pathe), Missouri Magazine (Selected).
Musical Program — "Selections from Rose Marie" (Symphony orchestra), "Andantino" (organ). On stage—Joe Cook and The Senator. Ossman & Shepp (banjo artists).

Loew's State Theatre—
Film Numbers—Black Cyclone (Pathe), Loew's State News and Views, Topics (Pathe).
Musical Program — Overture and popular numbers (Loew's State orchestra). On stage — Jack Denny and Band. Benny Davis (Popular song writer), Joanna (Mystery Girl), Arthur Kock (pianist).

Delmonte Theatre—
Film Numbers—The Police Patrol (Gotham Pro. S. R.), Revival of Gloria Swanson pictures. A new one each day. Delmonte news and views.
Musical Program—Orchestral overture and popular numbers. Vocal selections.

Grand -Central, West End Lyric and Capitol Theatres—
Film Numbers—Graustark (First National), Kinogram News and Views.
Musical Program—At Grand Central Conley-Silverman Band in "Chase Knights." At West End Lyric, Gene Rodemich and Gang in "The Schoolmaster." At Capitol, Joe Milsteen and Orchestra. Steve Cady (tenor).

William Goldman's Kings and Rivoli Theatres—
Film Numbers—Below the Line (Warner Brothers), William Goldman Magazine. The Caretaker's Daughter (Pathe).
Musical Program—Orchestral and vocal selections.

Three-column newspaper ad on "*Sun-Up*" (*Metro-Goldwyn*) at Loew's Aldine theatre, Pittsburgh.

MINNEAPOLIS

Aster Theatre—
Film Numbers— Capital Punishment (S. R.), Sweet Marie (Comedy), Fox News.
Musical Program — Organ Overture.

Garrick Theatre—
Film Numbers— The Tower of Lies (Metro-Goldwyn-Mayer), Baby Be Good (Educational), Garrick News.
Musical Program— Garrick Concert Orchestra, Organ, Emmett Long and his Golden Pheasant Orchestra.

Lyric Theatre—
Film Numbers — A Son of His Father (Paramount), Comedy (Selected), Pathe News.
Musical Program — Organ, White Brothers and Stendal (Vocal trio).

State Theatre—
Film Numbers — The Man Who Found Himself (Paramount), Life's Greatest Thrills (Universal), The First Hundred Years (Pathe), News Digest.
Musical Program—Wesley Barlow, soloist with State Concert Orchestra; Mary Songs, E. J. Dunstetter, organist; Alice Lilligren and Bennett Charles in Sunshine and Showers.

Strand Theatre—
Film Numbers— The Iron Horse (Fox), continued, Felix Trifles With Time (S. N.), Strand News.
Musical Program—Strand Concert Orchestra under Blaine Allen.

BUFFALO

Shea's Hippodrome—
Film Numbers— He's a Prince (Paramount), Beware (Educational), Current Events (from Fox News).
Musical Program—"Light Cavalry" (Orchestra), Fall Fashion Show staged in co-operation with the Wm. Hengerer Co.

Loew's State Theatre—
Film Numbers—The Trouble With Wives (Paramount), Educating Buster (Universal), Current Events (Pathe News).
Musical Program—Selections from "Suzanne" (orchestra).

Lafayette Square Theatre—
Film Numbers—The School for Wives (Vitagraph), Pathe Comedy, Current Events (Kinograms).
Musical Program—"Ukelele Lady"

Unusually distinctive and outstanding ad on "The Lucky Horseshoe" (Fox) at the Globe theatre in Kansas City.

Striking ad on "Sally of the Sawdust" (United Artists) by A. S. Rittenberg of the Fulton theatre, Jersey City.

(orchestra), Organ Solo. Five acts of vaudeville.

Olympic Theatre—
Film Numbers—Eve's Lover (Warner Brothers), Shattered Reputations (S. R.), Universal comedy. Current Events (International News).
Musical Program — Vocal selections by T. Jay Flannagan, radio artist. Organ solo.

Shea's North Park Theatre—
Film Numbers—Enticement (First National), Pathe comedy. Current Events (Fox and International News).
Musical Program — "Lady, Be Good" (Orchestra).

Palace Theatre—
Film Numbers—The Ranger of the Big Pines (Vitagraph), Universal comedy. Current Events (International News).
Musical Program—Medley of Popular Hits (organ).

KANSAS CITY

Newman Theatre—
Film Numbers—Wild, Wild Susan (Paramount). In the Movies (Educational), Newman Mirror of the World (Pathe, Kinograms and International News), Newman Current Events (Local Photography).
Musical Program—Syncopated Selections (Overture), Syncopated Fall Festival (Specialty), Janet Adler (Jazz Orchestra), Recessional (Organ Solos).

Liberty Theatre—
Film Numbers—Siege (Universal), Aesop's Fables (Pathe), On the Go (Fox), International News.

Globe — Lou Barton presents Tom Mix in "The Lucky Horseshoe"
DON'T MISS THIS!

Musical Program—"The Calif of Bagdad" (Overture), Recessional (Organ Solos).

Royal Theatre—
Film Numbers — The Freshman (Pathe), continued. Royal Screen Magazine (Pathe, Kinograms and International News), Royal Current Events (Local Photography).
Musical Program — "Collegiate Frolics" (Overture), Recessional (Organ Solos).

Mainstreet Theatre—
Film Numbers — Don Q. (United Artists), Pathe News and Educational Short Subjects.
Musical Program — Atmospheric Selections (Overture), Recessional (Organ Solos).

Pantages Theatre—
Film Numbers—If Marriage Fails (F. B. O.), Fox News and Fox Short Subjects.
Musical Program—Popular Selections (Overture), Recessional (Organ Solos).

MILWAUKEE

Alhambra Theatre—
Film Numbers — California Straight Ahead (Universal), International News, Milwaukee Chapter, "See America First" (Universal).
Musical Program—Medley of California Airs (Overture), Heinz Roembold's California Beach Revue (Stage Presentation).

Garden Theatre—
Film Numbers — Hell's Highroad (Prod. Dist. Corp.), Felix Cartoon (Educational), Topics of the Day (Pathe), Fox News.
Musical Program — Double Cross Word Puzzle (Organ Specialty).

Merrill Theatre—
Film Numbers—The Freshman (Pathe), Wild Beasts of Borneo (Educational), Kinograms.
Musical Program — Orchestra Overture.

Strand Theatre—
Film Numbers—The Trouble With Wives (Paramount), Felix Cartoon (Educational), Fair Warning (Educational), Prizma (S. R.), Kinograms.
Musical Program—Show Me the Way Home (Overture), Hello, People, Hello (Organ).

Wisconsin Theatre—
Film Numbers—A Slave of Fashion (Metro-Goldwyn-Mayer), The Movies (Educational), Twinkling Toes (Pathe), International News.
Musical Program—"Der Freischuetz" (Overture), "Traumerei" and "March Militaire" (On the Twin Organs), Terpsichorean Tid-bits (Lolo Girlie & Senia), "The Melvisto Phanto Revue" (Stage Presentation).

BALTIMORE

Century Theatre—
Film Numbers—The Man Who Found Himself (Paramount), Big Game Hunter (Fox), News Weekly (Fox).
Musical Program—"In the Clock Store" (Descriptive Fantasia

WHAT FOOLS MEN
LEWIS STONE
ALL THIS WEEK
PRINCESS

The Princess theatre in Hartford, Conn., used this four-columns ad recently on "What Fools Men" (First Nat'l).

Overture by Orchestra), "The Clown Revue" (Original Six Brown Brothers and Their Saxo Pals).

Garden Theatre—
Film Numbers—Gold and the Girl (Fox), Eighteen Carat (Universal Comedy), Life's Greatest Thrills (Universal International News), International News (Universal).
Musical Program—Five acts of vaudeville. Orchestra. Organ recessional.

Keith's Hippodrome—
Film Numbers—The Wild Bull's Lair (F. B. O.), News Weekly (Pathe), Aesop's Fable (Pathe), Uncle Tom's Gal (Universal).
Musical Program—Five acts of vaudeville. Orchestra, Organ recessional.

Metropolitan Theatre—
Film Numbers—Tracked in the Snow Country (Warner Brothers), Hungry Hounds (Pathe), News Weekly (Pathe), Oh Bridget (Educational), The Canyon of Champagnola (Pathe), Here Comes the Bride (Novelty).
Musical Program —, "Southern Rhapsody" (Overture) "Sometime" (Organ Selection), Orchestra.

New Theatre—
Film Numbers—The Ten Commandments (Paramount), News Weekly (Pathe).
Musical Program—Orchestra, Organ recessional.

Parkway Theatre—
Film Numbers—The Mystic (Metro-Goldwyn-Mayer), A Lucky Leap (Universal) Parkway Pictorial News (Educational Kinograms).
Musical Program—Popular Medley Introduction from opera "The Force of Destiny," "Indian Love Call" from "Rose Marie" and "At Dawning" (Overture). Organ recessional. Orchestra.

Rivoli Theatre—
Film Numbers—The Dark Angel (First National), Rivoli News (Pathe). Lucky Stars (Pathe Mack Sennett Comedy).
Musical Program—"Oberon" (Overture). On the Stage (Roy Smeck "Wizard of the Strings"), "Orpheus" and "Oh Boy What a Girl" (Organ Selections).

Exhibitors Box-Office Reports

Names of the theatre owners are omitted by agreement in accordance with the wishes of the average exhibitor and in the belief that reports published over the signature of the exhibitor reporting, is a dangerous practice.

Only reports received on specially prepared blanks furnished by us will be accepted for use in this department. Exhibitors who value this reporting service are urged to ask for these blanks.

Title of Picture	Population of Town	Location	Class of Patronage	Weather	Box Office Value	Checkup Percentage from other Reports
FAMOUS-PLAYERS						
Beggar on Horseback...	1800	Neb.	Small town	Clear	Fair	55
Coast of Folly, The...	772897	Mo.	1st run	Clear	Fair	67
	4450	Minn.	Mixed	Clear	Good	—
	506675	N. Y.	1st run	Clear	Good	—
Female, The...	1800	Neb.	Small town	Clear	Fair	63
Golden Princess, The...	506676	Cal.	1st run	Clear	Fair	70
He's A Prince...	796841	Ohio	1st run	Clear	Fair	70
In the Name of Love...	506676	Cal.	1st run	Clear	Fair	58
Lucky Devil, The...	15731	Iowa	General	Clear	Good	72
Man Who Found Himself	993678	Mich.	General	Clear	Good	63
Manicure Girl, The...	4450	Minn.	Mixed	Clear	Poor	54
Marry Me...	4450	Minn.	Mixed	Clear	Fair	51
	15731	Iowa	General	Clear	Fair	—
Night Life of New York..	1800	Neb.	Small town	Clear	Good	66
	15731	Iowa	General	Warm	Good	—
Not So Long Ago...	1800	Neb.	Small town	Clear	Poor	54
Paths to Paradise...	4450	Minn.	Mixed	Clear	Gro.5	68
Side Show of Life...	1800	Neb.	Small town	Clear	Fair	60
Son of His Father, A...	401247	Ohio	1st run	Clear	Fair	61
Street of Forgotten Men.	15731	Iowa	General	Clear	Good	65
	1800	Neb.	Small town	Clear	Big	—
Ten Commandments, The	4450	Minn.	Mixed	Clear	Big	87
Tomorrow's Love...	3000	Ga.	Mixed	Clear	Good	66
Top of the World...	1800	Neb.	Small town	Clear	Good	63
Wild Horse Mesa...	401247	Ohio	General	Clear	Fair	68
	4450	Minn.	Mixed	Clear	Good	—
	15731	Iowa	General	Clear	Good	—
Wild, Wild Susan...	1800	Neb.	Small town	Clear	Fair	61
F. B. O.						
Bloodhound, The...	15731	Iowa	General	Hot	Good	63
Lady Robinhood...	15731	Iowa	General	Clear	Good	70
Millionaire Cowboy, The	1621	Neb.	Rural	Clear	Fair	50
Parisian Nights...	314194	Ind.	General	Clear	Big	78
Smooth as Satin...	15731	Iowa	General	Hot	Good	70
White Fang...	15731	Iowa	General	Hot	Big	70
	1800	Neb.	Small town	Clear	Good	—
FIRST NATIONAL						
Desert Flower, The...	4450	Minn.	Mixed	Clear	Good	69
Fine Clothes...	733826	Md.	General	Warm	Good	89
Graustark...	324410	Ohio	1st run	Clear	Fair	78
Heart of a Siren...	3000	Ga.	Mixed	Clear	Fair	50
Her Sister from Paris...	15731	Iowa	General	Clear	Good	76
His Supreme Moment...	4450	Minn.	Mixed	Clear	Good	62
I Want My Man...	3000	Ga.	Mixed	Clear	Good	67
If I Marry Again...	4450	Minn.	Mixed	Clear	Fair	69
Knockout, The...	15731	Iowa	General	Clear	Good	60
Lost World, The...	15731	Iowa	General	Clear	Big	86
	350000	Wash.	General	Clear	Good	—
	401247	Ohio	General	Clear	Big	—
My Son...	4450	Minn.	Mixed	Clear	Fair	72
Necessary Evil...	3000	Ga.	Mixed	Clear	Good	58
Quo Vadis...	15731	Iowa	General	Warm	Good	78
	4450	Minn.	Mixed	Clear	Good	—
Sally of the Sawdust...	772897	Mo.	1st run	Clear	Fair	70
Sally...	1800	Neb.	Small town	Clear	Big	88
Scarlet West, The...	324410	Mo.	1st Run	St'rnyPoor		49
What Fools Men...	126468	Iowa	1st run	Clear	Good	72
Winds of Chance...	506675	Cal.	1st run	Clear	Big	82
FOX						
Arizona Romeo...	1021	Neb.	Rural	Clear	Fair	68
As No Man Has Loved...	350000	Wash.	General	Clear	Fair	63
	993678	Mich.	General	Clear	Good	—
Every Man's Wife...	350000	Wash.	General	Clear	Good	58
Fighting Heart, The...	350000	Wash.	General	Clear	Good	70
Fool of Vanity...	3000	Ga.	Mixed	Clear	Good	70
Fool, The...	506676	Cal.	1st run	Clear	Good	78
Great Diamond Mystery.	1021	Neb.	Rural	Clear	Fair	56
Havoc...	350000	Wash.	1st Run	Clear	Good	65
Lightnin'...	126468	Iowa	1st Run	Clear	Good	70
	733826	Md.	1st Run	Warm	Fair	—
Lucky Horseshoe...	350000	Wash.	General	Clear	Fair	43

Title of Picture	Population of Town	Location	Class of Patronage	Weather	Box Office Value	Checkup Percentage from other Reports
METRO-GOLDWYN-MAYER						
Beauty Prize, The...	1800	Neb.	Small town	Clear	Good	64
Cheaper to Marry...	1800	Neb.	Small town	Rain	Good	65
Chu Chin Chow...	1800	Neb.	Small town	Clear	Poor	54
Circle, The...	796841	Ohio	1st run	Clear	Fair	60
Daddy's Gone-a-Hunting	1800	Neb.	Small town	Clear	Good	61
Excuse Me...	1800	Neb.	Small town	Clear	Good	82
Greed...	1800	Neb.	Small town	Clear	Poor	54
Lady of the Night...	1800	Neb.	Small town	Clear	Fair	61
Never the Twain Shall Meet...	993678	Mich.	General	Clear	Big	70
Romola...	314194	Ind.	General	Clear	Big	78
Sun Up...	506675	N. Y.	1st run	Clear	Fair	55
Unholy Three, The...	324410	Mo.	1st run	St'rny	Good	72
Way of a Girl...	1800	Neb.	Small town	Clear	Fair	52
Wife of the Centaur...	1800	Neb.	Small town	Clear	Good	68
PATHE						
Black Cyclone, The...	506676	Cal.	General	Clear	Fair	76
Freshman, The...	401247	Ohio	1st Run	Clear	Big	92
	324410	Mo.	1st Run	St'rny	Big	—
	15731	Iowa	General	Clear	Big	—
	506675	N. Y.	1st Run	Clear	Big	—
	314194	Ind.	1st Run	Clear	Big	—
	126468	Iowa	1st Run	Clear	Big	—
STATE RIGHTS						
Breath of Scandal...	401247	Ohio	General	Clear	Fair	72
Capital Punishment...	15731	Iowa	General	Hot	Big	82
Crackerjack, The...	993678	Mich.	General	Clear	Big	—
Daring Youth...	1800	Neb.	Small town	Rain	Poor	45
Fighting the Flames...	733826	Md.	General	Warm	Good	43
Mansion of Aching Hearts	15731	Iowa	General	Clear	Big	70
Police Patrol, The...	324410	Mo.	General	St'rny	Fair	65
Price She Paid, The...	506675	N. Y.	General	Clear	Good	64
Speed...	15731	Iowa	General	Clear	Big	85
Super Speed...	15731	Iowa	General	Hot	Good	70
Trifiers, The...	15731	Iowa	General	Hot	Good	70
UNITED ARTISTS						
Don Q...	15731	Iowa	General	Clear	Big	94
Gold Rush, The...	772897	Mo.	1st Run	Clear	Big	91
	993678	Mich.	1st Run	Clear	Good	91
Sally of the Sawdust....	796841	Ohio	1st Run	Clear	Fair	70
UNIVERSAL						
California, Straight Ahead...	350000	Wash.	1st Run	Clear	Big	75
	324410	Mo.	1st Run	St'rny	Good	—
Goose Woman, The...	796841	Ohio	General	Clear	Fair	70
I'll Show You the Town...	15731	Iowa	General	Hot	Good	74
	733826	Md.	General	Hot	Good	—
	401247	Ohio	General	Clear	Fair	—
Raffles...	15731	Iowa	General	Clear	Fair	58
Spook Ranch, The...	733826	Md.	General	Hot	Good	55
Woman's Faith, A...	15731	Iowa	General	Hot	Big	53
VITAGRAPH						
School for Wives...	15731	Iowa	General	Rain	Good	56
Steele of Royal Mounted	1021	Neb.	Rural	Clear	Good	75
Unknown Lover, The...	15731	Iowa	General	Clear	Poor	55
Wildfire...	733826	Md.	General	Warm	Good	54
WARNER BROS.						
Dark Swan, The...	1800	Neb.	Small town	Clear	Poor	59
Her Marriage Vow...	15731	Iowa	General	Hot	Good	59
His Majesty Bunker Bean...	796841	Ohio	General	Clear	Fair	55
How Baxter Butted In...	506675	N. Y.	1st Run	Clear	Good	59
Kiss Me Again...	1621	Neb.	Rural	Clear	Good	67
Limited Mail, The...	733826	Md.	1st Run	Warm	Good	79
Wife Who Wasn't Wanted	350000	Wash.	1st Run	Clear	Good	55

CLASSIFIED AD SECTION

RATES: 10 cents a word for each insertion, in advance except Employment Wanted, on which rate is 5 cents.

CLASSIFIED SERVICE

A classified ad in MOTION PICTURE NEWS offers the full resources and circulation of the NEWS to the advertiser at a ridiculously low figure.

Whether you want to reach executives, branch managers, salesmen, or theatre managers, you can accomplish this quickly and economically through the NEWS Classified Columns.

Wanted

WANTED.—To rent or buy lease motion picture theatre. Anywhere. 400 seats up. Box A, Motion Picture News, 845 S. Wabash, Chicago.

THOROUGHLY experienced, practical, money making manager and booker (Gentile) open for engagement anywhere on two weeks notice. Chicago, Middle West or West Coast preferred. Box C, Motion Picture News, 845 S. Wabash, Chicago.

YOUNG MAN with initiative desires position as manager or assistant manager of motion picture house. Has had four years experience in Canada and the U. S., and is at present engaged in one of New York's leading houses. Box 410, Motion Picture News, New York City.

EXPERT OPERATOR and Electrician with 9 years' experience in big houses; married; wants to locate at once. Address, Operator, Box 282, Mason City, Iowa.

ORGANIST.—Experienced. References. Minimum, $60 six (6) days. Worth investigating. Now employed. Box 390, Motion Picture News, New York City.

PIANIST desires engagement for evenings to play alone in picture theatre within commuting distance from New York City. Box 400, Motion Picture News, New York City.

FEATURE THEATRE ORGANIST, married man, wishes to locate in first class theatre having modern organ. Have fine library and cue pictures intelligently. Box 380, Motion Picture News, New York City.

THEATRE IN TOWN OF 4,000 or better, anywhere in North Central states, Northern Indiana preferred. Can either give satisfactory security on lease or buy outright. Would consider buying interest in bona-fide proposition where owner wishes to retire. All replies absolutely confidential. Address Box 360, Motion Picture News, New York City.

For Sale

FOR SALE, Wyoming Theatre, Mullens, W. Va. $60,-000.00 cash. Now earning about $1,000.00 per month net. Owner retiring from business.

FOR SALE — Pathe Camera; good as new; with new Bell & Howell tripod; complete, $450; also new 200-foot Universal Camera with 7 magazines, $250, or both outfits for $600. H. Berger, 197 Hamilton St., Dorchester, Mass.

FOR SALE.—Theatre Equipment of all descriptions; Immediate shipment of used chairs, any quantity. Will also buy used chairs and equipment. Theatre Seating Company, 845 South State Street, Chicago, Illinois.

FOR SALE.—Hope Jones Wurlitzer type 135, excellent condition. Will trade for cheaper instrument with cash difference. A bargain if you are looking for a fine organ. H. E. Skinner, Box 882, Ogden, Utah.

IS THERE ROOM in your organization for a young man with initiative, energy, and proven ability? Ten years experience in the publishing business devoted to selling, consolidation, and publicity. Last five years as editor of a well-known motion picture house organ covering N. Y. State and Pennsylvania. Would like to associate myself with a sound organization either in New York or New England, where intelligent application and hard work will be recognized. Box 340, Motion Picture News, New York City.

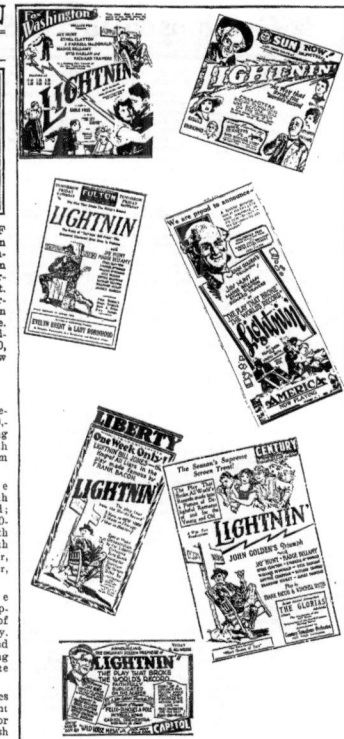

Ranging from stock cuts and type to the entirely hand-drawn display, the seven newspaper ads above give a fair idea of the way in which theatre managers throughout the country are announcing "Lightnin'" (Fox). The sources of these ads are as follows: A. S. Rittenberg, Fulton theatre, Jersey City; Liberty theatre, Kansas City; Fox-Washington theatre, Detroit; Sun theatre, Omaha; America theatre, Denver; Capitol theatre, Cincinnati, and the Century theatre, Baltimore.

Opinions on Current Short Subjects

"Good Morning, Madam"
(Pathe—Two Reels)

(Reviewed by Thomas C. Kennedy)

THIS looks like another Ralph Graves hit. There are sure-fire gags and a generally pleasant and entertaining air about the entire work. It concerns the experiences of a book agent who reaches the starvation point and goes further down the economic scale when he meets a young charmer who invites him to invite her and some girl friends to lunch. But he gets a break finally and wins the girl, the daughter of the man who "established the banks of the Wabash," we are told in one of A. H. Geibler's excellent group of titles.

The comedy is clean and clear-cut in its methods. It has a rich supply of effective gags, a sparkling quality to its presentation and excellent acting. Little more can be asked for in two reel comedies by either exhibitors or public than is offered in generous measure by "Good Morning, Madam." Lloyd Bacon's direction seems especially good, while Graves' acting and that of Marvin Lobach and Thelma Parr leaves nothing to be desired. The subtitles are by Mr. Geibler, who is always droll and never dull, but who seems to have been in rare form when he did the captions for this film.

The Cast

Book Agent	Ralph Graves
His Pal	Marvin Lobach
The Girl	Thelma Parr
Her Father	Wm. McCall

Story—Ralph and his pal, book agents who have not made a sale in weeks, are down to their last half dollar when they meet a society beauty who is collecting for a charity. She gets the lone coin as a donation and then invites herself to be their guest at lunch. But she soon discovers that her boy friend is broke and quietly pays the check. It is a case of love at first sight and the marriage takes place at the second meeting, when Ralph prevents her marriage to another chap endorsed by her father.

Summary.—A very entertaining two-reeler, offering clean, wholesome comedy and plenty of the gags that produce laughter. The picture has been finely directed and acted. An excellent choice for any exhibitor.

"Cuckoo Love"
(Pathe—Two Reels)

(Reviewed by Thomas C. Kennedy)

BATHING beauties are becoming more numerous on the Hal Roach lot. To this fact there is convincing evidence in "Cuckoo Love," a two-reeler featuring Glenn Tryon as a modern Romeo who finds that the "course of true love" is not the smoothest highway a man can travel. But the beauties! There are several of them shown in their one-piece suits at sprightly games of polo and swimming and diving contests. They do dress up the scenery a lot and we should be glad that they have been brought into the play, though their influence seems to go too deep into the fibre of the production.

From swimming tanks and polo fields, the action goes into a routine of gags about people sitting on pin cushions and cacti and bees—from which it emerges and forthwith plunges into some boudoir bantering in which a jealous husband becomes the dramatic "menace" to characters straying therein by error.

"Cuckoo Love" has its amusing moments and it will furnish satisfactory entertainment to the bulk of its audiences. Rather because of its treatment than any sophistication of idea in the story do we suggest that

the picture is better suited for the adult patronage than that of the youngsters.

Glenn Tryon, the featured player, has the support of an imposing cast, in which Katherine Grant, an actress who is making the most amazing progress in her work before the camera, Blanche Mehaffey, Chester Conklin, Jimmie Finlayson and Jane Sherman appear to decided advantage.

The production is a very dressy one and Fred Guiol's direction is better by far than the s o y material with which he had to work.t r

The Cast

Glen Tryon, Blanche Mehaffey, Katherine Grant, Chester Conklin, Jimmie Finlayson, Jane Sherman.

The Story—A letter from a former flame, enclosing a photograph, starts trouble between the engaged couple. The girl's father returns from Palm Beach with a bride and she proves to be the former flame of her sweetheart. The father is jealous and brings his gun into play when he sees the bride talking with his prospective son-in-law in the garden. A rival for the daughter's hand sees his opportunity and by a ruse sends the hero into the boudoire of the bride, a situation from which the hero extricates himself only after many exciting adventures.

Summary—Very elaborately produced and finely acted comedy is hampered by sketchy story and lack of anything clever in the way of gags. It is almost straight slapstick from start to finish.

"The Road From Latigo"
(Universal-Mustang—Two Reels)

(Reviewed by Chester J. Smith)

THERE is always that sameness about these two-reel Westerns and this one is not out of the ordinary, though it does have a twist or two that lifts it a little above the average. Edmund Cobb is the hero who accomplishes the usual rescues and overpowers the intriguing villains, whether there be one or a dozen.

He is the victim of a mistaken impression on the part of the girl whom he loves and she all but spills the beans in turning him over to the sheriff and posse as the real robber of the stage coach, but he thwarts even her and her information brings the true culprits to justice.

The Cast

Jeffy Donovan	Edmund Cobb

The Story. Jerry Donovan, keeper of the Half Way House thwarts the efforts of Black Dan's men to hold up the stage and assumes the delivery of the gold when the driver is wounded. With his horse and a donkey he arrives at the cabin of Janet Leigh, who has just been advised by the Sheriff there is a reward of $5000 for information regarding the whereabouts of Jerry. She discovers the gold bag and takes him for the stage robber. She substitutes bricks for the gold and Jerry goes on his way. She phones the Sheriff as Jerry is overtaken by the bandits. He passes the bag to them and the stones are revealed. The girl rides up demanding the reward, thinking the bandits are the sheriff's posse. She reveals to them where the gold is really hidden and they dash off to get it. The Sheriff's posse then overtakes and captures the gang, when it is revealed to the girl that the $5,000 reward for Jerry is offered by his wealthy father, who wants him to return home.

Summary. A Western of the usual type, whose story is somewhat above the average. There are some good riding shots and the picture is enlivened by some good fighting and fast action. It is well acted by a competent cast.

"Maid in Morocco"
(Educational—Two Reels)

(Reviewed by Chester J. Smith)

LUPINO LANE is the bright particular star of this good comedy, which shows Lane off to the same good advantage as he was seen in musical comedy and on the vaudeville stage. He is a versatile comedian and his pictures in this series, if this one is an indication, are bound to add to his popularity.

There seems to be nothing in the way of gymnastics and tumbling that is too hard of accomplishment for Lane and in this good story he is given every chance to show his full line of attractive wares, including his dancing specialty, when as a punch hitter for his young bride he struts his terpsichorean stuff in the harem to the delight of the Caliph.

If there is a fault to the picture it is that there is too much of the run-around stuff, but at that, there is hardly a foot of it when the comedian is not displaying some astonishing ability in one direction or another.

The Cast

The Groom	Lupino Lane
The Bride	Helen Foster
The Caliph	Wallace Lupino
The Favorite	Violet Blythe

A Jack White production, directed by Charles Lamont and photographed by Robert Doran.

The Story—The young bride and groom go to Morocco for their honeymoon and visit the harem of the Caliph, who becomes enamoured of the bride and would make her the newest member of his harem. She is made a prisoner as the groom is detected in the room with the Queen of the Harem. The enraged Caliph orders him tossed to the lions. After innumerable difficulties he makes his escape and takes his bride with him.

Summary—An exceptionally good comedy, well directed and well acted, with Lupino Lane displaying the full scope of his talents. There are a number of humorous situations with just enough slapstick to add to the two reels of fun. It is a comedy that should be appreciated in almost any type house.

"Solid Ivory"
(Pathe—One Reel)

EARL MOHAN and Billy Engle are here featured as the central characters of a slapstick contribution from the Hal Roach studios. The plot concerns the further adventures of a fighter and his manager introduced to picture audiences in previous films from the Roach plant. The reel reaches its climax in one of those comic boxing matches which have been so widely exploited on the screen that there is no telling at this date whether they are actually funny or just repetitions of gags that are not only stale but stupid as well. Of this work one can feel safe in reporting that there is action and speed and there is every apparent effort on the part of players and director to stage the action in as amusing a fashion as is possible.—T. C. KENNEDY.

"Scrambled Eggs"
(Educational—One Reel)

LITTLE out of the ordinary is on display in this one-reeler, which is of the usual slapstick type. It is the tale of a pair of correspondence marriages in which the couples on arrival of the train, become mixed up, with each getting the wrong partner. Jealousy develop as the action continues and complications come thick and fast. Phil Dunham, George Davis, Babe Landon and Helen Marlowe make up the misguided couples. Their antics are rather funny in spots and the picture may be good for a few laughs in the neighborhood houses.—CHESTER J. SMITH.

Short Subjects and Serials

Kinograms Inaugurates Prize Contest

IN order to stimulate interest its staff men and free lance cameramen in the news field, Kinograms, the newsreel released by Educational, has inaugurated a monthly prize offer of $100 for exclusive news pictures. The prize is divided into two parts. For the best exclusive picture sent in for the current month a $50 bonus is paid, and another $50 goes to the cameraman sending in the greatest number of exclusive pictures.

The first prize will be awarded October 31st and the succeeding prizes at the end of each month. The awarding of the prizes will be in the hands of an editorial committee consisting of Forrest Izard, managing editor and J. V. Fitz Gerald and H. E. Hancock, associate editors. The only restrictions placed on the cameramen are that the pictures must be based on news and that they must be original subjects obtained without any suggestion from the Kinograms editorial force.

Bernard Garcey Signed for Al Joy Comedies

Al Joy, head of Ricordo Films, producer of two-reel comedies in which he plays the leading roles, has engaged Bernard Garcey, who created the role of "Isaac Cohen" in "Abie's Irish Rose," to play prominent parts in his support.

Garcey will continue his stage engagements while working in the pictures. He is now rehearsing with an Arthur Hammerstein production soon to be presented in New York.

"Madame Sans Jane" is the title of Glenn Tryon's newest two-reel comedy produced for Pathe release by Hal Roach. These scenes are taken from the production.

Pathe Discusses 18th Program

Graves and Tryon Featured Comedians; Schedule Includes New "Sportlight" Reel

THE program which Pathe has announced for the week of October 18th covers a wide range of short subjects, the list including comedies, cartoons, Pathe Review, a serial episode and "Nazareth," a Biblical film, in addition to the regular issue of Pathe News and the "Topics of the Day" reel.

Ralph Graves and Glenn Tryon are the featured comedians appearing on this schedule. Graves will be seen in "Good Morning, Madam," a two-reeler produced by Mack Sennett under the direction of Lloyd Bacon. In his role as an enterprising but not very successful book agent, Graves is supported by Marvin Lobach, Thelma Parr, Wm. McCall and Bud Ross.

"Cuckoo Love" offers Glenn Tryon in a two-reel comedy from the Hal Roach studios. Katherine Grant, Chester Conklin, Jimmie Finlayson, Blanche Mehaffey, and Jane Sherman are the distinguished members of the cast. Fred L. Guiol directed.

"Ride 'Em, Cowboy" is the title of the fourth chapter of the Pathe serial "Wild West," featuring Jack Mulhall and Helen Ferguson.

"Clever Feet" is the newest Grantland Rice "Sportlight" release. In this reel producer J. L. Hawkinson shows how import-

ant clever feet are for the participants in all forms of athletics.

"Nazareth" is the second release of the "Pilgrimage to Palestine" series of Biblical films.

Pathe Review No. 42 presents three subjects: "The Gorges of Rocamadour," a mountainside village in Central France in Pathe color scenes; "Tree-Top Nurseries," first flashes of bird life; "Brides of the Northland," another of the "Here Comes the Bride" series.

"Air Cooled," one of the "Aesop's Film Fables"; "Topics of the Day," and two issues of the popular Pathe News complete the October 18th release schedule.

Release stills from "A Rainy Knight," a two-reel Mack Sennett comedy for the Pathe program.

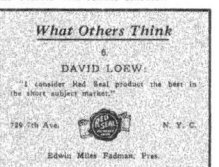

Resume of Current News Weeklies

PATHE NEWS NO. 81: Washington, D. C.—U. S. Franco debt negotiations end without definite settlement; Off Block Island, R. I.—Abandon hope of saving crew of sunken S-51; Fairmont, W. Va.—Striking miners in monster demonstration; Dearborn, Mich.—Ford starts planes on 1900-mile tour; London, England—Start 12,000-mile ocean trip in 30-foot yawl; Deadville, Colo.—Quilt carries names of all Presidents of U. S.; Cleveland, O. (Cleveland only)—World's largest cake donated to orphans; Worley, Tenn. (Memphis only)—One killed, 50 injured in train crash; New York (Philadelphia only)—J. E. Mastbaum, prominent theatre owner, returns from Europe; Charlestown, Mass.—Boy Scouts honorary members of Constitution crew; Niles, Mich.—Dempsey signs to box Wills; In the Andes, S. A.—Wales crosses Andes on visit to Chile; Washington, D. C.—Mitchell testifies before President's aerial inquiry board; Ruhr, Germany—Hindenburg visits Ruhr district; Providence, R. I. (Boston only)—Holy Name Societies march in sixth triennial procession; Collinsville, Ill. (St. Louis only)—Open new race track.

PATHE NEWS NO. 82: Quincy, Mass.—Launch America's largest airplane carrier; Racconigi, Italy — Princess Mafalda weds Prince Philip of Hesse; Honolulu, Hawaii—PN-9 makes first flight since 9-day drift in Pacific; Champaign, Ill.—Nebraska defeats Illinois in gridiron clash; Milwaukee, Wis.—LaFollette, Jr., wins Senate seat held by father; Exeter, England—"Back to the land" Lloyd George's cry in new campaign; Aberdeen, Md.—Complete giant gun for West Coast defense; Chattanooga, Tenn. (Memphis and Atlanta only)—Consecrate new Bishop Coadjutor of Episcopal diocese of South Florida; Santiago, Chile—Boy Scouts of Chile greet Prince of Wales; St. Louis, Mo.—Glenna Collett wins women's golf title for second time; Newark, N. J. (Newark only)—Shriners dedicate new mosque; Pittsburgh, Pa. (Pittsburgh only)—Lafayette springs football surprise and beats Pittsburgh 20 to 0; Annapolis, Md. (Washington only)—Navy sinks William and Mary team.

FOX NEWS VOL 7, NO. 1: San Francisco—Crew of PN-9 welcomed home; Pirates and Senators to meet in World Series; Newport, R. I.—John D. Rockefeller attends marriage of grandniece; Matteson, Ill.—Walter Hagen retains professional golf title; Locust Valley, L. I.—Display of fashion and wealth at Piping Rock horse show; London—Suklatala, communist member of Parliament barred

from U. S. posts for Fox News; Chicago, Ill.—One hundred thousand turn out to observe "Al Smith Day;" New York City—Cyclists race 50 miles at Breakneck speed; Phila., Pa.—Indians who played in "The Iron Horse" visit with stars of Athletic team; Buffalo, N. Y.—Buffalo Auto Club celebrated 17th birthday; Springfield, Ill.—Governor's Day held at Illinois State Fair; Amherst, Mass.—John Coolidge starts sophomore year at Amherst; Westbury, L. I.—Poloists compete for title at Meadowbrook Club; Off Block Island, R. I.—Rescuers work in vain effort to lift undersea craft sunk with crew in collision.

KINOGRAMS NO. 5123: Bochum, Germany—Great crowds greet Hindenburg on triumphal trip through Ruhr; Wayne, N. J.—Blind man builds himself a home (a Kinograms exclusive); Washington—U. S. is helpless in air war Mitchell tells aviation probe committee; Rome—Italy celebrates anniversary of union of Rome with kingdom; Mineola, N. Y.—Fair crowds see speedy trotters tear around track in one-mile championship races; Niles City, Mich.—Dempsey and Wills sign for bout in 1926—but who knows what may happen in the meantime?; St. Louis—Women golfers battle for national title.

KINOGRAMS NO. 5124: New York—Huge crowds block Wall street when army stages sham battle to celebrate aviation week; Racconigi, Italy—Princess Mafalda, King's second daughter is married to Prince Philip of Hesse; Santa Rosa, Cal—Burbank, plant wizard, denies he is to sell his wonder garden to Stanford University (a Kinograms exclusive); London—British girl athletes in exciting hurdle races; Aberdeen, Md.—Big guns, gas, smoke screens, and bombs form impressive spectacle for big crowds; New York—Scoot their way to championships, kiddies from public schools hold pushmobile finals in Central Park.

INTERNATIONAL NEWS NO. 82: Calcutta, India—Hold great religious festival; The Hague, Holland—Queen Wilhelmina reopens Dutch Parliament; Paris, France—Produce novelties in elaborate fireworks; Wash., D. C.—Colonel Mitchell appears before Coolidge's Air Commission; Wash., D. C. (Wash. only)—President congratulates Senators for winning second pennant; Milwaukee, Wis. (Milwaukee and Chicago only)—Cardinal Mundelein officiates at Golden jubilee of Archdiocese of Milwaukee; Philadelphia, Pa. (Phila. only)—Jules Mastbaum, film theatre magnate, returns from Europe; Seattle, Wash. (Seattle and Portland only)—Silver Foxes

treated like honored guests; Boston, Mass. (Boston only)—College boys test resistance and temperature of H₂O; N. Y. City—Advance hint on winter fashions; St. Louis, Mo. (St. Louis only)—Spectacular plays feature women's golf tourney; Niles, Mich.—Dempsey signs to battle Harry Wills; On the Pacific—Mighty battle fleet fights way thru storm.

INTERNATIONAL NEWS NO. 83: Santiago, Chile—Chilean army passes in review before Prince of Wales; Quincy, Mass.—Another giant carrier airplane for U. S. Navy; Fox Lake, Wis.—"Bob" LaFollette is youngest man ever elected to U. S. Senate; N. Y. City—Carl Laemmle, famous film man, returns from Europe; Near Shanghai, China—Newsreel man snaps "dog-face" man of China; Washington, D. C.—World parliament for universal peace begins sessions; Richmond, Va.—Railway tunnel caves in with fatal results; Aberdeen, Md.—"Leap for Life" in test of new anti-aircraft guns; Los Angeles, Cal. (Los Angeles only)—New million dollar ball park opened; Richmond, Cal.—Motorcyclists furnish thrills in hill climb event; An International Special—Thrilling moments in big gridiron battles as football season warms up.

F. B. O. Announces Short Subjects for November

F B. O. has announced eight short subject releases for the month of November, the program including two episodes of "The Adventures of Mazie," two Standard Fat Men comedies, a Blue Ribbon comedy, and three Bray cartoons.

November 1st is set as the release date for "A Ton of Fun in a Beauty Parlor," starring Fat Karr, Tiny Alexander and Kewpie Ross. The same day will also see the release of a Bray Cartoon as yet untitled.

On November 8th the fifth episode of "The Adventures of Mazie" starring Alberta Vaughn will be distributed.

The sixth Bray cartoon, as yet untitled, will be distributed on November 15th, as well as "Hold Tight" a two reel Blue Ribbon comedy starring Alice Ardell.

On November 22nd the sixth episode of "The Adventures of Mazie" will be ready for exhibitors.

A Standard Fat Men Comedy, as yet untitled, will be shown on November 29th, as well as a Bray Cartoon.

Three Episodes of "Mazie" Series Completed

The first three episodes of the "Adventures of Mazie," two-reel series being produced on the west coast by F. B. O. with Alberta Vaughn in the title role, have been completed. The pictures are being directed by Ralph Ceder and present Larry Kent, Al Cooke and Kit Guard in the principal supporting roles.

The stories, which are based on a series written by Nell Martin and were published in a magazine, depict the adventures in business and love of a young stenographer. There will be twelve episodes in the group.

Educational Celebrates New Studio Opening

Many of the best known leaders of filmland attended the reception which marked the opening of the new Educational studios in Los Angeles on October 8th, when the final stage was completed. With the completion of work the company now has five acres of stage space, according to Jack White, in charge of production at the Educational Studios on the west coast.

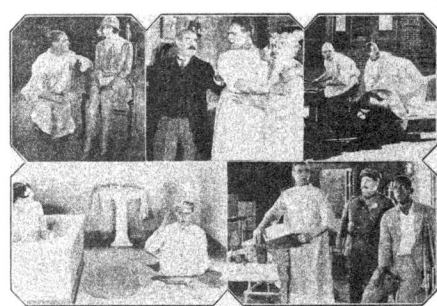

Ralph Graves in scenes from "Harry Doctor," a two-reel Mack Sennett comedy presented by Pathe.

Second Self-Protection Series Under Way

Leander de Cordova has started the direction of a new series of "The Scandal of America" for Self-Protection Pictures, Inc. The pictures are one-reelers dealing with the present national crime wave and show methods of self-defense whereby the weakest woman may learn to repel the attack of a powerful ruffian. Mme. Grace G. Girard, well known authority on the Japanese art of jiu jitsu is being featured in the series. Each story carries a plot and is complete in itself.

The producers have surrounded Mme. Girard with a cast that includes Tena Kamp, former Follies beauty; Jack Clemence and Tom Blake. Earl Rossman, producer and photographer of "Kivalina of the Icelands," has charge of the camera work for the series.

William Fox Signs New Comedy Leads

Georgie Harris and Barbara Luddy, pint-size comedians, have been signed to long term contract by Fox. They will have the leads in a new Irish-Jewish comedy series to be made at the west coast studios shortly. The first of these is "East Side, West Side," which has just been completed under the direction of Benjamin Stoloff.

Fox Starts New Helen and Warren Comedy

Fox has started production on "Hold Everybody," latest of the Helen and Warren series, under the direction of Albert Ray, Kathryn Perry and Hallam Cooley again have the leading roles. Sidney Bracey, Grace Darmond and Frank Rice have the leading supporting roles.

Scenes from "Transients In Arcadia," the O. Henry story adapted to the screen by Fox Film Corporation.

Eddie Gordon in scenes from "The Polo Kid," a two-reel Century Comedy released by Universal.

18 Comedies Completed By Fox

Six Production Units Now Working Under George Marshall's Supervision

THE SIX units producing Fox comedy pictures under the supervision of George E. Marshall have completed eighteen of the productions they are scheduled to make for the current season and six more are now in work. The progress made by the comedy division under Marshall's administration sets a new mark for the Fox studios in the production of the brief entertainments.

Two of the new series of Van Bibber Comedies, "The Sky Jumper" and "A Parisian Knight," were made under Marshall's personal direction. Robert P. Kerr has completed "The Big Game Hunter," "The Wrestler" and "The Feud" and is now preparing to film the sixth Van Bibber.

Daniel Keefe has just completed "Failure," third of the O. Henry series with Harvey Clark as Lawyer Gooteh and Kathryn McGuire as Tillie Jones.

Albert Ray is in the midst of filming "Hold Everything," fourth of the Helen and Warren married life Comedies based on Mabel Herbert Urner's stories.

Imperial Comedies, of which there will be twenty in the course of the season, are going forward rapidly. Robert Kerr was drafted from the Van Bibber lot to produce "The Brain Storm," with Sid Smith and Katherine Bennett in the leading roles and Larry Stears as the villain.

Benjamin Stoloff is directing Georgie Harris and Barbara Leddy in "East Side, West Side," the first of a series of Irish-Jewish comedies that will be released under the Imperial brand.

Lew Seiler has just finished filming "Strong For Love," with Sid Smith and Judy King in the leading roles and Stanley Blystone as the villain. Bryan Foy is hard at work on a new comedy as yet untitled.

Assemble Cast for "The Power God," Serial

Following conferences with J. Charles Davis, 2nd, on his recent visit to the coast, Ben Wilson has started casting "The Power God," to be filmed as a fifteen episode serial and distributed by Davis Distributing Division. Mary Brooklyn will be the star and important parts will be assigned to Mary Crane of Chicago and John Battaglia of New York, winners of a contest conducted by newspapers and magazines throughout the country in connection with "The Power God," an original story by Rex Taylor and Harry Haven.

Alice Day Starts Eighth Comedy for Pathe

Alice Day has completed "Gooseland," her seventh Sennett picture for Pathe release, and has started on her next production with Eddie Cline directing. The company is now at work on location scenes at San Pedro.

Ralph Graves also finished another two-reeler. This is entitled "Not So Fast" and shows the comedian as a cop. Thelma Parr is the leading lady.

Pre-release Reviews of Features

Children of the Whirlwind
(Arrow—Seven Reels)
(Reviewed by Thomas C. Kennedy)

LE ROY F. SCOTT'S story about a young crook who determines to "go straight" proves very adequate screen material as presented in this Whitman Bennett production. It offers a good plot, and with crook melodrama that is everything. We are on familiar ground, of course, but the action is quick and the number of complications sufficient to keep the heroic character in that position of uncertainty which never yet has failed to hold an audience.

A mighty good cast has been assembled to enact the play. Johnny Walker as the crafty and likable youth who steadfastly holds to his resolution to keep straight despite the attempts of both police and his former colleagues to "frame" him, furnishes a good characterization. Marguerite DeLaMotte, J. R. Toser, Lionel Barrymore and the others play with conviction and becoming earnestness. It is too long, but so too are ninety-nine out of every hundred features these days.

THEME. Crook melodrama dealing with adventures of young swindler who goes straight despite opposition of the cops and his former colleagues.

PRODUCTION HIGHLIGHTS. The quick action and good supply of effective melodramatic incident. The acting and sympathetic characters.

EXPLOITATION ANGLES. Feature first the cast. Author has been widely read and should be exploited. Bill as fast-moving and exciting crook melodrama.

DRAWING POWER. Good for "spot" wherever crook melodrama is popular.

SUMMARY. Well plotted and convincingly acted crook melodrama. It has action and is rich in melodramatic incident. Is interesting throughout.

THE CAST
Joe Ellison	Lionel Barrymore
Larry Brainerd	Johnny Walker
Maggie	Marguerite DeLaMotte
Hunt	J. R. Toser
"The Duchess"	Marie Haynes
Barney	Bert Tuey
Carlisle	Frank Montgomery

By Le Roy F. Scott. Directed by Whitman Bennett.

SYNOPSIS. Larry Brainerd returns to the rendezvous of his colleagues in crime after a "stretch" in jail and announces he will go straight. He escapes the detective who wants to "frame" him and also the crooks, later preventing the girl and her mentors from putting over a "badger game" on a wealthy youth, which wins him the girl and his chance to make good in legitimate enterprise.

A Lover's Oath
(Principal-Astor Distributing Corp. 5800 Feet)
(Reviewed by Edw. G. Johnston)

IF all the admirers of the Rubaiyat of Omar Khayyam, and there are many of them, could gather together and view this picture, they would acclaim it as a hit of the year but we do not believe that it will register as an all around attraction for the several different types of audiences, although the beauty of some of the backgrounds, the trick photography, the fine, practically all-star cast, offset some of its disadvantages.

Ramon Novarro and Kathleen Key are the stars, though Edwin Stevens easily runs away with the picture. As the old libertine of a Sheik, his acting is superb.

The Story is adapted from the Rubaiyat of Omar Khayyam and the old philosopher's verses are interwoven with the entire story.

THEME. A poetical melodrama adapted from the Rubaiyat of Omar Khayyam by Edward Fitzgerald and the efforts of a Sheik to gain possession of the betrothed of Ben Ali, Omar's son.

PRODUCTION HIGHLIGHTS. Artistic backgrounds, the trick photography and the fine handling of the entire production by Ferdinand P. Earle. The harem of the Sheik, Hassan ben Sabbath and the desert scenes.

EXPLOITATION ANGLES. Play up the names of Ramon Novarro and Kathleen Key. Arrange tie-up with book store on the Rubaiyat. The directing ability of F. P. Earle.

DRAWING POWER. Should draw well in houses catering to intelligent audiences.

SUMMARY. It was booked in New York City on a double feature day. Has an all star cast, is well directed and the settings are extremely artistic and beautiful.

THE CAST
Ben Ali	Ramon Novarro
Sherin	Kathleen Key
Omar Khayyam	Frederick Warde
Hassan Ben Sabbath	Edwin Stevens
His Wife	Hedwig Reicher
Omar's Servant	Snitz Edwards
Commander of the Faithful	Charles Post
Prince Yussuf	Arthur Edmund Carewe
Sheik Rustum	Paul Wigel
His Son	Phillipe de Lacy
Haja	Warren Rogers

Lionel Barrymore, who plays the lead in "Children of the Whirlwind," an Arrow release.

Children of the Whirlwind
(Arrow)
PRESS NOTICE

Le Roy F. Scott, whose crook stories have won him wide popularity, is the author of the play in which a notable cast will appear as the main attraction at the .... theatre on .... when "Children of the Whirlwind" is to be presented with Johnny Walker, Lionel Barrymore, Marguerite DeLaMotte and other well known screen players in the principal roles. The story is an exciting recital of the adventures of a young crook who succeeds in going straight despite the effort.

The hero not only triumphs over the many crafty plots to ruin him but as well saves the girl he loves and who was brought up to a life of crime.

CATCH LINES
Action, mystery and romance are skilfully blended in a stirring crook melodrama that will hold your interest unflaggingly from introduction to fadeout.

Ramon Novarro in "A Lover's Oath," released by Astor Distributing Corp.

A Lover's Oath
(Principal-Astor Dist. Corp.)
PRESS NOTICE

"A LOVER'S OATH", which will be the attraction at the ——— Theatre, was produced by a new process of revolutionary nature. Director Earle is solely responsible for this process in which backgrounds and sets are made in a unique and novel way. Ramon Novarro has never had a finer role nor one that fitted him better in Ben Ali, the greatest lover of all Persia. The picture was edited by one of today's foremost stars, Milton Sills and directed by Ferdinand P. Earle, noted painter, dramatist and motion picture producer de luxe.

CATCH LINES
Ramon Novarro as Ben Ali, the great lover, risks life for love. ——— and makes good in "A Lover's Oath." Ramon Novarro in a great role. Kathleen Key has never appeared sweeter or with more charm.

The Keeper of the Bees
(F. B. O.—6712 Feet)
(Reviewed by L. C. Moen)

IN the case of a book which has enjoyed the sale already chalked up by Gene Stratton-Porter's "Keeper of the Bees," any comment on the technical merits or shortcomings of the picturization is rather superfluous from a trade angle. Like "The Girl of the Limberlost," this can scarcely fail to do business—and mighty good business. At the same time, one cannot help feeling a little sorry that the inherent possibilities in the story were not brought out more sharply.

One expects nature study material in a Stratton-Porter story, and more footage devoted to the bees would not have been amiss. The hero's restoration to health and happiness through the example of that industrious and admirable creature, the bee, could have been made both fascinating and novel.

As it stands, most of the footage is devoted to the tangled marital relations of the hero, who is married and not a husband, and through rather inadequate direction many of these scenes are neither convincing nor unusual. However, the Gene Stratton-Porter fans in any community will make the nucleus of a man-sized audience, and this picture should appeal strongly to any save the more sophisticated audiences. But we'll always be sorry we didn't see more of the bees!

THEME.   Restoration to health of a disabled war veteran through his contact with nature, and his romance with a fair neighbor.

PRODUCTION HIGHLIGHTS.   Sincere performance by Robert Frazer. Natural characterization by Gene Stratton. The bee scenes. The storm.

EXPLOITATION ANGLES.   Play up the author heavily and tie up with bookstores and library on the book. Put a bee-hive, enclosed in glass, in the lobby. Tie up with grocers on honey.

DRAWING POWER.   Should draw well through popularity of book and strength of cast. Not especially good for sophisticated audiences.

SUMMARY.   Average picturization of popular novel, with excellent cast and laid in attractive settings.

THE CAST

James Lewis MacFarlane	Robert Frazer
The Bee Master	Josef Swickard
Margaret Cameron	Martha Mattox
Lolly	Clara Bow
Molly	Alyce Mills
The Little Scout	Gene Stratton

From the novel by Gene Stratton-Porter. Direction and continuity by J. Leo Meehan. Photographed by John Boyle.

SYNOPSIS. The hero, a disabled vet, runs away from army hospital when he learns he has short time to live. Befriends aged bee keeper, who dies and leaves him property. Healthy exercise and care of neighboring woman restore his vitality. Neighbor's daughter tricks him into marriage under her sister's name, to provide legal protection for erring sister. This girl dies in giving birth to child, and hero finds happiness with girl with whom he went through ceremony.

Exchange of Wives
(Metro-Goldwyn—6300 Feet)
(Reviewed by George T. Pardy)

THIS comedy is of pretty light texture as regards plot, even for a comedy, where thin stories are usually tolerated generously. An adaptation of one of Cosmo Hamilton's plays, the paring down process supposed to be necessary for the screen has reduced the narrative to a harmlessly amusing film, with some bright spots, but on the whole a rather weak production. Still many patrons will laugh over the adventures of the two wives, each attracted by the other's hubby, and the excellent acting of the entire cast. Renee Adoree is extremely captivating and saucily alluring as the coquettish Elise, Eleanor Boardman gives a remarkably fine performance as Margaret; while Lew Cody, as John Rathburn, and Creighton Hale, as Victor Moran, are decidedly effective in their respective roles.

From an artistic standpoint the feature ranks high. There are many handsome interiors with elaborate settings and the photography throughout is of first-class quality. Director Hobart Henley has kept the action moving swiftly throughout and the continuity links up smoothly.

THEME.   Domestic comedy in which two wives are temporarily attracted by each others' husbands.

PRODUCTION HIGHLIGHTS.   The excellent acting, colorful atmosphere, ornate settings, complications which ensue over the cooking arrangements and clever climax.

EXPLOITATION ANGLES.   The four principals mentioned in the cast are all worth featuring as they are well and favorably known to the fans. Play this up as a very funny comedy of domestic entanglements, with unique situations.

DRAWING POWER.   Should get by in most houses on strength of the title, the author's fame and strong cast, but is hardly likely to make big box office records.

SUMMARY.   Acting, settings, atmosphere O. K. Doesn't rank as a strong comedy, but is good enough to get by in most houses, provided it is properly exploited.

THE CAST

Margaret Rathburn	Eleanor Boardman
John Rathburn	Lew Cody
Elise Moran	Renee Adoree
Victor Moran	Creighton Hale

Author, Cosmo Hamilton. Director, Hobart Henley. Photographed by Benjamin F. Reynolds.

SYNOPSIS. Two couples, John and Margaret Rathburn, and Victor and Elise Moran are next-door neighbors. After being married a year they all reach a stage where they are for a time incompatible. Elise flirts desperately with John, while Victor finds consolation in the sympathy and excellent cooking of Margaret. The situation becomes intolerable and they resolve to test matters by going to camp, with each woman cooking for the other's husband. Many amusing and near tragic complications ensue, but finally everything is straightened out and all ends well.

The Keeper of the Bees (F. B. O.)

PRESS NOTICE

THE many admirers of Gene Stratton-Porter in this city will be delighted to learn that an entertaining motion picture adapted from her last novel will be the attraction at the ———— theatre on ————, according to announcement by the manager. This is "The Keeper of the Bees," based on the late author's last, and some say greatest, work.

A brilliant cast interprets the leading roles in the story, including Robert Frazer, Clara Bow, Alyce Mills, Martha Mattox, Josef Swickard and little Gene Stratton.

CATCH LINES

He ran away from the hospital to die by the sea, but instead he found renewed health and joy awaiting him as "The Keeper of the Bees."

Gene Stratton-Porter's greatest novel made into a beautiful and inspiring motion picture.

James Leo Meehan who directed "The Keeper of the Bees" an F.B.O. release.

Exchange of Wives (Metro-Goldwyn)

PRESS NOTICE

A WHIMSICAL comedy entitled "Exchange of Wives" will be the leading screen attraction at the ———— Theatre on ————. It concerns the marital troubles of two couples after being wedded one year. Each wife becomes temporarily attracted by the other's husband and although matters are straightened out in the end, there are any number of funny complications and near-tragedy incidents before peace reigns in each household.

The cast is practically an all star aggregation, consisting of Eleanor Boardman and Renee Adoree as the opposing wives; and Lew Cody and Creighton Hale in the husband roles.

CATCH LINES

Do you think domestic troubles could be solved by a partial exchange of wives for cooking purposes

Eleanor Boardman in "An Exchange of Wives," Metro-Goldwyn-Mayer.

A Regular Fellow

(Paramount—5027 Feet)
(Reviewed by George T. Pardy)

THE original title of this one was "He's A Prince," but as a matter of fact they could have called it any old thing and it would still stand out as one of the best comedies sponsored by Paramount in a dog's age. It would be hard to fancy a vehicle better suited to the talents of the star—versatile Raymond Griffith, there is a trifle more slap-stick stuff in the action than has previously been associated with the work of that breezy comedian, but the whirlwind humor is exactly in line with the story's absurdly farcical trend and it's all very amusing and a genuine, guaranteed cure for the blues.

Raymond Griffith has certainly never appeared to such good advantage as in this film and the support is excellent.

THEME. Farce comedy, with prince for hero who doesn't like his job, is forced into all kinds of royal activities, welcomes a revolution, is made president of New Republic and weds girl he loves.

PRODUCTION HIGHLIGHTS. Good direction and clever acting of star and support. Witty subtitles and fine continuity. Scene where prince presides at ship-launching, also that where dog keeps bringing back the bomb.

EXPLOITATION ANGLES. Boost as Griffith's first starring comedy. Call the fan's attention to the fact that he scored heavily in "Changing Husbands," "Forty Winks," "Miss Bluebeard," "The Night Club" and "Paths to Paradise."

DRAWING POWER. Should prove a winning box office attraction for all classes of theatres.

SUMMARY. A sure-fire hit comedy, one of the season's best, with Raynod Griffith getting the laughs all the way through, assisted by splendid cast. Ought to be a big box office magnet.

THE CAST

Prince	Raymond Griffith
Girl	Mary Brian
King	Tyrone Power
Prince's Valet	Edgar Norton
Revolutionist	Nigel de Brullere
Prime Minister	Gustav Von Seyffertitz
Girl's Companion	Kathleen Kirkham

Authors, Reginald Morris and Joseph Mitchell. Directed by Edward Sutherland. Photographed by Charles Boyle.

SYNOPSIS. Young European prince falls in love with girl but is prevented from meeting her by official duties which include ship-launchings, judging Baby shows, reviewing troops, etc. Whenever he gets a chance to talk to her, they are surrounded by hundreds who recognize him. One day he starts to run after her, is pursued by the Prime Minister and informed that his father is dead and he is the king. He arranges to have a revolution take place. It does, but they elect him president of the new Republic. But he gets the girl.

Raymond Griffith, who has the star role in "A Regular Fellow," produced by Paramount.

A Regular Fellow (Paramount)
PRESS NOTICE

THERE'S a real treat in store for the patrons of the ——— Theatre on ——— when "A Regular Fellow" comes to the screen. This film is the first comedy starring feature with Raymond Griffith as the bright and particular light, but the fans who have seen him in important roles in other productions will assuredly flock to witness his work in this one. The role fits Griffith perfectly, the picture has received unqualified praise from every critic in the country.

Griffith appears as a young European prince, sick of his job and in love with girl whom his royal duties prevent from meeting. It is a veritable whirlwind of fun. Mary Brian is the heroine, with a brilliant supporting cast.

CATCH LINES

His High Hat, Highness, The Prince of Laughter, is with us again. Be sure you are on hand when Raymond Griffith makes his appearance in "A Regular Fellow."

The Pace That Thrills

(First National—Seven Reels)
(Reviewed by Frank Elliott)

IT is hard to believe that Byron Morgan who turned out all those good Wallie Reid automobile stories, is responsible for the tale unreeled here. And while the plot is weak the manner in which it has been transplanted to the screen is even worse. It seems that an effort has been made to jam in everything. There is a ne'er-do-well dashing after his wife and baby with a pair of scissors and falling down stairs himself to an untimely end, there is a bull fight, a prize fight, an auto race and whatnot. There are many unconvincing situations.

THEME. Comedy drama of a youthful movie star who has to bear the brand of cowardice because he cannot afford to take chances as his mother needs him to aid in obtaining a pardon from jail.

PRODUCTION HIGHLIGHTS. The bull and prize fights. The auto race in which the hero goes thru the track. The dash from the city to the course where the hero arrives in time to get in the event.

EXPLOITATION ANGLES. Try and get a racing auto and put it on the streets with the driver in racing costume and with the car carrying appropriate advertising. Tie up with local auto dealers on this theme, "Enjoy the 'Pace That Thrills,' in a ——— Sedan." Play up the names of Ben Lyon and Mary Astor.

DRAWING POWER. Suitable for second class downtown houses, community theatres and towns.

SUMMARY. Much ado about nothing, but it may please some audiences in smaller houses. An unconvincing plot and a poorly produced picture with a big auto race as a saving factor.

THE CAST

Danny Wade	Ben Lyon
Doris	Mary Astor
Duke	Charles Beyer
Hezekiah Sims	Tully Marshall
The Director	Wheeler Oakman
John Van Loren, Sr	Thomas Holding
Jack Van Loren, Jr	Warner Richmond
Paula	Fritzi Brunette
Toreador	Paul Ellis

By Byron Morgan. Directed by Webster Campbell. Personal Supervision, Earl Hudson.

SYNOPSIS. Danny Wade, is unable to tell that the reason he will not take any chances in his pictures, is that he is working to get his mother out of jail where she was sent on perjured testimony accusing her of murdering her husband. Danny even refuses to drive in an auto race even though his reputation, future and "the" girl is at stake. His mother's case suddenly come up before the pardon board. He hastens to the hearing. His mother is freed. He then rushes for the race arriving in time to "get in," but is injured when the track gives way. He then proves to the world that it was not cowardice that made him refuse to take chances.

Ben Lyon, of "The Pace That Thrills," a First National production.

The Pace That Thrills
(1st Nat'l)
PRESS NOTICE

LOVERS of those popular Byron Morgan auto stories in which the late Wallace Reid won fame will welcome the announcement that Ben Lyon will appear at the ——— theatre on ——— in an original tale by this author which furnishes as many thrills as the most jaded fan could desire. Ben seems an ideal successor to Mr. Reid as a portrayer of exuberant youth. He is supported by beautiful Mary Astor, and a fine cast including Tully Marshall, Thomas Holding, Charles Beyer, Wheeler Oakman and others. The big thrill of the picture is the auto race.

CATCH LINES

Byron Morgan, who wrote 'em for Wally Reid, is the author of this thrill-drama. You'll be on the edge of the seat all thru it. It was made to thrill and it makes good. The fastest moving action film they've ever made. Speeding right at your heart!

"The Winding Stair"
(Fox—5700 Feet)
(Reviewed by Chester J. Smith)

THIS story, a mixture of intrigue, romance and fighting, nicely moulded together and rather tastefully dished up is almost sure fire stuff to the general run of picture patrons. The story is very implausible in spots and at times the cast is inclined to overact a bit, but these are things that can easily be overlooked in the continuous action. It is a war story, starting in Morocco and winding up in the trenches of the world war, where the hero vindicates himself, if vindication is necessary, for his desertion of the Moroccan forces.

Alma Rubens, Edmund Lowe and Mahlon Hamilton head the cast, and do generally good work, though Lowe is inclined at times to overact his heroic role. The work of Miss Rubens is an outstanding feature.

THEME. A romantic war story in which the hero, an officer of the French Foreign Legion, deserts for love of the girl and to save her from mutinous tribesmen, only later to re-establish himself as a hero of the world war.

PRODUCTION HIGHLIGHTS. The hand to hand fighting between the French Foreign Legion and the mutinous tribesmen. The realistic reproduction of world war scenes. Paul's heroic dash to reopen the gates for the returning soldiers.

EXPLOITATION ANGLES. The fierce fighting between the Legion and the tribesmen; the world war scenes, which have been realistically reproduced, and the exceptionally good cast.

DRAWING POWER. Should go well in almost any type house, but will be particularly attractive in all but the largest cities.

SUMMARY. This is a picture replete with action, having an abundance of suspense and particularly appealing in its battle scenes. It is well acted and the story is well sustained throughout.

THE CAST
Marguerite	Alma Rubens
Paul	Edmund Lowe
Petras	Warner Oland
Gerard	Mahlon Hamilton
Mme. Muller	Emily Fitzroy
Onery	Chester Conklin
Andrea	Frank Leigh

Story by A. E. W. Mason. Directed by John Griffith Wray.

SYNOPSIS. Paul Ravenal an officer in the French Foreign Legion deserts the Legion for love of Marguerite Lambert, who through unfortunate circumstances has been forced to become a cafe dancer in Morocco. The desertion is the result of Paul's knowledge that the girl is in imminent danger of being slain as a foreigner by a rebellious mob, who through a ruse have drawn the army from the city. Held as a deserter, Paul makes his escape and joins the American army in the world war. He becomes a hero and is decorated for his bravery. Wounded, he is rejoined in a hospital by Marguerite, who is serving as a Red Cross nurse. She takes her place as his wife.

Classified
(First National—6927 Feet)
(Reviewed by Thomas C. Kennedy)

FOR its brightness, pace and the telling appeal of its characters "Classified" deserves a high rating as screen entertainment. This most recent Corinne Griffith vehicle seems to this reviewer one of her best in a long while and there is a disposition to rate the picture this star's best box office bet since "Black Oxen."

"Classified," while totally dissimilar, has that swing and bright ness which we think won the applause of reviewers and fans for "Manslaughter." It is smart entertainment, with a buoyant quality of mirth rippling over the surface of a very substantial story of life-like and likeable people. It has its emotional appeal as well. Indeed, no hectic devices of roaring melodrama could stir the spectator to a keener interest in the characters or give more "punch" to the situation in which the heroine finally triumphs. Miss Griffith has excellent support from Jack Mulhall, capital as the hero, Ward Crane, Charlie Murray, Carroll Nye and the other principals of the east. The work is a glowing tribute to the taste and skill of Al Santell.

THEME. Comedy of New York dealing with a girl who lives in a tenement and uses her wits to enjoy the pleasures and luxuries of those who reside on Fifth Avenue.

PRODUCTION HIGHLIGHTS. The extraordinarily human and likeable characters and superb acting. The appeal of the story and its convincing portrayal of an interesting phase of New York life.

EXPLOITATION ANGLES. The star, of course, and her supporting cast. The author, Edna Ferber, who has a big following. Stress it as a very human vehicle.

DRAWING POWER. Seems capable of attracting big audiences everywhere.

SUMMARY. A sparkling comedy of New York life. Story is finely treated and acting and production just about perfect. One of the best pictures Miss Griffith has done.

THE CAST
Babs Comet	Corinne Griffith
Lloyd Whiting	Jack Mulhall
Spencer Clark	Ward Crane
Mart Comet	Carroll Nye
Old Man Comet	Charles Murray
"Maw" Comet	Edythe Chapman
Jeanette Comet	Jacqueline Wells
Weinstein	George Sidney
Bernstein	Bernard Randall

Story by Edna Ferber. Directed by Alfred A. Santell.

Synopsis. Deals with a girl who spends all her salary for clothes and bluffs her way into acquaintance with wealthy men about town. Her wits are always equal to the occasion which may arise but finally she gets into a compromising situation, walking home from the country where her escort's car "broke down." The escort is confronted by parents and he answers by asking their consent to his marriage with Babs. But Babs loves a garage mechanic and refuses wealth to marry him.

"The Winding Stair"
(Fox)
PRESS NOTICE

"THE WINDING STAIR," a Fox picture, which comes to the ————— Theatre next ———, is a thrilling tale of romance, intrigue and fighting, with the battle scenes laid in Morocco and the trenches of the World War. The story is enacted by a stellar cast which is headed by Edmund Lowe, Alma Rubens and Mahlon Hamilton.

This is out of the usual run of war pictures, though battle scenes of the world war have been accurately reproduced. It abounds in suspense with most of the action laid in Morocco. Both Edmund Lowe and Alma Rubens contribute sterling performances in their respective roles.

CATCH LINES
You have seen war pictures before, but not one of this type. It is gripping in every foot of film and will thrill you as you have rarely been thrilled by a picture before.

Edmund Lowe, who appears in "The Winding Stair," a Fox production.

Classified (First National)
PRESS NOTICE

A BRILLIANT adaptation of Edna Ferber's "Classified" will be offered on the screen of the ———— on ————, with Corrine Griffith in the role of the New York working girl who uses her wits to gain her acquaintance with men of wealth and position.

The picture has been commented upon as Miss Griffith's most appealing and interesting vehicle since "Black Oxen." It is a bubbling comedy concerning life-like people and endowed with many striking dramatic situations. The star is supported by Jack Mulhall, Ward Crane, Charles Murray, Edythe Chapman, Jacqueline Wells and George Sidney.

CATCH LINES
A sparkling comedy of New York life, filled with genuine, clean humor and moving dramatic episodes.
Corinne Griffith in the most interesting characterization she has ever done for the pictures.

Corinne Griffith, star of "Classified," a First National Feature.

The Fear Fighter
(Rayart Pictures—5000 Feet)
(Reviewed by George T. Pardy)

THE pugilistic arena has been utilized as the background for so many pictures of mediocre grade and inferior material that it comes as a pleasant surprise when one runs across such abright and entertaining film of gloveland as "The Fear Fighter." There are certain localities where this picture should go over big, there are others where some of the situations may be sneered at as over-melodramatic and impossible.

One thing is pretty certain, however, its admirers will outnumber the detractors. As to the ring episode, any old-time pugilist, or writer of the game can tell you of incidents where a man has battled for several rounds, "out on his feet," as they say, finally recovering from what amounts to a state of coma and coming home a winner.

The sporting element will like the feature sure, Billy Sullivan is as pretty a boxer and alluring hero as one could wish to see, and the ordinary fan will hail the yarn as a real thriller.

THEME. Comedy-drama. Hero young chap who learns the fighting game during a period when he is suffering from loss of memory, recovers after curious adventure, makes good and gets girl he wants.

PRODUCTION HIGHLIGHTS. Lively action, good stunt stuff, comedy touches, fight scenes, capable direction and great finish.

EXPLOITATION ANGLES. Play up hero Billy Sullivan as the young fellow who made good in the "Leather Pusher" and "Fast Stepper" series, as the fans are sure to remember his good work in both.

DRAWING POWER. Good for any house where patrons want quick action, fun and thrills for their money.

SUMMARY. A fast-moving bright comedy-drama where circumstances make a young chap a pugilist against his will. Plot has unusual twist, holds interest throughout and speeds into fine climax. Should do well at box office.

THE CAST
Billy Griffin	Billy Sullivan
Katherine Curtis	Ruth Dwyer
James Curtis	J. P. McGowan
Mother Griffin	Billy Bennett
Young Dillon	Phil Salvadore

Author, Grover Jones. Director, Albert Rogell. Photographed by Ross Fisher.

SYNOPSIS. Jim Curtis, boxing manager, refuses to allow Billy Griffin to wed his daughter Katherine, unless he proves he can fight for her. Billy, knowing nothing of the glove game, tackles Jim but is knocked out and loses his memory. A former ring champion, recognizing the value of Billy's undeveloped punch, takes the lad in hand. While still in a memory daze Billy encounters and defeats several good men. Finally Curtis matches him with Dillon. Just prior to the fight he injures his head and his memory returns. This results in his being nearly whipped, but Katherine wisely taunts him into fury and he knocks out Dillon. The lovers are united.

The Fear Fighter (Rayart)

Billy Sullivan, who is starred in "The Fear Fighter," a Rayart release.

Off the Highway
(Producers Distributing Corp.—7641 Feet)
(Reviewed by George T. Pardy)

IF the title of this picture is meant to suggest that it travels far off the beaten trail, there is no disputing its accuracy. For "Off the Highway" offers an ingenious and altogether unusual plot, handled with rare good judgment by director and players, an attraction registering undeniable audience appeal. The melodramatic effects may be stretched a bit, but that doesn't detract in the least from the entertaining powers of the film, which is beautifully photographed, well acted and a credit to all concerned in its production. John Bowers and Marguerite de La Motte do very fine work in the hero and heroine roles, but it must be conceded that the masterly work of William V. Mong in the dual portrayal of Caleb Fry and Tatterly stands out in bold relief.

THEME. Heart interest tale with melodramatic punches. Chief character miserly old uncle whose meanness almost blights lives of young lovers, but repents at end.

PRODUCTION HIGHLIGHTS. The capable direction, good acting of principals and supporting cast. The excellent photography, including really unique double exposure effects and lavish displays of life in artist quarter.

EXPLOITATION ANGLES. Play this one up not only as an unique story in which a man pretends to die in order to get a line on his relatives, but, as it deals with the struggles of a young artist, you would do well to have your throwaways cut in the shape of a pallette.

DRAWING POWER. Good investment for any house, big or little.

SUMMARY. Has general audience appeal, unusual plot and puts over some great emotional and melodramatic punches. Work of the cast especially deserving of praise.

THE CAST
Caleb Fry	William V. Mong
Tatterly	
Ella Tarrant	Marguerite De La Motte
Donald Brett	John Bowers
Hector Kindon	Charles Gerard
The Master	Joseph Swickard

Adapted from Tom Gallon's Novel, "Tatterly." Director, Tom Forman.

SYNOPSIS. Old Caleb Fry lives alone with Tatterly who resembles him strongly. Caleb is guardian of his nephew Donald Brett, who refuses to follow up a mercantile career, separates from his uncle and turns artist, incidentally falling in love with Ella Tarrant. Caleb, enraged, settles fortune on cousin Kindon, finds Tatterly dead and assumes his personality. In his disguise he is able to watch his relatives, finds that Kindon is a worthless scoundrel and Donald and Ella the only ones who treat him kindly. Finding Kindon hopelessly drunk, Caleb takes a large sum of money, a panic starts on the Exchange, Kindon wakes to find himself ruined, kills himself, Caleb sends the money to Donald and Ella, who wed immediately and he goes to them in the country.

Off the Highway (Prod. Dis. Corp.)

John Bowers in "Off the Highway," Producers Distributing Corp.

The Last Edition

(Emery Johnson Production-F. B. O.)
(Reviewed by Frank Elliott)

EMORY JOHNSON has scored again. This time, after doing the honors to the firemen, mailmen, railroad workers, etc., he has woven a stirring story around the business of getting out a big daily newspaper and in the telling takes the observer through every step the "story" goes in getting in on the street.

"The Last Edition," like other Johnson offerings, is loaded with sure-fire punch scenes. There is excitement galore as the newspaper seeks to bring to justice a notorious bootlegger who in turn has framed a bribe charge against the assistant foreman's son. The explosion in the newspaper plant and the subsequent fire which calls out the whole Frisco army of flame fighters is a climax few will forget.

THEME. A melodrama of newspaper life in which a bootlegger and a crooked assistant district attorney seeks to frame a bribery charge against the son of the assistant foreman of a newspaper composing room.

PRODUCTION HIGHLIGHTS. The scene in which young McDonald is arrested on a charge of bribery. The sequence showing "getting out" the "extra." The fight between McDonald and the bully foreman. The explosion and fire. The crash of the Chronicle building.

EXPLOITATION ANGLES. Arrange with your local newspaper to print a front page like the one the Frisco Chronicle got out, copy of which F.B.O. office will furnish.

DRAWING POWER. Exploitation possibilities should make this a box office winner in most any house. Has action that will entertain any audience.

SUMMARY. One of the best pictures F.B.O. has released in many, many moons. There is something doing every minute, the cast is well selected, there is a climax with a punch plus.

THE CAST

Dan McDonald	Ralph Lewis
Polly McDonald	Frances Teague
Rey McDonald	Ray Hallor
Mrs. McDonald	Lila Leslie
"Ink" Donavan	Billy Bakewell

By Emilie Johnson. Directed by Emory Johnson. Photographed by Gilbert Warrenton and Frank Evans.

SYNOPSIS. Dan McDonald, because of his age, looses out when a new foreman is appointed in the Chronicle composing room. Dan's son Rey is arrested on a trumped up charge of bribery, framed by a crooked district attorney's deputy who is mixed up with a notorious bootlegger. When the story comes out, Dan tries to wreck the presses to stop its publication. He is knocked out by "bull" Collins, the new foreman. The plant is blown up by "Red" McGann, but Dan is accused of the deed. Later the guilty persons are discovered by Polly McDonald, Dan's daughter, phone operator. Dan and Rey are freed. Dan is made foreman. A new newspaper plant is built.

The Last Addition (F. B. O.)
PRESS NOTICE

ONE of the best newspaper stories ever placed in screen form and well as the the most correct in detail, will come to the —————— theatre, commencing——————, when Manager —————— will present for the first time in this city, "The Last Edition," Emory Johnson's action-packed photoplay scenes which were taken in the new plant of the San Francisco Chronicle. Ralph Lewis, well known to movie fans, has the leading role in this puch picture. "The Last Edition," abounds in big scenes, while the climax showing the wrecking of a huge newspaper press and the explosion and burning of the entire plant together with the turning out of the entire Frisco fire department is a sure fire thrill.

CATCH LINES

A Thrilling Melodrama of the Roaring Presses. The Greatest Newspaper Story Ever Placed in Screen Form. See Ralph Lewis of "The Third Alarm" and "Westbound Limited" fame in the Greatest Role of His Career.

Ralph Lewis, Who appears in the F. B. O. production, "The Last Edition."

Wandering Fires

(Arrow—Seven Reels)
(Reviewed by Thomas C. Kennedy)

THIS picturization of Warner Fabian's "Wandering Fires" is cut to the popular pattern and it should register as a box office attraction everywhere. The play introduces the late war and goes into the trodden path by showing a character, who was thought killed in action, returning after several years of roaming as a victim of mental aphasia. But before this happens the author, and as regards the picture the director as well, has so involved the spectator's interest in a situation that is more novel and convincing, that the reaction to the Enoch Arden device is not one of apathy by any means.

Wallace MacDonald has the leading male role, which he does creditably on the whole but oversets considerably in spots. Constance Bennett does splendid work as the heroine and George Hackathorn contributes a telling performance as the soldier. The plot is an interesting one and has been handled very effectively. It is an excellent picture of its type, and we think it will score as a box office attraction.

THEME. Romantic melodrama concerning a girl whose lover was supposed killed in the war, but who returns years after when she is married to another.

PRODUCTION HIGHLIGHTS. Melodramatic power of scene in which heroine exposes herself to scandal to clear the name of her lover. Effective flashes of the war and a genuine air of conviction which pervades the entire work.

EXPLOITATION ANGLES. Play up author, Warner Fabian, who is famous for his "Flaming Youth" and "Sailors' Wives." Cast provides many good names for publicity purposes.

DRAWING POWER. Romantic melodrama of a type that should appeal. Should score in all types of theatres.

SUMMARY. A rather compelling melodrama employing many effective and unusual situations in combination with familiar devices introduced by plays dealing with the war. Well plotted and treated with considerable skill. It is a bit long-winded but has dramatic power.

THE CAST

Guerda Anthony	Constance Bennett
Raymond Carroll	George Hackathorne
Norman Yuell	Wallace MacDonald
Mrs. Carroll	Henrietta Crosman
Mrs. Satorius	Effie Shannon

By Warner Fabian. Directed by Maurice Campbell.

SYNOPSIS. Despite the scandal connected with her name, Norman Yuell, a youth of Puritan ideas, marries Guerda Anthony. The scandal resulted from her confession that she spent the entire night with Ray Carroll, to whom she was engaged, before he went overseas, where he was reported killed, subsequently. The confession was made to clear his name of a charge of giving information to the enemy, a charge brought by an enemy spy after the boy was reported dead. Ray returns after years of roaming as the victim of mental aphasia and he prevents the marriage of Guerda and Norman going on the rocks, because of a brooding jealousy which the husband develops.

Wandering Fires (Arrow)
PRESS NOTICE

A MODERN romance reflecting the late war and written by Warner Fabian, author of "Flaming Youth" and "Sailors' Wives," will be the main attraction at the —————— on ——————, when the Arrow Pictures production of "Wandering Fires" will be presented. This story is of the popular type and combines those elements which usually are found in the "best sellers" of the day.

Constance Bennett, one of the most promising of the newer leading women in pictures, plays the role of the heroine.

CATCH LINES

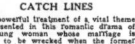

A powerful treatment of a vital theme is presented in this romantic drama of a young woman whose marriage is about to be wrecked when the former sweetheart, whose memory taunts the husband, unexpectedly returns and saves her happiness.

Constance Bennett, feminine lead in "Wandering Fires," an Arrow feature.

Paint and Powder
(Chadwick—7000 Feet)
(Reviewed by Thomas C. Kennedy)

THE story of the girl who forgives the sins of her sweetheart but whose own go unforgiven by him until it is too late, receives a sincere and earnest treatment in this presentation. This trait of sincerity and an adequate production give the picture a quality which makes it hold the interest despite an inherent lack of dramatic substance. It is a play which gets the characters nowhere in particular, the end showing the heroine bathing her bridal boquet with tears of bitterness over the fact that the man she loved and was faithful to had come back to her just a few moments after she had married another.

There is a glittering background of theatrical life, for it is a play concerned with a girl who starts as a dancer in an East Side saloon and later achieves stardom on Broadway. The author has been kind to theatrical managers.

Elaine Hammerstein has a very emotional role as the heroine and succeeds fairly with it. Theodore Von Eltz gives a consistent portrayal as the hero and John Sainpolis is interesting as the theatrical manager. Stuart Holmes does the villain role.

THEME. Melodrama about an actress who is misjudged by her sweetheart, though she has remained faithful to him even through his days of adversity and misfortune.

PRODUCTION HIGHLIGHTS. The acting and production, both of which are sincere. The several melodramatic situations and the glamor of the back-stage scenes. The appeal of the character of the actress.

EXPLOITATION ANGLES. Bill as a romance of the stage that remains faithful to the end to real life. A story that is different and that daringly adheres to realities.

DRAWING POWER. Has many qualities that will appeal, but is for adults of a sentimental trend. A fair program attraction.

SUMMARY. Is rather interesting but sentimental melodrama, well played and staged but story gets you nowhere in particular.

THE CAST

Mary Dolan	Elaine Hammerstein
Jimmy Evarts	Theodore Von Eltz
Mrs. Evarts	Mrs. Chas. G. Craig
Mark Kelsey	John Sainpolis
Phillip Andrews	Stuart Holmes
Mazie Hull	Derelys Perdue
Tim McCardle	Pat Hardigan
Riley	Russell Simpson
Cabman	Charles Murray

Story by Harvey Gates. Directed by Hunt Stromberg.

SYNOPSIS. Sweetheart of girl who dances at an East Side saloon steals a purse from a man who picked it from the pocket of a leading theatrical producer. He is caught and sent to jail but the dancer, now in a Broadway show remains faithful to him. Afterwards he spurns her because he finds her in compromising position at apartments of libertine. He roams about and then comes back to forgive Mary but is too late, for she has married the producer of the show.

Married?
(Jans Productions—Six Reels)
(Reviewed by Frank Elliott)

SHADES of the ten-twenty-thirty! How they will applaud when they sit in on this one and see the hero, lashed to a log, heading for the big buzz saw as the half breed girl swims through the treacherous stream and turns off the water power just as the teeth of said saw are about to give our hero a boyish bob and then some. What a treat the gallery gods of yesteryear would consider the climax of this film "meller." There is nothing new in the plot which once again shows the "cave man" carrying off the spoiled society girl into the wilderness to tame her. In the background of this theme is the battle for a large estate valuable for its water power resources.

THEME. A melodramatic romance of a marriage by proxy in which a head strong flapper is borne away by her husband into the big woods to be tamed.

PRODUCTION HIGHLIGHTS. The fights between the rival bands of woodmen. The wedding by telephone. The meeting of the husband and wife. The "kidnaping" of the bride.

EXPLOITATION ANGLES. Play up the names of Owen Moore and Constance Bennett. This is your best selling point. Try and get a couple to be married on your stage and tie up with local merchants to offer prizes to the newlyweds.

DRAWING POWER. Suitable for second class down-town houses, community theatres and towns. Also O. K. for houses playing double features.

SUMMARY. A fair program picture with a rather hackneyed plot and a climax that recalls the old "meller" days. Popularity of leading players will help you sell it.

THE CAST

Dennis Shawn	Owen Moore
Marcia Livingston	Constance Bennett
Mary Jane Paul	Betty Bilburn
Judge Tracey	John Costello
Chuck English	Antrim Short
Harvey Williams	Frank Walsh
Kate	Evangeline Russell

From the novel by Marjorie Bention Cooke. Directed by George Terwilliger. Scenario by Jean Conover. Photographed by Louis H. Dunmyre and Walter Blakely.

SYNOPSIS. Deals with the battle of two great interests to obtain title to a vast estate on which mountain streams furnish water power. An old lady living on an adjoining estate controls original title to all the holdings. Her manager, Dennis Shawn, advises her against selling out to rival interests, but the old lady, pretending illness, threatens to do so unless Dennis marries Marcia Livingston, spoiled heiress to the land. After many difficulties this is arranged. There is a phone wedding. Later the husband "kidnaps" his bride and takes her into the wilds to tame her. The rival interests attempt Dennis' life, but he is saved by a half breed girl. All ends happily.

Elaine Hammerstein, starred by Chadwick Pictures in "Paint and Powder."

Paint and Powder (Chadwick)
PRESS NOTICE

THE romance of a dancer, who wins fame as the star of a Broadway musical comedy is presented with a realism which mirrors life itself in "Paint and Powder," the feature attraction announced by the ———theatre for ———. No concessions to romance are made in this unusual picture, which shows the glamorous backgrounds of Broadway theatrical life during the unfolding of an appealing drama concerned with a dancer who forgives the sins of her sweetheart but lives to know the irony of having forgiveness withheld.

Elaine Hammerstein has a highly emotional role in that of Mary Dolan, a part that affords the actress a wide scope for her talent and personal charm.

CATCH LINES

A picture that will win your heart and engage your eye. Moving romance set against a background of glittering Broadway's theatrical life.

Owen Moore, who plays a featured role in "Married," a Jans production.

Married (Jans Prod.)
PRESS NOTICE

CONSTANCE BENNETT, who did such creditable work in "The Goose Hangs High," and "My Son," and Owen Moore, hero of countless picture successes, are co-starred in "Married," a melodramatic romance of the western timber country and New York's social whirl which will be shown in the ———theatre on ———. There is an abundance of dramatic incident in this action-packed tale.

The production abounds in attractive outdoor scenes, as well as views of the New York mansion interiors. The tenseness of the plot is relieved now and then by some clever comedy. There is an excellent supporting cast.

CATCH LINES

Rare drama, delightful outdoor scenes, a good story, an all-star cast. All here.

The man disliked the girl, the girl hated the man, but they were told they must marry. The story of a young couple who were not sure whether they were wed or not.

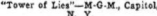

Newspaper Opinions on New Pictures

"Tower of Lies"—M-G-M., Capitol, N. Y.

Telegram: "Now and again we are privileged to behold an offering of the silent drama of such merit and character that our supplementary diet of pictorial piffle is almost forgotten in a floodtide of gratitude. Of such a rare order is 'The Tower of Lies.' Unlike most motion picture adaptations, characterizations has not been systematically reduced to action. There is none of the automatic 'going through the motions' when the director pulls the strings. We have four clearly defined studies of the four leading characters, each carefully conceived and sincerely portrayed. And the genius of Victor Seastrom, who credits the average spectator with a grain of intelligence and a suspicion of imagination, has combined them into one of the most harmonious and well constructed pictures that Broadway has seen in a long while."

Sun: "The talents of Victor Seastrom, bloom in their finest flower in 'The Tower of Lies,' a poetic, imaginatively staged photoplay. That should be considered in the nature of a command to attend one of its showings at the Capitol this week, where additional delight may be obtained through witnessing Lon Chaney and Norma Shearer in the distinctive acts of giving their finest performances."

Graphic: "The picture is a triumph of artistic directing and acting. While Lon Chaney has done more spectacular things, he has never been called upon to do anything which so indelibly stamps him as perhaps the greatest character artist on the screen. Norma Shearer as 'Glory is perfect. The role couldn't be better done. The same may be said of the mother, Claire McDowell."

Daily News: "Here, you feel, are great gifts. Rarely has a director put a story on the screen with such fine restraint, such poetical simplicity. 'The Tower of Lies' is drama at its best. It is realism coated with romance. Seastrom has set his moods with the wind and the rain and the sun, and achieves some unforgettable pictures. You are carried away to another land, other people, by the moving story and the fine characterizations by Lon Chaney and Norma Shearer."

Telegraph: "There is an outstanding fine bill at the Capitol Theatre this week. 'The Tower of Lies' is an exceptional moving picture, beautifully directed and a far cry from the hackneyed, trite stories which our producers glory in producing. To my mind the performance of Katrina, the mother, by Claire McDowell, is one of the finest bits of acting the screen has ever shown. Norma Shearer is splendid. Lon Chaney is very fine as the father, and William Haines is sincere as the young man."

World: "What this reviewer would wish to say at the earliest possible moment is that Lon Chaney's performance in 'The

Vera Reynolds in "Without Mercy," a Producers Distributing Corp. release.

Tower of Lies' is one of the most fascinating which he has seen in months. This serious-minded and prolific screen actor is one of the very best and certainly the foremost player of parts whose moods are primarily those of grotesque tragedy. Then there is the starry-eyed and wholly beautiful Norma Shearer. Let us advise the discerning to go and see this film and be pleased with the journey."

Evening World: "'The Tower of Lies' is an absorbing drama of the lives of simple folk, simply, beautifully and convincingly portrayed on the screen. It is a credit to all concerned in the making, but most of all to the director, Victor Seastrom. No outline can do justice to either the novel or the photoplay. Each deals with real people. Each is strong in the power of simplicity. Director Seastrom repeatedly uses the device of symbolism with telling effect. Intelligent and adequate direction and action reduces the need for subtitles."

American: "I have seldom seen anything finer than the work-ridden old peasant played by Claire McDowell. And what a performance Lon Chaney gives as Jan, the hard-working, poverty stricken farmer! Norma Shearer is excellent as Glory. Ian Keith gives a most creditable account of himself. In fact, all the characterizations are exceptionally well done, even the one of the boy, played by William Haines."

Post: "This film, featuring the work of that trio responsible for 'He Who Gets Slapped'—Lon Chaney, Norma Shearer and Director Victor Seastrom—is brilliantly conceived and acted with a sincerity that is impressive. Yes, impressive is the only word for it. Down to the smallest detail it is effectively worked out and executed with a smoothness not even encountered in week-to-week movie fare. So plausible, so inevitable, are the happenings of this tale, the reactions of its characters, that

all seems in harmony. Mr. Chaney and Miss Shearer do their best work in months,—in fact, it may very well be the best so far."

Brooklyn Eagle: "'The Tower of Lies' is as artistic and as moving a production as has appeared in some time. Victor Seastrom, who directed it, deserves a good deal of credit for the sincere artistry with which this tale has been picturized. He has been aided and abetted by the services of Lon Chaney and Norma Shearer."

"The Dark Angel"—1st National, Loew's State, L. A.

Times: "'The Dark Angel' really proves to be a winning dark horse on the race course of romantic film drama. Ronald Colman is superb as the soldier. Not only is his acting excellent, but for some reason or other he is romance incarnate on the screen. There is always something entirely inscrutable about him for one thing, despite his fire, magnetism and looks. Vilma Banky is exquisitely appealing."

Examiner: "'The Dark Angel' as done for the screen, proves a drama of intensive emotion and well balanced comedy and pathos. It is also an outstanding vehicle for Vilma Banky and Ronald Colman. Vilma Banky has beauty, grace and remarkable personality. Beside that she can act. Colman presents a splendid figure throughout the production, and takes advantage of his many opportunities with skill and artistry."

Express: "War and its aftermath have rarely been given a more sincere treatment than as found in the Dark Angel.' An intensely gripping story. The Dark Angel' is sentimental without being mawkish and romantic without being silly. It treats of the World War without spending too much time in the trenches."

Herald: "'The Dark Angel' is one of the few great war pictures. It is pure screen romance. Vilma Banky is a fine actress, playing her part with sympathy and power. As fine as Vilma Banky is, Ronald Colman's portrayal of Alan Trent is the outstanding feature of the picture. The understanding with which he plays the blind soldier is touching."

Record: "A powerful drama of love and devotion. Vilma Banky is an actress of genuine talent. She has a perfect screen personality. We consider her in the future's lineup of stars. And Ronald Colman gives a supreme performance. The heart interest is sustained throughout. The film is brimful of sentimental lure and is always convincing. It is beautifully photographed."

Times: "Quite in the foreground among the more romantic themes in the revival of interest in filming stories of European conflict is 'The Dark Angel.' Taste and sympathy are disclosed to an interesting degree in the treatment accorded the more serious scenes. Ronald Colman gives one of his finest performances. Colman's interpretation is quite an achievement in technique. Miss Banky is possessed of a radiant

refinement and loveliness. She may indeed be hailed as a truly notable screen 'find.'"

"The Freshman"—Pathe, Roosevelt, Chicago

Tribune: "I just love 'The Freshman'! Haven't seen its like in good, clean, original, spontaneously funny entertainment for an aeon—more or less. Do you know that you can almost bank on Harold Lloyd to turn out winners, and it doesn't take him three years, either. This time you see him in the humorously pitiful guise of what the press notices call a 'Sport model freshman'— and I know of no better description. The picture is full of thrilling, funny and pathetic incident, with all the folk in the supporting cast doing great work and the star outshining his always fresh self."

Herald - Examiner: "Gloom doesn't stand a chance against the line plunges of Harold Lloyd in 'The Freshman.' As the dumb hero of this comedy, Harold does his darndest for dear old Tate, and the final score is:

Gloom, 0; Joy, 106."

American: "Harold Lloyd's horn-rimmed glasses this time surround the eyes of one of the funniest of the many college boobs, who, although they do not attempt to give—or, at any rate, seldom succeed in giving—a true picture of campus life, have essayed to enliven an hour in the theatre. This overdone freshman is a genuine comic spectacle—or pair of spectacles."

Journal: "Balaban & Katz went rather out of their way to commend 'The Freshman,' showing at the Roosevelt, and in this commendation, as in other things, they prove they know what they are doing. Harold Lloyd after the fashion of Chaplin, gets his fun from being downtrodden—not in any big tragic way, but in the

Sally O'Neill in Metro-Goldwyn-Mayer's 'Sally, Irene and Mary.'

simple, heart-rending moments that come to most of us. There were times at the Roosevelt yesterday when I didn't know whether to ripple with laughter or sob, or go out to some collegiate campus and ask a lonely freshman to tea."

Post: "Harold Lloyd goes to college for his fun in this picture. It is his usual style of comedy, whimsical, gentle, shaded with pathos. His hero sets out with high ambitions for popularity in college, but he becomes the class 'boob' of the freshman class. The little drama has been worked out with great care. Each incident is neatly and expertly presented with its humorous possibilities brought out well. Slapstick as such has been avoided. No one tumbles and no one is struck to make you laugh. When such accidents do occur, they come in as part of the story. 'The Freshman' is very entertaining and has a charm all its own."

"Man on Box" — Warners, Warners, N. Y.

American: "I know very little of what constitutes a box office record, but I do know Syd Chaplin should come very near qualifying for that distinction. The theatre was packed to the doors. The audience laughed loudly at every comedy situation. Warners have enchanced the value of Harold McGrath's story rather than detracted from it. The direction of an involved comedy like this is the most difficult directorial feat in the world. And Chuck Reisner comes out with credit due by the deftness with which he plans his various situations. If you feel in need of a laugh take yourself to Warners Theatre."

Daily Mirror: "Syd Chaplin covers himself with glory and sends his audiences into gales of merriment. Even the Sphinx would shriek at Syd Chaplin's canny giftie o' fun, his clever acrobatics and female impersonation. Director Charles ('Chuck') Reisner has sustained the laughs until the final fadeout. He never permits the story to drag. Take our tip and put 'The Man On the Box' on your 'must' list."

Evening Journal: "Syd Chaplin as 'The Man On The Box' is a comedy riot. Yesterday's audiences shrieked at his exploits, and while Harold McGrath's novel was funny, this is one of those rare cases where a picture is an improvement on the original script. Chaplin is an excellent pantomimist. Toward the end of the film he disguises himself as a lady's maid, and if you thought he was good as Charley's Aunt you'll have a treat in store for you at this masquerade."

Evening Telegram: "Credit for the smoothness of the production is due in considerable measure to Charles Reisner, the director. With little straining after effect and not a few novel twists the picture romps along from start to finish in boisterous good humor. As an exponent of the gentle art of pantomiming the younger Chaplin has made quite a niche for himself in this latest comedy of his."

Morning Telegraph: "It is a pleasant, laugh-provoking farce, with enough merriment to please any audience. Alice Calhoun is quite lovely as the heroine. Hel-

ene Costello, daughter of the oldtime favorite, Maurice Costello, makes her film debut as Syd's sister. She is very beautiful and her screen success is hereby predicted. 'Chuck' Reisner and David Butler also contribute to the success of the picture. That the film is a success there can be no doubt. It is certainly highly amusing."

The Sun: "So far as I am concerned 'The Man On The Box' is every bit as worth while as was the screen version of 'Charley's Aunt,' through which the same Syd Chaplin bounced in petticoats. At yesterday's matinee Warners Theatre was filled to standing with an audience that seemed to relish the picture highly."

Evening Post: "It may be recommended as a picture with some very amusing scenes."

"Vanishing American" — Paramount, St. Francis, S. F.

Bulletin: "Magnificent in its setting, powerful in its realism, 'The Vanishing American' is more than a motion picture; it is an artistic historical chronicle of the American Indian; it tells of his rise and fall, and the picture is given just enough of romantic fiction to intensify interest and help impress indelibly upon the mind a true story of a race rapidly disappearing from the face of the earth."

Daily News: "Once more has Paramount selected San Francisco for the world premiere presentation of a superfeature and again has San Francisco placed upon that feature the stamp of its enthusiastic approval, if, in making this statement, the writer may be governed by his own impressions of 'The Vanishing American' and the crowds which he has seen storm the doors of the St. Francis theatre for the initial showings Saturday and Sunday. If there were no more to 'The Vanishing American' than the inspiringly beautiful scenes which picture the coming of the Redman as we know him and the emotion-gripping sequence which signalizes his passing, the picture would find a place in the forefront of film productions."

Chronicle "An epic of the Indian, his beginnings, his rise to power and glory, his fall and the tragic qualities of his existence today."

Examiner: "The Vanishing American' is destined to general popularity and ranks with the best of its type. Further, the music is worth going a long way to hear. It was composed especially by Charles Wakefield Cadman and its themes of Navajo chants with fluting and intricate drum rhythms are handled with exquisite feeling."

The Herald: "The credit for the success of 'The Vanishing American' — and it is unqualifiedly a success—must go to George B. Seitz, its director. The picture is superb. 'The Vanishing American' is destined to achieve general popularity and it's an important link in the chain of historical drama toward which picture producers are turning nowadays for their greater efforts."

Call: "Perhaps the most thrillingly picturesque photography as

yet displayed on the motion picture screen, backed up by a story of unusual pith and interest, to say nothing of its coherence, consistency and pathos, is to be seen in the world premiere screening of Zane Grey's powerful tale of the Great Southwest, entitled 'The Vanishing American.' The writer sat enthralled for upwards of 100 moments while this screen story of the semi-final chapters of the supremacy of the American Indian of the continent over which his forbears once held undisputed sway was unfolded before our eyes."

"Stella Dallas"—United Artists, West Coast, San Bernardino

Sun: "San Bernardino approves of 'Stella Dallas,' Belle Bennett is excellent in the role of Stella, mother of Laurel, played by six-teen-year-old Lois Moran. Their work raises the picture to a high standard and bids fair to make of it one of the sensations of the

coming winter season. To Ronald Colman and Alice Joyce high honors must be given for their work as Stephen Dallas and Helen Morrison."

"Stella Dallas"—United Artists, Florence, Pasadena

"'Stella Dallas' is destined to be the outstanding production of the year. If a preview-saturated city can view a picture and applaud it for full five minutes, that picture is a success. If a picture can hold every man, woman and child in the theatre, that picture is a success. If, throughout the preview, men and women permit tears to gather in their eyes, that picture is a success. If any actress can live her role so completely as Belle Bennett as Stella Dallas, that picture is a success. In all these phases 'Stella Dallas' excels. 'Stella Dallas' will make the nation weep; it will make the nation happy, and will cause discussions in every walk of life."

STATEMENT OF THE OWNERSHIP, MANAGEMENT, CIRCULATION, ETC., REQUIRED BY THE ACT OF CONGRESS OF AUGUST 24, 1912,

Of Motion Picture News published weekly at Albany, New York, for October 1, 1925.

STATE OF NEW YORK } ss.:
COUNTY OF NEW YORK }

Before me, a Notary Public in and for the State and county aforesaid, personally appeared Wm. A. Johnston, 729 7th Ave., N. Y. C. who, having been duly sworn according to law, deposes and says that he is the editor of the Motion Picture News and that the following is, to the best of his knowledge and belief, a true statement of the ownership, management (and if a daily paper, the circulation), etc., of the aforesaid publication for the date shown in the above caption, required by the Act of August 24, 1912, embodied in section 411, Postal Laws and Regulations, printed on the reverse of this form, to wit:

1. That the names and addresses of the publisher, editor, managing editor, and business managers are:

Name of publisher, Motion Picture News, Inc., Post office address, 729 Seventh Ave., New York City; Editor Wm. A. Johnston, 729 Seventh Ave., New York City; Managing Editors, J. S. Dickerson and Oscar Cooper, 729 Seventh Ave., New York City; Business Manager, Wm. A. Johnston, 729 Seventh Ave., New York City.

2. That the owner is: (if owned by a corporation, its name and address must be stated and also immediately thereunder the names and addresses of stockholders owning or holding one per cent or more of total amount of stock. If not owned by a corporation, the names and addresses of the individual owners must be given. If owned by a firm, company, or other unincorporated concern, its name and address, as well as those of each individual member, must be given.)

Percy S. Alden, 729 7th Ave.,

N. Y. C.; Motion Picture News, Inc., 729 7th Ave., N. Y. C.; Carll Tucker, 729 7th Ave., N. Y. C.; Wm. A. Johnston, 729 7th Ave., N. Y. C.; Dorothy Ovens Johnston, 729 7th Ave., N. Y. C.; E. Kendall Gillett, 729 7th Ave., N. Y. C.; Isabel G. Gillett, 729 7th Ave., N. Y. C.

3. That the known bondholders, mortgagees, and other security holders owning or holding 1 per cent or more of total amount of bonds, mortgages, or other securities are: (If there are none, so state.) None.

4. That the two paragraphs next above, giving the names of the owners, stockholders, and security holders, if any, contain not only the list of stockholders and security holders as they appear upon the books of the company but also, in cases where the stockholder or security holder appears upon the books of the company as trustee or in any other fiduciary relation, the name of the person or corporation for whom such trustee is acting, is given; also that the said two paragraphs contain statements embracing affiant's full knowledge and belief as to the circumstances and conditions under which stockholders and security holders who do not appear upon the books of the company as trustees, hold stock and securities in a capacity other than that of a bona fide owner; and this affiant has no reason to believe that any other person, association, or corporation has any interest direct or indirect in the said stock, bonds, or other securities than as so stated by him.

5. That the average number of copies of each issue of this publication sold or distributed, through the mails or otherwise, to paid subscribers during the six months preceding the date shown above is .... (This information is required from daily publications only.)

W. A. JOHNSTON.

Sworn to and subscribed before me this 29th day of September, 1925.

R. S. GEORGE.

(My commission expires March 30, 1926.)

Regional News from Correspondents

OSCAR NEUFELD, President and Sam Stiefel, Vice-President and Treasurer of the De Luxe Film Exchange have entered the real estate field in addition to their other activities. They have established the Neufeld Realty Company, with offices at 541 Market St., Camden, N. J., and expect to be able to interest motion picture men in the possibilities of New Jersey real estate with

Philadelphia

the new Delaware River bridge nearing completion.

N. J. Ayres, formerly manager of the local Independent Film Exchange, has been transferred to the Washington office in the same capacity.

Sidney Lowenstein, who has a nation wide reputation as a musical director, is now appearing as guest conductor at the new Stanley Theatre in Atlantic City.

Marcus Benn has recently installed a new $2,000 electric sign

over the marquee of the Benn Theatre in this city.

The four theatres recently acquired by the Stanley Company in Wilmington are being thoroughly renovated for the winter season.

Frank Cook has been appointed manager of Marcus Benn's Orient Theatre. William Harvey, who preceded him, is in charge of the Stanley Company's Arcadia Theatre in Wilmington.

Seattle

EXHIBITORS and film men over the entire territory were shocked last week to learn of the death of Claude A. Thompson, veteran theatre operator of Pomeroy, Wash., as a result of pernicious anemia. Mr. Thompson was 44 years of age, and had been interested in the theatre field in this state for twenty-five years. At the age of nineteen, he had managed the Seeley Opera House in Pomeroy, and the new Seeley Theatre in that city was built principally through his efforts. As a mark of respect to his memory, all business houses in Pomeroy remained closed for the hour of Mr. Thompson's funeral.

L. O. Lukan, manager of the local Universal exchange, and A. J. Kennedy, publicity, advertising and exploitation director, have just returned from Spokane, where they put across one of the Carl Laemmle Exhibitor Parties. Approximately 150 exhibitors of

the Eastern Washington territory attended the event.

H. W. Bruen's Arabian Theatre at Woodland Park Avenue and Seventy-Seventh Street in this city was opened with appropriate ceremonies the end of September, and has taken its place among the leading suburban houses of this territory.

Announcement was made last week to the effect that the lease on the Connell Theatre in Aberdeen, acquired last month by the Elbe Theatres Company, has just been disposed of to the Ed Dolan interests of that territory. Arthur Bishell, former manager of the Will Starkey Amusement Enterprises in Spokane, who was taken as manager of the Connell Theatre by the Elbe Company, has returned to this city, following the closing of the house by the Dolan organization. Further plans for the house have not yet been decided upon, it was reported.

Matt Apperton, well-known film salesman of this territory, left Manager W. H. Drummond's local Producers' Distributing Corporation exchange last week to take over the management of the Universal exchange in Salt Lake City. Mr. Apperton's position in a sales capacity here will be filled by "Cherry" Malotte, whose association with local film exchanges dates back for a number of years.

Roy Cooper, former manager of the Anzier Theatre in this city, last week announced his association with the John Danz interests. In his new capacity, Mr. Cooper will assist Harry Carey in the management and operation of the Roycroft Theatre, Mr. Danz's new suburban house in this city.

William C. Roach, owner and manager of the Sellwood and new Oregon Theatres in Portland, was a visitor on Film Row last week. The Oregon was opened by Mr. Roach only last month and repre-

sents one of the finest small theatres in the Oregon territory, according to reports.

A. A. Bruce, formerly associated in a sales capacity with Manager Al Rosenberg's De Luxe Feature Film Exchange, last week announced his resignation with that organization, and had joined the sales staff of Manager L. O. Lukan's local Universal office. It is expected that he will cover the Eastern Washington field for Universal, as he did for DeLuxe.

John Hamrick, owner and general manager of the Blue Mouse circuit of theatres in Seattle, Tacoma and Portland, announced last week that he plans to leave this city soon for a combined business and pleasure trip to New York City, where he will remain for several weeks the latter part of October.

New England

THE world famous Boston Theatre which for several generations has been the scene of music and drama, closed its doors for the last time Saturday night, Oct. 3. Bright and early Monday morning building wreckers started the demolition of the famous playhouse to make way for a modern business block. During recent years the theatre was under lease to the Keith-Albee interests.

Monday morning without any particular formalities, the New Boston Theatre, built by Keith-Albee interests, opened diagonally

across from the old Boston, at Washington and Essex streets.

Ben Laurie, for some time associated with the Franklin Film Co. at its Connecticut offices and more recently with Warner Brothers, has acquired the Keith Theatre in Campbello, Mass.

George Solomon of the Thompson Square Theatre in the Charlestown section of Boston, has taken over the Victoria Theatre in Lawrence, Mass., purchasing from Louis Rothenberg.

H. T. Skelly, general manager

of United Artists distribution for New England at Boston, has returned from a week's business trip in New York.

The new Lake Pleasant Theatre in Providence, R. I., is nearing completion and the finishing touches will be given within a few weeks. A. A. Spitz, who is owner of the Palace Theatre in Cranston, R. I., and the Park Theatre in Auburn, R. I., is owner of the new playhouse.

Philip Markell has added the Magnet Theatre in the Dorchester

District of Boston to his already extensive string of theatres.

Arthur J. Viano, owner of the Teel Square Theatre in Somerville and other playhouses in Suburban Boston, has purchased a site in Davis square, Somerville, Mass., and is planning the erection of a new theatre on the site.

Commencing this week, Gordon's Washington Street Olympia Theatre, Boston, changes its policy to four instead of three shows each day, with orchestra and vaudeville at each show.

Canada

J. E. LEDDEN, manager of the Papineau Theatre, Montreal, has a ball team that has earned a great record in baseball circles of the district during the past season. The Papineau Theatre team, headed by Ledden as catcher, won its 14th straight victory of the season when it captured an encounter with the Richilieu Club by the score of 4 to 3.

Cobalt, Ontario, one of the chief centres of the Northern Ontario

mining district, is to have a new moving picture house and hotel combined. Incorporation of a company under the laws of Ontario to be known as the Cobalt Hotel and Theatre Company, Limited, with headquarters at Cobalt, has been announced. The company is capitalized at $100,000.

William Mitchell, sales supervisor of First National Exhibitors, Toronto, has gone to Winnipeg, Manitoba, where he will

cover the territory out from that city. He was a guest at the September luncheon of the Manitoba Moving Picture Exhibitors Association.

Maurice Milligan, Canadian manager for Paramount, has been spending recent weeks at Winnipeg and in the Canadian Middle West in the interest of Famous-Lasky Film Service. Mr. Milligan formerly lived in Winnipeg.

Steve Ladas of Ottawa, On-

tario, a prominent local merchant, has entered into an arrangement with Montreal interests to take over the lease of the Family Theatre, Ottawa, one of the two local moving picture halls operated for years by the late Harry Brouse of First National fame. The Family, which is a downtown theatre, is to be resumed and will be re-opened after extensive renovating.

St. Louis

THE Missouri Theatre, Grand boulevard at Lucas avenue, St. Louis, owned by the Paramount-Balaban-Katz interests, has joined the national movement to encourage Saturday morning motion picture shows for children.

The New American Amusement Company, controlled by Oscar Lehr and relatives, has closed a deal for the New American Theatre, 2406 South Twelfth street, and the New Shenandoah Theatre, Broadway and Shenandoah avenue, St. Louis. The purchase was made from Samuel Lewis. The deal is said to have involved $50,000.

The members of the New American Amusement Company are Oscar Lehr, Marshall Lehr and Ida Lehr. They also control the Peerless, 1911 South Broadway; the Family, 1440 South Broadway, and the New

Broadway, 1719 South Broadway. The New American seats 704 persons and the New Shenandoah 1381. Both have airdomes. The other houses owned by the Lehrs range from 637 seats to 670 seats.

It is reported along Picture Row that George Skouras will add a prominent North St. Louis theatre to his increasing chain of amusement places. The deal is "on" but has not as yet been consummated those on the inside say.

Cons., uc, jon on George's beautiful new house at Southwest and Columbia avenues is well under way. It will rank with the city's best outlying house and contain about 1500 seats.

Work has started on the New Marshall Theatre, Sutton and Manchester avenues, Maplewood, Mo. It will cost about $150,000 and have 1500 seats. It was pro-

moted by Maplewood business men.

Contracts have been let on the Springfield, Ill., new Lincoln Square Theatre and Apartment building at Fifth and Jefferson streets.

The building will be three stories, 157 by 242 feet and the cost has been estimated at $1,000,000. The architects are Levin & Rupert, 822 West 79th street, Chicago, while the general contract was let to Kaiser & Ducett, Joliet, Ill.

The Lincoln Square Theatre Corporation, owner, has an office at 113 North Fifth street, Springfield. Louis Robert is in charge.

Plans for a building on a mammoth scale with motion picture theatre, restaurant, dance hall and garage are in preparation. The site is at the triangle formed by Skinker boulevard and Oakland and Clayton avenues at

the Southwestern entrance to Forest Park, St. Louis. The project calls for an expenditure of $1,000,000.

The identity of the syndicate behind the big deal has not been divulged by the Paul Jones Realty Company which acquired the site for the promoters. The lot fronts 364 feet on Clayton, 320 feet on Oakland, 200 feet on Central avenue and 26 feet on Skinker boulevard.

Tom McKean, manager for F. B. O. and Charley Goldman motored to Duquoin, Ill., to see Tom Reed.

Visitors seen along Picture Row were: John Rees, Wellsville, Mo.; John Marlowe, Herrin, Ill.; Mr. and Mrs. I. W. Rodgers, Cairo, Ill.; Jim Reilly, Alton, Ill.; O. E. Simon, Gem Theatre, Jefferson City, Mo., and Joe Hewitt, Robinson, Ill.

Baltimore

E. A. LAKE, manager of Loew's Hippodrome Theatre, here, is expected to return to his duties at that playhouse soon as he has been convalescing from his recent operation during the past week. During his absence W. J. McGowan, formerly manager of Loew's Valentine Theatre, Toledo, Ohio, acted in his place assisted by Elmer Free, the Hipp's publicity representative, who took his turn on the floor each night.

George Kollman, who formerly covered the Virginia territory for the Famous Players Lasky Corporation, has resigned his position to make a trip to Florida.

Clarence Eiseman, formerly covering the Baltimore territory for Producers' Distributing Corporation has gone over to Universal. Louis Bach, formerly manager of the Washington, D. C., office

for First National, Inc., then manager of the Canada Division of that company has returned to Washington, D. C., as manager of the Producers Distributing Corporation office there.

Arthur Melvin, who was a salesman with Fox Film Company for ten years and during that time handled the Baltimore territory for a number of years has resigned and is now with Metro-Goldwyn Mayer. He is succeeded in the Fox Company by Herndon Edmonds, who was with Metro-Goldwyn Mayer, for many years, who is now with Fox.

The Lafayette Theatre, (colored) 1423 West Lafayette avenue, which has a seating capacity of 550 persons, has been leased for a term of years by Peter Oletzky, proprietor of the Federated Film Exchange, and the Comedy and Waverly theatres.

Mr. Oletzky has had the Lafayette renovated and repainted.

Improvements to cost about $8,000 are being made now on the Broadway Theatre, 509 South Broadway, operated by the Associated Theatres Company, J. Louis Rome, general manager. New flooring is being laid and new seats being installed while a corps of painters are busy redecorating and painting the playhouse.

A week-end trip was taken to New York by Samuel Back on Saturday, October 3. Mr. Back is manager of the Rialto Theatre.

The Douglas Theatre, a colored playhouse on Pennsylvania avenue, now operated by a Philadelphia Company, was reopened to the public on Monday, September 28.

Three hundred window cards are being distributed in the neighborhoods of each of the following playhouses controlled by the Asso-

ciated Theatres Company, including: the Rialto, Capitol, Apollo and Broadway. The Poplar is not included in the list for window cards.

Harry Morstein, proprietor of the Queen Theatre, 666 West Lexington street, has left Baltimore for a vacation in California to last about eight months.

Another film salesman to go to Florida, is Stanley Spoehr who was formerly manager of the Vitagraph Exchange in Washington, D. C.

Florida has attracted Jack Osserman, Washington, D. C. office manager for Universal.

The Century Roof, atop the Century Theatre, both of which are operated by the Whitehurst Combined Interests, reopened to the public on Saturday night October 3. Dr. Milton Whitehurst is managing the Roof this year.

Denver

L. J. SCHLAIFER, District Manager for Universal, and L. B. Metzger, Complete Service Manager for Universal, arrived in Denver last Wednesday from the Western Coast. While in Denver, they spent the entire day at a local hotel holding a conference with Eugene Gerbase, local branch manager for Universal and his entire sales force which included not only all salesmen but the bookers and publicity men. Mr. Metzger left late Thursday for New York City.

Jack Tierney, Home Office representative of Pathe, has been visiting the local Pathe exchange for the past week. Mr. Tierney is efficiency man for the shipping and postal departments. He arrived in Denver last Monday from

Detroit and will leave soon for Salt Lake City.

The following individuals were visitors in film row during the past week: V. Barrett, one of the owners and operators of the Park Theatre, Greeley, Colorado; Jim Lynch, who owns and operates the theatre in Laramie, Wyoming, and who is also President of the New M. F. T. O. of Wyoming; J. J. Goodstein, owner of the Palm Theatre, Pueblo, and the Longmont Theatre, Longmont, Colorado. Mr. Goodstein arrived in Denver from Philadelphia and was accompanied by his Pueblo manager, C. H. Ernst.

Denver will have two new suburban houses celebrate their grand opening this week. On Friday night, October 2, the new Mena Theatre located at Alameda and

South Pearl Street opens, and on Saturday night, October 3rd, the new Alpine Theatre located at 33rd and Williams will also open. The Mena Theatre is owned and managed by William Menagh, and the Alpine Theatre was built and will be managed by Ed N. Nesbit.

Aaron Epstein, died suddenly at the breakfast table last Sunday morning. Mr. Epstein was the auditor for the Fox Theatres in Denver and one of the most popular men among Curtis Street exhibitors. His body was sent to Brooklyn, New York, his former home, at which place the funeral services will be held.

Homer Ellison, Jr., former manager of the Queen Theatre in Denver, has gone to Florida to try his luck in the real estate game. The theatre will soon be opened in Burns, Wyoming, by Messrs.

Smith and Storey. The new amusement house will be called the White City Theatre. The promoters of the theatre are businessmen in Burns and intend to operate under a community arrangement.

S. Z. Williams, Auditor, was in the city last week visiting the State Theatre, one of the houses owned and operated by the company he represents. After spending a few days in Denver, he left for Seattle, Washington.

Charles R. Gilmour has just resigned from a very successful sales trip in Cheyenne and Casper, Wyoming. Mr. Gilmour is the local branch manager for Warner Brothers.

J. A. Krum also made a hurried sales trip into the Arkansas Valley last week. He returned yesterday from Canon City, Colorado.

New York and New Jersey

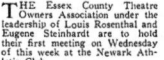

THE Essex County Theatre Owners Association under the leadership of Louis Rosenthal and Eugene Steinhardt are to hold their first meeting on Wednesday of this week at the Newark Athletic Club.

The opening of Filmland Theatre at Church and Nostrand Avenue, Brooklyn, a couple of weeks ago, has completed the final chapter of an interesting story. About two years ago the original promoter conceived the idea of erecting a strictly modern theatre in that section of Flatbush and started the scheme as a Community project. Owing to lack of funds the construction proceeded by fits and starts and for long periods there was no sign of work around the house. Messrs. Ryan and Buckley then organized Filmland Players, Inc. and, took over the task of re-organizing, financing and building and have at last presented the neighborhood with a beautiful new theatre.

Thomas J. Buckley is head of the Buckley Engineering Company with offices at 50 East 42nd Street, New York City. John L. Ryan is President of the Interboro Mortgage Company of 29 Broadway, City. The rest of the directors include several other names that are well known, one being that of the Hon. George W. Martin, Kings County Judge.

Fred J. Dollinger, well known showman, has been selected as manager of Filmland. Mr. Dollinger went on the stage at eight years of age and his experience in motion pictures theatres dates back to the days of the Nickelodeon. He was manager for twelve years at the Claramont theatre, 135th St. and Broadway, General Manager of the H. & S. Theatres, New York and assistant on many Broadway prologues for big feature photo-plays.

The balance of the executive staff include, Miss Virginia Early, Treasurer and House manager, Anthony Devodier, orchestra leader, Thomas McLucy, organist and John Palmerton, chief electrician.

Filmland is strictly up to the minute in every respect in the way of modern theatre construction with a seating capacity of about 1,700. A two manual Kramer organ has been installed. Typhoon ventilation system, novelty scenic stage settings and the lighting fixtures were installed by Lightolier. The seats were furnished by the Superior Seating Company.

Other important theatre openings that are scheduled for this territory within 'the next two weeks are Charlie Goldreyer's Manor, located at Ave K and Coney Island Ave., Brooklyn. Leo Brecher's New Boston Road theatre, at 167th Street, New York and the Berkshire Theatre, 60th St. and 8th Ave., Brooklyn, the latter owned and operated by Morris Ginsberg.

Ed. Carroll, the prize winning salesman who covers New Jersey territory for Associated Exhibitors, has returned from his summer home at Avon, N. J. to his apartment in Montclair where he will put up for the cold weather. Ed has recently purchased a piece of property in Montclair and contemplates building a home.

Sam Perry, hustling exhibitor from Englewood, N. J. was in town Tuesday and in addition to shopping for pictures was seeking information concerning a new electric sign for the front of his theatre.

Arron Schusterman, who operates the Cozy-Bijou at New Brunswick, N. J. is giving up his residence at that city and will make his home in New York City for the winter.

A. A. Adams, of Newark and Patterson theatres is en route to this country from Greece.

A. Padgett is the latest addition to the Pathe local sales force and will specialize on the two reelers. Mr. Pargett former connections were with the electrical supply business and has also worked out of Cleveland for Associated Exhibitors.

The new theatre at Madison, N. J. will open about the middle of October.

Joe. Stern has purchased property at Cranford, N. J. as a prospective theatre site. Cranford is the headquarters of Alec Okin who operates the Cranford theatre at that point. It is also reported that Mr. Stern is looking over ground at Rahway, where Louis Helman holds forth.

Roth Bros., of Morristown and Summit, N. J., have purchased from Messers. Bradder and Pollack, the theatre building that is at present under construction in Summit. The new house will have a seating capacity of about 1,500 and it is expected to be ready for business on November 15th. Manager Hoffman has been appointed managing director of all the Roth Bros. enterprises.

George Ellison, formerly with the Yost and the Proctor circuits for many years, is now the managing director of the Dyckman theatre at 207th St. and Sherman Ave.

Several more theatre openings are scheduled for this month and next. Rachmiel's New Ambassador in Brooklyn will open November 15th; The Forsyth, on the lower East Side, on October 15th, Alexander Fabian's new house in Patterson, on November 15th and Louis Rosenthal's Lyceum and Colonial in East Orange will be ready about October 15th.

Matthew Christmas has leased another theatre in Yonkers, this one being on Riverside Ave. This is the fourth one for Matthew this season and makes a total of eleven in the circuit at the present time.

Joe Hornstein and his staff at Howell's Cine Equinment Co. are keeping on the jump these days. Theatres recently equipped include Roth Bros. new house in Summit, Walter Reade's New Main St. theatre at Asbury Park, Rachmiel's New Ambassador in Brooklyn, the Forsyth, Bradler and Pollack's Hawthorne at Newark which will have its opening October 15th, the

Hollywood in Brooklyn, and Sol Brill's Inwood in the Dyckman Heights section. Joe is in receipt of a letter of thanks from Abe Fabian, of the Mosque Theatre, Newark, complimenting him on the services that he rendered on the opening night. Dave Soloman, a go-getter on Joe's sales staff has captured another prize, this one being the result of selling a lot of curtain control motors.

A luncheon at the Hofbrau House was tendered by F. B. O. to the New York salesmen of the company last Monday in celebration of the sale of 50% of the year's quota.

Charles Rosenzweig, manager of the New York exchange presided. Major H. C. S. Thomson, president of the F. B. O., Colvin W. Brown, vice-president, David Poucher, treasurer, Lee Marcus, sales manager, Nat. G. Rothstein, publicity and advertising director, Al Boasberg, sales promotion director and Cleve Adams, division manager of Chicago, attended. The F. B. O. salesmen who partook of the feast were G. William Wolf, H. Kram, Jack Ellis, L. C. Wechsler, Leo M. Fox, L. B. Cherwood, J. W. Holden, Phil Hodes and Frank Leonard, exploiteer, connected with the New York Exchange.

Major Thomson, in a brief talk, thanked the men for their loyalty and splendid service.

Manger Brodsky held a successful opening at his West End Theatre last Saturday. The West End is a 900 seat house.

Moe Kridel who operates the Globe at Irvington, N. J., has completed the extensive alterations to the old Victory theatre and will open this week. The new house will be know as the Congress and there is hardly a trace of the old theatre that shows.

Managers Daress of Boonton, N. J. and Coucolos of Elizabeth were visitors around the exchanges this week.

It is reported that Walter Reade, of the Walter Reade Enterprises, has purchased an interest in the Strand theatre at Freehold, N. J. Harold Burns has been the proprietor of the Strand.

Louis Boldberg of Mayer and Schneider, Milton Kronacker of Pathe and several others were observed in deep conference, Tuesday.

Joe Hornstein accompanied by W. C. Kunzman of the National Carbon Co. and Max Rubin of the Exhibitors Supply Co., Detroit, Michigan, left Saturday night to attend the meeting of the Society of Motion Picture Engineers at Roscoe, N. Y. They will be away until Thursday of this week. All are members of the S. M. P. E.

Henry Siegle is building a 2,000 seat theatre at Cedarhurst, L. I. and expects to complete the new house about Feb. 1st.

Minneapolis

VICTOR TORNQUIST of the Crystal theatre at Baxter, Ia., escaped death a little while ago when a film he was carrying on the outside of his car exploded.

Earl Skevdahl, 22, youngest manager in Iowa, is just about ready to reopen his Royal at Sioux City.

L. A. Hummell has succeeded Charles J. Howard in charge of the Associated Exhibitors branch in Minneapolis. He is an old timer on the sales force.

Sunday shows are being tried out at Hoffman, Minn., under direction of the town council, Davis and Johnson have the Princess theatre there.

Remodeling of the Palace theatre at Hector, Minn., is nearly completed under George W. Ryan who took it over from August Nelson.

Al Dubeau is looking around for new fields to conquer since selling his Caughren theatre at

Sauk Center to Clifford Getter of Staples.

The grand opening of the New Grand, newly built at Worthington, Minn., by George J. Ehlers is just over and a good time and good business are reported.

The Opera House at Egan, S. D., is dark. Poor patronage caused Randolph and Hodge to close.

Vienna, S. D., is to have its picture house. Axel Soderlund of Willow Lake, who presents occasional shows at Edwin, Bancroft and Melham, will open a new building there.

Castana, Ia., is planning a new show house.

Clarence Balzley will operate a theatre at Tracy, Ia.

Brownsdale is getting shows now through William Jamieson of Claramont and an arrangement with business men.

The new Metro theatre at Carlyle, Ia., is run by Park

Agnew, former Metro-Goldwyn booker at Des Moines.

Movement for a new community hall in Inkster, N. D., has received a big impetus since fire recently destroyed J. A. Hilden's Gem, the only theatre in town.

Once $14,000 loser after long efforts to make it pay, the T. B. Sheldon Memorial Auditorium, once the "white elephant" of Red Wing, Minn., is now trying to figure what to do with the $30,000 surplus now on hand. It was an expensive theatre given by the estate of T. B. Sheldon 20 years ago. At that time it was the only municipal theatre in the United States. G. W. Johnson put the theatre on a firm foundation after it burned out five years ago.

The Seventh Street theatre which long housed the Orpheum circuit in Minneapolis, is celebrating its 21st anniversary this week. Silas Hess is manager.

J. O. Johnson and George Gubbins, veteran theatre staff men in Minneapolis, are on a motor trip to Chicago.

Charles C. Perry, managing director of the Garrick, is back from Chicago where he has been booking music to go with his Metro-Goldwyn pictures.

L. N. Scott, manager of the Metropolitan theatres in St. Paul and Minneapolis, will include several big films among the bookings he is making on the present trip to New York.

Jack Segal of the Minneapolis Universal exchange is reported recovered from his automobile accident injuries sustained near Sauk Center.

Ground breaking for the new 1200 seat theatre at Minot to be built by J. M. Wilson of that North Dakota city, will probably not begin until next spring for the theatre is not to be finished till August, 1926.

Harold Cook, operator, who risked his life when a film exploded in the Family theatre, Davenport, Ia., is reported recovering from the burns he suffered.

Milwaukee

MAX STAHL, manager of the Milwaukee exchange of Educational, has returned to the city after spending the Jewish holidays at his old home in Farwell, Pa. While several of the local film men went out of town for the New Year's, Stahl took the long distance record of them all.

Morris Abrams, publicity director for Metro-Goldwyn in the Wisconsin and Minnesota territory, has come back to Milwaukee after spending the past two months in Minneapolis and the contiguous territory. He promises the Wisconsin exhibitors some real service during his sojourn in the state.

Ed. Tunstall, formerly head of the Tunstall Film Corporation of Milwaukee, and Milwaukee manager for Warner Bros., has been visiting with film men friends in

the city prior to returning East, where he is New England representative for the Arctic Nu-Air Co. Ed reports business as being very good with him, but although he's a busy man now-a-days, he can't forbear paying periodical visits to the Wisconsin boys, who always give him a hearty welcome.

Stan Brown, manager of Saxe's Strand Theatre, Milwaukee, is proudly calling the attention of all visitors this week to the brand new $30,000 Barton organ just installed in the house. The instrument is one of the finest in downtown Milwaukee and is capably played by Miss Terese Meyer.

Sam Sherman, Milwaukee manager for Metro-Goldwyn, has equipped himself with a shiny new bowling ball. Now he's ready to take on all comers and promises to give Tom Saxe, Eddie Keogh, and a lot of other exhibitors a

match they'll long remember. Bowling, by the way, is getting to be a popular topic among the local picture men, since the golf season is about over with.

Art Desormeaux, prominent Madison Exhibitor and general manager of the Strand Theatre Co., of that city, has put his final O.K. on the plans for the new Capitol Theatre in East Madison. Excavating for the new house started this week and the work is to be rushed. The new house will have 1,200 seats, and will be one of the finest theatres in the south central part of the state. It will be equipped with a full sized stage, adequate for accommodating any kind of production that comes along, but the principal feature will be pictures.

Charles H. Koch, former manager of the Garden Theatre while it was operated in conjunction

with the Alhambra Theatre, has returned to the former as assistant manager under O. J. Wooden, who assumed active charge of the house after Universal leased the Alhambra, which he had managed prior to that time. Koch has been taking a long needed vacation during the past few weeks and is now back in harness in good shape.

October 17 has been set as moving day by F. B. O., the Midwest Film Co., and the Ray Smith Co., who have heretofore composed the faithful triumverate to remain in the Old Film Exchange Building on Second Street. All three exchanges will be moved to a new structure erected for them at 147 Seventh Street by Oscar Brachman, secretary of the Wisconsin Theatre Co.

Cincinnati

M. B. DEVORE of the Palace Theater, Sabina, O., bought several large pictures while visiting the film buildings last week.

Izzy Schwartz, manager of the Dolly Garden Theater in this city, turned his house into a colored amusement palace on Saturday, October 3rd.

Mrs. J. Crone of the Ideal theater, Eastern Ave., Cincinnati, is the most consistent visitor to the exchanges in this city. She can be seen in the various exchanges every Saturday morning, and no matter how the business for the

week has been she always wears a pleasant smile.

William Kamp, an old timer in the film game, is reopening the Princess Theater in Dayton, Ky.

Harry Dodge, Paramount district manager with offices in Columbus, O., and Carl Weeks, Columbus branch manager for the same firm, spent several days at the local exchange last week.

R. N. Johnston of the It and Margaret Theaters, Huntington, W. Va., was in the city last week, purchasing supplies for his houses.

J. N. Fisher of the Lyric The-

ater, Versailles, Ky., and Chas. Groos of the Columbia, Dayton, O., were seen around the exchanges last week.

Ronald Moray is the new salesman for Paramount, taking the place of Dick Roach, who resigned last week. Moray comes here from Cleveland. To prove to him that the city appreciates him and wants him to stay, his car was stolen two days after he reached town.

Elston B. Dodge, exhibitor of New Richmond and Sharenville, O., spent a day at the exchanges

booking pictures for his several theaters.

University of Kentucky recently had a fire and have purchased new Power's projectors.

Manager Fisher of the Lyric Theatre, Versailles, Ky., was a visitor in Film Row this week.

M. A. Hewitt, at Bethel Theatre, Bethel, Ohio, has just purchased new equipment and is looking forward to having a prosperous year.

T. A. Elliot of the Sunset Theatre, Charleston, W. Va., was in town recently.

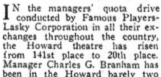

Atlanta

IN the managers' quota drive conducted by Famous Players-Lasky Corporation in all their exchanges throughout the country, the Howard theatre has risen from 141st place to 20th place. Manager Charles G. Branham has been in the Howard barely two months.

Mr. and Mrs. S. W. Taylor, opened the new Taylor theatre in Edenton, N. C., on September 28th. The Taylor theatre is reported to be a very attractive little house.

Jack Oswald, one of Paramounts' most popular travelling auditors, who is well-known to the exhibitors of this territory, has just received word here in Atlanta that he has been appointed assistant to Lem Stewart, director of publicity and advertising in Famous Players' theatre department.

Charles Kelly, formerly connected with the Journal, succeeds Mrs. Jacques Futrelle as director of publicity of the Howard theatre this week.

Several changes and promotions came about in Pathe's southern exchanges this week. Harry L. Knappen, who has been Pathe's special Harold Lloyd representative in this territory, took over the duties of managership in the New Orleans exchange last Monday.

Mr. Knappen succeeds P. A. Schmuck, former manager, who has been transferred to the Charlotte Branch; while E. E. Heller, formerly branch manager in Charlotte has been appointed special district serial representative here

the Southeast, entering on his duties immediately.

Jack Sellers, who produced the Telegraph Follies so successfully for the Rialto theatre, Macon, Ga., last year about this time, has recently entered a new field that has theatre exploitation work and producing prologues. Mr. Sellers is now manager of the Lincoln theatre, a Warner Bros. house, in Winston-Salem, N. C., and making good in his new position.

C. K. Howell, theatrical architect, formerly of Atlanta, and more recently of Richmond, Va., returned to Atlanta this week, where he will again open offices.

R. T. Hill, prominent exhibitor of Tennessee, and owner of the Strand theatre, Tullahoma, Tenn., among several others, was in Atlanta this week on a business trip.

T. F. Thompson (Chief), manager of the Palace theatre, Cedartown, Ga., was in Atlanta for a few days this week on business.

George F. Lenehan, Producers' popular district manager, arrived in Atlanta this week, from Charlotte, where he remained several days en route to Atlanta from his Washington headquarters.

Cowan Oldham, manager of Oldham's theatre, McMinnville, Tenn., arrived in Atlanta this week for a few days of business here.

E. Auger, formerly general sales manager of Vitagraph, stopped over in Atlanta this week on his way to Florida, where it is understood he will enter the real estate business.

Dan Roberts, popular film salesman of this territory, was in town this week on business matters.

C. K. Howell, widely-known theatre architect, arrived in Atlanta early this week to open his new offices here.

Arthur Dickenson, associated with the firm of Carson and Bradford, Miami, Fla., has been in Atlanta for the past several days visiting old friends.

Tom Little, branch manager of Producers, held a sales meeting this week to discuss plans for a big month's business. Those attending were Dixie Graham, L. G. Duncan, Jack Cook and (?) who left for their respective territories with renewed energy and pep.

Hank Hearn, Liberty's popular manager, returned to Atlanta from a business trip to Birmingham Monday.

Earl E. Griggs, exploiter for Universal, returned to the city Friday after having visited several points in the territory, this week.

P. A. Engler of the Famous theatre, Birmingham, Ala., whose name is known to thousands through Octavus Roy Cohen's popular stories based on its' locality, reports that business is better than ever, in keeping with Fall prosperity.

Ed Beech, formerly with Paramount in the Charlotte exchange, is now traveling the Georgia territory for Liberty Film Distributing Corporation.

J. W. Mangham, branch manager of the Atlanta Enterprise exchange, is due back from Florida this week, where he has been since August 1st selling Enterprise's product.

Howard Price Kingsmore,

formerly manager of the Howard theatre, Atlanta, who was transferred a short time ago to the Strand theatre, San Francisco, Calif., has resigned. Mr. Kingsmore's future plans are not yet known.

L. J. Duncan, formerly connected with the local Metro-Goldwyn exchange, is now connected with Producers in a similar capacity.

L. B. Remy district manager for Fox, was in Atlanta this week on business matters.

Charles Kranz, well-known to film folks of this territory, was in the city this week, on his way to Florida where he will engage in the real estate business.

H. E. Elder, district manager for Warner Bros., in this territory, was in Atlanta for a few days this week.

H. Griffin, of the Nicholas Power Company, was in the city during the week, and reported business was bright everywhere.

George McKean, son of Manager C. W. McKean of the St. Louis Fox Exchange, and under whom he has had valuable experience in exchange work, will be made manager of the Fox exchange in Memphis, to be opened sometime this month, it is announced.

Ernest Neiman, Producers district representative, arrived in Atlanta this week after having attended the big company meeting in Chicago. He reported many interesting developments in Producers plans for the future, which were of interest to Manager Tom Little and his salesmen.

Southeast

VERN JOHNSTON, General Manager of the Piedmont Amusement Company, of Winston Salem, N. C., has gone to Florida on a vacation.

E. E. Hellar, Manager of the Pathe Exchange, this city has received a promotion, being appointed as district sales representative for the serial department. He will be succeeded in the Charlotte office by M. Schmucker, who is being brought from New Orleans to fill this position.

E. L. Bean, of Shelby, N. C., was a Charlotte visitor the past week setting in dates and buying additional product for the coming season.

Webb Brothers, of Shelby, N. C., were Charlotte visitors the past week.

C. I. Gresham, of the Artcraft Theatre, Mooresville, N. C., was along Film Row the past week.

B. W. Bradford, of the Majestic Theatre, Fort Mill, S. C., who also owns the Imperial Theatre, Rock Hill, S. C., was along Film Row the past week looking over additional product for his theatres.

E. J. Smith, District Sales Man-

ager for Warner Brothers, is spending several days in Charlotte at the local exchange.

George Hendrickson, formerly with the Associated Exhibitors, has severed his connections and will carry a brief case for Metro-Goldwyn in the future.

Charlotte the past week has seen an influx of district managers, Claude Ezell of Associated Exhibitors is visiting in Charlotte and looking over general conditions and also to select a successor to Mr. Hendrickson, who resigned.

Chas. Picquet, Vice President, of the M.P.T.O., of North Carolina was a Charlotte visitor the past week. Mr. Picquet is very much enthused over the Fall meeting of the exhibitors and is doing everything possible to get as large a number of exhibitors to attend as possible. Mr. Picquet has invited the M.P.T.O. to meet at Pinehurst and is very anxious that this meeting be a success.

U. K. Rice, General Manager, and J. M. Davis, owner of the Capitol and Iris Theatres, Salisbury, N. C., were Charlotte visitors the past week. Mr. Davis stated that his new house the Cap-

itol, which is considered one of the prettiest and most up-to-date theatres in the South is doing a fairly nice business.

The Victory Theatre, Smithfield, N. C., owned by H. P. Howell suffered damage by fire the past week.

It is reported that there has been quite an exodus of motion

picture exhibitors from North Carolina and South Carolina to Florida. While they have not disposed of their theatre holdings in these communities they have turned them over to representatives to look after while they flirt with dame Fortune in the sunny clime of Florida.

Albany

AMONG film men in town during the past week, were George Roberts, division manager for Fox; Sidney Katz, the new assistant general sales manager for F. B. O., together with Charles Goetz and Murray Beier, of Dependable.

There was a meeting at the Film Board of Trade rooms last Saturday morning to consider plans for a Hallowe'en masquerade at the Hotel Kenmore in Albany on the night of October 31. J. H. MacIntyre is chairman of the entertainment committee of the Board of Trade.

Tom Clark has just been named as assistant manager of the Mark Strand theatre in Albany, and the way he is handling things at the house has caused many to predict an early advancement.

Frank Sardino, running the Crescent and Temple theatres in Syracuse and the Strand in Old Forge, was in Albany during the past week.

Herman Vineberg is putting the Albany and Regent theatres in Albany on an equal footing these days with other first-run houses, and receiving many compliments because of the spick and span appearance the two theatres now present.

Clyde Allen, of the Casino, in Antwerp, a delegate to the state convention of Kiwanis clubs in Albany last week, brought with him a large box of assorted cheese which he presented to C. R. Halligan, of the Universal exchange.

Although John Mattice, of the Novelty theatre, is located in Richmondville, he has installed a four-piece orchestra this fall, and is advertising for miles around.

Anniversary week at the Griswold in Troy, managed by Jake Golden, will start on October 18 instead of October 11, as was first planned. New seats are now being installed and the house is being re-carpeted throughout.

The Family theatre in Burnt Hills will be run this winter by the Knights of Pythias, with Mr. Hammond doing the booking. The Victory in Cambridge has been leased by William Curry of that place, who took over the house on October 5, planning to run it two nights a week. John A. Gillis took over the Star theatre in Salem on October 1.

While William Shirley, of Schenectady, returned from Florida last week, J. B. Harte, of the Harte theatre in Bennington, Vt., will leave for the south shortly.

H. C. McNamara, of Valatie, plans to open his new theatre in that village the latter part of October.

The Mark Strand theatre corporation of Albany received a permit from the city authorities last week for the erection of a $250,000 house in Pearl street. When completed, this will give the company four downtown houses, all located on the same street.

Ben Smith, formerly with Select, is now associated with the Warner brothers exchange in Albany. J. M. Klein, recently named as manager of the exchange, moved his family and household effects here last week from Lynn, Mass.

John Christy, of the Third Avenue theatre in Watervliet, has further improved his property during the past week or two by repainting the house as well as the new sidewalk.

Charles Sesonske, of the Grand in Johnstown, installed a ten-piece orchestra in his theatre last week, with Walter Smith conducting. From October 26, on, vaudeville will be run the first three days each week and pictures the last three days. Mr. Sesonske will

spend $5,000 next month in a new lobby and marquee.

Mike Freedman reopened the Rialto in Schenectady last Sunday, the house having been closed for the past six months. Mr. Freedman also owns the Woodlawn in the same city, being run at the present time with Ida B. Eisenberg.

A new theatre in course of erection in Coxsackie was saved from firebugs last week, owing to the fact that oil soaked rags found after the blaze had been discovered failed to make an impression on the green timber used in the side-walls.

Father Nolan has closed the theatre which he has been running the past summer in New Lebanon.

B. W. Griffin, running the Lyceum in Red Hook, had troubles of his own last week when he found that the building housing an ice cream and confectionery business which he runs had been quietly sold to New York city parties. Mr. Griffin is now endeavoring to acquire the building from its new owner.

Mrs. James Rose, wife of one of the best known exhibitors in Albany and Troy, is ill at the Albany hospital.

Sam Rochstim, owner of the Star theatre in Hudson, was in town last Friday.

Arthur Austin, former manager of the Pember theatre in Granville, is now running the Grange Hall in that village, two nights a week.

James F. Gilmore, organist at the Leland theatre in Albany, was named last week as organist and choir director at St. Patrick's church in Watervliet.

Although Arthur Whyte, of New York city, carried off one of the prizes in a recent golf tournament there, he has failed to re-

ply to the challenge issued by golfers along Film Row. The next time Mr. Whyte comes to Albany he is earnestly requested to bring his clubs with him.

Meyer Schine, one of the heads of the Schine chain of houses in New York state, and who was recently married, is now spending all of his time furnishing his home in Gloversville. Mr. Schine did manage to take a few days off, however, last week, indulging in a business trip to New York and Boston.

J. A. Fitzgerald, manager of the Strand in Hudson Falls, announces that vaudeville will be run with pictures at the house during the winter, and that road shows will also be booked.

The new Park theatre in Glens Falls, through Manager Conklin, announced a cut-rate admission for children fourteen years and under, at special matinees.

Michael Reznick is now covering this territory for Chase pictures in place of Mr. Sternman, who resigned.

The condition of Mrs. Elizabeth V. Colbert, member of the New York State Motion Picture Commission, and a resident of Albany, has materially improved of late.

The Bijou theatre, in Lowville, opened on October 5, as one of the Schine group of houses, having been leased from E. J. Wolfe, for a term of years. Mr. Wolfe, however, will continue to handle the house. L. J. Carkey, formerly of Carthage, and now district manager for the Schine brothers, was present and handled the opening night.

Seven years ago, L. L. Connors came to this section from Boston, and started in the motion picture business. Mr. Connors has leased his houses and is now employed as a salesman for F. B. O., out of Albany.

Des Moines

FUNERAL services for Nate Chapman, 34 years old, former resident of Des Moines, who died at his home at Iowa City, following an attack of heart disease, were held from the home of his parents, Mr. and Mrs. Solomen Chapman, 1411 West Eleventh street, last Friday.

The Ancient Craft lodge, No. 647 of the Masonic order officiated. Burial was in Jewish Glendale cemetery.

Mr. Chapman was manager and part owner of the Englert and Garden theatres at Iowa City, being associated in the enterprise with A. H. Blank.

Mr. Chapman had been in poor health for some time. He spent several weeks at different times at the Springs and in trips to Florida in order to recuperate his strength.

W. G. Smith, formerly salesman for the DesMoines branch of

Universal, has been transferred to the office of Universal in Pittsburg. It is probable that Harry Harsha who for several years was on the road in Iowa territory will take Mr. Smith's place. Mr. Harsha has been in the booking department of Universal most recently. Mr. L. J. Allison, who comes to DesMoines from Kansas City, will be the new booker for Universal.

Norman Lamb of Radcliffe, Iowa has bought the Electric Theatre at Hubbard. Fred Boeke, banker of Hubbard, has been the temporary owner.

Mrs. W. H. Gilbert, who had taken charge of most of the work of managing the Princess Theatre of which her husband was owner, with the death of Mr. Gilbert early in September, has taken the active management of the Princess. Mrs. Gilbert was in

DesMoines to arrange for bookings for the theatre.

The theatre at Carlyle, Iowa, rechristened the Metro, had its opening on Saturday under the management of Park Agnew, booker of the Metro-Goldwyn office. Mr. Agnew bought the theatre from D. T. Swan for whom H. C. Patterson had been managing the house. Mr. Patterson found his duties as a theatreman from D. T. Swan for whom H. C. Patterson had been managing the house. Mr. Patterson found his duties as a theatreman too heavy besides his work on the road as salesman of insurance. Mr. Agnew will run the theatres on Wednesdays and Saturdays as well as continuing as Metro-Goldwyn booker.

A. W. Nichols, district manager for Famous Players, came in to greet the Des Moines bunch last week.

Callers in Movie Row were L. D. Hendrix of the theatre at Mt. Vernon, E. C. Carragher of the Park theatre at Clear Lake, and William Thral of the Princess Theatre at Monteruma.

C. F. Baker, formerly at the Des Moines office of Universal as booker, is the proud daddy of a little girl born on September 14. Mr. Baker is now associate manager for Universal in San Francisco.

F. B. Rahn, special Lloyd representative, has been at the Pathe exchange for the past week.

The new staff of ushers at the Strand Theatre, Des Moines, of which Jes Day is manager, has made quite a hit. Mr. Day now employs a staff of boys. Up to this time the Des Moines was the only theatre to employ boy ushers.

Salt Lake City

JAMES R. KEITZ, Greater Features local manager, is back from Idaho. Keitz was the winner of a special prize of $25.00 given to the office turning in the bulk amount of business on certain productions during the months of July and August.

C. F. Parr, manager for Producers Distributing Corporation here, is making arrangements to welcome Mike Newman this month on his return trip from New York to the coast.

C. C. McDermond, selling out of the Producers Distributing Corporation exchange, is now making a clean-up trip in Cache Valley, Utah.

Melvin A. Brown has established a circuit in Southern Utah in three small towns namely Toquerville, Leeds and Springdale. These towns are located about seventy-five miles inland from a railroad in the region of the north rim of the Grand Canyon and Zions Canyon.

Steve Murgle of Mackay, Idaho, takes over the management of the American Theatre there on October 1st.

Carl A. Stearn, big chief for United Artists here, is making a loop through the state of Idaho.

The International Film Board of Trade held their regular meeting here September 28th at which time the resignation of Judge Loofbourow was accepted with regret. D. T. Lane was elected to succeed Judge Loofbourow as secretary and legal counsel.

George Leavy, Factory Representative of The Wurlitzer Organ Company, is over here attending to several deals in the Salt Lake territory.

Carsten Dahnkin, owner of the American Theatre in this city, has left for San Francisco for a short trip.

L. J. Schleifer, Western Division Manager for Universal, was in this city on his way to Denver from Butte, and is coming back the latter part of this week.

Lou Metzger, Sales Director of Complete Service Contracts, from Universal home office, was here this week. Metzger is visiting all of the branch houses.

L. A. Davis, manager for F. B. O. in this city, is leaving this week for a trip through the Montana territory.

Jos Soloman, F. B. O. Salesman, has been ill for the last few days and unable to leave the city. W. K. Bloom is working the Montana territory out of this office.

Vete Stewart selling out of the Associated First National office, is still in Montana.

W. F. Gordon has returned to his managerial chair at the Associated First National office here.

Ben Fish, Special Harold Lloyd Representative for Pathe, will be in this city from Denver this week. He is expected to remain in this territory for about a month.

R. S. Stackhouse, manager of the local Warner Brothers exchange, is leaving this week for Butte, Montana. George E. Jensen is now covering the Montana territory out of this office, and L. W. Hyde has just left for Southern Utah and Nevada.

Clyde H. Messinger, Educational chief here, has returned from his trip through Idaho.

George L. Cloward, in charge of the Metro-Goldwyn local exchange, is still in the Montana territory. C. L. Dillard, office manager here for Metro-Goldwyn, has been on a short trip to Blackfoot, Idaho, and returned this week.

A. G. Pickett, Famous Players-Lasky exchange manager here, has left for the Idaho branch.

The annual Golf tournament started here this week between a large number of theatre and exchange men. Those who qualified were Neil Schettler, Victory

Theatre orchestra leader, Ernest Jones, Victory Theatre drummer. Robert Runswick, Pantages Theatre orchestra leader, and George E. Carpenter, manager of the Paramount Empress Theatre. These four men will now fight to a finish for the cups and to prove who's who and why. Carl A. Porter announces that the cup is already theirs as far as his mind is concerned.

Among exhibitors visiting Film Row this week are: Nick Salevurakis, owner of the Lyric Theatre, Price, Utah; Harmon and Lou Peery of the Egyptian Theatre, Ogden, Utah; M. S. Stringham and H. E. Skinner of the Colonial Theatre, Ogden, Utah. Stringham is reported to be buying the entire interest of this theatre from Skinner who is said to be going to buy a gold mine; Mike Neilsen, formerly of Buhl, Idaho, is building a new theatre in Nampa, Idaho; C. R. Potter, owner of the Liberty and Strand theatres of Nampa, Idaho, has reopened the Majestic Theatre at Nampa after doing extensive decorating and after installing a large Kimball Organ. C. H. Archibald of the C. and A. Amusement Company of Pocatello, Idaho, and S. R. Rich, owner of the Rich Theatre, Montpelier, Idaho, were also here this week.

Central Penn

AN apartment building at Seventh and Turner streets, Allentown, has been purchased by Nicholas Iococca, former owner of the Franklin theatre, in that city. It is reported he plans the erection of a new theatre.

Improvements being made to the theatre recently purchased in Bethlehem by Lou Berman, of Philadelphia, include installation of a Solar cooling and ventilating system. This theatre is to be known as Savoy.

According to the Williamsport newspapers, the Chamberlain Amusement Enterprises, of Shamokin, who operates numerous theatres in Central Pennsylvania, have abandoned their intention of erecting a large new theatre on the site of the old Sterling Hotel, in Williamsport.

The seating capacity of the Freeland theatre, in Freeland, is to be increased from 500 to 1500, under an improvement and enlargement program now being worked out. A stage will be installed and the theatre equipped throughout so as to present vaudeville as well as motion pictures. The Freeland has been an exclusively picture house.

After some delay in the construction of the new Arcadia Theatre, Shamokin, due to difficulty in obtaining some of the materials promptly, it is now expected the house will be ready for formal opening in the Christmas holiday season. The new structure is on the site of the old Family theatre.

Lou Berman, now owner of the New Strand, in Shenandoah, has selected Orban E. Taylor, of New York City, to succeed Wash Weil, as manager of the theatre.

Improvements including the installation of a new organ are being made to the M. G. Pilosi Theatre, in Old Forge. A new organ is being placed in the theatre.

Announcement was made October 1 in the Lancaster newspapers that George M. Krupa, of that city, expects to open the Capitol Theatre, formerly the Oldine that was swept by flames on December 29, last—on or about Thanksgiving Day. Work is now being rushed to that end.

While the old Oldine had a seating capacity of 900, the new Capitol will seat 1,300.

Chicago

CHARLES CASANAVE has severed his connection with Lynch Theatres, Inc., to become associated with the Karzas-Cooney-Coston group of theatres and for the present is making his headquarters in the office of the 63rd Street Theatres at 845 S. Wabash Avenue.

Otto W. Bolle, manager of Famous Players-Lasky Detroit exchange, was a Chicago visitor this week and reports business good throughout his territory.

C. W. Spanuth, former Chicago exhibitor, is now operating the Majestic Theatre at Harvard, Illinois.

David Hellman of Reelcraft, is enjoying a two weeks' vacation in the Eagle River country and expects to bring back some record breaking muskies.

Wilbur Robinson, former popular film salesman, has practically regained his normal health following a long siege of illness caused by the serious automobile accident in which he was injured some months ago, and expects to get back in the film business at an early date.

A fall convention of Paramount executives will be held in Chicago, November 5, 6, and 7th at the Drake Hotel. About eighty executives from the home office, branch and district managers, are expected to be in attendance.

Irene Rich stopped off in Chicago for a few hours last week and before leaving for New York was at home to members of the press at the Blackstone Hotel.

At the last meeting of the Exhibitors Association of Chicago, it was decided to hold a motion picture ball some time in the near future and a committee, comprising Samuel Abrahams, chairman; James Plodna, L. Weil, Sam Meyers, Norman Fields, J. J. Daly and Earl Johnson was appointed to make plans for the event. It is several years since Chicago has had any similar function and it is the opinion of exhibitors that it will be a great success, especially if some of the leading stars can be present. It is probable that the ball will be held at the Trianon, Andrew Karzas' palace of dance on the south side.

COSTUMES FOR HIRE PRODUCTIONS EXPLOITATIONS PRESENTATIONS **BROOKS** 1437 Broadway Tel. 5580 Pen.

Butte

TOM McDONALD formerly a newspaper man associated for years with the Butte Miner and later with the Great Falls Tribune drifted into theatre work. He was for sometime manager of the American Theatre of Butte and also ran the Peoples Theatre making a popular success of both theatres. He was elected to the Montana legislature from Butte in 1921. He left Butte for California almost a year ago and now comes the news of his being chosen manager of the magnificent new Alexander Theatre, erected as the latest link in the West Coast-Langley chain, at Glendale, California.

There is a rumor current that the American Theatre, which was redecorated and made into a modern up-to-date Movie house late last year and is now known as the "Theatre Beautiful" is to be opened early in October. Manager W. J. Sullivan in a recent interview said the date had not been set for its opening but it would be opened early in October.

The Temple Theatre, the newest and most elaborate Theatre in the City is still closed with no promise of its opening.

Every indication points to a prosperous year in Montana and this has added impetus to all business enterprises and the theatres promise to share in the general good times. The Rialto theatre is playing to capacity house every night. Manager W. J. Sullivan is using every inducement to urge the pleasure-loving public to attend the Rialto program.

Montana is experiencing a lot of snow, and the cold weather has had a marked effect on all the places of amusement. so that once more there is a decided lure to the warm attractive theatres, where there are in all the houses splendid programs.

Pat Dowling representative of the Christie Film Company is in the City from Hollywood. He is making a seven weeks swing around the chief distributing centers of the country and has not overlooked Butte.

J. J. Harrington, former Booker for the First National exchange here, has been promoted to headsalesman for the Montana territory and manager of the shipping office in Butte. He arrived in Butte out of the Salt Lake office last week and left for the key cities of the state. Mr. Harrington is one of the genial, efficient salesmen that the busy theatre men enjoy meeting.

Wm. Hughardt, former manager for the Associated First National, has resigned his position in Montana to have charge of the Fox Exchange of Salt Lake City. Montana regrets the loss of Mr. Hughardt and Mrs. Hughardt.

R. C. Hudson, former manager of the Universal exchange in Butte has accepted a position with the Producers Distributing corporation in Portland and W. J. Heineman has been appointed to his position here. Mr. Heineman was formerly with the Warner Brothers here.

With the promotion of Jack Rue to the Portland office of the Producers Distributing corporation C. R. Wade accepted the managership of the Butte exchange.

Dave Frazer, who for several months was the executive of the Universal exchange in Butte and left to accept a similar position on the coast is now assistant to L. W. Weir, Western Division manager, Mr. Weir is returning to New York from the coast.

R. S. Stackhouse, Salt Lake, manager for Warner Brothers is in Montana in the interest of distribution.

Manager Davis of the Salt Lake Fox exchange is in Montana this week attending to the Fox products. Since the Fox office closed in Butte the business of the state is attended by the Salt Lake branch.

Kansas City

IT was a gay throng which welcomed home Frank L. Newman in Kansas City Thursday. Mr. Newman, now manager of a trio of Paramount theatres in Los Angeles, returned to close contracts for the sale of the Newman and Royal theatres, Kansas City, to Paramount. Leo Forbstein, former director of the Newman theatre orchestra, will accompany Mr. Newman on his return to Los Angeles where he will direct the orchestra of the Metropolitan theatre.

With all the details of Greater Movie Season now a thing of the past, C. E. "Doc" Cook, business manager of the M.P.T.O. Kansas-Missouri, will leave soon for a tour of the territory in behalf of the membership drive, which was cut short by an avalanche of routine details. The policy of inviting an exhibitor once—just once—to enter the organization will remain in force.

If there was as much business as there was "activity" along Kansas City's movie row last week it was a whale of a week for all concerned. The Standard Film Exchange found its quarters too small, so proceeded to lease more space at 113 West Eighteenth street. Harvey Day, general sales manager for Kinograms, was in Kansas City on a business tour.

Joe Klein, Chesterfield Picture Corp., representative, was busy calling on the independent distributors, while Mrs. G. K. Chetwood, Fox contract clerk, has a new Chevrolet coupe.

George Hartman, former First National salesman, has joined the Educational sales force, while C. F. Senning, Educational branch manager, returned from the territory with word that cool weather had made a great improvement among the smaller exhibitors.

C. J. Sonin, purchasing agent for the Metro-Goldwyn and Loew theatres, was a business visitor in Kansas City. Mrs. L. Mayhue, formerly Miss Lucille Hickman, Fox billing clerk, resigned Saturday to step into the home duties of married life.

Hollywood, the mecca for Kansas City's movie row, will move to a new location directly across the street from its present site on Eighteenth street, where a film club for out-of-town visitors and an up-to-date restaurant will be established.

Among the out-of-town exhibitors in the Kansas City market last week were: George Planck, Sedalia theatre, Sedalia, Mo.; C. M. Pattee, Pattee theatre, Lawrence, Kas.; M. W. Reinke, manager of Universal of St. Joseph, Mo.; C. R. Wilson, Liberty theatre, Liberty, Mo.

The Isis theatre, suburban house of Kansas City, in the future will have the first suburban run on all Fox product, according to M. A. Levy, Fox branch manager at Kansas City.

Roy Phipps, assistant treasurer of the Missouri theatre, Kansas City, and Miss Mary Frechin, formerly cashier at the Mainstreet theatre, Kansas City, were married the other day and left for Pittsburg, Pa., where Phipps will be assistant manager of Loew's Aldine theatre.

The opening of O. K. Mason's New Regent theatre in Winfield, Kas., last week took its place in the history of that town as an auspicious event. Film men from Kansas City and adjoining towns attended the opening, refreshments being served on the stage after the closing performance, followed by dancing. The New Regent formerly was the Grand theatre, but has undergone complete remodeling and now is one of the most modern theatres in Kansas.

San Francisco

BUILDING permit for a class A construction theatre at 39th and Telegraph Avenue was issued yesterday by A. S. Holmes, Oakland building inspector. The Alameda County Title Insurance Company is named as builder and contractor of the theatre which will be known as the Transbay Theatres, Inc. The total cost of the construction will be $175,000. A. A. Cantin is the architect.

The new $500,000 theatre, now rapidly nearing completion in Fresno, will be called the Wilson Theatre, and will formerly open its doors on Dec. 1st, it was announced by Ackerman & Harris, San Francisco theatrical firm which is building the Fresno theatre. The Wilson Theatre will feature first run film productions with elaborately staged prologues and vaudeville.

A new theatre will be built on Haight street, between Fillmore and Steiner, by the Golden State Theatre and Realty Corporation, it was announced. It will be the fourteenth community house under construction in a $2,000,000 program. The Golden State Theatre and Realty Corporation also has under construction in San Francisco the New Sunset, Irving Street, between 14th and 15th Avenues, and the State, Mission and Oliver Streets, and a site for another house has been acquired at Mission and Geneva Avenue.

R. M. Ford, for a large number of years associated theatrically in San Francisco and more recently at the Broadway Theatre in Oakland, has purchased the interest of Mortimer Thomas in this theatre which now makes him the heaviest stockholder in that house.

Walter W. Kofeldt, for many years connected with the Pathe Corporation on the Pacific Coast and for some years local manager of the Pathe corporation recently resigned to make a special trip to Paris and Germany for the Producers Film Corporation. Before Kofeldt left, a dinner was given him by his friends.

Cleveland

JOHN PALFI is remodelling his Princess theatre, Canton both inside and outside. He also has the Opera House in Canton.

Allen Simmons of the Allen and Dome theatre, Akron, has returned from an extensive fishing trip in Canada.

Public weddings are Sam Stein's best bet. Stein is manager of the Columbia theatre, Cleveland. He staged one last year. It was the biggest thing he ever put on. Now he's getting ready to stage another one and the whole neighborhood's excited about it. Advance notices of the public wedding, to be held on the stage of the theatre is advertising his house far and near.

William Selman, of the local Paramount sales force has been transferred from the Canton territory to the Toledo territory. And R. H. Ramsey, who formerly covered the Toledo territory, is now traveling in and about Canton.

Maurice Safier, manager of the Cleveland exchange for United Artists.

Lemotto Smith, head of the Smith Amusement Company of Alliance and Warren is home from a five month's trip abroad. During his travels Smith visited thirteen different countries, he says, but none of 'em look as good as the old U. S. A.

Christy Deibel, of the Liberty theatre, Youngstown, was in town all last week playing the Ohio State Golf Tournament.

Hal Smith, of the Cleveland Fox family, has joined Frank Drew's Detroit Fox family as city salesman. Al Goldman has succeeded Smith in the eastern Ohio territory.

The home office of the Standard Film Service Company has moved from the second floor of the Film Exchange Bldg. to the sixth floor, and is now combined with the Cleveland exchange of the company. The consolidation of the two offices makes for a big saving of time as well as of elevator service.

The Skirboll brothers, Bill and Harry, were in New Philadelphia to attend the formal opening of their Opera House. The theatre has been closed for several weeks while it underwent a complete transformation starting with the lobby entrance and going right through to the back door.

J. E. Beck, former local Vitagraph exchange manager, is now handling the city for Producers Distributing Corporation. This used to be Fred Schram's territory, prior to his recent resignation.

R. V. Anderson, sales manager for the International News reel has been in town for the past few days.

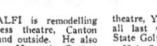
June Marlowe in "Below the Line" for Warners.

Bill Moore, son of George Robert Moore, who died suddenly last week, is running his father's Lion theatre in Bellevue, with marked success. Although only seventeen years old, local film men say that young Bill is showing a decided talent in the exhibition field. The Southern theatre in Bucyrus, another one of Moore's

houses, is being run by Dick Hertzer, who had previously been house manager for Moore.

The Gilger Opera House in Norwalk has changed everything, including its name. It is now called the Moose Theatre. The place has been thoroughly remodelled and has been newly decorated from start to finish. The Moose theatre is located on a side street, just off the main downtown business street of Norwalk. In order to attract attention from the main street, Manager Charles Frederick has put up a string of colored electric lights leading from his theatre entrance to the main street corner. Then at this corner, he has erected an electric sign pointing to his house. It's great stuff, and is doing him worlds of material good.

Henry Heifer, who owns the Opera House at Kenton, Ohio has recently acquired the Royal theatre of Kenton, also. The Royal formerly belonged to Messrs. Rose and Deardourff.

C. B. Moore has sold his interest in the Rex and Strand theatres to John Stoll. Stoll also has the Linwood Square theatre in Norwalk.

H. J. Walters is extending his motion picture interests. He has bought the Classic theatre in Mantua, Ohio from John Kleinfeld. Walters owns the Opera House in Butron, too.

Buffalo

MICHAEL SHEA, head of the Shea Amusement company of Buffalo, operating the Hippodrome, Court Street, North Park, and building the new Buffalo, has been elected president of the Buffalo branch of the Catholic Actors' Guild. Philomena Cavanaugh has been elected first vice president; Thomas Reese, second

Helen Lynch in "Bustin Through," Universal.

vice president; Helen Douris, social secretary; Dr. William Stapleton, executive secretary, and Margaret Crowley, recording secretary. Directors of the organization are: Al Beckerich, manager Loew's State; Basil Brady, manager Pathe exchange; Dr. Joseph Burke, William J. Conners, Jr., the Rev. Charles Duffy, Vincent R. McFaul, managing director, Shea's Hippodrome; Garry McGarry, John R. Oishei, Mayor Frank X. Schwab, John Laughlin, Mae Forrestel, Joseph Gavin, Clayton Sheehan, district manager, Fox Film company; Harry Yates, Mrs. Ruth Ashley Smith, Mrs. Orson Yeager, Alice Ryan, P. T. O'Connor, the Rev. C. J. Sloan, Mrs. J. J. Zimmerman, Mrs. John Lascelles and John Kloepfer.

Harry L. Knappen, former manager of the Buffalo First National exchange, has been appointed manager of the New Orleans Pathe office. Harry was in Buffalo recently on special sales work for the Pathe company.

The employes of the Buffalo Universal exchange held a gettogether party last Monday night in the form of a visit to Shea's Court street theatre and a supper afterwards at the Palais Royal. At the latter place Bob Murphy acted as head waiter, assisted by Elmer Lux, F. B. O. booker, who

was a guest. Al Barnett put on a Charleston. Branch Manager Earl L. Kramer arranged the proceedings.

It is reported that the Yellen family of Buffalo, of which Jack Yellen of popular song fame, is a member, is interested in a new motion picture theatre soon to be built in Tonawanda, N. Y. Well, if Jack does his stuff at each performance they ought to do business.

George Eastman and party, after hunting in Alaska and British Columbia, will arrive back in Rochester on October 11, according to word received. Good weather and fine hunting were encountered by the group which is made up of Mr. Eastman, the Rev. and Mrs. George E. Norton and Dr. Albert D. Kaiser. The party has been gone about two months.

Hiding in the cellar of the Capitol theatre, Syracuse, the other night, burglars waited until the performance was over and then after the place had been closed for the night, looted the house. The thieves left through the front door of the theatre, which was found open later by a patrolman. Little of value was stolen.

George T. Cruzen, manager of the Palace theatre in Lockport, N. Y., is going to inaugurate a series of Saturday morning programs

for children, similar to those presented by the Eastman in Rochester. The Lockport programs will begin October 10.

The return of regular time has brought a noticeable increase in business in western New York picture theatres. Daylight Saving is a terrible thing for exhibitors, especially in Buffalo. Many of the towns, however, do not recognize it and profit accordingly.

The little Hippodrome and Keith's theatres in lower Main street, Buffalo, are having a new fall dress put on their fronts, adding about 100 per cent. improvement in looks.

Three new specially built Simplex machines will be installed in the new Shea Buffalo theatre.

CONSTRUCTION & EQUIPMENT DEPARTMENT

Chapman's Alician Court Theatre is Model

California House Elaborately Decorated and Appointed; Has Unusual Features

CHAPMAN'S Alician Court theatre at Fullerton, Orange county, Calif., recently opened, represents the final word in architectural novelty and beauty as well as in modern equipment. Erected at a total cost, with the ground, of close to half a million dollars, the structure stands on the national highway between Canada and Mexico, where it is the cynosure of the eyes of thousands of motorists.

The entrance is a large court, near the center of which grows a mammoth fan-palm. Alternating with the arches on the sides are the attraction boards, each high-lighted, and shrubbery. Near the rear is a fountain constantly playing into a bed of lillies and ferns. Up one side runs a stone stairway connecting with a balcony which is used as one of the exits from the mezzanine and balcony proper.

The flasher announcement equipment is at one side while a single illuminated court panel at the rear announces only the star of the current attraction. On the roof of the stage is a triangular sign with flasher system containing close to nine hundred lamps. At the rear of the court entrance is a huge terra cotta urn with smoke-effects and also an old Greek theatrical mask with color illuminated eyes and mouth.

Through quaint, massive doors of old iron effect, one enters the foyer with its cement floor, squared and stained. In-

 ported rugs of rare pattern cover this room as well as that of the mezzanine above, some of them being fifteen feet square. The ceiling of the foyer is a marvel of decorating, blue and gold being the predominating tones. Stone benches and Italian table and lamps grace this room and further light is obtained from eight highly distinctive torchiers.

Two large entrances lead to the auditorium proper, the doorways being of Italian marble framed in Italian-colored velour curtains. On each side of the auditorium wall are three great mural paintings, depicting early California. A battery of colored lights plays on these canvasses from hidden niches in the ceiling, and this color scheme is changed constantly during the performance. The ceiling is laid off in Italian red and black squares while two gigantic chandeliers of original pattern hang midway back from the proscenium.

Almost every section of the auditorium can be illuminated by itself by the touch of a button, a lion's head here and an urn there, and other symbolical objects can be brought out into relief instantly. The entire lighting equipment is on

Three views of Chapman's Alician Court theatre, Fullerton, Orange County, Calif. showing, top, several of the mural paintings, left, a view of the mezzanine lounge and right, a view of the auditorium.

View of the auditorium of the Grand Riviera theatre, Detroit, which seats three thousand people. Notice the architecture at the side which is of Italian design.

Chapman's Alician Court Theatre is Model

(Continued from preceding page)

a dimmer system with corresponding superb effects. The 1,000 opera chairs run from 22 to 24 inches in width.

A grand stairway runs to the mezzanine with its dozen or more easy chairs and lounges, fireplace with glowing coals, phones, fountains, Oriental rugs and other attractions. From this mezzanine, the balcony and loge section are reached by easy ramps. The loges are in the front of the balcony and consist of two hundred wired wicker single and double chairs with massive cushions. Back of these is the balcony proper.

The stage is thirty-two feet in depth and sixty-five feet . wide with a proscenium sufficiently large and decorative to do justice to the finest theatres in the country. Ten dressing rooms, completely equipped with hot and cold water, shower baths, ventilating fans, individual wash bowls, individual stoves, etc., and a large club room with ironing board, sewing machine, lounges, etc., are beneath the stage. The latter is equipped to handle the largest road shows and the lighting system is extensive and modern. An automatic sprinkler system protects the entire stage and dressing rooms.

An orchestra is used on vaudeville road show days and for the picture programs, the theatre has a mammoth Marr and Colton organ with Tim Crawford, one of the cleverest young fellows in the business, at the console. The organ has one hundred stop controls and is in six different sections. An echo organ hidden midway back in the ceiling carries five ranks of pipes. This is the only echo in this part of the state.

Power's projectors with mirror reflectors are used in the booth which is in charge of Richard L. Martin.

Three mammoth gas furnaces furnish heat for the theatre, all automatically controlled. For ventilation, a ten foot fan drives the air through a large chamber shot through with sprays of cold water. This air is forced upwards and has an egress from under each seat in the entire house. The temperature in the hottest months never runs above 69 degrees. An automatic temperature regulator is one of the equipments of this amusement palace.

In conjunction with the theatre itself is the Fullerton branch of the famed Mary Louise cafe of Los Angeles, under direct supervision of the proprietors, Mr. and Mrs. Will C. Harris.

Chapman's Alician Court theatre is named after Alice Chapman, wife of C. Stanley Chapman, the builder and owner. Mr. Chapman has in this theatre, realized an ideal of years and his enterprise well merits the support that this entire section of the country is bestowing upon it. The Orange Belt Theatres, Inc., is the operating company, controlling also the Rialto theatre in Fullerton. Harry Lee Wilber is managing director of both houses. Meyer & Holler, who erected Grauman's Egyptian theatre at Hollywood, were the architects of Chapman's. The mural paintings were the work of C. F. Brunckhorst.

New Keith-Albee Theatre for Rochester, N. Y.

Work on the construction of a new $2,-000,000 theatre by the Keith-Albee interests will begin in Rochester next June. This company now operates the Temple theatre in Kodak Town. The site of the new house has not been announced although it has been rumored for some time that the company has been negotiating for the purchase of the Gordon theatre site in Clinton avenue north about two blocks from Main street east, presumably with the idea of erecting the new theatre on this property. With the building of the new theatre, it is not proposed to abandon the Temple. The property on which this house stands has been leased for a comparatively long term of years. When the new theatre is ready the Temple's policy may be changed to vaudeville and pictures. The new house will seat 2,500 and will be an exact replica of the Albee theatre in Brooklyn. The Temple has a seating capacity of 1,700. Harry Mitchell now is managing the Temple.

New Neighborhood Houses in San Francisco

Theatre competition in the beach end of the Park-Presidio district looms as a possibility with the announcement by the Oceanside Amusement Company of the building of a theatre to seat 1,000 on the corner of 48th avenue and Cabrillo street. This in addition to a theatre being built at 39th avenue and Cabrillo. Work on the Oceanside project is scheduled to start by Oct. 15th. Ten store compartments will be embraced in the building.

Plans are complete for a class "A" moving picture theatre with a seating capacity of about 2,000. The structure will be erected in Telegraph avenue between 38th and 40th streets, Oakland, and will probably cost $250,000. The Trans-Bay Theatres Corporation will be the owners.

Begin Work on Hippodrome at Portland, Ore.

Reports received here this week from Portland indicated that work was to begin immediately upon construction of the new $850,000 Hippodrome Theatre, which will be occupied on and after August 1, 1926, by the Ackerman and Harris circuit. The house will be operated under a combined motion picture and vaudeville policy, will seat 2,500 persons, and will include store rooms and office space in the building. Construction will be of reinforced concrete, and the theatre will be Spanish in design. The present Hippodrome Theatre will be occupied within a year by the Pantages Theatre shows, the latter's present showhouse being taken over then by Warner Brothers.

Theatre Building Will Be Erected in Magic City, Va.

Plans have been completed for the erection of theatre and office building on the northwest corner of the intersection of Jefferson street and Kirk avenue, Roanoke, Va. to cost between $1,000,000 and $1,250,000. Plans call for a ten story building, but will probably be fifteen stories when completed. When completed the theatre will have the largest seating capacity of any theatre in Virginia.

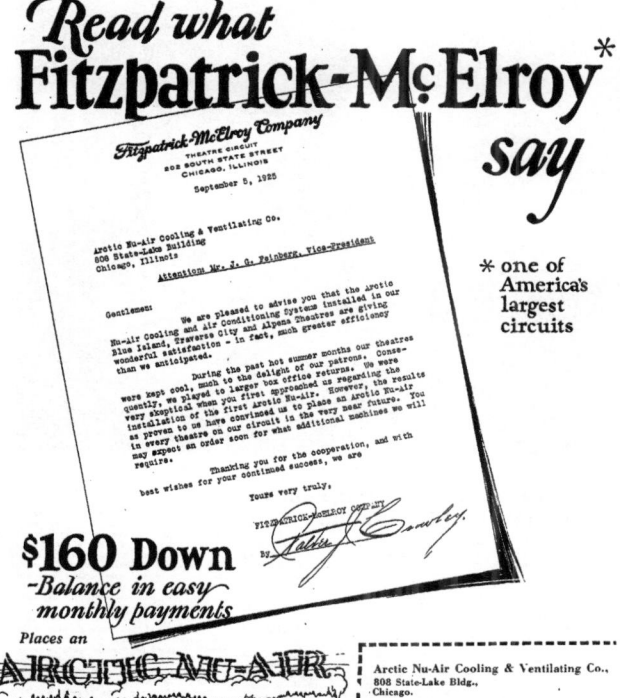

View of the Foyer leading into the interior of Gloria Gould's theatre, New York. Note the splendid appointments.

St. Francis Theatre, San Francisco, Follows Spanish Style of Decoration

ANOTHER magnificent theatre was added to the present group of motion picture palaces of San Francisco recently when the new St. Francis on Market opposite Mason was thrown open. The St. Francis occupies the site of the former Strand but it is in every respect a new theatre. Nothing but the four walls of the former structure have been used and those who remember the former theatre cannot recognize one feature that has been retained in the present palatial structure.

The general decorative scheme of the new theatre is carried out in strictly Spanish. The entire interior decorative scheme carries out the Spanish theme. All the walls are of decayed marble, giving a delicate pinkinsh tint. There are four large wall panels, two on each side of the main auditorium, which are partly covered with rich tapestry drapes, attached at the top with decorative shields. The ceiling is paneled with designs of Spanish heraldry and the lighting fixtures in entire harmony with the decorative scheme, are artistically arranged. There are no side boxes, an impressive Spanish grill occupying the position of the usual theatre boxes and covering the pipes of the large new organ.

A new ventilation system has been installed and there will be a vent under each seat. The seats are also to be of the newest type. The boxes to the rear on the first floor and the loges in front of the balcony are fitted with roomy chairs finished in Spanish leather. All seats in the theatre have Spanish leather finish.

The orchestra pit has been elevated and moved forward.

With the motion picture portion of the performance will be stage presentations. They will be arranged by Jack Partington and are to be not only elaborate in stage effects but will offer only the best talent.

Howard Price Kingsmore, the manager of the new St. Francis Theatre, was for some time manager of the well known Howard Theatre at Atlanta, Georgia.

Owner of New Star Theatre, Ark., to Build Another

D. W. Strong, who will open his new Star Theatre, at Gould, Ark., in the near future will also erect a new $10,000 theatre building at Pine Bluff, Ark.

Record Made in Renovating Loew's Colonial, Reading

A record for speed in effecting extensive improvements to the interior of the Colonial Theatre, Reading, was made by the Marcus Loew interests, who have acquired the house from the Carr & Schad, Inc., chain, when they renovated and considerably improved the picture house in the brief period of the week-end just prior to September 21, without interfering with any performances.

It was on September 21 that Loew took over operation of the theatre, showing as the first attraction, "Never the Twain Shall Meet." Part of the rapidly made improvements included installation of facilities for providing 40,000 additional watts of electricity for the theatre's daily use. This will be used chiefly in the large "Loew's Colonial" electric sign erected in front of the theatre. A new high-power projector and other improved mechanical devices were put in the projection booth, and more spot lights were placed in the orchestra pit.

The big organ has been repaired and retuned. A new concert orchestra will be in charge of Harry C. Fahrbach, and the organist will be Robert C. Henke. A feature of the first week's program was the presence of the Capitol Quartette, sent to Reading through the courtesy of Major Edward Bowes of Loew's Capitol Theatre, New York city.

Terminal Theatre, Brooklyn, Opened by Small-Strausberg Circuit

SMALL and Strausberg enabled 4th Avenue and Dean Street to come into its own on Wednesday, September 30th, when the Terminal Theatre held its premiere. The Terminal is controlled by the Fourth Avenue and Dean Street Corporation and under the personal supervision of the Small-Strausberg Circuit. The officers of the Fourth Avenue and Dean St. Corporation are S. Shotten, president, S. Strausberg, vice-president, W. Small, secretary and S. Kalkin, treasurer. William Small, Samuel Strausberg, Henry Rosenberg and Samuel Small are the officials of the Small-Strausberg Circuit. Most of these men mentioned were at the entrance of the theatre to take care of the patrons.

Lester Evans, under whose management the new house opened, is a showman in every sense of the word.

The Terminal is a modern, fireproof structure in every respect and was constructed from plans furnished by Eugene De Rosa of New York City. Building troubles were encountered with a piece of property on the corner which the owner refused to sell except at an exorbitant figure. However, Mr. De Rosa burrowed around it and the theatre is finished today. The seating capacity is about 1,800 and consists of two balconies and main floor.

Among those present at the premiere that are prominent in the exhibition and exchange circles of New York City, were Charlie Goldreyer, Chas. Steiner, Morris Goodman, Charles Schwartz, all well known exhibitors; Sam Moross, Sec'y of the T. O. C. C. of N. Y.; George Dillon, New York Exchange manager for Producers Dist. Corp.; Phil Meyer of Associated Exhibitors, Jack Bellman of Renown, Jack Goetz, Sol Edwards and Henry Siegel of Apollo, H. Thomas and Jack Levine of the Merit Exchange, Ben Levine and Jack Levy of Oxford, Louis Wexler and H. Kram of Film Booking Offices, Al Carloek of Educational, Fred Meyers and Jack Weinstein from the Warner Bros. Exchange and Harry Furst

of the Big U, Dave Gross, Gus Solomon, Ed Schnitzer and Bernard Scholtz, chaperoned by Miss Sadie Robinson, Harry Buxbaum's capable secretary, were also there.

The Terminal is equipped with a Rudolph Wurlitzer organ, lobby frames by the Libman Spanjer Corp., Automatic Ticket Register, and electric equipment by the Unit Electric Co. of New York City.

Installations of the Vallen Curtain Machines Gain

The many recent installations of the Vallen Automatic Curtain Machine and Noiseless Track clearly prove, according to reports from the company, the faith in the product and the growing realization of its value.

Among more than a score of installations during the month of August, the following are reported by the E. J. Vallen Electric Company: Strand theatre, Shreveport, La.; Alhambra theatre, Ogden, Utah; Strand theatre, Trenton, N. J.; Ambassador theatre, Cleveland; Casino theatre, Des Moines, Ia.; Grand theatre, Gary, Ind.; and the Mount Morris theatre, New York City.

Atlanta Supply Co. Moves to New Quarters

Theatre Supply and Equipment Company of Atlanta, Ga., recently moved into their new home at 102 Walton street, the former address of Pathe Exchange, which moved farther down on film row several months ago.

Theatre Supply and Equipment Company was formerly located at 158 Marietta street, where they have been engaged in business for the last ten years. They made the move to become more accessible to exhibitors visiting film row.

Attractive Theatre Planned for Reno, Nevada

Plans have been completed for the erection of a pretty new movie house to be erected on North Virginia street adjoining the Reno Hotel. It is to be 30-feet wide and 100 feet long, and its seating capacity will be 800. There will be only the highest class pictures shown according to the owner, George Simi.

2,000 Seat Theatre is Planned for West Bronx, N. Y.

Louis H. Kaplan, architect, plans to erect a theatre building at the southeast corner of University and Tremont Avenues, West Bronx, N. Y. The new theatre will have a seating capacity of 2,000. Owners of the new theatre are Louis H. Kaplan and Silverman, Willett & Ballatin.

Plans 1,000 Seat House for Philadelphia

Plans are being drawn by Hodgens & Hill, architects, for a 1,000-seat theatre, 7 stores and 14 apartments to be built at City and Bala avenues, Philadelphia, for the Bala Theatre Company.

The "H C" Reflector Arc Lamp built by Hall and Connolly, Inc.

Many "HC" Reflector Arcs Go Into Leading Houses

The "HC" Reflector Arc Lamp, the newest product of Hall & Connolly, Inc., 135 Grand St., New York City, has already been installed in a remarkably representative group of theatres, both in New York and elsewhere through the country.

Houses in New York City now using this reflector lamp include: Capitol, Strand, Embassy, State, Cohan, Lyric, Astor, Colony and Century. In addition, the lamp has been installed in all of the Loew houses, in New York and elsewhere, in Sol Brill's new Inwood theatre, New York, and the Mosque theatre, Newark, N. J.

$500,000 Picture Theatre for Milwaukee

Architects Dick & Bauer, 811 State street are drawing plans for the erection of motion picture theatre to be erected on Farwell avenue between Ivanhoe and Kenilworth, to cost approximately $500,000. The owner of the new theatre is the Mal Investment Company, Hy Weiss, Manager, located at 425 E. Water street, Milwaukee.

Plan Big House for Topeka, Kansas

Thomas W. Williamson, Architect, is drawing plans for the erection of a new motion picture theatre on Seventh street, Topeka, Kansas. The new theatre will have a seating capacity of from 1,000 to 1,500 persons. The theatre will adjoin the Hotel Jay Hawk at Seventh and Jackson streets.

Plans Announced by Sigried Malm Co. for Derby House

Derby, Conn., is to have a new motion picture theatre according to plans which have been recently announced. The new theatre will be erected on Elizabeth Street. The owner of the new theatre is the Sigried Malm Amusement Company.

Plans for Superstructure for Malden Theatre Completed

Plans for the superstructure for the new Middlesex Theatre in Malden, Mass., call for a structure 126 x 176 feet, to be located with entrances from Pleasant and Dartmouth streets. The structure will be of brick and cost about $300,000.

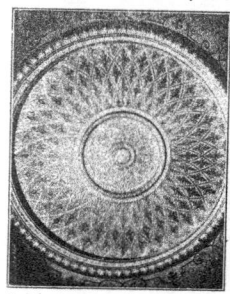

Decorative plaque in the ceiling of Gloria Gould's Embassy theatre, New York.

Safeguards negative quality—

EASTMAN
POSITIVE FILM

At Kodak Park every known precaution is exercised to make sure that every foot of Eastman Positive Film actually will reproduce tone for tone, all the detail of the negative.

Eastman experts safeguard for the screen the photographic quality your audiences are entitled to see there—and expect.

Look for the identification "Eastman" "Kodak" in black letters in the margin of prints you screen.

EASTMAN KODAK COMPANY
ROCHESTER, N. Y.

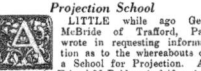

Projection
Optics, Electricity, Practical Ideas & advice

Inquiries and Comments

Projection School

LITTLE while ago Geo. McBride of Trafford, Pa., wrote in requesting information as to the whereabouts of a School for Projection. As we recall it, Friend McBride asked if such a school were located in New York City, though we may be wrong as to this item. Be that as it may, the reply stated that we were in ignorance of the existence of any such school and went on to describe the subjects which should be covered in order for such a school to effectively accomplish its purpose.

Evidently we must have erred in our belief concerning the non-existence of a projection school for O. Record, Royal Theatre, Grain Valley, Mo., takes us to task and refutes our statement swearing by all that is holy and sacred that there is such a school and gives its address to substantiate his claim. He neglects to mention, however, the official title or name so that we cannot directly verify it by sending a letter to the school in question in order to obtain further information concerning its curriculum.

If Record will do this—send the name of the school—we will follow it up by getting in touch with the conductor of the school and give it our approval, PROVIDING, it teaches what we believe to be essential to a complete course in Motion Picture Projection. How about it Friend Record, will you do this?

Record writes as follows:

Sirs:—I have read in the Mid-Week edition of MOTION PICTURE NEWS, August 29th, that Geo. McBride of Trafford, Pa., inquired about a Projection School and your reply that no such school was in existence.

I must state that there is such a school at 109 W. 18th Street, Kansas City, Missouri, and that this school teaches projection in all its branches and gives a thoroughly practical course in projection and electricity as applied to a theatre.

I cannot say whether or not this school has a correspondence course, but it has some of the best fitted men that can be procured as instructors. This course includes instruction in the handling of all types of projection apparatus.

New Fire Shutter Control

As this is my first letter, I won't make it tiresome but here is some dope on a fine shutter for either the Powers or Simplex projectors. I use a centrifugal type governor similar to the one regularly used by Powers on their projector with the difference that I place it *below* the lower idler sprocket.

The travel of the film over this sprocket causes the governor to revolve. The governor mechanism is connected, by means of a

long thin rod to the shutter lever so that when the governor is in operation this rod raises the fire shutter and when the governor slows down it lowers the shutter.

In case of film breaking or jamming the idler sprocket stops which causes the governor to slow down thus lowering the fire shutter. I have tested this device and found that it is positive in its action and that as soon as the film stops the shutter will close instantly.

Even should the lower, or takeup reel fail to work the shutter will close. To regulate the speed of the governor, it must be tightened on the ring shown in drawing.

This device has been submitted for patent application so that further information will be supplied on request.

Am attaching a very crude drawing illustrating just how this thing works.

Doubtful

As can probably be gleaned from Friend Record's description of his device it consists essentially of a governor patterned after the present Powers type with the difference that instead of placing the governor at the fire shutter location such as Powers and Simplex do he mounts it on the same shaft with the lower idler sprocket and then connects the governor to the fire shutter with a rod of suitable length.

The difference then is primarily one of location. Friend Record mentions that he has applied for a patent on this device. The question that rises in our mind, however, is this. What *improvement* results from changing the governing location from the fire shutter position to the lower sprocket? Is there any? What is wrong with the present practice followed by both Powers and Simplex. Do not both these governors do their work satisfactorily at their present location. If not, then your device will bear investigation as to its merits.

Patents

Concerning the patentability of an article or device, Friend Record, we would like to say a few things of a general nature. The writer is not an expert on patent affairs or procedures but there are a few common sense questions which should be asked before expense is incurred in filing a patent

application. A few of these questions are as follows:

1. Is the idea *new* and *original?*
2. Is there a *need* for such a device?
3. If the idea represents an improvement on an existing device is there any *actual improvement* in the way of better operation or reduced costs? In other words is there anything that would make people use *your* device in preference to others?
4. Will your device do the work you claim it will? In other words DOES IT WORK?

These are a few of the questions which should be answered before spending your good money for a patent. Incidentally it would also be advisable to secure the opinion of some person familiar with that line of work for which the device is intended.

You need not necessarily remain unprotected in doing this for all that is necessary to protect yourself is to write up a *clear, concise, complete* description of the device and how it works, supplemented by simple sketches or drawings and then have this sworn to by a notary public and signed by two witnesses. Also have it *dated.* This will establish your priority of conception of the idea so that even should a person file a patent application on your device before you do, you can prove the idea was *first* yours and so secure the patent.

Because an idea or device is granted a patent is no indication that it is valuable. The device must possess *real merit* for which people are willing to pay money. In other words, it must possess *sales value* Many people believe that once a patent has been granted they can sit back and watch others flock forward with money in either hand to buy the device.

Not so. A patent is merely the government's word that you will be protected in the exclusive rights to *manufacture* and *sell* the article in question for a certain period of time. In other words, in order to inspire new thought and original endeavor the government gives you the *edge*, so to speak, on other persons for a limited number of years which vary from 3½ years, I believe to 17 years, depending upon whether or not the idea is *basic.*

More often than not, in the case of patents or valuable ideas, the patent merely proves to be a governmental privilege to sue infringers at a considerable cost in the way of litigation. Many times the patent *plus* a great deal of money is required for proper protection of the patentee's rights.

Furthermore, you cannot, after securing a patent, squat idly on haunches and wait for the patent to be bought up or appreciate in value. ACTION is required if your patent rights are to remain valid and effective because if the patent is filed away in desk drawer and no steps are taken to constructively use it—that is, manufacture it or have some one else do so, another person, after about two years, I believe, can file for patent rights and it will then be up to you to prove that you have been constructively

(Continued on page 1854)

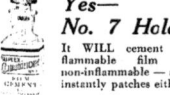

Lufkin, Tex., Theatre, Has Its Premiere

Opening of the Pines Theatre, Lufkin, Texas, with the auditorium filled to overflowing, with the stage decorated by a myriad of baskets of flowers, the gifts of admiring friends, the handsome new Pines Theatre was formally opened to the public Wednesday with a program consisting of speeches, special music and the first run Paramount picture. The Phil H. Pierce concerns. The Famous Players-Lasky Corp. The King Scenic Co., and many local concerns. The Famous Players-Lasky - Corp. and The First National Film Co. had representatives at the opening and sent handsome baskets of flowers. The opening program was featured by a concert on the big $10,000.00 Golden Voiced Barton organ by Dwight Brown, courtesy of the Palace Theatre of Dallas.

The theatre was erected at a cost of $110,000.00, fully equipped and is of face brick with interior of plaster inlaid with face brick, with velvet curtains and handsome brass chandeliers. The stage is fully equipped for road shows and vaudeville and has an automatic working velvet curtain in front of the big Gardinier Velet Gold Fibre screen. Simplex machines equipped with Mirror Arc lamps are installed in a concrete and brick fireproof projection room. The theatre is owned by the Lufkin Amusement Co. which owns the Palace and Victory also, and is under the management of Non Binion.

Peerless Reflector Lamps in Many Theatres

Reports from various theatres throughout the country concerning Peerless Reflector Arc Lamps, manufactured by The J. E. McAuley Company of Chicago, bear out the company's contention of many successful installations of its product, according to advices received by J. E. McAuley.

Peerless Reflector Arc Lamps are at present in use in the Rialto, Rivoli and Criterion theatres, New York. They are also used by the Stanley theatre, Philadelphia, where they took the place of high intensity arcs.

Judging from the fact that the Caribbean Film Company, Havana, Cuba, has installed two of these lamps in its Fausto theatre, Cuban exhibitors are evidently becoming aware of the need of good projection equipment.

Inquiries and Comments

(Continued from page 1850)

engaged in pursuing your rights under the patent.

The Government patent office does not tolerate inactivity on the part of patentees for any great length of time since they feel that such practice retards rather than promotes the general public welfare.

This is our general understanding of the patent laws, which, as stated before is not to be considered as expert but is merely given to enable you to pursue your rights in a little more intelligent manner.

As for your information on the Projection School, Friend Record, we wish to thank you and will look further into it upon receipt of the full address of this school.

Kissimee, Florida, to Have New Theatre

Work has just gotten under way on what is planned to be one of the finest theatres in the state at Kissimee, Florida.

Remodeling and rebuilding in part the old Casino Theatre and the entire block in which it stands to make a theatre just double in size, and a modern forty-room hotel, office building, etc. in the same building, has been undertaken by W. A. White and H. Gilbert, joint owners of a ninety-nine year lease on the old Greystone Casino Building, of which the Casino Theatre is a part.

C. C. Jordan, manager of the Casino, has obtained a five-year lease on the new theatre when completed. It is to be handsomely decorated

Automatic Ticket Co. to Equip Many Box Offices

Among recent orders to install automatic ticket machines is one for the new Madison Square theatre, of which Tex Rickard is President, which calls for a battery of six machines. These are of the Gold Seal type.

Fabian's new Mosque theatre, Newark, N. J., opened recently, is equipped with Gold Seal Ticket Registers, and they will also be used in the Metropolitan theatre, Boston, which will be opened early in October by Famous Players.

FEATURE RELEASE CHART

Productions are Listed Alphabetically and by Months in which Released in order that the Exhibitor may have a short-cut toward such information as he may need. Short subject and comedy releases, as well as information on pictures that are coming, will be found on succeeding pages. (S. R. indicates State Right release.)

Refer to THE MOTION PICTURE NEWS BOOKING GUIDE for Productions Listed Prior to March

MARCH

Feature	Star	Distributed by	Length	Reviewed
Adventurous Sex, The	Clara Bow	Assoc. Exhib	5039 feet	Mar. 21
Air Mail, The	Special Cast	Paramount	6976 feet	Mar. 28
Beauty and the Bad Man	Special Cast	Prod. Dist. Corp	5794 feet	May 9
Beyond the Border	Harry Carey	Prod. Dist. Corp	4469 feet	April 25
Billy, The Kid	Franklyn Farnum	Inde. Pict. Corp. (S. R.)	4800 feet	
Blood and Steel	Desmond Holmes	Inde. Pict. (S. R.)	5300 feet	
Border Justice	Bill Cody	Inde. Pict. Corp. (S. R.)	5432 feet	Nov. 8
Coast Patrol, The	Kenneth McDonald	Barsky (S. R.)	5000 feet	
Confessions of a Queen	Terry-Stone	Metro-Goldwyn	5820 feet	April 4
Crimson Runner, The	Priscilla Dean	Prod. Dist. Corp	4775 feet	June 6
Daddy's Gone A'Hunting	Joyce-Marmont	Metro-Goldwyn	5851 feet	Mar. 7
Denial, The	Special Cast	Metro-Goldwyn	4791 feet	Mar. 21
Double Action Daniels	Buffalo Bill, Jr	Weiss Bros. (S. R.)	4650 feet	
Dressmaker from Paris, The	Rod La Rocque	Paramount	7080 feet	Mar. 28
Fighting Romeo, A	Al Ferguson	Davis Dist. Div.(S.R.)	5000 feet	Aug. 15
Fighting the Flames	Haines-Devore	C. B. C. (S. R.)	5800 feet	
Forbidden Cargo	Evelyn Brent	F. B. O	4850 feet	April 11
Goose Hangs High, The	Constance Bennett	Paramount	6186 feet	Feb. 14
Great Divide, The	Terry-Tearle	Metro-Goldwyn	7811 feet	Feb. 21
Head Winds	House Peters	Universal	5600 feet	Mar. 28
Hunted Woman, The	Seena Owen	Fox	4954 feet	April 4
I Want My Man	Sills-Kenyon	First National	6175 feet	April 18
Jimmie's Millions	Richard Talmadge	F. B. O	5167 feet	Feb. 28
Just Traveling	Bob Burns	Sierra Pict. (S. R.)	4400 feet	
Last Laugh, The	Emil Jannings	Universal	6519 feet	Dec. 20
Let'er Buck	Hoot Gibson	Universal	5547 feet	Jan. 3
Mad Whirl, The	May McAvoy	Universal	6184 feet	Dec. 6
Marriage in Transit	Edmund Lowe	Fox Film	4800 feet	April 11
Men and Women	Special Cast	Paramount	6223 feet	Mar. 28
Monster, The	L. Chaney-J. Arthur	Metro-Goldwyn	6435 feet	Feb. 28
My Wife and I	Special Cast	Warner Bros	6700 feet	June 6
New Lives for Old	Betty Compson	Paramount	6796 feet	Mar. 7
New Toys	Richard Barthelmess	First National	7250 feet	Feb. 21
One Year to Live	Special Cast	First National	6064 feet	Feb. 28
Percy	Charles Ray	Assoc. Exhib	5384 feet	Feb 28
Playing With Souls	Special Cast	First National	5831 feet	Mar. 14
Price of Pleasure, The	Valli-Kerry	Universal	6618 feet	June 13
Recompense	M. Prevost-M. Blue	Warner Bros	7480 feet	May 2
Renegade Holmes, M.D	Ben Wilson	Arrow (S. R.)	4947 feet	
Riders of the Purple Sage	Tom Mix	Fox	5578 feet	Mar. 28
Romance and Rustlers	Yakima Canutt	Arrow (S. R.)	4994 feet	Nov. 15
Sackcloth and Scarlet	Alice Terry	Paramount	6732 feet	Mar. 7
Sally	Colleen Moore	First National	8636 feet	Mar. 28
Scar Hanan	Yakima Canutt	F. B. O	4684 feet	April 4
Scarlet Honeymoon, The	Shirley Mason	Fox	5080 feet	Mar. 21
Seven Chances	Buster Keaton	Metro-Goldwyn	5113 feet	Mar. 28
Sign of the Cactus, The	Jack Hoxie	Universal	4938 feet	Jan. 10
Sky Raider, The	Capt. Charles Nungesser	Assoc. Exhib.	6638 feet	April 4
Speed	Betty Blythe	Banner Prod. (S. R.)	6000 feet	May 30
Too Many Kisses	Richard Dix	Paramount	5759 feet	Mar. 14
Waking Up the Town	Jack Pickford	United Artists	4802 feet	April 11
Where Romance Rides	Dick Hatton	Arrow	4301 feet	
Zander the Great	Marion Davies	Metro-Goldwyn	5851 feet	May 16

APRIL

Feature	Star	Distributed by	Length	Reviewed
Adventure	P. Starke-T. Moore	Paramount	6713 feet	April 25
After Business Hours	Hammerstein-Tellegen	C B. C. (S. R.)	5800 feet	
Bandit Tamer, The	Franklyn Farnum	Inde. Pict. (S. R.)	5000 feet	
Border Vengeance	Jack Perrin	Madoc Sales (S. R.)	4300 feet	
Charmer, The	Pola Negri	Paramount	6076 feet	April 18
Code of the West	O. Moore-C. Bennett	Paramount	6777 feet	April 25
Courageous Fool, The	Reed Howes	Rayart (S. R.)		
Crowded Hour, The	Bebe Daniels	Paramount	6558 feet	May 9
Dangerous Innocence	LaPlante-E. O'Brien	Universal	6759 feet	Mar. 21
Declasse	Corinne Griffith	First National	7869 feet	April 4
Eyes of the Desert	Al Richmond	Sierra Prod. (S. R.)	4500 feet	
Fifth Avenue Models	Philbin-Kerry	Universal	6581 feet	Jan. 24
Fighting Parson, The	Al Ferguson	Davis Dist. Div.(S.R.)	5000 feet	
Fighting Sheriff, The	Bill Cody	Inde. Pict. (S. R.)	4500 feet	May 30
Friendly Enemies	Weber and Fields	Prod. Dist. Corp	6288 feet	May 9
Galloping Vengeance	Bob Custer	F. B. O	5095 feet	April 11
Getting 'Em Right	George Larkin	Rayart (S. R.)	4669 feet	
Gold and the Girl	Buck Jones	Fox	4521 feet	April 4
Go Straight	Gladys Hulette	B. P. Schulberg(S.R.)	6107 feet	May 23
Heart of a Siren, The	Barbara La Marr	First National	6700 feet	Mar. 21
How Baxter Butted In	M. Moore-D. Devore	Warner Bros	6650 feet	July 11
Justice Raffles	Henry Edwards	Cranfield & Clarke (S. R.)	6000 feet	
Kiss in the Dark, A	Special Cast	Paramount	5767 feet	April 18
Kiss Me Again	M. Prevost-M. Blue	Warner Bros	7200 feet	June 6
Love's Bargain	M. Daw-C. Brook	F. B. O	5641 feet	April 25
Madame Sans Gene	Gloria Swanson	Paramount	9994 feet	May 2
Man and Maid	Special Cast	Metro-Goldwyn	5307 feet	April 18
My Son	Nazimova-J. Pickford	First National	6500 feet	April 25
Night Club, The	R. Griffith-V. Reynolds	Paramount	5732 feet	May 16
One Way Street	Special Cast	First National	5596 feet	April 11
Proud Flesh	Special Cast	Metro-Goldwyn	5770 feet	April 25
Rearing Adventure, The	Jack Hoxie	Universal	4657 feet	Feb. 14
Ridin' Comet, The	Yakima Canutt	F. B. O	4354 feet	May 16
Rough Going	Franklyn Farnum	Indep. Pict. Corp. (S. R.)	4800 feet	
Shackled Lightning	Frank Merrill	Hercules Prod. (S. R.)		
She Wolves	Alma Rubens	Fox	5713 feet	May 9
Spaniard, The	Cortez-Goudal	Paramount	6676 feet	April 18
Sporting Venus	Special Cast	Metro-Goldwyn	5938 feet	May 23
Stop Flirting	Special Cast	Prod. Dist. Corp	5161 feet	June 6
Straight Through	Wm. Desmond	Universal	4867 feet	
Tale of a Thousand and One Nights	Special Cast	Davis Dist. Div. (S. R.)	6300 feet	Feb. 14
Tearing Through	Richard Talmadge	F. B. O.	4714 feet	May 23
That Devil Quemado	Fred Thomson	F. B. O.	4768 feet	April 4
Two-Fisted Sheriff, A	Yakima Canutt	Arrow (S. R.)	4149 feet	Dec. 6
Way of a Girl, The	Boardman-M. Moore	Metro-Goldwyn	5025 feet	April 18
Western Engagement, A	Dick Hatton	Arrow		
Wings of Youth	Madge Bellamy	Fox	5340 feet	May 16
Winning a Woman	Perrin-Hill	Rayart (S. R.)	4865 feet	

MAY

Feature	Star	Distributed by	Length	Reviewed
Alias Mary Flynn	Evelyn Brent	F. B. O.	5559 feet	May 30
Any Woman	Alice Terry	Paramount	5963 feet	June 13
Awful Truth, The	Agnes Ayres	Prod. Dist. Corp	5917 feet	July 11
Bandit's Baby, The	Fred Thomson	F. B. O.	5291 feet	June 20
Baree Son of Kazan	Wolf (dog)	Vitagraph	7 reels	May 2
Barriers of the Law	Holmes-Desmond	Indep. Pict. (S. R.)	5400 feet	
Burning Trail, The	William Desmond	Universal	4783 feet	April 18
Chickie	Mackaill-Bosworth	First National	7767 feet	May 9
Crackerjack, The	Johnny Hines	C. C. Burr (S. R.)	6500 feet	May 23
Every Man's Wife	Special Cast	Fox	4365 feet	July 4
Eve's Lover	Irene Rich	Warner Bros	6540 feet	Aug. 8
Eve's Secret	Betty Compson	Paramount	6305 feet	May 9
Fear Fighter, The	Billy Sullivan	Rayart (S. R.)		
Fighting Demon, The	Richard Talmadge	F B O	5470 feet	June 20
Fugitive, The	Ben Wilson	Arrow	4892 feet	
Golden Trails		Sanford Prod. (S. R.)	5 reels	
His Supreme Moment	B Sweet-R Colman	First National	6600 feet	April 25
Lilies of the Streets	J. Walker-V. L. Corbin	F. B. O.	7160 feet	April 25
Little French Girl, The	Alice Joyce	Paramount	5628 feet	June 13
Lunatic at Large, A	Henry Edwards	Cranfield & Clarke (S. R.)	6000 feet	
Makers of Men	Kenneth McDonald	Barsky Prod. (S. R.)	5000 feet	
Necessary Evil, The	Dana-Lyon	First National	6307 feet	May 23
Old Home Week	Thomas Meighan	Paramount	6888 feet	June 6
Phantom Rider, The	Al Richmond	Sierra Prod. (S. R.)	4750 feet	
Private Affairs	Special Cast	Prod. Dist. Corp	6132 feet	Aug. 15
Quick Change	George Larkin	Rayart (S. R.)		
Raffles, The Amateur Cracksman	House Peters	Universal	5557 feet	May 30
Rainbow Trail, The	Tom Mix	Fox	5251 feet	April 25
Red Love	Lowell-Russell	Lowell Film Prod. (S. R.)	6500 feet	May 23
Saddle Hawk, The	Hoot Gibson	Universal	5468 feet	Mar 7
Silent Sanderson	Harry Carey	Prod. Dist. Corp.	4841 feet	June 20
Scandal Proof	Shirley Mason	Fox	4400 feet	June 6
School for Wives	Tearle-Holmquist	Vitagraph	6750 feet	April 11
Shock Punch, The	Richard Dix	Paramount	6151 feet	May 23
Snob Buster, The	Reed Howes	Rayart (S. R.)		
Soul Fire	Barthelmess-B Love	First National	8262 feet	May 16
Speed Wild	Maurice B "Lefty" Flynn	F. B. O	4700 feet	June 20
Talker, The	A Nilsson-L Stone	First National	7861 feet	May 23
Texas Bearcat, The	Bob Custer	F. B. O	4770 feet	
Tides of Passion	Mae Marsh	Vitagraph	6279 feet	May 9
Up the Ladder	Virginia Valli	Universal	6023 feet	Jan 31
Welcome Home	Special Cast	Paramount	5909 feet	May 30
White Fang	Strongheart (dog)	F. B. O	6579 feet	June 20
White Thunder	Yakima Canutt	F B. O.	4550 feet	
Wildfire	Special Cast	Vitagraph	6 reels	June 20
Wolves of the Road	Yakima Canutt	Arrow	4375 feet	
Woman's Faith	Reubens-Marmont	Universal	6023 feet	Aug 15
Woman Hater, The	Helene Chadwick	Warner Brothers	7000 feet	Aug. 22

JUNE

Feature	Star	Distributed by	Length	Reviewed
Are Parents People?	Bronson-Vidor	Paramount	6586 feet	June 6
Dangerous Odds	Bill Cody	Inde. Pict. (S. R.)	4800 feet	
Desert Flower, The	Colleen Moore	First National	6837 feet	June 13
Double Fisted	Jack Perrin	Rayart (S. R.)		
Down the Border	Al Richmond	Sierra Prod. (S. R.)	4750 feet	
Faint Perfume	Seena Owen	B. P. Schulberg(S.R.)	6228 feet	July 11
Grounds for Divorce	Florence Vidor	Paramount	5712 feet	July 4
Happy Warrior, The		Vitagraph	6075 feet	July 18
Hearts and Spurs	Buck Jones	Fox	4600 feet	June 20
Human Tornado, The	Yakima Canutt	F. B. O.	4472 feet	
I'll Show You the Town	Reginald Denny	Universal	7400 feet	June 6
Introduce Me	Douglas MacLean	Assoc. Exhib.	5980 feet	Mar. 21
Just a Woman	Windsor-Tearle	First National	6500 feet	June 6
Light of Western Stars	Special Cast	Paramount	6652 feet	July 4
Lost—a Wife	Special Cast	Paramount	6420 feet	June 27
Making of O'Malley, The	Milton Sills	First National	7571 feet	July 4
Man from Lone Mountain, The	Ben Wilson	Arrow	4530 feet	
Man in Blue	Herbert Rawlinson	Universal	5706 feet	Feb. 21
Marry Me	Special Cast	Paramount	5586 feet	
Meddler, The	William Desmond	Universal	4890 feet	May 23
Mist in the Valley	Alma Taylor	Cranfield & Clarke (S. R.)	5500 feet	
My Lady's Lips	Clara Bow	B. P. Schulberg (S.R.)	6609 feet	Aug 15
Off the Highway	Bowers-De La Motte	Prod. Dist.	7641 feet	
Paths to Paradise	Compson-R. Griffith	Paramount	6741 feet	June 27
Pioneers of the West		Sanford Prod. (S. R.)	5 reels	
Ridin' Easy	Dick Hatton	Arrow	4483 feet	
Ridin' Thunder	Jack Hoxie	Universal	4354 feet	May 23

Feature	Star	Distributed by	Length	Reviewed
Rough Stuff	George Larkin	Rayart (S. R.)		
Shattered Lives	Special Cast	Gotham (S. R.)	6 reels	July 4
Smooth as Satin	Evelyn Brent	F. B. O	6003 feet	July 4
Texas Trail, The	Harry Carey	Prod. Dist. Corp	4720 feet	July 18
Tracked in the Snow Country	Rin-Tin-Tin (dog)	Warner Brothers	6900 feet	Aug. 1
White Monkey, The	La Marr-T. Holding	First National	6121 feet	July 4
Wild Bull's Lair, The	Fred Thompson	F. B. O.	5280 feet	Aug. 15
Youth's Gamble	Reed Howes	Rayart (S. R.)	5264 feet	

JULY

Feature	Star	Distributed by	Length	Reviewed
Bloodhound, The	Bob Custer	F. B. O	4789 feet	
Cold Nerve	Bill Cody	Inde. Pict. (S. R.)	5000 feet	
Danger Signal, The	Jane Novak	Columbia Pict. (S.R.)	5502 feet	Aug. 15
Don Daredevil	Jack Hoxie	Universal	4810 feet	
Drug Store Cowboy, The	Franklyn Farnum	Ind. Pict. Corp. (S.R.)	5100 feet	Feb. 7
Duped	Holmes-Desmond	Ind. Pict. (S. R.)	5400 feet	
Fighting Youth		Columbia Pict. (S.R.)		
Lady Who Lied, The	L. Stone-V. Valli	First National	7111 feet	July 18
Lady Robinhood	Evelyn Brent	F. B. O	5582 feet	Aug 22
Manicure Girl, The	Bebe Daniels	Paramount	5959 feet	June 27
Marriage Whirl, The	C. Griffith-H. Ford	First National	7672 feet	July 25
Mysterious Stranger, The	Richard Talmadge	F. B. O	5270 feet	
Night Life of New York	Special Cast	Paramount	6998 feet	July 4
Pipes of Pan	Alma Taylor	Cranfield & Clarke (S. R.)	6200 feet	
Ranger of the Big Pines, The	Kenneth Harlan	Vitagraph	5800 feet	Aug. 8
Scarlet West, The	Frazer-Bow	First National	8391 feet	July 25
Secret of Black Canyon, The	Dick Hatton	Arrow		
Strange Rider, The	Yakima Canutt	Arrow		
Taming the West	Hoot Gibson	Universal	5427 feet	Feb. 28
Trailed	Al Richmond	Sierra Prod. (S. R.)	4750 feet	
White Desert, The	Special Cast	Metro-Goldwyn	6345 feet	July 18

AUGUST

Feature	Star	Distributed by	Length	Reviewed
Beggar on Horseback, A	Ralston-Nissen	Paramount	6800 feet	June 20
Business of Love, The	E. Horton-M. Bellamy	Astor Dist. Corp		
Children of the Whirlwind	Lionel Barrymore	Arrow		
Drusilla With a Million	Special Cast	F. B. O	7391 feet	May 30
Evolution		Red Seal	4200 feet	Aug. 15
Fine Clothes	L. Stone-A. Rubens	First National	6971 feet	Aug. 15
Girl Who Wouldn't Work, The	Lionel Barrymore	B. P. Schulberg (S.R.)	5979 feet	Sept. 5
Gold Rush, The	Charles Chaplin	United Artists	8500 feet	Aug. 8
Halfway Girl, The	Doris Kenyon	First National	7570 feet	Aug. 8
Headlines	Alice Joyce	Assoc. Exhib	5600 feet	July 25
Her Sister From Paris	C. Talmadge	First National	7255 feet	Aug. 15
In the Name of Love	Cortez-Nissen	Paramount	5904 feet	Sept. 5
Isle of Hope, The	Richard Talmadge	Film Book. Offices	5800 feet	Sept. 5
Kivalina of the Ice Lands	Native Cast	Pathe	6 reels	July 11
Knockout, The	Milton Sills	First National	7450 feet	Sept. 19
Lightnin'	Jay Hunt	Fox	7979 feet	Aug. 1
Limited Mail, The	Monte Blue	Warner Brothers	6250 feet	
Love Hour, The	Ruth Clifford	Vitagraph	5900 feet	
Lover's Oath, The	Ramon Novarro	Astor Dist Corp		
Lucky Devil, The	Richard Dix	Paramount	5935 feet	July 18
Lucky Horseshoe, The	Tom Mix	Fox	5004 feet	Aug. 29
My Pal	Dick Hatton	Arrow		
Overland Limited, The		Gotham Prod. (S. R.)	6389 feet	Aug. 8
Parisian Love	Bow-Tellegen	B. P. Schulberg (S.R.)	6324 feet	Aug. 22
Quo Vadis	Emil Jannings	First National	8945 feet	Feb. 28
Range Justice	Dick Hatton	Arrow		
Romola	Gish Sisters	Metro-Goldwyn	10875 feet	Dec. 13
Rugged Water	Special Cast	Paramount	6015 feet	Aug. 1
Shining Adventure, The	Percy Marmont	Astor Dist. Corp		
Slave of Fashion, A	Special Cast	Metro-Goldwyn	5906 feet	Aug. 1
Speed Mad		Columbia Pict. (S.R.)	4442 feet	Sept. 19
Sporting Chance, The		Tiffany (S. R.)	6500 feet	July
Street of Forgotten Men	Special Cast	Paramount	6366 feet	Aug. 1
Ten Commandments	Special Cast	Paramount	9980 feet	Jan. 5-24
That Man Jack	Bob Custer	F. B. O	5032 feet	Aug. 22
Unholy Three	Lon Chaney	Metro-Goldwyn	6848 feet	Aug. 15
Unwritten Law, The		Columbia Pict. (S.R.)		
Wife Who Wasn't Wanted, The	Irene Rich	Warner Brothers	8400 feet	
Wizard of Oz	Larry Semon	Chadwick	6300 feet	Apr. 25
Wrongdoers, The	Lionel Barrymore	Astor Dist. Corp		

SEPTEMBER

Feature	Star	Distributed by	Length	Reviewed
Amazing Quest, The	Henry Edwards	Cranfield & Clarke	5500 feet	
American Pluck	George Walsh	Chadwick	5000 feet	July 11
Apache Love	Geo. Larkin	B'way Dist. Co	5000 feet	
As No Man Has Loved	Special Cast	Fox	7836 feet	Feb. 28
Batter, The	Kenneth McDonald	Bud Barsky (S. R.)	5000 feet	
Below The Line	Rin-Tin-Tin (dog)	Warner Brothers	6100 feet	
Black Cyclone	Rex (horse)	Pathe		May 30
Bobbed Hair	Prevost-Harlan	Warner Brothers	6700 feet	
California Straight Ahead	Reginald Denny	Universal		
Call of Courage, The	Art Acord	Universal	4661 feet	Sept. 19
Classified	Corinne Griffith	First National		
Coast of Folly	Gloria Swanson	Paramount		
Coming of Amos	Rod La Rocque	Prod. Dist. Corp	5677 feet	Sept. 19
Crack of Dawn	Reed Howes	Rayart (S. R.)		
Cyclone Cavalier	Reed Howes	Rayart (S. R.)	4928 feet	Sept. 26
Dark Angel, The	R. Colman-V. Banky	First National	7311 feet	Sept. 29
Don Q, Son of Zorro	Douglas Fairbanks	United Artists	10264 feet	June 27
Free to Love	C. Bow-D. Keith	B. P. Schulberg (S.R.)		
Freshman, The	Harold Lloyd	Pathe		July 25
Graustark	Norma Talmadge	First National	5900 feet	Sept. 19
Havoc	Special Cast	Fox	9200 feet	Aug. 29
Hell's Highroad	Leatrice Joy	Prod. Dist. Corp	6084 feet	Sept. 5
High and Handsome	"Lefty" Flynn	F. B. O.	5669 feet	
His Master's Voice	Thunder (dog)	Gotham Prod. (S. R.	6000 feet	
If Marriage Fails	J. Logan-C. Brook	F. B. O	6006 feet	May 23
Keep Smiling	Monty Banks	Assoc. Exhib	5400 feet	Aug. 1
Kentucky Pride	Special Cast	Fox	6597 feet	Sept. 19
Knockout Kid, The	Jack Perrin	Rayart Pict. Corp. (S. R.)	4901 feet	
Let's Go Gallagher	Tom Tyler	Film Book Offices	5182 feet	Oct. 3
Little Annie Rooney	Mary Pickford	United Artists		
Lost World, The	Special Cast	First National	9700 feet	Feb. 21
Man From Red Gulch	Harry Carey	Prod. Dist. Corp.		
Manhattan Madness	Dempsey-Taylor	Assoc. Exhib	5500 feet	July 25
Man Who Found Himself	Thomas Meighan	Paramount	7168 feet	Sept. 5
Mystic, The	Special Cast	Metro-Goldwyn		

Feature	Star	Distributed by	Length	Reviewed
Never the Twain Shall Meet	Stewart-Lytell	Metro-Goldwyn	8143 feet	Aug. 8
New Champion, The		Columbia Pict. (S.R.)		
Not So Long Ago	Betty Bronson	Paramount	6943 feet	Aug. 8
Other Woman's Story	Calhoun-Frazer	B. P. Schulberg		
Outlaw's Daughter, The	Josie Sedgwick	Universal	4375 feet	
Paint and Power	Elaine Hammerstein	Chadwick		
Parisian Nights	E. Hammerstein - L. Tellegen	F. B. O	6278 feet	June 20
Plastic Age, The	Special Cast	B. P. Schulberg (S. R.)		
Pretty Ladies	Zazu Pitts	Metro-Goldwyn	5828 feet	July 25
Primrose Path, The	Bow-MacDonald	Arrow	5475 feet	
Ridin' the Wind	Fred Thomson	Film Book. Offices		
Scandal Street	Kennedy-Welch	Arrow	6923 feet	
Sealed Lips		Columbia Pict. (S.R.)		
Seven Days	Lillian Rich	Prod. Dist. Corp.	6974 feet	
Shore Leave	Barthelmess-Mackaill	First National	6856 feet	Aug. 29
Siege	Virginia Valli	Universal	6424 feet	June 20
Son of His Father, A	Special Cast	Paramount	7009 feet	Sept. 19
Souls for Sables		Tiffany (S. R.)	7000 feet	
S. O. S. Perils of the Sea		Columbia Pict. (S.R.)		
Speed Madness	Frank Merrill	Hercules Film	4579 feet	
Spook Ranch	Hoot Gibson	Universal	5147 feet	May 2
Sun Up	Special Cast	Metro-Goldwyn		Aug. 29
Teaser, The	Laura La Plante	Universal	6967 feet	May 30
Three in Exile		Truart (S. R.)	5800 feet	
Three Weeks in Paris	M. Moore-D. Devore	Warner Brothers	5900 feet	
Three Wise Crooks	Evelyn Brent	Film Book. Offices		
Throwback, The	Special Cast	Universal		
Timber Wolf, The	Buck Jones	Fox	4809 feet	Sept. 26
Trouble With Wives, The	Vidor-T. Moore	Paramount	6489 feet	Aug. 15
Wall Street Whiz, The	Richard Talmadge	Film Book. Offices		
What Fools Men	Stone-Mason	First National		
Wheel, The	Special Cast	Fox	7264 feet	Aug. 29
White Outlaw, The	Jack Hoxie	Universal	4830 feet	June 27
Wild Horse Mesa	Special Cast	Paramount	7221 feet	Aug. 22
Wild, Wild Susan	Bebe Daniels	Paramount		
With This Ring	Mills-Tellegen	B. P. Schulberg	5333 feet	Oct. 3

OCTOBER

Feature	Star	Distributed by	Length	Reviewed
Borrowed Finery		Tiffany (S. R.)	6500 feet	
Bustin' Through	Jack Hoxie	Universal	4506 feet	
Cactus Trails	Jack Perrin	Madoc Sales	4800 feet	
Circle, The		Metro-Goldwyn		
Circus Cyclone, The	Art Acord	Universal	4609 feet	Aug. 22
Dollar Down	Ruth Roland	Truart (S. R.)	5800 feet	Aug. 29
Everlasting Whisper, The	Tom Mix	Fox		
Exchange of Wives, An	Special Cast	Metro-Goldwyn		
Fate of a Flirt, The		Columbia (S. R.)		
Fighting Heart, The	Geo. O'Brien	Fox	6978 feet	Oct. 3
Golden Princess, The	Bronson-Hamilton	Paramount	6395 feet	Sept. 19
Great Sensation, The	W. Fairbanks-P. Garon	Columbia (S. R.)	4470 feet	Sept. 26
Heads Up	Fred Thomson	F. B. O		
Heartless Husbands	Gloria Grey	Madoc Sales	5000 feet	
He's a Prince	Raymond Griffith	Paramount		
His Buddy's Wife	Glenn Hunter	Assoc. Exhib	5600 feet	July 2[illegible]
Iron Horse, The	O'Brien-Bellamy	Fox Film Corp.	10288 feet	Sept. 13
John Forrest	Henry Edwards	Cranfield&Clark(S.R.)	5000 feet	
Keeper of the Bees, The	Robert Frazer	F. B. O		
Lew Tyler's Wives		B. P. Schulberg (S. R.)		
Lights of Old Broadway	Marion Davies	Metro-Goldwyn		
Lovers in Quarantine	Daniels-Ford	Paramount		
Midshipman, The	Ramon Novarro	Metro-Goldwyn		
New Brooms	Hamilton-Love	Paramount		
Peacock Feathers	Logan-Landis	Universal	6747 feet	Aug. 29
Pony Express, The	Betty Compson	Paramount		
Prairie Pirate, The	Harry Carey	Prod. Dist. Corp.	4603 feet	Sept. 26
Sally of the Sawdust	Fields-Dempster	United Artists	9500 feet	Aug. 15
Silver Fingers	Geo. Larkin	B'way Dist. Co.	5000 feet	
Some Pun'kins	Chas. Ray	Chadwick	6500 feet	Sept. 19
Storm Breaker, The	House Peters	Universal	6064 feet	Sept. 26
Substitute Wife, The	Jane Novak	Arrow	5994 feet	
Thunder Mountain	Special Cast	Fox	7537 feet	
Tower of Lies	Chaney-Shearer	Metro-Goldwyn		
Tumbleweeds	Wm. S. Hart	United Artists		
Unchastened Woman, The	Theda Bara	Chadwick	6800 feet	
Under the Rouge	Tom Moore	Assoc. Exhib	6500 feet	July 25
Wandering Fires	Constance Bennett	Arrow		
Winds of Chance	A. Nilsson-B. Lyon	First National	9753 feet	Aug. 29
Without Mercy	Vera Reynolds	Prod. Dist. Corp	6550 feet	
Winding Stair, The	Special Cast	Fox		

NOVEMBER

Feature	Star	Distributed by	Length	Reviewed
After Marriage	Margaret Livingston	Madoc Sales	5000 feet	
Ancient Highway, The	Holt-Vidor	Paramount		
Best People, The	Special Cast	Paramount		
Blue Blood	George Walsh	Chadwick		
Calgary Stampede, The	Hoot Gibson	Universal		
Camille of the Barbary Coast	Busch-O. Moore	Assoc. Exhib	5600 feet	Aug. 1
Cobra	Valentino-Naldi	Paramount		
Daring Days	Josie Sedgwick	Universal	5 reels	
Don't	S. O'Neill-B. Roach	Metro-Goldwyn		
Durand of the Bad Lands	Buck Jones	Fox	5844 feet	
Fifty-Fifty	L.Barrymore-H.Hampton	Assoc. Exhib	5564 feet	June 20
Fight to a Finish, A		Columbia (S. R.)		
Flower of Night	Pola Negri	Paramount		
Fool, The	Edmund Lowe	Fox	9374 feet	April 25
King on Main St., The	Adolphe Menjou	Paramount		
Lazybones	Special Cast	Fox Film	7234 feet	
Little Bit of Broadway	Ray-Starke	Metro-Goldwyn		
Makers of Men	Special Cast	Bud Barsky (S. R.)	5500 feet	Oct. 3
Merry Widow	Mae Murray	Metro-Goldwyn		
People vs. Nancy Preston	Bowers-De La Motte	Prod. Dist. Corp.		
Perfect Clown, The	Larry Semon	Chadwick		
Price of Success, The	Alice Lake	Columbia (S. R.)		
Road to Yesterday, The	Joseph Schildkraut	Prod. Dist. Corp.		
Romance Road	Raymond McKee	Truart	5000 feet	
Simon the Jester	Rich-O'Brien	Prod. Dist. Corp.		
Stage Struck	Gloria Swanson	Paramount		
Tessie	McAvoy-Agnew	Arrow	6221 feet	
Thank U	Special Cast	Fox	6900 feet	Sept. 19
Time the Comedian		Metro-Goldwyn		
Transcontinental Limited	Special Cast	Chadwick (S. R.)		
Vanishing American, The	Dix-Wilson	Paramount		
Wedding Song, The	Leatrice Joy	Prod. Dist. Corp.		
Winner, The	Charles Ray	Chadwick (S. R.)		

DECEMBER

Feature	Star	Distributed by	Length	Reviewed
Braveheart	Rod LaRocque	Prod. Dist. Corp		
Dice Woman, The	Priscilla Dean	Prod. Dist. Corp.		
Lodge in the Wilderness, The		Tiffany (S. R.)	6500 feet	
Madam Behave	Eltinge-Pennington	Prod. Dist. Corp.		
Morals for Men	Tearle-Mills	Tiffany (S. R.)	6500 feet	
Prince of Broadway	George Walsh	Chadwick		
Sweet Adeline	Charles Ray	Chadwick		

JANUARY

Feature	Star	Distributed by	Length	Reviewed
Fifth Avenue	De La Motte	Prod. Dist. Corp.		
Lure of the Arctic, The		Prod. Dist. Corp.		
Million Dollar Handicap, The	Vera Reynolds	Prod. Dist. Corp.		
Steel Preferred	William Boyd	Prod. Dist. Corp.		
Three Faces East	Goudal-Ames	Prod. Dist. Corp.		

Comedy Releases

Feature	Star	Distributed by	Length	Reviewed
Absent Minded	Neely Edwards	Universal	1 reel	
Across the Hall	Edna Marian	Universal	2 reels	
Adventures of Adenoid	Aesop's Fables	Pathe	1 reel	April 26
After a Reputation	Edna Marian	Universal	2 reels	
Air Tight	Bobby Vernon	Educational	2 reels	June 13
Alice's Egg Plant	" Cartoon "	M. J. Winkler(S. R.)	1 reel	
Alice Stagestruck	Margie Gay	M. J. Winkler (S.R.)	1 reel	July 18
All at Sea	Smith-King	Fox		
Almost a Husband	Buddy Messinger	Universal	2 reels	
Amateur Detective	Earle Foxe	Fox	2 reels	
Andy in Hollywood	Joe Murphy	Universal	2 reels	
Andy's Lion Tale	" The Gumps "	Universal	2 reels	
Andy Takes a Flyer	" The Gumps "	Universal	2 reels	
Apache, The	Earle Foxe	Fox Film	2 reels	
Apollo's Pretty Sister		Fox	2 reels	
Are Husbands Human?	James Finlayson	Pathe	1 reel	April 11
Artists' Blues	G. Joy-J. Moore	Rayart (S. R.)	2 reels	
Ask Grandma	" Our Gang "	Pathe	2 reels	May 30
At the Seashore	Monkey	Fox	2 reels	
At the Zoo	Aesops Fables	Pathe	1 reel	
Baby Be Good		Educational	2 reels	
Baby Blues	Mickey Bennett	Educational	2 reels	
Bachelors	Special Cast	Universal		
Back to Nature	Charles Puffy	Universal	1 reel	
Bad Bill Brodie	Charles Chase	Pathe	2 reels	
Bad Boy	Charles Chase	Pathe	2 reels	April 11
Balboa Discovers Hollywood	" Red Head "	Sering D. Wilson(S.R.)	1 reel	
Bashful Jim	Ralph Graves	Pathe	2 reels	Mar. 21
Be Careful	Jimmie Adams	Educational Film	2 reels	Aug. 22
Below Zero	Lige Conley	Educational	2 reels	July 4
Beware	Lige Conley	Educational Film	2 reels	Aug. 1
Big Chief Ko-Ko (Out of the Inkwell)	" Cartoon "	Red Seal Pict.	1 reel	
Big Game Hunter, The	Earle Foxe	Fox	2 reels	
Bigger and Better Pictures	" Aesop's Fables "	Pathe	1 reel	
Big Kick, The	Engle-Mohan	Pathe	1 reel	
Big Red Riding Hood	Charley Chase	Pathe	1 reel	May 9
Black Gold Bricks	Roach-Edwards	Universal	1 reel	April 18
Black Hand Blues	" Spat Family "	Pathe	2 reels	April 18
Bobby Bumbs & Co	Cartoon	Educational	1 reel	July 4
Boobs in the Woods	Harry Langdon	Pathe	2 reels	
Boys Will Be Joys	" Our Gang "	Pathe	2 reels	July 25
Brainless Horsemen		Fox	2 reels	
Brass Button	Billy West	Arrow	2 reels	
Breaking the Ice	Ralph Graves	Pathe	2 reels	April 11
Bride Tamer, The	Milburn Moranti	Sierra Pict. (S. R.)	2 reels	
Bubbles	" Aesop's Fables "	Pathe	1 reel	Aug. 15
Bugville Field Day	" Aesop's Fables "	Pathe	1 reel	July 25
Buster Be Good	Trimble-Turner	Universal	2 reels	
Butterfly Man, The		Fox	2 reels	
By the Sea	Charles Puffy	Universal	1 reel	
California Here We Come	" The Gumps "	Universal	2 reels	
Cat's Shimmy, The	" Kid Noah "	Sering D. Wilson(S.R.)	1 reel	
Cat's Whiskers, The	Neely Edwards	Universal	1 reel	
Chasing the Chasers	Jas. Finlayson	Pathe	1 reel	July 4
City Bound	Charles Puffy	Universal	1 reel	
Clean-Up Week	" Aesop's Fables"	Pathe	1 reel	Mar. 7
Clear the Way	Buddy Messinger	Universal	2 reels	
Cleopatra and Her Easy Mark	" Cartoon "	Sering D. Wilson(S.R.)	1 reel	
Cloudhopper, The	Larry Semon	Educational	2 reels	June 6
Cloudy Romance, A	Special Cast	Fox	2 reels	
Columbus Discovers a New Whirl		Sering Wilson (S. R.)	1 reel	
Crime Crushers	Lige Conley	Educational	2 reels	
Crying for Love	Eddie Gordon	Universal	2 reels	Aug. 15
Cupid's Boots	Ralph Graves	Pathe	2 reels	July 25
Cupid's Victory	Wanda Wiley	Universal	2 reels	
Cure, The (Out of the Inkwell)	" Cartoon "	Red Seal Pict.	1 reel	
Curses	Al. St. John	Educational	2 reels	May 23
Daddy Goes A Grunting		Pathe	2 reels	July 18
Darkest Africa	" Aesop's Fables "	Pathe	1 reels	
Day's Outing, A	" The Gumps "	Universal	2 reels	
Deep Stuff	Aesop's Fables	Pathe	1 reel	April 25
Dinky Doodle and Cinderella	" Dinky Doodle "	F. B. O	1 reel	
Dinky Doodle and Robinson Crusoe	" Dinky Doodle "	F. B. O	1 reel	
Discord In " A " Flat	Arthur Lake	Universal	1 reel	July 25
Dog Days	" Our Gang "	Pathe	2 reels	Mar. 14
Dog Daze	Bowes-Vance	Educational		
Dog 'On It	Bobby Dunn	Arrow	2 reels	
Dome Doctor, The	Larry Semon	Educational	2 reels	
Don't Pinch	Bobby Vernon	Educational	2 reels	April 25
Don't Worry	Wanda Wiley	Universal	2 reels	Mar. 21
Dragon Alley	Jackie McHugh	Educational	2 reels	May 16
Dr. Pyckle and Mr. Pride	Stan Laurel	Film Booking Offices	2 reels	
Dry Up	Singleton Burkett	Universal	2 reels	July 25
Dumb and Daffy	Al. St. John	Fox	2 reels	
Dynamite Doggie	Al. St. John	Educational	2 reels	Mar. 21
East Side, West Side	Harris-Leddy	Fox		
Echoes From the Alps	Aesop's Fables	Pathe	1 reel	May 23
Educating Buster	Trimble-Turner	Universal	2 reels	
End of the World, The	Aesop's Fables	Pathe	1 reel	
Etiquette	Jimmy Aubrey	Film Book. Offices	2 reels	
Excuse My Glove	" Spat Family "	Pathe	2 reels	Mar 21
Expensive Ebony	"Ebenezer Ebony"	Sering Wilson (S. R.)	1 reel	
Fair Warning	Al St. John	Educational	2 reels	Sept. 26
Fares Please	Al. St. John	Educational	2 reels	May 16
Fast Worker, A	Aesop's Fables	Pathe	1 reel	
Felix the Cat Busts Into Business	" Cartoon "	Educational	1 reel	
Felix, the Cat on the Farm	Cartoon	Educational	1 reel	
Felix Full O'Fight	" Cartoon "	M. J. Winkler (S. R.)	1 reel	
Felix Gets His Fill	" Cartoon "	M. J. Winkler (S. R.)	1 reel	
Felix Grabs His Grub	" Cartoon "	M. J. Winkler (S. R.)	1 reel	
Felix the Cat on the Job	Cartoon	Educational	1 reel	
Fire Flies	" Hey, Fellas "	Davis Dist.	2 reels	
First Love	" Our Gang "	Pathe	2 reels	
Fishermen's Luck	"Aesop's Fables "	Pathe	1 reel	
For Hire	Edward Gordon	Universal		
For Love of a Gal	" Aesop's Fables "	Pathe	1 reel	July 25
Found World, The	" The Gumps "	Universal	2 reels	
Fun's Fun	Bowes-Vance	Educational	1 reel	June 6
Getting Trimmed	Wanda Wiley	Universal	2 reels	April 18
Giddap	Special Cast	Pathe	2 reels	Mar. 21
Going Great	Eddie Nelson	Educational	2 reels	June 13
Goldfish's Pajamas	" Kid Noah "	Sering D. Wilson(S.R.)	1 reel	
Good Morning Nurse	Ralph Graves	Pathe	2 reels	May 30
Good Scouts	" Reg'lar Kids "	M. J. Winkler (S. R.)	2 reels	
Great Guns	Bobby Vernon	Educational	2 reels	Feb. 21
Green-Eyed Monster, The	Arthur Lake	Universal	1 reel	
Gridiron Gertie	Wanda Wiley	Universal	2 reels	
Guilty Conscience, A	Eddie Gordon	Universal		
Gypping the Gypsies	" Ebonezer Ebony "	Sering Wilson (S. R.)	1 reel	
Half Fare	Arthur Lake	Universal	1 reel	
Half a Hero	Lloyd Hamilton	Educational	2 reels	Mar. 7
Half a Man	Stan Laurel	Pathe	2 reels	
Hard Boiled	Charley Chase	Pathe	2 reels	Mar. 21
Hard Working Loafer, The	Arthur Stone	Pathe		
Haunted Honeymoon	Tryon-Mehaffey	Pathe	2 reels	Feb. 28
Heart Breaker, The	Special Cast	Fox	2 reels	
Heart Trouble	Arthur Lake	Universal	1 reel	July 4
Heavy Swells	Special Cast	Fox	2 reels	
Hello, Goodby	Lige Conley	Educational	2 reels	May 30
Hello, Hollywood	Lige Conley	Educational	2 reels	Mar. 28
Helping Hand	Jimmy Aubrey	F. B. O	2 reels	
Help Yourself		Fox	2 reels	
Here's Your Hat	Arthur Lake	Universal	1 reel	May 9
Her Lucky Leap	Wanda Wiley	Universal	2 reels	
He Who Gets Crowned	Jimmy Aubrey	F. B. O	2 reels	
He Who Got Smacked	Ralph Graves	Pathe	2 reels	May 9
Hey! Taxi!	Bobby Dunn	Arrow	2 reels	
High Hopes	Bowes-Vance	Educational	1 reel	Feb. 14
High Jinx, A		Fox	2 reels	
His Marriage Wow	Harry Langdon	Pathe	2 reels	Mar. 7
Hold My Baby	Glenn Tryon	Pathe	2 reels	April 25
Home Scouts	Jimmie Aubrey	F. B. O.	2 reels	
Honeymoon Heaven		Sering Wilson (S. R.)	1 reel	
Horace Greeley, Jr	Harry Langdon	Pathe	2 reels	June 6
Horrible Hollywood		Lee-Bradford (S. R.)		
Hot and Heavy	Eddie Nelson	Educational	2 reel	July 18
Hot Dog	Animal	C B C (S. R.)	2 reels	
Hot Times in Iceland	Aesop's Fables	Pathe	1 reels	
House of Flickers, The		Fox	2 reels	
House that Dinky Built	(Cartoon)	F. B. O	1 reel	
Housing Shortage, The	" Aesop's Fables "	Pathe	1 reel	
Hurry Doctor	Ralph Graves	Pathe		
Hysterical History (Series)		Universal	1 reel	
Ice Boy, An	" Ebonezer Ebony "	Sering D. Wilson(S.R.)	1 reel	
Ice Cold	Arthur Lake	Universal	1 reel	June 13
In Deep	Bowes-Vance	Educational	1 reel	
In Dutch	Aesop's Fables	Pathe	1 reel	
Innocent Husbands	Charley Chase	Pathe	2 reels	Aug. 1
Inside Out	Bowes-Vance	Educational	1 reel	Mar. 28
Into the Grease	James Finlayson	Pathe	1 reel	June 27
Iron Mule	Al St. John	Educational	2 reels	April 18
Iron Nag, The	Billy Bevan	Pathe	2 reels	Aug. 15
Is Marriage the Bunk?	Charles Chase	Pathe	1 reel	April 4
Isn't Life Terrible?	Charles Chase	Pathe	2 reels	July 4
Itching for Revenge	Eddie Gordon	Universal	2 reels	Mar. 7
It's All Wrong	Karr-Engle	Universal		
James Boys' Sister		Wilson Sering (S. R.)	1 reel	
Jimminy Crickets	Wesley Edwards	Universal	1 reel	
Jungle Bike Riders	Aesop's Fables	Pathe	1 reel	Mar. 14.
Just in Time	Wanda Wiley	Universal	2 reels	July 11
Kicked About	Eddie Gordon	Universal	2 reels	Mar. 14.
Kidding Captain Kidd	" Cartoon "	Sering Wilson (S. R.)	1 reel	
King Cotton	Lloyd Hamilton	Educational	2 reels	May 9
King Dumb	Jimmy Aubrey	F. B. O	2 reels	
Klynick, The	" Hey, Fellas "	Davis Dict.	2 reels	
Knocked About	Eddie Gordon	Universal	2 reels	June 13
Ko-Ko Celebrates the Fourth (Out of the Inkwell)	" Cartoon "	Red Seal Pict.		
Ko-Ko Trains Animals (out of the Inkwell)	" Cartoon "	Red Seal Pict	1 reel	
Lead Pipe Cinch, A	Al Alt	Universal		
Lion Love		Fox	2 reels	Feb. 28
Lion and the Monkey	" Aesop's Fables "	Pathe		
Lion's Whiskers		Pathe	2 reels	April 18
Little Red Riding Hood	" Dinky Doodle "	F. B. O	1 reel	
Locked Out	Arthur Lake	Universal	1 reel	May 30
Looking for Sally	Charles Chase	Pathe	2 reels	May 9
Look Out	Bowes-Vance	Educational Film	1 reel	Aug. 1
Lost Cord, The	Bert Roach	Universal	1 reel	Feb. 21
Love and Kisses	Alice Day	Pathe	2 reels	
Love and Lions	Special Cast	Fox	2 reels	
Love Bug, The	" Our Gang "	Pathe	2 reels	April 4
Love Goofy	Jimmy Adams	Educational	2 reels	Mar. 7
Love and Kisses	Alice Day	Pathe	2 reels	Oct. 3
Love Sick	Constance Darling	Universal	2 reels	May 23
Love's Tragedy		Sering Wilson (S. R.)	1 reel	
Lucky Accident, The	Charles Puffy	Universal	1 reel	July 18
Lucky Leap, A	Wanda Wiley	Universal	2 reels	
Lucky Stars	Harry Langdon	Pathe	2 reels	Aug. 15
Madame Sans Jane	Glenn Tryon	Pathe	2 reels	
Marriage Circus, The	Ben Turpin	Pathe	2 reels	April 11
Married Neighbors	Engle-Darling	Universal	2 reels	July 4
Mary, Queen of Tots	" Our Gang "	Pathe	2 reels	Aug. 22
Meet the Ambassador	Jimmy Aubrey	F. B. O	2 reels	
Mellow Quartette	Pen & Ink Vaudeville	Educational	1 reel	April 4
Merrymakers	Bowes-Vance	Educational	1 reel	Mar. 28
Met by Accident	Wanda Wiley	Universal	2 reels	
Milky Way, The	Charles Puffy	Universal	1 reel	July 25
Min Walks in Her Sleep	" Gumps "	Universal		

Feature	Star	Distributed by	Length	Reviewed
Misfit Sailor, A	Dovley-Steadman	Educational	2 reels	Oct. 3
Miss Fixit	Wanda Wiley	Universal	2 reels	
Monkey Business	"Pen & Ink Vaude"	Educational	1 reel	May 9
Moonlight Nights	Gloria Joy	Rayart (S. R.)	2 reels	
Moonlight and Noses	Clyde Cook	Pathe	2 reels	Oct. 3
Movies, The	Lloyd Hamilton	Educational	2 reels	Oct. 3
Nearly Rich	Charles Puffy	Universal	1 reel	
Neptune's Stepdaughter		Fox	2 reels	
Nero's Jazz Band		Sering Wilson (S. R.)	1 reel	
Never Fear	Bowes-Vance	Educational	1 reel	
Never on Time		Lee-Bradford (S. R.)	2 reels	
Never Weaken	Lloyd reissue	Assoc. Exhib	2237 feet	
Nice Pickle, A	Edwards-Roach	Universal	1 reel	
Nicely Rewarded	Chas. Puffy	Universal	1 reel	June 27
Night Hawks		Educational Film	2 reels	
Nobody Wins	Arthur Lake	Universal	1 reel	
No Place to Go	Arthur Lake	Universal	1 reel	
Now or Never (reissue)	Harold Lloyd	Assoc. Exhib	3 reels	
Nursery Troubles	Edna Marian	Universal		
Nuts and Squirrels	"Aesop's Fables"	Pathe	1 reel	
Off His Beat	Walter Hiers	Educational	2 reels	
Office Help	"Aesop's Fables"	Pathe	1 reel	June 27
Officer 13	Eddie Gordon	Universal		
Official Officers	"Our Gang"	Pathe	2 reels	June 27
Oh, Bridget	Walter Hiers	Educational	2 reels	
Oh, What a Flirt	Jimmy Aubrey	Film Book. Offices	2 reels	
Oh, What a Gump	"The Gumps"	Universal	2 reels	
Old Family Toothbrush	"Kid Noah"	Sering Wilson (S. R.)	1 reel	
On Duty	Wanda Wiley	Universal	2 reels	
On the Go	Special Cast	Fox		
One Glorious Fourth	"Reg'lar Kids"	M. J. Winkler (S. R.)	2 reels	
One Wild Night	Neely Edwards	Universal	1 reel	
Orphan, The	Al Joy	Ricardo Films, Inc. (S.R.)		
Over the Bottom	Stan Laurel	F. B. O	2 reels	
Over the Plate	Aesops Fable	Pathe	1 reel	Aug. 22
Over Here	Harry Langdon	Pathe	2 reels	
Paging A Wife	Al Alt	Universal	2 reels	Aug. 1
Papa's Darling		Fox	2 reels	
Papa's Pet	Roach-Edwards	Universal	1 reel	April 11
Parisian Knight, A	Earle Foxe	Fox	2 reels	
Peggy in a Pinch	"Sheiks and Shebas"	Davis Dist.	2 reels	
Peggy's Pests	"Sheiks and Shebas"	Davis Dist.	2 reels	
Peggy's Putters	"Sheiks and Shebas"	Davis Dist.	2 reels	
Peggy the Vamp	"Sheiks and Shebas"	Davis Dist.	2 reels	Oct. 11
Permanent Waves	"Aesop's Fables"	Pathe	1 reel	
Permit Me	Bowes-Vance	Educational	1 reel	July 11
Pie-Eyed	Stan Laurel	F. B. O	2 reels	
Pie Man, The	"Aesop's Fables"	Pathe	1 reel	Mar. 21
Plain Clothes	Harry Langdon	Pathe	2 reels	Mar. 28
Plain and Fancy Girls	Charles Chase	Pathe	1 reel	Mar. 14
Plain Luck	Edna Marian	Universal	2 reels	
Pleasure Bound	Lige Conley	Educational	2 reels	Aug. 24
Plenty of Nerve	Edna Marian	Universal	2 reels	July 2
Polo Kid, The	Eddie Gordon	Universal	2 reels	July 18
Poor Sap, The		Fox	2 reels	
Powdered Chickens	Edna Marian	Universal	2 reels	Mar. 28
Props' Dash for Cash	Earl Hurd (Cartoon)	Educational	1 reel	
Putting on Airs	Edna Marian	Universal	2 reels	April 11
Puzzled by Crosswords	Eddie Gordon	Universal	2 reels	Mar. 7
Queen of Aces	Wanda Wiley	Universal	2 reels	May 16
Raid, The	Gloria Joy	Rayart Pict. (S. R.)	2 reels	
Rainy Knight, A	Special Cast	Pathe		
Raisin' Cain	Constance Darling	Universal	2 reels	April 4
Rapid Transit	Al. St. John	Educational	2 reels	
Rarin' Romeo	Walter Hiers	Educational	2 reels	Mar. 28
Raspberry Romance	Ben Turpin	Pathe	2 reels	Feb. 28
Red Pepper	Al. St. John	Educational	2 reels	Arpil 4
Regular Girl, A	Wanda Wiley	Universal	2 reels	
Riders of the Kitchen Range	Mohar-Engle	Pathe	1 reel	June 6
Remember When	Harry Langdon	Pathe	2 reels	April 25
Rip Without a Wink	"Redhead"	Sering Wilson (S. R.)	1 reel	
Ripe Melodrama, A		Sering Wilson (S. R.)	1 reel	
Rivals	Billy West	Arrow	2 reels	
Robinson Crusoe Returns on Friday	"Redhead"	Sering Wilson (S. R.)	1 reel	
Rock Bottom	Bowes-Vance	Educational	1 reel	May 9
Robbing the Rube		Lee-Bradford Corp.	2 reels	
Rolling Stones	Charles Puffy	Universal	1 reel	May 30
Rough Party	Al Alt	Universal	2 reels	
Royal Four-Flush	"Spat Family"	Pathe	2 reels	June 13
Runaway Balloon, The	"Aesop's Fables"	Pathe	1 reel	June 27
Runt, The	"Aesop's Fables"	Pathe	1 reel	June 6
Sailor Papa, A	Glenn Tryon	Pathe	2 reels	April 4
Salute	Alice Ardell	F. B. O.		
Saturday	"Hey Fellas"	Davis Dist. Div.	2 reels	
Say It With Flour		Fox	2 reels	
Scrambled Eggs	Bowes-Vance	Educational		
Sheiks of Bagdad		Pathe	1 reel	May 9
Sherlock Sleuth	Arthur Stone	Pathe	2 reels	July 11
Ship Shape	Vance-Bowes	Educational	1 reel	April 18
Shootin' Injuns	"Our Gang"	Pathe	2 reels	May 9
Short Pants	Arthur Lake	Universal	1 reel	Aug. 1
Should a Husband Tell?		Red Seal Pict.	1 reel	
Should Husbands Be watched?	Charles Chase	Pathe	1 reel	Mar. 14
Sir Walt and Lizzie		Sering Wilson (S. R.)	1 reel	
Sit Tight	Jimmie Adams	Educational	2 reels	May 30
Skinners in Silk		Pathe	2 reels	May 16
Sky Jumper, The	Earle Foxe	Fox	2 reels	
Skyscraper, The	Harry Langdon	Principal Pict. (S. R.)	2 reels	
Sleeping Sickness	Edwards-Roach	Universal	1 reel	May 30
Slick Articles	Engle-Karr	Universal	2 reels	May 30
Smoked Out	Lake-Hasbrouck	Universal	1 reel	April 13
Sneezing Beezers	Billy Bevan	Pathe	2 reels	July 18
Snow-Hawk	Stan Laurel	F. B. O.	2 reels	
Soap	"Aesop's Fables"	Pathe	1 reel	
Somewhere in Somewhere	Murray-Littlefield	Pathe	2 reels	Sept. 26
S. O. S.	"Aesop's Fables"	Pathe	1 reel	
Spanish Romeo, A (Van Bibber)		Fox	1 reel	
Speak Easy	Charley Puffy	Universal	1 reel	Aug. 22
Speak Sreely	Edna Marion	Universal	2 reels	
Spot Light		Educational	2 reels	
Stick Around	Bobby Dunn	Arrow	2 reels	
Stop, Look and Whistle		Fox	2 reels	
Storm, The (Out of the Inkwell)	"Cartoon"	Red Seal Pict.	1 reel	
Stranded	Edna Marian	Universal	2 reels	
Strong for Love	Special Cast	Fox	2 reels	
Super-Hooper-Dyne Lizzies		Pathe	3 reels	June 13
Sure Mike!	Martha Sleeper	Pathe	1 reel	May 23
Sweet Marie	Special Cast	Fox	2 reels	Aug. 29
Tame Men and Wild Women		Pathe	2 reels	Aug. 15
Taxi War, A	Eddie Gordon	Universal	2 reels	
Teaser Island	"Redhead"	Sering Wilson (S. R.)	1 reel	
Tee for Two	Alice Day	Pathe	2 reels	Aug. 1
Tell It To a Policeman	Glenn Tryon	Pathe	2 reels	May 23
Tender Feet	Walter Hiers	Educational	2 reels	May 23
Tenting Out	Roache-Edwards	Universal	1 reel	Mar. 23
This Week-End		Lee-Bradford (S. R.)		
Three Wise Goofs	Special Cast	F. B. O		
Thundering Landlords	Glenn Tryon	Pathe	2 reels	June 27
Ton of Fun in a Beauty Parlor, A		F. B. O		
Too Much Mother-in-Law	Constance Darling	Universal		
Too Young to Marry	Buddy Messinger	Universal	2 reels	
Tough Night, A	Jimmy Callahan	Aywon Film	2 reels	
Tourist, The	Harry Langdon	Educational Film	2 reels	Aug. 15
Tourists De Luxe	Hayes-Karr	Universal	2 reels	May 16
Transatlantic Flight, A	"Aesop's Fables"	Pathe	1 reel	
Twins	Stan Laurel	F. B. O	2 reels	
Two Cats and a Bird	"Cartoon"	Educational	1 reel	Mar. 14
Two Poor Fish	Earl Hurd cartoon	Educational	1 reel	May 30
Ugly Duckling, The	"Aesop's Fables"	Pathe	1 reel	Sept. 26
Uncle Tom's Gal	Edna Marian	Universal	2 reels	
Unwelcome	Charles Puffy	Universal	1 reel	June 27
Waiting	Lloyd Hamilton	Educational	2 reels	July 11
Wake Up	Bowes-Vance	Educational	1 reel	June 13
Watch Out	Bobby Vernon	Educational	2 reels	
Water Wagons	Special Cast	Pathe	2 reels	Feb. 21
Welcome Dangar	Bowes-Vance	Educational	1 reel	Feb. 23
West is West	Billy West	Arrow	2 reels	
Westward Ho	Charles Puffy	Universal	1 reel	Oct. 3
What Price Goofy	Charley Chase	Pathe	2 reels	June 6
When Dumbells Ring		Fox	2 reels	
When Men Were Men	"Aesop's Fables"	Pathe	1 reel	July 25
White Wing's Bride	Harry Langdon	Pathe	2 reels	July 11
Whose Baby Are You?	Glenn Tryon	Pathe	2 reels	
Who's Which	Bowes-Vance	Educational	1 reel	
Why Hesitate?	Neal Burns	Educational	2 reels	April 11
Why Sitting Bull Stood Up		Sering Wilson (S. R.)	1 reel	
Wide Awake	Lige Conley	Educational	2 reels	
Wild Papa	"Spat Family"	Pathe	2 reels	May 16
Wild Waves	Bowes-Vance	Educational	1 reel	May 23
Wine, Woman and Song	"Aesop's Fables"	Pathe	1 reel	
Winning Pair, A	Wanda Wiley	Universal	2 reels	
Wooly West, The	Buddy Messinger	Universal	2 reels	
Wrestler, The	Earle Foxe	Fox	2 reels	Aug. 29
Yarn About Yarn, A	Aesop Fable	Pathe	1 reel	Aug. 1
Yes, Yes, Nannette	Jas. Finlayson	Pathe	1 reel	Aug. 1
Your Own Back Yard	"Our Gang"	Pathe	2 reels	Oct. 3

Short Subjects

Feature	Distributed by	Length	Reviewed
Action (Sportlight)	Pathe	1 reel	
All Abroad (Helen and Warren)	Fox	2 reels	
All Under One Flag (Sportlight)	Pathe	1 reel	
Animal Celebrities (Sportlight)	Pathe	1 reel	June 27
Animated Hair Cartoon (Series)	Red Seal	1 reel	
Balto's Race to Nome (Special)	Educational	2 reels	May 23
Barbara Snitches (Pacemaker Series)	F. B. O.	2 reels	
Battle of Wits (Josie Sedgwick)	Universal	2 reels	July 18
Bashful Whirlwind, The (Edmund Cobb)	Universal	2 reels	
Beauty and the Bandit (Geo. Larkin)	Universal	2 reels	July 4
Beauty Spots (Sportlight)	Pathe	1 reel	April 18
Best Man, The (Josie Sedgwick)	Universal	2 reels	Aug. 15
Broken Trails	Denver Dixon (S.R.)	2 reels	
Boundary Line, The (Fred Humes)	Universal	2 reels	
Business Engagement, A (Helen & Warren)	Fox	2 reels	
Cabaret of Old Japan	M. J. Winkler (S.R.)	1 reel	
Color World	Sering Wilson (S. R.)	1 reel	
Captured Alive (Helen Gibson)	Universal	2 reels	July 25
Cinema Stars (Novelty)	Davis Dist	1 reel	
Close Call, The (Edmund Cobb)	Universal	2 reels	
Cocoon to Kimono	M. J. Winkler (S.R.)	1 reel	
Come-Back, The (Benny Leonard)	Henry Ginsberg-S.R.	2 reels	
Concerning Cheese (Varieties)	Fox	1 reel	
Covered Flagon, The (Pacemaker Series)	F. B. O	2 reels	
Cowpuncher's Comeback, The (Art Acord)	Universal	2 reels	
Crooked (Elinor King)	Davis Dist	2 reels	
Cross Word Puzzle Film (Comedy-Novelty)	Schwartz Enterprises (S. R.)	1 reel	
Cuba Steps Out (Variety)	Fox	1 reel	
Day With the Gypsies	Red Seal Pict.	1 reel	
Divertisement (Color Shots)	Sering Wilson (S. R.)	1 reel	
Don Coo Coo (Pacemakers)	Film Book. Offices	2 reels	
Do You Remember (Gems of Screen)	Red Seal	1 reel	
Dude Ranch Days (Sportlight)	Pathe	1 reel	May 30
Earth's Other Half (Hodge-Podge)	Educational	1 reel	June 6
East Side, West Side	DeForrest (S. R.)		
Failure (O. Henry) Marian Harlan	Fox	2 reels	
Fast Male, The (Pacemakers)	Film Book. Offices	2 reels	
Fighting Cowboy (Series)	Universal		
Fighting Ranger (Serial)	Universal	15 episodes	Feb. 7
Fighting Schoolmarm (Josie Sedgwick)	Universal	2 reels	Aug. 1
Film Facts	Red Seal	1 reel	
Fire Trader, The (Serial)	Universal	15 episodes	
Flirting With Death	Red Seal Pict.	2 reels	Sept. 26
Floral Feast, A	Sering Wilson (S.R.)	1 reel	
Frederick Chopin (Music Masters)	Jas. A. Fitzpatrick (S. R.)	1 reel	
From Mars to Munich (Varieties)	Fox	1 reel	April 4
Frontier Love (Billy Mack)	Denver Dixon	2 reels	
Fugitive Futurist	Cranfield & Clarke (S. R.)		
George F. Handel (Music Masters)	Jas. A. Fitzpatrick (S. R.)	1 reel	
Gems of the Screen	Red Seal	1 reel	
Ghost City, The (Serial)	Universal	15 episodes	
Golden Panther, The (Serial)	Pathe		
Gold Trap, The Fred Humes	Universal	2 reels	
Great Circus Mystery, The (Serial)	Universal	15 episodes	
Great Decide, The (Pacemakers)	Film Book. Offices	2 reels	
He Who Gets Rapped (Pacemakers)	Film Book. Offices	2 reels	
Hittin' the Trail (Fred Hank)	Sierra Pict. (S. R.)	2 reels	
How the Elephant Got His Trunk (Bray)	F. B. O		
Idaho (Serial)	Pathe	10 episodes	Feb. 28
If a Picture Tells a Story	Cranfield & Clarke (S. R.)		
In a China Shop (Variety)	Fox	1 reel	
In the Spider's Grip (Novelty)	Educational	1 reel	April 11

Feature	Star	Distributed by	Length	Reviewed
Invention, The (Elinor King)		Davis Dist.	2 reels	Oct. 3
I Remember		Short Films Synd.	2 reels	Sept. 26
It Might Happen to You (Evangeline Russell)		Davis Dist.	2 reels	
Jazz Fight, The (Benny Leonard)		Henry Ginsberg (S. R.)	2 reels	
Judge's Cross Word Puzzle (Novelty)		Educational	1 reel	Jan. 31
Just Cowboys	Corbett-Holmes	Universal	2 reels	
Klondike Today (Varieties)		Fox	1 reel	
Knicknacks of Knowledge (Hodge Podge)		Educational	1 reel	
Knockout Man, The (Mustang)		Universal	2 reels	July 11
Ko-Ko on the Run	(Ko-Ko Series)	Red Seal	1 reel	Oct. 3
Land of the Navajo (Educational)		Fox	1 reel	
Learning How (Sportlight)		Pathe	1 reel	July 18
Leopard's Lair		Universal	Serial	
Let's Paint		Cranfield & Clarke (S. R.)		
Life's Greatest Thrills		Universal	2 reels	Sept. 26
Line Runners, The (Arnold Gregg)		Universal	2 reels	
Little People of the Garden (Secrets of Life)		Educational	1 reel	
Little People of the Sea (Secrets of Life)		Educational	1 reel	Feb. 28
Lizzie's Last Lap		Cranfield & Clarke (S. R.)		
Loaded Dice (Edmund Cobb)		Universal	2 reels	April 4
Luna-cy (Stereoscopik)		Pathe	1 reel	
Mad Miner, A (Western)		Hunt Miller (S. R.)	2 reels	
Magic Hour, The		Red Seal Pict.	1 reel	
Man Who Rode Alone, The		Miller & Steen (S.R.)	2 reels	
Man Without a Scar		Universal	2 reels	
Marvels of Motion		Red Seal	1 reel	
Marvellous Manhattan		M. J. Winkler (S. R.)	1 reel	
Merry Kiddo, The (Pacemakers)		Film Book. Offices	2 reels	
Merton of the Goofies	"Pacemaker"	F. B. O.	2 reels	
Mexican Melody (Hodge-Podge)		Educational	1 Reel	
Mexican Oil Fields		M. J. Winkler (S. R.)	1 reel	
Movie Morsels (Hodge Podge)		Educational	1 reel	April 4
My Bonnie	(Ko-Ko Series)	Red Sea	1 reel	Oct. 3
My Own Carolina (Variety)		Fox	1 reel	Aug. 29
Mystery Box, The (Serial)		Davis Dist. Corp.	10 episodes	
Neptune's Nieces (Sportlight)		Pathe	1 reel	
New Sheriff, A (Western)		Hunt Miller (S. R.)	2 reels	
Olympic Mermaids (Sportlight)		Pathe	1 reel	
One Glorious Scrap (Edmund Cobb)		Universal	2 reels	
Only a Country Lass (Novelty)		Educational	1 reel	May 29
Ouch (Stereoscopik)		Pathe	1 reel	
Our Six-legged Friends (Secrets of Life)		Educational	1 reel	
Outings for All	(Sportlight)	Pathe	1 reel	
Outlaw, The (Jack Perrin)		Universal	2 reels	
Peacemakers, The	(Helen & Warren)	Fox	2 reels	
Paris Creations (Novelty)		Educational	1 reel	Feb. 7
Paris Creations in Color (Novelty)		Educational	1 reel	Feb. 28
People You Know (Screen Almanac)		Film Booking Offices.	1 reel	
Perfect View, The (Varieties)		Fox	1 reel	
Perils of the Wild (Serial)		Universal		
Pictorial Proverbs (Hodge Podge)		Educational	1 reel	Aug. 15
Plastigrams (Novelty)		Educational		
Play Ball (Serial)		Pathe	10 episodes	June 27
Power God, The (Serial)		Davis Dist. Div.	15 episodes	
Pronto Kid, The (Edmund Cobb)		Universal	2 reels	June 27
Queen of the Round-Up (J. Sedgwick)		Universal	2 reels	June 13
Race, The (Van Bibber)		Fox	2 reels	
Radio Detective, The		Universal	Serial	
Raid, The	Edmund Cobb	Universal	2 reels	
Record Breaker, The		Pathe	Serial	
Rim of the Desert (Jack Perrin)		Universal	2 reels	
River Nile, The (Variety)		Fox	1 reel	
Roaring Waters (Geo. Larkin)		Universal	2 reels	
Rock Bound Brittany (Educational)		Fox	1 reel	
Ropin' Venus, The (Mustang Series)		Universal	2 reels	July 11
R. Valentino and Eighty-eight Prize-winning American Beauties		Chesterfield (M. P. Corp.) (S. R.)	3 reels	
Runaway Taxi, A	(Stereoscopic)	Pathe	1 reel	Oct. 3
Rustlen of Boulder Canyon (Edmund Cobb)		Universal	2 reels	
Secrets of Life (Educational)		Principal Pict. (S. R.)	reel	Feb. 21
Seven Ages of Sport (Sportlight)		Pathe	1 reel	Aug. 22
Shadow of Suspicion (Eileen Sedgwick)		Universal	2 reels	
Shoes (O. Henry)		Fox	2 reels	
Shootin' Wild (Corbett-Holmes)		Universal	2 reels	
Show Down, The (Art Acord)		Universal	2 reels	
Silvery Art		Red Seal Pict.	2 reels	Sept. 26
Sky Tribe, The (Variety)		Fox	1 reel	
Smoke of a Forty-Five, The (Western)		Hunt Miller (S. R.)	2 reels	
Soft Muscles (Benny Leonard)		Ginsberg (S. R.)	2 reels	
Song Cartunes (Novelty)		Red Seal Pict.	1 reel	
Sons of Swat (Sportlight)		Pathe	1 reel	Aug. 15
Sporting Judgment (Sportlight)		Pathe	1 reel	May 9
Starting an Argument (Sportlight)		Pathe	1 reel	
Steam Heated Islands (Varieties)		Fox	1 reel	
Stereoscopic (Novelty)		Pathe	1 reel	May 16
Storm King (Edmund Cobb)		Universal	2 reels	
Story Teller, The (Hodge-Podge)		Educational	1 reel	Oct. 3
Straight Shootin' (Harry Carey)		Universal	2 reels	
Strangler Lewis vs. Wayne Munn		Educational	2 reels	July 4
Stratford on Avon (Gems of Screen)		Red Seal Pict	1 reel	
Sunken Silver (Serial)		Pathe	10 episodes	April 18
Surprise Fight, The (Benny Leonard)		Henry Ginsberg (S. R.)	2 reels	
Thundering Waters (Novelty)		Sering D. Wilson (S. R.)	1 reel	April 25
Tiger Kill, The (Pathe Review)		Pathe		
Toiling for Rest (Variety)		Fox	1 reel	
Too Many Bucks (Corbett-Holmes		Universal	2 reels	
Transiets in Arcadia (O. Henry)		Fox	2 reels	
Traps and Troubles (Sportlight)		Pathe	1 reel	Mar. 21
Travel Treasures (Hodge Podge)		Educational	1 reel	July 25
Turf Mystery (Serial)		Chesterfield Pict. Corp. (S. R.)	15 episodes	
Valley of Rogues (Western)		Universal	2 reels	April 18
Van Bibber and the Navy (Earle Foxe)		Fox	2 reels	
Village School, The (Hodge Podge)		Educational Film	1 reel	May
Voice of the Nightingale, The (Novelty)		Educational	1 reel	Mar. 28
Waiting For You (Music Film)		Hegerman Music Novelties (S. R.)		
Welcome Granger (Pacemakers)		Film Book. Offices	2 reels	
West Wind, The (Variety)		Fox	1 reel	
What Price Gloria (Pacemakers)		Film Book. Offices	2 reels	
Wheels of the Pioneers (Billy Mack)		Denver Dixon (S. R.)	2 reels	
Where the Waters Divide (Varieties)		Fox	1 reel	
White Paper (Varieties)		Fox	1 reel	
Wild West Wallop, The (Edmund Cobb)		Universal	2 reels	May 16
Wild West		Pathe	Serial	
With Pencil, Brush and Chisel (Variety)		Fox	1 reel	
Wonder Book, The (Series)		Sering D. Wilson	500 feet	April 25
Young Sheriff, The (Tom. Forman)		Miller & Steen (S. R.)	2 reels	
Zowie (Stereoscopik)		Pathe	1 reel	

Coming Attractions

Feature	Star	Distributed by	Length	Reviewed
Ace of Spades, The	Desmond-McAllister	Universal		
Age of Indiscretion		Truart (S. R.)	5800 feet	
Agony Column	Monte Blue	Warner Bros		
All Around the Frying Pan	Fred Thompson	F. B. O		
Aloma of the South Seas	Gilda Gray	Paramount		
American Venus, The	Special Cast	Paramount		
An Enemy of Men		Columbia Pict. (S. R.)		
Aristocrat, The	Special Cast	B. P. Schulberg (S. R.)		
Atlantis		First National		
Bad Lands, The	Harry Carey	Prod. Dist. Corp	5833 feet	Oct. 3
Barriers of Fire	Monte Blue	Warner Bros.		
Bat, The	Special Cast	United Artists		
Beautiful Cheat, The	Laura La Plante	Universal		
Beautiful City	R. Barthelmess	First National		
Before Midnight	Wm. Russell	Ginsberg (S. R.)	5895 feet	Aug. 8
Bells, The	Lionel Barrymore	Chadwick		
Beloved Pawn, The	Reed Howes	Rayart (S. R.)		
Ben Hur	Special Cast	Metro-Goldwyn		
Best Bad Man, The	Tom Mix	Fox		
Between Men	"Lefty" Flynn	F. B. O		
Big Parade, The	John Gilbert	Metro-Goldwyn		
Border Intrigue	Franklyn Farnum	Inde. Pict. (S. R.)	5 reels	June 6
Border Women	Special Cast	Phil Goldstone (S.R.)	5000 feet	
Broken Hearts of Hollywood	Harlan-Miller	Warner Brothers		
Broken Homes	Lake-Glass	Astor Dist		
Brooding Eyes		Ginsberg Dis. Corp. (S. R.)		
Cave Man, The	Harlan-Miller	Warner Brothers		
Charity Ball, The		Metro-Goldwyn		
Checkered Flag, The		Ginsberg Dist. Corp. (S. R.)		
Clean-Up, The	Richard Talmadge	F. B. O.		
Clod Hopper, The	Glenn Hunter	Assoc. Exhibitors		
Clothes Make the Pirate	Errol-D. Gish	First National		
College Widow, The	Syd Chaplin	Warner Brothers		
Compromise	Irene Rich	Warner Bros.		
Conquered	Gloria Swanson	Paramount		
Count of Luxembourg, The	Larry Semon	Chadwick		
Crashing Through	Jack Perrin	Ambassador Pict. (S. R.)	5000 feet	
Cyclone Bob	Bob Reeves	Anchor Film Dist.		
Cyrano de Bergerac	Special Cast	Atlas Dist. (S. R.)	9500 feet	July 18
Dance Madness	Pringle-Cody	Metro-Goldwyn		
Dangers of a Great City		Fox		
Dark Horse, The	Harry Carey	Prod. Dist. Corp.		
Daybreak		Fox		
Deerslayer, The		Weiss Bros. (S. R.)	4780 feet	
Daughter of the Sioux, A	Wilson-Gerber	Davis Dist. (S. R.)	5 reels	Oct. 3
Demon, The	Jack Hoxie	Universal		
Demon Rider, The	Ken Maynard	Davis Dist	5000 feet	Aug. 22
Detour		Prod. Dist. Corp.		
Devil Horse, The	Rex (horse)	Pathe		
Down Upon the Suwanee River	Special Cast	Lee Bradford (S. R.)		
Dumb Head		Tiffany (S. R.)	6500 feet	
East of the Setting Sun	Constance Talmadge	First National		
Eagle, The	Rudolph Valentino	United Artists		
Eden's Fruit		B. P. Schulberg (S.R.)		
Enchanted Hill, The	Special Cast	Paramount		
Ermine and Rhinestone		H. F. Jans (S. R.)		
Exquisite Sinner, The	Special Cast	Metro-Goldwin		
Face on the Air, The	Evelyn Brent	F. B. O.		
Fall of Jerusalem		Weiss Bros. (S. R.)	6800 feet	
False Pride		Astor Dist.		
Fast Pace, The	Special Cast	Arrow		
Fighter's Paradise, The	Rex Baker	Phil Goldstone	5000 feet	
Fighting Courage	Ken Maynard	Davis Dist. Div. (S.R.)	5 reels	July 11
Fighting Edge, The	Harlan-Miller	Warner Brothers		
Fighting Heart, The	Frank Merrill	Bud Barsky Prod. (S. R.)	5000 feet	
Fighting Smile, The	Bill Cody	Inde.Pict. Corp.(S.R.)	4630 feet	
First Year, The	Special Cast	Fox		
Flaming Waters		F. B. O.		
Flying Three	Al Wilson	Davis Dist. Corp.		
Flying Fool, The	Dick Jones	Sunset Prod. (S. R.)		
Forest of Destiny, The		Gotham Prod. (S. R.)		
Forever After	Corinne Griffith	First National		
Fort Frayne	Ben Wilson	Davis Dist.	5000 feet	Aug. 29
Free Lips	Norma Shearer	M-G-M		
Friends	Special Cast	Vitagraph		
Frivolity		B. P. Schulberg (S.R.)		
Galloping Dude, The	Franklyn Farnum	Inde.Pict.Corp.(S.R.)	4700 feet	
Going the Limit	Richard Holt	Gerson Pict. (S. R.)	5000 feet	Sept. 26
Golden Cocoon		Warner Bros.		
Goose Woman, The	Special Cast	Universal	7500 feet	Aug. 22
Go West	Buster Keaton	Metro-Goldwyn		
Great Love, The	Dana-Agnew	First National		
Grey Vulture, The	Ken Maynard	Davis Dist. Div.		
Gulliver's Travels		Universal		
Handsome Brute, The	Columbia Pict. (S. R.)			
Hassan		Paramount		
Haunted Range, The	Ken Maynard	Davis Dist. Div.		
Hearts and Fists		Assoc. Exhib.		
Hearts and Spangles		Gotham Prod. (S. R.)		
Hell Bent for Heaven		Warner Bros.		
Heir's Apparent	Special Cast	First National		
Her Father's Daughter		F. B. O.		
Hero of the Big Snows, A	Rin Tin Tn (dog)	Warner Brothers		
His Jazz Bride	Special Cast	Warner		
His Majesty Bunker Bean	M. Moore-Devore	Warner	7291 feet	Sept. 26
His Woman	Special Cast	Whitman Bennett	7 reels	
Hogan's Alley	Harlan-Miller	Warner		
Home Maker, The	Alice Joyce	Universal	7755 feet	Aug. 8
Honeymoon Express, The	M. Moore-D. Devore	Warner Brothers		
Horses and Women		B. P. Schulberg		
How to Train a Wife	Valli-O'Brien	Assoc. Exhib.		
Hurricane		Truart (S. R.)	5800 feet	
Husband Hunters		Tiffany	6500 feet	
Inevitable Millionaires, The	M. Moore-Devore	Warner Bros.		
Invisible Wounds	Sweet-Lyon	First National		
Irene	Colleen Moore	First National		
Justice of the Far North		C. B. C. (S. R.)	5500 feet	
Just Suppose	Richard Barthelmess	First National		
Kings of the Turf		Fox		

Feature	Star	Distributed by	Length	Reviewed
Kiss for Cinderella, A	Betty Bronson	Paramount		
La Boheme	Lillian Gish	Metro-Goldwyn		
Ladies of Leisure	Elaine Hammerstein	Columbia (S. R.)		
Lady Windermere's Fan	Special Cast	Warner Brothers		
Lariat, The	William Desmond	Universal		
Last Edition, The	Ralph Lewis	Film Book. Offices		
Lawful Cheater, The	Bow-McKee	B. P. Schulberg	4946 feet	
Lena Rivers	Special Cast	Arrow	6 reels	
Life of a Woman		Truart (S. R.)	6500 feet	
Lightning		Tiffany (S. R.)	6000 feet	
Lightning Jack	...ack Perrin	Ambassador Pict. (S.R.) 5000 feet		
Lightning Passes, The	Al Ferguson	Fleming Prod. (S.R.)		
Limited Mail, The	Monte Blue	Warner Bros.		
Little Girl in a Big City, A		Gotham Prod. (S. R.)		
Little Irish Girl, The	Special Cast	Warner Bros.		
Lodge in the Wilderness		Tiffany (S. R.)	6500 feet	
Lord Jim	Percy Marmont	Paramount		
Love Cargo, The	House Peters	Universal		
Lover's Island	Hampton-Kirkwood	Assoc. Exhib		
Love Gamble, The		Ginsberg Dist. Corp.		
		(S. R.)	5766 feet	July 11
Love Toy, The	Lowell Sherman	Warner Bros.		
Loyalties	Special Cast	Fox		
Lunatic at Large, The	Leon Errol	First National		
Lure of the North, The		Columbia Pict. (S. R.)		
Lure of the Wild	Jane Novak	Columbia (S.R.)		
Lying Wives	Special Cast	Ivan Abramson (S. R.) 7 reels		May 2
Man and the Moment		Metro-Goldwyn		
Mannequin, The		Paramount		
Man of Iron, A	L. Barrymore	Chadwick	6 reels	July 4
Man on the Box, The	Sydney Chaplin	Warner Bros	6856 feet	
Man She Bought, The	Constance Talmadge	First National		
Man Without a Conscience	Louis Sica	Warner Bros	6856 feet	May 2
Mare Nostrum	Special Cast	Metro-Goldwyn		
Married Cheats		Fox		
Married Hypocrites	Frederick-La Plante	Universal		
Marrying Money		Truart (S. R.)	5800 feet	
Martinique	Bebe Daniels	Paramount		
Masked Bride, The	Mae Murray	Metro-Goldwyn		
Memory Lane	Boardman-Nagel	First National		
Men of Steel	Milton Sills	First National		
Midnight Flyer, The	Landis-Devore	F. B. O.		
Miracle of Life, The	Busch-Marmont	Assoc. Exhib		
Midnight Flames		Columbia Pict. (S. R.)		
Miss Vanity	Mary Philbin	Universal		
Million Dollar Doll		Assoc. Exhib		
Miniature		First National		
Mocking Bird, The	Lon Chaney	M-G-M		
Modern Musketeer, A	Zeno Corrado	Bud Barsky (S. R.)	5000 feet	
Morganson's Finish		Tiffany (S. R.)		
Napoleon the Great		Universal		
My Own Pal	Tom Mix	Fox		
Night Cry, The	Rin-Tin-Tin (dog)	Warner Brothers		
Nightie Night Nurse	Syd Chaplin	Warner Brothers		
North Star, The	Strongheart (dog)	Assoc. Exhib		
Old Clothes	Jackie Coogan	Metro-Goldwyn		
Only Thing, The	Special Cast	Metro-Goldwyn		
Open Trail, The	Jack Hoxie	Universal	4800 feet	May 16
Pace That Thrills, The	Ben Lyon	First National		
Palace of Pleasure		Fox		
Pals		Truart (S. R.)	5800 feet	
Paris	Pauline Starke	Metro-Goldwyn		
Paris After Dark	Norma Talmadge	First National		
Partners Again		United Artists		
Passionate Quest, The	Marie Prevost	Warner Bros		
Passionate Youth	Special Cast	Truart (S. R.)	6 reels	July 11
Part Time Wife, The		Gotham Prod. (S. R.)		
Phantom of the Forest	Thunder (dog)	Gotham Prod.		
Phantom of the Opera	Lon Chaney	Universal	8464 feet	Sept. 19
Pinch Hitter, The	Glenn Hunter	Assoc. Exhibitors		
Pleasure Buyers, The	Irene Rich	Warner Brothers		
Police Patrol, The	James Kirkwood	Gotham Prod. (S.R.) 6000 feet		Sept. 19
Polly of the Ballet	Bebe Daniels	Paramount		
Pony Express, The	Special Cast	Paramount	9929 feet	Sept. 26
Prince, The	Philbin-Kerry	Universal		
Quality Street		Metro-Goldwyn		
Quicker 'n Lightning	Buffalo Bill, Jr.	Weiss Bros. (S. R.)	8 reels	June 13
Racing Blood		Gotham Prod. (S. R.)		
Rainbow Riley	Johnny Hines	First National		
Reckless Courage	Buddy Roosevelt	Weiss Bros. (S.R.) 4851 feet		May 2
Reckless Sex, The	Special Cast	Truart (S. R.)	6 reels	Feb. 14
Red Clay	William Desmond	Universal		
Red Dice	Rod La Rocque	Prod. Dist. Corp.		
Red Kimono, The	Mrs. Wallace Reid	Davis Dist. Div.		
Red Hot Tires	Monte Blue	Warner Bros.		
Return of a Soldier	Special Cast	Metro-Goldwyn		
Rims of the Ancient Marin-				
er, The		Fox Film		
Road to Glory, The		Fox		
Road That Led Home, The		Vitagraph		
Rocking Moon	Bowers-Tashman	Prod. Dist. Corp.		
Romance of an Actress		Chadw'ck		
Ropin' Venus, The	Josie Sedgwick	Universal		
Rose of the World	Special Cast	Warner Bros		
Sally, Irene and Mary	Special Cast	Metro-Goldwyn		
Salvage		Truart (S. R.)	58.. feet	
Sap, The	M. Moore-D. Devore	Warner Bros		
Satan in Sables	Lowell Sherman	Warner Bros		
Savage, The	Ben Lyon	First National		

Feature	Star	Distributed by	Length	Reviewed
Scarlet Saint, The	Lyon-Astor	First National		
Scraps	Mary Pickford	United Artists		
Sea Beast, The	John Barrymore	Warner Bros.		
Separate Rooms		Fox		
Seven Singers	Marie Prevost	Warner Bros.		
Seventh Heaven	Special Cast	Fox		
Shadow of the Wall		Gotham Prod. (S. R.)		
Shadow of the Mosque	Odette Taylor	Cranfield & Clarke		
		(S. R.)	6200 feet	
Shenandoah		B. P. Schulberg (S. R.)		
Ship of Souls	B. Lytell-L. Rich	Assoc. Exhib	6800 feet	
Shootin' Squares	Jack Perrin	Ambassador Pict. (S.R.)5000 feet		
Siegfried		Ufa		
Sign of the Claw		Gotham Prod. (S. R.)		
Silent Witness, The		Truart (S. R.)	5800 feet	
Silken Shackles	Irene Rich	Warner Bros.		
Silver Treasure, The	Special Cast	Fox		
Skinners Dress Suit	Reginald Denny	Universal		
Social Highwayman, The	Harlan-Miller	Warner Brothers		
Song and Dance Man, The	Tom Moore	Paramount		
Span of Life	Betty Blythe	Banner Prod. (S.R.)		
Speed Limit, The		Gotham Prod. (S. R.)		
Splendid Road, The	Anna Q. Nilsson	First National		
Sporting Life		Universal	6799 feet	Sept. 26
Stage Door Johnny	Raymond Griffith	Paramount		
Steele of the Royal				
Mounted		Vitagraph	6 reels	June 27
Stella Dallas		United Artists		
Stella Maris	Mary Philbin	Universal		
Still Alarm, The	Chadwick-Russell	Universal		
Stop, Look and Listen	Larry Semon	Pathe		
Strange Bedfellows		Metro-Goldwyn		
Streets of Sin		Fox		
Sunshine of Paradise Alley	Special Cast	Chadwick Pict.		
Super Speed	Reed Howes	Rayart (S. R.)		
Sweet Adeline	Charles Ray	Chadwick		
Tale of a Vanishing People		Tiffany (S. R.)	6800 feet	
Tattooed Countess, The	Pola Negri	Paramount		
Tearing Loose	Wally Wales	Weiss Bros. (S. R.) 4800 feet		June 13
Ten to Midnight		Prod. Dist. Corp.		
That Man from Arizona	F.Kerrit-W Fairbanks	F. B. O.		
That Royle Girl	Kirkwood-Dempster	Paramount		
This Woman	Special Cast	Fox		
Thoroughbred	George O'Brien	Fox		
Thoroughbred, The	Special Cast	Truart	5481 feet	Sept. 19
Three Bad Men	Special Cast	Fox		
Tony Runs Wild	Tom Mix	Fox		
Trailing Shadows	Edmund Lowe	Fox Film		
Travelin' Fast	Jack Perrin	Ambassador Pict. (S.		
		R.)	5800 feet	
Travis Coup, The		Tiffany (S.R.)	6500 feet	
Twin Sister, The	Constance Talmadge	First National		
Two Blocks Away	Special Cast	Universal		
Two Soldiers, The	Mildred Davis	Paramount		
Unguarded Hour, The	Sills-Kenyon	First National		
Unknown Lover, The	Elsie Ferguson	Vitagraph		
Up and at' Em	Jack Perrin	Ambassador Pict. (S.		
		R.)	5000 feet	
Vengeance of Durand, The	Irene Rich	Warner Brothers		
Viennese Medley	Special Cast	First National		
Volga Boatman, The		Prod. Dist. Corp.		
Wages for Wives	Special Cast	Fox		
Wanderer, The	William Collier, Jr.	Paramount		
Wandering Footsteps	Special Cast	Ginsberg Dist. Corp.		
Warrior Gap	Wilson-Gerber	Davis Dist.	4800 feet	Aug. 22
We Moderns	Colleen Moore	First National		
What Happened to Jones	Reginald Denny	Universal		
What Will People Say		Metro-Goldwyn		
When His Love Grew Cold		F. B. O.		
When Husbands Flirt	Dorothy Revier	Columbia		
Where the West Begins		Truart (S. R.)	5800 feet	
Whispering Canyon		Ginsberg Dist. Corp.		
		(S. R.)		
White Chief, The	Monte Blue	Warner Brothers		
White Mice	Jacqueline Logan	Sering D. Wilson (S. R.)		
Why Girls Go Back Home		Warner Brothers		
Why Women Love		First National		
Wild Girl		Truart (S. R.)	5800 feet	
Wild Justice	Peter the Great	United Artists	4 reels	Aug. 1
Wide Ridin'	Buck Jones	Fox		
Wide Open	Dick Jones	Sunset Prod. (S. R.)		
Wild West	Mulhall-Ferguson	Pathe		
Winning of Barbara Worth		Principal Pict. (S. R.)		
Wise Guy, The	Lefty Flynn	F. B. O.		
Wit Kit Carson Over the				
Great Divide	Special Cast	Sunset Prod. (S. R.)		
Wives for Rent		Universal		
Womanhandled	Richard Dix	Paramount		
Women		Banner Prod. (S. R.)		
Women and Wives		Metro-Goldwyn		
World's Illusion, The		Metro-Goldwyn		
Worst Woman, The	Special Cast	B. P. Schulberg (S. R.)		
Wreckage		Ginsberg Dist. Corp.		
Wrong Coat, The		Tiffany (S. R.)	6500 feet	
Ya-teee Senor, The	Tom Mix	Fox		
Yoke, The	Special Cast	Warner Brothers		
You Can't Live on Love	Reginald Denny	Universal		

Watch For October Issue of
BOOKING GUIDE
Containing Complete Information on Feature and Short Subjects

WILLIAMS PRESS, INC.
NEW YORK — ALBANY

Rothacker-Aller Laboratories, Hollywood, Calif.

Asher, Small and Rogers Present *Corinne Griffith* in *"Classified,"* by Edna Ferber. Written for the screen by June Mathis. The photography by Harold Rosson. Art direction by E. J. Shulter. Titles by Ralph Spence. Scott R. Beal, assistant director. Film edited by Cyril Gardner. The Excellent supporting cast includes Charley Murray, Jaqueline Wells, Edythe Chapman, Bernard Randall, Jack Mulhall, Ward Crane, Geo. Sidney. All directed by Mr. Al Santell. *A First National Picture.* **Rothacker Prints and Service.**

Corinne Griffith
in
"Classified"

Rothacker FILM MFG. CO. CHICAGO, U.S.A.

Look Better —
Wear Longer!

Founded 1910
by
Watterson R. Rothacker

and after he signed up for The Quality 52 he said: "I am a showman and I picked Metro-Gold wyn-Mayer because they talk my language on th e screen." And really af ter all this is a show man's business, isn't it?

Member Motion Picture Producers and Distributors of America, Inc.—Will H. Hays, President

LEE-BRADFORD CORPORATION

Present

"The
Blackguard"
Starring
JANE NOVAK
DIRECTED BY
GRAHAM CUTTS

From The Book
By Raymond Paton

Lee-Bradford Corporation
701 Seventh Ave.
New York

Pola's Perfect Paramount Picture!

America's most colorful star and America's most colorful novelist—*united!*

NEVER has Pola Negri flamed with the primitive fire and emotion that she displays in "Flower of Night." Well has America's most colorful novelist, Joseph Hergesheimer, wrought in providing her with this blazing Spanish-American romance as a vehicle. Here, at last, is the incomparable Pola at her best—as a fiery Spanish beauty smashing convention and flirting, frolicking, fighting for her man. Audiences will revel in this great love-drama. They'll go out proclaiming a new and mightier Pola Negri than ever;

Paramount Press Sheets — the Best in the Business

29 fine newspaper ads for you out of 11 press sheet cuts

The top row above reproduces the midget, one-, two-, three- and four-column ads from "The Pony Express" press sheet. The rest of the page shows how you make other good newspaper ads from the same cuts or mats to advertise your show. Cuts and mats at your Paramount exchange at very low cost. And you can get the same service out of every Paramount press sheet.

F.B.O.'s NEW STAR
TOM TYLER
[WITH HIS WONDERFUL HORSE AND DOG]
GOES OVER
WITH A SMASH !

Motion Picture News says

Tom Tyler, new F. B. O. cowboy star, makes his debut in LET'S GO GALLAGHER. Mr. Tyler is certainly "the goods." Wherever the fans like Western pictures this one should get the money, as it amply fulfills the demand for fast, furious action. Boost personality of new star, mention that he was selected out of one thousand other candidates by F. B. O. for Western pictures. You can praise the feature as melodrama of the kind that makes the spectators wild with enthusiasm over its forceful appeal. Good for any house where Western melodrama holds the patrons. Looks like a real attraction for the box office.

WESTERN UNION TELEGRAM

1925 Sep 25 AM 7 45

RECEIVED AT

N AS 75 NL 3 EXTRA SIOUXFALLS SDAK

LEE MARCUS, SALES MANAGER FILM BOOKING OFFICES OF AMERICA INC
723 7 AVE NEWYORK NY

WANT TO LET YOU KNOW YOUR NEW SURPRISE STAR TOM TYLER IN HIS FIRST
PICTURE LETS GO GALLAGHER OPENED HERE YESTERDAY AND GAVE EXCEPTIONAL
SATISFACTION STOP HE IS GOOD ACTOR GOOD RIDER AND SUPPORTING CAST
AND DIRECTION FINE STOP PATRONS COMMENTED ON LITTLE FRANKIE DARROW
AND HIS DOG AND PONY STOP SUGGEST YOU KEEP THIS COMBINATION WORKING
WITH TYLER FOR IT IS MY PREDICTION THAT THEY WILL BE VERY
POPULAR   H B REHFIELD   NEW ROYAL THEATRE

Distributed by
FILM BOOKING OFFICES OF AMERICA, INC.
723 Seventh Ave., New York, N. Y.
EXCHANGES EVERYWHERE

Exclusive Foreign Distributors,
R C Export Corporation
723 Seventh Avenue,
New York

"One Step Nearer . . . !"

All Wet!

he
ccessor

ittle
ld
ew
ork"

MA
Liq

When New York was a Village

The Riot at Tony Pastor's

RION DAVIES in

hts of Old Broadway

A MONTA BELL production

AUDIENCE delight! Oh, how they'll love it. The kind of sheer human joy and fun and drama that made *"Little Old New York"* a money-winner. Marion Davies proves herself one of the screen's greatest comediennes. A charming love story; thrilling, spectacular scenes of the exciting days when a metropolis was in the making; a production made by the showmen of Metro - Goldwyn - Mayer and backed by intensive, nationwide Cosmopolitan promotion—*here's the money!*

A Cosmopolitan Production

with
Conrad Nagel
based on the play
"Merry Wives of Gotham"
by Lawrence Eyre, *Adapted*
by Carey Wilson, *Directed*
by Monta Bell

One hit after another in Metro-Goldwyn-Mayer's

The Quality 52

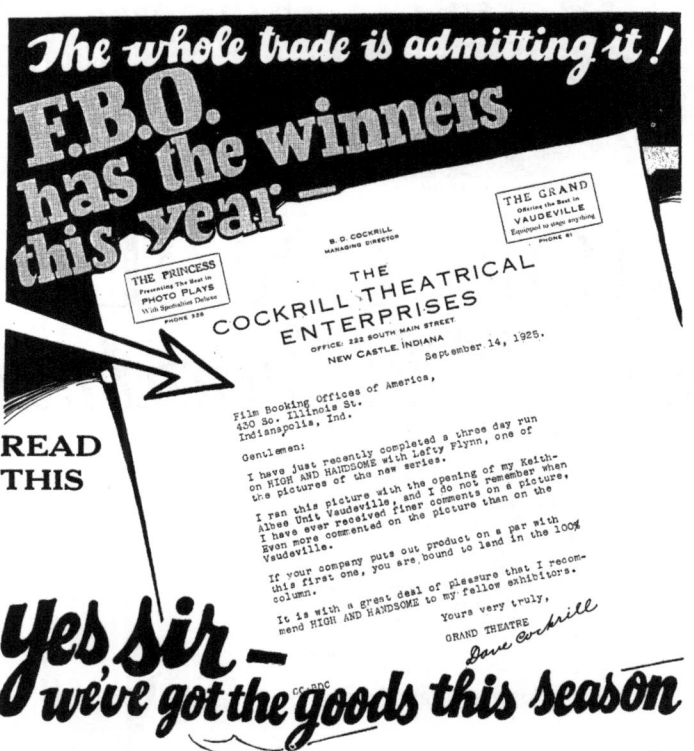

THE CONSTANT CO·STAR

CO-STARRING with every unit of your program is the eternal magic of music...magic to conjure up a thousand golden phantasies, to interpret every subtle emotion pictured on the screen, to transform a drab world into a highly bewitching land of Romance.

AUDIENCES, whose critical faculties have been sharpened by their familiarity with fine music, regard the *Robert Morton Unit Organ* as a permanent feature. Exhibitors, who realize the sound box-office value of good music, recognize it as an investment which pays assuredly perpetual dividends.

ROBERT MORTON ORGAN COMPANY

NEW YORK
1560 Broadway

CHICAGO
845 So. Wabash

LOS ANGELES
935 So. Olive

BERKELEY
California

Harry Nolan, First National franchise holder of Colorado, *Knows* pictures— Read this!

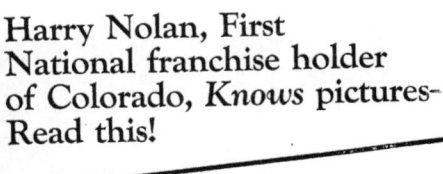

FIRST NATIONAL PICTURES INC.

2108 BROADWAY, DENVER, COLO.

PHONE: CHAMPA, 4304

September 20, 1925

Mr. William Fox
Fox Film Corporation
New York City

Dear Mr. Fox:—

Congratulations on "IRON HORSE" showing in Grand Junction and Greeley, Colo. This is one horse that runs true to form. Has our track record for Greeley and with one exception in Grand Junction.

Any Exhibitor who cannot make money with "THE IRON HORSE" ought not to be permitted to run a theatre.

Kindest regards,

Yours very truly,

(Signed) H. T. NOLAN

Try our IRON HORSE Records—fresh every week! Puts pep in your Box-Office's system!

Fox Film Corporation.

EVERY ELEMENT

SHOWMEN~
HOW EASY
PROVEN SUCCESS

William
A FIVE-FOLD

FIRST —
the play

LAZY

A Smashing Hit

SECOND —
the author

by **OWEN**
writer of countless
with

THIRD —
the cast

MADGE BELLAMY
ZASU PITTS~LESLIE
recognized

FOURTH —
the scenarist

FRANCES
a writer

FIFTH —
the director

FRANK
producer of

Fox Film Corporation.

T

MEN-
EASY
ICCESS
iam
'OLD
Y
Hit
N
itless
h
MY
LIE
nized
NCES
writer
NK
er of

# of SURE SUCCESS!

**YOU KNOW
IT IS TO SELL
TO YOUR PATRONS**

Fox *Presents*
SUCCESS

BONES

on Broadway

DAVIS
dramatic masterpieces

**CHARLES (BUCK) JONES
FENTON ~ JANE NOVAK**
stars every one

MARION
of renown

BORZAGE
picture triumphs

Fox Film Corporation.

Member Motion Picture Producers and Distributors of America, Inc. Will H. Hays, President.

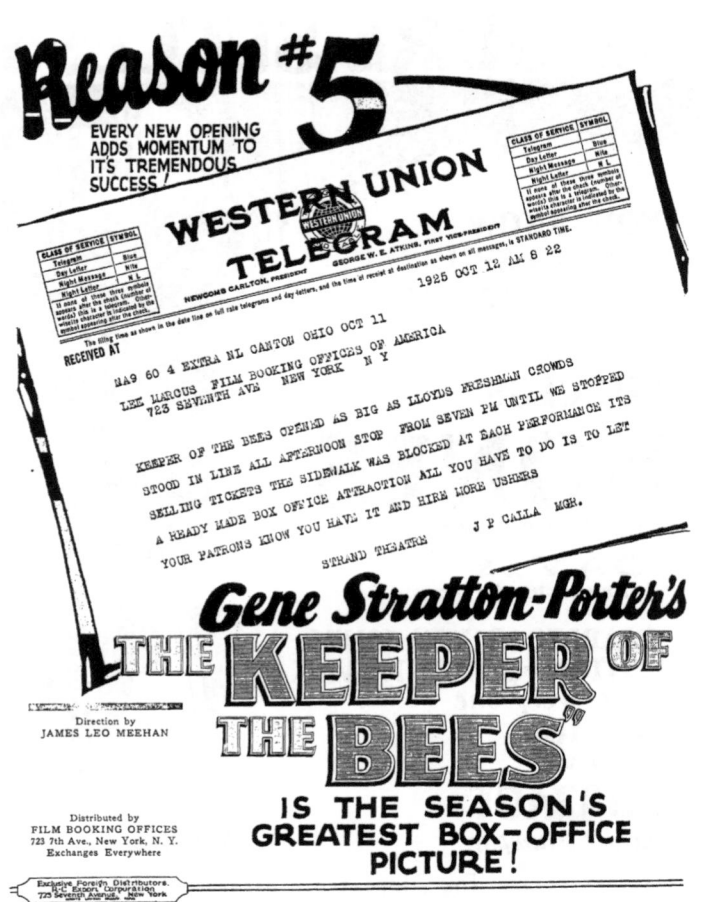

Reason #5

EVERY NEW OPENING
ADDS MOMENTUM TO
ITS TREMENDOUS
SUCCESS!

WESTERN UNION TELEGRAM

GEORGE W. E. ATKINS, FIRST VICE-PRESIDENT

NEWCOMB CARLTON, PRESIDENT

1925 OCT 12 AM 8 22

RECEIVED AT

MA9 60 4 EXTRA NL CANTON OHIO OCT 11

LEE MARCUS FILM BOOKING OFFICES OF AMERICA
723 SEVENTH AVE NEW YORK N Y

KEEPER OF THE BEES OPENED AS BIG AS LLOYDS FRESHMAN CROWDS
STOOD IN LINE ALL AFTERNOON STOP FROM SEVEN PM UNTIL WE STOPPED
SELLING TICKETS THE SIDEWALK WAS BLOCKED AT EACH PERFORMANCE ITS
A READY MADE BOX OFFICE ATTRACTION ALL YOU HAVE TO DO IS TO LET
YOUR PATRONS KNOW YOU HAVE IT AND HIRE MORE USHERS

J P CALLA MGR.

STRAND THEATRE

Gene Stratton-Porter's

THE KEEPER OF THE BEES

Direction by
JAMES LEO MEEHAN

IS THE SEASON'S GREATEST BOX-OFFICE PICTURE!

Distributed by
FILM BOOKING OFFICES
723 7th Ave., New York, N. Y.
Exchanges Everywhere

Exclusive Foreign Distributors.
R-C Export Corporation
723 Seventh Avenue, New York

"IMPOSSIBLE!"
---But Kinograms Did It!

The opening game of the World's Baseball series was over

Every theatre exhibitor in Pittsburgh was waiting feverishly to flash out a specially painted sign in his lobby announcing that news reel pictures of the great event had arrived

Every news reel (there are 4 of them) had a crew on the spot battling against time to get to the theatre first

And Who Do You Think Got There First?

KINOGRAMS - - - As Usual

Some time later after thousands of Kinogram fans had already seen Kinograms baseball pictures on the screen the exchange manager of a rival news reel heard about it

"Impossible," he said. "It couldn't be done!"

Of course we have to modestly admit that only a Kinograms crew could do it --- but it was far from "impossible."

In fact it was easy for KINOGRAMS

BOOK KINOGRAMS
The News Reel Built Like a Newspaper

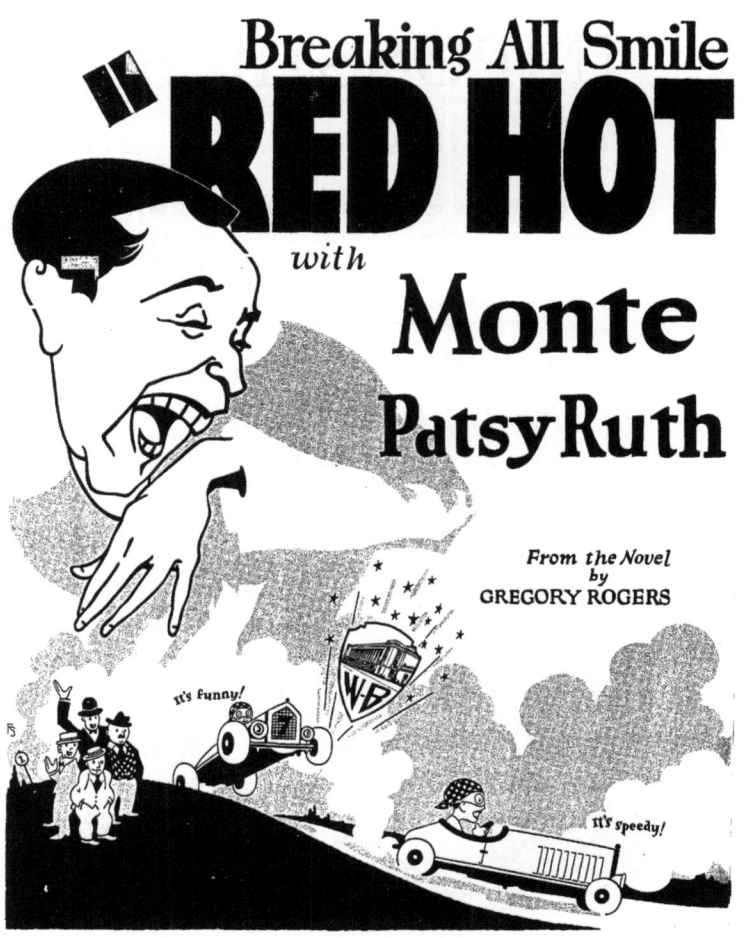

age Records!

TIRES

Blue
Miller

Directed by
Erle C. Kenton

Scenario by
Edward T. Lowe, Jr.

It's
peppy!

It's
zippy!

It's thrilly!

WARNER BROS
Classics of the Screen

MARY ANDERSON

STAR OF

"Bubbles"   "Too Much Married"   "Bluebeard, Jr."   "Wildness of Youth"

Now Under Contract With

RANDOLPH H. CLEMENT

To Make

Thomas Dixon's "The Black Hood" and Norman Houston's "Man Bait"

What a STAR
What a STORY
What a PICTURE
a *Wow*

ASSOCIATED EXHIBITORS, INC.
OSCAR A. PRICE, PRESIDENT

PRESENTS

Peggy Hopkins Joyce

IN
THE Sky
ROCKET
MARSHALL NEILAN PRODUCTION

The star known to every nation that reads ❦ In Adele
Rogers St. John's famous Cosmopolitan Magazine serial
and book novel success ❦ The sky-rocketting rise of a
waif of the tenements through struggles as a motion
picture extra girl to the dizzy heights of stardom ❦ With
a Neilan cast including Owen Moore, Earl Williams,
Gladys Hulette, Eddie Dillon, Gladys Brockwell,
Bull Montana ❦ Produced by Celebrity
Pictures, Inc., for the fans of the world

"The Sky Rocket" is a BIG ONE! The boldest of black type fails to convey an idea of its tremendous BOX-OFFICE VALUES ❦ The finest of gold lettering gives but a faint hint of its CLASS ❦ "The Sky Rocket" is destined to be the outstanding success of the coming season ❦ Peggy Hopkins Joyce, internationally famed beauty, by her sheer artistry in "The Sky Rocket" takes her place with the screen's four leading stars ❦ Marshall Neilan, the genius who gave the screen so many of its classics, contributes a new chapter of achievement ❦ THREE POSITIVE STATEMENTS OF POSITIVE FACT ❦ Wait until you SEE it ❦ It's a SENSATION!

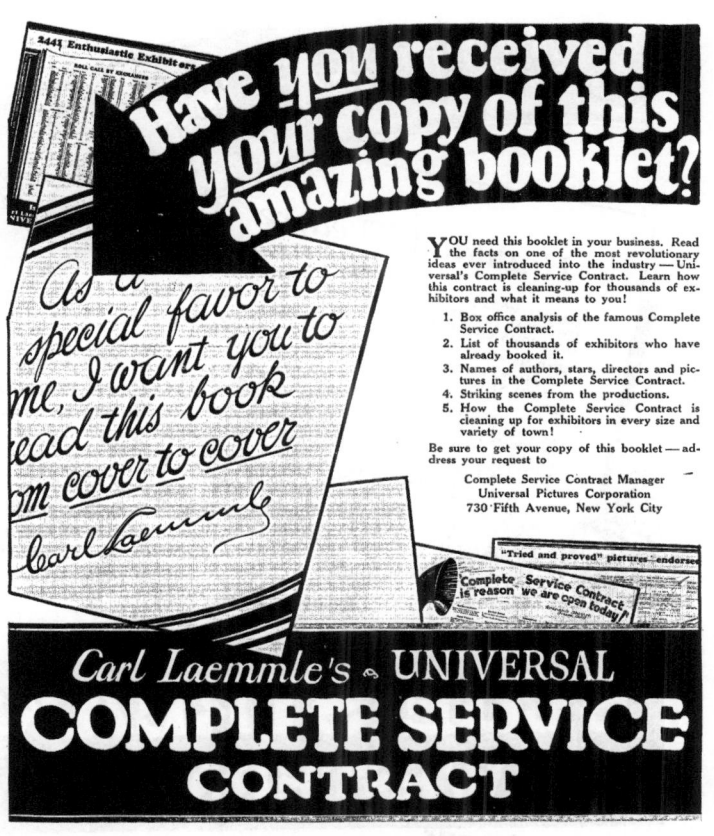

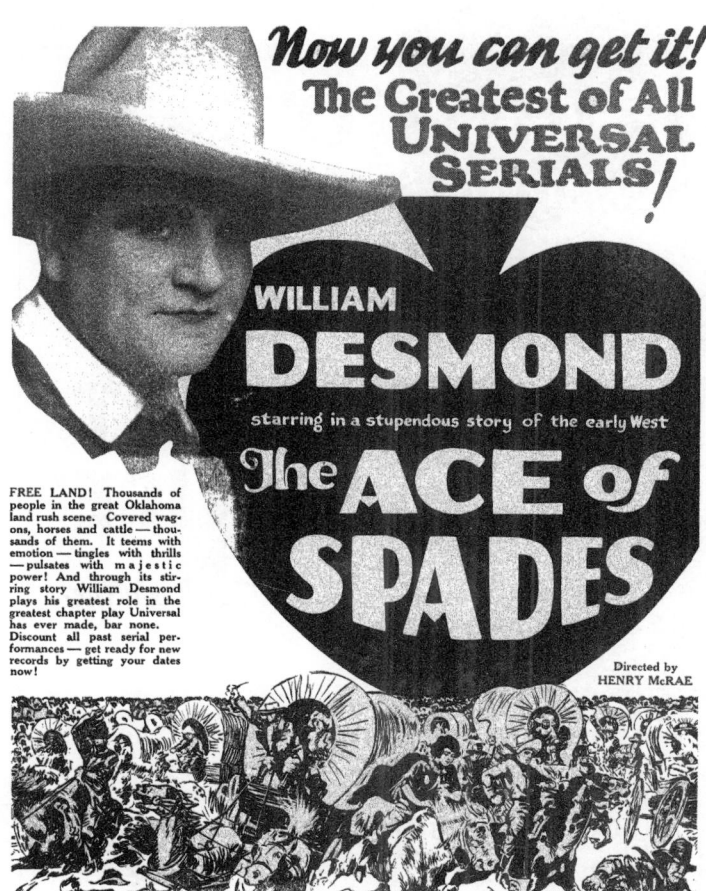

J. Charles Davis, 2nd.
Presents

PEGGY O'DAY
"The Thrill Girl"

"PEGGY
OF THE
SECRET
SERVICE"

A

Peggy O'Day Production

DAVIS DISTRIBUTING DIVISION, Inc.
J. Charles Davis, II. President
218 West 42nd. St.   New York.

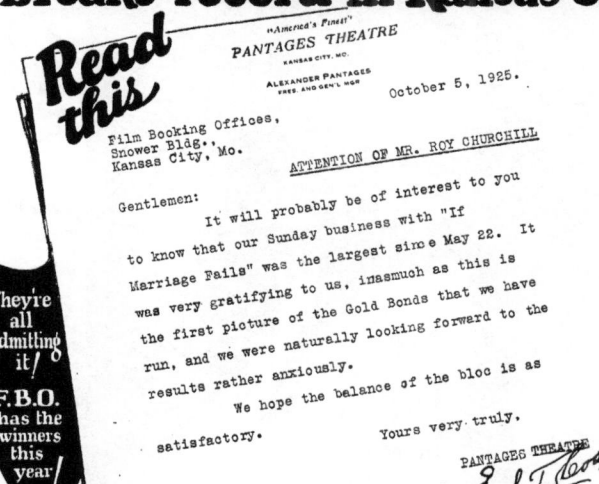
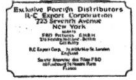

"Will make a barrel of money" says Quinn Martin in New York World

from N.Y. World

SAMUEL GOLDWYN

The George Fitzmaurice PRODUCTION

"The Dark Angel"

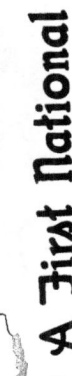

First National Pictures Inc. presents

"The PACE that THRILLS"

with BEN LYON MARY ASTOR
and TULLY MARSHALL

Here's a real breath taking intensely thrilling picture if there ever was one.

It's the story of a movie star— who refused to take chances and as a result was branded a coward.

The climax comes when he enters a great auto race and

by his daring proves to the girl he loves and all that he had a reason for his actions— his mother.

Something doing every minute from the first reel to the last.

Another great "Winner Group" picture.

Adapted from an original story by . . . BYRON MORGAN

Directed by
WEBSTER CAMPBELL
Produced under the supervision of
EARL HUDSON

Scenario by · RAYMOND HARRIS
Photographed by · T. D. McCORD
Art Director · MILTON MENASCO

Film Editor · ARTHUR TAVARES
Editorial Direction · MARION FAIRFAX
Supervised by · EARL HUDSON

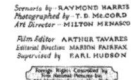

First National
Members of Motion Picture Producers

have the pictures
and Distributors of America Inc.~Will Hays President

Motion Picture News

Vol. XXXII   ALBANY, N. Y., AND NEW YORK CITY, OCTOBER 24, 1925   No. 17

A Plain Matter of Business

THERE are rumors of a collapse of the independent or state rights market. Which is not surprising; it has been predicted. Nor is it at all alarming. The state rights market, in the past twelve years, has been sharply up and down every year, and at times pronounced dead. We look for the usual revival—some time ahead. And we except those well established exchanges not over-stocked and concentrating on a few pictures and doing well.

The immediate crisis is that a number of exchanges are unable to lift negatives, even those of some recent first-rate productions. And the situation is due to such major causes as over-production and to the sharply competitive selling of the large national distributors—aimed by the way at each other, not at the independent exchanges.

Some time ago, in speaking of the entire independent group (as distinguished from the so-called Big Three), we said that the situation would be worked out along the straight lines of business economics. And so it has. It is a plain matter of the making and selling and buying of films; nothing else has counted at all.

The Milwaukee Convention has been, so far as we can see, a fizzle. Some independent producers—producing for the state rights market, are bitter; they say that because of the support promised they entered into heavy production cost and volume. And nothing has happened. The Play Date Bureau has sent out bulletins, the appeal of which has, naturally, scored no definite results at all. The association of independent producers and distributors has acquired membership, and that's about all. All the sentiment that has been spilled hasn't counted one iota. The exchanges—all of them, have been selling films; and the exhibitors—

all of them, have been buying films along purely unsentimental lines. We repeat—all exhibitors. If any at all have been sentimental toward the independent companies we will gladly correct this statement and give the facts; also we will be glad to report any sentiment toward exhibitors from any exchanges.

We might remark, in this connection, that the spillers of sentiment within a business have always good business motives, and only business motives. They deal in sentiment for what it does—for them. It's about time to recognize this truth and shape the future accordingly.

Since the Milwaukee Convention the film industry has gone on just exactly as it did before. This is a sharply competitive year. Selling is keen. If there is any collusion, as hinted by the irresponsible or uninformed, between some of the larger companies, we daresay their Sales Managers are not aware of it. They are too busy fighting each other. The industry is also getting into the era of big business. Capital counts, theatres, foreign organization, studio facilities, sales organizations—all count, and heavily. And the weaker exchanges have been caught—temporarily—between the millstones of business resources and efforts greater than their own. That's the sum and substance of it.

In the meantime the exhibitor is looking on dispassionately; he considers quality, advertising and price—especially price. Regardless of any other consideration he is buying low—too low in many cases, in the supine belief that people are going right on and make and distribute pictures for him when there has ceased to be any profit in the operation.

W. A. Johnston

AN EDITOR

The Week in Review

OFTEN you can look right into Hollywood from Broadway — and more clearly.

There's "Ben Hur," for instance. With the filming of the chariot races the big picture is all but finished; and we had wired and written Los Angeles, hoping to get an advance and inside story, a real appraisal of the picture by someone in the know—hoping, when along comes Marshall Neilan.

From Hollywood to Broadway.

He has seen the film, every bit of it, and seen the chariot races. And when I bumped into him, on Broadway, he had just seen Marcus Loew and had aired his opinions at length and emphatically.

View of a portion of the Circus Maximus set during the running of the chariot race for Metro-Goldwyn-Mayer's "Ben Hur."

"You can quote me," he said, "and you can go the limit."

So we take him at his word.

"Micky" Neilan is given somewhat to joking, himself; but he says that "Ben Hur" is the point where joking ceases. Somebody started making funny remarks about it—over its huge expense, the time it had taken, etc., and now it is the stock joke of the after-dinner speaker. "For all of which," said Mr. Neilan to Mr. Loew, "someone ought to be shot. Joking about 'Ben Hur' is as out of place as skylarking at a coronation or funny stories in a President's inaugural address."

For—and now take a good breath and take the estimate of "Ben Hur" as given by one of the most experienced, keenest and best producers in the business: take it or leave it.

"'Ben Hur' is the greatest of all pictures, past, present and future. It is so big that no one will ever attempt to outdo it. The most ambitious will say: 'there's "Ben Hur."' What's the use? It will go down in history as the great climax in magnificence of production.

"Its backgrounds are stupendous. That's the word. Overwhelming. The greatest efforts at atmosphere are as nothing beside this. It is 'way beyond the movie horizon. It not merely takes you out of yourself, but out of your country. I have sat in the projection room hour after hour and scarcely realized

I was breathing. The color scenes are beautiful—beyond description. It all is; it is just—great!

"I have just told Marcus Loew that simply to have his name on the picture he will regard as his greatest accomplishment—greater than all his enterprises and wealth, anything he has done."

"But the expense," I argued.

"Well, it cost three and a half million dollars," he replied. "That's staggering. But, if 'The Four Horsemen' grossed four and a half million, this picture should do eight million. People went to see 'The Four Horsemen' time and again. This picture has a similar quality of appeal—but vastly greater. It will last forever, and always be new. They won't approach it again, I tell you.

"You see, you've got to view its box-office by new standards. This picture could well open in Saint Patrick's Cathedral. Why not? That would be appropriate. It ought to play—it will—in every church that has a projection machine. All the theatres, halls and churches in the world, wherever people can be gathered. Its appeal is universal. It should run in Tex Rickard's stadium—over there, and be seen by the millions. Yes, you'll have to forget past standards of exhibition—with this picture. Not only will it break all past records, but it will demand new schemes of exhibition—and some mighty good ones. Somebody ought to get busy—" Mr. Neilan, now out of breath, waved his arms and walked rapidly away.

So we give—and literally—this Neilan review of "Ben Hur." Lest the cynical reader think he had something to do with the making of the picture, we append that he did not—except in this respect: he was first sent to Europe to report on the advisability of making the picture there. He reported that it should be made in Hollywood—as, finally, it was.

* * *

SPEAKING of Tex Rickard's big stadium—the new Madison Square Garden in West Forty-eighth Street, I understand it will seat twenty thousand people, and that Rickard is thinking of showing pictures there, along with dancing, at ten cents admission. Which is an item!

* * *

ANOTHER man-in-the-know arrived from Hollywood this week. He sees a lot of pictures before they reach the cutting room; and, generally, he picks them right. "'Tumbleweeds,' the new William S. Hart picture, looks fine and promising," he says. For which we are glad. It will be great to have Bill Hart back on the screen as he was, is and should be. And, according to the same source of information, Doctor Joe Schenck has done the right

ON BROADWAY

By William A. Johnston

of the business executive. He doesn't hesitate to ask advice, to court suggestions from all sides. He is an earnest student.

I am glad that he is to do—well, a big picture. Probably

thing with another star who also needed some management. The other picture our friend speaks enthusiastically of is "The Lone Eagle," Valentino's new production. "It should be fine," he says, and he added: "Vilma Banky also stands out. She's a coming star." And he added: "Of course, you've heard about 'The Viennese Medley.' By all the signs that will be a big one."

* * *

E RNST LUBITSCH is to do his first big American picture. He has just finished "Lady Windermere's Fan," which differs from his cycle of light comedy dramas in that it has an undertone of heavier drama. "It is light and sparkling," to use his own words, "but also it has the shadows—light and heavy shadows intermingled. I think it will have a broader appeal."

And now as to his big picture. "Please use quotations with 'big,'" suggested Mr. Lubitsch. "How shall we say that a picture is big? Certainly its length does not make it big. I think that we are in much the same position as years ago when pictures were made—all of them at so much per foot. If you made more feet you made a bigger picture. Then came pictures, big because they were better. Now with better pictures we call the big ones those that are exceptionally long. *But I believe that a picture should only be as long as it must be and not as it may be.* I hope that exhibitors today are not judging big pictures by their length. Surely an eight reel picture may be big, and a twelve reel picture may be tiresome.

"Then as to the cost. Messrs. Warner have asked me to set a cost figure for my big picture, and I know they will agree with whatever figure I suggest. But I have set no figure and I do not want to. There again—bigness is surely not a matter of cost. You will recall that, when I saw you in Hollywood, I said that the budget for exploitation was in my opinion quite as grave a question as the budget for production. That is another thing to consider. There are many things to consider with the so-called big picture. I am earnestly at work upon it—upon the whole matter.

"And now what shall the picture be? I have not decided. I have thought and planned about it a long time—and I know pretty well. But I am here in New York—it is a great inspiration, your city—and still thinking and listening, and planning. Well, we shall see."

It is a real pleasure to talk with Ernst Lubitsch. He is that rare combination of the artist and the sensible, even trained man of affairs. People are generally agreed as to his ability; they respect him highly and wholly, and I think for the above reason. He has no pose. He works with all the punctuality

he will do many. He has been waiting and studying. One idea he imparted in confidence is astounding. But he can do it. And it gives you a conception of the wonderful things the future has in store for motion pictures.

"The great trouble today," said he, "is that we borrow too much—from books, plays, magazines. We must think in motion pictures. Our great writers must conceive in motion pictures. Great advances are made in picture technique, but we lag behind in stories, in ideas for pictures, simply because it is a new language and we don't know how to use it for self expression. There are great things all about us —especially here in America—marvellous developments which we look at half blindly, apathetically, because pictures which can only express them, do not—that is, not adequately. We do not create—not enough, in and for motion pictures."

* * *

L AST week we "rumored" that J. D. Williams was building another "First National" in Great Britain. This week we hear from him direct and through the columns of the London *Daily Mail.* His first company has been organized and registered under the name: "British National Pictures, Ltd." and with the slogan: "British National Pictures demands for Britain her place on the screen." The company is all British, with the sole exception of the organizer. He will be back in this country in about six weeks and then return to begin a five-year contract with British National Pictures. He gives no details beyond the formation of the company, which we assume will engage in production; and we also assume that its relations with the market will be worked out on some franchise plan with the exhibitor.

(*Continued on next page*)

A close shot of one of the chariots figuring in the race scenes for "Ben Hur," staged recently at the Metro-Goldwyn-Mayer studios with 42 cameras trained on the Circus Maximus set.

MOTION PICTVRE
October 24
1925
NEWS
Vol. XXXII
No. 17

Founded in September 1913

Publication Office: Lyon Block, Albany, N. Y.

Editorial and General Offices: Branch Offices:
729 7th Ave., New York City   845 S. Wabash Ave., Chicago, Ill.
                                Room 616 Security Bldg., Hollywood,
                                Calif.

An Editor on Broadway
By *William A. Johnston*
(Continued from preceding page)

Members of the famous Hal Roach-Pathe "Our Gang" with Frank L. Newman, managing director of the Metropolitan, Rialto and Million Dollar, Los Angeles, and Robert McGowen, their director, when they made a personal appearance at the Metropolitan with "Mary, Queen of Tots."

"Well," said a prominent film man who happened to be in our office, and to whom we gave the news, "J. D. will put it over."

We happen to know that the international picture has long been one of Williams' cherished dreams. I was one of several who discussed the matter at length with him some years ago. And I'll say this, that his ideas are the best I have heard on the subject.

As to his solid ability as a promoter, no one questions that. But people, perhaps, do not stop and think that the man who promotes successfully in this peculiar business—and there have been few—must be an exceptional showman, a man of remarkable vision both as to pictures and theatres. Yes, and as to their successful relations, too.

We also have noted over a period of a dozen years that J. D. always foresaw the big moves of the industry and was in the lead when they happened. The big problem of the day is international film relations. We have a world film industry today, not merely an American. That's a certainty. And J. D. Williams is big enough to fit this bigger development.

* * *

ENCOUNTERED D. W. Griffith in the Astor. He is going back to big pictures and looks happy about it. He gives no details, but his repressed enthusiasm gives me the hunch that you'll see his name, next year, in big electric lights on the main thoroughfares. "Sorrows of Satan," the Corelli novel, is the vehicle, and he has had it in mind for years. Famous Players-Lasky will throw their heaviest resources back of it. The cost of production figure, we learn elsewhere, will be huge.

* *

"CLOTHES Make the Pirate," by all signs an exceptional picture, will set a stiff pace for Leon Errol's further pictures. But First National has picked two excellent vehicles: "Lunatic at Large" and Harry Leon Wilson's "Boss of Little Arcady." The latter, especially, should give full play to Errol's delightful whimsicality. "Clothes Make the Pirate," we predict, will put this excellent actor high in the screen world.

W. R. SHEEHAN, Vice President and General Manager of Fox Films, is back from Europe, looking rotund and happy over Fox's strong position in the field this year. "Nothing to say," said he. "That's our policy. We never announced this New York studio building until the walls were up. There are big developments in the offing, under way in fact. But we'll announce them when they're completed." He referred to the fact that the real estate holdings of the Fox Film Corporation exceed the capitalization, a remarkable and enviable position.

October 24, 1925   MOTION PICTURE NEWS   Vol. XXXII. No. 17
Published weekly by Motion Picture News, Inc., William A. Johnston, President; E. Kendall Gillett, Vice-President; William A. Johnston, Editor; J. S. Dickerson, Associate Editor; Oscar Cooper, Managing Editor; Fred J. Beecroft, Advertising Manager; L. H. Mason, Chicago Representative; William McCormack, Los Angeles Representative. Subscription price, $3 per year, post paid in United States, Mexico, Hawaii, Porto Rico, Philippine Islands and some other countries; Canada, $5; foreign, $10.00. Copyright 1925, by Motion Picture News, Inc., in the United States and Great Britain. Title registered in the United States Patent Office and foreign countries. Western Union cable address is "Picknews," New York. Entered as second-class matter January 31st, 1924, at the postoffice, Albany, N. Y., under the Act of March 3, 1879.

Unfair Type of Exhibitor is Scored by Laemmle

Universal Chief Defines Theatre Policy

By William A. Johnston

(Copyright, 1925, by Motion Picture News, Inc.)

UNIVERSAL has been buying a good many theatres. Also Carl Laemmle has a reputation for open and plain speaking. So, putting these two facts together and placing before him Mr. Zukor's explicit remarks on producer-owned theatres, I invited him to set forth his company's policy in this important respect. It was an interesting interview and a lively one.

"The single rotten thing about this business," said he, "is greed! Clean that up and we'll clean up our business and not before."

But I'll let him speak. Here, boiled-down, is what he had to say:

"I admire Mr. Zukor for his fearlessly frank statement. Nothing but good can result from it.

"There is not the least doubt that the exhibition end of this business is the best. Everybody who knows all three branches of the industry realizes that the producing and distributing departments require more investment and more work and worry for an equal return than the theatre department. I was an exhibitor before I became either a distributor or a producer, so I know. There is plenty of profit in the theatre business, provided the house is properly managed, well located and has the right kind of a show.

"I have felt many times that the producer is the goat of the business, especially when I have seen a handful of theatres making more net profit in a year than any producer made in the same period with a world-wide distributing and producing organization.

"I am strong for the fair exhibitor, but it is the unfair exhibitor who has made the producer the industry's pet goat. I'll confess there have been times when I felt like giving the unfair showman the battle of his life. I refer to the smart-aleck type who thinks it is good business to screw down rentals to a point where it is impossible for the producer to make a profit. I refer to the overly ambitious or grasping exhibitor who either controls a territory or has a vast buying power which he uses as a club on the producer's head. I refer to the man who pays less for a whole week's run of a picture than he takes in in one performance, and then gloats over the producer's discomfiture. Every producer in the business, great or small, has suffered bitterly from this type of exhibitor.

"But when it comes to the square shooter, the exhibitor who is willing to pay a fair price, it's another

—Photo, Underwood & Underwood, N. Y.

Carl Laemmle, President of the Universal Pictures Corporation.

story of course. He is entitled to prosper without interference, and I'll go the limit to see that he does.

"Universal will never disturb the peace and prosperity of that type of exhibitor, regardless of how much money he makes. We will never be tempted to own theatres that will hurt him. We have never yet built or bought a theatre which would compete with any customer who showed an honest desire to give us a fair break. We have built or bought only in those places where we were frozen out, and that's the course we intend to continue.

"There are still many places where Universal is deliberately shut out or offered starvation prices. I would be a mighty poor business man if I made no effort to get a fair representation in such places, and of course that's what I am going to do.

"I'll tell you one thing more. The evils of this industry are not due to producers alone nor to exhibitors alone. It's about a fifty-fifty split, and it is due in every case to one single rotten thing—greed. When we all reach the live-and-let-live frame of mind, we'll clean up our business and not before."

Joan Crawford, the Irene of "Sally, Irene and Mary" (Metro-Goldwyn-Mayer), takes lessons in the Charleston from Jimmy, the acknowledged studio champion in the art.

Dorothy Devore, who plays Primrose (after whom the well-known path was named) in "The Gilded Highway" (Warner Bros.), all dressed up in her Charleston clothes.

During the recent visit to Hollywood of Paula Gould, of the F. B. O. publicity department, she spent some little time with the "Adventures of Mazie" unit. The feminine members of the photo are, left to right: Miss Gould, Adamae Vaughn, Alberta Vaughn and Doris Anderson, continuity writer. Al Cooke, Kit Guard and Larry Kent may also be recognized.

PICTURES
AND
PEOPLE

W HAIL THE PRODUCTION MANAGER
HY is the production manager? Milton Hoffman, who occupies that post in connection with Cecil B. De Mille, and William Sistrom, general manager of Metropolitan pictures, step forward to explain.

Says Mr. Hoffman: "The production manager came logically in the wake of increased speculation. In the old days when directors were at the same time actors and even writers, functions overlapped. This was not good because while it gave the individual a general view of the whole field, the view was purely superficial. With the advent of specialists, came more intensive development of production and the deeper penetration and close study it entailed, so tied directors and scenarists to their studios and subdivisions as to dissociate them from the trend of the demand in the theatres which ultimately consume the product. As a result, these production specialists have welcomed the coming of a 'third party' whose chief value lines in his broad rather than specialized viewpoint. You might call the Production Manager the mirror of Sales Realities to which directors and writers appeal for the commercial reflection of their inspirations.

Says William Sistrom: "The Production Manager has come to fill in motion pictures the place held in other business corporations by the 'outside-minded' member of the Board of Directors."

The work of Production Manager Milton Hoffman is being watched with peculiar interest by the trade because of his re-association with Cecil DeMille for the purpose of taking from the producer-supervisor, production details of the current De Mille schedule which calls for twelve pictures during the ensuing season.

Thomas Meighan snapped in front of Blarney castle, Cork, Ireland, while filming exteriors for "Irish Luck" (Paramount), about to ascend and kiss the famous Blarney stone.

Lupino Lane, Educational's new comedy star, with Mrs. Lane and little Lauri, peer around the corner to see how the public takes to "Maid in Morocco."

This is the room in which Charles Wakefield Cadman, celebrated composer of Indian music, wrote the score for "The Vanishing American" (Paramount).

William Haines and Dale Fuller indulge in a novel terpsichorean travesty with all the trimmings between scenes of John M. Stahl's "Memory Lane" (First Nat's).

Dorothy Gish designed a Leon Errol Pirate Hat in honor of her co-star in Sam Rork's "Clothes Make the Pirate" (First Nat'l), which she is here wearing.

Maurice Costello, one of the first screen idols, who has been engaged by J. Stuart Blackton to direct Dolores Costello in "Maryland, My Maryland" (Warner Bros.).

One of the subjects taught the students of the Paramount Pictures school is practical make-up. This is Thelma Todd, one of the Junior Stars.

TALMADGE RESTING UP

RICHARD TALMADGE is taking a brief vacation in New York, where he expects to remain for three weeks. Incidentally, he is on the lookout for fresh story material, as he hopes to get back to Hollywood equipped with several yarns ready for immediate production.

After having witnessed a long series of Talmadge's wild stunt pictures, we'll say that he has earned a rest if ever a man did. At the Elk's Club the agile Richard made a short speech wherein he dwelt upon the risks he takes in making films, and stressed the fact that he has never used a double. Everyone in filmland will endorse that statement. They all know that Talmadge is the genuine article when it comes to risking his neck — incidentally it isn't so long ago that he broke the said neck, while executing a mad jump — but what would surely have killed the average citizen had little effect on robust Dick. He had to go to hospital, of course, but was out within half the period predicted by attending physicians, and back at work again. You can't call him a restful guy even when he's supposed to be resting. For instance, when leaving the Elk's Club, he spied a large automobile parked at the curb and executed a flying leap over the machine that gave the hundreds of spectators waiting for a glimpse of the F. B. O. star a real thrill.

A REAL NEWSPAPER PICTURE

IN our opinion F. B. O. has in "The Last Edition" a great exploitation picture.

Thrills, fast action, good action and a well knit story, the production has, too, but it is in the exploitation angle that "The Last Edition" shines. Every daily newspaper in the country, except maybe a few still printing on "flat beds," should jump at the chance of tieing up on "The Last Edition," not because they necessarily will want to help put over the picture just because it is a newspaper yarn, but because there is a great opportunity for the newspaper to get for itself a lot of prestige and advertising.

Emery Johnson has turned out some real tie-up pictures in the past, but this one has everything that "The Third Alarm," etc., contained and then some. It is clean, wholesome entertainment, plus opportunities for publicity smashes that have never been equaled.

WILLARD C. PATTERSON HERE

WILLIARD C. PATTERSON, manager of the Metropolitan Theatre, Atlanta, Ga., paid a flying visit to Gotham with a two-fold object, first on business for his house, secondly, to meet his wife, Mrs. Anna Aiken Patterson, publisher of the Weekly Film Review, who returned from foreign parts October 10, aboard the S. S. Ryndam, having completed a three months' tour of England and Continental Europe. Mr. and Mrs. Patterson expect to return to Atlanta shortly.

Monte Blue in his corner for "Hogan's Alley" (Warner Bros.), in regulation fighting togs. The others, left to right, are: Tommy Ryan, former middleweight champ, Roy Del Ruth, director, and James J. Jeffries, former holder of the heavyweight crown.

Margaret Quimby, to be seen in "The Radio Detective" (Universal), was a dancer in the Scandals, the Music Box and the El Fey club, and still retains her efficiency.

A charming study of Marion Davies, star of Metro-Goldwyn-Mayer's "Lights of Old Broadway," directed by Monta Bell, in which she has an unusually appealing role.

Painted decorations on the dimpled knee are not new, but Ralph Graves gives it a different twist in "Hurry Doctor," Mack Sennett-Pathe comedy. Thelma Parr is the girl.

*Director James P. Hogan (third from the right) and his staff on location
filming "S. O. S. Perils of the Sea," a Columbia production.*

THE NEW FILMS

OF the five new pictures on Broadway this week, "The Dark
Angel," First National's production, at the Strand Theatre, carries
off the honors in point of artistic excellence and genuine human appeal. It is a most touching story, with the World War for a background and a blind hero; replete with tense, pathetic situations, and
introducing Vilma Banky, Samuel Goldwyn's new star from Vienna.
The latter is an exquisite beauty and actress of great merit, with the
gift of moving her audience to tears by effective, simple pantomine.
As a matter of fact "The Dark Angel" is the sort of attraction sure
to please those who "take their pleasures sadly," for the note of
pathos is sustained to the finish, even if hero and heroine are finally
united.

At the Rivoli, Bebe Daniels, cute and vivacious, scores a palpable hit in a most amusing Paramount comedy entitled "Lovers In
Quarantine," with the able assistance of Harrison Ford as leading
man. A light, but unquestionably funny picture, certainly one of
the best features in which Miss Daniels has starred up-to-date.

Another good box office attraction is "The Midshipman," starring
Ramon Navarro, and holding forth at the Capitol under the Metro-
Goldwyn-Mayer banner. They certainly picked a dandy vehicle
for Navarro this trip, comedy and drama mingled in equal quantity,

colorful atmosphere, and excellent acting by the star and entire
supporting cast.

Tom Mix and his wonder horse, Tony, are seen at the Rialto
in one of those typical Mix melodramas of the West that stir
Thomas' admirers to frantic enthusiasm. It is "The Everlasting
Whisper," a Westerner of uncommon merit, quite up to the standard
of the best Mix offerings, and a credit to all concerned in its
production.

Warner's Theatre comes to the front with an exciting melodrama
of high and low life in Paris, a Warner Brothers production with
the alluring title of "Satan in Sables." It isn't explained just why
his Satanic Majesty should find it necessary to don furs in the
somewhat torrid climate where he is supposed to reside, but that
doesn't matter. It's a title pretty sure to catch the attention and
arouse the curiosity of the feminine contingent, so, what would you?
Lowell Sherman as a Russian prince, going the pace in Paris, is
the hero, and the story, while decidedly ultra-theatrical, moves fast,
supplies a natural note in the performance of petite Pauline Garon,
as an Apache girl, and registers as an offering likely to please a
majority of the fans.

LOEW'S INK

HAVE you seen that snappy little monthly entitled "Loew's
Ink" and devoted to the interests of the Loew-Metro-Goldwyn Club?
If not try and get hold of a copy, which isn't so easy unless you
can creep inside the magic circle wherein its wit and wisdom hold
sway. Brilliant paragraph stuff, gingery verse, clever editorial
musings — all to the good and smart as they make 'em. We don't
mind admitting in confidence that the editor of the sheet is none
other than R. W. Baremore, known to local fame under the
sobriquet of "The Vulture." Those who know him well, know
best why this title was conferred upon him in days long gone by.
The present scribe could throw considerable light upon the subject,
but what good would it do? The "Vult" is making good.

WE STAND CORRECTED

IN an article in our issue of October 10, the Weaver Studio was
mentioned as being located at Seattle. This was an error, and one
which aroused popular indignation around Tacoma. Mr. A. B.
Crain, manager Tacoma News Tribune Development, calls our attention to the fact that the Weaver Studio and General Ashton are
Tacoma property, and one hundred and twenty-five thousand Ta-
comans want that geographical fact made public. So here goes, so
far as our humble efforts can repair the mistake. There is real
activity ahead of Weavers, and it is perfectly proper that Mr. Crain
should see that Tacoma gets all the credit due that enterprising city.

*The luncheon to Richard Talmadge, F. B. O. stunt star, at the Ritz-Carlton hotel, New York City, last Friday. Sixty-five guests, including F. B. O.
executives, exhibitors and writers on the trade, fan and daily papers, were present. Talmadge did several novel and daring stunts to entertain
the guests.*

ERNEST VADJA ARRIVES

ERNEST VADJA, one of the advance guard of Hungarian playwrights who have been engaged to write original screen narratives for Famous Players-Lasky Corporation, arrived on the Mauretania, Friday. Mr. Vadja had four plays on Broadway recently, including "The Harem," "Grounds for Divorce," "Fata Morgana" and "The Little Angel." He is still a comparatively young man considerably under forty and speaks English perfectly.

Melchoir Lengyel, another of the famous Hungarian literary group came here about a month ago to attend rehearsals of his play "Antonia," a Charles Frohman production. The negotiations resulting in the engagement of these noted authors were made through Dr. Edmund Pauker, the representative of the Society of Hungarian Playwrights.

Jesse Lasky, first vice-president in charge of Famous productions recently said: "I believe that the theatres of Budapest and Vienna are storehouses of wonderful screen material that we have not touched. Originality of theme and treatment marks the work of the dramatists of middle Europe, and by bringing these men to this country to write directly for the screen, we hope to introduce a new note in film literature."

One of the alluring allegorical episodes in "The Viennese Medley," which First National is now making on an elaborate scale in Hollywood.

Vilma Banky, Valentino's leading woman in "The Lone Eagle" (United Artists), about to serve something from a "phoney" Russian wine-cellar to Clarence Brown, director, and Hans Kraely, scenarist.

"GREEN ARCHER" HITS THE MARK

AS announced last week, the Pathe studio party to the press scribes, in connection with filming of "The Green Archer," came off on schedule last Friday. Three large buses took the guests to the Long Island studio, where a novel, well filled program of amusement was provided. The guests danced, had tea with Allene Ray, the star, engaged in an archery contest, and otherwise amused themselves. Paul Yawitz, publicity director for the Ned Wayburn enterprises, brought Ruth Laird and Mildred Leisy, scheduled to appear in "Fez," who staged several exhibition dances. The wife of Walter Miller, formerly a vaudeville star, also danced several numbers. Miss Ray was crowned Queen of Serials, Burr McIntosh delivering the coronation address. Several of the Pathe executives dropped in later in the day, including Elmer R. Pearson and J. E. Storey. At the conclusion of the party the guests voted Edmund F. Supple, publicity director, a most thoughtful and efficient host.

YE WEDDING BELLS

SYLVIA HIRSH, daughter of Nathan Hirsh, President of Aywon Film Corporation, was married last Monday to Henry R. Arias, well known in the export end of the picture business. The wedding took place in the Crystal Room of the Ritz, and was attended by friends of both families, and many prominent members of filmdom. Mr. and Mrs. Arias will spend their moneymoon, and later reside in New York City. THE MOTION PICTURE NEWS extends congratulations to the happy pair.

WARNER BROTHER'S LUNCHEON

ERNST Lubitsch, director, and Irene Rich, star of the Warner Brothers' organization, were recently the guests of that company in this city, a luncheon in their honor at the Park Lane Hotel being attended by representatives of all the New York dailies and film magazines. They came from Toronto, where for several days the company producing the Oscar Wilde play — "Lady Windermere's Fan," had been making race course scenes. With Irene Rich were her daughters, Frances and Jane, and her mother. The four left October 17 for Europe, where the star will place the girls in a Switzerland school, her mother remaining with them. Miss Rich will then return to this country and go to California to appear in other Warner productions.

RED SEAL RECORD

DURING the week of September 6, Red Seal Pictures Corporation scored a decided hit by having three subjects on view on Broadway at the Capitol, Rivoli and Strand Theatres. These subjects were representatives of three of Red Seal's novelty series, "My Bonnie," a Ko-Ko Song Car-tune, appearing on the Capitol program; "Marvels of Motion" at the Rivoli; and "Ko-Ko on the Run" at the Strand. This is something of a record, and adds fresh luster to the Red Seal laurels as a purveyor of high-class novelties to the leading houses in the picture business.

Jack Mulhall, Helen Ferguson and other members of the cast of "Wild West" (Pathe), on location with performers of the Miller Brothers 101 Ranch Wild West show, who also appeared in many of the scenes of the Pathe serial.

Moderate Number of Producer-Owned Houses a Benefit, Says Exhibitor

KANSAS CITY just now is in the grip of a question, one so delicate that it has caused a factional division of opinion. The subject is mentioned only in guarded undertones. There is one exhibitor, however, Adolph M. Eisner, former president of the M. P. T. O. Kansas City and owner of the Circle theatre, Kansas City, who is prone to voice his sentiment without "coloring."
He says:

"Why all this howl if an exhibitor expresses an opinion on producer-owned theatres, which might conflict with the usual 'panic yell' voiced- If we think a conservative number of producer-owned theatres is such a terrible thing for the industry, why do we continue to sell our theatres to Universal and Paramount, who have been actively buying in the Kansas City territory of late? I have in mind not less than ten widely-known and prominent exhibitors in this territory, who in the past at some time have assisted in singing the 'death hymn' of producer-owned theatres. Today every one of them has sold at least one theatre to a producer within the last year. Do we expect people to take us seriously when our actions are so inconsistent? Are exhibitor organizations to be strictly an individual proposition, with the motto—'Wait till I get mine, then to hell with the others—in force?'

"One may say: 'It's only a comparatively few exhibitors who would sell their theatres to producers.' What 'one' really means is that it's only comparatively few theatres the producers want, but that they could buy from any exhibitor under the sun if the latter happened to need a buyer. Let's be honest about it. We—part of us, at least—are fighting among ourselves, trying to beat the other fellow to it by buying all the pictures that are made. Pretty soon we awaken and find that we are woefully over-booked, facing a big financial loss. We want to sell out. Do we think of the dear brother exhibitor who sat alongside of us at the meeting or convention and aided in passing a resolution against producer-owned theatres? It is to laugh. We would sell out to Jesse James if he had the cash.

"Personally I can see no harm, but a benefit, in a conservative number of producer-owned theatres in each territory. It will aid the owners of individual theatres to obtain better prices on rival product which must have an outlet. There are comparatively few theatres in each territory that producers want. Let them have them. It will make business all the better. The saddest thing of it all is that we exhibitors have to keep fighting among ourselves, with those who do the loudest bellowing usually the biggest hypocrites. If we must remain children all our lives, then the industry simply will have to wait until we catch up with it. It's time we sober up. We're overdue."

A. W. Eisner, owner of the Circle Theatre, Kansas City.

Propose Blue Law For Alabama

Sunday Closing Bill to Be Introduced at the Next State Legislative Session

A SUNDAY closing law, aimed at the operation of moving picture shows, vaudeville and delicatessens, looms as a subject to be bitterly fought during Governor Brandon's special legislative session next January in Alabama.

Forces advocating a Sunday blue law are said to be actively at work and said-to have strength has been mustered. Senator Bonner of Wilcox, leader of these forces, is expected to introduce the measure in the upper house. Bonner introduced a similar law during the 1923 session, which was defeated by only a few votes.

The coming of Gipsy Smith, Jr., noted evangelist, to Montgomery next month will have considerable influence in mustering strength for a Sunday observance law, religious leaders of Alabama state. Gypsy Smith is expected to throw considerable strength to the advocating forces and a general organization to seek the bill's passage may result, it is said.

Senator Bonner's bill in 1923 lacked only a few votes of passing. Before the session ended, Bonner claimed he had enough strength to pass it, but decided to let it remain on the adverse calendar until the next session.

Governor Brandon is not expected to include this bill in his call. The administration is said to be willing to leave this question to municipalities to settle within themselves. However, the legislature was divided in opinion at the general session.

If the measure is passed in January, it means that moving picture and vaudeville houses will be closed in every city throughout the state. Prominent religious workers of Montgomery will join forces with those of other cities in seeking passage of this bill, which will also seek to eliminate Sunday baseball and other amusements where an admission price is charged.

Miss Bauersfeld Appointed to Kansas Censor Board

A new member of the Kansas State Censor Board was appointed last week by Governor Ben. S. Paulen. She is Miss Fern Bauersfeld of Topeka, Kansas, who will succeed Miss Etta B. Beavers, who resigned.

Theatre Censorship Beaten in Atlanta Council

By a vote of 24 to 7 the City Council of Atlanta defeated an ordinance providing for a censorship of vaudeville shows, legitimate theatre attractions and special stage numbers at picture houses. The measure was supported by Councilman Horace Russell and John A. White. Opposition speeches were made by Alderman Jesse Armistead and Councilmen T. L. Slappey and A. J. Orme.

Mr. Orme said he "saw no reason to allow one group of people, or any one person, say what was good for everybody.

"I have never seen anything on the stage in Atlanta that called for such drastic action," he said. "As chairman of the police committee, I can say that nothing indecent will be tolerated here, and all people have to do is to call the chief of police and make complaints in order to get action if it is warranted."

Kansas-Missouri M. P. T. O. Directors to Meet

A meeting of the board of directors of the M. P. T. O. Kansas-Missouri has been called for Tuesday, October 13, at the Hotel Baltimore, Kansas City. The question of holding a semi-annual convention this fall and producer-owned theatres probably will be among the more important questions to be discussed. Sentiment among some of the exhibitors favors an annual convention instead of a semi-annual meeting. In that case the meeting would not be until next spring.

Pathe's Public Relations Director on Trip

Miss Regge Doran, director of Pathe's newly established Public Relations Department, has started on a trip that will take her to Chicago and Columbus, Ohio. At Chicago she will appoint a field representative to cooperate with exhibitors in the midwest territory. Miss Doran will attend the convention of the Child Conservation League of America, where she will address the league on the subject of "School Matinees."

To Discuss Tax Removal on October 24th

A TENTATIVE program of the hearing on revenue revision to be held by the House ways and means committee beginning October 19, has been prepared by Representative Green of Iowa, chairman, under which part of October 24 will be given over to discussion of the removal of the remaining admission tax. The witness for the motion picture industry will be Jack Connolly, Washington representative of the Motion Picture Producers and Distributors.

Representative of the Treasury Department will discuss their recommendations for tax changes at the beginning of the hearings, and will be followed by the various interests who are desirous of relief. Publicity of income tax returns will be considered on October 22.

F.P.-L. Denies Rumored Circuit Deals

Claim They Are Not Negotiating With Skouras and Butterfield Interests, Except for Booking Arrangement with Skouras

THAT Famous Players Theatres is involved in a deal with Colonel Butterfield regarding the taking over by Famous of the Michigan Circuit controlled by Colonel Butterfield, is denied by Famous, as is the deal which rumor says is on between Famous and the St. Louis Amusement Company, controlled by Skouras Brothers operating twenty theatres in St. Louis. The only item of authentic news is that Famous is negotiating for a booking arrangement with the Skouras interests for the Grand Central, West End Lyric and Capitol in St. Louis.

In denying the rumor regarding the St. Louis Amusement Company Spyros Skouras said that there was no deal under way involving a transfer in management of the twenty St. Louis theatres. He said:

"Skouras Brothers have no such idea in mind. We intend disposing of the management of our properties to nobody. We own the First National Franchise and have millions involved."

Regarding the rumors concerning the Michigan chain of Colonel Butterfield and the St. Louis proposition Famous says:

"There is no deal on between Famous Players Theatres and the Michigan circuit controlled by Colonel Butterfield. No such deal has ever been contemplated. There has been a move contemplated to add the downtown first run houses of the St. Louis Amusement Company to the Famous Players chain, but nothing has been definitely settled."

According to the rumor Famous is negotiating to take over the management of the Butterfield Circuit and the Skouras chain with the ultimate idea of merging these interests totalling sixty-six houses, in the new theatre corporation to be formed by Famous and B. & K.

In July the Skouras interests made a booking arrangement with William Goldman involving the King's, Garden and Rivoli, representing the Goldman interests and the Capitol, New Grand Central, West End Lyric and Lyric Skydome of the Skouras chain. This circuit practically dominates the theatre situation in St. Louis.

Meantime the St. Louis Amusement Company, controlled by Harry Koplar and Skouras Brothers have announced that subscriptions for an issue of 12,000 shares of Class A common stock of the company have been far in excess of the offering and that the shares will have to be pro rated to the prospective stockholders. The subscription price was $38 per share.

The Class A stock will have priority over Class B common to non-cumulative dividends of $4.50 per share in any one year. The authorized capitalization of the company is 40,000 shares of Class A with 20,000 shares outstanding and 30,000 shares of Class B with 30,000 shares outstanding.

The plans of the company contemplate the acquisition in the very near future of additional theatres in St. Louis and elsewhere and negotiations are now under way involving the transfer of eleven prominent St. Louis and suburban houses.

The earnings of the company for the two years prior to December 31, 1924, were sufficient to pay $3 per share on the Class A

A. M. P. A. Members Name Twelve Biggest Men

MEMBERS of the A. M. P. A. at the weekly meeting held at the Hofbrau House, New York, Thursday, October 8th, named the "twelve biggest men of the industry" as follows: Adolph Zukor, William Fox, General Will Hays, Sam Rothafel, Sam Katz, Carl Laemmle, Richard A. Rowland, Joe Schenck and Sidney Kent.

Each of the above candidates for the honor of classification as one of the twelve biggest men in the industry, will be invited to preside at forthcoming meetings of the association.

stock while for the six months ended June 27, 1925, the earnings were $45,246 or more than sufficient to pay $4.50 per share on the Class A stock.

A number of other deals involving many houses have been in negotiation during the past week.

The King Bee Theatre, 1710 North Jefferson avenue, St. Louis, for many years operated by Mike Nash, pioneer St. Louis motion picture exhibitor, has been taken under a 10-year lease by the King Bee Amusement Company, controlled by George P. Skouras.

D. Coston, one of the officers representing the Eastern Iowa Theatre Company, was in Des Moines booking pictures during the week and stated that they have secured options on a number of theatres which they are planning to add to their circuit. He did not wish, however, to be quoted upon the names of the theatres which the company is contemplating buying.

For some time it has been a mystery as to who would operate the new theatre in Quincy, Mass., which is being erected by ex-Mayor William A. Bradford and which will be one of the largest theatres in Massachusetts outside Boston. Announcement is now made that negotiations have been completed by the Moe Mark interests for a long lease of the house. It is expected that the playhouse will be completed and ready for opening about New Year's day.

The Buffalo Strand Theatre corporation has been incorporated in Albany with 500 shares of no par value. The policy of the company, as announced, is to conduct theatrical business and it is also stated that the incorporation was formed at this time merely to protect the name—Buffalo Strand. The directors are Walter Hays, Eugene L. Falk, Ira W. Smith, Stanley G. Falk, Raymond A. Williams and Lillian Olsen.

The Aldine Theatre, Wilmington, which was recently purchased by Loew's, Inc. from the Topkis-Ginns interests, has been acquired by the Stanley Company of America, being the last of the four Ginns houses in that city to pass into the Stanley Company hands. The house, which is now undergoing extensive alterations and improvements, will be opened in two or three weeks under the same policy now obtaining in other Stanley houses in Wilmington. The Loew's

are said to have paid $450,000 for the theatre, but the price at which the Stanley Company took it over has not been disclosed.

No sale has been consummated between the Whitehurst Combined Theatrical Interests of Baltimore, Md., and any out-of-town theatrical or film producing company for the theatres controlled by that company in the Monumental City up to this writing. The playhouses operated by that company include the Garden, New, Parkway and Century.

Rumors concerning the sale of the theatres have been flying thick and fast for a number of days and negotiations have been going on, it is said, between the Stanley Company of America and the Marcus Loew Interests. Mr. Loew has admitted that he has been negotiating for the properties but Jules Mastbaum has denied that his company is dickering for the theatres.

Two sums have been mentioned in connection with the proposed transaction. The first is $3,286,000 for all four of the playhouses while $1,859,000 is given as the price for the Century and Parkway. Mr. Loew is ready to accept either proposition, it is reported.

Reorganize Censor Board of British Columbia

An important reorganization of the British Columbia Board of Moving Picture Censors has been announced at Victoria, B. C., by Premier John Oliver, and, incidentally, a hot political situation has developed through the dismissal of one official.

The member of the board who has been released is John R. Foster, who is the president of the Motion Picture Operators Union at Victoria. The dismissal has been taken up rather warmly by the Victoria Trades and Labor Council, with which the Operators' Union is affiliated.

The new personnel of the board now includes two new members as well as two who had formerly held office. The two new men are J. H. Fletcher and J. H. Leslie, both of Vancouver, B. C. Mr. Fletcher is the proprietor of the Collingwood Theatre, and Mr. Leslie is a motion picture operator at the Dominion Theatre, Vancouver.

The two censors who have been retained are Joseph Walters and W. A. Oswald.

Test Vote Shows Sanborn Favors Sunday Movies

At a test election held last week in Sanborn, Iowa, to learn the sentiment in favor of Sunday shows, the shows won by a vote of 170 to 37. The council had previously agreed to pass Sunday pictures providing the majority wished such action. The test developed the fact that the majority were opposed to the ban and in favor of open Sundays.

The election followed a heated campaign between the liberal element, headed by Anna C. Jacobsen of the Princess theatre, and the reformers.

B. & K. Show "Her Sister from Paris" Despite Censor Board's Refusal of Permit

DESPITE the official ban of the Chicago Censor Board and efforts by that body to force Balaban and Katz to withdraw the picture "Her Sister from Paris," the First NaNtional feature starring Constance Talmadge was continued as the main attraction at the B & K Chicago theatre from Sunday until Thursday, up to which time the censors were unsuccessful in their endeavors to have the management withdraw the production from exhibition.

When a permit was refused by the board on October 8th, First National's attorney's appealed to Judge Pam for writ of mandamus to compel the board to grant a permit. Under this action two juries approved of the picture. The city served notice of appeal, automatically suspending the mandamus and on Saturday Corporation Counsel advised Police Chief Collins it was his duty to suppress the picture and that he could either seize the film, revoke the license of the theatre or cause the arrest of the management.

In defiance of this order Balaban and Katz opened their week's bill with the picture. On Tuesday Chief Collins declared he would telephone Mayor Dever at Pittsburgh, where the latter was attending the world series, and ask him to revoke the license of the Chicago theatre, but up to Thursday no action had been taken.

Should the city take any drastic action a long drawn legal battle seems assured, as both Balaban and Katz and First National are determined to fight for their rights in the court and in every other legitimate way.

M-G-M London Studio is Rumor

Reports American Producing Company Will Build Large Plant Persist in England

IN an article commenting on persistent rumors to the effect that two important American producing concerns would build large studios near London, "Kine," the London film trade publication, mentions Metro-Goldwyn-Mayer as one of the organizations referred to in connection with the reports.

"As regards one of the companies," the article states, "Metro-Goldwyn, we have been acquainted with certain facts which suggest that arrangements for this purpose are very far advanced.

"Our information is that, as a result of investigations made while Robert Rubin, the vice-president, was recently in London, Metro-Goldwyn has acquired a site and will shortly begin the erection of a studio close to North Acton station and that it will engage in production on a large scale in England.

"Acton, according to air Ministry statistics, suffers less from fog than any other London district and to this supporting circumstance should be added the further one, that of the several British producers who have just returned from the States, some are believed on the other side to be on a production mission for Metro."

In answer to an inquiry as to whether his company contemplated producing in England, Nicholas M. Schenck, of Metro-Goldwyn-Mayer, replied "I can neither confirm nor deny."

Fox-Defa Tie-up in Germany

Deutche Vereinsfilm A.-G. Productions to Be Released With American Features

CURRENT announcements in *Der Film*, a German film trade paper, indicate that Fox Film Corporation has entered into an arrangement for production in Germany in co-operation with Defa. The precise nature of the arrangement is not disclosed, but the pictures are advertised as German Fox films, and will include such prominent European players as Werner Krauss, Diomira Jacobini, Marcella Albani, Frieda Richard, ana Mierendorff and others.

The first titles to be announced are: "Troedler von Amsterdam" ("The Old Clothes Dealer of Amsterdam"), after the story by Dr. A. Schirokauer. Werner Krauss will play the title role, with Diomira Jacobini, ana Mierendorff and Hermann Picha supporting. Viktor Janson will direct. "Das Geheimnis der alten Mamsell" ("The Secret of the Old Housekeeper"), from the novel by Marlitt, directed by Dr. Paul Merzbach. Two others announced are "Der Mueller von Sanssouci" ("The Miller of Sanssouci") and "Gretchen."

It is also rumored that Warner Brothers will produce in Germany, and perhaps France. This has not been denied by the Warners, who have not, however, given out any statement as yet on the situation.

These various moves, others of which are rumored, are probably to be attributed to the "Kontingent" system.

Complete Hearings in "Ten Commandments" Suit

Testimony in the suit against Famous Players-Lasky Corporation by Mrs. Mattie Thomas Thompson for royalties claimed as author of "The Ten Commandments," which she alleges was written by her, was completed in the Federal Court at Atlanta last Saturday before Judge Samuel H. Sibley. The case will be re-opened for argument next Saturday.

Miss Jeanie MacPherson, scenarist, and Barrett C. Kiesling, director of publicity and advertising at the De Mille studios, were the star witnesses for the defense.

Camera Work Completed on Sam Rork Production

With the filming of elaborate scenes depicting a sea battle and the arrival in New York harbor of the pirate ship Sea Tiger, the camera work on "Clothes Make the Pirate," the new Sam Rork production starring Leon Errol, was completed recently. The film is now being assembled and titled.

Those who will be seen in support of Errol in this screen comedy, directed by Maurice Tourneur, are Dorothy Gish, Nita Naldi, Tully Marshall, George Marion, Edna Murphy, Reginald Barlow, Walter Law and James Rennie.

School for Screen Students at "U" City a Success

Raymond L. Schrock, general manager of Universal City has arranged for the extension of the school for screen students recently established there. The success of the venture is said to be so pronounced that its further development is considered advisable.

Among the lectures that have been conducted at the classes last week were addresses on "Screen Poise," given by Laura La Plante, and "The Screen Novice," delivered by Pat O'Malley.

Lieber Month Drive Booms First National Sales

The Lieber Month Drive of First National has been a tremendous success as far as it has progressed, according to First National. A large percentage of the branches have exceeded the quotas set for them. At the end of the third week Salt Lake City stood in first place, with New York second and Cleveland third, and Indianapolis and Montreal tied for fourth place.

Industry to Urge Tax Repeal Before House Committee

ARGUMENTS for the complete removal of the tax on theatre admissions will be made by representatives of the industry before the House Ways and Means Committee at Washington on Saturday, October 24. Charles C. Pettijohn, general counsel for the Hays organization, will appear for that body. On behalf of the Motion Picture Theatre Owners of America, the following committee will be present: Joseph M. Seider, chairman; R. F. Woodhull, Sydney S. Cohen and A. Julian Brylawski.

National headquarters of the M. P. T. O. A. are sending out 15,000 letters to exhibitors urging that they take up with their representatives in Congress the matter of admission tax repeal before the session opens.

The House Committee will hear some forty witnesses from all industries seeking the revision of various items in the revenue bill. For this reason it is probable that the time allotted to the picture representatives will be short.

The M. P. T. O. A. will also file a brief with the House Committee.

J. D. Williams Forms British Company

Well-Known American Film Executive Announces Initiation of Extensive Plans Abroad

AS foreshadowed in MOTION PICTURE NEWS last week, announcement has now been made by J. D. Williams of the formation of British National Pictures, Ltd. This information comes direct to William A. Johnston from Mr. Williams himself.

British National is the first of the companies to be formed by Mr. Williams in furtherance of his plan to put Britain definitely on the picture map. The company is an all-British concern, with the exception of Mr. Williams. Among his associates are Sir Harold De Courcy Moore, who is also interested in a newly-formed British producing company and was until recently a director of British First National and George C. Eaton.

Sir Harold Moore's company is W. & M. Ltd., the "W" standing for Herbert Wilcox, and it is now engaged in producing "Nell Gwynne," with Dorothy Gish as the star.

It is reported that J. D. Williams has made a deal for the American rights to "The Rat," the Graham Cutts production, with Ivor Novello and Mae Marsh.

The letter from Mr. Williams to the Editor of MOTION PICTURE NEWS says in part: "You have given a great deal of publicity in your paper recently regarding the European situation and there is no doubt that the time is now ripe for this country to be placed definitely on the picture map. Nearly two years ago (January, 1924 to be exact) I gave an interview in London in which I said:

"The next great move in the business, in my opinion, will be the internationalization of the industry. The American public is waiting for the big foreign picture, and the British producer must face the problem and devise ways and means to make British pictures acceptable for the market which is ready for them in their Colonies as well as in America and in the other parts of the world. Everyone engaged in the industry in Britain should work with this end in view and in a short time we shall find the British picture a welcome rival.'

"British National Pictures, Ltd. has been formed to carry out this idea."

With a view to educating the American public and American exhibitors on the subject of foreign pictures, Mr. Williams plans extensive advertising campaigns in trade papers as well as national mediums.

Non-Theatrical Pictures Lose in Kansas

AFTER a trial period covering several months, non-theatrical competition in Kansas apparently has been conquered. Under strict fire regulations of the state, covering projections booths, and an unwritten agreement with the Kansas City Film Board of Trade not to serve non-theatrical enterprises, exhibitors virtually are free from trouble of this source, if the small number of complaints coming into the M. P. T. O. Kansas-Missouri headquarters may be accepted as a barometer.

J. D. Williams, who has organized British National Pictures, Ltd.

Mr. Williams expects to be in New York in about a month or six weeks for a brief visit before returning to England to fulfil a five years' contract with British National.

The London *Daily Mail* of October 2 printed a lengthy article by Mr. Williams which read in part:

"All over the world the mark Made in England is regarded as a sign of quality that is supreme in many things. Few Americans of standing think of having anything but English cloth for their clothes. Sheffield cutlery is the standard of excellence, as the British car is the high-water mark of quality the world over.

"Unfortunately for Britain, this has not been the case with her motion pictures. It is not because you have not the material or the men; not because the frequently blamed climate is a handicap, for, indeed, it is not; not because you have not the actors or the stories. It is almost entirely because no one has so far attempted to organize what is, perhaps, the most technical business in the world on a sound and sufficiently large and stable basis.

"It is a fact that about 90 per cent of American-made films are produced under artificial light. Consequently climatic conditions no longer affect production.

"There are many British actors, directors, scenario writers, technical experts, camera men, and others at present working in America who could be induced to come back home if proper and permanent facilities existed here for the making of British motion pictures. And there are many others right here now who only need the opportunity to develop into as capable workers as those found anywhere.

"The motion picture does not belong to any one nation. The French and Italians

were the first to show us how to make motion pictures. I think the first really big picture success in America was 'Quo Vadis?' an Italian picture. 'Du Barry,' renamed 'Passion,' which was an enormous success in America, was a German-made picture of a French story. But up to the present time there has been no outstanding British picture.

"The American public, despite rumors to the contrary, are always looking for good pictures from any country. There are 16,000 exhibitors of films in the United States, the majority of whom would be glad to show really first-rate British pictures. When such pictures are made here they will be just as successful in America as those made in Hollywood."

India Production Shows Big Increase

A natural consequence of the increased popularity among Indians of the motion picture, states a recent Department of Commerce report from American Consul William Keblinger of Bombay, is the attempt to make pictures in the country with Indian capital, Indian artists and Indian direction.

It started in a very small way but in the last year the output has been greatly increased and gives promise of becoming a substantial industry in the near future. The pictures as now turned out by the Indian studios, however, lack many of the refinements of American pictures.

The Indian producing companies have been suffering from lack of capital and want of an organized method in distributing and it is stated that at times difficulty is experienced in continuing business. Until the pictures can be improved sufficiently to appeal to the better class of Indian it will be difficult to get theatres to run them. The admission at houses showing Indian pictures runs from Rs. 1-6-0 to 3 annas (from about 45 cents to 7 cents), but very few seats are sold at the higher price. Possibly the total admissions would average 6 to 8 annas per head (about 13 to 17 cents).

Montreal Theatre Tax of $323,014 Aids Charities

The manner in which the theatre-goers of Montreal, Quebec, the largest city in Canada, are assisting in the city's charities is shown in the annual report for the past fiscal year which has just been published by the city superintendent, Albert Chevalier.

The city's share of the amusement tax which is collected on all tickets of admission amounted in the past year to $323,014, all of which was turned over to local hospitals and other institutions. Under the laws of the Province of Quebec, there is no Provincial amusement tax, such as is collected in other Canadian Provinces or in other countries. The cities of the Provinces are empowered, however, to collect an amusement tax of their own, the proceeds to be devoted to local charities.

A. M. Botsford Heads New Department in Famous Players Theatre Unit

A. M. BOTSFORD, for several years advertising manager of the Famous Players-Lasky Corporation, has been appointed Director of Advertising Publicity and Exploitation for the new Theatre Corporation to be formed as a result of the deal between Paramount and Balaban & Katz.

Mr. Botsford will be succeeded as advertising manager of Famous Players by Russell Holman, who has been for some time the former's assistant, and is one of the best known advertising and publicity men in the industry.

The new department which Mr. Botsford will head will be operated separately. It is regarded as a very important post. In addition to directing the work of the advertising men in the various Paramount theatres, Mr. Botsford will also have charge of a national campaign of institutional advertising on behalf of the motion picture theatre, which, it is expected, will be along new lines and will be a creator of good-will on the part of the public toward the photoplay houses of the country.

Mr. Botsford will assume his new duties about November 1.

British Censorship Rules Are Made More Strict

New rulings providing for a stricter censorship of films dealing with crime have been issued by the British Board of Film Censors. The new rules regarding crime episodes in films are as follows:

(A) No serial dealing with crime will be examined except as a whole.

(B) No film in which crime is the dominant feature, and not merely an episode of the story, will receive a certificate.

(C) No film will be passed in which the methods of crime are shown or illustrated.

(D) No crime film will be passed, even in cases where, at the end of the film, retribution is supposed to have fallen on the criminal, or where actual crime is treated from the comic point of view.

Arkansas Exhibitors Convene

Eli Whitney Collins is Named President of Organization for Fourth Time

THE Arkansas M.P.T.O. held their semi-annual convention at T. F. Sharp's New Theatre in Little Rock last week and re-elected Eli Whitney Collins president for the fourth consecutive year. Cecil Cupp of Arkadelphia replaces H. D. Wharton as Vice-President and Wharton succeeds O. C. Hauber as secretary-treasurer. The directors elected were, W. L. Landers, E. H. Butler, E. C. Robertson, Walter Rainey, J. A. Collins, Sidney Nutt, L. B. Clark, H. D. Wharton and W. E. Blume.

Matters of considerable interest to the film industry in general were discussed at the session which lasted two days. Among the most important of these was in regard to the music tax. As a result of the compromise effected between Judge Felix D. Robertson of Texas, representing the American Society of Composers, Authors and Pub-

lishers, and the M.P.T.O., a considerable burden was reported lifted from the smaller exhibitors. Contemplated copyright infringement suits will not be filed and the seat tax of ten cents per seat per year, which the smaller exhibitors have contended was too large, will in all probability, be reduced.

A resolution was adopted endorsing the M.P.T.O.A. and pledging the support of the Arkansas organization to the national body. It was reported that seven new members had been admitted to the local organization.

Fire Destroys the Lyric In Reading. Penn.

The Lyric Theatre at Reading, Pennsylvania, was completely destroyed by fire early in the morning of October 8th. It is estimated it will take $500,000 to restore the theatre and equipment lost in the blaze. The house was one of the leading theatres of the chain operated by Carr & Schad, Inc., of which Dr. H. J. Schad, president of the Motion Picture Theatre Owners of Eastern Pennsylvania, Southern New Jersey and Delaware, is the active head.

Rex-Hedwig Laboratories in Contract With Vital

Wm. K. Hedwig and J. A. Kent, president and vice-president respectively of Rex-Hedwig Laboratories, Inc., and Vital Exchanges, last week entered a contract, covering a period of five years, to make prints for the Vital Exchanges, releasing the Davis Distributing Division's product. The laboratory company is enlarging its plant to handle the increase in business.

Charge Cotter Violated the Labor Statute

Not having been satisfied with seeing J. W. Cotter, owner of the Fourth Street theatre, Moberly, Mo., find $50 for violating the town's blue law ordinance for opening on Sunday, the county prosecutor of Randolph County has filed against Mr. Cotter a charge of violating the state's anti-Sunday labor statute. The first case has been taken to the supreme court.

School Head Endorses Children's Shows

MANAGER GEORGE T. CRUZEN started his Saturday Morning shows for children last Saturday at the Palace theatre in Lockport, New York, and the youth of the Lock City turned out en masse for the event. Superintendent of Schools, R. B. Kelley gave enthusiastic endorsement to the idea in a letter to Mr. Cruzen in which he said:

"I have examined with interest the information sent to me by the Motion Picture Producers and Distributors of America, Inc., with reference to the Saturday Morning Movie for boys and girls.

"In addition I have checked the titles of films to be used in connection with these movies. Educators for a long time have been anxious that film programs without objectionable features should be available to school pupils.

"With his present effort, Mr. Hays seems to have achieved just this. It is highly desirable that parents have the opportunity once a week of permitting their children to attend movie programs to which there can be no objection.

"I am glad, therefore, to endorse the inauguration of these Saturday Morning Movies at the Palace theatre in Lockport."

New Exhibitor Members of Kansas City Board Named

In line with the usual quarterly custom, a new arbitration board was appointed in Kansas City Monday. The exhibitor members, appointed by President R. R. Biechele of the M. P. T. O. Kansas-Missouri, are: K. L. Darnell, Alamo theatre, Kansas City; Frank Amos, New Diamond theatre, Kansas City, and A. F. Gibbons, Prospect theatre, Kansas City. The three distributor members, appointed by E. C. Rhoden, president of the Kansas City Film Board of Trade, are: Louis Reichert, Warner-Vitagraph; T. O. Byerle, First National, and M. A. Levy, Fox.

Marco Wolf Signed by West Coast Theatres Co.

West Coast Theatres, Inc., and Marco Wolf, San Francisco theatrical producer, have signed a three-year contract under which the latter will act as general stage director for houses in the West Coast circuit. The Fanchon and Marco revues are enjoying widespread popularity on the coast and are now being presented at San Jose, Stockton, San Diego, Pasadena, Long Beach, Santa Ana, San Bernardino, Pomona and four of the large neighborhood houses in Los Angeles.

Associated Field Force Has Conference

FOUR of the five special representatives of Associated Exhibitors were in conference for three days last week with General Manager John S. Woody and Sales Manager Jay A. Gove, when details of the company's new selling and administrative policy were outlined.

The special representatives were instructed with regard to the taking over of towns of less than 2,000 population, heretofore sold for Associated by Pathe, and for the employment of bookers and a greatly increased sales organization. In this respect were discussed many details of sales work and the entire distribution campaign for the remainder of the season. The special representatives in attendance were Claude C. Ezell, Floyd Lewis, Harry E. Lotz and Melville E. Maxwell. A number of the sixteen productions on the second half of Associated's schedule were previewed by those in attendance at the conference.

Seventeen Vital Exchanges To Open

Davis Distributing Division Announces Completion of System, With Fourteen Others to Open Shortly

D AVIS Distributing Division, Inc., and Vital Exchanges, Inc., who will handle their product, have completed the organization of an exchange system throughout the United States and Canada. It is announced by David R. Hochreich, President of Vital Exchanges, that exchanges are to be opened immediately in seventeen cities, and that the fourteen others completing the system, will be in operation within the next thirty days.

Coincident with the announcement of the beginning of actual distribution by Vital Exchanges, Hochreich also made known the officials of the organization as follows: David R. Hochreich, President; Arthur L. Price, Vice-President; Walter Cohen, Secretary-Treasurer; Leo A. Price, Chairman of the Board of Directors and Finance Committee, with the following Board of Directors: Leo A. Price, David R. Hochreich, Arthur L. Price, J. Charles Davis, 2nd, Walter Cohen, J. K. Adams, William Hedwig. Senator Abraham Kaplan is general counsel.

Leo A. Price makes his entrance into the picture industry through Vital Exchanges. He was formerly President of Rothenberg and Company and is now President of the Associated Banking Corporation. Arthur L. Price, his son, is Vice-President of the Associated Banking Corporation, with which Walter Cohen is also affiliated.

In discussing the organization of Vital Exchanges, President Hochreich said:

"I am delighted that Vital Exchanges, Inc., has been fortunate enough to secure the invaluable services of such men as Leo

Leo A. Price, chairman of the board of directors of Vital Exchanges, Inc., and a director of Davis Distributing Division, Inc.

A. Price, Arthur L. Price, Walter Cohen and Senator Kaplan. I consider that the entrance of these gentlemen into the motion picture industry is a tribute not only to Vital Exchanges, Inc., and the Davis Distributing Division, Inc., but to the motion picture industry itself, for they are recognized in the financial world as leaders in their chosen field and their affiliation with Vital Exchanges, Inc., is a tribute to that organization, its policies and product, as well as the Davis Distributing Division, Inc.

"Senator Abraham Kaplan, while a well-known lawyer, is recognized in the financial world and in the field of politics as one of

the ablest men in his chosen profession. He is an expert on motion picture matters.

"This reorganization of Vital Exchanges, Inc., in no way effects the association with Davis Distributing Division, Inc., whose product we will handle exclusively for the next five years and whom we look to with the utmost confidence for the supply of product of sufficient quantity and quality to make Vital Exchanges, Inc. one of the leading distributing organizations in the industry."

The Vital Exchanges which are now in operation and those opening within the week are: Philadelphia—Dave Segal; Pittsburgh—O. R. Kurtze; Buffalo—Richard C. Fox; Albany—Richard C. Fox; Milwaukee—Walter A. Baier; Cleveland—Harry A. Lande; Cincinnati—Harry A. Lande; Indianapolis—Harry A. Lande; St. John, N. B.—R. J. Romney; Toronto, Winnipeg, Montreal, Vancouver—R. J. Romney; Boston—Harry Segal; New York—Moe Kerman; Chicago—Si Greiver.

Mr. Hochreich is leaving on a trip immediately to arrange the opening of the other exchanges which are waiting the word to go. He will be joined on the Coast by Mr. Davis who will spend some time in California in the interest of productions and states that all production is to be speeded up in order to keep the newly opened exchanges fully supplied with quality product. Mr. Hochreich also states that his assistant, Milton Kempner, will accompany him on the trip and that the detail of all office management will be looked after by Max F. C. Goosman, assistant General Manager.

Connecticut Tax Rehearing is Denied

Decision Declares New Law Constitutional; Appeal is Prepared for Hearing in Supreme Court

T HE petition of motion picture interests for a rehearing of the Connecticut tax bill has been denied by the special Federal Court sitting for the purpose of hearing the appeal. The court, composed of Judges Henry Wade Rogers, Henry Goddard and Thomas W. Thatcher, last Friday handed down the decision which declared the new law constitutional and their decision was filed in the New Haven office of Charles E. Pickett, clerk of the U. S. District Court.

The decision did not come in the nature of a surprise, as it was not expected the three judges would grant the petition for another hearing. The action, however, paves the way for a hearing before the Supreme Court. Papers have been prepared for this petition and will probably be filed during the week. They were prepared by Benedict M. Holden of Hartford, counsel for the motion picture companies, in association with George W. Wickersham.

The text of the decision denying the plea for a rehearing in the special Federal Court follows:

"The motion for a re-argument is denied. The application is based on the theory that the court disposed of this case on the theory that the statute was passed in the exercise of the police power, but the court decided

that whether the act was passed in the exercise of the police power or the taxing power, it was valid."

The motion for re-argument was brought by the Fox Film Corporation of New York and the American Feature Film Company of Boston. It was contended that the court had decided the case on the basis that the act was passed under the police power of the state. The tax of ten dollars a reel, it was argued, could not be merely a fee to cover police supervision as it would bring a revenue several times larger than the cost of administration of the act.

A hearing on the constitutionality of the law was held in New Haven on July 10th and the court handed down a decision which favored the state and which denied the petition for an injunction. It was then argued that the court should pass upon the validity of the law as a revenue measure, rather than one coming under police powers of the state.

Meantime exhibitors and other executives in the picture industry in Connecticut, working in cooperation with the Hays organization are bending effort in a campaign calling for the repeal of the Durant law. Petitions have been distributed throughout the state and a majority of the legislators are said now to be in favor of such a repeal.

One of the best bits of propaganda in this direction was pulled by Clarence D. Burbank of the Franklin Theatre at Thompsonville when he persuaded Representative Harold J. Bromage to speak against the statute from the stage of his theatre. The Assemblyman said he voted against the bill and declared he would work for a special session of the Legislature to repeal the law. More than 1,200 residents of Thompsonville have signed "special session" cards which were distributed through the Franklin Theatres.

Tax Commissioner Blodgett has prepared a number of new regulations in connection with the operation of the tax law. The nature of the regulations has not yet been revealed, but the Commissioner stated they would not impose additional burden upon operators or exhibitors. He declared they would be of further assistance in ascertaining what films, if any, are being shown without the registration required by the statute.

The Commissioner discounts reports that independent distributors are doing any large volume of business in Connecticut. He has information to the effect that salesmen are trying to sell and that a small quantity of film has been contracted for.

Federal Trade Commission Appeals Eastman Decision to U. S. Supreme Court

A REVIEW of the decision of the United States Circuit Court of Appeals, holding that the Federal Trade Commission was without authority to order the Eastman Kodak Company to dispose of laboratories which the commission contended had been built as a means of coercing independent laboratories to use Eastman film exclusively, has been asked of the United States Supreme Court by the commission's counsel.

The circuit court concurred in the commission's opinion that an agreement between the Eastman Company and the laboratories that the former would refrain from operating its three laboratories so long as the latter used only American-made film was illegal and an unfair method of competition, but held that the Trade Commission Act did not confer upon the commission the power to require a citizen to sell property acquired in the course of business; and that as the Eastman Company had the unquestioned right to equip itself to enter the laboratory business, no court could require the sale by the company of the laboratories, holding invalid the commission's order requiring the company to dispose of the properties.

The court's view is contested by the commission's attorneys, who claim that the commission has authority under the law to make a provisional order requiring the disposition of the laboratories. The commission claims that the facts in the case disclose a deliberate purpose and intent to monopolize interstate commerce and to prevent the importation, in foreign commerce, of raw positive films; that acts otherwise lawful may become unlawful when done with an intent to violate the law, and that the sale of property acquired as part of a plan to restrict trade may be compelled.

Denial of the commission's petition is asked by the Eastman Kodak Company in a brief filed with the court, in which it is declared the acquisition and ownership of laboratories by the Eastman Company was not unlawful per se, and cannot be considered an unfair method of competition in interstate commerce. It is also contended that the commission has no power to order a sale of tangible physical property.

Walker Will Lay Cornerstone

Senator Will Preside at Ceremonies in Connection With New Fox Exchange

SENATOR James J. Walker, Democratic candidate for Mayor of New York, will lay the cornerstone of Fox Film Corporation's New York Exchange at 343-45 West 44th street on Wednesday, October 28th, according to announcement by James R. Grainger, general sales manager of the company. The event will bring together officials of the city and state, stars of the stage and screen and over 300 exhibitors of the metropolitan area.

Wilfred, Inc., are the architects of the building, which, it is said will be the most scientifically laid out exchange in the country. It will be equipped with every modern appliance for the handling and distribution of films and accessories. It will be absolutely fireproof, the building being of reinforced concrete with all steel partitions, a full sprinkling system and every other known safety appliance.

A beautiful lounge and reception room, opening out of a palatial projection room, will be fitted up for the comfort of visiting exhibitors on the third floor. There will also be vaults for the storage of films.

Harry Buxbaum, manager of the New York Exchange, will have his offices on the second floor, surrounded by the members of his staff. Plans call for large rest rooms on this floor for the office force. Lockers and other essential equipment will be found in these rooms.

A unique feature of the dedicatory ceremonies will be the placing of a can of films in the cornerstone instead of the usual papers. Great care is being taken to insure that the film will be typical of present day production.

Missouri Not to Tax Picture Theatres

THE motion picture theatres and other amusement places of Missouri will escape from the special 5 or 10 per cent tax Governor Sam A. Baker contemplated installing to provide a special fund for the maintenance of the public schools and high educational institutions of the state.

The Governor's conference will meet again in Jefferson City on October 19 to draft the proposed constitutional amendment to be submitted to the voters of the state in November 1926.

A sub-committee of the conference has drafted the proposed amendment. It will provide a 10 per cent tax on cigars and cigarettes, a severance tax on minerals mined in the state, transfer of the inheritance tax fund from general revenue to school revenue, transfer of present 5 cents per $100 property tax to school fund and similar treatment for the foreign insurance tax. It is estimated these will net $12,000,000 annually for the schools and colleges, etc.

Bert Ennis Opens Office to Handle Advertising

Bert Ennis, director of Publicity for Roxy Theatres Corporation and Sawyer-Lubin productions will open his own office for the purpose of handling general advertising, including national campaigns for commercial as well as motion picture organizations.

Ennis will conduct campaigns for Roxy Theatres, Sawyer-Lubin, Standard-Radio Corporation of Worcester, Mass., and other concerns from this office.

In and Out of Town

DAVE BADER, who has been representing Carl Laemmle in arranging Universal Theatre Parties, is back in New York after a ten weeks' trip.

JACK KAMINSKY, of Films Kaminsky, Paris, has arrived in New York.

GUS Schlesinger, foreign manager for Warner Bros., has gone to Los Angeles, preliminary to a European trip on which he will start in three or four weeks.

I. E. CHADWICK is expected in New York about October 25. He will bring the master-print of "The Count of Luxembourg."

HARRY T. NOLAN, of Denver, was a prominent exhibitor visitor in New York this week.

SAMUEL GOLDWYN has arrived from the Coast to arrange for the Broadway opening of "Stella Dallas."

AMONG the arrivals from the Hollywood film colony were Reginald Barker and Sidney Olcott.

W. J. MORGAN, sales manager for Producers Distributing Corp., returned to New York this week after an extended trip.

Musicians Return to Wells Theatres in Norfolk

Musicians of Norfolk, Va., and the management of the Wells theatres there have come to an agreement on the terms originally offered by the Wells Company, thus ending a strike which left the Colonial, Academy, Norva, Wells and Strand theatres without orchestras. The musicians returned to work Monday and with them the operators and stage employees who had been ordered out by their national officials on Saturday night.

Under the new agreement leaders draw $65 a week; men, $47.50, with the understanding that the Wells Company may employ any number of men when and where desired. Details regarding wage scales at combination houses, organists, pianists, etc., are to be entered in a formal agreement which the union is to present soon.

New Incorporations Week in New York State

Newly incorporated motion picture companies, chartered by the secretary of state, during the past week, included the following, the names of the directors and the amount of capitalization, when stated, being given: Beerbohm Corporation, $15,000, Harold P. Seligson, Edward S. Silver, Susanne Johnston, New York city; Chippewa Theatre Corporation, Joe Hart, Corona, L. I.; George Blake, Brooklyn; Edward M. Fay, Providence, R. I.; Craig's Wife, Inc., $1,000, Edward J. Clarke, Charles Berg, I. C. Weisman, New York city; George McFarlane Productions, E. C. Rafferty, Cecil Keller, Mae M. Lipp, New York city; Chester Beecroft Productions, Inc., $100,000, Henry E. Stohldreier, Esther Cohn, Edward Lemberger, New York city.

Film Golfers Have Great Session

Christie Deibel of Youngstown Gets Low Score at Fall Tournament Held on the Winged Foot Links

WITH ideal weather conditions, a perfect course over which to play and a "million dollar" club house for the banquet, the annual Fall golf tournament of the film industry, held Tuesday at Mamaroneck, N. Y. on the Winged Foot links, may be set down as another successful day's outing for the industry.

The attendance was not as large as in former events, owing no doubt to the holiday of Monday, but this probably added somewhat to the golfer's pleasures the two courses accommodating all those who desired to play without crowding. The banquet in the evening completed the schedule of the day's proceedings.

At this function, Christy Deibel, prominent exhibitor of Youngstown, O., acted as temporary toastmaster introducing E. A. Eschman of First National who finished the evening in this capacity.

The prize winners were announced by Mr. Eschman as follows:

Low net (Reuben Samuels Cup) by T. C. Young with a score of 75.

Low net runner-up (Pathe Exchange Cup) by Mitchell May at toss of coin with Walter Scheiber. Score, 77.

Low gross (Warner Bros. Cup) by Chris Deibel, with a score of 88.

Low gross runner-up (M. P. News Cup) by E. F. Curtis with a score of 91.

Leg on THE FILM DAILY Cup by Chris Deibel with a score of 88.

Jules Mastbaum Cup for lowest exhibitor score by Chris Deibel with a score of 88.

F. B. O. Cup for birdie by Walter Scheiber after toss of coin to decide between Scheiber, Paul H. Cohen, William H. Rabell and E. P. Curtis.

Carl Laemmle Cup for putting by Earl W. Hammons.

J. P. Muller Placque offered as special New York exhibitor prize by Harry Brandt after toss of coin on tie with Bernard Edulhertz.

Class A—range 70-100 (Watterson R. Rothacker Cup) by William H. Rabell with score of 92.

Class B—range 101-120 (Arthur W. Stebbins Cup) by Arthur S. Kane with score of 105.

Class C—range 121-170 (Jack Cosman Cup) by Hy Gainsboro with score of 121.

Winners of foursomes: Pat Garyn, Paul II. Cohen, G. E. Berry, W. K. Scott, Harry Brandt, Jacobo Glucksmann, Arthur Hirsh, Lee Gainsboro, Jack Kreh, George Wilson, Elmer Pearson, J. V. Ritchey, A. L. Pratchett, G. H. Oliphant, J. S. Dickerson, Bill Nolan, Dan W. Fish, F. W. Crosbie, Arthur G. Whyte, Walter Scheiber, Lee A. Ochs, D. J. Chatkin, E. P. Curtis, Earl W. Hammons, Stanley Hand, Kenneth Harris, E. A. Golden, C. C. Griffin, S. R. Burns, W. B. Frank, Gene Picker, Louis Brock and Mr. Casey.

Runners-up in their foursomes: Henry Creske, Arthur Brilant, Hyman Winik, Lou Geller, Eugene Hatscheck, Albert Sawtell, Nat G. Rothstein, John Theiss, Eddie Eschmann, John S. Spargo, Samuel Rubenstein, W. Scott, Richard Anderson, E. L. Smith, John Humm, Walter Futter, Chester F. Sawyer, Cy Fields, Joe Hornstein, W. F. Clarke, Mitchell May, Lon Young, Bobby North, Joe Miles, H. M. Scully and Messrs. Cummings, Mitchell, Bunn and Wheeler.

The duffers prize went to Jess Gourlay with a score of 168. Official handicapper Bruce Gallup of First National announced during the awarding of the prizes that there was a remarkable improvement in the skill of the golfers as a whole since the last tournament when high scores of 200 and over were made.

Mr. Gallup was the recipient of an extra prize, a silver cocktail shaker, donated by J. P. Muller. This award was by acclamation and a fine tribute to Mr. Gallup and recognition of his hard work during the many film tournaments of the past.

The Muller Agency donated a prize for the last tournament that was not awarded on account of the weather conditions and also had a new prize for Tuesday's event. The committee had decided to hold the latter over for a next competition but when Frank Hughes insisted that it be awarded it was decided to present it to Mr. Gallup.

98 Charters Issued In September

$422,473,961 is Capital Represented in Corporations Filing Papers During Month; Period Shows Slight Decline

A SLIGHT decline in the number of companies seeking charters to engage in all branches of the film industry is noted in the records for the month of September, according to a survey by The Film Daily, which reports that 98 companies, representing a total capital of $422,473,961, filed papers during that period.

The number of charters filed, the report continues, is the lowest since February, which had 86, although the amount of capital listed in September greatly exceeds that of the last two months.

Since Jan. 1, 1,346 companies were formed to do business in the industry, with a total active capital of $422,473,961. It is expected that the figure will exceed half a million by the end of the year. All of the 1,346 units formed since Jan. 1st do not, however, represent $422,473,961, because 403 listed capital stock instead of active capital. This means that only 943 companies listed by only 943 companies. A resume of corporate activity for the nine months of this year follows:

Month	No. of Co.	Capital	Not listing Capital
January	160	$68,809,000	154
February	86	21,941,00	23
March	228	36,946,440	63
April	115	42,582,500	30
May	233	29,010,721	14
June	135	108,640,300	34
July	146	27,591,000	42
August	145	31,991,000	51
September	98	62,656,000	33
Totals	1,346	$422,473,961	403

Several large corporations were chartered, most of them in Delaware. The Cine Manufacturing Corp. recorded the highest capital in September, $25,000,000. This is the third largest corporation, in point of capital, formed this year. The largest is North American Theatres, with a capital of $55,000,000, and next, Universal Pictures Co., Inc., with $32,000,000. Both are Delaware corporations. Following is a list of those units chartered in September with a capital of $1,000,000 or over:

Company	Capital	State chartered
Cine Mfg. Corp.	$25,000,000	Del.
Color Cinema Prod.	14,000,000	Del.
Far West Theatre Corp.	6,000,000	Del.
Northwest Theatre Cir.	4,751,000	Del.
Far West Theatre, Inc.	4,800,000	Del.
Assoc. Realty Operators.	2,350,000	Del.
Hansen Theatres, Inc.	1,000,000	Del.
San Fran. M. P. Corp.	1,000,000	Calif.
Schumann Heink Corp.	1,000,000	Del.

New York, as usual, leads in the number of companies formed. Delaware is first in the amount of capital listed. New York granted charters to 48 companies. In the latter classification, Delaware is second, with 20 new units, and California third, with nine. The Delaware charters listed $55,171,600 in capital, California is second listing $5,880,000 and New York, third, with $948,000. Twenty-two of the New York companies listed capital instead of active capital.

Two companies were chartered in England, and one in France. Below is a list of the September corporations, by states and countries:

State	No. of Co.	Capital	Not Listing Capital
Arkansas	1	$25,000	
California	9	5,880,000	2
Connecticut			1
Delaware	20	55,171,600	
Illinois	1	8,000	
Mississippi	1	1,200	
Missouri	1	31,000	1
New Jersey	7	575,000	2
New York	48	948,0 0	22
Ohio	3	11,000	
South Carolina	1	10,000	
Wyoming	1		
England	2		1
France	1		
Totals	98	$62,656,800	33

Fifteen Picture Theatres in Bombay

There are fifteen picture theatres in Bombay that might be placed in the first class, for India, states American Consul Wilbur. Keblinger, Bombay, India, in a recent report released by the Department of Commerce. These theatres, the report states, are comfortable in every way,.

Pictures dealing with the wild west in America were formerly exceedingly popular, but the craze for this type has somewhat subsided. Plays involving serious social problems are not generally liked and draw but small crowds.

M. de MIGUEL HERE

To Film "Don Quixote" in Spain

BRINGING with him a print of "Pedrucho" ("The Bull-Fighter"), filmed in Spain, M. de Miguel, pioneer Spanish distributor and producer, arrived in New York this week. This is from a story by the Duke of Tovar, and was filmed on his ranch. Senor de Miguel has already placed this in France, Germany, Italy and England.

He also announced upon his arrival that his company would film an elaborate version of the immortal novel, "Don Quixote," by Cervantes, which has been translated into more than sixty languages. This will be photographed in the actual settings of the story, with the co-operation of the Spanish government. An American director and cameraman, and perhaps an American star, are being considered for this.

Senor de Miguel is a pioneer in Spanish film circles, having been the distributor there of such pictures as "The Birth of a Nation," "Intolerance" and "Hearts of the World." His company, Repertorio M. de Miguel, the slogan of which is "La Aristocracia del Film," has offices in Barcelona, Madrid, Seville, Valencia, Bilbao, Paris, France, and Buenos Aires, in South America. He will arrange for other pictures while here.

He has done important work in Spain in establishing the motion pcture among the better class people as president of the Spanish Society of the Friends of the Cinema. His last program received diplomas from the Royal Club of Spanish Authors and the Club of Beaux Arts. He was host to Douglas Fairbanks and Mary Pickford on their last trip to Spain.

Mayer Addresses Fire Chiefs on "Flames"

LOUIS B. MAYER, head of the Metro-Goldwyn-Mayer studios addressed the annual convention of 2,000 fire chiefs from the United States and Canada at their annual session held in Louisville, Kentucky, last week. Mayer outlined to them plans for the production of "Flames," by C. Gardner Sullivan, to be produced by Hunt Stromberg. The picture is to be produced in the interest of fire protection and with the cooperation of every fire department in America and Canada.

A percentage of the profits from the picture are pledged to the treasury of the International Association of Fire Chiefs to be used in the promotion of fire prevention work. The film will be built purely from an entertainment standpoint, however, and will in no sense be a preachment, although its message will be clearly evident.

Mayer was warmly received in Louisville by civic and fire department officials.

Omaha Wins Laemmle Trophy

Takes First Annual Competition for Sales Made During Summer Months

THE Carl Laemmle Sales trophy offered to the Universal exchange making the best sales showing during the Summer months has been awarded to the Omaha Exchange, managed by Harry Lefholtz. It will remain in the possession of the exchange for the coming year. This was the first annual competition for the trophy.

The sales drive for the Laemmle Trophy was based on this summer's results in comparison with a similar period in 1924. Omaha showed surprising form in taking high honors in the contest, that exchange not having won a prize in a Universal sales contest for several years. Determined effort on the part of Lefholtz and especial efficiency on the part of his force, brought the mid-west exchange up to a high state of excellence.

The main idea behind the Trophy contest was to supply added incentive for Universal exchanges to keep up their speed during the summer months, a period which in the opinion of Mr. Laemmle is the most important in the entire year.

The Laemmle Trophy was designed by Black, Starr & Frost, jewelers of New York

City. It is of silver and stands four feet high on an attractive marble base encrusted with silver filigree work. The design embodies the Universal globe with its saturn rings, surmounted by a silver figurette copied after the famous Nike statue of Victory.

Lefholtz's force consists of H. L. Craig, A. B. Seymore, B. R. Greenblatt, J. McBride, G. H. McCool, salesmen; W. H. Strickland, booker; Lowell Dollen, poster clerk; Jack Edwards, exploiteer; Helen Whitmore, assistant cashier; Regina Molseed, contract clerk; Edythe Knigge, biller; James Peterson, shipper; Estelle Maguire, secretary; Mildred Peterson, head inspector; and Cora Mortensen, Margaret Mortensen and Anna Mraskoski, inspectors.

Columbia May Increase 1926-7 Schedule

AS a result of an optimistic report made by David A. O'Malley, secretary of Columbia Pictures Corporation, Jack Cohn and Joe Brandt may decide to increase even further the Columbia program for 1926-7.

Mr. O'Malley has just returned from a six weeks' trip covering all the Columbia exchanges throughout the country.

As announced last week, independent distributors now handling Columbia pictures have laid definite plans for a national organization for the exclusive distribution of Columbia product. They will meet in New York the coming week to decide definitely on new policies.

Hollywood Physician Plans Career on Screen

Dr. Tolento Nardini, a practising physician of Hollywood who made his debut as a screen actor in "The Merry Widow," is playing another role in "Free Lips," a Norma Shearer starring vehicle for Metro-Goldwyn-Mayer now being produced under the direction of Hobart Henley. Dr. Nardini, who was given his first acting opportunity by Erich von Stroheim, has played several small parts since his work in the "Merry Widow" and plans to give up the medical practice for a career in the photoplays.

Constance Bennett is Under Contract to M-G-M

Constance Bennett, featured player in productions by various companies, has signed a contract to appear exclusively in Metro-Goldwyn-Mayer pictures. Miss Bennett is now playing the role of Irene in "Sally, Irene and Mary," which Edmund Goulding is directing at the Culver City studios.

Rayart President Off for Coast Conference

W. Ray Johnston, President of Rayart Pictures Corporation, and Dwight C. Leeper, Vice-President of Richmount Pictures, who distribute Rayart product abroad, left for the coast last week, where Johnston will confer with Rayart producers regarding the second group of the different Rayart pictures for 1925-26. There are six companies shooting on Rayart pictures at present.

While on the coast Johnston will assist Billy West in casting his second feature length comedy, and will go over with B. Berger of Gerson Pictures Corporation the continuity and casting of "The Last Alarm," an Arthur Hoerl story, and "The Coast Guard Patrol," both of which will be started immediately following the editing of the Picture, "The Midnight Limited," starring Gaston Glass and Wanda Hawley.

Herrick Filming Feature for Davis Company

F. H. Herrick has started production of "Keep It Up," a feature-length comedy drama from a story by Alma June Leaman, at the Tee-Art Studios in New York. The picture will be released by Davis Distributing Division with Elinor King in the starred role. Reginald Sheffield and Hugh Wilson head the supporting cast.

Herrick made the "Fragments of Life" series for the Davis company. He began his career in pictures as a camera man, later graduating to directorial work.

De Luxe Buys Columbia Product for Canada

The entire Columbia program for 1925-26 has been purchased for Canada by the Film de Luxe company of Montreal, which is handling Banner productions and several other important independent programs in that territory. The contract was negotiated by Charles Lalumiere for the de Luxe company and Joe Brandt and Jack Cohn of the Columbia organization.

Waxman Joins Goldwyn as Exploiteer

A. P. Waxman, well known press agent, has been engaged to assist in the handling of the local exploitation campaign for "Stella Dallas," Samuel Goldwyn's production directed by Henry King, during its run at the Apollo theatre in New York. Waxman will work as associate to Victor M. Shapiro, publicity and advertising director for the company.

Jaffe Feature is Edited by Frances T. Patterson

Frances T. Patterson, instructor of photoplay composition at Columbia University, has completed the editing of "Broken Hearts," the Jaffe Art Film in which Lila Lee is starred. The story deals with immigrant life in America and was directed by Maurice Swartz, director of several important European films shown in this country.

Conway is Directing "The Reason Why"

Jack Conway has started production on "The Reason Why," the screen adaptation of Elinor Glyn's popular novel to be offered by Metro-Goldwyn-Mayer with Aileen Pringle and Edmund Lowe in the leading roles. The adaptation was written by Carey Wilson.

Bob De-Lacy is to Direct Tom Tyler Feature

Bob De Lacy has been engaged to direct Tom Tyler's next starring vehicle for F.B.O. De Lacy recently completed "Let's Go Gallagher," Tyler's last picture.

Ramon Novarro in scenes from "The Midshipman," his new starring vehicle for Metro-Goldwyn-Mayer.

Fox Production Still Booming

Sheehan on Visit to Coast Finds Great Activity by Studio Units

WINFIELD R. SHEEHAN, vice-president and general manager of Fox Film Corporation, who recently returned from a three months' tour of Europe, arrived last week at the studios of the company in Los Angeles and found the production units engaged on one of the most active schedules ever essayed by the organization. With five units preparing to begin camera work on new features, four important productions in the cutting room and two now in active production, the Fox feature forces are at the height of a production 'boom that is unprecedented in the history of the company.

Tom Mix has just finished filming "The Best Bad Man" under the direction of J. G. Blystone, and is starting work on "My Little Pal." Tom's new picture is based on Gerald Beaumont's story, "The Gallant Guardsman." Lillie Hayward wrote the scenario, and Blystone will direct.

Frank Borzage's film version of "Wages for Wives" is ready for screening and is now busy on his plans for launching "The First Year," in which Matt Moore is cast for the leading male role.

With "The Silver Treasure," based on Joseph Conrad's novel, "Nostromo," in the cutting room, Rowland V. Lee is preparing to film "Daybreak," an adaptation of the stage success "The Outsider."

Victor Schertzinger has been assigned to direct "The Golden Strain," another outdoor picture. It is the first of the four Peter B. Kyne stories to be filmed by Fox this season. Madge Bellamy and Kenneth Harlan will play the leads, while Ann Pennington, Hobart Bosworth, Frank Beal and Lawford Davidson will contribute import-

ant roles. Eve Unsell wrote the adaptation. Much of the picture will be made in Arizona.

"The Golden Butterfly" will be directed by Griffith Wray. It is an original story by Evelyn Campbell dealing with the redemption of a young girl whose conniving father has taught her the world owes her a living.

Buck Jones at present is out on location filming "Her Cowboy Prince," his fifth Fox starring vehicle this season. It is a romantic drama of the old West. R. William Neill is directing.

Henry Otto is still busy with "The Ancient Mariner," which is to be presented as a special Christmas season release. Emmett Flynn will wield the megaphone on a new romantic drama now in the course of construction.

George Marshall, supervising director of Fox comedies, announced completion of "Hold Everybody," fourth of the Helen and Warren married life comedies directed by Albert Ray, and "The Brain Storm," an Imperial Comedy directed by Robert P. Kerr.

Fill Cast of "Nightie Night Nurse"

Warner Bros. have about completed the cast which will appear in "Nightie Night Nurse," Syd Chaplin's next feature for that company. Those who have been assigned principal roles are Patsy Ruth Miller, Gayne Whitman, Pat Hartigan, Edith Yorke, David Torrence, Raymond Wells, Henry Barrowes and Ed Kennedy. The picture is in production under the direction of Charles F. Reisner.

Release stills from "Blue Blood," a Chadwick Picture production starring George Walsh.

Highlight scenes from the Paramount production, "New Brooms."

Ingram Making Final Scenes for "Mare Nostrum"

Rex Ingram is making the final scenes for "Mare Nostrum," a picturization of the novel of that title by Ibanez which is being filmed in France for Metro-Goldwyn-Mayer. He recently completed scenes at Fregus, France, in and about the famous cathedral there, and then went to Marseilles, where the picturesque waterfront was used as the location for several important sequences.

Denny and La Plante in "Skinner's Dress Suit"

Reginald Denny and Laura La Plante will be co-starred in a screen version of "Skinner's Dress Suit," which Universal will produce under the direction of William Seiter.

Casting will be finished within a day or so and it is expected that production will begin next week.

Warners Lend Harlan and Louise Fazenda

Warner Bros. have loaned Kenneth Harlan to the Fox company for the leading masculine role in "The Golden Strain," and Louise Fazenda to Famous Players-Lasky for a featured part in "Hassan," to be produced by Raoul Walsh.

Jere Austin Joins "Her Cowboy Prince" Cast

Jere Austin has been added to the cast of "Her Cowboy Prince," Buck Jones' fifth starring vehicle for Fox. R. William Neill is directing the picture.

Five From F.B.O. Next Month

"The Last Edition" Included in Group: Program Also Offers Eight Short Subjects

F. B. O. has announced five features for release during November, the program also including eight short subjects. The feature line-up will be headed by "The Last Edition," Emory Johnson's photoplay dealing with the newspaper profession and one of the group of Gold Bond Productions this company has announced for the current season.

November first will bring the release of "No Man's Law," an Independent Pictures Corporation production starring Bob Custer; and a western melodrama starring Tom Tyler and as yet untitled.

"All Around Frying Pan," based on the magazine story by Frank R. Pierce, will serve as Fred Thomson's next, and will be distributed on November 8th. David Kirkland directed from his own continuity. Clara Horton, James Marcus, William Courtwright, John Lince, Monte Collins, Elmo Lincoln and Newton Barber support Thomson.

"The Last Edition," written by Emilie Johnson, the mother of the young director-producer, will be released on November 8. The cast is headed by Ralph Lewis, with Lila Leslie, Ray Hallor, Frances Teague, Rex Lease, Lou Payne, David "Red" Kirby, Wade Boteler, Cuyler Supplee, Leigh Willard and Will Frank in support.

The second Texas Ranger production, starring Bob Custer, as yet untitled, will be shown on November 29th.

The eight short subjects scheduled for November include:

" 'A Ton of Fun' in a Beauty Parlor," a Standard Fat Man comedy; a Bray Cartoon from the pen of Walter Lantz, as yet untitled; the fifth episode of "The Adventures of Mazie," starring Alberta Vaughn; the sixth Bray Cartoon, as yet untitled; "Hold Tight," a two-reel Blue Ribbon comedy; the sixth episode of "The Adventures of Mazie"; a Standard Fat Man comedy, as yet untitled; and the seventh release in the Bray Cartoon series.

Greta Nissen is Added to "Lucky Lady" Cast

Greta Nissen has been added to the cast of "The Lucky Lady," a Famous Players-Lasky production with Lionel Barrymore, William Collier, Jr., Marc MacDermott, Mme. Daumery and So Jin in principal roles. The story is by Robert E. Sherwood and Bertram Block. Raoul Walsh is directing.

Custer Starts the Eighth for F. B. O. Program

Bob Custer has started work on "No Man's Law," his eighth western feature being produced by Jesse Goldburg for F.B.O. release. The story is by Walter F. Coburn. William E. Wing wrote the scenario and Forrest Sheldon is directing.

A trio of scenes from "The Ancient Highway," a Paramount production.

Frances Marion Has Finished "Simon the Jester"

The final editorial touches have been put on "Simon the Jester" by Frances Marion, producer of the picture which is scheduled for release through Producers Distributing Corporation. This is the initial offering of Frances Marion Productions.

The picture is an adaptation of the William J. Locke story and was directed by George Melford under Miss Marion's personal supervision. The cast includes Eugene O'Brien, Lillian Rich, Edmund Burns, Henry B. Walthall, Mary McAlister and Billy Platt.

Ethel Shannon Lead in "The Phantom Express"

Ethel Shannon has been chosen for the leading role in "The Phantom Express," a Royal feature to be distributed by Henry Ginsburg Distributing Corporation. The picture, which will be the third in the Royal series, will be directed by John Adolfi. David Butler and Frankie Darrow are others who have been cast for important roles.

Bernie Hyman Signs With Metro-Goldwyn-Mayer

Bernie Hyman, formerly general manager of Phil Goldstone and of Tiffany Productions, has joined the Metro-Goldwyn-Mayer organization under a long-term contract recently signed. Hyman will serve in an editorial capacity, working with Irving G. Thalberg, associate studio executive.

Scenes from "The People vs. Nancy Preston"; Producers Distributing Corp.

Production highlights from the Paramount picture, "The Vanishing American."

F. P. L. Program 4 Months Ahead

Winter Schedule About Complete: Start Work On Productions For New Season

THE twenty-three productions which Paramount will release during October, November, December and January have been completed and the studio forces of Famous Players-Lasky are now engaged on preliminary work for pictures that will be offered during the new season.

Productions already finished and the months of release follow:

October—"A Regular Fellow," Raymond Griffith's comedy; "Golden Princess," with Betty Bronson; "New Brooms," the William De Mille picture; "Lovers in Quarantine," with Bebe Daniels, Harrison Ford and Alfred Lunt; "The Pony Express," the new James Cruze feature; and "Seven Keys to Baldpate," an adaptation of the George M. Cohan stage success starring Douglas MacLean.

November—"Flower of Night," starring Pola Negri; "The Best People," directed by Sidney Olcott; "The King on Main Street," directed by Monta Bell; "The Ancient Highway," directed by Irvin Willat; "Stage Struck," starring Gloria Swanson; and "Cobra," with Rudolph Valentino.

December—"That Royle Girl," a D. W. Griffith attraction; and "A Kiss for Cinderella," Paramount's production for Christmas featuring Betty Bronson and Tom Moore.

Completing the winter schedule are these productions on which production is well advanced:

December—"Irish Luck," starring Thomas Meighan; "Lord Jim," directed by Victor Fleming; "Womanhandled," a Richard Dix vehicle directed by Gregory La Cava, and a new Pola Negri production as yet untitled.

January—A new William De Mille attraction tentatively titled "Magpie"; "Manne-

quin," the Fannie Hurst prize story being directed by James Cruze; "Hands Up," another Raymond Griffith comedy; "The Enchanted Hill," directed by Irvin Willat; and "The American Venus," which Frank Tuttle is directing.

On the advance program the cameras are clicking on "Behind the Front," with Mildred Davis; "The Song and Dance Man," with Herbert Brenon directing; "Aloma of the South Seas," which will star Gilda Gray; "The Lucky Lady," with Greta Nissen, Lionel Barrymore, William Collier, Jr., and Marc MacDermott.

Associated Exhibitors Will Release "Under the Rouge"

Associated Exhibitors will release "Under the Rouge," one of the biggest productions of the current program, on October 18th. The story is by A. P. Younger and has a cast that includes Tom Moore, Eileen Percy, Mary Alden and William H. Tooker. It was directed by Lewis H. Moomaw. A special exploitation campaign for the picture has been laid out by Robert E. Welsh, director of advertising and publicity for Associated.

Hal Crane Joins Scenario Staff of M-G-M

Hal Crane, well known author of several vaudeville sketches, will turn his creative talents to scenario work, which he will enter as one of the staff writers at the Metro-Goldwyn-Mayer studios on the coast. Crane, who is now in New York, will leave for the coast soon to start work under his new contract.

Kosloff Added to Cast of "Time, the Comedian"

Theodore Kosloff has been added to the cast of "Time, the Comedian," the Kate Jordan story being produced by Metro-Goldwyn-Mayer under the direction of Robert Z. Leonard with Mae Busch and Lew Cody in the leading roles. Besides Kosloff the supporting cast includes Gertrude Olmsted, Rae Ethelyn, Creighton Hale, Robert Ober, Paulette Duval, Roy Stewart, David Mir, Nellie Parker Spaulding, Templar Saxe, Frank Elliott, Shannon Day, George Periolat, Lillian Langdon, Gertrude Bennett and Jacques Abbott.

Bobby Watson Joins "Song and Dance Man" Cast

Herbert Brenon has added Bobby Watson to the cast of "The Song and Dance Man," his latest Paramount picture which features Tom Moore, Bessie Love, Harrison Ford and Norman Trevor. Watson is now playing opposite George M. Cohan in the latter's new Broadway production, "American Born."

Al Santell Starts Second Kane Production

Alfred Santell has started production of "Seven Wives of Bluebeard," Robert Kane's second feature for First National distribution. The film is being made at the Cosmopolitan Studios, New York, with Ben Lyon, Blanche Sweet, Dorothy Sebastian, Diana Kane, Sam Hardy and Betty Jewell playing the principal roles.

Marion Davies in scenes from "Lights of Old Broadway," a Cosmopolitan production, for Metro-Goldwyn-Mayer.

Maude Adams in Picture Field

Will Produce Kipling's "Kim" in Association With Meador-Robertson Firm

J. E. D. MEADOR, President of Meador-Robertson Pictures Corporation, accompanied by Maude Adams, celebrated stage star, and Joseph P. Bickerton, Jr., Secretary and general counsel of the corporation, sailed last week for Europe to consult with Rudyard Kipling on the production of his masterpiece, "Kim," to which Miss Adams has the screen rights. The picture will be produced by Meador-Robertson, in association with Miss Adams.

Miss Adams is not to appear in the picture, but will lend her talents in aid of the production which will be made with the assistance of Kipling on the actual locales in India called for in the story. John S. Robertson will direct the production following the completion of "Queen Calafia," the first Meador-Robertson production, which is about to be started in Nice, France.

Before sailing, Meador said that John Russell, novelist and screen writer, and Llewellyn Totman, Meador-Robertson scenarist, will be associated editorially with the production of "Kim."

While Meador is abroad he will complete arrangements for the production of "Queen Calafia," Blasco Ibanez's popular book success which is to be made in Spain, Monte Carlo and France. The cast is soon to go abroad, as shooting is scheduled by Robertson for an early start.

Joseph P. Bickerton, Jr., attorney and producer planned to arrange for a number of conferences abroad with leading English novelists, playwrights, government officials, motion picture producers and directors. It is said a number of prominent British officials already are quite favorably inclined toward a Government subsidy and active participation in film producing enterprises on account of the recent strong agitation in London against the so-called American monopoly of the world's picture producing and exhibiting activities.

Successful maturity of the plans of Mr. Bickerton, it is claimed, would result in the functioning of an organization whose scope and magnitude of operations would match those of the foremost American companies.

Archainbaud Will Direct "Men of Steel"

First National has assigned George Archainbaud to direct the production of "Men of Steel," to be filmed as a special with Milton Sills, who is the author of the story, in the starred role.

Important sequences are to be made in the steel mills at Gary, Indiana, Pittsburgh, at the iron mines and the docks of the big ore steamers in Duluth. The cast which will support the star includes Doris Kenyon, May Allison, Victor McLaglen, Claude Gillingwater, George Fawcett and John Philip Kolb.

Warner Bros. Assign New Players to Casts

Warners have made additions to the casts of "The Cave Man" and "The Agony Column," forthcoming features now in production at the studios in Hollywood. Phyllis Haver, Hedda Hopper, John Patrick and Myrna Loy have been assigned to the cast which will support Matt Moore and Marie Prevost in "The Cave Man," a Gillette Burgess story. To date the cast of "The Agony Column" includes Monte Blue and Dorothy Devore, co-features, Charles Conklin, Myrna Loy, Helen Dunbar and Otto Hoffman.

Production stills from "A Kiss For Cinderella."—Paramount.

Carey Western is Titled "Fighting Stranger"

Pathe has decided upon "The Fighting Stranger" as the title for Harry Carey's first feature western to be released by the company. Charles R. Rogers is producing this new series of Carey features at Universal City. The first picture is an adaptation of "Buck Up," by Basil Dickey and Harry Haven. Harvey Gates made the adaptation and prepared the continuity and Scott Dunlap is directing. In the supporting cast are Harriett Hammond, Ruth King, James Farley, Stanton Heck, Bert Woodruff, Raymond Nye and Joseph Gerard.

Julanne Johnston Joins Gilda Gray Cast

Julanne Johnston has been signed by Famous for the principal supporting role to Gilda Gray in "Aloma of the South Seas." Miss Johnston, who scored as leading lady with Doug Fairbanks in "The Thief of Bagdad" only recently returned from Europe. She will sail this week with William Powell, Joseph Smiley and nineteen Samoan natives to augment the company which Director Maurice Tourneur has taken to Porto Rico for exteriors.

"Stella Dallas" Premiere At Apollo, New York

"Stella Dallas," the Samuel Goldwyn production directed by Henry King, will have its world premiere in New York on November 15, when it will open for an extended run at the Apollo Theatre. The picture will be presented at two performances daily. "Stella Dallas" is Goldwyn's first production for United Artists release.

Mabel Van Buren Returns in "Free Lips"

Mabel Van Buren, stage and screen star who has played many featured parts in photoplays, will return to the pictures after an absence of two years as one of the principal supporting players in "Free Lips," in which Metro-Goldwyn-Mayer will star Norma Shearer.

Warners To Release Four Features This Month

WARNER BROTHERS have named four features for release during October. Syd Chaplin, Marie Prevost, Irene Rich, Monte Blue and Patsy Ruth Miller carrying the starring honors of the program for the month.

"Bobbed Hair," screened from the novel written by twenty authors, was released October 10th with Marie Prevost, Kenneth Harlan, Louise Fazenda, Francis J. McDonald and others in the principal roles. Syd Chaplin in "The Man on the Box" is the second offering, scheduled for October 17th.

Third on the program is "The Pleasure Buyers," released October 24th, with Irene Rich starred and made from the novel by Arthur Somers Roche under the direction of Chet Withey. Monte Blue and Patsy Ruth Miller are co-starred in the release for October 31st, titled "Red Hot Tires" and filmed under the direction of Erle C. Kenton.

Weiss Bros. to Enter the Short Subject Field

WEISS BROS. will enter the short subject field with a program of comedies, novelties and serials, it is announced by Louis Weiss, head of the organization.

The company will distribute a program of shorts during the coming year, Mr. Weiss stated. "We have for some time been making tentative arrangements with a number of people with a view towards the production of several series of two reel comedies and serials and will make further and more definite announcement of our future plans as they materialize," he said.

Turpin Added to "Steel Preferred" Cast

Ben Turpin has been added to the cast of "Steel Preferred" and will team up with Charlie Murray to supply the comedy relief to the many tense situations in the picture. The cast is headed by Vera Reynolds, William Boyd, Hobart Bosworth, Walter Long, Helene Sullivan, Nigel Barrie and William V. Mong. James Hogan is directing. The picture will be released through Producers Distributing Corporation.

Weight and Travers Return From Location Trip

Harmon Weight and Douglas Travers of the Associated Arts Corporation, F.B.O. producers, returned to the Hollywood studios of the company after a location tour of six of the foremost oil fields in Southern California. Locations were found for two weeks of outdoor shooting on "Flaming Waters," a melodrama of the oil fields, in which Mary Carr, Malcolm McGregor and Pauline Garon have the leading roles.

Tom Mix is Concluding "Best Bad Man"

Tom Mix is busy with the concluding scenes of "The Best Bad Man," his fourth starring vehicle of the season for Fox. It is an adaptation from the Max Brand story, "Senor Jingle Bells" and is being directed by J. G. Blystone. In the supporting cast are, Clara Bow, Cyril Chadwick, Paul Panzer and Judy King.

"Sea Horses" To Be Dwan's Next For Paramount

"Sea Horses," an adaptation from the novel by Francis Brett Young, will be Allan Dwan's next production for Paramount. The director will start camera work upon completion of the editing of "Stage Struck," Gloria Swanson's new feature on which he is now engaged.

Burr Completes Cast for Johnny Hines

C. C. Burr has completed the cast that will support Johnny Hines in "Rainbow Riley," the star's second picture for First National. In the principal roles will be Brenda Bond, as leading woman, J. Barney Sherry, Dan Mason and Bradley Barker. The exteriors are being made at Delaware Water Gap under the direction of Charles Hines.

Universal Production at Top Speed

Universal is making rapid progress with its feature productions. Two have just been completed, three are nearing completion and six others are to be put into work within the next two weeks. Edward Sloman has finished directing "His People," in which Rudolph Schildkraut and Rosa Rosanova are featured. "Stella Maris" has been finished with Mary Philbin in the starring role and Elliott Dexter playing opposite her.

The three pictures nearing completion are, "The Midnight Sun," a Dimitri Buchowetzki production; "Two Blocks Away," a Harry Pollard picture, and the untitled western being directed by Edward Sedgwick. The productions soon to get under way are, "Skinner's Dress Suit," starring Reginald Denny; "Wives for Rent," "The Brute," with House Peters; "The Big Gun," "The Perch of the Devil," starring Louise Dresser, and "Under Western Skies," starring Norman Kerry.

Jack Hoxie to Make "The Overland Trail" Next

Jack Hoxie, Universal Western star, will make "The Overland Trail," a romance dealing with the Black Hills gold rush as his next feature for that company. The leading feminine role will be played by Ena Gregory, recently signed to a long-term contract by Universal, and Francis Ford will appear in the heavy role.

Frank McGlynn Jr. Added to Fox Cast

Victor Schertzinger has added Frank McGlynn, Jr. to the cast of "The Golden Strain," which he is directing for Fox. It is an adaptation of the Peter B. Kyne story, "Thoroughbreds," which was published in the Cosmopolitan Magazine. Madge Bellamy, Kenneth Harlan, Ann Pennington and Hobart Bosworth play the important roles.

Dramatic episodes from "The Blackguard," a Lee-Bradford release.

First National Busy in East
Production in New York is Gaining
Momentum After Temporary Let-Down

PRODUCTION at the New York studios of First National will be going at top speed in a short time following a temporary let-down recently to permit the scenario department opportunity to catch up with the producing units, according to advices from Earl Hudson, supervisor of the eastern division of the company's studio organization.

"Men of Steel" will be the first picture to start. This will go into production between the 15th and 25th, according to present plans. The United States Steel Corporation has agreed to cooperate with First National in filming this picture. Milton Sills wrote the original story and will be seen in the starring role. George Archainbaud has been selected to direct. Doris Kenyon, May Allison, Claude Gillingwater, George Fawcett, Victor McLaglen and John Philip Kolb will comprise the principal players in this supporting cast.

Meanwhile work is being rushed for the starting of half a dozen other pictures which will be placed in production as rapidly as space at the studios will permit. Scenarios are being prepared by Olga Printzlau, John Fish Goodrich, Charles Whittaker, Jane Murfin and Harvey Thew.

John Goodrich is working on the script of "Men of Steel." Olga Printzlau is doing the script for "Pals First," which was first written as a novel by Francis Perry Elliot. Jane Murfin and Charles Whittaker are working together on the adaptation of "The Savage," an original story by Ernest Pascal. Harvey Thew is writing the script for "The Boss of Little Arcady," an adaptation of Harry Leon Wilson's magazine story. Earl Snell and C. L. Yearsley are writing the adaptation of "Mismates," the Myron C. Fagan play, and Jack Jungmeyer and Joseph Poland are working on another script not yet announced.

Kane Starts Second Production
Now Casting "Seven Wives of Bluebeard."
His Newest Feature for First National

WITH "The New Commandment," a screen adaptation of Frederick Palmer's novel "Invisible Wounds," completed, Robert T. Kane has started casting "Seven Wives of Bluebeard," his second production for First National release. At the same time, Mr. Kane has announced that "The Reckless Lady," one of the year's best sellers, has been selected as the fourth picture in the group which he will make this season.

"The New Commandment" was adapted for the screen by Howard Higgin and Sada Cowan. The cast assembled to interpret the characters in the Palmer story are Blanche Sweet, Ben Lyon, Effie Shannon, George Cooper, Pedro De Cordova, Diana Kane, Betty Jewell, Holbrook Blinn and others.

Katherine Ray, one of the featured beauties of Earl Carroll's "Vanities" has been engaged to play one of the wives in "Seven Wives of Bluebeard," which is to be directed by Alfred Santell. Other principals in the picture will be Blanche Sweet, Diana Kane, Dorothy Sebastian, Lucy Fox, Lois Wilson, Betty Jewell and Ben Lyon.

"The Reckless Lady," Mr. Kane's fourth production, will be based on a novel of the same title by Sir Philip Gibbs. It will be filmed at Kane's studios in New York. Production will be started following the completion of Michael Arlen's "The Dancer from Paris," which Kane will produce following "Seven Wives of Bluebeard."

Brooks Deserts Stage for De Mille Studio

Alan Brooks, actor and playwright, recently added to Cecil B. De Mille's personal staff has deserted the stage for pictures, where he thinks the possibilities for development far exceed those of the stage. Brooks has been given a roving commission with De Mille, in order that he may become acquainted with the various phases of studio work, before it is decided whether his dramatic ability or literary talent is to be capitalized.

At present Brooks is an interested spectator at the various conferences held on "The Volga Boatman," which will be De Mille's next personally directed production for release through Producers Distributing Corporation.

Four From First National Are Completed

Completed prints on "The New Commandment" and "The Beautiful City" are expected this week at the home office of First National Pictures. The former is Robert Kane's initial production for this company and the latter is Inspiration's new Richard Barthelmess feature.

Domestic negatives on "We Moderns," starring Colleen Moore, and "The Scarlet Saint," featuring Mary Astor and Lloyd Hughes, are due to be shipped about the middle of the month. Sam Rork's production, "Clothes Make the Pirate," starring Leon Errol, and John M. Stahl's "Memory Lane," will soon emerge from the cutting room.

Sam Sax Leaves for Coast Studios of Gotham

Sam Sax, president of Lumas Film Corp. and producer of Gotham Productions, is on his way to the studios in Los Angeles to complete details for the four remaining pictures on this year's schedule of Gotham. The pictures which remain to be filmed are "Hearts and Spangles," "Racing Blood," "The Speed Limit" and "The Sign of the Claw," in which "Thunder" the dog actor will be starred.

M-G-M Buys Screen Rights to "Altars of Desire"

The photoplay rights to "Altars of Desire," by Maria Thompson Davies, have been acquired by Metro-Goldwyn-Mayer and the work will be assigned to the company's scenario staff for adaptation soon. The screen version will be made on an elaborate scale, it is announced.

Maurice Costello is Now Warner Director

MAURICE COSTELLO, once popular screen idol, is to return to the pictures with Warner Brothers in the role of a director. His first directorial effort for Warner will be with his daughter, Dolores, as the star. The picture is "Maryland, My Maryland," a J. Stuart Blackton production.

Production work on the picture is to start almost immediately. In addition to Miss Costello the cast includes: John Harron, Otto Matieson, Sheldon Lewis and Tyron Power.

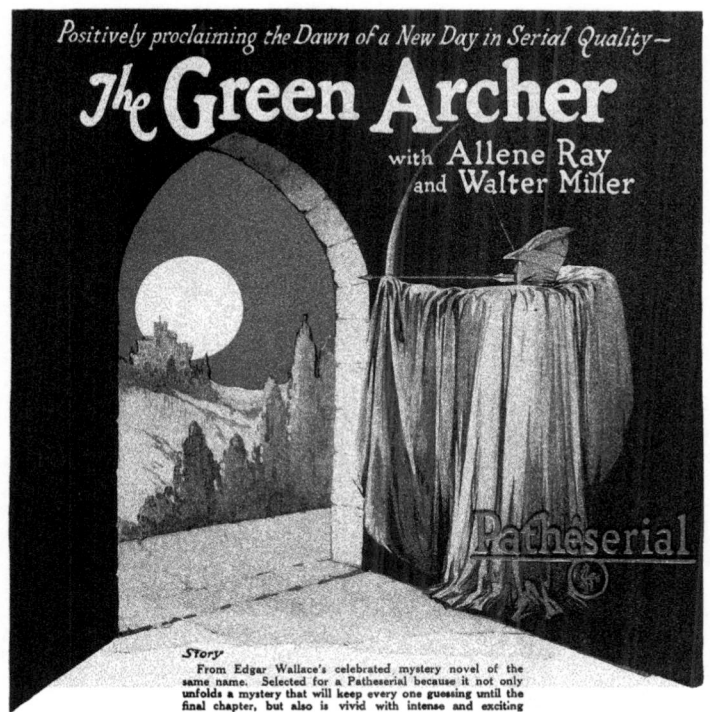

Positively proclaiming the Dawn of a New Day in Serial Quality—

The Green Archer

with Allene Ray
and Walter Miller

Pathéserial

Story

From Edgar Wallace's celebrated mystery novel of the same name. Selected for a Pathéserial because it not only unfolds a mystery that will keep every one guessing until the final chapter, but also is vivid with intense and exciting action.

Production

Absolutely strikes a new high note in serial production. In sets, mounting photography and locations EQUAL TO THE FINEST FEATURES.

Cast

In addition to the featured stars, Burr McIntosh, Frank Lackteen and a half dozen other unusually capable players are in the cast. THE ACTING IS ABOVE CRITICISM.

Direction

One hundred per cent in every respect, by Spencer Bennet. JUDGE IT FOR YOURSELF. JUST SEE IT—THAT'S TO YOUR INTEREST.

Scenario by FRANK LEON SMITH

Charlie

A

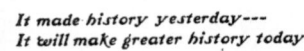

It made history yesterday---
It will make greater history today

Back in the days of the General Film, Chaplin was the surest box-office bet in the business. Even then he was the great outstanding figure of motion pictures. Even then they called out the police reserves when his latest was shown.

When the old Mutual Film Co. signed him on at unheard of figures, the whole business winked wisely and said, "Great as he is, WHO can make money at such prices?" But exhibitors cleaned up and made extraordinary profits—and so did Mutual.

Then came First National looking for a sure fire attraction. They signed Chaplin for one million

Chaplin

dollars for eight two reel pictures. Again the wise men shook their heads and grinned. Again exhibitors and distributors were amazed at the records hung up.

Chaplin has been away from the screen for three years. The boys and girls who saw Chaplin in "A Dog's Life" are seven years older, and have forgotten that picture. But they have not forgotten Chaplin. He has come back greater than ever, and the multitudes fight to see his latest feature. They will all want to see his big successes of the past.

SO PATHE PAYS A HALF A MILLION FOR THE PRIVILEGE OF RE-PRESENTING HIS FIRST FOUR PICTURES UNDER HIS FIRST NATIONAL CONTRACT.

Chaplin is Chaplin.

And "A Dog's Life," released November 22, is one of the greatest pictures he has ever made, a surer money-getter today than when Broadway and Main Street fought to see it!

Coming
during the season of 1925-6 in

the

Pathecolor

American Colleges in Pathecolor; American National Parks in Pathecolor; American Poetry in Pathecolor; Flower Studies in Pathecolor; Foreign Scenics in Pathecolor.

The above represent a rare treat for every house that wants the very best in quality "shorts." Pathecolor is truly incomparable.

Travel

THE BEEBE EXPEDITION to the Sargasso Sea; the exclusive story in pictures of the Scientific Expedition which has aroused wide interest.

Science

THE MAGIC EYE; the marvels of the world that are hidden to the naked eye. Wonderful pictures taken through a microscope.

ARCTIC EXPLORATION; with Knud Rasmussen in the uncharted wilderness of Greenland, Canada and extreme Northern Alaska.

DE PROROK EXPEDITION; exclusive pictures of the uncovering of the lost cities of North Africa.

Build your own home

A series of great practical and universal interest, showing how to build the home you desire at a cost within your means. Taken in co-operation with Secretary of Commerce Hoover.

Novelty

Continuing examples of the marvellous work of Alvin Knechtel's new Process Camera.

The above represents only a part of the subjects ready for the coming season. Every audience will enjoy every number of Pathe Review.

ONE REEL EVERY WEEK

Exhibitors Service Bureau

Manager F. J. Miller of the Modjeska theatre, Augusta, Ga., prepared a striking lobby display, specially painted, as shown here for the engagement of "The Freshman" (Pathe). A portrait of Lloyd as the college youth, colored pennants, and so on, made up the display.

Advisory Board and Contributing Editors, Exhibitors' Service Bureau

George J. Schade, Schade theatre, Sandusky.

Edward L. Hyman, Mark Strand theatre, Brooklyn.

Leo A. Landau, Lyceum theatre, Minneapolis.

C. C. Perry, Managing Director, Garrick theatre, Minneapolis.

E. R. Rogers, Managing Director, Tivoli theatre, Chattanooga, Tenn.

Stanley Chambers, Palace theatre, Wichita, Kan.

Willard C. Patterson, Metropolitan theatre, Atlanta.

E. V. Richards, Jr., Gen. Mgr., Saenger Amusement Co., New Orleans.

F. L. Newman, Managing Director, Famous Players-Lasky theatres, Los Angeles.

Arthur G. Stolte, Des Moines theatre, Des Moines, Iowa.

W. C. Quimby, Managing Director, Strand Palace and Jefferson theatres, Fort Wayne, Ind.

J. A. Partington, Imperial theatre, San Francisco.

George E. Carpenter, Paramount-Empress theatre, Salt Lake.

Sidney Grauman, Grauman's theatres, Los Angeles.

THE CHECK-UP

Weekly Edition of Exhibitors' Box Office Reports

Productions listed are new pictures on which reports were not available previously.

For ratings on current and older releases see MOTION PICTURE NEWS—first issue of each month.

KEY—The first column following the name of the feature represents the number of managers that have reported the picture as "Poor." The second column gives the number who considered it "Fair"; the third, the number who considered it "Good"; and the fourth column, those who considered it "Big." The fifth column is a percentage giving the average rating on that feature, obtained by the following method: A report of "Poor" is rated at 20%; one of "Fair," 40%; "Good," 70%; and "Big," 100%. The percentage rating of all of these reports on one picture are then added together, and divided by the number of reports, giving the average percentage—a figure which represents the consensus of opinion on that picture. In this way exceptional cases, reports which might be misleading taken alone, and such individual differences of opinion are averaged up and eliminated.

TITLE	Poor	Fair	Good	Big	Value	Length
FAMOUS PLAYERS						
Coast of Folly, The	—	2	10	1	68	6,840 ft.
Son of His Father, The	—	3	7	—	61	7,009 ft.
Wild Horse Mesa	—	5	11	2	65	7,221 ft.
Wild, Wild Susan	2	5	8	3	60	5,774 ft.
FIRST NATIONAL						
Shore Leave	—	—	8	4	80	6,856 ft.
FOX						
Iron Horse, The	—	1	6	5	80	11,335 ft.
UNITED ARTISTS						
Gold Rush, The	—	1	2	9	96	6,500 ft.

George E. Brown, Managing Director, Loew's Palace theatre, Memphis, Tenn.

Louis K. Sidney, Division Manager, Loew's theatres, Pittsburgh, Pa.

Geo. Rotsky, Managing Director, Palace theatre, Montreal, Can.

Eddie Zorn, Managing Director, Broadway-Strand theatre, Detroit.

Fred S. Myer, Managing Director, Palace theatre, Hamilton, Ohio.

Joseph Plunkett, Managing Director, Mark-Strand theatre, New York.

Ray Grombacher, Managing Director, Liberty theatre, Spokane, Wash.

Ross A. McVoy, Manager, Temple theatre, Geneva, N. Y.

W. S. McLaren, Managing Director, Capitol theatre, Jackson, Mich.

Harold B. Franklin, Director of Theatres, Famous Players-Lasky.

William J. Sullivan, Manager, Rialto theatre, Butte, Mont.

H. A. Albright, Manager, T. D. & L. theatre, Glendale, Calif.

Claire Meachine, Grand theatre, Westfield, N. Y.

Ace Berry, Managing Director, Circle theatre, Indianapolis.

See Complete "Check-Up" November 14

"A Woman's Faith" Given Canadian Campaign

"A Woman's Faith" at the Victoria theatre, Quebec, was given an unusually strong campaign. Since most of the action is laid near Quebec with the climax coming at the famous shrine of Ste. Anne de Beaupre, the theatre put up posters in French calling attention to this feature.

The engagement was started off by a special screening in the ballroom of the famous Chateau Frontenac at which many notables of the city were represented, including Justice Choquette. This is the first time that any picture has been permitted to be shown in the ballroom.

Slides were used ten days in advance; 5,000 heralds were mailed in house to house distribution; 500 half sheet window cards were taken, and a tie-up with the Chevrolet company put a car on the street three days ahead of the picture. Ten 24-sheets, 50 1-sheets, ten 3-sheets and five sixes were posted making an exceptional billing.

A drug store gave a window through the shaving soap angle. Marmont is seen shaving in the picture with a certain brand of soap. The window card read: "Even in the woods Williams Shaving cream is supreme. See it in A Woman's Faith at the Victoria theatre, Sunday, Monday and Tuesday."

Wrecked Auto in Street to Aid "The Lucky Devil"

The strongest selling unit of Manager Chas. F. Morrison's campaign on "The Lucky Devil," playing the Imperial, Jacksonville, was a wrecked Nash sedan loaned by a local garage.

With permission of the Police department, the car with its top and one side badly smashed was placed in the safety zone in front of the theatre, facing West. The mere fact that car was on wrong side of street aroused much comment. A large banner was placed on auto reading:

"Turned turtle twice and not a scratch on him—Wasn't he The Lucky Devil. See Richard Dix inside in the Paramount Picture of the same name."

Dramatic lobby, showing a scene from "Don Q" (United Artists), by Manager D. Roscoe Faunce of the Strand theatre, Birmingham.

"Don Q" Campaign Aimed at College Students

The strongest selling unit of Manager E. B. Roberts' campaign for "Don Q" at the Majestic theatre, Austin, was the direct appeal made to Texas University students.

On the opening day of the picture, which was also registration day at the University, lemonade was served to the students with the compliments of "Don Q." They were also handed an extra edition of theatre's Close-Up, printed in red ink, and accompanied by a telegram from F. P.'s' district manager stating that regular prices would prevail on this attraction.

The lemonade stunt met with such success that it was repeated later in the week at the first University rally, attended by approximately 5,500 people. At this meeting a telegram was read from Douglas Fairbanks in which he conveyed his best wishes to the entire student body.

The outstanding feature of the lobby display was a seventy-five foot announcement sign across marquee top.

Ticket Selling Tie-up is "Old Home Week" Stunt

A novel feature of manager J. P. Harrison's campaign for "Old Home Week" at the Hippodrome, Waco, was the advance sale of tickets for the attraction.

The United Daughters of the Confederacy handled this angle of the campaign on a percentage basis, selling tickets five days in advance of opening. They had booths in the largest department drug store in the city. Over each booth was a large card announcing the picture and urging that tickets be purchased in advance in order to secure good seats.

In the lobby was an old fashioned home set back on a green lawn with a small window cutout with a sign, advising passers-by to look inside. Upon satisfying their curiosity their read: "Thomas Meighan in his greatest picture 'Old Home Week.'" Though an old stunt, it worked to good advantage on this attraction, arresting the attention of many who passed the theatre.

A special prologue augmented the usual program. This was composed of a jazz orchestra of local chaps dressed as country boys who played rube selections. Their appearance met with a hearty reception at every performance.

Church Bulletin Exploits "As No Man Has Loved"

The Sept. 20th issue of the bulletin issued by the Church of The Redeemer, Newark, N. J., includes among its announcements, the following item. "Dr. Rose urges you to see 'As No Man Has Loved,' at the Fox Terminal theatre. It is a wonderful screen version of Edward Everett Hale's patriotic story: 'The Man Without A Country.'"

The Rev. Henry R. Rose, D. D., pastor of the Church of the Redeemer is well known as one of Newark's most public spirited and patriotic citizens. His inclusion of the picture notice among his regular parish announcements, was a splendid boost for the picture.

A cut-out from the 24-sheet on "The Coast of Folly" (Paramount) lent itself unusually well to use in this display, prepared by Don Nichols, manager of the Prais theatre, Durham, N. C., owned by Durham Amusement Company, Inc.

Keith Circuit Exploiting Pathe Short Subjects

The Keith-Albee circuit has launched a far-reaching advertising and exploitation campaign on Pathe comedies as a new feature of their big-time vaudeville programs. The lobbies and theatre fronts of the houses which are members of this circuit, now contain much of the regular publicity and accessories put out by Pathe and a great array of specially framed paintings and display material.

The comedy product is in the lights of the houses on his great circuit, in the newspaper advertising, window cards and special heralds, while exploitation stunts of various kinds are being used around the circuit to make known the fact that the comedies have a prominent spot on the vaudeville bills.

The big New York Hippodrome staged what is one of the first prologues ever produced for a two-reel picture in connection with the showing of "Your Own Back Yard." The prologue was put on by Alan Foster, the Hippodrome's producer. Six of the Hippodrome's chorus girls and two of Paul Whiteman's musicians were in the attraction. Up stage was a cottage set with a fence. Along the fence were the girls in country dress, singing with the two boys, the latter seated upon a bench. The song was "Stay In Your Own Back Yard," on which a special tie-up has been made between the Pathe exploitation department and the publishers. The Hippodrome intends to continue its prologue for the coming comedies.

"Your Own Back Yard" was played up in the Hippodrome lobby billing while a specially-painted announcement called attention of the patrons to the first run presentation of all the Hal Roach Pathe Comedies.

The Palace, New York's finest vaudeville theatre, has placed in the lobby a silver frame which will carry the black and white photos of the Pathe comedies. A large framed sign calls attention to the "Extra Added Comedy Feature" and lists the names of leading players in the various productions.

Decorated auto advertising "Lightnin'" (Fox) at the Strand theatre, St. Paul.

At the Bushwick theatre, in Brooklyn, the initial Pathe feature was ushered in with a special "Holiday Comedy Carnival." The first of the series of comedies played was "Your Own Back Yard," which was featured next to intermission.

At the Riverside, New York, "Our Gang" was given a prominent place in the list of vaudeville headliners while a comedy one-sheet was placed alongside the vaudeville billing on the theatre front. The opening scene of "Your Own Back Yard" was produced in the lobby. There was a back yard with a mechanical reproduction of the mammy of the picture washing clothes, a miniature cottage, fence, chickens, mule, goat, kids swinging on the gate, etc.

"Rainbow Trail" Sign Put in Repaired Street

Scottsbluff, Nebraska, may be considerably more than a stone's throw from the Great White Way, but its exploitation methods are not far behind Broadway's best.

The main street of Scottsbluff was recently treated to a new coat of asphalt, thereby closing the thoroughfare to all vehicular traffic, and isolating all theatres from the well known "carriage trade." This fact, however, did not deter Billy Ostenberg, Jr., from telling the world and particularly Scottsbluff that the Orpheum theatre which he manages would proffer "The Rainbow Trail."

"Goose Hangs High" Given Atmospheric Display

The lobby Manager H. J. Gould arranged for "The Goose Hangs High" at the Hippodrome, Fort Worth, was exceedingly nominal in cost.

The cottage used for "Welcome Home" was pressed into service, the house artist covering it with snow and icicles. A glass window was put in through which one saw a Xmas tree. On top of the cottage was a card reading: "The Goose Hangs High is a present day story of the American Family by James Cruze". This splendid display drew unusual attention.

Actionful Western Display for "Hurricane Kid"

For "The Hurricane Kid" at the Rex theatre, Sumter, Manager John Hannon arranged a lobby display which visualized the title.

Lobby was decorated with ropes, Western saddles, lariats, chaps, and so on. Suspended from ceiling was a six-sheet depicting Hoot Gibson on horseback trying to lasso a wild horse. A mounted three-sheet was also placed on either side of the lobby.

Loew's State theatre, Los Angeles, arranged for this window on "A Slave of Fashion" (Metro-Goldwyn) in one of the local Owl Drug company stores, which used a series of them on all prominent corners. Bob Locman, the theatre's publicity man, arranged with the studio to have Norma Shearer pose with Owl products.

Strong "Winds of Chance" Campaign in New York

"Winds of Chance" was booked for a two weeks' engagement recently at Warners theatre, New York City. Coincident with the opening date Frank Munsey's Evening Telegram commenced publication of the novel in serial form, preceded by an advertising campaign in its columns, stressing the importance of the author, the story and Frank Lloyd's film production of the same name.

Hearst's Daily Mirror, a pictorial tabloid, tied up with "Winds of Chance" on the first of the now popular "Lucky Deuce" contests, which proved to be a revelation to the newspaper world as a circulation builder. Daily stories were carried in the news columns of The Mirror illustrated with stills from the picture announcing that the "Lucky Deuces" would be handed out in change at the theatre box office.

This tie-up started four days before the opening of "Winds of Chance" and continued for fourteen days. The elements of chance and romance which figure so largely in this story of the Klondike lent themselves admirably to the tie-up. The Daily News, the other New York morning tab, also tied up with "Winds of Chance" in return for a theatre party for crippled kids—a pet charity of this newspaper.

A series of seven articles collectively labeled "Yukon Yarns," each a true story of the fortunes made in the Klondike, were prepared after exhaustive research by A. P. Waxman who handled the "Winds of Chance" campaign under the direction of Mr. Glenn. These seven articles totalling some ten thousand words were edited and approved by Mr. Beach who found it necessary to change but a few words in the entire series.

These "Yukon Yarns" written as preliminary press material for the publication of the serial story were carried in the Evening Telegram and have also been published in other cities, from coast to coast, serving their purpose of creating interest in the story and the picture by describing the true romantic stories of the sourdoughs and cheechakos who found fame and fortune in the frozen fastnesses of the Klondike.

We don't know the name of this fearsome looking animal posing with the dainty usherette, but it was used to exploit "The Lost World" (First National) with great effect at the Palace, San Antonio.

Bathing Beauties Ballyhoo "Fifth Avenue Models"

A Bathing Beauty and Model contest recently awakened much interest in the neighborhood of the Star theatre, Bronx, New York. The enterprising managers of the Star, Left and Begfichter, had more than one hundred girls in their contest, and as each beach beauty tripped across the stage, she carried a placard on the end of a gaily decorated stick giving advance notice on "Fifth Avenue Models." The winners of this contest were announced during the showing of the picture.

"Pop" Hartman, Big U's exploiteer, arranged for neighborhood dress shops to loan costumes for the amateur models. Each shop, of course, was credited with its apparel. Hartman also secured oil paintings of Universal stars and banners to decorate the lobby.

Tom Mix Hats Exploit Run of "Lucky Horseshoe"

The broad-brimmed Stetson hat which Tom Mix has made famous the world over, as part of his "cowboy dandy" attire, was used by the Kings theatre in St. Louis as an exploitation aid on "The Lucky Horseshoe."

Thousands of circulars were distributed broadcast through the city, bearing the following reading matter:

Win a $50 Tom Mix Hat Free. Five Tom Mix Stetson hats, the same as Mix presented to European royalty during his recent trip abroad, will be given away at the Kings absolutely Free. To win one, on the other side of this sheet—in 50 words or less—tell why Tom Mix is your favorite star. The best answer in each of these classes will win their writers a Mix hat; 1 to 6 years, 7 to 10, 11 to 15, 16 to 20, 21 to 60. Answers must be left at the Kings during the week Mix's "Lucky Horseshoe" is shown. Winners will be announced on the Kings screen during Circus week.

The balance of the sheet carried a brief sales talk on the picture, pictures of Mix and the hat, together with play date, etc. The back of the sheet was devoted to ruled space for the answer.

Incense Blown Onto Street for "Thief of Bagdad"

"The Thief of Bagdad," played the Galax, Birmingham, recently. In order to stimulate interest in the engagement, Manager Rodney Bush, in addition to his regular campaign, had a special display painted for the lobby.

The exhibit pictured Douglas Fairbanks flying over the city of Bagdad, with seven stills from the photoplay artistically arranged among the castles and clouds painted on the background. Illuminated by a spot light, the exhibit arrested attention.

A novel feature of the lobby display was the burning of incense in such a way that it was carried out on to the street by means of the ventilating fan. The exotic odor caused people to stop and eventually drew them into the lobby for a better look at the display.

Don Nichols, the enterprising manager of the Paris theatre at Durham, N. C., a Durham Amusement Company house, was responsible for this striking lobby display recently in connection with the engagement of "The Unholy Three" (Metro-Goldwyn).

"As No Man Has Loved" is Given Military Boost

When "As No Man Has Loved," played the Coliseum, Seattle, recently, the engagement took on all the aspects of a patriotic civic celebration, through the active participation of all the local military bodies, with parades and special performances. The first parade was staged a few nights after the opening, when the battleship Arizona arrived in the harbor. The officers and crew of the ship, responding to an invitation of the theatre management turned out in full force and marched to the theatre. A few nights later the full military personnel of Fort Lawton turned out in a body and saw the picture, and on another evening, the Marines from the Navy Yard barracks repeated the performance.

Other local military bodies that cooperated in the showing were the local posts of the American Legion, the G. A. R., the D. A. R., and the Boy Scouts. These organizations were tied in with the engagement through the medium of circular letters. The Scout bodies receiving heralds on the attraction through the mail with the official Scout organ.

The Superintendent of Schools in Seattle cooperated with the theatre to the extent of issuing with the daily circular that goes to Seattle's school-teachers, a request that the teachers urge their charges to see the picture. The students of the parochial schools were also circularized.

"East Lynne" Has Premiere in Cleveland

The world premiere of "East Lynne" took place recently at Keith's Palace theatre, Cleveland. The event was heralded by a very high class ballyhoo. Joe Shea, Fox publicity man, located an old fashioned surrey some forty miles out in the country. The double seated variety, with a cover that has a tan silk fringe all around it. You remember the kind. It is the kind that was very much in vogue at the time in which "East Lynne" is set.

A tandem bike in the lobby and an ancient gas buggy on the streets aided "Not So Long Ago" (Paramount) at Harry Gould's Hippodrome, Fort Worth, recently

Two very pretty young girls were secured who dressed up in Alma Rubens costumes,— the very costumes Miss Rubens wore when she made the picture, "East Lynne," which were shipped to Cleveland expressly for this ballyhoo. They rode in the back seat of the surrey, while two colored gentlemen, in cravats of fifty years ago, and wide brimmed silk high hats, occupied the front seat. This vehicle, horse drawn, of course, rode up and down Euclid avenue during the busy noon hour. It carried no sign. Nothing to indicate what it all was about. Crowds gathered on the curb to see a horse on Euclid avenue.

Crowds watched the girls being helped out of the surrey and going into a fashionable lunch room for refreshments. Traffic was impeded while the public asked who were the girls, and why were they appearing in these togs of their grandmothers. The second day that the vehicle appeared on the street, it carried a dignified banner, saying "East Lynne" was coming to the Palace.

Jungle Stage Setting for "Lost World" Showing

J. A. Jeffress of the Marshall theatre, Manhattan, Kans., conceived the idea for a weird and beautiful stage setting for "The Lost World," which gave his patrons something new to talk about.

Against a background of jungle, he placed cut-outs of the prehistoric monsters which appear in the photoplay, together with cut-outs of two of the human actors. As the curtain rose, the stage was illuminated with red and blue border and footlights. These were gradually dimmed until the setting was dark, with red and green spots and baby spots picking out the cut-outs. Thunder and lightning effects from back stage heightened the quality of weirdness inherent in the setting and the lighting.

The setting is one that can be duplicated at comparatively small expense by the exhibitor in any sized town. It is in keeping with the mood of the picture and will cause patrons to talk.

Brontosaurus is Oklahoma "Lost World" Boost

The brontosaurus which E. D. Brewer, First National's branch manager in Oklahoma City, had built to exploit "The Lost World" throughout the state of Oklahoma, has proved its value not only as a booster of First National, but as a ballyhoo for "The Lost World" at individual showings.

The huge, prehistoric animal is mounted on a Reo truck and is driven through the streets of the town where the photoplay is being shown.

For the second run of "The Lost World" in Oklahoma City, at the Empress theatre, the brontosaurus was called into play, and it attracted as much attention as a circus parade.

Manager J. F. Via of the Palace theatre, Blackwell, Okla., rented the brontosaurus for a street ballyhoo in his town with excellent results.

Advance lobby display, including a miniature locomotive and special art cards, for "The Iron Horse" (Fox) at the Majestic theatre, Little Rock, Ark., of which Gene Oliver is manager.

Strong Lobby Flash Given "Don Q" Engagement

Manager J. P. Harrison's campaign on "Don Q" at the Hippodrome, Waco, had many commendable features, one of which was his excellent lobby display.

Ticket window was encased in beaverboard painted with small "Don" in yellow and huge "Q" in red. Front of lobby was encased with beaverboard arch on which was painted the figure of "Don Q" brandishing a whip with a large "Q" at the end. The star's name appeared on banner in transparent lettering. The attention value of this brilliantly colored display was enhanced by the intermittent flashing of the whip and Q with the star's name.

Attached to side panels announcing the current program, were two crossed swords, such as used in the photoplay. These were donated to the theatre and provoked a lot of interest from passers-by. Special banner around marquee was done in red and yellow to correspond with balance of display.

Manager Harrison conceived a novel bally-hoo for the attraction by taking a Ford Chassis and encasing it in beaverboard with the figure of "Don Q," picture title, star's name, etc., done in the Spanish colors. Float was driven about town by a driver, who made periodic announcements through a bugle he carried. Both the week before and during the picture's showing, the bally attracted an unusual amount of attention.

Timely Cloudburst Boosts "Havoc" Engagement

It is not every exploitation man who can get an obliging cloudburst to come along and help exploit his picture, but that is what happened at Seattle, Washington, where the manager of the Liberty and the Fox exploitation representative sat down and tried to think up a new stunt for "Havoc."

Their deliberations were cut short by the news that the adjacent town of Wenatchee, had just been all but wiped out by a cloudburst. In fact the Seattle newsboys were already hawking extras on the streets.

Manager Bruce Fowler employed a dominating marquee display for "The Ten Commandments" (Paramount) at the Royal theatre, Kansas City, as pictured here.

shouting about the havoc wrought in Wenatchee. Then and there, an exploitation idea saw the light of day. It was but the work of a few minutes to despatch a still cameraman to the scene of the disaster, with instructions to shoot fast and furiously. The shots were made, the pictures developed in record time, and in twenty-five choice locations about Seattle, groups of people were gathered about the stills, and reading considerable about a picture called "Havoc" that was on its way to the Liberty.

"Sunshine" and "Carnation" bread, two Seattle products, also came forward and did their bit toward putting "Havoc" over, as 150,000 printed slips advising housewives to avoid the "Havoc" of home baking, etc., were wrapped up with the loaves.

"Avoid 'Havoc' In Your Filing Systems," was the slogan that sold the attraction to a local manufacturer of filing cabinets, and resulted in some exceptionally fine window tie-ups.

"Night Club" is Heralded at Wrestling Match

"The Night Club," playing recently at the Missouri, St. Louis, received some clever exploitation at the hands of Manager Herschel Stuart and Publicity Director William Saal.

At the Stecher-Zybysco match, which took place during the showing of this picture, a special crew of boys distributed 50,000 heralds announcing that "The Silk Hat King" was at the Missouri theatre in "The Night Club." This stunt was the means of successfully reaching a large number of potential patrons, the match drawing the largest attendance in the history of St. Louis.

Valuable publicity was also gained through the Wurlitzer company, who spent over a thousand dollars in advertising Barney Rapp and Band in conjunction with "The Night Club."

The regular newspaper and billing campaign was used, with 500 extra two-sheets.

Clever Lobby Display Aids "Learning to Love" Run

For his showing of "Learning to Love," Manager J. L. Cartwright of the Rialto, Chattanooga, conceived a unique display for the Rialto lobby which drew unusual attention.

This display conveyed the idea of a school where one could "learn how to love." In the center was a huge blackboard at top of which was a three-sheet cutout in the shape of a heart with the heads of Constance Talmadge and Antonio Moreno. Inscription on slate was along the lines of enrollment, with title, admission prices and performance hours cleverly tied-in. Three smaller boards were arranged on each side of the larger one, each carrying chalked copy of comedy lines indirectly tying-up with the picture.

A huge banner with the star's name and picture title was also placed directly above lobby doors.

The Liberty theatre's electrically illuminated lobby display in Portland, Ore., for the showing of "The Making of O'Malley" (First National).

Three More for Peggy Hopkins Joyce

Associated Exhibitors' Executives Enthuse Over Work of Star in "The Sky Rocket," Marshall Neilan's Production

SO pleased are the executives of Associated Exhibitors with the work of Peggy Hopkins Joyce in "The Sky Rocket," just completed under the direction of Marshall Neilan, that Miss Joyce will make three additional pictures for the company. Her second production, as yet unnamed, will be started on her return from Europe where she went last week for a rest of two months.

"The Sky Rocket," in which Miss Joyce made such a favorable impression on Associated officials, was written by Adela Rogers St. John and is based on the rise and fall of a movie star in Hollywood.

P. A. Powers, chairman of the Board of Directors of the Associated Exhibitors, was the first to see Miss Joyce's qualities as a film star. He thought enough of his convictions that he was willing to gamble a quarter of a million dollars on his judgment, it is said.

At this time Miss Joyce was appearing in a Broadway musical comedy at a high weekly salary and a percentage of the gross of the show. It took considerable financial coaxing on the part of Mr. Powers to lure Miss Joyce from the footlights, but finally this was accomplished and after getting the star's name to a contract the film magnate set about to find suitable story material.

In the course of seeking the right vehicle, over seven hundred plays, short stories, and novels were considered with the final selection of "The Sky Rocket," a book length novel which met with an overwhelming success in the Cosmopolitan Magazine.

Marshall Neilan was next engaged to direct the film, and without any fan-fare or red fire he surrounded himself with a strong supporting cast and quietly set about to make the picture. The complete absence of the circus type of publicity during the course of production was noted and commented on by the press all over the country.

But the big surprise, and a work of master showmanship on the part of Mr. Powers, came when Hollywood society primped itself up for the arrival of the beautiful Peggy Joyce, and Peggy didn't arrive. That is to say that Hollywood society saw little or nothing of the new star. The motion picture colony expected a series

Peggy Hopkins Joyce, star of "The Sky Rocket."
Associated Exhibitors release.

of Fourth of July celebrations and what they got was a "thunder of silence."

Even Los Angeles daily newspapers sat up and took notice. Reporters hit the trail to the studios where the Joyce picture was being filmed but very few of them saw the elusive Peggy and not a single one of them was able to interview her. It was really a masterful stroke on the part of the Powers organization.

While in Hollywood Miss Joyce was never seen at any of the public resorts and the Queen of England could not have been more carefully guarded.

With a star of unknown motion picture qualities on his hands and a story of which there couldn't be any doubt would make a successful screen drama, Marshall Neilan's next task was to find a cast that was sufficiently strong in name value and at the same time artists of ability to handle the parts.

The first two selected were Owen Moore and Earle Williams. These two stars have the outstanding parts second in importance to the role portrayed by Miss Joyce. Supporting these players are Gladys Hulette, Sammy Cohen, Bull Montana, Ed Dillon, and many others.

"The Sky Rocket" as a screen vehicle was actually in production almost three months. The actual shooting time covered a period of two months.

Following the completion of the picture Miss Joyce returned to New York and continued to remain in seclusion. The print of "The Sky Rocket" arrived in town three weeks ago for its final titling and editing.

With the arrival of the film it leaked out in film circles that the picture was a wonder and several of the leading distributors began angling for the picture. It was finally obtained for the Associated Exhibitors by Oscar Price and is scheduled for an early release.

In keeping with the plans outlined by P. A. Powers, over $150,000 will be spent on "The Sky Rocket" which will be released as a special and will not be included in the booking of the regular Associated Exhibitors product. Under the supervision of

John S. Woody, General Manager, a special sales force is being organized to handle the sale of the picture, while Robert F. Welsh, Director of Advertising and Publicity for Associated Exhibitors, is planning a special field force of exploitation men for the key cities and surrounding territory.

The first advertised official announcement for "The Sky Rocket" will be made next week with the release of a beautiful three colored insert in eight pages. This insert is only the beginning shot in the campaign and after having run in all the national motion picture trade newspapers and regional journals, it will be closely followed by a direct to the exhibitor series of broadsides.

The first of these is now in work and is founded on the beautiful gowns and wardrobe in the picture worn by Miss Joyce.

The second of the series of broadsides of which one each week will be released, is based on the endorsements of some of the world's greatest legitimate showmen and producers on Miss Joyce's ability as an actress.

The release of this broadside will be for the main reason of convincing the exhibitor that in Miss Joyce he has an artist of rare screen ability and that she is not capitalizing on the fact that she is a celebrity.

The art department in the offices of the Associated Exhibitors are busy at work on ideas for a gigantic campaign book. This compendium is planned to be three times as big as the ordinary press book containing among many ideas a full page of publicity written from the woman's standpoint, such as clothes and beauty hints.

Willard Louis Selected for "Don Juan" Cast

Willard Louis has been chosen to play a prominent role in "Don Juan," the Warner Bros. production in which John Barrymore will be starred. Louis will be seen as Pedrillo, probably the most important for which this actor has ever been cast. Mary Astor has the leading feminine part in the picture.

Burr McIntosh Plays Heavy Role in Pathe Serial

Burr McIntosh is playing the chief heavy role in "The Green Archer," the new Pathe serial now in production at the company's studios at Astoria, L. I. McIntosh, who is well known to the stage, screen and radio fans will be seen as Abel Bellamy in the chapter play in which Allene Ray and Walter Miller are co-featured.

"Uncle Tom's Gal" Goes to Exhibitors

"Uncle Tom's Gal," a two-reel Century comedy burlesquing "Uncle Tom's Cabin" and starring Edna Marian, has been released through all Universal exchanges. The picture was directed by William Watson.

"The Sky Rocket" to Go Direct to First Runs

IN a statement in which he denied the report that "The Sky Rocket," starring Peggy Hopkins Joyce, would be roadshowed, J. S. Woody, general manager of Associated Exhibitors, distributing the picture, said that the production would go direct to the big first run theatres and then to the entire field.

In connection with the denial of reports that "The Sky Rocket" would be road showed by a legitimate theatrical organization, it became known that certain newspapers had been premature in stating that the Marshall Neilan production may be shown at the Strand or the Capitol.

CLASSIFIED AD SECTION

RATES: 10 cents a word for each insertion, in advance except Employment Wanted, on which rate is 5 cents.

CLASSIFIED SERVICE

A classified ad in MOTION PICTURE NEWS offers the full resources and circulation of the NEWS to the advertiser at a ridiculously low figure.

Whether you want to reach executives, branch managers, salesmen, or theatre managers, you can accomplish this quickly and economically through the NEWS Classified Columns.

Wanted

WANTED.—To rent or buy lease motion picture theatre. Anywhere. 400 seats up. Box A, Motion Picture News, 845 S. Wabash, Chicago.

WANTED — Experienced motion picture theatre manager; married; theatre 40 minutes from New York; 2,000 seats; first run; state age, experience; reference and when available. Box 420, Motion Picture News, New York City.

EXPERT OPERATOR and Electrician with 9 years' experience in big houses; married; wants to locate at once. Address, Operator, Box 282, Mason City, Iowa.

ORGANIST.—Experienced. References. Minimum, $60 six (6) days. Worth investigating. Now employed. Box 390, Motion Picture News, New York City.

PIANIST desires engagement for evenings to play alone in picture theatre within commuting distance from New York City. Box 400, Motion Picture News, New York City.

FEATURE THEATRE ORGANIST, married man, wishes to locate in first class theatre having modern organ. Have fine library and cue pictures intelligently. Box 380, Motion Picture News, New York City.

THEATRE IN TOWN OF 4,000 or better, anywhere in North Central states, Northern Indiana preferred. Can either give satisfactory security on lease or buy outright. Would consider buying interest in bona-fide proposition where owner wishes to retire. All replies absolutely confi-

dential. Address Box 360, Motion Picture News, New York City.

For Sale

FOR SALE, Wyoming Theatre, Mullens, W. Va. $60,-000.00 cash. Now earning about $1,000.00 per month net. Owner retiring from business.

FOR SALE—400 veneered seats, $500; 2 Powers 6 B's, good condition, each $375; 1 Osborn Baby Grand Piano, $200; ½ horse 36 inch blower (new $575), $195; 4 16-inch wall fans, each $10; 1 Orpheum 14 ft. vertical sign with flasher, $150; in fact a complete set of equipment to be sold in line with above prices. S. O'Hare, Fairfield, Iowa.

FOR SALE—New modern movie theatre, 600 seats; exceptional proposition; quick sale; cheap; small town near Albany; no competition. Box 430, Motion Picture News, New York City.

FOR SALE—Six hundred veneered theatre chairs, A-1 condition; also all makes rebuilt projection machines and other equipment; write us your needs. Illinois Theatre Equipment Company, 12 E. Ninth St., Chicago.

FOR SALE—Moving picture theatre (valuable realty), in town near Camden, N. J.; seating capacity 486, etc. Frank DuFrayne, 20 S. 15th St., Philadelphia.

"*Graustark*" (*First National*) *is receiving some excellent newspaper advertising at the hands of various theatre managers throughout the country, as shown in the above lay-out of seven selected ads. The houses represented are: Capitol theatre, Cincinnati; Stillman theatre, Cleveland; Virginian, Charleston; Metropolitan theatre, Atlanta; Stillman, Cleveland (opening ad); Circle theatre, Indianapolis (anniversary ad); Mark Strand theatre, Albany. Ads were two, three and four columns wide in the original.*

With First Run Theatres

NEW YORK CITY

Mark Strand Theatre—
Film Numbers—The Dark Angel (First National), Mark Strand Topical Revue (Selected), Air Cooled (Pathe).
Musical Program—"Louise" (Overture, with "Depuis le jour" sung by soprano soloist), "Minute Waltz" (Dance solo Duo-Art piano), "Chanson du Coeur Brise" (Vocal solo), "Chanson Indoue" (Tenor solo), Tevis Huhn (Banjo virtuoso), "Prelude in G Minor" (Organ solo).

Warner's Theatre—
Film Numbers—Satan in Sables (Warner Bros.), Warner's News Weekly (Selected), The Lion Charges (Special reel), The Invisible Revenge (Cartoon).
Musical Program—"Orpheus in the Underworld" "Kinky Kids Parade" (Overture), "Ballet-Esque" (Dance solo), "An Operatic Sunrise" (Tenor solo).

Capitol Theatre—
Film Numbers—The Midshipman (Metro-Goldwyn-Mayer), Capitol Magazine (Selected), Felix Trips Thru Toyland (Educational).
Musical Program—Selections from "Pagliacci" (Overture), Fritz Zimmerman and Marcelle Grandville (Interpreters of old Swiss tunes and mountain yodels), "Dance of India" (Dance solo and ballet corps), "The Little Red Doll" (Dance solo), "Whirlwind" "Dance of the Toy Regiment" (Xylophone solo), Organ solo.

Rivoli Theatre—
Film Numbers—Lovers in Quarantine (Paramount), Rivoli Pictorial (Selected).
Musical Program—"Brown Eyes" (Organ), "In The Subway" (Reisenfeld's Classical Jazz).

Rialto Theatre—
Film Numbers—The Everlasting Whisper (Fox), Rialto Magazine (Selected), As You Like It (Pathe).
Musical Program — "Rubeville" (Ben Bernie and his gang), "Lamentations of the Long and Lean" (Organ).

Colony Theatre—
Film Numbers—The Freshman (Pathe), continued.

Cameo Theatre—
Film Numbers — Shore Leave (First National), continued.

Astor Theatre—
Film Numbers—The Phantom of the Opera (Universal), continued.

LOS ANGELES

Criterion Theatre—
Film Numbers—Sun-Up (Metro-Goldwyn-Mayer), Going Great (Educational), Glistening Wonderland (Scenic), Fox News.
Musical Program—Orchestra.

Forum Theatre—
Film Numbers—The Man on the Box (Warner Bros.), International News and Kinograms.

Musical Program—Musical Melange (Stage Revue).

Hillstreet Theatre—
Film Numbers—Under the Rouge (Asso. Exhib.), The Pacemakers (F. B. O.), Aesop's Fables (Pathe), International News.
Musical Program—Vaudeville.

Loew's State Theatre—
Film Numbers—Winds of Chance (First National), Marvels of Motion (Red Seal), Loew's State Pictorial News and Events (Selected).
Musical Program — Symphony selections (Orchestra), Mission Belles (Fanchon and Marco idea).

Metropolitan Theatre—
Film Numbers—He's a Prince (Paramount), Through Three Reigns (Red Seal), Pathe News.
Musical Program—"Il Guarany" (Overture).

Pantages Theatre—
Film Numbers—Lady Robinhood (F. B. O.), Pathe News.
Musical Program—Vaudeville.

Rialto Theatre—
Film Numbers—Phantom of the Opera (Universal), Pathe News.
Musical Program—Prologue to feature.

Million Dollar Theatre—
Film Numbers — The Freshman (Pathe), continued.
Musical Program — "On the Campus" (Overture).

BROOKLYN

Mark Strand Theatre—
Film Numbers—The Lost World (First National), Mark Strand Topical Review (Selected).
Musical Program—Concert arrangement of "Dixie" (piano solo), "Longing" (tenor solo, assisted by ballet), "Normandy" (soprano solo), "Hungarian Rag" (xylophone solo), "Oh How I Miss You Tonight" (tenor and soprano duet).

BOSTON

Beacon Theatre—
Film Numbers—Souls for Sables (S. R.), Lovers in Quarantine (Paramount), Comedy (Educational), News (Universal).
Musical Program—Organ, overture.

Fenway Theatre—
Film Numbers—Lovers in Quarantine (Paramount), Souls for Sables (S. R.), Comedy (Pathe), News (Pathe).
Musical Program—Organ novelty "Mamie" and other popular girl songs (Organ solo).

Gordon's Washington St. Olympia Theatre—
Film Numbers—The Pace That Thrills (First National), Love and Kisses (Pathe), News (Pathe).
Musical Program — Orchestra overture.

Loew's State Theatre—
Film Numbers—The Midshipman (Metro-Goldwyn), The Circle (Metro-Goldwyn-Mayer), Aesops Fables (Pathe), News (Pathe).
Musical Program—Overture.

CHICAGO

Chicago Theatre—
Film Numbers—Weekly News and Views (Pathe), Her Sister From Paris (First National), Comedy (Selected).
Musical Program—"Southern Rhapsody" (Overture), Miss Marie Herron, singing "Kiss Me Again" (Specialty), "Back Home," featuring Chicago Charleston Winners (Presentation), "Popular Selections" (Organ Solos).

Tivoli Theatre—
Film Numbers—Never the Twain Shall Meet (Metro-Goldwyn-Mayer), International News (Universal), Scenic Wonders, Cartoon.
Musical Program — "Under the Bridge" (Presentation), "Selections from the Merry Widow" (Overture), "The Son of the Desert" (Vocal Solo).

Uptown Theatre—
Film Numbers—Never the Twain Shall Meet (Metro-Goldwyn-Mayer), Comic Cartoon (Selected), International News (Universal).
Musical Program—"2nd Hungarian Rhapsody" (Overture), "A Sea

New Boston Theatre—
Film Numbers — The Fighting Heart (Fox), Comedy (Pathe), News (Pathe).
Musical Program — Orchestra, overture. Five acts vaudeville.

Modern Theatre—
Film Numbers—Souls for Sables (Paramount), Lovers in Quarantine (Paramount), Comedy (Educational), International News.
Film Numbers—Organ overture.

Fantasy" (Specialty). "Polonaise Militaire" (Organ Solo), "An Evening At Home" (Presentation).

Capitol Theatre—
Film Numbers—The Pony Express (Paramount), Capitol Scenic Review, Capitol World Events (Universal), Comedy Cartoon.
Musical Program — "American Fantasy" (Overture), "Kings of Syncopation" (Specialty), "The Magazine Girl" (Presentation), "Il Guarany" (Organ), Prologue to "The Pony Express" (Specialty).

Roosevelt Theatre—
Film Numbers — The Freshman (Pathe).

Orpheum Theatre—
Film Numbers — The Gold Rush (United Artists).

Monroe Theatre—
Film Numbers — Everlasting Whisper (Fox).

NEWARK

Capitol Theatre—
Film Numbers—Don Q, Son of Zorro (United Artists), Pictorial (Pathe).

Mosque Theatre—
Film Numbers — The Freshman (Pathe), News (International).
Musical Program—The Fortune Teller" (Overture), College Capers (prologue), "Momenta Chopin" (soloist, ballet and string ensemble).

Branford Theatre—
Film Numbers—Classified (First National), Comedy (Pathe), News (Pathe).
Musical Numbers — "You're in Love" (Overture), jazz band of midgets and soloist dancer.

Rialto Theatre—
Film Numbers — His Majesty, Bunker Bean (Warner Bros.), Street of Forgotten Men (Paramount), News (Kinograms).
Musical Program—Selection of old-time melodies.

Fox Terminal Theatre—
Film Numbers — Havoc (Fox), Comedy (Fox), News (Fox).
Musical Program—Selections by orchestra combined with jazz band.

BUFFALO

Shea's Hippodrome—
Film Numbers—The Ten Commandments (Paramount), Current Events (Fox and International News).
Musical Program — Hippodrome orchestra, playing the same musical score arranged for the New York presentation. Piano selections by Percy Grainger, Australian soloist.

Mr. Exhibitor! Ask at the Film Exchanges for the

It's little to ask for, but it's the only reliable aid you can give your musicians to help put the picture over

Olympic Theatre—
Film Numbers—The Freshman (Pathe), Life's Greatest Thrills (Universal), Current Events (International News).
Musical Program—Vocal selections by Lou Burr, the "Radio'a" girl. Organ overture, "The Student Prince."

Loew's State Theatre—
Film Numbers—The Everlasting Whisper (Fox), Daddy Goes A Grunting (Pathe), Current Events (Pathe News).
Musical Program—Vincent Lopez Debutantes in "Tinkling Tunes of the Time." Five acts of vaudeville.

Lafayette Square Theatre—
Film Numbers — Playing With Souls (First National), Comedy (Pathe), Current Events (Kinograms).
Musical Program—Selections from "The Greenwich Village Follies" Henry B. Murtagh playing his own compositions at the Wurlitzer.

Shea's North Park Theatre—
Film Numbers—A Slave of Fashion (Metro-Goldwyn-Mayer), Comedy (Pathe), Current Events (Fox and International News).
Musical Program—Selections from "The Red Mill" (Orchestra).

Palace Theatre—
Film Numbers—Riding the Wind (F. B. O.), Sherlock Sleuth (Comedy), Current Events (International News).

ROCHESTER

Eastman Theatre—
Film Numbers—The Iron Horse (Fox), Eastman Theatre Current Events (Selected).
Musical Program—"Storky in the Straw" (Overture), Prologue to "The Iron Horse" (Specialty).

BALTIMORE

Century Theatre—
Film Numbers—He's A Prince (Paramount), The Movie (Educational) News Weekly (Fox).
Musical Program — "Bohemian Girl" (Overture by Orchestra), The Eternal Flapper (Edna Wallace Hopper in Person). Orchestra. Organ Recessional.

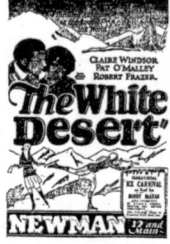

CLAIRE WINDSOR
PAT O'MALLEY
ROBERT FRAZER
"The White Desert"
REX CARNIVAL
NEWMAN 32 and Clean

The Newman theatre, Kansas City, advertised "The White Desert" (Metro-Goldwyn Mayer) in this way.

LOEW'S STATE
NOW PLAYING
The World's Sweetheart
MARY PICKFORD
LITTLE ANNIE ROONEY
"GARDEN OF DREAMS"
LOLA GIRLIE AND SENIA
THE SACRIFICE

Loew's State theatre, St. Louis, used this newspaper ad on "Little Annie Rooney" (United Artists).

Garden Theatre—
Film Numbers—The White Outlaw (Universal), Captain Suds (Universal), Monkeys With Magic (S. R.), International News (Universal).
Musical Program—Five acts of vaudeville. Orchestra. Organ recessional.

Keith's Hippodrome—
Film Numbers — Parisian Nights (F. B. O.), Aesop's Fable (Pathe), News Weekly (Pathe), Don't Tell Dad (Pathe).
Musical Program—Five acts of vaudeville. Orchestra. Organ recessional.

Metropolitan Theatre—
Film Numbers—The Trouble With Wives (Paramount), The Lion and the Monkey (Pathe), News Weekly (Pathe), Be Careful (Educational), Visiting Our Own America and Fireside Factories (Pathe).
Musical Program—"Fantasie Orientale" (Overture by Orchestra), "The Student Prince" (Organ Selection).

New Theatre—
Film Numbers—The Ten Commandments (Paramount), continued. News Weekly (Pathe).
Musical Program—Orchestra. Organ recessional.

Parkway Theatre—
Film Numbers — Girl of Gold (Producers Distributing Corporation), The Caretaker's Daughter (Pathe), Invisible Ink (Educational), Parkway Pictorial News (Educational Kinograms).
Musical Program — "Mignon" (Overture), Orchestra. Organ recessional.

Rivoli Theatre—
Film Numbers—The Live Wire (First National), Rivoli News (Pathe), Wild Beasts of Borneo (Educational).
Musical Program—Divertisement on the stage (Art Landry and His Orchestra), "Popular Hits of 1925" (Organ Selection), "Oh, Boy What a Girl" and "Collegiate" (Musical Themes for Feature Picture).

PHILADELPHIA

Stanley Theatre—
Film Numbers—Sally of the Sawdust (United Artists), News Weekly, Scenic.

Musical Program—"Echoes of the Metropolitan" (Organ selections), Orchestra and ballet.

Fox Theatre—
Film Numbers — East Lynne (Fox), Fox News.
Musical Program — "Poet and Peasant" (Orchestra).

Karlton Theatre—
Film Numbers — The Knockout (First National).

Palace Theatre—
Film Numbers—Coast of Folly (Paramount).

Victoria Theatre—
Film Numbers—The Half Way Girl (First National).

Capitol Theatre—
Film Numbers—The Desert Flower (First National).

Stanton Theatre—
Film Numbers—The Gold Rush (United Artists), continued.

Arcadia Theatre—
Film Numbers—Winds of Chance (First National), continued.

SAN FRANCISCO

California Theatre—
Film Numbers—Lightnin' (Fox), No Father to Guide Him (Pathe), International News.
Musical Program — "Morning. Noon and Night" (Overture), "Serenata" (Violin solo), "Sing 'Em Again" (Organ).

Loew's Warfield Theatre—
Film Numbers—An Exchange of Wives (Metro-Goldwyn-Mayer), The Misfit Sailor (Educational), Felix The Cat (Educational), International News.
Musical Program—"South Sea Ideas" (Panchon and Marco idea with singing and dancing), Novelle Brothers (Dancers).

Granada Theatre—
Film Numbers—Drusilla with a Million (F. B. O.), Moonlight and Roses (Pathe) Pathe News.
Musical Program — Syncopation Week.

Imperial Theatre—
Film Numbers — The Freshman (Pathe) continued.

Cameo Theatre—
Film Numbers—April Showers (Schulberg—S. R.), Cupid's Victory (Universal), International News.
Musical Program—"The World is Waiting for the Sunrise" (Baritone solo), Charleston Dancers (Colored leaders).

Union Square Theatre—
Film Numbers—Traffic in Hearts (S. R.), The Mysterious Stranger (Fox), Fox News.
Musical Program—Five vaudeville acts.

St. Francis Theatre—
Film Numbers—The Vanishing American (Paramount) continued.

DES MOINES

Capitol Theatre—
Film Numbers—Winds of Chance (First National). Fox News; Pals of My Cradle Days (Special).
Musical Program—"Vanity Doll" (song and dance number), "She's My Baby" (organ special).

DesMoines Theatre—
Film Numbers — Fine Clothes (First National), The Iron Knight (Educational), International News.
Musical Program — "Summer Nights" (organ feature).

Strand Theatre—
Film Numbers—Lovers in Quarantine (Paramount), Off His Beat (Educational), Kinograms.

KANSAS CITY

Newman Theatre—
Film Numbers—A Slave of Fashion (Metro-Goldwyn-Mayer), Newman Mirror of the World (Pathe, Kinograms and International News), Newman Current Events (Local Photography).
Musical Program—"Marche Slav" (Overture), "Fur Modes Revue" Novelty with cast of thirty), King Sisters (Specialty) Recessional (Organ solos).

Liberty Theatre—
Film Numbers — Little Annie Rooney (United Artists), Aesop's Fables (Pathe), International News.
Musical Program — Selections From "Eileen" (Overture), Recessional (Organ solos).

Royal Theatre—
Film Numbers—Romola (Metro-Goldwyn-Mayer), Royal Screen Magazine (Pathe, Kinograms and International News), Royal Current Events (Local Photography).
Musical Program — Royal Syncopators On Stage (Overture), Recessional (Organ solos).

Mainstreet Theatre—
Film Numbers—Classified (First National), Pathe News and Educational Short Subjects.
Musical Program—Popular Selections (Overture), Recessional (Organ solos).

Pantages Theatre—
Film Numbers—American Pluck (S. R.), Fox News and Fox Short Subjects).
Musical Program — Atmospheric Selections (Overture), Recessional (Organ solos).

CINCINNATI

Capitol Theatre—
Film Numbers—Classified (First National), Why Hesitate (Educational), Capitol News (Selected).
Musical Program—Orchestra.

Walnut Theatre—
Film Numbers — The Freshman (Pathe), continued.

Strand Theatre—
Film Numbers — California Straight Ahead (Universal), Felix Brings Home the Bacon (Educational), Pathe News.
Musical Program—Orchestra.

HOWARD
WHERE ATLANTA MEETS
Women say—'Isn't he just like a man?'
REX
THE WILD HORSE OF HAL ROACH'S
"BLACK CYCLONE"

The Howard theatre's ad in Atlanta for "Black Cyclone" (Pathe).

Lyric Theatre—
Film Numbers—Winds of Chance (First National), Kinograms.
Musical Program—Orchestra.
Gifts Theatre—
Film Numbers— Capital Punishment (Schulberg-S. R.), Piping Hot (Universal), Kinograms.
Family Theatre—
Film Numbers—The Lucky Horseshoe (Fox), Going Great (Comedy), Fox News.

INDIANAPOLIS

Circle Theatre—
Film Numbers— Classified (First National), Mermaid Comedy (Educational), Charleston (Pathe).
Musical Program—"The Red Mill" (Overture), "Cecilia" (Organ solo).
Apollo Theatre—
Film Numbers — The Coast of Folly (Paramount), Comedy (Educational), News Reel Weekly (Fox).
Musical Program — Orchestra, organist and Walter J. Schwartz (baritone).
Colonial Theatre—
Film Numbers—The Iron Horse (Fox), News Reel Weekly (Universal), Aesop Fable (Pathe).
Musical Program—American Harmonists.

MILWAUKEE

Alhambra Theatre—
Film Numbers—Don Q Son of Zorro (United Artists); International News.
Musical Program—Selections from "The Student Prince" (Overture), Atmospheric Prologue.
Garden Theatre—
Film Numbers—Souls for Sables (S. R.), Topics of the Day (Pathe), Fox News; Felix Cartoon.
Musical Program—Organ Overture.
Merrill Theatre—
Film Numbers—Romola (Metro-Goldwyn-Mayer), Kinograms, A Cat and Two Birds (Educational).
Musical Program — "Sandy" (Overture).
Strand Theatre—
Film Numbers—The Scarlet West (First National), Wake Up (Educational), Felix on the

Farm (Educational), Kinograms.
Musical Program—"Sandy" (overture and sung by James Durfee), "An Indian Fantasy" (Organ solo).
Wisconsin Theatre—
Film Numbers—Classified (First National), International News, Felix Cartoon.
Musical Program—"Aida" (Overture), Mario & Lazarin (Harmony Singers), Max Fischer and his California Jazz Syncopaters (Stage Presentation).

CLEVELAND

Stillman Theatre—
Film Numbers—The Gold Rush (United Artists) continued. International News (Orchestra).
Musical Program—"Forgotten Roses" (Overture).
Allen Theatre—
Film Numbers—Seven Keys to Baldpate (Paramount), Remember When (Pathe), Life's Greatest Thrills (Universal), Clever Feet (Pathe), Topics of the Day (Pathe), Pathe News.
Musical Program—"The Kiss I Can't Forget," symphonic phantasy (Overture), Charleston tunes, in celebration of Charleston week. Phil's Boys in "Tuning in on Charleston" (Specialty), Exhibition Charleston dancing.
State Theatre—
Film Numbers—The Pace that Thrills (First National), Cloudy Romance (Fox), Taxi War (Universal), Millionaires Without a Cent (S. R.), Pathe Review.
Musical Program—Organ Novelty (Overture), Vaudeville.
Park Theatre—
Film Numbers—Lovers in Quarantine (Paramount), Oh Bridget (Educational), Jumble in the Jungle (Educational), Topics of the Day (Pathe), Kinograms (Educational).
Musical Program — "Rosamunde" (Overture), Jazz Numbers: "Let's Wander Away," "Brown Eyes, Why Are You Blue," "I'm Gonna Charleston Back to Charleston."
Rheade's Hippodrome—
Film Numbers — T h e Lucky Horseshoe (Fox), Pathe Comedy, International News (Universal).
Musical Program—Popular Dance Medley (Overture), Vaudeville.
Keith's East 105th St—
Film Numbers—The Lucky Horseshoe (Fox), Betters Movies (Pathe), Aesop's Fables (Pathe), Pathe News.
Musical Program — "Blossom Time" (Overture), Vaudeville.
Circle Theatre—
Film Numbers—Off the Highway (Warner Bros.), Aesop's Fables (Pathe), Pathe News, Love and Lions (Fox).
Musical Program—"Orpheus" (Overture), "Indian Love Call" from "Rose Marie" and Sing Sing Birds on the Wing" (Vocal).

OKLAHOMA CITY

Criterion Theatre—
Film Numbers — The Freshman (Pathe), Felix The Cat in Trips Thru Toyland (Educational), Kinograms.

REX BEACH'S

"The GOOSE WOMAN"

With JACK PICKFORD CONSTANCE BENNETT and LOUISE DRESSER

Universal Jewel Presented by CARL LAEMMLE

NOW PLAYING AT AMERICA

Two-column ad on "The Goose Woman" (Universal) at the America theatre in Denver.

Musical Program—Organ recitals.
Empress Theatre—
Film Numbers—The Dark Angel (First National), Mix Fit Sailor (Educational).
Musical Program—Organ recitals.
Capitol Theatre—
Film Numbers—Tracked in the Snow Country (Warner Bros.), The Iron Nag (Pathe).
Musical Program—Organ recitals.
Majestic Theatre—
Film Numbers — The Alaskan (Paramount), Flickering Youth (Pathe).
Musical Program—Organ recitals.

HOUSTON

Queen Theatre—
Film Numbers—The Pony Express (Paramount). News (Pathe).
Musical Program—"Oh Suzanne" (Overture), Organ Numbers.
Isis Theatre—
Film Numbers—The Mystic (Metro-Goldwyn-Mayer), Comedy (Pathe), News (International).
Musical Program—"At Dawning" (Overture), Organ Numbers.
Capitol Theatre—
Film Numbers—Ten Commandments (Paramount), News (Kinograms).
Musical Program—Popular selections (orchestra), organ and piano numbers.
Majestic Theatre—
Film Numbers — The Iron Horse (Fox), Aesop's Fables (Pathe).
Musical Program—Concert orchestra numbers and organ specialty. Vaudeville and News (Pathe).
Rialto Theatre—

Film Numbers—The Goose Woman (Universal), Comedy (Educational), News (Fox).
Musical Program — Organ and piano selections.
Liberty Theatre—
Film Numbers—Below the Border (Warner), Comedy (Fox), Review (Pathe).
Musical Program—Piano and organ selections.

SEATTLE

Blue Mouse Theatre—
Film Numbers — Fighting the Flames (S. R.), All Aboard (Pathe), International News.
Musical Program — "Hungarian Fantasia" (Overture), "Everyone at Home is Asking For You" (Orchestra novelty), Victor Herbert Melodies (Organ solo).
Coliseum Theatre—
Film Numbers — The Knockout (First National), Unfriendly Enemies (Comedy), Kinograms and Pathe News.
Musical Program—"Bonquet of Roses" (Overture), Sans Souci Trio in vocal numbers.
Columbia Theatre—
Film Numbers—The Coming of Amos (Prod. Dist. Corp.), International News.
Musical Program—"William Tell" (Overture).
Heilig Theatre—
Film Numbers — The Calgary Stampede (Universal), Aesop's Fable (Pathe), Pathe Review), Topics of the Day (Pathe).
Musical Program—Popular Medley (Overture).
Liberty Theatre—
Film Numbers—The Freshman (Pathe), Pathe Review, International and Liberty News.
Musical Program—College medley (Overture, vocal and instrumental college special prologue).
Pantages Theatre—
Film Numbers—The Love Gamble (S. R.), Aesop's Fables (Pathe), Pathe News.
Musical Program—Vaudeville.
Strand Theatre—
Film Numbers—Just a Woman (First National), Horace Greeley, Jr. (Comedy), Fox News.
Musical Program — "Hungarian Rhapsodie" (Overture), Orchestral Numbers.

The World is Laughing at "THE FRESHMAN"

Harold Lloyd in the Freshman at the ROYAL

2nd EPOCHAL WEEK!

Novel and humorous ad on "The Freshman" at the Royal theatre, Kansas City.

Exhibitors Box-Office Reports

Names of the theatre owners are omitted by agreement in accordance with the wishes of the average exhibitor and in the belief that reports published over the signature of the exhibitor reporting, is a dangerous practice.

Only reports received on specially prepared blanks furnished by us will be accepted for use in this department. Exhibitors who value this reporting service are urged to ask for these blanks.

Title of Picture	Population of Town	Location	Class of Patronage	Weather	Box Office Value	Check-up Percentage from other Reports
ASSOC. EXHIBITORS						
Barriers Burned Away...	15000	Penna.	General	Clear	Good	65
Introduce Me..........	15000	Penna.	General	Clear	Good	82
FAMOUS PLAYERS						
Air Mail, The..........	12500	Tex.	Mixed	Clear	Good	70
Are Parents People?....	12500	Tex.	Mixed	Clear	Good	68
Coast of Folly, The.....	733826	Md.	1st Run	Clear	Big	75
	401247	Ohio	1st Run	Clear	Good	..
	120000	Fla.	1st Run	Clear	Good	..
	796841	Ohio	1st Run	Clear	Fair	..
Dressmaker From Paris.	12500	Tex.	Mixed	Clear	Good	72
He's A Prince..........	506000	Cal.	1st Run	Clear	Good	70
Little French Girl.......	8000	Maine	Mixed	Clear	Good	70
Lost, A Wife............	8000	Maine	Mixed	Clear	Fair	55
Madame Sans Gene.....	12500	Tex.	Mixed	Clear	Good	54
Man Who Found Himself, The................	772897	Mo.	1st Run	Rain	Fair	63
	324410	Mo.	1st Run	Clear	Good	..
Rugged Waters.........	772897	Mo.	1st Run	Rain	Fair	43
Sackcloth and Scarlet...	8000	Maine	Mixed	Clear	Good	63
Salome of the Tenements	8000	Maine	Mixed	Clear	Good	46
Son of His Father, A....	506675	N. Y.	1st Run	Clear	Fair	63
Thundering Herd, The..	12500	Tex.	Mixed	Clear	Big	80
Too Many Kisses.......	8000	Maine	Mixed	Clear	Good	65
Trouble With Wives.....	126468	Iowa	1st Run	Rain	Good	65
	993678	Mich.	1st Run	Clear	Good	65
	200000	Ga.	General	Clear	Good	65
Welcome Home..........	8000	Maine	Mixed	Clear	Good	60
Wild Horse Mesa........	350000	Wash.	General	Clear	Fair	66
F. B. O.						
Bandit's Baby, The.....	22000	N. Y.	General	Clear	Good	80
Cheap Kisses...........	200000	Ga.	General	Clear	Fair	63
Drusilla With a Million..	22000	N. Y.	General	Clear	Good	73
Midnight Molly.........	200000	Ga.	General	Clear	Fair	65
FIRST NATIONAL						
Dark Angel, The........	796341	Ohio	1st Run	Clear	Good	75
	414246	N. J.	1st Run	Clear	Good	..
Knockout, The..........	8000	Maine	Mixed	Clear	Good	60
	733826	Md.	General	Clear	Good	..
	772897	Mo.	1st Run	Rain	Good	..
	796841	Ohio	1st Run	Clear	Good	..
Live Wire, The.........	314194	Ind.	1st Run	Clear	Good	70
Lost World, The (2d wk.)	401247	Ohio	1st Run	Clear	Good	85
	993678	Mich.	General	Clear	Good	..
	126468	Iowa	1st Run	Rain	Good	..
Making of O'Malley.....	9500	Ill.	Mixed	Clear	Good	74
Pace That Thrills, The..	120000	Fla.	1st Run	Clear	Good	70
Scarlet West, The.......	8000	Maine	Mixed	Clear	Good	65
Shore Leave............	414246	N. J.	1st Run	Clear	Good	80
	9500	Ill.	Mixed	Clear	Good	..
Talker, The............	9500	Ill.	Mixed	Clear	Good	68
What Fools Men........	796841	Ohio	1st Run	Clear	Fair	70
White Monkey, The.....	414246	N. J.	General	Clear	Fair	52
FOX						
Iron Horse, The........	126468	Iowa	1st Run	Rain	Good	80
Lightnin'..............	350000	Wash.	General	Clear	Good	69
	324410	Mo.	1st Run	Clear	Good	..
Wheel, The............	993678	Mich.	1st Run	Clear	Good	72
	414246	N. J.	1st Run	Clear	Fair	..
METRO-GOLDWYN-MAYER						
Exchange of Wives......	414246	N. J.	1st Run	Clear	Good	70
Midshipman, The.......	506000	Cal.	1st Run	Clear	Good	75
Mystic, The............	350000	Wash.	1st Run	Clear	Fair	69
	120000	Fla.	1st Run	Clear	Good	..
Never The Twain Shall Meet................	200000	Ga.	General	Clear	Big	78
	993678	Mich.	1st Run	Clear	Big	..
Pretty Ladies..........	8000	Maine	Mixed	Clear	Fair	63
Rag Man, The..........	120000	Fla.	1st Run	Clear	Big	..
	733826	Md.	General	Clear	Good	89
Slave of Fashion, A.....	401247	Ohio	1st Run	Clear	Fair	65
	506675	N. Y.	1st Run	Clear	Fair	..
White Desert, The......	8000	Maine	Mixed	Clear	Good	..
Zander The Great......	506000	Cal.	General	Clear	Good	68
	350000	Wash.	General	Clear	Fair	72
PATHE						
Freshman, The.........	506675	N. Y.	1st Run	Clear	Big	92
	120000	Fla.	1st Run	Clear	Big	..
(2d week)	314194	Ind.	1st Run	Clear	Big	92
	401247	Ohio	1st Run	Clear	Good	..
	324410	Md.	1st Run	Clear	Big	..
Kivalina of Icelands.....	506000	Cal.	General	Clear	Good	70
PRODUCERS DIST. CORP.						
Bad Lands, The........	733826	Md.	1st Run	Clear	Fair	62
Charley's Aunt.........	6230	Ark.	Mixed	Clear	Big	92
Hell's Highroad........	506675	N. Y.	General	Clear	Fair	63
	993678	Mich.	General	Clear	Good	..
Roaring Rails..........	15000	Penna.	General	Clear	Good	79
	6230	Ark.	Mixed	Clear	Good	..
Seven Days............	796841	Ohio	General	Clear	Fair	70
STATE RIGHTS						
Black Lightning........	15000	Penna.	General	Clear	Good	70
Crackerjack, The.......	324410	Mo.	General	Clear	Fair	77
	18000	Penna.	General	Clear	Good	..
Do It Now.............	350000	Wash.	General	Clear	Fair	70
Souls for Sables........	126468	Iowa	1st Run	Rain	Fair	70
Sporting Chance, The...	772897	Mo.	1st Run	Rain	Good	..
Who Cares.............	401247	Ohio	General	Clear	Fair	62
Wizard of Oz..........	733826	Md.	General	Clear	Good	55
	8000	Maine	Mixed	Clear	Good	75
UNITED ARTISTS						
Don Q. Son of Zorro....	350000	Wash.	1st Run	Clear	Big	94
	120000	Fla.	1st Run	Clear	Big	..
	324410	Mo.	1st Run	Clear	Good	..
	200000	Ga.	1st Run	Clear	Good	..
Gold Rush, The........	414246	N. J.	1st Run	Clear	Fair	91
Little Annie Rooney.....	200000	Ga.	1st Run	Clear	Good	75
	772897	Mo.	1st Run	Rain	Big	..
UNIVERSAL						
California Straight Ahead	314194	Ind.	1st Run	Clear	Good	75
Don Daredevil..........	8000	Maine	Mixed	Clear	Fair	67
Goose Woman, The.....	350000	Wash.	General	Clear	Good	70
I'll Show You The Town.	6230	Ark.	Mixed	Clear	Good	74
Last Laugh, The........	6230	Ark.	Mixed	Clear	Poor	54
Let 'er Buck...........	8000	Maine	Mixed	Clear	Good	75
Mad Whirl, The........	8900	Maine	Mixed	Clear	Fair	60
Oh, Doctor............	8000	Maine	Mixed	Clear	Good	73
Outlaw's Daughter, The.	200000	Ga.	General	Clear	Good	69
Peacock Feathers.......	506675	N. Y.	General	Clear	Good	55
Taming The West.......	120000	Fla.	General	Clear	Good	70
Teaser, The............	6230	Ark.	Mixed	Clear	Fair	74
Tornado, The..........	733826	Md.	Mixed	Clear	Fair	73
	6230	Ark.	Mixed	Clear	Good	72
VITAGRAPH						
Baree, Son of Kazan....	9500	Ill.	Mixed	Clear	Good	74
Wildfire..............	9500	Ill.	Mixed	Clear	Good	67
WARNER BROS.						
Below the Line.........	796841	Ohio	General	Clear	Fair	65
	120000	Fla.	Mixed	Clear	Good	..
His Majesty Bunker Bean	350000	Wash.	1st Run	Clear	Good	40
Limited Mail, The......	120000	Fla.	General	Clear	Good	70
Man Without a Conscience..............	401247	Ohio	General	Clear	Fair	55
Wife Who Wasn't Wanted	733826	Md.	1st Run	Clear	Good	55

Short Subjects and Serials

Sennett's Komedy Kops to Return to Screen

Mack Sennett's famous komedy kops, famous in the Keystone comedy days, will stage a comeback to the screen in "Wandering Willies," a Pathe short feature release being produced at the Sennett studios with Billy Bevan, Andy Clyde, Ruth H att and Kewpie Morgan in principal roles. The picture was directed by Del Lord, who served as the patrol wagon driver at the time the "Keystone Kops" were at the height of their screen glory.

Other units now filming pictures at Sennetts are Harry Langdon, who is being directed in a forthcoming Pathe comedy by Harry Edwards; Alice Day, who is making a yachting comedy; Ralph Graves, playing a "fourflusher" role; and an all-star company in which Billy Bevan, Dave Morris, Evelyn Sherman, Natalie Kingston and Barbara Tennant are appearing.

New Juvenile Thespian in "Our Gang" Troupe

Hal Roach has added another youngster to his group of juvenile stars appearing in the "Our Gang" comedies, produced under the direction of Bob McGowan. The newcomer's name is Jay Smith and is distinguished for his freckles and diffident manner.

Clyde Cook is making a new comedy at the Roach studios under the direction of C. Richard Wallace. Mildred June, Frederic Kovert, Cesare Gravina and Fred Kelsey appear in prominent supporting roles.

Pathe, Ltd. to Distribute "Ko-Ko" Films in Britain

Pathe, Ltd., this week signed a contract with Edwin Miles Fadman, head of Red Seal, for the distribution of the Ko-Ko Song Car-Tunes, an animated series produced by Max Fleischer, in Great Britain.

Pathe, Ltd., concluded negotiations six months ago for the Great Britain rights to two other Red Seal series: the "Marvels of Motion," made via the Fleischer-Novagraph process, and the "Out-of-the-Inkwell" series in which the clown, Ko-Ko, was first introduced.

Century Starts on Third "Buster Brown" Comedy

CAMERA work has been started on "Oh Buster," third of the series of two-reel comedies based on R. F. Outcault's famous Buster Brown cartoons, at the Century studios in Hollywood. The picture is scheduled for release in December.

Gus Meins is directing "Oh Buster" and Arthur T Imble, who created the character on the screen, is in the name role. The first two pictures in the series, "Educating Buster" and "Buster be Good," have won widespread popularity according to reports from Universal, distributors of the Century product.

Mack Sennett presents an all star cast in "Over There-Abouts," a two-reel Pathe offering from which these scenes are taken.

Pathe Program For October 25

Roach and Sennett Comedies Head Schedule of Short Subjects: Serial Episode Included

THE Pathe release program of short features for the week of October 25th is headed by two-reel comedies from the Hal Roach and Mack Sennett Studios, and also includes a chapter of the Pathe serial "Wild West," a Hal Roach one-reel comedy, Pathe Review, "Topics of the Day," "Aesop's Film Fables" and two issues of Pathe News.

"A Punch in the Nose" is a two-reel Hal Roach Comedy with an all-star cast including Lucien Littlefield, Al St. John, "Husky" Hanes, Jimmie Finlayson, Lige Conley, Kewpie Morgan, Al Hallet, Martha Sleeper, Marjorie Whiteis and Dot Farley. The story concerns a stranded "Uncle Tom's Cabin" troupe.

"A Sweet Pickle" is a two-reeler featuring Alice Day and produced by Mack Sennett. In her new vehicle, Alice is employed in a bakery. Barney Hellum, Alma Bennett and Jack Richardson support Miss Day in providing the fun. Arthur Rosson directed.

"All Wool" is a Hal Roach one-reel comedy with Earl Mohan, Billy Engle and Katherine Grant in the leading roles. Mohan and Engle appear as tailors and Katherine Grant is an ambitious actress who wanted to play in "rain" but lost her umbrella. Tay Garnett directed.

"The Rustlers' Stampede" is the title of the fifth chapter of the current Pathe serial

"Wild West," which features Helen Ferguson and Jack Mulhall.

Pathe Review No. 43 presents "Makers of Men," showing how West Point builds military man-power, which was produced with the cooperation of the U. S. Military Academy and the New York Military Academy; "Fresh-Air Tonic," Pathecolor views of Mont Dore, France's favorite mountain resort; and "Sunlight, the World's Champion Producer of Energy," one of "The Magic Eye" series.

"Closer Than A Brother" is the latest of the Paul Terry creations of the "Aesop's Film Fables" series. "Topics of the Day" and two issues of Pathe News complete the October 25th Pathe release schedule.

Hawkinson is Off for New "Sportlight"

J. L. Hawkinson, producer of Grantland Rice "Sportlights" for Pathe, has departed for Whitehall, Montana, to make scenes for a forthcoming sport picture of mountain and outdoor life. He expects to get some exceptional shots of duck and bird shooting, lake fishing and big game hunting. He will return in time to photograph highlights of the big football games in the east.

Resume of Current News Weeklies

FOX NEWS VOL. 7, NO. 4: Omaha, Neb.—President Coolidge addresses American Legion convention; In the Day's News—Admiral Robison takes command of Fleet as Admiral Coontz retires; San Francisco—Whippets race for $5,000 prize; Railroads Hold Own World Series—Pennsylvania System's team defeats N. Y. Central champions; Napa, Cal.—Give old man of rock, a freak of nature, pipe to smoke; Santo Domingo—A visit to church where remains of Christopher Columbus lie; Mineola, L. I.—Crack flyers compete in National Air Meet; New York City—Big butter and egg men in convention; Sydney, N. S. W.—Men and women riders compete in ten-mile paper chase; The World's Series—Scenes on diamond where Senators and Pirates battle for baseball title.

INTERNATIONAL NEWS NO. 84: Pittsburg. Pa.—Washington vs. Pittsburg in World Series Baseball classic; N. Y. City—Eighteen-year-old American girl wins highest goal in Grand Opera; Freeport, Ill.—Dam Orphan Maid, champion pig mother of America, produces another brood of 15; Berlin, Germany—Bear dens at Berlin Zoo receive new additions; Ithaca, Wash.—Cranberry "scoopers" gathering biggest crop in years for Thanksgiving dinners; N. Y. City—Babies' footprints express mother's thanks to doctor; San Pedro, Cal.—Admiral Robison takes command of U. S. battle fleet; Frisco, Cal.—Lightning speed records in Whippet sweepstakes; Omaha, Neb. — President Coolidge thrills American Legion Convention in tribute to War Heroes.

INTERNATIONAL NEWS NO. 83: Allentown, Pa.—Explosion moves huge hillside; Palo Alto, Cal.—College boys clash in strenuous mud fight; Juanita, Wash.—Raid the busy bees' winter honey supplies; Wash. D. C.—Home-run hitting features world series contests; Portland, Ore.—"Ships" worth a fortune make a fine bonfire; Lisieux, France. (Phila. only)—Cardinal Dougherty leads in unique honors to Saint; St. Louis, Mo. (St. Louis only)—Veiled prophet rides in gorgeous night spectacle; Boston, Mass. (Boston only)—Boston's finest on parade; Mitchel Field, N. Y.—Speed of 248 miles an hour wins Pulitzer Air Classic; N. Haven, Conn.—Thrill football plays in Yale-Georgia battle; Providence, R. I.—(Boston and Phila. only)—Scenes from Pennsylvania-Brown game; N. Y.

City—Georgia "Tech" triumphs over Penn State; Off Morgan Island, Me.—MacMillan ship battles storm returning from Arctic trip.

KINOGRAMS NO. 5125: Pittsburgh—Washington wins first game of World's Series (Pre-released); Saranac Lake, N. Y.—But Christy Mathewson is not there to see world's champions triumph; Pittsburgh—Washington and Pittsburgh clubs pay tribute to Mathewson before second game of championship series; Paris—Great crowds greet Japanese airmen when they finish their flight from Tokio to Paris; Omaha—President Coolidge pleads for a spirit of tolerance in his speech before American Legion convention and then reviews parade of world war veterans with Mrs. Coolidge at his side; Great Neck, L. I.—Wields deadly bull whip on live target to show how lash is used in Australia; New York—Marion Talley, eighteen-year-old operatic sensation, joins Metropolitan Opera Company; San Francisco—Speedy dogs show almost as much speed as Man O' War in exciting races.

KINOGRAMS NO. 5126: Washington—Senators defeat Pirates in second World's Series game (Pre-released); Washington—MacMillan expedition returns from trip to Arctic regions; Lisieux, France—Church and people unite to honor "Little Flower" in magnificent rites elevating Carmelite nun to sainthood; Aberdeen, Scotland—King George visits Aberdeen, to open art gallery wing, wearing kilties; Haworth, N. J.—Miss Maureen Orcutt, woman Eastern golf champion, shows her skill and gives her twin brothers a lesson; St. Louis —Veiled prophet again visits St. Louis and gorgeous night parade is held in his honor; Danbury, Conn.—Auto daredevils thrill crowd in stirring race on dirt track; St. Louis—Four killed, 51 hurt in explosion (St. Louis only); Philadelphia—Senator Walker, New York Mayoralty candidate, and Mayor Kendrick of Philadelphia inspect subway construction (Philadelphia only); Salem, N. J.—Jersey celebrates founding of Salem with impressive pageant (Philadelphia only).

PATHE NEWS NO. 88: Omaha, Neb.—Coolidge receives ovation from American Legion; Valparaiso, Chile—Prince of Wales pays visit to Chile's principal Naval Academy; Havana, Cuba—Havana Yacht Club crew wins annual rowing regatta; Saranac Lake, N. Y.—Baseball fans throughout nation mourn death of Christy Mathewson; New York City—Amundsen returns, ready to try another polar

flight; Mitchel Field, N. Y.—French aviator wins Liberty trophy race in nation's aerial classic; Washington, D. C.—Pictorial record of World Series games; Kansas City, Mo. (Kansas City only.)—Start drive to organize national Girls' week.

PATHE NEWS NO. 84: Faribault, Minn.—Women's rodeo goes the men one better; Lisieux, France—Commemorate thirtieth anniversary of death of St. Theresa; San Francisco, Cal.—Speedy whippets compete in Pacific Coast Classic; Munich, Germany—Bavarians revive historical harvest festival; Paris, France—Set Japanese air record in Tokio-to-Paris flight; N. Y. City—One hundred years of men's styles betray the stunning evolution of Broadway's Beau Brummels; Mitchel Field, N. Y.—Army flier sets new mark in Pulitzer race; Pittsburgh, Pa.—Pirates win sixth game and tie with Senators for World's Series title; N. Y. City (Atlanta only)—Georgia Tech defeats Penn State.

Langdon Three-Reeler is Due November 29th

"THERE HE GOES," Harry Langdon's first three-reel special comedy released by Pathe, will go to the exhibitors on November 29th. It presents a complete plot and is said to abound in comedy situations and gags. The comedian is supported in the principal roles by Peggy Montgomery and Frank Watson. Harry Edwards who directed the comedian in a number of his comedy vehicles handled the megaphone on "There He Goes."

Lane's Brother to Support Him in Comedy

Wallace Lane, brother of Lupino Lane, star of a series of two-reel comedies being released by Educational, will play the role of the comedy heavy in a picture now being made with Lane as the star. The picture is being directed by William Goodrich. Virginia Vance, George Davis and Glen Cavender are others in the supporting cast.

Ann Pennington Appears in Pathe Review Reel

Ann Pennington, dancing star of several Ziegfeld Follies shows, appears in a series of scenes produced by the "Process Camera" presented in Pathe Review No. 40. Miss Pennington illustrates the "Charleston" and several other dances in this feature of the Review.

Johnny Arthur Has Finished Third Educational

Johnny Arthur has completed his third comedy for Educational, a two-reeler in which he will appear as a boy in love with a movie-struck girl and fascinated only by the handsome heroes of the screen. William Goodrich directed the picture.

Jack McHugh Returns to Educational Studios

Jack McHugh, featured in several Educational-Juvenile Comedies released last season, will again be seen in these comedies. He is being co-starred with Malcolm Sebastian in a two-reeler now being produced under the direction of Charles Lamont.

Scenes from "Baby Be Good," first of the 1925-26 Educational-Juvenile Comedies. Malcolm Sebastian, and Bonnie Barrett are featured.

Opinions on Current Short Subjects

"A Winning Pair"
(Universal-Century—Two Reels)
(Reviewed by Chester J. Smith)

WANDA WILEY has a rather clever little comedy in this one, which shows her first as a bathing girl and later as an equestrienne. She is as attractive in the one costume as she is for the lack of it in the other. Rather a versatile Miss, this Wanda Wiley and she takes many a hard knock to put a comedy situation over. But she does put them over.

There are some bathing scenes with a bevy of attractive girls in the opening scenes and some good high diving stunts before the story starts to unwind. And then it develops that this high dive is all a dream and Miss Wiley wakes up in a dive into a lot of sofa pillows.

There are some fairly humorous shots when the comedienne attempts to mount a horse of considerable proportions when she would start on the conquest of the man she really loves. She is also the victim of some nasty falls, but they accomplish her purpose both in the action of the story and the securing of laughs.

The Cast

The Girl......................Wanda Wiley

A Century Comedy, directed by Charles Lamont.

The Story. Wanda dreams she is a high diver and visualizes herself in the center of a bevy of beautiful bathing girls, making a beautiful swan-like dive for the edification of the man she loves. She awakens to find herself diving into an assortment of sofa cushions. She then joins the man in a horseback ride, feigns a runaway and a fall from the horse to arouse his sympathy. Apparently unconscious, she is revived by the kisses of her lover in the usual happy ending.

Synopsis. A series of interesting episodes in which Miss Wiley shows her versatility as a diving girl and an equestrienne. There is a bit of good comedy in the story, which is far better than the usual run of these comedy tales. It's a fairly interesting picture that should go well in the neighborhood houses.

"Spot Light"
(Educational-Mermaid—Two Reels)
(Reviewed by Chester J. Smith)

THIS comedy of the veriest hokum and slapstick and for the most part so silly that only the younger children will be able to appreciate the humor in it. It starts out promisingly enough with Lige Conley in the role of the sandwich man on high stilts, who is so frequently seen along Broadway exploiting some attraction. There is some fair comedy as it goes, when Lige becomes entangled with an auto and various other obstacles along the road, but when the scene shifts to the playhouse and the action becomes faster and more furious, the comedy ceases, though it strives hard enough to please.

Every backstage prop and every other form of hokum and slapstick is used to interrupt the acts on the stage. Hooks are applied, sand bags dropped, rain released instead of show on each succeeding act in an effort to get laughs, which will hardly be forthcoming except from the very young element in the house.

The Cast

Props......................Lige Conley
The Prima Donna..............Virginia Vance

A Jack White production, written and directed by Norman Taurog, photographed by Barney McGill.

The Story.—Lige Conley as Props first has the role of a sandwich man on high stilts, who becomes entangled with autos and motorcycles along the road. Later he handles the props as the show progresses. The act of each en-

tertainer is interrupted by the various devices used backstage and the audience finally leaves the house in disgust.

Summary.—A slapstick comedy, whose humor will be appreciated only by the youngsters. There is no story. It is merely a succession of rough gags used to interrupt the acts of performers on a vaudeville program.

"Nursery Troubles"
Universal-Century—Two Reels
Reviewed by Chester J. Smith

ASIDE from a nursery full of attractive looking babies, this comedy would have little to recommend it. There are some exceptionally good shots of these babes taking their bottles and they will bring exclamations of joy from almost any audience, particularly from the feminine customers.

Edna Marian heads the cast in a role that permits her to show all her vivaciousness, first as a female tramp disguised as a boy, and later as the nursery maid in the department store, where youngsters are checked as their mothers shop, and where the comedy develops when Edna passes out the wrong babies to the wrong mothers.

There is not much in the way of exceptional comedy to the picture. For the most part Miss Marian is chased by a cop, whom she has jolted off his pins as she makes her escape from a freight train. For a full reel she succeeds in escaping the minion of the law in the usual manner of these comedies. There is plenty of action such as it is, but it will hardly provide much in the way of laughter.

The Cast

The Maid......................Edna Marian

The Story. Edna, disguised as a boy, makes her escape from a brakebeam only to bump into a policeman who gives chase. She evades him when she changes into girls' clothes in a park. She then proceeds to get herself a job as nursery maid in a department store where babes are checked as the mothers shop. She hands the wrong babes to the wrong mothers, but succeeds in righting matters, with the result that she is promoted to the head of the department and wins the love of the boss.

Summary. This is a fairly fast moving comedy without much of a story and with but few situations that will be productive of laughs. Its attractiveness is in the nursery shots, where some exceptionally bright looking babies will win the admiration of almost any audience and just about put the picture over.

"The Ace of Spades"
(Universal Serial)
(Reviewed by Thomas C. Kennedy)

THE first three episodes of this ten-chapter serial play affirm Universal's claims regarding fast action, thrill stunts and stirring melodramatic incident. Beyond that the first three episodes serve to convince the reviewer that "The Ace of Spades" gets off to a flying start and offers a veritable bumper crop of those elements of screen entertainment which make a banquet of speedy movement, exciting situations and Homeric heroism for the confirmed serial fans.

There is very little in the way of sure-fire serial material which has escaped the scenarist, director and players in these opening chapters of "The Ace of Spades." The story is simple in outline and yet is supplied with sufficient plot matter to keep the action going for all ten episodes. We have the inevitable "papers"—this time in the form of an old French mineral survey, made before the sale of the Louisiana Territory by Napoleon, which is being sought by villains before the opening of the Oklahoma Land Rush. We have become reconciled to the "papers" in serial plots. They are an eco-

nomical device of the dramatist and simplify matters as much for the spectator as they do for the playwright. There is nothing confusing about action built around "papers" either the sympathetic characters have them, or they haven't, and so the struggle between villains and heroes goes back and forth, like a tug-of-war in which the course of the contest is always clear enough to permit onlookers to concentrate on the struggle itself.

Willim Desmond, whose long experience has filled his box of tricks to overflowing, is the hero—and a suitably commanding and intense hero he is. Mary McAllister is the heroine and others in an excellent cast are Albert J. Smith, a capital serial villain; William A. Steele, Cathleen Calhoun, Jack Pratt, Clark Comstock, Frank Lanning and others.

The play takes its title from the fact that the villainous band sends an ace of spades to those it has marked for its vengeance—a picturesque device and a contributor to the suspense which the story is ever striving to create and sustain.

Director Henry McRae, an experienced and capable hand at serial-making, has set his action to a snappy pace and throws about his characters and situations all the romantic and adventurous glamour necessary to achieve graphic, colorful melodrama. The story by Isadore Bernstein and William Lord Wright has been very capably scenarioized by Jacobson. Based on the evidence furnished by the first three episodes, we are urged unhesitatingly to pronounce "The Ace of Spades" a corking good choice for any theatre seeking a serial attraction.

The Cast

Dan Harvey.....................William Desmond
Oliver Heath...................Mary McAllister
Joe Dineen.....................Albert J. Smith
Jim Heath......................William A. Steele
"Poker Dice" Ann...............Cathleen Calhoun
Gideon Trask...................Jack Pratt
Martin Heath...................Clark Comstock
Francois Bonaparte.............Frank Lanning

Story by Isadore Bernstein and William Lord Wright. Scenario by Leigh Jacobson. Directed by Henry McRae.

The Story—Gideon Trask and his henchmen at the saloon in Arkansas City covet the mineral survey of the Louisiana Territory made for Napoleon before the sale of the Territory to the United States. This is in possession of the Heath Brothers, who seek to use it in staking their land when the Oklahoma territory, last of the Louisiana tract to be released by the Government, is opened to Homesteaders. They send Dan Harvey, who has protected the Heath brothers and Martin Heath's daughter from the gang, the "Ace of Spades," which means he is marked for death. Dan and his party set out for the Oklahoma territory and are overtaken by the band. They find shelter in a cave built by Indians as a temple to the Sun God and there make their stand against Trask and his henchmen—the episode which brings the third episode to a close.

Summary.—A finely produced and acted serial play offering a conventional plot but supplied with sufficient melodramatic incident to permit a steady flow of fast action. Picturesque backgrounds and interesting characters give material aid to the plot, which has been well constructed, so far at least as the first three episodes are concerned. It should score a big hit with the serial fans.

"A Sweet Pickle"
(Pathe—Two Reels)
(Reviewed by Thomas C. Kennedy)

HERE is a comedy creation from the Sennett studios which may be recommended as a sure laugh-getter for any theatre. It presents a veritable welter of "wow" gags done in the best Sennett style and aimed directly at the risibles of all the fans in Filmdom. It starts off with the conventional "love interest" and ends up with a series of thrill stunts and comedy moments that should have every audience roaring its response and appreciation.

Alice Day is starred, and grateful of the opportunities the director has afforded her and her support to hit the comedy mark clean and often, Miss Day comes through with an excellent performance as the little poor girl who gets invited to a very "swell" party at a very "swell" home. Miss Day has excellent support from Barney Hellum, Jack Richardson and Alma Bennett.

To Director Arthur Rosson must go great credit for the effectiveness of the gags. He has devised a stunt in which Alice hangs out a window on the end of a long strip of carpet, the carpet running back and forth as the heroine ascends and descends on the outside of the building according as the hero is able to pull her up or is forced to let go his hold on the other end of the strip. Around and about this device are several extraordinary clever and effective incidents —a notable one being that which shows a man carrying a trunk on his back as he walks furiously but gets nowhere treading in the direction opposite to that in which the carpet is running with its precious weight toward the street below.

"A Sweet Pickle" is easily the best picture Miss Day has had since her elevation to stardom and it is one that can be backed to make good on screens everywhere.

The Cast

The Girl	Alice Day
The Boy	Barney Hellum
The Villain	Jack Richardson
The Vamp	Alma Bennett

The Story.—Alice, handy girl at the bakery, delivers a cake at the home of a wealthy customer. Learning that there will be thirteen guests, the son of the house, insists his mother invite Alice to join the party. The rich girl, jealous because she loves the rich chap, dresses Alice up in a ridiculous outfit, making her the butt of the party, but the hero still likes the girl and risks his life to save her when a fight ensues and Alice falls out the window holding to the end of a strip of hall carpet.

Summary.—A brisk and bright slapstick comedy in which quick action and a series of decidedly effective gags have been skillfully injected. The picture is one of broad appeal and should register as uproarous entertainment.

"Baby Be Good"
(Educational-Juvenile—Two Reels)
(Reviewed by Chester J. Smith)

QUITE an attractive array of juveniles have been gathered together for this series, of which this is the first, and they go through some highly amusing antics. For the most part it is back alley stuff and particularly true to life. If any adverse criticism is to be found with this picture it is that the producers have tried too hard to cram it with humorous incidents and odd contraptions for the development of laughs.

There is enough of the element of the high class to the picture when the Van Pelton kid is introduced, to bring it out of the gutter and lend a little diversion to it, as well as to develop the story, if the whole thing can be termed a story. It is more a panorama of incidents than a story, but the producers need strive no harder than they have to gain popularity for the series. It is a type of comedy together with the various types of kids that is bound to make it alluring to the picture fans. Charles Lamont directed and George Spear is responsible for the photoplay.

The Story.—The Van Pelton swimming pool is at first revealed with the children of the aristocracy in all of their glory. Two of the gas house kids happen in and determine upon a similar pool down in their neighborhood. All sorts of contrivances are rigged up with a hathtub for a chute the chutes and 'he price of a chute one bottle. Mrs. Van Pelton happens in the neighborhood with her child and leaves the latter in the limousine. The child wanders to the swimming pool and is made one of the gang. She is discovered by her adoring mother in such a begrimed condition that only a mother could identify her.

Summary.—A good lively kid comedy with some exceptionally good types and almost too many humorous incidents. It is a type of picture that will appeal to all in all kinds of houses.

"Amazing Mazie"
(F. B. O.—Two Reels)
(Reviewed by Thomas C. Kennedy)

THE opening episode of "The Adventures of Mazie" series which F. B. O. is presenting, serves first and most importantly as sparkling, bright and pleasant screen comedy. And next it presents convincing evidence that F. B. O. has launched another eminently successful venture in production enterprise. Every hall-mark of the sure-fire success is found here in this first offering in the new series. We have a neatly contrived situation for the creation of sympathy and a set of characters filled with color and appeal.

"Amazing Mazie" introduces the girl who figures as the central character in the stories —a self-reliant, courageous girl seeking a job to support herself and her invalid brother. She is a product of the American city, trifle bold and boisterous, but a winning, extremely likable kid for all of that.

To Alberta Vaughn has been entrusted this role, and the assignment was wisely made, for Miss Vaughn has every qualification to act the part convincingly and entertainingly. Larry Kent is the hero, a young lawyer who needs Mazie's aggressiveness to help him in his business. Al Cooke and Kit Guard, well and favorably remembered for their characterizations in the previous series which F. B. O. presented, have important parts to do in the pictures.

Ralph Ceder's direction is most capable. His handling of the action shows the most effective timing of the gags and there is dash and color to the play as a result of his treatment.

There is no disposition to act the prophet nor to claim especial wisdom in the judgment of screen comedies on the part of this reviewer in venturing quite confidently the opinion that "The Adventures of Mazie" can be built up into a very profitable box office attraction by any exhibitor who will take the trouble to exploit these comedies as entertainment of the most popular and effective sort.

The Cast

Mazie	Alberta Vaughn
George Dorsey	Larry Kent
T-ing	Al Cooke
Pali	Kit Guard

The Story.—Mazie, a stenographer, needs a job and when the young lawyer to whom she has applied tells her he hasn't even money to pay the rent, she sets about to force the hardhearted landlord to defer action against the attorney. A plot is evolved which places the landlord in the position of being liable to a suit for $50,000 damages because a client has been delayed, because the elevator halts between floors, or compensating the lawyer for his loss by offering rent free for several months and giving him the landlord's legal work.

Summary.—A highly entertaining two-reel comedy based on the humorous adventures of a self-reliant stenographer. The characters are colorful and receive the finest handling by the players cast for them. There is brisk action and the gags have been neatly contrived. An excellent short attraction for any theatre.

"The Heart Breaker"
(Fox—Two Reels)
(Reviewed by Chester J. Smith)

THERE is a fair story on which this comedy is based, but it is rather slow in getting started, though it develops some fast action before the finish. It is based on a wager that the president of a bachelors' club cannot visit a certain inn without becoming engaged. The comedy in the Bachelors' club scenes is rather overstressed, but there should be some laughs when the second reel gets fairly under way.

The Cast

The Hero	Sid Smith
The Heroine	Judy King
The Villan	Jack Henderson

An Imperial comedy directed by Benjamin Stoloff.

The Story.—When the shortcomings of a member of the Bachelors' Club are revealed to him for becoming engaged, he wagers the club president that the latter cannot spend a week at a designated inn without becoming engaged. The president takes the bet and finds the inn run by women and with only women guests, most of them of the beauteous sort.

That she may avoid an unwelcome suitor, one of the guests is disguised as a boy. The bachelor persuades her to don girl's attire, thinking her a boy, and to represent herse f as being engaged to him, so that he may avoid the other girls. By the time he discovers she is really a girl he has fallen in love with her. He helps her to evade the rejected suitor and her father and mother, who have made the match for her. The girl and the bachelor are finally married in the middle of the lake at the height of the chase.

Summary.—This is a fairly fast comedy once it gets under way. It is a combination of hokum and situations in its appeal for laughs, of which it should get a fair number. Sid Smith and Judy King play their roles well and they are ably supported throughout the good story.

"Shootin' Wild"
(Universal-Mustang—Two Reels)
(Reviewed by Chester J. Smith)

THIS one is quite apart from the usual run of Westerns. Save for the atmosphere and the costumes there is little of the Western about it. It strives to be a comedy with Ben Corbett and Pee Wee Holmes in the featured roles, but it does not get far in that direction either.

The wildest kind of slapstick and hokum are employed throughout the two reels and the action is not nearly as humorous as it strives to be. Perhaps in some houses they will appreciate the comedy in a bull with boxing gloves on his horns serving as a sparring partner to a comedy boxer preparing for a bout.

The picture approaches the western in the last reel when the bandits plan a raid of the town while a fair and the boxing bout are in progress. They are routed by the two heroes who set off a batch of fireworks and the skyrockets shooting down the street play havoc with the intruders.

The Cast

Magpie Simpkins	Ben Corbett
Dirtyshirt Jones	Pee Wee Holmes

The Story.—Dirtyshirt Jones is being prepared for a Fourth of July boxing bout with the town terror as the main attraction of the fair. While the bout is on the bandit band plan a raid of the town. The signal is prematurely given for the raid and as the bandits approach Magpie Simpkins and Dirtyshirt Jones set a match to the fireworks lying on a table at the end of the main street. Skyrockets and devil chasers whip up the street to the consternation of the raiders and result in the complete rout of the latter, as Magpie and Dirtyshirt emerge heroes.

Summary.—There is not much that can be recommended in this two-reeler. The comedy is of the rough slapstick variety with the situations too ridiculous to provide much in the way of humor.

Pre-release Reviews of Features

Without Mercy
(Producers Distributing Corp —6550 Feet)
(Reviewed by George T. Pardy)

AN interesting story with the melodramatic sequences considerably exaggerated, but nevertheless a good buy for the average house, as the acting and tense action will hold the spectators. The picture leans hard on the emotional moments and has an especially strong appeal for feminine patrons, inasmuch as its plot hinges on a woman's revenge on a man for ill-treatment after a period of twenty years has elapsed, and her final triumph. Director George Melford has upholstered the feature handsomely, there are many fine interior settings and the British atmosphere and society glitter are artistically conceived and executed. It is, of course, largely hokum material, but the sort of hokum that scores with most of the fans when properly utilized, and in this case smooth team work between director and players helps amazingly in establishing conviction, even when the most lurid situations flame redly.

THEME. Society melodrama, English setting, tale of young girl's infatuation for unworthy suitor and mother's revenge on him for former sufferings.

PRODUCTION HIGHLIGHTS. The good acting, skilled direction, melodramatic punches and even continuity.

EXPLOITATION ANGLES. Play up the story's tense emotional appeal, melodramatic force; and feature Dorothy Phillips, Vera Reynolds, Lionel Belmore, Robert Ames.

DRAWING POWER. Suitable for average house.

SUMMARY. Has general audience appeal, a society melo, well acted, directed and handsomely mounted.

THE CAST
Mrs. Enid Garth.............................Dorothy Phillips
Sir Melmoth Craven.........................Rockliffe Fellowes
Margaret Garth..............................Vera Reynolds
John Orme...................................Robert Ames
Horace Massingham..........................Lionel Belmore
Author, John Goodwin. Directed by George Melford. Photographed by Charles G. Clarke.

SYNOPSIS. Sir Melmoth Craven and John Orme are political opponents for seat in English Parliament. Craven borrows money for campaign from Gordon, Ltd., a shady money-lending establishment. Margaret Garth, Orme's sweetheart, becomes infatuated with Melmoth. To save the girl, her mother narrates the history of her own sufferings at Melmoth's hands twenty years before. Mrs. Garth is behind the loan granted Craven and had it suddenly called in. Melmoth kidnaps Margaret, who is saved by Orme. Melmoth falls into trap prepared by Mrs. Garth and is jailed. Margaret and Orme are united.

Bustin' Through
(Universal—4506 Feet)
(Reviewed by George T. Pardy)

AN average Western which should make the box office grade generally speaking, and do especially well wherever Jack Hoxie is popular! The latter is undoubtedly one of the best looking of the cowboy-hero tribe, snaggles an engaging grin, is never averse to closeups, and to do him justice cuts quite an alluring figure before the camera. Also, he can ride and scrap in whirlwind fashion, and they give him plenty of rough-house tasks in "Bustin' Through," all of which he executes with such vigor and dispatch that the picture may be said to live fairly up to its title. The story's trend isn't particularly original, but director Cliff Smith, having tackled similar problems before, knew exactly how to overcome this handicap and "pepped" the situations up by dexterous handling, keeping the action whizzing at a lively pace, and attaining a smashing climax.

THEME. Western melodrama, young rancher hero, who defeats scheme of crooks to swindle father of girl he loves; and wins latter.

PRODUCTION HIGHLIGHTS. The fast action, riding and fighting stuff, Jack Hoxie's daring stunts and clever horsemanship, finale in which he pursues villain across country and captures him, romantic interest.

EXPLOITATION ANGLES. Feature Jack Hoxie. Tell the fans he is at his best in this fast-moving, brisk Western. Bill as intriguing romance of the open spaces.

DRAWING POWER. Good program attraction. Should win wherever they want straight Western films.

SUMMARY. Average Western, with Jack Hoxie working at top speed, romantic interest and plenty of action. Story not so original, but will pass as standard program attraction.

THE CAST
Jack Savage................................Jack Hoxie
Helen Merrit...............................Helen Lynch
Harvey Gregg...............................William Norton Bailey
John Merrit................................Alfred Allen
Rudolph Romano.............................Georgie Grandee
Scenario by Buckley Oxford. Director, Cliff Smith. Photographed by William Noble.

SYNOPSIS. Jack Savage refuses to sell his ranch to John Merrit, whom he does not know to be the father of Helen, the girl he loves. Merrit's lawyer, Gregg, is double-crossing his employer in the land deals the latter is making, intending to sell at a profit to a water company. Jack discovers and upsets Gregg's plans, but is temporarily obliged to run away. Later he returns, eludes the sheriff by a clever ruse, saves Helen in a runaway accident. He captures Gregg, exposes him, and wins Helen.

Vera Reynolds in "Without Mercy," a Producers Distributing Corp. release.

Without Mercy (Producers Dis. Corp)
PRESS NOTICE

A SOCIETY melodrama of intense force and emotional appeal, entitled "Without Mercy," is scheduled to be shown on the screen of the ———— Theatre on ————. The action takes place in England, the story dwells on the theme of a woman's revenge on a man who ill-treated her twenty years before, and with whom her daughter is temporarily infatuated. An unusual picture, attaining a great climax, beautifully mounted and photographed. The popular favorite, Dorothy Phillips, returns to the screen in this feature, playing the mother role, with Vera Reynolds as the daughter, Robert Ames the hero, and Rockliffe Fellowes, Lionel Belmore, Patricia Palmer, Fred Malatesta, Sidney D'Albrook in support.

CATCH LINES
A woman who deals with a man without mercy, generally has a good reason. See what it was in this case!

Jack Hoxie, star of "Bustin' Through," a Universal production.

Bustin' Through (Universal)
PRESS NOTICE

A DMIRERS of redblood Western melodrama have a treat in store for them on ———— at the ———— Theatre, when Jack Hoxie in "Bustin' Through" is the main screen attraction. Admirers of Hoxie know him as one of the most daredevil type of the cowboy hero brigade, and he fights, rides and executes any amount of nerve-racking stunts. The story shows Jack defeating the schemes of a crooked lawyer to fleece the father of the girl he loves, falsely accused, but overcoming his foes, and winning her.

Jack Hoxie is at his best in this picture, and supported by a talented cast, with Helen Lynch as the pretty heroine, and William Norton Bailey, Alfred Allen and Georgie Grandee filling important roles.

CATCH LINES
A stirring romance of the cattle country, full of thrilling scenes, fighting and love-making.

Three Wise Crooks
(F. B. O.—6074 Feet)
(Reviewed by George T. Pardy)

A FIRST-CHOP underworld yarn with sentiment, thrills, comedy and melodrama churned into the sort of attraction that nine out of ten fans will gloat over greedily, go home looking nervously about dark corners, yet wishing there had been more of it. The picture has mass appeal, there's no doubt about that, and Evelyn Brent "wins hands down" when it comes to portraying one of these sweetly fascinating crook ladies whose fingers are as nimble as their smiles are irresistible. There's a big market for this sort of entertainment, folks like to get a glimpse of what they suppose is the real seamy side of life, if overdrawn it makes little difference, so long as the director is on to his job, keeps the action fizzing furiously and gets the right support from his cast members.

THEME. Crook melodrama, with girl heroine and two helpers who finally all get under influence of kindly country persons, settle down and go straight.

PRODUCTION HIGHLIGHTS. Mystery and thrill atmosphere, bright comedy situations. Scene where the three confederates make their getaway after trimming diamond merchant.

EXPLOITATION ANGLES. Play this up as an admirable example of the sort of picture which has made Evelyn Brent famous from coast to coast. Also stamp it as the best of its kind, feature the star and dwell on the film's snappy comedy.

DRAWING POWER. Ought to prove fine box office attraction in all houses where forceful underworld melodramas are in favor.

SUMMARY. A swiftly moving underworld melodrama in which the star, Evelyn Brent, hits the treasury target hard. The picture is well acted, snappily directed and has general audience appeal.

THE CAST
Dolly	Evelyn Brent
Ma Dickenson	Fanny Midgley
Spug Casey	John Gough
Dan Pelton	Bruce Gordon
Grogan	William Humphrey

Au'hors, John Brownell and Fred Myton. Director F. Harmon Weight.

SYNOPSIS. Dolly Duvans, clever crook, pays a visit to Ma Dickinson in Greenville, the latter having being befriended by Dolly in the city. Finding out that the village banker Silas Wetherby and an oil promoter named Wadsworth are framing to cheat the towns-fclk out of their savings, she sends for two Pals Dan Pelton and Spug Casey. Detective Grogan comes to investigate Wadsworth's oil schemes. Wadsworth and Wetherby plan to leave the bank at night. But the safe is empty, Spug and Dolly having taken the money with the intention of returning it to the owners. Dan picks up an incriminating piece of paper left by Wetherby with which he c'ears Dolly when suspicion is directed to her. Dolly and Dan are united, Spug weds a village girl and all go straight.

Satan in Sables
(Warner Brothers—7260 Feet)
(Reviewed by George T. Pardy)

A MELODRAMA of life in the shadows and sunlight of Paris, with the inevitable Apache girl, now such a familiar figure on the American screen, as heroine, and a prince of the Russian blood-royal for hero. The whole atmosphere of the picture is ultra-theatrical, but just the same it looks like a good box office bet, being sumptuously mounted, well acted and exciting from beginning to end. To put it briefly, "Satan in Sables" belongs in the "popular entertainment" class and ought to bring the shekles into the exhibitor's treasury. Lowell Sherman heads the all-star cast. His performance is a bit stilted and artificial, but he certainly invests the role with a magnificent dignity which will probably satisfy the average fan's conception of how a prince in real life should conduct himself.

Pauline Garon is vivacious, natural and appealing as the Apache heroine, John Harron plays the part of the prince's younger brother remarkably well, and other members of the company render excellent support.

THEME. Melodrama of high and low life in Paris, with Apache heroine and Russian prince for hero, who finally weds her.

PRODUCTION HIGHLIGHTS. Party given by prince on night of Mardi Gras, when Apache heroine makes debut through window and astonishes guests by her dancing. The rich interiors, colorful atmosphere.

EXPLOITATION ANGLES. Title will fetch feminine patrons. Bill as exciting, melodramatic love story of Paris, play up the Apache atmosphere. Feature Lowell Sherman and Pauline Garon.

DRAWING POWER. Should do well in all classes of theatres.

SUMMARY. Melodrama of society and underworld life in Paris, plenty of love interest and thrills, story rather artificial, but will please most patrons as it is exciting from start to finish, well mounted and acted.

THE CAST
Michael Lyev Yervedoff	Lowell Sherman
Paul Yervedoff	John Harron
Colette Breton	Pauline Garon
Dolores Sierra	Gertrude Astor
Victor	Frank Butler
Emile	Francis J. MacDonald

Author, Bradley King. Directed by James Flood.

SYNOPSIS. Michael Yervedoff, Russian prince, leads a gay life in Paris. At a Mardi Gras party he gives, Colette, Apache girl, flits through an open window and astonishes all by her wild dancing. She and Michael are mutually attracted. Michael's discarded mistress, Dolores, seeks revenge by vamping Michael's beloved younger brother Paul. On the eve of marriage to Dolores, Paul suspects her former relations with Michael and visits the latter to learn the truth. In a frenzy of grief Paul drives his auto madly through the streets, it is overturned and Paul fatally injured. The shock changes Michael's life. He settles down and weds Colette.

Evelyn Brent, star of "Three Wise Crooks," an F. B. O. release.

Three Wise Crooks (F. B. O.)

PRESS NOTICE

EVELYN BRENT is due to appear at the ——— Theatre on ——— as the star of another of those thrilling underworld melodramas of the screen with which her name has become identified from New York to the Go'den Gate. The film in question is "Three Wise Crooks," a production crammed with sensational incident, romance and brilliant comedy. The plot shows how a successful criminal trio came so thoroughly under the kindly influence of an old lady in a country town that they finally abandoned their adventurous life and went straight for the future.

CATCH LINES

The shrill of police whistles and rush of feet, mysterious shadows looming across the dimly lighted pavement, glittering gems gone, the thieves disappeared! Wait till you see this, and what follows in "Three Wise Crooks!"

Lowell Sherman, star of "Satan in Sables," a Warner Bros. production.

Satan in Sables (Warner Bros.)

PRESS NOTICE

AN unique and exciting melodrama of society and underworld life in Paris, entitled "Satan in Sables," will be the main attraction on the screen of the ——— Theatre on ———. The story deals with a love affair which springs up between the hero, a Russian prince who leads a gay life, and Colette, an Apache girl. It is packed with suspense, thrills and magnificently mounted. Lowell Sherman plays the prince hero, with pretty Pauline Garon as the Apache girl, both giving splendid performances.

CATCH LINES

Prince Michael lived only for the social whirl and pleasures of life in the French capital. Then, came the strange fascination of a street gamin—a graceful, reckless dancing bit of a girl—and love claimed him.

The Midshipman
(Metro-Goldwyn-Mayer—7498 Feet)
(Reviewed by George T. Pardy)

YOU can call this navy propaganda and not be far out, and at the same time pronounce it bully screen entertainment without making any mistake. The Annapolis atmosphere is all that the most inveterate stickler for accurate detail could wish, real dignity being lent the story by the scenes showing the ancient buildings framed by the silver radiance of the glistening Severn. And at the same time we are given a story which not only carries the action, but rings in the human sympathy gag with tremendous vim. The plot is skimpy, but interesting. It concerns the rivalry between a naval cadet and a rich civilian for the affections of Patricia Lawrence. Freckle-faced Wesley Barry fills the role of Patricia's brother Ted, and there's a funny sequence based on the idea nourished by midshipman Navarro that the sister must resemble the unhandsome brother.

Navarro makes an excellent impression in the leading role. He doesn't overact or seem to be handicapped by the wearing of an unfamiliar uniform, something which in the past has sadly hampered the screen gyrations of many so-called stars.

THEME. Navy melodrama with genuine backgrounds, as exemplified by Annapolis scenes taken on the spot, with hero defeating enemies' schemes and winning girl he loves.

PRODUCTION HIGHLIGHTS. The accurate and charming Annapolis scenes and correct naval atmosphere. Excellent acting of principals and supporting cast.

EXPLOITATION ANGLES. You can play this up as a cracking melodrama, with fast action all the way, a capital and exact portrayal of life in the U. S. Naval Academy. Feature Novarro, Wesley Barry and Margaret Seddon.

DRAWING POWER. Should prove good card for big and little houses.

SUMMARY. A forceful melodrama, with navy propaganda ingeniously worked into story, without injuring entertainment values. A box office magnet for any theatre.

THE CAST
MIDSHIPMAN RANDALL	Ramon Novarro
Patricia Lawrence	Harriet Hammond
Ted Lawrence	Wesley Barry
Mrs. Randall	Margaret Seddon
Basil Courtney	Crawford Kent
Patricia's Aunt	Pauline Neff
Rita	Kathleen Key

Author, Carey Wilson. Director, Christy Cabanne. Photographed by Oliver Marsh.

SYNOPSIS. James Randall enters Annapolis Naval Academy and falls in love with Patricia, sister of freshman Ted Lawrence. Ted gets into bad company and is forced to sign Randall's name to a check. Randall faces the blackmailers and regains the check. Later, Patricia is kidnapped and imprisoned aboard a yacht. Randall goes to her aid, is overpowered and thrown overboard. He gets ashore and starts destroyers on the trail of the yacht. She is overhauled, Patricia rescued, and her bethrotal to Randall announced in due form.

The Midshipman (Metro-Goldwyn)
PRESS NOTICE

A FASCINATING romance of the U. S. Naval Academy, Annapolis, is offered in the presentation on the screen of the —— Theatre on —— of "The Midshipman", starring Ramon Novarro. This film was made with the direct assistance and co-operation of the Navy Department, and is therefore correct in every detail. It offers a story of breathless interest, full of thrills, suspense and romance, works up to an exciting climax and is in every way an unique and extraordinary production.

The tale dwells upon the troubles and triumphs of the life of an Annapolis graduate.

CATCH LINES

For the first time in film history, in the making of "The Midshipman," the U. S. authorities granted permission for the taking of authentic scenes at the Annapolis Naval Academy.

Ramon Novarro in "The Midshipman," released by Metro-Goldwyn-Mayer

Tessie
(Arrow Film Corp.—6800 Feet)
(Reviewed by George T. Pardy)

SNAPPY, bright, full of ginger, this comedy drama ought to prove a box office winner for the average house. It deals with everyday sort of folks, has a deal of human sympathy as well as humorous values and trips along at a merry gait with unhampered continuity and good acting by the entire cast. The sub titles are terse and witty, most of them taken verbatim from Sewell Ford's story on which the picture is based. Not the least of the feature's entertaining qualities is its ability to keep the spectators guessing as to what will be the outcome of the tangling-up of Tessie's two suitors, the auto salesman who jilts her for a wealthy widow, and the latter's son, who is rather an unlicked cub, but develops considerable determination at the close, when he carries off the gal in triumph.

This is good direction, and in fact the whole film is very well handled. Pretty May McAvoy is a most enticing Tessie, Bobby Agnew registers a hit as Roddy, the bashful chap who makes good at the last, Lee Moran scores as the bumptious salesman and the support is capital.

THEME. Comedy drama, with girl hotel clerk, sought by two suitors and wedding wealthy one at finish.

PRODUCTION HIGHLIGHTS. Excellent acting of May McAvoy and supporting cast. Ingenious mingling of little pathetic touches with comedy situations. Well sustained suspense and clever climax.

EXPLOITATION ANGLES. Play up as breezy, interesting comedy drama, with heart interest as well as lively humor. Feature May McAvoy, Bobby Agnew and Lee Moran.

DRAWING POWER. Should get the money in average house.

SUMMARY. Lots of snap and go to this comedy drama, which is well acted, moves briskly and has sympathetic and sharp humorous appeal. Direction capable, photography O. K.

THE CAST
Tessie	May McAvoy
Roddy Welles	Bobby Agnew
Barney Taylor	Lee Moran
Mrs. Welles	Myrtle Steadman
Mame McGuire	Gertrude Short
Aunt Maggie	Mary Gordon
Uncle Dan	Frank Perry

Author, Sewell Ford. Directed by Dallas M. Fitzgerald.

SYNOPSIS. Tessie is in charge of cigar and candy counter in large hotel. Her fiance is Barney Taylor, auto mechanic. Wealthy widow Mrs. Welles and son Roddy become guests. Urged by Tessie, Barney gets salesman's job and sells Mrs. Welles a car. Also, he captures the widow's heart. In revenge, Tessie accepts Roddy's attentions. The widow visits Tessie's home to buy her off, but fails. Barney appears, declares he still loves Tessie and that widow vamped him. But Roddy arrives, beats up Barney and carries Tessie off in triumph to wed.

Tessie (Arrow Films)
PRESS NOTICE

L AUGHTER and romance mingle freely in "Tessie," a comedy drama which comes to the screen of the —— Theatre on —— May McAvoy is the star, portraying a cute little hotel girl employed at the candy and cigar counter, who helps her auto-salesman fiance along in business until he makes a tenstrike with a rich widow, and jilts her. Tessie, in revenge, accepts the attentions of the widow's son and a most intriguing set of complications develop.

May McAvoy is said by the critics in general to be at her very best in the role of Tessie and is well supported, with Bobby Agnew, Myrtle Steadman, Lee Moran and Gertrude Short appearing in important parts.

CATCH LINES

Tessie's suitors were many but she was faithful to one, until he played her false. Then, she took a woman's revenge, and vamped the son of the widow her unreliable fiance fell for.

May McAvoy, starring in "Tessie," for Arrow Films.

Big Pal

(Ginsberg—5 Reels)

(Reviewed by Thomas C. Kennedy)

TO the credit of "Big Pal" and of William Russell, its star, it may be said that Russell puts up as honest a fight in the boxing match which marks the climax of this sentimental melodrama as ever was staged on the screen or in the squared circle itself. We have seen many fights in the photoplays, but not one which exhibited such earnestness nor one in which the hero of the proceedings gave and took such punishment as Bill Russell gives and takes in this picture.

The story, unfortunately, is hardly worthy such earnestness and sincerity as Russell gives forth. It is sentimental conventionalism in melodramatics, and lacks the incident and characterization to sustain it through five reels. Everything works up to the fight scenes, with the hero, a battler because it is his trade and because he needs money to send his ill mother on a health tour, forced into the position of winning the fight and saving his reputation for honesty or losing and regaining his nephew, kidnapped and held for this ransom. The fight scenes are excellent in their every detail and atmosphere but "Big Pal" is mechanical and unconvincing and loses its audience before the fight arrives.

THEME. A sentimental melodrama about a prize fighter and his romance with a girl of the "upper strata" of society.

PRODUCTION HIGHLIGHTS. The climax scenes, reproducing in faithful detail a prize fight. The acting and sincerity of the players.

EXPLOITATION ANGLES. Bill as a story of fighter who fights to gain the very things for which men in the most distinguished professions strive and work.

DRAWING POWER. For houses with the so-called "transient" patronage.

SUMMARY. A sentimental melodrama honestly played and produced but lacking in dramatic substance and convincing characterization.

THE CAST

Dan Williams	William Russell
Helen Truscott	Julanne Johnston
Mary Williams	Mary Carr
Johnny Williams	Mickey Bennett

Directed by John G. Adolphi.

SYNOPSIS. Prize fighter, honest to the core, is notified that unless he quits in the fifth round of a big bout his nephew, whom he loves better than life itself, will never be given up by the kidnappers who make him captive on the eve of the fight. Dan spares his opponent and is on the point of a knockout when the boy, who has escaped, runs up to the ringside and Dan then "cuts loose" and wins. He also wins the consent of his sweetheart to become his wife.

William Russell, star of the Ginsburg production, "Big Pal."

Ridin' the Wind

(F. B. O.—Six Reels)

(Reviewed by Thomas C. Kennedy)

FRED THOMSON contends with an inept conglomeration of melodrama and slapstick in this offering and finds the task a formidable one. The star, of course, registers a generally pleasant and attractive performance, but he has been left sadly in the lurch by the scenarist, who failed to invent the type of situations best suited for the display of Thomson's talents for humorous characterization and his skill in horsemanship. More "Ridin'" and less slapstick and sentimental hokum would have been better than this inexpert mixture of conventional drivel about a big brother whose charge turns out to be a crook despite the sacrifices which Jim has made in order to give Dicky a college education and all the advantages he knew his mother, who died when they were boys, would have wanted her youngest son to have.

Thomson is supported by Jacqueline Gadson, appealing as the school teacher whom the hero loves, Lewis Sargent, as the weak brother, and Betty Scott, in the role of a spinster who prays every night for Providence to send her a husband. The characters are unconvincing, but further than that the play jolts about from one extreme of the dramatic range to the other, hopping clumsily over the intermediate stages and moving at a snail's pace. It is not up to the standard of this star's former works.

THEME. Western melodrama about a big brother who sacrifices in interests of the younger and then finds that the boy is a member of a gang of notorious crooks.

PRODUCTION HIGHLIGHTS. Comedy scenes in which Thomson and "Silver King" star; the hero's riding and his fights with the villains.

EXPLOITATION ANGLES. Popularity of star offers best publicity angle. Concentrate on that.

DRAWING POWER. Will ride along on strength of star's previous work.

SUMMARY. A western melodrama hampered by sentimentality and ineffective slapstick as comedy relief. Unconvincing and action is leaden-footed. Star does his best to make his character interesting.

THE CAST

Jim Harkness	Fred Thomson
May Lacy	Jacqueline Gadson
Dick Harkness	Lewis Sargent
Dolly Dutton	Betty Scott
Gang Leader	David Dunbar

By Marion Jackson. Directed by Del Andrews.

SYNOPSIS. Jim Harkness makes every sacrifice to give his young brother a college education. The youth comes home to visit Jim and becomes involved in several notorious robberies. He is saved from disgrace through the heroic efforts of Jim in beating off the gang and returning the stolen goods to the owners. The boy reforms and Jim marries May Lacy, the sheriff's daughter.

Fred Thomson, Western star, whose latest is "Ridin' the Wind." F. B. O.

Fighting Youth
(Columbia Pictures Corp.—4781 Feet)
(Reviewed by George T. Pardy)

THERE'S quite a smart run upon pugilistic pets for screen heroes these days, and muscular, agile William Fairbanks shows to capital advantage as a mitt-wielder in this one. It's the kind of feature that should do very well in communities where they like the whirlwind action and highly colored romance type of picture without worrying about plot probabilities. The formula employed here has nothing uncommon about it, most of the situations having done loyal duty frequently in other productions dealing with the prize ring, but we're bound to admit that the director of "Fighting Youth" has turned out a bright, breezy film without any dull spots in it which will entertain a large percentage of the fans. Moreover, he hasn't spoiled the picture by padding it out to a superfluous length. It stays within the five reel limit where it belongs.

Bill Fairbanks battles vigorously, makes love ardently and indulges copiously in automobile, aeroplane and swimming stunts into the bargain. Pauline Garon, petite and vivacious, shines as heroine Jean Manley and the support is O. K.

THEME. Stunt melodrama of prize ring, hero young society chap with a hot temper, whose fondness for scrapping leads him into all sorts of scrapes.

PRODUCTION HIGHLIGHTS. The ring fights. Fairbanks' stunts. Comedy relief.

EXPLOITATION ANGLES. Boost the story as a real thriller chockful of action. Tell 'em about Bill Fairbanks' athletic feats, the auto, aeroplane and swimming situations.

DRAWING POWER. Should fill the bill nicely for neighborhood and smaller houses.

SUMMARY. Prize ring melo, with comedy relief and Bill Fairbanks scoring heavily as glove-battler and general stunt performer. Moves fast all the way and should make good wherever they want exciting action and plenty of it.

THE CAST
Dick Covington...................................William Fairbanks
Jean Manley......................................Pauline Garon
Judge Manley.....................................George Periolat
Harold Brentty...................................William N. Bailey
Paddy Ryan.......................................Pat Harmon
Murdering Mooney.................................Frank Hagney
Gangster...Tom Carr
Author, Paul Archer. Director, Reeves Eason. Photographed by George Meehan.

SYNOPSIS. Dick Covington, young society athlete, is upbraided by his fiancee, Jean Manley, for constantly getting into fights. He promises to keep the peace, but a rival steers him into accepting an offer to box at a charity show. Jean is furious until insulted by Dick's prospective opponent, when she bids him win. But his rival has Dick kidnapped and kept prisoner in a barn far out in the country. He makes a getaway in his guards' auto, which is wrecked, gets a lift from a kindly aviator whose plane cannot land at the fight stadium. Dick swims a lake and reaches the ringside in time to fight, is badly battered at first but finally knocks his man out, exposes his rival's treachery and wins Jean.

The Everlasting Whisper
(Fox—5611 Feet)
(Reviewed by George T. Pardy)

A TYPICAL Tom Mix yarn and one that will make his huge following whoop in admiration of their hero and—the never-to-be-forgotten horse Tony. Both Thomas and the famous steed deserve all the applause they get, the former, as usual, fights off his foes with careless abandon and success, while Tony bucks his hard hoofs against a bunch of wolves, holding them at bay until his master arrives and takes a hand in the game. Another big scene is that in which Tom gallops along a narrow mountain path and snatches the heroine from her horse just an instant before it plunges upon a broken bridge across a precipice. In fact, this is best described as real "Tom Mixian" melodrama. If one may be permitted to coin a phrase, and a box office winner wherever good Westerners are in favor.

Yet it would not be fair to class "The Everlasting Whisper" as just a Westerner, and let it go at that. The picture is distinctly high-grade in point of direction, acting and photography and should be listed as a super-product of the open-air, romance, adventure sort.

THEME. Western melodrama, with hero defeating swindlers who endeavor to steal secret of gold mine.

PRODUCTION HIGHLIGHTS. Tom Mix's smart acting, in combination with his wonder-horse Tony, who executes some marvelous stunts. The fast, sweeping action, melodramatic thrills and well developed romance.

EXPLOITATION ANGELS. Boost this as a regular Tom Mix melodrama, with a punch in every foot, alluring love interest, and Tony, the wonder horse, performing stunts that will make 'em all sit up and take notice.

DRAWING POWER. Has the general audience appeal slant, good for any house.

SUMMARY. Western melodrama, one of Tom Mix's real thrillers, packs a punch every other moment, moves fast, is strong on love angle. Should do well anywhere.

THE CAST
Mark King ....Tom Mix
Gloria Gaynor ....Alice Calhoun
Gratton ....Robert Cain
Old Honeycutt....................................George Berrell
Aswin Brody ....Walter James
Mrs. Gaynor ....Virginia Madison
Jarrold ....Karl Dane
Author, Jackson Gregory. Director J. G. Blystone.

SYNOPSIS. Mark King saves Gloria Gaynor from falling over a cliff when her horse stumbles. He rides with her to her mother's lodge. In the early morning they go together to the cabin of old Honeycutt, who holds the secret of a gold mine. In gratitude for King's kindness Honeycutt reveals the location of the mine. King prevents the marriage of Gloria to Gratton, a swindler and weds her himself. The gold is finally found and Gloria and her lover, in the everlasting whisper of the pines, start their pursuit of happiness.

William Fairbanks, the fighting star of "Fighting Youth," a Columbia picture.

Fighting Youth (Columbia Pictures)

Tom Mix, star of the Fox production, "The Everlasting Whisper."

The Everlasting Whisper (Fox)

Durand of the Bad Lands

(Fox—5900 Feet)

(Reviewed by Chester J. Smith)

HERE is a real smart Western with a well told and well acted story. Here and there it has a bit of the hackneyed tale characteristic of the western, but for the most part it fairly sparkles with action and suspense such as is rarely seen in pictures of this type.

Buck Jones fits into the role of Durand nicely and his acting brings all the sympathy necessary to the misunderstood and much maligned "bandit." But second to the work of the star is that of another Buck—Buck Black, a youngster who plays the part of Jimmy, the orphaned youth who aids Durand through many tough situations. Young Buck acts as naturally as Buck Jones and between them they will hold many an audience spellbound.

THEME. A Western melodrama in which the alleged "bad man" is ultimately revealed as the real hero and the sheriff is proven the real bad man.

PRODUCTION HIGHLIGHTS. The splendid performances given by Buck Jones, Buck Black and the entire cast. The fight between Durand and Sheriff Allison.

EXPLOITATION ANGLES. A bookstore tieup, as the picture was adapted from the well known story by Maibelle Heikes Justice. The name of Buck Jones is worth a lot from the box office angle.

DRAWING POWER. There are not many picture goers who would not get some kick out of this picture. They will eat it up where the Western is popular and they'll like it elsewhere.

SUMMARY. An exceptionally good Western with a well told and well acted story. It abounds in action and good situations and runs along smoothly.

THE CAST

Dick Durand	Buck Jones
Molly Gore	Marian Nixon
Clem Allison	Malcolm Waite
Pete Garson	Fred De Silva
Kingdom Come Knapp	Luke Cosgrove
John Boyd	George Lessley
Jimmie	Buck Black
Clara Belle Seesel	Ann Johnson

From the novel by Maibelle Heikes Justice. Directed by Lynn Reynolds.

SYNOPSIS. Durand is wanted in the West for a number of crimes attributed to him. He befriends Molly Gore, whose invalid father is unable to do any work around the farm. Pete Garson, evil genius of the town and Sheriff Allison plan a holdup of the Boyd gold on the way to the station. They pin the crime on Durand and trail him to the girl's cottage where he has taken the children of the murdered victims of the holdup. Durand makes his getaway and proceeds to the office of the U. S. Marshall, where he establishes his innocence and returns in time to rescue Boyd's daughter who is imprisoned in the mine and to establish the guilt of the real criminals. Durand, Molly Gore and the children ride off in the happy conclusion.

New Brooms

(William De Mille Production-Paramount—5443 Feet)

(Reviewed by Frank Elliott)

A LIGHT, airy offering requiring little exercise of the grey matter, but diverting withal. William DeMille has taken Frank Craven's play and transplanted it to the shadow stage in a fairly entertaining manner. It is a picture that will please most audiences because it is pure humor all through. The plot has to do with a self satisfied youth who thinks he knows more than dad about business and household affairs, so pater gives his son complete charge of both for a year, while the elder Bates is running around with the girls and idling. The son soon proves a flop at business as well as love making and in the end, so confesses to dad.

THEME. A comedy of American home life in which a father comes close to wrecking his business, but makes a man out of his son in doing it.

PRODUCTION HIGHLIGHTS. The laughable situation when the son, taking charge of the household, has to pay all the bills, which he formerly ran up with vigor. The son's adventures in the factory with the "Keep Smiling" sign eventually ending in the basket.

EXPLOITATION ANGLES. Tie up department and hardware store windows with new broom displays. Try and put over a "Clean Up Week" in your town. Give out toy brooms to children at special matinee.

DRAWING POWER. A good program picture, with some well known stars to help pull 'em in.

SUMMARY. An unpretentious but good little comedy which should be suitable material around which to build up an excellent all-comedy program. Well acted, possessing many laughs.

THE CAST

Thomas Bates, Jr.	Neil Hamilton
Geraldine Marsh	Bessie Love
Florence Levering	Phyllis Haver
Thomas Bates, Sr.	Robert McWade
Williams	Fred Walton
Margaret	Josephine Crowell
George Morrow	Larry Steers
Kneeland	James Neil

From the stage play by Frank Craven. Directed by William DeMille. Scenario by Clara Beranger. Photographed by L. Guy Wilky.

SYNOPSIS. After being called a grouch by his son and informed that his business methods are all wrong, Thomas Bates, Sr., decides to put his offspring in charge of said business for a year. Geraldine Marsh, daughter of an old friend, is taken into the home as a housekeeper. Tom Jr., falls in love with her and breaks his engagement to Florence Levering, his dad's ward. Tom suspects his dad of being in love with Geraldine and tells both to leave. They do. Tom is a "flop" as a businessman. At the end of a year Dad and Geraldine return. Tom finds she is not married to his Dad. He weds her. Dad takes over the reins again at the factory.

Simon the Jester
(Producers Distributing Corp.—5870 Feet)
(Reviewed by George T. Pardy)

LOOKED at from any angle this production measures up to the best standards. The plot, based upon a story by that fine literary craftsman—William J. Locke, fairly throbs with human interest, and has been developed into a picture of rare beauty and rich entertaining value. Director George Melford displays his usual skill in handling backgrounds and atmosphere, the English scenery seems every whit as charming as the real thing, and the circus life under the big tents is as picturesque and realistic as the most captious critic could demand. A vein of warm sympathy runs all through the feature, which is also strong in suspense and thrills. Of course, Simon's love affair with Lola is the most important thing in the film, and who can withhold pity from a hero whom we are informed at the first stage is ill from a malady bound to carry him off within a short period?

He doesn't die, however, and in this case the producers didn't change the book ending for the sake of attaining a happy finish, for the novel also presents Simon triumphantly recovered. In fact they've kept pretty close to the original story in filming it, so that lovers of Locke's delightful works will find the picture satisfying. The acting of principals and support is superb.

THEME. English drama. Hero ill of malady, doomed to die, falls in love with circus rider, weds, having recovered health.

PRODUCTION HIGHLIGHTS. Fine photography, clever acting, good direction, smooth continuity.—Sustained love interest, suspense, thrills. Circus atmosphere.

EXPLOITATION ANGLES. Feature Lillian Rich and Eugene O'Brien. Boost story's sympathetic values, fine sentiment and exciting situations.

DRAWING POWER. Good for big and small houses alike, and family trade.

Summary. A drama of great heart interest, beautifully photographed, acted and well directed. High-class production with general audience appeal.

THE CAST

Simon de Gex	Eugene O'Brien
Lola Brandt	Lillian Rich
Dale Kennersly	Edmund Burns
Brandt	Henry B. Walthall
Midget	William Platt

Author, William J. Locke. Directed by George Melford.

SYNOPSIS: Wealthy young Simon de Gex learns that he has a malady from which he must soon die. He leaves a fortune to his best friend, Dale Kennersly, requesting that he should marry Mazie Ellerton, to whom Dale is engaged, before he—Simon—dies. Dale is infatuated with Lola Brandt, circus rider. Simon goes with Dale to watch her perform. An unknown enemy shoots and kills her pet horse. Lola and her good friend Midget, the clown, vow revenge. Simon meets and is attracted by Lola. Later he is operated on and recovers his health. Lola's wastrel husband is shot by Midget, who also dies. Simon and Lola are united.

Lillian Rich, who appears in "Simon the Jester," a Prod. Dist. Corp. release.

Simon The Jester (Producers Dis. Corp.)
PRESS NOTICE

LOVERS of sentiment, romance, thrills and picturesque unfolding of life under the big circus tents will have something to look forward to in the coming of "Simon The Jester" to the screen of the ——— Theatre on ———. The hero of this story is a young Englishman who has been informed by physicians that he is doomed to die within a certain period. He falls in love with Lola Brandt, circus performer, and their subsequent adventures are detailed with sympathetic power.

Lillian Rich and Eugene O'Brien play the leads, with Edmund Burns, Henry B. Walthall, William Platt and others in support.

CATCH LINES

If you knew you had only a short time to live, what use would you make of the days remaining? This young Britisher solved the problem in a peculiar way.

Lovers in Quarantine
(Paramount—6570 Feet)
(Reviewed by George T. Pardy)

YOU can't get away from the alluring dash and sparkle of "Lovers in Quarantine" without acknowledging that here is absolutely the most entertaining picture in which fascinating Bebe Daniels has flashed her winsome smile up-to-date. As a cold matter of fact it is one of the most humorous things director Frank Tuttle has been responsible for in the silent drama, and Bebe, as the irresistible Diana, is away better than in anything else she has done. Her success in this role will surprise many who supposed her powers of characterization to be strictly limited to stock-in-trade stuff of the automatic order. She not only looks the part but plays it with such hilarious swing and fire that the audience is fairly carried away on a bright burning flame of enthusiasm.

It would have been fatally easy for the director to have run sex suggestiveness up to the limit in many of the scenes, but Frank Tuttle wasn't taking any chances on the censorship. He just slapped in touches of satire, little hints that made you think something was going to happen which didn't, and through it all steered his players as innocently as so many sheep.

THEME. Comedy, with heroine getting mixed up in elder sisters love affairs, and finally flirting herself into a match with desirable fiance.

PRODUCTION HIGHLIGHTS. Excellent direction. Bebe Daniel's splendid acting in heroine role. The fast action. Clever sub titles. Smooth continuity.

EXPLOITATION ANGLES. You can praise this as the best picture Bebe Daniels has starred in this season, without any fear of a comeback from your patrons. There's a strong supporting cast to feature and you can go the limit on the story's comedy values.

DRAWING POWER. Bebe Daniel's name will help to get 'em in and once in they'll stay and be satisfied. A good attraction for any theatre.

THE CAST

Diana	Bebe Daniels
Anthony Blunt	Harrison Ford
Mackintosh Josepha	Alfred Lunt
Pamela Gordon	Eden Gray
Amelia Pincent	Edna May Oliver
Lola	Diana Kane
Silent Passenger	Ivan Simpson
Mrs. Burroughs	Marie Shotwell

Adapted from F. Tennyson Jesse's Stage Play, "Quarantine". Director, Frank Tuttle. Photographed by J. Roy Hunt.

SYNOPSIS. Diana Gordon is a vivacious little tomboy who acts first and thinks afterwards. She is attracted by Tony Blunt, who imagines himself in love with Diana's older sister, the flirtatious Pamela and plans to elope with her on a steamer. Diana, thinking Tony is really infatuated with her, takes her sister's place through a clever stratagem, and three days pass before Blunt finds that he has eloped with the wrong girl. Finally the passengers are all quarantined. Subsequent developments reveal "who's who", and Tony and Diana are formally engaged.

Bebe Daniels, who is starred in "Lovers in Quarantine," a Paramount production.

Lovers in Quarantine (Paramount)
PRESS NOTICE

WATCH for cute Bebe Daniels in her latest picture—"Lovers in Quarantine". It is billed as the chief screen attraction at the ——— Theatre on ———. It is one of the most amusing things ever screened, filled with sly touches of irony, screams of mirth, breathless suspense and winding into a most surprising climax. Critics the country over have pronounced this film to be the greatest success ever attained by Miss Daniels.

This dainty star plays the part of a younger sister who falls in love with her elder's beau, vamps him successfully and finally steers him into a formal engagement

CATCH LINES

BEBE as a bride on a funnymoon trip. Imagine 'lovers in quarantine!
If you find yourself on board ship with the wrong girl, would you sink—or swim to the nearest exit?

Regional News from Correspondents

San Diego

G H. and J. F. Alcock, who ,have been operating the Dream Theatre at 755 Fifth street, have sold their interests to Frank Dorner, who has taken possession and will continue the house as a popular priced second-run film theatre.

Dwight L. Hill, formerly operating the Pickwick Theatre and more recently connected with the Pacific Southwest and National Theatres corporations, recently lost a $400 diamond from his ring while stopping at the U. S. Grant hotel.

Robert E. Hicks, formerly owner and manager of the Cabrillo and Balboa Theatres here, has been made president and general manager of the Mission Beach Amusement Corporation, which will operate the new amusement center at Mission Beach, a suburban pleasure resort. It is planned to have every detail of the beach playground completed in time for the opening of the 1926 season.

Des Moines

WITH the resignation of A. W. Kahn, manager of the Des Moines branch of Educational and Premier, Jimmy Winn of the Omaha office has been promoted to the managership of the Des Moines branch. Mr. Kahn who has been with Educational since its opening here and through the establishment of the headquarters of Premier pictures at the Des Moines office, is going into other lines of business.

The theatre at New London, Iowa, the Alamo, has been bought by J. O'Connor who is an old timer in the movie game. He started with pictures almost at the beginning. He ran the Derby theatre at Chesterton, Ind., eight years ago. The New London house was bought from Perkins and Martin. Mr. Martin has moved to Mineral Point, Wis., where he is a member of the firm of Hannah and Martin, operating the World theatre. Mr. Perkins is now in Milwaukee.

H. A. Jacobs who bought the Star Theatre at Dumont, Iowa, is a newcomer to the picture business. He bought the theatre from Joe Keefe who has not completed arrangements for buying another theatre.

Mrs. Harry Frankel, wife of Harry Frankel, salesman for Pathe, underwent an operation for appendicitis. She is recovering nicely.

R. G. Jones is opening up a new theatre in Des Moines. It is a suburban house located at Twenty-seventh street and Beaver avenue in a comparatively new addition. The building cost between $10,-000 and $15,000. The theatre seats four hundred. Mr. Jones, who until recently operated the Hiland Theatre in the Highland Park section of Des Moines, has not yet decided upon a name for his new theatre. The opening day has been set as November 10. The theatre will show every night.

The Women's Club of Malcolm, Iowa, has bought a motion picture machine for the presentation of special subjects as a part of their program.

Bert Reisman, formerly of the Des Moines office sales staff of Famous Players, has been added to the staff of Warner Brothers in Omaha.

The Frank Amusement Company has bought the Isis Theatre at Cedar Rapids. F. M. Honey who had the Isis has purchased the Moon Theatre at Tecumsah, Nebraska and the building which houses the Moon. L. M. Greene who operates the Moon has leased the building for three years.

The Rialto Theatre at Bedford was bought by Mr. Smith of Eagle Grove. H. Stanley sold to Mr. Smith.

C. F. Senning of the Kansas City office of Educational, visited Des Moines. He had not intended to come to Des Moines but said he could not find any place in Omaha to sleep on account of the American Legion convention there.

Mrs. Thelma Washburn, typist of the Pathe office, has been ill. Evelyn Lindbloom has been at Pathe during the absence of Mrs. Washburn.

E. H. Dickinston has bought the Empress Theatre at Chelsea from Frank Adamec.

Van Dyke and Young of Pella have sold the Alamo Theatre there to Chris Nelson.

Sam Blair, special representative for Pathe, has been at the Des Moines office.

Edna Johnson, film inspector for Pathe, has been the victim of an attack of 'flu.

The American Legion at Plainfield, represented by S. A. Orcutt, has bought a new machine.

Suits have been filed by the music society against three Sioux City exhibitors for the collection of the music tax. Two other theatres, located in towns near Sioux City, are also up on the same question.

Visitors in Movie Row were Wes Booth of Belle Plain, Messrs. Prusha and Bean of the Paramount Theatre at Winterset, and Wayne Dutton of the Plaza Theatre at Manchester.

Mr. Dunsmoor of the Lyric Theatre at Marshalltown and Ralph Pyler of Ladora attended the American Legion convention in Omaha.

Atlanta

SIG SAMUELS, managing director of the Metropolitan Theatre, on his arrival in Atlanta this week announced that in the future the Metropolitan Theatre would offer pretentious stage presentations on their programs.

One of the best known stage directors in the country has been engaged to supervise these productions, which will be put on about the middle of October.

Melvin P. Ogden, noted organist from the northwest, has taken the place of Charles J. Possa as organist at the Howard this week. Mr. Possa left late Saturday for New York.

W. J. Morgan, general sales manager of Producers Distributing Corporation, spent Monday in Atlanta going over the company's sales campaign with district manager George F. Lenehan and local manager Thomas A. Little. He left Monday night for Charlotte, Washington and New York.

Bill Wassman, who for the past year and a half has traveled Georgia for United Artists and previous to that traveled the Carolinas, will cover the Florida territory for Producers beginning next week.

Mr. and Mrs. Sig Samuels returned to Atlanta Monday after having completed an extended tour abroad. In Germany they visited Mr. Samuels' mother, remaining in that country for a short while.

J. N. Johnson, exhibitor of Jasper, Ala., was here this week for several days.

Adolph Gortatowsky, well-known exhibitor of Albany, Ga., and manager of the Liberty Theatre there, was in town this week and visited a number of his friends in the local film circle.

Phelps Sasseen, who has been a salesman with Liberty for the past two years, has been appointed manager of the Associated Exhibitors office in Charlotte, taking the place of George Hendrickson who is now connected with Metro-Goldwyn's Charlotte exchange.

Arthur Dickenson, former manager of Producers' Atlanta exchange, was in Atlanta again for a few days this week on his way back to Florida, after having visited his friends and family in Chattanooga, Tenn., last week.

R. B. Williams, branch manager for Universal, was in Birmingham this week on business. He returned to Atlanta Friday.

Rufus A. Davis, popular manager of Liberty's Charlotte exchange, arrived in Atlanta for a few days' stay this week. He returned to Charlotte Sunday.

Ray Beall, one of film row's members, has suffered an attack of tonsilitis for the past two weeks, and is just beginning to be seen about again.

S. C. Ware, Universal salesman for south Georgia and South Carolina, was in town over the week-end, leaving for his territory Monday evening.

Ed Beach, who was appointed to travel Georgia for Liberty, is another film row member confined to his home this week on account of illness. His sickness is not of a serious nature, however, and he expects to be back on the job again before long.

Earle E. Griggs, Universal exploiteer in this territory, left Atlanta Wednesday night for Jacksonville.

Harry E. Pearce, popular Educational salesman, was in the Atlanta office this week for a short visit. He left again for Alabama within a few days.

Mrs. Willingham Wood of the Strand Theatre, Washington, Ga., was here for several days this week, returning to her home town before the week-end.

Milwaukee

F. B. O. is going to hold open house for exhibitors at the fine new quarters on Seventh Street next week, and from "inside dope" of the plans it looks like a real party was brewing. M. J. Weisfeldt, district manager is scheduled to arrive Oct. 17, to help Sam Abrams and his local staff in conducting the housewarming.

Charles Koehler, assistant manager at Milwaukee for the Progress Pictures Company, beams proudly at pedestrians as he swishes by in his Maxwell all dolled in a new coat of paint.

And speaking of cars: Lyman Ballard, salesman for United Artists, has added a touch of color to Milwaukee's film row with his Chrysler coupe. Lyman works out of the Chicago office, parks his car in front of the Vells Street exchanges, where he gets a first chance at all visiting exhibitors.

Charles Lundgren, live-wire manager of the Milwaukee branch of the Producers Distributing Corporation, has just returned to his attractive new headquarters after a trip through the territory.

The Lyric Theatre at Tomahawk, Wis., was opened Friday to excellent business, according to Mrs. Ann Kuehling, managerette, who dropped in to tell Milwaukee friends about her latest achievement. The house has 700 seats and is a real adornment to the little city which it will grace.

Steve Doris, manager of the Star Theatre at Racine, Wis., came up to Milwaukee last week to tell the boys how nicely his latest project, the erection of a fine new theatre in Racine, was progressing.

J. G. Frackman, Milwaukee manager for the Progress Pictures Company, has returned from Chicago, where he conferred with his chief, Frank Zambreno.

John Lorentz, manager of the recently established branch office of the Fox Film Corporation in Milwaukee, has just returned from a trip through the territory, in the course of which he called on exhibitors in all the key cities.

Sam Therion, manager of the Bijou Theatre, Green Bay, Wis., was among the visitors to Milwaukee last week.

From Upper Michigan peninsula

came E. J. Bregger, manager of the Gem Theatre at Crystal Falls, to call at the Milwaukee offices for the purpose of booking the 1925-26 product for his house.

Dick Scheinbaum, F. B. O. salesman in the Northern Wisconsin and Upper Michigan territory, has just come back to the Milwaukee headquarters, from a four weeks trip through his territory.

Jimmie Zanieth, manager of the Jeffries and Apollo Theatres at Janesville, Wis., was in Milwaukee last week calling on the offices of the Saxe Amusement Enterprises, with which his houses are affiliated.

Thomas Saxe, who recently announced construction of three new theatres to cost in excess of $3,500,000, says Wisconsin's first exhibitor, having returned from the St. Louis Exposition with an idea that resulted in his opening a "Hale's Touring Car." Soon after, in conjunction with his brother John, he opened the old Theatorium, the first bona fide picture house in Milwaukee. The old Crystal Theatre soon followed and the Saxe Brothers started taking

the lead over competitors who sprang up like mushrooms.

Some fifteen years ago the picture industry, as well as the entire amusement world, was startled by the announcement that the Saxe brothers had leased the Alhambra, then the largest theatre in Milwaukee and long established as a home for legitimate road attractions. The inauguration of a picture policy in a house of this size was considered foolhardy by many, it being the largest picture house in the country at that time. However, the venture proved very successful and led to the rapid expansion of the Saxe interests and the establishment of one of the most profitable circuits in the Central West.

Throughout the history of their motion picture activities the Saxe's have maintained their reputation as shrewd but daring pioneers. Covering an entire city with key "uptown" theatres is by no means the least of their achievements, and promises to be the most important of recent developments in the Milwaukee picture house history.

San Francisco

E. C. CUNNINGHAM of Pacific Grove has disposed of his interest in the Iris Theatre to the Golden State Theatre & Realty Corporation. The Iris will be permanently closed and Cunningham will devote his personal attention to his other theatre at Carmel.

Ed Brumfield, manager of the Brumfield Electric Sign Co., was married August 30th to Miss Mildred Schultz, one of California's daughters.

Only a few days after the opening of the new San Mateo Theatre one of the Blumenfeld circuit of theatres, a fire, discovered in the nick of time, prevented possible destruction of the house. A cigarette stub left burning on one of the upholstered loge chairs smouldered all night, bursting into flame in the early morning, destroying several chairs and was discovered just in time to prevent a disastrous fire.

Nat Holt, manager of the California theatre and one of the real popular Western motion picture managers, has returned from his visit to Portland, Seattle and Canada.

Louis Reichert, former San Franciscan in charge of Selznick local exchange when the, closing of that distributing concern came about is now branch manager for Warner Bros. at Kansas City. Reichert has many friends in San Francisco who wish him success.

Clarence Laws, manager of the California Theatre in Watsonville, was the chairman of the social affair and dance given by the Exchange Club of his city.

Ed McGuire, well-known among the supply people of San Francisco, is in business for himself in Los Angeles, 1041 So. Olive St., where he represents W. G. Preddy of this city.

E. Rowell, one of the First National New York office officials, is making a tour of the Pacific Coast territory and paid San Francisco a visit of several days.

A theatre site at the corner of Robinson and Meyer streets in Oroville has been obtained by the T. & D. Jr., Corporation, who will erect a theatre costing upwards of $200,000. Plans have been drawn and work will commence at once.

Harry Lustig, popular district manager of Warner Bros., was shaking hands with friends and exhibitors who visited the local

Warner office recently. Lustig went south following a conference with Sam Warner and Manager Morgan Walsh.

Robert Morton Organ Co., through Mr. Schiller, closed a contract with Alexander Pantages for his new San Francisco house for a Robert Morton Unit Organ to cost $50,000.

Ward Morris of the White Theatre in Fresno, is now a member of the Playground Commission of his city.

Clem Pope of the T. & D. in Oakland has returned from a trip to Los Angeles.

The Senator Theatre in Sacramento celebrated its first anniversary the week of September 27th.

Frank Purkett of the Kinema Theatre is President of the Better Business Bureau in Fresno.

Central Penn

THE early fall business of the leading Harrisburg motion picture houses has been unprecedented, a fact that may be attributed to two principal causes: First, the fact that, pending the completion of the rebuilding of the Orpheum theatre, at an expenditure of $750,000, the city is without any "legitimate" shows as rival attractions to the movies, and, secondly, because of the exceptionally fine quality of the pictures that have been displayed in the picture houses.

Announcement made by the Wilmer & Vincent Theatre company, on October 9, that the rebuilding of the Orpheum will probably not be completed until about Christmas week, whereas it had been originally intended to have the theatre ready for opening at Thanksgiving time, means a further delay.

An increase of four in the number of inspectors employed to see that the rulings of the Pennsylvania State Board of Censors are enforced, has just been an-

nounced, in accordance with the wishes of Governor Pinchot. The addition of these inspectors to the Board of Censors' force makes the total eleven.

C. Floyd Hopkins, general manager of the Wilmer & Vincent theatres in Harrisburg and Reading, announces that the new State theatre, in Reading, which is being rebuilt, will be ready for formal opening sometime before the close of October.

Extensive improvements have just been completed in the Grand

theatre, Stroudsburg. The seating capacity has been increased to 500 and the exits have been enlarged. A new screen and two new projection machines have been installed.

Out-of-town organists have been substituting at the New Strand theatre, operated by the Nathan Appell interests, in the city of York, during the absence of John De Palma, the regular organist, who has been ill with typhoid fever.

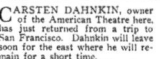

Salt Lake City

CARSTEN DAHNKIN, owner of the American Theatre here, has just returned from a trip to San Francisco. Dahnkin will leave soon for the east where he will remain for a short time.

L. J. Schlaifer, Division Manager for Universal, is in this city for four or five days with his wife.

Lou Metzger, Sales Manager of Complete Service Contracts for Universal, who stopped here for a day, is now on his way to New York.

Samuel Henley, manager for the Universal exchange in this city, is leaving this week for an extended trip throughout the territory.

M. Shiren, Universal's Traveling Auditor, is spending three or four weeks at the Salt Lake office.

L. A. Davis, manager of the local F. B. O. exchange, has returned from a very successful trip into Montana.

W. K. Bloom, who covers the Montana territory for F. B. O. is still in that section. J. K. Soloman is in Idaho.

Carl Stearn, local United Artists exchange manager, is back from Montana.

Joe Dowd is still in the Idaho territory, out of the United Artists office here.

Dave Schayer, Producers Distributing Corporation salesman, who has been in the city for a few days, is leaving for another ex tended trip into Idaho.

J. T. Sheffield, General Manager of Greater Features, is touring the Intermountain offices of his organization and is expected to be in this city some time in the near future.

W. F. Gordon, in charge of the Associated First National exchange here, is expecting to leave soon for a short trip to Butte, Montana.

R. S. Spackhouse, Warner Brothers local manager, is back from Butte, and is going to leave for the Idaho branch soon.

Harry Lustig, Division Manager for Warner Brothers, stopped at the Salt Lake office on his way to

the District Managers' convention in New York.

George Jensen, who covers the Montana territory out of the local Warner Brothers exchange, came in and left immediately for that section again. L. W. Hyde is still covering Southern Utah.

Jack Tierney, Special Representative from the Pathe Home offices, is in this city. Tierney is making all of the offices in the Western Division and is going to Butte, Montana, from here.

W. G. Seib, who has charge of the Pathe exchange here, is expecting Frank Harris, Pathe Western District Manager, to be in this city next week. Harris is returning from the sales convention which was held in New York the last of September.

Charlie Hamal, salesman in the Idaho territory for Pathe, has just left for a three weeks' trip. R. D. Boomer is now covering Southern Utah.

George L. Cloward, manager for Metro-Goldwyn here, has returned

from a trip through the Montana territory.

Harold Pickering, Famous Players-Lasky local Exploitation manager, is in Idaho for a few days. A. G. Pickett, manager of this exchange, has just returned from the Idaho territory.

Clyde H. Messinger, manager of the local Educational exchange has left for the coal camps of Southern Utah.

The Grand Prize donated by the Victory and Paramount-Empress theatres, for the Gold Tournament this year, was won by Neil Schettler, leader of the Victory Theatre orchestra.

Among exhibitors visiting the local exchanges this week were: The Peery Brothers, operating the Egyptian Theatre, Ogden, Utah; Tom Berta, owner of The Rialto Theatre, Rock Springs, Wyoming; S. H. Rich, of the Rich Theatre, Montpelier, Idaho, and J. Whitehead, owner of Recreation Hall, Eureka, Utah.

Philadelphia

THE board of managers of the M. P. T. O. A. of Eastern Pennsylvania, Southern New Jersey and Delaware is now making arrangements for a formal dinner dance to be held in the Benjamin Franklin Hotel on a Sunday evening the latter part of November. This will be the first formal dinner dance given by the organization and it is expected that it will be attended by all the prominent members of the film industry in the East.

Julia Barry who has been secretary to Percy A. Bloch, manager of the Philadelphia office of Paramount, was the guest of honor at a dinner tendered her by thirty-five employees of the exchange at the Arcadia Cafe. Miss Barry was presented with a sterling silver coffee set, the gift of her fellow workers. Miss Barry recently resigned from Paramount to become the bride of Dr. T. S. Col

lins, a prominent Philadelphia dentist.

George Rosenbaum, who has been a member of Edgar Moss' sales staff in the Philadelphia office of Fox, has been transferred to the home office in New York and will be sent out from there to the Boston exchange. Mr. Rosenbaum has been succeeded by Nat Fleisher, who was at one time connected with the old Goldwyn Company and later with Metro-Goldwyn.

A large delegation of Philadelphia motion picture men attended the formal opening of Len Berman's Savoy Theatre in Bethlehem. The opening was altogether an invitational one and Mr. Berman tendered the members of the film fraternity a dinner immediately after the close of the evening's performance. The Savoy is the third theatre recently acquired by Mr. Berman, who is planning

to extend his theatre holdings throughout the eastern part of Pennsylvania ultimately to include about fifteen houses.

The film community in Philadelphia took an active part in the campaign for greater safety during Fire Prevention Week and one of the outstanding features was a mass meeting held in the auditorium of the Catholic High School, which is almost in the heart of the film center. More than 300 exchange employees attended the meeting.

H. S. Powell, who is in charge of the Associated Exhibitors interests in Philadelphia, has recently added Peter Ryan and Joe McCreary to his sales force. Mr. McCreary was at one time publicity director for Carr & Schad in Reading and later was associated with Harry and Gene Marcus in the Twentieth Century ex-

change. Mr. Ryan has had considerable experience in motion picture circles, having for a time been connected with Real Art and World exchanges. Mr. McCreary will cover Southern New Jersey and Delaware towns and Mr. Ryan will be assigned to Harrisburg and York sections.

The Philadelphia interests of the Harold Lloyd Picture Corporation will be handled permanently by Ben Abrahams, a special representative who has been assigned to the Philadelphia office.

R. A. Bloch and W. E. Smith, branch manager and district manager, respectively, for Famous Players, will leave the first week in November to attend the semi-annual sales conference of district and branch managers of the Famous Players-Lasky Corporation, which is to be held November 6th to 8th, in the Hotel Drake, Chicago.

Cincinnati

L. B. WILSON, popular manager of the Liberty Theater, Covington, Ky., has added two more men to his jazz orchestra.

So many marriages have occurred at the Paramount offices lately that Many Nagle, assistant city salesman, has been forced to return to the booking counter. Many filled this job before and when Frances Brown his successor took up matrimony for a position there was nothing left for Many to do but get back into the harness till he trains some one else for the job.

Fred Middleburg, of the Hyman Theater interests of W. Va., was in the city for several days last week.

Claude Harding has purchased the Opera House at Ashland, Ky., and will reopen it under the name of the Ashland Theatre at an early date.

Chas. Trieble of the Pastime Theater, Maysville, Ky., booked several large pictures while visiting film row last week.

W. J. Curran of the Plaza Theater, Kings Mills, O., spent several days looking at pictures recently.

The local Universal offices have organized a club among the employees for the purpose of furnishing entertainments once a month. The name of the club is the Universal Film Joy Club. The offi-

cers are, Henrietta "Honey" Bocklew, President, Helen Weiler, Vice-President, Helen Cain, Secretary, and Mrs. Gus Geldreich, Treasurer. The first entertainment on the list for the season will consist partly of Charles Lowenburg, the exploiteer, in a song and dance act. Charlie was a vaudevillian before entering the movie game, and Al Sugarman, short subjects manager, in an Irish monologue.

Gladys Roemes, the pretty operator for Universal, will leave her post at the end of this week to become the bride of Albert Bohner on November 18. All who know Gladys wish her luck and happi-

ness for she is a most deserving and popular young lady.

Beatrice Prang of the Forum Theatre, Hillsborough, O., was a guest at Film Row last week. As usual she was royally entertained.

Chas. Reagan, district manager for Paramount, is one of the busiest men in the film game. Charlie is always on the go and the sales of the office prove that his missions are not in vain.

Bill Danziger, Paramount exploiteer was under the weather for several days last week.

Ann Keck, secretary to Pepplatt, Paramount Branch manager, made her first road trip last week, and her results most satisfactory.

New England

APPARENTLY the motion picture business in Florida will thrive this winter, judging from the number of New England exhibitors that have joined the Florida bound contingent. In a letter to one of the distributors in Boston, a former Bay State exhibitor said he found almost as many of his co-exhibitors in Florida as there were left in Massachusetts. He declared more New England people were in Florida than from any other section.

Three of the New England salesmen have joined the Florida gathering. They are "Chick" Varney and Jack Donovan, who were with the Producers Distributing Corporation of Boston and Charles Phillips who was with the Film Booking Office, Boston. They left this week and declared they would be in Florida indefinitely.

John Foley, who runs the Park Theatre at South Manchester, Conn., is expected back from a sojourn in Florida this week. He has been in the South for several weeks.

"Jake" Laurie is making extensive improvements and doing considerable remodelling of his theatres. As a result, the playhouses are temporarily closed but will reopen about Nov. 1st with the improvements completed. In the three playhouses the seating capacity will be increased by a total of 2300. At the Shawmut Theatre an additional 800 seats are being added; at the Jamaica Theatre 700 more seats will be provided and at the Roslindale Theatre 800 additional seats are being provided.

Mr. Laurie is also building a new theatre to be known as the Morton Street Theatre in Mattapan. This will have a seating capacity of more than 2,000. Work is to be pushed forward rapidly on this playhouse and it is expected to open early in the new year.

The Metropolitan is advertising its opening for Saturday morning, Oct. 17, and it is planned to commence each week's new program on Saturday instead of Monday. On Friday evening, Oct. 16, there will be an inspection of the new playhouse by invited guests.

In Salem, Mass., the Empire Theatre, which has for some years been playing stock, has closed. There is a rumor current that negotiations are under way for reopening the house as a motion picture theatre later in the season. The Palace Theatre in Bowdoin Square, Boston, is being remodeled by its owner, Louis Boas.

In addition to the Palace remodelling, much remodelling and work on the theatre fronts of the Bowdoin Square, Olympia and Star Theatres is being done in this same section of the city.

"Doc" Hermann has become affiliated with the Producers Distributing Corporation, Boston headquarters, as a salesman, where he is greeting old friends and rapidly making new ones.

Joseph Cloutier, formerly one of the well known salesmen in New England territory, has taken over the Modern Theatre in Manchester, N. H. and has changed the name of the playhouse to the Notre Dame Theatre. The theatre has opened to good business.

Philip Smith, who took over the National Theatre in Boston a couple of years ago and made a big success of it, and who disposed of it a short time ago, has now engaged in the insurance business in Albany where friends are predicting he will make the same success that he did in handling the National Theatre.

Frank Watton, who has successfully operated the Park Theatre in Lebanon, N. H., has just opened a new theatre at Williamsett, Mass., which is a prosperous town in Hamden county near Holyoke, Mass.

After eight years as a motion picture house, the Modern Theatre in Providence, R. I. has changed its policy to stock.

Abraham Spitz will open a new theatre in the outskirts of Providence in about a month's time.

It is reported that Nathan Yamins and Harry Horgan of Newport, R. I., have taken over the Colonial Theatre in that city. Mr. Horgan is at present operating the Opera House in Newport.

The St. James Theatre on Huntington Avenue, Boston, which has for some years been devoted to stock, will reopen early in November with motion pictures and vaudeville under the direction of the Keith-Albee interests. Extensive alterations and improvements are being made and this will give the Keith-Albee interests a Boston theatre in the Back Bay section of the city.

Arthur Viano, who has started the erection of a new theatre in Day square, Somerville, Mass., says that the house will have a policy of motion pictures and vaudeville and will open late in the winter.

"Jake" Laurie is making arrangements for some extensive feature advertising above the marquis of his theatres in Boston. He is spending between $12,000 and $15,000 for these displays at the Beacon, Modern, Dudley, Shawmut, Jamaica, and Roslindale Theatres.

At Newhall of the Strand Theatre, Lynn, Mass., is motoring about in a new Pierce Arrow sedan which is the envy of his friends.

Moe Silver of Moe Marks' Theatres and manager of the Waldorf Theatre, Lynn, is visiting the Row on a new Marmon car this fall.

A recent visitor to Boston was Pat Downing, publicity director for Metropolitan Pictures at Hollywood.

Mike Newman was a recent Boston visitor. Newman operated the Coast to Coast in Seven Days auto.

A new theatre in Roslindale, Mass. with a seating capacity of 900 is nearing completion and will be opened under the supervision of Stanley Sumner, who is in charge of the Community Theatre in Newton. The new playhouse will operate a straight picture policy.

The Broadway Theatre, Everett, has reopened after undergoing extensive alterations. Nathan Brown is in charge of the theatre and also of the Strand Theatre, in the same city.

The Premier Theatre in Fall River, which had been closed for several years, has been reopened by M. A. Dunn and is said to be having excellent success as a motion picture house. Mr. Dunn formerly owned the Academy of Music and the Palace Theatre and successfully operated them.

E. A. King, formerly of King & Rogers, is now in full control of the Colonial Theatre in Brockton, Mass., and is playing to capacity houses.

Denver

JAMES F. LYNCH, manager of the Empress Theatre, Laramie, Wyoming, has entered into a "tie up" with the Associated Students of the University of Wyoming for an entertainment to raise funds for the sending of the entire Wyoming Football Team on a ten day tour, on which they will play Montana State and Utah Aggies.

The new State Theatre closed Friday night, October 9th, because of its popularity with the fans. Seems queer, doesn't it. But here's the reason. The theatre will be closed for a two weeks' period in which time the stage of the theatre will be enlarged and fixed for the purpose of accommodating better and larger acts for the entertainment of the patrons in conjunction with their first run pictures.

James S. Hommel, manager for the local branch of Producers Distributing Corporation, has just returned from a four weeks' sales trip to the Southern territory. Jim returned yesterday after visiting nearly every town of any consequence which included Albuquerque, Santa Fe, Roswell and Jurex.

Eugene Gerbase, manager of the local Universal office, made a hurried trip to Salt Lake City the early part of the week returning Friday.

B. P. McCormick, owner and manager of the Rialto and Liberty Theatres, Florence, Colorado, and the Jones Theatre, Canon City, Colorado, was a welcome visitor in the city a few days ago. Welcome, because when Jim comes to town it means a lot more dates and new contracts for some exchanges.

Harry Lustig, Division Manager for Warner Brothers, arrived in the city today from Salt Lake City enroute to New York City. Mr. Lustig leaves for New York tomorrow.

The exhibitors visiting Denver during the past week were Ed. Marquand, manager of the Isis and Longmont Theatres, Longmont, Colorado; Stewart Tyo, manager of the Tyo Theatre, Wray, Colorado, stopped on his way back home from the American Legion Convention at Omaha; Mrs. Lee Mote, Acme Theatre, Riverton, Wyoming; A. V. Wessels, Orpheum Theatre, Steamboat Springs; Colorado; R. Murray, Eaton Theatre, Eaton, Colorado.

Seth Perkins, District Manager for Metro-Goldwyn, arrived in Denver early this week for a visit with Mr. R. J. Garland, the local branch manager of his organization.

Cleveland

THE local Pathe exchange is getting all ready for the fifteenth birthday celebration of the Pathe News service, which takes place the week of November 14th.

J. S. Jossey, head of Progress Pictures, has added to the dignity and comfort of his exchange by adding a new section to his sales department where exhibitors may sign contracts without danger of interruption. No, there are no bars to the office. Exhibitors may get out as well as get in.

Lou Rogers of Arrow Film Corporation has finished his missionary work in this territory and has moved on to Detroit.

William G. Smith, of Fidelity Pictures, New York, was in town and called on the independent exchange managers last week.

Jules Levy, Universal general manager, spent Saturday in Cleveland.

Sam Bullock, one-time exhibitor, and until recently, field manager for the Motion Picture Theatre owners of Ohio, has just returned from a trip to the auld countree. Bullock was on the other side about two months. If his trip had an official flavor, he has not mentioned it out loud, but it is understood that he went over on organization business of some sort.

The Governor's family were guests of Bill and Harry Skirboll at the official opening of the Opera House at New Philadelphia, last Friday. The New Philadelphia house, which they bought last season, was re-built during the summer, and is said to be one of the prettiest picture houses in this neck of the woods. And James McMahon forsook the management of his picture house in Willoughby, the McTodd, to offer a selection of songs. Many other prominent exhibitors were present at the opening, but they did not participate in the program. Forney Bowers continues as house manager of the Opera House.

Maurice Schwartz, director of "Broken Hearts," for Jaffe Art Film Corp.

When the old Toledo theatre in Toledo recovers from its $100,000 worth of alterations, it will be known as the New Palace. Howard Feigley, managing director of the Rivoli, will also manage the New Palace, which adjoins the Rivoli.

The Cleveland Motion Picture Exhibitors Association will hold a meeting on October 26th, to elect officers for the coming year.

W. J. Powell, of the Lo-Net theatre, Wellington, paid his personal respects to some of the local exchanges last week, and expressed himself as pleased with picture conditions as they are and as they promise to be during the coming months.

Mrs. Dolls, of Dolls theatre, Akron, one of the few women exhibitors in this territory, was in town last week to see the latest styles in pictures as well as the last word in feminine attire.

Bert Botzum, who owns the Orpheum theatre in Akron and the Strand in Canton, with his wife and family, is taking a holiday trip through Europe. He booked all the new pictures before he left.

The Empress theatre in Akron is no more. Charles Brill locked the front door of the house permanently on October 3d. That leaves Bill with just two houses in Akron,—the Miles Royal, which plays burlesque, and the old Grand Opera House which will play burlesque also when Brill gets through remodelling it.

Milton Bryer, who owns the Waldorf, People's, Ideal and Winter's theatres in Akron, in partnership with I. Friedman, was in town the other day and said that business in Akron is good. And what's more, Bryer said that the outlook for the winter is excellent.

Clint Kline, of the Arcade theatre, Akron, is all through with his annual visit to Cleveland for the year. Just about once a year Clint makes the twenty-mile grade. So it's an event when he comes and all the exchanges celebrate.

Louis Frisch of the Harbor Theatre at Ashtabula Harbor, while in town last week, told the exchangemen that business is picking up in his part of the country and that he's looking forward to a big season.

Howard Reiff and Percy Essick of the Scoville, Essick and Reiff circuit have made their wills all in favor of the third member of their firm before starting out to hunt wild animals in the Canadian woods. Both of them have demonstrated their ability as straight shooters but never before have they attempted auto shooting outside the Film building. "It looks so easy in the movies," Reiff said, "so we thought we'd like to try it ourselves." Scoville will run the circuit during the absence

Warner Baxter who will be seen in Paramount's "The Best People."

of his partners.

Mort Shea of New York and L. B. Cool of the Feiber and Shea circuit, spent a day last week visiting the Cleveland exchanges and filling in dates on pictures previously booked.

It is reported that Young brothers are building a new 800-seat movie house in Bowling Green. This isn't their first one. They also have the Delmar, Everybody's and Lyric.—all of them in Bowling Green.

Manager Halbert of the Odeon theatre, Canton, is all through with fishing for the season. He recently returned from his last trip to Michigan and has put away the fishing paraphernalia until another summer.

John Schleifenheimer is busy remodeling his Falls theatre, Chagrin Falls. There'll be a lot of new things to greet the eye when Schleifenheimer gets through. He was shopping for some of the things in Cleveland one day last week.

Messrs. Bly and Miller are in the act of building a new motion picture theatre in Conneaut, according to advices along the Film Rialto. They used to own and operate the Liberty at Geneva.

M. B. Horwitz, general manager of the Washington Circuit of Cleveland, was among the missing exhibitors the middle of last week. One guess where he was. Pittsburgh. Correct. "It was a great game" Moe told his less fortunate companions upon his return home.

Jake Stein, who has the Utopia theatre, Painesville, is just recovering from an illness which has kept him away from the film exchanges for several weeks.

Pete Theopolis used to serve entertainment to the patrons of the Pantheon theatre in Lorain.

Now he's serving sea food to the patrons of his popular restaurant on Euclid avenue at East 103d St.

George Fleishman, one of Toledo's most prominent exhibitors, while in Cleveland last week, stated that business was good in his town, and at his theatre. He had the World, Atlas and Ohio. Fleishman said that business was good at both uptown and downtown houses, but especially good downtown.

The Empress theatre in Toledo is closed. The lease on the theatre has expired and it will be converted into a series of store rooms. George Dixon, who managed the house has retired.

Joe Trunk and Max Schagrin drove up from Youngstown the other day. It was a business trip for Trunk, who is managing the Orpheum theatre. But it was a pleasure trip for Shagrin, who has sold his Orpheum theatre. As soon as building operations on the new house are begun, the Orpheum will be torn down and will be used as a lobby entrance to the new house.

Two new Keith houses will be ready in this territory no later than January 1st. One is in Youngstown and the other is in Akron.

It is reported that Loew is going to put up a big house in Canton.

Here's a new one. Yary and Frank Ptelka are brothers. They own and run the Union theatre, Cleveland. They work together all week. And they like to play together. So, in order to be able to play together, they close their theatre every Tuesday all the year round. Tuesday is their own day. And their patrons are used to waiting until Wednesday to see their favorite stars on the screen. In a seven days town, where the thought of Sunday closing is a nightmare, Ptelka brother's six days policy is extraordinary, to say the least. But they say the policy is quite satisfactory. It's all a matter of habit.

Howard Franke, has just acquired his third link in the picture theatre chain, which he is building in Ohio. Recently Frankel and Malott bought the Windsor theatre in Akron and the Weber theatre in Dover. Last week they purchased the Cinderella in Coshocton. Other purchases are in the wind.

The Film Bldg. Register showed the following out-of-town exhibitor guests for the past week:—Henry Rosenthal, Ohio theatre, Ravenna; W. L. Beckham, Artcraft, Toledo; D. M. Robbins. Dome, Youngstown; George Mock, Mock's theatre, Girard; E. C. Lair, Louisville theatre, Louisville; Garland Shetler, the new owner of the Opera House, Middlefield; Jim Platt, Lyric, Mt. Vernon; and T. J. Evans, Lyric and Strand theatres of Van Wert.

New York and New Jersey

Sol Brill, proprietor of the Inwood theatre, New York.

SLIGHTLY over twenty years ago, an earnest, hardworking young fellow, by the name of Sol Brill, started out in business in a little shop over in Brooklyn. The business was cloth shrinking and its capital consisted of three hundred dollars.

A few weeks ago, Sol Brill signed a lease on a suite of offices in the building atop Gloria Gould's Embassy theatre. Today, the letters on the entrance door, read "Meserole Securities Company," —and there is a vast difference between the capitalization of this company and that of the old cloth shrinking business.

Recently Sol Brill's "Inwood Theatre" in the Dyckman Heights section of New York City, held it Premiere. It is one of the most modern neighborhood houses in the city and a detailed description is given in the construction and equipment section of this issue.

Shortly after his venture in the cloth shrinking business, Mr. Brill became interested in a penny arcade located at number seven hundred Broadway, Brooklyn. It is interesting to note here that this entry into this form of the amusement business was to prove to be the nucleus that later on was the means of building up his fortune.

The penny arcade was started about nineteen years ago and it was at this time that the commercial possibilities of the "Nickelodeon" began to be talked about, and on the floor above the arcade, Mr. Brill constructed a two hundred seat theatre.

According to Mr. Brill's statements and those of his brother, Dave Brill, the present salesmanager of Universal's "Big U" Exchange, the first piece of film that was able to be run through a machine, was projected on a screen in this little theatre.

Along about this time Sol Brill became associated with William Fox and two more small theatres were built at 899 and 1100 Broadway, Brooklyn. These little places were for the most part, converted stores and a five cent admission was charged.

Following these ventures

Messrs Brill and Fox came over into New York City and opened up several more three hundred seat houses, among them the "Yorkville Comedy" whose show used to start at ten A. M. and last through to midnight. A ten cent admission was charged at this theatre. Then, these two men constructed the "Comedy" in Brooklyn, the first motion picture theatre to seat a thousand people.

About this time another prominent showman of today came into the field and joined forces with Fox and Brill. This man was B. S. Moss and with Sol Brill, he built the 86th Street theatre that is now owned by Loew, Inc. They followed the Jefferson 14th St. and Second Ave., and the Hamilton at 146th St. and Broadway, both now under the control of U. B. O. There was also the Meserole and Sumner in Brooklyn that are now operated by Small and Strassberg.

Sol Brill has continued in the exhibition and construction end of the industry and his present interests include the Strand at Rockaway, The Central at Cedarhurst, the Ogden and Lefferts in Brooklyn, Ferber's Strand at Lakewood, the Ritz and Liberty, Staten Island, the Globe and Central, Brooklyn, Cross Bay, Jamaica, and the Inwood, New York City. In addition to these named, Mr. Brill is financially interested in several theatrical enterprises in the Metropolitan district.

Two years ago Mr. Brill was a large stockholder in Warner Bros., but has since disposed of his holdings. He is a close friend of Carl Laemmle and showed the first single reel that was released by Universal. Mr. Brill is also a director of the Longacre Bank and is connected with the Prudence Bond Company; however, his efforts today are mostly confined to the construction and financing of motion picture theatres and he is ably assisted by his general manager, Harry Shiffman who has been with him for twenty years. Another associate of Mr. Brill's who has put in a matter of fifteen years service, is Harry Thomas, manager of the Rockaway Strand.

Prominent exhibitors and exchange men who were in attendance at the premiere of the Inwood include Lee Ochs, Harry and William Brandt of Brooklyn, Louis Blumenthal of New Jersey, Sam Lesselbaum, of Rachmiel and Lesselbaum, Charles Moses of Allwon circuit, Joe Weinstock, of the Freemont, Embassy and City Hall theatres, Harry Suchman, of Suchman Bros. Enterprises, Messrs. Grobe and Nobel, Matthew Christmas and Samuel Roth, Sam Friedman of the Regun, Al Steinman, of the Cosmo and Stadium, Manager Kaisestein from Bayonne, Al Harsten, Harry Buxbaum and Joe Lee, of the Fox Exchange, William Raynor, Manager of the Pathe New York branch, Moe Streimer, of United Artists, Joe Hornstein and Dave Solomon, Samuel Lash, of the Lee-Lash Studios, S. Strauss, "The Sign Man,"

and Lawrence Bologino, of the Consolidated Amusement Co. Members of the Aywon, Merit and Apollo exchanges were also present.

Albert L. Greene has been selected to manage the Inwood and although Mr. Greene is but twenty-six years of age, he has had a great deal of experience in the exhibition end of the industry, having been a Fox exploitation man and former manager of the Beverly and Premier theatres in Brooklyn, N. Y.

In his work as exploitation man and theatre manager, Greene has always distinguished himself by his unflagging energy and his ingenuity in publicizing both pictures and theatre along the lines of sound, sane showmanship. At the Inwood he will have an unusual opportunity for the carrying out on a wider scale of the same sort of high grade exploitation and capable management.

Another local theatre robbery took place last Sunday morning when burglars jimmied their way through the back doors of the Ogden theatre at 1431 Ogden Ave., New York City. Owing to the yegg-proof construction of the safe, the thieves managed only to burst through the first compartment and secured but six dollars for their trouble. In the inside compartment they overlooked three days' receipts. Moe Weinberg of the Apollo Exchange is the proprietor of the Ogden.

Charlie Goldreyer's new Manor theatre will hold its premiere on Thursday of this week. The Manor is located at Ave. K and Coney Island Ave., Brooklyn. J. Greene, who was formerly with the Paris Court theatre at 292 Court St., Brooklyn, and whose home is only two blocks away from the Manor, will be the new manager.

Mr. and Mrs. Harry Buxbaum recently carried off first prize at a costume ball held at Lawrence, L. I. The prize winning costumes were of Chinese design and there are many who believe that Harry is getting acquainted with Oriental customs in order to capture the Chinese trade in this city.

President Joseph M. Seider's two young sons are batting out balls at the rate of 1000 per cent up at their school. The younger one recently managed to get six hits out of six times up and the major league scouts are already looking them over as prospective Babe Ruths.

Milton Kronacher who has covered the lower East Side during the past ten years for Pathe has been given additional territory. In addition to the East Side, he will now take in all theatres in the section up to and including 116th Street. Milt also wants all his friends to know that he has on hand a strictly up to the minute stock of emblems for all lodges. These are on display at his desk in the Pathe exchange.

Bernard La Follette Scholtz, that enterprising young salesman who covers South Brooklyn for

Fox, has been appointed editor-in-chief for the house publication, "Fox Folks."

Max Fellerman, Pathe salesman who is contemplating matrimony about Xmas time, was observed on the curb Monday and accompanied by the future Mrs. Fellerman.

The friends of Robert Harris of the Pathe exchange will be glad to know that Mrs. Harris, who has been seriously ill for the past three months, is now getting along in fine shape.

Visitors among the exchanges on Tuesday included Cy Fabian, J. Kelly of Fort Lee, Louis Heiman of Rahway, H. W. Donnegan of Harry Hecht's Passaic, Henry P. Nelson, of the Capitol at Elizabeth, Jacob Unger of the Court theatre, Newark and Herman Metzger of the Park at Caldwell.

George Faulkner who has been with Producers Distributing Corp., in Washington, D. C., has recently joined his father and will help handle the Faulkner circuit of New Jersey.

Leo Brecher's new Boston Road theatre was opened to the public last Friday evening and in spite of the rain a capacity crowd jammed the house to the aisles. The Boston Road is another of the strictly up-to-the-minute neighborhood theatres that are lately being erected. It is of one floor design and every seat a good one. The seating capacity is about 2000.

Al Shiffman, managing director of the Leo Brecher houses, was in charge of the opening and presented a fine program. A number of prominent motion picture stars made their appearance and the usual gathering of well known local exchange men and exhibitors were also there. Refreshments were served in the reception room during and after the performance.

William and Harry Brandt are building another new theatre over on Sutter and Ralph Avenues, Brooklyn. It will be a 2000 seat house and it is expected to be ready about Feb. 1st.

The Gaiety at Trenton, controlled by the Ten Eyck's of the Orpheum in the same city, will open November 10th. The Gaiety will seat 1500.

Frank Becker's new theatre at Englewood, N. J., is nearly complete and the opening is being planned for November 15th. The new house will seat 2000 and will be devoted to feature pictures and vaudeville.

Harry M. Schwartz has a new theatre under construction at White Plains, N. Y. It is of 2500 seating capacity and will be ready on December 1st.

Joe Hornstein of Howell's is still putting over plenty of equipment. The latest list includes the two new Brandt houses, Ten Eyck's Gaiety at Trenton, Frank Becker's New Englewood theatre, and Harry Harris's new house in Mt. Vernon. William Gluck, chief engineer for Joe, has left for Boston to attend the opening of the Metropolitan, the new Famous-Players theatre.

Seattle

L. O. LUKAN and A. J. Kennedy, manager and publicity director, respectively, of the local Universal office, have just returned to this city from Yakima, where they staged the third of a series of Universal Theatre Parties for the exhibitors of the territory. As a feature of the program, J. M. Hone, secretary of the Motion Picture Theatre Owners of Washington, held a meeting with the exhibitors and urged their attendance at the M. P. T. O. W. convention in Seattle in November.

Les W. Weir, district manager of the Producers' Distributing Corporation exchange, spent several days here last week with W. H. Drummond, local manager, and from here proceeded to Portland to investigate the new office in that city. Mr. Weir was followed a few days later by Dave Frazer, his assistant, who is spending a number of days here with Mr. Drummond lining up Producers' new product for the fall and winter.

Announcements received here last week were to the effect that suburban houses in Portland have recently raised their general admission prices to twenty-five cents, with children's admissions raised to a dime. Newspaper advertisements heralding the raise were signed by the Alhambra, Bob White, Chaldean, Clinton, Colonial, Echo, Egyptian, Granada, Hawthorne, Highway, Irvington, Laurelhurst, Moreland, Oregon, Roseway, Sellwood,

Sunnyside, Venetian, Victoria, Walnut Park and Yeager Theatres. Increased costs of theatre operation and film purchasing were declared responsible for the raise by these leading suburban houses.

Joe Roberts, publicity and exploitation director of Al Finkelstein's Strand Theatre, last week announced that he had taken over the management of the "Seattle Amusement Guide," a small booklet published weekly in this city and distributed free through cigar stores, lunch counters and public places. The guide includes the programs from the first run picture houses and legitimate theatres of the city, and is financed through advertising of local firms. Mr. Roberts will continue his work at the Strand in conjunction with his new enterprise.

Louis Goldsmith, former owner and manager of the Society Theatre is now a full-fledged member of Seattle's Film Row, having joined forces last week with Al Rosenberg's De Luxe Feature Film Exchange. Mr. Goldsmith will represent De Luxe in a sales capacity in the Washington field.

Art Schmidt, Western district manager of the Film Booking Offices, spent a few days here last week in conference with A. H. Huot, manager of the F. B. O. enterprises in this territory. Mr. Schmidt, while here announced his recent appointment as special representative of the F. B. O. Home Office at the

Alan Hale, signed as a director by Cecil B. De Mille.

California studios, in addition to his present duties as division manager.

Among the visitors on Film Row last week were seen Bob White, of the Bob White Theatre in Portland; E. W. Grosbeck of Enumclaw and Buckley; and Walter Kraft of Aberdeen. All three of these Washington exhibitors were among those present at the opening of H. W. Bruen's

new Arabian Theatre early last week.

Cecil Gruwell, formerly associated with Manager W. H. Drummand's Producers' exchange in the capacity of booker, last week joined the booking department of C. M. Hill's Metro-Goldwyn exchange, where he works in conjunction with A. J. Sullivan, office manager and chief booker. Mr. Gruwell formerly worked in the same capacity with Mr. Sullivan when the latter was associated with the Producers' office.

J. F. Sheffield, associated with Jack Lannon in the Lannon-Sheffield Greater Features Exchanges, left recently for a business trip to the company's exchanges in Oregon and Montana, and expected to be gone for several week, during which time Mr. Lannon was scheduled to guide the destinies of the local office single-handed.

Bill Green, former salesman with Manager L. M. Cobb's Portland Pathe exchange, came to this territory recently and is now associated in a sales capacity with the local Pathe exchange. He covers the Eastern Washington territory, with headquarters in Spokane.

The Dolores Theatre, now in the course of construction in the North Park district of this city, was scheduled to open some time in November, according to information received recently from the Brown and Ross Company, who will own and operate the house. It will seat approximately 500 persons.

Kansas City

FRED SPEAR of the Orpheum theatre, Kansas City, felt contented with himself last week, having been first to the newspapers with the fact that his theatre would carry play-by-play detail of the world's series between the Pirates and Senators. But, in the meantime, Earl T. Cook, manager of the Pantages theatre, first run house, successfully countered with a special entertainment for the First Baptist Church Business Men's Bible class, while the Apollo theatre, suburban house, set the pace with a fashion revue of Paris gowns.

"They say competition is the spice of life, but I disagree," asserted Barney Dubinsky of the Regent theatre, Kansas City. "Since down town building improvements have swept away two rival motion picture theatres in the same block I have had better crowds and had far less trouble in buying films. That's that!"

Kansas City exhibitors and exchanges are co-operating in Fire Prevention Week, the exhibitors by running slides and the exchanges by posting posters in the various branch offices.

Exchange activities were many

last week. W. J. Morgan and C. D. Hill, general sales manager and district manager, respectively, were in Kansas City on a tour of the Middle West. Universal employees are jubilant over the fact that four of the five exchanges under W. E. Truog, district manager, finished in the first seven in the sales contest in June, July and August.

Earl Cunningham, Paramount exploiteer, is hard at work arranging "something special." Sam Stoll, formerly with Universal, has joined the Paramount sales force in Kansas City, while Leonard Allison, formerly assistant bookkeeper at the Universal branch, has been made chief booker at the Des Moines Universal office, being succeeded in Kansas City by Mark Gilbert.

Charles T. Sears, former president of the M. P. T. O., Missouri and now general manager of Universal theatres in the Kansas City territory, and Harry Taylor, Universal branch manager, left last week for Independence, Kas., to take charge of the Beldorf theatre, recently purchased by Universal.

From Joe Silverman, president,

down to the most humble employee, good feeling exists around the Independent Film Corporation office this week, due to several big sales last week. Ned Depinet and F. J. McConnell, southern division sales manager and short subjects manager, respectively, for Universal, were business visitors in Kansas City.

Several changes of management of theatres in the Kansas City territory have been announced. Lee Jones, manager of Universal theatres in Atchison, Kas., has been transferred to Independence, Kas., where he will manage the Beldorf theatre. Mr. Jones was succeeded in Atchison by A. R. Zimmer, who will assume charge of the Crystal and Royal theatres. The Garden theatre, Colony, Kas., has been purchased by T. H. Lauck from W. E. Bearce, owner of a chain of houses. The Robinson theatre at Robinson, Kas., has been purchased by Charles Pirkey from G. I. Rugg.

Amonst the out-of-town exhibitors in the Kansas City market this week were: G. L. Hooper, National theatre, Topeka, Kas.; W. H. Weber, Echo

and Lakin theatres, Great Bend, Kas.; Lawrence Brunninger, Cozy and Crystal, Topeka, Kas.; A. R. Zimmer, Crystal and Royal, Atchison, Kas.; H. B. Doering, People's theatre, Garnett, Kas.; Harry McClure, Strand, Emporia, Kas.; Edward Peskay, Rivola and Penn, St. Joseph, Mo., S. E. Wilhoit, Jefferson, Springfield, Mo.

A. E. Elliott is to become manager of the New Lewis and Elliott theatres in Independence, Mo., which recently were obtained by Glenn Dickinson, owner of a chain of houses.

An inter-exchange and exhibitors' golf tournament, to be staged at the Lakewood Golf and Country Club, Kansas City, next Monday, is the talk of movie row this week. A handsome trophy will be awarded the winner of the tournament, which will be a medal play event of eighteen holes.

A new Reproduco player pipe organ has been installed in the Gauntier theatre, Kansas City, Kas., owned by R. G. Liggett, while H. S. Beardsley had two new Simplex projectors installed in his new Legion theatre.

Buffalo

THE wrecking crew has started to raze the house at 464 Franklin street, on the site of which will rise the new Buffalo Paramount exchange, which, it is declared will be the last word in exchange buildings. It is hoped to have the building ready soon after the first of the year.

The Palace theatre opened in Syracuse on Monday evening, October 5. The program is being changed daily. The seating capacity is 1,289. Music is furnished by a large Wurlitzer organ. The house is at 2362 James street, corner Stafford avenue.

Eddie Lazinski, manager of the Park theatre, a north Buffalo community house, is sporting a new Buick roadster. When it rains, Eddie leaves his nice new boat in the garage and takes his dad's car to visit the film exchanges. Arnold Febrey, assistant booker at Pathe, was exhibiting one of the new Ford coupes the other day.

The Buffalo community theatre, which, it was reported, was to have been built by Barney Vohwinkle in association with the Shea Amusement company on Genesee street, will not have the Shea company behind it. Mr. Vohwinkle is expected to go ahead with the project himself.

G. K. Rudolph, publicity director of the Fox Film company, stopped off in Buffalo last Saturday to visit old friends along Film and Newspaper Rows. Jerry was en route to the west coast studios, where he expects to remain several months.

We hear that Jimmy Speer, former manager of the Buffalo Dependable exchange, has returned from Florida and is trying to sell exhibitors land in that boom country.

E. J. Hayes, former manager of the Buffalo First National office, and recently associated with the sales staff of Producers Distributing corporation and Bond Photoplays corporation, has entered a sanatorium to recover his health.

O. T. Schroeppel is now in charge of all the booking at the Fox office, where much rearranging has been underway in exchange layout. Harry Bailey, the new manager, has arrived and taken up his duties. J. Emerson Dickman, salesman par excellence, is now combing his hair straight back.

"Hub" Taylor, Pathe salesman, is getting out his snowshoes, shovel, boots, sledge and limbering up his Eskimo dogs, for his winter exploration along the Southern Tier. "Hub" is taking no chances this winter. He got stuck about once

Corinne Griffith, star of "Classified," a First National Feature.

a day last year in the drifts down around Jamestown, Elmira, Binghamton, etc.

Sydney Samson, manager of the Bond Photoplays exchange, is pre-

senting exhibitors with "business boosters."

C. W. Anthony, who recently resigned from the Warner Brothers staff to accept an appointment as Associated Exhibitors' representative in Buffalo, is now out in the sticks acquainting exhibitors with his product.

Manager H. M. Addison of the Binghamton theatre, Binghamton, N. Y., wants to know if there are any harmonica players in his city. If so, Mr. Addison is willing to offer cash prizes to the one who can play the best on Friday night, October 16. So Binghamton is going to hear some real music that night.

House Manager Morris of the Regent theatre, Rochester, tried an experiment this week and it was a big success. The experiment was Mark Daniels, baritone, formerly of Portland, Ore., and now a member of the Rochester American Opera company.

Mitchell Fitzer, and not Ben, as was announced, has taken over the new theatre being built in Kenmore, N. Y. The theatre will be one of the finest in western New York and will be ready for the public soon after the first of the year.

Houston

CURTIS DUNHAM, publicity director for Famous-Players in the South is now in town in interest of exploitation.

Milton S. Goss, theatre manager and director from Beaumont and Pt. Author was in Houston for several days this week. Mr. Goss is opening an office in the Auditorium Building which will be in charge of his wife Mrs. Milton S. Goss.

John Freadle and Paul Snider, director of Southern Enterprises, Inc., and supply manager for the same organization passed through Houston on a tour of inspection.

They spent a few days in Galveston and returned through Houston enroute to Dallas where headquarters are maintained.

Paul Snell, publicity and advertising man from the California "Movie Colony" spent a week in Houston with friends. Mr. Snell combined business with pleasure while in town.

Eddie Breamer, who has been local house manager of the Majestic theatre for several seasons has won a much deserved promotion. He is now business manager for the Interstate Amusement Company's theatres in Houston. He

has established an office in the Palace theatre building.

Bennet R. Flinn who directed the Palace theatre players last season will return to Houston next week to handle the directing of the new Palace Players who will open in' Houston for a winter season at an early date. Mr. Flinn is well known in Houston and is very popular with the public and his actors alike.

Work on the new Ritz Theatre is rapidly drawing to an end. This theatre will be ready for business before the turkey season arrives.

Hal Norfleet, Southerin representative for Fox Film Co. publicity department, is in town for a few days. Mr. Norfleet reports that the theatre business is on the upward go throughout his territory.

Abe Silverberg has been in Dallas for a week buying films for the late winter and spring season.

Ed. Collins, manager of the Queen and Tremont theatres at Galveston, Texas, was in town for a day early last week.

Canada

J. D. FLETCHER has returned to Toronto, Ontario, where he has taken the management of the York theatre, a well-established suburban house. He was in charge of the Algoma theatre at Sault Ste. Marie, Ontario, for a few weeks but the Algoma is now under the command of Ray Tubman who was manager of the Strand and Palace theatres in Calgary, Alberta, for some years.

Edith Yetta Gebertig, daughter of Mr. and Mrs. M. Gebertig of Toronto, was recently married to Norman M. Snider of Toronto in the Pompeian Room of the King

Edward Hotel. Mr. Gebertig is the owner of the Bluebell theatre, Toronto, and is a prominent worker in the Ontario Division of the Motion Picture Theatre Owners of America.

Manager Jack Allan of the Capital theatre, Kitchener, Ontario, has been laboring under a handicap with regard to poster advertising for the theatre. For some weeks past, he has been unable to secure a 24-sheet stand anywhere in the city, as all the locations have been taken up for commercial advertising. He hopes to get a look-in shortly, however.

Two theatres in Canada cooperated with fire and insurance organizations during the week of October 5, which was designated as "Fire Prevention Week". At Winnipeg, Manitoba, Manager D. E. L. Fisher of the Garrick theatre presented "Fighting the Flames" as a special feature for the week while at London, Ontario, Manager W. L. Stewart presented the same feature at the Patricia theatre.

The Rex theatre at Kindersley, Sask., has been undergoing comprehensive improvements. A new

floor has been laid in the auditorium and various conveniences have been added.

William Louis Aiken has been appointed organist of the Metropolitan theatre, Regina, Sask. Until recently, he was the organist of the Metropolitan theatre at Winnipeg, Man.

The Strand theatre, Brandon, Manitoba, formerly an Allen theatre, has been closed temporarily by Famous Players Canadian Corp. The manager, Charles L. Straw, has been placed in charge of a Winnipeg theatre.

Albany

ALTHOUGH a bowling league has been recently formed among the motion picture theatres of Troy, it now looks as though Ben Stern, manager of the Lincoln theatre, and one of the premier bowlers of the city, would not be able to participate. Since pitching in the baseball game three or four weeks ago between the Troy and Mark-Strand theatres, Mr. Stern has been suffering from a badly sprained back that may prevent his taking part in the bowling matches which are being rolled one night a week after the theatre is closed.

In order that employees of the Troy theatre might keep up to the minute in the World Series, Walter Roberts, manager of the house and also an ardent baseball fan, had a radio installed in one of the rooms beneath the stage.

Uly S. Hill, managing director of the Strand group of houses in Albany and Troy, is now using an announcement of coming attractions, which is being thrown on the screen and which supplements much the same announcement that is being carried in the newspapers.

The Charleston dance contests are now on their seventh week at the Griswold theatre in Troy, and with no evidence that the public is tiring of the same. In fact, Jacob Golden is finding it a hard matter to accommodate the crowds that flock to the theatre on the one night each week when the contests take place. At the conclusion of the series a silver loving cup will be given the winner, and there will also be a split of $100 in cash among the leaders. On election night Mr. Golden, realizing the intense interest in the local situation, will have a wire service installed furnishing complete returns to his audience.

It now looks as though Ben Apple, a former well known exhibitor in Troy, who went to Florida a month or two ago, and then returned, will remain this winter in Troy. Mr. Apple has been appointed as local representative for a large Florida real estate development.

There was a quick shift of managers at the Palace theatre in Troy, last week, resulting in Louis Saperstein, who was named only two or three weeks ago, tendering his resignation to Julius Derinstein, owner of the house.

Efforts are being made in Troy to feature Junior Movies this fall and winter at the Troy theatre, Walter Roberts having the matter in charge. These movies will be given under the auspices of the Parent-Teachers' association of the city and Mr. Roberts is hoping to enlist the interest of Lansingburg. The movies were held last winter and attracted thousands of youngsters to the theatre on Saturday mornings, with a ten cent admission prevailing.

Lauren Brown, a member of the orchestra at the Troy theatre, has resigned and with his wife, gone to Florida, where he will enter the real estate business with his father-in-law. His wife came to Troy from Miami on a visit, and later found employment as an usher at the Troy theatre. The two met and were later married and then received a letter from Mrs. Brown's parents, telling of the wonderful opportunities offered in the south and suggesting that the young couple come to Florida where Mrs. Brown's father is already in the real estate business.

With motion picture theatres in Albany, Troy and Schenectady, holding an amateur night each week, many of the amateurs in these cities are making a fine living these days in going from house to house, with an occasional side trip to some of the theatres in the Mohawk Valley.

Herman Stern, manager of the F. B. O. exchange in this city, and who is taking a vacation in New York this week, has arranged for a rather novel screening at the Leland theatre, on Monday night, October 19, following the usual show. To this screening, Mr. Stern has invited Governor Alfred E. Smith, as well as all newspaper representatives in Albany, exhibitors and members of the theatrical profession playing the city on that day.

William Shirley, of Schenectady, who has made two trips already to Florida, left for Miami last Wednesday, and according to his own assertions, will not be back north until he has made at least one-half a million dollars. Some of the boys along Film Row, in saying good-bye to Mr. Shirley, said that they did not expect to see him for some years to come.

F. W. Aldrich, of the Regent in St. Regis Falls, has informed Film Row that he will close his house for the winter on November 1. Vic Warren, of Massena, was in New York city during the week. Bob Landry, one of the best known exhibitors in northern New York, left during the week for Florida. The week also brought to town Ely Rosenbaum, of the Hippodrome in Ogdensburg.

John Maxwell, formerly connected with the Frontier Amuse-

Helen Lynch in "Bustin Through," Universal.

ment Company of Buffalo, is now handling the Liberty theatre in Herkimer, one of the Schine houses. And speaking of the Schine boys, Gloversville, which is the headquarters of the Schine circuit, has been dubbed "Schineville" along Film Row. The Schines are running a Fashion Show this week at the Glove theatre in Gloversville, along with the feature.

Among visitors along Film Row during the week were Earl Kramer, of Buffalo, Mrs. Fonda, of the Grand in Scotia and the Star in Schenectady and Margaret Sullivan of the San Souci in Watervliet. The week also brought to town Tom Kennedy of the Lyceum in Champlain and L. Shapiro, of Manchester, Vt., the latter, however, forgetting to bring along any maple syrup for the young ladies in the exchanges. J. B. Harte, of Bennington, Vt., also arrived in town in a brand new Packard. He will leave shortly for Fort Lauderdale, Fla.

Charles Henschel, district manager for Pathe, stopped over in Albany for a few hours one day last week, while on his way from New York to Boston.

Nick Dennis, of Utica, is planning to open the Auditorium in that city to pictures and Italian vaudeville on Nov. 2. Mr. Dennis has booked heavily of F. B. O. product and was present at a dinner given by Joe Raymond of the State theatre in that city, last week, at the Hotel Martin, with Harold Filkins, Ely Rosenbaum, and Herman Stern among those at the table.

George E. Loomis has just taken over the Savoy in Frankfort, reopening the house on October 7.

Another minister of the Gospel has been added, during the past week, to the ranks of exhibitors of New York state. Rev. H. H. Black has taken over the Central Bridge theatre and was along Film Row during the week, booking pictures.

Harry Nolan, who hails from the Middle West and an original First National franchise holder, stopped over in Albany during the week, for a visit with Alex Herman, local manager.

The boys along Film Row greeted Harvey Smith, of Wells, during the week. Mr. Smith does not make many trips to town, but now that he has a new car, will probably be seen oftener than in the past.

The Colonial theatre in Monroe has been taken over by J. J. Dimber, of Jersey City, from the K. and B. Amusement company.

George S. Jeffreys, special Harold Lloyd representative from New York city, is in town this week.

Announcement of Christy Mathewson's death came as a shock to Dave Seymour, owner of the Pontiac theatre in Saranac Lake, and one of the best showmen in this territory. During Mr. Mathewson's long stay in the Adirondack village, he and Mr. Seymour became fast friends and would often meet and talk over old times, for in years past Mr. Seymour was out with many a road company and knows the country from end to end.

Employees of the local Pathe exchange, are working hard these days toward accumulating a special fund that will provide the exchange with a victrola which will be used at private screenings and dances on the upper floor of the exchange. Up to the present time the fund has reached $7.50, so it may be some months before the victrola becomes a reality.

The new theatre in Lake Placid is making headway to the extent that the sidewalks are up.

Plans for the proposed Hallowe'en dinner and dance by the Albany Film Board of Trade have failed to materialize and as a result the party has been declared off.

There is a new salesman at the Fox exchange in the person of Morris Simon, who has been employed in both Rochester and New York city. He is scheduled to cover the southern tier.

William Smalley, of Cooperstown, has returned home from the Danbury Fair. Frank Briggs has been placed in charge of the Clinton Square theatre in Albany, with Alex Sayles managing both houses and doing the advertising for the one in Glens Falls, as well.

Junior Movies have started at the Empire in Glens Falls on Saturday mornings, with a ten cent admission.

Charles Gilmore, of Syracuse and Oswego, has leased the Temple as well as the Hohman theatres in Pulaski, assuming possession on November 1. Jacob A. Youngs will be retained as manager of the Temple, while a new manager will be named for the Hohman.

Mrs. Carpenter closed her theatre in Lake George last week. As soon as rather extensive alterations are completed, she will leave for the south to spend the winter.

Eleanor Boardman in "An Exchange of Wives," Metro-Goldwyn-Mayer.

Omaha

BEN C. MARCUS, who has been booker and assistant to Manager Sherman Fitch of the F. B. O., has been promoted to salesman.

F. A. Milhouse, owner of the Summer theatre at Summer, Neb., organized a party of twenty Legionnaires for a trip to the convention in Omaha, October 5 to 9.

L. J. McCarthy, general manager of Balaban and Katz, was in Omaha last week.

Mayer and Phil Monsky, owners of Liberty Films, Incorporated, celebrated their fifth anniversary September 25. They started out with only one picture, but in their five-year business life, they have picked many box office winners. In celebrating their anniversary, the Monsky brothers expressed their appreciation of the fine support theatre owners of Nebraska and Iowa have given them.

The Omaha Film Board of Trade has joined in the fire prevention campaign, October 4 to 10. At fifteen local film exchanges fire drills are held, stocks of film being removed in less than one minute.

W. J. Morgan, general sales manager for Producers Distributing Corporation, New York, and C. D. Hill, district manager, from St. Louis, were here Sunday and Monday.

E. J. Lipson, manager of the Des Moines office of the Producers Distributing Corporation, joined Mr. Morgan and Mr. Hill here for the week end.

Floyd Lewis, special representative for the Associated Exhibitors

in St. Louis, is here for a week.

Eddie Alperson, representative for the Associated Exhibitors here has resigned.

The Independent Film company of Omaha is contemplating opening a new office in Des Moines.

C. T. Lynch, manager for Metro-Goldwyn exchange, is spending the week in Red Oak, Clarinda and Atlantic.

J. L. Kelly, salesmen for Metro-Goldwyn, has just bought a new Chevrolet coupe.

Mrs. G. B. Uhler, formerly Lucille Watson, is taking the place of Nell Deal as stenographer for United Artists. Mrs. Uhler has had ten years' experience in film work and was formerly with United Artists at Atlanta, Georgia.

A $25,000 moving picture theater will be built by H. A. Hower at 520-524 No. Thirty-third street. Mr. Hower bought the property for $10,500.

George Monroe has just purchased the Oak theatre at Red Oak, Iowa, from Harry Simons.

J. L. Stearn, manager for the Independent Film Company of Omaha, has just returned from a trip to Des Moines and other key points.

The Universal exchange wound up its theatre parties with one held at the Majestic theatre at Lexington, Nebr., Sept. 28. Manager Harry F. Letholtz and others of the Omaha office made arrangements for the party, with the hearty cooperation of Ralph Falkinburg, manager of the theatre. Twenty-eight bonafide exhibitors

Ben Turpin, who has been added to the Metropolitan Production's cast of "Steel Preferred" for Producers Dist. Corp. release.

of western Nebraska were present, and the audience in addition contained members of their families and prominent citizens.

The Universal office is making plans to entertain visiting Legionnaire-exhibitors during the American Legion convention here October 5th to 9th.

John J. Gilmore, Fox Film Corporation exploitation man from New York city, is in town.

James Winn, manager of the Educational Film Company here, is going to Des Moines to take charge of that office.

Leo Blank, nephew of A. H. Blank of Des Moines, who has been a salesman for First National in Omaha, will become new manager for Educational.

C. P. Nedley, formerly with the Vitagraph exchange as assistant manager, is now covering the northern Iowa territory for Fox. Harry Musselman, has brought back the Auditorium theatre at Oscealo, Nebr.

The Omaha Film Board of Trade has abandoned temporarily the idea of putting on a central shipping room for all exchanges.

R. R. Booth, owner of the Paramount and Overland theatres in Nebraska City, is in town this week.

Joe Stark has resigned as Block B. salesman for Pathe here and has gone to join the St. Louis office.

Earl Meyers, representative for the Associated Exhibitors in Des Moines, was here visiting the Omaha branch for a week.

B. H. Shepers has become new owner of the Star theater at Callaway, Nebr. It was formerly owned by W. E. Scheringer and son.

J. M. Swenson, has just purchased the Opera house at Batavia, Iowa, from L. N. Frescoln.

Edwin Silverman, special representative for Warner Brothers, with offices in Chicago, visited here last week.

Chicago

MARIAN RICE, a daughter of H. E. Rice of the Jackson Park theatre, who was close to winning the recent Smart : Set Magazine beauty contest, and whose perfection of face and figure received favorable comment from the judges, is making personal appearances at the Capitol theatre this week.

The three thousand seat Harding theatre at Milwaukee and Sawyer, the first of the nine great houses under construction by Lubliner & Trinz to be opened since this firm's amalgamation with Balaban & Katz, threw its doors open to the public on Monday night and in line with the Lubliner & Trinz-Balaban & Katz policy, the house is one of great beauty and is magnificently equipped and furnished throughout, with a large stage. The Logan Square Business Men's Association and other improvement bodies staged a week carnival to celebrate the opening, and on the day of the premier performances throngs blocked the street surrounding the theatre and thousands were turned away.

The new Ambassador theatre at Division street and Mansfield, will have its official opening on October 20th, according to W. P. McCarthy, president of the M. & H. Theatres Corporation. An arrange-

ment has been entered into with Cooney Brothers National Theatres corporation, which insures the same high standard of entertainment for the Ambassador as that which has made the Capitol theater famous during the few months it has been operating.

Frank Schaefer of the Crystal theatre, accompanied by his wife, is enjoying a vacation in Asheville, North Carolina.

William Kleighe has assumed the ownership and management of the S. J. Gregory Theatrical company, the Hammond Amusement company and the East Chicago Amusement company, S. J. Gregory having severed all his connections with these enterprises, which operate the Parthenon, Orpheum and De Luxe theatres of Hammond; and the Forsythe and Lyric theaters of East Chicago. J. L. McCurdy, who for some time has been connected with the Gregory companies, has been named general manager and will be in complete charge of operation. No reason for the sudden change in the management has been given out, but it is understood that Mr. Gregory will continue active interest in his other theaters.

Manager Roy Alexander of Universal's Chicago exchange, is back again after a trip to the west coast headquarters of his company.

It is understood that Mr. Alexander has perfected plans for one of the most important advertising tie-ups in motion picture history. Among the visitors at the local exchange in the last few days were manager, and Lou Metzger, manager of the complete service department.

Samuel Halper and Harry Y. Dissen, operators of four Chicago theatres, and who will soon take over the Terminal, now being operated by Ascher Brothers, have organized the Ritz Theatre Company of Michigan, and will operate the new Ritz theatre, formerly the Globe in Flint, Michigan. The theatre is being completely redecorated, recarpeted and a large thirty foot electric sign and new marquee are being installed, as well as a new Barton organ with the console placed on a lift. Charles Garfield, old time theatre man, will be in charge of the house which is scheduled to open the middle of October, with a policy of first run photoplays and vaudeville at popular prices.

Henry Igel, well known Chicago projectionist, and son of Harry Igel, city hall representative of local film interests, reports the loss of his wife's father by sudden

death. He was William J. Ryan, president of the National Ice Company of Forest Park, and also president of the William J. Ryan Cinder Company. He left a widow and six grown children. Henry Igel is one of the executors of the will.

D. D. Cox is retiring from the active management of the Community theatre at Raymond, Illinois.

Floyd Brockell, general manager of Balaban & Katz Midwest Theatres, Inc., has returned from a short business trip to New York City.

Manager George Dembow, of Fox Film Corporation, has returned from New York where he attended the conference of sales executives.

Cooney Brothers state that they are not in a position to either deny or confirm reports that their company will shortly erect a big first run theatre in Chicago's loop. Cooneys, however, admitted that they may have something of interest to give out within a short time.

C. C. Pettijohn of the Hays Organization, was a Chicago visitor this week and made his headquarters at the Congress Hotel,

Is your theatre under this "New" Management?

A sign neatly displayed over the entrance to a theatre in which a new Simplex Projector had just been installed advised the public that the theatre was "Under New Management."

The Simplex Service man in that district dropped in to inquire as to policies of the new management.

"We have only one policy," said the manager. "That is a social one. We consider ourselves hosts to the whole community in which our theatre is located. Through the columns of a local newspaper we issued an invitation to this community to be our guests. It was a social invitation. We said nothing about the pictures we would show, nor about the prices we would charge. Just an invitation similar to ones used in social life.

"We believe our theatre has a definite place in the social activities of this community. We, as the hosts, are responsible for the comfort and pleasure of our patrons and we give as much consideration to their pleasure as any good host would give to the entertainment of his guests. We won't give our patrons broken chairs to sit on, and we'll pay as much attention to the manner in which pictures are presented as a hostess would pay to the dishes on which she serves refreshments.

"As evidence of that you will notice we have just installed new Simplex Projectors. That's our guarantee to patrons that pictures will be presented in the best possible manner." I said our policy was entirely social. It is—but we've found it excellent from a business standpoint too.

*   *   *   *   *   *

It has been proved many times that better projection draws so much more patronage to a theatre that the cost of the new equipment is soon paid for out of increased earnings.

Let us tell you what can be accomplished through the better projection obtained from Simplex Projectors.

CONSTRUCTION & EQUIPMENT DEPARTMENT

F.P.-L's Metropolitan, Boston, Opened

New House, With Seating Capacity of Forty-Six Hundred, Largest in New England

BOSTON'S new theatre, the Metropolitan, at Tremont and Hollis streets, opened Saturday, Oct. 10, taking its place as the largest theatre in New England, with a seating capacity of 4,600. It is a Paramount house under the management of Balaban & Katz and under the direction of Keith-Albee.

The Metropolitan marks the very latest word in completeness, luxury and appointment. From the outer lobby to the rooms back stage nothing has been omitted that makes for the comfort and enjoyment of the patrons and the employees.

The theatre itself occupies the entire block bounded by Tremont, Hollis, Dillaway and Dore streets and while the seating capacity is placed at 4,600, more widely spaced than in any other Boston playhouse, there is ample room for more than 2,500 more people to sit in the lounges, smoking rooms and parlors of the building. The marquee above the main entrance is so broad that it will permit fifteen automobiles to discharge passengers beneath its shelter at one time.

There will be no waiting of patrons in wet weather outside the theatre. The spacious lobby will care for any sized audience while awaiting their turn at the box office windows. These lobbies, as well as the lounges, parlors and the auditorium of the playhouse will be warmed in winter and cooled in summer.

In the lobbys will be an orchestra of 12 pieces which will furnish music distinct from the 55-piece orchestra in the auditorium. The grand lobby is 70 feet in height, decorated largely in gold and blue with relieving notes of lavender in the background. The ceiling is blue with allegorical paintings by Louis Amarosi of Chicago. Sixteen great pillars of rose jasper marble

range round this lobby, and set in the walls back of them are pilasters of the same stone. On the walls are panels of Botticino marble framed with rose tavernelle marble. All of the marble used came from Italy. Two crystal chandeliers and many floor torches are used in lighting this chamber.

The grand staircase at the end of the grand lobby is framed with deep valances of red velvet. The staircase gives access to two broad flights of steps to the single balcony. At the opposite end are two other flights of steps and nearby, at each end of the grand lobby, are pairs of staircases leading to the grand lounge.

The walls of the grand lounge are heavily panelled with carved walnut, classic leaf ornamental themes being used in the carvings. Opening from the lounge, as well as from the other levels of the playhouse, are retiring rooms for men and women, check rooms, telephone booths and similar services.

Patrons will not be sent hither and thither to find seats because the head usher, stationed at the main entrance, is at all times informed of vacant seats in all parts of the house by means of push buttons, operated by ushers of each section, which show by means of lights in an indicator panel beside the head usher, just where every vacant seat is located. Thus, if a party of eight arrives and wishes to be seated together, the head usher directs them without delay to a place where those seats are available.

The outer lobby is adorned with murals, copies of Titian's "Triumph of Venus" in Rome, painted by Amarosi. The murals in the grand lobby, also by Amarosi, are symbolic of the advance in drama and music. Encircling the ceiling of the main auditorium are a series of murals by Edmund Philo Kellogg of Chicago. The central mural is studded with 250 semi-precious jewels costing $10,000. Surrounding the central figure are five figures symbolizing ballad, operatic, dance, sacred and martial music; and five representing drama, pantomime, comedy, tragedy, history and romance.

There are three mezzanine promenades and one outside promenade. Two spacious elevators carry patrons from the main floor to the balconies. The mushroom system of ventilation is used. All of the loges are equipped with arm chairs. There is a red cross room with full hospital equipment, with a physician constantly in charge.

The 55-piece orchestra will be stationed upon an elevator platform so that it may be raised or lowered to any desired height.

There is an orchestra floor, mezzanine level from which entrance is gained to the mezzanine boxes, and balcony. The sight lines are as near perfect as science and *(Cont'd on page 1964)*

View of the grand lobby of Paramount's new Metropolitan theatre, Boston.

View of the entrance to the balcony of the new St. Francis theatre, San Francisco.

Brill's Inwood Combines Many Interesting and Novel Features

THE Inwood theatre, located in the Dyckman Street section of New York, with a seating capacity of two thousand, has a frontage of one hundred feet on Dyckman Street and runs back two hundred feet to Thayer Street. As designed by Architect Eugene De Rosa the layout of the house includes many new innovations.

In the portion of the building fronting on Dyckman Street is located the vestibule and entrance lobby to the theatre with four stores. The front is a mattglazed brick with granite base and granite terra cotta trimmings. The walls of the vestibule are lined with marble, the ceiling is of ornamental plaster, and the floors of terrazzo with border of marble mosaic.

Through doors glazed with plate glass divided into small panes the lobby is entered. The lobby is quite spacious having a width of 32 feet. The walls are of paneled marble in which gilded ornamental plaster panels are set in conjunction with mirrors trimmed in bronze and elaborate display panels. There is a richly decorated cornice and a coffered ceiling with ornamental plaster in relief in every panel. The floor is of terrazzo with marble mosaic border.

The auditorium has a length of 160 feet from the stage to the rear wall and a width of 100 feet. A low wainscott is carried around the side and rear walls and the surface above is laid off in panels, with an enriched cornice and froize at the ceiling line. The outstanding feature of the ceiling is a great circular dome 59 feet in diameter. In a cove running around this dome are concealed lights in different colors which may be used singly or in combinations producing most beautiful effects. The ceiling is otherwise decorated with panels, set pieces and running ornament in plaster relief which under the hands of the decorator lends itself to a scheme of decoration which is rich and beautiful in effect.

A small stage has been provided with a proscenium opening flanked with marble columns on either side, which is suitable for a singer or someone giving a recitation. At the back of the stage is the picture screen and at the proscenium opening is hung a curtain of rich material.

Marble staircase with wrought iron railing leading up from the promenade to the mezzanine story where the central space has been used for the projection, rewind and generator rooms where all the latest and best apparatus for showing the pictures will be found. The ladies' parlor, the men's smoking room, manager's office and ushers' room are also on this floor. The lounges provided for the ladies' and men open off into the auditorium with arched openings leading to ornamental balconies which provide an exceptional view of the screen and theatre. Care has been taken, by a study of sight lines and the elimination of all columns, to give everyone in the auditorium a clear and unobstructed view of the stage.

Great attention has also been given to the heating and ventilating of the auditorium so as to insure proper and comfortable conditions of the atmosphere for the patrons.

In the sides of the stage is located the supply fans and hot air ducts through which the heated air is introduced into the auditorium by means of registers of perforated plaster in the side walls. There is also in the basement the musicians' room, the boiler room and coal room.

The projection room, in charge of Julius Wetzler, is equipped with three Simplex machines, two Hertner generators (double 125), two Walsh curtain controls, a Brenkert double dissolver and Bausch and Lomb cinaphore lens. Howell's Cine Equipment Co. did the installation work.

Roofing and sheet metal material were installed by Sobel and Krauss, ornamental plastering by the Architectural Plastering Co., and electrical equipment by the Edwards Electrical Construction Co. Display frames by Markendorff, electric signs by Strauss, chairs by American Seating Co. and organ by the Moller Organ Co.

Instruments Ltd. to Distribute Ross F 2.4 Lens

Sole distribution throughout the United States and Canada for Ross F 2.4 projection lens, an important British mechanical development for the stereoscopic presentation of moving pictures, has been secured by Instruments, Limited, 240 Sparks street, Ottawa, Ontario, according to announcement by A. J. Ames, managing director of the company.

The first installation of the Ross lens was arranged by Donat Paquin for the Laurier Theatre, Hull, Quebec, while subsequent installations in Canada have been made by Manager Don Stapleton of the Centre Theatre, Ottawa, P. J. Nolan for the Rex Theatre and also in the Columbia Theatre, Ottawa. The new lens has made a distinct impression.

Files Plans for New Theatre in St. Louis

Plans for a $1,000,000 theatre and apartment building to be erected at Gravois and Ellenwood avenues, St. Louis, Mo. have been placed before the St. Louis Board of Aldermen by Rupert & Levine, Chicago architects. The owners desire the vacation of an alley to permit the erection of the house.

The new theatre will seat 3,800 and front 137 feet on Gravois avenue by 169 feet on Ellenwood. Six hundred feet of land nearby has been obtained for the apartment.

Reuben Levine of Chicago is the owner of the new project. He has stated that St. Louis theatre men will handle the theatre when it is completed.

Chicago to Have New Four Thousand Seat House

A company headed by Andrew Karzas plans to erect a great motion picture theatre at 79th and Cottage Grove Avenue. Plans for the house which will seat in the neighborhood of 4,000 persons, are practically complete and construction work will start immediately, according to those interested in the new house.

Plans Are Filed for New Buffalo Theatre

Plans have been filed with the Bureau of Buildings in Buffalo by the Farber & Yavno Holding company for a new motion picture theatre to be erected at 2275-2285 Genesee street. The house will cost $30,000.

Lobby of the new Embassy theatre, New York, which is under the management of Gloria Gould.

CAPITOL THEATRE, New York City
Seated by American Seating Company; Thomas W. Lamb, Architect

The Rewards of Leadership

Leadership in industry and business today requires organization, resources and a wealth of specialized experience and technical knowledge.

Because the American Seating Company has the organization, resources, the required experience and knowledge of real leadership, it is entrusted with the Seating of America's Foremost Theatres.

American Seating Company

| NEW YORK | CHICAGO | BOSTON | PHILADELPHIA |
| 115 W. 40th St. | 10 E. Jackson Blvd. | 77 O. Canal St. | 1211 K Chestnut St. |

Projection
Optics, Electricity, Practical Ideas & advice

Inquiries and Comments

Change-Over Troubles

 POINT which apparently receives but little attention on the part of the average projectionist is that of change-overs. It seems to be taken more or less as a matter of fact, yet nothing is more important to a smooth presentation than a changeover which cannot be detected as such on the screen by the average person.

The annoyance and irritation caused by a blank screen, or a dark screen, or an "End of Reel 5" marker, or anything else that indicates the projectionist is either lazy, indifferent, or on a "visiting" trip from the side of the warming-up projector where he belongs is seldom brought to the attention of the House Manager by the patrons but the fact remains that such interruptions in the thread of the story that is being woven on the screen tend to utterly dispel the illusion of reality which the producer has attempted to create and furthermore tend to result in anti-climaxes.

In view of the fact that this practice of making sloppy changeovers is unwarranted and really finds little to excuse it, the duty of the projectionist clearly lies in drilling himself so as to attain perfection in this point.

Evidently, J. G. Ashenfelter, Bridge Theatre, Petersburg, W. Va., feels the same as we do about the matter since he is evidently straining effort toward securing changeovers which the most practiced eye would have difficulty in observing.

Read for yourself.

"Dear Sir:—

"Ever since the installation of two projectors in this theatre, I have had trouble making changeovers because I could not get them smooth enough to be unnoticed by the average spectator.

"The first method that I used was to run a string from the handle of the dowser on one projector to the trigger that drops the dowser on the other projector, and vice versa, so that when I raise one dowser, the other is automatically dropped, but this did not seem to give the right effect. Oftimes there was slight margin of blank screen between the dropping of one dowser and the raising of the other. Again, the string would stretch when least expected, and both dowsers would be raised at the same time and the result would be a double picture, a sort of lap-dissolve on the screen for a fraction of a second until I would savagely jerk the string again, sometimes breaking it.

New Method

"The second method, which is more effective in a way which I just discovered the other day, is to fade one projector "out" and the other "in." This involved having the dowser raised on projector A and the lamp heated up, not full; but at about 8 amperes (What kind of a lamp is this? Ordinary arc, reflector arc, or Mazda?—Ed) and when the time for the changeover came, the man at projector B would throw the regulator handle back (Sounds like Mazda—Ed.) and projector A would be started and after the fire-shutter had raised the lamp would be brought on full.

"This appears to me to have at least one disadvantage. It takes lamp B too long to die down entirely to a point where projector A can begin to function and when projector A is started, the lamp has already been heated up to a point where the plainer part of the picture is discernible on the screen. Instead of "fading" in from nothing at all, this makes the white part of the picture appear on the screen in a dull red color.

"The only solution at which I can arrive, is for the various exchanges to put a four-foot fade-out trailer on the end of each reel, and a four-foot fade-in leader on the beginning of each reel after Reel 1.

"I would appreciate hearing your views on this subject, also the opinions of other projectionists."

Something Wrong

From the appearance of the above letter which is printed with no changes whatever in its construction or wording, Friend Ashenfelter appears to be a pretty intelligent sort of fellow. Be that as it may we have been trying to dope out just what sort of a set-up he is using. Mention of the regulator handle and to the "trigger" of the dowser seems to brand it as Mazda, so we will work on that assumption.

We had always thought that the changeover rigging for this outfit worked out pretty good, at least we have heard no complaints concerning it so had assumed that everything was "Jake." Are you sure, Friend Ashenfelter, that the jamming you mention is not being caused by bent "trigger" handles or the dowsers? Such would seem to be the case.

Furthermore, as for the string stretching, why that, we would say is purely a matter of choosing a string that won't stretch to the extent of refusing to work the dowsers. Heavy fish-line, about the size of light mason's twine we should think would be about the thing to use.

When nicely adjusted and balanced, the method of dowser control recommended for Mazda gives complete satisfaction and can be made to be quick and positive in action.

Dissolving Effect

Such a method of changing over abruptly from one reel to the next, however does not give the finished touch to the presentation. In other words it lacks the Master's touch which is a distinguishing characteristic of the work of all artists.

It might be mentioned in passing that if the reel in one projector is allowed to exhaust itself before the changeover period the result will be a "blank" screen, no matter what changeover method is used.

As for the dissolving effect, why that is a step in the right direction but the way you go at it, Friend Ashenfelter, leaves much to be desired.

Cutting down the intensity on one lamp while raising the screen intensity on the second lamp is the proper thing to do but this effect should not be secured by actually reducing the current flowing, through the lamps.

If this is done, as you have attempted to do, the natural result will be a very sloppy dissolving effect caused by the lag in lighting the filament up or cooling it off after the current has been turned on or off.

The right way to go about it is to leave both lamps burning full brightness and then place an iris diaphragm in each optic system. There are two locations in the optic systems where such a diaphragm could be placed to secure the desired results, viz., at the face of the *collecting lens* and over the mouth of the *objective lens* (toward screen).

An iris diaphragm placed at either of these locations would, if closed, gradually reduce the light intensity over the entire picture area and conversely, if opened would gradually raise the intensity over the entire picture area.

At the first location (next to collector lens) it would be difficult to secure dual control of the diaphragms and in the case of the Parabolic condenser on Mazda the diaphragm could not be used at all for lack of space.

The best location, therefore, would be at the mouth of the objective lens since then a metal rod joining both diaphragms could be fixed so as not to interfere with any other mechanism on the projectors.

When so placed, both lamps would be burning full brightness and the diaphragm on projector A would be wide open passing the full amount of the light whereas diaphragm B would be shut tight passing no light. The dowsers on both projectors would naturally be up and the fire-shutter on projector B would be down since this unit would not be working.

At the changeover period, selected beforehand from a cue sheet preferably, the motor switch on projector B would be closed and as soon as the fire-shutter had raised, the handle regulating both diaphragms would be pushed over thus opening B at the same time that A was being closed.

The result would be a dissolving or "vignetting" action which could be regulated as to speed merely by moving the control handle faster or slower.

As for the four foot leaders and tail pieces, Friend Ashenfelter, why that idea is as old as the hills and the only thing we can say about it is that every reel should have such a leader and tail piece attached to the ends of the film not only to assist in smooth changeovers but also to protect the film and aid in threading up the projector.

Million Dollar Theatre for Birmingham, Ala.

The Mudd and Colley Amusement Company, Inc., of Birmingham, Ala., announces this week the early erection of a million dollar motion picture house in that city.

The new theatre, not yet named, will be located on Second Avenue, North, in Birmingham, and covers a ground space of 75 feet by 140 feet deep. Contract for the erection was let recently and the work of dismantling the present buildings has been started.

The structure will be entirely of concrete and steel, and will incorporate as its prime features beauty, safety and comfort. All latest features in theatre design will be installed throughout, and the projection room will contain six projectors with the most modern equipment obtainable. A special ventilation system will be one of the important features.

The architect's plans call for a Spanish design interior of steel faced with granite finish terra cotta, with a polychrome terra

cotta trim. The orchestra will seat 1,000, with a large balcony, mezzanine and lounges. Interior to be designed in the Adam period, the auditorium to be hung with silken damask panels, and ornamented with Grecian figures in old ivory against a background of old blue and gold. Stage proper will be fully equipped and of adequate dimensions to allow for the most elaborate presentations.

Orpheum Theatre, Altoona, Redecorated

Elaborate improvements have just been completed in the Orpheum Theatre, Altoona, Pa., a Wilmer & Vincent house devoted to the presentation of "the best pictures" and musical revues. Decorators have wrought costly changes beginning with the marquee over the sidewalk and extending through foyers, stairways, mezzanine gallery, the main auditorium, stages, boxes, walls, ceilings and floors.

New draperies have been installed and the aisles and floors laid with fine Wilton carpets in gorgeous red. New lights have been added and these finely set off the brilliant coloring effects produced by the new decorations.

The management has also installed a new pipe organ. It has all the traps and combinations.

Louis A. Vaughn is the house manager while the theatre will be under the general direction of John F. Maloy, manager of the Wilmer & Vincent interests in Altoona.

Fred D. Burns Opens New House at Newport, Va.

Fred D. Burns recently opened his new Burns Theatre at Newport, Vt., replacing the old Premier formerly located on the same site.

Burns personally designed and supervised the construction of this theatre, which is fireproof throughout and complete in every detail, having a total of six hundred and fifty-six seats, five hundred and ten on the lower floor and one hundred and forty-six in the balcony. Seats built and placed by the local, Frost Veneer Seating Company, Newport, Vt.

The entrance is of Vermont granite and lobby decorations are finished with genuine South American walnut. The entire theatre and lobby are lighted throughout with orange tinted lights insuring quietness and comfort to all patrons.

New Willow Theatre at Willimansett Opened

Frank H. Wotton, formerly of the Park Theatre at Lebanon, N. H., has opened the New Willow theatre at Willimansett, Mass., which he has leased from the owner and builder, Mr. Reardon, local builder and contractor.

The Willow theatre is one of the most pretentious, fireproof and up-to-date theatres in this section of Massachusetts. Having 781 seats on one floor, the ceiling is thirty feet from the floor, insuring good ventilation and heating which is of the blower type, and complete changing of air every three minutes.

Suitable arrangements have been made for six piece orchestra and the policy of the theatre will be to show straight pictures of the very best.

New Comerford House for West Scranton, Penn.

Details have been announced concerning the plans for the new West Side Theatre, in West Scranton, upon which construction work has been begun by the Comerford Amusement Company. The contractors are Breig Brothers, and the estimated cost is $300,000. It will require about a year to complete the building which will cover a plot on North Main Avenue, 200 by 116 feet.

It will be a three-story building of brick and stone. A store room will be placed on either side of the lobby on the first floor and the two upper floors will be devoted to apartments. The auditorium will seat 2,000 and will be equipped with a stage, 80 by 30 feet, so that it will be possible to offer vaudeville and legitimate attractions, in addition to motion pictures, if at any time it is desired to do so.

Feldman to Build Theatre in Boston, Mass.

Mr. Feldman plans to erect a theatre on Broadway, Everett square, between Norwood and Church streets where he has already started erection of a business block. The plans call for converting two of the stores in the block into a theatre entrance and the auditorium will be located in the rear of the block, with seating capacity of about 1,500. Feldman plans to lease the theatre.

F. P. - L.'s Metropolitan, Boston, Opened

(Continued from page 1959)

study can make them. The curve of the seats is shallow and the screen is designed to give an undistorted effect from any seat in the theatre. The mezzanine boxes are on a level with the projection booth, but it is doubtful if many patrons will ever discover the location of the booth, which is well under the balcony and so placed that the lens is directly opposite the center of the screen, doing away with any distortion resulting from projection from the usual high angle. The booth is so located that no patron of the house will be obliged to look across the beam of light to view the picture.

A great dome, done in warm blue, touched with points of gold resembling stars, and with a gold sunburst in the center, will be the source of the concealed lighting. During the overture and other orchestral numbers, five 600-candle power lights will play on the orchestra. The sides of the auditorium have been framed with twelve great glass panels with glossy black backing, copies of the famous black mirrors of Versailles. The stage is said to be one of the highest stages of any theatre in the world.

Earl F. Crabb will be general manager of the theatre and he will have three department heads serving under his direction. One will be John Murray Anderson, producer of the first "Greenwich Village Follies," who will have the stage production part of the program. This will be an innovation to Boston and is arranged with much elasticity so that Mr. Anderson may have a wide variety of selection, ranging from a ballet to a special musical program or playlet.

Jeff Lazarus has been chosen as promotion and publicity director. Selection of the third department head who will have charge of the music, has not been made.

Paramount Managers' Class Visits Nicholas Power Company Plant

Studio at Trenton, Ontario, which combines fully equipped stage and laboratories. It is operated by Province of Ontario Pictures under Col. W. H. Price, K. C., provincial treasurer. G. E. Patton is the Director.

THE Paramount Managers' School spent three and a half hours in the Nicholas Power plant, N. Y. City, on October 6th as one of the sessions in the course which the students of this school are taking. The class is in charge of John F. Barry, director of the school, who with Harry Rubin, Chief Projectionist of the Rivoli, Rialto and Criterion theatres, were welcomed by P. A. McGuire, Advertising Manager of the Nicholas Power Company.

McGuire said that he had expected Bart F. Greene, Chief Examiner for electricity and moving picture licenses in the Department of Water Supply, Gas and Electricity, City of New York, to address the class, but Greene was unable to be present. Mr. McGuire stated that he had been authorized by Greene to make the following statement: "Protection of audiences by proper enforcement of the law in the motion picture theatres of the City of New York is the duty of the Department of Water Supply, Gas and Electricity. It is our duty to see that standard equipment is used, properly installed, maintained and placed in charge of competent projectionists. We are required to regularly inspect the equipment after installation and carefully examine all applicants for licenses to operate motion picture machines in New York City.

The class was divided into two groups, and one, under A. R. Schulze, of the Engineering Department of the Nicholas Power Company, were shown early models of Power's Edison, Lubin, Selig, Gaumont, and other projectors used in the formative period of the motion picture industry.

The other group under Mr. Wrede, of the Repair Department, were shown the projection room with three latest type Power's Projectors and three different modern types of lamps, Power's High Intensity, Power's Incandescent and Powerlite Low Intensity Reflector Arc.

After both groups had been shown the models and the projection room, they returned to the auditorium of the Power's testing laboratory and Mr. Schulze explained the special features of Power's Projectors. The members of the class took great interest in Schulze's talk and considerable discussion followed.

Joseph Abrams, who has been installation man for the Nicholas Power Company for nearly fifteen years, then gave a demonstration of the three types of illuminants, High Intensity, Incandescent and Low Intensity, which were shown successively on the screen and then all three at the same time. This was accomplished by superimposing the three lights upon each other but with a few inches of each extending on the side from the others so that the contrasting effect was clearly shown.

After this demonstration by Abrams and explanations by Schulze, Wrede delivered a very interesting talk on repairs and replacements and pointed out the importance of having emergency parts on hand in the projection room. The class was also supplied with an article written by Wrede which gave a list of the parts which should be carried on hand for Power's Projectors.

At the conclusion of Wrede's talk the class was divided into three groups, one under Schulze, one under Wrede, and one under Wickersheimer, Chief Inspector of the Nicholas Power Company, and were taken through the Power's factory. They were shown how large an equipment it takes to properly and efficiently manufacture a modern motion picture projector and, also, the exactness of the operations, measurements and inspection which enter into the making of Power's parts. In the various departments the groups stopped to watch the assembling of more important parts of the projector and were given explanations which would assist them in understanding the necessity for carefully looking after these particular parts.

The members of the Paramount Managers' School were deeply interested in all that was shown and told to them and asked many questions. Barry and Rubin expressed themselves as being very well pleased with their visit.

Newspaper Opinions on New Pictures

"An Exchange of Wives"— M-G-M, Capitol, N. Y.

Graphic: "An Exchange of Wives' is just as hectic as the title suggests. No French farce that ever found its way from the Place de Theatre to the Gay White Way ever afforded more thrills. The treatment is extremely modern and there are several new and highly amusing angles. The clever titles add not a little to the fun. How Eleanor Boardman arranges the exchange of wives and later straightens out the tangle forms the plot of the highly amusing and well directed comedy."

American: "'Exchange of Wives' is spicy, daring and skates along the edge of suggestion as far as it dares and still keeps within censorial bounds." It amuses those who are married and helps those who are single to stay that way and be thankful. Lew Cody does an effective bit of comedy in his moments of trying to square himself with his wife. 'Exchange of Wives' is well done. Hobart Henley has seen to that by doing a very good directorial job."

Journal: "It's an amusing comedy. Cody is a great comedian, and Eleanor Boardman does good work."

Times: "Eleanor Boardman is attractive and capable as Margaret. Renee Adoree is efficient as the constant flirt. Lew Cody is as good as John and Creighton Hale is effective as Victor."

"Go Straight"—Schulberg, Broadway, N. Y.

American: "If you get a kick out of crook melodrama, 'Go Straight' is your meat. You will have a feast and you will get the same excitement out of the suspense in this picture that you get out of reading a thrilling detective yarn."

Journal: "You'll enjoy it. Gladys Hulette does good work and Moore and the rest are well cast."

Daily News: "A well told colorful story with romantic Hedly

Fritz Lang, director of "Siegfried," the Ufa production.

wood helping along the narrative. It's told in a clean, straightforward, simple style. Yes 'Go Straight' is first rate. And it goes great."

Daily Mirror: "Director Frank O'Connor has checked in a crackerjack crook picture. 'Go Straight' unreels lively drama."

Telegraph: "A good, swiftly moving crook melodrama—well acted and logically developed. One of the most convincing stories of crook reformation yet presented on the screen."

Evening World: "If you enjoy a lively and intelligently presented crook play, 'Go Straight' is well worth seeing."

"Sally of the Sawdust"—United Artists, Empire, London, Eng.

Star: "'Sally of the Sawdust' makes you laugh with tears in your eyes. W. C. Fields is the discovery of the year."

Standard: "Dashes of broad comedy, some of it as full blooded as the old Chaplin-Keystone vintage."

Chronicle: "A recklessly comic picture lit with splendid humor."

Sunday Herald: "D. W. Griffith does, somehow, contrive to make people cry, and then make them laugh, and he does both in 'Sally of the Sawdust.'"

Referee: "Griffith has given us a genuine comedy, sentimental at times as only Griffith can be, and full of humor that is human."

News of World: "A film that will take a lot of beating. A real honest-to-goodness story with rich humor at every turn."

Observer: "Its humor is good and plentiful."

Express: "Griffith is a wizard of the humanities, and 'Sally of the Sawdust' is as clean and as refreshing as a gale from the sea."

Graphic: "'Sally' will rule the hearts of London picture-goers while she is with us."

Daily Chronicle: "The most satisfying film entertainment from Mr. Griffith since he gave us 'Way Down East.'"

"Little Annie Rooney"—United Artists, Marble Arch, London

Chronicle: "Mary Pickford in 'Little Annie Rooney' is a sheer joy."

Sketch: "From near the start to the finish the audience has nothing to do but laugh."

Times: "A short pause in the middle of 'Little Annie Rooney' would be useful to allow the spectators to catch breath before being plunged from one series of emotions into another."

Telegraph: "Mary's exploits with foot and fist provoke prolonged and boisterous merriment."

Star: "A quaint mixture of fun and pathos that was received with a succession of chuckles and laughs that fully demonstrated the audience's enjoyment of Mary Pickford's tomboy pranks."

Gazette: "Good entertainment in which The World's Sweetheart' repeats those delightful performances of tomboy exuberance."

Standard: "Mary Pickford makes a wonderful tomboy still."

"Little Annie Rooney"—United Artists, Stanley, Phila.

Daily News: "Mary Pickford's 'Little Annie Rooney' is charming. 'Our Mary' is a tomboy hoyden, with more than her share of Irish deviltry, and she leads her 'gang' through reels and reels of fights over and through back fences."

Public Ledger: "Mary Pickford has given us one of her old-time pictures. She has taken the hearts of the children again by storm. They laughed and applauded and sobbed. Neither were the children the only ones who laughed and applauded and whom we saw in tears."

Evening Ledger: "'Little Annie Rooney' is a good picture, and very much the type of picture Mary Pickford used to make. It has a remarkably dramatic story, with the humor of human nature allowed to be human naturally. There is bonafide thrill and excitement, and plenty of punch, especially as the film nears its climax. There is good acting in nearly every role."

Bulletin: "'Annie Rooney's' gang of small companions in Mary Pickford's 'Little Annie Rooney' is humorous. It is perhaps the greatest of this star's ability to act as a child with these children and she fulfils the requirements beautifully."

Inquirer: "'Our Mary' is just as charmingly youthful as she was a few years ago, 'Little Annie Rooney' is in all ways a charming picture."

"Keeping of Bees"—F. B. O., American, Salt Lake

News: "Salt Lake citizens are asked this week to give the first verdict on 'The Keeper of the Bees,' a picture destined to become known over the world. For those who love the Gene Stratton-Porter stories, which means millions, it is sufficient recommendation to say from a preview that what the author put in the book, Mr. Meehan and the cast have put in the picture—a notable achievement. How many of the readers of this book or others by the same author will be able to say definitely wherein lies the appeal or exactly what it was that brought the whimsical smile or the lump to the throat? Yet this intangible charm will carry the picture to the hearts of theatre goers."

Telegram: "Salt Lake City turned out to enjoy the world's premier yesterday at the American Theatre, and to honor J. Leo Meehan, former local newspaper man, who directed Gene Stratton-Porter's great novel 'The Keeper of the Bees.' The charm of the author has been preserved by Director Meehan in the screen version. Against the backgrounds of Southern California, a story more dramatic than the usual Gene Stratton-Porter tale moves smoothly to its climax."

Tribune: "The Keeper of the Bees,' should rate high in the popular estimation. The picture has just enough heart appeal to make it a success. Acting of high grade caliber and pleasing photography all contribute to make it an entirely meritorious production. Most of the scenes were taken at Santa Barbara just previous to the earthquake. The ocean and the rugged beach do much to enhance the picture. Coupled with the well planned and well done photography, the picture was directed by J. Leo Meehan, former Salt Lake newspaper man, and son-in-law of Mrs. Porter. Under his direction, the scenario has not deviated from the book."

Alfred Santell, director of 'Seven Wives of Bluebeard' for First National.

George E. Marshall, supervisor of Fox comedy productions.

FEATURE RELEASE CHART

Productions are Listed Alphabetically and by Months in which Released in order that the Exhibitor may have a short-cut toward such information as he may need. Short subject and comedy releases, as well as information on pictures that are coming, will be found on succeeding pages. (S. R. indicates State Right release.)

Refer to THE MOTION PICTURE NEWS BOOKING GUIDE for Productions Listed Prior to March

MARCH

Feature	Star	Distributed by	Length	Reviewed
Adventurous Sex, The	Clara Bow	Assoc. Exhib	5039 feet	Mar. 21
Air Mail, The	Special Cast	Paramount	6976 feet	Mar. 28
Beauty and the Bad Man	Special Cast	Prod. Dist. Corp	5794 feet	May 9
Beyond the Border	Harry Carey	Prod. Dist. Corp	4469 feet	April 25
Billy, The Kid	Franklyn Farnum	Inde. Pict. Corp. (S. R.)	4800 feet	
Blood and Steel	Desmond Holmes	Inde. Pict. (S. R.)	5300 feet	
Border Justice	Bill Cody	Inde. Pict. Corp. (S. R.)	5432 feet	Nov. 8
Coast Patrol, The	Kenneth McDonald	Barsky (S. R.)	5000 feet	
Confessions of a Queen	Terry-Stone	Metro-Goldwyn	5820 feet	April 4
Crimson Runner, The	Priscilla Dean	Prod. Dist. Corp	4775 feet	June 6
Daddy's Gone A'Hunting	Joyce-Marmont	Metro-Goldwyn	5851 feet	Mar. 7
Denial, The	Special Cast	Metro-Goldwyn	4791 feet	Mar. 21
Double Action Daniels	Buffalo Bill, Jr.	Weiss Bros. (S. R.)	4650 feet	
Dressmaker from Paris, The	Rod La Rocque	Paramount	7080 feet	Mar. 28
Fighting Romeo, A	Al Ferguson	Davis Dist. Div. (S.R.)	5000 feet	Aug. 15
Fighting the Flames	Haines-Devore	C. B. C. (S. R.)	5800 feet	
Forbidden Cargo	Evelyn Brent	F. B. O	4850 feet	April 11
Goose Hangs High, The	Constance Bennett	Paramount	6186 feet	Feb. 14
Great Divide, The	Terry-Tearle	Metro-Goldwyn	7811 feet	Feb. 21
Head Winds	House Peters	Universal	5600 feet	Mar. 28
Hunted Woman, The	Seena Owen	Fox	4954 feet	April 4
I Want My Man	Sills-Kenyon	First National	6175 feet	April 18
Jimmie's Millions	Richard Talmadge	F. B. O	5167 feet	Feb. 28
Just Traveling	Bob Burns	Sierra Pict. (S. R.)	4400 feet	
Last Laugh, The	Emil Jannings	Universal	6519 feet	Dec. 20
Let'er Buck	Hoot Gibson	Universal	5547 feet	Jan. 3
Mad Whirl, The	May McAvoy	Universal	6184 feet	Dec. 6
Marriage in Transit	Edmund Lowe	Fox Film	4800 feet	April 11
Men and Women	Special Cast	Paramount	6223 feet	Mar. 28
Monster, The	L. Chaney-J. Arthur	Metro-Goldwyn	6435 feet	Feb. 28
My Wife and I	Special Cast	Warner Bros	6700 feet	June 6
New Lives for Old	Betty Compson	Paramount	6796 feet	Mar. 7
New Toys	Richard Barthelmess	First National	7250 feet	Feb. 21
One Year to Live	Special Cast	First National	6064 feet	Feb. 28
Percy	Charles Ray	Assoc. Exhib	5384 feet	Feb 28
Playing With Souls	Special Cast	First National	5831 feet	Mar. 14
Price of Pleasure, The	Valli-Kerry	Universal	6618 feet	June 13
Recompense	M. Prevost-M. Blue	Warner Bros	7480 feet	May 2
Renegade Holmes, M.D.	Ben Wilson	Arrow (S. R.)	4947 feet	
Riders of the Purple Sage	Tom Mix	Fox	5578 feet	Mar. 28
Romance and Rustlers	Yakima Canutt	Arrow (S. R.)	4994 feet	Nov. 15
Sackcloth and Scarlet	Alice Terry	Paramount	6732 feet	Mar. 7
Sally	Colleen Moore	First National	8636 feet	Mar. 28
Scar Hanan	Yakima Canutt	F. B. O	4684 feet	April 4
Scarlet Honeymoon, The	Shirley Mason	Fox	5080 feet	Mar. 21
Seven Chances	Buster Keaton	Metro-Goldwyn	5113 feet	Mar. 28
Sign of the Cactus, The	Jack Hoxie	Universal	4938 feet	Jan. 10
Sky Raider, The	Capt. Charles Nungesser	Assoc. Exhib.	6638 feet	April 4
Speed	Betty Blythe	Banner Prod. (S. R.)	6000 feet	May 30
Too Many Kisses	Richard Dix	Paramount	5759 feet	Mar. 14
Waking Up the Town	Jack Pickford	United Artists	4802 feet	April 11
Where Romance Rides	Dick Hatton	Arrow	4301 feet	
Zander the Great	Marion Davies	Metro-Goldwyn	5851 feet	May 16

APRIL

Feature	Star	Distributed by	Length	Reviewed
Adventure	P. Starke-T. Moore	Paramount	6713 feet	April 25
After Business Hours	Hammerstein-Tellegen	C. B. C. (S. R.)	5800 feet	
Bandit Tamer, The	Franklyn Farnum	Inde. Pict. (S. R.)	5000 feet	
Border Vengeance	Jack Perrin	Madoc Sales (S. R.)	4500 feet	
Charmer, The	Pola Negri	Paramount	6076 feet	April 18
Code of the West	O. Moore-C. Bennett	Paramount	6777 feet	April 25
Courageous Fool, The	Reed Howes	Rayart (S. R.)		
Crowded Hour, The	Bebe Daniels	Paramount	6558 feet	May 9
Dangerous Innocence	LaPlante-E, O'Brien	Universal	6759 feet	Mar. 21
Declasse	Corinne Griffith	First National	7869 feet	April 4
Eyes of the Desert	Al Richmond	Sierra Prod. (S. R.)	4500 feet	
Fifth Avenue Models	Philbin-Kerry	Universal	6581 feet	Jan. 24
Fighting Parson, The	Al Ferguson	Davis Dist. Div. (S.R.)	5000 feet	
Fighting Sheriff, The	Bill Cody	Inde. Pict. (S. R.)	4500 feet	May 30
Friendly Enemies	Weber and Fields	Prod. Dist. Corp	6288 feet	May 9
Galloping Vengeance	Bob Custer	F. B. O	5095 feet	April 11
Getting 'Em Right	George Larkin	Rayart (S. R.)	4669 feet	
Gold and the Girl	Buck Jones	Fox	4521 feet	April 4
Go Straight	Gladys Hulette	B. P. Schulberg (S.R.)	6107 feet	May 23
Heart of a Siren, The	Barbara La Marr	First National	6700 feet	Mar. 21
How Baxter Butted In	M. Moore-D. Devore	Warner Bros	6650 feet	July 11
Justice Raffles	Henry Edwards	Cranfield & Clarke (S. R.)	6000 feet	
Kiss in the Dark, A	Special Cast	Paramount	5767 feet	April 18
Kiss Me Again	M. Prevost-M. Blue	Warner Bros	7200 feet	June 6
Love's Bargain	M. Daw-C. Brook	F. B. O	5641 feet	April 25
Madame Sans Gene	Gloria Swanson	Paramount	9994 feet	May 2
Man and Maid	Special Cast	Metro-Goldwyn	5307 feet	April 18
My Son	Nazimova-J. Pickford	First National	6500 feet	April 25
Night Club, The	R. Griffith-V. Reynolds	Paramount	5732 feet	May 16
One Way Street	Special Cast	First National	5596 feet	April 11
Proud Flesh	Special Cast	Metro-Goldwyn	5770 feet	April 25
Roaring Adventure, The	Jack Hoxie	Universal	4637 feet	Feb. 14
Ridin' Comet, The	Yakima Canutt	F. B. O	4354 feet	May 16
Rough Going	Franklyn Farnum	Indep. Pict. Corp. (S. R.)	4800 feet	
Shackled Lightning	Frank Merrill	Hercules Prod. (S. R.)		
She Wolves	Alma Rubens	Fox	57[illegible]3 feet	May 9
Spaniard, The	Cortez-Goudal	Paramount	6676 feet	April 18
Sporting Venus	Special Cast	Metro-Goldwyn	5938 feet	May 23
Stop Flirting	Special Cast	Prod. Dist. Corp	5161 feet	June 6
Straight Through	Wm. Desmond	Universal	4867 feet	
Tale of a Thousand and One Nights	Special Cast	Davis Dist. Div. (S. R.)	6500 feet	Feb. 14
Tearing Through	Richard Talmadge	F. B. O.	4714 feet	May 23
That Devil Quemado	Fred Thomson	F. B. O.	4768 feet	April 4
Two-Fisted Sheriff, A	Yakima Canutt	Arrow (S. R.)	4149 feet	Dec. 6
Way of a Girl, The	Boardman-M. Moore	Metro-Goldwyn	5025 feet	April 18
Western Engagement, A	Dick Hatton	Arrow		
Wings of Youth	Madge Bellamy	Fox	5340 feet	May 16
Winning a Woman	Perrin-Hill	Rayart (S. R.)	4865 feet	

MAY

Feature	Star	Distributed by	Length	Reviewed
Alias Mary Flynn	Evelyn Brent	F. B. O.	5559 feet	May 30
Any Woman	Alice Terry	Paramount	5963 feet	June 13
Awful Truth, The	Agnes Ayres	Prod. Dist. Corp	5917 feet	July 11
Bandit's Baby, The	Fred Thomson	F. B. O.	5291 feet	June 20
Baree Son of Kazan	Wolf (dog)	Vitagraph	7 reels	May 2
Barriers of the Law	Holmes-Desmond	Indep. Pict. (S. R.)	5400 feet	
Burning Trail, The	William Desmond	Universal	4783 feet	April 18
Chickie	Mackaill-Bosworth	First National	7767 feet	May 9
Crackerjack, The	Johnny Hines	C. C. Burr (S. R.)	6500 feet	May 23
Every Man's Wife	Special Cast	Fox	4365 feet	July 4
Eve's Lover	Irene Rich	Warner Bros	6540 feet	Aug. 8
Eve's Secret	Betty Compson	Paramount	6305 feet	May 9
Fear Fighter, The	Billy Sullivan	Rayart (S. R.)		
Fighting Demon, The	Richard Talmadge	F B O	5470 feet	June 20
Fugitive, The	Ben Wilson	Arrow	4892 feet	
Golden Trails		Sanford Prod. (S. R.)	5 reels	
His Supreme Moment	B Sweet-R Colman	First National	6600 feet	April 25
Lilies of the Streets	J. Walker-V. L. Corbin	F. B. O.	7160 feet	April 25
Little French Girl, The	Alice Joyce	Paramount	5628 feet	June 13
Lunatic at Large, A	Henry Edwards	Cranfield & Clarke (S. R.)	6000 feet	
Makers of Men	Kenneth McDonald	Barsky Prod. (S. R.)	5000 feet	
Necessary Evil, The	Dana-Lyon	First National	6307 feet	May 23
Old Home Week	Thomas Meighan	Paramount	6888 feet	June 6
Phantom Rider, The	Al Richmond	Sierra Prod. (S. R.)	4750 feet	
Private Affairs	Special Cast	Prod. Dist. Corp	6132 feet	Aug. 15
Quick Change	George Larkin	Rayart (S. R.)		
Raffles, The Amateur Cracksman	House Peters	Universal	5557 feet	May 30
Rainbow Trail, The	Tom Mix	Fox	5251 feet	April 25
Red Love	Lowell-Russell	Lowell Film Prod. (S. R.)	6500 feet	May 23
Saddle Hawk, The	Hoot Gibson	Universal	5468 feet	Mar 7
Silent Sanderson	Harry Carey	Prod. Dist. Corp.	4841 feet	June 20
Scandal Proof	Shirley Mason	Fox	4400 feet	June 6
School for Wives	Tearle-Holmquist	Vitagraph	6750 feet	April 11
Shock Punch, The	Richard Dix	Paramount	6151 feet	May 23
Snob Buster, The	Reed Howes	Rayart (S. R.)		
Soul Fire	Barthelmess-B Love	First National	8262 feet	May 16
Speed Wild	Maurice B "Lefty" Flynn	F. B. O	4700 feet	June 20
Talker, The	A Nilsson-L Stone	First National	7861 feet	May 23
Texas Bearcat, The	Bob Custer	F. B. O	4770 feet	
Tides of Passion	Mae Marsh	Vitagraph	6279 feet	May 9
Up the Ladder	Virginia Valli	Universal	6023 feet	Jan 21
Welcome Home	Special Cast	Paramount	5909 feet	May 30
White Fang	Strongheart (dog)	F. B. O	6579 feet	June 20
White Thunder	Yakima Canutt	F. B. O.	4550 feet	
Wildfire	Special Cast	Vitagraph	6 reels	June 20
Wolves of the Road	Yakima Canutt	Arrow	4373 feet	
Woman's Faith	Reubens-Marmont	Universal	6023 feet	Aug 15
Woman Hater, The	Helene Chadwick	Warner Brothers	7000 feet	Aug. 22

JUNE

Feature	Star	Distributed by	Length	Reviewed
Are Parents People?	Bronson-Vidor	Paramount	6356 feet	June 6
Dangerous Odds	Bill Cody	Inde. Pict. (S. R.)	4800 feet	
Desert Flower, The	Colleen Moore	First National	6837 feet	June 13
Double Fisted	Jack Perrin	Rayart (S. R.)		
Down the Border	Al Richmond	Sierra Prod. (S. R.)	4750 feet	
Faint Perfume	Seena Owen	B. P. Schulberg (S.R.)	6228 feet	July 11
Grounds for Divorce	Florence Vidor	Paramount	5712 feet	July 4
Happy Warrior, The		Vitagraph	6075 feet	July 18
Hearts and Spurs	Buck Jones	Fox	4600 feet	June 20
Human Tornado, The	Yakima Canutt	F. B. O.	4472 feet	
I'll Show You the Town	Reginald Denny	Universal	7400 feet	June 6
Introduce Me	Douglas MacLean	Assoc. Exhib.	5950 feet	Mar. 21
Just a Woman	Windsor-Tearle	First National	6500 feet	June 6
Light of Western Stars	Special Cast	Paramount	6652 feet	July 4
Lost—a Wife	Special Cast	Paramount	6420 feet	June 27
Making of O'Malley, The	Milton Sills	First National	7371 feet	July 4
Man from Lone Mountain, The	Ben Wilson	Arrow	4530 feet	
Man in Blue	Herbert Rawlinson	Universal	5706 feet	Feb. 21
Marry Me	Special Cast	Paramount	5586 feet	
Meddler, The	William Desmond	Universal	4890 feet	May 23
Mist in the Valley	Alma Taylor	Cranfield & Clarke (S. R.)	5500 feet	
My Lady's Lips	Clara Bow	B. P. Schulberg (S.R.)	6609 feet	Aug 15
Off the Highway	Bowers-De La Motte	Prod. Dist.	7641 feet	
Paths to Paradise	Compson-R. Griffith	Paramount	6741 feet	June 27
Pioneers of the West		Sanford Prod. (S. R.)	5 reels	
Ridin' Easy	Dick Hatton	Arrow	4483 feet	
Ridin' Thunder	Jack Hoxie	Universal	4354 feet	May 23

Feature	Star	Distributed by	Length	Reviewed
Rough Stuff	George Larkin	Rayart (S. R.)		
Shattered Lives	Special Cast	Gotham (S. R.)	6 reels	July 4
Smooth as Satin	Evelyn Brent	F. B. O	6003 feet	July 4
Texas Trail, The	Harry Carey	Prod. Dist. Corp	4720 feet	July 18
Tracked in the Snow Country	Rin-Tin-Tin (dog)	Warner Brothers	6900 feet	Aug. 1
White Monkey, The	La Marr-T. Holding	First National	6121 feet	July 4
Wild Bull's Lair, The	Fred Thompson	F. B. O.	5280 feet	Aug. 15
Youth's Gamble	Reed Howes	Rayart (S. R.)	5264 feet	

JULY

Feature	Star	Distributed by	Length	Reviewed
Bloodhound, The	Bob Custer	F. B. O.	4789 feet	
Cold Nerve	Bill Cody	Inde. Pict. (S. R.)	5000 feet	
Danger Signal, The	Jane Novak	Columbia Pict. (S.R.)	5502 feet	Aug. 15
Don Daredevil	Jack Hoxie	Universal	4810 feet	
Drug Store Cowboy, The	Franklyn Farnum	Ind. Pict. Corp. (S.R.)	5100 feet	Feb. 7
Duped	Holmes-Desmond	Ind. Pict. (S. R.)	5400 feet	
Fighting Youth		Columbia Pict. (S.R.)		
Lady Who Lied, The	L. Stone-V. Valli	First National	7111 feet	July 18
Lady Robinhood	Evelyn Brent	F. B. O	5582 feet	Aug 22
Manicure Girl, The	Bebe Daniels	Paramount	5959 feet	June 27
Marriage Whirl, The	C. Griffith-H. Ford	First National	7672 feet	July 25
Mysterious Stranger, The	Richard Talmadge	F. B. O	5270 feet	
Night Life of New York	Special Cast	Paramount	6998 feet	July 4
Pipes of Pan	Alma Taylor	Cranfield & Clarke (S. R.)	6200 feet	
Ranger of the Big Pines, The	Kenneth Harlan	Vitagraph	5800 feet	Aug. 8
Scarlet West, The	Frazer-Bow	First National	8391 feet	July 25
Secret of Black Canyon, The	Dick Hatton	Arrow		
Strange Rider, The	Yakima Canutt	Arrow		
Taming the West	Hoot Gibson	Universal	5427 feet	Feb. 28
Trailed	Al Richmond	Sierra Prod. (S. R.)	4750 feet	
White Desert, The	Special Cast	Metro-Goldwyn	6345 feet	July 18

AUGUST

Feature	Star	Distributed by	Length	Reviewed
Beggar on Horseback, A	Ralston-Nissen	Paramount	6800 feet	June 20
Business of Love, The	E. Horton-M. Bellamy	Astor Dist. Corp		
Children of the Whirlwind	Lionel Barrymore	Arrow		
Drusilla With a Million	Special Cast	F. B. O	7391 feet	May 30
Evolution		Red Seal	4200 feet	Aug. 15
Fine Clothes	L. Stone-A. Rubens	First National	6971 feet	Aug. 15
Girl Who Wouldn't Work, The	Lionel Barrymore	B. P. Schulberg (S.R.)	5979 feet	Sept. 5
Gold Rush, The	Charles Chaplin	United Artists	8500 feet	Aug. 8
Halfway Girl, The	Doris Kenyon	First National	7570 feet	Aug. 8
Headlines	Alice Joyce	Assoc. Exhib	5600 feet	July 25
Her Sister From Paris	C. Talmadge	First National	7255 feet	Aug. 15
In the Name of Love	Cortez-Nissen	Paramount	5904 feet	Sept. 5
Isle of Hope, The	Richard Talmadge	Film Book. Offices	5800 feet	Sept. 5
Kivalina of the Ice Lands	Native Cast	Pathe	6 reels	July 11
Knockout, The	Milton Sills	First National	7450 feet	Sept. 19
Lightnin'	Jay Hunt	Fox	7979 feet	Aug. 1
Limited Mail, The	Monte Blue	Warner Brothers	6250 feet	
Love Hour, The	Ruth Clifford	Vitagraph	5900 feet	
Lover's Oath, The	Ramon Novarro	Astor Dist. Corp		
Lucky Devil, The	Richard Dix	Paramount	5935 feet	July 18
Lucky Horseshoe, The	Tom Mix	Fox	5004 feet	Aug. 29
My Pal	Dick Hatton	Arrow		
Overland Limited, The		Gotham Prod. (S. R.)	6389 feet	Aug. 8
Parisian Love	Bow-Tellegen	B. P. Schulberg (S.R.)	6324 feet	Aug. 22
Quo Vadis	Emil Jannings	First National	8945 feet	Feb. 28
Range Justice	Dick Hatton	Arrow		
Romola	Gish Sisters	Metro-Goldwyn	10875 feet	Dec. 13
Rugged Water	Special Cast	Paramount	6015 feet	Aug. 1
Shining Adventure, The	Percy Marmont	Astor Dist. Corp		
Slave of Fashion, A	Special Cast	Metro-Goldwyn	5906 feet	Aug. 1
Speed Mad		Columbia Pict. (S.R.)	4442 feet	Sept. 19
Sporting Chance, The		Tiffany (S. R.)	6500 feet	July 4
Street of Forgotten Men	Special Cast	Paramount	6366 feet	Aug. 1
Ten Commandments	Special Cast	Paramount	9980 feet	Jan. 5-24
That Man Jack	Bob Custer	F. B. O	5032 feet	Aug. 22
Unholy Three	Lon Chaney	Metro-Goldwyn	6848 feet	Aug. 15
Unwritten Law, The		Columbia Pict. (S.R.)		
Wife Who Wasn't Wanted, The	Irene Rich	Warner Brothers	6400 feet	
Wizard of Oz	Larry Semon	Chadwick	6300 feet	Apr. 25
Wrongdoers, The	Lionel Barrymore	Astor Dist. Corp		

SEPTEMBER

Feature	Star	Distributed by	Length	Reviewed
Amazing Quest, The	Henry Edwards	Cranfield & Clarke	5500 feet	
American Pluck	George Walsh	Chadwick	5000 feet	July 11
Apache Love	Geo. Larkin	B'way Dist. Co	5000 feet	
As No Man Has Loved	Special Cast	Fox	7836 feet	Feb. 28
Batler, The	Kenneth McDonald	Bud Barsky (S. R.)	5000 feet	
Below The Line	Rin-Tin-Tin (dog)	Warner Brothers	6100 feet	
Black Cyclone	Rex (horse)	Pathe		May 30
Bobbed Hair	Prevost-Harlan	Warner Brothers	6700 feet	
California Straight Ahead	Reginald Denny	Universal		
Call of Courage, The	Art Acord	Universal	4661 feet	Sept. 19
Classified	Corinne Griffith	First National		
Coast of Folly	Gloria Swanson	Paramount		
Coming of Amos	Rod La Rocque	Prod. Dist. Corp	5677 feet	Sept. 19
Crack of Dawn	Reed Howes	Rayart (S. R.)		
Cyclone Cavalier	Reed Howes	Rayart (S. R.)	4928 feet	Sept. 26
Dark Angel, The	R. Colman-V. Banky	First National	7311 feet	Sept. 29
Don Q, Son of Zorro	Douglas Fairbanks	United Artists	10264 feet	June 27
Free to Love	C. Bow-D. Keith	B. P. Schulberg (S.R.)		
Freshman, The	Harold Lloyd	Pathe		July 25
Graustark	Norma Talmadge	First National	5900 feet	Sept. 19
Havoc	Special Cast	Fox	9200 feet	Aug. 29
Hell's Highroad	Leatrice Joy	Prod. Dist. Corp	6084 feet	Sept. 5
High and Handsome	"Lefty" Flynn	F. B. O.	5669 feet	
His Master's Voice	Thunder (dog)	Gotham Prod. (S. R.	6000 feet	
If Marriage Fails	J. Logan-C. Brook	F. B. O	6006 feet	May 23
Keep Smiling	Monty Banks	Assoc. Exhib	5400 feet	Aug. 1
Kentucky Pride	Special Cast	Fox	6597 feet	Sept. 19
Knockout Kid, The	Jack Perrin	Rayart Pict. Corp. (S. R.)	4901 feet	
Let's Go Gallagher	Tom Tyler	Film Book Offices	5182 feet	Oct. 3
Little Annie Rooney	Mary Pickford	United Artists		
Lost World, The	Special Cast	First National	9700 feet	Feb. 21
Man From Red Gulch	Harry Carey	Prod. Dist. Corp.		
Manhattan Madness	Dempsey-Taylor	Assoc. Exhib	5500 feet	July 25
Man Who Found Himself	Thomas Meighan	Paramount	7168 feet	Sept. 5
Mystic, The	Special Cast	Metro-Goldwyn		

Feature	Star	Distributed by	Length	Reviewed
Never the Twain Shall Meet	Stewart-Lytell	Metro-Goldwyn	8143 feet	Aug. 8
New Champion, The		Columbia Pict. (S.R.)		
Not So Long Ago	Betty Bronson	Paramount	5943 feet	Aug. 8
Other Woman's Story	Calhoun-Frazer	B. P. Schulberg		
Outlaw's Daughter, The	Josie Sedgwick	Universal	4375 feet	
Paint and Power	Elaine Hammerstein	Chadwick		
Parisian Nights	E. Hammerstein - L. Tellegen	F. B. O	6278 feet	June 20
Plastic Age, The	Special Cast	B. P. Schulberg (S. R.)		
Pretty Ladies	Zazu Pitts	Metro-Goldwyn	5828 feet	July 25
Primrose Path, The	Bow-MacDonald	Arrow	5475 feet	
Ridin' the Wind	Fred Thomson	Film Book. Offices		
Scandal Street	Kennedy-Welch	Arrow	6923 feet	
Sealed Lips		Columbia Pict. (S.R.)		
Seven Days	Lillian Rich	Prod. Dist. Corp.	6974 feet	
Shore Leave	Barthelmess-Mackaill	First National	6856 feet	Aug. 29
Siege	Virginia Valli	Universal	6424 feet	June 20
Son of His Father, A	Special Cast	Paramount	7009 feet	Sept. 19
Souls for Sables		Tiffany (S. R.)	7000 feet	
S. O. S. Perils of the Sea		Columbia Pict. (S.R.)		
Speed Madness	Frank Merrill	Hercules Film	4579 feet	
Spook Ranch	Hoot Gibson	Universal	5147 feet	May 2
Sun Up	Special Cast	Metro-Goldwyn		Aug. 29
Teaser, The	Laura La Plante	Universal	6967 feet	May 30
Three in Exile		Truart (S. R.)	5800 feet	
Three Weeks in Paris	M. Moore-D. Devore	Warner Brothers	5900 feet	
Three Wise Crooks	Evelyn Brent	Film Book. Offices		
Throwback, The	Special Cast	Universal		
Timber Wolf, The	Buck Jones	Fox	4809 feet	Sept. 26
Trouble With Wives, The	Vidor-T. Moore	Paramount	6489 feet	Aug. 15
Wall Street Whiz, The	Richard Talmadge	Film Book. Offices		
What Fools Men	Stone-Mason	First National		
Wheel, The	Special Cast	Fox	7264 feet	Aug. 29
White Outlaw, The	Jack Hoxie	Universal	4830 feet	June 27
Wild Horse Mesa	Special Cast	Paramount	7221 feet	Aug. 22
Wild, Wild Susan	Bebe Daniels	Paramount		
With This Ring	Mills-Tellegen	B. P. Schulberg	5333 feet	Oct. 3

OCTOBER

Feature	Star	Distributed by	Length	Reviewed
Borrowed Finery		Tiffany (S. R.)	6500 feet	
Bustin' Through	Jack Hoxie	Universal	4506 feet	
Cactus Trails	Jack Perrin	Madoc Sales	4800 feet	
Circle, The		Metro-Goldwyn		
Circus Cyclone, The	Art Acord	Universal	4609 feet	Aug. 22
Dollar Down	Ruth Roland	Truart (S. R.)	5800 feet	Aug. 29
Everlasting Whisper, The	Tom Mix	Fox		
Exchange of Wives, An	Special Cast	Metro-Goldwyn		
Fate of a Flirt, The		Columbia (S. R.)		
Fighting Heart, The	Geo. O'Brien	Fox	6978 feet	Oct. 3
Golden Princess, The	Bronson-Hamilton	Paramount	6395 feet	Sept. 19
Great Sensation, The	W. Fairbanks-P. Garon	Columbia (S. R.)	4470 feet	Sept. 26
Heads Up	Fred Thomson	F. B. O		
Heartless Husbands	Gloria Grey	Madoc Sales	5000 feet	
He's a Prince	Raymond Griffith	Paramount		
His Buddy's Wife	Glenn Hunter	Assoc. Exhib	5600 feet	July 25
Iron Horse, The	O'Brien-Bellamy	Fox Film Corp.	10288 feet	Sept. 13
John Forrest	Henry Edwards	Cranfeld&Clark(S.R.)	5000 feet	
Keeper of the Bees, The	Robert Frazer	F. B. O		
Lew Tyler's Wives		B. P. Schulberg (S. R.)		
Lights of Old Broadway	Marion Davies	Metro-Goldwyn		
Lovers in Quarantine	Daniels-Ford	Paramount		
Midshipman, The	Ramon Novarro	Metro-Goldwyn		
New Brooms	Hamilton-Love	Paramount		
Peacock Feathers	Logan-Landis	Universal	6747 feet	Aug. 29
Pony Express, The	Betty Compson	Paramount		
Prairie Pirate, The	Harry Carey	Prod. Dist. Corp.	4603 feet	Sept. 26
Sally of the Sawdust	Fields-Dempster	United Artists	9500 feet	Aug. 15
Silver Fingers	Geo. Larkin	B'way Dist. Co.	5000 feet	
Some Pun'kins	Chas. Ray	Chadwick	6500 feet	Sept. 19
Storm Breaker, The	House Peters	Universal	6064 feet	Sept. 26
Substitute Wife, The	Jane Novak	Arrow	5994 feet	
Thunder Mountain	Special Cast	Fox	7537 feet	
Tower of Lies	Chaney-Shearer	Metro-Goldwyn		
Tumbleweeds	Wm. S. Hart	United Artists		
Unchastened Woman, The	Theda Bara	Chadwick	6800 feet	
Under the Rouge	Tom Moore	Assoc. Exhib	6500 feet	July 25
Wandering Fires	Constance Bennett	Arrow		
Winds of Chance	A. Nilsson-B. Lyon	First National	9753 feet	Aug. 29
Without Mercy	Vera Reynolds	Prod. Dist. Corp	6550 feet	
Winding Stair, The	Special Cast	Fox		

NOVEMBER

Feature	Star	Distributed by	Length	Reviewed
After Marriage	Margaret Livingston	Madoc Sales	5000 feet	
Ancient Highway, The	Holt-vidor	Paramount		
Best People, The	Spec'al Cast	Paramount		
Blue Blood	George Walsh	Chadwick		
Calgary Stampede, The	Hoot Gibson	Universal		
Camille of the Barbary Coast	Busch-O. Moore	Assoc. Exhib	5600 feet	Aug. 1
Cobra	Valentino-Naldi	Paramount		
Daring Days	Josie Sedgwick	Universal	5 reels	
Don't	S. O'Neill-B. Roach	Metro-Goldwyn		
Durand of the Bad Lands	Buck Jones	Fox	5844 feet	
Fifty-Fifty	L.Barrymore-H.Hampton	Assoc. Exhib	5564 feet	June 20
Fight to a Finish, A		Columbia (S. R.)		
Flower of Night	Pola Negri	Paramount		
Fool, The	Edmund Lowe	Fox	9374 feet	April 25
King on Main St., The	Adolphe Menjou	Paramount		
Lazybones	Special Cast	Fox Film	7234 feet	
Little Bit of Broadway	Ray-Starke	Metro-Goldwyn		
Makers of Men	Special Cast	Bud Barsky (S. R.)	5500 feet	Oct. 3
Merry Widow	Mae Murray	Metro-Goldwyn		
People vs. Nancy Preston	Bowers-De La Motte	Prod. Dist. Corp.		
Perfect Clown, The	Larry Semon	Chadwick		
Price of Success, The	Alice Lake	Columbia (S. R.)		
Road to Yesterday, The	Joseph Schildkraut	Prod. Dist. Corp.		
Romance Road	Raymond McKee	Truart	5000 feet	
Simon the Jester	Rich-O'Brien	Prod. Dist. Corp.		
Stage Struck	Gloria Swanson	Paramount		
Tessie	McAvoy-Agnew	Arrow	6221 feet	
Thank U	Special Cast	Fox	6900 feet	Sept. 19
Time the Comedian		Metro-Goldwyn		
Transcontinental Limited	Special Cast	Chadwick (S. R.)		
Vanishing American, The	Dix-Wilson	Paramount		
Wedding Song, The	Leatrice Joy	Prod. Dist. Corp.		
Winner, The	Charles Ray	Chadwick (S. R.)		

DECEMBER

Feature	Star	Distributed by	Length	Reviewed
Braveheart	Rod LaRocque	Prod. Dist. Corp.		
Dice Woman, The	Priscilla Dean	Prod. Dist. Corp.		
Lodge in the Wilderness, The		Tiffany (S. R.)	6500 feet	
Madam Behave	Eltinge-Pennington	Prod. Dist. Corp.		
Morals for Men	Tearle-Mills	Tiffany (S. R.)	6500 feet	
Prince of Broadway	George Walsh	Chadwick		
Sweet Adeline	Charles Ray	Chadwick		

JANUARY

Feature	Star	Distributed by	Length	Reviewed
Fifth Avenue	De La Motte	Prod. Dist. Corp.		
Lure of the Arctic, The		Prod. Dist. Corp.		
Million Dollar Handicap, The	Vera Reynolds	Prod. Dist. Corp.		
Steel Preferred	William Boyd	Prod. Dist. Corp.		
Three Faces East	Goudal-Ames	Prod. Dist. Corp.		

Comedy Releases

Feature	Star	Distributed by	Length	Reviewed
Absent Minded	Neely Edwards	Universal	1 reel	
Across the Hall	Edna Marian	Universal	2 reels	
Adventures of Adenoid	Aesop's Fables	Pathe	1 reel	April 25
After a Reputation	Edna Marian	Universal	2 reels	
Air Tight	Bobby Vernon	Educational	2 reels	June 13
Alice's Egg Plant	" Cartoon "	M. J. Winkler (S. R.)	1 reel	
Alice Stagestruck	Margie Gay	M. J. Winkler (S.R.)	1 reel	July 18
All at Sea	Smith-King	Fox		
Almost a Husband	Buddy Messinger	Universal	2 reels	
Amateur Detective	Earle Foxe	Fox	2 reels	
Andy in Hollywood	Joe Murphy	Universal	2 reels	
Andy's Lion Tale	" The Gumps "	Universal	2 reels	
Andy Takes a Flyer	" The Gumps "	Universal	2 reels	
Apache, The	Earle Foxe	Fox Film	2 reels	
Apollo's Pretty Sister		Fox	2 reels	
Are Husbands Human?	James Finlayson	Pathe	1 reel	April 11
Artists' Blues	G. Joy-J. Moore	Rayart (S. R.)	2 reels	
Ask Grandma	" Our Gang "	Pathe	2 reels	May 30
At the Seashore	Monkey	Fox	2 reels	
At the Zoo	Aesops Fables	Pathe	1 reel	
Baby Be Good		Educational	2 reels	
Baby Blues	Mickey Bennett	Educational	2 reels	
Bachelors	Special Cast	Universal		
Back to Nature	Charles Puffy	Universal	1 reel	
Bad Bill Brodie	Charles Chase	Pathe	2 reels	
Bad Boy	Charles Chase	Pathe	2 reels	April 11
Balboa Discovers Hollywood	" Red Head "	Sering D. Wilson (S.R.)	1 reel	
Bashful Jim	Ralph Graves	Pathe	2 reels	Mar. 21
Be Careful	Jimmie Adams	Educational Film	2 reels	Aug. 22
Below Zero	Lige Conley	Educational	2 reels	July 4
Beware	Lige Conley	Educational Film	2 reels	Aug. 1
Big Chief Ko-Ko (Out of the Inkwell)	" Cartoon "	Red Seal Pict.	1 reel	
Big Game Hunter, The	Earle Foxe	Fox	2 reels	
Bigger and Better Pictures	" Aesop's Fables "	Pathe	1 reel	
Big Kick, The	Engle-Mohan	Pathe	1 reel	
Big Red Riding Hood	Charley Chase	Pathe	1 reel	May 9
Black Gold Bricks	Roach-Edwards	Universal	1 reel	April 18
Black Hand Blues	" Spat Family "	Pathe	2 reels	April 18
Bobby Bumbs & Co.	Cartoon	Educational	1 reel	July 4
Boobs in the Woods	Harry Langdon	Pathe	2 reels	
Boys Will Be Joys	" Our Gang "	Pathe	2 reels	July 25
Brainless Horsemen		Fox	2 reels	
Brass Button	Billy West	Arrow	2 reels	
Breaking the Ice	Ralph Graves	Pathe	2 reels	April 11
Bride Tamer, The	Milburn Moranti	Sierra Pict. (S. R.)	2 reels	
Bubbles	" Aesop's Fables "	Pathe	1 reel	Aug. 15
Bugville Field Day	" Aesop's Fables "	Pathe	1 reel	July 25
Buster Be Good	Trimble-Turner	Universal	2 reels	
Butterfly Man, The		Fox	2 reels	
By the Sea	Charles Puffy	Universal	1 reel	
California Here We Come	" The Gumps "	Universal	2 reels	
Cat's Shimmy, The	" Kid Noah "	Sering D. Wilson (S.R.)	1 reel	
Cat's Whiskers, The	Neely Edwards	Universal	1 reel	
Chasing the Chasers	Jas. Finlayson	Pathe	1 reel	July 4
City Bound	Charles Puffy	Universal	1 reel	
Clean-Up Week	" Aesop's Fables "	Pathe	1 reel	Mar. 7
Clear the Way	Buddy Messinger	Universal	2 reels	
Cleopatra and Her Easy Mark	" Cartoon "	Sering D. Wilson (S.R.)	1 reel	
Cloudhopper, The	Larry Semon	Educational	2 reels	June 6
Cloudy Romance, A	Special Cast	Fox	2 reels	
Columbus Discovers a New Whirl		Sering Wilson (S. R.)	1 reel	
Crime Crushers	Lige Conley	Educational	2 reels	
Crying for Love	Eddie Gordon	Universal	2 reels	Aug. 15
Cupid's Boots	Ralph Graves	Pathe	2 reels	July 25
Cupid's Victory	Wanda Wiley	Universal	2 reels	
Cure, The (Out of the Inkwell)	" Cartoon "	Red Seal Pict.	1 reel	
Curses	Al. St. John	Educational	2 reels	May 23
Daddy Goes A Grunting		Pathe	2 reels	July 18
Darkest Africa	" Aesop's Fables "	Pathe	1 reels	
Day's Outing, A	" The Gumps "	Universal	2 reels	
Deep Stuff	Aesop's Fables	Pathe	1 reel	April 25
Dinky Doodle and Cinderella	" Dinky Doodle "	F. B. O	1 reel	
Dinky Doodle and Robinson Crusoe	" Dinky Doodle "	F. B. O	1 reel	
Discord In " A " Flat	Arthur Lake	Universal	1 reel	July 25
Dog Days	" Our Gang "	Pathe	2 reels	Mar. 14
Dog Daze	Bowes-Vance	Educational		
Dog 'On It	Bobby Dunn	Arrow	2 reels	
Dome Doctor, The	Larry Semon	Educational	2 reels	
Don't Pinch	Bobby Vernon	Educational	2 reels	April 25
Don't Worry	Wanda Wiley	Universal	2 reels	Mar. 21
Dragon Alley	Jackie McHugh	Educational	2 reels	May 16
Dr. Pyckle and Mr. Pride	Stan Laurel	Film Booking Offices	2 reels	
Dry Up	Singleton Burkett	Universal	2 reels	July 25
Dumb and Daffy	Al. St. John	Fox	2 reels	
Dynamite Doggie	Al. St. John	Educational	2 reels	Mar. 21
East Side, West Side	Harris-Leddy	Fox		
Echoes From the Alps	Aesop's Fables	Pathe	1 reel	May 30
Educating Buster	Trimble-Turner	Universal	2 reels	
End of the World, The	Aesop's Fables	Pathe	1 reel	
Etiquette	Jimmy Aubrey	Film Book. Offices	2 reels	
Excuse My Glove	" Spat Family "	Pathe	2 reels	Mar 21
Expensive Ebony	"Ebenezer Ebony"	Sering Wilson (S. R.)	1 reel	
Fair Warning	Al St. John	Educational	2 reels	Sept. 26
Fares Please	Al. St. John	Educational	2 reels	May 16
Fast Worker, A	Aesop's Fables	Pathe	1 reel	
Felix the Cat Busts Into Business	" Cartoon "	Educational	1 reel	
Felix, the Cat on the Farm	Cartoon	Educational	1 reel	
Felix Full O'Fight	" Cartoon "	M. J. Winkler (S. R.)	1 reel	
Felix Gets His Fill	" Cartoon "	M. J. Winkler (S. R.)	1 reel	
Felix Grabs His Grub	" Cartoon "	M. J. Winkler (S. R.)	1 reel	
Felix the Cat on the Job	Cartoon	Educational	1 reel	
Fire Flies	" Hey, Fellas "	Davis Dist.	2 reels	
First Love	" Our Gang "	Pathe	2 reels	
Fishermen's Luck	"Aesop's Fables "	Pathe	1 reel	
For Hire	Edward Gordon	Universal		
For Love of a Gal	" Aesop's Fables "	Pathe	1 reel	July 25
Found World, The	" The Gumps "	Universal	2 reels	
Fun's Fun	Bowes-Vance	Educational	1 reel	June 6
Getting Trimmed	Wanda Wiley	Universal	2 reels	April 18
Giddap	Special Cast	Pathe	2 reels	Mar. 21
Going Great	Eddie Nelson	Educational	2 reels	June 13
Goldfish's Pajamas	" Kid Noah "	Sering D. Wilson (S.R.)	1 reel	
Good Morning Nurse	Ralph Graves	Pathe	2 reels	May 30
Good Scouts	" Reg'lar Kids "	M. J. Winkler (S. R.)	2 reels	
Great Guns	Bobby Vernon	Educational	2 reels	Feb. 21
Green-Eyed Monster, The	Arthur Lake	Universal	1 reel	
Gridiron Gertie	Wanda Wiley	Universal	2 reels	
Guilty Conscience, A	Eddie Gordon	Universal		
Gypping the Gypsies	" Ebenezer Ebony "	Sering Wilson (S. R.)	1 reel	
Half Fare	Arthur Lake	Universal	1 reel	
Half a Hero	Lloyd Hamilton	Educational	2 reels	Mar. 7
Half a Man	Stan Laurel	Pathe	2 reels	
Hard Boiled	Charley Chase	Pathe	2 reels	Mar. 21
Hard Working Loafer, The	Arthur Stone	Pathe		
Haunted Honeymoon	Tryon-Mehaffey	Pathe	2 reels	Feb. 28
Heart Breaker, The	Special Cast	Fox	2 reels	
Heart Trouble	Arthur Lake	Universal	1 reel	July 4
Heavy Swells	Special Cast	Fox	2 reels	
Hello, Goodby	Lige Conley	Educational	2 reels	May 30
Hello, Hollywood	Lige Conley	Educational	2 reels	Mar. 28
Helping Hand	Jimmy Aubrey	F. B. O	2 reels	
Help Yourself		Fox	2 reels	
Here's Your Hat	Arthur Lake	Universal	1 reel	May 9
Her Lucky Leap	Wanda Wiley	Universal	2 reels	
He Who Gets Crowned	Jimmy Aubrey	F. B. O	2 reels	
He Who Got Smacked	Ralph Graves	Pathe	2 reels	May 9
Hey! Taxi!	Bobby Dunn	Arrow	2 reels	
High Hopes	Bowes-Vance	Educational	1 reel	Feb. 14
High Jinx, A		Fox	2 reels	
His Marriage Wow	Harry Langdon	Pathe	2 reels	Mar. 7
Hold My Baby	Glenn Tryon	Pathe	2 reels	April 25
Home Scouts	Jimmie Aubrey	F. B. O.	2 reels	
Honeymoon Heaven		Sering Wilson (S. R.)	1 reel	
Horace Greeley, Jr.	Harry Langdon	Pathe	2 reels	June 6
Horrible Hollywood		Lee-Bradford (S. R.)		
Hot and Heavy	Eddie Nelson	Educational	2 reel	July 18
Hot Dog	Animal	C B C (S. R.)	2 reels	
Hot Times in Iceland	Aesop's Fables	Pathe	1 reels	
House of Flickers, The		Fox	2 reels	
House that Dinky Built	(Cartoon)	F. B. O	1 reel	
Housing Shortage, The	" Aesop's Fables "	Pathe	1 reel	
Hurry Doctor	Ralph Graves	Pathe		
Hysterical History (Series)		Universal	1 reel	
Ice Boy, An	" Ebonezer Ebony "	Sering D. Wilson (S.R.)	1 reel	
Ice Cold	Arthur Lake	Universal	1 reel	June 13
In Deep	Bowes-Vance	Educational	1 reel	
In Dutch	Aesop's Fables	Pathe	1 reel	
Innocent Husbands	Charley Chase	Pathe	2 reels	Aug. 1
Inside Out	Bowes-Vance	Educational	1 reel	Mar. 28
Into the Grease	James Finlayson	Pathe	1 reel	June 27
Iron Mule	Al St. John	Educational	2 reels	April 18
Iron Nag, The	Billy Bevan	Pathe	2 reels	Aug. 15
Is Marriage the Bunk?	Charles Chase	Pathe	1 reel	April 4
Isn't Life Terrible?	Charles Chase	Pathe	2 reels	July 4
Itching for Revenge	Eddie Gordon	Universal	2 reels	Mar. 7
It's All Wrong	Karr-Engle	Universal		
James Boys' Sister		Wilson Sering (S. R.)	1 reel	
Jimminy Crickets	Wesley Edwards	Universal	1 reel	
Jungle Bike Riders	Aesop's Fables	Pathe	1 reel	Mar. 14
Just in Time	Wanda Wiley	Universal	2 reels	July 11
Kicked About	Eddie Gordon	Universal	2 reels	Mar. 14
Kidding Captain Kidd	" Cartoon "	Sering Wilson (S. R.)	1 reel	
King Cotton	Lloyd Hamilton	Educational	2 reels	May 9
King Dumb	Jimmy Aubrey	F. B. O	2 reels	
Klynick, The	" Hey, Fellas "	Davis Dist.	2 reels	
Knocked About	Eddie Gordon	Universal	2 reels	June 13
Ko-Ko Celebrates the Fourth (Out of the Inkwell)	" Cartoon "	Red Seal Pict.		
Ko-Ko Trains Animals (out of the Inkwell)	" Cartoon "	Red Seal Pict.	1 reel	
Lead Pipe Cinch, A	Al Alt	Universal		
Lion Love		Fox	2 reels	Feb. 28
Lion and the Monkey	" Aesop's Fables "	Pathe		
Lion's Whiskers		Pathe	2 reels	April 18
Little Red Riding Hood	" Dinky Doodle "	F. B. O	1 reel	
Locked Out	Arthur Lake	Universal	1 reel	May 30
Looking for Sally	Charles Chase	Pathe	2 reels	May 9
Look Out	Bowes-Vance	Educational Film	1 reel	Aug. 1
Lost Cord, The	Bert Roach	Universal	1 reel	Feb. 21
Love and Kisses	Alice Day	Pathe	2 reels	
Love and Lions	Special Cast	Fox	2 reels	
Love Bug, The	" Our Gang "	Pathe	2 reels	April 4
Love Goofy	Jimmy Adams	Educational	2 reels	Mar. 7
Love and Kisses	Alice Day	Pathe	2 reels	Oct. 3
Love Sick	Constance Darling	Universal	2 reels	May 23
Love's Tragedy		Sering Wilson (S. R.)	1 reel	
Lucky Accident, The	Charles Puffy	Universal	1 reel	July 18
Lucky Leap, A	Wanda Wiley	Universal	2 reels	
Lucky Stars	Harry Langdon	Pathe	2 reels	Aug. 15
Madame Sans Jane	Glenn Tryon	Pathe	2 reels	
Marriage Circus, The	Ben Turpin	Pathe	2 reels	April 11
Married Neighbors	Engle-Darling	Universal	2 reels	July 4
Mary, Queen of Tots	" Our Gang "	Pathe	2 reels	Aug. 22
Meet the Ambassador	Jimmy Aubrey	F. B. O	2 reels	
Mellow Quartette	Pen & Ink Vaudeville	Educational	1 reel	April 4
Merrymakers	Bowes-Vance	Educational	1 reel	Mar. 28
Met by Accident	Wanda Wiley	Universal	2 reels	
Milky Way, The	Charles Puffy	Universal	1 reel	July 25
Min Walks in Her Sleep	" Gumps "	Universal		

Feature	Star	Distributed by	Length	Reviewed
Man's Sailer, A	Dorley-Steadman	Educational	2 reels	Oct. 3
Miss Fixit	Wanda Wiley	Universal	2 reels	
Monkey Business	"Peg & Ink Vaude"	Educational	1 reel	
Moonlight Nights	Gloria Joy	Bayart (S. R.)	2 reels	May 9
Moonlight and Noses	Clyde Cook	Pathe	2 reels	
Movies, The	Lloyd Hamilton	Educational	2 reels	Oct. 3
Nearly Rich	Charles Puffy	Universal	1 reel	
Neptune's Stepdaughter		Fox	2 reels	
Nero's Jazz Band		Sering Wilson (S. R.)	1 reel	
Never Fear	Bowes-Vance	Educational	1 reel	
Never on Time		Lee-Bradford (S. R.)	1 reel	
Never Weaken	Lloyd reissue	Assoc. Exhib.	2237 feet	
Nice Pickle, A	Edwards-Roach	Universal	2 reels	
Nicely Rewarded	Chas. Puffy	Universal	1 reel	June 27
Night Hawks		Educational Film	2 reels	
Nobody Wins	Arthur Lake	Universal	2 reels	
No Place to Go	Arthur Lake	Universal	1 reel	
Now or Never (reissue)	Harold Lloyd	Assoc. Exhib.	3 reels	
Nurse's Troubles	Edna Marian	Universal		
Nuts and Squirrels	"Aesop's Fables"	Pathe	1 reel	
Off His Beat	Walter Hiers	Educational	2 reels	
Office Help	"Aesop's Fables"	Pathe	1 reel	June 27
Officer 13	Eddie Gordon	Universal	2 reels	
Official Officers	"Our Gang"	Pathe	2 reels	June 27
Oh, Bridget!	Walter Hiers	Educational	2 reels	
Oh, What a Flirt	Jimmy Aubrey	Film Book. Offices	2 reels	
Oh, What a Queue	"The Queue"	Universal	1 reel	
Old Family Toothbrush	"Kid Noah"	Sering Wilson (S. R.)	1 reel	
On Duty	Wanda Wiley	Universal	2 reels	
On the Go	Special Cast	Fox		
One Glorious Fourth	"Reg'nr Kids"	M. J. Winkler (S. R.)	2 reels	
One Wild Night	Neely Edwards	Universal	1 reel	
Orphan, The	Al Joy	Ricardo Films, Inc.(S.R.)		
Permit Me	Bowes-Vance	Educational	1 reel	
Pie-Eyed	Stan Laurel	F. B. O.	2 reels	July 11
Pie Man, The	"Aesop's Fables"	Pathe	1 reel	Mar. 21
Plain Clothes	Harry Langdon	Pathe	2 reels	Mar. 14
Plain and Fancy Girls	Charles Chase	Pathe	2 reels	Mar. 14
Plain Luck	Edna Marian	Universal	2 reels	
Pleasure Bound	Lige Conley	Educational	2 reels	Aug. 1
Plenty of Nerve	Edna Marian	Universal	2 reels	July 4
Polo Kid, The	Eddie Gordon	Universal	2 reels	
Poor Sap, The		Fox	2 reels	
Powdered Chickens	Edna Marian	Universal	2 reels	
Props' Dash for Cash	Earl Hurd (Cartoon)	Educational	1 reel	April 11
Pulling on Aira	Edna Marian	Universal	2 reels	
Puzzled by Crosswords	Eddie Gordon	Universal	2 reels	Mar. 7
Queen of Aces	Wanda Wiley	Universal	2 reels	
Raid, The	Gloria Joy	Bayart Pict. (S. R.)	2 reels	
Rainy Knight, A	Special Cast	Fox	2 reels	
Rainin' Cain	Constance Darling	Universal	2 reels	April 4
Rapid Transit	Al St. John	Educational	2 reels	
Raris' Romeo	Walter Hiers	Educational	2 reels	
Raspberry Romance	Ben Turpin	Pathe	2 reels	Feb. 28
Red Pepper	Al St. John	Educational	2 reels	April 4
Regular Girl, A	Wanda Wiley	Universal	2 reels	
Riders of the Kitchen Range	Mohar-Engle	Pathe	1 reel	June 6
Remember When	Harry Langdon	Pathe	2 reels	April 26
Rip Without a Wink	"Redhead"	Sering Wilson (S. R.)	1 reel	
Ripe Melodrama, A	Billy West	Arrow	2 reels	
Rivals		Pathe		
Robinson Crusoe Returns on Friday	"Redhead"	Sering Wilson (S. R.)	1 reel	
Rock Bottom	Bowes-Vance	Educational	1 reel	May 9
Robbing the Raube		Lee-Bradford Corp.	2 reels	
Rolling Stones	Charles Puffy	Universal	1 reel	May 30
Rough Party	Al Alt	Universal	1 reel	
Royal Four-Flush	Spat Family	Pathe	1 reel	June 13
Runaway Balloon, The	"Aesop's Fables"	Pathe	1 reel	June 27
Rust, The	"Aesop's Fables"	Pathe	1 reel	June 20
Sailor Papa, A	Glenn Tryon	Pathe	2 reels	April 4
Salute	Alice Ardell	F. B. O.		
Saturday	"Hey Fellas"	Davis Dist. (S.R.)	2 reels	
Say It With Flour		Fox	2 reels	
Scrambled Eggs	Bowes-Vance	Educational		
Sheiks of Bagdad		Pathe	1 reel	May 9
Sherlock Sleuth	Arthur Stone	Pathe	2 reels	July 11
Ship Shape	Vance-Bowes	Educational	1 reel	April 18
Shoolin' Injuns	"Our Gang"	Pathe	2 reels	May 9
Shot! Pants	Arthur Lake	Universal	2 reels	
Should a Husband Tell?		Red Seal Pict.	1 reel	
Should Husbands Be Watched?	Charles Chase	Pathe	1 reel	Mar. 14
Sir Walt and Lizzie		Sering Wilson (S. R.)	1 reel	
'ist Tight	Jimmie Adams	Educational	2 reels	May 30
Skinnale in Silk		Pathe	2 reels	May 16
Sky Jumper, The	Earle Foxe	Fox	2 reels	
Skyscraper, The	Harry Langdon	Principal Pict. (S.R.)	2 reels	
Sleeping Sickness	Edwards-Roach	Universal	1 reel	May 30
Sick Abilities	Engle-Kart	Universal	2 reels	May 16
Smoked Out	Lake-HaatWouk	Universal	1 reel	April 12
Sneezing Beezers	Billy Bevan	Pathe	2 reels	July 18
Snow-Hawk	Stan Laurel	F. B. O.	2 reels	
Soap	"Aesop's Fables"	Pathe	1 reel	
Somewhere in Somewhere	Murray-Lifefield	Pathe	2 reels	Sept. 26
S. O. S.	"Aesop's Fables"	Pathe	1 reel	
Spanish Romeo, A (Van Bibber)		Fox	2 reels	
Sneak Easy	Charley Puffy	Universal	1 reel	Aug. 22
Sneak Freely	Edna Marion	Universal	2 reels	
Spot Light		Educational	2 reels	
Stick Around	Bobby Dunn	Arrow	2 reels	
Stop, Look and Whistle		Pathe	1 reel	
Storm, The (Out of the Inkwell)	"Cartoon"	Red Seal Pict.	1 reel	
Stranded	Edna Marian	Universal	2 reels	
Strong for Love	Special Cast	Fox	2 reels	
Sugar-Ho-ded'-Dyna Lizzies		Pathe	2 reels	June 13
Sal's Mitel		Pathe	1 reel	May 23
Sweet Marie	Special Cast	Fox	2 reels	Aug. 29
Tame Men and Wild Women		Pathe	2 reels	Aug. 22
Tam' War, A	Eddie Gordon	Universal	2 reels	May 30
'esert Island	"Redhead"	Sering Wilson (S. R.)	1 reel	
Tea for Two	Alice Day	Pathe	2 reels	Aug. 1

Feature	Star	Distributed by	Length	Reviewed
Tell It To a Policeman	Glenn Tryon	Pathe	2 reels	May 23
Tender Feet	Walter Hiers	Educational	2 reels	May 23
Tending Out	Roache-Edwards	Universal	1 reel	May 23
The Week-End		Lee-Bradford (S. R.)		
Three Wise Goofs	Special Cast	Fox	2 reels	
Three of Five Good Reasons		F. B. O.		
Thundering Landslide	Glenn Tryon	Pathe	2 reels	June 27
Time of Fun in a Beauty Parlor		F. B. O.		
Too Much Mother-In-Law	Constance Darling			
Too Young to Marry	Buddy Messinger	Universal	2 reels	
Tough Night, A	Jimmy Callahan	Arwon Film	2 reels	
Tourist, The	Harry Langdon	Educational Film	2 reels	Aug. 15
Tourists De Luxe	Hayes-Karr	Pathe	2 reels	May 16
Transatlantic Flight, A	"Aesop's Fables"	Pathe	1 reel	
Twins	Stan Laurel	F. B. O.	1 reel	
Two Cats and a Bird	"Cartoon"	Educational	1 reel	Mar. 14
Two Poor Fish	Earl Hurd cartoon	Educational	1 reel	May 30
Ugly Duckling, The	"Aesop's Fables"	Pathe	1 reel	Sept. 26
Uncle Tom's Gal	Edna Marian	Universal	2 reels	
Unwelcome	Charles Puffy	Universal	1 reel	June 27
Wailing	Lloyd Hamilton	Educational	2 reels	July 11
Wake Up	Bowes-Vance	Educational	1 reel	June 13
Watch Out	Bobby Vernon	Educational	2 reels	
Water Wagons	Special Cast	Pathe	2 reels	Feb. 21
Welcome Danger	Bowes-Vance	Educational	2 reels	Aug. 15
West of West	Billy West	Arrow	2 reels	
Westward Ho	Charles Puffy	Universal	1 reel	Oct. 3
What Price Goofy	Charley Chase	Pathe	2 reels	June 6
When Dumbells Ring		Pathe		
When Men Were Men	"Aesop's Fables"	Pathe	1 reel	July 25
While Wing's Bride	Harry Langdon	Pathe	2 reels	July 11
Whose Baby Are You?	Glenn Tryon	Pathe	2 reels	
Who's Which	Bowes-Vance	Educational	1 reel	
Why Hesitate?	Neal Burns	Educational	2 reels	
Why Sitting Bull Stood Up		Sering Wilson (S. R.)	2 reels	April 11
Wide Awake	Lige Conley	Educational	2 reels	
Wild Pass	"Spat Family"	Pathe	1 reel	May 23
Wild Waves	Bowes-Vance	Educational	1 reel	
Wine, Women and Song	"Aesop's Fables"	Pathe	1 reel	
Winning Pair, A	Wanda Wiley	Universal	2 reels	June 6
Woozy West, The	Buddy Messinger	Universal	2 reels	
Wrestler, The	Earle Foxe	Fox	2 reels	Aug. 29
Yarn About Yarn, A	"Aesop's Fables"	Pathe	1 reel	Aug. 1
Yes, Yes, Nannette	Jas. Finlayson	Pathe	2 reels	Aug. 1
Your Own Back Yard	"Our Gang"	Pathe	2 reels	Oct. 3

Short Subjects

Feature	Distributed by	Length	Reviewed
Action (Spotlight)	Pathe	1 reel	
All Abroad	(Helen and Warren) Fox	2 reels	
All Under One Flag (Spotlight)	Pathe	1 reel	
Animal Celebrities (Sportlight)	Pathe	1 reel	June 27
Animated Hair Cartoon (Series)	Red Seal	1 reel	
Sailor's Race to Rome (Special)	Educational	2 reels	May 30
Barbara Snitches (Pacemaker Series)	B. O.	2 reels	
Battle of Wits (Jone Sedgwick)	Universal	2 reels	July 18
Bashful Whirlwind, The (Edmund Cobb)	Universal	2 reels	
Beauty and the Bandit (Geo. Larkin)	Universal	2 reels	July 4
Beauty Spots (Sportlight)	Pathe	1 reel	April 18
Best Man, The (Josie Sedgwick)	Universal	2 reels	Aug. 15
Blazen Trails	Denver Dizon (S.R.)	2 reels	
Boundary Line, The (Fred Humes)	Universal	2 reels	
Business Engagement, A. (Helen & Warren)	Fox	2 reels	
Cabaret of Old Japan		1 reel	
Color World	Sering Wilson (S. R.)	1 reel	
Captured Alive (Helen Gibson)	Davis Dist.	2 reels	July 25
Cinema Stars (Novelty)	Pathe	1 reel	
Close Call, The (Edmund Cobb)	Universal	2 reels	
Cocoon to Kimono	M. J. Winkler (S.R.)	1 reel	
Come-Back, The (Benny Leonard)	Henry Ginsberg-S.R.	2 reels	
Concerning Cheese (Varieties)	Pathe	1 reel	
Cowred Flagon, The (Pacemaker Series)	B. O.	2 reels	
Cowpuncher's Comeback, The (Art Acord)	Universal	2 reels	
Crooked (Elinor King)	Davis Dist.	2 reels	
Cross Word Puzzle Film (Comedy-Novelty)	Schwartz Enterprises (S. R.)	1 reel	
Cuba Steps Out (Variety)	Pathe	1 reel	
Day With the Gypsies	Red Seal Pict.	1 reel	
Divertisement (Color Study)	Sering Wilson (S. R.)	1 reel	
Don Coo Coo (Pacemaker)	Film Book. Offices	2 reels	
Do You Remember (Gems of Screen)	Red Seal	1 reel	
Dude Ranch Days (Sportlight)	Pathe	1 reel	May 30
Earth's Other Half (Hodge-Podge)	Educational	1 reel	June 6
East Side, West Side	DeForrest (S. R.)		
Failure (O. Henry)	Fox	2 reels	
Fail Main, The (Pacemakers)	Film Book. Offices	2 reels	
Fighting Cowboy (Serial)	Universal	18 episodes	
Fighting Ranger (Serial)	Universal	18 episodes	Feb. 7
Fighting Schoolmarm (Josie Sedgwick)	Universal	2 reels	Aug. 1
Film Facts	Red Seal	1 reel	
Fitn Titnlel, The (Serial)	Universal	15 episodes	
Flirting With Death	Universal	2 reels	Sept. 26
Floral Feast, A	Sering Wilson (S.R.)	1 reel	
Frederick Chopin (Music Master's)	Jas. A. Fitzpatrick (S. R.)	1 reel	
From Mars to Munich (Varieties)	Pathe	1 reel	April 4
Frontier Love (Billy Mack)	Denver Dixon	2 reels	
Fugitive Futurist	Pathe	1 reel	
George F. Handel (Music Master's)	Jas. A. Fitzpatrick (S. R.)	1 reel	
Gems of the Screen	Red Seal	1 reel	
Good City, The (Serial)	Universal	15 episodes	
Golden Feather, The (Serial)	Universal	2 reels	
Gold Trap, The	Fred Humes	Universal	2 reels	
Great Circus Mystery, The (Serial)	Universal	15 episodes	
Great Decide, The (Pacemaker's)	Film Book. Offices	2 reels	
He Who Gets Rapped (Pacemakers)	Film Book. Offices	2 reels	
Hittin' the Trail (Fred Hart)	Surfs Pub. (S.R.)	2 reels	
How the Elephant Got His Trunk (Bray)	B. O.	1 reel	
Idaho (Serial)	Pathe	10 episodes	Feb. 28
If a Picture Tells a Story	Cranfield & Clarke (S. R.)	1 reel	
In a China Shop (Variety)	Fox	1 reel	
In the Spider's Grip (Novelty)	Educational	1 reel	April 11

Feature	Star	Distributed by	Length	Reviewed
Invention, The (Elinor King)		Davis Dist.	2 reels	Oct. 3
I Remember		Short Films Synd.	2 reels	Sept. 26
It Might Happen to You (Evangeline Russell)		Davis Dist.	2 reels	
Jazz Fight, The (Benny Leonard)		Henry Ginsberg (S. R.)	2 reels	
Judge's Cross Word Puzzle (Novelty)		Educational	1 reel	Jan. 31
Just Cowboys	Corbett-Holmes	Universal	2 reels	
Klondike Today (Varieties)		Fox	1 reel	
Knicknacks of Knowledge (Hodge Podge)		Educational	1 reel	
Knockout Man, The (Mustang)		Universal	2 reels	July 11
Ko-Ko on the Run	(Ko-Ko Series)	Red Seal	1 reel	Oct. 3
Land of the Navajo (Educational)		Fox	1 reel	
Learning How (Sportlight)		Pathe	1 reel	July 18
Leopard's Lair		Universal	Serial	
Let's Paint		Cranfield & Clarke (S. R.)		
Life's Greatest Thrills		Universal	2 reels	Sept. 26
Line Runners, The (Arnold Gregg)		Universal	2 reels	
Little People of the Garden (Secrets of Life)		Educational	1 reel	
Little People of the Sea (Secrets of Life)		Educational	1 reel	Feb. 28
Lizzie's Last Lap		Cranfield & Clarke (S. R.)		
Loaded Dice (Edmund Cobb)		Universal	2 reels	April 4
Luna-cy (Stereoscopik)		Pathe	1 reel	
Mad Miner, A (Western)		Hunt Miller (S. R.)	2 reels	
Magic Hour, The		Red Seal Pict.	1 reel	
Man Who Rode Alone, The		Miller & Steen (S.R.)	2 reels	
Man Without a Scar		Universal	2 reels	
Marvels of Motion		Red Seal	1 reel	
Marvellous Manhattan		M. J. Winkler (S. R.)	1 reel	
Merry Kiddo, The (Pacemakers)		Film Book. Offices	2 reels	
Merton of the Goofies	"Pacemaker"	F. B. O.	2 reels	
Mexican Melody (Hodge-Podge)		Educational	1 Reel	
Mexican Oil Fields		M. J. Winkler (S. R.)	1 reel	
Movie Morsels (Hodge Podge)		Educational	1 reel	April 4
My Bonnie	(Ko-Ko Series)	Red Sea	1 reel	Oct. 3
My Own Carolina (Variety)		Fox	1 reel	Aug. 29
Mystery Box, The (Serial)		Davis Dist. Corp.	10 episodes	
Neptune's Nieces (Sportlight)		Pathe	1 reel	
New Sheriff, A (Western)		Hunt Miller (S. R.)	2 reels	
Olympic Mermaids (Sportlight)		Pathe	1 reel	
One Glorious Scrap (Edmund Cobb)		Universal	2 reels	
Only a Country Lass (Novelty)		Educational	1 reel	May 29
Ouch (Stereoscopik)		Pathe	1 reel	
Our Six-legged Friends (Secrets of Life)		Educational	1 reel	
Outings for All	(Sportlight)	Pathe	1 reel	
Outlaw, The (Jack Perrin)		Universal	2 reels	
Peacemakers, The	(Helen & Warren)	Fox	2 reels	
Paris Creations (Novelty)		Educational	1 reel	Feb. 7
Paris Creations in Color (Novelty)		Educational	1 reel	Feb. 28
People You Know (Screen Almanac)		Film Booking Offices.	1 reel	
Perfect View, The (Varieties)		Fox	1 reel	
Perils of the Wild (Serial)		Universal		
Pictorial Proverbs (Hodge Podge)		Educational	1 reel	Aug. 15
Plastigrams (Novelty)		Educational		
Play Ball (Serial)		Pathe	10 episodes	June 27
Power God, The (Serial)		Davis Dist. Div.	15 episodes	
Pronto Kid, The (Edmund Cobb)		Universal	2 reels	June 27
Queen of the Round-Up (J. Sedgwick)		Universal	2 reels	June 13
Race, The (Van Bibber)		Fox	2 reels	
Radio Detective, The		Universal	Serial	
Raid, The	Edmund Cobb	Universal	2 reels	
Record Breaker, The		Pathe	Serial	
Rim of the Desert (Jack Perrin)		Universal	2 reels	
River Nile, The (Variety)		Fox	1 reel	
Roaring Waters (Geo. Larkin)		Universal	2 reels	
Rock Bound Brittany (Educational)		Fox	1 reel	
Ropin' Venus, The (Mustang Series)		Universal	2 reels	July 11
R. Valentino and Eighty-eight Prize-winning American Beauties		Chesterfield (M. P. Corp.) (S. R.)	3 reels	
Runaway Taxi, A	(Stereoscopic)	Pathe	1 reel	Oct. 3
Rustlen of Boulder Canyon (Edmund Cobb)		Universal	2 reels	
Secrets of Life (Educational)		Principal Pict. (S. R.)	reel	Feb. 21
Seven Ages of Sport (Sportlight)		Pathe	1 reel	Aug. 22
Shadow of Suspicion (Eileen Sedgwick)		Universal	2 reels	
Shoes (O. Henry)		Fox	2 reels	
Shootin' Wild (Corbett-Holmes)		Universal	2 reels	
Show Down, The (Art Acord)		Universal	2 reels	
Silvery Art		Red Seal Pict.	2 reels	Sept. 26
Sky Tribe, The (Variety)		Fox	1 reel	
Smoke of a Forty-Five, The (Western)		Hunt Miller (S. R.)	2 reels	
Soft Muscles (Benny Leonard)		Ginsberg (S. R.)	2 reels	
Song Cartunes (Novelty)		Red Seal Pict.	1 reel	
Sons of Swat (Sportlight)		Pathe	1 reel	Aug. 15
Sporting Judgment (Sportlight)		Pathe	1 reel	May 9
Starting an Argument (Sportlight)		Pathe	1 reel	
Steam Heated Islands (Varieties)		Fox	1 reel	
Stereoscopic (Novelty)		Pathe	1 reel	May 16
Storm King (Edmund Cobb)		Universal	2 reels	
Story Teller, The (Hodge-Podge)		Educational	1 reel	Oct. 3
Straight Shootin' (Harry Carey)		Universal	2 reels	
Strangler Lewis vs. Wayne Munn		Educational	2 reels	July 4
Stratford on Avon (Gems of Screen)		Red Seal Pict	1 reel	
Sunken Silver (Serial)		Pathe	10 episodes	April 18
Surprise Fight, The (Benny Leonard)		Henry Ginsberg (S. R.)	2 reels	
Thundering Waters (Novelty)		Sering D. Wilson (S. R.)	1 reel	April 25
Tiger Kill, The (Pathe Review)		Pathe		
Toiling for Rest (Variety)		Fox	1 reel	
Too Many Bucks (Corbett-Holmes		Universal	2 reels	
Transiets in Arcadia (O. Henry)		Fox	2 reels	
Traps and Troubles (Sportlight)		Pathe	1 reel	Mar. 21
Travel Treasures (Hodge Podge)		Educational	1 reel	July 25
Turf Mystery (Serial)		Chesterfield Pict. Corp. (S. R.)	15 episodes	
Valley of Rogues (Western)		Universal	2 reels	April 18
Van Bibber and the Navy (Earle Foxe)		Fox	2 reels	
Village School, The (Hodge Podge)		Educational Film	1 reel	May
Voice of the Nightingale, The (Novelty)		Educational	1 reel	Mar. 28
Waiting For You (Music Film)		Hegerman Music Novelties (S. R.)		
Welcome Granger (Pacemakers)		Film Book. Offices	2 reels	
West Wind, The (Variety)		Fox	1 reel	
What Price Gloria (Pacemakers)		Film Book. Offices	2 reels	
Wheels of the Pioneers (Billy Mack)		Denver Dixon (S. R.)	2 reels	
Where the Waters Divide (Varieties)		Fox	1 reel	
White Paper (Varieties)		Fox	1 reel	
Wild West Wallop, The (Edmund Cobb)		Universal	2 reels	May 16
Wild West		Pathe	Serial	
With Pencil, Brush and Chisel (Variety)		Fox	1 reel	
Wonder Book, The (Series)		Sering D. Wilson	500 feet	April 25
Young Sheriff, The (Tom. Forman)		Miller & Steen (S. R.)	2 reels	
Zowie (Stereoscopik)		Pathe	1 reel	

Coming Attractions

Feature	Star	Distributed by	Length	Reviewed
Ace of Spades, The	Desmond-McAllister	Universal		
Age of Indiscretion		Truart (S. R.)	5800 feet	
Agony Column	Monte Blue	Warner Bros		
All Around the Frying Pan	Fred Thompson	F. B. O		
Aloma of the South Seas	Gilda Gray	Paramount		
American Venus, The	Special Cast	Paramount		
An Enemy of Men		Columbia Pict. (S. R.)		
Aristocrat, The	Special Cast	B. P. Schulberg (S. R.)		
Atlantis		First National		
Bad Lands, The	Harry Carey	Prod. Dist. Corp.	5833 feet	Oct. 3
Barriers of Fire	Monte Blue	Warner Bros.		
Bat, The	Special Cast	United Artists		
Beautiful Cheat, The	Laura La Plante	Universal		
Beautiful City	R. Barthelmess	First National		
Before Midnight	Wm. Russell	Ginsberg (S. R.)	5893 feet	Aug. 8
Bells, The	Lionel Barrymore	Chadwick		
Beloved Pawn, The	Reed Howes	Rayart (S. R.)		
Ben Hur	Special Cast	Metro-Goldwyn		
Best Bad Man, The	Tom Mix	Fox		
Between Men	"Lefty" Flynn	F. B. O		
Big Parade, The	John Gilbert	Metro-Goldwyn		
Border Intrigue	Franklyn Farnum	Inde. Pict. (S. R.)	5 reels	June 6
Border Women	Special Cast	Phil Goldstone (S.R.)	5000 feet	
Broken Hearts of Hollywood	Harlan-Miller	Warner Brothers		
Broken Homes	Lake-Glass	Astor Dist		
Brooding Eyes		Ginsberg Dis. Corp. (S. R.)		
Cave Man, The	Harlan-Miller	Warner Brothers		
Charity Ball, The		Metro-Goldwyn		
Checkered Flag, The		Ginsberg Dist. Corp. (S. R.)		
Clean-Up, The	Richard Talmadge	F. B. O.		
Clod Hopper, The	Glenn Hunter	Assoc. Exhibitors		
Clothes Make the Pirate	Errol-D. Gish	First National		
College Widow, The	Syd Chaplin	Warner Brothers		
Compromise	Irene Rich	Warner Bros.		
Conquered	Gloria Swanson	Paramount		
Count of Luxembourg, The	Larry Semon	Chadwick		
Crashing Through	Jack Perrin	Ambassador Pict. (S. R.)	5000 feet	
Cyclone Bob	Bob Reeves	Anchor Film Dist.		
Cyrano de Bergerac	Special Cast	Atlas Dist. (S. R.)	9500 feet	July 18
Dance Madness	Pringle-Cody	Metro-Goldwyn		
Dangers of a Great City		Fox		
Dark Horse, The	Harry Carey	Prod. Dist. Corp.		
Daybreak		Fox		
Deerslayer, The		Weiss Bros. (S. R.)	4780 feet	
Daughter of the Sioux, A	Wilson-Gerber	Davis Dist. (S. R.)	5 reels	Oct. 3
Demon, The	Jack Hoxie	Universal		
Demon Rider, The	Ken Maynard	Davis Dist	5000 feet	Aug. 22
Detour		Prod. Dist. Corp.		
Devil Horse, The	Rex (horse)	Pathe		
Down Upon the Suwanee River	Special Cast	Lee Bradford (S. R.)		
Dumb Head		Tiffany (S. R.)	6500 feet	
East of the Setting Sun	Constance Talmadge	First National		
Eagle, The	Rudolph Valentino	United Artists		
Eden's Fruit		B. P. Schulberg (S.R.)		
Enchanted Hill, The	Special Cast	Paramount		
Ermine and Rhinestone		H. F. Jans (S. R.)		
Exquisite Sinner, The	Special Cast	Metro-Goldwin		
Face on the Air, The	Evelyn Brent	F. B. O.		
Fall of Jerusalem		Weiss Bros. (S. R.)	6800 feet	
False Pride		Astor Dist.		
Fast Pace, The	Special Cast	Arrow		
Fighter's Paradise, The	Rex Baker	Phil Goldstone	5000 feet	
Fighting Courage	Ken Maynard	Davis Dist. Div. (S.R.)	5 reels	July 11
Fighting Edge, The	Harlan-Miller	Warner Brothers		
Fighting Heart, The	Frank Merrill	Bud Barsky Prod. S. R.)	5000 feet	
Fighting Smile, The	Bill Cody	Inde.Pict. Corp.(S.R.)	4630 feet	
First Year, The	Special Cast	Fox		
Flaming Waters		F. B. O.		
Flying Three	Al Wilson	Davis Dist. Corp.		
Flying Fool, The	Dick Jones	Sunset Prod. (S. R.)		
Forest of Destiny, The		Gotham Prod. (S. R.)		
Forever After	Corinne Griffith	First National		
Fort Frayne	Ben Wilson	Davis Dist.	5000 feet	Aug. 29
Free Lips	Norma Shearer	M-G-M		
Friends	Special Cast	Vitagraph		
Frivolity		B. P. Schulberg (S.R.)		
Galloping Dude, The	Franklyn Farnum	Inde.Pict.Corp.(S.R.)	4700 feet	
Going the Limit	Richard Holt	Gerson Pict. (S. R.)	5000 feet	Sept. 26
Golden Cocoon		Warner Bros.		
Goose Woman, The	Special Cast	Universal	7500 feet	Aug. 22
Go West	Buster Keaton	Metro-Goldwyn		
Great Love, The	Dana-Agnew	First National		
Grey Vulture, The	Ken Maynard	Davis Dist. Div.		
Gulliver's Travels		Universal		
Handsome Brute, The	Columbia Pict. (S. R.)			
Hassan		Paramount		
Haunted Range, The	Ken Maynard	Davis Dist. Div.		
Hearts and Fists		Assoc. Exhib.		
Hearts and Spangles		Gotham Prod. (S. R.)		
Hell Bent for Heaven		Warner Bros.		
Heir's Apparent	Special Cast	First National		
Her Father's Daughter		F. B. O.		
Hero of the Big Snows, A	Rin Tin Tn (dog)	Warner Brothers		
His Jazz Bride	Special Cast	Warner		
His Majesty Bunker Bean	M. Moore-Devore	Warner	7291 feet	Sept. 26
His Woman	Special Cast	Whitman Bennett	7 reels	
Hogan's Alley	Harlan-Miller	Warner		
Home Maker, The	Alice Joyce	Universal	7755 feet	Aug. 8
Honeymoon Express, The	M. Moore-D. Devore	Warner Brothers		
Horses and Women		B. P. Schulberg		
How to Train a Wife	Valli-O'Brien	Assoc. Exhib.		
Hurricane		Truart (S. R.)	5800 feet	
Husband Hunters		Tiffany	6500 feet	
Inevitable Millionaires, The	M. Moore-Devore	Warner Bros.		
Invisible Wounds	Sweet-Lyon	First National		
Irene	Colleen Moore	First National		
Justice of the Far North		C. B. C. (S. R.)	5300 feet	
Just Suppose	Richard Barthelmess	First National		
Kings of the Turf		Fox		

Feature	Star	Distributed by	Length	Reviewed
Kiss for Cinderella, A	Betty Bronson	Paramount		
La Boheme	Lillian Gish	Metro-Goldwyn		
Ladies of Leisure	Elaine Hammerstein	Columbia (S. R.)		
Lady Windermere's Fan	Special Cast	Warner Brothers		
Lariat, The	William Desmond	Universal		
Last Edition, The	Ralph Lewis	Film Book. Offices		
Lawful Cheater, The	Bow-McKee	B. P. Schulberg	4845 feet	
Lena Rivers	Special Cast	Arrow (S. R.)	6 reels	
Life of a Woman		Truart (S. R.)	5300 feet	
Lightning		Tiffany (S. R.)	5300 feet	
Lightning Jack	Jack Perrin	Ambassador Pict. (S.R.) 5000 feet		
Lightning Passer, The	Al Ferguson	Fleming Prod. (S.R.)		
Limited Mail, The	Monte Blue	Warner Bros.		
Little Girl in a Big City, A		Gotham Prod. (S.R.)		
Little Irish Girl, The	Special Cast	Warner Bros.		
Lodge in the Wilderness		Tiffany (S. R.)		
Lord Jim	Percy Marmont	Paramount	6300 feet	
Love Cargo, The	House Peters	Universal		
Lover's Island	Hampton-Kirkwood	Assoc. Exhib.		
Love Gamble, The		Ginsberg Dist. Corp. (S. R.)		
Love Toy, The	Lowell Sherman	Warner Bros.	5766 feet	July 11
Loyalties	Special Cast	Pax		
Lunatic at Large, The	Leon Errol	First National		
Lure of the North, The		Columbia Pict. (S.R.)		
Lure of the Wild	Jane Novak	Columbia (S.R.) 5 reels		May 2
Lying Wives	Special Cast	Ivan Abramson (S. R.) 7 reels		
Man and the Moment		Metro-Goldwyn		
Mannequin, The		Paramount		
Man of Iron, A	L. Barrymore	Chadwick	6 reels	July 4
Man on the Box, The	Sydney Chaplin	Warner Bros.		
Man She Bought, The	Constance Talmadge	First National		
Man Without a Conscience, A	Louis Rich	Warner Bros.	6850 feet	May 2
Mare Nostrum	Special Cast	Metro-Goldwyn		
Married Cheats		Fox		
Married Hypocrites	Frederick-La Plante	Universal		
Marrying Money		Truart (S. R.)	5300 feet	
Martinique	Bebe Daniels	Paramount		
Masked Bride, The	Mae Murray	Metro-Goldwyn		
Memory Lane	Boardman-Nagel	First National		
Men of Steel	Milton Sills	First National		
Midnight Flyer, The	Landis-Devore	F. B. O.		
Miracle of Life, The	Special Cast	Assoc. Exhib.		
Midnight Flames		Columbia Pict. (S. R.)		
Miss Vanity	Mary Philbin	Universal		
Million Dollar Doll		Universal		
Mismates		Arrow. Exhib.		
Mocking Bird, The	Lon Chaney	First National		
Modern Musketeer, A	Zeno Corrado	M-G-M		
Morgenson's Finish		Tiffany (S. R.)	5300 feet	
Napoleon the Great		Tiffany (S. R.)	6500 feet	
My Own Pal	Tom Mix	Fox		
Night Cry, The	Rin-Tin-Tin (dog)	Warner Brothers		
Nightie, Night Nurse	Syd Chaplin	Warner Brothers		
North Star, The	Strongheart (dog)	Assoc. Exhib.		
Old Clothes	Jackie Coogan	Metro-Goldwyn		
Only Thing, The	Special Cast	Metro-Goldwyn		
Open Trail, The	Jack Hoxie	Universal	4800 feet	May 16
Pace That Thrills, The	Ben Lyon	First National		
Palace of Pleasure		Fox		
Pals		Truart (S. R.)	5300 feet	
Paris	Pauline Starke	Metro-Goldwyn		
Paris After Dark	Norma Talmadge	First National		
Perfect's Again		United Artists		
Passionate Quest, The	Marie Prevost	Warner Bros.		
Passionate Youth	Special Cast	Truart (S. R.)	5 reels	July 11
Part Time Wife, The		Gotham Prod. (S. R.)		
Phantom of the Forest	Thunder (dog)	Gotham Prod.		
Phantom of the Opera	Lon Chaney	Universal	8464 feet	Sept. 19
Pinch Hitter, The	Glenn Hunter	Asso. Exhibitors		
Pleasure Buyers, The	Irene Rich	Warner Brothers		
Police Patrol, The	James Kirkwood	Gotham Prod. (S.R.) 6000 feet		May 19
Polly of the Ballet	Bebe Daniels	Paramount		
Pony Express, The	Special Cast	Paramount	9929 feet	Sept. 26
Prince, The	Philbin-Kerry	Universal		
Quality Street		Metro-Goldwyn		
Quacker'n Lightning	Buffalo Bill, Jr.	Weiss Bros. (S.R.) 5 reels		June 13
Racing Blood		Gotham Prod. (S.R.)		
Rainbow Riley	Johnny Hines	First National		
Reckless Courage	Buddy Roosevelt	Weiss Bros. (S. R.) 4851 feet		May 2
Reckless Sex, The	Special Cast	Truart (S. R.)	6 reels	Feb. 14
Red Clay	William Desmond	Universal		
Red Dice	Rod La Rocque	Prod. Dist. Corp.		
Red Kimono, The	Mrs. Wallace Reid	Davis Dist. Div.		
Red Hot Tires	Monte Blue	Warner Bros.		
Return of a Soldier	Special Cast	Metro-Goldwyn		
Rime of the Ancient Mariner, The		Fox Film		
Road to Glory, The		Fox Film		
Road That Led Home, The		Vitagraph		
Rocking Moon	Bowers-Tashman	Prod. Dist. Corp.		
Romance of an Actress		Chadwick		
Ropin' Venus, The	Josie Sedgwick	Universal		
Rose of the World	Special Cast	Warner Bros.		
Sally, Irene and Mary	Special Cast	Metro-Goldwyn		
Salvage		Truart (S. R.)	5400 feet	
San, The	M. Moore-D. Devore	Warner Bros		
Satan in Sables	Lowell Sherman	Warner Bros		
Savage, The	Ben Lyon	First National		

Feature	Star	Distributed by	Length	Reviewed
Scarlet Saint, The	Lyon-Astor	First National		
Scraps	Mary Pickford	United Artists		
Sea Beast, The	John Barrymore	Warner Bros.		
Separate Rooms		Warner Bros.		
Seven Sinners	Marie Prevost	Warner Bros.		
Seventh Heaven	Special Cast	Fox		
Shadow of the Wall		Gotham Prod. (S. R.)		
Shadow of the Mosque	Odette Taylor	Cranfield & Clarke (S. R.)	6200 feet	
Shenandoah		B. P. Schulberg (S. R.)		
Ship of Souls	E. Lytell-L. Rich	Assoc. Exhib.	6800 feet	
Shootin' Square	Jack Perrin	Ambassador Pict. (S.R.)5000 feet		
Sign of the Claw		Ufa		
Silent Witness, The		Truart (S. R.)	5800 feet	
Silken Shackles	Irene Rich	Warner Bros.		
Silver Treasure, The	Special Cast	Fox		
Spinners Drives Surf	Reginald Denny	Universal		
Social Highwayman, The	Harlan-Miller	Warner Brothers		
Song and Dance Man, The	Tom Moore	Paramount		
Sons of Life		Special Cast		
Speed Limit, The	Betty Blythe	Banner Prod. (S. R.)		
Splendid Road, The	Anna Q. Nilsson	Gotham Prod. (S. R.)	6800 feet	
Sporting Life	Special Cast	First National		
Stage Door Johnny	Raymond Griffith	Paramount	5709 feet	Sept. 26
Stein of the Royal Mounted		Pathe		
Stella Dallas		Vitagraph	6 reels	June 27
Stella Maris	Mary Philbin	United Artists		
Still Alarm, The	Chadwick-Russell	Universal		
Slen, Love and Listen	Larry Semon	Universal		
Strange Bedfellows		Metro-Goldwyn		
Streets of Sin		Fox		
Sunshine of Paradise Alley	Special Cast	Chadwick (S. R.)		
Super Speed	Reed Howes	Rayart (S. R.)		
Sweet Adeline	Charles Ray	Chadwick		
Tale of a Vanishing People		Tiffany (S. R.)	6800 feet	
Tattooed Countess, The	Pola Negri	Paramount		
Tearing Loose	Wally Wales	Weiss Bros. (S. R.) 4900 feet		June 13
Ten to Midnight		United Dist. Corp.		
That Man from Arizona	D.Kevier-W.Fairbanks	F. B. O.		
That Royle Girl	Kirwood-Dempster	Paramount		
This Woman	Special Cast	Fox		
Thoroughbred	George O'Brien	Fox		
Thoroughbred, The	Special Cast	Truart	5451 feet	Sept. 19
Three Bad Men	Special Cast	Fox		
Tony Runs Wild	Tom Mix	Fox		
Trailing Shadows	Edmund Lowe	Fox Film		
Travelin' Fast	Jack Perrin	Ambassador Pict. (S. R.)		
Travis Cops, The		Truart (S. R.)	5800 feet	
Twin Rider, The	Constance Talmadge	First National	6300 feet	
Two Blocks Away	Special Cast	Universal		
Two Soldiers, The	Mildred Davis	Universal		
Unguarded Hour, The	Milton Sills	Paramount		
Unknown Lover, The	Elsie Ferguson	First National		
Us and At 'Em	Jack Perrin	Vitagraph		
		Ambassador Pict. (S. R.)	5000 feet	
Vengeance of Durand, The	Irene Rich	Warner Brothers		
Viennese Medley		First National		
Volga Boatman, The		Prod. Dist. Corp.		
Wages for Wives	Special Cast	Fox		
Wandering Fires		William Collier, Jr.		
Wandering Footsteps	Special Cast	Ginsberg Dist. Corp.	8172 feet	
Warrior Gap	Wilson-Gerber	United Dist.		
We Moderns	Colleen Moore	First National	6900 feet	Aug. 22
What Happened to Jones	Reginald Denny	Universal		
What Will People Say		Metro-Goldwyn		
When His Love Grew Cold		F. B. O.		
When Husbands Flirt	Dorothy Revier	Columbia		
Where the Worst Begins		Truart (S. R.)	5800 feet	
Whispering Canyon		Ginsberg Dist. Corp.		
White Chief, The	Monte Blue	Warner Brothers		
White Mice	Jacqueline Logan	Sering D. Wilson (S. R.)		
Why Girls Go Back Home		Warner Brothers		
Why Women Love		First National		
Wild Girl		Truart (S. R.)	5800 feet	
Wild Justice	Peter the Great	United Artists	5 reels	Aug. 1
Wild Rollin'	Buck Jones	Fox		
Wide Open	Dick Jones	Sunset Prod. (S. R.)		
Wild West	Mulhall-Ferguson	Pathe		
Winning of Barbara Worth		Principal Pict. (S. R.)		
Wise Guy, The	Lefty Flynn	F. B. O.		
With Kit Carson Over the Great Divide		Sunset Prod. (S. R.)		
Wives for Rent		Universal		
Womanhandled	Richard Dix	Paramount		
Women		Banner Prod. (S. R.)		
Women and Wives		Metro-Goldwyn		
World's Illusion, The		Metro-Goldwyn		
World Woman, The	Special Cast	B. P. Schulberg (S. R.)		
Wreckage		Ginsberg Dist. Corp.		
Wrong Coat, The		Tiffany (S. R.)	6500 feet	
Yankee Senor, The	Tom Mix	Fox		
Yoke, The		Warner Brothers		
You Can't Live on Love	Reginald Denny	Universal		

Watch For October Issue of
BOOKING GUIDE
Containing Complete Information on Feature and Short Subjects

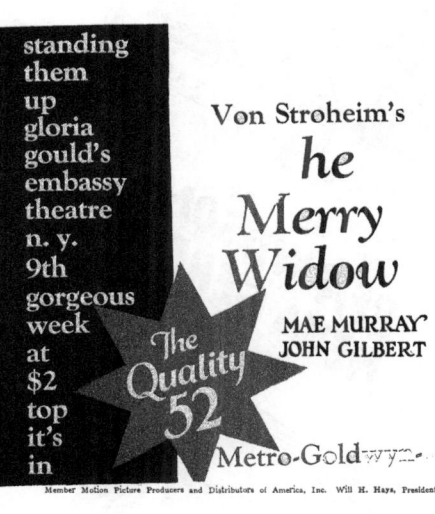

Guaranteed Pictures, Inc.
Presents

"WARRIOR GAP"

Book by GEN. CHARLES KING, U.S.A.

Starring

BEN WILSON & NEVA GERBER

A Ben Wilson Production

Distributed by Clifford S. Elfelt *through*

DAVIS DISTRIBUTING DIVISION, Inc.
J. Charles Davis, II, President
218 West 42nd Street · · · · New York, N. Y.

Released Thru **VITAL EXCHANGES, Inc.**
David R. Hochreich, President

in Albany, Buffalo, Cincinnati, Cleveland, Indianapolis, Milwaukee, Philadelphia, Pittsburgh and Canada.
Also ASTOR PRODUCTIONS, Boston; GREIVER PRODUCTIONS, Chicago; KERMAN FILMS, Inc., New York City

A Paramount Picture

SAN FRANCISCO, Cal.; Manitowoc, Wis.; and Marion, Ind., are just three of the many towns where "The Pony Express" has smashed all theatre records during the past two weeks. And all of these houses played "The Covered Wagon" and "The Ten Commandments" previously, too. This big special is the finest bargain exhibitors have been offered in years! A spectacular $2 road-show offered as a regular Greater Forty release!

— A —

JAMES CRUZE
PRODUCTION
WITH
BETTY COMPSON
RICARDO CORTEZ
ERNEST TORRENCE
WALLACE BEERY

BY HENRY JAMES FORMAN
AND WALTER WOODS

PRESENTED BY

ADOLPH ZUKOR AND JESSE L. LASKY

THE GREATEST of the GREATER FORTY are still to come

"BLESS my bright blue eyes, we have another of those pictures!" wires Bogart Rogers, general manager of Douglas MacLean Productions. And we'll say his b.b.e. don't deceive him! The man who made 'em chuckle in "The Hottentot", "Going Up", "Never Say Die" and the rest, will make 'em roar for joy in "7 Keys to Baldpate" — *his first for Paramount.*

DOUGLAS
MacLean

in

"7 KEYS TO BALDPATE"

George M. Cohan's greatest comedy

FROM THE NOVEL BY EARL DERR BIGGERS
DIRECTED BY FRED NEWMEYER

A Paramount Picture

THE
GREATEST
of the
GREATER
FORTY
are still to come

William de Mille's finest
since "Grumpy" is this
snappy picturization of the
year's-run New York stage
comedy success "New
Brooms".

with

BESSIE LOVE
NEIL HAMILTON
PHYLLIS HAVER

FROM THE PLAY BY
FRANK CRAVEN
SCREEN PLAY BY
**CLARA
BERANGER**

PRESENTED BY
ADOLPH ZUKOR
JESSE L. LASKY

William ᴬ de Mille
PRODUCTION

KINOGRAMS WINS THE
WORLD'S SERIES

As far as the news reels are concerned

Kinograms won every race to the screens of Pittsburgh and Washington during the world's series baseball games

Kinograms got out four specials --- *and was first in the theatres with all four*

Every special was packed full of news and pictorial values --- Kinograms has put over many a scoop,

But

THIS WAS A LANDSLIDE OF SCOOPS!!

They cost Kinograms a lot of money, *but not one extra cent to the exhibitor*

That's Kinograms' Service!

BOOK K I N O G R A M S
The News Reel Built Like a Newspaper

8,OOO Theatres Are Showing

A smashing record! With 8,000 theatres in the United States and Canada showing *Educational Pictures* this week, *Educational Pictures* set a mark that has seldom if ever been touched by any other program of pictures—the finest possible testimonial to the entertainment quality and box-office value of these great Short Subjects.

ducational Pictures This Week

Practically every one of America's Big Theatres is included in the great exchange city
houses named on these pages and in the
other key-city first-runs that have booked
Educational Pictures this week. Almost every
other theatre of any consequence in the land
is also on the list of bookings. No greater
indorsement could possibly be given to any
company's product.

STRAND
NEW YORK

EDUCATIONAL
FILM EXCHANGES, Inc.

E. W. Hammons
President

Member, Motion Picture Producers and
Distributors of America, Inc.
Will H. Hays, President.

"WHAT'S THE
WITH

(No. 457 Straight from the Shoulder Talk by Carl

What's The Matter With The Movies?

Nothing. Absolutely not a darned thing—**Provided You Get The Right Ones!**

If you get suggestive pictures and help to stir up censorship there's a lot the matter with the movies. If you get the all-star-no-story pictures it's your own fault. But—

If you get Reginald Denny in "Where Was I?" and "California Straight Ahead" and "What Happened to Jones", there will be **Nothing The Matter With Your Movies.**

If you get Hoot Gibson in "The Calgary Stampede", there will be **Nothing The Matter With Your Movies.**

If you get House Peters in "The Storm Breaker", there will be **Nothing The Matter With Your Movies.**

If you get Mary Philbin in "Stella Maris" (title to be changed) there will be **Nothing The Matter With Your Movies.**

If you get Louise Dresser in "The Goose Woman", there will be **Nothing The Matter With Your Movies.**

If you get Laura LaPlante in "The Teaser", there will be **Nothing The Matter With Your Movies.**

MATTER
THE MOVIES?"

aemmle, President of the Universal Pictures Corp.)

If you get Virginia Valli, Eugene O'Brien and Mary Alden in "Siege" there will be **Nothing The Matter With Your Movies.**

If you get Pat O'Malley and May McAv in "My Old Dutch" (title to be changed) there will be **Nothing The Matter With Your Movies.**

If you get Alice Joyce and Clive Brook in "The Home Maker" there will be **Nothing The Matter With Your Movies.**

If you get Bert Lytell and Marian Nixon in "Sporting Life" there will be **Nothing The Matter With Your Movies.**

If you get Helene Chadwick and William Russell in "The Still Alarm", there will be **Nothing The Matter With Your Movies.**

And so on, and on, and on with the whole Universal Second White List. It's white all through; it's sold on a white contract. This is what is putting Universal miles ahead of all others.

You don't have to apologize when you show Universal pictures. You'll never have to blush for shame, but you'll give your people every possible thrill and all possible "punch" and entertainment.

I am a Devil - I am
I am a Ghost - I am
I am the Greatest Scr

The Phanto

I am Breaking

A UNIVERS

the Country Over!

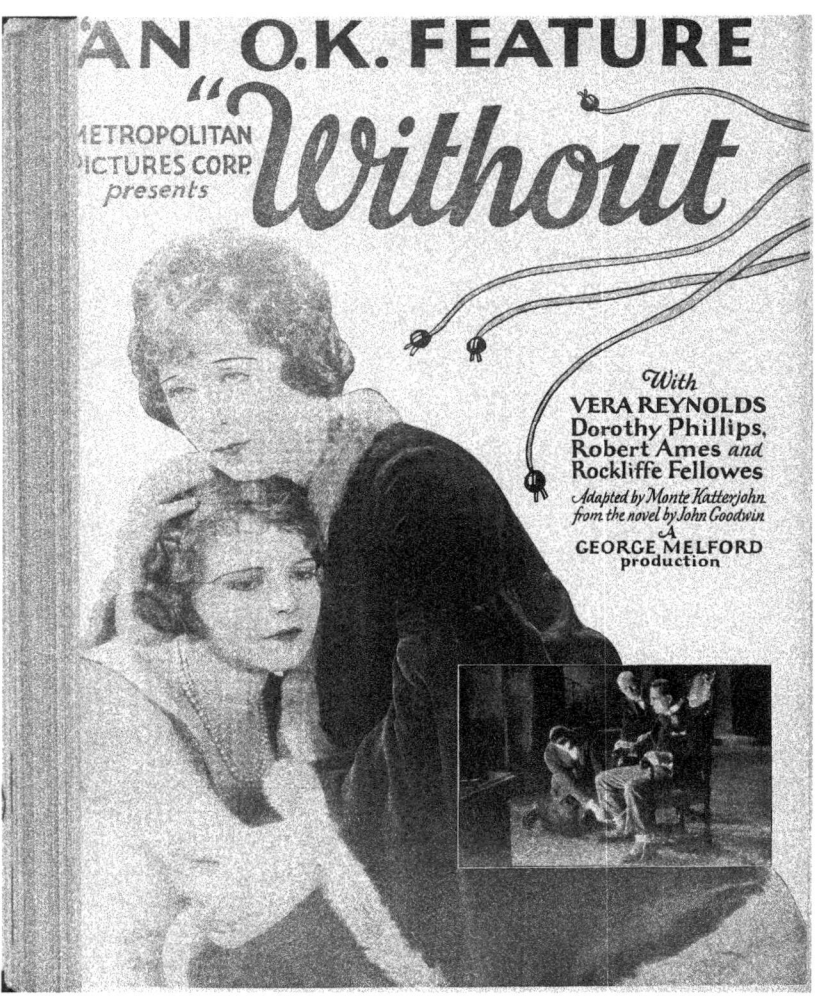

AN O.K. FEATURE

METROPOLITAN
PICTURES CORP.
presents

"*Without*

With
VERA REYNOLDS
Dorothy Phillips,
Robert Ames *and*
Rockliffe Fellowes

Adapted by Monte Katterjohn.
from the novel by John Goodwin.
A
GEORGE MELFORD
production

BET"
says VARIETY

"Mercy"

GOOD, honest Melodrama is the *BEST BOX OFFICE BET!* An exciting story—thrills—heart-throbs—and a happy ending—never fail to "get over" with an audience. "WITHOUT MERCY" has all these sure-fire ingredients— and then some! There are plots and intrigues, gripping dramatic moments a real romance—all culminating in a startling climax that will pull an audience right out of their seats.

"BOUND TO APPEAL" SAY REVIEWERS

Variety says: "Its well ordered production, competent direction and acting make it an okeh feature bet."

Film Daily says: "Dramatic offering that builds to good climax and includes varied forms of suspense. Very well acted and nicely directed."

Motion Pictures Today says: "It is bound to appeal to the critical audiences who weary of constant facsimiles and desire newness and freshness in a plot. * * * And it will also hold its appeal for the masses, in that it abounds with action and intrigue."

RELEASED BY
PRODUCERS DISTRIBUTING CORPORATION

F. C. MUNROE, President   RAYMOND PAWLEY, Vice-President and Treasurer   JOHN C. FLINN, Vice-President and General Manager

Member of Motion Picture Producers and Distributors of America, Inc.   Will H. Hays, President

THE KING OF
THRILL - BLA

The Idol of American Youth From

Presented By
Hunt Stromberg

THE real "American spirit" is the "spirit of the West." It is the spirit of "Young America"— virile, vibrant, adventurous and devil-may-care.

That's the spirit Harry Carey typifies on the screen — and that's why he's the idol of American youth — from eight to eighty.

Harry Carey, the screen's best loved cowboy, is famous for his broncho-bustin', square-shootin', reckless he-man type of characterizations that appeal to every healthy-minded movie fan. He is essentially the family favorite. Everybody, from seven-year-old Buddy to seventy-year-old Grandma, likes Carey. His pictures are clean, human and meaty with good old-fashioned thrills. The villain gets his just desserts and the hero wins the gal in Carey pictures.

An hour looking at a Carey picture is better than all the medicine in the world for that "tired feeling." Carey is the paprika in the movie bill-of-fare —he's the real "kick" in the screen cocktail.

TAKE A DOSE OF "DOC" CAREY'S WESTERNS
AND FORGET YOUR TROUBLES !

WESTERN ZERS

"Interpreter of the Eternal West"

8 to 80

HARRY CAREY

"THE NIGHT HAWK"
"THE LIGHTNING RIDER"
"TIGER THOMPSON"
"ROARING RAILS"
"THE FLAMING FORTIES"
"SOFT SHOES"
"BEYOND THE BORDER"
"SILENT SANDERSON"
"THE TEXAS TRAIL"
"THE BAD LANDS"
"THE PRAIRIE PIRATE"
"THE MAN FROM RED GULCH"

RELEASED BY
PRODUCERS DISTRIBUTING
CORPORATION

Member of Motion Picture Producers and Distributors of America, Inc.   Will H. Hays, President.

The Publicity Campaign

WILLIAM FOX

EAST

For sixty odd years the greatest of all love stories

EDMUND LOWE

ALMA RUBENS

LYDIA KNOTT

FRANK KEENAN

ERIC MAYNE

MARJORIE DAW

THE FIRST YEAR *with* Matt Moore
Frank Borzage *Production*

John Golden's Great Comedy Hit of Married Life

Fox Film Corporation.

Yes sir~

John Payette

Assistant General Manager,
CRANDALL CIRCUIT
Washington, D.C.

has bought

100% FOX
short subjects

he says~

"Without question Fox Comedies are the finest of their class. Never before has the public been offered such wonderful short subjects as those produced by Fox."

The man's right!

EARLE FOXE IN **VAN BIBBER** COMEDIES BY RICHARD HARDING DAVIS	THE MARRIED LIFE OF **HELEN AND WARREN** WITH HALLAM COOLEY-KATHRYN PERRY
O . HENRY COMEDIES	Imperial COMEDIES
FOX NEWS MIGHTIEST OF ALL	FOXVARIETIES THE WORLD WE LIVE IN

Are the best short subjects made

Fox Film Corporation.

Member Motion Picture Producers and Distributors of America, Inc. Will H. Hays, President.

ZIP go the records! "Go West" is coming. Chalk up a new score for the house! Buster knocks the old totals for a row of bank-deposits. "The Navigator" did the business. "Seven Chances" did the business. But wait 'till you count the gate on "Go West." And you can tell your audiences now that one of the funniest comedies ever made - bar none - is on its way to give them the treat of their lives. Go get the coin. Go get "Go West!"

BUSTER KEATON
in G WES

presented by   *directed by*
JOSEPH M. SCHENCK   BUSTER KEATON

Metro-Goldwyn-Mayer's

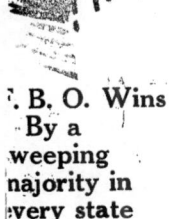

. B. O. Wins
By a
weeping
najority in
very state

12 Wonderful Chapters **2** Reels Each

of the highly popular

ADVENTURES OF MAZIE

Series Starring Cutie
ALBERTA VAUGHN
With Larry Kent—Al Cooke and Kit Guard

F. B. O. WINS

...u can't deny it - dispute it -

Have You Solved These Five Problems In Lighting Your Theatre?

You have five main problems to solve in planning your lighting and their effective solution means greater success to your theatre.

1. Lighting the front of your theatre to attract attention and dominate all surrounding displays.

2. Lighting your lobby to create an inviting atmosphere and to bring out your display announcements.

3. Lighting your foyer and lobby to enhance the decorative values of your furnishings.

4. Lighting your stage and auditorium to permit the play of color combinations and intensify gradations for effective stage presentations and musical accompaniments.

5. Special lighting touches here and there to bring out in relief any unusual architectural treatment and artistic features of your theatre.

These are problems that demand the attention of experts.

To all exhibitors who are interested in improving the lighting of their theatres Edison Lamp Works offers the free services of their staff of theatre lighting engineers.

These men will study your individual lighting requirements, make detailed recommendations and give you valuable information and advice pertaining to general lighting practice. Their services entail no obligation on your part.

Address your problems to the Lighting Service Department, Edison Lamp Works of General Electric Company, Harrison, New Jersey.

Supplementary to their advisory services our engineers have prepared a booklet on Theatre Lighting that is full of valuable information and suggestions.

A copy of this booklet will be sent to you free on request.

EDISON MAZDA LAMPS
A GENERAL ELECTRIC PRODUCT

MAIL THE ATTACHED COUPON

Publicity Department,
Edison Lamp Works
of General Electric Co.,
Harrison, N. J.
Please send me your free booklet
on theatre lighting.

NAME ....
THEATRE ....
ADDRESS ....

The Picture with the Double-

DRAMA

A woman horse – whipped by her own sister. An emotional scene never-to-be-forgotten

COMP
IRENE

Clive Brook Louise Fazenda
Pauline Garon Raymond McKee

Directed by
Alan Crosland

Story by Jay Gelzer
Scenario by **E. T. Lowe, Jr.**

Barrelled Appeal

WARNER BROS
Classics of the Screen

~ROMISE

RICH

A whole town wrecked by a
cyclone; 1000 people in a mad
dash for safety ~ ~ ~

THRILLS

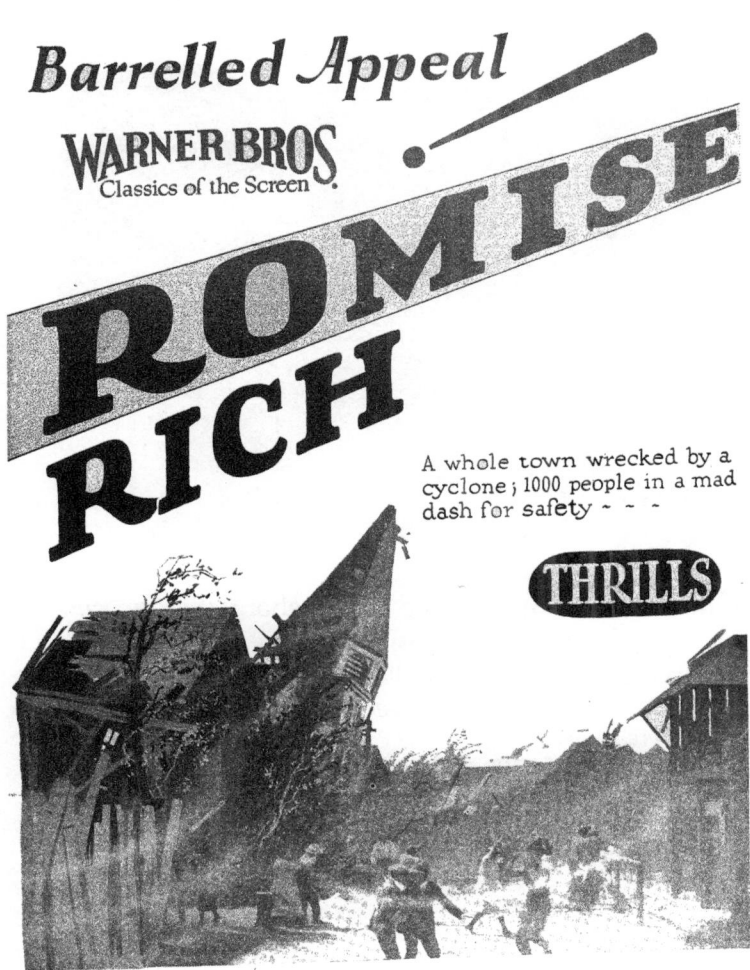

First National Pictures Inc.
presents
Sir Arthur Conan Doyle's
stupendous story

The
LOST
WORLD

By arrangement with
Watterson R. Rothacker
with
Bessie Love Lewis Stone
Wallace Beery Lloyd Hughes
Research and Technical Director
Willis H. O'Brien
Under the supervision of Earl Hudson

First
National
Pictures

One of the many *amazing* thrills about this *amazing* picture which are responsible for so many *amazing* reports from the "hard boiled" critics

A FEW OF WHICH WE REPRINT HERE . . . .

May Tinee in Chicago Tribune:
"Here's one that is different and a thriller, too. 'The Lost World' is something for you to see."

W. Ward Marsh in
Cleveland Plain Dealer:
". . . is an astounding photoplay."

Denver Post:
"No one should miss seeing 'The Lost World'."

Florence Lawrence in Los Angeles Examiner:
"No famed beauty or idol of the fans ever received greater attention than that bestowed by wondering and amazed crowds, as the parade of prehistoric animals marched across the screen."

Foreign Rights Controlled by
First National Pictures Inc.
383 Madison Avenue, New York

A First

Verne W. Bailey in
Portland Oregon Journal:

"No picture, in many months, has so broken away from the humdrum routine of 'just another movie' as has 'The Lost World' which is packing crowds this week into the Liberty like sardines in a sardine tin."

Detroit Free Press:

"To those who are looking for something new in the world, a picture of thrills and romance. 'The Lost World' will prove a 100 per cent picture. One of the most unusual pictures ever presented."

George Gerhard in
New York Eve. World:

"No words short of stupendous and marvelous will measure up to a description of its scenes."

Waco Texas Times Herald:

"You will acclaim it as the miracle motion picture of all time. The screen's greatest sensation to date and there may never be another to equal it."

Fairmont West Virginia Times:

" 'The Lost World' is here! And what a sensation it has created. It is an amazing picture."

Dayton Ohio Journal:

" 'The Lost World' marks an epoch in screen achievements. Rises to front ranks among the triumphs of screen achievements."

Peoria Ill. Journal:

" 'The Lost World'—a picture you'll never forget."

Philadelphia Evening Bulletin:

". . . is one of the most remarkable of all film achievements."

Picture

f America Inc.~Will Hays *President*

"CROWDED HOUSES PREVAILED"

from Morning Telegraph *Oct.*11*th*

JOHNNY HINES in "The LIVE WIRE" is by far the biggest laugh maker this star ever made. Another reason why FIRST NATIONAL'S "WINNER GROUP" leads in money-making pictures.

Adapted from "The Game of Light" by RICHARD WASHBURN CHILD—Directed by Charles Hines—Presented by C. C. Burr.

A First National Picture

Members of Motion Picture Producers and Distributors of America Inc.~Will Hays President

Motion Picture News

Vol. XXXII   ALBANY, N. Y., AND NEW YORK CITY, OCTOBER 31, 1925   No. 18

A New Department

"Theatre Management"

will be started in an early issue of

Motion Picture News

MOTION PICTURE NEWS *has long held the position of the industry's first-run trade paper. The creation of the "Theatre Management" department is an extension of the service given by this paper ever since its inception—service that is recognized as indispensable to better theatres everywhere.*

THIS department will be conducted by expert showmen. It will be practical in every sense of the word. It will contain material never before printed in a motion picture trade paper.

The inauguration of the "Theatre Management" department is in recognition of the fact that exhibition is rapidly growing in importance as a profession. The day of hit-or-miss methods in conducting the theatre is over. Theatre operation is now a definite business and, as such, it deserves a definite trade paper service along new lines.

Methods that have proved successful; new ideas from many sources; and, most important of all, the promotion of the theatre as a business institution second in importance to none—will be set forth in this regular weekly department of MOTION PICTURE NEWS.

The theatre manager is in the key-position in the industry. His success in the operation of the individual house—no matter how large the chain—is the determining factor in the whole business life of the motion picture.

Watch for Further Announcements

OUR FILMS

An Editorial

THE anti-American motion picture agitation in Europe, growing for some time, seems to be coming to a head. We are indebted to Mr. Ernest Fredman, editor of the British trade organ—*The Film Renter and Moving Picture News*—for an advance proof of his current editorial in which he says that the Americans have "only themselves to blame" for the Kontingent which he sees as the probable culmination of the "virulent campaign" about to be launched by the British lay press.

Mr. Fredman has, as he says, always championed in his country the American producer and distributor. He now says:

"Their policy in this country has been one of rapacious greed, and it is reaping its just reward. There has never been shown at any time the slightest sympathy towards the British film producing companies by any American distributing concern . . . All that we have had *ad nauseam* for the past five years is a succession of utterances from the leaders of the American industry mainly concerned with expressions of good will and constantly reiterated desires to take our pictures." Mr. Fredman deplores the inactivity of Will Hays and the lack of vision and business acumen of our leaders in general. Five years ago, he believes, something could have been done—namely, the marketing here of British pictures. Today, for lack of any reciprocity, the Kontingent System looms.

* * *

WELL, let us see.

To begin with, it is something of a relief to have the British Trade Press take off its gloves and talk bluntly. Nothing can be gained by smoothing over the question. And it is a momentous one—exceedingly so.

We disagree with Mr. Fredman as to the insincere utterances of Americans abroad. We, ourselves, have not been insincere in hoping that British pictures would be shown in American theatres. We do, however, agree that there has been a lack of vision in the matter. But that has been characteristic of the American film industry in many large respects—still is. It is too highly competitive, too infernally busy to see clearly its larger relations. What could have been done to build reciprocal film relations between America and Europe—done some years ago, we do not at the moment know. But at least we made no effort. That is true.

* * *

BUT to turn to the present situation.

First of all: we do not for the moment believe that Great Britain will impose a Kontingent upon American films.

For the simple reason that such a system is uneconomic—to an utter and preposterous degree.

A Kontingent is a radical and artificial trade barrier. Literally, the long arm of a government obtrudes in a crisis, and for radical reasons in radical times, turns upside down the good sound economic basis upon which all trade is, and only can be, established.

Let us not fool ourselves about a Kontingent. There is one in Germany today. It is controlled by the Ufa which in turn is owned by the Deutches Bank, which in turn is owned by the German government. If the latter—the German government—is determined to build up a film monopoly—at any cost, that is the German government's privilege. And its consequences upon German trade and Germany's financial and commercial relations with other countries remain to be seen. But we would not cite it as a just and successful and economic measure operating in the interests of mutual trade relations and an international trade balance.

Suppose the United States were to put a Kontingent system upon German made toys.

A Kontingent is not a tariff restriction. Far from it. That is quite another matter. Even so, a free trade country hesitates a long time before excepting certain goods for tariff protection. But what can be said of a Kontingent—an artificial trade barrier? Great Britain is very largely an exporting nation. We understand that at least three quarters of her annual business turnover is in export. Would she risk a trade war—a vast trade war, with a film Kontingent? We judge not. We can readily understand why Great Britain wants British pictures in the theatres of the world; but we do not for an instant believe that the agitation against American films in the British lay and trade press represents the mind of the British government when the agitation advocates the establishment of a Kontingent.

* * *

NOW as to the matter of fairness. We are accused of a lack of sympathy toward British production interests.

Let us be fair about this matter of fairness in trade. Does sympathy exist at all with any kind of goods involved in international trade relations? Are they not governed altogether by economic laws, by the status of supply and demand? In other words, by straight business consideration?

Take the rubber situation. The American film industry is a paltry affair as compared with the British rubber monopoly. The United States, I believe, uses about 75 per cent. of the world's crop of crude rubber. Last year our manufacturers paid as low as 20 cents a pound to the British control. This year the price fluctuates as high as $1.20, with the result that this country will send several hundred millions of dollars to Great Britain above last year's rubber bill. It is wrong, possibly, to call this "rapacious greed." But at least, no sympathy is given nor asked for. I note that one American manufacturer proposes to get his rubber in Liberia. That sounds like commendable enterprise.

AND EUROPE

By William A. Johnston

to say that British pictures are not as good as American? I do not care to raise the question here. So I make the amendment: "good for the American market."

* * *

A S a matter of fact, is there any British sympathy toward American goods? I spent a year in London as an advertising man, and saw many and many an American salesman go home baffled and beaten by the opposition to his goods—or to his sales methods. I saw one American product go finally over the top, but only because a large and well conducted advertising campaign to the public at length convinced the British housekeeper to insist that the British dealer stock up with this American made article. If an American manufacturer today tried to replace Bovril with an article of American make, he certainly could hope for no success unless he matched the other not merely in quality but with very large resources, chief among them a great advertising campaign to the trade and public.

Which brings us to the root of the matter—the public: the British public and the American public.

How can the American distributor force British films upon the American public, if the American public prefers American films? (In this connection, it is to be noted that the non-advertised American film cannot compete over here with those well advertised to the public.)

And why do 4,000 British picture theatres thrive—we hear they do thrive—on American pictures, if the latter are so unpopular with the British public as some British newspapers assert?

* * *

W E are not minded to present a brief here for American pictures. In the blind hurry of our industry here many—too many pictures are turned out without regard or respect to foreign taste, traditions, etc. They often offend; and there is no excuse for this. It is to be said, however, that pains are now being taken to remedy this fault, and possibly and shortly the day will come when no one can claim that our films give any offence to foreign audiences. It is also to be said that the present day American studio resources are such that there is no excuse for a bad picture and, already, if the resources do slip, the companies can and do throw these mistakes into the scrap heap (one American company this year scrapped eight productions, the total cost of which was well over a million dollars; it proved a good business move.)

But we do have a lot of mediocre product—too much. This market does not want it any more than the British market wants it. I do not defend the product, but I do point out that the only way these pictures can be profitably marketed is through block sales along with better product. Does Great Britain expect the American distributor to shelve his own mediocre merchandise to make way for pictures certainly no better—or at least no better for our American market?

Now I realize that this latter appraisal of British pictures is apt to raise a storm of protest. Who is

L ET us see what British pictures have done here —by the box-office reports. I have before me a list of twelve distributed here by our National Distributors (including United Artists and Metro-Goldwyn) since 1921. Only one shows box-office success—"Woman to Woman," featuring Betty Compson. "The Bohemian Girl" did fairly well. But, if these pictures had been made in America (with the same casts and direction) by independent producers, I question if they would have been as fortunate in finding national distribution.

We make no effort here to foster our own independent producers (I mean, of course, producers who do not own a national distributing machine). They have a tough time with our industrial machine. Scores of them—able and well financed, have come and gone in the past ten years. Right now they outnumber the British producers; they have, at call, the best of American studio facilities; they use our popular players. Yet, aside from those who use the State Rights market—and then back their wares for all they are worth, and aside from a very, very few good enough to land a contract with a big distributor, they take the chance of either no distribution at all or else one almost certain not to return negative cost. Famous Players, Fox, Metro-Goldwyn, Universal, Warners make the pictures they distribute. United Artists include only big stars and producers. First National alone has kept the door open to the best efforts of the independent producers; and of late this firm, too, has entered heavily into production.

Perhaps this is all wrong; without vision, business acumen, liberality, sympathy. Granted: but at least the blow—the business blow, has fallen most heavily by far upon the American producer, not upon the European. He is the one who has felt the grinding of the wheels of industrial development.

* * *

I N conclusion:
The British film industry, at a rough guess, is composed 90 per cent. of exhibitors, seven per cent. of renters, three per cent. of producers. The 90 per cent. part of the British market has a huge investment in brick and mortar which, in turn, has been rendered profitable by the 90 per cent. booking of American pictures. These pictures helped earn the theatre profits. And these pictures, in turn, were forthcoming from the highly speculative investment of millions upon millions of American capital. This industry is young. Its tremendous stride, its hold upon the world public today, came straight from American producing enterprise—and very little elsewhere. Now the three per cent. of the British industry ask the government to enact restrictive measures against the importation of American pictures for 4,000 British theatres.

(Continued on next page)

MOTION PICTVRE
October 31   Vol. XXXII
1925   **NEWS**   No. 18

Founded in September 1913

Publication Office: Lyon Block, Albany, N. Y.

Editorial and General Offices: Branch Offices:
729 7th Ave., New York City   845 S. Wabash Ave., Chicago, Ill.
                              Room 616 Security Bldg., Hollywood,
                                                        Calif.

Speaking Editorially

THE sales map is being charted today as never before. Distribution heads in New York are really the commanders of field armies. They do not confine themselves to mere staff work but go out, at frequent intervals, into the trenches. Talk with one of these commanders and you gain a lot of information—in detail—about film conditions in this city and that—all interesting and important, too. Which reminds us of a chat this week with Colvin Brown, sales generalissimo for F. B. O. Facts, figures and conditions at his finger-tips; direct shooting at the mark—and a very clear analysis of the field as it actually is, with particular application to F. B. O., of course—featured his comment.

* * *

AMONG the coming events marked on our calendar is the Fifteenth Anniversary Dinner of Pathe News to be held at the Hotel Plaza, New York, in November. Vice-President Dawes will be the guest of honor, and there will be a large attendance from official Washington. Looks like a redletter evening in which the whole industry will participate with great interest and pleasure.

* * *

HARRY WARNER makes some pointed remarks elsewhere in this issue on the subject of too much star-play and not enough team-play in the studios on the part of stars and directors. He comes right out with a lot of things. A sensational statement, in a way; sensational and timely.

* * *

SECRETARY MELLON advocates retaining the tax on theatre admissions. This is rather a surprise, as it had been understood that the Secretary was in favor of abolishing all the nuisance taxes. There is strong sentiment in Congress, however, for repeal of these taxes. Representative Tilson, of Connecticut, Republican Leader of the House, is for repeal, as noted exclusively in a recent issue.

* * *

TO THE imposing list of picture palaces has been added the Famous Players-Balaban & Katz theatre in Boston—the Metropolitan, which opened recently. One of the great houses of the country, it is the first to come conspicuously under the new Paramount-B. & K. arrangement and, for that reason, the premiere has a double interest. A large party of executives and others went from New York to attend. Incidentally, the Metropolitan puts on an elaborate revue and pageant staged by John Murray Anderson, an expert in this line. Theatre and per-

formance are topnotch in every respect. Surely, we have come a long way from the day of the store-show on the side-street.

* * *

LUNCHEONS in honor of the great of the picture industry are commonplace incidents in the lives of trade paper scribes, and speeches by those who really have a right to talk, are no longer novelties.

But we listened to Ernst Lubitsch as the honor guest at a luncheon given at the Lane Park by Warner Brothers, last Friday, with deep interest.

Mr. Lubitsch, responding to an invitation by Toastmaster Nathan Burkan, did not launch into high-flown rhetoric about his future plans or explain in detail his ideas concerning picture-making.

He just thanked the assembled guests for being present and promised to make the best pictures he knew how. Somehow the sincerity of the speaker, rather than the words spoken, made you feel that Lubitsch's "good as he knew how" will be quite enough.

It was a sensible speech and an honest one. It boosted this eminent director's stock with us a lot, and we've thought mighty well of him ever since he became a factor in American production.

* * *

Our Films in Europe
By *William A. Johnston*
(Continued from preceding page)

It is our opinion that some very clear thinking and weighing of facts should be done on this very large economic situation—done with vision, impartiality and business acumen, and done by the trade on each side of the water, not forgetting by any means the British exhibitor.

October 31, 1925   MOTION PICTURE NEWS   Vol. XXXII, No. 18
Published weekly by Motion Picture News, Inc., William A. Johnston, President; E. Kendall Gillett, Vice-President; William A. Johnston, Editor; J. S. Dickerson, Associate Editor; Oscar Cooper, Managing Editor; Fred J. Beecroft, Advertising Manager; L. H. Mason, Chicago Representative; William McCormack, Los Angeles Representative. Subscription price, $3 per year, post paid in United States, Mexico, Hawaii, Porto Rico, Philippine Islands and some other countries; Canada, $5; foreign, $10.00. Copyright 1925, by Motion Picture News, Inc., in the United States and Great Britain. Title registered in the United States Patent Office and foreign countries. Western Union cable address is "Pickfews," New York. Entered as second-class matter January 31st, 1924, at the postoffice, Albany, N. Y., under the Act of March 3, 1879.

For eleven years now Edwin Carewe (right), producer-director for First National, and Richard A. Rowland, general manager, have been associated.

PICTURES
AND
PEOPLE

BROADWAY PRESENTS—

AMONG the new films on Broadway this week, Annie Rooney, with Mary Pickford, United Artists, at the Mark Strand; "The Vanishing American," Paramount's great Indian epic, at the Criterion, and the same company's "Flower of Night," starring Pola Negri, at the Rivoli; occupy front rank as entertainment factors.

Miss Pickford returns to the sort of role that made her famous in a fine portrayal of a twelve-year old youngster on New York's East Side, leader of a kid gang. No hint of maturity detracts from the childish grace of her performance. Annie Rooney shines forth as a genuine slum product, ready for fight or sacrifice, mischievious and tender by turns, but always a real kid. The story combines comedy, melodrama and pathos, hokum stuff if you like, but just the sort of picture which should have a tremendous appeal to the masses, with Our Mary as they used to know her.

"The Vanishing American" registers as an extraordinarily colorful and historically vivid spectacle, with a well sustained note of human interest sounding through the production. It establishes a strong plea for the Red Man, its scenic beauty is marvelous, and the romantic angle well taken care of. From the time of the cliff dwellers up to the present the picture sweeps on in a succession of thrilling sequences, shown against magnificent backgrounds, a miracle of fine camera technique. The acting is at all times excellent, with the work of Lois Wilson, Richard Wilson, Richard Dix, Noah Beery and Malcolm McGregor standing out prominently.

Pola Negri in "Flower of Night" gives a wonderfully fine dramatic performance in the leading role. The part of the young Spanish-Mexican girl is exactly suited to the star's tempestuous, forceful style of acting, she is passionate and wistfully appealing, according as the situation demands, and never strikes a false or jarring chord

The first photo of Gilda Gray as she will appear in "Aloma of the South Seas" (Paramount), her first starring picture under her contract with that company.

Rex Lease, who plays a leading role in "The Last Edition" (F. B. O.), Emory Johnson's story of newspaper life, and is said to show considerable promise.

Another of Universal's See America First beauty contest winners, Dorothy Gulliver of Salt Lake City, who will be sent to Universal City on a six months' contract.

Mary Astor and Jockey Fred Steele, during the filming of scenes for "The Scarlet Saint" (First National) at the famed Empire race track recently.

The snappiest Hula dance we've seen to date is that furnished here by Bonnie Barrett, in "Baby Be Good," an Educational-Juvenile comedy. Bonnie, at the ripe age of four, has nearly this many years of screen experience behind her, and is a pianist, diver, dancer, etc., or what have you?

Jeanie Macpherson, scenarist for Cecil B. De Mille, who is in New York for a conference with officials of Producers Distributing corporation on stories.

Samuel Goldwyn, now producing for United Artists, and his wife, formerly Frances Howard, were seen off by a distinguished crew at the station on their recent departure for New York, including George Fitzmaurice, Marion Davies and Henry King.

throughout the feature. As a matter of fact, Miss Negri is the entire show, in a sense, for the story, which deals with the stormy days in California when the Vigilantes ruled, while colorful and alive with thrills, would lose fifty-per cent of its drawing power with the clever Polish actress out of the cast. Especial attention has been paid to correct detail regarding th ecostume and manners of the period and the scenes depicting Old San Francisco are remarkably well handled.

BUCK WINS FRESH LAURELS

AT a recent Fox projection room showing the reviewers were given a decided surprise, when Buck Jones, as the hero of "Lazybones" won fresh screen laurels by giving a finely sympathetic portrayal of a small-town youth, an entirely different sort of role from any in which he has previously appeared. We are used to Buck as a dare-devil rider, handy with a gun and ever performing deeds of valor, but this performance opened up a vista of new ideas concerning the star's talents. It establishes him as an actor of rare versatility, and one can expect great things from him in the future.

The picture, with its splendidly developed rural atmosphere proved a real knockout. Clean, wholesome sentiment, with the self-sacrifice angle prominent, was constantly in evidence. There was just one

Ernst Lubitsch, Warner Bros. director, and Mrs. Lubitsch, taken in front of the Executive office in Washington, D. C., just after they had been received by President Calvin Coolidge. (Henry Miller photo).

thrill, when Lazybones, then a soldier in the A. E. F., falls asleep and awakens suddenly to take a hand in repulsing a Hun attack. You got a glimpse of the old fighting Buck on that occasion, but the narrative switched quickly back to the even tenor of life in the hero's home-town. A film with undeniable audience appeal, the admirers of Buck Jones will surely respond favorably to the star's impressive work amid heretofore unfamiliar surroundings.

PARAMOUNT PEPPERS PERFORM

THE Belvedere room at the Hotel Astor, New York, was the setting for a peppy occasion on Wednesday night, when more than four hundred members (note the social significance of that "four hundred") of the Paramount Pep Club foregathered for the installation in office of Palmer Hall Stilson as president and Vincent Trotta as vice-president.

A well deserved tribute was paid to Harold B. Franklin when the club presented the director of Paramount theatres with a silver token signifying his appointment as honorary vice-president of the Pep Club. The only others on whom this has been bestowed are Jesse L. Lasky, Sidney R. Kent, Elek J. Ludvigh and Emil E. Shauer.

Arthur J. Dunne is the treasurer of the club, and Sally McLoughlin, secretary.

ADOLPH ZUKOR, II

EUGENE J. ZUKOR is wearing an unusually cheery expression these days around the 485 Fifth Avenue offices, thanks to the arrival on October 9 at his home of a son, who will carry the proud name of Adolph Zukor, 2nd. This, coupled with the fact that both Mrs. Zukor and the baby are doing exceedingly well, is being made the subject of numerous congratulations, in which the NEWS is glad to join.

Members of the trade, fan and daily press grouped about Allene Ray and Walter Miller at the Pathe "Green Archer" studio party, at which Miss Ray was crowned Queen of Serials.

EMORY ROLLS HIS OWN

PUBLICITY men are forever bewailing the fact that they have difficulty in obtaining co-operation from the director in such all-important matters as the shooting of proper stills, the preparation of special trailers, and so on, and not always without foundation. The director is not entirely to be blamed, since he is given a schedule of time and cost to which he must adhere, and he is limited in the co-operation which he can afford to give.

Nevertheless, it is those stills, trailers, and other publicity materials which are going to be the basis of selling his picture to the public, and it would seem as if a middle ground could be found that would benefit both the director and the publicity man.

One director who keenly appreciates this is Emory Johnson, who has just completed "The Last Edition" for Film Booking Offices, in proof of which it can be said that he is now personally preparing the trailer on this picture. He believes that this is time well spent in behalf of the exhibitor who books the picture, which it certainly should be.

SOMETHING NEW IN AUTHORS

MICHAEL ARLEN, the author, left New York on Friday for an indefinite stay in Hollywood, where he is to write original screen stories for Paramount. That, in itself, is not unique—but the statement given out by Arlen before leaving is nothing if not so.

"I realize," he said, "that the screen is a form of art apart from the arts of the stage and the printed word. I have consented to an adaptation of one of my stories, 'An Ace of Cads,' taken from my volume 'Mayfair.' But that is as far as I am willing to go now. I want to learn the rudiments of how pictures are made before I will attempt to write an original screen story. I want to say frankly, that if after being out there for some time I feel I cannot produce an original story fitted to the needs of the movies, I will long hesitate before attempting it."

Bravo, bravissimo, Mr. Arlen!

John L. Johnston assures us that this is the first time the entire Flugrath familly has appeared in one photo, the occasion being Viola (Dana)'s departure for New York to appear in Marshall Neilan-Producers Dist. Corp. picture; included are: Viola, Shirley Mason, sister Edna, their father and his bride, and Mabel Taliaferro, their old chum.

AN EDUCATIONAL TRIUMPH

A SPECIAL showing of four new releases on the Educational Pictures fall program was held Wednesday afternoon October 14. The presentation was arranged by President E. W. Hammons, and he certainly managed to lure as critical an audience as ever assembled in a projection room to the Wurlitzer Auditorium. There were present members of Will Hays' Public Relations group; of the Federation of Women's Clubs, reformers, clergymen, and representatives from the New York trade journals, dailies and fan magazines. When a string of comedy subjects can bring continuous and hearty laughter from a crowd consisting of such widely varying elements there can be scant doubt as to the high quality of the material offered. In this case the program stood the test and finished with flying colors. It included a "Felix the Cat trips through Toyland," Cartoon, by Pat Sullivan; Lloyd Hamilton in "The Movies"; "Wild Beasts of Borneo," a two-reel adventure special; and the first of the Lupino Lane comedy series, "Maid In Morocco."

All sure-fire mirth provokers; Our old friend Felix the Cat was never in better form, Lloyd Hamilton immense in a snappy burlesque of pictures in the making; and the scenes showing a camera party operating in the Borneo jungles, with occasional captures of pythons, bears, etc., were wonders of realism and suspense, all the more interesting because one knew them to be the genuine thing.

The noted British star, Lupino Lane, scored a decided hit in the screamingly funny melodramatic burlesque "Maid In Morocco," where as a gallant hero he outwits his dusky enemies, performs acrobatics extraordinary and saves the girl of his heart from the black potentate who would fain make her a harem ornament. Mr. Lane's pantomime is excellent, and in every way he lived up to the reputation he has made as one of England's foremost comedians.

Before the program started Mr. Hammons made a short, but very much to the point speech in which he stated that the object of the presentation was to call attention to the excellence of the comedies, novelties and specials being released by Educational as its contribu-

Theodore D. Robinson, assistant Secretary of the Navy, recently visited the Metro-Goldwyn-Mayer studios where "The Midshipman" was being completed. Left to right: Director Christy Cabanne, Kathleen Key, Mr. Robinson and Director Fred Niblo.

tion to a season of Greater Short Subjects for 1925—1926, just now getting under way. Also, that the briefer pictures are to-day playing a bigger part in film entertainment than they ever have done, since the advent of the multiple-reel feature.

A better selection of subjects in support of his remarks could not have been made, and the enthusiastic applause which greeted him at the close of the entertainment marked the affair as a real triumph for Educational-Film Exchanges, Inc.

CAN THIS BE?

CHANGING the titles of plays and books when they reach the screen has been made the subject of so many quips and jokes that it no longer elicits a smile. And, to be sure, the practice has been carried to extremes on more than one occasion.

Which makes all the more remarkable the fact that the first four Metropolitan productions will all reach the screen under their original titles—"Without Mercy," "Simon, the Jester," "Rocking Moon" and "Steel Preferred." William Sistrom believes that a story should be released as titled by the author.

ANOTHER EUROPEAN VOYAGER

HERMAN WOBBER, who has done yeoman service for Famous Players-Lasky as San Francisco district manager, was given a bon voyage luncheon by executives and department heads at the Hotel Roosevelt, New York City, on Thursday. He was to sail Saturday for a vacation in Europe.

Senor M. de Miguel, leading Spanish producer and distributor (at right), visits the office of Motion Picture News and talks over European conditions with William A. Johnston, the editor.

Mlle. Arlette Marchal, one of the most beautiful actresses of France, who appeared in "Madame Sans-Gene," and who arrived to join the Paramount stock company this week.

Left, A. M. Botsford, who resigned recently as advertising manager of Famous Players-Lasky to head the advertising department of the corporation to be formed for the operation of that company's theatres; and right, Russell Holman, formerly his aide, who succeeds him at Famous.

There's no need to ask what company Joyce Compton works for. Who could resist looking at the First National trademark in such a setting?

MARMONT IN RUSH ACT

PROBABLY the busiest morning of Percy Marmont's life was that of October 6. As he stepped from the 20th Century, he was notified by a Paramount official that he was scheduled to sail the briny main for Porto Rico at noon.

Marmont whirled into a buzz of activity that would have shamed a stunt star. Having retrieved his trunks, he hustled into the customs house for a passport, he being an English citizen, and Porto Rico a possession of the United States. Then to the boat, where forty-six members of the company which will make "Aloma of the South Seas," stood on deck and cheered as the star and his wife hit the gang plank just before it was hauled in.

THE ASTERISK QUINTETTE

FIVE golden stars were sprinkled over the film firmament (as a subtitle writer might say) by the National Board of Review for the week ending October 17. Two features and three short subjects were on the list of recommended films. (Have you noticed, by the way, how many of the short subjects are being asterisked? It speaks well for the rising standards in this field.)

The features starred were First National's "The Dark Angel," produced by Samuel Goldwyn, and the Paramount picture, "Flower of the Night." The short subjects included two Fox comedies, "Strong for Love" and "The Wrestler," and one Pathe release, Pathe Review No. 43.

A new camera study of Greta Garbo, the Scandinavian screen star who has been signed by Metro-Goldwyn-Mayer to appear under the direction of Mauritz Stiller.

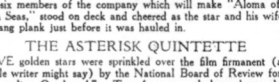

You'd have to take several good looks at this photo to realize that it is none other than Rod La Rocque in his makeup for "Braveheart" (Producers Dist. Corp.)

Among the 22 children of the film colony who helped celebrate the first birthday of Leatrice Joy, II, were the members of the Pathe-Roach "Our Gang."

We've run other photos of girl's knees being decorated, but lovely Helen Marlowe is ample excuse for using another. Cliff Bowes is the artist, and they appear in Educational-Cameo comedies.

Lew Cody gives his impression of Little Eva after her ascent, between scenes of "Free Lips" (Metro-Goldwyn-Mayer), his latest production.

Skouras Bros. Houses In Joint Deal

Goldman-Skouras Operation of Four: F. P.-L. May Acquire
Interest in Others; Many Circuit Moves Indicated

DEALS and rumors of deals concerning circuit expansion continued to fill the air this week, involving Famous Players-Lasky and Balaban & Katz, Skouras Brothers, the Saenger Amusement Company, the Cooper interests, Finkelstein & Ruben, the Shea Amusement Company, the Comerford circuit, the Mark Strand corporation, and other unnamed interests in Denver and middle-western points.

One of the principal developments of the week was the indication that Famous Players-Lasky and Skouras Brothers would enter into an agreement by which the Missouri theatre and the new Ambassador theatre now under construction in St. Louis will become Paramount first run houses under the management of Skouras Brothers, and definite announcement that the Grand Central, West End Lyric and Lyric Skydome, also owned by Skouras Brothers, and the William Goldman King's theatre, would pass into the hands of a corporation jointly owned by Goldman and Skouras Brothers.

The operating agreement covering the Skouras and Goldman deal was filed with Recorder of Deeds Tamme in St. Louis late Tuesday. A new corporation will operate the four houses. Spyros and Chas. Skouras will hold 55 per cent of the 1,000 shares of no par value stock and Goldman 45 per cent. The agreement is effective within thirty days after completion and opening of the Ambassador theatre being erected by Skouras Brothers and runs for ten years. It was dated March 18, 1925, but was held up pending outcome of a series of deals involving purchase by Skouras Brothers of a block of St. Louis Amusement Company stock held by Harry Koplar and the settlement of Goldman's suit against Koplar and the Metropolitan Theatre Corporation and others.

It also provides that if the Grand Central is leased to Universal Pictures Corporation under arrangements heretofore made Goldman shall receive 50 per cent of profits under such lease. He will be paid $12,500 annually and Skouras Brothers $8,750 each for managing the four theatres.

Official announcement that Skouras Brothers enterprises and Famous Players-Lasky Corporation have perfected an arrangement whereby the Missouri theatre and the new Ambassador theatre will become Paramount first-run houses under the management of Skouras Brothers is anticipated in St. Lou's film circles.

From a most reliable source it was learned that the papers for such a deal are now in the hands of attorneys for final inspection and it is rumored that the signatures needed to make the deal binding will be placed on the dotted l'ne within a week.

It has been impossible for obvious reasons to obtain official confirmation of the deal involving the Missouri and Ambassador theatres.

Spyros Skouras and Charles Skouras, president and first vice-president of Skouras Brothers Enterprises returned from New York on Friday evening, October 16. While in New York, Spyros Skouras denied that Famous Players or Balaban & Katz were negotiating for the purchase and control of all the Skouras Brothers houses, including

Stanley Company Not to File Brief

NO brief will be filed by the Stanley Company of America in connection with the demand of the Government's attorneys through the Federal Trade Commission that the company's exhibiting activities be divorced from its functions as a booking organization. This is the information forthcoming from Wolf, Patterson, Block and Schorr, attorneys for the Stanley Company.

The Stanley Company, with other defendants has been charged with operating in violation of the Sherman Anti-Trust Law. October 10th has been set as the date for the hearing. Famous Players have already separated their exhibiting activities from their producing and distributing operations. Attorneys for Famous and other co-defendants were allowed twenty days in which to reply to the complaint.

the St. Louis Amusement Company string of high-class neighborhood houses.

Skouras pointed out that Skouras Brothers Enterprises hold the First National franchise for the St. Louis territory and having many millions of dollars invested in their houses would entertain no proposition to sell out.

From an inside source it was learned that the first-run arrangement involving the Missouri and Ambassador will in no way affect the St. Louis Amusement Company chain.

Buffalo was another "storm center" during the week, with rumors of new houses and the entrance of Famous Players and Balaban & Katz into the field. Buffalo newspapers received a telegram from the New York offices of the Paramount theatre department stating that arrangements had been completed for the building of a house at 622-36 Main street, known as the Root property, which is owned by the McNaughton Realty company, which is headed by Michael Shea. While many doubt that such a house will be built almost next door to the new Shea Buffalo $2,000,000 house, now in the course of construction, it is understood that if such a move is made it will be in association with the Shea Amusement company. It can be stated, however, that the proposition is still in the negotiation stage.

It is possible, however, that there may be a new theatre near the Shea house and it is understood that plans are all set for the Comerford-Fox interests to place a vaudeville-picture house in the new business building to be erected at 606-614 Main street by Joseph and D. H. Coplon, work on which will start in February. This site is right at the corner of Main and Chippewa streets and between Shea's Hippodrome and the new Shea house. There has been talk of Comerford and Fox getting together on a Buffalo house for several months. Difficulty in placing first runs is believed to have hastened the deal so far as Fox is concerned. It is understood that $500,000 will be spent on the theatre part of the building.

Reports that the Mark-Strand company

will build on the old Browning-King store-site in Main street, directly across from Shea's Hippodrome are emphatically denied by Walter Hays, vice president of the Strand company. The incorporation of the Buffalo Strand corporation recently in Albany gave rise to this report. While no new house is contemplated at this time, Buffalo some day may again have a link in the Mark-Strand chain throughout the state, it is said.

Rumors of a deal between Finkelstein & Ruben and Famous Players in the Twin Cities, along the lines of the Balaban & Katz arrangement, were printed this week, but no statements were forthcoming from either party to give credence to the report.

A report from Omaha declared that the Cooper interests, which built a house for Famous Players in Lincoln, would also erect a house for that corporation in Grand Island. Universal has already announced a house for the latter city.

Famous Players is reported to have an interest in the theatre which the Saenger Amusement Co. is building in Havana, Cuba.

A charter has been issued to the Famous Players Realty corporation, which it is understood will be the holding corporation for the combined Paramount and Balaban & Katz houses. The incorporators were Elek J. Ludvigh, William H. English and Harold B. Franklin.

Announcement in Chicago threw additional light on the nature of the ten-year agreement between Famous Players-Lasky and B. & K. According to this statement, all of the Famous houses will pass into the hands of the new corporation, in which F. P.-L. will own all of the stock, Balaban & Katz to receive a participation in the profits. New houses to be acquired will be taken over by a second corporation, to be formed, the stock of which will be owned equally by B. & K. and Famous.

Allens Lease New House in Canada

The Allens of Toronto, formerly directing a chain of moving picture houses across Canada, have re-entered the Montreal amusement field once more and will shortly open a brand new moving picture and vaudeville palace in the new Amherst Block at the corners of St. Catherine, Amherst and St. Timothee Streets, Montreal. The business premises and the theatre are being built by the George Rabinovitch Investment Corporation of Montreal, the theatre structure being under lease for a long term of years to H. Allen, one of the members of the Allen family in Toronto. The new house, which is yet unnamed, will have a seating capacity of 1,800 and will be fitted in every way for both pictures and vaudeville presentations.

Jule and J. J. Allen and others had approximately 55 theatres in Canada several years ago under the name of Allen Theatres, Limited. The physical assets of this company were eventually acquired by Famous Players Canadian Corp., Toronto.

Fox Financial Statement Shows Big Earnings for First Six Months of Year

THAT the Fox Film Corporation is in an extremely healthy financial condition is shown by the statement issued for the six months ending June 27th, 1925, which shows net earnings for that period of $1,212,024, equivalent to $7.27 a share on the average amount of stock outstanding. The company's earnings, according to Wall Street reports, are said to be almost double so far this year over last year.

Fox now has 400,000 shares of Class A common stock and 100,000 shares of Class B. The control of the company is vested in Class B.

According to the balance sheet the corporation and its subsidiaries have total assets of $25,016,346, of which $15,629,728 represents current and working assets. The current liabilities are reported as $894,336. The statement show $8,200,000 cash on hand.

National Book Week Dates Set

National Committee Lists Films for Showing Week of November 8 to 14

CHILDREN'S Book Week and Motion Picture Book Week will be observed this year from November 8th to November 14th. Cooperating with the National Association of Book Publishers which promotes Children's Book Week are the American Library Association, the General Federation of Women's Clubs, the Boy Scouts of America and the National Board of Review of Motion Pictures.

The National Committee has issued a list of 137 selected films drawn from available published sources, which is being widely distributed to libraries, schools, bookstores, civic organizations, women's clubs and exhibitors. The list includes product of all companies. Among the companies and authors represented are:

Famous Players-Lasky—Joseph C. Lincoln, with "Rugged Water"; Arthur Richman, "Not So Long Ago"; Zane Grey, "Wild Horse Mesa" and "The Border Legion"; Kaufman and Connelly, "Beggar on Horseback"; Moreau and Sardou, "Madame Sans-Gene". Universal—Emerson Hough, "North of 36"; Lewis Beach, "The Goose Hangs High"; Samuel Hopkins Adams, "Siege"; Charles Guernon, "The Storm Breaker"; Rex Beach, "The Goose Woman"; Dorothy Canfield, "The Homemaker," Film Booking Offices—Jack London, "White Fang." First National—Struthers Burt, "The Interpreter's House (film title "I Want My Man"); Conan Doyle, "The Lost World." Fox—Channing Pollock, "The Fool"; Edwin C. Hill, "The Iron Horse"; Edward Everett Hale, "The Man Without a Country" (film title, "As No Man Has Loved"); Winchell Smith and Tom Cushing, "Thank You." Metro-Goldwyn-Mayer, Lula Vollmar, "Sun-up"; Leonid Andreyev, "He Who Gets Slapped"; Louis Joseph Vance, "Mrs. Paramor" (film title, "Married Flirts"); Katherine Newlin Burt, "The Way of a Girl." Producers Distributing—William J. Locke, "The Coming of Amos"; Thomas Gallon, "Off the Highway." Warner—A. S. M. Hutchinson, "The Happy Warrior"; Harriet Beecher Stowe, "My Wife and I"; Edwin Bateman Morris, "The Narrow Street"; Leonard Merrick, "The House of Lynch" (film title, "A School for Wives"); James Oliver Curwood, "Steele of the Royal Mounted." Unity—Edmond Rostand, "Cyrano de Bergerac." United Artists—K. and H. Prichard, "Don Q, Son of Zorro." Astor—Omar Khayyam, "The Rubaiyat" (film title, "The Lover's Oath").

Pathe—William Hamby, "The Desert Fiddler" (film title, "Percy").

Suggestions are also given with the list for stimulating public interest in good book-films and books both during Book Week and through the year. Thus the drive for Motion Picture Book Week is made an important part of the whole Better Films Movement. To encourage libraries in particular to continue the book-film tie-up the National Committee for Better Films is offering prizes of its current membership publications up to January 1927, which give advance information on the new selected films, to those libraries rendering the best reports of community cooperation in observance of Motion Picture Book Week in November.

Exhibitor Fined for Juvenile Violation

The Ottawa, Ontario, Juvenile Court opened an attack on several theatre proprietors in Ottawa on October 16, because of the habit of allowing unaccompanied children 15 years of age to enter their theatres, thus violating an Ontario statute. One exhibitor was haled to court, given a lecture and sentenced to pay a fine of $20 and costs or 10 days in jail. Magistrate Hopewell announced that he would raise the penalty for the next cinema manager who was found guilty on a charge of violating the juvenile regulation.

Decision Rendered in Denver Wage Scale Controversy

The State Industrial Commission of Colorado, has decided in favor of the Theatre Managers Association and against the trades-craft unions in the recent wage scale controversy. This marks the end of a fight which has extended over a period of two months and which at one time threatened to result in a general "walk-out" of all union employees. Early in August the unions demanded a twenty-five per cent increase in wages and shorter working time. These demands were denied by the theatre managers. Numerous conferences failed to bring about an agreement. A few days before the expiration of the old contract both sides agreed to submit to arbitration. The State Industrial Commission was selected, this body agreeing to act only on the promise that any award made would be final.

Arguments were presented on October 5th and to-day the decision upheld the contentions of the theatre managers in that the new contract should be substantially the same as the old contract; that present conditions do not warrant the increased demands of the union employees.

San Francisco House Robbed of $2,800

Prying open bars in a second story window and entering Manager C. A. Grissell's private office, expert yeggmen early on the morning of October 13th, robbed the safe of the Union Square Theatre. The strong box was opened and $2,800 stolen. The alarm was turned in by the night janitor, who, after sweeping the outer rooms, entered Grissell's office. All currency and silver, believed to have been the night's receipts was gone. Empty money bags and loose change were scattered about the floor. The bandits reached the windows by climbing down from the roof of the building. Officers believe the strong box was opened by one who knew the combination.

Announce Plans for New Theatre in Chicago

The $3,000,000 theatre to be erected at 79th and Maryland, Chicago, by the Woodlawn Theatre Company, of which Andrew Karras is the president, will seat three thousand and have a stage capable of accommodating the largest productions. The house will have a cantilever balcony.

Waddill Catchings is Named Chairman of Finance Committee of Warner Brothers

WADDILL CATCHINGS, member of the firm of Goldman, Sachs and Company, has been elected to the Board of Directors of Warner Brothers and named chairman of the Finance Committee. He will handle the financial affairs of the company and thus leave the four Warner brothers at liberty to devote their time to furthering the various ends of the business for which each of them is particularly adapted.

H. M. Warner, President of Warner Brothers, in announcing the acquisition of Mr. Catchings said:

"I feel that Mr. Catchings associating himself with our company is really the most important incident in our entire business career. Warner Bros. have been making such rapid progress, particularly in the past two years, that it required someone with an expert knowledge to advise on the finances of the company while my brothers and myself devoted our time to the production, and distribution of pictures and our theatre interests. With the election of Mr. Catchings this has been accomplished, and we are now prepared to step out unhampered on a scale larger than ever before.

Lasky Denies Program Curtailment

Fall and Spring Groups Will Total 73 Releases; No Material Reduction Planned Unless Sales Conditions Change

PUBLISHED reports to the effect that Famous Players-Lasky would cut its Spring group to 25 pictures, and that the 1926-27 releases would total only 52, were denied this week by Jesse L. Lasky, first vice-president in charge of production.

Present definite plans, he stated, calls for 33 pictures in the Spring group, making a total of 73 for the year, a figure not materially different from the program of the preceding 12 months.

"It should be borne in mind, said Mr. Lasky, "that the volume of production is controlled solely and directly by reports from the sales force in the field. It has been brought out repeatedly at sales conferences that approximately seventy-five pictures is the number which can be marketed to best advantage.

"If, at any time, conditions in the field should change and our sales force should report that an increase or decrease in the schedule was desirable, that change would be made. But until such a recommendation is received no such move will be considered.

"Any one who could have visited our studios during recent weeks would have realized how unfounded any talk of curtailment must be in connection with Famous Players-Lasky. At the Long Island studios, seven units were working at once during a recent week, and activity was also proceeding at top speed on the West Coast. That should be adequate answer to any report

Jesse L. Lasky.

that we are curtailing production.

"As matters now stand, we are further ahead of schedule than we have ever been, and are now working on Spring releases.

This is a most desirable condition, since it enables us to take the utmost care and thought with these pictures. But there is no basis at present for supposing that the releasing schedule will be materially curtailed."

A report published in a New York newspaper to the effect that B. P. Schulberg had signed as general production manager of Famous Players-Lasky was characterized as a misstatement of the facts by Mr. Lasky, who said:

"In the first place, Mr. Walter Wanger is the general manager of production for Famous, and you may say for me that he is doing very satisfactorily indeed. Therefore, there is no truth in any rumor which states that he is to be displaced.

"However, it is true that we have been negotiating with Mr. Schulberg in connection with a supervisory position at one of our studios, but his contractual status at the moment is such that he is not in a position to sign with us, or with any other company. This status might change at any time, of course, in which case the negotiations would doubtless be renewed. It is not true, however, that he has already signed with us.

"I should like particularly to emphasize that any move which might be made would not affect the position of Mr. Wanger, who is functioning most efficiently."

Blank Will Not Sell, Announcement

Acquires Nine Additional Houses; Sol Lesser Announces Formation of New $2,500,000 Corporation—Others Expanding

COINCIDENT with a statement in which he "most emphatically" denied a report that he was contemplating the sale of his theatres, A. H. Blank, head of the Blank circuit, announced that his organization had acquired nine additional theatres and has plans set for even more ambitious expansion operations. The contracts have been let for the building of the new Blank theatre in Omaha, to be erected at a cost of $1,000,000.

Among the new houses which have been added to the Blank string of over thirty theatres in Iowa, are the Strand and Lincoln in Chariton. Harry Mitznick, who has been manager of the Rialto Theatre at Des Moines has been transferred to Chariton to manage the new houses, which were purchased from W. H. Dewey.

According to an announcement from Sol Lesser from California, the new West Coast Junior Circuit, a $2,500,000 corporation recently formed between West Coast Theatres, Inc., and Michael Rosenberg, Arthur L. Bernstein and Harry Sugarman, will incorporate in the new system the houses of the West Coast Langley Circuit in Pasadena, Glendale, Tafet and Los Angeles, in addition to the thirty-five other houses in Southern California which will be taken over. Mr. Arthur L. Bernstein was the head of the Langley circuit. The West Coast Junior Cir-

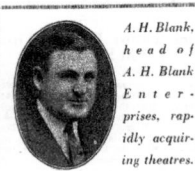

A. H. Blank, head of A. H. Blank Enterprises, rapidly acquiring theatres.

cuit will also combine the enterprises of the Junior Theatre Syndicate, the announcement states.

The theatres to be taken over in Los Angeles include the Royal, Crystal, Jewel, Riviera and Unique. The Whittier Theatre at Whittier is also included as one of the assets of the new syndicate.

One of the most important theatre transactions of the week was reported from Washington, where Fox has obtained the 4,000 seat house which will be part of the National Press Club building. According to reports when the theatre was first projected, Famous

was to have operated this house. The lease which Fox has on the theatre is for a term of 25 years. It is believed that Famous will start plans to acquire a theatre in Washington. In all probabilities the company will build one of its own there.

The pending sale of the Grand theatre, 8-10 Plymouth avenue North, Rochester, for the sum of $85,000, has been made public following the filing of papers to do with the transfer of the realty at the Court House. The prospective purchaser is given as the Sehine Theatrical Corporation. The owner of the property is Thomas G. Thompson, formerly of 393 Wellington avenue, adjudged incompetent nearly a year ago, and sent to an institution. Acting as a committee for Thompson were his daughter, Edith V. Thompson, and Attorney E. Reed Shutt. The committee acting in the interests of Thompson, found it best to dispose of the property, and an offer was made last August by the Sehine company. This offer was accepted with the provision that it must be approved by County Judge Willis K. Gillette. In the papers filed, Judge Gillette gives his approval of the report of Percival W. Gillette, referee in the proceedings. The purchase of the property will involve the taking over of a first mortgage for $16,000 held by the Monroe County Savings

(Continued on Next Page)

FLINN LEAVES FOR COAST
May Sign Stars, Directors

JOHN C. FLINN, Vice-President and General Manager of Producers Distributing Corporation left for the coast last week to confer with Cecil B. De Mille and the Christie Brothers on production plans for the 1926-27 season. It is said that a marked expansion of the company's production activities is contemplated for next season and during the stay of Flinn on the coast a number of prominent directors and stars will be signed to contracts.

Nothing definite has yet been arranged for next year's program, though an exchange of ideas has been going on for the past few months between the west coast producers and the executives of the Producers Distributing Corporation. These ideas will be consummated into definite form before the return of Flinn.

Charles Christie, who returned from Europe last week, is also en route for Los Angeles. Christie left New York on Saturday in order to stop over for one day in Chicago before joining Flinn, with whom he intended to travel from Chicago to Los Angeles.

Award Story Contest Prizes

Omaha Woman Offers Best Suggestion in Frank Lloyd-First National Quiz

THE prizes have been awarded in the Frank Lloyd-First National Pictures Story Suggestion Contest held for the purpose of finding screen stories which had not been previously filmed. Eight prizes were awarded, the first of which, $500 went to Mrs. Hazel Marie Bergh of 118 West Thirty-First Street, Omaha, Nebraska.

The nature of the story suggestion offered by Mrs. Bergh has not yet been revealed, except that it carries an Oriental locale. It will be produced by Mr. Lloyd who will make a special trip to the Orient to take up research work and study first hand the locale and characters in the story.

The other winners in the contest were, Mont Hurst, Dallas, Texas, $200; Mrs. Alien A. Keen, Allendale, N. J., $150; Mrs. G. W. Pliter, Santa Monica, California, $100; Miss Amalia Stetter, Milwaukee, $50, and the special prizes of $33.33 each to

R. T. Newton, Little Rock, Ark., Miss Charlotte Thorp, Spokane, and A. Methat, Montreal.

It was announced from the First National offices that 11,947 letters were entered in the contest and that they came from all parts of the world. There were letters from school boys and girls in the elementary grades, letters from authors, artists, lawyers, dressmakers and sailors.

More than a month was required to eliminate the suggestions which, for various reasons could not be considered. A number of suggestions were for the remaking of picture adaptations of well known classics. These could not be considered since the purpose of the contest was to find screen material which had not been previously filmed.

Mellon Recommends Tax Retention

RETENTION of the present tax on admissions to theatres was recommended on October 19 by Secretary of the Treasury Mellon in presenting his views on tax revision to the House committee on ways and means, in Washington, D. C.

"Admissions and dues brought in $31,-000,000 last year," he told the committee, and are estimated to bring in $33,000,000 this year. The tax applies only to admissions sold in excess of 50 cents. It does not seem that this tax is any particular burden and in the interests of the revenue it produces it ought to be retained."

The admission tax, however, was not the only one of the so-called nuisance taxes which the Secretary would retain, he also recommended the continuation of the tax on automobiles.

The repeal of the publicity provisions of the present law, as being "utterly useless" from a Treasury standpoint, was recommended.

Blank Denies Reports That He Will Sell Circuit

(Continued from preceding page)

Bank and a second mortgage for $42,000 held by the Fitzhugh Realty company. At the present time, the Glove City Amusement company holds a ten year lease on the building which will expire July 31, 1934. The amusement concern is given the privilege of either renewing the lease for another ten year span, or purchasing the building at any time for agreed price of $115,000.

The Gordon interests are said to be interested in a new theatre to be erected on Broadway, Everett, Mass. between Ellsworth anl Webster streets, which is introducing the innovation of providing a large parking space beside the theatre for autos of its patrons. The new theatre, according to plans now being drawn, will have a seating capacity of 2100 and the architecture and arrangement will conform to the municipal group of buildings adjoining. It will be ready early next summer. Monks & Johnson of Boston are drawing the plans. The theatre include a balcony seating 500. An organ will be installed and there will be full sized stage and orchestra pit.

Ohio Amusement Company Issues Statement

The following statement has been issued by the majority stockholders of the Ohio Amusement Company, Cleveland, regarding the minority stockholders' suit for dissolution:

The Ohio Amusement Company and stockholders owning two-thirds of its stock, on October 10th filed a motion in court to dismiss dissolution proceedings which have been brought by three employees and minority stockholders of the company, Messrs. Schumann, Fine and Kramer. The motions set forth that the company has since its organization been prosperous, has increased its number of theatres out of earnings from six to twelve and that the net operating profits during the month of September of this year amounted to $15,000.

The motions further charge that the petition of the minority stockholders was not filed in good faith, that they have no legal right to file the proceedings and that the proceedings were filed for the purpose of compelling stockholders of the company to sell their stock at less than its value and for purposes of gaining other advantages for the petitioners.

Officers of the company state that since the election of Mr. Leo Keller to succeed one of the complaining petitioners, Mr. Schumann, as President of the Ohio Amusement Company and since the majority of the stockholders of the company have undertaken a more active management of the company, the company is succeeding better than at any time in its history in spite of the embarrassment caused by the petition. They have the support of the Board of Directors in the present policies of the company and they see no reason why the present petition should be granted or why the complaints of the petitioners in this case should be given serious consideration, if matters should come to a final hearing in court.

Empress, St. John, N. B., is Totally Destroyed by Fire

The Empress Theatre in St. John, N. B., was totally destroyed by fire on October 15 when flames broke out in the projection room during a performance. There was only a small crowd in the theatre at the time and the spectators quickly escaped, although a couple of women fainted and had to be carried out. There was one near casualty when Louis McCourt, the projection machine operator, stuck to his post in an effort to subdue the flames with hand chemicals. In making his exit finally, he stumbled in the smoke and fell down the stairs, being rescued by firemen. The fire spread quickly through the whole structure. The building, which was owned by the City of St. John, was valued at $50,000.

Shores Assistant Director of Paramount School

Edwin C. King, manager of the Paramount Long Island Studio announces that Lynn Shores has been assigned to the Paramount Picture School, Inc., as assistant director. He will work under Sam Wood, who will direct the picture on which the Paramount Junior Stars will start production November 9th.

Wellenbrink Case Will Go to Jury

Fairness of Arbitration and Uniform Contract Brought Into Trial in New York Supreme Court This Week

FIRST steps toward some final action in the famous and long postponed case of the Apollo Exchange, Inc., vs. the Wellmont theatre, Montclair, N. J., were reached this week when Justice Proskauer of the Supreme Court of New York, special term, directed a jury trial to settle the point of whether or not the disputed contract was signed under duress. Both parties agreed to this, which will automatically bring it up in the regular November term.

The case came before Justice Proskauer on Tuesday morning. Apollo was represented by Louis Phillips, attorney for the Film Board of Trade, although the actual argument was presented by Edward P. Grosvenor of Cadwallader, Wickersham and Taft of counsel for the Hays organization in contract matters. Norman Samuelson, attorney for the M. P. T. O. of N. J., appeared for the defense.

Although the plaintiff's attorney was not inclined to admit that a test case was being made of the matter, observers point out that this is the first time that the Uniform Contract and the arbitration clause have been brought into court, and that therefore any legal action affecting them is likely to have an important future bearing on the negotiations for a new Uniform Contract.

As will be remembered by those who have followed the case, it is based upon Apollo's application for an order to enforce arbitration on a contract for 18 pictures which H. H. Wellenbrink, president of the Wellmont Theatre company, signed, and which he subsequently sought to cancel, after playing one picture, when the exchange tried to substitute "Her Marriage Vow" for "The Age of Innocence."

Seider Contract O.K.'d by Exhibitor Body

JOSEPH M. SEIDER, Chairman of the Contract and Arbitration Committee of the M. P. T. O. A., has made public a letter from the Motion Picture Theatre Owners of Eastern Missouri and Southern Illinois, endorsing the Standard Exhibition Contract recently drawn up by Mr. Seider. The letter from the exhibitor organization follows:

"Your very kind favor at hand and in reply will say that we had a meeting of the Executive Committee of the State organization yesterday and I read your letter; also the Standard Exhibition Contract and Set of Rules and will say that they have met with the approval of all who attended the meeting, and I wish to say that they do not see how they can be improved upon so far as we are position to judge as your Committee has gone into the matter more thoroughly and no doubt you have discussed the various points and have covered all that should be looked after. I cannot well improve upon the same. Trusting that the report of the Committee will be adopted and wishing you the best of success, I beg to remain.

Yours respectfully,
LOUIS C. HEHL,
Secretary.

T. O. C. C. May Reject Hays Contract

THE new uniform contract being drawn up by the Hays organization was the principal topic of discussion at the meeting of the Theatre Owners' Chamber of Commerce of New York on Tuesday, October 20.

Nathan Burkan told the exhibitors present that, in his opinion, the new Hays contract was too long and that it did not afford the exhibitor sufficient protection. It was decided to send a copy to each member of the T. O. C. C. The Board of Directors will meet Monday to discuss the matter and on Tuesday it will come up before the whole organization for settlement.

Sentiment in the T. O. C. C. is reported to be strong for rejecting the proposed contract in its present form.

There is also considerable sentiment in favor of the contract drawn by Joseph M. Seider, President of the M. P. T. O. of New Jersey and head of the M. P. T. O. A. Contract and Arbitration committee. The Seider contract incorporates the Burkan clause on the designation of playdates.

The joint arbitration board sat in the case last February and granted a judgment of $900 against the theatre by default, putting the theatre on a deposit basis with companies in the F. I. L. M. Club. Wellenbrink paid the deposits but declined to arbitrate or play the balance of the pictures on the contract. The action by Apollo is designed to force him, by legal means, to enter into the joint board and accept the decision of the joint board.

The chief claims stressed by Samuelson for the defense were:

1. That an exhibitor signing the Uniform Contract did so under duress or intimidation, knowing that unless he signed the contract containing the arbitration clause he would be refused film by all the companies in the F. I. L. M. clubs, making it impossible for him to obtain an adequate supply of acceptable product.

2. That the administration of the arbitration clause was unfair, since the individual exhibitor had no voice in the selection of the men who were to represent him, and no right of challenge.

It can probably be safely stated, in view of the statements made by Justice Proskauer on Tuesday, that the matter will largely hinge on these two points, that is, whether an exhibitor is forced to sign this contract whether he wishes to or not, and secondly, whether the arbitration boards as constituted are really an impartial tribunal.

In taking up the question of duress, Attorney Samuelson explained that the exhibitor, in order to obtain the product which he needed to keep his house open must sign the Uniform Contract. Justice Proskauer then turned to the plaintiff's attorney and said:

"Do you think that constitutes duress? Well, I do."

On the other hand, the justice favored the plaintiff on the second point, when, after Attorney Grosvenor stated that three of the members of the arbitration board were selected by an exhibitor body, he turned to Attorney Samuelson and reprimanded him for giving the impression that the arbitration board was wholly selected by the F. I. L. M. clubs. Samuelson then explained that this was a misapprehension, and that what he had intended to convey was that the board as now constituted cannot function impartially, and that the exhibitor members selected do not properly represent the defendant, since he has no voice in their selection and no right of challenge.

An affidavit by Joseph M. Seider was filed by the defense, bearing on the alleged unfairness of the arbitration system, which further tends to make a national issue of the case, since it brings the arbitration clause directly into it. He also took exception to the clause added to the contract which specifies that it may be replaced by any contract adopted and approved by the Hays organization.

The counsel for the Hays office and for the M. P. T. O. of N. J. conferred following the case and agreed on a jury trial, the alternative being to take the case to an appellate court.

Both sides expressed considerable satisfaction with the status of the case, and both expressed entire confidence in the outcome. The only material difference which trial by jury will make will be that Justice Proskauer will be assisted by a jury, and that the case will be argued out in court instead of settled on the basis of affidavits.

Ohio M. P. T. O. to Meet in December

Plans for the annual convention in Columbus, December 8, of the Ohio Motion Picture Theatre Owners are being taken care of by W. M. James, Columbus, president of the organization and P. J. Wood, business manager. A Chairman of the convention committee will be appointed at the executive committee meeting to be held at Columbus, November 10.

This organization, underwritten by a group of members to guarantee its sound financial standing, has been able to dispense with this underwriting because of the excellent showing of exhibitors.

A new secretary of the Joint Board of Arbitration and Film Board of Trade has been selected under a new arrangement with headquarters for both in Cleveland.

Charlotte Board of Trade Elects Officers

The Charlotte Film Board of Trade held their election the past week and Frank Bryan, of First National, was re-elected President. Hugh Owens, of Paramount, was elected Vice President. Jim Reynolds was elected Treasurer and Secretary. The following were elected an executive committee as follows: E. F. Dardine, Universal, Walter Price, Fox Film, and William Conn, F.B.O.

Schulberg Files Personal Bankruptcy Petition; Company Not Affected

B. P. SCHULBERG this week filed a personal petition in bankruptcy in the New York Federal Court. Liabilities are listed at $830,774 and assets at $1,420. The financial status of B. P. Schulberg Productions, Inc., is not affected by the petition according to a statement issued by J. G. Bachmann."

The principal creditors named and the amounts due them are: Standard Finance Corporation, Los Angeles, $300,000; Sol Fillin, $110,000; Standard Film Laboratories, Los Angeles, $90,030; Katherine MacDonald, $60,000; B. P. Fineman, Los Angeles, $48,500; David Jaffe, for loans, $30,000; W. F. Selig, Inc., The Pacific Southwest Trust and Savings Company, $25,000; and the United States Government for income taxes, $2,300.

The following statement was issued by Mr. Schulberg: "The indebtedness of $820,774, from which I am seeking relief by filing a voluntary petition in Bankruptcy, was not incurred by me personally nor used in my personal behalf. It was incurred by Preferred Pictures Corporation, and by myself as its agent in California. These obligations were assumed by me personally at the time Preferred Pictures Corporation (at the request of the Standard Film Laboratories of California, its largest creditor) went into the hands of an equity receiver.

"Since then I have made every possible effort to pay off this indebtedness from my personal earnings, but the attitude of certain creditors, in pressing me without giving me a fair chance to do that which I was under no actual legal or moral obligation to do, has left no other possible course open but to take this action."

Junior Movies Now Featured

Albany, Troy, Glens Falls, and Cleveland Popularizing Saturday Morning Shows

MORE prominent than ever before, Junior Movies will be featured this fall and winter in Albany, Schenectady, Troy, Glens Falls and other cities in central New York.

The Junior Movies in Albany this year are being held at Harmanus Bleecker Hall, with a seating capacity of 2,200, and with the Albany Mothers' Club handling much of the preliminary detail. There is a feature in connection with the movies in Albany this fall and winter, that is new. Such children as have talent to entertain will be afforded a half hour each Saturday morning to entertain the other children present, and as an incentive for other children to develop their dramatic, musical and comedy talent. Girl and Boy Scouts in Albany will act as ushers and assistants.

In Troy, the movies will be under the auspices of the Parent-Teachers' association, and will be given at the Troy theatre, the largest house in the city, and with Lansingburgh, probably included in the territory.

In Schenectady, the first of the Junior Movies was held last Saturday at the State theatre, and almost ended in a small boy riot. Owing to the fact that such movies have never been given in the city before, it was decided to distribute 15,000 circulars over the city, calling attention to the Saturday morning program for children. Over 6,000 boys and girls showed up and after the theatre had been filled, and 2,100 of the number had been taken care of, there still remained about 4,000 outside, begging for admission.

The Empire in Glens Falls announces a Junior Movie season, with a two hour show on Saturday mornings for a ten cent admission.

Special "matinee" performances for children will be offered in Loew's State theatre in Cleveland Saturday morning at ten o'clock.

This announcement came from Lora M. Kendall, press secretary of the Cleveland Cinema Club, which, in conjunction with the Motion Picture Producers and Distributors

of America, sponsors this program, and will continue to offer one every Saturday morning to the next year. Admission is set uniformly at ten cents for children: Adults will pay twenty-five cents.

$50,000 Fire Damage to Theatre in Madison

More than $50,000 damage was done by a fire that practically demolished the Parkway theatre at Madison, Wis., one of the well known old picture houses of the Badger capital. Only the front, with its offices, remains of the former theatre, which was operated by the Fischer Theatre Company, under the management of Leo Brown. Twelve hundred patrons of the house stampeded their way to safety, when the main curtain fell after it had been lowered, at the first alarm. It is considered a miracle that many persons were not killed or badly injured as a series of back-stage explosions threw the crowds into general confusion despite the efforts of the management and attaches to file them out in orderly fashion. A five year old child was painfully burned, when it fled to the stage instead of through the exit, but no other serious casualties were reported.

Injunction Closes Urbana's Theatres on Sundays

Urbana's two motion picture shows were dark on Sunday, October 18th because of a temporary injunction issued by the Champaign County Circuit Court late Saturday.

Circuit Judge Franklin H. Boggs will determine at the January term of court whether to make the injunction permanent.

In issuing his temporary injunction Judge Boggs stated there was not the slightest doubt that the legislature had given the right to city councils to regulate amusements and that under that grant of authority the council could prohibit Sunday shows.

New Companies Incorporated in New York State

Motion picture companies incorporating in New York state during the past week, included the following: Sidbill Company, Inc., capitalized at $10,000, with Sidney Clare, William Wolfson, New York city, Al Shayne, Freeport, L. I.; Springdale Dramatics, Inc., $10,000, B. M. L. Ernst, Clare, William Wolfson, New York city. Woodside Amusement Company, Inc., $5,000, M. R. Weinberger, S. H. Posner, Jerome Weinstein, New York city; Richard Herndon-Allan Dinehart Corporation, capitalization not specified, Richard Herndon, Allan Dinehart, New York city, Albert McGall, Orange, N. J.; Famous Players Realty Corporation, capitalization not specified, Elik Ludvigh, William H. English, New York city, Harold B. Franklin, New Rohelle.

New Building Will House Rogers Unit

Work is under way at Universal City upon a new building that will be devoted exclusively to the Charles R. Rogers organization, which will present Harry Carey in a series of Western features for Pathe release. In addition to the star's personal quarters, the building will house the executive quarters of the Rogers company, embracing Mr. Rogers' own suite and offices for the production, publicity and accounting departments.

Carey's first Pathe Western will be an adaptation of "Buck Up," a story by Basil Dickey and Harry Haven which Harvey Gates prepared for the screen. Scott Dunlap is directing. In the supporting cast are Harriett Hammond, Bert Woodruff, Ruth King, James Farley, Stanton Heck, Raymond Nye and Joseph Gerard.

Leaders to Celebrate With Pathe

Vice-President Dawes and Other Notables Will Attend Fifteenth Anniversary News Reel Dinner at Plaza

NATIONAL leaders of public affairs, including Vice-President Dawes, have accepted the invitation to celebrate with Pathe the dinner to be held at the Hotel Plaza in New York on November 14th marking the fifteenth anniversary of the Pathe Newsreel. Cabinet members, foreign ambassadors, governors of states, senators and congressmen have expressed their intention of participating in the ceremonies.

The Pathe list of illustrious men who have announced their intention of paying tribute to the news reel on November 14th, includes, in addition to the Vice-President of the United States, such notables as the Honorable Curtis D. Wilbur, Secretary of the Navy; Honorable Hubert Work, Secretary of the Interior; Senor Don Manuel C. Tellez, Mexican Ambassador to the United States; Baron Ago von Maltzan, German Ambassador; Ralph O. Brewster, Governor of Maine; Alfred E. Smith, Governor of New York; E. Lee Trinkle, Governor of Virginia; United States Senator Coleman DuPont; United States Senator Royal S. Copeland; Thomas A. Edison, noted pioneer film inventor; Chauncey Depew; Owen D. Young; Frank Hedley, President of the Interborough Rapid Transit Company; W. W. Atterbury, Pennsylvania Railroad; P. C. Crowley, New York Central Lines; William Greene, President American Federation of Labor; Dwight F. Davis, newly named Secretary of War; Mayor James M. Curley of Boston; Frank D. Waterman, Republican Mayorality Candidate for City of New York; James J. Walker, Democratic Mayorality nominee for City of New York; Dr. L. W. Rowe, Director-General of the Pan-American Union; Franklin Adams, Counsellor of the Pan-American Union; John Olive LaGorce, Associate Editor of the National Geographic Society, and Melville E. Stone, Counsellor of the Associated Press.

The United States Navy will be represented by Rear-Admiral Charles P.

Emanuel Cohen, Editor of Pathe News.

Plunkett, Commandant of the First Naval District; Admiral Robinson, Chief of Naval Operations; Rear-Admiral W. A. Moffett, Chief of the Bureau of Aeronautics; Admiral Leigh Palmer; Rear-Admiral William S. Benson, retired; Major General John A. Lejeune, Commandant Marine Corps; Captain Walter Gherardi, Aide to the Secretary of Navy; and Mr. T. V. O'Connor, Chairman of the United States Shipping Board.

The Army will be brilliantly represented by Major General John L. Hines, Chief of Staff; Major General Mason M. Patrick, Chief of the Air Service; Major General Charles P. Summerall, Commanding the Second Corps Area, which includes New York City.

A special train on the Pennsylvania Railroad has been chartered by Pathe News to convey the cabinet members, ambassadors, and other prominent officials to the dinner. This train will leave the Union Station in Washington at one o'clock on the afternoon of November 14th. It will return the following day. Two floors have been engaged in the Hotel Plaza for the convenience of the distinguished guests.

Emanuel Cohen, Editor of Pathe News, announces that the dinner at the Hotel Plaza is intended to emphasize the importance of the fifteenth Anniversary of news dissemination by motion pictures.

He said in part: "Twenty-five years ago the flickering and uncertain cinematograph showing the horse drawn fire engine responding to a fire aroused a wave of enthusiasm. Ten years later science had eliminated the eye-tiring, uncertain and cloudy projection of moving pictures. Charles Pathe was the pioneer in the news film field. He was the first to perceive the miraculous possibilities of the motion picture camera as the world's most accurate reporter. It was then that

the first attempt was made to organize a world-wide news film service.

"The development of the ordinary camera into motion picture portrayal has made the African jungles almost as familiar to the peoples of the world as the Strand in London or Broadway in New York. The news film has reached every corner of the world during the last fifteen years. The news film serves millions of subscribers in the farthest corners of the world. It speaks the universal language. It reaches all grades of mentality with the same perfection of accuracy. It has become the most accurate reporter of news and events that the world has ever known. It has ceased to be merely an entertainment. It is now an institution. It is to emphasize and honor this achievement that the dinner is tendered."

New Broadcasting Link for New York Capitol

Station K. S. D. of St. Louis has been added to the chain of radio stations broadcasting New York Capitol Theatre programs on Sunday evenings. This brings the total to eight stations now in the chain which relays the programs from the theatre every Sunday evening, followed by the supplementary studio program directed by Major Bowes.

The stations on the chain are W.E.A.F. New York, W.E.E.I. Boston, W.C.A.E. Pittsburgh, W.W.J. Detroit, W.C.A.P. Washington, W.J.A.R. Providence, W.T.A.G. Worcester and K.S.D. St. Louis.

Portland Exhibitors Have Trouble With Musicians

The Strand and Empire theatres, picture houses, owned by Abraham Goodside were without orchestras last week owing to a disagreement. A raise of ten dollars per week, longer rests between playing and the discharge of musicians hired outside the state are among the demands said to have been made by the musicians.

The musicians claim, however, that they were told to "get out." Organs have been continued in both houses during the week and it is expected that something in the way of orchestras will be secured before long.

Music Troubles Straightened Out in Schenectady

Things are once more running smoothly between the exhibitors of Schenectady and members of the musicians' union. After several conferences, the musicians decided to withdraw their demands for more wages, and as a result the same wage scale will prevail for another twelve months. Members of orchestras were asking two dollars a week more, while organists demanded $90 a week rather than $54, which they are now receiving.

Pathe Field Executives Win Promotions

SEVERAL promotions and changes are announced by Pathe in their field executives. R. S. Ballantyne, Des Moines branch manager has been made southern district manager, succeeding Oscar Morgan, who at his own request has been made branch manager of the Dallas office. D. J. Coughlin resigned in Dallas because of illness.

A. W. Kahn has been named as Ballantyne's successor at Des Moines. L. E. Kennedy, formerly special feature representative, has been appointed branch manager at San Francisco, succeeding W. W. Kofeldt, who resigned to take a position abroad. Kennedy relieved George Knowles, who has been serving as branch manager. The latter, at his request, has been transferred to Los Angeles as special comedy salesman.

On October 31st, the Washington Pathe branch, now a part of the Southern division, will come under the jurisdiction of the Eastern division, of which Charles Henschel is district manager.

Kansas - Missouri Exhibitors Advised to Pay Tax

"Like many other exhibitors we had neglected to take out our music license," writes Henry Tucker, owner of the Majestic and Tucker theatres, Liberal, Kan., "So inspectors were sent out and reported infringements and we were assessed $500. After sending my lawyer to Topeka, Kan., to confer with Newell & Wallace, attorneys for the music society, we succeeded in getting the amount cut to $400, which we paid rather than stand suit. And just to think a few months ago we could have taken out a license for $85."

Mr. Tucker's reference to "a few months ago" alludes to the agreement entered into by the M.P.T.O. Kansas-Missouri and the music society, in which members of the exhibitor organization received a 20 per cent reduction on amounts levied. The M.P.T.O. K.-M., which recently waged a bitter fight against the payment of music tax, has advised all its members to pay the tax.

Cast for Next Columbia Production Announced

Harry Cohn, head of the Waldorf studios announced the engagement of Forrest Stanley for the leading male role in "The Penalty of Jazz." He will support Dorothy Revier who is starred in this Columbia production. The rest of the cast consists of Tom Ricketts, Ethel Wales, Maude Wayne, Frank Wood and Erwin Connely.

"The Penalty of Jazz," which was written by Dorothy Azner and Paul Cangolin, goes into immediate production at the Waldorf Studios.

"Phantom of Forest" is Completed

Renaud Hoffman, supervising director has completed "The Phantom of the Forrest," eighth of the series of twelve Gotham productions to be released through Lumas Corporation. The picture stars Thunder the Marvel Dog, with Frank Davis, his owner and trainer in the heavy role. Others in the cast include Betty Francisco, Eddie Phillips, James Mason, Irene Hunt, Rhedy Hathaway and "White Fawn," Thunder's mate. Henry McCarty directed.

Davis Off to Coast for Production Plans

J. CHARLES DAVIS, II, president of the Davis Distributing Division leaves for the coast this week to confer with various producers of product to be distributed through his organization. Immediately upon the arrival of Davis, the second Al Wilson production will get under way.

"Peggy in Chinatown," second of the Peggy O'Day series will be cast and shooting started immediately. Davis will confer with Marilyn Mills on the third picture of her series, the title of which has not yet been announced. He will also consult with Guaranteed Pictures ,Inc., regarding "The Courage of Captain Plum," third of the series of James Oliver Curwood stories to be released about the first of the year.

Luncheon Will Follow Fox Ceremonies

FOLLOWING the laying of the cornerstone of the new $200,000 Fox Exchange building in New York City, Senator James J. Walker, Democratic candidate for Mayor will head the list of guests at the luncheon to be given in the Rose Room of the Hotel Astor on October 28th. James R. Grainger, general sales manager of the company will be the host.

The cornerstone will be laid promptly at noon at 343-45 West 44th street with appropriate ceremonies, in which civic officials, stars of stage and screen, and exhibitors will take part. Heading the list of city and state officials will be Senator Walker, Julius Miller, Manhattan Borough President, and Thomas J. Drennan, fire commissioner. Thomas Meighan, shepherd of the Lambs Club, will lead the delegation of stars representing stage and screen.

Father O'Reilly is Making Record With House

Father O'Reilly and Father Humphreys, the former of Rosendale, N. Y., and the latter in the neighboring village of New Paltz, are making quite a record for themselves these days as exhibitors. Father O'Reilly is running his theatre seven days a week and it is said that on Sunday night it is not uncommon to see more than 200 automobiles parked in the vicinity.

The house of 500 seats was remodeled by Father O'Reilly, who does all the booking and keeps a record not only of every picture that has been played at his theatre but also the hour the film was received and the hour that it was shipped in return. Father Humphreys is more of a newcomer in the business and until he becomes a bit more acquainted, Father O'Reilly will do his booking.

Musicians in Portland, Me., Houses Walk Out

Refused an increase of from $41 to $55 per week, longer rest periods and a walk-out of fifteen minutes each hour by Abraham Goodside, the musicians of the Strand, Empire and Jefferson theatres, Portland, Me., have quit. Fifteen are employed at the Strand and eleven at the Empire. Those at the Jefferson had not yet started work. Goodside declined to meet their demands on the grounds that they worked only five and a half hours a day with alternating twenty minute periods of work and rest.

Goodside also refused to discharge two organists he hired in Boston and New York, whom, he states, the musicians wanted replaced by Portland organists.

"Million Dollar Handicap" Cast Completed

Metropolitan Pictures has completed the cast for "The Million Dollar Handicap" and filming has started under the direction of Scott Sidney. Vera Reynolds has the leading role and in the supporting cast are Edmund Burns, Ralph Lewis, Walter Emerson, Ward Crane, Tom Wilson, Clarence Burton and Danny Hoy. The picture was adapted by F. McGrew Willis and Scott Sidney from the novel by W. A. Fraser.

Al Green Chosen to Direct First National's "Irene"

Word from John McCormick, of First National's West Coast studios, states that Al Green will direct Colleen Moore in "Irene," which, it is claimed, will be one of the most elaborate productions Miss Moore has made. George K. Arthur has been signed for the role of "Madame Lucy" and Lloyd Hughes will appear opposite the star. Charles Murray and Kate Price will also have important roles.

R. A. White Made Sales Manager of Florida Corporation

R. A. White, formerly General Sales Manager of Fox Films, has been made Sales Manager of the Delray office of the Mizner Development Corporation, Palm Beach, Fla., developers of Boca Raton, according to advices received from Harry Reichenbach. Delray is located eighteen miles south of Palm Beach and ten miles north of Boca Raton.

Del Andrews to Direct "No Man's Law" for F. B. O.

Del Andrews who recently directed a series of Fred Thompson starring vehicles for F.B.O. has been engaged to direct "No Man's Law," in which Bob Custer will be starred. Custer's support will include Adalyn Mayer, Ralph McCullough, Bruce Gordon and Ethan Laidlow.

The story is by Walter F. Coburn and William Wing prepared the script.

Sebastian Cast Completed for "Fifth Avenue"

Anna May Wong and Crauford Kent are the latest additions to the A. H. Sebastian cast for "Fifth Avenue," which will be released by Producers Distributing Corporation. Robert Vignola is directing and the cast includes Marguerite De La Motte, Allan Forrest, Louise Dresser, Sally Long, Josephine Norman and Lucille Lee Stewart.

"Other Woman's Story" is Next From Schulberg

B. P. Schulberg announces "The Other Woman's Story" as its next release. This production is the first directorial effort of B. F. Stanley, former newspaper man and writer of popular fiction.

"Roxy" to Stage Goldwyn's "Stella Dallas"

AS a special courtesy to Samuel Goldwyn producer of "Stella Dallas," S. L. Rothafel will stage and direct the presentation of that production when it opens at the Apollo theatre, New York, on November 15. Although generally understood that "Roxy," as president of the Roxy Theatres, Inc., would handle no interests other than those directly connected with the promulgation of his new theatre enterprise, it is claimed that the appeal of the production was too strong for the screen impressario to resist. Rothafel's associates, Messrs. Lubin and Atkinson, agreed that the vehicle merited his making an exception to the rule.

Too Many Stars, Says Harry Warner

Studio Workers All Gods in Their Own Minds and Think Only of Their Own Fame, He Declares

EXCESSIVE individualism and the insatiable desire for self aggrandizement on the part of those engaged in making pictures, is responsible for inefficiency in motion picture studios and at the bottom of many of the photoplay failures which issue from them, according to Harry M. Warner in a statement this week, in which he says that the most glaring fault in the studios today is that too many stars think they are gods.

"The 'star' attitude of mind," he says, "permeates the entire studio organization of every company producing pictures today. Instead of an organized force of specialists, each contributing a part to the work of turning out good pictures and functioning with that harmony which is essential to the achievement of an artistic unit composed of several widely different elements, we have in the studios a mass of individuals, concerned mostly with their own personal advancement and entirely blind to the fact that their professional welfare and that of the producer can best be served by co-operative effort in which they give their best and permit their fellow worker to give his best.

"From the office boy in a studio up to the very top of the organizations there is that one idea, 'self.' Each individual in the organization regards himself as the most im-

Harry M. Warner, president of Warner Bros.

portant personage in the studio, and convinced that he is 'IT,' thinks only of becoming more famous and more brilliant as a star.

"It is as though the star actor or actress, or star director or cameraman, or star scenarist or continuity clerk, alone counted when the picture had been completed. As a matter of fact no star can continue long as a real star if he or she appears in pictures which are not entertaining as a whole. The star's performance, no matter how brilliant the part nor how impressive the acting, cannot hold an audience if other important elements of the play are subordinated or entirely sacrificed for the sake of glorifying the star.

"If the Yale football team this year goes in for individual glorification as intensely as directors and actors are going in for it in the studios, I pity the chances at New Haven. It is a little bit humorous to watch the film makers at work on this account.

"Most of the assistant directors know more about picture-making than the directors in charge. The assistants get from $100 to $125 a week, while the directors draw salaries ranging from $1,000 a week to $5,000. In one case a director I know sent a prospective script on to his $125 assistant, who happened to be in New York. It was rejected by the assistant, and so the director refused to take it.

"The stars are intolerable in many instances. It is impossible to convince them that they are anything less than gods. We need a new crop of them, and we need them badly.

"The same idea is spreading beyond the studios. Today we have 'star critics' who think their own opinions on pictures are greater authority as to the merits of a screen production than the public for which it has been made. Critics have the right to express their own views of the pictures, but they have no right to tell the people they are crazy for liking these same pictures.

"A way will be found some day to bring organized effort into the making of pictures and the attitude now prevalent that 'I will make a picture' will be changed to one in which the producer, scenarist, director and players will proceed with the idea that 'we will make a picture,' and then more consistent work will be accomplished and the motion picture will be rid of many of the evils which beset it at present."

Washington M. P. T. O. Sets Convention

The third annual convention of the Motion Picture Theatre Owners of Washington was called for Wednesday, November 4, in communications sent out to all members last week by J. M. Hone, executive secretary with offices in Seattle. The convention will again be held in Seattle, and is expected to be attended by at least one hundred exhibitor members from the state.

John Hamrick, general manager of the Blue Mouse circuit, and president of the M. P. T. O. W. will preside, and active chairmanship will be taken over by Mr. Hone. Business meetings, entertainment features and a large banquet are already listed as the principal details of the program now being elaborately arranged.

Weaver Productions Are Reorganized

H. C. Weaver Productions, Inc., of Tacoma, Wash., was reorganized last week when a new executive board was chosen and officers elected. The personnel of the new board includes some of the most prominent financiers of the Northwest.

H. C. Weaver was chosen president of the company, with W. H. Rust, vice-president and Gen. James M. Ashton, secretary and treasurer. These three men, with Chester Thorne and J. T. Gregory constitute the board of trustees.

Plans for the company as announced by President Weaver include the production of about eighteen pictures, contracts for which already have been authorized by the Vital Exchanges and Associated Exhibitors.

Invites Wyoming to Join National Organization

A letter congratulating the Wyoming exhibitors upon the formation of a stage organization and inviting the body to join the National Organization of theatre owners, has been sent to James Lynch, president of the Wyoming association, by Eli Whitney Collins, head of the Arkansas M. P. T. O.

Mr. Collins extends his congratulations as an "exhibitor who has tested organization," and declares that the Wyoming exhibitors can enjoy National protection only through an alliance with the National organization.

Pathe Beauty Contest Winners Named

THE national beauty contest conducted by Pathe in conjunction with the showing of the company's serial, "Sunken Silver," has been concluded and the winner is Miss Ivene Whipple of Freeport, Maine. The release of the ten chapter serial was accompanied by a nation-wide newspaper and magazine advertising campaign built around the national beauty contest, which involved $3,000 in prize awards, as well as affording the winner an opportunity to play in a Patheserial.

The selection of the winners was made by a board of judges on the basis of photographs of candidates and letters written by them. The winners were determined on the basis of good looks, expression, intelligence and apparent screen effectiveness.

The winners, in addition to Miss Whipple were:

Laura Lacallade, N. Y. C.; Myrtle M. Cain, Miami, Fla.; Gay Coulton Ingold, Minneapolis, Minn.; Velta Lane, Griffith, Ga.; Hazel Fay Davis, Portland, Ore.; Helen M. Lambert, Seattle, Wash.; Marion Hill, Miami, Fla.; Gladys Tinker, Hollywood, Cal., Carlena Johnson, Dallas, Tex.; Pauline Christy, N. Y. C.; Doris Dumas, Jonesboro, Ark.; Florence Grote, Cincinnati, Ohio; Eugenia L. Lemerle, Washington, D. C.; Cornelia Reid, Hattiesburg, Miss.; Vera de Give, N. Y. C.; Annabelle Ross, Washington, Ind.; Edna Farrington, Sioux City, Iowa; Margaret Cage, Hutchinson, Kans.; Alma Kirch, Willisville, Ill.; Alvina Hofsommer, Breese, Ill.; Zelma Sanders, Cushing, Okla.; Gladys Snider, Cleveland, Ohio; Margaret Conway, Decatur, Mich.; Lucille Gray, Omaha, Neb.

Scenes indicative of the trend of the action in "The Circle," a Metro-Goldwyn-Mayer production.

Irish-Jewish Series For Fox

Popular Characters Will Be Launched in Eight Two-Reel Imperial Comedies

FOX FILM CORPORATION has launched a series of two-reel comedies based on the romance of a Jewish boy and an Irish colleen. There are to be eight of them in all, the first of which is titled, "East Side, West Side," which will be released Sunday, November 15th. Thereafter the comedies will be released under the Imperial brand at the rate of one every eight weeks.

Georgie Harris and Barbara Luddy have been engaged under long term contracts to portray the leading roles. Harris was a Jewish comedian in London before he succumbed to the lure of the motion pictures. Miss Luddy is a capable actress, well qualified to play the heroine role.

The best title writers available will interpret the wit and humor of the Irish and the Jews in the series. The intermingling of the two races as the result of the Irish-Jewish romance gives rise to hilarious situations and a chance for exceptional merit in title writing.

In "East Side, West Side" George Williams plays the Jewish father and Tom McGuire is the Irish father. Red Thompson is cast in the role of a crook.

Feelers sent out by the short subjects department of Fox Films are said to have brought back wide expressions of approval of the new series, which give promise of becoming exceptionally popular.

F. B. O. Fixes 1926-27 Program

Company Announces Twelve Specials and Six Star Series; Also Offers Short Reels

F. B. O. will have its entire next season's program arranged in the very near future according to an announcement issued by J. I. Schnitzer, vice-president in charge of productions. Though the titles of the various important productions are being withheld it is understood that at least twelve special attractions will be made, among them "The Life of Theodore Roosevelt."

There will be at least six star series, including productions starring Fred Thompson, Maurice (Lefty) Flynn, Dick Talmadge,

Tom Tyler, Bob Custer and it is likely that one or two of the first rank stars will be engaged for a series of special productions, continues the statement from Schnitzer.

F.B.O. will also continue active in the short subject field with another series titled "Fighting Hearts," to be put in production as soon as the current "Mazie" chapters are completed. Sam Hellman is the author of "Fighting Hearts." A series titled "Bill Grimms Progress," which detail the experiences of a taxi driver will be H. C. Witwer's contribution to the short subject program.

Dwan Will Produce "Sea Horses" on Coast

"Sea Horses" will go into production for Paramount shortly after the arrival of Allan Dwan on the coast. Dwan left New York last week. The picture is an adaptation from the novel by Francis Brett Young and was prepared for the screen by Becky Gardner. The leading roles will be played by Florence Vidor, Jack Holt, Noah Beery, George Bancroft, William Powell and Lawrence Gray.

Charleston Dancers in Bennett Production

Four couples, who are recognized in New York as the best exponents of the Charleston style of ball room dancing, according to Whitman Bennett, will take part in "Share and Share Alike," Bennett's latest production for Arrow release. To make the scene as realistic as possible, the couple adjudged to be the best dancers, will be presented with a silver challenge cup.

Mary O'Hara Writing Script for "Perch of the Devil"

Mary O'Hara is writing the adaptation of Gertrude Atherton's "Perch of the Devil," which Universal will produce. The picture is to be directed by King Baggot. Miss O'Hara made the scenario for "Black Oxen," another Gertrude Atherton work adapted to the screen.

Trio of highlights from "The Jester," a Prod. Dist. Corp. release.

Chadwick Starts Production on Railroad Drama

Chadwick Pictures Corporation has started production of the "Transcontinental Limited," a railroad drama which it is announced will be filmed on an elaborate scale. The picture will have Johnnie Walker in the star role, with Mary Carr, Eugenia Gilbert, Alec Francis and Bruce Gordon in principal supporting roles.

Among the spectacular features included in "Transcontinental Limited" will be a realistic railroad wreck. Nat Ross, director of many Universal productions, is directing the picture.

Austin Succeeds Panzer in "Her Cowboy Prince"

Fox has found it necessary to cast Jere Austin instead of Paul Panzer in the bandit role in "Her Cowboy Prince," the newest Buck Jones starring vehicle. The change was necessary because Panzer could not be spared from his work in the title role of "The Ancient Mariner," the special Fox Christmas release which is now in production.

Herrick Completes Cast for "Keep It Up"

The cast has been completed for "Keep It Up," F. Herrick Herrick's first picture for Davis Distributing Division, which is now in production. Eleanore King is the star, with Reginald Simpson playing opposite her. In the chief supporting roles are Hugh Wilson, Harry Stone, Ricca Allen, William Calhoun, Dennis Mullin, Al Stewart and Robert Billiours.

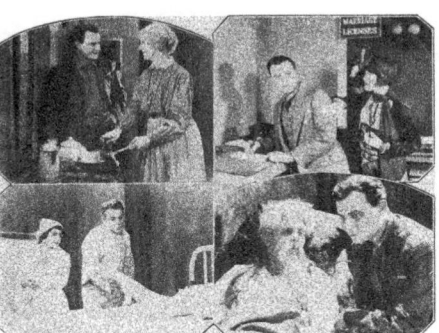

Production highlights from F. B. O.'s "The Keeper of the Bees."

George Walsh in "The Prince of Broadway," a Chadwick Picture.

Associated Product Is Titled

Program of Thirty Pictures Will Be Released as "The Triumphant Thirty"

"THE Triumphant Thirty" is the title chosen by Associated Exhibitors for the company's thirty pictures for the season. The first picture to be released under this title is "Counsel for the Defense," a melodrama of a small town and a keen girl lawyer. Betty Compson plays the stellar role with House Peters and Rockliffe Fellowes.

"Camille of the Barbary Coast," one of the biggest of the company's thirty, is scheduled for release November 1st. It features Mae Busch and Owen Moore. The stars are backed by a cast which includes Harry Morey, Dagmar Godowsky, Barr McIntosh, Fritzie Brunette, Dorothy King and Tammany Young. Hugh Dierker directed.

In addition to the scheduled thirty, several unusual specials will be released, one of which is already completed and is "The Sky Rocket," starring Peggy Hopkins Joyce. Marshall Neilan directed.

The first eight pictures have already been released, among them some prominent successes of moviedom. These were "Never Weaken," starring Harold Lloyd with Mildred Davis; "Headlines," starring Alice Joyce with Malcolm McGregor; "Keep Smiling," Monty Banks, with Ann Cornwall; "Manhattan Madness," starring Jack Dempsey and Estelle Taylor; "His Buddy's Wife," Glenn Hunter, with Edna Murphy; the great crook melodrama, "Under the Rouge," with Tom Moore and Eileen Percy; "Camille of the Barbary Coast," Mae Busch and Owen Moore; and "Fifty Fifty," with Lionel Barrymore and Hope Hampton.

Two Glenn Hunter pictures are scheduled for release in the near future. Pictures starring such well known players as Blanche Sweet, Ralph Lewis, Clara Bow, Percy Marmont, and many others of like calibre, in addition to other pictures by stars who already have appeared in the first eight, are in process of production.

"U" Announces Cast for "Skinner's Dress Suit"

The cast which will support Reginald Denny and Laura La Plante, co-stars of the picture, in "Skinner's Dress Suit" has been announced by Universal. Those who will be seen in principal roles are Ben Hendricks, Jr.; E. J. Ratcliffe, Arthur Lake, Henry A. Barrow, Hedda Hooper, Lionel Braham, William A. Strauss, Lisle Leslie, Betty Morrissey and Broderick O'Farrell. The picture is being directed by William A. Seiter.

Scenes from "The Golden Princess," Paramount's photoplay based on the Bret Hart story with Betty Bronson in the title role.

F. P.-L's Metropolitan Opened

Paramount Executives and Stars Present:
Boston House is Largest in New England

ALVAN T. FULLER, Governor of Massachusetts; James M. Curley, Mayor of Boston; Edward F. Albee, head of the Keith-Albee circuit; and John Murray Anderson, were the speakers at the invitation dedication of the new Metropolitan Theatre, Tremont and Hollis streets, Boston. This is New England's largest theatre. It is operated by Famous Players and Ballaban & Katz.

The invitation opening was on Friday evening, Oct. 16. Arrival of the Merchants Limited from New York started traffic trouble incidental to the initial opening of the playhouse. This train brought over from New York, in two special cars attached to the rear, film stars and luminaries. In the party were Adolph Zukor, Jesse Lasky, Mr. and Mrs. Harold B. Franklin and Charles E. McCarthy of the Famous Players-Lasky Corporation; Thomas Meighan, Harrison Ford, Bessie Love, Lois Wilson, Diana Kane and others.

By eight o'clock every seat in the big playhouse was filled. Practically every one in Greater Boston identified in any way with the theatrical and motion picture industries being present. Paramount officials occupied the spacious box at the left of the projection booth off the mezzanine floor. In the corresponding box at the right were the Paramount stars.

John Murray Anderson was master of ceremonies. The speakers were Governor Fuller, who extended the felicitations of the Commonwealth; Mayor Curley, who extended greetings on behalf of the city of Boston, and Edward F. Albee, who briefly outlined the work of construction of the theatre. All paid high compliment to the directing genius of William J. MacDonald. Mayor Curley presented Mr. Albee with a

gold key to the city, the highest honor paid by Boston.

Then, as curtain after curtain was drawn aside, each in turn drawing admiring applause, the entertainment commenced. It was the regular opening program. The 55-piece orchestra rose slowly from the orchestra pit into view on the specially constructed elevator-platform under the direction of Nathaniel W. Finston, formerly musical director of the Chicago and Uptown Theatre, Chicago, and with Arthur J. Martell at the organ. As the opening overture, "1812" was completed, the orchestra slowly receded into the orchestra pit again. There were vaudeville numbers, a combination film and stage production on the life of Chopin with the big orchestra again taking a leading part; a pageant specially staged by Mr. Anderson depicting early New England up to the present time, with more than 40 taking part, and finally the feature film. Owing to the delay occasioned by the traffic jam, the program was late in starting and it was one o'clock before the film was finished.

The scale of prices, which it is understood is the scale which is to prevail, is: 11 a. m. to 1 p. m. 35 cents; matinee to 6 p. m. 50 cents; evenings 65 cents except Saturday, Sunday and holiday evenings which will be 75 cents.

Metropolitan Signs Noted Studio Artist

Edward Withers, studio artist, has been signed by Metropolitan Pictures as assistant to art director Charles Cadwallader. Withers is a graduate of the Langham School of Art in London and studied under Linley Richardson of the Royal British Academy.

"A Savage in Silks" Rights Bought by Universal

Universal has purchased the screen rights to "A Savage in Silks," by Winifred Reeve, which is to be published as a novel. The work was bought as a starring vehicle for Mary Philbin. The leading role is said to offer Miss Philbin a part that differs greatly with any she has hitherto essayed and Universal states that the star made screen tests in the make-up and rehearsal of some scenes before the work was purchased. The author, Mrs. Reeve, is Universal's Editor-in-Chief and literary advisor.

Denig Directs New First National Department

A new special feature department has been created at First National and will be in charge of Lynde Denig, who for several years has been a member of the publicity staff of First National. Denig's duties will also include the handling of trade news. Frank Shields Jacobs, a Metropolitan newspaper man of fifteen years' experience, has been made city editor of the department. He will direct the gathering and dissemination of First National's news.

Blanche Mehaffey Joins Pola Negri Cast

Blanche Mehaffey has been making rapid progress as a screen actress, whose services are much in demand. She has been signed by Paramount for an important role in Pola Negri's new production.

Scenes from "Vanishing Millions," produced by Sierra Pictures, Inc.

Wray Starts Production on "Golden Butterfly"

John Griffith Wray has started production on "The Golden Butterfly," his second picture under his Fox contract. Alma Rubens and Bert Lytell head the cast which includes Frank Keenan, Huntley Gordon, Herbert Rawlinson, Vera Lewis and Carolynn Snowden. The picture is based on an original story by Evelyn Campbell, adapted by Bradley King.

F. B. O. to Start "Fighting Hearts" Series Soon

F.B.O. will start production of the new two-reel series, "Fighting Hearts," written by Sam Hellman, as soon as the "Adventures of Mazie" pictures are completed. The new series will be made in twelve episodes. The "Mazie" unit is now working on the sixth episode of the group, which will also consist of twelve episodes.

French Actress to Appear in Paramount Pictures

Mlle. Arlette Marchal, French actress and a noted beauty, will arrive here this week and will appear in Paramount productions, as a result of her work in "Madame Sans Gene" which was made in France, in which she played the role of Caroline. She will become a member of Paramount's stock company and her first picture will be announced shortly after her arrival.

Interesting moments from the Fox production featuring Edmund Lowe and Alma Rubens titled "The Winding Stair."

Scenes from "He's a Prince"—Paramount.

Seven Fox November Releases

Three Recent Broadway Stage Successes Due for Exhibitors Next Month

SEVEN feature pictures and a number of short subjects are included in the Fox November release schedule. Three of them are recent Broadway stage successes. "Thank You," "Lazybones" and "The Fool." A fourth well known stage success is "East Lynne." The other features will be Tom Mix in "The Best Bad Man" and Buck Jones in "Durand of the Bad Lands." A seventh feature will be announced later.

"Thank You," third of the John Golden plays will be released November 1st. It has already been well received in New York and Cleveland. Jacqueline Logan and George O'Brien have the leading roles. The other November 1st release will be Buck Jones in "Durand of the Bad Lands." Marian Nixon is the heroine and Malcolm Waite the villain.

"Lazybones," the Owen Davis stage success, will be released November 8th. Buck Jones again has the title role, but it is a vastly different one than any in which he has been seen before. In the supporting cast are Madge Bellamy, Jane Novak, Zasu Pitts and Leslie Fenton.

"The Fool" is next on the release schedule on November 15th. It is based on Channing Pollock's stage success. Edmund Lowe will be seen in the title role, with little Anne Dale as the crippled girl. The supporting cast includes Mary Thurman, Paul Panzer, Brenda Bond and Raymond Bloomer. Harry Millard directed.

"East Lynne" was produced under the direction of Emmett Flynn and the cast includes Alma Rubens, Edmund Lowe, Lou Tellegen, Paul Panzer, Frank Keenan, Leslie Fenton and Harry Seymour. It will be released November 22nd.

"The Best Bad Man," with Tom Mix, will be released November 29th. The story is by Max Brand who wrote "Just Tony" and "The Untamed." J. G. Blystone directed. In the supporting cast are Clara Bow, Cyril Chadwick, Paul Panzer, Frank Beal and Tom Kennedy.

Five two-reel comedies and three Fox Varieties are included in the month's releases. Earle Foxe will be seen in "The Wrestler," third of the new Van Bibber series, which will be released November 1st. "East Side, West Side," first of the new Irish-Jewish comedies is scheduled for November 15th. "The Peacemakers," third of the Helen and Warren comedies goes to the exhibitors November 15th. "Failure" of the O. Henry series is due November 29th. "The Sky Tribe," a one-reel Variety is set for November 1st, "White Paper" for November 15th and "The River Nile" for November 29th.

Sylvano Balboni to Direct for First National

John McCormick, general manager of the west coast activities of First National, this week announced that his company had promoted to a directorship Sylvano Balboni, eminent Italian artist and cameraman. His first directorial effort is to be "The Far Cry," a film version of Arthur Richman's stage play, the continuity for which is now being prepared by Katherine Kavanaugh. Blanche Sweet will play the leading feminine role.

Balboni's promotion is due to the valuable aid he gave June Mathis in superintending the production activities of the recently completed First National special "The Viennese Medley."

Marceline Day to Play Lead in "The Barrier"

Marceline Day has been signed to play Necia, the leading feminine role in "The Barrier," a Rex Beach story now in production under the direction of George Hill. The novel was adapted for the screen by Harvey Gates. It is a Metro-Goldwyn-Mayer release.

Norman Kerry plays Meade Burrell, the leading male role and Henry B. Walthall and Lionel Barrymore appear in prominent parts.

"Broken Homes" Completed by Macfadden

Final scenes for "Broken Homes," third of the "Macfadden Made Movies" of True Story Films, were shot last week at the Pathe Studio in New York. Alice Lake and Gaston Glass are starred in the picture, while in the supporting cast are Betty Jewel, J. Barney Sherry, and Jane Jennings. Hugh Dierker directed this picture as he did the first two of the series, "The Wrongdoers" and "False Pride."

Anthony Jowitt Assigned to "Magpie" Cast

Anthony Jowitt, young British actor has been assigned to one of the leading roles with Bebe Daniels in William de Mille's forthcoming Paramount production, temporarily titled "Magpie." Others in the cast include Neil Hamilton, Fred Walton, Ann Cornwall, Lloyd Corrigan and Mickey Mclan.

'Ralph Graves in scenes from "Good Morning Madam," a Mack Sennett comedy offered by Pathe.

New "Potash, Perlmutter" Picture Under Way

Henry King has started production on Samuel Goldwyn's third "Potash and Perlmutter" production for release through United Artists Corporation. It is titled, "Partners Again—with Potash and Perlmutter" and has George Sidney and Alexander Carr in the featured roles. The action in the coming story takes place in the haying, selling and demonstrating end of the airplane industry.

The script was written by Frances Marion in collaboration with Montague Glass, author and creator of the "Potash and Perlmutter" stories.

Maurice Sebastian is Made Production Manager

A. H. Sebastian has made his son, Maurice, production manager of the Sebastian producing organization, which is now making "Fifth Avenue" at the Metropolitan Studios in Hollywood for Producers Distributing Corporation release. The younger Sebastian has just completed an engagement as production manager of the Howard Estabrook Company.

"The Bride" Selected for Priscilla Dean

Priscilla Dean's first production for Metropolitan Pictures Corporation will be "The Bride," a play by Stewart Oliver and George Middleton. This vehicle was selected for the star by William Sistrom.

Weiss Bros. Will Continue Features

With the announced addition of a program of short subjects, Weiss Brothers have no intention of neglecting or curtailing their regular program of Western features. They will produce and deliver the twenty-four five-reel features under the Artclass branch. These consist of eight Buddy Roosevelts, eight Buffalo Bill's and enight with Wally Wales. In addition there will be eight with Leo Maloney under the Clarion trademark.

A number of these pictures have already arrived in New York. In the Buffalo Bill series the company has received, "Quicker'N Lightnin'," "The Desert Demon," "The Saddle Cyclone," "A Streak of Luck" and "Trumpin' Trouble."

In the Wally Wales series those already received are, "Tearin' Loose," "The Hurricane Horseman," "Galloping On," "The Roaring Rider" and "The Fighting Cheat," while those received in the Leo Maloney series are, "Win, Lose or Draw," and "Luck and Sand."

Gerald Beaumont Story Next for "Lefty" Flynn

"The Kitten and the King," a Gerald Beaumont story based on the life of a policeman has been acquired by Harry Garson as the next starring vehicle for Maurice (Lefty) Flynn. It will be the third policeman's role Flynn has played in this current series of starring productions for F.B.O. He is now making "Between Men," in which he plays a civil engineer.

Mack Named for "American Venus" Cast

Frank Tuttle has selected William B. Mack for an important role in "The American Venus," which he is directing for Paramount. Mack is at present playing the stage director in Herbert Brenon's "The Song and Dance Man," featuring Tom Moore, Bessie Love and Harrison Ford.

Three Added to "Golden Strain" Cast

Fox has added George Reed, Frank McGlynn, Jr., and Coy Watson to the cast of "The Golden Strain," the screen version of Peter B. Kyne's "Thoroughbreds," which has just been put into production at the West Coast studios.

Lloyd Making First for Paramount

HAROLD LLOYD'S first production for Paramount will be made under the working title of "For Heaven's Sake." It is an original story conceived by Lloyd and being developed by Ted Wilde, John Grey, Clyde Bruckman and Tim Whelan, with Sam Taylor directing.

The story deals in part with missionary endeavors in the slums and the comedian is now working on one of its most important sequences, scenes for which are being shot in the most congested districts of Los Angeles. Lloyd's supporting cast is again headed by Jobyna Ralston.

Schenck Signs Nobleman to Play Leads

Tullio Carminati, leading man and managing director for Eleanora Duse during her last tour in Italy, has signed a three year contract with Joseph M. Schenck to appear as leading man in productions including those starring Constance Talmadge. Carminati, whose full name is Count Tullio Carminati di Brambilla, though he has never used the full title, played leads in repertoire in Italy when but nineteen years of age. He afterwards co-starred with Leda Borelli and then formed his own company.

His first picture appearance was with Princess Matchiabelli; later he played in Ufa pictures in Germany. He came to this country recently to study picture conditions here. He will leave for the coast shortly with Schenck and will play opposite Constance Talmadge in one of her forthcoming productions.

Production Started on "The Agony Column"

Work was started this week on Monte Blue's next starring production for Warner Bros., "The Agony Column" with Dorothy Devore cast for the leading feminine role. The story, dealing with the "Personals" printed daily in the metropolitan newspapers, was written by Earl Dery Biggers. It is being directed by Roy Del Ruth.

Lillian Elliott Signs for "Partners Again"

Henry King has signed Lillian Elliott for the Samuel Goldwyn screen version of "Partners Again." Miss Elliott will have the role of Rosie, which she played in all of the Montague Glass "Potash and Perlmutter" stage plays. George Sidney and Alexander Carr have the title roles. United Artists Corporation will release the picture.

Mayo is to Direct "Money Talks" for M-G-M

According to an announcement made by Hunt Stromberg, associate studio executive for Metro-Goldwyn-Mayer, Archie Mayo will direct "Money Talks," a comedy drama by Rupert Hughes. Filming is to start at an early date. Hope Loring and Louis Leighton are now at work on the screen adaptation.

Corinne Griffith Finishes "Caesar's Wife"

"Caesar's Wife," Corinne Griffith's latest for First National, has been completed under the direction of Irving Cummings. While the film is in the hands of the cutters Miss Griffith will take a short rest, during which time another story will be selected to serve as her next vehicle.

Mary Carr Signed for Role in "Flaming Waters"

Mary Carr will play one of the leading roles in "Flaming Waters," an original story by E. Lloyd Sheldon with a continuity by Fred Kennedy Myton. It is a melodrama of the oil fields and is being produced by Associated Arts for release through F.B.O.

Production highlights from the Metro-Goldwyn-Mayer picture, "The Mystic."

F. B. O. Lot Hums With Action

Production Activities Continued Unabated With Schedule Being Maintained

F. B. O. is working at full blast on its extensive production schedule and there will be no letup in the activities until all of the pictures are completed. The program as arranged is keeping the production forces right on the proper schedule of work.

During the week "The Midnight Flyer" was completed. It is a railroad melodrama directed by Tom Forman and co-features Cullen Landis and Dorothy Devore. The release date is set for late in November.

The completion of "The Midnight Flyer" saw the starting of "Flaming Waters," an oil industry melodrama directed by Harmon Weight. Mary Carr, Malcolm McGregor and Pauline Garon are featured in the new production.

Within the next two weeks work will be started on "When His Love Grew Cold,"

from the old novel by Laura Jean Libbey. "A Poor Girl's Romance," by the same author, will also be filmed in the early future, as will "The Futurity Winner," a turf drama, by Louis Joseph Vance.

Fred Thomson has completed "All Around the Frying Pan" and is ready to start "The Tough Guy," which, however, is only a temporary title. Evelyn Brent, after a month's vacation in New York, will settle down at once to her next feature, "A Broadway Lady." Maurice Flynn has finished "Between Men" and "Heads Up," and will soon start another comedy melodrama.

Chester Conklin is in Pola Negri Cast

Chester Conklin has been signed by Paramount for an important comedy role in Pola Negri's next production, which has not yet been titled.

New Universal "Super" Being Edited

DIMITRI BUCHOWETZKI has completed camera work on "The Midnight Sun," the next super picture to be offered by Universal as a sequel to "The Hunchback" and "The Phantom."

The new production has an all-star cast in which Laura La Plante, Pat O'Malley, George Siegman, Theodore Kosloff, Cesare Gravina, Raymond Keane, Arthur Hoyt, Earl Metcalf and others appear.

The story is described as a dramatic tale of Russian life in the days of the Czar and afforded the producer exceptional opportunities for elaborate pictorial effects and massive ensemble scenes.

"Red Kimono" Completed by Mrs. Reid

Mrs. Wallace Reid has completed the last shots on her production, "The Red Kimono" and the picture is now being titled by Adela Rogers St. John, author of the story. Immediately upon its completion it will be shown to executives of the Davis Distributing Division and Vital Exchanges and the print will then be shipped east. The National premiere will take place in New York probably early in November at a theatre still to be decided upon.

M-G-M Signs Cedric Gibbons to Long Contract

From the Culver City studios of Metro-Goldwyn-Mayer comes the announcement that Cedric Gibbons, art director in chief, has been signed to a new long term contract with that organization. This was made known by Irving G. Thalberg, associate studio executive. Gibbons started as art director in pictures five years ago, with the Goldwyn company and continued in that capacity when Goldwyn merged with Metro and Mayer.

First National Purchases "Too Much Money"

First National has purchased screen rights to Israel Zangwill's stage play, "Too Much Money" and it is to be placed in production in the east under the supervision of Earl Hudson within the next two weeks with John Francis Dillon directing. Lewis Stone and Anna Q. Nilsson will be seen in the featured roles. Contracts have also just been closed by First National covering the purchase of motion picture rights to "The River," a play by Patrick Hastings.

Meighan's "Irish Luck" in Cutting Room

Thomas Meighan's new Paramount picture, "Irish Luck," is in the cutting room, where it will be one of the first to be titled under the supervision of John Peale Bishop, Paramount's new title editor. Assisting Bishop are Tom J. Geraghty, supervisor of Meighan productions, and Emmet Crozier, both of whom made the trip to Ireland with the star for the production of the picture. The production is scheduled for first run release November 16th.

The Constant Simp" is the title of the second episode in F. B. O.'s "Adventures of Mazie" series. These scenes are taken from the picture.

Wilson Completes "Power God" Cast

Ben Wilson has completed the casting for "The Power God," that will be released by Davis Distributing Division starting about the middle of December. Ben Wilson and Neva Gerber are the stars of the serial, while in the supporting cast are, Allan Garcia, Lafe McKee, Ruth Royce, Nelson McDowell, William Turner and Mary Crane. This fifteen episode serial was written by Rex Taylor and Harry Haven and the continuity was prepared by George W. Pyper. The picture will be edited by Earl Turner.

Brenon to Make "Dancing Mothers" for Paramount

Herbert Brenon is preparing to start filming of "Dancing Mothers," an adaptation of the stage play by Edgar Selwyn and Edmund Goulding, it was announced by Jesse Lasky. Conway Tearle will appear as the husband, Alice Joyce will play the role of the wife and the part of the daughter will be taken by Betty Bronson who will journey from Hollywood to the Paramount Long Island studios where Brenon will produce the picture.

Janet Gaynor Leading Lady in Universal Western

Janet Gaynor has been chosen to play the feminine lead in "Three Wise Men," a Western in which Ben Corbett and Gilbert Holmes have the featured roles. Other players in the cast are Ella McKenzie, Robert McKenzie, Frank Abbott and Vera James. Vin Moore is directing.

Warners Add to Casts of Two Features

The cast for "The Agony Column" Monte Blue's next starring vehicle for Warner Bros. has been enlarged with the addition of John Roche, Stanley Taylor, Carl Stockdale, Arthur Thalaso and Eve Southern. Miss Southern will replace Myrna Loy.

Matthew Betz will play a part in Syd Chaplin's second production on the current Warner schedule titled "Nightie Nightie Nurse," in which Patsy Ruth Miller plays opposite the star. Others in the cast are Gayne Whitman, David Torrence, Edith York and Raymond Wells. Charles Reisner is directing.

"Broken Hearts" Release Date Postponed

The Jaffe Art Film Company has found it necessary to postpone the release date of "Broken Hearts," which was originally set for October 25th. Upon final editing of the picture it was found a slight error in costuming had occurred. The scene was ordered retaken and that necessitated an entire new set. The actor who played the role was also busy with a new picture. Lila Lee has the starring role in "Broken Hearts."

Earl Hurd Returns With Bray Studios

Earl Hurd, cartoonist creator of Bobby Bumps and other cartoon characters, is again back at the Bray Studios. His first subject will be the third of the Unnatural History Comedies titled "The Camel's Hump," in which Walter Lantz and Frankie Evans, the child find, will enact the leading roles. Clyde Geronimi will handle the megaphone. The picture will be released early in November by F. B. O.

Robert Thornby Returns as Director

Robert Thornby, former screen comedian, returns to the studios after an absence of two years, in the role of director. He has signed with the Christie Film Company to make a series of comedies for Educational release. His first assignment will be with the Neal Burns unit.

Dena Reed Will Handle Ginsberg Publicity

Following an illness of several months' duration, Dena Reed has been placed in charge of publicity and advertising for the Henry Ginsberg Distributing Corporation and will publicize the Banner and Royal pictures.

Jeanie Macpherson in a New Role

CECIL B. DE MILLE has named Jeanie Macpherson production supervisor for Rod La Rocque's next starring vehicle, "Red Dice," an adaptation from the novel by Octavus Roy Cohan. In addition to her supervisorial duties Miss Macpherson will also write the continuity for "Red Dice," which will be directed by Alan Hale. Miss Macpherson has been associated with De Mille for the past ten years.

Exhibitors Service Bureau

A colorful lobby display, simple in design, was achieved by the manager of the Mojeska theatre, Augusta, Ga., for Paramount's "The Coast of Folly." The arrangement featured a cut-out from the 24-sheet, mounted in the center of the lobby, and a strip, representing a bathing beach, above the entrance doors.

Advisory Board and Contributing Editors, Exhibitors' Service Bureau

George J. Schade, Schade theatre, Sandusky.

Edward L. Hyman, Mark Strand theatre, Brooklyn.

Leo A. Landau, Lyceum theatre, Minneapolis.

C. C. Perry, Managing Director, Garrick theatre, Minneapolis.

E. R. Rogers, Managing Director, Tivoli theatre, Chattanooga, Tenn.

Stanley Chambers, Palace theatre, Wichita, Kan.

Willard C. Patterson, Metropolitan theatre, Atlanta.

E. V. Richards, Jr., Gen. Mgr., Saenger Amusement Co., New Orleans.

F. L. Newman, Managing Director, Famous Players-Lasky theatres, Los Angeles.

Arthur G. Stolte, Des Moines theatre, Des Moines, Iowa.

W. C. Quimby, Managing Director, Strand Palace and Jefferson theatres, Fort Wayne, Ind.

J. A. Partington, Imperial theatre, San Francisco.

George E. Carpenter, Paramount-Empress theatre, Salt Lake.

Sidney Grauman, Grauman's theatres, Los Angeles.

THE CHECK-UP

Weekly Edition of Exhibitors' Box Office Reports

Productions listed are new pictures on which reports were not available previously.

For ratings on current and older releases see MOTION PICTURE NEWS—first issue of each month.

KEY—The first column following the name of the feature represents the number of managers that have reported the picture as "Poor." The second column gives the number who considered it "Fair"; the third the number who considered it "Good"; and the fourth column, those who considered it "Big."

The fifth column is a percentage giving the average rating on that feature, obtained by the following method: A report of "Poor" is rated at 20%; one of "Fair," 40%; "Good," 30%; and "Big," 100%. The percentage rating of all of these reports on one picture are then added together, and divided by the number of reports, giving which represents the consensus of opinion on that picture. In this way exceptional cases, reports which might be outstanding taken alone, and such individual differences of opinion are averaged up and eliminated.

TITLE	Poor	Fair	Good	Big	Value	Length
FAMOUS PLAYERS						
Man Who Found Himself	—	3	8	—	62	7,168 ft.
METRO-GOLDWYN						
Never the Twain Shall Meet	—	4	4	3	67	8,143 ft.
Pretty Ladies	1	6	5	—	51	5,828 ft.
PATHE						
Freshman, The	—	—	2	18	97	6 reels
UNITED ARTISTS						
Don Q. Son of Zorro	—	3	7	9	91	10,264 ft.
UNIVERSAL						
California Straight Ahead	—	1	7	4	78	7,258 ft.
Teaser, The	—	3	9	—	63	5,967 ft.

George E. Brown, Managing Director, Loew's Palace theatre, Memphis, Tenn.

Louis K. Sidney, Division Manager, Loew's theatres, Pittsburgh, Pa.

Geo. Rotsky, Managing Director, Palace theatre, Montreal, Can.

Eddie Zorn, Managing Director, Broadway-Strand theatre, Detroit.

Fred S. Myer, Managing Director, Palace theatre, Hamilton, Ohio.

Joseph Plunkett, Managing Director, Mark-Strand theatre, New York.

Ray Grombacher, Managing Director, Liberty theatre, Spokane, Wash.

Ross A. McVoy, Manager, Temple theatre, Geneva, N. Y.

W. S. McLaren, Managing Director, Capitol theatre, Jackson, Mich.

Harold B. Franklin, Director of Theatres, Famous Players-Lasky.

William J. Sullivan, Manager, Rialto theatre, Butte, Mont.

H. A. Albright, Manager, T. D. & L. theatre, Glendale, Calif.

Claire Meschime, Grand theatre, Westfield, N. Y.

Ace Berry, Managing Director, Circle theatre, Indianapolis.

Here is an idea for your lobby display on "Pretty Ladies" (Metro-Goldwyn-Mayer), or any of the Follies stories. The "leg border" idea was worked out by Manager Frank Miller at the Modjeska, Augusta, Ga.

Stunts Sell "Our Gang" Comedy

Shea's Uses Letter Signed "Farina": Youngster's Ball Game Staged by Kessler

TWO rather novel exploitation stunts recently developed in connection with drives for the "Our Gang" comedies produced by Hal Roach for Pathe release, may be cited as evidence that stunt publicity may be applied effectively to short subjects and that for theatres which regularly show established comedy series this exploitation effort is a profitable venture.

The two examples to be pointed out in this connection include a stunt by the management of Shea's Hippodrome, Buffalo, N. Y., as a special drive for "Your Own Back Yard," a recent release in the "Our Gang" series.

To a list of prominent people a series of letters under the signature of Farina, the dusky star of the "Gang," were sent. These were written in the style illustrated in the following specimen:

"Dear Mister

"I have lots of trubbles becaus everybody pix on me but i will get even with them if you will tell the little boys and little girls that i will be at mister Shay's Hippodrum next Sunday and they made me cal my show 'Your Own Back Yard.'

"I just know how much you will like me and my gang and my show and pleas tell all yore frinds about me."

Manager Nyman Kessler of the Atlantic Theatre, Atlantic, Mass., called the week beginning September 7, "Our Gang Week" and gave wide publicity to the Pathe short comedies. Kessler arranged a baseball game in connection with the showing of "The Champeen." A Boy Scout Team met a nine from a Quincy School, Kessler umpiring the game and inviting all the players to be his guests after the contest. The winning team received a baseball bat, with auto-graphs of players in "Our Gang" and a catcher's glove.

The B. S. Moss' Franklin Theatre, New York, has printed a two-color 8 x 11, throwaway announcing to its patrons the fact that the entire output of Pathe's Hal Roach two-reel comedies will be an added feature to the Keith-Albee vaudeville program at that house during the coming season.

Good Teaser Copy for "Are Parents People"

The important feature of Manager Warren Irvin's campaign for "Are Parents People" at the Imperial, Charlotte, was the teaser campaign he started in the newspaper several days prior to opening.

Two column two inch ads were run with copy as follows: "Are Parents People?"—You'll Know Sunday. 'On Sunday, day before opening, these teaser ads were followed up by a large 3 x 11 inch display in the newspapers.

Three days prior to showing 1,000 postal cards, written in longhand, were mailed out. These carried the title only, with "I. T." (Imperial theatre) at bottom. This type of teaser aroused considerable interest in the picture.

Lehman Repeats "Charleston" Feature at Orpheum

So popular was the Charleston dance contest staged by the Orpheum theatre a few weeks ago that Lawrence Lehman, manager, decided to duplicate the feat this week. And he was not disappointed, the increase in attendance being well worth the effort, he says.

"Masked Marvel" Exploits "Don Q" in Spokane

A "movie ball" at the leading amusement park, with 7,000 persons in attendance, to see a "masked marvel" in a "Don Q" costume, was one of several exploitation bits put on by the management of the Liberty theatre, Spokane, Wash., when Douglas Fairbanks' new United Artists Corporation production was shown there.

A representative of the theatre made a speech in which he told the dancers Fairbanks had hoped to attend the ball and be present at the Northwest premiere of his new picture, but had been too deep in work on his next production.

There also was a special morning matinee for Boy Scouts and junior Y. M. C. A. members; a whip-cracking contest for boys under eighteen in a tieup with the Spokane Press, a special preview for 150 of the city's leading men and women; an automobile ballyhoo; and theatre attendants in Spanish costume, with several window displays.

"Freshman" Megaphones Distributed at Game

As the leading unit of his campaign for "The Freshman" at the Majestic, Austin, Tex., Manager E. B. Roberts had cowboys distribute 4,000 megaphones, bearing appropriate advance copy on the picture, at the football game between Texas University and Mississippi, which took place the Saturday before the Monday opening of the Harold Lloyd comedy at the Majestic.

The stunt was conducted in cooperation with a clothing shop, which paid for the printing of the megaphones in consideration of space advertising the concern. The tieup was extended to the display of "Freshmen" clothing in the store window, in which generous space was given to the billing for the theatre.

One of the girls Barry Burke, manager of the Palace, Dallas, Tex., sent out in connection with a publicity stunt for "The Coast of Folly," Paramount. Burke got considerable newspaper space on the story of a vogue for suspenders had been started by Gloria Swanson in "The Coast of Folly."

Auto Speeder Test Used to Sell "Seven Days"

Producers Distributing Corporation was very successful in its exploitation stunt for "Seven Days" in Minneapolis. The Daily Star gave generous first page space to Mike Newman and his car in which the cross-continent trip was made in seven days. Kick was given to the story by Newman's pulling a demonstration of the actual time saved in breakneck driving through traffic. With traffic policemen and newspaper men aboard he drove from the Gateway to Lake street in Minneapolis first observing all the rules and then drove back breaking most of them and crowding his way through. In the trip of three miles it was found the saving was less than two minutes which got both news and editorial notice in the paper with a good three-column picture of Mike's car.

"Peacock Feathers" Style Show at Small House

A well turned out fashion show was produced recently at the Cameraphone Theatre, East Liberty, Pa., by Richard Brown, manager of this popular little suburban house. With the assistance of Lon B. Ramsdell, exploiteer for Universal, East Liberty was flooded with exploitation for the "Fall Fashion Show," produced in conjunction with the Universal Jewel, "Peacock Feathers."

Six beautiful girls, attired in the latest of milady's garments ended their part of the performance by appearing on an illuminated runway that ran the entire length of the house. The setting was an old Moorish castle. It was a style show well worthy of a house more pretentious than the Cameraphone.

An especially attractive display for "Tracked In The Snow Country," Warner Bros. production, designed by Ollie Brownlee, manager of the Capitol Theatre, Oklahoma City.

Show "Lost World" In Airship

Feature Screened for German Notables Aboard Dirigible Sailing Over Berlin

BERLIN newspaper editors and personages in Germany's political sphere were the invited guests of the First National's offices in Central Europe at a novel advance showing of "The Lost World," which next week will attain to the distinction of being the first motion picture to be screened in a dirigible while in flight over Berlin.

While the stunt may be new to Germany, it was done previously in London, where Horace Judge, of First National's publicity staff in England, gave a showing of "The Lost World" in the clouds, as he called it.

When the idea was projected for use in Germany, the necessary permission of the Government was obtained and work immediately started to install a projection machine in the dirigible.

An added feature of the novel presentation was the inclusion of a musical accompaniment to be supplied by radio, equipment having been installed to furnish this important element of the modern motion picture entertainment.

The music is to be a surprise for this first afternoon audience, and is to be specially rendered by one of Germany's leading concert orchestras. The intervals will be timed exactly and the start will be arranged by telephone from the airdrome to the broadcasting station. The surface of the plane will be used as an antenna.

College Team in Football Togs See "Freshman"

Added attention was attracted to "The Freshman" in Maryville, through the attendance in a body of the Maryville College football team clad in their gridiron togs at the Palace theatre. The stunt was arranged by Manager J. E. Everett and through heavy advance billing of the event a highly effective publicity campaign was accomplished for the presentation of the Lloyd comedy.

Excellent window displays were secured. One with a department store in fall clothes for young men, one with a hardware store exhibiting football uniforms, and another with a drug company, displaying "Memory Books" for students. A feature of the standard campaign was a huge canvas football hung across the street in front of theatre, lettered with "Harold Lloyd in 'The Freshman' Mon., Tues. Wed."

Frank Newman got real display results on "Sally of the Sawdust" (United Artists) at the Rialto theatre, Los Angeles. The authorities don't permit cut-outs on the streets, so Newman mounted them on net and hung them back of the street line.

M - G - M Trackless Train Reaches Los Angeles

The Metro-Goldwyn-Mayer Trackless Train after a cross-country tour in which it exploited that company's pictures from the Atlantic to the Pacific Coast has arrived in Los Angeles. The event was celebrated with a huge pageant and other forms of celebration calculated to give the utmost publicity to the novel stunt.

The vehicle was met at the city limits by Mayor George Cryor and prominent city and county officials, including Boyle Workman, President of the City Council and L. Birnbaum, Chairman of the Police Commission. Irving G. Thalberg, Harry Rapf, Hunt Stromberg, associate studio executive and Edward J. Mannix, studio manager, rode at the head of the parade which included floats from the studio, from Loew's State Theatre, from Grauman's Egyptian, from various West Coast Theatres and from the local exchange. A large military escort from Fort McArthur accompanied the parade, in which stars and players from the Culver City studios rode in their own machines.

Enormous difficulties were encountered and successfully overcome on the train's trip. Muddy roads which made traveling exceedingly difficult for the heavy transport were encountered, especially in Oklahoma and northern Texas, where some of the heaviest rains recorded in these districts made the roads almost impassable. In Michigan a cloudburst carried away a bridge, making it necessary for the crew to choose between making a very long detour and constructing an emergency bridge. The latter course was taken, thereby enabling the train to arrive at its next stop, where crowds awaited it in the rain, with the loss of only two hours in time.

The special is shortly to extend its trip from Los Angeles to San Francisco.

Telegraph Co. Helps Him Exploit "Pony Express"

Acting Manager George Guise of the Fenway Theatre, Boston, made an effective

Special 36-foot cut-out, constructed and jointed for the engagement of "The Iron Horse" (Fox) at the Liberty theatre, Kansas City, the Palace, San Antonio.

tie-up with the Postal Telegraph offices in Boston and vicinity in connection with the presentation of "The Pony Express" with an especially effective window display in their various offices.

Miniature 'Open Spaces' in Display for Grey Film

The important feature of Manager F. J. Miller's campaign on "Light of the Western Stars" at the Modjeska, Augusta, was the shadow box display across the lobby front. This consisted of a background painted to represent a night scene with stars and a brilliant moon. In the center was a cutout of Jack Holt and Billie Dove embracing, while on each side were cutouts of cactus plants,

Elaborate Style Revue for "Trouble With Wives"

Through the combined efforts of Manager Barry Burke and publicity director Raymond B. Jones, of the Palace theatre, Dallas, an elaborate fashion show was staged in connection with the presentation of "The Trouble With Wives" at that house recently. The event attracted widespread notice, obtaining extensive extra publicity through the advertising efforts of the merchants who cooperated with the theatre.

"The Airways of Fashion," as the presentation was called, was given in three episodes. First, "Modish Mitzi," with a model displaying snappy street costumes. Second, a silk bazaar in a street in Persia, where mannikins paraded in brilliantly colored silk frocks. Third, against a rainbow sky setting, colorful evening gowns were shown on pretty models. Episode four, represented the entrance to the International Exposition of Decorative Art, Place de la Concorde, Paris, 1925. In this setting, gorgeous evening gowns and wraps were exhibited.

Newman Starts Drive for Take-a-Chance Week

Based on the success of last year, the Newman theatre, Kansas City's largest first run down town house, is making extensive plans for another take-a-chance week next week. A unique program arrangement of four pages has been issued, the front page being devoted to a list of famous men who "took a chance," along with the suggestion that it might not be amiss for the audience to also take a chance. Cuts of the stars in the picture, with their faces left blank, the ankles of other feminine members of the cast and a long series of question marks all add to make up an interesting and attractive medium of advertisement. This year's take-a-chance program, however, will be under the direction of Bruce Fowler, who is managing the Paramount controlled house, and Frank L. Newman, who is now managing three Paramount theatres in Los Angeles.

The entire window space of a large hardward store was given over to a display for First National's "The Lost World" in connection with its presentation at the Lyric theatre, San Angelo, Tex. The merchant just used firearms in this elaborate display, representing a jungle and giving the lion's share of the attractor to the picture.

present

L CE
y

in

"The Soapsuds Lady"

A tale of wooden shoes—and heads; of soft hearts and sappy domes; of an inn where anything might happen between midnight and dawn, and it all did.

Another fast one from Alice Day that goes around the end for a touchdown. As bubbly, bright and sparkling as its title, floating like a cake of soap on the tides of laughter.

CLYDE COOK

in   *"GET 'EM YOUNG"*
A Two Reel Comedy

"Gluttons for Great Names and Sensational Features" Found This One Good

"The picture is Hal Roach's 'Moonlight and Noses,' and being a short fun film it holds them very well considering that the Palace is the ace house of the world's music halls, and one whose patrons are gluttons for great names and sensational features."

N. Y. Graphic's review of the Bill for the Week of Sept. 30 in the Greatest Vaudeville House in the World, The Palace, New York City.

Watch the fellow with the india rubber legs and the long nose bounce his way through this one. If it can get big laughs in vaudeville's best house, it can get them in yours!

Hartford Campaign to Put "Lost World" Across

The Strand theatre, Hartford, recently played "The Lost World." Encouraged by New Haven's achievements, Hartford set out to go it one better and with the aid of First National's exploitation department under the direction of Allan S. Glenn, a farreaching campaign was conceived and effected in one week's time.

The Hartford Times and the Hartford Courant each co-operated on the engagement viewing of the picture as a distinct news event. Each paper carried a series of seven stories on their news pages, illustrated with stills from the picture, of scientific interest.

In addition The Hartford Courant carried a weight guessing contest in which a different story and photo of one of the "Lost World" monsters was carried daily with a prize for those guessing the weight of the beast. A half-page story in the feature section was used the day prior to the opening date describing and depicting the possible consequences of a visit to Hartford by one of the dinosaurs from "The Lost World."

The advertising budget was increased to allow for some quarter-page ads and an equally vigorous and liberal campaign was instituted via the billboards, rotogravure inserts, heralds and numerous novelties from First National's accessory department.

Lowell H. Stormont of First National's staff, assigned to assist the local management, in addition to his aid in preparing the material placed in the newspapers also effected a tie-up with the local taxi company who placed banners in the backs of all its cabs advising all and sundry in Hartford that "the cabs would take them to the Strand where the world's wonder picture 'The Lost World' was showing."

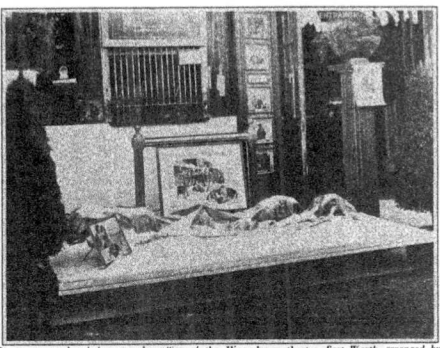

Miniature display before the box-office of the Hippodrome theatre, Fort Worth, arranged by Manager Barry Burke for the engagement of "The White Desert" (Metro-Goldwyn-Mayer).

"Iron Horse" Ballyhoo is Entered in Parade

The Greater Movie Season parade recently held at Seattle, Wash., was made doubly interesting by an "Iron Horse" ballyhoo of the Liberty theatre, which headed the procession.

The engine used to represent "The Iron Horse," was a real old time relic, 47 years old, which was dug up from the bone yard of one of the railroad companies. Several days were consumed working over the old thing, cleaning it and getting it in shape to run.

Securing permission to run the old engine on the municipally-owned tracks of the Seattle Street Railway company was about as formidable a task as inducing the old timer to show its speed, but both problems were eventually solved.

As the decrepit old relic swung into line at the head of the parade, it puffed, snorted and smoked as nothing ever did before. Several buildings along the line of march, had to be cleaned after the parade, because of the incrustation of smoke and grime that the ancient engine covered them with. The old horse also proved its equine relationship at several critical moments in the pageant, by pulling a real sure enough balk. Every time the horse went around a corner, it would jump a track. The engine was followed by a wrecking car from the street railway company, and every time the refractory engine would derail itself, the wrecking car would promptly put it back on the track and start it on its way again. The stunt created no end of amusement.

One corner of the outer lobby of the Heilig theatre, Seattle, during the run of "The Lucky Horseshoe" (Fox). The cut-out of Mix on Tony was mounted on rockers, operated by a motor, to make it "gallop."

"Light of Western Stars" Posters Illuminated

The most noteworthy unit of Manager R. Newton's splendid campaign on "The Light of Western Stars", was the placing of a beautifully hand-painted 24-sheet on the side of the Capitol theatre, Little Rock.

The four large stars, each carrying the name of one of the four featured players in the picture, were cut out and faced with paper with a light behind each. The picture title and author's name were printed on the display sheet, along with mention of the short comedy subject on the program.

Brilliantly illuminated at night, the sales value of the exhibit was tremendous.

LIBRARY TIE-UPS.

YOUR IDEA

A T a recent exploitation conference held by William N. Robson, Paramount exploiter at the Pittsburgh exchange, Miss K. S. Stamm, publicity director of the Pitts-

A highly artistic and atmospheric prologue was given in connection with the showing of "Romola" (Metro-Goldwyn) at the Tivoli theatre, Chattanooga, staged by Manager E. R. Rogers and pictured above.

burgh Public Library, read a brief on book tie-ups and library co-operation that we are printing here in full as an important contribution on the subject of exploitation. The assistance given by such progressive libraries as the Pittsburgh, Cleveland and other institutions deserves recognition. Miss Stamm said:

Co-operation between libraries and motion picture theatres is being knitted more closely throughout the country. The movie and the public library both influence large groups of people, and a close contact between them is bound to increase the usefulness of each to the community.

The people who visit the library are not always movie fans. Yet if they see a good play advertised by the library, and perhaps associate it with a favorite author, the desire is created to see the picture.

Regular attendants at movie houses do not always use the library, or know how it can serve them free of charge. Having the theatre suggest its use for other stories by the same author, such as was done by the Aldine theatre in Pittsburgh when Jack London's "Adventure" was being shown, or for books concerning the setting, as was was done by the Olympic and Liberty theatres while "The Covered Wagon" was being shown, creates a mutually advantageous bond.

During the past year, for the first time in its history, the Carnegie library of Pittsburgh has joined hands with local theatre owners in spreading publicity. The exploitation representatives of the theatres, and the publicity representatives of the library watch production schedules for a play which links up well with some good books—not only novels to be filmed, but books of travel as in the case of "The Ten Commandments," history as in the case of "Joan of Arc," biography as with "Abraham Lincoln," etc.

The joint publicity usually takes the form of a bookmark announcing a picture. Printed on the face is a short list of appropriate books concerning the film. The list is compiled by the library, and the local theatre pays for the printing. The markers are then distributed at the theatre a week before the production, and are given out with circulating books at the main and branch libraries. In the neighborhood of one thousand people visit the Central library alone in one day. Considering the nine branches in various parts of Pittsburgh, two sub-branch libraries, thirteen adult deposit stations, five high school libraries, 26 platoon school libraries, nine school deposit stations, and 95 classroom libraries, the circle influenced is quite large.

In the case of "The Little French Girl," besides the bookmark publicity, a pre-view of the film was arranged to be shown at the library's lecture hall for the director and library staff. The exploitation representative gave a short talk to the librarians, so that they might be informed in recommending the picture.

The Liberty theatre, Seattle, decorated its front brilliantly for "The Iron Horse" (Fox), making use of electric lighting to increase its effectiveness.

AND OURS

Usherettes of Loew's State theatre, Los Angeles, in a street stunt for "Shore Leave" (First National) in co-operation with a Navy Recruiting Week.

"Stills" are sometimes sent from the theatres for bulletin board display. I am thinking now of the appeal made by those from "Peter Pan." Reports from branches show that Barrie's books moved particularly well at that time. A poster, not too flagrantly commercial, is often used with an exhibit of books dealing with the picture advertised. In the case of one picture, I remember, bookmarks were put for distribution by the theatre's publicity man, into shops displaying advertising posters for the photoplay.

At special times of the year, the motion picture houses show slides for the library between their "Big picture" and the "comic." This was done this past year for Children's Book week in November, and for Library week in schools in May.

INGENUITY IN ADVERTISING

ONE of those little ingenious twists that help to make a theatre's advertising noticed and talked about was used in Winnipeg papers by H. M. Thomas, Western Canadian supervisor for F. P.-L., in advance of "The Ten Commandments" at the Capitol theatre.

Appropriate use was made of the numerals from "1" to "10" throughout the text of the one-column advertisement, the numbers being in proper series in large type from start to finish of the copy. The figures being prominently shown, the announcement reading as follows:

"1 picture you ought 2 see broke all records by playing to capacity crowds during 3 calendar years on Broadway. It will now be shown in Winnipeg 4 a run of six days. You will agree with the 5 or 6 million persons who have enjoyed it that it is a cinemasterpiece. Commandant Number 7 is given dramatic emphasis by Director Cecil B. DeMille which may explain why London, Paris, Vienna and New York 8 it up. 9 popular stars enact this melodrama which blends the orgies of ancient Egypt with the humors and tragedies of this jazz-mad age. Jeanie Macpherson wrote the story You'll enjoy the 10 Commandments. A Paramount Picture coming."

LET THEM WRITE YOUR ADS

SOME week, when there doesn't seem to be any particular outstanding exploitation angle in the picture lined up, let your customers write your advertising. In other words, tell them what the picture is all about, then offer a prize for the best ad which any person submits.

As a matter of fact, of course, plenty of them will resolve to write an ad and send it in, but very few of them will ever actually get arount to it. The important thing is, that in announcing the contest, you have an excuse to describe the picture in great detail, and because there is a prize offered, they will read this description with more interest than if it were merely the routine publicity yarn.

Another angle to this is that when you have an unfamiliar title or something about the picture that needs to be explained, it gives you a good chance to do it. For instance, when Manager Bert Crowe of the Capitol theatre, Peterboro, Ont., was playing "The Chechahcos," he used this contest as an excuse for explaining what a "Chechahco" was.

Like the Taka-Chance Week stunt it fits any picture and is well adapted for use with pictures of the sort that don't seem made for the usual tie-ups and advertising.

HEAVY SHORT SUBJECT CAMPAIGN

OF UNUSUAL scope and intensity is the big campaign being worked out for "Wild Beasts of Borneo," which Educational is releasing as a Special, with corresponding exploitation effort.

Several big news photo services and window display advertising service are broadcasting photographs showing some of the scenes of ferocious animals taken by Mr. and Mrs. Lou C. Hutt during their two year expedition into the darkest jungles of Borneo.

Educational is issuing a concise but complete press sheet to assist exhibitors in their local exploitation. Several advertising and publicity cuts are illustrated and the press sheet provides publicity stories for newspapers, suggestions for type ads, program paragraphs, etc., and a number of valuable suggestions for exploitation stunts.

Co-operation of the National Biscuit company, manufacturers of Barnum's Animal Crackers, has been obtained to arrange window display tie-ups with local grocers. The 2,200 salesmen of the National Biscuit company throughout the country are being instructed to assist grocers in arranging tie-ups which will exploit the animal crackers and "Wild Beasts of Borneo."

THE OLD AND THE NEW

ALTHOUGH the idea of exhibiting an old time film by way of contrast to the modern type of production has been done on several occasions, it was presented with particular attractiveness by Manager Harry Greenman of Loew's State theatre in St. Louis. Done as a feature of Greater Movie Season, it would be equally suitable at any other time.

He arranged a stage setting first of the exterior of an early day nickelodeon with the characteristic signs and the sing-song of the barker ticket seller.

Then when the audience had been sold the exterior of the odeon was shown with the screen in the front. It was an old style whistling, cheering, jeering, clapping audience that persisted in prompting and advising the screen stars.

The old-style movie was complete in every detail. Prior to the opening of the 2-reel feature picture the customary advertising slides were flashed upon the screen and also the union label of the operator.

The illustrated song was not overlooked and was "rendered" in the most approved style by a he-man tenor.

GOOD SUMMER SHOWS PAY

HARRISON SMOOTS of the Vine theatre, Mt. Vernon, O., told a film representative last week that this has been the best summer he has ever had in the picture business. Asked the reason for this he said: "Well, heretofore I have always laid down on the summer programs. I offered the weaker sister in the feature field, feeling that folks didn't want to attend picture shows in the summer time and that there was no use wasting the big picures on empty benches.

"This summer I tried the opposite tactics and the results have been astounding. I played the biggest pictures I could get. I put in the strongest productions on the market instead of the weakest. And the people came. And they kept on coming all summer. Now I'm planning to give my patrons the best of the new pictures. I'm getting ready to launch a big advertising campaign on Big Pictures, and I expect this to be the biggest winter I shall have had, just as it's been the biggest summer."

Painted flats and special still frames were featured in the lobby of the Rialto theatre, Colorado Springs, by Manager Pat August for "The Ten Commandments" (Paramount).

Historical Riddles Boost "As No Man Has Loved"

Labelled a nut-cracking contest, a means toward brushing up on American history has just been staged by the Rialto theatre, Charleston, West Virginia. That the list of brain twisters made a hit with local historians was evidenced by the number of replies received. The general excellence of the replies indicated as well, that Charleston's histories and reference books came in for a fine thumbing and combing during the week of the contest.

The Charleston Daily Mail did its patriotic bit toward the dissemination of our country's history by conducting the affair in a generous and public-spirited manner. The newspaper featured the contest in a prominent position each day, under a double column head. As the idea was launched to be one of the exploitation aids given the local engagement of "As No Man Has Loved," it can be appreciated that the picture came in for a lot of valuable free space.

A few of the thirteen queries propounded are as follows: 1. Who and what was Thomas Jefferson? Aaron Burr? 10. How many stars in the flag in 1807? and 1863? Who was president in the same years? 13. In what year was Philip Nolan condemned to be a man without a country? How long was he a man without a country? What was it he loved "As No Man Has Loved?"

Contestants sending the best answers were awarded the following prizes: First prize, $5 in gold; second prize, $3; third prize, $2. Honorable mention prizes consisting of six pairs of tickets were also awarded. Contestants were directed to send their answers, not to the newspaper offices, but to Lieutenant Nolan, Rialto theatre, Charleston.

Auto License Numbers Aid "I'll Show You the Town"

Any person whose automobile license number was printed in one of the ads on a double truck co-operative put out for "I'll Show You the Town" at the Kelley theatre in Iola, Kans., could collect two tickets for the show from the firm in whose advertisement he found it. That was the twist Bob Gary, Universal's exploitation man in Kansas City, worked out to make folks read the co-op.

He arranged a neat layout of his pages with a two and a half inch strip across the top of both pages telling of the free ticket stunt and an 8 x 12 space in the center of the page for the theatre's ad. Surrounding it were those of the fourteen merchants who had taken space.

"Last of Duanes" Scene is Reproduced in Lobby

Manager C. F. Creslin's lobby for "Last of the Duanes" at the Rialto theatre, Augusta, is noteworthy for two reasons. First, because of its faithful reproduction of an actual scene from the photoplay, and second for its action appeal.

Display consisted of a background painted to represent a house with a cut-out of Tom Mix and the heroine on Tony, the horse, leaping from the house into a pool of water below. The "leaping" effect was produced by suspending cut-out from a wire attached to top of shadow-box. The whole was mounted in a shadow-box painted to represent a desert with cactus, at top of which was printed "Tom Mix" and Tony make this leap in Zane Grey's "Last of the Duanes." Brilliantly lighted, the display arrested the attention of everyone.

Jewelry Window Display Advertises "Marry Me"

The outstanding unit of Manager John B. Carroll's campaign on "Marry Me" at the Victory, Tampa, was the tie-up he arranged with the Duval Jewelry company.

These jewelers had a beautiful window display of wedding gift suggestions with a large vase in the center filled with wedding rings. In the window was a one-sheet mat, stills and photos, with a miniature bride and groom in the center. Outer edges of window were decorated with old shoes, rice, etc.

The window attracted unusual attention, the contents getting valuable publicity both for the theatre and jewelry company.

A week in advance of opening date, wedding rings, each tied to a small card carrying picture title, were distributed at the theatre and on the streets.

By giving a ticket to see "Pretty Ladies" (Metro-Goldwyn-Mayer) at the Melba theatre, Dallas, Texas, to each purchaser of a hat, Manager Sid McDonald and Publicity Manager Raymond B. Jones, obtained this window tie-up on the picture.

Intensive Drive for "The Phantom" in Pittsfield

Backed by an intensive exploitation, advertising and publicity campaign, "The Phantom of the Opera" opened recently at the Union Square theatre, Pittsfield, Mass. The campaign was put across by General Manager Fred W. Homan and House Manager Benulin, assisted by a representative of the Universal Exploitation department.

More than a dozen windows in the most popular thoroughfares of Pittsfield were tied-up with "The Phantom," including furniture stores, millinery shops, drug stores, book shops, jewelry stores, textile emporiums and one double window in a vacant store. This, filled with oil paintings, art photos, cards, posters and the many accessories designed for the attraction, drew considerable attention.

Liberal newspaper advertising, extensive display of posters throughout Pittsfield and outlying districts, together with house to house distribution of the artistic "Phantom" heralds, all proved effective. In addition to the stock paper, Homan designed and had distributed several hundred special 1-sheets and window cards. Another effective medium was a specially-made herald distributed at the final game of the local baseball season.

Shoes for Babies is Stunt in "Goose Woman" Drive

C. E. Lounsbury, Denver exploitation man for Universal, evolved a clever tie-up for the America theatre in that city for the engagement of "The Goose Woman." Denver is in the midst of a civic drive which has "500,000 in 1930" as its slogan. Hooking up with the idea expressed in this campaign, Lounsbury induced a baby specialty shop to offer one pair of baby shoes to each baby born in the city on the day which the picture opened at the America.

The stunt had a wide appeal and several avenues of valuable publicity were opened up to it, with the result that the merchant realized on his advertising and the theatre was prominently mentioned and exploited in various ways. The shop assisted with a

As a result of a tieup on the Fox production of "Lightnin'," the Victory Theatre in Indianapolis was advertised in windows and on the wheels of the messengers of the Postal Telegraph Company's offices in that city.

big window display and the mailing of several hundred special heralds to a selected list.

Highway Traffic Signs Are Advertising for "Fool"

Automobilists on the main arterial highways in and about Ottawa, Ontario, have been getting plenty of admonition recently anent the perils of joy riding, through a new set of upright signs that made their appearance overnight at every dangerous street crossing. The signs, which were eight feet in height with a two foot square sign board at top and a three foot cross-piece half way down the sign-post, carried white lettering on a red surface, with the following copy:

The Fool takes chances. Slow Down. (See "The Fool" At The Regent Now.)

The signposts were part of the exploitation of "The Fool," which played at the Regent recently.

Futuristic Art in "Beggar on Horseback" Display

A "futuristic" lobby display, carrying out the bizarre effects in the dream sequence of the picture, proved a good attractor for the showing of "Beggar on Horseback" at the Galax theatre, Birmingham. The arrangement, which required nothing more than some compoboard and paint of various vivid hues, was designed by Rodney Bush, manager of the Galax.

The effect was produced by painting special door banner and three sheet frames with squares, triangles and overlapping circles, with a white panel in each for display copy. The one sheets were painted with uneven, broken letters of different colors and the red cow, two quart hat, musical frogs and huge necktie were all featured in the display.

The centerpiece was of compoboard showing Neil McRae in bathrobe and high silk hat riding a black horse with orange trappings. Sleepy Homer Cady, in a chair, was shown riding behind McRae, with the goddess money riding in the stirrup. To enhance the attention value of the exhibit, cutout circles in bright colors backed up these figures.

Crystal Gazer Parades for "The Mystic"

A sandwich man dressed as a Hindu carrying a small crystal ball on a small shelf in front of him attracted attention to a showing of "The Mystic" at the Haines theatre in Waterville, Me. The boards he carried were appropriately decorated with mystic signs and announcements of the showing.

A dry goods store contributed a window display featuring a card which read "There is no Mystery about our bargains—we leave that to 'The Mystic' at the Haines Theatre." One hundred special blocks in green and red on white were displayed prominently throughout the town, and a trailer was used. Twenty-five 1-sheets, six 3-sheets and three 6-sheets were posted. Floyd Stuart, Metro-Goldwyn exploiteer, waged this campaign.

Theatre display and ballyhoo used by the Liberty Theatre, McKeesport, Pa., for the engagement there of the Fox company's "The Iron Horse." The street demonstration consisted of a miniature engine mounted on a motor truck suitably bannered to exploit the attraction.

Exhibitors Box-Office Reports

Names of the theatre owners are omitted by agreement in accordance with the wishes of the average exhibitor and in the belief that reports published over the signature of the exhibitor reporting, is a dangerous practice.

Only reports received on specially prepared blanks furnished by us will be accepted for use in this department. Exhibitors who value this reporting service are urged to ask for these blanks.

Title of Picture	Population of Town	Location	Class of Patronage	Weather	Box Office Value	Checkup Percentage from other Reports
FAMOUS PLAYERS						
Beggar on Horseback...	993678	Mich.	General	Clear	Good	55
	414216	N. J.	1st Run	Clear	Good	—
Coast of Folly.........	350000	Wash.	General	Clear	Fair	66
Devils Cargo, The......	15000	Mich.	General	Clear	Big	65
Golden Princess, The...	796841	Ohio	General	Clear	Fair	49
He's a Prince.........	120000	Fla.	1st Run	St'my	Good	60
Lovers in Quarantine..	796841	Ohio		Clear	Fair	70
Man Who Found Himself	733826	Md.	1st Run	Clear	Good	60
	60000	Mont.	General	Clear	Good	—
	200000	Texas	1st Run	Clear	Good	—
	400000	Wash.	1st Run	St'my	Fair	—
Pony Express, The.....	414216	N. J.	1st Run	Clear	Fair	80
	250000	Texas	1st Run	St'my	Big	—
Seven Keys to Baldpate.	796841	Ohio	1st Run	Rain	Fair	40
Street of Forgotten Men	100000	Pa.	1st Run	Clear	Good	68
Ten Commandments, The	733826	Md.	1st Run	Clear	Big	87
	100000	Pa.	1st Run	Rain	Big	—
(2nd week)	250000	Texas	1st Run	St'my	Big	—
Top of the World......	15000	Mich.	General	Clear	Good	62
Trouble With Wives:...	772897	Mo.	General	St'my	Good	61
	250000	Texas	1st Run	Clear	Good	—
Vanishing American....	506676	Cal.	1st Run	Clear	Good	70
Wild, Wild Susan......	324410	Kans.	General	St'my	Good	61
F. B. O.						
If Marriage Fails......	324410	Kans.	1st Run	Clear	Fair	41
	200000	Texas	1st Run	Rain	Fair	—
Wild Bull's Lair.......	733826	Md.	1st Run	Rain	Fair	78
FIRST NATIONAL						
Born Rich.............	15000	Mich.	General	St'my	Poor	52
Classified............	796841	Ohio	General	Clear	Good	58
Dark Angel, The......	506676	Cal.	1st Run	Clear	Good	70
	733826	Md.	1st Run	Clear	Good	—
	993678	Mich.	General	Clear	Good	—
Fine Clothes..........	200618	Ga.	1st Run	St'my	Fair	58
Frivolous Sal.........	15000	Mich.	General	Hot	Poor	67
Graustark............	772897	Mo.	General	Rain	Big	78
	414216	N. J.	1st Run	St'my	Good	—
	401247	Ohio	General	Clear	Big	—
Half-Way Girl, The....	250000	Texas	General	Clear	Fair	64
Her Sister from Paris...	120000	Fla.	1st Run	Clear	Good	75
Husbands and Lovers...	15000	Mich.	General	Clear	Poor	75
Idle Tongues..........	15000	Mich.	General	Clear	Poor	60
Just a Woman.........	414216	N. J.	1st Run	Clear	Good	70
Knockout, The........	200000	Texas	1st Run	Rain	Big	66
Lady Who Lied, The....	350000	Wash.	General	Rain	Fair	64
Live Wire, The........	120000	Fla.	1st Run	Clear	Big	90
	796841	Ohio	General	Clear	Big	90
Lost World, The.......	993678	Mich.	General	Clear	Good	89
(3rd week)	401247	Ohio	1st Run	Rain	Fair	—
Marriage Whirl, The...	250000	Texas	General	Rain	Fair	62
Pace That Thrills, The..	796841	Ohio	1st Run	Clear	Good	70
Soul Fire............	60000	Mont.	General	Clear	Fair	69
What Fools Men.......	401247	Ohio	1st Run	Clear	Fair	60
White Monkey, The....	250000	Texas	1st Run	Clear	Poor	47
FOX						
Dick Turpin..........	200618	Ga.	1st Run	Clear	Big	75
East Lynne...........	350000	Wash.	General	Clear	Good	85
Fighting Heart, The....	796841	Ohio	General	Clear	Fair	60
Gerald Cranston's Lady.	200618	Ga.	1st Run	Clear	Fair	59
Gold and the Girl......	733826	Md.	1st Run	Rain	Good	73
Greater Than a Crown..	250000	Texas	General	Clear	Fair	50
Iron Horse, The.......	314194	Ind.	1st Run	St'my	Big	79
	993678	Mich.	General	Clear	Good	—
	450000	Minn.	1st Run	St'my	Good	—
	126468	Neb.	1st Run	Clear	Fair	—
	250000	Texas	1st Run	St'my	Big	79
Kentucky Pride........	350000	Wash.	General	Clear	Big	52
Lightnin'............	200000	Texas	1st Run	Clear	Big	73
	250000	Tex.	1st Run	St'my	Big	—

Title of Picture	Population of Town	Location	Class of Patronage	Weather	Box Office Value	Checkup Percentage from other Reports
Wheel, The...........	400000	Wash.	General	Clear	Fair	60
METRO-GOLDWYN-MAYER						
Midshipman, The......	200000	Texas	1st Run	Hot	Big	85
Mystic, The..........	733826	Md.	ost Run	Rain	Fair	58
	250000	Texas	1st Run	Clear	Good	—
Never the Twain Shall Meet..............	126468	Iowa	1st Run	St'my	Fair	67
Pretty Ladies........	993678	Mich.	General	Clear	Good	51
	401247	Ohio	1st Run	Clear	Fair	—
Sun Up..............	350000	Wash.	General	Clear	Fair	52
Tower of Lies, The....	414216	N. J.	1st Run	Clear	Big	70
	400000	Wash.	General	Rain	Good	—
Zander the Great......	126468	Neb.	1st Run	Clear	Fair	69
PATHE						
Black Cyclone........	772897	Mo.	General	Clear	Good	74
Freshman, The........	506676	Cal.	1st Run	Clear	Big	97
	314194	Ind.	1st Run	St my	Big	97
(3rd wk.)	324410	Kans.	1st Run	St'my	Big	97
	401247	Ohio	1st Run	Clear	Big	97
	250000	Texas	General	Clear	Big	97
Hot Water...........	15000	Mich.	General	Clear	Big	86
PRODUCERS DIST. CORP.						
Bad Lands, The.......	200618	Ga.	1st Run	Hot	Good	64
Chalk Marks..........	250000	Texas	1st Run	Clear	Fair	55
Hell's Highroad.......	506676	Cal.	1st Run	Clear	Fair	61
	60000	Mont.	General	Clear	Big	—
	350000	Wash.	General	St'my	Fair	—
Off The Highway......	796841	Ohio	1st Run	Clear	Good	55
Seven Days..........	506676	Cal.	1st Run	Rain	Good	70
Without Mercy.......	60000	Mont.	General	Hot	Big	60
STATE RIGHTS						
Lost in a Big City......	200618	Ga.	1st Run	Clear	Fair	75
One Glorious Night....	200618	Ga.	1st Run	Clear	Good	70
Police Patrol.........	772897	Mo.	General	Rain	Fair	45
Wizard of Oz, The.....	401247	Ohio	1st Run	St'my	Good	71
Wrongdoers..........	400000	Wash.	1st Run	Clear	Fair	50
UNITED ARTISTS						
Don Q...............	314194	Ind.	1st Run	Clear	Big	91
	324410	Kans.	1st Run	St'my	Good	—
	350000	Wash.	General	Clear	Good	—
(3rd wk.)	400000	Wash.	1st Run	Clear	Good	—
Gold Rush, The.......	200618	Ga.	1st Run	Clear	Good	96
	796841	Ohio	General	Clear	Big	—
(2d wk.)	796841	Ohio	1st Run	Clear	Good	—
	100000	Pa.	1st Run	Clear	Big	—
UNIVERSAL						
California Straight Ahead	120000	Fla.	1st Run	Clear	Good	77
Goose Woman, The....	250000	Texas	1st Run	Clear	Good	66
	993678	Mich.	General	Clear	Good	—
	200000	Texas	1st Run	Clear	Fair	—
Peacock Feathers......	400000	Wash.	General	Clear	Fair	85
Siege...............	324410	Kans.	1st Run	St'my	Good	66
Teaser, The..........	250000	Texas	General	Clear	Good	62
White Outlaw, The....	200618	Ga.	1st Run	Hot	Good	70
WARNER BROS.						
Below the Line........	772897	Mo.	General	Rain	Fair	63
	400000	Wash.	General	Hot	Big	—
Her Marriage Vow.....	15000	Mich.	General	Clear	Poor	59
His Majesty Bunker Bean..............	120000	Fla.	1st Run	St'my	Fair	50
How to Educate a Wife..	15000	Mich.	General	Hot	Poor	75
Lover's Lane.........	15000	Mich.	General	Clear	Poor	58
Man on the Box, The...	796841	Ohio	General	Rain	Fair	78
Tracked in the Snow Country...........	733826	Md.	1st Run	Rain	Big	70

With First Run Theatres

NEW YORK CITY

Rialto Theatre—
Film Numbers—The Best People (Paramount), Rialto Magazine (Selected), In the Movies (Lloyd Hamilton).
Musical Program—Ben Bernie and His Gang, "In Arabia," Organ Novelty, Orchestra Novelty.

Rivoli Theatre—
Film Numbers—Flower of Night (Paramount), Rivoli Pictorial (Selected), Wildcats of Paris (Aesop Fable).
Musical Program — "Il Guarany" (Overture), Bryce Canyon (Riesenfeld's), Organ Novelty, Rivoli Divertisements (Staff Artists).

Capitol Theatre—
Film Numbers — Fine Clothes (First National), Bryce Canyon (Art Color), Capital Magazine (Selected), On Many Shores (Travelogue).
Musical Program — "Orpheus" "Goin' Home" (Vocal Trio), "Red Rose" (Soloist and Ballet), "Una Voce Poco Fa" (Vocal Solo), "Pierrot's Serenade" (Ballet Corps), Organ Solo.

Warners Theatre—
Film Numbers—Red Hot Tires (Warner Bros.), Warner News Weekly (Selected), Pale Moon (Scenic), The Jail Bird (Cartoon subject).
Musical Program—Overture Special Orchestra—Popular Song Hits, "Mal De Mer" (Novelty Selection), Soloist and Danseuse.

Mark Strand Theatre—
Film Numbers — Little Annie Rooney (United Artists), Topical Review (Selected).
Musical Program—"Buffalmacco" (Overture), Prolog to Feature (Songs and dances), Organ Solo.

Cameo Theatre—
Film Numbers—A Regular Fellow (Paramount), Cameo Pictorial (Selected), Little Pills of Wisdom (Pathe), Ride on a Runaway Train (Novelty), Only A Country Lass (Novelty), Wilderness Tales (Scenic).
Musical Program—"Prince of Pilsen" (Overture), Organ Solo.

Astor Theatre—
Film Numbers—The Phantom of the Opera (Universal), Continued.

Criterion Theatre—
Film Numbers—The Vanishing American (Paramount), Continued.

Embassy Theatre—
Film Numbers—The Merry Widow (Metro-Goldwyn-Mayer), Continued.

Colony Theatre—
Film Numbers — The Freshman (Pathe), Continued.

BROOKLYN

Brooklyn Mark Strand Theatre—
Film Numbers—The Dark Angel (First National), "Richard Wagner," Famous Music Master Series (Fitzpatrick); Mark Strand Tropical Review (Selected).

AT LAST! ONE OF THE SEASON'S GREATEST PICTURES
New York City Acclaimed this photodrama. One Picture in a Million!

VIBRANT WITH THE LOVE LAUGHTER AND TEARS OF LIFE "
ALL STAR CAST

KENNETH HARLAN-
MARY CARR-PRISCILLA
BONNER.
Read what the critics say

COLUMBIA

The use of several reviews, combined with suitable pictorial material, resulted in this strong five-column ad on "Drusilla With a Million" (Film Booking Offices) on opening day at the Columbia, Dayton, Ohio.

Musical Numbers—"Pace Pace" from "La Forza del Destino" (soprano solo); popular medley (xylophone solo); "Goin' Home" (basso solo); "Faust Waltzes" (piano solo); "That Wonderful Mother of Mine" and "Mazushla" (tenor solos) and "Slavic Dance" (ballet number); and Mendelssohn "Allegro" (Sonata 4) as the recessional.

LOS ANGELES

Criterion Theatre—
Film Numbers—Souls for Sables (Tiffany), Scrambled Eggs (Educational Comedy), Scenic, Fox News.
Musical Program — "Sometime" (Overture).

Hillstreet Theatre—
Film Numbers — The Storm Breaker (Universal), Pacemakers (F. B. O.), Aesop Fable, International News.
Musical Program—Vaudeville.

Loew's State Theatre—
Film Numbers—Lights of Old Broadway (Metro-Goldwyn-Mayer), The Tourist (Educational), Pictorial News Events.
Musical Program—"No, No, Nanette" (Overture), Undersea Ballet, Fanchon and Marco.

Metropolitan Theatre—
Film Numbers—Flower of the Night (Paramount), Remember When (Pathe), Pathe News.
Musical Program—"William Tell" (Overture).

Pantages Theatre—
Film Numbers—The Crackerjack (C. C. Burr), Pathe News.
Musical Program—Vaudeville.

Forum Theatre—
Film Numbers—The Man on the Box (Warner Bros.), Continued.

Million Dollar Theatre—
Film Numbers—The Freshman (Pathe), Continued.

Rialto Theatre—
Film Numbers—Phantom of the Opera (Universal), Continued.

NEWARK

Capitol Theatre—
Film Numbers—Sally of the Sawdust (United Artists), Pictorial (Pathe).

Mosque Theatre—
Film Numbers—Second week of the Freshman (Pathe), News International).
Musical Program—"The Fortune Teller" (Overture), Colege Capers (Prologue), "Moments Chopin" (Soloist, ballet and string ensemble).

Brandford Theatre—
Film Numbers—Half Way Girl (First National), News (Pathe), Comedy (Pathe).
Musical Program—"Semiramide" (Overture), Van and Schenck, popular songs.

Rialto Theatre—
Film Numbers—Eve's Secret (Paramount), The Live Wire (First National), News (Kinograms).

Fox Terminal—
Film Numbers—Iron Horse (Fox), News (Fox).
Musical Numbers—"Lets Wander Away" by orchestra and tenor and soprano.

CHICAGO

Capitol Theatre—
Film Numbers — Capitol World Events (Universal), Scenic Review; Stepping Out (Comedy). A Punch In The Nose (Pathe).

Musical Program — "Slavische Rhapsodie," (Overture), "Climbing The Ladder of Roses," (Specialty), "Pierre & Pagie," (Divertissement), "Pal Of My Cradle Days" (Organ Solo), "Katinka," (Specialty).

Stratford Theatre—
Film Numbers — International News (Universal) Stratford Scenic Review, The Best People (Paramount) Comedy Cartoon.
Musical Program—"Emerald Isle," (Overture), "The Shamrock," (Specialty) "Some Old Time Irish Jigs," (Specialty) Sara Ann McCabe, soloist, singing "The Last Rose of Summer," and "Killarney," "Erin's Fairest Colleens in Immortal Song," (Organ Solo).

Chicago Theatre—
Film Numbers — Laughs of the Day (Prod. Dis. Corp.), Graustark (First National), Comedy (Selected) Weekly News and Views.
Musical Program—"Melodies of the Moment," (Overture) Bernard De Pace, soloist, playing "Mandolin Murmurs," (Specialty) "Bandinage," and "Dizzy Fingers," (Organ Solos) "A Nocturne," (Presentation).

Tivoli Theatre—
Film Numbers — International News (Universal), Scenic Wonders, An Exchange Of Wives (Metro-Goldwyn, Selected Comedy.
Musical Program—"A Southern Rhapsody," (Overture), "Pale Moon," "Charleston Strutters," Back Home In Charleston," (Presentation).

Uptown Theatre—
Film Numbers — Weekly News and Views, Shore Leave (First National), Lloyd Hamilton Comedy.
Musical Program—"The Merry Widow," (Overture) "The Son Of The Desert," (Specialty), "I Wonder If She Wonders Too," Organ Solo), "Under The Bridge," (Specialty).

Roosevelt Theatre—
Film Numbers — The Merry Widow, (Metro-Goldwyn).

Monroe Theatre—
Film Numbers—Thank You (Fox).

Orpheum Theatre—
Film Numbers—The Gold Rush (United Artists).

Randolph Theatre—
Film Numbers—Peacock Feathers (Universal), International News (Universal).

ALLEN

When the
Clock
Strikes
Midnight
on Gay
Broadway

See little Ann Pennington
do the Charleston

IN MONTA BELL'S

'PRETTY
LADIES'

The looming series after...

Tom Moore
Ann Pennington
Lilyan Tashman
Bernard Randall
Helena D'Algy
Conrad Nagel
Norma Shearer

Harry Langdon Comedy
"PLAIN CLOTHES"

ALLEN ORCHESTRA   PHIL'S JAZZ BAND

Two-column display used by the Allen Theatre, Cleveland, for "Pretty Ladies," a Metro-Goldwyn-Mayer production.

DETROIT

Madison Theatre—
Film Numbers—Pretty Ladies (Metro-Goldwyn), Detroit News and Pathe News, Aesop Fable (Pathe).
Musical Program—Orchestra and organ recessional. orchestra and Charleston dancers.

Capitol Theatre—
Film Numbers—The Dark Angel (First Natl.), Aesop Fables (Pathe), Detroit News and Pathe News.
Musical Program—Symphony orchestra and piano solos. Operatic star.

Broadway-Strand Theatre—
Film Numbers—The Goosewoman, (Universal), International News reel.
Musical Program—Organ recessional. Style show.

Fox Washington Theatre—
Film Numbers—Iron Horse (Fox), Fox news weekly.
Musical Program—Organ.

Adams Theatre—
Film Numbers—Lost World (First Natl.), Kinograms.
Musical Program—Orchestra and organ.

Grand Riviera Theatre—
Film Numbers—Beggar on Horseback (Paramount).
Musical Program—Orchestra.

WASHINGTON

Metropolitan Theatre—
Film Features—The Freshman (Pathe), Current Events (Pathe), Closer Than A Brother (Pathe), Wild Animals of Borneo (Educational).
Musical Program—"Campus Days" (Special Compilation). (Overture).

Palace Theatre—
Film Features—Seven Keys to

Baldpate (Paramount), Current Events (Pathe), Don't Tell Dad (Pathe), Hodge-Podge (Educational).
Musical Program—"The Student Prince" Selections (Overture).

Strand Theatre—
Film Features—With This Ring (S. R.), Current Events (Fox).

Rialto Theatre—
Film Features—The Phantom of the Opera (Universal), Current Events (Universal).
Musical Program—Finale from Tschaikovsky's Fourth Symphony (Overture), "Faust," (Duo from the first act; trio from last act), (Operatic Prologue).

Columbia Theatre—
Film Features—The King on Main Street (Paramount), Current Events (Universal), Topics of the Day (Pathe), Spotlight (Educational).

THREE JOYOUS DAYS!
STARTING TOMORROW...

SHE
WOLVES

ALMA RUBENS

EXTRAORDINARY STAGE SHOW
KEITH VAUDEVILLE FAVORITES
EVERYONE A BOMBSHELL OF SUBLIME ENJOYMENT

Kearse theatre ad in Charleston for "She Wolves" (Fox), four columns wide.

Musical Program—"What's Happened to Baby" (Medley overture), Pretty Baby "Oh Baby" "Yes Sir That's My Baby").

Earle Theatre—
Firm Features—Seven Days (Producers Distributing), Current Events (Educational).
Musical Program—"Rose Marie" Selections (Organ Solo), "Entrance of the Guards" (Overture), "Who Loved You Best" Exit March).

HOUSTON

Queen Theatre—
Film Numbers—The Pony Express (Paramount), Queen-Chronicle Review (Local), News (Pathe).
Musical Selections—Hawaiian Selections (Overture), Organ selections.

Majestic Theatre—
Film Numbers—The Iron Horse (Fox), Aesop's Fables (Pathe), news (Pathe).
Musical Selections—Popular hits, by orchestra (overture), organ selections, vaudeville.

Isis Theatre—
Film Numbers—The Mystic (Metro-Goldwyn-Mayer), comedy (Pathe), news (International).

Musical Selections—"Melody in 'F'" (Overture), Organ selection.

Rialto Theatre—
Film Numbers—The Love Hour (Vitagraph), comedy (Educational), news (Fox).
Musical Selections—Organ and Piano selections.

Capitol Theatre—
Film Numbers—Ten Commandments (Paramount), comedy (Educational), news (Kinograms).
Musical Selections—Popular hits (Orchestra), Organ and Piano selections.

Liberty Theatre—
Film Numbers—Chalk Marks (Producers), comedy (Educational) Review (Pathe).
Musical Selections—Organ and piano selections.

MILWAUKEE

Alhambra Theatre—
Film Numbers—Don Q, Son of Zoro (United Artists); International News.
Musical Program—Selections from "The Student Prince" (Overture); Atmospheric Prologue.

Garden Theatre—
Film Numbers—Without Mercy (Prod. Dis. Corp.); Shoes (Fox); Fox News; Topics of the Day.
Musical Program—"Normandy" (Organ Specialty).

Merrill Theatre—
Film Numbers—An Exchange of Wives (Metro-Goldwyn); Be Careful (Educational); Kinograms.

3rd
Rousing
Week!

Harold
Lloyd
in "The
Freshman"
COLLEGIATE FRENZY!

ROYAL

Two-column novelty ad on "The Freshman" (Pathe) at the Royal theatre, Kansas City.

Musical Program—Orchestra Overture.

Strand Theatre—
Film Numbers—He's A Prince (Paramount); Prisma; Skylad (S. R.); Misfit Sailor Educational); Kinograms.
Musical Program—"The King Isn't King Anymore" (Overture); "Concentration" (Organ).

Wisconsin Theatre—
Film Numbers—Shore Leave (First National); Robinson Crusoe (F. B. O.) International News; Kinograms; Fun From the Press.
Musical Program—The Merry Wives of Windsor" (Overture);

Thirty Pink Toes, The Girl in the Gilded Cage, Tommy Wonders, (Stage Presentation); Normandy (Organ).

CLEVELAND

Stillman Theatre—
Film Numbers—Don Q (United Artists), International News (Universal).
Musical Program—"Patria" (dramatic overture by Bizet to dedicate the Spanish Flag in 1874), "La Paloma" (vocal duet), Tango Dance (specialty number).

Allen Theatre—
Film Numbers—The Midshipman (Metro-Goldwyn), Beware (Educational), Topics of the Day (Pathe), Pathe News.
Musical Program—"Caprice Italinene" by Tschaikowsky (overture), The Mad scene from "Luceia" (vocal), "Serenade from "The Student Prince" and "Let's Wander Away" (Jazz).

State Theatre—
Film Numbers—Exchange of Wives (Metro-Goldwyn), Speedy Marriage (Universal), Heart Breakers (Fox), Pathe Review, Fun from the Press.
Musical Program—Organ Overture by Ernest Hunt, Vaudeville.

Park Theatre—
Film Numbers—New Brooms (Paramount), Wild Cat Willie (special), Topics of the Day (Pathe), Kinograms (Educational).
Musical Program—Waltzes of Yesterday and Today (overture, arranged by Angelo Vitale), Jazz: "Save Your Sorrow for Tomorrow", "Oh Boy What a Girl", "Sheikee", "Let's Wander Away" (saxophone trio).

Reade's Theatre—
Film Numbers—California Straight Ahead (Universal), Pathe comedy, Pathe News.
Musical Program—Popular Numbers of Today (medley, overture), Vaudeville.

Keith's 105th St. Theatre—
Film Numbers—California Straight Ahead (Universal), Cuckoo Love (Pathe), Aesop's Fables (Pathe), Pathe News.
Musical Program—Victor Herbert Hits (overture), Vaudeville.

TODAY & ALL WEEK

PRETTY
LADIES

DOES ANYTHING EVER
TAKE THE PLACE OF LOVE
IN A WOMAN'S HEART?

REGINALD DENNY

Strand

Striking silhouette ad on "Pretty Ladies" (Metro-Goldwyn-Mayer) at the Strand theatre, Cincinnatti.

CINCINNATI

Capitol Theatre—
He's a Prince (Paramount), "Ooch" Capitol News (Selected), Capitol Orchestra.

Walnut Theatre—
Lovers in Quarantine (Paramount), "Waiting", Fables, News (Pathe), Orchestra.

Strand Theatre—
The Trouble With Wives (Paramount), "Sit Tight," Pathe News Topics (Pathe), Orchestra.

Lyric Theatre—
The Gold Rush (United Artists), Kinograms, Orchestra.

Gifts Theatre—
Souls for Sables (S. R.), "A Winning Pair" (Universal), Kinograms.

Family Theatre—
Baree Son of Kazan (Vitagraph), "Felix Finishes First" Fox News.

BALTIMORE

Century Theatre—
Film Numbers—The Midshipman (Metro-Goldwyn-Mayer), Your Own Back Yard (Pathe, Our Gang comedy), News Weekly (Fox), Wonder Book No. 1 (S. D. Wilson).
Musical Program—Selections from "Floradora" (Medley Overture by Orchestra), Popular Selections (Eddie Miller and Ben Bernard), Organ Recessional.

Garden Theatre—
Film Numbers—The Lucky Horseshoe (Fox), Yearning for Love (Universal), Hot Dog (Trio Kraay Kat Cartoon Comic), International News (Universal).
Musical Program—Five Acts of vaudeville, Orchestra, Organ recessional.

Keith's Hippodrome—
Film Numbers—The Happy Warrior (Vitagraph), Aesop's Fable (Pathe), News Weekly (Pathe), Tea for Two (Pathe, Alice Day Comedy).
Musical Program—Five acts of vaudeville, Orchestra, Organ recessional.

Metropolitan Theatre—
Film Numbers—Lovers in Quarentine (Paramount), The Hero Wins (Pathe, Aesop's Fable), (Jem of Jura (Pathe color), Twinkle Toes, Topical Review

Three-column ad on "The Live Wire" (First Nat'l) at the Rivoli theatre, Baltimore.

(Pathe), Cuckoo Love (Pathe, Glenn Tryon comedy).
Musical Program—"At Dawning" and "By the Waters of the Minnetonka" (Overture by orchestra), Victor Herbert's Successes (Organ Selection).

New Theatre—
Film Numbers—The Unholy Three (Metro-Goldwyn-Mayer), A Misfit Sailor (Christie comedy), News Weekly (Pathe), Wonders in Art.
Musical Program—"Concert Fantasic" (Overture by Orchestra), Dancing Specialty on stage (Gravella and Theodore Caswell, Organ recessional.

Parkway Theatre—
Film Numbers—The Ten Commandments (Paramount), Parkway Pictorial News (Educational Kinograms).
Musical Program—Parkway Concert Ensemble, Organ recessional.

Rivoli Theatre—
Film Numbers—The Pace That Thrills (First National), Over There-abouts (Mack Sennett Pathe Comedy), Rivoli News (Pathe).
Musical Program—Divertisament on the stage (Art Landry and his Orchestra), "Popular Hits of 1925" (Organ Selection), Orchestra.

BUFFALO

Shea's Hippodrome—
Film Numbers—The Gold Rush (United Artists), Current Events (from Pathe and Fox News).

Vigorous action featured this ad on "The Freshman" (Pa he) at the Balaban & Katz Roosevelt, Chicago.

Music Program—"Taunhauser" (orchestra overture).

Lafayette Square—
Film Numbers—After Business Hours (S. R.) Pathe comedy, Current Events (from Kinograms).
Music Program—Selections from "Oh! Oh! Nurse,' (orchestra), Wurlitzer, Five acts of vaudeville.

Loew's State—
Film Numbers—The Mystic (Metro-Goldwyn) Baby Be Good (Juvenile comedy), Current Events (from Pathe News).
Music Program—"Poet and Peasant" (orchestra). Five acts of

Olympic—
Film Numbers—The Teaser (Universal), Three Wise Crooks F. B. O.), Current Events (from International News).
Music Program—Hits from the Greenwich Village Follies (Organ).

Shea's North Park—
Film Numbers—The Ten Commandments (Paramount), Current Events (from Pathe and Fox News).
Music Program—Selections from "Rose Marie" (orchestra).

Palace—
Film Numbers—The Night Ship (First Half), The Foolish Virgin (Last Half), Current Events (from International News).
Music Program—Vocal selections.

Novel background in the Circle theatre ad in Indianapolis for "The Marriage Whirl" (First Nat'l).

SAN FRANCISCO

California Theatre—
Film Numbers—Flower of the Night (Paramount), Shoes (Fox), Pathe Review, International News.
Musical Program—"Echoes of the Metropolitan Opera House" (Overture) "Legende" (Violin with Acempaniment), "Orchestra Novelty."

Golden Gate Theatre—
Film Numbers—Necessary Evil (First National), Why Hesitate (Educational), Two Poor Fish (Educational), Pathe Fable, Pathe News.
Musical Program—Six Vaudeville Acts.

Loew's Warfield Theatre—
Film Numbers—Graustark (First National), Maid in Morocco (Educational), International News.
Musical Program — "Futuristic Ideas" Singing and Dancing.

Granada Theatre—
Film Numbers—The Best People (Paramount), Hurry Doctor (Pathe), Pathe News.
Musical Program—Minstrel Show.

Imperial Theatre—
Film Numbers—The Freshman (Pathe), continued.

Cameo Theatre—
Film Numbers—She Wolves (Fox), Stolen Sweeties (Fox), Beyond the Border Line (Universal), vaudeville.

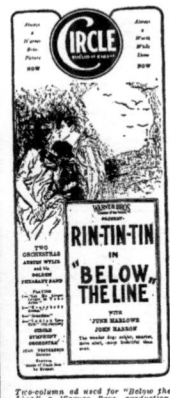

Two-column ad used for "Below the Line," a Warner Bros. production, by the Circle theatre, Cleveland.

Musical Program—Charleston Contest, "Oh The Bam Bam Bamy Shore," Baritone Solos.

Union Shore Theatre—
Film Numbers — Police Patrol (Gotham-S. R.), The Fight (Fox), Screen Snap Shots (All Star).
Musical Program—Five Acts of Vaudeville.

St Francis Theatre—
Film Numbers—The Vanishing American (Paramount), continued, 3d week.

SEATTLE

Blue Mouse Theatre—
Film Numbers—Bobbed Hair (Warner Bros.), Aesop Fable (Pathe), International News, (Universal).
Musical Program—"Pal of My Cradle Days" (Overture), "I Miss My Swiss" (Specialty).

Coliseum Theatre—
Film Numbers—He's a Prince (Paramount), White Wings Bride (Pathe Comedy), Kinograms and Pathe News.
Musical Program — "Cavalleria Rusticanna" (Overture).

Columbia Theatre—
Film Numbers—Phantom of the Opera (Universal), Hodge Podge (Comedy), International News.
Musical Program—"Second Hungarian Rhapsody" (Overture), Atmospheric Orchestral Prelude.

Liberty Theatre—
Film Numbers—The Freshman (Pathe), Continued.

Pantages Theatre—
Film Numbers—Deserted at the Altar (S. R.), Aesop Fable, Pathe News.
Musical Program—Vaudeville.

Strand Theatre—
Film Numbers — Fine Clothes (First National), The Movie Story Teler (Novelty).

DES MOINES

Capitol Theatre—
Film Numbers—Syncopation Week—Fox News, Dark Angel (First National), Sit Tight (Educational).
Musical Numbers—Syncopation from Musical Comedy, Bernadine DeGrave and Serge Leslie and their Charleston Steppers. Also Moore's Merrymakers orchestra.

DesMoines Theatre—
Film Numbers—Pathe News, Touchdowns of Fame, Sportlight (Pathe), The Gold Rush (United Artists).

Strand Theatre—
Film Numbers—Kinograms, Romola (Metro-Goldwyn).

ST. LOUIS

Grand Central, Kings and Capitol Theatres—
Film Numbers — The Freshman (Associated Exhibitors) Kinogram News and Views (Educational).
Music program—Orchestral and vocal number s. At Grand Central only "Collegiate." (Specialty).

Loew's State Theatre—
Film Numbers — The Tower of Lies (Metro-Goldwyn-Mayer), Your Own Back Yard (Pathe), Loew's State News and Views (Selected).
Music Program—Orchestral overture and popular numbers. On stage—6 U. S. S. Leviathan Band.

Missouri Theatre—
Film Numbers — The Pony Express (Paramount), Missouri Magazine.

Loew's Park and Mall Theatres, Cleveland, announced "The Circle" (Metro-Goldwyn-Mayer) with this two-column ad.

Music program—Symphony Orchestras. Organ accompaniments. (Dancer).

Delmonte Theatre—
Film Numbers— Wild, Wild Susan (Paramount), Youth for Sale, Delmonte News and Views.
Music Program—Orchestral and vocal selections.

West End Lyric—
Film Numbers—The Gold Rush (United Artists) Kinogram News.
Music P r o g r a m—"High Brow Stuff" assisted by (cellist) and (violinist).

MINNEAPOLIS

Aster Theatre—
Film Numbers—The Fighting Heart (Fox), A Cloudy Romance (Fox), Fox News.
Musical Program—Organ overture.

Garrick Theatre—
Film Numbers—The Midshipman (Metro-Goldwyn-Mayer), Felix Cat comedy (Educational), News Reel.
Musical Program—Garrick orchestra, "The Anvil Chorus" from Il Trovatore, Alice Lilligren and Charles Bennett, "A Dixie Romance".

Lyric Theatre—
Film Numbers—Why Women Love (First Nat.), Selected comedy, Pathe Weekly.
Musical Program—Organ Overture, Maurice Cook, "Normandy".

Star Theatre—
Film Numbers—Where Was I? (Universal), Spotlight (Educ.), News selected.
Musical Program—State Concert Orchestra, "From an Indian Pueblo", Organ Novelty, Jazz band.

Strand Theatre—
Film Numbers—The Freshman (Pathe), Strand News.
Musical Program—Strand Concert Orchestra, Baritone solo.

ATLANTA

Howard Theatre—
Film Numbers — He's a Prince (Paramount), International News Reel.
Musical Program—Organ Solo, Sextette from "Ducia". Fashion

NEVER HAS A PICTURE AROUSED SUCH ENTHUSIASM!!
7 MORE DAYS TO SEE THE PHOTOPLAY THAT IS CREATING A GENUINE FURORE
GASPING! THRILLING!
The LOST WORLD
MODERN LOVERS AMONG THE TEEMING, IN-DIFFUSION, MONSTERS

LEWIS STONE
BESSIE LOVE
WALLACE BEERY
LLOYD HUGHES

LYRIC
NEXT ATTRACTION / CHARLIE CHAPLIN in "the GOLD RUSH"

Strong action, with plenty of pictorial display, featured this four-column ad on "The Lost World" (First National) at the Lyric theatre in Cincinnati, used on the opening day of the second week.

Pageant, Violin Solo, "Caprice Viennois".

Metropolitan Theatre—
Film Numbers—Classified (First National), Fox News Reel, Sportlight (Pathe).
Musical Program—Overture, Song Hits from Past and Present, Prologue, "The Dance" (ballet).

Rialto Theatre—
Film Numbers—The Ten Commandments (Paramount).
Musical Program—Special Orchestra, Big Betel Choir.

Grand Theatre—
Film Numbers—Romola (Metro-Goldwyn-Mayer).
Musical Program—Five Acts Vaudeville.

Tudor Theatre—
Film Numbers—The Circus Cyclone" (Universal), Officer 13 (Universal).

Alamo Theatre No. 2—
Film Numbers—Siren of Seville (Producers), Uncle Tom's Gal (Universal); Last Saturday, Shackled Lightning (Progress).

ST. PAUL

Astor Theatre—
Film Numbers—The Live Wire (First Nat.), Baby Be Good, News Events.
Musical Program—Organ solo, "Jazz Week", Violin solo.

Capitol Theatre—
Film Numbers—Classified (First Nat.), Maid in Morocco (Pathe), Capitol Digest.
Musical Program—Capitol Symphony Orchestra, "Orchids of Songland".

Garrick Theatre—
Film Numbers—The Freshman (Pathe) Hodge Podge (Educational), News Reel.
Musical Program—Orchestra, "Evolution of the Charleston".

Princess Theatre—
Film Numbers—The Lost World (First Nat.), Felix Cat comedy Kinograms.
Musical Program—Organ Overture.

Strand Theatre—
Film Numbers—Thunder Mountain (Fox), Sweet Marie (Comedy), Kinograms.
Husbands (Pathe), Pathe News.
Musical Program—Organ Overture.

Tower Theatre—

Film Numbers—The Midshipman (Metro-Goldwyn-Mayer), Innocent Husbands (Pathe), Pathe News.
Musical Program—Orchestra selections from "Blossom Time".

KANSAS CITY

Newman Theatre—
Film Numbers—A Slave of Fashion (Metro-Goldwyn), Newman Mirror of the World (Pathe, Kinograms and International News), Newman Current Events (Local photography).
Musical Program—"Marche Slav" (Overture), Fur Modes Revue (Specialty With Cast of Thirty), King Sisters (Novelty) Recessional (Organ solos).

Liberty Theatre—
Film Numbers—Little Annie Rooney (United Artists), Aesop's Fables (Pathe), International News.
Musical Program—Selections from "Eileen" (Overture), Recessional (Organ solos).

Royal Theatre—
Film Numbers—Romola (Metro-Goldwyn), Royal Screen Magazine (Pathe Kinograms and International News), Royal Current Events (Local photography), Organ solos.

Mainstreet Theatre—
Film Numbers—Classified (First National), Pathe News and Educational Short Subjects.
Musical Program—Popular selections (Overture), Recessional (Organ solos).

Pantages Theatre—
Film Numbers—American Pluck (Chadwick, S. R.), Fox News and Fox short subjects.
Musical Program—Atmospheric Selections (Overture), Recessional (Organ solos).

SALT LAKE CITY

American Theatre—
Film Numbers — The Knockout (First National), International News, Cartoon (F. B. O.).

Kinema Theatre—
Film Numbers—Wildfire (Vitagraph), No Place To Go (Universal), Pathe Review.

Pantages Theatre—
Film Numbers — Exchange of Wives (Metro-Goldwyn-Mayer).

Harold Bell Wright novel featured in ad for screen adaptation of "A Son of His Father" (Paramount), used by the Strand theatre, Des Moines.

Opinions on Current Short Subjects

"A Punch in the Nose"
(Pathe—Two Reels)
(Reviewed by Thomas C. Kennedy)

THIS, as a parenthetical line below the title remarks, is not a love story. It is a series of punches in the noses and kicks in the pantzes of all the players in the cast—and what a cast it is. Among the many whose names stand for something quite worth while in short comedies appearing in this Hal Roach production directed by Jay Howe are Lucien Littlefield, Al. St. John, Lige Conley, Martha Sleeper, Dot Farley, "Husky" Hanes, Kewpie Morgan, Jimmie Finlayson, Al Hallett and Marjorie Whiteis.

With a line-up like that "A Punch In The Nose" seems entitled to the "all star" tag without any further question. But the significant thing is the comedy itself—and here, unfortunately, we are again taught that too many stars may spoil the picture, or rather, that all stars in the cast cannot make funny a series of incidents which have no comic merit of their own.

"A Punch in the Nose" is fast and furious as to the movement of its action and scenes, but little more than sheer movement develops. It is slapstick of the slam-bang style and seems always to strain for its comedy effects.

The Cast
Lucien Littlefield, Al. St. John, "Husky" Hanes, Jimmie Finlayson, Lige Conley, Kewpie Morgan, Al Hallet, Martha Sleeper, Dot Farley, Marjorie Whiteis.

The Story.—An "Uncle Tom's Cabin" road show gets stranded in a country town, where there is a sanitarium needing several specialists in swimming, massaging, cooking, etc. The troupe applies en masse for the jobs. They are all better actors than sanitarium specialists, even though they are not good actors. When the bruiser who runs the establishment learns that they have misrepresented themselves he sets after the whole crew, but by that time the actors have learned that the little slavey is the real owner of the sanitarium and they banish the villain.

Summary.—Few two-reelers boast casts made up of such well known comedians as are brought together here, but the players do not receive much support from the material and picture, owing to lack of effective gags, becomes a routine affair specializing in slapstick of a merely mechanical sort.

"The Boundary Line"
(Universal-Mustang—Two Reels)
(Reviewed by Chester J. Smith.)

A BOUNDARY line dispute with a Rebel war veteran on one side and a Union veteran on the other, and a family feud between them, furnishes the action on which this romantic western is based. Fred Humes is the hero and as usual, he acquits himself creditably. The story is rather a good one, a little out of the ordinary for the type of picture, but abounding in all of the usual action. In fact there is a little more action than usual with the climaxes developed naturally. The old soldiers are well played, as are all the other characters in the picture.

The Cast
Jack Barton Jones .... Fred Humes

A two-reel Mustang Western.

The Story. Colonel Jasper, Rebel war veteran, and Colonel Jones, old Union soldier are at the height of a boundary dispute with the arrival of Nellie Jones, granddaughter, from the east. She is compelled to drive alone from the station in a buckboard and in the ensuing runaway she is saved by Jack Barton Jones, grandson of the Southern Colonel. Later Jack also saves her from the unwelcome advances of Monte Boyle, ranch foreman, but Colonel Jasper orders him off the premises and forbids

---

the girl to associate with a Jones. Boyle, the foreman, seeks revenge, sneaks into the Jasper house and steals $4,000. Escaping he accosts the girl and tries to force her to accompany him. She is again rescued by Jack, who turns Boyle over to the sheriff, and the usual happy ending follows.

Summary. This is an entertaining and well acted story with a nice little love theme running through it. It fairly abounds in action and also has its humorous moments. It should go well where the short Western is appreciated.

"Working for the Rest"
(Bischoff, Inc.—Two Reels)
(Reviewed by Harold Flavin)

THIS is a take-off on the mother-in-law theme used so often and usually with excellent results as regards coining laughs. It is a sprightly affair with a number of good gags interspersed throughout the main business which has to do with the adventures experienced by a young newlywed who embarks on a vacation with his wife's entire family in tow.

From the start Johnny is hounded by his mother-in-law; nothing that he does seems right in her estimation so that he undergoes all the tortures of the damned in his efforts to conform to her method of keeping house, or rather camp, which is the form of vacation chosen.

The best bit of business in the production is the scene in which Johnny struggles through the woods with a canoe over his head which gives him the appearance of some strange animal. He is espied by two hunters who take pot-shots at him.

Another funny situation shows Johnny, in a dream as a result of being clouted by the mother-in-law, chasing a bevy of elusive bathing beauties who entice him into the water only to dive when he makes an attempt to catch them; he too dives but finds he is in an inch of water.

The cast all render good performances with Johnny Sinclair as the particular highlight of the production.

The Cast
Johnny Sinclair, Lois Boyd, Evleyn Thatcher, John Rand.

A Trem Carr production.

The Story—Johnny stars out on a camping trip accompanied by his wife and her mother with the usual collection of bundles. After many mishaps they arrive at their destination and Johnny's clumsy efforts at pitching camp arouse the mother-in-law's ire so that he is the object of her verbal and physical assaults. He finally escapes with his wife and they return home but just as he is about to declare himself "monarch of all he surveys" the mother-in-law, in some mysterious way, appears on the scene, so all becomes "as it was."

Summary—A rather lively comedy with some amusing gags utilized in a story that is of a conventional pattern. The cast turns in creditable performances and the direction is good.

"Cured Hams"
(Red Seal—Two Reels)
(Reviewed by Harold Flavin)

THE adventures of two ham-actors in a very small town, theatre forms the basis of the comedy in this Biff production featuring Jack Richardson and Al Alt. Their sequences in the theatre, showing the audience in different postures of repose should evoke a mirthful response. During the performances the two hams run through

---

the gamut of vaudeville routine appearing as musicians, acrobats, hand to hand balancers—even playing the Romeo and Juliet scene—all with very amusing results due to the faulty work of the stage hand and the very indifferent attitude of the audience.

There are several novel stage gags introduced—one showing one of the theatre patrons coming to the performance with a lounge which he places in the aisle—another showing the actor doing a bar gymnastic act which fails to get over because the assistants in the wings, who are holding the Jay ropes, are drawn through the air and on top of the Hams when they start to mount the bar.

This is a good bet for the entire family.

The Cast
Jack Richardson, Al Alt, Bud Fine and Dixie Lamont.

A Gold Medal Production.

The Story—Jack and Al, two actors, are due to perform in a small town 'Opry' house. They arrive and after a few mishaps succeed in getting started on their routine which consists of doing everything known to vaudeville from playing musicians to the 'dumb' or acrobatic act. Try as they do they can't seem to awaken the audience from its lethargic state. Having finished most of the work they go into a Bowery melodrama scene but during the performance the 'snow' catches fire and the actors become the unwelcome recipients of a variety of vegetables. The story closes with a scene showing the actors trying to sell that with which they were hit.

Summary—An amusing production with all manner of vaudeville gags used most of which should draw a laugh. The principals are good in their roles and the direction is fair.

"All Wool"
(Pathe—One Reel)

THIS Hal Roach production with Billy Engle and Earl Mohan in the leading roles is considerably above the average of one-reel comedies and may be recommended as effective entertainment. The principals are seen as a pair of misfit tailors, striving to make a living at a trade of which they appear to know precious little. Their efforts to please the man who wants his suit cleaned and pressed, the lady who wants to see a cloak exhibited on a living model before she will buy, and the demands of a hard-boiled customer who brings his "skirt" in to have a skirt made, make the way for a number of amusing items. The picture was directed by Tay Garnett.—T. C. KENNEDY.

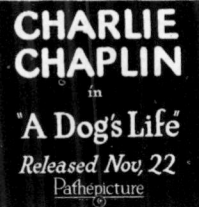

"A Goofy Gob"
(Educational-Christie—Two Reels)
(Reviewed by Chester J. Smith)

BILLY DOOLEY and Natalie Joyce have the leading roles in this two-reeler, which is well above the average for this type of comedy. The story is a fairly good one and supplies an abundance of humor both of the situation and slapstick variety. Dooley is a real comedian on the screen and goes through all sorts of evolutions that are bound to bring laughs. He gets some rough treatment in the exclusive girls' boarding school where he goes to deliver a ring for a superior officer, to conceal the latter's love for the daughter of the commander of the ship from the commander. There's a funny situation when Billy disguises himself as the punching bag in the gymnasium and there are numerous other funny ones as the action progresses to its humorous conclusion.

The Cast
A Goofy Gob	Billy Dooley
An Ensign	Jay Belasco
The Commander	Bill Blaisdell
Betty	Natalie Joyce

A Christie comedy from the story by Hal Conklin; directed by William Watson; photography by Paul Garnett and Frank Sullivan; cartoons by Norman Z. McLeod.

The Story.—The commander of the ship discovers on the finger of the ensign a ring similar to that he has given his daughter. The ensign denies it is the daughter's ring and the Commander leaves for the exclusive boarding school to ascertain the truth. Billy the gob volunteers to get the ring to the daughter before the arrival of her father. In the wild chase Billy arrives first, gains entrance to the school with difficulty, but has difficulty in finding the 'daughter. He is summarily dismissed from the premises a number of times, as the Commander waits the arrival of his daughter in the reception room. Eventually the girl is brought before her father who demands to see the ring. The girl, with her hands behind her backs before a huge grandfather's clock in which Billy is secreted. To her surprise he slips the ring on her finger and she proudly exhibits it for her father, who departs cursing himself for a suspicious old fool.

Summary.—This comedy is replete with humorous situations and with enough slapstick to allow Dooley to show his versatility. The action is fast and the story well above the average. It should go well in almost any type of house.

"Transients in Arcadia"
(Fox—Two Reels)
(Reviewed by Chester J. Smith)

IT'S a real pleasure to sit through a comedy of this type without the customary hokum and slapstick. It's a situation comedy pure and simple, an adaptation from the O. Henry story, which is a good enough guarantee for any story. It was directed by Daniel Keefe, who handled both subjects and players well.

It is really a delightful little tale and one that does not clamor for laughs, but gets them naturally. Mary Akin and Hugh Allan have the leading roles and they do them admirably. Not only is the picture well acted and the story well told, but is splendidly and almost lavishly produced. Miss Akin is the shop girl who saves her money for an entire year to pose as an aristocrat for one week at a fashionable summer resort. Allan is the collector for an installment payment house, who is at the same resort for the same purpose. The climaxes of the story are well worked up and the ending a perfectly natural one, without a false note to mar the telling.

The Cast
Mamie	Mary Akin
Farrington	Hugh Allan
Rosie	Yvonne Howell
Mrs. Beaumont	Marie Walcamp
Mr. Beaumont	Anthony Merlo

An O. Henry story, directed by Daniel Keefe. Supervised by George Marshall.

The Story.—Mamie is a New York shopgirl who saved for an entire year that she may pose at an exclusive Summer resort for one week as an aristocrat and perhaps win for herself a "Prince Charming." Farrington is collector for an installment payment concern who is at the resort for the same purpose. A series of humorous incidents invariably throw them together. In the end when Farrington calls at the shop for Mamie's installment each is revealed in his and her true character. They reveal their love for each other and start for a honeymoon at Coney Island.

Summary.—This is a real high class and real amusing comedy, whose humor is based on situations alone, and whose situations are so naturally brought about that the humor is spontaneous. This will not appeal to those who clamor only for slapstick and hokum in their comedies, but it will be highly amusing for those to whom a real comedy has an appeal.

"Roomers Afloat"
(Bischoff, Inc.—Two Reels)
(Reviewed by Harold Flavin.)

YOUR patrons should get many a laugh out of this comedy which details the efforts of a couple of young rent-dodgers to escape from their room unbeknownst to the landlady, in which effort they are successful but only after considerable trouble to themselves and a couple of strangers.

The opening scene shows them in their room about to arise but halted when they hear the landlady's knock on the door. They tear a sheet and tie it between the bed post and the door but when the landlady pulls open the door the bed folds up and they are 'hors de combat.' The lady of the house takes their clothes.

Espying two men on the street in front of their window the boys fashion grappling hooks out of sheets and clothes-hangers and, paying them out through the window, succeed in hooking the strangers and drawing them up to the room whence they strip them and clothe themselves. The director has worked up this gag to a laugh-producing affair as the boys in an effort to lower the disrobed strangers to the street start a see-saw affair finally hanging the strangers out the window and making their exit.

They are pursued and, having run into a modiste's shop, proceed to perform all kinds of stunts to elude their pursuers but are caught, disrobed and knocked out.

The bed room scenes and those in the modiste's shop should draw a mirthful response from your patrons.

(The Cast)
Jack Cooper, Jack Richardson, Ilona Marlowe and Agnes Steele.

The Story.—Tom and Jerry, unable to pay their rent, are left clothesless in their room by the landlady. Seeing two strangers on the street in front of their room they hook them up by means of torn sheets and clothes hangers and strip them of their clothes, leaving the disrobed ones dangling from the window ledge. Tom and Jerry leave the room but are pursued by the police and dodge into a modiste's shop. They are followed and a merry chase ensues in which Tom and Jerry perform all sorts of stunts in an effort to hide from the police, but they are finally caught, stripped and beaten and left in an alcove in the shop. They form an unconscious tableau when a mannequin draws back the curtains to display some gowns.

Summary.—An hilarious farce with many mirth-provoking gags interspersed throughout in this story. The production is well mounted and the direction is of good quality.

"Slippery Feet"
(Educational—Two Reels)
(Reviewed by Chester J. Smith)

BOBBY VERNON has some fast comedy stuff in this two reeler, which suffers only from repetition. The first reel is devoted almost entirely to comedy dancing which would be considerably funnier if there was only about half as much of it. Ditto for the second reel in which Bobby is disguised as Bad Dan Derby when Bad Dan puts in an appearance at the exclusive party and the guests become confused as to which is the real one. Both the deception and chase continue entirely too long in an effort to crowd in a few more laughs, which would be more readily forthcoming if they were not so eagerly sought. There is much wild slapstick throughout.

The Cast
Bobby	Bobby Vernon
Frances	Frances Lee
George	George Hall
Aunt Muscena	Blanche Payson

A Christy comedy, directed by Harold Beaudine; photography by Paul Garnett and Frank Sullivan; cartoons by Norman Z. McLeod.

The Story.—Bobby is the guest at the party given for Frances, and George is his rival. George connives so that Bobby is compelled to dance with Aunt Muscena, while he dances with Frances, but Bobby outwits him. George then bets Bobby he cannot disguise himself as Bad Dan Derby and deceive the party into believing he is the real Dan. Bobby dons the disguise as the real Dan appears. The guests are robbed of their jewels by Bobby, who returns them, and they are then taken by the real Dan, from whom Bobby steals them and again returns them. The police arrive and take Bobby for the real culprit, but after much confusion he turns over the real Dan to them.

Summary.—A rather fast moving comedy which would be more effective without so much of repetition. There are some humorous situations in it and an abundance of lapstick. All together it should be good for a few laughs in the neighborhood houses.

"A Taxi War"
(Universal-Century—Two Reels)
(Reviewed by Chester J. Smith)

EDDIE GORDON is featured in this two reeler, which is purely slapstick and not too entertaining. It is just a succession of alleged comedy situations that are almost too ridiculous to be really funny. It is first the old story of trying to dodge the landlady and later develops into a taxicab war between Gordon and his Pal who are working for rival companies.

The Story.—Eddie and his pal after repeatedly standing off the landlady, find the door of their room barricaded and escape cut off. Eddie endeavors to make his escape across a wire to a telegraph pole, but the wire breaks and he swings back into the room, breaking the barricade from the door. They make their getaway and Eddie sneaks into the garage and gets his cab, as his pal is fired for being late. The latter appeals to a rival company for a job promising to take all the business from his late pal. It is then a chase between them for customers with all sorts of devices resorted to to secure business.

Summary.—This is a slapstick comedy with a lot of knockabout stuff that will hardly get laughs except in some of the smaller neighborhood houses.

Film Facts "H"
(Red Seal—One Reel)

THIS number of the series deals with the ancient art of glass shaping by the blowing process and hand turning. The spectator is taken in to the factory and each step in the manufacturing of glass receptacles is shown from the molding to the final planing process. It is an entertaining and instructive number of the series.—HAROLD FLAVIN.

Short Subjects and Serials

Work Started on Second Half of Fox Comedies

There has been no let up in production at the Fox West Coast studios even though the halfway mark in comedy production was passed a few days ago. Under the general supervision of George E. Marshall, Tom Buckingham is engaged on a new Helen and Warren comedy as yet untitled. Charles Sellon and Tiny Sanford have been added to the cast. Earle Foxe is working on a Van Bibber, and Georgie Harris and Barbara Luddy are making the second Irish-Jewish comedy.

Carroll Nye, juvenile comedian, has been signed to play leads in the series of O. Henry comedies, under the direction of Robert Kerr.

Walter Hiers is Ready to Resume Work

Following an injury which compelled him to stop work for several weeks, Walter Hiers will return to the Christie studios next week to resume his comedies for Educational release. A number of his fingers were damaged while making a scene in a current production.

Gale Henry in Standard Fat Men Comedy

Gale Henry has been assigned to the feminine lead in Joe Rock's Standard comedy now in production for F.B.O. release. She will play opposite "Fat" Karr, "Kewpie" Ross and "Fatty" Alexander, the featured players. The comedy, a two-reeler, has not yet been titled.

Clyde Cook makes his debut as a Pathe comedy star in "Moonlight and Noses," a two-reeler produced by Hal Roach. The scenes are taken from the picture.

Alice Day is starred in "A Sweet Pickle," a two-reel Mack Sennett comedy from which these scenes are taken. Released by Pathe.

Succeeds With Short Subjects

Harrisburg, Pa., Broad Street Theatre Profits With First Experimental Program

THE first exclusively short subject program ever put on at a motion picture theatre in Harrisburg, Pa.—one of the few, in fact, ever presented in the Central Pennsylvania district—was tried as an experiment in the Broad street theatre, Third and Broad streets, that city, on Wednesday, October 14, and was declared by the management to have been a success beyond all expectations.

Oscar B. Feldser, one of the proprietors of the theatre, who is the house manager, declared that the short subject program, which consisted entirely of comedies, with the exception of a Fox news reel, brought entirely satisfactory returns and as a result of the one-day experiment the Broad street theatre will put on a similar program every other Wednesday as a permanent proposition.

None of the numbers on the program was of greater length than two reels. The numbers consisted of:

The two-reel "Our Gang" comedy, "Commencement Day," released by Pathe.

One reel of "Fun From The Press," (Literary Digest) released by the Producers Distributing Corporation.

Two-reel Mermaid comedy, "Motormad," Educational Pictures Incorporated.

One reel of Lyman Howe's travel pictures, "Earth's Oddities," including comedy

cartoons, Educational Pictures, Incorporated.

The two-reel Christie Comedy, "Step Fast," also released by Educational.

One reel of Fox News films.

In his newspaper advertisements Mr. Feldser mentioned each of the program numbers individually. He said in an interview afterward that he made the selection of each attraction on the basis of his own judgment, instead of depending on any individual booking concern to prepare the combined program.

Mr. Feldser, who is looked upon in Harrisburg as a particularly astute and progressive exhibitor, is a partner with Samuel Katzman, also of Harrisburg, in the ownership and operation of the theatre.

"For six months," said Mr. Feldser, "we had been considering the wisdom of experimenting with an exclusively short-subject program and finally decided to try it. It was my thought that the public would be slow to respond to the novelty but I was surprised beyond all expectations when we did 20 per cent more business than usual, on the first day of the try-out. That convinced me that the public wants that sort of program, and the Broad Street theatre is going to give it to them as long as the demand keeps up."

Resume of Current News Weeklies

PATHE NEWS NO. 85: New York City—Michelson wins Port Chester National Marathon; Pulham, England—Britain's dirigible R-33 in first flight since runaway trip last spring; Aneo Nueva Island, Cal.—Sea-lions from northern icy waters make their homes on protected island to rear young in warm clime; Washington, D. C.—Coolidge names Dwight F. Davis Secretary of War; Washington, D. C.—Elect new Fleet Corporation president; North Wales, Eng.—Pathe cameramen climbs steepest mountain in Wales; San Francisco, Cal.—Give football season a fiery reception; Locarno, Switzerland—Five European powers adopt pact against Rhine war; Venice Pier, Cal.—Daredevil motorcycle rider defies law of gravitation; Denver, Colo. (Denver only)—University of Denver Freshmen get severe initiation; Tiffin, Ohio (Cleveland only)—Ohio Knights Templars appear in competitive drills.

PATHE NEWS NO. 86: Tokio, Japan—Ten thousand homeless as result of huge flood; Washington, D. C.—Seek $300,000,000 income tax reduction; Hubertstock, Germany —Hindenburg 78 years young; New York City —Army bumbles Notre Dame in annual football game; London, England—Only woman ruler in India visits England; Philadelphia, Pa.—Scenes at Temple University campus pranks show why college boys are so hard on clothes; Newmarket, England—Girl jockey, 18, is first woman to win England's oldest race; Marino, Italy—A shock for Mr. Volstead—fountain pours wine for festival; Portland, Ore. —Pacific Coast aquaplane champions end season with thrilling exhibition.

INTERNATIONAL NEWS, NO. 86: Alecon, France—France decorates sturdy mother of 19 children; Pulham, England—Britain goes ahead with dirigible airship tests; Havana, Cuba (Boston only)—Ancients and Honorables make big hit in Cuba; Omaha, Neb. (Omaha only)—Ak-Sar-Ben parade provides brilliant night spectacle; Allentown, Pa.

(Philadelphia only) — Disastrous explosion wrecks 8-story building; Washington, D. C. (Washington only)—New Secretary of War, Dwight W. Davis, acting chief, appointed to succeed John M. Weeks, who quit because of illness; Colombes, France—Pole snaps as Olympic star tries for new vaulting record; Monkey Island, Milwaukee, Wis.—Toy balloons lure monkeys just like human kids; On the Atlantic—U. S. S. Republic battles gale to rescue crew on tiny ship helpless in grip of storm; Pittsburg, Pa.—Pittsburg wins World's Baseball Championship in sensational series finish.

INTERNATIONAL NEWS NO. 87: Yokohama, Japan—Flood wreaks havoc in Japan; Seattle, Wash.—Highest church honors for Bishop O'Dea; Indianapolis, Ind. (Indianapolis only)—Pay tribute to Sen. Ralston; Chicago, Ill.—Scientist claims he can bottle sunlight; Marino, Italy—Fountain pours forth wine for joyous feast; Seattle, Wash.—Herd of exiled reindeer arrives from the Arctic; Northfield, Vt.—Schoolboys in exhibition of rough riding; Football on Many Gridirons—An International News Reel special; Monkey Island, Milwaukee—Strenuous exercise gets monks ready for winter; Newmarket, Eng.—Girl jockeys compete in English turf classic; Baltimore, Md. (Washington only)—Princeton battles Navy's gridiron warriors.

FOX NEWS, VOL 7, NO. 6: Washington, D. C.—President Coolidge and his cabinet bid farewell to resigning Secretary of War John W. Weeks; New York City—Miss Congo, only female gorilla ever in captivity, arrives in America and goes to the Bronx Zoo; Paris, France—The high cost of taxes prompt this couple to ride to their wedding in a parade of push-carts; Chicago, Ill.—Thousands see thrilling gridiron game as Chicago and Ohio State battle to hard fought 3-3 tie; Guasti, Calif.— Harvest starts on state's vast crop of wine grapes which is expected to set record of 886,000 tons; Snoqualmie, Mont.—Nature submits to man's mastery at the falls here where drop greater than Niagara runs dynamos; El-paso, Tex.—J. C. Castner, new commander of Fort Bliss succeeding Gen. Howe, holds his first review; Cherokee, N. C.—Indians celebrate Fall Festival with ball game, a mixture of football, basketball and wrestling; Milan, Italy—One of Italy's splendors is the Duomo, the world's third largest cathedral and the most beautiful; Newark, N. J.—A scenic railway in the backyard; New Mexico—Vast drift of white sand, one of world's strangest desert formations, offers a thrill for motorcyclist; New York—The Jazz Barber Shop; New Yorker today can get a shave or a haircut to music of an orchestra.

Scenes from "Cuckoo Love," a two-reel Hal Roach Comedy released by Pathe.

Dick Sutherland in Cast of Hamilton Comedy

Dick Sutherland, screen "bad man," who made his debut in pictures in support of Harold Lloyd in "Grandma's Boy," has been selected for the cast which will appear with Lloyd Hamilton in Jack's next picture for Educational.

Marcella Daly is another prominent player who will be seen in this picture, being directed by Norman Taurog. Miss Daly, who has appeared in several features, including "Adam's Rib" and "The Ten Commandments," will make her debut in the short comedies with Hamilton in this Educational release.

Screen Comediennes Join Hal Roach Casts

Cissy Fitzgerald and Gale Henry, screen comediennes, are new members of Hal Roach comedy casts. Miss Fitzgerald is supporting Glenn Tryon in his latest comedy being directed by Fred L. Guiol, and Gale Henry has completed a role with Charley Chase in his latest two-reeler.

Allene Ray and Walter Miller Broadcast

The Pathe Serial stars, Allene Ray and Walter Miller, addressed the radio audience recently from Station W.R.N.Y., New York. Miller described his experiences during the filming of "Play Ball," a current Patheserial, in which he played the role of a rookie ball player. Miss Ray, interviewed on the air by Charles D. Isaacson, announcer of the station, related her entrance into pictures, why she preferred playing in serials and why she was particularly interested in her role in "The Green Archer," a Pathe-serial, the filming of which was completed recently.

"The Green Archer" will follow "Wild West" on the Pathe schedule.

Two New Beauties Join Educational Company

Winona Shirley and Anna Styers, newcomers to motion pictures, have been added to the aggregation of beauties who will appear in Educational Comedies.

Miss Shirley is a cousin of Buster Keaton and recently arrived in Hollywood from her home in Terre Haute, Indiana, where she completed her education a short time ago. Miss Styers is of the celebrated Dominguez family, which once owned the land on which San Pedro, Long Beach and Torrence, Cal., are located, under a land grant from the Spanish King when California was a Spanish colony.

Historic Figures In New Universal Serial

Alexander Graham Bell and Theodore N. Vail, whose genius contributed much to the development of the telephone, will be characterized in the new Universal serial titled "Strings of Steel," a ten-chapter play dealing with the invention and development of the telephone. Ted Duncan will impersonate the character of Vail and Alphonse Martel will appear as Bell. The picture is being directed by Henry McRae with William Desmond and Eileen Sedgwick in the featured roles.

Rock Making New Standard Comedy for F. B. O.

"Look Out Below" is the working title of the current Joe Rock Standard comedy featuring "Fat" Karr, "Kewpie" Ross and "Fatty" Alexander. Besides the featured players the cast will include Gale Henry and Lois Boyd, the latter a recent discovery of Rock's. Slim Summerville is handling the megaphone.

Upon completion of this vehicle Rock will begin production of a Blue Ribbon comedy featuring Alice Ardell.

Walter Lewis is Added to "Green Archer" Cast

Walter P. Lewis has been added to the cast of "The Green Archer," the new Pathe-serial now in production and featuring Allene Ray and Walter Miller. The serial is an adaptation of the Edgar Wallace novel prepared by Frank Leon Smith and directed by Spencer Bennett. It will be released following "Wild West" on the Pathe schedule.

Fox Starts Production on Two Two-Reelers

Two new comedies have been started by Fox in the Helen and Warren and O. Henry series. "The Silent Witness" is the title of the Helen and Warren two-reeler, based on another of Mabel Herbert Urner's stories. It is being directed by Tom Buckingham and again has Kathryn Perry and Hallam Cooley in the roles of Helen and Warren. They are supported by David Buther, Grace Goodall, Grace Darmond and Mickey Mc-Ban.

"Cupid a La Carte" is the new O. Henry picture being produced under the direction of Daniel Keefe. Florence Gilbert has the leading feminine role, with Carroll Nye cast as the hero. Maine Geary and Sidney de Grey have important supporting roles. Both comedies are being produced under the supervision of George Marshall.

Fleischer to Edit Series for Urban-Kineto

Max Fleischer, Out-of-the-Inkwell cartoonist, signed a contract this week with the Urban-Kineto Corporation, whereby he will be Editor-in-Chief of two new film series "Reelviews" and "Searchlights" for the corporation. "Reelviews" will be a film magazine of current topics and "Searchlights" a series of one-reelers on popular science. Fleischer will have a staff of cameramen reaching around the world ready at a moment's notice to take needed scenes. In addition to editing the reels Fleischer will also write the titles.

Urban-Kineto's studio and laboratory are at Irvington, New York.

"Our Gang" Making Xmas Comedy for Pathe

At the Hal Roach studios the "Our Gang" comedians are being directed by Bob McGowan in two-reeler with a Christmas flavor for release during the holiday season by Pathe.

Great production activity is in evidence at the Roach lot at present. Charley Chase, Clyde Cook and Glen Tryon are among the stars who are now engaged on new two-reelers. The all-star unit, being directed by James W. Horne, has "Husky" Hanes, Martha Sleeper, Jimmie Finlayson, Frank Butler, Vivian Oakland, Fred Malatesta and other well known comedians at work on a picture for early release by Pathe.

"Slim" Summerville Signs With Joe Rock

Joe Rock has signed "Slim" Summerville to direct his next Standard comedy for F.B.O. release. The picture, which has not yet been titled, is scheduled to go into production this week. Standard productions are two-reel comedies featuring the trio of fat men, "Fatty" Alexander, "Kewpie" Ross and "Fat" Karr.

Jimmie Adams Starts New Christie Comedy

William Watson is directing Jimmie Adams in a new Christie comedy under the working title, "A Busy Bum." Molly Malone again appears as Adams' leading lady.

Scenes from "Educating Buster," first of the series of "Buster Brown" comedies produced by Century and released by Universal.

Comedies Top Pathe Releases
Sennett Two-Reeler and "Our Gang" Vehicle Head Program for November 1st

ONE of Hal Roach's "Our Gang" comedies and a Mack-Sennett two-reeler head the Pathe list of short subject releases for the week of November 1st. "Better Movies" is the title of the "Our Gang" vehicle, which was directed by Robert McGowan. The "gang" find a deserted studio and proceed to stage their own comedies and thrillers. The "gang" is augmented for this release by Martha Sleeper and "Husky" Hanes.

"Dangerous Curves Behind" is the Mack Sennett two-reeler directed by Eddie Cline. In the cast are Ruth Taylor, Jack Cooper, Joseph Young and William McCall.

"The Diamond Girl" is the title of the sixth chapter of the Patheserial, "Wild West," which features Jack Mulhall and Helen Ferguson. Virginia Warwick and Eddie Phillips lend prominent support in this chapter.

"What Price Touchdown?" is the Grantland Rice "Sportlight" release. Rice shows

in this reel the course of training the big college teams must go through before they are ready for a game.

"The Sea of Galilee" is the third of "A Pilgrimage to Palestine" series and reveals scenes of Christ's early ministry. This series in addition to being both educational and entertaining, is particularly adapted for showings during the Christmas season.

Pathe Review No. 44 presents three subjects of wide appeal: "The Old Man of the Sea," an adventure of a Japanese fisherman; "Feminine Farmers." Pathecolor views of a manless town in Switzerland; and "Plundering the Sea," a camera record of the Arcturus Oceanographic Expedition, are released in co-operation with the New York Zoological Society.

"Wild Cats of Paris" is the latest of the "Aesop's Film Fables," "Topics of the Day," the reel of press humor, and two issues of Pathe News complete the November 1st schedule.

Christie Production At Peak
Twenty-Eight Two-Reel Comedies Under Way for Educational Release

THE Christie Comedy Company is busy with the greatest production schedule in the history of the organization, with twenty-eight two-reel comedy productions to be released through Educational Film Exchanges during the 1925-26 season. The new schedule includes four separate series with Bobby Vernon, Neal Burns, Jimmie Adams, Billy Dooley and Walter Hiers as the stars.

Variety of characterizations is the keynote of the new schedule. It is said the Christie comedians will be seen in entirely different roles than they have appeared in before. A new system in directorial assignments will also be in order. There will be an exchange of directors with each production.

Earl Rodney, erstwhile Christie comedian, has been elevated to the rank of director, and with William Watson, Robert Thornby and Harold Beaudine, comprises the directorial staff. Scott Sidney has been loaned to Metropolitan Pictures for one production, "The Million Dollar Handicap."

Frank Boland Conklin is editorial supervisor of the Christie forces and Sig Herzig and Hal Conklin are working with him. Norman McLeod is chief gagman at the studio.

Newspaper Opinions on New Pictures

"The Freshman"—Pathe, Southern, Columbus

Dispatch: "When football practice starts, the player never knows what may be expected of him. So yesterday I was not surprised to get an assignment to cover a movie with football atmosphere, Harold Lloyd in 'The Freshman,' at the Southern. If all movies were like this, the reviewer's life would be the life for me. This picture has just about everything and I want to recommend it with all my heart, to everybody on and off the campus."

Journal: "If you want to see a duplicate of Ohio Harley's 80-yard run for touchdown against Wisconsin in 1916, then don't fail to see Harold Lloyd in 'The Freshman' at the Southern all this week. Lloyd runs the length of the field for the winning counter in the best Harley manner sidestepping and straight-arming as well as the great Chic ever did."

Citizen: "'The Freshman' is a riot. It is the funniest picture we have seen in years. From the moment when Harold Lloyd meets Jobyna Ralston on train, while she's solving a crossword puzzle, to the finish of the picture there are laughs every minute. We asked Charlie Weidner to write his own notice of this picture (Charlie being the manager), but he was too busy herding the crowds in the lobby. Please see this picture."

"The Midshipman" — M-G-M., Capitol, N. Y.

Telegraph: "The picture gives Novarro opportunity for some excellent comedy scenes. He is splendid in them. The scenes in the mess hall, the boys' struggle for a pretty partner at the dances, and the spirit of comraderie and good fellowship among the men are deftly and at the same time amusingly portrayed, and the audience enjoyed it all hugely."

Brooklyn Eagle: "Ramon Novarro immaculately attired in the habiliments becoming a future admiral, presents a dashing and quite irresistible figure on the Capitol's screen. Harriet Hammond is seen opposite Novarro in a role to which she does complete justice with an unusual measure of good looks and a flare for dramatic interpretation, which should carry her far in pictures. The comedy in 'The Midshipman' is exceedingly bright. Yesterday afternoon these light touches aroused many a resounding peal of laughter in the packed theatre. Harriet Hammond is attractive as Patricia Lawrence, and Wesley Barry is amusing in the role of the young plebe. Crauford Kent gives an excellent performance in the heavy role. Christy Cabanne, who directed this picture, manifests a penchant for comedy, which he portrays with imagination."

Herald-Tribune: "'The Midshipman' is an entertaining picture, beautifully done. Whatever Mr. Novarro does is right. He is one of the most intelligent, yet ingratiating players on the screen. We

believe that the proper way to express what we mean is 'Take your boy friends to see him, girls—he's a wow.' Wesley Barry is very good as an almost grown-up midshipman."

Mirror: "Youthful America will adore this flag-waving story of Naval Academy life. It will warm the cockles of their hearts, and even inspire enthusiastic audiences to cheers. Novarro makes a husky, upstanding, wholesome midshipman. Slices of 'middy' life at Annapolis are revealed with an adroit combination of humor and pathos."

Telegram: "The audience applauded at the end of the picture, and more audiences battled in the lobby to get a glimpse of Ramon, who is shown as stroke of the crew and as an upright naval officer."

Evening World: "Annapolis makes a charming setting and the buildings and grounds provide beautiful scenes beautifully photographed. The big scenes were so arranged as to include the students, and the result is imposing."

"The Midshipman" — M-G-M., Loew's Palace, Washington, D. C.

Times: "They came through the rain and the puddles, in slickers and rubbers, under umbrellas or without them—but they came! And they—the Ramon Novarro fans—gave manager Larry Beatus one of the biggest days that Loew's Palace Theatre has ever enjoyed. Every performance of 'The Midshipman' was packed to the doors. The audience was not disappointed. The handsome Novarro appeals to the girls, and he's such a good actor that the males haven't anything against him, either."

Star: "Ramon Navarro has worn a great many uniforms in his screen career but none has set off his comely face and figure as does the garb of the midshipman in the new film, 'The Midshipman' which was given its premiere at the Palace yesterday. Novarro, let it be said, also is an actor as well, and his acting in 'The Midshipman' is excellent. The film is undoubtedly a true portrayal of the often fascinating development of a Navy officer."

Herald: "The conflict of love and duty interwoven with the esprit de corps of Annapolis has been chosen for the theme of Ramon Novarro's new picture. 'The Midshipman' will make a special appeal to the flapper and to the young man intending to enter a career in the navy. The audience seemed pleased with the picture and often broke forth into applause."

Post: "Mr. Novarro presents a sympathetic picture of what happens to a young man entering Annapolis and the life there. He managed so to absorb the atmosphere that his characterization of Dick Randall is most lifelike and appealing."

"The Mystic"—M-G-M., Park and Mall, Cleveland

Plain Dealer: " 'The Mystic' is another fine picture by Tod Browning, that surpasses his 'The Miracle Man' and perhaps equals the later and better production, 'The Unholy Three.' For interest and finesse of direction, it is probably one of the best pictures of the year. Aileen Pringle and Conway Tearle make the picture ring true with their startling, realistic characterizations. These two are personality personified and create the impression of not only acting their roles but of actually living their parts."

"The Unholy Three"— M-G-M., Chicago

Tribune: "Strange, sinister, human, inhuman, brilliantly acted, forcefully directed, with a compelling story that holds your interest like a magnet. A grim, fascinating story shot through with flashes of ghoulish humor that will return to haunt and wiggle an ear at you every time you visit the side shows of a circus. Lon Chaney is marvelous in his role. Mae Busch is darling! The others, all of them splendid!"

"Little Annie Rooney"—United Artists, Strand, New York

World: " 'Little Annie Rooney' is a film in which Mary Pickford returns to the type of playing with which she made her beginning, which, is and there can now be little question about, Mary Pickford at her best. I have never seen her more youthful nor lovelier. She is as wistfully juvenile as she was ten years ago, and every inch as adorable."

American: " 'Our Mary' is not only giving the world and his wife what they want in 'Little Annie Rooney,' but she is demonstrating beyond the shadow of a doubt that she can look like a little girl ten years old. I know 'Little Annie' is going to delight Miss Pickford's large army of admirers. It is the sort of character she plays so well, and in addition it has been most ably directed by William Beaudine. I cheerfully recommended this play to those who are shopping for pictures this week. Mary is back younger and more adorable than ever."

Daily News: "Here's your Mary Pickford—the Mary of the angelic smile and the golden curls and the fighting fists. Mary Pickford plays Marv Pickford and we like her best that way. Like 'Little Annie Rooney'? I think you'll love it. Mary and her gang are irresistible."

Mirror "The delicious Mary Pickford of 'Daddy Long Legs' returns to the screen in 'Little Annie Rooney.' The audience says it in peals of laughter. The box office saves it in huge figures. Mary Pickford is a marvel."

Times: "Capitulating to the desire of the vast majority of her public, Mary Pickford returns to cutie, short frocks and to the part of an East Side hoyden. 'Little Annie Rooney' is delightfully

filmed and Miss Pickford's characterization is emphatically pleasing. She look smaller than ever. She makes Annie a lovable, wistful little creature. This charming actress has not changed perceptibly since the early days of pictures."

Telegraph: "In 'Little Annie Rooney' Mary Pickford is captivating as the little gamin. There is lots of fun in this picture, and many laughs. Anything in which Miss Pickford appears is never boresome, and in this she is another of those lovable scamps which has endeared her to the public for years."

Herald-Tribune: "Those who have been wishing for the Nation's Sweetheart in childish roles should be amply satisfied with 'Little Annie Rooney.' We think there is not an actress oh the screen who can do anything better than Miss Pickford can do it. Probably 'Little Annie Rooney' will make millions of dollars. Plenty of people are delighted with it."

Journal: "The kind of picture in which everybody wants to see Mary Pickford, and she is seen in a role that is absolutely delightful. Mary looks amazingly young, and the 'gags' in the picture are uproariously funny. Don't miss it."

Graphic: "'Little Annie Rooney' is Mary Pickford as you love her —human, natural, hoydenish, generous and loving—she's great. Mary hasn't done anything half as good for a long time, and you'll like it. The story is cramful of heart interest, comedy and tense situations. The tears follow laughter in rapid fire succession."

Sun: "'Little Annie Rooney' brings back to the screen—after an absence of more than a year— America's first widely popular movie star, Mary Pickford, and judging by the cordial reception with which she was received— well, she is still 'Our Mary' as of long ago. From every angle the picture proved its worth. I should say that 'Little Annie Rooney' would entertain nearly everyone."

Post: "Mary Pickford romps through 'Little Annie Rooney' as a wild, wild tomboy of New York's East Side tenement district. It is Mary Pickford back in her old form."

Evening World: "Unless first indications are entirely misleading 'Little Annie Rooney' will be a popular Broadway attraction and even more popular as the film gets out to the neighborhood theatres where Mary's friends have been most numerous. The story has pathos, humor, comedy, tragedy and romance, and the role of Little Annie is exactly the kind of role which endeared Mary to the multitudes."

Telegram: "'Little Annie Rooney' has laughs and many tears and the vibration from the two are sympathetic vibrations, stirred alike by the happy impulse to please."

**"The Live Wire"—First National,
Broadway, New York**

Post: "A swift pace is maintained in 'The Live Wire' with apparently no effort at all. The comedy stunts, even the best ones, are not emphasized unduly nor played upon for more than their allotted time. Mr. Hines himself seems to be acquiring a steadily increasing facility in pantomime. At any rate he helps along many of the situations tremendously. The star is also blessed with a competent supporting cast."

Mirror: "'The Live Wire' is chuckful of gags. The comedy must be a merry hit, for the Broadway audiences gave vent to loud laughter throughout. Johnny is his usually energetic self."

American: "A fat man sat in back of me at the Broadway theatre and laughed so uproariously at Johnny Hines in 'The Live Wire,' I took a look at him to see if he had been placed there by the energetic management to help arouse enthusiasm. But a little later, I forgot my portly neighbor in my own amusement over Johnny Hines in the circus, as a tramp, and a little later, as an agent for electric signs. The gags are well thought out and the plot, while hokum, is the variety that flourishes among our most ardent movie patrons."

**"The Live Wire"—First National,
Circle, Indianapolis**

Star : "'The Live Wire' is the best picture Johnny Hines has had in a long time. There is an undercurrent of fun that bubbles and seethes throughout. It would better be described as a romance with comedy, although there are moments when it becomes a comedy with romance. Johnny has enough ideas to sink a barge and provide the best comedy that Hines has offered in months. The whole makes a delightful picture that is well worth watching."

**"The Live Wire"—First National.
Rivoli, Baltimore**

Sun: "Johnny Hines is the Fred Stone of the screen. Johnny's pictures are just as clean as Fred's shows, and that's saying something. What's more, they're just as speedy and full of 'pep.' Maybe Johnny can't jump through windows and do all the fancy dancing that sparkles from Fred's tootsies, but when it comes to keeping you laughing—not a mere chuckle or

two but downright button-busting roaring—you've got to hand it to Johnny."

**"The Live Wire"—First National,
Leland, Albany**

Times-Union: "There is absolutely nothing misleading about the title, 'The Live Wire,' Johnny Hines' latest film. This up and doing star is busier than ever in this tale of a circus performer, who turns tramp and then nerves himself into a good job with the daughter of the jolg-gives as the final reward. There is lots of fun in the circus sequences; in Johnny's adventures with a fractious cow and a trusting grocer to whom he sells the same pigs several times. Hines is brazen, but his audiences seem to enjoy it, and his antics are just wild farces, it does not matter."

**"Satan In Sables"—Warners,
Warners, New York**

American: "I listened for an opinion from the Warner audience and this is what I heard repeated word for word: 'Lowell Sherman is simply grand. I love him in this picture.' 'Mr. Sherman is a good actor and I like him very much.' Gertrude Astor, looking very lovely, is a new kind of blonde. Pauline Garon does very well as Colette and John Harron gave a creditable account of himself. I feel in my bones 'Satan In Sables' is a money-maker."

Morning Telegraph: "A colorful melodrama. James Flood in directing it has invested it with considerable charm. It moves along easily and consistently and there are bright little touches of humor. On the whole it is the sort of picture that Lowell Sherman fans, and audiences in general, will like. The star plays the hero in his usual suave fashion. Pauline Garon is charming as the little dancer. Johnny Harron and Gertrude Astor round out the cast nicely."

Evening Graphic: "Lowell Sherman, 'twould seem, never steps out of his character. Not that Mr. Sherman is the bad, bad man he portrays in pictures. But his mannerisms, his detached air, his nonchalance and aloofness are all with him off the screen as well as on. It's difficult to criticize his performance when one feels he's just being himself. As Colette little Pauline Garon is a delight. John Harron gives a splendid characterization. He is a very good actor and we predict that it won't be long before he's doing 'bigger and better things."

Sun: "Mr. Sherman is an actor who can hold an audience. He makes his role continually interesting."

"Vanishing American"— Paramount, Criterion, N. Y.

World: "One of the most beautiful and stirring things yet done in the films. There need be no secret of the fact that I am going to try to be a weekly patron of the Criterion for at least the next three months. In the broad and colorful curtain which serves as its background, in the exquisite camera work which has gone into the photographing of the far flung scenes, and in the remarkably true reproductions of its characters there is more than any man may

Vilma Banky, European star who is co-starred in "The Dark Angel" a First National release.

digest in a mere visit. The Vanishing American' is the finest thing of American history ever done in the cinema."

Times: "From a fleeting glimpse of the aborigines, one is taken to their skin-clad and paint bedaubed successors, and then to the more interesting but slothful cliff dwellers. The battle scene is a work of art, as one perceives the primitive spears being thrown helter-skelter among the lazy mass of cliff dwellers. Here, in spite of certain short-comings in the actions of some of the characters, is a photodrama which is a fine accomplishment."

Herald-Tribune: "Accompanied by the usual crowds of curious, are light, first nighters, policemen and stars, 'The Vanishing American' appeared on Broadway last night. The crowds were so dense that the wooden Indian stationed outside the theatre was scarcely able to resist the onslaught. We cheerfully recommend this latest Paramount picture. Its scenery is magnificent, its photography superb, its heroine charming. Its cast is perfect."

American: "It is a superb piece of work, covering as it does the various periods from the early cliff dwelling days down to the late war when the Indians marched away to do their bit."

Daily News: "It is like a full-throated war cry ringing down through the ages, this epic of the American Indian. A glorious moving picture that has caught the spirit of the Indian of today. Technically the picture is a marvel. Richard Dix scores a triumph. Noah Beery is the usual bland villain. Lois Wilson is effective as Marion. An impressive picture that is heartily recommended."

Mirror : "The Vanishing American' awed an enthusiastic first night audience at the Criterion last evening. In its subject matter 'The Vanishing American' is a great, humane, romantic picture. In its photographic presentation it scraptures, for cameramen C. Edgar Schoenbaum and Harry Perry have acquitted themselves splendidly."

Morning Telegraph : "The Vanishing American' may be considered a personal triumph for Richard Dix and Lois Wilson. I believe Richard Dix is permanently established as a star of the first rank, due to his excellent performance, and Miss Wilson, perfectly cast, plays her role with wisdom and restraint and is, in

fact, more interesting in this picture than in any the writer has witnessed in the past. 'The Vanishing American' is typically historical. Its appeal will last so long as the romance of the early days of this country lasts; it will be heralded by educators, scholars, mothers and fathers as one of the finest motion pictures of the day.

**"Drusilla With a Million "—
F. B. O., Capitol, New Bedford**

Standard: "The Capitol Theatre was sold out for the two evening shows at least yesterday to thrill every laugh-and-cry device in the show world. The picture was 'Drusilla With A Million . . . Mary Carr gives a good performance as the sad, tired-out little inmate."

**"Drusilla With a Million "—
F. B. O., Capitol, St. Paul**

Pioneer Press: "In 'Drusilla With A Million' featuring that most reliable of screen mamas, Mary Carr, the Capitol has a knockout picture. Highly recommended. In fact, it is one of the remarkable pictures of the year."

**"Drusilla With A Million "—
F. B. O., Terminal, Newark**

Star-Eagle: "'Drusilla With A Million' featuring Mary Carr of 'Over the Hill' fame, is a photoplay that will set your heart athrob as the tale unfolds. The Rev. Henry R. Rose of the Church of the Redeemer, in addressing a movie audience recently, declared that the theatre-goer needs a touch of pathos with movie diet. This picture will furnish the emotion. Crowded with tense moments."

The Call: "Seen at the opening performance yesterday, the picture appears to have all the heart appeal, human interest and fine acting of 'Over the Hill.' The film has been heralded as one having a soul and it is a relief from the usual offerings."

Anne Dale, who appears in the F. Herrick-Herrick serial titled "Fragments of Life," released through Davis Dist. Division.

William Haines who appears in the Metro-Goldwyn-Mayer production The Tower of Lies."

Pre-release Reviews of Features

Below the Line
(Warner Bros.—6053 Feet)
(Reviewed by George T. Pardy)

A SIMPLE and appealing story in which that famous canine actor Rin-Tin-Tin appears to splendid advantage. It is out and out melodrama, but well handled, the thrill punches going over like machine-gun bullets, and Rin-Tin-Tin always Johnny On The Spot, busily engaged in getting himself out of trouble, or leaping to the rescue of his young master and the heroine. Juveniles will be especially pleased with this picture, but adults will like it as well, and all dog-lovers stamp it first-chop entertainment. Among the many stunts so cleverly executed by the four-footed star, is that in which Rin-Tin-Tin climbs an old tree, pulling himself up from branch to branch, something we have never seen any of his four-footed screen contemporaries attempt. And his technique is peculiar to himself. This dog has real pantomimic gifts and it's no wonder that so many of his staunch fan admirers pronounce him king of the tribe.

THEME. Melodrama, with famous dog Rin-Tin-Tin for hero, saving his young master and girl from bloodhounds, tracking and killing villain and generally distinguishing himself.

PRODUCTION HIGHLIGHTS. Rin-Tin-Tin's fight with bloodhounds and slaying of villain and general stunts. The love story, good atmosphere and vibrant thrills.

EXPLOITATION ANGLES. Feature Rin-Tin-Tin, the fans all know him. Bill as one of his best adventure films.

DRAWING POWER. Good for all classes of theatres.

SUMMARY. Another Rin-Tin-Tin picture, with dog hero performing wonderfully intelligent feats. Good melodrama, interesting love tale. Should please most fans.

THE CAST
Rin-Tin-Tin .... Himself
Donald Cass .... John Harron
May Barton .... June Marlowe
Jamber Niles .... Pat Hartigan
Cuckoo Niles .... Victor Potel
Author, Charles A. Logue, Director, Herman Raymaker.

SYNOPSIS. Rin-Tin-Tin, famous fighting dog, falls off train, is found by village youth, Donald Cass, and grows to love new owner. Donald loves May Barton, minister's daughter. Wealthy young lady donates sum of money to church, is found murdered next day. Jamber Niles, a sinister character, knows money has been left in Donald's care, demands it, and is slowly choking him to death when Rin-Tin-Tin arrives and kills Jamber. A pack of bloodhounds sent out by Cuckoo Niles attack Donald and May, but are beaten off by Rin-Tin-Tin. The murder is traced to Jamber Niles Donald and May look forward to happy future.

June Marlowe who appears in "Below the Line" a Warner Bros. production.

Below the Line (Warner Bros.)
PRESS NOTICE

THE picture fans who know and admire canine actor Rin-Tin-Tin will be glad to know that the wonder dog will appear in a film entitled "Below The Line" at the ——— Theatre, on ———. This time Rin-Tin-Tin is the hero of a cracking melodrama, with an alluring love romance included. Among other feats, he fights off a pack of bloodhounds and kills the would-be master of his beloved master. A dandy story, replete with big punch situations.

As regards the human actors, John Harron plays the leading role of Donald Cass, while June Marlowe gives a fine performance in the sweetheart role. Others are Pat Hartigan, Victor Potel, Edith Yorke, Chas. Conklin, Gilbert Clayton.

CATCH LINES
A vicious dog made loyal and fine through tenderness of youth who loved him. Don't miss the big scene where Rin-Tin-Tin fights off the bloodhound pack, and saves his master's life.

The Primrose Path
(Arrow Pictures Corp.—6800 Feet)
(Reviewed by George T. Pardy)

THERE is a great deal more sympathetic interest interwoven into the plot of this picture than is usually found in the average melodrama. A straight story is told, without ringing in too many side issues and befogging the progress of events, but the suspense is well maintained without such doubtful aids, and director Harry O. Hoyt deserves credit for a very neat and compact bit of work. The hero's weakness is gambling, with the addition of a too well nourished liking for hootch, and it is through these faults that he finally finds himself locked in the booby-hatch, an accusation of murder hanging over him. There's a decided leaning toward arguments in favor of prohibition in the tale, but not enough to rank as actual propaganda, so that the exhibitor whose patrons' tastes don't jibe with the dry element, needn't be afraid of booking it. All-in-all, what with its clear-toned human note, murder mystery, and well-defined suspense this film ought to hold its own at the box office.

THEME. Melodrama with murder mystery and heart interest. Hero accused of the crime, but finally freed, and winning girl who has waited for him.

PRODUCTION HIGHLIGHTS. Scene where hero Bruce is forced through ill-luck at cards into diamond-smuggling scheme. The mystery of the killing and subsequent scenes with Bruce in jail accused of murder. Courtroom proceedings. The climax.

EXPLOITATION ANGLES. Make it plain that this is a forceful melorama, with deep sympathetic and romantic interest, a murder mystery and decisive thrills. Feature Wallace MacDonald and Clara Bow.

DRAWING POWER. Effective for the average house, with proper exploitation.

SUMMARY. A strong melodrama, with human interest developed well, a murder mystery, hero wrongly accused and girl who is faithful to him, possesses thrills and suspense, takes a shot at the over-abuse of liquor, but isn't propaganda.

THE CAST
Bruce Armstrong .... Wallace MacDonald
Marilyn Merrill .... Clara Bow
Helen .... Arline Pretty
Tom Canfield .... Stuart Holmes
Jimmy Armstrong .... Pat Moore
Big Jim Snead .... Tom Santschi
Mrs Armstrong .... Lydia Knott
Author, E. Lanning Masters. Cameraman, Andre Barlatier. Director, Harry O. Hoyt.

Clara Bow, starring for Arrow Films in "The Primrose Path."

The Primrose Path
(Arrow Picture Corp.)
PRESS NOTICE

IF you want to enjoy a story replete with pathos, a tender love affair, murder mystery, and crowded with breathless suspense and excitement, be sure you are present when "The Primrose Path" is flashed across the screen of the ——— Theatre on ———. This is a picture which the critics pronounce one of the most gripping films of the season, beautifully photographed, splendidly acted and a sure hit.

Wallace MacDonald plays the hero, unjustly accused of murder, thrown into jail, but with his sweetheart, mother and little brother ever loyal to him, until his innocence is proved. Others in the talented cast are Arline Pretty, Stuart Holmes, Clara Bow.

CATCH LINES
Youth treads the Primrose Path light-heartedly, unheeding what the goal may be.

Bobbed Hair
(Alan Crosland Production-Warner Brothers—6700 Feet)
(Reviewed by Frank Elliott)

LOVERS of action pictures will find this one to their liking. It is based on the novel written by twenty authors, each of whom wrote a single chapter. The title, however, is somewhat misleading as the picture is not a society tale but a mystery story dealing with mysterious theft of $50,000 and the adventures ensuing as its recovery is sought. There is an exciting auto chase in the early part which ends in one of the cars being wrecked. The crooks pursue the hero and the girl to a yacht where there are more battles.

The plot is not a very convincing one, the continuity is weak and the acting just fair. Marie Prevost, the star, is not called upon to do much more than look pretty. Kenneth Harlan is an acceptable hero and there are some good yegg types.

THEME. Crook mystery drama in which a society girl finds real love and much thrilling adventure in a chase for stolen booty.

PRODUCTION HIGHLIGHTS. The costume ball. The auto chase and the wreck of one of the cars. The battles aboard the yacht. The artistic interiors.

EXPLOITATION ANGLES. Play up the names of Marie Prevost and Kenneth Harlan. Emphasize the twenty authors idea. Tie up with beauty shops on the title.

DRAWING POWER. Should draw well through popularity of stars and good title. A good program picture.

SUMMARY. A fairly diverting mystery drama with lots of action. Well mounted and fairly well acted. Not especially convincing in plot or characterization

THE CAST
Connemara Moore	Marie Prevost
David Lacy	Kenneth Harlan
"Sweetie"	Louise Fazenda
Saltonstall Adams	John Roche
Aunt Celimena Moore	Emily Fitzroy
Bingham Carrington	Reed Howes
McTish	Otto Hoffman
The "Swede"	Pat Hartigan
"Doc"	Walter Long
"Pooch"	Francis McDonald
Mr. Brewster	Tom Ricketts
Mrs. Parker	Kate Toncray

Scenario by Lewis Milestone. Directed by Alan Crosland. Photographed by Byron Haskins.

SYNOPSIS. Connemara Moore plans to announce her engagement to one of two men bobbing her hair or leaving it long. But she appears in a nun's costume, covering her hair entirely. She then further postpones her decision by accepting a ride with a strange young man. This follows many exciting adventures including an auto wreck, a battle aboard a yacht for stolen booty, a battle with hi-jackers, etc. It all ends with Connie announcing her engagement to her newfound hero.

Kenneth Harlan, one of the co-stars in "Bobbed Hair" a Warner Bros. production

Little Annie Rooney
(United Artists—8850 Feet)
(Reviewed by George T. Pardy)

A PICKFORD picture of the good, old fashioned kind, the sort that won her the titles of "Our Mary" and "America's Sweetheart." Out of the shadows of heavily magnificent costume plays she emerges, once more the slim, wistful, but at times spit-fire kid that the fans loved and still keep on loving. Certainly the years have dealt kindly with her. Is there another actress on screen or stage who could impersonate a twelve-year old girl and act and look the part to such perfection? Not a single one, not if you fine-combed the U. S. for a double from the Golden Gate to the Statue of Liberty. As to the story, it has all the real flavor of Gotham's East Side, as realistic in atmosphere as it is compelling in heart interest, with rampant comedy which makes an audience rock with laughter. Lots of pure hokum, of course, but hokum with unfailing audience appeal. Make no mistake about it, this is a box office winner, a genuine Pickford triumph. And, incidentally how the kiddies will enjoy it!

THEME. Comedy-melodrama, East Side atmosphere, gangster stuff, humorous episodes, Mary Pickford as twelve-year old heroine.

PRODUCTION HIGHLIGHTS. Excellent direction. Mary Pickford's acting. Realistic East Side scenes. Dance-hall shooting. Episode where Mary gives blood for transfusion to save Joe's life. The pleasing finish.

EXPLOITATION ANGLES. Just tell patrons it's a Pickford picture with Mary playing a child role as convincingly and appealingly as she did in the old days. One love with first girl ha has ever seen. The melodramatic pathos and comedy.

DRAWING POWER. They'll flock to see this one wherever it is shown.

SUMMARY. A fine production and great box office bet. Mary Pickford back in the youngster type of role that made her famous. Wonderful East Side atmosphere, melodramatic thrills, pathos, bright comedy.

THE CAST
Little Annie Rooney	Mary Pickford
Joe Kelly	William Haines
Officer Rooney	Walter James
Able Levy	Spec O'Donnell
Tony	Carlo Schipa
Mamie	Vola Vale
Spider	Hugh Fay

Author, Katherine Hennessy. Directed by William Beaudine.

SYNOPSIS: Little Annie Rooney keeps house for her father-cop and brother Tim, and incidentally is leader of a gang of kids whom she heads in many brick-throwing and hand-to-hand scraps. She is a great admirer of big Joe Kelley whom she is fully determined to marry some day. During a dance-hall brawl officer Rooney is shot and killed and Joe Kelley blamed. Brother Tim avenges him further by putting a bullet in Joe. Annie, who knows him to be innocent, saves Joe's life by giving her blood for transfusion. All ends happily.

Mary Pickford, star of "Little Annie Rooney" a United Artists release

Red Hot Tires
(Warner Bros.—6600 Feet)
(Reviewed by George T. Pardy)

A CRAZILY funny farce comedy, as much a stunt picture as anything else, and carrying out the title's suggestion by hitting up a red hot pace from start to finish! There are enough thrills, accidents, automobile smashups in this feature to furnish material for a high-speed serial, it got a tremendous reception and kept the on-lookers in a continuous uproar of laughter during its initial showing at Warner's Theatre, New York; and gives every indication of being a money-maker wherever it is billed. Of course, it's all sheer "foolishment" but the masses will certainly like it, and there's additional lure in the development of the love affair between hero and heroine, which is ever in evidence all through a medley of exciting situations, crowded one upon the heels of another. Director Erle C. Kenton surely stepped on the gas when he made this one and the result is a cracking good audience film.

The principals, Monte Blue and Patsy Ruth Miller, are busier than bees in swarming time all the way through. Both do excellent work and are well supported. Photography is well up to standard mark.

THEME. Farce comedy. Young society man. driving auto, temporarily loses nerve through accident, regains it and has innumerable adventures chasing around after girl he falls in live with.

PRODUCTION HIGHLIGHTS. The fast action and slapstick comedy. Scene where Monte Blue pursues crooks who have seized girl, grabbing a fresh machine, whenever one he is driving breaks down. The amusing climax.

EXPLOITATION ANGLES. Play this up as a regular hurricane farce comedy, chockful of excitement, hair-raising accidents and so forth. Feature Monte Blue and Patsy Ruth Miller.

DRAWING POWER. Suitable for any house.

SUMMARY. Has whirlwind action, many thrills, smashup stunts galore. Is a sure box office bet wherever they want speed and undiluted farce comedy.

THE CAST
Al Jones	Monte Blue
Elizabeth Lowden	Patsy Ruth Miller
Hon. R. C. Lowden	Fred Esmelton
George Taylor	Lincoln Stedman
Coachman	Charles Conklin
Crook	Tom McGuire
Crook	William Lowry

Author, Gregory Rogers. Director, Erle C. Kenton.

SYNOPSIS. His attention drawn by a pretty girl Al Jones has an auto smashup and temporarily loses his driving nerve, taking to horse-back riding. The girl, Betty Lowden, while breaking speed laws, is the cause of Al getting bad fall from horse. Betty goes to jail for her escapade. Al joins her there, but is soon released. Innumerable accidents follow. Al regains his nerve when Betty is abducted by crooks, pursues in a machine and rescues her. Their romance ends happily.

Easy Going Gordon
(Gerson Pictures Corp.)
(Reviewed by George T. Pardy)

A NOTHER of Richard Holt's gingery pictures in which he puts his usual energy and agility into a number of clever stunts. It's snappy comedy-drama, not so much to the plot, but plenty of excitement running wild, lots of fun, and a queer twist to the general run of things when Richard suddenly gets hep that his girl is disgusted with his lack of ambition and his dad about to topple into bankruptcy. Whereupon he reforms and changes into a regular demon of speed and resourcefulness. It isn't the kind of film that members of the high brow contingent are apt to endorse, but it does furnish cheerful, brisk action entertainment, and as such, will please a large percentage of movie-goers. This should do well at the box office in the neighborhood and smaller houses. Duke Worne has done a nice job in directing this one, and has retained it within just the right limit of footage.

The star, besides his athletic feats, puts effective humor-seasoning into his portrayal of the hero role, Kathryn, as the heroine, is pretty, has little to do, but does that little well,

THEME. Comedy drama, enlivened by stunts of Richard Holt in hero role, he having suddenly resolved to make good with father and sweetheart, which he does, surprising everybody.

PRODUCTION HIGHLIGHTS. The big chasing scenes, from automobile to train, from train to ferry-boat, and finally to aeroplane, with hero keeping ahead, finally captured, but winning out in end and getting the girl.

EXPLOITATION ANGLES. Play up the novel idea of hero going into get-rich-quick business with two hold-up men. Feature Holt's stunts, the comedy and romance.

DRAWING POWER. O. K. for neighborhood and smaller houses.

SUMMARY. Typical Richard Holt picture, comedy drama, not quite so many stunts as in former productions, but enough to throw the thrills. Cheerful entertainment, will please lots of folks in average houses.

THE CAST
Gordon Palmer	Richard Holt
Aileen Merton	Kathryn McGuire
Slung Williams	Gordon Russell
Beef O'Connell	Fernando Galvez
Judson	Roy Cushing
George Elvin	Harris Gordon

Author, Grover Jones. Director, Duke Worne.

SYNOPSIS. Gordon Palmer, rich man's son, is slothfully lazy, until his sweetheart quarrels with him, and two hold-up men frisk them both for their jewelry, including Aileen's engagement ring. Gordon, at last aroused, pursues and scares thieves into returning ring. Later he goes into partnership with them in a get-rich-quick scheme. Financial ruin threatens his father and Gordon goes after proxies to save the situation. His crook friends, Gordon and proxies, all get tremendously mixed up in the chase, but Gordon triumphs and wins Aileen.

Monte Blue, star of "Red Hot Tires," a Warner Bros. release

Red Hot Tires (Warner Bros.)
PRESS NOTICE

WATCH for "Red Hot Tires," the screamingly funny farce comedy which comes to the screen of the ———— Theatre on ————. The hero, Al Jones, meets with auto smashup when his attention is diverted by Betty Lowden, loses his nerve and takes to horse-buck riding. He gets a bad fall when Betty drives by breaking speed-laws. Al chases all over after Betty, meeting with many adventures, and accidents innumerable.

He finally recovers his nerve when Betty is abducted by crooks, pursues in a machine and rescues her, with their romance ending happily. Monte Blue and Patsy Ruth Miller are the leads, with Fred Esmelton, Lincoln Stedman, Charles Conklin appearing in support.

CATCH LINES
A timid youth changes into a top-speed lover through influence of pretty girl.

Richard, Holt, star of the Gerson production titled "Easy Going Gordon"

Easy Going Gordon (Gerson Pictures)
PRESS NOTICE

RICHARD HOLT, the well-known comedy star and stunt performer, will be seen in his latest vehicle "Easy Going Gordon" at the ———— Theatre on ————. This is a bright comedy-drama, remarkable for its quick action, rapid-fire thrills and funny situations. The hero is a lazy, rich man's son, who takes life easily, until spurred into action by a quarrel with his sweetheart, who threatens to give him up. From then he becomes a human dynamo, mixes up with and gets the best of crooks, saves his father from financial disaster and regains girl's love.

Kathryn McGuire is the heroine, with Gordon Russell, Fernando Galvez, Roy Cushing, Harris Gordon and Ed A. Mills supporting.

CATCH LINES
One of the greatest chase episodes ever filmed shown in this one.

Flower of Night
(Paramount—6374 Feet)
(Reviewed by George T. Pardy)

JOSEPH HERGESHEIMER wrote this story especially for the purpose of starring Pola Negri, and succeeded in providing that brilliant actress with a role in which she shines resplendent. The action takes place in California in the days after the gold rush, when the Vigilantes arose to restore law and order in their own lawless, but unquestionably effective way. The tale doesn't differ a whole lot from scores of others dealing with that period, which have reached the screen, but it is none the less colorful, intense; and the combination of Paul Bern's skillful direction and Miss Negri's superb acting places this feature in the front rank of the season's most entertaining productions. Miss Negri, as Carlota, daughter of an old, impoverished Spanish Don, gives what many of her numerous admirers will consider her best performance on the screen. In her varying and subtly expressed moods of love, hate, terror and triumph, she is always convincing, swaying her audience as only a born actress could do.

THEME. Melodrama of California in year 1856. Heroine, daughter of improverished Spanish Don, who falls in love with young American and wins him after numerous adventures with Vigilantes.

PRODUCTION HIGHLIGHTS. The even continuity, sweeping action, colorful backgrounds. Carlota's adventures in dance hall. Scene where she saves lover after he is wounded defending mine from attack. The crashing finish.

EXPLOITATION ANGLES. Bill as Pola Negri's best screen performance. Play up names of supporting cast. Advertise film's tremendous melodramatic power

DRAWING POWER. Should get the money in any theatre.

SUMMARY. A great Pola Negri picture, with role which gives her best acting chance she has ever had, and of which she takes full advantage. Melodrama of Vigilante days in California, sweeping action, continuous thrills and love interest.

THE CAST
Carlota y Villalon	Pola Negri
Don Geraldo y Villalon	Joseph Dowling
John Basset	Youcca Troubetzkoy
Luke Rand	Warner Oland
Vigilante Leader	Gustav Von Seyffertitz
Josefa	Helen Lee Worthing

Author, Joseph Hergesheimer. Director, Paul Bern.

SYNOPSIS. Don Geraldo y Villalon detests Americans, who he thinks robbed him of his mine. Against his wishes, his daughter Carlota attends a dance at the mine. He kills himself. Carlota falls in love with mine superintendent Basset, who does not encourage her. She becomes a dance-hall girl in San Francisco and attracts Vigilante leader Luke Rand. To win her, Rand orders the mine confiscated. Carlota, repentant, joins Basset as he defends the mine. He is wounded and she conveys him out of danger. Later, Basset shoots and kills Rand. He is exonerated and returns Carlota's love.

Pola Negri, star of "Flower of the Night" a Paramount production

Flower of Night (Paramount)
PRESS NOTICE

A NEW Pola Negri picture is always a big event in filmland, and the coming of her latest success "Flower of Night," to the ———— Theatre on ———— will assuredly prove a treat to its patrons. The action takes place in California after the gold rush when the Vigilantes ruled. Miss Negri appears as the headstrong daughter of an impoverished Spanish Don, who falls in love with a young American mine superintendent, passes through a number of startling adventures, and is finally united to him. A great film, with Miss Negri at her best.

In support of the famous star are Joseph Dowling, Youcca Troubetzkoy, Warner Oland and other well-known players.

CATCH LINES

The tale of a flaming Spanish belle who fought for honor and the man she loved in the lawless days when the Vigilantes ruled California.

Lazybones
(Fox—7234 Feet)
(Reviewed by George T. Pardy)

QUITE different from the regulation Buck Jones pictures of straight adventure and riding feats, this picture is strongly sentimental, beautifully photographed and directed, aims at and hits squarely the heart target, and stands out in bold relief as one of the best attractions in which the star has figured. It's a sure box office card, has general audience appeal and registers as a credit to the versatile Mr. Jones and all concerned in its production. The small-town atmosphere is perfect, the types just the sort you can see in any burg of similar size, and the whole picture fairly radiates sympathy and human interest. Also, the director had the courage to finish up without straining for the traditional happy ending. For the hero doesn't wed the girl he intended to, but at the same time there's a hint of consolation for him from another source. The rural settings are true to life, and there's a war shot, with Lazybones in France, which is particularly well done.

Director Frank Borzage mixed his entertainment values nicely, for besides the dramatic scenes and pathetic touches, he has enlivened the action with timely comedy.

THEME. Dramatic romance, small-town atmosphere, hero easy-going youth, who adopts a motherless baby girl, loses his sweetheart, fights in France, returns to find girl grown, hopes to wed her, but fails.

PRODUCTION HIGHLIGHTS. The alluring small-town atmosphere and realism of rural life. The touching sentiment and hero's self-sacrifice.

EXPLOITATION ANGLES. Boost this as different from the regular Buck Jones film, but explain that it is one of his greatest roles. Praise story to limit.

DRAWING POWER. Should do good business at any house, large or small.

SUMMARY. A heart drama of intense power and sentimental lure. Different from Buck Jones' usual work, but a sure winner, with general audience appeal.

THE CAST
Lazybones	Buck Jones
Kit	Madge Bellamy
Mrs. Tuttle	Edythe Chapman
Ruth Fanning	ZaSu Pitts
Dick Ritchie	Leslie Fenton
Agnes Fanning	Jane Novak
Mrs. Fanning	Emily Fitzroy

Adapted from Owen Davis' Stage Play. Director, Frank Borzage. Photographed by Glen MacWilliams.

SYNOPSIS. Agnes Fanning's easy-going lover is known as Lazybones. Agnes' sister Ruth returns from school with a baby claiming to have wedded a sailor who was drowned. She tries suicide and is rescued by Lazybones. He adopts the baby girl. Because he refuses to surrender the child Agnes renounces him. Ruth dies. Years pass, war comes, Lazybones goes to France. Returning, he plans to marry his ward, now a grown girl. But she loves and marries another. The climax offers a hint that Agnes and Lazybones may yet be united.

Buck Jones in "Lazybones," a Fox production.

Lazybones (Fox)
PRESS NOTICE

BUCK JONES in "Lazybones" comes to the screen of the ———— Theatre on ————. This picture presents Mr. Jones in an entirely different role from any he has yet attempted, and the critics say that his impersonation of the lovable, easy-going hero is easily the best thing he has done on the screen. The story concerns the self-sacrifice of Lazybones, who refuses to give up the child of an unfortunate girl he has adopted, when his sweetheart so demands. She renounces him. When war breaks in after years he goes to the front and returns intending to wed his ward.

Supporting Mr. Jones are such popular favorites as Madge Bellamy, Jane Novak, ZaSu Pitts, Leslie Fenton and Edythe Chapman.

CATCH LINES

He was lazy but lovable and loyal to the core. When he adopted an orphan baby, he lost his sweetheart because he wouldn't give up the child.

The Mysterious Stranger

(F. B. O.—5270 Feet)

(Reviewed by George T. Pardy)

AS a general thing the plot values of Richard Talmadge's pictures are subordinated to the hair-raising stunts performed by that rubber-and-steel acrobat of the silent drama, yet they satisfy most of the fans who are out for the big thrills, and care little for anything else. In this instance the breath-taking stunts are as numerous as ever, but in addition they have fixed Dick up with an oddly interesting story. He appears as a young chap, who because of certain misfortunes which befell his father in the past, lives with him until over twenty in a house surrounded by great walls, and has never seen a woman or taken a step into the outside world. When he does get loose, strange things begin to happen, as might be imagined, and you can fancy what wild gyrations Talmadge indulges in under the circumstances. It's a film that's bound to amuse, loaded with burlesque touches, red-hot action, romance and wild adventure.

Talmadge is as wonderfully agile as ever and does some good acting into the bargain. The support is fine and photography of the best quality.

THEME. Comedy drama. Hero young fellow secluded from world for over twenty years, who finally emerges into a whirlwind of startling escapades.

PRODUCTION HIGHLIGHTS. Unique plot. Talmadge's astounding stunts. Scene where he walks in his sleep and is picked up by party masqueraders and falls in love with first girl he has ever seen. The melodramatic punches and romance.

EXPLOITATION ANGLES. Feature Talmadge's stunt work, but explain that there's an unusual plot in this picture which ranks it above his ordinary vehicles.

DRAWING POWER. Good for any house where star is favorite.

SUMMARY. Another swiftly moving Richard Talmadge stunt film, but offering a more unique and interesting plot than usual with this star's pictures. Has strong melo and brisk comedy values, as well as romance.

THE CAST

Paul Lesage	Richard Talmadge
Raoul Lesage	Joseph Swickard
April Lesage	Carmelita Geraghty
Herman Bennett	Lewis Sheldon
Helen Dresden	Duane Thompson
Arnold	Bert Bradley
Chauffeur	Robert Carleton

Scenario by James Bell Smith. Directed by Jack Nelson.

SYNOPSIS. Unjustly suspecting intimacy between his wife, April and Bennett, an artist, Raoul Lesage forsakes her and lives for over twenty years in a house surrounded by high walls, with his young son Paul. Latter has never seen a woman or the outside world. One night he walks in his sleep and gets out. Fate throws him into the company of Bennett, the latter's ward, Helen, with whom Paul falls in love, and April. After participating in a whirl of adventures, he foils Bennett and carries off Helen and April, who is reconciled to her husband, while Paul weds the girl he loves.

Richard Talmadge, star of "The Mysterious Stranger" an F. B. O. production

The Mysterious Stranger

(F. B. B.)

PRESS NOTICE

ANOTHER Richard Talmadge picture, alive with the extraordinary stunts for which this star is noted, but offering in addition a unique plot. This is "The Mysterious Stranger" which comes to the screen of the ———— Theatre on the ————. Talmadge portrays a young chap, who has lived secluded from the world for over twenty years with his father, and has never seen a woman in that time. One night he walks in his sleep, gets out—and then the thrills and funny situations come fast and thick. Talmadge works with his customary furious speed and acts better than he has ever done.

CATCH LINES

Supposing you had never gazed upon female beauty until over twenty, would you be likely to fall in love with first pretty girl you met? This hero did and won out in the end.

Hidden Loot

(Universal—4738 Feet)

(Reviewed by George T. Pardy)

A GOOD Western with a snappy plot which gets out of the common groove and gives Jack Hoxie something else to do besides shoot and ride. Not that the picture is lacking in thrills, or that Hoxie turns into a meek creature. But the leading role represents the star as a smooth-spoken, wise, not to say crafty, kind of chap, and the characterization is subtle and natural to a degree that makes a great impression on the spectators. Mr. Hoxie surely deserves credit for his fine work in this film. Incidentally, this story furnished Frank Mayo with a cracking good vehicle about four years ago, which was very successful. The narrative has undergone considerable changes, but the indications are that it will make as decisive a box office hit as its predecessor. The mystery enveloping the hero is cunningly handled, even the girl in love with him doesn't suspect his identity until the finale, when he stands revealed as a ranger officer.

Robert North Bradbury directed, and turned out a good job. The photography is pleasing throughout, including some magnificent bits of out-door scenery and the support is adequate, with Olive Hasbrouck excellent in heroine role.

THEME. Western melodrama. Mysterious stranger solves robbery of B. B. ranch and wins girl who is part-owner.

PRODUCTION HIGHLIGHTS. Well concealed mystery of hero's identity. Hoxie's good acting. Scene where he and girl hold off attacking party. Surprise climax.

EXPLOITATION ANGLES. Bill this as a Western with unusual, but exciting plot. Feature Jack Hoxie as playing a different role from those he has appeared in heretofore, and making a hit. Also, mention Olive Hasbrouck's good work.

DRAWING POWER. Should go over big wherever Westerns are popular.

SUMMARY. Western with plot out of ordinary, exciting, but showing Jack Hoxie in characterization role, differing from his usual presentations. A likely card.

THE CAST

Cranner (Slipper Tongue)	Jack Hoxie
Jean Hones	Olive Hasbrouck
Dick Hones	Edward Cecil
Big Bill Angus	Jack Kenny
Buck	Buck Connors
Manning	Bert DeMarc
Jordan	Charles Brinley

Author, William J. Neidig. Director, Robert North Bradbury. Photographed by William Nobles.

SYNOPSIS. Jean Bronson of the B. B. ranch encounters a mysterious stranger while out riding. Shifty Bill, head of a gang, steals ranch payroll bag. The stranger and his dog trail the thieves and recover the bag. He is captured, but escapes with dog's help. Later Jean falls in love with him, although suspecting his honesty. Trapped by the gang, they hold their own until rescued by sheriff's posse. Sheriff identifies stranger as ranger-detective. Jean confesses her love for him.

Olive Hasbrouck, who appears in "Hidden Loot," a Universal production.

Hidden Loot (Universal)

PRESS NOTICE

A "lively Western with unusual plot containing good mystery angle, "Hidden Loot," is billed as the big screen attraction at the ———— Theatre on ————. Jack Hoxie is starred as a mysterious stranger who falls in love with Jean Bronson of the B. B. ranch. When the ranch payroll bag is stolen, the stranger and his dog track the thieves and recover the loot. Later, with Jean, he holds off the attacking outlaws until the sheriff's posse comes to their aid. The sheriff introduces the stranger as a celebrated ranger-detective. Jean confesses her love for him. Olive Hasbrouck is the heroine, with Edward Cecil, Jack Kenny, and other well-known players in support.

CATCH LINES

He was such a slick, mysterious, smooth-spoken chap that the girl fell in love with him, although suspecting his honesty. But he cornered the thieves and turned out to be a famous detective.

Greater Than a Crown

(Fox—5000 Feet)
(Reviewed by George T. Pardy)

THE usual dashing young American and princess royal of a mythical kingdom figure as the chief characters in this romantic mystery melodrama, wherefore the plot isn't dazzlingly original. Nevertheless it affords pleasing entertainment likely to make a hit with the average fan, although not strong enough for a first-run, big-house bill. It is well directed, R. William Neill having managed the mystery angle neatly, so that the identity of the heroine isn't by any means apparent until well toward the finish. Also, he has kept the action swishing along at a zippy gait, and there are no dull moments in the whole picture. It gets off to a ripping start, with the hero and his pugilist friend being mixed up in a lively knock-'em-down-and-drag-'em-oft scrap in a London bar, shortly followed by another bout at fisticuffs when they meet and rescue the mysterious young lady from a couple of assailants.

Edmund Lowe shows up well as the Yankee hero and Dolores Costello registers as a very pretty and appealing heroine. Support adequate. Photography O. K.

THEME. Melodrama, with mystery side, mythical kingdom, American hero and princess heroine.

PRODUCTION HIGHLIGHTS. Suspense created by carefully covering up princess' identity through story's early stages. The smart action and thrills. Romantic developments. Clever climax.

EXPLOITATION ANGLES. Feature Edmund Lowe. Boost story's romance, mystery atmosphere. Play up as ardent love affair of princess and young American.

DRAWING POWER. A good card for neighborhood and smaller huses.

SUMMARY. Melodrama with mystery and love angles. Depicts adventures of Young American abroad, who woos and wins princess of mythical kingdom. Plot not original, but well handled. Will please average fan.

THE CAST

Tony Conway	Edmund Lowe
Isabel Francis	Dolores Costello
Molly Montrose	Margaret Livingston
Tiger Bugg	Ben Hendricks
Marquis Ferasti	Paul Panzer
King Danilo	Anthony Merlo
Count Seda	Robert Klein

Adapted from Victor Bridge's Novel, "The Lady from Longacre." Director, Roy Neill.

SYNOPSIS. Tom Conway, wealthy young American, and his pugilistic pal, Tiger Bugg, save a girl from assailants in London. She gives her name as Isabel Francis, and they take care of her for the night. Molly Montrose, actress and friend of Tom's loses her jewels, and at first Tom supposes Francis to be the thief. Later, she learns she is a foreign princess. She is abducted and taken to her own country. Tom and Molly follow. Isabel is rescued after many adventures, is united to Tom and Molly wins the man of her heart.

Greater Than a Crown (Fox)
PRESS NOTICE

ROMANCE, mystery and adventure mingle freely in "Greater Than A Crown," which will grace the screen of the —— Theatre on ——. Edmund Lowe is the star, portraying a wealthy young American, who, while in London, falls in love with a girl who later turns out to be a foreign princess. Royal spies abduct and take her back to her own country. The lover follows, and after a variety of surprising adventures, rescues and wins her.

The picture is replete with thrills and moments of breathless suspense, Edmund Lowe scoring heavily in the lead, with Dolores Costello a fascinating heroine. In support are Margaret Livingston, Ben Hendricks, Paul Panzer, Anthony Merlo, Robert Klein and Sidney Bracey.

CATCH LINES

What would you hold greater than a crown? Wealth, honor or love?

Edmund Lowe, who appears in "Greater Than a Crown," a Fox production.

Why Women Love

(First National—6570 Feet)
(Reviewed by George T. Pardy)

A STIRRING melodrama of the sea, with considerable heart interest and several tragic interludes, including the burning and blowing-up of an oil-laden schooner which registers as a very effective bit of realistic photography, and aftermath showing the waves aglow with the flaming compound while an old lighthouse keeper rows desperately to rescue the only survivor in sight, the captain's daughter. The melodramatic paint is laid on pretty thick, but nevertheless, the picture will make a strong appeal to those who like high-tension stuff kindled into a veritable furnace of emotions. The plot hinges on a seduction case, which may possibly be considered "too strong meat" by sticklers for strict propriety. But while not suitable entertainment for juveniles, a majority of adult fans will respond favorably to the absorbing human interest of the feature as developed by the fine acting of principals and supporting cast.

THEME. Marine melodrama, with lighthouse as principal locale, and romance of girl who waits faithfully for lover reported lost at sea.

PRODUCTION HIGHLIGHTS. Attractive marine atmosphere. Good photography. Scene where schooner blows up. Episode where Molla discovers Pearl is about to become a mother. Romantic appeal.

EXPLOITATION ANGLES. Boost as an exciting marine melo, with heart interest as conveyed by double love-affair, Pearl's betrayal. The burning vessel, and happy culmination of Molla's loyalty to fiance.

DRAWING POWER. Good for any house, except in communities where exhibitor caters to patrons who may not approve of seduction angle.

SUMMARY. A well-produced, beautifully photographed marine melo. Has strong heart interest and plot.

THE CAST

Molla Hansen	Blanche Sweet
Her Father	Bert Sprotte
Rodney O'Malley	Robert Frazer
Silas Martin	Russel Simpson
Pearl	Dorothy Sebastian
Charley Watts	Alan Roscoe
Ira Meers	Edward Earle

Adapted from Willard Robertson's Stage Play, "The Sea Woman." Director, Edwin Carewe.

SYNOPSIS. Oil schooner Viking burns at sea, captain's daughter, Molla Hansen, saved by old light-house keeper, who succumbs after exacting promise that she will care for his young orphan daughter Pearl. Molla takes charge of lighthouse. Her lover, Captain O'Malley, believing her dead, goes on long cruise. Two years pass. Pearl is seduced by rum-runner Watts, lies to Molla and implicates innocent man. Pearl learns that Watts is married. He comes, and while with Pearl in upper compartment of light, she turns on gas, causes explosion and Watts is killed. Pearl dies. O'Malley turns up, rescues Molla from flames and they wed.

Why Women Love (1st National)
PRESS NOTICE

A THRILLING melodrama of the sea. "Why Women Love" is scheduled as the chief attraction on the screen of the —— Theatre on ——. The story throbs with sensational thrills and includes two love affairs, one that of a ship-wrecked girl, who remains in a lighthouse, waiting for a long-lost lover, the other, an intrigue which results in a betrayal. There are some remarkably fine marine shots, and a lurid episode showing the blowing-up of an oil schooner. Intensely dramatic and full of human interest, this picture ranks as a great audience feature.

Beautiful Blanche Sweet plays the heroine role, one of her finest achievements, with Robert Frazer as hero. In support are, Dorothy Sebastian, Alan Roscoe and others

CATCH LINES

This girl waited for years for a lover who believed her dead. But her loyalty was rewarded, for he came at last. A tale of women's hearts, true love and false.

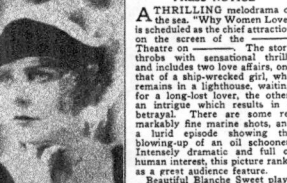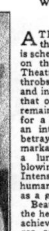

Blanche Sweet who appears in "Why Women Love," a First National release

The Circle

(Metro-Goldwyn-Mayer—5511 Feet)
(Reviewed by George T. Pardy)

THIS adaptation of W. Somerset Maughan's stage play starts off well but doesn't fulfill its promise, as it lags badly toward the middle and never quite recovers speed. It may suit as a program attraction, but there really isn't much to be said in its favor as an offering for critical audiences. In the early reels it develops some capital high comedy, and the subtitles are unusually witty and brilliant, helping the action along splendidly. But this happy mood dies out and thereafter, the narrative moves slowly, the characters seem artificial, despite the most strenuous efforts on the part of the players to instill life into them. The fact of the matter is that not one of them arouses sympathy, you can't feel particularly sympathetic toward the foolish young wife, who instead of profiting by the experiences of her husband's runaway mother, proposes to do the same thing with a friend of the family, and none of the rest moves the spectator's feelings to any great degree.

THEME. Drama of young wife undecided whether she will follow example of husband's mother who ran away with lover, or remain true to her own hubby.

PRODUCTION HIGHLIGHTS. Fine settings, colorful English atmosphere, good photography. High comedy stuff outlined in early reels. George Fawcett's acting.

EXPLOITATION ANGLES. Don't go too strong in boosting story's human interest. You have a practically all-star cast to play up, every name of which has box office value.

DRAWING POWER. Lists as fair program attraction for neighborhood and smaller houses.

SUMMARY. Drama with English society settings, colorful backgrounds, first half offers pleasing comedy, remainder rather uninteresting. Just an average program attraction.

THE CAST

Elizabeth	Eleanor Boardman
Edward Luton	Malcolm McGregor
Lord Clive Cheney	Alec Francis
Lady Catherine	Eugenie Besserer
Porteous	George Fawcett
Arnold	Creighton Hale
Dorker	Otto Hoffman

Adapted from Play by W. Somerset Maughan. Director, Frank Borzage. Photographed by Chester A. Lyons.

SYNOPSIS. Lord Cheney's wife elopes with his friend Porteous. Thirty years later his son Arnold is married and his wife Elizabeth plans to run away with one Luton. Elizabeth invites the old runaway pair to Cheney Castle. They come. Old Lord Cheney arrives, but greets the unusual guests calmly. Elizabeth at times is influenced by the sight of the ancient elopers to stay home, and again to fly with Luton. In the long run, however, her husband employs rough methods and Elizabeth stays.

Eleanor Boardman in "The Circle," Metro-Goldwyn-Mayer.

The Circle (Metro-Goldwyn-Mayer)

PRESS NOTICE

ADAPTED from a play by W. Somerset Maughan, "The Circle," a picture offering a dramatic and unusual story, is listed to be shown at the ———— Theatre on ————.

It deals with the temptation of a young wife, mistress of Castle Cheney, to run away with one Luton. Formerly, her husband's mother eloped. Elizabeth invites the old runaway pair on a visit. They come and odd complications ensue. Elizabeth at times is inclined to carry out her scheme, again, in doubt, she resolves to be true to her husband.

An all-star cast is headed by Eleanor Boardman and Malcolm McGregor.

CATCH LINES

She wanted to elope, but fate kept pulling her in contrary directions. How the problem was solved is told graphically in "The Circle."

The Unnamed Woman

(Arrow—6300 Feet)
(Reviewed by Edw. G. Johnston)

"THERE'S one good thing about divorce—it keeps women in circulation"—is one of the subtitles of this picture and it rather sums up the story. There are plenty of women in circulation, high pressure jazz parties, etc.

The story revolves around the efforts of two penniless girls to trap a husband for one of them. They succeed in this but find that their prize is debt ridden. An opportunity arises to frame the innocent wife of a wealthy, jealous member of their crowd and the plan is worked out with almost disastrous results.

A very good cast has been assembled and Katherine Mac Donald does good work in the role of the innocent wife. Likewise, does Herbert Rawlinson, as her husband. Wanda Hawley and Leah Baird work convincingly as the fortune hunters. John Miljan is well chosen in his role of the society waster.

THEME. A society drama dealing with the efforts of a penniless girl to capture a rich husband who later turns out to be as poor as she. They are bordering on divorce when the opportunity comes to frame an innocent wife of a wealthy man.

PRODUCTION HIGHLIGHTS. Katherine MacDonald's acting, the jazzy party, the fight between the husband and co-respondent and the final confession of the frame-up.

EXPLOITATION ANGLES. Play up the prominent stars in the cast. Bill it as a modern social tangle entertainingly presented.

DRAWING POWER. A suitable program picture with an excellent cast. The plot is old but one that is generally interesting to the average audience.

SUMMARY. A modern society drama with a divorce tangle. Has audience appeal and a collection of stars that lend strength to exploitation possibilities.

THE CAST

Flora Brookes	Katherine Mac Donald
Donald Brookes	Herbert Rawlinson
Doris Grey	Wanda Hawley
Billie Norton	Leah Baird
Archie Wesson	John Miljan

Author, Charles E. Blaney, Director, Harry O. Hoyt. Produced by Arthur F. Beck.

SYNOPSIS. Doris Grey, hounded by creditors, resolves to trap Archie Wesson, a society waster, into a proposal of marriage and enlists the aid of her friend Billie Norton. The marriage is loveless and soon border on divorce when Doris discovers that Archie is deep in debt. Doris takes her case to Donald Brookes. In the meantime Flora has spent the night at the Wesson home and awakened by burglars calls for help. Archie Wesson responds, the burglar escapes and Archie is caught in the act of holding the fainting Flora in his arms. Archie and his wife both size on this opportunity to frame Flora whose husband is wealthy. Wesson's chauffeur finally confesses to the attempted burglary and clears up the tangled situation. All are re-united.

Katherine McDonald who appears in "The Unnamed Woman" an Arrow release.

The Unnamed Woman (Arrow Picture Corp.)

PRESS NOTICE

A MODERN society drama that brings to the screen of the —— theatre such well know stars as Katherine MacDonald, Herbert Rawlinson, Wanda Hawley, Leah Baird and John Miljan. It is a story of how an innocent woman almost became separated from her husband thru the machinations of a money hunting couple. "The Unnamed Woman" is a modern society tangle with jazz and cocktail parties, a lover and a jealous husband.

This fascinating society drama was directed by Harry O. Hoyt, who has many successes to his credit, and is adapted from a story by the famous Charles E. Blaney. It should be a real treat for the fans.

CATCH LINES

The story of how an innocent wife almost paid the penalty—A whirl of, modern society life with a jealous husband and the eternal triangle.

Regional News from Correspondents

Milwaukee

FEBRUARY 15 has been tentatively set as the date of the formal opening of the new Bay View Theatre being erected for Walter A. Baier of the Walter A. Baier Film Company. The new house will be located in the rapidly developing Bay View section of the city. It will be fitted and equipped to take its place with the finest neighborhood theatres in the city.

E. J. Vollert, formerly manager of the Ideal Theatre at Fond du Lac, has purchased the Liberty Theatre at Milwaukee from Charles Washicheck. The house is well located and under Vollert's capable direction is expected to rank as one of the best bets in the outlying districts of the city.

E. C. Prinsen, general manager of the Fond du Lac Theatres Company of Fond du Lac, Wis., has resigned his position. His plans for the future have not been announced, but it is expected that he will seek new fields to conquer, without leaving the film industry.

Charles Bauman, manager of the Star Theatre at Oshkosh, Wis., visited his friends on the Milwaukee film row during the past week. He appeared optimistic about the season's prospects. ;

J. Stanley Wolf, traveling auditor for the Producers Distributing Corporation, has gone on to Minneapolis, after spending the past two weeks at the Milwaukee branch of the organization.

Edward Klein has been named manager of the poster department of the recently established Milwaukee branch of the Fox Film Corporation, which is now "hitting on all six."

Several major changes were made in the staff of the Milwaukee branch of the Producers Distributing Corporation during the past week. Tom McConnell, formerly with Paramount and Pathe,

has been assigned to the Fox River Valley sales territory for P. D. C., while Dave Levin of Detroit has been placed in the western Wisconsin territory. George Lemonoff, another salesman, has been transferred to P. D. C.'s Minneapolis branch.

Miss Eva Reichelm, formerly secretary to O. J. Wooden, manager of the Garden Theatre, has taken up new duties as private secretary to Charlie Lundgren, manager of the Milwaukee branch of the Producers Distributing Corporation.

Leon Goetz of Goetz Brothers, operators of a chain of picture houses in half a dozen Wisconsin cities, paid his periodical visit to the Milwaukee exchanges during the past week.

The Rex Theatre at Racine, Wis., will be reopened November 1, after having been extensively remodeled, according to Frank Steffen, who came to Milwaukee for a chat with his exchange men friends. Those who have seen the progress of the contractors in redecorating and rebuilding the house, declare it to be an excellent job.

Another house that has undergone changes for the better, is the Idlehour in Milwaukee. Max Krofta, its owner, has spent time, money and effort to make his house representative of the better class of theatres on the South Side, and apparently his efforts have been well repaid.

John Lorentz, manager of the Milwaukee branch of the Fox Film Corporation, has returned from another trip through northern Wisconsin and upper Michi-

gan, and reports that conditions in that section are improving.

Among the visitors at the Milwaukee branch of the Producers Distributing Corporation during the past week were Cecil Mayberry, district manager, who stopped over for two days en route to Minneapolis, and Fred Knispel, assistant district manager.

Jimmie Long has been appointed assistant house manager of Saxe's Wisconsin Theatre to succeed Elmer Zieman, who quit his post to go to the Coast with other members of his family.

The prize in the first annual outing and golf tournament of the Milwaukee Film Board of Trade, were awarded as follows: First prize in the driving contest to Parkis Waterbury, Idle Hour Theatre, Jefferson, Wis.; second, O. J. Wooden, Garden Theatre, Milwaukee; third, Charles Trampe, Rainbow and Climax theatres, Milwaukee; first prize in approaching and putting contest, N. T. Thompson, Lyric Theatre, Fort Atkinson, Wis.; second, Parkis Waterbury, Idle Hour Theatre, Jefferson, Wis.; low gross to O. J. Wooden, Garden Theatre, Milwaukee; low net to Ross Baldwin of the Pathe Exchange, Milwaukee; second, Sam Shurman, Metro-Goldwyn Exchange, Milwaukee; third, Harry Schuman, Associated Exhibitors, Milwaukee. The event was an unqualified success and will be made an annual event from now on, according to those who arranged it this year.

Neil Duffy of the Elite Theatre, Appleton, Wis., is going to have one fine winter season, if his predictions made at the Milwaukee

exchanges he visited last week come true.

Otto Meister, affable and affluent manager of the White House Theatre, Milwaukee, made a flying trip to Chicago, Sunday, being back at the theatre just six hours after leaving it and bearing a satisfied smile of achievement in regard to the business he set out to attend to. Just what the business was has not been disclosed, but it is understood that "O. L." has another big stunt up his sleeve.

Rapid progress is being made on the construction of the new theatre being erected on the East Side for Joe Cullen, former owner of the Jackson Theatre, Milwaukee. The new house will have 1,000 seats and will compare favorably with the other high class theatres recently erected in that prosperous section of the city.

E. P. Vollendorf, office manager for the Milwaukee branch of First National, now greets visitors from a Ritzic private office that has been equipped for him in the exchange quarters. The new arrangement has many business advantages and adds becoming dignity to Ed's daily grind.

F. B. O. is now established in its new Milwaukee branch quarters on Seventh Street, having finally severed the ties that bound it to the venerable Old Film Exchange Building on Second street. All this week Sam Abrams, branch manager, and Art Roberts, his first lieutenant, are extending a glad hand to visitors who are coming to offer congratulations on the fine new office lay-out. The new quarters are no larger than the old, but are infinitely superior as far as convenience and attractiveness are concerned. M. J. Weisfeldt, district manager, also spent a part of the week at the Milwaukee office to help in the "housewarming," which was attended to in grand old style.

St. Louis

A SLIGHT fire in the projection room of the Missouri Theatre, Grand boulevard at Lucas avenue, at 2.15 p. m. October 16 damaged film and apparatus about $500. The fire failed to interrupt the performance and the audience did not know a fire was in progress. Firemen were summoned by telephone and extinguished the blaze with chemicals. The blaze resulted from a short circuit in the projection machine. The loss was covered by insurance.

J. W. Miller, owner-manager of the Madison Theatre, Madison, Ill., died at his home in Madison on Thursday, October 15th. He had been ill for several months.

Edward Blanton has opened a new theatre at McKittrick, Mo.

The Kozy Theatre, Kahoka, Mo., has been purchased by James A. McLaughlin. It was formerly operated by Mrs. W. H. Felt.

D. D. Cox has given up the management of the Community Theatre at Raymond, Ill.

Visitors of the week included: Jack Pratt, Fulton, Mo.; Harry Mueller, Festus, Mo.; Jim Reilly, Alton, Ill.; J. McNamara of Virden, Ill.; and J. W. Cotter, Moberly, Mo.

Jack Underwood, manager of the St. Louis office of Enterprise Distributing Corporation, will leave for Dallas, Tex., on Sunday night, October 25, to assume charge of the Dallas office for Enterprise. Jack formerly lived and worked in Dallas and has many friends among the exhibitors of that territory. He is a wonderful chap and St. Louis hates to lose him.

Tom McKean, manager for the local F. B. O. office visited Hannibal, Quincy and vicinity during the week.

Felix F. Feist, general sales man-

ager for Metro-Goldwyn-Mayer, was a recent visitor to St. Louis. With J. E. Flynn, district manager for Metro-Goldwyn-Mayer and A. W. Smith, Jr., of the First National home office in New York, he was the guest of Charles Skouras at quite a banquet given at the Busch home on the Gravois road, St. Louis County.

Leslie B. Mace, First National salesman, sustained a fractured nose and other injuries when his automobile skidded on a wet road.

"Buns" Derby, contract chaser for F. B. O., spent a cheerful night in his Lizzie when the contraption skidded into a ditch while trying to negotiate some of Illinois' good roads. All highways are not concrete in the Prairie State.

Lew Bent of the F. B. O. sales organization returned from his va-

cation Monday, October 19, all pepped up for a big season.

Pending the return of Mr. Werner, J. E. Flynn, district manager for Metro-Goldwyn has appointed W. B. Scully as acting resident manager in St. Louis. He formerly was in charge of the Metro-Goldwyn office at New Haven, Conn., recently closed.

Commenting on his illness Mr. Werner said that he was feeling very much better. He also expressed his heartfelt thanks to the home office management of Metro-Goldwyn, the St. Louis office and his various friends among the exhibitors of this territory and elsewhere throughout the country and his fellow exchange men and film salesmen in St. Louis for the many cheering letters, telegrams and flowers he has received since his illness set in.

Atlanta

ANNA AIKEN PATTERSON, publisher of the Weekly Film Review, who landed in New York Saturday aboard the S. S. Ryndam after an extended trip abroad, was met by her husband, Willard C. Patterson, manager of the Metropolitan Theatre, and arrived in Atlanta Friday afternoon aboard the Piedmont Special.

Pat Dowling, director of publicity for Al. and Charles Christie, producers of the well-known Christie comedies, was in Atlanta this week on a visit to Producers and Educational exchanges, who handle Christie product in the Southeast.

T. F. Ware of the Star and Palace Theatres, Talladega, Ala., and T. C. Germain of the Peoples Theatre, have sold their interests to E. F. Ingram of the Ingram Theatre, Ashland, Ala., it was reported this week. The change in management took effect last Monday.

George F. Lenehan, district manager for Producers, was in Charlotte the first of the week and arrived in Atlanta Wednesday

night . It is not known how long he will remain here.

George W. Rollins, veteran showman, who has been coming to Atlanta for the past thirty years, is here this year as the guest of W. A. Sanges, manager of Progress Pictures.

A. H. Frazer, a district booker for Southern Enterprises in Charlotte, has served his connection with that company and was in the city this week. Mr. Frazer stated that his future plans were not entirely decided upon as yet.

Arthur C. Bromberg, president of Progress Pictures, had as his visitor last week-end his brother, Mr. F. W. Bromberg, a prominent jeweler of Birmingham, Ala.

Hank Hearn, manager of Liberty's Atlanta exchange, left last Sunday for a trip through south Georgia. He was expected back in the office Friday.

A. J. Borders, who has been traveling for Progress out of the Charlotte exchange, came to Atlanta this week and will hereafter travel south Georgia and south Alabama for his company, out of the Atlanta office.

Tom Little, local manager of Producers, left Wednesday night with his new salesman Bill Wassman for Florida. Manager Little will accompany Bill over the state in order to familiarize him with Producers' Florida territory.

C. E. Jones, who travels Tennessee and north Alabama for Progress, was recently married it is reported. The lady's name has not been learned as yet.

Jack Elwell, Tennessee representative for Metro, was in town last week-end, and left again for his territory after spending Monday in the office.

P. C. Parrish, manager of Southern Equipment Company was out of the city for a few days early in the week. He returned to his office Friday.

E. E. Geyer, exploiteer for Paramount, who left about ten days ago, reports that he is spending busy days in New Orleans and will not return to Atlanta for some three weeks yet. Mr. Geyer spent a short time in Augusta, Ga., en route to New Orleans.

L. J. Duncan, one of Producers' salesmen out of the local exchange,

was in town last week-end and remained through Monday. He left again for his territory all set for action and a successful trip.

H. E. Edenfield of the Dreamland Theatre, Augusta, Ga., was in town for several days this week. He left Atlanta Wednesday night.

D. L. Earnest, superintendent of the State Normal School at Athens, Ga., was here this week on one of his regular trips to purchase pictures for the school. He returned to Athens during the week-end.

F. A. Leatherman has just returned this week from Nashville, Tenn., where he spent several days on business.

Walter L. Brandenburg, popular exhibitor from Fort Valley, Ga., who came up to spend several days enjoying the Southeastern Fair, brought his bright young son Walter, Jr., along with him.

Fred Bryan, exhibitor from Cocoa, Fla., and well-known along Film Row, came up to Atlanta this week and remained for several days before returning to the land of perpetual sunshine.

Central Penn

SYDNEY J. GATES, of Harrisburg, Pa., youngest manager in charge of any motion picture theatre in the entire circuit controlled by the Marcus Loew interests, has received a new promotion. He received word on October 15 that he had been transferred from the post of managing director of Loew's Regent theatre, Harrisburg, and that he was instructed to report to the office in Pittsburgh, of Louis K. Sidney, division chief for the Loew theatres, which is in the district comprising Pittsburg, St. Louis, Reading and Harrisburg. It is understood the transfer of Mr. Gates means a material promotion for the young man, who, though only 24 years old, already has managed some of the most important theatres in the Loew

chain. Mr. Gates left Harrisburg on Sunday, October 18.

Mr. Gates' successor as managing director of Loew's Regent in Harrisburg, is Russell Bevim, who was transferred from a like post in Loew's Aldine theatre, Wilmington, Del. He already has taken charge in Harrisburg.

A picture theatre that will seat 600 will be a feature of a community building that will be erected by the Good Will Fire Company and Beneficial Association, of Hyde Park, a suburb of Reading. The structure will be completed early in 1926.

After having undergone extensive improvements the Poli theatre, Scranton, and the theatre of the same name in Wilkes-Barre, have been reopened and are being

devoted to photoplays and vaudeville. Both theatres are owned by the Union Theatre Company, of which Fred Herrman, of the Capitol theatre, Wilkes-Barre, is the director.

Alterations to the Pastime theatre, Lewistown, are rapidly nearing completion. A new ventilating system is being introduced and other changes being made, according to announcement by Isaac Berney, the proprietor.

Rev. F. W. Ruth, a Bernville pastor, negotiates the bookings for the town's only motion picture theatre, which is maintained in the Community Hall.

Flames were discovered in the projection room of the Hippodrome motion picture theatre, Pittston, on the afternoon of Oc-

tober 10. Considerable smoke began to pour from the building and the city firemen were summoned and put out the fire before it could extend to other parts of the building. The firemen were somewhat handicapped by fumes from burning films. The loss was confined to some films that were destroyed.

Peter Magaro, former owner of the Regent motion picture theatre, Harrisburg, which he sold to the Marcus Loew interests last spring, and former member-at-large of the executive committee of the Motion Picture Theatre Owners of America, was chairman of the reviewing stand committee of the annual Columbus Day parade held by the Italian societies in Harrisburg on October 12.

Butte

THE Tenth of October marked the opening of the American Theatre which has been closed since last June.

Manager W. J. Sullivan of the Silver Bow Amusement company, has remarked that among the hundreds of pictures he has reviewed in previews during the last three months that the best have been selected for future showing at the American and Rialto theatres for this winter season.

The Broadway theatre under the management of Merle Davis is one of the attractive amusement places

this season. The vaudeville program is a rare combination cleverly staged with strong photo play that brings compelling appeal to the theatre fans.

Active part in fire-prevention advocacy is being taken by the Montana Film Board of Trade, local representatives of the Motion Picture Distributors of America, by means of a committee of two film exchangemen and secretary Meyers of the Montana Board. This committee, according to the board, will carry out a program, in connection with Butte's observ-

ance of Fire Prevention Week, under the direction of Secretary Harry Meyers.

Mr. and Mrs. William Heineman of Universal fame are the proud parents of a wee baby girl born this week at the Murray hospital. Mrs. Heineman was formerly Miss Blanche Martin.

George L. Cloward is at present covering Montana territory from his office in Salt Lake where he is in Charge of the Metro pictures.

W. F. Gordon, Executive manager of the First National ex-

change of Salt Lake City has been in Montana touring the state and looking into the First National business. Vete Stewart, salesman, has been accompanying Mr. Gordon.

W. K. Bloom, F. B. O. salesman is spending a few weeks in Montana out of the Salt Lake office.

It is rumored that the beautiful new Temple theatre, that closed last summer is to be opened soon and that a big orchestra will be engaged and that only big first run pictures will be programmed.

Albany

FROM now on, it is expected that there will be more news forthcoming from the meetings of the Albany Film Board of Trade. Many of those connected with the Board have felt for some time past that if some of the action taken by the Board in session was permitted to reach exhibitors and others, that there would be less trouble encountered through violated contracts and other things. The Board did not meet on Columbus Day, as many of the managers were out of town, it being a half holiday along Film Row. The meeting was held on Saturday.

Clarence Gardner, who runs the Pine Hills theatre in Albany, a strictly residential house, is busily engaged at the present time in installing a new organ that will replace the piano and violin that have furnished music ever since the house was opened some years ago.

Julius Berinstein, running the Colonial and Hudson theatres in Albany, and the Palace in Troy, does not intend to take any chances either this fall or any other fall, for that matter, with coal shortage due to strikes. He has ordered oil burners installed in all three theatres at once.

Tony Veiller, manager of the Mark Strand in Albany, is saving himself hundreds of steps a day through a new office that has been installed on the second floor front of the theatre. This will give the use of the main office to Mr. Hill, and will do away with the necessity of Mr. Veiller chasing back stage every time he wishes to visit his own sanctum.

Ben Davis returned to Albany last week from a short visit to New York city. Mr. Davis has two or three propositions in view, the nature of which he is not disclosing for the moment, further than to say that he will continue to be connected with the theatrical business. Since leaving the Schine circuit of Gloversville, Mr. Davis has been making his home at the Hotel Ten Eyck in Albany.

Meyer Freedman, of Schenectady, having spent a thousand or more dollars in fixing up the Rialto theatre in that city, now has one

Marguerite McNulty in "Ermine and Rhinestones," a Jans production.

of the finest residential houses in these parts. Mr. Freedman, however, does not intend to devote his entire attention to the theatre, as he is still casting longing eyes towards Florida, and if William Shirley makes the connection he intends to, it is a safe bet that Mr. Freedman will shortly be receiving his mail around Miami.

Harry Hellman utilized the radio which he installed in his Royal theatre several months ago on the occasion of the World Series last week. Mr. Hellman advertised the fact and his matinees were well attended, the patrons receiving a report of the World Series as well as an afternoon of pictures for a dime. Mr. Hellman is still busy with his camp at Crooked Lake and has now built a very handsome fireplace in the living room.

W. W. Farley, of Albany, has recovered somewhat from his illness of two or three weeks ago and was able to journey to Binghamton the latter part of the week to register in connection with the fall campaign. Mr. Farley is one of the best known Democratic politicians in the state.

Harold Filkins, of the local F. B.O. exchange, is on a two weeks' trip through northern New York.

George Roberts, of Kingston, who has two theatres in that city, is now considering the advisability of buying a new car, and is inclined to talk automobile more than pictures when the film salesmen call. Mr. Roberts is running straight pictures in one of the theatres and pictures and vaudeville at the other.

Unless all signs fail, Robert Mochrie, manager of the Producers Distributing Co. exchange in Albany, will be on his way to Los Angeles in January through the record made by himself and his office force in the present cash sales contest. Last March the Albany exchange was in twenty-fifth place, but during the weeks and months that have followed, the exchange, under the able management of Mr. Mochrie, has advanced point by point until it now leads the entire country.

The many friends of James Rose, of Troy, will rejoice with him in the fact that Mrs. Rose is now on the road to recovery and left the hospital for her home a week or so ago.

Jerry Reap, well known in this city, where he was formerly connected with the Fox exchange, is now a salesman with the Famous Players office in Buffalo.

William Curry has not yet decided as to the policy of the Victory theatre in Cambridge, which he took over a few weeks ago. Under L. L. Connors, the house ran six nights a week. Mr. Curry believes that this is too much for a place the size of Cambridge, and that if the theatre was open but three nights a week, that the villagers would be more eager to see the pictures than otherwise.

Fred Mausert is having exceptionally good business at the State theatre in Glens Falls. Additional competition is in sight for all theatres in Glens Falls and after November 12, when the Rialto

will reopen with a program of vaudeville and pictures.

Tom Thornton, of Saugerties, has the agency for a couple of automobiles and between this and his theatre, in which he is running vaudeville one night a week, he is so busy that he rarely gets to Albany any more.

Elsie Cunningham, pianist at the Crescent theatre in Schenectady, for the last nine years, is now Mrs. Vernon Brand, but will continue at the theatre. Shortly before the wedding, Mrs. Brand was given a shower by Janet Noon, who formerly operated the theatre, and Miss Betty Feuer, the present operator.

Frank Braymeier, who managed the Barcli in Schenectady before it closed several months ago, is back at the old stand, now that the house has reopened under the Farley banner. Up to the present time no definite policy has been decided upon for the theatre. It is now given over to first-runs at a ten, fifteen and twenty-five cent admission, using up pictures booked but not run at either the Strand or the State theatres.

Arthur Adams, of the Happy Hour theatre in Lake Placid, and brother of Mrs. Elizabeth Walton, is back home from a most enjoyable trip with his family through western New York.

Jack Mathews, of Plattsburg; Claude Wade, of North Creek,

and Rae Candee, of Utica, are among the exhibitors who have unlimbered their heavy artillery at the opening of the deer hunting season. Film Row is anxiously awaiting the outcome, hoping against hope that venison may be included in some express package received by the exchanges.

Jerry LaRock, who runs Fairyland in Warrensburg, was among the recent visitors in Albany.

The American theatre in Schenectady was badly handicapped one night last week, when something went wrong with the transmission lines, and the theatre was left without lights during the entire evening. The house is operated by Claude Fish, who gave all patrons passes that could be used on the following day.

Jacob Feltman, and his son Alex. took over the Lincoln theatre in Schenectady just two months ago. They like the business so well and the theatre has proved so successful a venture that now they are making no bones of it in saying that they are looking around for another theatre, and in time they may become competitors of the Schine boys. The younger Mr. Feltman serves as the organist at the Lincoln and was formerly connected in a like capacity with the Hudson and Colonial theatres in Albany.

Cleveland

A VINCENT SEAS has sold the Miles theatre, which he was personally running, to Charles R. Bros. Bros bought the whole building in which the theatre was located.

LeMotto Smith, of The Smith Amusement Company, operating a chain of picture houses in Alliance and Warren, paid the Cleveland exchanges a visit last week.

Harry Charnas has bought out Mrs. George R. Moore's interest in the Southern theatre, Bucyrus. Charnas, who heads the Standard Film Service Company, largest independent distributors in the country, had an interest in the house previously.

Rose Levine, of the booking department of the Cleveland First National Exchange put one over her office associates by quietly marrying Louis Sattler on October 11th. The bride and groom are honeymooning in Detroit where they will remain a week. Rose will be back in the office after that to receive congratulations.

Genevieve Richmond, secretary to Universal exchange manager

Al Mertz has chosen Tuesday, October 20th, for her marriage to Arthur E. Engelbert, booker for the local Producers Distributors Corporation's office. They have a new home in Rocky River, a Cleveland suburb, all ready for them to move into, where the welcome signs will always hang out for their film friends.

William Banks, secretary of the Cleveland Motion Picture Exhibitors Association is taking a belated vacation of a week. His secretary, Rose Killelcy is running the office in his absence.

C. B. Dyar has concluded his student course in the local Fox exchange, and is now a regularly registered film man, associated with the Boston Fox office. Just so the Cleveland office will not get lonesome for students, G. J. Hermann has been sent out from New York to succeed Dyar.

W. C. Bachmeyer has returned unto the Metro-Goldwyn fold. For ten consecutive years Bachmeyer was central division manager for Metro, and then for Metro-Goldwyn. He resigned to fill a similar

post with Fox. He is now doing special work out of the Metro-Goldwyn home office in this territory.

W. F. Rogers, sales manager of the eastern division of Metro-Goldwyn paid the local exchange a brief visit last Thursday. Rogers has been making a tour of exchanges. He left Thursday night for New York.

R. S. Shrader, central division manager for Pathe was in town last week and held an important sales conference of the entire office. Shrader plans to hold similar meetings in each office that lies in his territory. That means Buffalo, Pittsburgh, Detroit, Cincinnati and Indianapolis.

The new $25,000 Wurlitzer organ recently installed in Loew's Alhambra theatre, was officially dedicated last Sunday with due ceremonies. Ernest H. Hunt, organist at the State theatre, presented an elaborate organ recital which included both classical and popular numbers, together with several original arrangements.

The Marquis Theatre, Craw-

ford Road, Cleveland, is once more resplendent with bright lights. Closed for several months under the ownership of B. C. Steele and his associates, it is now opening under the management of W. S. Glenn.

Frank Hard, for years and years in charge of publicity for the Standard Film Service Company, has resigned. His plans are not announced as yet. Neither is his successor.

Robert Cotton, division manager for P. D. C. is on a vacation trying to forget there ever were such things as motion pictures.

Martin Brown opened his New Lorain Theatre last Saturday. This is not a new theatre, but Brown has rebuilt it during the summer until it looks like new. He added 400 seats to the auditorium, redecorated it throughout, put in new equipment, built a new lobby with new electric light signs over the new marquee and then invited his patrons to come and have a look. Judging from appearances, they were all there on the opening night.

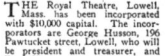

New England

THE Royal Theatre, Lowell, Mass. has been incorporated with $10,000 capital. The incorporators are George Husson, 196 Pawtucket street, Lowell, who will be president and treasurer, and Rose Husson.

The new Metropolitan Theatre, Boston's newest and largest theatre with approximately 5,000 seats, has adopted the same policy in vogue at the Fenway, Boston, of starting its week's program each Saturday. The other Boston houses commence their week's programs on Mondays.

Joseph Donahue of the Park Theatre, Woonsocket, R. I. was a recent visitor to Boston's Film Row.

Laurence Stuart, formerly manager of the Fenway Theatre, Boston, who was promoted to the

Theatre department of the Paramount organization in New York City, was welcomed to Boston for a brief return visit after several weeks elapsed since his transfer to the Metropolis.

Bob Cobe of the Merit Film Co., Boston, was a New York visitor during the week, going there on business.

Manager J. J. Scully of the Boston office of Educational Films, Inc., was in the New York City over the week end on business.

James Sheehy, formerly manager of the Allston Theatre, Boston, is to be the manager of Alfred Locatelli's new theatre, the Capitol, on Massachusetts avenue, Arlington, Mass., midway between Arlington Center and North Cambridge. It is expected that the Capitol will be completed and

ready for opening about Nov. 9.

The Jefferson Theatre, Springfield, Mass. has been incorporated with capital of $25,000. Louis Cohn of 254 Fort Pleasant avenue, Springfield, is president and treasurer of the corporation and Frederick Cohn is clerk.

Charles Morse, one of the best known men in Boston's Film Row, is to be married next June to Miss May Silver, daughter of Dr. and Mrs. B. M. Silver of Gloversville, N. Y., according to announcements issued by the young ladies' parents. Miss Silver is a graduate of the New England Conservatory of Music of Boston. Mr. Morse is a World War veteran.

Nathaniel Finston, director of the 55-piece orchestra of the new Metropolitan Theatre, Boston, comes to Boston from New York,

where he opened the Capitol Theatre. He is not a stranger to Boston, however, for he at one time played second violin in the old Boston Opera Company.

Boston secures another New York musician in the person of A. D. Richardson, who becomes organist at the new Keith-Albee house, the New Boston Theatre. Mr. Richardson has been organist at the Rialto Theatre, New York. Mr. Richardson will give a series of solos on the $50,000 Wurlitzer for the present at the new playhouse.

Samuel Lerer, owner of the Rialto Theatre building in Maynard, Mass. has sold the property to Gruber Brothers of that town. The transaction involves nearly $50,000.

Canada

SAM COPLAN, proprietor of the Princess Theatre, Ottawa, Ontario, has been elected president of the congregation of the Rideau Street Synagogue, Ottawa. Mr. Coplan is also directly interested in the Imperial Theatre, Ottawa, which is under the management of his son David Coplan, with another son, Joseph Coplan, assistant manager. Both the Princess and Imperial theatres are strictly independent moving picture houses.

Oral Cloakey, former manager of the Regent Theatre, Ottawa, and previously with large moving picture houses in Hamilton, Ontario, Calgary and Winnipeg, is now on a business tour of the United States which is taking

him as far as Florida and California. Mr. Cloakey is now identified with the new gold fields at Rouyn, in Northern Quebec.

Peter Kehayes and associates of Ottawa and Montreal reopened the Capital Theatre, Ottawa, Ontario, on October 19, this having previously been the Franklin Theatre. The policy under the new name and management includes the presentation of a complete film programme coupled with five acts of vaudeville, programmes changing every week, the change date being Monday. Three performances are given daily and the top price is 40 cents. Mr. Kehayes was formerly manager of the Casino

Theatre, Ottawa, and various theatres in Montreal.

Col. John A. Cooper, Toronto, president of the Motion Picture Distributors and Exhibitors of Canada, has made arrangements whereby all literature of the Motion Picture Producers and Distributors of America, Inc., New York, with which the Canadian body is affiliated, is distributed regularly among the newspaper editors of Canada, clergymen, social workers, educationists and others directly interested. "The Motion Picture," the monthly booklet of the Hays organization, is chiefly distributed in this way, although special bulletins are included at times.

The Classic Theatre at Stratford, Ontario has undergone substantial changes, the theatre front having been remodelled particularly. The manager of the Classic is John V. Ward, one of the best known veteran exhibitors in the Dominion. The Classic operates under the auspices of the Famous Players Canadian Corp.

Phil. Kaufman, general sales manager of Regal Films, Limited, one of the leading film distributors of Canada, has just recovered from a serious operation for internal troubles at the Toronto General Hospital. Mr. Kaufman has been identified with the moving picture business in Toronto for many years.

Minnesota

SAM SHAPIN, the Warner Brothers auditor from New York is doing his stuff with the Minneapolis branch books.

Lou Hummel is hard at work at his new job managing Associated Exhibitors Minneapolis business.

Ted Quandell and G. W. Turner are new men on the sales force of Associated here.

Morris Abrams of the Metro-Goldwyn offices here is doing all the exploiting he can at Milwaukee just now.

It isn't often that the head booker gets a trip around the territory but Al Anderson at the Paramount office has just got back from a little whirl among the accounts.

John Sholseth of Sioux Falls must be doing a real business at his Princess Theatre. He drove down to the Twin Cities recently in a Hudson of pre-war vintage and went back in a brand new Cadillac.

Ralph Branton of the Educational offices of the district suffered the loss of his father, Robert Branton, for many years connected with the Chamber of Commerce, last week.

Three of the four salesmen in the Paramount contest list for the United States are working out of the Minneapolis office. They are Fred Benno, Frank Thayer and James Cobb. Cobb's performance is particularly remarkable as he has only been in the film business four months, having come from the correspondence school line.

A. W. Nicolls, district manager of Paramount, for this section, heads the highest group in the contest, leading the nation by a safe margin.

Miss Annebe Barstow of Anoka has taken the place of Mrs. Lucia Comer as secretary to A. V. Leak, Paramount manager here. Mrs. Comer has gone to Chicago.

C. H. McClintock has gone to Des Moines to take the assortment of the Famous Players office.

Dan Roach, publicity man for Producers' is in Minneapolis with Newman and Cecil Mayberry, district manager, has also been visiting here this week.

Mrs. Luella Boehne a former school teacher of Aneta, N. D., has taken over the Bijou Theatre there as of December 1 and will make her first venture into the entertainment world.

J. E. O'Toole, as president of the Film Board of Trade in Minneapolis, gave a luncheon for William Dunlap of the Los Angeles board of education who was brought to Minneapolis by a group of women's clubs to discuss the influence of the motion picture upon school children.

Ed Bregger of the Gem Theatre at Crystal Falls, N. D., paid a visit to the Twin Cities last week.

George Leninoff of the Milwaukee office of Producers has been transferred to Minneapolis and will have northern Minnesota territory.

George Cobry, assistant manager of Producers has been laid up for a week and a half.

N. L. Shaw, formerly of Los Angeles, is the new manager of the Garden Theatre, Minneapolis, for Finkelstein & Ruben. He succeeds Harry Sternberg.

William Prass, Universal exploiteer, helped George Ehlers open his new theatre at Worthington. It is called the New Grand and is completely equipped even to a brand-new pipe organ.

M. E. Montgomery of Warner Brothers office here is back from a trip to Northern Minnesota where he had the experience of getting stuck in a snowstorm for the first time this winter.

Earl Lorenz, salesman for the Paramount offices in Minneapolis, has been having a bitter fight with pneumonia.

Jack Hellman, Paramount exploiteer, was all packed up to go to Cleveland, Ohio, to take charge of the exploitation there for his company when he received notice to stay where he was for the time being and so he will remain in Minneapolis.

That was a great trip that Jack O'Toole got back from the other day. Not content with being pulled out of the mud and snow after spending half the night marooned in his car between Hayward and Ashland, Wis., he decided to engage in a little public demonstration for one of the Producers' films in Eau Claire. Herman Swan and Cecil Mayberry, Jack's immediate superior, decided to pull one on him and they had him arrested for using a siren on the automobile. (It was Mike Newman's car, by the way, with Mike driving.) They did some tall explaining and some taller swearing but they were forced to sit in the "hoosegow" three hours before the chief of police could be found to admit them to bail. They spent most of the time studying the Eau Claire traffic laws.

Ben Friedman of the Friedman Film Corporation is up and around again minus a pair of tonsils that he decided to have removed.

Theodore Hays, veteran Minneapolis theater man, who is one of the ace's in the Finkelstein & Ruben organization, has been laid up for several days.

First National's Minneapolis branch staged a fire drill last week in which the place was emptied in nearly a minute flat.

Prosper F. Schwic, long Finkelstein & Ruben manager in Duluth, is coming back to the Twin Cities. He has assumed management of the Tower Theatre in St. Paul, owned by Joseph Friedman. Billy Mick is expected to take Schwie's place in Duluth.

In spite of a petition carrying 120 names, Madelia, Minn., has turned down the proposal of a Sunday theater closing ordinance.

At a recent session of the Minneapolis arbitration board the only case not won by a distributor was one which was thrown out because there was no arbitration clause in the contract. One exhibitor, Max Torodor, Old Mill Theatre, Minneapolis, was denied cancellation of his contract in spite of the fact that he had been unable to get from Fox the film contracted for although it had been more than a year since the contract was signed.

Because of fire hazard the state fire marshal recently halted a proposed motion picture show in a church hall at Holdingford, Minn.

McCarthy Enterprises of Fargo has taken over the Royal at Badger and the Princess at Roseau, both Minnesota theatres.

The dance-hall-theatre combination will be used in Graceville, Minn., by B. J. Benfield who now operates the Strand at Morris. He has plans for a new 400 seat house.

Twin City distributors learned with sorrow of the death of Nate Chapman, veteran manager of the Englert Theatre, Iowa City.

H. N. Davies of Spencer, Ia., was in Minneapolis last week.

'Art Roberts, F.O.B. assistant manager at Milwaukee, has been in Minneapolis all week at the bedside of his mother.

E. G. Tunstall, former Warner Brothers man for Wisconsin lost his mother last week in Minneapolis.

Film Booking Offices has taken on Joseph Schwartzbein, formerly of Universal. He will cover Wisconsin.

Ben Marcus, of Omaha, is helping Harry Weinberg at Sioux Falls in F. B. O. sales this week during the illness of C. W. Nobling.

The Opera house at Doland, S. D., formerly operated by W. W. Welch is now run by Robert Redburn.

Sam Levinsohn, operating the Cedar Theatre, Minneapolis, and manager of the United Theatre Equipment company here, is the father of a girl born last week.

The Orpheum at Grand Forks is brilliant with a new electric sign. Shows will be given twice a week at Johnson hall, Braham, Minn.

The Magic Theatre of Pierson, Ia., has been taken over from R. G. Ruch by H. G. Anderson of Ravina, S. D.

Shortly before his illness Theodore Hays of Finkelstein & Ruben looked over the company's new State theatre at Sioux Falls, S. D., and said it would be ready Jan. 1.

Rapid City, S. D., will have a new theatre, the Palace, November 1. It will be operated by Brown & Watterson known in Aberdeen, Watertown and Butts as well as in Rapid City.

The Legion theatre at Blunt, S. D., has gone under the management of Al Schriever, who has theatres at Onida and Agar. A. W. Martin was formerly manager.

Women seem to be invading this theatre business. Mrs. Fred Haas and Miss Katie Fischer are the newest additions to the ranks in North Dakota, having taken over the Foto Pla at Hazen.

The Electric theatre has been reopened by Frank Smith at Clear Lake, Ia.

William E. Mick, who has been in charge of the Lyric theatre here for the last six weeks, has just been installed as general manager of the various Finkelstein & Ruben playhouses in Duluth, and also will have supervision of vaudeville at the Palace theatre, Superior. He succeeds to the position held by P. F. Schwie for the last five years.

All vaudeville bills at the Lyric in the future will start from Duluth on their tour of F. & R. houses through to the Pacific coast. Mr. Mick, who will have offices at the Garrick building, will make monthly visits to Chicago to choose the Lyric bookings.

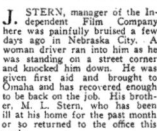

Omaha

J. STERN, manager of the Independent Film Company here was painfully bruised a few days ago in Nebraska City. A woman driver ran into him as he was standing on a street corner and knocked him down. He was given first aid and brought to Omaha and has recovered enough to be back on the job. His brother, M. L. Stern, who has been ill at his home for the past month or so returned to the office this week.

J. E. Flynn, district manager for the Metro-Goldwyn corporation, with office in St. Louis, is in town for a few days.

A. Burrus, manager of the Lyric theatre in Crete, Nebraska, was here last week inspecting the North Star theatre, said to be the model suburban theatre of Omaha. It is under direction of J. Erle Kirk. Mr. Burrus is contemplating the erection of a new theatre.

W. N. Peterson, son of H. O. Peterson, exhibitor at Geneva, Nebraska, has become salesman for Pathe here.

James Patrick Shea has been named new manager for the Associated Exhibitors at the Omaha branch taking the place of Eddie Alperson. Mr. Alperson resigned recently to become special repre-

sentative for Warner Brothers. He was formerly branch manager for First National and later branch manager for Universal with offices in St. Louis.

Lloyd Willis, special representative of Warner Brothers' home office, was in Omaha last week.

Sam Stern, youngest brother of Joe Stern, and M. L. Stern, owners of the Independent Film Company of Omaha, has been made salesman covering the Nebraska territory. He was formerly in charge of the poster department.

P. E. Doe, manager of the Electric theatre in Arcadia, Nebraska, was visiting along the row Monday.

Fred Hunt is now salesman for Premiere Pictures here.

A. W. Smith, Jr., of the New York office of First National, was here Friday and Saturday. He went Sunday, Monday and Tuesday in Des Moines and left Tuesday night for a three weeks' trip through this territory before returning to the East.

Abe Rose, manager for First National here, has returned from a business trip to Des Moines with A. W. Smith, Jr. They held a conference with A. H. Blank.

F. F. Weiss, owner of the Plaza

Leo Blank, new exchange manager for Educational Films in Omaha, Nebr.

theatre at Fort Dodge, Iowa, was a visitor here last Monday.

R. R. Booth, formerly of the Paramount, Overland and Empress theatres at Nebraska City, was a caller at the Metro-Goldwyn office early this week.

A. F. Jenkins of the Community theatre, David City, Nebraska, dropped into Omaha last Monday to spend the day.

Charles Prokop, manager of the Rex theatre at Wahoo, Nebraska, paid a visit here Monday.

A. G. Miller of the Miller theatre in Atkinson, Nebraska, was here attending the Legion convention.

M. S. Frankel and L. A. Burson, formerly owner of the Sun theatre at Gothenburg, Nebraska, have been added to the sales staff of the United Artists.

Floyd Lewis, special representative for Associated Exhibitors in New York, is here for a couple of days.

Among the many out-of-town exhibitors here attending the American Legion convention were: H. F. Kennedy of the Lyric theatre, Broken Bow, Nebraska; J. M. Reynolds, Opera House, Elwood, Neb.; J. T. Grotenhuis, Cottage theatre, Tilden, Iowa; L. J. Shurwood from Moorhead, Iowa; E. T. Dunlap, Hawarden, Iowa and Mr. and Mrs. Elmer Gailey of the Crystal theatre, Wayne, Nebraska.

Glenn Rogers and Edgar Cox are now salesmen for the Associated Exhibitors Film Company.

Baltimore

THE Brodie Theatre, 1118 Light street, with a seating capacity of 600 persons, was reopened to the public on Thursday, October 22, after having been completely remodeled at a cost of $25,000, according to Joseph Brodie.

Work on the playhouse was done after the plans of J. Lowther Forrest, architect, and the construction work was done by the Mervis Construction Company. The front is in Spanish Mission style.

The Riviera Amusement Company is now operating the theatre and the entire playhouse is practically new. It is a residential house.

A large circular, cushioned seat has been placed in the inner foyer of the Rivoli Theatre. It is lo-

cated directly under the art-glass dome in the center of the ceiling.

Guy L. Wonders, manager of the Rivoli Theatre, is limping around on a cane these days with a game leg, having sprained several ligaments recently when he accidentally fell while going down the concrete steps in his home.

The by-laws of the Motion Picture Theatre Owners of Maryland will have some changes made in them according to a decision which was made at a meeting of the Board of Directors on Wednesday, October 14.

A committee of three was appointed to look into the matter. The members of this committee are: William M. Whitehurst,

chairman; Frank H. Durkee and J. Louis Rome.

Abram Eskin, formerly Baltimore representative for Paramount in Baltimore, has resigned to go to New York. He has been succeeded by Joe Ostahan who formerly covered the Eastern Shore of Maryland for Paramount.

R. Ayers has returned to Washington, D. C., as manager of the Independent Film Exchange of that city. He was formerly in Washington and then in Philadelphia for the same company.

Rudolph Berger, Manager of the Washington, D. C. exchange for Metro-Goldwyn-Mayer and H. Mendelsohn, District Manager of that company, visited Baltimore

last week and looked over the field.

Ushers and doormen in the larger houses of Baltimore practically all are wearing their new fall uniforms. Greys and dark blue are the predominating colors.

A charter has been given the Metropolitan Theatre, Morgantown, W. Va., by the Secretary of State and it will still retain the same name as a corporation of which the capital stock is $500,000. All the incorporators are from Morgantown including George P., Henry P. and John P. Communtzis, Norma Lough and Louis F. Tanner.

Services with motion pictures have been resumed at the Associate Congregational Church, Baltimore.

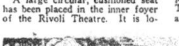

Houston

J. W. WILLIAMS president of the Independent Film Service, with home offices in Dallas Texas, was in Houston this week on a business trip. Mr. Williams is also connected with the Home State Film Company.

John McCarty special pep man for Paramount pictures is in Houston and this territory for a two weeks' tour. Mr. McCarty is making the tour in an especially

built truck and will help exploit Paramount pictures wherever they are playing.

Ed. Collins city manager for Southern Enterprises in Galveston stopped off in Houston early this week enroute home from Dallas. Mr. Collins was called to north Texas on account of his mother's health, however she was out of danger before he left for Galveston.

Ben Broyles Fox Film Service representative is in town for a few days' business trip. After leaving Houston Mr. Broyles will go to Dallas the home office of the Fox interest.

Theatre owners from South Texas and the San Antonio district were guests of the Richard Dix, Paramount, Company last week. They arrived in a body

and went direct to the Bassett ranch.

Rain and stormy weather has hampered the work on the new million dollar theatre being erected by Jesse H. Jones. They have only been able to put in about half time the past ten days. It is hoped that the basement will be completed before Thanksgiving arrives.

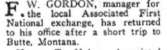

Kansas City

FROM all corners of the Kansas City territory they came, those golfers, with clubs polished agleaming for the abundance of prizes awarded in the annual exhibitors' and inter-exchange golf tournament, which was played over the Lakewood Golf and Country Club course, Kansas City, Monday.

So plentiful were the prizes—given by various theatres and exchanges—that virtually each contestant had a "story" for the wife that night. Following the nine holes of the morning, a round which was for the purpose of determining the handicaps for the 18-hole round of the afternoon, there was a banquet, at which merriment was made and hurled to the winds. C. R. Rhoden, manager of Midwest Film Distributors, Inc., was toastmaster. In order to provide a little "spice" to the event, the scores of a couple of well known exhibitors, the names of whom have been concealed as carefully as a "scales" hip pocket, were contested, they being accused of little short of embezzlement. The joke, so the story goes, went over great until one of the "accused" called forth his anger to defend his dignity—then it was all off.

The winners of the more important prizes:

No. 1—Silver loving cup, given by the Newman theatre for the lowest net score, won by Harry Taylor, Universal branch manager at Kansas City.

No. 2—Silver cigarette container, given by Pathe for the lowest gross score, won by Leon Abraham, Pathe.

No. 3—Wrist watch, given by the Mainstreet theatre on blind bogey event, won by T. O. Byerle, Kansas City First National branch manager.

No. 4—Golf bag, given by Liberty theatre, Kansas City, for low net score on first nine holes, won by Roland Thompson, Midwest Film Distributors, Inc.

No. 5—Driver, given by Globe theatre, Kansas City, for low net on second nine holes, won by Edward Dubinsky, manager of the Regent theatre, Kansas City.

No. 6—Driver, given by Pantages theatre for low score against par on any hole, won by O. H. Lambert, Metro-Goldwyn.

No. 7—Driver, given by Electric theatre, Kansas City, Kans., for blind bogey event, won by C. A. Schultz, P. D. C. branch manager at Kansas City.

No. 8—Golf bag, given by Isis theatre on blind hole event, won by R. C. Libeau, Paramount district manager.

When Adolph Eisner, former president of the M. P. T. O. Kansas City, opened the Circle theatre, Kansas City, and started a "rush on the gate" with 10-cent admission, he set a precedent.

Brisk steps and facial expressions smacking of big business were in vogue along Kansas City's movie row this week. N. E. Depinet and F. J. McConnell, Universal southern division sales manager and short subject sales manager, respectively, held a lively sales meeting in Kansas City, while B. H. Goldstein, treasurer and general manager of Universal, Julius Singer and A. E. Fair, head of the theatre department, were in conference with Charles T. Sears, former M. P. T. O. Missouri president and now midwest manager of Universal theatres.

C. M. Parkhurst, formerly with Warner-Vitagraph, now is with the Kansas City F. B. O. sales force, while James Bradford of the P. D. C. sales force left for Omaha, Neb., to accept a similar position with the same company in that city.

J. F. Burke, traveling auditor for Educational, was a busy Kansas City visitor.

E. O. Brooks, serial sales manager for Pathe, conducted a sales meeting at the Kansas City exchange.

H. O. Bartels, former Denver exhibitor and Associated Exhibitor's branch manager of Los Angeles, has been added to the Pathe sales force in Kansas City. T. W. Edwards, formerly with the Salt City Pathe branch, also has been added to the Kansas City staff of that company.

Improvements aplenty are in progress at the Fox branch. Not only is M. A. Levy, branch manager, having the interior repointed, but opera chairs have been installed in the projection room.

J. E. Flynn, Metro-Goldwyn district manager, was a Kansas City visitor, as was W. G. Bishop, Metro-Goldwyn exploiteer of St. Louis.

New decorations for the interior, installation of new vestibule partitions and other improvements are being made on the Best theatre, Parsons, Kas., according to Walter Finney, manager of the Universal owned house.

Among the out-of-town exhibitors in the Kansas City market this week were: G. L. Rugg, Opera House, Troy, Kas.; Walter Finney, Best theatre, Parsons, Kas.; Charles T. Sears, manager of Universal theatres in the Kansas City territory; Ben Levy, Hippodrome, Joplin, Mo.

Salt Lake City

F W. GORDON, manager for the local Associated First National exchange, has returned to his office after a short trip to Butte, Montana.

Harry T. Nolan, Associated First National District Manager, is in New York City at the present time. He said before leaving here that he was going there to work, but Manager Gorgon is of the impression that he really went to see the ball game.

Vete Stewart, who covers the Montana territory out of the Associated First National exchange in this city, is working his way back from that section. Outside of tipping his car over, the trip was uneventful.

W. G. Seib has left his managerial chair at the local Pathe office for a few days during a short trip to Northern Utah and the Idaho branch. Seib was accompanied by Ben Fish, Special Feature representative.

Ed C. Mix, in charge of the Associated Exhibitors office in this city, is leaving for a short trip into Cache Valley and other Northern Utah points.

Lon Hoss, who was for a short time connected with Preferred Pictures here, has recently joined the selling forces of Associated Exhibitors, and is now covering the coal camps of Utah out of this office. Hoss will have all of the state of Utah as his territory. Associated Exhibitors are now planning to put on another salesman to work exclusively in Idaho.

Warner Brothers' local manager, R. S. Stackhouse, is now in Boise, Idaho. George Jensen is covering Montana out of this office, and L. W. Hyde is still in Southern Utah.

L. A. Davis, who has charge of the F. B. O. exchange in this city, is expecting to leave this week for a short trip into Cache Valley, Utah.

A. A. Schmidt, Western representative for the Film Booking Offices, will shortly pay a visit to Salt Lake City from Los Angeles.

W. K. Bloom is due back from Montana where he has had a very successful trip with his F. B. O. product. After a few days' rest he will make a trip into Southern Utah. Joe K. Soloman left this week for a trip into the Nevada territory out of this office.

Samuel Henley has left his managerial desk at the local Universal exchange, for a trip into North Western Idaho.

L. J. Schlaifer, Universal Division Manager, left here this week for Butte, Montana.

M. Aparton has been added to the Universal sales force, this last week, and is now doing his stuff in Northern Idaho.

Joe McElhenney, salesman out of the local Universal exchange, has left for North Western Nevada.

George Mayne, owner of the Preferred Pictures and Super-Feature Independent exchange in this city, is planning to make a trip through Idaho which he expects to be the longest trip he has ever made. Mayne is leaving next week.

All of the open situations in Nevada were closed recently by J. A. Tidwell, Fox salesman, who expects to return to the local office the later part of this week.

H. Bradley Fish, Fox exchange manager in this city, is in Boise, Idaho, for a few days.

Carl Stearn, in charge of the local United Artists exchange, has returned from a trip to a number of Utah towns.

A new salesman has been added to the sales force of United Artists in the person of M. K. Cohn. Cohn was formerly connected with the Universal office here, and has been manager of various exchanges in Salt Lake and Denver.

James R. Keitz has just returned to the local Greater Features exchange of which he is manager, from Pocatello, Idaho.

J. T. Sheffield, General manager of Greater Features Incorporated, is expected to make a visit to this city within the next few weeks.

Andy Anderson, formerly with Fox, is the new shipping clerk for Greater Features here.

Clyde H. Messinger, manager for Educational in this city, has returned from his trip through Southern Utah, and leaves next week for Idaho.

An Educational drive is to begin October 25th, and the local office expects to go over the top.

Exhibitors visiting Exchange Row this week were: John Ruger, owner of the American theatre of Park City, Utah; Mell Stringham, operating the Colonial theatre, Ogden, Utah; Garl Ridgeway, owner of the Star theatre, Kimberley, Idaho; The Peery Brothers of the Egyptian theatre, Ogden, Utah, and C. M. Pace, owner of the Pace theatre, Delta, Utah.

CLASSIFIED AD SECTION

RATES: 10 cents a word for each insertion, in advance
except Employment Wanted, on which rate is 5 cents.

CLASSIFIED SERVICE

A classified ad in MOTION PICTURE NEWS offers the
full resources and circulation of the NEWS to the advertiser at a ridiculously low figure.

Whether you want to reach executives, branch managers,
salesmen, or theatre managers, you can accomplish this
quickly and economically through the NEWS Classified
Columns.

Wanted

PIANIST would like to play alone, evenings, in picture theatre, within commuting distance from New York City. Box 400, Motion Picture News, New York City.

WANTED to lease theatre for suitable combination house in Eastern State. Write Box 440, Motion Picture News, New York City.

THEATRE WANTED in thriving town within 150 miles of Toledo, Ohio, preferred; will buy, lease or rent. Send particulars. Waid Zeis, 1358 Elmwood Ave., Toledo, Ohio.

WANTED.—To rent or buy lease motion picture theatre. Anywhere. 400 seats up. Box A, Motion Picture News, 945 S. Wabash, Chicago.

EXPERT OPERATOR and Electrician with 9 years' experience in big houses; married; wants to locate at once. Address, Operator, Box 282, Mason City, Iowa.

ORGANIST.—Experienced. References. Minimum, $60 six (6) days. Worth investigating. Now employed. Box 390, Motion Picture News, New York City.

PIANIST desires engagement for evenings to play alone in picture theatre within commuting distance from New York City. Box 400, Motion Picture News, New York City.

THEATRE IN TOWN OF 4,000 or better, anywhere in North Central states, Northern Indiana preferred. Can either give satisfactory security on lease or buy outright. Would consider buying interest in bona-fide proposition where owner wishes to retire. All replies absolutely confi-

dential. Address Box 360, Motion Picture News, New York City.

For Sale

FOR SALE, Wyoming Theatre, Mullens, W. Va. $60,-000.00 cash. Now earning about $1,000.00 per month net. Owner retiring from business.

FOR SALE—400 veneered seats, $500; 2 Powers 6 B's, good condition, each $375; 1 Osborn Baby Grand Piano, $200; ½ horse 36 inch blower (new $575), $195; 4 16-inch wall fans, each $10; 1 Orpheum 14 ft. vertical sign with flasher, $150; in fact a complete set of equipment to be sold in line with above prices. S. O'Hare, Fairfield, Iowa.

FOR SALE—New modern movie theatre, 600 seats; exceptional proposition; quick sale; cheap; small town near Albany; no competition. Box 430, Motion Picture News, New York City.

FOR SALE—Six hundred veneered theatre chairs, A-1 condition; also all makes rebuilt projection machines and other equipment; write us your needs. Illinois Theatre Equipment Company, 12 E. Ninth St., Chicago.

FOR SALE—Moving picture theatre (valuable realty), in town near Camden, N. J.; seating capacity 486, etc. Frank DuFrayne, 20 S. 15th St., Philadelphia.

Newspaper displays that have been used for Paramount's "The Coast of Folly," showing the wide variety in which stock and original materials were employed with this picture by the following theatres, whose ads are shown above:. Des Moines Theatre, Des Moines, Ia.; Hippodrome, Joplin, Mo.; Palace, Dallas, Tex.; Strand Theatre, Birmingham, Ala.; Century Théatre, Baltimore, Md., and the Howard, Atlanta, Ga.

Buffalo

Y EGGS pried open an exit door in the Broadway theatre, a Buffalo community house, the other night, advanced on Manager Ben Wallerstein's office, souped the safe and escaped with the contents. When asked how much the bandits got, Ben replied, "I should tell how much business I do and get a boost in rentals." Sayin' which he polished up his 10-karat diamond and continued on his way.

The new 800-seat house which Farber & Yavno will build at 2275 Genesee street, Buffalo, will be named the Ambassador. The house which will show pictures exclusively, will feature a large organ.

William Calihan, formerly manager of the Regent, Rochester, is now a member of the Eastman executive staff. L. Morris has succeeded Mr. Calihan as manager of the Regent. Bert Caley, formerly a member of the Eastman staff, is now managing the Piccadilly.

When the print of "The Iron Horse," which was scheduled to open at the Strand theatre in Binghamton the other night, was burned in the baggage room at East Aurora, Manager H. M. Addison, of course, became much upset. So did Dave Cohn and Ned Kornblite, owners of the house. In fact all three dashed for the phones, telegraph offices, etc., to get in touch with the Buffalo office of the Fox Film Company. Officials there got busy at once, engaged Lieut. Donald F.

Goold of the firm of McCurie & Goold, commercial aviators of Buffalo, and in a few hours had delivered another print of the picture to the Southern Tier city in time for the evening show. Lieut. Goold left Buffalo at 3 P. M. and was in Binghamton at 5 o'clock. The audience, which had waited several hours during the afternoon, during which time other films were shown, received tickets good for the evening showing, so no one was disappointed.

Al Beckerich, manager of the Loew State, Buffalo, put over a good one this week, when for the first time, local street cars used ads on their stern and bow telling the world about the show at Al's house.

Helen Kozanowski, sister of Hilda and Stanley Kozanowski, managers of the Rivoli theatre, Buffalo, died last week. Helen had been cashier at the big community house.

Michael Shea, head of the Shea Amusement Company of Buffalo, and Vincent R. McFaul, managing director of Shea's Hippodrome, journeyed to Boston last week for the opening of the new Metropolitan theatre in the Hub city.

Jack Stevens, formerly with the Schine Theatrical corporation, as manager of houses down state, has accepted the management of the new Grand theatre in Westfield, N. Y., operated by the Zicofe corporation of Buffalo. He will also continue to book for the

Elk theatre, Buffalo, which house he has been managing of late.

Jack Muldoon will celebrate the first anniversary of the Academy, Buffalo, under his management during the week of November 9.

John Henderson, aged 24, of 16 Russell street, Rochester, who with a pocket comb case, attempted to hold up Frank M. Smith of the Eastman theatre as he was cashing up for the night ten days ago, has waived examination and has been held for the grand jury on a charge of attempted robbery, first degree.

The new Shea Buffalo theatre will open the middle of January. The exterior work is complete and the interior is coming along in fine shape. The house will be the last word in decoration, furnishings, equipment, construction and convenience.

Richard C. Fox, president of Freedom Film corporation, 257 Franklin street, Buffalo, will be in charge of the Vital exchanges in Buffalo and Albany. Headquarters in Buffalo will be in the Freedom office.

Harry Gibbs, manager of the New Haven Fox office, is in Buffalo promoting sales and now is touring the territory with G. Emerson Dickman. Carl Fahrenhola, managing director of the shipping department, wishes to deny that he will double for George O'Brien in that star's hazardous stunts. Clarence Ross has resigned as cashier.

E. S. Flynn has arrived in Buf-

falo from Philadelphia to take over the management of the United Artists exchange, succeeding William L. Sherry, who has gone to Florida.

Colvin Brown, vice president of F. B. O., was in Buffalo last week end and during his stay here he took occasion to congratulate Local Mar--er Harry T. Dixon on the fine sales showing made by the exchange.

Al Teschmacher, for many years booker at the Pathe office, is back in the game as booker for Associated Exhibitors. Al is continuing, however, to operate the Casino theatre, an east side community house.

Dolly McMillan, beautiful inspector at the F. B. O. office, is the happy possessor of the $1,000 check awarded her as first prize winner in the Buffalo Evening Times popularity contest. We suppose Dolly soon will be on her way to Hollywood.

Herk Webster, now that the snow is falling and golfing means flirting with the doctor, has turned to radio. To show that he is a real DX fan, he is planning on making a survey of the neighborhood to try and find wherefrom comes that dern interference.

The Hi-Art theatre in Lockport has returned to a straight picture policy and it is understood that the new Palace, Paramount leased, has reduced prices to 25 cents. Harold B. Franklin was in Lockport last week looking ov - the Palace.

Seattle

O NE of the outstanding musical events of the fall season was presented by Manager Frank Steffy of the Coliseum Theatre recently, when he arranged for the appearance as a special added attraction on one of his programs of a musical aggregation of Seattle women that have established a unique and enviable reputation in the Pacific Northwest.

Word was received on Film Row last week to the effect that the famous "Seven Days" exploitation car will arrive here early in November for a two or three day visit in the Washington territory. Manager W. H. Drummond of the Producers' Distributing Corporation exchange in this city is already planning a gala reception for the Christie vehicle, which will come here direct from Salt Lake City and Portland following its Eastern tour.

Calvin Heilig, director of the Heilig Theatre circuit in Washington and Oregon spent a few days here recently with Charles W. McKee, manager of the local house, during which time plans

for the coming season were made.

Reopening of the American Theatre in Butte for the fall and winter season was announced here last week by Louis Dreibelbis, Montana financier and owner of the house. First run feature pictures and musical specialties under the direction of Ted Rose and his Orchestra will comprise the new policy.

Friends of Leonard Hagen, director of the Blue Mouse Music Masters playing at John Hamrick's Blue Mouse Theatre in this city were glad to see him again in charge of the orchestra last week, following an enforced absence from the playhouse as a result of a serious illness.

I. M. Binnard, theatre owner and manager of Lewiston, Idaho, spent a few days on Film Row last week. Much of his time was spent in buying and booking pictures for the remainder of the fall season.

Harry Eagles, publicity and exploitation director of Manager George P. Endert's local Famous Players exchange, returned re-

cently from Spokane, where he arranged a mammoth Autumn Tea and Motion Picture Style Show to be held at the Davenport Hotel.

Latest reports received on Film Row indicated that Cliff Kaplinger, associated with his father in the Bellingham Theatres, Inc., at Bellingham, was rapidly recovering from the effects of a serious operation performed early in October. Transfusion of blood by his sister was necessitated by the severity of the case, but a complete recovery is expected soon.

Following his recent opening of the New Arabian Theatre in this city, H. W. Bruen, managing director of the Pacific Theatres Company, is already hard at work on plans for his next new theatre, the Woodlawn. It is expected that the house will be ready for a gala opening about January 1. It is located in the North End of the city, in one of the prominent new residential districts.

Another Christmas or New Year opening, as planned at present, is scheduled by E. A. Hallberg of Mt. Vernon, who is rush-

ing work on his new theatre in that territory. The house will be located in the main business district, and will be entirely modern in design, equipment and detail of every kind.

Three cases were brought before the Film Board of Arbitration of this city last week, with the following results: United Artists Corporation, in a suit against W. L. Casey of Bonner's Ferry, Idaho, were instructed to make out their contract according to their application form, thus denying their charges of non-fulfillment of contract against Casey; First National were awarded a decision against C. D. Gillespie of Brewster, Washington, specifying that Mr. Brewster either pay or play his thirty-nine First National pictures; I. M. Binnard, bringing a claim against First National for price adjustment on several films, was advised that the Board had no jurisdiction whatever over contract prices, and that as far as it was concerned, the exhibitor and exchange both must live up to their part of the contract.

Denver

ANOTHER new D & R theatre will be opened Sunday night October 18th. This time it is the Highland D & R located at 42nd and Lowell Blvd. an excellent location. The new theatre although containing only 650 seats has every convenience of a major first run house. It is the second D & R theatre to open in Denver the Washington Park D & R on South Gaylord Street having opened its doors about six weeks ago. Another, The Egyptian, is nearing completion and will open in a short time. The D & R theatres are being built by the Western Enterprises, a company in which Rick Ricketson and Dick Dickenson are the chief stockholders and general managers. The opening of the Highland D & R will make the eighth of a chain of theatres now being operated in Colorado by the Western Enterprises, two in Denver and others in outlying points.

James Pace, owner and manager of the Pace Theatre, Chadron Nebraska, has now completely replaced all equipment in his projection booth which was recently destroyed by fire.

Claude Ezell, special representative for Associated Exhibitors, was a visitor with H. L. Burnham, local representative of that organization, at the Pathe Ex-

View showing general offices of Fox Film Corporation's Detroit exchange, located at 66 Sibley Street.

change, during the last week. Mr. Ezell left Denver for Oklahoma City, Dallas and New Orleans, after which he will again return to Denver and remain for a longer period of time.

Arthur O'Connell, head shipper

for Universal, and Addie Mooncy of the contract department in the First National office, were married Saturday night, October 17th. Immediately after the ceremony, they left for a honeymoon trip to Salt Lake City,

after which they will return to Denver and take up their residence. Arthur O'Connell has been employed by the Universal Film Exchange for the past eight years and is probably one of the most widely known shippers among the exhibitors of the territory.

The following exhibitors were visitors in Denver during the past week: Otis P. Fish of the Iris Theatre, Lander, Wyoming; J. M. Cook, Crowley Theatre, Crowley, Colorado; Arthur Van, formerly of the Pixie Theatre, Golden, Colorado, who also opened a theatre in Olney Springs, Colorado; W. A. Clemens, Yoder Theatre, Yoder, Wyoming; D. Bratton, Ovid Theatre, Ovid, Colorado; Orson Clark who will open a new 700 seat theatre in Salt Creek, Wyoming.

Dan Rush, former manager of the Colonial Theatre, Pueblo Colorado, has been employed by the Denver Theatre Supply Company as representative.

The Stratton Home, Colorado Springs, has recently installed equipment for the showing of film to the inmates of the home.

Thatcher School, Pueblo, Colorado, has also made the necessary installments for the showing of Educational film to the pupils.

Southeast

W. M. SAAL, Booking Supervisor for Southern Enterprises, was a Charlotte visitor the past week setting in bookings for their theatres.

C. C. Pettijohn, General Counselor of the Film Board of Trade, was in Charlotte the past week to meet with the Charlotte board.

Phelps Sasseen, former salesman with Liberty Film Company has been appointed manager of the Associated Exhibitors office in Charlotte, taking the place of George Hendrickson, who is now connected with the Metro-Goldwyn Charlotte office as salesman.

The Taylor Theatre at Edenton, N. C. has opened. This is said to be a very attractive little house.

Arthur Lucas, owner of the Educational franchise for the South, and who also owns the Charlotte theatre, Charlotte, N. C., was a Charlotte visitor the past week. Mr. Lucas has transferred

his brother, Harry Lucas, to Raleigh to look after his theatres at that point and Jack Revielle, manager at that point has been transferred to Charlotte as manager of the Charlotte theatre.

H. T. Elder, District Manager of Warner Brothers, has been in Charlotte for a week or ten days making a change in the managers of that office. Mr. E. P. Pickler, former manager, has resigned and Mr. M. W. Davis, former salesman with Universal's Charlotte office, and who also at one time was manager of the Paramount office, at Memphis, has been appointed to manage the Warner branch.

Ed Beach, former Paramount salesman, has left that company and become affiliated with the Liberty Film Exchange, of Atlanta, as salesman.

H. H. Drake, of Fayetteville, N. C., one of the first exhibitors to

have a theatre in this city has died. Mr. Drake some time ago was compelled on account of illness, to sell his holdings to the National Theatres, at Greensboro, on which Mr. Leitch is general manager. Mr. Drake was well known throughout the Carolinas and has been very active at all times in the interest of exhibitors and the motion picture industry.

Sailor Harvey, of the Hays organization, was a Charlotte visitor going over exchanges and checking up on the fire hazard of the different offices.

George Linchan, district manager of Producers & Distributors, was a Charlotte visitor the past week.

A. F. Sams, President of the Piedmont Amusement Company, of Winston-Salem, and also a senator from his district in the state legislature, was a Charlotte visitor the past week. Mr. Sams is a

staunch friend of the motion picture industry and has been very active at the state legislature in assistin' to stop any adverse legislation to the industry.

A. B. Cheatham, who has been general manager of the Ideal and Ottoway theatres, at Charlotte, for a number of years, will sever his connections with that company on Saturday, October 17, when we understand he will enter into the distributine end again by accepting a position with Progress pictures. The Film Fraternity at Charlotte, wish him success in his new ventures as Mr. Cheatham is well liked and has a wonderful personality.

E. H. Fraser, formerly booker for Famous Players, passed through Charlotte several days ago on his way to Florida. We understand Mr. Fraser has severed his connections with the Famous Players organization.

Detroit

MISS Caroline Butterfield, daughter of W. S. Butterfield, owner of many theatres in Michigan, is playing in stock in Grand Rapids.

Arthur D. Baehr of the Crystal Crystal Theatre, Detroit, is recovering from injuries received

when his automobile was hit by a truck.

J. B. Hunter of Grand Haven leaves October 26 to spend the winter in California.

Robert Cotton, district manager for Producers Distributing Company, visited old friends in

Detroit recently. He now has his offices in Cleveland.

Phil Gleichman, former exhibitor in Detroit who now maintains headquarters in Cleveland, maintains an office in Detroit to look after his interests in that city.

The DeLuxe Theatre on Octo-

ber 25 will revert to a strictly film program, dropping vaudeville. At the same time admission will be cut one-half, to 25 cents. The Cinderella and Roosevelt, also owned by the James N. Robertson Enterprises, will continue with vaudeville and pictures.

New York and New Jersey

CHALK up another handsome neighborhood theatre for New York City. Last Thursday evening the Manor at Coney Island Ave. and Avenue K was opened to the public by Charlie Goldreyer, Maurice Fleischman and William Fleischman.

The building was erected by the realty corporation of which Isaac Miller is president. Dave Berk, of Berk and Moross, handled the sale of the property to the present owners.

There is an exceptionally long throw, about 208 feet and almost equaling the distance at the Capitol theatre in New York City. However, in spite of the distance the projection on the opening night was remarkably clear.

Harry Scholl will be in charge of the projection room and Howell's Cine Equipment Company followed out their usual custom of taking charge on the first night. William Glick, chief engineer of Howell's, Dave Narcy and Dave Solomon were in attendance. The equipment consists of Simplex machines equipped with Peerless reflectors and using about 20 amperes. Further specification include Hertner generators, curtain controls and a gold fibre screen.

Members of the trade who were present at the Manor's premiere include William and Harry Brandt, Herman Rachmiel, Sam Moross, John Mannheimer, Charles Steiner, Harry Suchman, Isaac Seider, Dave Berk, Bernard Scholtz, Jack Bellman, Herman Kram, William Glick, Dave Solomon, Dave Narcy, Tom Hamlin, Dave Gross and Harry Thomas.

The next meeting of the M. P. T. O. of N. J. will be held at Camden, N. J. on October 27th, when the members will be the guests of Dr. Benjamin Schindler.

Louis Heiman has announced that he will reopen the Lyric theatre at Rahway, in the near future. The Lyric has been closed since last December and at the present time extensive alterations are in progress in order to install modern equipment and also to make the theatre attractive in gen-

As the New Fox Exchange on West 44th St. will appear when completed.

eral. Mr. Heiman, who also operates the Empire in the same city, further states that the policy of the Lyric will adhere strictly to motion pictures.

The Grand theatre at Paterson, N. J., is now under the ownership of Sam Altholz. Louis Ginsberg is the new manager.

Sam Perry of Englewood was in town Tuesday and sporting a new polka-dot tie.

Last week these columns made mention that Frank Becker's theatre in Englewood was almost completed and that it was soon to be opened. It is stated on good authority that this is not the case and that it will be February or March before the theatre will hold its opening.

Pathe and Associated Exhibitor salesmen, headed by William Raynor, attended the Army-Notre Dame football game last Saturday. Al Sautelle, the Volstedian, was also there.

Fred Cross of Ridgefield Park,

Hugh Otis of Hackensack and Aaron Schusterman of New Brunswick were visitors at the exchanges this week.

William Brandt, of the Brandt theatres in Brooklyn tells us that there is to be something entirely new in the design of the Carleton that is in the course of construction on Flatbush Avenue, Brooklyn.

Floyd Vogt, Pathe salesman for South Jersey, suffered considerable damage to his home when a big elm tree fell on the roof during the wind storm of about a week ago.

William McChesney of the Walter Reade Circuit, who is one of the enterprising commuters between South Jersey and New York, has a new traveling companion these days in the person of George Faulkner who has recently joined his father on the Faulkner circuit of New Jersey. They say that the younger Faulkner is a fast pinochle player.

Previous to the opening of the new, big Famous-Players Metropolitan theatre at Boston, William Glick, chief engineer of Howell's, was called over for consultation on a projection problem. Part of the beam of light struck the lower part of the balcony and Glick finally had to rip up part of the floor in order to get a clear path. Mr. Glick was also in attendance on the opening night.

The many acquaintances of Al Moley, who handles the booking sheets at the Prudential Film Delivery offices will regret to hear of a loss that Al suffered last Saturday noon. Al's mother is dead after an illness of two weeks. She passed away at her home at 227 West 115th St., New York City. Friends in the film trade contributed a beautiful floral wreath.

They say Bill Raynor of Pathe won a bet on last Saturday's football game, but dropped it on a Sunday golf match although Mr. Raynor has long been associated with the "birdie" class.

It is reported that Charlie Stombaugh of the Newark Pathe branch is getting ready to entertain the sales staff in his brand new apartment.

The Seventh Avenue theatre, formerly the Atlantic Playhouse, at Seventh Avenue and 51st Street, Brooklyn, has opened up under new management. The new manager was at one time the operator at the United theatre at Flatbush Extension and Myrtle Avenue.

Sam Roth, general manager with Christmas and Roth, has announced his engagement to the most beautiful girl in Westchester County. Sam contemplates the final knot about Xmas time.

Joseph Stern's New Royal theatre at Bloomfield, N. J., will open about November 15th.

Samuel Zierler, President of The Commonwealth Film Corporation, will stage a Hallowe'en party on Friday evening, October 30th, in the offices of the Commonwealth.

Cincinnati

THE Film Exchange managers annual ball will take place at the Gibson Hotel Ball Room on Saturday evening October 24. At least by the time this issue is out it will have happened. Morris Straus, manager for Progress, is chairman of the affair and he is doing all in his power to make the affair a huge success. Others on the committee are Stanley Jacques of Pathe and J. V. Allen of Warner Brothers. Tickets are selling for one dollar and a half and a large crowd is assured. Freda Sanker and her orchestra will do the playing for the dancing as well as the accompanying for the various acts that are to be a feature of the evening.

Nick Shaefer, manager for

Producers has resigned. His place at the present writing has not as yet been filled.

J. S. Jassey, president of Progress Pictures Corporation was in the city last week and spent some time with Morris Strauss, local manager, discussing their new product.

John Gregory of the Colonial theatre, Springfield, O., spent several days around film row.

V. E. Gilfoil of the Virginia theatre, Wellston, O., was another exhibitor who honored the film building with his presence last week.

J. S. Davis of the Westland theatre, Portsmouth, O., bought several features while here last week.

There is always a great deal of commotion around the film buildings when Ed Paul, representing the Gus Sun interests of Springfield, O., comes around. This time it was no exception, but the effort is always worth the while for Paul usually books many pictures on each visit.

Many out of town exhibitors attended the second annual ball given by the Film Managers Association. It must have been a case of Johnny the head usher you run the theatre while I dance, for practically all of the prominent exhibitors from the surrounding territory were here, and a good time was had by all.

Chas. Reagan, district manager

for Paramount has moved his offices to Indianapolis. Charlie is married and wants to be at home more and it is in Indianapolis that Charlie's family lives.

Mildred Boclege, former secretary to Chas. Reagan, district manager for Famous Players has become secretary to C. E. Peppiatt, branch manager. She took up her duties after the resignation of Miss Keck, the former secretary.

Fred Tines of the Columbia theatre, Portsmouth, O., was seen around film row last week.

Rena Leaky, the most popular young lady at the Paramount offices has taken up horseback riding for a pastime.

Chicago

MANAGER WALLACE of United Artists' Chicago office, in order to give best possible service to exhibitors and keep in closer touch with the large territory under the jurisdiction of the Chicago exchange, has appointed three territorial sales supervisors. Lyman Ballard, former Wisconsin salesman, as sales supervisor of Wisconsin with headquarters in Milwaukee; Fred Martin, sales supervisor of Indiana with headquarters in Chicago; and Frank Young, sales supervisor for Illinois, with headquarters in Chicago. E. A. McLain has arrived from Los Angeles to join the local sales staff and has been assigned to Northern Indiana, and W. T. Cuddy, formerly publicity manager, goes to Wisconsin as a salesman.

H. P. Wolfberg, former Chicago film executive with a host of friends in this city, now connected with Metro-Goldwyn, with headquarters in New York City, was a visitor during the week.

Eddie Trinz has taken over the Calumet Theatre at 92nd and South Chicago Avenue and will operate it as a combined picture and vaudeville house. For some time the theatre had been operating as a stock house. Mr. Trinz is manager of Lubliner & Trinz's big north side Pantheon, and, it is understood, will continue in that capacity.

Mitchell & Allen have set October 27th as the general date for their new five hundred seat motion picture house, the Westmount at Westmount, Illinois.

Roy Alexander, who came from Kansas City one year ago October 19th to take over the management of Universal's Chicago exchange, has renewed his contract as manager for one year, starting January 1st, 1926. During the twelve months that Mr. Alexander has occupied the manager's chair at the Chicago exchange, he has made a splendid record in the amount of business produced. It may also be said that he has won for himself a host of friends among exhibitors.

J. R. McPherson is now connected with the Chicago office of the ational Screen Service, Inc. Mr. Pherson up to two years ago, was located in this city, where he was treasurer of Balaban & Katz's Tivoli Theatre, from where he went to Hollywood to appear in pictures.

I. L. Leserman, who for many years was manager of the Chicago office of Universal Film exchange, Inc., has been visiting along film row for the past two weeks. He is now connected with the Tamiami Realty Company of Tampa, Fla.

Jack Sampson of F. B. O., who is president of the Film Board of Trade, has returned from a visit to New York in the interests of the Film Board of Trade. While there he conferred with Will Hays and Charles Pettijohn, and executives of the leading film companies.

Ellis Rees, a newcomer in the film business, has purchased the

Ethel Shannon, engaged for the leading feminine role in "The Phantom Express," a Royal picture for release by Henry Ginsberg Distributing Corporation.

Gem Theatre at Plymouth, which has been closed for some time, and is remodeling and redecorating the house, which he expects to open at an early date. Mr. Rees is the ex-postmaster of Winnemac, Ind.

Ben Lukasewski, proprietor of the Honeymoon Theatre, South

fiend, has taken over and reopened the Century Theatre in Mishawaka, Indiana.

Sanf Warwick, popular Sheldon, Illinois, theatre man has gone to Florida where he will spend the winter.

Walter Brown, for the last year, booker at F. B. O., has been promoted to salesman and assigned to the Illinois territory formerly covered by G. G. Gregory, resigned. Mark Koenig, who started as assistant shipping clerk of F. B. O.'s Chicago exchange and worked himself up, takes Mr. Brown's job as booker.

The Lincoln Theatre, Valpariso, which was closed owing to financial troubles, has been taken over by Manager Nichols who will operate it on a high class picture policy.

Cress Smith, for the past year, United Artists' district manager, with headquarters in Chicago has been transferred to United Artists' home office in New York City.

According to real estate editors of the daily papers, the announcement that Andrew Karzas would erect a big motion picture house at 79th and Cottage Grove Avenue, have caused great activity in nearby property and already a three story apartment and office building to cost in the neighborhood of $150,000, has been announced for the corner across the street from the proposed motion picture theatre.

Des Moines

PACE and Bauma have bought the Princess Theatre at West Union. The Opera House at Corning, formerly owned by Hal Kelly has also changed hands.

A. W. Kahn was established as the new manager of the Des Moines office of Pathe on October 12, succeeding R. F. Ballentyne who won a very nice promotion to the position of district manager in the southern part of the country. Mr. Kahn has been manager of Educational for the past four or five years, ever since the opening of the office in Des Moines. Mr. Kahn took with him to the Pathe organization one of his star salesmen, O. H. Garland, who will take charge of the sale of two reel subjects in the

southern part of the state. The northern part of the state is covered by Mr. McEwen. Mr. Garland is an addition to the sales staff of Pathe.

J. W. Ross, formerly salesman for Universal has joined the staff of First National and will cover Iowa territory for them. No plans are made by Universal to put a man in Mr. Ross' place. Mr. Allison, who came from the Kansas City office to take the place of booker, has on his staff Al Yarowsky who recently won promotion from the shipping department. It is the general impression that Al worked hard and deserved this recognition of his endeavors. Harry Stephens now wrestles the boxes in the shipping department.

Another change in the Universal office is in the cashier's cage where Elsworth Hull was replaced by M. Lee, recruited from outside the film business. Mr. Hull has signed up with another film exchange.

G. H. Young of Pella has taken over the Monroe Theatre at Monroe. He bought the house from G. H. Dehoet.

Helen Ditzler who used to be with Pathe in the stenographic department and was transferred to the Chicago office, has returned to Des Moines. She left last June.

Grace Gannon has returned to the office of F. B. O. where she formerly held the office of stenographer.

Mr. Blair, special representative from the home office, has been visiting Pathe.

Fern Derting is now the head inspector for Universal. She takes the place of Hazel George who accepted an offer made by the First National office to take the place as head inspector there.

Visitors in Movie Row were John Anderson, of Boone, who was still in good spirits after having attended the American Legion convention in Omaha, Bill Treloar of the Opera House at Ogden and Mr. C. C. Dunsmoor of Marshalltown who brought Mrs. Dunsmoor with him.

F. C. Aiken, district manager of Pathe, visited the Des Moines office. He went from Des Moines to the Omaha exchange.

San Francisco

THE newly organized Children's theatre will give a series of plays each Saturday at the Players' Guild theatre, 1715 Bush street. Mrs. John I. Cuddy is the director of the theatre and prominent children's motion picture plays will be shown.

A marriage license was recently issued to George Milton Lip-

schultz, orchestra leader at Loew's Warfield and Mrs. Joan Schirmer.

A new $25,000 theatre will rise on the site of the present Ocean View theatre. It has just been announced. All the latest improvements possible will be put into this small house.

Salesmanager Patridge of the local Paramount office has returned from a trip in Central California.

Herman Wobber, district manager for Paramount in this section was given a nice send off by his friends before he started for his European trip.

Max Dolin, considered by many the leading violinist on the Coast and leader of the famous California orchestra, was asked to olay 'Kol Nidra' at one of the recent Jewish temples at one of the recent Jewish holidays. He did so to the pleasure of the many who attended and also played on another day.

CONSTRUCTION & EQUIPMENT DEPARTMENT

Valuable Papers Read at S.M.P.E. Meeting

Program of Speakers and Entertainment Makes Convention Success; New Officers Elected

A VERY successful convention of the Society of Motion Picture Engineers came to an end October 8th, the members and guests having enjoyed a very pleasant four day meeting at the Lakewood Farm Inn, Roscoe, N. Y. The program of papers which was presented by prominent engineers on the various phases of motion picture engineering added another volume to the Library of technical data and general information that the Society has made available to the motion picture industry during its six years of activities. Also diversion was furnished the members and guests through an interesting program of sports, banquets, dancing, etc.

The various papers which were read by their authors before the Society are as follows:

"Handling of Motion Picture Film in the Field under Climatic Conditions," R. J. Flaherty; "Washing of Motion Picture Film," Kenneth Hickman; "Effects of Scratches on Strength of Motion Picture Film," S. E. Shepard and S. S. Sweet; "Importance of Village Theatre," F. H. Richardson; "Color Photography Patents," William V. D. Kelley; "A New Camera for News Screen Cinematographers," J. H. McNabb; "A New Incandescent Spot Light," L. C. Porter; "The Questionable Educational Value of the Motion Pictures," A. W. Abrams; "Movies for-Teaching: The Proof of Their Usefulness," Rowland Rogers; "Exhibitors Problem in 1925," E. T. Clark; "A Prefocusing Base and Socket for Projection Lamps," R. S. Burnap; "Transmission of Pictures Over Telephone Lines," Dr. H. E. Ives; "The High Intensity Arc," Dr. Frank Benford; "Reflector Arc Projection, Some Limitations and Possibilities in Theory and Practice," S. Stark; "Importance of Proper Splicing," E. J. Dennison; "Rack Marks and Air Bells roduced in the Development of Motion Picture Films" by J. I. Crabtree; "The Pathe Camera and Projector," W. R. Daniel.

An election of officers was held, the results showing Willard Cook of the Pathescope Company, president; M. W. Palmer, Famous Players-Lasky Corporation, Long Island City, vice-president; J. A. Summers, Edison Lamp Works, Harrison, N. J., secretary (re-elected); W. C. Hubbard of the Cooper Hewitt Co., New York City, treasurer; R. S. Peek, Director of the Canadian Motion Picture Bureau, Ottawa, Ontario, and J. H. Theis with the Dupont Company, Board of Governors.

Several of the members were fortunate in winning very desirable prizes. First prize of the Golf Tournament was awarded to

Willard B. Cook, President, S. M. P. E.

Jack Theis, Dupont Company; second prize to C. A. Ziebarth of Chicago and third

prize which was tied for by Joe Hornstein and Mr. J. A. Summers, being won by Joe Hornstein through a match-off.

The Trap Shooting contest was won by L. C. Porter of Edison Lamp Works.

High bridge honors were held by Dr. Kenneth Hickman, Royal College of Science, London, and the second honor by L. A. Jones of the Eastman Kodak Company. Among the ladies in bridge, Mrs. L. A. Jones won first prize and Mrs. L. C. Porter, second prize.

Among the high spots of the meeting was the paper presented by Dr. Herbert E. Ives of the Bell Telephone Laboratories, N. Y., on "Transmission of Pictures Over Telephone Lines." This lecture was given an added interest through use of many illustrations and photographs. Also the banquet held on Wednesday night was an affair that was greatly enjoyed by every one, along with a special motion picture show and dance.

In general, the meeting proved very successful, though the attendance was somewhat lower than at the last meeting.

View of the proscenium and organ lofts, Chapman's Alician Court theatre, Fullerton, Cal.

Paramount Student Theatre Managers at the Edison Lighting Institute

THE Class of the Paramount Theatre Managers Training School recently spent a week at the Edison Lighting Institute getting a complete course of instruction and practice in theatre lighting, arranged by John F. Barry, director of the School, with the engineers and lighting specialists of the Edison Lamp Works. The work done at the Edison Lighting Institute will complement what the students are doing at the school and at the local theatres where their practical training is held.

The week at the Edison Lighting Institute was decided upon so that advantage could be taken of the demonstration facilities that are provided there. Each lecture was accompanied by practical demonstrations of the particular principles or type of theatre lighting under discussion. Demonstrations were made with the equipment of the various departments of an up-to-date motion picture theatre. The students, therefore, were not only given thorough instruction in the principles that govern the correct lighting of theatres but were shown how these principles are practically applied.

The first part of the course reviewed the progress made in theatre lighting practice from the early periods to the present day. A detailed outline of the development of the incandescent lamp was given and an inspection made of lamp manufacturing plants. The characteristics and purposes of each type of lamp manufactured were explained so that the students have adequate knowledge of what style or type of lamp most efficiently fills each lighting requirement.

Lectures on the fundamentals of electrical engineering and on the mechanics of lighting design gave the necessary technical information applied in planning and developing individuality in the lighting of theatres.

The lighting requirements of each department of the theatre were explained in detail and typical illustrations of the recommended systems and arrangements reproduced in the Institute's demonstration rooms.

Lectures on foyer lighting dealt with the use of luminaires, pedestal lamps, and cornice lighting; the selection of hangings and wall decorations to harmonize with desired color lighting effects and the various schemes of rest room lighting that give proper predominance to decorative and restful elements.

Talks on lounge room lighting emphasized particularly the value of light as a decorative medium. Instructions were given in the art of combining colors through the use of portable lamps, spot lights, etc. to obtain desirable contrast and touches of high light.

The lighting of auditoriums was outlined and the general principles that are essential in every lighting scheme applied in this department of the theatre. This included the use of indirect and direct lighting, the application of colored light for psychological effects, orchestral lighting and the relation of light and music. It also included a special discussion on safety lighting.

Lectures and demonstrations on stage lighting covered the usage and operation of foot lights, border lights, flood lamps, "effect" apparatus, switchboard, and wiring; the production of colored lighting and the effects of colors on the appearance of objects.

The sales value of light was fully discussed in its relation to the lighting of the marquee, sign, side walls, poster boards, flood lighting, show window lighting, and other special advertising effects. The students were given special instruction in the use of the electric sign as an advertising medium. Lectures on this subject included the fundamental principles of sign lighting; the proper use of different types of electric signs; designing and spacing of letters; effect of letter size on readability of signs; general considerations in the selection of lamps for sign lighting, and wiring calculations.

Time was given to the study of projection to complement the thorough course in Projection which will be given at the school by Harry Rubin, projection expert of the Famous Players-Lasky Corporation Theatre Department. The theory of various projection devices now in use and the fundamental phenomena of optics were explained. The study of optics covered reflection, refraction, the use of parabolic reflectors, spherical mirrors, and other reflecting projection devices; the control of lighting by lenses, chromatic apparatus, etc. and a study of the tonal quality of light emitted from different projection sources. The adaptability of incandescent lamp projection to various sizes of theatres, tests of optical systems and the operation of incandescent lamp projection equipment was given special attention.

The course is intensely practical and contained much material directly applicable by the theatre manager. For example, in the concluding session a talk was given on "Lighting for Stage Prologues" in which actual demonstrations were made of standard stage equipment in service and details given on very simple methods by which numerous effects such as twinkling stars, lightning, rainbows, etc. can be produced at practically no expense. Another topic in this session was "Light and Music." This is a subject to which much thought has been given and one of vital interest to the motion picture organization. On the miniature stage available at the Lighting Institute is equipment for producing fine gradations of color. This was utilized in connection with music. Of course, for the symphony orchestra a phonograph must be substituted, but nevertheless the demonstration is exceedingly effective. Several well known compositions were analyzed as to motives and the most appropriate color treatment, and then the principles set forth visualized in actual use.

The students, accompanied by Mr. Barry and Mr. Myrick of the Paramount School, reported each morning of the week at the Lighting Institute and spent the entire day there.

New Daytona Theatre Has Premiere

The Florida Theatre, of Daytona Beach, Fla., beautiful new Famous Players house, opened recently with a program indicative of the high type of entertainment they expect to offer, and an array of prominent speakers to give the new house a most fitting send-off.

The house seats over 1,800, with a large balcony arrangement. It is built on the Colonial Spanish type. The lobby is done in mahogany, with walls of stone and a beamed ceiling, and the floor is laid with pink Tennessee marble. The foyer and auditorium are heavily carpeted in a mulberry shade, and the color scheme for the interior is principally ivory and grey with border effects in polychrome having a touch of gold. The lighting equipment, considered only secondary in importance today to the music of a theatre, is in three colors which may be changed imperceptibly to amber, red or blue. The degree of illumination used in the auditorium is many times greater than used to be considered sufficient for the interior of a house, but in no way destroys the efficiency of the projection, since all lighting is indirect, diffused, and well-shaded. The lobby is brightly illuminated, but there are no bulbs in view. The light comes from a 1,000 watt electric bulb placed at the top of the box office providing indirect but thorough illumination.

Photo snapped on the roof of the Nicholas Power plant when the Paramount theatre managers school met there recently for a special series of lectures on projection. Seated in the center is P. A. McGuire of Nicholas Power and on his immediate left is J. F. Barry, director of the School and Harry Rubin, chief projectionist of the Rivoli, Rialto and Criterion theatres, New York

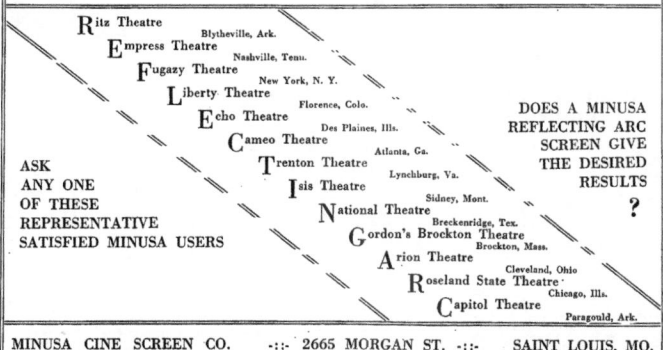

Projection
Optics, Electricity, Practical Ideas & advice

Inquiries and Comments

An Editorial Bid

UY E. McALLAN who hails from Millicent, Alta. (Canada) and signs himself Motion Picture Projection Engineer writes in offering his services as Associate Editor in conducting a "Hints to Projectionists" column, providing we pay him his "usual rate." He doesn't state, however, what his "usual rate" is so we are somewhat in the dark concerning this important point.

Here is his letter:

"Dear Sir—I am writing you to see if you can use a series of helps for projectionists as per enclosed samples. I ran such a series for about eight months in the 'Canadian Moving Picture Digest' during 1924."

We are sorry, Friend McAllan, but the Officers of this Journal feel that having one Projection Editor on the payroll is just about all the game can stand. Sometimes the results of even this one editor are doubtful, for projectionists are notoriously poor correspondents and practically the only indication as to whether or not the stuff is getting across is from the way inquiries for information and offer of ideas come in to the office.

The average person is quick to criticize but loathe to help.

Advertise Yourself

We feel that by offering the use of these columns to projectionists for discussions and debates that we are giving them a good chance to advertise themselves in a national way, which, in the long run is worth far more than slight monetary benefits which might be obtained by their shopping around for someone to buy their ideas and editorial services.

McAllan sent in a couple of his "ideas" as samples and we are taking the liberty of giving them here for what they are worth —having written him beforehand of course, that we intended to do so.

Idea number one has to do with the glare from e it lights and states that it can often be reduced without impairing the visibility by inserting a sheet or two of orange colored glass behind the red glass of the sign. The orange glass, he states, can be obtained from any dealer in photographic supplies.

Toning High Intensity Light

The second idea relates to improving the color quality of the light from the high intensity are which, as is commonly known, is of a harsh chalky white and renders the true reproduction of colors and tonal values in the original print practically impossible.

According to McAllan, "a slight trace of amber color will tone down the white and give it a more pleasing tone. A ray filter for this purpose can be easily made as follows: Get an old photographic plate and remove all trace of the emulsion by washing in hot soda water. When thoroughly dry and clean it may be given a bath of orange color as follows:

"Obtain some orange diamond dye and make up a solution which should be allowed to flow over the plate until it has the proper degree of color. The proper shade of orange can only be determined by experiment, as the color density will vary with the amperage being used. Just enough color should be used to get away from the rather greenish white of the high intensity arc.

"When the plate is ready, mount it up against the front of the projection lens . . ."

If space permitted we could offer a few ideas of our own for tempering the white light of the high intensity arc in addition to describing some interesting stunts tried out by other people. However, we will have to pass this up until some other time.

As far as we are able to determine offhand, McAllan's "cure" should be all right up to a certain point. It might or it might not work. He doesn't state whether his particular "dyed plate" idea has actually been tried, or not. Somewhat similar efforts have already been made with varying degrees of success—and failure. However, let it ride —for the moment.

Where Can He Get It?

John F. Kraczek, Milwaukee, Mo., is exceedingly anxious to learn where he can purchase a copy of "Motion Picture Projection," by James R. Cameron.

He states that he has placed an order for one of these handbooks with his local dealer and, after a wait of two months, has not yet received it.

As far as we know this book is being sold, or distributed, only by dealers in motion picture supplies, so if your local dealer hasn't it, the obvious thing to do is to write to a dealer in another town. We would

suggest, therefore, Friend Kraczek, that you try the supply companies of Chicago or New York, if you still desire this particular book.

Who's "Ad" Was This?

That wonderful little part of our anatomy, called the brain, sometimes plays us tricks by refusing to function when most necessary. It appears that Harry S. Miller, Ford City, Pa., is in this predicament, as you can judge from his letter.

"Dear Sir:—I wish to ask a favor of you. Some months ago I noticed an 'ad' in your section of a concern that specialized in cleaning and renovating screens. Somehow I lost that issue and cannot recall just what issue carried this ad. Furthermore, I cannot even remember the name or address of the company whose ad that was.

"My screen rather needs painting badly, and as I have a gold fibre screen, I would like to get the address of the company who sells this painting material for screens."

Step Up, Advertisers!

Well, Friend Miller, we do not know the particular company who advertised that screen preparation, so we are broadcasting your appeal through these columns in the hope that the particular advertiser in question will step forth and announce himself. If he doesn't, you may rest assured that others will.

Motiograph Issues New Projector Catalogue

The Enterprise Optical Company, manufacturers of the Motiograph DeLuxe Projectors and projection equipment have recently issued a finely arranged and attractive catalogue. It is a work of art in itself and tells in detail about the new model projectors, are lamps, lamp housings, high intensity lamps, etc. Full specifications are also given.

Hertner Electric Company Reports Increase

The Hertner Electric Company reports that there is a very marked increase in the purchase of Transverters for the coming season.

The company have just recently received orders from the following theatres:

Bluebird Theatre, Baltimore, Md.; Merlin Theatre, Duquesne, Penn.; Midwood Theatre and Park Theatre, both at Brooklyn, N. Y., and Bellevue Theatre at West Roxbury, Mass.

These orders originate through N. C. Haefele and Company, Baltimore, Md.; Hollis, Smith, Morton Co., Pittsburgh, Pa.; Howells Cine Equipment Co., New York, and United Theatre Equipment Co., Boston, Mass.

Stern Enterprises Building in New Jersey

In addition to the chain of theatres already established by the Joseph Stern Theatrical Enterprises its plans call for one house to be constructed and five now being erected which will be opened shortly after the first of the year.

The houses in construction at present are the Ritz, Springfield Ave., Newark, a two thousand seat house which will open on February first, the Royal theatre, Bloomfield, a two thousand seat house which will run both vaudeville and pictures, open Jan. 1, the Sanford theatre. Irvington, also with a vaudeville and picture policy which seats eighteen hundred to open Jan. 15, the Red Bank in Red Bank, vaudeville and pictures with a two thousand seating capacity which opens March 1, and the Cranford, a fifteen hundred seat house which will run pictures only.

A site has been secured at 63-73 Kearny Ave. and 52-56 Maple Street, Kearny, N. J. which plot comprises 150 x 200 feet; an eighteen hundred seat vaudeville and picture house with six stores will be erected at a cost of $275,000, and will be opened March first.

Blackstone Amusement Co. Negotiate Lease

R. L. Willis, who is erecting one of the largest suburban motion picture theatres at Thirty-eighth and Main streets, Kansas City, took title to the building site last week. The property, 165 x 65 feet, was deeded by John B. Kassebaum to Mr. Willis. Mr. Willis is erecting the theatre to comply with the terms of a 25-year lease to the Blackstone Amusement Company, of which George Trinastich is president. The lease, filed for record, calls for an annual rental of $16,500 for the first five years of the term and

$18,000 a year for the remainder of the twenty-five years. Footings and foundation of the theatre already have been completed. The theatre will be a Spanish type building, designed by the architectural firm of DeFoe & Beseeke and will have a seating capacity of 3,000. An attempt will be made to have the house in operation by January 1. The Blackstone Amusement Company also operates the Isis theatre of Kansas City. Jack Roth, manager of that house, also will be in charge of the new theatre.

Ray Fernstrom with his camera equipped with a two inch f-1. 9 Ultrastigmat lens.

Stern Enterprises Building in New Jersey

The $2,000,000 St. Louis Theatre, Grand boulevard at Morgan street, the grand opening of which has been delayed from time to time, is scheduled to throw open its doors within a very short time now according to the latest advices.

The building was erected by the Metropolitan Theatres Corporation of which David Sommers is president; Sam Koplar, vice-president; Emil S. Strauss, treasurer, and Lambert E. Walther, director. It will seat 4,200 persons.

Several months ago the theatre was leased to the Orpheum circuit and will be used as a combination vaudeville and picture house. It adjoins the Grand Central Theatre, owned by Skouras Brothers Enterprises, while but across Lucas avenue is the Missouri Theatre, owned by Paramount and Balaban & Katz. Walther is also a director in the St. Louis Amusement Company controlled by Skouras Brothers and Harry Koplar.

Andrew Pegu to Build New Vermont Theatre

Contracts were awarded this week for the new theatre in St. Johnsbury, Vt., to be built by Andrew Pegu of that city at a cost of between $140,000 and $150,000. Architects Haynes & Mason of Fitchburg, Mass., drew the plans. The theatre will be one of the largest in the Green Mountain state and it is expected that it will be completed in about a year. John Bergeron of Keene, N. H., has the building contract.

Two of the murals in Paramount's Metropolitan theatre Boston. The figure on the left represents "Pantomime" and that on the right "Sacred."

Theatre Construction On Increase in St. Louis Zone

THE Arsenal Theatre, Grand boulevard at Arsenal street, St. Louis, Mo., plans to erect a handsome steel canopy in front of the house. It commands South Grand boulevard for many blocks. The St. Louis Amusement Company are the owners.

The Jonesboro Amusement Company, Ark., will soon take bids on a $100,000 motion picture and vaudeville theatre to be erected at Church and Monroe streets.

The house will be 75 by 120 feet and of steel, stone, concrete and terra cotta construction. E. J. Wolpert is the architect.

Tony Sudekum, president of the Crescent Amusement Company, Nashville, Tenn., has had plans prepared for a $50,000 theatre for Shelbyville, Tenn. It will be erected on the site of the present opera house.

William Schrader plans to erect a $75,000 motion picture and vaudeville house in Sterling, Ill. The plans prepared by Bradley & Bradley, 520 Brown Building, Sterling, call for a house two-story and basement, 50 by 135 feet. It will be of brick, concrete and stone construction.

The Columbia Theatre at Sixth and St. Charles street and the adjoining Strand Theatre will be demolished shortly to make way for a four-story store building for the McCrory Stores Corporation of New York. The company recently obtained a 99-year lease on the property at an annual rental of $110,000. The fee is owned by the Columbia Theatre Company and the Supreme Realty Company controlled by Frank Tate and Charley Cella.

T. W. Sharp of Little Rock, Ark., has awarded the contracts on his new theatre to be erected at 620 Beech street. Jenkins & Apple, 215 West Second street, Little Rock, are the contractors. The house will be two-story, 44 by 140 and cost about $50,000.

World Ticket Supply Co. Report New Sales

The World Ticket and Supply Company are reporting an increase on the sale of Simplex Ticket Registers this season. They have been installed in many of the new theatres which include the Capitol at Newark, Pollack and Bratter's Hawthorne, Newark, N. J., The Kinema, Brooklyn, N. Y., and Charlie Goldreyer's New Manor, Brooklyn, N. Y.

It is claimed that the new model register has several improvements over the past one and the sales force is being enlarged in anticipation of a big season ahead.

Advertising in the Equipment Department Pays

FEATURE RELEASE CHART

Productions are Listed Alphabetically and by Months in which Released in order that the Exhibitor may have a short-cut toward such information as he may need. Short subject and comedy releases, as well as information on pictures that are coming, will be found on succeeding pages. (S. R. indicates State Right release.)

Refer to THE MOTION PICTURE NEWS BOOKING GUIDE for Productions Listed Prior to March

MARCH

Feature	Star	Distributed by	Length	Reviewed
Adventurous Sex, The	Clara Bow	Assoc. Exhib.	5039 feet	Mar. 21
Air Mail, The	Special Cast	Paramount	6976 feet	Mar. 28
Beauty and the Bad Man	Special Cast	Prod. Dist. Corp	5794 feet	May 9
Beyond the Border	Harry Carey	Prod. Dist. Corp	4469 feet	April 25
Billy, The Kid	Franklyn Farnum	Inde. Pict. Corp. (S. R.)	4800 feet	
Blood and Steel	Desmond Holmes	Inde. Pict. (S. R.)	5300 feet	
Border Justice	Bill Cody	Inde. Pict. Corp. (S. R.)	5432 feet	Nov. 8
Coast Patrol, The	Kenneth McDonald	Barsky (S. R.)	5000 feet	
Confessions of a Queen	Terry-Stone	Metro-Goldwyn	5820 feet	April 4
Crimson Runner, The	Priscilla Dean	Prod. Dist. Corp	4775 feet	June 6
Daddy's Gone A'Hunting	Joyce-Marmont	Metro-Goldwyn	5851 feet	Mar. 7
Denial, The	Special Cast	Metro-Goldwyn	4791 feet	Mar. 21
Double Action Daniels	Buffalo Bill, Jr.	Weiss Bros. (S. R.)	4650 feet	
Dressmaker from Paris, The	Rod La Rocque	Paramount	7080 feet	Mar. 28
Fighting Romeo, A	Al Ferguson	Davis Dist. Div. (S.R.)	5000 feet	Aug. 15
Fighting the Flames	Haines-Devore	C. B. C. (S. R.)	5800 feet	
Forbidden Cargo	Evelyn Brent	F. B. O	4850 feet	April 11
Goose Hangs High, The	Constance Bennett	Paramount	6186 feet	Feb. 14
Great Divide, The	Terry-Tearle	Metro-Goldwyn	7811 feet	Feb. 21
Head Winds	House Peters	Universal	5600 feet	Mar. 28
Hunted Woman, The	Seena Owen	Fox	4954 feet	April 4
I Want My Man	Sills-Kenyon	First National	6175 feet	April 18
Jimmie's Millions	Richard Talmadge	F. B. O	5167 feet	Feb. 28
Just Traveling	Bob Burns	Sierra Pict. (S. R.)	4400 feet	
Last Laugh, The	Emil Jannings	Universal	6519 feet	Dec. 20
Let'er Buck	Hoot Gibson	Universal	5547 feet	Jan. 3
Mad Whirl, The	May McAvoy	Universal	6184 feet	Dec. 6
Marriage in Transit	Edmund Lowe	Fox Film	4800 feet	April 11
Men and Women	Special Cast	Paramount	6223 feet	Mar. 28
Monster, The	L. Chaney-J. Arthur	Metro-Goldwyn	6435 feet	Feb. 28
My Wife and I	Special Cast	Warner Bros	6700 feet	June 6
New Lives for Old	Betty Compson	Paramount	6796 feet	Mar. 7
New Toys	Richard Barthelmess	First National	7250 feet	Feb. 21
One Year to Live	Special Cast	First National	6064 feet	Feb. 28
Percy	Charles Ray	Assoc. Exhib	5384 feet	Feb 28
Playing With Souls	Special Cast	First National	5831 feet	Mar. 14
Price of Pleasure, The	Valli-Kerry	Universal	6618 feet	June 13
Recompense	M. Prevost-M. Blue	Warner Bros	7480 feet	May 2
Renegade Holmes, M.D.	Ben Wilson	Arrow (S. R.)	4947 feet	
Riders of the Purple Sage	Tom Mix	Fox	5578 feet	Mar. 28
Romance and Rustlers	Yakima Canutt	Arrow (S. R.)	4994 feet	Nov. 15
Sackcloth and Scarlet	Alice Terry	Paramount	6732 feet	Mar. 7
Sally	Colleen Moore	First National	8636 feet	Mar. 28
Scar Hanan	Yakima Canutt	F. B. O	4684 feet	April 4
Scarlet Honeymoon, The	Shirley Mason	Fox	5080 feet	Mar. 21
Seven Chances	Buster Keaton	Metro-Goldwyn	5113 feet	Mar. 28
Sign of the Cactus, The	Jack Hoxie	Universal	4938 feet	Jan. 10
Sky Raider, The	Capt. Charles Nungesser	Assoc. Exhib.	6638 feet	April 4
Speed	Betty Blythe	Banner Prod. (S. R.)	6000 feet	May 30
Too Many Kisses	Richard Dix	Paramount	5759 feet	Mar. 14
Waking Up the Town	Jack Pickford	United Artists	4802 feet	April 11
Where Romance Rides	Dick Hatton	Arrow	4301 feet	
Zander the Great	Marion Davies	Metro-Goldwyn	5851 feet	May 16

APRIL

Feature	Star	Distributed by	Length	Reviewed
Adventure	P. Starke-T. Moore	Paramount	6713 feet	April 25
After Business Hours	Hammerstein-Tellegen	C. B. C. (S. R.)	5800 feet	
Bandit Tamer, The	Franklyn Farnum	Inde. Pict. (S. R.)	5000 feet	
Border Vengeance	Jack Perrin	Madoc Sales (S. R.)	4500 feet	
Charmer, The	Pola Negri	Paramount	6076 feet	April 18
Code of the West	O. Moore-C. Bennett	Paramount	6777 feet	April 25
Courageous Fool, The	Reed Howes	Rayart (S. R.)		
Crowded Hour, The	Bebe Daniels	Paramount	6558 feet	May 9
Dangerous Innocence	LaPlante-E. O'Brien	Universal	6759 feet	Mar. 21
Declasse	Corinne Griffith	First National	7869 feet	April 4
Eyes of the Desert	Al Richmond	Sierra Prod. (S. R.)	4500 feet	
Fifth Avenue Models	Philbin-Kerry	Universal	6581 feet	Jan. 24
Fighting Parson, The	Al Ferguson	Davis Dist. Div. (S.R.)	5000 feet	
Fighting Sheriff, The	Bill Cody	Inde. Pict. (S. R.)	4500 feet	May 30
Friendly Enemies	Weber and Fields	Prod. Dist. Corp	6288 feet	May 9
Galloping Vengeance	Bob Custer	F. B. O	5095 feet	April 11
Getting 'Em Right	George Larkin	Rayart (S. R.)	4669 feet	
Gold and the Girl	Buck Jones	Fox	4521 feet	April 4
Go Straight	Gladys Hulette	B. P. Schulberg (S.R.)	6107 feet	May 23
Heart of a Siren, The	Barbara La Marr	First National	6700 feet	Mar. 21
How Baxter Butted In	M. Moore-D. Devore	Warner Bros	6650 feet	July 11
Justice Raffles	Henry Edwards	Cranfield & Clarke (S. R.)	6000 feet	
Kiss in the Dark, A	Special Cast	Paramount	5767 feet	April 18
Kiss Me Again	M. Prevost-M. Blue	Warner Bros	7200 feet	June 6
Love's Bargain	M. Daw-C. Brook	F. B. O	5641 feet	April 25
Madame Sans Gene	Gloria Swanson	Paramount	9994 feet	May 2
Man and Maid	Special Cast	Metro-Goldwyn	5307 feet	April 18
My Son	Nazimova-J. Pickford	First National	6500 feet	April 25
Night Club, The	R. Griffith-V. Reynolds	Paramount	5732 feet	May 16
One Way Street	Special Cast	First National	5596 feet	April 11
Proud Flesh	Special Cast	Metro-Goldwyn	5770 feet	April 25
Roaring Adventure, The	Jack Hoxie	Universal	4657 feet	Feb. 14
Ridin' Comet, The	Yakima Canutt	F. B. O	4354 feet	May 16
Rough Going	Franklyn Farnum	Indep. Pict. Corp. (S. R.)	4800 feet	
Shackled Lightning	Frank Merrill	Hercules Prod. (S. R.)		
She Wolves	Alma Rubens	Fox	5713 feet	May 9
Spaniard, The	Cortez-Goudal	Paramount	6676 feet	April 18
Sporting Venus	Special Cast	Metro-Goldwyn	5938 feet	May 23
Stop Flirting	Special Cast	Prod. Dist. Corp	5161 feet	June 6
Straight Through	Wm. Desmond	Universal	4867 feet	
Tale of a Thousand and One Nights	Special Cast	Davis Dist. Div. (S. R.)	6500 feet	Feb. 14
Tearing Through	Richard Talmadge	F. B. O.	4714 feet	May 23
That Devil Quemado	Fred Thomson	F. B. O.	4768 feet	April 4
Two-Fisted Sheriff, A	Yakima Canutt	Arrow (S. R.)	4149 feet	Dec. 6
Way of a Girl, The	Boardman-M. Moore	Metro-Goldwyn	5025 feet	April 18
Western Engagement, A	Dick Hatton	Arrow		
Wings of Youth	Madge Bellamy	Fox	5340 feet	May 16
Winning a Woman	Perrin-Hill	Rayart (S. R.)	4865 feet	

MAY

Feature	Star	Distributed by	Length	Reviewed
Alias Mary Flynn	Evelyn Brent	F. B. O.	5559 feet	May 30
Any Woman	Alice Terry	Paramount	5963 feet	June 13
Awful Truth, The	Agnes Ayres	Prod. Dist. Corp	5917 feet	July 11
Bandit's Baby, The	Fred Thomson	F. B. O.	5291 feet	June 20
Baree Son of Kazan	Wolf (dog)	Vitagraph	7 reels	May 2
Barriers of the Law	Holmes-Desmond	Indep. Pict. (S. R.)	5400 feet	
Burning Trail, The	William Desmond	Universal	4783 feet	April 18
Chickie	Mackaill-Bosworth	First National	7767 feet	May 9
Crackerjack, The	Johnny Hines	C. C. Burr (S. R.)	6500 feet	May 23
Every Man's Wife	Special Cast	Fox	4365 feet	July 4
Eve's Lover	Irene Rich	Warner Bros	6540 feet	Aug. 8
Eve's Secret	Betty Compson	Paramount	6305 feet	May 9
Fear Fighter, The	Billy Sullivan	Rayart (S. R.)		
Fighting Demon, The	Richard Talmadge	F B O	5470 feet	June 20
Fugitive, The	Ben Wilson	Arrow	4892 feet	
Golden Trails		Sanford Prod. (S. R.)	5 reels	
His Supreme Moment	B Sweet-R Colman	First National	6600 feet	April 25
Lilies of the Streets	J. Walker-V. L. Corbin	F. B. O.	7160 feet	April 25
Little French Girl, The	Alice Joyce	Paramount	5628 feet	June 13
Lunatic at Large, A	Henry Edwards	Cranfield & Clarke (S. R.)	6000 feet	
Makers of Men	Kenneth McDonald	Barsky Prod. (S. R.)	5000 feet	
Necessary Evil, The	Dana-Lyon	First National	6307 feet	May 23
Old Home Week	Thomas Meighan	Paramount	6888 feet	June 6
Phantom Rider, The	Al Richmond	Sierra Prod. (S. R.)	4750 feet	
Private Affairs	Special Cast	Prod. Dist. Corp	6132 feet	Aug. 15
Quick Change	George Larkin	Rayart (S. R.)		
Raffles, The Amateur Cracksman	House Peters	Universal	5557 feet	May 30
Rainbow Trail, The	Tom Mix	Fox	5251 feet	April 25
Red Love	Lowell-Russell	Lowell Film Prod. (S. R.)	6500 feet	May 23
Saddle Hawk, The	Hoot Gibson	Universal	5468 feet	Mar 7
Silent Sanderson	Harry Carey	Prod. Dist. Corp	4841 feet	June 20
Scandal Proof	Shirley Mason	Fox	4400 feet	June 6
School for Wives	Tearle-Holmquist	Vitagraph	6750 feet	April 11
Shock Punch, The	Richard Dix	Paramount	6151 feet	May 23
Snob Buster, The	Reed Howes	Rayart (S. R.)		
Soul Fire	Barthelmess-B Love	First National	8262 feet	May 16
Speed Wild	Maurice B "Lefty" Flynn	F. B. O	4700 feet	June 20
Talker, The	A Nilsson-L Stone	First National	7861 feet	May 23
Texas Bearcat, The	Bob Custer	F. B. O	4770 feet	
Tides of Passion	Mae Marsh	Vitagraph	6279 feet	May 9
Up the Ladder	Virginia Valli	Universal	6023 feet	Jan 31
Welcome Home	Special Cast	Paramount	5909 feet	May 30
White Fang	Strongheart (dog)	F. B. O	6579 feet	June 20
White Thunder	Yakima Canutt	F. B. O.	4550 feet	
Wildfire	Special Cast	Vitagraph	6 reels	June 20
Wolves of the Road	Yakima Canutt	Arrow	4375 feet	
Woman's Faith	Reubens-Marmont	Universal	6023 feet	Aug 15
Woman Hater, The	Helene Chadwick	Warner Brothers	7000 feet	Aug. 22

JUNE

Feature	Star	Distributed by	Length	Reviewed
Are Parents People?	Bronson-Vidor	Paramount	6586 feet	June 6
Dangerous Odds	Bill Cody	Inde. Pict. (S. R.)	4800 feet	
Desert Flower, The	Colleen Moore	First National	6837 feet	June 13
Double Fisted	Jack Perrin	Rayart (S. R.)		
Down the Border	Al Richmond	Sierra Prod. (S. R.)	4750 feet	
Faint Perfume	Seena Owen	B. P. Schulberg (S.R.)	6228 feet	July 11
Grounds for Divorce	Florence Vidor	Paramount	5712 feet	July 4
Happy Warrior, The		Vitagraph	6075 feet	July 18
Hearts and Spurs	Buck Jones	Fox	4600 feet	June 20
Human Tornado, The	Yakima Canutt	F. B. O.	4472 feet	
I'll Show You the Town	Reginald Denny	Universal	7400 feet	June 6
Introduce Me	Douglas MacLean	Assoc. Exhib.	5980 feet	Mar. 21
Just a Woman	Windsor-Tearle	First National	6300 feet	June 6
Light of Western Stars	Special Cast	Paramount	6652 feet	July 4
Lost—a Wife	Special Cast	Paramount	6420 feet	June 27
Making of O'Malley, The	Milton Sills	First National	7571 feet	July 4
Man from Lone Mountain, The	Ben Wilson	Arrow	4530 feet	
Man in Blue	Herbert Rawlinson	Universal	5708 feet	Feb. 21
Marry Me	Special Cast	Paramount	5586 feet	
Meddler, The	William Desmond	Universal	4890 feet	May 23
Mist in the Valley	Alma Taylor	Cranfield & Clarke (S. R.)	5500 feet	
My Lady's Lips	Clara Bow	B. P. Schulberg (S.R.)	6609 feet	Aug 15
Off the Highway	Bowers-De La Motte	Prod. Dist.	7641 feet	
Paths to Paradise	Compson-R. Griffith	Paramount	6741 feet	June 27
Pioneers of the West		Sanford Prod. (S. R.)	5 reels	
Ridin' Easy	Dick Hatton	Arrow	4483 feet	
Ridin' Thunder	Jack Hoxie	Universal	4351 feet	May 30

Feature	Star	Distributed by	Length	Reviewed
Rough Stuff	George Larkin	Rayart (S. R.)		
Shattered Lives	Special Cast	Gotham (S. R.)	6 reels	July 4
Smooth as Satin	Evelyn Brent	F. B. O	6003 feet	July 4
Texas Trail, The	Harry Carey	Prod. Dist. Corp	4720 feet	July 18
Tracked in the Snow Country	Rin-Tin-Tin (dog)	Warner Brothers	6900 feet	Aug. 1
White Monkey, The	La Marr-T. Holding	First National	6121 feet	July 4
Wild Bull's Lair, The	Fred Thompson	F. B. O.	5280 feet	Aug. 15
Youth's Gamble	Reed Howes	Rayart (S. R.)	5264 feet	

JULY

Feature	Star	Distributed by	Length	Reviewed
Bloodhound, The	Bob Custer	F. B. O.	4789 feet	
Cold Nerve	Bill Cody	Inde. Pict. (S. R.)	5000 feet	
Danger Signal, The	Jane Novak	Columbia Pict. (S.R.)	5502 feet	Aug. 15
Don Daredevil	Jack Hoxie	Universal	4610 feet	
Drug Store Cowboy, The	Franklyn Farnum	Ind. Pict. Corp. (S.R.)	5100 feet	Feb. 7
Duped	Holmes-Desmond	Ind. Pict. (S. R.)	5400 feet	
Fighting Youth		Columbia Pict. (S.R.)		
Lady Who Lied, The	L. Stone-V. Valli	First National	7111 feet	July 18
Lady Robinhood	Evelyn Brent	F. B. O	5582 feet	Aug 22
Manicure Girl, The	Bebe Daniels	Paramount	5959 feet	June 27
Marriage Whirl, The	C. Griffith-H. Ford	First National	7672 feet	July 25
Mysterious Stranger, The	Richard Talmadge	F. B. O	5270 feet	
Night Life of New York	Special Cast	Paramount	6998 feet	July 4
Pipes of Pan	Alma Taylor	Cranfield & Clarke (S. R.)	6200 feet	
Ranger of the Big Pines, The	Kenneth Harlan	Vitagraph	5800 feet	Aug. 8
Scarlet West, The	Frazer-Bow	First National	8391 feet	July 25
Secret of Black Canyon, The	Dick Hatton	Arrow		
Strange Rider, The	Yakima Canutt	Arrow		
Taming the West	Hoot Gibson	Universal	5427 feet	Feb. 28
Trailed	Al Richmond	Sierra Prod. (S. R.)	4750 feet	
White Desert, The	Special Cast	Metro-Goldwyn	6345 feet	July 18

AUGUST

Feature	Star	Distributed by	Length	Reviewed
Beggar on Horseback, A	Ralston-Nissen	Paramount	6800 feet	June 20
Business of Love, The	E. Horton-M. Bellamy	Astor Dist. Corp		
Children of the Whirlwind	Lionel Barrymore	Arrow		
Drusilla With a Million	Special Cast	F. B. O	7391 feet	May 30
Evolution		Red Seal	4200 feet	Aug. 15
Fine Clothes	L. Stone-A. Rubens	First National	6971 feet	Aug. 15
Girl Who Wouldn't Work, The	Lionel Barrymore	B. P. Schulberg (S.R.)	5979 feet	Sept. 5
Gold Rush, The	Charles Chaplin	United Artists	8500 feet	Aug. 8
Halfway Girl, The	Doris Kenyon	First National	7570 feet	Aug. 8
Headlines	Alice Joyce	Assoc. Exhib	5600 feet	July 25
Her Sister From Paris	C. Talmadge	First National	7255 feet	Aug. 15
In the Name of Love	Cortez-Nissen	Paramount	5904 feet	Sept. 5
Isle of Hope, The	Richard Talmadge	Film Book. Offices	5800 feet	Sept. 5
Kivalina of the Ice Lands	Native Cast	Pathe	6 reels	July 11
Knockout, The	Milton Sills	First National	7450 feet	Sept. 19
Lightnin'	Jay Hunt	Fox	7979 feet	Aug. 1
Limited Mail, The	Monte Blue	Warner Brothers	6250 feet	
Love Hour, The	Ruth Clifford	Vitagraph	5900 feet	
Lover's Oath, The	Ramon Novarro	Astor Dist Corp		
Lucky Devil, The	Richard Dix	Paramount	5935 feet	July 18
Lucky Horseshoe, The	Tom Mix	Fox	5004 feet	Aug. 29
My Pal	Dick Hatton	Arrow		
Overland Limited, The		Gotham Prod. (S. R.)	6389 feet	Aug. 8
Parisian Love	Bow-Tellegen	B. P. Schulberg (S.R.)	6324 feet	Aug. 22
Quo Vadis	Emil Jannings	First National	8945 feet	Feb. 28
Range Justice	Dick Hatton	Arrow		
Romola	Gish Sisters	Metro-Goldwyn	10875 feet	Dec. 13
Rugged Water	Special Cast	Paramount	6015 feet	Aug. 1
Shining Adventure, The	Percy Marmont	Astor Dist. Corp		
Slave of Fashion, A	Special Cast	Metro-Goldwyn	5906 feet	Aug. 1
Speed Mad		Columbia Pict. (S.R.)	4442 feet	Sept. 19
Sporting Chance, The		Tiffany (S. R.)	6500 feet	July 4
Street of Forgotten Men	Special Cast	Paramount	6366 feet	Aug. 1
Ten Commandments	Special Cast	Paramount	9980 feet	Jan. 5-24
That Man Jack	Bob Custer	F. B. O	5032 feet	Aug. 22
Unholy Three	Lon Chaney	Metro-Goldwyn	6848 feet	Aug. 15
Unwritten Law, The		Columbia Pict. (S.R.)		
Wife Who Wasn't Wanted, The	Irene Rich	Warner Brothers	6400 feet	
Wizard of Oz	Larry Semon	Chadwick	6300 feet	Apr. 25
Wrongdoers, The	Lionel Barrymore	Astor Dist. Corp		

SEPTEMBER

Feature	Star	Distributed by	Length	Reviewed
Amazing Quest, The	Henry Edwards	Cranfield & Clarke	5500 feet	
American Pluck	George Walsh	Chadwick	5000 feet	July 11
Apache Love	Geo. Larkin	B'way Dist. Co	5000 feet	
As No Man Has Loved	Special Cast	Fox	7836 feet	Feb. 28
Batter, The	Kenneth McDonald	Bud Barsky (S. R.)	5000 feet	
Below The Line	Rin-Tin-Tin (dog)	Warner Brothers	6100 feet	
Black Cyclone	Rex (horse)	Pathe		May 30
Bobbed Hair	Prevost-Harlan	Warner Brothers	6700 feet	
California Straight Ahead	Reginald Denny	Universal		
Call of Courage, The	Art Acord	Universal	4861 feet	Sept. 19
Classified	Corinne Griffith	First National		
Coast of Folly	Gloria Swanson	Paramount		
Coming of Amos	Rod La Rocque	Prod. Dist. Corp	5677 feet	Sept. 19
Crack of Dawn	Reed Howes	Rayart (S. R.)		
Cyclone Cavalier	Reed Howes	Rayart (S. R.)	4928 feet	Sept. 26
Dark Angel, The	R. Colman-V. Banky	First National	7311 feet	Sept. 29
Don Q, Son of Zorro	Douglas Fairbanks	United Artists	10264 feet	June 27
Free to Love	C. Bow-D. Keith	B. P. Schulberg (S.R.)		
Freshman, The	Harold Lloyd	Pathe		July 25
Graustark	Norma Talmadge	First National	5900 feet	Sept. 19
Havoc	Special Cast	Fox	9200 feet	Aug. 29
Hell's Highroad	Leatrice Joy	Prod. Dist. Corp	6084 feet	Sept. 5
High and Handsome	"Lefty" Flynn	F. B. O.	5669 feet	
His Master's Voice	Thunder (dog)	Gotham Prod. (S. R.	6000 feet	
If Marriage Fails	J. Logan-C. Brook	F. B. O	6006 feet	May 23
Keep Smiling	Monty Banks	Assoc. Exhib	5400 feet	Aug. 1
Kentucky Pride	Special Cast	Fox	6597 feet	Sept. 19
Knockout Kid, The	Jack Perrin	Rayart Pict. Corp. (S. R.)	4901 feet	
Let's Go Gallagher	Tom Tyler	Film Book Offices	5182 feet	Oct. 3
Little Annie Rooney	Mary Pickford	United Artists		
Lost World, The	Special Cast	First National	9700 feet	Feb. 21
Man From Red Gulch	Harry Carey	Prod. Dist. Corp.		
Manhattan Madness	Dempsey-Taylor	Assoc. Exhib	5500 feet	July 25
Man Who Found Himself	Thomas Meighan	Paramount	7168 feet	Sept. 5
Mystic, The	Special Cast	Metro-Goldwyn		

Feature	Star	Distributed by	Length	Reviewed
Never the Twain Shall Meet	Stewart-Lytell	Metro-Goldwyn	8143 feet	Aug. 8
New Champion, The		Columbia Pict. (S.R.)		
Not So Long Ago	Betty Bronson	Paramount	6943 feet	Aug. 8
Other Woman's Story	Calhoun-Frazer	B. P. Schulberg		
Outlaw's Daughter, The	Josie Sedgwick	Universal	4375 feet	
Paint and Power	Elaine Hammerstein	Chadwick		
Parisian Nights	E. Hammerstein - L. Tellegen	F. B. O	6278 feet	June 20
Plastic Age, The	Special Cast	B. P. Schulberg (S. R.)		
Pretty Ladies	Zazu Pitts	Metro-Goldwyn	5828 feet	July 28
Primrose Path, The	Bow-MacDonald	Arrow	6475 feet	
Ridin' the Wind	Fred Thomson	Film Book. Offices		
Scandal Street	Kennedy-Welch	Arrow	6923 feet	
Sealed Lips		Columbia Pict. (S.R.)		
Seven Days	Lillian Rich	Prod. Dist. Corp.	6974 feet	
Shore Leave	Barthelmess-Mackaill	First National	6856 feet	Aug. 29
Siege	Virginia Valli	Universal	6424 feet	June 20
Son of His Father, A	Special Cast	Paramount	7009 feet	Sept. 19
Souls for Sables		Tiffany (S. R.)	7000 feet	
S. O. S. Perils of the Sea		Columbia Pict. (S.R.)		
Speed Madness	Frank Merrill	Hercules Film	4579 feet	
Spook Ranch	Hoot Gibson	Universal	5147 feet	May 2
Sun Up	Special Cast	Metro-Goldwyn		Aug. 29
Teaser, The	Laura La Plante	Universal	6967 feet	May 30
Three in Exile		Truart (S. R.)	5800 feet	
Three Weeks in Paris	M. Moore-D. Devore	Warner Brothers	5900 feet	
Three Wise Crooks	Evelyn Brent	Film Book. Offices		
Throwback, The	Special Cast	Universal		
Timber Wolf, The	Buck Jones	Fox	4809 feet	Sept. 26
Trouble With Wives, The	Vidor-T. Moore	Paramount	6489 feet	Aug. 16
Wall Street Whiz, The	Richard Talmadge	Film Book. Offices		
What Fools Men	Stone-Mason	First National		
Wheel, The	Special Cast	Fox	7264 feet	Aug. 29
White Outlaw, The	Jack Hoxie	Universal	4830 feet	June 27
Wild Horse Mesa	Special Cast	Paramount	7221 feet	Aug. 22
Wild, Wild Susan	Bebe Daniels	Paramount		
With This Ring	Mills-Tellegen	B. P. Schulberg	5333 feet	Oct. 3

OCTOBER

Feature	Star	Distributed by	Length	Reviewed
Borrowed Finery		Tiffany (S. R.)	6500 feet	
Bustin' Through	Jack Hoxie	Universal	4506 feet	
Cactus Trails	Jack Perrin	Madoc Sales	4800 feet	
Circle, The		Metro-Goldwyn		
Circus Cyclone, The	Art Acord	Universal	4609 feet	Aug. 22
Dollar Down	Ruth Roland	Truart (S. R.)	5600 feet	Aug. 29
Everlasting Whisper, The	Tom Mix	Fox		
Exchange of Wives, An	Special Cast	Metro-Goldwyn		
Fate of a Flirt, The		Columbia (S. R.)		
Fighting Heart, The	Geo. O'Brien	Fox	6978 feet	Oct. 3
Golden Princess, The	Bronson-Hamilton	Paramount	6395 feet	Sept. 19
Great Sensation, The	W. Fairbanks-P. Garon	Columbia (S. R.)	4470 feet	Sept. 26
Heads Up	Fred Thomson	F. B. O		
Heartless Husbands	Gloria Grey	Madoc Sales	5000 feet	
He's a Prince	Raymond Griffith	Paramount		
His Buddy's Wife	Glenn Hunter	Assoc. Exhib	5800 feet	July 26
Iron Horse, The	O'Brien-Bellamy	Fox Film Corp.	10288 feet	Sept. 18
John Forrest	Henry Edwards	Cranfield&Clark(S.R.)	5000 feet	
Keeper of the Bees, The	Robert Frazer	F. B. O		
Lew Tyler's Wives		B. P. Schulberg (S. R.)		
Lights of Old Broadway	Marion Davies	Metro-Goldwyn		
Lovers in Quarantine	Daniels-Ford	Paramount		
Midshipman, The	Ramon Novarro	Metro-Goldwyn		
New Brooms	Hamilton-Love	Paramount		
Peacock Feathers	Logan-Landis	Universal	6747 feet	Aug. 29
Pony Express, The	Betty Compson	Paramount		
Prairie Pirate, The	Harry Carey	Prod. Dist. Corp.	4603 feet	Sept. 26
Sally of the Sawdust	Fields-Dempster	United Artists	9500 feet	Aug. 15
Silver Fingers	Geo. Larkin	B'way Dist. Co.	5000 feet	
Some Pun'kins	Chas. Ray	Chadwick	6500 feet	Sept. 19
Storm Breaker, The	House Peters	Universal	6064 feet	Sept. 26
Substitute Wife, The	Jane Novak	Arrow	5994 feet	
Thunder Mountain	Special Cast	Fox	7537 feet	
Tower of Lies	Chaney-Shearer	Metro-Goldwyn		
Tumbleweeds	Wm. S. Hart	United Artists		
Unchastened Woman, The	Theda Bara	Chadwick	6800 feet	
Under the Rouge	Tom Moore	Assoc. Exhib	6500 feet	July 26
Wandering Fires	Constance Bennett	Arrow		
Winds of Chance	A. Nilsson-B. Lyon	First National	9753 feet	Aug. 29
Without Mercy	Vera Reynolds	Prod. Dist. Corp	6550 feet	
Winding Stair, The	Special Cast	Fox		

NOVEMBER

Feature	Star	Distributed by	Length	Reviewed
After Marriage	Margaret Livingston	Madoc Sales	5000 feet	
Ancient Highway, The	Holt-Vidor	Paramount		
Best People, The	Special Cast	Paramount		
Blue Blood	George Walsh	Chadwick		
Calgary Stampede, The	Hoot Gibson	Universal		
Camille of the Barbary Coast	Busch-O. Moore	Assoc. Exhib	5800 feet	Aug. 1
Cobra	Valentino-Naldi	Paramount		
Daring Days	Josie Sedgwick	Universal	5 reels	
Don't	S. O'Neill-B. Roach	Metro-Goldwyn		
Durand of the Bad Lands	Buck Jones	Fox	5844 feet	
Fifty-Fifty	L. Barrymore-H. Hampton	Assoc. Exhib	5564 feet	June 20
Fight to a Finish, A		Columbia (S. R.)		
Flower of Night	Pola Negri	Paramount		
Fool, The	Edmund Lowe	Fox	9374 feet	April 25
King on Main St, The	Adolphe Menjou	Paramount		
Lazybones	Special Cast	Fox Film	7234 feet	
Little Bit of Broadway	Ray-Starke	Metro-Goldwyn		
Makers of Men	Special Cast	Bud Barsky (S. R.)	5500 feet	Oct. 3
Merry Widow	Mae Murray	Metro-Goldwyn		
People vs. Nancy Preston	Bowers-De La Motte	Prod. Dist. Corp.		
Perfect Clown, The	Larry Semon	Chadwick		
Price of Success, The	Alice Lake	Columbia (S. R.)		
Road to Yesterday, The	Joseph Schildkraut	Prod. Dist. Corp.		
Romance Road	Raymond McKee	Truart	5090 feet	
Simon the Jester	Rich-O'Brien	Prod. Dist. Corp.		
Stage Struck	Gloria Swanson	Paramount		
Tessie	McAvoy-Agnew	Arrow	6221 feet	
Thank U	Special Cast	Fox	6900 feet	Sept. 19
Time the Comedian		Metro-Goldwyn		
Transcontinental Limited	Special Cast	Chadwick (S. R.)		
Vanishing American, The	Dix-Wilson	Paramount		
Wedding Song, The	Leatrice Joy	Prod. Dist. Corp.		
Winner, The	Charles Ray	Chadwick (S. R.)		

DECEMBER

Feature	Star	Distributed by	Length	Reviewed
Braveheart	Rod LaRocque	Prod. Dist. Corp.		
Dice Woman, The	Priscilla Dean	Prod. Dist. Corp.		
Lodge in the Wilderness, The		Tiffany (S. R.)	6500 feet	
Madam Behave	Eltinge-Pennington	Prod. Dist. Corp.		
Morals for Men	Tearle-Mills	Tiffany (S. R.)	6500 feet	
Prince of Broadway	George Walsh	Chadwick		
Sweet Adeline	Charles Ray	Chadwick		

JANUARY

Feature	Star	Distributed by	Length	Reviewed
Fifth Avenue	De La Motte	Prod. Dist. Corp.		
Lure of the Arctic, The		Prod. Dist. Corp.		
Million Dollar Handicap, The	Vera Reynolds	Prod. Dist. Corp.		
Steel Preferred	William Boyd	Prod. Dist. Corp.		
Three Faces East	Goudal-Ames	Prod. Dist. Corp.		

Comedy Releases

Feature	Star	Distributed by	Length	Reviewed
Absent Minded	Neely Edwards	Universal	1 reel	
Across the Hall	Edna Marian	Universal	2 reels	
Adventures of Adenoid	Aesop's Fables	Pathe	1 reel	April 25
After a Reputation	Edna Marian	Universal	2 reels	
Air Tight	Bobby Vernon	Educational	2 reels	June 13
Alice's Egg Plant	"Cartoon"	M. J. Winkler (S. R.)	1 reel	
Alice Stagestruck	Margie Gay	M. J. Winkler (S.R.)	1 reel	July 18
All at Sea	Smith-King	Fox		
Almost a Husband	Buddy Messinger	Universal	2 reels	
Amateur Detective	Earle Foxe	Fox	2 reels	
Andy in Hollywood	Joe Murphy	Universal	2 reels	
Andy's Lion Tale	"The Gumps"	Universal	2 reels	
Andy Takes a Flyer	"The Gumps"	Universal	2 reels	
Apache, The	Earle Foxe	Fox Film	2 reels	
Apollo's Pretty Sister		Fox	2 reels	
Are Husbands Human?	James Finlayson	Pathe	1 reel	April 11
Artists' Blues	G. Joy-J. Moore	Rayart (S. R.)	2 reels	
Ask Grandma	"Our Gang"	Pathe	2 reels	May 30
At the Seashore	Monkey	Fox	2 reels	
At the Zoo	Aesops Fables	Pathe	1 reel	
Baby Be Good		Educational	2 reels	
Baby Blues	Mickey Bennett	Educational	2 reels	
Bachelors	Special Cast	Universal		
Back to Nature	Charles Puffy	Universal	1 reel	
Bad Bill Brodie	Charles Chase	Pathe	2 reels	
Bad Boy	Charles Chase	Pathe	2 reels	April 11
Balboa Discovers Hollywood	"Red Head"	Sering D. Wilson (S.R.)	1 reel	
Bashful Jim	Ralph Graves	Pathe	2 reels	Mar. 21
Be Careful	Jimmie Adams	Educational Film	2 reels	Aug. 22
Below Zero	Lige Conley	Educational	2 reels	July 4
Beware	Lige Conley	Educational Film	2 reels	Aug. 1
Big Chief Ko-Ko (Out of the Inkwell)	"Cartoon"	Red Seal Pict.	1 reel	
Big Game Hunter, The	Earle Foxe	Fox	2 reels	
Bigger and Better Pictures	"Aesop's Fables"	Pathe	1 reel	
Big Kick, The	Engle-Mohan	Pathe	1 reel	
Big Red Riding Hood	Charley Chase	Pathe	1 reel	May 9
Black Gold Bricks	Roach-Edwards	Universal	1 reel	April 18
Black Hand Blues	"Spat Family"	Pathe	2 reels	April 18
Bobby Bumbs & Co.	Cartoon	Educational	1 reel	July 4
Boobs in the Woods	Harry Langdon	Pathe	2 reels	
Boys Will Be Joys	"Our Gang"	Pathe	2 reels	July 25
Brainless Horsemen		Fox	2 reels	
Brass Button	Billy West	Arrow	2 reels	
Breaking the Ice	Ralph Graves	Pathe	2 reels	April 11
Bride Tamer, The	Milburn Moranti	Sierra Pict. (S. R.)	2 reels	
Bubbles	"Aesop's Fables"	Pathe	1 reel	Aug. 15
Bugville Field Day	"Aesop's Fables"	Pathe	1 reel	July 26
Buster Be Good	Trimble-Turner	Universal	2 reels	
Butterfly Man, The		Fox	2 reels	
By the Sea	Charles Puffy	Universal	1 reel	
California Here We Come	"The Gumps"	Universal	2 reels	
Cat's Shimmy, The	"Kid Noah"	Sering D. Wilson (S.R.)	1 reel	
Cat's Whiskers, The	Neely Edwards	Universal	1 reel	
Chasing the Chasers	Jas. Finlayson	Pathe	1 reel	July 4
City Bound	Charles Puffy	Universal	1 reel	
Clean-Up Week	"Aesop's Fables"	Pathe	1 reel	Mar. 7
Clear the Way	Buddy Messinger	Universal	2 reels	
Cleopatra and Her Easy Mark	"Cartoon"	Sering D. Wilson (S.R.)	1 reel	
Cloudhopper, The	Larry Semon	Educational	2 reels	June 6
Cloudy Romance, A	Special Cast	Fox	2 reels	
Columbus Discovers a New Whirl		Sering Wilson (S. R.)	1 reel	
Crime Crushers	Lige Conley	Educational	2 reels	
Crying for Love	Eddie Gordon	Universal	2 reels	Aug. 15
Cupid's Boots	Ralph Graves	Pathe	2 reels	July 25
Cupid's Victory	Wanda Wiley	Universal	2 reels	
Cure, The (Out of the Inkwell)	"Cartoon"	Red Seal Pict.	1 reel	
Curses	Al. St. John	Educational	2 reels	May 23
Daddy Goes A Grunting		Pathe	2 reels	July 18
Darkest Africa	"Aesop's Fables"	Pathe	1 reels	
Day's Outing, A	"The Gumps"	Universal	2 reels	
Deep Stuff	Aesop's Fables	Pathe	1 reel	April 25
Dinky Doodle and Cinderella	"Dinky Doodle"	F. B. O	1 reel	
Dinky Doodle and Robinson Crusoe	"Dinky Doodle"	F. B. O	1 reel	
Discord In "A" Flat	Arthur Lake	Universal	1 reel	July 25
Dog Days	"Our Gang"	Pathe	2 reels	Mar. 14
Dog Daze	Bowes-Vance	Educational		
Dog 'On It	Bobby Dunn	Arrow	2 reels	
Dome Doctor, The	Larry Semon	Educational	2 reels	
Don't Pinch	Bobby Vernon	Educational	2 reels	April 25
Don't Worry	Wanda Wiley	Universal	2 reels	Mar. 21
Dragon Alley	Jackie McHugh	Educational	2 reels	May 16
Dr. Pyckle and Mr. Pride	Stan Laurel	Film Booking Offices	2 reels	
Dry Up	Singleton Burkett	Universal	2 reels	July 25
Dumb and Daffy	Al. St. John	Fox	2 reels	
Dynamite Doggie	Al. St. John	Educational	2 reels	Mar. 21
East Side, West Side	Harris-Leddy	Fox		
Echoes From the Alps	Aesop's Fables	Pathe	1 reel	May 23
Educating Buster	Trimble-Turner	Universal	2 reels	
End of the World, The	Aesop's Fables	Pathe	1 reel	
Etiquette	Jimmy Aubrey	Film Book. Offices	2 reels	
Excuse My Glove	"Spat Family"	Pathe	2 reels	Mar 21
Expensive Ebony	"Ebenezer Ebony"	Sering Wilson (S. R.)	1 reel	
Fair Warning	Al St. John	Educational	2 reels	Sept. 26
Fares Please	Al. St. John	Educational	2 reels	May 16
Fast Worker, A	Aesop's Fables	Pathe	1 reel	
Felix the Cat Busts Into Business	"Cartoon"	Educational	1 reel	
Felix, the Cat on the Farm	Cartoon	Educational	1 reel	
Felix Full O'Fight	"Cartoon"	M. J. Winkler (S. R.)	1 reel	
Felix Gets His Fill	"Cartoon"	M. J. Winkler (S. R.)	1 reel	
Felix Grabs His Grub	"Cartoon"	M. J. Winkler (S. R.)	1 reel	
Felix the Cat on the Job	Cartoon	Educational	1 reel	
Fire Flies	"Hey, Fellas"	Davis Dist.	2 reels	
First Love	"Our Gang"	Pathe	2 reels	
Fishermen's Luck	"Aesop's Fables"	Pathe	1 reel	
For Hire	Edward Gordon	Universal		
For Love of a Gal	"Aesop's Fables"	Pathe	1 reel	July 25
Found World, The	"The Gumps"	Universal	2 reels	
Fun's Fun	Bowes-Vance	Educational	1 reel	June 6
Getting Trimmed	Wanda Wiley	Universal	2 reels	April 18
Giddap	Special Cast	Pathe	2 reels	Mar. 21
Going Great	Eddie Nelson	Educational	2 reels	June 13
Geldfish's Pajamas	"Kid Noah"	Sering D. Wilson (S.R.)	1 reel	
Good Morning Nurse	Ralph Graves	Pathe	2 reels	May 30
Good Scouts	"Reg'lar Kids"	M. J. Winkler (S. R.)	2 reels	
Great Guns	Bobby Vernon	Educational	2 reels	Feb. 28
Green-Eyed Monster, The	Arthur Lake	Universal	1 reel	
Gridiron Gertie	Wanda Wiley	Universal	2 reels	
Guilty Conscience, A	Eddie Gordon	Universal		
Gypping the Gypsies	"Ebenezer Ebony"	Sering Wilson (S. R.)	1 reel	
Half Fare	Arthur Lake	Universal	1 reel	
Half a Hero	Lloyd Hamilton	Educational	2 reels	Mar. 7
Half a Man	Stan Laurel	Pathe	2 reels	
Hard Boiled	Charley Chase	Pathe	2 reels	Mar. 28
Hard Working Loafer, The	Arthur Stone	Pathe		
Haunted Honeymoon	Tryoq-Mehaffey	Pathe	2 reels	Feb. 28
Heart Breaker, The	Special Cast	Fox	2 reels	
Heart Trouble	Arthur Lake	Universal	1 reel	July 4
Heavy Swells	Special Cast	Fox	2 reels	
Hello, Goodby	Lige Conley	Educational	2 reels	May 30
Hellq, Hollywood	Lige Conley	Educational	2 reels	Mar. 28
Helping Hand	Jimmy Aubrey	F. B. O	2 reels	
Help Yourself		Fox	2 reels	
Here's Your Hat	Arthur Lake	Universal	1 reel	May 9
Her Lucky Leap	Wanda Wiley	Universal	2 reels	
He Who Gets Crowned	Jimmy Aubrey	F. B. O	2 reels	
He Who Got Smacked	Ralph Graves	Pathe	2 reels	May 9
Hey! Taxi!	Bobby Dunn	Arrow	2 reels	
High Hopes	Bowes-Vance	Educational	1 reel	Feb. 14
High Jinx, A		Fox	2 reels	
His Marriage Wow	Harry Langdon	Pathe	2 reels	Mar. 7
Hold My Baby	Glenn Tryon	Pathe	2 reels	April 25
Home Scouts	Jimmie Aubrey	F. B. O.	2 reels	
Honeymoon Heaven		Sering Wilson (S. R.)	1 reel	
Horace Greeley, Jr.	Harry Langdon	Pathe	2 reels	June 6
Horrible Hollywood		Lee-Bradford (S. R.)		
Hot and Heavy	Eddie Nelson	Educational	2 reel	July 18
Hot Dog	Animal	C B C (S. R.)	2 reels	
Hot Times in Iceland	Aesop's Fables	Pathe	1 reels	
House of Flickers, The		Fox	2 reels	
House that Dinky Built	(Cartoon)	F. B. O	1 reel	
Housing Shortage, The	"Aesop's Fables"	Pathe	1 reel	
Hurry Doctor	Ralph Graves	Pathe		
Hysterical History (Series)		Universal	1 reel	
Ice Boy, An	"Ebenezer Ebony"	Sering D. Wilson (S.R.)	1 reel	
Ice Cold	Arthur Lake	Universal	1 reel	June 13
In Deep	Bowes-Vance	Educational	1 reel	
In Dutch	Aesop's Fables	Pathe	1 reel	
Innocent Husbands	Charley Chase	Pathe	2 reels	Aug. 1
Inside Out	Bowes-Vance	Educational	1 reel	Mar. 28
Into the Grease	James Finlayson	Pathe	1 reel	June 27
Iron Mule	Al St. John	Educational	2 reels	April 18
Iron Nag, The	Billy Bevan	Pathe	2 reels	Aug. 15
Is Marriage the Bunk?	Charles Chase	Pathe	1 reel	April 4
Isn't Life Terrible?	Charles Chase	Pathe	2 reels	July 4
Itching for Revenge	Eddie Gordon	Universal	2 reels	Mar. 7
It's All Wrong	Karr-Engle	Universal		
James Boys' Sister		Wilson Sering (S. R.)	1 reel	
Jimminy Crickets	Wesley Edwards	Universal	1 reel	
Jungle Bike Riders	Aesop's Fables	Pathe	1 reel	Mar. 14
Just in Time	Wanda Wiley	Universal	2 reels	July 11
Kicked About	Eddie Gordon	Universal	2 reels	Mar. 14
Kidding Captain Kidd	"Cartoon"	Sering Wilson (S. R.)	1 reel	
King Cotton	Lloyd Hamilton	Educational	2 reels	May 9
King Dumb	Jimmy Aubrey	F. B. O	2 reels	
Klynick, The	"Hey, Fellas"	Davis Dist.	2 reels	
Knocked About	Eddie Gordon	Universal	2 reels	June 13
Ko-Ko Celebrates the Fourth (Out of the Inkwell)	"Cartoon"	Red Seal Pict.		
Ko-Ko Trains Animals (out of the Inkwell)	"Cartoon"	Red Seal Pict	1 reel	
Lead Pipe Cinch, A	Al Alt	Universal		
Lion Love		Fox	2 reels	Feb. 28
Lion and the Monkey	"Aesop's Fables"	Pathe		
Lion's Whiskers		Pathe	2 reels	April 18
Little Red Riding Hood	"Dinky Doodle"	F. B. O	1 reel	
Locked Out	Arthur Lake	Universal	1 reel	May 30
Looking for Sally	Charles Chase	Pathe	2 reels	May 9
Look Out	Bowes-Vance	Educational Film	1 reel	Aug. 1
Lost Cord, The	Bert Roach	Universal	1 reel	Feb. 21
Love and Kisses	Alice Day	Pathe	2 reels	
Love and Lions	Special Cast	Fox	2 reels	
Love Bug, The	"Our Gang"	Pathe	2 reels	April 4
Love Goofy	Jimmy Adams	Educational	2 reels	Mar. 7
Love and Kisses	Alice Day	Pathe	2 reels	Oct. 3
Love Sick	Constance Darling	Universal	2 reels	May 23
Love's Tragedy		Sering Wilson (S. R.)	1 reel	
Lucky Accident, The	Charles Puffy	Universal	1 reel	July 18
Lucky Leap, A	Wanda Wiley	Universal	2 reels	
Lucky Stars	Harry Langdon	Pathe	2 reels	Aug. 15
Madame Sans Jane	Glenn Tryon	Pathe	2 reels	
Marriage Circus, The	Ben Turpin	Pathe	2 reels	April 11
Married Neighbors	Engle-Darling	Universal	2 reels	July 4
Mary, Queen of Tots	"Our Gang"	Pathe	2 reels	Aug. 22
Meet the Ambassador	Jimmy Aubrey	F. B. O	2 reels	
Mellow Quartette	Pen & Ink Vaudeville	Educational	1 reel	April 4
Merrymakers	Bowes-Vance	Educational	1 reel	Mar. 28
Met by Accident	Wanda Wiley	Universal	2 reels	
Milky Way, The	Charles Puffy	Universal	1 reel	July 25
Min Walks in Her Sleep	"Gumps"	Universal		

Feature	Star	Distributed by	Length	Reviewed
Misfit Sailor, A	Dovley-Steadman	Educational	2 reels	Oct. 3
Miss Fixit	Wanda Wiley	Universal	2 reels	
Monkey Business	"Pen & Ink Vaude"	Educational	1 reel	May 9
Moonlight Nights	Gloria Joy	Rayart (S. R.)	2 reels	
Moonlight and Noses	Clyde Cook	Pathe	2 reels	Oct. 3
Movies, The	Lloyd Hamilton	Educational	2 reels	Oct. 3
Nearly Rich	Charles Puffy	Universal	1 reel	
Neptune's Stepdaughter		Fox	2 reels	
Nero's Jazz Band		Sering Wilson (S. R.)	1 reel	
Never Fear	Bowes-Vance	Educational	1 reel	
Never on Time		Lee-Bradford (S. R.)	2 reels	
Never Weaken	Lloyd reissue	Assoc. Exhib	2237 feet	
Nice Pickle, A	Edwards-Roach	Universal	1 reel	
Nicely Rewarded	Chas. Puffy	Universal	1 reel	June 27
Night Hawks		Educational Film	2 reels	
Nobody Wins	Arthur Lake	Universal	1 reel	
No Place to Go	Arthur Lake	Universal	1 reel	
Now or Never (reissue)	Harold Lloyd	Assoc. Exhib	3 reels	
Nursery Troubles	Edna Marian	Universal		
Nuts and Squirrels	"Aesop's Fables"	Pathe	1 reel	
Off His Beat	Walter Hiers	Educational	2 reels	
Office Help	"Aesop's Fables"	Pathe	1 reel	June 27
Officer 13	Eddie Gordon	Universal		
Official Officers	"Our Gang"	Pathe	2 reels	June 27
Oh, Bridget	Walter Hiers	Educational	2 reels	
Oh, What a Flirt	Jimmy Aubrey	Film Book. Offices	2 reels	
Oh, What a Gump	"The Gumps"	Universal	2 reels	
Old Family Toothbrush	"Kid Noah"	Sering Wilson (S. R.)	1 reel	
On Duty	Wanda Wiley	Universal	2 reels	
On the Go	Special Cast	Fox		
One Glorious Fourth	"Reg'lar Kids"	M. J. Winkler (S. R.)	2 reels	
One Wild Night	Neely Edwards	Universal	1 reel	
Orphan, The	Al Joy	Ricardo Films, Inc.(S.R.)		
Over the Bottom	Stan Laurel	F. B. O	2 reels	
Over the Plate	Aesops Fable	Pathe	1 reel	Aug. 22
Over Here	Harry Langdon	Pathe	2 reels	
Paging A Wife	Al Alt	Universal	2 reels	Aug. 1
Papa's Darling		Fox	2 reels	
Papa's Pet	Roach-Edwards	Universal	1 reel	April 11
Parisian Knight, A	Earle Foxe	Fox	2 reels	
Peggy in a Pinch	"Sheiks and Shebas"	Davis Dist.	2 reels	
Peggy's Pests	"Sheiks and Shebas"	Davis Dist.	2 reels	
Peggy's Putters	"Sheiks and Shebas"	Davis Dist.	2 reels	
Peggy the Vamp	"Sheiks and Shebas"	Davis Dist.	2 reels	Oct. 11
Permanent Waves	"Aesop's Fables"	Pathe	1 reel	
Permit Me	Bowes-Vance	Educational	1 reel	July 11
Pie-Eyed	Stan Laurel	F. B. O	2 reels	
Pie Man, The	"Aesop's Fables"	Pathe	1 reel	Mar. 21
Plain Clothes	Harry Langdon	Pathe	2 reels	Mar. 28
Plain and Fancy Girls	Charles Chase	Pathe	1 reel	Mar. 14
Plain Luck	Edna Marian	Universal	2 reels	
Pleasure Bound	Lige Conley	Educational	2 reels	Aug. 24
Plenty of Nerve	Edna Marian	Universal	2 reels	July 2
Polo Kid, The	Eddie Gordon	Universal	2 reels	July 18
Poor Sap, The		Fox	2 reels	
Powdered Chickens	Edna Marian	Universal	2 reels	Mar. 28
Props' Dash for Cash	Earl Hurd (Cartoon)	Educational	1 reel	
Putting on Airs	Edna Marian	Universal	2 reels	April 11
Puzzled by Crosswords	Eddie Gordon	Universal	2 reels	Mar. 7
Queen of Aces	Wanda Wiley	Universal	2 reels	May 16
Raid, The	Gloria Joy	Rayart Pict. (S. R.)	2 reels	
Rainy Knight, A	Special Cast	Pathe		
Raisin' Cain	Constance Darling	Universal	2 reels	April 4
Rapid Transit	Al. St. John	Educational	2 reels	
Rarin' Romeo	Walter Hiers	Educational	2 reels	Mar. 28
Raspberry Romance	Ben Turpin	Pathe	2 reels	Feb. 28
Red Pepper	Al. St. John	Educational	2 reels	Arpil 4
Regular Girl, A	Wanda Wiley	Universal	2 reels	
Riders of the Kitchen Range	Mohar-Engle	Pathe	1 reel	June 6
Remember When	Harry Langdon	Pathe	2 reels	April 25
Rip Without a Wink	"Redhead"	Sering Wilson (S. R.)	1 reel	
Ripe Melodrama, A		Sering Wilson (S. R.)	1 reel	
Rivals	Billy West	Arrow	2 reels	
Robinson Crusoe Returns on Friday	"Redhead"	Sering Wilson (S. R.)	1 reel	
Rock Bottom	Bowes-Vance	Educational	1 reel	May 9
Robbing the Rube		Lee-Bradford Corp.	2 reels	
Rolling Stones	Charles Puffy	Universal	1 reel	May 30
Rough Party	Al Alt	Universal	2 reels	
Royal Four-Flush	"Spat Family"	Pathe	2 reels	June 13
Runaway Balloon, The	"Aesop's Fables"	Pathe	1 reel	June 27
Runt, The	"Aesop's Fables"	Pathe	1 reel	June 6
Sailor Papa, A	Glenn Tryon	Pathe	2 reels	April 4
Salute	Alice Ardell	F. B. O.		
Saturday	"Hey Fellas"	Davis Dist. Div.	2 reels	
Say It With Flour		Fox	2 reels	
Scrambled Eggs	Bowes-Vance	Educational		
Sheiks of Bagdad		Pathe	1 reel	May 9
Sherlock Sleuth	Arthur Stone	Pathe	2 reels	July 11
Ship Shape	Vance-Bowes	Educational	1 reel	April 18
Shootin' Injuns	"Our Gang"	Pathe	2 reels	May 9
Short Pants	Arthur Lake	Universal	1 reel	Aug. 1
Should a Husband Tell?		Red Seal Pict.	1 reel	
Should Husbands Be Watched?	Charles Chase	Pathe	1 reel	Mar. 14
Sir Walt and Lizzie		Sering Wilson (S. R.)	1 reel	
Sit Tight	Jimmie Adams	Educational	2 reels	May 30
Skinners in Silk		Pathe	2 reels	May 16
Sky Jumper, The	Earle Foxe	Fox	2 reels	
Skyscraper, The	Harry Langdon	Principal Pict. (S. R.)	2 reels	
Sleeping Sickness	Edwards-Roach	Universal	1 reel	May 30
Slick Articles	Engle-Karr	Universal	2 reels	May 30
Smoked Out	Lake-Hasbrouck	Universal	1 reel	April 13
Sneezing Beezers	Billy Bevan	Pathe	2 reels	July 18
Snow-Hawk	Stan Laurel	F. B. O.	2 reels	
Soap	"Aesop's Fables"	Pathe	1 reel	
Somewhere in Somewhere	Murray-Littlefield	Pathe	2 reels	Sept. 26
S. O. S.	"Aesop's Fables"	Pathe	1 reel	
Spanish Romeo, A (Van Bibber)		Fox	1 reel	
Speak Easy	Charley Puffy	Universal	1 reel	Aug. 22
Speak Freely	Edna Marion	Universal	2 reels	
Spot Light		Educational	2 reels	
Stick Around	Bobby Dunn	Arrow	2 reels	
Stop, Look and Whistle		Fox	2 reels	
Storm, The (Out of the Inkwell)	"Cartoon"	Red Seal Pict.	1 reel	
Stranded	Edna Marian	Universal	2 reels	
Strong for Love	Special Cast	Fox	2 reels	
Super-Hooper-Dyne Lizzies		Pathe	2 reels	June 13
Sure Mike!	Martha Sleeper	Pathe	1 reel	May 23
Sweet Marie	Special Cast	Fox	2 reels	Aug. 29
Tame Men and Wild Women		Pathe	2 reels	Aug. 15
Taxi War, A	Eddie Gordon	Universal	2 reels	
Teaser Island	"Redhead"	Sering Wilson (S. R.)	1 reel	
Tee for Two	Alice Day	Pathe	2 reels	Aug. 1
Tell It To a Policeman	Glenn Tryon	Pathe	2 reels	May 23
Tender Feet	Walter Hiers	Educational	2 reels	May 23
Tenting Out	Roache-Edwards	Universal	1 reel	Mar. 23
This Week-End		Lee-Bradford (S. R.)		
Three Wise Goofs	Special Cast	F. B. O		
Thundering Landlords	Glenn Tryon	Pathe	2 reels	June 27
Ton of Fun in a Beauty Parlor, A		F. B. O		
Too Much Mother-in-Law	Constance Darling	Universal		
Too Young to Marry	Buddy Messinger	Universal	2 reels	
Tough Night, A	Jimmy Callahan	Aywon Film	2 reels	
Tourist, The	Harry Langdon	Educational Film	2 reels	Aug. 15
Tourists De Luxe	Hayes-Kart	Universal	2 reels	May 16
Transatlantic Flight, A	"Aesop's Fables"	Pathe	1 reel	
Twins	Stan Laurel	F. B. O	2 reels	
Two Cats and a Bird	"Cartoon"	Educational	1 reel	Mar. 14
Two Poor Fish	Earl Hurd cartoon	Educational	1 reel	May 30
Ugly Duckling, The	"Aesop's Fables"	Pathe	1 reel	Sept. 26
Uncle Tom's Gal	Edna Marian	Universal	2 reels	
Unwelcome	Charles Puffy	Universal	1 reel	June 27
Waiting	Lloyd Hamilton	Educational	2 reels	July 11
Wake Up	Bowes-Vance	Educational	1 reel	June 13
Watch Out	Bobby Vernon	Educational	2 reels	
Water Wagons	Special Cast	Pathe	2 reels	Feb. 21
Welcome Dangar	Bowes-Vance	Educational	1 reel	Feb. 23
West is West	Billy West	Arrow	2 reels	
Westward Ho	Charles Puffy	Universal	1 reel	Oct. 3
What Price Goofy	Charley Chase	Pathe	2 reels	June 6
When Dumbells Ring		Fox	2 reels	
When Men Were Men	"Aesop's Fables"	Pathe	1 reel	July 25
White Wing's Bride	Harry Langdon	Pathe	2 reels	July 11
Whose Baby Are You?	Glenn Tryon	Pathe	2 reels	
Who's Which	Bowes-Vance	Educational	1 reel	
Why Hesitate?	Neal Burns	Educational	2 reels	April 11
Why Sitting Bull Stood Up		Sering Wilson (S. R.)	1 reel	
Wide Awake	Lige Conley	Educational	2 reels	
Wild Papa	"Spat Family"	Pathe	2 reels	May 16
Wild Waves	Bowes-Vance	Educational	1 reel	May 23
Wine, Woman and Song	"Aesop's Fables"	Pathe	1 reel	
Winning Pair, A	Wanda Wiley	Universal	2 reels	
Wooly West, The	Buddy Messinger	Universal	2 reels	
Wrestler, The	Earle Foxe	Fox	2 reels	Aug. 29
Yarn About Yarn, A	Aesop Fable	Pathe	1 reel	Aug. 1
Yes, Yes, Nannette	Jas. Finlayson	Pathe	1 reel	Aug. 1
Your Own Back Yard	"Our Gang"	Pathe	2 reels	Oct. 3

Short Subjects

Feature	Distributed by	Length	Reviewed
Action (Sportlight)	Pathe	1 reel	
All Abroad (Helen and Warren)	Fox	2 reels	
All Under One Flag (Sportlight)	Pathe	1 reel	
Animal Celebrities (Sportlight)	Pathe	1 reel	June 27
Animated Hair Cartoon (Series)	Red Seal	1 reel	
Balto's Race to Nome (Special)	Educational	2 reels	May 23
Barbara Snitches (Pacemaker Series)	F. B. O.	2 reels	
Battle of Wits (Josie Sedgwick)	Universal	2 reels	July 18
Bashful Whirlwind, The (Edmund Cobb)	Universal	2 reels	
Beauty and the Bandit (Geo. Larkin)	Universal	2 reels	July 4
Beauty Spots (Sportlight)	Pathe	1 reel	April 18
Best Man, The (Josie Sedgwick)	Universal	2 reels	Aug. 15
Broken Trails	Denver Dixon (S.R.)	2 reels	
Boundary Line, The (Fred Humes)	Universal	2 reels	
Business Engagement, A (Helen & Warren)	Fox	2 reels	
Cabaret of Old Japan	M. J. Winkler (S.R.)	1 reel	
Color World	Sering Wilson (S. R.)	1 reel	
Captured Alive (Helen Gibson)	Universal	2 reels	July 25
Cinema Stars (Novelty)	Davis Dist	1 reel	
Close Call, The (Edmund Cobb)	Universal	2 reels	
Cocoon to Kimono	M. J. Winkler (S.R.)	1 reel	
Come-Back, The (Benny Leonard)	Henry Ginsberg-S.R.	2 reels	
Concerning Cheese (Varieties)	Fox	1 reel	
Covered Flagon, The (Pacemaker Series)	F. B. O	2 reels	
Cowpuncher's Comeback, The (Art Acord)	Universal	2 reels	
Crooked (Elinor King)	Davis Dist	2 reels	
Cross Word Puzzle Film (Comedy-Novelty)	Schwartz Enterprises (S. R.)	1 reel	
Cuba Steps Out (Variety)	Fox	1 reel	
Day With the Gypsies	Red Seal Pict.	1 reel	
Divertisement (Color Shots)	Sering Wilson (S. R.)	1 reel	
Don Coo Coo (Pacemakers)	Film Book. Offices	2 reels	
Do You Remember (Gems of Screen)	Red Seal	1 reel	
Dude Ranch Days (Sportlight)	Pathe	1 reel	May 30
Earth's Other Half (Hodge-Podge)	Educational	1 reel	June 6
East Side, West Side	DeForrest (S. R.)		
Failure (O. Henry) Marian Harlan	Fox	2 reels	
Fast Male, The (Pacemakers)	Film Book. Offices	2 reels	
Fighting Cowboy (Series)	Universal		
Fighting Ranger (Serial)	Universal	15 episodes	Feb. 7
Fighting Schoolmarm (Josie Sedgwick)	Universal	2 reels	Aug. 1
Film Facts	Red Seal	1 reel	
Fire Trader, The (Serial)	Universal	15 episodes	
Flirting With Death	Red Seal Pict.	2 reels	Sept. 26
Floral Feast, A	Sering Wilson (S.R.)	1 reel	
Frederick Chopin (Music Masters)	Jas. A. Fitzpatrick (S. R.)	1 reel	
From Mars to Munich (Varieties)	Fox	1 reel	April 4
Frontier Love (Billy Mack)	Denver Dixon	2 reels	
Fugitive Futurist	Cranfield & Clarke (S. R.)		
George F. Handel (Music Masters)	Jas. A. Fitzpatrick (S. R.)	1 reel	
Gems of the Screen	Red Seal	1 reel	
Ghost City, The (Serial)	Universal	15 episodes	
Golden Panther, The (Serial)	Pathe		
Gold Trap, The Fred Humes	Universal	2 reels	
Great Circus Mystery, The (Serial)	Universal	15 episodes	
Great Decide, The (Pacemakers)	Film Book. Offices	2 reels	
He Who Gets Rapped (Pacemakers)	Film Book. Offices	2 reels	
Hittin' the Trail (Fred Hank)	Sierra Pict. (S. R.)	2 reels	
How the Elephant Got His Trunk (Bray)	F. B. O		
Idaho (Serial)	Pathe	10 episodes	Feb. 28
If a Picture Tells a Story	Cranfield & Clarke (S. R.)		
In a China Shop (Variety)	Fox	1 reel	
In the Spider's Grip (Novelty)	Educational	1 reel	April 11

Feature	Star	Distributed by	Length	Reviewed
Invention, The (Elinor King)		Davis Dist	2 reels	Oct. 3
I Remember		Short Films Synd.	2 reels	Sept. 26
It Might Happen to You (Evangeline Russell)		Davis Dist	2 reels	
Jazz Fight, The (Benny Leonard)		Henry Ginsberg (S. R.)	2 reels	
Judge's Cross Word Puzzle (Novelty)		Educational	1 reel	Jan. 31
Just Cowboys	Corbett-Holmes	Universal	2 reels	
Klondike Today (Varieties)		Fox	1 reel	
Knicknacks of Knowledge (Hodge Podge)		Educational	1 reel	
Knockout Man, The (Mustang)		Universal	2 reels	July 11
Ko-Ko on the Run	(Ko-Ko Series)	Red Seal	1 reel	Oct. 3
Land of the Navajo (Educational)		Fox	1 reel	
Learning How (Sportlight)		Pathe	1 reel	July 18
Leopard's Lair		Universal	Serial	
Let's Paint		Cranfield & Clarke (S. R.)		
Life's Greatest Thrills		Universal	2 reels	Sept. 26
Line Runners, The (Arnold Gregg)		Universal	2 reels	
Little People of the Garden (Secrets of Life)		Educational	1 reel	
Little People of the Sea (Secrets of Life)		Educational	1 reel	Feb. 28
Lizzie's Last Lap		Cranfield & Clarke (S. R.)		
Loaded Dice (Edmund Cobb)		Universal	2 reels	April 4
Luna-cy (Stereoscopik)		Pathe	1 reel	
Mad Miner, A (Western)		Hunt Miller (S. R.)	2 reels	
Magic Hour, The		Red Seal Pict.	1 reel	
Man Who Rode Alone, The		Miller & Steen (S.R.)	2 reels	
Man Without a Scar		Universal	2 reels	
Marvels of Motion		Red Seal	1 reel	
Marvellous Manhattan		M. J. Winkler (S. R.)	1 reel	
Merry Kiddo, The (Pacemakers)		Film Book. Offices	2 reels	
Merton of the Goofies	"Pacemaker"	F. B. O.	2 reels	
Mexican Melody (Hodge-Podge)		Educational	1 Reel	
Mexican Oil Fields		M. J. Winkler (S. R.)	1 reel	
Movie Morsels (Hodge Podge)		Educational	1 reel	April 4
My Bonnie	(Ko-Ko Series)	Red Sea	1 reel	Oct. 3
My Own Carolina (Variety)		Fox	1 reel	Aug. 29
Mystery Box, The (Serial)		Davis Dist. Corp.	10 episodes	
Neptune's Nieces (Sportlight)		Pathe	1 reel	
New Sheriff, A (Western)		Hunt Miller (S. R.)	2 reels	
Olympic Mermaids (Sportlight)		Pathe	1 reel	
One Glorious Scrap (Edmund Cobb)		Universal	2 reels	
Only a Country Lass (Novelty)		Educational	1 reel	May 29
Ouch (Stereoscopik)		Pathe	1 reel	
Our Six-legged Friends (Secrets of Life)		Educational	1 reel	
Outings for All	(Sportlight)	Pathe	1 reel	
Outlaw, The (Jack Perrin)		Universal	2 reels	
Peacemakers, The	(Helen & Warren)	Fox	2 reels	
Paris Creations (Novelty)		Educational	1 reel	Feb. 7
Paris Creations in Color (Novelty)		Educational	1 reel	Feb. 28
People You Know (Screen Almanac)		Film Booking Offices.	1 reel	
Perfect View, The (Varieties)		Fox	1 reel	
Perils of the Wild (Serial)		Universal		
Pictorial Proverbs (Hodge Podge)		Educational	1 reel	Aug. 18
Plastigrams (Novelty)		Educational		
Play Ball (Serial)		Pathe	10 episodes	June 27
Power God, The (Serial)		Davis Dist. Div.	15 episodes	
Pronto Kid, The (Edmund Cobb)		Universal	2 reels	June 27
Queen of the Round-Up (J. Sedgwick)		Universal	2 reels	June 13
Race, The (Van Bibber)		Fox	2 reels	
Radio Detective, The		Universal	Serial	
Raid, The	Edmund Cobb	Universal	2 reels	
Record Breaker, The		Pathe	Serial	
Rim of the Desert (Jack Perrin)		Universal	2 reels	
River Nile, The (Variety)		Fox	1 reel	
Roaring Waters (Geo. Larkin)		Universal	2 reels	
Rock Bound Brittany (Educational)		Fox	1 reel	
Ropin' Venus, The (Mustang Series)		Universal	2 reels	July 11
R. Valentino and Eighty-eight Prize-winning American Beauties		Chesterfield (M. P. Corp.) (S. R.)	3 reels	
Runaway Taxi, A	(Stereoscopic)	Pathe	1 reel	Oct. 3
Rustlen of Boulder Canyon (Edmund Cobb)		Universal	2 reels	
Secrets of Life (Educational)		Principal Pict. (S. R.)	reel	Feb. 21
Seven Ages of Sport (Sportlight)		Pathe	1 reel	Aug. 22
Shadow of Suspicion (Eileen Sedgwick)		Universal	2 reels	
Shoes (O. Henry)		Fox	2 reels	
Shootin' Wild (Corbett-Holmes)		Universal	2 reels	
Show Down, The (Art Acord)		Universal	2 reels	
Silvery Art		Red Seal Pict.	2 reels	Sept. 26
Sky Tribe, The (Variety)		Fox	1 reel	
Smoke of a Forty-Five, The (Western)		Hunt Miller (S. R.)	2 reels	
Soft Muscles (Benny Leonard)		Ginsberg (S. R.)	2 reels	
Song Cartunes (Novelty)		Red Seal Pict.	1 reel	
Sons of Swat (Sportlight)		Pathe	1 reel	Aug. 15
Sporting Judgment (Sportlight)		Pathe	1 reel	May 9
Starting an Argument (Sportlight)		Pathe	1 reel	
Steam Heated Islands (Varieties)		Fox	1 reel	
Stereoscopic (Novelty)		Pathe	1 reel	May 16
Storm King (Edmund Cobb)		Universal	2 reels	
Story Teller, The (Hodge-Podge)		Educational	1 reel	Oct. 3
Straight Shootin' (Harry Carey)		Universal	2 reels	
Strangler Lewis vs. Wayne Munn		Educational	2 reels	July 4
Stratford on Avon (Gems of Screen)		Red Seal Pict	1 reel	
Sunken Silver (Serial)		Pathe	10 episodes	April 18
Surprise Fight, The (Benny Leonard)		Henry Ginsberg (S. R.)	2 reels	
Thundering Waters (Novelty)		Sering D. Wilson (S. R.)	1 reel	April 25
Tiger Kill, The (Pathe Review)		Pathe		
Toiling for Rest (Variety)		Fox	1 reel	
Too Many Bucks (Corbett-Holmes		Universal	2 reels	
Transiets in Arcadia (O. Henry)		Fox	2 reels	
Traps and Troubles (Sportlight)		Pathe	1 reel	Mar. 21
Travel Treasures (Hodge Podge)		Educational	1 reel	July 25
Turf Mystery (Serial)		Chesterfield Pict. Corp. (S. R.)	15 episodes	
Valley of Rogues (Western)		Universal	2 reels	April 18
Van Bibber and the Navy (Earle Foxe)		Fox	2 reels	
Village School, The (Hodge Podge)		Educational Film	1 reel	May
Voice of the Nightingale, The (Novelty)		Educational	1 reel	Mar. 28
Waiting For You (Music Film)		Hegerman Music Novelties (S. R.)		
Welcome Granger (Pacemakers)		Film Book. Offices	2 reels	
West Wind, The (Variety)		Fox	1 reel	
What Price Gloria (Pacemakers)		Film Book. Offices	2 reels	
Wheels of the Pioneers (Billy Mack)		Denver Dixon (S. R.)	2 reels	
Where the Waters Divide (Varieties)		Fox	1 reel	
White Paper (Varieties)		Fox	1 reel	
Wild West Wallop, The (Edmund Cobb)		Universal	2 reels	May 16
Wild West		Pathe	Serial	
With Pencil, Brush and Chisel (Variety)		Fox	1 reel	
Wonder Book, The (Series)		Sering D. Wilson	500 feet	April 25
Young Sheriff, The (Tom. Forman)		Miller & Steen (S. R.)	2 reels	
Zowie (Stereoscopik)		Pathe	1 reel	

Coming Attractions

Feature	Star	Distributed by	Length	Reviewed
Ace of Spades, The	Desmond-McAllister	Universal		
Age of Indiscretion		Truatt (S. R.)	5800 feet	
Agony Column	Monte Blue	Warner Bros		
All Around the Frying Pan	Fred Thompson	F. B. O		
Aloma of the South Seas	Gilda Gray	Paramount		
American Venus, The	Special Cast	Paramount		
An Enemy of Men		Columbia Pict. (S. R.)		
Aristocrat, The	Special Cast	B. P. Schulberg (S. R.)		
Atlantis		First National		
Bad Lands, The	Harry Carey	Prod. Dist. Corp	5833 feet	Oct. 3
Barriers of Fire	Monte Blue	Warner Bros.		
Bat, The	Special Cast	United Artists		
Beautiful Cheat, The	Laura La Plante	Universal		
Beautiful City	R. Barthelmess	First National		
Before Midnight	Wm. Russell	Ginsberg (S. R.)	5895 feet	Aug. 8
Bells, The	Lionel barrymore	Chadwick		
Beloved Pawn, The	Reed Howes	Rayart (S. R.)		
Ben Hur	Special Cast	Metro-Goldwyn		
Best Bad Man, The	Tom Mix	Fox		
Between Men	"Lefty" Flynn	F. B. O		
Big Parade, The	John Gilbert	Metro-Goldwyn		
Border Intrigue	Franklyn Farnum	Inde. Pict. (S. R.)	5 reels	June 6
Border Women	Special Cast	Phil Goldstone (S.R.)	5000 feet	
Broken Hearts of Hollywood	Harlan-Miller	Warner Brothers		
Broken Homes	Lake-Glass	Astor Dist		
Brooding Eyes		Ginsberg Dis. Corp. (S. R.)		
Cave Man, The	Harlan-Miller	Warner Brothers		
Charity Ball, The		Metro-Goldwyn		
Checkered Flag, The		Ginsberg Dist. Corp. (S. R.)		
Clean-Up, The	Richard Talmadge	F. B. O.		
Clod Hopper, The	Glenn Hunter	Assoc. Exhibitors		
Clothes Make the Pirate	Errol-D. Gish	First National		
College Widow, The	Syd Chaplin	Warner Brothers		
Compromise	Irene Rich	Warner Bros.		
Conquered	Gloria Swanson	Paramount		
Count of Luxembourg, The	Larry Semon	Chadwick		
Crashing Through	Jack Perrin	Ambassador Pict. (S. R.)	5000 feet	
Cyclone Bob	Bob Reeves	Anchor Film Dist.		
Cyrano de Bergerac	Special Cast	Atlas Dist. (S. R.)	9500 feet	July 18
Dance Madness	Pringle-Cody	Metro-Goldwyn		
Dangers of a Great City		Fox		
Dark Horse, The	Harry Carey	Prod. Dist. Corp.		
Daybreak		Fox		
Deerslayer, The		Weiss Bros. (S. R.)	4780 feet	
Daughter of the Sioux, A	Wilson-Gerber	Davis Dist. (S. R.)	5 reels	Oct. 3
Demon, The	Jack Hoxie	Universal		
Demon Rider, The	Ken Maynard	Davis Dist	5000 feet	Aug. 22
Detour		Prod. Dist. Corp.		
Devil Horse, The	Rex (horse)	Pathe		
Down Upon the Suwanee River	Special Cast	Lee Bradford (S. R.)		
Dumb Head		Tiffany (S. R.)	6500 feet	
East of the Setting Sun	Constance Talmadge	First National		
Eagle, The	Rudolph Valentino	United Artists		
Eden's Fruit		B. P. Schulberg (S.R.)		
Enchanted Hill, The	Special Cast	Paramount		
Ermine and Rhinestone		H. F. Jans (S. R.)		
Exquisite Sinner, The	Special Cast	Metro-Goldwin		
Face on the Air, The	Evelyn Brent	F. B. O.		
Fall of Jerusalem		Weiss Bros. (S. R.)	6800 feet	
False Pride		Astor Dist.		
Fast Pace, The	Special Cast	Arrow		
Fighter's Paradise, The	Rex Baker	Phil Goldstone	5000 feet	
Fighting Courage	Ken Maynard	Davis Dist. Div. (S.R.)	5 reels	July 11
Fighting Edge, The	Harlan-Miller	Warner Brothers		
Fighting Heart, The	Frank Merrill	Bud Barsky Prod. (S. R.)	5000 feet	
Fighting Smile, The	Bill Cody	Inde. Pict. Corp. (S.R.)	4630 feet	
First Year, The	Special Cast	Fox		
Flaming Waters		F. B. O.		
Flying Three	Al Wilson	Davis Dist. Corp.		
Flying Fool, The	Dick Jones	Sunset Prod. (S. R.)		
Forest of Destiny, The		Gotham Prod. (S. R.)		
Forever After	Corinne Griffith	First National		
Fort Frayne	Ben Wilson	Davis Dist.	5000 feet	Aug. 29
Free Lips	Norma Shearer	M-G-M		
Friends	Special Cast	Vitagraph		
Frivolity		B. P. Schulberg (S.R.)		
Galloping Dude, The	Franklyn Farnum	Inde. Pict. Corp. (S.R.)	4700 feet	
Going the Limit	Richard Holt	Gerson Pict. (S. R.)	5000 feet	Sept. 26
Golden Cocoon		Warner Bros.		
Goose Woman, The	Special Cast	Universal	7500 feet	Aug. 22
Go West	Buster Keaton	Metro-Goldwyn		
Great Love, The	Dana-Agnew	First National		
Grey Vulture, The	Ken Maynard	Davis Dist. Div.		
Gulliver's Travels		Universal		
Handsome Brute, The	Columbia Pict. (S. R.)			
Hassan		Paramount		
Haunted Range, The	Ken Maynard	Davis Dist. Div.		
Hearts and Fists		Assoc. Exhib.		
Hearts and Spangles		Gotham Prod. (S. R.)		
Hell Bent for Heaven		Warner Bros.		
Heir's Apparent	Special Cast	First National		
Her Father's Daughter		F. B. O.		
Hero of the Big Snows, A	Rin Tin Tin (dog)	Warner Brothers		
His Jazz Bride	Special Cast	Warner		
His Majesty Bunker Bean	M. Moore-Devore	Warner	7291 feet	Sept. 26
His Woman	Special Cast	Whitman Bennett	7 reels	
Hogan's Alley	Harlan-Miller	Warner		
Home Maker, The	Alice Joyce	Universal	7755 feet	Aug. 8
Honeymoon Express, The	M. Moore-D. Devore	Warner Brothers		
Horses and Women		B. P. Schulberg		
How to Train a Wife	Valli-O'Brien	Assoc. Exhib.		
Hurricane		Truart (S. R.)	5800 feet	
Husband Hunters		Tiffany	6500 feet	
Inevitable Millionaires, The	M. Moore-Devore	Warner Bros.		
Invisible Wounds	Sweet-Lyon	First National		
Irene	Colleen Moore	First National		
Justice of the Far North		C. B. C. (S. R.)	6500 feet	
Just Suppose	Richard Barthelmess	First National		
Kings of the Turf		Fox		

Feature	Star	Distributed by	Length	Reviewed
Kiss for Cinderella, A	Betty Bronson	Paramount		
La Boheme	Lillian Gish	Metro-Goldwyn		
Ladies of Leisure	Elaine Hammerstein	Columbia (S. R.)		
Lady Windermere's Fan	Special Cast	Warner Brothers		
Lariat, The	William Desmond	Universal		
Last Edition, The	Ralph Lewis	Film Book. Offices		
Lawful Cheater, The	Bow-McKee	B. P. Schulberg	chié feet	
Lena Rivers	Special Cast	Arrow	6 reels	
Life of a Woman		Truart (S. R.)	6500 feet	
Lightning		Tiffany (S. R.)	6500 feet	
Lightning Jack	Jack Perrin	Ambassador Pict. (S.R.) 5000 feet		
Lightning Passes, The	Al Ferguson	Fleming Prod. (S.R.)		
Limited Mail, The	Monte Blue	Warner Bros.		
Little Girl in a Big City, A		Gotham Prod. (S. R.)		
Little Irish Girl, The	Special Cast	Warner Bros.		
Lodge in the Wilderness		Tiffany (S. R.)	5500 feet	
Lord Jim	Percy Marmont	Paramount		
Love Cargo, The	House Peters	Universal		
Lover's Island	Hampton-Kirkwood	Assoc. Exhib.		
Love Gamble, The		Ginsberg Dist. Corp.		
		(S. R.)	5766 feet	July 11
Love Toy, The	Lowell Sherman	Warner Bros.		
Loyalties	Special Cast	Fox		
Lunatic at Large, The	Leon Errol	First National		
Lure of the North, The		Columbia Pict. (S. R.)		
Lure of the Wild	Jane Novak	Columbia (S.R.)		
Lying Wives	Special Cast	Ivan Abramson (S. R.) 7 reels		May 2
Man and the Moment		Metro-Goldwyn		
Mannequin, The		Paramount		
Man of Iron, A		Chadwick	6 reels	July 4
Man on the Box, The	Sydney Chaplin	Warner Bros.		
Man She Bought, The	Constance Talmadge	First National		
Man Without a Conscience	Louis-Rich	Warner Bros.	6650 feet	May 7
Mare Nostrum	Special Cast	Metro-Goldwyn		
Married Cheats		Fox		
Married Hypocrites	Fredericks-La Plante	Universal		
Marrying Money		Truart (S. R.)	5800 feet	
Martinique	Bebe Daniels	Paramount		
Masked Bride, The	Mae Murray	Metro-Goldwyn		
Memory Lane	Boardman-Nagel	First National		
Men of Steel	Milton Sills	First National		
Midnight Flyer, The	Landis-Devore	F. B. O.		
Miracle of Life, The	Busch-Marmont	Assoc. Exhib		
Midnight Flames		Columbia Pict. (S. R.)		
Miss Vanity		Universal		
Million Dollar Doll	Mary Philbin	Assoc. Exhib		
Mismates		First National		
Mocking Bird, The	Lon Chaney	M-G-M		
Modern Musketeer, A	Zeno Corrado	Bud Barsky (S. R.) 5500 feet		
Morganson's Finish		Tiffany (S. R.)	5500 feet	
Napoleon the Great		Universal		
My Own Pal	Tom Mix	Fox		5096 feet
Night Cry, The	Rin-Tin-Tin (dog)	Warner Brothers		5580 feet
Nights, Night Nurse	Syd Chaplin	Warner Brothers		
North Star, The	Strongheart (dog)	Assoc. Exhib.		
Old Clothes	Jackie Coogan	Metro-Goldwyn		
Only Thing, The	Special Cast	Metro-Goldwyn		
Open Trail, The	Jack Hoxie	Universal	4800 feet	May 16
Pace That Thrills, The	Ben Lyon	First National		
Palace of Pleasure		Fox		
Pals		Truart (S. R.)	5800 feet	
Paris	Pauline Starke	Metro-Goldwyn		
Paris After Dark	Norma Talmadge	First National		
Partners Again		United Artists		
Passionate Quest, The	Marie Prevost	Warner Bros.		
Passionate Youth	Special Cast	Truart (S. R.)	6 reels	July 11
Part Time Wife, The		Gotham Prod. (S. R.)		
Phantom of the Forest	Thunder (dog)	Gotham Prod.		
Phantom of the Opera	Lon Chaney	Universal	8464 feet	Sept. 19
Pinch Hitter, The	Glenn Hunter	Assn. Exhibitors		
Pleasure Buyers, The	Irene Rich	Warner Brothers		
Police Patrol, The	James Kirkwood	Gotham Prod. (S.R.) 6000 feet		Sept. 19
Polly of the Ballet	Bebe Daniels	Paramount		
Pony Express, The	Special Cast	Paramount	9929 feet	Sept. 26
Prince, The	Philbin-Kerry	Universal		
Quality Street		Metro-Goldwyn		
Quicker 'n Lightning	Buffalo Bill, Jr.	Weiss Bros. (S. R.)	5 reels	June 13
Racing Blood		Gotham Prod. (S.R.)		
Rainbow Riley	Johnny Hines	First National		
Reckless Courage	Buddy Roosevelt	Weiss Bros. (S.R.) 4851 feet		May 2
Reckless Sex, The	Special Cast	Truart (S. R.)	6 reels	Feb. 14
Red Clay	William Desmond	Universal		
Red Dice	Rod La Rocque	Prod. Dist. Corp.		
Red Kimono, The	Mrs. Wallace Reid	Davis Dist. Div.		
Red Hot Tires	Monte Blue	Warner Bros.		
Return of a Soldier	Special Cast	Metro-Goldwyn		
Rime of the Ancient Mari-				
ner, The		Fox Film		
Road to Glory, The		Fox		
Road That Led Home, The		Vitagraph		
Rocking Moon	Bowers-Tashman	Prod. Dist. Corp.		
Romance of an Actress		Chadwick		
Ropin' Venus, The	Josie Sedgwick	Universal		
Rose of the World	Special Cast	Warner Bros.		
Sally, Irene and Mary	Special Cast	Metro-Goldwyn		
Salvage		Truart (S. R.)	5800 feet	
Sap, The	M. Moore-D. Devore	Warner Bros.		
Satan in Sables	Lowell Sherman	Warner Bros.		
Savage, The	Ben Lyon	First National		
Scarlet Saint, The	Lyon-Astor	First National		
Scraps	Mary Pickford	United Artists		
Sea Beast, The	John Barrymore	Warner Bros.		
Separate Rooms		Fox		
Seven Sinners	Marie Prevost	Warner Bros.		
Seventh Heaven	Special Cast	Fox		
Shadow of the Wall		Gotham Prod. (S. R.)		
Shadow of the Mosque	Odette Taylor	Cranford & Clarke		
		(S. R.)	6200 feet	
Shenandoah		B. P. Schulberg (S. R.)		
Ship of Souls	D. Lytell-L. Rich	Assoc. Exhib.	5800 feet	
Shootin' Square	Jack Perrin	Ambassador Pict. (S.R.)5000 feet		
Siegfried		Ufa		
Sign of the Claw		Gotham Prod. (S. R.)		
Silent Witness, The		Truart (S. R.)	5800 feet	
Sixteen Shackles	Irene Rich	Warner Bros.		
Silver Treasure, The	Special Cast	Fox		
Skinners Dress Suit	Reginald Denny	Universal		
Social Highwayman, The	Haclan-Miller	Warner Brothers		
Song and Dance Man, The	Tom Moore	Paramount		
Span of Life	Betty Blythe	Banner Prod. (S. R.)		
Speed Limit, The		Gotham Prod. (S. R.)		
Splendid Road, The	Anna Q. Nilsson	First National		
Sporting Life	Special Cast	Universal	6798 feet	Sept. 26
Stage Door Johnny	Raymond Griffith	Paramount		
Steele of the Royal				
Mounted		Vitagraph	6 reels	June 27
Stella Dallas		United Artists		
Stella Maris	Mary Philbin	Universal		
Still Alarm, The	Chadwick-Russell	Universal		
Stop, Look and Listen	Larry Semon	Pathe		
Strange Bedfellows		Metro-Goldwyn		
Streets of Sin		Fox		
Sunshine of Paradise Alley	Special Cast	Chadwick		
Super Speed	Reed Howes	Rayart (S. R.)		
Sweet Adeline	Charles Ray	Chadwick		
Tale of a Vanishing People		Tiffany (S. R.)	6500 feet	
Tattooed Countess, The	Pola Negri	Paramount		
Tearing Loose	Wally Wales	Weiss Bros. (S. R.)	4800 feet	June 13
Ten to Midnight		Prod. Dist. Corp.		
That Man from Arizona	D. Revier-W.Fairbanks	F. B. O.		
That Royle Girl	Kirkwood-Dempster	Paramount		
This Woman	Special Cast	Fox		
Thoroughbred	George O'Brien	Fox		
Thoroughbred, The	Special Cast	Truart	6451 feet	Sept. 19
Three Bad Men	Special Cast	Fox		
Tony Runs Wild	Tom Mix	Fox		
Trailing Shadows	Edmund Lowe	Fox		
Travelin' Fast	Jack Perrin	Ambassador Pict. (S.		
		R.)		
Travis Coup, The		Tiffany (S. R.)	5800 feet	
Two Sister, The	Constance Talmadge	First National		
Two Blocks Away	Special Cast	Universal		
Two Soldiers, The	Special Cast	Universal		
Unguarded Hour, The	Sills-Kenyon	First National		
Unknown Lover, The	Elsie Ferguson	Vitagraph		
Up and At 'Em	Jack Perrin	Ambassador Pict. (S.		
		R.)	5000 feet	
Vengeance of Durand, The	Irene Rich	Warner Brothers		
Viennese Medley	Special Cast	First National		
Volga Boatman, The		Prod. Dist. Corp.		
Wages for Wives	Special Cast	Fox		
Wanderer, The	William Collier, Jr.	Paramount	8173 feet	
Wandering Footsteps	Special Cast	Ginsberg Dist. Corp.		
Warrior Gap	Wilcox-Gerber	Davis Dist.	4900 feet	Aug. 22
We Moderns	Colleen Moore	First National		
What Happened to Jones	Reginald Denny	Universal		
What Will People Say		Metro-Goldwyn		
When His Love Grew Cold		Metro-Goldwyn		
When Husbands Flirt	Dorothy Revier	Columbia		
Where the Worst Begins		Truart (S. R.)	5800 feet	
Whispering Canyon		Ginsberg Dist. Corp.		
		(S. R.)		
White Chief, The	Monte Blue	Warner Brothers		
White Mice	Jacqueline Logan	Sering D. Wilson (S. R.)		
Why Girls Go Back Home		Warner Brothers		
Why Women Love		First National		
Wild Girl		Truart (S. R.)	5800 feet	
Wild Justice	Peter the Great	United Artists	6 reels	Aug. 1
Wild Jubin'	Buck Jones	Fox		
Wide Open	Dick Jones	Sunset Prod. (S. R.)		
Wild West	Mulhall-Ferguson	Pathe		
Winning of Barbara Worth		Principal Pict. (S. R.)		
Wise Guy, The	Lefty Flynn	F. B. O.		
With Kit Carson Over the				
Great Divide	Special Cast	Sunset Prod. (S. R.)		
Wives for Rent		Universal		
Womanhandled	Richard Dix	Paramount		
Women		Banner Prod. (S. R.)		
Women and Wives		Metro-Goldwyn		
World's Illusion, The		Fox		
Worst Woman, The	Special Cast	B. P. Schulberg (S. R.)		
Wreckage		Ginsberg Dist. Corp.		
Wrong Coat, The		Tiffany (S. R.)	6500 feet	
Yankee Senor, The	Tom Mix	Fox		
Yoke, The	Special Cast	Warner Brothers		
You Can't Live on Love	Reginald Denny	Universal		

Watch For October Issue of

BOOKING GUIDE

Containing Complete Information on Feature and Short Subjects

WILLIAMS PRESS, INC.
NEW YORK — ALBANY

Rothacker-Aller Laboratories, Hollywood, Calif.

Inspiration Pictures, Inc.
Presents Richard Barthelmess
With delightful Dorothy Gish in
"The Beautiful City." Written for
The screen by Edmund Goulding—
Adapted by Violet E. Powell. Scenario
And titles by Don Bartlet and C.
Graham Baker. Photographed by Roy
Overbaugh and Stewart Kelson. The
Settings by Tec-Art Studios, Inc. Art
Titles by H. E. R. Studios. Film edited
By William Hamilton. Everything
Directed by Mr. Kenneth Webb
A First National Picture.
Rothacker Prints and Service.

Richard Barthelmess
and
Dorothy Gish
in
"The Beautiful City."

Look Better—
Wear Longer!

Founded 1910
by
Watterson R. Rothacker